Turkish
Standard Dictionary

Turkish – English • English – Turkish

Berlitz Publishing
New York · Munich · Singapore

Original edition edited by the Langenscheidt editorial staff

Based on a dictionary by Resuhi Akdikmen

Book in cover photo: © Punchstock/Medioimages

Berlitz Publishing
193 Morris Avenue
Springfield, NJ 07081
USA

Printed in Germany
ISBN 978-981-268-522-3

09 10 11 12 13 5. 4. 3. 2. 1.

Contents
İçindekiler

How to use this dictionary
Sözlüğün Kullanımı

Turkish - English

1. The tilde (~) replaces the headword, example:
   vadeli...: **~ _hesap_** = vadeli hesap

2. The short hyphen (-) preceding declension and conjugation suffixes replaces the headword and indicates the writing in one word; example:
   vade...: **_-si gelmek_** = vadesi gelmek

3. The -*i* case of Turkish nouns and adjectives is, if necessary, given in an abbreviated form; example:
   vahşet **_-ti_**
   vakıt **_-kfı_**

4. The present tense (geniş zaman) of a Turkish verb is indicated by means of the suffix of the third person; example:
   varmak (-_ır_) = varır
   yanmak (-_ar_) = yanar

5. A long vowel of a headword is marked by a line placed on top of the respective vowel, which is seperately given in brackets; example:
   vahşi [ī]
   yani [ā]
   suret **_-ti_** [ū]

6. The character of the syllable, whether short, long or stressed, is indicated by the following symbols [.], [-], [x]; examples:
   vanilya [.x.] (= all syllables are short, the second syllable is stressed)
   viran [- -] (= both syllables are long)

7. Phrases and proverbs are listed following the different meanings of the headword.

8. A voiceless consonant at the end of a verbal root becomes voiced when a suffix beginning with a vowel is added. This change is indicated in the following way:
   git-mek (-_der_) = gider

5

English - Turkish

I. English Headwords	I. İngilizce Madde Başı Sözcükleri

1. The alphabetical order of the headwords has been observed throughout, including the irregular forms.

1. Düzensiz şekilleri de dahil olmak üzere madde başı sözcüklerin alfabetik sırasına baştan sona dikkat edilmiştir.

2. Centred dots or stress marks within a headword indicate syllabification.

2. Madde başı bir sözcükteki noktalar veya vurgu işaretleri heceleymeyi göstermektedirler.

e.g. **cul.ti.vat.ed... cul.ti'va.tion**

örnek: **cul.ti.vat.ed ... cul.ti'va.-tion**

3. In hyphenated compounds a hyphen coinciding with the end of a line is repeated at the beginning of the text.

3. Tire ile ayrılmış bileşik sözcüklerde satır sonuna gelen tire, diğer satırın başında tekrarlanmıştır.

4. The tilde (∼) represents the repetition of a headword.

4. Tekrar işareti (∼), madde başı sözcüğün tekrarını gösterir.

a) In compounds the tilde in bold type (∼) replaces the catchword.

a) Bileşik sözcüklerdeki siyah tekrar işareti (∼) asıl sözcüğün yerini alır

e.g. **aft.er ... '∼.birth** (= afterbirth)

örnek: **aft.er ... '∼.birth** (= afterbirth)

b) The simple tilde (∼) replaces the headword immediately preceding (which itself may contain a tilde in bold type).

b) Açık renkli tekrar işareti (∼) kendisinden hemen önce gelen siyah harfli sözcüğün yerini alır.

e.g. **dis.tance... *at a* ∼** = at a distance
day... '∼.light ... ∼-*saving time* = daylight-saving time

örnek: **dis.tance... *at a* ∼** = at a distance
day... '∼.light ... ∼-*saving time* daylight-saving time

5. When the initial letter changes from small to capital or vice versa, the usual tilde is replaced by ♀.

5. Bir sözcüğün ilk harfi küçük harften büyük harfe veya büyük harften küçük harfe dönüştüğünde ♀ veya ♀ tekrar işaretleri konulmuştur.

e.g. **foot..: ... ♀ Guards** = Foot Guards.

örnek: **foot..: ... ♀ Guards** = Foot Guards.

II. Pronunciation

1. The pronunciation of English headwords is given in square brackets by means of the symbols of the International Phonetic Association.

2. To save space the tilde (∼) has been used in many places within the phonetic transcription. It replaces any part of the preceding complete transcription which remains unchanged.

e.g. **as.so.ci.a.ble** [ə'səuʃjəbl] ...
as'so.ci.ate 1. [-ʃieit] ... **2.** [-ʃiit]
... **as.so.ci.a.tion** [-si'eiʃən] ...

II. Telaffuz

1. İngilizce madde başı sözcüklerin telaffuzları. Uluslararası Fonetik Kuruluşunun sembolleriyle köşeli ayraclarda verilmiştir.

2. Yerden kazanmak için tekrar işare ti (∼) fonetik yazımda da pek çok yer lerde kullanılmıştır. Bu işaret, fonetik yazımın değişmeyen kısmının yerine geçmektedir.

örnek: **as.so.ci.a.ble** [ə'səuʃjəbl]
... **as'so.ci.ate 1.** [-ʃieit] ... **2.**
[-ʃiit] ... **as.so.ci.a.tion** [-si'ei-ʃən] ...

III. Grammatical References

1. In the appendix you will find a list of irregular verbs.

2. (*irr.*) following a verb refers to this list, where you will find the principal parts of this particular verb.

3. A reference such as (*irr.* **fall**) indicates that the compound verb is conjugated exactly like the primary verb as given in the list of irregular verbs.

4. An adjective marked with □ takes the regular adverbial form, *i.e.* by affixing ...ly to the adjective or by changing ...le into ...ly or ...y into ...ily.

5. (∼*ally*) means that an adverb is formed by affixing ...ally to the adjective.

6. When there is only one adverb for adjectives ending in both ...ic

III. Gramatik Başvurular

1. Sözlüğün ek kısmında düzensiz fiillerin bir listesini bulacaksınız.

2. Bir fiili izleyen (*irr.*), söz konusu fiilin ikinci ve üçüncü şekillerinin olduğu bu listeye ilişkindir.

3. Örneğin (*irr.* **fall**), söz konusu bileşik fiilin düzensiz fiil listesinde verilen esas fiil gibi çekildiğini göstermektedir.

4. □ işaretli bir sıfat, kendisine ...ly eklenerek veya ...le ...ly'e veya ...y ...ily'e dönüştürülerek düzenli zarf şeklini alır.

5. (∼*ally*), bir zarfın sıfata ...ally eklenerek yapıldığını göstermektedir.

6. Sonu ...ic veya ...ical ile biten sıfatlar için yalnızca bir zarf ol-

and ...ical, this is indicated in the following way:

his.tor.ic, his.tor.i.cal □ *i.e.* historically is the adverb of both adjectives.

duğunda, bu şu şekilde gösterilmektedir.

his.tor.ic, his.tor.i.cal □, yani «historically» her iki sıfatın da zarfıdır.

IV. Translations

1. Translations of a headword have been subdivided by Arabic numerals to distinguish the various parts of speech. Words of similar meanings have been subdivided by commas, the various senses by semicolons.

2. Explanatory additions have been printed in italics.

e.g. **whip**... *v/t.* ... çalkamak, çırpmak (*yumurta*); ... bastırmak (*kumaş*); döndürmek, çevirmek (*topaç*) ...

3. Prepositions governing an English catchword (verb, adjective, noun) are given in both languages.

e.g. **con.vers.a.ble** ... **con.verse** ... **3.** [kən'vəːs] *vb.* konuşmak, görüşmek, sohbet etm. (***with** ile*)...

IV. Sözcüklerin Anlamları

1. Madde baş bir sözcüğün anlamları, sözcüklerin türlerine göre rakamlarla ayrılmıştır. Anlamdaş sözcükler virgüllerle, ayrı anlamlı sözcükler noktalı virgüllerle ayrılmışlardır.

2. Açıklayıcı ek sözcükler italik olarak verilmiştir.

örnek: **whip** ... *v/t.* ... çalkamak, çırpmak (*yumurta*); ... bastırmak (*kumaş*); döndürmek, çevirmek (*topaç*) ...

3. İngilizce bir sözcüğün (fiil, sıfat, isim) aldığı edatlar her iki dilde de verilmiştir.

örnek: **con.vers.a.ble** ... **con.-verse** ... **3.** [kən'vəːs] *vb.* konuşmak, görüşmek, sohbet etm. (***with** ile*)...

Abbreviations
Kısaltmalar

a.	also	*keza*
abbr.	abbreviation	*kısaltma*
abl.	ablative	*-den hali*
acc.	accusative	*-i hali*
adj.	adjective	*sıfat*
adv.	adverb	*zarf*
AGR	agriculture	*ziraat, tarım*
Am.	Americanism	*Amerikan dili*
ANAT	anatomy	*anatomi, yapibilim*
ARCH	architecture	*mimarlık*
AST	astronomy	*astronomi, gökbilim*
attr.	attributively	*niteleyici olarak*
AVIA	aviation	*havacılık*
b-de		*biri(si)nde*
b-den		*biri(si)nden*
b-i		*biri(si)*
BIOL	biology	*biyoloji, dirimbilim*
b-le		*biri(si)yle*
b-ne		*biri(si)ne*
b-ni		*biri(si)ni*
b-nin		*biri(si)nin*
BOT	botany	*botanik, bitkibilion*
b.s.	bad sense	*kötü anlamda*
b-ş.		*bir şey*
bşde		*bir şeyde*
bşden		*bir şeyden*
bşe		*bir şeye*
bşi		*bir şeyi*
bşin		*bir şeyin*
bşle		*bir şeyle*
caus.	causative	*ettirgen*
CHEM	chemistry	*kimya*
cj.	conjunction	*bağlaç*
co.	comical	*komik*
COM	commercial term	*ticari terim*
comb.	combining form	*tamlama*
contp.	contemptuously	*aşağılayıcı olarak*
ECCL	ecclesiastical	*dini*
ELECT	electrical engineering	*elektrik mühendisliği*

9

esp.	especially	*özellikle*
etc.	et cetera	*ve saire*
F	colloquial language	*konuşma dili*
FENC	fencing	*eskrim*
fig.	figuratively	*mecazi olarak*
gen.	genitive	*-in hali*
GEOGR	geography	*coğrafya*
GEOL	geology	*jeoloji, yerbilim*
ger.	gerund	*isim-fiil*
GR	grammar	*gramer, dilbilgisi*
HIST	history	*tarih*
HUNT	hunting	*avcılık*
ICHTH	ichthyology	*balıklar bilimi*
inf.	infinitive	*mastar, eylemlik*
int.	interjection	*ünlem*
Ir.	Irish	*İrlanda dili*
iro.	ironically	*alaylı*
irr.	irregular	*düzensiz, kural dişi*
isl.	İslamic	*İslami*
IT	IT, computing	*enformatik*
JUR	jurisprudence	*hukuk*
k-de		*kendi(si)de*
k-den		*kendi(si)nden*
k-le		*kendi(si)yle*
k-ne		*kendi(si)ne*
k-ni		*kendi(si)ni*
k-nin		*kendi(si)nin*
lit.	literary	*edebi, yazınsal*
LOG	logic	*mantık*
MATH	mathematics	*matematik*
MEC	mechanics	*mekanik*
MED	medicine	*tıp*
METEOR	meteorology	*meteoroloji, havabilgisi*
mf.	men's forename	*erkek ismi*
MIL	military term	*askeri terim*
MIN	mineralogy; mining	*mineraloji, mineralbilim; madencilik*
MOT	motoring	*otomobilcilik*
MOUNT	mountaineering	*dağcilik*
mst.	mostly	*çoğunlukla*
MUS	musical term	*müzik terimi*
MYTH	mythology	*mitoloji, efsanebilim*
n.	noun	*isim*
NAUT	nautical term	*denizcilik terimi*
n. pl.	plural noun	*çoğul isim*
obs.	obsolete	*eski*
oft.	often	*genellikle*
OPT	optics	*optik*
ORN	ornithology	*ornitoloji, kuşbilim*
o.s.	oneself	*kendi(si); kendi kendine*

P	provincialism	*taşra dili*
PAINT	painting	*ressamlık*
PARL	parliamentary term	*parlamento terimi*
part.	particularly	*özellikle*
pass.	passive	*edilgen*
pej.	pejorative	*aşağılayıcı*
PHARM	pharmacy	*eczacılık*
PHLS	philosophy	*felsefe*
PHOT	photography	*fotoğrafçılık*
PHYS	physics	*fizik*
PHYSIOL	physiology	*fizyoloji*
pl.	plural	*çoğul*
poet.	poetry; poetic	*şiir sanatı; şiirsel*
POL	politics	*siyaset*
POST	postal affairs	*postacılık*
p.p.	past participle	*-mış yapılı ortaç*
p.pr.	present participle	*-en yapılı ortaç*
pred.	predicatively	*yüklem olarak*
pret.	preterite	*-di'li geçmiş zaman*
pr.n.	proper noun	*özel isim*
pron.	pronoun	*zamir*
prp.	preposition	*edat, ilgeç*
PSYCH	psychology	*psikoloji, ruhbilim*
RAIL	railway, railroad	*demiryolu*
rare	rare, little used	*az kullanılan*
RHET	rhetoric	*sözbilim, konuşma sanatı*
s.	see	*bakınız*
sg.	singular	*tekil*
sl.	slang	*argo*
s.o.	someone	*biri(si)*
s.th.	something	*bir şey*
sup.	superlative	*enüstünlük derecesi*
surv.	surveying	*yeri ölçme bilimi*
syn.	synonym	*eşanlam*
TEL	telegraphy	*telgrafçılık*
TELEPH	telephony	*telefonculuk*
THEAT	theatre	*tiyatro*
TYP	typography	*basımcılık*
UNIV	university	*üniversite*
V	vulgar	*kaba, ayıp*
v/aux.	auxiliary verb	*yardımcı fiil*
v.b.		*ve benzeri*
vb.	verb	*fiil, eylem*
VET	veterinary medicine	*veterinerlik*
v/i.	verb intransitive	*geçişsiz fiil*
v/t.	verb transitive	*geçişli fiil*
wf.	women's forename	*kadın ismi*
ZOO	zoology	*zooloji, hayvanbilim*
		kelimenin aslı

The International Phonetic Alphabet
Uluslararası Fonetik Alfabesinin Kullanımı

Ünlüler ve Diftonglar

[ɑː]   Türkçedeki (a) sesinin uzun şekli gibidir: *far* [fɑː], *father* [ˈfɑːðə].

[ʌ]   Türkçedeki (a) sesinin kısa ve sert şeklidir: *butter* [ˈbʌtə], *come* [kʌm], *colour* [ˈkʌlə], *blood* [blʌd], *flourish* [ˈflʌriʃ].

[æ]   Türkçedeki (a) sesi ile (e) sesi arasında bir sestir. Ağız, (a) diyecekmiş gibi açılır, daha sonra ses (e)'ye dönüştürülür: *fat* [fæt], *man* [mæn].

[ɛə]   Türkçedeki (e) sesinin uzun ve yumuşak şeklidir: *bare* [bɛə], *pair* [pɛə], *there* [ðɛə].

[ai]   Türkçedeki (ay) sesi gibidir: *I* [ai], *lie* [lai], *dry* [drai].

[au]   Dudaklar önce (a) sesi çıkartmak için açılacak, daha sonra (u) sesi için uzatılacaktır: *house* [haus], *now* [nau].

[e]   Türkçedeki (e) sesi gibidir: *bed* [bed], *less* [les].

[ei]   Türkçedeki (ey) sesi gibidir: *date* [deit], *play* [plei], *obey* [əˈbei].

[ə]   Türkçedeki (ı) sesi gibidir: *about* [əˈbaut], *butter* [ˈbʌtə], *connect* [kəˈnekt].

[əu]   Dudaklar önce (o) sesi çıkartmak için yuvarlaklaştırılır, daha sonra (u) sesi için uzatılır: *note* [nəut], *boat* [bəut], *below* [biˈləu].

[iː]   Türkçedeki (i) sesinin uzun şeklidir: *scene* [siːn], *sea* [siː], *feet* [fiːt], *ceiling* [ˈsiːliŋ].

[i]   Türkçedeki (i) sesi gibidir: *big* [big], *city* [ˈsiti].

[iə]   Dudaklar önce (i) sesi çıkartmak için açılacak, daha sonra ses (ı)'ya dönüştürülecektir: *here* [hiə], *hear* [hiə], *inferior* [inˈfiəriə].

[ɔː]   Türkçedeki (o) sesinin uzun şeklidir: *fall* [fɔːl], *nought* [nɔːt], *or* [ɔː], *before* [biˈfɔː].

[ɔ]   Türkçedeki (o) ile (a) sesleri arasında bir sestir. İngiliz İngilizcesinde (o) sesine, Amerikan İngilizcesinde ise (a) sesine daha yakındır: *god* [gɔd], *not* [nɔt], *wash* [wɔʃ], *hobby* [ˈhɔbi].

[ɔi]   Türkçedeki (oy) sesi gibidir: *voice* [vɔis], *boy* [bɔi], *annoy* [əˈnɔi].

[əː]   Türkçedeki (ö) sesi gibidir: *word* [wəːd], *girl* [gəːl], *learn* [ləːn], *murmur* ['məːmə].

[uː]   Türkçedeki (u) sesinin uzun şeklidir: *fool* [fuːl], *shoe* [ʃuː], *you* [juː], *rule* [ruːl], *canoe* [kəˈnuː].

[u]   Türkçedeki (u) sesi gibidir: *put* [put], *look* [luk].

[uə]   Dudaklar önce (u) sesi çıkartmak için uzatılır, daha sonra ses (ı) sesine dönüştürülür: *poor* [puə], *sure* [ʃuə], *allure* [əˈljuə].

Ünsüzler

[r]   Türkçedeki (r) sesi gibidir: *rose* [rəuz], *pride* [praid].

[ʒ]   Türkçedeki (j) sesi gibidir: *azure* ['æʒə], *vision* ['viʒən].

[dʒ]   Türkçedeki (c) sesi gibidir: *June* [dʒuːn], *jeep* [dʒiːp].

[tʃ]   Türkçedeki (ç) sesi gibidir: *chair* [tʃɛə], *church* [tʃəːtʃ].

[ʃ]   Türkçedeki (ş) sesi gibidir: *shake* [ʃeik], *washing* ['wɔʃi ŋ], *she* [ʃiː].

[θ]   Bu ses Türkçede yoktur. Dilin ucu üst kesicidişlere dokundurulup (t) sesi çıkarılır: *thank* [θæŋk], *thin* [θin], *path* [pɑːθ], *method* ['meθəd].

[ð]   Bu ses de Türkçede yoktur. Dilin ucu üst kesicidişlere dokundurulup (d) sesi çıkarılır: *there* [ðɛə], *father* ['fɑːðə], *breathe* [briːð].

[ŋ]   Bu ses de Türkçede yoktur. Dil damağa dokundurularak genizden (n) sesi çıkarılır: *ring* [riŋ], *sing* [siŋ].

[s]   Türkçedeki (s) sesi gibidir: *see* [siː], *hats* [hæts], *decide* [diˈsaid].

[z]   Türkçedeki (z) sesi gibidir: *rise* [raiz], *zeal* [ziːl], *horizon* [hɔˈraizn].

[w]   Bu ses Türkçede yoktur. Dudaklar yuvarlaklaştırılıp (v) sesi çıkartılır: *will* [wil], *swear* [swɛə], *queen* [kwiːn].

[f]   Türkçedeki (f) sesi gibidir: *fat* [fæt], *tough* [tʌf], *effort* ['efət].

[v]   Türkçedeki (v) sesi gibidir: *vein* [vein].

[j]   Türkçedeki (y) sesi gibidir: *yes* [jes], *onion* ['ʌnjən].

[p]   Türkçedeki (p) sesi gibidir: *pen* [pen].

[b]   Türkçedeki (b) sesi gibidir: *bad* [bæd].

[t]   Türkçedeki (t) sesi gibidir: *tea* [tiː].

[d]   Türkçedeki (d) sesi gibidir: *did* [did].

[k]   Türkçedeki (k) sesi gibidir: *cat* [kæt].

[g]   Türkçedeki (g) sesi gibidir: *got* [gɔt].

[h]   Türkçedeki (h) sesi gibidir: *how* [hau].

[m]   Türkçedeki (m) sesi gibidir: *man* [mæn].

[n]   Türkçedeki (n) sesi gibidir: *no* [nəu].

[l]   Türkçedeki (l) sesi gibidir: *leg* [leg].

Spelling of American English
Amerikan İngilizcesinin Yazımı

İngiltere'de konuşulan İngilizcenin yazımından farklı olarak Amerikan İngilizcesinin yazımında başlıca şu özellikler vardır:

1. İki sözcüğü birleştiren çizgi çoğunlukla kaldırılır, örneğin: cooperate, breakdown, soapbox.
2. **-our** ekindeki **(u)** harfi Amerikan İngilizcesinde yazılmaz, örneğin: color, harbor, humor, favor.
3. **-re** ile biten birçok sözcük Amerikan İngilizcesinde **-er** olarak yazılır, örneğin: center, theater, fiber.
4. **(l)** ve **(p)** harfleri ile biten fiillerin türetmelerinde son ünsüz harf ikilenmez, örneğin: traveled, quarreled, worshiped.
5. **-ence** ile biten sözcükler Amerikan İngilizcesinde **-ense** ile yazılır, örneğin: defense, offense, license.
6. Fransızcadan gelen ekler çoğu kez kaldırılır veya kısaltılır, örneğin: dialog(ue), program(me), envelop(e), catalog(ue).
7. **ae** ve **oe** yerine çoğu kez yalnız **(e)** yazılır, örneğin: an(a)emia, man(o)euvers.
8. **-xion** yerine **-ction** kullanılır, örneğin: connection, reflection.
9. Söylenmeyen **(e)** harfi, judg(e)ment, abridg(e)ment, acknowledg(e)ment gibi sözcüklerde yazılmaz.
10. **en-** öneki yerine **in-** öneki daha çok kullanılır, örneğin: inclose.
11. Amerikan İngilizcesinde although yerine altho, all right yerine alright, through yerine thru biçimleri de kullanılabilir.
12. Tüm bunlardan başka, özel yazım biçimleri olan bazı sözcükler vardır, örneğin;

English	**American**
cheque	check
cosy	cozy
grey	gray
moustache	mustache
plough	plow
sceptic	skeptic
tyre	tire

Pronunciation of American English
Amerikan İngilizcesinin Söylenişi

American İngilizcesi (AE) ile İngiliz İngilizcesi (BE) arasında söyleniş bakımından bazı ayrılıklar vardırki, en önemlileri şöyledir:

1. İngiliz İngilizcesinde (ɑː) olarak söylenen ses, Amerikan İngilizcesinde (æ) veya (æː) olarak söylenir: pass [BE pɑːs = AE pæ(ː)s], answer [BE 'ɑːnsə = AE 'æ(ː)nsər], dance [BE dɑːns = AE dæ(ː)ns], half [BE hɑːf = AE hæ(ː)f], laugh [BE lɑːf = AE læ(ː)f].

2. İngiliz İngilizcesinde (o) olarak söylenen ses, Amerikan İngilizcesinde (a)'ya yakın olarak söylenir: dollar [BE'dɔlə = AE 'dɑlər], college [BE 'kɔlidʒ = AE 'kɑlidʒ], lot [BE lɔt = AE lɑt], problem [BE 'prɔbləm = AE 'prɑbləm].

3. Sonda olup bir ünlüden sonra gelen veya bir ünlü ile bir ünsüz arasında bulunan (r), İngiliz İngilizcesinde söylenmez. Buna karşın Amerikan İngilizcesinde söylenir: car [BE kɑː = AE kɑːr], care [BE kɛə = AE kɛr], border [BE 'bɔːdə = AE 'bɔːrdər].

4. Vurgulu hecedeki (u) sesi, İngiliz İngilizcesinde (juː) olarak söylenir. Fakat bu ses Amerikan İngilizcesinde (uː) olarak söylenmektedir: Tuesday [BE 'tjuːzdi = AE 'tuːzdi], student [BE 'stjuːdənt = AE 'stuːdənt]. Fakat (music) ve (fuel) sözcükleri her iki söylenişte de aynıdır: [BE, AE = 'mjuːzik] [BE, AE = 'fjuːəl].

5. (p) ve (t) sesleri, Amerikan İngilizcesinde iki ünlü arasında olduklarında (b) ve (d) olarak söylenirler: property [BE 'prɔpəti = AE 'prɑbərti], united [BE juː'naitid = AE juː'naidid].

6. İki veya daha fazla heceli sözcükler, Amerikan İngilizcesinde ana vurgudan sonra daha hafif ikinci bir vurgu alırlar: secretary [BE 'sekrətri = AE 'sekrə'tɛri], dictionary [BE 'dikʃənri = AE 'dikʃənɛri].

7. Sözcük sonundaki (-ile) hecesi, İngiliz İngilizcesinde (-ail) olarak söylendiği halde, Amerikan İngilizcesinde (-əl) veya (-il) olarak söylenir: futile [BE 'fjuːtail = AE 'fjuːtəl], textile [BE 'tekstail = AE 'tekstil].

8. Sözcük sonundaki (-ization) hecesi, İngiliz İngilizcesinde [-ai'zeiʃən] olarak söylendiği halde, Amerikan İngilizcesinde [-i'zeiʃən] olarak söylenir: civilization [BE sivəlai'zeiʃən = AE sivəli'zeiʃən].

9. (-able) ve (-ible) eklerinde bulunan (e) okunmamasına karşın, Amerikan İngilizcesinde (b) ile (l) arasında bir (ı) varmış gibi okunur; possible [BE = 'pɔsəbl = AE 'pɑsəbəl], admirable [BE 'ædmərəbl = AE 'ædmərəbəl].

Turkish – English

A

A 1. MIL = *alay*; **2.** PHYS = *amper.*

a¹ [ā] *int.* O!, Oh!, Ah!, Ha!

a² [ā] *iro.* nonsense!, certainly not!

a³ [ā] *pers. connective in various archaic compounds. e.g.* **lebalep, peyapey,** etc.

a⁴ [ā], **e** (*after 2nd person conditional, imperative with impatient tone*) **alsana!** there, take it!; **baksana!** look here!; **söylesenize!** tell, then!

a⁵ (*emphatic, confirms a statement*) **olur a!** these things happen!; **söyledik a!** we told you!

-a (*dative suffix*) to, towards, for.

A.A. *abbr. for* **Anatolia News Agency.**

aa, aah F no!, impossible!, not at all!, not a bit of it!

ab, -bı [-] *obs.* water.

aba 1. coarse wool(l)en material; **2.** coat *or* cloak made of such material; **~ altından değnek göstermek** *fig.* to threaten with soft words, to use an iron hand in a velvet glove; **~ gibi** coarse and thick (*material*); **~ kebe** rough and old clothes, tatters; **-nın kadri yağmurda belli olur** *pro.* you appreciate the value of s.th. when its necessity arises; (*b-ne*) **-yı yakmak** to fall desperately in love with *s.o.*, to be gone on *s.o.*

abacı maker *or* seller of **aba.**

abadi [- - -] kind of valuable yellow glazed paper, Manila paper.

abajur lampshade.

abalı 1. wearing coarse wool(l)en garments (*s.* **aba**); **2.** *fig.* weak, poor, wretched; **vurya!** hit him when he's down!

abandone *sports*: concession; **~ etm.** to concede defeat.

abani [- - -] **1.** a fine cotton material embroidered with yellow silk; **2.** made of this cloth.

abanmak 1. to lean forward, to push forward with one's weight; **2.** *sl.* *b-ne* to live at s.o.'s expense.

abanoz 1. ebony; **2.** made of ebony; **~ ağacı** ebony-tree; **~ gibi 1.** black as ebony; **2.** very hard; **~ kesilmek** *fig.* to become as hard as ebony; **~ yürekli** hardhearted.

abartı exaggeration.

abartıcı a person who exaggerates; boaster.

abartma exaggeration, overstatement.

abartmak to exaggerate.

Abaza Abkhasia(n).

Abazaca Abkhasian (language).

abazan *sl.* **1.** hungry, craving; **2.** starved for sex.

Abbas *mf.*; **~ yolcudur duramaz** said of s.o. who must leave.

Abbasi [. - -] Abbaside.

ABD (*abbr. for* **Amerika Birleşik Devletleri**) U.S.A.

abe P Hey!

abes 1. silly, stupid, useless, vain; **2.** unreasonable; nonsense, absurdity; **~ kaçmak** to be improper; **-le uğraşmak** to exert o.s. in vain, to fool around.

abıhayat, -tı [- . . . -] **1.** water of life; **2.** elixir; **~ içmiş** *fig.* healthy and young-looking; long-lived.

abıru [- . -] hono(u)r, glory, pride; **~ dökmek** to abase o.s., to implore humbly.

abi (*sl. for* **ağabey**) older brother.

abide monument, memorial, edifice.

abideleşmek *fig.* to be memorialized, to become an hono(u)red symbol.

abidevi [- . . .] monumental.

abis GEOGR abyss.

abit, -bdi 1. *obs.* servant; **2.** *fig.* slave; **3.** God's creature, human being.

âbit, **-di** devotee; worshipper.

abla [x .] **1.** older sister; **2.** F Miss!

ablak round, chubby-faced.

ablatya [. x .] large fishing net.

abli [x .] NAUT vang, gaff-balancer rope on a trisail; **-yi bırakmak** (or **kaçır-mak**) fig. to become confused, to lose one's bearings.

abluka [. x .] blockade; ~ **bölgesi** blockade zone; ~ **etm.** or **-ya almak** to blockade; **-dan kurtarmak** to free s.o. or s.th. from blockade; **-yı kaldır-mak** to raise a blockade; **-yı yarmak** to run a blockade.

abone **1.** subscriber; **2.** subscription; **3.** subscription fee; ~ **bedeli** subscrip-tion fee; ~ **fiyatı** price; ~ **olm.** (bşe) to subscribe (to), to become a sub-scriber (to); ~ **şeraiti** (or **şartları**) terms of subscription; ~ **ücreti** = ~ **be-deli**; **~yi kesmek** to cancel a subscrip-tion.

abonman **1.** subscription; **2.** season ticket (or pass).

aborda [. x .] NAUT alongside; ~ **etm.** to come up alongside (a dock, pier, an-other ship, etc.).

abraş **1.** speckled, dappled, piebald (horse); **2.** having colo(u)rless spots (face, leaf); **3.** leprous.

abraşlamak to become spotted.

abse s. **apse.**

absorbe absorbed; ~ **etm.** **-i** to absorb.

abstrakt, **-tı** s. **abstre.**

abstre abstract; ~ **sayı** MATH abstract number.

abuk sabuk **1.** incoherent, nonsensi-cal; **2.** inconsiderate, rash; ~ **insan** il-logical, incoherent person; ~ **konuş-mak** to talk nonsense, to talk incoher-ently.

abullabut sl. **1.** boorish; **2.** dunce.

abullabutluk sl. boorishness, stupidi-ty.

abur cubur **1.** all sorts of food; **2.** hap-hazard, confused, incongruous; ~ **ye-mek** to eat greedily (without regard to kind or quality).

abus [ū] unfriendly, cross-looking, grim, frowning.

acaba **1.** (in a question) I wonder (if); ~ **gitsem mi?** I wonder if I should go?; ~ **sonu ne olacak?** I wonder what the outcome is going to be?; **2.** (showing disbelief) Indeed!, I wonder!

acaip, **-bi** [. - .] **1.** **acaibisebalâlem** the Seven Wonders of the World; **2.** s.

acayip.

acar **1.** clever, cunning; enterprising; **2.** fearless, bold; **3.** new.

acayip, **-bi** **1.** strange, peculiar, curi-ous; **2.** How strange!, Odd!; (b-nin) **acayibine gitmek** to find s.th. strange.

acele **1.** hurry, haste; **2.** urgent (tele-gram, etc.): **3.** hurriedly, hastily; ~ **etm.** to hasten, to be in a hurry, to hur-ry up; ~ **ile** in a hurry, hastily; ~ **işe şeytan karışır** pro. haste makes waste; haste is the Devil's work; **-si yok** there is no hurry; **-ye boğmak** (bşi) to use haste to cloud or confuse an issue; **-ye gelmek** to be done hast-ily and carelessly; **-ye getirmek 1.** to profit from s.o.'s need for quick ac-tion; **2.** to do s.th. sloppily and hastily.

aceleci hustler, impatient person; al-ways on the go.

acelelestirmek **-i** to hasten, to speed s.th. up.

Acem a Persian; ~ **gömleği** type of shirt, overall; ~ **kılıcı** two-edged sword; ~ **kılıcı gibi** two-faced, double dealing; ~ **mübalağası** excessive ex-aggeration.

Acemce Persian (language).

acemi **1.** untrained, inexperienced, raw; **2.** recruit, beginner; ~ **caylak** F tyro, clumsy person; ~ **er** MIL raw re-cruit; ~ **oğlanı** HIST conscript boy (se-lected to be raised as a Janissary); ~ **öğretmeye vaktim yok** I won't argue with s.o. who doesn't know what he's talking about, I have no time to argue with fools; ~ **şansı** beginner's luck.

acemilik inexperience, lack of experi-ence; ~ **çekmek** to suffer from inexpe-rience.

Acemistan F Persia, Iran.

acenta, acente [. x .] **1.** agent, repre-sentative; **2.** agency.

acentalık, acentelik agency; ~ **etm.** to represent.

acep F s. **acaba.**

aceze pl. of **âciz** the destitute, needy.

acı **1.** bitter, acrid; **2.** hot, peppery; **3.** sharp (taste, smell or flavo(u)r); **4.** painful; **5.** pitiful, pitiable; **6.** pain, ache; **7.** hurtful, biting (words); ~ ~ **bağırmak** to cry out in pain; ~ **bir tees-sürle haber almak** to regret to learn; ~ **çekmek** to suffer, to feel pain; ~ **çiğ-dem** BOT meadow saffron; ~ **damko-**

ruğu BOT bitter houseleek; *~ dil* reproach, bitter words; *~ düleks. acıhıyar*; *~ göl* salt lake; *~ görmüş* undergone suffering; *~ ılgın* BOT bitter tamarisk; *~ kahve* coffee made without sugar; *~ kahve içmek* fig. to invite s.o. to one's home; *~ kök* quassia; *~ manyak* bitter manioc; *~ marul* dandelion; *~ patlıcanı kırağı çalmaz pro.* (*lit.* frost doesn't touch bitter eggplants) ill weeds grow apace, only valuable things get lost; *~ söylemek* to tell the painful truth bluntly; *~ soğuk* bitter cold; *~ su* bitter, brackish water; *~ su sabunu* hard water soap; *~ süt otu* BOT bitter milkwort; *~ yitimi* MED pain killer, analgesia; *-sı tepemden çıktı* I nearly passed out from pain; *-sı yüreğine çıkmak* (*bşin*) to be overcome with grief; *-sını çekmek* to pay the consequence for; *-sını çıkarmak* to get revenge for, to get back at s.o. for s.th.; *-sını koymamak s. acısını çıkarmak.*

acıağaç *-cı* BOT bitter wood, quassia.
acıbadem bitter almond; *~ kurabiyesi* almond cooky.
acıbakla BOT white horse bean.
acıelma BOT colocynth, bitter apple.
acıhıyar BOT **1.** bitter cucumber, colocynth; **2.** squirting cucumber.
acık 1. grief, sorrow, tragedy; **2.** mourning.
acıklı sorrowful, pathetic, tragic, touching; sentimental.
acıklılık mournfulness, grief.
acıkmak to feel (*or* become) hungry; *karnım acıktı* I'm hungry.
acıkmış hungry.
acılanmak, acılaşmak 1. to become bitter, rancid, sour *or* hot; **2.** to become sorry *or* regretful.
acılı 1. spicy, having a bitter taste; **2.** grieved, mourning.
acılık degree of bitterness, spiciness *etc.*
acıma *verbal noun of* **acımak** pity, compassion.
acımak 1. to hurt, to feel pain, to ache; **2.** (*b-ne*) to feel sorry for, to take pity on; **3.** to become bitter, to turn rancid (*butter, oil, etc.*); **4.** to begrudge; *paraya acıyor* he can't bring himself to spend the money.
acımasız cruel, merciless, pitiless.
acımış rancid.
acımsı, acımtırak somewhat bitter.
acınacak pitiable, heart-rending; re-

grettable.
acındırmak to arouse compassion for o.s.
acınmak *-e* to be pitied; to become sorry for, to feel pity for.
acırak *s.* **acımsı.**
acırga BOT horseradish.
acısız 1. painless; **2.** not bitter, without pepper, *etc.*
acıtmak 1. to hurt, to cause pain; **2.** to make s.th. bitter, *etc.*; to make s.th. go sour.
acıyonca BOT bitter clover (*leaves used in certain medicines*).
acibe [ī] strange thing, curiosity.
âcil 1. critical, urgent, requiring immediate attention; **2.** swift; **3.** transitory, fleeting.
âcilen without delay; urgently.
aciz *-czi* **1.** inability; **2.** helplessness; **3.** JUR insolvency; *~ kemiği s. sağrı kemiği.*
âciz weak, incapable, impotent, helpless; *~ kalmak -den* to be incapable of, to be unable to.
âcizane humbly, modestly.
acul, -lü always in a hurry, very impatient.
acun AST cosmos, universe.
acunsal AST cosmic, universal.
acur 1. BOT hairy cucumber; **2.** = *ajur.*
acuze [ū] hag; shrew, vixen.
acyo [x .] agio, premium.
acyocu dealer in agiotage.
acyoculuk agiotage.
aç, -çı 1. hungry; **2.** destitute; **3.** greedy, insatiable; **4.** (*bşe*) hungry (for); *~ ~ ile yatınca arada dilenci doğar* when two hungry people marry a beggar is born; *~ -ına* on a hungry stomach; *~ ayı oynamaz pro.* (*lit.* hungry bears won't dance) if you want s.o. to work you must feed him adequately, a discontented man won't work well; *~ bırakmak* (*or* **koymak**) to starve (*a person*), to let s.o. go hungry, to fail to feed; *~ biilâç* starving, utterly destitute; *~ çıplak* hungry and naked, destitute; *~ doyurmak* to feed the poor (*or* hungry); *~ durmak* to go without food, to do without food; *~ gezmektense tok ölmek yeğdir pro.* it is better to die full than to live hungry; *~ kalmak 1.* not to eat, to go hungry, to be left hungry; *2.* to be poor; *~ karnına* on an empty stomach; *~ kurt aslana saldırır pro.* (*lit.*

a hungry wolf will attack lions.) hunger makes a person desperate; ~ **kurt gibi** *fig.* like a hungry wolf, with overwhelming greed *or* ambition; ~ **susuz** without food and water; ~ **tavuk k-ni arpa ambarında sanır** *pro.* (*lit.* a hungry chicken thinks it's in the barley barn.) wishful thinking; **acından ölmek** to starve to death.

açacak 1. opener; **2.** key; **3.** pencil sharpener.

açalya [. x .] BOT azalea.

açan 1. opener; **2.** ANAT extensor, tensor.

açar 1. key; **2.** aperitif; **3.** appetizer.

açgözlü greedy, covetous, avaricious.

açgözlülük greed; ~ **etm.** to act greedily.

açı 1. MATH angle; **2.** point of view; ~ **uzaklığı** AST visual angle.

açıcı 1. opener; **2.** relieving; **3.** customs inspector.

açık 1. open, not closed; **2.** uncovered; naked, bare; **3.** clear, unoccupied, empty (*space*); **4.** lucid, easy to understand; **5.** unhidden, not secret, in the open; **6.** clear; **7.** light (*colo(u)r*); **8.** obscene; **9.** audible; **10.** blank; **11.** clear, cloudless, fine; **12.** frank(ly), open(ly); **13.** gap; **14.** unobstructed, free; **15.** open for business; **16.** defenseless, unprotected (*city*); **17.** not enclosed; **18.** vacancy; **19.** deficit, shortage; **20.** outskirts; **21.** open sea; **Marmara açıklarında** offshore in the Marmara; **Yeşilköy açıklarında** off Yeşilköy; ~ ~ openly, frankly; ~ ~ **konuşmak** to have a heart-to-heart talk, to talk frankly and freely; ~ **ağızlı** imbecile, stupid; ~ **alınlı** *fig.* with clear conscience; ~ **arazi** open country; ~ **artırma** sale by public auction; ~ **ateş** MIL direct fire; ~ **baş 1.** bare-headed, bald; **2.** *fig.* immoral; ~ **bono** *a. fig.* blank check; ~ **bono vermek** to give (a person) a blank check; ~ **bulundurmak** (*or* **tutmak**) to keep open, to keep free; ~ **ciro** blank endorsement, general endorsement; ~ **deniz** high seas; ~ **denize çıkmak** to enter the high seas; ~ **doru** light chestnut (*horse*); ~ **durmak** to stand aside, not to interfere; ~ **eksiltme** public bidding for a contract; ~ **elli** open-handed, generous; ~ **fikirli** broad-minded, liberal; ~ **ge!** *sl.* **1.** Stand away!; **2.** Come on, out with

it!; ~ **gelmek** *sl.* to stay away, not to come near; ~ **hava 1.** clear weather; **2.** open air, the outdoors; fresh air; ~ **hava tiyatrosu** (**sineması**) open air theatre (cinema); ~ **hava toplantısı** public protest meeting; ~ **hece** open syllable; ~ **imza** signature at the bottom of a blank piece of paper (*given to s.o. who can be trusted*); ~ **kalmak** to stay open; ~ **kalpli** open-hearted, guileless; ~ **kanat** MIL open wing; ~ **kapı** open door; ~ **kapı bırakmak** to leave the door open (*for further opportunities*); ~ **kapı siyaseti** open-door policy; ~ **konuşmak** to talk frankly; ~ **kredi** open credit, blank credit; ~ **liman 1.** unprotected port; **2.** free port; **3.** port subject to bad weather conditions; ~ **maaş** half pay (*given to an official who has been temporarily removed from office*); ~ **mavi** light-blue; ~ **mektup** open letter; ~ **mevzi** MIL exposed position; ~ **mukavele** open agreement; ~ **ordugâh** bivouac; ~ **oturum** panel discussion; ~ **oy** open vote; ~ **öz tok söz** *fig.* pure and honest; ~ **saçık** indecent, immodest, obscene; ~ **saçık gezmek** to move about too freely, too openly (*of a woman*); ~ **saçık yayın** pornography; ~ **seçik** distinct, clear; ~ **söylemek** to speak openly, to speak frankly, to speak without leaving anything unclear; ~ **şehir** MIL open city; ~ **şehir ilân etm.** to declare to be an open city; ~ **teşekkür** public acknowledgement, public thanks; ~ **vermek 1.** to show a deficit; **2.** to lay o.s. open to criticism; ~ **vicdanla** with free conscience; ~ **yer** vacancy; ~ **yürekle** without concealing anything, without deception; ~ **yürekli** sincere, openhearted; ~ **yüzlü** fair-faced, with an honest face, undeceitful; ~ **zincir serisi** CHEM aliphatic molecular structure; (**açığa**): ~ **çıkarmak 1.** to remove (*or* fire) from a government office; **2.** to bring out into the open; ~ **çıkmak 1.** to be removed from office; **2.** to become known, to be revealed; ~ **satış** public sale; ~ **vermek** (*or* **vurmak**) to reveal, to disclose; ~ **vurmak** to become apparent; **açığı çıkmak** to have a deficit; **açığı kapatmak 1.** to get rid of a deficit; **2.** to close a gap; **açıklar livası** *co.* brigade of the unemployed; (**açıkta**): **1.** in the open air, outdoors, exposed;

2. in the offing, offshore; **3.** unemployed; **~ bırakmak 1.** to leave s.o. without home *or* employment; **2.** to leave s.th. out in the open; **3.** to leave out, to exclude (*a person from a privilege*); **~ kalmak 1.** to be without home *or* employment; **2.** to be exposed to the elements; **3.** to be left out (*of a generally provided benefit*); **4.** to be left outside; **~ olm. s. ~ kalmak; ~ yatmak** to camp out; (**açıktan**): **1.** from a distance; **2.** additional, extra; **3.** without having worked for it; **~ açığa** openly, frankly, publicly; **~ para kazanmak** to get a windfall, to get an unearned and unexpected addition to one's income; **~ satış** short sale; **~ tayin edilmek** (*or* **atanmak**) to be transferred from outside an organization, *etc.*

açıkça [. x .] openly, without concealment, clearly; **-sı** in plain words, in short, frankly speaking, to tell the truth.

açıkçı short seller, bear (*on the Stock Market*).

açıkgöz(lü) 1. sharp, cunning, clever; **2.** trickster.

açıkgöz(lü)lük slyness, cunning, trickery; **~ etm.** to be shrewd, to jump at an opportunity.

açıklama 1. explanation, statement; **2.** disclosure; **3.** announcement; commentary.

açıklamak 1. to explain; **2.** to disclose, to reveal; **3.** to announce, to make public.

açıklayıcı explanatory.

açıklı: ~ koyulu with light and dark colo(u)rs.

açıklık 1. being open, free *or* clear; **2.** opening, aperture; **3.** nakedness, nudity, indecency; **4.** lightness (*of colo(u)r*); **5.** degree of articulation *or* comprehensibility; **6.** space, gap, distance, open space; **7.** AST azimuth.

açıkmeşrep, -bi overfree, licentious.

açıksözlü frank, outspoken.

açılama *cinema*: shooting a scene from several angles.

açılır kapanır collapsible, folding; **~ geçit parmaklığı** roadway barrier; **~ köprü** drawbridge; swing bridge.

açılış 1. opening; **2.** inauguration; **~ töreni** opening ceremony.

açılma 1. MIL deployment; **2.** = **açılış**.

açılmadık unopened; **örtüsü ~ sırlar**

deep secrets; **yakası ~ küfürler** heavy curses; **yakası ~ usuller** completely untried methods.

açılmak 1. *pass. of* **açmak; 2.** to open, to open up; **3.** to become clear, to improve (*of the weather, etc.*); **4.** to open out (*-e* into); **5.** to bloom; **6.** to become relaxed, to be at ease; **7.** (*b-ne*) to confide (**in** *s.o.*); **8.** to become wider, etc.; **9.** to become vacant, empty, etc.; **10.** to cheer up; **11.** to cast off, to set sail, to put to sea; **açılıp saçılmak** to be immodestly dressed.

açıölçer protractor.

açısal angular.

açış opening, inauguration.

açkı 1. burnishing; **2.** smith's tool for widening a hole; **3.** key.

açkıcı 1. polisher; burnisher; **2.** key maker.

açkılamak to polish; to burnish.

açkılı polished, glossy.

açlık 1. hunger; **2.** famine; **3.** poverty; **~ grevi** hunger strike; **-tan kırılmak** to be starving, to be dying of hunger; **-tan nefesi kokmak** to be poverty-stricken.

açma 1. opening; **2.** clearing; **3.** kind of pastry.

açmak 1. to open; **2.** to construct and open (*a road, etc.*); **3.** to draw aside, to lift (*a covering, etc.*); **4.** to open out, to unfold; **5.** to set (*a sail*); **6.** to unfurl (*a flag*); **7.** to uncover; **8.** to roll out; **9.** to undo, to untie (*a knot, etc.*); **10.** to unlock; **11.** to turn on (*switch, light, radio, etc.*); **12.** to widen (*the space between*); **13.** to explain fully; **14.** to begin, to open (*a meeting, a conversation, etc.*); **15.** to disclose; **16.** to make lighter (*colo(u)r*); **17.** to suit, to go well with; **18.** to whet, to sharpen (*one's appetite*); **19.** to open (*flower*); **20.** to clear up (*weather*); **açtı ağzını yumdu gözünü** he became angry and started cursing wildly, he spoke without reflection.

açmaz 1. will not open; **2.** secretive; **3.** difficult position, impasse, dilemma; **4.** *chess*: pin: **-a düşmek** (*or* **gelmek**) to fall into an impasse; **-a getirmek** to dupe, to entrap, to deceive.

açmazlık 1. difficulty; **2.** secrecy.

ad¹, -dı 1. name; **2.** first name; **3.** reputation, fame; **~ almak** to become well-known; **~ koymak** (*or* **vermek**) to name, to give a name (*-e* to); **~ tak-**

mak to nickname, to give a nickname (*-e* to); (adı) ~ *batası* (*or* *batsın*)! damn!, (may he) be damned!; ~ *batmak* to become unknown, to pass into oblivion; ~ *belirsiz* unknown, obscure; ~ *bile okunamamak* to be a nobody, to be insignificant; ~ *bozulmak* to lose one's reputation; ~ *çıkmak* 1. to get a bad name, to become notorious; 2. to become noted; ~ *geçen* above mentioned, the aforesaid; ~ *sanı* one's name and reputation; ~ *şimdi dilime gelmiyor* I can't remember his name for the moment; ~ *üstünde* its name makes everything clear; *adını çıkarmak* to discredit, to bring into discredit; *adını koymak* co. set the price (*-in* of); *adını vermek* 1. *fig*. to broadcast, to advertise, to spread around; 2. to name *s.o.* or s.th.; *adiyle saniyle* s. *adlı sanlı*.

ad², *-ddi* estimation, esteeming, deeming, considering, *s. a.* **addetmek**.

ada 1. island; 2. ward of town, etc.; 3. lot, plot of land; city block; ~ *gibi* very large (*ship*).

adabalığı, *-nı* zoo tench.

adabımuaşeret, *-ti* [- - . . - - . .] etiquette, rules of good behavio(u)r.

adacık islet.

adaçayı, *-nı* BOT garden sage; ~ *tütsüsü* 1. fumigation with garden sage; 2. inhaling the vapo(u)rs of garden sage.

adadiyoz *sl*. shabby, ragged.

adak 1. vow; 2. votive offering.

Adalardenizi s. *Ege denizi*.

adale ANAT muscle.

adaleli muscular.

adalet, *-ti* [. - .] 1. justice; 2. the courts; 3. equity; fairness; righteousness; ♀ *Bakanı* Minister of Justice; ♀ *Bakanlığı* Ministry of Justice; ♀ *Divanı* the International Court of Justice; *-in pençesi* *fig*. the long arm of the Law.

adaletli just, fair.

adaletsiz unjust, unfair.

adaletsizlik injustice.

adalı islander.

Adalı Aegean islander.

adalı [ī] muscular.

adam 1. man; 2. human being; 3. person, individual; 4. a brave, capable, good, *etc*. person; 5. man-servant, employee, worker; 6. minion; 7. partisan; 8. agent; 9. all, everyone; 10. P husband, man; ~ *başına* per person, apiece, each; ~ *boyu* a man's height;

~ *etm*. 1. to make a man of; 2. to raise well; 3. to turn into s.th. useful or good, to set s.th. in order; ~ *evlâdı* well-bred, a person of good family; ~ *gibi* 1. manly, like a man; 2. correctly, properly; ~ *içine gitmek* (*or* *çıkmak*) to mix with important people; ~ *kaldırmak* JUR to kidnap, to abduct; ~ *öldürme* JUR homicide, manslaughter; ~ *sarrafı* a good judge of character; ~ *sen de!*, come off it!, don't worry!; ~ *sırasına geçmek* (*or* *girmek*) to become an important person; ~ *yerine koymak* to count as important or of consequence; *-dan saymak* not to disregard; s. ~ *yerine koymak*.

adamak 1. to devote, to vow, to promise; 2. to dedicate o.s. (*-e* to); *-la mal tükenmez* pro. it costs nothing to make a promise.

adamakıllı 1. proper, duly, as required; 2. thorough(ly).

adamcağız 1. good fellow; 2. poor chap.

adamlık humanness, humanity.

adamsendecilik indifference, callousness.

adamsız 1. alone, without help; 2. without servants; ~ *kalmak* to be without servants or help.

adamsızlık 1. lack of good help or servants; 2. lack of protection.

adap, *-bı* (*pl. of edep*) 1. regular customs; 2. accepted ways; ~ *erkân* customary practice or observance; *adaba aykırı* contrary to rules of accepted ways; *adabı umumiye* public morals.

adaptasyon 1. adaptation (*of a play, novel, etc.*); 2. an adapted work.

adapte adapted (*novel or play*); ~ *etm*. to adapt, to make an adaptation.

adasoğanı, *-nı* BOT squill, sea onion.

adaş namesake, person sharing the same proper name.

adatavşanı, *-nı* European rabbit, cony.

aday candidate, nominee; ~ *adayı* candidate for nomination.

adaylık candidacy.

adçekme 1. drawing of lots; 2. drawing straws.

addetmek [x . .] to count, to enumerate; to esteem.

adem 1. non-existence, nothingness; 2. lack, absence; *-i emniyet* insecurity; *-i kabiliyet* inability; *-i tecavüz* non-aggression.

Âdem *pr. n.* Adam; ~ **elması** Adam's apple; ~ **evladı** (*or* **oğlu**) man, mankind, human being.

Aden *pr. n.* Eden; **cenneti** ~ the garden of Eden; paradise.

adese 1. lens; **2.** lenticel.

adet 1. number; **2.** unit.

âdet, -ti 1. custom, practice; **2.** habit; **3.** menstrual period; ~ **bezi** (*or* **bağı**) hygienic pad; ~ **budur en sonra gelir bezme ekâbir** custom precedes all; ~ **çıkarmak** to start a new custom; ~ **edinmek** to form a habit (*-i* of); ~ **görmek** to menstruate; ~ **üzere** according to custom; ~ **yerini bulsun diye** for the sake of custom; *-ten kesilmek* to reach menopause.

adeta [x . -] **1.** nearly, almost; **2.** simply, merely; **3.** rather, sort of; ~**!** walk! (*riding command*).

adetçe in number.

adıl pronoun.

adım 1. step; **2.** pace; **3.** *fig.* step; ~ **açmak** to increase the pace; ~ ~ step by step; ~ **atmak** to take the first step, to begin; ~ **başın(d)a 1.** at every step; **2.** everywhere; ~ **uydurmak** to follow the example (*-e* of).

adımlamak 1. to pace off; **2.** to measure by pacing.

adımlık pace, distance; **üç** ~ a distance of three paces.

adi [- -] **1.** customary, usual; **2.** ordinary, common; **3.** vulgar, base, low, mean, ornery; ~ **adım** MIL break step; ~ **hisse senedi** common stock; ~ **iflas** JUR non-fraudulent bankruptcy; ~ **itiraz** JUR simple objection; ~ **mektup** ordinary letter; ~ **suç** ordinary crime; ~ **şirket** (*or* **ortaklık**) JUR unincorporated association.

adilik vulgarity, baseness.

âdil just, dealing justly.

âdilâne [- . - .] justly, equitably.

adlandırma 1. naming; **2.** classification.

adlandırmak 1. to name; **2.** to rate, to classify.

adlanmak 1. to be named; **2.** to become famous, to get a bad reputation.

adlı 1. with the name of; named; **2.** famous; ~ **sanlı** well-known, famous, celebrated.

adli [î] judicial, legal; ~ **hata** legal error; ~ **sicil** record of previous convictions; ~ **subay** provost marshal; ~ **tıp**

forensic medicine; ~ **yıl** court year.

adliye 1. (administration of) justice; court system; **2.** courthouse; ♀ **Vekâleti** *s.* **Adalet Bakanlığı**; ~ **mahkemeleri** JUR ordinary courts of justice; ~ **sarayı** courthouse; *-nin pençesi* *s.* **adaletin pençesi.**

adliyeci specialist in judicial affairs; a legal authority.

adrenalin adrenalin.

adres address; ~ **rehberi** directory, address book; ~ **sahibi** addressee.

Adriyatik (Denizi) *pr. n.* Adriatic (Sea).

adsız 1. nameless; **2.** unknown, obscure.

adsızparmak ring finger.

aerodinamik 1. aerodynamics; **2.** aerodynamic; ~ **biçim** streamlined.

af, -ffı 1. pardon, forgiving, forgiveness; **2.** amnesty; **3.** exemption; **4.** discharge of obligation, etc.; **5.** liquidation of a debt; ~ **dilemek** to beg pardon, to apologize; **affı umumi** *s.* **umumi af.**

afacan rascal, urchin, wild or restless child.

afakan boredom; *-lar basmak* to be severely depressed.

afaki [- - -] **1.** objective; **2.** superficial.

afal 1. stupid; **2.** startled; ~ ~ **bakmak 1.** to look stupidly; **2.** to look startled.

afallamak, afallaşmak to be amazed, to be taken aback, to be disconcerted, to be bewildered.

aferin [ā] [x . .] congratulations!, bravo!, well done!, very good!; ~ **almak** to receive hono(u)rable mention.

afet, -ti 1. calamity, disaster, catastrophe; **2.** F bewitching person; **3.** MED tissue damage; ~ **gibi** very beautiful (*woman*).

afetzede victim of a disaster.

affetmek [x . .] **1.** to pardon, to excuse, to forgive; **2.** to exempt (*-den* from); **3.** to release (*from an obligation, etc.*); **affedersiniz!** I beg your pardon!, excuse me!

affolunmaz inexcusable, unpardonable.

Afgan *pr. n.* Afghan.

Afganistan *pr. n.* Afghanistan.

Afganlı *pr. n.* Afghani, from Afghanistan.

afif [. -] chaste, uncorrupted.

afili *sl.* swaggering, showy.

afiş poster, placard, bill.

afişe etmek to make a public spectacle (-*i* of).

afiyet, -ti [ā] **1.** good health, well-being; **2.** appetite; ∼**(ler) olsun!** I hope you enjoy it, good appetite! (*said when offering food to s.o.*).

afiyetlemek to wish s.o. a good appetite.

aforoz excommunication; ∼ *etm.* **1.** to excommunicate; **2.** *fig.* to put on ice, to relegate to the background.

aforozlamak s. *aforoz etm.*

aforozlu 1. excommunicated; **2.** *fig.* shelved.

Afrika *pr. n.* Africa.

Afrikalı *pr. n.* African.

afsun [ū] spell, charm, incantation.

afsuncu spellmaster, charmer, magic user.

afsunculuk spell-weaving, witchcraft, sorcery.

afsunlamak to bewitch, to charm, to enchant.

afsunlu charmed, enchanted, bewitched.

afyon 1. opium; **2.** ♀ *Karahisar city in Western Anatolia*, ∼ *ruhu* tincture of opium.

afyonkeş opium addict.

afyonkeşlik opium addiction.

afyonlu (*a. fig.*) containing opium.

agâh 1. informed, aware; **2.** vigilant, on guard; ∼ *etm.* to put on guard, to inform, to make aware.

agrandisman PHOT enlargement.

agrandisör PHOT enlarger.

agreman agreement.

agu *term of endearment used towards babies;* ∼ *bebek* darling child.

agucuk s. *agu.*

agulamak to make baby-like noises.

ağ 1. net (*a. fig.*); **2.** tailoring gore, gusset; **3.** network; **4.** (*spider's*) web; -*lar* the nets (*behind the goal in soccer*).

ağa 1. lord, master, chief, boss, landowner; **2.** = -*bey;* **3.** Mister (*used after a proper name when addressing an old and/or illiterate person*).

ağababa 1. *familiar term used to address an old man;* **2.** grandfather, oldest man in the family.

ağabey [=bi] **1.** older brother; **2.** *familiar term of respect used to address any male somewhat older than o.s.*

ağaç, -cı 1. tree; **2.** shrub; **3.** timber, wood; **4.** wooden support, pillar, piece, part, etc.; **5.** wooden; ∼ *çivi*

peg; ∼ *kabuğu* bark; ∼ *kaplama* wooden wainscoting; ∼ *kova* wooden bucket; ∼ *kovuğu* hollow of a tree; ∼ *kurdu* wood borer; ∼ *olmak* sl. to stand and wait a long time; ∼ *oyma* wood carving; ∼ *sıpa* wood(en) horse; ∼ *tıpa* wooden dowel, peg, stopper; ∼ *tokmak* wooden hammer; ∼ *yaş iken eğilir pro.* you cannot teach an old dog new tricks.

ağaçbiti, -ni ZOO termite.

ağaççileği, -ni BOT raspberry.

ağaçkakan ZOO woodpecker.

ağaçkavunu, -nu BOT citron.

ağaçlamak 1. to afforest, to plant trees in an area; **2.** to cover with timber.

ağaçlı having trees, wooded.

ağaçlık 1. clump of trees; **2.** woods; -*lı* wooded, forested.

ağalanmak to lord it over, to become overweening.

ağalık 1. being an *ağa;* **2.** generosity, nobility; **3.** pride, conceit; **4.** territory of an *ağa.*

ağarmak 1. to get bleached, to whiten; **2.** to become visible in the distance; **3.** to dawn.

ağartı 1. barely visible shadow in the darkness; **2.** milk product.

ağartmak 1. to make s.th. become gray, pale, white, etc.; **2.** to bleach, to blanch.

ağda 1. semi-solid sweet, syrup; **2.** epilating wax; ∼ *kullanmak* (or *yapıştırmak*) to use *ağda* to remove hair from the skin.

ağdalanmak, ağdalaşmak 1. to become thick, to begin to thicken; **2.** *fig.* to become heavy, slow, cumbersome, pompous.

ağdalı 1. thick as a syrup; **2.** *fig.* heavy, pompous, bombastic.

ağı poison, venom.

ağıl 1. pen, sheep fold; **2.** halo.

ağılamak to poison.

ağıllanmak 1. to be put in a pen or fold; **2.** to be surrounded by a halo (*moon*).

ağım instep.

ağımlı high in the instep.

ağır 1. heavy; **2.** heavy, difficult (*work*); **3.** significant; **4.** weighty; **5.** difficult, troublesome; **6.** serious, grave (*sickness*); **7.** difficult to digest, rich, heavy (*food*); **8.** unfavo(u)rable, unhealthy (*climate*); **9.** unpleasant, disagreeable; **10.** offensive, painful; **11.** slow, indolent; **12.** slowly-moving; **13.** stuffy; smelly; **14.** valuable, precious; ~ ~ **1.** slowly; **2.** (*to weigh*) at the very most; ~ **almak** (*bir işi*) to work slowly; ~ **basmak 1.** to have influence; **2.** (*b-ni*) to give nightmares (**to**), to oppress; **3.** to be heavy; **4.** to be important, to have priority; ~ **canlı** phlegmatic, lazy, inactive; ~ **ceza** JUR major punishment; ~ **ceza işleri** JUR indictable offenses; ~ **ceza mahkemesi** JUR criminal court for major cases; ~ **davranmak 1.** to react slowly; **2.** to move slowly; ~ **ezgi, fıstıki makam** F **1.** slowly and surely; **2.** ponderously; ~ **gelmek 1.** to be difficult to bear; **2.** to offend, to hurt; **3.** to be difficult to digest; ~ **hapis** imprisonment for five years or more; ~ **hastalık** heavy illness, serious disease; ~ **hava 1.** unwholesome climate; **2.** slow or sad melody; **3.** kind of slow folk dance; ~ **hıyanet** JUR high treason; ~ **ihmal** (*or* **kusur**) JUR gross negligence; ~ **iş** hard work; ~ **işitmek** (*a fig.*) to be hard of hearing; ~ **kazan geç kaynar** *pro.* important things take time; ~ **makineli tüfek** MIL heavy machine gun; ~ **ol! 1.** slow down!, take it easy!, calm down! **2.** get serious!; ~ **oturmak** *fig.* to behave with dignity, to be costly; ~ **sanayi** heavy industry; ~ **satmak** (*k-ni*) to emphasize one's own importance; ~ **sıklet** *boxing:* heavy weight; ~ **söz** harsh words; ~ **takımdan** F distinguished, aristocratic: ~ **tutmak** *fig.* to be unwilling (to do): ~ **yaralı** seriously wounded, gravely injured.

ağırayak pregnant, with child; about to give birth.

ağırbaşlı 1. prudent; **2.** deserving; **3.** sedate, staid; **4.** respectable; **5.** virtuous (*woman or girl*).

ağırkanlı 1. slow, lazy, indolent; **2.** numbed, insensate.

ağırküre barysphere.

ağırlamak 1. to slacken, to slow down; **2.** to treat (*a guest*) well, to show hospitality.

ağırlaşmak 1. to become heavy; **2.** to become important; **3.** to become serious (*illness*); **4.** to slow down; **5.** *to* spoil (*food*); **6.** to get harder, to become more difficult.

ağırlaştırmak *caus.* of **ağırlaşmak**; **ağırlaştıran sebepler** (*or* **nedenler**) JUR grievous circumstances.

ağırlık 1. weight, heaviness; **2.** significance, importance; **3.** prudence; **4.** respectability; **5.** difficulty; **6.** slowness (*of motion or action*); **7.** indigestibility; **8.** oppressiveness (*of the weather*); **9.** drowsiness, lethargy; **10.** burden, responsibility; **11.** severity (*of a disease*); **12.** baggage, luggage; **13.** MIL munitions, supplies; **14.** nightmare; **15.** dowry; ~ **merkezi** PHYS center of gravity; **ağırlığınca altın değmek** to be worth its weight in gold; **üzerime** ~ **bastı 1.** I had a nightmare; **2.** I felt sleepy; **3.** I felt uncomfortable.

ağırşak 1. disk; **2.** bobbin; **3.** round and/or swollen thing; ~ **kemiği** kneecap.

ağıt 1. dirge, funeral song; **2.** wailing, lamentation; ~ **yakmak** to lament for the dead, to wail.

ağız, -ğzı 1. mouth; **2.** snout, muzzle; **3.** bill, beak; **4.** nozzle; **5.** opening; **6.** entrance; **7.** beginning; **8.** outlet; **9.** first thick milk (*at birth*); **10.** edge, blade (*of a knife, etc.*); **11.** crossing point, corner (*of roads*); **12.** local style (*of music*); **13.** accent; **14.** dialect; **15.** MUS key; **16.** time; **17.** *mst pl.* (**-lar**) gossip; **18.** flattery; **19.** rim, brink; ~ **açmak 1.** to open one's mouth; **2.** to abuse; **3.** to gape with astonishment; ~ **açmamak 1.** not to open one's mouth; **2.** to stay without saying a word; ~ **ağıza dolu** completely full; ~ **ağıza vermek** to whisper privately; ~ **aramak** (*or* **yoklamak**) **1.** to get opinions; **2.** to learn intentions; ~ **armonikası** harmonica; ~ **atmak** to brag, to boast; ~ **dalaşı** bickering, quarrel; ~ **değiştirmek 1.** MUS to change key; **2.** to change one's tune; ~ **dolusu 1.** mouthful; **2.** at the top of one's voice; ~ **dolusu küfür** unrestrained swearing; ~ **etm. 1.** to speak out freely; **2.** to try to persuade; **3.** to make boastful speeches; ~ **kavafı** troublesome chatterbox, one who overinsists with much talking; ~ **kavgası** = ~ **dalaşı**; ~ **sakızı** *fig.* endless chatter; ~ **suyu** saliva, spittle; ~ **şakası** joke; ~ **tadı** *fig.* enjoyment, pleasure, harmony; ~ **tadı ile 1.** with enjoyment; **2.** enjoying the flavo(u)r; **-dan kapmak 1.** to elicit a secret; **2.** to overhear; **-dan kulağa söylemek** to whisper; **-dan sakız avlamak** *fig.* to sound out (*a person's opinion*); *-larda bir parmak bal olm.* to be talked about; (ağza): ~ *alınmaz* 1. uneatable; 2. unspeakable, obscene, very vulgar; ~ *almak* to mention; ~ *düşmek* to be talked about, to be a subject of common gossip; (ağzı): ~ *açık* 1. startled; 2. stupid, idiotic; 3. open, without a cover; ~ *bir* all telling the same story; ~ *bozuk* foulmouthed; vituperative; ~ *büyük* boastful, bragging; ~ *gevşek* chatterbox; indiscreet; ~ *havada* 1. proud; 2. exorbitant; 3. thoughtless, negligent; ~ *ile aslan tuttuğunu söylemek* to be an unbearable chatterbox; ~ *ile kuş tutmak* to be very capable; ~ *örtülü küp* covered clay pitcher; ~ *pis* foulmouthed; ~ *sıkı* untalkative, secretive; ~ *sulandı* his mouth watered; ~ *süt kokuyor* *fig.* he's still wet behind the ears; ~ *teneke kaplı* *fig.* his mouth is insensitive to hot food, *etc.*; ~ *var dili yok* close mouthed; ~ *varmak* (*bşi söylemeğe*) to bring o.s. to say; (ağzına): ~ *bakmak* (*b-nin*) 1. to hang on s.o.'s words; 2. to wait to see what s.o. will say; 3. to act according to s.o.'s instruction; ~ *bir parmak bal çalmak* 1. to put off with sweet words; 2. to speak with tongue in cheek; ~ *kedi ciğere bakar gibi bakıp dinlemek* (*b-nin*) to hang on s.o.'s every word (*like a cat with its eye on a piece of liver*); ~ *layık* delicious; first-class; (ağzında): ~ *bakla ıslanmaz* (*or baklayı* ~ *ıslatmaz*) he can't keep a secret; ~ *gevelemek* (*lakırdıyı, sözü lafı*) to beat around the bush; (ağzından): ~ *baklayı çıkarmak* to say what's really on one's mind, to let the cat out of the bag; ~ *çıkanı kulağı işitmemek* *fig.* not to even hear what he's saying, to speak without listening to himself; (ağzını): ~ *açmak* 1. to begin to speak; 2. to begin to swear; ~ *aramak* (*or yoklamak*) to collect opinions; ~ *bıçak açmıyor* uncommunicative; ~ *bozmak* to start to swear; ~ *havaya* (*or poyraza*) *açmak* to be cut out, to be left out, to be left empty-handed; ~ *hayra aç!* speak no evil!; ~ *kapamak* 1. to shut up; 2. to pay not to talk; 3. to cover up, to conceal; ~ *öpeylm* (*or seveyim*)*!* well-said!; ~ *silmek* 1. to wipe one's mouth; 2. to shut up; ~ *tıkamak* 1. to stop up the mouth;

2. to keep one from speaking; ~ *tutmak* 1. to keep one's piece; 2. to avoid saying s.th. bad; ~ *yormak* to waste time talking; (ağzının): ~ *içine bakmak* (*b-nin*) to hang on *s.o.'s* every word; ~ *suyu akıyor* he wants s.th. very badly, his mouth is watering; ~ *suyunu akıtmak* to make one's mouth water; ~ *tadını almak* (*bşden*) to have a bad experience; ~ *tadını bilmek* to know what one likes; to be a gourmet; ~ *tadını bozmak* to spoil the enjoyment (*-in* of); *ağzınızdan çıkanı kulaklarınız işitsin!* mind what you say!; *ağzınızı değiştiriniz!* I won't have that!; *ağzınızı düzeltiniz!* I won't listen to that kind of talk; *ağzınla kuş tutsan bile nafile!* even if you do the impossible, it's useless!

ağızbirliği, -ni agreement on what is to be said.

ağızboşluğu, -nu mouth cavity.

ağızlık 1. cigarette holder; 2. mouthpiece (*of a pipe, instrument, etc.*); 3. muzzle; 4. cover of leaves (*over a basket of fruit*); 5. circle of stones at the top of a well; 6. funnel.

ağızsız submissive, docile.

ağkepçe landing net

ağlamak 1. to cry, to weep; 2. to grieve; 3. to complain, to whine; 4. (*sap in trees*) to rise, to flow; *ağlamayan çocuğa meme vermezler* pro (*lit.* the baby who doesn't cry isn't fed) the squeaking wheel gets the grease.

ağlama(k)lı tearful, ready to cry.

ağlaşmak 1. to weep together; 2. to cry continuously.

ağnam [. -] flocks; ~ *vergisi* JUR sheep tax.

ağrı 1. ache, pain; 2. travail.

Ağrıdağı, -nı *pr. n.* Mount Ararat.

ağrı(k)lı diseased; painful.

ağrımak to ache, to hurt.

ağrısız painless; without pain.

ağsı BIOL netlike.

ağtabaka retina.

ağucuk *s.* agucuk.

ağustos August; ~ *gülü* BOT dog-rose; *-ta suya girse balta kesmez buz olur* pro. he's very unlucky, he's always unfortunate.

ağustosböceği, -ni ZOO cicada.

ağyar [. -] others, strangers.

ağzıpek discreet, rather silent.

ah 1. Ah!, Oh!, Alas!; 2. sigh, groan; 3. complaint; 4. curse; ~ *almak* to be cursed for one's cruelty; ~ **çekmek** to sigh; **-a gelmek** (or **uğramak**) **1.** = ~ **almak**; **2.** to suffer retribution; **-ı çıkmak** (for one's curse) to take effect; **-ı yerde kalmamak** to have one's curse take effect; **-ı tutuyor** (b-ne) for one's curse to be realized (against another).

aha P here, there.

ahali [. - .] **1.** inhabitant(s); **2.** population; **3.** public; ~ **mübadelesi** exchange of populations.

âhar obs. different.

ahbap, -bı 1. acquaintance; friend; **2.** My friend! (used to attract the attention of a person); ~ **çavuşlar** co. inseparable friends, pals.

ahbaplaşmak 1. to become friendly; **2.** to chum up to.

ahbaplık friendship, acquaintance.

ahçı 1. cook; **2.** proprietor of a small restaurant; **3.** HIST title of a janissary chief; ~ **baltası** cleaver; ~ **dükkânı** low-class restaurant; ~ **kadın** female cook; ~ **yamağı** cook's assistance, kitchen boy.

ahçılık 1. cooking; **2.** profession of being a cook; ~ **etm.** to work as a cook.

ahdetmek [x . .] to swear an oath, to undertake, to promise o.s.

ahenk, -gi [ā] **1.** MUS harmony; **2.** concord, accord; **3.** musical gathering (of oriental music); **4.** GR agreement; ~ **kaidesi** vowel harmony (in Turkish phonetics); ~ **tahtası** sounding board (on a stringed instrument).

ahenkli [ā] **1.** MUS in tune; **2.** in unison; **3.** good-natured.

ahenksiz [ā] **1.** MUS out of tune; **2.** inharmonious, discordant.

aheste slow; calm.

ahfeş: -in keçisi gibi ne söyleseler başını sallar he agrees with everything that s.o. says.

ahım şahım 1. beautiful, bright; **2.** fig. conspicuous

ahır stable, shed, barn; ~ **gibi** filthy and confused (place); **-a çekmek** to lead to stable; **-a çevirmek** to mess up.

âhir last; final; latter; ~ **vakit** last days of one's life.

ahiren [ī] obs. **1.** lastly; **2.** recently.

ahit, -hdi 1. vow, resolution; **2.** agreement, pact, treaty; contract; **3.** period, era.

ahitleşmek to enter into solemn agreement.

ahiz, -hzi obs. **1.** receiving; **2.** reception; ~ **kabiliyeti** reception sensitivity.

ahize receiver.

ahkâm (pl. of **hüküm**) judg(e)ments; dispositions; laws; inferences; ~ **çıkarmak** to draw arbitrary conclusions, to put forward absurd suppositions; ~ **kesmek** to make judg(e)ments without restraint; **ahkâmı cezaiye** (kanunu) obs. Criminal Law; **ahkâmı şahsiye** JUR personal statute.

ahlak, -kı (pl. of **hulk**) **1.** morals; **2.** PHLS ethics; **3.** character; ~ **düşkünlüğü** moral lapse; ~ **hocalığı** etm. to be a teacher of ethics; ~ **âdap** JUR good morals.

ahlakçı 1. moralist; **2.** teacher of ethics.

ahlakî [ī] moral, ethical; pertaining to morals; ~ **zabıta** Morals Squad (police).

ahlaklı of good conduct, decent.

ahlaksız 1. immoral; **2.** unethical; **3.** amoral, asocial.

ahlamak to sigh, to moan.

ahlat, -tı BOT wild pear; ~ **ağa** boor, fool; **-ın** (or **armudun**) **iyisini ayı yer** pro. (lit. the best pears are eaten by bears) the best things fall to those who don't deserve them.

ahmak fool, idiot; ~ **ıslatan** F fine drizzle.

ahret, -ti the next world, the future life; ~ **evi** the other world; ~ **suali sormak** (b-ne) F to ask endless questions, to cross-examine; **-i boylamak** sl. to kick the bucket; **-te on parmağım yakasında olacak** I'll get even if it's in the next world.

ahretlik 1. adopted girl; **2.** otherworldly.

ahşap, -bı 1. wooden; **2.** made of wood.

ahtapot, -tu 1. ZOO octopus; **2.** MED polyp, cancerous ulcer; **3.** sl. parasite, sponger.

ahu [- -] ZOO gazelle.

ahubaba 1. ghost; **2.** talkative old man.

ahududu, -nu BOT raspberry.

ahval, -li [. -] **1.** conditions, circumstances; **2.** incidents, affairs, events, occurrences; **ahvali şahsiye** JUR personal circumstances.

aidat, -tı [- . -] subscription, membership fee; contribution; allowance.

aile 1. family; **2.** F wife; **3.** grouping of people; **4.** grouping by language, culture, etc.; **5.** animal or plant grouping; ~ *efradı* members of a family; ~ *malları* family property; ~ *reisi* head of the family; ~ *sofrası* family table; ~ *terbiyesi* fig. well-bred.

ailevî [- . . .-] regarding the family, domestic.

ait, -di 1. concerning, relating to; belonging to, pertaining to; **2.** descended from.

ajan 1. (political) agent; **2.** (commercial) agent, representative; **3.** political representative.

ajanda date book, engagement calendar.

ajans 1. press agency; **2.** press release; **3.** branch office (*of a bank*); ~ *bülteni* news bulletin.

ajur 1. mesh, hemstitch; **2.** embroidery frame.

ajurlu 1. with an embroidered edge; **2.** embroidered (*stocking*).

ak, -kı 1. white; **2.** clear, unspotted; **3.** white spot; ~ *akçe kara gün içindir* pro. save for a rainy day; ~ *arap* white Arabian (*horse*); ~ *babaya dönmek* to become entirely white; ~ *bıyık* fig. advanced in years, old; ~ *düşmek* (*saça, sakala*) gradually to become gray or white (*hair, beard*); ~ *pak* **1.** completely clean; **2.** aged; ~ *yüz ile* successfully and hono(u)rably; ~ *karayı seçememek* to be unable to tell black from white, to have no intelligence at all.

akabinde immediately after.

akademi 1. academy; **2.** picture made from a live nude model.

akademik 1. academic; **2.** in the form of an academy.

akademisyen member of an academy.

akağaç (white) birch.

akaju acajou.

akala a hybrid cotton developed in Turkey.

akamet, -ti [. - .] **1.** sterility; **2.** failure; *-e uğramak* to fail.

akanyıldız AST meteor.

akar[1] [. -] rental property, real estate.

akar[2] flowing, fluid, liquid; ~ *amber* **1.** BOT amber-tree; **2.** liquid ambergris; **3.** solution of musk; ~ *ı (yok), kokarı yok!* F completely blameless!

akarat, -tı, akaret, -ti [. - .] property rented out and bringing income.

akarsu 1. GEOGR flowing stream; **2.** wa-

tercourse; **3.** single strand pearl or diamond necklace; ~ *pis tutmaz* pro. water under the bridge.

akaryakıt, -tı fuel oil.

akasma BOT white bryony.

akasya [. x .] BOT **1.** acacia; **2.** locust.

akbaba ZOO vulture.

akbasma MED cataract.

akbenek white speck in the eye.

akciğer lung(s).

akça rather white; ~ *pakça* pretty fair or attractive (*woman*); completely clean.

akçaağaç, -cı BOT maple.

akçakavak BOT white poplar.

akçayel southeast wind.

akçe 1. money; **2.** HIST a small silver coin; ~ *düşkünü* greedy, stingy; ~ *etmez* worthless; ~ *farkı* premium, agio; ~ *ile bohça ile* fig. by bribery; ~ *kesmek* fig. to be very rich.

Akdeniz pr. n. the Mediterranean.

akdetmek [x . .] **1.** to conclude (*a contract*); **2.** to hold (*a meeting, session, etc.*); **3.** to negotiate (*a loan*).

akdiken BOT buckthorn.

akgözlü fig. mean, low, common.

akgünlük incense.

akgürgen BOT white alder.

akı PHYS flux, flow.

akıbet, -ti 1. end, consequence, result, outcome; **2.** destiny, fate; **3.** eventuality; *-ini tayin etm.* to determine the fate of s.th.

akıcı 1. fluid, liquid; **2.** fluent; ~ *ünsüz* liquid consonant.

akıcılık fluency.

akıl, -klı 1. reason, intellect, mind; **2.** intelligence; **3.** idea, thought, sense; **4.** iro. bright idea; **5.** recollection, remembrance; **6.** wisdom, discretion; ~ *almak* to get opinions; ~ *almaz* unbelievable; ~ *bu ya!* iro. what a story!; ~ *danışmak* (*b-ne*) to consult *s.o.*; ~ *etm.* (*bşi*) to think of, to dream up; ~ *fikir* complete attention; ~ *fikir dağıtmak* (*or bırakmamak*) to distract totally; ~ *hastalıkları* mental disorders: ~ *hocası* **1.** one who gives good advice; **2.** iro. one who gives pretentious, pointless, etc. advice; ~ *kârı olmamak* to be unreasonable (to do); ~ *kumkuması* (*or kutusu*) trusty adviser, mine of wisdom; ~ *melakâtı* mental facilities; ~ *öğrenmek* **1.** to get good advice; **2.** iro. to be given useless advice; ~ *öğretmek* (*b-ne*) **1.** to give good advice; **2.** *iro.* to give pointless, useless advice; **3.** to put idea into s.o.'s head; ~ **satmak** *iro.* to give useless advice; ~ **sormak** to inquire, to consult; ~ **var, izan** (*or* **yakın** *or* **mantık**) **var 1.** with a little bit of intelligence one can understand it; **2.** *iro.* why don't you wise up?; ~ **yaşta değil baştadır** *pro.* intelligence does not depend on age; ~ **zayıflığı** mental deficiency; (akla): ~ **hayale sığmayan** unthinkable, unimaginable; ~ **sığmak** to be evident, to be obvious; ~ **yakın** plausible, reasonable; (aklı): ~ **almak** (*bşi*) **1.** to understand. to grasp; **2.** to believe; ~ **başına gelmek 1.** to come to one's senses; **2.** to come to; ~ **başında** sensible, rational; ~ **başından gitmek** to be overwhelmed, to be beside o.s.; ~ **çalık 1.** light-minded, frivolous; **2.** crazy, out of one's head; ~ **durmak** to be perplexed, to be dumbfounded; ~ **ermek** (*bşe*) to understand *s.th.*; ~ **kesmek** to decide, to judge; ~ **kıt** (*or* **kısa**) half-witted; ~ **oynamak 1.** to be crazy; **2.** to go insane; ~ **sıra** *iro.* as one hopes, as one believes; ~ **sonradan geldi 1.** it later occurred to him; **2.** he was too wise too late; ~ **tepesinden yukarı** thoughtless, foolish, absent-minded; ~ **yatmak** (*bşe*) **1.** to understand, to grasp; **2.** to be convinced; **3.** to find reasonable; ~ **zıvanasından çıkmış görünüyor** he seems to be out of his head; **aklı başına yar ise** if he knows what's good for him; (aklına): ~ **gelmek 1.** to come to one's mind; **2.** to recall; ~ **getirmek** to recollect, to call to mind; ~ **koymak 1.** to make up one's mind, to be determined; **2.** to suggest; **3.** not to forget; ~ **sığdırmak 1.** to comprehend; **2.** to make s.o. understand; (aklını): ~ **başına almak** (*or* **toplamak**) **1.** to come to one's senses; **2.** to sober up; **3.** to think better of; ~ **çelmek** (*or* **değiştirmek**) to change one's mind; ~ **çelmek** (*b-nin*) **1.** to mislead; **2.** to put *s.o.* off doing.

akılçı 1. rationalistic; **2.** rationalist.

akılcılık PHLS rationalism.

akıldışı, -nı irrational.

akıldişi, -ni wisdom tooth.

akıllanmak 1. to become wiser; **2.** to have learned one's lesson.

akıllı 1. intelligent, reasonable, wise; **2.** clever, shrewd; ~ **davranmak** to act

wisely; ~ **geçinmek** to pass for a wise man.

akılsız stupid; unreasonable; ~ **başın zahmetini ayak çeker** *pro.* little wit in the head makes much work for the feet.

akılsızlık 1. stupidity; **2.** foolishness.

akım 1. current; **2.** trend, movement.

akın 1. sudden rush; **2.** MIL (roving) expedition, raid; **3.** (*air*) attack; **4.** run (*of fish*); ~ ~ wave after wave, surging; ~ **etm. 1.** to raid, attack and pillage; **2.** to surge (*of a crowd*); ~ **halinde** *s.* ~ ~.

akıncı 1. raider; **2.** plunderer; **3.** *sports*: forward; **4.** enterprising, energetic.

akıntı 1. current, flow; **2.** stream; **3.** MED flux; **4.** gradient, fall, descent; **-ya kapılmak** to get caught in the current; **-ya kürek çekmek 1.** to row upstream; **2.** to waste one's efforts.

akış 1. flow, current, course; **2.** MEC outlet, outfall.

akışkan fluid.

akide [ī] **1.** dogma; **2.** confession of faith, creed; **3.** (**şekeri**) sugar candy; **-yi bozmak 1.** to apostatize; **2.** *fig.* to stray from the true path.

akik GEOL agate.

akim [ī] **1.** sterile; **2.** unsuccessful, ineffective, in vain; ~ **bırakmak** to thwart, to frustrate; ~ **kalmak** to be unsuccessful, to be thwarted.

akis, -ksi 1. reflection; **2.** MATH inversion; **3.** LOG conversion; **4.** echo; **5.** reaction; **6.** reversion.

akit, -kdi 1. closing, conclusion; **2.** marriage contract; **3.** undertaking (*of a loan*); **4.** agreement, contract, treaty, arrangement; ~ **yapma va'di** JUR preliminary agreement; **akdi nikâh etm.** *s.* **nikâh kıymak.**

akitleşmek to conclude (*a contract, etc.*).

akkarınca termite, white ant.

akkavak BOT white poplar.

akkefal ZOO bleak.

akkor CHEM, PHYS **1.** incandescent; **2.** incandescence.

aklamak 1. to clear one's hono(u)r, to clear s.o. of responsibility; **2.** to make white.

aklan GEOGR slope, slant.

aklen [x .] rational.

aklı white-spotted; ~ **karalı 1.** pepper-and-salt; **2.** spotted.

aklıselim [ī] commonsense.

akli [ī] **1.** intellectual; **2.** mental, rational; ~ **denge** mental balance; ~ **mele-kât** mental faculties.

akliye 1. mental illnesses; **2.** psychiatric clinic; **3.** PHLS rationalism; ~ **hekimi** psychiatrist.

akmak, (-ar) 1. to flow; **2.** to leak; **3.** to be shed (*blood*); **4.** to run (*faucet, water*); **5.** F to slip away; **6.** to unravel (*textile*); **7.** to fall (*shooting star*); **akacak kan damarda kalmaz** *pro.* one can't escape fate; **akan sular durur** it broaches no argument; **akmazsa da damlar** *pro.* anything is better than nothing; **akmış çorap** laddered stocking; **akmış kumaş** frayed.

akmaz 1. stagnant, stale; **2.** standing water.

akordeon 1. accordion; **2.** accordion pleats.

akort, -du 1. MUS accord; **2.** MUS being in key; **akordu bozuk** *fig.* out of tune, out of key, inharmonious.

akortçu (piano) tuner.

akortlamak (or **akort etm.**) to tune (*a musical instrument*).

akraba 1. relative(s); **2.** related.

akrabalık kinship, affinity.

akran [. -] equal, peer, match; **kendi akranıyle** with one's match or equal.

akreditif COM letter of credit.

akrep, -bi 1. ZOO scorpion; **2.** hour hand (*of a clock*); **3.** ♀ AST Scorpio.

akrobasi 1. acrobatics; **2.** stunt flying.

akrobat, -tı 1. acrobat; **2.** stunt flier.

akrobatlık 1. acrobatics; **2.** stunt flying.

akropol, -lü 1. acropolis; **2.** ♀ *pr. n.* The Acropolis (*in Athens*).

aksak 1. lame, limping; **2.** crippled; ♀ **Timur** Tamerlane.

aksakal 1. old, aged; **2.** village elder; ~ **karasakal** *fig.* the high and the low; **-dan yok sakala gelmek** to become very aged.

aksaklık 1. lameness, limp; **2.** lopsidedness; **2.** flaw, defect, disturbance, trouble; ~ **göstermek** not to work right, to run wrong.

aksamak 1. to be lame; to limp; **2.** *fig.* not to work right, to run wrong, to develop a hitch.

aksan accent, stress.

akse 1. MED fit, attack; **2.** BIOL reflex.

akselator MEC accelerator, gas pedal.

akseptans COM acceptance.

aksesuar 1. accessory; **2.** stage prop.

aksetmek [x . .] **1.** to be reflected; **2.** to echo; **3.** to reverberate; **4.** to resound; **5.** to come to one's ear, knowledge or attention.

aksırık sneeze; ~ **tozu** sneezing powder; **-lı tıksırıklı 1.** sneezing and coughing; **2.** *fig.* old and in bad health.

aksırmak to sneeze.

aksi 1. opposite, contrary, opposed; **2.** disagreeable, unpleasant; **3.** adverse, untoward; ~ **akıntı** countercurrent; ~ **gibi** F unfortunately; ~ **halde** otherwise; ~ **mütalâa** (or **fikir**) contrary opinion; ~ **olarak** on the contrary; ~ **takdirde** otherwise; ~ **tesadüf 1.** mischance; **2.** unluckily; **işlerim aksi gidiyor** I'm having a run of bad luck.

aksilik 1. bad luck, misfortune; **2.** unpleasantness, disagreeableness; **3.** crossness, bad temper, obstinacy; ~ **etm.** to be obstinate; to raise difficulties.

aksiseda [. . . -] echo, reflection; ~ **vermek** to give an echo, to reverberate.

aksitesir [. . - -] reaction, opposite effect.

aksiyom axiom.

aksiyon 1. share; **2.** activity, occupation, business; **3.** stage business.

aksiyoner shareholder.

aksöğüt, -dü BOT white willow.

aksu *s.* **akbasma.**

aksülamel reaction, counter-effect.

aksülümen CHEM sublimate.

akşam 1. evening; **2.** in the evening; **3.** last night; **4.** the sunset hour, the time of the evening prayer; ~ **demez sabah demez 1.** all day long; **2.** he comes at any time of day or night, considerate; ~ **etm.** to finish up the day; ~ **ezanı 1.** evening prayer-call; **2.** evening time; ~ **gazetesi** evening newspaper; ~ **olm.** to become evening; ~ (or **-ki**) **yediğini sabah unutmak** to become exceedingly forgetful; ~ **yemeği** the evening meal, dinner; **-a doğru** (or **karşı**) towards evening; **-dan kalmış** (or **kalma**) hung over; **-dan sonra merhaba** *fig.* to say s.th. too late and thus uselessly; **-lar hayrolsun!** good evening!

akşamcı 1. one who spends all his evenings drinking; **2.** night-worker; **3.** one whose turn of duty falls in the evening; **4.** night student.

akşamcılık habit of drinking every evening.

akşamgüneşi, -ni 1. setting sun; **2.** yellowish-pink; **3.** autumn of one's years; ~ **gibi** rapidly vanishing.

akşamki of the evening, in the evening.

akşamlamak 1. to stay until evening; **2.** to spend the evening in a place.

akşamleyin in the evening.

akşamlı sabahlı all the time, morning and evening.

akşamlık intended for evening use.

Akşamyıldızı, -nı evening star, Venus.

aktar haberdasher, mercer; ~ **dükkânı** haberdasher's shop, mercery.

aktarma 1. *vn. of* **aktarmak**; **2.** transfer; **3.** transfer, change (*of trains. etc.*): **4.** quotation, plagiarism; **5.** plowing a field for the first or second time; **6.** *sports*: pass; ~ **bileti** transfer ticket; ~ **eşyası** transit goods; ~ **etm. 1.** to carry over, to transfer; **2.** to transpose, to shift (*into another form*); **3.** *s.* **aktarmak**; ~ **limanı** transit port; ~ **merkezi** (*or* **yeri**) MIL transfer point; ~ **yapmak** to change (*trains, etc.*).

aktarmak 1. to transfer; to move; **2.** to transship; **3.** to carry over; **4.** to quote (*a passage from another book, etc.*); **5.** *rare* to bring into disorder; **6.** to reassign; **7.** to reload; **8.** to review; **9.** to transmit, to convey; **10.** *sports*: to pass; **11.** to retile (*a roof*); **12.** to plow (*new ground*); **13.** MED to transplant.

aktarmalı having a connection (*flight, etc.*); ~ **bilet** transfer ticket.

aktavşan ZOO jerboa.

aktif 1. active; **2.** COM assets; **3.** effective.

aktör actor.

aktris actress.

aktüalite 1. the news of the day; **2.** popular subject; **3.** (*film*) newsreel; ~ **filmi** newsreel; ~ **haline gelmek** to become a subject for popular discussion.

aktüel actual; present; current.

akupliman MEC coupling, clutch.

akustik acoustic(s).

akü, akümülatör storage battery.

akvam [. -] *pl. of* **kavim**; ♀ **Cemiyeti** HIST League of Nations.

akvaryum aquarium.

akyuvar BIOL white blood corpuscle.

akzambak BOT Madonna lily.

al¹ 1. scarlet, crimson, vermillion, red; **2.** chestnut (*horse*); **3.** bright red; **4.** rouge; **5.** MED erysipelas; ~ **at** sorrel (*horse*); ~ **basmak** (**loğusayı**) MED

to suffer puerperal fever; ~ **kanlar içinde revan** (*or* **puyan**) in a pool of blood; **alı alına moru moruna 1.** all flushed in the face; **2.** out of breath; **allar giymek** to rejoice.

al² deceit, intrigue.

âl, -li 1. family, dynasty; **2.** high-born; **âli Osman** Ottoman Dynasty.

ala 1. colo(u)rful; **2.** light brown; **3.** *s.* **alabalık**; ~ **kaz** white-cheeked goose.

âlâ first-rate, excellent, very good.

alabalık ZOO trout.

alabanda [. . x .] **1.** bulwarks; **2.** broadside; **3.** *sl.* obtrusive; ~ **etm. 1.** to put the helm hard over; **2.** to tip over; ~ **vermek** (*b-ne*) to give *s.o.* a real scolding; ~ **yemek** to get a real scolding.

alabildiğine maximum, extremely, the most possible; ~ **şişman bir adam** an incredibly fat man.

alabora NAUT capsizing, overturn; ~ **etm.** NAUT to overturn; ~ **olm.** to capsize, to turn over.

alaca 1. *s.* **ala**; **2.** bad temper(ed); **3.** *kinds of variegated cloth*; ~ **at** piebald (*horse*); ~ **bulaca 1.** loud (colo(u)red); **2.** incongruously colo(u)red; ~ **dostluk** insincere friendship; ~ **gre** speckled sandstone; ~ **karanlık** twilight; ~ **karga** ZOO **1.** jackdaw; **2.** rook; **3.** magpie; ~ **kargaya borçlu** up to his ears in debt; **-sı içinde** crafty, deceitful, fraudulent.

alacadoğan ZOO peregrine falcon.

alacak 1. JUR claim, demand; **2.** credit; ~ **davası** JUR personal action; ~ **olan** receiver; ~ **senedi** promissory note, debenture; **alacağı olsun!** he'll pay for this! I'll show him; **alacağım elli lira** I've got fifty liras coming.

alacaklı creditor; ~ **bakiye** credit balance; ~ **taraf** credit side.

alacalanmak 1. to become colo(u)rful *or* spotted; **2.** to blush.

alacalı *s.* **ala 1.** ~ **bulacalı** loud (colo(u)r); ~ **kuntaşı** *s.* **alaca gre**.

alacalık 1. motleyness; **2.** *fig.* deceit; ~ **etm.** to be deceitful.

alaçam BOT spruce.

aladoğan *s.* **alacadoğan**.

alafranga [. . x .] in the European style; ~ **musiki** European music; ~ **tuvalet** Western style toilet.

alafrangacı follower of European custom.

alafrangacılık preference for European styles.

alafrangalaşmak to adopt Western ways.

alafrangalık European mode of living.

alagarson boyish bob.

alageyik zoo fallow deer.

alaimisema [. - . . . -] rainbow.

alaka 1. interest; **2.** affection; **3.** relation; **4.** claim; **5.** CHEM affinity; **~ göstermek** to show interest; to take an interest (-*e* in); **~ uyandırmak** to arouse interest; **~ verici** captivating, fascinating; **-sı var** there is a connection; he has an interest; **-sını kesmek** to terminate one's association, to break off relations (*ile* with).

alakadar [. - . -] **1.** connected; concerned; **2.** interested; **3.** responsible; **~ etm.** -*i* **1.** to interest (*ile* in); **2.** to concern; **~ olm. 1.** to be interested (*ile* in); **2.** to be concerned (*ile* with).

alakalanmak 1. to be interested (*ile* in); **2.** to be enamo(u)red (*ile* of, with).

alakalı 1. interested; **2.** enamo(u)red; **3.** authoritative; standard; **4.** associated; **5.** participating, participant.

alakarga zoo **1.** spotted crow; **2.** jackdaw; **3.** magpie; **4.** jay.

alakasız 1. disinterested, indifferent; **2.** uninteresting; **3.** not related.

alakasızlık 1. indifference; **2.** lack of interest.

alako(y)mak *s.* **alıko(y)mak.**

Alaman *s.* **Alman.**

alamana [. . x .] NAUT **1.** lugger; **2.** large trawl net.

alamet, -ti 1. sign, mark, symbol; **2.** *a.* MIL badge; **3.** monstrous, enormous, (*anything conspicuous by its size*); **-i farika 1.** trademark; **2.** NAUT emblem.

alan 1. PHYS field; **2.** MATH area; **3.** PHLS field, sphere, domain; **4.** (public) square; **5.** plain, space; **6.** airport.

alan talan F in complete confusion; **~ etm.** to mess up.

alarga [. x .] **1.** in the Turkish style: **~ 1270'te** in 1270 (*old calendar*); **~ mü-**

F stand off!, keep away!; **~ durmak** *sl.* to keep off, to keep away; **~ etm. 1.** to enter the high seas; **2.** *sl.* to keep one's distance; **-da** anchored offshore.

alarm 1. alarm; **2.** state of emergency; **~ işareti 1.** warning sign; **2.** MIL warning signal.

alaşağı etm. 1. to pull down; **2.** to overthrow, to depose.

alaşım alloy.

alaturka [. . x .] in the Turkish style: **~**

zik Turkish music; **~ yemek** Turkish (*or* Oriental) cuisine or style of cooking.

alaturkacı F **1.** partisan of Turkish style (*esp. old Turkish music*); **2.** performer or singer of Turkish music.

alavere [. . x .] **1.** complete confusion; **2.** passing or throwing about (*from hand to hand*); **3.** coal chute; **~ dalavere** dirty tricks; **~ tulumbası** suction pump.

alay 1. procession; **2.** MIL regiment. squadron, group; **3.** large quantity, all of (*a group*); **4.** solemnity; **5.** mockery, sarcasm. teasing; **~ ~** row upon row, in large crowds; **~ etme!** don't mock!; **~ etm.** (*b-le*) to make fun (**of**), to mock; **~ geçmek** *sl. s.* **~ etm**; **~ malay** F the whole outfit; **-a almak** F to deride, to ridicule, to mock; **-ında olm.** (*bşin*) not to take *s.th.* seriously, to take *s.th.* as a joke.

alaycı 1. mocking, sarcastic, ironic; **2.** mocker.

alayiş [- - .] pomp, show.

alaylı 1. MIL from the ranks; **2.** *fig.* uneducated, unschooled; **3.** mocking; **4.** ceremonious.

alaz flame.

alazlanmak 1. to be singed; **2.** to get red areas on the skin.

albastı MED puerperal fever.

albatr alabaster.

albatros albatross.

albay 1. MIL colonel; **2.** NAUT captain.

albeni charm, attractiveness.

albüm album

albümin albumen.

alçacık [x . .] very low.

alçak 1. low; **2.** vile, mean, low, base, abject; **3.** cowardly; **~ basınç** low pressure; **~ gönüllü** humble, modest, unpretentious; **~ gönüllülük** modesty, humility.

alçakça 1. rather low; **2.** [. x .] shamefully, viciously.

alçaklık 1. lowness; **2.** shamefulness, vileness; **~ etm.** to behave viciously.

alçalma 1. decline, descent; **2.** ebb tide; **3.** degradation.

alçalmak 1. to become low; to decline; to go down; **2.** to descend, to lose altitude; **3.** to degrade o.s.; to lose esteem.

alçaltıcı degrading.

alçarak somewhat low.

alçı gypsum. plaster of Paris; **~ kalıbı**

plaster mo(u)ld; *-ya koymak* to put in a plaster cast.

alçıtaşı, *-nı* GEOL gypsum, parget.

aldaç trick, ruse.

aldanç easily fooled.

aldangıç trick, cheat.

aldanmak 1. to be deceived. to be taken in: **2.** to be mistaken, to be wrong.

aldatıcı deceptive, misleading.

aldatılmak to be deceived.

aldatma deception, deceiving.

aldatmaca deception, trick.

aldatmak 1. to deceive, to dupe, to cheat; **2.** to mislead; **3.** to mislead s.o. by appearance; **4.** to be unfaithful (*-i* to).

aldırış attention, care; ~ *etmemek* not to mind, not to pay any attention (*-e* to).

aldırışsız indifferent.

aldırmak 1. *caus. of almak*; **2.** to mind, to take notice (*-e* of), to pay attention (*-e* to); *aldırmamak s. aldırış etmemek.*

alegori allegory.

alelacayip very peculiar, odd.

alelacele hastily, in a big hurry.

alelade ordinary, usual, normal.

alelhesap as an advance (*payment*), on account.

alelumum in general, generally.

alelusul as a formality.

alem 1. flag, banner; **2.** peak (*of a minaret*); **3.** *obs.* proper name.

âlem 1. world, universe; **2.** realm; **3.** condition, state (of); **4.** field, sphere; **5.** the world of people, the public; **6.** revel, orgy; ~ *yapmak* to have a wild party; *-i var mı?* is it really proper?

alemdar [. . -] **1.** standard-bearer; **2.** *fig.* leader.

âlemşümul, *-lü* [ū] worldwide, universal; ~ *bir şöhret* a worldwide fame.

alenen [x . .] openly, publicly.

alengirli *sl.* showy.

aleni [ī] open, public; ~ *müzayede s. açık artırma*; ~ *satış* public sale.

aleniyet, *-ti* publicity.

alerji MED allergy.

alerjik MED allergic.

alert, *-ti* alert, alarm.

alesta [. x .] **1.** ready!, stand by!; **2.** *sl.* ready; **3.** *sl.* right away, right now; ~ *beklemek* to stand by.

alet, *-ti* [ā] **1.** tool, instrument, implement, device; **2.** apparatus, machine; **3.** *fig.* tool, means, instrument, agent;

4. ANAT organ; ~ *edevat* tools, implements; ~ *etm* (*b-ni*) to make a tool of s.o.; ~ *olm.* to be an instrument (*-e* to), to be a tool (*-e* to), to lend o.s. (*-e* to), to stooge (*-e* for); *-li jimnastik* apparatus gymnastics.

alev 1. flame; **2.** pennant (*on a lance*); **3.** ♀ *wf.*; ~ *almak* **1.** to catch fire; **2.** *fig.* to flare up, to blaze up, to flame out, to flare out; ~ *cihazı* MIL flame thrower; ~ *kesilmek* to blaze up, to flame out; ~ *saçağı* (*or bacayı*) *sardı* things have gone too far, danger has gone beyond control; *-lere yem olm.* to fall a victim to the flames.

Alevi [. . -] partisan of the Caliph Ali; Shiite.

Alevilik Shiism.

alevlendirmek 1. to make (*the fire*) flame up; **2.** *fig.* to inflame, to incite, to exacerbate.

alevlenmek 1. to flare, to blaze up; **2.** *fig.* to flame up, to flare up, to flame out; **3.** to glisten.

alevli 1. flaming, in flames; **2.** *fig.* violent, furious.

aleyh against; *-inde, -ine* against him; *-inde bulunmak* to talk against, to backbite, to run down; *-te olm.* to be in opposition.

aleyhtar opponent.

aleyhtarlık opposition.

aleykümselam peace be upon you (*said in reply to the greeting selamünaleyküm*).

alfabe 1. alphabet; **2.** primer; **3.** *fig.* the ABC (*of*).

alfabetik alphabetical; ~ *sıra* alphabetical order.

algı perception; sensation; impression.

algılama perception, comprehension.

algılamak to perceive, to comprehend.

alıcı 1. buyer, customer, purchaser; **2.** MEC receiver, recipient; **3.** movie camera; **4.** the Angel of Death (*Azrail*); ~ *gözüyle bakmak* to look meticulously; ~ *kuş* bird of prey; ~ *radyo makinesi* radio receiver; radio set; ~ *verici* **1.** one who takes back a present he has given; **2.** MEC two-way radio.

alık clumsy, stupid, imbecile, silly; ~ ~ stupidly.

alıklaşmak to be astounded, to be taken aback.

alıklık stupidity, imbecility.

alıko(y)mak 1. to hold s.o. in a place; **2.** to keep back, to detain, to restrain, to prevent (*-den* from); **3.** to set aside, to reserve.

alım 1. taking; **2.** purchase, buying; **3.** attractiveness; ~ **satım** trade, business; purchase and sale.

alımlı attractive, charming; ~ **çalımlı** eye-catching, charming.

alımsız unattractive.

alın, -lnı 1. forehead, brow; **2.** MIN face; ~ **akı** hono(u)r, integrity; ~ **çatmak** to frown, to scowl; ~ **damarı** shame; ~ **damarı çatlamak** to lose all sense of shame; ~ **karası** shame, disgrace; ~ **teri** *fig.* effort, work, labo(u)r; ~ **teri dökmek** *fig.* to toil. to sweat (*over*), to struggle; ~ **teri ile kazanmak** to turn an honest penny; **-dan ter boşanmak** *fig.* to sweat blood; **alnı açık yüzü ak** blameless, irreproachable; **alnı davul derisi** *fig.* unabashed, shameless; **alnında yazılmış olm.** to be one's fate, to be destined; **alnını karışlarım! 1.** I'll show you!; **2.** I dare you!; **alnını karışlayayım!** he is no threat; **alnının akı ile** hono(u)rably, with no shadow of blame, without a blemish.

alındı receipt.

alındılı registered (*mail*).

alıngan touchy, irascible, choleric, testy.

alınganlık touchiness, testiness.

alınlı 1. having a forehead; **2.** *fig.* saucy, cheeky, *Am. sl.* fresh.

alınlık 1. ornament worn on the forehead; **2.** facade, frontal.

alınmak 1. *pass. of* **almak**; **2.** to take offence (*-e, -den* at), to resent.

alıntı quotation; ~ **yapmak** to quote.

alınyazısı, -nı *fig.* destiny, ordinance, predestination.

alış 1. taking, receiving; **2.** purchase, buying; ~ **fiyatı** purchase price; ~ **valfı** inlet valve.

alışagelmek to be accustomed (*-e* to).

alışık accustomed (*-e* to), used (*-e* to).

alışıklık 1. habit; **2.** familiarity.

alışılmış ordinary, usual, accustomed.

alışkan accustomed (*-e* to), used (*-e* to).

alışkanlık 1. habit; **2.** force of habit; **3.** familiarity.

alışkı habit, practice, usage.

alışkın *s.* **alışık.**

alışmak 1. to get used (*-e* to), to get accustomed (*-e* to); to become familiar (*-e* with); **2.** to accustom o.s. (*-e* to); **3.** to come to fit; **4.** to become addicted (*-e* to); **5.** P to catch fire.

alıştırma 1. exercise; **2.** training.

alıştırmak 1. to accustom (*-e* to), to familiarize; **2.** to domesticate, to tame; to train; **3.** to allow s.o. to become addicted (*-e* to); **4.** MEC to break in, to make s.th. work smoothly; **5.** to set on fire; (*b-ne*) **alıştırarak haber vermek** to break the news gently to s.o.

alışveriş 1. shopping; buying and selling, trade, business, commerce; **2.** *fig.* dealings, relations: ~ **yapmak 1.** to shop. to go shopping; **2.** (*b-le*) to do business with s.o.; **-i olmamak** (*b-le*) to avoid contact with s.o., not to have anything to do with s.o.; **-ten dönmek** to return from shopping; **dostlar -te görsün!** for the sake of appearances.

Ali *mf.*; ~ **paşa vergisi** *iro.* a present which is taken back; **-nin külahını Veli'ye Veli'nin külahını Ali'ye giydirmek** F to rob Peter to pay Paul.

âli *obs.* **1.** high, exalted, sublime; **2.** *mf.*; **zatı âliniz** your worship, you; **ismi âliniz nedir?** what is your name?

âlicenap, -bı noble-hearted, magnanimous.

âlicenaplık magnanimity.

alicengiz oyunu F a dirty trick.

alıkıran başkesen F bully, despot.

alim all-knowing, omniscient.

âlim 1. scholar; **2.** wise, learned.

alimallah! by God!

âlimlik 1. scholarship; **2.** erudition.

alivre COM short (*sale*).

alize trade wind.

alkali CHEM alkali.

alkaloit CHEM alkaloid.

alkım METEOR rainbow.

alkış applause, clapping; ~ **tufanı** flood of applause; ~ **tutmak 1.** to clap (*-e* for); **2.** to cheer.

alkışçı *contp.* **1.** applauder; **2.** flatterer, toady.

alkışlamak to clap (*-i* for), to acclaim, to applaud.

alkışlanmak *pass. of* **alkışlamak** to be clapped, to be greeted with applause; **ayakta** ~ to be given a standing ovation.

alkol, -lü alcohol.

alkolik alcoholic.

alkolizm alcoholism.

alkollü 1. alcoholic, spirituous, intoxi-

cating; **2.** drunk; **3.** while drunk.
alkolsuz non-alcoholic, soft (*drink*).
Allah [. -] **1.** God; **2.** o God!; **3.** how wonderful!, really!; **~ acısın!** may God have pity on him!; **~ afiyet versin!** may God give you success!; **~ ~ 1.** good Lord!, goodness gracious!; **2.** Turkish battle cry; **~ aşkına! 1.** for God's sake!, for heaven's sake!; **2.** how wonderful!; **~ bağışlasın** God bless him; **~ belâsını versin!** damn him!; **~ bilir!** God knows!; **~ bir kapıyı kaparsa, başka kapıyı açar** *pro.* when one door shuts, another opens; **~ canını alsın!** God damn you!; **~ cezanı vermesin** (*or* **~ cezanı versin**) God damn you; **~ dağına göre kar verir** *pro.* God tempers the wind to the shorn lamb; **~ derim!** all I can say is 'o God'; **~ esirgesin!** God forbid!; **~ göstermesin!** God forbid!; **~ hakkı için!** in God's name; **~ (seni) inandırsın ...** take it from me that ..., take my word ...; **~ korusun!** God forbid!; **~ layığını versin!** damn you (*or* him)!; **~ müstahakını versin!** *s.* **~ layığını versin**; **~ ömürler versin!** may God give you a long life!; **~ rahatlık versin!** good night!; **~ rahmet eylesin!** may God have mercy on him; **~ rahmetine kavuşmak** to meet one's Maker, to die; **~ versin! 1.** may Good help you!; **2.** may you enjoy it!; (Allaha); **~ ısmarladık** good-bye!; **~ şükür!** thank God!; **Allahı(nı) seversen** for God's sake; (Allahın): **~ belası** nuisance, pest, trial; **~ cezası** damn, damned; **~ günü** every darn day; **~ ondurmadığını, Peygamber sopa ile kovar** *pro.* misfortunes never come singly; **~ tembeli** bone-lazy; (Allahtan): **1.** luckily, fortunately; **2.** from birth; **~ bulsun!** let God punish him!; **~ korkmaz** cruel, unmerciful, ruthless; **~ umut kesilmez** while there is life there is hope.
Allahlık 1. harmless, simpleton, simple man; **2.** left to God, unpredictable.
Allahsız 1. atheist; **2.** *fig.* unmerciful, merciless.
Allahuekber [. - . . .] God is almighty.
allak 1. untrustworthy, fickle; **2.** deceitful.
allak bullak 1. topsy-turvy, pell-mell; **2.** in great confusion; **~ etm. 1.** to make a mess (-*i* of), to upset; **2.** *fig.* to confuse, to bewilder.

allame *obs.* **1.** scholar, learned man; **2.** learned.
allasen [. - .] [. x .] = **Allahı seversen.**
allegretto MUS allegretto.
allegro MUS allegro.
allem kallem tricks, dodges; **allem etti, kallem etti** he tried all sorts of wiles.
allı pullu spangled, showily dressed.
allık 1. redness; **2.** rouge.
almaç TELEPH receiver.
almak, (-ır) 1. to take; **2.** to get, to obtain, to procure; **3.** to buy; **4.** to receive; to accept; **5.** to steal; **6.** to marry (*a girl*); **7.** to take along, to call for; **8.** to hold, to contain, to take; **9.** to capture, to conquer; **10.** to take in, to shorten (*a dress*); **11.** to pluck out, to remove, to take away; **12.** to clean, to sweep, to dust; **13.** to have, to take (*a bath*); **14.** to lead; **15.** to drink; to smoke; **16.** to last, to take (*a period of time*); **17.** to swallow, to take (*medicine*); **18.** to cover, to travel (*a distance*); **19.** to catch (*cold, fire*); **20.** to employ, to hire, to take on; **21.** to move; **22.** to sense, to smell, to hear; **23.** to put on, to throw over o.s. (*garment*); **24.** to take (*water*); **25.** to carry away, to destroy (*flood*); **26.** to overwhelm, to sweep through (*smoke, fear*); **27.** to begin all at once (*rain*); **al birini vur ötekine** tarred with the same brush; **alıp satmak** to trade, to commerce; **alıp vermek 1.** to exchange; to trade; **2.** to have one's heart beat wildly; **3.** to dwell on a matter; **alıp yürüdü** it has made headway.
Alman German; **~ hükümeti** German government.
almanak almanac.
Almanca [. x .] German, the German language; **~ gramer** German grammar; **~ öğretmeni** teacher of German; **~ sözlü bir film** a film in German; **bunun -sı nedir?** what does it mean in German?
almangümüşü German silver, albata.
Almanya [. x .] *pr. n.* Germany.
Almanyalı German; from Germany.
alo! [x .] (*telefon*) hello!
Alp, Alpler *pr. n.* the Alps.
alpaka ZOO alpaca.
alpyıldızı BOT edelweiss.
alt, -tı 1. bottom, underside, lower part; **2.** buttocks, rump, bottom; **3.** contin-

uation, the rest; **4.** the farther; **5.** the lower, inferior; **6.** (*altına, altında*) under, beneath, below; ~ *alta* one under the other; ~ *alta üst üste* rough-and--tumble; ~ *alta üst üste boğuşma* rough-and-tumble fight; ~ *aşağı vurmak* to cast down, to overthrow, to conquer; ~ *başından* from the very bottom (of); ~ *etm.* to beat, to defeat, to overwhelm; ~ *kat* **1.** downstairs; **2.** first (*or* ground) floor; ~ *olm.* to be defeated, to be overcome (-*e* by); ~ *taraf* the lower part; the underside; ~ *tarafı çıkmaz sokak* F this business is a blind alley; ~ *yazı* footnote, postscript; -*ı alay, üstü kalay* gaudy, showy, tawdry; -*ı çizilmiş kelime* underlined word; -*ı kaval, üstü şişhane* odd-looking; (altına): ~ *almak* to throw s.o. down; ~ *etm.* (*or koyvermek or kaçırmak*) to wet *or* soil one's clothes a little; -*ında kalmak* to have no retort. to be unable to reply; -*ından girip üstünden çıkmak* to squander, to blow, to blue, to play ducks and drakes with (*money*); -*ını üstüne getirmek* **1.** to turn upside down; **2.** to search high and low; *altta kalanın canı çıksın!* woe to the vanquished!, vae victis!, the devil take the hindmost!; *altta kalmak* to be defeated, to be beaten, to lose.

altbilinç PSYCH the subconscious.

altçene the lower jaw.

altderi ANAT corium, derma.

alternatif 1. alternative; **2.** alternate; ~ *akım* ELECT alternating current.

alternatör generator, alternator.

altes his highness, her highness.

altgeçit underpass.

altı six; ~ *köşe(li)* **1.** six-cornered; **2.** MATH hexagon; ~ *okka etm.* (*b-ni*) to carry s.o. by having people lift his arms and legs; -*da bir* one sixth; -*nı çizmek* fig. to underline.

altıgen MATH hexagon.

altılı 1. *cards:* six; **2.** MUS sextet, sextette.

altın 1. gold; **2.** gold coin; **3.** golden; ~ *adını bakır etm.* fig. to degrade o.s., to disgrace o.s.; ~ *anahtar* fig. money; ~ *anahtar her kapıyı açar* money talks; ~ *babası* moneybags, well-heeled; ~ *bilezik* **1.** gold bracelet; **2.** fig. a skill one can use to support o.s.; ~ *çağı* golden age; ~ *kaplama* **1.** gold-plating; **2.** gold-plated; ~ *kesmek* to be

coining (*or* minting) money, to make pots of money; ~ *kıymeti şartı* JUR gold clause; ~ *pas tutmaz* pro. a good character cannot be harmed by slander; ~ *sarısı* golden blond; ~ *varak* gold-leaf; ~ *yıldönümü* golden anniversary (*or* wedding); ~ *yumurtlayan tavuk* person with a generous income.

altınbaş 1. gold-headed; **2.** BOT muskmelon, cantaloupe; ~ *kefal* ZOO golden mullet.

altıncı[1] sixth.

altıncı[2] goldsmith.

altınlamak to gild; to ornament with gold.

Altınordu pr. n. HIST Golden Horde.

altınsuyu, -nu CHEM aqua regia.

altıntop, -pu BOT grapefruit.

altıparmak 1. six-fingered; having six toes; **2.** ZOO large bonito.

altıpatlar six-shooter, revolver.

altışar six each, six apiece; ~ ~ six by six.

altız sextuplet.

altlık 1. support, base; **2.** pad, coaster.

altmış sixty.

altmışaltı sixty-six (*a card game*); -*ya bağlamak* sl. to put s.o. off with promises.

altmışıncı sixtieth.

altmışlık 1. containing sixty; **2.** sixty years old, sexagenarian.

alto[x.] MUS **1.** viola; **2.** alto; **3.** alto saxophone.

altşube subbranch.

altulaşım underground transportation.

altuni [. - -] golden, gold colo(u)red.

altüst, -tü topsy-turvy, upside down; ~ *etm* **1.** to turn topsy-turvy, to mess up, to turn upside down, to upset; **2.** to damage, to ruin, to wreck; ~ *olm.* pass. of ~ *etm.*

altyapı 1. substructure; **2.** infrastructure.

altyazı subtitle.

aluvyon alluvium.

alüfte 1. promiscuous (*woman*); **2.** prostitute, whore.

alümin CHEM alumina, alumin.

alüminyum aluminium, *Am.* aluminum.

alyans wedding ring.

alyuvar ANAT erythrocyte.

am sl. cunt, pussy, vulva.

ama [x .] **1.** but, still, yet; **2.** above all; absolutely; **3.** truly, really; -*sı ma-*

ması yok! there are no buts about it!, but me no buts!; **amma da yaptın ha!** *a. iro.* how can it be!, not really!.

âmâ blind.

amaç aim, goal, target, object, objective, purpose, end; ~ **gütmek** to pursue a goal; **amacına ulaşmak** to attain one's object.

amaçlamak to aim (-*i* at), to intend, to purpose.

amaçlı purposeful.

amaçsız purposeless, aimless.

amade [- - -.] ready, prepared (-*e* for); **emre~ olm.** to be ready; to be at s.o.'s disposal.

amal, -li [- -.] *obs. pl. of amel* works, deeds, actions; **amali erbaa** *obs. s.* **dört işlem.**

aman [. -] **1.** oh!, mercy!, help!; **2.** please; **3.** for goodness sake; **4.** heavens!, my!; **5.** mercy; ~ **Allah çağırmak** *fig.* to be much distressed; ~ **aralık vermemek** not to give any respite; ~ **dedirtmek** (*b-ne*) to make *s.o.* give up, to make *s.o.* yield; ~ **demek** (*or* **dilemek**) to ask for mercy; to surrender; ~ **vermek** to grant one his life, to spare one's life; **-a gelmek** to come to terms, to give in, to give up and submit; **-a getirmek** *s.* ~ **dedirtmek**; **-ı zamanı yok** there is no trying to get out of it, you must; **-ını tüketmek** to exhaust.

amanın F oh my!, what now!

amansız 1. merciless; **2.** inexorable, cruel; **3.** incurable (*disease*).

amatör amateur.

amazon 1. amazon; **2.** equestrienne.

ambalaj 1. packing, wrapping; **2.** package; ~ **kâğıdı** wrapping paper; ~ **yapmak** to pack, to wrap up.

ambalajlamak to pack, to wrap up.

ambale olm. to be overwhelmed and confused.

ambar 1. granary; grain silo; **2.** warehouse, storehouse, magazine; **3.** express company, trucking firm; **4.** hold (*of a ship*); ~ **ağzı** NAUT hatchway; ~ **kapağı** NAUT hatch (cover); ~ **memuru** storekeeper, warehouse official.

ambarcı 1. trucker, express agent; **2.** *s.* **ambar memuru.**

ambargo [. x .] embargo; ~ **koymak** to impose an embargo (-*e* on); **-yu kaldırmak** to lift the embargo.

ambarlama storage.

amber 1. ambergris; **2.** *s.* **akar amber.**

amberbalığı, -nı ZOO sperm whale, cachalot.

amberbaris [. . - .] BOT barberry.

amberçiçeği, -ni BOT musk-mallow.

amboli embolism.

ambülans ambulance.

amca [x .] **1.** (paternal) uncle; **2.** sir (*polite form of address to an older man*); ~ **kızı** girl cousin; ~ **oğlu** male cousin.

amcalık 1. unclehood; **2.** step uncle; ~ **etm.** to be avuncular (-*e* towards), to act like an uncle.

amcazade cousin.

amel 1. act, action, deed, work; **2.** performance, practice; **3.** diarrhea; ~ **olm.** to have diarrhea.

amele worker, workman; ~ **çavuşu** foreman.

amelebaşı, -nı foreman.

amelelik workmanship.

ameli practical, applied.

amelimanda disabled, retired; invalid.

ameliyat, -tı 1. practice, performance; **2.** MED surgical operation; ~ **etm.** MED to operate (-*i* on); ~ **olm.** to be operated on, to have an operation.

ameliyathane [.....-.] operating room (*or* theatre).

ameliye process, procedure, operation.

amenna! [- x -] **1.** we believe!; **2.** admitted!, agreed!; ~ **demek** F to admit, to accept, to agree.

amentü [ä] I believe; credo.

Amerika 1. *pr. n.* America; **2.** *sl.* well-heeled, rich, rolling in money; ~ **Birleşik Devletleri** the United States of America, U.S.A.

Amerikalı 1. American; **2.** an American.

amerikalılaşmak to become Americanized.

amerikalılaştırmak to Americanize.

Amerikan 1. American; **2.** an American; ~ **bar** bar; ~ **fıstığı** BOT peanut; ~ **şekeri** fine ground sugar.

amerikanbezi, -ni unbleached calico.

amfi amphitheater, lecture room.

amfibi amphibian.

amfiteatr *s.* **amfi.**

amigo cheerleader.

amil factor, agent, motive, reason, cause; doing, active.

amin [ä] amen.

amip, -bi ZOO ameba, amoeba.

amipli amebic; ~ **dizanteri** MED amebic dysentery.

amir 1. commander; **2.** superior, chief; ~ **hükümler** JUR imperative provisions.

amiral, -li admiral; ~ **gemisi** flagship.

amirallik admiralship, admiralty.

amirane [- . - .] *rare* **1.** imperiously, commandingly; **2.** imperious (*action*).

amirlik 1. authority, superiority in rank; **2.** air of authority; ~ **taslamak** to behave arrogantly.

amit CHEM amide.

amiyane 1. colloquial; **2.** common, ordinary.

amma s. **ama.**

amme 1. the public; **2.** public, general; ~ **davası** JUR public prosecution; ~ **hizmeti** public service; ~ **menfaati** JUR public interest; ~ **nizamı** public policy.

amonyak CHEM ammonia (water).

amonyum CHEM ammonium; ~ **karbonatı** salt of hartshorn.

amorti 1. *lottery*: the smallest prize; **2.** redemption of a bond issue; ~ **etm.** to amortize, to redeem, to pay off.

amortisman 1. amortization; **2.** the redemption of a bond; ~ **akçesi** depreciation fund; ~ **sandığı** sinking-fund.

amortisör MEC **1.** shock absorber; **2.** damper.

amper ELECT ampere.

amperaj amperage.

ampermetre, amperölçer ELECT ammeter.

ampersaat, -ti ampere-hour.

ampirik empirical.

amplifikasyon MEC amplification.

amplifikatör MEC amplifier.

ampul, -lü 1. ELECT electric bulb; **2.** MED amp(o)ule; **3.** *sl.* boob.

amudi [ū, ī] vertical, perpendicular.

amudufikari [. - .. - -] backbone, spinal column.

amut, -du [ū] perpendicular; **amuda kalkmak** to do a hand stand.

amyant, -tı asbestos.

an [ā] **1.** moment, instant; **2.** boundary (*between fields*).

ana 1. mother; **2.** mother animal, dam; **3.** protector, patroness; **4.** principle, main, basic, fundamental; **5.** COM capital, stock; principal; ~ **akçe** principal; ~ **baba** parents, father and mother; ~ **baba bir** (**kardeş**) having the same father and mother; ~ **baba eline bakar**

he depends on his parents for his support; ~ **baba evladı** beloved child; ~ **baba günü** pandemonium, tumult; ~ **baba sevgisi** parental love; ~ **defter** ledger; ~ **demiryolu** main railway; ~ **direk** NAUT lower mast; ~ **fikir** central theme; ~ **hat** main (*or* truck) line; ~ **hatlar** the main lines, the outline; ~ **kısmı** kindergarten; nursery-school; ~ **kucağı** *fig.* mother's bosom; ~ **kuzusu 1.** very small baby, dear child; **2.** sissy, milksop, mollycoddle; ~ **makinesi** incubator; ~ **mesele** main subject; ~ **sermaye** original capital; ~ **ses** PHYS keynote; ~ **şaft** MEC cardan shaft; ~ **tem** MUS main theme; **-dan doğduğuna pişman olm.** *fig.* to be sorry to have been born, to feel very miserable; **-dan doğma 1.** stark naked; **2.** from birth; congenital; **-m babam!** *sl.* oh dear!, oh my!; **-mdan emdiğim süt burnumdan fitil fitil geldi** I went through extreme hardship; **-n yerinde kadın** the woman as old as your mother; **-sı danası** F his mother and the rest of the family, the whole bunch; **-sına bak kızını al, kenarına bak bezini al** *pro.* what is bred in the bone will never come out of the flesh, the sack is known by the sample; **-sını satayım!** I don't care two hoots!, I don't give a damn!; **-sının ak sütü gibi helal** (**olsun**)**!** you are welcome to it!; **-sının çocuğu** like mother like child; **-sının gözü** *sl.* sly, cunning, tricky, shifty; **-sının ipini pazara çıkarmış** *fig.* wicked, vicious; **-sının körpe kuzusu** mother's darling (*or* pet); **-sının nikâhını istemek** *fig.* to charge s.o. an arm and a leg, to make s.o. pay through the nose.

anacık darling mother.

anaç 1. matured (*animal*); **2.** fruit-bearing, mature (*tree*); **3.** experienced, shrewd; **4.** tough, huge.

anadil parent language.

anadili mother tongue, native language.

Anadolu *pr. n.* Anatolia; ~ **Ajansı** *pr. n.* Anatolian Agency; ~ **yakası** Anatolian quarter.

Anadolulu 1. an Anatolian; **2.** Anatolian.

anaerki matriarchy.

anaerkil matriarchal.

anafor 1. eddy, countercurrent, back current; **2.** *sl.* illicit gain, windfall; **-a**

konmak *sl.* to get s.th. for nothing; ~ (*or* **-dan**) **gelmek** (*b-ne*) *sl.* to fall into one's lap, to come easily.

anaforcu *sl.* **1.** freeloader, parasite, sponger; **2.** opportunist, cheater.

anaforculuk *sl.* **1.** freeloading; **2.** cheating.

anaforlamak*sl.* to pinch, to swipe, to steal.

anahtar 1. key; **2.** spanner, *Am.* wrench; **3.** ELECT switch; **4.** clef; ~ **deliği** keyhole; ~ **sözcük** IT keyword (*for website*); ~ **uydurmak** to match up a key (*to a lock*).

anahtarcı 1. locksmith; **2.** *sl.* thief who picks locks.

anahtarlık key ring (*or* holder).

anakara continent.

analı having a mother; ~ **kuzu kınalı kuzu** *fig.* a child whose mother is alive is clean and well cared for; **iki** ~ **kuzu** *fig.* two-job man, dual wage--earner.

analık 1. maternity, motherhood; **2.** stepmother, adoptive mother; **3.** maternal love; **4.** motherliness; ~ **etm.** (*b-ne*) to be a mother to *s.o.*

analitik analytical; ~ **geometri** analytical geometry.

analiz analysis; ~ **etm.** to analyze.

analizlemek CHEM to analyze.

anamal capital.

anamalcı 1. capitalist; **2.** capitalistic.

anamalcılık capitalism.

ananas pineapple.

anane tradition; **-siyle anlatmak** *fig.* to tell in detail.

ananeperest, -ti traditionalist.

ananeperestlik traditionalism.

ananet, -ti MED sexual impotence.

ananevi [ī] traditional.

anaokulu kindergarten, infant school, nursery school.

anapara capital.

anarşi anarchy.

anarşist, -ti anarchist.

anarşizm anarchism.

anason 1. aniseed; **2.** anise; **-lu** containing aniseed.

anatomi anatomy.

anatomik anatomical.

anavatan *s.* **anayurt.**

anayasa constitution.

anayasal constitutional.

anayol main (*or* trunk) road.

anayön cardinal point (*of the compass*).

anayurt, -du mother country, homeland.

anbean [ā, ā] with every moment, gradually.

anca [x .]: ~ **beraber kanca beraber** we will stick together through thick and thin.

ancak [x .] **1.** only, solely, merely; **2.** hardly, just, barely; **3.** but, however, on the other hand; **4.** not until, only.

ançüez anchovy.

andaç souvenir, gift, keepsake, memento.

andavallı *sl.* imbecile, idiot, fool, simpleton.

andetmek [x . .] to swear, to take an oath.

andırışma 1. resembling; **2.** ambiguity.

andırmak 1. to resemble, to be reminiscent (*-i* of); **2.** to bring to mind.

andızotu BOT elecampane.

andiçmek [x . .] to take an oath, to swear.

andilya [. x .] BOT endive.

ane [ā] pubic bone; ~ **biti** ZOO crab--louse.

anekdot, -tu anecdote.

anestezi MED anesthesia.

angaje 1. occupied, reserved; **2.** hired, employed, engaged; **3.** tied (*-e* to), bound (*-e* to); ~ **etm.** to employ, to engage.

angajman engagement, employment, undertaking; ~ **yapmak** to reach a formal agreement (*ile* with).

angarya, angarye [. x .] **1.** forced labo(u)r, corvée; **2.** angary; **3.** drudgery.

angı memory.

angın famous.

angıt 1. ZOO ruddy, sheldrake; **2.** *sl.* fool, idiot.

Anglikan *pr. n.* Anglican.

Anglosakson *pr. n.* Anglo-Saxon.

angudi [ī] ruddy.

angut *s.* **angıt.**

anı memory.

anık apt (*-e* to), ready (*-e* to), inclined (*-e* to).

anılmak *pass.* of **anmak** to be remembered, to be mentioned.

anımsamak to remember, to recall.

anırmak to bray.

anıt, -tı monument.

anıtkabir, -bri 1. mausoleum; **2.** ♀*pr. n.* tomb of Atatürk in Ankara.

anıtmezar mausoleum.

anıtsal monumental.

anız stubble.

ani [ī] **1.** sudden, instantaneous, unexpected; **2.** suddenly, all of a sudden.

aniden suddenly, all of a sudden.

anjin angina.

Anka 1. *pr. n.* phoenix; **2.** *sl.* well-heeled, moneybags; ~ *gibi* nonexistent.

ankesman paying in, collection (*of payment*).

ankesör public call-office, coin telephone.

anket, -ti questionnaire, (opinion) poll, public survey; ~ *yapmak* to take a poll.

anketçi pollster.

anlak PSYCH intelligence.

anlam 1. meaning, sense; **2.** connotation; **-ına gelmek** to mean, to amount (**to**).

anlamak 1. to understand, to comprehend, to conceive; **2.** to find out; **3.** (*bşden*) to know about *s.th.*, to have knowledge of *s.th.*; **4.** to deduce; to realize; **5.** (*bşden*) *sl.* to appreciate *s.th.*, to enjoy *s.th.*; **6.** *sl.* to try, to sample (*a delicacy*); **anladımsa, Arap olayım!** it is all Greek to me, I am unable to make head or tail of it!; **Anlayana sivrisinek saz, anlamayana davul zurna az** *pro.* a word is enough to the wise.

anlambilim semantics.

anlamdaş 1. synonymous; **2.** synonym.

anlamdaşlık synonymy, synonymity.

anlamlandırmak to explain.

anlamlı meaningful, expressive.

anlamsal semantic.

anlamsız meaningless.

anlamsızlık meaninglessness.

anlaşamamazlık 1. disagreement, conflict; **2.** misunderstanding.

anlaşılmak *pass. of anlamak* to be understood; **anlaşılan ...** it appears that ...

anlaşılmaz incomprehensible, unintelligible.

anlaşma 1. agreement, understanding; **2.** pact, treaty; **-ya varmak** to come to an agreement.

anlaşmak 1. to understand each other; **2.** to come to (*or* reach) an agreement.

anlaşmalı arranged by agreement.

anlaşmazlık 1. disagreement, conflict, incompatibility; **2.** misunderstanding.

ing.

anlatı narration.

anlatım expression, exposition.

anlatımlı expressive.

anlatmak *caus. of anlamak* **1.** to explain, to expound; **2.** to narrate, to relate, to tell; **3.** to describe; **4.** to show s.o., to learn s.o.

anlayış 1. understanding, comprehension; **2.** intelligence, perceptiveness; **3.** sympathy; **4.** mind, intellect; ~ *göstermek* to be tolerant (*-e* towards).

anlayışlı 1. understanding; **2.** intelligent.

anlayışsız 1. insensitive, inconsiderate; **2.** lacking in understanding.

anma 1. remembrance; **2.** commemoration; ~ *töreni* commemorative ceremony.

anmak 1. to call to mind, to remember, to think (*-i* of); **2.** to commemorate; **3.** to call, to name, to distinguish.

anmalık keepsake, souvenir.

anne [x .] mother; ~ *olm.* to become a mother; **-ler günü** Mother's Day.

anneanne grandmother.

anneciğim! mum!, mummy!

annelik motherhood; ~ *etm.* (*b-ne*) to be a mother to *s.o.*

anofel ZOO anopheles.

anonim 1. anonymous; **2.** incorporated; ~ *şirket* joint-stock company.

anons announcement; ~ *etm.* to announce; to page (*in a hotel, etc.*).

anorak anorak.

anormal abnormal.

anormalleşmek to become abnormal.

anormallik abnormality.

anot anode.

ansefalit, -ti MED encephalitis.

ansızın suddenly, all of a sudden, without warning.

ansiklopedi encyclopedia.

ansiklopedik encyclopedic.

ant, -dı 1. oath, vow; **2.** resolution; ~ *içmek* to take an oath, to swear; ~ *vermek* to importune *s.o.* with pleading oaths; **andını bozmak** to break one's oath.

antant, -tı agreement; ~ *kalmak* to come to an agreement.

antarktik Antarctic.

anten aerial, antenna (*a.* ZOO).

antepfıstığı, -nı pistachio.

antet, -ti letterhead.

antibiyotik antibiotic.

antidemokratik antidemocratic.

antifeding *radio*: antifading.
antifriz MEC antifreeze.
antika [. x .] **1.** antique; **2.** F queer, funny, eccentric; **3.** hemstitch.
antikacı antique-dealer.
antikalık 1. antiquity; **2.** F queerness, eccentricity.
antikite antiquity; **-ler** antiques.
antikor BIOL antibody.
antilop ZOO antelope.
antimon CHEM antimony.
antipati antipathy.
antipatik antipathetic; ~ **bulmak** to dislike.
antiseptik MED antiseptic.
antişambr antechamber.
antitez antithesis.
antitoksin BIOL antitoxin.
antlaşma pack, treaty.
antlaşmak to come to a solemn agreement.
antlı under oath, sworn.
antoloji anthology.
antrakt intermission, interval.
antrasit, -ti anthracite.
antre entrance, doorway, vestibule.
antrenman *sports*: training, exercise, work-out; ~ **yapmak** to work out, to exercise, to go into training.
antrenör *sports*: trainer, coach.
antrepo bonded warehouse, entrepôt.
antropoloji anthropology.
antrparantez parenthetically, in parenthesis.
anudane [. - - .] stubborn(ly), obstinate(ly).
anus [x .] ANAT anus.
aort, -tu ANAT aorta.
apaçık [x . .] as plain as the nose on one's face, clear, evident.
apak [x .] snow-white, pure white, all white.
apandis ANAT appendix.
apandisit, -ti ANAT appendicitis; ~ **olm.** to suffer from appendicitis.
apansız [x . .], **apansızın** [. x . .] at the drop of a hat, suddenly, all of a sudden, out of the blue.
aparmak 1. to carry away; **2.** *sl.* to make off (-i with).
apartman block of flats, apartment house; ~ **dairesi** flat, apartment.
apar topar posthaste, pell-mell, headlong, helter-skelter.
apaşikâr as plain as the nose on one's face.
apaydın [x . .] very bright, well lit.

apayrı [x . .] as different as chalk and cheese, as like as chalk to cheese, completely different.
apaz 1. cupped hand; **2.** handful.
aperitif apéritif, appetizer.
apış the inner sides of the thighs; ~ **açmak** to straddle; ~ **arası** the space between the thighs.
apışık holding its tail between its legs.
apışıklık gore, gusset.
apışmak 1. to spread its legs apart and collapse (*animal*); **2.** *fig.* to give up, to stand helpless; **apışıp kalmak** to be nonplussed.
apiko [. x .] **1.** NAUT apeak; **2.** *sl.* alert, ready, quick; **3.** *sl.* handsome, spruce, smart.
apikoluk *sl.* spruceness.
aplik, -ği wall lamp (*or* fixture).
aplikasyon 1. appliqué; **2.** *surv.* staking out.
aplike = **aplikasyon.**
apolet, -ti epaulet.
apostrof apostrophe.
apre 1. size, finish; **2.** sizing.
apse MED abscess.
apşak 1. bowlegged; **2.** sluggish; fagged out.
aptal silly, stupid, fool, simpleton; ~ **oğlu** ~ fucker.
aptalca 1. stupid (*act*); **2.** stupidly.
aptallaşmak 1. to become stupid; **2.** *fig.* to be taken aback.
aptallık stupidity, foolishness.
aptes 1. ritual ablution; **2.** feces; ~ **almak** to perform an ablution; ~ **bozacağı gelmek** to be taken short; ~ **bozmak** to relieve nature, to go to the toilet; ~ **etm.** = ~ **bozmak**; ~ **vermek** *fig.* to scold, to reprimand; **-i kaçtı** he ceased to need to go to the toilet; **-i olm.** (*or* **gelmek**) to be taken short.
apteshane [. . - .] toilet, water closet, latrine.
aptessiz canonically unclean; ~ **yere basmamak** *fig.* to be very strict in one's religious practices.
apul apul waddlingly.
ar[1] are (*100 m[2]*).
ar[2] [ā] shame; ~ **damarı** sense of shame; ~ **etm.** to be ashamed.
ara 1. distance; **2.** interval; gap; **3.** relation; **4.** break (*in a game*); intermission; interlude; **5.** space, spacing; **6.** intermediate, intermediary; **7.** time; **8.** **arasına, arasında** between; among; ~ **bozmak** to destroy the

friendship (between); ~ *bulmak* to reconcile, to mediate; ~ *hattı* diving (*or* parting) line; ~ *imtihanı* intermediate examination; ~ *seçimi* by-election; ~ *sıra* sometimes, now and then, from time to time, occasionally; ~ *vermek* (*bşe*) to take a break, to stop doing *s.th.* for a while, to pause; (arada) between; among; ~ *bir* from time to time, seldom, rarely; ~ *gitmek* to pass unnoticed; ~ *kalmak* to be mixed up in an affair; ~ *kaynamak* to pass unnoticed; ~ *sırada s.* ~ *sıra*; (aradan) ~ *çıkarmak* to remove; ~ *çıkmak* not to interfere; *görüşmeyeli ~ uzun zaman geçti* long time no see; (aralar) ~ *açıktır* they are at odds, they are at loggerheads; ~ *açıldı* they are on bad terms; ~ *bozuldu* they are on strained terms; ~ *iyileşti* they became reconciled; ~ *soğudu* a coolness has arisen in their friendship; ~ *şekerrenk* their relations are strained; ~ *yağbal* they are on good terms, they stand well with each other; *-nda dağlar kadar fark olm.* to be as different as black and white, to be as different as chalk and cheese; *-nda kan olm.* to have a blood feud (between); *-ndan kara kedi geçmek* *fig.* to be cross with each other, to bear resentment against each other; *-ından su sızmaz* *fig.* they are on intimate terms with each other; *-nı açmak* to create a rift (between): *-nı bulmak* to reconcile; *-nı düzeltmek* to reconcile; (arası) ~ *geçmeden* without delay; ~ *soğumak* (*bşin*) to lose *its* importance with the passage of time; *-nı bulmak* to reconcile; (araya) ~ *girmek* to meddle, to interfere; ~ *gitmek* 1. to go to waste; 2. F to be lost in the confusion; ~ *koymak* (*b-ni*) to ask *s.o.* to mediate, to put in *s.o.* as intermediary.

âra [ā] *obs. pl. of* **rey** 1. votes; 2. opinions.

araba 1. car, automobile; 2. cart, carriage; 3. cartload, wagonload; truckload; ~ *devrilince yol gösteren çok olur* *pro.* it is easy to be wise after the event; ~ *vapuru* car ferry, ferryboat; ~ *yolu* carriageway; *-sını düze çıkarmak* *fig.* to overcome difficulties, to put matters straight; *-yı çekmek* *sl.* to piss off, to clear out, to beat it, to scram.

arabacı 1. driver; coachman; 2. cartwright.

arabalık 1. coach-house; cart shed; 2. carload, wagonload; truckload; 3. garage.

arabesk arabesque.

Arabi [i] 1. Arabic, Arabian; 2. Arabic, the Arabic language.

Arabistan *pr. n.* Arabia; ~ *çölü* the Arabian desert.

arabozan mischief-maker.

arabozanlık mischief-making.

arabozucu mischief-maker.

arabozuculuk mischief-making.

arabulma mediation, reconciliation.

arabulucu mediator, peacemaker, go-between.

arabuluculuk mediation, intervention; ~ *etm.* to mediate.

aracı 1. go-between, mediator; 2. middleman.

aracılık mediation, intervention; ~ *etm.* to mediate.

araç 1. means; 2. tool, implement; 3. vehicle.

araçlı indirect.

araçsız direct.

Araf [- -] *isl.* MYTH purgatory.

arakçı *sl.* pilferer, thief.

arakçılık *sl.* pilferage, theft.

arakesit *-ti* MATH intersection.

arakıye [. - . .] 1. a soft felt cap; 2. a small oboe-like instrument.

araklamak *sl.* to pilfer, to pinch, to filch, to walk off (*-i* with), to swipe, to nick, to nip.

aralamak 1. to leave ajar (*door*); 2. to open out, to space; 3. to separate.

aralanmak 1. *pass. of* **aralamak**; 2. *sl.* to piss off, to toddle off.

aralık 1. space, interval, gap, opening; 2. time, moment, interval; 3. ajar (*door*); 4. corridor; passageway; 5. toilet, loo; ~ ~ now and then, occasionally; ~ *ayı* December; ~ *bırakmak* 1. to leave ajar (*door*); 2. to leave a space; ~ *etm.* to leave ajar, to open part way; ~ *hattı* dividing (*or* parting) line; ~ *vermeden* uninterruptedly, on and on; ~ *vermek* to take a break, to pause, to halt.

aralıklı 1. spaced, having intervals; 2. at intervals, on and off.

aralıksız 1. continuous; 2. continuously, on end, on and on.

arama *vn. of* **aramak** search, exploration; ~ *tarama* body search; police search; ~ *yapmak* to search.

aramak 1. to look (*-i* for), to hunt (*-i* for), to seek; **2.** to search; **3.** to miss, to long (*-i* for); **4.** F to look for trouble; **5.** to ask (*-i* for), to demand; **6.** to drop in on; *ara ki bulasın!* you can never find it!; *arama!* it is too much to expect; *Arayan belasını da bulur, Mevlasını da pro.* he that seeks finds.

aranjman MUS arrangement.

aranmak 1. *pass. of aramak*; **2.** to be in demand, to be sought after; **3.** to be missed; **4.** to search one's own clothes and pockets; **5.** F to look for trouble.

Arap, -bı 1. Arab; **2.** Arabian; **3.** F Negro; ~ *aklı* primitive thought; ~ *Birliği pr. n.* Arabic League; ~ *uyandı* F we have learned our lesson.

Arapça the Arabic language, Arabic.

arapsabunu, -nu soft soap.

arapsaçı, -nı 1. fuzzy hair; **2.** *fig.* tangled affair, mess; *-na döndürmek* to confound.

arapzamkı, -nı gum arabic.

ararot, -tu BOT arrowroot (starch).

Arasat, -tı [. . -] *isl.* MYTH the place of the Doomsday.

arasız continuously, on end, on and on.

arasöz digression.

araştırıcı 1. researcher, investigator; **2.** inquisitive, curious; **3.** investigative.

araştırma investigation, research.

araştırmacı researcher.

araştırmak to research, to investigate, to explore; to search.

aratümce GR parenthetical clause.

arayıcı 1. seeker; searcher; searching; **2.** customs inspector; **3.** AST finder.

araz symptoms.

arazi [. - -] land; estate(s); ~ *açmak* to clear land; ~ *olm. sl.* to take to one's heels, to beat it; ~ *sahibi* landowner; ~ *vergisi* land tax; *-ye uymak sl.* to lay low.

arazî accidental, extrinsic.

arbede tumult, riot, uproar, brawl.

arbitraj arbitrage.

arda 1. (marking) stake; **2.** lathe chisel.

ardala 1. camel bell; **2.** pillion, cushion.

ardıç, -cı BOT juniper.

ardıçkuşu, -nu ZOO fieldfare.

ardıl 1. consecutive; **2.** successor.

ardın ardın backwards.

ardınca behind, following, shortly afterwards.

ardışık MATH consecutive.

ardiye 1. warehouse; **2.** storage rent.

arduvaz slate.

arena arena.

argaç, -cı woof, weft.

argaçlamak to weave.

argalı argal(i).

argın tired, weak, feeble.

argınlık weakness, feebleness.

argo [x .] **1.** slang, cant; **2.** argot, jargon.

arı[1] ZOO bee; ~ *beyi* queen bee; ~ *gibi* busy as a bee; ~ *kovanı* **1.** beehive; **2.** BOT foxglove; ~ *kovanı gibi işlemek* to hum with people; ~ *sürüsü* swarm of bees.

arı[2] **1.** pure; **2.** clean; **3.** innocent; ~ *su* pure water.

arıcı beekeeper, apiarist.

arıcılık beekeeping, apiculture.

arık 1. lean, thin; **2.** lean (*meat*).

arıkuşu, -nu ZOO bee eater.

arılamak to absolve.

arılaşmak to become pure.

arılaştırmak to purify.

arılık 1. purity; **2.** innocence; **3.** cleanliness.

arındırmak to purify.

arınmak to be purified.

arısütü, -nü royal jelly.

arış 1. warp; **2.** pole (*of a car*).

arıtımevi refinery.

arıtmak 1. to refine; **2.** to purify, to clean.

arız happening; ~ *olm.* to happen, to occur, to befall (*-e* to).

arıza 1. breakdown, defect, failure, obstruction; **2.** unevenness, roughness; **3.** MUS accidental; ~ *yapmak* to break down.

arızalanmak to break down.

arızalı out of order, defective.

arızi 1. accidental, casual; **2.** temporary.

Ari [ā] Aryan.

ari 1. free (*-den* of); **2.** lacking; **3.** naked, bare.

arif 1. wise, knowing, sagacious; **2.** ♀ *mf.*

arifane wisely.

arife eve.

aristokrasi aristocracy.

aristokrat, -tı 1. aristocrat; **2.** aristocratic.

aristokratlık aristocracy.

aritmetik 1. arithmetic; **2.** arithmetical.

ariyet. *-ti* [ā] on loan, lent; ~ *almak* to borrow; ~ *vermek* to lend.

ariyeten as a loan.

arizamik [. - . -] thoroughly.

Arjantin *pr. n.* Argentina.

Arjantinli an Argentine; Argentinean.

ark. *-kı* irrigation trench, canal; ~ *lambası* arc-lamp.

arka 1. the back; **2.** back part, rear, reverse; **3.** buttocks, rump, fanny; **4.** hind, back, posterior; **5.** *fig.* backer, supporter; pull, influence; **6.** sequel; **7.** *arkasına, arkasında* behind; ~ *-ya* one after the other; ~ *-ya vermek* to back each other, to join forces; ~ *-ya beş gün* five days in succession, five days running; ~ *çantası* knapsack, rucksack; ~ *çıkmak* (*b-ne*) to back *s.o.* up; ~ *kapı* back door; ~ *plan* background; ~ *sokak* back street; ~ *taraf* back side, reverse; ~ *üstü yatmak* to lie on one's back; ~ *vermek* to lean one's back (*-e* against); ~ *yüz* back side, reverse; *-da bırakmak* to leave behind, to outstrip; to outdistance; *-da kalanlar* the bereaved; *-da kalmak* **1.** to stay behind; to be outdistanced; **2.** *fig.* to be overshadowed; *-dan* **1.** from behind, in the back; behind the back; **2.** afterwards; *-dan -ya* under the counter, secretively; *-dan söylemek* to backbite; (arkası) ~ *gelmedi* it didn't last (*or* continue); ~ *kesilmek* to run out, to peter out; ~ *sıra* right after, on one's heels; ~ *var* to be continued; ~ *yere gelmemek* not to be defeated; ~ *yufka!* there is not much to follow!; *-na düşmek* **1.** to follow up (*a matter*); **2.** to follow, to dog, to tail *s.o.*; *-nı almak* to bring to an end; *-nı bırakmamak* to follow up, to stick to; *-nı dayamak* (*b-ne*) to build (*or* rely) on *s.o.*; *-nı getiremedim* I was unable to carry through it; *-nı kesmek* to stop, to cut off; *-nı vermek* **1.** to lean one's back (*-e* against); **2.** *fig.* to rely (*or* build) on (*-e* on).

arkadaş friend, companion; ~ *olm.* to become friends; *-ını söyle, kim olduğunu söyleyeyim pro.* men are known by the company they keep, birds of a feather flock together.

arkadaşlık friendship; ~ *etm.* **1.** to accompany; **2.** to be a friend (*ile* of).

arkaik archaic.

arkalamak 1. to hoist *s.th.* onto one's back; **2.** *fig.* to back up, to protect, to support.

arkalanmak 1. *pass. of* **arkalamak; 2.** to rely (*or* count *or* depend) on.

arkalı *fig.* having a backing, having a friend at court.

arkalık 1. a sleeveless jacket; **2.** back (*of a chair*); **3.** porter's back pad; **4.** carrier (*of a bicycle*).

arkeolog archeologist.

arkeoloji archeology; ~ *müzesi* archeological museum.

arkeolojik archeological.

arklı arc …; ~ *lamba* arc-lamp.

arktik Arctic; ~ *kuşak* GEOGR Arctic Zone.

arlanmak to feel ashamed.

arma [x .] **1.** coat of arms, armorial bearings; **2.** NAUT rigging; **3.** *sl.* jewel(-le)ry; ~ *donatmak* NAUT to rig a ship; ~ *soymak* NAUT to unrig a ship.

armador NAUT rigger.

armağan 1. present, gift; **2.** prize, award; ~ *etm.* to present (*-e* to).

armatör shipowner.

armatur 1. armature; **2.** condenser plate.

armoni MUS harmony.

armonik(a) 1. harmonica, mouth organ; **2.** accordion.

armoz NAUT seam, joint.

armudi [ū, ī] pear-shaped.

armut. *-du* **1.** BOT pear; **2.** *sl.* blockhead; ~ *piş, ağzıma düş demek* to expect things to fall into one's lap without doing anything; *armudun sapı var, üzümün çöpü var demek fig.* there is no garden without its weed.

armuz NAUT seam, joint.

Arnavut. *-du* Albanian; ~ *biberi* red pepper.

arnavutciğeri. *-ni* fried liver.

Arnavutça Albanian (language).

arnavutkaldırımı rough cobblestone pavement.

Arnavutluk 1. the character of an Albanian; **2.** *pr. n.* Albania.

arozöz sprinkler, watering truck.

arpa BOT barley; ~ *boyu* very short distance; ~ *boyu kadar gitmek* to show little progress; ~ *ektim, darı çıktı fig.* I did not get what I expected.

arpacı[1] seller of barley; ~ *kumrusu gibi düşünmek* to be in a brown study.

arpacı[2] *sl.* thief, pilferer.

arpacık 1. MED sty; **2.** front sight (*of a gun*).

arpalık 1. barley field; 2. barley bin; 3. *fig.* sinecure; 4. = *başmaklık.*

arsa building-ground, building-site, vacant lot.

arsenik CHEM arsenic.

arsıulusal international.

arsız 1. saucy, cheeky, impudent, insolent, shameless; 2. vigorous (*plant*).

arsızlanmak to act shamelessly, to be saucy.

arsızlık impudence, insolence; ~ *etm.* to behave shamelessly.

arslan *s. aslan.*

arş¹: ~*!* MIL march!

arş² 1. *isl.* MYTH the highest heaven; 2. trolley pole.

arşe violin bow.

arşın yard, cubit (*a former Turkish unit of length, 60-70 cm.*).

arşınlamak 1. to measure by the yard; 2. to stride through.

arşidük, -*kü* archduke.

arşidüşes archduchess.

arşiv archives.

art, -*dı* 1. back, rear, behind; hind; 2. sequel; ~ *arda* one after another; ~ *düşünce* hidden intent; ~ *niyet s.* ~ *düşünce*; *ardı arası kesilmeden* uninterruptedly; *ardı ardına* one after another, continually; *ardı arkası gelmeyen* endless, never-ending; *ardı kesilmek* to run out; *ardı sıra* 1. (along) behind; 2. immediately after; *ardına düşmek* 1. to follow in the steps of; 2. to follow up, to tail, to pursue; *ardına kadar açık* wide open (*door, window*); *ardına koymamak fig.* to revenge *o.s.* (*on*); *ardınca* behind; *ardında gezmek* (*or dolaşmak*) to run after; *ardını almak* to complete; *ardını bırakmamak* to follow up, to stick to; *artta kalmak* 1. to remain (*or stay*) behind, to be left behind; 2. to survive.

artağan exceptionally fruitful.

artakalan remainder.

artakalmak to be left over, to remain.

artan remaining, left over.

artçı MIL rear guard.

artdamak hard palate.

arter artery.

artezyen artesian well.

artı MATH plus.

artık 1. left (over), remaining; 2. remainder, remnant, residue, leavings; 3. extra, superfluous, redundant; 4. now, well then; 5. finally; from now on; 6. (*with negative*) any more; ~ *başlayalım!* let's start!; ~ *mal göz çıkarmaz pro.* a little extra does no harm.

artıkgün AST leap(-year) day.

artıklık superabundancy.

artıkyıl AST leap year.

artırım economy, saving, frugality.

artırma 1. auction; 2. saving, economizing.

artırmak 1. to increase, to expand, to add (*to*), to augment, to step up; 2. to save, to economize (*money*); 3. to overbid (*at an auction*); 4. to go too far.

artış increase, augmentation, mark--up.

artist, -*ti* 1. artist; 2. actor, actress.

artistik artistic; ~ *patinaj* artistic skating.

artkafa back of the head, occiput.

artmak, (-*ar*) 1. to increase, to go up (*price*); 2. to remain, to be left over.

artsız arasız uninterrupted, perpetual.

aruz [ū] prosody.

arya [x .] MUS aria.

arz¹ the earth.

arz² 1. width; 2. latitude; ~ *dairesi* parallel of latitude.

arz³ presentation, representation, demonstration; petition; ~ *etm.* 1. to present; 2. to show; 3. to offer; ~ *ve talep* supply and demand; *arzı hürmet(ler)* (*ederim*) yours faithfully; *arzı veda etm.* (*b-ne*) to bid farewell to *s.o.*, to say good-bye to *s.o.*

arzî¹ earthly.

arzî² GEOGR terrestrial.

arzu [ū] wish, desire, longing; ~ *etm.* to wish (-*i* for), to desire, to long (-*i* for); ~ *üzerine* on request; *kalmak -sundadır* he wishes to stay.

arzuhal, -*li* [. . -] petition.

arzuhalci scrivener.

arzukeş desirous.

arzulamak to desire, to wish (-*i* for), to long (-*i* for), to want.

arzulu *s. arzukeş.*

as¹ zoo ermine, stoat.

as² 1. *cards*: ace; 2. ace, champion.

as- sub-

asa scepter, stick, baton, staff.

asabi 1. nervous, irritable, on edge; 2. neural.

asabileşmek to get nervous.

asabilik nervousness, irritability.

asabiye1. nervous diseases; **2.** neurology, neuropathology.

asabiyeci nerve specialist, neurologist.

asabiyet, -ti nervousness, irritability; **-e kapılmak** to get nervous.

asal basic, fundamental; ~ **sayı** MATH prime (or odd) number.

asalak 1. BOT, ZOO parasite; **2.** fig. hanger-on, sponger, parasite.

asalaklık1. parasitism; **2.** fig. freeloading, sponging.

asalet, -ti [. - .] **1.** nobility, nobleness; **2.** definitive appointment.

asaleten [. - .] acting as principal.

asaletli [. - . .] noble.

asamble assembly.

asansör lift, Am. elevator.

asansörcü liftman, liftboy.

asap, -bı ANAT nerves; ~ **bozukluğu** nervous upset; ~ **cümlesi** ANAT nervous system; **asabı bozulmak** to get nervous; **asabına dokunmak** to get on one's nerves.

asar [ā] obs. pl. of **eser** monuments, works.

asarıatika antiquities, ancient monuments.

asayiş [- - .] repose, public peace (or security).

asayişsiz troubled, insecure, unsafe.

asbaşkan vice-president, deputy chief.

asbest, -ti GEOL asbestos.

aselbent storax.

asepsi asepsis.

asetat, -tı acetate.

asetilen CHEM acetylene.

aseton acetone.

asfalt, -tı1. asphalt; **2.** asphalt highway, paved road.

asfaltlamak to asphalt.

asgari [ī] minimum, least, smallest; ~ **fiyat** minimum price; ~ **ücret** minimum wage.

ashap, -bı [. -] obs. pl. of **sahip** possessors, masters.

ası¹**: -da olm.** (or **kalmak**) to be in the air, to hang in the balance, to be in suspense.

ası² profit, benefit.

asık 1. sulky; **2.** hanging; ~ **suratlı** (or **yüzlü**) sulky, sullen, grouchy.

asıl1. (the) original; **2.** origin; **3.** truth, reality; basis; **4.** actual, true; real, essential; **5.** main, the most important; **6.** actually, essentially; ~ **maksatları**

their main purpose; ~ **sayılar** GR cardinal numbers; (aslı) ~ **astarı yok** it is unfounded, it is not true; ~ **çıkmak** to prove to be true; ~ **faslı yok** there is no truth in it; ~ **nesli bellisiz** whose origin is unknown; ~ **var** it is true; ~ **yok nesli yok** s. ~ **astarı yok; bu söylentinin ~ yok** this rumo(u)r is not true.

asılı hanging, suspended.

asılmak 1. pass. of **asmak; 2.** to be hanged; **3.** to insist; **4.** to pull hard; **5.** (b-ne) to pester s.o., to bother s.o.

asılsız unfounded, groundless (news, rumo(u)r).

asılsızlık groundlessness.

asılzade [. . - .] **1.** nobleman, aristocrat, peer; **2.** sl. pander, pimp, procurer.

asılzadelik nobility, peerage.

asıntı 1. delay; **2.** pestering, bothering; **-da kalmak** to hang in the air; **-ya bırakmak** to delay, to postpone.

asır, -srı 1. century; **2.** era, epoch, age, time, period.

asırlık a century old.

asi [ī] **1.** rebellious, refractory; **2.** rebel, insurgent.

aside [ī] dish made of okra with ground meat and flour.

asil 1. noble, aristocrat; **2.** hono(u)rable, praiseworthy, noble (action); **3.** permanent (official); **4.** JUR principal; ~ **kan** blue blood.

asileşmek to rebel, to be unruly.

asilik 1. rebelliousness; **2.** rebellion.

asillik nobility, blue blood.

asistan1. assistant; **2.** assistant doctor.

asistanlık assistantship.

asit, -di CHEM acid.

asitli containing acid.

asker1. soldier; troops; **2.** military service; **3.** militant, valiant; **4.** sl. tin, dough; ~ **kaçağı** deserter; ~ **olm.** to join the army; **-den kaçmak** to desert; **-e alınmak** to be drafted; **-e çağırmak** to draft, to call up; **-e çağrılmak** to be called up; to be drafted; **-e gitmek** to go into the army.

askerce soldierly, military.

askeri military; ~ **bando** military band; ~ **fabrika** war (or armament) factory; ~ **hastane** military hospital; ~ **inzibat** military police (or policeman); ~ **lise** cadets school; ~ **mahkeme** military court, court-martial; ~ **mıntıka** military zone; ~ **müze** military museum; ~ **öğrenci** cadet; ~ **zabıta** military police.

askerileşmek to become militarized.

askerileştirmek to militarize.

askerlik military service; ~ **şubesi** local draft office, recruiting office; ~ **yoklaması** roll call.

askı 1. hook, hanger; **2.** braces, *Am.* suspenders; **3.** coat rack; **4.** MED sling; **5.** the posting (*of an announcement*); **6.** necklace *or* gold chain; **-da bırakmak** to leave in the air, to shelve; **-da kalmak** to hang in the balance, to remain in suspense; **-ya almak 1.** to prop up temporarily (*house*); **2.** to lift by lines from other ships; **-ya çıkarmak** to post (*the banns*).

asla [x -] never, by no means, in no way.

aslan[1] **1.** ZOO lion; **2.** *fig.* plucky person, brave man; ~ **ağzında olm.** *fig.* to be very hard to get; ~ **gibi 1.** like a lion (*person*); **2.** healthy, in the pink; ~ **payı** the lion's share; ~ **terbiyecisi** lion-tamer; ~ **yürekli** *fig.* lion-hearted; **-ım!** my lad!

aslan[2] *s.* **aslen**.

Aslan[3] AST Leo.

aslanağzı, -nı BOT snapdragon.

aslen fundamentally, essentially, basically, originally.

asli [i] fundamental, essential, original, principal; ~ **adet** cardinal number; ~ **maaş** basic salary; ~ **nüsha** original text; ~ **vazife** principal duty.

asliye ~ **mahkemesi** JUR court of first instance.

asma[1] BOT **1.** vine; **2.** grapevine; ~ **kütüğü** vine stock; ~ **yaprağı** vine leaf.

asma[2] **1.** hanging, suspended; **2.** suspension; ~ **kat** mezzanine; ~ **kilit** padlock; ~ **köprü** suspension bridge; ~ **saat** wall clock.

asmabahçe hanging garden.

asmak (-ar) 1. to hang up (**-e** on), to suspend; **2.** to hang (*a person*); **3.** *sl.* to play truant (*or* hooky), to skip, to cut (*school*); **4.** *sl.* to neglect; **5.** *sl.* to skip out (**-i** on); **6.** *sl.* to refuse to pay back (*a debt*); **asıp kesmek** to play the tyrant; **astığı astık kestiği kestik** what he says goes.

asmakabağı, -nı BOT long edible squash.

aspiratör 1. exhaust (*or* suction) fan; **2.** MED aspirator.

aspirin aspirin.

asri modern, up-to-date.

asrileşmek to be modernized.

asrilik modernity.

assubay MIL noncommissioned officer.

asşuur subconscious.

ast, -tı 1. MIL sub, under; **2.** subordinate.

astar 1. lining; **2.** priming, undercoat (*before painting*); **3.** caulking; ~ **boyası** undercoat, priming; **-ı yüzünden pahalı** it costs more than it is worth.

astarlamak 1. to line (*a garment*); **2.** to prime.

asteğmen MIL second lieutenant.

astım MED asthma.

astigmat MED astigmatic.

astragan astrakhan.

astroloji astrology.

astronomi astronomy.

astronomik astronomical; ~ **fiyat** astronomical price.

astronot astronaut.

asude [ü] calm, quiet, tranquil.

asuman [ā, ā] sky, the heavens.

Asya *pr. n.* Asia.

Asyalı *pr. n.* Asiatic.

aş cooked food; ~ **deliye kalıyor** the person who does not get involved in an argument profits; ~ **kabı** MIL mess tin, *Am.* mess kit; **-ta** (*or* **çorbada**) **tuzu bulunmak** (*b-nin*) to make a contribution, however small.

aşağı 1. bottom, the lower part; **2.** lower; **3.** inferior, low; **4.** common, mean, commonplace; **5.** down, downstairs; ~ **atmak** to pay no attention (**to**), to disregard; ~ **görmek** to look down (**-i** on), to despise; ~ **kalmak** to fall short (**-den** of); ~ **mal** inferior goods; ~ **yukarı** more or less, about, approximately; **-daki** below; **-dan almak** to ingratiate *o.s.*; **Mehmet** ~ **Mehmet yukarı** it is 'Mehmet' all the time, nothing but 'Mehmet'.

aşağılamak to run down, to lower, to degrade, to denigrate.

aşağılık 1. coarse, vulgar; **2.** vulgarity; ~ **duygusu** (*or* **kompleksi**) inferiority complex.

aşama 1. degree, rank, level, position, grade; **2.** stage, step.

aşarî [- - -] *obs.* MATH decimal.

aşçı *s.* **ahçı**.

aşçılık *s.* **ahçılık**.

aşevi, -ni 1. restaurant; **2.** soup kitchen; **3.** temporary kitchen.

aşhane [. - .] *s.* **aşevi**.

aşı 1. vaccine; **2.** vaccination, inoculation; **3.** budding, grafting; **4.** scion, graft, bud; ~ **kâğıdı** certificate of vaccination; ~ **olm.** to be inoculated; ~ **yapmak 1.** to inoculate, to vaccinate; **2.** to graft, to bud.

aşıboyası, -nı 1. red ocher; **2.** brick red.

aşıcı 1. vaccinator; **2.** grafter (*of trees*).

aşık ANAT astragalus, talus, anklebone, hucklebone; ~ **atmak 1.** to play knucklebones; **2.** *fig.* to vie, to compete (*ile* with); **aşığı bey** (*or* **çift** *or* **cuk**) **oturuyor** he is having everything smoothly.

aşık 1. in love (*-e* with); **2.** lover, suitor; **3.** bard, troubadour; **4.** absent-minded person; ~ **olm.** to fall in love (*-e* with); **-lısı** lover (**of**), devotee.

âşıkane 1. amorously; **2.** amorous (*act*).

âşıktaş sweetheart.

aşılamak 1. to inoculate (*a. fig.*), to vaccinate; **2.** to bud, to graft; **3.** to infect; **4.** *fig.* to inculcate, to instill, to inoculate (*ideas*) (*-e* in).

aşındırmak 1. to abrade, to wear away; **2.** CHEM to corrode; **3.** *fig.* to frequent (*a place*).

aşınma 1. corrosion; **2.** wear and tear; **3.** erosion.

aşınmak 1. to wear away, to be corroded, to be abraded, to be eroded; **2.** to depreciate.

aşırı 1. extreme, excessive; **2.** extremely, excessively; **3.** beyond, over; **4.** every other; ~ **gitmek** to exceed the limit, to go beyond bounds, to overshoot the mark; ~ **solcu** extreme leftist; **gün** ~ every other day.

aşırıdoyma CHEM supersaturation.

aşırıduyu hyperesthesia.

aşırılık excessiveness.

aşırma 1. *vn.* of **aşırmak**; **2.** theft, pilfering; **3.** stolen, pilfered; **4.** P bucket; ~ **kayış** (drive) belt.

aşırmak 1. (*bir yerden*) to pass over (*a place*); **2.** F to swipe, to nick, to nip, to pinch; **3.** *sl.* to get rid (of); **4.** to plagiarize.

aşifte [ā] loose woman.

aşikâr [ā] clear, evident, manifest, open.

aşina [ā, ā] **1.** familiar, well-known; **2.** acquaintance; **3.** knowing, acquainted (*-e* with).

aşinalık acquaintance, intimacy; ~ **etm.** to bow, to greet by a gesture.

aşiret, -ti [ī] tribe.

aşk, -kı love, passion; ~ **etm.** to land, to inflict (*a blow*); **-a gelmek** to go into a rapture, to be enraptured; **aşkınıza!** to your health!

aşkın 1. more than, over, beyond; **2.** excessive; **işi başından -dır** he is up to his ears in work; **yaşı elliyi -dır** he is over fifty.

aşkolsun! 1. bravo!, well done!; **2.** shame on you!

aşlamak to mix hot water with (*cold water*).

aşlık 1. provisions; **2.** wheat.

aşmak, (-ar) 1. to pass (**over**), to go (**beyond**); **2.** to exceed, to surpass; **3.** to cover (*a mare*); **4.** *sl.* to slip away, to sneak away.

aşna fişne *sl.* secret love affair.

aşure [ū] *pudding made with cereals, sugar and raisins.*

aşüfte [ā] *s.* **aşifte.**

at, -tı ZOO horse; ~ **başı beraber** (*or* **bir**) neck and neck; ~ **çalındıktan sonra ahırın kapısını kapamak** to lock the stable door after the horse has been stolen; ~ **hırsızı** rustler; ~ **koşusu** (*or* **yarışı**) horse-racing; ♀ **Meydanı** *pr. n.* Hippodrome; **-a binmek** to ride a horse; **-ı alan Üsküdar'ı geçmek** to miss the bus (*or* boat); **-ı eşkin, kılıcı keskin** *fig.* he is powerful.

ata 1. father; **2.** ancestor; **3.** ♀ *pr. n. abbr.* for **Atatürk**; **-lardan kalma** ancestral.

atacılık BIOL atavism, reversion.

ataerki, -nı patriarchy.

ataerkil patriarchal.

atak 1. rash, reckless, boastful (*person*); **2.** *football*: attack.

ataklık rashness.

atalanı, -nı hippodrome.

atalet, -ti [. - .] **1.** laziness, lassitude; **2.** unemployment; **3.** PHYS inertia; ~ **kanunu** PHYS principle of inertia.

atalık fatherliness.

atamak to appoint (*-e* to).

ataman ataman, hetman.

atanmak to be appointed (*-e* to).

atardamar ANAT artery.

atasözü, -nü proverb.

ataşe attaché.

Atatürk *pr. n. founder and first president of the Turkish Republic.*

Atatürkçü *pr. n.* Kemalist.

Atatürkçülük *pr. n.* Kemalism.

atavik atavistic.

atçı horse breeder.

atçılık horse breeding.

ateh dotage, senility; ~ **getirmek** to dote.

ateizm atheism.

atelye 1. workshop; **2.** studio, atelier.

aterina [. . x .] zoo silversides, atherine.

ateş 1. fire; **2.** MED temperature, fever; **3.** vehemence, fervo(u)r, zeal, ardo(u)r; **4.** *fig.* vivacity, exuberance; **5.** MIL gunfire; artillery fire; **6.** a light (*for a cigarette*); **7.** danger; catastrophe; ~ **açmak** MIL to open fire (*-e* on); ~ **almak 1.** to catch (*or* take) fire; **2.** MIL to be fired (*gun*); **3.** to be alarmed; ~ **etm.** MIL to fire (*-e* on), to shoot (*-e* at); ~ **gibi 1.** piping hot; **2.** agile, intelligent; ~ **gibi yanmak** to run a temperature; ~ **hattı** (*or* **boyu**) MIL firing line; ~ **kesilmek** *fig.* to become industrious and active; ~ **kesmek** to cease fire; ~ **koymak** to set on fire; ~ **olmayan yerden duman çıkmaz** *pro.* there is no smoke without fire, where there is smoke there is fire; ~ **pahasına** very expensive; ~ **püskürmek** *fig.* to spit fire (*-e* at), to go up in the air; ~ **vermek** to set on fire, to burn; **-e körükle gitmek** *fig.* to add fuel to the flames; **-e vermek 1.** to set fire (*-i* to); **2.** to panic, to upset; **3.** to ravage, to devastate (*a country*); **-i başına vurmak** to blow one's top; **-i çıkmak** (*or* **yükselmek**) to run a temperature; **-le oynamak** to play with fire (*or* edged tools); **-ler içinde** feverish; **-ten gömlek** ordeal.

ateşbalığı, -nı sardine.

ateşböceği, -ni zoo firefly, glowworm.

ateşçi fireman, stoker.

ateşkes cease-fire, armistice, truce.

ateşleme ELECT ignition.

ateşlemek 1. to set fire (*-i* to), to ignite, to light; **2.** *fig.* to provoke, to incite.

ateşlendirmek 1. to enliven; **2.** to stir up, to aggravate (*trouble*).

ateşlenmek 1. *pass. of* **ateşlemek**; **2.** to run a temperature; **3.** *fig.* to get angry.

ateşli 1. MED feverish; **2.** *fig.* fiery; **3.** *fig.* fervent, vivacious; **4.** MIL fire ...; ~ **silah** firearm.

ateşlik 1. firepan; **2.** fit for burning.

atfen [x .] **1.** ascribed (*-e* to); **2.** based (*-e* on).

atfetmek [x . .] **1.** to attribute (*-e* to), to ascribe (*-e* to), to impute (*-e* to); **2.** to direct, to turn (*-e* to) (*one's glance*).

atıcı 1. marksman; **2.** *fig.* fibber.

atıcılık 1. marksmanship; **2.** *fig.* mendacity, fibbing.

atıf, -tfı attribution.

atıfet, -ti [ā] affection, sympathy.

atık small churn.

atıl 1. lazy; **2.** idle; **3.** PHYS inert.

atılgan 1. dashing, bold, plucky; **2.** enterprising.

atılganlık 1. audacity, boldness; **2.** enterprise.

atılım, atılış 1. advance, progress; **2.** *sports:* attack.

atılmak 1. *pass. of* **atmak**; **2.** to attack, to go (*-e* at); **3.** *sl.* to butt in, to cut in; **4.** to begin, to go (*-e* into).

atım range (*of a gun*).

atımlık the quantity of powder for one charge; **iki ~ barut** two charges of powder.

atış 1. throwing; **2.** firing, shooting; **3.** beating (*of the heart*); ~ **menzili** range.

atışmak 1. (*b-le*) to quarrel with *s.o.*, to have a tiff with *s.o.*; **2.** *to* try to make up (*-e* with); **3.** to indulge in poetic repartee.

atıştırmak 1. *caus. of* **atışmak**; **2.** to bolt, to gobble (*food*); **3.** to drizzle, to spit (*rain, snow*).

ati the future; **-deki** in the future.

atik¹ alert, agile.

atik², -kı ancient.

Atina *pr. n.* Athens.

Atinalı *pr. n.* an Athenian.

atkafalı dumb, stupid.

atkestanesi, -ni [. . - . .] BOT horse chestnut.

atkı 1. shawl, stole; **2.** weft, woof; **3.** shoe strap; **4.** pitchfork; **5.** lintel.

atkılamak to weave the woof in.

atkuyruğu, -nu 1. BOT mare's-tail; **2.** ponytail.

atlama jump; ~ **taşı** steppingstone; ~ **taşı yapmak** *fig.* to use as a steppingstone.

atlamak 1. to jump; **2.** to jump down (*-den* from), to leap (*-den* from); **3.** to jump (*-e* into) (*a taxi*); **4.** to skip, to miss, to leave out; **5.** *journalism:* to miss a scoop; **6.** to be misled, to be mistaken (*-de* in); **7.** *sl.* to screw, to stuff, to fuck.

atlambaçleapfrog.

atlanmak 1. *pass. of atlamak*; **2.** to mount a horse; **3.** to get a horse.

Atlantik*pr. n.* Atlantic.

atlas1. atlas, map book; **2.** ANAT atlas; **3.** satin.

atlasçiçeği *-ni* BOT cactus.

atlatmak*caus. of atlamak* **1.** to make *s.o.* jump; **2.** to overcome, to weather (*crisis, danger, etc.*); **3.** to put off, to get rid of (*a person*).

atlayışleap.

atlet *-ti* **1.** athlete; **2.** muscular, well--developed; **3.** (*a.* ~ *fanilası*) undershirt, vest.

atletikathletic.

atletizmathletics.

atlı rider, horseman; mounted on horseback; ~ *araba* horse cart, wagon.

atlıkarıncamerry-go-round, carousel, roundabout.

atmacazoo sparrow-hawk.

atmak (-ar) 1. to throw; **2.** to drop; **3.** to send away; **4.** to put out, to extend; **5.** to fire (*a gun, a shot*); **6.** to postpone, to put off; **7.** to throw on, to put on (*a garment*); **8.** to impute, to throw (*-e* on), to put (*-e* on) (*blame*); **9.** to expel *s.o.* (*-den* from); **10.** to discard, to throw away; **11.** to reject, to expel; **12.** to blow up, to demolish; **13.** F to lie, to fib; **14.** F to drink; **15.** to fluff (*cotton*); **16.** to split crack, to come loose; **17.** to pulsate, to beat, to throb (*heart, artery*); **18.** to send, to post (*letter*); **19.** to let out (*cry, scream*); **20.** to abandon, to give up; **21.** *sl.* to perform (*a dance*); **22.** *sl.* to sing (*a song*); **23.** to land (*a blow*); **24.** to write (*one's signature, the date*); *at martini Debre'li Hasan!* don't try to pull my leg!; *atıp tutmak* (*or savurmak*) **1.** to run down; **2.** to talk big, to boast; *atma Recep, din kardeşiyiz!* don't try to pull my leg!; *attığı tırnak olamamak* (*b-nin*) *fig.* can't hold a candle to *s.o.*

atmasyon*sl.* **1.** lie; **2.** false, made up.

atmasyoncu*sl.* **1.** liar; **2.** mendacious.

atmasyonculuk*sl.* lying, mendacity.

atmosferatmosphere.

atol *-lü* atoll.

atomatom; ~ *bombası* atomic bomb, A-bomb, *sl.* nuke; ~ *çağı* atomic age; ~ *çekirdeği* (atomic) nucleus; ~ *enerjisi or -lar arası enerjisi* atomic energy.

atomalatomic.

atraksiyon number in a floor show, feature.

atsineği *-ni* zoo horsefly, forest fly.

av 1. hunt(ing), chase; shooting; fishing; **2.** game, prey; catch (*fish*); **3.** *fig.* victim, prey; ~ *alayı* MIL fighter wing (*or* group); ~ *aramak* to look for game; ~ *köpeği* hound, hunting dog; ~ *kuşu* **1.** fowling hawk; **2.** game bird; ~ *takımı* hunting equipment; ~ *tüfeği* fowling-piece, shotgun; *-a giden avlanır pro.* the biter is sometimes bit.

avadan*rare* set of tools.

avadanlık1. set of tools; **2.** *sl.* cock and bollocks.

aval[*, -li* **1.** endorsement of a bill of exchange by a third party; **2.** endorser.

aval²*sl.* half-witted, stupid.

aval aval*sl.* stupidly.

avam[. -] *pl. of amme* common people, lower classes; ♀ *Kamarası pr. n.* the House of Commons.

avanak*sl.* gullible, simpleton.

avanaklık*sl.* gullibility.

avans advance (*of money*), earnest (*-money*); ~ *almak* to get an advance; ~ *vermek* to advance money.

avanta[. x .] *sl.* illicit profit; *-dan* for nothing, gratis.

avantacı*sl.* freeloader, sponger, bum.

avantacılık*sl.* freeloading.

avantajadvantage, profit, gain.

avara[. x .] NAUT shoving off; ~ *etm.* to shove off; ~ *kolu* MEC switch lever.

avarevagabond, good-for-nothing, out of work.

avarız[. - .] *pl. of arıza* roughness.

avarya[. x .] NAUT average.

avaz[. -] shout, cry; ~ ~ *bağırmak or -ı çıktığı kadar bağırmak* to shout at the top of one's voice.

avcı 1. hunter, huntsman; **2.** MIL rifleman, skirmisher; ~ *uçağı* fighter; ~ *zağarı* **1.** hound; **2.** *fig.* hanger-on.

avcılık 1. hunting, huntsmanship, shooting; **2.** *fig.* woman-chasing.

avdet *-ti* return; ~ *etm.* to return.

aveneaccomplices, gang.

avgındrain hole (*in a wall*).

avisto[. x .] COM at sight.

avize[i] chandelier.

avizeağacı *-nı* BOT yucca.

avizo[. x .] NAUT dispatch boat.

avlakhunting ground.

avlamak1. to hunt, to shoot; **2.** *fig.* to

dupe, to deceive.
avlanmak 1. *pass. of* **avlamak; 2.** to go hunting.
avlu court(yard).
Avrasya *pr. n.* Eurasia.
avrat, -tı *contp., sl. or* P **1.** woman; **2.** wife.
avret, -ti private parts, genitals.
Avrupa [. x .] *pr. n.* Europe.
Avrupai European (style).
Avrupalı European.
Avrupalılaşmak to become Europeanized.
avt, avut *football:* out.
avuç, -cu 1. the hollow of the hand; **2.** handful; ~ **açmak** to beg, to cadge; ~ ~ **1.** handful to each; **2.** by the handful, lavishly; ~ **dolusu** plenty of, a lot of; ~ **dolusu para tutmak** to cost an arm and a leg; ~ **içi kadar 1.** skimpy; **2.** narrow (*place*); **avucu gidişmek** (*or* **kaşınmak**) *fig.* to anticipate getting money; **avucuna saymak** to pay in hand (*cash*); **avucunu yalamak** to be left empty-handed; **avucunun içi gibi bilmek** to know like the back of one's hand; **avucunun içindedir** *fig.* he is at her command.
avuçiçi bilgisayar ıт handheld, PDA (= *personal digital assistant*).
avuçlamak 1. to grasp; **2.** to take by handfuls.
avukat, -tı lawyer, solicitor, advocate, barrister.
avukatlık 1. advocacy, barristership; **2.** *fig.* unnecessary defense.
avunç consolation, comfort.
avundurmak to console, to comfort.
avunmak 1. to be consoled (*ile* with), to be cheered up; **2.** to be preoccupied (*ile* with); **3.** to be bred, to become pregnant (*animal*).
avuntu consolation.
avurt, -du pouch of the cheek; ~ **etm.** to put on airs; ~ **kesmek** to give *o.s.* airs; ~ **satmak** (*or* **şişirmek**) to brag, to talk big; ~ **zavurt etm. 1.** *s.* ~ **satmak**; **2.** to threaten (*or* browbeat) others; **avurdu avurduna göçmek** to have sunken cheeks.
avurtlamak *s.* **avurt etm.**
Avustralya [.. x .] *pr. n.* Australia.
Avustralyalı [. . x . .] **1.** Australian; **2.** an Australian.
Avusturya [. . x .] *pr. n.* Austria.
Avusturyalı [.. x . .] **1.** Austrian; **2.** an Austrian.

avut *s.* **avt.**
avutmak 1. to soothe, to distract; to delude, to quieten; **2.** to console, to comfort; **3.** to attract and amuse.
ay¹ 1. moon; crescent; **2.** month (*of the year*); ~ **aydını** (*or* **aydınlığı**) moonlight; ~ **dede** the moon; ~ **ışığı** moonlight; ~ **modülü** moon module; ~ **parçası** a beauty; ~ **tutulması** lunar eclipse; ~ **yıldız** star and crescent (*Turkish emblem*); **-da yılda bir** once in a blue moon; **-ın on dördü** full moon; **-ın on dördü gibi** very beautiful (*woman*).
ay² 1. oh!; **2.** ouch!
aya palm of the hand.
ayak 1. foot; **2.** leg; **3.** pedestal, base, footing; **4.** outlet (*of a lake*); **5.** step; **6.** treadle (*of a sewing machine*); **7.** shaft (*of a loom*); **8.** tributary; **9.** pace, gait; **10.** rhyme; **11.** foot (*measure*); ~ **atmak 1.** to go for the first time; **2.** to take a step; ~ ~ **üstüne atmak** to cross one's legs; ~ **bağı** hindrance, impediment; ~ **basmak 1.** (*bir yere*) to set foot in (*or* on) *somewhere*; **2.** to arrive (*-e* at, in), to enter; ~ **bileği 1.** ankle; **2.** ANAT tarsus; ~ **değiştirmek** to get into step by changing one's foot (*in marching*); ~ **diremek** to put one's foot down, to insist; ~ **işi** errands and small deals; ~ **kirası** messenger's tip; ~ **parmakları** toes; ~ **patırdısı** tramping of feet; ~ **uydurmak 1.** to fall in step; to keep in step (*-e* with); **2.** *fig.* to keep pace (*-e* with); ~ **üstü** in haste, without sitting down; **ayağa fırlamak** to jump to one's feet; **ayağa kaldırmak** to incite, to stir up to rebellion; **ayağa kalkmak 1.** to stand up, to rise to one's feet; **2.** to get excited, to be aroused; **3.** to get about, to get round, to go about; (ayağına): ~ **çabuk** swift of foot; ~ **çağırmak** to call into one's presence; ~ **kadar gelmek** to condescend to visit *s.o.*; ~ **gitmek** to visit personally (*as an act of deference*); ~ **karasu inmek** to be on one's last legs; (ayağını): ~ **çabuk tut!** shake a leg!; ~ **çelmek** to trip up; ~ **denk almak** to watch one's step, to keep one's eyes skinned; ~ **kaydırmak** to cut the ground from under s.o.'s feet; ~ **öpeyim!** I beg (*or* implore) you!; ~ **vurmak** (*ayakkabı*) to pinch, to chafe one's foot; ~ **yorganına göre uzatmak** *pro.* to cut one's coat according

to one's cloth; **-nın tozu ile** having just arrived; **ayakta 1.** standing, on one's feet; **2.** *fig.* excited, aroused; **3.** MED ambulatory; **ayakta durmak** to stand; **ayakta kalmak 1.** to be left without a seat; **2.** to remain standing; to have lasted; **ayakta tedavi** MED ambulatory treatment; **ayakta uyumak** to be dead on one's feet.

ayakaltı, -nı much frequented place; **-nda dolaşmak** to get under foot, to be in the way.

ayakkabı, -yı shoe; footwear.

ayakkabıcı 1. shoemaker; **2.** shoe--dealer.

ayakkabıcılık 1. shoemaking; **2.** shoe trade.

ayaklamak to measure by pacing.

ayaklanma rebellion, mutiny, revolt.

ayaklanmak 1. *pass. of* **ayaklamak; 2.** to rebel, to revolt; **3.** to begin to walk (*child*).

ayaklı footed, legged; **~ canavar** naughty child; **~ kütüphane** *fig.* very learned person.

ayaklık 1. pedal, treadle; **2.** stilts; **3.** place to step on.

ayaktakımı, -nı rabble, mob.

ayakteri, -ni tip given to a messenger.

ayaktopu, -nu football, soccer.

ayakucu, -nu 1. foot (*of a bed*); **2.** tip-toe.

ayakyolu, -nu toilet, water closet, loo.

ayan [. -] clear, evident, plain, manifest; **~ beyan** very clear.

âyan [- .] **1.** notables; **2.** senators; **~ meclisi** the senate.

ayar 1. standard (*of time*); **2.** adjustment for accuracy (*watch*); **3.** adjustment, set-up (*machine*); **4.** fineness; karats (*gold, silver*); **5.** *fig.* quality, character (*person*); **~ etm.** to adjust, to fix, to regulate, to set; **-ı bozuk 1.** out of order; **2.** *fig.* of bad character.

ayarlamak 1. to adjust, to fix, to regulate, to set; **2.** to arrange, to put in order; **3.** to test, to assay, to gauge.

ayarlı 1. regulated (*clock*); **2.** of standard fineness; **~ bomba** time bomb.

ayarsız 1. out of adjustment; **2.** unassayed; below standard; **3.** *fig.* unbalanced (*person*).

ayartmak to lead astray, to seduce, to tempt, to entice, to pervert.

Ayasofya [. . x .] *pr. n.* Hagia Sophia.

ayaz 1. dry cold, nip in the air; frostiness; **2.** cold, frosty (*air, night*); **~ al-**

mak to get nothing; **~ kesmek** *fig.* to be exposed to the cold for a long time; **~ olm.** to be frosty; **~ paşa kola çıkmış** (*or* **kol geziyor**) F Jack Frost is going the rounds, it is freezing weather; **-a kalmak** s. **~ almak; -a çekmek** to turn cold (*weather*).

ayazlamak 1. to become clear and cold (*weather*); **2.** to become cold in the freeze; **3.** *sl.* to wait in vain.

ayazlanmak to be cooled.

ayazma [. x .] ECCL sacred spring.

aybaşı, -nı menstruation, menses, the curse.

ayçiçeği, -nı BOT sunflower; **~ yağı** vegetable oil, sunflower oil.

aydın 1. well lighted; **2.** lucid, clear; **3.** intellectual, enlightened person; **4.** (*in expressions*) joyous, happy.

aydınlanmak 1. to brighten up, to become luminous; **2.** to be enlightened, to become informed (*on a subject*); **3.** to become clear.

aydınlatıcı 1. illuminating; **2.** informative, enlightening.

aydınlatmak 1. to illuminate, to illumine; **2.** to clarify, to explain; **3.** to enlighten.

aydınlık 1. light; **2.** bright, luminous; **3.** clear, brilliant; **4.** luminousness; **5.** clarity; **6.** light shaft.

ayet, -ti [- .] verse of the Koran.

aygın: ~ baygın 1. languid; **2.** languishing (-*e* for); **3.** languidly.

aygır 1. stallion; **2.** *fig.* lout.

aygıt, -tı 1. apparatus, instrument, device; tool; **2.** BIOL system.

ayı 1. ZOO bear; **2.** *fig.* jerk; **~ gibi** bearish; **-ya dayı demek** *fig.* to cajole *s.o.*; **-ya kaval çalmak** to try in vain to explain *s.th.* to a blockhead.

ayıbalığı, -nı ZOO seal.

ayıcı 1. bear leader; **2.** *fig.* rude, rough, coarse.

ayık 1. sober; **2.** *fig.* wide-awake, alert.

ayıklamak 1. to pick over, to clean off, to sort, to select; **2.** to shell (*peas, beans*); **ayıkla pirincin taşını!** *fig.* that is a fine (*or* pretty) kettle of fish!

ayıklanma BIOL selection.

ayılmak 1. to sober up; **2.** to come to, to come round; **3.** to come to one's senses, to see the light; **~ bayılmak** *fig.* to be wild (-*e* about), to be nuts (-*e* about, over).

ayıltmak to sober up.

ayıp, -bı 1. shame, disgrace; **2.** shameful, disgraceful; **3.** defect, fault; **4.** shame on you!; ~ **etm.** (or **yapmak**) to behave shamefully; **-tır söylemesi** if you will excuse my French.

ayıplamak to condemn, to censure, to blame. to vilify.

ayıplı faulty, defective.

ayıpsız intact, free from defects.

ayırım discrimination; ~ **yapmak** to discriminate.

ayırmak 1. to separate, to part, to sever (*-den* from); **2.** to select, to pick, to choose; **3.** to discriminate (between); **4.** to distinguish (*-den* from); **5.** to divide, to sunder; **6.** to set apart; **7.** to save, to spare, to reserve (*-e* for); **8.** to isolate (*-den* from).

ayırt etm. to distinguish, to discriminate, to discern (*-den* from).

ayin [ī] **1.** rite; **2.** ceremony; **ayini ruhani** church worship.

aykırı 1. contrary; **2.** contrary (*-e* to), against, in violation of; **3.** diverging, divergent; ~ **düşmek** to be contrary (*-e* to), to be incongruous (*-e* with); ~ **olm.** to be contrary, to be opposite (*-e* to).

aykırılaşmak to become contrary.

aykırılık incongruity; difference, disagreement.

aylak idle, unemployed; ~ ~ **dolaşmak** to fool around (or about).

aylakçı casual labo(u)rer.

aylaklık idleness, unemployment.

aylık 1. monthly; **2.** monthly salary (or pay); **3.** … months old (*baby*); **4.** lasting … months; **5.** enough for … months; ~ **almak** to be on salary; ~ **bağlamak** (*b-ne*) to put s.o. on salary.

aylıkçı salaried employee.

aylıklı salaried.

aymak to come to, to awake.

aymaz unaware.

ayn 1. exact copy, counterpart; **2.** JUR thing, res; **3.** s. **aynı**.

ayna 1. mirror, looking glass; **2.** telescope; **3.** NAUT sextant; **4.** panel (*of a door*); **5.** blade (*of an oar*); **6.** kneecap (*of a horse*); **7.** sl. perfect; ~ **gibi 1.** mirror-like, lustrous; **2.** glassy (*water*).

aynacı 1. maker of mirrors; **2.** fig. trickster.

aynalı 1. having a mirror; **2.** sl. beautiful; ~ **dolap** wardrobe fitted with mirrors.

Aynaroz pr. n. Mount Athos.

aynasız 1. sl. bad, unpleasant; **2.** sl. policeman, pig, cop, bobby.

aynen [x .] exactly, likewise, textually.

aynı the same, identical; ~ **kapıya** (or **yola**) **çıkmak** to amount (or **come**) to the same thing; ~ **şekilde** in the same way, likewise; ~ **şey** it makes no difference; ~ **zamanda** at the same time, simultaneously; meanwhile.

aynılık sameness, identity.

aynıyle without any change, as it is.

ayni in kind; ~ **kıymet** JUR real value.

ayniyat, -tı goods. property, belongings.

ayniyet, -ti identity.

ayol [x .] well!, hey!, you!

ayraç GR bracket, parenthesis; parentheses.

ayran 1. *a drink made of yogurt and water*; **2.** buttermilk; ~ **ağızlı** (or **budalası** or **delisi**) F stupid, simpleton; **-ı kabarmak** sl. **1.** to fly off the handle; **2.** to be sexually aroused; **-ım ekşi diyen olmaz** pro. nobody confesses to the shortcomings of his own work.

ayrı 1. different, distinct; **2.** separate, apart; **3.** exceptional; ~ ~ **1.** separate, distinct; **2.** individual; **3.** one by one, separately; ~ **gayrı bilmemek** to have all things in common; ~ **koymak** to put aside; ~ **seçi olm.** to withdraw one's property. to divide out; ~ **seçi yapmak** to discriminate; ~ **tutmak** to discriminate (between); **-sı gayrısı olmamak 1.** = ~ **gavrı bilmemek**; **2.** to make no discriminations.

ayrıbasım offprint, reprint.

ayrıca [x .] **1.** separately; **2.** specially; **3.** besides, also, moreover, furthermore, in addition.

ayrıcalı 1. privileged; **2.** exceptional.

ayrıcalık privilege.

ayrıcalıklı privileged.

ayrıcinsten heterogeneous.

ayrık 1. separated; **2.** exceptional; **3.** LOG disjunctive.

ayrıkotu, -nu BOT couch grass.

ayrılanmak 1. to separate out; **2.** to be isolated.

ayrılaşmak to become outstanding.

ayrılık 1. separateness; **2.** separation, rupture; **3.** difference; **4.** deviation; **5.** JUR legal separation; ~ **davası** JUR action for legal separation.

ayrılmak 1. pass. of **ayırmak**; **2.** to part, to separate from one another; **3.** to split, to crack, to open up; **4.** to leave, to depart (*-den* from); **5.** to split (*-e* into); **6.** JUR to divorce.

ayrım 1. difference; **2.** differentiation; **3.** section, part, chapter; **4.** *cinema*: sequence.

ayrımlı 1. different; **2.** divided into sections.

ayrıntı detail; *-lar* details.

ayrıntılı detailed, in details.

ayrışık 1. decomposed; **2.** different, various.

ayrışım CHEM decomposition.

ayrışmak CHEM to be decomposed.

ayrıştırmak CHEM to decompose, to analyze.

ayrıt, *-tı* MATH edge.

aysar moonstruck.

aysberk, *-ki* iceberg.

Ayşe *wf.*; ♀ *kadın fasulyesi* French (*or* string *or* green) bean.

ayva BOT quince; ~ *tüyü* fuzz on a youth's cheek; *-yı yemek sl.* to be in the soup, to be in hot (*or* deep) waters.

ayvalık quince orchard.

ayvaz 1. footman; **2.** NAUT hospital aide on a ship; ~ *kasap her bir hesap* it makes no difference.

ayyaş drunkard, toper, sot.

ayyaşlık dipsomania, drunkenness.

ayyuk, *-ku* [ū] the highest point of the sky; *-a çıkarmak fig.* to praise to the skies, to vaunt; *-a çıkmak 1.* to be very loud (*sound*); **2.** to be widely known (*event*).

az 1. little, small (*amount*); **2.** few; **3.** seldom, rarely; **4.** less (*-den* than); ~ ~ little by little, gradually; ~ *buçuk* **1.** scanty, hardly enough; **2.** somewhat, a little; ~ *bulmak* to consider insufficient; ~ *buz şey değil!* F it is no small matter!; ~ *çok* more or less; ~ *daha* almost, nearly; ~ *gelmek* not to be enough; ~ *görmek* to find insufficient; ~ *kaldı* (*or* *kalsın*) almost, nearly, all but; ~ *maz* F more or less; ~ *olsun öz olsun!* let it be little but good!; ~ *tamah çok ziyan getirir pro.* grasp all, lose all; ~ *yağlı* low fat (*foods*); *-a çoğa bakmamak* to be satisfied with what one gets; *-ı çoğa tutmak fig.* to take the will for the deed.

aza [- -] **1.** member, participant; **2.** ANAT limbs, organs.

azade [- - .] **1.** free, untrammeled; **2.** free, released (*-den* from); **3.** ♀ *pr. n.*

wf.

azalmak to lessen, to diminish, to be reduced, to be decreased.

azaltmak to lessen, to diminish, to reduce, to decrease, to lower.

âzam *obs.* greatest, largest.

azamet, *-ti* **1.** greatness, grandeur, majesty; **2.** *fig.* conceit, arrogance.

azametlenmek to give *o.s.* airs.

azametli 1. grand, great, august; **2.** *fig.* conceited, haughty, arrogant.

azami [ī] maximum, greatest, utmost; ~ *fiyat* maximum price; ~ *hızla* at full (*or* top) speed; ~ *sürat* top speed.

azap, *-bı* [. -] pain, torment, torture; ~ *çekmek* to suffer torments; ~ *vermek* to torment.

azar reprimand, reproach, scolding; ~ *işitmek* to get it in the neck, to be scolded.

azar azar little by little.

azarlamak to scold, to reproach, to reprimand, to rebuke, to give what for.

azat, *-dı* [- -] **1.** emancipation, liberation, setting free; **2.** dismissal (*from school*); ~ *etm.* **1.** to set free, to free; **2.** to dismiss (*from school*).

azatlamak *s.* **azat etm.**

azca rather little (*or* few).

azcık *s.* **azıcık.**

azdırmak 1. to irritate, to inflame; **2.** to tease; **3.** to excite sexually; **4.** to spoil, to indulge (*a child*); **5.** to lead astray, to corrupt.

Azeri [ā] Azerbaijani.

azgelişmiş underdeveloped; ~ *ülke* underdeveloped country.

azgın 1. wild, mad, furious; fierce, ferocious; **2.** tender, sensitive (*skin*); **3.** naughty, mischievous (*child*); **4.** oversexed; **5.** in heat, in rut (*animal*).

azgınlaşmak 1. to get wild; **2.** to become oversexed, to become lecherous.

azgınlık 1. wildness, fierceness; **2.** naughtiness (*in a child*).

azıcık 1. very small (*amount*); **2.** just a little bit; **3.** for a moment; ~ *aşım kaygısız başım!* it is good to live simply.

azıdişi, *-ni* *s.* **azı.**

azık 1. provisions; **2.** food.

azıklanmak to provide *o.s.* with provisions.

azıklık 1. provisions; **2.** nosebag.

azılı ferocious, wild, savage, inhuman.
azım, -zmı *obs. s.* **kemik.**
azımsamak 1. to consider too little; **2.** to underestimate, to undervalue.
azınlık minority; **-ta kalmak** to be in the minority.
azışmak to grow vehement, to intensify.
azıtmak 1. to get wild, to get out of control; **2.** to drive away; **3.** to make worse, to aggravate, to exacerbate.
azil, -zli dismissal, removal.
azim, -zmi determination, resolution; **-le** resolutely.
azîm 1. great, immense, vast; **2.** powerful, glorious.
azimet, -ti [ī] departure; **~ etm.** to set out on a journey.
azimkâr resolute, determined.
azimli *s.* **azimkâr.**
aziz [ī] **1.** dear, beloved, precious; **2.** saint; **3.** ♀ [x .] *mf.*
azizlik 1. sainthood; **2.** *fig.* practical joke, trick; **~ etm.** to play a trick (*-e* on).
azletmek [x . .] to dismiss from office, to fire.
azlık 1. scarcity; **2.** *s.* **azınlık.**

azlolunmak to be fired, to be dismissed.
azma 1. *vn. of* **azmak**; **2.** hybrid, half--bred.
azmak¹ 1. dry well (*or* pit); **2.** puddle; **3.** ditch.
azmak² 1. to get wild, to romp, to become unmanageable; **2.** to get rough (*sea*); **3.** to be on heat, to rut; **4.** to get inflamed (*wound*); **5.** to be of mixed blood; **6.** to be in flood (*river*).
azman 1. overgrown, enormous; **2.** heavy log; **3.** *s.* **azma 2.**; **adam -ı** giant, hulk.
azmetmek [x . .] to resolve (*-e* upon), to persevere.
aznavur: **~ gibi** terror-inspiring, fierce-faced.
azot, -tu CHEM nitrogen.
azotik nitrous; **~ asit** nitric acid.
azotlamak CHEM to nitrify, to nitrogenize.
azotlu nitrogenous.
Azrail [. - -] *isl.* MYTH Azrael; **-e bir can borcu olm.** *fig.* **1.** to free *o.s.* from debt; **2.** to resign *o.s.* to one's eventual death; **-in elinden kurtulmak** to be saved from death.

B

B 1. MUS = **baso**; **2.** = **bor**; **3.** = **Bay.**
baba 1. father; **2.** forefathers; **3.** abbot; **4.** benefactor; **5.** venerable man; elderly man; **6.** head of a religious order; **7.** NAUT bollard; bitt; **8.** newel post; **9.** knob; **-larım** my forefathers; **-larımı ayağa kaldırma!** *fig.* don't infuriate me!; **-m mezardan kalksd** never!; **-na rahmet!** bravo!, well done!, bless your father!; **-sı tutmak 1.** to fly into a rage; **2.** to have an epileptic fit; **-sına rahmet okumak** *fig.* to have bad intentions toward; **-sının hayrına** without following one's selfish interest, just for love, in a disinterested manner; **-sının oğlu** like father like son.
babaanne paternal grandmother, father's mother.
babacan good-natured, fatherly (*man*).
babacanlaşmak to behave in a fatherly way.
babaç 1. big (*turkey, cock or other*

fowl); **2.** swaggering.
babaçko F strong; imposing (*woman*).
babafingo NAUT topgallant.
babalanmak *s.* **babası tutmak 1.**
babalı 1. having a father; **2.** epileptic; **3.** irascible, irritable.
babalık 1. fatherhood, paternity; **2.** stepfather; **3.** father-in-law; **4.** adoptive father; **5.** F simple old man; **~ etm.** to act as a father (*-e* to); **~ fırın has işler!** *iro.* a father's oven produces good bread (*said regarding a young man who spends his father's money*).
babayani [. . - .] **1.** fatherly; **2.** unpretentious, free and easy, plain, simple.
babayiğit, -di brave, virile; brave lad, strong fellow.
Babıâli [- . - .] **1.** *pr. n.* HIST the Sublime Porte; **2.** *name of a quarter in Istanbul where many publishing houses are found.*
Babil [ā] *pr. n.* Babylon, Babel.

baca 1. chimney; flue; NAUT funnel; **2.** skylight; smoke hole; **3.** (mine) shaft; **~ başı** stone mantelpiece; **-sı tütmez olm.** *fig.* to be destitute (*or* impoverished *or* impecunious *or* left without resources).

bacak 1. leg; shank; **2.** *cards*: jack, knave; **~ ~ üstüne atmak** to cross one's legs, to sit with one's legs crossed; **~ kadar** tiny, short, knee-high; **~ kadar boy 1.** smallness; **2.** insignificance; **~ kadar boyuyla** *iro.* so small and pretentious.

bacaklı 1. ... legged; **2.** long-legged; **3.** *obs.* Dutch ducat; **~ yazı** large, plain and clear handwriting.

bacaksız 1. without legs; **2.** short-legged, dwarfish; **3.** *iro.* urchin, brat.

bacanak brother-in-law (*husband of one's wife's sister*).

bacı 1. negro nurse; **2.** F (elder) sister; **3.** F wife.

baç, çı HIST **1.** tribute; tax; **2.** toll.

badana whitewash, limewash; **~ etm.** (*or* **vurmak**) to whitewash.

badanacı whitewasher.

badanalamak *s.* **badana etm.**

badanalı 1. whitewashed; **2.** over made-up (*woman*).

badaşmak *s.* **bağdaşmak.**

badem [ā] almond; **~ ezmesi** almond paste, marchpane, marzipan; **~ şekeri** sugared almonds.

bademcik [ā] ANAT tonsil.

bademlik [ā] almond orchard.

bademyağı [ā] almond oil.

badi ZOO duck; **~ ~ bacak** short-legged; **~ ~ yürümek** to waddle.

badik 1. duck; gosling; **2.** *sl.* short, tiny.

badiklemek *s.* **badi badi yürümek.**

badire [ā] unexpected calamity, unforeseen danger.

badya [x .] tub; a wooden *or* glass vessel.

bagaj 1. luggage, baggage; **2.** MOT trunk, boot; **~ dairesi** luggage office.

bağ¹ 1. vineyard; **2.** garden, orchard; **~ bozmak** to harvest grapes; **~ budamak** to prune a vineyard; **~ kütüğü** vine stock.

bağ² 1. tie, cord, string, lace; bandage; **2.** NAUT knot; **3.** bunch; bundle; **4.** bond, connection, link; affection; **5.** impediment, restraint; **6.** GR conjunction; **7.** ANAT ligament.

bağa 1. tortoise-shell; **2.** tumo(u)r; **~ gözlük** horn-rimmed spectacles.

bağbozumu, -nu 1. vintage; **2.** autumn, fall.

bağcı viticulturist; grape grower.

bağcık cord, string, strap.

bağcılık viniculture, viticulture.

bağdadi [. - -] (*walls or ceiling*) made of lath and plaster.

bağdalamak to trip (up).

bağdamak 1. to intertwine; **2.** to deadlock.

bağdaş sitting cross-legged; **~ kurmak** to sit cross-legged.

bağdaşmak 1. to suit, to agree, to get along (*ile* with); **2.** to choose one's partner (*in children's games*); **3.** *obs.* to embrace one another; **4.** P to sit cross-legged.

Bağdat, -dı *pr. n.* Baghdad; **~ harabol-du** *co.* I am hungry; **Bağdadı tamir etm.** *co.* to eat one's meal.

bağı spell, charm.

bağıcı 1. sorcerer, sorceress, witch, magician; **2.** attractive; **3.** seductive; **4.** seducer.

bağıl PHYS relative.

bağıldak, bağırdak the strap with which a baby is kept safe in its cradle.

bağım dependence.

bağımlaşma interdependence.

bağımlı dependent (*-e* on).

bağımlılık dependence.

bağımsız independent.

bağımsızlaşmak to become independent, to gain one's independence.

bağımsızlık independence.

bağıntı relation(ship) (*-e* to).

bağır, -ğrı 1. breast, bosom; **2.** heart; **3.** liver, lungs; **4.** middle part (*of an archery bow*); saddle (*of a mountain*); **~ yeleği** jacket worn under armo(u)r; (**bağrı**): **~ açık** with one's shirt opened; **~ çökük** hollow-chested; **~ yanık** *fig.* heartsick, distressed; **-na basmak 1.** to embrace, to fondle, to hug; **2.** to shelter, to protect, to sponsor; **-na taş basmak** *fig.* to bear suffering with great patience, to suffer patiently.

bağır bağır bağırmak *s.* **bar bar bağırmak.**

bağırlar ANAT viscera.

bağırış shouting, clamo(u)r.

bağırmak to shout, to yell. to cry out; **bağırıp çağırmak** to clamo(u)r, to make a fuss, to make a lot of noise.

bağırsak *s.* **barsak.**

bağırtı shout, yell, outcry.

bağış gift, donation, grant.
bağışlama JUR donation.
bağışlamak 1. to donate, to give gratis; **2.** to forgive, to pardon; **3.** to spare.
bağlaç GR conjunction.
bağlaçlı having a conjunction; **~ yantümce** subordinate clause.
bağlama 1. vn. of **bağlamak**; **2.** folk instrument with three double strings and a long neck; **3.** tied, bound; **4.** MEC coupling, connecting; **5.** ARCH crossbar; **~ borusu** connecting tube; **~ limanı** home port, port of registry.
bağlamacı 1. a person who makes or sells a **bağlama**; **2.** a person who plays a **bağlama**.
bağlamak 1. to tie, to fasten, to bind; to connect; **2.** to chain, to tie up, to fetter; **3.** to bandage; **4.** to wrap up; to make a knot, to tie; **5.** to conclude, to finish (speech, etc.); **6.** to make secure, to settle (by contract, etc.); **7.** to appropriate, to assign (salary, etc.); to invest (capital), to engage, to lock up in (money); **8.** to hinder, to obstruct, to paralyze, to frustrate; **9.** to form (skin, crust, etc.); **10.** to form (seeds, head, fruit); **11.** to bind by a charm or spell.
bağlan ZOO ruddy shelduck.
bağlanış MEC connecting, coupling.
bağlanmak pass. of **bağlamak 1.** to be tied (-e to); to be obliged (-e to); **2.** to be dedicated (-e to); **3.** fig. to undertake; to engage or commit one's self.
bağlantı 1. tie, connection; **2.** liaison; **3.** MEC connecting; **4.** IT link (in Internet sense).
bağlaşık allied.
bağlaşmak 1. to agree, to come to terms, to unite; **2.** to harmonize; **3.** to form an alliance (ile with); **4.** to be at one, to be agreed.
bağlayıcı 1. connective, connecting; **2.** binding, in force.
bağlı 1. bound (-e to), tied (-e to), chained, fastened, attached (-e to); **2.** dependent (-e on); **3.** having ties, strings, etc.; **4.** faithful, devoted (-e to); **5.** closed, locked; **6.** made impotent.
bağlılık 1. devotion, attachment, loyalty, faithfulness, affection; **2.** dependence; **3.** solidarity; **~ akçesi** forfeit.
bağnaz fanatical, bigoted.
bağnazlık fanaticism, bigotry.

bağrışma outcry, shout, yell, scream, shriek.
bağrışmak 1. to cry out together, to yell at each other; **2.** to scold each other noisily.
bahadır [. - .] brave, gallant, valiant; hero, champion.
bahane [. - .] pretext, excuse; **~ etm.** to plead, to use as an excuse.
bahar[1] 1. spring; **2.** flowers, blossoms; **3.** fig. youth, the prime (of life); ♀ **Bayramı** the Spring Festival (1st May); **~ noktası** AST spring equinox.
bahar[2] spice.
baharat, -tı [. - .] spices.
baharatçı [. - - .] spice-seller.
baharlı spiced, aromatic, spicy.
bahçe garden; park; **~ mimarisi** landscape gardening.
bahçe-sokak street with a garden.
bahçeci (landscape) gardener.
bahçecilik horticulture, gardening.
bahçeli having a garden or gardens; **~ evler** garden city.
bahçelik 1. full of gardens; **2.** garden-plot.
bahçıvan gardener; **~ kovası** watering can; **~ takımları** gardener's tools.
bahçıvanlık gardening; horticulture.
bahis, -hsi 1. subject, topic; **2.** bet, wager; **3.** rare inquiry, search, investigation; **4.** rare discussion, argument, dispute, debate; **~ açmak** to bring up (a subject); **~ konusu** theme, subject of discussion; **~ koymak** to bet, to wager; **~ tutuşmak** or **bahse girişmek** to wager, to bet; **bahsi geçen** aforementioned, above-mentioned; **bahsi müşterek** pools.
bahri ZOO kingfisher.
bahrî maritime, naval, nautical; **~ imparatorluk** maritime predominance.
bahriye 1. navy; **2.** ZOO turtle; **~ feriki** HIST vice-admiral.
bahriyeli sailor; naval officer.
bahsetmek [x . .] -den **1.** to treat (of a subject), to talk (about), to mention, to speak of; **2.** to wager, to bet; **3.** rare to discuss.
bahşetmek [x . .] to give, to endow, to grant.
bahşiş 1. tip, bakhshish; **2.** rare present, gift; **~ atın dişine bakılmaz** pro. never look a gift horse in the mouth; **~ vermek** to tip.
baht, -tı 1. luck, fortune, destiny; **2.** good fortune, good luck; **~ işi** a mat-

ter of luck, a turn of fortune; ~ **yıldızı** lucky star; **-ı açık** lucky, fortunate; **-ı kara** unlucky, unfortunate; **-ın gür olsun!** good luck!

bahtiyar [. . -] lucky, fortunate; happy.

bahtsız unfortunate, unlucky, ill--starred.

bahusus [- . -] especially.

baka s. **beka.**

bakadurmak, bakakalmak s. **bakmak.**

bakalit, -ti Bakelite.

bakalorya bachelor's degree.

bakan minister, state secretary; **-lar kurulu** cabinet, council of ministers.

bakanlık ministry.

bakara baccarat.

bakarkör 1. a blind person whose eyes appear normal, part. stone-blind; **2.** fig. inattentive, careless, absent--minded.

bakaya obs., pl. of **bakıye 1.** remnants; **2.** arrears, outstanding taxes; **3.** MIL deserter.

bakı GEOGR exposure.

bakıcı 1. attendant, guard; nurse; **2.** soothsayer, fortuneteller.

bakılmak to be attended to, to be looked after, to be taken care of.

bakım 1. care, attention, upkeep; **2.** point of view, viewpoint; **3.** glance, look; ~ **evi** nursing home, dispensary, polyclinic; **birdan** (or **-a**) in one respect; **bu -dan** from this point of view.

bakımından from the point of view (**of**).

bakımsız neglected, unkempt, disorderly.

bakıncak the back sight of a gun.

bakındı [x . .] int. just look!, gee!

bakınmak 1. to look about, to look around; **2.** to be examined (medically) (**by**).

bakır 1. copper; **2.** of copper, copper ...; **3.** copper utensil; ~ **çalmak** to be contaminated with verdigris (food); ~ **pası** verdigris.

bakırcak copper vessel.

bakırcı coppersmith.

bakış glance, look; view; care.

bakışık symmetrical.

bakışım symmetry.

bakışımlı symmetric.

bakışımsız asymmetric.

bakışımsızlık asymmetry.

bakışmak to look at one another.

baki [- -] **1.** permanent, everlasting, enduring; **2.** MATH remainder; **3.** still val-

id, not yet ended; **4.** remaining; remnant, surplus; **5.** ♀ pr. n. (Turkish poet in 16th century).

bâki rain cloud; raining.

bakir [ā] virginal, untouched; ~ **orman** virgin forest; ~ **toprak** virgin soil.

bakire [ā] virgin, girl, maiden.

bakiye 1. remainder, remnant, residue; **2.** COM arrears (of a debt), balance.

bakkal 1. grocer; **2.** grocery.

bakkaliye 1. groceries; **2.** grocery shop.

bakkam 1. logwood; **2.** fading colo(u)r; ~ **boya 1.** = **bakkam 2; 2.** fig. spurious, false.

bakla¹ BOT broad-bean, horse bean; ~ **atmak** (or **dökmok**) to throw beans (for fortunetelling), to tell fortunes by beans; ~ **kadar** big, large (louse, flea, etc.); **-yı ağızdan çıkarmak** fig. to spill the beans, to let the cat out of the bag; **-yı ağızında ıslatmaz** fig. he is an indiscreet talker, he is a chatterbox.

bakla² chain link.

baklaçiçeği, -ni a dirty yellowish white colo(u)r.

baklagiller BOT leguminous plants.

baklakırı, -nı dappled gray.

baklava sweet pastry made of flake pastry, nuts, and honey; ~ **biçimi** diamond-shaped.

bakliyat, -tı [. . -] pulses (peas, beans, etc.).

bakmak, (-ar) 1. to look (**-e** at), to pay attention (**-e** to), to consider; **2.** to face, to front (**-e** towards); **3.** to examine, to investigate, to look into; **4.** to look for; **5.** to take care (**-e** of), to look after, to see to, to tend; **6.** to treat; **7.** to be in charge (of); **8.** to depend (on); **9.** to be dependent (on); **10.** to verge (on another colo(u)r); **11.** to serve (waiter); **bakadurmak** to stare at constantly, to keep looking (at); **bakakalmak** to stand in astonishment; **bakalım** (or **bakayım**) **1.** let's see; we'll see; **2.** well now!, oh!; **bakar mısın(ız)?** hey!, I say!; **bakarsın** possibly, perhaps; **bakıp durmak** s. **bakadurmak; baksan(ız)a!** hey!, look here!, I say!, listen to me!

bakraç, -cı copper bucket.

bakteri bacterium.

bakteriyoloji bacteriology.

bal, -lı 1. honey; **2.** BOT nectar; ~ **alacak çiçeği bulmak** (or **bilmek**) fig. to know which side one's bread is buttered; ~ **başı** the purest honey; ~ **dök de yala!** *fig.* spick-and-span; ~ **gibi 1.** honey-sweet; like honey; **2.** in spite of it all, very well; **3.** all the more; ~ **sağmak** to take honey (*from the hive*); ~ **tutan parmağını yalar** *pro.* (*lit.* one who touches honey licks his finger) one who has *s.th.* to do with a big deal will get some profit out of it.

bala *rare* child, babe.

balaban 1. husky (*person*), great, huge; **2.** tame bear; **3.** large drum.

balabankuşu, -nu zoo bittern.

balabanlaşmak to become very large.

balad ballad.

balak young animal, cub, *part.* buffalo calf.

balalayka balalaika.

balans balance; ~ **ayarı** MOT wheel balance.

balansuvar (*koltuğu*) rocking-chair.

balar shingle, joist, rafter, beam.

balarısı, -nı zoo (honey)bee.

balast, -tı ballast.

balastlamak to ballast.

balata MOT brake lining.

balayı honeymoon; ~ **seyahati** honeymoon trip.

balcı dealer in honey.

balcılık apiculture.

balçak guard of a sword hilt.

balçık clay, mud; ~ **hurması** crushed dates.

baldır ANAT calf; back of the shank; ~ **bacak meydanda** showing her bare legs; ~ **kemiği** tibia, shinbone.

baldırak lower part of a trouser leg.

baldıran BOT poison hemlock.

baldırıçıplak rowdy, tough, ruffian.

baldırıkara BOT maidenhair fern.

baldırsokan stable fly.

baldız sister-in-law (*sister of the wife*).

bale ballet.

balerin ballerina.

balet, -ti ballet.

balgam mucus, phlegm; ~ **atmak** *fig.* to drop a malicious hint; ~ **çıkarmak** (*or* **sökmek**) to expectorate.

balgamtaşı, -nı meerschaum.

balık 1. fish; **2.** ♀ AST Pisces, the Fishes; ~ **ağı** fishing-net; ~ **avı** fishing; ~ **avlamak** to fish; ~ **baştan kokar** *pro.* (*lit.* the fish begins to stink at the head) corruption starts at the top; ~ **kavaga çıkınca** (*or* **çıktığı zaman**) *fig.* never;

~ **nefesi** spermaceti; ~ **oltası** fishing line; ~ **pazarı** fish market; ~ **pulu** fish scale; ~ **tutmak** to fish, to angle; ~ **yumurtası** hard roe, spawn; ~ **yuvası** spawn place; **balığa çıkmak** to go out fishing; **balığın belkemiğini bulmak** *fig.* to discover.

balıkadam skin diver.

balıkçı 1. fisherman; **2.** fish pedlar, fish-monger; ~ **yaka** turtle-neck, pole-neck.

balıkçıl 1. piscivorous; **2.** zoo heron, egret, bittern.

balıkçılık fishery, fishing.

balıkçın zoo tern.

balıketi, -ni balıketinde, balıketli plump, matronly.

balıkhane [. . - .] central establishment for the marketing and taxation of fish.

balıklama 1. *vn. of* **balıklamak**; **2.** header; **3.** headlong; ~ **atlamak** to take a header.

balıklamak to writhe in agony.

balıklava good fishing ground.

balıklı abounding in fish.

balıksırtı, -nı 1. camber, ridge; **2.** ridged, hogbacked (*road, roof*).

balıkyağı, -nı 1. fish oil; **2.** cod-liver oil.

baliğ [ā] **1.** adolescent; adult; **2.** perfect, mature; ~ **olm.** -e to amount to, to reach.

balina [. x .] **1.** whale; **2.** whalebone.

balinagiller whales, dolphins.

balistik ballistics.

balkabağı, -nı 1. BOT winter squash; **2.** *fig.* blockhead, brainless.

balkan thickly wooded mountain rage; ♀ **Yarımadası** the Balkan Peninsula.

Balkanlar the Balkans.

Balkar Balkar.

Balkarca the Balkar dialect of Turkish.

balkon balcony.

ballandırmak *fig.* to praise extravagantly, to make one's mouth water (**for**).

ballanmak 1. to become covered with honey, to become thick like honey; **2.** *fig.* to ripen; to get ripe and sweet (*fruit*).

ballı honeyed, containing honey.

ballıbaba BOT dead-nettle.

ballıbasra an insect pest on figs.

balmumu, -nu wax; ~ **müzesi** waxworks; ~ **yapıştırmak** *fig.* to mark, to notice and remember (*words*).

balo [x .] ball, dance; ~ **vermek** to give a ball.

balon balloon; ~ **uçurmak** fig. to fly a kite.

baloz low-class cabaret.

balotaj POL. ballotage.

balözü, -nü nectar.

balsıra honeydew; mildew.

balta axe, Am. ax, hatchet; ~ **asmak** fig. to pester, to annoy; to blackmail; ~ **değmemiş** (or **girmemiş** or **görmemiş**) **orman** virgin (or untouched) forest; ~ **ile girişiyor** fig. he is like a bull in a china shop; ~ **ile yontulmuş** fig. unpolished, uncouth, rough; ~ **olm.** (b-ne) fig. to pester, to keep on at s.o., to harass; -**yı kapıya asmak** fig. to be tiresome, to bore; -**yı taşa vurmak** fig. to put one's foot in it, to blunder.

baltabaş NAUT. straight-stemmed.

baltaburun 1. s. **baltabaş**; **2.** sl. hook--nosed.

baltacı 1. maker or seller of axes; **2.** woodcutter; **3.** fireman equipped with an axe; **4.** HIST. halberdier attached to the sultan's palace.

baltalama 1. vn. of **baltalamak**; **2.** part. sabotage; -**dan gitmek 1.** to act violently; **2.** to pronounce words barbarously.

baltalamak 1. to cut down with an axe, to hew down; to cut away; **2.** fig. to sabotage, to paralyze, to torpedo, to block.

baltalı 1. furnished with an axe; armed with a halberd; **2.** = **gammalı.**

baltalık 1. district in which the inhabitants of a village have the right of woodcutting; **2.** coppice, copse.

Baltık the Baltic; ~ **Denizi** the Baltic sea; ~ **devletleri** the Baltic countries.

balya [x .] bale, packet; ~ **bezi** pack--cloth; ~ **yapmak** to bale, to make into bales.

balyemez HIST. long-range battering gun.

balyos HIST. Bailo.

balyoz sledge-hammer; ~ **gibi** very heavy.

bambaşka [x ..] utterly (or quite) different.

bambu BOT. bamboo.

bamburuk; -larını sökmek to maul, to batter.

bamteli, -ni 1. bass-string; **2.** imperial; **3.** fig. vital point, sore spot; -**ne bas-mak** (or **dokunmak**) -in fig. to tread on s.o.'s corns.

bamya [x .] BOT. gumbo, okra; ~ **tarlası** sl. churchyard, cemetery.

bana (to) me; ~ **bak(sana)!** look here!, hey!; ~ **bakma!** don't count on me!. never mind what I do!; ~ **gelince** as to me, for me; ~ **göre hava hoş!** F it is all the same to me, it makes no difference to me; ~ **kalırsa** as far as I am concerned; ~ **mısın dememek** fig. to be thick-skinned; to have no effect, to show no reaction (**to**).

bandaj bandage; -**lı** bandaged.

bandıra [x .] flag, colo(u)rs.

bandıralı having a flag; sailing under the colo(u)rs of.

bandırmak s. **banmak.**

bando [x .] MUS. band.

bandrol, -lü revenue stamp.

bangır bangır sobbingly, at the top of one's voice; ~ **ağlamak** = **hüngür hüngür ağlamak**; ~ **bağırmak** to shout loudly, to bawl.

bangırdamak s. **bangır bangır bağırmak.**

bangoboz sl. fool, idiot, simpleton.

bani 1. builder, constructor; **2.** founder.

bank 1. = **banka**; **2.** bench (in a public place).

banka [x .] bank.

bankacı 1. banker; **2.** bank clerk.

bankacılık banking.

bankalık bankable.

bankamatik ATM.

banker 1. banker; stockbroker; **2.** fig. immensely rich person.

banket, -ti hard shoulder (of a road).

banknot, -tu banknote, paper money.

bankiz ice field, ice pack.

banko [x .] **1.** bench; **2.** counter; **3.** int. gambling: bank!

banliyö suburb; ~ **treni** suburban train, commuter's train.

banmak to dip (-e into).

banotu, -nu BOT. henbane.

bant, -dı 1. band. tape; **2.** ribbon; **3.** radio: wave-band; **4.** billiards: cushion; ~ **izole** ELECT. insulating tape.

banyo [x .] **1.** bath; **2.** bathroom; **3.** bathtub; **4.** spa; **5.** PHOT. developer; ~ **etm.** to develop (film); ~ **yapmak** to take (or have) a bath; to bathe.

bap, -bı [ā] **1.** = **kapı**; **2.** section, chapter; **3.** theme, subject; **bu -ta** on this matter; in this respect; in this connection.

bar¹ *name of a folk dance in Eastern Anatolia.*

bar² **1.** dirt, tarnish; **2.** fur (*on the tongue*).

bar³ bar, night club.

bar bar: ~ *bağırmak* to shout at the top of one's voice.

baraj 1. dam; **2.** MIL barrage; **3.** *football*: wall; *-ı aşmak* to pass (*the examination*); ~ *ateşi* MIL barrage, curtain fire.

barak 1. *obs.* plush; long-piled cloth; **2.** P long-haired dog.

baraka [. x .] hut, shed.

barbakan barbican.

barbar barbarian; barbarous.

barbarizm barbarism.

barbarlık barbarism, brutality.

barbunya [. x .] **1.** ZOO red mullet; **2.** BOT a kind of bean.

barbut, -tu a kind of dice game.

barda [x .] cooper's adze.

bardacık a fresh fig.

bardak 1. glass, goblet, cup, mug; **2.** P jug, pitcher.

bardakeriği, -ni egg-plum, greengage.

barem 1. classification of salaries; **2.** ready reckoner; ~ *cetveli* fixed schedule of salaries; ~ *kanunu* law regulating official salaries.

barfiks *sports*: horizontal bar.

bargam fish of the bass family.

barhana 1. impractically large mansion; **2.** baggage, luggage, movables; ~ *gibi* colossal (*house*).

barı P garden wall, fence.

barınak 1. shelter, refuge, hiding place; **2.** home.

barınmak 1. to take refuge (*or* shelter) in; **2.** to get along.

barış peace; reconciliation; ~ *görüş olm.* to become reconciled, to make peace (*ile* with).

barışçı(l) peace-loving, pacific, peaceable.

barışık reconciled, at peace.

barışıklık mutual peace, reconciliation.

barışmak to make peace (*ile* with), to become reconciled.

barışsever pacifistic, peace-loving.

barıştırmak to reconcile, to conciliate.

bari [ā] at least, for once.

barikat, -tı barricade; *-la kapatmak* to barricade, to block *or* defend with a barricade.

barikatlamak *s.* **barikatla kapatmak.**

barisfer barysphere.

bariton MUS baritone.

bariz prominent, manifest, glaring; clear, obvious.

bark, -kı house, home, dwelling.

barka [x .] NAUT barge.

barklanmak to have a household, to set up house.

barko [x .] NAUT bark, barque.

barlam ZOO hake.

barmen barman, bartender.

baro [x .] bar, the body of lawyers.

barok baroque.

barometre barometer.

baron baron.

barparalel parallel bars.

barsak intestine, bowel, gut, entrail.

barsakçı intestine-dealer.

barsam ZOO sting fish.

barudi [. - -] slate-colo(u)red.

barut, -du (*or -tu*) gunpowder; ~ *ambarı* (*or deposu*) gunpowder store; ~ *gibi* **1.** irascible; **2.** too hot *or* sour; ~ *hakkı* powder charge; ~ *kesilmek* (*or olm.*) *fig.* to fly into a rage.

baruthane [. . - .] **1.** powder mill; **2.** powder magazine.

barutluk 1. powder flask (*or* horn); **2.** powder magazine.

baryum barium.

basamak 1. step, stair; **2.** tread, round; **3.** running board; **4.** MATH order, degree: ~ *yapmak* *fig.* to use as a stepping-stone.

basarık 1. treadle; pedal; **2.** bolt (*of a gate*).

basbayağı [x . .] **1.** quite common(ly), ordinary; **2.** simply, just; without hesitation.

bası printing, impression.

basıcı printer.

basık 1. low; **2.** flat; **3.** compressed; pressed down.

basılı printed.

basılış printing, impression.

basım printing, impression.

basımcı printer.

basımevi, -ni printing house, press.

basın press, newspapers (*syn.* **matbuat**); ~ *ataşesi* press attaché; ~ *toplantısı* press conference.

basınç, -cı PHYS pressure (*syn.* **tazyik**).

basiret, -ti [ī] prudence, understanding, insight, discernment; caution, circumspection, care, attention; *-i bağlanmak* to become blind (*to a danger*).

basiretkâr, basiretli prudent, sagacious; cautious, circumspect.

basiretsiz imprudent.

basit, -ti 1. simple, easy, plain, elementary; **2.** common, ordinary.

basitleşmek to be simplified, to become simple.

basitleştirmek to simplify, to make simple.

basitlik simplicity, simpleness.

basketbol, -lü basketball.

baskı 1. press; **2.** constraint, restraint, oppression; **3.** stamp; **4.** printing; **5.** edition; **6.** hem; **7.** circulation (*of a newspaper*); ~ **altında** under pressure (*or* discipline); ~ **altında tutmak** a. MIL to suppress, to oppress.

baskılık paper-weight.

baskın 1. raid, sudden attack; **2.** unexpected visit; **3.** overpowering, superior; **4.** heavy, oppressing; ~ **çıkmak** to get the upper hand (*-den* over), to be superior (*-e* to); ~ **vermek** to be attacked, to be raided; ~ **yapmak** to raid, to swoop down (*-e* on).

baskıncı raider.

baskül weigh-bridge; scales, weighing machine.

basma 1. *vn. of* **basmak; 2.** printed goods; printed matter; **3.** printed cotton, calico; **4.** a card game; **5.** GEOL transgression.

basmak, (-ar) 1. to tread (*-e* on), to stand (*-e* on); **2.** to press a (*-e* on); to weigh down; **3.** to set (**the foot on**); **4.** to enter (**upon** *a year or age*); **5.** to impress, to stamp; to print; to coin; **6.** to swoop down (**on**), to overwhelm, to overpower; to raid, to surprise; to flood; **7.** to crowd in; **8.** to set in (*darkness, pain, cold*); **9.** to bring down (*a blow*); to let out (*cry*); **10.** to settle, to sag; **11.** to sit (*on eggs*); **12.** *a.* **basıp gitmek** *sl.* to go off, to go away, to walk off; **13.** *sl.* = **faka basmak.**

basmakalıp, -bı 1. trite, cliché, conventional; **2.** pressure-molded; **3.** stereotyped.

basso [x .] MUS bass.

bastarda [. x .] **1.** HIST bastard; **2.** HIST flag-ship; **3.** foremast.

bastı vegetable stew.

bastıbacak 1. short-legged, bandy-legged, knock-kneed; **2.** gamin, urchin, squat.

bastırmak *caus. of* **basmak 1.** to have

printed, to publish; **2.** to suppress, to crush, to extinguish; **3.** to appease, to satisfy, to stay (*hunger*); **4.** to hem; **5.** to surpass; **6.** to quell, to force down (*rebellion*); **7.** to set in, to settle in, to close in (*cold, etc.*); **8.** = **baskın çıkmak; 9.** to go unannounced, to take *s.o.* unawares; **10.** to drown out (*a sound*); **11.** to hide, to hush up (*scandal, etc.*); **12.** NAUT to splice.

bastika NAUT a hole in a spar.

baston 1. (walking-)stick, cane; **2.** NAUT jib-boom; ~ **yutmuş gibi** as stiff as a poker.

basur [- -] MED piles, hemorrhoids; ~ **memesi** hemorrhoidal swelling.

bâsübedelmevt, -ti [- . - . .] resurrection.

baş 1. head; **2.** chief, head, leader; warden; **3.** beginning, commencement; first, initial; **4.** summit, top; **5.** knob; **6.** bulb (*of a plant*); cyme; **7.** NAUT prow, bow, fore-part; **8.** lump (*of cheese, crude sugar, etc.*); **9.** head (*of cattle, etc.*); **10.** skein, hank (*of silk, etc.*); **11.** river head. spring; **12.** main, chief, principal; **13.** COM agio, premium on bills; **14.** *wrestling*: first class; **15.** end, extremity; ~ **ağrısı 1.** headache; **2.** *fig.* trouble, nuisance; ~ **aşağı gelmek** (*or* **gitmek**) to go steadily down; ~ **-a 1.** face to face, privately; **2.** together, tête-à-tête; ~ **-a vermek** to have a tête-à-tête, to collaborate, to put their heads together; ~ **belası** trial, pest, nuisance, trouble-maker; ~ **edememek** (*b-le*) to be unable to cope with *s.o.*; ~ **göstermek** to appear, to arise; to break out (*revolt, etc.*); ~ **göz yarmak** to cause havoc; ~ **kaldırmak** to rebel (*-e* against); ~ **kaldırmamak** to keep one's nose to the grindstone; ~ **kaldırtmamak** *fig.* to suppress; ~ **kesmek** to bow; ~ **korkusu** fear for one's life; ~ **sallamak** to nod, to agree (with); ~ **tacı 1.** crown; **2.** a greatly respected and loved person; ~ **taraf** beginning, commencement; ~ **üstüne!** with pleasure!; ~ **vurmak 1.** to apply (*-e* to), to consult; **2.** to bite (*fish*); (başı:) ~ **açık 1.** bare-headed; **2.** obvious, evident, clear; ~ **açılmak** to go bald, to get thin on top (*hair*); ~ **bağlı** married, betrothed; ~ **bozuk 1.** civilian; **2.** irregular; ~ **sert** hard headed, obstinate; **başımla beraber** with pleasure, gladly, willingly;

başın(ız) sağ olsun! may your life be spared; (başına): **~ belâ kesilmek** to pester, to annoy; **~ buyruk** independent; **~ çıkmak** to plague, to become a trial (*-in* to); **~ devlet kuşu konmak** to have a stroke of great luck; **~ dikilmek** to stand over *s.o.*, to supervise; **~ gün doğmak** to have unhoped-for luck; **~ hal gelmek** to be in great trouble, to get into hot water; **başıma hal geldiği taktirde** in case *s.th.* happens to me; **~ kakmak** to rub it in, to cast *s.th.* in one's teeth; **~ teller takınmak** to be overjoyed; (başından): **~ atmak** to get rid (*-i* of); **~ geçmek** to happen to *s.o.*, to go through, to undergo; **~ savmak** (*or* **savuşturmak**) to turn away, to get rid (*-i* of); (başını): **~ dik tutmak** to hold one's head high; **~ ezmek** *fig.* to crush; **~ gözünü yarmak 1.** to handle roughly; **2.** to speak badly, to murder (*language, etc.*); **~ ortaya koymak** to challenge death, to risk one's life; **~ sallamak** to nod, to agree (with); **~ taşa vurmak** to repent greatly, to regret; (baştan): **1.** from the beginning; **2.** again, once more; **~ aşağı** from top to bottom, from head to foot, from end to end, throughout; **~ aşmak** to be too much for *s.o.*; **~ atmak** to get rid (of); **~ çıkarmak** to tempt, to lead astray, to corrupt, to seduce; **~ çıkmak** to be led astray, to be corrupted.

başabaş 1. only just enough; **2.** COM at par.

başak 1. ear (*of grain*), spike; **2.** gleanings; **~ bağlamak** (*or* **tutmak**) to come into ear; **~ etm.** to glean.

Başak AST Virgo.

başakçı gleaner.

başaklı 1. with gleanings left; **2.** eared, in ear.

başaltı, -nı ı. *wrestling*: second class; **2.** steerage.

başarı success; accomplishment; **~ elde etm.** to have success, to succeed; **~ göstermek** to show success; **-lar dilemek** to wish success.

başarılı successful.

başarısız unsuccessful.

başarısızlık failure.

başarmak to succeed (*-i* in), to accomplish, to achieve.

başasistan chief intern (*in a hospital*).

başat dominant.

başatlık dominance, dominancy.

başbakan prime minister, premier.

başbakanlık prime ministry, premiership.

başbuğ *rare* commander-in-chief.

başçavuş MIL sergeant-major.

başçı 1. foreman; **2.** seller of cooked sheep's heads.

başgedikli MIL sergeant-major.

başgöz: ~ etm. to marry; **~ olm.** to marry.

başhakem chief referee.

başhekim head doctor (*in a hospital*).

başıboş 1. untied, free, independent; **2.** untamed; **3.** uncared-for, neglected (*child*); **~ bırakmak** to allow *s.o.* to run wild, to leave uncontrolled; **~ kalmak** to run wild; to be independent.

başıkabak 1. bald; **2.** bare-headed.

başka 1. other, another, different (**from**); **2.** except, apart (*-den* from), other (*-den* than); **~ ~ 1.** separately, one by one; **2.** different; **-ları** others, the other people; **-sı** another, someone else.

başkaca 1. somewhat different; **2.** besides, furthermore, moreover, otherwise.

başkalamak to alter, to change, to vary.

başkalaşım metamorphism.

başkalaşmak 1. to change, to grow different, to alter; **2.** to metamorphose.

başkalık 1. difference; **2.** alteration, change, diversity.

başkan president; chief; chairman.

başkanlık presidency; chairmanship; **~ etm.** to preside.

başkâtip, -bi head clerk.

başkent capital.

başkomutan commander-in-chief.

başkomutanlık supreme military command.

başkonsolos consul general.

başkonsolosluk consulate general.

başkumandan commander-in-chief.

başlamak to begin, to start, to commence.

başlangıç, -cı 1. beginning, start, commencement; **2.** preface, foreword; **~ noktası** starting point.

başlanmak 1. *pass. of* **başlamak**; **2.** to cyme, to bulb (*plant*).

başlıbaşına separate, independent, in itself; independently, by himself, on one's own.

başlıca main, principal, chief.

başlık 1. cowl, cap, headgear; crown; helmet; head-harness; **2.** capital (*of a column*); **3.** truss; **4.** title; headline; crosshead, heading (*of a column*); **5.** war head (*of a torpedo*); **6.** heading, superscription; **7.** caption (*of a page*); **8.** MEC hub, nave (*of a wheel*); **9.** head-ship, presidency; **10.** money paid by the bridegroom to the bride's family; **11.** hood; ~ *atmak* to write a headline.

başmak shoe; slipper.

başmakale [. . - .] editorial, leading article, leader.

başmakçı 1. shoemaker; **2.** person in charge of shoes that are taken off at the door of a mosque.

başmaklık HIST fief conferred on the royal women of the sultan's family.

başmuharrir editor, editorial writer.

başmüddeiumumi attorney general.

başmüfettiş chief inspector.

başmühendis chief engineer.

başmüşavir [. . - .] chief counsel(l)or, chief advisor.

başoyuncu co-star, featured actor *or* actress.

başöğretmen (school) principal.

başörtü(sü) head-scarf, kerchief.

başparmak 1. thumb; **2.** big toe.

başpehlivan wrestling champion.

başpiskopos archbishop.

başpiskoposluk archbishopric.

başrol lead, leading role.

başsağı, başsağlığı condolence; *başsağı* (*or başsağıları or başsağlığı*) *dilemek* to offer one's condolences.

başsavcı attorney-general.

başsız 1. headless; **2.** having no chief.

başsızlık 1. lack of government; **2.** anarchy.

başşehir, -hri capital.

baştanbaşa entirely; from first to last.

baştankara ZOO great titmouse.

baştarda *s. bastarda.*

başucu, -nu 1. head end (*of a bed*); AST zenith; *-mda* at my bedside; *-na dikilmek* *fig.* to afflict incessantly.

başvekâlet, -ti *s. başbakanlık.*

başvekil *s. başbakan.*

başyaver [. - .] first aide-de-camp.

başyazar editor, editorial writer.

başyazı editorial, leader, leading article.

başyazman head clerk.

batak 1. bog, marsh, swamp; **2.** marshy, boggy, swampy; **3.** floundering, unstable, unsound; **4.** pond; tank for immersion.

batakçı 1. fraudulent borrower; bankrupt; **2.** swindler, cheat, crook.

batakhane [. . - .] **1.** gambling den; **2.** den of thieves; **3.** *sl.* joint.

bataklık bog, marsh, swamp, fen, moor.

batar P = *zatürrie.*

batarya [. x .] **1.** ELECT & MIL battery; **2.** NAUT the guns of one deck.

bateri battery.

baterist drummer (*in a jazz band*).

batı 1. west; western; **2.** west wind; **3.** West, Occident; Western, Occidental; ~ *Avrupa(sı)* western Europe.

batıcı 1. stinging, pricking, hurting; **2.** Westernizer.

batık 1. sunk(en), hollow; **2.** submerged (*submarine*); **3.** wrecked, ruined.

batıl superstitious, vain, false, useless, non-valid; ~ *itikat* superstition.

batılı Western(er), Occidental.

batılılaşmak to westernize, to adopt European practices.

batın, -tnı 1. abdomen; **2.** gestation; **3.** generation; *bir -da* at a birth.

batırmak 1. to sink, to submerge; **2.** to plunge, to dip; to ruin; **3.** to stick (*into*). to prick; **4.** to lose (*capital, etc.*); **5.** to speak ill (*of*), to decry, to run down; **6.** to dirty.

bati [ī] *rare* slow; slothful, lazy.

batma *vn. of batmak part.* breakdown, collapse.

batmak, (-ar) 1. to sink (*-e* into), to go to the bottom; to be plunged (into); **2.** to set (*sun, etc.*); **3.** to be lost sight (of); **4.** to go bankrupt, to be ruined; **5.** to penetrate; **6.** to hurt. to prick, to sting; **7.** to dirty; **8.** to get on the nerves (of), to irk; **9.** to be lost (*money*), to perish, to go to pieces; **10.** NAUT to run aground, to founder; **11.** to pass out of existence; *bata çıka* dragging *o.s.* along; *battı balık yan gider* in for a penny, in for a pound.

batman batman.

batri MUS percussion instruments, drums.

batonsale breadstick.

battal 1. useless. worthless; void, non--valid. abrogated, canceled; obsolete, out of use; **2.** over-size, large and clumsy; ~ *etm.* **1.** to cancel, to render null and void; **2.** to abrogate, to abolish, to do away with.

battaniye [. - . .] blanket.

batur brave; hero.

bavul suitcase, trunk.

Bavyera [. x .] *pr. n. rare* Bavaria.

Bavyeralı Bavarian.

bay 1. gentleman; **2.** Mr., Sir; **3.** P rich.

bayağı 1. ordinary, common, plain; **2.** mean, vulgar, banal, rough, coarse; **3.** quite, simply; ~ **gün** weekday.

bayağıkesir common fraction.

bayağılaşmak to become vulgar.

bayan 1. lady, madame; **2.** Mrs., Miss; *-lar, baylar!* ladies and gentlemen!

bayat, -tı 1. stale. not fresh; **2.** trite, old, insipid, out-of-date.

bayatlamak to get stale.

baygın 1. faint, languid; **2.** fainted, unconscious; **3.** amorous; **4.** drooping (*plant*); **5.** heavy (*smell*).

baygınlık faintness, swoon, fainting.

bayılmak 1. to faint, to swoon; **2.** to fall for, to tumble for, to be enraptured (**by**); **3.** *sl.* to shell out (*money*); **4.** to droop (*plant*); *gülmekten* ~ to roll in the aisles; *susuzluktan* ~ to die of thirst.

bayıltmak 1. to make faint; **2.** MED to narcotize, to anesthetize.

bayındır prosperous, developed, cultivated.

bayındırlık prosperity, development, public works; ℈ *Bakanlığı* Ministry of Public Works.

bayır 1. slope; ascent; **2.** hill; ~ *aşağı* downhill.

bayi, -ii 1. vendor, seller; **2.** supplier, outlet.

baykuş zoo owl.

bayrak flag, standard, colo(u)rs; ~ *açmak* **1.** to unfurl a flag; **2.** to recruit volunteers; **3.** to revolt; *-ları açmak* to become abusive and insolent; *-ları indirmek* to lower (*or* dip) the flag; *-ları yarıya indirmek* to fly the flag at half-mast.

bayraktar standard (*or* flag) bearer.

bayram religious festival, Bayram; holiday; festival, festivity; ~ *etm.* (*or* **yapmak**) *fig.* to feast, to be very delighted; ~ *haftasını mangal tahtası anlamak* to misunderstand completely; ~ *tatili* festive holiday; *-ınız kutlu olsun!* happy Bayram!, happy feast!; *-dan -a fig.* once in a blue moon, on occasion.

bayramlaşmak to exchange greetings at a holiday, to celebrate the Bayram together.

bayramlık 1. fit for a festival; **2.** present given on a festival; **3.** one's best dress, festive dress.

baytar veterinary surgeon, veterinarian.

baz CHEM base.

bazal CHEM basic.

bazalt basalt.

bazan, bazen [- .] [x .] sometimes, now and then.

bazı 1. some, a few, certain; some of; **2.** = **bazen**; *-larınca* for some people.

bazilika 1. basilica; **2.** royal palace.

bazlama(ç) flat bread baked on an iron sheet.

bazu *s.* **pazı²**.

bazubent *s.* **pazıbent**.

bazuka [. x .] MIL bazooka.

be! F hi!, I say!, hey!; ~, *çocuk!* hey, you! (*to a child*).

bebe P baby.

bebecik little baby, little darling.

bebek 1. baby; **2.** doll; **3.** ANAT pupil (*of the eye*); ~ *beklemek* to expect a baby, to be pregnant; ~ *karyolası* cot, crib.

bebeklik babyhood; infancy; ~ *etm.* to be childish.

beberuhi dwarfish man.

becayiş [ā] exchange of posts between two officials.

becelleşmek to argue, to quarrel.

beceri skill, dexterity, adroitness.

becerik *rare* skill.

becerikli skillful, adroit, resourceful, capable, clever.

beceriklilik skill, adroitness, dexterity.

beceriksiz clumsy, incapable, maladroit, unskillful.

beceriksizlik clumsiness, unskillfulness, incapability.

becermek 1. to do skillfully, to carry out successfully, to manage cleverly; **2.** *iro.* to spoil, to ruin, to make a mess (*of*); **3.** *fig.* to rape.

bed 1. bad, ill, evil; **2.** ugly, unseemly.

bedahet, -ti [ā] **1.** obviousness; **2.** improvisation.

bedava [x . .] gratis, for nothing, free; *-dan ucuz* dirt-cheap.

bedavacı F freeloader, sponger, bum.

bedavet, -ti [ā] nomad life, nomadism.

bedbaht, -tı unfortunate, unhappy, unlucky, miserable.

bedbahtlık unhappiness.

bedbin [ī] pessimistic.

bedbinlik pessimism.

beddua curse, malediction, imprecation; ~ **etm.** to curse, to put a curse (-e on); **-sını almak** to be an object of malediction.

bedel 1. equivalent (-e of); **2.** value, worth; price; **3.** substitute (-e for); in lieu of, for, in exchange for; **4.** = **bedeli nakdî; -i nakdî** JUR sum paid for exemption from military service; ~ **vermek** to pay the government a fee (*in lieu of regular military service*).

bedelsiz free, without charge.

beden 1. body; **2.** trunk; **3.** wall (*of a castle*); **4.** size; ~ **eğitimi** physical education (*or training*).

bedenen physically.

bedeni bodily, corporal, physical, somatic.

bedesten covered market (*for the sale of valuable goods*).

bedevi [ī] **1.** Bedouin; **2.** nomadic.

bedhah malevolent, malicious.

bedihî [ī, ī] self-evident, obvious.

bediî 1. esthetic; **2.** rhetorical.

bedir, -dri (*a.* **bedri tam**) full moon.

bedmest, -ti intoxicated.

bednam [ā] ill-famed, notorious.

begüm begum.

beğence commendatory preface.

beğendi a dish of aubergines; mashed eggplant.

beğeni affinity, taste, zest, gusto.

beğenmek 1. to like, to admire; to approve (-i of); **2.** to choose; to prefer.

beğenmezlik disapproval.

beha *s.* **paha**.

behemehal, -li [. x . .] in any case, whatever happens, for sure, absolutely.

beher to each, for each, per; **-ine** per person *or* piece.

behey *int.* hey!, o!

behimi [ī, ī] animal (*feelings*), bestial, brutish.

behre lot, share, portion, part.

beis, -e'si harm; ~ **görmemek** to see no harm in it; ~ **yok** never mind!, no harm!, no matter!

bej beige.

bek¹, -ki soccer: back.

bek², -ki gas burner.

beka [ā] permanence, eternalness; sequel; lasting; ~ **bulmak** to last, to be permanent.

bekar MUS the natural sign.

bekâr 1. unmarried, bachelor, single; **2.** grass widower.

bekâret, -ti 1. virginity, maidenhood; **2.** hymen, maidenhead; **3.** *fig.* purity; **-ten almak** to deflower.

bekârlık bachelorhood, celibacy; ~ **sultanlıktır** *fig.* a bachelor is as comfortable and independent as a sovereign.

bekas ZOO woodcock.

bekçi (night)watchman; sentry, guard; lookout; ~ **köpeği** watchdog.

bekçilik etm. to stand guard.

bekhent, -di *tennis:* backhand stroke.

bekleme waiting; ~ **odası** (*or* **salonu**) waiting room.

beklemek 1. to wait (-i for), to await, to hope (-i for), to look (-i for); **2.** to expect (-den from); **3.** to watch (-i over), to attend, to guard.

beklen(il)mek to be expected.

beklenmedik unexpected, unforeseen.

bekletmek 1. to cause to wait; **2.** to delay, to postpone.

bekri toper, sot, tippler; ♀ **Mustafa** *sl.* *name of a famous drunkard, hero of many anecdotes.*

Bektaşi [ā] dervish of the Bektashi order; ~ **sırrı** F unfathomable secret.

bektaşiüzümü, -nü BOT gooseberry.

bel¹ 1. waist; **2.** loins; the small of the back; **3.** mountain pass, defile, notch; **4.** NAUT midship body; **5.** semen, spunk, come, sperm; ~ **bağlamak** to rely (-e on), to trust; ~ **bölgesi** ANAT lumbar region; ~ **gevşekliği** MED incontinence; ~ **vermek** to bulge, to sag; **-i çökmek** to become humpbacked.

bel² spade; digging fork.

bel³: ~~ bakmak to stare (-e at), to goggle (-e at).

bel⁴ mark, sign.

bela trouble, misfortune, calamity, evil, curse; ~ **aramak** to trail one's coat, to look for trouble; ~ **çıkarmak** to stir up trouble, to make a scene; **-lar mübareki** the last straw; **-sını bulmak** to get one's deserts; to get into trouble; **-sını çekmek** to suffer for, to pay for; **-ya çatmak** (*or* **girmek** *or* **uğramak**) to run into trouble; **-yı satın almak** to invite trouble.

belagat, -ti 1. eloquence; **2.** rhetoric.

belahat, -ti foolishness, stupidity, idiocy.

belalı 1. troublesome, calamitous, tiresome; **2.** quarrelsome, brawling; **3.**

bent

bully, pimp.

Belçika *pr. n.* Belgium.

Belçikalı Belgian.

belde city, town.

beledi 1. municipal, urban; **2.** local; town-made; **3.** a kind of locally-made cotton material.

belediye municipality; ~ **meclisi** town council; ~ **reisi** mayor; ~ **seçimi** municipal election.

belediyeci municipal officer.

belermek to stare (*eyes*), to be wide open.

beleş *sl.* gratis, for nothing, free (of charge).

beleşçi *sl.* freeloader, sponger, bum, hanger-on.

belge document, certificate; ~ **almak** to be expelled from school, to flunk out.

belgelemek to document; to confirm, to prove.

belgeli 1. confirmed, proved; **2.** dismissed (*from school*).

belgesel documentary; ~ **film** documentary film.

belgin clear.

belgisiz GR indefinite; ~ **adılı** indefinite pronoun; ~ **sıfat** nonrestrictive adjective.

beliğ [ī] eloquent.

belirgin clear, evident, prominent, manifest.

belirginlik clarity.

belirlemek to determine, to fix.

belirleyici characteristic, diagnostic.

belirli determined, definite, precise, specific.

belirmek 1. to appear, to become visible, to come into sight; **2.** = **belirmek.**

belirsiz 1. indefinite, undetermined, unknown, uncertain; **2.** imperceptible.

belirteç GR adverb.

belirten GR modifier, defining word.

belirti symptom; sign, symbol.

belirtmek *caus. of* **belirmek** to state, to make clear, to expound; to determine.

beliyye trouble, evil, calamity, affliction.

belkemiği, -ni 1. backbone, spine; **2.** *fig.* pillar, fundamental part.

belki [x .] perhaps, maybe.

belladon 1. BOT deadly nightshade; **2.** PHARM belladonna, atropine.

bellek memory.

belleme 1. *vn. of* **bellemek**; **2.** horse blanket, numnah.

bellemek 1. to commit to memory, to learn by heart, to memorize; **2.** to suppose, to think; **3.** to dig with a spade, to spade.

belleten bulletin, notice.

belletici tutor.

belli 1. evident, clear, obvious, known; visible; **2.** certain, definite; ~ **başlı 1.** clear, definite, proper; **2.** eminent, notable, well-known; main, chief; ~ **belirsiz** hardly visible; ~ **etm. 1.** to make clear; **2.** to show; to be unable to hide; ~ **günler** certain days.

belsoğukluğu, -nu MED gonorrhea, *sl.* clap.

bembeyaz [x . .] snow-white, pure white.

bemol. -lü MUS flat; **ml** ~ E flat.

ben[1] I, me.

ben[2] **1.** mole; beauty-spot, birthmark; **2.** bait, lure.

bence [x .] in my opinion, as to me, as for me.

bencil selfish; ~ **olm.** to be selfish.

bencileyin like me.

bencillik egotism; ~ **etm.** to be selfish.

bende[1] *abl. of* **ben**[1].

bende[2] *rare* slave; servant; bondsman; **-niz** your humble servant, I.

benek spot, speck, freckle; ~ ~ speckled; ~ **sakal** imperial.

benekli spotted, speckled.

beni[1] *acc. of* **ben**[1].

beni[2] *rare* the sons of; ~ **İsrail** children of Israel, the Jews; ~ **nevi** mankind.

benim[1] [. x] *gen. of* **ben**[1] my; mine; ~ **için** for me; ~ **var** I have.

benim[2] [x .] I am, it is I.

benimki mine.

benimsemek to adopt, to appropriate to *o.s.*, to make one's own, to identify *o.s.* with, to welcome.

beniz, -nzi colo(u)r of the face; **benzi atmak** to blanch, to grow (*or* turn) pale; **benzi bozuk** pale.

benli spotted, freckled.

benlik 1. egotism; **2.** personality, ego; **3.** conceit; ~ **davasında olm.** to be self-assertive; ~ **sahibi kimse** conceited person; **benliğinden çıkmak** to change one's personality.

bent, -di 1. dam, dike, dyke, weir, barrage, aqueduct; **2.** reservoir; **3.** paragraph; article; **4.** *obs.* newspaper article; **5.** stanza (*in a poem*).

benzemek to resemble, to be like, to look like, to seem like, to look as if.

benzer similar, like; resembling; **-i yok** unique.

benzerlik similarity, resemblance.

benzeşmek to resemble each other.

benzetmek *caus. of* **benzemek 1.** to liken (*-e* to); **2.** to compare (*-e* with); **3.** to mistake (*-e* for), to mix up (*-e* with); **4.** *iro.* to ruin, to bust, to smash, to wreck; **5.** F to thrash, to wallop.

benzeyiş resemblance.

benzin petrol, *Am.* gasoline; benzine; **~ borusu** petrol pipe; **~ deposu** petrol tank; **~ istasyonu** petrol station, filling station; **~ pompası** pump feeding petrol into carburetor.

beraat, -tı [ā] acquittal, innocence, non-guilt; **~ etm.** to be acquitted; **~ ettirmek** to acquit.

beraber [ā] **1.** together; **2.** equal; level, abreast, even, in a line; **~ kalmak** to be in company with; **~ olm. 1.** to be together (*ile* with); **2.** to be on the same level (*ile* with); **-e kalmak** to draw, to tie; **-inde** together, with one; **bununla ~** nevertheless, however, still, yet; **... olmakla ~ 1.** (al)though; **2.** ... as well as ..., both ... and ...

beraberlik [ā] **1.** draw, tie; **2.** unity, co-operation, solidarity; **~ golü** equalizing goal.

beraet *s.* **beraat.**

berat, -tı patent, warrant; ♎ **Gecesi** (*or* **Kandili**) *Moslem feast, celebrating the night of the revelation of his mission to Mohammed.*

berbat, -dı 1. ruined, spoilt, injured; **2.** filthy, soiled, dirty; dreadful, disgusting; **~ etm. 1.** to spoil, to ruin, to corrupt, to make a mess of, to mess up; **2.** to dirty, to soil; **~ olm.** *pass. of* **~ etm.**

berber barber; hairdresser.

Berberi *pr. n.* a Berber.

berdevam [ā] going on, continuing.

berduş vagabond, tramp, vagrant.

bere¹ beret.

bere² bruise; dent.

bereket, -ti 1. blessing; **2.** abundance, plenty; fruitfulness; **3.** fortunately, luckily; **4.** P rain; **~ versin!** fortunately!, luckily!, thank God!; God bless you!, thank you!

bereketli fruitful; fertile; abundant; blessed.

bereketsiz infertile; unfruitful;

scanty; bringing no good luck.

berelemek to bruise; to dent, to batter, to cause bruises (*-i* on).

bereli bruised; dented, battered.

berhane impractically large mansion, rambling house.

berhava blown up; **~ etm.** to blow up; **~ olm. 1.** to explode; **2.** to go for nothing.

berhayat [. . -] living, alive.

berhudar [ā] happy, prosperous, successful; **~ ol!** God bless you!, thank you!

beri 1. the near side. this side, hither, here, hithermost; **2.** *-den* since; **-de** on this side.

beriki the nearest, the nearer one; the last mentioned; this one.

berjer easy chair.

berk hard, firm, strong, solid, tight, fast.

bermuda Bermuda shorts.

bermutat, -dı [ū, ā] as usual.

berrak, -kı *or* **-ğı** clear, limpid, transparent.

bertaraf aside, apart, out of the way; **~ etm.** to put aside, to do away (**with**), to get rid (**of**), to remove.

berzah 1. GEOGR isthmus, neck of land; **2.** *fig.* precipice, chasm, abyss.

besbedava [x . - .] dirt cheap.

besbelli [x . .] *emph. of* **belli.**

besbeter [x . .] *emph. of* **beter.**

besi 1. nourishing, nutrition; **2.** fattening, feeding up; **3.** prop, shim; **-ye çekmek** to fatten (*an animal*).

besici fattener (*of livestock*).

besili fat(ted), well-fed, fleshy, plump.

besin nutriment, nourishment, food.

besleme 1. *vn. of* **beslemek; 2.** foster child; **3.** MEC feed(ing); **4.** MEC base, support.

beslemek 1. to feed, to nourish; **2.** to fatten (*animal*); **3.** to support, to keep, to maintain; **4.** to rear (*animal*); **5.** to bear (*grudge, etc.*), to nourish (*hope, etc.*); **6.** MEC to prop, to shim up, to reinforce; **7.** MEC to feed.

besleyici nutritious, nourishing, nutritive.

besmele the formula *bismillahirrahmanirrahim*; **~ çekmek** (*or* **okumak**) to pronounce this formula.

besmelesiz *sl.* bastard; good-for-nothing.

beste musical composition, tune, melody.

besteci, bestekâr composer.

bestelemek to compose, to set to music.

beş five; ~ *aşağı* ~ *yukarı* close bargaining; ~ *aşağı* ~ *yukarı aynı* almost the same; ~ *duyu* the five senses; ~ *kardeş(ler)* co. slap; ~ *para etmez* worthless, rubbishy; ~ *parasız* broke, penniless, skint; ~ *vakit namaz* the complete schedule of daily prayers; *-i bir yerde* ornamental coin worth five Turkish gold pounds; *-te bir* one fifth.

beşbıyık BOT medlar.

beşer¹ five each, five apiece.

beşer² man, mankind.

beşeri human; ~ *coğrafya* anthropogeography.

beşeriyet, -ti 1. human nature; 2. humanity, mankind.

beşgen MATH pentagon.

beşibirlik = *beşi bir yerde*.

beşik cradle (*a. fig.*); ~ *kertme nişanlı* (*or* ~ *kertiği or* ~ *kertmesi*) engaged to one another while yet in the cradle.

beşinci fifth.

beşiz quintuplets.

beşizli fivefold.

beşlemek to quintuple; to raise its quantity to five.

beşli 1. fivefold; 2. MUS quintain; 3. *card games*: the five.

beşlik 1. five-kurush piece; 2. perception to five.

beşpençe ZOO starfish.

beşuş smiling; cheerful; merry.

beşyüz five hundred.

beşyüzlük 1. five-hundred lira bill; 2. containing five hundred.

bet, -ti face; ~ *beniz* colo(u)r of the face; *-i benzi atmak* to go pale from fear; *-i bereketi olmamak* to grow scarce, to run out.

betimlemek to describe.

beton concrete.

betonarme reinforced concrete.

bevil, -vli urine.

bevliye urology.

bevliyeci urologist.

bey 1. gentleman, sir; Mr., bey (*used after the first name*); 2. chief, head, ruler, master, prince; 3. husband; 4. notable, country gentleman; 5. *card games*: ace; ~ *baba* father.

beyan [ā] 1. declaration, expression; 2. GR explanation; 3. clearness, distinctness; ~ *etm.* to declare, to announce, to express; *-da bulunmak* to give an explanation, to deliver a speech.

beyanat, -tı [. - -] (*pl. of* **beyan**) statement, declaration; *-ta bulunmak or* ~ *yapmak* to make a statement.

beyanname [ā, ā] written statement, declaration; COM manifest.

beyarı *s. arıbeyi.*

beyaz 1. white; 2. fair copy; 3. fair-skinned; ~ *etm.* to make a fair copy (*of*); ~ *harp* war of nerves; ♀ *Saray pr. n.* the White House (*in Washington*); *-a çekmek* to make a fair copy (*of*).

beyazımsı, beyazımtırak whitish.

beyazlatmak to whiten, to bleach.

beyazlık whiteness.

beyazperde 1. movie screen; 2. the cinema.

beyazpeynir white cheese.

beyefendi sir; Mr. (*after name*).

beygir 1. horse; packhorse, cart horse; 2. gelding; ~ *gibi* clumsy, stupid, awkward.

beygirgücü, -nü horsepower.

beyhude [ū] in vain; useless, vain; ~ *yere* in vain, uselessly.

beyin, -yni 1. brain; 2. intelligence, brains; mind; ~ *sarsıntısı* MED concussion of the brains; ~ *sektesi* MED cerebral apoplexy; ~ *tavası* brain fritters, fried brain, baked brains; ~ *yıkamak* to brainwash; *beyni atmak* to fly off the handle, to fly into a rage; *beyninden vurulmuşa dönmek* to be greatly upset.

beyincik ANAT cerebellum.

beyinli 1. ... brained, having brains; 2. intelligent, sensible.

beyinsiz *fig.* brainless, stupid.

beyit, -yti 1. verse, couplet, distich; 2. *obs.* house.

beyiye commission.

beylerbeyl, -ni HIST governor-general.

beylik 1. *title or status of* **bey**; 2. state-owned; 3. commonplace, conventional, trite; 4. principality, district governed by a **bey**; 5. thin, small soldier's blanket; ~ *lakırdı* cliché; ~ *satmak* to give o.s. airs.

beynamaz person who does not perform the canonical prayers.

beynelmilel international.

beynelmileicilik internationalism.

beynelmileliyet, *-ti* international character.

beysbol baseball.

beyyine JUR proof, evidence, argument.

beyzi [ī] oval, ellipse; elliptical.

bez[1] cloth, duster, dustcloth, diaper; canvas; **-den bebek 1.** rag doll; **2.** *fig.* lazy, useless person; **o taraflarda -i yok** *fig.* he has nothing to do with that.

bez[2] ANAT gland.

bezdirmek *caus. of* **bezmek** to disgust, to sicken, to weary, to annoy, to plague.

beze 1. gland; **2.** lump of dough.

bezek ornament; decoration.

bezekçi 1. decorator; **2.** lady's maid.

bezelye [. x .] BOT pea(s).

bezemek to adorn, to deck, to embellish.

bezen *contp.* ornament, embellishment.

bezenmek 1. to decorate o.s.; **2.** to be ornamented.

bezesten *s.* **bedesten.**

bezgin disgusted, wearied; depressed, discouraged.

bezginlik weariness, lethargy.

bezik bezique.

bezir, **-ri zri 1.** flaxseed; **2.** (*yağı*) linseed oil.

bezirgân 1. greedy merchant (*part. Jewish*); **2.** merchant.

bezm banquet; feast.

bezmek (*bşden*) to get tired of *s.th*, to become disgusted with *s.th*., to become sick of *s.th*.

bıcıl 1. ANAT knucklebones; **2.** game of dice.

bıçak knife; **~ ağzı** the sharp edge of a knife; **~ altına yatmak** to go under the knife; **~ çekmek** to draw a knife (*-e* on); **~ bıçağa gelmek** to be at daggers drawn (*ile* with); **~ kemiğe dayanmak** *fig.* to become unbearable, to reach the limit; **~ sırtı kadar fark** a hairbreadth's difference; **~ yarası onulur, dil yarası onulmaz** words cut more than swords; **~ yemek** to get knifed.; **bıçağın ağzında olm.** *fig.* to be on a razor's edge.

bıçakçı cutler, dealer in knives.

bıçaklamak to stab, to knife.

bıçkı two-handed saw, bucksaw, crosscut saw.

bıçkıcı sawyer.

bıçkın F rascal, rowdy, bully, vagabond.

bıdık short and tubby.

bıkkın bored, tired, disgusted.

bıkkınlık disgust, boredom.

bıkmak (*bşden*) to tire of *s.th.*, to get bored with *s.th.*, to grow tired of *s.th.*

bıktırıcı tiresome, irksome, annoying, boring.

bıldır (= *bir yıldır*) **1.** last year; **2.** a year ago.

bıldırcın 1. zoo quail; **2.** *sl.* plump little woman.

bıllık bıllık buxom, roundish, plump.

bıngıl bıngıl 1. = **bıllık bıllık; 2.** well nourished. fat.

bıngıldak ANAT fontanel.

bıngıldamak to quiver like jelly.

bırakmak, (*-ır, rare -ar*) **1.** to leave; to quit, to abandon; to desert; **2.** to let, to allow, to permit, to tolerate; **3.** to put down (*or* aside), to lay down; **4.** to put off, to postpone, to defer, to adjourn; **5.** to give up, to relinquish (*habit*); **6.** to grow (*beard*); **7.** to let off, to let go, to release, to set free, to liberate, to emancipate; **8.** (*karı*) to divorce; **9.** to fail (*in an examination*); **10.** to entrust, to confide; to deposit; **11.** to assign (*-e* to), to transfer, to bequeath; **12.** to come unstuck, to come away (*from*) **13.** to yield, to bring (*profit*).

bıyık 1. moustache, *Am.* mustache; **2.** zoo whiskers; **3.** tendril; **~ altından gülmek** to laugh up one's sleeve; **~ bırakmak** to grow a moustache; **~ burmak 1.** to twist the moustache; **2.** *fig.* to swagger, to put on airs.

bıyıklı having a moustache, moustached.

bızdık nipper.

bızır ANAT clitoris.

biat, **-tı** homage; **~ etm.** to do (*or* pay) homage (*-e* to).

biber 1. pepper; **2.** paprika; **~ dolması** stuffed peppers; **~ ekmek** to pepper; **~ tanesi** peppercorn; **~ turşusu** pickled green pepper.

biberiye BOT rosemary.

biberli peppery, peppered.

biberlik pepper pot, pepperbox, pepper shaker.

biberon feeding bottle.

biblo knick-nack, trinket, curio.

biçare [ī, ā] poor, wretched, pitiable, helpless.

biçerbağlar reaper, binder, harvester.

biçerdöver combine(-harvester), reaper-thresher.

biçim 1. shape, form; manner, way; **2.** elegant form, well-proportioned shape; **3.** *tailoring*: cut; **4.** harvest; ~ *almak* to take shape; *-e sokmak* (*or* ~ *vermek*) to shape; *bu ne* ~ *iş?* this is odd!, what's this?

biçimlendirmek to shape, to put into a form.

biçimlenmek to take shape (*or* form).

biçimli shapely, well-shaped, trim, well-cut.

biçimsel formal.

biçimsiz 1. ill-shaped, ugly; **2.** unlovely; ~ *haber* F bad news.

biçki cutting out (*clothes*); ~ *dikiş yurdu* tailoring school.

biçme 1. *vn. of biçmek*; **2.** MATH prism.

biçmek 1. to cut; to cut out (*or* up); **2.** to reap, to mow; **3.** to assess, to fix (*price*).

bidayet, -ti [ā] beginning, commencement.

bide bidet.

bidon can, drum, barrel.

biftek beefsteak, steak.

bigâne stranger (*-e* to), detached (*-e* from).

bigudi hair curler.

bihaber unaware (*-den* of), ignorant (*-den* of).

bihakkın 1. rightly; **2.** truly, fully.

bikarbonat, -tı CHEM bicarbonate.

bikes [ī] friendless, destitute; orphan.

bikini bikini.

bikir, -kri virginity, maidenhood; *bikrini izale etm.* (*bir kızın*) to deflower.

bilahara later, afterwards.

bilaistisna without exception.

bilakaydüşart, -tı unconditionally.

bilakis [x . .] on the contrary.

bilanço [. x .] balance (sheet).

bilardo [. x .] billiards.

bilâvasıta [. - - .] directly.

bilbedahe [ā] *rare* extempore, extemporaneously.

bilcümle all, entire; in all; totally, entirely.

bildik 1. known; **2.** acquaintance; *bildiğinden şaşmamak* to get one's own way; *bildiğini okumak* to go one's own way; *bildiğini yapmak* to do what one wants.

bildirge 1. report; **2.** tax report.

bildiri communiqué.

bildirim declaration; announcement, notice.

bildirmek *caus. of bilmek* to notify, to make known (*-e* to), to communicate, to inform.

bile 1. even; **2.** *obs.* together; **3.** *s. bilye.*

bileği whetstone, grindstone, hone.

bileğitaşı whetstone.

bilek 1. wrist; **2.** pastern (*in an animal*); ~ *kuvveti* brute force (*or* strength); ~ *saati* wrist watch; *bileğine güvenmek* to rely on one's fists.

bilemek to sharpen, to whet, to grind.

bileşik 1. composed; **2.** CHEM compound; ~ *faiz* compound interest; ~ *kesir* compound fraction; ~ *sözcük* compound word.

bileşim CHEM composition.

bileşke resultant.

bileşmek CHEM to be compounded (*ile* with), to combine.

bilet, -ti ticket; ~ *gişesi* ticket window (*or* office), box office, ticket booth.

biletçi conductor, ticket collector, ticket man.

bileyici knife-grinder.

bilezik 1. bracelet; **2.** *sl.* handcuffs, nippers; **3.** MEC metal ring.

bilfarz [x .] supposing; supposedly.

bilfiil [x . .] in fact, actually.

bilge learned; wise.

bilgi 1. knowledge; learning; **2.** (branch of) science; **3.** information; ~ *edinmek* to be informed, to get information.

bilgiç 1. pedant(ic); **2.** *obs.* sage.

bilgili learned; well-informed.

bilgin scholar, savant; scientist, learned man, expert.

bilgisayar computer.

bilgisiz ignorant.

bilgisizlik ignorance.

bilhassa [x . .] especially, in particular, particularly; ~ *ve* ~ above all.

bilim science; knowledge, learning.

bilimkurgu science fiction.

bilimsel scientific.

bilinç the conscious.

bilinçaltı, -nı the subconscious.

bilinçdışı, -nı the unconscious.

bilinçlendirmek to make s.o. conscious of s.th.

bilinçli conscious.

bilinçsiz unconscious.

bilinmek to be known.

bilirkişi expert; ~ *raporu* expertise.

billah, billahi [x . .] by God!

billur 1. crystal; **2.** rock crystal; **3.** cut

billuriye

glass.

billuriye cut-glass ware.

billurlaş(tır)mak to crystallize.

bilmece riddle, enigma; puzzle.

bilmedik [x . .] unknown.

bilmek, (-ir) 1. to know; to be aware (*or* informed); **2.** to understand; **3.** to consider, to deem; to suppose, to think, to believe; **4.** to learn; to hear; to guess; to recognize; **5.** to hold responsible; **6.** to appreciate, to value; to experience; **7.** to be able to *inf.*; **görebilmek** to be able to see; **görmeyebilmek** to be unable to see; **bile bile** on purpose, intentionally, wittingly.

bilmemezlik ignorance; **-ten gelmek** to feign ignorance, to act innocent, to pretend not to know.

bilmez ignorant.

bilmisil in a like manner.

bilmukabele [ā] in return, in retaliation, in reciprocation.

bilumum [x . .] on the whole, in general; all.

bilvasıta [x - . .] indirectly.

bilvesile [. . - .] taking this opportunity, profiting by the occasion.

bilya, bilye [x .] **1.** marble; **2.** MEC ball.

bilyon a thousand million, *Am.* billion.

bin¹ thousand; **~ bir 1.** one thousand and one; **2.** *fig.* innumerable, a great many; **~ can ile** with heart and soul; **~ dereden su getirmek** to beat about the bush; **~ kalıba girmek** to change permanently; **~ pişman olm.** to regret greatly; **~ tarakta bezi var** he has too many irons in the fire; **~ yaşa(sın)!** may you live a thousand years!, long live!; **-de bir** scarcely, once in a blue moon; **-i bir para(ya) 1.** dirt-cheap; **2.** worthless; **3.** abundant, numberless, countless; **-in yarısı beşyüz** *fig.* a penny for your thoughts!; **-lerce** thousands of.

bin² *rare* son of.

bina [ā] **1.** building, edifice, structure; construction; **2.** chapter on indeclinable words in Arabic grammar; **3.** GR voice; **~ etm. 1.** to build, to construct; **2.** to base (**upon**).

binaen [ā] in consequence (of), on account (of), based (on); **buna ~** consequently, therefore, hereupon.

binaenaleyh [. - . . . .] [. x . . .] = **buna binaen.**

binbaşı MIL major; commander; squadron leader.

bindallı purple velvet embroidered with silver thread.

bindirme *vn. of* **bindirmek** *part.* **1.** MIL loading, shipping; **2.** MEC overlapping; joint; **~ iskelesi** port of embarkation.

bindirmek *caus. of* **binmek 1.** to cause to mount; to load; **2.** to collide (*-e* with), to run (*-e* into), to ram; **3.** to add on; **4.** MEC to overlap.

binek saddle beast, mount (*horse*); **~ atı** saddle horse.

biner a thousand each; **~ ~** by thousands.

bingözotu, -nu BOT scammony.

binici rider, horseman; equestrian.

binicilik horsemanship, horse-riding; **~ müsabakası** equestrian contest.

bininci the thousandth.

biniş 1. act of riding; **2.** ancient ceremonial riding dress; **3.** long cloak worn by certain dignitaries.

binişmek 1. to get out of line (*muscles*); **2.** to get on the same vehicle.

binlik 1. a thousand-lira note; **2.** large bottle holding 1000 drams.

binme *vn. of* **binmek**; **~ iskelesi** boarding pier.

binmek, (-er) 1. to mount, to embark, to board, to get on, to go on (*a train, etc.*); **2.** to ride (*a horse, a bicycle, etc.*); **3.** to overlap; **4.** to be added (*-e* to); **5.** to rise, to increase (*price*); **bindiği dalı kesmek** to cut (*or* slit) one's (own) throat.

biperva [ī, ā] **1.** intrepid, fearless, daredevil; **2.** fearlessly.

bir 1. one; a, an; **2.** unique; **3.** the same, equal, alike; **4.** once; **5.** mere, only; merely; just; **6.** so, in such a way; **günün inde** one day; **~ ağızdan** in unison, with one voice; **~ an evvel** as soon as possible; **~ arada 1.** all together; **2.** at the same time; **~ araya gelmek** to come together; to clash; **~ aşağı ~ yukarı dolaşmak** to walk up and down; **~ avazı yerde ~ avazı gökte** *fig.* to shout with all one's might; **~ ayağı çukurda olm.** to have one foot in the grave; **~ baltaya sap olm.** *fig.* to find a job, to be employed; **~ bardak suda fırtına koparmak** *fig.* to raise a tempest in a teapot; **~ cihetten** in a way, in one way; **~ çırpıda** without interruption, at once; **~ çiçekle bahar** (*or* **yaz**) **olmaz** *pro.*

one swallow does not make a summer; ~ **çift söz** a word or two; ~ **çifte** (*kayık, sandal*) rowing-boat; ~ **daha 1.** once more, once again; **2.** one more; ~ **de** also, in addition, furthermore; ~ **dediğini iki etmemek** (*b-nin*) to dance attendance on *s.o.*, to be at *s.o.'s* beck and call; ~ **deri** ~ **kemik** only skin and bones, a bag of bones; ~ **düziye** continuously, incessantly; ~ **elin nesi var, iki elin sesi var** *pro.* united we stand, divided we fall; ~ **hoş olm. 1.** to feel embarrassed; **2.** to feel sad; ~ **hoşluğu olm.** to be out of sorts; ~ **içim su 1.** a gulp of water; **2.** very pretty (*woman*); ~ **iki** one or two, very few; ~ **kafada** of the same opinion; ~ **kalemde** in one go; ~ **kapıya çıkmak** to come to the same thing; ~ **kulağından girip öbür kulağından çıkmak** to go in at one ear and out at the other; ~ **miktar** a little, some; ~ **nice** a good many; ~ **parça 1.** a little, a bit; **2.** one piece, a whole; ~ **şey değil!** not at all!, you are welcome!; ~ **şeyler** something, several things; ~ **şeyler olm.** to become strange; to put on airs; ~ **tahtası eksik olm.** *fig.* to have a screw loose; ~ **tarafa koymak 1.** to save, to put aside (*or* away), to lay aside (*or* by); **2.** to overlook, to disregard; ~ **taşla iki kuş vurmak** *fig.* to kill two birds with one stone; ~ **tesadüf eseri** by chance; ~ **türlü 1.** somehow, in one way or another; **2.** in no way; **3.** just as bad; ~ **vakit** at one time; ~ **varmış** ~ **yokmuş** once upon a time; ~ **yana** aside from, apart from; ~ **yastığa baş koymak** to be husband and wife; ~ **yiyip bin şükretmek** to call o.s. happy, to be very thankful; **-e on katmak** to exaggerate too much; **-e geldi** it is one o'clock; **-e kadar** by one o'clock, till one o'clock.

bira [x .] beer; ~ **fabrikası** brewery; ~ **mayası** barm, yeast.

biracı brewer.

birader [ā] **1.** brother; **2.** fellow; hey you!; **3.** Mason.

birahane [. . - .] beer-house.

biraz [x .] a little, some, somewhat; ~ **sonra** soon after, after a short while.

birazcık [x . .] a little bit.

birazdan [x . .] a little later, after a while; in a little while.

bir(i)biri, **-ni** one another, each other; ~ **ardınca** one after the other; **-ne**

düşürmek to set persons by the ears, to play one person off against another, to set at loggerheads, to set at odds; **-ne girmek 1.** to start quarrelling; **2.** to be stirred up.

birçok [x .] many, a lot (of); ~ **kimse** (**-ler**) many people; **-ları** = ~ **kimseler**.

birden 1. suddenly; **2.** at a time, in one lot; together.

birdenbire [. x . .] suddenly, all of a sudden, out of the blue.

birdirbir oynamak to play leapfrog.

birebir most effective (*remedy*).

birer one each, one apiece; ~ ~ one by one, singly.

birey individual.

bireysel individual.

biri someone, somebody, one person; one of them.

biricik unique, sole, the only.

birikim accumulation, buildup.

birikinti accumulation, heap, mass, assemblage.

birikmek to come together, to accumulate, to assemble, to collect, to form a puddle.

biriktirmek 1. to gather, to pile up, to assemble, to accumulate, to amass; **2.** to save up (*money*); **3.** to collect; **4.** MEC to store up.

birim unit; **-ler** MATH units.

birinci 1. the first; **2.** first-class; **3.** champion; ~ **elden** COM at first hand; ~ **gelmek** to be best; ~ **mevki** first class (*in a train*, *bus*), cabin class (*on a ship*).

birincil primary.

birkaç, **-çı** a few, some, several; ~ **kitap** a few books; **-ı** some of them.

birkaçıncı umpteenth.

birle [x .] **1.** *obs.* with; **2.** = **gibi**.

birleşik united, joint; ♀ **Amerika Devletleri** United States of America; ~ **oturum** joint meeting; ~ **sözcük** compound word.

birleşme *vn. of* **birleşmek** *part.* **1.** BIOL, BOT copulation; **2.** CHEM combination; **3.** JUR fusion, amalgamation, merger; ~ **noktası** (point of) intersection; ~ **parçası** extension.

birleşmek 1. to unite, to merge, to join together; **2.** to meet; **3.** to agree; **4.** to converge; **Birleşmiş Milletler** *pr. n.* United Nations.

birleştirici uniting, unifying.

birleştirme *vn. of* **birleştirmek**; ~ **çizgisi** hyphen.

birleştirmek to unite, to connect, to put together, to merge, to join.

birli 1. *cards:* ace; **2.** *dominoes:* the one.

birlik 1. unity, oneness; accord; **2.** sameness; equality; similarity; identity; **3.** union; association; corporation; **4.** MIL unit; **5.** MUS semibreve.

birlikli common, joint.

birlikte together, in company.

birsam [ā] hallucination.

birtakım some, a certain number of, a quantity ~ *kimseler* some people.

bis! da capo!, encore!

bisiklet, *-ti* bicycle, cycle, bike; ~ *yolu* cycle track; *-e binmek* to bicycle, to cycle, to bike, to ride a bicycle.

bisikletçi bicyclist, cyclist.

bisküvi, bisküvit, *-ti* biscuit, cracker.

bismillah in the name of God; ~ *demek* *fig.* to start an undertaking by invoking the name of God.

bisturi lancet.

bit, *-ti* louse; ~ *sirkesi* nit; *-i kanlanmak* *fig.* to become well off (*or* lousy).

bitap, *-bı* [- -] exhausted, feeble; ~ *düşmek* to get exhausted.

bitaraf [ī] neutral; impartial.

bitaraflık [ī] neutrality.

bitek AGR fertile.

biteksiz AGR infertile.

bitevi [x . .], **biteviye** [x . . .] **1.** continuously, incessantly, monotonously, uninterruptedly; **2.** all of a piece, whole, complete.

bitey flora.

bitik exhausted, worn out, broken down.

bitim end(ing).

bitirim 1. *vn. of* **bitirmek; 2.** *sl.* smart, topping, appealing; **3.** *sl.* gambling den.

bitirmek 1. to finish, to complete, to terminate, to bring to an end; to eat up; **2.** to accomplish; **3.** to exhaust, to use up; to kill; to destroy.

bitirmiş F experienced, versed in all vices; cunning.

bitiş end.

bitişik 1. touching, neighbo(u)ring, contiguous, adjacent, joining; attached; **2.** next door.

bitişmek to join, to grow together, to become contiguous; to adhere.

bitiştirmek to join, to unite, to attach.

bitki plant.

bitkimsi plant-like, phytoid.

bitkin exhausted, worn out, dead tired;

~ *düşmek* to collapse from exhaustion.

bitkinlik exhaustion, fatigue.

bitkisel vegetal, vegetable; ~ *yaşam* life without consciousness.

bitlemek 1. to delouse, to clear of lice; **2.** *sl.* to angle for a quarrel.

bitlenmek 1. to be infested with lice, to get lice, to become lousy; **2.** to clear o.s. of lice.

bitli lousy, infested with lice.

bitmek[1] **1.** to end, to come to an end, to finish, to terminate; to be settled, to be completed; **2.** to be all gone; to be exhausted; **3.** to be ruined (*or* destroyed); **4.** to fall for, to tumble for; *bitmedi* to be continued; *bitmez tükenmez* infinite, endless, vast, never ending.

bitmek[2] to grow, to sprout.

bitnik beatnik.

bitpazarı, *-nı* flea market, rag-fair.

bittabi [x . .] of course, sure, naturally, certainly.

bitter [x .] **1.** a kind of bitter beer; **2.** bitter chocolate.

bityeniği *-ni* *fig.* catch, s.th. fishy.

biyografi biography.

biyokimya biochemistry.

biyoloji biology.

biyolojik silah bioweapon.

biyopsi biopsy.

biyoşimi biochemistry.

biz[1] we; ~ *-e by* ourselves, without outsiders.

biz[2] awl.

Bizans *pr. n.* Byzantium.

Bizanslı *pr. n.* Byzantine.

bizar [- -] tired; weary, disgusted, sick (*of*); ~ *olm.* to be disgusted (*-den* of).

bizatihi [ā] [. x . .] in himself, in itself, of itself, by itself.

bizce according to us, in our opinion.

bizden 1. *abl. of biz 1 & 2*; **2.** *sl.* sly, cunning, crafty, wily.

bizim *gen. of biz 1.* our; ours; ~ *için* for us.

bizimki 1. ours; **2.** my wife; my husband.

bizon ZOO bison.

bizzat [x .] in person, personally.

blog blog (*web diary where a person can post their thoughts*).

blok 1. block; **2.** writing pad; **3.** POL bloc.

blokaj 1. blockage, blocking; **2.** covering.

bloke blocked; stopped; ~ *etm.* to close, to stop; ~ *hesap* blocked account.

blokhavs [x .] **1.** blockhouse; **2.** MIL bunker, pillbox.

bloklaşmak to form a bloc.

bloknot, -tu [x .] writing pad, memorandum block.

bloküs blockade.

blont, -du blond(e), fair.

blöf bluff; ~ *yapmak* to bluff.

blöfçü bluffer.

blucin (blue) jeans.

blum a card game.

bluz blouse.

Bn. = *bayan.*

boa 1. (*yılanı*) ZOO boa; **2.** feather-boa.

bobin 1. PHYS reel, spool, bobbin; **2.** ELECT coil; **3.** PHOT roll of film, spool.

bobinaj winding.

bobstil dandy; snob.

boca [x .] **1.** NAUT lee (side); **2.** turning over, tilting, canting over; ~ *etm.* **1.** NAUT to bear away to leeward; **2.** to cant over, to tilt, to turn over.

bocalamak 1. NAUT to veer, to bear away; **2.** to falter, to vacillate, to reel, to stagger, to get confused.

bocurgat, -tı capstan, crab.

bodoslama 1. NAUT stempost; sternpost; **2.** *sl.* nose.

bodrum cellar, dungeon; ~ *katı* basement.

bodur dumpy, squat; dwarf.

boğa 1. bull; **2.** AST Taurus; ~ *güreşcisi* toreador; ~ *güreşi* (*or dövüşü*) bullfight.

boğaca *s. poğaça.*

boğak MED angina.

boğası thin twill used for linings.

boğaz 1. throat; gullet, esophagus; **2.** neck (*of a bottle, etc.*); **3.** mountain pass, defile; **4.** strait; **5.** ♀ = *Boğaziçi*; **6.** mouth of a river; **7.** board, food, maintenance; **8.** a mouth to feed; eating, food; appetite; **9.** sore throat; ~ *açılmak* to develop an appetite, to become hungry; ~ *-a gelmek* to be at each other's throat, to be at daggers drawn; ~ *derdine düşmek* to struggle for a living; ~ *olm.* to have a sore throat; ~ *tokluğuna çalışmak* to work in return for food; *-ına dizilmek* to stick in one's throat; *-ına düşkün* gourmet, gastronome, glutton, gourmand; *-ına kadar* up to one's neck; *-ına kadar tok* full; *-ından geç-*

memek to stick in one's throat; *-ını çıkarmak* to earn just enough for one's food; *-ını yırtmak* to shout at the top of one's voice.

Boğaziçi, -ni *pr. n.* the Bosp(h)orus.

boğazkesen defensive fortress commanding a strait, *part.* Rumeli Hisarı (*on the Bosp(h)orus*).

boğazlamak to cut the throat of, to strangle, to slaughter.

Boğazlar *pr. n.* the straits (*Bosp(h)orus and Dardanelles*); ~ *Rejimi* control of the straits.

boğazlaşmak 1. to cut each other's throats; **2.** *fig.* to fight violently.

boğazlı gluttonous.

boğmaca MED whooping-cough, pertussis, croup.

boğmak[1] 1. to strangle, to choke; **2.** to suffocate; **3.** to drown; **4.** to overwhelm (with), to swamp (with); **5.** to constrict by binding; **6.** to conceal (*under a flood of words, jokes, etc.*).

boğmak[2] node, joint, articulation.

boğucu sultry, suffocating; ~ *gaz* poison-gas; ~ *sıcak* oppressive heat, stifling heat.

boğuk hoarse, raucous; muffled; ~ ~ hoarsely; with a muffled sound; ~ *sesli* hoarse-voiced.

boğulmak *pass. of boğmak* **1.** to become hoarse (*voice*); **2.** MOT to be flooded; **3.** *sl.* to be fleeced.

boğum 1. BOT knot, joint, node; **2.** internode; **3.** ANAT ganglion.

boğuntu 1. profiteering, swindling, cheating, duping; **2.** oppression, suffocation; ~ *yeri sl.* gambling-den; *-ya getirmek* to swindle money out of s.o.

boğuşma scramble, romp, scuffle, fray.

boğuşmak 1. to fly at one another's throats, to be at each other's throats; **2.** to romp, to scruffle, to scramble.

bohça 1. wrapping cloth; bundle; **2.** small bale of fine tobacco; **3.** *sl.* buttocks, ass, arse; *-sını bağlamak* to pack up one's belongings; *-sını koltuğuna vermek fig.* to give s.o. the sack, to fire.

bohçacı woman pedlar of small draperies.

bohçalamak to wrap up in a bundle.

bohem bohemian.

bok, -ku *sl.* **1.** shit, crap; excrement,

dung, ordure, feces; **2.** rubbish, dirt; worthless, shit; ~ **atmak** *sl.* to throw dirt (*-e* on), to slander, to defame, to blacken, to calumniate; ~ **etm.** *sl.* to spoil; ~ **püsür** *sl.* **1.** rubbish, nonsense; **2.** details; *-u çıktı sl.* it has come to light.

boklamak *sl.* **1.** to shit, to crap; **2.** to ruin, to louse up, to spoil, to mismanage; **3.** to soil, to befoul; **4.** to besmirch, to calumniate, to defame, to blacken.

bokluca bülbül 1. zoo wren; **2.** a pert (*or* saucy) child.

bokluk *sl.* **1.** dunghill; **2.** filthy place, dump; **3.** state of disorder, bad state.

boks boxing; ~ **maçı** boxing-match; ~ **yapmak** to box.

boksör boxer.

boktan *sl.* made of rubbish, useless, worthless.

bol[1] **1.** wide, loose; loose-fitting; **2.** abundant, copious, ample; ~ **ağızdan** (*or* **keseden** *or* **paçadan**) **atıp tutmak** to scatter promises around, to make extravagant promises; ~ **biçmek** *fig.* to estimate lavishly; ~ ~ abundantly, amply, generously; ~ **doğramak 1.** to squander, to blow (*money*); **2.** to be lavish in promises; ~ **keseden** generously.

bol[2], **-lü** [-] bowle, fruit punch, claret cup.

bol[3] [-] bowls.

bolca 1. fairly abundant, rather amply; **2.** somewhat wide.

boliçe [. x .] Jewish woman.

bollanmak, bollaşmak 1. to become wide (*or* loose), to widen; **2.** to become abundant (*or* copious).

bollatmak, bollaştırmak 1. to widen; **2.** to make abundant (*or* plentiful).

bolluk 1. wideness, looseness; **2.** abundance, plenty; **3.** plenteous (*country*).

Bolşevik Bolshevik.

Bolşeviklik Bolshevism.

Bolşevist, -ti, Bolşevistlik *s.* **Bolşevik(lik).**

Bolşevizm *s.* **Bolşeviklik.**

bom 1. *int.* boom!, bang!; **2.** *sl.* lie, humbug; ~ **atmak** *sl.* to lie.

bomba [x .] **1.** bomb; **2.** barrel; **3.** bomb-shaped metal container; ~ **atmak** to throw (*or* drop) bomb(s); ~ **gibi** F in the pink, in good condition.

bombacı [x . .] **1.** bombardier; **2.** bomb-maker; **3.** bomber.

bombalamak to bomb.

bombardıman bombardment, bombing; ~ **etm.** to shell, to bombard; ~ **uçağı** bomber.

bombasalan mortar.

bombe arch.

bombok *sl.* utterly spoiled, very bad, quite useless.

bomboş [x .] quite empty.

bomcu *sl.* liar.

bon: ~ **şans!** good luck!

bonbon candy, bonbon, sweet-meat.

boncuk 1. bead; **2.** F Negro, Negress; ~ **gibi** beady (*eyes*); ~ **illeti** MED infantile convulsions; fit; ~ **mavisi** turquoise blue.

bone 1. bonnet, lady's hat; **2.** bathing cap.

bonfile sirloin steak.

bonjur! good morning!

bonmarşe department store.

bono [x .] bond, bill/check; *-nun vadesi geldi* the bill is due.

bonservis testimonial, certificate of good service, written character.

bora [x .] **1.** tempest, hurricane, gale, squall, storm; **2.** *sl.* violent scolding; ~ **patlatmak** *sl.* to break out in a fury, to storm.

borak barren, sterile (*land*).

boraks borax.

borani [ā] dish of stewed and fried vegetables with yogurt.

borazan 1. trumpet; **2.** trumpeter; ~ **başı** first trumpeter; ~ **çalmak 1.** to trumpet, to play a trumpet; **2.** *fig.* to let everybody know.

borcetmek [x . .] to get into debt, to become indebted.

borç, -cu 1. debt; loan; **2.** obligation, duty; **3.** debit; ~ **almak** to borrow (*money*); ~ **gırtlağa çıkmak** (*or* **paçadan akmak**) *fig.* to be head over heels in debt, to be over head and ears in debt; ~ **harç** getting money by hook or by crook; ~ **vermek** to lend; **borca girmek** to get into debt; **borcunu kapatmak** to settle one's debt.

borçlanmak to get into debt, to become indebted (*-e* to).

borçlu 1. debtor; **2.** indebted, under obligation (*-e* to).

borda [x .] **1.** board, broadside, ship's side; **2.** beam; **3.** *sl.* = **yan.**

bordalamak to board.

bordro [x .] payroll; docket; list, register, roll.

bordür bordure, border; edging; frame.

bornoz, bornuz [x .] bath-robe.

borsa [x .] (stock) exchange, bourse; ~ **acentesi** stockbroker; ~ **rayici** exchange rate; ~ **oyunu** speculation.

borsacı stock-broker, speculator.

boru 1. tube, pipe; **2.** trumpet; horn; **3.** speaking trumpet; phonograph horn; **4.** *sl.* nonsense, idle tale, empty talk; **5.** *sl.* boaster, vain; ~ **çalmak 1.** to sound a trumpet; **2.** to hoot, to honk (*car*); ~ **değil bu!** *sl.* that's no small matter!; **-su ötmek** *fig.* to be the «big noise», to have a say in, to wear the trousers.

borucu 1. trumpeter; **2.** maker *or* seller of pipes, tubes, horns *or* trumpets; **3.** leader of the pump squad of a fire brigade.

borucuk ANAT tubule, tubulus.

boruçiçeği, -ni BOT downy thornapple; morning-glory.

borumsu BIOL tubiform.

boruyolu, -nu pipeline.

Bosna [x .] *pr. n.* Bosnia; ~ **Saray = Saraybosna.**

bostan 1. market garden, truck garden, vegetable garden, truck farm; **2.** melon; watermelon; **3.** melon field; ~ **dolabı** noria, irrigation water-wheel; ~ **korkuluğu 1.** scarecrow; **2.** *fig.* a mere puppet.

bostancı 1. market gardener; **2.** HIST member of the Imperial guard; ~ **başı** commander of the Sultan's bodyguards.

boş 1. empty, empty-handed; blank; hollow; **2.** uninhabited; **3.** vacant (*post*); **4.** free (*seat*); **5.** futile, frivolous, unfounded; **6.** ignorant, superficial (*person*); **7.** unoccupied; unemployed, out of work, idle; **8.** neutral (*gear*); **9.** loose, slack (*rope*); **10.** not in use (*machine*); **11.** unsown, uncultivated (*land*); **12.** divorced (*woman*); **13.** TYP space; ~ **atıp dolu tutmak** *fig.* to hit the mark at a venture, to make a lucky shot, to draw a bow at a venture; ~ **bulunmak** to be taken unawares; ~ **çıkmak** (*lottery*) to hit a blank; ~ **dönmek** to come back empty-handed; ~ **durmak** to be unoccupied, to idle; ~ **düşmek** (*or* **olmak**) to be considered as divorced; ~ **gezenin boş kalfası** *co.* do-nothing, idler, loafer; ~ **gezmek** to loaf, to laze, to wander about idly; to

be unemployed; ~ **kafalı** silly, empty-headed; ~ **vermek** *sl.* not to give a damn, to pay no attention; ~ **yere 1.** in vain; **2.** groundlessly; *s. a.* **boşta, boşuboşuna, boşuna**; **-a çıkmak** to fall flat, to fall to the ground (*hope, etc.*); **-a gitmek** to go for nothing, to come to nothing, to be to no end.

boşalım discharge, release.

boşalmak 1. to be emptied; to empty itself, to run out; **2.** to become free, to become vacant; **3.** to get loose (*animal*); **4.** to unwind itself, to be unwound (*rope*); **5.** to be discharged (*gun*).

boşaltım BIOL excretion; ~ **aygıtı** excretory organ.

boşaltmak *caus. of* **boşalmak 1.** to empty, to pour (out); **2.** to evacuate; to vacate, to move out (*house*); **3.** to discharge (*gun*); **4.** to unload, to discharge (*cargo, ship*); **5.** to land, to disembark (*troops*); **6.** to unbosom o.s.; **7.** to vomit, to bring up.

boşamak to divorce, to repudiate (*one's wife*).

boşanma divorce(ment); ~ **davası** JUR divorce case (*or* suit).

boşanmak 1. to be divorced (**-den** from); **2.** to be loosed, to be set at large; to break loose; **3.** to pelt down, to teem (*rain, etc.*); **4.** to burst forth (*tears, blood*); **5.** to rush out; **6.** to pour out one's heart.

boşanmış divorced.

boşatmak to make a wife be divorced.

boşboğaz garrulous, indiscreet, blab.

boşboğazlık indiscretion, idle talk; ~ **etm.** to talk indiscreetly, to blab.

boşlamak *sl.* **1.** to ignore, to neglect; to let alone; **2.** to let go.

boşluk 1. emptiness; **2.** blank; cavity; **3.** vacuum.

Boşnak, -kı Bosnian.

Boşnakça Bosnian (language).

boşta 1. unemployed, non-employed, idle; **2.** MOT in neutral gear, not in gear; ~ **kalmak** (*or* **oturmak**) to be unemployed, to loaf.

boşuboşuna in vain, uselessly; ~ **gayretler** vain efforts.

boşuna in vain, for nothing, uselessly.

bot¹, -tu boat, dinghy.

bot², -tu boot.

botanik 1. botany; **2.** botanic(al).

botanikçi botanist.

boy¹ clan, tribe; ~ **beyi** chieftain of a

clan.

boy² 1. height; stature; 2. length; 3. size; 4. edge (*of a road*), bank (*of a river*); 5. PHOT full-length; ~ *almak* (*or at-mak*) to grow in height; to shoot up; ~ *aptesti* ritual bathing of the body; ~ *aynası* cheval-glass, full-length mirror; ~ ~ assorted, of various sizes; of various qualities; ~ *göstermek* to cut (*or* dash) a figure, to show o.s. off; ~ *ölçüşmek* to compete (*ile* with); ~ *satmak* to put on airs; ~ *vermek* 1. to be above one's head (*water*); 2. to grow taller; *-a çekmek* to shoot up (*child*); *-dan -a* all over, from end to end; *-u beraber* as tall as himself; *-u bosu yerinde* tall and well made; *-u devrilsin!* may he die!; *-unun ölçüsü-nü almak* fig. to get one's deserts: to be disappointed (*by* s.o.'s indifference).

boya 1. paint; 2. dye; colo(u)r; 3. make-up; 4. fig. varnish; ~ *atmak* to fade; ~ *tabancası* spray-gun; air brush; ~ *tutmak* 1. to take paint (*wood, etc.*); 2. to take a dye (*fabric*); ~ *vurmak* to paint; *-sı atmak* to fade.

boyacı 1. shoeblack, shoeshine boy; 2. housepainter; dyer; 3. dealer in paints; ~ *küpü* dyer's vat; ~ *küpü değil ya hemen daldırıp çıkarasın!* it is not so easy as all that!

boyahane [. . - .] dye-house, dyer's shop.

boyalamak to cover with paint.

boyalı 1. painted; dyed; colo(u)red; 2. made-up (*woman*).

boyama 1. action of painting; 2. painted, colo(u)red; dyed; 3. colo(u)red handkerchief.

boyamak to paint, to dye, to colo(u)r.

boyanmak 1. *pass. of* **boyamak** 2. to make up, to put on make-up.

boyarmadde CHEM pigment, colo(u)r-ing matter, dye.

boyasız 1. unpainted; 2. undyed, un-colo(u)red; unpolished (*shoe*); 3. without make-up (*woman*).

boyca 1. as regards height; 2. length-wise, longitudinally; ~ *akran olm.* to be of the same height; ~ *evlat* a prac-tically grown-up child; ~ *günaha gir-mek* to go deep into sin; ~ *kefil olm.* to vouch fully.

boydaş 1. of the same height, equal in stature; 2. equal, peer.

boykot, *-tu* boycott; ~ *etm.* to boycott.

boykotaj boycott.

boykotçu boycotter.

boylam AST longitude.

boylamak 1. traverse lengthwise; 2. (*bir yeri*) to end up (*in*), to land up (*in*); 3. to measure the length *or* height (*of*); 4. to fall prone (*upon the ground*); 5. to escape, to run away.

boylanmak 1. to grow in height, to be-come taller *or* longer; 2. to go on, to walk on; 3. *pass. of* **boylamak**.

boyler boiler.

boylu 1. tall, high; long; 2. of high stat-ure; ~ *boslu* tall and well-built, hand-some; ~ *boyuna* (*or boyunca*) 1. at full length; 2. from end to end.

boynuz 1. horn, antler; 2. horn, trum-pet; 3. cupping horn; 4. antenna (*of insects, etc.*); ~ *taktırmak* sl. to cuck-old; ~ *vurmak* to gore.

boynuzlamak 1. to gore; 2. sl. to cuck-old.

boynuzlanmak 1. to grow horns, to become horned; 2. to be gored; 3. sl. to be cuckold.

boynuzlu 1. horned; 2. sl. cuckold (*man*).

boynuzsuz hornless, polled; ~ *koyun* fig. harmless person.

boyotu, *-nu* BOT cumin.

boyskavt, *-tı* boy scout.

boysuz short, not tall.

boyun, *-ynu* 1. neck; 2. GEOGR pass, de-file; 3. fig. responsibility; ~ *borcu* honorary obligation, binding duty; ~ *çeviren* ZOO wryneck; ~ *eğmek* to submit; to humiliate o.s.; ~ *kesmek* to bow the head; ~ *vermek* to surren-der; to submit; (boynu): ~ *altında kalsın!* may he die!; ~ *kıldan ince* fig. ready to accept any decision; *-na almak* to take upon o.s.; *-na at-mak* to put the blame (on); *-na atıl-mak* to fall on s.o.'s neck; *-na binmek* to pester, to dun; *-nu vurmak* to be-head, to decapitate.

boyuna 1. lengthwise; longitudinally; 2. [x . .] incessantly, continually.

boyunbağı, *-nı* necktie.

boyunca 1. along; 2. lengthwise; 3. throughout, during.

boyunduruk 1. yoke (*a. fig.*); 2. *wres-tling*: headlock; ~ *altına almak* (*or bo-yunduruğa vurmak*) to put under the yoke, to enslave.

boyut, *-tu* dimension.

boz 1. gray; roan; 2. rough, waste, uncultivated (*land*).

boza boza (*drink made of fermented millet*); ~ *gibi* thick (*liquid*).

bozacı maker *or* seller of boza.

bozarmak 1. to turn pale; 2. to become gray.

bozca 1. grayish; 2. uncultivated soil.

bozdoğan 1. zoo merlin; 2. (*a. boz-dağan*) iron war-mace.

bozdurmak 1. *caus. of bozmak*; 2. to change (*money*), to get change for.

bozgun 1. rout, defeat; 2. routed, defeated; ~ *vermek* (*or -a uğramak*) to get clobbered, to be routed; *-a uğratmak* to clobber, to rout, to defeat.

bozguncu defeatist.

bozgunculuk defeatism.

bozkır steppe, wold.

bozkurt, *-du* gray wolf.

bozma 1. *vn. of bozmak*; 2. made out (*-den* of); 3. pervert, proselyte; 4. descendant of mixed blood; 5. JUR cassation, abrogation, quashing.

bozmacı second-hand dealer, junk dealer.

bozmak, (*-ar*) 1. to spoil, to ruin, to destroy; 2. to change (*money*); 3. to upset (*stomach, plans, etc.*); 4. to undo, to disintegrate; 5. to take to pieces, to take down (*tent*), to demolish, to scrap; 6. to disturb (*peace*); 7. to disorganize; 8. to defeat, to clobber, to rout (*enemy*); 9. to deform; to taint, to make putrid; 10. to adulterate; to deprave, to corrupt; to cause to wither; 11. to erase, to cross out, to deface, to obliterate; 12. to break (*oath, custom*), to cancel (*agreement*); 13. JUR to quash (*by cassation*); 14. to deflower, to violate; 15. to disconcert; to embarrass, to humiliate; 16. to break, to change for the worse (*weather*); 17. to be crazy (*about*), to be wild (*about*).

bozrak grayish, greyish.

bozuk 1. destroyed, spoilt, broken; gone bad; 2. out of order, out of repair; 3. depraved, bad, corrupt; 4. bad (*weather*); 5. (small) change; ~ *çalmak* to be in a bad mood; ~ *para* small change; ~ *para gibi harcamak* to use a person in a demeaning way.

bozukdüzen 1. irregular, disordered; 2. unsettled conditions.

bozukluk 1. vice; defeat; 2. small change, coins.

bozulmak 1. *pass. of bozmak*; 2. to be

spoilt, to be destroyed, to become tainted (*or* putrid); 3. to become corrupt (*or* depraved); to wither; to become thin and sallow; 4. to break down (*car, etc.*); 5. to look vexed, to resent, to be humiliated, to be disconcerted; 6. to go bad (*meat, etc.*); *bozulmaz denge* PHYS indifferent (*or* neutral) equilibrium; *bozulup kalmak* to be discomfited.

bozum 1. *sl.* discomfiture, humiliation, embarrassment; 2. *sl.* pecuniary embarrassment, going broke; ~ *etm sl.* to embarrass; ~ *havası sl.* atmosphere of embarrassment; ~ *olm. sl.* to be embarrassed, to lose face, to be discomfited.

bozumca a kind of lizard.

bozunma CHEM disintegration, decomposition.

bozunmak CHEM to disintegrate, to decompose.

bozuntu 1. discomfiture, embarrassment; 2. F caricature (of), mere parody (of); 3. scrap, refuse; *-ya vermemek* to keep up appearances.

bozuşmak to break with one another, to fall out (*ile* with).

bozuşuk on unfriendly terms, on bad terms.

böbrek ANAT kidney; ~ *iltihabı* nephritis.

böbürlenmek to boast, to be arrogant, to strut, to brag, to be puffed up.

böcek 1. zoo insect; 2. bug, beetle; worm; 3. louse; 4. lobster; crayfish; 5. HIST detective; ~ *zehiri* pesticide.

böcekçil BIOL insectivorous.

böcekkabuğu, *-nu* greenish blue with a metallic luster.

böceklenmek to become infested with vermin, to get buggy.

böğür, *-ğrü* 1. side, flank (*of the body*); 2. side-piece of a saddle frame.

böğürmek to bellow, to low; to moo.

böğürtlen 1. BOT blackberry, bramble; 2. *sl.* = *kusmuk*.

böğürtü bellow, roar; moo.

bölen MATH divisor.

bölge 1. zone, district, region; 2. section; part; line of division.

bölgeci regionalist.

bölgesel regional.

bölme 1. *vn. of bölmek*; 2. partition, dividing wall; 3. MATH division; 4. compartment; 5. NAUT bulkhead.

bölmek 1. to separate; to cut up; 2.

MATH to divide (*-e* into).
bölmeli partitioned.
bölü MATH divided by.
bölücü 1. MATH divider; **2.** separationist, intriguer, plotter.
bölücülük divisive behavio(u)r.
bölük 1. MIL company; squadron; **2.** MATH order, place; **3.** part, division, subdivision; compartment; **4.** body, group (*of men*); **5.** one of two braids of hair; **6.** HIST detachment, squad; ~~ in groups; ~ *komutanı* MIL captain; ~ *pörçük* in bits.
bölüm 1. MATH quotient, dividing; **2.** portion, slice, division, chapter, part, episode, section.
bölümlemek to classify, to sort out.
bölünebilme MATH divisibility.
bölünen MATH dividend.
bölünme 1. *vn. of* **bölünmek**; **2.** BIOL division.
bölünmek to be divided (*-e* into), to be separated.
bölünmez indivisible.
bölüntü part, section.
bölüşmek to divide up, to share out.
bölüştürme division, distribution.
bön naive, silly, imbecile, simple; *bakmak* to stare foolishly.
bönlük naiveté, imbecility, foolishness.
börek pastry, pie.
börekçi maker *or* seller of *börek*.
börtmek to boil slightly.
börülce BOT cowpea, black-eyed bean.
böyle so, thus, in this way; such; ~ *iken* (*or ise de*) anyhow, while this is so, notwithstanding the circumstances; *bundan* ~ henceforth; *bunlar kim* ~? who on earth are they? *nereden* (*nereye*) ~? where are you coming from? (where are you going?)
böylece [x . .] thus, in this way.
böylelikle [. . x .] = *böylece*.
böylesi the like, such a one, this kind.
brakisefal, -li brachycephalic.
branda [x .] sailor's hammock; ~ *bezi* canvas.
branş branch, department, field of work.
bravo! *int.* bravo!, well done!
bre! *int.* P **1.** you!, hey!, you chap!, fellow! **2.** oh!, ah!, gee!
Brezilya [. x .] **1.** *pr. n.* Brazil; **2.** ♀ brazilwood; ~ *kestanesi* brazil-nut.
brıçka [x .] buggy.
briç, -ci *cards*: bridge.

brifing briefing.
brik¹, -gi NAUT brig.
brik², -ki a horse carriage.
briket, -ti briquette.
briyantin brilliantine, pomade.
broderi embroidery.
broderili embroidered.
brokar brocade.
brom 1. CHEM bromine; **2.** BOT brome grass.
bromür CHEM bromide.
bronş ANAT bronchus.
bronşçuk ANAT bronchiole.
bronşit, -ti bronchitis.
bronz bronze; ~ *tel* bronze wire.
broş brooch.
broşür brochure, pamphlet.
bröve pilot's license; testimonial, certificate.
Brüksel *pr. n.* Brussels; ~ *lahanası* Brussels sprouts.
brülör burner, combustion unit.
brüt gross.
bu this; ~ *arada* **1.** meanwhile, in the meantime; **2.** among other things, in passing; ~ *aralıkta* at this moment (*or* instant); ~ *cihetten* in this respect; from this point of view; ~ *cümleden* as an instance of this ~ *defa* this time; and now; ~ *gece* tonight; ~ *gibi* like this, such, of this kind; ~ *ne perhiz bu ne lahana turşusu!* *fig.* what a contrast!, how inconsistent!; ~ *sabah* (*akşam*) this morning (evening); ~ *sefer s.* ~ *defa*; ~ *yakınlarda* **1.** recently; **2.** in the near future; **3.** hereabouts; *-nda bir iş var* there is s.th. fishy in it, there is a catch in it; *-ndan başka* besides, moreover, furthermore, in addition; *-ndan böyle* from now on, henceforth; *-ndan dolayı* (*or ötürü*) because of this, for this reason, therefore, that is why; *-ndan iyisi sağlık* (*or can sağlığı*) this is the best; *-ndan sonra* (*or böyle*) **1.** henceforth, from now on, in future, from today; **2.** after this.
bucak 1. corner, nook; **2.** POL sub-district (*syn. nahiye*); ~~ here and there, high and low; *dünyanın dört bucağına* to the four corners of the earth; *yurdun her bucağında* all over the country.
bucurgat *s.* **bocurgat.**
buç end, limit.
buçuk half (*after numerals*); *dört* ~ **1.** four and a half; **2.** it is half past four.

bulaşkan

buçuklu having halves *or* fractions.
budak 1. knot (*in timber*), burr; **2.** twig, branch; ~ **özü** young shoot.
budaklanmak to become knotty; to send forth shoots; **dallanıp ~** *fig.* to become complicated.
budaklı knotty, gnarled.
budala 1. silly, imbecile; foolish; **2.** crazy (*about*), wild (*about*), mad (*about*).
budalalık 1. stupidity, foolishness; **2.** madness, craze.
budamak 1. to prune, to lop, to trim; **2.** *fig.* to diminish, to decrease, to lessen.
budanmak 1. *pass. of* **budamak**; **2.** to apply o.s. assiduously to s.th.
Budist, -ti Buddhist.
Budizm Buddhism.
budun nation, people.
budunlararası international.
bugün [x .] today; ~ **yarın** soon, at any time; **-den** from today; **-den tezi yok** right away; **-e ~** don't forget that; unquestionably, sure enough; **-ler** these days: **-lerde** nowadays, in these days; **-ün işini yarına bırakma** never put off until tomorrow what you can do today.
bugünkü [x . .] of today, today's; ~ **günde 1.** today; **2.** under present conditions; ~ **tavuk yarınki kazdan iyidir** a bird in the hand is worth two in the bush.
bugünlük [x . .] for today; ~ **yarınlık** that may happen any moment.
buğday wheat; ~ **benizli** dark-skinned.
buğdaygiller BOT gramineae, poaceae.
buğdaypası, -nı wheat rust.
buğu 1. vapo(u)r, steam, fog, mist; **2.** moisture, dew.
buğuevi, -ni fumigating station.
buğulamak to steam up, to mist up.
buğulanmak 1. *pass. of* **buğulamak**; **2.** to be steamed up, to mist over.
buğulu steamed up, fogged.
buhar steam, vapo(u)r; ~ **gemisi** steamship; ~ **kazanı** boiler; ~ **makinesi** steam engine.
buharlaşma evaporation.
buharlaşmak to evaporate, to vapo(u)rize.
buharlaştırmak to vapo(u)rize.
buharlı steamy, vaporous.
buhran [ā] crisis; **mali ~** financial crisis.
buhranlı critical, stressful.

buhur [. -] incense, fumigatory.
buhurdan(lık) = **buhurluk**.
buhurlamak to fumigate with incense, to cense.
buhurluk 1. censer; **2.** incense box.
buhurumeryem BOT cyclamen.
buji MOT spark plug.
bukadar [x . .] **1.** this much, that much, so many; **2.** that's all; **3.** odd; **bin ~ yıl önce** a thousand odd years ago; **-ı da fazla!** enough's enough!
bukağı fetter; hobble.
bukağılamak to fetter.
bukağılı fettered.
bukalemun ZOO & *fig.* chameleon.
buket, -ti bouquet, bunch of flowers.
bukle lock, curl of hair.
bukleli curly.
bulak P spring, fountain, river-head.
bulama 1. *vn. of* **bulamak**; **2.** grape-juice (*boiled down to the consistency of honey*).
bulamaç, -cı thick soup (*made with flour, butter and sugar*).
bulamak 1. to roll (*in flour*); to besmear, to bedaub (-*e* with); to smear (-*e* on); **2.** to dirty.
bulandırıcı 1. causing nausea; **2.** agitator, instigator.
bulandırmak 1. to render turbid (*or* muddy), to muddy, to roil; **2.** to turn (*the stomach*).
bulanık turbid, roily; cloudy, overcast; dim; ~ **hava** overcast (*or* cloudy) weather; ~ **suda balık avlamak** *fig.* to fish in troubled waters.
bulanıklık turbidity; dimness.
bulanmak 1. *pass. of* **bulamak**; **2.** to become cloudy; to become turbid; **3.** to be stirred, to be upset, to get confused; **4.** to be dimmed; **5.** to become bloodshot (*or* opaque) (*eye*); **midesi ~** to become nauseated.
bulantı 1. nausea, queasiness; **2.** turbidity.
bulaşıcı infectious, contagious.
bulaşık 1. smeared, soiled, bedaubed; tainted; **2.** contagious, infected (*disease*); **3.** dirty dishes, dirty kitchen utensils; **4.** *sl.* saucy, pert (*person*); **5.** irregular; ~ **bezi** dish-cloth; ~ **deniz** dangerous waters; ~ **makinesi** dishwasher; ~ **suyu** dishwater; ~ **suyu gibi** wishywashy (*soup, tea, etc.*).
bulaşıkçı dishwasher.
bulaşkan 1. sticky, adhesive; **2.** combative (*person*).

bulaşmak 1. to become dirty, to be smeared; **2.** to soil, to become smeared (*-e* on), to get sticky; **3.** to be spread by contagion, to communicate itself (*-e* to) (*disease*); **4.** to be involved (*-e* in), to interfere (*-e* in); **5.** to molest, to pester, to annoy; **6.** to take in hand (*work*).

bulaştırmak 1. to smear, to stick on, to dirty; **2.** to spread, to infect (*disease*); **3.** to involve (*-e* in).

buldok bulldog.

buldozer bulldozer.

Bulgaristan [. x . .], **Bulgarya** [. x .] *pr. n.* Bulgaria.

bulgu 1. finding, discovery; **2.** invention; **3.** diagnosis.

bulgur boiled and pounded wheat; ~ *pilavı* dish of boiled pounded wheat.

bulmaca crossword puzzle.

bulmak, **(-ur) 1.** to find; **2.** to discover; to invent; **3.** to hit, to reach; **4.** to meet (**with**); **5.** to find (*fault*) (*-e* with), to blame (*-e* on); **6.** to amount to (*a sum*); **7.** to recall; **buldu da bunadı** he always wishes for more; **bulup buluşturmak** to be adroit in providing; **bulup çıkarmak** to find out.

buluğ puberty; **-a ermek** to reach puberty.

bulundurmak *caus. of* **bulunmak** to make available, to provide, to have present, to have waiting, to keep in stock.

bulunmak 1. *pass. or refl. of* **bulmak**; **2.** to be found, to be discovered; **3.** to be present, to exist, to be; **4.** to take part (*-de* in), to be present (*-de* at), to participate (*-de* in).

bulunmaz unobtainable; rare, choice; ~ *Hint kumaşı fig.* rarity, a very rare thing; *bu, bulunmaz Hint kumaşı değil ya!* it is not certainly a rarity!

buluntu 1. a rare find; **2.** foundling.

buluş 1. invention; discovery; finding; **2.** idea, original thought.

buluşma meeting, rendezvous; ~ *yeri* rendezvous, meeting place.

buluşmak to meet, to rendezvous, to come together.

bulut, **-tu 1.** cloud; **2.** *sl.* pissed as a newt, as drunk as a lord; ~ *gibi* (*sarhoş*) = *bulut 2*; *-tan nem almak* (*or kapmak*) *fig.* to be very touchy (*or* suspicious).

bulutlanmak to become cloudy.

bulutlu 1. cloudy, overcast; **2.** opaque, turbid.

bulutsu AST nebular, nebulous.

bulvar boulevard.

bumbar 1. sausage casing; **2.** sausage (*made of rice and meat stuffed in a large gut*); **3.** weatherstripping.

bumbulanık [x . . .] quite turbid.

bumburuşuk [x . . .] very creased, wrinkled all over.

bunak dotard.

bunaklık dotage.

bunalım 1. crisis; **2.** depression, stupefaction.

bunalmak 1. to be stupefied. to be suffocated (*-den* with); **2.** to be depressed (*or* bored).

bunaltıcı 1. sultry, stupefying, suffocating, oppressive, stifling; **2.** depressing, boring.

bunaltmak 1. to stupefy, to stifle, to oppress; **2.** to depress, to bore.

bunama dotage.

bunamak to dote, to be in one's dotage.

bunca [x .] this much, so much; ~ *zaman* for such a long time.

bunda *loc. of* **bu.**

bundan *abl. of* **bu**; ~ *başka* besides, moreover, furthermore, in addition; ~ *böyle* henceforth; ~ *dolayı* therefore, that is why, thereof; ~ *ötürü s.* ~ *dolayı*; ~ *sonra* **1.** after this; **2.** from now on, henceforth.

bunlar *pl. of* **bu** these.

bunsuz without this.

bunu *acc. of* **bu.**

bunun *gen. of* **bu**; ~ *için* therefore, that is why; ~ *üzerine* thereupon; *-la beraber* (*or birlikte*) nevertheless.

bura this place, this spot; ~ *adamları* the men of this place; *-da* here; *-dan* from here, hence; *-sı neresi?* what place is this?; *-ya* to this spot, here, hither.

burağan METEOR whirlwind.

buralı native of this place.

buram buram in whirls (*snow*), in clouds (*smoke*), in great quantities (*smell, sweat*); ~ *duman çıkıyor* it is steaming; ~ *kokmak* to smell very much; ~ *terlemek* to sweat profusely; ~ *tütmek* to smoke in clouds.

buran *s.* **burağan.**

burani *s.* **borani.**

burcu burcu fragrantly, smelling sweetly.

burç, **-cu 1.** tower; bastion; **2.** sign of

the zodiac; **3.** BOT mistletoe.

burçak BOT common vetch.

burçin, burçun hind.

burgacık [x . .] *s.* **kargacık.**

burgaç, -cı whirlpool.

burgu 1. auger, gimlet, drill; **2.** corkscrew; ~ **yapmak** AVIA to go into a spin.

burgulamak to drill, to bore.

burjuva bourgeois.

burjuvazi bourgeoisie.

burkmak to sprain, to wrench; to twist.

burkulma sprain, wrench.

burkulmak to be sprained, to be wrenched.

burma [x .] **1.** *vn. of* **burmak**; **2.** screwed, twisted, spiral; screw, convolution; **3.** castrated by twisting; **4.** cock, tap, faucet; **5.** P bracelet; **6.** gripe of colic; **7.** *s.* **sarığı burma.**

burmak 1. to twist, to screw; to wring; **2.** to castrate; **3.** to gripe (*bowels*); **4.** (*ağzını*) to cause an acrid feeling in the mouth; **bura bura sıkmak** to wring out.

burnaz hawk-nosed, large-nosed.

burs scholarship, bursary; ~ **öğrencisi** scholar, bursar.

bursiye = **burs öğrencisi.**

buruk 1. acrid, astringent, puckery; **2.** sprained, twisted; **3.** oversensitive, touchy (*person*).

burukluk 1. pungency, acridity; **2.** resentment, being upset.

burulmak 1. *pass. of* **burmak**; **2.** to writhe; **3.** (*bşe*) to resent *s.th.*, to take offence at *s.th.*

burum burum: ~ **burulmak** to gripe repeatedly.

burun (*acc.:* **burunu;** *poss. suffix* **burnu**) **1.** nose; **2.** bill, beak; **3.** tip; **4.** GEOGR promontory, cape, headland, point; **5.** *fig.* arrogance, pride; ~ **boşluğu** nasal cavity; ~ **buruna gelmek** to run into; ~ **burmak** to turn one's nose up (-*e* at); ~ **deliği nostril**; ~ **kıvırmak** to turn one's nose up (-*e* at), to sniff (-*e* at); ~ **maskesi** muzzle; ~ **silmek** to blow one's nose, to wipe one's nose; (**burnu**): ~ **bile kanamadan** *fig.* with (*or* in) a whole skin; ~ **büyük** *fig.* conceited, arrogant; ~ **havada** *fig.* nose-in-the-air; ~ **havada olm.** to be on one's high horse; ~ **kırılmak** to eat humble pie, to be humiliated; **-na girmek** *fig.* to come too close (-*in* to); **-nda tütmek** *fig.* to long

for; **-ndan düşen bin parça olur** he is very sulky; **-ndan düşmüş** the spit and image of, the dead spit of; **-ndan** (**fitil fitil**) **gelmek** *fig.* to be spoiled completely, to do penance for; **-ndan kıl aldırmamak** to be untouchable; to be very conceited and unapproachable; **-dan solumak** to go up in the air; **-nu çekmek 1.** to sniff; **2.** *fig.* to be the loser, to go without, to be bereft of; **-nu sokmak** to poke one's nose (-*e* into), to meddle (-*e* in), to snoop (-*e* into); **-nu sürtmek** to eat humble pie; **-nun dibinde** right under one's (very) nose; **-nun dikine** (*or* **doğrusuna**) **gitmek** to follow one's nose; **-nun direği kırılmak** *fig.* to be suffocated by bad smell; **-nun doğrusundan ayrılmamak** to follow one's nose; **-nun ucunu görememek** *fig. sl.* to be pissed as a newt, to be as drunk as a lord.

burunduruk barnacle.

burunlu 1. ... nosed; ... pointed; **2.** *fig.* proud, snooty.

burunluk nose-ring (*of a bull*); iron toe-cap (*of a boot*).

burunsalık muzzle.

buruntu colic.

buruşmak 1. to wrinkle, to crease, to pucker up, to crumple; **2.** to have the teeth set on edge.

buruşturmak to crease, to wrinkle, to pucker, to crumple, to contort, to ruffle.

buruşuk wrinkled, puckered, crumpled, ruffled, contorted, shrivel(l)ed.

buruşukluk pucker, crease, wrinkle.

buse [ū] kiss.

but, -du thigh, rump, the buttocks.

butik boutique.

butlan [ā] invalidity, nullity, voidness; ~ **davası** JUR action for nullity, action for voidance.

buut, -u'du 1. dimension; **2.** distance.

buymak 1. to freeze to death; **2.** to freeze, to be chilled to the bone.

buyot, -tu hot-water bottle.

buyruk order, command, decree; **başına ~ olm.** to be one's own master (*or* man).

buyrultu 1. order, decree; **2.** mandate, rescript.

buyurmak 1. to order, to decree; **2.** to command, to rule; **3.** to come, to enter, to pass; **4.** to take, to have, to eat, to drink; **5.** to say, to utter; **6.** to be so kind as to, to condescend (**to** *inf.*), to deign; **buyurun cenaze namazına!** we are done for!

buy(u)run(uz)! 1. please!; **2.** come in!; **3.** sit down!; **4.** help yourself!

buz 1. ice; **2.** frozen, very cold; ~ **bağlamak** to ice up, to freeze; ~ **gibi 1.** icy, ice-cold; **2.** regular, good and proper; **3.** fat and firm (*meat*); ~ **kesilmek 1.** to freeze; **2.** *fig.* to be stunned, to stand aghast (at); ~ **kesmek** *fig.* to freeze, to feel very cold; ~ **tutmak** to ice up, to ice over, to freeze; ~ **üstüne yazı yazmak** *fig.* to write in (*or* on) water, to build on sand.

buzağı calf; fawn.

buzağılamak to calve.

buzdağı, -nı iceberg.

buzdolabı, -nı refrigerator, fridge, ice-box.

buzhane [ā] **1.** ice house; ice factory; **2.** cold storage plant.

buzkıran ice-breaker.

buzlanmak to ice up (*or* over), to get icy.

buzlu 1. iced, icy; **2.** dulled, clouded; **3.** frosted, ground (*glass*).

buzlucam frosted (*or* ground) glass.

buzluk 1. = **buzhane**; **2.** ice-box; ice cube tray.

buzul glacier; ~ **devri** glacial period, ice age.

buzullaşma glaciation.

bücür squat, short, dwarf, stocky.

büfe 1. sideboard; **2.** buffet, refreshment stall, bar.

büfeci barkeeper.

büfecilik barkeeping.

büge, büğelek gadfly.

bühtan [ā] calumny, slander; ~ **etm.** (*b-ne*) to slander, to calumniate.

büklüm 1. twist, curl, fold, coil; **2.** ANAT plica; **3.** bend; ~ ~ curly, in curls.

bükme 1. *vn. of* **bükmek**; **2.** cord, braid, (twisted) thread, twine.

bükmek 1. to bend; **2.** to twist, to curl, to contort; **3.** to fold; **4.** to spin; to twine; **5.** to flex (*muscle*).

Bükreş *pr. n.* Bucharest.

bükük twisted, bent, curved.

bükülgen flexible.

bükülme bending, curvature.

bükülmek 1. *pass. of* **bükmek**; **2.** to twist, to curl; to bend; to fold.

bükülü bent, twisted, crooked, curled, spun.

büküm curl, twine, twist, bend, torsion, fold.

bükünmek to writhe (*with pain*).

büküntü 1. bend, fold, twist; **2.** colic; **3.** hem.

bülbül nightingale; ~ **dişi** a kind of fine needlework; ~ **gibi** fluently; ~ **gibi okumak** to read fluently; ~ **kesilmek** to spill the beans.

bülent, -di 1. high, elevated; **2.** tall, lofty; **3.** ♀ *mf.*

bülten bulletin.

bülûg s. **buluğ**.

bünye 1. structure (*a.* GR), constitution; **2.** edifice, building; **3.** construction (*of a building*).

bürç, -cü s. **burç**.

bürçük curl of hair.

bürgü kerchief; scarf; veil; woman's cloak.

bürhan [ā] **1.** indisputable argument; **2.** evidence, proof.

büro [x .] bureau, office; ~ **şefi** head clerk.

bürokrasi bureaucracy, red tape.

bürülü wrapped, enfolded, enveloped.

bürüm 1. roll, fold; **2.** BOT involucre.

bürümcek anything wrapped up like a cocoon.

bürümcük 1. raw silk gauze; **2.** BOT involucel.

bürümeden superficially.

bürümek 1. to wrap, to enfold; **2.** to cover up, to clothe, to infest, to invade, to fill; **gözünü kan** ~ to see red.

bürünmek *pass. or refl. of* **bürümek** to wrap o.s. up (*-e* in), to be clothed (*-e* in); to wrap around o.s.; to be filled (*-e* with).

büsbütün [x ..] altogether, quite, completely, wholly.

büst, -tü bust; portrait.

bütan butane.

bütçe budget; ~ **yılı** budget year.

bütün 1. whole, entire, complete, total; all; **2.** undivided, unbroken; **3.** altogether, wholly; **4.** MATH sum, total; ~ ~ = **büsbütün**.

bütünleme *vn. of* **bütünlemek**; ~ **sınavı** make-up examination.

bütünlemek 1. to complete; to complement; to make up, to supplement; **2.** to mend, to repair.

bütünlemeli having a make-up examination.

bütünler supplementary; ~ **açı** MATH supplementary angle.

bütünlük entirety, universality, fullness, wholeness; ~ **harbi** *rare* total war.

büve(lek) zoo gadfly; ~ **sokmuşa dönmek** *fig.* to rage as if stung.

büvet, -ti refreshment stall.

büyü magic, spell, incantation, sorcery, charm; ~ **bozmak** to break a spell; ~ **yapmak** to cast a spell (-*e* over), to put a spell (-*e* on), to practice sorcery.

büyücek somewhat large.

büyücü sorcerer, witch, magician.

büyücülük sorcery; witchcraft.

büyük 1. big, large; **2.** great, high; **3.** important, serious, major; **4.** elder, older, senior, eldest; ~ **aptes** feces; ~ **atardamar** aorta; ⚯ **çarşı** *pr. n.* Grand Bazaar; ~ **çizgi** dash; ~ **harf** capital (letter); ~ **laf etm.** to talk big; ⚯ **Millet Meclisi** *pr. n.* the Grand National Assembly; ~ **ölçüde** on a large scale; ~ **söylemek** to dogmatize, to talk big, to boast.

büyükana, büyükanne grandmother.

büyükamiral, -li full admiral, Admiral of the Fleet.

Büyükayı AST Big Dipper, Ursa Major.

büyükbaba grandfather.

büyükbaş cattle.

büyükelçi ambassador.

büyükelçilik embassy.

büyüklü küçüklü everybody, old and young.

büyüklük 1. greatness, largeness; seniority; **2.** gravity, importance; **3.** size; ~ **göstermek** to act nobly; ~ **taslamak**

to put on airs.

büyüksemek to overrate, to enlarge; to exaggerate.

büyülemek to bewitch (*a. fig.*); to charm, to fascinate.

büyülenme fascination.

büyültme PHOT blow-up, enlargement.

büyültmek 1. to lengthen, to prolong, to extend; **2.** PHOT to enlarge, to blow up; **3.** to enlarge.

büyülü bewitched, charmed, enchanted, magic.

büyüme growing up, development.

büyümek 1. to grow (up); **2.** to prosper, to thrive; **3.** to become large: **büyümüş de küçülmüş** precocious (*child*).

büyüteç magnifying glass.

büyütme 1. *vn. of* **büyütmek**; **2.** foster child; **3.** PHOT blow-up, enlargement.

büyütmek *caus. of* **büyümek 1.** to bring up (*child*), to rear, to raise; **2.** to exaggerate; to magnify; **3.** to enlarge.

büzgü smocking, shirr, gather, pucker.

büzgülü smocked, shirred, gathered.

büzme 1. *vn. of* **büzmek**; **2.** drawn together.

büzmek to gather, to constrict, to pucker.

büzük 1. contracted, puckered, constricted; **2.** *sl.* asshole, arsehole, anus; **3.** *sl.* courage.

büzülmek 1. *pass. of* **büzmek**; **2.** to shrink, to shrivel up; **3.** to crouch, to cower; **büzülüp oturmak** to sit shyly; **ezile büzüle** cap in hand.

C

caba [x .] **1.** free (of charge), gratis, without payment; **2.** thrown into the bargain, over and above, on (the) top of it.

cabacı [x ..] F sponger, parasite, toady.

cabadan [x ..] for nothing, gratis, gratuitously, free (of charge).

cacık *a dish consisting of chopped cucumber, garlic and dill in yoghurt.*

cadaloz a spiteful old hag; nagging woman, shrew.

cadde main road, street, avenue; **-yi tutmak 1.** *sl.* to clear out; **2.** to close off the street.

cadı 1. ghost, specter, vampire; **2.** witch; **3.** old and ugly woman, hag; **~ kazanı** den of intrigue.

cafcaf F **1.** ostentatious, showy talk; **2.** pompousness, showiness.

cafcaflı pompous, showy.

cahil [ā] **1.** ignorant; **2.** uneducated, illiterate; **3.** untaught; inexperienced; *fig.* greenhorn, beginner; **4.** not knowing, ignorant (**of**).

cahillik [ā] **1.** ignorance; **2.** a stupid act; **3.** inexperience; youth; **~ etm.** to act foolishly.

caiz [ā] lawful, permitted; admissible, permissible, allowable, valid.

caize [ā] **1.** HIST reward, present (*given to a poet for a laudatory poem*); **2.** mark, tick; **3.** *pl.* quotation-marks, inverted commas.

caka [x .] *sl.* brag, boast; ostentation; swagger; **~ satmak** *sl.* to show off, to boast, to brag, to swagger.

cakacı [x ..] *sl.* boaster, braggart, swaggerer. bounder.

cakalı [x ..] *sl.* boastful; showy, ostentatious. swaggering.

câli [- -] artificial, affected; false, not genuine; insincere.

cam 1. glass; **2.** of glass; **3.** window (*pane*); **4.** PHOT plate; **5.** optical lens; **~ takmak 1.** to glaze, to install panes; **2.** to replace lenses.

camadan 1. double-breasted velvet waistcoat; **2.** NAUT reef.

cambaz 1. rope-dancer, tight-rope walker, acrobat; roughrider, circus rider; **2.** horse dealer; **3.** sly, cunning,

crafty, wily, juggler, trick rider, swindler.

cambazhane [. . - .] **1.** circus; **2.** variety theatre.

camcı glazier.

camcılık glaziery.

camekân 1. shop-window, show-case; **2.** glass cupboard; **3.** greenhouse, hothouse; **4.** dressing room of a Turkish bath; **5.** *sl.* specs.

camgöbeği, -ni glass-green.

camgöz 1. zoo tope, shark; **2.** *fig.* greedy, insatiable, avaricious, stingy, miser; **3.** one who has a glass eye.

camız zoo water buffalo.

cami -ii (*a. frequently* **-si**) mosque; **~ yıkılmış ama mihrap yerinde** *fig.* there may be snow on the roof but there is still fire in the furnace.

camia [- . .] **1.** community, body, group; **2.** PHYS collector.

camlamak to cover with glass.

camlık 1. glassed-in place; **2.** small greenhouse, hotbed, hothouse.

camyünü, -nü fiberglass, glass wool.

can 1. soul; **2.** life; **3.** vitality, energy, zeal, vigo(u)r; **4.** darling, love; **5.** person, individual; **6.** intimate friend, confidant; **7.** a member of an order, ECCL *a.* friar; **8.** dear, sympathetic; **~ acısı** acute pain; **~ acısıyle** with fear of death; **~ acıtmak** to pain (*or* hurt) a person, to cause a person pain; to oppress; **~ alacak yer** (*or* **nokta**) **1.** tender spot, the most sensitive spot; **2.** central point (*or* issue), key (**of**); **~ atmak** (*bşe*) to desire passionately, to crave; **~ beslemek** to feed o.s. well; **~ çekişme** death-struggle, being in the throes of death; **~ damarı** vital point; **~ derdine düşmek** to struggle for one's life; **~ dostu** a very close friend. dear friend; **~ düşmanı** deadly enemy, mortal enemy; **~ evi 1.** the seat of life (*heart, pit of stomach*): **2.** the vital spot. sensitive point; **~ korkusu** fear of death; *fig.* mortal dread; **~ kulağıyle dinlemek** to be all ears, to listen intently (-*i* to); **~ pazarı** a matter of life and death; **~ sıkıntısı 1.** boredom, tediousness, ennui, vexation;

2. oppression, anguish, anxiety; ~ **vermek 1.** to die, to perish; **2.** *fig.* to desire passionately; **3.** to grant spiritual strength; **4.** to resuscitate again, to give life again (*-e* to); ~ **yakmak 1.** to do violence to, to violate; **2.** to torture, to torment; **3.** to cause great injure, to hurt; *-a* ~ **katmak 1.** to enhance the joy of life, to refresh, to increase the vitality; **2.** to invigorate, to strengthen; **3.** to intensify; *-a yakın* lovable. amiable, sympathetic(ally), likable; agreeable; (canı): ~ **ağzına gelmek** to be half-dead (*from anxiety, fear*), to be frightened to death; ~ **çekmek** to desire, to crave for, to long for; ~ **çıkmak 1.** to die; **2.** to be killed, to perish; **3.** *fig.* to get very tired; **4.** *fig.* to be worn out (*clothes*); ~ **pek** tenacious of life, tough, stout; ~ **sıkılmak 1.** to feel angry, to feel vexed (*by*); **2.** to be restless; **3.** to be bored (*-e* by); to be annoyed; ~ **yanmak 1.** to suffer (*-den* from); **2.** to be deeply sad (*or* grieved) (*at, about*); *canım* **1.** my darling!; **2.** my dear; *canıma minnet!* **1.** what more could I want!, so much the better; **2.** I do it with great pleasure; (canına): ~ **kıymak 1.** to kill without mercy; **2.** to commit suicide; *canla başla* with heart and soul.

canan [- -] beloved, sweetheart.

canavar 1. wild beast, brute, monster; **2.** *fig.* brutish person; **3.** *co.* young scamp (*or* rascal), little unruly devil; **4.** *rare* dragon; ~ **düdüğü** (warning) siren; ~ **ruhlu** brutal, inhuman.

canavarlık savagery, ferocity.

canciğer 1. intimate friendship, very close relation; ~ **kuzu sarması** *fig.* inseparable friend, intimate friend.

candan 1. sincere, wholehearted, hearty, cordial; **2.** sincerely, wholeheartedly.

caneriği, -ni green plum.

canfes taffeta.

cangıl cungul 1. tinkle, clink; **2.** ding- -dong.

canhıraş heart-reading, harrowing, bitter.

cani [- -] criminal, murderer.

cankurtaran 1. life-saving remedy; **2.** life-saver; **3.** *a.* ~ **filikası** life-boat; **4.** *a.* ~ **arabası** ambulance; ~ **yeleği** life-belt; ~ **yok mu!** help!

canlandırmak *caus. of* **canlanmak 1.** to invigorate, to animate; **2.** THEAT to (im)personate, to perform.

canlanmak 1. to revive; **2.** to come to life; **3.** to become active (*or* lively).

canlı 1. alive, living; **2.** lively, active; **3.** vigorous, powerful; **4.** living creature, living being; **5.** (*in compounds*) fond of, mad after, bent on; ~ **bebek** *fig.* charming, lovely: nice, *Am.* cute; ~ **canavar** naughty and mischievous, urchin; ~ **cenaze** wan and worn-out person; ~ **yayın** live broadcast.

canlılık liveliness, vigo(u)r.

cansız 1. lifeless, dead, inanimate; **2.** feeble, weak; F lame; **3.** stagnant (*market conditions*); **4.** dull, spiritless; **5.** listless; ~ **düşmek** to become poor in health.

cansiperane self-sacrificing (*act*).

capcanlı vivacious, brisk.

car[1] woman's shawl (*or* cloak).

car[2] P cry, wail.

car car noisily.

carcar F chatterbox.

carcur P cartridge clip.

cari [- -] **1.** flowing, running; **2.** COM current; **3.** usual, customary; **4.** valid; effective; ~ **fiyat** current price; ~ **hesap** current account.

cariye [- . .] female slave; concubine.

cartadak! [x . .] bang!

cascavlak [x . .] **1.** stark naked; **2.** bald- -headed; ~ **etm.** to plunder, to empty; ~ **kalmak** *fig.* to be in low water, to be on the rocks.

casus [â] **1.** spy; **2.** agent.

casuslamak [- . . . .] to spy, to explore.

casusluk [â] espionage, spying.

cavalacoz *sl.* worthless.

cavlak 1. naked, nude, bare; **2.** bald(- -headed), hairless, featherless; *cavlağı çekmek* *sl.* to peg out.

caydırmak *caus. of* **caymak** to dissuade s.o. from s.th. to cause to renounce, to make s.o. change his purpose.

cayır cayır furiously, fiercely: willy- -nilly; ~ **yanmak** to burn in full blaze, to be ablaze; ~ **yırtılmak** to get torn in rags completely.

cayırdamak to creak, to rattle; to grate (*voice*).

cayırtı creak, rattle, crash; yell, roar, shout; *-yı basmak* (*or* **koparmak**) to start shouting furiously.

caymak to retire from an undertaking, to back out to change one's mind, to renounce (*-den* from), to give up.

caz jazz; jazz band.

cazırdamak 1. to crackle (*fire*); 2. *fig.* to sound off.

cazibe [ā] 1. attractive power, gravitation the force of gravity; 2. charm, attraction, appeal.

cazibeli [- . . .] charming, attractive.

cazip attractive, attracting; alluring, appealing.

cazzadak whizzing, hissing.

CD CD; **~-çalar** CD player; **~-ROM** CD-ROM.

cebbar [ā] 1. violent, brutal; despotic, tyrannical; tyrant; 2. F capable (*woman*).

cebellezi [. x . .] *sl.* pinch, swipe.

Cebelitarık, -kı [ā] Gibraltar.

ceberut, -tu [ū] 1. omnipotence of God; 2. arrogance, haughtiness, presumption; 3. tyranny; 4. despotic, tyrannical, tyrant.

cebir, -bri 1. force, compulsion, violence; 2. MATH algebra.

cebire [. - .] splint.

Cebrail [. - -] the Archangel Gabriel.

cebren [x .] by force.

cebretmek [x . .] 1. to force, to enforce (*part. legal*), to compel, to urge; 2. to impose upon forcibly.

cebri 1. forcible, violent, compulsory, forced; 2. MATH algebraic; **~ tedbirler** violent measures; **~ yürüyüş** MIL forced march.

cebrinefis, -fsi [. . x .] self-victory, self--control, self-restraint.

cefa [ā] 1. ill-treatment, cruelty, severity, tormenting; *fig.* vexation; 2. pain, suffering; **~ çekmek** to suffer, to be subject to suffering; **~ etm.** to ill-treat, to abuse, to torment, to inflict pain (*-e* on).

cefakâr long-suffering.

cehalet, -ti [ā] ignorance, inexperience.

cehdetmek [x . .] to exert o.s., to strive, to struggle.

cehennem hell, inferno (*a. fig.*); **~ azabı** hellish torture; **~ ol!** go to hell!, clear out!; **~ zebanisi** demon, brute, devil.

cehennemlik 1. worthy of hell, deserving hell; 2. furnace, stokehole (*of a Turkish bath*).

cehennemtaşı, -nı silver nitrate.

cehre spindle, spool, reel.

cehri BOT 1. dyer's weed, yellow weed; buckthorn.

ceht, -di effort, endeavo(u)r; strain; zeal, eagerness, enthusiasm.

ceket, -ti jacket, sports coat, jacket of a suit.

ceketatay morning coat.

celal, -li 1. glory, majesty of God; 2. ♀ *mf.*

celallenmek to get into a rage.

celbe net bag used by hunters.

celbetmek [x . .] 1. to attract, to pull, to draw; 2. to summon, to cite; MIL to call up, *Am.* to draft, to induct; 3. to give rise to, to call forth. to cause.

celep, -bi cattle-dealer, drover.

cellat, -dı 1. executioner; 2. *fig.* cruel, pitiless, merciless.

celp, -bi 1. JUR summons; 2. attraction; 3. MIL call(ing) up, *Am.* draft, induction.

celpname [ā] JUR summons, written citation.

celse 1. session; 2. JUR hearing, sitting; **-yi açmak** to open the session.

cemaat, -ti [. - .] 1. congregation, group, community at divine service; 2. religious community; 3. crowd; **-e uymak** to conform.

cemal, -li 1. beauty, grace; 2. perfection (of God).

cem'an altogether; **~ yekûn** sum total, in all.

cemetmek [x . .] 1. to collect, to gather, to bring together; 2. MATH to add up.

cemi, -m'i 1. collecting, bringing together; 2. MATH sum, addition, total; 3. GR plural.

cemile [ī] kindness, friendliness, courtesy, attentiveness, compliment.

cemilekâr [ī] kind, obliging, amiable, loveable.

cemiyet, -ti 1. society; association; 2. social gathering; 3. union, assembly; 4. ceremony, party, wedding.

cemiyetli 1. full of people, crowded; 2. significant, expressive, meaningful, comprehensive.

cemre 1. *obs.* glowing ashes; 2. increase of warmth in February (*a short-time before beginning of spring*).

cenabet, -ti [ā] 1. ritual impurity, uncleanliness; 2. ritually impure (*person*); 3. *fig.* nauseous, foul, disgusting; nasty, unpleasant.

cenah [ā] wing (*a.* MIL, ARCH, POL, SPORTS).

cenap, -bı [ā] 1. high personality; excellency, majesty; **2.** ♀ [x .] *mf.*; **Cenabı Hak** God, Lord; **Sefir Cenapları** His Excellency the Ambassador.

cenaze [ā] **1.** corpse, (dead) body; **2.** funeral; ~ *alayı* funeral procession.

cendere 1. (roller) press, cylinder, mangle; press, screw; **2.** narrow pass, defile, valley; *-ye koymak* (*or* **sokmak**) *fig.* give a person a hard time, to put under pressure, to torture.

Cenevizli a Genoese.

Cenevre [. x .] Geneva.

cengâver 1. warlike, heroic; **2.** brave, courageous.

cengâverlik heroism.

cengel jungle.

Cengiz *pr. n.* **1.** Genghis Khan; **2.** *mf.*

cenin [ī] f(o)etus, embryo; **cenini sakıt 1.** abortive fruit; **2.** miscarriage, abortion.

cenk, -gi fight, battle, combat; war; ~ *etm.* to fight, to struggle: to make war.

cenkleşmek to fight; to quarrel.

cennet, -ti 1. *obs.* garden, park; **2.** paradise, heaven (*a. fig.*); ~ *gibi* heavenly; ~ *öküzü* simpleton, good-hearted but simple person.

cennetkuşu, -nu bird of paradise.

cennetli late, deceased, defunct, blessed, happy.

cennetlik 1. pious, religious, faithful, believing; deserving of heaven; **2.** defunct.

Cenova [x . .] Genoa.

centilmen (**adam**) gentleman.

centilmence gentlemanlike; in a gentlemanly way.

centilmenlik gentlemanliness; gentle behavio(u)r.

cenubi [. - -] southern, south ...

cenup, -bu 1. south; **2.** south ...; ♀ **Amerika(sı)** South America; ♀ **Kutbu** South Pole; **cenubu garbi** southwest ..., south-western; **cenubu şarkî** south-east, south-eastern.

cep, -bi 1. pocket; **2.** MIL pocket, break-through; ~ *harçlığı* pocket money; ~ *saati* pocket watch; ~ *sözlüğü* pocket dictionary; ~ *telefonu* *Am.* cellphone; mobile phone; **cebi boş** (*or* **delik**) **1.** beggar; **2.** penniless, broke; **cebi para görmek** to earn money.

cephane [ā] **1.** ammunition, munitions; **2.** *obs.* powder magazine; **3.** *sl.* opium.

cephanelik [ā] ammunition depot, store; arsenal.

cephe 1. front(side), facade; **2.** MIL front-line; **3.** *fig.* side, face; ~ *almak* to turn against, to take sides (*-e* against).

cepken short embroidered jacket.

cepkitabı, -nı pocketbook.

cer, -rri pulling, dragging; ~ *atelyesi* railway repair shop.

cerahat, -ti [. - .] matter, pus; ~ *bağlamak* (*or* **toplamak**) to suppurate.

cerahatlanmak [. - . . .] to suppurate.

cerahatlı [. - . .] suppurating.

cerbeze 1. eloquence, quick-wittedness; **2.** ability to win one's way into favo(u)r.

cerbezeli convincing.

cereme *s.* **cerime.**

cereyan [ā] **1.** flowing, stream; **2.** ELECT current; **3.** course; **4.** movement, trend; **5.** draught; ~ *etm.* **1.** to flow, to run, to pass; **2.** to take place, to happen, to occur.

cerh 1. wounding, hurt, injury; **2.** refutation, confutation; ~ *etm.* **1.** to wound, to injure; **2.** to refute, to disprove.

ceride [ī] *obs.* **1.** newspaper, journal; **2.** diary; daybook, account book; **3.** register.

cerime [ī] **1.** penalty; **2.** JUR fine; *-sini çekmek* to pay the penalty of ...

Cermen HIST Teuton.

cerrah [ā] **1.** surgeon; **2.** *obs.* dresser of wounds.

cerrahi [ā] surgical; ~ *müdahale* operation.

cerrahlık surgery.

cerrar [ā] obtrusive beggar.

cerretmek [x . .] **1.** to pull through, to drag.

cesamet, -ti [ā] **1.** size, largeness, bulkiness; (*absolute*) greatness.

cesametli huge, bulky.

cesaret, -ti [ā] **1.** courage, daring, boldness; **2.** audacity, daredevilry, impudence; ~ *almak* to summon up courage, to take heart; ~ *bulmak* to become bold (*or* impudent *or* audacious); ~ *etm.* to venture, to dare.

cesaretlenmek [ā] **1.** to take courage, to summon up courage; **2.** to become bold (*or* impudent).

cesaretli [ā] **1.** courageous, brave, bold, daring; **2.** audacious, impudent.

ceset, -di 1. (dead) body, corpse; **2.** *obs.* body.

ceste ceste little by little, gradually;

by instal(l)ments; piece by piece, bit by bit.

cesur = **cesaretli.**

cet, -ddi 1. grandfather; 2. ancestor, forefather.

cetvel 1. (**tahtası**) ruler; 2. scale; 3. printed form, blank form, list, roll, register, record, schedule; 4. TYP writing frame; 5. watering canal, trench.

cevaben [ā] in reply (-e to).

cevabi [. - -] replying; ~ **nota** reply note; ~ **ziyaret** return visit.

cevahir [ā] (*pl. of* **cevher**) precious stone, gem, jewels, jewel(le)ry; ~ **yumurtlıyor** *iro.* he speaks wisely and well.

cevap, -bı answer, reply; return (*a. fig.*); JUR defense; ~ **vermek** -*e* to answer, to reply, to return; ~ **ziyareti** return visit.

cevaplandırmak to answer.

cevaplı 1. having an answer; 2. with reply coupon; 3. reply-paid (*telegram*).

cevapsız unanswered; without a reply; ~ **bırakmak** to leave unanswered; to refuse to reply; *fig.* to keep silent.

cevaz [ā] 1. admissibility; lawfulness; 2. permission; ~ **görmek** to be judged as permissible; ~ **vermek** to allow, to permit.

cevelân 1. circulation (*a.* MED); 2. walk, stroll, drive round (*a town, etc.*); ~ **etm.** to circle, to revolve, to rotate, to circulate.

cevher 1. BIOL substance, matter; 2. PHLS essence, substance; 3. nature; 4. talent, ability; 5. precious stone, gem; 6. MIN ore; -**ini tüketmek** to be at one's wits' end.

cevherli 1. gifted, talented; 2. set with jewels.

cevir, -vri maltreatment, cruelty, tormenting.

ceviz 1. BOT walnut; 2. (**ağacı**) walnut-tree; 3. walnut ...; ~ **içi** 1. kernel; 2. shelled walnuts; ~ **kabuğu** walnut shell; ~ **kabuğu doldurmaz** *fig.* ridiculous, very unimportant, insignificant, slight.

cevretmek [x . .] (*b-ne*) to torment, to torture.

cevval, -li [ā] living, alive, lively, brisk, active, quick.

ceylan ZOO gazelle, antelope; ~ **bakışlı** having alluring eyes.

ceza [ā] punishment, penalty; fine; ~ **almak** to be punished; to be fined;

~ **çekmek** to serve a sentence (-*den* for), to complete one's sentence, to serve one's time; ~ **görmek** to be fined; to be punished; ~ **kanunu** criminal code; ~ **sahası** *sports*: penalty area ~ **vermek** 1. to punish; to fine; 2. JUR to pay a fine; ~ **vuruşu** *sports*: penalty kick; ~ **yemek** to be fined; to be punished; -**sını bulmak** to get one's due punishment; -**sını çekmek** 1. to do penance (**for**), to atone (**for**), to be fined for; 2. to serve a sentence.

cezaen [ā] *obs.* as a punishment.

cezaevi, -ni prison.

cezalandırmak [. - . . .] to punish.

cezalanmak [. - . .] to be punished.

Cezayir *pr. n.* 1. Algiers; 2. Algeria; ~ **dayısı** military governor of Algeria; ~ **dayısı** (*or* **kadısı**) **gibi kurulmak** *co.* to strike an attitude.

cezbe (mystical) ecstasy, rapture.

cezbetmek [x . .] 1. to draw, to attract, to draw to one, *fig.* to take hold of; 2. *fig.* to charm, to fascinate, to infatuate; 3. to absorb, to suck up.

cezir, -zri 1. BOT, MATH, GR root; 2. CHEM radical; 3. ebb (tide); ~ **hareketi ebb.**

cezmetmek [x . .] 1. *obs.* to amputate; 2. to decide, to determine, to resolve.

cezp, -bi 1. attraction; 2. charm, grace, allurement; 3. suction.

cezri 1. radical, fundamental, basic(ally); 2. CHEM basic element.

cezve pot (*for making Turkish coffee*).

cezvit *s.* **cizvit.**

chat odası chat room.

cıcık: **cıcığı çıkmış** worn-out, in pieces, old; **cıcığını çıkarmak** to make useless and wear out, to damage by use.

cıgara [x . .] P cigarette; ~ **böreği** *a kind of long, thin pastry*; ~ **içmek** to smoke cigarette; ~ **kâğıdı gibi** filmy, flimsy; ~ **tablası** ashtray.

cılız meager, lean, feeble, weak, thin, undersized, puny, delicate.

cılk 1. rotten (*egg*); 2. purulent, inflamed, festering (*wound*); ~ **çıkmak** 1. to be addled, to be spoiled; 2. *fig.* to turn out to be a washout, to come to naught (*affair*).

cılkava *fur made of pieces from the neck of wolves or foxes.*

cımbız 1. (a pair of) tweezers; 2. nap, pile (*cloth*); 3. *fig.* bitter words.

cırboğa 1. ZOO jerboa; 2. *fig.* meager, weak child.

cırcır annoying chatterbox; babbler; gossip.

cırcırböceği, -ni cricket; cicada.

cırlak 1. creaking, screechy, shrill, squeaking, chirping; **2.** = **cırcırböceği**; **3.** zoo cricket.

cırıt! harsh!, screeching sound.

cırtlak 1. = **cırlak**; **2.** braggart, boaster.

cırtlamak to make a screeching sound.

cıva [x .] mercury, quicksilver; **~ gibi** fig. very restless.

cıvadra [. x .] naut bowsprit.

cıvata [. x .] **1.** bolt, screw; **2.** naut ring bolt; **~ anahtarı** spanner.

cıvık 1. greasy, soft, runny, wet, sticky; **2.** fig. importunate, obtrusive, impertinent.

cıvıklanmak 1. to become wet (or sticky); **2.** to get impudent.

cıvıl cıvıl 1. twittering; **2.** peeping (chick).

cıvıldamak 1. to twitter, to chirp; **2.** to peep.

cıvıltı twittering, chirping sound.

cıvımak 1. to become wet (or sticky); **2.** fig. to become insipid (or tiresome); **3.** sl. to become impertinent (or obtrusive).

cıyak cıyak with a shrill voice (cry).

cıyaklamak to cry with a shrill voice.

cıyırdamak to make a creaking sound when torn (paper, cloth, etc.).

cıyırtı sound as of cloth tearing.

cız 1. baby's language: fire; **2.** sizzling noise; **~ etm.** to make a sizzling noise; to have a pang.

cızbız grilled meat (part. **köfte**).

cızık 1. = **çizgi**; **2.** grieves; **~ ~ bağırmak** to shout with the fear of death (mice).

cızıktırmak F to scribble, to scrawl, to smear.

cızır cızır 1. with a sizzling noise; **2.** with a creaking noise (glass); **3.** with a scratching noise (feather).

cızırdamak 1. to sizzle; **2.** to creak; **3.** to scratch.

cızırtı sizzling (or creaking) noise.

cızlamak 1. = **cızırdamak**; **2.** = **cız etm.**

cibilli [. . -] natural, innate, inborn.

cibilliyet, -ti disposition, nature, temperament, character.

cibilliyetsiz 1. common, unprincipled; **2.** avaricious, stingy, mean, niggardly, ignoble.

cibinlik mosquito-net.

cibre [x .] husks of grapes, residue of fruits after pressing.

cici baby's language: good, pretty, nice; toy, plaything; **~ bey** a proper man; **-m!** my darling!, my sweet!, my dear!; **-m pilicim!** my sweet darling!

cicianne grandma.

cici bici nice, sweet, Am. cute.

cicili bicili gaudy, glaringly ornamented, dressed up glaringly.

cicim light carpet woven on a hand loom.

cicoz sl. **1.** not at hand, not present, nothing left; **2.** away!, gone!, off!.

cicozlamak sl. to beat it, to go away at once.

cidal, -li [ā] **1.** fight, combat, battle; **2.** quarrel, dispute, argument, discussion.

cidar anat, phys wall, inner side, inside.

cidden [x .] **1.** seriously; **2.** really, truly, actually, in fact; **3.** very, exceedingly, extremely, greatly.

ciddi 1. serious, earnest; **2.** true, real, actual; **3.** sincere, upright, trustworthy, reliable; **~ mi söylüyorsun?** are you serious?; **-ye almak** to take s.th. seriously.

ciddileşmek 1. to become serious, to become aggravate; **2.** to become threatening.

ciddilik seriousness.

ciddiyet, -ti seriousness.

cif com abbr. for coast, insurance and freight.

cife [ī] **1.** carrion, carcass; **2.** fig. nauseous, disgusting; nasty.

cigara s. **cıgara**.

ciğer 1. lung(s); **2.** liver; **3.** vitals, essential parts as heart, lungs and liver; **4.** internal parts; **5.** courage; **6.** darling; **7.** = **~ takımı**, **-i beş para etmez** a bad egg. a worthless fellow, despicable; **-i yanmak** (or **sızlamak**) to feel great compassion (-e for); to suffer greatly (-den from); **-im!** my darling!

ciğerci seller of liver and lungs.

ciğerpare [ā] darling.

cihad [ā] holy war.

cihan [ā] world, universe; **~ harbi** world war.

cihangir [. - -] **1.** world conqueror; **2.** ♀ mf.

cihanşümul [ā, ū] worldwide, global, mondial; **~ şöhretli** world-renowned, world-famed, universally known.

cihar [ā] *dice*: four; **-du** four and two; **-üse** four and three; **-üyek** four and one.

cihaz [ā] **1.** = **çeyiz**; **2.** CHEM, PHYS apparatus, equipment; **3.** BIOL organs, system.

cihazlamak [. - . .] to equip, to provide, to supply (*ile* with).

cihazlandırmak [. - . . .] = **cihazlamak**.

cihazlanmak [. - . .] *pass. of* **cihazlamak**.

cihet, **-ti 1.** side, direction. quarter: **2.** aspect, point of view, viewpoint, respect, regard, consideration; **3.** cause, on grounds of, based on: **4.** modality; **... diği cihetle** because, since, in view of, considering.

cila **1.** shellac, lacquer. varnish: polish: **2.** *fig.* whitewash, varnish; ~ **etm.** = **cilalamak**, ~ **sürmek** (or **vurmak**) to polish, to burnish, to varnish, to lacquer.

cilacı varnisher, finisher.

cilalamak to polish, to varnish, to shine, to finish.

cilalı polished, varnished, finished; shining.

cilasız unpolished, unvarnished, unfinished.

cilasun: ~ **gibi** tall and handsome, brave, mighty.

cilbent, **-di 1.** *obs.* large pocket-book, portfolio; **2.** *obs.* set of surgical instruments; **3.** *rare* letter-file; **4.** large folder (*for drawing, etc.*).

cildiye **1.** dermatology; **2.** skin disease.

cildiyeci dermatologist.

cilt, **-di 1.** skin; **2.** binding, cover (*of a book*); **3.** volume, tome; ~ **hastalığı** skin disease.

ciltçi bookbinder.

ciltlemek to bind (*a book*).

ciltevi, **-ni** bindery.

ciltli bound (*book*).

ciltsiz unbound, in paper cover, stitched.

cilve **1.** grace, coquetry, charm; **2.** appearance; manifestation, attestation.

cilvelenmek to coquet, to flirt.

cilveleşmek to flirt with each other; **2.** to tease mutually, to chaff reciprocally.

cilveli graceful; coquettish, flirtatious.

cim *a letter of the old alphabet*; ~ **karnında bir nokta** a matter of no importance.

cima, **-aı** [ā] **1.** sexual intercourse, coitION; **2.** BOT copulation. fecundation; ~ **etm.** to have (sexual) intercourse with.

cimbakuka [. . x .] thin and ugly, puny: gnomish, gnomelike.

cimcime **1.** small and delicious watermelon; **2.** small and sweet.

cimnastik **1.** gymnastics; **2.** practise.

cimnastikhane [. . . - .] **1.** gym(nasium); **2.** gymnastics hall.

cimri niggardly, stingy, mean, miserly, parsimonious.

cimrileşmek to become stingy.

cimrilik stinginess.

cin[1] gin.

cin[2], **-nni** (*wicked*) genie, demon, spirit, evil; ~ **fikirli** clever and crafty; ~ **tutmak** to lose one's mind, to go mad; ~ **yavrusu** mischievous, little child, imp, urchin; **-ler(i) başına çıkmak** (or **toplanmak** or **üşüşmek**) *fig.* to get furious (or violent); **-ler** (or **in cin** or **ecinniler**) top (or **cirit**) **oynuyor** to be completely deserted.

cinaî [. - -] criminal.

cinas [ā] **1.** play on words, pun; **2.** personal remark, suggestiveness; equivocal allusion.

cinaslı [ā] suggestive; personal.

cinayet, **-ti** [ā] crime, murder; ~ **işlemek** to commit murder.

cingil a stalk of a bunch of grapes.

cingöz = **cin fikirli**.

cinli haunted.

cinmısırı, **-nı** popcorn.

cinnet, **-ti** insanity, madness; ~ **getirmek** to lose one's mind, to go mad, to become insane.

cinni = **cin**[2].

cins **1.** BOT, ZOO race, species, genus; **2.** sex; **3.** GR gender; **4.** category, group, kind, type, sort; **5.** thoroughbred, breed (*horse*); first-class; ~ ~ of various kinds, various; ~ **ismi** GR common noun.

cinsel, cinsi **1.** sexual; **2.** generic.

cinsellik sexuality.

cinsiyet, **-ti 1.** sex; **2.** sexuality.

cinslik sex; sexuality.

cinsliksiz asexual.

cip [ī] jeep.

ciranta [. x .] COM endorser, indorser.

cirim, **-rmi 1.** (*inanimate*) body; **2.** size, largeness, extension, expansion, dimension, volume; **kendi cirmi kadar** on his strength of.

cirit, **-di 1.** javelin, dart (*without head*);

2. the game of jereed; **3.** spear, javelin; ~ *atma* javelin-throw(ing); ~ *oynamak* **1.** to organize a jereed game; **2.** *fig.* to move around freely.

ciro [x .] COM endorsement, transfer note; ~ *etm.* to endorse; to transfer.

cisim, -smi 1. body, substance; **2.** material thing, matter, object.

cisimcik 1. corpuscle; **2.** particle, atom.

cisimlenmek to take a material form.

cismani [.--] **1.** corporeal; material; **2.** ECCL worldly; ~ *ceza* corporal punishment; ~ *zarar* JUR (*grievous*) bodily harm.

cismen [x .] bodily, material; in size.

civan [ā] **1.** young, youthful, juvenile; **2.** handsome young man.

civankaşı, -nı *embroidery*: zigzag ornamentation.

civanmert, -di [ā] brave, noble(-minded), generous, knightly.

civanperçemi, -ni [ā] BOT yarrow.

civar [ā] **1.** neighbo(u)rhood, vicinity, surroundings, environs; **2.** neighbo(u)ring; *-ında* **1.** near; **2.** about. approximately.

civciv 1. chick(en); **2.** twitter, chirp.

civcivli 1. hen; **2.** animated, merry, gay, funny; **3.** lively, crowded, busy, intensive.

civelek 1. lively, fresh, playful, vivacious; **2.** HIST young man in the service of the Janissaries; **3.** agricultural labo(u)r, farm hand, day-labo(u)rer.

civeleklik liveliness, vivacity.

cizvit, -ti 1. Jesuit, Jesuitic(al); **2.** *fig.* instigator, agitator, tricky, sly.

cizye HIST poll tax.

coğrafi geographical.

coğrafya [. x .] geography.

coğrafyacı [. x . .] **1.** geographer; **2.** F geography teacher.

cokey [x .] jockey.

cokeylik work of a jockey.

compact disk compact disc, CD.

conta [x .] MEC joint, packing, seal, gasket.

cop, -pu 1. thick stick (*with round head*); **2.** (*rubber*) truncheon, *Am.* club, F billy, nightstick.

coplamak to beat s.o. with a nightstick, to truncheon.

corum shoal, flow together; *balık -u* shoal of fish.

coşku enthusiasm, strong excitement.

coşkulu enthusiastic.

coşkun 1. fiery, lively, ebullient, exuberant, boiling over, enthusiastic; **2.** agitated, animated; **3.** overflowing its banks (*river*); **4.** very vehement, very violent, very strong, very heavy (*wind, rain*).

coşkunluk enthusiasm; overflowing.

coşmak 1. to be(come) fiery (*or* enthusiastic), to boil over; **2.** to turn out to be a strong movement (*sea*); **3.** to overflow its bank, to rise (*river*); **4.** to become violent (*wind*).

coşturmak to inspire, to fill with enthusiasm, to excite, to stimulate, to incite.

cömert, -di 1. liberal, generous, munificent **2.** fruitful.

cömertleşmek to become generous.

cömertlik generosity, munificence.

cönk, -kü 1. ship, vessel; **2.** anthology, collection of poems, collection of various essays.

cudam pitiful simpleton, stupid blunderer, clumsy fool.

cuma Friday.

cumartesi, -ni *or* **-yi** Saturday.

cumba [x .] **1.** bay-window, bay-stor(e)y; **2.** lattice-window.

cumbadak [x . .] **1.** *int.* plop!, splash!; **2.** head over heels; very sudden, abrupt.

cumbalak somersault.

cumbul cumbul 1. gurgling; gargling (*water*); **2.** rumbling, resounding; **3.** too watery, diluted (*food*).

cumbuldamak 1. to make a plopping sound, to make a gurgling sound (*water*); **2.** to rumble, to resound; **3.** to plop, to flop, to thud.

cumburlop! *int.* plop!

cumburtu 1. gurgle, gargle (*water*); **2.** flop, plop, thud.

cumhur [. -] **1.** the mass of the people, the public, populace; **2.** dervish hymn.

cumhurbaşkanı, -nı president of a republic.

cumhuriyet, -ti [. - . .] **1.** republic; **2.** *sl. obs.* a paper bank-note; ♀ *Bayramı* celebration of being a republic (*October 28-30*); ~ *Senatosu* (Turkish) Senate.

cumhuriyetçi [. - . . .] republican.

cumhurluk republic.

cunda [x .] NAUT end of a gaff, peak.

cunta POL junta.

cuntacı POL member of a junta.

cup! plop!, splash!

cuppadak s. **cumbadak.**

cura 1. two *or* three-stringed *bağlama*; **2.** a small, shrill-voiced hawk; **3.** *sl.* the last drag on a cigarette.

curcuna [. x .] **1.** noisy dance in a drunken revel, carousal; **2.** noisy confusion, confused medley; *-ya çevirmek* (*or döndürmek or vermek*) (*bir yeri*) to fill with noise and fuss, to raise an uproar (*in a place*); *-ya kalkmak* **1.** to behave frolicsome; **2.** to start a quarrel.

curnal 1. denunciation; **2.** report of an informer; *~ etm.* (*or vermek*) to denounce, to inform against, to report (*-e* to).

curnalcı denouncer, informer, police--spy.

curnata an onrush of quail.

cuşiş exuberance.

cüce dwarf.

cücelik 1. dwarfish growth; **2.** dwarfishness.

cücük 1. *obs.* sweet, tender, tasty; **2.** heart of an onion; **3.** tuft of beard, imperial.

cücüklenmek to sprout.

cüda [ā] far, distant, remote, separate(d): *~ düşmek* to get separated (*-den* from): to long for.

cühela *pl. of.* **cahil,** ignorant people.

cülus accession (*to the throne*); *~ etm.* to access (*to the throne*).

cümbür cemaat the whole kit and caboodle.

cümbüş 1. (*music, dance*) pleasure, enjoyment, carousal; **2.** kind of mandolin *or* guitar with a metal body; *~ etm.* (*or yapmak*) to carouse, to revel, to enjoy, to divert, to amuse (*with music*).

cümle 1. all (of them), total, whole; **2.** BIOL system; **3.** GR phrase, sentence, clause; **4.** MATH group; **5.** CHEM period-ical system; *~ kapısı* main door; *-miz* all of us, we all; *-si* all of; *bu -den* for example, for instance.

cümlecik GR clause.

cümleten all together.

cümudiye [ū] glacier; iceberg.

cünha [ā] crime, serious offence.

cünun [ū] insanity.

cünüp, -nbü, -mbü canonically unclean (*from sexual act*).

cüppe robe (*with full sleeves and long skirts*); *~ gibi* long and loose (*garment*).

cüret, -ti 1. courage, boldness, daring, daredevilry, audacity; **2.** *contp.* boldness, impudence, insolence; F sauciness; *~ etm.* **1.** to venture. to dare, to take the liberty of doing; **2.** *contp.* to have the impudence.

cüretkâr, cüretli 1. courageous, brave, audacious, daring; **2.** bold, impudent, insolent.

cüretkârlık 1. boldness, bravery; **2.** insolence.

cüretsiz timid.

cüruf [ū] slag, dross, scoria.

cürüm, -rmü crime, felony, offence; *~ işlemek* to commit a crime: *cürmümeşhut halinde* JUR caught in the act, in flagrante delicto; *cürmümeşhut yapmak* to set a trap for, to lay a trap to catch s.o. red-handed.

cüsse 1. body (*build, figure*); **2.** big, strong body.

cüsseli big-bodied; huge.

cüz, -z'ü 1. part, section; **2.** a thirtieth part of the Koran; **3.** (*book*) number, single volume, fascicle (*print work*).

cüzam [ā] MED leprosy.

cüzamlı [ā] MED leprous; leper.

cüzdan [ā] **1.** wallet; **2.** account-book; (*bank*) pass-book; **3.** portfolio.

cüzi 1. very few, very little, trifling; **2.** partial.

Ç

çaba zeal, eagerness, exertion; effort; **~ göstermek** to work hard.

çabalamak 1. to strive, to struggle, to do one's best, to flounder; **2.** to exert o.s., to try, to put forth effort.

çabalanmak to flounder with one's arms and legs.

çabucacık [x . . .], **çabucak** [x . .] quickly, in all haste, immediately, forthwith.

çabuk 1. quick, fast, swift, hasty, agile; **2.** quickly, soon; **~ ~** quickly; **~ olm. 1.** to hurry, to make haste; **2.** to be finished; **~ parlayan ~ söner** pro. what flares up fast dies down fast.

çabuklaşmak to accelerate, to hasten, to speed up.

çabuklaştırılmak to get accelerated, to be speeded up.

çabuklaştırma speeding up.

çabuklaştırmak to speed up, to expedite, to hasten.

çabukluk speed, haste; quickness, fastness, rapidity, promptness.

çaça 1. (balığı) zoo sprat; **2.** old and experienced sailor; **3.** the cha-cha; **4.** sl. madam (brothel-keeper).

çaçaron F talkative, garrulous, chatterbox.

çaçaronluk being a chatterbox.

çadır tent; ~ bezi tent canvas; **~ kurmak** to pitch a tent.

çadırcı tentmaker.

çadırcılık tentmaking.

çadırçiçeği, -ni BOT bindwind.

çadıruşağı, -nı BOT gum ammoniacum.

çağ 1. time, date; **2.** age, period, epoch; **3.** the right time (for s.th.); **~ açmak** to open a period; **~ dışı olm.** to be dropped from the roll of military reserves because of old age.

çağında in the period (of), at the age (of).

çağanak 1. castanet; **2.** small gypsy tambourine.

çağanoz zoo crab; **~ gibi** crooked and humpbacked (man).

Çağatay Jagatai, Chagatai.

Çağatayca the Jagatai language.

çağcıl modern, up-to-date.

çağcılık modernism.

çağcıllaşmak to become modern.

çağcıllaştırmak to modernize.

çağdaş contemporary.

çağdaşlaşmak to become contemporary.

çağdaşlık being contemporary.

çağdışı 1. anachronistic; **2.** not of draft age.

çağıl çağıl with a babbling, murmuring or crashing sound (water).

çağıldamak to babble, to burble, to murmur, to dabble.

çağıltı the babbling sound, the burbling sound, the murmur of running water.

çağırıcı person sent to invite or summon s.o.

çağırış way of calling, inviting or summoning.

çağırma calling, inviting.

çağırmak 1. to call; to invite (-e to); **2.** to shout, to call out, to cry; **3.** MIL to call up; PARL to convoke; to convene; to sing.

çağırtı call, shout.

çağırtkan 1. decoy bird; **2.** decoy whistle.

çağırtmaç town crier.

çağırtmak 1. to have s.o. called; **2.** to have s.o. sing.

çağla green almond eaten in the shell; **~ yeşili** almond green.

çağlamak to burble, to murmur, to rustle, to roar, to splash, to crash (falling water).

çağlar s. **çağlayan.**

çağlayan cascade, small waterfall.

çağlayık bubbling spring; hot spring.

çağmak (sun) to beat down (-e on).

çağrı 1. invitation, summons, citation, convocation, request (to accession); **2.** interjection; **3.** GR vocative; **4.** MIL call.

çağrıcı summoner.

çağrılı invited (person).

çağrılık invitation (card).

çağrılmak to be invited, to be called.

çağrım the reach of a voice.

çağrışım PSYCH association.

çağrışımcılık PSYCH associationism.

çağrışmak 1. to cry out together, to shout together; 2. *rare* to sing in unison; 3. to call (out)to one another.

çakal 1. zoo jackal; 2. *sl.* helpless, weak; 3. *sl.* cunning, crafty, wily; 4. *sl.* shady person, underhanded person.

çakaleriği, *-ni* BOT sloe, wild plum; unripe plum.

çakaloz HIST a swivel gun.

çakar dragnet for catching mackerel; ~ almaz 1. lighter; 2. *sl.* pistol that won't fire; 3. useless, good for nothing.

çakı pocketknife; ~ gibi lively, active, alert, quick by the hands.

çakıl 1. pebble; 2. gravel, grit; ~ döşemek 1. to pave with pebbles; 2. to gravel; ~ taşı rounded pebble.

çakıldak 1. mill clapper; 2. rattle; 3. chatterbox, babbler; 4. ball of dried dung hanging on an animal's tail.

çakıldamak to rattle, to rustle, to clatter.

çakıldatmak to rattle, to shake s.th. noisily.

çakılı fixed, nailed (-*e* to).

çakıllı pebbly.

çakıllık 1. place paved with pebbles; 2. gravel pit.

çakılmak 1. to be driven into place (*nail, peg*); 2. to be pegged down, to be nailed down.

çakıltı rattle, rustle, clatter.

çakım, çakın 1. lightning; 2. spark.

çakır[1] 1. grayish blue, bluish; 2. = çakırdoğan.

çakır[2] *obs.* wine.

çakır[3]: ~ çukur 1. uneven, rough, bumpy; *fig.* stumbling; 2. rattling noise.

çakırdiken BOT burdock, burr.

çakırdoğan zoo goshawk.

çakırkanat zoo teal.

çakırkeyf F half-tipsy, slightly-tipsy, mellow, *Am.* happy.

çakırpençe 1. having a hawk-like grip; 2. greedy, avaricious, stingy, mean.

çakışmak 1. *rare* to fit into one another; 2. to beat (*or* strike) one after (*or* upon) another; 3. to compete in impromptu verse; 4. MATH to be congruent.

çakıştırmak 1. *caus. of* çakışmak; 2. to drink, to carouse, to tipple.

çakma 1. *vn. of* çakmak; 2. nailed on; 3. embossed; 4. mo(u)ld for embossing.

çakmak[1] 1. flash of fire; 2. steel for striking on a flint; 3. (cigarette, pocket) lighter.

çakmak[2] 1. to drive in s.th. with blows; 2. to nail on; 3. to bind, to tie up; 4. *sl.* to palm off s.th. on s.o.; 5. *sl.* to strike, to hit; 6. *sl.* to cotton on, to get the notion (*or* idea), to perceive, to grasp; 7. *sl.* to know (-*den* about); 8. to flash (up) (*lightning*); 9. *sl.* to drink, to booze; 10. *sl.* to fail (*an examination, a subject*). to be 'plowed' (*in an examination*), *Am.* to flunk; 11. to snap (at) all of a sudden; 12. to fire (off), to discharge.

çakmakçı repairer *or* maker of lighters.

çakmaklı flintlock gun.

çakmaklık lighter (*fluid*).

çakmaktaşı 1. GEOL flint; 2. artificial flint.

çakşır 1. (*long, wide*) trousers (*with light leather boots at the ankles*); 2. shank feather.

çakşırlı with feathered shanks (*pigeon*).

çaktırılmak to be nailed down.

çaktırmak to have (a nail) hammered down.

çalak swift, nimble.

çalakalem: ~ yazmak to write in haste *or* without deliberation, to scribble down.

çalakaşık: ~ yemek F to tuck in.

çalakürek: ~ çekmek to row with all one's might.

Çalap, *-bı* God.

çalapaça dragging s.o. along by force.

çalar 1. alarm, striking mechanism (*of a clock*); 2. equipped with an alarm mechanism (*clock*); ~ saat 1. alarm clock; 2. repeater; 3. musical clock.

çalçene chatterbox, babbler, gossip.

çaldırmak 1. *caus. of* çalmak; 2. to lose by theft.

çalgı 1. music; 2. musical instrument; 3. orchestra, band; ~ çağanak with music and noise; ~ çaldırmak to have s.o. *or* a band play musical instrument(s); ~ çalmak 1. to play a musical instrument; 2. to play music.

çalgıcı 1. musician, instrumentalist; 2. producer *or* seller of musical instruments.

çalgıcılık being a professional musician.

çalgıcıotu, *-nu* BOT hedge mustard.

çalgıç plectrum.

çalgılı offering entertainment (*restaurant, etc.*), with music.

çalı 1. bush, shrub; **2.** underwood, scrub, *Am.* brush; thicket; ~ **çırpı** brushwood; sticks and twigs.

çalıfasulyesi, -ni climbing kidney-beans.

çalık 1. oblique, crooked; **2.** cut slanting (*cloth*); **3.** restive (*animal*); **4.** faded (*cloth, etc.*); **5.** whose name is struck off the roll; **6.** pock-marked; **7.** pock-mark; **8.** mange; **9.** deranged in the mind.

çalıkkavak BOT a kind of poplar whose branches are used in wickerwork.

çalıkuşu, -nu 1. ZOO goldcrest kinglet; **2.** ZOO wren; **3.** *fig.* inconstant, fickle, unstable; **4.** *fig.* lively.

çalılık thicket; brushwood.

çalım 1. *obs.* blow, stroke; **2.** edge (*sabre*); **3.** swagger, boasting, big talk; **4.** *soccer:* adroit movements; ~ **etm.** (*or* **satmak**) to behave arrogantly, to boast; **-ına getirmek** *fig.* to find a favo(u)rable time *or* position to achieve *or* obtain.

çalımlamak *soccer:* adroitly to keep the ball from.

çalımlanmak 1. *to* swagger; **2.** *soccer:* to be kept away from the ball.

çalımlı 1. pompous; **2.** NAUT narrow-built and with a high bow.

çalınmak *pass. of* **çalmak.**

çalıntı 1. stolen goods; **2.** plagiarized matter, plagiarism.

çalışkan industrious, hard-working, diligent, studious.

çalışkanlık diligence.

çalışma work; study; ♀ **Bakanlığı** Ministry of Labo(u)r; ~ **müsaadesi** working permit.

çalışmak 1. to try, to strive; **2.** to be in the employ of, to work for; **3.** to be in activity; to run (*machine*); **4.** to exert o.s.; **5.** to study; **çalışıp çabalamak** to do one's best, to try hard.

çalıştırıcı trainer, coach.

çalıştırılmak to get run.

çalıştırmak 1. to operate, to use; **2.** to make run, to make work; **3.** to employ; **4.** to tutor; **5.** *sl.* to make fun of; **6.** *sl.* to shell out (*money*).

çalkagı cotton gin.

çalka(la)mak 1. to rinse, to wash off (*or* up *or* out); **2.** to shake, to jog; **3.** to stir up; **4.** to beat, to whip (*egg*);

5. to churn (*milk*); **6.** to disturb and addle (*an egg of a brooding hen*); **7.** to winnow (*corn, grain*); **süt, çocuğu çalka(la)dı** milk turned the baby's stomach.

çalka(la)nmak 1. *pass. of* **çalka(la)mak;** **2.** to be shaken; **3.** to be rough (*sea*); **4.** to be talked about everywhere; **5.** to be tossed around; **6.** to shake o.s.

çalkantı 1. violent shock; **2.** remaining chaff; **3.** MED diarrh(o)ea, vomiting; **4.** strong internal excitement; **5.** wave (*sea*); **6.** beaten eggs.

çalkar 1. *obs.* anything that upsets the stomach; **2.** cotton gin; **3.** MED laxative, purgative.

çalma 1. *vn. of* **çalmak;** **2.** stolen; **3.** beaten up, shaken; **4.** a turban; **5.** chiseled (*metal object*).

çalmak, (-ar) 1. to hit, to strike, to knock on, to give a blow to **2.** to add, to mix in; **3.** to make (*yoghurt*); **4.** to spread (*butter, honey, etc.*); **5.** to steal, to take away (*-den* from); **6.** to spoil, to taint; **7.** to play (*a musical instrument*); **8.** to chase, to engrave (*a design on a metal*); **9.** to cut on the bias; **10.** to sweep hard; **11.** to taste of, to have a flavo(u)r of, to tend to resemble; **12.** to ring, to toll, to strike, to put in action (*clock, bell*); **13.** to strike (*the hour*); **14.** to knock (*at the door*); **bunu al da başına çal!** *iro.* may it do you no good!; **çalmadan oynamak 1.** to be very lively and happy; **2.** to be always ready (*to do s.th.*), to be officious; **çalıp çırpmak** to steal whatever is in sight.

çalpara 1. castanet; **2.** ZOO lady crab; **3.** MEC guide-box.

çalyaka seizing by the collar; ~ **etm.** to collar s.o.

çam 1. BOT pine; fir; **2.** *any of several types of tall tree with thin sharp leaves that do not drop off in winter, found esp. in colder parts of the world*; ~ **devirmek** F to blunder, to drop a brick, to put one's foot in it; ~ **yarması gibi** enormous, giant (*person*).

çamaşır 1. linen, underwear, underclothing; **2.** laundry; **3.** washing; ~ **değiş(tir)mek** to change one's underwear; ~ **dolabı** dresser; ~ **ipeği** silk embroidery thread; ~ **ipi** clothesline; ~ **makinesi** washing machine; ~ **yıkamak** to wash clothes, to do the laundry.

çamaşırcı washerwoman; laundry-man; laundress.

çamaşrevi, -ni, çamaşırhane [. - - -.] laundry room, washhouse.

çamaşırlık 1. = *çamaşrevi*; **2.** suitable material for underwear manufacturing.

çamça roach (*small fresh-water fish*).

çamçak wooden dipper.

çamfıstığı, -nı pine nut, pine kernel.

çamlık pine grove.

çamsakızı, -nı 1. pine resin; **2.** *fig.* (*a ~ gibi*) importunate, obtrusive, troublesome, bothersome, annoying (*person*); ~ *çoban armağanı* small present.

çamuka [. x .] kind of sardine, sand smelt.

çamur 1. mud, mire; **2.** argillaceous earth; **3.** dirt, filth; **4.** mortar, plaster; **5.** mixture of clay; **6.** *sl.* brazen, impertinent, obtrusive; ~ *atmak* **1.** to sling mud (*-e* at); **2.** *fig.* to calumniate, to defame; *a.* JUR to slander; ~ *etm.* to dirty; *fig.* to soil; ~ *olm.* to get muddy; *-a bulaşmak* F to be down on one's luck; *-a yatmak sl.* **1.** to default on a debt; **2.** not to keep a promise.

çamurcuk a small carp.

çamurcun ZOO teal.

çamurlamak 1. to smear with mud; **2.** *fig.* to defame, to calumniate.

çamurlanmak to get muddy.

çamurlaşmak 1. to turn into mud; **2.** to become aggressive, to begin to pick a quarrel.

çamurlatmak to have s.th. plastered with mud.

çamurlu 1. muddy, miry; **2.** dirty; ~ *yer* marsh, slough.

çamurluk 1. mudguard, *Am.* fender; **2.** running-board, foot-board; **3.** trough; **4.** muddy place; **5.** gaiter, legging; **6.** waterproof boots; **7.** footscraper; **8.** metal fittings.

çan bell, church bell; ~ *çalmak* **1.** to ring a bell; **2.** *fig.* to trumpet, to noise abroad; **3.** to ring; ~ *kulesi* belfry, bell tower; *-ına ot tıkamak fig.* to put a spoke in one's wheel.

çanak 1. earthenware pot; **2.** BOT calyx; ~ *ağızlı* **1.** having a large mouth; **2.** *fig.* blabbermouth; ~ *anten* satellite dish; ~ *çömlek* earthenware pots; ~ *tutmak* to ask for (*trouble*); ~ *yalamak* to flat-

ter; ~ *yalayıcı* parasite, sponger; toady, sycophant.

çanakçı potter; seller of pottery.

çanakçılık making or selling earthenware.

Çanakkale Boğazı *pr. n.* the Dardanelles, the Hellespont.

çanaklık 1. depository; **2.** NAUT masthead.

çanaksı BIOL calyciform.

çanakyaprağı, -nı sepal.

çancı 1. maker or seller of bells; **2.** bell ringer.

çançan F loud and stupid idle talk, twaddle.

çançiçeği, -ni BOT bellflower.

çangal branch, limb.

çangallı having branches.

çangıl çungul with a clattering and crashing sound.

çangırdamak to clang, to clatter, to jangle.

çangırtı clattering (or crashing) sound.

çanıltı the clanging of a bell.

çanta [x .] **1.** bag; **2.** handbag; **3.** briefcase; **4.** purse; **5.** knapsack; **6.** suitcase; *-da keklik fig.* in hand, in the bag; already gained.

çap, -pı 1. MATH diameter; **2.** *a.* MIL caliber, bore; **3.** size, largeness, scale, extent, volume; **4.** quality, worth; **5.** plan showing the size and boundaries of a plot; *-tan düşmek* to go downhill, to decline, to be undersized.

çapa [x .] **1.** hoe, mattock; **2.** NAUT anchor; **3.** bilge plank.

çapacı 1. hoer; **2.** maker or seller of hoes.

çapaçul F disorderly, slovenly, untidy.

çapaçulluk untidiness.

çapak 1. dried rheum round the eye, crust; **2.** wire edge, burr; fin, beard (*of a casting*).

çapaklanmak to become gummy (*eye*).

çapaklı 1. crusty, having dried rheum round the eye; **2.** with fins or burrs (*from casting*); **3.** *print.* having a flaw in the casting (*letter*).

çapalamak to hoe up.

çapanoğlu, -nu unpleasant or difficult situation that might appear, a hidden difficulty.

çapar 1. a kind of boat used in the Black Sea; **2.** spotted, mottled; **3.** albino; **4.** HIST mounted courier.

çaparı trawl, trotline.

çaparız F **1.** obstacle; **2.** inverted, reversed, upside down, untoward, adverse, inconvenient; **3.** NAUT being athwarthawse.

çapçak 1. wooden bowl; **2.** open barrel.

çapkın 1. *obs.* swift (*horse*); **2.** *obs.* vagabond, vagrant, tramp; **3.** womanizer, philanderer, casanova; **4.** young scamp (*or* rascal); **5.** sensual, greedy, covetous (*look*).

çapkınlaşmak to turn into a skirt-chaser.

çapkınlık profligacy; debauchery.

çapla cold chisel.

çaplamak to gauge, to measure the diameter of, to calibrate.

çaplı 1. having a diameter (of); calibered; **2.** large sized, of large caliber; **3.** F husky, strapping.

çapmak 1. to run, to trot, to gallop; **2.** to ride (*horse*) fast; **3.** to raid, to pillage.

çaprak saddle-cloth.

çapraşık 1. complicated, tangled, intricate; **2.** crosswise.

çapraşıklaşmak to get confused and chaotic.

çapraşıklık confusion, chaos.

çapraşmak 1. to get complicated; **2.** to cross each other.

çapraz 1. crossing, transverse, crosswise; **2.** diagonal; **3.** saw set, saw file; **4.** *tailoring*; double-breasted; **5.** *wrestling*: a clinch; ~ **kelime bulmacası** crossword puzzle.

çaprazlama 1. diagonally; **2.** chiasmus.

çaprazlamak to cross obliquely, to put crosswise (-*e* to).

çaprazlaşmak to become confused and involved.

çaprazlık being in crosswise arrangement.

çaprazölçer set gauge (*for saw teeth*).

çapul raid, sack, loot, pillage; booty, spoil.

çapulcu looter, marauder, pillager.

çaput, -tu P **1.** rag; **2.** coarse cloth.

çar czar, tsar.

çarçabuk [x . .] as quick as lightning, with lightning speed, very quickly.

çarçur dissipation, waste, squandering; ~ **etm.** to throw out of the window (*money*), to squander; ~ **olm.** to be squandered.

çardak arbo(u)r, hut, pergola.

çare [ā] means, way; solution; remedy, medicament, cure; help; ~ **aramak** to look for a remedy; **-sine bakmak** to settle, to see (to); **bundan başka çare yok** there is no other way out, this is the only thing to do.

çaresiz [ā] **1.** helpless, poor; **2.** unalterable, irrevocable, imperious, commanding; **3.** willy-nilly.

çaresizlik helplessness, lack of means; poverty.

çareviç [x . .] czarevitch, tsarevitch.

çarık 1. rural footwear, rawhide sandal; **2.** brake-shoe, brake-block; **3.** *sl.* wallet; ~ **çürük** s. **çürük** ~.

çarıklı 1. wearing rawhide sandals; **2.** *fig.* rural, rustic; ~ **diplomat** (*or* **erkânıharp**) a sly rustic, a wily rustic.

çariçe czarina, tsarina.

çark, -kı 1. wheel (*of a machine*); **2.** wheelwork, gear(ing); **3.** disk, plate; **4.** MIL wheel, pivoting maneuver; **5.** fate, destiny; **6.** firmament; **7.** NAUT paddle wheel; **8.** fly-wheel; ~ **etm. 1.** MIL to turn; **2.** to change one's resoluteness (*a. fig.*); **-a vermek** (*or* **çektirmek**) to put (*a blade*) to the grindstone; **-ı bozulmak** *fig.* to have one's affairs upset, to meet misfortune; **-ına etm.** (*or* **okumak**) F to bungle; to ruin one.

çarkçı 1. machinist, engine operator; **2.** knife-grinder; **3.** NAUT engineer, mechanic.

çarkçılık 1. NAUT occupation of an engineer; **2.** knife-grinding.

çarkıfelek 1. sky, heaven; **2.** moonlight; **3.** destiny, fate; **4.** pinwheel; **5.** BOT passion flower.

çarlık czardom, tsardom.

çarliston charleston (*dance*).

çarmıh, çarmık cross (*for crucifying*); **çarmıha germek** to crucify.

çarmık NAUT shrouds.

çarnanar [- - -] willy-nilly.

çarpan MATH multiplier.

çarpanbalığı, -nı ZOO greater weever.

çarpı 1. whitewash; **2.** MATH ... times, multiplied by.

çarpık oblique, crooked, distorted, bent; slanting; ~ **bacaklı** bow-legged; ~ **çurpuk** crooked and oblique; deformed.

çarpılan MATH multiplicand.

çarpılma 1. being hit, collision; **2.** becoming crooked.

çarpılmak 1. *pass. of* **çarpmak**; **2.** to

take s.th. ill (*or* amiss), to take offence at, to resent; **cezaya ~** to be punished.

çarpım MATH product; **~ tablosu** multiplication table.

çarpınma 1. convulsion, spasm; **2.** a struggle to find a way to get s.th. done.

çarpınmak 1. *fig.* to struggle, to try every possible means; to exert o.s.; **2.** to move agitatedly.

çarpıntı 1. violent beating (*or* palpitation) of the heart; **2.** strong excitement.

çarpışık 1. collided; **2.** irregular.

çarpışma 1. fight, combat, battle; **2.** collision, clash.

çarpışmak 1. to collide, to strike one another; **2.** to fight; **3.** to be in conflict.

çarpıtmak to distort (*a face*), to wrench.

çarpma 1. impact, shock (*a.* MIL); **2.** stroke, blow; **3.** MATH multiplication; **4.** embossed; **5.** s.th. produced by beating; **6.** stolen.

çarpmak, (-ar) 1. to strike, to knock against; **2.** to throw (at); **3.** to strike, to smite, to paralyze, to distort (*evil spirit*); **4.** *sl.* to steal cleverly; **5.** MATH to multiply; **6.** to affect violently (*sun, disease*); **7.** to go one's head (*wine*); **8.** to beat, to palpitate (*heart*); **9.** to slam (*a door*); **10.** to collide with.

çarptırmak 1. to make (*two things*) collide; **2.** to have one's pocket picked.

çarşaf 1. sheet of a bed; **2.** veiled dress (*formerly worn by Turkish women in public*); **~ gibi** as calm as a millpond, calm (*sea*); **~ kadar** very large (*said for s.th. supposed to be small*).

çarşaflamak to fasten a sheet.

çarşaflanmak to have a cover fastened on it.

çarşaflı wearing a veiled dress.

çarşamba Wednesday; **~ karısı** hag, hell-cat; **~ pazarı gibi** a place in disorder and confusion.

çarşı shopping district, permanent market, bazaar, street with shops; **~ pazar dolaşmak** to go on a shopping expedition; **-ya çıkarmak** to (put on the) market; **-ya gitmek** to go shopping.

çarşılı tradesman.

çaşıt spy.

çaşıtlamak to spy.

çat, -tı *int.* crash!, bang!; **~ kapı** unexpectedly there was a knock at the

door; **~ orda ~ burda, ~ kapı arkasında** now here now there (*said for s.o. or s.th. always in a different place*); **~ pat 1.** abrupt, disjointed; **2.** very little; now and then, rarely.

çatadak [x . .] with a sudden cracking noise.

çatak 1. valley; **2.** *fig.* complicated, intricate; **3.** twins, double (*fruits*); **4.** nagging, quarrelsome.

çatal 1. forked, bifurcated; **2.** fork; **3.** bifurcation; **4.** *fig.* dilemma; **5.** horns, antlers (*deer*); **6.** difficult, hard, complicated, intricate; **7.** having a double meaning (*word*); **~ görmek 1.** to squint; **2.** *fig.* to make a mistake; **~ tırnaklı** cloven hoofed.

çatalağız, -ğzı delta (*river*).

çatallanmak to bifurcate, to fork.

çatallaşmak 1. *rare* = **çatallanmak; 2.** to get complicated; **3.** to become cracked (*voice*).

çatallı 1. forked, bifurcated; **2.** badly arranged, difficult to survey, complicated; **3.** GR disjunctive; **4.** cracked (*voice*).

çatana [. x .] NAUT small steam boat.

çatapat, -tı small toy explosive that goes off when stepped on.

çatı 1. roof; **2.** framework of a roof; **3.** attic; **4.** ANAT pubis; **5.** GR voice; **~ katı** (*or arası* **or altı**) attic, penthouse.

çatık 1. frowning, sulky, stern (*face*); **2.** stacked (*rifles*); **~ kaşlı** beetle--browed, frowning.

çatır çatır 1. with a cracking (*or* crashing) noise; with a crackling and snapping noise (*fire*); with a creaking (*or* popping) noise (*wood, bones*); **2.** by force; like it or not; **3.** fluently, easily.

çatırdamak 1. to crackle, to snap; to creak, to pop; **2.** to chatter (*teeth*).

çatırtı crackle, snap; clattering, chattering.

çatışık contradictory, clashing.

çatışma 1. MIL skirmish; **2.** dispute; argument; **3.** PSYCH state of conflict.

çatışmak 1. to clash, to collide (*ile* with); **2.** to contradict, to clash, to be in conflict (*ideas*); **3.** to have a quarrel; **4.** (*dogs, camels*) to mate; **5.** to coincide (*ile* with) (*time*).

çatkı 1. stack of rifles; **2.** cloth headband; **3.** frame, skeleton; **4.** basting.

çatkın 1. = **çatık; 2.** favo(u)rite, protégé.

çatlak 1. split, slit, fissured; **2.** crack,

fissure, crevice; **3.** chapped (*hand*); **4.** cracked (*voice*); **5.** *fig.* cracked, not all there; **6.** *fig.* mad, crazy.

çatlaklık 1. crack; **2.** *fig.* craziness.

çatlamak 1. to crack, to split; **2.** to chap (*hand*); **3.** to burst with impatience; **4.** to die from overeating (*or* exhaustion).

çatlatmak 1. to split, to crack; **2.** F to drive crazy.

çatma 1. *vn. of* **çatmak**; **2.** framework of a building; **3.** JUR picking a quarrel.

çatmak, (-ar) 1. to stack (*arms*); **2.** to fit together; **3.** to baste (*or* tack) together; **4.** to tie; **5.** to load (*on an animal*); **6.** to inveigh (-*e* against), to lash out (-*e* against, at); **7.** to collide (-*e* with), to knock (-*e* against), to bump up (-*e* against); **8.** to meet (**with** *trouble*), to come up (**against** *a difficulty*); **9.** to win favo(u)r of s.o.

çatra patra [x . x .] incorrectly and brokenly (*speaking a language*).

çavdar BOT rye; ~ **ekmeği** rye-bread.

çavdarmahmuzu, -nu BOT rye ergot.

çavlan waterfall.

çavlı young untrained hawk.

çavuş 1. MIL sergeant; **2.** guard; **3.** herald, messenger.

çavuşkuşu, -nu ZOO hoopoe.

çavuşüzümü, -nü BOT sweet-water.

çay¹ 1. tea; **2.** tea plant; **3.** tea party, reception; ~ **demlemek** to steep (*tea*).

çay² 1. brook, rivulet, creek, stream; -*ı* **görmeden paçaları sıvamak** to count one's chickens before they are hatched.

çaycı 1. seller of tea; tea merchant; **2.** keeper of a teahouse; **3.** drinker of tea.

çaydanlık teapot, teakettle.

çayevi, -ni teahouse.

çayhane [. . -] teahouse.

çayır 1. meadow; pasture; **2.** pasture grass; green (*or* fresh) fodder; -*a* **çıkarmak** to pasture, to graze.

çayırkuşu, -nu ZOO skylark.

çayırlanmak to graze, to pasture.

çayırlık meadowland, pasture.

çayırotu, -nu BOT **1.** grass; fodder; **2.** timothy grass.

çaylak 1. ZOO kite; **2.** *fig.* green, tiro, fledgling.

çeç, -çi heap of winnowed grain.

çeçe ZOO tsetse fly.

çedik morocco slipper; ~ **pabuç** lady's house slippers.

çehre 1. face, countenance; **2.** aspect, appearance; **3.** sour face; ~ **asmak** (*or* **etm.** *or* **çatmak**) to pull a long face; ~ **zügürdü** ugly-faced.

çek, -ki cheque, *Am.* check; ~ **defteri** chequebook; ~ **yazmak** to make out a cheque.

Çek, -ki Czech.

Çekçe Czech.

çekçek small four-wheeled handcart.

çekecek shoehorn.

çekek NAUT slip.

çekememezlik envy, jealousy.

çeki a weight of 250 kilos; ~ **taşı** a stone weight of 230 kilos; ~ **taşı gibi** ponderous; -*ye* **gelmez 1.** it is too heavy; it is unbearable; **2.** it is disorderly, it is untidy.

çekici *fig.* attractive, charming.

çekicilik *fig.* attractiveness, charm.

çekiç, -ci 1. hammer; **2.** ANAT malleus; ~ **atma** throwing the hammer.

çekiçhane [ā] steamhammer shop of a factory.

çekiçkemiği, -ni ANAT hammer, malleus.

çekiçlemek to hammer.

çekidüzen tidiness, orderliness; ~ **vermek** to tidy up, to put in order.

çekik 1. slanting (*eyes*); **2.** drawn out; **3.** drawn in; ~ **gözlü** slit-eyed.

çekiliş drawing (*in a lottery*).

çekilmek 1. *pass. of* **çekmek**; **2.** to withdraw, to draw back, to recede; **3.** to retreat; **4.** to resign; **5.** (*oyundan*) to give up; **6.** to flex (*muscle*); **çekil oradan!** F clear out of there!

çekilmez unbearable, intolerable, unendurable.

çekim 1. PHYS attraction; **2.** GR inflection, declination, conjugation; **3.** *cinema*: shot, take; **4.** *sl.* sniff (*of snuff*); ~ **eki** GR termination.

çekimlemek 1. GR to inflect, to decline, to conjugate; **2.** PHYS to attract.

çekimli 1. attractive, graceful; **2.** GR inflectional.

çekimser 1. abstaining; **2.** uncommitted.

çekimserlik abstention.

çekince 1. drawback; **2.** risk.

çekingen timid, shy, hesitant, bashful.

çekingenlik timidity, shyness.

çekinik BIOL recessive.

çekinmek 1. to beware (-*den* of), to refrain (-*den* from), to recoil (-*den* from), to hesitate to do, to be timid;

2. to put on (*eye make-up*).

çekinti hesitation.

çekirdek 1. pip, seed, stone (*of a fruit*); **2.** nucleus; **3.** nuclear; **4.** kernel (*a. fig.*); ~ *kahve* coffee beans; *-ten yetişme* trained from the cradle.

çekirdeklenmek to from seeds, to seed.

çekirdeksel PHYS nuclear.

çekirdeksiz seedless.

çekirge 1. ZOO grasshopper, locust; **2.** cricket.

çekişme argument, quarrel.

çekişmek 1. to argue, to quarrel, to dispute; **2.** to pull in opposite directions; **3.** to draw mutually (*knife*); **4.** to try hard (*as a group*); *çekişe çekişe pazarlık etm.* to haggle.

çekişmeli 1. contentious; **2.** hard, difficult.

çekiştirmek 1. *caus. of çekişmek*; **2.** to back bite, to run down.

çekme 1. *vn. of çekmek*; **2.** drawer, tilt; **3.** overalls; **4.** shapely, well-shaped; **5.** plucked (*instrument*); **6.** stunted (*tree*); **7.** chinning-up (*an exercise*); ~ *demir* rolled iron; ~ *halatı* tow rope; ~ *taşıtı* recovery vehicle.

çekmece 1. drawer; tilt; **2.** coffer.

çekmek, (-er) 1. to pull; **2.** to draw, to haul, to drag, to tug; **3.** to hoist (*flag*); **4.** to pull on (*boots, trousers*); **5.** to drive, to move (*car*); **6.** NAUT to tow; **7.** to draw (*knife, gun*); **8.** to extract, to pull out (*tooth*); **9.** to draw (*magnet*); **10.** to attract, to charm, to fascinate; **11.** to absorb; **12.** to bear, to suspend (*weight, load*); **13.** to bear, to pay for, to stand (*expense*); **14.** to bear, to endure, to put up with, to go through, to suffer, to undergo (*experience, sorrow, pain*); **15.** to breathe in; to suck in; to sniff; **16.** to withdraw, to draw out (*money*); **17.** to withdraw, to draw back (*troops*); **18.** to suck up, to pump out (*liquid*); **19.** to distill; **20.** to draw (*chimney*); **21.** to draw (*line*); **22.** to extend, to lengthen; **23.** to build (*fence, wall*); to stretch out, to hang (*curtain*); **24.** to lay (*cable*); **25.** to stretch (*wire, rope*); **26.** to weigh; **27.** to draw (*lots*); **28.** to copy; **29.** to prepare, to draw up (*protest, policy*); **30.** to send (*telegram*); **31.** to photograph, to take (*photograph*); **32.** to grind (*coffee*); **33.** (*b-ne*) to resemble *s.o.*, to take after *s.o.*; **34.** to shrink (*cloth*); **35.** to

paint, to give (*a coat of paint*); **36.** GR to conjugate (*verb*); **37.** *sl.* to drink, to wet one's whistle; **38.** to give (*a banquet*); *çek* (*or çek arabanı*)! *sl.* clear out!, beat it!, hop it!; *çekip çekiştirmek* to backbite, to run down; *çekip çevirmek* to manage; *çekip çıkarmak* to pull (*or* pluck) out; *çekip gitmek* to go away; *çekip uzatma* prolixity.

çekmekat, -tı penthouse.

Çekoslovak, -kı *pr. n.* Czechoslovakian.

Çekoslovakya *pr. n.* Czechoslovakia.

çekül plumb line.

çelebi 1. educated, well-bred; **2.** gentleman; **3.** *obs.* prince; **4.** *title given to men of certain religious orders.*

çelenç *sports*: challenge.

çelenk, -gi wreath; garland; ~ *koymak* to lay a wreath.

çelik[1] steel; ~ *gibi* as tough as a leather.

çelik[2] **1.** short piece of tapered wood; **2.** cat (*in tipcat*); **3.** cutting; **4.** NAUT marlinespike; carling.

çelikçomak tipcat.

çelikhane [ā] steel works, steel foundry.

çelikleşmek 1. to become steel; **2.** to become as tough as a leather.

çelim stature, form, shape.

çelimsiz puny, misshapen, scraggy, frail.

çelişik contradictory.

çelişki contradiction.

çelişmek (*bşle*) to be in contradiction with *s.th.*

çelme 1. *vn. of çelmek*; **2.** tripping; ~ *atmak* (*or takmak*) to trip up.

çelmek 1. to cut on the bias; **2.** to divert, to change another's course; **3.** to wipe out, to negate, to void; **4.** (*aklını or zihnini*) to pervert, to dissuade, to talk *s.o.* into doing *s.th.*, to seduce; **5.** to be in contradiction (*with*).

çelmelemek (*b-ni*) to trip *s.o.* with one's foot.

çeltik rice in the husk.

çember 1. MATH circle; **2.** hoop; rim; **3.** child's hoop; barrel hoop; **4.** strap; **5.** hoop-shaped; **6.** *basketball*: basket, hoop; **7.** MIL encirclement; ~ *çevirmek* to trundle (*or* roll) a hoop; ~ *içine almak* MIL to encircle; ~ *sakal* round trimmed beard.

çemberlemek 1. to hoop, to strap; **2.**

MIL to encircle, to surround.

çemberli strapped; hooped.

çemen BOT cumin.

çemre(le)mek 1. to tuck up (one's garments, sleeves, etc.); **2.** to squeeze the end of s.th. together.

çemrenmek to roll up one's sleeves (a. fig.).

çene 1. chin; **2.** jaw; **3.** jaw bone; **4.** fig. garrulity, talkativeness; **~ çalmak** to chat, to natter, to chatter; **~ kavafı** talkative; **~ sakızı** fig. a saying that is always in one's mouth; **~ yarışı** talkfest; **-n pırtı!** shut up!; **-si atmak** to drop one's jaw in dying, to die; **-si düşük** chatter-box, garrulous, chatty; **-ye kuvvet** by dint of talking.

çenebaz talkative, garrulous.

çenebazlık talkativeness.

çenek 1. BOT, ZOO valve; **2.** ANAT mandible.

çeneli fig. talkative, chatty.

çengel hook; **~ takmak** to get one's claws (-e into), to be a nuisance (-e to).

çengellemek to hook.

çengellenmek 1. pass. of **çengellemek**; **2.** to be hung on a hook.

çengelli hooked.

çengelliiğne safety pin.

çengelsakızı, -nı chewing gum (made from the juice of cardoon).

çengi dancing girl.

çenk, -gi primitive harp.

çentik 1. notch; nick; **2.** notched; nicked; **3.** incisure.

çentiklemek to notch; to nick.

çentikli notched; nicked.

çentmek 1. to notch; to nick; **2.** to chop up (onions).

çepçevre [x . .], **çepeçevre** [. x . .] all around.

çepel 1. muddy, dirty, foul; **2.** gloomy, dull, disagreeable; **3.** rubbish.

çeper 1. bamboo fence; **2.** immoral; **3.** BIOL membrane.

çepiç year-old goat.

çepken s. **cepken**.

çerçeve 1. frame; **2.** sash, window frame; **3.** rim (of glasses); **4.** shaft (of a loom); **5.** parallel bars; **6.** fig. framework.

çerçeveci picture-framer.

çerçevelemek to frame, to put in a frame.

çerçi sundries pedlar.

çerçöp 1. twigs; **2.** sweepings, rubbish;

3. odds and ends.

çerden çöpten flimsy, jerry-built.

çerez 1. tidbits, nuts, snack; **2.** appetizers, hors d'oeuvres.

çerezci seller of appetizers (or tidbits).

çerezlenmek 1. to eat appetizers; **2.** fig. to take advantage of opportunities.

çerge makeshift (or gypsy's) tent.

çeri obs. troops, army.

çeribaşı obs. **1.** gypsy chief; **2.** commander of troops.

Çerkez pr. n. Circassian; **~ tavuğu** chicken with walnut.

çerviş 1. inferior cooking fat; **2.** the juicy part of a cooked dish.

çeşit, -di 1. kind, sort, variety (a. BIOL); **2.** assortment; **3.** COM sample; **~ ~** assorted; **~ düzmek** (or **yapmak**) to buy various sorts of a thing.

çeşitleme MUS variation.

çeşitlemek to increase the variety of.

çeşitli different, various, assorted.

çeşitlilik variety, diversity.

çeşme fountain.

çeşni 1. taste, flavo(u)r; **2.** sample, specimen; **3.** enjoyment, special flavo(u)r; **-sine bakmak** (bşin) to taste s.th., to test the flavo(u)r of s.th.

çeşnilemek to make palatable (or tasty).

çeşnilik seasoning.

çete [x .] band of rebels, guerrillas or brigands; **~ harbi** guerrilla warfare; **~ reisi** guerrilla leader.

çeteci [x . .] guerrilla, brigand, marauder.

çetecilik brigandage, marauding.

çetele [x . .] tally (stick); **~ tutmak** to keep tally.

çetin 1. hard, difficult, harsh; **2.** perverse, intractable; **~ ceviz** fig. hard (or tough) nut to crack.

çetinleşmek to get difficult; to become intractable.

çetrefil 1. confused, complicated; **2.** bad, incorrect, ungrammatical (language).

çetrefilleşmek to get complicated.

çevgen 1. polo stick; **2.** polo.

çevik nimble, agile, swift.

çeviklik agility, nimbleness.

çeviren translator.

çevirgeç PHYS commutator.

çeviri translation.

çevirici translator.

çevirim filming.

çevirme 1. vn. of **çevirmek**; **2.** translation; translating; **3.** translated; **4.** meat roasted on a spit; **5.** MIL encirclement.

çevirmek 1. to turn; **2.** to rotate, to turn; **3.** to translate (-e into); **4.** to return, to reject, to refuse, to turn down (offer, etc.); **5.** to manage; **6.** to interpret, to explain (another's words); **7.** to turn inside out (garment); **8.** to surround, to enclose; **9.** to pull (a trick); **çevir kazı yanmasın** F turn cat in pan.

çevirmen translator.

çevre 1. surroundings; **2.** circumference; contour, circuit, periphery; **3.** environment, milieu; ~ **dostu** eco-friendly, environmentally friendly; **4.** embroidered handkerchief.

çevrelemek to encircle, to surround, to enclose; to circumscribe.

çevren AST horizon.

çevresel environmental.

çevri 1. GEOGR whirlwind; whirlpool; **2.** forced interpretation.

çevrik 1. turned (around); **2.** surrounded; **3.** whirlpool; whirlwind; waterspout.

çevrili 1. bordered, surrounded; **2.** facing, turned towards.

çevrilmek pass. or refl. of **çevirmek**.

çevrim period, cycle.

çevrimsel CHEM cyclic, periodic.

çevrinti 1. rotation, eddy, whirl; **2.** whirlpool; whirlwind.

çevriyazı, -yı GR transcription, transliteration.

çeyiz trousseau; ~ **çemen** complete trousseau; ~ **düzmek** to prepare a trousseau.

çeyrek 1. quarter, one fourth; **2.** quarter (of an hour).

çıban boil, furuncle, abscess; pustule; ~ **başı 1.** head of a boil; **2.** fig. delicate matter; ~ **işlemek** to ooze pus (boil); **-ın başını koparmak** fig. to bring matters to a head.

çıdam patience.

çıfıt 1. contp. Jew; **2.** fig. miser, stingy; **3.** fig. tricky.

çığ avalanche; ~ **gibi büyümek** fig. to snowball.

çığa (balığı) ZOO sturgeon.

çığıltı confused noise of animal cries.

çığır, -ğrı 1. track left by an avalanche; **2.** path; track, rut; **3.** fig. epoch; ~ **açmak** to mark a new epoch, to break new (or fresh) ground; **çığrından**

çıkmak to go off the rails.

çığırtkan 1. = **çağırtkan**; **2.** barker, tout.

çığlık cry, scream, shriek; ~ **atmak** (or **basmak** or **koparmak**) to shriek, to scream.

çıkagelmek to appear suddenly, to burst in.

çıkar interest, profit, advantage; ~ **sağlamak** to exploit, to profit by; ~ **yol 1.** way out; **2.** fig. solution to a difficulty; **-ına bakmak** to look after number one; **-ının nerede olduğunu bilmek** to know which side one's bread is buttered.

çıkarcı opportunist, exploiter.

çıkarcılık opportunism, avarice.

çıkarma 1. MATH subtraction; **2.** MIL landing.

çıkarmak 1. to take out, to get out, to bring out, to push out, to expel, to send out; **2.** to extract, to remove, to take out (stain); **3.** to take out, to obtain, to procure (patent); **4.** to publish; **5.** to omit, to strike out; **6.** to export; **7.** MATH to subtract; **8.** to land, to unload; **9.** (telefonda) to get through; **10.** (b-ni) to place s.o.; **11.** to vomit, to throw up (food); **12.** to take off (garment); **13.** to deduce, to derive; **14.** to make out, to decipher; **15.** to take it out (-den on), to vent one's anger (-den on); **16.** to cause, to be the source of; **17.** to offer, to serve; **çıkarıp atmak** to throw off (garment); **sizi çıkaramadım** I can't place you.

çıkarsama LOG inference.

çıkartma sticker, decal.

çıkartmak caus. of **çıkarmak**.

çıkı P small bundle.

çıkık 1. dislocated, out of joint (bone); **2.** dislocation; **3.** projecting, protruding.

çıkıkçı bonesetter.

çıkın knotted bundle.

çıkıntı 1. projecting (or salient) part; **2.** marginal note.

çıkış 1. exit; **2.** MIL sortie, sally; **3.** races: start, **4.** scolding; ~ **imtihanı** leaving (or final) examination; ~ **vizesi** POL exit visa.

çıkışlı graduate (of a school).

çıkışma reprimand, rebuke.

çıkışmak 1. (b-ne) to scold s.o., to rebuke s.o., to chide s.o., to inveigh against s.o.; **2.** to be enough, to suffice (money).

çıkma 1. *vn. of* **çıkmak**; **2.** projection; promontory; **3.** marginal note; **4.** come out; appeared; **5.** separated (*from a group*).

çıkmak, (-ar) 1. to come out, to go out, to emerge; **2.** to move out (*of a house*), to vacate; **3.** to graduate (*-den* from); **4.** to withdraw (*-den* from), to leave, to quit; **5.** to be made (*or* produced) (*-den* from); **6.** to depart (*-den* from), to leave; **7.** to be subtracted (*-den* from), **8.** to turn out to be, to prove, to come true; **9.** to go up, to climb, to ascend, to step on (*-e* to); **10.** to come off; **11.** to break out (*war, fire, etc.*); **12.** to fall to one's lot; **13.** to cost, to amount (to); **14.** to lead (*-e* to) (*street*); **15.** to set (*or* start) off; **16.** to run, to come out (*colo(u)r*); **17.** to be dislocated (*limb*); **18.** to get about (*rumo(u)r*); **19.** to rise, to come out (*sun, moon*); **20.** to appear, to become visible; **21.** to be published, to come out, to appear (*book*); **22.** to come out, to be removed (*stain*); **23.** to be audible; to be detectible; **24.** to come on the market, to become available, to appear; **25.** to sprout; **26.** to be over (*month, season*); **27.** to go up, to increase (*fever, prices*); **28.** to be issued (*order, law*); **29.** to be announced (*promotion*); **30.** to appear (*before the court*); **31.** to apply in person (*to a high official*); **32.** to go out (*ile* with), to date; **33.** to go to the toilet; **34.** *sl.* to fork out, to pay up (*money*); **çıkmadık canda ümit vardır** *pro.* while there is life, there is hope.

çıkmaz 1. blind alley, dead-end street, impasse; **2.** *fig.* dilemma, deadlock; ~ **ayın son çarşambası** F Greek calends; **-a sokmak** (*b-ni*) to place *s.o.* in a dilemma.

çıkra thick scrub.

çıkrık 1. windlass; **2.** spinning wheel (*or* jenny); **3.** sheave, pulley wheel.

çılbır 1. dish of poached eggs with yogurt; **2.** leading rein.

çıldırasıya madly, passionately.

çıldır çıldır brightly; ~ **bakmak** to look with bright and shining eyes; ~ **yan mak** to burn brightly.

çıldırmak 1. to go mad, to lose one's wits, to go off one's head; **2.** *fig.* (*için*) to be nuts (**over**), to be wild (**obut**).

çıldırtmak to drive crazy.

çılgın mad, insane, crazy, raving, frenzied.

çılgınca madly; ~ **eğlenmek** F to whoop it up.

çılgınlık madness, frenzy, craziness.

çıma [x .] NAUT hawser, rope's end.

çımacı [x . .] quayside hand.

çımkırık bird's feces.

çın true, real.

çınar (*ağacı*) BOT plane tree.

çın çın: ~ **ötmek** to make a continuous ringing sound.

çıngar *sl.* row, quarrel, brawl; ~ **çıkarmak** *sl.* to make a scene, to kick up (*or* make) a row.

çıngıl a bunch of undeveloped grapes.

çıngırak 1. small bell; **2.** rattle; **çıngırağı çekmek** *sl.* to kick the bucket, to die.

çıngıraklıyılan ZOO rattlesnake.

çıngır çıngır with a rattling sound.

çıngırdak 1. = **çıngırak**; **2.** rattle.

çıngırdamak to ring, to tinkle.

çıngırtı tinkle.

çınlamak 1. to give out a tinkling sound; **2.** to ring (*ear*); **3.** to echo.

çıpıldak naked.

çıplak 1. naked, nude; bare; **2.** *fig.* destitute, needy; ~ **gözle** with the naked eye.

çıplaklık nakedness, nudity.

çıra [x .] pitch-pine.

çırak apprentice; ~ **çıkarmak** (*or* **etm.**) to free (*an apprentice*) to work on his own.

çıraklık 1. apprenticeship; **2.** apprentice's fee; ~ **etm.** to work as an apprentice.

çıralı resinous.

çıramoz torch-holder (*for attracting fish by night*).

çırçıplak [x .] stark naked, in the altogether, in one's birthday suit.

çırçır 1. cotton gin; **2.** trickling spring; **3.** *s.* **cırcırböceği.**

çırçırbalığı, -nı ZOO wrasse.

çırılçıpıldak [. x . . .], **çırılçıplak** [. x . .] *s.* **çırçıplak.**

çırpı 1. chip, clipping, shaving; **2.** chalk line; ~ **ipi 1.** carpenter's chalk line; **2.** mason's leveling line; ~ **vurmak** to mark a straight line with the chalk line; **-ya getirmek** to line up.

çırpınma struggle, fluttering.

çırpınmak 1. to flutter, to struggle; **2.** to be all in a fluster; **3.** to struggle desperately.

çırpıntı 1. flurry; 2. slight agitation (*of the sea*).

çırpıntılı slightly agitated (*sea*).

çırpışmak to flutter (*birds*).

çırpıştırmak 1. to tap, to beat lightly; 2. F to do superficially.

çırpmak, (*-ar*) 1. to beat, to strike, to tap, to pat; 2. to beat (*carpet*); 3. to clap (*hands*); 4. to flutter (*wings*); 5. to rinse (*laundry*); 6. to full (*cloth*); 7. to trim, to clip; 8. *fig.* to steal, to pilfer; 9. to stir; to beat (*food*).

çırt, *-tı* irrigation pump powered by an animal.

çıt, *-tı* crack, cracking sound; ~ **çıkmamak** to be dead silent; ~ **yok** there is a dead silence.

çıta [x .] lath.

çıtçıt snap fastener, press-stud, popper.

çıtı pıtı F dainty.

çıtır çıtır with a crackling sound; ~ **etm.** to crackle.

çıtırdamak to crackle.

çıtır pıtır prattling, babbling sweetly.

çıtırtı crackle.

çıtkırıldım 1. fragile, overdelicate; 2. *fig.* dandy, sissified, effeminate.

çıtlamak to crackle.

çıtlatmak 1. to crack; 2. *fig.* to drop a hint.

çıtpıt, *-tı* percussion cap (*which goes off when trodden on*).

çıvgar auxiliary animal (*for plowing*).

çıyan 1. zoo centipede; 2. *fig.* disgusting blond person.

çızıktırmak F to dash off, to knock off, to tear off.

çiçek 1. flower, blossom; 2. MED smallpox, variola; 3. *fig.* fickle and tricky person; 4. CHEM flowers; ~ **açmak** to blossom, to bloom, to come into flower; ~ **aşısı** vaccination; ~ **çıkarmak** (*or* **dökmek**) MED to have smallpox; ~ **gibi açılmak** to blossom; ~ **tozu** pollen; **çiçeği burnunda** brand new, very fresh.

çiçekbozuğu, *-nu* 1. pockmark; 2. pock-marked.

çiçekçi florist.

çiçekçilik floriculture, floristry.

çiçeklemek 1. to plant with flowers; 2. to decorate with flowers.

çiçeklenmek to flower, to blossom, to come into flower.

çiçekli flowered, in bloom.

çiçeklik 1. (flower) vase; flower stand; 2. flower bed; 3. flower garden; 4. greenhouse; 5. BOT receptacle.

çiçeksimek CHEM to effloresce.

çiçeksiz without flowers.

çift, *-ti* 1. pair, couple; double; 2. duplicate; 3. pincers; ~ **camlı pencere** double-glazed window; ~ ~ by (*or* in) pairs; ~ **çubuk** farming implements; ~ **koşmak** to harness to a plow (*horses, etc.*); ~ **meclis sistemi** POL two-chamber system; ~ **priz** ELECT two-pin plug; ~ **sürmek** to plough, *Am.* to plow; ~ **tıklamak** IT to double-click.

çiftçi farmer, agriculturalist.

çiftçilik agriculture, farming.

çifte 1. double, paired; 2. kick (*of a horse*); 3. shotgun, double-barreled gun; 4. double-oared boat; ~ **atmak** to kick (*horse, etc.*); ~ **dikiş** *sl.* repeater (*in a class*); ~ **kumrular** *fig.* two inseparable chums; ~ **şamdan** two-branched candlestick.

çiftehane [. . - .] pairing cage (*for birds*).

çifteker bicycle.

çiftelemek to kick.

çifter çifter in pairs.

çiftetelli a kind of solo folk dance.

çiftleşmek 1. to become a pair; 2. to mate.

çiftleştirmek 1. to make a pair; 2. to mate (*two animals*).

çiftlik farm, plantation.

çiftsayı MATH even number.

çiğ[1] 1. raw, uncooked; 2. green, crude, fresh, soft (*person*); 3. crude, unfitting (*word, act*); 4. crude (*colo(u)r*); 5. P immature, unripe (*fruit*); uncultivated (*land*); ~ **kaçmak** *fig.* to be crude; ~ **yemedim ki karnım ağrısın!** *fig.* I have done nothing that I should be blamed!

çiğ[2] dew.

çiğde BOT jujube (tree).

çiğdem BOT crocus, meadow saffron.

çiğindirik shoulder yoke.

çiğit cotton seed.

çiğlik 1. rawness; 2. *fig.* crudeness.

çiğnemek 1. to chew; 2. to run over (*a person in car accident*); 3. to trample down, to tread under foot; 4. *fig.* to violate (*rule, law*).

çiklet, *-ti* chewing-gum.

çikolata [. . x .] chocolate.

çil[1] zoo hazel grouse; ~ **yavrusu gibi**

dağılmak to scatter like a covey of partridges.

çil² 1. freckle; 2. spot (*on a mirror*); 3. freckled, speckled; 4. root hair; 5. bright, shiny (*coin*).

çile¹ 1. hank, skein; 2. bowstring.

çile² ordeal, trial, sufferance; **~ çekmek** (*or* **çıkarmak** *or* **doldurmak**) to pass through a severe trial, to suffer greatly; **-den çıkarmak** to infuriate, to exasperate; **-den çıkmak** to lose one's temper.

çilecilik asceticism.

çilek BOT strawberry (plant).

çilekeş 1. long-suffering; 2. religious ascetic; 3. ascetical.

çileli 1. suffering, enduring; 2. full of suffering.

çilemek to sing (*nightingale*).

çilenti drizzle.

çilingir 1. locksmith; 2. *sl.* lockbreaker, burglar; **~ sofrası** F small table with rakı and light snacks.

çilingirlik locksmithery.

çillenmek to become freckled (*or* speckled).

çilli freckled, speckled.

çim lawn, garden grass.

çimbali, çimbalo MUS cymbal.

çimdik 1. pinch; 2. a pinch (of); 3. *fig.* an unfriendly remark; **~ atmak** (*or* **basmak**) to pinch.

çimdiklemek 1. to pinch; 2. to crumble.

çimen 1. wild grass; 2. = **çemen.**

çimenlik 1. grassy; 2. meadow, lawn.

çimento [. x .] cement.

çimentolamak to cement.

çimlemek to plant with grass.

çimlendirmek to grass over.

çimlenmek 1. to sprout, to germinate; 2. to become grassy; 3. *co.* to get pickings.

çimmek to duck under water, to dip down (*in water*).

Çin *pr. n.* China.

Çinakop, -pu ZOO young of the bluefish.

Çince *pr. n.* Chinese, the Chinese language.

çinçilya ZOO chinchilla.

Çingene¹ [x . .] *pr. n.* Gypsy; the Gypsies; **~ borçları** petty debts; **~ çergesi** 1. Gypsy tent; 2. dump; **~ düğünü** 1. Gypsy wedding; 2. *fig.* riotous and disorderly assembly.

çingene² *fig.* miser, stingy person.

Çingenece *pr. n.* the Romany language.

çingeneleşmek to pinch pennies.

çingenelik 1. miserliness, stinginess; 2. paltriness, shabbiness; 3. vagabondage.

çingenepalamudu, -nu ZOO the young of the bonito.

Çin Halk Cumhuriyeti *pr. n.* People's Republic of China.

çini 1. tile, encaustic (*or* glazed) tile; 2. tile, tiled; 3. porcelain, china; **~ döşemek** to tile; **~ mürekkebi** India ink.

çinici maker of tiles.

çinicilik the art of tile-making.

çinili tiled.

çinko [x .] 1. zinc; zinc sheet; 2. zincograph; 3. payoff (*in a lotto game*).

çinkograf zincographer.

çinkografi zincography.

Çinli *pr. n.* 1. Chinese; 2. a Chinese.

çintan, çintaniye, çintiyan wide trousers worn by peasant women.

çipil 1. gummy, bleary, dirty (*eye*); bleary-eyed; 2. = **çepel.**

çipo [x .] NAUT anchor stock.

çipura [. x.] ZOO gilt-head bream.

çiriş paste, glue; size.

çirişlemek to smear with paste.

çirişli pasted; pasty, gluey; sized.

çirişotu, -nu BOT asphodel.

çirkef 1. filthy (*or* foul) water; 2. *fig.* disgusting, loathsome (*person*).

çirkin 1. ugly; 2. unseemly, unbecoming, ugly, shameful.

çirkinleşmek to get ugly.

çirkinlik ugliness.

çirkinsemek to consider ugly.

çiroz 1. salted and dried thin mackerel; 2. *fig.* a bag of bones.

çis BOT manna.

çise drizzle.

çiselemek to drizzle, to spit.

çisenti drizzle.

çiskin 1. wet by a drizzle; 2. drizzle.

çiş urine, pee, peepee; **~ etm.** to pee; **-i gelmek** to want to pee.

çişik leveret, bunny.

çit, -ti 1. hedge; fence; 2. chintz; 3. kerchief.

çitari ZOO salpa.

çiti rubbing, scrubbing (*laundry*).

çit(ile)mek to rub together (*clothes*).

çitili rubbed, scrubbed (*laundry*).

çitişmek 1. to interlace; 2. to occlude well (*teeth*).

çitlembik BOT nettle tree berry; **~ gibi**

small and dark (*girl*).

çitlemek 1. to hedge, to fence; **2.** to crack between one's teeth (*dried seeds*).

çitmik 1. *s.* **çıngıl**; **2.** a pinch.

çitsarmaşığı, -nı BOT convolvulus, bindweed, corn lily.

çivi 1. nail; **2.** pin, peg; **3.** tubercle, stud, knob; ~ **çakmak** to drive in nails; ~ **-yi söker** *pro.* set a thief to catch a thief, an old poacher makes the best keeper; ~ **dişi** canine tooth; ~ **gibi 1.** healthy, strong; **2.** stiff with cold (*finger*); ~ **kesmek** F to freeze, to feel very cold.

çivici 1. seller of nails; **2.** *sports*: smasher.

çividi [. - -] (*mavi*) indigo blue.

çivileme 1. *vn. of* **çivilemek**; **2.** feet-first jump; **3.** *sports*: smash.

çivilemek 1. to nail; **2.** *fig.* F to stab.

çivilenmek 1. *pass. of* **çivilemek**; **2.** *fig.* (*bir yere*) to be rooted (*to a spot*).

çivili 1. nailed; **2.** having nails.

çivit, -di indigo, blue dye; ~ **mavisi** indigo

çivitlemek 1. to dye with indigo; **2.** to blue (*laundry*).

çivitli blued (*laundry*).

çivitotu, -nu BOT **1.** indigo plant; **2.** woad.

çiviyazısı, -nı cuneiform writing.

çiy dew; ~ **düşmek** (*or* **yağmak**) to fall (*dew*).

çiyli dewy.

çizecek scriber.

çizelge chart.

çizem diagram, plan; outline.

çizemsel diagrammatic, schematic.

çizge diagram, curve, graph.

çizgi 1. MATH line; **2.** stripe; striation; **3.** scratch, mark, scar; **4.** dash; **5.** part (*in a person's hair*); ~ **çekmek** (*or* **çizmek**) to draw a line; ~ ~ striped; ~ **hakemi** *sports*: linesman; ~ **resim** drawing.

çizgilemek to mark with lines, to lineate.

çizgili 1. ruled, marked with lines; **2.** striped, striated; **3.** scratched; ~ **çek** COM crossed check; ~ **kâğıt** ruled paper.

çizgilik straightedge.

çizgisiz unlined; unstriped; unmarked; ~ **kâğıt** plain-paper.

çizi 1. = **çizgi**; **2.** furrow.

çizik 1. = **çizgi**; **2.** = **çizili**.

çizikli lined.

çiziktirmek to scrawl.

çizili 1. ruled, lined; **2.** scratched, marked; **3.** drawn, delineated; **4.** cancelled, crossed out; **5.** (*altı*) underlined.

çizim MATH construction.

çizinti 1. scratch; **2.** part crossed off.

çizme 1. *vn. of* **çizmek**; **2.** high (*or* top) boot; **-den yukarı çıkmak** to be over-wise.

çizmeci bootmaker.

çizmek, (-er) 1. to draw; to mark; to score; **2.** to sketch, to draw; **3.** to cross out, to strike off, to cancel; **4.** to scarify, to scratch.

çizmeli booted.

çoban 1. shepherd, herdsman; **2.** *fig.* rustic, boor; ~ **armağanı çam sakızı** *pro.* a shepherd's present is pine resin (*expression of modesty, in giving a present*); ~ **itikadı** simple and firm faith; ~ **köpeği** sheep dog.

çobanaldatan ZOO goatsucker, night-jar.

çobanlama *lit.* pastoral.

çobanlık *etm.* to shepherd.

Çobanyıldızı, -nı AST Venus.

çocuğumsu childish.

çocuk 1. child, infant; **2.** childish; ~ **aldırmak** MED to have an abortion; ~ **arabası** pram, *Am.* baby carriage; ~ **bahçesi 1.** children's playground; **2.** playpen; ~ **bakımevi** day nursery, crèche; ~ **bezi** nappy, *Am.* diaper; ~ **büyütmek** to bring up children; ~ **canlısı** fond of children; ~ **dili** child's language; ~ **doğurmak** to give birth to a child, to bear a child; ~ **doktoru** pediatrician; ~ **düşürme** MED abortion, miscarriage; ~ **düşürmek** MED to abort, to miscarry; ♀ **Esirgeme Kurumu** Society for the Protection of Children; ~ **felci** infantile paralysis, polio; ~ **gibi** childish(ly); childlike; ~ **mahkemesi** JUR juvenile court; ~ **odası** nursery; ~ **oyuncağı 1.** toy; **2.** *fig.* child's play, pushover; ~ **yuvası** nursery school; ~ **zammı** child allowance; **-tan al haberi!** *pro.* a child will tell the truth!

çocukbilim pedology, paidology.

çocukbilimci pedologist, paidologist.

çocukça 1. childish (*act*); **2.** childishly.

çocukcağız poor little child.

çocuklaşmak to become childish; to act childishly.

çocukluk 1. childhood; 2. childishness; folly; ~ etm. to act childishly.
çocuksu childish.
çoğalmak to increase, to multiply.
çoğaltım reproduction, copying.
çoğaltmak 1. to increase, to augment; 2. to reproduce.
çoğu, -nu 1. most (of); 2. mostly, usually; ~ zaman usually.
çoğul GR plural; ~ ekleri plural endings.
çoğulcu pluralist.
çoğullaştırmak GR to pluralize.
çoğulluk plural form.
çoğun(ca) often.
çoğunluk majority.
çoğunlukla 1. with a majority of votes; 2. usually.
çok 1. many, much; 2. often, long (time); 3. too; too much; too many; too long; 4. very; ~ çocuklu having many children; ~~ at (the) most; ~ defa often; ~ fazla far too much; ~ geçmeden soon, before long; ~ gelmek 1. to be too much (-e for); 2. to become unbearable; ~ görmek 1. to consider to be too much; 2. to begrudge; ~ olm. to go too far, to overstep the limit; ~ şey! how strange!; ~ şükür! thank God!; ~ taraflı JUR multilateral; ~ yaşa! long live!, hurrah!; çoğa kalmaz (or varmaz or varmadan) before long, soon; çoğa oturmak (or varmak) to cost dearly.
çoka [x .] s. çığa balığı.
çokal plate armo(u)r, coat of mail.
çokayaklılar zoo myriapoda.
çokbiçimli polymorphic.
çokbilmiş 1. cunning, sly; 2. precocious.
çokça a good many, somewhat abundant.
çokçuluk PHLS pluralism.
çokdüzlemli MATH polyhedral.
çokevli polygamous.
çokevlilik polygamy.
çokfazlı PHYS polyphasal.
çokgen MATH polygon.
çokkarılı polygynous.
çokkocalı polyandrous.
çokluk 1. abundance; 2. majority; 3. often; mostly.
çoktanrıcılık polytheism.
çoktanrılı polytheist.
çokterimli MATH polynomial.
çokyüzlü MATH 1. polyhedral; 2. polyhedron.

çolak with one arm; crippled in one hand.
çolpa clumsy, uncouth.
çoluk çocuk 1. wife and children, household, family; 2. (pack of) children; çoluk çocuğa karışmak to get married and have children.
çomak 1. cudgel, truncheon; short thick stick; 2. stick, bat (in tipcat).
çomar 1. mastiff, large watchdog; 2. sl. old tavern-keeper; 3. P hornless sheep.
çopra 1. backbone (of a fish); 2. impenetrable scrub.
çoprabalığı, -nı zoo loach.
çopur 1. pock-marked; 2. pockmarks.
çopurina zoo picarel.
çor 1. illness, disease; 2. P murrain, anthrax.
çorak 1. arid, barren; 2. brackish, bitter (water); 3. saltpeter bed; 4. an impervious kind of clay.
çoraklaşmak to become arid.
çoraklaştırmak to make arid (or barren), to destroy the fertility of (land).
çoraklık 1. aridity, barrenness (of land); 2. brackishness (of water).
çorap sock, stocking, hose; ~ kaçmak to ladder, Am. to run (stocking); ~ örmek 1. to knit stockings; 2. fig. to plot (aganist s.o.), to get s.o. into trouble; ~ söküğü gibi fig. in rapid succession, easily and quickly; ~ şişi knitting needle.
çorapçı hosier.
çorapçılık the hosiery business.
çorba 1. soup; 2. fig. mess; ~ içmek to eat soup; ~ etm. fig. to make a mess (of); ~ gibi fig. in a mess, confused; ~ kaşığı tablespoon; -da tuzu bulunmak fig. to participate in a small way; -ya dönmek fig. to become a mess.
çorbacı 1. maker or seller of soup; 2. the form of address used by sailors when addressing the ship's owner; 3. Christian notable in Turkish towns; 4. sl. boss.
çorbalık suitable for making soup.
çotira zoo triggerfish.
çotra [x .] flat wooden bottle.
çotuk 1. tree stump; 2. stock of a vine.
çöğür 1. lute; 2. seedling.
çökek 1. hollow, low spot; 2. bog.
çökelek 1. cheese made of curds; 2. CHEM precipitate.
çökelmek CHEM to precipitate, to settle.

çökelti CHEM s. *çökelek 2.*
çökeltmek CHEM to precipitate.
çökertme 1. *vn. of* *çökertmek;* 2. a kind of fishing-net; 3. MIL break--through.
çökertmek 1. to make kneel down (*camel*); 2. to cause to collapse.
çökkün 1. collapsed, broken down; 2. PSYCH depressed.
çökkünlük breakdown; depression.
çökmek, (-er) 1. to collapse, to fall in (*or* down); to break down; to give way; 2. to sit down suddenly; 3. to come down (*fog, smoke*); 4. to fall (*darkness*); 5. (*diz*) to kneel; 6. to cave in, to become sunk and hollow; 7. to settle, to precipitate; 8. to descend on one (*sorrow*); 9. to be prostrated (*by age or fatigue*), to break down.
çökük 1. collapsed, fallen in; 2. caved in, sunken (in); 3. prostrated (*by age*).
çöküntü 1. debris, wreckage; 2. deposit, sediment; 3. depression; subsidence (*of land*).
çöküş collapse, fall (*a. fig.*).
çöküşmek to sit down together; to gather.
çöl desert; wasteland, wilderness.
çölfaresi, -ni ZOO jerboa.
çöllük 1. desert tract of country; 2. arid, barren.
çömelmek to squat down.
çömez 1. *boy who works in return for board and lodging*; 2. *fig.* follower, disciple.
çömlek earthen pot; ~ *hesabı fig.* calculation of an illiterate person; crude scheme.
çömlekçi potter; ~ *çamuru* potter's clay.
çömlekçilik pottery.
çöp, -pü 1. straw, chip; 2. matchstick; 3. stalk, peduncle (*of a fruit*); 4. rubbish, litter, trash, garbage, sweepings; ~ *arabası* garbage truck; ~ *atlamaz fig.* meticulous, punctilious; ~ *dökmek* to tip, to dump (*rubbish*); ~ *dökmek yasaktır* no rubbish to be tipped here; ~ *gibi* skinny; ~ *tenekesi* garbage can, dustbin, litterbin; -*ten direk fig.* unsound undertaking.
çöpçatan matchmaker.
çöpçatanlık matchmaking.
çöpçü 1. dustman, street sweeper, scavenger; 2. garbage collector.
çöpçülük garbage collecting.
çöpleme BOT bear's foot.

çöplenmek 1. to pick up scraps for a meal; 2. *fig.* to get pickings.
çöplüce bülbül ZOO wren.
çöplük tip, dump (*a. fig.*); ~ *horozu fig.* debauchee, profligate.
çöpsüz 1. free from rubbish; 2. seedless.
çörek 1. cookie; 2. disc.
çöreklenmek 1. to coil itself up (*snake*); 2. to settle down and stay.
çöre(k)otu, -*nu* BOT black cumin, seeds of Nigella sativa.
çöven 1. BOT soapwort; 2. polo (stick).
çözelti CHEM solution.
çözgü warp.
çözgün 1. untied, unfastened; 2. dissolved, dispersed; gone.
çözme 1. *vn. of* *çözmek;* 2. a kind of cotton sheeting.
çözmek, (-er) 1. to untie, to unfasten; 2. to unbutton; 3. to solve (*problem*); 4. to unravel, to disentangle, to undo (*knot*); 5. CHEM to dissolve.
çözücü solvent.
çözük 1. untied, loose; 2. unraveled.
çözülmek 1. *pass. of* *çözmek;* 2. to thaw (*ice*); 3. to be scattered, to lose its unity; 4. to become feeble, to lose its strength; 5. MIL to withdraw; to become routed (*or* scattered); 6. *sl.* to run away.
çözülüm 1. MIL disengagement; rout; 2. PSYCH dissociation.
çözüm solution.
çözümleme analysis.
çözümlemek to analyze.
çözümsel analytic(al).
çözünmek CHEM to dissolve; to decompose.
çözünüm PSYCH dissociation.
çözüşme CHEM dissociation.
çözüşmek CHEM to dissociate.
çubuk 1. rod, bar; 2. staff, wand; 3. shoot, twig; sapling; 4. cigarette holder; 5. stripe, rib (*in cloth*); 6. NAUT upper mast; *çubuğu tellendirmek fig.* to take it easy.
çubuklamak to beat (*carpet*).
çubuklu 1. barred; 2. striped, ribbed (*cloth*).
çuha broadcloth.
çuhaçiçeği, -*ni* BOT cowslip.
çuhçuh choo-choo (*train*).
çukur 1. pit, hole, hollow, ditch; dent; cavity; 2. concave; depressed; low; 3. dimple; 4. cesspool; 5. *fig.* grave; 6. *sl.* buttocks; ~ *açmak* to dig a pit; ~ *göz-*

lü hollow-eyed; ~ *tabak* soup-plate; **-unu kazmak** (*b-nin*) *fig.* to plot against *s.o.*

çukurlaşmak to become hollowed (*or* bowl-shaped); to be dented.

çukurlatmak 1. to pit; **2.** to depress, to make concave.

çukurlu pitted; dented.

çukurluk 1. concavity, hollowness; **2.** pit, hole.

çul 1. haircloth; **2.** horsecloth; **3.** clothes; ~ *çuval* haircloth sack; ~ *çürütmek* *fig.* to sit a long time (*guest*); ~ *tutmaz* spendthrift, shiftless; **-u tutmak** to grow rich.

çulha weaver.

çulhakuşu, -nu zoo penduline titmouse.

çullamak to furnish (*or* cover) with a horsecloth.

çullanmak 1. *pass. of* **çullamak**; **2.** (*b-ne*) to jump on *s.o.*; **3.** (*b-ne*) *fig.* to pester *s.o.*, to bother *s.o.*

çulluk zoo woodcock.

Çulpan AST s. **Çobanyıldızı.**

çulsaz *fig.* penniless, skint.

çultar quilted saddle-cloth.

çurçur (*balığı*) s. **çırçır** (*balığı*).

çuval 1. sack; **2.** *sl.* fat (*person*); ~ *gibi* loose, untidy (*clothes*).

çuvaldız packing needle.

çuvallamak 1. to bag, to put in sacks; **2.** *sl.* to fail the class, to flunk.

çük penis.

çünki s. **çünkü.**

çünkü [x .] because.

çürük 1. rotten, spoilt, decayed; **2.** unstable; **3.** unfounded; untenable; **4.** bruise, discolo(u)ration, black-and--blue spot; **5.** rotten, bad (*egg*); **6.** carious (*tooth*); **7.** disabled (*soldier*); ~ *çarık* worn out, useless; ~ *gaz* MEC exhaust fumes; **çürüğe çıkarmak 1.** to discard as useless; **2.** MIL to invalid out (*soldier*).

çürükçül saprophyte.

çürüklük 1. rottenness, putrefaction; **2.** garbage dump; **3.** *fig.* graveyard.

çürümek 1. to rot, to decay, to putrefy; **2.** to be refuted, to be disproved (*claim, etc.*); **3.** to be bruised (*or* discolo(u)red); **4.** to become worn out (*or* unsound) (*material*); **5.** to become infirm (*because of aging*).

çürütmek *caus. of* **çürümek**, *part.* **1.** to make decay; **2.** to refute, to disprove (*one's argument*); **3.** to season, to age (*meat*).

çüş 1. whoa!; **2.** *sl.* you fool!, you ass!

D

da 1. also, too; **2.** and; **3.** but; **4.** in, at, on, upon; **5.** within, in; **6.** in the possession of, with; **7.** having, of; **8.** denominator (*in fractions*).

-da *particle forming the locative case*; *s.a.* **-de, -ta, -te.**

da [ā] *obs.* illness, disease.

dadanmak 1. (*bşe*) *mst contp.* to acquire a taste for *s.th.*; **2.** (*bir yere*) to frequent, to visit (*a place*) frequently.

dadaş P **1.** brother; **2.** pal, comrade; **3.** youth, youngster.

dadı nurse(maid), nanny.

dafi, -ii [ā] *rare* **1.** that repels, wards off; **2.** God.

dağ[1] **1.** stigma, brand; **2.** MED cautery, cauterization, mark; **3.** branding iron; ~ *basmak* to brand, to cauterize.

dağ[2] **1.** mountain; **2.** mound, heap; **3.** wild; ~ *adamı* **1.** mountaineer, highlander; **2.** boor; ~ *başı* **1.** summit, mountain top; **2.** wilds, remote place; ~ *deviren* a bull in a china shop; ~ *eteği* foothills, hillside, skirts of a mountain; ~ *harbi* mountain warfare; ~ *silsilesi* mountain range; ~ *taş* all around, as far as the eye can see; ~ *yürümezse, abdal yürür* if the mountain will not come to Mohammed, Mohammed must go to the mountain; *-a çıkmak* to take to the hills; *-a kaldırmak* to kidnap, to elope (*with*); *-lara taşlara!* may such a thing be far from us!; *aralarında -lar kadar fark var* they are as different as chalk and cheese.

dağarcık 1. leather sack (*or* pouch); **2.** *fig.* knowledge.

dağcı alpinist, mountaineer, mountain climber.

dağcılık mountaineering, mountain climbing.

dağdağa tumult, turmoil.
dağdağalı tumultuous.
dağılım 1. dissociation; **2.** dispersion; **3.** distribution.
dağılış 1. dispersal; **2.** fall, collapse.
dağılmak 1. to scatter; to disperse, to separate; **2.** to spread, to be disseminated (*rumo(u)rs*); **3.** to dissolve; to fall to pieces; **4.** to become untidy; **5.** to be distributed.
dağınık 1. untidy; disorganized; **2.** scattered, dispersed.
dağınıklık untidiness; dispersion.
dağıtıcı 1. deliverer, deliveryman; distributor; **2.** divisive.
dağıtıcılık delivery; distribution.
dağıtım distribution; delivery.
dağıtımevi, -ni distributor.
dağıtmak 1. to scatter, to disperse; **2.** to distribute, to deliver, to serve out; **3.** to mess up, to disorder (*room, etc.*); **4.** to break into pieces; **5.** to dissolve, to annul (*parliament, business, etc.*); **6.** (*k-ni*) to go to pieces; **7.** to divert, to distract (*attention*).
dağkeçisi zoo chamois.
dağlamak 1. to brand; to cauterize, to sear; **2.** to burn, to scorch (*sun, wind*); **3.** *fig.* to grieve, to afflict, to take to heart.
dağlı¹ 1. branded; **2.** scarred; **3.** hurt to the quick, sore.
dağlı² 1. mountaineer, highlander; **2.** *cards*: king; **3.** unmannerly, uncouth, discourteous, unmannered.
dağlıç a kind of stump-tailed sheep.
dağlık mountainous, hilly.
dağsıçanı, -nı marmot.
daha 1. more (*-den* than), further; and, plus; **2.** still, so far, yet; **3.** only; *~ neleri* how absurd!; *-sı var* that is not all, to be continued; *bir ~* once more.
dahdah gee-gee.
dahi also, too, even.
dâhi genius.
dahil 1. inside, the interior; **2.** including; included; *~ etm.* to include; to insert; *~ olm.* to be included, to join, to participate (*-e* in).
dahilen inwardly, internally.
dahili internal, inner; *~ deniz* inland sea; *~ harp* civil war; *~ işler* internal affairs, domestic affairs; *~ merkez* hypocentrum; *~ nizamname* JUR internal regulations; POL standing orders.
dahiliye [â] **1.** home (*or* internal) affairs; **2.** internal diseases; **3.** = **Dahili-**

ye Vekâleti; **4.** department of buildings and grounds; ♎ **Vekâleti** (*or* **Nezareti**) Ministry of the Interior.
dâhiyane [- . - .] ingenious, brilliant.
dahletmek [x . .] to interfere (*-e* with), to meddle (*-e* in); to blame.
daima [- . .] always, continually, perpetually.
daimi [- . -] constant, permanent, perpetual; *~ encümen* standing committee; *~ kadro* permanent staff.
daimilik [â] permanency.
dair [ā] concerning, about, relating (*-e* to).
daire [ā] **1.** circle; circumference; **2.** office, department; **3.** limit, range; **4.** flat, apartments; **5.** MUS tambourine.
dairesel circular.
dairevi [- . . -] circular.
dakik, -ki [ī] **1.** punctual, time-minded, exact, particular, thorough, painstaking; **2.** fine, subtle.
dakika, dakka minute; *-sı -sına* punctually, to the very minute; *-sında* at once, instantly.
daktilo [x . .] **1.** typewriting; **2.** typist (*person*); **3.** *a.* ~ **makinesi** typewriter; *~ etm.* to type; *~ ile yazılmış* typewritten, typed.
daktilograf typist.
daktilografi typewriting, typing.
daktiloskopi fingerprinting.
dal¹ 1. branch, bough, twig; **2.** *fig.* branch, subdivision, ramification; *~ budak salmak* **1.** to shoot out branches; **2.** *fig.* to spread, to become wide-spread; *~ gibi* slender, graceful; *-dan -a atlamak* *fig.* to jump from one thing to the other, to ramble; *-dan -a konan* *fig.* fickle, inconstant.
dal² 1. back; shoulder; *-ına basmak* (*b-nin*) to tread on *s.o.*'s corns (*or* toes); *-ına binmek* (*b-nin*) to pester *s.o.*, to put pressure on *s.o.*
dal³ naked, bare.
dalak 1. spleen; milt; **2.** honeycomb.
dalalet, -ti heresy, deviation, aberration; *-e düşmek* to deviate, to go astray.
dalamak 1. to bite; **2.** to prick, to sting; to burn, to sear; to scratch; to chafe.
dalaş dogfight, brawl, row.
dalaşmak 1. to fight savagely (*dogs*); **2.** *fig.* to wrangle.
dalavere [. . x .] F trick, intrigue, swindle, deception, deceit; *~ çevirmek* to intrigue, to plot; *-li iş* sharp practice.

dalavereci trickster, intriguer, sharper, swindler.

dalbastı big and fine in quality (*cherry*).

dalburun nosy, inquisitive.

daldırma 1. *vn. of* **daldırmak**; **2.** layered (*branch*); layer.

daldırmak *caus. of* **dalmak 1.** to layer (*a shoot*); **2.** to plunge (-*e* into), to dip (-*e* into); **3.** *fig.* to disparage.

dalga 1. wave, ripple; undulation, corrugation; **2.** watering (*on silk*); **3.** wave (*of hair*); **4.** ELECT wave; **5.** *sl.* distraction; **6.** *sl.* trick, intrigue; **7.** *sl.* dope; ~ **boyu** PHYS wavelength; ~ ~ **1.** in waves; **2.** wavy (*hair*); **3.** striped. in light and dark (*colo(u)rs*); ~ **geçmek** *sl.* **1.** to woolgather; **2.** (*b-le*) to make fun of *s.o.*, to make mock of *s.o.*

dalgacı 1. F woolgatherer; **2.** *sl.* trickster, swindler; ~ **Mahmut** F dodger.

dalgakıran breakwater, mole.

dalgalanmak 1. to wave, to surge, to billow, to undulate; **2.** to fluctuate (*prices*); **3.** to get rough (*sea*); **4.** to become uneven (*dye*); **5.** to get watered (*silk*); **6.** MEC to get corrugated (*metal sheet*).

dalgalı 1. rough (*sea*); undulated; **2.** wavy (*hair*); **3.** corrugated (*metal*); **4.** watered (*silk*).

dalgıç, -cı 1. diver; **2.** ZOO grebe; ~ **elbisesi** diving suit (*or dress*).

dalgın 1. absent-minded, contemplative, abstracted, plunged in thought, preoccupied; **2.** unconscious (*sick person*), comatose.

dalgınlık 1. absent-mindedness, abstractedness, preoccupation, reverie.

dalkavuk toady, bootlicker, hanger-on, leech, lickspittle; sycophant, parasite.

dalkavukluk flattery, toadyism, fawning; sycophancy; ~ **etm.** to toady, to fawn, to truckle, to cringe.

dalkılıç with naked sword.

dallandırmak 1. to cause to ramify; **2.** to complicate, to render difficult; **3.** to exaggerate.

dallanmak 1. to shoot out branches, to branch out, to ramify, to become branched; **2.** to spread, to become complicated.

dallı 1. branched, ramified; **2.** ornamented with branches; ~ **budaklı 1.** ramified; **2.** *fig.* complicated, intricate, knotty.

dalmak, (-ar) 1. to dive, to plunge (-*e* into); **2.** to be intent (-*e* on); **3.** to burst (-*e* into), to blow (-*e* into), to plunge (-*e* into); **4.** to be lost in thought; **5.** to become absorbed (-*e* in); **6.** to drop off, to doze off; to become unconscious (*sick person*); **dala çıka** F sinking or rising, with the greatest difficulty.

daltaban 1. barefooted; **2.** *fig.* destitute, wretched; **3.** *fig.* contemptible (*person*).

dalya dahlia.

dalyan fishing weir; ~ **gibi** well-built, well set-up.

dalyarak *sl.* booby, boob.

dam[1] 1. roof; **2.** outhouse; roofed shed; **3.** stable; **4.** P house; **5.** *sl.* jail, stir, cooler; ~ **altı** loft, attic, garret; **-dan düşer gibi** out of the blue, out of a clear (blue) sky.

dam[2] 1. lady partner (*in dance*); **2.** *cards*: queen.

dama [x .] 1. game of draughts, *Am.* game of checkers; **2.** *draughts*: king; ~ **tahtası** draughtboard, *Am.* checkerboard; ~ **taşı 1.** *draughts*: man; **2.** *fig.* one who is often reassigned.

damacana demijohn, large bottle.

damak palate.

damaklı having a palate.

damaksıl palatal.

damalı chequered, *Am.* checkered.

damar 1. BIOL vein, blood-vessel; **2.** ANAT vessel, vas; **3.** GEOL seam; **4.** BOT vein; **5.** MIN vein, streak; lode; **6.** *fig.* obstinacy, wil(l)fulness; **7.** *fig.* temper, nature, disposition; **8.** *fig.* streak; ~ **sertliği** MED arteriosclerosis; ~ **tıkanıklığı** embolism; **-ına basmak** (*b-nin*) to touch one's sore spot, to tread on *s.o.*'s corns; **-ını bulmak** to find the weak spot (*in a person*).

damarlı 1. veined, veiny; **2.** vascular; **3.** *fig.* obstinate.

damarsız 1. having no veins; **2.** *fig.* docile, biddable.

damasko [. x .] damask.

damat, -dı son-in-law; bridegroom.

damdazlak [x . .] completely bald.

damga 1. stamp, mark; hallmark; **2.** (rubber-)stamp; **3.** *fig.* stain, stigma; ~ **basmak** to stamp; ~ **pulu** revenue stamp; ~ **resmi** stamp duty; ~ **vurmak** to stamp.

damgalamak 1. to stamp; **2.** *fig.* to brand, to stigmatize.

damgalanmak 1. *pass of* **damgalamak**; **2.** *fig.* to be branded, to be stigmatized.

damgalı 1. stamped, marked; **2.** *fig.* branded, stigmatized.

damıtık distilled.

damıtmak to distil(l).

damız stable.

damızlık 1. animal kept for breeding; **2.** yeast, ferment.

damla 1. drop; MED drops; **2.** bit; **3.** medicine dropper; **4.** paralytic stroke; **5.** gout; ~ ~ drop by drop, little by little, bit by bit; ~ *inmek* (*b-ne*) to have a stroke.

damlalık 1. MED dropper; **2.** eaves-trough; **3.** dripstone.

damlamak 1. to drip, to trickle; **2.** *sl.* to turn up, to show up; *damlaya damlaya göl olur* pro. many a little makes a mickle.

damlatmak to drip, to pour out drop by drop; to distil(l).

damlayakut, -tu fine kind of ruby.

damperli kamyon dump-truck.

damping dumping; ~ *yapmak* to dump.

-dan[1]**1.** from; (out) of; due to, because of; since; **2.** than; **3.** through, by way of, via, by.

-dan[2] [ā] case of, receptacle of.

-dan[3] [ā] who knows.

dan dun! bang! bang!

dana calf; ~ *eti* veal; *-lar gibi bağırmak* to bawl, to shout blue murder; *-nın kuyruğu kopacak! fig.* the crucial moment will come.

danaburnu, -nu ZOO mole cricket.

dandini [x . .] **1.** *expression used when dandling a baby*; **2.** in a mess, untidy; ~ *bebek* childish person.

dangalak F blockhead, boor, dumb, loutish.

dangalaklık F idiocy, stupidity.

dangıl dungul boorish; ~ *konuşmak* to drivel.

danış consultation; conversation.

danışık 1. = *danış*; **2.** mutual agreement.

danışıklı sham, prearranged; ~ *dövüş fig.* **1.** sham fight; **2.** put-up job.

danışma information; inquiry; ~ *bürosu* information office.

danışmak (*bşi b-ne*) **1.** to consult *s.o.* about *s.th.*; **2.** to confer (*about*), to discuss.

danışman adviser, consultant, counselor.

Danıştay Council of State.

Danimarka [. . x .] *pr. n.* Denmark.

Danimarkalı Dane; Danish.

daniska [. x .] F the best, the finest; *-sı* (*bşin*) *sl.* the best of *s.th.*; *o, işin -sını bilir* he knows this from A to Z, he knows the A to Z of this.

dank: beynine (*or* **kafasına**) ~ *demek* (*or* **etmek**) to dawn (**upon**).

dans dance; ~ *etm.* to dance; ~ *salonu* ballroom.

dansör dancer (*man*).

dansöz dancer (*woman*), belly-dancer, danseuse.

dantel(a) lace(-work).

dantelli ornamented with lace.

dapdaracık [x . . .] *emph. of* **dar**(**acık**) very narrow (*or* tight).

dar 1. narrow; tight; **2.** scanty, scant; **3.** *fig.* straits, difficulty; **4.** *fig.* with difficulty, barely, only just; ~ *açı* MATH acute angle; ~ *bogaz fig.* bottle-neck; ~ *hat* narrow-gauge line; ~ *kafalı* narrow-minded; ~ *yetişmek* to cut it fine; *-a bogmak* **1.** to take advantage of s.o.'s difficulties; **2.** to rush, to bring pressure (on); *-da bulunmak* (*or* *kalmak*) to be in financial straits.

dâr dwelling place, house, habitation.

-dar [ā] that has, possesses, holds.

dara [x .] tare; *-sını almak* to deduct the tare (*-ın* of).

daraban [. . -] throbbing, palpitation; pulsation.

daracık *emph. of* **dar** rather narrow (*or* tight).

daradar barely, very narrowly, only just.

darağacı, -nı gallows.

daralmak 1. to narrow, to become narrow (*or* tight); to shrink; **2.** to become scanty; to become restricted (*or* difficult); *vaktimiz daraldı* we are pushed for time.

daraltmak to narrow, to make narrower, to take in (*dress*), to reduce.

darbe blow, stroke; *bir* ~ *indirmek* to strike; *hükümet -si* coup d'état.

darbelemek *mst fig.* to sabotage.

darbetmek [x . .] **1.** to strike, to hit; **2.** to coin (*money*); **3.** to pulsate, to throb, to palpitate.

darbevari [. . - -] MIL abrupt.

darbımesel proverb; ~ *kabilinden* proverbial.

darbuka [. x .] clay drum.

dardağan in utter confusion.

dardarına very narrowly, barely, only just.

dargın angry, irritated, cross, sulky.

darginlık anger, irritability, sulk.

darı BOT 1. millet; 2. P corn, maize; *-sı başınıza!* may your turn come next!, may you follow suit!.

darılgan easily offended (*or* hurt), huffy.

darılmak 1. to be offended (*-e* with), to take offence (*-e* at), to get cross (*-e* with), to get sulky (*-e* with); 2. to resent; 3. to scold; *darılmaca yok!* no offence!

darıltmak to give offence (*-e* to), to offend.

darlaşmak 1. to narrow; 2. to become tight; 3. to be limited, to be in straits.

darlaştırmak 1. to narrow, to make narrow; 2. to restrict.

darlatmak *s.* **darlaştırmak.**

darlık 1. narrowness; 2. *fig.* poverty, need, destitution.

darmadağan, darmadağın in utter confusion, in a terrible mess.

darp, -bı 1. blow; 2. coining (*money*); 3. MUS stroke; 4. MATH multiplication.

darphane mint.

darülaceze [- . . . .] poorhouse, hospice, workhouse.

darülfünun [- . . . -] *obs.* university.

darülharb [- . .] the countries outside the dominion of Islam.

Darüşşafaka [- . . . . -] *pr. n. name of a school for orphans in Istanbul.*

dasnik *sl.* pimp.

-daş *suffix implying fellowship or participation:* **dindaş** coreligionist.

daülfil [- . . -] MED elephantiasis.

daülkelp, -bi [ā] MED rabies, hydrophobia.

daülrakıs, -kısı [- . . . .] MED St. Vitus's dance.

daüssıla [- . . . .] homesickness, nostalgia.

dava 1. suit, lawsuit, action, case; 2. trial; 3. claim; assertion, allegation; complaint; 4. thesis, preposition; matter, cause, problem, question; 5. MATH theorem; problem; *~ başı* main argument; *~ eden* JUR plaintiff, claimant; litigant; *~ edilen* JUR defendant; litigant; *~ etm.* (*b-ni*) to sue for *s.o.*, to bring *s.o.* to court, to go to law against *s.o.*; *~ vekili* lawyer, attorney, barrister.

davacı JUR plaintiff, claimant; litigant.

davalı JUR 1. defendant; 2. litigant; 3. contested, in dispute.

davar 1. sheep *or* goat; 2. sheep *or* goats.

davet, -ti [ā] 1. invitation; 2. party, feast; 3. JUR summons; 4. COM convocation; 5. call; request; *~ etm.* 1. to invite, to call, to summon; to convoke; 2. to provoke; 3. to request; *~ yapmak* to give a party, to feast.

davetiye [ā] 1. invitation card; 2. JUR summons, citation.

davetli invited (guest).

davetname invitation card.

davetsiz uninvited; gatecrasher.

davlumbaz 1. paddlebox; 2. chimney hood; *~ kılıklı fig.* dressed up to the nines, dolled up.

davranış behavio(u)r, attitude.

davranmak 1. to behave, to act; 2. to take action, to set about, to bestir o.s.; 3. to make (for), to reach (for); 4. to take pains.

davudi [- - -] bass (*voice*).

davul drum; *~ çalmak* (*or* **dövmek**) 1. to beat the drum; 2. *fig.* to trumpet, to noise abroad; *~ gibi* swollen; *~ zurna* drum and pipe, with pomp; *-un sesi uzaktan hoş gelir pro.* distance lends enchantment.

davulcu drummer.

Davut, -du *pr. n.* 1. David; 2. *mf.*

dayak 1. beating, hiding, cudgeling, thrashing; 2. MEC prop, support, shore; *~ atmak* (*b-ne*) to give *s.o.* a beating (*or* hiding *or* thrashing); *~ kaçkını* one who deserves a beating; *~ yemek* to get a hiding (*or* beating *or* thrashing).

dayaklık 1. deserving a beating; 2. MEC suitable as a prop.

dayalı 1. leaning (*-e* against); 2. propped up, shored; *~ döşeli* furnished (*house*).

dayamak 1. to lean (*-e* against), to rest (*-e* on); to base (*-e* on); to hold (*-e* against); to draw up (*-e* against); 2. to shore up, to prop up, to support; 3. to present immediately; 4. to thrust resolutely, to fling offensively; 5. *s.* **döşemek.**

dayanak 1. (**noktası**) MIL base; 2. support; 3. PHLS substratum.

dayanıklı strong, resistant, lasting, enduring.

dayanıksız weak, not lasting, not resistant.

dayanıksızlık weakness.

dayanılmaz1. irresistable; **2.** unbearable.

dayanışma solidarity.

dayanışmak to act with solidarity.

dayanmak1. *rare pass. of dayamak*; **2.** to lean (*-e* against, on); to push, to press (*-e* against, on); **3.** to rest, to be based (*-e* on, upon); **4.** to rely (*-e* on, upon), to be backed (by); to confide, to trust (*-e* in); **5.** to resist, to hold out; **6.** to endure, to last; **7.** to bear, to tolerate, to endure, to put up (*-e* with), to support; **8.** (*bir yere*) to reach, to arrive (*-e* in, at), to get (*-e* to); **9.** to step (*-e* on); **10.** to set about s.th. energetically; **11.** to go a long way, to last, to be enough; **12.** to arrive at the door (of); **13.** to be drawn up (*-e* against).

dayatmak 1. *caus. of dayamak*; **2.** to insist (*on*).

dayı 1. maternal uncle; **2.** *sl.* policeman, pig, cop; **3.** protector; **4.** pull, protection; **5.** HIST dey; *-sı dümende* he has a friend at court, he has friends in high places.

dayızade [. . - .] cousin.

daz1. bald(-headed); **2.** bare (*country*).

dazara dazar, dazıra dazır in a great hurry, speedily.

dazlak 1. bald; **2.** bare, barren (*country*); *~ kafalı* bald-headed.

dazlaklık baldness.

de *s. da*; *... se ~* even if, although.

-de *s. a.* **-de, ta, -te.**

debagat *-ti* [. - .] **1.** the trade of a tanner; **2.** tanning.

debarkman MIL disembarkation.

debboy depot.

debdebe splendo(u)r, pomp, display.

debdebeli splendid, magnificent, resplendent, showy.

debelenmek1. to thrash about, to kick about, to fidget about, to flounder; **2.** *fig.* to struggle desperately.

debriyaj MEC clutch; *~ pedalı* clutch pedal.

dede 1. grandfather; **2.** ancestor, forefather; **3.** old man; **4.** sheikh.

Dedeağaç, -cı *pr. n.* Alexandroupolis.

dedik (one's) word, promise, what one says; *dediği ~ olm.* (*b-nin*) to abide by what one says, to be an obstinate fellow.

dedikodu gossip, tittle-tattle; backbit-

ing; *~ etm.* (*or yapmak*) to gossip; to backbite.

dedikoducu gossip, gossiper, backbiter.

dedikodulu gossipy (*news*).

dedirgin unsettled, troubled, stirred up.

def 1. *s. tef*; **2.** *s. defi.*

defa time, turn; *-larca* again and again, repeatedly, time after time; *birkaç ~* on several occasions; *çok ~* often.

defalık *bu ~* for this time.

defetmek [x . .] **1.** to repel, to repulse, to drive away, to push back, to rebuff; **2.** to expel, to eject, to dismiss; **3.** PHYS to repel.

defi, -f'i 1. repulsion, driving away; **2.** PHYS repulsion; **3.** JUR defense; **4.** *rare* refutation; *defi bela kabilinden* F so as to ward off an evil; *defi hacet etm.* to go to the toilet; *defi tabii* bowel movement, stool.

defile fashion show.

defin, -fni interment, burial.

define [ī] **1.** buried treasure; treasure; treasure-trove; **2.** *fig.* unexpected wealth.

definceci [. - . .] treasure-seeker.

deflasyon deflation.

defne [x . .] BOT bay-tree, laurel.

defnetmek [x . .] (*bir yere*) to bury, to inter.

defo flaw.

defolmak [x . .] to piss off, to clear out, to go away, to blow; *defol!* off with you!, piss off!

defolu flawed.

defter1. notebook, exercise book, copybook; **2.** register, inventory; **3.** (account) book; **4.** *-ler* the rolls; **5.** list, catalogue; *~ açmak* to open a subscription list; *~ tutmak* to keep the books; *-e geçirmek* to enter in the book; *defteri âmal isl.* MYTH list of an individual's good and bad acts; *defteri kebir* ledger.

defterdar [ā] **1.** accountant; **2.** HIST minister of finance.

değer 1. value, worth; **2.** price; *~ biçmek* to evaluate, to assess, to assay, to appraise; *~ vermek* to esteem, to appreciate, to respect.

değerbilir appreciative.

değerbilmez inappreciative.

değerlemek to esteem highly, to respect.

değerlendirmek 1. to appraise, to

delege

evaluate, to assess; **2.** to estimate; **3.** to utilize, to turn to (good) account, to put to good use.

değerlenmek 1. *pass. of değerlemek*; **2.** to appreciate, to increase in value.

değerli 1. valuable, precious; **2.** worthy, talented; **3.** estimable.

değersiz worthless, valueless.

değersizlik worthlessness.

değil 1. not; **2.** no; **3.** not only, let alone; **4.** not caring.

değin until, till; **bugüne ~** until today, up to now.

değinmek to touch (-*e* on).

değirmen 1. mill; **2.** grinder, grinding machine; **3.** *sl.* watch.

değirmenci miller, millwright.

değirmentaşı millstone.

değirmi 1. round, circular; **2.** square (*cloth*).

değiş exchange; **~** (*or* **~ tokuş**) etm. (*bşi bşle*) to exchange *s.th.* for *s.th.*, to barter *s.th.* for *s.th.*

değişen changeable; **~ hareket** (*or* **devim**) PHYS irregular motion.

değişici changeable.

değişik 1. different, changed; **2.** novel, original; **3.** varied; **4.** exchanged, substituted.

değişiklik 1. difference; **2.** change, variation, amendment, alteration; **~ olsun diye** for a change.

değişim variation.

değişken 1. changeable, changeful, mutable; **2.** MATH variable.

değişkenlik changeableness, changefulness, mutability.

değişkin modified.

değişmek 1. to change, to alter, to vary, to be replaced; **2.** to substitute; **3.** to exchange, to barter (*ile* for).

değişmez unchangeable, invariable; constant, stable.

değiştirgeç converter; transformer.

değiştirmek 1. to change, to alter, to shift, to modify; **2.** to exchange (*ile* for).

değme 1. contact, touch; **2.** every, any.

değmede [x . .] unlikely.

değmek, (-er) 1. to touch; **2.** to reach, to hit, to attain; **3.** to be worth, to be worthwhile; **4.** (*yüreğine or içine*) to take to heart, to affect.

değnek 1. stick, rod, cane, wand; **2.** thrashing, hiding; **~ yemek** to get the cane.

değneklemek to cane, to give the cane.

deh! giddap!; **~ deyip salıvermek** F to kick out.

deha [ā] genius, sagacity; **~ sahibi** ingenious.

dehakâr [. - -] ingenious.

dehalet, -ti [ā] submission.

-de hali GR locative.

dehlemek 1. to urge on, to drive on (*animal*); **2.** F to send s.o. packing, to fire, to oust, to give s.o. the sack.

dehlenmek 1. to be urged on (*animal*); **2.** F to be fired, to get the sack.

dehliz 1. corridor, entrance-hall; **2.** ANAT ear-passage; vestibule.

dehşet, -ti 1. terror, horror, awe, dread; **2.** marvel(l)ous; **3.** wow!, well, I'm blowed!; **~ saçmak** to horrify, to terrorize.

dehşetli 1. terrible, dreadful, horrible, awful; **2.** marvel(l)ous, formidable, tremendous.

dejenere degenerate; **~ etm.** to make degenerate; **~ olm.** to degenerate.

dejenereleşmek to degenerate.

dek until, as far as.

dekagram MATH decagram.

dekalitre MATH decaliter.

dekametre MATH decameter.

dekan dean (*of a faculty*).

dekanlık 1. deanship; **2.** dean's office.

dekar measure of land (*0.247 acres*).

dekatlon *sports*: decathlon.

deklanşör PHOT trigger, shutter release button.

dekolte 1. low-neck, low-cut, décolleté; **2.** licentious, indecent, immodest; **~ konuşmak** *fig.* not to mince matters.

dekont, -tu statement of account, deduction.

dekor décor, setting; scenery.

dekorasyon decoration.

dekoratif decorative.

dekoratör decorator.

dekorcu (set) designer.

dekovil narrow-gauge railroad.

dekupaj *film*: scenario, *Am.* script.

delalet, -ti 1. guidance; **2.** indication; denotation; signification; **3.** mediation; **~ etm. 1.** to guide (-*e* to); **2.** to show, to indicate, to denote; **... -iyle** through, by the agency of; care of (*c/o*).

deldirmek to have s.th. bored.

delegosyon delegation.

delege delegate, representative.

delgeç punch.

delgi drill, gimlet.

deli 1. mad, insane, lunatic, crazy; **2.** whimsical, eccentric; **3.** foolish, inconsiderate; rash, foolhardy; ~ *alacası* motley, variegated; ~ *baş* obstinate, wil(l)ful; ~ *çıkmak* **1.** to go mad; **2.** *fig.* to fly into a rage, to blow one's top; ~ *divane* crazy (about); wild (about), nuts (over); ~ *etm.* to drive one out of one's wits, to drive s.o. mad; ~ *gibi* like mad, madly; ~ *ırmak* torrential river; ~ *olm.* **1.** to be crazy (-*e* about), to be wild (-*e* about), to be nuts (-*e* over); **2.** to fly into a rage; ~ *saçması* tommy-rot; ~ *pazarı* in a pickle; -*ye dönmek* to throw one's hat in the air.

delibozuk unbalanced, fitful; inconstant.

delice 1. somewhat mad, crazy; **2.** madly, crazily; **3.** crazy, mad (*act*); **4.** wild (*plant*); **5.** (*otu*) BOT darnel, rye grass; ergoted rye.

delicesine 1. madly, crazily; **2.** passionately (*love*).

delidolu indiscreet, inconsiderate, thoughtless, rash, reckless.

deliduman reckless, daredevil, foolhardy.

delifişek unbalanced, flippant, flighty, giddy.

delik 1. hole, opening, orifice; **2.** pierced, bored; **3.** ANAT foramen; **4.** *sl.* prison, cooler, stir, clink, choky; ~ *açmak* to hole, to bore, to pierce; ~ *deşik* full of holes; ~ *deşik etm.* to riddle; *deliğe girmek sl.* to go to clink; *deliğe tıkamak sl.* to put into clink, to jug.

delikanlı youth, young man, youngster.

delikanlılık youth; youthfulness.

delikli 1. holey; **2.** sieve, skimmer, strainer.

delikliler ZOO foraminifera.

deliksiz 1. without a hole; **2.** *fig.* sound (*sleep*); ~ *çıkarmak fig.* to carry out faultlessly.

delil [ī] **1.** JUR proof, evidence; **2.** guide; **3.** indication, sign; ~ *göstermek* to adduce proofs.

delilenmek to become mad, to behave madly, to act crazily.

delilik 1. madness, insanity; mania; **2.** folly, foolishness, eccentricity.

delinmek 1. *pass. of* **delmek**; **2.** to be

holed (*or* perforated); to become worn through; to burst; **3.** to be pierced; **4.** to get a puncture, to be punctured.

deliorman a vast and dense forest.

deliotu BOT alyssum, madwort.

delirmek to go mad, to become insane.

delirtmek to drive mad.

delişmen madcap, spoiled, over-impulsive, flighty, giddy.

delişmenlik impulsiveness, giddiness.

delk, -*ki* PHYS friction.

delme 1. *vn. of* **delmek**; **2.** bored, pierced, perforated, punched; **3.** P waistcoat; ~ *kudreti* MIL penetrating power.

delmek, (-*er*) to hole, to pierce, to bore, to break through (*a.* MIL); *delip geçmek* to pierce through, to penetrate.

delta GEOGR delta.

deltakası ANAT deltoid muscle.

dem¹ blood, hemorrhage; ~ *dökmek* to menstruate.

dem² 1. breath; gust, blast; **2.** time, moment, instant; **3.** alcoholic drink; **4.** sip, draught; ~ *çekmek* **1.** (*of birds*) to warble; **2.** *co.* to drink; ~ *tutmak* MUS to accompany music; ~ *vurmak* (*bşden*) to talk at random about *s.th.*

dem³ steeping; ~ *çekmek* to steep (*tea*); -*i çok* well steeped, strong (*tea*).

demagog demagogue.

demagoji demagogy.

deme 1. *vn. of* **demek**; **2.** meaning; -*m o* ~ *değil* that is not what I mean, that is not my meaning.

demeç statement; speech; -*te bulunmak* to make a statement.

demek¹ 1. to say (-*e* to); **2.** to tell, to mention (-*e* to); **3.** to think, to be of the opinion; **4.** to call, to name; **5.** to mean; *deme yahu!* you don't say so!; oh, don't!; *dememek* not to pay attention, not to heed; *demeye kalmamak* no sooner than, as soon as; *derken* **1.** while saying; **2.** while trying to, when intending to; **3.** just at that moment; then; *desene, desenize* F that means, that is to say, then; *deyip geçmek* to underrate, to underestimate; *diyecek yok* (*bşe*) it's fine, it's OK.

demek², *demek ki* so, thus, in this case, therefore, that means (to say).

demet, -*ti* **1.** bunch, bouquet (*flowers*); **2.** bundle, faggot; **3.** sheaf (*of grain*), wisp; **4.** PHYS bundle (*of rays*); **5.** BOT corymb; ~ ~ in bunches, in sheaves.

demetlemek to bunch, to sheaf.

demevî [ī] full-blooded; sanguine.

demin [x .] just now, a second ago.

demincek [x . .] *emph. of* **demin.**

deminden [x . .] = **demin.**

deminki [x . .] foregoing, of a second ago.

demir 1. iron; **2.** anchor; **3.** iron part of anything; **4.** made of iron; **5.** heel plate; **6.** irons, fetters; **7.** grille (*of a window*); **8.** bar (*of a door*); **9.** ♀ *mf.*; ~ **almak 1.** NAUT to weigh anchor; **2.** F to go away, to hop it; ~ **atmak 1.** NAUT to let go (*or* drop *or* cast) the anchor, to anchor; **2.** *fig.* to overstay one's welcome; ~ **gibi 1.** strong, iron-like; **2.** very cold; ~ **kırı** iron gray (*horse*); ~ **kırıntısı** scrap iron; ~ **leblebi** *fig.* tough (*or* hard) nut to crack; ~ **resmi** anchorage; ~ **taramak** NAUT to drag the anchor; ~ **tavında dövülür** *pro.* strike while the iron is hot; *-de* **yatmak** NAUT to lie at anchor; *-e* **vurmak** to fetter, to chain.

demirbaş 1. furnishings, inventory, fixtures; **2.** old timer, fixture (*person*); **3.** inflexible; obstinate.

demirci blacksmith, iron-monger, *Am.* hardware dealer; ~ **ocağı** smithy, forge.

demircilik 1. ironworking; **2.** hardware business.

demirhane [ā] ironworks, iron-foundry.

demirhindi 1. BOT tamarind; **2.** *sl.* stingy, mean, niggardly.

demiri iron-gray.

demirkapan magnet.

Demirkazık North Star, Polaris, Polestar.

demirlemek 1. to bolt and bar (*door*); **2.** NAUT to anchor.

demirli 1. NAUT anchored, at anchor; **2.** ferriferous, containing iron; **3.** bolted; chained; **4.** barred.

demirlibeton reinforced concrete.

demirpası, *-nı* iron rust (colo(u)r).

demirperde POL Iron Curtain.

demiryeri, *-ni* berth, anchorage, moorage.

demiryol *s.* **demiryolu.**

demiryolcu railwayman.

demiryolculuk railwaymanship.

demiryolu, *-nu* railway, railroad.

demlemek to steep, to brew (*tea*).

demlendirmek *s.* **demlemek.**

demlenmek 1. to be steeped (*tea*); **2.** *co.* to carouse, to imbibe.

demli well steeped, strong (*tea*).

demlik teapot.

demode outmoded, out-of-date, old-fashioned, démodé.

demografi demography.

demokrasi democracy.

demokrat, *-tı* democrat(ic); ♀ *Parti* Democrat Party.

demokratik democratic.

demokratlaşmak to become democratic.

demokratlık democracy.

demontabl MEC demountable.

demontaj MEC disassembly, dismantlement.

demonte disassembly, dismantlement; ~ **etm.** to disassemble, to dismantle.

-den *s.a.* *-dan,* *-tan,* *-ten.*

denaet, *-ti* [ā] baseness, cowardice, meanness, vileness.

denaetkâr mean, vile.

denden ditto mark.

denek 1. *obs.* proved, tried; **2.** PSYCH subject (*of an experiment*).

denektaşı, *-nı* touch-stone.

deneme 1. trial, test, experiment; **2.** essay.

denemeci essayist.

denemek 1. to test, to try, to experiment; to attempt; **2.** to tempt.

denenmek *pass. of* **denemek.**

denet 1. control, supervision; **2.** inspection; audit; **3.** trial projection (*of a finished film*).

denetçi controller, supervisor; inspector, auditor.

denetim 1. control, supervision; **2.** inspection; auditing.

denetlemek to check, to oversee, to supervise, to control.

deney CHEM, PHYS test, experiment.

deneyim experimentation.

deneykap CHEM test tube.

deneysel experimental; empirical.

deneyselcilik experimentalism; empiricism.

deneyüstü PHLS transcendental.

denge balance, equilibrium.

dengelemek to balance, to equilibrate, to stabilize.

dengeli balanced; stable, stabilized.

dengesiz unbalanced, out of balance; unstable.

-den hali GR ablative.

deni [ī] *rare* base, despicable, vile.

denilmek *pass. of* **demek 1.** to be said; **2.** to be called, to be named; **denilen** so-called, would-be.

deniz 1. sea; ocean; **2.** maritime, marine, naval, nautical; **3.** waves; high sea; swell; **4.** *fig.* expanse, tract; ~ **baskını** high tide; tidal wave, tsunami; ~ **birliği** naval unit; ~ **buzulu** ice floe; ~ **feneri** lighthouse; ~ **kurdu** *fig.* old salt, sea dog; ~ **kuvvetleri** naval forces; ~ **mili** nautical (*or* sea) mile; ~ **sigortası** maritime insurance; ~ **subayı** naval officer; ~ **tutmak** (*b-ni*) to get seasick; ~ **üssü** naval base; ~ **yolları** maritime lines; *-de* **balık** *fig.* a bird in the bush; *-de* **kum, onda para** he is lousy with money, he has got pots of money; *-den bir* **avuç su gibi** like a drop in the bucket (*or* ocean); *-den çıkmış balığa dönmek* to feel like a fish out of water; *-e düşen yılana sarılır* pro. a drowning man will clutch at a straw.

denizaltı, -nı 1. submarine; **2.** submerged; **3.** deep-sea (*current*).

denizaltıcı submariner.

denizanası ZOO jellyfish, medusa.

denizaşırı overseas.

denizatı, -nı ZOO seahorse.

denizayısı, -nı ZOO manatee, sea cow.

denizbilim GEOGR oceanography.

denizcöceği ZOO shrimp.

denizci seaman, sailor.

denizcilik 1. navigation, sailing; **2.** seamanship.

denizçakısı, -nı ZOO razor clam.

denizçulluğu, -nu ZOO sanderling.

denizdanteli, -ni ZOO millepore.

denizel GEOGR marine; naval.

denizgergedanı, -nı ZOO narwhal.

deniziğnesi, -ni ZOO European pipe-fish.

denizineği, -ni ZOO sea cow.

denizkaplumbağası, -nı ZOO sea turtle.

denizkestanesi, -ni ZOO sea urchin.

denizkırlangıcı, -nı ZOO tern.

denizkızı, -nı MYTH mermaid, siren, nixie, nymph.

denizkulağı, -nı lagoon.

denizsel GEOGR maritime.

denizyıldızı, -nı starfish.

denk, -gi 1. bale; **2.** in equilibrium, equal, balanced; **3.** suitable; match; **4.** MATH equivalent; **5.** counterpoise;

trim; ~ **etm. 1.** to balance, to equilibrate; **2.** NAUT to trim (*a boat*); ~ **gelmek** to balance, to be in equipoise; to be suitable, to be timely; **dengiyle karşılamak** to retaliate, to pay s.o. in his own (*or* the same) coin, to reciprocate.

denklem MATH equation.

denklemek 1. to make up in bales, to tie up; **2.** to balance.

denkleşmek to become well balanced, to be in equilibrium.

denkleştirmek 1. to bring into balance, to equalize; **2.** to find, to put together (*money*).

denli tractable, tactful; ~ **densiz söz söylemek** to talk out of turn, to speak offhandedly.

denmek *pass. of* **demek.**

densiz tactless, lacking in manners.

densizleşmek to become tactless.

densizlik tactlessness.

denyo *sl.* fool, ass, idiot.

deontoloji deontology.

depar flying start.

deplasman: ~ **maçı** away match.

depo [x .] **1.** depot; **2.** store, warehouse; ~ **etm.** to store.

depocu warehouseman; stockman.

depolamak to store.

depozit(o) deposit, security.

deppoy *s.* **debboy.**

deprem earthquake; ~ **bölgesi** seismic zone.

deprembilim seismology.

depremyazar seismograph.

depresyon PSYCH depression.

depreşmek to move, to rise, to reappear.

depreştirmek to stir, to reawaken, to renew.

derakap [x . .] instantly, immediately afterwards.

derayman derailment; ~ **etm.** to derail (*train*).

derbeder 1. vagrant, tramp, vagabond; **2.** untidy, slovenly, disorderly, irregular.

derbederlik vagrancy, vagabondage.

derbent, -di defile, pass.

dercetmek [x . .] to insert, to include.

derç, -ci insertion, inclusion.

derdetmek [x . .] to grieve.

dere 1. brook, runnel, rivulet, stream, creek; **2.** valley; ~ **tepe** up hill and down dale; ~ **tepe demeyip** over hedge and ditch; *-den tepeden ko-*

nuşmak to have a chitchat, to have a small talk.

derebeyi, -ni 1. feudal lord; **2.** *fig.* bully, tyrant.

derebeylik 1. local despotate; **2.** feudalism.

derece 1. degree, grade; **2.** stage, step, stair, rank; **3.** F thermometer; **4.** so ... (that); ~ ~ by degrees, gradually.

derecelenmek to become graded.

dereceli graded.

dereke *rare* low stratum.

dereotu, -nu BOT dill.

dergâh dervish convent.

dergi magazine, periodical, review.

derhal [x .] at once, immediately, right away.

deri 1. skin, hide; **2.** leather; **3.** peel, rind; **-sine sığmaz** *fig.* he is too big for his boots; **-sini yüzmek 1.** to skin, to flay; **2.** *fig.* to strip, to rob; **3.** to torture to death.

derialtı, -nı ANAT subcutaneous.

deribilim dermatology.

derici leather dealer.

dericilik leather trade.

derilenmek to heal up (*wound*).

derin 1. deep; depth; **2.** profound; ~ ~ deeply, soundly (*sleep*); ~ ~ **dalmak** to be plunged in thought; ~ ~ **düşünmek** to be in a brown study; ~ **saygılarımı sunarım** yours faithfully, very truly yours.

derinlemesine, derinliğine in depth, deeply.

derinleşmek 1. to deepen, to get deep; **2.** to specialize (-*de* in); **3.** to fade away with distance (*sound*).

derinleştirmek to deepen (*a. fig.*).

derinlik 1. depth; deepness; depths; **2.** profundity; **3.** PHOT depth of focus.

derişik concentrated.

derk, -ki *rare* comprehension.

derkenar [ā] marginal note, postscript.

derleme 1. compilation, miscellany; **2.** collected, selected; **3.** anthology.

derlemek to compile, to collect, to gather; ~ **toplamak** to tidy up, *Am.* to straighten up, to put in order, to clear away.

derlenmek 1. *pass. of* **derlemek**; **2.** to compose o.s., to pull o.s. together; **derlenip toplanmak 1.** to pull o.s. together, to compose o.s.; **2.** to get ready.

derleyici compiler; anthologist.

derli toplu tidy, in order; well coordinated.

derman [ā] **1.** strength, energy, power; **2.** remedy, cure, medicine; ~ **aramak** to seek a remedy; ~ **bulmak** to find a remedy (-*e* for); ~ **olm.** to be a remedy, to cure (-*e* for); **-ım yok** I am bushed.

dermansız [ā] **1.** exhausted, feeble, weak, bushed; **2.** incurable, irremediable.

dermansızlaşmak to get feeble.

dermansızlık 1. exhaustion, feebleness; **2.** incurability, debility.

derme 1. *vn. of* **dermek**; **2.** collection; **3.** gathered, compiled, collected; ~ **çatma 1.** hastily put up, jerry-built; **2.** scraps, odds and ends.

dermek to pick (*flower*), to gather, to compile, to pick up.

dermeyan [ā] *rare* in the midst, under discussion; ~ **etm.** to put forward.

dernek association, club, society.

derpiş etm. [ī] to put forward, to consider, to bear in mind, to take into consideration.

ders 1. lesson, class, lecture; **2.** warning, example, moral; ~ **almak 1.** to take lessons (-*den* from); **2.** to learn a lesson (-*den* by); **3.** to take warning (-*den* from); ~ **anlatmak** to give a lesson, to teach, to lecture; ~ **çalışmak** to study; ~ **kitabı** textbook, schoolbook; ~ **odası** classroom; **-i asmak** to cut a class, to skip class; **bu sana** ~ **olsun** let this be a warning to you.

dershane [ā] **1.** classroom, schoolroom; **2.** private institute offering specialized courses.

dert, -di 1. pain, suffering, disease, illness, malady; **2.** trouble, sorrow, grief, cares, worries, affliction, woe; annoyance, grievance; **3.** tumo(u)r, boil; ~ **çekmek** to suffer; ~ **dökmek** to unbosom o.s.; ~ **ortağı** confidant, fellow-sufferer; ~ **yanmak** *fig.* to unbosom o.s.; **derde girmek** to get into trouble, to get into hot water; **derdine düşmek** (*bşin*) to be quite taken up with *s.th.*; **derdini dökmek** to unbosom o.s., to air one's grievances.

dertlenmek to be pained (**by**), to be sorry (**because of**), to have troubles.

dertleşmek to have a heart-to-heart talk (*ile* with).

dertli 1. pained; sorrowful, wretched; **2.** aggrieved, complaining; **3.**

troubled.

dertop: ~ **etm.** to gather together; ~ **olm.** to roll into a ball.

dertsiz untroubled, free from trouble.

derttaş confidant.

deruhte etm. to undertake, to take upon o.s.

derun [ū] *rare* inside, interior; mind, soul, heart.

deruni [. - -] *rare* **1.** internal, inner; **2.** cordial, sincere.

derviş 1. dervish; **2.** *fig.* humble, contented, tolerant; *-in fikri ne ise, zikri de odur* he has a bee in his bonnet; *sabreden* ~ *muradına ermiş* everything comes to him who waits.

dervişmeşrep, -bı unconventional; tolerant, modest.

derya [ā] **1.** sea, ocean; **2.** *fig.* very learned man.

desen 1. design; ornament; **2.** drawing.

desenli figured.

desigram decigram.

desilitre deciliter.

desimetre decimeter.

desinatör stylist.

desise [ī] trick, intrigue, device, plot; ~ **çevirmek** to plot, to intrigue, to trick.

despot, -tu despot(ic).

despothane office and residence of a despot.

despotluk despotism.

dessas [ā] trickster, intriguer.

destan [ā] **1.** story, legend, epic; **2.** ballad, song; ~ **olm.** *contp.* to become very famous.

destanlaşmak to become legendary.

destar [ā] turban.

deste 1. bunch, bouquet; packet; wisp; **2.** a quire of paper; **3.** handle, hilt; ~ **başı** choice specimen put on the top of a package of goods; ~~ in bunches; in packets; by dozens.

destek 1. support; **2.** prop; beam; **3.** NAUT crutch; **4.** MIL reinforcement; ~ **vurmak** to put a prop (-e to), to prop up, to shore up.

desteklemek 1. to support, to prop, to shore up; **2.** to root for (*a team*).

destekli supported, propped up.

destelemek to bundle (up).

destroyer [. x .] destroyer.

destur [ū] **1.** permission; leave; **2.** *int.* by your leave!, make way!, gangway!

desturun [x . .] begging your pardon!

deşarj discharge; ~ **olm. 1.** to be discharged; **2.** *fig.* to unbosom o.s.

deşelemek to scratch up.

deşik 1. pierced, burst open; **2.** hole; **3.** *s.* **delik deşik.**

deşilmek 1. *pass. of* **deşmek**; **2.** to be lanced, to open.

deşmek 1. to lance (*boil*); **2.** *fig.* to open up, to rake up (*a painful subject*); **3.** to dig up, to dig into.

detay detail.

detektif detective.

detektör ELECT detector.

deterjan detergent.

determinant MATH determinant.

determinizm determinism.

dev 1. ogre; demon, fiend, devil; **2.** giant; gigantic; ~ **gibi** gigantic, huge, enormous.

deva [ā] remedy, cure, medicine.

devali [. - -] MED varicose.

devalüasyon devaluation.

devam [ā] **1.** continuation, permanence; **2.** duration; **3.** attendance, frequenting; **4.** constancy, assiduity; **5.** *int.* go on!; ~ **etm. 1.** to go on, to last; to continue, to keep on; to carry on, to go on (-e with); **2.** to attend, to follow (*classes*); **3.** to extend (-den, -e kadar from, to); **4.** to persevere; ~ **eden** on-going; *-ı var* to be continued.

devamlı [ā] **1.** continuous, lasting, steady, unbroken, uninterrupted; **2.** constant, assiduous; regular; ~ **sulh** continuous peace.

devamlılık continuity; assiduousness.

devamsız 1. discontinuous; **2.** inconstant; **3.** irregular (*in attendance*).

devamsızlık discontinuity; absenteeism.

devasa [. - -] *rare* gigantic, giant-like.

devaynası, -nı convex (*or magnifying*) mirror.

deve ZOO camel; ~ **gibi** huge and awkward; ~ **kini** *fig.* deep-seated ranco(u)r; ~ **olm.** F to disappear (*money, etc.*); ~ **yapmak** *co.* to embezzle; ~ **yürekli** coward; *-de kulak* a drop in the bucket (*or ocean*).

devebağırtan *fig.* steep and stony road.

deveci 1. camel driver, cameleer; **2.** camel owner.

devedikeni BOT thistle.

devekuşu, -nu ZOO ostrich.

develope etm. PHOT to develop.

deveran [ā] **1.** rotation, circulation; **2.** revolution; ~ **etm.** to circulate, to rotate.

deveranıdem blood circulation.

devetabanı, nı BOT philodendron, monstera.

devetımarı, -nı *fig.* superficial.

devetüyü 1. camel hair; **2.** camel colo(u)red.

devim BIOL, PHYS movement, motion, flux.

devingen mobile, dynamic, active.

devinim movement, motion, action.

devinmek to move.

devir, -vri 1. period, epoch, era; **2.** cycle, rotation; **3.** circuit, circumference, periphery; **4.** tour, turn, revolution; **5.** transfer, turning over; **devri âlem seyahati** globe-trotting.

devirli periodic.

devirmek 1. to overturn, to knock down, to turn over; **2.** to overthrow, to throw down; **3.** to upset, to capsize; **4.** to tilt to one side; **5.** to drink down, to toss off, to drink to the dregs **6.** to read from cover to cover (*a book*).

devlet, -ti 1. state; government; power; **2.** prosperity, success, good luck; ~ **adamı** statesman; ~ **başkanı** president; ~ **hazinesi** state treasury, Exchequer; ~ **hizmeti** government (*or* public *or* civil) service; ~ **kuşu** windfall, unexpected good luck; ~ **memuru** civil servant. government official: ~ **reisi** head of state: ~ **tahvili** state bond; **-le!** good luck to you!

devletçe on the part of the government.

devletçi partisan of state control, favo(u)ring state control, etatist.

devletçilik etatism, state control.

devletleştirmek to nationalize, to collectivize.

devralmak to take over.

devran [ā] **1.** time, age, epoch; **2.** fate, wheel of fortune; ~ **sürmek** to live happily in prosperity.

devre 1. period; term, epoch; **2.** session (*of Parliament*); **3.** cycle; **4.** ELECT circuit; **5.** *sports*: half time.

devren [x .] as a sublet, as a sublease, by cession. by continuation of the present contract: ~ **kiralık** subletting.

devretmek [x . .] **1.** to turn over, to transfer (-*e* to); **2.** to sublet.

devri 1. rotatory; **2.** CHEM, MATH periodic(al), cyclical.

devrik 1. folded, turned over; **2.** inverted (*sentence*) **3.** overthrown; ~ **yaka** turn-down collar.

devrilmek 1. *pass. of* **devirmek**; **2.** to be overturned; to capsize; to be overthrown (*government*).

devrim 1. revolution; reform; **2.** folding; curve, bend.

devrimci revolutionary, revolutionist.

devrimcilik revolutionism.

devrisi = **ertesi**.

devriye 1. anniversary; **2.** beat, patrol, police round; ~ **arabası** patrol car; ~ **gezmek** to go the rounds, to walk the beat, to patrol.

devşirmek 1. to collect, to pick, to gather; **2.** to fold, to roll up.

devvar [ā] revolving, rotating; ~ **köprü** swing-bridge.

deyim idiom, phrase, expression.

deyiş 1. way of speaking; **2.** a kind of folk song; poem; **3.** expression; statement, report.

deyyus [ū] pander, cuckold.

dezenfekte disinfected; ~ **etm.** to disinfect.

dılı, -l'ı 1. *geom.* side; **2.** ANAT rib.

dımdızlak [x . .] **1.** naked, bare, nude; **2.** destitute; empty-handed; **3.** *sl.* stony-broke.

dırdır grumbling; nagging; ~ **etm.** to nag, to grumble.

dırdırcı nag, nagger, grumbler, carper.

dırdırlanmak to murmur, to babble, to grouch, to mutter to o.s.

dırıltı 1. grumbling, snarling; **2.** squabble; ~ **çıkarmak** to cause a squabble.

dırlanmak to complain, to talk annoyingly, to gripe.

dırlaşmak to squabble in undertones.

dış 1. outside, exterior; **2.** outer space; **3.** external, outer; **4.** foreign; **5.** *geom.* circumscribed; ~ **haberler** foreign news: ~ **hat 1.** external line; **2.** international line (*a.* TELEPH); ~ **kapının dış mandalı** *fig.* a very distant relative; ~ **lastik** MOT tyre, *Am.* tire, casing; ~ **taraf** outside; ~ **ticaret** foreign trade.

dışadönük PSYCH extrovert.

dışalım importation.

dışarı 1. out; outside, exterior; **2.** outdoor; out of doors; **3.** provinces; the country; **4.** abroad, foreign lands; ~ **gitmek 1.** to go out; **2.** to go abroad; **-da** outside; abroad; **-dan** from the outside; from abroad; **-ya** abroad; towards the outside.

dışbükey convex.

dışderi 1. ectoderm; **2.** BOT exodermis.

dışık CHEM scoria.

dışişleri, -ni POL foreign (*or* external) affairs; ♀ **Bakanlığı** Ministry of Foreign Affairs.

dışkı feces.

dışkılık cloaca.

dışmerkez GEOL epicenter.

dışmerkezli *geom.* eccentric.

dışplazma BIOL ectoplasm.

dışsatım exportation.

dız buzz, hum, whizz; **~ etm.** to buzz, to hum, to whizz.

dızdız 1. = **dız; 2.** *sl.* swindling, trickery.

dızlanmak to keep on humming to o.s.

diba [- -] brocade; silk tissue.

dibek large stone *or* wooden mortar; **~ kahvesi** coffee ground in a mortar.

Dicle *pr. n.* Tigris.

didaktik 1. didactic; **2.** didactics.

didik teased out, pulled to shreds; **~ ~ etm. 1.** *s.* **didiklemek; 2.** to pull to pieces; **~ ~ doğramak** to shred, to cut to shreds.

didiklemek 1. to tear to pieces; **2.** to pick into fibers and shreds; **3.** to put in disorder.

didinmek 1. to toil, to wear o.s. out; **2.** to fret.

didişmek to scrap, to scuffle, to quarrel, to bicker (*ile* with).

diferansiyel MOT differential gear.

difteri diphtheria.

diftong GR diphthong.

diğer 1. other, another; different; **2.** next, succeeding; **~ taraftan** on the other hand.

dijital digital; **~ fotoğraf** digital photo; **~ fotoğraf makinesi** digital camera; **~ gösterici** digital projector; **~ kablo** digital cable.

dik 1. perpendicular; **2.** upright, straight, stiff; **3.** steep; **4.** fixed, intent, penetrating (*look*); **5.** *geom.* right; **6.** obstinate, contrary; **~ açı** MATH right angle; **~ aşağı** straight down; **~ baş(lı)** pig-headed, obstinate; **~ ~ bakmak** to stare (-*e* at), to glare (-*e* at), to gaze (-*e* at), to look daggers; **~ ~ cevap vermek** to retort, to answer back; **~ dörtgen** MATH rectangle; **~ kafalı** pig-headed, obstinate, cussed; **~ üçgen** *geom.* right triangle; **-ine dalan uçak** dive-bomber; **-ine gitmek** (*b-nin*) to do just the opposite of what one is asked for; to be pig-headed; **-ine tıraş 1.** shaving against the grain; **2.** F utterly boring talk.

diken 1. thorn; spine; **2.** sting; **3.** thorn-bush; **4.** *fig.* obstacle, hindrance; **~ üstünde oturmak** *fig.* to be on tenterhooks.

dikence ZOO stickleback.

dikendudu, -nu BOT blackberry.

dikenli thorny, prickly; **~ tel** barbed wire.

dikensi spinoid, spinelike.

dikensiz without thorns; spineless; **~ gül olmaz** there is no rose without a thorn.

dikey *geom.* vertical, perpendicular.

dikici 1. cobbler, shoe-repairer; **2.** tailor.

dikili 1. sewn; stitched; **2.** planted, set; **3.** erected, set up.

dikilitaş obelisk.

dikilmek 1. *pass. of* **dikmek; 2.** to stand stiff, to post to o.s., to plant o.s.; **3.** to become erect (*penis*).

dikim *vn. of* **dikmek** sewing; planting; **~ evi** (*or* **yurdu**) sewing workshop; **~ zamanı** planting time.

dikimhane [ā] = **dikim evi.**

dikine vertically, upright.

dikiş *vn. of* **dikmek** *part.* **1.** sewing, stitching; seam; **2.** ANAT suture: **3.** gulp: **~ dikmek** to sew; **~ iğnesi** sewing needle; **~ kaynağı** MEC welding seam; **~ kutusu** sewing box; **~ makinesi** sewing machine; **~ yeri 1.** seam; **2.** MED stitch scars.

dikişçi seamstress, dressmaker.

dikişli sewed, stitched; spliced.

dikişsiz seamless.

dikit GEOL stalagmite.

dikiz *sl.* peeping, look; **~ aynası** rear view mirror; **~ etm.** (*or* **geçmek**) to peep.

dikizci *sl.* peeping Tom, voyeur.

dikizlemek *sl.* to peep.

dikkat, -ti 1. attention, care; **2.** take care!, look out!; **~ çekmek** to attract attention, to call attention (-*e* to); **~ etm. 1.** to pay attention (-*e* to), to note, to notice, to mind; **2.** to be careful (-*e* with); **~ kesilmek** to be all ears; **-e almak** to take note (-*i* of), to take into consideration; **-e şayan** note-worthy, remarkable; **-i çekmek** to attract attention.

dikkatle carefully, with care.

dikkatli attentive, careful, painstaking; **-ce** carefully, attentively.

dikkatsiz careless, inattentive; thoughtless.

dikkatsizlik carelessness, inattentiveness; thoughtlessness.

diklenmek, dikleşmek 1. to become steep; **2.** to get stubborn; **3.** to stand erect.

dikme 1. vn. of **dikmek**; **2.** geom. perpendicular; **3.** seedling; **4.** derrick; prop; **5.** pole, post.

dikmek, (-er) 1. to sew; to stitch; **2.** to set up, to erect; **3.** to plant; **4.** to stare, to fix (eyes); **5.** to prick up (ears); **6.** to drain, to drink off; **7.** to station (a guard); **8.** to build, to construct, to put up; **9.** to set down (a ball) for play.

diksiyon diction; intonation.

dikta dictate.

diktafon dictaphone.

diktatör dictator.

diktatörlük dictatorship.

dikte dictation; ~ **etm. 1.** to dictate (letter); **2.** fig. to dictate to, to force (up-) on (order).

dil 1. tongue; **2.** language; dialect; **3.** GEOGR promontory, spit; **4.** MEC bolt (of a lock); **5.** MEC tenon (of a mortise); **6.** NAUT sheave (of a block or pulley); **7.** index (of a balance); **8.** reed (of a wind instrument); **9.** MIL prisoner of war captured for interrogation; ~ **çıkarmak** to put one's tongue out; ~ **dalaşı** quarrel; ~ **dökmek** to talk s.o. round (or over); ♀ **Devrimi** Language Reform; ~ **sürçmesi** slip of the tongue; ♀, **Tarih ve Coğrafya Fakültesi** pr. n. the College of Languages, History and Geography; ~ **uzatmak** to assail (with), to malign, to defame; **-e** (or **-lere**) **düşmek** to become a subject of common talk, to be on everyone's tongue; **-e düşürmek** to set tongues (or chins or beards) wagging; **-e getirmek 1.** to cause to talk; **2.** to express, to give utterance to; **-e kolay** easier said than done; **-e vermek** to divulge, to denounce; **-i çözülmek** to find one's tongue; **-i dolaşmak** to mumble, to stumble; **-i ensesinden çekilsin!** may his tongue be pulled out; **-i kayıyor** he is making a slip of the tongue; **-i tutuk** tongue-tied; **-i uzun** impudent, insolent; **-imin ucunda** on the tip of my tongue; **-inde tüy bitmek** to talk till one is blue in the face; **-inden düşürmemek** to keep on and on (-i about); **-ine dolamak** to keep on and on (-i about); **-ini kesmek** to shut up; to silence; **-ini tutmak** to hold one's

tongue (or peace); **-ini yutmak** to have lost one's tongue; **-inin altında bir bakla** (or **şey**) **var** there is s.th. he hasn't come out with yet; **-inin ucunda olm.** to have s.th. on the tip of one's tongue; **-lerde dolaşmak** to be the subject of common gossip.

dilak ANAT clitoris.

dilaltı, -nı 1. sublingual, hypoglossal; **2.** pip (in fowls).

dilbalığı, -nı zoo sole.

dilbasan MED spatula.

dilbaz [ā] eloquent.

dilber beautiful, beloved.

dilberdudağı, -nı a kind of Turkish pastry.

dilbilgisi, -ni grammar.

dilbilim linguistics.

dilci linguist.

dilcik 1. BOT ligula; **2.** = **dilak**; **3.** = **kurbağacık 4**; **4.** pip (of fowl); **5.** P uvula.

dilek 1. wish, desire; **2.** request, petition, demand; ~ **kipleri** GR optatives; ~ **şart kipi** GR conditional optative; **-te bulunmak** to make a wish.

dilekçe petition, formal request.

dilekçi petitioner.

dilemek 1. to wish (for), to desire, to long (for); **2.** to ask (for), to beg, to request; **özür**~ to ask pardon, to apologize.

dilenci beggar, cadger; ~ **değneğine dönmek** to become a bag of bones; ~ **vapuru** steamer that stops at every port of call; **-ye hıyar vermişler de, eğri diye beğenmemiş** beggars can't be choosers.

dilencilik begging, beggary, mendicancy.

dilenmek 1. pass. of **dilemek**; **2.** to beg, to cadge; **3.** to ask (for), to plead (for).

dilhâh rare heart's desire, beloved object.

di'li: ~ **geçmiş zaman** GR past tense.

dilim 1. slice; strip; **2.** leaf (of a radiator); ~ ~ in slices, in strips.

dilimlemek to cut into slices, to slice.

dilinim GEOL cleavage.

dillemek rare **1.** to touch or lick with the tongue; **2.** fig. to backbite, to censure.

dillenmek 1. pass. of **dillemek 2.** to loosen one's tongue, to begin to talk; **3.** to become chatty; **4.** to be on everyone's tongue.

dilleşmek to chat.

dilli 1. ... tongued; **2.** bolted; sheaved;

3. *fig.* talkative, chatty.
dillidüdük 1. talkative, chatterbox, windbag; **2.** reed whistle.
dilmek to slice, to cut into slices.
dilsel lingual, linguistic.
dilsiz 1. dumb, mute; **2.** *fig.* docile, easygoing; **~ kaval** German flute.
dilsizlik dumbness.
dimağ brain, mind; intelligence.
dimağçe ANAT cerebellum.
dimaği [. - -] cerebral.
dimdik [x .] *emph. of dik part.* bolt upright, erect, stiff.
din¹ PHYS dyne.
din² religion; belief, faith; creed; **-i bir uğruna** for the sake of Islam; **-i bütün** religious; **hay -ine yandığım!** the cursed!, damned!
dinamik dynamic(s).
dinamit dynamite.
dinamitlemek to dynamite.
dinamizm dynamism.
dinamo dynamo.
dinar dinar.
dincelmek to become vigorous, to recover one's strength.
dinci [- .] clerical.
dincierki theocracy.
dinç 1. vigorous, robust; **2.** calm, untroubled.
dinçleşmek to become robust.
dinçleştirmek to strengthen, to invigorate.
dinçlik vigo(u)r, vivacity, robustness.
dindar [- -] religious, pious, devout, godly, god-fearing.
dindarlık religiousness, devotion, piety, godliness.
dindaş [ī] coreligionist.
dindışı secular, temporal, civil.
dindirmek to stop (*pain, etc.*); to slake (*thirst*).
dineri [. x .] diamonds.
dingil MEC axle, axletree.
dingildemek 1. to rattle, to wobble; to sway; **2.** to tremble (*with fear*).
dingin 1. calm; **2.** CHEM inactive; **3.** inactive (*volcano*); **4.** exhausted, bushed.
dinginleşmek to calm down, to get calm.
dinginlik calm, quietness.
dini [- -] religious; pertaining to religion; **~ ayin** divine service; **~ nikâh** ecclesiastical wedding.
dinleme *vn. of dinlemek part.* auscultation; **~ aleti** MED stethoscope; **~ hiz-**

meti MIL listening service.
dinlemek 1. to listen (*-i* to), to hear; **2.** to pay attention (*-i* to); to obey, to conform (*-i* to); **3.** to auscultate.
dinlence 1. restful thing; **2.** holiday, vacation.
dinlendirici relaxing.
dinlendirmek 1. to (let) rest; **2.** to leave (*a field*) fallow; **3.** to set aside; **4.** to put out (*fire, light, etc.*).
dinlenme rest, relaxation; **~ kamçı** holiday camp; **~ yeri** resort, vacation place; road house; **~ yurdu** recreation home.
dinlenmek 1. *pass. of dinlemek*; **2.** to rest, to relax; **3.** to be set aside (*wine, etc.*).
dinletmek *caus. of dinlemek* to have s.o. listen *or* obey; **k-ni ~** to make o.s. heard.
dinleyici listener; **-ler** audience.
dinmek, (**-er**) to stop, to cease, to leave off (*rain, etc.*); to die down, to get better, to calm down, to pass off (*pain*).
dinöncesi prereligion, preanimism.
dinsel religious, pertaining to religion.
dinsiz [- .] **1.** irreligious, ungodly, impious, unbelieving, atheistic; **2.** cruel, tyrant; **-in hakkından imansız gelir** *pro.* set a thief to catch a thief, take hair of dog that bit you, an old poacher makes the best keeper.
dinsizlik 1. irreligion, atheism; **2.** cruelty.
dip, -bi 1. bottom; foot, lowest part; **2.** the far end, back; **~ göstermek** (*or sömürmek*) to drink to the dregs; **dibinden budamak 1.** to cut from the bottom; **2.** to nip in the bud; **dibine darı ekmek** to use up, to finish off.
dipçik butt (*of a rifle*).
dipçiklemek to club with a rifle butt.
dipdiri [x . .] **1.** full of life, energetic, active; **2.** shapely; **3.** fresh.
dipkoçanı, -nı stub, counterfoil.
diplemek *sl.* to flunk, to fail (*in school*).
diploma [. x .] diploma, certificate; degree.
diplomalı graduate; qualified.
diplomasız 1. having no diploma; **2.** without a license.
diplomasi diplomacy.
diplomat, -tı diplomat.
diplomatik diplomatic.
dipnot footnote.
dipsiz 1. bottomless; **2.** *fig.* unfounded,

false; **3.** unfathomable; ~ **kile boş ambar 1.** he spends everything he gets; **2.** it will never be of any use; ~ **testi** *fig.* spendthrift, squanderer.

dirayet, -ti [ā] **1.** ability; **2.** skillfulness; **3.** perception, discernment.

dirayetli 1. capable, effective; **2.** skillful; **3.** perceptive.

dirayetsiz 1. incapable; **2.** unskilled; **3.** imperceptive.

direk 1. pole, post; **2.** mast; **3.** beam, rafter; **4.** column, pillar; **5.** *football*: goalpost, crossbar; **6.** *fig.* pillar, mainstay; ~ **bağırmak** to shout at the top of one's voice; **ailenin direği** mainstay of the family.

direksiyon 1. steering-wheel; **2.** *fig.* guidance; ~ **boşluğu** play in the steering; **-da** at the wheel; **-u idare etm.** to steer, to drive; **-u kırmak** to swerve.

direkt, -ti 1. direct, nonstop; **2.** directly.

direktif directive, instruction, order.

direktör director; principal.

direktörlük directorship.

diremek 1. to support, to hold up, to sustain; **2.** to resist.

diren pitchfork.

direnç PHYS resistance.

dirençli 1. resistant; **2.** tough.

dirençsiz having low resistance.

dirençsizlik low resistance.

direnek MIL bulwark.

direngen stubborn, obstinate.

direngenlik obstinacy.

direniş 1. resistance, opposition; **2.** boycott.

direnme 1. resistance; **2.** persistence.

direnmek 1. to insist (*-de* on); **2.** to resist, to hold out; **3.** to put one's foot down.

direşken persistent, determined, insistent.

direşmek P **1.** to persevere; to be determined; **2.** to resist.

diretmek to put one's foot down, to insist (*-de* on), to show obstinacy.

direy fauna.

dirgen *s.* **diren.**

dirhem drachma; **k-ni** ~ ~ **satmak** to make a great show of reluctance.

diri 1. alive, living; **2.** vigorous, lively, energetic; **3.** fresh; **4.** undercooked; rare.

diriksel animal, physiological.

dirilik 1. life, liveliness; **2.** freshness.

diriliş revival, invigoration; resurgence.

dirilmek 1. to come (*or* return) to life; **2.** to be revived, to gain fresh vigo(u)r.

diriltmek to revive, to bring to life.

dirim life.

dirlik 1. peace, peaceful coexistence; **2.** affluence; ~ **düzenlik** harmony in social relations, peace; ~ **vermemek** (*b-ne*) to give *s.o.* no rest.

dirliksiz cantankerous, cross.

dirsek 1. elbow; **2.** bend, turn (*in a line, road or river*); **3.** (*pipe*) elbow; **4.** NAUT prop; ~ **çevirmek** (*b-ne*) *fig.* to drop *s.o.* socially, to throw *s.o.* over; ~ **çürütmek** to study long and hard.

dirseklemek to elbow.

disiplin discipline.

disiplinli disciplined.

disiplinsiz undisciplined.

disk, -ki 1. *sports*: discus; ~ **atma** throw the discus; **2.** record; **3.** MEC disk; ~ **sürücü** IT disk drive.

diskalifiye disqualified; ~ **etm.** to disqualify; ~ **olm.** to be disqualified.

diskotek, -ği 1. discotheque; **2.** collection of recorded music.

dispanser dispensary.

distribütör ELECT distributor.

diş 1. tooth; **2.** tusk; **3.** tooth (*of a saw, comb*); **4.** cog (*of a wheel*); **5.** ward (*of a key*); **6.** thread (*of a screw*); **7.** clove (*of garlic*); **8.** head (*of cloves*); **9.** *sl.* dope, hashish; ~ **ağrısı** toothache; ~ **bakımı** dental care; ~ **bilemek** (*b-ne*) to watch for a change to take revenge on *s.o.*; ~ **çekmek** to extract (*or* pull out) a tooth; ~ **çektirmek** to have a tooth extracted (*or* pulled out); ~ **çıkarmak** to cut a tooth, to teethe; ~ **doldurmak** to fill (*or* stop) a tooth; ~ **fırçası** toothbrush; ~ **geçirmek** *fig.* to be able to influence (*a powerful person*); ~ **gıcırdatmak** *fig.* to gnash one's teeth; ~ **göstermek** *fig.* to snow one's teeth; ~ **hekimi** dentist; ~ **hekimliği** dentistry; ~ **kamaştırmak** to set one's teeth on edge; ~ **kemiği** dentine; ~ **kovuğu** cavity; ~ **macunu** toothpaste; ~ **pası** tartar, scale; ~ **siniri** dental nerve; ~ **tababeti** dentistry; ~ **tabibi** dentist; **-e dokunur** worthwhile; **-inden tırnağından artırmak** to pinch and scrape, to scrimp and save; **-ine göre** within one's power; **-ini sıkmak** to grit one's teeth, to endure, to bare; **-ini tırnağına takmak** to work tooth and nail, to try every means.

dişbudak BOT ash tree.

dişçi 1. dentist; **2.** *sl.* one who robs graves for gold teeth.

dişçilik dentistry.

dişeti, -ni gum.

dişi 1. female, she; **2.** woman; **3.** feminine; **4.** MEC female; **5.** malleable (*metal*); ~ **anahtar** hollow key; ~ **kopça** an eye for a hook.

dişil 1. female; **2.** GR feminine.

dişileşmek to become feminine.

dişilik feminine gender, female sex.

dişiorgan BOT pistil.

dişlek bucktoothed, having protruding teeth.

dişlemek 1. to bite, to nibble, to gnaw; **2.** MEC to tooth, to serrate.

dişli 1. toothed, serrated; notched, jagged; cogged; **2.** MEC cogwheel, gear; **3.** sprocket; **4.** *fig.* formidable, influential; ~ **tırnaklı** red in tooth and claw, very aggressive and fierce.

dişsel dental.

dişsiz 1. toothless; **2.** unserrated.

ditmek, (-er) 1. to card, to tease (*cotton, wool*); **2.** to shred.

divan [- -] **1.** sofa, divan, couch; **2.** collection of stamps; **3.** POL council of state; ~ **durmak** to stand in a respectful position with hands folded in front; ♀ **Edebiyatı** classical Ottoman poetry; **dıvanı haysiyet, haysiyet dıvanı** court of hono(u)r.

divane [- - .] crazy, mad, insane; **-si olm.** (*bşin*) to be nuts over *s.th.*, to be wild about *s.th.*

divanelik craziness.

divanhane [- - - .] large hall.

divanıharp, -bi court-martial, military court.

divik ZOO termite, white ant.

divit, -ti a pen-case with an inkholder, ink-and-pen case.

diyabet, -ti diabetes.

diyafram ANAT, PHYS, PHOT diaphragm.

diyagram 1. graph; **2.** diagram.

diyakoz [. x .] deacon.

diyalekt dialect.

diyalektik dialectic(s).

diyalog dialog(ue).

diyanet, -ti [ā] **1.** piety, devoutness; **2.** religion; ~ **işleri** religious affairs.

diyanetkâr, diyanetli [ā] religious, pious.

diyani [. - -] religious; ~ **tesis** JUR religious foundation.

diyapazon diapason, tuning fork.

diyar [ā] country, land.

diye (= **diyerek**) **1.** so that; lest; **2.** because; **3.** by saying; **4.** on the assumption that; by mistake; **5.** named, called.

diyecek s.th. to say; **diyeceği olmamak** to have no objection; to have nothing to say.

diyet¹, -ti diet.

diyet², -ti blood money, wergeld.

Diyet³, -ti Diet.

diyez MUS sharp.

diz 1. knee; **2.** lap; ~ **boyu** knee-deep, up to the knees; ~ **çökmek** to kneel (down); ~ **çöktürmek 1.** to make s.o. kneel down; **2.** to bring s.o. to his knees; ~ **kırmak 1.** to bend one's knees; **2.** to curtsy; ~ **üstü** on one's knees, kneeling; **-e gelmek** to fall on one's knees; to give up, to surrender; **-e getirmek** (*b-ni*) to bring *s.o.* to heel; **-ini dövmek** *fig.* to repent bitterly; **-inin bağı çözüldü** *fig.* he is on his last legs.

dizanteri MED dysentery.

dizbağı, -nı garter; ~ **nişanı** the Order of the Garter.

dizbarko [. x .] JUR unloading (*of a ship*).

dizdirmek 1. to have s.th. typeset; **2.** to have things strung on a cord; **3.** to have things arranged in order.

dize line (*of poetry*).

dizel diesel engine.

dizgi composition, typesetting.

dizgici typesetter, compositor.

dizgin rein, bridle; ~ **vurmak** to bridle; **-ini çekmek** (*or* **kısmak**) *fig.* to keep a tight rein (on); **-leri ele almak** to take the reins; **-leri ele vermek** (*or* **başkasına kaptırmak**) *fig.* to let another take the reins; **-leri salıvermek** *fig.* to give the reins (to); **-lerini toplamak** to rein in, to check off.

dizginlemek 1. to bridle (*a horse*); **2.** *fig.* to restrain.

dizginsiz *fig.* uncontrolled, unbridled.

dizi 1. string (*of beads*); **2.** line, row; **3.** series; **4.** MUS scale; **5.** MATH progression; series; **6.** MIL file (*of soldiers*); ~ **kol nizamında** in single (*or* Indian) file.

dizici TYP typesetter, compositor.

dizili 1. strung (*beads*); **2.** TYP set.

diziliş arrangement.

dizilmek 1. to be arranged (*-e* in); **2.** to

be strung (*-e* on); **3.** to line up; **4.** TYP to be set.

dizim typesetting, composition.

dizin index.

dizkapağı, -nı kneecap; ~ **kemiği** ANAT kneepan, kneecap, patella.

dizlik 1. knee-guard; **2.** knee-breeches.

dizmek 1. to line up, to arrange in a row; **2.** to string (*beads*); **3.** TYP to set.

dizmen typesetter, compositor.

dizüstü bilgisayar laptop.

do MUS **1.** do, doh; **2.** C.

doanahtarı MUS key of C.

dobra dobra [x . x .] bluntly, frankly.

doçent, -ti lecturer, assistant professor, associate professor.

doçentlik associate professorship, lectureship.

doğa nature.

doğacı animist.

doğal natural; ~ **ayıklanma** natural selection; ~ **bilimler** the natural sciences; ~ **kaynaklar** natural resources; ~ **olarak** naturally.

doğallık naturalness.

doğan ZOO falcon.

doğaötesi, -ni 1. metaphysics; **2.** metaphysical.

doğarlık birth-rate.

doğaüstü, -nü supernatural.

doğma 1. *vn. of* **doğmak**; **2.** born; ~ **büyüme İstanbullu** born and bred in Istanbul.

doğmak, (-ar) 1. to be born; **2.** AST to rise (*sun, moon*); **3.** to emerge, to appear, to arise; **4.** (*b-ne*) to occur to *s.o.*; **doğduğu yer** birthplace; **doğduğuna pişman** tired of life, miserable, unhappy; **içime doğdu** I felt it in my bones.

doğmalık congenital.

doğram slice; ~ ~ in slices.

doğrama 1. *vn. of* **doğramak**; **2.** woodwork, joinery.

doğramacı joiner, carpenter.

doğramacılık joinery.

doğramak to cut into pieces (*or* slices); to carve, to chop to bits.

doğru 1. straight; **2.** true; **3.** suitable, proper; **4.** honest, good (*person*); **5.** correct, accurate; **6.** the truth; **7.** MATH line; **8.** truly, correctly; **9.** straight, directly; **10.** towards, in the direction of; **11.** toward, near the time of; **12.** that's true!; **13.** F correct answer (*in a test*); ~ **akım** ELECT direct current; ~ **bulmak** to approve (*-i* of), to see fit; ~ **çıkmak**

to come true, to prove to be right; ~ **durmak 1.** to stand straight; **2.** to sit still, to keep quiet; ~ **dürüst** F **1.** properly; **2.** genuine, proper, real; ~ **orantılı** MATH directly proportional; ~ **oturmak** to sit still, to behave o.s.; **-dan -ya** directly.

doğruca [x . .] **1.** more or less right; **2.** straight, directly.

doğrucu truthful, veracious.

doğrulamak to verify, to confirm, to corroborate.

doğrulmak 1. to straighten out; to be straightened; to become erect (*or* straight); **2.** to sit up; **3.** to be righted; to be put right; **4.** F to be earned; **5.** to direct o.s. (*-e* towards), to head (*-e* for).

doğrultmak 1. to straighten, to put straight; **2.** to correct; **3.** to aim, to point (*-e* at), to direct; **4.** F to get, to take in (*money*).

doğrultu direction.

doğruluk 1. truth; honesty, uprightness; **2.** straightness; ~ **kâğıdı** certificate of conduct.

doğrusal linear.

doğrusu the truth of the matter; to speak honestly, to be quite frank about it; **-nu isterseniz** to tell the truth; **daha** ~ as a matter of fact, to be more exact.

doğu 1. east; **2.** eastern; **3.** the East, the Orient; the eastern provinces of Turkey; **4.** AST equinoctial sunrise point; ~ **Afrika(sı)** East Africa.

doğulu 1. easterner; **2.** Oriental.

doğum 1. birth; **2.** year of birth; **3.** = **doğarlık**; **4.** confinement; **5.** delivery, parturition; ~ **günü** birthday; ~ **hali** nascent condition; ~ **kontrol hapı** the pill, contraceptive pill; ~ **kontrolu** birth control; ~ **kütüğü** birth-register; ~ **sancısı 1.** labo(u)r pain; **2.** *fig.* birth pangs; ~ **yapmak** to give birth to a child, a bear.

doğumevi, -ni maternity hospital.

doğumlu born in such and such a year; **1940 -lar** born in 1940.

doğumsal natal.

doğurgan prolific, fecund.

doğurganlık prolificacy, fecundity.

doğurmak 1. to give birth (**to**) to, to bear; **2.** *fig.* to give birth to, to cause, to bring about, to bring forth.

doğurtmak to assist (*a mother*) at childbirth.

doğuş 1. birth; **2.** AST rise; **3.** emergence; **-tan** innate; from birth; congenital.

dok, -ku NAUT dock, wharf.

doka *s.* **duka.**

doksan ninety.

doksanar ninety each.

doksanıncı ninetieth.

doksanlık 1. containing ninety; **2.** ninety years old.

doktor 1. doctor, physician; **2.** person with a doctorate; ~ **çıkmak** (*or olm.*) **1.** to become a doctor; **2.** to take one's degree.

doktora 1. doctorate; **2.** doctoral examination; ~ **talebesi** postgraduate; ~ **tezi** thesis.

doktorluk 1. = **doktora**; **2.** profession of a doctor; ~ **etm.** to work as a doctor.

doktrin doctrine.

doku ANAT tissue.

dokubilim histology.

dokuma 1. *vn. of* **dokumak**; **2.** woven; **3.** textile; **4.** cotton cloth; ~ **makinesi** loom.

dokumacı weaver; textile worker.

dokumacılık textile industry.

dokumak 1. to weave; **2.** to knock down (*fruit from a tree*).

dokunaklı touching, moving, biting, harmful, harsh, insinuating.

dokundurmak 1. to make s.th. touch another thing; **2.** to hint (**about**).

dokunmak 1. *pass. of* **dokumak**; **2.** to touch, to make contact (*-e* with); **3.** to take in one's hand, to touch; **4.** to disturb, to upset, to meddle (*-e* with); **5.** to take and use; **6.** to disagree (*-e* with), to upset (*one's health*); **7.** to affect; **8.** to move, to cut (*or* touch) s.o. to the quick; **9.** to touch (*-e* on), to deal (*-e* with).

dokunulmazlık POL immunity.

dokunum BIOL sense of touch.

dokurcun 1. stack of hay *or* grain; **2.** a game played with nine small stones.

dokuz nine; ~ **doğurmak** *fig.* to sweat blood, to be on pins and needles; ~ **düğüm altında** under lock and key; ~ **yorgan eskitmek** *fig.* to have a very long life.

dokuzar nine each.

dokuzlamak to increase to nine.

dokuzlu 1. containing nine; **2.** *cards:* the nine; **3.** made up of nine-line stanzas.

dokuztaş a game played with nine

small stones.

dokuzuncu ninth.

doküman document; ~ **fotoğraf** documentary photograph.

dokümanter documentary; ~ **film** documentary film.

dolak puttee.

dolam 1. one turn of any coiled thing; **2.** enough for a turn.

dolama 1. *vn. of* **dolamak**; **2.** dolman; **3.** whitlow, felon.

dolamak 1. to twist, to wind (*-e* on); **2.** to wrap around (*one's arms*).

dolambaç 1. curve, bend; **2.** ANAT labyrinth; **3.** = **dolambaçlı.**

dolambaçlı 1. sinuous, winding, meandering; **2.** *fig.* tangled, involved, intricate; ~ **yollardan gitmek** *fig.* to prevaricate, to shuffle, to dodge.

dolamık trap, snare, net.

dolan deception, deceit.

dolandırıcı swindler, embezzler, deceiver, cheat.

dolandırıcılık swindle, fraud, deceit.

dolandırılmak to be swindled.

dolandırmak 1. = **dolaştırmak**; **2.** to cheat, to swindle, to defraud, to deceive.

dolanmak 1. *pass. of* **dolamak**; **2.** to be wrapped (*-e* around); **3.** to be wound on (*-e* to); **4.** to hang about (*or* around), to wander about, to rove, to roam about.

dolap, -bı 1. cupboard; wardrobe; **2.** water wheel; **3.** treadmill; **4.** Ferris wheel; merry-go-round; **5.** stall in the Covered Market in Istanbul; **6.** MUS musical box; **7.** *fig.* plot, trick, intrigue; ~ **çevirmek** *fig.* to pull a trick, to set a trap.

dolar dollar.

dolaşık 1. roundabout, indirect, meandering, sinuous (*road, way*); **2.** confused tortuous, tangled, intricate (*matter*); ~ **yol** detour, roundabout way.

dolaşıklık 1. entanglement, intricateness, crookedness; **2.** indirectness; **3.** tortuosity.

dolaşıksız 1. direct; **2.** directly.

dolaşım BIOL circulation.

dolaşlı winding; twining; *fig.* having obstacles.

dolaşmak 1. to stroll, to wander, to walk around; **2.** to go the long way round, to make a roundabout way; **3.** to be indirect (*road*); **4.** to get tangled (*hair, thread*); **5.** to go around, to get around (*rumo(u)r, news*); **6.** to patrol (*soldier*); **7.** to go on the beat (*police*); **8.** to get about, to wander around (*a place*).

dolaştırmak *caus. of* **dolaşmak** *part.* **1.** to take s.o. for a walk, to make s.o. go around; to show s.o. around; **2.** to wind (*or* tangle) s.th. around s.th. else.

dolay 1. vicinity, environment, surroundings; **2.** suburbs, outskirts; **3.** turn, bend (*in a road*).

dolayı 1. = **dolay**. **2.** because of, due to, on account of, thanks to, owing to; **3.** as, because; **bundan** ~ therefore, that's why, for that reason.

dolayısıyle [. . . - .] **1.** consequently, so; **2.** because of, on account of, owing to, due to.

dolaylı 1. indirect; **2.** indirectly; ~ **tümleç** GR indirect object.

dolaysız 1. direct; **2.** directly.

doldurma 1. loading, filling; **2.** PHYS charging; ~ **makinesi** charging machine.

doldurmak 1. to fill (up), to stuff; **2.** to complete (*sum or period of time*); **3.** to charge (*a battery*); **4.** to load (*firearm*); **5.** to fill out, to fill in (*a printed form*); **6.** (*b-ni*) to turn *s.o.* against s.o. else.

doldurtmak to have s.th. filled (out).

dolgu 1. act of filling (*out*); **2.** filling, stopping; ~ **yapmak** to fill, to stop; ~ **yaptırmak** to have a tooth filled (*or* stopped).

dolgun 1. full, filled, stuffed; **2.** plump, buxom; **3.** high (*salary*); **4.** abundantly endowed (*with information or knowledge*); ~ **maaşlı** high salaried; ~ **mide** full stomach; ~ **yüzlü** round--faced.

dolgunlaşmak to get plump.

dolgunluk 1. fullness; **2.** plumpness.

dolma 1. *vn. of* **dolmak**; **2.** filled up, reclaimed (*land*); **3.** stuffed (*food*); **4.** *sl.* lie, tall story, humbug; ~ **yutmak** *sl.* to be duped, to be humbugged; ~ **yutturmak** *sl.* to dupe, to humbug, to hoax.

dolmak, (-ar) 1. to get full, to become full, to be filled; **2.** to be packed (*ile* with); **3.** to expire (*term, period*); **4.** *fig.* to be ready to burst (*from anger*), to be exasperated.

dolmakalem fountain-pen.

dolmuş 1. jitney, shared-taxi, collec-

tive-taxi, dolmush (*a taxi which only starts when it is filled up with passengers*); **2.** full, filled, stuffed.

dolmuşçu driver of a shared-taxi.

dolmuşçuluk driving a shared-taxi.

dolu[1] **1.** full, filled; **2.** abounding in, teeming (*ile* with), alive (*ile* with); **3.** loaded (*gun*); **4.** charged (*battery*); **5.** solid; **6.** oversensitive; **7.** a glass (*containing a drink*); **8.** *fig.* about to blow up (*with anger*); ~ ~ plentifully, in abundance; ~ **tüfek** *fig.* choleric person.

dolu[2] hail; ~ **tanesi** hailstone; ~ **yağıyor** it is hailing.

doludizgin at full speed, galloping, at a full gallop.

doluk goatskin bottle.

doluluk fullness, plenitude.

dolunay full moon.

doluşmak to crowd (*into a place*).

domalan BOT truffle.

domalıç humped; bulging; bulbous; protruding.

domalika [. . x .] shellac.

domalmak 1. to bulge out, to stand out, to rise; **2.** to squat down in a humped position.

domaniç *s.* **domalıç.**

domaran *s.* **domalan.**

domates [. x .] BOT tomato; ~ **suyu** tomato juice.

dombalan *s.* **domalan.**

dombay zoo water buffalo.

dombaz *s.* **tombaz.**

domino 1. dominoes (*game*); **2.** domino (*costume*).

domuz 1. zoo pig, hog, swine; **2.** *fig.* obstinate; spiteful, malicious; **3.** you fink!, you swine!; ~ **derisi** pigskin; ~ **eti** pork; ~ **gibi** F **1.** vicious(ly); **2.** for certain; ~ **yağı** lard; ~ **yavrusu** pig; **bu** ~ **karı** *sl.* this swine broad.

domuzayağı, -nı wormer used for with drawing the charge from a gun.

domuzdamı gallery of a mine supported by wooden props.

domuzlan zoo bombardier beetle.

domuzlaşmak to become malicious.

domuzluk 1. viciousness; **2.** water wheel casing.

don[1] **1.** pair of drawers, underpants; **2.** coat, colo(u)r (*of a horse*); **-una etm.** (*or* **kaçırmak**) to wet *or* soil one's underwear; **-una yapmak 1.** to wet *or* soil one's underwear (*child*); **2.** *fig.* to shake in one's shoes.

don[2] frost, freeze; ~ *çözülmek* to thaw; ~ *tutmak* to freeze.

donakalmak, (-ır) to stand aghast (*at*), to be petrified with horror *or* astonishment.

donamak to decorate, to embellish, to adorn.

donanım NAUT rigging, tackle.

donanma 1. *vn. of* **donanmak; 2.** fleet, navy, naval force; **3.** fireworks; flags and bunting; **2.** illumination; ~ *fişeği* rocket, skyrocket.

donanmak 1. to dress up; **2.** to be decorated; **3.** to be equipped; **2.** to be illuminated.

donatan rigger.

donatım 1. equipping; **2.** equipment, outfit; **3.** MIL procurement of ordnance; **2.** incidental details.

donatımcı progman, property man.

donatmak 1. to dress up; **2.** to ornament, to deck out, to illuminate, to decorate; **3.** NAUT to equip (*a ship*); to rig; **4.** to set lavishly (*table*); **5.** *sl.* to insult, to abuse, to swear (*at*).

dondurma 1. *vn. of* **dondurmak; 2.** ice-cream; **3.** (made) frozen, solidified.

dondurmacı ice-cream vendor, ice-cream seller; maker of ice-cream.

dondurmak to freeze (*a. fig.*).

dondurucu freezing; cold, chilling.

dondurulmuş 1. frozen; **2.** fixed.

Donkişotluk quixotism, quixotry.

donma freezing; ~ *noktası* freezing point.

donmak, (-ar) 1. to freeze; **2.** to freeze to death; **3.** to freeze, to feel very cold; **4.** to set, to harden, to solidify (*concrete, etc.*); **5.** to freeze, to remain motionless.

donsuz *fig.* destitute, needy; vagabond.

donuk matt, dull, lusterless, lifeless.

donuklaşmak to be dull, to be lifeless.

donukluk dimness, dullness.

donyağı, -nı 1. tallow; **2.** *fig.* cold fish, disagreeable person; *donyağıyle pekmez fig.* incompatible.

dopdolu [x . .] chockfull, full up.

doru chestnut (*horse*).

doruk 1. summit, peak, apex, top; **2.** *fig.* zenith; ~ *çizgisi* watershed, water parting.

doruklamak to brim, to fill to the brim.

dosa NAUT gangplank.

dosdoğru [x - .] *emph. of* **doğru** straight ahead; perfectly correct.

dost, -tu 1. friend; comrade, confidant, intimate; **2.** friendly; **3.** lover; mistress; ~ *devlet* friendly state; ~ *düşman* friend and foe, everybody; ~ *edinmek* **1.** to make friends (with); **2.** to take a lover *or* a mistress; ~ *kara günde belli olur pro.* a friend in need is a friend indeed; ~ *olm.* to become friends; *-a düşmana karşı* in front of everybody; in the eyes of everybody, publicly; *-lar başına!* may the same befall all my friends!; *-lar başından ırak!* I wouldn't wish such a thing on my friends!

dostane [ā] friendly.

dostça = **dostane**.

dostluk friendship; ~ *etm.* (*or* **göstermek**) to be friends (*-e* with); ~ *kurmak* to make friends (*ile* with).

dosya [x .] **1.** file, dossier; **2.** file folder; *indirilen* ~ IT download; *yüklenen* ~ IT upload.

dosyalamak to file, to put in a file.

dosyalanmak *pass. of* **dosyalamak** to be filed.

dosye *s.* **dosya**.

doyasıya to one's heart's content, to repletion, as much as one can.

doygun 1. satiated; **2.** saturated.

doygunluk 1. satiation; **2.** saturation.

doyma saturation (*a.* CHEM).

doymak 1. to eat one's fill, to be full up, to be satiated; **2.** (*bşe*) to be satisfied with *s.th.*; **3.** CHEM to be saturated (*-e* with); *doya doya* to one's heart's content, to repletion.

doymaz greedy, insatiable.

doymazlık greed, insatiability.

doymuş CHEM saturated.

doyum satiety, satisfaction; *buna* ~ *olmaz* one never gets tired of this, one cannot have enough of it.

doyumluk enough to satisfy.

doyurmak 1. to fill up, to satisfy, to satiate, to allay one's hunger; **2.** CHEM to saturate.

doyurucu 1. satisfying, filling (*food*); **2.** *fig.* convincing, persuasive.

doz MED dose; *-unu kaçırmak* to overdo, to go too far.

dozer bulldozer.

dökme 1. *vn. of* **dökmek; 2.** poured; **3.** cast (*metal*); **4.** spilled, scattered; **5.** COM in bulk; ~ *demir* cast iron.

dökmeci foundryman, founder.

dökmecilik foundry work.

dökmehane [ā] foundry.

dökmek (-er) 1. to pour (out); **2.** to spill; **3.** to throw out; **4.** to scatter; **5.** to shed; **6.** to cast; **7.** to empty; **8.** to let (one's hair) hang freely; **9.** to pour out (one's troubles); **10.** to fail, to flunk (students in a class); **11.** to have (spots, freckles) break out on one's skin; **12.** (kâğıda) to write down, to commit to paper.

döktürmek 1. caus. of **dökmek**; **2.** sl. to do a swell job.

dökük 1. nicely hanging (cloth); **2.** loose, free (hair); **3.** F shabby, seedy.

döküksaçık 1. rough, untidy (hair); **2.** shabby, ragged.

dökülmek 1. pass. of **dökmek**; **2.** to go out in large numbers (people); **3.** to disintegrate; **4.** to drape, to drop off; **5.** to get ragged; **6.** sl. to be dead tired, to be bushed. to be worn out; **7.** to be miserable; **dökülüp saçılmak 1.** to unburden o.s. to unbosom o.s., to make a clean breast of it; **2.** to blow, to blue, to squander (money).

döküm 1. casting, cast; **2.** dropping; **3.** enumeration (of an account); **4.** inventory; **5.** MATH addition; **6.** mo(u)lting; shedding; **7.** sl. ugly (woman); **8.** sl. sloppily dressed; ~ **kalıbı** casting mo(u)ld.

dökümcü foundryman.

dökümcülük foundry work.

dökümevi, dökümhane [ā] MEC foundry, ironworks.

dökümlü well-fitting (clothing).

dökünmek refl. of **dökmek** part. to throw over o.s. (water, etc.).

döküntü 1. remains, remnants, leavings, debris, remainder; **2.** stragglers; **3.** skin eruption, exanthema; **4.** drifters; **5.** reef (of rock); ~ **erler** MIL stragglers.

döl 1. seed, germ, semen, sperm; **2.** young, offspring, issue, new generation; **3.** new plant, seedling; **4.** descendants, posterity; **5.** generation; **6.** race, stock, origin; ~ **döş** children, family, descendants, progeny; ~ **tutmak** to become pregnant (animal); ~ **vermek** to give birth, to bring forth young, to reproduce.

döllemek BIOL to inseminate, to make pregnant, to fertilize, to fecundate.

döllenme insemination, fecundation, fertilization.

döllenmek pass. of **döllemek** to be inseminated, to be fertilized, to be fecundated.

dölüt BIOL fetus.

dölyatağı, -nı ANAT uterus, womb.

dölyolu, -nu ANAT vagina.

döndürmek 1. to turn round, to reverse, to rotate, to spin; **2.** to send back; **3.** to drive s.o. (wild, crazy); **4.** to fail, to flunk (a student); **5.** to pull (a. trick).

döneç PHYS rotor.

dönek fickle, untrustworthy, inconstant, changeable.

döneklik fickleness, inconstancy; ~ **etm.** to go back on one's word.

dönem 1. period (of time), era; **2.** PARL term; **3.** school term; **4.** boxing: round; ~ **sonu sınavları** end-of-term examinations.

dönemeç bend, curve (in a road).

dönemeçli winding, curved (road).

dönence 1. AST tropic; **2.** turning point.

döner turning, revolving; ~ **kapı** revolving door; ~ **kebap** pressed lamb roasted on a large vertical spit; ~ **koltuk** swivel chair; ~ **merdiven** spiral stairs; ~ **sermaye** revolving fund, circulating capital.

döngel BOT medlar.

döngü circle (s. **kısır döngü**).

dönme 1. vn. of **dönmek**; **2.** converted to Islam; ~ **dolap 1.** Ferris wheel, big wheel; **2.** revolving cupboard.

dönmek, (-er) 1. to turn, to revolve, to rotate, to spin; **2.** to return, to go back, to come back; **3.** to turn (-e towards); **4.** to turn (-e into), to become; **5.** to fail; **6.** to be converted (to another religion); **7.** to change (weather, etc.); **8.** to be going on (s.th. tricky); **9.** to swerve (from a course); **10.** (sözünden) to break (one's promise), to go back on one's word; **11.** (kararından) to change one's mind; **döne döne çıkmak** to ascend in a spiral; **dönüp dolaşıp** in the long run, after all; **dönüp dolaşmak** to walk back and forth.

dönük 1. turned (-e to, towards), facing; **2.** aimed (-e at), addressed (-e to).

dönüm 1. a land measure of about 920 m²; **2.** turning, returning; **3.** rotating, revolving; **4.** (round) trip; ~ **noktası** turning point.

dönüş 1. turning; **2.** return(ing); **3.**

sports: pivoting turn.

dönüşlü GR reflective.

dönüşmek 1. to change (-*e* into), to turn (-*e* into), to be transformed (-*e* into); **2.** to mutate.

dönüştürmek 1. to change (-*e* into), to transform (-*e* into); **2.** to cause a mutation (*in*).

dönüşüm 1. transformation; **2.** metaplasia.

döpiyes two-piece.

dörder four each; ~ ~ by fours.

dördüncü fourth; ~ *zaman* GEOL Quaternary.

dördüz quadruplet.

dört, -dü four; ~ *ayak üstüne düşmek* to land on one's feet, to fall on one's feet; ~ *başı mamur fig.* in perfect condition, prosperous, flourishing; ~ *bucakta* everywhere, high and low; ~ *duvar arasında kalmak* to be shut in; ~ *elle sarılmak* **1.** (*bir işe*) to stick heart and soul (-*e* at), to be wrapped up (-*e* in); **2.** (*b-ne*) to cling to *s.o.*; ~ *gözle beklemek* to wait eagerly (-*i* for), to look forward (-*i* to); ~ *işlem* MATH the four operations.

dörtayak 1. quadruped; **2.** on all fours.

dörtcihar [ā] *dice*: double four.

dörtgen MATH quadrangle, quadrilateral.

dörtkenar *s.* **dörtgen.**

dörtlemek to quadruplicate.

dörtlü 1. *cards*: four; **2.** quartet.

dörtlük 1. MUS quarter note; **2.** quatrain; **3.** AST quarter (*of the sky*); ~ *es* MUS crotchet-rest.

dörtnal gallop.

dörtnala at a gallop, galloping.

dörtyol crossroads; ~ *ağzı* crossroads, junction, intersection.

döş 1. breast, bosom; **2.** brisket, breast.

döşek mattress, bed; ~ *esiri olm.* to be bedridden, to be confined to bed, *Am.* to be bedfast.

döşeli 1. furnished; **2.** floored, laid; *dayalı* ~ completely furnished (*house*).

döşeme 1. floor(ing), pavement; **2.** furniture; **3.** upholstery; covering.

döşemeci 1. upholsterer; **2.** furniture dealer.

döşemecilik 1. upholstery; **2.** furniture trade.

döşemek 1. to spread, to lay down; **2.** to floor, to pave; **3.** to furnish, to upholster; *dayayıp* ~ to furnish completely (*house*).

döşenmek 1. *pass. of* **döşemek**; **2.** (*b-ne*) to scold *s.o.*; **3.** (*bş. hakkında*) to write a diatribe against *s.th.*; **4.** F to take to one's bed, to be bedridden.

döşeyici installer; fitter; plumber; electrician.

dövdürmek to have s.o. beaten.

döven threshing sled; flail.

döviz 1. foreign currency, foreign exchange; **2.** motto, slogan, device; **3.** placard; ~ *kontrolu* exchange control.

dövme 1. *vn*, *of* **dövmek**; **2.** tattoo; **3.** forging, **4.** wrought (*iron*); **5.** dehusked wheat.

dövmek, (-er) 1. to beat, to flog, to thrash; **2.** to thresh (*grain*); **3.** to hammer, to forge (*hot metal*); **4.** to beat (*laundry*); **5.** to pound to a powder, to crush up; **6.** to beat (*eggs*); **7.** to tamp, to pound down; **8.** to shell, to bombard; **9.** to beat, to pound (*waves*, *rain*).

dövülgen MEC malleable.

dövülgenlik MEC malleability.

dövülmek *pass. of* **dövmek** *part.* to be beaten, to be pounded, to be threshed, to be forged.

dövünmek 1. to beat o.s., to beat one's breast; **2.** *fig.* to lament, to be frantic with sorrow.

dövüş 1. beating; **2.** fight, brawl, scuffle.

dövüşçü fighter.

dövüşken bellicose, combative, belligerent.

dövüşkenlik bellicosity, pugnacity.

dövüşmek 1. to fight, to struggle; **2.** to clash (*armed forces*); **3.** to box.

dövüştürmek to pit (*fighters*, *animals*) against each other.

drahmi drachma.

drahoma [x . .] dowry.

draje 1. sugar-coated pill; **2.** chocolate-coated nuts.

dram 1. THEAT drama; **2.** tragedy, tragic event.

dramatik 1. dramatic; **2.** tragic.

drenaj drainage.

dresuvar sideboard.

dretnot, -tu dreadnought.

dua [ā] prayer, blessing; ~ *etm.* to pray, to bless; *-sını almak* (*b-nin*) to have the blessing of *s.o.*

duacı well-wisher.

duayen doyen.

duba [x .] pontoon, barge; ~ *gibi* paunchy, very fat.

dubara [. - .] **1.** *dice*: double deuce; **2.** *sl.* trick, fraud.

dubaracı *sl.* trickster, cheat.

dublaj dubbing; ~ **yapmak** to dub.

duble 1. double (*spirits, beer*); **2.** lining (*of a garment*); **3.** slip, underdress; ~ **etm.** to line (*a garment*).

dubleks duplex (*house*).

dublör stunt-man; body double (*person who looks exactly like another*).

duçar [- -] subject (*-e* to), afflicted (*-e* with), exposed (*-e* to); ~ **olm.** to be subject (*-e* to), to be exposed (*-e* to), to be afflicted (*-e* with).

dudak lip; ~ **boyası** lipstick; ~ **bükmek** to curl one's lip; ~ **dudağa** lip to lip; ~ **sarkıtmak** to hang the lip, to sulk; **dudağı yarık** hare-lipped; **dudağını ısırmak** to bite one's lip.

dudaksıl labial.

dudu 1. old Armenian woman; **2.** *title given to women*; **3.** = ~ **kuşu**; ~ **gibi konuşmak** to prattle, to chat; ~ **kuşu** parrot.

duhul, -lü [. -] **1.** entering, entrance; **2.** penetration; **3.** JUR a man's consummating the sexual act; ~ **hakkı** JUR right of free entrance; ~ **imtihanı** *obs.* entrance examination.

duhuliye [. - . .] **1.** entrance fee; **2.** import duty.

duka [x .] **1.** *obs.* duke; **2.** ducat.

dul [ū] **1.** widow; widower; **2.** widowed; ~ **kalmak** to be widowed; ~ **karı enciği** F chatterer.

dulavratotu, -nu BOT burdock.

duman 1. smoke; fumes; **2.** mist, fog, haze; **3.** F bad, hopeless (*condition*); **4.** *sl.* hashish, dope; ~ **attırmak** *sl.* to intimidate; ~ **çökmek** to settle down (*smoke or mist*); ~ **etm.** *sl.* **1.** to spoil, to break up; **2.** to clobber, to defeat; ~ **olm.** *sl.* to be very bad (*situation*); **-a boğmak** to smoke up; **-ı üstünde** *fig.* very fresh, brand new.

dumanlamak 1. to smoke up, to fill with smoke; **2.** to smoke, to cure; **3.** (*kafayı*) to get fuddled.

dumanlanmak 1. *pass. of* **dumanlamak**; **2.** to get smoky; **3.** to become cloudy (*eyes*); **4.** to get confused (*mind*), to get fuddled; **5.** to be smoked, to be cured.

dumanlı 1. smoky; fumy; **2.** misty, foggy; **3.** (*kafası*) tipsy, fuddled.

dumansız smokeless.

dumdum dumdum bullet.

dumur [. -] atrophy; **-a uğramak** to be atrophied.

dun [ū] *rare* lower, inferior.

dupduru crystal clear.

duraç¹, -cı ZOO francolin.

duraç², -cı base, pedestal (*of a statue*).

durağan fixed, stable.

durağanlık stability.

durak 1. stop; **2.** halt, pause, break; **3.** tonic note; **4.** caesura.

durakı BOT nectarine.

duraklama 1. pause; **2.** hesitation; **3.** MIL standstill.

duraklamak 1. to stop, to pause, to halt; **2.** to hesitate.

duraklı PHYS stationary.

duraksama hesitation.

duraksamak to hesitate.

dural PHLS static, unchanging.

duralama hesitation, pause.

duralamak 1. to pause, to halt, to come to a stop; **2.** to hesitate.

durdinlen pause, halt, break; ~ **yok** there is no time for a break.

durdurmak to stop, to halt, to bring to a halt.

durgun 1. calm, quiet, still; **2.** stagnant, stationary; **3.** subdued, withdrawn; ~ **su** standing (*or* stagnant) water.

durgunlaşmak 1. to get calm, to calm down; **2.** to become dull, to become torpid.

durgunluk 1. calmness; **2.** dullness, heaviness; **3.** stagnation, standstill.

durmak, (-ur) 1. to stop, to cease; **2.** to last, to endure, to continue to exist; **3.** to stand; to lie; **4.** to be, to remain (*at a place*); **5.** to exist as a possession, to (still) have; **6.** to suit, to go, to appear, to look; **7.** to behave (*in a specified way*); **8.** (*bir nokta üzerinde*) to dwell on (*a subject*): **dur(un)!** wait!, stop!; **dur! kimdir o?** MIL stop! who goes there?; **durakalmak** to be taken aback; **duracak yer** standing-place; **durmaksızın** *or* **durmadan** continuously, on end; **durmuş oturmuş** staid, sedate; **durup dururken 1.** suddenly, out, of the blue; **2.** with no reason, without provocation.

duru clear, limpid.

durulama *vn. of* **durulamak** rinsing; ~ **suyu** rinse water; ~ **tesisatı** purification plant.

durulamak to rinse.

durulaşmak to become clear (*or* transparent).

durulmak 1. to become clear and limpid; **2.** to settle down, to quiet down, to calm down.

duruluk clearness, limpidity.

durum 1. state, condition, situation, circumstances, position, occasion; **2.** behavio(u)r, attitude.

duruş 1. rest, stop; **2.** posture, attitude.

duruşma JUR trial, hearing (*of a case*).

duruşmak to confront one another.

duş 1. shower, shower-bath; **2.** shower nozzle; ~ **yapmak** to have (*or* take) a shower.

dut, -tu, -du 1. mulberry; **2.** *sl.* tipsy, pissed; ~ **gibi olm.** *sl.* **1.** to be pissed, to be as drunk as a lord; **2.** to be greatly ashamed; ~ **yemiş bülbüle benzemek** (*or* **dönmek**) to be tongue-tied, to become sad and taciturn.

duvak 1. bridal veil; **2.** large stone lid (*for covering a cistern*); ~ **düşkünü** young widow; **duvağına doymamak** to be widowed *or* die while still young (*bride*).

duvaklı veiled.

duvar 1. wall; **2.** barrier (*between two people*); **3.** *sports*: blocking, defensive barrier; ~ **gibi** stone-deaf, as deaf as a post; ~ **kâğıdı** wallpaper; ~ **örmek** to put up a wall; ~ **resmi** fresco; ~ **saati** wall clock; **-a yazıyorum!** *fig.* mark my words!

duvarcı 1. bricklayer; stonemason; **2.** *sl.* burglar.

duvarcılık bricklaying; stonemasonry.

duy ELECT socket.

duyar sensible, sensitive.

duyarga ZOO antenna.

duyarlı sensitive.

duyarlık sensitiveness; sensitivity.

duygu 1. feeling, attitude; **2.** emotion; **3.** sensation, sense; perception; **4.** impression; **5.** sentiment.

duygudaş sympathizer.

duygudaşlık sympathy.

duygulamak to affect, to touch, to move.

duygulandırmak to move, to affect, to touch.

duygulanmak to be affected, to be touched, to be moved.

duygulu 1. sensitive; **2.** impressionable, emotional.

duygululuk sensitivity.

duygun sensitive.

duygunluk sensitivity.

duygusal 1. emotional; **2.** romantic, sentimental.

duygusuz unfeeling, hardhearted, callous, insensitive, apathetic.

duygusuzluk insensitivity, heartlessness.

duymak, (-ar) 1. to hear; **2.** to get word of, to learn; **3.** to be aware of; **4.** to feel, to sense, to perceive, to experience; **5.** to have the sensation of; **6.** to feel (*pride, pleasure, etc.*).

duyu sense.

duyulmak *pass. of* **duymak.**

duyum sensation; ~ **eşiği** PSYCH threshold of consciousness.

duyumölçer esthesiometer.

duyumsal sensorial.

duyurmak *caus. of* **duymak** *part.* to announce, (*b-ne bşi*) to let *s.o.* hear (*or* learn) *s.th.*

duyuru announcement; notification.

duyusal sensorial.

duyuş 1. hearing; **2.** perception; **3.** impression, feeling.

duziko F rakı.

dübeş *dice*: fives.

dübür *rare* the hinder part of anything; F the buttocks; *sl.* the anus, ass, arse.

düçar [ā] *s.* **duçar.**

düdük 1. whistle, pipe, flute, hooter; **2.** *sl.* stupid, empty-headed, brainless; ~ **gibi kalmak** to be left entirely alone; ~ **makarnası 1.** macaroni; **2.** *sl.* silly, dull, imbecile; **düdüğü çalmak 1.** to succeed; **2.** *fig.* to become happy; **-le beraber** *football*: with the whistle.

düdüklemek *sl.* to screw, to stuff.

düdüklü having a whistle; ~ **tencere** pressure cooker.

düello duel; ~ **etm.** to duel.

düet MUS duet.

düğme 1. button; **2.** ELECT switch; **3.** bud.

düğmeci maker *or* seller of buttons.

düğmelemek to button up.

düğmeli buttoned.

düğüm 1. *a.* BOT, PHYS knot, bow; **2.** *fig.* knotty problem; **3.** *lit.* climax; **4.** PHYS node; ~ **atmak** to knot, to tie in a knot; ~ **istasyonu** railway junction; ~ **noktası** *fig.* crucial (*or* vital) point; ~ **olm.** to get knotted.

düğümlemek to knot, to tie in a knot.

düğümlenmek *pass. of* **düğümlemek**, *part.* to get tangled.

düğümlü knotted.

düğün 1. wedding feast; **2.** circumcision feast; ~ **bayram etm.** *fig.* to be as happy as the day is long, to be as happy as a sandboy; ~ **dernek, hep bir örnek** F it's always the same old thing; ~ **yapmak** to hold a wedding.

düğünçiçeği, -ni BOT buttercup.

dük, -kü duke; ♎ **dö Windsor** duke of Windsor.

dükkân 1. shop; **2.** sl. gambling house; ~ **açmak** to open shop, to set up business.

dükkâncı shopkeeper.

düldül sl. **1.** nag, broken-down horse; **2.** lizzie, jalopy, crate.

dülger carpenter; builder.

dülgerbalığı, -nı zoo John Dory, dory.

dülgerlik carpentry.

dümbelek 1. tabor, timbal; **2.** sl. idiot.

dümbelekçi drummer.

dümdar [ā] MIL rear guard; ~ **muharebeleri** rear guard action.

dümdüz [x.] **1.** perfectly smooth, quite level; **2.** straight ahead; **3.** sl. simple, plain (person).

dümen 1. rudder, helm; **2.** sl. trick, humbug; **3.** fig. control, administration; ~ **çevirmek** F to play tricks, to humbug; ~ **erbaşı** steersman; ~ **kırmak** NAUT to veer; ~ **kolu** rudder bar; ~ **kullanmak 1.** to steer; **2.** fig. to be on one's guard; ~ **neferi** fig. the last or laziest (person); ~ **suyundan gitmek** (b-nin) to follow in s.o.'s wake; ~ **tutmak** to steer; ~ **yapmak** sl. to trick, to deceive, to cheat; ~ **yekesi** NAUT tiller; **-i eğri** co. walking sideways; **-i kırmak** sl. to slip away, to clear out, to beat it, to make off.

dümenci 1. helmsman, steersman; **2.** sl. the last or laziest (student); **3.** sl. trickster, cheat.

dümencilik 1. steering; **2.** sl. the tail end; being the last; **3.** sl. trickiness.

dün 1. yesterday; **2.** the past; ~ **akşam** last night, yesterday evening; ~ **bir, bugün iki** it is still too soon; ~ **değil evvelki gün** the day before yesterday.

dünden 1. from yesterday; **2.** eagerly; ~ **bugüne** in a short time, overnight; ~ **hazır** eager; ~ **ölmüş** listless, without zest; ~ **teşnedir** fig. he is over-eager.

dünkü 1. yesterday's, of yesterday; **2.** fig. raw, inexperienced, green, tiro; ~ **çocuk** greenhorn, tyro.

dünür 1. the father-in-law or mother-in-law of one's child; **2.** = **dünürsü**; ~ **gezmek** to search for a suitable bride for a suitor.

dünürcü woman sent out to see about a prospective bride.

dünürsü, dünüş the mother-in-law of a woman's child.

dünya 1. world, earth; **2.** universe; **3.** everyone, people; ~ **âlem** F everyone, all the world; ~ **başına yıkılmak** fig. to be very miserable; ~ **durdukça** for ever and ever; ~ **evine girmek** to get married; ~ **harbi** world-war; ~ **kadar** a world of, loads of, pots of; ~ **şampiyonu** sports: world champion; ~ **yıkılsa umurunda olmamak** not to give a damn; **-da** never in this world; **-dan elini eteğini çekmek** to go (or retire) into one's shell; **-nın dört bucağı** the four corners of the earth; **-ya gelmek** to be born, to come into the world; **-ya getirmek** to give birth to, to bring into the world; **-ya gözlerini kapamak** to die, to pass away, to pass on; **-ya kazık çakmak** (or **kakmak**) fig. to live to a ripe old age; **-yayı tozpembe görmek** to see the world through rose-colo(u)red spectacles.

dünyevi worldly.

düpedüz [x..] **1.** openly; **2.** sheer, absolute, downright, utter.

dürbün 1. binoculars, field glasses; **2.** small telescope.

dürmek to roll up, to fold.

dürtmek 1. to prod, to goad, to nudge; **2.** fig. to incite, to stir up, to provoke, to urge on, to instigate.

dürtü PSYCH impulse, compulsion, drive.

dürtüklemek to nudge.

dürtüşmek to push (or prod) one another.

dürülmek pass. of **dürmek**.

dürüm roll, fold, pleat.

dürüm dürüm in rolls.

dürüst, -tü 1. honest, straightforward; **2.** fig. flawless.

dürüstlük honesty.

dürüşt, -tü harsh, coarse, severe, brutal.

Dürzi pr. n. Druse.

dürzü sl. scoundrel.

düse [-.] dice: double three.

düstur [ū] **1.** norm; rule; **2.** code of laws; **3.** CHEM, MATH formula; **4.** principle.

düş 1. dream; **2.** aspiration, hope; ~ **görmek** to have a dream; ~ **kırıklığı** disappointment; ~ **kurmak** to daydream.

düşes duchess.

düşeş 1. *dice*: double six; **2.** *fig.* windfall; bargain.

düşey MATH perpendicular, vertical.

düşgelmek to chance (*-e* on), to come across, to come (*-e* upon).

düşkün 1. addicted (*-e* to), given (*-e* to), devoted (*-e* to); **2.** deeply devoted (*-e* to), wrapped up (*-e* in); **3.** down--and-out, who has seen better days; **4.** worn-out, washed-out; **5.** unchaste, fallen, loose (*woman*).

düşkünleşmek 1. to come down in the world, to fall upon hard times; **2.** (*of women*) to go on (or walk) the streets.

düşkünlük 1. poverty, decay; **2.** excessive addiction.

düşman enemy, foe, adversary; **~ ağzı** calumny; **~ olm.** to become an enemy (*-e* of).

düşmanca in a hostile manner.

düşmanlık enmity, hostility, animosity.

düşme 1. *vn. of* **düşmek**; **2.** PHYS fall.

düşmek, (-er) 1. to fall; **2.** to drop, to go down, to decrease, to fall; **3.** to subtract; to deduct; **4.** to be born dead (*fetus*); **5.** to fall (*-e* into) (*doubt, worry, trouble*); **6.** to get (*tired, weak*); **7.** to suit, to match, to go (*-e* with); **8.** to be up (*-e* to), to lie within one's responsibility; **9.** to lie (*in a direction*); **10.** to fall (*on a certain day*); **11.** to fall to one's lot; **12.** to come (*-e* to) by chance; **13.** to be left out (*-den* of), to be omitted, to be skipped; **14.** to wind up (*-e* in), to end up (*-e* in), to land up (*-e* in) (*prison, court, hospital*); **15.** to drop (*in value*); **16.** to fall (*government, fort*); **17.** (*birbirine*) to be set by the ears; **18.** to drop (*fever*); **düş önüme!** come along with me!; **düşe kalka** struggling along, with difficulty; **düşenin dostu olmaz** *pro.* laugh, the whole world will laugh with you; cry, and you will cry alone; **düşüp kalkmak** (*b-le*) to live with *s.o.*, to live together, to shack up with *s.o.*

düşsel oneiric.

düşük 1. fallen, drooping; **2.** low (*price, quality*); **3.** unchaste, fallen, loose (*woman*); **4.** GR misconstrued (*sentence*); **5.** MED miscarriage, abortion; **~ etek** *fig.* slipshod, sloppy (*woman*).

düşüm fall, decline.

düşümdeşlik PHLS coincidence.

düşün thought.

düşünce 1. thought; **2.** idea, opinion, reflection; **3.** anxiety, worry; **-ye dalmak** to be lost in thought.

düşünceleme PHLS ideation.

düşünceli 1. thoughtful, considerate; **2.** worried, anxious, depressed; **3.** pensive, lost in thought.

düşüncesiz 1. thoughtless, inconsiderate, tactless; careless; **2.** unworried; carefree.

düşüncesizlik thoughtlessness, tactlessness, inconsiderateness.

düşündürmek *caus. of* **düşünmek**.

düşündürücü thought-provoking.

düşünme 1. thinking, thought; **2.** PHLS introspection.

düşünmece problem, brain-twister, *Am.* quiz.

düşünmek 1. to think (*-i* of); **2.** to consider, to think (*-i* about), to ponder (*üzerinde* over); **3.** to worry (*-i* about); **4.** to remember; **düşünüp taşınmak** to consider at length, to mull over.

düşünülmek *pass. of* **düşünmek**.

düşünür thinker, intellectual.

düşünüş mentality, way of thinking, reflection.

düşürmek *caus. of* **düşmek** *part.* **1.** to drop, to let fall, to bring down; **2.** to reduce; **3.** to miscarry, to abort (*child*); **4.** to pass (*from the body*); **5.** to get at a bargain; **6.** to overthrow, to bring down (*government*); **7.** (*birbirine*) to set at loggerheads, to play *one person* off against *another*.

düşüş 1. fall, falling; **2.** decrease.

düşüt aborted fetus.

düt toot.

düttürü [x . .] **1.** oddly dressed; **2.** odd *or* tight dress.

düve zoo heifer.

düven threshing sled; **~ sürmek** to thresh.

düyun [ū] *pl.* debts.

düz 1. smooth, even; flat, level; **2.** straight; **3.** simple, plain; without ornament, plain-colo(u)red; **4.** level area, plain; **~ tümleç** GR direct object.

düzayak 1. without stairs, on one floor; **2.** on a level with the street.

düzce [x .] fairly smooth (*or* level); **-si** frankly, to tell the truth.

düzelmek 1. to be put in order, to be arranged; **2.** to improve, to get better;

3. to straighten out; **4.** to get well, to get about.

düzeltici 1. corrective; **2.** proofreader.

düzelticilik proofreading.

düzeltme *vn. of* ***düzeltmek*** *part.* **1.** proofreading; **2.** correction; **3.** reform; **~ işareti** circumflex.

düzeltmek *caus. of* ***düzelmek*** **1.** to smooth, to make smooth; to straighten; **2.** to put in order, to repair; **3.** to correct; **4.** to proofread.

düzeltmen proofreader.

düzem CHEM formula, recipe.

düzen 1. order, harmony, regularity, orderliness; arrangement; **2.** the social order, the system; **3.** MUS tuning; **4.** *fig.* trick, swindle; **~ kurmak** *fig.* to set a trap, to prepare a trick, to resort to deception; **~ vermek** (*or* **-e koymak** *or* **-e sokmak**) to put in order, to tidy up.

düzenbaz, düzenci trickster, cheat, humbug.

düzenek 1. plan; **2.** mechanism.

düzengeç PHYS regulator.

düzenleme *vn. of* ***düzenlemek*** arrangement; preparation.

düzenlemek 1. to put in order; **2.** to arrange, to hold (*a meeting*); to prepare.

düzenlenmek *pass. of* ***düzenlemek.***

düzenli 1. tidy, orderly, in order; **2.** *fig.* systematic.

düzenlilik orderliness, tidiness.

düzensiz 1. out of order, untidy, disorderly, tumultuous; **2.** *fig.* unsystematic.

düzensizlik disorder, untidiness.

düzenteker PHYS flywheel.

düzey 1. level; **2.** rank; **3.** contour line.

düzgün[1] **1.** smooth, level; **2.** orderly, well-arranged, tidy; **3.** correct; **4.** MATH regular; **5.** smoothly, regularly.

düzgün[2] a liquid make-up for the face.

düzgünlük order, regularity, smoothness.

düzgüsel PHLS normative.

düzgüsüz PHLS abnormal.

düzine 1. dozen; **2.** dozens of, lots of.

düzlem MATH plane; **~ geometri** plane geometry.

düzlemek 1. to smooth, to level, to flatten; **2.** to mill, to machine.

düzlemküre planisphere.

düzleşmek to become smooth (*or* level *or* straight).

düzletmek to smooth, to flatten.

düzlük 1. smoothness, flatness, levelness; **2.** evenness, uniformity; **3.** plainness; **4.** level (*or* flat) place, plain.

düzme 1. *vn. of* ***düzmek***; **2.** false, fake; forged.

düzmece = ***düzme 2.***

düzmeci forger, faker, cheat.

düzmecilik forgery; deception, deceit.

düzmek, (-er) 1. to arrange, to compose; to prepare; **2.** to invent, to fabricate (*a story*); **3.** to forge, to counterfeit; **4.** *sl.* to rape; ***düzüp koşmak*** to arrange, to compose.

düztaban 1. flat-footed; **2.** *fig.* ill-omened, Jonah; **3.** flatfoot; **4.** rabbet plane.

düztabanlık flat-footedness.

düzülmek 1. *pass. of* ***düzmek***; **2.** *s.* **yola ~.**

düzyazı prose.

DVD DVD; **~-ROM** DVD-ROM.

E

e 1. (*in request or question*) well, all right; **2.** then; **3.** *s. a* (**4**); **4.** now then, now; **5.** oh! (*surprise*).

-e (*ending of dat*).

-e hali GR dative (case).

ebat [ā] **1.** dimensions; **2.** size.

ebe 1. midwife; **2.** it (*in children's games*): ~ **hekim** obstetrician; **-nin örekesi** F pack of nonsense.

ebeden [x . .] **1.** ever, eternally; **2.** (*followed by negative verb*) never.

ebedi eternal, without end, never-ending.

ebediyen [ī] [. . x . .] **1.** eternally, for ever, in perpetuity; **2.** (*in negative sentences*) not at all, by no means.

ebediyet, -ti eternity.

ebegümeci, -ni BOT mallow.

ebekuşağı, -nı rainbow.

ebet eternity without end.

ebeveyn parents.

e-bilet IT e-ticket.

ebleh stupid, foolish, silly; imbecile.

ebonit, -ti ebonite.

ebru [ū] **1.** marbling (*of variegated paper*); marbled (*paper*); **2.** watering (*of fabrics*).

ebrulamak [. - . .] **1.** to marble (*paper*); **2.** to water (*a fabric*).

ecdat [. -] ancestors.

ece queen.

ecel 1. JUR appointed term; **2.** death, decease, appointed hour of death; ~ **teri dökmek** to be in mortal fear, to be in a cold sweat, to be in fear and trembling; **-i gelmek** to have one's fated time of death arrive; **-ine susamak** to be fool hardy, to be daredevil; **-iyle ölmek** to die a natural death; **eceli kaza** accidental death.

ecinli, ecinni P = *cin²*.

ecir, -cri 1. reward, recompense; **2.** pay, wage, remuneration; ~ **sabır dilemek** to condole (**with**).

eciş bücüş 1. out of shape, crooked, distorted, contorted; **2.** eccentric, odd, unusual; **3.** wizened (*person*).

ecnebi 1. foreigner, stranger, alien; **2.** foreign, strange; ~ **matbuat** (**-ı**) foreign press.

ecza, -aı [ā] **1.** parts; **2.** MATH submulti-

ple; **3.** drugs, medicines, chemicals; **4.** PHOT developer; **5.** in paper cover, unbound.

eczacı [ā] chemist, druggist, pharmacist.

eczacılık [ā] pharmacy (*profession*).

eczalı [ā] prepared with chemicals; containing chemicals; ~ **pamuk** medical cotton.

eczane [ā] pharmacy, chemist's shop, drugstore.

eda [ā] **1.** payment; **2.** execution, fulfil(l)ment, performance; **3.** behavio(u)r, conduct, manner, style, tone, affectation; **4.** arrogance, insolence; **5.** representation, articulation; ~ **etm. 1.** to fulfil(l), to perform (*a duty*); **2.** to articulate (*word or letter*); **3.** to represent; **4.** to pay (*a debt*).

edalı [ā] **1.** having an air; **2.** charming, gracious; **3.** arrogant, affected, pretended.

edat, -tı [ā] **1.** instrument, implement; **2.** GR particle, preposition.

edebi literary.

edebikelâm euphemism.

edebiyat, -tı [ā] literature; ~ **dekoru** rhetorical ornamentation; ∼ **Fakültesi** Faculty of Arts, the College of Literature and Arts; ~ **yapmak** to use a pompous language.

edebiyatçı [ā] man of letters, literary man, writer.

edep, -bi 1. good breeding, good manners, politeness, respect, modesty; rule custom; **2.** = **ayıp**; ~ **erkân** good manners; etiquette; ~ **yeri** private parts, genitals; **edebini takınmak** to behave *o.s.*, to be polite; **-tir söylemesi** P excuse the expression.

edepli well-behaved, well-mannered, with good manners.

edepsiz ill-mannered, rude, shameless, insolent.

eder price.

edevat, -tı [ā] **1.** tools, instruments, implements; **2.** GR particles; ~ **deposu** tools store.

edibane [. - - .] **1.** = **edepli**; **2.** in a literary manner; worthy of a literary man.

edilgen GR passive; ~ **fiil** GR passive.

edilmek *pass. of* **etmek.**

edinmek to get, to have, to procure, to acquire.

edip [ī] man of letters, literary man, writer; **2.** = **edepli.**

Edirne *pr. n.* Edirne, Adrianople.

editör 1. publisher; **2.** editor.

efe¹ 1. elder brother; **2.** brave chap, courageous lad; **3.** guer(r)illa, irregular; **4.** village hero, swashbuckling village dandy.

efe² *rare* effect.

efekt, -ti MEC effect.

efektif cash, ready money.

efelik swagger, dash; ~ **satmak** (*or* **yapmak**) to swagger, to strut, to boast.

efendi [. x .] **1.** *title given to literate people, members of the Clergy, Ottoman princes, army officers up to major*; **2.** master; Mr. (*after the first name*); **3.** *pej.* strange, odd, peculiar (*person*); **4.** (*a. -den*) gentleman; ~ **adam** gentleman.

efendim 1. yes? (*as an answer to a call*); **2.** I beg your pardon?; **3.** sir; ma'am; **4.** *added to a sentence for politeness.*

Efes Ephesus.

Efgan(istan) *s.* **Afgan(istan).**

efkâr (*pl. of* **fikir**) **1.** thoughts, ideas, opinions; **2.** intentions; **3.** worry, anxiety; ~ **dağıtmak** to cheer o.s. up.

efkânumumiye public opinion.

efkârlanmak F to become wistfully sad.

efkârlı worried, anxious.

Eflâtun [ū] *pr. n.* Plato.

eflâtun [ū] (*renkli*) lilac-colo(u)red.

efor effort, exertion.

efrat, -dı [ā] (*pl. of* **fert**) **1.** individuals, people; **2.** MIL private soldiers. the ranks, rank and file; **3.** members.

efsane [ā] **1.** legend; fable, tale, myth; **2.** *pej.* idle tale.

efsanevi [ā] legendary.

efsun charm, spell, enchantment.

eften püften flimsy.

Ege Aegean Sea; ~ **Denizi** Aegean Sea; ~ **havzası** Aegean territory.

ege master guardian.

egemen sovereign, dominant.

egemenlik sovereignty, dominance.

egoist egoist, selfish.

egoistlik egoism, selfishness.

egoizm egoism, selfishness.

egosantrizm egocentricity.

egzama [x . .] eczema.

egzersiz exercise, practice.

egzistansialist, -ti existentialist.

egzos, egzost, -tu MEC exhaust; ~ **borusu** exhaust pipe; ~ **gazı** exhaust gas.

egzotik exotic.

eğe¹ file.

eğe² ANAT rib.

eğelemek to file.

eğer [x .] **1.** if, whether; when; **2.** *s.* **eyer.**

eğik 1. MATH oblique; **2.** inclined, sloping down.

eğilim tendency, inclination, affinity; ~ **göstermek** to show tendency (-*e* to).

eğilme MATH, PHYS inclination, dip.

eğilmek 1. *pass. of* **eğmek**; **2.** to bend; to incline; to curve; to warp; **3.** to bow (down), to stoop; **4.** to submit, to yield; **5.** to get down to (*a job*); **eğilip bükülmek** to wind.

eğim 1. slope, declivity; **2.** MATH dip, grade, gradient.

eğin, -ğni back, shoulders; **eğne binmek** *fig.* to bully, to tyrannize.

eğinç, -ci tumo(u)r.

eğinik leaning, inclined.

eğinim inclination, tendency, affinity.

eğinti filings.

eğirmek to spin.

eğirmen spindle, distaff.

eğitbilim pedagogy.

eğitici 1. pedagogue; **2.** educational, instructive.

eğitim education, training, instruction.

eğitimci educator, educationalist, pedagogue.

eğitimli educated, trained, instructed.

eğitmek 1. to educate; **2.** to train, to break in.

eğitmen educator; instructor.

eğitsel educational.

eğlemek 1. to retard, to delay, to hold back; **2.** to amuse.

eğlence 1. diversion, amusement, enjoyment, entertainment, fun; **2.** butt of derision, laughing-stock, joke; **3.** entertaining party; ~ **yeri** pleasure ground, amusement park, recreation ground.

eğlenceli amusing, diverting, entertaining.

eğlencelik 1. titbits, tidbits; **2.** *fig.* laughing-stock.

eğlendirmek to entertain, to amuse,

to divert.

eğlenmek 1. to be amused, to amuse o.s., to enjoy o.s., to have a good time; **2.** (*b-le*) to make fun of *s.o.*, to joke with *s.o.*, to make a mock of *s.o.*, to ridicule; **3.** to while away, to loaf.

eğlenti blow-out, amusement, feast, party, entertainment.

eğmek to bend, to incline, to curve, to bow.

eğre saddlecloth.

eğrelti, eğreltiotu, -nu BOT fern, bracken.

eğreti 1. artificial, false: **2.** borrowed; **3.** provisional, temporary, makeshift; **~ almak** (*bşi b-den*) to borrow; **~ ata binen tez iner** *pro.* he who rides a borrowed horse must soon dismount; **~ oturmak** to sit on the edge of *s.th.*

eğri 1. crooked, bent, curved; **2.** oblique, slanting, inclined, awry, askew; **3.** MATH curve, bend, angle; **4.** perverse, wrong, unjust, untrue; **5.** NAUT rib; **~ bakmak 1.** to look at *s.th.* slantwise; **2.** to leer (*-e* at); **~ gitmek** *fig.* to deviate, to go wrong; **~ oturmak** to sit informally; **~ söylemek 1.** to say maliciously; **2.** to fib, to tell fibs.

eğribacak bow-legged, bandy-legged, knock-kneed.

eğribüğrü [- . . . .] **1.** bent and crooked, contorted, twisted, gnarled, devious; **2.** pitiful, pitiable, miserable.

eğrili MATH curvilinear.

eğrilik 1. crookedness; curvature; **2.** dishonesty; **3.** obliquity, slope, incline; **4.** MATH bend(ing).

eğrilmek to become bent, to incline, to arch, to slope, to bow.

eğriltmek to make crooked, to bend, to twist.

eh *int.* well, all right, come on, enough.

ehemmiyet, -ti importance, significance; **~ vermek** (*bşe*) to attach importance to *s.th.*; **-le kaydetmek** to render prominently, to emphasize; **-le rica etm.** to entreat, to beseech, to implore, to adjure.

ehemmiyetli important, significant.

ehemmiyetsiz unimportant, insignificant.

ehil, -hli 1. community, people; **2.** competent; **3.** gifted, talented; **4.** husband; wife; spouse; **5.** possessor, owner, proprietor; **ehli olm.** (*bşin*) to be endowed with *s.th.*, to be versed in *s.th.*

ehli tame, domestic(ated).

ehlibeyt, -ti the Prophet's family.

ehlihibre (*sg. or pl.*) expert.

ehliislam Muslim(s).

ehlikeyf self-indulgent, pleasure-seeking.

ehlileştirmek to tame.

Ehlisalip, -bi HIST Crusaders; **~ Seferleri** HIST Crusades.

ehlivukuf *s.* **ehlihibre.**

ehliyet, -ti 1. capacity, competence, efficiency; **2.** (= **~ vesikası**) driving license, driver's license; **~ sahibi** expert, specialist; **ehliyeti fenniye vesikası** certificate of qualification, certificate of competence.

ehliyetli 1. able, capable; gifted, talented; **2.** competent, qualified; **3.** licensed.

ehliyetname [ā] **1.** driving license, driver's license; **2.** certificate of competence, certificate of qualification.

ehram [ā] **1.** the Pyramids; **2.** Pyramid.

ehven 1. cheap(est), inexpensive; **2.** the better; **ehveni şer** the lesser of two evils.

ejder, ejderha [ā] dragon.

ek, -ki 1. addition; appendix; **2.** extension; **3.** supplement; **4.** seam, scar, knot (*tree*); **5.** wing; **6.** join(t); **7.** GR inflexion-ending; **8.** GR suffix, affix, prefix; **~ pük** odds and ends, bits and pieces; **~ yeri** seam, scar; body joint; **-ini belli etmemek** *fig.* to cover up, to dissimulate, to dissemble.

ekâbir the great; important people; VIP's, F bigwig, big shot, big pot.

ekalliyet, -ti minority; **-ler hukuku** JUR Law of Minorities; **-te kalmak** to be in the minority.

e-kart IT e-card.

ekber 1. greatest, very great, highest; **2.** older, oldest.

ekici sower.

ekili sown, planted (*field*).

ekim 1. sowing, planting; **2.** (*ayı*) October.

ekin 1. crops, growing grain; **2.** culture, civilization; **~ biçmek** to reap, to harvest.

ekinci 1. sower; cultivator; **2.** farmer.

ekip, -pi team (*a. sport*), crew, gang, company.

e-kitap IT e-book.

eklem ANAT joint, articulation.

eklemek 1. to add, to join; **2.** to lengthen; **3.** to put together, to compose, to compound, to assemble; **4.** to combine, to merge, to consolidate, to fuse; **5.** *sl.* to knock down, to fell.

eklenmek to be joined (*-e* to), to be added (*-e* to).

eklenti 1. GR suffix; **2.** annex.

ekler[1] BIOL annexa.

ekler[2] zip fastener, zip(per).

ekli pieced, put together; ~ **püklü** patchy.

ekmek[1] **1.** to sow; **2.** to till, to cultivate (*field*); **3.** to scatter, to sprinkle, to spread; **4.** *sl.* to squander, to blue, to blow (*money*); **5.** *sl.* to pass, to overtake, to outstrip; **6.** *sl.* to put s.o. off, to get rid of s.o.

ekmek[2] **1.** bread; **2.** bread and butter, bread-winning, living, livelihood; **3.** food; **4.** job; ~ **çiğne(n)meden yutulmaz** *pro.* you have to chew the bread to swallow it; ~ **kabuğu** crust of a loaf; ~ **kapısı** *fig.* the place where one works for one's living; ~ **ufağı** breadcrumb; **ekmeği dizinde** *fig.* submissive, servile, ungrateful; **ekmeğine yağ sürmek** *fig.* to play into s.o.'s. hands.

ekmekçi 1. baker; **2.** bakery.

ekmeklik 1. breadbasket; **2.** suitable for bread making; **3.** *sl.* simpleton, dupe, fool, easy victim, easy mark.

ekoloji ecology.

ekonomi economy; ♀ **Bakanlığı** Ministry of Economy; ~ **politik** political economy.

ekonomik economic(al); ~ **coğrafya** economic geography.

ekose plaid, tartan.

ekran 1. screen; **2.** PHOT filter.

eksantrik eccentric; ~ **mili** MEC eccentric rod.

ekselans Excellency.

eksen 1. axis; **2.** axle.

ekser[1] large nail, spike; **-i oynamış** *fig.* mad, nuts.

ekser[2] [x .], **ekseri** [x . .] majority, the greater part; **ekser(i) ahvalde** mostly, generally; **ekserisi** usually.

ekseriya [x . .] generally, mostly, usually, often.

ekseriyet, -ti majority; **-le** generally, usually, mostly.

eksi MATH minus; **yedi** ~ **üç** seven minus three.

eksibe sand dunes.

eksik 1. missing, lacking, absent, defect, wanting; **2.** less (than); **3.** defi-

cient, incomplete, defective, imperfect; **4.** deficit; ~ **etmemek** to keep always in stock, always to have, never to omit; ~ **gedik** small necessities, deficiencies; ~ **gelmek** to be insufficient; ~ **olma(-yın)!** thank you very much!; ~ **olsun!** no, thank you!; ~ **olmamak** always to turn up, always to be available; **eksiğini tamamlamak** to fill the gap, to make good a deficiency, to complement, to supplement.

eksiklik 1. deficiency, defectiveness; lack, absence; **2.** shortcoming, defect, fault.

eksiksiz 1. complete, perfect; **2.** permanent; **3.** without defect, faultless.

eksilmek 1. to decrease, to lessen, to diminish, to dwindle; **2.** to be absent, to disappear.

eksiltme bid, tender.

eksiltmek to diminish, to reduce, to lessen, to decrease.

eksiz 1. seamless (*a.* MEC); **2.** GR without a suffix.

ekskavatör excavator, steam shovel.

eksos *s.* **egzos(t)**.

eksper expert, valuer.

ekspres express train *or* steamer.

ekstra [x .] extra, first quality; ~ ~ the very best, best of all.

ekşi 1. sour, acid, tart; **2.** *fig.* sour-faced, unfriendly; ~ **surat** long (*or* surly *or* sullen) face; **-ye çalmak** to taste sour.

ekşilik 1. sourness, acidity, tartness; **2.** *fig.* unfriendliness.

ekşimek 1. to (become) sour, to turn sour; **2.** to ferment; **3.** *sl.* to be disgraced, to fall into disgrace, to be disconcerted; **4.** to be upset (*stomach*); **5.** to become cross (*or* disagreeable).

ekşimik a kind of soft cheese.

ekşimsi, ekşimtırak sourish.

ekşitmek to sour; *part. sl.* to compromise.

ekvator equator.

el[1] **1.** hand; **2.** forefoot; **3.** grip, handle; **4.** handful; **5.** help, assistance, aid; **6.** handwriting; **7.** possession; **8.** shot, discharge (*of a fire-arm*); **9.** hand, deal (*of cards*); **10.** power; ~ **açmak** to beg (for), to go begging; ~ **altında** handy, on hand, available, ready; ~ **altından** under the counter, underhandedly, secretly; ~ **arabası 1.** wheel-barrow, hand-cart, push-cart;

2. *sl. school*: wank; ~ **atmak** (*bşe*) **1.** to lay hands (on), to seize, to usurp; **2.** to attempt, to undertake, to take over, to assume; **3.** to intervene, to interfere; ~ **çekmek** (*bşden*) to withdraw, to give up, to relinquish, to leave off, to desist (from); ~ **koymak** (*bşe*) **1.** to take *s.th.* in hand; **2.** to seize, monopolize, to confiscate; ~ **ulağı 1.** messenger boy; **2.** helper, assistant; ~ **uzatmak 1.** to stretch out the hand, to reach (for); **2.** (*b-ne*) *fig.* to help *s.o.* (out), to give (*or* lend) *s.o.* a hand; ~ **yazısı 1.** handwriting; **2.** manuscript; **-de bulunmak** to be available, to be at *s.o.*'s disposal; **-de etm. 1.** to get hold of, to obtain, to get, to secure, to achieve, to attain; **2.** to win *s.o.* over; **-den 1.** by oneself, in person; **2.** by hand, by a messenger; **-den ağıza yaşamak** to live from hand to mouth; **-den çıkarmak** to sell, to dispose (of), to get rid (of); **-den düşme** secondhand; **-den -e** from hand to hand; **-den geçirmek 1.** to review, to go over, to examine, to look through; **2.** to overhaul; **-den gelmek 1.** to be able to do, to be within one's capabilities; **2.** *sl.* to fork out, to tip, to pay up; **-e geçirmek 1.** to get hold (of), to obtain, to secure; **2.** to conquer; **-e vermek** to hand over, to give away, to betray, to put the finger on; **-i açık** open-handed, generous, liberal; **-i ağır 1.** heavy-handed, slow; **2.** heavy-fisted, strong-fisted; **-i ayağı tutmak** to be alive and kicking, to be in the pink (of health); **-i bayraklı** quarrelsome, insolent, shrew, virago; scold, vixen; **-i çabuk** adroit, nimble-fingered; **-i dar(-da)** hard up; **-i hafif** light-handed; **-i maşalı** shrew, virago, scold, vixen, termagant, amazon; **-i sıkı** close-fisted; **-i uzun** light-fingered; **-i varmamak** not to have the heart (to do *s.th.*); **-i yatkın** deft, handy; **-i yüzü düzgün** presentable; **-inde** in the hands of, in *s.o.*'s hands; **-inde bulunmak 1.** to be at *s.o.*'s disposal; **2.** to be owned (by); **-inden tutmak** *fig.* **1.** to help (out); **2.** to patronize, to protect; **-ine bakmak 1.** to depend (-*in* on), to be dependent (-*in* on), to be supported (-*in* by); **2.** to look at *s.o.*'s hands to see what has been brought; **-ine geçmek 1.** to earn, to get; **2.** to meet, to come across; **3.** to find; **-ine su dökemez** (*b-nin*) can't

hold a candle to *s.o.*; **-ini çabuk tutmak** to hurry up; **-ini kolunu bağlamak** (*b-nin*) to tie (*or* bind) *s.o.* hand and foot; **-ini veren kolunu alamaz** (*b-ne*) give him an inch and he'll take a yard; **-ini yüzünü yıkamak** (*bşden*) to wash one's hands of *s.th.*; **-ler yukarı!** hands up!; **-leri yanına gelmek** to die; **-lerinizden öperim** I kiss your hands.

el² 1. land, country; **2.** people; **3.** stranger, alien; **4.** others; ~ **ağziyle çorba yemek** to slander *s.o.*; ~ **gün = elalem**; ~ **kapısı** a stranger's house; ~ **kapısında çalışmak** to work in another's house; ~ **oğlu = elalem**; **-e güne karşı** in the eyes of everybody.

ela hazel (eyes).

elado etm *sl.* to snatch away.

elalem people, all the world, everybody, strangers; **-e kepaze olm.** to become the laughing-stock of people.

elaman 1. *rare* mercy, pardon; **2.** enough!, I am fed up!

el'an [ā] now, at present; still, yet.

elastik(i) elastic.

elastikiyet elasticity.

elbet, -ti [x .], **elbette** [x .] *or* [. x .] certainly, decidedly, surely.

elbirliği co-operation.

elbise 1. clothes, clothing, garments; **2.** dress, suit (*of clothes*); ~ **askısı** coat-hanger.

elçi envoy; ambassador.

elçilik embassy; legation.

eldiven glove.

elebaşı 1. *contp.* ringleader; **2.** captain (*in a game*).

elek sieve; **-ten geçirmek** to sift (*a. fig*).

elektrifikasyon electrification.

elektrik 1. electricity; **2.** *obs.* electric; ~ **akımı** electric current; ~ **düğmesi** switch; ~ **fabrikası** (electric) power station.

elektrikçi electrician.

elektrikleştirmek 1. to electrify; **2.** to inspire, to thrill.

elektrikli electric; live (*wire*); ~ **koltuk** (*or* **sandalye**) electric chair.

elektrokardiyografi electrocardiography.

elektrokardiyogram ECG.

elektromanyetik electromagnetic.

elektromıknatıs electromagnet.

elektron electron.

elektronik electronic(s); ~ **beyin** computer.

elem pain, suffering; sorrow, care; illness, ailment; affliction, grief; ~ **çekmek** to suffer.

eleman 1. element, part, component; **2.** personnel, staff member, performer, worker; **3.** ELECT battery cell.

elemanter elementary.

eleme 1. *vn. of* **elemek**; **2.** sifted, sieved; selected; **3.** elimination; ~ **imtihanı** (*or* **sınavı**) preliminary examination.

elemek 1. to sift, to sieve; **2.** *fig.* to eliminate, to select, to pick out; 3. to wind into hanks (*yarn*).

element element.

elemli painful, grievous, sorrowful.

Elen 1. Hellene; **2.** Greek, Hellenic.

elenika- *-sını bilmek* (*bşin*) to have s.th. at one's fingertips.

eleştiri criticism.

eleştirici 1. critic; **2.** critical.

eleştirim criticism.

eleştirimci critic.

eleştirme criticism.

eleştirmek to criticize.

eleştirmen critic.

elfatiha *name of the opening chapter of the Koran.*

elhamdülillah [. x . . -] *rare* Thank God!

elhasıl in short, in brief, to sum up.

elif *name of the first letter of the Arabic alphabet;* **-i -ine** exactly, just, sharply; **-i görse mertek** (*or* **direk**) **sanır** he knows not a «B» from a bull's foot.

elifba, elifbe the Arabic alphabet.

elim painful, grievous, deplorable, sorrowful

elinsaf! have a heart!, be reasonable!

elişi 1. handicraft, manual labo(u)r; **2.** hand-made.

elkitabı handbook, manual.

elleme 1. *vn. of* **ellemek**; **2.** *part.* hand-picked charcoal.

ellemek to handle, to feel with the hand, to touch with the hand.

elleşmek (*b-le*) **1.** to push and shove; **2.** to shake hands; **3.** to try one another's strength by hand grips; **4.** to come to blows (*or* grips); **5.** to disturb, to trouble, to molest, to annoy, to bother.

elli[1] ... handed; having hands.

elli[2] fifty; ~ **altı 1.** fifty-six; **2.** *sl.* slap; a beating; ~ **dirhem otuz** *sl.* pissed, pickled.

ellilik 1. a banknote for fifty liras; **2.** quinquagenarian, fifty years old.

ellinci fiftieth.

ellişer fifty each; fifty at a time.

elma BOT apple; ~ **ağacı** apple tree; ~ **kürk** *fur made of the cheek pieces of fox skin;* ~ **şarabı** cider; ~ **şekeri** candied apple.

elmacık cheekbone, zygomatic bone.

elmalık apple orchard.

elmas 1. diamond; **2.** diamond glass cutter; **3.** diamond ...; **4.** precious, beloved.

elmasçı seller *or* cutter of diamonds, diamond-merchant.

elmasiye [ā] fruit jelly.

elmastıraş 1. diamond glass cutter; **2.** cut glass, cut diamond; **3.** diamond-cutter.

eloğlu, -nu stranger.

elti sister-in-law (*relationship between the wives of two brothers*).

eltopu, -nu *sports:* handball.

elulağı, -nı helper.

elveda, -aı [ā] farewell, good-bye; ~ **etm.** to say good-bye, to bid farewell.

elverişli 1. sufficient; **2.** profitable; **3.** suitable, convenient, useful, well-adapted, handy.

elverişsiz unsuitable, inconvenient.

elverişsizlik inconvenience, unsuitability.

elvermek 1. to suffice, to be enough; **2.** to be suitable, to be convenient.

elyaf fibres, *Am.* fibers.

elyevm *rare* today, at the present time.

elzem indispensable, imperative, essential, most necessary.

em'a entrails, bowels, intestines.

emanet, -ti [ā] **1.** a trust, deposit, anything entrusted to s.o.; **2.** HIST government office; **3.** left luggage office, *Am.* baggage room; ~ **almak** to take over; ~ **etm.** to entrust, to commit (*-e* to).

emanetçi [ā] depositary, trustee.

emaneten [ā] on deposit; as a trust, for safekeeping.

emare [ā] *rare* sign, mark, token, indication; clue; JUR circumstantial evidence.

emaret, -ti HIST emirate; chieftainship, leadership.

emaye 1. enameled; **2.** glazed.

embriyon ANAT embryo.

embube [ū] tube, canal.

emcik P teat; nipple.

emece *s.* **imece.**

emek 1. work, labo(u)r; **2.** trouble,

pains, fatigue; **~ çekmek** or **vermek** to labo(u)r, to take great pains; **emeği geçmek** to contribute efforts.

emekbirliği, -ni co-operation.

emekçi 1. worker, labo(u)rer; **2.** proletarian.

emeklemek 1. to crawl (or creep) on all fours; **2.** to attempt, to try (as a beginner); **emekliye emekliye** with great difficulty.

emekli 1. retired; pensioner; **2.** = **emektar**; **3.** rare troublesome, hard, laborious; **4.** inactive (sportsman); **-ye ayırmak** to pension off, to retire; **-ye ayrılmak** to retire, to be pensioned off.

emeklilik retirement.

emeksiz effortless, easy, free from labo(u)r.

emektar [ā] old and faithful; veteran.

emektarlık [ā] loyal service, loyalty.

emel longing, desire, wish, coveting, ambition, ideal; **~ beslemek** (or **edinmek**) to long (**for**), to aspire (**to, after**).

emeroit, -ti hemorrhoid.

emilmek pass. of **emmek**.

emin [ī] **1.** safe, secure; **2.** sure, certain; firm, strong; **3.** trustworthy; **4.** steward, custodian, trustee; **5.** HIST superintendent; **6.** God; **7.** ♀ [x .] mf.; **~ olm.** to be sure (-den of), to be confident (-den of).

emir¹, -mri 1. order, command; decree; **2.** rare matter, business; event, case; **3.** (kipi) GR imperative (mood); **~ neferi** (or **eri**) MIL orderly, batman; **emre amade** (or **müheyya**) ready, at one's service (or disposal); **emrinde olm.** to be at s.o.'s disposal (or command); **emri ahîre kadar** until further notice.

emir² emir, chief, prince, leader, ruler, commander.

emirber MIL orderly, batman.

emirlik emirate.

emirname [ā] written command, decree.

emisyon 1. COM issue; **2.** transmission.

emişkamış olm. F to be familiar, to be intimate.

emlak, -ki (pl. of **mülk**) lands, possessions, real estate; **~ alım vergisi** purchase tax on real estate; **~ komisyoncusu** estate agent; **~ vergisi** property tax.

emme vn. of **emmek**; **~ tulumba** suction pump.

emmek 1. to suck; **2.** to absorb; **3.** sl. to swindle money out of s.o.

emniyet, -ti 1. security, safety; **2.** confidence, belief; **3.** reliance; **4.** safety-catch; **5.** the police, the law; **~ altına almak** to secure, to make safe, to ensure; **~ edilir** reliable, dependable, trustworthy; **~ etm. 1.** to trust; **2.** to entrust; **~ kemeri** safety belt; **~ supabı** MEC safety valve, bypass valve.

emniyetli 1. safe; **2.** reliable, trustworthy.

emniyetsiz 1. unsafe, insecure; **2.** distrustful, untrustworthy.

emniyetsizlik lack of confidence, untrustworthiness.

emperyalist POL **1.** imperialist; **2.** imperialistic.

emperyalizm POL imperialism.

empresyonizm impressionism.

empoze imposition; **~ etm.** to force (up)on, to impose.

emprime print fabric.

emretmek [x . .] to order, to command.

emrihak, -kkı 1. God's will; **2.** euph. death; **~ vaki olm.** to die, to pass away.

emrivaki, -li [ā] fait accompli, accomplished fact.

emriyevmî MIL order of the day.

emsal, -li [ā] **1.** similars, equals; **2.** peer, compeer; **3.** precedent; **4.** MATH coefficient; **-i bulunmaz** (or **görülmedik**) matchless, incomparable, unprecedented, unparalleled; **-i misillû** in the same way.

emsalsiz [ā] peerless, unequalled, matchless.

emtia (pl. of **meta**) rare goods, merchandise, wares.

emval, -li [ā] (pl. of **mal**) goods, property.

emzik 1. baby's bottle, feeding bottle; **2.** nipple, teat; **3.** (a. **~ memesi**) dummy, Am. pacifier; **4.** P spout; **5.** P cigarette-holder.

emzirmek to suckle, to nurse, to breast-feed.

en¹ width, breadth; **-i boyu bir** as wide as it is long; **-i sonu** or **-inde sonunda** in the end, at last, eventually; **-ine boyuna 1.** tall and well-built, husky, hefty, huge; **2.** in length and breadth; **3.** fully, completely, thoroughly.

en² most (superlative); **~ az(dan)** at least; **~ başta** at the very beginning; **~ birinci** first of all; **~ çok 1.** mostly; **2.** at (the) most, at the outside; **3.** at the latest; ~ **güzel** most beautiful; ~ **mühim bir mesele** most important matter; ~ **önce** first of all; ~ **sonra** finally; ~ **yüksek** maximum.

en'am [ā] **1.** *pl. of* **nimet**; **2.** Koran anthology.

enaniyet, -ti [ā] *rare* self-centeredness.

enayi *sl.* sucker, fool, idiot, gullible; ~ **dümbeleği** a prize idiot.

enayilik foolishness, gullibility.

encam [ā] *rare* end, conclusion, result, extremity, termination; **-ı kâr** obs. finally, at the end.

encek, encik pup, cub, whelp.

encümen council, committee, commission.

endaht, -tı 1. *obs.* a throwing; **2.** a firing, discharge (*of a firearm*); ~ **etm. 1.** *obs.* to throw; **2.** to fire, to shoot, to discharge.

endam [ā] shape, figure, body, stature; ~ **aynası** full-length mirror.

endamlı [ā] shapely, well-proportioned, graceful.

endaze [ā] **1.** measure; proportion; **2.** *obs. linear measure* (= **0,65 m.**); **-ye vurmak 1.** to measure; **2.** *fig.* to calculate, to consider.

ender (*comp. of* **nadir**) very rare; rarely.

enderun [ū] *rare* gynaeceum, women's apartments of a palace.

enderuni [ū, ī] *rare* inner, interior.

endişe [ī] **1.** anxiety, perplexity, care, disquietude; **2.** worry, fear, suspicion; thought; ~ **etm.** to worry, to be anxious.

endişelenmek [ī] to become anxious, to be troubled, to feel anxiety (**-den** about); to be thoughtful.

endişeli [. - . .] thoughtful, anxious, troubled, worried.

endişesiz [. - . .] carefree, unworried, calm.

endüstri industry.

endüstrileştirmek to industrialize.

enek P castrated.

enemek to castrate.

enerji energy; ~ **santralı** power station (*or* plant); **-nin sakımı** PHYS preservation of energy.

enerjik energetic.

enfarktüs MED heart attack.

enfes (*comp. of* **nefis**) delightful, delicious, excellent, wonderful.

enfiye snuff; ~ **çekmek** to snuff, to take snuff; ~ **kutusu** snuff-box.

enflasyon inflation.

enfüsi [ī] subjective.

engebe unevenness of ground; broken ground, rough country.

engebeli GEOGR steep and broken, uneven, rough.

engebesiz even, smooth.

engel obstacle, difficulty, hindrance, handicap; ~ **imtihanı** second check; ~ **olm.** to hinder, to prevent.

engellemek to hinder, to hamper, to prevent.

engelli: ~ **koşu** (*or* **yarış**) **1.** hurdles; **2.** steeple-chase.

engerek zoo adder, viper.

engin 1. vast, boundless, open, wide; **2.** the high sea, the open sea, offing; **3.** P ordinary, common, low; cheap; **4.** base, mean; ~ **deniz** the high seas, the open sea; **-lere dalmak** to brood, to ponder, to pore (**over**).

enginar BOT artichoke.

enginlik vastness, vastitude, wideness.

engizisyon the Inquisition.

enik P whelp, cub, puppy.

enikonu quite, thoroughly, fully, at length.

enine [x . .] in width, breadthwise, crosswise, transversally.

enişte [x . .] husband of an aunt *or* sister, brother-in-law, uncle.

enjeksiyon injection.

enjektör injector.

enkaz ruins; debris; wreck(age).

enlem parallel, line of latitude.

enli wide, broad.

enlilik breadth, width.

enmuzeç, -ci *rare* model, sample.

ense 1. back of the neck, nape; **2.** *sl.* buttocks, bottom, rump; ~ **kökü** nape of the neck; ~ **yapmak** *sl.* to goof off; **-si kalın 1.** willful, obstinate, stiff-necked; **2.** well-to-do, prosperous, well-off, well-heeled; **-sinde boza pişirmek** (*b-nin*) *sl.* to drive hard, to over-tire and torment; **-sinden gitmek** to follow close (upon); **-sine binmek** (*b-nin*) to persecute *s.o.*, to tyrannize *s.o.*

enselemek *sl.* to nick.

ensiz narrow.

ensizlik narrowness.

enstantane snapshot.

enstitü institute.

enstrüman instrument.

ensülin insulin.

entari [ā] **1.** loose robe; **2.** dress.

entbent F confused, disconcerted, perplexed; ~ *olm.* to be taken aback.

entelektüel intellectual.

entegrasyon integration.

enteresan interesting.

enternasyonal 1. international; **2.** POL International.

enterne etm. to intern.

enterüptör MEC interruptor.

entipüften *sl.* flimsy.

entrika [. x .] intrigue, trick; ~ *çevirmek* to intrigue, to scheme.

entrikacı schemer, trickster.

enüstünlük GR superlative degree.

envanter 1. inventory; **2.** stock-taking.

envestisman investment.

epeski [x . .] very old, ancient.

epey a good many, a good deal of; pretty well, fairly; ~ *zaman* long time.

epeyce pretty well, fairly.

epher ANAT aorta.

epidemi epidemic.

epik epic(al).

epkem *obs.* dumb, mute, silent.

e-posta *pr.n.* & *v/t.* e-mail; ~ *adresi* e-mail address.

er[1] = *erken*; ~ *veya geç* = *ergeç.*

er[2] **1.** man, male; **2.** MIL private; **3.** brave man; **4.** capable man, able man; **5.** P husband; ~ *oğlu* ~ hero, brave man; *-e gitmek* (*or varmak*) P to marry a man; *-e vermek* to give in marriage.

eramil [ā] *pl. rare* widows.

erat, *-tı* MIL privates, recruits.

erbap, *-bı* [ā] expert, specialist.

erbaş MIL non-commissioned officer.

erdem virtue.

erdemli virtuous.

erdemsizlik lack of virtue.

erdirmek *caus. of* **ermek** to cause to reach *or* attain.

erek aim, end, goal.

ereklik PHIL finality.

erenler 1. those who have arrived at the divine truth; **2.** mode of address among dervishes.

ergeç sooner or later.

ergen 1. marriageable; **2.** unmarried, single, celibate; ~ *olm.* to be old enough to marry.

ergenlik 1. singleness, bachelorhood; **2.** youthful acne; ~ *dişi* wisdom-tooth.

ergime fusion.

ergimek to melt.

ergin 1. mature, adult, ripe; **2.** JUR major.

erginleşmek to mature.

erginlik maturity, puberty; JUR majority.

erguvan [ā] BOT **1.** Judas-tree, redbud; **2.** purple.

erguvani [. . - -] purple.

erik BOT plum.

eril GR masculine.

erim[1] *obs.* reach, range.

erim[2]; ~ ~ *erimek* to pine away.

erimek 1. to melt, to fuse, to dissolve; to pass away; **2.** to wear out (*textiles*); **3.** to pine away; **4.** to be greatly embarrassed.

erirlik CHEM solubility.

erişmek 1. (*bşe*) to arrive, to attain, to reach; **2.** to mature, to reach the age of marriage; **3.** to come.

erişte vermicelli.

eritmek 1. to melt, to dissolve; **2.** to squander (*money*).

eriyik CHEM solution.

erk power, faculty; authority.

erkân (*pl. of rükûn*) **1.** great men, high officials, pillars of the state; **2.** generals; **3.** rules of conduct, way, method; *-ı harp* MIL general staff.

erkeç ZOO he-goat, billy-goat.

erkek 1. man, male; **2.** manly, courageous, virile, honest and true; **3.** P husband; **4.** good, hard (*metal*); **5.** MEC male; ~ *berberi* men's hairdresser, barber; ~ *dul* widower; ~ *kopça* hook for an eye.

erkekçe manly; manfully.

erkeklik 1. masculinity; manliness; courage; **2.** sexual potency, virility.

erkeksi tomboyish, masculine; ~ *kadın* amazon, mannish woman.

erkeksiz 1. without husband; **2.** alone, lonely (*woman*).

erken early.

erkence rather early, a little early, somewhat early.

erkenci early riser, early comer.

erkenden early.

erkin 1. free, independent; **2.** ♀ *mf.*

erklik power.

erlik 1. manliness, bravery, courage; **2.** soldiership.

ermek (*-ir*) **1.** to attain; to reach; **2.** to ripen, to mature; **3.** to come of age; **4.** to reach spiritual perfection.

Ermeni Armenian; ~ *gelini gibi kırıtmak* **1.** to hang back; **2.** to be affected, to attitudinize.

Ermenice Armenian (language).

Ermenistan *pr. n.* Armenia.
ermiş saint, holy person.
eroin heroin, junk.
eroinman junky, junkie.
erozyon erosion.
ersiz without husband.
ertak! *sl.* let's go!
erte the next, the following (*s.a.* **erte-si**).
ertelemek to postpone, to defer, to adjourn, to put off.
ertesi the next, the following; ~ **gün** the next day, the following day; ~ **se-ne** the next year, the following year, the year after.
ervah spirits, souls; **-ına yuf olsun!** damn him!
erzak [ā] (*pl. of* **rızk**) provisions, food.
erzats ersatz, substitute.
es MUS rest; ~ **geçmek** *sl.* to disregard.
esame [ā] HIST muster roll (*or* roster) of the Janissaries.
esameli [ā] **1.** registered in **esame; 2.** previously convicted; **3.** notorious, ill-famed.
esami [. - -] (*obs.. pl. of* **isim**); ~ **üze-rine yoklama** MIL roll-call; **-si okun-mamak** *fig.* to be disregarded, to be of no consequence.
esans essence, perfume.
esaret 1. slavery; captivity; **2.** yoke.
esas 1. foundation, base, basis; **2.** basic, fundamental, principle, essential; **3.** true state; **4.** CHEM base; ~ **itibariyle** in principle, as a matter of fact, essentially, basically; ~ **nokta** main point; ~ **sermaye** (original) stock, capital deposit.
esasen [ā] [. x .] **1.** fundamentally, in principle, essentially; **2.** anyhow.
esasi [.- -] fundamental, essential, basic (*a.* CHEM).
esaslı [ā] **1.** based, founded; **2.** fundamental, main; **3.** real, true, sure, reliable; **4.** sound, solid, concrete; ~ **bir noktaya dokunmak** to hit the mark; ~ **malumat** thorough information.
esassız [ā] baseless, unfounded, groundless.
esatir [. - -] *pl.* legends, myths, tales, stories.
esatirî [. - - -] mythological.
esbab, **-bı** [ā] (*obs., pl. of* **sebep**) causes, reasons; **-ı mucibe** JUR motives.
esef regret; ~ **etm.** to be sorry, to pity, to feel regret (for); **-e şayan** regretta-ble, deplorable.

esefle regretfully, deplorably.
esefli regrettable, deplorable.
eselemek ~ **beselemek** to leave no stone unturned, to leave nothing undone.
esen hearty healthy, robust, sound; ~ **kal(-ınız)** so long!
esenlik health, soundness, welfare.
eser 1. work (of art); **2.** trace, sign, mark; **3.** remains, monuments; ~ **sa-hibi** author.
esermek ~ **besermek** to bring about laboriously.
esham [ā] (*pl. of* **sehim**) share, bonds, securities; ~ **ve tahvilât borsası** stock exchange.
esinlenmek to be inspired (*-den* by).
esinti breeze.
esintili breezy.
esir [ī] **1.** captive, prisoner of war; **2.** slave; **3.** infatuated with, gone on; ~ **almaca** prisoners' base; ~ **almak** to take prisoner; ~ **düşmek** (*or* **olm.**) (*b-ne*) to be taken prisoner; ~ **etm.** to enslave, to take prisoner; ~ **kampı** prison(ers') camp; ~ **ticareti** slave trade.
esir ether, aether.
esirci slave trader.
esircilik slave trade.
esirgemek 1. to protect (*-den* from), to spare; **2.** to grudge; to withhold (*-den* from); **Allah esirgesin!** may God protect us!, God forbid!
esirlik captivity; slavery.
eski 1. old, ancient; **2.** former, ex-; **3.** worn out, old; **4.** second-hand; **5.** out of date; **6.** chronic (*disease*); ~ **çamlar bardak oldu** (*or* **kürek ol-muş**) *fig.* a lot of water has flowed (*or* passed *or* gone) under the bridge; ~ **defterleri karıştırmak** to rake over the ashes, to rake up the past; ~ **göz ağrısı** an old flame; ~ **hamam, eski tas** the same old thing, just the same as ever; ~ **hayratı berbat etmek** to make s.th. worse by trying to improve it; ~ **kafalı** old fogy; ~ **kurt** old hand; ~ **püskü** old and tattered things, castoffs, junk; ~ **toprak** *fig.* old-timer; ~ **zaman(-lar) 1.** antiquity; **2.** olden times, the past; **-si gibi** as of old, as before.
eskici 1. oldclothes man, ragman; **2.** shoe-repairer, cobbler.
eskiçağ prehistoric period.

eskiden formerly, in the past, in old days; ~ *kalma* handed down, passed down.

eskiler 1. the ancients; **2.** castoffs.

eskileşmek 1. to go out (of date); **2.** to wear out.

eskilik oldness.

eskime *vn. of eskimek*; ~ *ve aşınma* MIL natural attrition, wear and tear.

eskimek 1. = *eskileşmek*; **2.** to become chronic; **3.** to become gray-headed.

Eskimo [. x .] Eskimo.

eskişehirtaşı, -nı meerschaum.

eskitmek to wear out, to wear up.

eskiz draft, sketch, model.

eskrim fencing; ~ *meçi* foil.

eskrimci fencer.

esmek 1. to blow (*wind*); **2.** *fig.* to come into the mind of s.o., to occur to s.o.; *esip savurmak* F **1.** to brag, to boast, to show off, to talk big; **2.** to rage, to storm and bluster.

esmer brunette, swarthy, dark complexioned; ~ *güzeli* dark brown beauty, dark complexioned belle.

esmerleşmek to tan, to get brown.

esna [ā] *rare* moment, instant, time, course, interval; *harb -sında* during the war; *o -da* at that time, meanwhile; *-da* while; *-sında* in the course of, during.

esnaf [ā] (*pl. of sınıf*) **1.** trades, guilds; **2.** tradesmen, artisans; **3.** *sl.* prostitute, whore, bitch, tart.

esnek 1. elastic, flexible; **2.** ambiguous.

esneklik elasticity, flexibility.

esnemek 1. to yawn, to gape; **2.** to bulge, to bend, to give (*board, etc.*); **3.** to stretch (*material*).

esnetmek *caus. of esnemek a.* to vex, to annoy, to bore.

espri wisecrack, witticism, wit; ~ *yapmak* to wisecrack.

esprili witty.

esrar [ā] (*obs., pl. of sır*) **1.** secrets; mysteries; **2.** hashish; ~ *kumkuması* (or *kutusu* or *küpü*) secretive or mysterious person, a locked door; ~ *çekmek* to smoke hashish; to take drugs; ~ *tekkesi* opium den.

esrarengiz [. - . -] mysterious.

esrarkeş [ā] hashish addict; doper.

esrarlı [ā] **1.** = *esrarkeş*; **2.** mysterious.

esselâmünaleyküm = *selâmünaleyküm*.

estağfurullah [. x . . .] **1.** *rare* God forbid!; **2.** don't mention it!, not at all!

estek: ~ *köstek etm.* or ~ *etm. köstek etm.* to make all sorts of excuses to get out of doing s.th.

ester¹ *rare* mule.

ester² CHEM ester.

estetik 1. esthetics; **2.** esthetic.

esvap clothes; garment; dress; suit.

eş 1. one of a pair, mate, fellow; **2.** husband; wife; partner; **3.** a similar thing, match; ~ *dost* friends and acquaintances; ~ *tutmak* to choose a partner; *-i görülmedik* peerless, matchless, unique.

eşanlam synonym.

eşanlamlı synonymous.

eşarp, -pı scarf; stole, sash.

eşcinsel homosexual; ~ *evlilik* gay marriage.

eşdeğer equivalence.

eşdeğerli equivalent.

eşek 1. donkey, ass; **2.** jackass, boor; ~ *başı fig.* superior without authority; ~ *başı mısın?* why don't you use your authority?; ~ *herif* jackass; ~ *kadar oldu sl.* he is big enough to know what's what; ~ *sudan gelinceye kadar dövmek* to tan s.o.'s hide, to beat the hell out of s.o., to beat to a pulp; ~ *şakası* practical joke, horseplay; *eşeğe ters bindirmek fig.* to pillory, to brand, to denounce, to show s.o. up.

eşekarısı, -nı ZOO wasp, hornet.

eşekçe(sine) coarsely; stupidly.

eşekhıyarı, -nı *s.* acıhıyar.

eşeksırtı, -nı gable roof.

eşeksineği, -ni ZOO horsefly, gadfly.

eşekzeytini, -ni a kind of large olive.

eşelemek (*bşi*) **1.** to scrape, to scratch; **2.** *fig.* to stir up, to rake up, to rummage, to hunt (**for**).

eşey sex.

eşeysel sexual.

eşhas [ā] (*pl. of şahıs*) persons; characters (*in a play*).

eşik 1. threshold, doorstep; **2.** bridge (*of a violin, etc.*); **3.** *fig.* verge, brink; *eşiğine gelmek* (*b-nin*) **1.** to petition; **2.** to molest, to pester; *eşiğini aşındırmak* (*b-nin*) to frequent constantly.

eşinmek to scratch, to paw.

eşit 1. equal, equivalent, match; the same; **2.** MATH equals.

eşitlik equality.

eşkâl, -li [. -] **1.** features and appearance, description **2.** shapes, figures.

eşkenar MATH equilateral.

eşkıya [ā] (*pl. of* **şaki**) **1.** brigands; **2.** brigand, thug, bandit; ~ **yatağı 1.** den of robbers, hide-out; **2.** accomplice.

eşleme 1. pairing; **2.** cinema; synchronization.

eşlemek 1. to pair, to match; **2.** to synchronize.

eşleşmek 1. to be partners (*in a game*); **2.** (*animals*) to mate with each other.

eşlik 1. partnership; **2.** MUS accompaniment; ~ **etm.** to accompany.

eşmek 1. to dig lightly; to scratch up the ground; **2.** to search and investigate.

eşofman 1. tracksuit; **2.** warming up.

eşeğlu eşek *sl.* silly ass, louse.

eşraf [ā] (*pl. of* **şerif**) notables (*of a town, etc.*).

eşref (*comp. of* **şerif**) *rare* most noble; ~ **saati** propitious moment, opportune time.

eşsesli homonym.

eşsiz 1. matchless, peerless, unique; **2.** unpaired.

eşya [ā] (*pl. of* **şey**) **1.** things, objects; **2.** furniture; luggage; belongings; goods.

eşyalı furnished.

eşyasız unfurnished.

eşzamanlı isochronal.

et, -ti 1. meat; **2.** flesh; **3.** pulp (*of a fruit*); **4.** skin; ~ **bağlamak 1.** to close up, to heal up (*wound*); **2.** to put on weight, to get fat; ~ **but** (*or* **can**) **tutmak** to put on weight, to get stout; ~ **suyu 1.** meat broth, bouillon; **2.** gravy; ~ **tırnaktan ayrılmaz** *pro.* blood is thicker than water; ~ **yığını** *fig.* fleshy; **-i budu yerinde** *or* **-ine dolgun** plump, buxom, roly-poly, matronly.

etabli settled, naturalized.

etajer dresser, whatnot; shelves, bookcase.

etap *sports*: lag, stage; distance between laps.

etçil BIOL carnivorous.

etek 1. skirt; **2.** foot (*of a mountain*), hillside; **3.** fringe; **4.** private parts, genital area; ~ **dolusu** *or* ~ ~ loads of, plenty of, in abundance; ~ **öpmek** *fig.* to flatter, to toady; ~ **silkmek** (*bşden*) to dissociate *o.s.* from *s.th.*; **eteği belinde** industrious, diligent (*woman*); **eteği düşük** slovenly, sloppy, slipshod (*woman*); **-leri tutuşmak**

to be exceedingly alarmed; **-leri zil** (*or* **ıslık**) **çalıyor** he is up in the air, he is walking on air.

eteklemek 1. to kiss *s.o.*'s skirt; **2.** to flatter.

eteklik 1. skirt, frock; **2.** material for a skirt.

etelemek: ~ **betelemek** to treat unfriendly.

eter CHEM ether.

etıbba [ā] (*pl. of* **tabip**) doctors.

Eti Hittite.

e-ticaret IT e-commerce.

etiket, -ti 1. label, ticket; **2.** etiquette.

etiketlemek to label.

etilen ethylene.

etimoloji etymology.

etkafalı blockhead, dumb, dizzy, thick-headed.

etken 1. agent, factor; **2.** effective; **3.** GR active.

etki 1. effect, influence; **2.** impression, impact; ~ **alanı** domain (*in Internet sense*).

etkilemek to affect, to influence.

etkili effective, influential, effectual.

etkin active, effective.

etkinlik 1. activity; **2.** efficiency, effectiveness.

etlenmek to grow fat.

etli 1. fleshy, plump; **2.** pulpy, fleshy (*fruit*); **3.** meaty; ~ **butlu** plump, buxom; ~ **kemikli** corporeal; ~ **yemek** meaty dish; **-ye sütlüye karışmamak** to mind one's own business, to avoid getting involved.

etmek (**eder**) **1.** to do, to make; **2.** to be worth, to be of value; **3.** to come to, to amount to; **4.** to act, to behave; **5.** to live, to be alive, to exist; **6.** to reach; **7.** to deprive (*or* rob) of; **8.** to do *s.th.* to *s.o.*; **9.** to urinate *or* to defecate; **eden bulur** one pays for what one does; **ettiğini yanına bırakmamak** not to let *s.o.* get away with *s.th.*, to get revenge on *s.o.*

etmen factor.

etnik ethnic.

etoburlar ZOO carnivorous animals.

etol, -lü stole.

etraf [ā] (*pl. of* **taraf**) **1.** sides, ends; **2.** surroundings; **3.** relatives; **4.** directions, regions; **5. -ına, -ında** around; **6. -ında** concerning, with regard to, in respect of; **-a haber vermek** to trumpet (forth), to noise abroad; **-ını almak** (*or* **çevirmek** *or* **sarmak**) to surround, to encircle; **-lyle** detailed, in detail; **-ta** in the neighbo(u)rhood, in the vicinity, around; **-tan** from all around, from all directions.

etraflı(ca) detailed, in detail, fully.

etsineği, -ni ZOO blowfly.

etsiz 1. without meat; fleshless; **2.** thin, weak, puny.

ettahiyat, -tı [. . . -] *name of a certain Muslim canticle*.

ettirgen GR causative (*verb*).

ettirmek to cause to do.

etüt, -dü 1. study, essay, research; **2.** MUS preliminary study; **3.** study hall.

etüv 1. CHEM drying-out cupboard; **2.** sterilizer.

etyaran whitlow.

Etyopi, Etyopya [. x .] *pr. n.* Ethiopia.

ev 1. house, dwelling; **2.** home, household; **3.** office, institution; **4.** *fig.* family, clan; ~ **açmak** to set up house; ~ **bark** house and home, household; ~ **bark sahibi** family man; ~ **ekmeği** homemade bread; ~ **eşyası** furniture, effects; ~ **halkı** household, family; ~ **hanımı** hostess; ~ **idaresi** housekeeping; ~ **işletmek** to run a brothel; ~ **işi** housework; ~ **kadını** housewife; ~ **kadınlığı** housewifery; ~ **sahibi 1.** host; **2.** landlord; ~ **tutmak** to rent a house; ~ **yıkmak** to break up a home; **-de kalmış** *fig.* on the shelf; **-lere şenlik** happiness to homes!, joy to houses!

evani [. - -] *pl. rare* pots, dishes, vessels.

evce, evcek with the whole family.

evci 1. homebody; **2.** weekly boarder.

evcil domesticated, tame.

evcilik: ~ **oynamak** to play mothers and fathers.

evcilleştirmek to domesticate, to tame.

evcimen, evciment, -di home-lover, domesticated.

evedi *s.* **ivedi.**

evelemek *s.* **gevelemek.**

evemek to hasten, to hurry.

evermek P to marry off, to give in marriage.

evet, -ti yes, certainly; ~ **efendim!** yes!, sure!, certainly!; ~ **efendimci** yes-man; ~ **efendim, sepet efendim, güzel efendim demek** to say amen.

evetlemek to say 'yes', to okay.

evham [ā] (*pl. of* **vehim**) delusions, apprehensions, illusions; **-a kapılmak** to become suspicious, to be hypochondriac.

evhamlı [ā] hypochondriac, suspicious.

evirmek to change, to alter; **evire çevire** thoroughly, soundly; ~ **çevirmek 1.** to turn s.th. over and over; **2.** *fig.* to turn s.th. over in one's mind.

eviye (*pl. of* **via**) ANAT vessels.

evkaf (*pl. of* **vakıf**) **1.** pious foundations; estates in mortmain; **2.** the government department in control of estates in mortmain.

evla *rare* best, most suitable, preferable, better (**than**).

evladiyelik heirloom.

evlat, -di [ā] (*pl. of* **velet**) **1.** child, son, daughter; **2.** children, descendants; ~ **acısı** grief for one's deceased child; ~ **canlısı** very fond of his *or* her children; ~ **edinmek** to adopt a child; ~ **sevgisi** love for one's children.

evlatlık 1. adopted child; **2.** foster child; **-tan ret** (*or* **çıkarma**) disownment.

evlek 1. furrow (*in a field*); **2.** a quarter of **dönüm**; **3.** *sl.* a ten-lira note; **4.** water-channel, drainage ditch.

evlendirmek *caus. of* **evlenmek** to marry (off), to give in marriage.

evlenme *vn. of* **evlenmek** marriage; ~ **dairesi** registry office; ~ **kâğıdı** JUR marriage certificate (*or* lines).

evlenmek to marry; to get married.

evleviyet, -ti *rare* preference; **-le** all the more, so much the sooner.

evli married; ~ **hayat** married life; ~ **kadın** married woman.

evlilik marriage; ~ **birliği** JUR conjugal community.

evliya [ā] (*pl. of* **veli**) saint; ~ **gibi** saintly, gentle.

evrak, -kı [ā] **1.** *obs.*, BOT leaves; **2.** documents, papers; ~ **çantası** brief-case, portfolio; ~ **kalemi** record office, registry; ~ **memuru** registrar; **-ı müsbite** document of proof.

evre phase.

evren 1. universe; **2.** cosmos; **3.** environment; **4.** time; **5.** great.

evrensel universal.

evrim evolution.

evrimsel evolutionary.

evsaf [ā] (*pl. of* **vasıf**) *rare* qualities, qualifications; **birinci -ta askerler** highly qualified soldiers.

evvel 1. first; ago; before, earlier, of

old; initial; **2.** the first part, the beginning; ~ **emirde** first of all; ~ **zaman içinde** once upon a time; **bundan** ~ before this, previously; **iki sene -sine nazaran** compared to (or in comparison with) the time two years ago.

evvela [x . .] firstly, first of all, to begin with.

evvelce formerly, previously.

evvelden previously, formerly, beforehand; ~ **sezmek** to foresee, to anticipate.

evveli 1. in the old days; **2.** the previous.

evveliyat, -tı [ā] antecedents, first stages, first principles, beginnings.

evvelki, evvelsi 1. the previous; **2.** the (year, month, week) before last; ~ **gün** the day before yesterday; ~ **sene** the year before last.

evza [ā] (pl. of vazı) rare **1.** gestures; **2.** acts, conduct, behavio(u)r; **3.** position, postures.

ey 1. o!; **2.** now see here!; **3.** so?, so what?

eyalet, -ti [ā] province; state.

eyer saddle; ~ **takımı** saddle and harness; ~ **takmak** (or **vurmak**) to put a saddle on, to saddle.

eyerci saddler.

eyerlemek to saddle.

eyerli saddled.

eyersiz unsaddled; bareback.

eylem 1. action, deed; **2.** operation; **3.** verb; ~ **tümcesi** GR verbal sentence; **-e geçmek** to put into operation.

eylemci activist.

eylemcilik activism.

eylemek s. **etmek.**

eylül, -lü September.

eytam [ā] (pl. of yetim) rare orphans.

eyvah [ā] alas!; ~ **çekmek** to sigh; **-lar olsun!** alas!, what a pity!

eyvallah [x . -] **1.** thank you!, thanks!; **2.** good bye!; **3.** all right!; ~ **demek** to agree, to accept; ~ **etm. 1.** to comply with s.o.'s wish; **2.** to flatter, to adulate; **-ı olmamak** (b-ne) to be obliged to no one.

eyyam [ā] (pl. of yevm) **1.** time, period; **2.** better days, prosperous days; **3.** power, influence; **4.** NAUT favo(u)rable wind; ~ **efendisi** (or **ağası** or **reisi**) opportunist, timeserver; ~ **görmüş** (or **sürmüş**) who has seen better days; ~ **ola!** NAUT may wind and weather be favo(u)rable to you!; **-ı ba-**

hur dog-days.

eza [ā] annoyance, vexation; pain, torment, torture.

ezan [ā] call to prayer.

ezani [. - -]: ~ **saat** the hour as reckoned from sunset.

ezber 1. by heart; **2.** memorization; lesson to be memorized.

ezberci who learns parrot fashion.

ezberden 1. by heart; **2.** without knowing; ~ **okumak** to recite by heart.

ezbere 1. by heart; **2.** superficially; ~ **iş görmek** to act without due knowledge, to do s.th. superficially.

ezberlemek to learn by heart, to memorize, to commit to memory.

ezcümle [x . .] **1.** among other things; for instance, for example; **2.** in short; **3.** especially, particularly.

ezel rare past eternity; **-denberi** from eternity, all along.

ezeli without beginning, eternal; ~ **ve ebedi** eternal; without beginning or end.

ezeliyet, -ti [ā] past eternity.

ezgi 1. MUS tune, note, melody; **2.** fig. style, tempo; **3.** worry, anxiety.

ezgin = **ezik.**

ezici crushing, overwhelming.

ezik 1. crushed, squashed; **2.** worried, anxious; **3.** bruise.

eziklik 1. worry; depression; **2.** feeling of hunger.

ezilmek 1. pass. of **ezmek** to be crushed, to be oppressed; **2.** (with **mide, yürek** or **iç**) to have a sinking feeling; **ezildi büzüldü 1.** he was embarrassed; **2.** he felt a great deal of pain, he was racked with pain.

eziyet, -ti injury, pain, torture, torment; hurt, fatigue, suffering; cruelty, ill-treatment; ~ **çekmek** to suffer fatigue; ~ **etm.** (or **vermek**) to torment, to torture, to cause pain.

eziyetçi tormentor, torturer.

eziyetli fatiguing, painful, tiring, vexatious.

eziyetsiz easy, untroublesome.

ezkaza [. . -] by chance, accidentally.

ezme 1. vn. of **ezmek**; **2.** purée, paste.

ezmek, (-er) 1. to crush, to pound, to powder, to bruise, to squash, to mash; **2.** to trample down, to tread down; **3.** to over-exert, to over-strain, to suppress; **4.** to overcome, to overpower, to overwhelm (enemy); **5.** to run over;

6. F to dissipate (*money*); **7.** to melt, to dissolve (*sugar*); **8.** *fig. sport*: to trounce; *ezip suyunu içi* it is abso-

lutely worthless!
Ezrail *s.* **Azrail.**

F

fa MUS fa.
faal, -li [. -] **1.** active, industrious; **2.** serviceable.
faaliyet, -ti [. - . .] **1.** activity, energy; **2.** serviceableness; ~ *göstermek* to function; ~ *sahası* **1.** scope, field of activity; **2.** *obs.* line of business; *-e geçmek* **1.** to begin to operate; **2.** to take action.
faanahtarı, -nı MUS bass clef.
fabrika [x . .] factory, mill, plant, works; ~ *işi* machine made; ~ *mamulatı* manufactured (*or* factory-made) goods *or* article; ~ *tesisatı* manufacturing plant.
fabrikacı manufacturer, factory owner, industrialist.
fabrikacılık **1.** factory ownership; **2.** industrial production; **3.** manufacture.
fabrikator, fabrikatör *s.* **fabrikacı.**
facia [- . .] **1.** calamity, disaster, catastrophe; **2.** drama, tragedy.
facialı [- . . . .] tragic, terrible, disastrous, catastrophic.
facianüvis [- . . . . -] *obs.* dramatist, tragedian.
faça [x .] **1.** NAUT a ship's facing the wind with the topsail aback; **2.** *sl.* mug, face; **3.** *sl.* the bottommost card, the card at the bottom of a pack; **4.** *sl.* clothing, clothes, dress; *-sını almak (aşağıya)* *sl.* to ridicule, to make fun (*-in* of).
façeta [. x .] facet.
façuna [. x .] NAUT the serving *or* whipping (*of a rope*).
fağfur **1.** *ancient title of the Emperor of China*; **2.** porcelain.
fahim, -hmi great, grand, illustrious, glorious.
fahime intelligence; understanding.
fahiş [ā] **1.** excessive, exorbitant; **2.** *rare* obscene, immoral.
fahişe [ā] prostitute, whore, harlot, *sl.* bitch, tart.
fahrenhayt, -tı Fahrenheit.
fahri **1.** honorary; **2.** **Fahri** [x .] *mf.*; **3.** voluntary, volunteer.

faide *s.* **fayda.**
faik, -kı [ā] **1.** superior; **2.** *rare* outstanding, excellent; **3.** ♀ *mf.*
faikıyet, -ti [ā] superiority.
fail [ā] **1.** agent, author; **2.** perpetrator, author (*of a crime*); **3.** BIOL effective; **4.** GR subject; *-i muhtar* free agent, independent.
failiyet, -ti [ā] **1.** *rare* effect, effectiveness; **2.** efficiency, activity.
faiz [ā] interest; ~ *fiyatı* (*or* nispeti) rate of interest; ~ *yürütmek* to calculate interest; *-e ~ yürütülmesi* calculation of compound interest; *-e vermek* (*or* yatırmak) to lend at interest; *-i işlemek* (*bşin*) to yield interest, to bear interest; *-i mürekkep* (*or* bir-leşik ~) compound interest.
faizci [ā] usurer, moneylender.
faizcilik [ā] usury.
faizli [ā] interest-bearing, at interest.
faizsiz [ā] interest-free.
fak, -kı P snare, trap; *-a basmak* to be duped.
fakat, -tı [x .] but, however, only, merely.
fakfon German silver.
fakih **1.** Moslem jurist; **2.** [faki] learned man.
fakir [ī] **1.** poor, pauper, needy, destitute; beggar; **2.** *obs.* your humble servant; ~ *düşmek* to become poor; ~ *fukara* the poor.
fakirhane [. - - .] **1.** poorhouse; **2.** my house.
fakirleşmek to become poor.
fakirlik poverty.
faksimile facsimile.
faktör factor.
fakülte faculty (*of a university*).
fakülteli university student.
fal, -lı [ā] **1.** fortune; omen, augury; **2.** fortune-telling, soothsaying; ~ *açmak* (*or* atmak) to tell fortunes; ~ *çıktı* the prophecy was fulfilled; ~ *taşı a pebble or bean from which an omen is taken*; ~ *tutmak* to have one's fortune told; *-a bakmak s.* ~ *açmak.*

falaka [x . .] bastinado; **-ya çekmek** to bastinado.

falan F **1.** so and so, such and such; **2.** and so on; **3.** and such like; about, approximately; **~ festekiz** (or **feşmekan** or **fıstık** or **filan**) mst iro. = **falan 2.**

falanca F = **falan 1.**

falanıncı F the nth, the umpteenth.

falbala furbelow.

falcı fortune-teller.

falcılık fortune-telling.

falçete [. x .] curved shoemaker's knife.

falez precipice.

falihayır [- . . . .] good omen.

falname [- - .] oracular book used in fortune-telling.

falso [x .] **1.** MUS discord, dissonance, false note; **2.** fig. blunder, false step, slip; **3.** billiards: side, Am. English; **~ basmak** (or **etm.**) to blunder, to make a slip, F to put one's foot in it; **~ vermek 1.** = **~ etm.**; **2.** billiards: to put English on.

falsolu 1. discordant, dissonant; **2.** awkward, clumsy, maladroit; **3.** billiards: with English on.

familya [. x .] **1.** a. BOT, GEOL, BIOL family; **2.** rare wife.

fanatik fanatic.

fanatizm fanaticism.

fan dergisi fanzine.

fanfan 1. slur; **2.** unintelligible (chatter).

fani [ī] transitory, perishable; mortal.

fanila [. x .] **1.** flannel; **2.** undershirt, vest.

fantastik fantastic.

fantaziye [. x . .] fantasy, fancy, imagination.

fantezi 1. MUS fantasia; **2.** fancy, de luxe, pompous; **3.** fancy, imagination; **~ yelek** fanciful waistcoat.

fanus [ā] **1.** lantern; lamp-glass; **2.** obs. lighthouse.

fanya [x .] wide-meshed part of a fish-net.

far 1. MOT headlight; **2.** eye-shadow.

faraş dustpan.

faraza [x . .] supposing that . . ., assuming . . .

farazi [ī] hypothetical.

faraziye hypothesis, supposition, assumption; **~ yürütmek** to make supposition.

farbala s. **falbala**.

fare [ā] ZOO mouse; rat; **~ kapanı**

mouse-trap; **~ zehiri** rat poison.

farfara empty-headed, braggart; windbag.

farfaralık idle brag, frivolity.

farımak 1. to grow old; **2.** to weaken; **2.** to wear out.

fariğ [ā] rare **1.** unemployed, non-employed; **2.** exempt (-den from), free (-den from); **3.** JUR transferor, assignor.

farik, -kı [ā] rare distinguishing, separating, distinctive.

farika [- . .] **1.** typical, distinguishing; **2.** MATH characteristic.

Farisî [- . -] the Persian language; Persian.

fariza sacred duty, obligation.

fark, -kı 1. difference, distinction; **2.** discrimination; **3.** disparity; **~ etm. 1.** to notice, to perceive; to realize, to discriminate, to distinguish, to discern; **2.** to differ, to change; **3.** to matter; to make a difference; **~ gözetmek** to discriminate; **-ına varmak** (bşin) to become aware of s.th., to notice s.th., to perceive s.th.; **-ında olm.** (bşin) to be aware of s.th., to notice s.th.; **-ında olmamak** (bşin) to be unaware of s.th.

farklanmak 1. to differentiate; **2.** to rise (price).

farklı 1. different, changed; **2.** better; dearer; **~ farksız** hardly distinguishable; **~ tutmak** to discriminate, to differentiate.

farklılık difference.

farksız indistinguishable, without difference, same, equal.

farmakolo|i pharmacology.

farmason 1. freemason; **2.** F irreligious, ungodly, atheist; **~ locası** freemasons' lodge.

farmasonluk freemasonry.

Fars Persian.

Farsça Persian (language).

fart[1], **-tı** rare excess, overdoing, exaggeration.

fart[2], **-tr. ~ furt** brag; empty threats.

farta [x .]: **fartafurtasız** F tactless, inconsiderate; awkward, clumsy; **-sı furtası olmamak** to speak inconsiderately.

farz 1. rare supposition, hypothesis; **2.** ECCL precept; **~ etm.** to suppose, to assume, to imagine; **farzedelim ki** . . . let us suppose, supposing . . .

farzımuhal, -li [. . . .] supposing the impossible that …; ~ *olarak* as a possible example.

Fas *pr. n.* **1.** Morocco; **2.** Fez.

fasafiso [. . x .] *sl.* trash, twaddle, prattle, nonsense.

fasahat, -ti [. - .] correctness, purity, cleanness, clearness (*of speech*), eloquence.

fasarya [. x .] *sl.* **1.** = *fasafiso*; **2.** coquetry, coquettishness.

fasıl[1]**, -slı 1.** division, chapter, section; **2.** solution; **3.** *obs.* season; **4.** *a concert program all in the same makam*; **5.** THEAT act; **6.** gossip; slander.

fasıl[2] *rare* separating, dividing.

fasıla 1. separation; **2.** interval, interruption; ~ *vermek* to interrupt, to break.

fasılasız continuous, uninterrupted, unceasing.

fasih [ī] correct and clear (*speech*); eloquent, fluent, lucid.

fasikül fascicle, section (*of a book*).

fasile [ī] BOT, ZOO family.

fasit, -di 1. vicious, wicked, evil, corrupt; **2.** perverse; ~ *daire* vicious circle.

faska [x .] wrapper cloth (*for babies*).

fasletmek [x . .] **1.** to separate; **2.** to divide; **3.** to decide; **4.** to gossip, to malign, to traduce.

fason 1. fashion, style, cutting; MEC trimming, bordering.

fasulye [. x .] BOT bean; *taze* ~ string beans.

faşır faşır in gushes.

faşist Fascist.

faşizm Fascism.

fatih conqueror, victor.

fatiha *the opening chapter of the Koran*; ~ *okumak* **1.** to recite the *fatiha*; **2.** *fig.* (*bşe*) to give up hope.

fatura invoice; ~ *düzenlemek* to invoice; ~ *kesmek* to make out an invoice.

faturalamak to write an invoice for.

faul *sports*: foul.

favori 1. whiskers, side-burns; **2.** favorite.

fayans tile.

fayda use, profit, advantage; *-sı dokunmak* (*bşin*) to come in handy, to come in useful, to be of help.

faydalanmak to profit (*-den* by), to make use (*-den* of), to utilize, to benefit (*-den* from).

faydalı useful, profitable, advanta-

geous; ~ *malumat* **1.** useful information; **2.** informative knowledge.

faydasız useless, unprofitable, in vain.

fayrap [x .] NAUT fire up!; ~ *etm.* **1.** NAUT to get up steam; **2.** *fig.* to speed up.

fayton phaeton.

faytoncu coachman.

faz [ā] PHYS phase; ~ *kalemi* circuit-tester.

fazilet, -ti [. -] virtue, grace; merit, superiority.

faziletli virtuous, excellent.

fazla 1. excessive; superfluous; **2.** remainder; **3.** more (than); **4.** too (much); very much; too many; **5.** a lot; plenty; ~ *gecikmek* to be overdue, to be too late; ~ *olarak* besides, moreover, furthermore; ~ *olm.* **1.** to be superfluous, to be too much; **2.** to go too far; ~ *tazyik* MEC over-pressure; *-siyle* abundantly, amply.

fazlalaşmak to increase.

fazlalık 1. excess; **2.** abundance; **3.** surplus.

fecaat, -ti [. -.] calamity, tragedy, catastrophe.

feci, -li [ī] painful, tragic, terrible, catastrophic.

fecir, -cri dawn.

feda, -aı [ā] sacrifice; ransom; ~ *etm.* to sacrifice; ~ *olm.* (*pass. of* ~ *etm.*) to be sacrificed; ~ *olsun!* let it be sacrificed!

fedai [. - -] **1.** bodyguard, bouncer; **2.** patriot.

fedakâr [. - -] self-sacrificing, devoted, loyal.

fedakârlık [. - -.] **1.** self-sacrifice, devotion; **2.** great difficulties and expense.

federal federal.

federasyon federation, association.

federatif federative.

federe federate; ~ *devlet* JUR federal state; canton.

feding *radio*: fading.

fehamet, -ti [ā] highness.

fehim, -hmi comprehension, understanding.

fehmetmek [x . .] to understand, to comprehend.

fehva [ā] *rare* tenor, import, meaning, sense.

fek, -kki *rare* **1.** severing, detaching, separation; **2.** solving (*a difficulty*); **3.** JUR redemption.

fekketmek [x . .] *rare* **1.** to sever, to detach, to separate; to break open; **2.** to undo, to raise.

fekül fecula.

felah 1. prosperity, happiness; **2.** deliverance.

felaket, -ti disaster, catastrophe, calamity; ~ **haberi** bad news; **-e uğramak** to have a disaster.

felaketli 1. disastrous, fatal, sinister, ominous, calamitous; **2.** = **felaketzede.**

felaketzede victim (of a disaster).

felç, -ci MED paralysis; **çocuk felci** infantile paralysis; **felce uğramak** to be paralyzed (a. fig.).

felçli paralytic, paralyzed.

feldmareşal, -li [x . . .] MIL field marshal.

felek 1. firmament, heavens; **2.** fate, destiny; **3.** the universe; **feleğin çemberinden geçmiş** gone through the mill: **-ten kâm almak** fig. to have a very good time.

Felemenk, -gi [x . .] pr. n. Holland, the Netherlands.

Felemenkli pr. n. Dutch; Dutchman.

felfelek a kind of small butterfly.

fellah 1. fellah, Egyptian farmer; **2.** F Negro.

fellek fellek or **fellik fellik** running hither and thither; ~ **aramak** to search high and low (-i for).

felsefe philosophy; ~ **yapmak** (or **yürütmek**) to philosophize.

felsefi philosophical.

feminist, -ti feminist.

fen, -nni 1. natural sciences; **2.** technics, art; ~ **fakültesi** faculty of science; ~ **heyeti** technical commission; **-ni harp** obs. the art of war.

fena 1. bad, unpleasant; evil; **2.** ill, sick; **3.** awful, terrible, miserable; **4.** extremely, terribly; ~ **değil!** not bad!; ~ **etm. 1.** to treat badly, to ill-treat; **2.** to do evil; **3.** to make s.o. feel sick; ~ **halde** badly, extremely; ~ **muamele** ill-treatment; ~ **olm. 1.** to feel sick; **2.** to be upset; ~ **puan** bad mark; **-sına gitmek** (b-nin) to be exasperated; **-ya çekmek** (or **almak**) to take s.th. amiss (or ill); **-ya sarmak** (or **varmak**) to get worse, to take a turn for the worse.

fenâ rare death, extinction, annihilation.

fenalaşmak 1. to get worse, to deteriorate; **2.** to turn faint; **3.** to become more serious.

fenalaştırmak to worsen, to make worse.

fenalık 1. evil, badness; injury, harm; **2.** fainting; ~ **etm.** (or **yapmak**) **1.** to do evil; **2.** (b-ne) to harm s.o.; ~ **geçirmek** to feel faint.

fenci 1. scientist; **2.** F science teacher.

fener 1. lantern; street-lamp; **2.** lighthouse; **3.** coffee tray with handle on top; **4.** MEC pinion (of a shaft); ~ **alayı** torchlight procession; ~ **resmî** lighthouse dues.

fenerbalığı, -nı angler.

Fenike pr. n. Phoenicia.

fenienmiş F early-ripe, precocious (girl).

fenni scientific, technical, expert; ~ **terimler** technical terms.

fenol, -lü phenol.

fenomen phenomenon.

fent, -di trick, ruse; feint.

feodal feudal.

feodalite feudalism.

fer 1. brightness, radiance, lustre, Am. luster, brilliancy; **2.** vividness.

ferace [. - .] a kind of overall (formerly worn by Turkish women).

feragat, -ti [. - .] **1.** self-sacrifice, abnegation; **2.** JUR renunciation, abandonment (of a right), cession, waiver; abdication; ~ **etm.** to renounce, to give up, to abandon, to cede; to abdicate (-den from); ~ **göstermek** to show self-denial, to act altruistically; ~ **sahibi** altruistic, unselfish.

feragatname [. - . - .] certificate of renunciation.

ferağ [ā] **1.** cession (of property), transfer; **2.** obs. leisure, rest, withdrawing from work; ~ **etm.** to cede, to withdraw (-den from).

ferah 1. spacious, open, roomy, wide; **2.** joy, pleasure, cheerfulness, gladness; ~ ~ **1.** easily, abundantly, amply; **2.** at least; **içi** ~ cheerful, in a good humo(u)r; **-a çıkmak** to feel relieved.

ferahi [. - -] **1.** HIST gorget; **2.** crescent-shaped metal collar plate formerly worn by police guards.

ferahlamak 1. to become spacious or airy; to clear up; **2.** to become cheerful, to feel relieved.

ferahlık 1. spaciousness, airiness; **2.** cheerfulness; relief.

feraset, -ti [ā] **1.** obs. horsemanship; **2.** sagacity, intuition; understanding, intelligence.

ferasetli [ā] perceptive.

ferç, -ci vulva.

ferda [ā] *rare* **1.** the morrow, the next day; **2.** the future; eternity; **3.** the Day of Judg(e)ment.

ferdasız [ā] *fig.* hopeless.

ferde *rare* bale.

ferdi 1. individual; **2.** personal; **~ teşebbüs** individual enterprise.

ferdiyet, -ti individuality.

ferdiyetçi individualist.

ferdiyetçilik individualism.

fere P chick of a game bird; chicken.

feri, -r'i 1. branch, subdivision; **2.** accessory circumstance, particular point, detail, item.

fer'i derived, secondary; subordinate; accessory.

feribot, -tu [x . .] train *or* car ferry, ferryboat.

ferih [ī] *rare* cheerful, merry; **~ fahur** in abundance; in comfort.

ferik 1. pullet; **2.** kind of apple.

ferik *obs.* MIL Divisional General.

ferma [ā] pointing, setting; **~ etm.** (*or* **durmak**) to point, to set (*hound*).

ferman [ā] **1.** firman, imperial edict; **2.** *rare* command, order, decree; **~ dinlememek** to ignore the law.

fermejüp, -pü snap-fastener, press-stud, popper.

fermene [. x .] short embroidered vest.

fermetür, fermuar zip-fastener, zip (-per).

ferraş *rare* **1.** mosque sweeper; **2.** carpet-layer, servant.

fersah parasang (*5 ½ km*); **~ ~** greatly, very far.

fersiz lusterless, dull, dim.

fersude [ū] *rare* worn out, old, ragged.

ferş *rare* laying, spreading; **~ etm.** to lay down, to spread out (*carpets*).

ferşiyat, -tı [ā] the laying (*of rails, pipes, etc.*).

fert, -di 1. person, individual; **2.** BOT particular specimen.

fertçi individualist.

fertçilik individualism.

fertik [x .]: **fertiği çekmek** (*or* **kırmak**) *sl.* **1.** to run away, to make off; **2.** *rare* to peg out.

fertiklemek *sl.* = **fertiği çekmek**.

feryat, -dı [ā] **1.** cry, wail, scream, yell, shriek; **2.** *fig.* complaint; **~ etm. 1.** to lament, to cry out, to wail, to yell, to scream, to shriek; **2.** to complain.

ferz *chess*: queen.

fes fez; **~ ibiği** fez tassel.

fesat, -dı [ā] **1.** depravity, corruption, malice, intrigue, duplicity, mischief; **2.** mischievous, intriguer; **3.** *rare* sedition, disturbance, disorder; **4.** POL unrest; **5.** rebellion, revolt; **6.** JUR plot, conspiracy; **~ başı** ring-leader, main plotter (*or* intriguer); **~ çıkarmak** to cause trouble, to plot mischief, to conspire; **~ kumkuması** (*or* **kutusu**) mischief-maker, conspirator; **~ tohumu saçmak** to sow the seeds of intrigue: **fesada vermek** to plot, to conspire.

fesatçı insurgent, conspirator, rebel, instigator, agitator, mischief-maker.

feshetmek [x . .] **1.** to annul, to cancel, to abolish, to rescind, to revoke; **2.** to dissolve (*parliament*).

fesih, -shi 1. abolition, cancellation, annulment; **2.** dissolution.

fesrengi, -ni deep red.

festekiz *s.* **falan.**

festival, -li 1. festival; **2.** *sl.* fiasco, utter failure.

fesuphanallah [. . - . -] oh my God!

feşafeş *rare* swish, a rustling noise.

feşmekan *s.* **falan.**

fetha 1. ANAT opening, orifice; **2.** *vowel sign for* **a, e** *in Arabic script.*

fethetmek [x . .] to conquer.

fethimeyyit, -ti autopsy.

fetih, -thi conquest.

fetihçi 1. *rare* = **fatih**; **2.** imperialist(ic).

fetiş fetish.

fettan [ā] tempting, seductive, alluring; **~ civelek** good-for-nothing.

fetva [ā] ECCL decision (*on religious matter given by a mufti*); **~ vermek 1.** to deliver a **fetva**; **2.** *co* to express an opinion.

fevç, -ci crowd, a stream of people, a flow of people; **~ ~** (*or* **fevçafevç**) in streams, in crowds.

feveran [ā] **1.** boiling, effervescence; **2.** flying into a temper, flaring up, rage; **3.** excitement; **4.** eruption (*volcano*); **~ etm.** to boil over with anger, to flare up, to fly off the handle.

fevk, -kı top, upper part, superior to.

fevkalade [x . - .] **1.** extraordinary, unusual; **2.** unusually, exceptionally, exceedingly, excessively; **3.** wonderful, excellent; **~ ağır** over-weight; **~ delege** special delegate; **~ haller** exceptional circumstances; **~ nüsha** special edition.

fevkalbeşer [x . . .] superhuman.

fevkattabla supernatural.

fevren [x .] promptly, at once; impulsively, hastily.

fevri 1. speedy, sudden; **2.** impulsive.

fevt, -ti *rare* **1.** irreparable loss; going by; **2.** death; ~ *etm.* to let slip, to miss, to lose; ~ *olm.* **1.** *pass. of* ~ *etm.*; **2.** to die.

fevz *rare* success, victory, triumph.

feyezan [ā] **1.** overflowing, flood, inundation; **2.** *rare* abundance.

feyizli abundant; prosperous; bountiful, productive.

feylesof philosopher.

feyyaz [ā] *rare* **1.** munificent, generous; **2.** overflowing, abounding, flourishing.

feyz 1. abundance; prosperity; bountifulness, fertility; **2.** enlightenment; **3.** bounteous gift; ~ *almak* **1.** *fig.* to make headway, to get ahead; **2.** to be enlightened (-*den* by), to learn (-*den* from); ~ *bulmak* = ~ *almak* **1.**

feza [ā] space, universe.

fezahat, -ti vulgarity, meanness.

fezleke 1. summary; **2.** police report.

fıçı cask, barrel; tub; ~ *balığı* salted fish in barrels; ~ *birası* draught beer, *Am.* draft beer; ~ *gibi* corpulent, squat.

fıçıcı cooper.

fıçılamak to barrel, to put in a barrel.

fıkara *s.* **fukara.**

fıkı *s.* **sıkı fıkı.**

fıkıh, -khı Muslim canonical jurisprudence.

fıkır fıkır 1. with a bubbling noise; **2.** coquettish.

fıkırdak 1. coquettish; **2.** restless, fidget.

fıkırdamak 1. to boil up, to bubble; **2.** to behave coquettishly; to giggle.

fıkra 1. anecdote; **2.** short column (*in a newspaper*); **3.** paragraph; passage; **4.** ANAT vertebra; ~ *başı* new paragraph.

fıkracı 1. anecdotist; **2.** columnist.

fıldır fıldır rolling (*eyes*).

fındık hazel-nut, filbert; ~ *altını* **1.** name of a gold coin; **2.** *fig.* small and valuable thing; ~ *kabuğunu doldurmaz* trifling, unimportant; nonsensical; ~ *kurdu gibi* tiny and roly-poly (*woman*).

fındıkçı 1. seller of nuts; **2.** F flirtatious woman.

fındıkfaresi, -ni common house-mouse.

fındıkkıran nutcrackers.

fındıkkurdu, -nu nut maggot.

fır whirr; ~ ~ = *fırıl fırıl.*

Fırat, -tı *pr. n.* the Euphrates.

fırça 1. brush; **2.** paint-brush; ~ *çekmek sl.* to dress down.

fırçalamak to brush, to dust.

fırdolayı [x . . .] all around; round about.

fırdöndü 1. swivel; **2.** MEC lathe carrier; **3.** gambler's top; **4.** *fig.* inconstant, fickle, changeable.

fırıl fırıl whirling, around and around.

fırıldak 1. ventilator; **2.** weathercock; **3.** spinning-top; whirligig; **4.** windmill (*child's toy*); **5.** *fig.* intrigue, deception, trick, ruse; ~ *çevirmek* to intrigue, to be up to some mischief.

fırılda(n)mak to spin around.

fırın 1. oven; **2.** bakery; **3.** kiln; **4.** furnace.

fırıncı baker.

fırınlamak MEC to kiln-dry.

fırınlanmış MEC kiln-dried.

fırka 1. POL party; **2.** MIL division; NAUT squadron; **3.** group.

fırlak protruding, sticking out, overhanging.

fırlama *sl.* bastard; brat.

fırlamak 1. to fly off, to fly out; to leap up; **2.** to rush; **3.** to protrude, to stick out, to overhang; **4.** *fig.* to scar, to sky-rocket (*price*).

fırlatmak *caus. of* **fırlamak** *part.* to hurl, to shoot, to throw, to fling, to cast.

fırsat, -tı opportunity, chance; occasion; ~ *bu* ~*!* this is my (your, his) chance!; ~ *düşkünü* opportunist; -*ı ganimet bilmek* to seize the opportunity; -*ı kaçırmak* to miss the opportunity; -*tan istifade* taking advantage of an opportunity.

fırsatçı opportunist.

fırt fırt continually, incessantly, unremittingly.

fırtına 1. gale, storm, tempest; **2.** *fig.* vehemence, violence; ~ *kopmak* **1.** to break suddenly (*storm*); **2.** *fig.* to break out in noisy arguments; -*ya tutulmak* to be caught in a storm.

fırtınalı stormy (*a. fig.*).

fıs: ~ *geçmek* to whisper.

fısı fıs in whispers, in a whisper.

fısıl fısıl = **fıs fıs.**

fısıldamak to whisper.

fısıltı whisper.

fısır fısır with a crackling noise, with a hissing noise.

fıskıye jet of water, fountain.

fıslamak 1. to whisper; **2.** to tip the wink, to tip off.

fıstık[1] pistachio nut; ground nut; peanut; ~ **çamı** BOT pine; ~ **gibi** F **1.** buxom, plump, stout; **2.** as pretty as a picture.

fıstık[2] *emph.* of *falan* or *filan.*

fıstıki [ī] pistachio green, light green; ~ **makam** *co.* slowly, unhurriedly, ponderously.

fış fış or **fışıl fışıl** or **fışır fışır 1.** with a rustling noise (*silk clothes*); **2.** with a splashing noise (*water*).

fışırdamak to gurgle, to rustle.

fışkı horse dung; manure.

fışkılamak to dung (*horse*).

fışkılık dunghill.

fışkırmak 1. to gush out, to spurt out, to squirt forth, to jet; **2.** to spring up (*plant*).

fışkırtmak to spurt, to splash.

fıta 1. skiff; **2.** = **futa.**

fıtık hernia, rupture; ~ **bağı** MED truss; ~ **olm. 1.** to get a hernia; **2.** *sl.* to become irritated.

fıtır the ending of a religious fast.

fıtnat, -tı natural intelligence.

fıtrat, -tı 1. *obs.* creation; **2.** nature, constitution.

fıtraten [x . .] by nature, naturally; by birth, congenitally.

fıtri [ī] **1.** natural, innate, congenital; **2.** PHLS native.

fiber fibreboard, *Am.* fiberboard.

fiberglas fibreglass, *Am.* fiberglass.

fidan young plant; sapling; ~ **boylu** tall and slender; ~ **gibi** slim (*girl*).

fidanlık nursery.

fide [x .] seedling plant.

fidelemek to plant out seedlings.

fidelik nursery bed.

fidye, fidyeinecat, -tı [ā] ransom.

fifre [x .] fife.

figan [ā] wail, lamentation; ~ **etm.** to lament.

figür figure.

figüran extra, supernumerary; THEAT super.

fiğ BOT vetch.

fihrist, -ti index; catalogue, list.

fiil, -li 1. act, action, deed; **2.** CHEM, PHLS activity; **3.** GR verb; **-e gelmek 1.** to be carried out; **2.** to become a fact; **-e getirmek** to carry out, to execute; **-i bozuk** immoral; **-i şeni** indecent assault; **-I teşemmüs** sunstroke.

fillen 1. actually, really; **2.** JUR in act; **3.** POL de facto.

filli 1. actual, real; **2.** de facto; **3.** acting; **4.** GR verbal; ~ **hizmet** active service.

filliyat, -tı [ā] **1.** *pl.* acts, deeds; **2.** practice; **-ta** in practice, de facto.

fikir, -kri thought, idea; opinion, mind; ~ **adamı** intellectual, savant, thinker; ~ **edinmek** to have an idea; to form an opinion (about); ~ **işçisi** white-collar worker; ~ **vermek** to give an idea (about); ~ **yürütmek** to opine; **fikre getirmek** to recall; **fikri dağınık** distracted, absent-minded; **fikrince** in one's opinion; **fikrinde tutmak** to keep (*or* bear) in mind; **fikrine koymak 1.** to make up one's mind (about); **2.** to put into the mind of; **fikri sabit; sabit fikir** fixed idea, fixation.

fikirli 1. having ideas; **2.** rich in ideas, intelligent, thoughtful.

fikirsiz 1. lacking in ideas; **2.** thoughtless, heedless.

fikren [x .] in ideas, in thought, intellectually.

fikri mental, intellectual.

fikriyat, -tı [ā] **1.** intellectual aspects (*of a matter*); **2.** ideology.

fikstür *sport:* fixture.

fil 1. elephant; **2.** *chess:* bishop; ~ **gibi** greedy, voracious; huge, enormous.

filan *s.* **falan;** ~ **fıstık** and so on, this and that, and so forth.

filanca *s.* **falanca.**

filandra *s.* **flandra.**

filanıncı *s.* **falanıncı.**

filarmonik philharmonic; ~ **orkestra(sı)** philharmonic orchestra.

fildekos lisle.

fildişi, -ni ivory.

file 1. net (*or* string) bag; **2.** netting; **3.** hair-net.

fileto [x .] fillet; loin.

filhakika [x . - .] in fact, actually, truly, in truth.

Filibe *pr. n.* Philippopolis, Plovdiv.

filibit, -ti MED phlebitis.

filigran watermark (*in paper*).

filika [. x .] NAUT life-boat, ship's boat.

filinta [. x .] carbine, short gun; ~ **gibi** handsome.

Filipinler *pr. n.* Philippines.

fitil

Filistin [. x .] *pr. n.* Palestine.

Filistinli [. x . .] Palestinian.

filiz 1. tendril, young shoot, bud, sprout, scion; **2.** MIN ore; **~ gibi** slender.

filizi bright green.

filizlenmek 1. to sprout; to send forth shoots, to shoot; **2.** *fig.* to burgeon.

film 1. film (*for a camera*); **2.** film, movie; **~ çekmek 1.** to film; **2.** to X-ray; **~ çevirmek 1.** to make a movie, to film; **2.** *sl.* to swagger, to show off; **~ koparmak** *sl.* to talk rubbish; **~ makinesi** movie camera; **~ oynatmak** so show; **~ yıldızı** film star; **-e çekmek** to film; **-ini almak 1.** to film; **2.** to X-ray.

filo [x .] **1.** fleet; squadron; **2.** NAUT reef sails!

filoloji philology.

filotilla [. . x .] flotilla.

filozof 1. philosopher; **2.** *fig.* philosophical.

filozofi philosophy.

filozofluk the quality of a philosopher; being a philosopher; *part. co.* indifference.

filtral filtering; **~ tesisatı** purification plant.

filtre [x .] filter, sieve; **~ etm.** to filter.

filvaki [x - .] in fact, actually.

Fin *pr. n.* Finn; Finnish; **~ hamamı** sauna.

final, -li 1. *sports:* final; **2.** MUS finale; **-e kalmak** *sports:* to go on to the finals.

finalist, -ti *sports:* finalist.

finance finance; **~ etm.** to finance.

finansman financing.

fincan 1. cup; **2.** ELECT porcelain insulator; **~ tabağı** saucer; **~ zarfı** metal cup holder.

fingir fingir coquettishly.

fingirdek coquettish, frivolous.

fingirdemek to behave coquettishly, to coquet.

finiş *sport:* finish.

fink: ~ atmak (*or* **atıp gezmek**) F to saunter about and enjoy o.s., to flirt around, to gallivant.

Finlandiya [. x . .] *pr. n.* Finland.

fino [x .] pet (*or* lap) dog.

firak, -kı [. -] separation.

firaklı sad, melancholy.

firar [ā] flight; MIL desertion; **~ etm. 1.** to run away, to flee; **2.** MIL to desert.

firari [. - -] **1.** fugitive, runaway; **2.** MIL deserter.

firavun 1. Pharaoh; **2.** *fig.* haughty,

despotical (*person*).

fire [x .] JUR loss, decrease, diminution; wastage; shrinkage; **~ vermek** to suffer wastage; to diminish; to shrink.

firigo *sl.* disagreeable, unpleasant (*person*).

firik P roasted unripe wheat.

firkat, -tı separation, absence.

firkateyn NAUT frigate.

firkete [. x .] hair-pin.

firketelemek [. x . . .] to pin up (*one's hair*).

firma [x .] **1.** firm; **2.** trade name.

firuze [ū] turquoise.

fisebilillah [- . - . -] (*lit.* in the way of God) expecting nothing in return.

fiske 1. flick, flip (*with the finger*); **2.** pinch; **3.** pimple; **~ vurmak = fiskelemek.**

fiskelemek to give a flip (**to**), to flick.

fisket, -ti boatswain's pipe; whistle.

fiskos whispering; gossip.

fistan 1. dress, petticoat, skirt; **2.** kilt.

fisto [x .] decorative scalloped ribbon.

fistül fistula.

fiş 1. slip of paper, card; **2.** ELECT plug; **3.** form; **4.** chip, receipt; **5.** counter (*games*): **~ açmak** to prepare a file card.

fişek 1. cartridge; **2.** rocket; **3.** roll of coins; **4.** fireworks; **~ atmak 1.** to fire (*or* let fly) a rocket; **2.** *sl.* to put the cat among the pigeons; **3.** *sl.* to have sexual relations (-*e* with); **~ gibi** quickly, speedily; **~ gibi girmek** to burst in, to blow in.

fişekçi 1. cartridge-maker; **2.** pyrotechnist.

fişekhane [ā] cartridge factory.

fişeklik cartridge belt; bandolier; ammunition pouch; cartridge box.

fişlemek 1. to prepare an index card (-*i* on); **2.** (*the police*) to open a file (-*i* on).

fit¹ -ti instigation; incitement; **~ çıkarmak** (*or* **vermek**) to instigate, to incite.

fit², -ti 1. ready; consenting; **2.** (*bşe*) *sl.* quits; **~ olm.** *sl.* to be quits, to settle for.

fit³, -ti [ī] MEC feed.

fitçi agitator, instigator, intriguer.

fitil 1. wick; **2.** MED seton, tent; **3.** MIL fuse; **4.** piping; **5.** a kind of card game; **~ (gibi)** as drunk as a lord; **~ vermek** to infuriate, to exasperate, to incite, to stir up; **-i almak** to flare up, to become alarmed.

fitillemek 1. to light (*the fuse of a mine*); **2.** to attach a fuse *or* wick to; **3.** = *fitil vermek.*

fitlemek to instigate, to excite, to incite, to denounce, to set one person against another.

fitne 1. instigation; mischief-making; **2.** *obs.* sedition, disorder, rebellion; **3.** = *fitneci*; ~ *basmak* (*or kopmak*) to break out (*unrest*); ~ *etm.* **1.** to incite, to intrigue; **2.** to revolt; ~ *fücur* dangerous agitator; ~ *kumkuması* dangerous intriguer; ~ *sokmak* (*or koymak*) to set people at loggerheads, to set s.o. against s.o.; ~ *vermek* **1.** to mislead, to lead astray; **2.** to make a mischievous suggestion.

fitneci intriguer, agitator.

fitnelemek to calumniate, to inform (*on*), to denounce, to peach, to betray.

fitre alms (*given at the close of Ramadan*).

fitret, -ti *rare* interregnum.

fiyaka [. x .] *sl.* showing off, ostentation, swagger, swank, pretension; ~ *satmak* *sl.* to show off, to swank, to swagger; *-yı bozmak* to ridicule s.o.'s swagger.

fiyakacı *sl.* swank, swaggerer.

fiyakalı *sl.* showy, nobby, ostentatious.

fiyasko fiasco, washout, failure; ~ *vermek* to end in fiasco.

fiyat, -tı price; ~ *biçmek* to estimate a price (*-e* for); ~ *farkı* price difference; ~ *indirimi* reduction; ~ *kırmak* to reduce the price, to discount; ~ *koymak* to fix the price (*-e* of); ~ *vermek* to quote a price (*-e* for).

fiyatlanmak to get expensive, to go up in price.

fiyatlı expensive, dear, costly.

fiyonga [. x .], **fiyonk 1.** bow tie; **2.** bowknot, bow.

fiyort, -du fiord.

fizik 1. physics; **2.** physical; ~ *tedavisi* physiotherapy.

fizikçi physicist.

fiziki physical.

fizikötesi, -ni 1. metaphysics; **2.** metaphysical.

fiziksel physical.

fizyoloji physiology.

fizyolojik physiological.

fizyonomi physiognomy.

flama 1. pennant, streamer, colo(u)rs, banners; **2.** stadia (*or* surveyor's) rod.

flamingo, flamankuşu, -nu ZOO flamingo.

flandra [x .] **1.** NAUT pennant; **2.** ZOO red bandfish.

flaş PHOT **1.** flash; **2.** flash bulb.

flavta [x .] *obs.* flute.

flebit, -ti MED phlebitis.

flok, -ku NAUT jibsail.

Floransa [. x .] *pr. n.* Florence.

floresan fluorescent; ~ *lamba* fluorescent lamp.

florin florin, guilder.

floş 1. floss silk; **2.** *cards*: flush.

flöre FENC foil.

flört, -tü 1. flirtation; **2.** girl (*or* boy) friend; ~ *etm.* to flirt.

flû PHOT blurred, weak.

flüorışı fluorescence.

flüt, -tü flute.

flütçü flutist, flautist.

fob COM f.o.b., free on board.

fobi [x .] phobia.

fodra [x .] lining, padding.

fodul vain, presumptuous.

foga [x .] *obs.* fire!; ~ *etm.* to fire.

fok, -ku ZOO seal.

fokurdamak to boil up, to bubble.

fokur fokur boiling up, bubbling noisily.

fokurtu bubbling sound.

foküs focus.

fol nest egg.

folklor, -ru [x .] folklore; folk dancing.

folkon NAUT frame-liner, timber-band (*of a wooden ship*).

folluk nesting-box.

folya [x .] ZOO eagle ray.

fon 1. fund, asset; **2.** PAINT background colo(u)r; **3.** THEAT décor, setting; ~ *müziği* background music, accompaniment.

fonda [x .] NAUT let go the anchor!; ~ *etm.* to let go the anchor.

fondan fondant; ~ *çikolata* vanilla chocolate.

fondo [x .] *obs.* stock; bond; funds.

fonem GR phoneme.

fonetik 1. phonetics; **2.** phonetic.

fonksiyon function.

fonograf phonograph.

fonojenik phonogenic.

font, -tu cast (*or* pig) iron.

fora NAUT open it!, unfurl (*the sail*)!; ~ *etm.* **1.** NAUT to open, to unfurl; **2.** *sl.* to pull off (*bşi* s.th.).

foravelâ [.. x .] *obs.*, NAUT to make sail.

form form; *-a girmek* *sports*: to get into

shape; **-unda olm.** *sports*: to be in (good) form.

forma [x .] **1.** forme, folio; **2.** uniform; **3.** form; **4.** colo(u)rs (*of a sporting club*); **5.** *football*: shirt; ~ ~ in parts.

formalist, -ti formalist.

formalite formality; red tape; ~ **düşkünü** formalist; ~ **gereği** as a matter of form.

formasyon 1. formation; **2.** training education.

formika formica.

formsuz *sports*: out of form, off form.

formül 1. *a.* MATH, CHEM formula; **2.** = **formüler.**

formüle: ~ **etm.** to formulate.

formüler formulary.

foroz haul (*of fish*).

fors 1. NAUT admiral's flag at the main; personal flag flown on a ship; **2.** flag (*or* pennant) of office; **3.** F power, esteem, influence, prestige; **-u olm.** F to have influence.

forsa [x .] **1.** galley slave; **2.** TYP pressure.

forseps MED forceps.

forslu influential, powerful.

forsmajör force majeure; compulsion.

forum forum.

forvet, -ti *sports*: forward.

fos *sl.* rotten, putrid, bad, false, shaky, groundless; ~ **dalga** *sl.* malice, treachery.

fosfat, -tı phosphate.

fosfor phosphorus.

fosforışı phosphorescence.

fosforlu phosphorous; phosphoric.

fosil fossil.

foslamak *sl.* to fail, to be upset, to turn up bad *or* false.

fosseptik cesspool, cesspit.

fosur fosur in puffs.

fota [x .] cask (*for making wine*).

fotin *s.* **potin.**

foto 1. photo; **2.** photographer; ~ **muhabiri** newspaper photographer.

fotografi, fotografya [. . x .] photography.

fotoğraf 1. photograph; **2.** photography; ~ **çekmek** to take a photograph, to photograph; ~ **makinesi** camera; **-ını çektirmek** to have one's photograph taken.

fotoğrafçı 1. photographer; **2.** photographer's studio.

fotoğrafçılık photography.

fotoğrafhane [. . . . - .] photographer's

studio.

fotojenik photogenic.

fotokopi photocopy, photostat (copy), Xerox; ~ **makinesi** photocopier, photostat.

fotometre photometer.

fotomontal photomontage.

fotoroman photo-story.

fotosentez photosynthesis.

foya [x .] **1.** foil (*for setting off a gem*); **2.** *fig.* eyewash, fraud; ~ **vermek** *fig.* to give o.s. away; **-sı bozuk 1.** deceitful, fraudulent; **2.** charlatan, quack, mountebank; **-sı meydana** (*or* **ortaya**) **çıkmak** to give the show away.

fötr felt; ~ **şapka** felt hat.

fragman fragment; *cinema*: trailer.

frak, -kı tail-coat, tails.

francala [x . .] white bread; roll.

frank, -gı franc.

Fransa [x .] *pr. n.* France.

Fransız 1. French; **2.** Frenchman.

Fransızca French (language).

frapan striking, flamboyant.

frekans frequency.

fren brake; ~ **ayarı** brake adjustment; ~ **balatası** brake lining; ~ **çubuğu** brake rod; ~ **pedalı** brake pedal; ~ **tutmadı** the brakes failed to grip; ~ **yapmak** to brake.

frenci brake(s)man.

frengi [x .] syphilis, pox.

Frenk, -gi European.

frenkarpası, -nı pearl barley.

frenkasması, -nı Virginia creeper.

frenkeriği, -ni greengage plum.

frenkgömleği, -ni shirt.

frenksalatası, -nı rampion.

frenküzümü, -nü red currant.

frenlemek 1. to brake; **2.** *fig.* to moderate, to check.

frensiz 1. brakeless; **2.** *fig.* unrestrained (*person*).

freze [x .] milling cutter; ~ **etm.** to mill.

frezeci workman skilled in milling.

frigorifik frigorific, refrigerated.

frijider refrigerator, ice-box.

frikik *football*: free kick.

friksiyon friction, massage.

fuar [. x] fair, exposition.

fuaye THEAT foyer.

fuhşiyat, -tı [ā] prostitution; obscenities, immoralities; **-a tahrik** JUR soliciting.

fuhuş, -hşu prostitution.

fukara [. . . -] **1.** the poor; **2.** poor, destitute, needy, pauper; **3.** dervish.

fukaralık poverty, destitution.
fukaraperver charitable; benevolent.
ful, -lü BOT **1.** broad bean; **2.** syringa.
fular cravat.
fulya [x .] BOT jonquil.
funda [x .] **1.** thicket, shrub; **2.** BOT heath; ~ **toprağı** humus of heath.
fundalık scrub, underwood, brush.
funya [x .] primer.
furgon luggage-van, freight-car.
furş fork of a bicycle.
furta *s.* **farta.**
furun *s.* **fırın.**
furya [x .] rush; glut.
fus BIOL lobe.
futa [x .] **1.** loin-cloth; **2.** = **fıtaı 3.** = **fota.**
futbol, -lu football, soccer; ~ **bahsimüştereki** football-pools; ~ **maçı** football match; ~ **meraklısı** football fan.
futbolcu footballer.
fuzulen [. - .] superfluously; without right; unjustly.
fuzuli [. - -] **1.** unnecessary, needless,

superfluous; **2.** officious; **3.** excessive; **4.** unnecessarily; ~ **gayretkeş** over--zealous; ~ **tasarruflar** JUR dispositions (*or* contracts) made without authority.
fücceten [x . .] suddenly; ~ **ölmek** to die a sudden death.
füme smoked; ~ **etm.** to smoke.
fümuvar smoking room.
füniküler suspension railway, (aerial) cableway.
fürce 1. ANAT fissure; **2.** *rare* breach, gap; **3.** *rare* leisure.
füsun [ü] charm, enchantment, spell, magic.
fütuhat, -tı [. - -] victories; conquests.
fütuhatçı [. - - .] conqueror; imperialist.
fütur [. -] languor; abatement; ~ **getirmek** to get tired (*of*), to lose zeal.
fütursuz [. - .] **1.** indifferent; **2.** undeterred.
füze [x .] rocket, missile.
füzen charcoal pencil (*or* drawing).

G

gabardin gabardine.
gabari loading gauge.
gabavet, -ti [. - .] stupidity, obtuseness.
gabi thick-headed, stupid, obtuse.
gabilik *s.* **gabavet.**
gabin JUR fraud, cheating (*on a sale*).
gabro gabbro.
gabya [x .] NAUT topmast, topsail.
gacırdamak to creak.
gacır gucur producing a continuous creaking noise.
gaco *sl.* woman; sweetheart; ~ **eskisi** *sl.* English pound.
gaddar [. -] cruel, perfidious, tyrant.
gaddare [. - .] a heavy double-edged scimitar.
gaddarlık cruelty, perfidy, tyranny.
gadir, -dri 1. cruelty; **2.** injustice; tyranny.
gadolinyum CHEM gadolinium.
gadretmek [x . .] (*b-ne*) **1.** to do wrong to *s.o.*, to treat unjustly towards *s.o.*; **2.** to treat cruelly towards *s.o.*
gaf blunder, gaffe, faux pas; ~ **yapmak** to blunder.
gafçı blunderer.
gafil [ā] unaware (*-den* of); careless,

inattentive, unmindful; ~ **avlamak** to catch unawares, to take by surprise; ~ **bulunmak** (*or* olm.) to take no heed.
gafiet, -ti heedlessness, carelessness; **-e düşmek** to be careless, to act heedlessly.
gafieten unawares, inadvertently.
gaga 1. beak, bill; **2.** *sl.* mouth, trap; ~ **burun** hook-nosed, aquiline; ~ **-ya vermek** to bill and coo; **-sından yakalamak** *fig.* to catch by the nose; **kapa -nı!** *sl.* shut your trap!
gagalamak 1. to peck; **2.** *fig.* to scorn, to rebuke.
gagalaşmak 1. to peck one another; **2.** to bill and coo.
gagalı beaked.
gâh *s.* **kâh.**
gaile [ā] trouble, anxiety, worry, difficulty.
gaileli 1. troubled, worried; **2.** troublesome.
gailesiz 1. untroubled; **2.** trouble-free, carefree.
gailesizlik untroubledness.
gaip, -bi [ā] **1.** absent, invisible; missing, lost; **2.** the invisible world; **-ten**

haber vermek to foretell, to divine.

gaiplik [ā] JUR disappearance; ~ *kararı* JUR declaration of death.

gaita [- . .] feces.

gakl caw! (*of a crow*).

gaklamak to caw.

Gal *pr. n.* Wales.

gala [x .] 1. gala, première; 2. state dinner; ~ *gecesi* gala night.

galat, -tı error, mistake; *galatı hilkat* freak of nature, monster.

galatıhis, -ssi illusion.

galatımeşhur commonly accepted error (*in language*).

galdır guldur with an uneven, heavy, rolling gait.

galebe 1. victory; 2. supremacy, predominance; ~ *çalmak* to conquer, to overwhelm; ~ *etm.* 1. to get the upper hand; 2. to overcome, to overwhelm.

galen GEOL galena.

galeri 1. gallery; 2. art gallery; 3. gallery, working drift; 4. THEAT gallery, balcony; 5. showroom (*or* display lot) (*for automobiles, etc.*).

galeta [. x .] bread stick, rusk; ~ *tozu* bread crumbs; ~ *unu* fine white flour.

galeyan [. . -] 1. rage, agitation, excitement; 2. ebullition; *-a gelmek* to get worked up, to be agitated.

galiba [- .-] [x .-] 1. most probably, presumably; 2. I think so.

galibiyet, -ti [ā] victory, win.

galip, -bi [ā] 1. victorious; 2. victor, vanquisher; 3. overwhelming, superior; ~ *çıkmak* to emerge victorious (*-den* from); ~ *gelmek* (*b-ne*) to defeat *s.o.*, to overcome *s.o.*; ~ *ihtimale göre* = *ağlebi ihtimal*.

galiz [ī] 1. filthy, dirty; 2. obscene, indecent.

galon 1. gallon; 2. gas can.

galoş galosh.

galsame ANAT gill (*of a fish*).

galvaniz galvanization.

galvanize galvanized; ~ *etm.* to galvanize.

galvanizlemek to galvanize.

galvanizli galvanized.

galyum CHEM gallium.

gam[1] MUS scale.

gam[2] grief, anxiety, worry; ~ *çekmek* to grieve; ~ *değil* it does not matter; ~ *yememek* not to worry.

gamalı HIST comprising a gamma; ~ *haç* swastika, gammadion.

Gambiya *pr. n.* Gambia.

gambot, -tu 1. gunboat; 2. ICHTH small mullet.

gamet, -ti BIOL gamete.

gamlanmak to worry (*-e* about).

gamlı worried, sorrowful, grieved.

gamma gamma; ~ *ışınları* gamma rays.

gammaz [. -] sneak, informer, telltale.

gammazlamak to inform (**against**), to tell on, to tell tales (**about**), to denounce, to peach (**against, on**).

gammazlık tale-bearing, spying, informing.

gamsele [x . .] raincoat, oilskin, mackintosh.

gamsız carefree, lighthearted, happy-go-lucky.

gamsızlık lightheartedness, untroubledness.

gamze 1. dimple; 2. coquettish glance, twinkle.

Gana *pr. n.* Ghana.

gangster gangster, gunman.

gangsterlik gangsterism.

gani [ī] 1. abundant; 2. rich; ~ ~ abundantly; ~ *gönüllü* generous; *-si olm.* to have enough, not to be in need of.

ganimet, -ti [ī] 1. spoils, booty, loot; 2. windfall, godsend; 3. ♀ *wf.*; ~ *bilmek* (*or görmek*) to look on as a godsend; to seize (*an opportunity*).

Ganj *pr. n.* Ganges.

gant, -tı *sports*: boxing glove.

ganyan the winner (*horse*); winning ticket.

gar large railway station; ~ *şefi* station-master.

garabet, -ti strangeness, oddity.

garaip, -bi [. - .] strange things.

garaj garage.

garam [. -] passion, love; eager desire.

garami lyric(al).

garanti 1. guaranty, guarantee; 2. F sure, certain; certainly, without doubt; ~ *etm.* to guarantee.

garantilemek 1. to guarantee; 2. to make certain, to make sure (*-i* of).

garantili 1. guaranteed; 2. *fig.* certain, sure.

garaz 1. grudge, ranco(u)r, malice, animosity; 2. aim, object, goal, purpose; ~ *bağlamak* (*b-ne*) to hold a grudge against *s.o.*; ~ *beslemek* (*or tutmak*) to nourish a spite; ~ *olm.* (*b-ne*) to bear a grudge against *s.o.*, to bear *s.o.* malice.

garazkâr rancorous, spiteful.
garazkârlık spitefulness.
garazsız unbiased, unprejudiced, disinterested.
garben [x .] westwards.
garbi [ī] western.
gardenparti [x . . .] garden party.
gardenya BOT gardenia.
gardıfren brakeman.
gardırop, -bu 1. wardrobe, armoire; 2. cloakroom.
gardiyan gaoler, warder, *Am.* jailer.
garez *s.* **garaz.**
gargar water jug with a filter.
gargara 1. gargle; 2. mouthwash; ~ **yapmak** to gargle; **-ya getirmek** *sl.* to deflect on purpose.
gariban pitiable, pathetic (*person*).
garibe strange thing, curiosity.
garip, -bi [ī] 1. strange, odd, peculiar, unusual; 2. destitute, needy; 3. stranger; **garibine gitmek** (*b-nin*) to strike as odd, to appear strange to *s.o.*
gariplik strangeness, oddity.
garipsemek 1. to find strange (*or* curious); 2. to feel lonely and homesick.
gark, -kı drowning; ~ **etm.** to overwhelm; ~ **olm.** to be overwhelmed (*-e* with), to be submerged.
garnitür 1. garnish, garniture, trimmings (*of a dish*); 2. trimmings (*of a dress*).
garnizon 1. garrison; 2. garrison town; ~ **komutanı** (*or* **kumandanı**) garrison commander.
garp, -bı 1. west; 2. Europe.
garpçı Westernizer.
garplı Westerner, Occidental.
garplılık Occidentalism.
garson waiter.
garsoniye service charge.
garsoniyer bachelor's establishment.
gaseyan [. . -] 1. nausea; 2. vomiting; ~ **etm.** to vomit.
gasıp[1], **-spı** usurpation, seizure by violence.
gasıp[2] [ā] usurper.
gasil, -sli washing of the dead.
gasletmek [x . .] to wash (*the dead*).
gaspetmek [x . .] to seize by force, to usurp.
gassal washer of the dead.
gastrit, -ti gastritis.
gastrula BIOL gastrula.
gaşiy, -şyi ecstasy, rapture.
gaşyetmek [x . .] to enrapture.
gaşyolmak [x . .] to be enraptured.

gauss PHYS gauss.
gâvur 1. giaour, unbeliever, non-Moslem, infidel, Christian; 2. *fig.* merciless, cruel; obstinate; ~ **etm.** F to squander, to blow (*money*); ~ **inadı** pigheadedness, obstinacy; ~ **ölüsü gibi** as heavy as lead.
gâvurca 1. in a European language; 2. heartlessly, cruelly.
gâvurcasına mercilessly.
gâvurluk 1. unbelief; 2. *fig.* cruelty; ~ **etm.** to act cruelly.
gaybubet, -ti [ū] absence; **-inde** in the absence of.
gayda [x .] MUS bagpipe.
gaydacı MUS bagpiper.
gaye [ā] aim, object, end, goal; ~ **edinmek** (*bşi*) to aim at *s.th.*; **-siyle** for the purpose of; **-ye ulaşmak** to attain the aim, to succeed.
gayet, -ti [ā] very, extremely, greatly.
gaygay with a shrill grating sound.
gaygaylı shrill.
gayr someone else; **-e muhtaç olmamak** not to be in need of anyone.
gayret, -ti 1. zeal, energy, ardo(u)r, effort, perseverance; 2. solicitude, protectiveness; ~ **etm.** to endeavo(u)r, to try hard; ~ **vermek** 1. to encourage; 2. to console; **-e gelmek** 1. to get into working spirit; 2. to become enthusiastic, to show zeal; **-i elden bırakmamak** to keep trying, to persist; **-ten düşmek** to become discouraged.
gayretkeş 1. zealous; 2. zealot; 3. partisan.
gayretlenmek 1. to get into working spirit; 2. to display zeal.
gayretli 1. zealous; 2. hard-working, persevering.
gayretsiz slack, without enthusiasm, lacking zeal.
gayrı 1. now, well then, at length, finally; 2. *emph. of* **ayrı**; 3. (not) any more, (no) longer.
gayri 1. other (*den* than), besides, apart from; 2. (*before adjectives*) un-, non-; ~ **ihtiyari** involuntarily; ~ **kabil** impossible; ~ **menkul** 1. immovable, real (*property*); 2. real estate; ~ **meşru** illegitimate; unlawful; illicit (*gain*); unjust (*war*); ~ **muntazam** 1. irregular(ly); 2. disorderly; ~ **müslim** non--Moslem; ~ **resmi** unofficial; informal; ~ **safi** COM gross; ~ **tabil** unnatural, abnormal, strange.
gayya a well in hell; ~ **kuyusu** place of

confusion.

gayzer geyser, hot spring.

gaz[1] gauze.

gaz[2] **1.** kerosene; **2.** PHYS gas; **3.** flatus; **~ bombası** gas bomb; **~ hali** gaseous state; **~ lambası** kerosene lamp; **~ maskesi** gas mask; **~ ocağı** kerosene cookstove; **~ sobası** kerosene heater; **-a basmak 1.** MOT to step on the gas, to accelerate; **2.** *sl.* to go away, to scram; **-ı kesmek** MOT to throttle back (*gas*).

gazal, -li [. -] zoo gazelle; antelope.

gazap, -bı wrath, rage; **-a gelmek** to get in a rage.

gazaplı wrathful, infuriated.

gazdan(lık) oil-can, oiler.

gazel[1] **1.** lyric poem of a certain pattern; **2.** extemporaneous vocal **taksim.**

gazel[2] autumn leaf.

gazete [. x .] newspaper; **~ çıkarmak** to publish a newspaper.

gazeteci 1. journalist, newspaperman; **2.** newspaper seller, news-vendor, newsboy, paperboy; **3.** owner of a newspaper.

gazetecilik journalism.

gazhane [. - .] gasworks.

gazışıl PHYS luminescent.

gazi [- -] **1.** ghazi; **2.** fighter for Islam. **Gazi** Atatürk.

gazino [. x .] casino, café.

gazlamak 1. to smear (*or* sprinkle) with kerosene; **2.** MOT to accelerate; **3.** *sl.* to run away.

gazlanmak 1. *pass. of* **gazlamak**; **2.** to be flatulent.

gazlaştırmak to gasify.

gazlı 1. gaseous; **2.** containing kerosene; **~ bez** gauze.

gazoil, gazoyl diesel oil.

gazojen gas generator.

gazolin gasoline.

gazoma [. x .] seam around the edge of a stitched sole.

gazometre gasometer.

gazoz soda pop, fizzy lemonade.

gazozcu seller of **gazoz.**

gazölçer gas meter.

gazyağı, -nı kerosene.

gebe pregnant, expectant; **~ bırakmak** (*or* **etm.**) to make pregnant; **~ kalmak** to fall pregnant, to become pregnant (**-den** by); **~ olm.** (*bşe or bş için*) *fig.* to be pregnant with *s.th.*

gebelik pregnancy; **~ önleyici** contraceptive.

geberik *contp.* dead.

gebermek *contp.* to die, to croak, to kick the bucket, to perish.

gebertmek *contp.* to kill, to bump off.

gebeş 1. dumpy, squat; **2.** *sl.* idiot, blockhead.

gebre[1] haircloth glove (*for grooming horses*).

gebre[2] BOT caper.

gece 1. night; **2.** at night; last night; to-night; **~ gündüz** night and day, continuously; **~ kasası** night safe; **~ kuşu 1.** bat; **2.** *fig.* night owl, night bird, nighthawk; **~ lambası** night-light; **~ vakti** at night; **~ yarısı** midnight; **~ yatısı** overnight visit; **-ler gebedir** nights are pregnant with new events; **-niz hayrolsun!** good night!; **-yi gündüze katmak** to work night and day.

gececi worker on a night shift.

geceki nocturnal.

gecekondu shanty; **~ bölgesi** shanty-town.

gecelemek to spend the night (*in a place*).

geceleyin [. x . .] by night.

geceli: ~ gündüzlü day and night, continuously.

gecelik 1. nightdress, nightgown, nightshirt; **2.** pertaining to the night; lasting the night; **3.** fee for the night.

gecesefası, -nı BOT four-o'clock.

gecikme delay.

gecikmek to be late, to be delayed.

geciktirmek to delay, to retard.

geç late, delayed; **~ kalmak** to be late; **~ vakit** late in the evening.

geçe past (*time*); **beşi on ~** 10 minutes past five.

geçeğen temporary, transitory.

geçen past, last; **~ gün** the other day; **~ sefer** last time; **~ yıl** last year.

geçende, geçenlerde lately, recently.

geçenek corridor.

geçer 1. current, in circulation; **2.** desired, in demand.

geçerli valid.

geçerlik validity, currency.

geçersiz invalid, null; **~ saymak** to annul; to cancel.

geçersizlik invalidity.

geçici 1. temporary, transitory, passing; **2.** contagious; **~ hükümet** caretaker government; **~ madde** temporary article; **~ olarak** temporarily; **~ tutku** passing fad (*or* whim).

geçilmek *pass. of* geçmek 1. to pass, to traverse; 2. to be left aside; geçilmez! no passage!; geçilmemek (*bşden*) to have a great abundance of *s.th.*; to have too much of *s.th.*

geçim 1. livelihood, living; 2. harmony, getting alone with one another; ~ derdi the struggle to make a living; ~ indeksi cost of living index; ~ masrafı cost of living; ~ seviyesi the standard of living; ~ yolu means of subsistence.

geçimli affable, easy to get along with.

geçimlik livelihood.

geçimsiz fractious, quarrelsome, shrewish, unsociable.

geçimsizlik fractiousness.

geçindirmek to support (*a person*), to maintain.

geçinecek 1. income; 2. livelihood, living.

geçinge budget.

geçinim, geçinme subsistence, getting by.

geçinmek 1. to live (*ile* on), to subsist (*ile* on); 2. to rub along (*ile* with), to get on well (*ile* with), to get along (*ile* with); 3. to pretend to be, to pass (for); 4. (*b-den*) to live on *s.o.*, to sponge on *s.o.*; 5. P to die.

geçirgen PHYS permeable.

geçirgenlik PHYS permeability.

geçirimli permeable.

geçirimsiz impermeable.

geçirimsizlik impermeability.

geçirmek *caus. of* geçmek *part.* 1. to infect (*s.o. with a disease*); 2. to fix, to fit, to insert (*glass into a frame*); 3. to slip on (*a cover on a book, etc.*); 4. to spend, to pass (*time*); 5. to enter, to register (*in an account*); 6. to undergo (*an operation*); 7. to copy out; 8. to get over (*a disease*); 9. to accompany s.o., to see s.o. out; 10. to see s.o. off; 11. to have (*an attack*); 12. to pass (*s.th. through s.th.*); 13. to transmit (*heat*); 14. *sl.* to fuck, to screw.

geçiş 1. passing, crossing; 2. change, transfer; 3. MUS transition; ~ üstünlüğü right of way.

geçişli GR transitive.

geçişmek to intermix, to be diffused.

geçişsiz GR intransitive.

geçiştirmek 1. *caus. of* geçişmek; 2. to pass over lightly; 3. to get over (*an illness*); 4. to escape with little harm.

geçit, -di 1. mountain pass; 2. passageway, passage; 3. ford; 4. parade; 5. AST transit; ~ resmi (*or* töreni) parade; ~ vermek to be fordable.

geçkin 1. elderly; 2. overripe (*fruit*); 3. overmatured (*wood*); otuzu ~ over thirty.

geçkinlik 1. elderliness; 2. overripeness (*fruit*).

geçme 1. *vn. of* geçmek; 2. dovetailed; telescoped; 3. tenon.

geçmek, (-çer) 1. to pass (-*den* over, along), to cross, to traverse; 2. to undergo, to go through; 3. to pass by; 4. to give up on, to renounce; 5. to move (-*e* to); 6. to penetrate, to affect; to influence; 7. to come into (*power*); 8. (*b-den b-ne*) to spread from *s.o.* to *s.o.*; 9. (*b-den b-ne*) to pass from *s.o.* to *s.o.* through heredity; 10. to be recorded (*in a book*); 11. (*tarihe*) to go down in history; 12. to exceed, to pass; to cross, to go past; 13. to omit, to skip, to leave out; 14. to pass (*time*); 15. to be mentioned; 16. to be current, to be in force; 17. to be popular, to be the fad; 18. to pass, to come to an end, to end (*season, period, illness*); 19. to pass one's class; to pass (*an exam*); 20. to be overripe (*fruit*); to spoil, to go stale; 21. to practice (*music*); 22. (*k-den*) to faint; geç! (*or* geç efendim!) F leave it!, it is not worth talking about!; (*gün*) geçtikçe as the day goes on, in the course of time.

geçmelik toll.

geçmiş 1. past; 2. the past; 3. overripe, spoiled; ~ ola (*or* olsun) I I wish you a speedy recovery!; ~ olsuna gitmek to visit s.o. who has been ill; ~ zaman GR past tense; -i kandilli (*or* tenekeli) F damned (*for a person*); -i olm. (*b-le*) to have known *s.o.* in the past.

gedik 1. gap, breach; 2. fault, defect; 3. mountain pass; 4. privilege; ~ açmak to make a breach (-*de* in); ~ kapamak to fill the gap.

gedikli 1. breached; gapped; notched; 2. constant frequenter, patron; 3. MIL regular non-commissioned officer (NCO); ~ çavuş MIL sergeant; warrant officer.

geğirmek to belch, to burp, to eructate.

geğirti belch, burp, eructation.

geğrek lower (*or* false) rib; ~ batması stitch in the side.

gelberi poker, rake; ~ etm. *sl.* to swipe,

to nick, to pilfer.

gele *backgammon*: blank throw.

gelecek 1. future; **2.** next, coming; ~ **sefer** next time; ~ **zaman** GR future tense; ~ **zaman ortacı** GR future participle.

gelecekbilim futurology.

gelecekbilimci futurologist.

gelecekçi futurist.

gelecekçilik futurism.

geleğen tributary (*river*).

gelembe sheepfold.

gelen 1. comer; **2.** PHYS incident; ~ **ge-çen(ler)** passer(s)-by; ~ **giden(ler)** visitor(s), comer(s); ~ **gidene rahmet okutur** (*or* ~ **gideni aratır**) *fig.* the new is often worse than the old.

gelenek tradition.

gelenekçi traditionalist.

gelenekçilik traditionalism.

gelenekli, geleneksel traditional.

geleneksellik traditionalism.

geleni ZOO meadow mouse.

gelgeç fickle, inconstant.

gelgelelim but, only.

gelgit, -ti 1. tide, flood-tide; **2.** useless coming and going.

gelin 1. bride; **2.** daughter-in-law; ~ **alayı** bridal procession; ~ **güvey olm.** (*kendi k-ne*) to build castles in Spain; ~ **odası** bridal chamber; ~ **odası gibi** attractive and very tidy (*room*); ~ **olm.** to get married (*girl*); ~ **teli** silver tinsel.

gelinböceği, -ni ZOO ladybug.

gelince [. x .] *-e* as for, regarding.

gelincik 1. BOT poppy; **2.** ZOO weasel; **3.** (*illeti*) P hectic fever; dropsy; sty.

gelinfeneri, -ni BOT winter cherry.

gelinhavası, -nı fine weather.

gelinkuşu, -nu ZOO pencilled lark.

gelinlik 1. wedding-dress; **2.** nubile, marriageable (*girl*).

gelinsaçı, -nı BOT dodder.

gelir income, revenue; ~ **dağılımı** income distribution; ~ **gider** income and outgo; ~ **vergisi** income tax.

geliş coming.

gelişigüzel superficial(ly), by chance, at random; haphazard, desultory.

gelişim development, progress.

gelişme 1. development; **2.** growing, maturing.

gelişmek 1. to grow up; to mature; to grow healthy (*or* fat); **2.** to develop, to prosper, to thrive; **gelişmekte olan ülke** developing country.

gelişmiş 1. developed; **2.** grown-up (*person*).

geliştirmek to develop, to improve, to advance.

gelme *vn. of* **gelmek** *part.* **1.** arrival; **2.** *optics:* incidence; **3.** originating (*-den* from); derived (*-den* from); **yeni** ~ newcomer.

gelmek, (-ir) 1. to come; **2.** *-e* to seem, to appear; **3.** *-e* to suit, to fit; **4.** to come up to; **5.** to cost; **6.** to be felt, to come to one; **7.** to affect; **8.** to come around (*-e* to); **9.** *-den* to pretend, to feign; **gel gelelim** all the same, however, and yet; **gele gele** eventually, finally; **gelip çatmak** to come round at last, to be finally at hand (*a time*); **gelip geçici** transient, passing; **gel zaman git zaman** long afterwards; **gelip gitmek** to frequent, to come and go.

gem bit (*of a horse*); ~ **almak** to take the bit (*horse*); ~ **almaz** unbridled; ~ **vurmak** *-e* to curb; to bridle; **-i azıya almak** to take the bit between the teeth (*a. fig.*); **-ini kısmak** *fig.* to rein in.

gemi ship, boat, vessel; ~ **aslanı** F stuffed dummy; ~ **ızgarası** shipway, ways; ~ **işletimi** cabotage, coasting trade; ~ **izi** wake; ~ **kafilesi** convoy; ~ **karaya oturmak** to go (*or* run) aground; ~ **kiralamak** to charter a ship; ~ **leşi** shipwreck; ~ **mürettebatı** crew; ~ **tezgâhı** stocks, dockyard; ~ **yatağı** ship's berth, port of shelter; **-de teslim** COM free on board, f.o.b.; **-ye binmek** to embark, to go on board.

gemici sailor, mariner; ~ **feneri** barn lantern.

gemicilik 1. seamanship; **2.** navigation; seafaring.

gemilik dockyard, shipyard.

gemlemek to bridle (*a. fig.*).

gen¹ BIOL gene; ~ **tedavisi** gene therapy.

gen² broad, vast; untouched (*ground*).

gencecik [x . .] very young.

genç, -ci young, youthful; youngster; ~ **yaşında** in his youth; **-ler** the young, youth.

gençleşmek to become youthful, to be rejuvenated.

gençleştirmek to rejuvenate.

gençlik 1. youth, youthfulness; **2.** the young, youth.

gençten young.

gene [x.] **1.** again; **2.** still, nevertheless; **~ görüşelim!** see you soon!, be seeing you!; **-de** but still; yet again.

genel general; **~ af** amnesty; **~ merkez** headquarters; **~ müdür** general director; ♀ **Müdür** CEO (= *chief executive officer of a company*); **~ olarak** in general, generally; **~ prova** dress rehearsal; **~ seçim** general election; **~ seferberlik** general mobilization; **~ sekreter** secretary general.

genelev brothel.

genelge circular, notice.

genelkurmay MIL general staff.

genelkurul general meeting.

genelleme generalization.

genellemek to generalize.

genelleşme generalization.

genelleşmek to become general.

genelleştirme generalization.

genelleştirmek to generalize.

genellik generality.

genellikle generally, in general, usually.

general, -li MIL general.

generallik MIL generalship.

genetik genetics; **~ kod** genetic code; **~ mühendisliği** genetic engineering.

gengüdüm MIL strategy.

geniş 1. wide. broad; **2.** extensive, spacious, vast: **3.** carefree (*person*); **~ açı** MATH obtuse angle; **~ bant** IT broadband; **~ fikirli** *fig.* broad-minded, **~ gönüllü** (*or* **yürekli**) *fig.* easygoing, serene; **~ mezhepli** very tolerant; **~ ölçüde** on a large scale; **~ yapraklı** BOT broad-leaved; **~ zaman** GR simple present tense, aorist; **~ zaman ortacı** GR present participle.

genişlemek 1. to widen, to broaden; to expand; **2.** to ease up.

genişletmek to widen, to broaden; to expand, to enlarge.

genişlik 1. width, wideness; extensiveness; **2.** abundance, wealth, comfort.

geniz, -nzi nasal passages (*or* fossae); **-den konuşmak** to speak through the nose; **-e kaçmak** to go down the wrong way (*food*); **genzi yakmak** to stifle, to choke on.

genleşme dilatation.

genleşmek to dilate, to be dilated.

genlik 1. comfort; **2.** PHYS amplitude.

genom genome.

gensoru POL interpellation.

genzel nasal.

geometri geometry.

geometrik geometric(al); **~ dizi** geometrical progression.

gepegenç very young.

gerçek 1. real, true, genuine; **2.** reality, truth; **3.** really, in truth; **gerçeğe gözlerini yummak** to blink the facts.

gerçekçi 1. realist; **2.** realistic.

gerçekçilik realism.

gerçekdışı unreal.

gerçeklemek 1. to confirm; **2.** to verify.

gerçekleşme realization, fulfillment.

gerçekleşmek to come true, to materialize, to turn out to be true.

gerçekleştirmek to realize; to certify, to verify.

gerçekli real, true.

gerçeklik reality, truth.

gerçekten really, truly.

gerçeküstü surrealistic.

gerçi [x.] although, though, it is true that.

gerdan 1. neck, throat; **2.** double chin; dewlap; **~ kırmak** *fig.* to put on coquettish airs.

gerdanlık necklace, neckband.

gerdek bridal chamber; **~ gecesi** wedding (*or* nuptial) night; **gerdeğe girmek** to enter the bridal chamber.

gerdel wooden (*or* leather) bucket.

gerdirmek to have *s.o.* make *s.th.* taut.

gereç requisite, material, necessaries.

gereğince in accordance with, following.

gerek 1. necessary, needed; **2.** requisite, need, necessity; **~ ... ~** whether ... or; both ... and; **gereği gibi** as is due, properly; **gereği yok** it is not necessary.

gerekçe 1. reason, justification; **2.** corollary.

gerekçeli justifiable, justified.

gerekçesiz unjustifiable, unjustified.

gerekli necessary, required, needed.

gereklik need, necessity; **~ kipi** GR necessitative mood.

gereklilik necessity, need.

gerekmek, (-ir) to be necessary, to be needed, to be required; **gerekince** when necessary; **gerekirse** if need be.

gerekseme necessity, need.

gereksemek to need, to consider necessary.

gereksinim, gereksinme necessity, need.

gereksinmek to need, to consider necessary.

gereksiz unnecessary, superfluous.

gerektirmek 1. to necessitate, to require; **2.** to imply, to entail.

geren clayey soil.

gergedan zoo rhinoceros.

gergef embroidery frame; ~ *işlemek* to embroider with a frame.

gergi 1. curtain; **2.** stretcher.

gergin 1. tight, stretched, taut; **2.** tense; strained (*relations*).

gerginleşmek 1. to get stretched; **2.** *fig.* to become tense.

gerginleştirmek 1. to tighten; **2.** *fig.* to strain, to make tense.

gerginlik tightness, tension.

geri 1. back, rear; **2.** the rest; **3.** backward, to the rear; **4.** *fig.* backward, reactionary; **5.** slow (*clock*); **6.** (go) back!; **7.** *sl.* fool; ~ *almak* **1.** to get (*or* take) back; **2.** to take back, to withdraw (*word, order*); **3.** to back up; **4.** to put back (*clock*); ~ *basmak* to back up, to move backwards; ~ *bırakmak* to postpone, to put off, to defer; ~ *çekilmek* to withdraw (-*den* from), to back away (-*den* from); ~ *çevirmek* to turn down, to turn away, to throw out, to toss out (*a request*); ~ *dönmek* to come (*or* go) back, to return, to turn back; ~ *durmak* to refrain, to abstain (-*den* from); ~ *gitmek* **1.** to go back, to return; **2.** to be slow, to lose time (*clock*); **3.** *fig.* to take a turn for the worse; ~ *göndermek* to send back; ~ ~ *hizmet* MIL supply service behind the front; ~ *kafalı* *fig.* reactionary, fogey, fogy; ~ *kalmak* **1.** to stay (*or* remain) behind; **2.** to be slow (*clock*); **3.** = *geri durmak*; ~ *kazanılabilir* recyclable (*waste, materials*); ~ *tepmek* to recoil, to kick (*gun*); ~ *vermek* to give back, to return; ~ *vites dişlisi* MOT reverse (gear); -*de bırakmak* to leave behind, to pass; to surpass; -*den bakmak* *fig.* to look from a distance (-*e* at); to be an onlooker; -*si aydın havası!* *fig.* the rest is of no avail!

gerici reactionary.

gericilik reaction.

geridon round pedestal table.

gerileme *vn.* of **gerilemek** *part.* regression; retrogression.

gerilemek 1. to regress; to recede; to retreat; **2.** to be on the wane (*sickness*); **3.** to fall behind, to be left behind.

gerili stretched, taut, tight.

gerilik backwardness.

gerilim 1. PHYS tension; **2.** ELECT voltage; **3.** MED blood pressure; **4.** tension (*vocal cords*).

gerilimli tense; under tension.

gerilimsiz slack; relaxed.

gerilla guerrilla.

gerillacı guerrilla.

gerilme tension.

gerilmek 1. to be tightened (*or* stretched); **2.** to be tensed.

gerinmek to stretch.

gerisingeriye backwards.

geriz sewer.

germanyum CHEM germanium.

germek, (-er) 1. to tighten, to stretch; **2.** to extend (*muscle, limb*).

germen BIOL germen.

getir, -tri gaiter, spat.

getirmek to bring, to give, to yield.

getirtmek 1. to send for; **2.** to order, to import (-*den* from).

gevelemek 1. to chew, to mumble; **2.** *fig.* to hum and haw, to mumble.

geveze talkative, chattering, chatterbox, babbler; indiscreet.

gevezelik 1. chatter, chat, chitchat; **2.** chattering, prattling; ~ *etm.* **1.** to chatter, to chat, to babble, to prattle; **2.** to blab.

geviş rumination, cud; ~ *getirmek* to ruminate, to chew the cud.

gevişgetirenler zoo ruminants.

gevmek to mumble, to chew.

gevrek 1. crisp, brittle, crackly; **2.** crisp cake (*or* biscuit); ~ ~ *gülmek* to laugh in an easy and lively way.

gevrekçi seller of **gevrek.**

gevreklik crispness.

gevremek 1. to become crisp, to be dry (*or* brittle); **2.** P to starve.

gevşek 1. loose, slack, lax; **2.** *fig.* soft, lax, lacking in backbone; ~ *ağızlı* indiscreet; ~ *davranmak* to be lax, to act in a lukewarm manner.

gevşeklik looseness, slack.

gevşemek 1. to loosen, to slacken; to become lax; **2.** to relax, to become calm (*nerves*).

gevşetici relaxative.

gevşetmek 1. to loosen, to slacken; **2.** to relax.

geyik 1. zoo deer, stag, hart; **2.** *sl.* pander; ~ *etine girmek* to take on the physical appearance of a woman (*growing girl*); -*ler kırkımında co.*

on the Greek calends.

geyikdikeni, -ni BOT buckthorn.

geyikotu, -nu BOT white dittany.

gez[1] **1.** notch (*in an arrow*); **2.** rear sight (*of a gun*).

gez[2] rope with knots at intervals for measuring ground.

gez[3] plumb line.

gez[4] (*ağacı*) BOT tamarisk tree.

gezdirmek *caus. of* **gezmek** *part.* **1.** to show around, to take about, to take through, to lead about, to conduct; **2.** to sprinkle (*as oil on salad*).

gezegen planet.

gezelemek 1. to pace up and down; **2.** *fig.* to hesitate.

gezente, gezenti roving, peripatetic (*person*).

gezer mobile.

gezge patrol.

gezgin 1. wandering, roving; **2.** travel(l)er, tourist; **~ satıcı** pedlar, hawker.

gezginci 1. roving, wandering; **2.** itinerant (*pedlar*).

gezgincilik travel(l)ing; roving; itinerancy.

gezi[1] **1.** excursion, outing; tour; **2.** promenade; **-ye çıkmak** to go on a trip.

gezi[2] silk and cotton material.

gezici itinerant; **~ esnaf** pedlar(s); **~ kütüphane** bookmobile.

gezicilik peddling.

gezim tourism.

gezimsel touristic.

gezinmek 1. to stroll, to go about; **2.** MUS to pass slowly from one *makam* to another while improvising; **3.** *Internet:* to surf the net.

gezinti 1. stroll, walk, outing; tour; **2.** corridor, floor; **3.** MUS slowly passing from one *makam* to another while improvising; **~ yeri** promenade.

gezlemek 1. to measure a place; **2.** to aim (*-i* at).

gezlik 1. sword edge; **2.** pocketknife.

gezme 1. *vn. of* **gezmek**; **2.** patrol; **3.** watchman.

gezmek, (-er) 1. to stroll, to walk, to get about, to go about, to get round, to take about; **2.** to go out; **3.** to tour (*a place*); to walk around (*a place*); **4.** to look round (*a place*); **gezip tozmak** to gallivant, to gad about (*or* around); **gezmeğe gitmek** to pay a visit.

gezmen tourist, travel(l)er.

gıcık 1. tickling sensation in the throat; **2.** *sl.* pain (in the neck); **~ olm.** to be irritated (*-e* by); **~ tutmak** to have a tickle in the throat.

gıcıklamak 1. to tickle; **2.** *fig.* to raise one's suspicion.

gıcıklanmak 1. to tickle; **2.** *fig. -den* to suspect.

gıcır 1. gum of sarsaparilla used as chewing gum; **2.** *sl.* new.

gıcırdamak to creak, to squeak, to rustle.

gıcırdatmak 1. to grind, to gnash (*one's teeth*); **2.** to make creak.

gıcır gıcır 1. very clean; **2.** brand-new; **~ ~ etm.** to creak, to squeak.

gıcırtı creak, squeak.

gıda [ā] food, nourishment; nutriment; **~ maddeleri** foodstuffs.

gıdaklamak to cackle.

gıdalı nutritious, nourishing.

gıdasız undernourished; **~ kalmak** to be undernourished.

gıdgıd gıdak cackle, cluck (*of a hen*).

gıdık 1. tickling; **2.** under part of the chin.

gıdıklamak to tickle.

gıdıklanmak to tickle, to have a tickling sensation.

gıgı under part of the chin.

gık: ~ demek to be sick (*-den* of); **~ dedirtmemek** to listen to no objections; **~ dememek** not to say a word not to object.

gıldır gıldır with a roaring sound.

gına [ā] **1.** wealth; **2.** sufficiency; **~ gelmek** (*or* getirmek) to be sick (*-den* of), to be fed up (*-den* with), to be tired (*-den* of).

gıpta envy, longing; **~ etm.** (*bşe*) to envy *s.th.*

gır: ~ atmak (*or* kaynatmak) *sl.* to chat; to gossip; **~ geçmek** *sl.* to shoot the breeze, to chatter; **~ ~ geçmek** *sl.* to make fun (*or* mock) (*ile* of); **~ -a almak** *sl.* to hoax, to mock.

gırgır 1. tiresome noise; **2.** carpet sweeper; **3.** a clay jug for drinking water; **4.** large bag shaped fishing net; **5.** raucously, annoyingly.

gırgırlamak to use a carpet sweeper (*-i* on).

gırla [x .] F amply, abundantly; incessantly, to the utmost; **~ gitmek** F to be abundant.

gırnata MUS clarinet.

gırt, -tı tearing sound; **~ ~** *or* **~ diye** with

a tearing sound.

gırtlak throat, larynx; **~ gırtlağa gelmek** to be at each other's throat, to be at daggers drawn; **~ kemiği** ANAT Adam's apple; **gırtlağına basmak** (*b-nin*) to get *s.o.* by the throat; **gırtlağına düşkün** greedy, gluttonous; **gırtlağına kadar borcu olm.** to be up to one's neck in debt; **gırtlağından kesmek** to cut back on one's food expenses.

gırtlaklamak to strangle.

gırtlaklaşmak to be at each other's throats.

gışa [. -] membrane.

gıyaben [ā] [. x .] **1.** in one's absence, in absentia; **2.** by name (*or* repute); **3.** JUR by default; **~ tanımak** (*b-ni*) to know *s.o.* by name.

gıyabi [. - -] **1.** in absentia; **2.** JUR defaulting; **~ hüküm** (*or* **karar**) JUR judg(e)ment by default.

gıyap, -bı [ā] absence, default; **gıyabında** in one's absence.

gıybet, -ti slander, calumny, defamation; **~ etm.** to slander, to calumniate.

gıybetçi slanderer, backbiter.

gibi 1. like, similar; **2.** nearly, almost, somewhat; **-sine gelmek** to seem, to appear; **bunun ~** like this.

gibice somewhat like.

gideğen outlet (*of a lake*).

gider expenditure, expense, outgo, outlay.

giderayak just before leaving, at the last moment.

giderek gradually.

giderici remover.

gidermek to remove, to exterminate, to eradicate.

gidi 1. pander; **2.** *in the exclamations:* **seni ~ seni!** you little rascal!

gidici 1. on his way out, goer; **2.** about to die.

gidiş 1. departure, going, leaving; **2.** conduct, manner of living, way of life; **~ dönüş bileti** return ticket, *Am.* round-trip ticket; **~ o ~** that was the last that was seen of him.

gidişat, -tı [ā] **1.** conduct, goings-on, behavio(u)r; **2.** the course of events.

gidişgeliş coming and going; traffic.

gidişmek to itch.

gidon handlebar (*of a bicycle*).

Gine *pr. n.* Guinea.

girdap, -bı [ā] whirlpool.

girdi input.

girgin sociable, gregarious.

girginlik sociability, gregariousness.

girift, -ti involved, intricate.

giriftar 1. captive (of); **2.** victim (of), afflicted (with).

girilir entrance, way in.

girilmek enter; **girilmez** no entrance, no admittance.

girim entrance.

girimlik entrance ticket.

girinti indentation, recess.

girintili indented; **~ çıkıntılı** wavy, toothed, zigzag.

giriş 1. entrance, entry; **2.** going in; **3.** introduction; **~ çıkış** entrance and exit; going in and out; **~ serbesttir** admission free; **~ sınavı** entrance examination; **~ ücreti** price of admission.

girişik intricate; complex; **~ tümce** GR complex sentence.

girişim 1. enterprise, iniatiative; **2.** PHYS interference.

girişimci entrepreneur.

girişimölçer interferometer.

girişken enterprising, pushing, pushy.

girişkenlik enterprise, initiative.

girişli çıkışlı movable, sliding.

girişlik introduction.

girişmek 1. to interfere, to meddle, to mix up (*-e* in); **2.** to undertake, to attempt; to set about, to go about.

Girit, -ti *pr. n.* Crete.

giritlalesi, -ni BOT ranunculus, crowfoot, buttercup.

Giritii Cretan.

girive [. - .] **1.** rocky hill; **2.** ravine; abyss; **3.** *fig.* impasse.

girizgâh [. - -] introduction, prologue.

girmek, (-er) 1. *-e* to enter, to go in, to come in; **2.** to join, to participate (*-e* in); **3.** to fit (*-e* into); **4.** to begin, to come (*season, time*); **5.** to spread (*-e* into) (*contagion*); **6.** to be enrolled; **7.** to become, to turn; **8.** to comprehend, to understand; **girdisi çıktısı 1.** the ins and outs (of); **2.** intimacy; **girip çıkmak 1.** to pay a flying visit; **2.** to frequent; **girmiş çıkmış** *fig.* with a screw loose.

girmelik entrance fee.

gişe ticket window, pay desk; cashier's desk; booking office; THEAT box office.

gitar guitar.

gitarcı, gitarist, -ti guitarist.

gitgide [x . .] more and more, gradually.

gitmek (*-der*) **1.** to go (*-e* to); **2.** to lead, to go (*road*); **3.** to suit, to fit, to go well (*-e* with), to harmonize (*-e* with); **4.** to last, to be enough for, to suffice; **5.** (*b-le*) to accompany *s.o.*; **6.** to be spent, to be used up, to go; **7.** to travel, to go; **8.** to go away, to leave; **9.** to work (*machine*); **10.** to pass, to end; **11.** to turn to, to have recourse to; **12.** to disappear; to die; **13.** to get worn out; *git çişini et yat!* have a pee and go to bed!; *gitti gider* he's (*or* it's) gone forever.

gittikçe [. x .] gradually, little by little, by degrees, more and more.

giydirici dresser.

giydirmek *caus. of* **giymek** *part.* **1.** to dress, to clothe; **2.** *fig.* to dress down, to abuse.

giyecek clothes, clothing, dress.

giyim clothing, dress, attire; **~ eşyası** clothing, clothes; **~ kuşam** dress and finery, garments, attire; **-i kuşamı yerinde** carefully dressed, chic.

giyimevi, -ni clothing store.

giyimli dressed.

giyinik dressed.

giyinmek 1. to dress o.s.; **2.** to put on (*hat, clothes, shoes*); **3.** *fig.* to resent; **giyinip kuşanmak** to put on one's Sunday best, to dress o.s. up.

giymek 1. to put on, to wear; **2.** *fig.* to listen silently to (*abuse*).

giyotin guillotine.

giysi garment, dress; clothes, clothing; **~ dolabı** wardrobe, armoire.

giz mystery.

gizdüzen conspiracy.

gizem mystery.

gizemci mystic.

gizemcilik mysticism.

gizemli mystical, mysterious.

gizil PHYS potential, latent.

gizilgüç PHYS potential energy.

gizlemek to hide, to conceal, to secrete; to dissemble, to dissimulate (*one's feelings*).

gizlenmek *pass. or refl. of* **gizlemek 1.** to hide o.s.; **2.** to be kept secret (*-den* from).

gizli 1. secret, confidential; **2.** concealed, hidden; **3.** occult; **4.** secretly; **~ celse** (*or* **oturum**) secret session; **~ kapaklı** clandestine, obscure; **~ oy** secret vote, vote by ballot; **~ pençe** half sole; **~ sıtma 1.** dormant malaria; **2.** *fig.* insidious; **~ tutmak** (*bşi*) to keep

s.th. dark; *-den -ye* in the dark, in all secrecy.

gizlice in the dark, in secrecy, secretly.

gizlilik secrecy, stealth.

gladyatör gladiator.

glase patent leather.

glayöl BOT gladiola.

glikojen CHEM glycogen.

glikol glycol.

glikoz glucose.

glikozit, -ti glucoside.

gliserin glycerin(e), glycerol.

glokoni GEOL glauconite.

glüten gluten.

gnays GEOL gneiss.

goblen Gobelin stitch.

gocuk sheepskin cloak.

gocundurmak to offend.

gocunmak to take offence (*-den* at).

godoş *sl.* pimp.

gofre puckered (*material*).

gofret a waffle-like chocolate cookie.

gogo *sl.* hashish.

gol, -lü *football*: goal; **~ atmak** (*or* **yapmak**) to score (*or* kick) a goal; **~ yemek** to let in a goal.

golcü *football*: scorer.

golet, -ti NAUT schooner.

golf golf; **~ pantolon** plus-fours, knickerbockers.

golfstrim Gulf Stream.

gollük *football*; good for making a goal.

gomalak shellac.

gonca bud.

gondol, -lü gondola.

gondolcu gondolier.

gonk, -gu gong.

goril ZOO gorilla.

gotik Gothic; **~ sanat** Gothic art; **~ yazı** Gothic.

Gotlar *pr. n.* Goths.

goygoycu blind beggar.

göbek 1. navel; **2.** potbelly, paunch; **3.** the middle, heart, central part; **4.** generation; **5.** hub (*of a bicycle wheel*); **~ adı** name given to a child when its umbilical cord is cut; **~ atmak 1.** to belly dance; **2.** *fig.* to be wild with joy; **~ bağı** infant's belly band; **~ bağlamak** to develop a potbelly; **~ havası** music for a belly dance; **~ taşı** central massage slab; **göbeği çatlamak** *fig.* to have a hard time; **göbeği sokakta kesilmiş** *fig.* **1.** gadabout; **2.** streetwalker, prostitute.

göbeklenmek 1. to get a potbelly, to

become paunchy; **2.** to develop a heart (*vegetables*).

göbekli 1. paunchy, potbellied; **2.** navel(l)ed; with a central boss; ~ *salata* lettuce.

göbel 1. street urchin (*or* arab); **2.** bastard; **3.** mound (*in a field used as a marker*).

göbelek mushroom.

göbelez terrier.

göç, -çü 1. migration, emigration, immigration; **2.** transhumance; **3.** goods and chattels of migrating people; ~ *etm.* **1.** to migrate, to emigrate, to immigrate; **2.** to pass away.

göçebe 1. nomad; wanderer; **2.** nomadic; migrant, migratory.

göçebelik nomadic life; migration, emigration.

göçelge P migrant settlement.

göçer *s.* **göçebe.**

göçeri, göçerkonar nomadic, wandering.

göçermek to run over, to transfer.

göçertmek to demolish, to knock down.

göçkün dilapidated.

göçmek, (-çer) 1. to migrate, to move off, to move (*-e* to); to move out; **2.** to migrate seasonally; **3.** to cave in, to fall down (*building*); **4.** to pass away, to die.

göçmen immigrant, settler, refugee; ~ *hücre* BIOL migratory cell; ~ *kuşlar* migratory birds.

göçmenlik migration.

göçü 1. migration; **2.** landslip, landslide.

göçük GEOL subsidence.

göçüm BIOL taxis.

göçünmek P to pass away, to die.

göçürmek *caus. of* **göçmek** *part.* **1.** to cause to move off (*-e* to), to make migrate; **2.** to make collapse (*roof, etc.*); to make subside (*land*); **3.** F to gobble up (*or* down).

göçürtmek 1. to cause to migrate; **2.** to make collapse.

göçüş 1. migration; **2.** collapse.

göden blind gut, caecum; rectum; large intestine.

gödeş *s.* **ödeş.**

göğüs, -ğsü 1. breast, chest; bosom; **2.** NAUT bow; ~ *bağır açık* with one's shirt open; ~ *cerrahisi* thoracic surgery; ~ *darlığı* asthma; ~ *geçirmek* to sigh, to groan; ~ *germek* to face,

to stand up (*-e* to, against); ~ *göğüse gelmek* to come face to face; ~ *hastalıkları* chest (*or* thoracic) diseases; ~ *kafesi* rib cage; ~ *kemiği* ANAT breastbone, sternum; ~ *tahtası* **1.** = *göğüs kemiği*; **2.** MUS soundboard, belly; *göğsü kabarmak* to swell with pride, to be proud.

göğüslemek 1. to breast; **2.** to block, to interpose o.s.

göğüslü 1. broad-chested; full-bosomed; **2.** NAUT having a flared bow.

göğüslük 1. bib, pinafore; apron; **2.** breastplate.

gök, -ğü 1. sky, heavens, firmament; **2.** azure, (sky) blue; aquamarine; ~ *gözlü* **1.** blue-eyed; **2.** *fig.* injurious, malevolent; *gürlemesi* (*or* gürültüsü) (a clap of) thunder; ~ *gürlüyor* it is thundering; ~ *kandil* *sl.* dead drunk, pissed; ~ *kubbe* the sky, the vault of heaven; *göklere çıkarmak* *fig.* to praise to the skies; *göklere çıkmak* *fig.* to rise to the sky; *gökten zembille inmemiş ya!* what's so special about him!

gökada AST galaxy.

gökbilim AST astronomy.

gökbilimci AST astronomer.

gökbilimsel AST astronomical.

gökcismi, -ni celestial (*or* heavenly) body.

gökçe 1. celestial, heavenly; **2.** sky-blue; aquamarine; **3.** pretty, beautiful (*person*).

gökdelen skyscraper.

Gökhan AST Uranus.

gökkır blue-roan (*horse*); blue-gray (*hair*).

gökkuşağı, -nı rainbow.

gökküresi, -ni AST celestial sphere.

gökmen P blue-eyed and blond.

göksel celestial, heavenly.

göktaşı, -nı 1. AST meteor, meteorite, aerolite; bolide; **2.** turquoise.

Göktürk *pr. n.* Gök Turk.

Göktürkçe *pr. n.* the language of the Gök Turks.

gökyolu, -nu Milky Way.

gökyüzü, -nü sky, firmament.

göl lake; ~ *ayağı* outlet of a lake; ~ *olm.* to form a lake.

gölalası ZOO lake trout.

gölbaşı, -nı inlet.

gölcük pond; small lake.

gölcül lacustrine.

gölek pond; puddle; small lake.

gölermek P to form a pond (or puddle).

gölet P **1.** pond; puddle; **2.** tank.

gölge shadow, shade; ~ **düşürmek** *fig.* to overshadow, to obscure; ~ **etm. 1.** to shade, to cast a shadow (-*e* on); **2.** *fig.* to bother, to molest; ~ **gibi** shadowy; ~ **oyunu** (or **tiyatrosu**) shadow play; ~ **vurmak** to shade; -*de* **bırakmak** *fig.* to eclipse, to outshine, to overshadow; -*sinden* **korkmak** *fig.* to be afraid of one's (own) shadow.

gölgebalığı, -*nı* ZOO grayling.

gölgecil BOT shade-loving.

gölgelemek 1. to overshadow (a. *fig.*); **2.** *art.* to shade in.

gölgelendirmek to shade, to overshadow (a. *fig.*).

gölgelenmek 1. to be shaded, to grow shadowy; **2.** to sit or lie in the shade.

gölgeli shady, shaded, shadowy.

gölgelik 1. shady spot; **2.** arbo(u)r, bower; **3.** awning.

gölgeolay PHLS epiphenomenon

göllenmek, göllemek to form a lake (or pond or puddle).

gölük pack animal.

gömgök [x .] **1.** dark blue, quite blue; **2.** *fig.* extremely.

gömlek 1. shirt; **2.** woman's slip; **3.** book jacket; **4.** smock; **5.** generation; **6.** gas mantle; **7.** level, degree; **8.** shade (of colo(u)r); **9.** MEC sleeve; **10.** slough (of a snake); **11.** BIOL coat, covering, tunic; **12.** ANAT integument; ~ **değiştirmek 1.** (for a snake) to cast off its skin, to slough off; **2.** *fig.* to change one's opinion, to be changeable; ~ **eskitmek** *fig.* to live a long life; **gömleği kalın** *fig.* well-to-do, well--off.

gömlekçi maker or seller of shirts.

gömlekçilik making or selling of shirts.

gömlekli wearing a shirt.

gömleklik shirting.

gömme 1. *vn.* of **gömmek**; **2.** built-in, set-in, sunken, recessed; buried; embedded, inlaid; ~ **banyo** sunken bathtub; ~ **dolap** built-in cupboard; ~ **kilit** inset lock.

gömmek, (-er) 1. to bury, to inter; **2.** to install, to build in, to set in.

gömü buried treasure.

gömük buried.

gömülmek 1. *pass.* or *refl.* of **gömmek**, *part.* to be buried; **2.** to sink deeply (-*e* into).

gömülü 1. buried, underground; **2.** sunk (-*e* into); grown (-*e* into).

gömüt tomb, grave.

gömütlük cemetery.

gön rawhide.

gönder 1. pole, staff; **2.** ox-goad.

gönderen sender.

gönderi sendoff.

gönderilmek *pass.* of **göndermek**, *part.* to be sent (-*e* to).

göndermek, (-ir) 1. to send, to dispatch, to forward; **2.** to see off; to send away.

gönen 1. moisture; humidity; **2.** moist (soil).

gönence comfort, ease.

gönenceli comfortable.

gönenç prosperity, comfort.

gönençli prosperous.

gönenmek to prosper.

gönül, -*nlü* **1.** heart; mind; **2.** affection, inclination, willingness, desire; **3.** ♀ *wf.*; ~ **acısı** pangs of love; ~ **almak 1.** to please; **2.** to apologize and make up; ~ **avcısı** lady-killer; ~ **bağı** the ties of love; ~ **bağlamak** to set one's heart (-*e* on); ~ **darlığı** distress, foreboding; ~ **eğlendirmek** to amuse o.s.; ~ **eri** broad-minded; ~ **ferahlığı** contentment; ~ **hoşluğu** ile (or ~ **rızasiyle**) willingly; ~ **işi** love affair; ~ **kırmak** to break s.o.'s heart; ~ **tokluğu** contentment; ~ **vermek** (or **bağlamak**) to lose one's heart (-*e* to); (**gönlü**): ~ **açık 1.** openhearted, frank; **2.** carefree; ~ **alçak** modest, unpretentious; ~ **bulanmak 1.** to be nauseated, to have heartburn; **2.** *fig.* to suspect; ~ **çekmek** to desire; ~ **olm. 1.** (*bşde*) to be in love with s.th.; **2.** (*bşe*) to agree to s.th.; ~ **tez** impatient; ~ **tok** satisfied, contented; ~ **yufka** soft-hearted, tender-hearted; ~ **zengin** generous; -*nce* to one's heart's content; -*nden geçirmek* to think (-*i* of); -*ne doğmak* to have a foreboding, to feel it in one's bones, to have a presentiment; -*nü etm.* (or **yapmak**) (*b-nin*) **1.** to please *s.o.*; **2.** to win *s.o.'s* assent, to persuade *s.o.*

gönüldeş sympathizer.

gönüllü 1. volunteer; **2.** (*bşin*) -*sü* keen on *s.th.*, eager for *s.th.*; **3.** lover; ~ **kıtası** MIL volunteer corps.

gönüllülük willingness.

gönülsüz 1. = **alçak gönüllü**; **2.** unwilling, disinclined.

gönülsüzce unwillingly.

gönülsüzlük unwillingness, disinclination.

gönye [x .] triangle; *-sinde olm.* to be at right angles.

göre according (*-e* to), as (*-e* to), in respect (*-e* of), considering, regarding, respecting.

görece relative.

göreceli relative.

göreli relative.

görelik PHLS relation.

görenek custom.

göreneksel customary, conventional.

göresimek to miss, to yearn (*-i* for).

görev 1. duty, obligation; **2.** function; **3.** office; *-den alınmak* **1.** to be removed from office; **2.** to be demoted; *-den kaçmak* to shirk, to goldbrick.

görevlendirmek to commission, to charge, to entrust (*ile* with).

görevlenmek to be assigned (*or* commissioned).

görevli 1. assigned, commissioned, charged; **2.** official, employee, jobholder; **3.** on duty.

görevsel functional.

görevsiz unemployed, out of work.

görgü 1. etiquette, good manners; **2.** experience; **3.** witnessing; *~ tanığı* eyewitness.

görgülü polite, well-mannered.

görgüsüz impolite, rude, ill-mannered.

görgüsüzlük impoliteness, rudeness, lack of manners.

görkem splendo(u)r, magnificence, pomp.

görkemli splendid, magnificent, pompous.

görme 1. *vn. of görmek*; **2.** vision, sight.

görmek, (-ür) 1. to see; **2.** to realize, to recognize, to see; **3.** to talk (*-i* with), to see; **4.** to spot; **5.** to regard, to consider, to see, to judge; **6.** to live through, to experience, to undergo, to see; **7.** to take (*lessons*); **8.** to perform (*a duty*); **9.** to pay (*an expense*); **10.** to receive, to get; **11.** to face; *göreyim seni!* **1.** just you try it! (*threat*); **2.** let's see if you can; *görmüş geçirmiş* worldly-wise, experienced.

görmemiş 1. upstart, parvenu; **2.** = *görgüsüz.*

görmezlik, görmemezlik pretending

not to see; *-ten gelmek* (*b-ni*) to cut *s.o.* dead, to turn one's blind on to *s.o.*

görmüşlük having seen before; *bu adamı görmüşlüğüm var* I have seen this man before; *~ duygusu* paramnesia.

görsel visual.

görsel-işitsel audio-visual.

görücü matchmaker, female go-between.

görücülük matchmaking.

görüldüğünde COM at sight (*draft, etc.*).

görülmek *pass. of görmek* to be seen.

görülmemiş never seen before.

görüm 1. vision; **2.** house call, hospital visit (*of a physician*).

görümce [. x .] sister of the husband, sister-in-law (*of the wife*).

görümlük 1. physician's fee for a house call *or* hospital visit; **2.** display window; **3.** = *yüzgörümlüğü.*

görünmek 1. to be seen, to be visible; to appear, to come in sight; **2.** to seem; **3.** (*b-ne*) *fig.* to scold *s.o.*; *göründü Sivas'ın bağları! iro.* what we feared is starting to happen!

görünmez invisible; unforeseen, unexpected; *~ kaza* unforeseen accident; *~ olm.* to disappear.

görüntü 1. phantom, specter; **2.** image.

görüntülemek to project.

görünüm 1. appearance, view; **2.** GR aspect.

görünür(ler)de in appearance (*or* sight); *~ yok* not in sight.

görünüş appearance, sight, view, spectacle; aspect; *-e aldanmamalı pro.* all that glitters is not gold; *-e göre* (*or bakılırsa*) apparently, as far as can be seen.

görünüşte apparently, on the surface.

görüş 1. sight; **2.** opinion, point of view; *~ açısı* point of view; *~ ayrılığı* difference of opinion, conflict; *~ birliği* agreement, consensus.

görüşme 1. *vn. of görüşmek*; **2.** interview; **3.** discussion, negotiation; **4.** meeting.

görüşmeci visitor.

görüşmek 1. to meet; to converse, to have an interview; **2.** to see (*or* visit) each other; **3.** to talk over, to discuss; *görüşeni karışanı olmamak* (*b-nin*) to be free from interference.

görüştürmek to arrange a meeting (*for*).

gösterge 1. PHYS indicator; **2.** table, chart, index.

gösteri 1. show, display; **2.** showing (*of a film*), performance (*of a play*); **3.** demonstration; ~ *yürüyüşü* demonstration march.

gösterici 1. projector; **2.** demonstrator.

gösterim projection.

gösteriş 1. showing, demonstrating; **2.** showing off, ostentation; **3.** striking (*or imposing*) appearance; ~ *yapmak* to show off.

gösterişçi show-off, ostentatious; pretentious.

gösterişçillik showing off, ostentation.

gösterişli stately, imposing, showy.

gösterişsiz unimposing, poor-looking, inconspicuous.

göstermek, (-ir) 1. to show; to indicate, to denote; **2.** to show, to manifest, to evidence, to evince, to demonstrate; **3.** to teach, to instruct, to show; **4.** to assign, to show; **5.** to expose (*to light, etc.*); **6.** (*b-ne*) to get even with *s.o.*, to show *s.o.*, to learn *s.o.*; **7.** to appear, to seem to be

göstermelik 1. specimen, sample, showpiece; **2.** non-functional; **3.** scenery put up before the beginning of *Karagöz*.

göt, -tü *sl.* **1.** ass, arse; **2.** *fig.* courage, guts; **3.** silly arse; ~ *üstü oturmak sl.* to be in a jam; *-üne kına yak! sl.* kick him now that he's down!; *-ünü yalamak* (*b-nin*) *sl.* to lick *s.o.'s* arse; on*u yapmaya* ~ *ister! sl.* it takes guts to do it!

götlek *sl.* passive pederast.

götün götün *sl.* backwards.

götürmek, (-ür) 1. to take (away), to carry, to convey; **2.** to remove, to destroy, to carry off; **3.** to accompany; **4.** to kill (*illness*); **5.** to bear, to put up with, to stand for; **6.** to lead (*-e* to); **7.** to take off to jail.

götürü by the piece (*or* job), in a lump sum; ~ *çalışmak* to work by the job, to do piecework; ~ *fiyat* job lot (*or* contract) price; flat rate; ~ *iş* piecework, job work; ~ *pazarlık* JUR contracting by the job.

gövde 1. body, trunk, stem; **2.** GR stem, theme; **3.** whole carcass; ~ *gösterisi*

public demonstration; *-ye atmak* (*or indirmek*) F to gulp down.

gövdebilim anatomy.

gövdebilimci anatomist.

gövdelenmek 1. to get husky; **2.** to develop a trunk (*tree*).

gövdeli husky.

gövdesel corpor(e)al.

gövermek P **1.** to turn green; **2.** to turn blue.

göynük 1. burnt; **2.** rotten, decayed, putrid; **3.** overripe.

göynümek to be burned (*or* scorched).

göz 1. eye; **2.** sight; **3.** eye (*of a needle*); **4.** division, drawer, compartment, cubbyhole; **5.** spring (*water*); **6.** *fig.* the evil eye; **7.** love; esteem; friendship; **8.** bud; **9.** pan (*of a balance*); ~ *açıp kapayıncaya kadar* in the twinkling of an eye; ~ *açtırmamak* to give no respite (*-e* to); ~ *ağrısı* **1.** eye-strain; **2.** ilk ~ *ağrısı* first love; ~ *alabildiğine* as far as the eye can see; ~ *alıcı* eye-catching, striking, dazzling; ~ *almak* to dazzle; ~ *aşinalığı* a slight acquaintance; ~ *atmak* to scan, to run an eye (*-e* over), to glance (*-e* at); ~ *bankası* eye bank; ~ *boyamak* to throw dust in s.o.'s eyes; ~ *dikmek* (*bşe*) to covet *s.th.*; ~ *doktoru* oculist; ~ *etm.* to wink (*-e* at); ~ *gezdirmek* to cast an eye (*-e* over), to run one's eye (*-e* over); ~ *göre* (*or* ~ *göre göre*) openly, publicly; knowingly; ~ *görmeyince gönül katlanır pro.* what the eye doesn't see, the heart doesn't grieve over; ~ *hapsi* surveillance; ~ *kamaştırmak* **1.** to dazzle; **2.** *fig.* to fascinate; ~ *kararı* by rule of thumb; visual estimation, judg(e)ment by the eye; ~ *kırpmak* to wink (*a. fig.*), to blink; ~ *kırpmamak* not to sleep a wink, not to have a wink of sleep, not to bat an eyelid; ~ *koymak* to covet; ~ *kulak olm.* to keep an eye (*-e* on); ~ *önünde* in front of one's eyes; ~ *önünde bulundurmak* (*or tutmak*) to take into consideration (*or* account); ~ *önüne getirmek* to envisage, to envision; ~ *yaşı* tear; ~ *yaşı dökmek* to shed tears, to weep; ~ *yummak fig.* to close one's eyes (*-e* to), to turn a blind eye (*-e* to), to wink (*-e* at); ~ *yuvası* ANAT eye socket; *-den çıkarmak* to sacrifice; *-den düşmek* to fall out of favo(u)r, to fall into disfavo(u)r; **-den geçirmek** to scrutinize, to look (or go) over; **-den ırak olan gönülden de ırak olur** pro. out of sight, out of mind; **-den kaçmak** to be overlooked; **-den kaybolmak** to vanish from sight; **-e almak** to risk, to venture; **-e batmak 1.** to be very inappropriate; **2.** to attract attention; **3.** to be exasperating (or maddening); **-e çarpmak** to stand out, to strike one's eyes; **-e girmek** to curry favo(u)r; **-e ~, dişe diş** an eye for an eye a tooth for a tooth, tit for tat; **-leri bağlı** blindfolded; **-leri fal taşı gibi açılmakı** to be moon--eyed; **-leri yollarda kalmak** to wait a long time for s.o. to come; **-lerine inanamamak** cannot believe one's eyes; **-lerinizden öperim** kind regards; **-ü açık** wide awake, shrewd; sharp; **-ü bağlı 1.** blindfolded; **2.** fig. unconscious; **3.** fig. bewitched; **-ü dalmak** to stare into space, to gaze vacantly; **-ü dönmek** to see red; **-ü gibi sevmek** (b-ni) to regard s.o. as the apple of one's eye; **-ü görmeyen** blind; **-ü ısırmak** (b-ni) not to be unfamiliar to s.o.; **-ü kalmak** (bşde) to long for s.th.; **-ü keskin** sharp-eyed, sharp--sighted; **-ü kör olsun!** damn it!, curse it!; **-ü olm.** (bşde) to have designs on s.th., to have one's eyes on s.th.; **-ü pek** brave, bold, daring; **-ü tok** contented; **-ü tutmamak** (b-ni) not to appeal to s.o.; **-üm!** (or **-ümün nuru!**) darling!, beloved!; **-ünde tütmek** to long for; **-üne girmek** (b-nin) to find favo(u)r in s.o.'s eyes, to curry favo(u)r; **-ünü açmak 1.** to keep one's eye open, to keep one's eyes peeled (or skinned); **2.** (b-nin) to undeceive s.o.; **-ünü dikmek** to fasten (or fix) one's eyes (-e on); **-ünü dört açmak** to be all eyes; **-ünü kan bürümek** to see red; **-ünü kapamak 1.** to pretend not to see; **2.** to die; **-ünü korkutmak** to daunt, to intimidate; **-ünün bebeği gibi sevmek** (b-ni) to love s.o. like the apple of one's eye; **-ünün ucuyle bakmak** to look out of the corner of one's eye; **-ünün yaşına bakmamak** fig. to have no pity (-in on).

gözakı, -nı the white of the eye.

gözaltı, -nı (house) arrest; **~ etm.** (or **-na almak**) **1.** to put under house arrest; **2.** to take into custody.

gözaşısı, -nı BOT bud graft.

gözbağı, -nı sleight of hand.

gözbebeği, -ni 1. ANAT pupil; **2.** fig. apple of the eye, honey, pet.

gözcü 1. watchman, sentry, observer, scout; **2.** oculist.

gözcülük 1. observing, scouting; **2.** medical treatment of the eyes; **~ etm.** to watch.

gözdağı, -nı intimidation, threat; **~ vermek** to intimidate, to threaten.

gözde favo(u)rite, pet.

gözdemiri, -ni NAUT bower anchor.

gözdikeği, -ni object, aim, purpose.

gözdişi, -ni eyetooth, canine tooth.

göze 1. ANAT cell; **2.** spring, source.

gözemek 1. to patch, to mend; **2.** to embroider with silk thread.

gözenek 1. stoma, pore; **2.** window; **3.** hemstitch; **4.** AST granulation; **5.** beekeeper's mask.

gözer coarse sieve.

gözerimi 1. horizon; **2.** (range of) sight.

gözetici guard, protector; observer.

gözetim supervision; care, watch.

gözetleme vn. of **gözetlemek**, part. MIL observation; **~ deliği 1.** peephole, spyhole (in a door); **2.** MIL observation slit; **~ yeri** MIL observation point, lookout.

gözetlemek to peep (-i at), to spy (-i on), to observe.

gözetleyici MIL observer; lookout.

gözetmek, (-ir) 1. to guard, to protect; to mind, to look after, to take care (-i of); **2.** to consider, to respect; to regard, to observe (law, rule).

gözevi, -ni eye-socket.

gözkapağı, -nı eyelid.

gözlem observation.

gözlemci observer.

gözlemcilik observation.

gözleme 1. vn. of **gözlemek**, part. **1.** MIL or AST observation; **3.** pancake.

gözlemek 1. to watch (-i for), to wait (-i for), to keep an eye (-i on); **2.** to observe; **3.** to prick with holes.

gözlemen observer.

gözlemevi, -ni observatory.

gözlemlemek to watch (-i **for, over**).

gözleyici observer.

gözlü 1. -eyed; **2.** having drawers or pigeonholes.

gözlük (eye)glasses, spectacles; **~ camı** spectacle lens; **~ çerçevesi** frames (or rim) for glasses; **~ takmak** (or **kullanmak**) to wear glasses.

gözlükcü optician.

gözlüklü wearing glasses.

gözlüklüyılan zoo hooded snake.

gözpınarı, -nı inner corner of the eye.

gözsüz 1. without pigeonholes *or* compartments; **2.** blind.

göztaşı, -nı copper sulphate.

gözükmek, (-ür) 1. to appear, to be visible (*or* seen); **2.** to show o.s., to turn up.

grado [x .] **1.** proof (spirit); **2.** degree, grade.

grafik 1. graph, diagram; **2.** graphic; ~ *sanatlar* graphics, graphic arts.

grafit, -ti GEOL graphite.

grafoloji graphology.

gram gram(me).

gramaj weight in grams.

gramer grammar; ~ *yönünden* grammatically.

gramerci grammarian.

gramkuvvet, -ti gram force.

gramofon phonograph.

grandi [x .] NAUT mainmast.

grandük, -kü grand duke.

grandüşes grand duchess.

granit, -ti granite.

granül ANAT granule.

granüle granulated.

granülit, -ti GEOL granulite.

gravür engraving.

gravürcü engraver.

gravyer (peyniri) Gruyère cheese.

Grek *pr. n.* Greek.

Grekçe *pr. n.* the ancient Greek language.

grekoromen Greco-Roman wrestling.

grena GEOL garnet.

grenadin grenadine.

gres (yağı) MEC lubricating grease.

grev strike; ~ *gözcüsü* picket; ~ *hakkı* right of strike; ~ *yapmak* to strike, to go on strike; *-i bozmak* to break the strike.

grevci striker.

greyder bulldozer.

greyfrut BOT grapefruit.

gri grey, *Am.* gray.

grip, -bi influenza, flu, grippe; ~ *olm.* to have influenza; *gribe tutulmak* to come down with flu.

grizu firedamp, pit gas, methane; ~ *patlaması* firedamp explosion.

grogren grosgrain.

gros gross; ~ *ağırlık* gross weight.

grosa *obs.* gross (= *12 dozen*).

grup, -bu 1. group; **2.** MIL section; ~~ in

groups; ~ *olm.* to form a group.

gruplandırmak to group.

gruplaşmak 1. to separate into groups; **2.** to gather into groups.

guano GEOL guano.

Guatemala *pr. n.* Guatemala.

guatr MED goitre, *Am.* goiter.

guatrlı MED goitrous.

gudde ANAT gland.

gudubet, -ti like the back (end) of a bus.

gufran [. -] God's mercy (*or* pardon).

guguk zoo cuckoo; ~ *yapmak* *fig.* to make mock (*-e* of).

guguklu having a cuckoo; ~ *saat* cuckoo clock.

gulfe foreskin, prepuce.

gulu(k) P turkey.

gulyabani [ü, ı] ogre, ogress.

gurbet, -ti 1. foreign land; **2.** F absence from one's home; ~ *çekmek* to be homesick, to suffer absence from home; ~ *eli* (*or diyarı*) foreign land; *-e* (*or ~ ellere*) *düşmek* to be in a foreign land.

gurbetçi stranger.

gureba [ä] the poor and destitute; ~ *hastanesi* hospital for the poor.

gur gur rumbling sound; ~ *etm.* to rumble.

gurk, -ku 1. broody (*hen*); **2.** turkey cock; ~~ *etm.* to cluck (*broody hen*).

gurklamak to be broody (*hen*).

guruldamak to rumble, to growl.

gurul gurul rumbling sound; *karnı* ~ *ötüyor* his stomach is rumbling (*or* growling).

gurultu rumble.

gurup, -bu sunset, sundown.

gurur [. -] **1.** pride; **2.** conceit, vanity; ~ *duymak* to feel proud (*-den* of), to take pride (*-den* in); ~ *gelmek* (*b-ne*) *or* ~ *getirmek* (*b-i*) to be proud (of); to be conceited (about); *-unu kırmak* (*b-nin*) to hurt the pride of s.o.; *-unu okşamak* *fig.* to play on s.o.'s pride, to flatter s.o.'s pride.

gururlanmak to pride o.s. (*ile* on), to pique o.s. (*ile* on), to preen o.s. (*ile* on).

gururlu arrogant, vain, haughty, conceited.

gusletmek [x . .] to take a ritual bath.

gusto [x .] gusto, zest; taste.

gusül, -slü *isl.* total ablution of the body; ~ *abdesti* total ablution; ~ *abdesti almak* to perform a total ablution.

gusülhane [ā] bathroom for ritual washing.

guşa [x .] *s.* **guatr.**

gut MED gout.

guvaş gouache.

gübre dung, manure, fertilizer, droppings; ~ **şerbeti** manure tea, liquid manure.

gübrelemek to manure, to fertilize, to dung.

gübreli manured, fertilized.

gübrelik dunghill.

gücendirmek to offend, to hurt.

gücenik offended, hurt, resentful.

gücenmek to resent, to take offence (-*e* at), to be offended (*or* hurt) (-*e* by).

gücü sley, weaver's reed.

gücün [x .] **1.** just barely, hardly; **2.** by force, forcibly.

güç[1], **-cü 1.** strength; **2.** power; **3.** force; **4.** energy; ~ **birliği** cooperation; **-ten düşmek** to get weak; **gücü yetmek** to be strong enough; **gücü yettiği kadar** as well as he can, with all his might; **gücünü yenmek** to suppress one's anger.

güç[2], **-cü 1.** difficult, hard; **2.** difficulty; ~ **gelmek** (*b-ne*) to seem difficult to *s.o.*; ~ **halle** (*or* **gücü gücüne**) with much effort, with great difficulty; ~ **ile** with difficulty, with great trouble; **güce sarmak** to get hard, to become difficult; **gücüne gitmek** to be offended, to be hurt, to take offence; **gücüne koşmak** to do s.th. the hard way.

güçbela with great difficulty, hardly.

güçlendirmek to strengthen.

güçlenmek to get strong, to strengthen.

güçleşmek to grow difficult.

güçleştirmek to render difficult, to complicate, to impede.

güçlü strong, powerful; ~ **kuvvetli** very strong and healthy.

güçlük difficulty, pain, trouble; ~ **çekmek** to experience difficulty; ~ **çıkarmak** (*or* **göstermek**) to make difficulties (-*e* for); **güçlüğü yenmek** to overcome difficulties.

güçlülük strength, power.

güçsüz weak, feeble, strengthless.

güçsüzlük weakness, feebleness, strengthlessness.

güderi 1. chamois (leather), chammy, shammy; **2.** made of chamois; ~ **eldiven** chamois glove.

güdü motive, incentive; drive, push.

güdücü shepherd; cattle drover.

güdük 1. deficient, incomplete; **2.** docked; tailless; **2.** F thick-set, dumpy, squat; ~ **kalmak** F to be stunted; ~ **tavuk 1.** hen without tail feathers; **2.** *fig.* nobody.

güdükleşmek to become stunted; to become truncated.

güdüleyici incentive.

güdüm guidance, direction, management.

güdümbilim cybernetics.

güdümlü controlled, directed; ~ **mermi** guided missile.

güfte words of a song, lyrics.

güğüm large jug.

güherçile CHEM saltpetre, *Am.* saltpeter.

gül 1. BOT rose; **2.** ♀ *wf.*; ~ **ağacı** rosewood; ~ **gibi** swimmingly; ~ **gibi geçinmek** to get along swimmingly; ~ **goncası** rosebud; ~ **reçeli** rose jam; ~ **rengi** rose pink; ~ **üstüne ~ koklamak** to be disloyal to one's darling by loving another person; **-ü seven dikenine katlanır** pro. he that would have eggs must endure the cackling of hens, take the rough with the smooth.

güldeste anthology of poems.

güldür güldür with a crashing sound; ~ **akmak** to brawl (*river*).

güldürmek *caus. of* **gülmek** to make laugh, to amuse.

güldürü THEAT comedy, farce.

güldürücü comic, funny.

güleç smiling, joyful.

gülhatmi BOT hollyhock.

gülistan [ā] rose garden.

gülizar *poet.* rosy-cheeked.

gülkurusu, -nu violet-pink.

güllabi(ci) 1. warden (*in a lunatic asylum*); **2.** *fig.* flatterer, coaxer.

güllaç, -cı starch wafer.

gülle 1. cannon ball; shell; **2.** *sports*: shot; weight; ~ **atma** *sports*: shot put; ~ **atmak** *sports*: to put the shot; ~ **gibi** as heavy as lead; ~ **kaldırmak** *sports*: to lift weights; ~ **yağdırmak** to shell, to bombard.

gülleci *sports*: shot-putter.

güllük rose garden (*or* bed); ~ **gülistanlık** *fig.* a bed of roses.

gülme laughing, laughter; ~ **almak** to have a fit of laughter.

gülmece F funny story *or* novel.

gülmek, (-er) 1. to laugh; **2.** (*b-ne*) to

laugh at *s.o.*, to deride *s.o.*; **3.** to be pleased; *güle güle!* **1.** good-bye!; **2.** good luck!; *güle güle gidin!* have a good trip!; *güle güle kullan!* enjoy using it!; *güle oynaya* merrily, joyously; *güleceği tuttu* he had a fit of laughter; *güler yüz* cheerful, smiling face; *güler yüz göstermek* to behave cheerfully and hospitably (*-e* towards); *güler yüzlü* cheerful, affable, merry; *gülmekten çatlamak* to split one's sides laughing; *gülmekten kırılmak* to be doubled up with laughter; *gülüp oynamak* *fig.* to have a good time.

gülmez sullen, sour-faced; unsmiling.
gülsuyu, -nu rose water.
gülücük smile.
gülümseme smile.
gülümsemek to smile.
gülünç, -cü ridiculous, ludicrous, laughable, funny.
gülünçleştirmek to caricature.
gülünçlü funny, comical.
gülünçlük funniness, comicality.
gülünmek 1. *pass.* of *gülmek*; **2.** to laugh.
gülüş laughter.
gülüşmek to laugh together; to laugh at each other.
gülyağı, -nı attar of roses.
güm 1. bang!; **2.** *sl.* fishy-story, tall-story; ~ *atmak sl.* to pull a fast one; ~ *etm.* to boom, to resound, to reverberate; ~ *atmak* to throb (*heart*); *-e gitmek sl.* or F **1.** to go for nothing; **2.** to die in vain, to peg out.
gümbedek [x . .] **1.** with a booming sound; **2.** out of the blue, all of a sudden.
gümbürdemek 1. to boom, to thunder, to reverberate; **2.** *sl.* to peg out, to pop off.
gümbür gümbür with a booming noise.
gümbürtü boom, rumble, crash, thunder.
gümeç, -ci honeycomb; ~ *balı* honey in the comb.
gümlemek 1. to bang, to boom, to rumble; **2.** *sl.* = *güme gitmek*.
gümrah [ā] abundant, dense, copious.
gümrük 1. customs (house); **2.** duty; tariff; ~ *almak* to collect duty (*-den* on); ~ *kaçağı* smuggled (*goods*); ~ *kaçakçısı* smuggler; ~ *komisyoncusu* customs broker; ~ *kontrolü* customs

inspection (*or* control); ~ *memuru* customs officer; ~ *resmi* customs charges; ♀ *ve Tekel Bakanlığı* the Ministry of Customs and Monopolies; *-ten muaf* duty-free; *gümrüğe tabi* dutiable, subject to duty.
gümrükçü 1. customs officer; **2.** customs agent.
gümrüklenmek to be cleared through customs.
gümrüklü 1. subject to customs duties; **2.** with customs duties paid.
gümrüksüz duty-free.
gümüş silver; ~ *kaplama* silver-plated; silver plating; ~ *madeni* silver mine; ~ *takımı* silver (plate).
gümüşbalığı, -nı zoo sand-smelt, silversides, atherine.
gümüşçü silversmith.
gümüşi [ī], **gümüşü** silvery, silver-gray, silver-colo(u)red.
gümüşlemek to silver-plate.
gümüşlü 1. containing silver; **2.** ornamented with silver.
gümüşservi moonlight shining on water.
gün 1. day; daytime; **2.** period; time; age; **3.** happy (*or* better) days; **4.** lady's at-home day; **5.** sun; light; **6.** date; **7.** feast day; ~ *ağarmak* to break (*dawn*); ~ *ağarması* daybreak; ~ *batımı* sunset, sundown; ~ *bugün!* now is the right time!; ~ *doğmak* **1.** to rise, to dawn (*sun*); **2.** (*b-ne*) *fig.* to give *s.o.* an unexpected opportunity; ~ *doğuşu* sunrise, sun-up; ~ *geçmek* (*b-ne*) to get a sunstroke; ~ *geçtikçe* as the day goes on; ~ *görmez* sunless (*place*); ~ *görmüş* **1.** who has seen better days; **2.** experienced; ~ *tutulması* eclipse of the sun; ~ *yapmak* to give an at-home; *-den -e* from day to day; *-lerce* for days; *-lerden bir gün* once upon a time; *-leri sayılıdır* his days are numbered; *-ü -üne* punctually; to the very day; *-ün birinde* one day, some day; *-ünü ~ etm.* to enjoy *o.s.* thoroughly.
günah [ā] **1.** sin; **2.** isn't it a crime!, shame!; ~ *benden gitti* it is no longer my responsibility; ~ *çıkartmak* to confess one's sins (*to a priest*); ~ *işlemek* to sin, to commit a sin; ~ *olm.* to be a crime; *-a girmek s.* ~ *işlemek*; *-a sokmak* **1.** to tempt; **2.** to drive to blasphemy; *-ı* (*or* *vebali*) *boynuna!* the moral responsibility rests upon

you (*or* him)!; **-ını çekmek** to suffer for one's sins; **-ını vermez** *fig.* he is very miser.

günahkâr 1. sinner; culprit, wrongdoer; **2.** sinful, impious; culpable.

günahkârlık sinfulness.

günahlı = **günahkâr 1 & 2.**

günahsız sinless, innocent.

günahsızlık sinlessness, innocence.

günaşırı every other day.

günaydın good morning.

günbatısı, -nı west.

güncek P umbrella.

güncel current, up-to-date; **~ olaylar** current events.

güncelleşmek to become current.

güncelleştirmek to make contemporary, to bring up-to-date.

güncellik currency.

günçiçeği, -ni BOT sunflower.

gündelik 1. daily; **2.** daily wage (*or* fee); **~ gazete** daily (paper); **~ ücret** daily wage; **-le çalışmak** to work by the day.

gündelikçi day labo(u)rer, hired man; **~ kadın** charwoman, *Am.* hired woman.

gündelikçilik day labo(u)r.

gündem agenda; **-e almak** to put on the agenda; **-e geçmek** to be put on the agenda.

gündeş happening on the same day.

gündoğ(r)usu, -nu 1. NAUT east; **2.** easterly wind.

gündönümü, -nü equinox, solstice.

gündüz 1. daytime; **2.** by day (*or* daylight), in the daytime; **~ feneri** *co.* Negro; **~ gözüyle** by the light of day; **~ vakti** in the daytime, during the day; **-leri** in the daytime, during the day.

gündüzcü 1. on day duty; **2.** day student; **3.** day drinker.

gündüzlü 1. day (*school*); **2.** = **gündüzcü 2.**

gündüzsefası, -nı BOT bindweed.

gündüzün [x . .] by (*or* during the) day.

günebakan BOT sunflower.

güneş 1. sun; **2.** sunshine; **~ açmak** to become sunny; **~ almak** (*or* **görmek**) to let in the sun; **~ banyosu** sun bath(-ing); **~ batması** sunset, sundown; **~ çarpması** sunstroke; **~ doğmak** to rise (*sun*); **~ gözlüğü** sunglasses; **~ ışını** sunbeam, sunray; **~ saati** sundial; **~ sistemi** solar system; **~ tutulması** solar eclipse; **~ yanığı** sunburn;

~ yılı solar year; **-e göstermek** to expose to the sun; **-i balçıkla** (*or* **çamurla**) **sıvamak** *fig.* to try to hide the truth; **-in alnında** (*or* **altında**) in full sun; **-te yanmak** to be sunburned; to be tanned.

güneşle(n)mek to sunbathe.

güneşli sunny, sunlit.

güneşlik 1. sunny place; **2.** sunshade, sunblind; **3.** sun hat; visor (*of a cap*); **4.** sun-visor (*in a car*); **5.** lens cover (*for a camera*).

güneşsiz sunless.

güney 1. south; **2.** southern; **1.** south wind; **4.** sunny side; **~ kutbu** South Pole.

Güney Afrika Cumhuriyeti *pr. n.* Republic of South Africa.

güneybatı southwest.

güneydoğu southeast.

güneyli 1. southerner; **2.** southern.

günlü dated.

günlük¹ 1. daily; **2.** ... days old (*baby*); **3.** sufficient for ... days; **4.** diary; **5.** everyday, usual; **~ emir** MIL order of the day; **~ gazete** daily paper; **~ güneşlik** sunny; **~ kur** COM current rate of exchange; **~ rapor** daily report, bulletin; **~ yumurta** fresh egg.

günlük² incense, frankincense, myrrh.

günlükçü diarist.

günöte AST apogee.

günübirlik, günübirliğine for the day.

güpegündüz [. x . .] in broad daylight.

gür 1. abundant, dense, thick; rank; **2.** gushing.

gürbüz sturdy, robust, healthy.

gürbüzlük sturdiness, robustness.

Gürcistan *pr. n.* Georgia.

Gürcü Georgian.

güreş wrestling; **~ etm.** (*or* **tutmak**) to wrestle.

güreşçi wrestler.

güreşçilik wrestling.

güreşmek to wrestle (*ile* with).

gürgen (**ağacı**) BOT hornbeam, horn beech.

gürlemek 1. to thunder; to roar; **2.** *fig.* to roar with rage; **3.** *sl.* to peg out, to pop off.

gürleşmek to become abundant (*or* dense).

gürlük 1. abundance, luxuriance; **2.** bountifulness.

güruh [ü] gang, group, lot, band, mob.

gürüldemek to thunder.

gürül gürül with a brawling sound; ~~ **akmak** to brawl (*river*).

gürültü 1. noise, uproar; **2.** *fig.* brawl, row; ~ **çıkarmak** (*or* etm. *or* **yapmak**) to make a row; ~ **koparmak** to kick up (*or* make) a row; ~ **patırtı** noise, commotion; -**ye boğmak** to cause to be lost in the confusion; -**ye gelmek** to be lost in the confusion; -**ye gitmek** to be the victim of the confusion; (**kuru**) -**ye pabuç bırakmamak** not to be intimidated by mere threats.

gürültücü noisy, troublesome.

gürültülü noisy, tumultuous, clamorous.

gürültüsüz noiseless, quiet.

gürz HIST mace.

gütaperka [. . x .] gutta-percha.

gütmek, (-der) 1. to herd, to drive (*animal*); **2.** *fig.* to cherish, to nourish, to nurse (*grudge, aim, ambition*); **3.** to impel.

güve ZOO clothes moth; ~ **yemiş** moth-eaten; ~ **yeniği** moth hole.

güveç, -ci casserole; hotpot.

güvelenmek to be moth-eaten.

güven 1. trust, confidence, reliance; **2.** security, safety; -**i olm.** to have confidence (-*e* in); -**i sarsılmak** to lose confidence (in); -**ini kazanmak** (*b-nin*) to win *s.o.'s* confidence.

güvence guarantee.

güvenç *s.* **güven.**

güvenışığı PHOT safelight.

güvenilir trusty, trustworthy, dependable.

güvenli dependable, trusty.

güvenlik 1. security, safety; **2.** confidence; ♀ **Konseyi** Security Council.

güvenmek to trust (-*e* in), to rely (-*e* on); to confide (-*e* in); **güvendiği dağlara kar yağmak** *fig.* to be let down.

güvenoyu, -nu vote of confidence; ~ **almak** to win a vote of confidence; ~ **vermek** to give a vote of confidence.

güvensiz distrustful.

güvensizlik distrustfulness, lack of confidence.

güvercin ZOO pigeon; ~ **postası** pigeon post.

güvercinboynu, -nu multicolo(u)red, shot; dove colo(u)red.

güvercinlik dovecote, pigeon-loft.

güverte [. x .] NAUT deck.

güvey 1. bridegroom; **2.** son-in-law; ~ **olmadık, ama kapı dışında bekledik** *co.* although we weren't there we know quite a lot about it.

güveyfeneri, -ni BOT winter cherry.

güveyotu, -nu BOT marjoram.

güvez purplish red.

güya 1. supposedly; **2.** as if, as though.

güz autumn, *Am.* fall.

güzçiğdemi, -ni BOT autumn crocus, meadow saffron.

güzel 1. beautiful, pretty, nice; **2.** beauty, belle; **3.** fine!, good!; **4.** excellent, good; ~ ~ calmly, gently; ~ **hava** fine weather; ~ **sanatlar** fine arts; ~ **mi güzel!** of breath-taking beauty, very beautiful; ♀ **Sanatlar Akademisi** *pr. n.* the Academy of Fine Arts; -**im 1.** darling, honey; **2.** that beautiful (*thing or person*).

güzelavratotu, -nu BOT belladonna, deadly nightshade.

güzelce 1. pretty, fair; **2.** thoroughly.

güzelleme a kind of folk song of praise for a special person.

güzelleşmek to become beautiful.

güzelleştirmek to beautify.

güzellik 1. beauty, prettiness; **2.** gentleness, kindness; ~ **kraliçesi** beauty queen; ~ **salonu** beauty-parlo(u)r, beauty-salon; ~ **yarışması** beauty contest.

güzellikle gently, with gentleness.

güzergâh route.

güzey GEOGR shady side.

güzide [î] select, distinguished, outstanding; choice.

güzlük autumn ..., *Am.* fall ...; ~ **ekim** autumn (*or* fall) sowing.

güzün [x .] in the autumn, *Am.* in the fall.

H

ha 1. what a …!, wow!; **2.** o yes!, I see!; **3.** come on now!; **4.** look here!; **5.** F eh?, huh?; **6.** P yes; **7.** either, or; **8.** on and on; **~ bire** uninterruptedly; **~ deyince** at a moment's notice.

habaset, -ti [. - .] villainy, wickedness.

habazan F starved, ravenous.

habbe grain, seed, kernel; **-yi kubbe yapmak** F to make a mountain out of a molehill.

habe [ā] sl. bread; **~ etm.** (or kaymak or uçlanmak) sl. to get enough to eat.

habeci [ā] sl. fool, idiot, fucker.

habeden [ā] sl. for nothing, gratis.

haber 1. news, information, word, message; **2.** knowledge; **3.** GR obs. predicate; **~ ajansı** news agency; **~ alma** MIL intelligence; **~ almak** (bşi) to learn s.th., to get word of s.th., to hear s.th.; **~ göndermek** to send a message (-e to); **~ kaynağı** news source; **~ merkezi 1.** news bureau; **2.** information bureau; **3.** command post; **~ salmak** F to send news (-e to); **~ sütunu** news column; **~ toplamak** to gather news; **~ uçurmak** to send a message secretly or urgently (-e to); **~ vermek 1.** to let s.o. know; **2.** to inform, to announce; **-i olm.** (bşden) to be informed of s.th., to know about s.th.; **-im var** I know about it; **-im yok** I know nothing about it, I haven't heard it.

haberci herald, harbinger (a. fig.); forerunner, messenger; **guguk kuşu baharın -sidir** the cuckoo is a harbinger of spring.

haberdar [. . -] informed; **~ etm.** (b-ni bşden) to inform s.o. of s.th.; **~ olm.** to know (-den about); to find out (-den about), to possess information (-den about).

haberleşme communication.

haberleşmek to communicate (ile with), to correspond (ile with).

haberli 1. informed; **2.** having notified.

habersiz 1. uninformed, ignorant (-den of); **2.** without warning.

habersizce without warning, secretly.

Habeş pr. n. Abyssinian, Ethiopian; **~ maymunu** zoo sacred baboon.

Habeşi s. **Habeş.**

Habeşistan pr. n. Abyssinia, Ethiopia.

habis 1. malicious, evil; **2.** malignant (tumo(u)r).

hac, -ccı pilgrimage to Mecca; **-ca gitmek** to go on the pilgrimage to Mecca.

hacamat, -tı 1. bloodletting by cupping; **2.** sl. stabbing, knifing; **~ şişesi** cupping glass.

haccetmek [x . .] to go on the pilgrimage to Mecca.

hacet, -ti [ā] **1.** need, necessity, requirement; **2.** feces; urine; **~ görmek 1.** to deem necessary; **2.** F to go to the toilet; **~ kalmamak** to be no longer necessary; **~ kapısı** (or penceresi) door (or window) of a saint's tomb; **~ yeri** toilet; **~ yok** it's not necessary.

hacı hadji; pilgrim; **~ ağa** contp. parvenu, upstart, nouveau riche; **~ baba 1.** elderly hadji; **2.** F venerable old man; **~ bekler gibi beklemek** to wait impatiently (-i for); **~ pintorosa kavuşmak** sl. to get a good hiding; **-sı hocası** F everyone.

hacılaryolu, -nu the Milky Way.

hacıyatmaz 1. tumbler, roly-poly (toy); **2.** resilient person.

hacim, -cmi 1. volume, capacity; bulk; **2.** NAUT tonnage.

hacimli voluminous, bulky.

hacir, -cri JUR putting under restraint.

Hacivat, -tı pr. n. one of the main characters of the Karagöz shadow play.

haciz, -czi seizure, sequestration, distraint; **~ altına almak** to sequestrate; **~ kararı** warrant of distraint; **~ koymak** to sequestrate.

hacizli sequestered, sequestrated.

haczetmek to sequestrate, to seize.

haç, -çı the cross, crucifix; **~ çıkarmak** to cross o.s.; **-ı suya atma yortusu** Epiphany.

haçlamak to crucify.

Haçlılar pr. n. HIST Crusaders.

Haçlı seferleri HIST the Crusades.

had, -ddi 1. limit, boundary, degree, point; **2.** MATH, LOG term; **-di hesabı olmamak** to be boundless (or bountiful); **-di olmamak** (b-nin) not to have the right to, not to be up to *s.o.*; **-di zatında** actually, essentially; **-dinden fazla** excessive, overmuch; **-dini aşmak** to go too far; **-dini bildirmek** (*b-ne*) to put *s.o.* in his place, to tell *s.o.* where to get off; **-dini bilmek** to know one's place.

hâd, -ddi 1. sharp, pointed; 2. MED acute; 3. *fig.* critical, acute.

hadde 1. wire-drawer's plate; 2. rolling machine; ~ **fabrikası** rolling mill; **-den geçirmek** *fig.* to examine minutely.

haddehane [. . - .] rolling mill.

hademe caretaker, *Am.* janitor.

hadım eunuch; ~ **etm.** to castrate.

hadımağası, -nı HIST chief eunuch in the sultan's palace.

hadi *s.* **haydi.**

hadim 1. manservant; 2. serving.

hadis 1. hadith; 2. the study of hadiths.

hadise event, incident, occurrence, happening; ~ **çıkarmak** to make a scene, to stir up trouble.

hadiseli eventful.

hadisene F come on!

hadisesiz smoothly, eventless.

hadsiz unbounded, unlimited; ~ **hesapsız** countless, innumerable.

haf *sports:* half-back.

hafakan sudden exasperation; **-lar boğmak** (*or* **basmak**) to be bored stiff.

hafazanallah [. . . . .-] may God protect us from such a misfortune!

hafız [ā] 1. hafiz; 2. *sl.* fool, silly; 3. *sl.* swot, grind, crammer.

hafıza memory.

hafızıkütüp librarian.

hafızlamak *sl.* to swot up, to mug up, to grind, to cram, to bone up on.

hafızlık 1. being a hafiz; 2. *sl.* swotting; 3. *sl.* stupidity.

hafi [ī] secret, hidden.

hafif 1. light; 2. easy; 3. frivolous, flighty; 4. slight; 5. slightly; 6. insignificant, unimportant; ~ **atlatmak** to escape (*or* get off) lightly; ~ **çay** weak tea; ~ **giyinmek** to dress lightly; ~ ~ gently, slowly; ~ **müzik** light music; ~ **sanayi** light industry; ~ **tertip** 1. small-scale; 2. slightly, a little; **-e almak** to make light (*-i* of); **-ten almak** to trifle (*-i* with), to make light (*-i* of).

hafifçe lightly.

hafiflemek 1. to get lighter; 2. to subside, to diminish; 3. to be relieved.

hafifleşmek 1. to get light; 2. *fig.* to become flighty (*or* light-headed).

hafifleştirmek, hafifletmek 1. to lighten; 2. to abate, to diminish; 3. to relieve.

hafifletici 1. extenuating; 2. giving relief; ~ **sebepler** JUR extenuating circumstances.

hafiflik 1. lightness, slightness; 2. relief, ease of mind; 3. *fig.* flightiness.

hafifmeşrep, -bi loose, flighty, frivolous.

hafifsemek to make light (*-i* of), to trifle (*-i* with).

hafifsiklet, -ti welterweight.

hafiften lightly, gently.

hafiye detective, investigator, spy.

hafriyat, -tı [. . -] excavation(s).

hafriyatçı [. . . -] excavator.

hafta week; ~ **arasında** (*or* **içinde**) during the week; ~ **başı** the first day of the week; ~ **sonu** (*or* **tatili**) weekend; **-larca** for weeks; **-sına** a week later; **-sına kalmaz** within a week; **-ya** in a week's time, next week; **-ya bugün** this day week.

haftalık 1. weekly; 2. weekly wage; 3. lasting ... weeks; ~ **mecmua** weekly; **iki ~ bir çalışma** a two-week work.

haftalıkçı wage earner (*paid by the week*).

haftaym [- .] [x .] *sports:* half time.

hah there!, now!, exactly!; ~ **şöylet** there, that's good!

haham ECCL rabbi.

hahambaşı, -nı ECCL the chief rabbi.

hahamhane [. . - .] rabbinate.

hahha [. -], **hahhah** [x .] ha!, haha!

hail [ā] barrier, screen, curtain.

haile [ā] tragedy.

hain [ā] 1. traitor; 2. treacherous, traitorous; 3. malicious; ~ ~ maliciously.

hainleşmek to become (*or* act) treacherous, to become malicious.

hainlik 1. treachery, perfidy; 2. malice; ~ **etm.** to act treacherously (*-e* towards).

Haiti *pr. n.* Haiti.

haiz [ā] 1. containing, having; 2. provided (*-i* with); ~ **olm.** to possess, to obtain, to have.

hak¹, -kkı 1. justice; 2. right; due, share; 3. fairness; 4. true, right; 5. remuneration, fee, pay; ~ **etm.** to deserve, to merit; ~ **iddia etm.** to claim; ~ **kazanmak** to deserve, to have a right (*-e* to); ~ **sahibi** holder of a right; ~ **vermek**

(*b-ne*) to acknowledge *s.o.* to be right; **~ yemek** to be unjust; **~ yemez** rightful; **...hakkı için** for the sake of ...; **hakkı olm. 1.** to have a right to; **2.** to be justified; **hakkı var** he is right; **hakkından gelmek 1.** to get the better (*-in* of); **2.** (*b-nin*) to get even with *s.o.*, to pay *s.o.* back; **hakkını almak** to get one's due; to take one's share; **hakkını vermek** to give s.o. his due, to remunerate; **hakkını yemek** (*b-nin*) to do an injustice to *s.o.*

hak² **-kki 1.** engraving, incising; **2.** erasing by scraping.

Hak, -kkı (*a.* **Cenabı Hak**) God; **Hakkın rahmetine kavuşanlar** the dead, the deceased; **Hakkın rahmetine kavuşmak** to die, to go to meet one's Maker.

hâk, -ki *obs.* earth, soil; **~ ile yeksan etm.** to raze to the ground, to bring down.

hakan [-.] khan, Turkish ruler; emperor.

hakaret, -ti [. - .] insult, contempt; **~ etm.** to insult; **~ görmek** *pass. of* **~ etm.**

hakça [x .] **1.** truthfully, truly; **2.** justly.

hakem 1. arbitrator; **2.** *sports*: referee, umpire; **~ kararı** JUR arbitral award, arbitration; **~ kurulu** arbitration committee.

hakemlik umpirage; arbitration; **~ etm. 1.** to arbitrate; **2.** *sports*: to umpire, to referee.

hakeza [- .-] [x . -] likewise.

haki [ā] khaki.

hakikat, -ti [ī] **1.** truth, reality; **2.** truly, really; **~ olm.** to come true; *-te* in fact.

hakikaten [ī] [. x ..] truly, really.

hakikatli [. - . .] loyal, faithful.

hakikatsiz [. - . .] disloyal, unfaithful.

hakiki 1. true, real; **2.** genuine; **3.** sincere (*friend*); **~ mermi** live cartridge; **~ şahıs** JUR natural person; **~ Türk tütünü** genuine Turkish tobacco.

hakim 1. sage; **2.** philosopher.

hâkim 1. dominating, ruling; **2.** dominant, supreme; **3.** ruler; **4.** JUR judge; **5.** overlooking, dominating; **~ olm. 1.** to rule; **2.** to dominate; **3.** to overlook; **~ denize ~ bir ev** a house overlooking the sea.

hâkimiyet, -ti sovereignty; rule, domination; **hâkimiyeti milliye** (*or mst* **millî hâkimiyet** *or* **ulusal egemenlik**) sovereignty of the nation.

hâkimlik judgeship.

hakir vile, worthless, mean; **~ görmek** to despise.

hakkâk, -ki engraver; **~ kalemi** scriber, engraver's chisel.

hakkaniyet, -ti [. - . .] justice, equity; **~ göstermek** to do justice (*-e* to).

hakketmek [x . .] **1.** to engrave, to incise (*-e* on); **2.** to scrape away, to erase.

hakkıhıyar JUR option.

hakkıhuzur daily allowance, *Am.* per diem.

hakkında about, regarding, concerning; **dil ~ yazı** an article about language.

hakkısükût, -tu hush money.

hakkıyle 1. thoroughly, properly; **2.** rightfully.

haklamak 1. to overcome, to beat, to suppress, to crush; **2.** F to eat up, to gulp down.

haklaşmak to settle mutual rights *or* claims, to be quits.

haklı 1. right, just; **2.** rightful; **~ çıkarmak** to justify; **~ çıkmak** to turn out to be right; **~ olm.** to be in the right.

haklılık justice, rightfulness.

haksever just.

hakseverlik justness.

haksız 1. unjust, wrong; **2.** unjustifiable, in the wrong; **~ çıkmak** to turn out to be in the wrong; **~ fiil** JUR wrong; **~ rekabet** unfair competition; **~ yere** unjustly, wrongfully.

haksızlık injustice, wrongfulness; **~ etm. 1.** to act unjustly; **2.** to do an injustice (*-e* to).

hakşinas [.. -] just, fair, rightful.

haktanır just, righteous.

hakuran dove; **~ kafesi gibi** F tumble-down (*place*).

hal¹ 1. condition, state; **2.** circumstances, state of affairs; **3.** attitude, behavio(u)r; **4.** GR case; **5.** energy, strength; **6.** *fig.* trouble; **7.** the present time; **~ böyle iken** and yet, nevertheless; **~ çaresi** remedy; **~ hatır sormak** to enquire (*or* inquire) after s.o., to ask after s.o.; **~ tercümesi 1.** biography; **2.** curriculum vitae; *-den anlamak* to sympathize; *-e bak!* how terrible!, how strange!; *-e yola koymak* to put in order; *-i duman* (*or* **harap**) **olm.** to fall into dire straits, to be in hot water; *-i kalmamak* to be exhausted; *-i vakti yerinde* (*b-nin*) well-off, wealthy; **-im yok** I am under the weather; **-ine köpekler gülüyor** F he is a laughingstock.

hal², **-li** covered market-place.

hal³, **-lli 1.** MATH solution, resolution; **2.** melting, dissolving.

hala [x .] paternal aunt.

hâlâ [x -] still, yet.

halas salvation, deliverance; **~ etm.** to save, to deliver; **~ olm.** (or **bulmak**) to be saved; to escape (**-den** from).

halaskâr savio(u)r, deliverer.

halat, **-tı** rope, hawser; **~ çekme** tug of war.

halavet, **-ti** sweetness, cuteness.

halay a folk dance performed by holding hands in a circle; **~ çekmek** to dance the **halay.**

halayık, **-kı** concubine.

halazade [. . - .] cousin.

halbuki [x . .] or [. x .] whereas, however, but.

haldeş [ä] in the same boat (another person).

haldır haldır speedily and noisily.

hale [ä] **1.** halo; **2.** ANAT areola; **3.** ♀ wf.

halef successor; **~ selef olm.** to succeed.

halel harm, injury, damage; **~ gelmek 1.** to be harmed; **2.** to be blemished; **~ getirmek** (or **vermek**) to harm, to injure, to spoil.

haleldar [. . -] injured, harmed; **~ etm.** to injure, to harm.

halelenmek to form a halo.

halen [ä] [x .] at present, now, presently.

Halep, **-bi** pr. n. Aleppo; **~ çamı** BOT Aleppo (or Jerusalem) pine; **~ orada ise arşın burada!** well, prove it!

halet, **-ti** [ä] condition, situation, aspect; **haleti ruhiye** mood, state of mind.

haletmek [x . .] to dethrone (a sultan).

halfa(otu) BOT esparto (grass).

halhal, **-li** anklet, bangle.

halı carpet, rug; **~ döşemek** to lay a carpet.

halıcı carpet maker or seller.

halıcılık the rug business.

hali [- -] **1.** empty, vacant; **2.** deserted, uninhabited.

haliç, **-çi 1.** inlet, bay, estuary; **2.** ♀ pr. n. the Golden Horn.

halife [î] HIST caliph.

halifelik HIST caliphate.

halihazır [ä, ä] the present (time); **-da** at present.

halik, **-kı** [ä] **1.** creator; **2.** creative; **3.** the Creator, God.

halim mild, gentle; **~ selim** docile, biddable.

halis [ä] pure, unmixed, genuine; **~ muhlis** genuine, true.

halisane [- . - .] sincere(ly).

halita [î] CHEM alloy; **~ yapmak** to alloy.

haliyle [- - .] **1.** as it is, without change; **2.** naturally, consequently.

halk, **-kı 1.** people, nation; **2.** populace, people; **3.** the common people; **~ ağzı** vernacular; **~ dili** colloquial language, vernacular; **~ edebiyatı** folk literature; **~ müziği** folk music; **~ oyunu** folk dance; **~ şarkısı** folk song, ballad; **-a dönük** popular.

halka 1. hoop; **2.** circle; **3.** link; **4.** (finger) ring; earring; **5.** ring-shaped biscuit; **~ ~ 1.** in circles; **2.** in rings; **3.** in links; **~ olm.** to form a circle; **~ oyunu 1.** round dance; **2.** quoits, hoop-la; **-yı burnuna takmak** to bring into submission.

halkalamak 1. to encircle; **2.** to fasten with a ring.

halkalı ringed, linked.

halkalıdamar BOT annular vessel.

halkavcılığı demagogy.

halkavcısı demagogue.

halkbilgisi, **-ni** folklore.

halkbilimci folklorist.

halkçı populist.

halkçılık populism.

halkoylaması, **-nı** referendum.

halkoyu, **-nu** public opinion.

hallaç, **-cı** wool or cotton fluffer; **~ pamuğu gibi atmak** fig. to scatter about.

hallenmek [ä] **1.** to acquire a new form or condition; **2.** to feel faint; **3.** sl. to desire, to want.

halleşmek [ä] to have a heart-to-heart talk.

halletmek [x . .] **1.** to solve, to resolve; **2.** to dissolve; **3.** to finish up, to complete, to settle.

hallice somewhat better (**-den** than).

hallihamur olm. to conform, to accustom o.s. to circumstances.

hallolunmak 1. to be solved; **2.** to be settled; **3.** to be dissolved.

halojen CHEM halogen; **~ lambası** halogen reflector.

halsiz weak, exhausted, tired out; **~ düşmek** to be exhausted (or tired out).

halsizlik weakness.

halt, -tı 1. mixup; **2.** impertinence; ~ *etm.* to do s.th. rude; to say s.th. improper; ~ *karıştırmak* (*or yemek*) to do s.th. rude, to make a great blunder; *ne ~ etmeye oraya gittin?* what the dickens did you go there for?; *ona ~ düşer* he has no right at all to interfere.

halter *sports*: dumbbell, barbell.

halterci weight lifter.

haluk, -ku 1. good-natured; **2.** ♀ [x .] *mf.*

halvet, -ti 1. solitude; **2.** a very hot bathing cubicle in a public bath; ~ *gibi* like an oven; ~ *olm.* to meet in private; *-e dönmek* to become like an oven (*room, etc.*).

ham 1. unripe, green; **2.** crude, raw, unrefined; **3.** *fig.* unrefined (*person*); **4.** unrealistic (*aim, ambition, etc.*); **5.** *sports*: out of shape (*or condition*); ~ *çelik* crude steel; ~ *deri* untanned leather; ~ *fikir* absurdity; ~ *ipek* raw silk; ~ *meyve* unripe fruit; ~ *pamuk* raw cotton; ~ *petrol* crude oil; ~ *teklif* unacceptable suggestion; ~ *toprak* uncultivated land; ~ *ümit* unrealizable hope.

hamail [. - .] **1.** baldric; **2.** amulet, charm.

hamak hammock.

hamakat, -ti [. - .] stupidity; ~ *etm.* (*or göstermek*) to act like a stupid.

hamal porter, carrier; stevedore; ~ *camal* F mob, rabble; ~ *ücreti* (*or parası*) porterage.

hamaliye [. - . .] porterage, porter's fee.

hamallık 1. porterage; **2.** porter's fee, porterage; **3.** *fig.* unnecessary burden; *hamallığını etm.* (*bir işin*) to do the dull and tiring part of (*a job*).

hamam 1. Turkish (*or public*) bath; **2.** bathroom; **3.** *fig.* very hot room; ~ *gibi* like an oven (*room*); ~ *takımı* set of supplies for the Turkish bath; ~ *yapmak* to have a bath.

hamamanası, -nı 1. manageress in a public bath for women; **2.** *fig.* huge and shrewish woman.

hamamböceği, -ni zoo cockroach.

hamamcı 1. proprietor *or* keeper of a public bath; **2.** ECCL unclean and in need of a ritual bath; ~ *kadın = hamamanası.*

hamamotu, -nu depilatory agent.

hamamtası, -nı metal bowl.

hamarat, -tı hard-working, deft, industrious.

hamaratlaşmak to be industrious (*woman*).

hamaratlık deftness, industriousness.

hamaset, -ti [. - .] heroism, valo(u)r.

hamasi [. - -] heroic. epic (*story, poem*).

Hamburg *pr. n.* Hamburg.

hamdolsun! [x . .] God be praised!, thanks be to God!

Hamel AST Aries.

hamhalat, -tı rough, boorish, loutish (*man*).

ham hum F hemming and hawing; ~ *etm.* F to hem and haw; ~ *şaralop sl.* empty words, a lot of nonsense.

hamız CHEM acid.

hami [- -] **1.** guardian, protector; **2.** sponsor, patron.

hamil, -mli 1. COM bearer; **2.** bearing, possessing; **3.** prop, support; ~ *olm.* to have, to possess; *-ine* COM (pay) to bearer.

hamile pregnant (*woman*); ~ *bırakmak* to impregnate, to make pregnant; ~ *elbisesi* maternity dress; ~ *kalmak* **1.** to get pregnant; **2.** (*b-den*) to be with child by *s.o.*; ~ *olm.* to be pregnant.

hamilelik pregnancy.

haminne [. x .] (= *hanım nine*) F grandma.

haminto [. x .] *sl.* swindle, illicit gain.

hamiş postscript.

hamiyet, -ti patriotism.

hamiyetli patriotic.

hamla [x .] NAUT stroke (*of the oars*).

hamlaç CHEM blowpipe.

hamlamak, hamlaşmak to get out of condition, to get rusty, to get out of practice.

hamle 1. attack, assault, onslaught; **2.** dash, élan; **3.** *chess & draughts*: turn; ~ *etm.* (*or yapmak*) to make an attack; to dash.

hamleci enterprising, venturesome.

hamletmet [x . .] to attribute (*-e* to), to impute (*-e* to), to ascribe (*-e* to).

hamlık 1. unripeness, rawness, greenness; crudeness; **2.** being out of shape.

hammadde raw material.

hampa *s.* **hempa.**

hamsi zoo anchovy.

hamt giving praise to God; ~ *olsun!* praise be to God!, thank God!

hamule [ū] load, freight; ~ *senedi* waybill, bill of lading.

hamur 1. dough, paste, leaven; **2.** grade, quality (*of paper*); **3.** half-cooked (*bread*); **4.** paper pulp; **5.** clay (*for pottery*); ~ *açmak* to roll out dough; ~ ~ *gibi* **1.** overcooked, soggy, mushy; **2.** doughty, undercooked; **3.** F bushed, done up, worn out, exhausted; ~ *işi* pastry; ~ *olm.* to become doughty; ~ *tahtası* pastry board; ~ *teknesi* kneading trough.

hamurlamak 1. to cover with dough; **2.** to lute.

hamurlaşmak to get doughy (*or* soggy).

hamursu doughy.

hamursuz unleavened (bread); ♀ *Bayramı* Passover.

hamurumsu s. **hamursu.**

hamut, -tu horse collar.

han¹ [ā] khan, sovereign, ruler.

han² [ā] **1.** inn; caravansary, caravanserai, khan; **2.** large commercial building; ~ *gibi* spacious, vast; ~ *hamam sahibi* a man of property.

hancı innkeeper.

hancılık innkeeping.

hançer dagger, stab, khanjar.

hançere ANAT larynx.

hançerlemek to stab, to knife.

handikap handicap.

handiyse [x..] F **1.** all but, very nearly; **2.** any moment, soon.

hands-free hands-free (*car phone, device*).

hane [ā] **1.** house; **2.** household; **3.** square (*of a chessboard*): **4.** section, division; **5.** blank (*in a printed form*).

hanedan [-.-] **1.** dynasty; **2.** generous, hospitable.

Hanefi [..-] *pr. n.* Hanafi, Hanafite.

haneli [ā] **1.** comprising ... houses; **2.** having ... places (*number*).

hanelik of ... houses.

hanende [ā] singer.

hangar hangar.

hangi [x.] which: ~ *biri?* which one?; ~ *dağda kurt öldü?* fancy your doing it!; ~ *rüzgâr attı?* fancy seeing you here!, what on earth brought you here?; ~ *taşı kaldırsan, altından çıkar* he has a finger in every pie.

hangisi which of them, which one.

hanım 1. lady; **2.** (*after a first name*) Mrs.; Miss; **3.** wife; **4.** mistress (*of a household*); **5.** ladylike; ~ *abla* sister; ~ *evladı sl.* **1.** mother's boy, milksop, mollycoddle; **2.** bastard; ~ *hanımcık* ladylike; ~ *kızınız* your daughter.

hanımböceği, -ni zoo ladybug.

hanımefendi 1. lady, gentlewoman; **2.** madam, ma'am.

hanımefendilik ladyship, being a lady.

hanımeli, -yi BOT honeysuckle, woodbine.

hanımgöbeği, -ni ring-shaped syrupy pastry.

hanımlık ladyship, quality of a lady.

hani¹ (*balığı*) zoo sea bass, cabrilla.

hani² [x.] **1.** so where is ...?; **2.** why ... not ...?; **3.** you know!, you remember ...?; **4.** let's suppose that ...; **5.** in fact, besides; **6.** actually, to tell the truth; ~ *yok mu?* **1.** if only ...; **2.** very nearly; ~ *-dir* for ages, for a long time.

hanlık 1. khanate; **2.** sovereignty, rulership.

hanos zoo sea bass, cabrilla.

hantal 1. clumsy, coarse; **2.** huge, bulky.

hantallaşmak to become clumsy (*or* coarse).

hantallık 1. clumsiness, coarseness; **2.** bulkiness.

hant hant ötmek to crave.

Hanya Canea, Khania; *-'yı Konya'yı göstermek* (*b-ne*) to teach *s.o.* a lesson, to show *s.o.* what's what.

hap, -pı [x.] **1.** pill; **2.** *sl.* dope; *-ı yutmak* F to be in the soup, to be in hot waters.

hapçı *sl.* **1.** drug addict; **2.** opium addict, doper.

hapır hapır, hapır hupur; ~ ~ *yemek* to wolf down, to munch.

hapis, -psi **1.** imprisonment, confinement; **2.** prison, gaol, *Am.* jail; **3.** prisoner, gaoler, *Am.* jailer; **4.** imprisoned; ~ *cezası* prison sentence; ~ *giymek* (*or* *yemek*) to be sentenced to prison; ~ *hakkı* JUR right of retention; ~ *yatmak* to be in prison; *hapse tıkmak* F to put *s.o.* in gaol, *Am.* to put *s.o.* in jail.

hapishane [..-.] prison, gaol, *Am.* jail; ~ *kaçkını* **1.** criminal still at large; **2.** *fig.* scoundrel; *-yi boylamak* to end up (*or* land up) in gaol.

hapislik imprisonment.

hapsetmek [x..] **1.** to gaol, *Am.* to jail; to imprison; **2.** to lock up (*-e in*); **3.** to confine; **4.** *fig.* to retain, to detain.

hapşırmak to sneeze.

hapşu! atishoo!, *Am.* achoo!

hapt etm. [x . .] F to silence.

har: ~ **gür** 1. noisy squabble; 2. tumultuously; ~~ violently, strongly; ~ **akmak** to brawl; ~ **hur** chaos, confusion; ~ **vurup harman savurmak** F to play ducks and drakes (-i with), to squander; -ı **başına vurmak** to go wild; -ı **geçmek** 1. to calm down, to cool down, to cool off, to simmer down; 2. to lose one's enthusiasm.

hara [x .] stud (farm).

harabat, -tı [. - -] 1. ruins; 2. *Ottoman lit.*: wineshops, taverns.

harabati [. - - -] unkempt, slovenly, untidy.

harabe [. - .] 1. ruins, remains; 2. tumbledown house.

haraç, -çı 1. tribute; 2. protection money; 3. *obs.* tax paid by non-Moslems; ~ **mezat satmak** to auction; ~ **yemek** *sl.* to sponge on another; **haraca bağlamak** to lay s.o. under tribute, to force s.o. to pay protection, money; **haraca çıkarmak** to put up to auction.

haraççı 1. extortioner who exacts protection money; 2. *obs.* collector of tribute.

harakiri hara-kiri.

haram [. -] forbidden by religion, unlawful, wrong; ~ **etm.** *fig.* to take the pleasure out of s.th for s.o.; ~ **mal** ill gotten gains; ~ **olm.** *pass.* of ~ **etm.** to be spoiled; ~ **olsun!** may you get no benefit from it!; ~ **yemek** to get illegally or illegitimately; **-a uçkur çözmek** F to live in sin, to commit adultery.

harami [. - -] robber.

haramzade [. - - .] bastard.

harap, -bı [. -] 1. ruined, in ruins, devastated; 2. bushed, done up, worn out, exhausted; ~ **etm.** to ruin, to destroy, to devastate, to vandalize; ~ **olm.** 1. to be ruined (or destroyed or devastated), to fall into ruin; 2. to be bushed, to be worn out (or exhausted).

haraplaşmak to fall into ruin.

haraplık ruin, desolation.

harar large haircloth sack.

hararet, -ti [. - .] 1. heat, warmth; 2. temperature, fever; 3. thirst; 4. *fig.* vehemence, fervo (u)r, exaltation; ~ **basmak** to feel very thirsty; ~ **kes-**

mek (or **söndürmek**) to quench one's thirst; ~ **vermek** to make thirsty.

hararetlendirmek *fig.* to excite.

hararetlenmek [. - . . .] to get warm (or excited or heated).

hararetli [. - . .] vehement, excited, lively, heated.

haraşo [. x .] *sl.* Russian woman.

haraza 1. *sl.* quarrel, row; 2. gallstone (of a cow or ox).

harbe short lance.

harbi 1. ramrod; 2. *sl.* correct, straight; ~ **konuşmak** *sl.* to speak straightforwardly.

harbiye 1. military affairs; 2. ♀ War Academy.

harbiyeli cadet.

harcama 1. *vn.* of **harcamak**; 2. outgo, outlay, expenditure.

harcamak 1. to spend; 2. to use (up); 3. to sacrifice; 4. *sl.* to kill, to finish off.

harcı cheap, affordable, inexpensive.

haciâlem 1. ordinary, common; 2. unoriginal cliché.

harcırah travel allowance, travelling expenses.

harç[1], **-cı** 1. mortar; 2. plaster; 3. ingredients; 4. trimming (of a garment); 5. AGR compost; **harcı olm.** (b-nin) to be within one's power.

harç[2], **-cı** 1. outgo, outlay, expenditure; 2. customs duty; **harcını vermek** *sl.* to scold, to rebuke.

harçlı 1. containing mortar or plaster; 2. trimmed (garment); 3. with the government fee paid; liable to duty.

harçlık pocket-money, allowance.

hardal mustard.

hardaliye [. - . .] grape juice flavo(u)red with mustard.

hare [- .] 1. moiré, water (of cloth); 2. moiréd cloth.

harekât, -tı MIL operation(s), campaign.

hareket, -ti 1. movement, motion; 2. act, deed; behavio(u)r, conduct; 3. departure; 4. activity, stir; 5. tremor, earthquake; 6. MUS tempo; 7. *sports*: exercise(s), exercising; 8. RAIL traffic; ~ **cetveli** RAIL timetable; ~ **dairesi** dispatcher's office; ~ **otm.** 1. to move, to act, to stir; 2. to behave, to act; 3. to set out (or off); to depart (-den from); 4. to leave (-e for); ~ **kolu** starting handle; crank; ~ **noktası** starting point; **-e geçmek** to begin (to act), to start; **-e getirmek** 1. to set in motion; **2.** to stir up.

hareketlendirmek to put into motion.

hareketlenmek to get into motion.

hareketli 1. active, moving; **2.** animated, vivacious.

hareketlilik 1. activity; **2.** vivacity, animation.

hareketsiz motionless, inactive.

hareketsizlik immobility.

harelemek to moiré, to water (*cloth*).

harelenmek to have a sheen.

hareli [ā] moiréd, watered, wavy; ~ **Ipek** watered silk, moiré.

harem 1. harem, women's apartments; **2.** wife; ~ **ağası** black eunuch in the sultan's palace.

haremlik 1. wifehood; **2.** harem; ~ **se-lâmlık olm.** *fig.* to sit in two groups, the women being separate from the men.

harf, -fi letter; ~ **atmak** to pester, to bother; **-i -ine** word for word, to the letter, literatim.

harfiyen word for word, to the letter, literatim.

harharyas zoo man-eater, a kind of shark.

harıl harıl 1. incessantly, continuously; **2.** with great effort; ~ **çalışmak** to work like mad; ~ **yanmak** to burn furiously.

harıltı roar (*of a fire*); ~ **gürültü** din.

harın 1. intractable (*horse*); **2.** *fig.* obstinate, pig-headed.

haricen externally, outwardly.

harici [ā] **1.** external, exterior; **2.** foreign.

hariciye [ā] **1.** foreign affairs; **2.** external diseases; ♀ **Vekâleti** *obs.* Ministry of Foreign Affairs; ♀ **Vekili** *obs.* Minister of Foreign Affairs.

hariciyeci [- . . . .] **1.** diplomat; **2.** MED specialist in external diseases.

hariç, -ci [ā] **1.** outside, exterior; **2.** abroad; **3.** except (*for*), excluded, apart (*from*), besides; ~ **olm.** (*bşden*) to be excluded from *s.th.*; **-ten gazel okumak** (*or* **atmak**) to butt in.

harika [- . .] **1.** wonder, miracle; **2.** *fig.* marvelous, extraordinary; ~ **çocuk** infant prodigy; **-lar yaratmak** to work miracles, to do wonders.

harikulade [- . . - .] **1.** wonderful, marvelous; **2.** unusual, extraordinary.

haris [ī] greedy, avaricious, ambitious, acquisitive.

harita map.

haritacı cartographer.

haritacılık cartography.

harlamak 1. to burn furiously; **2.** *fig.* to flare up.

harlatmak to poke up (*fire*).

harlı burning in flames.

harman 1. threshing (floor); **2.** harvest (time); **3.** stack of grain (*ready for threshing*); **4.** blending; **5.** blend (*tea, tobacco*); ~ **çorman** mixed up; ~ **dövmek** to thresh grain; ~ **etm.** (*or* **yapmak**) **1.** to thresh; **2.** to blend (*tea, tobacco*); ~ **makinesi** thresher; ~ **savurmak** to winnow grain; ~ **sonu 1.** the end of the threshing season; **2.** gleanings; **3.** *fig.* remnants (*of a fortune or business*).

harmancı 1. thresher; **2.** blender (*of tea or tobacco*).

harmancılık 1. threshing; **2.** blending.

harmandalı, -nı a folk dance (*in Izmir and vicinity*).

harmani [. - -], **harmaniye** [. - . .] long cape.

harmanlamak 1. to blend; **2.** to go in circles; **3.** NAUT to go in a circle.

harmoni MUS harmony.

harmonik, harmonili MUS harmonic.

harmonisiz MUS inharmonious.

harmonyum MUS harmonium.

harnup BOT carob (tree).

harp¹, -pı MUS harp.

harp², -bi war; battle, fight; ~ **açmak** to start a war; ~ **esiri** prisoner of war; ~ **filosu** war fleet; ~ **gemisi** warship; ~ **malulü** war casualty; ~ **meydanı** battlefield; ♀ **Okulu** the Turkish Military Academy; ♀ **Şûrası** Supreme War Council; ~ **tazminatı** war indemnity; ~ **zengini** war profiteer.

harrangürra [x . x .] in a disorderly and noisy manner.

hars *obs.* culture.

hart: ~ **diye** with a loud crunch.

hartadak, hartadan [x . .] with a loud crunch.

hartası hurtası olmamak to show disrespect.

hart hart, hart hurt with a crunching sound.

hartuç, -cu cartridge, shell.

harup, -bu *s.* **harnup.**

has, -ssı [ā] **1.** peculiar (*-e* to); belonging (*-e* to); special (*-e* to); **2.** royal, belonging to the sultan; **3.** pure, unmixed, unadulterated; ~ **boya** fast dye; ~ **işlemek** *sl.* to gobble up another's food without permission.

hasa (bezi) heavy cambric.

hasar [. -] damage, loss; ~ **görmek** (or -a **uğramak**) to suffer damage; ~ **yapmak** to cause damage.

hasat, -dı harvest, reaping.

hasatçı reaper.

hasatçılık harvesting.

hasbahçe private garden of the sultan.

hasbıhal, -li [. . -] chitchat; ~ **etm.** to have a chitchat.

hasbi [ī] **1.** voluntary, volunteer; **2.** without reason; ~ **geçmek** sl. not to care at all.

hasebiyle [. . - .] because of, by reason of.

hasep merits, personal qualities.

haset, -ti jealousy, envy; ~ **etm.** to envy.

hasetçi jealous, envious.

hasetlenmek to feel envy.

hasetlik envy.

hasıl grain still green in the field.

hâsıl resulting; produced; ~ **etm.** to produce; ~ **olm.** to result, to be produced, to be obtained (-**den** from).

hâsıla [- . .] result, outcome.

hâsılat, -tı [- . -] **1.** products; produce; **2.** returns, revenue; proceeds.

hâsılı [x . .] in brief (or short), in a word, to sum up; ~ **kelam** the long and the short of it.

hasıllanmak 1. to grow up; **2.** to mature (crop).

hasım, -smı 1. opponent; **2.** enemy, adversary.

hasımlık enmity, antagonism.

hasır 1. rush mat; matting; canework; wickerwork; **2.** cane ..., wicker ...; ~ **altı etm.** to sweep s.th. under the carpet (or rug); ~ **işi** wickerwork; ~ **koltuk** wicker chair; ~ **şapka** boater, straw (or Panama) hat; -**lara sarılmak** (or **yatmak**) sl. to take a day off (taxi driver).

hasırlamak to cover with matting, to cane.

hasırlı 1. caned, covered with matting; **2.** large bottle covered with wickerwork.

hasırotu, -nu BOT rush.

hasis [ī] **1.** miserly, stingy, niggardly; **2.** base, low, vile.

hasislik stinginess.

hasiyet, -ti [â] **1.** special virtue (or quality); **2.** wholesomeness.

hasiyetli wholesome (food).

haslet, -ti trait, virtue.

haspa F minx, baggage.

hasret, -ti longing, yearning; nostalgia, homesickness; ~ **çekmek** to long (-e for), to yearn (-e for); ~ **gitmek** to die longing (-e for); ~ **kalmak** to feel the absence (-e of), to miss; -**ini çekmek** to long to see again; to miss.

hasretli 1. longing, yearning; **2.** homesick.

hasretlik 1. longing, yearning; **2.** homesickness.

hasretmek [x . .] to devote (-e to), to consecrate (-e to), to appropriate (-e for).

hassa peculiarity; quality; ~ **askeri** bodyguard.

hassas [. -] **1.** sensitive, delicate, responsive; **2.** touchy, oversensitive; **3.** susceptible (-e to).

hassasiyet, -ti [. - .] **1.** sensitivity, sensitiveness; **2.** touchiness, oversensitivity.

hassaten [- . .] [x . .] particularly, especially.

hasse s. **hasa.**

hasta 1. sick, ill; **2.** patient; **3.** addicted (to), fond (of); ~ **düşmek** to get sick, to fall (or be taken) ill; ~ **etm.** to make ill; ~ **koğuşu** MIL sickroom; ~ **olm.** to get sick, to become ill; ~ **yatağı** sickbed; -**sı olm.** (bşin) F to be a fan of s.th., to be nuts over s.th., to be wild about s.th.; -**ya bakmak** to nurse (or look after) a patient.

hastabakıcı nurse's aide.

hastalanmak to fall ill, to get sick.

hastalık 1. illness, sickness; **2.** disease; **3.** addiction; ~ **almak** (or **kapmak**) to catch a disease; ~ **geçirmek** to have an illness, to be sick; ~ **hastası** hypochondriac; ~ **sigortası** health insurance; **hastalığa tutulmak** to get sick; **hastalığa yakalanmak** to fall (or be taken) ill.

hastalıklı sickly, ailing.

hastane [. - .] hospital.

hastanelik requiring hospitalization; ~ **etm.** (b-ni) F to wallop s.o.

hasut, -du [ū] jealous.

haşa MIL saddlecloth.

hâşa [x -] God forbid!; ~ **huzur(unuz-)dan** if you'll excuse my French.

haşarat, -tı [. . -] **1.** vermin, insects; **2.** fig. the mob, the rabble.

haşan 1. impish, naughty, mischievous

(*child*); **2.** ungovernable (*animal*).
haşarılaşmak to become impish (*or* naughty).
haşarılık naughtiness, impishness.
haşat *sl.* **1.** worn-out car; **2.** worn-out; **3.** in the soup, in hot waters.
haşere insect.
haşhaş BOT opium poppy.
haşıl sizing (*for cloth*).
haşırdamak to rustle.
haşır haşır, haşır huşur with a scraping sound.
haşin [i] rough, harsh, rude.
haşinlik harshness, rudeness.
haşir, -şri doomsday, Last Judg(e)ment; ~ **neşir olm.** (*b-le*) to be cheek by jowl with *s.o.*
haşiş hashish.
haşiv, -şvi redundancy, padding.
haşiye [ā] footnote, postscript; annotation.
haşlama 1. *vn. of* **haşlamak**; **2.** boiled.
haşlamak 1. to boil; **2.** to scald; **3.** to sting all over (*insect*); **4.** F to scold, to rebuke.
haşlanmak *pass. of* **haşlamak** to be boiled; to be scalded.
haşmet, -ti majesty, pomp, grandeur.
haşmetli 1. majestic, grand, splendid, pompous; **2.** His Majesty.
haşmetmeap [. . . -] His Majesty.
haşyet, -ti fear.
hat, -ttı 1. line; **2.** contour (*of a face*); **3.** handwriting; calligraphy; ~ **çekmek** to install a line; ~ **işçisi** lineman; trackman.
hata [. -] mistake, error, fault; ~ **etm.** (*or* **işlemek**) to make a mistake, to err; ~ **yapmak** to make a mistake; **-ya düşmek** to fall into error, to err.
hatalı [- -.] **1.** faulty, defective, erroneous; **2.** at fault, in the wrong.
hatasız [. - .] **1.** flawless, faultless, errorless; **2.** unerring; ~ **kul olmaz** nobody is perfect.
hatıl crossbeam, horizontal beam.
hatır [ā] **1.** memory, mind; **2.** sake; **3.** feelings, sensitivities; **4.** consideration, influence, weight; ~ **almak** to please, to delight; ~ **gönül** personal consideration; ~ **senedi** accommodation bill; ~ **sormak** to ask (*or* inquire) after *s.o.*; ~ **yapmak** to please, to delight; **-a gelmemek** not even to occur to one; **-ı için** for *s.o.*'s sake; **-ı kalmak** (*b-nin*) to feel hurt (*or* offended); **-ı sayılır 1.** considerable; **2.** respected;

-ına bir şey gelmesin as the actress said to the bishop; **-ına gelmek** to occur to one, to come to mind; **-ında kalmak** to remember; **-ında olm.** to have in mind; **-ında tutmak** to keep in mind; **-ından çıkmak** to pass out of one's mind; **-ından geçmemek** not even to think (of); **-ını kırmak** to offend, to give offence; **-ını saymak** (*b-nin*) to show one's respect; **-ını yapmak** to please, to delight.
hatıra 1. memory, recollection, reminiscence; **2.** keepsake, souvenir, memento, remembrance; ~ **defteri** diary; **-larını yazmak** to write one's memoirs; **-sı olarak** in memory of.
hatıralık *s.* **hatıra 2.**
hatırat, -tı memoirs.
hatır hatır, hatır hutur crunch crunch, with a crunching sound; **hatır hutur yemek** to munch, to crunch.
hatırlamak to remember, to recollect, to recall.
hatırlatmak (*b-ne bşi*) to remind *s.o.* of *s.th.*
hatırlı [ā] influential, esteemed.
hatırşinas [- . . . -] considerate, obliging, courteous.
hatim, -tmi recitation of the Koran from beginning to end; ~ **indirmek** to finish repeating the whole Koran.
hatime epilogue.
hatip, -bı [i] **1.** orator; **2.** ECCL preacher.
hatmetmek [x . .] **1.** to recite from beginning to end (*the Koran*); **2.** *co.* to read from cover to cover.
hatmi BOT marsh mallow.
hatta [x -] even, to the extent that; besides, moreover.
hattat, -tı [. -] calligrapher.
hattatlık calligraphy.
hattıhareket, -ti way of procedure, line of action.
hatun [ā] **1.** woman; **2.** lady (*after a given name*); **3.** wife.
hav nap, pile (*of cloth*).
hava 1. air, atmosphere; **2.** weather; **3.** climate; **4.** the sky; **5.** wind, breeze; **6.** desire, whim, fancy; **7.** MUS pitch of a note; **8.** JUR air rights; **9.** tune, melody, air; **10.** style; **11.** (social) environment; **12.** airs, affectation; **13.** F nothing; ~ **açmak** (*or* **açılmak**) to clear up; ~ **akımı** draught, *Am.* draft; ~ **akını** air raid (*or* attack); ~ **almak 1.** to breathe fresh air; **2.** to take in (*or* absorb) air; **3.** *sl.* to whistle for it; ~ **at-**

mak sl. **1.** to put on airs, to give o.s. airs; **2.** to speak claptrap; ~ *basıncı* atmospheric pressure; ~ *basmak* = ~ *atmak*; ~ *boşluğu* **1.** air pocket; **2.** air shaft (*in a building*); ~ *bozdu* it turned stormy *or* rainy; ~ *bulandı* (*or bulutlandı*) it turned rainy; ~ *cereyanı* draught, *Am.* draft; ~ *deliği* **1.** ventilation hole; **2.** ventilation conduit (*in a building*); ~ *filosu* air fleet; ~ *fişeği* rocket; ~ *freni* air (*or* pneumatic) brake; ~ *geçirmez* airtight; ~ *hoş olm.* (*b-ne*) to be all the same to *s.o.*; ~ *kabarcığı* bubble; ~ *kaçırmak* to lose air; ~ *kapanmak* to be overcast (*sky*); ~ *karadı* it got dark; ~ *kirliliği* air pollution; ~ *korsanı* hijacker; ~ *köprüsü* airlift; ~ *kuvvetleri* air force; ~ *meydanı* airport, airfield; ~ *oyunu* speculative trading in futures; ~ *parası* lump cash payment (*demanded of a renter before he is given possession*); ~ *raporu* weather report; ~ *tahmini* weather forecast; ~ *üssü* air base; ~ *vermek* **1.** to give air, to fill with air; **2.** to aerate (*s.o.'s lungs*); *-da kalmak* **1.** to be up too high; **2.** to be left in suspense; *-dan* **1.** free. for nothing, as a windfall; **2.** empty, worthless; *-dan sudan* at random, randomly; *-dan sudan konuşmak* to have a chitchat; *-sına uymak* to adapt o.s. (*-in* to), to fit in (*-in* with); *-sını bulmak* to get into a good mood; *-ya gitmek* to go for nothing; *-ya pala* (or *kılıç*) *sallamak* to beat the air, to plow the sand(s); *-ya savurmak* to make the money fly.

havaalanı, nı- airport, airfield.

havaaltı, nı- GEOL subaerial.

havacı airman, pilot, aviator, flyer, flier.

havacılık aviation.

havacıva 1. BOT alkanet; **2.** *sl.* trivial, nought; **3.** *sl.* nonsense, rubbish.

havadar airy, well-ventilated.

havadis news.

havagazı, -nı 1. coal gas; **2.** *sl.* rubbish.

havai [. - -] **1.** aerial; **2.** fanciful, flighty; irresponsible, **3.** meaningless, nonsense; **4.** (*a.* ~ *mavi*) sky-blue; ~ *fişek* skyrocket; ~ *hat* overhead railway; funicular; ~ *sözler* idle talk.

havailik flightiness, inconstancy.

havaküre atmosphere.

havalandırma ventilation.

havalandırmak 1. to air, to ventilate;

2. to take up into the air (*airplane*); **3.** to fly (*kite*).

havalanmak 1. to be aired (*or* ventilated); **2.** AVIA to take off; **3.** to become frivolous.

havale [. - .] **1.** assignment, referral; **2.** money order; bill of exchange; **3.** MED eclampsia; **4.** hoarding; ~ *çekmek* to fence off; ~ *etm.* **1.** to transfer, to assign; to endorse over (*-e* to); **2.** to refer (*-e* to); ~ *gelmek* MED to have an attack of eclampsia; ~ *göndermek* (*or yollamak*) to send a money order.

havaleli [. - . .] **1.** top-heavy; **2.** MED eclamptic; **3.** fenced, enclosed.

havalename [. - . - .] money order.

havalı 1. airy; well-ventilated; breezy; **2.** eye-catching, showy; swanky; **3.** restless; **4.** pneumatic; ~ *korna* (or *klakson*) air (*or* pneumatic) horn.

havali [. - -] vicinity, environs, neighbo(u)rhood.

havalimanı, -nı airport.

havan mortar; ~ *dövücünün hınk deyicisi* *iro.* flatterer who agrees with all that another says; ~ *topu* MIL (trench) mortar, howitzer; *-da dövmek* to pestle; *-da su dövmek* *fig.* to beat the air.

havaneli, -ni pestle.

havaölçer 1. barometer; **2.** aerometer.

havari [. - -] **1.** apostle, disciple; **2.** assistant.

havâs the senses.

havasız 1. airless; **2.** stuffy.

havasızlık 1. airlessness; **2.** stuffiness.

havasızyaşar 1. anaerobic; **2.** anaerobe.

havayolu, -nu airline; ~ *ile* by air.

havayuvarı, -nı atmosphere.

havhav bow-wow, doggie.

havi including, containing; ~ *olm.* to include, to contain.

havil, -vli fear; *can havliyle* fearing for one's life.

havlamak to bark, to bay.

havlı 1. downy, nappy, piled; **2.** *s. hav-lu.*

havlu towel.

havlucu towel-dealer.

havluluk 1. toweling; **2.** towel rack; **3.** towel cupboard.

havra [x .] **1.** synagogue; **2.** *fig.* bedlam.

havsala 1. ANAT pelvic cavity, pelvis; **2.** *fig.* intelligence, comprehension; *-sı almamak* to be unable to comprehend; *-sı geniş* tolerant, accommodating; **-sına sığmamak** (*b-nin*) to be hard for *s.o.* to believe.

havşa MEC countersink.

havuç, -cu BOT carrot.

havut, -tu camel's packsaddle.

havuz 1. pool; pond; 2. dry dock; ~ **balığı** ZOO goldfish; **-a çekmek** NAUT to dock (*a ship*).

havuzcuk ANAT calyx.

havuzlamak NAUT to dock (*a ship*).

Havva [. -] *pr. n.* Eve.

havya [x .] MEC soldering iron.

havyar caviar; ~ **kesmek** *sl.* to idle around, to moon away.

havza GEOGR river basin, catchment area; sphere, domain.

hay what a ...!, alas!; ~ **Allah!** my God!; ~ **anasını!** F what a pity!; ~ ~ *!* certainly!, by all means!; ~ **lanet kör şeytan!** damn it all!; **-dan gelen huya gider** *pro.* easy come easy go.

haya [-.] testicle.

hayâ shame.

hayal, -li [. -] 1. image; 2. imagination, fancy; 3. PHYS image; reflection; 4. daydream; 5. ghost, spectre, *Am.* specter, phantom; ~ **âlemi** the realm of the imagination; ~ **etm.** to imagine; ~ **gibi** 1. like a dream; 2. a bag of bones (*person*); ~ **gücü** imaginative power; ~ **kırıklığı** disappointment, let-down; ~ **kırıklığına uğratmak** to disappoint, to let *s.o.* down; **kurmak** to dream; ~ **mahsulü** imaginary, fancied; ~ **meyal** vaguely; ~ **oyunu** shadow play (*or* show); ~ **peşinde koşmak** to build castles in the air (*or* in Spain); **-e dalmak** to daydream; **-e kapılmak** to build high hopes, to be given to fancy; **-inden geçirmek** (*bşi*) to dream of *s.th.*, to think of *s.th.*

hayalci [. -.] 1. unrealistic; 2. visionary, dreamer; 3. puppeteer in shadow plays.

hayalet, -ti [. -.] ghost, phantom, apparition, spectre, *Am.* specter.

hayalhane [. - - .] imagination, imaginative power.

hayali [. - -] 1. imaginary, fantastic, visionary, chimerical; 2. = **hayalci 3.**

hayalifener [. - . . .] *fig.* skinny (*person*).

hayalperest, -ti 1. fanciful; 2. visionary, daydreamer.

hayalperestlik fancifulness, daydreaming.

hayâsız shameless, impudent.

hayat, -tı [. -] 1. life; 2. P courtyard (*of a house*); 3. P veranda, porch; ~ **adamı** man of the world; ~ **arkadaşı** life partner; ~ **kadını** prostitute, whore; ~ **memat meselesi** matter of life and death; ~ **mücadelesi** (*or* **kavgası**) life struggle; ~ **pahalılığı** high cost of living; ~ **standardı** standard of living; ~ **sigortası** life insurance; ~ **sürmek** to live a life; ~ **vermek** to enliven; **-a atılmak** to begin to work; **-a gözlerini yummak** (*or* **kapamak**) to depart this life, to die; **-a küsmek** to be weary of life; **-ı kaymak** *sl.* to go to the dogs; **-ı zindan etm.** (*b-ne*) *fig.* to make *s.o.'s* life a hell; **-ım!** my love!, my darling!; **-ın baharı** the prime of life; **-ına mal olm.** (*b-nin*) to cost *s.o.* his life; **-ını kazanmak** (*or* **temin etm.**) to earn one's living, to make a living; **-ını yaşamak** to lead a life of ease; **-ta olm.** to be living (*or* alive).

hayatağacı, -nı 1. ANAT arborvitae; 2. family tree, genealogical chart.

hayati [. - -] 1. vital; 2. ♀ *mf.*

hayatiyet, -ti [. - . .] 1. vitality, vigo(u)r; 2. liveliness.

haybeci *sl.* sucker.

haybeden *sl.* free, gratis, for nothing.

hayda 1. giddap!; 2. what on earth!

haydalamak to urge (*or* drive) on (*an animal*).

haydamak. 1. = **haydalamak**; 2. *sl.* to sack, to fire.

haydi [x .], **hadi** 1. come on!; 2. let's say; 3. OK, all right; 4. come off it!, rubbish!; ~ **bakalım** come on then, hurry up; ~ **canım sen de!** F 1. that's bunk!, you're talking crap!; 2. who do you think you're fooling?; ~ **gidelim** come along, let's go; ~ **git! off** with you!; ~ ~ 1. cut it short!, there are no flies on us!; 2. easily, amply; 3. hurry up!; 4. at the very most; ~ **oradan** 1. clear out!, piss off!; 2. who do you think you're fooling?

haydin [x .] F come on all of you, hurry up!

haydindi F come along!, hurry up!

haydisene [. . x .] F come on!

haydut, -du brigand, bandit, robber; ~ **yatağı** brigands' den, robbers' roost, bandits' hide-out.

haydutluk brigandage.

hayhay by all means!, certainly!

hayhuy 1. tumult; confusion; 2. *fig.* fruitless struggle.

hayıf, -yfı 1. injustice; **2.** what a pity!

hayıflanmak to lament; to regret, to repent.

hayır¹ [x .] no; ~ **demek** to say no.

hayır², -yrı 1. charity, philanthropy; **2.** fortune; **3.** use(fulness); ~ **etm.** to do good (-e to), to be of use; ~ **gelmemek** to be of no help; ~ **görmemek** (bşden) not to benefit from s.th.; ~ **işlemek** to do good, to be charitable; ~ **kalmamak** to be of no more use; ~ **kurumu** charitable foundation, philanthropic institution; ~ **ola** (or **hayrola**)! what's up?, I hope nothing is wrong; ~ **sahibi** benefactor, philanthropist; ~ **yok** (b-den) he's of no use; **hayra alamet** good (or auspicious) sign; **hayra alamet değil** it bodes no good; **hayra yormak** to interpret favo(u)rably, to regard as auspicious (dream, omen); **hayrı dokunmak** to be of use (-e to), to be a help (-e to); **hayrı yok** it is good for nothing; **-dır inşallah! 1.** I hope all is well!; **2.** I hope the dream is a good sign!; **hayrını görün!** may it bring you good luck!, enjoy using it!

hayırdua [. . . -] benediction, blessing.

hayırhah [. . -] benevolent, well-wishing.

hayırlaşmak to exchange good wishes after having concluded a bargain.

hayırlı 1. good, auspicious beneficial, advantageous, favo(u)rable; **2.** good, happy (journey); ~ **haberler** good news; ~ **yolculuklar** have a good trip; **-sı** (olsun)! let's hope for the best!

hayırperver benevolent.

hayırsever charitable.

hayırsız 1. good for nothing, useless; **2.** unfaithful, disloyal.

hayız, -yzı menstruation, period; ~ **görmek** to menstruate; **-dan kesilme** menopause.

haykırı 1. outcry, scream; **2.** GR exclamation, interjection; ~ **işareti** exclamation mark.

haykırış shout, cry.

haykırışmak to scream (or shout) together.

haykırmak 1. to cry out, to bawl, to scream, to shout; **2.** to protest loudly.

haylamak 1. = **haydalamak**; **2.** to shove, to prod (a person); **3.** sl. to pay attention (to), to heed.

haylaz 1. idle, lazy; **2.** loafer, idler, lazybones.

haylazlaşmak 1. to get lazy, to loaf; **2.**

to make mischief.

haylazlık idleness, laziness; ~ **etm. 1.** to loaf; **2.** to make mischief.

hayli [x .] many, much; a good deal, very; fairly; **bir** ~ = ~.

haylice considerably, somewhat, much.

haymana prairie, pasture; ~ **beygiri gibi dolaşmak** to gad (or knock) about; ~ **mandası** (or **öküzü** or **sığırı**) fig. hulk, do-nothing, sluggard.

haymatlos stateless.

hayran [. -] **1.** admirer, lover, adorer, fan; **2.** astonished, perplexed; ~ **bırakmak** (or **etm.**) (b-ni) to charm s.o., to entrance s.o.; ~ **kalmak** (or **olm.**) (bşe) to be entranced by s.th., to admire s.th., to be astonished (or perplexed).

hayranlık [. - .] admiration, appreciation; adoration.

hayrat, -tı [. -] **1.** pious foundation; **2.** charities, pious deeds.

hayret, -ti 1. astonishment, amazement, surprise; **2.** how surprising!; ~ **etm.** to be surprised (-e at), to be astonished (-e at); ~ **verici** amazing, astonishing; **-e düşmek** to be astounded; **-te bırakmak** to astound; **-te kalmak** to be lost in amazement.

hayrola s. **hayır ola.**

haysiyet, -ti self-respect, dignity, hono(u)r, amour-propre; ~ **divanı** (or **kurulu**) discipline committee; ~ **sahibi** self-respecting; **-iyle** because of.

haysiyetli self-respecting, dignified.

haysiyetsiz without dignity, lacking in self-respect.

hayta [x .] **1.** obs. mercenary cavalryman; **2.** fig. vagabond; **3.** F street urchin.

haytalık fig. vagabondage.

hayvan 1. animal; **2.** fig. beast, brute; ~ **alım satımı** livestock market; ~ **gibi 1.** asinine, stupid; **2.** brutally, coarsely; ~ **hırsızı** rustler.

hayvanat, -tı [. - .] **1.** animals; **2.** obs. zoology; ~ **bahçesi** zoo. zoological garden.

hayvanbilim zoology.

hayvanca(sına) bestially, brutishly, brutally.

hayvancık animalcule.

hayvancılık 1. stockbreeding; **2.** cattle-dealing.

hayvani [. - -] **1.** brutal, brutish, animal-like, bestial; **2.** carnal, sensual; ~ **kuvvet** brute force.

hayvankömürü, -nü boneblack, animal charcoal.

hayvanlaşmak to become bestial (*or* brutal), to be brutalized.

hayvanlık 1. animalism; **2.** *fig.* bestiality, brutishness; ~ *etm.* to act like a turd.

hayvansal animal ... (*product*).

haz, -zzı delight, pleasure, gusto, enjoyment; ~ *duymak* to be greatly gratified (*-den* by).

hâzâ [- -] F perfect, complete.

hazakat, -ti skill, ability.

hazan autumn, *Am.* fall.

hazar peace.

Hazar *pr. n.* Khazar; ~ *Denizi* Caspian Sea.

hazcı hedonist(ic).

hazcılık hedonism.

hazfetmek [x . .] to remove, to delete.

hazık, -kı [â] skillful, expert (*doctor*).

hazım, -zmı digestion; *hazmı güç* indigestible.

hâzım digestive.

hazımlı *fig.* tolerant, patient.

hazımsız *fig.* irritable, touchy.

hazımsızlık MED indigestion.

hazır 1. ready, prepared; **2.** ready-made (*garment*); **3.** present, in attendance; **4.** seeing that, now that, since; ~ *bulunmak* (*or olm.*) **1.** to be present (*-de* at); **2.** to be ready; ~ *etm.* to prepare, to get ready; ~ *giyim* ready-made clothing; ~ *ol!* MIL attention!; ~ *para* ready money, cash; ~ *yiyici* one who lives on his capital; *-a konmak* *fig.* to enjoy the fruits of others' labo(u)rs; *-dan yemek* to live on one's capital.

hazırcevap, -bı ready-witted, quick at repartee.

hazırcı seller of ready-made clothing, outfitter.

hazırlamak 1. to prepare, to make ready; **2.** CHEM to dispense.

hazırlanmak 1. *pass. of* **hazırlamak; 2.** to get ready.

hazırlık 1. readiness; **2.** preparation; ~ *görmek* to get things ready, to make preparations; ~ *okulu* prep (*or* preparatory) school; ~ *sınıfı* preparatory year; ~ *tahkikatı* (*or soruşturması*) JUR preliminary investigations.

hazırlıklı (well) prepared; ~ *olm.* to be prepared.

hazırlop, -pu 1. hard-boiled (*egg*); **2.** *fig.* effortless.

hazin [î] sad, tragic, touching, pathetic, melancholic.

hazine [î] **1.** treasure (*a. fig.*); **2.** treasury, strongroom; **3.** national treasury; **4.** treasure-trove; **5.** depot; cistern; **6.** ANAT uterus, womb.

hazinedar [. - . -] treasurer.

haziran [î] June.

hazmetmek [x . .] **1.** to digest; **2.** *fig.* to stomach, to swallow.

hazne *s.* **hazine.**

haznedar [. . -] *s.* **hazinedar.**

hazret, -ti 1. Excellency; **2.** *co.* old fellow; *-leri* (*after a title*) His Excellency.

hazzetmek [x . .] to like, to enjoy.

he! P yes!, yeah!; ~ *demek* (*bşe*) to accept *s.th.*, to consent to *s.th.*; ~ *mi?* P is that all right?

heba [â] waste, loss; ~ *etm.* to waste, to spoil.

hebenneka idiot, fool.

heccav [â] *rare* satirist.

hece GR syllable; ~ *vezni* syllabic meter.

hecelemek to spell.

heceli ... syllabled.

hecin [î] (*devesi*) ZOO dromedary.

hedef 1. target, mark; **2.** *fig.* aim, object, goal; ~ *almak* to aim (*-i* at); ~ *olm.* (*bşe*) to be the butt of *s.th.*; *-e isabet etm.* **1.** to hit the target; **2.** *fig.* to attain one's object.

heder loss, waste; ~ *etm.* to waste; ~ *olm.* to be wasted.

hediye 1. present, gift; **2.** price (*of a sacred book*); ~ *etm.* to give as a gift (*-e* to).

hediyelik fit for a present.

hegemonya hegemony.

hekim [î] doctor, physician.

hekimlik [. - .] **1.** doctorship; **2.** medicine, medical science.

hektar hectare.

hektogram hectogram(me).

hektolitre hectolitre, *Am.* hectoliter.

hektometre hectometre, *Am.* hectometer.

hela toilet, loo, water closet, privy.

helak, -ki 1. death; murder; **2.** destruction; **3.** fatigue, exhaustion; ~ *etm.* **1.** to kill, to finish off; **2.** *fig.* to tire out, to exhaust; ~ *olm.* **1.** to perish; **2.** *fig.* to be bushed.

helal, -li 1. permissible, canonically lawful; **2.** *fig.* F lawful spouse; ~ *etm.* (*bşi b-ne*) to give up *s.th.* to *s.o.*; ~ *olsun!* take it with my blessings!, no need to thank!; ~ **süt emmiş** trustworthy; **-ü hoş olsun!** let it be yours to have and enjoy!; **-inden** lawfully, legitimately, honestly.

helallaşmak to forgive each other mutually.

helalli = **helal 2**.

helallik obs. **1.** = **helal 2**; **2.** waiving (rights, etc.); ~ **dilemek** to ask forgiveness for an unlawful act.

hele [x .] **1.** especially, above all; **2.** you had better not; **3.** if (only); **4.** look here!; ~ **bak!** just look!; ~ **bir 1.** you had better not …; **2.** let's wait until …; ~ ~ now tell me the truth; ~ **şükür!** thank goodness!, at last!

helecan palpitation.

Helen Greek, Grecian.

helezon 1. spiral, helix; helicoid; **2.** MED spiral.

helezoni [ī] spiral, helical; helicoidal; ~ **merdiven** spiral (or winding) staircase; ~ **yay** spiral spring.

helezonlanmak to form a spiral.

helikoit helicoid.

helikon helicon.

helikopter helicopter.

helis MATH helix.

helke pail, bucket.

helme thick liquid (made by boiling starchy substances); ~ **dökmek** to become thick and soupy (cooking water).

helmelenmek = **helme dökmek**.

helmeli thick and soupy.

helva halva(h); ~ **demesini de biliriz**, **halva demesini de** fig. I can speak politely, but at a pinch I can also speak rudely.

helvacı maker or seller of halva(h).

helvacıkabağı, -nı BOT pumpkin.

helvahane [. . - .] shallow pan used for cooking halva(h).

helyosta [. x .] heliostat.

helyum CHEM helium.

hem 1. both … and; **2.** and also, besides, too; **3.** even; (**ve**) ~ **de** and besides, moreover, and also, both … and, as well as; ~ **de nasıl!** and how!; ~ **nalına**, ~ **mıhına vurmak** fig. to waver between two sides; ~ **suçlu**, ~ **güçlü** offensive though at fault; ~ **ziyaret**, ~ **ticaret** it's a combination of business and pleasure.

hematit, -ti hematite.

hematoloji hematology.

hemayar equal; of the same kind.

hemcins equal, fellow; of the same kind.

hemdert, -di fellow sufferer, confidant.

hemen [x .] **1.** right away; right now, immediately, at once; **2.** almost, nearly; about; ~ ~ **1.** almost, very nearly; **2.** pretty soon; ~ **sonra 1.** immediately after, right after; **2.** immediately afterwards; ~ **şimdi** at once, right now.

hemencecik [. x . .] F at once.

hemencek [x . .] F = **hemencecik**.

hemfikir of the same opinion, like-minded.

hemhal, -li [ā] in the same boat.

hemhudut, -du contiguous.

hemoglobin BIOL hemoglobin.

hemoroit, -di h(a)emorrhoids, piles.

hempa accomplice, confederate.

hemşeri 1. fellow townsman (or countryman), fellow citizen, compatriot; **2.** hey friend!

hemşerilik citizenship.

hemşire [ī] **1.** nurse; **2.** sister.

hemşirelik 1. nursing; **2.** sisterhood.

hemşirezade [. . - . .] nephew, niece (of one's sister).

hemze GR hamza.

hendek ditch, trench, dike, dyke, moat.

hendese geometry.

hendesi geometrical.

hengâme tumult, uproar.

hentbol, -lü handball.

henüz [x .] **1.** (only) just, a minute or so ago; **2.** (in negative sentences) yet.

hep, -pi 1. all, the whole; **2.** always; ~ **beraber** all together; ~ **bir ağızdan** in unison, with one voice; ~ **birlikte** all together; **-imiz** all of us.

hepçil omnivorous.

hepsi, -ni [x .] all of it; all of them.

hepten F entirely.

hepyek, -ki dice: double one.

her every, each; ~ **an** at any moment; ~ **bakımdan** in every respect; ~ **bir** each, every single; ~ **biri** each one, every one (of); ~ **daim** always; ~ **defa** (or **defasında**) each time; ~ **derde deva** cure-all, panacea, nostrum; ~ **durumda** in any case; ~ **gördüğün sakallıyı baban sanma** pro. all that glistens (or glitters or glisters) is not gold; ~ **gün** every day; ~ **günkü** everyday; ~ **günlük** everyday clothes; ~ **halde 1.** in any case; **2.** in all probability; for sure; ~ **horoz kendi çöplüğünde öter** pro.

every cock crows on his own dunghill; ~ *hususta* in all respects in every way, from all points of view; ~ *ihtimale karşı* just in case; ~ *inişin bir yokuşu, her yokuşun bir inişi vardır* pro. every flow must have its ebb, and every ebb has its flow; ~ *işe burnunu sokmak* to poke one's nose into everything; ~ *işte bir hayır vardır* pro. every cloud has a silver lining; ~ *kim* whoever; ~ *kim olursa olsun* no matter who it is, whoever it may be; ~ *nasılsa* somehow or other; ~ *ne* whatever; ~ *ne hal ise* anyway, anyhow; ~ *ne ise* 1. so anyhow; 2. anyway; let's forget it; 3. whatever the cost; ~ *ne kadar* although however much; ~ *ne pahasına olursa olsun* at any cost; ~ *nerede* wherever; ~ *ne zaman* whenever; ~ *nedense* somehow, I don't know why; ~ *şey* everything; ~ *şeye burnunu sokmak* = ~ *işe burnunu sokmak*; ~ *tarafta* (or *yerde*) everywhere, all around; ~ *taraftan* from everywhere; ~ *tarakta bezi olm.* to have a finger in every pie; ~ *zaman* always.

hercai [. - -] 1. watered, shot (*silk*); 2. *fig.* fickle, inconstant.

hercailik [. - - .] inconstancy.

hercaimenekşe [. - - . . .] вот pansy.

hercümerç, -ci tumultuous, confused, disordered.

herek, -ki stake, pale.

hereklemek to stake (*vine, plant*).

hergele 1. unbroken horse; 2. *fig.* scoundrel, rake, rascal.

herhangi whichever, whatever; (*in negative sentences*) whatsoever, any; ~ *bir* (just) any; ~ *biri* anyone, anybody.

herif 1. *contp.* fellow, rascal; 2. P man, gent; 3. P husband, hubby.

herifçioğlu, -nu *sl.* the fellow.

herk, -ki fallow field.

herkes [x .] everyone, everybody.

Herkül Hercules.

herrü: ya herrü ya merrü! we will have to take the consequences!

Hersek pr. n. Herzegovina.

heryerdelik omnipresence.

herze nonsense, rubbish; ~ *yemek* F to make a blunder.

herzevekil busybody, nosy parker.

hesabi [. - -] economical, thrifty, close-fisted.

hesap, -bı [ā] 1. arithmetic; 2. account; 3. calculation, computation; 4. bill,

Am. check; 5. estimate; 6. expectation, plan; ~ *açmak* to open an account; ~ *bakiyesi* balance; arrears; ~ *cetveli* slide rule; ~ *cüzdanı* bankbook, passbook; ~ *çıkarmak* to make out the accounts; ~ *etm.* 1. to calculate, to add up, to compute, to count; 2. to estimate, to reckon, to project; 3. to expect, to plan; ~ *etmek kitap etm.* to think twice; ~ *görmek* 1. to pay (or foot) the bill; 2. to settle accounts; ~ *günü* doomsday; ~ *istemek* to ask for the bill (or account); ~ *kitap* F 1. after careful calculation; 2. after full consideration; ~ *makinesi* calculator, calculating machine, adding machine; ~ *müfettişi* auditor; ~ *sormak* (*b-den*) to call *s.o.* to account; ~ *tutmak* 1. to keep the books, to do the bookkeeping; 2. to keep a record; ~ *uzmanı* trained accountant; ~ *vermek* (*b-ne*) to give *s.o.* an account; (hesaba): ~ *almak* to take into account; ~ *almamak* to leave out of account; ~ *çekmek* (*b-ni*) to call *s.o.* to account; ~ *geçirmek* to enter in an account; ~ *geçmek* to debit *s.o.'s* account; ~ *gelmez* 1. countless; 2. unexpected, unforeseen; ~ *katmak* to take into account (or consideration); (hesabı): ~ *kapa(t)mak* to pay one's debt; ~ *kesmek* 1. to stop doing business (*ile* with); 2. *fig.* to cut all relations (*ile* with); ~ *kitabı yok* *fig.* it has no limits, it is uncontrolled; ~ *kuvvetli* good at figures; ~ *yok* innumerable; *-na gelmek* (*b-nin*) to fit *one's* views (or interest), to suit; *-nı bilmek* *fig.* to be economical; *-nı görmek* 1. to pay the bill; 2. to settle accounts; *hesaptan düşmek* 1. to deduct; 2. to write off (*a person, etc.*).

hesapça [. x .] according to calculation, supposedly.

hesapçı 1. thrifty; 2. accountant.

hesaplamak = *hesap etm.*; ~ *kitaplamak* = *hesap etmek kitap etm.*

hesaplaşmak 1. to settle accounts mutually; 2. *fig.* to settle (or square *or* balance) accounts (*ile* with), to get even (*ile* with).

hesaplı 1. economical, affordable; 2. thrifty (*person*); 3. well considered (*or* calculated); 4. *fig.* moderate, rational, reasonable.

hesapsız 1. undocumented; 2. innumerable, countless, incalculable; 3.

not properly considered; **4.** excessively; ~~ *kitapsız* **1.** undocumented, unrecorded (*expenses*); **2.** *fig.* thoughtlessly, casually, at random.

heterogen CHEM heterogeneous.

hevenk, -gi hanging bunch of fruit.

heves 1. desire, spirit, inclination, enthusiasm; **2.** fad, fancy, passing whim, crush; ~ *etm.* (*bşe*) to have a desire (*or* fancy *or* liking) for *s.th.*; **-i kaçmak** to lose interest; **-ini almak** to satisfy one's desire; **-ini kaçırmak** to dishearten, to discourage.

heveskâr *s.* **hevesli.**

heveslendirmek to arouse s.o.'s interest.

heveslenmek to desire, to long (*-e* for).

hevesli 1. desirous (*-e* of), eager (*-e* for), enthusiastic (*-e* about, over); **2.** = *amatör.*

hevessiz uninterested, disinclined.

hey! hey (you)!, look here!; o ...!

heyamola [. . x .] NAUT heave, ho!; ~ *ile* F with great difficulty.

heybe saddlebag.

heybet, -ti grandeur, majesty, awe.

heybetli awesome, awe-inspiring, grand, majestic, imposing.

heyecan [ā] **1.** excitement; **2.** enthusiasm; ~ *duymak* **1.** to get excited; **2.** to be enthusiastic; **-a gelmek** (*or* kapılmak) to get excited.

heyecanlandırmak to excite, to thrill.

heyecanlanmak [. . - . .] **1.** to get excited, to be enthusiastic; **2.** to be upset.

heyecanlı 1. excited, thrilled; **2.** excitable; lively; **3.** exciting, thrilling.

heyecansız 1. unexcited, calm; **2.** unexciting, unemotional.

heyelan landslide.

heyet, -ti 1. committee, commission; delegation; board; **2.** *obs.* astronomy; **-iyle** as it is, as a whole; **heyeti umumiye** the whole.

heyhat, -tı [. -] alas!

heyhey nervous upset, jitters; **-ler geçirmek** (*or* **-leri tutmak**) to suffer from nervous fits; **-leri üstünde olm.** to have the jitters.

heykel statue; ~ *gibi* statuesque.

heykelci *s.* **heykeltıraş.**

heykelcilik *s.* **heykeltıraşlık.**

heykeltıraş sculptor.

heykeltıraşlık sculpture.

heyula [. - -] **1.** chaos; **2.** specter, bogy.

hezaren [ā] BOT **1.** rattan palm; **2.** lark-spur.

hezel parody, burlesque.

hezeyan [ā] **1.** nonsensical talk; **2.** delirium, raving; ~ *etm.* to drivel, to piffle.

hezimet, -ti [ī] rout; **-e uğramak** to get clobbered; **-e uğratmak** to rout, to clobber.

hı F yes.

hıçkıra hıçkıra sobbingly.

hıçkırık 1. hiccup, hiccough; **2.** sob; ~ *tutmak* to have the hiccups (*or* hiccoughs); **-la ağlamak** to sob.

hıçkırmak 1. to hiccup, to hiccough; **2.** to sob.

hıdrellez 1. beginning of summer (*May 6th*); **2.** the half year from May 6th to November 8th.

hıfız, -fzı 1. protection, preservation; **2.** memorization.

hıfzetmek [x . .] **1.** to protect, to preserve; **2.** to memorize.

hıfzıss'hha hygiene.

hık hiccup, hiccough; ~ *demiş anasının burnundan düşmüş* F he is the spit and image of his mother, he is the spitting image of his mother; ~ *mık etm.* F to hem and haw.

hılt, -tı BIOL humo(u)r.

hım F hmm, I see.

hımbıl sluggish, indolent.

hım hım nasally; ~ *konuşmak* to nasalize.

hımhım one who nasalizes.

hımış MEC timber construction with brick filling.

hıncahınç [x . .] jammed, packed, chock-a-block.

hınç, -cı grudge, ranco(u)r, hatred; **-ını almak** to revenge; **-ını çıkarmak** to vent one's spleen (*-den* on), to take revenge (*-den* on).

hındım *sl.* orgy, carousal.

hındımlamak *sl.* to jump on, to attack.

hınk deyici F one who pretends to be helpful.

hınt *sl.* stupid, crazy.

hınzır F swine.

hınzırlık 1. nastiness; **2.** mischief; ~ *etm.* to behave nastily.

hır *sl.* row, quarrel; ~ *çıkarmak* *sl.* to kick up a row.

hırbo [x .] *sl.* oafish, loutish.

hırçın 1. ill-tempered, peevish, cross; **2.** *fig.* tempestuous (*sea*).

hırçınlaşmak to show a bad temper.

hırçınlık peevishness, irritability.

hırdavat, -tı 1. hardware; **2.** junk.

hırdavatçı 1. hardware-seller; **2.** junkdealer, ironmonger.

hırdavatçılık ironmongery.

hırgür F squabble, row; **~ çıkarmak** F to make a row (or scene).

hırıldamak to wheeze.

hırıltı 1. wheeze; **2.** snarl; **3.** fig. F squabble, row.

hırıltıcı fig. F quarrelsome.

hırıltılı wheezy.

hırızma [. x .] nose ring.

Hıristiyan pr. n. Christian.

Hıristiyanlaşmak to become a Christian.

Hıristiyanlaştırmak to Christianize.

Hıristiyanlık pr. n. **1.** Christianity; **2.** Christendom.

Hıristo teyeli cross-stitch.

hırka cardigan.

hırlamak 1. to snarl (at), to growl (at); **2.** to wheeze; **3.** F to rail (at).

hırlanmak to grumble, Am. to grouch.

hırlaşmak 1. to snarl at each other (dogs); **2.** F to rail at each other.

hırlı: ~ mıdır, hırsız mıdır bilmiyorum I don't know whether he is honest or not.

hırpalamak 1. to buffet; to ill-treat, to misuse; **2.** fig. to manhandle, to rough up.

hırpani [. - -] F ragged, in tatters, unkempt.

hırs 1. greed; **2.** anger, rage, fury; **-ını alamamak** to be unable to control one's anger; **-ından çatlamak** to be ready to burst with anger; **-ını çıkarmak** (b-den) to vent one's spleen on s.o.

hırsız thief, burglar, robber; **~ çetesi** gang of thieves; **~ gibi** stealthily; **~ yatağı 1.** den of thieves; **2.** fence.

hırsızlama stealthily, surreptitiously.

hırsızlık theft, burglary, robbery; JUR larceny; **~ etm.** (or yapmak) to commit theft, to steal; **~ malı** stolen goods.

hırslandırmak to infuriate, to anger.

hırslanmak to get angry, to become furious.

hırslı 1. angry, furious; **2.** fig. greedy, avaricious.

hırt, -tı sl. conceited blockhead, pretentious fool.

hırtapoz sl. s. **hırt.**

hırtı pırtı F junk rubbish, lumber.

hırtlamba F shabby, dressed in rags; **~ gibi giyinmek** to be dressed in several

layers of shabby clothes; **-sı çıkmış 1.** in rags and tatters; **2.** thin and bony.

Hırvat, -tı pr. n. **1.** Croat; **2.** Croatian.

Hırvatça pr. n. Croatian, the Croat language.

Hırvatistan pr. n. Croatia.

hısım 1. relative, kin; **2.** in-law; **~ akraba** kith and kin.

hısımlık kinship.

hış hış with a rustling sound; **~ etm.** to rustle.

hışıldamak to rustle.

hışıltı rustle; froufrou.

hışım, -şmı rage, anger, fury; **hışmına uğramak** (b-nin) to be the object of s.o.'s rage.

hışır 1. unripe melon; **2.** rind of a melon; **3.** sl. uncouth; **-i çıkmak** F **1.** to be worn out (or tattered); **2.** to be bushed (or worn out).

hışırdamak to rustle, to grate.

hışırdatmak to rustle.

hışır hışır s. **hış hış.**

hışırtı rustle.

hışlamak s. **hışıldamak.**

hıyanet, -ti [ā] **1.** treachery, perfidy, infidelity; **2.** JUR treason; **3.** F disloyal, faithless (person).

hıyar[1] 1. BOT cucumber; **2.** sl. dolt, blockhead, swine.

hıyar[2] [ā] JUR option.

hıyarağa sl. swine, dolt.

hıyarcık, hıyarcıl MED bubo, adenoma, glandular tumo(u)r.

hıyarlaşmak sl. to begin to act like a swine.

hız 1. speed; **2.** momentum, impetus; **3.** velocity; **~ almak** to get up speed, to take a running start; **~ vermek 1.** (bşe) to speed s.th. up; **2.** to urge on; **-ını alamamak 1.** to be unable to slow down, to be out of control; **2.** to be unable to get up to speed; **-ını almak 1.** to slow down; **2.** to calm down, to subside.

hızar MEC large (or pit) saw.

hızarcı pit sawyer.

Hızır isl. MYTH; **~ gibi yetişmek** to come as a godsend, to be heaven-sent.

hızlandırmak to accelerate, to speed up.

hızlanmak to gain speed (or momentum), to be accelerated.

hızlı 1. speedy, rapid, quick, swift; **2.** loud; **3.** strong (blow); **4.** forcefully, strongly; **~ konuşmayınız, rica ederim!** be quiet, please!; **~ yaşamak** F to live fast, to live it up.

hızlılık speed, velocity.

hızölçer MEC anemometer.

hibe donation, gift; ~ **etm.** to donate.

hicap, -bı shame, embarrassment; bashfulness; ~ **duymak** to feel ashamed, to be embarrassed.

Hicaz [ā] *pr. n.* the Hejaz.

hicaz [. -] MUS a **makam.**

hicazkâr [. . -] MUS a **makam.**

hiciv, -cvi satire; lampoon.

hicivci satirist; lampooner.

hicran [. -] **1.** separation; **2.** sadness.

hicret, -ti 1. emigration; **2.** ECCL the Hegira; ~ **etm.** to migrate.

hicri of the Hegira; ~ **takvim** the Moslem calendar.

hicvetmek [x . .] to satirize; to lampoon.

hicviye satirical poem; lampoon.

hiç, -çi 1. never, not at all; **2.** nothing (at all); **3.** (*in negative sentences and questions*) ever; at all; **4.** MATH zero, nil; ~ **bir** not even one; ~ **biri** none of them; ~ **bir surette** in no way, by no means; ~ **bir şey** nothing (at all); ~ **bir yerde** nowhere; ~ **bir zaman** never; ~ **de** not at all; ~ **değil** no, not at all; ~ **değilse** at least; ~ **kimse** nobody, no one; ~ **kuşku yok** beyond a doubt, undoubtedly; ~ **mi hiç** really never; ~ **olmazsa** at least; ~ **öyle şey olur mu?** is it possible?. it won't do; ~ **yoktan** for no reason at all; ~ **yoktan iyi** better than nothing at all; ~ **yoktan kavga çıkarmak** to kick up a row for no reason; **-e saymak** to make light (*-i* of), to disregard.

hiçleşmek to become insignificant.

hiçlik 1. nullity, nothingness; **2.** poverty.

hiçten 1. worthless; **2.** unnecessarily.

hidayet, -ti [ā] **1.** the way to Islam, the right way; **2.** ♀ *mf. or wf.*; **-e ermek** to become a Moslem.

hiddet, -ti anger, fury, rage.

hiddetlendirmek to anger.

hiddetlenmek to get angry (*or* furious).

hiddetli angry, furious.

hidrasit CHEM hydracid.

hidrat, -tı CHEM hydrate.

hidrobiyoloji hydrobiology.

hidrodinamik hydrodynamic(s).

hidroelektrik hydroelectric; ~ **santralı** hydroelectric power plant.

hidrofil 1. hydrophilic; **2.** absorbent; ~

pamuk absorbent cotton.

hidrofobi hydrophobia.

hidrofor pressure tank for a water supply.

hidrojen CHEM hydrogen; ~ **bombası** hydrogen bomb, H-bomb.

hidrokarbon CHEM hydrocarbon.

hidroklorik asit CHEM hydrochloric acid.

hidroksil CHEM hydroxyl group.

hidroksit, -ti CHEM hydroxide.

hidrolik hydraulic(s); ~ **fren** hydraulic brake.

hidroliz hydrolysis.

hidroloji hydrology.

hidromekanik 1. hydromechanics; **2.** hydromechanical.

hidrometre hydrometer.

hidrosfer hydrosphere.

hidroskopi water-divining, dowsing, rhabdomancy.

hidrostatik hydrostatic(s).

hidroterapi hydrotherapy.

higrometre hygrometer.

higroskop, -pu hygroscope.

hikâye 1. story, tale, narration; **2.** F tall story, whopper; ~ **bileşik zamanı** GR compound tense formed by adding the past tense; ~ **etm.** to narrate, to tell, to relate.

hikâyeci 1. storyteller, narrator; **2.** short story writer.

hikâyecilik 1. the art of storytelling; **2.** short story writing.

hikâyeleme narration.

hikmet, -ti 1. wisdom; **2.** philosophy; **3.** hidden (*or* inner) meaning; **4.** purpose, point; **5.** the unknowable intentions of God; **6.** *obs.* physics; **7.** ♀ *mf. or wf.*; **-inden sual olunmaz** Heaven only knows why.

hilaf 1. opposite, contrary; **2.** F lie; ~ **olmasın!** F if I'm not mistaken!; ~ **söylemek** to tell a lie; **-ına** contrary (*-in* to), in opposition (*or* contravention) (*-in* to).

hilafet, -ti Caliphate.

hilafsız for sure, surely, undoubtedly.

hilal, -li 1. crescent moon; **2.** crescent; **3.** *obs.* pointer (*once used by children learning to read*); ~ **gibi** narrow and arched (*eyebrow*).

hile [ī] **1.** trick, ruse, deceit, wile, fraud; **2.** adulteration; ~ **hurda bilmez** (*or* **-si hurdası yok**) there is nothing tricky about him; ~ **yapmak 1.** to cheat, to swindle, to trick; **2.** to adulterate.

hilebaz, hilekâr s. **hileci.**

hileci [- . .] **1.** deceitful, tricky, dishonest; **2.** swindler, trickster, fraud.

hilecilik trickery, fraud.

hilekârlık s. **hilecilik.**

hileli [- . .] **1.** tricky; JUR fraudulent; **2.** adulterated, impure; ~ **iflas** JUR fraudulent bankruptcy.

hilesiz 1. honest, upright; **2.** aboveboard, free of fraud (or trickery); **3.** unadulterated, pure.

hilkat, -ti 1. creation; **2.** natural disposition; nature; ~ **garibesi** monstrosity, freak.

himaye [ā] **1.** protection, defense; **2.** support, patronage; ~ **etm.** to protect; to patronize; **-sinde** (b-nin) under the protection of s.o.; **-sine almak** (b-ni) to take s.o. under one's protection, to take s.o. under one's wing.

himayecilik [ā] JUR protectionism.

himayeli [ā] **1.** protected; **2.** MIL escorted (ship, etc.).

himayesiz [ā] **1.** unprotected; **2.** MIL unescorted (ship, etc.).

himmet, -ti 1. auspices, help, favo(u)r; **2.** effort, labo(u)r, zeal; ~ **etm.** to help, to exert o.s. (-e for); **-in var olsun!** all thanks for your help!; **-inizle** thanks to you, by your help.

hindi ZOO turkey; ~ **gibi kabarmak** fig. to be full of o.s.

hindiba [ā] BOT chicory, succory.

Hindistan [ā] pr. n. India.

hindistancevizi, -ni BOT **1.** coconut (palm); **2.** nutmeg (tree).

Hindu pr. n. Hindu.

hinoğluhin F **1.** devil; shyster; **2.** very sly (or tricky).

Hint, -di 1. Indian; **2.** India; ~ **Avrupa dilleri** Indo-European languages; ~ **fakiri** fakir; ~ **Okyanusu** Indian Ocean.

hintarmudu, -nu BOT guava tree.

hintbademi, -ni BOT cacao tree.

hintbezelyesi, -ni BOT horse grain (or gram).

hintdarısı, -nı BOT pearl millet.

hinterlant, -dı hinterland.

hintfıstığı, -nı BOT physic nut.

hintgüreşi, -ni sports; Indian wrestling.

hinthıyarı, -nı BOT cassia, drumstick tree.

hinthurması, -nı BOT palmyra.

hintkamışı, -nı BOT rattan palm.

hintkeneviri, -ni BOT (Indian) hemp, bhang, cannabis.

Hintli Indian.

hintyağı, -nı castor oil.

hiperbol, -lü MATH hyperbola.

hiperbolik MATH hyperbolic.

hiperboloit MATH hyperboloid.

hipermetrop, -pu farsighted, hypermetropic.

hipertansiyon MED hypertension, high blood pressure.

hip-hop MUS hip-hop.

hipnotizma hypnosis, hypnotism.

hipnoz hypnosis.

hipodrom hippodrome.

hipofiz the pituitary gland.

hipopotam ZOO hippopotamus.

hipotansiyon MED low blood pressure.

hipotenüs MATH hypotenuse.

hipotez hypothesis.

hippi hippy, hippie.

hippilik hippiness.

his, -ssi 1. feeling, emotion, perception; **2.** sensation, feeling, sentiment; **3.** sense; **-lerine kapılmak** to be ruled by one's emotions; **-sini vermek** to give the impression that.

hisar [ā] **1.** fort, fortress, castle; **2.** MUS B flat.

hislenmek to be touched (or affected or moved).

hisli sensitive, sentimental, emotional.

hisse 1. share, lot, part, allotted portion; **2.** fig. lesson; ~ **çıkarmak** to take offence (-den at); ~ **kapmak** to draw a lesson (-den from); ~ **sahibi** shareholder; joint owner; ~ **senedi** COM share.

hissedar [ā] = **hisse sahibi.**

hisseişayia [. . . - . .] JUR co-ownership.

hisseişayialı [. . . - . .] JUR jointly owned.

hisseli divided into shares; jointly owned.

hisset, -ti miserliness.

hissetmek [x . .] to feel, to sense, to perceive; **hissedilir** perceptible, noticeable.

hissettirmek (b-ne bşi) **1.** to cause s.o. to perceive s.th.; **2.** to let s.o. know about s.th.

hissi emotional, sentimental; sensible, sensorial.

hissiselim [. . . -] common sense.

hissiyat, -tı [ā] feelings; emotions; **-a kapılmak** to be ruled by one's emotions.

hissiz 1. unfeeling, insensitive, callous; **2.** numb, asleep.

hissizlik 1. insensitivity; **2.** numbness.

histeri hysteria.

histoloji MED histology.

hişt, hişt, -ti F hey!, look here!

hitabe [ā] address, speech.

hitaben [ā] addressing, speaking (*-e* to); addressed (*-e* to).

hitabet, -ti [ā] oratory, rhetoric, eloquence.

hitam [ā] end, conclusion, close; completion; *~ bulmak* (*or -a ermek*) to come to a conclusion; *~ vermek* to bring to an end.

hitap, -bı [ā] address, speech, discourse; *~ etm.* to address.

Hitit, -ti *pr. n.* Hittite.

Hititçe *pr. n.* Hittite (language).

hiyerarşi hierarchy.

hiyeroglif hieroglyph.

hiza [ā] line, level; *-sına kadar* up to level (*-in* of); *-ya gelmek* **1.** to line up, to form a line; **2.** *fig.* F to get into line, to shape up; *-ya getirmek* **1.** to line up (*people*); to straighten, to align; **2.** *fig.* F (*b-ni*) to bring *s.o.* into line.

hizalamak to become aligned.

hizip, -zbi clique, faction (*group*).

hizipçi factionary.

hizipçilik cliquishness.

hizipleşmek to separate into factions.

hizmet, -ti 1. service; **2.** duty; employment; **3.** care, maintenance; *~ akdi* JUR contract of service; *~ eri* MIL orderly batman; *~ etm.* to serve, to render service; *~ görmek* to serve, to render service; *~ e girmek* **1.** to be put into service (*or* operation); **2.** to begin working in the civil service; *-inde bulunmak* (*b-nin*) to be in the service of *s.o.*; *-ine girmek* (*b-nin*) to be in *s.o.'s* employment.

hizmetçi servant, maid, maidservant; *~ kadın* charwoman; *~ kız* maidservant; *~ tutmak* to put in a maid.

hizmetçilik working as a maid.

hizmetkâr manservant.

hizmetkârlık working as a manservant.

hizmetli caretaker.

hobi hobby.

hoca [x .] **1.** ECCL hodja; **2.** teacher; *-nın dediğini yap, yaptığını yapma* *pro.* do as I say, not as I do.

hocalık 1. ECCL rank and duties of a hodja; **2.** teaching.

hodan BOT borage.

hodbehot [x ..] of one's own accord.

hodbin [ī] egoistic, selfish.

hodkâm = **hodbin.**

hodpesent, -ti conceited.

hodri [x .]: *~ meydan!* come and try!, I dare you!

hohlamak to breathe (*-e* on), to blow one's breath (*-e* upon).

hokey *sports*: hockey.

hokka 1. inkwell, inkpot, inkstand; **2.** pot, cup; *~ gibi oturmak* to fit like a glove (*clothes*).

hokkabaz 1. juggler, conjurer; **2.** *fig.* shyster, cheat.

hokkabazlık 1. juggling, sleight of hand; **2.** *fig.* put-up job; trickery.

hol, -lü entrance hall, vestibule.

holding COM holding company.

Hollanda [. x .] *pr. n.* Holland, the Netherlands.

Hollandalı *pr. n.* Dutchman.

holmiyum CHEM holmium.

homo F homo, homosexual.

homogen, homojen homogeneous.

homoseksüel homosexual.

homurdanmak to grumble (*-e* at), to mutter to o.s.

homur homur in a muttering way.

homurtu 1. mutter(ing); **2.** growl (*of a bear*).

hop, -pu 1. all of a sudden; **2.** jump, skip; **3.** oops!; *~ ~!* stop!, whoa!; *~ ~ sıçramak* to jump for joy; *~ oturup ~ kalkmak* to be like a cat on hot bricks.

hoparlör loudspeaker.

hoplamak 1. to jump; to skip along; **2.** to jump for joy.

hoplatmak *caus. of* **hoplamak**, *part.* to dandle; to bounce on one's knee (*a child*).

hoppa *flighty*, frivolous (*woman*).

hoppala [x ..] **1.** upsy-daisy!; **2.** how odd!, what an idea!; **3.** that's just it!; **4.** baby's play-chair hung by a spring; *~ bebek* a childish person.

hoppalık levity, flightiness, frivolity.

hopurdatmak to slurp.

hor contemptible, despicable; *~ bakmak* (*or görmek*) to look down on; *~ kullanmak* to be hard (*-i* on), to misuse; *~ tutmak* to mistreat; *-a geçmek* to be welcome.

hora [x .] a round dance; *~ tepmek* **1.** to

dance a round dance; **2.** *fig.* to stamp noisily.

horan a folk dance of the Black sea region.

horanta [. x .] P household, family.

horda horde.

horgörü contempt.

horhor water flowing noisily.

horlamak 1. to snore; **2.** *fig.* to insult, to treat with contempt, to ill-treat.

hormon BIOL hormone.

hornblent GEOL hornblende.

horoz 1. ZOO cock, rooster; **2.** hammer (*of a gun*), cock; **3.** bridge (*of a lock*); ~ **akıllı** (*or* **kafalı**) harebrained, brainless; ~ **döğüşü** cockfight; ~ **şekeri** lolipop in the shape of a rooster; **-dan kaçmak** to avoid the company of men (*woman*); **-lar öttü** morning has broken; **-u çok olan köyde sabah geç olur** *pro.* too many cooks spoil the broth.

horozayağı, -nı cartridge extractor.

horozlanmak to swagger, to bluster, to strut about.

horezsıklet, -ti *sports*: featherweight.

hortlak ghost, specter.

hortlamak 1. to rise from the grave and haunt people; **2.** *fig.* to rearise (*trouble, etc.*).

hortum 1. ZOO trunk, proboscis; **2.** MEC hose; **3.** METEOR whirlwind, waterspout; ~ **gibi** long (*nose*); ~ **sıkmak** to direct a fire hose (*-e at*).

hortumlu 1. having a trunk; **2.** ZOO proboscidian; **3.** MEC with a hose attached.

hortumlular ZOO proboscidea.

horuldamak *s.* **horlamak** *1.*

horul horul snoring loudly.

horultu snore, snoring.

hostes stewardess; air hostess.

hoş 1. pleasant, nice, lovely; **2.** for that matter, as far as that's concerned; **3.** fine, but ...; ~ **bulduk!** thank you! (*said in reply to a welcoming greeting*); ~ **geçinmek** (*b-le*) to get on well with *s.o.*; ~ **geldiniz!** welcome!; ~ **görmek** to tolerate, to overlook; ~ **tutmak** (*b-ni*) to treat *s.o.* warmly; **-a gitmek** to be pleasing; **-una gitmek** to please, to be agreeable (*-in* to).

hoşaf stewed fruit; ~ **gibi** bushed, worn-out; **-ın yağı kesilmek** (*b-de*) to be flabbergasted, to be at a loss for words; **-ına gitmek** F to please.

hoşbeş small talk; ~ **etm.** to have small talk, to chitchat.

hoşça [x .] pretty well, somewhat pleasant; ~ **kalın!** so long!, bye!, cheers!

hoşgörü tolerance.

hoşgörülü tolerant.

hoşgörüsüz intolerant.

hoşgörüsüzlük intolerance.

hoşhoş bow-wow, woof-woof, doggy, doggie.

hoşlanmak to like, to enjoy, to be pleased (*-den* with).

hoşlaşmak 1. to become pleasant and agreeable; **2.** to like each other.

hoşluk 1. pleasantness; **2.** strangeness.

hoşnut, -du [ū] pleased, satisfied, contented (*-den* with); ~ **etm.** (*b-ni*) to please *s.o.*; ~ **olm.** to be pleased (*-den* with).

hoşnutluk contentment, satisfaction, pleasure.

hoşnutsuz displeased, discontented.

hoşnutsuzluk discontent, dissatisfaction.

hoşor *sl.* plump and pretty (*woman*).

hoşsohbet, -ti conversable, conversationalist.

hoşt, -tu shoo!, scram!

hoşur 1. worthless; **2.** uncouth, crude.

hotoz 1. crest, tuft; **2.** bun, topknot (*of hair*); **3.** *obs.* headdress (*for women*).

hovarda 1. spendthrift, profligate; **2.** womanizer, rake; **3.** womanizing, rakish.

hovardalaşmak 1. to become a spendthrift; **2.** to become a womanizer.

hovardalık 1. profligacy; **2.** womanizing; ~ **etm. 1.** to womanize; **2.** to spend money extravagantly.

hoyrat, -tı rough, coarse (*person*).

hödük boorish, uncouth.

höpürdetmek to slurp.

höpürtü slurp.

hörgüç, -cü ZOO hump.

hörgüçlü humped.

höst, -tü 1. whoa!; **2.** *sl.* hey you bastard!

höt, -tü boo!; ~ **demek** to bark (*-e at*), to speak sharply (*-e* to); ~ **zöt** browbeating.

höyük tumulus, artificial hill (*or* mound).

hu [-] **1.** hey there!; **2.** He (*God*).

hububat, -tı [. - -] grain, cereals.

Huda [ā] God.

hud'a trick.

hudayinabit, -ti [ā, ā] wild, self-sown,

volunteer (*plant*).

hudut, -du [. -] **1.** boundary, border, frontier; **2.** end, limit; **~ dışı etm.** (*b-ni*) to expel s.o. from the country.

hudutlandırmak to limit, to put a limit (**to**).

hudutlu limited.

hudutsuz unlimited, boundless.

hukuk, -ku [. -] **1.** law, jurisprudence; **2.** JUR rights; **3.** friendship; **4.** = **Hukuk Fakültesi**; **~ davası** civil lawsuit; **~ doktoru** doctor of law; ♀ **Fakültesi** law school; **~ mahkemesi** civil court; **~ müşaviri** legal adviser.

hukukçu jurist.

hukuki [. - -] legal, juridical; **~ muamele** legal action.

hukuklu law student.

hulasa 1. summary, résumé; **2.** in short (*or* brief), summing up; **3.** CHEM extract; **~ etm.** to sum up, to summarize.

hulliyat, -ti [ā] valuable jewelry.

hulül, -lü 1. penetration; infiltration; **2.** osmosis; **3.** arrival, beginning (*of a season*).

hulus sincerity, purity of heart; **~ çakmak** F (*b-ne*) to curry favo(u)r with s.o.

huluskâr 1. sincere, genuine; **2.** flatterer.

hulya [ā] daydream, fancy; **-ya dalmak** to daydream.

hulyalı [ā] dreamy, romantic; fanciful.

humar [ā] hangover (*from drink*); loginess (*from sleep*).

humma MED fever.

hummalı MED feverish (*a. fig.*)

humus humus.

hunhar [. -] bloodthirsty.

hunharca [. - .] **1.** cruelly, brutally; **2.** brutal, savage.

hunharlık bloodthirstiness.

huni funnel.

hunnak, -kı [ā] MED quinsy.

hura hurray!, hurrah!

hurafe [ā] superstition.

hurç, -cu large leather saddlebag.

hurda 1. scrap iron (*or* metal), junk; **2.** scrap (*metal*); **3.** *fig.* worn-out; **~ demir** scrap iron; **~ fiyatına** very cheaply; **-sı çıkmış** worn-out.

hurdacı scrap iron dealer, junk dealer, secondhand metal dealer.

hurdahaş [ā] bashed up, crushed; **~ etm.** to smash to bits; **~ olm. 1.** to be smashed to bits; **2.** *fig.* to become bushed; **araba kazadan sonra ~ oldu** the car was a write-off after the accident.

huri [ū] *isl.* MYTH houri; **~ gibi** as pretty as a picture (*girl*).

hurma BOT date; **~ agacı** BOT date palm; **~ tatlısı** a date-shaped sweet.

hurmalık date grove.

huruç [. -] departure, exodus.

hurufat, -tı [. - -] TYP type(face); **~ dökmek** to cast type; **~ kasası** type case.

husuf [. -] eclipse (*of the moon*).

husul, -lü [. -] occurrence, appearance, coming into existence; **~ bulmak** (*or* **-e gelmek**) to occur, to come into existence; **-e getirmek** to bring about, to accomplish.

husumet, -ti [. - .] hostility, enmity; **~ beslemek** to nourish hostility (**-e** towards).

husus [. -] **1.** subject, matter, question; case; **2.** particularity, peculiarity; relation, respect; **-unda** regarding, with reference to, in connection with; **bu -ta** in this matter (*or* connection).

hususi [. - -] **1.** particular, special, distinctive, characteristic; **2.** personal, private; **3.** reserved (*seat*); **4.** F privately owned automobile.

hususiyet, -ti [. - . .] **1.** characteristic, peculiarity, trait; **2.** intimacy.

hususyla [. - - .] [. - x .] particularly, especially.

husye MED testis, testicle.

huş BOT birch.

huşu, -u [. -] **1.** modesty, humility; **2.** submission to God.

huşunet, -ti [. - .] severity, harshness.

hutbe ECCL khutbah (*sermon delivered at the noon prayer on Friday and on certain other occasions*).

huy 1. habit, temper, disposition, temperament; **2.** nature; **~ edinmek** (*or* **etm.** *or* **kapmak**) to get into the habit (**of**), to take to; **-u suyu** (*b-nin*) one's nature and disposition; **-una çekmek** (*b-nin*) to take after s.o., to resemble s.o.; **-una suyuna gitmek** to humo(u)r, to indulge.

huylandırmak 1. to upset, to molest; **2.** to frighten, to startle (*animal*).

huylanmak 1. to be irritated, to get nervous, to become uneasy; **2.** to get excited; **3.** to shy (*animal*).

huylu 1. ... tempered; **2.** bad-tempered, irritable, touchy, cross; **3.** suspicious.

huysuz bad-tempered, irascible; petulant, peevish.

huysuzlanmak to fuss, to fret (*child*).

huysuzlaşmak to become fretful (*child*); to become peevish.

huysuzluk fractiousness, bad temper, petulance; **~ etm.** to show bad temper; **huysuzluğu tutmak** to have a fit of bad temper.

huzme PHYS **1.** bundle, bunch; **2.** light beam.

huzur [. -] **1.** peace of mind, repose, comfort, quiet; **2.** presence, attendance; **3.** presence, access (*of an emperor*); **~ ve asayiş** peace and security; **~ vermek** (*b-ne*) **1.** to leave *s.o.* alone, not to bother *s.o.*; **2.** to bring *s.o.* comfort and joy, to soothe *s.o.*; **-una çıkmak** (*b-nin*) to have access to *s.o.*; **-unda** in the presence (*-in* of); **-unu kaçırmak** to trouble, to disturb.

huzurevi, -ni rest home.

huzurlu 1. peaceful, tranquil; **2.** happy, untroubled.

huzursuz troubled, uneasy.

huzursuzluk uneasiness, disquiet.

hüccet, -ti (legal) document; argument, proof.

hücra [. -] remote, solitary (*place*).

hücre 1. BIOL cell; **2.** cell; chamber, room; **3.** niche, alcove.

hücrelerarası, -nı BIOL & ANAT intercellular.

hücum [ū] **1.** attack, assault; charge; **2.** sudden crowding, rush; **3.** lash of criticism, verbal attack; **~ etm. 1.** to attack, to storm; **2.** *fig.* to mob, to rush to (*a place*); **~ kıtası** (*or* **kolu**) MIL storm troops; **-a uğramak** to be attacked (*or* assailed).

hücumbot, -tu MIL assault boat.

Hüda [. -] God.

hükmen [x.] *sports:* by the decision of a referee; **~ galip** *sports:* won by the decision of a referee.

hükmetmek [x..] **1.** to rule, to govern, to dominate; **2.** to decide, to conclude.

hükmi [ī] **1.** legal; judicial; **2.** nominal; **~ şahıs** (*or* **şahsiyet**) JUR legal person.

hüküm, -kmü 1. judg(e)ment, decision, decree, sentence; **2.** jurisdiction, sovereignty, sway, rule; **3.** opinion, thought, assumption; **4.** legality, validity, authority; **5.** influence, importance, effect; **6.** grip, force, hold; **~ giydirmek** to pass sentence (*-e* on);

~ giymek to be condemned (*or* sentenced); **~ sürmek 1.** to reign, to rule; **2.** *fig.* to prevail; **~ vermek 1.** to bring in a verdict; **2.** to pass sentence, to condemn; **hükmü geçmek 1.** to have authority (*-e* over), to carry weight (*-e* with); **2.** to expire (*validity*), to be over with; **hükmü kalmadı** (*or* **yoktur**) it is invalid; **hükmünde olm.** to be considered (**as**), to be of the same effect (**as**); **hükmünü geçirmek** to assert one's authority (*-e* over); **hükümden düşmek** to be invalid.

hükümat, -tı *sl.* prison warden.

hükümdar [ā] ruler, monarch, sovereign.

hükümdarlık 1. rulership, sovereignty; **2.** empire, kingdom.

hükümet, -ti 1. government, administration, state; **2.** government building (*or* office); **~ darbesi** coup d'état; **~ kapısı** government office; **~ konağı** government office; **~ merkezi** capital, seat of government; **~ sürmek** to rule, to reign, to govern; **-i devirmek** to overthrow the government; **-i kurmak** to form a government.

hükümlü 1. sentenced, condemned; **2.** convict.

hükümran [ā] sovereign.

hükümranlık [ā] sovereignty.

hükümsüz invalid, null; **~ kılmak** to invalidate, to nullify, to annul.

hükümsüzlük nullity.

hülle *obs.* interim marriage necessary before a divorced couple could remarry.

hümanist, -ti humanist(ic).

hümanizm humanism.

hümayun [. - -] HIST royal, imperial.

hüner skill, talent, ability, dexterity; **~ göstermek** to show skill (*or* proficiency) (*-de* in).

hünerli 1. skillful, talented, dexterous, proficient; **2.** done with skill.

hünersiz unskilled.

hüngürdemek to sob violently, to wail loudly.

hüngür hüngür sobbingly; **~ ağlamak** to sob, to blubber, to boohoo.

hüngürtü sob.

hünkâr HIST sovereign, sultan.

hünnap, -bı BOT jujube.

hünsa [ā] BIOL, BOT, ZOO **1.** hermaphrodite; **2.** hermaphroditic.

hür free; unconstrained, untrammeled; **~ düşünce** free thought.

hürmet, -ti respect, regard, veneration; ~ etm. to respect, to hono(u)r, to venerate; -le respectfully; -lerimle respectfully yours, with my respects.
hürmeten [x . .] out of respect.
hürmetkâr respectful.
hürmetli 1. respectful, deferent; respected; 2. fig. huge, large, considerable.
hürmetsiz disrespectful.
hürmetsizlik disrespect; ~ etm. to be disrespectful (-e to).
hürriyet, -ti freedom, liberty; -i seçmek to throw off the yoke.
hürya [x .] in a rush; ~ etm. to rush out (or in).
hüsnühal, -li [ā] good conduct; ~ kâğıdı certificate of good conduct, reference.
hüsnükabul, -lü [. . . .] warmly reception; ~ göstermek (b-ne) to receive s.o. warmly.

hüsnükuruntu co. wishful thinking.
hüsnüniyet, -ti good intention (or will or faith); ~ sahibi goodwilled.
hüsnütelakki favo(u)rably biased interpretation.
hüsnüyusuf BOT sweet william.
hüsran [. -] 1. disappointment, frustration, let-down; 2. loss, damage; -a uğramak to be disappointed (or let down).
hüsün, -snü obs. beauty.
hüthüt, -tü ZOO hoopoe, hoopoe.
hüviyet, -ti 1. identity (card); 2. fig. character, quality; ~ cüzdanı identity card, ID card.
hüzün, -znü sadness, sorrow, grief, melancholy.
hüzünlendirmek to sadden.
hüzünlenmek to feel sad, to sadden.
hüzünlü sad, sorrowful.
Hz. abbr. of Hazretleri.

I

ıcık: ıcığını cıcığını çıkarmak F to go over with a fine-tooth comb.
ığıl! P still water.
ığıl ığıl slowly; ~ akmak to flow slowly, to gurgle.
ığrıp, -bı trawl (net); ~ çevirmek fig. to make the best use of s.th.; ~ kayığı trawler.
ıh! cry used to make a camel kneel.
ıhlamak to groan, to moan.
ıhlamur 1. BOT linden tree, lime-tree; 2. linden-flower (tea).
ıhmak to kneel down (camel).
ıkıl ıkıl in gasps, gaspingly; ~ nefes almak to gasp for breath.
ıkınmak 1. to strain while defecating; 2. to grunt, to moan; ıkınıp sıkınmak F 1. to grunt and strain; 2. to try hard.
ıklamak 1. to huff and puff, to breathe heavily; 2. to sob; ıklaya sıklaya with the greatest effort.
ıklım tıklım up to the brim; brimful.
ılgar 1. gallop; 2. cavalry raid; ~ etm. to raid.
ılgarlamak to raid, to foray.
ılgım mirage.
ılgın BOT tamarisk.
ılgıt ılgıt gently, lightly.
ılıca hot spring, spa.

ılıcak tepid, warm, lukewarm.
ılık tepid, lukewarm; warmish, mild.
ılıklaşmak to become tepid (or lukewarm), to warm up slightly.
ılıklaştırmak to make lukewarm.
ılıklık tepidity, warmness.
ılım moderation.
ılımak s. ılıklaşmak.
ılıman temperate; ~ bölge Temperate Zone.
ılımlı moderate, middle-of-the-road.
ılımlılık moderateness.
ılınmak s. ılıklaşmak.
ılıştırmak to make lukewarm.
ılıtmak s. ılıklaştırmak.
ımızganma 1. dozing; 2. wavering, indecision; 3. smoldering; ~ halleri PSYCH hypnagogic images (or hallucinations).
ımızganmak 1. to doze, to be half asleep; 2. to waver (between two opinions); 3. to die down, to smolder (fire).
ıpıslak completely wet, soaked.
ıpıssız very desolate, entirely uninhabited.
ır song; tune.
ıra characteristic, trait.
ırabilim characterology.

ırak far, distant, remote.
Irak, -kı pr. n. Iraq.
ırakgörür telescope.
ıraklaşmak to go (or move) away.
Iraklı pr. n. Iraqi.
ıraklık distance.
ıraksak MATH & PHYS divergent.
ıraksama 1. vn. of ıraksamak; 2. MATH & PHYS divergence.
ıraksamak to consider improbable.
ıralamak to characterize.
ıramak to go (or move) away (-den from)
ırgalamak 1. to shake, to rock; 2. sl. to interest, to concern.
ırgamak to shift, to move, to budge.
ırgat, -tı 1. day-labo(u)rer, workman; 2. windlass, winch; ~ başı foreman, overseer; ~ gibi çalışmak fig. to sweat blood; ~ pazarı labo(u)r market.
ırgatlık day-labo(u)r.
ırk, -kı 1. race; 2. lineage, blood; ~ ayrımı racial discrimination.
ırkçı racist.
ırkçılık racialism, racism.
ırki racial.
ırkiyat, -tı ethnology.
ırktaş of the same race.
ırlamak to sing.
ırmak river.
ırz chastity, purity, hono(u)r; ~ düşmanı rapist; ~ ehli virtuous, chaste, honest; -a geçme (or tecavüz) JUR rape; -ına geçmek (or tecavüz etm.) 1. (b-nin) to rape s.o., to violate s.o.; 2. fig. to bastardize, to debase, to adulterate.
ıs (legal) owner.
ısdar [ā] loom.
ısı 1. heat, warm; 2. temperature; ~ dam Turkish bath; ~ kuşak tropical zone.
ısıalan CHEM endothermal, endothermic.
ısıdenetir thermostat.
ısıldeğer thermal value.
ısın PHYS calorie.
ısınma warming; ~ koşusu sports: warm-up run.
ısınmak 1. to grow warm; 2. to warm o.s.; 3. fig. to warm (-e to), to get accustomed (-e to).
ısıölçer 1. thermometer; 2. calorimeter.
ısırgan 1. BOT stinging nettle; 2. snappish, snappy (animal).
ısırgın heat rash, prickly heat.

ısırıcı 1. biting (cold); 2. snappish (animal); 3. scratchy (cloth).
ısırık 1. bite; 2. a bite (or mouthful).
ısırmak 1. to bite; 2. fig. to scratch, to irritate (cloth); ısıran it dişini göstermez pro. barking dogs seldom bite.
ısıtıcı heater.
ısıtmak to warm, to heat.
ısıveren CHEM exothermic, exothermal.
ıska sl. miss, muff; ~ geçmek sl. 1. to miss, to fail to hit; 2. fig. to overlook, to ignore.
ıskaça NAUT step (of a mast).
ıskala [. x .] MUS scale.
ıskarça [. x .] 1. NAUT congestion (in a harbo(u)r); 2. packed, crowded.
ıskarmoz 1. NAUT rib; 2. NAUT oarlock, thole (pin); 3. ZOO barracuda.
ıskarta [. x .] 1. cards: discard; 2. discarded; 3. COM waste; ~ etm. (or -ya çıkarmak) to discard; ~ mal waste goods; -ya çıkmak to be discarded.
ıskat, -tı 1. dropping; 2. alms given on behalf of the dead as compensation for their neglected religious duties.
ıskatçı 1. person receiving alms from mourners; 2. beggar at the graveside.
ıskonto [. x .] 1. COM discount; 2. price reduction; ~ etm. (or yapmak) 1. to reduce the price of; 2. COM to discount.
ıskota [. x .] NAUT sheet; clew line.
ıskuna [. x .] NAUT schooner.
ıslah [ā] 1. improvement, correction, reform; 2. amendment, rectification; ~ etm. 1. to amend, to improve; 2. to discipline, to reform; ~ olmaz F incorrigible.
ıslahat, -tı [. - -] reform, improvement, amendment; ~ yapmak to make reforms.
ıslahatçı [. - - .] reformer, reformist.
ıslahevi, -ni [. . - . .] reformatory, approved (or reform) school.
ıslahhane s. ıslahevi.
ıslak wet; damp.
ıslaklık wetness; dampness.
ıslamak s. ıslatmak 1.
ıslanmak to get wet, to be wetted.
ıslatmak 1. to wet; to dampen; to moisten; 2. sl. to cudgel, to thrash; 3. F celebrate by a booze-up, to wet.
ıslık 1. whistle; 2. hiss; ~ çalmak 1. to whistle; 2. to hiss (snake); 3. to whistle (-e at, to).
ıslıklamak to boo, to give s.o. the bird,

to hiss.

ıslıklı whistling, hissing (*sound*); **~ ünsüz** GR sibilant.

ısmarlama 1. *vn. of* **ısmarlamak; 2.** made-to-order, bespoke, custom made, made-to-measure; **3.** slapdash, superficial; **~ elbise** tailor-made (*or* custom-made) suit.

ısmarlamak 1. (*b-ne*) to order s.th. from *s.o.*; to have *s.o.* make s.th.; **2.** (*b-ne*) to treat *s.o.* to (*drink, food*); **3.** to entrust to s.o.; **4.** (*b-ne*) to warn *s.o.* to behave (*in a certain manner*).

ıspanak 1. BOT spinach; **2.** *sl.* imbecile, idiot.

ıspavli NAUT cord, twine.

ıspazmoz convulsion, spasm.

ısrar [ā] insistence, persistence; **~ etm.** to insist (*-de* on), to persist (*-de* in).

ısrarla [. - .] insistently.

ısrarlı [. - .] insistent.

ıssız desolate, forlorn, solitary.

ıssızlaşmak to become desolate.

ıssızlık desolation, forlornness, solitariness.

ıstakoz ZOO lobster.

ıstampa [. x .] **1.** stamp; **2.** ink (*or* stamp) pad.

ıstavroz cross, crucifix; **~ çıkarmak** to cross o.s.

ıstıfa, -aı [ā] selection.

ıstılah [ā] technical term.

ıstırap, -bı [ā] **1.** pain; anguish, misery; **2.** bodily suffering; **~ çekmek** to suffer; **~ vermek** to make s.o. suffer, to afflict.

ıstıraplı [ā] suffering; miserable, anguished.

ışığadoğrulum BOT phototropism.

ışık 1. light; **2.** any source of light, *part.* lamp; **~ almak** PHOT to be fogged (*or* exposed); **~ oyunu** play of light; **~ saçmak** to shine, to give off light; **~ tutmak 1.** to light the way (*-e* for); **2.** to shine alight (*-e* on); **3.** *fig.* to shed (*or* throw) light (*-e* on); **~ yılı** light year; **ışığı altında** in the light of.

ışıkçı THEAT electrician.

ışıkgöçüm BOT phototaxy, phototaxis.

ışıkkesen PHOT light trap.

ışıkküre photosphere.

ışıklandırma lighting, illumination.

ışıklandırmak to light up, to illuminate.

ışıklı illuminated, lighted up, floodlit; **reklam** neon sign.

ışıklılık luminance.

ışıkölçer PHYS photometer; light (*or* exposure) meter.

ışıkölçümü, -nü photometry.

ışıksız unlit, without light.

ışıkyuvarı, -nı AST photosphere.

ışılamak *s.* **ışıldamak.**

ışıldak 1. bright, sparkling; **2.** searchlight, spotlight, projector, floodlight.

ışıldamak to shine, to sparkle, to gleam, to twinkle.

ışıl ışıl sparklingly, glitteringly.

ışılküf BOT actinomycete.

ışıltı flash, spark, glitter, twinkle.

ışıltılı sparkling, glittering, flashy.

ışıma 1. glowing; **2.** PHYS radiation.

ışımak 1. to glow, to radiate light; **2.** to become light (*or* illuminated).

ışın MATH & PHYS ray; **~ demeti** pencil of rays.

ışınetki radioactivity.

ışınetkin radioactive.

ışınım radiation.

ışınımölçer AST bolometer.

ışınlama radiation.

ışınlı 1. radiant; **2.** radiolarian.

ışınölçer radiometer.

ışıtmak to illuminate.

ışkı drawknife, spokeshave.

ışkırlak cap worn by **Karagöz.**

ıştın clay lamp.

ıtır, -trı attar, essence, perfume; **~ çiçeği** BOT geranium.

ıtırlı fragrant, aromatic.

ıtnap, -bı [ā] verbiage.

ıtri perfumed, fragrant.

ıtriyat, -tı [ā] perfumes, essences, attars.

ıtriyatçı [ā] perfumer, perfumier.

ıttıla, -aı [ā] knowledge, information.

ıvır zıvır 1. bits and pieces, bobs and trinkets, baubles; **2.** F nonsensical, rubbish; junky, trifling; **3.** F nonsense, hooey.

ızbandut huge and terrifying man, hulk; **~ gibi** burly, strapping (*man*).

ızgara [x . .] **1.** grate, grating; **2.** grill, grid, gridiron; **3.** grilled (*fish, meat, etc.*); **~ köfte** grilled meat balls; **~ yapmak** to grill.

ızrar [ā] *obs.* harming; **~ etm.** to harm.

i

iade [ā] **1.** return(ing), giving back; **2.** refusal, rejection; **3.** restoration, restitution; **~ etm. 1.** to return (-e to), to give back (-e to); **2.** to refuse, to reject; **3.** to restore; **iadei ziyaret etm.** (b-ni) to return s.o.'s call.

iadeli [ā] reply-paid (letter); **~ taahhütlü mektup** registered and reply-paid letter.

iane [ā] **1.** subsidy, donation; **2.** help, aid; **~ toplamak** to collect contributions.

iare [ā] loan.

iaşe [ā] feeding, victualing; **~ etm.** to feed, to sustain; **~ ve ibate** room and board, board and lodging.

ibadet, **-ti** [ā] worship, prayer; **~ etm.** to worship.

ibadethane [ā, ā] temple, sanctuary.

ibadullah [ā, ā] abundant.

ibare [ā] sentence; expression; paragraph.

ibaret, **-ti** [ā] composed (-den of), consisting (-den of); **~ olm.** to consist (-den of), to be composed (-den of), to be made up (-den of).

ibate [ā] sheltering, giving lodging to; **~ etm.** to house, to shelter.

ibda, **-aı** [ā] creating; **~ etm.** to create.

ibibik ZOO hoopoe.

ibik 1. ZOO comb (of a fowl); **2.** ANAT crista; **3.** red tassel (of a fez).

ibikli crested (bird).

ibiş name of the foolish servant in certain old Turkish plays; **~ gibi** comically foolish.

iblağ 1. delivery; communication; **2.** increase, augmentation; **~ etm. 1.** to communicate, to transmit; to deliver; **2.** to increase (-e to).

iblis [. -] **1.** satan, the Devil; **2.** fig. demon, devil, imp.

ibne sl. fag, gay, queen, queer.

ibra [ā] acquittance; **~ etm.** to release (from debt); **~ kâğıdı** quittance.

ibraname [ā, ā] quittance, release.

ibrani [. - -] pr. n. Hebrew.

ibranice [. - - .] [. - x .] pr. n. the Hebrew language.

ibraz [ā] presentation, showing; **~ etm.** to present, to show (a document).

ibre MEC needle, pointer.

ibret, **-ti 1.** warning, lesson, admonition; **2.** P strange, queer; **~ almak** (bşden) to take warning from s.th., to learn a lesson from s.th.; **~ olm.** to be a warning (-e to); **-in kudreti** F strange and hideous.

ibrik ewer, pitcher.

ibrişim silk thread; **~ kurdu** ZOO silkworm.

icabet, **-ti** [ā] acceptance (of an invitation), attendance (at a gathering); **~ etm. 1.** to accept (an invitation); **2.** to accede (to a request).

icap, **-bı** [- -] **1.** necessity, requirement, demand; **2.** LOG affirmation; **~ etm.** to be necessary; **-ına bakmak 1.** to do what is necessary, to see to; **2.** fig. F to take care of, to kill; **-ında** if needed, at a push (or pinch).

icar [- -] rent; **-a vermek** to lease, to let.

icat, **-dı** [- -] invention; **~ etm. 1.** to invent; **2.** to fabricate, to trump up.

icaz [- -] concision, succinctness.

icazet, **-ti** [ā] **1.** permission; **2.** obs. madrasa diploma.

icazetname [ā, ā] obs. madrasa diploma.

icbar [ā] compulsion, coercion; **~ etm.** to force, to compel, to coerce.

icik F: **iciğini ciciğini çıkarmak** to go over (or through) s.th. with a fine-tooth comb.

icmal, **-li** [ā] summary; **~ etm.** to summarize.

icra [ā] **1.** execution, performance, carrying out; **2.** (dairesi) court for claims; **3.** MUS performance; **~ etm. 1.** to carry out, to execute; **2.** MUS to perform; to play; to sing; **~ heyeti 1.** executive board (or committee); **2.** MUS performers; **~ kuvveti** executive power; **~ memuru** bailiff; **~ vekili** minister, member of the cabinet; **-ya vermek** (b-ni) to take s.o. to court.

icraat, **-tı** [ā, ā] performances; operations, actions.

iç, **-çi 1.** inside, interior; **2.** inner, internal; **3.** in; among; **4.** internal organs of the body; **5.** domestic; home; **6.** fig. mind, heart, will; **~ açı** MATH interior angle; ~ **açıcı** heartwarming; ~ **aç-mak** to cheer up; ♀ **Anadolu** Inner Anatolia; ~ **bezelye** shelled peas; ~ **bulantısı** nausea; ~ **çamaşırı** underwear; ~ **çekmek 1.** to sigh; **2.** to sob; ~ **deniz** inland sea; ~ **donu** underpants; ~ **etm.** F to swipe, to pocket; ~ **geçirmek** to sigh; ~ **gıcıklamak** to arouse one's lust; ~ **gömleği** slip; ~ **hat 1.** domestic line; **2.** domestic communications; ~ **içe 1.** one inside the other, nested; **2.** one opening into another (*room*); ~ **lastik** inner tube; ~ **merkez** focus (*of an earthquake*); ~ **organlar** internal organs, viscera; ~ **pazar** domestic (*or* home) market; ~ **pilav** pilaf prepared with currants, pine nuts, spices and liver; ~ **piyasa** s.; ~ **pazar**; ~ **savaş** civil war; ~ **sıkıcı** dull, boring, tedious; ~ **sıkıntısı** boredom; ~ **sular** inland rivers and lakes; ~ **ticaret** domestic (*or* home) trade; (**içi**): ~ **açılmak** to feel relieved, to be cheered up; ~ **almamak** (*or* **kabul etmemek**) not to feel like eating; ~ **bayılmak** to feel faint with hunger, to be starving; ~ **bulanmak 1.** to feel nauseated; **2.** *fig.* to get suspicious; ~ **burkulmak** to be very unhappy; ~ **çekmek** (*bşi*) to have a longing for *s.th.*, to desire *s.th.*; ~ **çıfıt çarşısı** *fig.* evil-minded; ~ **dar** (*or* **tez**) impatient, restless (*person*); ~ **daralmak** to be depressed (*or* distressed); ~ **dışı bir** unaffected, sincere; ~ **dışına çıkmak** to be nauseous; ~ **erimek** to be greatly grieved; ~ **ezilmek** to feel hungry, to have a sinking feeling; ~ **geçmek 1.** to doze; **2.** F to be worn out; **3.** to become overripe (*fruit*); ~ **geniş** *fig.* F easygoing, carefree; ~ **gitmek 1.** to have diarrhea (*or* the squirts); **2.** to starve (*-e* for), to hunger (*-e* for); ~ **içine sığmamak** to be up in the air; ~ **içini yemek** (*or* **kemirmek**) to eat one's heart out; ~ **kalkmak** to have a feeling of nausea; ~ **kan ağlamak** to be deeply grieved, to be in great sorrow; ~ **kararmak** to be dismayed; ~ **kazınmak** to feel very hungry, to starve; ~ **paralanmak** to be greatly upset; ~ **rahat etm.** to be relieved; ~ **sıkılmak** to feel bored; ~ **sızlamak** to be very unhappy (*-e* about); ~ **sürmek** MED to have diarrhea; ~ **yağ bağlamak** to be filled with joy; ~ **yanmak 1.** to be very thirsty; **2.** *fig.* to be very

upset; (**içinde**): ~ **yüzmek** to be rolling in (*money, etc.*); (**içinden**): ~ **çıkmak** to accomplish, to solve, to carry out; ~ **geçirmek** to think about, to consider; ~ **geçmek** (*b-nin*) to occur to *s.o.*, to cross *one's* mind; ~ **gülmek** (*b-ne*) to laugh up one's sleeve at *s.o.*; ~ **okumak 1.** to read to o.s.; **2.** *sl.* to swear under one's breath (*-e* at); ~ **pazarlıklı** backstabbing, two-faced; (**içine**): ~ **almak** to contain, to hold; to include, to encompass; ~ **atmak 1.** to keep to o.s. (*problem*); **2.** to brood over (*an insult*); ~ **çekmek** to inhale; ~ **doğmak** to feel in one's bones, to have a presentiment (*or* hunch); ~ **etm.** (*bşin*) *sl.* to make a hash (*or* mess) of *s.th.*; ~ **işlemek 1.** to cut s.o. the quick; **2.** to chill s.o. to the bone (*cold*); to soak s.o. to the skin (*rain*); ~ **kapanık** introverted, withdrawn; ~ **kurt düşmek** to suspect; ~ **sıçmak** s. ~ **etm.**; ~ **sokacağı gelmek** (*b-ni*) to be nuts over *s.o.*, to be wild about *s.o.*; (**içini**): ~ **bayıltmak 1.** to make s.o. feel sick; **2.** to talk s.o.'s head off; ~ **boşaltmak** s. ~ **dökmek**; ~ **çekmek** to sigh; ~ **dökmek** to unburden o.s., to unbosom o.s., to make a clean breast of; (**içinin**): ~ **yağı erimek** to pine away with anxiety; **içler acısı** heart-rending, heartbreaking; **içten içe** underhandedly, secretly.

içbükey concave.

içderi endoderm(is).

içebakış PSYCH introspection.

içecek 1. beverage, drink; **2.** potable, drinkable (*water*); ~ **su** drinking water.

içedoğma presentiment.

içedönük introverted.

içek GR infix.

içekapanık 1. schizoid; **2.** autistic.

içeri, içerisi, -ni 1. inside, interior; **2.** inner; **3.** in; ~ **atmak** (*or* **tıkmak**) *fig.* F to put in clink; ~ **buyurun!** please come in!; ~ **dalmak** to barge in, to burst into; ~ **düşmek** *sl.* to go to clink; ~ **girmek 1.** to go in, to enter; **2.** F to make a loss; **3.** F to go to clink; **içerde 1.** losing; **2.** F in clink (*or* stir); **içerde olm.** F **1.** to lose, to be out, to be to the bad (*money*); **2.** to be in clink (*or* stir).

içerik 1. content(s); **2.** LOG implicit.

içerlek 1. sitting back (*building*); **2.** indented (*line*).

içerlemek to resent.

içermek 1. to contain, to include, to comprise; **2.** LOG to imply.

içgeçit tunnel.

içgözlem introspection.

içgüdü instinct.

içgüdüsel instinctive.

içgüvey, içgüveyisi, -*ni* man who lives with his wife's parents; **-den** (*or* **-sinden**) **hallice** *fig.* so so.

içici drunkard, alcoholic.

içim 1. sip; **2.** taste, flavo(u)r.

içimli 1. having ... taste (*cigarette*, *etc.*); **2.** pleasant to the taste (*cigarette*, *etc.*).

için 1. for; **2.** because; **3.** so that, in order that; **4.** in order to, so as to, to; **5.** concerning, about; **bunun ~** for this reason.

içinde 1. in, inside; **2.** within, in; **3.** under (*circumstances*); **4.** having, full of, all; **~ olm.** to be included.

içindekiler contents.

için için 1. internally; **2.** secretly; **~ ağlamak** to weep inwardly.

içirmek *caus. of* **içmek** to make s.o. drink.

içişleri, -*ni* POL internal (*or* home) affairs; **♀ Bakanı** Minister of Internal Affairs; **♀ Bakanlığı** Ministry of Internal Affairs.

içken tippler, boozer, alcoholic.

içki 1. drink, liquor, booze; **2.** drinking; **~ âlemi** orgy, booze-up, spree; **~ içmek** (*or* **kullanmak**) to drink, to tipple; **~ yasağı** prohibition of alcoholic beverages; **-ye düşkün** addicted to drink.

içkici 1. liquor dealer; **2.** drunkard, tippler.

içkili 1. intoxicated; **2.** licensed to sell (*or* serve) alcoholic drinks.

içkin 1. immanent; **2.** intrinsic, inherent.

içkulak ANAT inner ear.

içlem LOG comprehension, connotation, intension.

içlenmek to be affected (*-den* by), to take to heart.

içli 1. having an inside (*kernel*, *pulp*, *etc.*); **2.** oversensitive.

içlidışlı intimate, bosom, cheek by jowl; **~ olm.** to be bosom friends, to be on intimate terms.

içlik 1. interior; **2.** undergarment.

içme 1. *vn. of* **içmek**; **2.** mineral spring; **~ suyu** fresh (*or* drinking) water.

içmek, (-çer) 1. to drink; **2.** to smoke; **3.** to drink, to tipple; **4.** to absorb, to imbibe (*fluid*); **içtikleri su ayrı gitmez** *fig.* they are hail-fellow-well-met with each other.

içmeler mineral springs.

içmimar interior decorator.

içplazma BIOL endoplasm.

içsalgı hormone.

içsel 1. internal, inner; **2.** spiritual.

içten 1. from within; **2.** sincere, from the heart; **~ gelen** sincere; **~ yanmalı** MOT internal-combustion.

içtenlik sincerity.

içtepi PSYCH compulsion.

içtihat [. . -] opinion, conviction.

içtima, -*aı* [ā] **1.** meeting, gathering; assembly; **2.** MIL muster; **3.** AST conjunction; **~ etm. 1.** to meet, to assemble; **2.** MIL to muster.

içtimal [. . - -] social.

içtimaiyat, -*tı* [ā, ā] sociology.

içtinap [. . -] abstention, avoidance; **~ etm.** to refrain (*-den* from), to abstain (*-den* from), to avoid.

içtüzük bylaws, internal regulations, standing rules.

içyağı, -*nı* suet.

içyapı internal structure.

içyarıçap, -*pı* MATH apothem.

içyüz the inside story, the hidden side, the real truth, true colo(u)rs.

içzar BOT intine.

idadi [- - -] HIST senior high school.

idam [- -] **1.** capital punishment; **2.** execution of a death sentence; **~ cezası** death sentence; **~ etm.** to execute, to put to death; **~ hükmü** (*or* **kararı**) sentence of death; **-a mahkûm etm.** to condemn to death.

idame [ā] continuation; **~ etm.** to continue.

idamlık 1. capital (*crime*); **2.** condemned to death.

idare [ā] **1.** administration, management, direction; **2.** thriftiness, economy; **~ amiri** chief, head administrator; **~ etm. 1.** to manage, to administer, to direct, to conduct, to lead; to govern; to control; **2.** to economize, to make ends meet; **3.** to be enough, to suffice; **4.** F (*b-ni*) to handle *s.o.* with kid gloves; **5.** F to hush up, to cover up; **6.** to drive, to use (*car*); **7.** to stretch (*resources*); **~ etmez** it doesn't pay; **~ heyeti** (*or* **meclisi**) administrative committee; board of directors; **~ hukuku** administrative law.

idareci [ā] **1.** manager, administrator, organizer; **2.** tactful.

idarecilik [ā] **1.** administration; **2.** tact.

idarehane [ā, ā] administrative office.

idareimaslahat. *-tı* [. - . . . . .] muddling through.

idareli [ā] **1.** efficient, good at managing; **2.** thrifty; **3.** economical; **~ kullanmak** to economize, to husband.

idaresiz 1. inefficient, incompetent; **2.** wasteful, uneconomical.

idareten on a day-to-day basis, temporarily.

idari [. - -] administrative, managerial.

idbar [ā] adversity.

iddia [ā] **1.** claim, assertion, thesis; **2.** insistence; **3.** pretension; **4.** bet, wager; **~ etm. 1.** to claim; to assert, to allege; **2.** to insist; **3.** to pretend; **~ makamı** JUR the public prosecutor; **~ olunan şey** JUR question at issue; **-ya girişmek** (*or* **tutuşmak**) to bet, to wager.

iddiacı obstinate, assertive.

iddialı 1. assertive, presumptuous; **2.** disputed.

iddianame [ā, ā] JUR indictment.

iddiasız unassertive; unpretentious; simple, modest.

ideal, *-li* **1.** ideal; **2.** ideal, perfect.

idealist, *-ti* idealist(ic).

idealizm idealism.

identik MATH identical.

identiklik MATH identity.

ideoloji ideology.

ideolojik ideological.

idi 1. (*he, she, it*) was; **2.** and so on (*or* forth); like, such as.

idil *lit.* idyll.

idiş 1. gelding; **2.** gelded, castrated.

idman [ā] **1.** workout, training, exercise(s); **2.** fitness; **~ yapmak** to work out, to exercise, to train.

idmancı [ā] **1.** athlete in training; **2.** gymnast, gym teacher.

idmanlı [ā] **1.** fit, in good shape; **2.** (*bşe*) *fig.* experienced in *s.th.*

idrak, *-ki* [ā] **1.** perception, comprehension, understanding; **2.** attainment, reaching; **~ etm. 1.** to perceive, to apprehend, to comprehend; **2.** to attain, to reach.

idrakli [ā] perceptive, intelligent.

idraksiz dull-witted, unintelligent.

idrar [ā] urine; **~ torbası** (urinary) bladder; **~ yolu** urethra; **~ zorluğu** dysuria.

idrisağacı, *-nı* BOT St. Lucie's cherry, mahaleb (cherry).

İETT (*abbr. for* **İstanbul Elektrik, Tünel, Tramvay İşletmesi**) the Istanbul Electric Power, Funicular and Streetcar Board.

ifa [- -] fulfil(l)ment, performance; **~ etm.** to fulfil(l), to execute, to carry out, to perform.

ifade [ā] **1.** expression, explanation; **2.** statement; **3.** JUR deposition; **4.** *sl.* affair, business; **~ etm. 1.** to be of value (*or* significance); **2.** to explain, to express; **~ vermek** JUR to give evidence, to testify; **-sini almak 1.** JUR to interrogate, to grill, to cross-examine; **2.** *sl.* to beat up, to wallop.

ifadelendirmek [ā] to make meaningful (*or* expressive).

iffet, *-ti* **1.** chastity; **2.** honesty, uprightness.

iffetli 1. chaste, virtuous; **2.** honest, upright.

iffetsiz 1. unchaste; **2.** dishonest.

iflâh restoration, recovery; **~ olm.** to get well (*or* better); **~ olmaz 1.** incorrigible (*person*); **2.** hopeless (*situation*); **-ı kesilmek** F to be exhausted (*or* done for); **-ını kesmek** F to wear down.

iflas 1. bankruptcy, insolvency; **2.** *fig.* failure; **~ dairesi** bankruptcy office; **~ etm. 1.** to go bankrupt; **2.** *fig.* to fall flat (*idea, plan*); **~ kararı** decree of bankruptcy, adjudication of insolvency; **~ masası** bankrupt's assets.

ifrat, *-tı* [ā] **1.** excess, overdoing; **2.** exaggeration; **-a kaçmak** to overdo.

ifraz [ā] **1.** separation; **2.** JUR allotment; **3.** BIOL secretion; **~ etm. 1.** JUR to allot; **2.** BIOL to secrete.

ifrazat, *-tı* BIOL secretions.

ifrit, *-ti* [.-] malicious demon; **~ kesilmek** (*or* **olm.**) to fly off the handle.

ifsat, *-dı* [ā] **1.** subversion; **2.** corruption.

ifşa [ā] disclosure, divulgence; **~ etm.** to disclose, to divulge, to reveal, to expose.

iftar [ā] ECCL **1.** breaking one's fast; **2.** the evening meal during Ramadan; **~ etm.** to break one's fast; **~ topu** *gun fired at sunset during Ramadan as a signal for breaking the fast.*

iftarlık [ā] **1.** snack eaten when breaking the fast; **2.** suitable for eating when breaking the fast; **3.** *fig.* very little.

iftihar [ā] (laudable) pride; ~ *etm.* to take pride (*ile* in), to be proud (*ile* of); *-a geçmek* to get on the hono(u)r roll.

iftira [ā] slander, calumny; ~ *etm.* (*or* **atmak**) to slander, to calumniate, to blacken.

iftiracı [ā] slanderer.

iğ spindle.

iğbirar [ā] resentment.

iğde BOT oleaster, wild olive.

iğdemir MEC carpenter's chisel.

iğdiş 1. gelding; 2. castrated, gelded (*animal*); ~ *etm.* to castrate, to geld.

iğfal, *-li* [ā] rape; ~ *etm.* to rape.

iğne 1. needle; 2. pin; safety pin; 3. brooch, pin; 4. MEC pointer, needle; 5. ZOO stinger; 6. BOT style; 7. fish-hook; 8. syringe; 9. MED injection, shot; 10. *fig.* pinprick; ~ *atsan yere düşmez fig.* it is packed-out; ~ *deliği* the eye of a needle; ~ *deliğinden Hindistan'ı seyretmek fig.* to read between the lines; ~ *ile kuyu kazmak fig.* 1. to do a hard job without proper means; 2. to work on a slow and difficult task; ~ *ipliğe dönmek fig.* to become skin and bones, to be worn away to a shadow; ~ *vurmak* (*or yapmak*) (*b-ne*) to give *s.o.* an injection; ~ *yemiş köpeğe dönmek fig.* to become a bag of bones; *-den ipilğe kadar* down to the smallest detail; *-yi kendine batır, sonra çuvaldızı başkasına pro.* do as you would be done by.

iğneardı, *-nı* backstitch.

iğnedenlik *s.* **iğnelik**.

iğnelemek 1. to pin (*-e* to); 2. *fig.* to speak sarcastically.

iğnelenmek 1. *pass. of* **iğnelemek**; 2. to have pins and needles.

iğneleyici biting, sarcastic; ~ *söz* biting word.

iğneli 1. having a needle (*or* pin *or* thorn *or* sting); 2. pinned; 3. *fig.* biting, sarcastic (*words*); ~ *fıçı fig.* hot water; ~ *fıçıda olm.* to be in hot water; ~ *söz* sarcastic remark.

iğnelik pincushion.

iğneyapraklılar BOT Coniferales.

iğrenç, *-ci* detestable, repulsive, odious, loathsome, disgusting.

iğrendirmek to disgust.

iğrengen easily disgusted.

iğrenme *s.* **iğrenti**.

iğrenmek (*bşden*) to feel disgust at

s.th., to be disgusted with *s.th.*, to loathe.

iğrenti disgust, loathing.

ihale [ā] tender, bid; ~ *etm.* to let a contract to.

-i hali GR accusative case.

ihanet, *-ti* [ā] 1. treachery; 2. unfaithfulness, infidelity; ~ *etm.* 1. to betray; 2. to be unfaithful (*-e* to).

ihata [. - .] surrounding, enclosing; 2. comprehension; ~ *etm.* to surround.

ihatalı 1. vast; 2. knowledgeable.

ihbar [ā] denunciation, tip-off; ~ *etm.* 1. to denounce, to tip off, to inform (*-i* against); 2. to inform, to notify.

ihbarcı [ā] informer.

ihbariye [ā] 1. official notice, notification; 2. reward for informing against s.o.

ihbarlı informed; ~ *konuşma* TELEPH person-to person call.

ihbarname [ā, ā] = **ihbariye 1**.

ihdas [ā] creating, invention; ~ *etm.* to invent, to create, to introduce.

ihlal, *-li* infringement, violation; ~ *etm.* to infringe, to violate, to break (*law, treaty, etc.*).

ihmal, *-li* [ā] negligence, omission; ~ *etm.* to neglect, to omit.

ihmalci, **ihmalkâr** [ā] negligent, neglectful.

ihmalkârlık [ā] neglectfulness.

ihracat, *-tı* [. - -] exportation, exporting; ~ *malları* exports; ~ *yapmak* to export.

ihracatçı [ā, ā] exporter.

ihracatçılık [ā, ā] exporting, the export business.

ihraç, *-cı* [ā] 1. expulsion; 2. COM exportation, export; ~ *bankası* bank of issue; ~ *etm.* 1. to expel; 2. COM to export.

ihram [ā] 1. garment worn by pilgrims in Mecca; 2. Bedouin cloak; 3. cover (*for a sofa, etc.*); *-a girmek* to put on the pilgrim's garb.

ihraz [ā] obtainment; ~ *etm.* to obtain, to attain.

ihsan [ā] favo(ur), kindness, benevolence; ~ *etm.* to grant, to bestow.

ihsas [ā] 1. hint, insinuation, indication; 2. PHYS perception; ~ *etm.* to insinuate, to indicate.

ihtar [ā] warning; ~ *cezası* admonition; ~ *etm.* to warn, to remind; ~ *vermek* (*or -da bulunmak*) to warn, to remind.

ihtarname [ā, ā] **1.** official warning; **2.** JUR = **protesto**.

ihtifal, **-li** commemorative ceremony.

ihtikâr profiteering.

ihtilaç, **-cı** convulsion.

ihtilaf conflict, difference, disagreement, dispute; **-a düşmek** to conflict (ile with), to disagree (ile with).

ihtilaflı controversial.

ihtilal, **-li 1.** revolution, rebellion, riot; **2.** disturbance, disorder; **~ yapmak** to raise a rebellion.

ihtilalci rebel, revolutionary.

ihtilam [ā] nocturnal emission.

ihtilas embezzlement; **~ etm.** to embezzle.

ihtilat, **-tı 1.** MED complication; **2.** social intercourse (or relations); **~ etm.** MED to lead to complication.

ihtimal, **-li** [ā] **1.** probability; **2.** probably; **~ vermek** to consider likely, to regard as possible; **-ki** probably; **her -e karşı** just to be safe.

ihtimali [ā] probable.

ihtimam [ā] care, carefulness; **~ etm.** (or **göstermek**) to take great pains (-e over, with).

ihtimamlı [ā] painstaking, meticulous.

ihtimamsız [ā] careless.

ihtira, **-aı** [ā] invention; **~ beratı** patent (right).

ihtirak, **-kı** [ā] combustion.

ihtiram [ā] veneration, reverence; **~ bölüğü** guard of hono(u)r; **~ duruşu** standing at attention.

ihtiras [ā] ambition, greed, passion.

ihtiraslı [ā] ambitious, greedy, passionate.

ihtiraz [ā] avoidance; wariness, caution; **~ kaydı** reservation.

ihtisar [ā] abbreviation.

ihtisas [ā] specialization, specialty; **~ yapmak** to specialize (-de in), to major (-de in).

ihtişam [ā] splendo(u)r, magnificence, pomp, grandeur.

ihtişamlı [ā] splendid, magnificent, pompous.

ihtiva [ā] inclusion, containment; **~ etm. 1.** to contain, to hold; **2.** to include, to comprise.

ihtiyaç, **-cı** [ā] **1.** need, necessity, want; **2.** poverty; **~ duymak** to feel the need (-e for); **-ı karşılamak** to serve (or meet) a need; **-ı olm.** (bşe) to need s.th., to be in need (or want) of s.th.

ihtiyar[1] [ā] **1.** old, aged (person); **2.** old

person, Am. old-timer **~ meclisi** (or **heyeti**) JUR village council.

ihtiyar[2] [ā] selection, choice, option; **~ etm. 1.** to choose, to select; **2.** to endure, to put up with, to bear with.

ihtiyari [. . - -] optional.

ihtiyarlamak to grow (or get) old, to age.

ihtiyarlatmak to age.

ihtiyarlık old age, senility; **~ sigortası** social security, old-age insurance.

ihtiyat, **-tı** [ā] **1.** precaution, caution; **2.** reserve; **~ akçesi** reserve fund, nest egg; **~ kaydı ile** with some doubt; **~ kuvvetleri** reserve forces.

ihtiyaten [ā] **1.** as a reserve; **2.** as a precaution.

ihtiyati [. . - -] precautionary; **~ haciz** JUR provisional distraint; **~ tedbirler** precautionary measures.

ihtiyatkâr [ā] cautious, prudent, foresighted.

ihtiyatlı s. **ihtiyatkâr**; **~ davranmak** to act prudently.

ihtiyatsız imprudent, incautious, rash; improvident.

ihtizaz [ā] vibration; tremor.

ihvan [ā] **1.** friends; **2.** brethren, fellow members.

ihya [ā] **1.** revitalization, resuscitation; **2.** fig. revival; **~ etm. 1.** to revitalize, to enliven; **2.** fig. to revive, to revivify.

ihzar [ā] preparation.

ihzari [. - -] preparatory.

ikame [ā] **1.** substitution; **2.** establishment, appointment; **3.** opening (a law case); **~ etm. 1.** to substitute; **2.** to establish, to appoint; **3.** to open (a law case).

ikamet, **-ti** [ā] residence, dwelling; **~ etm.** to live, to reside, to dwell; **~ tezkeresi** JUR residence permit.

ikametgâh [ā] (place of) residence, legal domicile; **~ kâğıdı** (or **ilmühaberi**) residence paper.

ikaz [- -] warning; **~ etm.** to warn.

ikbal, **-li** [ā] **1.** prosperity, success; **2.** obs. wish, desire; **~ düşkünü** person who has fallen from riches to poverty.

iken while, whilst.

iki two; **~ ahbap çavuşlar** F inseparable friends; **~ arada kalmak** to be at a loss as to whom to believe; **~ aslan bir posta sığmaz** pro. two stars keep not their motion in one sphere; **~ ateş arasında kalmak** to be caught between two fires; **~ ayağını bir pabuca**

sokmak F to put in a flurry; **~ büklüm olm.** *fig.* to double up; **~ cami arasında kalmış beynamaz** *fig.* fallen between two stools; **~ çift laf** (*or* **söz**) a word or two; **~ dirhem bir çekirdek** F dressed to kill, dressed (up) to the nines, dressed up like a dog's dinner; **~ eli kanda olsa** *fig.* no matter how pressed he is; **~ elim yanıma gelsin!** I swear I'm telling the truth; **gözü ~ çeşme ağlamak** to cry buckets; **~ günde** in (*or* within) two days; **~ kat olm.** to double up; **~ misli** twofold; **~ nokta colon**; **~ ucunu bir araya getirememek** to be unable to make both ends meet; **~ yakası bir araya gelmemek** to be unable to make both ends meet; **~ zamanlı motor** MEC two-stroke engine; **-de bir** (*or* **birde**) frequently, all the time; **-miz** the two of us; **-si aynı kapıya çıkar** it is as broad as it is long; **-ye ayırmak** to halve.

ikianlamlı ambiguous, equivocal.
ikicanlı pregnant.
ikicinsli, ikicinslikli bisexual.
ikideğerli bivalent.
ikidilli bilingual.
ikidüzlemli MATH dihedral.
ikieşeyli bisexual.
ikikatlı duplex apartment.
ikilem *log* dilemma.
ikilemek 1. to make two (*or* a pair); **2.** to plow twice (*field*).
ikileşmek to become two, to be doubled.
ikili 1. having two parts; **2.** double, dual; **3.** bilateral; **4.** *cards*; two; **5.** MUS duet; **6.** MUS duo; **~ anlaşma** bilateral treaty.
ikilik 1. discord, disagreement; **2.** MUS half note.
ikinci 1. second; **2.** secondary; **3.** vice-, sub-; **~ bir emre kadar** until further notice; **~ hamur kâğıt** lightly glazed paper; **~ mevki** (*or* **sınıf**) **1.** second-class; **2.** the second-class section (*in a boat, etc.*).
ikincil secondary.
ikindi midafternoon; **~ ezanı** the call to afternoon prayer; **~ kahvaltısı** afternoon tea, snack; **~ namazı** *isl.* the afternoon prayer.
ikindiyin [. . x .] F in the afternoon.
ikişekilli dimorphic, dimorphous.
ikişer two at a time; two each; **~ ~** two by two, in twos.
ikiyanlı bilateral.

ikiyaşayışlı BIOL amphibian, amphibious.
ikiyüzlü 1. *fig.* two-faced, hypocritical; **2.** double-faced (*cloth*).
ikiyüzlülük hypocrisy.
ikiz 1. twins; **2.** a twin; **3.** twinned; **~ doğurmak 1.** to twin; **2.** *fig.* to have a devil of a hard time.
ikizkenar MATH isosceles; **~ üçgen** isosceles triangle; **~ yamuk** isosceles trapezoid.
ikizler AST the Twins, Gemini.
ikizli 1. having twins; **2.** with two handles; **3.** of two kinds; **4.** LOG ambiguous.
iklim climate.
iklimleme aygıtı air conditioner.
iklimsel climatic.
ikmal, -li [ā] **1.** completion; **2.** replenishment, supplying; **3.** MIL reinforcement; supply; **4.** (*imtihanı*) make-up examination; **~ etm. 1.** to finish, to complete; **2.** to replenish, to supply; **-e kalmak** to have to take a make-up examination.
ikna, -aı [ā] persuasion; **~ etm.** to persuade, to convince; **~ olm.** to be persuaded.
ikon icon.
ikrah [ā] disgust, detestation, abhorrence; **~ etm.** to detest, to loathe, to abhor; **~ getirmek** to begin to detest.
ikrahlık = ikrah.
ikram [ā] **1.** hono(u)ring; **2.** discount; **3.** s.th. offered a guest (*food, drink*); **~ etm. 1.** to offer, to serve, to help s.o. to (*food, drink*); **2.** to discount.
ikramiye [ā] **1.** bonus, gratuity; **2.** prize (*in a lottery*).
ikramiyeli [ā] **1.** with a premium; **2.** with a prize.
ikrar [ā] avowal, declaration, confession; **~ etm.** to confess, to declare, to attest.
ikraz [ā] loan; **~ etm.** to lend (*money*).
iksir [. -] elixir.
iktibas [ā] quotation; **~ etm.** to quote.
iktidar [ā] **1.** power, capacity, ability; **2.** POL the ruling party, government; **3.** potency, virility; **~ mevkii** the position of being in power; **~ partisi** the party in power; **-da olm.** POL to be in power.
iktidarlı [ā] powerful, capable.
iktidarsız 1. weak; incompetent; **2.** impotent.
iktidarsızlık 1. weakness; incapacity; **2.** impotence.

iktifa [ā] contentment; ~ *etm.* to be content (*ile* with).

iktisadi [. . - -] 1. economic; 2. economical; ~ *devlet kuruluşu* (*or teşekkülü*) corporation in which the government is the majority stock-holder; ~ *ve ticari ilimler akademisi* academy of economic and commercial sciences.

iktisadiyat, *-tı* [ā, ā] economy, economic state (*of a country*).

iktisap, *-bı* [ā] acquisition; ~ *etm.* to acquire.

iktisat, *-dı* [ā] 1. economics, economy; 2. economy, thrift, saving; ♀ *Fakültesi* the School of Economics.

iktisatçı economist.

iktiza [ā] necessity, need; ~ *etm.* to be necessary.

il 1. province; 2. country, nation; ~ *genel meclisi* provincial assembly; ~ *özel idaresi* the administration of a province.

ila [. -] from ... to ..., between ... and ...; *üç ~ beş kişi* between three and five people.

ilaç, *-cı* 1. medicine, drug; 2. CHEM chemical; 3. cure, remedy; 4. insecticide, pesticide; ~ *içmek* to take medicine.

ilaçbilim pharmacology.

ilaçlamak 1. to apply medicine (to); 2. to disinfect; 3. to apply insecticide (to).

ilaçlı 1. medicated; 2. treated (*with pesticide*).

ilah god, deity.

ilahe goddess.

ilahi 1. [. - -] hymn, psalm; 2. [. x .] my God!

ilahî divine, heavenly.

ilahîleştirmek to deify.

ilahiyat, *-tı* [ā, ā] theology, divinity; ♀ *Fakültesi* the School of Theology.

ilahiyatçı theologian.

ilam [- -] writ.

ilamaşallah 1. until God knows when; 2. bravo!

ilan [- -] 1. notice; ~ *tahtası* message board *on a website*; 2. advertisement; 3. proclamation, declaration; ~ *etm.* 1. to declare, to announce; 2. to advertise; 3. to proclaim, to declare; ~ *vermek* to insert an advertisement (*in a newspaper*); *-ı aşk* declaration of love; *-ı aşk etm.* to declare one's love (*-e* to).

ilancılık advertising.

ilarya zoo a kind of mullet.

ilave 1. addition, increase; 2. supplement; ~ *etm.* to add (*-e* to).

ilaveten in addition, additionally.

ilbay *s. vali.*

ilçe administrative district (*within an il*), borough.

ilçebay *s. kaymakam.*

ile 1. with, together with; 2. and; 3. by means of, by.

ilelebet forever.

ilenç curse, malediction.

ilenmek to curse, to execrate.

ilerde *s. ileride.*

ileri 1. front part; 2. forward; 3. fore, front, forward; 4. *fig.* advanced, progressive; 5. fast (*clock*); 6. forward!; ~ *almak* 1. to move forward; 2. to put forward (*clock*); 3. to promote (*a person*); ~ *atılmak* 1. to rush ahead, to spring forward; 2. *fig.* to act with courage; ~ *gelenler* notables; ~ *gelmek* to result (*-den* from), to be due (*-den* to); ~ *gitmek* 1. to go forward, to advance; 2. to be running fast (*clock*); 3. *fig.* to go too far; ~ *karakol* MIL advance outpost, outlying picket; ~ *kol* MIL vanguard; ~ *sürmek* 1. to drive forwards; 2. to put forward (*idea*); 3. to insist (on); *-yi görmek* *fig.* to take the long view, to be farsighted (*or* farseeing).

ilerici progressive.

ilericilik progressiveness.

ileride 1. in the future, later on; 2. ahead, further on; 3. in front.

ilerlek advanced, developed.

ilerlemek 1. to go forward, to move ahead, to advance; 2. to improve, to get better; 3. to progress, to develop; 4. to pass, to go by (*time*).

ileti 1. message; 2. communiqué.

iletim transmission, transmittal.

iletimli transmitted; ~ *yayın* live broadcast.

iletişim communication.

iletken 1. PHYS conductor; 2. PHYS conductive.

iletkenlik PHYS conductivity.

iletki MATH protractor.

iletmek 1. to transmit, to convey; 2. PHYS to conduct.

ilga [ā] 1. annulment, nullification; 2. abolition; 3. repeal; ~ *etm.* 1. to annul; 2. to abolish; 3. to repeal.

ilgeç GR postposition.

ilgi 1. relation, connection; **2.** interest, concern; **3.** GR relational, relative; **4.** CHEM affinity; ~ **çekici** interesting; ~ **çekmek** to draw attention, to arouse interest; ~ **duymak** to be interested (-e in); ~ **göstermek** to show an interest (-e in); ~ **toplamak** to arouse interest, to attract attention; ~ **zamiri** GR relative pronoun.

ilgilendirmek 1. to interest; to concern; **2.** to arouse s.o.'s interest (ile in).

ilgilenmek (bşle) to be interested in s.th., to pay attention to s.th., to show concern for s.th.

ilgili 1. interested (ile in); **2.** concerned (ile with), involving; **3.** relevant, involved, concerned; ~ **olm.** to involve, to be concerned (ile with); to pertain (ile to); **-ler** those concerned.

ilginç interesting.

ilgisiz 1. indifferent; **2.** irrelevant.

ilgisizlik 1. indifference; **2.** irrelevance.

ilhak, -kı [ā] annexation; ~ **etm.** to annex, to add (-e to).

ilham [ā] inspiration; ~ **almak** to be inspired (-den by); ~ **etm.** to inspire; ~ **perisi** muse; ~ **vermek** to inspire.

ilhan 1. emperor; **2.** ♀ mf.

ilik, -ği 1. ANAT bone marrow; **2.** buttonhole; button loop; ~ **gibi 1.** delicious; **2.** sl. as pretty as a picture (girl); ~ **gibi pişmiş** (or **olmuş**) done to a turn; **iliğine işlemek** (or **geçmek**) **1.** to penetrate to one's marrow (cold); **2.** to drench to the skin; **3.** to touch to the quick; **iliğine kadar ıslanmak** to be soaked to the skin, to get wet through; **iliğini kemirmek** (b-nin) to affect s.o. deeply; **iliğini kurutmak** (b-nin) fig. to wear s.o. out.

iliklemek to button up.

ilikli 1. containing marrow; **2.** buttoned up.

ilim, -imi science; ~ **adamı** scientist.

ilimcilik scientism.

ilinti 1. relevance, connection; **2.** distress.

ilintili 1. related, connected; relevant; **2.** distressed, upset.

ilişik 1. attached, enclosed; **2.** related, connected; **3.** connection, relation; **ilişiği kalmamak** to be through (ile with), to have no further connection (ile with); **ilişiği olm.** to be related (ile to), to be connected (ile with); **ilişiğini kesmek 1.** to sever one's con-

nection (ile with); **2.** to dismiss, to discharge (ile from).

ilişkili related, concerned, connected.

ilişiksiz unattached, free, independent.

ilişki 1. relation, connection; **2.** communications; ~ **kurmak** to establish relations (ile with).

ilişkili related (ile to).

ilişkin concerning, regarding, relating (-e to).

ilişkisiz unrelated.

ilişmek 1. to graze, to touch; **2.** to meddle (-e with), to touch; **3.** to point out; **4.** to bother, to disturb; **5.** to perch, to sit on the edge.

iliştirmek to attach, to fasten (-e to).

ilk, -ki 1. (the) first; **2.** initial; **3.** primary; ~ **adım** first step; ~ **ağızda** the first time, at the first attempt; ~ **defa** for the first time; ~ **fırsatta** at the first opportunity; ~ **görüşte** at first sight; ~ **göz ağrısı 1.** first child; **2.** F first love, old flame; ~ **tahkikat** JUR preliminary inquiry; ~ **yardım** first aid; ~ **yardım çantası** first aid kit.

ilkah [ā] fertilization, fecundation, insemination; ~ **etm.** to fecundate, to impregnate.

ilkbahar spring.

ilkçağ antiquity.

ilke 1. principle, tenet; **2.** element; **3.** postulate, assumption; **4.** fundamental, essential.

ilkel 1. primitive; **2.** primary.

ilkeleştirmek to adopt as a principle.

ilkelleştirmek to make primitive.

ilkellik primitiveness.

ilkgirişim initiative.

ilkin [x .] **1.** in the first place, first; **2.** at first.

ilkkânun obs. December.

ilkokul primary school.

ilköğretim primary education.

ilkönce first (of all).

ilkteşrin obs. October.

illa [x -], **illaki 1.** whatever happens, come what may; **2.** or else; **3.** especially, particularly; ~ **ve lakin** on the other hand, nevertheless.

illallah [x . -] I'm fed up!; ~ **demek** to be fed up.

ille [x .] s. **illa.**

illet, -ti 1. illness, disease; **2.** defect, fault; **3.** addiction; **4.** PHLS reason, cause.

illetli 1. sickly, diseased; **2.** faulty, defective.

illiyet, -ti causality.

ilmek[1] **1.** to fasten (*or* tie) loosely; **2.** to knot; **3.** to graze.

ilmek[2] *s.* **ilmik.**

ilmen scientifically speaking.

ilmi scientific.

ilmihal, -li [ā] catechism.

ilmik 1. loop; **2.** noose; ~ **atmak** to loop.

ilmiklemek to loop.

ilmühaber 1. certification, certificate of proof; **2.** receipt.

iltibas [ā] **1.** confusion (*between two similar things*); **2.** ambiguity; **-a yol açmak** to give rise to confusion.

iltica [ā] taking (*or* seeking) refuge; ~ **etm.** to take refuge (**-e** with, in), to seek asylum (**-e** in); ~ **hakkı** right of asylum.

iltifat, -tı [ā] **1.** favo(u)r; **2.** compliment; ~ **etm. 1.** to compliment; to flatter; **2.** to enjoy, to like.

iltihak, -kı [ā] adherence, joining; ~ **etm.** to join, to attach o.s. (**-e** to).

iltihap, -bı [ā] MED inflammation.

iltihaplanmak [. . - . .] MED to get inflamed (*or* infected), to fester.

iltihaplı MED inflamed, infected.

iltimas [ā] protection, patronage, favo(u)ritism, pull; ~ **etm.** to show favo(u)ritism (**-e** towards), to favo(u)r; **-ı olm.** to have s.o. at one's back, to have a pull.

iltimasçı [ā] backer, patron, protector.

iltimaslı favo(u)red, privileged.

iltizam [ā] **1.** favo(u)ritism, partiality; **2.** finding necessary; **3.** tax farming; ~ **etm.** to favo(u)r.

İlyada the Iliad.

im sign, signal; symbol.

ima [- -] hint, allusion, innuendo; ~ **etm.** to hint (**at**), to imply, to allude (**to**).

imaj image.

imal, -li [ā] **1.** manufacture, production; **2.** product; ~ **etm.** to manufacture, to produce, to make.

imalat, -tı [- - -] **1.** products, manufactured goods; **2.** production.

imalatçı manufacturer.

imalathane [- - - - .] workshop, factory, shop.

imalı [- - .] allusive, implicit.

imam 1. imam; **2.** religious leader; **3.** successor to the Prophet; ~ **hatip okulu** secondary school for the training of Islamic religious personnel; ~

imla

kayığı *sl.* coffin; ~ **nikâhı** wedding performed by an imam; ~ **suyu** *sl.* raki.

imambayıldı *a dish of eggplants with oil and onions.*

imame [ā] junction bead in a string of prayer beads.

iman [- -] **1.** faith, belief; **2.** religion; ~ **getirmek** to become a Muslim; ~ **sahibi** man of faith, believer; ~ **tahtası** F breastbone; **-a getirmek** (*b-ni*) **1.** to convert *s.o.* to Islam; **2.** *fig.* to persuade *s.o.* by force, to subdue *s.o.*; **-ı gevremek** (*or* **ağlamak**) F to wear o.s. out; **-ı yok! 1.** damn him!; **2.** the callous swine!; **-ım** *sl.* hey, you!; **-ına kadar** up to the brim; **-ına yandığım** F damned; **-ını gevretmek** to wear out.

imanlı [- - .] religious, faithful.

imansız 1. unbelieving, atheist; **2.** unbeliever; **3.** *fig.* cruel, unjust, wicked.

imar [- -] public works, development; ~ **etm.** to improve, to render prosperous; ~ **planı** zoning and construction plan; ♀ **ve İskân Bakanlığı** Ministry of Development and Housing.

imaret, -ti [ā], **imarethane** [ā] soup kitchen (*for the poor*).

imbat, -tı daytime summer sea breaze.

imbik still, retort; **-ten çekmek** to distill.

imdat, -dı [ā] **1.** help, assistance, aid; **2.** help!; ~ **freni** RAIL emergency brake; ~ **işareti** SOS signal; ~ **kapısı** emergency exit; **-ına yetişmek** (*b-nin*) to come to *s.o.'s* rescue.

imdi [x .] **1.** therefore, so, thus; **2.** now.

imece cooperation for the community or one of its members.

imge 1. image; **2.** dream.

imgelemek to imagine.

imgesel imaginary.

imha [ā] destruction, eradication; ~ **etm.** to destroy, to eradicate, to annihilate, to obliterate.

imik ANAT throat.

imkân 1. possibility; **2.** opportunity, chance; ~ **dahilinde** as far as possible; ~ **vermek** to give an opportunity, to give a chance, to make possible; **-ı yok!** it's impossible (*or* out of question)!

imkânsız impossible.

imla 1. spelling, orthography; **2.** dictation; **3.** filling up; ~ **etm. 1.** to dictate; **2.** to fill (up); ~ **yanlışı** spelling mistake; **-sı bozuk 1.** bad at spelling; **2.** misspelled; **-ya gelmemek** *fig.* to go beyond all reason.

imlemek 1. to indicate; **2.** to hint (**at**), to imply.

imparator [. . x .] emperor.

imparatoriçe [. . . x . .] empress.

imparatoriuk 1. empire; **2.** emperorship.

imrendirmek to arouse s.o.'s appetite (*or* desire) (*-e* for).

imrenmek 1. to long (*-e* for), to feel an appetite (*-e* for); **2.** to desire, to envy, to covet.

imrenti desire, envy.

imsak, -kı [ā] **1.** fasting, abstinence; **2.** hour at which the daily Ramadan fast begins.

imsel symbolic.

imtihan [ā] examination, test, trial; **~ etm.** to test, to examine; **~ olm.** to take (*or* sit for *or* go in for) an examination; **~ vermek 1.** to pass an examination; **2.** *fig.* to get off scot-free; **-da kalmak** to fail (*or* flunk) in an examination.

imtina, -aı [ā] avoidance; **~ etm.** to avoid, to refrain (*-den* from).

imtiyaz [ā] **1.** privilege; **2.** government concession, franchise; **~ sahibi 1.** concessionaire, concessioner; **2.** licensee; **~ vermek** to give s.o. the privilege.

imtiyazlı 1. privileged; **2.** licensed.

imtizaç harmony, compatibility; **~ etm. 1.** to harmonize; **2.** to get on well together.

imyazım stenography.

imza [ā] signature; **~ atmak** (*or* **etm.**) to sign; **~ sahibi** signatory; **~ toplamak** to gather signatures.

imzalamak to sign.

imzalı signed.

imzasız unsigned.

in¹ **1.** den, lair; **2.** cave.

in²: **~ cin yok** (*or* **top oynuyor**) there is nobody around, there isn't a soul around.

inadına [x - . .] out of obstinacy (*or* spite).

inan 1. belief; **2.** faith, confidence, trust; **~ olsun!** take it from me!, take my word!

inanç, -cı 1. belief; **2.** trust, confidence.

inançlı believing, faithful.

inançsız unbelieving.

inandırıcı convincing, plausible.

inandırmak to convince, to persuade.

inanılır believable, credible.

inanılmaz unbelievable, incredible.

inanmak 1. to believe, to trust; **2.** to have faith in (*God*).

inansız faithless.

inat, -dı [ā] **1.** obstinacy, stubbornness; **2.** F obstinate, stubborn, pigheaded; **~ etm.** to be obstinate; **-ı,~** F as stubborn as a mule; **-ı tutmak** to have a fit of obstinacy.

inatçı obstinate, stubborn, pigheaded.

inatçılık obstinacy, stubbornness.

inatlaşmak to behave stubbornly towards each other.

inayet, -ti [ā] kindness, benevolence; **~ etm.** to do a favo(u)r (*-e* to); **~ ola!** may God help you!

inayetli [ā] kind, gracious.

ince 1. slender, slim; **2.** thin, fine, small; **3.** refined, graceful, subtle; **4.** delicate, intricate; **5.** sensitive, delicate; **6.** dainty; **7.** high-pitched (*voice*); **8.** front (*vowel*); **~ elemek** to sift fine; **~ eleyip sık dokumak** *fig.* to split hairs; **~ görüşlü** sharp-witted; **~ kesim** small boned; **~ ses** high (*or* treble) voice; **-den -ye** meticulously.

inceağrı twinge.

incebağırsak small intestine.

incecik very slender (*or* thin).

inceleme *vn. of* **incelemek**, *part.* examination, investigation.

incelemek to examine, to inspect, to scan, to scrutinize.

incelik 1. thinness, slenderness, slimness; **2.** delicacy, fineness; **3.** tact, finesse, delicacy; **4.** subtlety; **5.** detail.

incelmek 1. to become thin; **2.** to be thinned (*paint*); **3.** to lose weight; **4.** F to try to appear refined.

inceltici thinner.

inceltmek 1. to make thin; **2.** to thin (*paint*).

incesaz MUS *group of musicians who perform classical Turkish music.*

inci pearl; **~ avı** pearl fishing; **~ avcısı** pearl fisher (*or* diver); **~ gibi** pearly (*teeth*).

inciçiçeği, -ni BOT lily-of-the-valley.

incik 1. hurt, injured; **2.** ANAT shin; **3.** P shinbone; **4.** P ankle.

incik boncuk cheap tawdry jewelry.

İncil *pr. n.* **1.** the New Testament; **2.** Gospel, Evangel.

incili pearly, pearled.

incinmek 1. to be hurt (*or* injured); **2.** to be strained (*muscle*); **3.** *fig.* to be

insaflı

offended (*-den* by).

incir BOT fig (tree); ~ **çekirdeğini dol-durmaz** *fig.* trifling, insignificant.

incitici painful, offensive.

incitmebeni P cancer.

incitmek 1. to hurt, to injure; to strain; **2.** *fig.* to offend.

indeks index.

indi subjective, personal.

indifa, -aı [ā] eruption; ~ **etm.** to erupt.

indirgeme reduction.

indirgemek MATH, CHEM to reduce.

indirim discount, reduction.

indirimli 1. reduced, discount (*price*); **2.** at a reduced price; ~ **satış** sale.

indirmek *caus. of* **inmek**, *part.* **1.** to lower, to bring down, to get down, to take down; **2.** to land, to deliver, to plant (*slap, blow*); **3.** to reduce (*price, etc.*); **4.** to destroy, to wreck; **5.** IT to download; **indirilen dosya** download.

indiyum CHEM indium.

İndonezya *pr. n.* Indonesia.

indükleç ELECT inductor.

indükleme PHYS induction.

indüklemek PHYS to induce.

ineç, -ci GEOL syncline.

inek 1. ZOO cow; **2.** *sl.* swot, *Am.* grind; **3.** *sl.* loose woman, tart.

ineklemek *sl.* to swot up, *Am.* to grind, to bone.

ineklik 1. cowshed; **2.** *sl.* imbecility.

infaz [ā] execution, carrying out; ~ **etm.** to execute, to carry out.

infial, -li [ā] indignation, resentment.

infilak, -kı explosion, ~ **etm.** to explode, to burst.

İngiliz [x . .] **1.** Englishman; English-woman; **2.** English; ~ **anahtarı** MEC monkey wrench, spanner; ~ **lirası** pound sterling; ♀ **Uluslar Birliği** the British Commonwealth of Nations.

İngilizce 1. English, the English lan-guage; **2.** in English.

İngiltere [. . x .] *pr. n.* **1.** England; **2.** F Great Britain.

ingin[1] low.

ingin[2] (head) cold.

inginlik 1. lowness; **2.** *fig.* weakness.

-in hali GR the genitive case.

inhiraf [ā] deviation deflection; ~ **etm.** to deviate, to be deflected (*-den* from).

inhisar [ā] **1.** restriction, limitation; **2.** monopoly; ~ **etm.** to be restricted (*or* limited) (*-e* to); **-a almak** to monopo-

lize.

inik 1. pulled down, lowered (*curtain, etc.*); flat (*tire*); **2.** *s.* **encek**, ~ **deniz** GEOGR low tide.

inikâs 1. PHYS reflection; **2.** echo; **3.** COM reaction; ~ **etm.** PHYS to echo.

inildemek to groan, to moan, to whim-per.

inilti groan, moan, whimper.

inim inim: ~ **inlemek** to whimper (*or* moan *or* groan) bitterly.

inisiyatif initiative.

iniş 1. *vn. of* **inmek**; **2.** downward slope; ~ **aşağı** downhill, downwards; ~ **çıkış 1.** descent and ascent; **2.** COM rise and fall, fluctuation; ~ **takımı** AVIA undercarriage, undercart, land-ing gear.

inişli sloping downwards; ~ **çıkışlı** (*or* **yokuşlu**) hilly (*road*).

inkâr denial; ~ **etm.** to deny.

inkıbaz [ā] constipation.

inkılap, -bı revolution.

inkılapçı revolutionary.

inkıraz [ā] collapse, end, extinction; ~ **bulmak** collapse, to end, to fall.

inkıta, -aı cessation; **-a uğramak** to cease.

inkisar [ā] **1.** refraction; **2.** curse, mal-ediction; ~ **etm.** to curse.

inkişaf [ā] development (*a.* MATH); ~ **etm.** to develop.

inlemek 1. to groan, to whimper, to moan; **2.** to resound.

inletmek 1. *caus. of* **inlemek**; **2.** *fig.* to torture, to torment.

inme 1. *vn. of* **inmek**; **2.** MED stroke, ap-oplexy, paralysis; **3.** GEOGR ebb tide; ~ **inmek** MED to have a stroke.

inmek, (-er) 1. to descend, to come (*or* go) down; **2.** to get off (*a bus, plane, train, ship*); to get out of (*a car*); to dismount from (*a horse*); **3.** to dimin-ish, to decrease, to recede. to die down; **4.** to land (*-e* at) (*plane*); **5.** to move down (*-e* to); **6.** to stay at (*a hotel*); **7.** MED to be paralyzed; **8.** to collapse (*wall, etc.*); **9.** to reduce (*price*); **10.** to fall (*prices*); **11.** *sl.* to hit, to strike.

inmeli MED paralyzed, apoplectic.

inorganik CHEM inorganic.

insaf [ā] **1.** justice, fairness; **2.** have a heart!; ~ **etm. 1.** to take pity (*-e* on); **2.** to have a heart; **-ına kalmış** it's up to his discretion.

insaflı [ā] equitable, just, fair.

insafsız 1. unmerciful, merciless; **2.** unjust, unfair.

insan [ā] **1.** person, human being; **2.** person, man; **3.** moral, decent, good; **4.** *fig.* upright (*or* decent) person; ~ **doğduğu yerde değil, doyduğu yer- de** *pro.* not where one is bred, but where he is fed; ~ **hakları** human rights; ~ **müsveddesi** inhuman person; ~ **sarrafı** a good judge of people; **-ın adı çıkacağına canı çıksın** *pro.* give a dog a bad name (and hang him).

insanbilim anthropology.

insanca [. - .] **1.** humanely, decently; **2.** humane (*act*).

insancıl 1. humanistic; **2.** domestic (*animal*).

insani [. - -] **1.** human; **2.** humane; **3.** humanely.

insaniyet, -ti [ā] **1.** humanity, mankind; **2.** humaneness, kindness.

insaniyetli humane, kind, benevolent.

insaniyetsiz inhuman.

insanlık [ā] *s.* **insaniyet;** ~ **bilmez** inhuman, cruel; **-tan çıkmak 1.** to become a bag of bones; **2.** to become inhuman.

insanoğlu, -nu man, human being.

insanüstü, -nü [ā] superhuman.

insicam [ā] consistency, coherence.

insicamlı [ā] consistent, coherent.

insicamsız [ā] inconsistent, incoherent.

insiyak, -kı [ā] instinct.

insiyaki [. . - -] instinctive.

inşa [ā] **1.** construction; **2.** writing, literary composition; ~ **etm.** to build, to construct.

inşaat, -tı [ā, ā] (*pl. of* **inşa**) building, construction; ~ **mühendisi** civil engineer.

inşaatçı [ā, ā] builder, contractor.

inşallah [x . -] **1.** I hope that ...; **2.** I hope so.

inşat, -dı [ā] recitation; declamation; ~ **etm.** to recite; to declaim.

integral MATH integral.

intelek intellect.

intelektüalizm intellectualism.

internet IT Internet, F net; **-te gezin- mek** to surf the net.

İnterpol, -lü Interpol.

intiba, -aı [ā] impression; ~ **bırakmak** to make an impression (*-de* on).

intibak, -kı [ā] **1.** adaptation, adjustment, conformation, accommodation; **2.** suitability; ~ **etm.** to adjust

o.s. (*-e* to), to accustom o.s. (*-e* to); to conform (*-e* to).

intibaksız maladjusted.

intifa, -aı [ā] benefit, advantage, gain; ~ **etm.** (*bşden*) to profit from *s.th.*; ~ **hakkı** usufruct; ~ **senetleri** preferred shares.

intihar [ā] suicide; ~ **bombacısı** suicide bomber; ~ **etm.** to commit suicide.

intikal, -li [ā] **1.** transition, passage; **2.** comprehension, grasp; **3.** inference; **4.** transfer (*by inheritance or sale*); ~ **devresi** transition period; ~ **etm. 1.** to pass to another place; **2.** to perceive, to grasp; **3.** to pass by inheritance, to be inherited (*by*).

intikam [ā] revenge, vengeance; ~ **al- mak** to take revenge (*-den* on), to revenge o.s. (*-den* on), to avenge o.s. (*-den* on).

intikamcı [ā] vengeful, vindictive.

intisap, -bı [ā] joining; affiliation; membership; ~ **etm.** to join, to become a member (*-e* of).

intişar [ā] **1.** diffusion; **2.** publication, dissemination; ~ **etm. 1.** to spread, to radiate; **2.** to be published, to come out.

intizam [ā] order, orderliness, tidiness; **-a sokmak** to tidy up.

intizamlı [ā] tidy, orderly, regular.

intizamsız [ā] untidy, disorderly, irregular.

intizamsızlık [ā] untidiness, disorder.

intizar [ā] **1.** curse; **2.** expectation; ~ **etm.** to curse.

inzibat, -tı [ā] **1.** military police; **2.** discipline; ~ **eri** military policeman.

inziva [ā] seclusion; **-ya çekilmek** to seclude o.s.

ip, -pi 1. rope, string, cord; **2.** P thread; ~ **atlamak** to jump rope, to skip; ~ **cambazı** ropedancer, tightrope walker; ~ **kaçkını** bad egg, tough; ~ **merdi- ven** rope ladder; ~ **takmak** to try to harm s.o. behind his back; **-e çekmek** to hang; **-e gelesice!** damned!; **-e sa- pa gelmez** inconsistent, nonsensical; **-e un sermek** *fig.* to make vain excuses; **-i çürük** *fig.* undependable; **-i kırmak** *sl.* to run away, to take to one's heels; **-ini çekmek** (*b-nin*) *fig.* to keep s.o. under control; **-ini kırmak** *sl.* to get out of hand; **-iyle kuyuya inilmez** you can't count on him; **-le çekmek** to look forward (*to*), to be counting the days until; *-leri birinin elinde olm.* to pull strings; *-ten kazıktan kurtulmuş* gallows bird.

ipek 1. silk; **2.** silken; ~ *gibi* silky.

ipekböceği, -ni zoo silkworm.

ipekböcekçiliği, -ni sericulture.

ipekçilik sericulture.

ipekli 1. of silk, silk; **2.** silk cloth.

ipince [x . .] very thin (*or* slender).

iplemek *sl.* to heed, to mind.

iplememek *sl.* not to give a damn (*for*), not to care 2 hoots, not to give a rap (*for*).

iplik 1. thread; yarn; **2.** fiber, filament; **3.** string (*in a bean pod*); ~ *eğirmek* to spin yarn; ~~ *olm.* to become threadbare; *ipliği pazara çıkmak* (*b-nin*) to come to light (*one's faults*).

iplikhane [ā] spinning mill.

ipnotize hypnotized; ~ *etm.* to hypnotize.

ipnotizma hypnotism.

ipnotizmacı hypnotizer.

ipnoz hypnosis.

ipotek mortgage.

ipotekli mortgaged.

ipsiz 1. ropeless; **2.** *sl.* vagabond; ~ *sapsız* **1.** senseless, meaningless (*words*); **2.** ne'er-do-well; vagabond; shiftless.

iptal, -li [ā] **1.** cancellation; **2.** JUR annulment; ~ *etm.* **1.** to cancel; **2.** JUR to annul.

iptida [ā] **1.** beginning, commencement, start; **2.** [x . .] at first, in the beginning.

iptidal [. . - -] **1.** primitive; **2.** primary, elementary.

iptila addiction.

ipucu, -nu 1. clue; **2.** hint, indication; ~ *vermek* to give a clue.

irade [ā] **1.** desire, will; **2.** command, decree; **3.** PSYCH volition.

iradedışı, -nı PSYCH involuntary.

iradeli [ā] **1.** strong-willed, strong-minded, forceful, resolute; **2.** voluntary, volitional.

iradesiz [ā] **1.** irresolute, weak; **2.** involuntary.

iradi [. - -] voluntary, volitional.

İran [- .] *pr. n.* Iran.

İranlı [ī] [x . .] Iranian.

irat, -dı [- .] income, revenue; ~ *getirmek* to bring in revenue.

irdeleme investigation, examination.

irdelemek to consider at length, to examine, to scrutinize.

irfan [ā] **1.** comprehension, understanding, insight; **2.** knowledge; **3.** ♀ [x .] *mf.*

iri 1. large, huge, big; voluminous; **2.** coarse (-grained); ~ *kum* gravel; ~ *taneli* large-grained, large berried; coarse-grained.

iribaş zoo tadpole.

irice 1. fairly large, largish, siz(e)able; **2.** fairly coarse.

iridyum CHEM iridium.

irikıyım 1. coarsely chopped; **2.** *fig.* huge, burly.

irileşme 1. *vn. of irileşmek;* **2.** BIOL hypertrophy.

irileşmek 1. to grow large; **2.** BIOL to hypertrophy.

irili ufaklı big and little.

irilik largeness, bigness.

irin pus; ~ *toplamak* to suppurate.

irinlenmek to suppurate, to fester.

irinli purulent.

iris [x .] ANAT iris.

iriyarı burly, strapping, husky, portly.

irkilmek 1. to be startled; to start; **2.** MED to be inflamed, to tumefy.

irkinti 1. puddle; **2.** start.

İrlanda *pr. n.* Ireland, Eire.

İrlandalı *pr. n.* **1.** Irishman; Irishwoman; **2.** Irish.

irmik semolina; ~ *helvası* dessert made of semolina.

irs heredity, inheritance.

irsal, -li [ā] sending, forwarding.

irsaliye [. - . .] COM waybill.

irsen [x .] through heredity, by inheritance.

irsi hereditary.

irsiyet, -ti heredity.

irşat, -dı [ā] guidance; ~ *etm.* to guide.

irtibat, -tı [ā] **1.** communications, contact; **2.** link, connection; ~ *kurmak* to get in touch (*ile* with); ~ *subayı* MIL liaison officer.

irtica, -aı [ā] reaction.

irticai [. . - -] reactionary.

irticalen [ā] extempore, extemporaneously.

irtifa, -aı [ā] AST, GEOGR, MATH altitude, elevation.

irtifak sharing, access; ~ *hakkı* easement, right of access.

irtihal, -li [ā] death, passing away; ~ *etm.* to die, to pass away.

irtikâp bribery, corruption.

is soot; lampblack; ~ *kokmak* to give off a scorched smell; *-e tutmak* to blacken with soot.

İsa [- -] *pr. n.* **1.** (*a.* **Hazreti İsa**) Jesus; **2.** *mf.*

isabet, -ti [ā] **1.** hitting (*the mark*); **2.** happy encounter; **3.** falling by chance to; **4.** thing done right; **5.** well done!; ~ **almak** to be hit (*by a missile*); ~ **etm. 1.** to hit (*the mark*); **2.** to fall to (*one's share*); ~ **ki** luckily; ~ **oldu** it worked out well.

isabetli [ā] very fitting (*or* appropriate).

isabetsiz [ā] inappropriate, ineffective.

ise 1. if; **2.** as for; ~ **de** although; even if.

İsevi [- . -] Christian.

İsevilik [- . - .] Christianity.

isfenks sphinx.

isfilt, -ti ice field.

ishakkuşu, -nu zoo short-eared owl.

ishal, -li [ā] diarrh(o)ea, the runs; ~ **olm.** to have diarrh(o)ea (*or* the runs).

isilik prickly heat, heat rash; ~ **olm.** to have heat rash.

isim, -smi 1. name; **2.** title; **3.** GR noun; ~ **cümlesi** noun clause; ~ **hali** GR case (*of a noun*); ~ **koymak** (*or* **vermek**) to name, to call; ~ **takımı** GR genitive (*or* possessive) case; ~ **takmak** to nickname; ~ **yapmak** *fig.* to make a name for o.s.; **ismi geçen** aforementioned, above-mentioned; **ismi var cismi yok** titular; **isminiz nedir?** what is your name?

isimfiil GR **1.** gerund; **2.** infinitive.

iskambil 1. playing card; **2.** any card game; ~ **kâğıdı 1.** playing card; **2.** deck of cards; ~ **oynamak** to play cards.

iskân settling, inhabiting; ~ **etm. 1.** to settle, to inhabit; **2.** to house.

iskandil 1. NAUT sounding, plumb; **2.** sounding line; **3.** *fig.* investigating; ~ **etm. 1.** NAUT to sound, to fathom, to plumb; **2.** to investigate; **3.** *sl.* to put out feelers; **4.** *sl.* to sound out.

İskandinav *pr. n.* Scandinavian.

İskandinavya *pr. n.* Scandinavia.

iskarpela [. . x .] carpenter's chisel.

iskarpin woman's shoe.

iskele 1. quay, wharf, pier, dock; **2.** gangplank; **3.** port (town); **4.** scaffold(ing); **5.** port side of a ship; ~ **babası** bollard; ~ **vermek** to lower the gangplank.

iskelekuşu, -nu zoo kingfisher, halcyon.

iskelet, -ti 1. skeleton; **2.** framework; ~

gibi like a skeleton, a bag of bones; ~**i çıkmak** to become skin and bone(s).

iskemle 1. chair; stool; **2.** coffee (*or* end) table.

İskender *pr. n.* Alexander (the Great).

İskenderiye *pr. n.* Alexandria.

İskenderun [ū] *pr. n.* Iskenderun.

iskete [. x .] zoo titmouse.

İskoç, -çu 1. Scottish, Scots; Scotch; **2.** Scot, Scotsman.

İskoçya [. x .] *pr. n.* Scotland.

iskonto discount; ~ **yapmak** to give a discount.

iskorbüt, -tü scurvy.

iskorpit, -ti zoo scorpion fish.

İslam *pr. n.* **1.** Islam; **2.** Islamic; **3.** Muslim; **-a gelmek** to become a Muslim.

İslamiyet, -ti [. - . .] *pr. n.* the Islamic religion.

İslamlaşmak to become a Muslim.

İslav *pr. n.* **1.** Slav; **2.** Slavic, Slavonic.

İslavca *pr. n.* Slavic.

islemek 1. to soot, to blacken with soot; **2.** to smoke (*fish, etc.*); **3.** to burn slightly (*pudding, etc.*).

isli 1. sooty; **2.** smoked.

islim steam; ~ **arkadan gelsin** *fig.* let's do it just any old way.

ismen [x .] by name.

ismet, -ti 1. chastity, purity; **2.** ♀ *mf.* & *wf.*

isnat, -dı 1. attribution, ascription; **2.** imputation; ~ **etm. 1.** to attribute, to ascribe; **2.** to impute.

İspanya [. x .] *pr. n.* Spain.

İspanyol *pr. n.* **1.** Spanish; **2.** Spaniard.

İspanyolca [. . x .] *pr. n.* **1.** Spanish, the Spanish language; **2.** in Spanish.

ispanyolet, -ti espagnolette.

ispat, -tı [ā] **1.** proof, evidence; **2.** proving; ~ **etm.** to prove; **ispatı vücut etm.** to appear in person.

ispati [. x .] *cards:* clubs.

ispatlamak to prove.

ispenç, -ci zoo bantam; ~ **horozu** *fig.* hop-o'-my-thumb and cocky man.

ispinoz 1. zoo chaffinch; **2.** *sl.* gabby, talkative.

ispiralya [. . x .] NAUT cabin skylight.

ispirto [. x .] grain (*or* ethyl) alcohol; ~ **lambası** spirit lamp; ~ **ocağı** spirit stove.

ispirtolu alcoholic, containing alcohol.

ispiyonlamak *sl.* (*b-ni*) to inform on s.o., to squeal on s.o., to peach on s.o., to squeak.

israf [ā] extravagance, wastage, dissipation; ~ **etm.** to waste, to dissipate, to squander.

İsrail [. - -] *pr. n.* **1.** Israel; **2.** Israeli.

İsrailli [. - . .] *Israeli.*

İstanbul *pr. n.* Istanbul; ~ **Boğazı** the Bosp(h)orus; ~ **kazan ben kepçe** *fig.* I left no stone unturned in Istanbul.

İstanbullu *pr. n.* native of Istanbul, Istanbulite.

istasyon (railway) station; ~ **şefi** stationmaster.

istatistik statistic(s).

istatistikçi statistician.

istavrit, -ti zoo horse mackerel, scad; ~ **azmanı** zoo bluefin.

istavroz cross, crucifix; ~ **çıkarmak** to cross o.s.

istek 1. wish, desire; **2.** request; **3.** appetite, inclination; ~ **duymak** to want, to desire, to long (-*e* for); ~ **kipi** GR optative (mood).

isteka 1. *billiards*: cue; **2.** TYP stick.

isteklendirmek to encourage, to motivate.

istekli desirous, willing.

isteksiz unwilling, reluctant, apathetic.

istem 1. request, demand; **2.** volition, will.

istemek 1. to want, to wish, to desire; **2.** (*b-den bş*) to ask *s.o.* for *s.th.*; **3.** to be necessary; to require; **4.** (*kız*) to ask for a woman in marriage; *ister istemez* willy-nilly, perforce; *ister... ister...* whether ... or ...

istemli 1. optional; **2.** voluntary.

istemsiz involuntary.

isten(il)mek 1. to be desired, to be in demand; **2.** to be asked for.

istep, -pi steppe.

istepne MOT spare tire.

isteri MED hysteria.

isterik MED hysterical.

istiap, -bı [ā] holding, containing; ~ **haddi 1.** load limit, capacity; **2.** NAUT tonnage; **3.** passenger capacity.

istiare [ā] *lit.* metaphor.

istibdat, -dı [ā] despotism.

istida [ā] petition.

istidat, -dı [. - -] aptitude, endowment.

istidatlı [. - - .] apt, capable, talented.

istidatsız [. - - .] inept, incompetent.

istidlal, -li deduction, inference.

istif stowage; ~ **etm.** to stow; *-ini bozmamak* *fig.* to keep up appearances.

istifa [. - -] resignation; ~ **etm.** to resign; *-sını vermek* to hand in one's resignation.

istifade [ā] profit, advantage, gain; ~ **etm.** to benefit (-*den* from), to profit (-*den* from).

istifadeli [ā] advantageous, profitable.

istifçi 1. stacker; stevedore; **2.** *fig.* hoarer.

istiflemek = *istif etm.*

istifrağ [ā] vomit; ~ **etm.** to vomit, to bring up.

istihale [ā] **1.** change of form; **2.** BIOL & GEOL metamorphosis; ~ **etm. 1.** to change form; **2.** BIOL & GEOL to undergo metamorphosis.

istihbarat, -tı [ā, ā] **1.** news, information; **2.** intelligence; ~ **bürosu** information bureau; ~ **dairesi** intelligence department; ~ **servisi** *newspaper:* news desk; ~ **subayı** intelligence officer; ~ **şefi** news editor.

istihdam [ā] employment; ~ **etm.** to employ.

istihfaf [ā] contempt; ~ **etm.** to despise.

istihkak, -kı [ā] merit, deserts; ration.

istihkâm 1. fortification, stronghold; **2.** military engineering; ~ **subayı** engineer officer.

istihlak, -kı consumption; ~ **etm.** to consume, to use up.

istihsal, -li [ā] production; ~ **etm.** to produce.

istihza [ā] sarcasm, ridicule, irony; ~ **etm.** (*b-le*) to ridicule *s.o.*

istikamet, -ti [ā] **1.** direction; **2.** straightness, integrity; ~ **vermek** to direct.

istikbal, -li [ā] the future.

istiklal, -li independence; ~ **marşı** the Turkish national anthem.

istikrah [ā] aversion; ~ **etm.** to loath.

istikrar [ā] stability, stabilization; ~ **bulmak** to become stabilized.

istikrarlı [ā] stable, stabilized; steady; settled.

istikrarsız [ā] unstable; inconsistent; unsettled; unsteady.

istila [. - -] **1.** invasion, occupation; **2.** infestation; ~ **etm. 1.** to invade; **2.** to infest.

istilacı [. - - .] **1.** invading, occupying (*army*); **2.** invader.

istim 1. steam; **2.** *sl.* booze.

istimator customs evaluator.

istimbot, -tu steamboat.

istimlak, -ki expropriation, confiscation, condemnation; ~ *etm.* to expropriate, to confiscate, to condemn.

istimna masturbation.

istinaden [ā] based (-*e* on), supported (-*e* by).

istinaf [. - -] JUR appeal; ~ *mahkemesi* court of appeals.

istinat, *-dı* [ā] **1.** resting on, leaning against; **2.** relying on, depending on; ~ *duvarı* retaining (*or* supporting) wall; ~ *etm.* **1.** to rest (-*e* on), to lean (-*e* against); **2.** to rely (*or* depend) (-*e* on).

istinkâf abstention; ~ *etm.* to abstain (-*den* from).

istintaç, *-cı* [ā] deduction, inference.

istirahat, *-ti* [. . - .] rest, repose; ~ *etm.* to rest, to relax, to repose.

istirdat, *-dı* [ā] restitution; ~ *davası* JUR action for restitution; ~ *etm.* to retake.

istirham [ā] plea, petition; ~ *etm.* to plead, to petition.

istiridye [. . x .] ZOO oyster.

istismar [ā] exploitation; ~ *etm.* **1.** to exploit; **2.** to utilize.

istismarcı [ā] exploiter.

istisna [ā] exception; ~ *etm.* to except, to exclude; *-lar kaideyi bozmaz* the exception proves the rule.

istisnai [. . - -] exceptional.

istisnasız [. . - .] without exception, unexceptionally.

istişare [ā] consultation; ~ *etm.* to consult; ~ *kurulu* advisory council.

istişari [. . . -] consultative, advisory.

istiva [ā] levelness, evenness.

istop stoppage; ~ *etm.* **1.** to stop; **2.** *football:* to stop (*the ball*).

istor **1.** roller blind; **2.** roller (*or* window) shade.

İsveç, *-ci* pr. n. Sweden.

İsveççe pr. n. **1.** Swedish; **2.** in Swedish.

İsveçli pr. n. Swede.

İsviçre [. x .] pr. n. Switzerland.

İsviçreli pr. n. Swiss.

isyan [ā] rebellion, revolt; mutiny; ~ *etm.* rebel, to revolt, to mutiny.

isyancı [ā] **1.** rebel; **2.** rebellious.

isyankâr rebellious.

iş **1.** work, labo(u)r; **2.** employment, job, work; **3.** occupation, (line of) work; **4.** duty, job; **5.** trade, business, commerce; **6.** affair, matter, business, commerce; **7.** *sl.* trick, swindle; ~ *arkadaşı* colleague, co-worker, fellow-worker, collaborator; ~ *başında* **1.**

on the job; **2.** during work time; ~ *bilmek* to be skilled; ~ *bitirmek* to complete a job successfully; ~ *çıkarmak* **1.** to do a lot of work; **2.** *fig.* to cause trouble; ~ *eri* skilled worker; ~ *görmek* **1.** to work; **2.** to be of use (*or* service); ~ *güç* occupation; ~ *-ten geçti!* it is too late!; ~ *sahibi* employer; ~ *yok* *fig.* it is no use (*or* good); -*e girmek* to become employed, to get a job; -*e yaramak* to be of use, to come in handy; -*i azıtmak* *fig.* to go too far, to overstep the mark; -*i başından aşkın olm.* to be up to one's ears in work; -*i* ~ *olm.* to go very well; -*i olm.* **1.** to have work to do; **2.** to turn out well; -*in başı* the crux; -*in içinde* ~ *var* there are wheels within wheels, there is *s.th.* fishy in it; -*inden olm.* to lose one's job, -*ine gelmek* (*b-nin*) to suit *one's* interests; -*ini bitirmek* (*b-nin*) *fig.* to finish *s.o.* off, to bump *s.o.* off; -*ini sağlamak* (*or* *sağlam kazığa*) *bağlamak* to make a matter safe; -*ten atmak* F to fire, to dismiss, to give the sack; -*ten el çektirmek* to remove from office.

işadamı, *-nı* businessman.

işaret, *-ti* [ā] **1.** sign; **2.** mark; **3.** signal, gesture; ~ *etm.* to point out, to indicate, to mark; ~ *fişeği* signal rocket; ~ *sıfatı* GR demonstrative adjective; ~ *vermek* to signal, to give a signal; ~ *zamiri* GR demonstrative pronoun.

işaretçi [ā] signaler, flagger.

işaretlemek [ā] **1.** to mark; **2.** to point out, to denote.

işaretli [ā] marked, tagged.

işaretparmağı, *-nı* index finger, forefinger.

işbaşı, *-nı* hour at which work begins; ~ ~ *yapmak* to begin work.

işbırakımcı striker.

işbırakımı, *-nı* strike.

işbıraktırımı, *-nı* lockout.

işbirliği, *-ni* cooperation.

işbirlikçi **1.** comprador; **2.** collaborationist.

işbirlikli cooperative, collective.

işbölümü, *-nü* division of labo(u)r.

işbu [x .] this.

işçi **1.** worker, workman, labo(u)rer; **2.** *sl.* trickster, cardsharp; ~ *sınıfı* working class, proletariat; ~ *sigortası* worker's insurance; ~ *ücreti* wages.

işçilik **1.** workmanship; **2.** worker's pay.

işemek to urinate, to piss, to pee, to spend a penny.

işgal, **-li** [ā] **1.** occupation; **2.** distraction; ~ **altında** under military occupation, occupied; ~ **etm. 1.** to occupy; **2.** to take up, to occupy (*space*); **3.** MIL to occupy, to take over; ~ **kuvvetleri** MIL occupation forces.

işgalci [ā] **1.** occupier; **2.** occupying.

işgücü, **-nü** COM **1.** productive power; **2.** work force (*of a nation*).

işgüder POL chargé d'affaires.

işgünü, **-nü** weekday, workday.

işgüzar [ā] officious, obtrusive.

işitme *vn. of* **işitmek**; ~ **aleti** hearing aid.

işitmek 1. to hear; **2.** to learn (-*i* of).

işitmemezlik not hearing; **-ten** (*or* **-liğe**) **gelmek** to pretend not to hear, to feign deafness.

işitsel auditory.

işittirmek (*b-ne*) to cause *s.o.* to hear *s.th.*

işkembe 1. ZOO rumen, paunch; **2.** tripe (*food*); ~ **çorbası** tripe soup; **-si-ni şişirmek** F to make a pig of o.s.

işkembeci 1. tripe seller; **2.** tripe restaurant.

işkence 1. torture, torment; **2.** MEC carpenter's clamp; ~ **etm.** to torture, to torment.

işkil suspicion, doubt.

işkolu, **-nu 1.** the work force; **2.** department.

işlek 1. busy; **2.** flowing, cursive (*handwriting*).

işlem 1. MATH operation; **2.** process; **3.** transaction, procedure.

işleme 1. *vn. of* **işlemek**; **2.** embroidery, handwork; **3.** embroidered.

işlemeci embroiderer.

işlemek 1. to work up, to process, to treat; **2.** to operate, to function, to perform; **3.** to embroider; **4.** to penetrate, to soak (-*e* into); **5.** to cultivate (*land*); **6.** to carry traffic (*road*); **7.** to ply (*ship, bus. etc.*); **8.** to discuss, to treat (*subject*); **9.** to be enforced (*or* effective) (*law*); **10.** to fester (*boil*); **11.** *sl.* to steal, to swipe.

işlemeli embroidered.

işlenmemiş raw, untreated.

işletici operator.

işletme *vn. of* **işletmek**, *part.* business enterprise; ~ **fakültesi** school of business administration; ~ **malzemesi** rolling stock; ~ **vergisi 1.** excise tax;

2. sales tax.

işletmeci administrator, manager; business executive.

işletmecilik 1. business administration; **2.** managership.

işletmek *caus. of* **işlemek**, *part.* **1.** to run, to operate; **2.** *sl.* hoodwink, to pull s.o.'s leg, to have s.o. on, to hoax, to kid.

işlev function.

işlevsel functional.

işlevsiz nonfunctional.

işleyim industry.

işli embroidered; ornamented; ~ **güç-lü 1.** having business; **2.** very busy.

işmar [ā] signal, gesture; wink; nod; ~ **etm.** to signal, to gesture, to wink.

işporta [. x .] **1.** pedlar's pushcart; **2.** basket, box (*used by pedlars*); ~ **malı** shoddy goods.

işportacı pedlar, peddler, pitchman.

işportacılık yapmak to peddle.

işret, **-ti** carousal; ~ **etm.** to carouse, to booze; ~ **meclisi** carousal, booze-up.

işsiz unemployed, out of work; ~ **güç-süz** idle.

işsizlik unemployment; joblessness; ~ **sigortası** unemployment insurance.

iştah 1. appetite; **2.** desire, urge; ~ **açıcı** appetizing; ~ **açmak** to whet one's appetite; ~ **kapamak** (*or* **kesmek** *or* **tıkamak**) to spoil (*or* kill) one's appetite; ~ **kapanmak** (*or* **kesilmek**) to lose one's appetite; ~ **-ım yok** I have no appetite; **-la yemek** to eat hungrily.

iştahlanmak 1. to get pleasantly hungry; **2.** to get a craving (-*e* for).

iştahlı 1. having an appetite; **2.** *fig.* desirous.

iştahsız without appetite.

iştahsızlık lack of appetite.

işte 1. here!, here it is!; **2.** look!, see!, behold!; **3.** as you see; ~ **böyle** such is the matter.

iştigal, **-li** [ā] occupation; ~ **etm.** (*bşle*) to occupy o.s. with *s.th.*, to be busy with *s.th.*

iştirak, **-ki** [ā] **1.** participation; **2.** partnership; ~ **etm. 1.** to participate (-*e* in), to join in (-*e* on); **2.** to share, to agree (-*e* with).

iştirakçi [ā] participant.

iştiyak, **-kı** [ā] longing, desire; ~ **duymak** to long (-*e* for).

işve coquettishness, coquetry.

işveli coquettish, flirtatious.

işveren employer.

işyeri, -ni place of employment, practice.

it, -ti 1. ZOO dog, cur; **2.** *fig.* cur, swine, son of a bitch, bastard, punk; ~ **canlı** tough and strong; ~ *gibi çalışmak* to sweat blood; ~ *oğlu* ~ *sl.* cur, son of a bitch; ~ *sürüsü fig.* rabble.

ita [- -] **1.** delivery; **2.** payment; ~ *etm.* **1.** to give; **2.** to pay.

itaat, -ti [. - .] obedience; ~ *etm.* to obey.

itaatli obedient.

itaatsiz disobedient.

itaatsizlik disobedience.

italik TYP italic.

İtalya [. x .] *pr. n.* Italy.

İtalyan *pr. n.* Italian.

İtalyanca *pr. n.* **1.** Italian; **2.** in Italian.

itboğan BOT autumn crocus, meadow saffron.

itburnu, -nu BOT dog rose.

iteklemek F to manhandle, to shove.

itelemek 1. to shove, to nudge; **2.** PHYS to repel.

itenek MEC piston.

itfa [ā] **1.** extinguishing, putting out; **2.** COM redemption, amortization; ~ *akçesi* (*or bedeli*) sinking fund; ~ *etm.* to pay off (*debt*), to redeem (*bond*).

itfaiye [ā] fire brigade, *Am.* fire department; ~ *eri* fireman.

itfaiyeci [ā] fireman.

ithaf [ā] dedication; ~ *etm.* to dedicate (*-e* to).

ithal, -li [ā] importation; ~ *etm.* to import; ~ *malı* imported goods.

ithalat, -tı [. - -] **1.** importation; **2.** imports.

ithalatçı [. - - .] importer.

ithalatçılık importation.

itham [ā] accusation, imputation; ~ *etm.* to accuse.

ithamname [ā, ā] indictment.

ithıyarı, -nı *s.* **acıhıyar.**

itibar [- .-] **1.** esteem, hono(u)r, consideration, regard; **2.** COM credit; ~ *etm.* to esteem, to show consideration; ~ *görmek* **1.** to be respected; **2.** to be in demand; **-a almak** to consider; **-dan düşmek** to fall from esteem; **-ı olm. 1.** to be held in esteem; **2.** to have credit.

itibaren [- . - .] [- . x .] from ... on, beginning from, dating from.

itibarıyla [-. - - .] **1.** concerning, consid-

ering; **2.** as of ...

itibarî [- . - -] COM **1.** nominal; **2.** conventional; ~ *kıymet* nominal value.

itibarlı [- . - .] **1.** esteemed, valued; influential; **2.** redeemable, acceptable (*bill*).

itibarsız [- . - .] unesteemed.

itici propulsive.

itidal, -li [- . - .] **1.** moderation; **2.** mildness, sobriety; ~ *bulmak* to calm down, to become moderate; ~ *sahibi* calm, composed, self-possessed.

itidalli [- . - .] calm; moderate.

itikat, -dı [- . - .] belief, faith, creed; ~ *etm.* to believe (*-e* in).

itilâf [- . -] entente.

itilim, itilme PSYCH repression.

itimat, -dı [- . - .] trust, confidence, reliance; ~ *etm.* to trust, to rely (*-e* on), to have confidence (*-e* in).

itimatlı [- . - .] trustworthy.

itimatname [- . - - .] letter of credence, credentials.

itimatsızlık [- . - . .] distrust, mistrust.

itina [- . - .] care, attention; ~ *etm.* (*or göstermek*) to take great care (*-e* in), to take pains (*-e* to); ~ *ile* carefully.

itinalı [- . - .] careful, painstaking.

itinasız [- . - .] careless, inattentive, slipshod.

itiraf [- . - .] confession, admission; ~ *etm.* to confess, to admit, to acknowledge.

itiraz [- . -] **1.** objection, disapproval; **2.** JUR protest; ~ *etm.* to object (*-e* to); ~ *götürmez* incontestable.

itirazcı objector.

itirazsız [- . - .] without any objection.

itişmek 1. to push one another; **2.** to scuffle, to tussle; *itişip kakışmak* to scuffle, to push and shove one another.

itiyat, -dı [- . - .] habit; ~ *edinmek* to get into the habit (*of*), to make a habit.

itizar [- . - .] apology; ~ *etm.* to apologize.

itki PSYCH motive, drive.

itlaf destruction; ~ *etm.* to destroy, to kill.

itlik *fig.* dirty trick, villainy.

itmam [ā] completion; ~ *etm.* to complete.

itmek, (-er) 1. to push, to shove; **2.** to persuade, to compel; *ite kaka* pushing and shoving.

itriyum CHEM yttrium.

ittırat, -dı [ā] regularity.

ittifak, -kı [ā] **1.** alliance, agreement; **2.** accord, concord; **~ Devletleri** HIST the Central Powers; **~ etm.** to agree, to come to an agreement.

ittifakla [ā] unanimously.

ittihat, -dı [ā] union; **~ etm.** to unite; **2 ve Terakki Cemiyeti** HIST the Committee of Union and Progress.

itüzümü, -nü BOT black nightshade.

ivaz JUR consideration.

ivdirmek 1. to accelerate; to hasten; **2.** to hurry, to urge on.

ivedi 1. haste; **2.** hasty.

ivedileşmek to become urgent.

ivedili urgent.

ivedilik urgency; **-le** urgently.

ivgi hatchet.

ivinti speed, rapidity; **~ yeri** GEOGR rapids.

ivme 1. haste; **2.** PHYS acceleration.

ivmek to hurry.

iye possessor, owner.

iyelik possession, ownership; **~ eki** possessive suffix; **~ zamiri** GR possessive pronoun.

iyi 1. good; **2.** well, in good health; **3.** abundant, plentiful; **~ etm. 1.** to heal, to cure; **2.** to do well; **3.** sl. to rob; **4.** (b-ni) sl. to give s.o. his comeuppance, to get even with s.o.; **~ gelmek 1.** to help, to work (medicine, etc.); **2.** to fit, to suit; **~ gitmek 1.** to go well; **2.** to suit; **~ gün dostu** fair-weather friend; **~ hal kâğıdı** certificate of good conduct; **~ hoş amma...** that's all very well but ...; **~ kalpli** good-hearted, kind; **~ ki** luckily, fortunately; **~ kötü** mediocre, not bad; **~ olm. 1.** to recover; **2.** to go well; **3.** to be good (or favo(u)rable); **~ saatte olsunlar** the djinns; **-den ~** etm. completely, thoroughly; **-si mi** the best thing to do is ...

iyice 1. [x . .] rather well, pretty good, fairly good; **2.** [. x .] completely, thoroughly.

iyicene [. x . .] F thoroughly.

iyicil well-wishing, benevolent.

iyileşmek 1. to recover (from illness); **2.** to improve, to get better.

iyileştirmek 1. to cure; **2.** to repair, to improve.

iyilik 1. goodness; **2.** favo(u)r, kindness; **3.** advantage, benefit; **4.** good health; **~ etm.** to do a kindness (or favo(u)r); **~ güzellik** (or **sağlık**) everything is all right; **-le** kindly, gently.

iyilikbilir grateful, thankful.

iyilikçi, iyiliksever kind, benevolent, good.

iyimser optimistic.

iyimserlik optimism.

iyon PHYS ion.

iyonlaşmak PHYS to ionize.

iyot, -du CHEM iodine.

iz 1. footprint, track; **2.** fig. mark, trace, clue, evidence; **3.** MATH trace; **~ düşürmek** MATH, PHYS to project; **~ sürmek** to follow a trail; **-i belirsiz olm.** to leave no trace; **-inden yürümek** (b-nin) to follow in s.o.'s footsteps; **-ine basmak** (b-nin) to tail s.o., to follow s.o.; **-ine dönmek** to change one's mind; **-ine uymak** (b-nin) fig. to tread in s.o.'s footsteps.

izaç, -cı [ā] vexation, worry; **~ etm.** to vex, to harass.

izafet, -ti [ā] **1.** GR nominal compound; **2.** PHLS relativity.

izafeten [ā] after, in hono(u)r of.

izafi [. - -] **1.** relative; **2.** PHLS nominal; **3.** PHYS specific.

izafiyet, -ti [ā] relativity.

izah [- -] explanation; **~ etm.** to explain.

izahat, -tı [- - -] explanations; **~ vermek** to give an explanation.

izale [ā] removal; **~ etm.** to remove, to wipe out.

izam [- -] exaggeration; **~ etm.** to exaggerate.

izan [ā] understanding, intelligence; **~ etm.** to be considerate.

izbe 1. hovel; **2.** out-of-the-way.

izbiro [. x .] rope sling (used in lifting cargo).

izci 1. scout; **2.** boy (or girl) scout.

izcilik scouting.

izdiham [ā] throng, crush, crowd.

izdivaç, -cı [ā] marriage, matrimony; **~ etm.** to get married; **~ teklifi** marriage proposal.

izdüşüm MATH, PHYS projection.

izdüşümsel MATH, PHYS projectional.

izhar [ā] display, manifestation; **~ etm.** to display, to reveal, to show.

izin, -zni 1. permission; **2.** leave (of absence); vacation; **3.** MIL discharge; **~ almak** to get permission (or leave); **~ koparmak** F = **~ almak**; **~ vermek 1.** to give permission; **2.** MIL to discharge; **-e çıkmak** to take a vacation, to go on vacation (or leave); **iznini kullanmak** to take one's vacation;

to use one's leave.

izinli on vacation (*or* leave).

izinsiz 1. without permission; **2.** *school:* kept in; **3.** detention.

İzlanda *pr. n.* **1.** Iceland; **2.** Icelandic.

İzlandalı *pr. n.* Icelander.

izlem observation.

izlemci observer.

izlemek 1. to follow, to trace, to pursue; **2.** to watch, to view; to observe

izlence program(me).

izlendirmek to make an impression (**on**).

izlenim impression.

izlenmek 1. *pass. of* **izlemek**; **2.** to get an impression.

izleyici spectator, onlooker; viewer.

izmarit, -ti 1. cigarette butt (*or* end); **2.** zoo sea bream.

izmihlâl, -li destruction, annihilation.

izobar GEOGR isobar.

izohips GEOGR contour line.

izolasyon ELECT insulation.

izole insulated; ~ **bant** electric (*or* friction) tape; ~ **etm.** ELECT, PHYS to insulate, to isolate.

izoterm GEOGR isotherm.

izotop, -pu PHYS isotope.

izzet, -ti 1. glory, might, hono(u)r, excellence; **2.** ♀ *mf.*

izzetinefis, -fsi self-respect, self-esteem, amour propre.

J

jaguar zoo jaguar.

jaketatay cutaway.

jaluzi Venetian blind.

Jamayka *pr. n.* **1.** Jamaica; **2.** Jamaican.

Jamaykalı *pr. n.* Jamaican.

jambon ham.

jandarma [. x .] **1.** gendarme, police soldier; **2.** gendarmerie, constabulary.

jant, -tı MOT rim (*of a wheel*); ~ **kapağı** hubcap.

Japon *pr. n.* Japanese.

Japonca [. x .] *pr. n.* Japanese.

japongülü, -nü BOT camellia.

Japonya [. x .] *pr. n.* Japan.

Japonyalı *pr. n. s.* **Japon**.

jarse 1. jersey cloth; **2.** jersey jacket.

jartiyer garter.

jelatin 1. gelatin(e); **2.** *a.* ~ **kâğıdı** cellophane (paper).

jelatinli gelatinous.

jeneratör PHYS **1.** generator; **2.** boiler.

jeofizik geophysics.

jeofizikçi geophysicist.

jeolog geologist.

jeoloji geology.

jeolojik geologic(al).

jest, -ti 1. gesture; **2.** beau geste, gesture.

jet, -ti jet (airplane).

jeton token, slug; ~ **düştü** *sl.* the penny (has) dropped, *Am.* now it is registered; ~ **geç düştü** *sl.* it took a while for me to catch on.

jigolo gigolo.

jile jumper.

jilet, -ti razor blade, safety razor.

jimnastik 1. gymnastics; **2.** gymnastic.

jimnastikçi gymnast.

jinekolog, -gu gynecologist.

jorjet, -ti georgette, Georgette crepe.

jöle jelly, *Am.* jello.

jön 1. handsome youngster; **2.** actor playing the role of a young lover.

jönprömiye *s.* **jön 2**.

Jöntürk HIST Young Turk.

judo judo.

judocu judoka.

jurnal report of an informer; ~ **etm.** to denounce, to inform (**on**), to report.

jurnalcı informer, denouncer.

jübile jubilee.

Jüpiter Jupiter.

jüpon underskirt, slip, petticoat.

jüri jury; ~ **üyesi** juror.

jüt, -tü jute (fiber).

K

kaba 1. puffed up, puffy; **2.** *fig.* boorish, coarse, rough, rude; unmannerly, uncouth; **3.** *fig.* vulgar, common; **4.** crudely made; **5.** coarse-grained; **6.** buttocks; ~ *et(ler)* buttocks; ~ *iş* rough (*or* unskilled) work; ~ *saba* **1.** rough and uneducated; **2.** crudely made, rough-and-ready ~ *sıva* roughcast; ~ *sofu* bigoted; *-sını almak* **1.** to roughhew, to trim roughly; **2.** *fig.* to tidy up roughly, to clean up quickly.

kababurun ZOO a kind of small fish.

kabaca 1. roughly, rather crudely, coarsely, in a rude way; **2.** biggish, somewhat grown up.

kabadayı 1. rough fellow, tough, bully, hooligan; **2.** intrepid, undaunted fellow; **3.** the best (*of anything*).

kabadayılık bravado, swagger; ~ *etm.* to swagger; ~ *taslamak* to act as if a tough, to play the tough.

kabahat, *-ti* [. - .] fault, defect; offence, guilt, sin, transgression, blame; ~ *bende* it is my fault; ~ *bulmak* to carp (*or* cavil) (*-de* at), to find fault (*-de* with); ~ *işlemek* (*or* *etm.*) to commit an offence, to offend, to do s.th. wrong.

kabahatli guilty, blameworthy, culpable, in the wrong.

kabahatsiz innocent, not guilty, inculpable.

kabahatsizlik innocence.

kabak 1. BOT squash, pumpkin, gourd; **2.** hashish pipe; **3.** *fig.* inexperienced, rude, rough, boorish; **4.** unripe (*melon*); **5.** *fig.* bald, closeshaven, hairless; **6.** without hat; **7.** worn out (*tire*); ~ *bastısı* stewed vegetable marrow; ~ *başına patlamak* (*b-nin*) *fig.* to carry the can; ~ *çekirdeği* pumpkinseed; ~ *çıkmak* to turn out to be unripe (*melon*); ~ *çiçeği gibi açılmak* *fig.* to display free and easy behavio(u)r; ~ *dolması* stuffed squash; ~ *gibi* bare, naked; ~ *kafalı* bald, hairless; *fig.* stupid; ~ *tadı vermek* to become boring gradually, to lose its appeal.

kabakgiller BOT Cucurbitaceae.

kabaklamak to prune (*a tree*).

kabaklaşmak to go bald.

kabaklık 1. unripeness (*melon*); **2.** baldness; **3.** boorishness, rudeness.

kabakulak MED mumps, parotitis.

kabala cabala.

kabalaşmak 1. to become coarse (*or* vulgar); **2.** to act rudely.

kabalık rudeness, discourtesy, coarseness, vulgarity, impoliteness; sponginess.

kaban hooded (*or* casual) jacket.

kabara [. x .] **1.** hobnail; **2.** ornamental brass-headed stud.

kabaralı hobnailed.

kabarcık 1. MED bulla, bleb, blister; **2.** bubble; **3.** pimple, pustule.

kabare cabaret; ~ *tiyatrosu* revue.

kabarık 1. swollen, blistered, puffy; **2.** swelling; ~ *deniz* high tide.

kabarma *vn. of* **kabarmak**, *part.* high tide.

kabarmak 1. to swell up, to become fluffy; **2.** to rise (*dough, paste*), to bubble up (*liquid*); **3.** to increase considerably; **4.** to stand on end, to bristle (*hair*); **5.** *fig.* to be puffed up (**with**) (*turkey*); **6.** *fig.* to get furious (*-e* at); **7.** to increase, to swell (*expenses, figures*); **8.** to become linty (*or* nappy) (*cloth*); **9.** to blister (*paint*); **10.** to boast, to be arrogant, to swell; **11.** to get rough (*sea*).

kabartı swelling, bulge; blister.

kabartma 1. *vn. of* **kabartmak**; **2.** embossed, (en)chased, stamping, in relief; **3.** relief ..., embossed ...

kabartmak *caus. of* **kabarmak**.

kabasakal bushy-bearded.

kabataslak roughly sketched out; in outline, without details.

Kâbe *pr. n.* the Kaaba at Mecca.

kabız, *-bzı* MED **1.** constipation; **2.** constipated; ~ *olm.* to be constipated.

kabızlık MED constipation; ~ *çekmek* to suffer from constipation.

kabil [ā] possible (*-e* for), practicable, capable (*-e* of), feasible; *gayrikabil* impossible.

Kabil [ā] *pr. n.* Cain (*Bible*).

kabil kind, sort, type; *bu* ~ (*or* *-den*) such, of such a kind, this sort of.

kabile[1] [ā] midwife.

kabile[2] 1. tribe; 2. BOT genus; ~ **reisi** tribal chieftain.

kabiliyet, -ti [ā] ability, capacity, aptitude, talent, capability, competence, possibility.

kabiliyetli [ā] capable (-e of), able (-e to), fit (-e for), qualified, talented, gifted, skil(l)ful (-e at, in), clever (-e at), adroit.

kabiliyetsiz [ā] unskil(l)ful, incapable, incompetent, untalented.

kabiliyetsizlik [ā] unskil(l)fulness, incapability, incapacity, incompetence.

kabin 1. cabin (of an airplane or ship or spacecraft); 2. changing cubicle (at a beach).

kabine 1. cabinet (a. POL.), Cabinet Council; 2. surgery, consulting room (of a doctor); 3. small room; 4. toilet; 5. changing cubicle (at a beach, in a store); ~ **çekilmek** (for a government) to resign; ~ **düşmek** (for a government) to fall; ~ **reisi** prime minister; ~ **toplantısı** cabinet meeting.

kabir, -bri grave, burial-place, tomb; ~ **azabı çekmek** to suffer agonies; ~ **suali** F endless questioning.

kablo [x .] ELECT cable, cord, line; ~ **döşemek** to lay down a cable; ~ **gemisi** cable ship.

kabotaj NAUT cabotage.

kabristan [. . -] churchyard, cemetery, graveyard.

kabuk, -uğu 1. BOT bark; skin, shell, rind, peel, pod, husk, cod; 2. MED crust, scab (wound); 3. outer covering; ~ **bağlamak** to form a crust (or scab) (wound); **kabuğuna çekilmek** to withdraw o.s. into solitude, to withdraw into one's shell; **kabuğunu soymak** to peel, to skin.

kabuklanmak 1. to form a crust (or scab) (wound); 2. to grow bark.

kabuklu 1. barky; 2. ... shelled; crustaceous.

kabuklubit, -ti ZOO cochineal insect.

kabuklular ZOO Crustacea.

kabuksuz shelled, peeled; without bark.

kabul, -lü [ū] 1. acceptance; 2. reception; 3. confession, consent, admission, avowal; 4. agreement, assent; 5. agreed!; ~ **etm.** 1. to accept; 2. to receive; 3. to put up with; 4. to admit, to confess, to avow; 5. to approve (of); 6. to agree, to consent to; ~ **günü** at-home; ~ **havzası** GEOGR catchment basin; ~ **resmi, resmi** ~ official solemn reception; ~ **salonu** reception room; -ü **olm.** to accept willingly.

kabullenmek 1. to appropriate, to take away, to seize; 2. to accept unwillingly; 3. = **kabul etm.**

kaburga 1. rib; 2. ANAT thorax, chest; 3. skeleton (or frame) (of a ship); -ları **çıkmak** (or **sayılmak**) to be only skin and bones.

kâbus [- -] nightmare; ~ **çökmek** (üzerine) or ~ **geçirmek** to have a nightmare.

kâbuslu [- - .] nightmarish.

kabza 1. grip, grasp, hold; heft, handle; 2. butt (end) (gun); 3. sl. a handful of hashish.

kabzımal fruit and vegetable wholesaler, middleman in fruit and vegetable.

kaç, -çı 1. how many?; how much?; ~ **defa** 1. how many times?, how often?; 2. many times, frequently, so often; ~ **para eder?** what's it good for?, what's the use?; ~ **paralık** (adam or şey) ki! F he (or it) is absolutely worthless!, he (or it) is good for nothing!; ~ **parça olayım?** F which of all these jobs can I cope with?; ~ **yaşındasın?** how old are you?; -**a?** what is the price?, how much is it?; -**ın kur'ası** fig. crafty, fox, wily fellow, old hand.

kaçaburuk shoemaker's awl.

kaçak 1. runaway, fugitive, truant (pupil), deserter; 2. contraband, smuggled (goods); 3. leakage, leak, escape (of gas); ~ **içki** F moonshine.

kaçakçı smuggler.

kaçakçılık smuggling; ~ **yapmak** to smuggle.

kaçaklık 1. desertion, fugitiveness; truancy; 2. tax or duty evasion.

kaçamak 1. neglect of duty, 2. evasion, flight, subterfuge, pretext, equivocation; 3. place of refuge, asylum, sheepfold; 4. F having a bit on the side; ~ **yapmak** 1. to shirk, to dodge, to goldbrick (a duty); 2. to prevaricate, to shuffle, to dodge; ~ **yolu** excuse, pretext; evasion.

kaçamaklı evasive, elusive.

kaçar how many at a time?, how many ... each?, how much per ...?, how many to each?

kaçarola, kaçarula frying-pan, casserole.

kaçık 1. batty, mad (**on**), crazy (**for, about**), foolish, eccentric; **2.** ladder, *Am.* run (*in a stocking*); **3.** having a ladder (*stocking*); **4.** crooked, warped.

kaçıklık craziness, battiness.

kaçılmak *fig.* to get out of the way.

kaçımsamak to goof off.

kaçımsar evasive.

kaçıncı which ... (*in a series*).

kaçınık reclusive.

kaçınılmaz inevitable, unavoidable, ineluctable.

kaçınmak to abstain (*-den* from), to avoid, to steer clear (*-den* of), to get out of the way, to stand aside, to shirk, to dodge, to shun, to evade.

kaçıntı leakage, leak.

kaçırma *vn.* of **kaçırmak**, JUR abduction, kidnapping; hijacking.

kaçırmak *caus.* of **kaçmak**, *part.* **1.** to make (*or* let) escape, to get away, to drive away; **2.** to leak (*air, gas, etc.*); **3.** *fig.* to rob (*or* deprive) s.o. of s.th.; **4.** to conceal, to hide; **5.** to cause s.o. to go away (*or* leave); **6.** to miss (*a vehicle, school, chance*); **7.** to kidnap, to abduct; to hijack; **8.** to smuggle; **9.** to withhold s.th. from s.o.; **10.** to soil, to wet; **11.** to go mad (*or* crazy); to lose one's mind; **12.** to get overdrunk; **13.** to overlook, to omit, to skip.

kaçış flight, escape, desertion.

kaçışmak to disperse, to flee in confusion, to run away in various directions.

kaçkın fugitive (*a. fig.*), deserter; truant.

kaçlı 1. from which number? (*card*); **2.** from which annual set? (*of birth, graduation*).

kaçlık 1. at what price?; **2.** contains how many?; of what size?; **3.** how old?; *bu adamı kaçlık tahmin edersiniz?* How old do you think this man is?

kaçmak, (**-ar**) **1.** to escape, to flee, to run away (*-den* from), to desert, **2.** not to appear, not to show up, to shun; **3.** to avoid, to shirk, to get out of the way, to stand aside, to steer clear; **4.** to leak, to leak out; **5.** to shift, to get out of place, to slip; **6.** to ladder, *Am.* to run (*stocking*); **7.** to withdraw without noticed; **8.** to make haste, to hurry; **9.** to disappear, to vanish, to come to nothing, to be frustrated; F

to go to pot (*rest, joy, etc.*); **10.** to turn out, to prove, to be (*good, bad, etc.*); **11.** to draw near; **12.** to slip into, to get into (*water, dust, etc.*); **13.** to elope (*ile* with); *kaçacak delik aramak* to look for a place to hide; *kaçanın anası ağlamamış* safety is in being cautious; *-tan kovalamaya vakit olmamak* to have no time for lesser things because of important matters.

kaçmaz runproof, non-laddering, *Am.* non-running (*stocking*).

kadana [. x .] **1.** *name of a kind of horse breed;* **2.** *sl.* huge woman; F dragon.

kadar 1. as much as, as far as, so long as, as big as; **2.** to; up to; **3.** about, say *Am.* around, like; **4.** so much; *bir ay öncesine* ~ up to a month ago; *istediğin ~ al!* take as much (*or* many) as you like; *gözün görebildiği* ~ as (*or* so) long as eye reaches.

kadastro [. x .] cadastration, land survey, land registry; *-ya geçmek* to be registered in a cadaster.

kadavra [. x .] cadaver, corpse, carcass.

kadayıf dry dough (*for various kinds of sweet pastry*).

kadeh glass, cup; wineglass, goblet; ~ *arkadaşı* drinking companion; ~ *kaldırmak* to raise one's glass in a toast; ~ *tokuşturmak* to clink glasses.

kadem 1. foot, pace; **2.** good luck, good foreboding; ~ *basmak* to set foot on (*or* in); ~ *getirmek* to bring good luck.

kademe 1. stage, level, grade, rank, degree; **2.** AVIA, MIL echelon, squadron; ~ *birliği* AVIA, MIL squadron formation; ~ ~ **1.** step by step, gradually, by degrees; **2.** MIL in echelons.

kademelendirmek MIL to stagger.

kademeli 1. MIL articulated, in echelons; **2.** stepped, graded.

kademhane [. . - .] (water-)closet, lavatory, toilet.

kademli bringing luck, lucky, fortunate.

kademsiz unlucky, fatal, baneful, bringing bad luck.

kademsizlik inauspiciousness, ill omen.

kader destiny, fate, predestination; *-in cilvesi* the irony of fate; *-in sillesi* the buffet of fate.

kadercilik fatalism.

kadı Moslem judge, cadi, kadi.

kadın 1. woman; **2.** matron; **3.** *a title*

used after the names of older women; **4.** maid, charwoman; ~ *berberi* ladies' hairdresser; ~ *doktoru* gynecologist; ~ *-a* (*meeting, party, etc.*) with only women present; ~ *-cık* ideal housewoman; ~ *milleti* F womankind, women; ~ *olm.* **1.** to lose her virginity; **2.** to be a good housewife; ~ *oyuncu* actress; ~ *sporcu* sportswoman; ~ *terzisi* dressmaker; *-lar hamamı gibi* fig. like a bear garden.

kadınbudu, *-nu* meat ball with eggs and rice.

kadıncık poor woman.

kadıncıl woman-chaser, womanizer.

kadıngöbeği, *-ni* sweet dish made with semolina and eggs.

kadınlık 1. womanhood; **2.** good housekeeping; **3.** womankind, women; ~ *gururu* womanly pride; ~ *hormonları* woman hormones; ~ *uzvu* vagina.

kadınsı womanish, effeminate, sissy.

kadıntuzluğu, *-nu* BOT barberry.

kadırga [. x .] obs. galley.

kadırgabalığı, *-nı* ZOO whale, cachalot.

kadife [ī] velvet; corduroy; ~ *gibi* velvety.

kadim [ī] old, ancient (*times*), through eternal.

kadir[1], *-dri* **1.** worth, value; **2.** AST magnitude; ♀ *gecesi* the Night of Power (*the 27th of Ramadan, when the Koran was revealed*); ~ *gecesi doğmuş* **1.** he is married to a very fine woman; **2.** he is a very lucky person.

kadir[2] [ā] able (*-e* to), capable (*-e* of), fit (*-e* for), powerful, mighty (*God*).

kadirbilir appreciative (*of value or merit*).

kadirbilirlik appreciation.

kadirşinas [. . . .] appreciative (*of value or merit*).

kadirşinaslık appreciation.

kadit, *-di* [ī] **1.** skeleton; **2.** skin and bone, a mere skeleton; **3.** jerked meat; *-i çıkmak* to turn into skin and bones.

kadmiyum CHEM cadmium.

kadran 1. MEC dial (plate); face; **2.** scale (*radio, etc.*); **3.** quadrant.

kadril quadrille (*the dance and its music*).

kadro [x .] **1.** personnel, staff; workers; teaching staff; roll; **2.** MIL cadre, establishment; **3.** framework; **4.** a permanent position; ~ *dışı* not on the permanent staff, temporary; not employed; ~ *mevcudu* MIL authorized strength; *-ya dahil* on the permanent staff; *-ya girmek* to be put on the permanent staff.

kadrolu on the permanent staff.

kadrosuz not on the permanent staff; temporarily employed.

kafa 1. head, skull; **2.** sight, view, opinion; **3.** intelligence, understanding; **4.** marble (*children's toy*); ~ *değiştirmek* to change one's mind, to change one's way of thinking; ~ *dengi* like-minded, intimate, kindred spirit; ~ *göz yarmak* fig. to be clumsy; ~ *-ya vermek* to put their heads together; ~ *kalmamak* not to be able think because of being worn out; ~ *oyunu* puzzle; ~ *patlatmak* to rack one's brain (*-e* over); ~ *sallamak* to be a yes-man, to approve everything; ~ *şişirmek* to talk s.o.'s head off, to talk the pants off one; ~ *tutmak* **1.** to oppose, to resist, to struggle against, to contradict, to be rebellious, to be contrary; **2.** (*b-ne*) to rebel, to revolt against s.o.; ~ *ütülemek* sl. to talk s.o.'s head off, to talk to s.o. to death; ~ *yormak* to rack one's brains (*-e* over), to ponder; *-dan atmak* to take a shot in the dark, to shoot off the belly; *-dan gayri müsellah* co. stupid, dull, nutty, obtuse; *-dan kontak* sl. having a screw loose, screwy, nutty; *-sı almamak* **1.** not to be able to understand (*or* grasp); **2.** not to be receptive any more; **3.** not to be able to believe; *-sı bozulmak* to get angry; *-sı bulanmak* to get confused; *-sı dönmek* fig. to get perplexed, to fly into a broad passion; *-sı dumanlı* **1.** tipsy, in one's cups; **2.** confused and perplexed; *-sı durmak* to be too tired to think; *-sı işlemek* to be on the ball; *-sı kazan olm. s. -sı şişmek, -sı kızmak* to blow one's top, to get angry; *-sı şişmek* to be ringing (*from noise*); to feel fuddled; *-sı taşa çarpmak* fig. to suffer for one's mistake; *-sı yerinde olmamak* to woolgather; *-sı yerine gelmek* to regain self-control, to pull o.s. together; *-sına dank etm.* to dawn on one at last; *-sına koymak* to make up one's mind, to be determined to …; *-sına sığmamak* not to be able to conceive (*of*), to find unacceptable; **-sına vur, ekmeğini elinden al** he can't say boo to a goose; **-sına vura vura** by force; **-sında şimşek çakmak** to have a brainwave, to dawn on one suddenly; **-sını kırmak** fig. to knock s.o.'s block off; **-sını kullanmak** to use one's loaf; **-sını kurcalamak** to obsess; **-sını taştan taşa çarpmak** to regret bitterly; **-sının dikine gitmek** to behave stubbornly, to go one's own way; **-yı bulmak** sl. to be in one's cups; **-yı çekmek** sl. to be on the booze; **-yı tütsülemek** sl. to get tight; **-yı (yere) vurmak** to get tight; **-yı (yere) vurmak** to get laid up in bed; **-yı vurup yatmak** F to hit the sack.

kafadanbacaklılar ZOO Cephalopoda.

kafadar like-minded; kindred spirit, buddy.

kafaiçi, -ni ANAT brain, intercranial.

kafakâğıdı, -nı F identity card, ID card.

kafalı 1. ... headed; **2.** fig. intelligent, brainy.

kafasız stupid, dull, obtuse.

kafasızlık stupidity.

kafatasçı racist.

kafatasçılık racism.

kafatası, -nı ANAT skull, cranium.

kafein caffeine.

kafes 1. cage; coop; **2.** lattice, grating, latticework; **3.** sl. clink; **4.** framework (wooden house); **5.** skeleton (of a ship); **~ gibi 1.** a more skeleton; **2.** (entirely) perforated; **~ ~** full of holes, perforated; **~ tamiri** a thoroughly overhauling of a building; **-e girmek** sl. to be duped (or tricked); **-e koymak** sl. to trick, to deceive, to make a dupe (of).

kafesçi 1. maker or seller of cages or latticework; **2.** sl. deceiver.

kafeslemek sl. to deceive, to trick, to con.

kafesli latticed.

kafeterya cafeteria.

kâfi [- -] sufficient, enough (-e for); **~ gelmek** (or olm.) to be enough (or sufficient), to suffice.

kafile [ā] **1.** caravan, troop, band; **2.** MIL convoy, escort; **3.** sending, part.

kâfir [ā] **1.** unbeliever, infidel, misbeliever, non-Muslim; **2.** fig. chap, bloke, Am. guy; **seni ~ seni!** you mad chap!

kâfirlik infidelity, impiousness.

kafiye [ā] rhyme.

kafiyeli [ā] rhyming, rhymed.

kafiyesiz [ā] unrhymed.

Kafkas (Dağları), Kafkasya pr. n. Caucasus.

Kafkasyalı pr. n. Caucasian.

kaftan robe, caftan; **~ giymek** to receive a robe of hono(u)r.

kâfur [- -] **kâfuru** [- ..] CHEM camphor.

kâgir built of stone or brick; stone ..., brick ...

kağan khan, ruler.

kağanlık khanate.

kâğıt, -dı 1. paper; **2.** slip (of paper), note; **3.** letter; **4.** (playing) card; **5.** document, report; **6.** one lira; **7.** paper ...; **~ açmak** to turn up the trump card; **~ dağıtmak** to deal cards; **~ fener** Chinese lantern; **~ gibi olm.** (b-nin yüzü) to turn pale in the face; **~ oynamak** to play cards; **~ oyunu** card game; **~ para** paper money; **~ sepeti** waste paper basket; **~ üzerinde kalmak** to exist on paper only (plan, etc.); **~ üzerine koymak** to commit to paper; **kâğıda dökmek** to write s.th. down; **kâğıdı kim yaptı?** who had the deal?

kâğıtbalığı, -nı ZOO ribbonfish, dealfish.

kâğıtçı stationer.

kâğıthelvası disk-shaped wafers.

kâğıtlamak to paper.

kâğıtlık 1. paper case (or chest or stand); **2.** suitable for making paper.

kağnı two-wheeled ox-cart; **~ gibi (gitmek)** (to go) at a snail's pace.

kağşak near to collapse; out of repair, dilapidated.

kağşamak 1. to become shaky, to become tottery; F to come apart (furniture); **2.** fig. to become old and feeble.

kâh sometimes, now and then, occasionally; **~ ... ~** sometimes ... sometimes.

kahır, -hrı 1. great, sorrow, grief; **2.** unjust treatment; **~ çekmek** to bear difficulties for a long time, to endure, to put up with ...; **kahrı çekilir** bearable; **kahrı çekilmez** unbearable; **kahrından ölmek** to die of grief; **kahrını çekmek** to lump (it), to endure.

kahırlanmak to be grieved (or distressed).

kahırlı extremely sad, deeply distressed, wretched.

kâhin soothsayer, seer.

kâhinlik 1. soothsaying; **2.** prophecy.

kahir [ā] overwhelming, irresistible, overpowering; ~ **ekseriyet** overwhelming majority.

Kahire [ā] *pr. n.* Cairo.

kahkaha peal of laughter, loud laughter; ~ **atmak** (*or* **koparmak**) to burst out laughing; ~ **tufanı** peals of laughter.

kahkahaçiçeği, -ni BOT morning-glory.

kahpe 1. whore, prostitute; **2.** *sl.* fickle, inconstant, faithless, perfidious, base, mean; **-nin dölü** *sl.* son of a bitch.

kahpelik 1. prostitution, being a whore; **2.** villainy, knavish trick; ~ **etm. 1.** to be a prostitute; **2.** to behave villainously.

kahraman 1. hero, gallant; heroine; **2.** *fig.* brave, heroic (*affair, etc.*).

kahramanlık 1. heroism, valo(u)r; **2.** heroic deed, exploit.

kahretmek [x . .] **1.** to crush (to death), to overcome, to overpower, to overwhelm, to ruin, to destroy, to wreck; **2.** *fig.* to be distressed, to torture; **3.** to grieve; **4.** to curse, to execrate.

kahrolmak [x . .] to grieve, to be depressed; **Kahrolsun!** damned!, to hell with him!

kahvaltı 1. (*a.* **sabah kahvaltısı**) breakfast; **2.** afternoon coffee; **3.** (*cold*) snack; ~ **etm. 1.** to (have) breakfast; **2.** to have a snack.

kahvaltılık 1. … for breakfast; **2.** food for breakfast.

kahve 1. (*a.* **kuru kahve**) coffee, coffee-beans; **2.** coffee (*as drink*); **3.** Oriental coffee-house, café; ~ **çekmek** to grind coffee-beans; ~ **değirmeni** coffee-mill, coffee-grinder; ~ **dolabı** cylindrical coffee roaster; ~ **fincanı** coffee cup; ~ **ocağı** *room where coffee, tea, etc. are made;* ~ **parası** tip, gratuity.

kahveci 1. grower *or* seller of coffee; **2.** the owner *or* lessee of an Oriental coffee-house; **3.** coffee-boiler, coffee-maker.

kahvehane Oriental coffee-house, café.

kahverengi, -yi, -ni brown.

kâhya 1. (landowner's) steward, major-domo, bailiff, superintendent; **2.** warden of a trade guild; **3.** *fig. contp.* overseer; **4.** *fig.* busybody; **5.** parking lot attendant; (*Birinin başına*) ~ **kesilmek** to meddle in affairs.

kâhyalık 1. stewardship; **2.** duty of a steward *or* a parking lot attendant; **3.** money paid to the parking lot attendant; **4.** *fig.* meddling in affairs; ~ **etm. 1.** to work as a steward *or* a parking lot attendant; **2.** *fig.* to meddle in affairs.

kaide [ā] **1.** basis, foundation; **2.** foot, base, pedestal; **3.** rule, principle (*a.* MATH); **4.** norm, standard; **5.** *geom.* base-line; **6.** cardinal number; **7.** doctrine, teaching, theory; **8.** *sl.* buttocks, rump.

kaidesiz irregular.

kail [ā] **1.** (*bşe*) convinced, positive; **2.** agreed! (with); **3.** speaker; ~ **olm.** to convince, to agree.

kaim [ā] **1.** extant, lasting, existing, present; **2.** taking the place of; ~ **olm. 1.** to exist, to be extant; **2.** to take the place of.

kaime [ā] **1.** official list (*or* document); **2.** *obs.* paper-money.

kâin 1. being, existent; **2.** situated.

kâinat, -tı [- . -] **1.** the universe, the cosmos; **2.** *fig.* everyone, everybody, the whole world.

kak¹, -kı 1. dried fruit; **2.** *fig.* meagre, *Am.* meager, skinny.

kak², -kı puddle, pool.

kaka (*child's language*) **1.** bad, ugly, bratty; **2.** dirt, filth, excrement; ~ **yapmak** to defecate, to go potty (*child*).

kakalamak 1. to push *or* strike continuously; **2.** = **kaka yapmak**; **3.** *fig.* to put across (*or* one over on) (*in shopping*).

kakao BOT cocoa; ~ **yağı** cocoa butter.

kakavan 1. stuck-up and stupid; **2.** *sl.* old and ugly.

kakıç gaff, a kind of harpoon.

kakılmak to be shoved and pushed; **kakılıp kalmak** to be stuck, to have to wait, to be rooted to (the spot).

kakım ZOO ermine, stoat.

kakımak to blame, to reprove, to censure, to denounce, to criticize.

kakınç reproach; (*başına*) ~ **etm.** to rub it in.

kakırdamak 1. to rattle, to rustle, to crackle, to snap; **2.** *sl.* to die, to peg out.

kakırtı crackling sound, crackle, soft crack.

kakışmak to push and shove mutually, to keep nudging (*ile* with).

kakıştırmak to cuff, to thump, to push,

to nudge.

kakma 1. *vn. of* **kakmak 2.** repousse work, chased work, relief work.

kakmacı inlayer.

kakmacılık repoussage, ornamental inlaying.

kakmak, (-ar) 1. to push, to shove, to drive in, to nail, to ram in; **2.** to encrust, to inlay; **3.** to chase.

kakmalı inlayed.

kaknem *sl.* **1.** meager and misery; **2.** ugly, mean, bad-tempered.

kaktüs [ā] BOT cactus.

kakule [ā] BOT cardamom.

kâkül forelock, bangs, fringe.

kâküllü having forelock.

kal[1] **1.** refining, purification (*from metal*); **2.** CHEM cupellation.

kal[2]**, -li** [ā] word, talk, speech; **-e almak** to mention, to discuss, to take into consideration; **-e almamak** to consider insignificant (*or* negligible), to take no notice (-*i* of).

kala -e to (*for time*); before (*a time*); **saat ona beş ~** at five to ten; **köye iki kilometre ~** two kilometers from the village; **on gün ~** ten days before.

kalaazar kala-azar, dumdum fever.

kalaba crowd, mass.

kalabalık 1. crowd, throng, press; **2.** crowded; **3.** numerous (*luggage*); big (*family*); **4.** overcrowded (*bus*); overpopulated (*city*); **~ etm. 1.** to crowd, to take up, to occupy (*a place*), to be in the way (*object*); **2.** F to stand about uselessly.

kalabalıkça a little crowded.

kalabalıklaşmak 1. to get crowded; **2.** to get cluttered.

kalafat, -tı 1. NAUT caulking; **2.** turban (*headdress worn by commander-in-chiefs and Janisseries*); **~ yeri** caulking wharf; **-a çekmek** to careen for caulking.

kalafatçı caulker.

kalafatlamak 1. to caulk, to careen; **2.** *fig.* to repair, to restore.

kalafatsız uncaulked, caulkless.

kalak 1. nostril (*of animals*); **2.** winnings stones (*children's game*).

kalakalmak 1. to be petrified, to be surprised, to be taken aback, to stand perplexed; **2.** to have a hard time.

kalamar ZOO squid, cuttle-fish.

kalan 1. remaining; **2.** MATH remainder; **3.** the rest; **4.** staying.

kalantor well-heeled and ostentatious man.

kalas beam, plank, timber.

kalastra lifeboat chock on the deck of ships.

kalay 1. tin; **2.** *fig.* varnish; **3.** *sl.* swear, curse; **-ı basmak** *sl.* to swear a blue streak, to chew out.

kalaycı tinsmith, tinner; tinker.

kalaylamak 1. to tin; **2.** *sl.* to insult, to call s.o. names, to abuse; **3.** *fig.* to conceal by sham (*fault, etc.*).

kalaylı 1. tinned; **2.** containing tin; **3.** *fig.* sham.

kalaysız 1. untinned; **2.** containing no tin.

kalben 1. sincerely, wholeheartedly; **2.** ethical, spiritual, mental.

kalbi [. -] sincere, heartfelt, warm, cordial.

kalbur sieve, riddle; **~ gibi** riddled, full of holes; **~ kemiği** ANAT ethmoid bone; **-a çevirmek** to fill with holes, to riddle; **-a dönmek** to be riddled, to be filled with holes; **-dan geçirmek** to sieve, to sift, to screen; **-la su taşımak** *fig.* to exert o.s. to purposeless work, to plow the sand(s).

kalburcu 1. maker *or* seller of sieves; **2.** sifter.

kalburlamak to sift, to sieve, to screen.

kalburüstü, -nü *fig.* select, elite, prominent; **-ne gelmek** (*or* **kalmak**) to become outstanding.

kalcı refiner of metals.

kalça [x .] ANAT hip; **~ çevresi** hip-measurement; **~ kemiği** ANAT hip-bone.

kalçalı 1. hipped; **2.** with big hips, broad across the beam.

kalçasız 1. without hips; **2.** with narrow hips.

kalçete NAUT gasket.

kalçın long felt hose.

kaldıraç lever, crowbar.

kaldıran ANAT levator.

kaldırıcı jack.

kaldırım pavement, *Am.* sidewalk, causeway; **~ çiğnemek** *fig.* to be experienced in the ways of the world, to be worldly-wise; **~ döşemek** to pave; **~ mühendisi** *co.* loafer, idler; **~ süpürgesi** (*or* **yosması**) streetwalker, prostitute; **~ taşı** paving stone; **-a düşmek 1.** to lose its value; **2.** to be sold cheap in the street.

kaldırımcı 1. paver; **2.** *sl.* swindler,

crook, pickpocket.

kaldırımsız unpaved.

kaldırımsı BIOL squamous (epithelium).

kaldırma *vn. of* **kaldırmak;** ~ **cihazı** forklift.

kaldırmak *caus. of* **kalkmak 1.** to lift, to elevate, to raise; **2.** to move away, to remove, to clear away; **3.** to clear (*table*); **4.** to scare; **5.** to abolish, to do away with; **6.** to wake; **7.** to cause to recover (from); **8.** to bear, to endure, to tolerate; **9.** to erect, to stand; **10.** F to steal, to pinch, to swipe; **11.** to start (*a motorcar*); **12.** to buy in bulky quantities; **13.** to kidnap; **14.** to carry the corpse to grave; **15.** to take the ill to hospital.

kale 1. fortress, castle, citadel; **2.** MIL bunker, pillbox; **3.** *fig.* bulwark, bastion; **4.** *chess:* castle, rook; **5.** *sports:* goal; ~ **gibi 1.** big, plain and solid (*building*); **2.** trustworthy and strong, portly (*person*); ~ **sahası** goal area.

kalebent, -di castle convict.

kaleci goalkeeper.

kalem 1. (lead) pencil, colo(u)red pencil, fountain-pen, writing reed; **2.** (government) office, chancellery; **3.** style, (im)personation, representation; **4.** chisel; **5.** carving knife; **6.** COM item, entry, sum; **7.** AGR graft; **8.** paintbrush; ~ **açmak** to sharpen a pencil; (*üstüne*) ~ **çekmek** to cross out, to cancel; ~ **efendisi** clerk in a government office; ~ **işi 1.** hand-painting; **2.** hand-carved; ~ **kaşlı** having thin and long eyebrows; ~ **kulaklı** having small, upright ears (*horse, deer, etc.*); ~ **oynatmak 1.** to write; **2.** to correct, to edit; **3.** to spoil by altering (*article, etc.*); ~ **parmaklı** having long, slim, tapering fingers; ~ **sahibi** author, writer, man of letters; **-e almak** to write, to draw up, to indite; **-e gelir 1.** describable; **2.** reasonable; **-e gelmemek** to be indescribable; **-e** (*or* **kâğıda**) **sarılmak** to take pen in hand, to start to write promptly; (**herhangi bir nitelikte**) **-i olm.** to write well on any subject; **-inden çıkmak** to be written by s.o.; **-inden kan damlamak** *fig.* **1.** to write effectively; **2.** to write bitterly and harmfully; **-iyle yaşamak** (*or* **geçinmek**) to make a living by writing, to live by one's pen.

kalemaşısı, -nı graft, scion.

kalembek 1. aloes; **2.** a kind of maize.

kalemis civet (cat).

kalemkâr [. . -] **1.** decorator; **2.** engraver, chase-worker.

kalemlik 1. pencil box; **2.** penholder, pen rack.

kalemşor *co.* polemical writer.

kalemtıraş pencil sharpener.

kalender 1. wandering, mendicant friar; **2.** *fig.* unconventional, easy-going, easily satisfied.

kalenderce 1. unconventional and easy going, bohemian; **2.** philosophical.

kalenderleşmek to behave *or* live in an unconventional way.

kalenderlik 1. unconventionality; **2.** a Bohemian existence.

kalevi alkaline.

kaleydeskop kaleidoscope.

kalfa [x .] **1.** assistant master; qualified workman; **2.** building contractor; **3.** chief palace maid-servant; **4.** *obs.* assistant (*of a primary school teacher*).

kalgımak 1. to leap up, to jump up, to rise, to scar up (*dolphin*); **2.** to rear, to rise, to prance (*horse*); **3.** to jump up angrily.

kalhane [. - .] MEC smelter(y).

kalıcı permanent, lasting.

kalıcılık 1. permanence; **2.** PHYS retentivity.

kalıç sickle.

kalık 1. defective, incomplete; **2.** spinster.

kalıklık defectiveness, deficiency.

kalım survival, duration, life.

kalımlı everlasting, perpetual, permanent; immortal.

kalımlılık 1. permanence; **2.** immortality.

kalımsız transient, impermanent.

kalın[1] **1.** thick, stout; **2.** viscous, stiff; **3.** *sl.* rich, wealthy, well-heeled; **4.** *obs.* coarse, uneducated; **5.** velar; ~ **kafalı** thickheaded, thickwitted, obtuse, stupid, dull; ~ **kafalılık** dullness; ~ **ses** deep voice; ~ **ünlü** back vowel (*a, ı, o, u*).

kalın[2] *present given by the bridegroom to the bride.*

kalınbağırsak ANAT great gut, large intestine.

kalınca somewhat thick.

kalınlaşmak to become thick (*or* stout), to thicken.

kalınlaştırmak to thicken, to make

s.th. thick.

kalınlatmak = **kalınlaştırmak.**

kalınlık 1. thickness (*a.* MATH); **2.** viscousness (*gas, fluid*); **3.** *fig.* coarseness; **4.** deepness (*voice*).

kalınmak to stay, to rest, to stop.

kalıntı 1. remnant, remainder, leftovers, leavings; **2.** ruin, ruins, debris, relic; **3.** mark, trace.

kalınyağ lubricating oil.

kalıp, -bı 1. mo(u)ld, press form; **2.** matrix, model; **3.** shoemaker last; **4.** block (*hat*); **5.** bar, bolt (*cheese or scap*); **6.** external appearance; model, pattern; ~ **gibi** still, without moving; ~ **gibi oturmak** to fit like a glove (*suit, dress*); ~ **gibi serilmek** (*or* **yatmak**) to lie stretched out like a log; ~ **gibi uyumak** to sleep like a log; ~ **kesilmek** to stand aghast, to be petrified; ~ **kıyafet** outer appearance; ~ **sigarası** machine-made cigarette; **-a dökmek** to cast, to mo(u)ld; **-a vurmak** to put on a block (*or* last) (*hat, etc.*); **-ı kıyafeti yerinde** imposing and well dressed man; **-ı değiştirmek** (*or* **dinlendirmek**) *sl.* to die, to pop off; **-ını basmak** *fig.* to give (*or* provide) security, to stand surety; **-ının adamı olmamak** not to be the man as expected from his appearance; **-tan -a girmek** *fig.* to be fickle (*or* inconstant *or* volatile) for one's benefit.

kalıpçı 1. maker *or* seller of mo(u)lds; **2.** mo(u)lder, blocker.

kalıplamak to form, to block, to mo(u)ld.

kalıplaşmak to get fixed in one form (*or* type), to become stereotyped.

kalıplaşmış 1. stereotyped; **2.** clichéd; ~ **iyelik** GR stereotyped possessed form.

kalıplı shaped by mo(u)lds.

kalıpsız out of shape.

kalıt, -tı 1. inheritance; **2.** inherited characteristic.

kalıtçı heir, inheritor.

kalıtım 1. BIOL (genetic) heritage; **2.** inheritance, heritage.

kalıtımbilim genetics.

kalıtımsal hereditary.

kalıtsal hereditary.

kalibre caliber.

kalifiye qualified, skilled.

kaliforniyum californium.

kalinos ICHTH a kind of sea bass.

kalite quality, class; ~ **kontrolü** quality control (*or* test).

kaliteli 1. high-quality, of good quality; **2.** of high value, high-class, high--grade.

kalitesiz poor-quality, shoddy.

kalitesizlik lack of quality, shoddiness.

kalkan 1. shield; **2.** ZOO turbot; **3.** *fig.* defender.

kalkanbezi, -ni ANAT thyroid gland.

kalker GEOL limestone.

kalkerleşmek to calcify.

kalkerli calcareous.

kalkık 1. pointing upwards; **2.** upturned (*brim, collar, etc.*); **3.** peeled off (*paint, polish, etc.*); **4.** pulled up (*curtain*); **5.** high (*eyebrow*); **6.** standing on end (*hair*); **7.** retroussé (*nose*).

kalkındırmak to develop, to improve, to cause to recover, to lead towards progress.

kalkınış developing, improving.

kalkınma 1. development, progress improvement; **2.** recovery; **3.** ascent; ~ **hızı** rate of economic development; ~ **planı** development plan.

kalkınmak to develop, to make progress, to advance.

kalkış 1. rising; **2.** departure; **-a geçmek** AVIA to take off.

kalkışmak to attempt, to (dare to) undertake (**-meğe** to do s.th.), to try (--meğe to do s.th.).

kalkmak, (-ar) 1. to stand up, to rise to go up; **2.** to get loose (*polish*); **3.** to get up, to get out of bed; **4.** to depart, to leave, to set out (*or* off), to start; **5.** to rear (*horse*); **6.** to be taken off (*cloth, lid*); **7.** to recover (*from an illness*), **8.** to be annulled, to be abolished, to be repealed; **9.** to be cleared (*or* removed); **10.** to set about, to undertake (*to do s.th.*), to venture; **11.** to disappear, to vanish; **12.** to rebel; **13.** to be reaped (*or* gathered); **14.** to move to; **15.** to go out of circulation (*money*); **Kalk borusu** MIL reveille; **Kalkıp kalkıp oturmak** to show one's anger by movements, to be hopping mad.

kallavi [. - -] **1.** ceremonial turban (*formerly worn by viziers*); **2.** F huge, very big.

kalleş F unreliable, treacherous, faithless, perfidious, backstabbing.

kalleşçe treacherously.

kalleşlik treachery, backstabbing, faithlessness, disloyalty, perfidiousness, perfidy; ~ *etm.* to play s.o. a dirty trick.

kalma 1. *vn. of* **kalmak**; **2.** remaining, left; **3.** handed down, inherited (*-den* from), descended (*-den* from).

kalmak. (*-ır*) **1.** to remain, to be left; **2.** to continue to exist, to survive; **3.** to dwell, to stay; **4.** not to make progress; **5.** (*sınıfta*) not to get one's remove, to fail (*a class*); **6.** to be detained, to be put off; **7.** to be inherited (*-den* from); **8.** to be postponed; **9.** to be on s.o.'s duty, to be incumbent on s.o., to rest with s.o.; **10.** to be kept from doing *s.th.*; **11.** to be contented with; **12.** to halt; **13.** to cease; **14.** to drop (*wind*). *Kala kala* there only remains, all that is left; *kaldı ki* besides, moreover; (*şundan or bundan*) *Kalır yeri yok* it is indistinguishable, it is perfectly the same; (*Şuna or buna*) *Kalsa* (*or Kalırsa*) **1.** if you ask (*my, his, etc.*) opinion; **2.** if it were left up to (*s.o.*); *kalsın!* **1.** leave it!, forget it!; **2.** it is not important any more.

kalmalı locative; ~ *tümleç* GR locative noun phrase with adverbial force.

kaloma [. x .] NAUT **1.** slack of a hawser; **2.** loose end of rope.

kalomel calomel.

kalori calorie.

kalorifer 1. central heating; **2.** radiator; ~ *dairesi* furnace room; ~ *kazanı* boiler.

kaloriferci 1. furnaceman; **2.** stoker, fireman.

kalorimetre calorimeter.

kaloş overshoe, galosh.

kalp¹ *-bi* **1.** ANAT heart; **2.** heart disease; **3.** *fig.* affection; **4.** *fig.* feeling, sense; **5.** centre, innermost part; ~ *ağrısı* lover's grief, heartache; ~ *atışı* heartbeat; ~ *çarpıntısı* beating (*or palpitation*) of the heart; ~ *kazanmak* (*or fethetmek*) to win the heart (of); ~ *kırmak* to hurt s.o.'s feelings, to break s.o.'s heart; ~ *krizi* heart attack from cardiac weakness; ~ *olmamak* (*b-de*) not to have sympathy, to be merciless; ~ *sektesi* heart attack; ~ *yetersizliği* (*or kifayetsizliği*) cardiac insufficiency; *-den yaralı* sad, grieved (at, about); *-e doğmak* to have a presentiment; ~ *-e karşıdır* feelings are mutual; *-i çarpmak* **1.** to palpitate (*or beat*) fast; **2.** to palpitate with excitement; *-i fesat* **1.** envious, jealous;

2. suspicious; *-i kırık* broken-hearted; *-ine doğmak* s. *-e doğmak*; *-ine girmek* to win s.o.'s heart; *-ine göre* after one's own heart; *-ini açmak* to pour out one's troubles, to let one's hair down, to bare one's soul (*-e* to).

kalp² change, transformation.

kalp³, *-pı* **1.** not genuine, spurious, false, forged; **2.** *fig.* untrustworthy, liar.

kalpak fur cap.

kalpazan 1. counterfeiter, forger, faker; **2.** *fig.* swindler, cheat, crook, liar.

kalpazanlık 1. counterfeiting; **2.** swindling, cheating, trickery.

kalplaşmak to lose one's strength (*or agility or diligence*).

kalplık 1. falsity, spuriousness; **2.** aversion to work.

kalpli having heart disease.

kalpsiz heartless, pitiless, merciless.

kalpsizlik heartlessness, pitilessness.

kalseduan chalcedony.

kalsit, *-ti* calcite.

kalsiyum calcium.

kaltaban 1. swindler, crook, tricky, unreliable; **2.** *obs.* dishonest, without hono(u)r, pander.

kaltabanlık deceitfulness, dishonesty.

kaltak 1. saddle frame; **2.** *sl.* whore, prostitute, slut, hussy.

kaltaklık 1. prostitution; **2.** mean behavio(u)r (*of a woman*).

kalubeladan beri [- - . - x . .] from time immemorial.

kalya 1. potash; **2.** *squash or eggplant cooked with meat, onion and butter.*

kalyon galleon, galley.

kalyoncu 1. armed member of galley; **2.** seaman, sailor.

kam shaman.

kâm wish, desire; ~ *almak* (*bşden*) to get what one desires.

kama [x .] **1.** dagger, dirk; **2.** wedge; **3.** breechblock; ~ *basmak* to win a game.

kamacı artillery mechanic (*or artificer*).

kamalamak 1. to stab (*with a dagger*); **2.** MEC to fasten with wedges.

kamanço etm. *sl.* to burden s.o. with s.th., to exchange, to hand over.

kamara [x . .] **1.** ship's cabin; **2.** ♀ House (*of Lords or Commons*); **3.** joint edge (*sole*).

kamarilla [. . x .] camarilla, clique.

kamarot, *-tu* ship's steward.

kamaşmak 1. to be dazzled, to be blinded, to become dull; **2.** to be set on edge (*teeth*).

kamaştırmak 1. to dazzle; **2.** to set on edge (*teeth*).

Kamber 1. *pr. n.*; **2.** *obs.* faithful servant; *-siz düğün olmaz* he can't be left out.

kambiyo [x . .] COM **1.** foreign exchange (dealing); **2.** foreign exchange *or* currency (office); **~ kuru** foreign exchange rate.

kambiyocu foreign exchange dealer.

kambiyoculuk foreign exchange speculation.

kambur 1. humpback(ed), hunchback(ed); **2.** hump(back), hunch(back); **3.** bulge, curvature, projection; **4.** bulging, projecting; **5.** *fig.* trouble, grief; **~ felek** adverse destiny, bad luck, misfortune; **~ üstüne** (*or* **~ üstüne**) one trouble after another; **~ zambur** (*or* **~ kumbur**) crooked and hunchbacked, bumpy, over hedge and ditch; *-u çıkmak* **1.** to become hunchbacked; **2.** *fig.* to be discredit; **3.** *fig.* to be having been worked very much (*at work that requires bending, lifting*); *-unu çıkarmak* to hunch one's back.

kamburlaşmak 1. to become hunchbacked; **2.** to become arched, to become warped, to become bulged.

kamburlaştırmak *caus.* of **kamburlaşmak.**

kamburluk 1. being hunchbacked; **2.** protuberance.

kamçı 1. whip; **2.** NAUT pendant, tail; **3.** BIOL flagellum; **~ çalmak** (*or* **vurmak**) to whip; **~ şaklatmak** to crack a whip.

kamçılamak 1. to whip, to flog, to flagellate; **2.** *fig.* to stimulate, to whip up.

kamelya BOT camellia.

kamer moon; **~ yılı** lunar year.

kamera 1. camera; **2.** = **kameraman.**

kameraman cameraman.

kameri [. . -] lunar.

kameriye arbo(u)r, bower.

kamet, -ti [ā] **1.** height, stature; **2.** muezzin's call signal(l)ing the beginning of the **namaz; ~ getirmek** to recite the **kamet.**

kamış 1. BOT reed; cattail, reed-mace; bamboo; **2.** reed ...; **3.** fishing rod (*or* pole); **4.** penis, prick, dick; **~ kalem** reed pen; *-ı kırmak* *sl.* to catch gonorrhea.

kamışçık jewel(l)er's blowpipe.

kamışkulak long-eared horse.

kamışlı reedy.

kamışlık reed bed.

kâmil 1. perfect, complete; **2.** mature; **3.** ♀ *mf.*

kâmilen [x . .] entirely, fully, completely.

kamineto [. . x .] single-burner.

kamp, -pı 1. camp; **2.** camping; **3.** campground; **~ kurmak** to pitch camp, to camp; **~ yeri** campsite, campground; *-a girmek* *sports*: to go into camp.

kampana [. x .] bell.

kampanacı *sl.* quack, charlatan, mountebank.

kampanya [. x .] **1.** campaign, drive; **2.** cropping season; **~ açmak** to start a campaign.

kampçı camper.

kamping campsite, campground.

kamu the public; **~ düzeni** public order, the peace; **~ hizmeti** public service; **~ kesimi** (*or* **sektörü**) the public sector; **~ personeli** civil servants; **~ yararı** the public interest.

kamuflaj camouflage.

kamufle camouflaged; **~ etm.** to camouflage.

kamulaştırma nationalization.

kamulaştırmak to nationalize.

kamuoyu, -nu public opinion; **~ yoklaması** opinion poll.

kamus [- -] lexicon.

kamusal public.

kamutanrıcılık PHLS pantheism.

kamutay joint session of the Turkish National Assembly.

kamyon 1. lorry, *Am.* truck; **2.** *sl.* prostitute, hooker.

kamyoncu truck driver.

kamyonet pickup (truck).

kan 1. blood; **2.** lineage, family; **~ ağlamak** *fig.* to shed tears of blood; **~ akıtmak 1.** to sacrifice an animal; **2.** *fig.* to shed blood; **~ akrabalığı** blood relationship, consanguinity; **~ alacak damarı bilmek** to know which side one's bread is buttered; **~ almak** to take blood (*-den* from), to bleed; **~ bağı** blood tie; **~ bankası** blood bank; **~ beynine sıçramak** *fig.* to burst a blood vessel, to blow one's top, to see red; **~ çanağı gibi** bloodshot (*eyes*); **~ damarı** blood vessel; **~ davası** blood feud, vendetta; **~ dolaşımı**

circulation of the blood; ~ **dökmek** to shed blood; ~ **emici** blood-sucking; ~ **gelmek** to bleed; ~ **gölü** blood bath; ~ **gövdeyi götürmek** to be shed (*blood*); ~ **grubu** blood group (*or* type); ~ **istemek** to want blood revenge; ~ **kaybetmek** to lose blood; ~ **kaybı** loss of blood; ~ **kırmızı** blood-red, crimson; ~ **kusmak 1.** to vomit blood; **2.** *fig.* to be extremely grieved; ~ **lekesi** bloodstain; ~ **merkezi** blood transfusion centre; ~ **muayenesi** blood test; ~ **nakli** blood transfusion; ~ **revan içinde** blood-bespattered; ~ **tahlili** blood analysis; ~ **vermek 1.** to give a blood transfusion (*-e* to); **2.** to donate blood; **-a ~ istemek** to want blood revenge; **-a susamak** to thirst for blood; **-a susamış** bloodthirsty; **-ı donmak** *fig.* s.o.'s blood runs cold; **-ı kaynamak 1.** to be hot-blooded; **2.** (*b-ne*) to warm to *s.o.*; **-ı kurumak** to be exasperated; **-ına dokunmak** to make s.o.'s blood boil; **-ına girmek 1.** to have s.o.'s blood on one's hands; **2.** to get a girl into trouble; **-ına susamak** (*kendi*) to court death.

kana NAUT load line.

kanaat, -ti [. - .] **1.** opinion, conviction; **2.** satisfaction, contentment; ~ **etm.** to be satisfied (*or* contented) (*ile* with); ~ **getirmek** to be of the opinion that; ~ **notu** mark based on the observation of the teacher; **-i olm.** to have an opinion; **-imce** in my opinion.

kanaatkâr, kanaatli contented; satisfied with what he has.

Kanada pr. n. Canada.

Kanadalı pr. n. Canadian.

kanağan credulous, gullible.

kanaktarım blood transfusion.

kanal 1. canal; **2.** ANAT duct, canal; **3.** MEC channel; ~ **açmak** to canalize.

kanalizasyon sewer system, sewerage, drains, sewers; ~ **borusu** sewer.

kanama bleeding, hemorrhage.

kanamak to bleed.

kanara [. x .] slaughterhouse.

kanarya [. x .] ZOO canary; ~ **sarısı** canary yellow.

kanat, -tı [. -] **1.** wing; **2.** ICHTH fin; **3.** leaf (*of a door*); **4.** vane; **5.** panel (*of a curtain*); ~ **alıştırmak** fig. to practice; ~ **çırpmak** to flutter; ~ **germek** (*b-nin üstüne*) fig. to take *s.o.* under one's protection; **-ı altına almak**

(*b-ni*) fig. to take *s.o.* under one's wing.

kanata [. x .] mug, tumbler.

kanatlanmak to take wing, to fly away.

kanatlı 1. winged; **2.** finned.

kanatmak to make bleed.

kanatsız wingless, apterous.

kanava [. x .], **kaneviçe** embroidery canvas.

kanca [x .] **1.** hook; **2.** grapnel; **-yı takmak** (*or* **atmak**) fig. to set one's cap (*-e* at), to get one's hooks (*-e* into).

kancalamak 1. to hook; **2.** to grapple.

kancalı hooked; ~ **iğne** safety pin.

kancık 1. bitch; **2.** fig. sneaky, low-down; **3.** sl. woman.

kançılar POL official in a consular *or* embassy secretariat.

kandaş cognate, consanguineous.

kandırıcı 1. deceptive, beguiling; **2.** convincing; **3.** thirst-quenching.

kandırmaca bluff; ~ **yapmak** to bluff.

kandırmak 1. to deceive, to fool, to cajole, to take in; **2.** to convince, to persuade; **3.** to quench (*thirst*).

kandil 1. oil-lamp; **2.** kerosene lamp; **3.** isl. one of five Islamic holy nights *when the minarets are illuminated*; **4.** sl. pissed, drunk; ~ **gecesi** isl. = ~ **3**; ~ **yağı** poor quality olive oil; **-in yağı tükenmek** fig. to breathe one's last breath.

kandilci tender of oil lamps (*in a mosque*).

kandilli 1. illuminated by an oil lamp; **2.** sl. pissed; ~ **küfür** resounding oath; ~ **temenna** (*or* **selam**) bowing and scraping.

kanepe[1] sofa, couch, settee.

kanepe[2] canapé.

kangal 1. coil; skein; **2.** ANAT loop, ansa.

kangallamak to coil up.

kangren MED gangrene; ~ **olm.** to have gangrene.

kanguru ZOO kangaroo.

kanı opinion, view.

kanık content, satisfied.

kanıksamak, kanıksımak 1. to become inured (*-e* to); **2.** to become surfeited (*-e* with), to become sick (*-e* of).

kanırtmak to twist or bend loose.

kanış opinion.

kanıt, -tı evidence, proof.

kanıtlamak to prove.

kani, -li [â] convinced; ~ **olm.** to be convinced (*-e* of).

kaniş poodle.

kankurutan BOT mandrake.

kanlamak to blood.

kanlanmak 1. to become blood-stained; **2.** to become vigorous; **3.** to get bloodshot (*eyes*).

kanlı 1. bloody, bloodstained; **2.** bloodshot (*eyes*); **3.** sanguinary, bloody; **4.** bloodguilty; **5.** robust, vigorous; ~ **basur** dysentery; ~ **bıçaklı olm. 1.** to get into a bloody fight; **2.** to be out for each other's blood; ~ **canlı** robust, vigorous; ~ **katil** bloodthirsty criminal.

kanmak 1. to be fooled (*or* taken in); **2.** to believe; **3.** to be contented (*or* satisfied) (*ile* with); **4.** to have had one's fill (-*e* of); **kana kana içmek** to drink thirstily, to quaff, to drink to one's heart's content.

kano canoe.

kanon MUS canon.

kansa craw, maw, crop.

kanser cancer; ~ **olm.** to have cancer; to become cancerous.

kanserli cancerous.

kansız 1. bloodless; anemic; **2.** *fig.* spineless, cowardly.

kansızlık anemia.

kantar 1. scales, weighbridge; **2.** steelyard; **3.** kantar, cantar; ~ **kavunu** a large kind of muskmelon; ~ **resmi** (*or* **parası**) weighing fee; ~ **topu** ball of a steelyard; -*a* **çekmek** (*or* **vurmak**) to weigh (*a. fig.*); -*a* **gelmek** to be weighable; -*ı* **belinde** F alert, sly, cunning; -*ın* **topunu kaçırmak** *fig.* to overstep the limit, to go to extremes.

kantariye [. - . .] tax levied on weighable things.

kantarlı 1. heavy, severe; **2.** resounding oath; ~ **küfür** resounding oath; -*yı* **atmak** (*or* **basmak** *or* **savurmak**) *sl.* to cuss a blue streak.

kantaron BOT centaury.

kantaşı, -nı 1. bloodstone, heliotrope; **2.** alum.

kantin canteen, snack bar.

kanto [x .] MUS fin-de-siècle cabaret song.

kantocu fin-de-siècle cabaret chanteuse.

kanton canton.

kanun [- -] **1.** law, statute, act; **2.** MUS zitherlike instrument; ~ **dışı** illegal, outlaw; ~ **gücü** legal force (*or* power); ~ **maddesi** article of a law; ~ **nazarın-da** in the eyes of the law; ~ **tasarısı** bill, draft of a law; ~ **teklifi** bill; ~ **yapmak** to enact a law; ~ **yolu ile** by legal means; -*a aykırı* illegal, outlaw; -*a uygun* legal, licit, lawful; -*i esası* JUR constitution.

kanunen [- - .] legally, by law, according to law.

kanuni [- - -] **1.** legal, lawful, legitimate, statutory; **2.** **kanun**-player; **2** **Sultan Süleyman** Suleiman the Magnificent; ~ **yollara baş vurmak** to take legal steps.

kanuniyet, -ti [- - . .] legality; ~ **kesp etm.** to become a law.

kanunlaşmak to become a law.

kanunlaştırmak to legalize.

kanunname [- - - .] statute book, code of laws.

kanunsuz illegal, unlawful.

kanunsuzluk illegality, unlawfulness, lawlessness.

kânunuevvel [- - . . .] *obs.* December.

kânunusani [- - . . .] *obs.* January.

kanyak cognac, brandy.

kanyon canyon.

kaos chaos.

kap, -bı 1. pot, vessel; **2.** cover; case; container, receptacle; **3.** dish, plate (*of food*); ~ **kacak** pots and pans.

Kapadokya *pr. n.* Cappadocia.

kapak 1. lid, cover; **2.** tap, stopper; **3.** cover (*of a book*); **4.** ANAT valve; ~ **kızı** cover girl; **kapağı atmak** F to escape (-*e* to).

kapakçık ANAT valvule, valvula.

kapaklanmak 1. to fall flat on one's face; **2.** to capsize, to overturn.

kapaklı covered.

kapaksız coverless; lidless.

kapalı 1. closed, shut; covered; **2.** roofed, covered; **3.** overcast (*sky*); **4.** blocked (*road*); **5.** oblique, indirect (*words*); **6.** secret (*meeting*); ~ **celse** closed (*or* executive) session; ~ **duruşma** closed hearing; ~ **geçmek** to pass over, to slide over, to slur over (*a point*); ~ **gişe oynamak** to play to a full house; ~ **kutu** *fig.* inscrutable person, pussyfooter; ~ **oturum** *s.* ~ **celse**; ~ **sözler** hints, innuendoes; ~ **tribün** covered grandstand; ~ **zarf usulü ile** by sealed tender.

Kapalıçarşı *pr. n.* the Grand Bazaar, the Covered Bazaar.

kapama 1. *vn. of* **kapamak**; **2.** lamb and onion stew; **3.** *obs.* complete suit of ready-made clothes.

kapamak 1. to close, to shut; **2.** to block (*road*); **3.** to stop up, to plug up; **4.** to shut down, to close down (*business*); to abolish, to suppress (*organization*); **5.** to hide, to cover, to conceal, to obscure; to veil; **6.** to turn off (*radio, faucet, electricity, etc.*); **7.** to lock up; **8.** to pay up, to settle (*account*); **9.** to drop (*matter*); **10.** to hoard, to stockpile; **11.** to draw (*curtain*).

kapan 1. trap; snare; **2.** *fig.* trap, trick; ~ **kurmak** to set a trap; **-a düşmek** to fall into a trap; **-a düşürmek** to entrap; **-a kısılmak** to be caught in a trap.

kapanık 1. closed, shut; **2.** *fig.* gloomy, oppressive (*place*); **3.** confined, shut in; **4.** overcast (*weather*); **5.** unsociable, shy.

kapanış closure; ~ **saati** closing time.

kapanmak 1. *pass. or refl. of* **kapamak**; **2.** (*bir yere*) to seclude o.s. in (*a place*); **3.** to veil herself; **4.** to heal (*wound*); **5.** to cease; **6.** to become cloudy (*or* overcast) (*sky*); **7.** (*üstüne*) to hunch down (*over*).

kapari [x . .] вот caper (plant).

kaparo [. x .] deposit, earnest money.

kaparoz *sl.* swag, pickings, spoils.

kapasite capacity.

kapatma 1. *vn. of* **kapatmak**; **2.** concubine, mistress; **3.** *basketball*: blocking.

kapatmak 1. *caus. of* **kapamak**; **2.** to close, to shut; to cover; **3.** to get very cheap; **4.** to keep (*mistress*); **5.** to close down; to abolish, to suppress; **6.** to hang up (*telephone*).

kapçak large hook with a long handle.

kapçık 1. small container; **2.** shell; **3.** вот capsule, pod.

kapı 1. door; **2.** gate; **3.** possibility; **4.** *backgammon*: point; ~ **açmak** to mention, to bring up; ~ **almak** *backgammon*: to block a point; ~ **baca açık** *fig.* unprotected (*place*); ~ **dışarı etm.** (*b-ni*) to show *s.o.* the door, to throw *s.o.* out; ~ **duvar** no one answered the door; ~ **gibi** portly, full-bodied; ~~ **dolaşmak** to go from door to door; ~ **kolu** door handle; ~ **komşu** next-door neighbo(u)r; ~ **kuzusu** wicket; ~ **mandalı** door latch; ~ **numarası** street number (*of a house*); ~ **tokmağı** (door) knocker; **-sı herkese açık olm.** to keep open house; **-sını çalmak** (*b-nin*) *fig.* to resort to *s.o.*;

-ya dayanmak *fig.* to heave into sight; **-yı kırıp odun etm.** *fig.* to kill the goose that lays the golden egg(s); **-yı** (*or* **-ya**) **vurmak** to knock at (*or* on) the door.

kapıcı doorkeeper, doorman; caretaker, janitor.

kapıkulu, -nu *obs.* Janissary guard.

kapılanmak to find a job (**-e** with).

kapılgan 1. susceptible; **2.** easily deceived; **3.** quick to fall in love.

kapılmak 1. *pass. of* **kapmak**; **2.** to be carried (*or* washed) away (**-e** by); **3.** to be entranced (*or* carried away) (**-e** by).

kapış snatch; ~~ **gitmek** to be sold like hot cakes; ~~ **yemek** to gobble up, to wolf down.

kapışılmak *s.* **kapış kapış gitmek**.

kapışmak 1. to snatch (**at**), to scramble (**for**); **2.** to rush to purchase; **3.** (*b-le*) to get to grips with *s.o.*; **4.** *sl.* to kiss each other, to bill and coo.

kapik kopeck, kopek.

kapital, -li capital.

kapitalist, -ti capitalist.

kapitalizm capitalism.

kapitone quilted (*cloth*); tufted (*upholstery*).

kapitülasyon capitulation.

kapkaç purse-snatching.

kapkaççı purse-snatcher; snatch-and-run thief.

kapkara [x . .] pitch-dark; pitch-black.

kapkaranlık completely dark.

kaplam LOG extension, extent.

kaplama 1. *vn. of* **kaplamak**; **2.** coat; plate; **3.** coating; plating; **4.** crown; **5.** veneer; **6.** coated, plated, covered; ~ **diş** crowned tooth.

kaplamacı 1. metal plater; **2.** veneerer.

kaplamak 1. to cover; **2.** to coat, to plate; to veneer; **3.** to bind; to line; **4.** to spread over, to envelop; **5.** to encase, to cover.

kaplan zoo tiger.

kaplı 1. covered; plated; coated; **2.** bound (*book*).

kaplıca 1. hot spring, thermal spring; hot spring resort, spa; **2.** вот einkorn wheat.

kaplumbağa [. x . .] zoo turtle, tortoise.

kapma 1. *vn. of* **kapmak**; **2.** seized, snatched.

kapmak, (-ar) 1. to snatch, to grasp, to seize, to catch, to snap up; **2.** to grab and devour; **3.** to catch (*disease*); **4.** to catch and mangle (*machine*); **5.** to pick up, to get the hang (of); **6.** to get, to develop, to acquire (*habit*).

kaporta 1. MOT bonnet, *Am.* hood; **2.** NAUT hatch(way), companion, skylight.

kapris caprice, whim, fancy; ~ *yapmak* to behave capriciously.

kaprisli capricious.

kapsam 1. scope, radius, embrace, sphere; **2.** LOG extent, extension.

kapsamak to contain, to comprise, to include.

kapsamlı extensive, comprehensive.

kapsız coverless.

kapsol percussion cap.

kapsül BOT, MED, CHEM, ANAT capsule.

kapşon hood.

kaptan captain (*a. sports*), skipper; ~ *köşkü* (or *köprüsü*) NAUT bridge; ~ *pilot* AVIA chief pilot.

kaptanlık captaincy, captainship; ~ *etm.* to captain.

kaptıkaçtı 1. minibus; **2.** purse-snatching; **3.** a card game.

kaptırmak 1. *caus. of* **kapmak**; **2.** to get (*a part of one's body*) caught in (*a machine*).

kapuska [. x .] cabbage stew.

kaput, -tu 1. military greatcoat; **2.** condom, contraceptive, sheath, rubber; **3.** bonnet, *Am.* hood; ~ *gitmek* to flunk all one's exams.

kaputbezi, -ni canvas, sail cloth.

kar snow; ~ *fırtınası* snowstorm; ~ *gibi* snowwhite; ~ *topu* snowball; ~ *topu oynamak* to have a snowball fight; ~ *tutmak* to stick (*snow*); ~ *yağmak* to snow; *-dan adam* snowman.

kâr 1. profit; **2.** benefit; ~ *bırakmak* to yield a profit; ~ *etm.* to profit, to make a profit; ~ *getirmek* = ~ *bırakmak*; ~ *haddi* profit limit; ~ *kalmak* to remain as profit; ~ *payı* dividend; ~ *ve zarar* profit and loss; *-ı olmamak* (*b-nin*) not to be up (*or* equal) to); *bu, benim kârım değil* I am not equal to this; *-ını tamam etm. fig.* to kill, to polish off.

kara¹ 1. land, shore; **2.** terrestrial; ~ *kuvvetleri* MIL land forces, army; ~ *vapuru* F train; ~ *yolculuğu* overland journey; *-da* on land (*or* shore), ashore; *-dan* by land; *-ya ayak basmak* to go ashore, to disembark; *-ya çıkmak* to land, to go ashore, to disembark; *-ya düşmek* to run aground;

-ya oturmak to run aground; *-ya vurmak* to run ashore.

kara² 1. black; **2.** swarthy; **3.** PHOT negative; **4.** *fig.* unlucky; bad; ~ *benizli* swarthy, dark-complexioned; ~ *cahil* illiterate; ~ *cümle* co. the four arithmetical operations; ~ *çalmak* to slander, to calumniate; ~ *et* lean meat; ~ *gün dostu* true friend, a friend in need; ~ *haber bad news*: ~ *haber tez duyulur pro.* bad news travels fast; ~ ~ *düşünmek* to brood, to be in a brown study; ~ *listeye almak* to blacklist; ~ *mizah* black humo(u)r; ~ *oğlan* **1.** swarthy boy; **2.** gypsy; ~ *sürmek fig.* to slander, to blacken, to calumniate; ~ *tahta* blackboard; ~ *talih* bad luck, misfortune; ~ *toprak* black soil, chernozem; ~ *yağız* swarthy (*young man*); *-lar bağlamak* (*or giymek*) to put on (*or* wear) mourning, to be dressed in black.

karaağaç, -cı BOT elm.

karabasan 1. nightmare; **2.** depression.

karabaş 1. monk; **2.** confirmed bachelor; **3.** BOT French lavender; **4.** P Anatolian sheep dog.

karabatak ZOO cormorant.

karabet, -ti [. - .] **1.** affinity; **2.** relationship, kinship.

karabiber 1. BOT black pepper; **2.** *fig.* cute brunette.

karabina [. . x .] carbine; blunderbuss.

karaborsa black market; *-ya düşmek* to go on the black market.

karaborsacı black marketeer.

karaborsacılık black-marketeering.

karaboya sulphuric acid.

karabuğday BOT buckwheat.

karabulut, -tu black (*or* rain) cloud, nimbus.

karaca¹ blackish; dark; ~ *kemiği* ANAT humerus.

karaca² ZOO roe (deer).

karacı 1. soldier; **2.** *fig.* slanderer; **3.** gypsy.

karaciğer ANAT liver.

karaçalı BOT blackthorn.

karaçam BOT black pine.

karaçıban MED carbuncle.

Karadağ *pr. n.* Montenegro.

karadamga smirch, stain, blot.

Karadeniz *pr. n.* the Black Sea; *-de gemilerin mi battı?* why are you in the dumps (*or* doldrums)?, why so worried?

karadut BOT black mulberry.
karaduygu melancholia.
karaelmas coal.
karafaki [. . x .] small carafe (or decanter).
karafatma ZOO cockroach, blackbeetle.
karagöz 1. ZOO sargo; **2.** ♀ Turkish shadow play; **3.** Turkish Punch; ~ *oyunu* shadow play.
karagül karakul.
karağı 1. poker; **2.** blindness.
karahumma MED typhoid (or enteric) fever.
karaiğne ZOO red ant.
karakaçan black donkey.
karakalem 1. charcoal; **2.** charcoal drawing.
karakehribar black amber, jet.
karakış the dead of winter.
karakol police station; ~ *gemisi* coast-guard ship, patrol vessel; ~ *gezmek* to patrol his beat.
karakolluk olm. F to have to be taken to the police station.
karakoncolos 1. bugbear, black bogy, vampire, bugaboo; **2.** fig. person like the back (end) of a bus.
karakter character; ~ *oyuncusu* character actor; ~ *rolü* character part; ~ *sahibi* person of firm character.
karakteristik characteristic, distinctive.
karakterli of good character.
karaktersiz characterless.
karakulak ZOO caracal.
karakuş 1. ZOO black eagle; **2.** farcy.
karalama 1. vn. of **karalamak**; **2.** calligraphic exercise; **3.** scribble, doodle; **4.** (rough) draft; **5.** slander; ~ *defteri* exercise book.
karalamak 1. to scribble, to doodle; **2.** to cross out; **3.** to draft, to sketch out; **4.** fig. to slander, to blacken, to calumniate.
karalaşmak to blacken.
karalı spotted with black.
karalık blackness; darkness.
karaltı 1. indistinct figure; **2.** silhouette; **3.** smudge.
karamak[1] to slander, to run down.
karamak[2] to look after, to take care of.
karaman fat-tailed sheep.
karambol 1. billiards: cannon, carom, billiard; **2.** F collision, smashup.
karamela [. . x .] caramel.
karamsar pessimistic.

karamsarlık pessimism.
karamsı blackish.
karamuk 1. BOT corncockle; **2.** MED roseola infantum.
karanfil BOT **1.** carnation; **2.** clove (tree).
karanlık 1. dark; **2.** darkness, the dark; **3.** bad, wicked; **4.** obscure, unclarified; **5.** dangerous; ~ *basmadan* before nightfall (or dark); ~ *basmak* to fall (darkness); ~ *etm.* to block the light, to stand in s.o.'s light; ~ *oda* PHOT darkroom; ~ *olm.* to get dark; *karanlığa kalmak* to be benighted; *-ta göz kırpmak* fig. to wink in the dark.
karantina [. . x .] quarantine; ~ *bayrağı* quarantine flag; *-ya almak* to quarantine.
karar 1. decision, resolution, determination; **2.** stability, predictability; **3.** JUR verdict; **4.** estimate, approximation; ~ *almak* to make a decision; ~ *kılmak* (bşde) to decide on s.th.; ~ *vermek 1.* to decide (-e to); **2.** to make a decision; *-a bağlamak* to make a decision about; *-a varmak 1.* to arrive at (or reach) a decision; **2.** JUR to bring in a verdict (of).
karargâh MIL headquarters.
kararlama 1. vn. of **kararlamak**; **2.** estimated by guess, by rule of thumb.
kararlamadan at a guess.
kararlamak 1. to estimate by eye; **2.** to make a rough estimate.
kararlaşmak to be decided (or agreed on).
kararlaştırmak to decide, to agree (on), to resolve (on); to determine, to fix (date).
kararlı decisive, determined, resolute.
kararlılık 1. decisiveness, determination, resolution; **2.** stability.
kararmak 1. to get dark; to turn black, to darken; **2.** to fade (light).
kararname [. . - .] decree.
kararsız 1. indecisive, undecided; **2.** unstable, changeable; ~ *olm.* to be indecisive, to shilly-shally.
kararsızlık 1. indecision; **2.** instability.
karartı 1. darkness; **2.** smudge.
karartma blackout.
karartmak 1. to darken; **2.** to black out.
karasaban primitive plough, Am. plow.
karasal terrestrial, territorial.
karasevda 1. passionate love; **2.** mel-

ancholia; *-ya düşmek* (*or tutulmak*) to be passionately in love.

karasevdalı 1. passionately in love; **2.** melancholic.

karasığır ZOO water buffalo.

karasinek ZOO housefly.

karasu MED glaucoma.

karasuları, -nı territorial waters.

karatavuk ZOO blackbird.

karate karate.

karateci karateist.

karavan caravan, trailer.

karavana [.. x .] **1.** MIL cauldron, mess-tin; **2.** MIL food, chow; mess; **3.** miss; ~ *borusu* mess call; *-dan yemek* MIL to mess together.

karavanacı MIL mess carrier.

karayazı evil fate, ill luck.

karayel northwest wind.

karayıkım disaster.

karayolu, -nu highway, road; overland route.

karbon CHEM carbon; ~ *dioksit* carbon dioxide; ~ *kâğıdı* carbon paper; ~ *monoksit* carbon monoxide.

karbonat, -tı CHEM **1.** carbonate; **2.** sodium bicarbonate.

karbonatlamak CHEM to carbonate.

karbonhidrat, -tı CHEM carbohydrate.

karbonik CHEM carbonic; ~ *asit* carbonic acid.

karbonlaştırmak CHEM to carbonize, to char.

karbonlu CHEM carbonaceous, carboniferous.

karbüratör MEC carburet(t)or; ~ *ayan* carburet(t)or adjustment; ~ *memesi* carburet(t)or nozzle.

kardan Cardan (*or* universal) joint; ~ *mili* Cardan shaft.

kardaş s. *kardeş.*

kardelen BOT snowdrop.

kardeş brother; sister; sibling; ~ *payı yapmak* to go halves.

kardeşçe(sine) 1. in a brotherly manner, fraternally; in a sisterly manner; **2.** brotherly, fraternal; sisterly.

kardeşlik brotherhood; sisterhood.

kardinal, -li cardinal.

kardinallik cardinalate.

kardiyografi MED cardiography.

kardiyogram cardiogram.

kare square; *-sini almak* to square.

karekök, -kü square root; *-ünü almak* to extract the square root (*-in* of).

kareli chequered, *Am.* checkered, checked.

karfiçe [. x .] finishing nail.

karga ZOO crow; ~ *bok yemeden sl.* bright and early, at (the) crack of dawn; *-yı bülbül diye satmak* F to swindle.

kargaburnu, -nu MEC round-nose pliers.

kargaburun hawk-nosed.

kargabüken BOT nux vomica (tree).

kargacık burgacık 1. scrawly; **2.** in a scrawl; ~ ~ *yazmak* to write in a scrawl.

kargaşa 1. tumult, disorder; turmoil; anarchy; **2.** chaos, confusion, scramble; **3.** hullabaloo, commotion; ~ *çıkarmak* to kick up a row.

kargaşalı tumultuous.

kargaşalık = *kargaşa.*

kargatulumba carrying by arms and legs; ~ *etm.* to carry by arms and legs.

kargı pike; javelin; lance.

kargılık cartridge belt; bandoleer.

kargımak to curse.

kargın large carpenter's plane.

kargo [x .] cargo.

karha MED ulcer.

karı 1. wife, spouse; **2.** *sl.* broad, woman; ~ *almak* to marry; ~ *kısmı* womankind, weaker sex; ~ *kızan* P wife and children; ~ *koca* husband and wife, married couple; ~ *koca hayatı* married life; ~ *kocalık* matrimony; ~ *milleti* = ~ *kısmı*; *-sı ağızlı co.* henpecked (*husband*).

karık 1. snow blindness; **2.** snow-blind; **3.** furrow.

karılaşmak to become effeminate.

karılık wifehood; wifeliness.

karın, -rnı 1. abdomen; **2.** stomach, belly; **3.** womb; **4.** *fig.* mind, head, loaf; **5.** PHYS loop, antinode; ~ *ağrısı* **1.** stomach ache, colic; **2.** *fig.* a pain in the neck (*person*); **3.** F what-do-you-call-it, whatyoumay jigger; ~ *boşluğu* abdominal cavity; (karnı): ~ *aç* hungry; ~ *ağrımak* to have a stomach ache; ~ *burnunda* F in the (pudding) club, very much in the family way; ~ *geniş* easygoing, nonchalant; ~ *-na geçmiş* skeleton, a bag of bones; ~ *tok* full; ~ *tok, sırtı pek* well-off and contented with life; ~ *zil* (*or dümbelek*) *çalmak* to growl from hunger, to feel peckish; *-ndan söylemek* F to make up a yarn; *-nı şişirmek* (*b-nin*) F to put *s.o.* in the club.

karınca 1. zoo ant; **2.** min blowhole; ~
asidi chem formic acid; ~ **belli** wasp-
-waisted; ~ **duası gibi** very illegible
(*handwriting*); ~ **kararınca** (*or* **kade-
rince**) as much as one can; ~ **yuvası**
ant nest, anthill; ~ **yuvası gibi kaynamak** *fig.* to teem (*or* be swarming)
with people; **-yı bile incitmez** he will
not say 'boo' to a goose.

karıncalanmak 1. to be crawling with
ants; **2.** to have pins and needles; **3.**
mec to develop blowholes.

karınlamak naut to pull up alongside.

karınlı potbellied.

karınmak 1. to be mixed (together); **2.**
to mate (*fowls*).

karınsa molting (season) (*birds*).

karıntı whirlpool.

karınzarı, -nı anat peritoneum; ~
yangısı peritonitis.

karış span, handspan; ~ ~ **1.** every inch
(*of a place*); **2.** with a fine-tooth comb.

karışık 1. mixed; miscellaneous, assorted, heterogeneous; motley; **2.**
adulterated; **3.** disorganized,
jumbled, confused; **4.** complex; complicated.

karışıklık 1. confusion, disorder; **2.** tumult, civic turmoil; ~ **çıkarmak** to stir
up trouble, to kick up a row.

karışım 1. chem mix, mixture, blend; **2.**
med complication.

karışlamak to span.

karışmak 1. to mix (*ile* with); to be dispersed (*ile* in); **2.** to interfere (*-e* in), to
meddle (*-e* in); **3.** to get mixed up, to
become confused (*or* jumbled); **4.** to
join; **5.** to flow into (*another river*); **6.**
to be in charge (*-e* of), to be responsible (*-e* for).

karıştırıcı 1. mixer; blender; **2.** *fig.*
trouble-maker.

karıştırmak *caus. of* **karışmak 1.** to
mix, to stir; to blend; **2.** to confuse
(*ile* with); **3.** to get confused (*in mind*);
4. to rummage through; to thumb
through; **5.** (*burnunu*) to pick one's
nose.

karides [. x .] zoo shrimp; prawn.

karikatür 1. caricature; **2.** cartoon;
comic strip; **3.** takeoff; **-ünü yapmak**
to caricature.

karikatürcü caricaturist.

karikatürist = **karikatürcü.**

**karikatürize etm., karikatürleştirmek
1.** to caricature; **2.** to take off.

karina [. x .] naut bottom (*of a ship*); ~

etm. (*or* **-ya basmak**) to careen (*a vessel*).

karine 1. evidence, trace; **2.** clue; ~ **ile
anlamak** to infer, to conjecture, to deduce from the available information.

kariyer career; ~ **yapmak** to build a career.

karkas mec concrete skeleton (*of a
building*).

karlamak to snow.

karlı snowy; snow-clad; snow-capped.

kârlı profitable, advantageous; ~
çıkmak to make a profit, to come
out ahead; to turn out profitable.

karlık snow-pit.

karma 1. *vn. of* **karmak; 2.** mixed; **3.** co-
educational; ~ **eğitim** coeducation; ~
ekonomi mixed economy; ~ **okul** co-
educational school.

karmak 1. to mix, to blend; **2.** *cards:* to
shuffle.

karmakarış [x . .], **karmakarışık** [x . . .
.] promiscuous, in utter confusion; ~
etm. to mess up.

karman çorman *s.* **karmakarışık.**

karmanyola [. . x .] robbery; ~ **etm.** to
rob, to mug.

karmanyolacı robber, mugger.

karmaşa 1. complexity, confusion; **2.**
psych complex.

karmaşık complicated, complex.

karmaşıklık complexity.

karmuk big hook.

karnabahar, karnabit, -ti bot cauli-
flower.

karnaksı *s.* **karın ağrısı.**

karnaval carnival.

karne 1. (student's) report card; **2.**
card.

karnıyarık *dish of aubergines stuffed
with mincemeat.*

karni chem retort.

karo *cards:* diamond.

karoser mot body.

karpit chem (calcium) carbide.

karpuz 1. bot watermelon; **2.** globe; ~
fener Chinese lantern.

karpuzcu watermelon-seller; water-
melon-grower.

karsak zoo corsac.

kârsız unprofitable, profitless.

karşı 1. opposite; **2.** opposing; **3.** anti-,
counter-; **4.** in the direction (*-e* of),
facing, towards; **5.** against, contrary
(*-e* to); **6.** in return (*-e* for); **7.** in response (*-e* to); **8.** as a cure (*-e* for),
as a countermeasure (*-e* to), against;

~ **çıkmak** (*b-ne*) **1.** to oppose *s.o.*; **2.** to object to *s.o.*; ~ **durmak** to resist, to oppose; ~ **gelmek** (*b-ne*) to defy *s.o.*, to go against *s.o.*; ~ **görüşlü** opponent; ~ **hücum** counterattack; ~ **hücuma geçmek** to counterattack; ~ **-ya** face to face; ~ **koymak** to resist, to oppose; ~ **olm.** to be against; ~ **taarruz** MIL counteroffensive; ~ **takım** opposing team; ~ **taraf** opposite side; ~ **teklif** counterproposal; counteroffer; **-dan bakmak** *fig.* to watch idly; **-dan -ya** across; *bu ani kaza karşısında* in face of this sudden accident.

karşıcasus counterspy.

karşıgelim BIOL antagonism.

karşıki (the) opposite, facing.

karşılama *folk music played or sung when meeting a bridal procession.*

karşılamak 1. to go to meet, to welcome; **2.** to pay, to cover; to be enough (*for*), to suffice, to meet (*a need*); **3.** to defray (*expenses*); **4.** to respond (*or* react) (*to*); **5.** to prevent; to remedy.

karşılaşma *vn. of* **karşılaşmak**, *part.* **1.** *sports:* game, match; **2.** CHEM reaction.

karşılaşmak 1. to meet; **2.** to run (*ile* into), to meet; **3.** to face, to be up (*ile* against), to be confronted (*ile* with); **4.** *sports:* to play each other.

karşılaştırılabilir comparable.

karşılaştırma 1. comparison; **2.** confrontation.

karşılaştırmak *caus. of* **karşılaşmak**, *part.* **1.** to compare (*ile* with); **2.** to confront (*ile* with).

karşılaştırmalı comparative; ~ **dilbilim** comparative linguistics.

karşılık 1. reply, retort, response, answer; **2.** reaction, response; **3.** equivalent, translation; **4.** appropriation; **5.** contrary, opposite; **6.** in response (*-e* to); **7.** in contrast (*-e* to); **8.** in payment (*-e* for); ~ **olarak 1.** in return; **2.** in reply (*-e* to); ~ **vermek** to retort, to answer back, to talk back.

karşılıklı 1. mutual, reciprocal; **2.** opposite; ~ **olarak** mutually; ~ **sigorta** mutual insurance.

karşılıksız 1. complimentary, gratis; **2.** dishono(u)red (*check*); **3.** unanswered (*love*); **4.** unreturned, unrequited; ~ **çıkmak** to bounce (*check*).

karşın in spite of (*-e* of).

karşıt, -tı 1. opposite, contrary (*-e* to); **2.** anti-, counter-; **3.** opposed, in disagreement; ~ **anlamlı** antonymous.

karşıtdeğerli ambivalent.

karşıtduygu antipathy.

karşıtlı GR adversative.

karşıtlık 1. contrast; **2.** disagreement.

kart¹, -tı 1. old; **2.** hard, tough; ~ **kız** old maid, spinster.

kart², -tı 1. card; **2.** visiting (*or* calling) card; **3.** postcard.

kartal ZOO eagle; ~ **yavrusu** eaglet.

kartalağacı, -nı BOT eaglewood.

kartaloş, kartaloz *sl.* over the hill, past it.

kartel¹ cartel.

kartel² keg.

kartlaşmak to grow old, to get past it.

kartlık 1. oldness; **2.** staleness.

kartograf cartographer.

kartografi cartography.

karton pasteboard; cardboard; ~ **kapak** cover.

kartonpiyer papier-mâché.

kartpostal postcard.

kartuk large rake.

kartuş cartridge.

kartvizit, -ti visiting (*or* calling) card.

Karun [- -] **1.** *pr. n. a rich man mentioned in the Koran;* **2.** *fig.* Croesus.

karyağdı pepper-and-salt.

karyola bed, bedstead.

kas muscle; ~ **kasılması** muscular contraction; ~ **teli** muscular fiber; ~ **tutukluğu** muscle cramp.

kasa [x .] **1.** safe, strongbox; **2.** cash register, till; **3.** safe-deposit box; **4.** case, crate (*for bottles*); **5.** MEC body; **6.** *games:* the bank; **7.** *gymnastics:* horse; **8.** door frame; window frame; ~ **açığı** cash shortage, deficit; ~ **dairesi** strongroom; ~ **defteri** cashbook; ~ **hesabı** cash ac count; ~ **hırsızı** safecracker, safebreaker; ~ **soymak** to break (*or* crack) a safe.

kasaba small town.

kasadar cashier, teller.

kasap, -bı 1. butcher (*a. fig.*); **2.** butcher shop, butcher's.

kasaphane [. . - .] slaughterhouse.

kasaplık 1. butchery; **2.** fit for slaughter (*animal*).

kasara [. x .] NAUT castle; ~ **altı** steerage; ~ **üstü** poop deck.

kasatura [.. x .] sword bayonet.

kasavet, -ti [. - .] worry, sorrow.

kasavetlenmek [. - . . .] to become

worried.

kasbilim myology.

kasdoku muscle tissue.

kâse 1. bowl; **2.** *sl.* rump.

kasık 1. ANAT groin; **2.** inguinal; **~ kemiği** ANAT pubis; **kasığı çatlamak** (*b-nin*) to get a hernia.

kasıkbağı, -nı truss for a hernia.

kasıkbiti, -ni ZOO crab louse.

kasıksal inguinal.

kasıl ANAT, MED muscular.

kasılduyumlar PSYCH muscular sensations.

kasılmak 1. *pass. of* **kasmak**; **2.** to contract, to flex; **3.** to shorten; **4.** *fig.* to put on airs, to swank, to show off, to swagger.

kasım November.

kasımpatı, -nı BOT chrysanthemum.

kasınç cramp, spasm.

kasınmak 1. to become cramped (*muscle*); **2.** *fig.* to give o.s. airs.

kasıntı 1. stitching used to shorten a garment; **2.** *fig.* swagger, swank.

kasır, -srı mansion, pleasure-house.

kasırga whirlwind, tornado; cyclone.

kasıt, -stı 1. purpose, intention; **2.** evil intent; **kastı olm.** to harbo(u)r evil intentions (*-e* against).

kasıtlı deliberate, intentional; premeditated.

kaside qasida.

kasis open drainage ditch (*cut across a road*).

kasiyer cashier.

kaskatı [x . .] as hard as a stone, as hard as nails.

kasket, -ti cap.

kasko automobile insurance.

kaslı muscular, brawny.

kasmak, (-ar) 1. to take in (*garment*); **2.** to reduce, to curtail (*amount*); **3.** to shorten (*tie, etc.*); **4.** to oppress; **kasıp kavurmak 1.** to tyrannize, to terrorize; **2.** (*ortalığı*) to ruin, to destroy.

kasnak 1. rim, hoop; **2.** tambour; **3.** wrestling hold; **~ kayışı** MEC belt.

kasnaklamak 1. to hoop; **2.** to hug.

kaspanak *sl.* by force, willy-nilly.

kastanyola [. . x .] NAUT pawl, ratchet, detent.

kastarlamak to bleach.

kasten [x .] on purpose, intentionally, deliberately.

kastetmek [x . .] **1.** to mean; to intend, to purpose; **2.** to have designs (*-e* on, against).

kasti [ī] deliberate, intentional, premeditated.

kastor beaver (*fur*).

kasvet, -ti gloom, depression.

kasvetli gloomy.

kaş 1. eyebrow; **2.** projection, brow; **3.** pommel (*of a saddle*); **~ atmak** (*or* **etm.**) to raise one's eyebrows (*as a signal*); **~ göz etm.** to wink (*-e* at); **~ yapayım derken göz çıkarmak** *fig.* to aggravate matters while trying to be helpful; **-la göz arasında** in the twinkling of an eye, in a trice; **-larını çatmak** to frown, to knit one's brows.

kaşağı currycomb.

kaşağılamak to curry, to groom.

kaşalot 1. ZOO cachalot; **2.** *sl.* dunce, imbecile.

kaşamak *s.* **kaşağılamak.**

kaşan urinating, staling.

kâşane [- - .] mansion.

kaşanmak to stop and stale.

kaşar 1. (*peyniri*) sheep cheese; **2.** kosher; **3.** *sl.* clever, sly (*gambler*).

kaşarlanmak to become hackneyed.

kaşarlanmış hackneyed.

kaşe cachet.

kaşer *s.* **kaşar.**

kaşık 1. spoon; **2.** spoonful; **~ atmak** (*or* **çalmak**) eat heartily; **~ düşmanı** *co.* one's wife, the missus; **~ ~** by spoonfuls; **-la yedirip sapıyle** (*gözünü*) **çıkarmak** to spoil a good deed with a bad one.

kaşıkçı elması *the largest diamond in the Ottoman jewel collection.*

kaşıkçıkuşu, -nu ZOO pelican.

kaşıklamak to spoon out.

kaşımak to scratch.

kaşındırmak to make itch.

kaşınmak 1. to itch, to scratch o.s.; **2.** *fig.* to be itching for a beating.

kaşıntı itch, pruritus.

kaşıntılı itchy, pruritic.

kâşif explorer; discoverer.

kaşkariko [. . x .] *sl.* trick, deceit.

kaşkaval 1. yellow cheese; **2.** *sl.* dimwitted.

kaşkol scarf, neckerchief.

kaşkorse camisole.

kaşmer, kaşmerdikoz *sl.* clown; oddball.

kaşmir cashmere.

kat, -tı 1. storey, *Am.* story, floor; **2.** layer, stratum; fold; **3.** coat (*of paint*); **4.** set (*of clothes*); **5.** time(s); **6.** presence; **7.** MATH multiple; **~ çıkmak** to add a storey (*to a building*); ~ ~ **1.** in layers; **2.** many times more, much more; ~ *mülkiyeti* condominium; ~ *yeri* crease, fold.

katafalk, *-kı* catafalque.

katakofti [. . x .] *sl.* lie.

katakulli [. . x .] *sl.* trick, ruse; ~ *yapmak sl.* to swindle; to dupe; *-ye gelmek sl.* to be taken in.

kataliz catalysis.

katalizatör catalyst.

katalog catalogue.

katana artillery horse; ~ *gibi* F portly (*woman*).

katar 1. train (*of wagons or animals*); **2.** caravan (*of vehicles*); **3.** convoy (*of military vehicles*); ~ *kılavuzu* donkey at the head of a file of camels.

Katar *pr. n.* Qatar.

katarakt, *-tı* MED cataract.

katarlamak to form into a line (*animals, vehicles*).

katedral, *-li* cathedral.

kategori category.

katetmek [x . .] **1.** to travel (*over*), to traverse, to cover; **2.** to out (*off*), to terminate; **3.** to intersect.

katgüt, *tü* catgut.

katı[1] **1.** hard, rigid, stiff; **2.** *fig.* tough, unbending; stern; insensitive; **3.** CHEM, PHYS solid; ~ *yumurta* hard-boiled egg; ~ *yürekli* hardhearted.

katı[2] gizzard (*of birds*).

katık anything eaten with bread.

katılaşmak 1. to harden (*a. fig.*); to stiffen; **2.** CHEM, PHYS to solidify.

katılaştırmak to harden.

katılgandoku ANAT connective tissue.

katılık 1. hardness; stiffness, rigidity; **2.** *fig.* hardheartedness; **3.** CHEM, PHYS solidity.

katılmak[1] **1.** *pass. of* **katmak**; **2.** to join (*a group*); to enter (*-e* into), to participate (*-e* in); **3.** (*b-ne*) to agree with *s.o.*

katılmak[2] to be out of breath (*from laughing or weeping*); *katıla katıla ağlamak* to choke with sobs; *katıla katıla gülmek* to split one's sides laughing, to choke with laughter, to be convulsed with laughter.

katım 1. adding, mixing; **2.** *s.* *koç katımı.*

katıntı mixture.

katır 1. mule; hinny; **2.** *fig.* mulish, obstinate; ~ *gibi inatçı* as stubborn as a mule.

katırcı muleteer.

katır kutur; ~ *yemek* to crunch, to munch.

katırtırnağı, *-nı* BOT broom, besom.

katışık mixed.

katışıksız unmixed, pure, unadulterated.

katışmak to join (*a group*).

katıştırmak to add (*-e* to).

katıyağ CHEM machine (*or* lubricating) grease.

kati definite, absolute, final; decisive; ~ *karar* unappealable decision; ~ *olarak* definitely; ~ *suretle* absolutely; ~ *teklif* firm offer.

katil[1]*, -tli* murder, homicide.

katil[2] [â] **1.** murderer; **2.** lethal, deadly; ~ *kadın* murderess.

katileşmek [î] to become definite.

kâtip, *-bi* clerk; secretary.

kâtiplik clerkship; ~ *yapmak* to clerk.

katiyen [î] [. x .] **1.** never, by no means; **2.** definitely, absolutely.

katiyet, *-ti* definiteness, finality, decisiveness.

katkı 1. help, assistance, aid; **2.** contribution, addition, supplement; **3.** additive; alloy; *-da bulunmak* to contribute (*-e* to).

katkılı alloyed.

katkısız unalloyed; pure.

katlamak to fold (up).

katlanır folding, collapsible.

katlanmak 1. *pass. of* **katlamak**; **2.** to endure, to bear, to put up (*-e* with); *... yapmak zahmetine* ~ to take the trouble to do ...

katletmek [x . .] to murder (*a. fig.*).

katlı 1. folded; **2.** ... storied (*building*).

katliam massacre.

katma 1. *vn. of* **katmak**; **2.** added; ~ *bütçe* supplementary budget; ~ *değer vergisi* value-added-tax.

katmak, (*-ar*) **1.** to add, to mix (*-e* in); **2.** to send with; **3.** to annex (*-e* to); **4.** (*birbirine*) to set *a person* against *a person.*

katman *geol.* GEOGR layer; stratum; seam, bed.

katmanbulut, *-tu* METEOR stratus.

katmanlaşmak to stratify.

katmer 1. flaky pastry; **2.** layer; ~ ~ one on top of the other; one after the other.

katmerleşmek to become layered.

katmerli 1. in layers; **2.** double (*flower*); **3.** manifold, multiplied; ~ *yalan*

whopping lie.
Katolik *pr. n.* Catholic.
Katoliklik *pr. n.* Catholicism.
katra [x .] drop.
katran tar; ~ *gibi* tarry.
katranağacı, -nı BOT terebinth.
katrançamı, -nı BOT Georgia pine.
katranlamak to tar.
katranlı tarry, tarred.
katranruhu, -nu MED (wood) creosote.
katrilyon quadrillion.
katsayı MATH coefficient.
kauçuk 1. rubber; caoutchouc; **2.** BOT rubber plant; ~ *ağacı* BOT rubber tree.
kav tinder, punk.
kavaf cheap, ready-made shoes dealer; ~ *işi* shoddy; ~ *malı* shoddy goods.
kavak BOT poplar.
kavakinciri, -ni purple fig.
kaval shepherd's pipe, flageolet; ~ *kemiği* ANAT tibia; ~ *tüfek* smoothbored gun.
kavalcı piper.
kavallanmak *sl.* to pester.
kavalye escort, male partner (*in a dance*).
kavalyelik etm. to escort.
kavanço [. x .] **1.** NAUT shifting (*of a sail, etc.*); **2.** *sl.* landing (*s.o. with a job*).
kavanoz jar, pot.
kavara [. x .] *sl.* outburst, noise.
kavas HIST kavass.
kavata [. x .] **1.** BOT sour green tomato; **2.** large wooden bowl.
kavela [. x .] NAUT treenail, trunnel.
kavga 1. fight, brawl; row, quarrel; **2.** struggle; ~ *aramak* to look for trouble; ~ *çıkarmak* to kick up (*or* make) a row, to pick a fight; ~ *etm.* to fight (*ile* with); to quarrel (*ile* with); ~ *kaşağısı* instigator, agitator; *-ya girişmek* (*or tutuşmak*) to take up a quarrel (*ile* with).
kavgacı 1. quarrelsome, pugnacious; **2.** puncher.
kavgalı 1. angry (*ile* with); **2.** disputed.
kavgasız 1. peaceable, peace-loving; **2.** peacefully, without a quarrel.
kavi [ī] strong; sound.
kavil, -vli 1. *obs.* word; **2.** agreement.
kavilleşmek to agree, to reach an understanding.
kavim, -vmi people; tribe.
kavis, -vsi curve, arc.
kavkı ZOO shell.
kavlak 1. barkless; **2.** peeled off (*skin*).
kavlamak 1. to scale off (*bark*); **2.** to

peel, to desquamate (*skin*).
kavlıç, -cı 1. hernia, rupture; **2.** ruptured.
kavmantarı, -nı BOT punk, amadou.
kavram[1] *s.* **karınzarı.**
kavram[2] LOG concept.
kavrama 1. comprehension, grasp; **2.** MOT clutch (pedal); **3.** crosspiece, strut.
kavramak 1. to grasp, to clutch; **2.** *fig.* to comprehend, to grasp.
kavramcılık conceptualism.
kavramsal conceptual.
kavrayış PSYCH comprehension, grasp.
kavrayışlı quick-witted.
kavrayışsız slow-witted.
kavruk 1. scorched; **2.** *fig.* undersized, wizened, stunted.
kavrulmak 1. *pass. of* **kavurmak**; **2.** to be scorched.
kavrulmuş roasted; ~ *kahve* roasted coffee.
kavşak crossroads, junction, intersection.
kavuk 1. turban; **2.** bladder; ~ *sallamak* (*b-ne*) to fawn on *s.o.*, to toady to *s.o.*
kavuklu 1. turbaned; **2.** ♀ a character in the **ortaoyunu.**
kavun BOT muskmelon.
kavuniçi, -ni pale (*or* yellowish) orange.
kavurga roasted chickpeas, wheat *or* corn.
kavurma 1. *vn. of* **kavurmak**; **2.** roasted; **3.** fried meat.
kavurmaç, -cı roasted wheat.
kavurmak 1. to roast; **2.** to scorch, to parch (*sun*); **3.** to blight, to blast (*wind, cold*).
kavurucu parching, scorching (*heat*).
kavuşma 1. *vn. of* **kavuşmak**; **2.** BOT isogamy.
kavuşmak 1. to be reunited (*-e* with); **2.** to reach, to arrive (*-e* at); **3.** to meet, to overlap; **4.** to join (*roads*); **5.** to flow (*-e* into) (*rivers*).
kavuşum conjunction.
kay, -yyı vomit.
kaya 1. rock; reef; **2.** palisade, rock cliff (*or* precipice); **3.** ♀ *mf.*; ~ *gibi* rocky; *-lara bindirmek* to run on the rocks.
kayabalığı, -nı ZOO goby.
kayağan slippery, slick.
kayağantaş GEOL slate.
kayak 1. ski; **2.** skiing; ~ *yapmak* to ski.
kayakçı skier.

kayakçılık skiing.

kayalık 1. rocky, reefy; **2.** rocky place; rock cliff.

kayalifi, -ni asbestos.

kayan mountain torrent.

kayar 1. path, goat trail; **2.** reusing an old horseshoe.

kayasa cinch, girth (*of a saddle*).

kayatuzu, -nu GEOL rock salt, halite.

kaybetmek [x . .] to lose.

kaybolmak [x . .] to be lost; to vanish, to disappear.

kaydetmek [x . .] **1.** to register, to enroll; **2.** to enter, to write down, to record (*a.* with a tape recorder); **3.** *sports:* to score, to chalk up; **4.** to bear in mind.

kaydıhayat, -tı: -la (*or* ~ **şartıyle**) as long as one lives, for life.

kaydırak 1. slide; **2.** skid, stoneboat; **3.** hopscotch.

kaydırmak *caus. of* **kaymak 2.**, to slide, to skid.

kaydiye registration fee.

kaygan slippery, slick.

kaygana omelet(te).

kaygı anxiety, worry.

kaygılandırmak to worry.

kaygılanmak to worry, to be anxious.

kaygılı worried, anxious, uneasy.

kaygın slippery, slick.

kaygısız carefree, untroubled.

kaygısızlık untroubledness.

kayık 1. boat, caique, skiff; **2.** slipped to one side; ~ **salıncak** boat shaped swing; ~ **tabak** oval dish; ~ **yarışı** boat race; *-la gezmek* to go boating.

kayıkçı boatman.

kayıkhane [. . - .] boathouse.

kayın¹ brother-in-law.

kayın² BOT beech.

kayınbaba = **kayınpeder.**

kayınbirader brother-in-law.

kayınpeder father-in-law.

kayınvalide [. . - . .] mother-in-law.

kayıp, -ybı 1. loss; losses; **2.** MIL casualties; **3.** lost, missing; ~ **eşya bürosu** lost property office; ~ **listesi** casualty list; *-lara karışmak co.* to vanish into thin air, to disappear (*or* go off) into the blue.

kayır sandbank, sandbar.

kayırıcı patron, protector.

kayırıcılık favo(u)ritism.

kayırmak 1. to protect, to sponsor; **2.** to favo(u)r.

kayısı BOT apricot.

kayış¹ belt, strap, watch band; ~ **gibi 1.** as tough as leather (*meat*); **2.** heavily sun-tanned (*skin*); *-a çekmek* to strop (*a razor*).

kayış² *vn. of* **kaymak.**

kayışçı 1. strap maker *or* seller; **2.** *fig.* trickster, con man.

kayışdili, -ni strong language.

kayıt, -ydı 1. registration, enrollment; **2.** entry; **3.** recording; **4.** restriction, limitation, restraint; **5.** giving importance (to); **6.** noting down; ~ **altında** restricted; ~ **defteri** register, record book; ~ **ücreti** registration fee; **kayda değer** noteworthy, remarkable; **kayda geçirmek** to register; **kaydını silmek** to delete; to expunge.

kayıtlı 1. registered, enrolled; **2.** entered, recorded; noted down; **3.** restricted.

kayıtsız 1. unregistered, unrecorded; **2.** unrestricted; **3.** *fig.* indifferent, carefree, unconcerned; ~ **kalmak** to be indifferent (*-e* to); ~ **şartsız** unconditionally; ~ **şartsız teslim** unconditional surrender.

kayıtsızlık indifference, unconcern.

kayma 1. *vn. of* **kaymak;** **2.** landslide; **3.** *cinema:* misframe.

kaymaç, -cı slanting (*eye*).

kaymak¹ cream; ~ **altı** skim milk; ~ **bağlamak** to form cream; ~ **gibi 1.** snowwhite; **2.** creamy and delicious.

kaymak², (-ar) to slip, to slide, to skid.

kaymakam kaimakam, head official (*of a district*).

kaymaklanmak = **kaymak bağlamak.**

kaymaklı creamy; ~ **dondurma** (creamy) ice cream.

kaymaktaşı, -nı alabaster, gypsum.

kayme P paper lira.

kaynaç GEOL geyser.

kaynak 1. source, fountainhead; spring; **2.** origin source; **3.** MEC weld; **4.** patch (*on rubber*); ~ **yapmak 1.** MEC to weld; **2.** to patch (*rubber*).

kaynakça bibliography.

kaynakçı welder.

kaynakçılık welding.

kaynaklamak 1. MEC to weld; **2.** to patch (*rubber*).

kaynaklı 1. MEC welded; **2.** patched (*rubber*).

kaynama *vn. of* **kaynamak;** ~ **noktası** boiling point.

kaynamak 1. to boil; **2.** to ferment; **3.** to teem, to swarm; **4.** to knit (*bone*); **5.**

to surge up, to seethe; **6.** MEC to become welded; **7.** to fidget; **8.** *sl.* to be wasted (*lesson*).

kaynana mother-in-law.

kaynanadili, -ni BOT cactus.

kaynanazırıltısı, -nı clacker, rattle.

kaynar 1. boiling (*water*); **2.** *sl.* hashish.

kaynarca [. x .] **1.** hot spring, spa; **2.** fountainhead; spring.

kaynaşma *vn. of* **kaynaşmak**, *part.* uproar.

kaynaşmak 1. to fuse, to join (*ile* with); **2.** to go well (*ile* with), to blend (*ile* with); **3.** to teem, to swarm; **4.** CHEM to combine; **5.** *fig.* to become bosom friends.

kaynata [x . .] father-in-law.

kaynatmak 1. *caus. of* **kaynamak**; **2.** to boil; **3.** MEC to weld; **4.** *sl.* to swipe, to nick, to pinch; **5.** (*dersi*) *sl.* to waste (*a lesson hour*) talking; **6.** *sl.* to gad about.

kaypak 1. slippery, slick; **2.** *fig.* slippery, shifty.

kayrak 1. ski area (*or* slope); **2.** slate.

kayran glade.

kayser [x .] (*Roman*) caesar; (*German*) kaiser.

kayşa landslide.

kayşamak to slide, to slip (*land*).

kayşat, -tı GEOL debris.

kaytan cotton *or* silk cord; **~ bıyıklı** pointed mustachioed.

kaytarıcı shirker, goldbricker.

kaytarmak 1. to reject, to turn down; **2.** to shirk, to goldbrick (*work*).

kayyım 1. caretaker of a mosque; **2.** JUR trustee, administrator.

kaz 1. ZOO goose; **2.** *fig.* dumbbell, dolt; **~ gelen yerden tavuk esirgenmez** *pro.* you must lose a fly to catch a trout, throw out a sprat to catch a mackerel; **~ kafalı** F dumb. doltish; **~ kazla, daz dazla, kel tavuk topal horozla** *pro.* birds of a feather flock together; **~ palazı** gosling; **-ı koz anlamak** to get wrong, to misunderstand; **-ın ayağı öyle değil** it isn't like that at all.

kaza [. -] **1.** accident; misfortune; **2.** borough, county; district; **3.** *isl.* late performance of an act of worship; **~ geçirmek** to have an accident; **~ ile** by accident; **~ kurşunu** stray bullet; **~ sigortası** accident (*or* casualty) insurance; **-ya uğramak** to have (*or* meet with) an accident.

kazaen [. - .] **1.** by accident; **2.** by chance.

Kazak[1] Kazakh; Cossack.

kazak[2] pullover, sweater.

kazak[3] dominating, despotic (*husband*).

Kazakistan *pr. n.* Kazakhstan.

kazalı [. - .] **1.** dangerous, unsafe; **2.** with ... boroughs.

kazamat, -tı MIL casemate.

kazan 1. cauldron; **2.** boiler; furnace; **~ dairesi** boiler room; **İstanbul ~ ben kepçe** I left no stone unturned in Istanbul.

kazanç, -cı 1. gain, earnings; profit; **2.** benefit, advantage.

kazançlı profitable.

kazançsal economic.

kazançsız unprofitable, profitless.

kazandırmak *caus. of* **kazanmak.**

kazandibi, -ni *milk pudding slightly burnt on the bottom.*

kazanmak 1. to earn; **2.** to win; **3.** to acquire, to gain, to get.

kazara [. - .] [. x .] **1.** by accident; **2.** by chance.

kazasker HIST military judge.

kazayağı, -nı 1. BOT goosefoot, pigweed; **2.** NAUT three-ended rope.

kazazede [. - . .] **1.** victim, casualty (*of an accident*); **2.** shipwrecked; struck (*by an accident*).

kazboku, -nu chartreuse.

kazein casein.

kazı excavation; **~ yapmak** to excavate, to dig.

kazıbilim archeology.

kazıbilimci archeologist.

kazıcı excavator (*person*).

kazık 1. stake, pale; pile, picket; **2.** *sl.* swindle, trick; **3.** *sl.* exorbitant (*price*); **~ atmak** F to overcharge, to fleece, to soak, to put it on, to rook; **~ gibi 1.** as stiff as a ramrod; **2.** as stiff as a board; **~ kadar** grown-up; **~ marka** too expensive; **~ yemek** *sl.* to be rooked (*or* soaked); **~ yutmuş gibi** as stiff as a ramrod; **kazığa oturtmak** HIST to impale.

kazıkçı swindler, trickster.

kazıklamak 1. to pile, to picket, to stake; **2.** HIST to impale; **3.** *sl.* to overcharge, to soak, to put it on, to fleece, to rook.

kazıma 1. *vn. of* **kazımak**; **2.** curettage.

kazımak 1. to scrape (off); **2.** to shave; **3.** to incise, to engrave; **4.** *sl.* to clean out, to pluck.

kazınmak 1. to scrape o.s.; **2.** to scratch o.s. hard; **3.** to give o.s. a very close shave

kazıntı scrapings.

kazıyıcı road grader.

kaziye LOG proposition.

kazma 1. *vn. of* **kazmak**; **2.** pick, pick-ax; mattock; **3.** excavated, dug; **4.** in-cised, engraved.

kazmacı MIL sapper.

kazmaç excavator.

kazmadiş bucktoothed (*person*).

kazmak, (-ar) to dig, to excavate, to trench.

kazmir cassimere, kerseymere.

kazulet, -ti *sl.* grotesque, portly.

kebap, -bı 1. shish kebab; **2.** roasted; broiled; ~ **şişi** *sl.* dagger; ~ **yapmak** to roast; to broil.

kebe 1. felt jacket; **2.** embroidered felt.

kebir 1. big; great; **2.** elderly, old.

kebze shoulder blade, scapula.

keçe 1. felt; **2.** mat.

keçeleşmek 1. to become matted (*hair, etc.*); **2.** *fig.* to become numb.

keçeli made of felt; ~ **kalem** felt-tip pen, felt-tipped pen.

keçi 1. ZOO goat; **2.** nanny goat, she-goat; **3.** *fig.* stubborn, obstinate; ~ **ağızlı** *fig.* gluttonous; ~ **çobanı** goat-herd; ~ **derisi** goatskin; ~ **yavrusu** kid; **-leri kaçırmak** F to go nuts.

keçiboynuzu, -nu BOT carob, St. John's bread; ~ **gibi** insipid.

keçileşmek F to become mulish (*or* pigheaded).

keçisakal goatee.

keçiyolu, -nu path.

keder sorrow, grief; ~ **vermek** to grieve, to sadden.

kederlenmek to be grieved.

kederli sorrowful, grieved.

kedersiz free from grief.

kedi ZOO cat; ~ **ciğere bakar gibi bak-mak** to stare covetously; ~ **yetişeme-diği ciğere pis dermiş** pro. that's sour grapes; **-yi sıkıştırırsan üstüne atılır** pro. even a worm will turn.

kedibalığı, -nı ZOO ray, stake.

kedigözü, -nü 1. taillight; **2.** cat's-eye.

kediotu, -nu BOT valerian.

kefal 1. ZOO gray (*or* striped) mullet; **2.** *sl.* cigarette butt.

kefalet, -ti [ā] bail; **-le salıvermek** to release on bail.

kefaletname bail bond, guaranty,

surety bond.

kefaret, -ti [ā] atonement, expiation; **-ini ödemek** to expiate, to atone (*-in* for).

kefe¹ pan. scale (*of a balance*).

kefe² haircloth bag (*used for grooming horses*).

kefeki 1. travertine, calsinter, scale; **2.** tartar, scale (*on teeth*).

kefen shroud, winding sheet; ~ **soyu-cu** grave robber; **-i yırtmak** *fig.* to turn the corner, to pass the danger point safely.

kefenci 1. shroud seller; shroud mak-er; **2.** *sl.* grave robber.

kefenlemek to shroud.

kefere non-Muslims; unbelievers.

kefil [ī] guarantor, sponsor, surety; bondsman; ~ *olm.* to sponsor.

kefillik sponsorship, suretyship.

kefir kefir, kephir.

kefiye kaffiyeh.

kehanet, -ti [ā] prediction; ~ **etm.** (*or* **-te bulunmak**) to predict, to foretell.

kehkeşan [ā] AST the Milky Way.

kehle ZOO louse.

kehlibar, kehribar [ā] amber; ~ **balı** clear yellow honey.

kek, -ki cake.

kekâ, kekâh [x-] F: **oh** ~! this is the life!

keke stammering, stuttering (*person*).

kekelemek 1. to stammer, to stutter; **2.** to hem and haw.

kekeme stammering, stuttering (*per-son*).

kekemelik stutter.

kekik BOT thyme.

keklik ZOO partridge, acrid.

kekre astringent.

kekremsi 1. somewhat acrid; **2.** *fig.* sour-faced.

kel 1. bald; **2.** MED favus, ringworm; **3.** *fig.* bare, denuded; ~ **başa şimşir ta-rak** *fig.* out of place luxury; ~ **kâhya** *fig.* busybody; **-i körü toplamak** to as-semble a band of incompetents.

kelam 1. remark, utterance; **2.** the Ko-ran; **3.** Islamic theology.

Kelamıkadim [ī] the Koran.

kelebek 1. ZOO butterfly; moth; **2.** MED distomatosis; **3.** MEC butterfly (*or* wing) nut; **4.** MEC butterfly valve; ~ **cam** butterfly window; ~ **gözlük** pince-nez; ~ **kulacı** butterfly stroke; ~ **somun** MEC butterfly (*or* wing) nut.

kelek 1. unripe melon; **2.** hairless; **3.** underdeveloped; **4.** *sl.* dunderhead;

~ *herif* sl. a bad hat (or egg).
kelepçe [. x .] **1.** handcuffs; **2.** MEC pipe clip; ~ **vurmak** (or **takmak**) (b-ne) to handcuff s.o.
kelepçelemek to handcuff.
kelepçeli handcuffed.
kelepir 1. bargain, steal; **2.** dirt-cheap.
keler ZOO lizard.
keleş F **1.** beautiful; handsome; **2.** bald.
kelime GR word; ~ **hazinesi** vocabulary; ~ ~ word by word; ~ **oyunu** pun; **kelimel şahadet** isl. the confession of faith; -**si** -**sine** word for word, literally.
kelle 1. contp. head, nut, crumpet, nob; **2.** boiled sheep's head; **3.** head (of cabbage); **4.** ear, head (of grain); ~ **götürür gibi** helter-skelter; -**sini koltuğuna almak** fig. to take one's life in one's hands; -**sini uçurmak** (b-nin) to behead s.o., to decapitate s.o.; -**yi vermek** to sacrifice one's life; **İngiltere kazanırsa kellemi keserim!** F I'll eat my hat if England wins!
kelli since, seeing that.
kellifelli well-dressed and dignified (person).
kellik 1. baldness; **2.** ringworm, favus.
keloğlan name of a popular hero of Turkish folk tales.
Kelt pr. n. Kelt, Celt.
kem evil, malicious.
kemal, -**li** [ā] **1.** perfection; **2.** maturity; ripeness; **3.** the highest price; **4.** ♀ [x .] mf.; -**e ermek 1.** to reach perfection; **2.** to reach maturity.
Kemalist Kemalist.
Kemalizm Kemalism.
keman [ā] **1.** violin; **2.** archery: bow; ~ **çalmak** to play the violin; ~ **yayı** violin bow.
kemancı [ā] violinist.
kemençe [. x .] kemancha, kit.
kement -**di** lasso.
kementlemek sl. to swindle.
kemer 1. belt; **2.** arch; vault; **3.** waist (of a garment); **4.** aqueduct; **5.** ANAT arch; **6.** Roman (nose); ~ **altı** vaulted bazaar; -**ini** (or -**leri**) **sıkmak** to tighten one's belt.
kemerli 1. girdled; **2.** arched; vaulted.
kemerlik leather belt (used for holding tools, etc.).
kemerpatlıcan long, thin aubergine.
kemgöz evil eye.
kemik 1. bone; **2.** osseous; ~ **atmak**

(b-nin önüne) fig. to throw s.o. a sop; ~ **gibi 1.** as hard as a bone; **2.** bone-dry; ~ **iltihabı** osteitis; ~ **yalayıcı** fig. bootlicker, toady; -**leri sayılmak** to be a bag of bones.
kemikbilim osteology.
kemikçik ossicle.
kemikdoku bone tissue.
kemikleşmek to ossify.
kemikli bony.
kemiksiz boneless.
kemircik cartilage, gristle.
kemirdek tail bones.
kemirgen rodent.
kemirgenler ZOO Rodentia.
kemirici 1. rodent; **2.** corrosive.
kemirmek 1. to gnaw, to nibble; **2.** to corrode.
kemiyet, -**ti** quantity.
kem küm etm. to hem and haw.
kenar [ā] **1.** edge; border; margin; hem; brink; **2.** isolated; **3.** suburb; ~ **çekmek** to edge, to hem, to border; ~ **mahalie** slums; -**a çekilmek** to get out of the way; -**a çekmek** to pull in, to pull over (or off) (vehicle); -**da kalmak** fig. to remain aside; -**da köşede** in nooks and crannies.
kenarlı edged.
kendi 1. self, oneself; **2.** own; **3.** he; she; **4.** in person; ~ **başına 1.** of one's own accord; **2.** by oneself, single-handedly; ~ **bildiğini okumak** fig. to get one's own way; ~ **derdine düşmek** to be preoccupied with one's own troubles; ~ **düşen ağlamaz** pro. you've made your bed and you must lie on it; ~ **halinde** innocuous, inoffensive (person); ~ **haline bırakmak** (b-ni) to leave s.o. to his own devices; ~ -**ne 1.** by oneself; **2.** to oneself; **3.** on one's own accord; ~ -**ni yemek** to eat one's heart out; ~ **kuyusunu** ~ **kazmak** fig. to dig one's own grave; ~ **payıma** as for me, for my part; ~ **yağıyle kavrulmak** fig. to get by on one's own means; -**nden geçmek** to faint; -**ne gel! 1.** behave yourself!, come to your senses!; **2.** pull yourself together!; -**ne gelmek 1.** to come to (or round); **2.** to behave o.s., to pull o.s. together; -**ne yediremmek** to be unable to stomach; -**ni beğenmek** to be full of o.s.; -**ni bir şey sanmak** to be too big for one's boots; -**ni dev aynasında görmek** to think no small beer of o.s.; -**ni göstermek** to prove

one's worth; *-ni gülmekten alamamak* can't help laughing; *-ni kaptırmak fig.* to let o.s. get carried away (*-e* by); *-ni kaybetmek* **1.** to lose consciousness; **2.** to fly into a rage; *-ni vermek* (*bşe*) to put one's heart into *s.th.*; *-sinden bahsettirmek* to make a noise in the world.

kendiliğinden 1. by oneself; **2.** automatically; **3.** of one's own accord.

kendilik entity.

kendince 1. subjective, personal; **2.** in one's opinion.

kendir BOT hemp.

kene ZOO tick; ~ *gibi yapışmak fig.* to stick like a leech.

kenef 1. bog, toilet; **2.** filthy.

kenegöz small-eyed (*person*).

kenet, *-di* MEC metal clamp, cramp iron.

kenetlemek 1. to clamp; **2.** to lock (*jaws*).

kenevir *s.* **kendir.**

kent, *-ti* city, town.

kental, *-li* quintal.

kentbilim urbanology.

kentilyon quintillion.

kentleşmek to become urbanized.

kentli city-dweller.

kentsel urban.

Kenya *pr. n.* Kenya.

kep, *-pi* **1.** cap; **2.** mortarboard.

kepaze [ā] **1.** ridiculous, vile, contemptible; **2.** disgraceful, shameless; ~ *etm.* to disgrace; ~ *olm.* to become a laughingstock.

kepazelik ignominy, degradation, vileness.

kepbastı double-netted fishing weir.

kepçe 1. ladle; **2.** dip (*or* scoop) net; **3.** butterfly net; **4.** NAUT buttock; ~ *gibi* sticking out (*ears*).

kepçekulak having outstanding ears.

kepçeli having a ladle.

kepek 1. scurf, dandruff; **2.** bran; ~ *ekmeği* whole-wheat bread; ~ *unu* whole-wheat flour.

kepeklenmek to become scurfy.

kepekli scurfy (*hair*).

kepenek 1. ZOO flour (*or* wheat) moth; **2.** shepherd's felt cloak.

kepenk rolling (*or* roll-down) shutter.

kerahet, *-ti* [ā] repugnance, nastiness; ~ *vakti co.* drinking-time.

keramet, *-ti* [ā] miracle, marvel; ~ *buyur dunuz* your words are wonderful; ~ *göstermek* to work miracles.

kerametli [ā] holy.

kerata 1. shoehorn; **2.** F cuckold; **3.** F son of a gun, dog.

Kerbela *pr. n.* Karbala; ~ *gibi* waterless (*place*).

kere time(s); *iki* ~ *okudum* I read it twice, *üç* ~ *beş* three times five.

kerecik *diminutive of* **kere**; *bir* ~ (only) just once.

kerem beneficence, kindness.

kereste [. x .] **1.** timber, lumber; **2.** *sl.* swine.

keresteci timber (*or* lumber) merchant.

keresteli [. x . .] P portly (*man*).

kerevet, *-ti* **1.** plank-bed; **2.** *cinema*: dolly.

kerevides [. . x .] ZOO crayfish, crawfish.

kereviz 1. ZOO celery, celeriac; **2.** *sl.* dunce.

kerez *sl.* food or drink offered a guest.

kerhane [ā] brothel, cathouse.

kerhaneci [ā] **1.** brothel keeper; **2.** *sl.* son of a bitch, bastard.

kerhen [x .] **1.** reluctantly, unwillingly; **2.** disgustedly.

kerih [ī] disgusting, detestable.

kerim [ī] **1.** gracious, kind, munificent; **2.** ♀ [x .] *mf.*

kerime [ī] *rare* daughter.

keriz 1. *s.* **geriz; 2.** *sl.* sucker.

kerkenez ZOO kestrel.

kerki large axe.

kerliferli *s.* **kellifelli.**

kermes 1. fete, kermis; **2.** festival.

kerpeten pincers, pliers; forceps.

kerpiç, *-ci* **1.** sundried (*or* mud) brick, adobe; **2.** made of sundried bricks.

kerrake [ā] *obs.* a kind of light cloak; *şimdi anlaşıldı Vehbi'nin kerrakesi!* now all is clear!

kerrat, *-tı* *obs.* times; ~ *cetveli* times (*or* multiplication) table.

kertan *sl.* risky.

kerte 1. notch, score; **2.** rhumb; **3.** state, degree; *-sine getirmek* to bring to the very best time.

kerteli gradual.

kertenkele ZOO lizard.

kerteriz NAUT bearing.

kertik notch, tally, score, gash.

kertiklemek to notch.

kertikli notched.

kertmek, (-er) 1. to notch; **2.** to scrape.

kervan caravan; *-a katılmak fig.* to go with the crowd.

kervanbaşı, -nı leader of a caravan.
kervancı organizer or leader of a caravan.
Kervankıran *pr. n.* AST Venus.
kervansaray caravanserai, caravansary.
kes sneaker.
kesafet, -ti [ā] density.
kesat, -dı [ā] **1.** slack, stagnant, flat; **2.** slackness.
kesatlık *s.* **kesat 2.**
kesbetmek [x..] to acquire, to take on, to assume.
kese¹ 1. moneybag, purse; **2.** ZOO marsupium, pouch; **3.** MED cyst, sac, bursa; **3.** coarse glove-like cloth; **5.** *fig.* wealth, purse; **~ sürmek** to rub with a *kese*; **-nin ağzını açmak** to loosen the purse strings; **-nin dibi görünmek** to run out of money, to be short of money; **-sine güvenmek** to be able to afford, to be within one's purse; **-sine hiç bir şey girmemek** not to benefit at all.
kese² short cut; **~ yol** short cut.
kesecik ANAT saccule.
kesedar [ā] HIST treasurer, keeper of the purse.
kesek clod.
kesekâğıdı, -nı paper bag.
keselemek *s.* **kese sürmek.**
keselenmek to rub o.s. with a *kese*.
keseli ZOO marsupial.
keseliler ZOO Marsupialia.
kesen *geom.* secant.
kesenek deduction.
kesenkes P absolutely.
keser adze.
kesici 1. incisive, incisory, cutting; **2.** cutter; **3.** butcher.
kesicidiş incisor.
kesif [î] dense, thick.
kesik 1. cut; **2.** off (*electricity, water, etc.*); **3.** curdled; **4.** *geom.* truncated; **5.** clipping; **6.** interrupted, broken off; **~ ~** gaspingly.
kesikli discontinuous, intermittent.
kesiksiz 1. uninterrupted, continuous; **2.** continuously, on and on.
kesilme *vn. of* **kesilmek**, *part.* exhaustion.
kesilmek 1. *pass. or refl. of* **kesmek**; **2.** to be tired out (*or* bushed); **3.** to curdle, to sour; **4.** to be cut off (*electricity, water, etc.*); **5.** to stop, to die down, to let up (*rain, etc.*); **6.** to lose (*appetite, strength*); **7.** *sl.* to fall for.

kesim 1. slaughter; **2.** section (*a.* MED); sector; **3.** period (*of time*).
kesimevi, -ni slaughterhouse.
kesin definite, certain.
kesinleşmek to become definite.
kesinleştirmek to make definite.
kesinlik certainty, certitude.
kesinlikle definitely, certainly.
kesinti 1. deduction; **2.** interruption; **-ye almak** (*b-ni*) F to make fun of *s.o.* behind his back.
kesintisiz 1. uninterrupted, continuous; **2.** without deductions.
kesir, -sri 1. MEC fraction; **2.** MED fracture.
kesirli MATH fractional.
kesişen *geom.* intersecting.
kesişmek 1. to intersect, to cross; **2.** to come to an agreement; **3.** to exchange amorous glances.
kesit, -ti MATH crosscut.
keski 1. billhook, coulter; **2.** chisel; **3.** hatchet.
keskin 1. sharp; **2.** acute, keen; **3.** pungent; **4.** severe; **~ gözlü** eagle-eyed; **~ nişancı** marksman, dead shot; **~ sirke küpüne** (*or* **kabına**) **zarar** a bad temper harms its possessor most; **~ viraj** sharp (*or* hairpin) curve.
keskinleşmek to get sharp.
keskinleştirmek to sharpen.
keskinlik sharpness, keenness.
kesme 1. *vn. of* **kesmek**; **2.** tin snips; **3.** cut, faceted; **4.** sector; **5.** *cinema*: cut; **6.** cube-shaped; **7.** fixed (*price*); **~ almak** F to pinch one's cheek; **~ işareti** apostrophe.
kesmece 1. for a lump sum; **2.** at the same price.
kesmek, (-er) 1. to cut (off); to cut down, to fell (*tree*); **2.** to slice, to cut up; **3.** to slaughter, to butcher; **4.** to stop, to interrupt; **5.** to turn off (*electricity, water, gas*); **6.** to determine, to fix; **7.** to deduct; **8.** to cut (*cards*); **9.** to coin, to issue (*money*); **10.** to block; to hinder, to impede; **11.** to take away, to kill (*pain, etc.*); **12.** *sl.* to shut up, to cut the cackle; **13.** *sl.* to shoot the bull; **14.** *sl.* to ogle at (*a girl*); **kesip atmak** to settle offhand, to settle once and for all; **kesip biçmek** to bluster; **kestiği tırnak olamamak** (*b-nin*) can't hold a candle to *s.o.*
kesmelik quarry.
kesmeşeker lump (*or* cube) sugar.
kesmik 1. chaff; **2.** curds.

kesret, -ti abundance.
kestane [ā] BOT chestnut (tree); **~ ke-babı** roast chestnuts; **~ şekeri** marron glacé, candied chestnuts.
kestaneci [ā] chestnut man.
kestanecik [ā] MED prostate gland.
kestanefişeği, -ni firecracker.
kestanelik [ā] chestnut grove.
kestirme 1. vn. of **kestirmek; 2.** estimate; **3.** short cut; **4.** concise, direct (answer); **~ yol** short cut; **-den gitmek** to take a short cut.
kestirmek 1. caus. of **kesmek; 2.** to estimate, to guess, to predict; **3.** to take a nap, to nap, to doze off; **4.** to curdle.
keş 1. dry curd; skim-milk cheese; **2.** sl. idiotic; **~ etm.** sl. to humiliate, to shame.
keşfetmek [x . .] **1.** to discover, to explore; **2.** to uncover, to find out (secret); **3.** MIL to reconnoiter.
keşide [ī] drawing; **~ etm.** to draw.
keşideci [ī] COM drawer.
keşif, -şfi 1. discovery, exploration; **2.** investigation; **3.** MIL reconnaissance; **~ kolu** reconnaissance patrol; **~ uçağı** MIL reconnaissance plane.
keşiş monk.
keşişhane [ā] monastery.
keşişleme 1. southeast wind; **2.** NAUT southeast point (of the compass).
keşke, keşki [x .] I wish, if only, would that …!; **~ gelseydin** if only you'd come!
keşkül milk pudding with coconut.
keşlemek sl. to take no notice (-e of).
keşmekeş disorder, rush.
keşşaf [ā] obs. MIL military scout.
ket¹ = nişasta.
ket², -ti obstacle; **~ vurmak** to put back, to handicap, to hinder, to impede.
ketçap ketchup, catchup, catsup.
keten 1. linen; **2.** BOT flax; **~ bezi** linen cloth.
ketenhelvası, -nı cotton candy.
ketenkuşu, -nu ZOO linnet.
ketentohumu, -nu linseed, flaxseed; **~ yağı** linseed oil.
keton CHEM ketone.
ketum [ū] tightlipped, discreet.
ketumiyet, -ti [ū] reticence, discretion.
kevgir 1. skimmer; **2.** colander.
Kevser isl. MYTH name of a river in Paradise; **~ gibi** nectarous.
keyfetmek to enjoy o.s., to have fun.
keyfi arbitrary, discretionary.

keyfiyet, -ti 1. situation; **2.** condition, nature; **3.** affair matter.
keyif, -yfi 1. pleasure, delight, joy, enjoyment, merriment; **2.** humo(u)r, mood, spirits, disposition; **3.** high, kef; **4.** PSYCH euphoria; **~ çatmak** to enjoy o.s., to have a good time; **~ halinde** tipsy; **~ için** for pleasure (or fun); **~ sürmek** to live the good life; **~ vermek** to make tipsy; **keyfi bilmek** to do as one pleases; **keyfi bozuldu** (or **kaçtı**) he is out of spirits; **keyfi gelmek** to get into a happy mood; **keyfi olmamak** to feel under the weather; **keyfinden dört köşe olm.** to be as happy as the day is long; **keyfine bakmak** to enjoy o.s.; **keyfine gitmek** (kendi) to do as one pleases; **keyfini çıkarmak** (bşin) to get a kick out of s.th.
keyiflenmek 1. to become merry; **2.** to get tipsy.
keyifli 1. merry, joyous, in good spirits; **2.** tipsy.
keyifsiz 1. indisposed, under the weather; **2.** in bad humo(u)r.
keyifsizlik indisposition; depression.
kez time; **bu ~** this time; **dört ~** four times.
keza [x -], **kezalik** [. x .] [ā] **1.** the same, ditto; **2.** likewise; **3.** also, too.
kezzap, -bı [ā] aqua fortis, nitric acid.
kıble 1. kiblah, the direction of Mecca; **2.** south wind; **-ye dönmek** to turn towards Mecca.
Kıbrıs pr. n. Cyprus.
Kıbrıslı pr. n. Cyprian, Cypriote.
kıç, -çı 1. buttocks, butt, bottom, rump, behind; **2.** NAUT poop, stern; **3.** back, hind; **~ atmak 1.** to kick (animal); **2.** fig. to long (-e for); **~ güverte** quarter-deck; **~ üstü oturmak** F to remain helpless; **-ına kına yakmak** F to gloat; **-ına tekmeyi atmak** sl. to give s.o. the boot, to boot out; **-ını yırtmak** sl. to rant and rave; **-ının kılları ağarmış** sl. old, past it.
kıçın kıçın backwards; astern.
kıdem 1. seniority, priority, precedence; **2.** length of service; **~ tazminatı** severance (package) (for employee being laid off).
kıdemli senior (in service); **~ onbaşı** MIL lance corporal.
kıdemsiz junior (in service).
kığ, kığı sheep, goat or camel droppings.

kıh dirty.

kıkırdak 1. ANAT cartilage, gristle; **2.** greaves, crackling.

kıkırdakdoku ANAT cartilaginous (or gristly) tissue.

kıkırdaklı cartilaginous, gristly.

kıkırdamak 1. to giggle, to chuckle; **2.** to be freezing; **3.** sl. to croak, to peg out, to pop off.

kıkır kıkır gigglingly.

kıkırtı giggle ,chuckle.

kıl 1. hair; bristle; **2.** goat hair; ~ **çekmek** sl. flatter, to soft-soap; ~ **çuval** haircloth sack; ~ **gibi** thin as a hair; ~ **kaldı ödülü kazanacaktı** he was within an ace (or inch) of winning the prize; ~ **payı 1.** hairbreadth; **2.** by the skin or one's teeth; ~ **payı kalmak** to come within an inch (of); ~ **şaşmadan** painstakingly; ~ **testere** MEC fretsaw, scrollsaw; **-ı kıpırdamamak** not to turn a hair; **-ı kırk yarmak** to split hairs; **-ını bile kıpırdatmamak** = **-ı kıpırdamamak**.

kılağı burr.

kılaptan silvered cotton thread.

kılavuz 1. guide; **2.** NAUT pilot; **3.** matchmaker, go-between.

kılavuzluk 1. guidance; **2.** NAUT pilotage.

kılburun GEOGR promontory.

kılcal BIOL capillary; ~ **damar** ANAT capillary.

kılçık 1. fishbone; **2.** string (of beans); **kılçığını çıkarmak 1.** to bone (fish); **2.** to string (beans).

kılçıklı 1. bony (fish); **2.** string (beans).

kılçıksız 1. boneless (fish); **2.** stringless (bean).

kılıbık henpecked (husband).

kılıbıklaşmak to become henpecked.

kılıcına edgewise.

kılıç, -cı sword; saber; ~ **çekmek** to draw one's sword; ~ **kabzası** sword hilt; ~ **kuşanmak** to gird on a sword; ~ **oynatmak** to rule over; **-tan geçirmek** to put to the sword.

kılıçbacak bowlegged, bandylegged.

kılıçbalığı, -nı ZOO swordfish.

kılıççı sword maker or seller.

kılıçlama 1. = **kılıcına; 2.** crosswise.

kılıf 1. case, cover; **2.** holster; **3.** BIOL sheath; **4.** ANAT, ZOO tunic.

kılıflamak to encase.

kılık 1. appearance, shape; **2.** costume, dress; ~ **kıyafet** attire, dress; ~ **kıyafet düşkünü** dressed in shabby clothes.

kılıklı dressed like ...; ~ **kıyafetli** well dressed.

kılıksız shabby.

kılkıran alopecia.

kılkuyruk F shabby and penniless.

kıllanmak to become hairy.

kıllı hairy; bristly; ~ **bebek** fig. big baby.

kılmak, (-ar) 1. to render, to make; **2.** to perform.

kılsız hairless.

kımılda(n)mak to stir, to budge.

kımıldatmak caus. of **kımıldamak** to move, to shake.

kımıltı 1. movement, motion, agitation; **2.** facial gesture.

kımız k(o)umiss.

kın 1. sheath, scabbard; **2.** BOT ocrea, stipule; **-ına koymak** to sheathe; **-ından çıkarmak** to unsheathe.

kına henna; ~ **yakmak** (or **koymak** or **vurmak** or **sürmek**) to henna; **-lar yakmak** (sevincinden) fig. to gloat, to rejoice.

kınaçiçeği, -ni BOT garden balsam.

kınagecesi, -ni party during which a bride-to-be has her fingers hennaed.

kınakına [. . x .] BOT cinchona.

kınalamak to henna.

kınalı 1. hennaed; **2.** henna-colo(u)red.

kınama condemnation, censure.

kınamak to condemn, to censure.

kınamsımak to find fault with, to criticize.

kınnap, -bı twine, string, packthread.

kıpık half-closed (eyes).

kıpırda(n)mak to move, to stir, to quiver, to vibrate, to fidget.

kıpırdaşmak to stir, to fidget.

kıpırdatmak to stir, to budge.

kıpır kıpır fidgetingly.

kıpırtı stirring, quiver.

kıpkırmızı [x . . .] crimson, carmine.

kıpkızıl s. **kıpkırmızı.**

kıpmak, (-ar) to wink (an eye); to blink (one's eyes).

kır¹ grey, Am. gray; ~ **düşmek** (saçına, sakalına) to turn grey.

kır² the country, countryside, rural area; ~ **çiçeği** wildflower; ~ **gezisi** country outing; ~ **koşusu** cross-country race.

kıraat, -tı [. - .] **1.** reading; **2.** reading-book, reader; ~ **etm.** to read.

kıraathane [. . . - .] café.

kıraç 1. arid (land); **2.** sterile, unproductive, waste (*land*).

kırağı frost, hoarfrost; ~ **çalmak** to become frostbitten (*plant*); ~ **düşmek** (*or* **yağmak**) to frost.

kırağılı frosty.

kıran 1. edge; shore; bank; **2.** murrain; pestilence.

kıranta [. x .] grayhead.

kırat, -tı 1. carat; **2.** *fig.* value, character, quality.

kırba waterskin; ~ **olm.** to swell up.

kırbaç, -cı whip; ~ **vurmak** to whip, to flog; ~ **yemek** to be whipped (*or* flogged).

kırbaçlamak to whip, to flog.

kırcın murrain.

kırçıl graying (*hair, beard*).

kırçıllaşmak to gray.

kırçoz *sl.* = **kıranta.**

kırgın hurt, offended, resentful.

kırgınlık hurt, offense; resentment.

Kırgız *pr. n.* Kirghiz.

Kırgızistan *pr. n.* Kirghizia.

kırıcı hurtful, offensive (*word, etc.*).

kırık 1. broken; **2.** MED fracture, break; **3.** hybrid; mongrel; **4.** (broken) piece; **5.** failing grade; **6.** *fig.* hurt, offended, resentful; ~ **almak** to get a failing grade; ~ **dökük 1.** broken, worn out; **2.** odds and ends; ~ **ışın** refracted ray; ~ **not** failing grade; ~ **tahtası** MED splint.

kırıkçı bonesetter.

kırıkkırak breadstick.

kırıklık 1. brokenness; **2.** fatigue; soreness.

kırılgan 1. breakable, fragile; **2.** *fig.* touchy.

kırılım refraction.

kırılmak 1. *pass. of* **kırmak**; **2.** (*b-ne*) to resent *s.o.*, to be hurt (*or* offended) by *s.o.*; **3.** PHYS to be refracted; **4.** to die, to perish; **kırılıp dökülmek** to speak in a flirtatious way.

Kırım *pr. n.* Crimea.

kırım 1. slaughter, massacre, genocide, carnage; **2.** fold, pleat.

kırım kırım flirtatiously, coquettishly.

kırınım PHYS diffraction.

kırıntı 1. fragment, piece; **2.** crumb.

kırışık 1. wrinkly, wrinkled; **2.** wrinkle, pucker.

kırışmak 1. to get wrinkled, to pucker, to crumple; **2.** to bet with each other; **3.** to divide among *or* between themselves; **4.** F to flirt with each other.

kırıştırmak 1. to wrinkle, to crumple,

to pucker; **2.** to flirt (*ile* with), to carry on (*ile* with).

kırıtkan coquettish, flirtatious, mincing.

kırıtmak to mince, to coquet.

kırk, -kı forty; ~ **bir kere maşallah!** touch wood!; ~ (*or* **bin**) **dereden su getirmek** to beat about the bush; ~ **tarakta bezi olm.** to have too many irons in the fire; ~ **yılda bir** *fig.* once in a blue moon; ~ **yılın başında** = ~ **yılda bir.**

kırkambar 1. general store; **2.** *fig.* omniscient person; **3.** NAUT mixed cargo.

kırkar forty at a time; forty to each.

kırkayak ZOO **1.** centipede; **2.** millipede; **3.** crab louse.

kırkbayır omasum, manyplies.

kırkı shearing.

kırkım shearing (season).

kırkıncı fortieth.

kırklık 1. forty-year-old; **2.** layette; **3.** P shears.

kırkmak, (-ar) 1. to shear, to clip (*animal*); **2.** to trim.

kırkmerak nosy, inquisitive.

kırkmerdiven *fig.* very steep slope.

kırlağan pestilence, plague.

kırlangıç, -cı 1. ZOO swallow; **2.** (house) martin; **3.** *fig.* quack eye doctor; **4.** HIST light galley; ~ **kuyruğu** dovetail.

kırlangıçbalığı, -nı ZOO red gurnard.

kırlangıçdönümü, -nü early October.

kırlaşmak to turn gray.

kırlık open country.

kırma 1. *vn. of* **kırmak**; **2.** pleat, fold; **3.** folding, collapsible; **4.** groats; **5.** ZOO hybrid, mongrel.

kırmak, (-ar) 1. to break; **2.** to split, to chop (*wood*); **3.** to fold; **4.** to destroy, to break (*resistance, pride, desire, etc.*); **5.** to reduce (*price*); **6.** to offend, to hurt; **7.** (*direksiyon*) to swerve; **8.** to mitigate, to abate, to break; **9.** *sl.* to run away, to clear out; **kırıp geçirmek 1.** to wipe out, to slay; **2.** (*gülmekten*) to have people rolling in the aisles.

kırmalı pleated.

kırmataş gravel, ballast.

kırmızı red; crimson; carmine; ~ **balık** ZOO goldfish; ~ **dut** BOT red mulberry; ~ **oy** negative vote.

kırmızıbiber BOT red (*or* cayenne) pepper.

kırmızılaşmak to redden, to turn red.

kırmızılık redness, ruddiness; flush.

kırmızımsı, kırmızımtırak reddish.
kırmızıturp, -pu BOT radish.
kırpık clipped, shorn.
kırpıntı 1. clippings; **2.** bit, scrap.
kırpıştırmak to blink (eyes).
kırpmak, (-ar) 1. to shear, to clip; to trim; **2.** to wink (eye).
kırsal rural, rustic, country; pastoral.
kırtasiye [ā] stationery.
kırtasiyeci [ā] **1.** stationer; **2.** pettifogger, bureaucrat.
kırtasiyecilik [ā] **1.** the stationery business; **2.** red tape, bureaucracy.
kırtıpil sl. shabby, common, mean.
kısa short; ~ **boylu** squat, short; ~ **dalga** radio: short wave; ~ **devre** PHYS short circuit; ~ **geçmek** to refer briefly; ~ **kesmek** to cut short (talk); ~ **kollu** short-sleeved; ~ **mesaj** text-message; ~ **mesaj göndermek** to text; ~ **ömürlü** short-lived, ephemeral; ~ **sürmek** to take a short time; ~ **vadeli** short-term.
kısaca 1. squat; **2.** [. x .] in short, shortly, briefly; **-sı** [. x ..] in a word; in brief.
kısacık very short.
kısalık shortness.
kısalmak 1. to shorten; **2.** to shrink.
kısaltma 1. abbreviation; **2.** abridg(e)-ment.
kısaltmak 1. to shorten; **2.** to abbreviate, to abridge, to condense; **3.** to take up (garment).
kısaltmalı shortened, abbreviated.
kısas [ā] retaliation, reprisal; **-a** ~ an eye for an eye, tit for tat.
kısık 1. hoarse (voice); **2.** turned down (radio, lamp); **3.** slitted, narrowed (eyes).
kısıklık hoarseness.
kısılma 1. vn. of **kısılmak**; **2.** reduction; **3.** MED heart contraction.
kısılmak 1. pass. of **kısmak**; **2.** to get hoarse (voice); **3.** to be caught (in a trap); **4.** to contract (muscle); **5.** to be slitted (or narrowed) (eyes).
kısım, -smı 1. part, section, division, portion; **2.** kind; ~ ~ in parts (or sections); **kadın kısmı** womankind.
kısınmak to refrain (-den from), to abstain (-den from).
kısıntı reduction, cutback, restriction.
kısır 1. sterile, barren; **2.** unproductive; ~ **döngü** LOG vicious circle.
kısırganmak (bşi) to grudge s.th.
kısırlaşmak to be sterilized, to become barren (or unproductive).

kısırlaştırmak MED to sterilize.
kısırlık sterility, barrenness.
kısıt, -tı seizure, distraint.
kısıtlamak to restrict.
kısıtlayıcı restrictive.
kısıtlı restricted.
kıskaç, -cı 1. pincers, pliers; forceps; **2.** claw, chela, pincer; **3.** stepladder; ~ **gözlük** pince-nez.
kıskanç, -cı jealous.
kıskançlık jealousy.
kıskandırmak to arouse s.o.'s jealousy.
kıskanmak 1. to be jealous (-i of); **2.** (b-den bşi) to grudge s.o. s.th., to envy s.o. s.th.
kıs kıs gülmek to laugh up one's sleeve, to snicker, to snigger.
kıskıvrak [x . .] very tightly; ~ **bağlamak** to bind tightly.
kısmak, (-ar) 1. to lessen, to reduce; to shorten; **2.** to lower (voice, sound); **3.** to cut (expenses); **4.** to turn down (lamp, light); **5.** to narrow (eyes).
kısmen [x .] partly, partially.
kısmet, -ti 1. destiny, fate, fortune, luck, kismet; **2.** change of marriage; **3.** perhaps!, if fortune wills it!; ~ **ise** if fate so decrees; ~ **olm.** to be on the cards; **-i çıkmak** to receive a marriage proposal; **-inde ne varsa kaşığında o çıkar** pro. you can't avoid your destiny.
kısmetli lucky, fortunate.
kısmetsiz unlucky, unfortunate.
kısmi [ī] partial; ~ **seçim** by-election.
kısrak zoo mare.
kıssa tale, story; anecdote; **-dan hisse almak** to draw a moral from a story.
kıstak GEOGR isthmus.
kıstas [ā] criterion.
kıstelyevm deduction from wages (for absence).
kıstırmak caus. of **kısmak**, part. to squeeze, to pinch; **parmağımı kapıya kıstırdım** I pinched my finger in the doorway.
kış[1] winter; ~ **basmak** to set in (winter); ~ **günü** wint(e)ry day; ~ **kıyamet severe** winter; ~ **ortasında** in the dead of winter; ~ **uykusu** zoo hibernation; ~ **uykusuna yatmak** zoo to hibernate; **-ı geçirmek** to winter.
kış[2] shoo!, scat!; ~ ~ **etm.** to shoo away.
kışın [x .] in (or during) the winter.
kışır, -şrı 1. bark; peel; rind; **2.** GEOL crust.

kışkırtı instigation, incitement, provocation, agitation.

kışkırtıcı 1. provocative; 2. instigator, fomenter, agitator.

kışkırtmak 1. to incite, to provoke, to stir, to agitate; 2. to shoo away (animals).

kışla [x .] MIL barracks; ~ hapsi detention in barracks; ~ hizmeti fatigue; -ya yerleştirmek to barrack.

kışlak winter quarters.

kışlamak 1. to set in (winter); 2. to winter.

kışlık 1. wint(e)ry; 2. winter residence.

kıt, -tı 1. scarce; 2. insufficient, inadequate; ~ kanaat geçinmek to live from hand to mouth, to make both ends meet; -ı -ına idare etm. to get by on a shoestring, to scrape by.

kıta 1. GEOGR continent; 2. MIL detachment; 3. lit. quatrain, stanza; ~ ~ in sections; ~ sahanlığı continental shelf.

kıtık stuffing, tow.

kıtıpiyos sl. no-account, good-for-nothing.

kıtır 1. popcorn; 2. F lie, fib; ~ atmak (or yuvarlamak) F to fib.

kıtırbom sl. lie.

kıtırdamak to crackle.

kıtır kıtır: ~ doğramak (or kesmek) to kill in cold blood; ~ yemek to munch.

kıtırtı crackle.

kıtlaşmak to become scarce, to run short.

kıtlık 1. scarcity, shortage; 2. famine; kıtlığına kıran girmek to become as scarce as hen's teeth; -tan çıkmış gibi yemek to wade (or tuck) into the meal.

kıvam [ā] 1. thickness, density, consistency; 2. the right moment (or stage); -ında 1. of the proper consistency; 2. at the most suitable time; 3. in top shape.

kıvanç 1. pride; 2. pleasure, joy; ~ duymak to take pride (-den in).

kıvançlı 1. proud; 2. pleased, glad.

kıvılcım spark; ~ saçmak to spark.

kıvılcımlanmak to spark.

kıvırcık curly; kinky; frizzy; ~ salata lettuce.

kıvır kıvır in curls; ~ yapmak to curl, to frizz.

kıvırmak 1. to curl, to twist, to coil; 2. to turn up (cuffs); 3. to fold back; 4. to crimp; 5. F to make up, to fabricate

(lies); 6. F to pull off, to bring off.

kıvır zıvır 1. trifling, piddling; 2. kickshaw, odds and ends, bits and pieces.

kıvracık [x . .] P orderly (place).

kıvrak 1. brisk, supple, agile; 2. fluent (speech, writing); 3. neat, elegant, spruce (clothing, etc.).

kıvraklık 1. briskness, agility; 2. fluency; 3. neatness.

kıvramak to kink.

kıvranmak to writhe (-den with), to double up (-den with).

kıvrık 1. curled, twisted; 2. curly (hair); 3. cuffed (trousers).

kıvrılmak 1. pass. of kıvırmak; 2. to curl, to twist; 3. to curl up; to coil up.

kıvrım 1. curl, twist, undulation, convolution, fold (a. GEOL); 2. bend (of a road); 3. ringlet (of hair); 4. ANAT plica, fold; ~ ~ 1. very curly (hair); 2. twisty (road); ~ ~ kıvranmak to be doubled up with pain.

kıvrımlı curled, twisted, folded.

kıvrıntı 1. = kıvrım; 2. turn, twist (of a road).

kıyafet, -ti [ā] 1. dress, attire, clothes, costume; 2. appearance; ~ balosu fancy dress (or costume) ball; -ini değiştirmek to change one's clothes.

kıyaletli [ā] dressed in …

kıyafetsiz [ā] ill-dressed, untidy, shabby.

kıyak F great, super, swell.

kıyam [ā] 1. standing up; 2. endeavo(u)r, attempt; 3. rebellion, mutiny, revolt.

kıyamet, -ti [ā] 1. Doomsday, the Day of Judg(e)ment; 2. fig. ruction, tumult, uproar; ~ gibi (or kadar) heaps of, pots of; ~ günü Doomsday; ~ kopacak F there will be ructions, there will be hell to pay; ~ mi koptu? what the devil does it matter?; -e kadar till Doomsday, till kingdom come, till hell freezes over; -ı (or -leri) koparmak to raise hell, to make a hell of a fuss.

kıyas [ā] 1. comparison; 2. JUR analogy; 3. LOG syllogism; ~ etm. to compare (ile with); ~ kabul etmez incomparable; -la in comparison (-e to, with).

kıyasen [ā] by comparison (-e to).

kıyasıya 1. cruelly, mercilessly; 2. murderous, savage.

kıyasi [. - -] 1. regular; 2. analogical; 3. syllogistical.

kıyaslamak to compare.

kıyı 1. shore, coast; bank; **2.** edge, side; **3.** outskirts; **~ balıkçılığı** inshore fishing; **~ sıra** inshore; **-da bucakta** (or **köşede**) in nooks and crannies; **-ya çıkmak** to go ashore, to land.

kıyıcı 1. beachcomber; **2.** cutter; **3.** fig. cruel.

kıyılamak to coast.

kıyılmak 1. pass. of **kıymak**; **2.** fig. to ache.

kıyım massacre, genocide.

kıyınmak 1. to starve, to feel peckish; **2.** to ache.

kıyıntı 1. languor; **2.** scrap.

kıyışmak 1. to come to an agreement; **2.** to compete (ile against).

kıyma 1. vn. of **kıymak**; **2.** mince, mincemeat, minced meat; **~ makinesi** mincer.

kıymak, (-ar) 1. to mince, to chop up; **2.** to part (-e with), to spare, to let go (-e of); **3.** to slaughter, to massacre, to slay; **4.** to perform (marriage); **paraya kıyıp kendime yeni bir elbise alacağım** I'll treat myself to a new dress.

kıymalı with mincemeat.

kıymet, -ti value, worth; **~ biçmek** to value, to evaluate; **~ koymak** (or **takdir etm.**) to value, to appraise, to assess; **~ vermek** to value, to esteem; **-ini bilmek** to appreciate, to value; **-ten düş(ür)mek** to depreciate.

kıymetlendirmek to raise the value (of), to utilize.

kıymetlenmek to appreciate.

kıymetli valuable, precious.

kıymetsiz worthless, valueless.

kıymık splinter, sliver.

kıymıklanmak to splinter.

kız 1. girl; **2.** daughter; **3.** virgin, maiden; **4.** cards: queen; **~ alıp vermek** to intermarry; **~ bozmak** to deflower; **~ evlât** daughter; **~ gibi 1.** girlish, sissy; **2.** brand-new; **3.** shy; **~ kaçırmak 1.** to kidnap a girl; **2.** to elope with a girl; **~ kardeş** sister; **~ kurusu** old maid, spinster; **~ lisesi** girls' high school; **~ oğlan ~** virgin, maiden; **~ tarafı** the bride's family; **~ vermek** to give a girl in marriage (-e to); **-ını dövmeyen dizini döver** pro. spare the rod and spoil the child.

kızak 1. sledge; sled; toboggan; sleigh; bobsled; **2.** skid; **3.** NAUT stocks, ways; ground (or sliding) ways; **4.** MEC way; **~ kaymak** to slide, to sledge, to sled,

to sleigh; **~ yapmak** to skid (vehicle); **kızağa çekmek 1.** NAUT to put on the stocks; **2.** fig. to put on the shelf; to kick upstairs; **-tan indirmek** to launch (ship).

kızaklamak to skid (vehicle).

kızamık MED measles, rubeola; **~ çıkarmak** to develop measles; **~ olm.** to have measles.

kızamıkçık MED German measles.

kızamıklı MED measly.

kızan P **1.** boy, lad; **2.** hellraiser.

kızarmak 1. to redden, to turn red; **2.** to blush, to flush; **3.** to fry; to toast; to roast; **4.** to glow (coals); **kızarıp bozarmak** to blush as red as a rose; **kızarmış ekmek** toast.

kızartı red spot (or place).

kızartma 1. vn. of **kızartmak**; **2.** fried (food).

kızartmak caus. of **kızarmak**, part. to fry; to roast; to toast.

kızböceği, -ni ZOO dragonfly.

kızdırmak 1. to anger, to irritate, infuriate, to exasperate; **2.** to heat.

kızgın 1. red-hot; **2.** angry; **3.** estral, in heat (or rut) (animal); **~ ~** angrily.

kızgınlaşmak 1. to get angry; **2.** to become red-hot.

kızgınlık 1. anger, rage, fury; **2.** rut; heat.

kızıl 1. red; **2.** fig. communist, red; **3.** MED scarlet fever, scarlatina; **~ cahil** as ignorant as they come; **~ kıyameti koparmak** to raise a hell of a row; **~ saçlı** redheaded.

Kızılay pr. n. the Red Crescent.

kızılca reddish; **~ kıyameti koparmak** to raise a hell of a row.

kızılcık BOT cornelian cherry; **~ sopası** fig. hiding, caning; **~ sopası yemek** F to get caned.

Kızıldeniz pr. n. the Red Sea.

Kızılderili Red (or American) Indian.

Kızılhaç, -çı pr. n. the Red Cross.

kızıllaşmak to turn red, to redden.

kızıllık 1. redness; **2.** alpenglow.

Kızılordu the Red Army.

kızılötesi, -ni PHYS infrared.

kızıltı reddish gleam (or glow).

kızılyıldız AST Mars.

kızışmak 1. to become fierce; **2.** to become violent (or lively); **3.** to beat down (sun); **4.** to go into rut (animal).

kızıştırmak 1. to enliven, to liven up; **2.** to incite, to egg on; **3.** to make red--hot.

kızkuşu, -nu zoo lapwing, pewit.

kızlık girlhood, maidenhood, virginity; ~ **adı** maiden name; ~ **zarı** hymen, maidenhead.

kızmak, (-ar) 1. to get angry; **2.** to get hot; **3.** to go into rut (*or* heat) (*animal*).

kızmemesi, -ni F grapefruit.

ki 1. who, which, that: **bir çocuk ki çok yaramaz** a child who is very naughty; **2.** so … that, such … that: **öyle pahalı ki alamıyorum** it is so expensive that I cannot afford it; **3.** seeing (*or* considering) that; **4.** as, though; **5.** when: **henüz televizyonu açmıştım ki telefon çaldı** I'd just turned on the television when the telephone rang; **6.** …, I wonder?: **bilmem ki ne desem?** what should I say, I wonder?; **7.** in; of: **Türkiyede'ki İngilizler** the English in Turkey; **bugünkü Türkiye** Turkey of today.

kibar [ā] polite, courteous, well-bred.

kibarca [ā] politely.

kibarlaşmak [ā] to become polite (*or* courteous).

kibarlık [ā] politeness, courtesy, refinement.

kibir, -bri arrogance, haughtiness; pride; **kibrine dokunmak** to wound s.o.'s pride; **kibrini kırmak** to take s.o. down a peg or two, to humiliate.

kibirlenmek to become haughty (*or* arrogant).

kibirli arrogant, haughty; proud.

kibrit, -ti match; ~ **çakmak** to strike a match; ~ **çöpü** matchstick; ~ **kutusu** matchbox.

kibritçi 1. match seller; **2.** *fig.* miserly, niggardly.

kifayet, -ti [ā] sufficiency; ~ **etm. 1.** to be enough, to suffice; **2.** (*bşle*) to be satisfied (*or* contented) with *s.th.*

kifayetli [ā] sufficient, adequate, enough.

kifayetsiz [ā] insufficient, inadequate.

kik, -ki 1. NAUT gig; **2.** *sl.* nose, snout, conk.

kikirik F beanpole (*person*).

kiklon cyclone.

kil clay.

kile kileh.

kiler pantry, larder, storeroom.

kilim kilim; **-i kebeyi sermek** F to settle down (*in a place*).

kilise [. x .] church.

kilit, -di 1. lock; padlock; **2.** linchpin; **3.** clevis, shackle; ~ **altında** under lock and key; ~ **noktası** key position (*or* point); ~ **vurmak** to lock.

kilitçi locksmith.

kilitlemek 1. to lock (up); **2.** to dovetail; to interlock.

kilitli 1. locked; **2.** dovetailed; interlocked.

kilitsiz unlocked.

kiliz BOT reed, rush.

killi clayey, argillaceous.

kilo [x .] kilo(gram(me)); ~ **almak** to put on weight; ~ **vermek** to lose weight.

kilogram kilogram(me).

kilohertz PHYS kilocycle.

kiloluk weighing … kilos.

kilometre [. . x .] kilometre, Am. kilometer; ~ **doldurmak** *sl.* to kill time; ~ **kare** square kilometer; ~ **saati 1.** speedometer, odometer; **2.** taximeter; ~ **taşı** kilometer stone.

kilosikl PHYS kilocycle.

kilovat, -tı kilowatt; ~ **saati** kilowatt-hour.

kils limestone.

kim 1. who; **2.** whoever; ~ **bilir?** who knows?; ~ **-e, dum duma** nobody knows anything about it; ~ **o?** who is it?; **-i** (*or* **-isi**) some (of them); **o ~ kibarlık ~** he is wanting in courtesy.

kimi, -ni some; some people; some things; ~ **kez** sometimes; ~ **köprü bulamaz geçmeye, ~ su bulamaz içmeye** *pro.* water is a boon in the desert, but the drowning man curses it; ~ **zaman** sometimes; **-miz** some of us; **-si** some of them; some people.

kimlik identity (card); ~ **cüzdanı** identity (*or* ID) card.

kimono kimono.

kimse 1. somebody, someone; **2.** anyone, anybody; **3.** (*with negative*) nobody, no one.

kimsecik not a soul; **-ler yok** there's not a soul here.

kimsesiz without relations *or* friends; ~ **çocuklar** homeless children, waifs and strays.

kimya [ā] chemistry; ~ **fakültesi** department of chemistry; ~ **mühendisi** chemical engineer; ~ **sanayii** chemical industry.

kimyacı [ā] **1.** chemist; **2.** teacher of chemistry.

kimyager [ā] chemist.

kimyasal chemical; ~ **madde** chemical.

kimyevi [. . -] chemical.
kimyon BOT cumin.
kin [ī] grudge, malice, ranco(u)r; ~ **beslemek** to nurse (or bear or nourish) a grudge (-e against).
kinaye [ā] allusion, hint; innuendo, insinuation.
kinci [- .], **kindar** [- -] vindictive, revengeful, rancorous.
kinetik kinetic(s).
kinin MED quinine.
kinizm Cynicism.
kip, -pi 1. type; 2. GR mood; 3. LOG, PHLS mode.
kir dirt, filth; ~ **götürmek** (or **kaldırmak**) not to show dirt; ~ **tutmak** to show dirt easily.
kira [ā] rent, hire; ~ **bedeli** rent; ~ **ile tutmak** to rent; ~ **kontratı** lease; **-da oturmak** to live in a rented flat (or house); **-ya vermek** to let, to rent.
kiracı [ā] renter, lessee; tenant.
kiralamak [. -. .] 1. (b-ne) to rent to s.o., to let to s.o., to lease to s.o.; 2. (b-den) to rent from s.o., to lease from s.o.; to charter from s.o. (vehicle).
kiralık [ā] to let, for rent; ~ **kasa** safe-deposit box; ~ **katil** hired gun (or assassin), goon.
kiraz BOT cherry; ~ **dudaklı** cherry-lipped.
kirde a kind of maize bread.
kireç, -ci lime; ~ **gibi olm.** to turn pale; ~ **kuyusu** lime pit; ~ **ocağı** limekiln.
kireçkaymağı, -nı bleaching powder.
kireçlemek 1. to lime; 2. to whitewash.
kireçlenme 1. calcification; 2. MED calcinosis.
kireçlenmek 1. to be limed; 2. to calcify.
kireçleşmek to calcify.
kireçli limy, calcareous.
kireçtaşı, -nı limestone.
kiremit tile; ~ **kaplamak** to tile; ~ **ocağı** tile kiln; ~ **rengi** tile (or brick) red.
kiremitçi tiler.
kiremitli tiled.
kiriş 1. joist; rafter; beam; girder; 2. geom. chord; 3. MUS string (of an instrument); 4. bowstring (of a shooting bow); **-i kırmak** sl. to take to one's heels.
kirişli 1. joisted; 2. tendinous.
kirizma [. x .] trenching (the soil); subsoiling.
kirlenmek 1. to (get) dirty, to foul; to

become polluted; 2. fig. to be defiled (or sullied) (hono(u)r); 3. to menstruate, to have the curse; 4. to be raped, to lose one's cherry.
kirletmek 1. to dirty ,to soil, to foul; to pollute; 2. fig. to foul, to sully, to stain, to blot, to besmirch (hono(u)r); 3. to rape.
kirli 1. dirty, filthy, soiled; polluted; 2. fig. blemished, disreputable (hono(u)r); 3. menstruating (woman); 4. dirty laundry; ~ **çamaşır** dirty clothes, laundry; ~ **çamaşırlarını ortaya dökmek** fig. to wash one's dirty linen in public; ~ **çıkı(n)** fig. wealthy niggard; ~ **sepeti** laundry basket.
kirlikan venous blood.
kirlilik dirtiness, filthiness, foulness; pollution.
kirpi ZOO hedgehog.
kirpik 1. eyelash; 2. BIOL cilium.
kispet, -ti leather pants (worn by a greased wrestler).
kist, -ti MED cyst.
kisve attire, apparel; dress, garb.
kişi person (a. GR), human being; one.
kişileştirmek to personify.
kişilik 1. personality; 2. individuality; 3. for ... persons.
kişiliksiz characterless, styleless.
kişioğlu, -nu highborn person.
kişisel personal.
kişizade [ā] highborn.
kişmiş a kind of raisin grape.
kişnemek to neigh, to whinny.
kişniş BOT coriander.
KİT (abbr. for Kamu İktisadi Teşekkülü) state-owned economic enterprise.
kitabe [ā] inscription, legend: epitaph.
kitabet, -ti [ā] 1. rhetoric; 2. secretaryship.
kitabevi, -ni bookstore, bookshop.
kitabi 1. bookish, book-learned; 2. stilted.
kitap, -bı book; ~ **delisi** bibliomaniac; ~ **ehli** People of the Book; ~ **kurdu** book worm; **kitaba el basmak** to swear on the Koran.
kitapçı 1. bookseller; 2. F bookstore.
kitapçılık bookselling.
kitaplık 1. bookcase; bookstand, bookrack; 2. library.
kitapsarayı, -nı public library.
kitapsız 1. bookless; 2. F heathen; pagan.
kitara [. x .] MUS guitar.
kitle mass; ~ **iletişimi** mass media.

kitlemek *s*. **kilitlemek.**
kitli *s*. **kilitli.**
kiyaset, -ti [â] cleverness.
KKK (*abbr. for* **Kara Kuvvetleri Komutanlığı**) Commandership of the Ground Forces.
klakson horn; **~ çalmak** to hoot.
klan clan.
klapa lapel.
klarnet, -ti clarinet.
klarnetçi clarinetist.
klas F first-rate, ace, A1.
klasik 1. classic; **2.** classic(al).
klasman *sports*: rating, classifying.
klasör file.
klavye keyboard; **-si kuvvetli** skillful (*typist, etc.*).
kleptoman kleptomaniac.
kleptomani kleptomania.
klik clique.
klima (cihazı) air conditioner.
klinik 1. clinic; **2.** clinical.
klips (spring) clip.
klipsli clip-on.
kliring COM clearing.
klişe 1. TYP cliché, plate; **2.** *fig*. trite, hackneyed.
klişeleşmek to become a cliché (*or* hackneyed).
klon clone.
klonlama cloning.
klonlamak to clone.
klor chlorine.
klorlamak to chlorinate.
klorlu chlorinated.
klorofil BOT chlorophyll.
kloroform CHEM chloroform.
kloş bell-shaped (*skirt*).
klüz GEOGR gap, col.
koalisyon coalition; **~ hükümeti** coalition government.
kobalt, -tı CHEM cobalt.
kobay ZOO guinea pig, cavy.
koca¹ husband, hubby; **~ bulmak** to find a hubby; **-ya kaçmak** to elope; **-ya varmak** to marry; **-ya vermek** to marry off (*a woman*).
koca² 1. large, very big; **2.** grand, great; **3.** adult; aged, old; **~ herif olm.** F to be fully grown; **~ oğlan** *co*. bear.
kocakarı *sl*. hag, crone; **~ ilacı** nostrum; **~ soğuğu** cold spell in mid-March.
kocamak to age.
kocaman huge, enormous.
kocasız husbandless; widowed.

kocatmak to age, to put years on.
koç, -çu 1. ram; **2.** *fig*. sturdy youngster; **~ burunlu** hook-nosed.
Koç, -çu Aries, the Ram.
koçan 1. corncob; **2.** stump; **3.** heart (*or* stem) (*of a vegetable*).
koçu 1. a kind of horse-drawn carriage; **2.** granary (*built up on poles*).
kod, -du code.
kodaman *co*. **1.** big cheese (*or* shot *or* pot), bigwig; **2.** powerful, influential; **-lar** *co*. the big pots, the bigwigs.
kodeks codex.
kodes *sl*. clink, jug, cooler, stir, chokey; **-e tıkmak** *sl*. to throw in the clink.
kodoş *sl*. pimp, pander.
kof 1. hollow; **2.** weak; **3.** ignorant; ineffectual.
kofana [. x .] ZOO large bluefish.
koflaşmak 1. to become hollow; **2.** to get weak.
kofti [x .] *sl*. lie.
koğuş dormitory; hospital ward.
kok, -ku (*a*. **~ kömürü**) coke.
kokain cocaine.
kokak smelly, fetid, whiffy.
kokarca [. x .] ZOO polecat, skunk.
kokart, -tı cockade.
koket, -ti coquettish.
koklamak to smell, to sniff.
koklaşmak *fig*. to neck, to pet.
koklatmak *caus. of* **koklamak**; **koklatmamak** *sl*. not even to give a very tiny bit of.
kokmak, (-ar) 1. to smell; **2.** to stink, to putrefy, to whiff; **3.** *fig*. to reek (**of**).
kokmuş 1. smelly, whiffy, putrid; **2.** *fig*. bone-idle, bone-lazy.
koko coconut macaroon.
kokoreç, -ci roasted sheep's intestines.
kokoroz 1. BOT corn; **2.** *sl*. person like the back (end) of a bus.
kokorozlanmak to become defiant.
kokoz *sl*. broke, penniless.
kokteyl cocktail (party).
koku 1. smell, scent, odo(u)r; **2.** perfume; **3.** *fig*. the tiniest bit of, a mote of; **-su çıkmak** to be divulged; **-sunu almak** (*bşin*) *fig*. to scent *s.th*., to get wind of *s.th*.
kokulu sweet smelling, fragrant, odoriferous, odorous, perfumed.
kokusuz scentless, odo(u)rless.
kokuşmak to putrefy, to whiff.
kokutmak 1. to make smell; **2.** to make

stink; **3.** to break wind.

kol 1. arm; **2.** sleeve; **3.** MEC handle, bar; lever; **4.** limb (*of a tree*); **5.** crank; **6.** MUS neck (*of an instrument*); **7.** branch, division; **8.** club (*in a school*); **9.** patrol; **10.** MIL column; **11.** troupe; gang; **12.** side; ~ **askısı** MED sling; ~ **demiri** iron bar; ~ **düğmesi** cuff link; ~ **gezmek 1.** to patrol; **2.** *fig.* to lurk, to prowl around; ~ **kanat olm.** *fig.* to take under one's wing; ~ **kapağı** shirt cuff; ~ **-a** arm in arm; ~ **-a girmek** to link arms; ~ **nizamı** MIL column; ~ **saati** wristwatch; **-larını sıvamak** *fig.* to roll up one's sleeves; **-u uzun** *fig.* powerful, influential; **-una girmek** (*b-nin*) to take *s.o.*'s arm.

kola [x .] **1.** (laundry) starch; **2.** starch paste; ~ **yapmak** to starch.

kolaçan etm. to prowl, to have a look- -see round.

kolalamak to starch.

kolalı starched, starchy.

kolan 1. stout band; **2.** cinch, girth; **3.** rope of a swing.

kolay 1. easy, simple; **2.** easily; ~ **gelsin!** may it be easy!; ~ ~ easily; **-da** handy; **-ına bakmak** (*bir işin*) to look for the easiest way (*of doing s.th.*); **-ını bulmak** (*bşin*) to find an easy way to do *s.th.*

kolayca [. x .] **1.** easily; **2.** fairly easy.

kolaycacık [. x ..] very easily.

kolaylamak to break the back of (*a job*).

kolaylaşmak to get easy.

kolaylaştırmak to facilitate, to ease.

kolaylık 1. easiness; **2.** facility, means; **3.** convenience, labo(u)rsaving device; ~ **göstermek** to make things easier (*-e* for).

kolcu guard, watchman.

kolçak 1. mitten; **2.** armlet, armband; **3.** sleevelet; **4.** chair arm.

koldaş colleague, co-worker.

kolej private high school.

koleksiyon collection; ~ **yapmak** to collect.

koleksiyoncu collector.

koleksiyonculuk collecting.

kolektif collective, joint; ~ **ortaklık** unlimited company.

kolektör ELECT collector.

kolera cholera.

kolesterol MED cholesterol.

koli parcel, packet.

kolibasil coli (*or* colon) bacillus.

kollamak 1. to watch (*or* look out) for, to be on the alert for; **2.** to look after, to protect; **3.** to scan.

kollu 1. ... sleeved; **2.** having ... arms; **3.** MIL of ... columns; **4.** MEC handled; **kısa** ~ short-sleeved.

kolluk 1. cuff; **2.** sleevelet; **3.** armband, armlet.

Kolombiya *pr. n.* Colombia.

kolon 1. column; **2.** riser, conduit; **3.** ANAT colon; **4.** MEC (loud)speaker.

koloni colony.

kolonya cologne.

kolordu MIL army corps.

koltuk 1. armchair, easy chair; **2.** armpit; **3.** *fig.* flattery; **4.** out-of-the-way spot; **5.** out-of-the-way shop; **6.** *fig.* patronage, pull, favo(u)ritism; **7.** *sl.* brothel; ~ **altı** armpit; ~ **değneği** crutch; ~ **değneğiyle gezmek** to go about on crutches; ~ **vermek** to flatter to his face; **-ları kabarmak** to swell with pride; **-ta olm.** *co.* to sponge on *s.o.*

koltukçu 1. maker *or* seller of armchairs; **2.** *fig.* flatterer.

koltuklamak 1. to tuck under one's arm; **2.** to take s.o.'s arm; **3.** *fig.* to flatter.

koltukluk dress shield.

kolye necklace.

kolyoz [x .] ZOO chub mackerel.

kolza [x .] BOT rape.

koma [- .] MED coma; **-dan çıkmak** to come out of a coma; **-ya girmek** to go into a coma; **-ya sokmak** *sl.* to beat to a pulp.

komak *s.* **koymak.**

komalık *sl.* **1.** enraged; **2.** badly beaten up; ~ **etm.** *sl.* to beat the tar out of s.o.

komandit, -ti (*or* ~ **şirket**) limited (*or* special) partnership; commandite.

komando commando.

kombine combined.

kombinezon 1. slip; **2.** scheme, plan, arrangement.

komedi, komedya comedy.

komedyacı [. x ..] fakey, charlatanic.

komedyen comedian; comedienne.

komi busboy.

komik 1. comical, funny; **2.** comedian, comic.

komikleşmek to become comical.

komiklik funniness, comicality.

komiser superintendent of police.

komisyon 1. commission, committee; **2.** commission, percentage.

komisyoncu 1. commission agent, middleman, broker; **2.** house agent, *Am.* realtor.

komita revolutionary committee.

komitacı comitadji.

komitacılık activities of an underground revolutionary.

komite committee.

komodin commode, bedstand.

komodor NAUT commodore.

komot, -du dresser, chest of drawers.

kompartıman compartment.

kompas calipers, caliper compass.

kompetan expert, authority.

komple 1. full, filled up; **2.** complete, full, entire.

kompleks PSYCH complex.

kompleksli PSYCH having a complex.

komplikasyon MED complication.

komplike complicated.

kompliman compliment; ~ *yapmak* to compliment.

komplo plot, conspiracy; ~ *kurmak* to plot, to conspire.

komplocu conspirator, plotter.

komposto compote.

kompozisyon composition (*a. art,* MUS).

kompozitör MUS composer.

komprador comprador.

kompres MED compress.

kompresör MEC compressor.

komprime tablet.

kompütür computer.

komşu 1. neighbo(u)r; **2.** neighbo(u)ring, adjacent; ~ *memleketler* neighbo(u)ring countries; ~ *olm.* to become neighbo(u)rs; **-nun tavuğu komşuya kaz görünür** *pro.* the grass is greener on the other side of the hill (*or* fence).

komşuluk 1. neighbo(u)rhood; **2.** neighbo(u)rliness.

komut, -tu MIL order, command; ~ *vermek* to command.

komuta MIL command; ~ *etm.* to command.

komutan MIL commander.

komutanlık MIL commandership.

komünist, -ti communist; ~ *partisi* communist party.

komünistlik, komünizm communism.

komütatör MEC commutator.

konak 1. mansion; **2.** stopping place; ~ *gibi* stately (*house*).

konaklamak to pass (*or* spend) the night, to stay over night.

konca 1. flower bud; **2.** *sl.* good-quality hashish.

konç, -cu JUR (*of a boot or stocking*).

konçerto [. x .] MUS concerto.

kondansatör MEC condenser.

kondisyon 1. physical fitness; **2.** condition.

kondurmak 1. *caus. of* **konmak**; **2.** to tack (*-e* on), to stick (*-e* on); **3.** to label s.o. a ... put s.o. down as a ...; **4.** suddenly to land (*-e* on) (*blow*); suddenly to place (*-e* on) (*kiss*).

kondüktör conductor.

konfederasyon confederation.

konfederatif confederal, confederative.

konfedere confederated.

konfeksiyon ready-to-wear clothing.

konferans 1. lecture; **2.** POL conference; ~ *salonu* lecture theatre, assembly room, auditorium; ~ *vermek* to give a lecture.

konferansçı lecturer.

konfeti confetti.

konfor comforts, conveniences.

konforlu comfortable, comfy.

kongre [x .] congress.

koni *geom.* cone.

konik *geom.* conic(al).

konjonktür economic situation (*of a country*).

konkasör MEC rock crusher.

konkav concave.

konken cooncan, coon king.

konkordato [. . x .] **1.** JUR composition of debts; **2.** concordat.

konkur competition, contest.

konkurhipik riding competition.

konmak 1. to stay for the night (*-e* at); **2.** to camp (*-e* in); to bivouac (*-e* in); **3.** to (a)light (*-e* on), to settle (*-e* on), to perch (*-e* on); **4.** F to have s.th. fall in one's lap.

konsantrasyon concentration.

konsantre concentrated; ~ *olm.* to concentrate (*-e* on).

konsa gizzard.

konsept, -ti concept.

konser concert; ~ *vermek* to give a concert.

konservatuvar conservatory, conservatoire.

konserve tinned (*or Am.* canned) food.

konsey council.

konsol 1. chest (of drawers); **2.** console, corbel, bracket; **3.** console table;

~ **saati** bracket (or mantel) clock.
konsolidasyon COM consolidation.
konsolide COM consolidated.
konsolit, -ti consol, consolidated annuity.
konsolos consul.
konsolosluk consulate.
konsomasyon food or drink.
konsomatris B-girl.
konsorsiyum COM consortium.
konsültasyon MED consultation.
konşimento COM bill of lading.
kont, -tu count: earl; ~ **gibi yaşamak** to live like a lord.
kontak 1. short (circuit); **2.** sl. nutty, cracked; ~ **anahtarı** car (or engine) key; **kontağı açmak** to start the engine, to switch on the motor; **kontağı kapamak** to shut off the engine.
kontenjan quota.
kontes countess.
kontluk countship, earldom.
kontra [x .] **1.** counter, against; **2.** plywood.
kontrast, -tı contrast.
kontrat, -tı contract.
kontratak sports: counterattack.
kontrbas MUS contrabass.
kontrol, -lü 1. control; inspection; **2.** inspector, controller; ~ **etm.** to control, to check, to inspect; ~ **kalemi** circuit-tester; ~ **kulesi** AVIA control tower.
kontrolcu controller, inspector.
kontrplak plywood.
konu topic, subject; matter, theme.
konuk guest.
konukçu host; hostess.
konukevi, -ni guest house.
konuklamak to host, to put up, to entertain (a guest).
konu komşu neighbo(u)rhood, the neighbo(u)rs.
konuksever hospitable.
konukseverlik hospitality.
konum location, site.
konuşkan talkative, loquacious, chatty.
konuşkanlık talkativeness, loquacity, chattiness.
konuşma 1. vn. of **konuşmak**; **2.** speech, talk, lecture; **3.** conversation; discussion; ~ **dili** colloquial language, everyday speech; ~ **yapmak** to make a speech.
konuşmacı 1. lecturer; **2.** speaker, announcer.

konuşmak 1. to speak (ile to), to talk (ile to); **2.** to converse, to chat; **3.** to communicate; **4.** to discuss, to talk (-i about); **5.** to be on speaking (or friendly) terms (ile with) **6.** F to look sharp, to be eye-catching.
konuşturmak caus. of **konuşmak**, part. to make talk (a musical instrument).
konuşucu lecturer, speaker.
konut, -tu 1. house, dwelling, residence; **2.** domicile.
konveks convex.
konvektör convector.
konvoy convoy.
konyak cognac, brandy.
kooperatif cooperative, co-op.
kooperatifçi 1. member of a co-op; **2.** manager of a co-op.
kooperatifçilik economic cooperation, cooperative system.
kooperatifleşmek to become a cooperative.
koordinasyon coordination.
koordinat, -tı MATH coordinate.
kopanaki bobbin (lace).
koparmak caus. of **kopmak**, part. **1.** to break (or tear) off; **2.** to pluck, to pick, to snap off; **3.** to let out, to set up (noise); **4.** (b-den bşi) F to get (or wangle) s.th. out of s.o.
kopça hook and eye.
kopçalamak to hook, to fasten.
kopil sl. street Arab, urchin, gamin.
kopkolay [x . .] as easy as pie.
kopmak, (-ar) 1. to break, to snap; **2.** to break out (storm, war, etc.); **3.** to ache violently.
kopoy hound.
kopsi kefali etm. sl. to behead.
kopuk 1. broken (or snapped) off; **2.** F tramp, bum, punk; ~ **alayı** band of vagabonds.
kopuz lute-like instrument.
kopya 1. copy; **2.** cheating; ~ **çekmek** to copy, to cheat; ~ **defteri** copybook; ~ **etm.** to copy; ~ **kâğıdı** carbon paper; ~ **mürekkebi** copying ink; **-sını çıkarmak** to copy.
kopyacı 1. copier; **2.** cheater, cribber.
kor¹ MIL corps.
kor² 1. ember; **2.** fiery red; ~ **dökmek** to form a bed of glowing coals; ~ **gibi** red-hot.
koramiral, -li vice admiral.
kordele ribbon.
kordiplomatik corps diplomatique,

diplomatic corps.

kordon 1. cord (*a.* ELECT), cordon, braid; **2.** cord, rope; pull; **3.** cordon, stringcourse; **4.** cordon (*of police*); ~ *altına almak* to cordon off, to isolate.

Kore *pr. n.* Korea.

Koreli *pr. n.* Korean.

Korgeneral, -li lieutenant general, corps commander.

koridor corridor.

korkak 1. cowardly, fearful, timid; **2.** coward, poltroon.

korkaklık cowardice, fearfulness.

korkmak, (-ar) to be afraid (*or* scared) (*-den* of), to fear, to dread.

korku fear, dread, terror; phobia; fright; ~ *filmi* horror film; ~ *saçmak* to spread terror; ~ *vermek* to terrorize.

korkulu 1. scary, dreadful; **2.** dangerous, perilous.

korkuluk 1. scarecrow; **2.** balustrade, banister; parapet; **3.** *fig.* figurehead, cipher.

korkunç, -cu 1. terrible, awful, dreadful; **2.** tremendous, terrific, rightful; **3.** terrifically, awfully.

korkusuz 1. fearless, intrepid; **2.** safe.

korkutmak *caus. of* **korkmak**, *part.* **1.** to scare, to frighten, to threaten; to intimidate; **2.** to scare off (*or* away).

korna [x .] horn; ~ *çalmak* to hoot, to honk.

korner *football:* corner (kick).

kornet, -ti MUS cornet.

korniş cornice.

korno [x .] **1.** MUS French horn; **2.** powder horn.

koro [x .] chorus, choir.

koroydo [. x .] *sl.* idiotic, foolish.

korporasyon corporation.

korsa corset; girdle.

korsan pirate, corsair; ~ *gemisi* pirate ship; ~ *radyo* pirate radio station.

korsanlık piracy.

korse = **korsa**.

kort, -tu court.

korta, korte courting; flirting; ~ *etm.* to court; to flirt (*ile* with).

kortej cortege.

koru grove, coppice, copse.

korucu forest watchman.

korugan MIL blockhouse.

koruk unripe grape; ~ *lüferi* small bluefish (*caught in August*).

koruluk grove, coppice, copse.

koruma *vn. of* **korumak**; ~ *görevlisi*

bodyguard, bouncer; ~ *polisi* police bodyguard.

korumak 1. to protect, to guard, to watch over, to shield; to defend; **2.** to cover (*expense*).

korunak shelter.

koruncak case, box.

korunga BOT trefoil.

korunmak *pass. or refl. of* **korumak**, *part.* to safeguard (*or* protect) o.s. (*-den* against); to escape, to avoid.

koruyucu 1. protective; **2.** protector, defender.

kosinüs MATH cosine.

koskoca [x . .] very big (*or* great).

koskocaman [x . . .] enormous, huge.

kostüm 1. suit; **2.** THEAT costume.

koşaltı yoking *or* harnessing two animals together.

koşmaca tag.

koşmak, (-ar) 1. to run; **2.** (*ardından, arkasından, peşinden*) to pursue, to run after, to chase; **3.** (*yardımına*) to run to s.o.'s assistance (*or* aid); **4.** (*şart*) to make it a condition, to stipulate; **5.** to harness, to hitch (*-e* to); **6.** to hitch up (*horse*); **7.** to put to work; *koşar adımlarla* at a run; *koşar adım marş!* run!

koşturmak *caus. of* **koşmak**, *part.* **1.** to send s.o. on (*an errand*); to hurry s.o.; **2.** to race (*horse*).

koşu race; ~ *alanı* hippodrome; ~ *atı* racehorse; ~ *yolu* racecourse, racetrack; *bir* ~ *yardım getir* run for help.

koşucu runner.

koşuk verse.

koşul condition, stipulation, provision.

koşullandırmak PSYCH to condition.

koşullanmak PSYCH to be conditioned.

koşullu 1. PSYCH conditioned; **2.** conditional.

koşulsuz unconditional.

koşum harness.

koşuntu 1. supporters, followers; **2.** accomplices.

koşuşmak 1. to run (*or* rush) together; **2.** to run hither and thither, to run about.

koşuşturmak to run hither and yon, to bustle about.

koşut, -tu parallel.

kot, -tu (blue) jeans, denims.

kota COM quota.

kotarmak 1. to dish up (*food*); **2.** *fig.* to

finish, to complete.
kotlamak to spell out (*word*).
kotlet, -ti cutlet.
kotletpane breaded cutlet.
kotonperle pearl cotton.
kotra NAUT cutter.
kova 1. bucket, pail; **2.** ♎ AST Aquarius.
kovalamaca tag.
kovalamak to chase, to pursue, to run after.
kovan 1. (bee)hive; **2.** cartridge case.
kovboy [x .] cowboy; **~ filmi** western, cowboy film.
kovcu 1. backbiting; **2.** talebearing.
kovlamak 1. to run down, to disparage; **2.** to tell (*or* inform) (**on**).
kovmak, (-ar) 1. to dismiss, to drive away, to repel; **2.** to expel, to get rid of.
kovuk hollow, cavity.
kovuşturma JUR prosecution, investigation; **~ yapmak** to prosecute.
kavuşturmak JUR to prosecute, to investigate.
koy cove, small bay.
kovacak container.
koyak valley.
koymak 1. to put, to place (-*e* in); **2.** to let go; **3.** *fig.* to upset, to bother, to affect; to move; **4.** to set aside, to appropriate.
koyu 1. thick (*liquid*); **2.** dense (*fog*); **3.** deep, dark (*colo(u)r*); **4.** *fig.* fervid, extreme, rabid, dyed-in-the-wool; **~ kırmızı** dark red; **~ yeşil** dark green.
koyulaşmak 1. to thicken (*liquid*); **2.** to darken (*colo(u)r*).
koyulaştırmak 1. to thicken (*liquid*); **2.** to darken (*colo(u)r*).
koyulmak to set to (*or* about), to embark (-*e* upon).
koyuluk 1. thickness (*liquid*); **2.** deepness, darkness (*colo(u)r*); **3.** *fig.* extremeness, rabidity.
koyun¹ 1. ZOO sheep; **2.** F simpleton; **~ bakışlı** silly, simpleton (*in look*); **~ eti** mutton; **-un bulunmadığı yerde keçiye Abdurrahman Çelebi derler** *pro.* in the country of the blind, the one--eyed man is king.
koyun², -ynu 1. bosom, breast; **2.** *fig.* arms, embrace; **~ koyuna** in each other's arms; **koynuna girmek** (*b-nin*) to go to bed with *s.o.*, to sleep with *s.o.*; **koynunda yılan beslemek** *fig.* to nurse a viper in one's bosom, to have a snake in the grass.
koyungözü, -nü BOT feverfew.

koy(u)vermek, to set free, to let go.
koz 1. walnut; **2.** *cards*; trump (*a. fig.*); **~ kırmak 1.** to play a trump card; **2.** F to be up to no good; **-u kaybetmek** *fig.* to come out the loser; **-unu oynamak** *fig.* to play one's trump (*or* best) card; **-unu paylaşmak** *fig.* to settle (*or* square *or* balance) accounts (*ile* with).
koza [x .] **1.** cocoon; **2.** pod; boll.
koza(la)k 1. = **koza**; **2.** cone; **3.** unripe fruit.
kozalaklı coniferous.
kozalaklılar BOT Coniferae.
kozalaksı pineal; **~ bez** pineal gland (*or* body).
kozmetik cosmetic.
kozmik cosmic.
kozmonot, -tu cosmonaut.
kozmopolit, -ti cosmopolitan.
kozmos AST cosmos.
köçek 1. ZOO foal (*of a camel*); **2.** boy dancer; **3.** *fig.* light-minded person.
köfte meatball; croquette.
köfteci maker and seller of meatball.
köftehor *co.* lucky dog.
köfter a kind of grape sweet.
köftün oil meal.
köhne 1. old, ramshackle, dilapidated; **2.** outmoded, outdated.
kök, -kü 1. root (*a.* MATH); **2.** origin; **3.** CHEM radical; **~ işareti** MATH radical sign; **~ salmak** to take root (*a. fig.*); **~ söktürmek** (*b-ne*) to make things warm for *s.o.*; **-ünden** root and branch; **-ünü kazımak** to root out, to exterminate, to eradicate, to extirpate.
kökboyası, -nı 1. BOT madder plant; **2.** madder (*root*); alizarin.
kokçü herbalist.
köken 1. origin, source; **~ kodu** IT source code; **2.** homeland, place of origin; **3.** GR root (form).
koklemek 1. to uproot; **2.** to quilt, to tuft (*mattress*); **3.** to tune (**saz**).
köklenmek, kökleşmek to take root (*a. fig.*).
köklü rooted (*a. fig.*)
köknar BOT fir (tree).
köksel radicular.
koksüz rootless (*a. fig.*)
kökten radical, fundamental.
köktencilik radicalism.
kökteş cognate (*word*).
köle slave.
kölelik slavery, servitude, bondage.
kölemen HIST Mameluke.

kömür 1. coal; **2.** charcoal; **3.** coal--black; ~ **gibi** coal-black; ~ **gözlü** with coal-black eyes; ~ **işçisi** collier, coal miner; ~ **ocağı** coal mine.

kömürcü 1. coal dealer; **2.** stoker; ~ **çırağına dönmek** to get black all over.

kömürleşmek to coalify, to char.

kömürlük 1. coal cellar; coalbin; **2.** NAUT bunker.

köpek 1. ZOO dog; **2.** sl. cur; ~ **gibi** cringingly; **köpeği öldürene sürütür- ler** pro. it is the guilty one who suffers.

köpekbalığı, -nı ZOO shark.

köpekdişi, -ni cuspid, canine tooth.

köpeklemek 1. to be dog-tired; **2.** fig. to be humiliated.

köpeklenmek, köpekleşmek to fawn, to cringe, to grovel.

köpekmemesi, -ni large bubo.

köpoğlu, -nu [x - .] (a. ~ **köpek**) F **1.** bastard; **2.** fox.

köprü 1. bridge; **2.** hasp (of a lock); ~ **altı çocuğu** guttersnipe; ~ **başı 1.** MIL bridgehead; **2.** fig. foothold.

köprücü 1. bridge builder; **2.** MIL pontooning (unit).

köprücük (a. ~ **kemiği**) ANAT collarbone, clavicle.

köpük foam, froth; suds.

köpüklü foamy, frothy; sudsy.

köpürmek 1. to foam, to froth, to spume; **2.** fig. to foam at the mouth.

kör 1. blind; **2.** dull, blunt (knife, etc.); **3.** dim (light); **4.** fig. evil; unlucky; ~ **kütük** fig. pissed, corked, as drunk as a lord; ~ **olası!** damn it!; ~ **talih** bad (or hard) luck, evil destiny; ~ **topal** F after a fashion; **-le yatan şaşı kalkar** pro. the rotten apple injures its neighbo(u)rs, who keeps company with the wolf will learn how to howl; **-ü -une** blindly, at random.

körbağırsak ANAT c(a)ecum, blind gut.

kördügüm fig. Gordian knot.

körebe blindman's buff.

körelmek 1. BIOL to atrophy; **2.** to get dull (or blunt) (knife, etc.); **3.** to die down (fire).

köreltmek to dull, to blunt (knife, etc.).

körfez gulf; bay; inlet.

körkandil = kor kütük.

körkuyu dry well.

körlemeden blindly, at random.

körlenmek, körleşmek 1. to become dull (or blunt) (knife, etc.); **2.** to go dry (well); **3.** fig. to decline, to become blunt (mental power).

körleştirmek, körletmek 1. to dull, to blunt (knife, etc.); **2.** to cause to fail (mental power); **3.** to make go dry (well).

körlük 1. blindness; **2.** bluntness, dullness (of a knife, etc.)

Köroğlu. -nu 1. pr. n. name of a hero in Turkish folktales; **2.** F wife, the missus.

körpe fresh, tender.

körpecik emph. of **körpe** very fresh (or tender).

körpelik freshness; tenderness.

körük 1. bellows; **2.** accordion coupling (on a bus or train).

körüklemek 1. to fan with bellows; **2.** fig. to incite.

körükleyici fig. instigative.

kös big drum; ~ **dinlemiş** fig. thick--skinned, hardened.

köse beardless; ~ **sakal** very sparse bard.

kösele stout leather; ~ **gibi** leathery (food); ~ **suratlı** F shameless.

köseletaşı, -nı 1. sandstone; **2.** lapstone; **3.** whetstone.

kösemen lead goat (or ram); bellwether.

kös kös looking neither right nor left.

köskötürüm [x . . .] completely paralyzed.

kösnümek to be in heat (or rut).

köstebek 1. ZOO mole; **2.** MED scrofula.

köstek 1. hobble; **2.** watch (or key) chain; **3.** fig. obstacle, impediment; ~ **olm** to hinder, to impede; ~ **vurmak** to hobble (horse); **kösteği kırmak** fig. to beat it.

kösteklemek 1. to hobble, to fetter (horse); **2.** fig. to hamper, to impede.

köşe 1. corner; **2.** fig. nook; ~ **başı 1.** street corner; **2.** corner ...; ~ **bucak** every nook and cranny; ~ **kadısı** stay-at-home; ~ **kapmaca** puss in the corner; **-sine çekilmek** to retire into one's shell; **-yi dönmek** F to strike it rich.

köşebent MEC **1.** angle iron; **2.** cornerpiece.

köşegen MATH diagonal.

köşeleme diagonally.

köşeli cornered, angled; ~ **ayraç** TYP (square) bracket.

köşk, -kü villa, pleasure-house.

kötek beating; ~ **atmak** to cane; ~ **yemek** to get the cane.

kötü 1. bad; **2.** worthless; **3.** wicked, evil; **4.** F terribly; **~ beslenme** malnutrition; **~ günler** hard times; **~ huy** bad habit; **~ kadın** prostitute; **~ kişi olm.** to be in s.o.'s bad books; **~ söylemek** (*b-i için*) to speak ill of *s.o.*; **~ yola düşmek** (*or* **sapmak**) to go on (*or* walk) the streets; **-ye kullanmak** to misuse, to abuse.

kötücül malicious, evil, malevolent.

kötülemek to speak ill (*-i* of), to run down.

kötüleşmek 1. to become bad, to deteriorate; **2.** to be on the streets.

kötülük 1. badness, wickedness; **2.** harm, wrong; **~ etm.** (*b-ne*) to do *s.o.* harm.

kötülükçü evil, wicked.

kötümsemek to belittle, to disparage, to think ill (*-i* of).

kötümser pessimistic.

kötümserlik pessimism.

kötürüm paralyzed, crippled.

kötürümleşmek to become paralyzed.

köy village; ♀ **İşieri Bakanlığı** Ministry of Village Affairs; **~ muhtarı** village headman.

köydeş fellow villager.

köylü villager, peasant; fellow villager.

köyodası, -nı village social room.

köz ashes, embers.

közlemek to broil (*or* roast) over charcoal.

kral 1. king; **2.** *fig.* super, A1, top-notch.

kraliçe queen.

kraliçelik queenship, queenhood.

kraliyet, -ti 1. kingdom; **2.** kingship; **~ ailesi** royal family.

krallık 1. kingdom; **2.** kingship.

kramp, -pı MED cramp; **~ girmek** (*ayağına*) to be seized with cramp.

krampon screw-in stud.

krank, -kı MEC crankshaft.

krater crater.

kravat, -tı (neck)tie.

kredi credit; **~ kartı** credit card; **~ mektubu** letter of credit.

krem cream.

krema [x .] cream; icing.

kremkaramel crème caramel.

kremlemek to apply cream (*-i* to).

kremşantiyi crème chantilly.

krep, -pi crepe.

krepon crepon; **~ kâğıdı** crepe paper.

kreş day nursery, crèche.

kriket, -ti *sports*: cricket.

kriko [x .] jack; **-ya almak** to jack up.

kriminoloji criminology.

kristal, -li crystal.

kriter criterion.

kritik 1. critique; **2.** critical (*a.* MED), crucial.

kriz 1. crisis; **2.** fit, attack; **3.** fit of hysterics; **~ geçirmek** to have a fit of hysterics.

krizalit, -ti BIOL chrysalis.

kroke croquet.

kroki [x .] sketch; **-sini almak** (*or* **yapmak**) to sketch, to outline.

krom chrome, chromium.

kromozom BIOL chromosome.

kronik chronic.

kronoloji chronology.

kronometre [. . x .] chronometer, stopwatch.

kros cross-country race.

kroşçu cross-country runner.

kroşe *boring*: hook.

krupiye croupier.

kruvaze double-breasted (*garment*).

kruvazör NAUT cruiser.

kubbe dome, cupola.

kubbeli domed.

kubur 1. drain-hole; drainpipe; **2.** quiver; **3.** holster.

kuburluk 1. holster; **2.** powder flask.

kucak 1. embrace; lap; **2.** armful; **~ açmak** (*b-ne*) to receive *s.o.* with open arms; **~ çocuğu** babe in arms; **~ dolusu** armful; **~ kucağa** in each other's arms; **~ ~** by the armloads (*or* armfuls); **kucağına düşmek** to fall into the midst (*-in* of).

kucaklamak 1. to embrace, to hug; **2.** to surround.

kucaklaşmak to embrace (*or* hug) each other.

kuçukuçu doggy, bow-wow.

kudret, -ti 1. power, strength, might; **2.** omnipotence (*of God*); **3.** capacity, ability; **4.** the wherewithal; **~ hamamı** Turkish bath; **~ helvası** manna; **-ten** natural.

kudretli powerful, mighty.

kudretsiz powerless, incapable.

kudurgan wild, uncontrollable (*person*).

kudurmak 1. to become rabid, to go mad; **2.** *fig.* to be foaming at the mouth, to be beside o.s. with anger; **3.** *fig.* to go wild, to romp.

kuduruk 1. rabid, mad; **2.** *fig.* wild

(*person*).

kuduz 1. rabies, hydrophobia; **2.** rabid, hydrophobic.

Kudüs *pr. n.* Jerusalem.

kuğu zoo swan.

kuğurmak to coo (*pigeon*).

kuintet, -ti mus quintet.

kuka ball.

kukla [x .] **1.** puppet; marionette; **2.** puppet show; **3.** *fig.* puppet, tool; ~ **hükümet** puppet government.

kuklacı puppeteer.

kuku zoo cuckoo.

kukuleta [. . x .] hood; cowl.

kukuletalı hooded.

kukulya [. x .] silkworm cocoon; ~ **fırtınası** *storm occurring about the middle of April.*

kukumav zoo owlet; ~ **gibi** all alone.

kul 1. slave; **2.** mortal, man, human being (*in relation to God*); ~ **köle olm.** *fig.* to be at s.o.'s beck and call; ~ **yapısı** manmade.

kula [x .] dun-colo(u)red (*horse*).

kulaç 1. fathom; **2.** *swimming:* stroke; crawl; ~ **atmak** to crawl; to swim a stroke.

kulaçlamak 1. to fathom; **2.** to crawl.

kulağakaçan zoo earwig.

kulak 1. ear; **2.** zoo gill (*of a fish*); **3.** mus tuning peg; **4.** lug, handle, handgrip; ~ **asmak** to lend one's ear(s); ~ **asmanak** *fig.* to turn a deaf ear (*-e* to); ~ **dolçunluğu** knowledge picked up here and there; ~ **erimi** earshot; ~ **kabartmak** to prick up one's ears; ~ **kepçesi** anat earlap; ~ **kesilmek** to be all ears; ~ **kiri** earwax; ~ **misafiri olm.** to overhear, to eavesdrop; ~ **tıkamak** to stop one's ears (*-e* to); ~ **uğultusu** ringing in the ears; ~ **vermek** to give (*or* lend an) ear (*-e* to); ~ **yolu** anat auditory canal; **kulağı ağır işitmek** to be hard of hearing; **kulağı delik** quick of hearing; **kulağı okşamak** to be pleasant to the ear; **kulağına çalınmak** to come to one's ears; **kulağına girmek** (*b-nin*) to take note (*of*), to heed; **kulağına küpe olm** to be a lesson (*-in* to), to serve as a warning (*-in* to); **kulağını çekmek** (*b-nin*) to pull *s.o.*'s ear; **kulağını doldurmak** (*b-nin*) to put *s.o.* in the know, to fill *s.o.* in; **-ları çınlasın!** I hope his ears are burning!; **-larına kadar kızarmak** to blush to the top of one's ears; **-larını dikmek** *fig.* to prick up its ears

(*animal*); **-tan dolma** picked up (*knowledge*); **-tan kulağa** on the grapevine.

kulakaltı, -nı parotid; ~ **bezi** parotid gland.

kulakçı ear specialist.

kulakçık anat atrium, auricle.

kulakçın ear(f)lap.

kulaklı eared.

kulaklık 1. earphone, headphone; earpiece; **2.** hearing aid; **3.** = **kulakçın.**

kulakmemesi, -ni earlobe.

kulaksız earless.

kulakzarı, -nı eardrum.

kulampara [. x . .] pederast.

kule tower; turret.

kuleli towered; turreted; ♀ **Askeri Lisesi** Kuleli Military High School.

kulis 1. theat backstage, wings; **2.** com curb exchange; ~ **yapmak** to lobby, to work behind the scenes.

kullanılmış used, secondhand.

kullanım 1. use; **2.** gr usage.

kullanış using; ~ **tarzı** usage, way of using.

kullanışlı useful, handy; serviceable.

kullanışsız useless, unhandy; unserviceable.

kullanmak 1. to use; **2.** to employ; **3.** to drive (*car*); to fly (*plane*); to steer (*ship*); **4.** to take, to consume, to use.

kullap, -bı [ā] hasp.

kulluk 1. slavery, servitude; **2.** worship, adoration.

kulp, -pu 1. handle; **2.** *fig.* pretext; ~ **takmak** to find a pretext; **-unu bulmak** (*bir işin*) to find a way out of *s.th.*

kulplu handled; ~ **beygir** *sports:* pommel horse.

kuluçka [. x .] **1.** broody; **2.** hen bird; ~ **devri** incubation period; ~ **makinesi** incubator; **-ya oturmak** (*or* **yatmak**) to brood, to incubate, to set.

kulun newborn foal.

kulunç 1. shoulder pain; **2.** colic; **3.** cramp.

kulübe 1. hut, shed, cottage; shanty, shack; **2.** mil sentry box; **3.** telephone box (*or* booth); **4.** tollbooth.

kulüp, -bü 1. club; **2.** clubhouse.

kulvar lane.

kum 1. sand; **2.** med gravel (*in the kidneys*); ~ **çölü** sandy desert; ~ **gibi** loads of; ~ **saati** hourglass; ~ **torbası** sandbag; **-da oynamak** *fig.* to whistle for it.

kuma fellow wife.

kumanda [. x .] MIL command; ~ *etm.* to command, to be in command (*-e* of).

kumandan commander.

kumandanlık commandership.

kumanya [. x .] **1.** food (*to be eaten while traveling*); **2.** MIL soldier's (*or* field) rations.

kumar gambling (*a. fig.*); ~ *masası* gaming table; ~ *oynamak* to gamble, to game.

kumarbaz, kumarcı gambler.

kumarhane [. - .] gaming-house, gambling-house.

kumaş cloth, fabric, material.

kumbara [x ..] **1.** piggy bank, money-box; **2.** coin (*or* token) box (*of a pay telephone, etc.*); **3.** obs. (bomb) shell.

kumbaracı obs. bombardier.

kumkuma 1. jug, vase; **2.** fig. instigator, spreader.

kumlu sandy.

kumluk sandy (place).

kumpanya 1. COM company, firm; **2.** THEAT troupe; **3.** fig. gang, band, bunch.

kumpas s. **kompas**.

kumral 1. brown (*hair*); **2.** brown-haired (*person*).

kumru ZOO (turtle)dove; ~ *göğsü* iridescent.

kumsal sandy (beach).

kumsallık sandiness.

kumtaşı, -nı sandstone.

kumul (sand) dune.

kunda ZOO a kind of poisonous spider.

kundak 1. swaddling clothes; **2.** gunstock; **3.** bundle of rags; ~ *sokmak* **1.** to set fire (*-e* to); **2.** to sabotage, to wreck; **3.** (*arasına*) fig. to set *persons* by the ears.

kundakçı 1. arsonist, incendiary, firebug; **2.** fig. mischief-maker.

kundakçılık arson, incendiarism.

kundaklamak 1. to swaddle; **2.** to set fire (to); **3.** fig. to sabotage, to wreck.

kundaklı swaddled.

kundura [x ..] shoe; ~ *tamircisi* shoe-repairer, cobbler.

kunduracı 1. shoemaker; **2.** shoe-repairer, cobbler; **3.** seller of shoes.

kunduz ZOO beaver.

kunt, -tu stout, solid.

kupa[1] [x .] **1.** cup; **2.** cards: heart; ~ *finali* cup final.

kupa[2] [x .] coupé.

kupkuru [x ..] emph. of **kuru**, bone-dry, as dry as a bone.

kupon coupon.

kupür clipping.

kur[1] **1.** COM rate of exchange; **2.** course (*of studies*).

kur[2] courtship, flirtation; ~ *yapmak* (*b-ne*) to court *s.o.*, to pay court to s.o.

kura 1. drawing of lots; **2.** lot; **3.** MIL conscription; ~ *çekmek* to draw lots; *-sı olm.* (*bir yılın*) MIL to be among those conscripted in (*a certain year*).

kurabiye [ā] cooky, cookie.

kurak dry, rainless, arid.

kuraklık drought.

kural rule, regulation.

kuraldışı exceptional.

kurallı GR regular.

kuralsız GR irregular.

kuram theory.

kuramcı theorist, theoretician.

kuramsal theoretical.

Kuran pr. n. Koran, the Quran; *-ı Kerim* the Holy Koran.

kurander draught, Am. draft.

kurbağa ZOO frog; ~ *adam* frogman.

kurbağacık 1. froglet; **2.** small monkey wrench; **3.** handgrip.

kurbağalama swimming: breast stroke.

kurban [ā] **1.** sacrifice; **2.** victim (*of an accident*); **3.** ♀ (*Bayramı*) isl. the Feast of the Sacrifice, the Greater Bayram; **4.** fig. martyr; **5.** ♙ hey!, hello mate!; ~ *etm.* to sacrifice (*-e* to); ~ *gitmek* to fall victim (*or* a prey) (*-e* to); ~ *kesmek* to kill an animal as a sacrifice.

kurbanlık sacrificial (*animal*).

kurcalamak 1. to monkey about (*or* tamper) (*-i* with); **2.** to rub, to irritate, to scratch; **3.** fig. to delve into, dwell on (*a matter*).

kurdele ribbon.

kurdeşen (nettle) rash, urticaria.

kurgu 1. knob, winder; clock (*or* watch) key; **2.** MEC installation; **3.** PHLS speculation; **4.** assembly and editing (*of a film*).

kurgubilim science fiction.

kurgusal theoretical, speculative.

kurlağan MED whitlow, felon.

kurmak, (-ar) 1. to set up, to assemble, to put together; **2.** to wind (*clock*); **3.** to set, to lay (*table*); **4.** to pitch (*tent*); **5.** to set (*trap*); **6.** to cock (*gun*); **7.** to found, to establish; to form; **8.** to plan, to plot; **9.** to ponder, to dwell (on); **10.** to indulge in (*daydreams*).

kurmay MIL staff; ~ **subay** staff officer.
kurna [x .] marble basin.
kurnaz cunning, foxy, sly.
kurnazca cunningly, foxily.
kurnazlık cunning, foxiness.
kuron crown.
kurs¹ course; ~ **görmek** to take a course.
kurs² disk (a. AST)
kursak 1. crop, craw; **2.** F maw, stomach.
kurşun 1. CHEM lead; **2.** bullet; **3.** lead seal; ~ **atmak** to fire a gun; ~ **dökmek** to melt lead and pour it into cold water over the head of a sick person (in order to break an evil spell); ~ **gibi** as heavy as lead; ~ **işlemez** bullet-proof; ~ **yağdırmak** to shower bullets (-e on); ~ **yarası** bullet wound; -a **dizmek** to execute by shooting.
kurşuni [. - -] leaden, gray.
kurşunkalem (lead) pencil.
kurşunlamak 1. to lead; **2.** to shoot.
kurşunlu leaden.
kurt, -du 1. ZOO wolf; **2.** worm, maggot; **3.** fig. fox; ~ **dökmek** to pass worms; ~ **dumanlı havayı sever** pro. a person who is up to no good loves a chaotic situation; ~ **gibi** fig. foxy, shrewd; ~ **sürüsü** a pack of wolves; ~ **yemiş** worm-eaten; -**larını dökmek** to have one's fling, to have the time of one's life; -**unu kırmak** to satisfy one's whims.
kurtarıcı 1. savio(u)r; **2.** MOT wrecker, breakdown lorry, tow truck.
kurtarmak 1. to save, to rescue; **2.** to extricate from (trouble); **3.** to redeem (s.th. pawned); **4.** to recover (losses); **5.** to be enough to satisfy the seller; **daha aşağısı kurtarmaz** I can't sell it for less.
kurtçuk larva.
kurtköpeği, -ni Alsatian, German shepherd.
kurtlanmak 1. to get wormy; **2.** fig. to fidget; **3.** fig. to go stir crazy.
kurtlu 1. wormy; **2.** fig. fidgety; ~ **peynir** fig. fidgety child.
kurtmasalı, -nı cock-and-bull story.
kurtulmak 1. to escape; to be saved (or rescued); **2.** to get (or break) loose (animal), **3.** to slip (or fall) out (of); **4.** to be completed (or finished); **5.** to get rid of (s.th. or s.o. unpleasant); **6.** to give birth.
kurtuluş 1. liberation; **2.** salvation; **3.**

escape; ♀ **Savaşı** the Turkish War of Independence.
kuru 1. dry; dried; **2.** bare, unfurnished, unadorned; **3.** empty, vain, hollow; **4.** dead (plant); **5.** thin, emaciated; **6.** curt (utterance); ~ **fasulye** kidney (or haricot) bean; ~ **gürültü** much ado about nothing; ~ **hastalık** P tuberculosis; ~ **hava** dry air; ~ **iftira** sheer calumny; ~ **incir** dried fig; ~ **kafes** fig. skin and bones; ~ **meyve** dried fruit(s); ~ **öksürük** dry cough; ~ **sıkı 1.** blank (shot); **2.** fig. bluff; ~ **soğuk** dry cold; ~ **temizleme** dry cleaning; ~ **temizleyici** dry cleaner; ~ **üzüm** raisins; ~ **yemiş** nuts; -**nun yanında yaş da yanar** pro. the innocent suffers with the guilty.
kurucu founder; ~ **meclis** constitutional assembly (or convention).
kurukafa 1. skull; **2.** fig. dope.
kurukahve (roasted and ground) coffee.
kurukahveci seller of ground coffee.
kurul committee.
kurulamak to dry, to wipe dry.
kurulanmak pass. or refl. of **kurulamak**, part. to dry o.s.
kurulmak 1. pass. of **kurmak**; **2.** to nestle (or snuggle) down (-e in); **3.** to swagger, to show off.
kurultay general meeting (or assembly).
kuruluk dryness.
kuruluş organization, institution, establishment.
kurum 1. institution, foundation, association; **2.** soot; **3.** fig. swagger; ~~ **kurulmak** to be stuck-up; ~ **satmak** to put on airs.
kurumak 1. to dry, to get dry; **2.** to dry up (stream); **3.** to die (plant); **4.** to become skinny.
kurumlanmak 1. to put on airs; **2.** to get sooty.
kurumlaştırmak to institutionalize.
kurumlu 1. sooty; **2.** fig. conceited, stuck-up.
kurumsal institutional.
kurunmak to dry o.s.
kuruntu delusion, illusion, fancy.
kuruntulu neurotic, hypochondriac.
kuruş kurush, piastre, Am. piaster.
kuruşlandırmak to itemize.
kurutma kâğıdı blotting paper.
kurutmak 1. to dry; **2.** to wither (plant); **3.** to blot; **4.** to dehumidify;

to desiccate.

kurye POL courier.

kuskun crupper; *-u düşük* *fig.* in disgrace, out of favo(u)r.

kuskus couscous.

kusmak, **(-ar)** to vomit, to throw (*or* bring) up, to spew, to puke.

kusmuk vomit.

kusturmak to puke.

kusturucu emetic.

kusur [. -] fault, defect, flaw: shortcoming; drawback; *~ etm.* to be at fault; *-a bakmamak* to overlook, to pardon, to let it pass; *-a bakma!* I beg your pardon!, excuse me!

kusurlu 1. faulty, defective; 2. at fault, in the wrong.

kusursuz flawless, faultless, perfect.

kuş 1. zoo bird; 2. *sl.* wet behind the ears; 3. *sl.* penis, pecker, cock; *~ beyinli* bird-brained, nit-witted, dizzy; *~ gibi* as light as a feather (*or* air *or* thistledown); *~ kafesi gibi* small and beautiful (*house*); *~ kanadıyle gitmek* to go like a bird, to go off at a terrific bat; *~ uçmaz kervan geçmez bir yer* desolate place; *~ uçurmamak* *fig.* not to allow anyone *or* anything to escape; *-a benzetmek* to mess up, to spoil.

kuşak 1. sash; girdle, loin-cloth; cummerbund; 2. generation; 3. strap; 4. brace; 5. GEOGR zone; 6. AST Saturn.

kuşaklamak 1. to band, to tie up; 2. to brace.

kuşam s. *giyim kuşam.*

kuşane [ā] aviary.

kuşanmak 1. to gird (*or* put) on (*sword, etc.*); 2. s. *giyinip kuşanmak.*

kuşatma *vn.* of *kuşatmak*, part. MIL siege.

kuşatmak 1. to gird (*ile* with); 2. to surround; to besiege (*country*).

kuşbakışı, *-nı* bird's-eye view.

kuşbaşı, *-nı* 1. in small chunks (*meat*); 2. in big flakes (*snow*).

kuşbilim ornithology.

kuşekâğıdı, *-nı* glossy paper.

kuşet, *-ti* berth; couchette.

kuşkonmaz BOT asparagus.

kuşku suspicion, doubt; *-ya düşmek* to feel suspicious.

kuşkucu suspicious, skeptical.

kuşkulanmak to get suspicious.

kuşkulu 1. suspicious, distrustful; 2. unlikely, doubtful.

kuşkusuz 1. unsuspecting, trusting; 2.

certainly, for sure.

kuşlamak *sl.* to swot up, *Am.* to grind.

kuşlokumu small cookie.

kuşluk midmorning.

kuşmar bird trap.

kuşpalazı, *-nı* MED diphtheria.

kuşsütü, *-nü* any unobtainable thing; *~ ile beslemek* to nourish with the choicest of food; *-nden başka her şey var* there's everything you can think of to eat.

kuştüyü, *-nü* down; *~ yatak* feather bed.

kuşüzümü, *-nü* currant.

kutlama 1. congratulation; 2. celebration; *~ töreni* celebration.

kutlamak 1. to congratulate; 2. to celebrate.

kutlu lucky; blessed; *bayramınız ~ olsun!* have a happy Bayram!

kutlulamak = *kutlamak.*

kutsal holy, sacred; ♀ *kitap* the (Holy) Bible.

kutsallık holiness, sacredness.

kutsamak to sanctify; to bless; to hallow; to consecrate.

kutsi [ī] = *kutsal.*

kutu box, case; *~ gibi* small but cozy (*house*).

kutup, *-tbu* 1. pole; 2. axle; 3. *fig.* authority, expert; *~ ayısı* polar bear; *~ dairesi* polar circle; *~ kuşağı* GEOGR polar (*or* frigid) zone.

kutuplaşmak to be polarized.

Kutupyıldızı, *-nı* AST North Star, Polaris.

kutur, *-tru* MATH 1. diameter; 2. diagonal.

kuvaför hairdresser, coiffeur.

kuvars quartz.

Kuvayı Milliye HIST the Nationalist Forces.

Kuveyt, *-ti pr. n.* Kuwait.

kuvöz incubator.

kuvve 1. potential; 2. MIL the effective forces and equipment (*of a unit*); *-den fiile çıkarmak* to put into action.

kuvvet, *-ti* strength, power (*a.* MATH); force; vigo(u)r; *~ ilacı* tonic; *~ macunu* aphrodisiac with fruit and nuts; *~ vermek* 1. to strengthen; 2. to hearten, to encourage; *-le* 1. by force; 2. emphatically; *-ten düşmek* to weaken.

kuvvetlendirmek to strengthen.

kuvvetlenmek to strengthen, to become strong.

kuvvetli strong, powerful; vigorous;

forceful.

kuvvetsiz weak, feeble.

kuyruk 1. tail; **2.** queue, *Am.* line; **3.** *fig.* follower; suite, retinue; **4.** ponytail; **5.** train (*of a dress*); **6.** corner (*of the eye*); ~ **sallamak 1.** to wag its tail; **2.** *fig.* to fawn (*-e* over), to play up (*-e* to); **kuyruğu kapana kısılmak** F to have one's back against the wall; **kuyruğu titretmek** *sl.* to kick the bucket; **kuyruğunu kısmak** *fig.* to tuck one's tail.

kuyrukkakan zoo (stone)chat.

kuyruklu 1. tailed; **2.** zoo scorpion; ~ **kurbağa** tadpole; ~ **piyano** grand piano; ~ **yalan** whopper, walloping lie.

kuyrukluyıldız ast comet.

kuyruksallayan zoo yellow wagtail.

kuyruksokumu, -nu coccyx.

kuyruksuz tailless.

kuytu 1. snug, remote, secluded; **2.** out-of-the-way.

kuyu 1. well; **2.** pit; **3.** min shaft; ~ **açmak** to dig a well (*or* pit); ~ **bileziği** wellcurb; **-sunu kazmak** (*b-nin*) *fig.* to set a trap for *s.o.*

kuyucu well digger (*or* driller).

kuyum *obs.* jewel(le)ry.

kuyumcu jewel(l)er.

kuyumculuk jewel(le)ry.

kuzen cousin.

kuzey 1. north; **2.** northern.

kuzeybatı northwest.

kuzeydoğu northeast.

kuzeyli northerner.

kuzgun zoo raven; **-a yavrusu şahin görünür** pro. all his geese are swans.

kuzguncuk small iron grate.

kuzguni [. - -] as black as pitch (*or* ink).

kuzgunkılıcı, -nı bot gladiolus.

kuzin cousin.

kuzu lamb; ~ **derisi** lambskin; ~ **dolması** stuffed and roasted lamb; ~ **gibi** *fig.* as meek as a lamb; **-m!** F dear!, honey!

kuzudişi, -ni milk (*or* baby) tooth.

kuzukestanesi, -ni small chestnut.

kuzukulağı, -nı bot sorrel.

kuzulamak 1. to lamb; **2.** to crawl on all fours (*baby*).

kuzulu pregnant (*ewe*).

kuzumantarı, -nı bot a kind of mushroom.

Küba *pr. n.* Cuba.

kübik cubic(al).

küçücük [x . .] tiny, wee.

küçük 1. small, little; **2.** young, little; **3.**

petty, small(-minded); **4.** minor, petty; **5.** petite, dainty; **6.** small-scale, miniature; **7.** hey little one!; ~ **aptes** urination, piss, pee; ~ **dağları ben yarattım demek** *fig.* to think no small beer of o.s.; ~ **düşmek** to lose face; ~ **düşürmek** to disgrace, to mortify, to humiliate; ~ **görmek** to belittle, to underrate, to underestimate, to undervalue; ~ **harf** minuscule; ~ **köyün büyük ağası** *iro.* he thinks he is something!; ~ **parmak** little finger *or* toe; ~ **su dökmek** to piss, to pee, to urinate; **-ten beri** ever since childhood.

Küçükayı ast Ursa Minor, the Little Bear.

küçükbaş sheep, goat, *etc.*; ~ **hayvanlar** sheep, goats, *etc.*

küçükdil anat uvula; **-ini yutmak** *fig.* to fall off one's chair.

küçükhindistancevizi, -ni bot nutmeg (tree).

küçüklemek P to slight, to despise.

küçükleşmek 1. to grow smaller; **2.** to humiliate o.s.

küçüklü büyüklü 1. big and small; **2.** young and old.

küçüklük 1. littleness, smallness; **2.** childhood; **3.** *fig.* meanness, pettiness.

küçüksemek to despise, to belittle.

küçülmek 1. to shrink; **2.** to be humiliated.

küçültme *vn.* of **küçültmek**, *part.* **1.** humiliation; **2.** deprecation; ~ **eki** gr diminutive suffix.

küçültmek *caus.* of **küçülmek 1.** to make smaller; to shrink, to reduce, to diminish; **2.** to deprecate; to underrate; **3.** to humiliate.

küçültücü derogatory, deprecatory.

küçümen tiny, peewee.

küçümsemek to despise, to lessen, to look down (*-i* on).

küf mo(u)ld; mildew; ~ **bağlamak** (*or* **tutmak**) to mo(u)ld, to get mo(u)ldy; ~ **kokmak** to smell musty; ~ **kokusu** musty smell.

küfe 1. pannier; **2.** *sl.* fanny, ass.

küfelik 1. basketful; **2.** *fig.* blotto, under the table, well-oiled, lit up.

küflenmek 1. to mo(u)ld, to get mo(u)ldy; to mildew; **2.** *fig.* to become fogyish (*or* fusty); **3.** *fig.* to rot, to get rusty.

küflü 1. mo(u)ldy; musty; mildewy; **2.** *fig.* fogyish, fusty, mo(u)ldy.

küfran [ā] ingratitude.

küfretmek [x . .] to swear, to curse.

küfür, -frü 1. cuss, swearword, oath; **2.** blasphemy, impiety; **~ etm.** (*or savurmak or küfrü basmak*) to swear, to cuss.

küfürbaz foulmouthed.

küfürbazlık swearing.

küfür küfür: ~ esmek to puff.

küfüv, -ffü peer, equal, match.

küheylan Arabian horse.

kükremek 1. to roar (*lion*); **2.** *fig.* to bellow, to roar.

kükürt CHEM sulphur, *Am.* sulfur.

kükürtçiçeği, -ni flowers of sulfur.

kükürtlemek to dust with sulfur.

kükürtlü sulphurous, *Am.* sulfurous.

kül¹, -lü ash; **~ etm.** *fig.* to ruin; **~ gibi** ashen (*face*); **~ tablası** ashtray; **~ yutmak** *fig.* to get taken for a ride; **-ünü savurmak** *fig.* to play ducks and drakes with; **ben ~ yutmam** there are no flies on me.

kül², -lli all, the whole.

külah 1. conical hat; **2.** paper cone; **3.** *fig.* trick, deceit; **~ kapmak** to get an important job by chicanery; **-ıma anlat!** tell that to the marines!; **-ını havaya atmak** *fig.* to throw one's hat in the air; **Ali'nin -ını Veli'ye, Veli'nin -ını Ali'ye giydirmek** to rob Peter to pay Paul.

külbastı grilled cutlet.

külçe 1. nugget, lump; **2.** ingot; **~ gibi oturmak** *fig.* to flop (*or* plop) down, to plunk o.s. down.

külek tub.

külfet, -ti burden, onus, bother; **... yapmak külfetine katlanmak** to be at pains to do ...

külfetli burdensome, troublesome.

külfetsiz untroublesome, easy.

külhan stokehole (*of a bath*).

külhanbeyi, -ni rowdy, toughie, hood(lum), hooligan.

küllenmek 1. to become ashy; **2.** *fig.* to cool (*or* die) down (*anger, etc.*)

külli [ī] total, complete.

külliyat, -tı [ā] complete works (*of an author*).

külliye complex of buildings (*adjacent to a mosque*).

külliyen entirely, totally.

külliyet, -ti completeness.

külliyetli a good many.

küllü ashy.

küllük ashtray.

külot, -tu 1. (*women's*) panties; (*men's*) underpants, briefs, undershorts; **2.** breeches; **-lu çorap** tights, *Am.* panty hose.

külrengi, -ni ashen; gray.

külte 1. = **külçe**; **2.** bunch; **3.** GEOL rock formation.

kültivatör AGR cultivator.

kültür culture; **~ sahibi** cultured, cultivated.

kültürel cultural.

kültür fizik free exercise.

kültürlü cultured, cultivated.

kültürsüz uncultured.

külünk pick(ax).

külüstür ramshackle; junky-looking; **araba** crate, jalopy, rattletrap.

kümbet, -ti dome, cupola.

küme 1. pile, heap, mound; **2.** *sports:* league; **3.** group; **~ ~** in heaps (*or* groups).

kümebulut, -tu cumulus cloud.

kümelemek to heap (*or* pile) up.

kümelenmek 1. MIL to group; **2.** to cluster (*-e* around).

kümeleşmek to group.

kümes 1. coop; **2.** *fig.* tiny house; **~ hayvanları** poultry.

künde 1. hobble, fetter; **2.** *wrestling:* hold; **-den atmak** *fig.* to trip up.

künk, -kü pipe; tile.

künye 1. personal data; **2.** identification bracelet; identification (*or* dog) tag; **~ defteri** personnel roster; **-si bozuk** with a blot on one's escutcheon.

küp¹, -pü 1. earthenware jar; **2.** *sl.* pissed, lit up; **~ gibi** as fat as a pig; **-lere binmek** *fig.* to go up in the air, to blow one's top; **-ünü doldurmak** to feather one's nest.

küp² MATH **1.** cube; **2.** cubic.

küpe 1. earring; **2.** ANAT dewlap, wattle.

küpeçiçeği, -ni BOT fuchsia.

küpeli earringed.

küpeşte [. x .] **1.** NAUT rail(ing); gunnel; **2.** banister, handrail.

kür health cure.

kürdan toothpick.

kürdanlık toothpick holder.

küre 1. GEOGR globe, sphere; **2.** MIN smelter; **~ kuşağı** zone.

kürecik globule.

kürek 1. shovel; **2.** oar; paddle; **3.** (*baker's*) peel; **~ çekmek** to row; **~ kemiği** ANAT shoulder blade, scapula; **~~** by the shovelful; **~ yarışı** boatrace, rowing competition.

kürekçi 1. oarsman, rower; **2.** stoker (*on a boat*).

küremek to shovel up.

küresel MATH spherical; global; ~ **ısınma** global warming.

küreselleşme *vn. of küreselleşmek* globalization; ~ **karşıtı** anti-globalist.

küreselleştirmek *caus. of küreselleşmek* to globalize (*commerce*).

küret, -ti MED curette.

kürevi [i] spherical.

kürk, -kü fur.

kürkçü furrier.

kürklü (be)furred.

kürsü 1. lectern, rostrum, podium; pulpit; **2.** (*teacher's*) desk; **3.** *fig.* professorship, chair.

Kürt, -dü *pr. n.* **1.** Kurd; **2.** Kurdish.

kürtaj MED curettage.

kürtün 1. large packsaddle; **2.** snowdrift.

küs sullen.

küseğen 1. touchy; **2.** BOT sensitive plant.

küskü crowbar.

küskün offended, disgruntled, peeved.

küs küs sullenly.

küsküt, -tü BOT dodder.

küskütük [x . .] **1.** as stiff as a board; **2.** *fig.* blind, dead (*drunk*).

küsmek, (-er) to sulk, to pout, to be offended (*-e* by).

küspe bagasse; residue.

küstah insolent, impudent, cheeky, pert.

küstahlık insolence, impudence, cheek.

küstere 1. (*carpenter's*) plane; **2.** grindstone.

küstümotu, -nu BOT mimosa.

küstürmek to offend.

küsur [ü] **1.** remainder; **2.** odd; *beş yüz* ~ five hundred odd.

küsurat, -tı remainder.

küsüşmek to get cross with each other.

küt, -tü 1. stubby; **2.** blunt, dull; ~ *diye kapatmak* to slam (*door*).

küt küt ~ *atmak* to pound, to thump, to throb (*heart*).

kütle mass.

kütleşmek to get blunt (*or* dull).

küttedek [x . .] with a thud (*or* clonk).

kütük 1. trunk; stub stump; **2.** log; **3.** ledger, register.

kütüphane 1. library; **2.** bookcase; **3.** bookshop.

kütüphaneci librarian.

kütürdemek 1. to crunch; **2.** to crack, to snap.

kütürdetmek 1. to crunch; **2.** to crack, to snap.

kütür kütür 1. crunchingly; **2.** crunchy (*fruit*).

kütürtü 1. crunch; **2.** snap, crack.

küvet, -ti 1. bath(tub); **2.** basin, sink; **3.** PHOT developing tray; **4.** bedpan.

L

la MUS la; A.

labada BOT patience.

labirent, -ti labyrinth.

laborant, -tı laboratory assistant.

laboratuvar laboratory.

lacivert dark (*or* navy) blue, ultramarine.

laçka 1. NAUT untying a rope; **2.** *fig.* loose, lax; disorganized; indifferent, careless; **~ etm.** to slacken, to cast off; **~ olm.** *fig.* to get slack, to slacken off.

laçkalaşmak *s.* **laçka olm.**

laden BOT cistus.

lades a bet with a wishbone; **~ kemiği** ANAT wishbone; **~ tutuşmak** to pull a wishbone with one another.

laf 1. word, remark; **2.** empty words, hot air; **3.** talk, chat; **4.** that's bull!; **~ anlamaz** thickheaded; obstinate; **~ aramızda** between you, me and the gatepost, between you and me; **~ atmak 1.** to chat; **2.** to proposition; **~ etm.** (*b-le*) to chat with *s.o.*; **2.** (*bşi*) to gossip about *s.th.*; **~ işitmek** to be on the carpet; **~ -ı açar** one topic leads to another; **~ olsun diye** just for *s.th.* to say; **~ söyledi balkabağı!** you're talking crap!; **-a tutmak** (*b-ni*) to engage *s.o.* in conversation; **-ını** (*or* **-ınızı**) **balla kestim** excuse me for interrupting you; **-ını bilmek** to weigh one's words; **-ını etm.** (*bşin*) to talk about *s.th.*; **-la peynir gemisi yürümez** actions speak louder than words.

lafazan, lafçı talkative, windy, chatty.

lafebesi, -ni talkative, garrulous.

lafız, -fzı utterance, word.

lağap *s.* **lakap.**

lağar skinny (*animal*).

lağım 1. sewer, drain; **2.** MIL mine; underground tunnel; **~ açmak** to dig a drain; **~ atmak** to explode a mine; **~ çukuru** cesspool, sinkhole; **~ kuyusu** = **~ çukuru**; **~ sıçanı** ZOO brown rat; **~ suları** sewage; **-la atmak** to blast.

lağımcı sewerman.

lağıv, -ğvı abolition.

lağvetmek [x ..] to abolish, to do away (*-i* with).

lahana [x ..] BOT cabbage.

lahavle [- x .] my God!

lahika 1. appendix, addendum; **2.** GR suffix.

lahit, -hdi 1. sarcophagus; **2.** walled tomb.

lahmacun *a kind of meat pizza.*

lahza instant, moment, trice, second.

lailaheillallah there is no god but God.

lak, -kı *s.* **laka.**

laka [x .] lac; shellac; lacquer, varnish.

lakap, -bı nickname; **~ takmak** to nickname.

lakayt indifferent, unconcerned; nonchalant; **~ kalmak** (*bşe or bşe karşı*) to be indifferent towards *s.th.*, to remain unmoved by *s.th.*

lakaytlık indifference, unconcern; nonchalance.

lake lacquered; shellacked.

lakerda salt bonito.

lakırdı 1. word(s), talk; **2.** conversation, chat; **3.** gossip; **~ altında kalmamak** to give as good as one gets, to be quick to retort; **~ etm. 1.** to chat, to talk; **2.** to gossip; **~ taşımak** to tell tales; **-ya boğmak** (*bir konuyu*) to drown a subject in a flood of words; **-yı ağzına tıkamak** (*b-nin*) to shut *s.o.* up.

lakırdıcı talkative, chatty.

lakin [x .] but, however.

laklak *fig.* chatter; clatter; **~ etm.** to yak, to clatter, to natter, to prattle.

lal, -li 1. ruby; garnet; **2.** red ink.

lala HIST manservant (*who took care of a boy*).

lalanga [. x .] a kind of pancake.

lale 1. BOT tulip; **2.** forked stick; ♀ **Devri** HIST the Tulip Period (*1718-1730*); **~ soğanı** tulip bulb.

lalelik vase.

lalettayin 1. at random, indiscriminately; **2.** any … whatsoever; unexceptional.

lam[1] (micro)slide.

lam[2]: -ı cimi yok I don't want any ifs and buts.

lama 1. ZOO llama; **2.** lama.

lamba[1] 1. lamp; **2.** tube; **~ şişesi** lamp chimney; **-yı açmak** to run up the wick (*of a lamp*).

lamba² rabbet.

lambalamak to candle (*eggs*).

lame lamé.

lamise 1. the sense of touch; **2.** zoo antenna.

lan 1. hey, you!; **2.** say man!; **3.** listen, buster!

lanet, -ti 1. curse, imprecation; **2.** damnable, cursed, damned; ~ **etm.** (*or* **okumak**) to curse, to damn; ~ **olsun!** damn!

lanetlemek to curse, to damn.

lanetli = **lanet 2.**

langır lungur 1. rattling and banging; **2.** brusquely; loutishly.

langırt, -tı 1. pinball; **2.** foosball.

langust, -tu zoo langouste.

lanolin lanolin(e).

lanse launched; ~ **etm.** to launch, to introduce.

lantan CHEM lanthanum.

lap, -pı flop, plop; ~ **dlye** with a flop; ~~ with a smacking sound.

lapa porridge; poultice, blister; ~ **gibi** soft, mushy; ~~ **kar yağıyor** it is snowing in large flakes; ~ **koymak** (*or* **vurmak**) to poultice; to blister.

lapacı 1. fond of **lapa**; **2.** *fig.* flabby, languid.

lappadak with a plop.

largetto MUS larghetto.

largo MUS largo.

larp, -pı: ~ **diye** out of the blue.

larpadak *s.* **larp diye.**

laser laser.

laskine lansquenet.

laso lasso.

lasta [x .] NAUT last.

lasteks Lastex.

lastik 1. rubber; **2.** tyre, *Am.* tire; **3.** galosh, rubber, overshoe; **4.** rubber band; elastic band; **5.** rubber, *Am.* eraser; ~ **çizme** waders, wellington (boot); ~ **hortum** rubber hose.

lastikli 1. made of rubber; **2.** flexible, elastic; ~ **konuşmak** *fig.* to speak in double entendres.

lata [x .] lath.

latarna, laterna [. x .] hand (*or* barrel) organ.

latif [. -] nice, pleasant, lovely; amiable; dainty.

latife [. - .] joke, quip, leg-pull; ~ **etm.** to joke, to wisecrack; ~ **latif gerek** *pro.* politeness should not be neglected even in a joke.

latifeci witty (*person*).

latilokum *s.* **lokum.**

Latin *pr. n.* **1.** Latin; **2.** Romance (*language*); ~ **Amerika** Latin America; ~ **harfleri** Latin characters; ~ **yelkeni** lateen sail.

Latince [x . .] *pr. n.* Latin.

latinçiçeği, -ni BOT nasturtium.

laubali [- . - -] saucy, pert, free-and-easy.

laubalileşmek to become saucy.

laubalilik sauciness, pertness.

lav GEOGR lava.

lava [x .] NAUT pull! (*on the oars*).

lavabo washbasin, lavatory, *Am.* sink.

lavaj 1. MIN washing; sluicing; **2.** MED lavage.

lavanta [. x .] **1.** BOT lavender; **2.** lavender water.

lavdanom [x . .] PHARM laudanum.

lavman MED **1.** enema; **2.** enemator.

lavta¹ [x .] MUS lute.

lavta² [x .] MED **1.** obstetrical forceps; **2.** obstetrician.

layık, -ğı 1. worthy (*-e* of); fit to be; **2.** suitable, proper, appropriate; ~ **görmek** (*b-ni bşe*) to deem *s.th.* worthy of *s.o.*; ~ **olm.** to deserve, to be worthy (*-e* of), to suit; **layığını bulmak 1.** to find a suitable mate; **2.** to get one's deserts.

layıkıyle properly, adequately.

layiha JUR proposal, memorandum.

layik, -ki secular, nonclerical.

layikleştirmek to secularize, to laicize.

layiklik secularism, laicism.

layter NAUT lighter.

Laz *pr. n.* Laz.

laza small trough (*for honey*).

lazer laser; **-le ameliyat** laser surgery.

lazım 1. necessary, needed; **2.** GR intransitive (*verb*); ~ **olm.** (*or* **gelmek**) to be necessary (*or* needed).

lazımlık potty, (chamber) pot.

leb: ~ **demeden leblebiyi anlamak** to be able to read *s.o.*'s thoughts.

lebaleb [x - .] brimful.

lebiderya 1. on the sea, seaside (*building*); **2.** seashore.

leblebi 1. roasted chickpeas; **2.** *fig.* bullet.

ledün, -nnü knowledge of the nature of God.

leğen 1. washtub; washbowl; **2.** ANAT pelvis.

Leh *pr. n.* **1.** Pole; **2.** Polish.

leh in favo(u)r of, for; **-inde bulunmak**

to speak in favo(u)r (-in of); **-inde olm.** to be in favo(u)r (-in of); **-te oy vermek** to vote for; **-te ve aleyhte** pro and con, for and against.

Lehçe pr. n. Polish.

lehçe dialect.

lehim solder.

lehimci solderer.

lehimlemek to solder.

lehimli soldered.

Lehistan pr. n. Poland.

lehtar [ā] JUR beneficiary.

leke 1. stain (a. fig.), blot (a. fig.), spot; **2.** blemish, fleck, spot; birthmark; ~ **etm.** to stain; ~ **getirmek** (b-ne) fig. to blacken s.o., to besmirch s.o.; ~ **olm.** to become stained; ~ **sürmek** fig. to blacken, to besmirch; ~ **yapmak** to stain, to leave (or make) a stain (on).

lekelemek 1. to stain; to soil; **2.** fig. to blacken, to besmirch, to sully.

lekeli 1. stained, spotted; **2.** fig. of bad repute, dishono(u)red.

lekelihumma typhus.

lekesiz 1. spotless; **2.** fig. of repute.

leksikografi lexicography.

lenduha [ū] hulking.

lenf(a) lymph.

lenfatik MED lymphatic.

lenger 1. large deep dish; **2.** NAUT anchor.

lengüistik linguistics.

lento 1. lintel; **2.** MUS lento.

leopar ZOO leopard.

lepiska [. x .] flaxen (hair).

lesepase laissez-passer.

leş carcass; ~ **gibi 1.** stinking to high heaven; **2.** bone-lazy; **-ini çıkarmak** (b-nin) to beat the tar out of s.o.; **-ini sermek** (b-nin) to do s.o. in, to bum s.o. off.

leşkargası, -nı ZOO hooded crow.

letafet, -ti [ā] charm, grace, winsomeness; delicacy.

Levanten pr. n. Levantine.

levazım [ā] impedimenta, supplies, provisions.

levha sign(board); panel, slab.

levye rod, lever, crowbar.

levrek ZOO sea bass.

leydi lady.

leylak, -kı BOT lilac.

leylek ZOO stork.

leyli boarding; ~ **mektep** boarding school ~ **talebe** boarder.

leziz delicious, tasty, tasteful.

lezzet, -ti 1. taste, flavo(u)r; **2.** pleasure; ~ **almak** (or **duymak**) (bşden) to enjoy s.th., to find pleasure in s.th.

lezzetlenmek to become tasty.

lezzetli delicious, tasty, tasteful.

lezzetsiz tasteless.

lığ GEOL alluvium.

lığlı GEOL alluvial, alluvian.

lıkırdamak to glug, to gurgle.

lıkır lıkır with a gurgle.

liberal, -li liberal.

liberalizm liberalism.

libre [x .] **1.** pound; **2.** libra.

libretto MUS libretto.

Libya pr. n. Libya.

lider [x .] **1.** leader; **2.** leading, first-rate.

liderlik leadership.

lif [ī] **1.** fibre, Am. fiber; **2.** BOT luffa, loofah.

lifli fibrous.

lig, -gi sports: league.

lika [x .] lac(ca).

liken BOT, MED lichen.

likidasyon COM liquidation.

likide etm. COM to liquidate.

likidite COM liquidity.

likit fluid, liquid.

likorinoz smoked fish.

likör liqueur.

liman harbo(u)r; (sea)port.

limanlamak 1. to come into harbo(u)r; **2.** to die down (wind).

limanlık 1. suitable for a harbo(u)r; **2.** windless; **3.** calm (sea).

limba [x .] NAUT barge.

limbo [x .] s. **limba.**

lime [ī]: ~ ~ in tatters (or rags).

limit, -ti limit.

limitet, -ti COM limited; ~ **şirket** limited company.

limon BOT lemon; ~ **gibi** pale (face); ~ **sarısı** lemon yellow; ~ **sıkmak** fig. to wet-blanket (a conversation).

limonata [. . x .] lemonade; ~ **gibi** cool and pleasant (weather).

limonatacı lemonade seller.

limoni [. - -] **1.** lemon (or pale) yellow; **2.** fig. bad, sour (relations); **3.** fig. snappish, fractious.

limonküfü bluish green.

limonluk 1. greenhouse; **2.** lemon squeezer; **3.** parapet.

limontozu, -nu, limontuzu, -nu citric acid.

linç, -çi lynching; ~ **etm.** to lynch.

link, -ki trot: ~ **gitmek** to trot.

linolyum linoleum.
linotip, -pi linotype.
linyit, -ti lignite.
liposuction MED liposuction.
lir MUS lyre.
lira (*Turkish*) lira (*or* pound).
liralık worth … liras.
liret, -ti (*Italian*) lira.
lirik *lit.* lyrical.
lisan language, tongue; **-a gelmek** to begin to speak (*for s.th. nonhuman*).
lisans 1. licence, *Am.* license; certificate; **2.** bachelor's degree; **3.** import *or* export license; **4.** license to manufacture; **~ yapmak** to study for a bachelor's degree.
lisanslı licensed; certified.
lisansüstü (post)graduate.
lise [x .] high school.
liseli high-school student.
liste [x .] list; **-ye geçirmek** to list.
litografya, litografi lithography.
litre [x .] litre, *Am.* liter.
liva *obs.* **1.** MIL brigade; **2.** MIL brigadier general; **3.** banner, flag.
livar fishweir, fishgarth.
liyakat, -ti [. - .] merit, worthiness, suitability; competence; **~ göstermek** to prove capable.
liyakatli [. - . .] worthy, deserving; competent.
liynet, -ti looseness (*of the bowels*).
lizol, -lü Lysol.
lobi lobby (*a* POL)
lobut, -tu 1. *sports:* Indian club; **2.** club, cudgel.
loca [x .] **1.** THEAT box; **2.** Masonic lodge.
lodos 1. southwest wind; **2.** south; **~ poyraz** *fig.* he blows hot and cold.
logaritma MATH logarithm.
loğ roller.
loğlamak to roll with a roller.
loğusa woman in childbed.
loğusalık childbed, confinement.
lojistik MIL logistics.
lojman lodging (*for workers and employees*).
lokal, -li 1. local headquarters, clubroom; **2.** local (*a.* MED); **3.** rendezvous, haunt.
lokanta [. x .] restaurant.
lokantacı [. x . .] restaurateur.
lokavt, -tı lockout.
lokma 1. morsel, bite; **2.** ANAT condyle; **3.** a kind of syrupy friedcake; **4.** MEC wrench; **-sını dökmek** (*b-nin*) to

make friedcake in memory of *s.o.* who has died.
lokmanruhu, -nu CHEM ether.
lokomotif RAIL locomotive, engine.
lokum Turkish delight.
lololo *sl.* nonsense, bull.
lombar NAUT gunport.
lomboz NAUT porthole, scuttle.
lonca [x .] guild.
Londra [x .] *pr. n.* London.
Londralı *pr. n.* Londoner.
long-play long-playing record, LP.
lop, -pu 1. round and soft; **2.** ANAT lobe; **~ ~ yutmak** to bolt down; **~ yumurta** hard-boiled egg.
loppadak [x . .] with a plop.
lopur lopur yemek to bolt down.
lort 1. lord; **2.** F nabob, moneybags; *Lortlar Kamarası* the House of Lords.
lostra [x .] shoe polish; **~ salonu** shoeshine shop (*or* parlour).
lostracı [x . .] shoeshiner, shoeblack.
lostromo [. x .] NAUT boatswain, bosun.
losyon lotion.
loş dim, murky, dark, gloomy.
loşluk dimness, murkiness, gloom.
lotarya [. x .] lottery.
Lozan *pr. n.* Lausanne.
lök, -kü 1. awkward, clumsy; **2.** male camel.
lökün lute.
lösemi MED leukemia.
lumbago [x . .] MED lumbago.
lunapark, -kı fair, amusement park.
lustur *sl.* shoeshiner.
lutr ZOO otter (fur).
Lübnan [ā] *pr. n.* Lebanon.
Lübnanlı [ā] *pr. n.* Lebanese.
lüfer ZOO bluefish.
lügat, -tı 1. dictionary; **2.** word; **~ paralamak** to use a pompous language.
lügatçe glossary.
lüks 1. luxury; **2.** luxurious; **3.** lantern; **~ mevki** luxury class; **~ vergisi** luxury tax; **şehrin en lüks otelleri** the most luxurious hotels of the city.
Lüksemburg *pr. n.* Luxemb(o)urg.
lüle 1. curl, bob, fold, ringlet, lock (*of hair*); **2.** spout (*of a fountain*); **3.** clay bowl; **~ ~** in curls (*or* ringlets).
lületaşı, -nı GEOL meerschaum.
lüp, -pü *sl.* **1.** windfall; **2.** kernel, essence, marrow; **~ diye yutmak** to bolt down.
lüpçü *sl.* freeloader, parasite, hanger-

on.
lütfen [x .] please.
lütfetmek [x . .] to condescend, to deign, to be so kind as to; to oblige.
lütuf, -tfu kindness, favo(u)r; *lütfunda bulunmak* to be so good as to, to be so kind as to.

lütufkâr gracious, kind.
lüzum necessity, need; ~ *görmek* to deem necessary; *-unda* at a pinch (*or* push), when it's necessary.
lüzumlu necessary, needed.
lüzumsuz unnecessary, unneeded.

M

maada [- . -] **1.** except, apart from; **2.** besides, in addition to; *-sı* the rest; *bundan* ~ furthermore.
maaile with the whole family.
maalesef [. x . .] unfortunately.
maarif [. - .] **1.** education, public instruction; **2.** ♀ the Ministry of Education; ~ *müdürü* superintendent of schools.
maaş salary, stipend, pay; pension; ~ *bağlamak* to salary, to put on a salary.
maaşlı salaried.
maatteessuf regrettably, I regret to say.
maazallah [. x . -] God forbid!
mabat [- -] continuation, sequel.
mabet temple, place of worship.
mablak spatula; putty knife.
mabut [- -] **1.** God; **2.** god, deity; idol.
Macar[1] *pr. n.* Hungarian; ~ *salamı* salami.
macar[2] *sl.* louse.
Macarca [. x .] *pr. n.* Hungarian.
Macaristan *pr. n.* Hungary.
macera [- . -] adventure; ~ *filmi* adventure film; ~ *romanı* adventure novel; ~ *peşinde koşmak* to seek adventure; *-ya atılmak* to get involved in a risky business.
maceracı adventuresome, adventurous.
maceralı adventurous.
maceraperest, -ti *s. maceracı.*
macun [ā] **1.** putty; **2.** paste; **3.** MED paste; electuary.
macunlamak [- . . . .] to putty.
maç, -cı match; ~ *yapmak* to hold a match.
maça [x .] *cards:* spade; ~ *beyi* jack of spades; ~ *beyi gibi kurulmak* to sprawl; ~ *kızı* queen of spades.
maçuna [. x .] MEC crane.
madalya medal; *-nın ters tarafı* (*or yüzü*) the other side of the coin.

madalyon locket, medallion.
madam Madame.
madama Ma'am, Lady.
madara *sl.* **1.** worthless; **2.** vulgar, common; ~ *olm. sl.* to feel ashamed.
madde 1. matter, substance; **2.** article, clause, paragraph; **3.** item, entry; **4.** component, material; **5.** matter, topic, question; ~~ article by article, item by item.
maddeci materialist.
maddecilik materialism.
maddesel material.
maddeten [x . .] materially.
maddi [ī] material, physical.
maddiyat, -tı materiality.
madem [x .], **mademki** [. x .] [ā] since, as, seeing that.
maden [ā] **1.** MIN mine; **2.** CHEM metal; **3.** mineral; ~ *çevheri* ore; ~ *damarı* lode, vein; ~ *işçisi* miner; ~ *kuyusu* mine shaft; ~ *mühendisi* mining engineer; ~ *ocağı* mine, pit; ~ *ocağı işçisi* pitman; ~ *yatağı* ore bed.
madenci [ā] miner.
madencilik [ā] mining.
madeni [ā] **1.** metal(lic); **2.** mineral; ~ *para* coin, specie.
madenkırmız CHEM kermesite.
madenkömürü, -nü hard coal, anthracite.
madensel *s. madeni.*
madensuyu, -nu mineral water.
madik 1. marbles (*game*); **2.** *sl.* trick; ~ *atmak* to pull a fast one (*-e* on).
madrabaz cheat, swindler.
maestro MUS maestro.
Mafia Maf(f)ia.
mafiş 1. a kind of fritter; **2.** F nothing left, not to be found.
mafsal joint.
mafsallı articulate.
magazin magazine.
magma GEOL magma.

magnezyum CHEM magnesium.

Magosa [x . .] *pr. n.* Famagusta.

mağara cave, cavern.

mağaza large store.

mağdur [ū] wronged; JUR injured party.

mağduriyet, -ti [ū] unjust treatment.

mağfiret, -ti forgiveness of God.

mağfur [ū] whose sins have been forgiven by God.

mağlubiyet, -ti defeat, beating; **-e uğramak** to get a beating, to be defeated.

mağlup, -bu defeated, beaten, overcome; ~ **etm.** to defeat, to beat; ~ **olm.** to be defeated (*or* beaten).

mağrıp, -bi 1. the west; **2.** ♀ *pr. n.* the Maghreb.

magrur [ū] **1.** haughty, conceited; **2.** proud.

mahal, -lli place, spot, locality, site; ~ **kalmamak** to be no longer necessary; **-inde** on the spot, in situ.

mahalle neighbo(u)rhood, quarter; district, ~ **bekçisi** night watchman; ~ **çapkını** timid womanizer; ~ **çocuğu** urchin, gamin; ~ **karısı** fishwife.

mahallebi *s.* **muhallebi.**

mahalli local; ~ **idare** local government.

maharet, -ti [. . .] skill, proficiency.

maharetli skillful, proficient.

maharetsiz unskillful.

mahcubiyet, -ti [ū] shyness, bashfulness.

mahcup, -bu [ū] **1.** shy, bashful; **2.** ashamed; ~ **etm.** to shame, to put to the blush; ~ **olm.** to be ashamed.

mahcur [ū] JUR under interdiction.

mahcuz [ū] JUR seized, distrained.

mahdum [ū] *rare* son.

mahdut, -du [ū] **1.** limited, restricted, definite; **2.** bordered (*or* bounded) (*ile* by).

mahfaza case, box, cover.

mahfe howdah.

mahfil *obs.* **1.** club, rendezvous; **2.** maksoorah.

mahfuz [ū] **1.** protected, sheltered; **2.** guarded; ~ **hisse** JUR legal (*or* compulsory) portion.

mahfuzen [ū] under guard.

mahıv, -hvı destruction.

mahir [ā] **1.** skil(l)ful, expert; **2.** ♀ *mf.*

mahiyet, -ti [ā] **1.** reality; true nature, character; **2.** the heart (*of a matter*).

mahkeme 1. law court; **2.** trial, hear-

ing; ~ **celpnamesi** summons, citation; ~ **kadıya mülk değil.** *pro.* place and power are not everlasting; ~ **kararı** judg(e)ment, verdict; **-de dayısı olm.** to have a friend at court, to have friends in high places; **-ye düşmek** to be taken to court; **-ye vermek** (*b-ni*) to go to law against *s.o.*, to have the law on *s.o.*, to bring *s.o.* to court.

mahkemelik matter for the courts; ~ **olm.** to go to court.

mahkûm 1. JUR sentenced, condemned; **2.** convict; **3.** forced (*or* obliged) (*-e* to); **4.** destined (*or* doomed) (*-e* to); ~ **etm.** to sentence (*-e* to), to condemn (*-e* to).

mahkûmiyet, -ti sentence, condemnation.

mahlas pen name, pseudonym.

mahlep, -bi BOT mahaleb.

mahluk, -ku creature.

mahlukat, -tı [. - -] creatures.

mahlul, -lü 1. JUR escheated (*property*); **2.** CHEM solution.

mahmude [ū] BOT scammony (resin).

mahmur [ū] **1.** logy, groggy (*from sleep*); **2.** fuddled (*from drink*); **3.** half-closed (*eye*); **4.** heavy-eyed, sleepy-eyed; **5.** lovesick, languishing (*look*).

mahmurluk 1. grogginess, loginess; **2.** listlessness.

mahmuz [ū] **1.** spur; **2.** NAUT ram, rostrum.

mahmuzlamak to spur.

mahpus [ū] **1.** prisoner; **2.** imprisoned; captive.

mahpushane [ū] prison, gaol, *Am.* jail.

mahpusluk [ū] imprisonment.

mahreç, -ci 1. outlet; **2.** source, origin; **3.** MATH denominator.

mahrek, -ki AST orbit.

mahrem 1. confidential, secret, intimate, private; **2.** confidant(e).

mahremiyet, -ti confidentiality, intimacy, privacy.

mahrukat, -tı [. - -] fuel; combustibles.

mahrum [ū] deprived (*-den* of), bereft (*-den* of), destitute (*-den* of); ~ **etm.** (*or* **bırakmak**) (*b-ni bşden*) to deprive *s.o.* of *s.th.*, to bereave *s.o.* of *s.th.*; ~ **kalmak** (*or* **olm.**) (*bşden*) to be deprived (*or* bereft) of *s.th.*; **bundan** ~ **kaldı** he was deprived of this.

mahrumiyet, -ti [ū] deprivation, bereavement; ~ **bölgesi** hardship area.

mahsuben [ū] to the account (*-e* of), reckoning that …

mahsul, -lü [ū] 1. crop, yield, produce; product; 2. *fig.* product, result.

mahsup, -bu [ū] entered in an account; ~ *etm.* to enter in an account.

mahsur [ū] 1. stuck; 2. surrounded; 3. confined (*-e* to), limited (*-e* to); ~ *kalmak* to be stuck. (*-de* in).

mahsus 1. peculiar (*-e* to), unique (*-e* to), special (*-e* to); 2. reserved (*-e* for), set aside (*-e* for); 3. on purpose, intentionally, deliberately; 4. as a joke, jokingly; 5. particularly, especially.

mahşer 1. *isl.* MYTH the place where people will gather on the Day of Judgment; 2. *fig.* throng, press; ~ *günü* Day of Judg(e)ment.

mahşeri tremendous, huge (*crowd*).

mahut [- -] known.

mahvetmek [x . .] to destroy, to ruin; to wipe out, to obliterate.

mahvolmak [x . .] *pass. of* **mahvetmek.**

mahya *lights strung between minarets during Ramazan to form words or pictures.*

mahzen cellar, underground storeroom.

mahzun [ū] sad, depressed, dejected, grieved.

mahzunlaşmak to become sad, to sadden.

mahzunluk sadness.

mahzur [ū] 1. drawback, objection; 2. obstacle, snag; ~ *görmek* to object (*-de* to).

mahzurlu objectionable; ill-advised, unwise.

mail [ā] 1. slanting, leaning; 2. with a bent (*-e* for); 3. fond (*-e* of).

maişet, -ti [i] livelihood, means of subsistence.

maiyet, -ti 1. suite, entourage; 2. employ, service; *-inde* (*b-nin*) in *s.o.'s* suite, at *s.o.'s* side.

majeste His (*or* Her) Majesty; *-leri* (His, Her, Your) Majesty.

majör MUS major.

majüskül majuscule.

makadam macadam.

makale [. - .] article.

makam [. -] office, post, portfolio, position ~ *arabası* official car; ~ *şoförü* chauffeur.

makamlı [. - .] harmonious.

makamsız [. - .] inharmonious, discordant.

makara reel; bobbin; spool; pulley; drum, barrel; ~ *gibi konuşmak* to talk nonstop; *-ları koyuvermek* to burst into laughter; *-ya almak* to make fun (*-i* of); *-yı takmak* (*b-ne*) to pull *s.o.'s* leg.

makarna [. x .] macaroni; spaghetti.

makas 1. scissors; shears; 2. MOT spring; 3. RAIL switch, points; 4. *sl.* pinch (*on one's cheek*); ~ *almak* (*b-den*) to pinch *s.o.'s* cheek; ~ *ateşi* MIL crossfire; ~ *dili* switch (*or* point) rail; ~ *hakkı* the remnants of cloth; ~ *vurmak* to put the scissors (*-e* to), to cut.

makasçı 1. scissors man; 2. RAIL switchman, pointsman.

makaslama 1. *vn. of* **makaslamak;** 2. crosswise; 3. *swimming:* scissors kick.

makaslamak 1. to scissor; 2. *sl.* to pinch (*s.o.'s cheek*).

makastar cutter.

makat, -tı anus; buttocks, rump.

makber grave.

makbul, -lü [ū] welcome, acceptable; satisfactory, liked; *-e geçmek* to be welcome, to touch the spot.

makbuz [ū] receipt; ~ *kesmek* to write a receipt, to receipt.

Makedonya [. . x .] *pr. n.* Macedonia.

maket, -ti maquette.

maki maquis, scrub.

makine [x . .] 1. machine; 2. motor, engine; mechanism; 3. P car; 4. *sl.* pistol; ~ *dairesi* NAUT engine room; ~ *gibi* 1. efficient; mechanical; 2. mechanically; ~ *gibi adam* efficient man; ~ *mühendisi* mechanical engineer; ~ *yağı* machine (*or* lubricating) oil; *-yi bozmak* co. to get diarrhea (*or* the squirts).

makineci mechanic, machinist.

makineleşmek 1. to become mechanized; 2. to become machinelike.

makineleştirmek to mechanize.

makineli [x . . .] fitted with a machine; ~ *tüfek* machine-gun.

makinist, -ti 1. engine-driver; 2. machinist.

makrama 1. tassel; 2. head scarf.

maksat, -dı purpose, intention, aim, object, end; ~ *gütmek* to cherish a secret intention.

maksatlı purposeful.

maksi maxi; ~ *etek* maxi skirt.

maksim place containing a large reservoir.

maksimum maximum.

maksure [ū] maksoorah.

maksut, -du [ū] intention, purpose.

maktu, -uu [ū] 1. fixed (*price*); 2. for a lump sum; ~ *fiyat* fixed price.

maktul, -lü [ū] killed, murdered; ~ *düşmek* to be murdered (*or* killed).

makul, -lü [ū] sensible, reasonable; ~ *konuşmak* to talk sense.

makyaj make-up; ~ *yapmak* to make up, to put on make-up.

mal 1. goods, merchandise; 2. property, possession; 3. wealth, riches; assets; 4. cattle; 5. *sl.* loose (*woman*); 6. *sl.* heroin, skag; 7. *sl.* bastard, scoundrel; ~ *beyanı* JUR declaration of property; ~ *bulmuş Mağribi gibi* as happy as a king; ~ *canın yongasıdır pro.* it is hard to part with anything one owns; ~ *canlısı* greedy, avaricious; ~ *edinmek* 1. to acquire wealth; 2. to appropriate; ~ *etm.* 1. (*k-ne*) to appropriate for *o.s.*; 2. to produce (*-e* at); ~ *kaçırmak* JUR to smuggle goods; ~ *müdürü* head of the finance office (*in a district*); ~ *mülk* property, goods; ~ *olm.* to cost; ~ *sahibi* landlord, landowner, proprietor; ~ *sandığı* financial office; *-ın gözü* 1. tricky, sly, shifty; 2. loose, promiscuous (*woman*).

mala [x .] trowel.

malak calf.

malalamak to trowel.

malama *sl.* gold lira.

malarya [. x .] malaria.

malca [x .] as far as wealth is concerned, as to goods (*or* property).

Malezya *pr. n.* Malaysia.

mali financial; fiscal; ~ *buhran* financial crisis; ♀ *İşler Müdürü* CFO (= *chief financial officer*); ~ *yıl* fiscal year.

malihulya [ā, ā] 1. groundless fear; 2. melancholy.

malik, -ki [ā] 1. owner, possessor; 2. owning, possessing; ~ *olm.* to possess, to have, to own; *kendine ~ değildir* he is beside himself.

malikâne [ā] stately home, country estate, mansion.

maliye 1. finance; 2. the Exchequer, the Ministry of Finance, the Treasury; ♀ *Bakanı* Chancellor of the Exchequer, Minister of Finance; ♀ *Bakanlığı* the Exchequer, Ministry of Fi-

nance.

maliyeci [ā] financier; economist.

maliyet, -ti [ā] cost; ~ *fiyatı* cost price, prime cost.

malkıran VET cattle-plague.

malt, -tı malt.

Malta *pr. n.* Malta.

Maltalı *pr. n.* Maltese.

maltaeriği, -ni BOT loquat.

maltahumması, -nı Malta fever.

maltataşı, -nı Malta stone.

Maltız = Maltalı.

malul, -lü 1. invalid, disabled; 2. victim (*of war, disease*); ~ *gazi* disabled veteran.

maluliyet, malullük disability, invalidity.

malum [- -] 1. known; 2. GR active (*voice*); ~ *olmak* to feel in one's bones, to sense; ~ *olduğu üzere* as everybody knows; *-unuz* as you know.

malumat, -tı [- - -] information, knowledge; ~ *almak* (*or* **edinmek**) to get information; ~ *sahibi* knowledgeable person; ~ *vermek* to inform (*hakkında* of), to give information (*-e* to); *-ı olm.* (*bşden*) to know about *s.th.*, to be in the know; *-ım yok* I know nothing about it.

malumatfuruş [- - . . -] pedantic.

malumatlı [- - . .] well-informed, knowledgeable.

malumatsız [- - . .] uninformed.

malzeme material, necessaries, supplies; ingredients; equipment.

mama¹ 1. baby food; 2. (*baby talk*) food; ~ *bezi* bib.

mama² *sl.* madam (*of a brothel*).

mamafih [- - .] nevertheless, however.

mamaliga [. . x .] dish made of corn flour.

mamul, -lü [- -] 1. product, manufacture; 2. made (*-den* of), manufactured (*-den* from).

mamulat, -tı [- - -] products, manufactures.

mamur [- -] prosperous, flourishing (*place*); well-cultivated (*land*).

mamut, -tu ZOO mammoth.

mana 1. meaning; sense; significance; 2. expression (*of the face, etc.*); ~ *çıkarmak* to interpret amiss, to misunderstand; ~ *vermek* to interpret, to make sense (*-e* of); *-sına gelmek* to mean, to signify.

manalı 1. meaningful; 2. expressive, allusive, significant.

manasız 1. meaningless, senseless; pointless, **2.** out of place, inappropriate.

manastır monastery.

manav 1. greengrocer, fruiterer; **2.** greengrocer's, greengrocery.

manca [x .] pet food.

mancana [. x .] NAUT scuttle.

mancınık catapult; mangonel; ballista.

manda¹ ZOO water buffalo; ~ *gibi* hulk.

manda² POL mandate.

mandal 1. clothes-peg, *Am.* clothespin; **2.** latch; tumbler; catch; **3.** MUS tuning peg (*of a violin. etc.*); **4.** MEC pawl.

mandalina [. . x .] BOT tangerine, mandarin.

mandallamak 1. to peg up, *Am.* to pin up (*laundry*); **2.** to latch (*door*).

mandapost, -tu postal money order.

mandarin = **mandalina**.

mandater: ~ *devlet* mandatory.

mandepsi *sl.* trick, deceit; -*ye basmak sl.* to be duped (*or* tricked).

mandıra [x . .] dairy (farm), cheesery.

mandıracı dairyman; dairywoman.

mandolin MUS mandolin.

manej manège.

manen [x .] spiritually; ~ *ve maddeten* in body and in spirit.

manevi [ī] spiritual, moral; ~ *destek olm.* to give moral support; ~ *evlat* adopted child; ~ *işkence* JUR mental cruelty.

maneviyat, -tı [- . . -] morale, spirit; -*ı bozulmak 1.* to feel low; **2.** to lose heart.

manevra [. x .] **1.** manoeuvre, *Am.* maneuver (*a.* MIL, NAUT, *fig.*); **2.** RAIL shunting; ~ *fişeği* MIL blank (cartridge); ~ *lokomotifi* RAIL shunting engine, shunter; ~ *yapmak 1.* MIL to manoeuvre, *Am.* to maneuver; **2.** RAIL to shunt.

manga [x .] **1.** MIL squad; **2.** NAUT mess.

mangal brazier; ~ *kömürü* charcoal; -*da kül bırakmamak sl.* to talk big.

manganez, mangan CHEM manganese.

mangır *sl.* money, dough, tin.

mangırsız *sl.* penniless, broke, without a bean.

mangiz *sl.* money, dough, tin; ~ *tutmak sl.* to be in funds.

mani¹ [ā] ballad.

mani² PSYCH mania.

mâni 1. obstacle, impediment, hindrance; **2.** hindering, preventing; ~ *olm.* to prevent, to hinder.

mânia [- . .] obstacle, hindrance, barrier.

mânialı [- . . . .] rough, uneven (*country*); ~ *koşu* hurdle race; steeplechase.

manidar [- . -] *s.* **manalı.**

manifatura [. . . x .] drapery, *Am.* dry goods.

manifaturacı draper.

manifesto [. . x .] NAUT manifest.

manikür manicure.

manikürcü manicurist.

maniple [. x] TEL sending (*or* signal(-l)ing) key.

manita [. x .] *sl.* **1.** girlfriend, bird, *Am.* chick; **2.** swindle.

manivela [. . x .] lever, crank, crowbar, handspike; ~ *kolu* lever-arm.

mankafa [x . .] blockheaded, thickheaded.

manken model; mannequin, manikin, dummy, lay figure.

manolya [. x .] BOT magnolia.

manometre manometer.

mansiyon hono(u)rable mention.

Manş Denizi *pr. n.* the English Channel.

manşet, -ti 1. newspaper headline; **2.** cuff.

manşon muff.

mantar 1. mushroom; fungus; toadstool; **2.** (bottle) cork; **3.** muzzle, snout; **4.** cork (*for a popgun*); **5.** *sl.* lie; ~ *atmak sl.* to lie, to fib; ~ *gibi yerden bitmek* to mushroom; ~ *tabancası* popgun; -*a basmak sl.* to be duped (*or* taken in).

mantarlı corked (*bottle*).

mantarmeşesi, -ni BOT cork oak.

mantı¹ *a ravioli-like dish served with yogurt.*

mantı² NAUT pulley (*for hoisting the topsail yard*).

mantık logic.

mantıkçı logician.

mantıkdışı, -nı alogical.

mantıki [ī] logical.

mantıklı logical.

mantıksız illogical.

manto [x .] (*woman's*) coat.

manya MED mania.

manyak 1. MED maniac; **2.** F crazy, nutty.

manyaklık F craziness, nuttiness.

manyetik magnetic; ~ *alan* magnetic field.
manyetizma magnetism.
manyeto magneto.
manyezit, *-ti* magnesium silicate.
manzara 1. scene, view; scenery, panorama; 2. appearance.
manzaralı scenic.
manzum *lit.* written in verse.
manzume [ü] 1. *lit.* poem, verses; system.
maral zoo doe.
marangoz joiner, carpenter, cabinetmaker.
marangozbalığı, *-nı* zoo sawfish.
marangozluk joinery, carpentry.
maraton marathon.
maraz 1. *rare* disease, sickness; 2. *fig.* grouchy, bad-tempered.
maraza [- . .] quarrel, row.
marazi [î] pathological.
marda cullage, discarded goods.
mareşal, *-li* MIL (field) marshal.
mareşallik MIL marshalship.
margarin margarine.
margarit, *-ti* BOT marguerite.
marifet, *-ti* [ã] 1. skill, talent, craft; 2. *iro.* piece of work, little masterpiece.
marifetli [ã] skilled, talented, skil(l)ful.
mariz[1] sick(ly), ill.
mariz[2] *sl.* beating; ~ *atmak* (*b-ne*) *sl.* to give *s.o.* a beating.
marizlemek *sl.* to beat up. to tan s.o.'s hide.
marj margin.
marjinal, *-li* COM marginal.
mark, *-kı* mark.
marka [x .] 1. trademark; 2. brand, make; 3. *football*: blocking; 4. token; 5. sign, mark.
markalamak 1. to trademark; 2. to mark.
markalı 1. trademarked; 2. marked.
markasız unmarked.
marki marquis, marquess.
markiz marquise, marchioness.
markizet, *-ti* marquisette.
Marksist, *-ti pr. n.* Marxist.
Marksizm *pr. n.* Marxism.
Marmara Denizi, *-ni pr. n.* the Sea of Marmara.
marmelat, *-tı* marmalade.
maroken morocco (leather)
marpuç, *-cu* tube of a nargileh.
mars etm. *backgammon*: to skunk.
Mars AST Mars.

Marsilya *pr. n.* Marseilles.
marş 1. MIL forward, march!; 2. MOT starter; 3. MUS march; ~ ~*!* 1. MIL run!; 2. F get going!; *-a basmak* to press the starter.
marşandiz goods (*or* freight) train.
marşpiye MOT footboard.
mart, *-tı* March; ~ *havası* changeable (*or* unpredictable) weather; ~ *kapıdan baktırır, kazma kürek yaktırır pro.* cast not a clout ere May be out.
martaval *sl.* humbug, bull, hot air, guff, baloney; ~ *atmak* (*or okumak*) *sl.* to bullshit, to talk nonsense.
martavalcı *sl.* bullshitter, liar.
martı zoo (sea) gull.
martini martini.
maruf [- -] (well-)known, famous.
marul cos, romaine, lettuce.
maruz [- -] exposed (*or* subject) (*-e* to); ~ *bırakmak* to expose (*-e* to); ~ *kalmak* to be exposed (*or* subjected) (*-e* to); *güneşe* ~ *kalmak* to be exposed to the sun.
maruzat, *-tı* [- - - -] petitions, representations.
marya zoo 1. ewe; 2. female animal.
mas, *-ssı* AST, PHYS suction; soakage; absorption.
masa [x .] 1. table; 2. desk; ~ *başında* at table; ~ *örtüsü* tablecloth.
masaj massage; ~ *yapmak* to massage.
masajcı masseur; masseuse.
masal 1. story, tale; fable; 2. *fig.* bull, cock-and-bull story; ~ *okumak* (*or anlatmak*) F to give a cock-and-bull story.
masalcı storyteller.
masat (*butcher's*) steel.
masatenisi, *-ni* table tennis, ping-pong.
mask (*actor's*) mask.
maskara 1. clown, buffoon, laughingstock; 2. silly, ridiculous, ludicrous; 3. droll person; cutup; 4. mascara; ~ *etm.* (*b-ni*) to make *s.o.* a laughingstock, to pillory; ~ *olm.* to become a figure of fun; *-ya çevirmek* (*b-ni, bşi*) to make a fool of *s.o., s.th.*
maskaralanmak to clown around, to play the buffoon.
maskaralık 1. clowning (around), buffoonery; 2. disgrace; ~ *etm.* to play the buffoon, to clown around.
maske [x .] mask; *-sini atmak fig.* to let one's mask drop, to show one's true colo(u)rs; *-sini kaldırmak* (*b-nin*)

fig. to show *s.o.* up, to expose *s.o.*, to unmask *s.o.*

maskelemek to mask.

maskeli masked; ~ *balo* masked (*of fancy dress*) ball, masquerade.

maskot, -tu mascot.

maslahat, -tı business, affair.

maslahatgüzar [. . . . -] POL chargé d'affaires.

maslak 1. pipe; **2.** stone trough.

masmavi [x - .] very (*or* deep) blue.

mason Freemason, Mason.

masonluk Freemasonry, Masonry.

masör masseur.

masöz masseuse.

masraf 1. expense(s), expenditure(s), outlay, outgoings; ~ *etm.* to go to expense, to spend money; ~ *görmek* to shell out some money; ~ *kapısı açmak* to cause expenses; *-a girmek* to go to expense; *-a sokmak* to put to expense; *-ı çekmek* to bear the expenses; *-ı kısmak* to reduce (*or* cut) expenses; *-tan kaçmak* to avoid expense; *-tan kaçmamak* to spare no expense.

masraflı expensive, costly, dear.

masrafsız inexpensive, cheap.

massetmek [x . .] to suck (*or* soak) up, to absorb.

mastar 1. GR infinitive; **2.** gage, template.

mastika [. x .] mastic.

masturbasyon masturbation; ~ *yapmak* to masturbate.

masum [- -] **1.** innocent, guiltless; **2.** little child.

masumane [- - - .] innocently.

masumiyet, -ti [- - . .] innocence.

masun [ū] **1.** guarded, protected (*-den* from); safe; **2.** JUR inviolable.

masuniyet, -ti [ū] **1.** safety, security; **2.** JUR immunity; inviolability.

masura [. x .] **1.** bobbin; **2.** spout.

maşa 1. (pair of) tongs; **2.** *fig.* cat's-paw, tool, dummy, front; ~ *gibi* dark and thin (*person*); ~ *gibi kullanmak* (*b-ni*) *fig.* to use *s.o.* as a cat's paw; ~ *kadar* teeny-weeny (*baby*); ~ *varken elini yakmak* *fig.* to burn one's fingers; *-sı olm.* (*b-nin*) *fig.* to be *s.o.'s* cat's paw (*or* tool).

maşalamak to crimp with a curling iron (*hair*).

maşallah [- . .] [x . .] **1.** may God preserve him from evil!; **2.** magnificent!, wonderful!; *-ı var* he is unusual today.

maşatlık non-Muslim cemetery.

maşlah long and open-fronted cloak.

maşrapa mug; dipper.

mat[1], -tı *chess:* (check)mate; ~ *etm.* **1.** to checkmate; **2.** *fig.* to silence; ~ *olm.* **1.** to be checkmated; **2.** *fig.* to be silenced.

mat[2], -tı mat(t), *Am.* matte, dull, lusterless.

matador matador.

matah *contp.* prize package, great shakes.

matara [. x .] canteen, flask, water-bottle.

matbaa printing house, press.

matbaacı printer.

matbaacılık printing.

matbu, -uu [ū] printed (*matter*).

matbua [ū] printed matter.

matbuat, -tı [. - -] the press; ~ *hürriyeti* freedom of the press.

matem [ā] mourning; ~ *havası* (*or* *marşı*) funeral march; ~ *tutmak* to mourn.

matematik mathematics.

matematikçi 1. mathematician; **2.** F mathematics teacher.

matemli [ā] **1.** in mourning; **2.** mournful.

materyalist, -ti materialist.

materyalizm materialism.

materyel material, supplies.

matine matinée.

matiz[1] *sl.* dead drunk, pissed, soused.

matiz[2] NAUT making a long splice.

matkap, -bı drill; auger; gimlet.

matlaşmak to become dull.

matlaştırmak to dull.

matlup, -bu [ū] COM credit, receivable account.

matmazel Miss, Mademoiselle.

matrah category of taxed goods, standard.

matrak *sl.* funny, droll, amusing; ~ *geçmek* *sl.* to make fun (*or* mock) (*ile* of).

matris TYP, MATH matrix.

matuf [- -] aimed (*-e* at), directed (*-e* towards).

maun BOT mahogany.

maval *sl.* cock-and-bull story; ~ *okumak* *sl.* to give a cock-and-bull story.

mavi [- .] blue; ~ *boncuk* blue bead; ~ *kâğıt almak* to get fired; *-ye çalmak* to be bluish.

mavileşmek to turn blue.

mavilik blueness.

mavimsi [ā], **mavimtırak** [- . . .] bluish.

maviş blue-eyed.

mavna [x .] barge, lighter.

mavzer Mauser rifle.

maya 1. yeast, ferment; leaven; **2.** *fig.* origin, essence, marrow, blood; **-sı bozuk** no-good, corrupt (*person*).

mayalamak to yeast, to leaven.

mayalı yeasted; leavened.

mayasıl eczema.

mayasız unleavened, unfermented.

maydanoz BOT parsley.

mayhoş 1. sourish, tart; **2.** *fig.* cool (*relations*).

mayın MIL mine; **~ dökmek** to mine, to lay mines (*-e* in); **~ tarama gemisi** minesweeper; **~ tarlası** minefield.

mayınlamak MIL to mine.

mayıs May.

mayısböceği, -ni ZOO cockchafer.

mayışmak *sl.* to get drowsy.

mayi [- -] liquid, fluid.

maymun 1. ZOO monkey; ape; **2.** *fig.* droll (*person*); **~ gözünü açtı** *fig.* he has learned his lesson; **~ iştahlı** inconstant, fickle; **~ suratlı** like the back (end) of a bus.

maymuncuk skeleton key, picklock.

mayo [x .] **1.** bathing suit, swimsuit; trunks; **2.** leotard.

mayonez mayonnaise.

maytap, -bı small fireworks, sparkler; **-a almak** (*b-ni*) to take the mickey out of *s.o.*

mazbata official report, protocol, minutes.

mazbut, -tu [. -] **1.** disciplined, orderly; **2.** well-built, solid (*building*); **3.** recorded.

mazeret, -ti [ā] excuse.

mazeretli [ā] excusable, justifiable.

mazeretsiz unjustifiable, unwarranted.

mazgal crenel, embrasure.

mazhar 1. the object of (*hono(u)rs, favo(u)r, etc.*); **2.** ♀ *mf.*; **~ olm.** (*bşe*) to be the object (*or* recipient) of *s.th.*

mazı 1. BOT arborvitae; **2.** gallnut, gall-apple.

mazi [- -] **1.** the past, bygones; **2.** GR the simple past tense; **-ye karışmak** to belong to bygone days.

mazlum [ū] **1.** oppressed, wronged; **2.** *fig.* inoffensive, compliant; **3.** ♀ [x .] *mf.*

mazmun [ū] *lit.* witticism, pun.

maznun [ū] JUR **1.** suspected, accused; **2.** suspect.

mazot, -tu diesel oil (*or* fuel).

mazur [- -] excused; excusable; **~ görmek** to excuse, to pardon, to hold excused.

meal, -li [ā] meaning, purport.

meblağ amount, sum (*of money*).

mebni [ī] based (*-e* on), because (*-e* of).

mebus deputy, member of parliament.

mebusluk deputyship.

mebzul, -lü [ū] abundant, lavish.

mecal, -li [ā] power, strength; **~ bırakmamak** *fig.* to wear out.

mecalsiz [ā] weak, exhausted, powerless.

mecaz [ā] figure of speech, trope; metaphor.

mecazen [ā] figuratively; metaphorically.

mecazi [. - -] figurative; metaphorical.

mecbur [ū] forced (*-e* to), compelled (*-e* to), obliged (*-e* to); **~ etm.** to force, to oblige, to compel; **~ olm.** (*or* **kalmak**) to be forced (*or* obliged *or* compelled) (*-e* to).

mecburen [ū] [. x .] compulsorily, out of necessity, perforce.

mecburi [. - -] compulsory, obligatory; **~ iniş** AVIA forced landing, crash-landing; **~ istikamet** one way.

mecburiyet, -ti [ū] compulsion, obligation; **~ halinde** at a push (*or* pinch).

meccanen [ā] free, gratis.

meccani [. - -] free, gratuitous.

mecelle 1. volume, book; **2.** JUR civil code.

mecidiye, mecit HIST silver coin.

meclis 1. assembly, council; **2.** meeting; **Meclisi Mebusan** the Ottoman Parliament.

mecmu, -uu [ū] **1.** whole, all; **2.** MATH sum, total.

mecmua [ū] magazine, periodical.

mecnun [ū] **1.** mad, insane, crackers; **2.** love-crazed.

mecra [ā] **1.** watercourse, conduit; **2.** *fig.* the course (*of events*).

Mecusi [. - -] *pr. n.* Zoroastrian, Mazdean.

meczup, -bu [ū] insane, crazy.

meç FENC foil, rapier.

meçhul, -lü [ū] **1.** unknown; **2.** GR passive.

medar [ā] **1.** AST orbit; **2.** GEOGR tropic; **3.** support, help; **4.** means; reason, cause; **~ olm.** to help, to aid.

meddah [ā] **1.** public storyteller; **2.** eulogist.

meddücezir, -zri ebb and flow, tide.

medeni 1. civilized; **2.** JUR civil; **~ haklar** civil rights; **~ hal** marital status; **~ hukuk** civil law; **~ kanun** civil code; **~ nikâh** civil marriage.

medenileşmek to become civilized.

medenileştirmek to civilize.

medeniyet, -ti civilization.

medeniyetsiz uncivilized.

medet help, aid; **~ Allah!** help me, God!; **~ beklemek** (or **ummak**) to hope for help (**-den** from).

medih, -dhi prise, eulogy.

medikososyal medico-social.

Medine pr. n. Medina.

medrese HIST medresseh, madrasa, madrasah.

medreseli student at a medresseh.

medüz ZOO medusa, jellyfish.

medyum medium.

medyun [ū] indebted.

mefhum [ū] concept.

mefkûre ideal.

mefkûrecilik idealism.

mefluç, -cu paralyzed.

mefruşat, -tı [. - -] **1.** furnishings; **2.** fabrics.

meftun [ū] charmed, captivated; infatuated; **~ olm.** to be charmed (or captivated) (**-e** by).

megafon megaphone.

megaloman megalomaniac.

megavat, -tı. PHYS megawatt.

meğer [x .] it seems that ..., apparently ..., but, however.

meğerki [x . .] unless.

mehil respite, grace period, extension, delay.

Mehmetçik pr. n. the Turkish 'Tommy'.

mehtap, -bı [ā] moonlight, moonglow.

mehtaplı [ā] moonlit.

mehter member of a Janissary band; **~ takımı** Janissary band.

mekân 1. place; **2.** residence, abode; **3.** PHLS space.

mekanik 1. mechanics; **2.** mechanical.

mekanizm PHLS mechanism.

mekanize MIL mechanized.

mekanizma [. . x .] mechanism.

mekik shuttle; **~ dokumak** to shuttle.

Mekke pr. n. Mecca.

mekruh [ū] abominable.

Meksika pr. n. Mexico.

Meksikalı pr. n. Mexican.

mektep, -bi school; **~ arkadaşı** schoolmate; **~ kaçağı** truant; **~ medrese görmüş** educated; **mektebi asmak** to play truant (or hooky), to cut school.

mektepli student, pupil, schoolkid.

mektup, -bu letter; **~ atmak** to mail (or post or send) a letter; **~ üstü** address on a letter.

mektuplaşmak to correspond (ile with).

melaike angels.

melal, -li boredom; tedium.

melamin melamine.

melankoli melancholy.

melankolik melancholic.

melce sanctuary, refuge, asylum.

melek 1. angel; **2.** ♀ wf.

meleke 1. aptitude, knack, bent; **2.** faculty; **3.** skill.

melemek [- . .] to bleat.

melez 1. hybrid, crossbred; **2.** of mixed race (or blood).

melezlemek to crossbreed, to hybridize.

melezlik hybridity, hybridism.

melhem s. **merhem.**

melik, -ki 1. sovereign, ruler, king; **2.** ♀ mf.

melike 1. queen, ruler, sovereign; **2.** ♀ wf.

melodi melody.

melodik melodic.

melodram melodrama.

melon (şapka) bowler, derby (hat).

melun damned, cursed.

melül, -lü sad, blue, low-spirited.

memba, -aı spring; fountainhead, source (a. fig.).

meme 1. breast, boob, ANAT mamma; **2.** dug, udder; **3.** MEC nozzle; **~ başı** (or **ucu**) teat, nipple; **~ çocuğu** suckling; **~ emmek** to suck, to nurse; **~ vermek** to suckle; **-den kesmek** (çocuğu) to wean (a child).

memeli ZOO mammiferous; **~ hayvanlar** mammals.

memeliler ZOO mammals.

memeş slaver, slobber.

memişhane F loo, john.

memleket, -ti 1. country, land; **2.** home town; **3.** fatherland.

memleketli fellow countryman, compatriot.

memnu, -uu [ū] forbidden, prohibited.

memnun [ū] pleased, delighted, glad, contented, satisfied; **~ etm.** to please, to satisfy; ~ **olm.** to be pleased (*or* satisfied), to be glad.

memnuniyet, -ti [ü] pleasure, gladness, gratitude, delight, content, satisfaction; ~ **verici** satisfactory, pleasurable, delightful.

memnuniyetle [ü] with pleasure, gladly.

memorandum [.. x .] memorandum.

memul, -lü [- -] hoped, expected; ~ **etm.** to hope, to expect.

memur civil servant, jobholder, official; employee; ~ **etm.** (*b-ni bşe*) to commission *s.o.* to do *s.th.*, to charge *s.o.* with *s.th.*

memure female civil servant; female employee.

memuriyet, -ti [- - - .] government job, civil service post.

men, -ni prohibition.

menajer manager.

mendebur 1. good-for-nothing (*person*); **2.** F bastard.

menderes GEOGR meander.

mendil handkerchief, hanky; ~ **sallamak** to wave one's handkerchief.

mendirek breakwater, mole.

menekşe 1. BOT violet; **2.** *sl.* asshole.

menenjit, -ti MED meningitis.

menetmek [x ..] to prohibit, to forbid.

meneviş moire, water.

menfaat, -ti advantage, interest, benefit.

menfaatçı self-seeking.

menfaatperest *s.* **menfaatçı.**

menfez hole, vent.

menfi [ī] negative; ~ **cevap** negative answer.

menfur [ü] abhorrent, loathsome.

mengel P anklet.

mengene [x . .] **1.** vice, *Am.* vise; **2.** press; **3.** clamp.

menhus [ü] unlucky, ill-omened.

meni BIOL sperm, semen.

menkıbe legend, tale.

menkul, -lü [ü] **1.** movable, conveyable, transferable; **2.** conveyed, transported; ~ **kıymetler** JUR stocks and bonds; ~ **mallar** JUR movable goods.

menolunmak [x . . .] *pass. of* **menetmek.**

menopoz MED menopause.

mensucat, -tı [. - -] textiles.

mensup, -bu [ü] **1.** belonging (*-e* to), connected (*-e* to), related (*-e* to); **2.** member; ~ **olm.** to belong (*-e* to).

mensur [ü] (in) prose.

menşe, -ei place of origin, source; ~ **şahadetnamesi** COM certificate of origin.

menteşe hinge.

mentol, -lü menthol.

mentollü mentholated.

menü menu.

menzil 1. range; **2.** stage, leg.

mera [ā] pasture.

merak, -kı [ā] **1.** curiosity; **2.** worry, anxiety; **3.** passion, whim, interest, liking; ~ **etme!** don't worry!; ~ **etm.** (*bşi*) **1.** to be curious about *s.th.*; **2.** to be anxious about *s.th.*; ~ **getirmek** to suffer from melancholia; **-ı kalkmak** to become filled with curiosity; **-tan çatlamak** to be dying of curiosity, to be burning with curiosity.

meraklanmak 1. to worry (*-e* about), to be anxious (*-e* about); **2.** to be aroused (*s.o.'s* curiosity).

meraklı 1. curious, inquisitive; **2.** interested (*-e* in), fond (*-e* of); **3.** scrupulous, particular.

meraksız 1. incurious, uninquisitive; **2.** unworried, unanxious.

meram [ā] intention, purpose, goal, aim; ~ **etm.** to intend, to wish; **-ın elinden bir şey kurtulmaz** *pro.* where there is a will there is a way; **-ını anlatmak** to express o.s.

merasim [ā] **1.** ceremony; **2.** formalities; ~ **kıtası** MIL guard of hono(u)r, hono(u)r guard.

merbut, -tu [ü] **1.** devoted (*-e* to); **2.** attached (*or* connected) (*-e* to); **3.** dependent (*-e* upon).

mercan [ā] ZOO coral.

mercanada atoll.

mercanbalığı, -nı ZOO red sea bream.

mercek lens.

merci, -ii reference, recourse; competent authority.

mercimek BOT lentil; **mercimeği fırına vermek** *co.* to carry on with.

merdane [ā] **1.** cylinder, roller; **2.** mangle, wringer; **3.** rolling pin.

merdiven 1. stairs, staircase; steps; **2.** ladder; ~ **basamağı** step, stair; ~ **dayamak** *fig.* to push (*a certain age*); ~ **sahanlığı** landing.

meret, -ti damn.

merhaba [x ..] F hello!, hi!; **-yı kesmek** (*b-le*) to break off with *s.o.*

merhabalaşmak to greet one another.

merhale stage, phase; ~~ gradually, by stages.

merhamet, -ti mercy, pity, compassion; **~ etm.** (or **göstermek**) to pity, to have mercy (-e on); **-e gelmek** to become merciful.

merhametli merciful, compassionate.

merhametsiz merciless, pitiless.

merhem ointment, salve.

merhum [ū] deceased, the late, the departed; **~ olm.** to die, to pass away.

merhume [ū] deceased, the late, the departed (*woman*).

mer'i [ī] *obs.* in force, valid.

meridyen meridian.

Merih [ī] *pr. n.* AST Mars.

merinos [. x .] (*koyun*) Merino sheep.

meriyet, -ti validity; **-e girmek** to come into force.

merkep donkey.

merkez 1. centre, *Am.* center; **2.** headquarters; **3.** police station.

merkezci centralist.

merkezcil kuvvet PHYS centripetal force.

merkezcilik centralism.

merkezi central.

merkezileşmek to centralize.

merkeziyet, -ti centralism.

merkezkaç kuvvet PHYS centrifugal force.

mermer marble.

mermi missile, projectile.

merserize mercerized.

mersi! thanks!, cheers!

mersin 1. BOT myrtle; **2.** (*balığı*) ZOO sturgeon.

mersiye elegy.

mert 1. brave, manly; **2.** trustworthy.

mertebe 1. stage, step, degree; **2.** rank, position.

mertek beam.

Meryem Ana *pr. n.* the Virgin Mary.

mesafe [ā] distance, interval, space.

mesaha [. - .] **1.** surveying; **2.** area; **~ memuru** (land) surveyor.

mesai [. - -] efforts, work, pains; **~ arkadaşı** colleague; **~ saatleri** working hours; **~ yapmak** (or **-ye kalmak**) to work overtime.

mesaj message.

mesame [ā] BIOL pore.

mesane [ā] ANAT bladder.

mescit masjid, small mosque.

mesel saying, proverb, parable.

mesela [x. -] for instance, for example.

mesele question, problem, matter; issue; **~ çıkarmak** to make a fuss; **~ yapmak** (*bşi*) to make a to-do about *s.th.*

meserret, -ti joy.

meshetmek [x . .] to wipe with the wet palm of one's hand.

Mesih [ī] the Messiah, Christ.

mesire [ī] promenade.

mesken dwelling, residence, house; JUR domicile; **~ masuniyeti** JUR domiciliary inviolability.

meskûn inhabited; **~ kılmak** to populate.

meslek 1. profession; **2.** occupation, line of work; **~ okulu** trade (or vocational) school; **~ sahibi** professional (*person*).

mesleki 1. professional; **2.** occupational, vocational.

mesleksiz having no profession, out of work.

meslektaş colleague, co-worker, associate.

mesnet, -di 1. support, prop; **2.** position, office.

mest¹, -ti enchanted, captivated; **~ olm.** to be in the seventh heaven.

mest², -ti light soleless boot.

mesul, -lü [ū] responsible (-den for); **~ tutmak** (*b-ni bşden*) to hold *s.o.* responsible for *s.th.*

mesuliyet, -ti [ū] responsibility; **~ kabul etmemek** to decline responsibility; **~ sigortası** JUR liability insurance.

mesuliyetli [ū] responsible.

mesut [ū] **1.** happy; **2.** ♀ [x .] *mf.*

meşakkat, -ti trouble, hardship, fatigue; **~ çekmek** to suffer hardship.

meşale cresset; torch.

meşe BOT oak; **~ odunu 1.** oak wood; **2.** *fig.* blockhead.

meşebüken *fig.* strong, brawny.

meşgale occupation, activity, pastime.

meşgul, -lü [ū] **1.** busy (*ile* with), preoccupied (*ile* with), concerned (*ile* with), **2.** TELEPH busy, engaged (*line*); **~ etm.** to busy, to occupy; to distract; **~ olm.** to be busy, to busy o.s. (*ile* with).

meşguliyet, -ti [ū] occupation, activity, pastime, concern.

meşhur [ū] **1.** famous, well-known; **2.** celebrity; **~ olm.** to become famous.

meşhut, -du [ū] witnessed.

meşin leather.

meşk, -ki 1. practice; **2.** piece of calligraphy; **~ etm.** to practice, *Am.* to practice.

meşrep, -bi temperament, disposition.

meşru, -uu [ū] legal, lawful, legitimate.

meşrubat, -tı [. - -] beverages, drinks.

meşruten [ū] conditionally; **~ tahliye** JUR release on probation.

meşruti [. - -] POL constitutional; **~ krallık** constitutional monarchy.

meşrutiyet, -ti [ū] POL constitutional monarchy.

meşum [ū] ill-starred, inauspicious.

meşveret, -ti consultation.

met, -ddi flood (or high) tide.

meta, -aı [ā] goods, merchandise.

metabolizma BIOL metabolism.

metafizik 1. metaphysics; **2.** metaphysical.

metal, -li metal.

metalurji metallurgy.

metan CHEM methane.

metanet, -ti [ā] fortitude, backbone.

metanetsiz spineless; weak.

metazori [. . x .] sl. by force.

metelik F bean, red cent; **~ vermemek** (bşe) fig. not to give a damn about s.th.; **meteliğe kurşun atmak** F not to have a bean (or red cent), to be flat broke.

meteliksiz without a bean (or red cent), penniless, flat broke.

meteoroloji meteorology.

meteortaşı, -nı AST meteorite.

metfen grave.

metfun [ū] buried.

methal, -li 1. entrance; **2.** introduction; **-l olm.** (b-nin bir işte) to be involved in s.th., to have a hand in s.th.

methaldar [. . .] involved (-e in).

methetmek to praise, to extol, to laud.

methiye panegyric.

metin[1], **-tni** text.

metin[2] **1.** firm, solid, strong; **2.** ♀ [x .] mf.

metis BIOL hybrid.

metodoloji methodology.

metot method.

metrdotel headwaiter.

metre [x .] **1.** metre, Am. meter; **2.** meterstick; **~ kare** square meter; **~ küp** cubic meter.

metres mistress.

metrik metric; **~ sistem** metric system.

metris MIL breastwork.

metro underground, tube, Am. subway.

metronom MUS metronome.

metruk, -kü [ū] abandoned, deserted.

mevcudat, -tı [. - -] assets.

mevcudiyet, -ti [ū] **1.** existence; **2.** presence.

mevcut, -du [ū] **1.** existing; present, extant; **2.** supply, stock; **3.** MIL the strength (of a unit); **~ olm. 1.** to exist, to be; **2.** to be present.

mevduat, -tı [. - -] COM deposits; **~ hesabı** deposit account.

mevki, -ii 1. place, location; **2.** position, portfolio, rank; **3.** class; **4.** situation, position.

mevkuf [ū] under arrest.

mevla obs. master, patron.

Mevla pr. n. God.

Mevlevi [ī] pr. n. Mevlevi.

mevlit the night of the birth of the Prophet Mohammed; **~ kandili** the religious celebration held on the evening of the Prophet Mohammed's birth; **~ okumak** to chant the **mevlit**.

mevsim season.

mevsimlik seasonal.

mevsimsiz 1. untimely, ill-timed; **2.** prematurely.

mevzi, -ii MIL position; **~ almak** MIL to take up a position.

mevzii localized; scattered.

mevzilenmek MIL to take up a position.

mevzu, -uu [ū] subject, topic; **-a girmek** to come to the point.

mevzuat, -tı [. - -] **1.** the laws; **2.** containers.

mevzubahis, -hsi subject under discussion.

mevzun [ū] **1.** shapely, well-proportioned; **2.** lit. metrical (verse); rhythmical (prose).

mey wine.

meyan[1] [ā] = **meyankökü.**

meyan[2] [ā] **1.** middle, centre, Am. center; **2.** interval; **bu -da** while ..., among them.

meyanbalı, -nı licorice extract.

meyancı [ā] go-between, mediator.

meyane [ā] **1.** a kind of sauce; **2.** correct degree of thickness (for halvah); **-si gelmek** to reach the right degree of thickness.

meyankökü, -nü [ā] BOT licorice.

meydan [ā] **1.** open space; **2.** public square; **3.** field; **4.** ring; arena; **5.** opportunity, occasion; possibility; **~ almak** to spread, to advance; **~ bulmak** to find an opportunity; **~ dayağı** public beating; **~ korkusu** MED agoraphobia; **~ okumak** to challenge, to defy; **~**

savaşı MIL pitched battle; **~ vermek** to give a chance; **-a atmak** to bring up, to broach, to suggest; **-a çıkarmak 1.** to make public, to reveal, to disclose, to divulge; **2.** to bring to light; to expose to view; **-a çıkmak** to come to light, to be revealed; **-a gelmek** to happen, to occur; to come into existence; **-a getirmek** to bring forth, to produce; **-a vurmak** to make public, to reveal; **-da 1.** in sight, around; **2.** obvious, clear, evident; **-ı boş bulmak** to seize an opportunity to do s.th.

meydanlık open space, square.

meyhane [ā] pub, café, joint, dive.

meyhaneci [ā] publican, barkeep(er).

meyil, -yli 1. slope, slant, incline; **2.** PHYS inclination, tendency; **3.** fig. penchant, predilection, fondness, liking.

meyletmek 1. to slant, to slope (-e towards); to lean (-e towards); **2.** to be inclined (-e to); **3.** fig. to have a liking (-e for).

meymenet, -ti fortune, auspiciousness.

meymenetsiz 1. unlucky, inauspicious; **2.** disagreeable (person).

meyus [ū] hopeless, desperate.

meyve fruit; **~ bahçesi** orchard; **~ suyu** fruit juice; **~ vermek** to fruit.

meyveli 1. fruit-laden, fruited; **2.** fruit ...

meyvelik orchard, grove.

meyvesiz fruitless, unfruitful.

meyyal, -li [ā] inclined (-e to); fond (-e of).

mezalim [ā] cruelties, atrocities.

mezar [ā] grave, tomb; **~ kaçkını** fig. person with one foot in the grave; **~ kitabesi** epitaph.

mezarcı gravedigger.

mezarlık [ā] cemetery, graveyard.

mezat [ā] auction; **~ malı** fig. bargain; **-a çıkarmak** to put up for auction.

mezatçı auctioneer.

mezbaha slaughterhouse, abattoir.

mezbele dump, pigsty, pigpen.

meze [x.] snack, appetizer, hors d'oeuvre.

mezgit, -ti zoo whiting.

mezhep, -bi denomination, creed, religion; **-i geniş** too tolerant.

meziyet, -ti virtue, merit, excellence.

meziyetli excellent, superior, virtuous.

mezkûr aforementioned.

mezmur [ū] psalm.

Mezopotamya pr. n. Mesopotamia.

mezun [- -] **1.** graduate; **2.** graduated (-den from); **3.** authorized (-meğe to inf.); **~ olm.** to graduate (-den from).

mezuniyet, -ti [- - . .] **1.** graduation; **2.** authorization, permission; **~ imtihanı** leaving (or Am. final) examination.

mezura [. x .] tape measure.

mezzosoprano MUS mezzo-soprano.

mıcır 1. fine gravel; **2.** small bits of coal; **3.** sl. bad egg (person)

mıh nail.

mıhladız s. **mıknatıs.**

mıhlamak 1. to nail; **2.** to set, to place (precious stone); **3.** sl. to skewer, to stab.

mıhsıçtı sl. very niggardly (or stingy).

mıknatıs magnet.

mıknatısi [ī] magnetic.

mıknatısiyet, -ti magnetism.

mıknatıslamak to magnetize.

mıknatıslı 1. magnetic; **2.** magnetized; **~ iğne** magnetic needle.

mıncıklamak 1. to make squishy; **2.** to pinch and squeeze.

mıncık mıncık squashed to a pulp; **~ etm. 1.** to squash to a pulp; **2.** to pinch (a cheek).

mıntıka zone, region, area, district.

mırılda(n)mak to mutter, to murmur, to mumble.

mırıl mırıl with a mutter, in low.

mırıltı mutter, mumble.

mırın kırın etm. F to hem and haw, to grumble.

mırlamak to purr.

mır mır with a mutter, in low.

mırnav! meow!

mısır BOT maize, corn; **~ buğdayı** popcorn; **~ ekmeği** corn bread (or pone); **~ koçan** corncob.

Mısır pr. n. Egypt.

Mısırlı pr. n. Egyptian.

mısırözü yağı corn oil.

mısıryağı, -nı corn oil.

mıskal syrinx, panpipe.

mısra, -aı [ā] line (of poetry).

mışıl mışıl soundly; **~ uyumak** to sleep soundly.

mıymıntı sluggish.

mızıka MUS **1.** harmonica, mouth-organ; **2.** brass band.

mızıkacı MUS harmonica player.

mızıkçı F spoilsport, killjoy, bad loser.

mızıkçılık etm. not to play the game.

mızıklanmak = **mızıkçılık etm.**

mızmız fussbudgety, persnickety,

mimarlık

whiny.

mızmızlanmak to whine, to fuss.

mızrak spear, lance; ~ *çuvala girmez* (*or* *sığmaz*) *pro.* there are some things which cannot be kept secret.

mızrap, *-bı* plectrum, quill, pick.

mi¹ (*mı, mu, mü*) *interrogative particle, sometimes adding emphasis*; *cahil mi cahil!* he is ignorant beyond words; *geldi mi?* has he come?; *yapar mı yapar* you can bet your bottom dollar he'll do it.

mi² MUS mi; E.

miat, *-dı* **1.** wear life (*of an object*); **2.** fixed period; **3.** deadline; due date; *miadı dolmak* to expire, to terminate.

mibzer AGR sower, seeder.

miço [x .] **1.** young deckhand; **2.** cabin boy.

mide [ī] stomach, belly; ~ *borusu* esophagus; ~ *bozukluğu* (*or* *fesadı*) indigestion; ~ *bulantısı* nausea; ~ *iltihabı* gastritis; ~ *kanaması* gastric bleeding; *-si almamak* (*or* *kabul etmemek*) to have no appetite (*-i* for); *-si bozulmak* to have indigestion; *-si bulanmak* **1.** to feel nauseated; **2.** *fig.* to smell a rat; *-si ekşimek* to have heartburn; *-si kazınmak* to feel peckish, to have a sinking feeling; *-ye oturmak* to lie heavy on the stomach.

midesiz [- . .] **1.** eating anything; **2.** *fig.* having bad taste.

midevi gastric, gastral.

midi midi; ~ *etek* midi skirt.

midilli [. x .] pony.

midye [x .] ZOO mussel; ~ *dolması* stuffed mussel; ~ *tavası* fried mussel.

migren migraine.

miğfer helmet.

mihenk touchstone, test.

mihmandar [. - -] host; hostess.

mihnet, *-ti* trouble, hardship; ~ *çekmek* to suffer.

mihrace [. - .] maharaja(h).

mihrak, *-kı* [ā] PHYS focus.

mihrap, *-bı* [ā] mihrab, altar.

mihver axis; axle, pivot.

mika [x .] GEOL mica.

mikado mikado.

mikâp, *-bı* s. *küp.*

miki (fare) Mickey Mouse.

mikroçip microchip.

mikrofilm microfilm.

mikrofon microphone.

mikrolif micro fiber.

mikrometre micrometer.

mikron micron.

mikroorganizma microorganism.

mikrop, *-bu* **1.** germ, microbe; **2.** *fig.* viper, bad lot.

mikroplu germy, contaminated.

mikropsuz germless.

mikropsuzlandırmak to disinfect, to decontaminate.

mikroskobik microscopic.

mikroskop, *-pu* microscope.

miktar [ā] **1.** amount, quantity; **2.** portion, part.

mikyas [ā] scale, proportion.

mil¹ MEC pivot, pin; axle; shaft; spindle.

mil² mile.

mil³ GEOL silt.

mil⁴ *obs.* thousand, mille; ~ *mersi!* thank you very much!

miladi [- - -] of the Christian era; ~ *takvim* the Gregorian calendar.

milat, *-dı* [- -] birth of Christ; *-tan önce* B.C., before Christ; *-tan sonra* A.D., anno Domini.

milföy mille-feuille, napoleon.

miligram milligram(me).

milim millimetre, *Am.* millimeter.

milimetre millimetre, *Am.* millimeter.

milis militia; ~ *kuvvetleri* militia forces, militia.

militan militant.

millet, *-ti* nation, people; ♀ *Meclisi* the Turkish National Assembly.

milletlerarası, *-nı* international.

milletvekili, *-ni* deputy, M.P.

millî national; ~ *bayram* national holiday; ♀ *Eğitim Bakanı* the Minister of Education; ♀ *Eğitim Bakanlığı* the Ministry of Education; ♀ *Güvenlik Kurulu* the National Security Council; ♀ *İstihbarat Teşkilatı* the National Intelligence Organization; ~ *marş* national anthem; ~ *takımı* national team.

millîleştirmek to nationalize.

milliyet, *-ti* nationality.

milliyetçi nationalist.

milliyetçilik nationalism.

milyar milliard, *Am.* billion, a thousand million.

milyarder billionaire.

milyon million.

milyoner millionaire.

mimar [- -] architect.

mimari [- - -] architectural.

mimarlık [- - .] architecture.

mimber pulpit, mimbar.
mimik facial expression.1
mimlemek to mark down, to blacklist.
mimli marked, blacklisted.
minare [ā] minaret; ~ *gibi* as tall as a lamp-post; *-yi çalan kılıfını hazırlar pro.* if you venture to do s.th. illegal, you must plan it carefully in advance.
minder cushion; mattress, mat (*a. sports*); ~ *çürütmek* to sit idly, to be a bench warmer; ~ *sermek* to outstay one's welcome.
mine [x.] **1.** enamel; **2.** dial (*of a clock*); **3.** ♀ *wf.*
minelemek to enamel.
mineli enameled.
mineral, *-li* mineral.
mini mini; ~ *etek* miniskirt.
minibüs minibus.
minicik [x..] teeny, tiny, wee.
minik **1.** tiny and cute; **2.** tot, toddler.
minimini teen(s)y-ween(s)y, itty-bitty.
minimum minimum.
minkale protractor.
minnacık = *minimini*.
minnet, *-ti* gratitude, indebtedness, obligation; ~ *altında kalmak* to be obligated; ~ *etm.* to grovel, to plead.
minnettar [ā] grateful (*-e* to), indebted (*-e* to), obliged (*-e* to).
minnettarlık [ā] gratitude.
minnoş F little darling, honey.
minör MUS minor.
mintan shirt.
minüskül minuscule.
minval, *-li* [ā] manner, way.
minyatür miniature.
minyon petite, mignon.
mir leader, chief; *-îm!* governor!, my dear fellow!
mira surveyor's rod.
miraç, *-cı* [- -] *the Prophet Mohammed's ascent to heaven.*
miralay MIL colonel.
miras [- -] inheritance, legacy; heritage; ~ *yemek* to inherit; *-a konmak* to inherit a fortune; *-tan ıskat* disinheritance; *-tan mahrum etm.* to disinherit.
mirasçı [- -.] heir, inheritor, legatee.
mirasyedi **1.** one who has inherited a fortune; **2.** *fig.* extravagant.
mis[1] musk; ~ *gibi* **1.** fragrant; **2.** super, first-rate.
mis[2] **1.** miss; **2.** Miss.
misafir [ā] **1.** guest, visitor; **2.** ANAT nebula; ~ *etm.* to put up, to entertain, to

have down; ~ *gibi oturmak co.* to sit in a constrained posture; ~ *odası* drawing room, guest room; ~ *sanatçı* guest artist.
misafirhane [ā] **1.** guesthouse; **2.** hostelry, inn.
misafirlik visit; *misafirliğe gitmek* **1.** to pay a visit (*-e* to); **2.** to go on a visit.
misafirperver [ā] hospitable.
misafirperverlik [ā] hospitality.
misak, *-kı* [- -] pact, treaty.
misal, *-li* [ā] example, model, exemplar; precedent.
misil, *-sli* **1.** equal, like, counterpart; **2.** as much again; *misli görülmemiş* unique, matchless; *misliyle mukabele* JUR retaliation, retortion.
misilleme retaliation, retortion.
misina fishline.
misk *s.* *mis[1]*.
miskal, *-li* [ā] *obs.* miskal.
misket, *-ti* **1.** marble; **2.** (grape)shot; shrapnel ball.
miskin **1.** indolent, supine, shiftless; **2.** poor, wretched; **3.** leprous, lazarous.
miskinleşmek to become indolent (*or* supine).
miskinlik supineness, shiftlessness.
mister Mister, Mr.
mistik mystic(al).
misyon mission.
misyoner missionary.
-miş'li geçmiş zaman GR the inferential past tense.
mit, *-ti* myth.
miting meeting, demonstration; ~ *yapmak* to hold a meeting.
mitingçi demonstrator.
mitoloji mythology.
mitralyöz machine-gun.
miyar [- -] **1.** CHEM reagent; **2.** standard.
miyav! meow!
miyavlamak to miaow, *Am.* to meow.
miyop nearsighted, shortsighted, myopic.
miyopluk nearsightedness, shortsightedness, myopia.
mizaç, *-cı* [ā] disposition, temperament, nature.
mizah [ā] humo(u)r; ~ *dergisi* humo(u)r magazine.
mizahçı [ā] humorist.
mizahi [.- -] humorous.
mizan [- -] **1.** scales, balance; **2.** MATH proof.
mizana [.x.] NAUT mizzenmast.
mizanpaj TYP **1.** layout; **2.** paging up,

make-up.
mizanpli set.
mizansen mise-en-scène.
mobilya [. x .] furniture; ~ *mağazası* furniture store.
mobilyacı maker *or* seller of furniture.
mobilyalı furnished.
mobilyasız unfurnished.
moda [x .] **1.** fashion, vogue, style; **2.** fashionable, stylish; ~ *olm.* to come into vogue, to be in; *-sı geçmek* to go out of fashion (*or* vogue), to be out, to become démodé; *-ya uymak* to keep up with fashions.
modacı stylist; couturier.
model **1.** model; **2.** pattern; **3.** fashion magazine; **4.** type, model, style; **5.** F spitting image; ~ *değiştirmek sl.* to wreck one's car.
modelci patternmaker.
modellik being a model.
modern modern.
modernize modernized; ~ *etm.* to modernize.
modernleştirmek to modernize.
modistra [. x .] seamstress.
modül module.
modülasyon MUS modulation.
Moğol *pr. n.* Mongol.
Moğolistan *pr. n.* Mongolia.
moher mohair.
mokasen moccasin.
mola [x .] **1.** break, rest, pause, stop-over; **2.** NAUT ease it off!; ~ *etm.* NAUT to ease off (*rope*); ~ *vermek* to stop (*or* lay) over.
molekül molecule.
molla *obs.* mullah, mollah.
molotofkokteyli Molotov cocktail.
moloz **1.** rubble, debris; **2.** *sl.* swine.
moment, *-ti* PHYS moment.
monarşi monarchy.
monden pleasure-loving.
monogami monogamy.
monoki, *-lü* monocle.
monolog monologue.
monopol monopoly.
monoray monorail.
monoton monotonous.
monotonluk monotony.
monşer mon cher.
montaj assembly, mounting.
monte etm. to assemble, to put together.
mor violet, purple; ~ *etm. sl.* to put to the blush; ~ *olm. sl.* to turn red in the face.

moral, *-li* morale; ~ *vermek* (*b-ne*) to boost *s.o.*'s morale; *-i bozuk* low-spirited, down; *-ini bozmak* (*b-nin*) to get *s.o.* down, to destroy *s.o.*'s morale, to demoralize *s.o.*
morarmak **1.** to turn purple; **2.** to turn black-and-blue.
morartı bruise.
moratoryum [. . x .] moratorium.
morfem GR morpheme.
morfin morphine.
morfinoman morphine addict.
morfoloji morphology.
morg morgue.
morlaşmak to turn purple.
morötesi, *-ni* ultraviolet.
mors[1] ZOO walrus.
mors[2]: ~ *alfabesi* Morse code.
mortlamak *sl.* to kick the bucket, to peg out, to pop off.
mortlatmak *sl.* **1.** to bump off, to do in, to kill; **2.** to clean out, to pluck.
morto [x .] *sl.* corpse, stiff; *-yu çekmek sl.* = *mortlamak.*
mortocu **1.** driver of a hearse; **2.** pall-bearer.
mortu *s.* **morto.**
mortucu *s.* **mortocu.**
moruk *sl.* old man, dotard.
moruklaşmak *sl.* to get old (*or* decrepit).
morumsu, morumtırak purplish.
Moskof *pr. n.* Russian.
Moskova [x . .] *pr. n.* Moscow.
mosmor [x .] **1.** deep purple; **2.** black and blue all over.
mostra [x .] sample, pattern, model; ~ *olm.* to be caught with one's pants down; *-sını bozmak* (*b-nin*) *sl.* to show *s.o.* up.
mostralık [x . .] **1.** sample, model; **2.** prize example (*or* package).
motel motel.
motif motif.
motivasyon motivation.
motopomp, *-pu* motor-driven pump.
motor **1.** motor; engine; **2.** = *motor-bot*; **3.** = *motosiklet*; **4.** *sl.* loose (*woman*); **5.** *sl.* dunce, fool; ~ *açmak* MOT to run in.
motorbot, *-tu* motorboat.
motorcu motorman.
motorin diesel fuel (*or* oil).
motorize MIL motorized; ~ *etm.* to motorize.
motorlu motorized (*a.* MIL), motor-driven.

motorsuz motorless.
motosiklet, -ti motorcycle.
motör, s. **motor.**
motörcü s. **motorcu.**
motris RAIL motor car.
mozaik mosaic.
mozole mausoleum.
M.Ö. B.C.
möble furniture.
möbleli furnished.
mönü menu.
mösyö Monsieur.
M.S. A.D.
muadelet, -ti [ā] equality.
muadil [ā] equivalent.
muaf [ā] **1.** exempt (-*den* from), free (-*den* from); **2.** MED immune; ~ **tutmak** to exempt (-*den* from).
muafiyet, -ti [ā] **1.** exemption; **2.** MED immunity.
muahede [ā] treaty, pact.
muaheze [ā] criticism, censure; ~ **etm.** to criticize.
muallak, -kı 1. hung, suspended; **2.** up in the air, undecided; **-ta kalmak** (*or olm.*) to be in the air, to hang in the balance.
muallim teacher, preceptor.
muallime schoolmistress.
muamele [ā] **1.** transaction, processing, procedure; **2.** conduct, behavio(u)r, treatment; **3.** trading, dealing; **4.** CHEM reaction; ~ **etm.** (*b-ne*) to treat *s.o.*
muamma [. x -] **1.** enigma, mystery; **2.** riddle.
muammalı enigmatic.
muare moiré.
muarız [ā] opposed (-*e* to).
muasır [ā] contemporary.
muaşeret, -ti [ā] social intercourse; ~ **adabı** etiquette.
muavenet, -ti [ā] help, assistance; ~ **etm.** to help, to assist.
muavin [ā] assistant, helper.
muayene [ā] inspection, examination (*a.* MED); ~ **etm.** to examine, to inspect.
muayeneci [ā] **1.** customs officer; **2.** examiner.
muayenehane [ā, ā] surgery, consulting room.
muayyen fixed, determined, definite.
muazzam 1. huge, enormous; **2.** F terrific, magnificent.
mubah [ā] permissible, fair.
mubayaa [. - . .] buying; ~ **etm.** to buy,

to purchase.
mubayaacı [. - . . .] stockbroker.
mucibince [- . x .] in accordance with, as required by.
mucip, -bi [ü] cause, reason; ~ **olm.** to necessitate, to entail.
mucit [ü] **1.** inventor; **2.** inventive, creative.
mucize [ü] miracle; **-ler yaratmak** to work miracles.
mucizevi [- . . .-] miraculous, miraculous.
mucur 1. bits of coal; **2.** fine gravel; **3.** trash, debris, rubbish.
muço s. **miço.**
mudi, -ii COM depositor.
mufassal detailed.
mufassalan [. x . .] in detail.
muflon ZOO mouflon.
mugayir [ā] contrary (-*e* to).
muğlak, -kı obscure, abstruse, recondite.
muhabbet, -ti 1. chat; **2.** love, affection; ~ **etm.** to chat; ~ **tellalı** pimp, procurer.
muhabbetçiçeği, -ni BOT mignonette.
muhabbetkuşu, -nu ZOO lovebird, parakeet.
muhabbetli affectionate.
muhaberat, -tı [ā, ā] correspondence, communications.
muhabere [ā] correspondence; communications; ~ **etm.** to correspond (*ile* with); to communicate (*ile* with); ~ **sınıfı** Signal Corps.
muhabir [ā] correspondent, reporter.
muhaceret, -ti [ā] immigration.
muhacir [ā] immigrant, emigrant, refugee.
muhafaza [. - . .] protection, care; maintenance, preservation; ~ **altına almak** to protect, to safeguard; ~ **etm.** to protect, to preserve, to guard.
muhafazakâr [. - . . -] conservative.
muhafazakârlık conservatism.
muhafız [ā] (body)guard, guardsman; ~ **alayı** MIL troop of guardsmen.
muhakeme [ā] **1.** trial; adjudication; **2.** judg(e)ment, discernment; ~ **etm. 1.** JUR to try; **2.** to judge, to reason.
muhakkak 1. certain, sure; **2.** certainly, without doubt, undoubtedly.
muhalefet, -ti [ā] **1.** opposition; **2.** POL the Opposition; ~ **etm.** to oppose; ~ **partisi** Opposition party.
muhalif [ā] **1.** contrary (-*e* to), against, adverse; **2.** opposing; Opposition …
muhallebi pudding; ~ **çocuğu** milk-

sop, namby-pamby, mollycoddle.

muhammem COM estimated (value, etc.).

Muhammet, -di (a. **Hazreti ~**) Mohammed.

muhammin COM appraiser.

muharebe [ā] battle, war, combat; **~ etm.** to fight, to battle; **~ meydanı** battlefield.

muharip, -bi [ā] MIL **1.** warrior, combatant; **2.** belligerent; combat ...

muharrem 1. Muharram; **2.** ♀ mf., wf.

muharrik, -ki 1. moving, motive ...; **2.** fig. inciter, instigator.

muharrir writer, author.

muhasara [. - . .] MIL siege; **~ etm.** to besiege, to beleaguer; **-yı kaldırmak** to raise a siege.

muhasebe [ā] accountancy, bookkeeping; **~ memuru** accountant, bookkeeper.

muhasebeci [ā] accountant, bookkeeper.

muhasebecilik [ā] accountancy, bookkeeping.

muhasım [ā] hostile, enemy; opponent.

muhasip, -bi [ā] accountant, bookkeeper.

muhatap, -bı [. - .] **1.** collocutor; **2.** COM drawee.

muhatara [. - . .] danger, risk.

muhataralı [. - . . .] dangerous.

muhavere [ā] conversation, talk; **~ etm.** to converse.

muhavvile ELECT transformer.

muhayyel imaginary.

muhayyer 1. COM on trial (or approval); **2.** MUS a **makam.**

muhayyile imagination, fancy.

muhbir 1. informer; **2.** reporter, correspondent.

muhit, -ti [ī] **1.** surroundings, environment, milieu; **2.** area, district, neighbo(u)rhood.

muhkem solid, tight, firm.

muhlis 1. sincere; **2.** ♀ mf.

muhrip, -bi destroyer.

muhtaç, -cı [ā] needy, poor, destitute, indigent; **~ olm.** to be in need (or want) (-e of), to need.

muhtar 1. [. -] autonomous, self-governing; **2.** [. .] mukhtar, headman.

muhtariyet, -ti [ā] autonomy, self-government.

muhtarlık 1. being a mukhtar; **2.** the mukhtar's office.

muhtasar short, brief, concise.

muhtasaran [. x . .] briefly, concisely.

muhtekir profiteer.

muhtelif various, diverse.

muhtelit, -ti 1. mixed; **2.** MATH complex; **~ mahkeme** JUR mixed court.

muhtemel likely, probable.

muhtemelen probably.

muhterem respected, hono(u)red, esteemed, venerable.

muhteris passionate.

muhteriz shy, timid.

muhteşem splendid, magnificent, imposing, grand.

muhteva [ā] content(s).

muhtevi [ī] containing.

muhteviyat, -tı [ā] contents.

muhtıra 1. POL note, warning; **2.** diary; **3.** memorandum; **~ defteri** notebook.

mukabele [ā] **1.** retaliation, response, reciprocation; **2.** comparison; **~ etm.** to retaliate, to reciprocate.

mukabil [ā] **1.** counter ...; **2.** counterpart; **3.** in return (-e for); **4.** in response (-e to); **buna ~** in return for this; **~ dava** JUR counterclaim; **~ taarruz** MIL counterattack; **-inde** by way of return.

mukaddeme preface, introduction.

mukadder predestined, fated, foreordained.

mukadderat, -tı [. . . . -] destiny, fate.

mukaddes holy, sacred; blessed.

mukaddesat, -tı [ā] sacred things.

mukallit, -di imitator.

mukavele [ā] agreement, contract; **~ yapmak** to make a contract.

mukaveleli [ā] bound by contract.

mukavelename [. - . - . .] contract, agreement; deed.

mukavemet, -ti [ā] **1.** resistance; endurance; **2.** PHLS nolition; **~ etm.** to resist; **~ yarışı** long-distance race.

mukavemetçi [ā] POL resistance fighter.

mukavemetli [ā] resistant.

mukavemetsiz [ā] irresisting.

mukavim [ā] resistant.

mukavva cardboard.

mukayese [ā] comparison; **~ etm.** to compare.

mukayeseli [ā] comparative.

mukayyet, -di 1. recorded, registered; **2.** bound (ile by), limited (ile by); **~ olm.** to mind, to look after.

mukim [ī] who resides (or dwells) (-de in).

muktedir 1. capable, able; 2. potent, virile; ~ *olm.* to be able (*-e* to), to be capable (*-e* of).

mulaj 1. moulage (*a.* MED); 2. impression, cast.

multipleks multiplex (*cinema*).

mum 1. candle; 2. wax; 3. ELECT candlepower; watt; ~ *dibine ışık vermez pro.* one who helps others sometimes is unable to help himself; ~ *direk* ramrod straight; ~ *gibi* 1. = ~ *direk*; 2. well-behaved; ~ *ışığı* candlelight; ~ *olm.* 1. to become obedient; 2. *sl.* to be willing to do s.th.; *-a döndürmek* (*or* çe-virmek) to make obedient; *-la ara-mak* fig. to crave (*or* hanker) for.

mumcu candlemaker, chandler.

mumlamak to wax.

mumlu waxed; ~ *kâğıt* stencil.

mumya [x .] mummy.

mumyalamak to mummify, to embalm.

mumyalaşmak to be mummified.

munafık, *-kı* [ā] mischief-maker.

mundar *s.* *murdar.*

munis [ū] 1. sociable, friendly; 2. well-known, familiar; 3. tame.

munkabız constipated.

muntazam 1. regular, even, uniform; 2. regularly; 3. methodical; orderly.

muntazaman regularly, orderly.

munzam added; supplementary; additional.

murabaha [. - . .] JUR usury.

murabba¹, *-aı* MATH square.

murabba² [. . -] preserved fruit.

murahhas delegate; ~ *heyet* delegation.

murakabe [. - . .] 1. inspection, supervision; 2. contemplation; ~ *etm.* to inspect.

murakıp, *-bı* [ā] 1. inspector; 2. COM auditor.

murat, *-dı* [ā] 1. desire, wish; aim, intention, goal; 2. ♀ *mf.*; *muradına er-mek* to attain one's desire, to reach one's goal.

murdar dirty, filthy; ~ *ilik* spinal cord.

Musa [- -] *pr. n.* 1. Moses; 2. *mf.*

musahhih proofreader.

musahhihlik proofreading.

musakka moussaka.

musalla [. . -] 1. public place for prayer; 2. area within a mosque for performing a funeral service, ~ *taşı* stone on which the coffin is placed during the funeral service.

musallat, *-tı* worrying, annoying; ~ *etm.* (*b-ni b-ne*) to set *s.o.* to pester *s.o.*, to cause *s.o.* to plague *s.o.*; ~ *olm.* to pester, to bother, to pick on; to infest; to plague.

musandıra [. x ..] large cupboard.

musannif *obs.* 1. compiler (*of a book*); 2. classifier.

Musevi [- . -] 1. Jew; 2. Jewish.

Musevilik [- . - .] Judaism.

Mushaf the Koran.

musibet, *-ti* (*i*) 1. calamity, disaster; 2. F a pain in the neck, pest; 3. *fig.* ill--omened.

musikar [- . -] 1. panpipe; 2. a kind of mythical bird.

musiki [- . -] music.

musikişinas [- . - . . -] 1. musician; 2. lover of music.

muska amulet, charm.

muslin muslin.

musluk 1. tap, faucet, spigot; 2. F washbasin, lavatory; ~ *taşı* stone sink.

muslukçu 1. plumber; 2. *sl.* pickpocket.

muson METEOR monsoon.

mustarip, *-bi* suffering.

muşamba [. x .] 1. oilcloth; oilskin; 2. linoleum; 3. raincoat, slicker; ~ *gibi* very dirty (*clothes*).

muşmula [x . .] 1. BOT medlar; 2. *sl.* antique, old person; ~ *suratlı* who has a wrinkled face.

muşta [x .] 1. blow with the fist; 2. brass knucks (*or* knuckles).

muştu good news.

mut, *-tu* happiness.

mutaassıp, *-bı* fanatical, bigoted, strict.

mutaassıplık fanaticism, bigotry.

mutabakat, *-tı* [. - . .] 1. agreement, conformity, correspondence, congruity; 2. MATH identity; *-a varmak* to come to an agreement.

mutabık, *-kı* [ā] 1. in agreement, agreeing, conformable; 2. appropriate (*-e* to), suited (*-e* to); ~ *kalmak* to come to an agreement (*-de* on).

mutaf [ū] weaver of goat's-hair articles.

mutarıza bracket, parenthesis.

mutasarrıf 1. JUR owner, possessor; 2. HIST governor of a *sancak.*

mutasavvıf Sufi; mystic.

mutat customary, habitual.

mutavassıt, *-tı* go-between, intermediary.

muteber [ū] **1.** valid, in force (or effect); **2.** esteemed, eminent; **3.** trustworthy; believable; ~ *olm.* to be valid, to be in force (or effect).

muteberan [- . . -] big shots, bigwigs.

mutedil [ū] **1.** moderate, mild, temperate; **2.** CHEM neutral.

mutekit, -*di* [ū] religious, pious.

mutemet, -*di* [ū] **1.** paymaster, fiduciary **2.** trustworthy.

mutena [- . -] **1.** select, refined; **2.** delicate; **3.** carefully done.

mutfak **1.** kitchen; **2.** cuisine.

mutlak, -*kı* **1.** absolute, unconditional; **2.** absolutely, surely; by all means; ~ *ekseriyet* absolute majority.

mutlaka [x . -] absolutely, certainly, surely, definitely; undoubtedly; by all means.

mutlakıyet, -*ti* **1.** absolutism; **2.** autocracy.

mutlu **1.** happy; **2.** lucky, fortunate; *ne mutlu Türküm diyene!* he is a lucky person who can call himself a Turk!

mutluluk happiness.

mutsuz unhappy.

mutsuzluk unhappiness.

muttasıl **1.** adjoining; **2.** continuously.

muvacehe [ā] confrontation; -*sinde* in the face (-*in* of).

muvafakat, -*ti* [. - . .] consent; ~ *etm.* to consent (-*e* to).

muvaffak, -*kı* successful; ~ *olm.* to succeed (-*de* in), to be successful (-*de* in).

muvaffakiyet, -*ti* success.

muvaffakiyetli successful.

muvaffakiyetsiz unsuccessful.

muvaffakiyetsizlik unsuccess, failure.

muvafık, -*kı* [ā] suitable, appropriate, fit.

muvahhit monotheist.

muvakkat, -*ti* temporary, provisional; interim.

muvakkaten [. x . .] temporarily.

muvasala [. - . .] communication.

muvazaa [. - . .] JUR collusion.

muvazaalı [. - . . .] JUR collusive, collusory.

muvazene [ā] **1.** balance, equilibrium; **2.** MED sense of balance, equilibrium sense.

muvazeneli [ā] balanced, in equilibrium.

muvazenesiz [ā] unbalanced.

muvazi [. - -] parallel.

muvazzaf **1.** MIL regular; **2.** charged

(*ile* with); ~ *subay* MIL regular (or active) officer.

muylu MEC hub.

muz BOT banana; ~ *gibi olm. sl.* to be rattled.

muzaffer **1.** victorious, triumphant; **2.** ♀ *mf.*

muzafferiyet, -*ti* victory, triumph.

muzır, -*rrı* **1.** mischievous, naughty; **2.** injurious, harmful.

muzırlık **1.** mischievousness; **2.** harmfulness.

muzip, -*bi* [ū] plaguing, tormenting; mischievous.

muziplik [ū] kidding, teasing; ~ *etm.* to kid, to tease.

mübadele [ā] exchange, barter, trade; ~ *etm.* to exchange, to trade, to swap.

mübadil [ā] exchangee.

mübalağa exaggeration; ~ *etm.* to exaggerate.

mübalağacı exaggerator.

mübalağalı exaggerated, blown-up.

mübarek, -*ki* [ā] **1.** blessed; sacred, holy; **2.** confounded, blasted; **3.** F you son of a gun!; ~ *olsun!* may it be blessed!

mübaşir [ā] usher, crier.

mübayenet, -*ti* [ā] conflict.

mübrem inescapable.

mücadele [ā] struggle, fight, contention, fray, combat, strife; ~ *etm.* to struggle, to fight, to strive, to contend (*ile* with).

mücadeleci [ā] striver, fighter, contender.

mücahit, -*di* [ā] combatant, fighter, champion.

mücbir compelling; ~ *sebepler* JUR force majeure.

mücehhez **1.** equipped (*ile* with) fitted out (*ile* with); **2.** ready, prepared (*ile* with).

mücellit, -*di* bookbinder.

mücellithane [ā] bookbindery.

mücerret, -*di* **1.** abstract; **2.** unmarried; **3.** GR the nominative case; **4.** [x . .] F only, solely.

mücessem **1.** personified; **2.** three-dimensional.

mücevher jewel.

mücevherat, -*tı* [ā] jewel(le)ry.

mücevherci jewel(l)er.

mücmel concise.

mücrim **1.** guilty; **2.** criminal, felon.

mücver croquette.

müdafaa [. - . .] defence, *Am.* defense;

~ *etm.* to defend; ~ *hakkı* JUR right of defense; ~ *hattı* MIL line of defense.
müdafaasız [. - . . .] defenceless, *Am.* defenseless, undefended.
müdafi, -ii [ā] **1.** defender; **2.** *football*: back.
müdahale [. - . . .] interference, intervention; ~ *etm.* to interfere, to intervene, to step in.
müdana [. - -] gratitude, thankfulness.
müdavim [ā] frequenter, habitué.
müddei [ī] JUR plaintiff.
müddeiumumi [. . - . - -] JUR public prosecutor.
müddeiumumilik public prosecutorship.
müddet, -ti period, duration, space of time, interval, while; *bir* ~ for a while.
müderris 1. *obs.* professor; **2.** HIST teacher in a *medrese.*
müdevver 1. circular, round, spherical; **2.** transferred.
müdire [ī] **1.** headmistress; **2.** manageress, directress.
müdiriyet, -ti [. - . .] *s.* **müdürlük.**
müdrik, -ki perceiving, comprehending; ~ *olm.* to perceive, to comprehend.
müdür 1. director, head, chief; manager; **2.** principal, headmaster.
müdürlük 1. directorate; **2.** directorship.
müebbeden [. x . .] forever, eternally.
müebbet, -di 1. perpetual, eternal, endless; **2.** life, lifelong; ~ *hapis* JUR life (sentence).
müellif writer, author.
müessese [. x . .] institution, foundation, establishment, organization.
müessif regrettable; sad.
müessir 1. touching, heart-moving; **2.** influential, effective; **3.** CHEM active; ~ *fiil* JUR assault and battery.
müessis founder, establisher.
müeyyide JUR sanction.
müezzin *isl.* muezzin.
müfettiş inspector, supervisor.
müfettişlik inspectorship; inspectorate.
müflis bankrupt, insolvent.
müfredat, -tı [ā] items (*of a list*); ~ *programı* (*bir okulun*) curriculum.
müfreze MIL detachment, platoon.
müfrit, -di excessive.
müfsit, -di seditious.
müfteri [ī] slanderer, calumniator.
müftü *isl.* mufti.

müge 1. BOT lily of the valley; **2.** ♀ *wf.*
mühendis engineer.
mühendislik engineering.
mühim, -mmi important.
mühimmat, -tı [ā] munitions.
mühimsemek to consider important, to regard as important.
mühlet, -ti period, respite, delay, extension.
mühre 1. stone used for polishing *or* grinding; **2.** decoy.
mührelemek to grind with a *mühre.*
mühtedi [ī] convert to Islam.
mühür, -hrü 1. seal, signet; signet ring; **2.** stamp; ~ *basmak* to seal; to stamp; ~ *mumu* sealing wax; *mührünü basmak fig.* to vouch (-*e* for); *mührünü yalamak fig.* to go back on one's word.
mührcü engraver of seals.
mührdar [ā] HIST private secretary of a high official.
mührlemek 1. to seal; to stamp; **2.** to seal up, to padlock (*a place*).
mührlü sealed.
müjde good news; ~ *vermek* to give a piece of good news.
müjdeci harbinger, herald.
müjdelemek to give a piece of good news.
müjdelik present given to s.o. who brings good news.
mükâfat, -tı [. - -] reward; prize, recompense; ~ *almak* (*or kazanmak*) to win a prize; ~ *vermek* (*b-ne*) to give *s.o.* a prize (*or* reward).
mükâfatlandırmak [. - - . . .] to reward, to recompense.
mükâleme 1. conversation; **2.** diplomatic conference, **3.** MIL parley; ~ *memuru* (*or subayı*) MIL officer with the flag of truce.
mükellef 1. obliged (-*mekle* to *inf.*), charged (*ile* with); **2.** elaborate, grand; **3.** taxpayer.
mükellefiyet, -ti obligation, liability.
mükemmel excellent, perfect, superb, consummate.
mükemmeliyet, -ti mükemmellik perfection.
mükerrer repeated, reiterated; ~ *ıskonto* COM rediscount; ~ *sigorta* COM reinsurance.
müktesep, -bi acquired; ~ *hak* JUR vested right.
mülahaza consideration; observation; ~ *etm.* to think twice; -*sıyla* in consid-

mürettebat

eration of.

mülahazat, -tı [. - . -] observations; thoughts; **~ hanesi** blank space; **~ hanesini açık bırakmak** *fig.* to reserve comment.

mülakat, -tı [. - -] interview, audience; **~ yapmak** to have an interview (*ile* with).

mülayemet, -ti 1. docility; **2.** looseness in the bowels.

mülayim 1. docile, gentle, mild; **2.** suitable, reasonable.

mülazım 1. *obs.* probationer; **2.** MIL lieutenant.

mülhem inspired.

mülk, -kü property, real estate, possession; **~ almak** to buy landed property; **~ sahibi** property owner.

mülki [ı] civil(ian).

mülkiye 1. civil service; **2.** ♀ (**Mektebi**) the School of Political Science.

mülkiyet, -ti ownership, proprietorship, possession; **~ hakkı** JUR property right.

mülteci [ı] refugee.

mültefit courteous, attentive.

mültezim HIST tax farmer.

mültimilyoner multimillionaire.

mümbit, -ti fertile.

mümessil 1. representative, agent; **2.** prefect, monitor.

mümeyyiz 1. examiner; **2.** distinctive.

mümin [- .] *isl.* believer, Muslim.

mümkün possible; **~ kılmak** to render possible; **~ mertebe** *or* **~ olduğu kadar** as far as possible.

mümtaz [ā] **1.** select, distinguished; **2.** privileged, special; **3.** ♀ *mf.*

münakale [. - . .] transport.

münakaşa [. - . .] argument, dispute, debate; wrangle, quarrel; **~ etm.** to argue, to dispute; to quarrel.

münasebet, -ti [ā] **1.** relation; **2.** connection, tie-in; **3.** opportunity; **4.** reason; means; **5.** fitness; **~ almaz** it isn't fit; **~ kurmak** to establish a relationship (*ile* with); **-iyle** on the occasion of, because of; **-te bulunmak 1.** to have relations (*or* dealings) (*ile* with); **2.** to go to bed (*ile* with).

münasebetli [ā] **1.** opportune, favo(u)rable; **2.** appropriate; **~ münasebetsiz** without considering whether it is suitable or not.

münasebetsiz [ā] **1.** unfavo(u)rable, inopportune; **2.** inappropriate; unseemly: **3.** tactless, inconsiderate.

münasip 1. suitable, proper, fit; **2.** opportune, reasonable, convenient; **~ görmek** to see fit.

münavebe [ā] alternation, turn; **~ ile** by turns.

münazaa [. - . .] quarrel, dispute.

münazara [. - . .] debate, discussion.

münderecat, -tı [ā] contents.

münebbih 1. stimulative; **2.** (*saat*) *obs.* alarm clock.

müneccim *obs.* astrologer.

münekkit, -di critic.

münevver 1. enlightened, intellectual, cultivated; **2.** ♀ *wf.*

münfail offended.

münferit, -di separate, alone, isolated; **~ hücre** solitary cell.

münfesih 1. dissolved, broken off; **2.** abolished, annulled.

münhal, -li 1. vacant, vacated; **2.** CHEM soluble; **3.** CHEM dissolved.

münhasır limited (*-e* to), restricted (*-e* to).

Münih *pr. n.* Munich.

münkir 1. denier; **2.** atheist.

müntahabat, -tı [. . . -] anthology.

müntahap, -bı select, choice.

münteha [ā] end, limit.

müntesir published.

münzevi [ı] reclusive, hermitic.

müphem vague, uncertain, indefinite.

müphemiyet, -ti vagueness.

müptela 1. addicted (*-e* to); **2.** in love (*-e* with); **3.** afflicted (*-e* with); **~ olm.** to become addicted (*-e* to).

müptezel vulgar, common.

müracaat, -tı [. - . .] **1.** application; **2.** reference, recourse; **3.** information desk (*or* office); **~ etm. 1.** to apply (*-e* to); **2.** to resort (*-e* to), to turn (*-e* to).

müracaatçı applicant.

mürai [. - -] two-faced, hypocritical.

mürdolmak [x . .] to die.

mürdümeriği, -ni BOT damson (plum).

mürebbiye governess.

müreffeh well-off, well-heeled.

mürekkep¹, -bi ink; **~ hokkası** inkwell; **~ lekesi** inkstain; **~ yalamış** *fig.* well educated.

mürekkep² composed (*-den* of), made up (*-den* of).

mürekkepbalığı, -nı ZOO cuttlefish.

mürekkeplemek to ink.

mürekkepli inky; ink-stained.

mürekkeplik inkwell.

mürettebat, -tı [ā] crew.

mürettebatsız [ā] unmanned.

mürettip, **-bi** compositor, typesetter.

mürettiphane [ā] TYP composing room.

mürit, **-di** [ī] disciple.

mürşit, **-di 1.** guide; mentor; **2.** sheikh.

mürteci, **-ii** reactionary.

mürtet, **-ddi** apostate Muslim.

mürur [ü] passage, transit.

mururiye **1.** laissez-passer; **2.** toll.

müruruzaman [. - . . . -] JUR prescription; limitation.

mürüvvet, **-ti 1.** joy (felt by parents when they see their children reach certain stages in life); **2.** generosity; **-ini görmek** to see one's children grow up and do well.

mürver BOT elder(berry).

müsaade [. - . .] permission; leave; ~ **etm.** to permit, to let, to allow; **-nizle!** with your permission (or leave)!

müsabaka [. - . .] contest, competition.

müsabık, **-kı** [ā] competitor, contestant.

müsademe [ā] **1.** collision, clash; **2.** MIL skirmish.

müsadere [ā] JUR confiscation, seizure; ~ **etm.** to seize, to confiscate.

müsait, **-di** [ā] suitable, favo(u)rable, convenient.

müsamaha [. - . .] tolerance, lenience, indulgence; ~ **etm.** (or **göstermek**) **1.** (b-ne) to be lenient with s.o., to tolerate s.o.; **2.** (bşe) to overlook s.th., to disregard s.th.

müsamahakâr müsamahalı tolerant, lenient, indulgent.

müsamere [ā] show.

müsavat, **-tı** [. - -] equality.

müsavi [. - -] equal.

müsebbip, **-bi** cause(r).

müseccel registered; ~ **marka** registered trademark.

müsekkin MED sedative, tranquilizer.

müselles MATH **1.** triangle; **2.** triangular.

müshil MED laxative, aperient; purgative, cathartic.

müskirat, **-tı** alcoholic drinks, intoxicants.

Müslim Muslim.

Müslüman Muslim.

Müslümanlık **1.** Islam; **2.** the Moslem world.

müsmir fruitful, productive.

müspet, **-ti 1.** positive, affirmative; **2.** proved, established; ~ **cevap** positive

(or affirmative) answer.

müsrif wasteful, extravagant, spendthrift, prodigal.

müsriflik wastefulness, extravagance.

müstacel [ā] urgent.

müstaceliyet, **-ti** [ā] urgency.

müstahak, **-kkı 1.** condign; **2.** worthy (-e of), deserving (-e of); **-ını bulmak** to get one's deserts.

müstahdem employee, servant, caretaker, Am. janitor.

müstahkem MIL fortified.

müstahsil producer.

müstahzar preparation.

müstahzarat, **-tı** [. . . .] preparations.

müstakbel (the) future.

müstakil, **-lli 1.** independent; autonomous; **2.** detached, self-contained, separate; ~ **ev** detached house.

müstamel [ā] used; secondhand.

müstear [ā] **1.** borrowed; **2.** pseudo.

müstebit, **-ddi** despotic, tyrannical.

müstebitlik despotism.

müstecir [. - .] tenant, renter.

müstehcen obscene; pornographic, off colo(u)r.

müstehlik, **-ki** COM consumer.

müstehzi [ī] mocking, sarcastic, ironical.

müstekreh loathsome.

müstemleke colony.

müstemlekeci colonialist.

müstemlekecilik colonialism.

müstenit, **-di** based (-e on), relying (-e on).

müsterih [ī] at ease; ~ **olm.** to be set at ease.

müstesna [ā] **1.** exceptional, extraordinary; **2.** except for, with the exception for.

müsteşar [ā] **1.** undersecretary; **2.** counselor.

müsteşarlık [ā] **1.** undersecretaryship; **2.** counselorship.

müsteşrik, **-kı** orientalist.

müstevi [ī] **1.** MATH plane; **2.** level, flat.

müsvedde **1.** draft, rough copy; **2.** manuscript; typescript; **3.** fig. parody; ~ **defteri** notebook.

müşahede [ā] observation; ~ **altında** under medical observation; ~ **etm.** to observe, to see.

müşahhas concrete.

müşahit, **-di** observer.

müşavere [ā] consultation.

müşavir [ā] consultant, adviser.

müşerref **1.** hono(u)red, exalted; **2.** ♀

mf., wf.; ~ **olm.** to be (*or* feel) hon-o(u)red; ~ **oldum** I am hono(u)red to meet you.

müşfik kind, tender; compassionate.

müşir *s.* **müşür.**

müş'ir MEC gauge, indicator.

müşkül 1. difficult, hard; **2.** difficulty, problem, trouble.

müşkülat, -tı difficulties, problems; ~ **çıkarmak** (*or* **göstermek**) (*b-ne*) to raise difficulties for *s.o.*

müşkülpesent, -di fastidious, fussy, hard to please, particular.

müşrik, -ki polytheist.

müstak¹, -kkı derived.

müstak², -kı longing (*or* pining) (*-e* for).

müşteki [ī] complainant.

müstemilat, -tı outbuildings; additions, annexes.

müşterek, -ki common, joint; cooperative, combined; ~ **bahis** pari-mutuel; ~ **duvar** party wall; ~ **mülkiyet** co-ownership.

müştereken [. x . .] in common, jointly.

müşteri customer, buyer, purchaser, client; ~ **avlamak** to try to attract customers by artifice.

Müşteri AST Jupiter.

müşür (field) marshal.

mütalaa [. - . .] **1.** study; **2.** observation, opinion; ~ **etm. 1.** to study, to peruse; **2.** to ponder, to deliberate.

mütareke [ā] armistice, truce.

müteaddit numerous, many.

müteahhit builder, contractor.

müteakiben 1. afterwards, subsequently; **2.** after, following.

mütebessim smiling.

mütecanis [ā] homogeneous.

mütecaviz [ā] **1.** exceeding, over; **2.** aggressive.

mütecessis inquisitive, nosy, curious.

mütedavil [ā] **1.** current, in circulation; **2.** working (*capital*); ~ **sermaye** working capital.

müteessif grieved, sorry, regretful; ~ **olm.** to be grieved, to regret.

müteessir 1. depressed, saddened; pained, hurt; **2.** influenced; affected; ~ **olm.** (*bşden*) **1.** to be saddened (*or* depressed) by *s.th.*; **2.** to be influenced (*or* affected) by *s.th.*

mütefekkir thinker.

müteferrik, -kı scattered, dispersed; diverse, sundry.

müteferrika petty cash.

müteharrik, -ki 1. mobile, moving; **2.** powered (*or* driven) (*ile* by).

mütehassıs specialist, expert.

mütehassis touched, moved; ~ **etm.** to touch, to move; ~ **olm.** to be touched (*or* moved).

mütehayyir amazed, taken aback.

mütekabil 1. mutual, reciprocal; ~ **dava** JUR cross action.

mütekabiliyet, -ti [ā] reciprocity.

mütekait, -di [ā] pensioner; retired.

mütekâmil mature.

mütekebbir haughty, arrogant.

mütemadi [. . - -] continuous.

mütemadiyen [ā] [. . x . .] continuously, continually.

mütenahi [. . - -] MATH, PHLS finite.

mütenasip, -bi [ā] **1.** proportional; **2.** well-proportioned, shapely.

mütenavip, -bi [ā] alternate.

mütenevvi, -ii various, diverse.

müteradif [ā] synonymous.

müterakim [ā] accumulated.

mütercim translator.

mütereddit, -di hesitant, undecided, indecisive.

müteselsil 1. continuous, successive; **2.** JUR joint; ~ **alacaklılar** JUR joint creditors; ~ **borçlular** JUR joint debtors; ~ **mesuliyet** JUR joint liability; ~ **suç** JUR crime involving another crime.

müteşebbis 1. enterprising (*person*); **2.** entrepreneur.

müteşekkil composed (*-den* of).

müteşekkir grateful, thankful.

mütevazı, -ıı modest, humble.

müteveccih 1. aimed (*-e* at), directed (*-e* towards); **2.** sympathetic (*-e* to).

müteveccihen [. . x . .] in the direction (*-e* of), headed (*-e* towards), bound (*-e* for).

müteveffa [ā] the deceased.

mütevekkil who puts his trust in God.

mütevelli [ī] trustee (*of a* **vakıf**), mutawalli; ~ **heyeti** board of trustees (*of a* **vakıf**).

mütevellit, -di caused (*-den* by), resulting (*-den* from).

müthiş 1. terrible, awful, dreadful, terrific, frightful; **2.** *fig.* amazing, astounding.

müttefik, -ki 1. ally; **2.** allied; ~ **devletler** the allied powers, the allies.

müttehit, -di united.

müvekkil client.

müverrih historian.

müvezzi, -*li* 1. distributor; **2.** paperboy; postman.

müzakere [ā] **1.** discussion, deliberation, negotiation; **2.** oral test, recitation; ~ *etm.* to discuss, to debate, to talk over, to deliberate.

müzakereci [ā] tutor.

müzayede [ā] auction; ~ *ile satış* sale by auction; *-ye koymak* to put up for auction.

müze [x .] museum.

müzeci museum curator.

müzecilik museology.

müzehhep, -*bi* gilded, gilt.

müzelik [x . .] **1.** museum ...; **2.** *fig. co.* ancient, antiquated.

müziç, -*ci* troublesome, vexatious.

müzik music.

müzikal musical.

müzikçi musician.

müzikhol, -*lü* music hall.

müziksever 1. music lover; **2.** music-loving, fond of music.

müzisyen musician.

müzmin chronic (*disease*); ~ *bekâr* confirmed bachelor.

müzminleşmek to become chronic.

N

na! *sl.* **1.** take it!; **2.** there it is; ~ *kafa!* what a fool I was!

naaş, -*a'şı* corpse, body.

nabız, -*bzı* pulse; ~ *yoklamak fig.* to put out feelers; *nabzına göre şerbet vermek fig.* to feel one's way with a person; *nabzını tutmak* to take s.o.'s pulse; *nabzını yoklamak* (*b-nin*) *fig.* to sound s.o. out.

nacak hatchet.

naçar [- -] **1.** helpless; **2.** hopeless.

naçiz [- -] **1.** insignificant, worthless; **2.** humble.

naçizane [-. -.] **1.** humble (*opinion*); **2.** humbly; **3.** = *naçiz 1.*

nadan [- -] unmannerly, rude, boorish.

nadas fallow; ~ *etm.* to fallow; *-a bırakmak* to leave the land fallow.

nadide [- - -.] **1.** rare, curious, precious; **2.** ♀ [x . .] *wf.*

nadim regretful; ~ *olm.* to regret.

nadir [ā] **1.** rare, scarce; **2.** rarely; **3.** ♀ *mf.*

nadirat, -*tı* [-. -] rarities; *-tan olm.* to be a rarity.

nadiren [ā] [x . .] rarely.

nafaka 1. JUR alimony; **2.** livelihood, living; ~ *bağlamak* to assign a subsistence.

nafıa [- . .] public works.

nafile [ā] **1.** vain, useless, futile; **2.** in vain, for nothing; ~ *namaz isl.* supererogatory prayer; ~ *yere* in vain.

nafiz [ā] **1.** *fig.* influential; **2.** ♀ *mf.*

naftalin CHEM naphthalene.

naftalinlemek to put naphthalene (*-i* among).

nağme 1. tune, melody, air; **2.** tone; **3.** song; **4.** *fig.* sham protestation; *-yi değiştirmek fig.* to change one's tune.

nah *s. na.*

nahak, -*kkı* unjust; ~ *yere* unjustly, unjustifiably.

nahif [ī] gaunt, emaciated.

nahiv, -*hvi* GR syntax.

nahiye [ā] **1.** subdistrict; **2.** region (*a.* ANAT): district; ~ *müdürü* governor of a subdistrict.

nahoş [ā] unpleasant, nasty, disagreeable; ~ *bir sürpriz* an unpleasant surprise.

nail [ā] **1.** who receives (*or gains*); **2.** ♀ *mf.*; ~ *olm.* to obtain, to attain, to acquire.

naip, -*bi* [ā] regent, viceroy.

naiplik [ā] regency, viceroyalty.

nakarat, -*tı* [. . .] **1.** MUS refrain, burden; **2.** *fig.* the same old refrain.

nakavt, -*tı* boxing: knockout; ~ *etm.* to knock out.

nakden [x .] in cash (*or ready money*).

nakdi monetary, pecuniary; ~ *ceza* fine; ~ *teminat* JUR pecuniary warrant.

nakıs 1. minus, less; **2.** MATH negative (*number*); **3.** incomplete, deficient.

nakış, -*kşı* 1. embroidery, needlework; **2.** miniature; **3.** MUS a kind of song; ~ *işlemek* to embroider.

nakışlamak = *nakış işlemek.*

nakışlı embroidered.

nakız, -*kzı* 1. violation, breach; **2.** overthrowing (*of a court decision*); **3.** abrogation (*of a treaty*).

nakil, **-kli 1.** transport, transfer; **2.** transferring s.o. to a new post; **3.** telling, recounting (*story*); **4.** moving to (*another residence*); **5.** MED transplanting; ~ *vasıtası* transport vehicle.

nâkil **1.** transporter; **2.** teller, narrator; **3.** PHYS conductor.

nakit, **-kdi** cash, ready money.

nakkaş [. -] **1.** muralist; frescoist; **2.** miniaturist.

naklen [x .] live; ~ *yayın* live broadcast (*or* telecast).

nakletmek [x . .] **1.** to transport (-*e* to); to convey (-*e* to), to transfer (-*e* to); **2.** to move (-*e* to); **3.** to narrate, to recount, to tell.

nakliyat, **-tı** [. . -] transport, shipment, freighting, forwarding; ~ *şirketi* transport (*or* shipping *or* forwarding) company.

nakliyatçı freighter, shipper.

nakliye **1.** freight(age); **2.** transport, shipping; ~ *gemisi* troopship, transport; ~ *senedi* COM waybill; ~ *uçağı* troop carrier, transport plane; ~ *ücreti* freight(age), carriage.

nakliyeci freighter, shipper; forwarding agent.

nakşetmek [x . .] to engrave (*in one's memory*).

nakzen [x .]: ~ *görmek* (*davayı*) to re-examine *a case*; ~ *iade etm.* (*davayı*) to send *a case* back.

nakzetmek [x . .] **1.** to violate, to break; **2.** to annul, to abrogate (*treaty*); **3.** JUR to overthrow, to overturn (*the decision of a lower court*)

nal horseshoe; ~ *çakmak* to shoe (*a horse*); **-ları dikmek** *sl.* to kick the bucket, to peg out, to pop off.

nalbant, **-dı** blacksmith, farrier, horseshoer.

nalbur iron-monger, hardwareman, hardware dealer; ~ *dükkânı* hardware store.

nalburiye hardware store.

nalça metal piece, iron tip (*on a boot*).

naldöken stony (*road*).

nalet, **-ti** F cursed, damned; ~ *olsun!* God damn him!

nalın bath clog.

nallamak **1.** to shoe (*a horse, etc.*); **2.** *sl.* to bump off, to kill.

nam [ā] **1.** name; **2.** reputation, fame, renown; ~ *almak* (*or kazanmak or vermek*) to make a name for o.s.; **-ına 1.** on behalf of; in s.o.'s name;

2. in the way of; **-ında** named, called; *namı diğer* alias.

namağlup, **-bu** undefeated.

namahrem canonically a stranger.

namaz prayer, namaz; ~ *kılmak* to perform the namaz, to pray; ~ *seccadesi* prayer rug; ~ *vakti* time of the namaz, prayer time; **-ı kılındı** he is dead.

namazgâh open-air prayer place.

namazlık prayer rug.

namazsız (*woman*) who is menstruating.

namdar [- -] famous, celebrated.

name [ā] **1.** (love) letter; **2.** document, certificate.

namert, **-di 1.** cowardly; **2.** despicable, contemptible.

namertlik **1.** cowardliness; **2.** despicableness.

namlı famous, celebrated.

namlu **1.** barrel (*of a rifle, etc.*); **2.** blade (*of a sword*).

namuhesabına (*b-nin*) on *s.o.'s* behalf, on behalf of *s.o.*

namus [- -] **1.** hono(u)r, integrity, probity; **2.** chastity, virtue; ~ *borcu* debt of hono(u)r; ~ *sözü* word of hono(u)r; **-una dokunmak** (*b-nin*) to touch *s.o.'s* hono(u)r; **-uyla yaşamak** to keep to the straight and narrow, to live honestly.

namuslu [ā] **1.** hono(u)rable, upright; **2.** virtuous, chaste.

namussuz [ā] **1.** dishonest, dishono(u)rable; **2.** unvirtuous, unchaste; **3.** rotten bastard, damned thing.

namünasip [- . - .] inappropriate; unsuitable; inconvenient.

namütenahi [- . . - -] endless, boundless.

namzet **1.** candidate, prospect; nominee; **2.** betrothed, fiancé(e); ~ *göstermek* to nominate, to put forward as a candidate.

namzetlik candidacy; *namzetliğini koymak* to put o.s. forward as a candidate (-*e* for); to stand (-*e* for), *Am.* to run (-*e* for).

nanay *sl.* there isn't ...; *bende para* ~ I haven't a bean.

nane [ā] **1.** BOT (pepper)mint; **2.** mint tea; ~ *suyu* peppermint water; ~ *yemek* F to make a blunder.

naneli [ā] (pepper)minty.

nanemolla [- . . . .] weak Willy, cream puff.

naneruhu, **-nu** [- . - .] peppermint oil,

essence of peppermint.

naneşekeri, **-ni** [- . . . .] peppermint drop.

nanik: ~ **yapmak** to cock a snook (-*e* at), to thumb one's nose (-*e* at).

nankör ungrateful, unthankful, thankless.

nankörlük ungratefulness, ingratitude; ~ **etm.** to act ungratefully.

nar BOT pomegranate; ~ **gibi** well toasted (*or* roasted).

nara [- .] shout, cry, yell; ~ **atmak** to shout out, to yell; **-yı basmak** to let out a yell.

narçiçeği, **-ni** grenadine red.

narenciye [ā] BOT citrus fruits.

nargile hookah, nargileh, water pipe, hubble-bubble.

narh officially fixed price; ~ **koymak** to put a fixed price (-*e* on).

narin [ā] delicate, slim, slender.

narkotik narcotic.

narkoz narcosis; ~ **vermek** to anesthetize.

nasbetmek [x . .] to appoint (-*e* to).

nasıl [x .] **1.** how?; **2.** how (much); **3.** what sort of ...?; **4.** in the just same way; **nasılsınız?** how do you do?; ~ **ki** just as ... so ...; ~ **olsa** in any case, somehow or other.

nasılsa [x . .] = **nasıl olsa**.

nasır corn, clavus; callus, wart; ~ **bağlamak** to become calloused; **-ına basmak** (*b-nin*) F to tread on *s.o.*'s toes.

nasırlanmak = **nasır bağlamak**.

nasırlı calloused, warty; horny.

nasihat, **-ti** [ī] advice, counsel, admonition; ~ **etm.** (*or* **vermek**) to advise, to give advice, to counsel.

nasip, **-bi** [ī] portion, share, lot; ~ **olm.** to fall to one's lot; ~ **olursa** all being well; **nasibini almak** to enjoy.

Nasrani [. - -] Christian.

naşi [- -] owing (-*den* to), because (-*den* of).

naşir [ā] **1.** publisher; **2.** propagator.

natamam [- . -] incomplete, unfinished.

natıka [- . .] eloquence.

natır female bath attendant.

natokafa *sl.* numskull.

natüralist, **-ti** naturalist.

natüralizm naturalism.

natürel natural.

natürmort, **-tu** still life.

navlun freight(age).

naylon [x .] **1.** nylon; **2.** plastic.

naz coyness, reluctance; ~ **etm.** (*or* **yapmak**) to feign reluctance; ~ **ını çekmek** (*b-nin*) to put up with *s.o.*'s whims.

nazar 1. glance, look; **2.** opinion; **3.** the evil eye; ~ **boncuğu** blue bead, amulet; ~ **değmek** to cause misfortune by the evil eye, to hex; ~ **değmesin!** touch wood!; **-ı dikkate almak** to take into consideration; **-ı dikkatini çekmek** to attract *s.o.*'s attention; **-ı itibara almak** to take into consideration; **-ıyla bakmak** to regard as, to consider.

nazaran [x . .] **1.** in comparison (-*e* to); **2.** according (-*e* to).

nazari [ī] theoretical, speculative.

nazariye theory.

nazarlık amulet, charm.

nazenin [- . -] **1.** of delicate build; **2.** hussy, minx; son of a gun; **3.** coy.

nazım, **-zmı** verse; versification.

nâzım 1. regulatory; **2.** PHYS regulator; **3.** writer of verse; **4.** ♀ *mf*.

nazır [ā] **1.** overlooking, facing, looking out on; **2.** minister.

Nazi *pr. n.* Nazi.

nazik, **-ki** [ā] **1.** polite, courteous; **2.** delicate, fragile.

nazikleşmek [ā] **1.** to become polite (*or* courteous); **2.** to become delicate.

naziklik [ā] **1.** politeness, courteousness, courtesy; **2.** delicacy.

nazir [ī] **1.** equal, counterpart; **2.** AST nadir.

nazire [ī] *a poem written to resemble another poem in form and subject.*

nazlanmak *s.* **naz etm.**

nazlı 1. reluctant; **2.** coy, arch, coquettish; **3.** petted, coddled.

ne 1. what?; **2.** whatever; **3.** what a ...!, how ...!; ~ **âlemdesiniz?** how are you?, how are things with you?; ~ **buyurdunuz?** what did you say?; ~ **çıkar?** what does it matter?; ~ **de olsa** nevertheless, still; ~ **demek?** what does it mean?; ~ **dese beğenirsiniz?** guess what he said to me!; ~ **diye?** why ...?, for what purpose ...?; ~ **ekersen onu biçersin** *pro.* as you sow, so shall you reap; ~ **gibi?** what, for example?, like what?; ~ **görsem beğenirsiniz?** guess what I saw!; ~ **haber?** what's the news?, how goes it?; ~ **hacet?** what need is there!; ~ **hali varsa görsün** let him stew in his own juice; ~ **halt etmeye** F why in the hell ...?; ~ **hikmetse** heaven knows why!; ~ *ise* in any case, at any rate, anyway; ~ *kadar güzel!* how beautiful!; ~ *karın ağrısı!* what a pain in the neck he is!; ~ *malum?* how do you know?; ~ *mümkün!* impossible!; ~ *münasebet?* of course not!; ~ *oldu?* 1. what happened?; 2. what is the matter with ...?; ~ *oldum delisi* parvenu; ~ *olur* ~ *olmaz* just in case; ~ *pahasına olursa olsun* at any costs, at all costs; ~ *sinir şey!* what a pain in the neck it is!; ~ *vakit* (*or zaman*) when?, at what time?; ~ *var?* what's the matter?; ~ *var ki* only; but; however; ~ *yalan söyleyeyim* to tell you the truth, ...; ~ *yapıp yapıp* by hook or by crook, in some way or other; ~ *yazık!* what a pity!; *-me lazım?* what's it to me?

nebat, *-tı* [ā] plant.
nebatat, *-tı* [. - -] 1. plants; 2. botany; ~ *bahçesi* botanical garden.
nebati [. - -] botanical, vegetable; ~ *yağ* vegetable oil.
nebi [ī] prophet.
nebülöz AST nebula.
nebze bit, particle.
necat, *-tı* [ā] salvation, safety.
nece [x .] what language ...?
neci: *o, -dir?* what's his job?, what does he do?; *sen* ~ *oluyorsun?* what's it to you?
necip, *-bi* [ī] 1. noble; 2. ♀ [x .] *mf.*
nedamet, *-ti* [ā] regret, remorse; ~ *etm.* (*or getirmek*) to regret.
nedbe MED scar.
neden 1. why?, what for?; 2. reason, cause; ~ *olm.* to cause; *-iyle* because of, owing to; because; *bu -le* for this reason. because of this.
nedense for some reason or other, I don't know why, but ...
nedensel causal.
nedensellik causality.
nedim [ī] 1. intimate friend; 2. ♀ [x .] *mf.*
nedime [ī] 1. lady-in-waiting; 2. ♀ [x ..] *wf.*
nefaset, *-ti* [ā] excellence, exquisiteness.
nefer 1. individual, person; 2. MIL private.
nefes 1. breath; 2. draw, puff, drag (*on a cigarette*); 3. moment, instant; 4. *sl.* hash(ish); ~ *aldırmamak* (*b-ne*) to give *s.o.* no rest, not to give *s.o.* any respite; ~ *almak* 1. to breathe; to in-

hale; 2. *fig.* to catch one's breath, to take a short break, to rest; ~ *borusu* ANAT trachea; ~ *çekmek* 1. to take a puff (*or draw or* drag) (*on a cigarette*); 2. *sl.* to smoke some hash; ~ *darlığı* 1. shortness of breath; 2. asthma; ~ *etm.* (*b-ne*) to blow one's breath upon *s.o.* (*to cure him of an ailment*); ~ *-e* out of breath; ~ *-e kalmak* to gasp for breath, to pant; ~ *tüketmek* to waste one's breath; ~ *vermek* to breathe out, to exhale; *-i kesilmek* to gasp for breath, to catch one's breath.
nefeslemek *s.* **nefes etm.**
nefesli 1. MUS wind (*instrument*); 2. long-winded (*person*); ~ *çalgı* MUS wind instrument.
nefeslik vent(hole), air hole.
nefis[1], *-fsi* 1. self; essence; 2. the body, the flesh; 3. soul, life; *nefsine uymak* to yield to the flesh, to sin; *nefsine yedirememek* to be unable to bring o.s. (*to do s.th.*); *nefsini körletmek* (*or öldürmek*) 1. to take the edge off one's desire; 2. to stave off one's hunger; *nefsini yenmek* to master o.s.
nefis[2] excellent, choice, exquisite.
nefly, *-fyi* 1. JUR banishment, exile; 2. denial; negation; ~ *edatı* GR negative (particle).
nefret, *-ti* hate, hatred, detestation, abhorrence; aversion; ~ *etm.* to hate, to detest, to abhor, to loathe.
nefrit, *-ti* MED nephritis.
nefsani [. - -] carnal, fleshly, bodily.
nefsaniyet, *-ti* [ā] enmity, malice.
neft, *-ti* (*yağı*) naphtha.
nefyetmek [x . .] 1. to exile; 2. GR to negate.
negatif MATH, PHOT, ELECT negative.
neglije negligee.
nehari [. - -] day (*student, school*); ~ *mektep* day school; ~ *talebe* day student.
nehir, *-hri* river; ~ *yatağı* riverbed.
nehiy, *-hyi* 1. prohibition; 2. PSYCH inhibition.
nehyetmek [x . .] to prohibit, to forbid.
nekahet, *-ti* [ā] convalescence.
nekes stingy, mean.
nekeslik stinginess.
nekre witty.
nektar BOT nectar.
neli what ... made of?
nem 1. damp(ness), moisture; 2. humidity; 3. dew.

nema [ā] **1.** growth; **2.** interest.

nemelazımcı indifferent.

nemelazımcılık indifference.

nemlendirici moisturizer; humidifier.

nemlendirmek to moisten; to humidify; to moisturize.

nemlenmek to become damp, to moisten.

nemli damp, humid, moist; dank.

Nemrut, -du [ū] **1.** *pr. n.* Nimrod; **2.** ♀ cruel, grim (*person*).

nenin *s.* **neyin.**

neogen GEOL the Neogene.

neolitik (*çağ*) Neolithic.

neon neon; ~ **lambası** neon lamp (*or* tube).

Neptün AST Neptune.

nere [x .] where ...?, what place ...?; **buranın ~ olduğunu biliyor musunuz?** do you know what place this is?; **burası neresi?** what place is this?

nerede [x . .] where?; wherever ...?

nereden [x . .] (from) where?, whence ...?; ~ **geliyorsun?** where are you coming from?; ~ **nereye!** what a coincidence!

neredeyse [x . . .] **1.** almost, nearly, all but; **2.** (pretty) soon, before long; ~ **gelir** he'll come pretty soon.

nereli [x . .] where ... from?; **siz nerelisiniz?** where are you from?; **benim nereli olduğumu biliyor musunuz?** do you know where I am from?

nereye [x . .] where ...?; wherever ...?; ~ **gidiyorsunuz?** where are you going?

nergis BOT narcissus.

nesep, -bi ancestry, genealogy, lineage.

nesiç, -sci (*a.* BOT, MED) tissue.

nesil, -sli 1. generation; **2.** race, line; **3.** offspring, progeny; **nesli tükenmek** to die out.

nesir, -sri prose.

nesne 1. thing; **2.** GR object.

nesnel objective.

nesneleştirmek to objectify.

nesnelleşmek to become objective.

nesnellik objectivity.

neşe merriment, gaiety, joy; **-si yerinde** he is in good spirits.

neşelendirmek to render merry, to put s.o. in good spirits.

neşelenmek to become merry.

neşeli merry, cheerful, joyful, joyous.

neşesiz low-spirited, out of sorts (*or* spirits), downcast.

neşet, -ti 1. origination; emergence; **2.** ♀ *mf.*; ~ **etm. 1.** to originate (*-den* from), to arise (*-den* from); **2.** to graduate (*-den* from).

neşetli who graduated in (*a certain year*).

neşir, -şri 1. publication; **2.** dissemination, diffusion; **3.** broadcasting.

neşren through the mass media; in print.

neşretmek [x . .] **1.** to publish; **2.** to diffuse, to spread; **3.** to broadcast.

neşriyat, -ti [ā] publications.

neşter MED lancet.

neşvünema [ā] growth, development; ~ **bulmak** to grow.

net, -ti 1. clear, sharp; **2.** net.

netameli [ā] **1.** sinister; **2.** accident-prone.

netice [ī] result, consequence, outcome; end; **-de** in the end; **-sinde** as a result of ...

neticelendirmek to bring to an end, to conclude.

neticelenmek to come to an end, to end; to result (*ile* in).

neticesiz inconclusive, useless, fruitless, futile.

neuzübillah! God help us!

nevale [ā] provisions, food, victuals; **-yi düzmek** to provide food.

nevazil [ā] (common) cold, catarrh.

nevi, -v'i kind, sort, variety; **bu nevi** (*-den*) of this kind; **nev'i beşer** mankind; **nev'i şahsına münhasır** unique.

nevir, -vri the colo(u)r of s.o.'s face; **nevri dönmek** to fly off the handle.

nevralji MED neuralgia.

nevresim protective case (*made of sheeting*).

nevroloji neurology.

nevroz neurosis.

ney reed flute; ~ **çalmak** (*or* **üflemek**) to play the **ney.**

neye why?; ~ **doğruyu söylemiyorsun?** why aren't you telling the truth?

neyin *gen. of* **ne.**

neyle = **ne ile.**

neyse = **ne ise.**

neyzen ney player.

nezafet, -ti [ā] cleanliness.

nezaket, -ti [ā] courtesy, politeness; tact, delicacy; ~ **kesp etm.** to become delicate.

nezaketen [ā] [. x . .] as a matter of courtesy, out of politeness.

nezaketli [ā] courteous, polite; tactful.

nezaketsiz [ā] discourteous, impolite.

nezaret, -ti [ā] 1. superintendence, supervision; 2. surveillance; 3. direction, administration; 4. *obs.* ministry; ~ *altında* 1. under surveillance; 2. in police custody; ~ *etm.* to superintend, to oversee, to supervise; -*e almak* 1. to take into custody; 2. to put under surveillance.

nezarethane [. - . - .] lockup, jail.

nezih [ī] 1. decent, clean; 2. ♀ [x .] *mf.*

nezir, -*zri* vow.

nezle (common) cold, catarrh; ~ *olm.* to catch cold, to get a cold.

nezretmek [x . .] to vow; to pledge (-*e* to).

nıkris [ī] MED gout.

nısfiye short *ney.*

nısıf, -*sfı* half; ~ *daire* semicircle; ~ *kutur* radius; ~ *küre* hemisphere.

nışadır CHEM salamoniac; ammonia.

nışadırruhu, -*nu* CHEM ammonia.

nice [x .] how many …!, many a …!, so many …!; ~ ~ very many, a great many; ~ *senelere!* many happy returns of the day!

nicel quantitative.

nicelik quantity.

niçin [- .] [x .] why?, what for?

nida [ā] 1. cry, exclamation, shout; 2. GR exclamation, interjection; ~ *etm.* to exclaim; ~ *işareti* exclamation mark (*or* point).

nifak, -*kı* [ā] discord, strife, dissension; ~ *sokmak* to sow the seeds of discord.

nihai [. - -] final, decisive; ~ *karar* JUR final decision.

nihayet, -*ti* [ā] 1. end, conclusion; finish; 2. finally, at last; in the end; ~ *bulmak* to come to an end, to end, to finish; ~ *vermek* to conclude, to terminate, to bring to an end.

nihayetlendirmek [ā] to put an end to; to bring to an end.

nihayetlenmek [ā] to come to an end, to end.

nihayetsiz [ā] endless, unending; infinite, vast.

nikâh marriage (ceremony); ~ *altına almak* to marry; ~ *dairesi* marriage office; ~ *düşmek* (*for a marriage*) to be legally possible; ~ *etm.* (*bir kadını*) to marry *a woman* (-*e* to); to give *a woman* in marriage (-*e* to); ~ *kıymak* to perform a marriage ceremony; ~ *şahidi* witness at a marriage.

nikâhlamak 1. = *nikâh etm.*; 2. = *nikâh kıymak.*

nikâhlanmak to get married; to marry.

nikâhlı married, wedded.

nikâhsız unmarried, unwed.

nikbin [- -] optimistic.

nikbinlik [- - .] optimism.

nikel nickel.

nikelaj 1. nickeling; 2. nickel plate.

nikotin nicotine.

Nil *pr. n.* the Nile.

nilüfer [ī] 1. BOT water lily; 2. ♀ *wf.*

nim [ī] half; semi.

nimbus [x .] nimbus.

nimet, -*ti* [ī] 1. blessing; 2. the staff of life, bread; 3. ♀ *mf.*, *wf.*

nimresmi [- . .] semiofficial.

nine 1. grandmother, grandma, granny; 2. old woman.

ninni lullaby; ~ *söylemek* to sing a lullaby.

nisaiye gynecology.

nisan April.

nisanbalığı, -*nı* April fool.

nispet, -*ti* 1. proportion, ratio, rate; 2. relation(ship); 3. spite; ~ *etm.* 1. to compare; 2. to act spitefully; ~ *vermek* (*or* *yapmak*) to say *or* do s.th. out of spite.

nispetçi spiteful.

nispeten [x . .] 1. comparatively, relatively; 2. in comparison (-*e* to), compared (-*e* to).

nispi 1. proportional; 2. relative, comparative.

nişan [ā] 1. sign, indication, mark; 2. target; 3. engagement, betrothal; 4. engagement ceremony (*or* party); 5. POL medal, decoration, order; ~ *almak* 1. to aim (-*e* at), to take aim (-*e* at); 2. POL to receive a decoration; ~ *koymak* to make a mark; ~ *merasimi* (*or* *töreni*) engagement ceremony; ~ *takmak* 1. to put an engagement ring (-*e* on); 2. to pin a decoration (-*e* on); ~ *vermek* to bestow a decoration (-*e* on); ~ *yapmak* to have an engagement ceremony (*or* party); ~ *yüzüğü* engagement ring; -*dan dönmek* to break off an engagement.

nişancı [ā] sharpshooter, marksman.

nişane [ā] = *nişan 1.*

nişangâh [ā] 1. target; 2. rear sight (*of a gun*).

nişanlamak 1. to engage, to affiance,

to betroth; **2.** to take aim (-e at).
nişanlanma engagement, betrothal.
nişanlanmak 1. pass. of **nişanlamak**, to get engaged; **2.** to be marked.
nişanlı engaged, betrothed, intended; fiancé(e).
nişanlılık engagement.
nişasta CHEM (corn)starch, amylum.
nite [x .] obs. how?
nitekim [x . .] just as; as a matter of fact; in just the same way.
nitel qualitative.
niteleme vn. of **nitelemek**, qualification; ~ **sıfatı** GR descriptive adjective.
nitelemek 1. to describe, to characterize; **2.** GR to modify, to qualify.
nitelik quality, characteristic, attribute.
nitelikli 1. well-qualified; **2.** of ... quality.
niteliksiz of poor quality.
nitrat, -tı nitrate.
nitrikasit nitric acid.
nitrojen CHEM nitrogen.
niyabet, -ti [ā] regency; viceroyalty.
niyaz [ā] entreaty, supplication, plea; ~ **etm.** to plead, to entreat.
niye why?, what for?
niyet, -ti 1. intention, purpose, aim; **2.** fortune (written on a slip of paper); ~ **etm.** to intend, to aim, to mean; ~ **tutmak** to think of the matter about which one is inquiring when consulting a fortuneteller; **-i bozuk** having evil intentions; **-inde olm.** (bşi yapmak) to be intent on doing s.th.
niyetçi person who lets his rabbit or bird draw a **niyet 2.**
niyetlenmek s. **niyet etm.**
niyetli 1. intent; **2.** who intends to fast.
niza, -aı [ā] quarrel, dispute.
nizam [ā] **1.** order, arrangement, system, method, organization; **2.** regulation, rule; law; **-a sokmak** (or **koymak**) to put in order.
nizami [. - -] **1.** regulative, regulatory; legal; **2.** systematic, orderly, methodical.
nizamlı [ā] **1.** orderly, organized, systematic; **2.** lawful, legal.
nizamname [. - - .] regulations, statutes.
nizamsız [ā] **1.** disorderly, disordered, unsystematic; **2.** unlawful, illegal.
No. (abbr. for **numara**) No.
nobran harsh, rude, churlish.
Noel Christmas; ~ **ağacı** Christmas

tree; ~ **baba** Father Christmas, Am. Santa Claus.
nohudi [. - -] buff-colo(u)red, manila.
nohut, -du BOT chickpea; ~ **oda, bakla sofa** small house.
noksan [ā] **1.** deficient, defective, missing; **2.** deficiency, defect, shortcoming; **3.** want, lack.
noksanlık 1. deficiency, defect(iveness), shortcoming, **2.** lack, want.
noksansız 1. complete; **2.** flawless, perfect.
nokta 1. point (a. MATH), dot; **2.** speck, spot; **3.** GR full stop, Am. period; **4.** MIL sentry, post; ~ **koymak 1.** to put a full stop (or period); **2.** to wind up, to finish; ~ **olm.** sl. **1.** to get lost, to beat it; **2.** (for a dope-taker) to be so high he cannot move a muscle; **-sı -sına** exactly, in every way; **noktai nazar** viewpoint, point of view.
noktalama punctuation; ~ **işaretleri** punctuation marks.
noktalamak 1. to punctuate; **2.** to dot, to mark.
noktalı dotted; speckled; ~ **virgül** semicolon.
noktasız undotted.
nonoş little darling, honey.
norm norm.
normal, -li normal (a. MATH).
normalleşmek to become normal.
Norveç pr. n. Norway.
Norveçli pr. n. Norwegian.
nostalji nostalgia, homesickness.
not, -tu 1. note, memorandum; minute; **2.** school: mark, grade; ~ **almak 1.** to take (or make) notes; **2.** to get a grade; ~ **atmak** to record a grade; ~ **defteri** notebook; ~ **düşmek** to write down a note; ~ **etm** to note down; ~ **kırmak** to give low grades; ~ **tutmak** to take notes; ~ **vermek 1.** to give a grade (-e to); **2.** to pass judgment (-e on).
nota [x .] MUS & POL note.
noter notary public.
noterlik 1. notary public's office; **2.** notaryship.
nöbet, -ti 1. turn (of duty); **2.** watch (of a sentry); **3.** shift; **4.** MED onset, fit, attack; ~ **beklemek 1.** to stand guard; to keep watch; to be on duty; **2.** to await one's turn; ~ **değiştirmek** to change guard; ~ **gelmek** (b-ne) to have a fit; ~ **tutmak** s. ~ **beklemek 1.**
nöbetçi 1. sentry, watchman; **2.** on duty; ~ **eczane** pharmacy on night-duty;

~ kulübesi sentry box; **~ subayı** MIL duty officer.

nöbetçilik guard-duty.

nöbetleşe by turns.

nöbetşekeri, -ni sugar-candy.

nöron BIOL neuron.

nötr 1. neutral; **2.** neuter.

nötrlemek to neutralize.

nötrleşmek to become neutral.

nötron neutron; **~ bombası neutron** bomb.

Nuh [ü] *pr. n.* Noah; **~ der peygamber demez** he is as stubborn as a mule; **~ Nebi'den kalma** out of the ark; **-un gemisi** Noah's Ark.

numara [x . .] **1.** number; **2.** size, number (*shoe, etc.*); **3.** grade; **4.** *sl.* ruse, trick, stratagem; **~ koymak** to number; **~ yapmak** to fake, to pretend; **-sı yapmak** to pretend to be, to fake, to pose as; **-sını vermek** (*b-nin*) *fig.* to form a bad opinion of *s.o.*

numaracı *sl.* poseur, faker, phony.

numaralamak to number.

numaralı [x . . .] numbered; **yerler -dır** the seats are numbered; **iki numaralı ev** the house number two.

numarasız numberless, unnumbered.

numune sample, model, pattern.

numunelik sample, specimen.

nur [ü] **1.** light, brilliance; radiance; **2.** ♀ *mf., wf.*; **~ içinde yatsın** (*or* **toprağı ~ olsun**)**!** may he rest in peace; **~ ol!** bravo!, well done!; **~ topu gibi** very healthy and cute (*child*); **~ yüzlü** benevolent looking (*old man*).

nurani [- - -], **nurlu** [- .] bright, radiant.

nursuz [- .]; **~ pirsiz** *sl.* ugly and unlovely.

nutuk, -tku speech, oration, address; **~ atmak** (*or* **çekmek**) to sermonize, to hold forth; **~ söylemek** (*or* **vermek**) to make a speech; **nutka gelmek** to begin to speak; **nutku tutulmak** to be tongue-tied.

nü nude.

nüans nuance.

nüfus [ü] **1.** population, inhabitants; **2.** people, persons; **~ cüzdanı** (*or* **kâğıdı**) identity card (*or* booklet); **~ dağılımı** distribution of the population; **~ fazlalığı** overpopulation; **~ kütüğü** state register of persons; **~ memurluğu** public registration office; **~ sayımı** (population) census.

nüfusça as regards persons; **~ kayıp yoktur** there is no loss of human life.

nüfuslu 1. having … inhabitants; **2.** made up of … persons (*family*); **altı ~ bir aile** a family of six persons; **500.000 ~ bir şehir** a city of 500.000 people.

nüfuz [ü] **1.** influence, power, weight, pull; **2.** penetration; permeation; **~ etm. 1.** to penetrate; to permeate; **2.** to influence; **~ sahibi** influential, powerful (*person*).

nüfuzlu [. - .] influential, powerful, dominant.

nükleer nuclear; **~ silah** nuclear weapon.

nüksetmek [x . .] to relapse, to recur (*disease*).

nükte witticism, wisecrack; **~ yapmak** to wisecrack.

nükteci, nüktedan [ä] **1.** witty; **2.** wit, wisecracker.

nükteli witty.

nükûl, -lü withdrawal, abstention; **~ etm.** (*sözünden*) to withdraw, to go back on (*one's promise*).

nümayiş [ä] **1.** demonstration; **2.** show, pomp.

nümayişçi [ä] demonstrator.

nüsha 1. copy, specimen, transcript, duplicate; **2.** issue, number (*of a magazine, etc.*); **iki ~ olarak** in duplicate.

nüve nucleus.

nüzul, -lü [ü] apoplexy, stroke.

O

o¹ [-] ah!, oh!, o!, I say!

o² *-nu* **1.** he, she, it; **2.** that, those; **3.** the former, previous; **~ anda** at that moment; **~ bu** whether this or that; everybody; **~ denli** so much, that much; **~ duvar senin, bu duvar benim** to walk along rolling (*drunk*); **~ gün bu gün(dür)** since then, from that day on; **~ halde** in that case, therefore, hence, thus, so, consequently; **~ kadar** so much, so … that; **~ kapı senin bu kapı benim dolaşmak** to gallivant, to wander around; **~ saat 1.** at that hour; **2.** at once, immediately, directly, forthwith, straight, at that very moment, right away; **~ sırada** at that straight moment; **~ taraflı olmamak** not to pay attention to; **~ tarakta bezi olmamak** not to have anything with …, not to be interested in …; **~ vakit** (*or zaman*) **1.** then, after that; **2.** at that time; **3.** in that case; **~ yolda** in that way, like that; **~ yolun yolcusu 1.** to live immorally; **2.** he is in such a situation that he is going to end up with death; **~ nun için** that's why.

oba 1. large nomad tent; **2.** nomad family; **3.** temporary nomad camp.

obartı exaggeration.

obartıcı exaggerator.

obartılmak to be exaggerated.

obartma exaggeration, hyperbole.

obartmak to exaggerate.

obartmalı exaggerated.

obelisk, -ki obelisk.

obje object, thing.

objektif 1. objective; **2.** PHOT lens, objective.

objektivist objectivist.

objektivizm objectivism.

obligasyon COM bond.

obruk 1. PHYS concave; **2.** funnel-shaped; **3.** hollow ground.

observatuvar observatory.

obstrüksiyon 1. hindering, preventing, obstruction; **2.** *sports*: blocking.

obua oboe.

obuacı oboist.

obur gluttonous, greedy, voracious.

oburca greedily.

oburlaşmak to become gluttonous (*or* greedy).

oburluk gluttony, voracity.

obüs 1. shell; **2.** howitzer.

ocak¹ January; **~ ayı** January.

ocak² 1. fireplace, hearth; **2.** forge; **3.** (gas)burner; **4.** cooker, oven, range; **5.** furnace; **6.** distillery; **7.** mine, kiln, pit; **8.** quarry; **9.** bed, plantation; **10.** centre, focus, starting-point; **11.** (local) club, local branch (*of a party, etc.*); **12.** family, home; **13.** dynasty; **14.** military organization; **~ kaşı** stone stand for saucepans *etc.* in front of the hearth; **ocağı batmak** to be exhausted, to be ruined; **ocağı tütmek** to keep continuing one's family; **ocağına düşmek** (*b-nin*) to take s.o.'s refuge, to plead with s.o. for help; **ocağını söndürmek** to destroy the family (*-in* of); to exhaust one's family, to ruin.

ocakçı 1. stoker; **2.** chimney-sweep.

ocakçılık being a stoker (*or* chimney-sweep).

ocaklı 1. with a fireplace; **2.** s.o. who belongs to a specific organization (*Janissary*).

ocaklık 1. family estate given by the sovereign; **2.** fireplace; **3.** (supporting) beam; **4.** kitchen; **5.** chimney.

od fire; **~ yok ocak yok** *fig*. he is a poor devil (*or* wretch).

oda 1. room; **2.** board, chamber, association, society; **3.** *obs*. office; **4.** room, space, hall; **~ müziği** chamber music; **~ takımı** suite of furniture.

odabaşı, -nı s.o. in charge of the rooms in an inn.

odacı servant (*at an office or public building*).

odak 1. PHYS focus, focal point; **2.** *fig*. starting-point.

odaklama focusing.

odaklamak to focus.

odaklaşma focalization.

odaklaşmak to focalize.

odaklaştırma focalization.

odaklaştırmak to focalize.

odaklayıcı assistant cameraman, lenser.

odaksız afocal.

odalı which has certain number of rooms.

odalık concubine, odalisque (*up to 1908*).

oditoryum [. . x .] auditorium.

odun 1. firewood, log; 2. *fig.* (*a.* ~ *aleyhisselam*) foolish and rough fellow; 3. a sound thrashing; ~ *gibi* blockhead, rude, rough; ~ *kırmak* to chop wood, to split firewood; ~ *yarıcı* woodchopper.

oduncu 1. wood-cutter; 2. seller of firewood.

odunkömürü, *-nü* charcoal.

odunlaşma lignification.

odunlaşmak 1. to lignify; 2. *fig.* to get rough, to become insensitive to others.

odunluk 1. woodshed; 2. tree ready to be cut and used as firewood; 3. *fig.* rudeness, insensitivity to others.

odyometre audiometer.

odyovizüel audio-visual.

of! 1. oof!; 2. ow!, alas!, ah!, ouch!, oh!

ofis office, department, bureau.

oflamak to say 'ugh'; *oflayıp puflamak* to moan and groan, to huff and puff.

oflaz excellent, superb.

ofris twayblade.

ofsayt, *-dı* sports: offside.

ofset, *-ti* 1. (*baskısı*) offset (printing); 2. (*makinesi*) offset printing machine.

oftalmoloji ophthalmology.

oftalmoskop ophthalmoscope.

oğalamak *s.* *ovalamak.*

Oğan God.

oğdurmak *s.* *ovdurmak.*

Oğlak 1. AST Capricorn; 2. ♀ ZOO kid.

oğlan 1. boy, lad; 2. *cards*: knave; 3. catamite.

oğlancı pederast.

oğlancılık pederasty.

oğmaç *s.* *ovmaç.*

oğmak *s.* *ovmak.*

oğul, *-ğlu* 1. son; 2. ZOO swarm of bees; ~ *balı* virgin honey.

oğulcuk 1. dear little son; 2. embryo.

oğulluk 1. sonship; 2. stepson, adopted son.

oğulotu, *-nu* BOT bee balm, lemon balm.

oğunmak *s.* *ovunmak.*

oğuşturmak *s.* *ovuşturmak.*

Oğuz 1. an Oghuz Turk; 2. of the Oghuz Turks.

oğuz 1. young bull; 2. honest, sincere; 3. brave, valiant; 4. severe, rigorous; 5. provincial, peasant, villager; 6. ♀ *mf.*

Oğuzca the Turkish spoken by the Oghuz Turks.

oh oh!, ah!, indeed!; ~ *çekmek* to be malicious (*or* gloating), to rejoice over another's misfortune; ~ *demek* to (take a) rest, to have a breather; ~ *olsun!* it serves him right!

oha [x -] 1. *sl.* whoa!, hey you!; 2. whoa (*said to stop cattle*).

oje fingernail polish.

ojit augite.

ok, *-ku* 1. arrow; 2. pole, beam; 3. plowtail; 4. MATH sine versus; 5. prick, quill; ~ *atmak* to shoot an arrow; ~ *gibi* (*yerinden*) *fırlamak* to rush out of (*a place*); ~ *meydanı* archery ground; ~ *meydanında buhurdan yakmak* 1. to try to heat a big place with an inadequate mean of heater; 2. to try to use inadequate facilities to accomplish an important job; ~ *yaydan çıktı* *fig.* what's done is done, there's no turning back.

okaliptüs BOT eucalyptus.

okçu 1. archer; 2. maker *or* seller of arrows.

okçuluk 1. archery; 2. making *or* selling of arrows.

okka obs. (*Turkish weight measure*) oke, oka (= *1283* GR = *400 dirhem*); ~ *çekmek* to weigh heavier than it looks; ~ *dört yüz dirhem* facts are facts; *-nın altına gitmek* to bear the brunt, to be the victim.

okkalamak 1. to estimate the weight of s.th. by weighing it in hand; 2. *fig.* to flutter.

okkalı 1. heavy; 2. important, profitable; 3. big; 4. significant; ~ *kahve* big cup of Turkish coffee.

okkalık which weighs … okes.

oklamak 1. to shoot with an arrow; 2. to dart like an arrow.

oklanmak to get shot with an arrow.

oklava rolling pin; ~ (*or baston*) *yutmuş gibi* standing as if a stick were swallowed.

okluk quiver.

oklukirpi zoo porcupine.

okramak (*for a horse*) to whinny (*for water or food*).

oksalat CHEM oxalate.

oksijen 1. oxygen; 2. hydrogen peroxide.

oksijenlemek 1. CHEM to add oxygen into a compound, to oxygenize; **2.** to turn hair yellow with diluted oxygen.

oksijensizlik anoxia.

oksilit chemical substance containing peroxides of sodium and potassium.

oksit oxide

oksitlemek to oxidize.

oksitlenme oxidation.

oksitlenmek to get oxidized.

okşamak 1. to stroke, to caress, to pat, to fondle; **2.** to touch lightly; **3.** to resemble; **4.** sl. to beat up, to trash; **5.** to please, to flatter.

okşanmak to be caressed.

okşantı caress.

okşatmak caus. of **okşamak.**

okşayıcı pleasing (word, behave, etc.).

okşayış 1. caressing, fondling; **2.** way of caressing; **3.** caress.

oktan octane.

oktant, -tı octant, mariner's quadrant.

oktav octave.

oktruva [x . .] octroi, excise, city customs.

okul school.

okuldaş schoolmate.

okullu student, pupil.

okulöncesi, -ni 1. preschool; **2.** preschool period.

okulsonrası, -nı 1. post-school; **2.** period relating to post-school.

okuma reading; ~ **kitabı** primer, reader; ~ **yazma** reading and writing; ~ **yitimi** word blindness, alexia.

okumak 1. to read; **2.** to learn, to study; **3.** to recite; **4.** to sing; **5.** to call, to invite; **6.** to review (book); **7.** sl. to curse, to swear; **8.** to ruin s.o.; **9.** to decipher; **10.** to exorcise.

okumamış illiterate.

okume okoume, Gaboon mahogany.

okumuş educated, learned.

okumuşluk being educated.

okunaklı legible, readable.

okunaksız difficult to read, illegible.

okunmak 1. to be read (or recited); **2.** to be sung.

okuntu invitation (card).

okunuş way of reading (or singing).

okur reader.

okuryazar literate.

okuryazarlık literacy.

okutmak caus. of **okumak 1.** to have s.o. educate; **2.** to instruct s.o. in

s.th.; **3.** to teach s.o. s.th.; **4.** sl. to sell, to dispose of.

okutman lecturer, reader.

okuyucu 1. reader; **2.** singer; **3.** exorcist; **4.** s.o. sent around to invite people to a wedding.

oküler PHYS ocular, eyepiece.

okyanus GEOGR ocean.

Okyanusya [. . x .] pr. n. Oceania.

okyılanı, -nı ZOO water snake; viper.

ol obs. = **o²**

olabilir possible.

olabilirlik possibility.

olacak 1. suitable, appropriate; **2.** which will happen; **3.** inevitable, unavoidable; **4.** so-called; ~ **gibi degil** impossible, it doesn't look s.th. will happen.

olagelmek to happen now and then (or often), to continue, to go on.

olağan 1. common, usual, ordinary, normal; **2.** frequent, commonly happening.

olağandışı, -nı unusual, exceptional, strange, out of the common, abnormal.

olağanlaşmak to become commonplace.

olağanlık normality.

olağanüstü, -nü 1. extraordinary; unusual, uncommon; **2.** unexpected, exceptional; **3.** excellent, stunning, wonderful.

olağanüstülük extraordinariness.

olamaz [. x .] impossible, impracticable.

olanak possibility; ~ **sağlamak** to provide (the) opportunity for (or to).

olanaklı possible.

olanaksız impossible.

olanaksızlaşmak to become impossible.

olanaksızlaştırmak to make s.th. impossible.

olanaksızlık impossibility.

olanca [. x .] utmost, all of ...; ~ **kuvvetiyle** with all his might.

olası probable.

olasıcılık PHLS probabilism

olasılı based on probability.

olasılık probability.

olay 1. event, occurrence, incident; **2.** PHYS phenomenon; ~ **çıkarmak** to cause trouble, to provoke an incident.

olayanlatım narration.

olaybilim phenomenology.

olaycılık phenomenalism.

olaylı eventful; marked by unpleasant events.

olaysız uneventful.

olçum 1. quack doctor; **2.** quack; **3.** skilful.

oldu okay!, all right!, yes!

oldubitti fait accompli; **-ye** (or **olup-bittiye**) **getirmek** to confront s.o. with a fait accompli.

oldukça [. x .] rather, pretty, to some extent.

oldum olası s. **olmak.**

oldurgan GR causative (verb).

oldurmak 1. to cause to happen, to be; **2.** to ripen, to mature.

olefin CHEM olefin.

oleik CHEM oleic.

olein CHEM olein.

olgu 1. PHLS fact; **2.** MED case.

olgucu positivist.

olguculuk positivism.

olgun 1. ripe (fruit); mature (human being); **2.** experienced, mature.

olgunlaşma maturation.

olgunlaşmak 1. to become ripe; **2.** to become mature.

olgunlaştırmak to mature.

olgunluk ripeness; maturity; ~ **çağı** (or **yaşı**) age of maturity; ~ **sınavı** obs. university entrance examination.

oligarşi oligarchy.

oligoklaz oligoclase.

oligosen Oligacene, the period between Miocene and Eocene.

olijist GEOL hematite.

olimpiyat the Olympic games, the Olympics.

olivin GEOL olivine.

olmadık [x . .] **1.** unprecedented; **2.** incredible, unheard-of; **3.** out of place, inappropriate, insulting (word); **4.** impossible.

olmak, (-ur) 1. to be, to exist; **2.** to become, to happen, to occur, to take place, to come off; **3.** to be practicable, to be feasible, to be admissible; **4.** to ripen; to mature; **5.** to be prepared; **6.** to fade (away) (time); **7.** to come on (or near) (holiday); **8.** to have, to possess; **9.** to get, to catch (disease); **10.** to fit s.o., s.th., to suit s.o.; **11.** various verbal forms of it are used as helping verbs; **12.** (b-ne bş) to happen to s.o.; **13.** v/aux. to have, to get; **14.** pass. of **etmek; 15.** sl. to get drunk; **16.** to lose (opportunity, etc.); **ola ki** let's say …; **olan biten** (or **olup biten**) everything

that took place; **olan oldu** it is too late now, there is nothing to do; **oldu olacak kırıldı nacak** it is too late to do anything about s.th.; **oldu olanlar** all the worst things happened to s.o.: **oldum bittim** (or **oldum olası** or **oldum olasıya**) as long as s.o. remembers, always; **olsa olsa!** (or **olsun olsun**) at (the) most; ... **olsun,** ... **olsun** both ... and ..., all ..., **olup olacağı** that's all; **olur olmaz 1.** ordinary, whatsoever; **2.** unnecessary, unimportant. inappropriate.

olmamış 1. unripe, immature; **2.** s.th. hasn't been worked out well; **3.** s.th. which didn't happen.

olmayacak 1. impossible; **2.** inappropriate, unsuitable.

olmaz 1. impossible!, that will not do!; **2.** incredible, unheard-of; ~ ~ nothing is impossible.

olmazlı LOG absurd.

olmazlık LOG absurdity.

olmuş ripe, mature; ~ (or **pişmiş**) **armut gibi eline düşmek** to get s.th. without any effort.

olta [x .] fishing line; ~ **balığı** line-fish ~ **iğnesi** fish-hook; ~ **yemi** bait; **-ya vurmak 1.** to bite (fish); **2.** fig. to take the bait.

oluk 1. gutter-pipe, eaves; **2.** channel, chamfer; groove; **3.** transmittal; ~ **gibi** (or ~ ~) **akmak** to stream out, to flow in abundance (water, money, etc.).

olukçuk 1. small groove; **2.** MED sulculus.

oluklu 1. grooved; **2.** s.th. which has **oluk** attached to; ~ **kalem** gauge, engraver's tool; ~ **sac** corrugated iron sheet.

olumlama LOG affirmation.

olumlamak LOG to affirm.

olumlu 1. positive, affirmative; **2.** proved, useful; **3.** constructive, supportive; ~ **eylem** affirmative verb; ~ **tümce** affirmative sentence.

olumluk curriculum vitae.

olumluluk 1. positiveness; **2.** constructiveness.

olumsal LOG possible.

olumsallık LOG possibility, contingency.

olumsuz 1. negative; **2.** not constructive, negatory; ~ **eylem** negative verb; ~ **tümce** negative sentence.

olumsuzluk negativeness; ~ **eki** negative suffix.

olunmak *pass. of olmak.*

olupbitti *s. oldubitti.*

olur 1. possible, thinkable; **2.** all right!; ~ *olmaz* **1.** as soon as …, just after s.th. happens; **2.** anybody; **3.** any; ~ *şey* common, ordinary; ~ *şey* (*or iş*) *değil!* it is incredible!, it's impossible!; *-una bakmak* to try to see if s.th. is possible to (be) do(ne); (*bir işi*) *-una bırakmak* (*or bağlamak*) to let s.th. take its course; *-uyla yetinmek* to be contented with, to be satisfied with.

olurluk possibility.

oluş 1. way and nature of becoming; formation, genesis; **2.** event, happening.

oluşma formation, organization.

oluşmak to come into being, to be formed.

oluşturma formation, constitution.

oluşturmak to form, to constitute, to organize.

oluşuk GEOL formation.

oluşum 1. formation, constitution; **2.** GEOL & AST formation period.

om PHYS ohm.

om, oma 1. protuberance, tubercle; **2.** MED coccyx.

omaca 1. = *om*; **2.** stump of a tree.

ombra umber.

omça 1. part of the hip-bone; **2.** vine.

omlet, -ti omelet(te).

omur ANAT vertebra.

omurga 1. ANAT backbone, spine; **2.** NAUT keel; **3.** *fig.* vital part, base.

omurgalılar ZOO Vertebrata.

omurgasızlar ZOO Invertebrata.

omurilik ANAT spinal marrow (*or* cord).

omuz, -mzu shoulder; ~ *başı* end of the shoulder; ~ *çevirmek* to cold--shoulder; ~ *kaldırmak* to pretend not to know; ~ *-a* **1.** shoulder to shoulder; **2.** *fig.* supportive, together; ~ *öpüşmek* to be almost equal; ~ *silkmek* to shrug the shoulders; ~ *vermek* **1.** to press against s.th. with shoulder; **2.** to support, to help; *-da taşımak* to hono(u)r, to hold in high esteem; *-ları çökmek* to get exhausted, to get ruined; *-una binmek* (*b-nin*) to be a burden to *s.o.*

omuzdaş *contp.* accomplice.

omuzdaşlık mutual support, cooperation, solidarity.

omuzlamak 1. to shoulder; **2.** to press s.th. with shoulder; **3.** *sl.* to steal, to walk off with; **4.** *fig.* to support, to help.

omuzluk 1. shoulder strap, epaulet; **2.** shoulder yoke; **3.** NAUT quarter.

on ten; ~ *kez* (*or defa or kere*) ten times; ~ (*or beş*) *para etmez* worthless; ~ *paralık etm.* (*b-ni*) to insult *s.o.*, to put *s.o.* into a bad position; ~ *parasız* penniless, flat broke; ~ *parmağında* ~ *hüner* (*or marifet*) very skillful, capable, clever; ~ *parmağında* ~ *kara* slanderous.

ona to him; to her; to it; ~ *buna dil uzatmak* to speak tactlessly; ~ *sebep* P for that reason, therefore, that is why.

onaltılık MUS sixteenth note.

onama approval; certification.

onamak 1. to approve; **2.** = *onaylamak.*

onanizm masturbation.

onanmak to be approved; to be certified.

onar ten each, ten apiece; ~ ~ ten at a time, in tens, by tens.

onarılmak to be repaired, to be mended, to be fixed, to be restored.

onarım 1. repair(s); **2.** restoration.

onarımcı repairer, restorer.

onarma repair; restoration.

onarmak 1. to repair; **2.** to restore; **3.** *fig.* to make amendments, to make up for, to compensate.

onat, -tı 1. proper; **2.** useful; **3.** honest, straightforward.

onay 1. suitable, convenient; **2.** approval; *-ını almak* (*b-nin*) to get *s.o.*'s approval (*or* consent).

onayaklılar Decapoda.

onaylama 1. approval; **2.** ratification.

onaylamak 1. to approve; **2.** to ratify; to certify.

onaylı approved; ratified; certified.

onaysız unapproved; unratified; uncertified.

onbaşı, -yı MIL corporal.

onbaşılık 1. being a corporal; **2.** corporalship.

onca [x .] **1.** according to him (*or* her); **2.** so many; so much.

onculayın 1. according to him (*or* her); **2.** like him (*or* her).

onda tenth.

ondalık 1. a tenth; ten per cent compensation; **2.** HIST a tax paid at the rate of ten per cent on crops; **3.** MATH decimal; **~ kesir** decimal fraction; **~ sayı** decimal number.

ondalıkçı one who works on a ten per cent commission.

ondurmak 1. to improve; **2.** to cure; to heal.

ondüle 1. curly, wavy (*hair*); **2.** waterwave, permanent wave, F perm.

ogun 1. very productive; **2.** developed, prosperous, flourishing; **3.** happy; **4.** lucky; **5.** totem; **6.** armorial bearings; **~ besisuyu** BOT nourishment carried from the leaves to the rest of the plant.

ongunculuk totemism.

ongunluk 1. prosperity; **2.** productivity; **3.** happiness.

onikiparmakbağırsağı, -nı ANAT duodenum.

onikitelli twelve-stringed guitar-shaped instrument.

oniks meerschaum.

onlar *pl. of* **o**, they.

online IT *adj. & adv.* online; **~ alışveriş** online shopping; **~ bankacılık** online banking.

onlu 1. *cards*: the ten; **2.** having ten parts.

onluk 1. of ten parts; **2.** ten kuruş piece, ten lira bill.

onmak 1. to improve, to get better; **2.** to heal (up), to recover (**from**), to get well; **3.** to find happiness.

ons ounce (28, 35. *gramme*).

onsuz without him (*or* her *or* it).

ontoloji ontology.

onu him, her, it.

onulmak *pass. of* **onmak.**

onulmaz incurable.

onun his, her, its.

onuncu tenth; in the tenth order.

onur 1. hono(u)r; **2.** sense of hono(u)r, dignity, pride, self-respect; **~ kurulu** discipline committee; **~ üyesi** honorary member; **-una dokunmak** (*b-nin*) to hurt *s.o.*'s pride; **-una yedirememek** not to be able to stomach.

onurlandırmak to hono(u)r, to do hono(u)r to, to hono(u)r s.o. with one's presence.

onurlanmak to acquire hono(u)r, to be hono(u)red; to feel proud.

onurlu self-respecting, dignified, proud.

onursal honorary; **~ başkan** honorary president; **~ üye** honorary member.

onursuz without dignity, lacking in self-respect.

onursuzluk lack of self-respect.

oosfer oosphere.

oosit, -ti oocyte.

opal, -li opal.

opera [x . .] MUS **1.** opera; **2.** opera house.

operakomik comic opera.

operasyon 1. MED operation; **2.** operation.

operatör 1. MED surgeon; **2.** operator (*of a machine*); **3.** TYP type-setter; **4.** cameraman.

operet, -ti operetta.

oportünist, -ti opportunist.

oportünizm opportunism.

optik 1. optics; **2.** optical.

optimist, -ti optimist.

optimizm optimism.

optimum optimum; the most suitable (*or* favo(u)rable).

opus opus.

ora [x .] that place; **~ senin bura benim dolaşmak** (*or* **gezinmek**) to go around from place to place; **-da** there; **-da burada** here ad there; **-dan** from there; **-larda** there(abouts); **-larda olmamak** not to listen to; to pretend not to hear (*or* know); **-ya** there, thither.

oracıkta just over there.

orak 1. sickle; **2.** *fig.* harvest time.

orakböceği, -ni ZOO cicada.

orakçı reaper.

oralı [x . .] of that place; **~ olmamak** *fig.* not to pay attention, not to take notice of; to feign indifference.

oramiral, -li vice-admiral.

oran 1. proportion (*a.* MATH); ratio; **2.** indifferent proportion; **3.** estimate; **4.** measure, scale.

orangutan ZOO orangutan.

oranla relatively, spitefully, in comparison with.

oranlamak 1. to calculate, to measure; **2.** to estimate; **3.** to compare (*ile* with).

oranlı 1. proportioned; **2.** symmetrical; **3.** appropriate.

oransız 1. badly proportioned; **2.** unsymmetrical.

oransızlık lack of proportion.

orantı MATH proportion.

orantılı 1. balanced, well-proportioned; **2.** MATH proportional.

orası, -nı 1. that place; **2.** that aspect of the matter.

oratoryo [. . x .] oratorio.

ordinaryus [. . x .] senior professor holding a chair in a university, distinguished (*professor*).

ordinat, *-tı* MATH ordinate.

ordino [. x .] delivery order; COM certificate of ownership; boarding slip.

ordonat, *-tı* MIL supply service.

ordövr hors d'oeuvres.

ordu 1. army; 2. army arrangement; 3. crowd.

ordubozan 1. P varicose veins; 2. public enemy; 3. spoilsport.

ordubozanlık being a spoilsport.

orduevi, *-ni* officers' club.

ordugâh MIL military camp; bivouac.

org, *-gu* MUS organ.

organ 1. ANAT & POL organ; 2. publication, organ.

organaktarımı transplantation.

organik organic; ~ *kimya* organic chemistry; ~ *kütle* organic rock.

organizasyon organization.

organizatör organizer.

organizma [. . x .] organism.

organlaşmak BIOL to develop organs, to become an organ.

organze organza.

orgazm climax.

orgeneral, *-li* MIL full general.

orijin source, origin.

orijinal, *-li* 1. original (*picture, etc.*); 2. *contp.* specific, peculiar; 3. original (*parts, etc.*).

orijinallik 1. originality; 2. *fig.* unusualness, differentness.

orkestra MUS orchestra.

orkide [. x .] BOT orchid.

orkinos [x . .] ZOO tuna, tunny-fish.

orkit, *-ti* orchitis.

orman forest, wood; ~ *gibi* thick (*hair, eyebrow, etc.*); ~ *kebabı* stew (*made of mutton and vegetables*); ~ *kibarı iro.* rude fellow, boor, ruffian; ~ *taşlamak fig.* to sound s.o.

ormancı 1. forester; 2. forestry specialist.

ormancılık 1. forestry; 2. being a forester.

ormanborozu, *-nu* blackcock.

ormanlaşmak to become forested.

ormanlık woodland; thickly wooded.

ormansıçanı *-nı* ZOO wood mouse.

ormansız forestless.

ornatmak to substitute.

ornitolog ornithologist.

ornitoloji ornithology.

orojeni GEOL orogeny.

orospu prostitute, whore, harlot; ~ *çocuğu sl.* 1. bastard, son of a bitch; 2. cunning, crafty, wily.

orospuluk 1. prostitution; 2. dirty trick, treachery.

orostopolluk *sl.* trick, ruse.

orsa [x .] NAUT the weather side, luff; ~ *alabanda* down with the helm!; ~ *etm.* to luff up; ~ *poca* (*or baca*) 1. luffing and falling off; 2. *fig.* struggling along.

orsalamak NAUT to hug the wind, to luff.

orta 1. middle, centre; 2. PHYS place, field; 3. MATH proportion; 4. environment, culture, medium; 5. middle ..., central ..., intermediate ...; 6. average, medium; ~ *boy* medium size, medium length; ~ *boylu* of medium height ~ *dalga* PHYS medium wave; ~ *dikme* MATH perpendicular bisector; ~ *halli* from middle-class; ~ *hizmetçisi* housemaid; ~ *işi* housework; ~ *karar* of middling quality, moderate, somewhat appropriate; ~ *malı* 1. common property; 2. common, usual; 3. prostitute, whore; ~ *şekerli* 1. having sugar neither too much nor too little (*coffee*); 2. moderate, so so (*situation*); ~ *terim* LOG middle term; ~ *yaşlı* middle-aged; *-da* 1. in the middle; 2. seizable, visible, obvious; 3. in public, publicly; *-da bırakmak* to abandon, to desert, to leave in the lurch; *-da fol yok yumurta yok* F there is no apparent reason whatsoever; *-da kalmak* 1. to be left without home; 2. to be in a two-alternative situation; *-da olm.* to have to be considered; *-dan kaldırmak* 1. to hide; 2. to remove, to abolish, to do away with; 3. *fig.* to kill; *-dan kalkmak* 1. to disappear, to vanish; 2. to be removed, to be ruined; 3. to get killed; *-dan kaybolmak* to disappear, to vanish; *-dan söylemek* to speak in a group without mentioning anyone, to drop hints; *-nın sağı* POL group which is to the right of centre; *-nın solu* POL group which is to the left of centre; *-ya almak* 1. to circle, to surround; 2. *fig.* to press s.o. hard; *-ya atılmak* 1. to be proposed, to be suggested; 2. to volunteer; *-ya atmak* to bring up, to throw up, to suggest; *-ya bir balgam atmak b.s.* to throw up a malicious hint that upsets things; **-ya çıkarmak** to prove, to reveal, to bring to light; **-ya çıkmak 1.** to arise, to come into being; **2.** to appear, to emerge; **-ya dökmek 1.** to display, to disclose; **2.** to explain, to tell; **-ya düşmek** to become a prostitute; **-ya koymak 1.** to put forward; **2.** to expose, to present for consideration.

ortaağırlık 1. middleweight (*boxer, etc*.); **2.** a class in boxing (*between 71-75 kg*); a class in wrestling, weight-lifting and shot (*between 72-79 kg*).

ortaç GR participle, verbal adjective.

ortaçağ the Middle Ages.

ortadamar BOT the large vein in the middle of a leaf.

ortaderi mesoderm.

ortadirek *fig.* middle class.

Ortadoğu the Middle East.

ortaelçi minister plenipotentiary.

ortak 1. companion, COM partner, associate, copartner; **2.** *contp.* accomplice; **3.** fellow wife; **4.** common; ~ **olm.** to participate in, to share in; ~ **ölçülmez sayılar** MATH incommensurable numbers; ~ **tam bölen** MATH common divisor.

ortakçı 1. s.o. who assists a farmer in return for a share of the crop; **2.** BIOL commensal.

ortakkat, -tı MATH common multiple.

ortaklaşa 1. in common, jointly; **2.** joint business; **3.** common, joint, shared, collective.

ortaklaşacı collectivist.

ortaklaşacılık collectivism.

ortaklaşmak to enter into partnership with s.o., to become partners.

ortaklık 1. partnership; **2.** COM company, firm, corporation.

ortakulak ANAT middle ear, tympanum.

ortakyapım joint production.

ortakyaşama BIOL symbiosis.

ortakyaşar BIOL symbiont.

ortakyönetim coalition.

ortalama 1. average, mean; **2.** right through; **3.** in the middle.

ortalamak 1. to reach the middle of; **2.** to divide in the middle; **3.** to put in the midst.

ortalık 1. surroundings, the area around; **2.** PHYS medium; **3.** people, world, the public; ~ **ağarmak** (*for the dawn*) to break; ~ **düzelmek** to improve, to get better; ~ **kararmak** to get

dark, (*for night*) to fall; ~ **karışmak** to be upside down, to be topsy-turvy; ~ **yatışmak** to calm down, to be restored; **ortalığı birbirine katmak** to cause tumult, to cause confusion and excitement, to make a mess; **ortalığı ... götürmek** to cover the whole place; **-ta** in sight, around, within view.

ortam 1. environment, surroundings; **2.** atmosphere.

ortanca[1] **1.** second eldest (*for three brothers or sisters*); **2.** middle, middling.

ortanca[2] BOT hydrangea.

ortaokul secondary school, middle school.

ortaoyunu, -nu a theatrical genre once popular in Turkey.

ortaöğretim secondary education.

ortaparmak middle finger.

ortayuvar mesosphere.

Ortodoks Orthodox.

Ortodoksluk Orthodoxy.

ortoklaz GEOL orthoclase.

ortopedi orthopedics.

ortopedik orthopedic.

ortopedist orthopedist.

ortoz *s.* **ortoklaz.**

oruç, -cu ECCL fasting, fast, the Moslem daytime fast during the month of Ramazan; ~ **açmak** to break the fast (*at sunset*); ~ **bozmak** to break the fast (*at an improper time, before sunset*); ~ **tutmak** to fast; ~ **yemek** not to fast.

oruçlu fasting.

oruçsuz not fasting.

orun 1. private place; **2.** place, abode, office.

orya [x .] *cards*: diamond.

oryantal Oriental.

oryantalist, -ti Orientalist.

Osmanlı 1. an Ottoman (Turk); **2.** Ottoman; **3.** *fig.* brave and noble.

Osmanlıca the Ottoman Turkish language.

Osmanlılık 1. being an Ottoman; **2.** the period of Ottoman empire.

osmiyum CHEM osmium.

osurgan s.o. who farts a lot.

osurganböceği, -ni ZOO stag beetle.

osurmak to fart, to break wind.

osuruk *sl.* fart; **osuruğu cinli** *sl.* ill-humo(u)red, very touchy, easily effervesced.

oşinografi GEOGR oceanography.

ot, **-tu 1.** herb, plant; **2.** (*a. yeşil* ~) grass; **3.** (*a. kuru* ~) hay; **4.** weed; **5.** poison; **6.** medicine; **7.** depilatory; **8.** *sl.* hashish; **9.** stuffed with grass (*pillow, cushion, etc.*); **10.** fodder; ~ **tutunmak** to rub a depilatory on one's body; ~ **yiyenler** zoo herbivorous; ~ **yoldurmak** (*b-ne*) to give *s.o.* a hard time, to put *s.o.* to trouble.

otağ, otak pavilion, large nomad tent.

otalamak **1.** to poison; **2.** to treat medically.

otamak to treat medically.

otantik authentic.

otarmak to pasture.

otarşi autarky.

otçul zoo herbivorous.

otel hotel.

otelci hotel-keeper, hotelier.

otelcilik hotel industry; hotel management.

otizm PSYCH autism.

otlak pasture, grassy area, pastureland.

otlakçı *sl.* sponger, parasite.

otlakçılık *sl.* being a sponger.

otlakıye [ā] tax (*paid by those who pasture their animals on government land*).

otlamak **1.** to graze, to pasture; **2.** *sl.* to sponge; **3.** *sl.* to pitch, to steal.

otlanmak **1.** to graze, to pasture; **2.** to be grazed over.

otlatılmak *pass. of* **otlatmak.**

otlatmak to put out to graze.

otlubağa zoo toad.

otluk **1.** pastureland, grassy area; **2.** hayrick, haystack; **3.** hay-barn.

oto[1] *prefix* with the meaning of «self».

oto[2] motorcar, car, auto, automobile.

otoban highway, autobahn.

otobiyografi autobiography.

otobüs bus, motor coach, autobus.

otobüsçü **1.** *s.o.* who owns and runs a line of buses; **2.** bus driver.

otodidakt, **-tı** self-taught person, autodidact.

otoerotizm autoerotism.

otogar bus station.

otokar large motorcar, bus.

otoklav autoclave.

otokrasi autocracy.

otokrat, **-tı** autocrat.

otokritik self-criticism, autocriticism.

otolit, **-ti** otolith, ear stone.

otoman **1.** ottoman (*a kind of coach*); **2.** ottoman (*fabric*).

otomasyon automation.

otomat, **-tı 1.** automaton, robot; **2.** flash heater, geyser; **3.** system in which electric lights are switched on manually and switched off automatically.

otomatik automatic.

otomatikman automatically.

otomatikleşmek to become automatic.

otomatizm automatism.

otomobil car, automobile.

otomotiv automotive industry.

otonom autonomous.

otonomi autonomy.

otopark, **-kı** car park; parking lot; parking building.

otoplasti MED autoplasty.

otopsi autopsy, postmortem examination.

otoray autorail, rail-car.

otorite **1.** authority, standing; **2.** authority (*scientifically*); **3.** JUR supreme (*or* executive) power.

otoriter authoritarian.

otosist, **-ti** otocyst.

otostop, **-pu** hitchhiking; ~ **yapmak** to hitch-hike.

otostopçu hitchhiker.

otoyol super highway, autobahn.

otçu, otsul BOT herbaceous.

oturacak seat.

oturak **1.** chamberpot; **2.** seat, foot, bottom; **3.** residence; **4.** oar-bench, thwart; ~ **âlemi** a drinking party with belly dancers.

oturaklı **1.** solidly constructed, with solid foundation; **2.** *fig.* grave, sober, serious; **3.** striking, appropriate (*word*).

oturaklılık sedateness, dignity, sobriety.

oturma **1.** sitting; **2.** residing; ~ **belgesi** residence permit; ~ **grevi** slow-down strike; ~ **odası** living room.

oturmak **1.** to sit down on; **2.** to sit; **3.** to live; to dwell in, to reside; **4.** to fit; **5.** to loaf, to laze; **6.** to sink; **7.** NAUT to run ashore; **8.** CHEM to precipitate; **9.** to settle; **10.** F to cost; **11.** to come to an agreement; **12.** to take up (*a post*); **13.** to take root, to be accepted; **oturup kalkmak** to act on.

oturmuş *fig.* rooted, settled.

oturtma **1.** *vn. of* **oturtmak**; **2.** *a dish made with ground meat and vegetables.*

oturtmak *caus. of* **oturmak 1.** to place,

to put (*vase, etc.*); **2.** to seat, to sit s.o. down; **3.** to set, to mount, to emboss; **4.** NAUT to run aground on.

oturtmalık ARCH basement, stereobate.

oturulmak *impersonal pass.* **1.** to sit; **2.** to live, to dwell in.

oturum 1. sitting, session; **2.** JUR hearing; **~ açmak** IT to log in *a.* on (*to*); **~ kapamak** IT to log out (*from*).

oturuş way of sitting.

oturuşmak to calm down; to slow down.

otuz thirty; **-bir** a card game; **-bir çekmek** *sl.* to wank off, to jerk off, to masturbate, to beat one's meat.

otuzar MATH thirty at a time, thirty each.

otuzuncu thirtieth.

ova grassy plain, meadow.

oval, -li oval.

ovalamak 1. to grind, to rub, to powder, to pulverize, to crumble, to press with the hands; **2.** to massage, to knead.

ovalı s.o. who lives in a plain.

ovalık grassy land, plain, level and extensive (*area*).

ovmak 1. to massage, to knead, to rub; **2.** to rub, to scrub, to scour; **3.** to polish.

ovogon BOT oogonium.

ovolit, -ti GEOL oolite.

ovulmak 1. to be kneaded, to be massaged, to be rubbed; **2.** to be scoured, to be scrubbed.

ovuşturmak to massage, to rub, to knead, to wipe one's eyes.

oy 1. opinion, view, sight; **2.** vote; **3.** voting; **~ birliği 1.** unanimity; **2.** unanimous vote; **~ birliğiyle** unanimously; **~ çokluğu** majority; **~ hakkı** the right of voting; **~ sandığı** ballot box; **~ vermek** to vote for; **-a koymak** (*bşi*) to put *s.th.* to the vote.

oya pinking, embroidery; **~ gibi** fine and dainty.

oyacı maker *or* seller of embroidery.

oyalamak 1. to distract one's attention; **2.** to detain; **3.** to delay, to put off, to hold out; **4.** to keep busy, to amuse; **5.** to pink, to embroider.

oyalanmak 1. *pass of* **oyalamak; 2.** to make o.s. merry; **2.** to kill time, to dawdle.

oyalayıcı amusing, keeping busy.

oyalı edged with embroidery.

oydaş of the same opinion, like-minded.

oylama voting, poll.

oylamak to vote on, to put s.th. to the vote.

oylanmak to be voted on.

oyluk thigh; **~ kemiği** femur, thighbone.

oylum 1. volume, size; **2.** hollowed out, carved; **3.** depth, three dimensional effect (*painting*); **~~** curling (*smoke*), saw-toothed.

oylumlama modeling, giving s.th. three-dimensional shape (*fine arts*).

oylumlu bulk, voluminous; **2.** *fig.* large, great.

oyma 1. *vn. of* **oymak; 2.** craving, engraving, wood-carving, fretwork, stamping, sculpture; **3.** carved, engraved, stamped, sculptured, hollowed out.

oymabaskı engraving (*printing process using the engraved plates*).

oymacı sculptor, engraver.

oymacılık the art of engraving (*or* carving).

oymak¹ 1. to scoop out, to dig out; **2.** to engrave, to carve.

oymak² 1. subdivision, tribe; **2.** troop of boy scouts; **~ beyi** scoutmaster.

oymalı carved, engraved, chisel(l)ed; **~ yaprak** BOT lobate leaf.

oynak 1. frisky, restless (*horse*); **2.** playful; **3.** unstable; **4.** MEC loose, having much play; **5.** capricious, wayward; **6.** coquettish; **7.** ANAT joint.

oynaklık 1. liveliness, being restless; **2.** capricious behavio(u)r.

oynamak 1. to play, to amuse o.s.; **2.** to frisk, to skip (*horse*); **3.** to be loose (*tooth, etc.*); **4.** COM to fluctuate; **5.** to play (*cards, game, etc.*); **6.** to dance; **7.** to perform (*a play*); **8.** (*bşle*) to stake, to jeopardize; **9.** to trifle with, to risk; **10.** to be on (*film, play, etc.*); **11.** to flicker, to vibrate; **12.** to fool with, to tamper with; **13.** to show differences (*price*); **14.** to slip (*of the ground*); **Oynama!** (*negative*) **1.** do not dawdle! **2.** do not touch that!, do not play with it!; **oynaya oynaya** with great pleasure, joyfully.

oynaş lover, lovemate.

oynaşmak 1. to play with one another; **2.** to have a love affair.

oynatmak 1. *caus. of* **oynamak; 2.** to cause to play; **2.** to keep amused (*child*); **3.** to cause to move, to stir; **4.** to make s.o. dance; **5.** to lose one's mind, to go off one's nut.

oysa(ki) [x . .] but, yet, however, whereas.

oyuk 1. hollowed out; **2.** cave, cavity, hole.

oyulga tacking, basting.

oyulga(la)mak to tack together, to bast together.

oyulgan ulcer.

oyulmak *pass. of* **oymak.**

oyum 1. hollowing; **2.** cutting, carving, engraving; **3.** cavity, cave hole.

oyun 1. game (*a. fig.*); **2.** THEAT performance; **3.** (stage) play; **4.** dance; **5.** wrestling (*match*); **6.** wrestling technic; **7.** cheat, swindle; **8.** gambling; **9.** trick; ~ *almak* to win a game; ~ *çıkarmak sports:* to play a game; ~ *etmek* (*or oynamak*) to play a trick on, to fool, to dupe; ~ *havası* MUS melody, tone, tune (*folk dances*); ~ *kağıdı* playing card; ~ *vermek* to lose a game; *-a çıkmak* THEAT to appear on the stage; *-a gelmek* to be deceived, to be duped; *-a getirmek* to deceive, to swindle, to dupe; *-u almak* to win

the game; *Bizans -u* trick, fraud, wile, intrigue.

oyunbaz 1. *obs.* playful, frolicsome; **2.** swindler; **3.** tricker.

oyunbazlık trickery, deceitfulness.

oyunbozan spoil-sport, kill-joy, intruder, troublemaker.

oyunbozanlık being a spoil-sport; ~ *etm.* to be a spoil-sport.

oyuncak 1. toy, plaything; **2.** *fig.* trifle, child's play, easy job; **3.** *fig.* sport, plaything.

oyuncakçı maker *or* seller of toys.

oyuncakçılık the toy business.

oyuncu 1. player; **2.** actor, player, actress; **3.** dancer; **4.** *s.* **oyunbaz**; **5.** gambler.

oyunculuk 1. being a player; **2.** acting, being an actor (*or* actress); **3.** trickery.

oyunevi, -ni theatre, *Am.* theater.

oyuntu hollow, hole, cavity.

ozalit Ozalid.

ozan 1. poet; **2.** wandering minstrel.

ozanca like a poet, in a poetic manner.

ozanlık 1. being a poet; **2.** poetic talent.

ozansı poetastrical.

ozon CHEM ozone.

Ö

ö [-] boo!, ugh!, phew!, oof!

öbek heap, pile, group, crowd; ~ ~ in groups, in heaps, in crowds.

öbür [x .] **1.** the other (*of two*); **2.** the former; ~ *gün* the day after tomorrow; ~ *dünya* the hereafter, the next world; ~ *hafta* the week after next.

öbürkü F *s.* **öbürü.**

öbürü, -nü the other one (*person or thing*).

öcü (*child's language*) bad man, evil, ogre, bogyman.

öç, -cü revenge, vengeance; ~ *almak* (*or çıkarmak*) (*b-den*) **1.** to revenge *o.s.* (*or* be revenged) on *s.o.*; **2.** to get revenge.

öd, -dü gall, bile; *-ü kopmak* (*or patlamak*) to be frightened to death, to be scared out of one's wits; *-ünü koparmak* (*or patlatmak*) to frighten to death, to scare s.o. out of his wits.

ödağacı, -nı BOT agalloch tree.

ödem MED edema.

ödeme payment, disbursement; ~ *emri* JUR default summons, writ of execution; ~ *kabiliyeti* solvency; *-lerin tatili* suspension of payment.

ödemek 1. to pay, to disburse; **2.** to indemnify, to compensate; **3.** COM to amortize, to redeem.

ödemeli 1. cash on delivery payment, *Am.* collect; **2.** (*to send s.th.*) cash on delivery (*c.o.d.*); **3.** TELEPH reversed charge.

ödenek appropriations, allotments, allowance.

ödenmek *pass. of* **ödemek.**

ödenti 1. membership fee; **2.** proceeds, receipts, income.

ödeşmek to settle (*or* square) accounts with each other.

ödetmek *caus. of* **ödemek.**

ödev 1. duty, obligation, liability, task, assignment, job; **2.** homework.

ödevbilim deontology.

ödkesesi, -ni gall bladder.

ödlek 1. frightened, scared; **2.** cowardly, timid.

ödül 1. prize; **2.** reward, recompense, premium.

ödüllendirmek to award s.o. a prize, to give s.o. a prize.

ödün compensation, equalization, restitution, amends **(for)**, indemnity; **~ vermek** to compensate, to indemnify, to make a concession.

ödünç, -cü 1. lent, loaned; **2.** borrowed, on loan; **~ almak** to borrow; **~ para** loan; **~ vermek** to lend.

ödünleme compensation, concession.

ödünlemek to compensate, to make up **(for)**.

öf phew!, ugh!, boo!, how nauseous!, how disgusting!, alas!, oh!, oof!

öfke anger, rage, wrath, fury; **~ baldan tatlıdır** it is to shout at when you are angry; **~ topuklarına çıkmak** *(b-nin)* to fill with great rage; **-si burnunda** hot-headed; **-sini çıkarmak** *(or al-mak) (b-den)* to vent one's anger on *s.o.*; **-sini yenmek** to control one's temper, to get hold of *o.s.*

öfkelendirmek to anger, to bring into a rage, to make angry, to infuriate.

öfkelenmek to get angry, to grow angry *(-e* at).

öfkeli choleric, hotheaded, angry, furious, *Am.* mad **(with)**.

öğe element, component.

öğle noon; **~ paydosu** *(or tatili or din-lencesi)* lunch break; **~ üstü** *(or üze-ri)* about noon; **~ yemeği** lunch; **-(n)den önce** *(or evvel)* in the morning, before noon; **-(n)den sonra** in the afternoon.

öğlen 1. F noon, midday; **2.** AST meridian.

öğlende at noon, about midday.

öğleyin *s.* **öğlende**.

öğmek *s.* **övmek**.

öğrenci student, pupil.

öğrencilik being a student.

öğrenim education, study, formation.

öğrenme learning.

öğrenmek 1. to learn; **2.** to become familiar with; **3.** to hear, to inquire.

öğrenmelik scholarship.

öğreti[1] doctrine, principles.

öğretici educational, didactic, instructive *(film, etc.)*

öğretim instruction, lessons; **~ bilgisi** didactics; **~ görevlisi** lecturer; **~ iz-lencesi** curriculum; **~ üyesi** universi-

ty teacher; **~ yardımcıları** university teachers who are not lecturers and below in the rank than of associate professors; **~ yılı** school year.

öğretmek 1. to teach, to impart, to instruct, to give lessons; **2.** to teach, to show *(treat, menace).*

öğretmen teacher.

öğretmenlik teaching, being a teacher.

öğünmek *s.* **övünmek**.

öğür 1. of the same age; **2.** familiar, intimate; **3.** used to, accustomed to; **4.** group, class, party; **~ olm.** to get used to, to get very familiar with.

öğürmek 1. to retch; **2.** to bellow; **öğü-receği gelmek** *fig.* to feel very disgusted.

öğürtmek *caus. of* **öğürmek**.

öğürtü 1. retching; **2.** retching sound.

öğüt, -dü advice, counsel, admonition, lesson, warning; **~ vermek** *(or -te bu-lunmak)* to advise, to counsel.

öğütlemek to advise, to counsel *(s.o. to do s.th.).*

öğütmek 1. to grind; **2.** *fig.* to digest.

öğütücü 1. grinder; **2.** digestive …

öğütücüdiş molar (tooth).

öğütülmek *pass. of.* **öğütmek**.

öhö coughing sound.

ökçe 1. heel; **2.** heel *(of a boot)*; **3.** heel leather.

ökçell heeled, high heeled *(shoe)*.

ökçesiz heelless, flat-soled.

öke genius.

ökse 1. birdlime; **2.** *fig.* attractive woman; **~ çubuğu** stick smeared with birdlime; **-ye basmak** to make a mistake *or* to lose carelessly.

ökseotu, -nu BOT mistletoe.

öksürmek to cough, to clear one's throat, to have a cough; **öksürmek tıksırmak** to cough.

öksürtmek to cause to cough.

öksürtücü urging to cough, causing cough.

öksürük cough, clearing one's throat.

öksürüklü *s.o.* who has a cough, coughing all the time, coughing slightly; **~ tıksırıklı** F sickly.

öksürükotu, -nu BOT coltsfoot.

öksüz 1. motherless, orphan; **2.** *fig.* alone (in the world), single, without friends; **~ babası** *fig.* good benefactor; **~ kalmak 1.** to lose one's both father and mother; **2.** to be left alone; **~ sevindiren** a common tawdry thing.

öküz 1. zoo ox; **2.** *fig.* fool, stupid, *Am.* sap(head), oaf; **3.** *sl.* loaded dice, die; **~ arabası** ox-cart; **~ arabası gibi** very slowly; **~ gibi** stupid, fool; **~ gibi bakmak** to stare like a fool; **~ trene bakar gibi bakmak** to stare like a fool (*or* stupidly); **-e boynuzu yük olmaz** (*or* **ağır gelmez**) it is not a burden to help one's friends; **-ün altında buzağı aramak** to hunt for s.th. in the most unlikely place.

öküzbalığı, -nı zoo walrus.
öküzburnu, -nu zoo hornbill.
öküzdili, -ni BOT bugloss.
öküzgözü, -nü arnica.
öküzlük *fig.* incredible stupidity.
öl moistness, wetness.
ölçek 1. measure, scale, standard; **2.** grain measure equal to four okka.
ölçer poker, fire-rake.
ölçmek, (-er) 1. to measure; **2.** *fig.* to weigh; **ölçüp biçmek** to consider carefully, to think s.th. over carefully.
ölçü 1. measure; **2.** unit of measurement; **3.** dimensions; **4.** *fig.* in reason; **5.** MUS time, measure; **6.** *poet.* meter; **7.** *fig.* regard; **~ almak 1.** to measure; **2.** to compare; **~ vermek** to give the measurements of (*dress, shoe, etc.*); **-yü kaçırmak** to behave excessively (*or* beyond reason).
ölçülmek to be measured.
ölçülü 1. measured; **2.** *poet.* metrical; **3.** *fig.* moderate, temperate; **4.** proportionally distributed; **~ biçili**, elaborated; **~ balon** CHEM gauge glass.
ölçülülük moderation.
ölçüm 1. measuring; **2.** measurement; **3.** appraisal.
ölçümlemek 1. to reason s.th. out, to consider s.th. carefully; **2.** to evaluate.
ölçüsüz 1. unmeasured; **2.** immeasurable, immense; **3.** excessive; **4.** immoderate, excessive, unbridled; **5.** without consideration.
ölçüşmek (*b-le*) to compete (*or* grapple) with *s.o.*
ölçüt, -tü criterion.
öldüresiye ruthlessly, murderously.
öldürmek 1. to kill, to murder, to slay (*a. time*); **2.** to remove the strong taste of (*onion. etc.*); **3.** to torture, to treat harshly; **4.** to exhaust, to wear out.
öldürtmek *caus. of* **öldürmek.**
öldürücü 1. mortal, fatal, deadly, lethal; **2.** suffocating.
öldürülmek to be killed.

ölesiye excessively, intensely.
ölgün 1. not fresh anymore, faded, withered; **2.** tired, exhausted, worn out; **3.** calm (*sea*).
ölmek, (-ür) 1. to die; **2.** to fade, to wither; **3.** to suffer great grief (*or* anxiety); **4.** to perish; **~ var dönmek yok** to come hell or high water; **ölüp ölüp dirilmek** to sweat blood; **ölür müsün, öldürür müsün?** to be between the rock and hard place.
ölmez 1. immortal, eternal; **2.** indestructible, tough.
ölmezoğlu, -nu indestructible, tough.
ölmüş 1. dead; **2.** dead (*person*).
ölü 1. dead; **2.** feeble, faint, weak, fatigued, motionless; **3.** dead (*body*); **4.** dead (*person*); **5.** out of fashion, not used any more; **6.** *sl.* marked playing cards, loaded die; **~ açı** MIL dead angle; **~ dalga** low wave, swell; **~ deniz** swell; **~ fiyatına** dirt cheap; **~ gözü gibi** pale, weak (*light*); **~ mevsim** dead season; **~ nokta** dead point (*a.* MIL); **~ salı** wooden bench on which a corpse is washed; **~ veya sag** dead or alive; **-sü kandilli** (*or* **kınalı**) *sl.* the damned scoundrel, the wretch; **-sü ortada kalmak** not to be claimed by anybody (*corpse*); **-yü güldürür** very funny.
ölük weak, exhausted, feeble, faint.
ölüm death, decease, case of death; **~ Allah'ın emri** death is the will of God; **~ döşeği** deathbed; **~ kalım meselesi** matter of life or death; **~ sessizliği** deathly silence; **~ var dirim var** death is an ever-present contingency; **-e bağlı tasarruflar** JUR testamentary decrees (*or* orders); **-le burun buruna gelmek** to have a close brush with death; **-ü göze almak** to act in the face of death; **-üne susamak** to court death.
ölümcül 1. fatal, mortal; **2.** dying.
ölümlü mortal; **~ dünya** (this) mortal world.
ölümsü deathlike, deathly.
ölümsüz immortal.
ölümsüzlük immortality.
ömür, -mrü 1. life, existence; **2.** duration of life; **3.** happy life; **4.** *fig.* wonderful, marvel(l)ous; **~ adam 1.** a fine fellow; **2.** odd fellow; **~ boyunca** all one's life; **~ çürütmek** to spend one's time and energy in vain; **~ geçirmek** to live, to spend one's life; **~ sürmek** to lead a comfortable and happy life;

~ tehlikesi danger of life; **~ törpüsü** a long and exhausting job; **ömre bedel** worth a life (*beautiful, excellent*); **-ler olsun!** may you live long!; **ömrü billah 1.** up to now; **2.** never; **ömrü vefa etmemek** to die before attaining one's goal; **ömründe** never (*in one's life*); **ömrüne bereket!** may you live long!

ömürlü long-lived, long-lasted.

ömürsüz short-lived.

ön 1. front; **2.** front (side), **3.** foremost; **4.** the future; **~ ayak olm.** to be (the) pioneer, to be (the) first in doing s.th.; **~ plana geçmek** to come to the fore; **-de gelmek** to be in (the) most important place; **-e almak** to give preference (to); **-e düşmek** to march in front, to lead the way; **-e sürmek 1.** to propose, to suggest; **2.** to put forward (*idea*); **-ü alınmak** to be prevented; **-ü sıra** at a small distance ahead (of); **-ünde, -üne** in front of; **-üne bak!** look out!, take care!, be careful!; **-üne bakmak** to hang one's head in shame; **-üne geçmek** to prevent, to avert; **-üne gelen** anybody; **-ünü almak 1.** to prevent, to avert, to obviate; **2.** to dam up (*a. fig.*), to embank; **-ünü ardını düşünmemek** not to act circumspectly; **-ünü kesmek** to dam up, to embank.

önad GR adjective.

önavurt ANAT alveolar ridge.

önce [x .] **1.** before, previously; **2.** first, at first, first of all; **3.** the past, pre. ...

önceden [x . .] in the beginning, at first, beforehand, first of all.

önceki the preceding, the former, the previous.

öncel predecessor, ancestor; **~ düzen** PHLS the theory of pre-established harmony.

önceleri [x . . .] previously, formerly.

öncelik priority.

öncelikle first of all, before all else.

öncesiz eternal, without beginning.

öncesizlik past eternity.

öncü 1. MIL vanguard; **2.** advance courier; **3.** avant-garde; **4.** leader.

öncül PHLS premise.

öncülük leadership.

öndamak ANAT palate.

öndelik COM payment in advance.

önder leader, chief.

önderlik leadership.

öndeyiş prologue.

önek GR prefix.

önel extension, delay, fixed period of time, due date; respite.

önem importance, consequence, significance; **~ vermek** to consider important, to esteem, to appreciate.

önemli important, considerable.

önemsemek to consider important.

önemsiz unimportant, insignificant.

önemsizlik unimportance, insignificance.

önerge proposal, motion.

öneri offer, suggestion, proposal.

önermek to propose, to motion, to offer.

önerti LOG antecedent.

öngörmek 1. to provide for, to foresee; **2.** to consider, to bear in mind.

öngörü far-sightedness, prescience.

öngörülü foresighted, prescient.

öngün eve.

önkol ANAT forearm.

önlem precaution, measure, action; **~ almak** to take the necessary measurements.

önlemek 1. to prevent, to avert, to obviate, to guard against; **2.** to stop, to forestall.

önleyici preventive.

önlük 1. apron; **2.** pinafore; **3.** smock.

önseçim primary election.

önsel a priori.

önses GR first sound of a word; **~ düşmesi** GR elision of the first sound of a word.

önsezi presentiment, foreboding.

önsöz preface, foreword.

öntasar(ı) preliminary draft.

önyargı prejudice.

önyargılı prejudiced.

önyüz front (*a.* MIL).

önyüzbaşı, -yı MIL a senior captain, lieutenant commander.

öpmek, (-er) to kiss; **~ babanın elini!** we are done for!; **-üp te başına koymak** to be thankful for small favo(u)rs, to accept s.th. with pleasure.

öpücük kiss; **~ göndermek** (*or* **yollamak**) to blow kisses, to cast kisses to.

öpülmek to be kissed.

öpüş kissing.

öpüşmek to kiss one another.

ördek 1. ZOO duck; **2.** urinal (*for use in bed*); **3.** sl. extra passenger picked up on the way; **~ yürüyüşü** duckwaddle.

ördekbaşı, -nı greenish-blue.

ördekgagası, -nı reddish-yellow.

ördürmek to have s.th. knitted.

öreke distaff.

ören ruins.

örf custom, convention, common usage, sovereign right.

örfi [î] conventional, customary, consuetudinary; ~ *idare* JUR state of siege, martial law.

örge motif.

örgen BIOL organ.

örgü 1. plaited *or* knitted work, plait; **2.** knitting; **3.** knitted *or* plaited; **4.** tress, plait (of hair) **5.** ANAT plexus; **6.** rush mat; ~ *şişi* knitting-needle.

örgün organic.

örgüt, -tü organization.

örgütçü organizer.

örgütlemek to organize.

örgütlendirmek to organize.

örgütlenmek to be organized.

örgütleyici organizer.

örgütlü organized.

örgütsel organizational.

örgütsüz unorganized.

örme 1. *vn. of* **örmek 2.** knitting, plaiting; **3.** plaited, knitted; **4.** braided (*hair*).

örmek, (-er) 1. to plait, to knit; **2.** to tie, to knot, to crochet; **3.** to darn, to mend (*linen, etc.*); **4.** to build, to erect (*wall*); **5.** to braid, to plait (*hair*); **6.** *fig.* to make, to execute (*a.* THEAT)

örneğin for example, for instance.

örnek 1. sample, design, pattern, specimen; **2.** example, prototype; **3.** equivalent (*to*), of the same value, like; **4.** type, model; **5.** typical ..., model ...; **6.** form, blank (form); **7.** copy, TYP proof; ~ *almak* (*b-den*) to take *s.o.* as one's model, to take a lesson from *s.o.*; ~ *olmak* to be a model; *örneğini almak* (*bşin*) to draw the design *or* model of *s.th.*; *örneğini çıkarmak* to make a copy of.

örneklemek to give an example of, to illustrate.

örs anvil.

örselemek 1. to use badly, to maul, to batter, to handle roughly, to damage, to spoil, to rumple; **2.** to use *s.o.* ill, to play *s.o.* a nasty trick; **3.** to exhaust, to weaken (*illness*).

örselenmek *caus. of* **örselemek.**

örtbas etm. to suppress, to hush up.

örtenek ANAT mantle.

örtmek, (-er) 1. to cover (*a.* MIL, COM, boxing), to veil, to mask, to disguise (*a. fig.*); **3.** to shut, to close; **4.** to shovel, to cast; **5.** to wrap; **6.** to hush up.

örttürmek *caus. of* **örtmek.**

örtü 1. cover, wrap **2.** blanket; **3.** roof.

örtük covered, closed.

örtülmek 1. to be covered, to be wrapped up; **2.** to be closed; **3.** to be hushed up.

örtülü 1. covered, wrapped up; **2.** roofed; **3.** closed, shut; **4.** hushed up, concealed; ~ *ödenek* discretionary fund in the government budget (*used to finance secret projects*).

örtünmek to cover o.s., to veil o.s.

örtüsüz uncovered, unveiled.

örü 1. plaited *or* knitted work; **2.** building, edifice, **3.** mending, repair; **4.** enclosed place.

örücü 1. knitter; **2.** darner, mender; **3.** stonemason, bricklayer.

örülü 1. knitted; **2.** darned, mended; **3.** braided.

örümce zoo a fig. moth.

örümcek 1. zoo spider; **2.** (*ağı*) cobweb; ~ *bağlamak* **1.** to get covered with cobwebs; **2.** to be left without being used for a long time; ~ *kafalı* *pej.* reactionary, stone-conservative, old fashioned; (*bir yeri*) ~ *sarmak* to get covered with cobwebs.

örümcekkuşu, -nu zoo shrike.

örümceklenmek 1. to get covered with cobwebs; **2.** *fig.* to be left without being used; **3.** MED to become coated with dry mucous (*around eyes, mouth, nostrils*).

örümcekler zoo Araneida.

örümcekli covered with cobwebs; ~ *kafa* *fig.* old-fashioned, reactionary.

östaki ANAT Eustachian; ~ *borusu* Eustachian tube.

öşür, -şrü 1. MATH tenth (part); **2.** tithe.

öşürcü tithe collector.

öte 1. the farther side; the other side; **2.** other, farther; **3.** the rest; ~ *gün* a few days ago, the other day, recently; ~ *de beride* here and there; *-den beri* from of old, at all times, *-den beriden* from here and there, from this and that; *-si berisi* **1.** one's goods and possessions; **2.** one's various places, various things; *-si var mı?* stick that in your pipe and smoke it!; *-sinde berisinde* here and there of ...; *-sini beri etm.* (*bşin*) to leave no stone unturned (*to*); *-ye beriye* here and there.

öteberi this and that, various things.

öteki, **-ni 1.** the other; **2.** the farther; **3.** the next but one; **~ beriki** anybody and everybody.

ötekisi, **-ni** the other one.

ötleğen zoo warbler.

ötleği zoo lammergeier.

ötmek (**-er**) **1.** to sing (bird), to crow (cock); **2.** to sound, to echo; **3.** to ring, to tinkle, to sound; **4.** sl. to speak incessantly; **5.** sl. to vomit, to puke.

öttürmek **1.** caus. of **ötmek**; **2.** to boast, to brag (**of**).

ötücü which sings habitually (bird).

ötürü because of, by reason of, on account of.

ötüş way of singing.

ötüşmek to sing at the same time (birds).

öveç two or three-year old ram.

övendire oxgoad.

övgü eulogy, panegyric.

övgücü flatterer.

övme praising, laudation.

övmek, (**-er**) to praise, to extol.

övülmek to be praised.

övünç pride; **~ çizelgesi** hono(u)r roll.

övüngen boastful, boasting, braggart, boaster.

övünmek **1.** to boast; **2.** to praise o.s., to boast, to brag, to bluster, to talk big, to show off; **~ gibi olmasın** if I do say so myself ..., I don't mean to boast but ...

öykü story.

öykücü **1.** story-teller; **2.** short-story writer.

öykünme imitating, imitation, mimicking.

öykünmek to imitate, to mimic.

öyle **1.** such, such a, such a kind; **2.** so, in such a way, like that; **~ ise** if so, in that case; (b-ne) **~ gelmek** it seems to ..., to have the impression that ...; **~ olsun** all right, it is okay; **~ şey** (or **yağma) yok!** (s.o. is) not going to get away with that, it's out of the question; **~ ya** of course, certainly.

öylece [x ..], öylelikle [x ...] in such a manner, thus, in this way, so that, so.

öylesi such ..., like ...

öz **1.** (one's own) self; **2.** kernel, essence, heart substance; **3.** bot pith; **4.** core; **5.** own, proper; **6.** genuine, real; **7.** essential; **8.** cream; **9.** marrow; **10.** brook, stream; **~ hayat** private life; **~ odun** heartwood; **~ kardeş** full

brother (or sister); **-ü sözü bir** decent, sincere, honest, genuine, frank.

özbağışıklık MED autoimmunity.

Özbek **1.** Uzbek; **2.** Uzbek, of the Uzbeks.

Özbekçe the Uzbek language.

Özbekistan Uzbekistan.

özbeöz real, genuine, true.

özdek **1.** material; **2.** goods, merchandise; **3.** PHLS matter.

özdekçi PHLS materialist.

özdekçilik PHLS materialism.

özdeksel PHLS materialist.

özden **1.** genuine, true, sincere; **2.** ANAT thymus.

özdeş identical (a. PHLS & MATH).

özdeşlemek **1.** to equate; **2.** to identify.

özdeşlik **1.** identity; **2.** identicalness.

özdevim automation.

özdevinim automatism.

özdeyiş epigram, aphorism.

özdışı, **-ni** PHLS extrinsic.

özdirenç PHYS resistivity.

öze PHLS peculiar to, special.

özek center; **~ ağacı** central pole of a four-wheeled cart.

özekdoku parenchyma.

özel s. **hususi.**

özeleştiri self-criticism.

özellik peculiarity, characteristic.

özellikle specially, especially, particularly.

özen care, carefulness, pains, trouble, attention; **~ göstermek** to take great care (**in**), to take pains to.

özenç wishing, longing.

özendirmek caus. of **özenmek.**

özengen amateur.

özenli **1.** with particular care, painstaking; **2.** careful.

özenmek **1.** to take pains about, to desire ardently; **2.** to feel like; **3.** to imitate, to ape; **özene bezene** carefully, willingly, painstakingly; **özene özene** with utmost care; **özenip bezenmek** to take great pains.

özensiz **1.** superficial, casual; **2.** careless, negligent.

özenti pretended, alleged, ostensible, pseudo-, swindle, fraud, cheat, false, counterfeit(ed), spurious, not genuine, fake(d), imitation.

özentili very careful, painstaking.

özentisiz **1.** careless; **2.** casual.

özerk POL autonomous.

özerklik POL autonomy.

özet, -ti 1. summary, résumé, synopsis; **2.** subject; **3.** extract.

özetlemek to sum up, to summarize, to recapitulate.

özge 1. other (than), apart from; **2.** different, distinctive, unusual.

özgeci altruist.

özgecil altruistic, unselfish.

özgecilik altruism.

özgeçmiş biography.

özgü special, peculiar to, unique to.

özgül specific, special; ~ *ağırlık* specific gravity.

özgün 1. specific, peculiar; **2.** original; creative; **3.** authentic, genuine.

özgünlük originality.

özgür free, independent.

özgürce freely, independently.

özgürleşmek to become free.

özgürleştirmek to free.

özgürlük freedom, liberty.

özgürlükçü partisan of freedom, which aims to promote freedom.

özgüven self-confidence.

özışın BOT medullary rays.

özindükleme PHYS self-induction.

özlem 1. longing, yearning; **2.** inclination, aspiration, ardent desire.

özlemek to long for, to yearn for, to miss, to wish for.

özleşmek 1. to become purified; **2.** to get ripen.

özletmek to make s.o. long for.

özleyiş longing, yearning.

özlü 1. marrowy, pithy; **2.** pulpy, substantial; **3.** having kernel.

özlük 1. nature, character; **2.** person, individual, employee; ~ *işleri* matters pertaining to personnel.

özne GR & PHLS subject.

öznel GR & PHLS subjective.

öznelci PHLS subjectivist.

öznelcilik PHLS subjectivism.

öznellik subjectivity.

özsaygı self-respect.

özsel essential.

özseverlik narcissism.

özsu 1. BOT sap; **2.** BIOL juice.

özümleme BIOL assimilation.

özümlemedokusu, -nu BOT plant issue in which photosynthesis takes place.

özümlemek BOT to assimilate.

özümlenmek BOT to be assimilated.

özümseme s. *özümleme.*

özümsemek s. *özümlemek.*

özümsenmek s. *özümlenmek.*

özünerosluk autoeroticism.

özünlü intrinsic.

özür, -zrü 1. excuse, apology; **2.** defect, shortcoming, infirmity; ~ *dilemek* **1.** to apologize (to *s.o.*; *for s.th.*), to ask pardon; **2.** to refuse, to decline; *özrü kabahatinden büyük* his excuse is worse than his fault.

özürlü 1. defective, flawed; **2.** handicapped; **3.** having an excuse.

özürsüz 1. flawless, perfect, nondefective; **2.** lacking an excuse.

özveren self-sacrificing, self-denying.

özveri self-sacrifice, self-denial.

özverili self-sacrificing, self-denying.

özyaşamöyküsü, -nü autobiography.

P

pabuç, -cu 1. shoe; 2. ARCH base, pedestal; ~ bırakmamak (bşe) fig. not to be discouraged by s.th.; -tan aşağı despicable, low-down; -u dama atılmak fig. to lose favo(u)r, to fall into discredit; -unu eline vermek (b-nin) to give s.o. the boot (or the push).

pabuççu shoemaker, cobbler.

paça 1. lowest part of a trouser leg; 2. trotter; -sı düşük untidy, down-at--heels; -sından tutup atmak to give s.o. the chuck; -yı kurtarmak to elude, to evade.

paçavra [. x .] 1. rag; 2. fig. worn-out, worthless thing; ~ hastalığı F influenza, flu; -ya çevirmek (or döndürmek) to botch, to make a mess of.

paçavracı [. x .] ragman, ragpicker.

paçoz sl. prostitute.

padavra [. x .] shingle; -sı çıkmış fig. so thin that you can count his ribs.

padişah [- . -] padishah, sultan, ruler, sovereign.

padişahlık [- . . .] sovereignty, sultanate.

pafta [x .] 1. section of a map; 2. MEC diestock; 3. metal decoration (on a horse's harness).

pagan pagan.

paha [. -] price, value; ~ biçilmez priceless, invaluable; ~ biçmek to set a value (-e on), to price, to evaluate; -sına at the cost of; -ya çıkmak to rise in price, to become expensive.

pahacı who sells at a high price.

pahalanmak s. pahalılaşmak.

pahalı expensive, dear, costly; -ya oturmak to cost an arm and a leg.

pahalılanmak s. pahalılaşmak.

pahalılaşmak to become expensive, to increase in price.

pahalılık 1. expensiveness, costliness; 2. dearth.

pak, -ki [ā] 1. clean, pure; 2. fig. pure--hearted.

paket, -ti 1. pack(et); 2. package, parcel; 3. sl. ass. buttocks; ~ etm. to package; to wrap up; ~ postanesi parcel post office.

paketlemek to package, to wrap up.

Pakistan [- . -] pr. n. Pakistan.

Pakistanlı [- . - .] pr. n. Pakistani.

paklamak [- . .] 1. to clean, to purify; 2. F to deserve; 3. F to kill, to bump off.

paklık cleanness.

pakt, -tı pact, treaty.

pala 1. scimitar; 2. blade; ~ çalmak (or sallamak) to strive, to try hard.

palabıyık having a handlebar moustache.

palamar NAUT hawser; ~ parası dockage, buoyage; -ı çözmek (or koparmak) sl. to show a clean pair of heels, to take to one's heels.

palamut, -tu 1. ZOO bonito; 2. BOT valonia oak.

palan a kind of saddle.

palanga [. x .] NAUT pulley, tackle.

palas 1. sumptuous hotel; 2. palace.

palaska [. x .] MIL bandolier, cartridge belt.

palas pandıras pell-mell, helter-skelter.

palavra [. x .] bunk, palaver, bullshit, baloney, humbug; ~ atmak (or savurmak or sıkmak) to talk bunk (or rot), to be full of bull.

palavracı braggart, bull-shooter.

palaz duckling, gosling, squab.

palazla(n)mak 1. to grow strong (or plump); 2. to grow up (child); 3. sl. to become lousy.

paldır küldür pell-mell, headlong.

paleontoloji paleontology.

palet, -ti 1. track, caterpillar tread; 2. flipper; 3. (artist's) palette.

palikarya [. . x .] Greek rowdy.

palmiye BOT palm (tree).

palto [x .] (over)coat.

palyaço [. x .] clown, buffoon.

palyoş poniard, stiletto.

pami [x .] sl. let's get going!

pamuk BOT cotton; ~ ağacı cotton tree; ~ atmak to fluff cotton (with a bow and mallet); ~ barutu guncotton; ~ gibi soft as cotton; ~ ipliği cotton thread; ♀ Prenses Snow White; ~ tarlası cotton field.

pamukbalığı, -nı ZOO blue shark.

pamuklu 1. cotton ...; 2. cotton (cloth).

panayır fair; ~ yeri fairground.

pancar BOT beet; ~ **kesilmek** (*or* ~ *gibi olm.*) to turn as red as a beetroot, to go beet red; ~ **şekeri** beet sugar.

pancur *s.* **panjur.**

panda ZOO panda.

pandantif pendant.

pandispanya [. . x .] sponge cake.

pandomima [. . x .] pantomime.

pandûl pendulum.

panel panel discussion.

pangodoz *sl.* drunkard (*old man*).

panik panic; ~ **yaratmak** to arouse (*or* create) panic; **paniğe kapılmak** to panic, to be seized with panic; **paniğe kapılmış** panic-stricken.

panjur shutter.

pankart, -tı placard, banner.

pankreas¹ pancreas.

pankreas² a kind of wrestling.

pano 1. wall panel; **2.** bulletin (*or* notice) board; panel.

panorama panorama.

pansiyon boarding house, pension, digs, lodgings.

pansiyoner boarder, lodger.

pansuman MED dressing; ~ **yapmak** to dress (*a wound*).

panter ZOO panther, leopard.

pantolon trousers, pants.

pantufla [. x .] pantofle, felt slippers.

panzehir antidote.

papa the Pope.

papağan ZOO parrot.

papalık the Papacy.

papara 1. *dish made from pieces of dry bread and broth*; **2.** F scolding; ~ **yemek** F to get it in the neck, to cop it, to catch it.

paparazzi *sg.* (*pl.* **paparazziler**) paparazzi *pl.*

papatya [. x .] BOT daisy; camomile.

papaz 1. priest, minister; **2.** *cards*: king; **-a kızıp perhiz bozmak** to cut off one's nose to spite one's face.

papazlık priesthood.

papel *sl.* one Turkish lira.

papirüs papyrus.

papura heavy plow (*drawn by two yoke of oxen*).

papyebuvar blotting paper.

papyekuşe glossy paper.

papyon bow tie.

para money; ~ **babası** moneybags; ~ **bağlamak** to lock up (-*e* in); ~ **basmak** to mint, to print (*money*); ~ **bozmak** to change money; ~ **canlısı** money-lover; ~ **canlısı olm.** to have an

itching palm; ~ **cezası** fine; ~ **cüzdanı** wallet, billfold; ~ **çantası** money-bag, purse; ~ **çekmek 1.** to draw money (*from a bank*); **2.** *fig.* to squeeze money out of s.o.; ~ **dökmek** to pour money (-*e* into); ~ **etm.** to be worth s.th., to be valuable; ~ **içinde yüzmek** to be wallowing in money; ~ **ile değil** *fig.* it is dirt cheap; ~ **kesmek 1.** = ~ **basmak**; **2.** *fig.* to rake it in; ~ **-yı çeker** *pro.* money breeds (*or* begets) money; ~ **pul** money and assets; ~ **sızdırmak** (*b-den*) to squeeze money out of s.o.; ~ **tutmak 1.** to save money; **2.** to cost; ~ **yardımı** monetary aid, subsidy, donation; ~ **yatırmak 1.** to invest (-*e* in); **2.** to deposit money (-*e* in); ~ **yedirmek** to bribe, to grease s.o.'s palm; ~ **yemek 1.** to play ducks and drakes with money; **2.** to accept a bribe; **-dan çıkmak** to have to spend money; **-nın üstü** change; **-yı veren düdüğü çalar** *pro.* pay the piper and call the tune.

parabellum Parabellum.

parabol, -lü MATH parabola.

parafe initialed; ~ **etm.** to initial (*a document*).

parafin paraffin (wax).

paragöz money-grubber.

paragraf paragraph.

paraka [. x .] groundline, setline.

paralamak 1. to tear to pieces; **2.** to wear to pieces.

paralanmak 1. *pass.* of **paralamak**; **2.** to wear (*or* lay) o.s. out; **3.** to strain every nerve; **4.** F to become lousy.

paralel 1. parallel; **2.** *sports*: parallel bars.

paralelkenar parallelogram.

paralı 1. rich, well-heeled, moneyed; **2.** requiring payment; ~ **asker** mercenary; ~ **yol** turnpike, toll road.

parametre MATH parameter.

paramparça [. x . .] in tatters, ragged; smashed to bits; ~ **etm.** to smash to bits, to tatter, to tear to rags.

parantez parenthesis; ~ **açmak** *fig.* to digress.

parapet, -ti 1. NAUT bulwarks; **2.** parapet.

parasal monetary.

parasız 1. penniless, poor, moneyless; **2.** gratis, free (of charge); ~ **yatılı öğrenci** boarding student, boarder.

parasızlık pennilessness, poverty.

paraşüt, -tü parachute.

paraşütçü parachutist, parachuter, paratrooper.

paratifo MED paratyphoid.

paratoner lightning rod (*or* conductor).

paravan(a) (folding) screen.

parazit, -ti 1. BIOL parasite (*a. fig.*); **2.** MEC interference, static, atmospherics.

parça 1. piece, bit, fragment; **2.** *lit.*, MUS passage; piece; **3.** item; **4.** *sl.* dope; **5.** *sl.* nice piece of goods, pretty woman; ~ **başına ücret** piece-wage; ~ **mal** piece goods; ~ ~ **1.** in bits and pieces, in smithereens; **2.** in rags, tattered; ~ ~ **etm.** to break (*or* tear) into pieces.

parçacı 1. seller of piece goods; **2.** seller of spare parts.

parçalamak to tear (*or* smash *or* break) into pieces.

parçalanmak 1. *pass. of* **parçalamak**; **2.** *fig.* to lay (*or* wear) o.s. out.

parçalı 1. pieced, in parts; **2.** patchwork(ed); ~ **bulutlu** cloudy in patches.

pardesü, pardösü (over)coat.

pardon pardon me, excuse me.

pare [ā] piece, fragment, bit.

parfüm perfume.

parıldamak to gleam, to glitter; to sparkle; to twinkle, to flash.

parıl parıl gleamingly, glitteringly.

parıltı gleam, glitter; sparkle; twinkle, flash.

Paris [ā] [x .] *pr. n.* Paris.

parite COM parity.

park, -kı 1. park (*a.* MIL); **2.** car park, *Am.* parking lot; **3.** playpen; ~ **etm.** (*or* **yapmak**) to park; ~ **sayacı** parking meter; ~ **yapılmaz** no parking.

parka parka, windcheater.

parke 1. parquet(ry); **2.** cobblestone pavement; ~ **döşeme** parquet floor.

parkur (race)course.

parlak 1. bright, brilliant; luminous, radiant; **2.** *fig.* brilliant, great; successful; **3.** *sl.* sissy, sissified.

parlaklık brightness, brilliance (*a. fig.*).

parlamak 1. to shine, to glisten, to gleam; **2.** to flame up, to flare up (*a. fig.*).

parlamenter 1. member of parliament; **2.** parliamentary.

parlamento parliament.

parlatmak 1. *caus. of* **parlamak**, to pol-

ish, to rub up, to burnish; **2.** *sl.* to toss off, to knock back (*booze*).

parmak 1. finger; **2.** toe; **3.** spoke (*of a wheel*); **4.** inch; **5.** rail, bar; ~ **basmak 1.** to draw attention (*-e* to); **2.** to put one's thumbprint (*-e* on); ~ **emmek** to suck one's finger; ~ **hesabı 1.** counting on the fingers; **2.** *lit.* syllabic meter; ~ **ısırmak** to be taken aback, to be dumbfounded; ~ **izi** fingerprint; ~ **kadar** mere slip of (*a child*); ~ **kadar çocuk** hop-o'-my-thumb; ~ **kaldırmak** to raise one's hand; **parmağı ağzında kalmak** to be astounded, to fall off one's chair; **parmağı olm.** (*b-nin bir işte*) *fig.* to have a finger in *s.th.*; **parmağında oynatmak** (*b-ni*) *fig.* to twist *s.o.* round one's little finger.

parmakçı *fig.* agitator, inciter.

parmaklamak 1. to eat with one's fingers; **2.** to finger, to goose.

parmaklık railing, balustrade; grating, grate, grill.

parodi parody.

parola [. x .] password, watchword.

pars ZOO leopard.

parsa [x .] money, collection; *-yı başkası toplamak* to reap the benefits of your work.

parsal *s.* **partal.**

parsel plot, lot, parcel.

parsellemek to divide into parcels, to subdivide.

parşömen parchment, vellum.

partal shabby, worn-out.

parter THEAT parterre.

parti 1. party (*a.* POL); **2.** COM consignment (*of goods*); **3.** MUS part; **4.** game, match; ~ **vermek** to give a party.

partici POL party member.

partisip, -pi GR participle.

partisyon MUS full score.

partizan partisan.

partizanlık partisanship.

parya outcast, pariah.

pas[1] **1.** rust, corrosion, tarnish; **2.** fur (*on the tongue*); ~ **tutmak** to rust, to corrode, to tarnish; ~ **tutmaz** rust-proof.

pas[2] *sports, cards:* pass; ~ **geçmek** to disregard; ~ **vermek** *sl.* to give the glad eye (*woman*).

pasaj 1. arcade with shops; **2.** passage.

pasak dirt, filth.

pasaklı dirty, filthy; slovenly.

pasaparola [. . . x .] MIL password.

pasaport, -tu passport; **~ çıkartmak** to have a passport taken out; **-unu eline vermek** *fig.* to give s.o. the boot (*or* the bullet *or* the chop).

pasavan laissez-passer.

pasif 1. passive; **2.** COM liabilities.

paskal funny, clownish.

paskalya [. x .] Easter.

paslanmak 1. to rust, to corrode, to tarnish; **2.** to fur (*tongue*); **3.** *fig.* to become rusty.

paslanmaz rustproof, tarnishproof, non-corrodible; **~ çelik** stainless steel.

paslaşmak 1. *football*: to pass the ball to each other; **2.** *sl.* to give each other the glad eye.

paslı rusty.

paso [x .] pass.

paspas doormat.

paspaslamak to mop.

pasta [x .] **1.** cake, pastry, tart; **2.** fold, pleat.

pastacı maker *or* seller of pastry.

pastane [. - .] pastry shop, bakery.

pastel pastel.

pastırma pastrami-like beef; **~ yazı** Indian Summer.

pastil pastille, troche, lozenge.

pastoral 1. pastoral; **2.** MUS pastorale.

pastörize pasteurized; **~ etm.** to pasteurize.

paşa 1. pasha; **2.** sedate, well-behaved (*child*); **~ ~** sedately.

pat¹, -tı flat, snub (*nose*).

pat² bam!, whop!, thud!; **~ diye** with a thud; **~ ~** pit-a-pat.

pat³, -tı BOT aster.

patagos *sl.* five-kurush coin.

patak F beating, hiding.

pataklamak to beat, to thrash, to give a beating (*or* hiding).

patates [. x .] BOT potato.

patavatsız indiscreet, tactless.

paten 1. ice skate; **2.** (*a.* **tekerlekli ~**) roller skate.

patent, -ti 1. patent; **2.** NAUT bill of health.

patentli patented.

patırdamak to patter, to clatter.

patır patır with a pattering sound.

patırtı 1. clatter, patter; noise; **2.** tumult, row, disturbance; **~ çıkarmak** to make a row, to raise a ruckus; **-ya pabuç bırakmamak** not to be scared off by empty threats; **-ya vermek** to put into confusion.

patik bootee.

patika [. x .] path, track, trail.

patinaj 1. ice skating; **2.** MOT skidding, slipping; **~ yapmak 1.** to skate; **2.** mot. to skid, to slip, to spin; **~ zinciri** anti-skid (*or* tire) chain.

patis a fine kind of batiste.

patiska [. x .] cambric, cotton batiste.

patlak 1. burst; cracked; **2.** MOT puncture; **~ gözlü** popeyed, bug-eyed; **~ vermek 1.** to break out (*war, etc.*); **2.** to be discovered (*or* divulged) (*secret*).

patlama *vn. of* **patlamak**, *part.* explosion.

patlamak 1. to explode, to burst, to blow up; **2.** to break out (*war, etc.*); **3.** to burst (*or* split) open; **4.** *fig.* to explode, to burst out (*with anger, etc.*); **5.** F to cost.

patlamalı: ~ motor MEC internal-combustion engine.

patlangaç popgun; peashooter.

patlatmak *caus. of* **patlamak**, *part.* **1.** to blow up, to blast, to explode; **2.** to infuriate; **3.** to fire (*weapon*); **4.** to crack (*joke*); **5.** to land, to slap, to plant (*blow*).

patlayıcı explosive.

patlıcan BOT aubergine, *Am.* eggplant.

patoloji pathology.

patrik patriarch.

patron 1. boss, employer; **2.** (*tailor's*) pattern.

patrona [. x .] HIST vice-admiral.

pattadak, pattadan suddenly, all of a sudden.

pavurya [. x .] ZOO hermit crab.

pavyon 1. night club; **2.** pavilion.

pay 1. share, portion, lot; **2.** MATH numerator; **3.** *tailoring*: margin; **4.** equal part; **~ biçmek 1.** to take as an example; to compare; **2.** to deduce, to judge (*-den* from); **~ etm.** to share, to divide; **~ vermek** to answer back, to sass; **-ını almak 1.** to get one's share; **2.** to be scolded, to get told off.

payanda [. x .] prop, shore, support; **~ vurmak** to prop up, to shore; **-ları çözmek** to run away, to beat it.

payda MATH denominator.

paydaş shareholder.

paydos [x .] **1.** break, rest; **2.** it's break time!; **~ etm.** to knock off, to quit work, to stop working.

paye rank, position; **~ vermek** to show deference (*-e* to), to esteem.

payidar permanent, constant; **~ olm.**

to be permanent, to last.

payitaht, -tı *obs.* capital (city).

paylamak to scold, to tell off, to rebuke, to reprimand.

paylaşmak to share, to go shares.

paytak 1. knock-kneed; bowlegged, bandy-legged; **2.** *chess*: pawn; **~ ~ yürümek** to waddle.

payton phaeton.

pazar 1. market (place); bazaar; **2.** Sunday; **3.** trade; **~ bozmak** to close an open-air market; **~ günü** on Sunday; **~ kayığı gibi** heavily loaded, top-heavy (*vehicle*); **~ kurmak** to set up an open market; **~ ola!** good luck! (*said to sellers*); **~ tatili** Sunday rest; **~ yeri** market place; **-a çıkarmak** to put up for sale, to put on sale.

pazarbaşı, -nı warden of a market.

pazarcı seller in a market.

pazarlama marketing.

pazarlamacı marketing expert, commercial travel(l)er.

pazarlamak to market.

pazarlaşmak to bargain, to haggle.

pazarlık bargain, haggle; **~ etm.** to bargain, to haggle.

pazartesi, -yi [. x . .] Monday.

pazen [ā] flannel.

pazı[1] BOT chard.

pazı[2] ANAT biceps; **~ kemiği** ANAT humerus.

pazıbent, -di armband, armlet.

pazval (*shoemaker's*) knee-strap.

pazvant, -tı night watchman.

peçe veil.

peçelemek *fig.* to camouflage.

peçeli veiled.

peçete napkin, serviette.

pedagog pedagogist.

pedagoji pedagogics.

pedal pedal, treadle.

peder father.

pederane fatherly.

pederşahi patriarchal.

pedikür pedicure.

pehlivan wrestler.

pehpeh! bravo!, well done!

pehriz *s.* **perhiz.**

pejmürde shabby, worn-out, ragged.

pek, -ki 1. very, extremely; **2.** a great deal, very much; **3.** firm, hard; **4.** sound, strong; **5.** very fast; **~ çok 1.** quite a few, a lot of, a great many; **2.** very much, a great deal; **~ gözlü** courageous, bold; **~ ~** at the very most; **— yürekli** hardhearted; **~ yüzlü** shameless, brazen.

pekâlâ [x - -] **1.** all right, okay, very well; **2.** very good, quite adequate; **3.** most certainly.

peki [x .] **1.** all right, okay; **2.** if that's so, then …

pekin certain.

pekişmek 1. to harden; **2.** to strengthen.

pekiştirmek 1. to strengthen, to consolidate, to reinforce, to intensify; **2.** to harden, to stiffen.

peklik constipation; **~ çekmek** to be constipated.

pekmez 1. grape molasses; **2.** *sl.* blood.

peksimet, -ti hardtack, ship biscuit.

pelerin cape, cloak.

pelesenk, -gi balm, balsam.

pelesenkağacı, -nı BOT balm of Gilead.

pelikan ZOO pelican.

pelin BOT wormwood.

pelit, -ti BOT valonia; camata.

pelte jelly, gelatin(e).

peltek lisping.

peltekleşmek to lisp.

pelteklik lisp.

peltelenmek, pelteleşmek to gel.

pelür onionskin.

pelüş plush.

pembe pink; **~ görmek** *fig.* to see through rose-colo(u)red (*or* rosy) spectacles.

pembeleşmek to turn pink.

pembemsi pinkish.

penaltı, -yı *sports*: penalty.

pencere [x .] window.

pencüdü a five and a two.

pencüse a five and a three.

pencüyek a five and a one.

pençe 1. paw, claw; **2.** grip, clutches; **3.** sole (*of a shoe*); **~ vurmak** to sole (*a shoe*).

pençelemek 1. to paw, to claw, to maul; **2.** to sole (*a shoe*).

pençeleşmek 1. to paw (*or* claw) at each other; **2.** *fig.* to grapple (*ile* with), to wrestle (*ile* with), to battle (*ile* with), to struggle (*ile* against).

pençeli 1. having a paw (*or* claw); **2.** resoled (*shoe*); **3.** *fig.* aggressive; **4.** *fig.* powerful.

pendifrank, -kı *sl.* clout, sock, punch.

penguen ZOO penguin.

penisilin penicillin.

peniz *etm. sl.* to disclose (*a secret*).

pens[1] **1.** pliers; **2.** pincers; tweezers;

nippers; **3.** forceps; **4.** pleat.
pens[2] pence.
pense [x .] pliers.
pentation *sports*: pentathlon.
pepe stammerer, stutterer.
pepelemek to stutter, to stammer.
pepelik stutter.
perakende [ā] retail.
perakendeci [ā] retailer.
perçem 1. bangs; **2.** forelock (*of a horse*); **3.** scalp lock.
perçin rivet, clinch bolt.
perçinlemek 1. to rivet, to clinch; **2.** *fig.* to consolidate.
perçinli riveted, clinched.
perdah 1. polish, sheen, finish, glaze; **2.** finishing shave; ~ **vurmak** to glaze, to polish, to finish, to burnish.
perdahlamak 1. to finish, to polish, to burnish; to glaze, to buff; **2.** to shave a second time (*beard*); **3.** *sl.* to swear at; **4.** *sl.* to fast-talk.
perdahlı burnished, polished, glazed.
perdahsız unburnished, unpolished, unglazed.
perde 1. curtain, drape; **2.** THEAT act; **3.** (movie) screen; **4.** MUS fret; **5.** pitch; **6.** ZOO web; **7.** MED cataract (*on the eye*); ~ **arası** intermission, interval; ~ **arkası** *fig.* the hidden side (*of a matter*); ~ **arkasından** *fig.* behind the scenes, backstage; ~ **ayaklı** ZOO web-footed.
perdelemek 1. to curtain; **2.** *fig.* to conceal, to veil.
perdeli 1. curtained; **2.** THEAT having ... acts; **3.** MUS fretted; **4.** ZOO webbed.
perende [. x .] somersault, flip; ~ **atmak** to somersault, to turn a somersault; ~ **atamamak** (*b-nin yanında*) *fig.* can't hold a candle to *s.o.*
perese 1. plumb line; **2.** *fig.* state, condition, **-sine getirmek** to choose the right moment to do s.th.; **-ye almak** to take into consideration.
perestiş worship, adoration; ~ **etm.** to worship, to adore.
performans *sports*: performance.
pergel pair of compasses; **-leri açmak** F to shake a leg, to take long steps.
pergellemek 1. to measure with a pair of compasses; **2.** to pace off (*a distance*); **3.** *fig.* to consider all the angles of (*a matter*).
perhiz 1. diet; **2.** Christian *or* Jewish fast; ~ **etm. 1.** to diet; **2.** to fast; **-i bozmak** to violate one's diet.
perhizli 1. on a diet; **2.** fasting.

peri fairy; sprite, pixie; nymph; ~ **gibi** fairylike; ~ **masalı** fairy story (*or* tale).
peribacası, -nı 1. fairy chimney; **2.** GEOL earth pillar, demoiselle.
perili haunted; ~ **köşk** haunted house.
periskop, -pu periscope.
perişan [. - -] **1.** perturbed, upset, miserable, wretched, distraught; **2.** scattered; untidy, disordered; ~ **etm. 1.** to upset, to perturb, to ruin; **2.** to scatter, to rout; ~ **olm. 1.** to become miserable (*or* wretched); **2.** to be scattered (*or* routed).
periton ANAT peritoneum; ~ **kovuğu** ANAT peritoneal cavity.
peritonit, -ti MED peritonitis.
perma, permanant, -tı perm, permanent (wave).
permanganat, -tı CHEM permanganate.
permeçe NAUT small hawser.
permi 1. COM permit; **2.** RAIL pass.
peroksit CHEM peroxide.
peron RAIL platform.
persenk, -gi refrain.
personel personnel, staff.
perspektif perspective.
perşembe Thursday; **-nin gelişi çarşambadan bellidir** *pro.* coming events cast their shadows before.
pertavsız magnifying glass.
Peru *pr. n.* Peru.
peruka wig.
perva [ā] **1.** fear; **2.** attention, heed.
pervane [ā] **1.** propeller; **2.** screw; **3.** fanner; **4.** ZOO moth; ~ **olm.** (*b-ne*) to be *s.o.*'s shadow.
pervasız [ā] fearless, unafraid, undauntable; unconcerned.
pervaz [ā] **1.** cornice, fringe, architrave; **2.** border, edging.
peryodik 1. periodic; **2.** periodical.
pes[1] **1.** this is the last straw!; **2.** uncle!; ~ **demek** to submit, to give in, to say «uncle»; ~ **etm.** to yield, to submit, to give in.
pes[2] low, soft (*voice*); ~ **perdeden konuşmak** *fig.* to speak softly.
pesek tartar (*on teeth*).
pesimist, -ti pessimist.
pespaye [ā] vulgar, despicable.
pespembe rose-pink.
pestenkerani [ā] [. . . x .] nonsensical, idiotic.
pestil pressed and dried fruit pulp; ~ **gibi olm.** *fig.* to be too tired to move, to be bushed; **-i çıkmak** *fig.* to be worn

to a frazzle, to be dog-tired; **-ini çıkar-mak** (*b-nin*) *fig.* **1.** to beat *s.o.* to a pulp; **2.** to wear *s.o.* a frazzle; **3.** (*bşin*) to crush *s.th.* to a pulp.

pesüs oil lamp.

peş the back, the rear; **~ -e** one after another; **-i sıra** right behind; **-inde koşmak** to run after; **-inden gitmek** (*b-nin*) *fig.* to follow in the footsteps of *s.o.*; **-ine düşmek 1.** to follow *s.o.* around; **2.** to run after, to be after *s.th.*; **-ine takılmak** (*b-nin*) to tail after *s.o.*, to follow *s.o.* around; **-ini bırak-mak** to stop following.

peşin 1. paid in advance, ready (*money*); **2.** in advance, beforehand; earlier, in the first place; **~ almak** to buy for cash; **~ cevap** answer that anticipates a question; **~ hüküm** (*or yargı*) prejudg(e)ment; **~ para** cash, ready money, advance payment; **~ söyle-mek** to tell in advance, to prognosticate.

peşinat [. - -] **1.** cash; downpayment; **2.** advance payment.

peşinen [î] *s.* **peşin 2.**

peşkeş: ~ çekmek (*b-ne bşi*) to make *s.o.* a present of *s.th.* that does not belong to one.

peşkir 1. (table) napkin, serviette; **2.** (hand) towel.

peşrev 1. MUS overture, prelude; **2.** the entry of wrestlers on to the wrestling field.

peştamal loincloth, waist cloth.

peştamallık COM goodwill.

petek honeycomb; **~ balı** honey in the comb.

petekgöz compound eye (*of insects*).

petrokimya petrochemistry.

petrol, -lü petroleum, crude oil; **~ hattı** oil pipeline; **~ kuyusu** oil well; **~ şir-keti** oil (*or* petroleum) company.

petrolcü oilman.

petunya [. x .] BOT petunia.

pey deposit, earnest money; **~ sürmek** (*or vurmak*) to make a bid.

peyda [â] visible, manifest; **~ etm. 1.** to beget, to give birth to; **2.** to produce; **~ olm.** to appear, to crop up, to spring up.

peydahla(n)mak 1. to give birth to, to sire; **2.** to produce; **3.** to acquire, to pick up.

peyderpey 1. bit by bit, step by step, little by little; **2.** in succession.

peygamber prophet.

peygamberlik prophethood, prophecy.

peyk, -ki 1. AST, POL satellite; **2.** *fig.* adherent, follower.

peyke wooden bench.

peyklik being a satellite.

peylemek to reserve, to book, to engage.

peynir cheese.

peynirhane cheesery.

peynirli containing cheese; **~ sandviç** cheese sandwich.

peyzaj landscape (picture).

pezevenk, -gi 1. procurer, pimp; **2.** scoundrel, bastard, son of a bitch.

pezevenklik procuring, pimping; **~ etm.** to procure, to pimp.

pezo 1. peso; **2.** *sl.* procurer, pimp.

pıhtı clot, coagulate, coagulum.

pıhtılanmak, pıhtılaşmak to clot, to coagulate.

pıhtılaştırmak to clot, to coagulate.

pılı pırtı 1. junk, trash, traps; **2.** belongings, bag and baggage.

pınar spring.

pır whir; **~ diye uçtu** it whirred away.

pırasa [. x .] BOT leek; **~ bıyıklı** having a handlebar moustache.

pırıldak signal (*or* dark) lantern; heliograph.

pırıldamak to gleam, to glitter, to shine.

pırıl pırıl 1. gleaming, glittering; **2.** spick-and-span.

pırıltı gleam, glitter, sparkle.

pırlak lure, decoy.

pırlamak 1. to whir away, to flutter; **2.** *fig.* to take to one's heels.

pırlangıç, -cı humming-top.

pırlanta [. x .] brilliant; **~ gibi** F top-notch, first-rate.

pırnal BOT holly (*or* holm) oak.

pırpır tri-car, put-put.

pırpırı womanizer, skirt-chaser.

pırpıt, -tı 1. useless, worn-out; **2.** a kind of coarse cloth.

pırtı 1. junk, traps; **2.** bag and baggage, belongings.

pırtık torn, ragged.

pısırık faint-hearted, pusillanimous, diffident.

pıt, -tı drip!; **~ yok** you can hear a pin drop.

pıtırdamak to patter.

pıtır pıtır with a patter.

pıtırtı patter.

pıt pıt with a patter, pit-a-pat; **~ atmak**

to go pit-a-pat (*one's heart*).

pıtrak BOT burdock.

piç 1. bastard; **2.** *fig*. brat, bratty child; ~ *etm.* to ball up, to make a balls-up of s.th.; ~ *kurusu* bratty child, brat; ~ *olm.* to be balled up (*or* spoiled).

piçlik bastardy.

pide [x .] pizza-like bread; ~ *gibi* very flat.

pijama [. x .] pyjamas, *Am*. pajamas.

pik (demir) MEC pig (*or* cast) iron.

pikap[1] MUS record player, gramophone, phonograph.

pikap[2] pickup (truck).

pike[1] piqué.

pike[2] AVIA nosedive; ~ *yapmak* **1.** AVIA to nosedive; **2.** *billiards*: to make a massé shot.

piknik picnic; ~ *yapmak* to picnic, to have a picnic.

piko picot.

pil ELECT battery.

pilaki [. x .] **1.** *stew of beans or fish with oil and onions*; **2.** *sl*. idiot.

pilav rice.

piliç, -ci 1. chick, pullet, fryer, broiler; **2.** *sl*. chick, a bit of skirt, babe.

pilot, -tu pilot.

pim MEC pin, gudgeon.

PIN numarası PIN number.

pineklemek to doze, to slumber.

pingpong ping-pong, table tennis.

pinti stingy, niggardly, miserly, closefisted.

pintileşmek to get stingy.

pintilik stinginess, tightness.

pipet, -ti CHEM pipette.

pipo [x .] pipe; ~ *içmek* to smoke a pipe; ~ *tütünü* pipe tobacco.

pîr [î] **1.** master, patron saint; **2.** thoroughly, completely.

piramit, -di pyramid.

pire ZOO flea; ~ *gibi* very agile; ~ *için yorgan yakmak* to cut off one's nose to spite one's face; *-yi deve yapmak* to make a mountain out of a molehill; *-yi nallamak* *fig*. to attempt the impossible.

pirelenmek 1. to become flea-ridden; **2.** *fig*. to smell a rat.

pirina [. x .] oil cake.

pirinç[1], *-ci* brass.

pirinç[2], *-ci* BOT rice.

pirit, -ti GEOL pyrite.

pirüpak, -ki [- . -] spotless, immaculate.

pirzola cutlet, chop.

pis 1. dirty, filthy, foul; **2.** nasty, vile, foul; **3.** obscene, foul, profane; ~ *kokmak* to stink; ~ *koku* stink; ~ ~ *bakmak* to leer (*-e* at); ~ ~ *gülmek* to grin, to chuckle; *-i -ine* for nothing, in vain.

pisbıyık *sl*. scraggly moustache.

pisboğaz greedy.

pisi pussycat, kitty; ~ ~ here kitty, kitty, kitty!

pisibalığı, -nı ZOO plaice.

pisin swimming pool.

pisipisi 1. pussycat, kitty; **2.** here kitty, kitty, kitty!

piskopos bishop.

pislemek 1. to foul; **2.** to dirty, to soil.

pislenmek to get dirty.

pisletmek 1. to foul up, to make a balls-up of; **2.** to soil, to dirty.

pislik 1. dirt, filth; **2.** dirtiness, filthiness.

pissu sewage.

pist[1], *-ti* scat!

pist[2], *-ti* **1.** running track; **2.** AVIA runway; **3.** dance floor.

piston 1. MEC piston; **2.** *fig*. friend at court; ~ *kolu* MOT connecting rod, piston-rod.

pistonlu 1. MEC having a piston; **2.** *fig*. having a friend at court.

pisuar urinal.

pişik heat rash, prickly heat.

pişirmek 1. to cook, to bake; **2.** to ripen, to mature; **3.** to fire (*pottery*); **4.** to heat-treat (*metal*); **5.** to learn well.

pişkin 1. well-cooked, well-done; **2.** *fig*. experienced, worldly-wise; **3.** *fig*. brazen; **4.** used (*-e* to), accustomed (*-e* to).

pişkinlik 1. indifference to criticism; **2.** experience; maturity; **pişkinliğe vurmak** to brazen out.

pişman [ā] regretful, remorseful, penitent; ~ *olm.* to regret, to repent.

pişmaniye *candy made of sugar and oil with soapwort whipped into fibers*.

pişmanlık [ā] regret, repentance, remorse, penitence; ~ *duymak* to feel regret (*or* remorse).

pişmek, (-er) 1. to be cooked; **2.** to mature, to ripen; **3.** to be fired (*pottery*); **4.** to become worldly-wise; **pişmiş aşa soğuk su katmak** *fig*. to throw (*or* pour) cold water on; **pişmiş kelle gibi sırıtmak** to grin like a Cheshire cat, to simper.

pişti a card game.

piştov pistol.

piton ZOO python.
pitoresk, -ki picturesque.
piyade [â] **1.** MIL infantry; **2.** infantryman, foot soldier; **3.** *chess*: pawn.
piyanço [. x .] *sl.* louse.
piyango [. x .] lottery, raffle; ~ *bileti* lottery (*or* raffle) ticket; ~ *çekmek* to draw a lottery ticket.
piyanist, -ti pianist.
piyano [. x .] piano; ~ *çalmak* to play the piano; ~ *resitali* piano recital.
piyasa [. x .] **1.** market; **2.** the market, trading; **3.** the market price; **4.** promenading; ~ *etm.* to stroll about, to promenade; *-ya çıkarmak* to put on the market; *-ya çıkmak* **1.** to come on the market; **2.** to go out for a stroll; *-ya düşmek* **1.** to be on the market in abundance; **2.** *fig.* to go on the streets.
piyata [. x .] dinner plate.
piyaz **1.** bean salad; **2.** chopped onions; **3.** *sl.* flattery.
piyes THEAT play.
piyiz *sl.* rakî.
piyon *chess*: pawn.
piyoniye *fig.* pioneer.
pizza pizza.
plaçka [x .] loot, plunder, booty.
plaj beach, plage.
plak record.
plaka [x .] **1.** MOT license plate, number plate; **2.** MEC plaque, tablet.
plaket, -ti plaquette.
plan plan, scheme, project; ~ *kurmak* to plan, to scheme.
plançete [. x .] *surv.* plane table.
plankton plankton.
planlamak to plan.
planlı **1.** planned; **2.** premeditated (*crime*).
planör glider.
planörcü glider pilot.
planörcülük gliding.
plantasyon plantation.
planya [x .] carpenter's plane.
planyalamak to plane.
plasman COM investment.
plaster plaster, band-aid.
plastik plastic; ~ *ameliyat* plastic surgery; ~ *sanatlar* the plastic arts; ~ *tutkal* plastic glue.
platform platform (*a.* GEOGR), rostrum.
platin **1.** platinum; **2.** MOT points.
plato GEOGR plateau.
platonik platonic.
plazma plasma.
pli **1.** pleat; **2.** pleated.

plise **1.** pleating; **2.** pleated; ~ *yapmak* to pleat.
plonjon *football*: *dive made by a goalkeeper to block a shoot.*
poca NAUT leeward.
podüsüet, -ti suede.
podyum podium, dais, platform.
pof sss!; ~ *diye* with a hiss.
pofurdamak to snort.
pofur pofur in great puffs.
pofyos *sl.* **1.** hollow, empty; **2.** no-count, worthless.
poğaça [. x .] flaky pastry.
pohpoh flattery, soft soap.
pohpohçu flatterer.
pohpohlamak to flatter, to pamper.
poker poker; ~ *çevirmek* F to play poker.
pokerci poker player.
polarma PHYS, CHEM polarization.
polarmak PHYS, CHEM to polarize.
polemik polemic; *polemiğe girmek* to joust.
poliçe **1.** COM draft, bill of exchange; **2.** insurance policy.
poligami polygamy.
poligon **1.** polygon; **2.** MIL gunnery (*or* artillery) range.
poliklinik polyclinic.
polim *sl.* lie; ~ *atmak* *sl.* to tell lies.
polis **1.** the police; **2.** policeman.
polisiye detective ...; ~ *film* detective movie; ~ *roman* detective novel, whodunit.
polislik policemanship.
politik political.
politika **1.** politics; **2.** policy.
politikacı **1.** politician; **2.** *fig.* politic (*person*).
poliüretan polyurethane.
poliyester polyester.
polo polo.
Polonya [. x .] *pr. n.* Poland.
Polonyalı *pr. n.* **1.** Pole; **2.** Polish.
pomat MED pomade.
pompa [x .] pump.
pompalamak to pump.
pompuruk *sl.* old, decrepit (*man.*).
ponpon **1.** pompon, pom-pom; **2.** powder puff.
ponza [x .] (*taşı*) pumice.
poplin poplin.
pop (müzik) pop (music).
popo bottom, buttocks, fanny.
popüler popular.
pornografi pornography.
porselen porcelain.

porsiyon helping, portion (*of food*).
porsuk zoo badger.
porsukağacı, -nı bot yew (tree).
portakal orange; **~ rengi** orange.
portatif portable, movable, collapsible; **~ karyola** camp bed, *Am.* cot.
porte 1. scope, range; **2.** mus stave, staff.
Portekiz *pr. n.* Portugal.
portföy wallet, billfold.
portmanto hallstand, hatstand.
portör med carrier.
portre portrait.
posa [x .] residue, pulp, bagasse.
posbıyık having a bushy moustache.
post, -tu 1. skin, hide, pelt; **2.** *fig.* office, position, post; **~ elden gitmek** to be killed (*or* bumped off); **~ kapmak** to get an office; **~ kavgası** struggle over official positions; **-u kurtarmak** to save one's skin; **-u sermek** *fig.* to outstay one's welcome; **-una oturmak** *fig.* to put on airs.
posta [x .] **1.** post, mail; **2.** the post office, postal service; **3.** mil orderly; **4.** mail train; mail truck; mail steamer; **5.** crew, team; **6.** trip, run; **~ etm.** to take to the police station; **~ güvercini** carrier pigeon; **~ havalesi** (postal) money order; **~ koymak** to dupe, to con; **~ pulu** postage stamp; **~ yapmak** to ply; **-ya vermek** to post, *Am.* to mail; **-yı kesmek** *fig.* to cut relationships.
postacı [x ..] postman; postwoman.
postal 1. mil combat (*or* half) boot; **2.** F hussy, trollop.
postalamak to post, *Am.* to mail.
postane [ā] post office.
postrestant, -tı poste restante, general delivery.
poşet, -ti pochette.
pot¹, -tu the pot, the pool.
pot², -tu 1. pucker, wrinkle; **2.** blunder, blooper, slip of the tongue; **~ gelmek** (*iş*) to go wrong; **~ kırmak** to put one's foot in it, to drop a brick, to blunder; **~ yeri** *fig.* the sticky part (*of a matter*).
pot³ -tu raft, punt.
pota [x .] chem crucible.
potansiyel potential.
potas chem potash.
potasyum chem potassium.
potin boot.
potpuri mus medley, potpourri.
potur 1. puckered, wrinkled; **2.** Turkish breeches.

poyra [x .] mec hub (*of a wheel*).
poyraz Boreas, northeast wind.
poz 1. pose; **2.** phot exposure; **~ vermek** to pose.
pozitif positive.
pozometre [.. x .] phot exposure (*or* light) meter.
pöf phew!, ugh!
pörsük flaccid, wizened, withered.
pörsümek to wizen, to shrivel up.
pösteki sheepskin, goatskin; **~ saymak** *fig.* to be engaged in a tedious task; **-sini çıkarmak** (*or* **sermek**) *fig.* to beat to death; **-yi sermek** *fig.* to outstay one's welcome.
prafa [x .] a card game.
pranga [x .] fetters, irons, shackles; **-ya vurmak** to shackle, to fetter.
pratik 1. practical; handy; **2.** practice, application; **3.** applied; **~ yapmak** to practise, *Am.* to practice.
pratikleşmek to become practical.
pratisyen hekim med general practitioner.
prelüd mus prelude.
prens prince.
prenses princess.
prensip, -bi principle.
prenslik princedom, principate.
pres mec press.
presbit, -ti presbyopic.
prese mec (com)pressed.
prestij prestige.
prevantoryum [.. x .] med preventorium.
prezantabl presentable.
prezante etm. to introduce.
prezervatif condom, rubber.
prifiks com fixed price.
prim 1. premium; **2.** bonus.
priz elect socket, wall plug, power-point, jack.
prizma prism.
problem problem (*a.* math); **~ çocuk** problem child.
prodüktör producer.
profesör professor.
profesörlük professorship.
profesyonel professional.
profesyonellik professionalism.
profil profile.
program 1. program(me); **2.** schedule.
programcı 1. programmer; **2.** program(me) director.
programlamak to program.
programlı programmed.
proje project.

projeksiyon projection.
projectör projector, searchlight, spotlight.
proletarya proletariat.
prolog prologue.
propaganda propaganda; ~ *yapmak* to propagandize.
propagandacı propagandist.
prospektüs 1. instructions; **2.** prospectus.
prostat, -tı MED prostate.
protein protein.
Protestan *pr. n.* Protestant.
Protestanlık *pr. n.* Protestantism.
protesto [. x .] protest, outcry; ~ *etm.* (*bşi*) to protest against, *s.th.*
protez 1. MED prosthesis; **2.** denture, dental prosthesis.
protokol, -lü protocol.
protoplazma protoplasm.
prototip, -pi prototype.
prova [x .] **1.** rehearsal; **2.** TYP proof; **3.** fitting; **4.** *s. pruva.*
prömiyer premiere.
Prusya [x .] *pr. n.* Prussia.
pruva [x .] NAUT bow, head.
psikanaliz psychoanalysis.
psikiyatri psychiatry.
psikiyatrist, -ti psychiatrist.
psikolog psychologist.
psikoloji psychology.
psikolojik psychological.
psikopat, -tı psychopath.
psikoterapi psychotherapy.
puan 1. point; **2.** dot; ~ *almak* to score (points).
puanlamak to grade.
puantiye dotted (*cloth*).
puding pudding.
pudra powder.
pudralamak to powder.
pudralık compact.
pudraşeker powdered sugar.
pudriyer compact.
puf hassock, pouf, ottoman.
pufla [x .] **1.** ZOO eider; **2.** (eider)down; ~ *gibi* fluffy, downy.
puflamak to snort.
puhu (kuşu) ZOO eagle owl.
pul 1. stamp; **2.** *games*: piece, counter; **3.** MEC washer; nut; **4.** scale (*of a fish*); **5.** sequin, spangle; ~ *koleksiyonu* collection of stamps.
pulcu 1. seller of stamps; **2.** philatelist.
pullamak 1. to stamp; **2.** to decorate with spangles.
pullu stamped.

pulluk plough, *Am.* plow.
pulsuz unstamped, stampless.
puluç impotent.
puma ZOO puma.
punç, çu punch.
punt, -du 1. NAUT position; **2.** appropriate time; ~ *tayini* NAUT calculating a ship's position; ~*una getirmek* (*or* -*unu bulmak*) to find a suitable opportunity.
punto [x .] TYP size.
pupa [x .] NAUT **1.** stern; **2.** astern; ~*gitmek* **1.** to sail with the wind directly astern; **2.** *fig.* to go straight ahead; ~ *yelken gitmek* to go in full sail.
puro [x .] cigar.
pus[1] inch.
pus[2] **1.** mist, haze; **2.** gum; **3.** bloom (*on fruit*); **4.** crust (*on the nipple of a ewe*).
pusarık 1. misty, hazy; **2.** mirage.
pusat, -tı 1. equipment, gear; **2.** armo(u)r, arms.
puset, -ti stroller.
pusla *s. pusula.*
puslanmak to get misty (*or* hazy).
puslu misty, hazy.
pusmak to crouch down.
pusu ambush; ~ *kurmak* to lay an ambush; -*ya düşürmek* to ambush; -*ya yatmak* to lie in ambush, to lurk.
pusula [x ..] **1.** NAUT compass; **2.** memorandum, note; -*yı şaşırmak* *fig.* to be at a loss what to do, to be at sea.
puşt, -tu son of a bitch, bastard.
put, -tu 1. idol, effigy; **2.** the cross; ~ *gibi* as still as a statue; ~ *kesilmek* to become as still as a statue.
putperest, -ti idolater, pagan.
putperestlik idolatry, paganism.
putrel iron beam.
puvan *s. puan.*
püf puff, breath; ~ *noktası* (*bir işin*) the most delicate part (*of a matter*).
püflemek to blow on.
püfür püfür gently and coolingly; ~ *esmek* to blow gently, to puff.
pünez drawing pin, thumbtack.
pürçek lock, curl.
püre purée, mash.
pürgatif MED purgative.
pürneşe bright and merry.
pürtük knob.
pürüz 1. unevenness, roughness; **2.** *fig.* difficulty, snag, hitch.
pürüzlenmek 1. to get uneven (*or* rough); **2.** *fig.* to get snagged up, to

go awry.

pürüzlü 1. uneven, rough; **2.** *fig.* difficult, marked by snags.

pürüzsüz 1. even, smooth; **2.** *fig.* free of snags (*or* hitches).

püskül tassel.

püsküllü tasseled; ~ *bela* F a peck of trouble, damnable nuisance.

püskürgeç, -ci atomizer; sprayer.

püskürmek 1. to spray from one's mouth; **2.** to erupt (*volcano*); **3.** to spew out, to spume forth (*lava*).

püskürteç 1. atomizer; spray gun, sprayer; **2.** aerosol (bomb).

püskürtmek 1. *caus. of püskürmek*, to spray; to dust; **2.** MIL to repel, to drive back, to repulse.

püskürtü lava.

püsür 1. botherment, headache; **2.** petty; **3.** pain in the neck (*person*).

pütürlenmek to chap (*skin*).

pütürlü chapped, cracked.

pütür pütür chapped, cracked (*skin*).

R

Rab, -bbi God, the Lord.

Rabbena [. . -]: ~ *hakkı için* by God.

Rabbi(m) my God!

rabıt, -ptı connection.

rabıta [- . .] **1.** relation, connection, tie, bond; **2.** conformity; **3.** system, method, order.

rabıtalı [- . . . .] **1.** orderly; well-conducted; **2.** level-headed (*person*); **3.** coherent, consistent.

rabıtasız [- . . . .] **1.** disorderly, untidy; **2.** incoherent, inconsistent.

raca raja(h).

raci, -ii [ā] returning; ~ *olm.* to concern, to touch.

racon *sl.* **1.** custom, rule; **2.** swagger; ~ *kesmek* to swagger, to show off.

radar [x .] radar.

radarcı 1. radar operator; **2.** *sl.* talebearer, sneak.

radde degree, point; *-lerinde, -sinde* around, about.

radikal radical.

radyasyon PHYS radiation.

radyatör radiator.

radyo 1. radio, wireless; **2.** radio (station); ~ *dinlemek* to listen to the radio.

radyoaktif radioactive.

radyoculuk radio broadcasting.

radyoevi, -ni broadcasting station.

radyofonik radio ...; ~ *piyes* radio play.

radyofoto radiophotograph.

radyografi radiography.

radyogram radiogram.

radyotelefon radiotelephone.

radyotelgraf radiotelegram.

radyoterapi radiotherapy.

radyum CHEM radium.

raf shelf; *-a koymak* (*or kaldırmak*) to shelve (*a. fig.*).

rafadan 1. soft-boiled (*egg*); **2.** *sl.* naive; ~ *pişirmek* to soft-boil (*egg*).

rafine refined; ~ *etm.* to refine.

rafineri refinery.

rağbet, -ti 1. demand, inclination, desire; **2.** popularity; ~ *etm.* **1.** to demand, to like; **2.** to esteem; ~ *görmek* **1.** to be in demand; **2.** to be popular; *-ten düşmek* **1.** to be no longer in demand; **2.** to be out of favo(u)r.

rağbetli in demand.

rağbetsiz not in demand.

rağmen [x .] in spite (*-e* of).

rahat, -tı 1. comfort, ease; **2.** peace; **3.** comfortable; **4.** easy, at ease, untroubled; **5.** MIL at ease!; **6.** easygoing (*person*); ~ *bırakmamak* (*or vermemek*) to pester, to annoy, to devil; ~ *durmak* to behave o.s.; ~ *etm.* **1.** to be at ease; **2.** to rest, to take it easy; ~ ~ comfortably; easily; ~ *yüzü görmemek* to have no peace; *-ına bakmak* to mind one's own comfort, to see to one's pleasures; *-ını kaçırmak* to annoy, to pester, to molest.

rahatça 1. easily; **2.** comfortably.

rahatlamak to feel relieved (*or* better); to feel at ease, to cheer up.

rahatlık 1. peace, quiet; **2.** ease, comfort; **3.** easygoingness.

rahatsız 1. uncomfortable; **2.** uneasy, anxious; **3.** unwell, under the weather, indisposed; ~ *etm.* **1.** to annoy, to disturb, to trouble, to bother; **2.** to pay a visit; ~ *olm.* **1.** to feel uncomfortable; **2.** to be under the weather, to feel in-

disposed.
rahatsızlanmak to feel ill (*or* unwell).
rahatsızlık 1. discomfort, uneasiness; **2.** illness, sickness.
rahibe [ā] nun.
rahibelik [ā] nunhood.
rahim, -hmi womb, uterus.
Rahîm the Merciful.
rahip, -bi [ā] **1.** priest, minister, pastor; **2.** monk.
rahle low reading-desk.
Rahman [. -] the Compassionate.
rahmet, -ti 1. God's mercy (*or* compassion); **2.** *fig.* rain; **~ düşmek** (*or* **yağmak**) to rain; **~ okumak 1.** to pray for the soul (-*e* of); **2.** to regret the loss (-*e* of); **~ okutmak** to be a greater nuisance (-*e* than); **-ine kavuşmak** to pass away, to go to meet one's Maker.
rahmetli(k) the deceased, the late; **~ olm.** to pass away, to die.
rahne fissure, breach.
rahvan amble; **~ gitmek** to amble (*horse*)
rakam 1. number, figure; **2.** numeral, digit.
raket, -ti 1. racket, racquet; **2.** snowshoe.
rakı raki, arrack.
rakım altitude, elevation.
rakıs, -ksı 1. dance; **2.** PHYS oscillation.
rakip, -bi rival.
rakit, -di [ā] still, stagnant (*water*).
rakkas [. -] pendulum.
rakkase [. - .] belly dancer.
rakor MEC joint, union (*of pipes*).
raksetmek [x . .] to dance.
ralanti MOT idling; **-de çalışmak** MOT to tick over, to idle; **-ye almak** MOT to idle.
rali rally.
ram: ~ etm. to master, to subjugate.
ramak, -kı: ~ kalmak to be within an ace (*or* inch) (-*e* of).
Ramazan 1. Ramazan; **2.** *mf.*; **~ bayramı** the Ramazan festival.
rampa [x .] **1.** slope, incline, grade; **2.** loading ramp; **~ etm. 1.** to sidle up (-*e* to); **2.** *sl.* to latch (-*e* onto).
rampalamak *s.* **rampa etm.**
randevu appointment, rendezvous, tryst, engagement, date; **~ almak** to get an appointment (-*den* from); **~ vermek** (*b-ne*) to make an appointment with *s.o.*
randevuevi, -ni unlicensed brothel.
randıman output, yield, production.

randımanlı productive.
randımansız unproductive.
rant, -tı COM unearned income.
rantabl COM profitable.
ranza [x .] **1.** bunk bed; **2.** AVIA, RAIL berth.
rap MUS rap (*music*).
rapido drawing pen.
rapor report.
raporcu reporter.
raporlu on sick leave.
raportör reporter.
rap rap striking the ground smartly.
rapsodi MUS rhapsody.
raptetmek [x . .] to attach, to fasten.
raptiye drawing pin, *Am.* thumbtack.
raptiyelemek to thumbtack.
rasat, -dı AST observation.
rasathane [. . - .] observatory.
rasgele [x . .] haphazardly, at random; by chance.
rasıt, -dı AST observer.
raspa [x .] **1.** scraper; **2.** *sl.* gluttony; **~ etm.** to scrape.
rast: ~ gelmek 1. to chance (-*e* upon), to meet by chance; **2.** to come (-*e* across), to meet (-*e* with), to encounter; **3.** to coincide (-*e* with), to fall (-*e* on); **~ getirmek 1.** to come across (*or* upon); **2.** to approach, to collar s.o. (*at the right time*); **3.** to hit the target; **4.** to cause to succeed (*God*); **~ gitmek** to go well, to turn out well.
rastık kohl.
rastlamak *s.* **rast gelmek.**
rastlantı coincidence, chance, accident.
rastlaşmak 1. to chance upon each other; **2.** to coincide.
rasyonalizm rationalism.
rasyonel rational.
raşitizm MED rickets, rachitis.
raunt *s.* **ravnt.**
ravnt *boxing:* round.
ray rail; track; **-dan çıkmak 1.** RAIL to jump the rails, to go off the rails; **2.** *fig.* to go awry (*or* haywire); **-ına oturtmak** to set to rights.
rayiç, -ci COM market (*or* current) value; **~ fiyat** market (*or* current) price.
rayiha [- . .] fragrance.
razakı a kind of white grape.
razı [ā] willing, content; **~ etm.** (*b-ni bşe*) to get *s.o.* to agree to *s.th.*, to get *s.o.* round to *s.th.*; **~ olm.** to consent (-*e* to), to agree (-*e* to).
re MUS re; D.

reaksiyon reaction.
reaktör reactor.
realist, -ti realist(ic).
realite reality.
realizm realism.
Recep, -bi 1. Rajab; **2.** *mf.*
reçel jam.
reçete 1. prescription; **2.** recipe.
reçine [. x .] resin, rosin.
reçineli resinous.
redaksiyon redaction.
reddetmek [x . .] **1.** to refuse, to reject, to refute, to repudiate; **2.** to disown, to cast off.
redingot, -tu frock coat.
refah [ā] welfare, prosperity, well-being; **~ içinde yaşamak** to live in prosperity, to be in easy circumstances.
refakat, -ti [. - .] accompaniment (*a. MUS*), companionship; **~ etm.** to accompany (*a. MUS*); to escort; **-inde** in the company (*-in* of).
refakatçi companion (*who stays with a patient while he is in hospital*).
referandum [. . x .] POL referendum.
referans reference, letter of recommendation.
refetmek [x . .] to remove, to abolish.
refik, -kı [ī] **1.** friend, companion; **2.** ♀ [x .] *mf.*
refika [ī] **1.** wife; **2.** ♀ [x . .] *wf.*
refleks reflex.
reflektör reflector.
reform reform.
reformcu 1. reformer; **2.** reformist(ic).
refüj MOT (traffic) island, refuge.
refüze etm. to refuse, to turn down.
regaip, -bi [ā]: **~ kandili** the 12th of Recep. anniversary of the conception of Mohammad.
regülatör MEC regulator.
rehabilitasyon MED rehabilitation.
rehavet, -ti [ā] languor, lassitude.
rehber 1. guide; **2.** guidebook; **3.** (telephone) directory.
rehberlik 1. guidance; **2.** guiding; **~ etm.** to guide.
rehin pawn, pledge, security, collateral; **-e koymak** to pawn, to hock, to pop, to pledge.
rehine hostage.
reis [ī] head, chief, leader; president; chairman; **~ vekili** vice-president.
reisicumhur president.
reislik leadership, chieftaincy; presidency; chairmanship; **~ etm.** to preside.

reji 1. the Regie; **2.** THEAT, *cinema*: direction.
rejim 1. POL regime; **2.** MED diet; **~ yapmak** to diet.
rejisör director.
rekabet, -ti [ā] rivalry, competition; **~ etm.** (*b-le*) to rival *s.o.*, to compete against *s.o.*, to vie with *s.o.*
rekâket, -ti stammer, stutter.
rekât, -tı isl. complete act of worship with the prescribed postures.
reklam advertisement.
reklamcılık advertising.
rekolte [. x .] COM harvest, crop.
rekor record; **~ kırmak** to break a record; **~ sahibi** record-holder.
rekorcu, rekortmen record-breaker.
rektifiye etm. MEC to rectify.
rektör UNIV rector, president, chancellor.
rektörlük UNIV rectorship, rectorate.
remil, -mli geomancy.
remiz, -mzi symbol, sign.
remmal, -li [ā] geomancer.
rencide [ī] hurt, offended, wounded; **~ etm.** to hurt (*s.o.'s feelings*).
rençper 1. farmer; **2.** farmhand.
rende 1. (*carpenter's*) plane; **2.** grater.
rendelemek 1. to plane; **2.** to grate.
rengârenk, -gi colo(u)rful, multicolo(u)red.
rengeyiği, -ni ZOO reindeer.
renk, -gi 1. colo(u)r, hue; **2.** *fig.* character, colo(u)r; **~~** colo(u)rful, multicolo(u)red; **~ vermek** (*or* **katmak**) to enliven, to liven up; **~ vermemek** to keep up appearances; **-i atmak** (*or* **uçmak**) **1.** to fade; **2.** to go pale; **-i çalık** faded, discolo(u)red; **-ten -e girmek** *fig.* to go all shades of red.
renkgideren decolo(u)rant, bleach.
renkkörlüğü, -nü colo(u)r blindness.
renkkörü, -nü colo(u)r-blind.
renklendirmek 1. to make colo(u)rful, to give colo(u)r; **2.** *fig.* to enliven, to liven up.
renkli 1. colo(u)red; **2.** colo(u)rful, amusing, lively; **~ film** colo(u)r film; **~ fotoğraf** colo(u)r photograph; **~ işitme** PSYCH colo(u)r hearing.
renkseçmezlik colo(u)r blindness.
renksemez achromatic (*lens*).
renksiz 1. colo(u)rless, uncolo(u)red; **2.** faded, pale; **3.** *fig.* lackluster, non-descript.
repertuvar repertoire, repertory.
replik THEAT rejoinder.

re'sen [x .] on one's own account, independently.

resepsiyon reception (desk).

reseptör ELECT receiver.

resif GEOGR reef.

resim, -smi 1. picture; photograph; drawing; painting; illustration; **2.** tax, duty, impost; **3.** ceremony; ~ *çekmek* to take a photograph, to photograph; ~ *dersi* art lesson; ~ *sergisi* exhibition of pictures; ~ *yapmak* to paint; to draw; *resmini çekmek* to take a picture (*-in* of).

resimci 1. photographer; **2.** illustrator; artist; **3.** art teacher.

resimlemek to illustrate.

resimli illustrated, pictorial; ~ *roman* comic (strip).

resimlik 1. photograph album; **2.** picture frame.

resital, -li MUS recital.

resmen [x .] officially, formally.

resmetmek [x . .] **1.** to picture, to draw; **2.** to depict, to delineate, to describe, to represent.

resmi 1. official, government ...; **2.** authorized, official; **3.** formal, ceremonious, official; ~ *dil* official language; ~ *elbise* uniform; ~ *gazete* official gazette; ~ *nikâh* civil marriage.

resmiyet, -ti 1. formality, ceremony; **2.** officialism, officiality; *-e dökmek* to officialize.

ressam painter, artist.

rest, -ti: ~ *çekmek* **1.** to stake all; **2.** *fig.* to have the last word.

resto *sl.* stop!, that's enough!

restoran restaurant.

restorasyon restoration.

restore etm. to restore.

resul, -lü [ü] prophet.

resülmal, -li [- . -] COM capital.

reşit, -di [ī] **1.** of age, adult; **2.** ♀ [x .] *mf.*; ~ *olm.* to come of age.

ret, -ddi 1. refusal, rejection; **2.** repudiation, disownment.

reva [ā] suitable, worthy; ~ *görmek* to deem proper.

revaç, -cı 1. salability, marketability; **2.** current (*or* market) price; ~ *bulmak* to be in demand; to be in vogue; ~ *vermek* to cause to be in demand.

revani [. - -] *a sweet made with semolina.*

reverans curts(e)y, bow; ~ *yapmak* to curtsy (*-e* to); to bow (*-e* to).

revir infirmary, sick bay.

revizyon MEC overhaul; *-dan geçirmek* MEC to overhaul.

revolver revolver.

revü THEAT revue, review.

rey 1. vote; **2.** view, opinion; *-e koymak* to put to the vote.

reye striped (*cloth*).

reyon department.

rezalet, -ti [ā] **1.** disgrace, outrage, scandal; **2.** disgraceful, scandalous; ~ *çıkarmak* to create a scandal.

reze 1. pintle hinge; **2.** hasp.

rezene BOT fennel.

rezerv(e) reserve.

rezervasyon reservation; ~ *yapmak* to make a reservation.

rezerve reserved; *-etm.* to reserve, to book.

rezervuar reservoir.

rezil [ī] disgraceful, outrageous, scandalous; ~ *etm.* to disgrace, to pillory; ~ *olm.* to be disgraced.

rezillik [ī] disgrace, scandal, outrage.

rezistans ELECT resistance.

rıhtım quay, pier, wharf.

rıza [ā] **1.** consent, approval, assent; **2.** volition, choice; **3.** ♀ [x .] *mf.*; ~ *göstermek* to consent (*-e* to); *-sını almak* (*b-nin*) to get *s.o.'s* consent.

rızk, -kı one's daily bread, food; *-ını çıkarmak* to earn one's daily bread.

riayet, -ti [ā] **1.** obedience, compliance, observance; **2.** respect, esteem; regard; **3.** hospitality; ~ *etm.* **1.** to comply (*-e* with), to obey; to observe; **2.** to respect; **3.** to show hospitality (*-e* to).

riayetkâr [ā] **1.** obedient; **2.** respectful.

riayetsiz [ā] **1.** disobedient; **2.** disrespectful.

riayetsizlik [ā] **1.** disobedience, noncompliance; **2.** disrespect.

rica [ā] request; ~ *ederim!* not at all!, please!; ~ *etm.* (*b-den bşi*) to request *s.th.* of *s.o.*

rical, -li [ā] men of importance; dignitaries.

ricat, -tı MIL retreat; ~ *etm.* to retreat.

rikkat, -ti 1. pity, compassion; mercy; **2.** gentleness, tenderness.

rimel mascara.

rina ZOO stingray.

ring, -gi *sports*: ring.

ringa ZOO herring.

risale [ā] treatise, pamphlet, booklet.

risk, -ki risk; *-e girmek* to take (*or* run) a risk.

ritim, -tmi rhythm.

ritmik rhythmic.

rivayet, -ti [ā] rumo(u)r, hearsay; ~ **etm.** to relate.

riya [ā] hypocrisy, two-facedness.

riyakâr [ā] hypocritical, two-faced.

riyal, -li ri(y)al.

riyaset, -ti [ā] headship, presidency; ~ **etm.** to preside (-e over).

riyaseticumhur presidency.

riyazet, -ti [ā] asceticism.

riyaziye [ā] obs. mathematics.

riyaziyeci [ā] obs. mathematician.

riziko [x . .] risk.

rizikolu [x . . .] risky.

roba 1. dress; **2.** yoke (of a garment).

robdöşambr dressing gown.

robot, -tu robot.

roka BOT (garden) rocket.

roket, -ti rocket.

roketatar bazooka.

rokoko rococo.

rol, -lü role, part; ~ **almak** to have a role (or part) (in a play); to perform; ~ **kesmek** F to put on an act, to playact; ~ **oynamak** (bşde) to play a part in s.th., to figure in s.th.; ~ **yapmak** = ~ **kesmek.**

rom rum.

Roma [x .] pr. n. Rome.

Romalı pr. n. Roman.

roman novel.

romancı novelist.

romantik romantic.

romantizm romance, romanticism.

Romanya [. x .] pr. n. Rumania.

Romanyalı pr. n. Rumanian.

romatizma [. . x .] rheumatism.

romatizmalı rheumatic.

Romen: ~ **harfleri** TYP Roman letters; ~ **rakamları** Roman numerals.

rondela MEC washer.

rop, -bu dress, robe.

rosto [x .] roast.

rot, -tu MOT rod.

rota [x .] NAUT course; **-yı değiştirmek** to change course (a. fig.).

roza [x .] rose (diamond).

rozbif roast beef.

rozet, -ti 1. rosette; **2.** emblem, badge.

rölöve statistical survey.

rölyef relief.

römork, -ku trailer.

römorkör tug(boat).

rönar fox fur.

Rönesans the Renaissance.

röntgen 1. X-ray; **2.** sl. peeping, voyeurism; **-ini çekmek** to X-ray.

röntgenci 1. X-ray specialist; **2.** sl. Peeping Tom, voyeur.

röportaj report (of a newspaperman).

rötar delay.

rötarlı delayed (train, bus, etc.).

rötuş retouching; ~ **yapmak** to touch up.

rövanş sports: return match (or game).

ruam [ā] MED glanders.

rubai [. - -] quatrain.

ruble [x .] ruble.

rugan patent leather.

ruh 1. soul, spirit; **2.** animation, life, spirit; **3.** PSYCH psyche; **4.** CHEM essence, spirit; **5.** heart, essence (of a matter); **6.** spirit (of a dead person); ~ **doktoru** psychiatrist; ~ **çağırma** necromancy; ~ **göçü** metempsychosis; ~ **haleti** (or **hali**) mood, state of mind; ~ **hastası** mental patient; ~ **hekimi** psychiatrist; ~ **hekimliği** psychiatry; **-unu teslim etm.** to give up the ghost.

ruhani [- - -] spiritual.

ruhbilim psychology.

ruhbilimci psychologist.

ruhen [- .] spiritually, in spirit.

ruhi [- -] **1.** psychological, mental; **2.** ⚲ [x .] mf.

ruhiyat, -tı [- . -] psychology.

ruhlanmak to become animated, to revive.

ruhlu spirited, lively, energetic.

ruhsal psychological, mental.

ruhsat, -tı 1. permission, authorization; **2.** license, permit; registration (or log) book.

ruhsatiye s. **ruhsatname.**

ruhsatlı 1. authorized, permitted; **2.** licensed.

ruhsatname [. . - .] permit, license; registration (or log) book.

ruhsatsız 1. unauthorized; **2.** unlicensed.

ruhsuz spiritless, lifeless, inanimate.

ruj lipstick.

rulet, -ti roulette.

rulman MEC bearing.

rulo roll (of paper).

Rum Greek.

rumba r(h)umba.

Rumca [x .] Greek (language).

Rumen Romanian.

rumuz [. -] **1.** symbol, sign; **2.** pseudonym, alias.

Rus Russian.

Rusça [x .] the Russian language, Russian.

Rusya [x .] *pr. n.* Russia.

rutubet, -ti [. - .] humidity, damp(ness).

rutubetlenmek to become humid.

rutubetli [. - . .] humid, damp.

ruva [. x] *cards:* king.

ruzname [- - .] **1.** diary, journal; **2.** agenda.

rücu, -uu [ū] **1.** recision; **2.** withdrawal; ~ **hakkı** JUR right of recovery.

rüçhan [ā] **1.** preference, preemption; **2.** ♀ *mf., wf.*; ~ **hakkı** JUR (right to) preference.

rükün, -knü mainstay, pillar, prop.

rüküş comically dressed.

rüsum [ū] *pl. of* **resim**, duties, taxes.

rüsup, -bu [ū] sediment.

rüşt, -tü JUR majority; **-ünü ispat etm.** *fig.* to evidence one's maturity.

rüştiye HIST junior high school.

rüşvet, -ti bribe, graft; bribery; ~ **al-**

mak to take (*or* accept) a bribe, to graft; ~ **vermek** to give a bribe, to bribe; ~ **yemek** to take bribes, to bribe; ~ **yemek** to take bribes, to graft.

rüşvetçi grafter, taker of bribes.

rüşvetçilik bribery.

rütbe MIL rank.

rüya dream; ~ **görmek** to dream, to have a dream; **-sında görmek** to dream of, to see in one's dreams; **-sını tabir etm.** to interpret s.o.'s dream.

rüyet, -ti seeing, vision.

rüzgâr wind, breeze; ~ **almak** to be exposed to the wind; ~ **ekip fırtına biçmek** to sow the wind and reap the whirlwind; ~ **ile gitmek** to sail with the wind.

rüzgârgülü, -nü compass rose.

rüzgârlı windy, breezy.

rüzgârlık windbreaker, windcheater.

S

saadet, -ti [. - .] **1.** happiness; **2.** ♀ *wf.*; **-le!** good luck!

saat, -ti 1. hour; **2.** watch, clock; **3.** time; **4.** meter; taximeter; speedometer; ~ **ayarı** time signal; ~ **başı** on the hour; ~ **kaç?** what time is it?, what is the time?; ~ **kulesi** clock tower; ~ **on birde 1.** at eleven o'clock; **2.** *fig.* very late in life; ~ **tutmak** to time; ~ **vurmak** to strike the hour (*clock*); **-i kurmak** to wind a watch *or* clock; **-i uymamak** to chop and change.

saatçi 1. watchmaker; watch repairer; **2.** seller of watches *or* clocks.

saatçilik making, selling *or* repairing watches *or* clocks.

saatli fitted with a clock; ~ **bomba** time bomb.

saatlik lasting … hours.

sabah 1. morning; **2.** in the morning; ~ **akşam** all the time; ~ **gazetesi** morning paper; ~ **kahvaltısı** breakfast; ~ **oldu** it's morning, morning's come; ~ ~ early in the morning; **-a çıkmamak** not to live through the night; **-a doğru** towards morning; **-ın köründe** at the crack of dawn; **-lar hayrolsun!** good morning!; **-lardan bir** ~ one morning.

sabahçı 1. person who works on a

morning shift; **2.** pupil who goes to school in the mornings; **3.** person who sits up all night.

sabahki morning's.

sabahlamak to sit up (*or* work) all night; **hasta çocuğunun başında sabahladı** she kept vigil over her sick child.

sabahleyin [. x . .] in the morning.

sabahlı akşamlı mornings and evenings.

sabahlık 1. dressing gown, housecoat; **2.** enough for … mornings.

saban plough, *Am.* plow; ~ **demiri** ploughshare, *Am.* plowshare; ~ **izi** furrow; ~ **sürmek** to plough, *Am.* to plow

sabık, -kı [ā] previous, former, last, ex-; ~ **kral** ex-king.

sabıka [- . . .] JUR previous conviction, past offence.

sabıkalı [- . . . .] JUR previously convicted; recidivist.

sabır, -brı patience; forbearance; ~ **taşı** very patient person; **sabrı taşmak** (*or* **tükenmek**) (*for one's patience*) to come to an end; **sabrın sonu selamettir** patience is rewarded.

sabırlı patient; forbearing.

sabırsız impatient.

sabırsızlanmak to grow impatient.
sabırsızlık impatience.
sabit, -ti [ā] **1.** fixed, stationary; constant; stable; **2.** fast (*dye, colo(u)r*); **3.** fixed (*stare*); **4.** proved; ~ *balon* captive balloon; ~ *fikir* fixed idea, crank; ~ *fiyat* fixed price.
sabitleşmek to become fixed; to stabilize.
sabo clog.
sabotaj sabotage; ~ *yapmak* to sabotage.
sabotajcı saboteur.
sabote etm. to sabotage.
sabretmek [x . .] to show patience, to be patient; *sabreden derviş muradına ermiş pro.* everything comes to him who waits.
sabuk *s.* **abuk sabuk.**
sabuklama delirium.
sabun soap; ~ *köpüğü* lather.
sabuncu soap maker; soap seller.
sabunlamak to soap, to lather.
sabunlanmak to soap o.s.
sabunlu soapy.
sabunluk soap dish.
sac *s.* **saç 2.**
saçayağı, -nı, sacayak trivet.
saç¹, -çı hair; ~ *bağı* hair band; ~ *boyası* hair dye; ~ *dibi* hair bed; ~ *filesi* hair-net; ~ *kurutma makinesi* hair drier; ~ *örgüsü* plait; ~ *örmek* to braid the hair; ~ *-a baş başa gelmek* to come to blows; ~ *sakal ağartmak* to work on s.th. for a long time; *-ına ak düşmek* to turn gray; *-ını başını yolmak* to tear one's hair, to beat one's breast; *-ını süpürge etm.* to exert o.s. (*woman*); *-ları diken diken oldu* his hair stood on end; *-ları iki türlü olm.* to get old.
saç², -cı, -çı MEC sheet iron.
saçak 1. eave(s) (*of a building*); **2.** fringe.
saçakbulut, -tu cirrus (cloud).
saçaklı 1. eaved (*building*); **2.** fringed.
saçkıran MED alopecia, loss of hair.
saçlı ... haired.
saçma 1. *vn. of* **saçmak; 2.** (buck)shot; **3.** cast(ing) net; **4.** (*a.* ~ *sapan*) nonsensical, absurd; ~ *sapan konuşmak* to talk crap, to drivel, to talk nonsense.
saçmak, (-ar) to scatter, to strew; *saçıp savurmak* to play ducks and drakes with (*money*), to squander.
saçmalamak to talk nonsense (*or* rot

or crap), to drivel, to piffle, to ramble, to twaddle.
saçmalık piece of nonsense.
sada *s.* **seda.**
sadak quiver.
sadaka alms; ~ *istemek* to beg, to cadge; ~ *vermek* to give alms.
sadakat, -ti [. - .] loyalty, fidelity, devotion, allegiance; ~ *borcu* JUR loyalty; ~ *göstermek* to show loyalty (*-e* to); ~ *yemini* oath of allegiance.
sadakatli [. - . .] loyal, faithful, devoted.
sadakatsiz [. - . .] disloyal, unfaithful.
sadakatsizlik disloyalty, unfaithfulness, infidelity.
sadakor raw silk.
sadalı *s.* **sedalı.**
sadaret, -ti [. - .] HIST grand vizierate (*or* viziership); ♀ *Dairesi* HIST the Sublime Porte.
sadasız *s.* **sedasız.**
sade [ā] **1.** plain, simple; **2.** black and unsweetened (*coffee*); **3.** merely, only, solely, just; ~ *suya çorba* clear soup.
sadece [ā] *s.* **sade 3.**
sadedil [ā] simple-hearted, guileless.
sadeleşmek [ā] to become simple (*or* plain).
sadeleştirmek [ā] to simplify, to purify.
sadelik [ā] simplicity, plainness.
sadet, -di main topic (*or* point); *-e gelmek* to come to the point; *-ten ayrılmak* to get off the subject.
sadeyağ clarified (*or* run) butter.
sadık, -kı [ā] **1.** loyal, faithful, devoted, fast; **2.** true, veracious; **3.** ♀ *mf.*; ~ *kalmak* to remain loyal (*-e* to).
sadist, -ti sadist(ic).
sadistlik, sadizm sadism.
sadme shock (*a. psych*), jolt; collision.
sadrazam [. - .] HIST grand vizier.
sadrazamlık HIST grand viziership (*or* vizierate).
saf¹, -ffı 1. row, line; **2.** MIL rank, line; ~ *bağlamak* to form a line; ~ ~ in rows (*or* ranks *or* lines).
saf² 1. pure, unadulterated; **2.** credulous, naïve, gullible.
safa [. -] **1.** ease, peace, untroubledness; **2.** delight, enjoyment, pleasure; **3.** entertainment, party; **4.** ♀ [x .] *mf.*; ~ *bulduk!* thank you! (*said in reply to the greeting* ~ *geldiniz!*); ~ *geldiniz!* welcome!; ~ *sürmek* to enjoy o.s., to have a good time.

safer safar.

saffet, -ti 1. purity; **2.** ♀ *mf.*, *wf.*

safha phase, stage.

safi [- -] **1.** pure, unadulterated; **2.** net; **3.** only, merely, solely.

safir sapphire.

safkan [- .] purebred, thoroughbred (*horse*).

saflaştırmak [- . . .] to purify; to refine.

saflık 1. purity; **2.** credulousness, naiveté.

safra¹ NAUT ballast; ~ **atmak** to get rid of troublesome people *or* things.

safra² ANAT bile, gall; ~ **bastırmak** to have a snack; ~ **kesesi** gall bladder; **-sı kabarmak** (*or* **bulanmak**) to be seasick.

safran BOT saffron.

safsata sophistry, casuistry.

safsatacı sophist, casuist.

sağ¹ **1.** right; **2.** POL right-wing; ~ **gözünü sol gözünden kıskanmak** to be extremely jealous; **-a bak!** MIL eyes right!; **-a sola** hither and thither; **-dan gidiniz!** keep to the right!; **-dan soldan** from the right and from the left; **-ı solu olmamak** *fig.* to chop and change; **-ını solunu şaşırmak** not to know what to do.

sağ² **1.** alive, living; **2.** healthy, well; **3.** *s.* **sağlam;** ~ **kalanlar** the survivors; ~ **kalmak** to remain alive, to survive; ~ **ol!** thanks!, cheers!; ~ **salim** safe and sound, scot-free.

sağaçık *football*: outside right.

sağanak shower, downpour, cloudburst.

sağbek, -ki *football*: right back.

sağcı POL rightist, right-winger.

sağdıç bridesmaid; groomsman.

sağduyu common sense.

sağgörü foresight.

sağgörülü foresighted.

sağhaf [. -] *football*: right halfback.

sağılmak 1. *pass. of* **sağmak; 2.** to uncoil itself (*snake*); **3.** to fray, to ravel (*cloth*).

sağın exact, precise.

sağır 1. deaf; **2.** blank, blind (*wall-etc.*); **3.** muted, muffled (*sound*); ~ **sultan bile duydu** everybody from here to China knows about it.

sağırlaşmak to grow deaf.

sağırlık deafness.

sağiç, -çi *football*: right centre (*or Am.* center).

sağlam 1. strong, sound; well-built,

well-made; secure; **2.** healthy, strong; **3.** reliable, trustworthy, dependable; ~ (*or* **sağ**) **ayakkabı değildir** he is unreliable; ~ **kaba kotarmak** (*bşi*) *fig.* to make *s.th.* profitable; ~ (*or* **sağ**) **kazığa bağlamak** *fig.* to make safe (*or* sure).

sağlama 1. *vn. of* **sağlamak; 2.** *part.* MATH proof, cross-check.

sağlamak 1. to provide, to get, to find, to obtain; **2.** to guarantee, to ensure; **3.** MATH to prove, to cross-check; **4.** MOT to move to the right side (*of the road*).

sağlamlamak to strengthen, to fortify, to reinforce.

sağlamlaşmak to become strong.

sağlamlaştırmak to strengthen, to fortify, to reinforce, to consolidate.

sağlamlık strength, soundness.

sağlı sollu 1. on both sides of; **2.** using first one hand and then the other.

sağlıcakla [. . x .] in good health, happily.

sağlık¹ health; ~ **bilgisi** hygiene; ~ **ocağı** village clinic; ~ **olsun!** never mind!; ~ **raporu** health report; ♀ **ve Sosyal Yardım Bakanlığı** the Ministry of Health and Social Services; ~ **sigortası** health insurance; ~ **yoklaması** general medical checkup, physical examination; ~ **yurdu** convalescent home; **sağlığında** in his lifetime, while he is alive; **sağlığınıza!** cheers!, to your health!

sağlık² *s.* **salık.**

sağlıklı 1. healthy, in good health; **2.** *fig.* sound, reliable.

sağlıksız sickly.

sağmak, (-ar) 1. to milk (*an animal*); **2.** to extract from the hive (*honey*); **3.** to unwind, to unravel (*threads*); **4.** *sl.* to mulct, to milk.

sağmal 1. milch (*animal*); **2.** *sl.* fit to be fleeced (*person*); ~ **inek** milch cow (*a. fig.*).

sağrı rump (*of an animal*); ~ **kemiği** ANAT rump bone, sacrum.

sah, -hhı stet; ~ **çekmek** to stet.

saha [- .] field (*a. sports*), area, zone, region.

sahaf [. -] dealer in secondhand books, bouquiniste.

sahan copper pan; **-da yumurta** fried egg.

sahanlık 1. landing (*on a staircase*); **2.** platform.

sahi [ī] really, truly.

sahibe [- . .] proprietress; mistress.

sahici genuine, real.

sahiden really, truly.

sahife *s.* **sayfa.**

sahil [ā] shore, coast; bank; **~ kordonu** GEOGR (sand)bar.

sahip, -bi [ā] owner, possessor, proprietor, master; proprietress, mistress; **~ çıkmak 1.** (*bşe*) to claim *s.th.*; **2.** (*b-ne*) to look after *s.o.*, to see to *s.o.*; **~ olm. 1.** to own, to possess, to have; **2.** to get under control.

sahipsiz ownerless, unclaimed, unappropriated.

sahne 1. stage; **2.** THEAT scene; **~ olm.** to be the scene (*-e* of); **-ye çıkmak** to appear; **-ye koymak** to stage, to put on (*a play*).

sahra [. -] **1.** open plain; **2.** desert; **3.** MIL field ...; **~ topu** MIL field gun.

sahre GEOL rock mass.

sahte 1. false, fake, counterfeit, spurious, phony; **2.** feigned, pretended.

sahtekâr forger, faker, falsifier.

sahtekârlık forgery, falsification; imposture.

sahtiyan morocco (leather).

sahur [ū] *isl.* meal before dawn (*during Ramazan*).

saik, -kı [ā] motive.

saika[1] [- . .] motive; incentive.

saika[2] [- . .] *obs.* lightning.

sair [ā] other.

saka water seller.

sakakuşu, -nu zoo (gold)finch.

sakağı MED glanders.

sakal beard; whiskers; **~ bırakmak** (*or* **koyuvermek** *or* **salıvermek** *or* **uzatmak**) to grow a beard; **-ı bitmek** (*bir işin*) to be in the balance; **-ı ele vermek** *fig.* to allow o.s. to be led by the nose; **-ımı değirmende ağartmadım** *fig.* I am not an old fool; **-ına gülmek** to laugh up one's sleeve.

sakallı bearded; whiskered.

sakalsız beardless.

sakamonya [. . x .] BOT scammony.

sakandırık chin strap.

sakar 1. blaze (*on an animal's forehead*); **2.** butterfingered, clumsy, accident-prone.

sakarin saccharin.

sakarlaşmak to become butterfingered.

sakarlık clumsiness, awkwardness.

sakat, -tı 1. disabled, invalid, handi-

capped; **2.** *fig.* unsound, crippled, defective.

sakatat, -tı [. . -] offal.

sakatlamak to disable, to mutilate, to maim, to cripple.

sakatlanmak to become disabled (*or* crippled).

sakatlık 1. disability, handicap, impairment; **2.** *fig.* flaw, defect.

sakın don't, beware!; **~ söylediklerimi unutmayın!** don't forget what I said.

sakınca drawback, objection.

sakıncalı objectionable, inadvisable; unwise.

sakıngan cautious, prudent.

sakınma *vn. of* **sakınmak**; **-sı olmamak** to be heedless.

sakınmak 1. to avoid, to shun, to keep away (*-den* from), to steer clear (*-den* of); **2.** to watch out (*-den* for); to guard (*-den* against); **3.** to protect (*-den* from).

sakırga zoo tick.

sakıt, -tı 1. falling; fallen; **2.** MED stillborn; **3.** JUR invalid.

Sakıt, -tı AST Mars.

sakız (gum) mastic; **~ gibi 1.** sticky; **2.** very white and clean; **~ rakısı** raki flavo(u)red with mastic.

Sakız Adası, -nı *pr. n.* Chios.

sakızkabağı, -nı vegetable marrow.

saki cupbearer.

sakin [ā] **1.** calm, tranquil, quiet, serene; **2.** resident, inhabitant, dweller.

sakinleşmek to become calm, to calm down.

sakinleştirmek to calm, to soothe, to tranquilize.

sakinlik calmness, tranquility, serenity.

sakit, -ti silent.

saklamak 1. to hide, to conceal; **2.** to keep dark; **3.** to save (*or* keep) (*-e* for), to set aside (*-e* for); **4.** to store, to keep (*-de* in).

saklambaç hide-and-seek.

saklanmak *pass. or refl. of* **saklamak**, to hide (*or* conceal) o.s.

saklı 1. hidden, concealed; **2.** JUR legally guaranteed (*right*).

saksağan zoo magpie.

saksı flowerpot.

saksofon MUS saxophone.

sal, -lı raft.

sala *isl.* call to prayer *or* to a funeral.

salacak bench on which a corpse is washed.

salah 1. improvement; **2.** goodness, soundness; **~ bulmak** to improve.

salahiyet, -ti authority, power, authorization; competence; **~ vermek** to authorize.

salahiyetli 1. authoritative; competent (-e for); **2.** authorized (-meye to inf.).

salahiyetname [. - . . . -.] credentials.

salahiyettar [. - . . . -] s. **salahiyetli.**

salak silly, doltish, dunderheaded, half-witted.

salaklık silliness, dunderheadedness.

salam salami.

salamura [. . x .] **1.** brine, pickle; **2.** pickled.

salapurya [. . x .] NAUT small lighter.

salaş temporary wooden shed.

salat, -tı isl. ritual prayer.

salata [. x .] **1.** salad; **2.** lettuce.

salatalık cucumber.

salavat, -tı [. . . -] s. **salat.**

salbetmek [x .] **1.** to hang; **2.** obs. to crucify.

salça [x .] tomato sauce (or paste).

salçalı gravied, covered with sauce.

salçalık sauceboat, gravy boat.

saldırgan aggressive, belligerent, truculent.

saldırı attack, assault; aggression.

saldırmak 1. to attack, to assault, to assail; to charge (at); to rush; **2.** CHEM to act (-e on); to dissolve.

saldırmazlık nonaggression; **~ antlaşması** (or **paktı**) nonaggression treaty.

salep, -bi [ā] salep (a. BOT).

salgı BIOL secretion.

salgın 1. epidemic (disease); **2.** epidemic, outbreak (of a disease); **3.** epidemic invasion (of insects); **~ hastalık** epidemic disease.

salhane [. - .] slaughterhouse.

salı Tuesday.

salık advice; **~ vermek** to advise, to recommend.

salıncak 1. swing; **2.** hammock.

salıncaklı: ~ koltuk rocking chair.

salınım 1. PHYS oscillation; **2.** AST libration of the moon.

salınmak 1. pass. of **salmak; 2.** to sway; to oscillate; **salına salına yürümek** to walk along swaggeringly.

salıntı 1. swaying motion; **2.** swell, undulation (of the sea).

salıvermek to let go, to release, to set free.

salih [ā] **1.** suitable (or good) (-e for);

2. authorized (-e to); **3.** ♀ mf.

salim [ā] **1.** healthy, sound; **2.** secure, safe.

salip, -bi [ī] cross.

salkım 1. bunch (of grapes); **2.** bunch, cluster; **3.** BOT wisteria; **~ küpe** ear pendant; **~ saçak** hanging down in rags.

salkımak to hang down loosely.

salkımsı racemose.

salkımsöğüt BOT weeping willow.

sallabaş afflicted with an involuntary shaking of the head.

sallamak 1. to swing, to shake, to rock; to wave, to wag; **2.** to nod (one's head); **3.** to brandish (sword); **4.** fig. to put off, to postpone.

sallamamak sl. to pay no attention (-i to), not to care about.

sallandırmak 1. caus. of **sallanmak; 2.** F to hang, to make s.o. swing.

sallanmak 1. pass. or refl. of **sallamak; 2.** to sway, to swing; to wobble, to rock, to totter; **3.** to be loose (tooth); **4.** fig. to fool around; **5.** fig. to be about to get the sack.

sallantı swaying, swinging, rocking; **-da bırakmak** to leave up in the air.

sallasırt etm. to shoulder, to hoist onto one's shoulder(s).

salma 1. vn. of **salmak; 2.** a kind of stew with rice; **3.** HIST policeman; **4.** loft, cote; **5.** running (water).

salmak, (-ar) 1. to let go, to set free, to release; **2.** to dispatch, to send; **3.** to put forth (or out) (roots); **4.** to turn an animal out to graze; to direct, to channel (-e into); **5.** to let attack, to turn loose (-e on); **6.** to add (-e to); **7.** to attack (animal).

salmalık pasture.

salmastra [. x .] MEC gasket.

salon 1. hall; **2.** drawing-room; **~ takımı** drawing-room suite.

saloz sl. dunderheaded, stupid.

salpa loose, slack.

salt, -tı 1. mere, pure, simple; **2.** simply, merely, solely; **~ çoğunluk** absolute majority.

salta[1] [x .]: **~ durmak** to stand on its hind legs (dog).

salta[2] [x .] bolero.

saltanat, -tı 1. reign, sovereignty, rule, dominion; **2.** sultanate; **3.** fig. pomp, magnificence, splendo(u)r; **~ sürmek 1.** to reign; **2.** fig. to live in great splendo(u)r.

saltık absolute.

salvo [x .] salvo.

salya [x .] saliva; slaver, slobber, drool.

salyangoz ZOO snail.

saman straw; chaff; ~ *altından su yürütmek* fig. to be as sly as a fox; ~ *gibi* insipid tasteless; ~ *nezlesi* hay fever; ~ *sarısı* straw yellow.

samankâğıdı, -nı tracing paper.

samankapan amber.

samanlık hayloft, haymow.

samanrengi, -ni straw (yellow).

samanyolu, -nu AST the Milky Way

samba samba.

Sami [ā] 1. Semite; 2. Semitic.

samia [- .] MED hearing.

samimi [. - -] 1. intimate, close; 2. sincere, genuine; heartfelt.

samimiyet, -ti 1. intimacy, closeness, 2. sincerity.

samsa a kind of pastry.

samur ZOO sable; ~ *kaşlı* having bushy eyebrows; ~ *kürk* sable fur.

samyeli, -ni samiel, simoom, sirocco.

san 1. repute, fame, reputation; 2. title, appellation.

sana to you; for you; ~ *gelince* as for you.

sanat, -tı 1. art; 2. trade, craft, skill; 3. craftsmanship, skill, craft; ~ *eseri* work of art; ~ *filmi* art film; ~ *okulu* trade (*or* industrial) school.

sanatçı, sanatkâr 1. artist; 2. craftsman, artisan.

sanatkârlık 1. artistry; 2. craftsmanship, artisanship.

sanatoryum sanatorium.

sanatsever art lover, lover of art.

sanayi, -ii [. - .] industry; ~ *odası* association of manufacturers.

sanayici industrialist.

sanayileşmek to become industrialized.

sanayileştirmek to industrialize.

sancak 1. flag, banner, standard; 2. NAUT starboard; 3. HIST sanjak, sub--province; ~ *açmak* to unfurl a flag.

sancakbeyi, -ni HIST governor of a sanjak.

sancaktar [. . -] standard-bearer.

sancı 1. pain, gripes, twinge, stitch; 2. labo(u)r pain, travail.

sancılanmak 1. to have a pain; 2. to have labo(u)r pains (*pregnant woman*).

sancımak to ache, to twinge.

sandal[1] sandal.

sandal[2] sendal, brocade.

sandal[3] sandalwood.

sandal[4] rowboat.

sandalet, -ti sandal.

sandalye 1. chair; 2. *fig.* office, post; ~ *kavgası* struggle for a post; ~ *sazı* rush for caning chairs.

sandık 1. chest, trunk; 2. coffer, strongbox; 3. bank; credit union; 4. crate; ~ *emini* treasurer, cashier; ~ *eşyası* clothes, *etc.* (*kept in a hope chest*); ~ *lekesi* stain made by mildew; ~ *odası* lumber room, storeroom; ~ *sepet* bag and baggage.

sandıklamak to box, to crate.

sanduka sarcophagus.

sandviç, -ci sandwich.

sanem idol.

sangı dazed, confused.

sanı supposition, surmise, imagination.

sanık JUR suspect; accused.

sani [- -] second.

saniye [ā] second.

saniyelik [ā] taking a very short time.

sanki [x .] as if, as though; supposing that; *sanki Fransızca'yı çok iyi bilirmiş gibi konuşuyor* he speaks as if he knew French very well.

sanlı famous.

sanmak, (-ır) to suppose, to think, to imagine.

sanrı hallucination.

sanrılamak to hallucinate.

sansar ZOO marten; ~ *gibi* sly.

sansasyon sensation.

sansasyonel sensational.

sansör censor.

sansür censorship; ~ *etm.* to censor.

sansürlemek to censor.

santigram centigram(me).

santigrat centigrade.

santilitre centilitre, *Am.* centiliter.

santim 1. centimetre, *Am.* centimeter; 2. centime.

santimetre [. . x .] centimetre, *Am.* centimeter.

santra sports: centre, *Am.* center.

santrafor s. **santrfor.**

santrahaf s. **santrhaf.**

santral, -lı 1. switchboard, telephone exchange; 2. powerhouse; ~ *memuru* telephonist, (telephone) operator.

santrfor sports: centre forward, *Am.* center forward.

santrfüj 1. centrifuge; 2. centrifugal; ~ *kuvvet* PHYS centrifugal force.

santrhaf *sports*: centre halfback, *Am.* center halfback.

santur MUS dulcimer, santour.

santuri [. - -] MUS dulcimer player.

sap, *-pı* **1.** handle; **2.** BOT stem; stalk; **3.** peduncle, pedicel; **4.** *sl.* prick, cock, dick; *-ına kadar* to the backbone (*or* core).

sapa out-of-the-way (*place*); ~ *düşmek* to be off the beaten track.

sapak turning, turnoff.

sapaklık PSYCH abnormality.

sapan catapult. *Am.* slingshot.

sapanorya [. . x .] *sl.* very ugly.

saparta [. x .] NAUT broadside (*a. fig.*).

sapasağlam [x . . .] in the pink, very strong.

sapık **1.** pervert; **2.** perverted.

sapıklaşmak to become perverted.

sapıklık perversion.

sapır sapır: ~ *dökülmek* to rain down from every side; ~ *titremek* to shiver and shake.

sapıtmak **1.** *caus. of* **sapmak**; **2.** to go haywire (*or* nuts); **3.** to talk crap, to drivel.

saplamak to stick (*-e* into), to thrust (*-e* into), to pierce (*-e* into).

saplanmak **1.** *pass. of* **saplamak**; **2.** to be fixed (*or* rooted) (*-e* to); **3.** *fig.* to be obsessed (*-e* by), to be hipped (*-e* on).

saplantı fixed idea; obsession.

saplı **1.** ... handled; **2.** BOT stemmed; stalked.

sapmak, (*-ar*) **1.** to turn (*-e* to), to swerve (*or* veer) (*-e* to); **2.** to deviate (*or* depart) (*-den* from); to digress (*-den* from); **3.** to resort (*-e* to).

sapsağlam *s.* **sapasağlam**.

sapsarı [x . .] **1.** bright yellow; **2.** very pale (*face*).

saptamak **1.** to fix, to determine, to establish; **2.** to stabilize, to fix.

saptırmak **1.** *caus. of* **sapmak**; **2.** *fig.* to wrench, to distort (*facts*).

sara MED epilepsy; *-sı tutmak* to have an epileptic fit.

saraç, *-cı* saddler.

sarahat, *-ti* [. - .] clarity, clearness.

sarahaten [. - . .] clearly.

sarak ARCH stringcourse.

saraka ridicule, mock; *-ya almak* to mock, to ridicule.

saralı epileptic.

sararmak **1.** to turn yellow; **2.** to pale, to grow (*or* turn) pale; *sararıp sol-*

mak to pine away, to grow pale.

sarartmak to yellow.

saray **1.** palace; **2.** government house; ~ *lokması* a kind of sweet.

sardalye [. x .] ZOO sardine, pilchard.

sardunya [. x .] BOT geranium.

sarf **1.** expenditure; **2.** GR morphology; ~ *etm.* **1.** to spend (*money*); **2.** to use up, to consume, to expend (*time, effort*); **3.** to use (*words*).

sarfınazar apart from, regardless of; ~ *etm.* **1.** to disregard, to overlook; **2.** to relinquish, to give up.

sarfiyat, *-tı* [. . -] **1.** expenditure, expenses, outgo; **2.** consumption; wastage.

sargı bandage.

sargılı bandaged.

sarhoş **1.** drunk, high, blotto, intoxicated; **2.** *fig.* drunk (*with joy, etc.*).

sarhoşluk drunkenness, intoxication.

sarı **1.** yellow; **2.** blond; **3.** yolk, yellow (*of an egg*); **4.** MEC brass; **5.** pale, wan, pallid (*face*); ~ *çizmeli Mehmet Ağa* F some Joe Doakes or other.

sarıçalı BOT barberry.

sarıçam BOT Scotch pine.

sarığıburma a sweet pastry.

sarıhumma MED yellow fever.

sarık turban (cloth).

sarıklı turbaned.

sarılgan BOT climbing, twining (*plant*).

sarılı[1] **1.** bandaged; **2.** wrapped; **3.** surrounded (*ile* by).

sarılı[2] mixed with yellow colo(u)r.

sarılık **1.** yellowness; **2.** MED jaundice, icterus.

sarılmak **1.** *pass. of* **sarmak**; **2.** to embrace, to hug; **3.** to coil (*or* twine) (*-e* around); **4.** to cling (*-e* to), to hold fast (*-e* to); **5.** to take up.

sarımsak *s.* **sarmısak**.

sarımsı, sarımtırak yellowish.

sarınmak to wrap o.s. up (*-e* in).

sarısabır **1.** BOT aloe; **2.** aloes.

sarışın blond(e).

sari [- -] infectious, contagious (*disease*).

sarih [ī] clear, explicit, evident.

sarkaç pendulum.

sarkık pendulous, flabby.

sarkılmak to hang down.

sarkıntılık molestation; ~ *etm.* to molest.

sarkıt, *-tı* GEOL, ARCH stalactite.

sarkıtmak **1.** *caus. of* **sarkmak**; **2.** to dangle; to lower; **3.** *sl.* to hang, to make s.o. swing.

sarkmak 1. to hang (down); to hang out; to lean out of (*a window*); to dangle; **2.** to drop by; **3.** to be left over.

sarma 1. *vn. of* **sarmak**; **2.** *dish made of rice and meat wrapped up in grape leaves*; **3.** *a wrestling maneuver.*

sarmak, (-ar) 1. to wrap up, to wind; to encircle; **2.** to surround; **3.** to bandage; **4.** to wind (*or* coil) up; **5.** to embrace; **6.** to cover, to envelop; **7.** to climb, to twine around (*vine*); **8.** to infest (*insects*); **9.** F to interest, to captivate; **sarıp sarmalamak** to wrap up.

sarmal spiral, helical.

sarmalamak to wrap up.

sarmaş: ~ dolaş olm. to be locked in a close embrace.

sarmaşık BOT ivy.

sarmaşmak to embrace one another.

sarmısak BOT garlic.

sarnıç, -cı 1. cistern; **2.** tank; **~ gemisi** tanker; **~ vagonu** tank car.

sarp, -pı 1. steep, precipitous; **2.** *fig.* difficult, hard; **-a sarmak** to become complicated.

sarraf moneychanger; moneylender.

sarsak shaky, quavery.

sarsılmak to be shaken (*or* jolted).

sarsıntı 1. shake, tremor, jolt; **2.** (*brain*) concussion; **3.** *psych.* shock.

sarsmak, (-ar) 1. to shake, to jolt, to jar; **2.** to upset; to weaken (*one's health*); **3.** to give a shock, to shock.

sataşmak to annoy, to tease, to provoke, to aggravate.

saten satin.

sathi [î] superficial, cursory; shallow.

satı sale; **-ya çıkarmak** to put up for sale.

satıcı seller; salesman; saleswoman; pedlar, *Am.* peddler.

satıh, -thı surface.

satılık for (*or* on) sale; **satılığa çıkarmak** to put up for sale.

satım sale.

satın almak to buy, to purchase.

satır¹ line.

satır² ** chopper, cleaver; **~ atmak to slay.

satırbaşı, -nı paragraph indentation, head of a paragraph.

satış sale; **~ fiyatı** selling price.

satmak, (-ar) 1. to sell; **2.** to pretend, to put on a show of; **3.** *sl.* (*b-ni*) to get rid of *s.o.*; **satıp savmak** to sell all one has.

satranç, -cı chess; **~ ~** checkered, checked; **~ tahtası** chessboard; **~ taşı** chessman; **~ turnuvası** chess tournament.

satrançlı checkered, checked.

Satürn AST Saturn.

sauna sauna.

sav 1. assertion, claim; **2.** JUR indictment, allegation.

savaş 1. war, battle; **2.** struggle, fight; **~ açmak** to go to war (-e against), to start a war.

savaşçı warrior, combatant, fighter.

savaşmak to fight (*a. fig.*), to battle.

savcı public prosecutor; attorney general.

savlet, -ti assault, onslaught.

savmak, (-ar) 1. to get rid of, to dismiss, to drive away; **2.** to get over (*an illness*); **3.** to penetrate (*cold*).

savruk 1. inattentive, careless; **2.** untidy, messy.

savsak 1. neglectful, negligent; **2.** slipshod, careless.

savsaklamak 1. (*bsi*) to neglect *s.th.*; to put off (*doing s.th.*); **2.** (*b-ni*) to put *s.o.* off.

savul! gangway!, get out of the way!

savulmak to draw (*or* stand) aside, to get out of the way.

savunma defence, *Am.* defense.

savunmak to defend.

savurgan extravagant, wasteful, spendthrift, prodigal.

savurganlık extravagance, prodigality.

savurmak 1. to throw, to fling, to hurl, to hurtle; **2.** to winnow (*grain*); **3.** to land (*blow, kick*); **4.** to fling, to let fly (*curse*); **5.** to brandish (*sword*); **6.** to waste, to squander; **7.** to bluster, to brag.

savuşmak 1. to slip away, to sneak off; **2.** to pass (*illness*).

savuşturmak 1. to get rid of, to ward off; **2.** to deflect, to parry (*a blow*).

say effort, work.

saya vamp.

sayaç meter, counter.

saydam transparent.

saydamlık transparency.

saye [â] **1.** shade, shadow; **2.** protection, assistance, favo(u)r; **-sinde** thanks to; **bu -de** hereby, by this.

sayfa page; **-yı çevirmek** to turn over the leaf.

sayfiye summer resort (*or* house).

saygı respect, esteem; **~ göstermek** to

show respect, to pay tribute, to venerate, to revere; *-larımla* yours faithfully.

saygıdeğer estimable, venerable.

saygılı respectful.

saygın respected, esteemed.

saygınlık respect, esteem.

saygısız disrespectful.

saygısızlık disrespect(fulness).

sayı 1. number; **2.** issue, number (*of a magazine*); **3.** *sports*: point(s); **4.** *basketbal*: basket.

sayıklamak 1. to talk in one's sleep, to rave, to wander; **2.** to dream (*of s.th. longed for*).

sayılı 1. numbered, counted; **2.** limited; few and far between, **3.** best, topnotch.

sayım enumeration, census, count.

sayın esteemed, hono(u)rable; dear (*in a letter*).

sayısal numerical.

sayısız countless, numberless, innumerable.

Sayıştay *pr. n.* the Government Accounting Bureau.

saylav *s.* **mebus.**

saymak, (-ar) 1. to count; **2.** to respect, to value; **3.** to consider, to take into account; **4.** to reckon, to deem, to regard, to look upon as; **5.** to enumerate, to list.

sayman accountant.

saz 1. BOT rush, reed; **2.** MUS musical instrument; **3.** group of musicians; ~ *benizli* pale-faced; ~ *şairi* minstrel; ~ *takımı* group of musicians (*who play traditional Turkish music*).

sazan (*balığı*) ZOO carp.

sazlık 1. rushy, reedy (*place*); **2.** reedbed.

se *dice*: three.

seans 1. session, sitting; **2.** performance (*of a play*); **3.** treatment; **4.** *cards*: game.

sebat, -tı [ā] perseverance, firmness, constancy; ~ *etm.* to persevere, to show resolution.

sebatkâr steady, constant, steadfast.

sebebiyet, -ti: ~ *vermek* to cause, to bring about.

sebep, -bi reason, cause; ~ *olm.* to bring about, to cause; *-iyle* because of, owing to.

sebeplenmek to get a share of the pie.

sebepsiz without any reason, causeless.

sebil [ī] **1.** free distribution of water; **2.** public fountain; ~ *etm.* **1.** to distribute s.th. free; **2.** *fig.* to ladle out.

sebze vegetable.

sebzeci vegetable seller.

seccade [ā] prayer rug.

secde prostrating o.s.; ~ *etm. or -ye kapanmak or -ye varmak* to prostrate o.s.

seciye character, disposition.

seçenek alternative.

seçi selection.

seçici selector; ~ *kurul* selection committee.

seçim POL election; ~ *bölgesi* (*or çevresi*) election district; ~ *sandığı* ballot box.

seçkin select, choice, prominent.

seçme 1. *vn. of* **seçmek; 2.** select, choice, distinguished; *-ler* selections.

seçmek, (-er) 1. to choose, to select; **2.** POL to elect; **3.** to perceive, to discern, to distinguish; **4.** to be particular (*or choosy*) about.

seçmeli optional.

seçmen voter, elector; ~ *kütüğü* electoral roll.

seda 1. voice; **2.** echo.

sedalı voiced, vocal.

sedasız voiceless, unvoiced.

sedef mother-of-pearl, nacre; ~ *hastalığı* MED psoriasis.

sedefli decorated with mother-of-pearl.

sedir[1] divan.

sedir[2] BOT cedar.

sedrebeki nonsense, rot.

sedye [x .] stretcher, litter.

sefa *s.* **safa.**

sefahat, -tı [ā] dissipation, debauch.

sefalet, -ti [ā] **1.** poverty; **2.** misery; ~ *çekmek* to suffer privation; *-e düşmek* to be reduced to poverty.

sefaret, -ti [ā] POL **1.** ambassadorship, envoyship; **2.** embassy.

sefarethane [ā, ā] embassy, legation.

sefer 1. journey, voyage; **2.** MIL campaign, expedition; **3.** time, occasion; *bu* ~ this time; *on* ~ ten times.

seferber mobilized (*for war*); ~ *etm.* to mobilize.

seferberlik mobilization.

sefertası, -nı travel(l)ing food box.

sefih [ī] dissolute, dissipated.

sefil [ī] **1.** poor, miserable, destitute; **2.** *fig.* mean, despicable.

sefir POL ambassador; envoy.

sefire POL ambassadress.

seğirmek to twitch.

seher 1. daybreak, dawn; **2.** ♀ *wf*.

sehpa [ā] **1.** coffee (*or* end) table; **2.** tripod; **3.** gallows; **4.** easel; *-ya çekmek* to hang, to string up.

sehven [x .] by mistake.

sek, -ki dry, neat (*wine*).

seki 1. stone base; **2.** doorsteps, stoop; **3.** GEOL terrace, bench.

sekiz eight.

sekizer eight apiece (*or* each); ~~ eight at a time.

sekizgen octagon.

sekizinci eighth.

sekizli 1. *cards*: the eight; **2.** MUS octet.

sekizlik MUS eighth note.

sekmek 1. to hop; **2.** to skip; **3.** to ricochet.

sekreter secretary.

sekreterlik secretaryship.

seks sex; ~ *filmi* skin flick.

seksek hopscotch.

seksen eighty.

sekseninci eightieth.

seksenlik octogenarian.

seksoloji sexology.

seksüel sexual.

sekte stoppage, interruption, suspension, cessation; ~ *vermek* to cease, to come to a halt; ~ *vurmak* to put back, to interrupt, to impede.

sektirmek to cause to hop (*or* skip).

sektör sector.

sel flood, torrent, inundation.

selam 1. greeting, regards, salutation, hello; **2.** MIL salute; **3.** F hello!, hi!; ~ *dur!* MIL present arms!; ~ *etm.* to send one's regards; ~ *söylemek* (*or* *yollamak*) to send (*or* give) one's regards (*-e* to), to say hello (*-e* to); ~ *vermek* to greet; *-ı sabahı kesmek* to break off relations (*ile* with).

selamet, -ti 1. security, safety; well-being; **2.** healthiness, soundness; **3.** salvation, deliverance; ~ *bulmak* to reach safety; *-le* **1.** safe and sound; **2.** God speed!

selamlamak 1. to greet; **2.** MIL to salute.

selamlaşmak to exchange greetings, to greet each other.

selamlık 1. the part of a Moslem house reserved for the men; **2.** HIST public procession of the sultan to a mosque at noon on Fridays.

selamünaleyküm [. x . . x .] peace be with you; ~ *demeden* *fig*. without so much as by your leave.

Selanik *pr. n.* Salonika.

selaset, -ti fluency.

Selçuk Seljuk.

sele saddle, seat (*of a bicycle*).

selef predecessor.

selektör 1. selector; **2.** MOT dimmer; ~ *yapmak* MOT to dim (*or* blink) the headlights.

selfservis self-service.

selim [ī] **1.** sound, healthy; safe; **2.** MED benign; **3.** ♀ *mf*.

selman etm. *sl.* to beg.

soleteyp Scotch (*or* cellophane) tape.

selp etm. to destroy, to take away.

selüloz cellulose.

selülozik cellulosic.

selvi BOT cypress.

sema [ā] **1.** firmament, sky; **2.** ♀ *wf*.

semafor semaphore.

semahat, -ti [. - .] **1.** generosity; **2.** ♀ *wf*.

semai [. - -] a poetic form.

semantik semantics.

semaver [ā] samovar, urn.

semavi [. - -] celestial, firmamental.

sembol, -lü symbol.

sembolik symbolic(al).

sembolleştirmek to symbolize.

semen corpulence, fatness.

semer 1. packsaddle; **2.** stout, pad; **3.** *sl.* buttocks; ~ *vurmak* to put a packsaddle (*-e* on).

semere fruit, outcome, consequence.

semereli fruitful.

seminer seminar.

semirgin fat and lazy.

semirmek to get (*or* grow) fat.

semirtmek to fatten.

semiz fat.

semizlemek *s.* **semirmek.**

semizotu, -nu BOT purslane.

sempati 1. attraction, liking; **2.** PSYCH sympathy; ~ *duymak* to take to, to take kindly to; ~ *sinirleri* ANAT sympathetic nerves.

sempatik 1. attractive, likable, simpatico; **2.** sympathetic.

sempatizan sympathizer.

sempozyum symposium.

semt, -ti 1. neighbo(u)rhood, district, quarter; **2.** AST azimuth; ~ ~ in every neighbo(u)rhood; *-ine uğramamak* to darken s.o.'s door(s).

semtürreis, -e'si AST zenith.

semum [ū] simoom.

sen you; ~ *de* you too; *-ce* in your opinion; **-den** from you.

sena [ā] praise; ~ **etm.** to praise.

senarist, -ti scenarist, script-writer.

senaryo [. x .] scenario, screenplay, script.

senaryocu s. **senarist.**

senato [. x .] senate.

senatör senator.

senatörlük senatorship.

sendelemek 1. to stagger, to totter, to lurch, to reel; **2.** *fig.* to be shocked, to be taken aback.

sendik JUR receiver.

sendika trade (*or* labo(u)r) union.

sendikacı trade unionist.

sendikacılık trade unionism.

sendikalaştırmak to unionize.

sene year; **1961 -sinde** in the year 1961.

senelik 1. lasting ... years; **2.** yearly, annual; **3.** annual payment.

senet voucher; security; promissory note; ~ **vermek** *fig.* to guarantee.

senetli certified.

senevi [ī] yearly, annual.

senfoni symphony.

seni *acc. of* **sen**, you; ~ **it oğlu it!** *sl.* you bastard!

senin *gen. of* **sen**, your; ~ **için** for you; **-le** with you.

seninki yours.

senlibenli familiar, intimate, free-and-easy; ~ **olm.** to be hail-fellow-well-met (*ile* with).

sentaks syntax.

sentetik synthetic.

sentez synthesis.

sepet, -ti 1. basket; **2.** sidecar (*of a motorcycle*); ~ **havası çalmak** (*b-ne*) *sl.* to give *s.o.* the boot.

sepetlemek 1. to basket; **2.** *sl.* to send *s.o.* packing; to fire.

sepettopu, -nu basketball.

sepilemek to tan (*a hide*).

sepmek to sprinkle; to scatter.

septik skeptical.

septisemi MED septicemia.

ser 1. head; **2.** summit, top; ~ **verip sır vermemek** to die rather than disclose a secret.

ser(a) greenhouse, hothouse, conservatory.

seramik 1. ceramics; **2.** ceramic.

seramikçi ceramist, ceramicist.

serap, -bı [ā] mirage.

serasker HIST Minister of War.

serazat, -dı [. - -] *obs.* unrestricted, free.

serbest, -ti 1. free, independent, unrestricted; **2.** unconstrained; unconfined; **3.** open, unobstructed; ~ **bırakmak** to set free, to free, to release; ~ **bölge** free zone; ~ **güreş** catch-as-catch-can (wrestling); ~ **meslek sahibi** self-employed person.

serbesti [ī] s. **serbestlik.**

serbestlik 1. freedom; independence; **2.** unconstraint.

serçe ZOO sparrow.

serçeparmak little finger.

serdar [ā] commander-in-chief.

serdengeçti who sacrifices his life.

serdetmek [x . .] to put forward, to assert.

serdümen NAUT **1.** helmsman; **2.** quartermaster.

seremoni ceremony.

seren NAUT yard; boom.

serenat serenade.

serencam [ā] **1.** conclusion, end; **2.** occurrence, adventure.

sereserpe: ~ **yatmak** to sprawl.

sergi 1. exhibition, show, display; **2.** mat, rug.

sergilemek to exhibit, to display, to put on display.

sergin 1. laid (*or* spread) out; **2.** bedridden, bedfast; ~ **vermek** to lie sick in bed.

sergüzeşt, -ti adventure.

serhat, -ddi frontier, border.

seri[1] series; ~ **bağlama** ELECT series connection; ~ **imalat** mass production.

seri[2], **-li** [ī] swift, quick, speedy, rapid.

serilmek 1. *pass. of* **sermek**; **2.** to sprawl o.s. out.

serin cool; chill(y).

serinkanlı cool-headed, imperturbable.

serinlemek 1. to cool off, to get cool; **2.** *fig.* to feel relieved.

serinleşmek to cool off, to get cool (*or* chilly).

serinlik 1. coolness; **2.** cool(ness), chill(iness).

serj serge.

serkeş rebellious, unruly.

serlevha title, heading.

sermaye [ā] **1.** capital; **2.** cost price; production cost; **3.** *fig.* wealth; **4.** *sl.* prostitute; ~ **koymak** to invest capital (*-e* in).

sermayedar [ā] capitalist.

sermek, (-er) 1. to spread, to lay; **2.** (*işi*) to neglect (*one's job*); **3.** (*yere*) to beat down to the ground.

sermest, -ti drunk.

serpantin serpentine (*a.* GEOL)

serpelemek to sprinkle down.

serpilmek 1. *pass. of* **serpmek; 2.** (*for a child*) to grow.

serpinti 1. sprinkle, drizzle (*of rain*); **2.** spray; **3.** vestiges.

serpiştirmek 1. (*yağmur*) to drizzle, to mizzle, to sprinkle down; **2.** (*kar*) to spit down; **3.** to scatter, to sprinkle.

serpme 1. *vn. of* **serpmek; 2.** scattered about; **3.** cast net.

serpmek 1. to sprinkle, to scatter; **2.** *s.* **serpiştirmek 1, 2.**

serpuş [ū] headgear.

sersefil very miserable.

sersem 1. stunned, dazed; **2.** scatter-brained, silly, muddleheaded; ~ **etm.** (*or* -*e çevirmek*) to daze, to stupefy.

sersemlemek 1. to become dazed (*or* stupefied); **2.** to become muddle-headed.

sersemletmek 1. to daze, to stupefy, to stun; **2.** to confuse, to addle.

serseri 1. vagrant, vagabond, tramp, hobo; **2.** good-for-nothing, ne'er-do-well, loafer, bum, layabout; ~ **kurşun** stray bullet; ~ **mayın** floating mine.

serserilik vagrancy, vagabondage.

sert, -ti 1. hard, tough; **2.** harsh, severe, rough; **3.** potent, strong; pungent; ~ **konuşmak** to speak harshly.

sertabip, -bi head doctor.

sertifika certificate.

sertleşmek 1. to harden, to toughen; to harshen; **2.** to turn bad (*weather*).

sertleştirmek to harden, to toughen; to harshen.

sertlik 1. hardness, toughness; **2.** harshness, severeness.

serum MED serum.

serüven adventure.

servet, -ti 1. wealth, riches, fortune; **2.** ♀ *mf.*, *wf.*; -*e konmak* to come into a fortune.

servetli wealthy.

servi *s.* **selvi.**

servis 1. service (*a.* sports); **2.** service charge; **3.** department, section; ~ *at-mak* sports: to serve the ball; ~ *yap-mak* **1.** to serve food (-*e* to); **2.** sports: to serve the ball.

serzeniş reproach.

ses 1. sound; **2.** voice; **3.** noise; ~ *çıkar-*

mak **1.** to voice one's opinion; **2.** to say s.th.; ~ *çıkarmamak* **1.** to raise no objection, to condone; **2.** to keep quiet; ~ ~ *düşmesi* hyphaeresis; ~ *etm.* to shout (-*e* to), to call; ~ *seda yok* not a sound is heard; -*i ayyuka çıkmak* to shout to high heaven; -*i çıkmaz* taciturn; -*ini kesmek* **1.** (*kendi*) to shut (*or* clam) up; **2.** (*b-nin*) to shut *s.o.* up; -*ini kısmak* to turn down.

sesbilgisi, -ni phonetics.

sesbilim phonology.

sesçil phonetic.

seslemek to give ear, to hearken.

seslendirmek 1. *caus. of* **seslenmek; 2.** to dub.

seslenmek 1. to call out (-*e* to); **2.** to address, to speak (-*e* to).

sesli 1. voiced; **2.** GR vowel; ~ *film* sound motion picture, talkie.

sessiz 1. silent, quiet; **2.** taciturn; **3.** GR consonant; ~ *film* **1.** silent movie; **2.** F charades.

sessizlik silence, quietness.

set¹, -ti sports: set.

set², -ddi dam, dyke, dike, levee; wall; ~ *çekmek* to dike.

setir, -tri hiding, concealing.

setretmek [x . .] to hide, to conceal; to cover.

sevap, -bı [ā] **1.** good deed; **2.** merit, reward, credit; ~ *işlemek* (*or kazan-mak*) to acquire merit; *sevaba gir-mek* to acquire merit in God's sight.

sevda [ā] love, passion; ~ *çekmek* to be passionately in love.

sevdalanmak [ā] to fall in love (-*e* with), to lose one's heart (-*e* to).

sevdalı [ā] lovesick.

sevdiceğim my darling.

sevecen compassionate, kind.

sevgi love, affection.

sevgili 1. darling, dear, beloved; **2.** sweetheart, beloved; **3.** dear (*in a letter*).

sevici lesbian.

sevicilik lesbianism.

sevimli lovable, cute; likable.

sevimsiz unlovable; unlikable.

sevinç, -ci delight, joy, pleasure.

sevinçli joyful.

sevindirmek to please, to delight, to rejoice.

sevinmek to be pleased (-*e* with), to feel glad, to rejoice.

sevişmek 1. to make love; **2.** to love each other.

seviye 1. level, plane; **2.** standing, footing, level.

sevk, -kı 1. sending; **2.** impulse; **3.** dispatch; ~ *etm.* **1.** to send; **2.** to ship; to dispatch; ~ *ve idare* management, conduct.

sevkıyat, -tı [ā] **1.** dispatch (*of troops*); **2.** consignment (*of goods*).

sevkulceyş MIL strategy.

sevmek, (-er) 1. to love; to like; **2.** to caress, to fondle; *seve seve* willingly.

seyahat, -ti [. - .] journey, travel, trip; voyage; ~ *acentesi* travel agency; ~ *çeki* traveler's check; ~ *etm.* to travel; *-e çıkmak* to go on a trip.

seyahatname [. - . - .] travel book.

seyek *dice*: three and one.

seyelan flow; ~ *etm.* to flow.

seyir, -yri 1. course, progress; movement; **2.** show, spectacle; **3.** onlooking, observation; ~ *jurnalı* NAUT log(-book); ~ *yeri* place of amusement; *seyre çıkmak* to go for a walk *or* ride.

seyirci spectator, onlooker, viewer; ~ *kalmak* to stand on the sidelines.

seyis stableman, groom, hostler.

Seylan *pr. n.* Ceylon.

seylap, -bı flood.

seyran [ā] **1.** outing; promenade; **2.** observation, onlooking; ~ *etm.* to make an excursion.

seyrek 1. widely set; **2.** sparse; **3.** rare, uncommon, seldom.

seyrekleşmek, seyrelmek 1. to thin out (*or* down); to become sparse; **2.** to become infrequent.

seyretmek [x . .] **1.** to watch, to look at, to see; **2.** to progress, to proceed; **3.** to develop (*illness*).

seyrüsefer traffic.

seyyah [ā] travel(l)er, tourist.

seyyal, -li [ā] fluid.

seyyar [ā] **1.** itinerant, peripatetic; **2.** movable, portable; mobile; ~ *satıcı* pedlar, *Am.* peddler, hawker.

seyyare [ā] AST planet.

seyyie 1. wickedness; **2.** sin.

Sezar *vr. n.* Caesar; *-ın hakkını -a vermek* to render to Caesar the things that are Caesar's.

sezaryen MED cesarean.

sezdirmek to cause to sense, to imply.

sezgi intuition.

sezi *s.* **sezgi.**

sezin(le)mek to sense, to feel, to anticipate.

sezmek, (-er) to sense, to perceive, to

discern, to feel, to anticipate.

sezon season.

sfenks sphinx.

sıcacık [x . .] warm and cozy.

sıcak 1. hot, warm (*a. fig.*); **2.** heat; ~ *dalgası* heat-wave; ~ *tutmak* to keep warm; *sıcağı sıcağına* while the iron is hot.

sıcakkanlı 1. warm-blooded (*animal*); **2.** *fig.* friendly, companionable, genial.

sıcaklık warmth, heat.

sıçan ZOO rat; mouse.

sıçandişi, -ni hemstitch.

sıçankırı, -nı mouse-gray.

sıçankuyruğu, -nu rattail file.

sıçanotu, -nu arsenic.

sıçanyolu, -nu sewer.

sıçmak *sl.* to shit.

sıçrama 1. *vn. of* **sıçramak**; **2.** jump; ~ *tahtası* springboard; diving board.

sıçramak 1. to jump, to leap, to spring; **2.** to be startled, to start; **3.** to splash; to spatter.

sıçratmak 1. to splash; to spatter, to splatter; **2.** to startle.

sıdık, -dkı 1. truth; **2.** sincerity; *sıdkı sıyrılmak* (*b-den*) to lose faith in *s.o.*

sıfat, -tı 1. capacity, position, role; **2.** GR adjective; **3.** F appearance, face; **4.** F title, honorific; *-iyle* in the capacity of, as.

sıfır 1. zero; naught, nil; **2.** *fig.* nothing; *-dan başlamak* to start from scratch (*or* square one).

sığ shallow.

sığa PHYS capacity.

sığamak to roll up.

sığdırmak *caus. of* **sığmak**, *part.* to make s.th. fit (*-e* into).

sığınak shelter, bunker.

sığınmak to take shelter (*-e* in), to shelter.

sığır cattle; ~ *eti* beef.

sığırcık ZOO starling.

sığırtmaç herdsman, herder, drover.

sığışmak to squeeze o.s. (*-e* into).

sığıştırmak to squeeze (*-e* into).

sığlık 1. shallowness; **2.** shallow.

sığmak, (-ar) to fit (*-e* into).

sıhhat, -ti 1. health; **2.** soundness, correctness; *-inize!* to your health!, cheers!; *-ler olsun!* good health to you!; *-te bulunmak* to be in good health.

sıhhatli healthy.

sıhhi [ī] **1.** hygienic, sanitary; health

...; **2.** wholesome, salubrious, healthful.

sıhhiye sanitary matters.

sıhhiyeci 1. public health official; **2.** MIL medic.

sıhriyet, -ti affinity.

sık 1. dense, thick; **2.** close; **3.** frequent; ~ ~ frequently, often.

sıkboğaz etm. (*b-ni*) to keep on at *s.o.*, to push *s.o.*, to importune *s.o.*

sıkı 1. tight; firm; **2.** close (*weave*); **3.** tightly; **4.** strict; **5.** stingy, closefisted; ~ **basmak** to put one's foot down; ~ **çalışmak** to work hard; ~ **fıkı 1.** intimate; **2.** on intimate terms, palsy-walsy; ~ **tutmak** (*b-ni*) to hold tightly; **2.** *fig.* to do with care; **-ya koymak** (*b-ni*) to urge *s.o.*, to push *s.o.*; **-yı yemek** to get it in the neck.

sıkıca tightly.

sıkıcı boring, tiresome, irksome, tedious, bothersome, wearisome.

sıkılamak 1. to wad; **2.** *fig.* to put pressure on.

sıkılgan shy, timid, bashful.

sıkılganlık shyness, bashfulness.

sıkılık tightness.

sıkılmak 1. *pass. of* **sıkmak**; **2.** to get bored; **3.** to feel embarrassed; **4.** to be pushed for money.

sıkılmaz shameless, brazen.

sıkım 1. squeeze; **2.** fistful.

sıkınmak to restrain o.s.

sıkıntı 1. trouble, difficulty, distress; worry, annoyance; **2.** boredom; **3.** financial straits; ~ **çekmek 1.** to have (*or* experience) difficulty; **2.** to experience distress; ~ **vermek** to annoy, to bother; to worry; **-da olm.** to be in straits, to be on the rocks; **-ya gelememek** to be unable to stand the gaff.

sıkıntılı 1. troubled; out of sorts; worried; **2.** worrisome, difficult.

sıkışık 1. tight; jammed; congested; **2.** hard up (*for money*); **3.** pushed (*for time*).

sıkışmak 1. to be pressed together; to be congested; **2.** to be hard up (*for money*); **3.** to be pinched (*-e* in), to get caught (*-e* in); **4.** to be taken short.

sıkıştırmak *caus. of* **sıkışmak**, *part.* **1.** to tighten, to compress; **2.** to squeeze, to crowd, to jam, to wedge; **3.** to pinch, to squeeze; **4.** to catch, to pinch (*one's finger*) (*-e* in); **5.** to press, to pressure.

sıkıt[1], -tı abortus.

sıkıt[2], -tı CHEM tablet.

sıkıyönetim martial law.

sıklaşmak to happen often, to become frequent.

sıklet, -ti 1. weight; **2.** *fig.* burden; ~ **vermek** to bore, to depress.

sıklık 1. frequency; **2.** density.

sıkmak, (-ar) 1. to squeeze, to press; **2.** to tighten; **3.** to wring; **4.** to bother, to annoy; **5.** to fire, to shoot (*bullet*).

sıla reunion; **-ya gitmek** to go home.

sımak, (-ar) to break.

sımsıkı very tight.

sınai [. - -] industrial; ~ **kuruluş** industrial enterprise.

sınamak to test, to try out.

sınav examination, test; ~ **vermek** to pass a test; **-a girmek** to take (*or* sit for *or* go in for) an examination.

sındı scissors.

sınıf 1. class (*a.* ZOO, BOT), category; **2.** classroom; **3.** MIL corps; ~ **arkadaşı** classmate; **-ta kalmak** (*or* **çakmak**) to fail, to flunk.

sınıflamak, sınıflandırmak to classify.

sınık 1. broken; **2.** defeated; **3.** scattered.

sınır frontier, border.

sınırdaş bordering.

sınırdışı etm. to deport.

sınırlamak, sınırlandırmak to limit.

sınırlı limited, restricted.

sınırsız limitless, boundless, unlimited.

sınmak *pass. of* **sımak 1.** to get broken; **2.** to be scattered; **3.** to be defeated.

sıpa 1. colt, foal; **2.** P = **sehpa.**

sır[1] glaze.

sır[2], -rrı secret; mystery; ~ **küpü** pussyfooter; ~ **saklamak** (*or* **tutmak**) to keep a secret; **-ra kadem basmak** *co.* to vanish into thin air.

sıra 1. row, line; queue; file; **2.** turn; **3.** order, sequence; **4.** desk; **5.** bench; **6.** moment, time, point; ~ **bizim!** it's our turn!; ~ **evler** row houses; ~ **malı** run-of-the-mill things; ~ ~ in rows; **-dan** ordinary; **-sı değil** this isn't the right time; **-sı gelmişken** by the way; **-sıyla** respectively.

sıraca MED scrofula.

sıradağ(lar) mountain range, chain of mountains.

sıralamak 1. to arrange in rows, to line up; **2.** to enumerate, to tick off; **3.** to file, to arrange; **4.** (*for a child*) to begin to walk (*by holding on to one thing* *after another*).

Sırbistan *pr. n.* Serbia.

sırça glass; ~ **köşkte oturan başkasına** (*or* **komşusuna**) **taş atmamalı** *pro.* people who live in glass houses should not throw stones.

sırdaş confidant.

sırf 1. pure, utter; **2.** only.

sırık pole; stake; ~ **gibi** lanky; **-la atlama** *sports*: pole vaulting.

sırılsıklam [. x . .] *s.* **sırsıklam.**

sırım whipcord, thong, strap; ~ **gibi** wiry.

sırıtkan given to grinning.

sırıtmak 1. to grin; **2.** *fig.* to show up, to come out.

sırlamak 1. to glaze; **2.** to silver (*a mirror*).

sırlı 1. glazed; **2.** silvered (*mirror*).

sırma 1. silver thread; **2.** MIL stripes; ~ **saçlı** golden-haired.

sırnaşık saucy, pert, pertinacious.

sırnaşmak to importune.

Sırp *pr. n.* Serb(ian).

sırrolmak [x . .] to vanish into thin air.

sırsıklam [x . .] soaking (*or* sopping *or* wringing) wet; ~ **âşık** madly in love; ~ **olm.** to get wet through, to be soaked to the skin.

sırt, -tı 1. back; **2.** ridge (*of a hill, etc.*); **3.** the blunt side (*of a knife, etc.*); ~ **çantası** knapsack, rucksack; ~ **çevirmek** (*b-ne*) to turn one's back on *s.o.*, to give *s.o.* the cold shoulder; ~ **omurları** ANAT dorsal vertebrae; ~ **-a vermek 1.** to stand back to back; **2.** *fig.* to support each other; ~ **üstü** on one's back; **-ı kaşınmak** to ask for it, to itch for a beating; **-ı pek** warmly clad; **-ı yere gelmek** *fig.* to bite the dust; **-ına almak 1.** to shoulder; **2.** to put on; **-ından çıkarmak** (*b-nin*) to saddle *s.o.* with the bill for; **-ından geçinmek** (*b-nin*) to sponge on *s.o.*, to live off *s.o.*; **-ını dayamak** (*b-ne*) *fig.* to have *s.o.* at one's back.

sırtarmak 1. to get one's dander (*or* hackles) up; **2.** to mass, to pile up (*clouds*).

sırtlamak to shoulder.

sırtlan ZOO hyena.

sıska puny, thin and weak, scrawny.

sıtma MED malaria; ~ **görmemiş ses** rich and deep voice; ~ **tutmak** to get malaria.

sıtmalı malarious, malarial.

sıva plaster.

sıvacı plasterer.

sıvalamak to plaster.

sıvalı 1. plastered; **2.** rolled up (*sleeves, etc.*).

sıvamak 1. to plaster; **2.** to smear (*-e on*); **3.** to roll up (*sleeves, etc.*).

sıvanmak 1. *pass. of* **sıvamak**; **2.** (*bir işe*) to roll up one's sleeves and set to doing *s.th.*

sıvaşmak 1. to get smeared (*-e on*); **2.** *fig.* to get sticky (*or* gooey).

sıvazlamak to stroke, to pet, to caress.

sıvı liquid, fluid.

sıvık 1. sticky; **2.** *sl.* importunate.

sıvılaştırmak to liquefy.

sıvırya [. x .] continually.

sıvışık 1. sticky, gooey; **2.** *fig.* troublesome.

sıvışmak to slip (*or* run) away, to sneak off, to take to one's heels.

sıyanet, -ti [ā] protection; ~ **etm.** to protect.

sıyga GR mood; **-ya çekmek** F to cross-examine.

sıyırmak 1. to graze, to scrape, to skin; **2.** to strip (*or* peel *or* take) off; **3.** to pick (*or* gnaw) clean (*bone*); **4.** to draw (*a sword*); **5.** *fig.* to get s.o. out of (*a predicament*).

sıyrık 1. graze, scrape; **2.** grazed, scraped; **3.** *fig.* brazen.

sıyrılmak 1. *pass. of* **sıyırmak**; **2.** (*bşden*) to get shut of *s.th.*, to squeak through *s.th.*

sıyrıntı 1. scrapings; **2.** strip of cloth.

sızdırmak 1. *caus. of* **sızmak**, *part.* to leak; **2.** *fig.* to squeeze (*or* wangle) money out of *s.o.*, to extort money from *s.o.*

sızdırmaz leakproof.

sızı ache, pain.

sızıltı complaint; discontent.

sızım sızım: ~ **sızlamak** to ache intensely.

sızıntı leakage, ooze; seepage; ~ **yapmak** to leak.

sızlamak 1. to hurt, to ache; **2.** *s.* **sızlanmak.**

sızlanmak to complain, to moan, to lament.

sızmak, (-ar) 1. to leak, to ooze, to trickle; **2.** to leak out (*secret*); **3.** MIL to infiltrate; **4.** to pass out (*after getting drunk*).

si MUS ti.

siber... cyber...

Sibirya *pr. n.* Siberia.

sicil 1. register; 2. dossier, employment record, file.

sicilli 1. registered; 2. *fig.* previously convicted.

Sicilya *pr. n.* Sicily.

sicim string, twine, packthread.

sidik urine; ~ *borusu* ureter; ~ *söktürücü* diuretic; ~ *torbası* ANAT bladder; ~ *yarışı* iro. futile rivalry.

sidikli enuretic.

sidikyolu, -nu urethra.

sidikzoru, -nu dysuria.

sif COM C.I.F. (*cost, insurance and freight*).

sifon 1. siphon; 2. flush tank.

sifos *sl.* useless.

siftah 1. first sale of the day; handsel; 2. for the first time.

sigara cigarette; ~ *içilmeyen* smoke-free (*zone, building*); ~ *içmek* to smoke; ~ *kâğıdı* cigarette paper; ~ *tablası* ashtray; -yı *bırakmak* to give up smoking.

sigaralık 1. cigarette-holder; 2. cigarette box.

sigorta [. x .] 1. insurance; 2. ELECT fuse; ~ *etm.* to insure; ~ *olm.* to be insured; ~ *poliçesi* insurance policy; ~ *şirketi* insurance company.

sigortacı [. x ..] insurer, insurance agent, underwriter.

sigortalamak to insure.

sigortalı [. x ..] insured.

sigorya [. x .] *sl.* by all means.

siğil wart.

sihir, -hri magic, sorcery, witchcraft; charm.

sihirbaz magician, sorcerer.

sihirlemek to bewitch.

sihirli 1. bewitched, enchanted; 2. magical; 3. charming, bewitching.

sik *sl.* cock, dick, prick, penis.

sikişmek *sl.* to fuck, to screw.

sikke coin.

siklamen BOT cyclamen.

siklememek *sl.* not to give a fuck (*or* shit *or* damn).

siklon cyclone.

sikmek, (-er) *sl.* to fuck, to screw.

siktir! *sl.* fuck off!

silah weapon, arm; ~ *atmak* to fire a weapon; ~ *başına!* MIL to arms!; ~ *çekmek* to draw (*or* pull out) a weapon; ~ *omuza!* MIL shoulder arms!; -a *davranmak* (*or* sarılmak) to go for a weapon.

silahendaz [. . . . -] MIL marine.

silahhane [. . - .] armo(u)ry, arsenal.

silahlamak, silahlandırmak to arm.

silahlı armed; ~ *kuvvetler* armed forces.

silahsız unarmed.

silahsızlandırmak to disarm.

silahsızlanma POL disarmament.

silahşor man-at-arms, musketeer.

silecek 1. bath towel; 2. MOT windscreen (*or* Am. windshield) wiper.

silgi 1. eraser, duster; 2. rubber, eraser; 3. doormat; 4. mop; 5. *s.* silecek 2.

silgiç *s.* silecek 2.

silik 1. indistinct; rubbed out, worn; 2. *fig.* colo(u)rless.

silikat, -tı silicate.

silikon silicone.

silindir 1. cylinder; 2. road roller; ~ *şapka* top hat.

silindiraj rolling.

silinmek 1. *pass. of* silmek; 2. to wipe o.s. dry, to rub o.s.

silinti wipings.

silis silica.

silkelemek 1. to shake (out); 2. *sl.* to drop off.

silkinmek 1. (*bşden*) to rid o.s. of *s.th.*; 2. to shake o.s.

silkinti start.

silkişmek to shake itself.

silkmek, (-er) 1. to shake (out); 2. to shrug (*one's shoulders*).

sille 1. slap, box, cuff; 2. *fig.* buffet; ~ *atmak* to slap, to cuff.

silme 1. *vn. of* silmek; 2. ARCH mo(u)lding; 3. full to the brim.

silmek, (-er) 1. to wipe (up), 2. to dry; 3. to rub out, to erase; 4. to clean, to rub; *silip süpürmek* 1. to clean from stem to stern; 2. to polish off, to put away, to end (*or* finish) off.

silo [x .] silo.

silsile 1. chain, series; 2. ancestry, lineage; 3. (mountain) range.

silsilename [â] genealogical tree.

siluet, -ti silhouette.

sim silver.

sima [- -] 1. face; 2. figure, personage.

simetri symmetry.

simetrik symmetrical.

simge symbol, embodiment (a. *fig.*).

simgelemek to symbolize.

simgesel symbolical.

simit, -di 1. cracknel (*in the shape of a ring*); 2. NAUT life buoy (*or* ring).

simitçi seller *or* maker of *simits*.

simsar [â] broker, middleman, commission agent.

simsariye [ā] brokerage, commission.

simsiyah [x . .] jet-black, pitch-dark, pitch-black.

simya [ā] alchemy.

simyager [ā] alchemist.

sin[1] grave, tomb.

sîn[2], **-nni** age.

sinagog synagogue.

sinameki [ā] вот senna; ~ **gibi** tiresome and persnickety (*person*).

sinara [. x .] fishhook.

sinarit, **-ti** zoo dentex.

sincabi [. - -] dark gray.

sincap, **-bı** zoo squirrel.

sindirim digestion; ~ **sistemi** digestive system.

sindirmek *caus. of* **sinmek**, *part.* **1.** to digest; **2.** to cow, to intimidate.

sine breast, bosom; **-ye çekmek** to take s.th. lying down.

sinek 1. (house)fly; **2.** *cards*: club; ~ **avlamak** to potter about, to twiddle one's thumbs.

sinekkaydı very close (*shave*).

sineklik flyswatter.

sineksıklet, **-ti** featherweight class.

sinema cinema, the pictures, the movies.

sinemacı 1. moviemaker; **2.** movie distributor; **3.** cinema actor *or* actress.

sinemasever movie fan (*or* buff).

sinemaskop cinemascope.

sini round metal tray.

sinik[1] crouching.

sinik[2] cynical.

sinir 1. nerve; **2.** sinew, tendon; **3.** P quirk; **4.** P equanimity; ~ **argınlığı** neurasthenia; ~ **harbi** war of nerves; **-ine dokunmak** (*b-nin*) to give *s.o.* the pip, to get on *one's* nerves.

sinirlendirmek to irritate, to make nervous.

sinirlenmek to get nervous, to become irritated, to get in a state.

sinirli 1. nervous, edgy; quick-tempered, angry; **2.** tendinous, sinewy.

sinirsel neural.

sinmek, **(-er) 1.** to crouch down, to cower; **2.** to penetrate, to pervade.

sinonim 1. synonym; **2.** synonymous.

sinsi stealthy, insidious, sly.

sinsice slyly, stealthily, insidiously.

sinüs 1. мАТН sine; **2.** ANAT sinus.

sinüzit, **-ti** sinusitis.

sinyal, **-li 1.** signal; **2.** мот indicator

light; ~ **vermek** to signal.

sipahi [. - -] ниsт cavalry soldier.

sipariş [ā] order; ~ **almak** to receive an order; ~ **etm.** (*or* **vermek**) to order, to place an order.

siper 1. мiL trench, foxhole; **2.** shelter; shield; **3.** visor, peak, bill (*of a cap*); ~ **almak** to take shelter; ~ **etm.** to use as a shield; **-e almak** to take under one's protection.

siperisaika [. . . . - .] lightning rod.

siperlenmek мiL to take shelter.

siperlik 1. canopy; awning; **2.** visor, peak, bill (*of a cap*).

sipsi 1. NAUT boatswain's whistle; **2.** *sl.* cigarette, fag.

sipsivri [x . .] very sharp; ~ **kalmak** to be deserted by everyone.

sirayet, **-ti** [ā] propagation, contagion, infection; ~ **etm.** to spread.

siren siren, hooter.

sirk, **-ki** circus.

sirkat, **-ti** theft.

sirke[1] vinegar.

sirke[2] nit.

sirkülasyon circulation.

sirküler circular.

siroz мED cirrhosis.

sirrus [x .] мeteor cirrus.

sirto [x .] a dance.

sis fog, mist, haze; ~ **basmak** (*for the fog*) to come in; ~ **bombası** smoke bomb; ~ **düdüğü** foghorn; ~ **lambası** fog light (*or* lamp).

Sisam *pr. n.* Samos.

sislenmek 1. *pass. of* **sislemek**; **2.** to get foggy.

sisli foggy, misty, hazy.

sismograf seismograph.

sistem system.

sistematik systematic.

sistemleştirmek to systematize.

sistemli 1. systematic; **2.** systematically.

sistemsiz 1. unsystematic; **2.** unsystematically.

sistit, **-ti** мED cystitis.

sitayiş [ā] praise; ~ **etm.** to praise.

sitayişkâr [ā] laudatory, praiseful.

site 1. housing estate (*or* development), building, complex; **2.** ниsт city-state.

sitem reproach; ~ **etm.** to reproach.

sitemkâr, **sitemli** reproachful.

sitil large bucket.

sittinsene donkey's years.

sivil 1. civilian; **2.** in civilian clothes, in

mufti; **3.** F stark naked, in the altogether; ~ **polis** plainclothes policeman.

sivilce pimple, pustule.

sivilceli pimply, pimpled.

sivişmek s. **sıvışmak.**

sivri sharp; ~ **akıllı** eccentric.

sivribiber BOT hot pepper.

sivrilmek 1. to become pointed; **2.** fig. to stand out.

sivriltmek to sharpen, to point.

sivrisinek ZOO mosquito.

siya [x .] NAUT rowing backwards; ~ ~ **gitmek** fig. to backwater.

siyah 1. black; **2.** dark; **3.** Negro, Black; **4.** TYP boldface (letter); **5.** sl. opium; ~ **beyaz** black-and-white.

siyahımsı, siyahımtırak blackish.

siyahi [. - -] Black, Negro.

siyahlaşmak to turn black.

siyahlık blackness.

siyakusibak, -kı [ā, ā] context.

Siyam pr. n. Siam; ~ **kedisi** Siamese cat.

siyanür cyanide.

siyasa s. **siyaset.**

siyasal political; 2 **Bilgiler Fakültesi** pr. n. the School of Political Science.

siyaset, -ti [ā] politics.

siyasetçi [ā] politician.

siyasi [. - -] **1.** political; **2.** politician.

siyatik MED sciatica.

siyek ANAT urethra.

siymek to urinate, to pee (cat, dog).

Siyonist, -ti pr. n. Zionist.

Siyonizm pr. n. Zionism.

siz you; ~ **bilirsiniz 1.** as you like; **2.** the decision is up to you; ~ **sağ olun!** never mind!

sizin your; yours; ~ **için** for you.

sizinki yours.

skandal scandal.

skeç, -çi sketch, skit.

ski skiing; ~ **yapmak** to ski.

Skoç, -çu Scotch.

skor score.

slayt slide, transparency.

slip, -pi briefs.

slogan slogan; ~ **atmak** to shout slogans.

smokin [x .] tuxedo, dinner jacket.

snop, -bu snobby, snobbish.

soba [x .] stove; ~ **borusu** stovepipe.

sobe 1. home free!; **2.** you're out!

sobelemek 1. to put a player out; **2.** to reach base before s.o. else.

soda [x .] **1.** sodium carbonate; **2.** soda water.

sodyum sodium.

sof 1. wool(l)en cloth; **2.** silkaline.

sofa hall, anteroom.

sofizm sophism.

sofra table; ~ **başına geçmek** to sit down to a meal; ~ **başında** at the table; ~ **kurmak** to set the table; ~ **örtüsü** tablecloth; ~ **takımı** set of dinnerware; ~**sı açık** hospitable; ~**yı kaldırmak** (or **toplamak**) to clear the table.

softa 1. obs. Muslim theological student; **2.** very pious; **3.** fig. blind follower.

sofu religious, devout, puritanical.

soğan BOT onion.

soğuk 1. cold; **2.** cold weather, the cold; **3.** fig. cold, unfriendly, frosty; **4.** MED frigid; ~ **algınlığı** (common) cold; ~ **almak** to catch cold; ~ **damga** embossed stamp; ~ **davranmak** (b-ne) to give s.o. the cold shoulder; ~ **harp** cold war; ~ **hava deposu** cold store, cold-storage depot; ~ **nevale** cold fish.

soğukkanlı cool-headed, calm.

soğukkanlılık cool-headedness, calmness.

soğuklamak to catch cold.

soğukluk 1. cold(ness); **2.** fig. chill; **3.** MED frigidity.

soğumak 1. to get cold, to cool; **2.** fig. to lose one's love; to go off.

soğurmak CHEM to absorb.

soğutmak 1. to cool, to chill; **2.** fig. to put off.

soğutucu refrigerator, fridge.

sohbet, -ti chat, conversation, talk; ~ **etm.** to chat, to talk, to converse.

sokak street; ~ **başı** beginning of a street; ~ **çocuğu** guttersnipe, street Arab, urchin, gamin; ~ **kadını** streetwalker; ~ **kapısı** street door; ~ **köpeği** tyke, cur; **sokağa atsan beş lira eder** it's worth at least five liras; **sokağa çıkma yasağı** curfew; **sokağa çıkmak** to go out; **sokağa düşmek** to go on the streets.

soket, -ti sock.

sokmak, (-ar) 1. to insert (-e in), to put (-e in); to shove (-e in), to thrust (-e in), to stick (-e in); **2.** to admit, to let in; **3.** to bite, to sting (insect); **4.** to smuggle (-e into).

sokman a high boot.

sokra NAUT butt seam.

sokulgan sociable, friendly, companionable.

sokulmak 1. *pass. of* **sokmak**; **2.** to insinuate o.s. (-*e* into), to slip (-*e* into), to work one's way (-*e* into); **3.** to draw near (-*e* to).

sokur 1. mole; **2.** sunken (*eye*); **3.** blind.

sokuşmak to squeeze (-*e* into), to sneak (-*e* in).

sokuşturmak 1. to squeeze (-*e* into); **2.** *fig.* to put it across, to put it over (-*e* on).

sol¹, -lu 1. left; **2.** left side; **3.** POL the left; **~ tarafından kalkmak** to get out of bed on the wrong side; **~ yapmak** to steer to the left; **-da sıfır** unimportant, a mere nothing; **-umda** on my left.

sol², -lü MUS **1.** sol; **2.** G.

solaçık *football*: left wing.

solak left-handed.

solanahtarı, -nı MUS treble clef.

solbek *football*: left back, fullback.

solcu POL leftist, lefty.

solculuk POL leftism.

solfej MUS solfege.

solgun 1. pale, faded; **2.** wilted (*flowers*).

solhaf [ā] *football*: left halfback.

soliç, -çi *football*: left inner.

solist, -ti soloist.

sollamak to pass a vehicle on its left side.

solmak, (-ar) 1. to fade, to get pale; **2.** to wilt (*flowers*).

solmaz unfading, fast (*colo(u)r*); colo(u)rfast (*cloth*).

solo solo.

solucan ZOO **1.** worm; **2.** ascarid, roundworm; **~ gibi** pale and thin.

soluğan 1. wheezy (*animal*); **2.** swell (*of the sea*).

soluk¹ *s.* **solgun**; **~ beniz** paleface.

soluk² breath; ~ aldırmamak to give no respite; **~ almak 1.** to breathe; **2.** *fig.* to take a breather, to rest; **~ borusu** ANAT windpipe, trachea; **~ soluğa** out of breath, panting for breath; **soluğu kesilmek** to get out of breath.

soluklanmak to rest, to take a breather.

solumak to pant, to snort.

solungaç ANAT gill.

solunmak to breathe.

solunum respiration; **~ sistemi** respiratory system.

solüsyon CHEM solution.

som¹ 1. solid; **2.** unalloyed, pure.

som² the part of a dock located above water.

som³ (*balığı*) ZOO salmon.

somak BOT sumac.

somaki [. - -] porphyry.

somata [. x .] a kind of sweet.

somun 1. loaf (*of bread*); **2.** MEC nut.

somurdanmak to grumble to o.s.

somurtkan sulky, grouchy.

somurtmak to sulk, to grouch, to pout.

somut, -tu concrete.

somutlamak to concretize.

somutlaşmak to concretize.

somutlaştırmak to concretize.

somya, somye [x .] spring mattress.

son 1. end, termination, conclusion; **2.** final; last; **3.** afterbirth; **~ bulmak** to come to an end, to end; **~ defa** (for the) last time; **~ derece** extremely; **~ gülen iyi güler** *pro.* he laughs best who laughs last; **~ kozunu oynamak** to play one's last card; **~ nefesini vermek** to breathe one's last; **~ vermek** to put an end (-*e* to), to abolish; to bring to an end; **-a ermek** to finish, to end; **-a kalan dona kalır** *pro.* first come, first served; **-dan bir evvelki** next to the last, penultimate; **-una kadar** to the last; **-unda** in the end, finally; **-unu getirmek** (*bşin*) to bring *s.th.* to a successful conclusion, to accomplish *s.th.*

sonat, -tı MUS sonata.

sonbahar autumn, *Am.* fall.

sonda [x .] **1.** MED probe, sound; **2.** MEC drill.

sondaj 1. MEC drilling; **2.** NAUT sounding; **3.** *fig.* sounding out; **~ yapmak 1.** MEC to drill, to bore; **2.** NAUT to sound, to fathom; **3.** *fig.* to sound out.

sondajcı MEC driller.

sondalamak 1. NAUT to sound, to fathom; **2.** MEC to drill; **3.** MED to probe.

sonek, -ki GR suffix.

sonkânun [ū] *obs.* January.

sonra [x .] **1.** then, later, afterwards; **2.** after; **3.** the rest; **4.** or else, otherwise; **-ya atmak** (*or* **bırakmak**) to postpone, to put off; **ondan ~** after that.

sonradan [x . .] later, subsequently; **~ görme** parvenu, upstart, nouveau riche.

sonraki [x . .] subsequent, following.

sonraları [x . . .] afterwards, later on.

sonsuz 1. endless, eternal; **2.** infinite; **-a dek** eternally.

sonsuzluk 1. eternity; **2.** infinity.
sonteşrin [ī] *obs.* November.
sonuç, -cu result, conclusion, outcome; ~ *olarak* consequently; *sonucuna katlanmak* to take the consequences.
sonuçlandırmak to conclude, to bring to a conclusion.
sonuçlanmak to come to a conclusion; to result.
sonuncu last, final; latter.
sopa [x .] **1.** stick, cudgel, club; **2.** *fig.* beating; ~ *atmak* (*or* **çekmek**) (*b-ne*) to give *s.o.* a beating, to give *s.o.* the cane; ~ *yemek* to get a beating, to get the cane.
soprano MUS soprano.
sorgu interrogation, cross-examination; *-ya çekmek* to interrogate, to cross-examine, to grill.
sorguç, -cu crest, tuft.
sormak[1], (-ar) 1. to ask; **2.** to ask (*or* inquire) about; to ask after; *sora sora Bağdat* (*or* **Kâbe**) *bulunur pro.* you can find any place you want to go to by asking for directions; *öyle bir sıcak oldu ki sormayın!* you cannot imagine how hot it was!
sormak[2], (-ur) to suck.
sorti ELECT outlet.
soru question; ~ *işareti* question mark; ~ *sormak* to ask a question.
sorum responsibility.
sorumak *s.* **sormak 2.**
sorumlu responsible (*-den* for).
sorumluluk responsibility.
sorumsuz irresponsible.
sorumsuzluk irresponsibility.
sorun problem, matter, question; issue.
soruşmak[1] P to dry up.
soruşmak[2] to question each other.
soruşturma 1. *vn. of* **soruşturmak**; **2.** investigation; **3.** questionnaire; ~ *açmak* to open an investigation.
soruşturmak to investigate, to inquire about.
sos sauce.
sosis hot dog, frankfurter, wiener.
sosyal, -li social; ~ *sigorta* social insurance.
sosyalist, -ti socialist.
sosyalizm socialism.
sosyete society, the smart set.
sosyetik society ...
sosyolog sociologist.
sosyoloji sociology.

sote sauté(ed).
Sovyet, -ti Soviet; ~ *Sosyalist Cumhuriyetleri Birliği* the Union of Soviet Socialist Republics.
soy 1. race; **2.** line(age), family; **3.** high-bred; ~ *sop* family, relations; *-a çekmek* to take after one's family.
soya BOT soybean.
soyaçekim heredity.
soyadı, -nı family name, surname.
soydaş of the same race.
soygun 1. robbery, holdup; stick-up; **2.** = *soyguncu*; **3.** ill-gotten gain.
soyguncu robber.
soykırım(ı) genocide.
soylu noble, highborn.
soymak 1. to peel (*fruit, etc.*); **2.** to undress; **3.** to skin (*an animal*); **4.** to rob, to strip; *soyup soğana çevirmek* to clean out, to pluck, to take to the cleaners.
soysuz 1. of bad race; **2.** base, good-for-nothing (*person*).
soysuzlaşmak to degenerate.
soytarı clown, buffoon.
soyunmak to undress o.s., to strip, to peel off, to take off one's clothes; *soyunup dökünmek* to change into casual clothes.
soyut, -tu abstract.
soyutlamak to abstract.
söbe oval.
söğüş cold meat; boiled meat.
söğüt BOT willow.
sökmek, (-er) 1. to dismantle; to undo, to rip, to unstitch; to unravel; **2.** to uproot, to pull up (*or* out); to rip out; **3.** to decipher, to read (*handwriting*); **4.** to learn to read (*alphabet*); **5.** to appear, to come out; **6.** to break through (*obstacle*); **7.** to flow (*mucus*); **8.** *sl.* to make a dent (*-e* on).
sökük 1. unstitched; unraveled; **2.** dropped stitch.
sökülmek 1. *pass. of* **sökmek**; **2.** *sl.* to shell (*or* fork) out (*money*).
sökün etm. to come one after the other.
söküntü rip.
sölpük flabby, lax.
sölpümek to hang flabbily.
sömestr semester.
sömikok (*kömürü*) semicoke.
sömürge colony.
sömürgeci colonialist(ic).
sömürgecilik colonialism.
sömürmek 1. to exploit (*a. fig.*); **2.** to

eat up, to gobble down; **3.** to suck (*a liquid*).

sömürü exploitation.

söndürmek *caus. of* **sönmek 1.** to extinguish, to put out (*fire*); **2.** to turn (*or* switch) off (*light*); **3.** to deflate; **4.** to reduce, to diminish (*passion, fever*).

söndürücü fire extinguisher.

sönmek, (-er) 1. to go out, to die down (*fire*); **2.** to go out, to fade (*light*); **3.** to go flat (*tire*); **4.** to die down (*anger, etc.*); **5.** to go into a decline.

sönük 1. extinguished (*fire, light*); **2.** flat (*tire*); deflated (*balloon*); **3.** dim, faint; **4.** inactive, extinct (*volcano*); **5.** dull, uninspired, lifeless (*person*).

sör [-] sister.

söve doorpost.

sövgü swearword, curse, cussword.

sövmek, (-er) to swear, to curse (-*e* at); **sövüp saymak** to swear a blue streak (-*e* at).

sövüşlemek *sl.* to swindle.

sövüşmek to swear at each other.

söylemek 1. to say, to utter; to tell; **2.** to sing (*a song*); to recite (*a poem*); **3.** to speak (-*e* to); **söyleyecek kelime bulamıyorum** I am at a loss for words.

söylenmek 1. *pass. of* **söylemek; 2.** to grumble, to mutter to o.s.

söylenti rumo(u)r, hearsay.

söyleşi chat.

söyleşmek to chat, to converse.

söylev speech, address; oration.

söz 1. remark, utterance; word; statement; **2.** rumo(u)r; **3.** promise; **~ anlamak** to show understanding; **~ aramızda** between you and me; **~ arasında** in the course of the conversation; **~ bir, Allah bir!** I am a man of my word!; **~ dinlemek** to follow advice; **~ etm. 1.** to talk about; **2.** to gossip; **~ geçirmek** to assert o.s.; **~ götürmez** indisputable, beyond doubt; **~ işitmek** to be told off; **~ kavafı** F garrulous; **~ kesmek** to agree to give in marriage; **~ konusu** in question; **~ konusu etm.** to discuss; **~ olm.** to be the subject of gossip; **~ sahibi** who has a say (*in a matter*); **~ vermek** to promise; **-ü ağzına tıkamak** to squelch, to silence; **-ü geçen** aforementioned, said, aforesaid; **-ü geçmek 1.** to assert o.s.; **2.** to be mentioned; **-ü uzatmak** to be long-winded (*or* wordy); **-üm**

meclisten dışarı (*or* **yabana**) present company excepted; **-ün gelişi** context; **-ün kısası** in short, the long and the short of it is that; **-ünde durmak** to keep one's word; **-den dönmek** to go back on one's word, to backpedal; **-ünü esirgememek** to call a spade a spade, not to mince words; **-ünü kesmek** to interrupt; **-ünü tutmak 1.** (*b-nin*) to take the advice of *s.o.*; **2.** (*kendi*) to keep *one's* word; **-ünün eri** man of his word; **sizin evde kimin sözü geçer?** who wears the trousers in your house?

sözbirliği, -ni agreement.

sözcü spokesman.

sözcük word.

sözde 1. so-called, would-be; **2.** supposedly.

sözdizimi, -ni syntax.

sözgelimi, sözgelişi for instance, for example.

sözleşme 1. *vn. of* **sözleşmek; 2.** agreement, contract.

sözleşmek 1. to promise each other; **2.** to make an appointment.

sözleşmeli contractual.

sözlü 1. oral, verbal; **2.** engaged to be married; **3.** fiancé; fiancée; **~ sınav** oral examination.

sözlük dictionary.

sözlükbilgisi, -ni lexicography.

sözlükçü lexicographer.

sözlükçülük lexicography.

sözümona *s.* **sözde.**

spam IT spam (mail).

spekülasyon speculation.

spekülatif speculative.

spekülatör speculator.

sperma sperm.

spesiyal, -li special.

spiker announcer.

spiral 1. spiral; **2.** MED coil.

spor 1. sport; **2.** sport(s); **~ araba** sports car.

sporcu sportsman.

sporsever sports fan.

sportif sports …

sportmen 1. sportsman; **2.** sportsmanlike.

sportoto the football pools, the pools.

sprey 1. spray; **2.** sprayer.

stabilize stabilized; **~ etm.** to stabilize; **~ yol** gravel (*or* macadam) road.

stad, stadyum stadium.

staj apprenticeship; internship; **~ yapmak** to undergo training; to serve

one's internship.
stajyer trainee; houseman, intern.
standart standard.
statü statutes.
statüko the status quo.
steno 1. shorthand, stenography; **2.** steno(grapher).
stenograf stenographer.
stenografi shorthand, stenography.
step, -pi steppe.
stepne MOT spare tyre (*or Am.* tire).
stereo stereo.
steril sterile.
sterilize etm. to sterilize.
sterlin (pound) sterling.
steyşin estate car. *Am.* station wagon.
stil style.
stilo [x .] fountain pen.
stok, -ku stock; ~ **etm.** to stock.
stokçu stockpiler.
stop, -pu stop!; ~ **etm.** to stop.
stopaj stoppage at source.
stoplazma cytoplasm.
strateji strategy.
stratejik strategical.
stratus [x .] METEOR stratus.
striptiz striptease.
striptizci stripteaser, stripper.
stüdyo [x .] studio.
su, -yu 1. water; **2.** river, stream; **3.** juice; **4.** sap; **5.** gravy; broth; **6.** temper (*of steel*); ~ **akarken testiyi doldurmalı** *pro.* strike while the iron is hot, make hay while the sun shines; ~ **almak** to leak, to make water (*boat*); ~ **baskını** flood; ~ **basmak** to flood, to inundate; ~ **birikintisi** puddle; ~ **bölümü çizgisi** GEOGR watershed; ~ **cenderesi** hydraulic press; ~ **çekmek** to draw water; ~ **dökmek** to make water, to urinate; ~ **gibi akmak** to fly (*time*); ~ **gibi bilmek** to know perfectly; ~ **gibi para harcamak** to spend money like water; ~ **götürmez** indisputable; ~ **içinde** at least; ~ **koyuvermek** *fig.* to overstep the mark; ~ **tabancası** water pistol (*or gun*); ~ **testisi su yolunda kırılır** *pro.* the pitcher goes too often to the well; ~ **vermek 1.** to water; **2.** MEC to temper, to quench (*steel*); ~ **yüzüne çıkmak** to come to light; *-dan ucuz* dirt cheap; *-larında* about, around; *-ya düşmek* *fig.* to fall to the ground, to go phut; *-ya sabuna dokunmamak* to avoid meddling; *-ya salmak* *fig.* to throw away (*money*); *-yu görmeden paçaları sıvamak*

fig. to count one's chickens before they are hatched; *-yunca gitmek* *fig.* to comply with s.o.'s wishes; *-yunu çekmek* *fig.* to run out (*money*); *-yunun suyu* only a remote connection.
sual, -li [ā] question; inquiry; ~ **açmak** to interrogate; ~ **etm.** to question; ~ **sormak** to ask a question.
sualtı, -nı underwater.
suare evening performance (*of a play*); evening showing (*of a movie*).
suaygırı, -nı ZOO hippopotamus.
subaşı, -nı HIST **1.** police superintendent; **2.** farm manager.
subay MIL officer.
subilim hydrology.
subra [x .] dress shield.
subye [x .] strap.
sucu water seller.
sucuk 1. sausage; **2.** sweetmeat (*made of grape juice, nuts, etc.*); ~ **gibi olm.** (*or* **ıslanmak**) to get wet through, to get drenched; **sucuğunu çıkarmak** *fig.* **1.** to beat the tar out of; **2.** to tire out.
suç, -çu 1. offence, *Am.* offense; guilt; fault; **2.** crime; ~ **atmak** (*b-nin üstüne*) to put the blame on *s.o.*; ~ **işlemek** to commit an offence *or* crime; ~ **ortağı** accomplice, accessory; *-unu bağışlamak or -undan geçmek* to pardon, to forgive an offence.
suçiçeği, -ni chicken pox, varicella.
suçlamak (*b-ni bşle*) to accuse *s.o.* of *s.th.*
suçlandırmak to find guilty.
suçlu 1. guilty; **2.** criminal, felon, offender; ~ **çıkarmak** to find guilty; *-ların iadesi* JUR extradition.
suçsuz not guilty, innocent.
suçüstü, -nü red-handed, in the act; ~ **yakalamak** to catch red-handed.
sudak ZOO zander.
sudan trivial, weak.
Sudan [- -] *pr. n.* Sudan.
sudolabı, -nı waterwheel.
sufi [- -] Sufi.
suflör THEAT prompter.
sugeçirmez waterproof.
suiistimal, -li [- . . . .] misuse, abuse; ~ **etm.** to misuse, to abuse.
suikast, -tı 1. conspiracy; **2.** assassination; *-ta bulunmak* **1.** to conspire; **2.** to assassinate.
suikastçı 1. conspirator; **2.** assassin.
suiniyet, -ti [ü] malice.

suizan, -nnı [ū] suspicion.

sukabağı, -nı BOT dipper gourd.

sukemeri, -ni aqueduct.

sukut, -tu [. -] fall; ~ etm. to fall; -u hayal disappointment; -u hayale uğramak to be disappointed; -u hayale
uğratmak to disappoint, to let down.

suküre hydrosphere.

sulak 1. watery, well-watered; 2.
marshy.

sulama vn. of sulamak, part. irrigation.

sulamaç sprinkler.

sulamak 1. to water; to irrigate; 2. sl.
to shell out (money).

sulandırmak 1. caus. of sulanmak; 2.
to water (down); 3. to dilute, to thin.

sulanmak 1. pass. of sulamak; 2. (bşe)
sl. to hanker after s.th.; 3. (b-ne) sl. to
make improper advances to s.o.

sulfata, sulfato [. x .] P quinine sulfate.

sulh peace; ~ hâkimi justice of the
peace; ~ mahkemesi justice court;
~ olm. to settle their differences.

sulhçu 1. peace-loving; 2. pacifist.

sulhname [ā] peace treaty.

sulhperver, sulhsever s. sulhçu.

sulp, -bü 1. hard, tough; 2. loins; sul-
bünden gelmek to be the offspring
(-in of).

sulta authority.

sultan 1. sultan; 2. sultana.

sultanlık sultanate; sultanship.

sulu 1. watery; dilute; 2. juicy; 3. fig.
importunate, saucy, pert; ~ gözlü 1.
tearful, lachrymose; 2. crybaby.

suluboya watercolo(u)r.

suluk 1. water cup; 2. MED infantile
seborrhea.

sulusepken sleet; ~ yağmak to sleet.

sumak BOT sumac.

sumen writing-pad, blotting-pad.

suna drake.

sundurma shed, lean-to.

sungu 1. gift; 2. sacrifice.

sungur ZOO white falcon.

suni [ī] artificial, false; imitation.

sunmak, (-ar) 1. to present, to offer; to
submit; 2. to perform; to play; to sing.

sunta fiberboard.

sunturlu awful, whopping.

sunucu compère, emcee.

sup(anglez) chocolate pudding.

supap, -bı MEC valve.

suphanallah! heavens above!, great
Scott!

suples flexibility.

sur¹ rampart, city wall.

sur² isl. MYTH good luck.

surat, -tı face; ~ asmak to pull (or
make) a long face; ~ bir karış sour-
-faced; ~ düşkünü ugly; ~ etm. to pull
a long face; -ı asık sour-faced, sulky;
-ından düşen bin parça olur fig. very
sour-faced; -ını ekşitmek to put on a
sour face.

suratlı sour-faced, sulky.

suratsız 1. sour-faced; 2. ugly; 3. bad-
-tempered.

surdin MUS mute.

sure [ū] sura (of the Koran).

suret, -ti [ū] 1. copy, transcript; 2. form,
figure, shape; 3. way, manner, fashion; ~ almak (or çıkarmak) to make
a copy of, to transcribe; -ine girmek
to assume the form of; bu -le thus, so.

sureta [- . -] [x . -] 1. assumed, affected;
2. outwardly.

Suriye pr. n. Syria.

sus! be quiet!, silence!

susak 1. thirsty; 2. dipper.

susam BOT sesame.

susamak 1. to get thirsty; 2. fig. to
thirst (-e for).

susamuru, -nu ZOO otter.

susığırı, -nı ZOO water buffalo.

suskun quiet, taciturn.

susmak, (-ar) to stop talking, to be
quiet, to become silent, to hold one's
tongue; sus payı hush money.

suspansuvar jock(strap).

suspus: ~ olm. to be silenced; to be as
quiet as a mouse.

susta [x .] safety catch; ~ durmak 1. to
stand on its hind legs (dog); 2. fig. to
stand to heel.

sustalı switchblade.

susturmak to silence, to hush, to shut
up.

susturucu 1. silencer (of a gun); 2. MOT
silencer, muffler.

susuz waterless.

susuzluk 1. waterlessness; 2. thirst.

sut, -du soda.

sutopu, -nu water polo.

sutyen bra, brassiere.

Suudi Arabistan pr. n. Saudi Arabia.

SUV SUV (= sports utility vehicle).

suvare evening showing (of a movie);
evening performance (of a play).

suvarmak to water (an animal).

suvat, -tı watering place.

suyolu, -nu 1. waterline; 2. watermark

(*in paper*).
suyosunları, -nı BOT algae.
suyosunu, -nu seaweed, alga.
suyuk fluid.
suziş [ü] heartache, anguish.
suzişli [ü] full of anguish.
sübek urinal (*for a baby*).
sübjektif subjective.
sübut, -tu [ü] realization; ~ *bulmak* to become a reality.
sübyan children.
sübyancı F pedophiliac.
sübye [x .] **1.** a kind of sweet; **2.** CHEM emulsion.
sücut [ü] prostration; ~ *etm.* to prostrate o.s. in worship.
südremek to get drunk.
süet, -ti suede.
süfli [î] **1.** contemptible, low-down; **2.** shabby.
sühulet, -ti [ü] ease, facility.
sühunet, -ti [ü] METEOR, PHYS temperature.
süje subject (*a.* GR).
süklüm püklüm cap in hand, in a hangdog manner.
sükna [â] residence; ~ *hakkı* JUR right of residence.
sükse success, hit; ~ *yapmak* to be a hit (*or* success).
sükûn, sükûnet, -ti calm, quiet, rest, repose; ~ *bulmak* to quiet down.
sükût, -tu silence; ~ *etm.* to remain silent; ~ *hakkı* hush money; *-la geçiştirmek* to pass over in silence.
sükûti [î] silent.
sülale family, line.
sülfat, -tı sulphate, *Am.* sulfate.
sülfit, -ti sulfite.
sülfür sulphide, *Am.* sulfide.
sülfürik sulphuric, *Am.* sulfuric.
sülük 1. ZOO leech; **2.** BOT tendril; ~ *gibi yapışmak* to stick like a leech.
sülün ZOO pheasant; ~ *gibi* tall and graceful.
sümbül BOT hyacinth.
sümbüli [î] overcast, cloudy (*sky*).
Sümer *pr. n.* Sumer.
sümkürmek to blow one's nose.
sümmettedarik [â] last-minute.
sümsük shiftless, supine.
sümük mucus; snot; slime.
sümükdoku mucous membrane.
sümüklü snotty; snotty-nosed; slimy.
sümüklüböcek ZOO slug.
sümüksü mucoid.
sünepe shiftless, supine.

sünger sponge; ~ *avcılığı* sponge fishing; ~ *avcısı* sponge fisherman; ~ *geçirmek* (*bşin üzerinden*) to pass the sponge over *s.th.*; ~ *gibi* spongy.
süngerci 1. sponge fisherman; **2.** sponge seller.
süngerdoku BOT spongy parenchyma.
süngertaşı, -nı pumice.
süngü 1. bayonet; **2.** poker (*for a fire*); *-sü depreşmesin ama ...* I don't like to speak ill of the dead, but ...; *-sü düşük* depressed, down in the dumps.
süngülemek to bayonet.
süngülü with fixed bayonets.
sünnet, -ti *isl.* **1.** the Sunna; **2.** circumcision; ~ *düğünü* circumcision feast; ~ *etm.* to circumcise; ~ *olm.* to be circumcised.
sünnetçi circumciser.
sünnetlemek P to eat up.
sünnetli circumcised.
sünnetsiz uncircumcised.
Sünni [î] Sunni.
Sünnilik [. - .] the Sunni branch of Islam.
süper super; ~ *benzin* high-octane gasoline.
süpermarket, -ti supermarket.
süpersonik supersonic.
süpozituvar MED suppository.
süprüntü sweepings, rubbish, trash (*a. fig.*).
süprüntücü 1. dustman, street sweeper; **2.** *fig.* junkman.
sünrüntülük dump, rubbish heap.
süpürge broom.
süpürgeci 1. maker *or* seller of brooms; **2.** street sweeper.
süpürgelik baseboard, mopboard.
süpürgeotu, -nu BOT heath.
süpürmek 1. to sweep; **2.** *fig.* to sweep away.
sürahi [. - .] decanter, jug, carafe.
sürat, -ti speed, velocity; ~ *motoru* speedboat; *-ini artırmak* to accelerate, to speed up; *-le* speedily, quickly.
süratlendirmek to accelerate, to speed up.
süratlenmek to speed up, to gain speed, to go faster.
süratli speedy; rapid, quick.
sürç, -cü; -ü lisan slip of the tongue.
sürçmek, (-er) 1. to stumble; **2.** *fig.* to make a slip of the tongue.
sürdürmek 1. *caus. of* **sürmek**; **2.** to carry on, to continue, to maintain.
süre period; extension.

süreç process, progression.

süredurum PHYS inertia.

süregelmek to have gone on for a long time.

süreğen chronic.

sürek 1. duration, continuation; 2. drove (of cattle); ~ avı drive.

sürekli continuous, continual.

süreksiz transitory, transient.

süreksizlik transitoriness.

süreli periodic.

sürerlik continuousness.

Süreyya [ā] pr.n. 1. AST the Pleiades; 2. mf., wf.

sürfe larva.

sürgü 1. bolt; 2. bedpan; 3. harrow; 4. (plasterer's) trowel.

sürgülemek to bolt.

sürgülü bolted; ~ cetvel slide rule.

sürgün 1. BOT shoot, sucker; 2. exile, banishment; 3. MED diarrhea; ~ avı drive; ~ etm. to exile, to banish; -e gitmek to go into exile; -e göndermek to send into exile.

sürme 1. vn. of sürmek; 2. drawer; 3. latch; 4. kohl; 5. sliding; ~ kapı sliding door.

sürmedan(lık) [ā] container for kohl.

sürmek, (-er) 1. to drive (a vehicle, an animal) 2. to exile; 3. to plough, Am. to plow (a field); 4. to put into circulation (money); to put on the market (goods); 5. to rub, to smear; 6. to go on, to continue, to last; 7. to lead (a good life); 8. BOT to shoot out.

sürmelemek to bolt.

sürmelik s. sürmedan(lık).

sürmenaj nervous breakdown, neurasthenia.

sürpriz surprise; ~ yapmak (b-ne) to surprise s.o.

sürre the presents sent annually by the Sultan to Mecca and Medina; ~devesi gibi iro. overdressed woman.

sürrealist, -ti surrealist.

sürşarj surcharge (on a stamp).

sürtmek, (-er) 1. to rub (-e against); 2. to loiter, to wander about.

sürtük 1. gadabout (woman); 2. streetwalker.

sürtünme vn. of sürtünmek, part. PHYS friction.

sürtünmek 1. to rub o.s. (-e against); 2. fig. to seek a quarrel.

sürtüşmek 1. to rub against each other; 2. to vex (or irritate) each other.

sürur [ū] delight, joy.

sürü herd, drove, flock; ~ içgüdüsü PSYCH the herd instinct; ~ sepet F the whole kit and caboodle, the whole lot; -den ayrılmak fig. to go one's own way; -süne bereket a lot of, heaps of.

sürücü 1. drover; 2. driver, motorist.

sürüklemek 1. to drag; 2. to hold one's attention, to carry with one; 3. to drag (-e into).

sürüklenmek 1. pass. of sürüklemek; 2. to drag o.s.; 3. to drag on (or out).

sürükleyici fascinating, engrossing.

sürüm COM demand, sale.

sürümek to drag.

sürümlü in demand.

sürüm sürüm: ~ sürünmek to suffer great misery.

sürünceme: -de bırakmak to procrastinate; -de kalmak to drag on, to be left hanging in the air.

süründürmek caus. of sürünmek, part. to drive from pillar to post.

sürüngen reptile.

sürünmek 1. to crawl, to creep, to grovel; 2. to rub (-e against); 3. fig. to live in misery.

sürüşmek to rub (or smear) on each other.

sürüştürmek to rub (or spread) slowly (-e on).

sürütme 1. vn. of sürütmek; 2. trawl(-net).

sürütmek caus. of sürümek.

sürveyan supervisor.

süs 1. ornament, decoration; 2. ornamentation; ~ püs frippery, finery; -e düşkün dressy; ... süsü vermek (k-ne) to pass o.s. off as ..., to set up as ..., to pose as ...

süsen BOT iris; ~ kökü orris(root).

süslemek 1. to adorn, to decorate, to embellish; 2. to doll up, to deck out; süsleyip püslemek to doll up fit to kill, to prank.

süslenmek pass. or refl. of süslemek, to deck o.s. out, to doll o.s. up; süslenip püslenmek to doll o.s. up fit to kill, to primp and preen, to prank o.s. up.

süslü 1. ornately, decorated, adorned; 2. fancy, ornate, dressy; ~ püslü dolled up fit to kill.

süsmek to butt, to gore.

süspansiyon MEC suspension.

süssüz undecorated, unadorned.

süt, -tü 1. milk; 2. latex; 3. sl. petrol,

juice; ~ **çalmak** (*çocuğu*) to make (*a nursing baby*) ill; ~ **çocuğu** 1. nursling; 2. *fig.* mollycoddle, babe in the woods; ~ **dökmüş kedi gibi** in a crestfallen manner; ~ **gibi** white and clean; ~ **kesilmek** to sour, to go off (*or* bad); ~ **kuzusu** 1. suckling lamb; 2. *fig.* baby; tot, toddler; ~ **tozu** milk powder; ~ **vermek** to suckle, to breast-feed, to nurse; **-ten ağzı yanan yoğurdu üfleyerek yer** *pro.* once bitten twice shy; **-ten kesmek** to wean; **-ü bozuk** *fig.* no-good, villain; **-üne havale etm.** (*bir işi b-nin*) to leave (*a matter*) to s.o.

sütana, **sütanne** wet nurse.
sütbaşı, **-nı** cream.
sütbeyaz milk white.
sütçü milkman.
sütçülük being a milkman.
sütdişi, **-ni** milk (*or* baby) tooth.
sütkardeş foster brother *or* sister.
sütkırı, **-nı** milk-white (*horse*).
sütkızı foster daughter.
sütlaç rice pudding.
sütleğen BOT spurge.
sütliman dead calm, as calm as a millpond, halcyon.
sütlü 1. milky, in milk; 2. made with milk (*food*); 3. full (*ear of grain*); ~ **kahve** white coffee, coffee with milk.
sütmavisi, **-ni** light sky-blue.

sütnine wet nurse.
sütoğul, **-ğlu** foster son.
sütre MIL cover.
sütsüz milkless.
sütun [ü] column; post; pillar; ~ **başlığı** ARCH capital of a column.
sütyen *s.* **sutyen**.
süvari [. - -] 1. cavalryman; 2. rider, horseman; 3. NAUT captain; ~ **alayı** cavalry regiment.
süve *s.* **söve**.
süveter sweater.
Süveyş [. x] *pr. n.* Suez; ~ **Kanalı** Suez Canal.
süyek MED splint.
süzek strainer; filter.
süzeni a kind of embroidery.
süzgeç, **-ci** 1. strainer; filter; sieve; 2. PHOT colo(u)r (*or* light) filter; ~ **kâğıdı** filter paper.
süzgün 1. languorous (*look*); 2. gaunt, thin.
süzme 1. *vn. of* **süzmek**; 2. filtered; strained; 3. *sl.* fox, rascal.
süzmek, **(-er)** 1. to filter; to strain; 2. to give the once-over; 3. to scan.
süzülmek 1. *pass. of* **süzmek**; 2. to glide; 3. to flow, to run; 4. to get thin; 5. to steal (*or* slip) in; 6. to be about to close (*eyes*).
süzüntü 1. filtrate; 2. residue, dregs.

Ş

şa [ä]: ~ ~ ~ hip, hip, hurrah!
şaban[1] [- -] 1. *isl.* Sha'ban; 2. ♀ *mf.*
şaban[2] *sl.* dumb, nitwitted.
şablon pattern, template, former.
şad [ä] happy; joyful; ~ **olm.** to rejoice.
şadırdamak to plash (*water*).
şadırvan fountain.
şafak dawn, twilight; ~ **atmak** to dawn on s.o.; ~ **sökmek** (*for dawn*) to break.
şaft, **-tı** MEC shaft.
şah[1]: **-a kalkmak** to rear (*horse*).
şah[2] [ä] 1. shah; 2. *chess*: king; ~ **iken şahbaz olm.** *co.* to get even worse; **ben şahımı bu kadar severim** *fig.* I'll help my boss to this extent only.
şahadet, **-ti** [. -.] 1. witness, attestation; 2. martyrdom; ~ **getirmek** to repeat the Islamic testimony of faith; **-te bulunmak** to bear witness, to testify.
şahadetname [. - . - .] 1. diploma; 2.

certificate.
şahadetparmağı, **-nı** index finger, forefinger.
şahane [- - .] 1. splendid, magnificent, superb; 2. imperial, royal.
şahap, **-bı** [. -] 1. AST shooting star; 2. ♀ *mf.*
şahbaz 1. ZOO royal falcon; 2. courageous, brave.
şahdamarı, **-nı** ANAT carotid artery, jugular vein.
şaheser masterpiece, masterwork.
şahıs, **-hsı** 1. person (*a.* GR), individual; 2. THEAT character; ~ **zamiri** GR personal pronoun.
şâhıs surveyor's rod.
şahika 1. summit; 2. ♀ *wf.*
şahin [ä] 1. ZOO falcon; 2. ♀ *mf.*
şahit, **-di** [ä] (eye)witness; ~ **olm.** to witness.

şahitlik [ā] witnessing, testimony; ~ **etm.** to testify, to bear witness.

şahlanmak 1. to rear up (*horse*); **2.** *fig.* to become angry and threatening.

şahlık shahdom.

şahmerdan MEC pile-driver; drop hammer.

şahniş(in) [- . -] bay window.

şahrem şahrem in strips (*or* shreds).

şahsen [x .] **1.** personally, in person; **2.** for my part, personally; **3.** by sight.

şahsi [ī] personal, private; ~ **eşya** personal effects, belongings.

şahsiyet, -ti 1. personality; **2.** individuality; **3.** personage.

şahsiyetli having personality.

şahsiyetsiz who lacks personality.

şaibe [ā] stain, blot.

şair [ā] poet.

şairane [- . - .] poetic(al).

şairlik poetship.

şak¹, -kı smack!

şak², -kkı split, fissure.

şaka joke, leg-pull, jest; gag; ~ **bir tarafa** (*or* **yana**) joking apart; ~ **etm.** to kid; ~ **gibi gelmek** to seem like a joke (-*e* to); ~ **götürmez bir iş** it is no joking matter; ~ **iken kaka olm.** to turn into a quarrel; to backfire; ~ **kaldırmak** to be able to take a joke; ~ **maka** (**derken**) imperceptibly; ~ **söylemek** to joke; **-dan anlamak** to take a joke; **-sı yok** it is no joke; **-ya boğmak** to turn into a joke; **-ya gelmek** to be able to take a joke; **-ya vurmak** to pretend to take as a joke.

şakacı joker.

şakacıktan 1. jokingly, as a joke; **2.** inadvertently, unwittingly.

şakadan jokingly, as a joke.

şakak ANAT temple.

şakalaşmak to joke with one another.

şakayık, -kı, -gı BOT peony.

şakımak to warble, to trill.

şakırdamak 1. to clatter, to rattle; **2.** to snap (*fingers*); **3.** to jingle; **4.** to crack (*whip*); **5.** to drum, to beat, to patter (*rain*).

şakırdatmak 1. to rattle, to clatter; **2.** to jingle; **3.** to crack (*a whip*); **4.** to snap (*fingers*).

şakır şakır 1. with a patter; **2.** with a rattle (*or* jingle).

şakır şukur clatteringly, with a rattle.

şakırtı 1. clatter, rattle; **2.** patter, plash; **3.** crack, snap; **4.** jingle.

şaki robber, brigand.

şakirt, -di [ā] student.

şaklaban 1. jester, buffoon; **2.** *fig.* sycophantic.

şaklamak to crack, to snap, to pop.

şaklatmak to crack, to snap.

şakrak mirthful, merry.

şakrakkuşu, -nu ZOO bullfinch.

şakramak *s.* **şakımak.**

şakşak 1. slapstick; **2.** applause.

şakul, -lü [ā] plumb line.

şakuli [- . -] perpendicular.

şakullemek 1. to plumb, to plumb-line; **2.** *fig.* to sound out.

şal shawl.

şalgam BOT turnip.

şallak naked; ~ **maliak** stark naked.

şalter ELECT switch; (circuit) breaker.

şalupa [. x .] NAUT sloop.

şalvar baggy trousers, shalwar; ~ **gibi** very baggy.

Şam *pr. n.* Damascus.

şama [x .] wax taper.

şamama [. . -.] muskmelon; ~ **gibi** small and cute-looking.

Şaman *pr. n.* shaman.

şamandıra [. x . .] **1.** NAUT buoy, float; **2.** cork float.

şamar slap, box on the ear; ~ **atmak** to slap; to give a box on the ear; ~ **oğlanı** whipping boy, scapegoat; ~ **yemek** to get a slap on the face.

şamata whoopee, commotion, uproar, clamo(u)r; ~ **yapmak** to make whoopee, to make a commotion.

şamatacı noisy, boisterous.

şambriyel MOT inner tube (*of a tire*).

şambrnuar PHOT darkroom.

şamdan candlestick.

şamfıstığı, -nı pistachio (nut).

şamil [ā] **1.** all-inclusive, comprehensive; **2.** ♀ *mf.*; ~ **olm.** to include, to cover.

şamme [ā] BIOL (sense of) smell.

şampanya [. x .] champagne.

şampiyon champion.

şampiyona championship.

şampiyonluk championship.

şampuan shampoo.

şan¹ [ā] glory, reputation, fame; ~ **vermek** to become famous; **-ına düşmek** (*or* **yakışmak**) to befit one's dignity; **-ından olm.** to befit.

şan² singing; ~ **resitali** recital given by a vocalist.

şangırdamak to crash.

şangır şungur with a crash.

şangırtı crash.

şanjan iridescence.

şanjman MOT gearbox, shift.

şanlı glorious, illustrious; ~ **şöhretli** illustrious and famous.

şano [x .] THEAT stage.

şans luck; chance; ~ **tanımak** to give a chance; **-ı yaver gitmek** to have good luck, to be lucky enough.

şansız unrenowned.

şanslı lucky, fortunate.

şanssız unlucky.

şanssızlık unluckiness.

şantaj blackmail, extortion; ~ **yapmak** to blackmail.

şantajcı blackmailer.

şantiye 1. building (or construction) site; **2.** shipyard.

şantör chanteur, male singer.

şantöz chanteuse, female singer.

şanziman, şanzuman s. **şanjman.**

şap[1], **-pı** CHEM alum; ♀ **Denizi** pr. n. the Red Sea; ~ **hastalığı** foot-and-mouth disease; **-a oturmak** fig. to get in a pickle (or quandary).

şap[2] smack.

şapırdamak to smack.

şapırdatmak to smack (one's lips).

şapır şapır or **şapır şupur** smacking one's lips loudly.

şapırtı smack.

şapka [x .] **1.** hat; **2.** truck (of a mast); **3.** cowl, cap (of a chimney); **-sını çıkarmak** to take off one's hat; **-sını glymek** to put on one's hat.

şapkacı hatter.

şapkalık hatstand, hat rack.

şaplak whang.

şaplamak[1] to land with a smack.

şaplamak[2] CHEM to treat with alum.

şappadak [x .] all of a sudden, out of the blue.

şaprak saddlecloth.

şapşal 1. slovenly, untidy, shabby; **2.** stupid, lunkheaded.

şarabi [. - -] wine-red.

şarampol shoulder (of a road).

şarap, -bı wine.

şaraphane [. . - .] **1.** winehouse; **2.** winery.

şarapnel MIL shrapnel.

şarbon MED charbon.

şarıldamak to splash.

şarıl şarıl splashingly.

şarıltı splash.

şarj 1. ELECT charge; **2.** football: rush; ~ **etm.** to charge.

şarjör (cartridge) clip, charger.

şark, -kı the east; the East, the Orient.

şarkadak [x . .] with a whop (or thump).

şarkı song; ~ **okumak** (or **söylemek**) to sing a song.

şarkıcı singer.

şarki [î] eastern.

şarklı easterner.

şarküteri delicatessen.

şarlatan charlatan.

şarlatanlık charlatanry.

şarpi NAUT sharpie.

şar şar splashingly.

şart, -tı condition, stipulation, provision; ~ **koşmak** to make a condition (or stipulation), to stipulate; ~ **şurt tanımaz** F he refuses to be bound by any conditions.

şartlandırmak to condition.

şartlanmak to be conditioned.

şartlaşmak to agree to conditions.

şartlı conditional; stipulated.

şartname [. - .] list of conditions.

şartsız unconditional; unconditioned.

şaryo [x .] carriage (of a typewriter).

şasi chassis.

şaşaa splendo(u)r; glitter; brilliance.

şaşaalı splendid, pompous, grand, brilliant.

şaşakalmak, şaşalamak to be bewildered, to be taken aback.

şaşı cross-eyed, squint-eyed; ~ **bakmak** to squint.

şaşılaşmak to get cross-eyed.

şaşılık cross-eye, squint.

şaşırmak 1. to be confused (or puzzled), to be at a loss; **2.** to lose (one's way).

şaşırtma vn. of **şaşırtmak,** part. transplanting (of seedlings).

şaşırtmaca tongue-twister, puzzle.

şaşırtmak caus. of **şaşırmak,** part. **1.** to confuse, to bewilder, to mislead, to puzzle, to amaze; **2.** to transplant (seedlings).

şaşkaloz sl. **1.** cross-eyed; **2.** confused.

şaşkın 1. confused, bewildered, at a loss; **2.** silly, stupid; **-a çevirmek** to confuse, to bewilder; **-a dönmek** to be stupefied.

şaşkınlık confusion, bewilderment, daze; ~ **içinde** in a daze.

şaşmak, (-ar) 1. to be astonished (or amazed) (-e at); **2.** to deviate (-den from), to depart (-den from); **3.** (for a missile) to miss (its object); **4.** to be mistaken; **5.** to lose (one's way).

şat, -tı NAUT lighter.

şatafat, -tı display, show, ostentation.

şatafatlı showy, ostentatious, splendiferous.

şato [x .] castle, château.

şavalak F stupid, thick, dense.

şayan [- -] worthy (-e of), deserving; **-ı itimat** trustworthy; **-ı merhamet** pitiful.

şayet [ā] if (by chance), if perchance.

şayi, -li [ā] **1.** widespread; **2.** JUR shared in common.

şayia [- . .] rumo(u)r.

şaz [ā] irregular; exceptional.

seamet, -ti [ā] bad luck.

şeametli [ā] unlucky, ill-omened.

şebboy BOT **1.** wallflower; **2.** gillyflower, stock.

şebek 1. ZOO baboon; **2.** *fig.* ugly.

şebeke 1. network; **2.** identity card (*of a university student*).

şebnem dew.

şecaat, -ti [. - .] courage.

şecaatli [. - . .] courageous.

şecere family tree, pedigree.

şef chief, leader; **~ garson** head waiter.

şefaat, -ti [. - .] intercession; **~ etm.** (*b-ne*) to intercede with *s.o.*

şeffaf [ā] transparent.

şeffaflık [ā] transparency.

şefik, -kı [ī] **1.** tender(hearted), kind, compassionate; **2.** ♀ [x .] *mf.*

şefkat, -ti kindness, compassion, tenderness.

şefkatli kind, compassionate, tender(-hearted).

şeftali [ā] BOT peach.

şeftren RAIL guard, conductor.

şehevi [ī] carnal.

şehik, -kı [ī] BIOL inhalation, inspiration.

şehinşah [ā] the Shahinshah.

şehir, -hri city, town.

şehirci city planner.

şehirlerarası, -nı 1. intercity, interurban; **2.** TELEPH long-distance.

şehirli townsman, city dweller.

şehit, -di martyr; **~ düşmek** to die a martyr.

şehitlik 1. martyrdom; **2.** cemetery for Turkish soldiers.

şehla having a slight cast in the eye.

şehremaneti, -ni [ā] municipality.

şehremini, -ni mayor.

şehriye vermicelli; **~ çorbası** vermicelli soup.

şehvani [. - -] carnal, libidinal.

şehvet, -ti lust, concupiscence; **~ düşkünü** lewd, prurient.

şehvetli lustful, concupiscent, libidinous.

şehvetperest, -ti lustful.

şehzade [ā] prince, shahzadah.

şek, -kki suspicion, doubt.

şekavet, -ti [ā] brigandage.

şeker 1. sugar; **2.** candy; **3.** MED diabetes; **4.** *fig.* darling, sweet; **♀ Bayramı** the Lesser Bayram; **~ gibi** darling, sweet; **~ hastası** diabetic; **~ hastalığı** diabetes; **~ kellesi** sugarloaf; **~ pancarı** sugar beet; **-im** F honey, sweetie, darling.

şekerci confectioner; candymaker; candyseller.

şekercilik confectionery.

şekerkamışı, -nı BOT sugar cane.

şekerleme 1. *vn. of* **şekerlemek; 2.** candied fruit; **3.** nap, doze; **~ yapmak** to have (*or* take) a nap, to doze off.

şekerlemek 1. to sugar; **2.** to candy (*fruit*).

şekerleşmek 1. to turn into sugar, to sugar; **2.** *fig.* to become sweet.

şekerli 1. sugared; **2.** diabetic; **~ kahve** well-sugared coffee.

şekerlik 1. sugar basin (*or* bowl); **2.** candy bowl (*or* dish).

şekerrenk, -gi cool, uncordial.

şekersiz unsugared, unsweetened.

şekil, -kli 1. shape; **2.** figure, diagram; illustration; **3.** manner, way; **4.** sort, kind; **şeklini değiştirmek** to transform.

şekilbilgisi, -ni morphology.

şekilci formalist(ic).

şekilcilik formalism.

şekillendirmek to shape.

şekillenmek to take on a shape.

şekilsiz shapeless.

şeklen [x .] in shape (*or* appearance).

şekva [ā] complaint.

şelale waterfall.

şema [x .] diagram, scheme, plan; outline.

şemacılık [x . . .] schematism.

şematik schematic.

şempanze ZOO chimpanzee.

şemse sunburst (design).

şemsiper visor.

şemsiye 1. umbrella; parasol; **2.** umbel.

şemsiyelik umbrella stand.

şen happy, merry, cheerful, joyous.

şenaat, **-ti** [. - .] vileness, wickedness.

şendere 1. veneer; **2.** barrel stave; **3.** zoo red mullet.

şeneltmek to populate.

şeni, **-li** vile, foul; wicked.

şenia [ī] immorality.

şenlendirmek 1. to cheer up, to enliven; **2.** to populate.

şenlenmek 1. to be cheered up; **2.** to be populated.

şenlik 1. gaiety, cheerfulness; **2.** merriment; festival, festivity; **3.** prosperity.

şer, **-rri** evil, wickedness.

şerait, **-ti** [ā] conditions, stipulations.

şer'an [x .] in accordance with canon law, canonically.

şerare [ā] PHYS spark.

şerbet, **-ti** sherbet, sweet drink.

şerbetçiotu, **-nu** BOT hop.

şerbetli 1. immune to snakebite; **2.** fig. incorrigible.

şerç, **-ci** ANAT anus.

şeref 1. hono(u)r; **2.** ♀ mf.; **~ defteri** honorary-book; **~ madalyası** plume; **~ misafiri** guest of hono(u)r; **~ sözü** word of hono(u)r; **~ vermek** to hono(u)r; **-inizel** cheers!, to your health!

şerefe balcony.

şerefiye betterment tax.

şereflendirmek to hono(u)r.

şereflenmek to be hono(u)red.

şerefli hono(u)red.

şerefsiz dishono(u)rable.

şergil naughty.

şerh explanation; **~ etm.** to explain.

şeriat, **-tı** [ī] Islamic (or canon) law.

şerif[1] [ī] **1.** sacred; **2.** ♀ [x .] mf.

şerif[2] sheriff.

şerik, **-ki** [ī] partner.

şerir [ī] evil, wicked.

şerit, **-di 1.** ribbon, tape; band; **2.** MOT lane; **3.** MIL stripe; **4.** zoo tapeworm; **~ metre** tape measure.

şeş six; **-i beş görmek** to be completely mistaken.

şeşbeş six and five.

şeşcihar six and four.

şeşüdü six and two.

şeşüse six and three.

şeşüyek six and one.

şetaret, **-ti** [ā] gaiety, merriness.

şetim, **-tmi** execration, cursing.

şetmetmek [x . -] to curse, to execrate.

şev 1. slope, decline; **2.** slant; bevel.

şevk, **-ki** enthusiasm, eagerness, ardo(u)r, fervo(u)r; **-e gelmek** to become eager.

şevket, **-ti 1.** majesty, grandeur; **2.** ♀ mf.

şevval, **-li** [ā] isl. Shawwal.

şey 1. thing; **2.** what-do-you-call-it; thingumbob, thingummy.

şeyh sheik(h).

şeyhülislam Sheikh ul-Islam.

şeytan [ā] **1.** Satan, the Devil; **2.** fig. fiend, demon, devil; **~ azapta gerek** fig. it serves him right; **~ çekici** little devil, clever urchin; **~ gibi** as cunning as a fox; **~ kulağına kurşun!** touch wood!; **~ tüyü** fig. talisman supposed to give personal attraction; **-a çarık giydirmek** fig. to be clever enough to cheat the devil himself; **-a uyma** don't yield to temptation; **-ın bacağını kırmak** fig. to get the show on the road at last.

şaytanarabası, **-nı** cluster of feathery seeds floating in the air.

şeytanca 1. devilish; **2.** devilishly.

şeytanet, **-ti** [ā] s. **şeytanlık**.

şeytani [. - -] devilish.

şeytanlık 1. devilry; **2.** devilment, mischief.

şezlong, **-gu** chaise longue, deck chair.

şık[1], **-kı** smart, chic, neat, elegant, fashionable; **~ mı ~!** she is dressed to kill.

şık[2], **-kkı** choice, option; alternative.

şıkırdamak to clink, to rattle, to jingle.

şıkırdatmak to rattle, to jingle, to clink.

şıkırdım sl. lad, kid.

şıkır şıkır 1. with a clinking noise; **2.** jingling (coins, etc.); **3.** glittery, shiny.

şıkırtı clink, rattle, jingle.

şıklık smartness, chic, elegance.

şıllık loose woman, gaudily dressed woman.

şımarık spoiled.

şımarmak to get spoiled.

şımartmak to spoil, to pamper.

şıngırdamak to clink, to rattle.

şıngır şıngır with a rattling sound.

şıngırtı rattle, clink.

şıp, **-pı: ~ diye** in a trice, all of a sudden; **~ ~** with a dripping sound.

şıpıdık scuff, slipper.

şıpır şıpır continuously, without letup.

şıpırtı splash.

şıppadak [x . .] all of a sudden, out of the blue.

şıpsevdi susceptible.

şıpşıp s. **şıpıdık**.

şıra [x .] grape must.

şırak crack!, crash!, pop!

şırakkadak [. x . .] all of a sudden.

şırfıntı tramp, slut, floozy.

şırıldamak to plash, to purl, to ripple.

şırıl şırıl with a plash.

şırıltı plash, purl, ripple.

şırınga syringe; ~ *yapmak* to syringe.

şırlağan 1. sesame oil; **2.** flow.

şırlamak *s.* **şırıldamak.**

şırlop eggs served with yogurt.

şırp: ~ *diye kesmek* to cut off with a snip (*of scissors*).

şırpadak *s.* **şıppadak.**

şırvan, şırvanı loft, attic, garret.

şıvgın 1. shoot, twig; **2.** pine, fir.

Şia the Shi'a.

şiar [ā] **1.** mark, sign, token; **2.** password.

şibîh, -bhi resemblance.

şiddet, -ti 1. intensity; violence, severity; vehemence; **2.** harshness, stringency; ~ *olayı* act of terrorism; **-e** *başvurmak* to resort to brute force; **-le 1.** violently, severely; **2.** passionately; vehemently.

şiddetlendirmek to intensify.

şiddetlenmek to become more intense, to intensify.

şiddetli intense; violent, severe; passionate, vehement; ~ *geçimsizlik* JUR extreme incompatibility.

şifa [ā] recovery, healing; ~ *bulmak* to recover one's health, to get well; **-lar olsun!** may it give you health!; **-yı** *bulmak* (*or kapmak*) to fall ill.

şifahen [ā] orally, verbally.

şifahi [. - -] oral, verbal; ~ *imtihan* oral examination.

şifalı [ā] restorative, healing, curative; ~ *ot* medicinal plant.

şifon chiffon.

şifoniyer chiffon(n)ier.

şifre [x .] cipher, code; ~ *anahtarı* key to a code; **-yi açmak** (*or çözmek*) to decode, to break a code, to decipher.

şifrelemek to encode, to encipher.

şifreli in cipher; ~ *kilit* combination lock.

Şii [- -] Shi'i.

Şiilik [- - .] *s.* **Şia.**

şiir 1. poem; **2.** poetry, verse.

şiirsel poetic(al).

şikâyet, -ti complaint; gripe, grouse; ~ *etm.* to complain; to gripe, to grouse; ~ *hakkı* JUR right of petition.

şikâyetçi complainer, complainant; griper, grouser; ~ *olm.* to have a complaint to make (-*den* against).

şikâyetname [ā] written complaint.

şike chicane(ry); ~ *yapmak* to chicane.

şikemperver gluttonous.

şilem *bridge*: slam.

şilep, -bi freighter, cargo ship (*or* liner).

Şili *pr. n.* Chile.

şilin shilling.

şilt, -ti plaque.

şilte thin mattress.

şimal, -li [ā] north.

şimalen [ā] on the north.

şimali [ā] northern.

şimdi [x .] now; ~ *bile* still, yet; **-ye kadar** up to now.

şimdicik [x . .] just now.

şimdiden [x . .] already, right now; ~ *sonra* from now on, henceforth; ~ *te-zi yok* right now, at once.

şimdik *s.* **şimdicik.**

şimdiki [x . .] of today, of the present time; ~ *zaman* GR the present continuous tense.

şimdilik [x . .] for now, for the time being, for the present.

şimendifer 1. railway, railroad; **2.** train.

şimik chemical.

şimşek lightning; ~ *çakmak* (*for lightning*) to flash; ~ *gibi* like lightning, with lightning speed.

şimşeklenmek (*for lightning*) to flash.

şimşir BOT boxwood, boxtree.

şinanay F **1.** tra-la-la; **2.** whoopee!, hurrah!

şipşak *sl.* in an instant, in a flash.

şipşakçı street photographer.

şipşirin [. - -] very sweet.

şirden ZOO abomasum.

şirin [- -] **1.** sweet, charming, cute, cunning; **2.** ♀ *wf.*

şirk, -ki polytheism; ~ *koşmak* to attribute a partner to God.

şirket, -ti company, firm; partnership; ~ *kurmak* to found (*or* establish) a company.

şirpençe [ī] MED carbuncle.

şirret, -ti shrew, dragon, battle-ax, virago.

şirürji surgery.

şiryan [ā] ANAT artery.

şist, -ti GEOL schist.

şiş[1] **1.** spit, skewer; **2.** knitting needle; ~ *kebap* shish kebab; **-e geçirmek** to skewer, to spit.

şiş[2] **1.** swelling; **2.** swollen.

şişe 1. bottle; flask; 2. cupping glass; 3. chimney (*of a lamp*); 4. lath; ~ **çekmek** to apply a cupping glass (*-e* to).

şişeci maker *or* seller of bottles.

şişek yearling (lamb).

şişelemek to bottle.

şişirmek *caus. of* **şişmek** 1. to inflate, to blow up; to distend; 2. to billow (*sails, etc.*); 3. F to exaggerate; 4. F to do hastily and carelessly; 5. *sl.* to stab.

şişkin swollen, puffed up, puffy.

şişkinlik 1. swelling; bulge, protuberance; 2. puffiness; 3. bloated feeling.

şişko [x .] *co.* fat(ty), paunchy.

şişlemek 1. to spit, to skewer; 2. *sl.* to stab.

şişlik *s.* **şişkinlik 1 & 2.**

şişman fat, obese, portly.

şişmanlamak to get (*or* grow) fat.

şişmanlık fatness, obesity.

şişmek, (**-er**) 1. to swell, to get swollen; 2. to billow (*in the wind*); 3. to feel too full (*owing to overeating*); 4. to get winded, to become out of breath; 5. to get fat; 6. *sl.* to feel sheepish, to be embarrassed; 7. F to give o.s. airs.

şive [î] 1. accent; 2. coquetry.

şiveli [- . .] coy, coquettish.

sivesiz [- . .] with a bad accent.

şizofreni MED schizophrenia.

şofaj heating system.

şofben geyser, flash heater.

şoför driver, chauffeur.

şok, **-ku** shock.

şoke: ~ **etm.** to shock; ~ **olm.** to be shocked.

şom: ~ **ağızlı** who always predicts misfortune.

şorolo *sl.* queen, homosexual.

şorolop P 1. in a gulp; 2. lie.

şort, **-tu** shorts.

şose [x .] paved road.

şoset, *ti* sock.

şoson galosh, overshoe.

şov show.

şoven chauvinist.

şovenlik chauvinism.

şöhret, **-ti** 1. fame, reputation, renown; 2. celebrity.

şöhretli famous, famed.

şölen feast, banquet.

şömine fireplace.

şövale easel.

şövalye knight, chevalier.

şöyle 1. thus(ly), in this way; like this; 2. such; this kind of; of that sort; ~ **bir**

baktı he just glanced at it; ~ **böyle** 1. so-so; 2. approximately; ~ **dursun** let alone ..., never mind about ...; ~ **ki** such that.

şöylece [x . .] thus(ly), in this way; like that.

söylesi this sort of ...; such a ... as that.

şu, **-nu** that, this; ~ **günlerde** in these days; ~ **halde** in that case; ~ **var ki** however, only; **-na bak!** just look at him!; **-ndan bundan konuşmak** to talk of this and that; **-nu bunu bilmemek** not to accept any excuses; **-nun şurasında** just, only.

şua, **-aı** [â] beam, ray.

şubat, **-tı** February.

şube [û] 1. branch (office); office; 2. division, section.

şuf'a JUR preemption.

şuh [û] coquettish, pert.

şule [û] flame.

şunca [x .] this (*or* that) much.

şura [x .] this (*or* that) place.

şûra council.

şuracık [x . .] just there.

şurada over there.

şuradan from there; ~ **buradan** of this and that.

şuralı [x . .] inhabitant of that place.

şurası [x . .] that place; this fact; ~ **muhakkak ki** this much is certain.

şuriş disorder, tumult.

şurup, **-bu** syrup.

şut, **-tu** *football:* shoot; ~ **çekmek** to shoot.

şuur [. -] the conscious, consciousness.

şuuraltı, **-nı** (the) subconscious.

şuurlu conscious.

şuursuz unconscious.

şükran [â] 1. gratitude, thanks(giving); 2. ♀ *wf.*; ~ **borcu** debt of gratitude.

şükretmek [x . .] 1. to thank God; 2. to give thanks (*-e* to).

şükür, **-krü** 1. gratitude, thankfulness; 2. I thank God that ...

şümul, **-lü** [û] 1. scope, sphere, inclusiveness; 2. LOG extension.

şümullendirmek [û] to extend.

şümullü [û] extensive, comprehensive.

şüphe 1. suspicion, doubt; 2. uncertainty; ~ **etm.** to suspect, to doubt; ~ **kurdu** gnawing doubt; ~ **yok!** there is no doubt about it!; **-ye düşmek** to become suspicious.

şüpheci suspicious; skeptic.

şüphelenmek to suspect, to doubt, to

be in doubt (*den* about).
şüpheli 1. suspicious, questionable; **2.** doubtful; **3.** uncertain.
şüphesiz 1. certain, sure; **2.** doubtless,

surely, certainly.
şüt, -tü *s.* **şut.**
şüyu, -uu [ü] publicity; ~ **bulmak** to be noised abroad.

T

T cetveli, -ni T square.
ta [ā] even until; even as far as; ~ **eski-den beri** from time immemorial; ~ **kendisi** his very self; ~ **ki** so that even.
taabbüt, -dü worship; ~ **etm.** to worship.
taaccüp, -bü astonishment; ~ **etm.** to be astonished.
taahhüt, -dü engagement, obligation, contract, commitment; ~ **etm.** to undertake, to commit o.s.; ~ **senedi** contract.
taahhütlü registered (*letter*).
taahhütname [. . . -.] written contract.
taalluk, -ku relation, connection; ~ **etm.** to be related (-*e* to), to concern; **-u olm.** = ~ **etm.**
taallukat, -tı [. . . -] relatives, kin.
taallül evasion, subterfuge; ~ **etm.** to evade.
taammüden [. x .] JUR premeditatedly, deliberately.
taammüm generalization, spread; ~ **etm.** to spread.
taarruz attack, assault; ~ **etm.** to attack, to assault; **-a geçmek** to begin to attack.
taarruzi [î] offensive.
taassup, -bu bigotry, fanaticism.
taayyün 1. manifestation, becoming clear; **2.** determination; ~ **etm. 1.** to become manifest; **2.** to become determined.
tab, -b'ı *s.* **tabı.**
taba tobacco.
tabaat, -tı [. - .] printing.
tababet, -ti [. - .] **1.** medical science; **2.** the medical profession.
tabak¹ plate, dish; ~ **yalamak** fig. F to idle.
tabak² [. -] tanner.
tabaka¹ 1. layer, stratum; **2.** sheet (*of paper*); **3.** group, category, class (*of people*).
tabaka² tobacco box.
tabakalaşma GEOL stratification.
tabakhane [. . - .] tannery.

tabaklamak to tan.
tabaklık¹ tanning.
tabaklık² 1. plate-rack; **2.** dish drainer.
taban 1. sole (*of a shoe or foot*); **2.** floor; **3.** flat top (*of a hill, etc.*); **4.** pedestal, base (*a.* MATH); **5.** bed (*of a river*); **6.** fine steel; **7.** P roller; **8.** COM floor; ~ **fiyat** the minimum price; ~ **tepmek** (*or* **patlatmak**) to walk, to hoof it, to tramp, to trapes, to traipse; ~ **-a zıt** diametrically opposite (-*e* to), antipodal (-*e* to); **-a kuvvet** by dint of hard walking; **-ları kaldırmak** iro. to run like anything; to make tracks; **-ları yağlamak** F to take to one's heels, to show a clean pair of heels.
tab'an [x .] naturally.
tabanca [. x .] **1.** pistol, revolver; **2.** sprayer, spray gun; **3.** *sl.* bottle of raki *or* wine; ~ **atmak** to fire a pistol (-*e* at); ~ **boyası** spray paint; ~ **çekmek** to draw a pistol (-*e* on); ~ **kılıfı** pistol holster.
tabanlı soled.
tabansız 1. soleless; **2.** *fig.* cowardly, lily-livered.
tabanvay co.; **-la gitmek** to foot it, to hoof it, to go on foot.
tabasbus fawning, cringing; ~ **etm.** to fawn, to cringe, to grovel.
tabela [. x .] **1.** sign; **2.** list of food (*in schools, hospitals, etc.*); **3.** card of treatment, chart.
tabelacı sign painter.
tabetmek [x . .] to print.
tabı, -b'ı 1. print, edition, impression; **2.** character, nature.
tabi¹, -ii [ā] printer; publisher.
tabi², -ii 1. subject (-*e* to); bound (-*e* by); **2.** dependent (-*e* on), contingent (-*e* on); **3.** citizen; national; **4.** tributary (*of a river, etc.*); ~ **kılmak** to subject; ~ **olm.** (*b-ne*) to depend on *s.o.*, to be dependent on *s.o.*; ~ **tutmak** (*bşe*) to subject to *s.th.*, to make dependent on *s.th.*
tabiat, -tı [. - .] **1.** nature; **2.** character,

nature; **3.** taste, refinement; **4.** regularity (*of the bowels*); **5.** habit; **~ bilgisi** nature study; **~ kanunu** law of nature.

tabiatıyla 1. naturally; **2.** by his very nature.

tabiatsız ill-tempered.

tabiatsızlık ill-temperedness.

tabiatüstü, -nü supernatural.

tabii [. - -] **1.** natural; **2.** customary, habitual; **3.** unadulterated, pure; **4.** of course, naturally; **~ afet** natural disaster; **~ borçlar** JUR natural obligations.

tabiilik naturalness.

tabiiyat, -tı [. - . -] the natural sciences.

tabiiye [. - . .] PHLS naturalism.

tabiiyet, -ti nationality, citizenship.

tabiiyetsiz stateless (*person*).

tabip, -bi [ī] doctor, physician.

tabir 1. expression, term, phrase; idiom; **2.** interpretation (*of a dream*); **~ caizse** if I may say so; **~ etm. 1.** to express in words, to verbalize; **2.** to interpret (*a dream*); **tabiri diğerle** in other words.

tabirname [- . - .] book on the interpretation of dreams.

tabiye MIL tactics.

tabiyeci MIL tactician.

tabla [x .] **1.** circular tray; **2.** ashtray; **3.** disc; **4.** pan (*of a balance*); **5.** panel (*of a door*); **6.** metal pan or tray (*put under a stove*).

tabldot, -tu table d'hôte.

tablet, -ti tablet.

tablo [x .] **1.** painting, picture; **2.** panorama, view, picture; **3.** table; **4.** tableau; **5.** MOT instrument board (*or panel*).

tabu taboo.

tabur 1. MIL battalion; **2.** *fig.* row, line, file.

taburcu 1. discharged (*from a hospital*); **2.** *sl.* released from jail; **~ etm.** to discharge, to dismiss; **~ olm.** to be discharged.

tabure 1. stool; **2.** footstool; ottoman.

tabut, -tu 1. coffin; **2.** egg crate.

tabutlamak to put into a coffin.

tabutluk place where empty coffins are stored.

tabülatör tabulator.

tabya [x .] MIL bastion, redoubt.

tacil [- .] speeding up, hastening; **~ etm.** to speed up, to hasten, to expedite.

tacir [ā] merchant.

taciz [- -] annoyance, harassment; **~ etm.** to annoy, to harass, to bother.

tacizlik harassment, bothering; **~ getirmek 1.** to complain (-*den* about); **2.** to get fed up (-*den* with); **~ vermek** to bother, to annoy, to harass.

taç, -cı 1. crown; coronet; **2.** crest, crown (*of a bird*); **3.** BOT corolla, petal; **4.** AST corona; **5.** *football:* touchdown; **~ giyme töreni** coronation; **~ giymek** to be crowned.

taçlı crowned.

taçsız uncrowned.

taçyapraklı BOT petal(l)ed, petalous.

tadım taste.

tadımlık just enough to taste.

tadil [- -] alteration, adjustment, modification; amendment; **~ etm.** to change, to alter, to amend.

tadilat, -tı [- . -] *pl. of* **tadil**, changes, alterations; amendments.

taflan BOT cherry laurel.

tafra pomposity, conceit; **~ satmak** to talk big.

tafracı big talker.

tafsil [ī] detailed explanation; **~ etm.** to detail.

tafsilat, -tı details, particulars; **~ vermek** to detail; **-a girmek** (*or* **girişmek**) to go into detail; **-iyle** in detail.

tafsilatlı detailed.

tafta taffeta.

tagaddi [ī] nourishment; **~ etm.** to feed; to be nurtured.

tagallüp, -bü 1. tyranny; **2.** usurpation; **~ etm.** to tyrannize (-*e* over).

taganni [ī] singing; **~ etm.** to sing.

tagayyür change, alteration; **~ etm.** to change, to alter.

tağdiye feeding; **~ etm.** to feed, to nourish.

tağşiş [ī] adulteration; **~ etm.** to adulterate.

tağyir [ī] change, alteration; **~ etm.** to change, to alter.

tahaddüs arising, coming into being; **~ etm.** to arise, to come into being.

tahaffuz guarding o.s.; **~ etm.** to guard o.s.

tahaffuzhane [. . . . - .] quarantine station.

tahaffuzi [ī] precautionary.

tahakkuk, -ku 1. realization; **2.** verification; **3.** accruement, accrual; **~ etm. 1.** to be realized, to come true; **2.** to prove true; **3.** to fall due (*interest, tax*); **~ memuru** tax assessor; **~ tarihi**

due date (*of a tax, interest*).

tahakküm tyranny; domination; ~ **etm.** (*b-ne*) to tyrannize over *s.o.*; to dominate over *s.o.*

tahallül CHEM dissolution; dissociation; ~ **etm.** to dissolve; to dissociate.

tahammül 1. patience, endurance, forbearance; 2. durability (*of a thing*); ~ **etm.** to endure, to bear, to put up (*-e* with); ~ **olunamayacak derecede** unbearably.

tahammülfersa [. . . . .] *rare* unbearable, unendurable.

tahammüllü patient.

tahammülsüz impatient, intolerant.

tahammür fermentation; ~ **etm.** to ferment.

taharet, **-ti** [. - .] 1. cleanliness, purity; 2. canonical purification (*of the body*); ~ **kâğıdı** toilet paper.

taharri [ī] 1. investigation, research; 2. search; ~ **etm.** 1. to investigate; 2. to search; ~ **memuru** plainclothesman.

taharrüş MED itching; irritation; ~ **etm.** to itch; to be irritated.

tahassul, **-lü** resulting, emerging; ~ **etm.** to result, to emerge.

tahassür longing, yearning; ~ **etm.** to long (*-e* for), to yearn (*-e* for).

tahassüs sensation.

tahaşşüt, **-dü** concentration (*of troops*); ~ **etm.** to be concentrated (*or* amassed) (*troops*).

tahavvül change, conversion; ~ **etm.** to change.

tahayyül 1. imagination; fancy; 2. daydreaming; ~ **etm.** 1. to imagine; 2. to fantasize; to daydream.

tahdidat, **-tı** [. - -] *pl. of* **tahdit** limitations; restrictions.

tahdit, **-di** [ī] 1. limitation; restriction; 2. demarcation, delimitation; ~ **etm.** 1. to limit; to restrict; 2. to demarcate, to delimit.

tahıl 1. grain; 2. cereal; ~ **ambarı** granary.

tahin [- .] sesame oil; ~ **helvası** hal(a)vah.

tahini [- . -] tan(-colo(u)red).

tahkik, **-ki** [ī] investigation; ~ **etm.** to investigate.

tahkikat, **-tı** [. - -] *pl. of* **tahkik** inquiry; probe, investigation; ~ **yapmak** to conduct an investigation.

tahkim [ī] 1. fortification; 2. strengthening; 3. JUR resolution of a dispute by arbitration; ~ **etm.** 1. to fortify;

2. to strengthen; 3. JUR to resolve by arbitration.

tahkimat, **-tı** [. - -] MIL fortifications.

tahkimli [. - .] fortified.

tahkir [ī] insult, scorn; ~ **etm.** to insult, to despise, to scorn.

tahlif [ī] swearing (*a witness*); ~ **etm.** to swear (*a witness*).

tahlil [ī] analysis; ~ **etm.** to analyze.

tahlili [. - -] analytical.

tahlisiye [. - ..] lifeboat service; ~ **sandalı** lifeboat; ~ **simidi** life buoy; ~ **yeleği** life jacket.

tahliye 1. evacuation (*of people*); 2. emptying; 3. discharging, unloading (*cargo*); 4. vacating (*a building*); 5. releasing (*a prisoner*); ~ **etm.** 1. to evacuate (*people, a place*); 2. to empty; to unload, to discharge (*cargo*); 3. to vacate (*a building*); 4. to release, to set free (*a prisoner*).

tahmil [ī] 1. loading; 2. imposition (*of a task*); 3. imputation, (*of blame, etc.*) ~ **etm.** 1. to load; 2. to impose (*a task*) (*-e* on); 3. to lay (*the blame*) (*-e* on).

tahmin [ī] 1. guess, conjecture, surmisal; 2. estimation; prediction; ~ **etm.** 1. to guess, to conjecture, to surmise; 2. to estimate, to reckon, to judge; to predict, to forecast.

tahminen [ī] [. x .] approximately; roughly.

tahmini [. - -] approximate; conjectural.

tahminlemek [ī] *s.* **tahmin etm.**

tahnit, **-ti** [ī] embalmment; ~ **etm.** 1. to embalm (*a corpse*); 2. to stuff (*a dead animal*).

tahra P pruning hook.

Tahran [. -] *pr. n.* Tehran.

tahribat, **-tı** [. - -] damage, destruction; ~ **yapmak** to damage, to destroy.

tahrif [ī] distortion, falsification; misrepresentation (*of facts*); ~ **etm.** to distort (*a meaning*); to misrepresent (*facts*).

tahrifat, **-tı** [. - -] distortions; misrepresentations.

tahrik, **-ki** [ī] incitement, instigation, provocation, fomentation; ~ **etm.** 1. to incite, to instigate, to provoke, to foment; 2. to stimulate, to excite, to arouse, to stir; 3. to propel, to drive; to move.

tahrikât, **-tı** *pl. of* **tahrik** POL incitements, provocations, instigations.

tahrikçi instigator, provocator, fomenter.

tahril stripe, line.

tahrip, -bi [i] destruction, devastation, demolition; ~ **etm.** to destroy, to ruin, to devastate; to demolish.

tahripçi [. - .], **tahripkâr** [. - -] destructive.

tahrir [i] 1. composing, writing down; 2. registration; 3. essay, composition; ~ **etm.** to compose, to write down, to draft; **-i nüfus** population census.

tahriri [. - -] written.

tahriş MED irritation; ~ **edici** irritative; ~ **etm.** to irritate.

tahsil [i] 1. education, study; 2. collection (of money); ~ **etm.** 1. to study, to get an education; 2. to collect (money, taxes); ~ **görmek** to get an education, to study.

tahsilat, -tı revenue, money received.

tahsildar [. - -] 1. receiving teller (in a bank); 2. tax collector.

tahsis [i] assignment, appropriation, allotment; ~ **etm.** to assign, to appropriate, to allot.

tahsisat, -tı [. - -] pl. of **tahsis**, appropriation, allotment, allowance; ~ **ayırmak** to appropriate money (-e for).

tahşit, -di [i] concentration, amassing (of troops); ~ **etm.** to concentrate, to amass (troops).

taht, -tı throne; **-a çıkarmak** (or **oturtmak**) to enthrone; **-a çıkmak** (or **geçmek** or **oturmak**) to ascend the throne; **-tan indirmek** to dethrone.

tahta 1. board, plank; batten; 2. blackboard; 3. sheet (of metal); 4. wooden ...; 5. bed (in a garden); ~ **perde** board fence, hoarding; **-dan** wooden; **-sı eksik** co. screwy, nutty, balmy.

tahtabiti, -ni s. **tahtakurusu.**

tahtaboş wooden balcony.

tahtakoz sl. policeman, fuzz, cop.

tahtakurusu, -nu zoo bedbug.

tahtalı 1. boarded; planked; 2. zoo ringdove; ~ **köy** sl. cemetery, boneyard; ~ **köyü boylamak** sl. to kick the bucket, to peg out, to go to one's long account.

tahtapuş s. **tahtaboş.**

tahtelhıfız, -fzı under guard; in custody.

tahterevalli [. . . . x .] seesaw, teeterboard, teeter-totter.

tahteşşuur subconscious.

tahtezzemin [i] underground, subterranean.

tahtırevan [. . . -] 1. howdah; 2. palanquin.

tahvil [i] 1. transformation; transfer; conversion; 2. COM bond, debenture; ~ **etm.** to transform; to transfer; to convert.

tahvilat, -tı COM bonds, debentures, securities.

taife [- . .] s. **tayfa.**

tak¹, -kı [ā] arch.

tak² thump, knock; ~ ~ **kapı vuruldu** there was a knock on the door.

taka 1. small sailing boat; 2. sl. jalopy, rattletrap.

takaddüm 1. precedence; 2. antecedence; ~ **etm.** 1. to have precedence (-e over); 2. to antecede; 3. to act before s.o. else does.

takanak s. **takıntı.**

takarrüp, -bü approach; ~ **etm.** to approach, to near.

takarrür 1. establishment; 2. being decided; ~ **etm.** 1. to be established; 2. to be decided.

takas 1. barter, swap, exchange; 2. COM clearing; ~ **etm.** 1. to barter, to swap, to exchange; 2. COM to clear; ~ **tukas etm.** to square accounts with each other.

takat, -ti [- .] strength (a. PHYS); ~ **getirmek** to endure; **-i kalmamak** (or **kesilmek** or **tükenmek**) to be exhausted (or worn out).

takatlı strong.

takatsız [- . . .] weak, debilitated.

takatuka [. . x .] 1. noise, tumult, commotion; 2. spittoon; 3. TYP quoin.

takayyüt, -dü 1. attentiveness, attention, care; 2. vigilance; ~ **etm.** 1. to pay attention (-e to), to take care (-e of); 2. to be vigilant.

takaza [. - -] taunt; ~ **etm.** to taunt, to rub it in.

takbih [i] disapproval; ~ **etm.** to disapprove.

takdim [i] 1. introduction; 2. presentation; ~ **etm.** 1. to present, to tender, to offer; 2. (b-ni) to introduce s.o. to another; ~ **tehir** inversion.

takdimci compère, emcee.

takdir [i] 1. appreciation; 2. judg(e)ment, discretion; 3. commendation, approval, applause; 4. predestination, fate; ~ **etm.** 1. to appreciate; 2. to commend, to approve, to applaud; 3. to evaluate, to value; 4. (for God) to predestine, to foreordain; ~ **hakkı** JUR judicial discretion; ~ **toplamak** to win general approval; **-de** in the event of ..., if ...; **-e bağlı muamele** JUR discretionary act; **-ine bırakmak** (b-nin) to leave (a matter) to s.o.'s judg(e)ment; **öldüğü -de** in the event of his death.

takdirkâr [ī] 1. appreciative; 2. appreciator.

takdirname [. - - .] letter of commendation (or appreciation).

takdis [ī] 1. sanctification, consecration; 2. veneration; ~ **etm.** 1. to bless, to sanctify, to consecrate, to hallow; 2. to venerate, to revere; 3. to glorify (God).

takı 1. wedding present; 2. GR particle.

takılgan teaser.

takılı 1. GR affixed; 2. attached (-e to), fastened (-e to).

takılmak 1. pass. of **takmak**; 2. to kid, to tease, to rally, to pull s.o.'s leg; 3. fig. (bş. üzerinde) to get stuck on s.th., to get snagged on s.th., to get hung up on s.th. 4. to get hung up in, to be delayed in (a place).

takım 1. team, group, band, gang, crew, troop; 2. set (of things); 3. BOT, ZOO order; 4. MIL platoon; 5. MEC train; ~ **elbise** suit; ~ **mukavelesi** JUR collective agreement; ~ **taklavat** F the whole kit and caboodle, the whole push; ~ **tutmak** to support a team, to root for a team.

takımada archipelago.

takımyıldız AST constellation.

takınmak 1. to assume (an air); 2. to put on (ornaments).

takıntı 1. ramification; 2. outstanding debt; 3. dealings, relationship; 4. F subject which a student has flunked; 5. piece of jewelry.

takırdamak to clatter, to rattle, to bang.

takırdatmak to rattle, to clatter.

takır takır 1. with a rattling noise; 2. very stale (food); 3. hard and dry.

takırtı rattle, clatter; clop-clop.

takır tukur with a clattering noise.

takışmak 1. to tease each other; 2. to quarrel with each other.

takıştırmak to deck o.s. out in jewels.

takızafer [- . . . .] triumphal arch.

takibat, **-tı** [- - -] legal proceedings (or action); prosecution (of a case).

takip, **-bi** [- -] 1. following; pursuit; 2. JUR legal proceedings; prosecution

(of a case); ~ **etm.** 1. to follow, to pursue, to trail; 2. to follow, to succeed; 3. to keep up with, to follow (a fashion).

takke skullcap.

takla somersault; cartwheel; ~ **atmak** (or **kılmak**) 1. to turn a somersault, to somersault; 2. fig. to jump for joy.

taklak s. **takla**.

taklidi [. - -] imitative.

taklit, **-di** [ī] 1. imitation; 2. counterfeit, imitated, sham; 3. imitative; 4. mockery, impersonation; ~ **etm.** 1. to imitate, to copy, to duplicate, to reproduce; 2. to imitate, to ape; 3. to fake, to counterfeit; 4. to impersonate, to mimic, to mock.

taklitçi 1. imitator, copier; 2. impersonator; mimic.

takma 1. vn. of **takmak**; 2. artificial (tooth, eye); false (beard); 3. prefabricated; ~ **ad** 1. nickname; 2. pen name; ~ **diş** false teeth; ~ **motor** outboard motor; ~ **saç** wig.

takmak, **(-ar)** 1. to attach, to fasten, to put on, to affix, to fit; 2. to nickname; 3. to pick on; 4. sl. school: to fail, to flunk; 5. to put on; to wear; **takıp takıştırmak** to deck o.s. out in jewelry.

takmamak sl. to take no notice (-i of), to pay no heed (-i of).

takoz 1. wedge, chock; 2. shore, prop; 3. plug.

takozlamak 1. to shore up; 2. to put a wedge under or behind s.th.

takriben [ī] [. x .] approximately, about.

takribi [. - -] approximate.

takrir [ī] 1. explaining, expounding; 2. report, memorandum; 3. proposal, motion; ~ **etm.** to present, to expound.

takriz [ī] laudatory preface to a book.

taksa [x .] postage due; ~ **pulu** postage-due stamp.

taksi [x .] taxi, cab; ~ **durağı** taxi rank, cabstand.

taksim [ī] 1. division; partition, distribution; 2. slash (mark), diagonal, virgule; 3. MATH division sign; 4. MUS instrumental improvisation; ~ **etm.** 1. to divide up; to share out, to distribute; 2. MUS to improvise; ~ **geçmek** = ~ **etm.** 2; ~ **işareti** slash (mark), diagonal, virgule.

taksimat, **-tı** [. - -] divisions, sections, parts.

taksimetre taximeter.

taksir [ī] **1.** cutting short; **2.** failure in duty, remissness; ~ **etm. 1.** to cut short, to curtail; **2.** to be remiss.

taksirat, **-tı** [. - -] **1.** sins; **2.** F fate, destiny.

taksit, **-ti** instal(l)ment; ~ ~ in instal(l)-ments; **-le** in instal(l)ments.

tak tak *s.* **tak²**.

taktik 1. tactic, manoeuvre, *Am.* maneuver; **2.** MIL tactics.

taktir [ī] distillation; ~ **etm.** to distil(l).

tak tuk knock! knock!

takunya, **takunye** [. x .] clog, patten.

takvim [ī] calendar; ~ **yılı** calendar year.

takviye reinforcement (*a.* MIL); ~ **etm.** to reinforce (*a.* MIL); to strengthen.

takyit, **-di** [ī] restriction; ~ **etm.** to restrict, to limit.

talak, **-kı** *isl.* JUR divorce.

talan pillage, plunder, sack; ~ **etm.** to pillage, to plunder, to sack.

talaş 1. sawdust; wood shavings; **2.** metal filings.

talaşlamak to sprinkle sawdust over (*a place*).

talaz 1. wave (*in the sea*); **2.** ripple, undulation (*in a piece of silk*).

talebe student, pupil.

talebelik being a student *or* pupil.

talebetmek [. x .] to demand, to want, to require, to request.

talep, **-bi** demand, request; ~ **etm.** to demand, to want, to require, to request.

tali secondary; subordinate; ~ **cümle** GR subordinate clause; ~ **komisyon** subcommittee

talih [ā] luck, good fortune; ~ **kuşu** good luck; **-i olmamak** to be unlucky; **-i yaver gitmek** to be lucky; **-ine küsmek** to curse one's luck.

talihli [ā] lucky, fortunate.

talihsiz [ā] unlucky.

talihsizlik [ā] bad luck, lucklessness, mischance.

talik, **-kı** [- -] **1.** postponement; **2.** depending on, hinging on; **3.** calligraphic style; ~ **etm. 1.** to postpone, to put off; **2.** to depend (**-e** on), to hinge (**-e** on).

talika [. x .] a small, horsedrawn vehicle.

talim [- -] **1.** instruction, training; **2.** practice, drill, exercise; **3.** MIL drill; ~ **etm. 1.** to teach, to instruct; **2.** to

practice; **3.** MIL to drill; ~ **fişeği** blank (cartridge); ~ **meydanı** MIL drill field; ~ **ve terbiye** training.

talimat, **-tı** [- - -] instructions, directions; ~ **vermek** to instruct, to give instructions.

talimatname [-.....] regulations book.

talimgâh [- . -] MIL training centre.

talimhane [- . - .] MIL drill field.

talimli [ā] trained; instructed; practiced.

talimname [- . - .] **1.** MIL field manual; **2.** technical manual.

talip, **-bi 1.** desirous, wishful; **2.** suitor, wooer; **3.** applicant; **4.** customer; ~ **çıkmak** to become the suitor (**-e** of); ~ **olm. 1.** to desire, to want, to seek; **2.** to seek the hand of a woman in marriage.

talk, **-kı** GEOL talc(um); ~ **pudrası** talc, talcum powder.

tallahi [x . .] by God!

taltif [ī] **1.** favo(u)r, kindness; **2.** recompense; ~ **etm. 1.** to gratify, to please, to win the heart of; **2.** to reward.

talveg [x .] (*hattı*) GEOGR thalweg.

tam 1. complete, perfect; full, whole; **2.** fully, completely; **3.** exactly; immediately; ~ **açı** MATH perigon; ~ **adamını bulmak** to choose the very man (*for the job, etc.*); ~ **iki kilo** a full two kilos; ~ **pansiyon** full pension; ~ **-ına** (*or* **-ı -ına**) completely; in full; ~ **tertip** thoroughly; ~ **teşekküllü bir hastane** a fully equipped hospital; ~ **üstüne basmak** to hit the nail right on the head; ~ **vaktinde** right on time; ~ **yetki** full authority; ~ **yol** at full (*or* top) speed.

tamah greed, avarice, cupidity.

tamahkâr 1. greedy, avaricious; **2.** miserly, stingy, tight.

tamam 1. complete, finished; ready; **2.** the whole of the ... all of the ...; **3.** correct; **4.** O.K.!, all right!; **5.** fully; for a whole; ~ **etm. 1.** to finish, to complete, to terminate; **-ı -ına** completely; in full.

tamamen [. - .] [. x .] completely, wholly, entirely, quite.

tamamiyet, **-ti** [. - . .] completeness, entirety.

tamamıyla *s.* **tamamen.**

tamamlamak to complete, to finish; to complement.

tamamlayıcı complementary, complemental; supplementary, supplemental.

tambur MUS *a kind of stringed instrument similar to the mandolin.*

tambura [. x .] any stringed instrument.

tamburi [. - -] player of a *tambur.*

tamim [- -] **1.** circular; **2.** generalization; **3.** circularization; ~ *etm.* **1.** to circularize; **2.** to generalize; **3.** to diffuse.

tamir [- -] repair; restoration; ~ *etm.* to repair, to mend, to fix; ~ *görmek* to be repaired (*or* mended *or* fixed); *-e vermek* (*bşi*) to have *s.th.* repaired.

tamirat, *-tı* [- - -] repairs.

tamirci [ā] repairman, repairer.

tamirhane [- . - .] repair shop.

tamlama GR **1.** noun phrase; **2.** prepositional phrase.

tamlayan GR modifier.

tampon **1.** MOT bumper; **2.** RAIL buffer; **3.** MED tampon, plug, pack; **4.** CHEM buffer; **5.** blotter; ~ *devlet* buffer state.

tamsayı MATH whole number.

tamtakır [x .] absolutely empty; ~ *kuru bakır* absolutely empty.

tamtam tom-tom.

tan dawn, daybreak; ~ *ağarmak* to dawn, (*for day*) to break.

tanassur conversion to Christianity; ~ *etm.* to become a Christian.

Tanca *pr. n.* Tangier(s).

tandans tendency.

tandır **1.** oven (*made in a hole in the earth*); **2.** heating arrangement; ~ *kebabı* dish of meat roasted in an oven.

tandırname [. . - .] old wives' tale.

tane [ā] **1.** kernel, grain; **2.** grain (*of salt, sand, sugar, etc.*); **3.** item, piece, ~ ~ in separate pieces; ~ ~ *konuşmak* to speak distinctly; ~ *tutmak* (*or -ye gelmek*) to ear (up), to form ears.

tanecik [ā] **1.** granule (*of sand, salt, sugar, etc.*); **2.** tiny kernel; **3.** particle.

tanecikli [ā] granular.

tanecil [ā] zoo granivorous (*animal*).

tanelemek [ā] **1.** to granulate; **2.** to shell.

tanelenmek [ā] **1.** *pass. of tanelemek*; **2.** to ear (up), to form ears (*cereal plant*).

taneli [ā] grainy.

tanen CHEM tannin.

tanga very skimpy bikini, G-string.

tangırdamak to clatter, to clang.

tangırdatmak to clatter, to clang.

tangır tangır clatteringly.

tangırtı clatter, clang, racket.

tangırtılı clattery, clattering.

tangır tungur with a clatter.

tango [x .] **1.** MUS tango; **2.** *sl.* loudly dressed woman.

tanı diagnosis.

tanıdık acquaintance; ~ *çıkmak* to have met before.

tanık (eye)witness; ~ *olm.* to witness.

tanıklık testimony, witness; ~ *etm.* to testify.

tanılamak to diagnose.

tanım definition.

tanıma *vn. of tanımak*, *part.* JUR recognition, acknowledgement.

tanımak **1.** to recognize, to know; **2.** to be acquainted, to know; **3.** to be able to distinguish, to recognize, to know; **4.** to recognize, to acknowledge; **5.** to listen to, to pay attention to; to respect; **6.** to hold responsible.

tanımlama definition.

tanımlamak to define.

tanımsal definitional.

tanınmak **1.** to be (well-)known; **2.** to be known for; **3.** to be acknowledged (*or* recognized); *dürüstlüğüyle tanınır* he is known for his honesty.

tanınmış **1.** famous, well-known, famed, reputable; **2.** known for; *doğru ~ bir hâkim* a judge who's known for his honesty.

tanış F acquaintance; ~ *çıkmak* to have met before.

tanışık: ~ *çıkmak* to have met before.

tanışıklık acquaintance(ship).

tanışmak to get acquainted (*ile* with), to be acquainted (*ile* with), to make the acquaintance (*ile* of); to know one another.

tanıştırmak to introduce.

tanıt, *-tı* proof, evidence.

tanıtıcı introductory.

tanıtım **1.** introduction, presentation; **2.** advertisement.

tanıtlamak to prove.

tanıtmacı COM salesman, sales representative.

tanıtmak **1.** to introduce, to present; **2.** to advertise, to publicize.

tanjant, *-tı* MATH tangent.

tank, *-kı* tank.

tankçı MIL tanker.

tanker tanker.

tanksavar MIL **1.** antitank; **2.** antitank weapon.

tanrı 1. god, deity; **2.** ♀ God; **~ hakkı için** for God's sake; **~ kayrası** Providence; **~ misafiri** unexpected guest; **-nın günü** every blessed (*or* doggone) day.

Tanrıbilim theology.

Tanrıbilimci theologian.

Tanrıcılık theism.

tanrıça goddess.

tanrılaşmak to become a god, to become divine.

tanrılaştırmak to deify.

tanrılık divinity, godhood.

tanrısal divine.

tanrısız godless, atheistic.

Tanrıtanımazlık atheism.

tansiyon 1. MED blood pressure; **2.** tension; **~ aleti** sphygmomanometer; **~ düşüklüğü** MED hypotension; **~ yüksekliği** hypertension.

tantana pomp, display; grandiosity.

tantanalı pompous, grand; grandiose.

tan tuna gitmek *sl.* to be killed; to be done for.

tanyeli, -ni dawn breeze.

tanyeri, -ni dawn; **~ ağarmak** (*for dawn*) to break.

tanzifat, -tı [. . -] street-cleaning.

tanzim 1. organizing, arranging; **2.** regulating; reorganizing; **3.** drafting, drawing up, preparing; **~ etm. 1.** to organize, to arrange, to determine; **2.** to regulate; to reorganize; to put in order; **3.** to draft, to draw up, to prepare; **~ satışı** sale of foodstuffs by a municipality in order to regulate prices.

Tanzimat, -tı [. - -] *pr. n. the political reforms made in the Ottoman state in 1839.*

tapa [x .] **1.** stopper; cork; plug; bung; **2.** fuse (*for a bomb*).

tapalamak to stopper, to put a stopper (-ı on).

tapalı stoppered.

tapı god, deity.

tapınak temple, place of worship.

tapınmak, (-ır), tapmak, (-ar) 1. to worship; **2.** to idolize, to adore.

tapon F shoddy, fourth-rate, crummy, sorry.

taptaze [x .] very fresh.

tapu 1. (title) deed; **2.** (*dairesi*) deed (*or* land) office; **~ kütüğü** register of title deeds; **~ senedi** (title) deed.

tapulamak 1. to register with a title deed, to get title for (*a piece of land*); **2.** to issue a title deed for (*a piece of*

land).

tapyoka [. x .] tapioca.

taraça [. x .] terrace.

taraf 1. side; part, portion; **2.** region, area; direction; **3.** party; litigant; **4.** behalf; **~ tutmak** to take sides; **-a olm.** (*b-den*) to side with *s.o.*, to be for *s.o.*; **-ını tutmak** (*b-nin*) to side with *s.o.*

tarafeyn the two parties; the prosecution and the defense.

tarafgir [ī] partial, biased.

taraflı 1. -sided, -edged; **2.** supporter, adherent; **3.** person from a certain region; **sen ne taraflısın?** what part of the country are you from?

tarafsız 1. neutral; noncommittal; **2.** impartial, unbiased.

tarafsızlık 1. neutrality; **2.** impartiality.

taraftar [. . -] supporter, adherent, follower, advocate, partisan; **~ olm.** to support, to be in favo(u)r (-e of).

taraftarlık 1. adherence, advocacy; **2.** partiality, partisanship.

tarak 1. comb; **2.** hackle, hatchel; **3.** reed; **4.** rake; harrow; **5.** gill (*of a fish*); **6.** ANAT instep, metatarsus (*of the foot*); **7.** ZOO crest (*of a bird*); **8.** ZOO scallop; cockle; **9.** dredge; **10.** dragnet; **~ dubası** dredger; **~ gemisi** dredge; **~ vurmak** to comb.

tarakişi, -ni serrated embroidery.

taraklamak 1. to comb; **2.** to rake; **3.** to dredge; **4.** to hackle; to card, to comb (*wool*).

taraklı 1. crested (*bird*); **2.** serrated (*cloth*); **3.** wide (*foot*).

tarakotu, -nu BOT teasel.

taralı 1. combed; **2.** raked; **3.** dredged.

tarama 1. *vn. of* **taramak; 2.** MED & *computer* scan; **3.** hachure; **4.** red caviar.

taramak 1. to comb; **2.** to rake, to harrow; **3.** to hackle; to card, to comb; **4.** to dredge; **5.** to search thoroughly, to comb; **6.** to scan, to give the once--over; **7.** to (cross)hatch; to hachure (*a map*); **8.** to scan (*computers, medically*).

taranmak 1. *pass. of* **taramak; 2.** to comb one's hair.

tarantı 1. combings; **2.** rakings; **3.** dredgings.

tarassut, -du AST, MIL observation; surveillance; **~ etm.** to observe; to keep under surveillance.

tarator *sauce made with vinegar and*

tasalı

walnuts.
taravet, *-ti* [. . -.] freshness; tenderness.
tarayıcı MED & *computer* scanner.
taraz ravels, ravelings, fuzz; **~~ olm.** *s.*
tarazlanmak.
tarazlamak to remove the ravelings
from.
tarazlanmak 1. to ravel, to fuzz; **2.** (*for
hair*) to frizz.
tarçın cinnamon.
tardetmek [x . .] **1.** to expel (*-den*
from); to dismiss (*-den* from), to discharge (*-den* from); **2.** MIL to repulse,
to drive back.
taret, *-ti* MIL turret.
tarh 1. MATH subtraction; **2.** imposition
(*of a tax*); **3.** (*a.* **çicek tarhı**) flower
bed.
tarhana [x . .] *preparation of yogurt
and flour dried in the sun*; **~ çorbası**
soup made with **tarhana.**
tarhetmek [x . .] **1.** to subtract; **2.** to impose (*a tax*).
tarhun BOT tarragon, estragon.
tarım agriculture, farming.
tarımcı agriculturist.
tarımsal agricultural.
tarif [- -] **1.** description; **2.** definition; **3.**
recipe; **~ edilemez** indescribable; **~
etm. 1.** to describe; **2.** to define; *-e uymak* to match the description, to answer to the description.
tarife [ā] **1.** tariff; **2.** timetable, schedule; **3.** directions, instructions; **4.** recipe.
tarih [ā] **1.** history; **2.** date; **3.** chrono-
gram; **~ atmak** (*or* **koymak**) to date;
-e geçmek to go down in history as;
-e karışmak to become a thing of
the past.
tarihçe [ā] short history.
tarihçi [ā] **1.** historian; **2.** history teacher.
tarihi [- . -] historic(al).
tarihli [ā] dated; **20 Nisan ~ bir mektup** a letter dated 20 April.
tarihöncesi, *-ni* [ā] **1.** prehistory; **2.**
prehistoric(al).
tarihsel [ā] historic(al).
tarihsiz [ā] **1.** undated; **2.** historyless.
tarik, *-kı* **1.** road; **2.** way of life, path.
tarikat, *-tı* [ī] **1.** *isl.* tarekat, tariqa, dervish order; **2.** tariqa(t), Sufi path.
tarikatçı [ī] *isl.* member of a tariqa,
dervish.
tariz [- -] **1.** allusion, hint, innuendo; **~
etm.** to get in a dig (*-e* at), to allude

(*-e* to).
tarla [x .] field; **~ açmak** to clear a
piece of land; **~ sürmek** to plough,
Am. to plow.
tarlafaresi, *-ni* ZOO vole.
tarlakuşu, *-nu* ZOO skylark.
tarpan tarpan.
tarsin [ī] strengthening; **~ etm.** to
strengthen.
tart[1], *-tı* pie.
tart[2], *-dı* **1.** expulsion; discharge, dismissal; **2.** MIL repulse, repulsion.
tartaklamak to rough up, to manhandle.
tartar CHEM tartar.
tartı 1. weight, heaviness; **2.** balance,
scales; **3.** NAUT line; **4.** *poetry:* meter;
~ aleti weighing device, scale; *-ya gelmemek* to be unweighable; *-ya vurmak* to weigh.
tartıcı weigher.
tartıl CHEM quantitative.
tartılı 1. weighed; **2.** well-considered;
3. metrical (*poem*).
tartışma *vn. of* **tartışmak**, *part.* debate, discussion; dispute, argument.
tartışmacı debater, discussant, dispu-
tant.
tartışmak to debate, to dispute, to argue, to discuss.
tartışmalı disputatious.
tartmak, (*-ar*) **1.** to weigh (*a. fig.*); **2.** to
sound (*or* feel) out; **3.** to evaluate, to
size up.
tartura [. x .] lathe wheel.
tarumar [- . -] confused, jumbled, topsy-turvy; **~ etm.** to disarray, to make a
mess of.
tarz 1. manner, way, sort, kind; **2.** style.
tarziye apology; **~ vermek** to apologize (*-e* to).
tas cup, bowl; porringer; **~ gibi** bald
(*head*); **~ kebabı** goulash (*a stew
made of meat and vegetables*); *-ı tarağı toplamak* fig. to pack one's bags,
to pack up one's belongings (*or
traps*).
tasa worry, anxiety; **~ etm.** (*or* **çekmek**) to worry, *-mın on beşi!* F I don't
care!, what is it to me!; *-sı sana mı
düştü?* what is it to you?, it's no concern of yours!
tasaddi attempt; **~ etm.** to attempt, to
try.
tasalandırmak to worry.
tasalanmak to worry.
tasalı worried, anxious, troubled.

tasallut, *-tu* 1. molestation; 2. attack; ~ **etm.** 1. to molest; 2. to attack.

tasallüp, *-bü* hardening; ~ **etm.** to harden.

tasannu, *-uu* simulation, pretense; artificiality.

tasar plan.

tasarı 1. plan, project, scheme; 2. bill, draft law; proposal.

tasarım 1. conception, envisagement; 2. concept, idea; 3. PHLS presentation.

tasarımlamak to imagine, to conceive, to envisage.

tasarlamak 1. to envisage, to envision, to plan, to project; 2. to rough out, to roughhew; **tasarlayarak öldürmek** JUR to murder premeditatedly.

tasarruf 1. JUR disposition, disposal; possession; management, administration; 2. economy, thrift; saving (*money*); 3. savings; ~ **bankası** savings bank; ~ **bonosu** a kind of savings bond; ~ **etm.** 1. to save (up), to save money, to economize; 2. to have the use of; ~ **hesabı** savings account; ~ **mevduatı** savings deposit; ~ **sandığı** savings bank.

tasarruflu thrifty, economical, frugal.

tasasız carefree, lighthearted.

tasasızlık carefreeness, lightheartedness.

tasavvuf *isl.* Sufism, Islamic mysticism.

tasavvufi *isl.* Sufistic, Sufic.

tasavvur 1. imagination, conception, envisagement; 2. concept, idea; ~ **etm.** to imagine, to conceive, to envisage.

tasdi, *-ii* [ī] discommoding, inconveniencing; ~ **etm.** to discommode, to inconvenience.

tasdik, *-kı* [ī] 1. confirmation; certification; 2. ratification; ~ **etm.** to confirm, to certify, to ratify, to affirm.

tasdikli certified, ratified.

tasdikname [. . - .] 1. certificate; letter of confirmation; 2. certificate of attendance (*given to a student who leaves a school without graduating*).

tasdiksiz uncertified.

tasfiye 1. COM liquidation; 2. purification; 3. discharge, elimination (*of the employees*); ~ **etm.** 1. to purify, to clarify, to refine; 2. COM to liquidate; 3. to discharge, to eliminate (*employees*); ~ **memuru** JUR liquidator; *-ye gitmek* COM to go into liquidation.

tasfiyeci purist.

tasfiyehane [. . . . - .] refinery.

tashih [ī] correction; rectification, amendment; ~ **etm.** to correct; to rectify, to amend.

tasımlamak 1. to plan; 2. to estimate, to reckon.

taslak 1. draft, sketch, outline; 2. model, maquette; 3. *contp.* would-be; **şair taslağı** would-be poet.

taslamak 1. to pretend, to make a show of, to feign, to fake, to simulate, to sham; 2. to hew.

tasma 1. collar; 2. strap (*of clogs*); 3. *sl.* sucker, pushover; ~ **takmak** to put a collar (*-e* on).

tasni, *-ii* [ī] fabrication, invention; ~ **etm.** to fabricate, to make up, to concoct, to devise.

tasnif [ī] classification; ~ **etm.** to classify.

tasrif [ī] GR inflection; conjugation; ~ **etm.** to inflect, to conjugate.

tasrih [ī] clear expression; ~ **etm.** to explain clearly, to specify.

tastamam [x . .] absolutely complete; altogether perfect.

tasvip, *-bi* [ī] approval; sanction; ~ **etm.** to approve, to give one's approval; to sanction.

tasvir [ī] 1. description, depiction; 2. P picture; ~ **etm.** to describe, to portray, to depict; ~ **gibi** as pretty as a picture.

tasviri [ī] descriptive.

taş 1. stone; rock; 2. playing piece, counter; 3. stone, gem (*in a piece of jewelry*); 4. MED calculus, stone; 5. *fig.* dig, allusion, innuendo; ~ **arabası** *sl.* blockhead, dodo; ~ **atmak** to get in a dig (*-e* at), to make an allusion (*-e* about); ~ **bebek** doll; ~ **çatlasa** by no means, whatever happens; ~ **çıkartmak** (*b-ne*) to be able to run rings around *s.o.*, to be far superior to *s.o.*; ~ **devri** HIST the Stone Age; ~ **gibi** 1. as hard as a rock; 2. stonyhearted, hardhearted; ~ **kesilmek** *fig.* to be dumbfounded; ~ **ocağı** stone quarry; ~ **tahta** slate; ~ ~ **üstünde bırakmamak** to leave no stone standing, to level with the ground; ~ **tutmak** *sl.* to have money; *-a tutmak* to stone, to stone to death; *-ı gediğine koymak* to hit the nail on the head; *-ı sıksa suyunu çıkarır* *fig.* he is very strong; *-tan ekmeğini çıkarmak* *fig.* to be able to make a living out of anything.

taşak testicle, testis, ball, nut.

taşbaskı lithography.

taşbasması, **-nı** lithograph.

taşçı 1. quarryman, quarrier; **2.** stone-cutter; **3.** stonemason.

taşeron subcontractor.

taşıl fossil.

taşıllaşmak to fossilize.

taşım: ~ **kaynamak** (*for a liquid*) to come to the boil.

taşıma 1. *vn. of* **taşımak; 2.** transport.

taşımacı transporter, carrier; forwarder.

taşımacılık transportation, shipping.

taşımak 1. to carry, to transport; **2.** to bear, to support, to sustain, to hold up (*a weight*); **3.** to carry, to bear, to possess (*a name, etc.*).

taşınır movable, portable, transferable, conveyable.

taşınmak 1. *pass. of* **taşımak; 2.** to move (*-e* to), to remove (*-e* to); **3.** to go too often (*-e* to).

taşınmaz immovable, real (*property*).

taşırmak to overflow.

taşıt, **-tı** vehicle, conveyance, means of transportation; ~ **giremez** no entry; ~ **kazası** traffic accident.

taşıyıcı 1. porter, carrier; stevedore; **2.** conveyor

taşkın 1. overflowing; **2.** rowdy, boisterous, exuberant; **3.** flood, inundation.

taşkınlık rowdiness, boisterousness, impetuosity.

taşkömür(ü) (pit)coal.

taşlama 1. *vn. of* **taşlamak; 2.** satirizing; **3.** satire; lampoon.

taşlamacı 1. satirist; **2.** honer.

taşlamak 1. to stone; **2.** to stone to death; **3.** *fig.* to satirize; to lampoon; **4.** to hone; **5.** to pave with stones; **6.** *fig.* to get in a dig (*-i* at).

taşlaşmak to petrify, to turn to stone.

taşlı 1. stony; **2.** set with stones.

taşlık 1. stony place; **2.** gizzard (*of a bird*).

taşmak, **(-ar) 1.** to overflow, to run over; **2.** to boil over; **3.** *fig.* to lose one's patience, to blow one's stack.

taşra [x .] the provinces, the sticks.

taşralı [x ..] provincial.

taşyürekli stonyhearted, hardhearted.

tat, **-dı 1.** taste, flavo(u)r; **2.** sweetness; **3.** relish, pleasure, delight; ~ **almak** to relish, to get a kick (*-den* out of), to

find pleasure (*-den* in); ~ **vermek** to flavo(u)r; **-ı damağında kalmak** to remember s.th. with relish; **-ı tuzu kalmamak** to lose its charm, to be no longer pleasurable; **-ı tuzu yok** it is insipid, it has no flavo(u)r at all; **-ına bakmak** to taste, to sample; **-ına doyum olmamak** to be very tasty; **-ına varmak** *fig.* to get the full flavo(u)r (*-in* of), to enjoy; **-ında bırakmak** *fig.* not to overdo, **-ını çıkarmak** (*bşin*) to make the most of *s.th.*, to enjoy *s.th.*; **-ını kaçırmak** to spoil; to cast a damper (*-in* on).

tatar 1. HIST mounted courier; postrider; **2.** ♀ Ta(r)tar.

tatarböreği, **-ni** a kind of pastry.

tatarcık zoo sandfly; ~ **humması** MED sandfly fever.

tatarımsı, **tatarsı** half-cooked, underdone (*food*).

tatbik, **-ki** [i] application; adaptation; ~ **etm. 1.** to apply; to put into effect (*or* practice); **2.** to compare (*-e* with); ~ **sahasına koymak** to put into effect (*or* practice).

tatbikat, **-tı** [. - -] **1.** application; practice; **2.** MIL manoeuvres, *Am.* maneuvers, exercises; **-ta** in practice.

tatbiki [. - -] applied; ~ **sanatlar** applied arts.

tatil [- -] **1.** holiday, vacation; **2.** break (*for a meal*); **3.** suspension, temporary cessation; ~ **etm. 1.** to close temporarily; **2.** to suspend; ~ **günü 1.** holiday; **2.** off day, day off; ~ **köyü** holiday village; ~ **olm.** to be closed (*for a holiday*); ~ **yapmak** to take a holiday (*or* vacation), to holiday.

tatlandırmak to flavo(u)r.

tatlanmak to flavo(u)r, to sweeten.

tatlı 1. sweet; **2.** nice, pleasant, sweet; delicious; melodious, dulcet; **3.** sweet, dessert, ~ **dil** soft words; ~ **dil yılanı deliğinden çıkarır** *pro.* a soft answer turns away wrath; ~ **dilli** softspoken; ~ **kaşığı** dessert spoon; ~ **su** fresh water; **-ya bağlamak** to settle amicably.

tatlıca sweetish.

tatlıcı 1. maker *or* seller of sweets; **2.** fond of sweets, sweet-toothed.

tatlılaşmak to get sweet, to sweeten.

tatlılaştırmak to make sweet, to sweeten.

tatlılık 1. sweetness; **2.** *fig.* niceness, pleasantness, sweetness; delicious-

ness; **-la** with kindness; amicably.
tatlımsı sweetish.
tatlısulevreği, -ni zoo perch.
tatmak, (-ar) 1. to taste; **2.** *fig.* to go through, to experience, to taste.
tatmin [ī] satisfaction, gratification; ~ **etm.** to satisfy, to gratify, to content; ~ **olm.** to be satisfied (*or* gratified *or* contented).
tatminkâr satisfactory.
tatsal gustatory, gustatorial, gustative.
tatsız 1. tasteless, insipid, vapid; **2.** unsweet; **3.** *fig.* unpleasant, disagreeable; ~ **tuzsuz** insipid.
tatula [. x .] BOT datura.
taun [- -] plague, pestilence.
tav 1. anneal (*of steel, etc.*); **2.** the exact state of heat *or* dampness; **3.** *fig.* opportune moment; **4.** *sl.* trick, deception; ~ **olm.** *sl.* to fall for s.o.'s trick; ~ **vermek** to dampen; **-a düşürmek** *sl.* to trick, to hoodwink; **-ına getirmek** to bring to the right condition.
tava 1. frying pan, skillet, frypan; **2.** fried (*food*); **3.** ladle (*for melting metal*); **4.** trough (*for slaking lime*); **5.** bed (*for young plants*).
tavaf [. -] circumambulation (*of the Kaaba*); ~ **etm. 1.** to circumambulate (*the Kaaba*); **2.** *fig.* to wander around.
tavan ceiling; ~ **arası** attic, garret, loft; ~ **fiyat** ceiling price; ~ **süpürgesi** long-handled broom (*for ceilings*).
tavassut, -tu mediation; interposition, intervention; ~ **etm.** to mediate, to interpose, to intervene.
tavazzuh becoming clear; ~ **etm.** to become clear.
taverna nightclub, tavern.
tavır, -vrı 1. manner, attitude, air; **2.** airs, affectation, put-on; pose; ~ **satmak** to give o.s. airs.
taviz [- -] **1.** concession; **2.** compensation; ~ **vermek** to make a concession, to stretch a point.
tavla¹ [x .] backgammon; ~ **atmak** F to play backgammon.
tavla² [x .] stable (*for horses*).
tavlamak 1. to dampen; **2.** to anneal (*steel, etc.*); **3.** *sl.* to trick, to hoodwink, to bamboozle; **4.** *sl.* to charm, to snow, to beguile.
tavsamak to abate, to moderate, to slacken.
tavsif [ī] characterization; designation, qualification; ~ **etm.** to characterize; to designate, to qualify.

tavsifi [. - -] descriptive.
tavsiye recommendation, commendation; ~ **etm.** to recommend, to advise, to commend; ~ **mektubu** letter of recommendation; **-ye şayan** recommendable.
tavsiyeli 1. recommended; **2.** supported, backed.
tavşan¹ zoo rabbit, hare; ~ **kız** Bunny (girl); ~ **uykusu** rabbit's sleep; ~ **yavrusu** young hare, leveret; ~ **yürekli** timid; **-a kaç, tazıya tut demek** to run with the hare and hunt with the hounds; **-ı araba ile avlamak** *fig.* to do s.th. calmly and unhurriedly; **-ın suyunun suyu** *fig.* a very distant connection.
tavşan² cabinetmaker.
tavşancıl zoo vulture; eagle.
tavşandudağı, -nı harelip.
tavşandudaklı harelipped.
tavşankanı, -nı dark and strong (*tea*).
tavşanlık rabbit hutch.
tavuk zoo hen, chicken; ~ **kümesi** chicken coop; ~ **suyu** chicken broth.
tavukçu 1. poulterer; **2.** chicken farmer.
tavukgöğsü, -nü *a pudding made of rice flour and very finely shredded chicken.*
tavukgötü, -nü wart.
tavukkarası, -nı night blindness.
tavus, tavuskuşu, -nu zoo peacock, peafowl.
tavzif [ī] appointing s.o. to a duty; ~ **etm.** (*b-ni bşle*) to appoint s.o. to s.th., to entrust s.o. with s.th.
tavzih [ī] explanation, elucidation; ~ **etm.** to explain, to elucidate.
tay¹ zoo colt, filly, foal.
tay² 1. one of a pair, fellow, mate; **2.** peer, equal; ~ **durmak** (*for a baby*) to stand upright; ~ ~! up, up! (*said to a baby just learning to walk*).
tay³, -yyı removal, deletion, expunction.
taya nursemaid, nanny.
tayf 1. apparition, specter; wraith; **2.** PHYS spectrum.
tayfa [x .] **1.** crew; **2.** crewman, sailor; **3.** gang, bunch, band, troop.
tayfun typhoon.
tayın MIL ration.
tayin [- -] **1.** appointment; **2.** indication; **3.** designation; ~ **etm. 1.** to appoint; **2.** to fix, to determine; **-ı çıkmak** to be appointed (*or* assigned).

taylan tall and well-set-up (*man*).

Tayland *pr. n.* Thailand.

Taymis *pr. n.* the Thames.

tayyare [. - .] airplane; ~ **gemisi** aircraft carrier; ~ **meydanı** airfield, aerodrome.

tayyareci [. - . .] **1.** pilot; **2.** airman.

tayyarecilik [. - . . .] pilotry; aviation.

tayyetmek [x . .] to remove, to delete, to expunge.

tayyör tailleur, (*woman's*) tailor-made suit.

tazallüm complaint, lamentation; ~ **etm.** to complain, to lament.

tazammum 1. including, comprising, embracing; **2.** PHLS implication; ~ **etm. 1.** to include, to comprise, to embrace; **2.** PHLS to imply.

tazarru, -uu supplication; ~ **etm.** to supplicate.

taze [ā] **1.** fresh; **2.** new; young; **3.** newly, freshly; **4.** young girl; ~ **biber** green pepper; ~ **ekmek** fresh bread; ~ **fasulye** green beans.

tazelemek [ā] **1.** to freshen, to renew; **2.** to add water and reheat.

tazeleşmek [ā] to be rejuvenated.

tazelik [ā] freshness, newness, youth.

tazı greyhound; ~ **gibi** lean and agile (*person*); -ya **dönmek 1.** to get very thin, to get as thin as a rail; **2.** to get soaked to the skin.

tazim [- -] hono(u)ring, respect; ~ **etm.** to hono(u)r, to revere.

taziye [ā] condolence; ~ **etm.** (*or* -**de bulunmak**) to offer one's condolences, to condole; ~ **mektubu** letter of condolence.

taziz [- -] **1.** cherishing; **2.** exaltation; **3.** *Christianity*: conferring sainthood upon; ~ **etm. 1.** to cherish; **2.** to exalt; **3.** *Christianity*: to confer sainthood (-*i* upon).

tazmin [ī] indemnification; ~ **etm.** to indemnify; to make up for (*a mistake*).

tazminat, -tı [. - - -] JUR **1.** indemnity, damages, compensation, reparations; **2.** separation pay; ~ **davası** JUR action for damages.

tazyik, -ki [ī] pressure; ~ **etm.** to press, to put pressure on, to pressure.

tazyikli [. - .] **1.** compressed (*air*); **2.** under compression.

TBMM (*abbr. for* **Türkiye Büyük Millet Meclisi**) the Turkish National Assembly.

TC (*abbr. for* **Türkiye Cumhuriyeti**) the Republic of Turkey.

TCDD (*abbr. for* **Türkiye Cumhuriyeti Devlet Demiryolları**) Turkish Rail.

TDK (*abbr. for* **Türk Dil Kurumu**) the Turkish Language Association.

teadül [ā] equivalence; ~ **etm.** to be equivalent (-*e* to).

teakup, -bu [ā] succession; ~ **etm.** to follow one another in succession.

teali [. - -] rise, ascent; ~ **etm.** to rise, to ascend.

teamül [ā] **1.** practice, custom; **2.** CHEM reaction; ~ **hukuku** JUR consuetudinary law.

tearuz [ā] conflict, contradiction.

teati [. - -] exchange; ~ **etm.** to exchange.

teavün [ā] cooperation; ~ **etm.** to cooperate.

tebaa 1. citizen; subject; **2.** citizens; subjects.

tebadül [ā] **1.** exchange; permutation; **2.** BIOL mutation; ~ **etm.** to undergo permutation *or* mutation.

tebahhur vaporization, evaporation; ~ **etm.** to vaporize, to evaporate.

tebarüz [ā] becoming clear (*or* evident); ~ **etm.** to become clear (*or* evident); ~ **ettirmek** to make clear, to show clearly.

tebcil [ī] exaltation, glorification; ~ **etm.** to hono(u)r, to exalt, to glorify.

tebdil [ī] **1.** exchange, alteration; **2.** in disguise, incognito; ~ **etm.** to change, to alter, to exchange; ~ **gezmek** to go around in disguise, to travel incognito; -*ı* **hava** change of air; -*i* **mekan** **etm.** to move (house).

tebeddul alteration, exchange, replacement; ~ **etm.** to be changed (*or* altered).

tebelleş P pestiferous, importunate (*person*).

tebellür 1. crystallization; **2.** *fig.* becoming clear; ~ **etm. 1.** to crystallize; **2.** *fig.* to become clear.

teber 1. HIST battle-ax; **2.** knife (*for cutting leather*).

teberru, -uu donation, gift, contribution; ~ **etm.** to donate.

tebessüm smile; ~ **etm.** to smile.

tebeşir chalk.

tebeyyün becoming evident (*or* manifest); ~ **etm.** to become evident (*or* manifest).

tebligat, -tı [. - -] *pl. of* **tebliğ 1.** notifications, communiqués; **2.** notification, communiqué.

tebliğ [ī] **1.** communicating, notifying; **2.** communication, notification, communiqué; ~ **etm.** to communicate, to notify.

tebrik, *-ki* [ī] **1.** congratulation; **2.** congratulatory card; ~ **etm.** to congratulate; ~ **kartı** greeting (*or* congratulatory) card.

tebriye JUR acquittal, exoneration; ~ **etm.** to acquit, to exonerate.

Tebriz [ī] *pr. n.* Tabriz.

tebyiz [ī] **1.** making a fair copy of (*a document*); **2.** whitening; ~ **etm. 1.** to make a fair copy of (*a document*); **2.** to whiten.

tecahül [ā] feigning ignorance; ~ **etm.** to feign ignorance.

tecanüs [ā] homogeneity.

tecavüz [ā] **1.** aggression, attack; **2.** JUR molestation; rape, assault; **3.** JUR violation, infringement; encroachment; transgression; ~ **etm. 1.** to attack; **2.** to molest, to assault, to rape; **3.** to violate, to infringe; to transgress; to encroach; to trespass (*-e* on); **4.** to surpass, to exceed.

tecavüzi [. - . -] aggressive, offensive.

tecdit, *-di* [ī] renewal; restoration, renovation, refurbishment; ~ **etm.** to renew; to restore, to renovate, to refurbish.

teceddüt, *-dü* **1.** renewal; innovation; **2.** renaissance; ~ **etm.** to be renewed, to renew itself.

tecelli [ī] **1.** manifestation; revelation; **2.** destiny, fate; ~ **etm.** to become manifest; to be revealed.

tecemmu, *-uu* **1.** assembling, gathering; **2.** MIL concentration (*of troops*); ~ **etm. 1.** to assemble, to gather; **2.** MIL (*for troops*) to be concentrated.

tecerrüt, *-dü* **1.** isolation; **2.** abstraction; ~ **etm. 1.** to isolate o.s. (*-den* from); **2.** to free o.s. (*-den* from), to set aside (*a prejudice, etc.*); **3.** to abstract.

tecessüm 1. embodiment; **2.** appearance; ~ **etm. 1.** to become embodied (*or* tangible); **2.** to appear, to become apparent.

tecessüs 1. curiosity, inquisitiveness, nosiness, snoopiness; **2.** spying; ~ **etm. 1.** to inquire pryingly; **2.** to spy (*-i* on).

tecil [. - -] postponement; deferment; ~

etm. to postpone; to defer.

tecim commerce, trade.

tecrit, *-di* [ī] isolation, separation, insulation; ~ **etm.** to isolate, to separate, to set apart, to insulate; to quarantine; ~ **kampı** POL isolation camp; ~ **siyaseti** isolationism.

tecrübe 1. experience; **2.** CHEM, PHYS experiment, trial, test; ~ **etm. 1.** to experience, to test, to experiment; **2.** to attempt, to try; ~ **sahibi** experienced; ~ **tahtası** *fig.* corpus vile, guinea pig.

tecrübeli experienced.

tecrübesiz inexperienced.

tecrübesizlik inexperience.

tecrübi [ī] experimental.

tecvit, *-di* [ī] recitation of the Koran with proper rhythm.

tecviz [ī] permitting, allowing; ~ **etm.** to permit, to allow.

tecziye punishment; ~ **etm.** to punish.

teçhiz [ī] equipment; ~ **etm.** to equip, to outfit.

teçhizat, *-tı* [. - -] equipment, gear, apparatus.

tedafüi [. - . -] defensive; ~ **harp** defensive war.

tedahül [ā] **1.** interpenetration; permeation; **2.** delay in payment; **3.** PHYS interference; *-de kalmak* (*or* *-e binmek*) (*for a payment*) to be overdue, to be in arrears.

tedai [. - -] PSYCH association.

tedansan tea dance, thé dansant.

tedarik, *-ki* [ā] **1.** procurement, obtainment; **2.** preparation; **3.** accumulation; ~ **etm. 1.** to procure, to obtain, to provide; **2.** to accumulate; *-te bulunmak* to make preparations (*-e* for), to get ready (*-e* for)

tedarikli [ā] prepared, ready.

tedariksiz [ā] unprepared, unready.

tedavi [. - -] MED treatment, cure; therapy; ~ **etm.** to treat, to cure; ~ **görmek** (*or* ~ **olm.**) to be treated.

tedavül [ā] circulation; ~ **bankası** bank of circulation (*or* issue); ~ **etm.** to be in circulation; *-den çekmek* (*or* **çıkarmak**) to withdraw from circulation, to call in; *-den kalkmak* to go out of circulation; *-e çıkarmak* to put into circulation, to issue.

tedbir [ī] measure, step, precaution, action; ~ **almak** to take measures (*or* steps).

tedbirli provident, cautious, forethoughtful, prudent.

tedbirsiz improvident, unforethoughtful, imprudent.

tedbirsizlik improvidence, imprudence.

tedenni [ī] decline; ~ **etm.** to decline, to fall off.

tedfin [ī] burial, interment; ~ **etm.** to bury, to inter.

tedhiş [ī] terror, terrorization; ~ **etm.** to terrorize.

tedhişçi terrorist.

tedhişçilik terrorism.

tedip, -bi [- -] disciplining; chastisement; ~ **etm.** to discipline, to chastise.

tedirgin uncomfortable, uneasy, troubled, anxious, worried; ~ **etm.** to disquiet, to discompose.

tedirginlik disquiet, uneasiness, anxiety, worry.

tediyat, -tı [- . .] pl. of **tediye** payments.

tediye [- . .] payment, disbursement; ~ **dengesi** balance of payments; ~ **etm.** to pay, to disburse; ~ **günü** pay-day.

tedricen [ī] [. x .] gradually, by degrees, by stages.

tedrici [. - -] gradual.

tedris [ī] instruction, teaching; ~ **etm.** to teach.

tedrisat, -tı [. - -] instruction, teaching.

tedvin [ī] **1.** JUR codification (of laws); **2.** compilation; ~ **etm. 1.** JUR to codify (laws); **2.** to compile.

tedvir [ī] **1.** rotation; **2.** fig. administration, management; ~ **etm. 1.** to rotate, to turn, to revolve; **2.** fig. to administer, to manage, to direct.

teehhür delay; ~ **etm.** to be delayed.

teemmül careful consideration, deliberation; ~ **etm.** to think carefully, to deliberate.

teenni [ī] deliberation, caution; ~ **etm.** to exercise caution, to proceed slowly and carefully.

teessüf regret, sorrow, sadness; ~ **etm.** to feel sorry (-e about); to regret; ~ **ederim** it makes me very sad; I never expected you to do s.th. like this.

teessür 1. sorrow, sadness; **2.** emotion.

teessüs 1. establishment; **2.** foundation; ~ **etm. 1.** to become established (or rooted); **2.** to be founded.

teeyyüt, -dü confirmation, substantiation; ~ **etm.** to be confirmed (or substantiated).

tef tambourine; ~ **çalmak** to play the tambourine; ~ **çalsan oynayacak** fig. it's all topsy-turvy, what a mess!;

-e koymak (or **-e koyup çalmak**) (b-ni) fig. to make fun of s.o., to run s.o. down.

tefcir [ī] drainage; ~ **etm.** to drain.

tefeci usurer.

tefecilik usury.

tefehhüm coming to understand; ~ **etm.** to come to understand.

tefekkür consideration, reflection, contemplation; thought; ~ **etm.** to think, to consider, to contemplate; **-e dalmak** to be lost in thought, to contemplate.

teferruat, -tı [ā] details.

teferruatlı [ā] detailed.

teferrüc, -cü walk, excursion, outing.

teferrüt, -dü being unique, standing alone; ~ **etm.** to be unique, to stand alone.

tefessüh rot, decay (a. CHEM); ~ **etm.** to rot, to decay.

tefevvuk, -ku superiority; ~ **etm.** (b-ne) to be superior to s.o.

tefhim [ī] JUR pronouncement (of a sentence); ~ **etm.** JUR to pronounce (a sentence).

tefrik, -ki [ī] distinction; ~ **etm.** to distinguish; to differentiate.

tefrika 1. serial; **2.** disagreement, discord.

tefriş [ī] **1.** spreading over; **2.** furnishing; ~ **etm. 1.** to spread; **2.** to furnish; **3.** to pave; to cover.

tefrit, -ti [ī] remissness.

tefsir [ī] **1.** interpretation; **2.** commentary on the Koran; ~ **etm. 1.** to interpret; to explain; to expound; **2.** to comment (on a sura of the Koran).

teftiş [ī] inspection; ~ **etm.** to inspect.

teğelti saddle blanket.

teğet, -ti MATH tangent; ~ **olm.** to be tangent (-e to).

teğmen MIL lieutenant.

teğmenlik MIL lieutenancy.

tehacüm [ā] **1.** concerted attack; **2.** rush; ~ **etm. 1.** to make a concerted attack; **2.** to rush.

tehdit, -di [ī] threat, menace; ~ **etm.** to threaten, to menace; ~ **savurmak** to bluster out threats.

teheyyüç, -cü emotional excitement; ~ **etm.** to get emotionally excited, to get worked up.

tehir [- -] **1.** delay, postponement, deferment, deferral; **2.** JUR adjournment; ~ **etm. 1.** to delay, to postpone, to defer; **2.** JUR to adjourn.

tehirli delayed, late.

tehlike danger, hazard, peril, risk; **~ atlatmak** to get through a dangerous situation successfully; **-ye atmak** to put in danger; **-ye atılmak** to court danger, to go into danger; **-ye koymak** (*or* **sokmak**) to endanger, to imperil, to put in danger.

tehlikeli dangerous, hazardous, perilous, risky.

tehlikesiz undangerous, dangerless, unhazardous, unperilous, riskless.

tehyiç, -ci [ī] excitation; **~ etm.** to excite.

tehzil [ī] ridiculing, making fun of; **~ etm.** to ridicule, to make fun of.

tek, -ki 1. one, sole, single, solitary, only; **2.** unique, unrivaled; **3.** one of a pair, fellow, mate; **4.** MATH odd (*number*); **5.** only, solely; **~ atmak** F to knock back a drink; **~ başına** alone, on one's own; **~ başına kalmak** to be left alone; **~ meclisli hükümet sistemi** JUR unicameral system of government; **~ motorlu** single-engined; **~ taraflı** unilateral; **~ ~ one** by one; **~ tük** only a few; **~ yönlü** one-way.

tekabül [ā] correspondence, equivalence; **~ etm.** to correspond.

tekâmül 1. evolution; **2.** maturation; **~ etm. 1.** to evolve; **2.** to mature.

tekâsüf 1. condensation, inspissation; concentration; **2.** opacification; **~ etm. 1.** to condense, to inspissate, to thicken; **2.** to opacify; **3.** (*for a crowd*) to gather, to congregate.

tekaüt, -dü [ā] **1.** retirement; **2.** F retired (*person*); **3.** retired person, pensioner; **~ etm.** (*or* **-e sevk etm.**) to retire, to pension off; **~ maaşı** retirement pay, pension; **~ olm.** to retire; **~ sandığı** retirement fund.

tekaütlük [ā] retirement.

tekbencilik PHLS solipsism.

tekçe individual.

tekçilik PHLS monism.

tekdeğerli CHEM univalent.

tekdir [ī] reprimand, dressing down; **~ etm.** to reprimand, to dress down, to upbraid.

tekdüze(n) monotonous.

tekdüzelik, tekdüzenlik monotony.

teke ZOO **1.** he-goat, billy goat; **2.** shrimp; prawn.

tekeffül guaranteeing; **~ etm.** to guarantee; to go bond (*-e* for).

tekel monopoly; **-ine almak** to monopolize.

Tekel *pr. n.* the Turkish State Liquor and Tobacco Monopoly.

tekelci monopolist.

tekelcilik monopolism.

tekellüf 1. empty show, false display; **2.** formality, ceremoniousness.

tekellüflü ornate, sumptuous.

tekellüfsüz plain.

tekellüm speech; **~ etm.** to speak.

tekemmül maturation; **~ etm.** to reach maturity.

teker wheel; **~ meker yuvarlanmak** to roll over and over.

tekerklik monarchy.

tekerlek 1. wheel; **2.** *sl.* homosexual, fag, queer; **~ kırıldıktan sonra yol gösteren çok olur** *pro.* it is easy to be wise after the event; **~ pabucu** skidpan, drag shoe; **~ parmağı** spoke of a wheel; **tekerleğine çomak sokmak** to put a spoke in one's wheel.

tekerlekli wheeled; **~ sandalye** wheelchair.

tekerleme 1. *vn. of* **tekerlemek; 2.** rigmarole; **3.** tongue-twister; **4.** repartee.

tekerlemek to roll.

tekerlenmek 1. *pass. of* **tekerlemek; 2.** to roll.

tekerli wheeled.

tekerrür 1. repetition; **2.** recurrence; **~ etm. 1.** to be repeated; **2.** to recur.

tekevlilik monogamy.

tekevvün coming into existence, origination; **~ etm.** to come into existence.

tekfin [ī] (en)shrouding (*a corpse*); **~ etm.** to (en)shroud (*a corpse*).

tekfir [ī] *isl.* accusing s.o. of being an infidel; **~ etm.** to accuse s.o. of being an infidel.

tekfur HIST Christian princelet.

tekil GR singular.

tekin 1. deserted, empty (*place*); **2.** auspicious; **3.** ♀ *mf.;* **~ değil** inauspicious, ill-omened, sinister.

tekinsiz 1. unlucky, of ill omen; **2.** taboo.

tekir 1. tabby; **2.** (*balığı*) surmullet, red mullet; **~ kedi** tabby-cat.

tekke 1. dervish lodge, tekke; **2.** *sl.* hashish den.

tekleme 1. *vn. of* **teklemek; 2.** MEC misfiring.

teklemek 1. to thin (*seedlings*); **2.** MEC to miss, to misfire; **3.** *sl.* to stammer, to

telefon

stutter.

teklif [ī] **1.** proposal, offer, motion; **2.** formality, ceremony; ~ *etm.* to propose, to offer, to suggest; ~ *kutusu* suggestion box; ~ *sahibi* **1.** mover (*of a motion*); **2.** bidder; ~ *tekellüf* formality; ~ *yok* there's no need for ceremony.

teklifli formal, ceremonious.

teklifsiz informal, unceremonious.

teklifsizce unceremoniously, familiarly, casually.

teklifsizlik informality, casualness.

teklik **1.** oneness; **2.** *sl.* lira.

tekme kick; ~ *atmak* to kick; ~ *yemek* to get kicked, to get a kick.

tekmelemek to kick.

tekmil [ī] **1.** completion; **2.** all, the whole; ~ *etm.* to complete, to finish; ~ *haberi* MIL oral report; ~ *vermek* MIL to give an oral report.

tekne **1.** trough; vat; **2.** boat, vessel; **3.** hull (*of a ship*); **4.** TYP galley; **5.** GEOL basin; ~ *kazıntısı* co. the youngest child of the family, born when his *or* her parents are no longer young.

teknik **1.** technique; **2.** technical; ~ *destek* technical support; ~ *resim* drafting; ~ *ressam* draughtsman, *Am.* draftsman; ~ *terim* technical term.

tekniker technician.

teknikokul technical school.

teknoköğretim technical education.

teknisyen technician.

teknoloji technology.

teknolojik technological.

tekrar [x -] **1.** repetition, repeat, reiteration; **2.** recurrence; **3.** again, over again, once more; ~ *etm.* to repeat, to reiterate; ~ ~ repeatedly, again and again.

tekrarlamak to repeat, to reiterate.

tekrarlanmak **1.** *pass. of* tekrarlamak; **2.** to recur.

teksif [ī] **1.** concentration; condensation, inspissation; **2.** opacification; ~ *etm.* **1.** to concentrate, to densen, to thicken, to condense, to inspissate; **2.** to opacify.

teksir [ī] **1.** duplication; **2.** augmentation, increase, multiplication; ~ *etm.* **1.** to duplicate, to copy; **2.** to augment, to increase, to multiply; ~ *kâğıdı* paper used for making duplicates; ~ *makinesi* duplicating machine, duplicator, mimeograph.

tekst, *-ti* text.

tekstil textile; ~ *sanayii* textile industry.

tektanrıcılık monotheism.

tekyazım monograph.

tekzip, *-bi* [ī] denial, disclaimer; ~ *etm.* to deny, to disclaim, to declare false.

tel **1.** wire; **2.** string (*of a musical instrument*); **3.** thread; strand; fibre, *Am.* fiber; **4.** screen cloth, screening; window screen; door screen; **5.** F telegram, wire, cable; ~ *çekmek* **1.** to enclose with wire; **2.** F to telegraph, to send a wire, to cable, to wire; ~ *çivi* brad, wire-tack; ~ *fırça* wire brush; ~ *kadayıf* a kind of sweet pastry; ~ *kafes* wire cage; ~ *kırmak* **1.** to blunder; **2.** *sl.* to tread on s.o.'s toes; ~ *örgü* wire fence; ~ *şehriye* vermicelli; *-ler takınmak* fig. to rejoice greatly.

tela [x .] interfacing.

telaffuz pronunciation; ~ *etm.* to pronounce.

telafi [. - -] compensation; ~ *etm.* to compensate, to make up for; *-si imkânsız* irreparable, irremediable.

telakki [. . -] **1.** consideration, evaluation; **2.** view(point); ~ *etm.* to regard, to view.

telaş **1.** flurry, flutter, commotion, hurry, bustle, to-do; **2.** agitation; ~ *etm.* to bustle, to behave agitatedly; ~ *içinde* in a bustle (*or* hurry); *-a düşmek* to get agitated, to get in a swivet; *-a vermek* to get (*everybody in a place*) agitated, to alarm.

telaşçı nervous, restless (*person*).

telaşlandırmak (*b-ni*) to get *s.o.* agitated.

telaşlanmak to get agitated.

telaşlı agitated.

telaşsız unagitated, unruffled, steady, calm.

telatin Russia, Russia leather.

telcik fibril.

teldolap screen safe.

telef **1.** waste; **2.** death; ~ *etm.* **1.** to waste, to throw away, to squander; **2.** to kill, to do away with; ~ *olm.* **1.** to be wasted (*or* thrown away); **2.** to die.

telefat, *-tı* [ā] losses, casualties; ~ *verdirmek* to inflict losses (*-e* on); ~ *vermek* to suffer losses.

teleferik telpher, teleferic.

telefon **1.** telephone, phone; **2.** telephone (*or* phone) call; ~ *etm.* to telephone, to phone, to ring (up), to call (up); ~ **kartı** phone-card; ~ **kulübesi** telephone box; ~ **rehberi** telephone directory (*or* book); ~ **santralı** telephone exchange, switchboard; *-la* **aramak** (*b-ni*) to give *s.o.* a ring; *-u* **kapamak** to hang up.

telefoncu 1. telephone lineman; installer of telephones; **2.** telephonist, operator.

telefonlaşmak to talk on the telephone (*ile* with).

telefoto, **telefotografi 1.** telephotography; **2.** phototelegraphy.

teleke zoo remex.

telekomünikasyon telecommunication.

telekonferans teleconference.

teleks telex; ~ **çekmek** to telex.

telem teletype(writer), teleprinter.

telemetre [. . x .] telemeter.

teleobjektif PHOT teleobjective, telephoto (lens), telelens.

telepati telepathy.

telepatik telepathic.

telepazarlama telemarketing.

teles threadbare.

telesekreter voice mail; *-de not bırakmak* to leave a message on a voice mail.

telesimek 1. to pant; **2.** to get thin; to pine away.

telesinema telephotography.

teleskop, *-pu* telescope.

televizör television set.

televizyon 1. television; **2.** television (set), TV, telly; ~ **alıcısı** television set (*or* receiver); ~ **vericisi** television transmitter; ~ **yayını** telecast; *-la* **öğretim** telecourse; *-la yayınlamak* to telecast, to televise.

televizyoncu maker, seller *or* repairer of television sets.

televizyonculuk making, selling *or* repairing television sets.

telgraf 1. telegraph; **2.** telegram, wire, cable; ~ **çekmek** to telegraph, to telegram, to wire, to cable.

telgrafçı telegrapher, telegraphist.

telgrafçılık telegraphy.

telgrafhane [. . - .] telegraph office.

telif [- -] **1.** reconciliation; **2.** compilation; ~ **etm. 1.** to reconcile; **2.** to compile (*a book*); ~ **hakkı** copyright.

tel'in [ī] damnation; ~ **etm.** to damn, to curse.

telkâri filigreed with gold *or* silver.

telkin [ī] inspiration, inculcation, suggestion; ~ **etm.** to inspire, to inculcate, to instill.

tellak bath attendant.

tellal 1. (town) crier; **2.** barker; hawker; crier; **3.** middleman, broker.

tellemek 1. to string wires on; **2.** to deck out; **3.** to embellish (*a story*); **4.** to send a telegram, to wire; *telleyip pullamak* **1.** to deck out, to prank, to fig out; **2.** *fig.* to praise to the skies.

tellendirmek to smoke, to enjoy a smoke.

telli 1. wired; **2.** adorned with gold *or* silver wires; ~ **bebek** *fig.* frivolous; ~ **cam** wire(d) glass; ~ **çalgılar** MUS stringed instruments, strings; ~ **pullu** decked out; showy.

telliturna zoo demoiselle crane.

telmih [ī] allusion, reference; ~ **etm.** to allude, to refer to.

telsi fibrous.

telsiz 1. wireless; **2.** radio, wireless; ~ **telefon** radiophone; wireless phone; ~ **telgraf** radio, wireless telegraph; *-le bildirmek* to radio.

telsizci 1. radiotelephonist; **2.** radiotelegraphist.

telsizcilik 1. radiotelephony; **2.** radiotelegraphy.

teltik 1. defect; **2.** deficiency; **3.** deficient, insufficient, lacking, short.

telve coffee grounds; ~ **falı** fortune-telling by the appearance of coffee grounds.

tema 1. theme, topic, subject; **2.** MUS theme, thema.

temadi [. . - -] continuation; ~ **etm.** to continue.

temaruz [ā] feigning illness; ~ **etm.** to feign illness, to pretend to be ill, to sham ill.

temas [ā] **1.** contact, touch; **2.** contact, communication; ~ **etm. 1.** to touch; **2.** to touch on (*a subject*); **3.** (*b-le*) to get in touch with *s.o.*, to contact *s.o.*; ~ **kurmak** to establish contact (*ile* with); ~ **noktası** point of contact; *-a geçmek* to get in touch (*ile* with), to contact; *-ta bulunmak* (*or* **olm.**) (*b-le*) to be in touch with *s.o.*

temaşa [. - -] **1.** pleasure excursion, promenade; **2.** play, show, scene; the theatre; ~ **etm.** to view, to contemplate.

temayül [ā] **1.** tendency, inclination, propensity; **2.** affection, liking, fondness; ~ **etm. 1.** to have a tendency (-*e* to), to be inclined (-*e* to); **2.** to have a liking (-*e* for).

temayüz [ā] becoming distinguished; ~ **etm.** to become distinguished, to stand out, to excel.

tembel lazy, indolent, supine, slothful.

tembelhane [ā] den of idlers (*or* loafers).

tembelleşmek to get (*or* grow) lazy.

tembellik laziness, indolence, supinity, sloth.

tembih [ī] **1.** warning, admonition, caution; **2.** PSYCH stimulation; ~ **etm. 1.** to warn, to caution, to admonish; **2.** PSYCH to stimulate.

tembihlemek *s.* **tembih etm. 1.**

temcit, -di [ī] **1.** *canticle intoned from minarets before dawn*; **2.** *meal eaten just before dawn during the month of Ramazan*; ~ **pilavı gibi ısıtıp ısıtıp öne sürmek** *fig.* to keep bringing up the same topic time after time.

temdit, -di [ī] extension, prolongation; ~ **etm.** to extend, to prolong.

temel 1. foundation; **2.** *fig.* basis; ground (work); **3.** fundamental, basic; **4.** main, principal, chief; ~ **atmak** to lay the foundation; ~ **cümle** GR main clause; ~ **direk** main post (*in a building*); ~ **kakmak** (*bir yere*) to settle down in (*a place*) for good; ~ **taşı** foundation stone, cornerstone (*a. fig.*); ~ **tutmak** to become firmly fixed; **-inden** at bottom, fundamentally.

temellenmek to become firmly fixed (*or* established).

temelleşmek *s.* **temellenmek.**

temelli 1. having a foundation; **2.** permanent; **3.** permanently, for good; **4.** completely, wholly; ~ **bir iş** a permanent job; ~ **gitti** he has gone for good.

temellük, -kü taking possession of; ~ **etm.** to take possession of.

temelsiz unfounded, groundless, baseless.

temenna(h) [ā] Oriental salute; ~ **etm.** to salute.

temenni [ī] wish, desire; ~ **etm.** to wish, to desire.

temerküz 1. concentration; **2.** POL coalition; ~ **etm.** to be concentrated (-*de* on), to centre, *Am.* to center (-*de* on); ~ **kabinesi** POL coalition government; ~ **kampı** concentration camp.

temerrüt, -dü 1. obstinacy, perverseness; **2.** JUR default (*in payment*); ~

etm. to be obstinate (*or* perverse); ~ **faizi** COM moratory interest.

temessül 1. coming to resemble; **2.** BIOL assimilation; ~ **etm. 1.** to come to resemble; **2.** BIOL to assimilate.

temettü, -üü 1. profit; **2.** COM dividend; ~ **etm.** to profit; ~ **hissesi** COM dividend; ~ **vergisi** tax on profits.

temevvüç fluctuation; ~ **etm. 1.** to fluctuate; **2.** to swell, to heave.

temeyyüz standing out, becoming distinguished; ~ **etm.** to stand out, to become distinguished.

temhir [ī] sealing up; ~ **etm.** to seal up, to padlock (*a place*).

temin [- -] **1.** assurance; **2.** procurement; ~ **etm. 1.** to assure, to ensure; **2.** to secure, to achieve, to bring about; **3.** to obtain, to procure, to get.

teminat, -tı [- . -.] **1.** guarantee, guaranty; **2.** assurance.

teminatlı [- . - .] guaranteed, secured.

teminatsız unsecured, insecure.

temiz 1. clean; **2.** fresh (*air*); **3.** *fig.* decent, clean-living; chaste, virtuous; **4.** net (*amount of money*); **5.** *sl.* poker; ~ **çevirmek** *sl.* to play poker; ~ **hava almak** to get some fresh air; ~ **pak** spotlessly clean; ~ **raporu** clean bill of health; ~ **süt emmiş** F decent, trustworthy; **-e çekmek** to make a fair copy (-*i* of); **-e çıkarmak** (*b-ni*) to put *s.o.* in the clear, to clear *s.o.*, to exonerate *s.o.*; **-e çıkmak** to be in the clear, to be cleared (*or* exonerated); **-e havale etm.** *sl.* **1.** to finish in a jiffy; **2.** to kill, to bump off; **3.** to eat up, to polish off, to put away (*food*).

temizkan 1. arterial blood; **2.** purebred, pedigree (*animal*).

temizlemek 1. to clean, to purify; **2.** to clean, to gut, to dress (*fish, etc.*) **3.** F to finish; **4.** F to eat up, to put away, to polish off (*food*); **5.** *sl.* to clean out, to rob; **6.** *sl.* to kill, to bump off, to put away, to polish off.

temizlenmek 1. *pass. of* **temizlemek**; **2.** to clean o.s. (up).

temizleyici 1. cleanser, purificant; **2.** dry cleaner; **3.** cleaner.

temizlik 1. cleanliness; **2.** purity, pureness; **3.** purification; ~ **işleri** street-cleaning, scavenging; ~ **yapmak** to do the cleaning, to clean.

temizlikçi charwoman, cleaning woman; cleaner.

temkin [ī] **1.** self-possession, poise; **2.** deliberation, deliberateness.

temkinli [. - .] **1.** self-possessed, poised; **2.** deliberate.

temlik, -ki [ī] JUR alienation, transferral (*of a property, right*); **~ edilemeyen haklaı** JUR unassignable rights; **~ etm.** to alienate, to transfer, to convey (*property, etc.*).

temmuz July.

tempo [x .] MUS tempo, time; **~ tutmak** to keep (*or* beat) time.

temren arrowhead; spearhead.

temrin [ī] **1.** practice; **2.** exercise.

temriye BOT, MED lichen.

temsil [ī] **1.** representation; **2.** THEAT performance; **3.** analogy, comparison; **4.** BIOL assimilation; **5.** P for example; **~ etm. 1.** to represent; **2.** THEAT to perform, to put on; **3.** BIOL to assimilate.

temsilci representative, agent.

temsilcilik representation.

temsili [. - -] **1.** representative; **2.** imaginative; **3.** composite; **~ hükümet** POL government by representation.

temyiz [ī] **1.** discernment, distinguishing; **2.** JUR appeal; **~ etm. 1.** to discern, to distinguish, to recognize; **2.** JUR to appeal (*a case*); **~ kudreti** JUR power of discernment; **~ mahkemesi** court of appeal.

ten 1. complexion; **2.** flesh, skin; **3.** body; **~ fanilası** undershirt.

tenafür [ā] cacophony.

tenakus [ā] decrease, diminution; **~ etm.** to decrease, to diminish.

tenakuz [ā] LOG contradiction.

tenasüh [ā] transmigration of souls, metempsychosis.

tenasül [ā] procreation, generation, reproduction; **~ aletleri** genitals, genitalia.

tenasüp, -bü [ā] **1.** proportion; **2.** symmetry.

tencere [x . .] saucepot, saucepan, stewpot, stewpan; **~ dibin kara, seninki benden kara** the pot calling the kettle black; **~ yuvarlanmış, kapağını bulmuş** birds of a feather flock together.

tender [x .] RAIL tender.

tendürüst, -tü robust (*person*).

teneffüs 1. respiration; **2.** recess, break (*in a school*); **~ etm.** to breathe, to respire.

teneke 1. tin, tinplate; **2.** can, canister;

~ çalmak (*arkasından*) *fig.* to boo s.o., to jeer at s.o.; **~ kaplamak** to tin; **~ mahallesi** shantytown, favela; **-sini eline vermek** F to fire s.o., to give s.o. the boot.

tenekeci tinsmith, tinman, tinner.

tenekecilik tinsmithery.

teneşir wooden bench on which a corpse is washed; **~ kargası** *fig.* bag of bones; **-e gelmek** *fig.* to kick the bucket, to die, to croak.

teneşirlik 1. place for washing corpses; **2.** *sl.* about to die, at death's door.

tenevvü, -üü variety, diversity; **~ etm.** to vary.

tenevvür enlightenment; **~ etm.** to become lit (*or* enlightened).

tenezzüh excursion, outing, promenade; **~ gemisi** cruise ship.

tenezzül condescension; **~ buyurmak** to be so kind as to; **~ etm. 1.** to condescend (*-e* to), to deign (*-e* to); **2.** (*for prices*) to go down, to fall.

tenfiz [ī] JUR execution, implementation (*of a court order*); enforcement (*of a law*); **~ etm.** to carry out, to execute, to implement (*a court order*); to enforce (*a law*).

tenha [ā] lonely, solitary, unfrequented, uncrowded, isolated.

tenhalaşmak [ā] to become empty.

tenhalık [ā] **1.** loneliness, solitude, isolation; **2.** lonely (*or* solitary) place.

tenis [x .] tennis; **~ kortu** tennis court; **~ raketi** tennis racket; **~ topu** tennis ball.

tenisçi tennis player.

tenkıye 1. enema, cyster; **2.** enemator.

tenkil [ī] getting rid of, doing away with; **~ etm.** to get rid of, to do away with.

tenkit¹ 1. criticism; **2.** (critical) review, critique; **~ etm. 1.** to criticize; **2.** to write a critical review (*-i* of), to review.

tenkit², -ti [ī] punctuation; **~ etm.** to punctuate.

tenkitçi 1. critic, reviewer; **2.** critic, faultfinder; **3.** critical, censorious (*person*).

tenor MUS tenor.

tenperver fond of comfort.

tenrengi, -ni flesh-colo(u)red, flesh-pink.

tensel 1. fleshly, bodily; **2.** material, corporeal.

tensik, -kı 1. putting in order; reorgan-

terbiye

ization; **2.** MIL regroupment (of troops); ~ **etm. 1.** to put in order; to reorganize; **2.** MIL to regroup (troops).

tensip, -bi [ī] seeing fit; ~ **etm.** to see fit.

tente [x .] awning.

tenteli [x . .] awninged.

tentene [x . .] lace.

tentür tincture.

tentürdiyot tincture of iodine.

tenvir [ī] **1.** illumination; **2.** fig. enlightenment; ~ **etm. 1.** to illuminate, to light; **2.** fig. to enlighten, to inform.

tenvirat, -tı [. - -] illumination; ~ **resmi** municipal tax imposed on citizens living in areas illuminated at night by streetlights.

tenya [x .] ZOO tapeworm, tenia.

tenzil [ī] **1.** lowering; **2.** reduction, decrease; ~ **etm. 1.** to lower; **2. to** reduce, to decrease.

tenzilat, -tı [. - -] reduction (of prices); ~ **yapmak** to make a reduction in price.

tenzilatlı reduced, discount (price); ~ **satış** sale.

teokrasi theocracy.

teoloji theology.

teorem MATH theorem.

teori theory.

teorik theoretic(al).

tepe 1. hill; **2.** top; **3.** crest, crown (of a bird); **4.** MATH vertex; **-den bakmak** to look down (-e on), to look down one's nose (-e at), to despise; **-den inme 1.** unexpected, sudden; **2.** from above, coming from one of the big guns; **-den tırnağa kadar** from head to toe (or foot), cap-a-pie; **-si aşağı gitmek** fig. to go downhill, to hit the skids, to fall flat on one's face; **-si atmak** to lose one's temper, to blow one's stack, to fly off the handle, to blow one's top; **-sinden kaynar su dökülmek** fig. to be left aghast, to be stunned; **-sine binmek** fig. to bedevil, to bug to death.

tepecamı, -nı skylight; bull's-eye.

tepecik hillock.

tepegöz 1. low-browed; **2.** ZOO cyclops.

tepeleme 1. vn. of **tepelemek**; **2.** heaping portion of, heap of.

tepelemek 1. to give s.o. a severe beating, to wallop; **2.** to clobber; **3.** to kill.

tepeli crested (bird).

tepetaklak 1. headlong, headfirst; **2.** upside down.

tephir [ī] vaporization, evaporation; ~ **etm.** to vaporize, to evaporate.

tephirhane [. - - .] fumigator; fumatorium.

tepinmek 1. to stamp; **2.** to kick and stamp; **3.** to jump for joy.

tepişmek 1. to kick at each other; **2.** fig. to push and shove.

tepke reflex.

tepki 1. reaction; response; **2.** recoil (of a firearm); ~ **göstermek** to react.

tepkili reactive; ~ **motor** reaction engine (or motor); ~ **uçak** jet (plane).

tepkime reaction (a. CHEM).

tepkimek to react (a. CHEM).

tepkisiz unreactive, inert.

tepme 1. vn. of **tepmek**; **2.** kick.

tepmek, (-er) 1. to kick; **2.** to turn down, to reject, to decline, to throw away (an opportunity, etc.); **3.** to recoil, to kick (gun); **4.** to tread on, to trample; **5.** to crop up again, to recur; **tepe tepe kullanmak** to use as roughly as one pleases.

tepsi tray.

ter sweat, perspiration; ~ **alıştırmak** to cool off a little, to rest a bit; ~ **basmak** to break out in a sweat; ~ **boşanmak** to sweat like a pig; ~ **dökmek** to sweat (a. fig.), to perspire; **-e batmak** to be covered with sweat; **-e yatmak** to make o.s. sweat; **-ini soğutmak** to cool off, to rest a bit.

terakki [ī] progress, advance(ment); ~ **etm.** to progress, to advance.

terakkiperver [ī] **1.** progressive; **2.** progressive-minded.

teraküm [ā] collection, accumulation; ~ **etm.** to collect, to accumulate, to gather.

terane [ā] **1.** melody, air, tune; **2.** fig. same old story, tired old refrain.

terapi therapy.

teras terrace; ~ **katı** penthouse.

teravi [. - -] prayer special to the nights of Ramazan.

terazi [ā] **1.** balance, scales; **2.** ♀AST Libra; ~ **gözü** pan (or scale) of a balance.

terbıyık youth whose moustache has just begun to sprout.

terbi, -ii [ī] AST quarter (of the moon); ~ **etm.** MATH to quadruple.

terbiye 1. (good) manners; **2.** education, training (of a person); **3.** taming, training (of an animal); **4.** seasoning for food; sauce; **5.** rein (of a horse);

~ **etm. 1.** to teach s.o. good manners; **2.** to train, to educate; **3.** to train, to tame (an animal); ~ **görmek** to be trained (or educated); **-sini bozmak** to forget one's manners, to be rude; **-sini vermek** (b-nin) to give s.o. a dressing down.

terbiyeci 1. educator, educationist; **2.** trainer, tamer.

terbiyeli 1. well-mannered, polite, courteous, well-bred; **2.** flavo(u)red (with a sauce).

terbiyesiz ill-mannered, impolite, unmannerly, rude, discourteous, unmannered.

terbiyesizlik impoliteness, rudeness, unmannerliness; ~ **etm.** to behave rudely, to be impolite.

terbiyevi [. . . . -] educational, educative; pedagogic(al).

tercih [ī] preference; ~ **etm.** to prefer.

tercihen [ī] by preference, preferably.

tercüman interpreter, translator.

tercümanlık interpretership; ~ **yapmak** to interpret; to be an interpreter.

tercüme translation; ~ **etm.** to translate.

tercümeihal, -li [ā] biography.

tere BOT cress.

terebentin turpentine.

tereci seller of cress; **-ye tere satmak** to try to teach one's grandmother to suck eggs, to carry coals to Newcastle.

tereddi [ī] degeneration, decline; ~ **etm.** to degenerate, to decline.

tereddüt, -dü hesitation, indecision; ~ **etm.** to hesitate; to falter, to waver.

tereddütlü hesitant; indecisive.

tereddütsüz unhesitant.

terek P shelf.

tereke estate.

terekküp, -bü 1. composition; **2.** formation; ~ **etm.** to be composed (-den of).

terelelli [. . x .] F crazy, nutty.

terementi [. . x .] turpentine, resin; ~ **ağacı** BOT turpentine tree.

teres 1. son of a bitch, bastard; **2.** procurer, pimp, pander.

teressüp, -bü being incumbent, on, falling to; ~ **etm.** to be incumbent (-e on), to fall (-e to).

tereyağı, -nı 1. butter; **2.** sl. stupid (person); **-ndan kıl çeker gibi** as easy as taking candy from a baby, as easy as falling off a log.

terfi, -ii [ī] promotion; ~ **etm.** to be promoted; ~ **ettirmek** to promote.

terfian [ī] by way of promotion.

terfih [ī] making prosperous; ~ **etm.** to make prosperous, to bring prosperity to.

terfik, -kı [ī] sending s.o. alongside another as an escort; ~ **etm.** to send s.o. alongside another as an escort.

terhin [ī] pawning, hocking; ~ **etm.** to pawn, to hock.

terhis [ī] MIL discharge, demobilization; ~ **etm.** to discharge, to demobilize; ~ **olm.** to be discharged (or demobilized), to get demobbed; ~ **tezkeresi** discharge (certificate).

terilen terylene.

terim term (a. MATH, LOG).

terimsel terminological.

terk, -ki abandonment, desertion; ~ **etm.** to abandon, to leave, to quit; to desert; to forsake; **terki hayat etm.** to die, to depart this life.

terki 1. the back part of a saddle; **2.** croup (of a horse); **-sine almak** to sit s.o. behind him.

terkibi [. - -] synthetic(al).

terkip, -bi [ī] **1.** combination; **2.** CHEM, PHLS synthesis; **3.** compound, union; **4.** CHEM compound; ~ **etm. 1.** to compound, to put together; to combine; **2.** CHEM, PHLS to synthesize.

terlemek 1. to sweat, to perspire; **2.** (for a window) to fog (or steam) up; **3.** (for one's moustache) to sprout; **4.** fig. to work hard, to sweat.

terli sweaty, perspiry.

terlik slipper, scuff.

termal, -li thermal.

termik PHYS, CHEM thermic, thermal; ~ **santral** thermoelectric power plant.

terminal, -li terminal.

terminoloji terminology.

terminüs terminus.

termoelektrik 1. thermoelectricity; **2.** thermoelectric(al).

termofor hot-water bottle.

termokimya thermochemistry.

termometre thermometer.

termonükleer thermonuclear.

termos [x .] thermos (bottle), vacuum bottle.

termosfer thermosphere.

termosifon 1. hot-water heater; **2.** thermosiphon.

termostat, -tı thermostat.
terör terror.
terörist, -ti terrorist.
terörizm terrorism.
ters 1. back reverse; converse; inverse, opposite; **2.** blunt edge (*of a cutting implement*); **3.** inverted, turned inside out; **4.** MATH opposite (*angle*); **5.** P feces, excrement; **6.** wrong, opposite (*road, direction*); **7.** *fig.* bad-tempered, peevish, ornery, cantankerous, cross-grained; **8.** sharp, curt, brusque; cross (*answer, word*); **9.** backwards, in the opposite direction; **10.** sharply, curtly, brusquely; **~ anlamak** to misunderstand, to misinterpret; **~ bakmak** to leer (*-e* at); **~ düşmek** to run counter (*-e* to), to go against; **~ gitmek** to go wrong, to turn out badly; **~ tarafından kalkmak** *fig.* to get out of bed on the wrong side; **~~ bakmak** to look daggers (*-e* at); **-i dönmek** to lose one's bearings.
tersane [ā] shipyard.
tersine on the contrary.
terslemek 1. (*b-ni*) to snap at *s.o.*, to bite *s.o.*'s head off; **2.** to dung.
terslenmek 1. *pass.* of **terslemek; 2.** to growl (*-e* at), to be short (*-e* with), to talk sharply (*-e* to).
terslik 1. hitch, set-back; **2.** ill-temperedness, peevishness.
tersyüz: ~ etm. to turn inside out.
tertemiz [x . .] spotless, spotlessly clean.
tertibat, -tı [. - -] **1.** arrangement, setup; **2.** mechanism, apparatus; **3.** MIL disposition (*of troops, etc.*); **~ almak** to take measures.
tertip, -bi [ī] **1.** arrangement, setup; contrivance; **2.** MIL disposition (*of troops, etc.*) **3.** TYP typesetting; **4.** MED recipe, prescription; **5.** MATH ordinate; **~ etm. 1.** to arrange, to set up, to organize, to contrive; **2.** MIL to dispose (*troops, etc.*); **3.** TYP to typeset.
tertipçi 1. arranger, planner; **2.** TYP typesetter.
tertiplemek to arrange, to set up, to organize, to contrive, to plan.
tertipleyici organizer, arranger, planner, contriver.
tertipli tidy, neat, orderly; organized.
tertipsiz untidy, messy; disorganized.
tertipsizlik untidiness, messiness; disorganization.
terütaze [ā] very fresh.

terviç, -ci [ī] supporting (*an idea*); **~ etm.** to support, to advocate (*an idea*).
terzi 1. tailor, dressmaker; **2.** tailor's shop.
terzihane [ā] tailor's shop.
terzil [ī] disgracing; **~ etm.** to disgrace.
terzilik tailorship, tailory.
tesadüf [ā] **1.** chance event, accident; happenstance; coincidence; **2.** chance, hazard; **~ etm. 1.** to meet by chance, to chance upon, to come across, to come upon, to happen upon; **2.** to coincide with.
tesadüfen [ā] [. x . .] by chance, by accident, by coincidence, coincidentally.
tesadüfi [. - . -] accidental, chance, casual, fortuitous, coincidental.
tesahup, -bu [ā] **1.** claiming to be the owner of; **2.** protection; **~ etm. 1.** to claim to be the owner (*-e* of). **2.** to protect.
tesanüt, -dü [ā] solidarity.
tesbit *s.* **tespit.**
tescil [ī] registration; **~ etm.** to register.
tescilli [ī] registered; **~ marka** registered trademark.
teselli [ī] consolation, comfort, solace; **~ etm.** (*or* **vermek**) to console, to comfort, to give consolation; **~ mükâfatı** consolation prize.
tesellüm receiving; taking delivery; **~ etm.** to receive; to receive a consignment of (*goods*); to take delivery on (*a shipment*).
teselsül concatenation; chain; **~ etm.** to continue without interruption.
teshil [ī] facilitation; **~ etm.** to facilitate.
teshin [ī] heating; warming; **~ etm.** to heat; to warm.
teshir [ī] bewitching, charming, enchanting; **~ etm.** to bewitch, to charm, to enchant.
tesir [- -] effect, influence; impression; **~ etm.** to affect, to act upon; to influence, to make an impression (*-e* on).
tesirli [- . .] effective, effectual, efficacious; impressive.
tesirsiz ineffective, ineffectual, inefficacious.
tesis [- -] **1.** foundation, establishment; **2.** institution, association, establishment, foundation; **3.** facility; **4.** installation, system; **~ etm.** to found,

to set up, to establish; to institute.

tesisat, *-tı* [- . -] **1.** installation; **2.** institutions, establishments, foundations; **3.** facilities.

tesisatçı installer.

tesit, *-di* [ī] celebration; ~ *etm.* to celebrate.

teskere [x . .] **1.** *obs.* stretcher, litter; **2.** handbarrow.

teskereci stretcher-bearer (*a.* MIL).

teskin [ī] tranquilization; ~ *etm.* to tranquilize, to calm, to allay, to pacify.

teslih [ī] armament; ~ *etm.* to arm.

teslihat, *-tı* [. - -] **1.** armament; **2.** armaments, arms, weaponry.

teslim [ī] **1.** delivery; **2.** submission, surrender, capitulation; **3.** concession; **4.** surrender!, give up!; ~ *almak* **1.** to take delivery of, to receive; **2.** MIL to possess, to seize control of (*a place*); ~ *bayrağı çekmek* F to strike one's flag, to throw in the sponge; ~ *etm.* **1.** to deliver, to hand over; **2.** to surrender; **3.** to admit, to concede; ~ *olm.* to give in, to yield, to submit, to surrender; ~ *ve tesellüm* delivery and receipt.

teslimat, *-tı* [. - -] goods delivered, deliveries.

teslimiyet, *-ti* [. - . . .] submission; ~ *göstermek* to submit (*-e* to).

tesmiye naming; ~ *etm.* to name.

tespih prayer beads, rosary; ~ *çekmek* to tell one's beads.

tespihböceği, *-ni* ZOO wood louse, sow bug.

tespit, *-ti* determination, fixation; stabilization; ~ *banyosu* PHOT fixing bath; ~ *davası* JUR declaratory action; ~ *etm.* **1.** to fix; **2.** to establish, to determine; **3.** to fix, to set (*prices*).

tesri, *-li* [ī] acceleration, speeding up; ~ *etm.* to accelerate, to speed up.

test, *-ti* test.

testere [x . .] saw.

testerebalığı, *-nı* ZOO sawfish.

testi pitcher, jug.

tesviye 1. smoothing, flattening, leveling; **2.** paying (*a debt*); **3.** pass (*given to travel(l)ing soldiers*); ~ *aleti* level; ~ *etm.* **1.** to smooth, to level, to flatten, to grade, to even, to plane; **2.** to pay (*a debt*).

tesviyeci (pipe) fitter.

tesviyeruhu, *-nu* (spirit) level.

teşbih [ī] **1.** *lit.* simile; **2.** comparison; ~ *etm.* to compare; *-te hata olmaz* (*or*

olmasın)*!* pardon the crude expression!

teşdit, *-di* [ī] **1.** intensification; **2.** harshening; ~ *etm.* **1.** to intensify; **2.** to harshen.

teşebbüs 1. enterprise, undertaking, attempt; **2.** initiative, enterprise; ~ *etm.* to undertake, to set about, to enter upon, to attempt; *-e geçmek* to set about, to set to; *-ü ele almak* to take the initiative.

teşekkül 1. formation; **2.** consisting of, being made up of; **3.** organization, unit, body, group; ~ *etm.* **1.** to be formed; to take shape; **2.** to consist (*-den* of), to be made up (*-den* of).

teşekkür thanking; ~ *ederim!* thank you!; ~ *etm.* to thank.

teşekkürname [ā] letter of thanks.

teşerrüf being hono(u)red; ~ *etm.* **1.** to be hono(u)red; **2.** to feel hono(u)red to meet s.o., to have the hono(u)r of meeting s.o.

tesevvüş confusion.

teşhir [ī] **1.** display, exhibition; **2.** *fig.* pillorying; ~ *etm.* **1.** to display, to exhibit, to expose; **2.** *fig.* to pillory.

teşhis [ī] **1.** MED diagnosis; **2.** recognition, identification; **3.** *lit.* personification; ~ *etm.* **1.** MED to diagnose; **2.** to recognize, to identify; ~ *koymak* MED to diagnose.

teşkil [ī] formation; ~ *etm.* to form; to constitute.

teşkilat, *-tı* organization; *teşkilatı esasiye kanunu* JUR constitution.

teşkilatçı organizer.

teşkilatçılık organizing.

teşkilatlandırmak to organize.

teşkilatlanmak to be organized.

teşkilatlı organized.

teşkilatsız unorganized.

teşne thirsty (*a. fig.*); ~ *olm.* (*bşe*) *fig.* to thirst for *s.th.*

teşrif [ī] **1.** visit; **2.** hono(u)ring; **3.** going to; ~ *etm.* (*or buyurmak*) **1.** to visit, to hono(u)r; **2.** to go (*-e* to); ~ *nereye?* where are you going?

teşrifat, *-tı* [. - -] **1.** protocol; **2.** formality, ceremonial.

teşrifatçı 1. master of ceremonies; **2.** protocolist.

teşrih [ī] **1.** MED dissection; **2.** anatomy; **3.** P skeleton; ~ *etm.* to dissect.

teşrihhane [. - - .] dissecting room.

teşrii [. - -] legislative; ~ *kuvvet* legislative power; ~ *masuniyet* legislative immunity.

teşrik, -ki [ī] making s.o. a partner; ~ **etm.** (*b-ni*) to make *s.o.* a partner (*-e* in).

teşrikimesal [. - . . - -] cooperation; collaboration; ~ **etm.** to cooperate (*ile* with), to collaborate (*ile* with).

teşrinievvel [. - . . .] *obs.* October.

teşrinisani [. - . - -] *obs.* November.

teşvik, -ki 1. encouragement; **2.** incitement, provocation; ~ **etm. 1.** to encourage, to spur on, to inspire; **2.** to incite, to provoke.

teşviş confusing; ~ **etm.** to confuse.

teşyi [ī] seeing s.o. off; ~ **etm.** (*b-ni*) to see *s.o.* off.

tetabuk, -ku [ā] agreement; coincidence; correspondence; ~ **etm.** to be in harmony (*ile* with), to agree (*ile* with), to coincide (*ile* with).

tetanos [x . .] MED tetanus, lockjaw.

tetebbu, -uu investigation, research; ~ **etm.** to investigate, to research.

tetik 1. trigger (*of a gun*); **2.** alert, vigilant; **3.** delicate; ~ **davranmak** to act quickly; **tetiğini bozmamak** to keep one's cool, to keep a cool head; **-te olm.** to be on the alert, to be on the qui vive.

tetkik, -ki [ī] investigation, examination; scrutiny; ~ **etm.** to investigate, to examine; to scrutinize.

tetkikat, -tı [. - -] investigations, examinations; scrutinies.

tevafuk, -ku [ā] accordance; ~ **etm.** to accord (*-e* with), to agree (*-e* with).

tevakkuf 1. stopping; pausing; sojourning; **2.** depending on; ~ **etm. 1.** to stop; to pause; to sojourn, to stay; **2.** to depend (*-e* on), to be subject (*-e* to).

tevali [. - -] **1.** succession, sequence; **2.** continuation; ~ **etm.** to continue without letup.

tevarüs [ā] inheriting; ~ **etm.** to inherit.

tevazu, -uu [ā] humility, humbleness; modesty; ~ **göstermek** to behave humbly.

tevazün [ā] balance, equilibrium; ~ **etm.** to be balanced, to be in equilibrium.

tevbih [ī] reprimand; ~ **etm.** to reprimand.

tevcih [ī] **1.** turning towards; **2.** pointing, aiming, directing; **3.** bestowing, conferring; ~ **etm. 1.** to turn (*-e* to-

wards); **2.** to point (*-e* at), to aim (*-e* at), to direct (*-e* to); **3.** to bestow, to confer, to grant.

tevdi, -ii [ī] entrusting, consigning; depositing; ~ **etm. 1.** to entrust, to consign, to commit; to confide; **2.** to deposit (*money*).

tevdiat, -tı [. - -] deposits; **-ta bulunmak** to make a deposit, to deposit some money in (*a bank*).

teveccüh 1. kindness, consideration, favo(u)r; **2.** directing one's attention to; ~ **etm. 1.** to be directed (*-e* toward); **2.** to betake o.s. (*-e* to); ~ **göstermek** to show kindness (*-e* to); **-ünü kazanmak** (*b-nin*) to win favo(u)r in *s.o.'s* eyes; **-ünüz efendim!** that's very kind of you!

tevehhüm imagining; ~ **etm.** to imagine.

tevekkel P happy-go-lucky.

tevekkeli F for no reason, for nothing; ~ **değil** it is not just a matter of chance that …

tevekkül resignation; ~ **etm. 1.** to put o.s. in God's hands; **2.** to resign o.s. to one's fate.

tevellüt, -dü 1. birth; **2.** date of birth.

tevellütlü born in …

tevessü, -üü expansion, enlargement; spreading; ~ **etm.** to widen, to expand, to enlarge; to spread.

tevessül 1. having recourse to; **2.** undertaking, attempting; ~ **etm. 1.** to have recourse (*-e* to); **2.** to undertake, to attempt.

tevettür tension.

tevfik, -ki [ī] **1.** divine guidance and assistance; **2.** adaptation; **3.** ♀ [- .] *mf.*

tevfikan [- . .] in accordance (*-e* with), in conformity (*-e* to).

tevhit, -di [ī] **1.** unification; combination; **2.** monotheism; ~ **etm.** to unify, to unite; to combine.

tevil [- -] forced interpretation; ~ **etm.** to misinterpret intentionally.

tevkif [ī] **1.** arrest; custody, detention; **2.** stopping, halting; ~ **etm. 1.** to arrest, to take into custody, to take under detention; **2.** to stop, to halt; to detain; ~ **müzekkeresi** JUR warrant of arrest.

tevkifhane [. - - .] gaol, *Am.* jail, lock-up.

tevkil [ī] making s.o. one's proxy; ~ **etm.** (*b-ni*) to make *s.o.* one's proxy.

tevlit, -di [ī] **1.** giving birth to (*a child*);

2. *fig.* producing, bringing about; ~ **etm. 1.** to give birth to (*a child*); **2.** *fig.* to produce, to bring about.

tevliyet, -ti trusteeship of a *vakıf*.

Tevrat, -tı [ā] *pr. n.* **1.** the Torah; **2.** the Old Testament.

tevsi, -ii [ī] extension, enlargement; ~ **etm.** to widen, to enlarge, to extend, to expand.

tevsik, -ki [ī] documentation; ~ **etm.** to document.

tevzi, -ii [ī] **1.** distribution; **2.** delivery (*of letters, etc.*); ~ **etm. 1.** to distribute; **2.** to deliver (*letters, etc.*).

tevziat, -tı [. - -] **1.** distributions; **2.** deliveries.

teyakkuz vigilance; circumspection; ~ **etm.** to be vigilant.

teyel basting.

teyellemek to baste, to tack.

teyelli basted, tacked.

teyit, -di [- -] **1.** strengthening; **2.** confirmation, corroboration; ~ **etm. 1.** to strengthen; **2.** to confirm, to corroborate.

teyp tape recorder; *-e almak* to tape, to tape-record.

teyze maternal aunt.

tez[1] **1.** quick, speedy; **2.** quickly, speedily; ~ *beri* P easily; ~ *canlı* impetuous, precipitate; ~ *elden* without delay, quickly; ~ *olm.* to hurry (up).

tez[2] thesis.

tezahür [ā] **1.** appearing; **2.** sign, manifestation; ~ **etm.** to appear, to become visible.

tezahürat, -tı [. - . -] **1.** cheering; ovation; applause; **2.** demonstration; **3.** signs, manifestations; ~ *yapmak* to cheer (*-e* for), to root (*-e* for).

tezat, -dı [ā] **1.** contrast; oppositeness; **2.** contradiction; *-a düşmek* to contradict o.s.

tezayüt, -dü [ā] increase; ~ **etm.** to increase.

tezebzüp, -bü 1. disorder, confusion; **2.** indecision, vacillation.

tezek dried dung.

tezelzül shaking; ~ **etm.** to shake, to quake.

tezene P plectrum, pick.

tezgâh 1. counter; **2.** workbench; **3.** loom; **4.** stocks, ways, shipway; ~ *başı yapmak* F to stand at the bar and have a drink; *-ından geçmek* sl. (*for a woman*) to have sex with, to go to bed with.

tezgâhlamak to concoct, to cook up, to plan.

tezgâhtar shop assistant, *Am.* (sales) clerk, salesman, saleswoman, shopgirl, *Am.* salesgirl.

tezgâhtarlık clerking; ~ **etm.** to clerk.

tezhip, -bi [ī] gilding; ~ **etm.** to gild.

tezkere [x . .] **1.** message, note; **2.** MIL discharge papers; **3.** permit; license; *-sini eline vermek* fig. to fire, to give s.o. his walking papers.

tezkereci MIL discharged soldier.

tezkiye 1. purification; **2.** praise.

tezlemek P to speed up.

tezlenmek 1. *pass. of* **tezlemek**; **2.** to hurry, to hasten.

tezlik 1. quickness, speed, haste; **2.** impatience, impetuosity.

tevzir [ī] **1.** malicious misrepresentation; **2.** trickery, deceit.

tezyin [ī] ornamentation, embellishment, decoration; ~ **etm.** to adorn, to embellish, to ornament.

tezyinat, -tı [. - -] adornments, ornamentations, decorations.

tezyini [. - -] ornamental, decorative.

THY (*abbr. for* **Türk Hava Yolları**) Turkish Airlines.

tıbben medically, from a medical point of view.

tıbbi [ī] medical.

tıbbiye medical school, school of medicine.

tıbbiyeli medical student.

tıfıl, -flı child.

tığ 1. crochet-hook; **2.** awl; **3.** plane iron; ~ *gibi* wiry.

tığlamak 1. to lance (*a wound*); **2.** to pierce with a needle; **3.** to slaughter (*animal*); **4.** sl. to stab, to knife, to bayonet.

tığmak, (-ar) sl. to make o.s. scarce, to split.

tıka basa as full as possible, crammed full; ~ *yemek* to make a pig of o.s.

tıkaç, -cı plug, stopper; gag.

tıkalı stopped (up); clogged, congested.

tıkamak to plug, to stop; to clog, to congest.

tıkanık stopped (up); clogged, congested.

tıkanıklık stoppage; cloggage, congestion.

tıkanmak 1. *pass. of* **tıkamak**; **2.** to gasp for breath; **3.** to lose one's appetite.

tıkılmak 1. *pass. of* **tıkmak**; **2.** to jump

into (*a place*).

tıkınmak F to cram it in, to pack it away, to tuck in.

tıkır: ~ ~ like clockwork; **-ında gitmek** to go like clockwork.

tıkırdamak to rattle, to clink.

tıkırtı rattle, click, clack, tap.

tıkışık crammed, squeezed.

tıkışıklık crowdedness.

tıkışmak (*for people*) to cram (*or* squeeze) themselves into (*a place*).

tıkıştırmak 1. to cram, to squeeze, to jam; **2.** to bolt down (*food*).

tıkız 1. hard, too tightly stuffed; **2.** underdone, undercooked (*bread*).

tıklım tıklım very crowded, jammed, packed; ~ **dolu** jam-packed.

tıkmak, **(-ar)** to cram, to jam, to thrust, to stick (**-e** into).

tıknaz plump, dumpy.

tıknefes 1. short of breath, short-winded, pursy; **2.** shortness of breath.

tıksırık sneeze (*made with one's mouth shut*).

tıksırmak to sneeze (*with one's mouth shut*).

tılsım talisman, charm, amulet.

tılsımlı enchanted.

tımar 1. grooming (*a horse*); **2.** dressing (*of wounds*); **3.** pruning (*of trees*); **4.** HIST fief; ~ **etm.** to groom, to curry.

tımarhane [. . - .] insane asylum, nut house, bughouse; ~ **kaçkını** fig. nut, kook.

tımarlamak to groom, to curry.

tımarlı groomed (*horse*).

tın tın sl. dim-witted.

tınaz haystack.

tıngadak [x . .] with a metallic clang.

tıngır 1. clanging sound; **2.** sl. penniless, flat broke; **3.** sl. money, tin, dough.

tıngırdamak 1. to rattle, to clang; **2.** sl. to die, to croak, to peg out.

tıngırdatmak to thrum, to strum, to twang (*a stringed instrument*).

tıngır mıngır 1. with a clanging sound; **2.** slowly.

tıngırtı clang, rattle.

tıngır tıngır 1. with a clanging sound; **2.** completely empty.

tınlamak to resound, to resonate, to ring, to clink.

tınmak to make a sound.

tınmamak fig. to take no notice (**-e** of).

tınnet, **-ti** tone, timbre.

tıp, **-bbı** medicine, medical science.

tıpa stopper, cork.

tıpatıp [x . .] perfectly, exactly.

tıpırdamak 1. to patter; **2.** to go pit-a--pat.

tıpırtı (pitter-)patter.

tıpır tıpır 1. with a pattering sound; **2.** pit-a-pat.

tıpış tıpış: ~ **gitmek** (*or* **yürümek**) to patter, to toddle.

tıpkı [x .] **1.** just like, in just the same way as; **2.** spitting image; ~ **-sına** exactly like.

tıpkıbasım facsimile.

tıp tıp pit-a-pat.

tırabzan stair rail(ing), banister; ~ **babası 1.** newel; **2.** fig. ineffectual father.

tırak bang; ~ **diye** with a bang.

tıraş 1. shave, shaving; **2.** haircut; **3.** sl. pulling s.o.'s leg, having s.o. on; **4.** sl. boring talk, palaver; ~ **bıçağı** razorblade; ~ **etm. 1.** to shave; **2.** to cut (*hair*); **3.** sl. to pull s.o.'s leg, to have s.o. on; **4.** sl. to talk s.o.'s head off; ~ **fırçası** shaving brush; ~ **kremi** shaving cream; ~ **losyonu** after-shave (lotion); ~ **makinesi 1.** (safety) razor; **2.** electric shaver; ~ **olm. 1.** to shave; **2.** to get (*or* have) a shave; ~ **sabunu** shaving soap; ~ **takımı** shaving things; **-ı gelmek** (*or* **uzamak**) to need a shave.

tıraşlamak 1. to plane, to prune; **2.** sl. to pull s.o.'s leg, to have s.o. on; **3.** sl. to talk s.o.'s head off.

tıraşlı 1. shaved, shaven; **2.** needing a shave.

tıraşsız 1. unshaved, unshaven; **2.** needing a shave.

tırık rattle; ~ **diye** with a rattle.

tırıl sl. **1.** naked; **2.** penniless, stone--broke.

tırıs trot; ~ **gitmek** to trot; **-a kalkmak** to begin to trot.

tırkaz bolt, bar.

tırmalamak 1. to scratch, to claw; **2.** fig. to grate on, to irritate.

tırmanma vn. of **tırmanmak**, ~ **şeridi** MOT climbing lane.

tırmanmak 1. to climb; **2.** to increase, to escalate.

tırmık 1. scratch; **2.** rake.

tırmıklamak 1. to scratch, to claw; **2.** to rake.

tırnak 1. nail; fingernail; toenail; **2.** claw, hoof; **3.** quotation mark, quote, inverted comma; **4.** MEC ratchet, click, pawl; **5.** fluke, palm (of an anchor); ~ **boyası** (or **cilası**) nail varnish, Am. nail polish; ~ **göstermek** fig. to show one's claws; ~ **işareti** quotation mark, quote, inverted comma; ~ **makası** nail scissors; ~ **törpüsü** nail file; ~ **yeri** fingerhold; **-larını yemek** to bite one's nails.

tırnakçı sl. pickpocket.

tırnaklamak to claw, to scratch.

tırpan scythe; ~ **atmak 1.** to kill off, to slay; **2.** to get rid (-e of), to weed out.

tırpanlamak to scythe.

tırtık nick; notch.

tırtıklamak sl. to steal, to nick, to swipe.

tırtıklı 1. nicked; notched; **2.** jaggy, jagged.

tırtıl 1. zoo caterpillar; **2.** caterpillar tread; **3.** serration (on a knife blade); **4.** perforation (of a stamp); **5.** rowel; jagging wheel; **6.** sl. sponger, freeloader.

tırtıllı 1. jagged; serrated; **2.** milled.

tıs hiss; ~ **yok** there is not a sound to be heard.

tıslamak to hiss.

tıynet, -ti nature, character, makeup (of a person).

ti [-] MIL bugle call; ~ **işareti** bugle call; **-ye almak** (b-ni) sl. to make fun of s.o., to poke fun at s.o.

Tibet, -ti pr. n. Tibet.

ticaret, -ti [ā] trade, commerce, traffic; ~ **anlaşması** trade agreement; ~ **ataşesi** commercial attaché; ♀ **Bakanlığı** Ministry of Commerce; ~ **bankası** commercial bank; ~ **borsası** exchange; stock exchange; ~ **filosu** merchant (or mercantile) marine; ~ **gemisi** merchant ship, merchantman; ~ **hukuku** commercial law; ~ **odası** chamber of commerce; ~ **unvanı** trade name (of a firm); ~ **yolu** trade route.

ticaretgâh [ā] centre of commerce, trading centre.

ticarethane [. - . - .] trading establishment, firm, business.

ticari [. - -] commercial, trade.

tifo [x .] MED typhoid fever.

tiftik mohair, angora.

tiftiklenmek to fuzz, to become fuzzy (cloth).

tifüs [x .] MED typhus (fever).

tik, -ki tic.

tiksindirici repugnant, repellent, loathsome.

tiksindirmek to revolt, to fill with disgust.

tiksinmek to be disgusted (-den with), to loathe, to revolt, to abominate, to abhor.

tiksinti revulsion, repugnance, disgust, loathing, abomination.

tilavet, -ti chanting (the Koran); **-le okumak** to chant (the Koran).

tilki 1. zoo fox; **2.** fig. fox, cunning person, slyboots; ~ **gibi** foxy, sly, crafty; **-nin dönüp dolaşıp geleceği yer kürkçü dükkânıdır** pro. at length, the fox is brought to the furrier.

tilkileşmek to get foxy (or crafty).

tim [ī] sports: team.

timbal, -li MUS kettledrum, timbal, tymbal.

timsah zoo crocodile; alligator.

timsal, -li [ā] symbol.

tiner thinner.

tinsel spiritual.

tin tin very quietly; on tiptoe.

tip, -pi 1. type, sort; **2.** unusual, odd; **3.** fig. geezer.

tipi snowstorm, blizzard.

tipik typical.

tipsiz sl. ugly, unattractive.

tipografya letterpress, typography.

tirad s. **tirat**.

tiraj circulation (of a newspaper).

tiramola NAUT tacking; ~ **etm.** to tack.

tirat THEAT tirade.

tirbuşon corkscrew.

tirbuton buttonhook.

tire¹ hyphen; dash.

tire² cotton thread.

tirendaz [- . -] **1.** archer; **2.** fig. skil(l)ful, adroit; **3.** fig. elegant.

tirfil BOT trefoil, clover.

tirfillenmek to become threadbare.

tirfon large screw.

tirhos zoo sardine.

tirildemek to quiver, to shiver, to tremble.

tiril tiril 1. gauzy, filmy, gossamery (cloth); **2.** spotlessly clean.

tirit bread soaked in gravy; ~ **gibi** as old as the hills.

tiriz lath, batten.

tirlin ruling (or drawing) pen.

tiroit, -di ANAT thyroid.

tirpidin small mattock.

tirsi (balığı) zoo shad.

tirşe 1. bluish green; **2.** vellum; parchment.

tir tir titremek to be all of a tremble, to shiver, to quiver, to tremble, to quake.

tiryaki [. - -] addict; **-si olm.** (*bşin*) to be addicted to *s.th.*

tiryakilik [. - . .] addiction.

tişört, -tü T-shirt, tee shirt.

titiz 1. fastidious, hard to please, finicky, picky, pernickety; **2.** particular, choosy; **3.** meticulous.

titizlenmek 1. to become hard to please, to get finicky; **2.** to become particular (*or* choosy); **3.** to become meticulous.

titizlik 1. fastidiousness, persnicketiness; **2.** particularity, choosiness; **3.** meticulousness.

titrek shaky, tremulous.

titremek 1. to shiver, to tremble, to shake, to quake, to quiver; **2.** to flicker (*light*); **3.** to be very afraid (*-den* of).

titreşim 1. PHYS vibration; **2.** MUS vibrato.

titreşimli 1. PHYS vibratory, vibratile; **2.** voiced.

titreşimsiz 1. PHYS vibrationless; **2.** unvoiced.

titreşmek 1. to tremble, to quake, to shake, to quiver; **2.** to vibrate.

tiyatro [. x .] theatre, *Am.* theater.

tiyatrocu [. x . .] **1.** theatre owner; **2.** actor; actress.

tiyatrolaştırmak to dramatize for the stage.

tiz [ī] **1.** shrill; **2.** MUS high(-pitched); sharp.

tizleşmek [ī] **1.** to become shrill; **2.** MUS to sharp.

TL (*abbr. for* **Türk Lirası**) Turkish Lira.

toğrul ZOO goshawk.

tohum 1. seed; **2.** sperm; **3.** fertilized egg; **4.** family, stock; ~ **atmak** to sow; ~ **bağlamak** to go to seed; ~ **ekmek** to sow seed, to seed; **-a kaçmak** to go to seed (*a. fig.*); **-u dökülmek** to reach the menopause.

tohumlamak 1. to inseminate artificially; **2.** to fertilize; **3.** to seed.

tok, -ku 1. full; **2.** thick (*cloth*); **3.** deep (*voice*), ~ **karnına** on a full stomach; ~ **sözlü** blunt; plainspoken, outspoken.

toka¹ [x .] **1.** buckle; **2.** barette (*for the hair*).

toka² [x .] **1.** shaking hands; **2.** clinking glasses; ~ **etm. 1.** to shake hands; **2.** to clink glasses (*while toasting*); **3.** NAUT

to make taut, to draw tight; **4.** *sl.* to pay, to plank down.

tokaç, -cı clothes stick (*used for beating washing*).

tokalaşmak to shake hands.

tokat¹, -tı slap, cuff; ~ **atmak** (*or* **aşketmek** *or* **yapıştırmak**) to slap, to cuff; ~ **yemek** to be slapped.

tokat², -tı sheepfold; pen.

tokatlamak to slap; to cuff.

tokgözlü contented.

toklaşmak (*for a voice*) to deepen.

toklu yearling sheep.

tokluk 1. fullness; **2.** deepness (*of voice*).

tokmak 1. mallet; tamper; beetle; gavel; **2.** knocker (*for a door*); **3.** wooden pestle.

tokmakçı *sl.* gigolo.

tokmaklamak to beat with a mallet; to tamp.

toksik toxic.

toksin toxin.

toktağan constant; ~ **karlar** perennial snow.

tokurdamak to bubble.

tokurtu bubble.

tokuşmak 1. (*for animals*) to butt each other; **2.** to collide.

tokuşturmak 1. *caus. of* **tokuşmak**; **2.** to clink (*glasses*).

tokuz *s.* **tok 2.**

Tokyo *pr. n.* Tokyo.

tokyo thong, flip-flop.

tolerans tolerance (*a.* MEC).

tolga war helmet.

tomak 1. wooden mace; **2.** wooden ball; **3.** a kind of boot.

tomar 1. roll (*of paper, etc.*); **2.** a great deal of, a lot of, a wad of; **3.** rammer.

tombala tombola, lot(t)o; ~ **çekmek** to draw a number (*while playing tombola*).

tombalacı lotto man.

tombalak plump, chubby.

tombaz 1. flat-bottomed barge, lighter; **2.** pontoon, float (*of a pontoon bridge*); ~ **köprü** pontoon bridge.

tombul plump.

tombullaşmak to get plump.

tombulluk plumpness.

tomruk 1. log; **2.** bud (*of a plant*); **3.** ingot (*of cast metal*); **4.** *obs.* gaol, *Am.* jail.

tomson Thompson.

tomurcuk bud.

tomurcuklanmak to bud.

ton[1] ton (= *1000 kg.*); **-la** tons of.

ton[2] tone (*a.* MUS).

tonaj tonnage.

tonalite tonality.

tonbalığı, -nı ZOO tunny.

tonga [x .] *sl.* trick, fast one; **-ya basmak** (*or* **düşmek** *or* **oturmak**) to be duped, to be taken in, to fall for; **-ya bastırmak** to dupe, to con, to trick.

tonik MED tonic.

tonilato [. . x .] NAUT tonnage.

tonlama intonation.

tonoz ARCH vault.

tonton darling, sweet, dear.

top, -pu 1. ball; 2. cannon; 3. roll, bolt (*of cloth*); 4. ream (*of paper*); 5. round(ed); **~ arabası** MIL gun carriage; **~ ateşi** cannon fire; gunfire, artillery fire; **~ çehre** round face; **~ gibi gitmek** to go at once; **~ oynamak** to play football; **~ sakal** full, round beard; **-a tutmak** to bombard; **-u atmak** *sl.* 1. to go bankrupt, to go bust; 2. to flunk a grade, to fail a year; **-u -u** in all, all told, altogether; **-un ağzında** *fig.* at the lion's mouth, on the edge of the volcano.

topaç, -cı 1. (peg) top; teetotum; 2. rounded loom (*of an oar*); 3. round basket; **~ çevirmek** to whip a top; **~ gibi** plump and sturdy (*child*).

topak 1. ball, lump; 2. fetlock; 3. *metall.* pellet.

topaklamak *metall.* to pelletize.

topal lame, crippled; **~ ~ yürümek** to limp.

topallamak to limp.

topallık lameness.

topaltı, -nı terreplein of a fort.

toparlak 1. round; 2. MIL limber.

toparlamak 1. to collect, to gather together; 2. to summarize, to put in a nutshell; 3. to tidy o.s. up, to smarten o.s. up; 4. to tidy, to pick up; 5. to pull (*or get*) o.s. together.

toparlanmak 1. *pass. of* **toparlamak**; 2. to pull o.s. together; to shape up; 3. to recover, to get back on one's feet (*after an illness*).

topatan a kind of melon.

topçeker 1. gunboat; 2. artillery (*animal, vehicle*).

topçu 1. MIL cannoneer; artilleryman; 2. MIL the artillery; 3. *sl.* student who has flunked a grade; **~ sınıfı** MIL the artillery branch; **~ subayı** MIL artillery officer.

topçuluk gunnery.

tophane [ā] HIST 1. cannon foundry, arsenal; 2. artillery school.

toplaç ELECT collector.

toplam MATH total; **~ olarak** in all, all told.

toplama *vn. of* **toplamak**, *part.* MATH addition; **~ işareti** MATH plus sign; **~ kampı** concentration camp; **~ makinesi** adding machine.

toplamak 1. to collect, to gather; 2. MATH to add (up), to total; 3. to pick, to harvest; 4. to accumulate, to amass; 5. to tidy (*or pick*) up, to straighten up; 6. to clear (*the table*); 7. to convene, to convoke; 8. to put on (*or gain*) weight.

toplanmak 1. *pass. of* **toplamak**; 2. to gather, to assemble, to congregate; 3. to shape up; 4. to put on (*or gain*) weight.

toplantı meeting, gathering; **~ salonu** meeting room, assembly hall.

toplardamar ANAT vein.

toplu 1. collected, gathered, assembled; 2. tidy, neat (*place*); 3. plump; 4. collective; 5. F pin; 6. cumulative; **~ konut** housing estate; **~ mezar** mass grave; **~ sigorta** group insurance; **~ tabanca** six-shooter; **~ taşıma** mass transport(ation).

topluca 1. as a group; 2. plumpish.

topluiğne pin.

topluluk 1. group; 2. community; **~ adı** GR collective noun.

toplum society, community.

toplumbilim sociology.

toplumbilimci sociologist.

toplumcu socialist.

toplumdışı extrasocial.

toplumsal social, societal.

toplumsallaştırmak to socialize.

toplusözleşme collective agreement.

topografi topography.

toprak 1. earth, soil; dirt; 2. land; 3. ELECT earth, ground; 4. earthen(ware); 5. unpaved, dirt (*road*); **~ aşınması** GEOL soil erosion; **~ doyursun gözünü!** nothing on earth can satisfy you!; **~ kayması** landslide, slump; **~ reformu** land reform; **~ rengi** earth-colo(u)red; **~ sahibi** landowner; **~ yol** dirt road; **toprağa bakmak** *fig.* to be at death's door, to have one foot in the grave; **toprağa vermek** to bury, to inter, to lay to rest; **toprağı bol ol-**

sun may he rest in peace.

toprakaltı, -nı subsoil, underground.

toprakboya 1. oxide red; **2.** earth colo(u)r.

topraklamak 1. to cover *or* fill with earth; **2.** to dirty; **3.** ELECT to ground.

toptan 1. wholesale; **2.** all at once, all at the same time.

toptancı wholesaler.

toptancılık wholesaling.

topuk 1. heel; **2.** GEOGR bar (*of a river*); **topuğuna basmak** (*b-nin*) *fig.* to be at *s.o.'s* heels; **-larına kadar** up to the ankles.

topuklamak to heel.

topuklu high-heeled (*shoe*).

topuksuz flat-heeled, low-heeled (*shoe*).

toput CHEM deposit.

topuz 1. mace; **2.** bun, knot (*of hair*); **3.** doorknob; **4.** head (*of a walking stick*).

topyekûn 1. in all, all told, altogether; **2.** total, all-out; **~ harp** total war.

tor 1. fine-meshed net; **2.** *fig.* inexperienced, green (*youth*).

toraman 1. sturdy child; **2.** sturdy (*child*).

torba 1. bag, sack; **2.** MED cyst; **3.** ANAT scrotum; **-ya koymak** to acquire, to get.

torbalamak to bag.

torbalanmak 1. *pass. of* **torbalamak**; **2.** to bag, to become baggy.

torik 1. ZOO large bonito; **2.** *sl.* acumen, brains; **toriğini çalıştırmak** (*or* **işletmek**) *sl.* to use one's loaf.

torna [x .] lathe; **~ etm.** to lathe, to turn.

tornacı [x . .] latheman, turner.

tornacılık turnery.

tornavida [. . x .] screwdriver.

tornistan [x . .] **1.** NAUT stern-way; **2.** turning inside out (*a garment*); **~ etm. 1.** NAUT to go astern; **2.** to turn (*a garment*).

Toros Dağları *pr. n.* the Taurus Mountains.

torpido [. x .] NAUT torpedo boat; **~ gözü** MOT glove compartment; **~ muhribi** torpedo-boat destroyer.

torpidobot, -tu torpedo boat.

torpil 1. torpedo; **2.** *sl.* pull, influence; **3.** *sl.* big gun, a friend at court; **~ patlatmak** *sl.* to pull, to pull strings (*or* wires).

torpilbalığı, -nı ZOO torpedo fish.

torpillemek 1. to torpedo; **2.** *sl.* to flunk a grade.

tortop, -pu as round as a top (*or* ball).

tortu sediment, deposit, dregs, precipitate.

tortul sedimentary.

tortullaşma sedimentation.

tortulu turbid.

tortusuz free of sediment, clear.

torun grandchild; **~ torba** (*or* **tosun**) **sahibi olm.** to have children and grandchildren.

tos butt; **~ vurmak** to butt.

tosbağa ZOO turtle, tortoise.

toslamak 1. to butt; **2.** to bump lightly (*-e* against); **3.** *sl.* to pay out to fork over (*money*); **4.** *sl.* to fail, to flunk.

tost, -tu toasted sandwich.

tostoparlak as round as a ball.

tosun 1. bullock; **2.** *fig.* lad.

tosuncuk big, healthy, newborn baby.

totaliter POL totalitarian.

totem totem.

toto the pools, the football pools.

toy[1] inexperienced, green.

toy[2] ZOO bustard.

toy[3] feast, banquet.

toydan ZOO great bustard.

toyluk inexperience, greenness.

toynak hoof.

toynaklı hoofed.

toz 1. dust; **2.** powder; **3.** *sl.* heroin, skag; **~ almak** to dust; **~ bezi** dustcloth, dustrag; **~ biber** ground pepper; **~ etm. 1.** to crush, to pulverize, to annihilate; **2.** to raise dust; **~ kondurmamak** not to allow anything to be said (*-e* against); **~ koparmak** to raise dust; **~ olm.** *sl.* to get lost, to beat it; **-u dumana katmak 1.** to raise clouds of dust; **2.** *fig.* to kick up a dust, to raise a ruckus; **-unu silkmek** (*b-nin*) *fig.* to dust *s.o.'s* jacket.

tozboya powder paint.

tozkoparan very windy place.

tozlanmak to get dusty.

tozlu dusty.

tozluk 1. gaiter; spat; **2.** *sports*: sock.

tozpembe pale pink; **~ görmek** to see the world through rose-colo(u)red glasses.

tozşeker granulated sugar.

tozumak to give off dust.

tozutmak 1. to raise dust; to make dusty; **2.** *sl.* to go nuts.

töhmet, -ti imputation; **~ altında bırakmak** to implicate, to incriminate.

tökezlemek to stumble.

tömbeki Persian tobacco (*smoked in hookahs*).

töre custom(s), consuetudo.

törebilim ethics.

törebilimci ethician, ethicist.

törebilimsel ethical.

töredışı amoral, nonmoral.

törel ethical, moral.

tören ceremony, ritual; rite.

törenli ceremonial.

törensel ceremonial, ceremonious, ritual.

töresel customary, consuetudinary.

töresiz unethical, immoral.

törpü file, rasp.

törpülemek to file, to rasp.

tövbe repentance, penitence; forswearing; ~ *etm.* **1.** to forswear, to swear off; **2.** to repent, to vow not to do s.th. again; *-ler -si!* (*or -ler olsun!*) not on your life!, never again!

tövbekâr [. .] penitent, repentant.

tövbeli repentant, penitent.

Trablus [x .] *pr. n.* Tripoli.

Trabzon *pr. n.* Trabzon.

trabzonhurması, -nı BOT persimmon, kaki.

trafik traffic; ~ *işareti* traffic sign; ~ *kazası* traffic accident; ~ *lambası* traffic light; ~ *polisi* traffic policeman; ~ *şeridi* traffic lane; ~ *tıkanması* traffic jam, snarl-up.

trafo ELECT transformer.

trahom MED trachoma.

trajedi tragedy.

trajik tragic.

traktör tractor.

Trakya [x .] *pr. n.* Thrace.

Trakyalı [x . .] Thracian.

trampa [x .] barter, swop; ~ *etm.* to barter, to swop.

trampet, -ti side (*or* snare) drum.

tramplen **1.** diving board; springboard; **2.** trampolin(e).

tramvay tram(car), streetcar, trolley.

transatlantik transatlantic (liner).

transfer transfer; ~ *etm.* to transfer; ~ *olm.* to be transferred.

transformasyon transformation.

transformatör ELECT transformer.

transistor ELECT transistor.

transistorlu ELECT transistorized, transistor; ~ *radyo* transistor radio.

transit, -ti transit; ~ *geçmek* to go through in transit; ~ *vizesi* transit vi-

sa; ~ *yolcu* in-transit passenger; ~ *yolu* through highway.

transkripsiyon transcription.

transmisyon MEC transmission.

transplantasyon MED transplant(ation).

transport transport.

transportasyon transportation.

trapez trapeze.

trapezci trapezist.

traş *s.* **tıraş**.

trata [x .] small seine net.

travers RAIL sleeper, crosstie.

travma MED trauma.

travmatoloji MED traumatology.

tren train; ~ *istasyonu* train (*or* railway) station; ~ *tarifesi* train timetable.

trençkot mackintosh, mack, trench coat, raincoat.

trete textbook.

treyler trailer.

tribün (grand)stand.

trigonometri trigonometry.

trigonometrik trigonometric.

triko [x .] machine-knit fabric, tricot.

trikotaj knitting; ~ *sanayii* knitting industry.

trilyon trillion, quintillion.

trinketa NAUT foresail.

tripo [x .] *sl.* gambling den.

triportör **1.** three-wheeler; **2.** tricycle.

triyo MUS trio.

triyör sorter; separator.

troleybüs trolley-bus.

trombon MUS trombone.

trompet, -ti MUS trumpet.

trompetçi MUS trumpet player, trumpeter.

tropik(a) GEOGR tropic.

tropikal, -li tropical; ~ *kuşak* tropical zone.

trotuvar pavement, *Am.* sidewalk.

tröst, -tü COM trust.

TRT (*abbr. for* **Türkiye Radyo Televizyon Kurumu**) Turkish Radio and Television Company.

trup, -pu THEAT troupe.

Truva *pr. n.* Troy; ~ *atı* Trojan horse.

tu [ü] ugh!, oof!

tuba MUS tuba.

tufa *sl.* gravy.

tufacı *sl.* robber.

tufan [- -] **1.** flood, deluge; **2.** torrential rain, deluge; **3.** ♀ the Flood.

tufeyli [î] **1.** BIOL parasite; **2.** parasite; leech.

tugay brigade.

tuğ MIL horsetail.

tuğamiral, -li rear admiral.

tuğgeneral, -li brigadier (general).

tuğla [x .] brick.

tuğra HIST Sultan's signature.

tuğyan [ā] rising up, springing up.

tuh oof!, ugh!

tuhaf 1. strange, odd, queer, curious; **2.** funny; ridiculous; **-ına gitmek** (*b-nin*) to seem strange to *s.o.*

tuhafiye sundries, notions, haberdashery.

tuhafiyeci haberdasher.

tuhaflaşmak to get odd, to become queer.

tuhaflık strangeness, oddity, queerness.

tul, -lü [ū] **1.** length; **2.** longitude; **~ dairesi** GEOGR meridian.

tulu, -uu AST rising (*of the sun, etc.*); **~ etm.** AST (*for the sun, etc.*) to rise.

tuluat, -ti [. - -] a kind of improvisatorial theatre; **~ yapmak** to improvise, to ad-lib.

tulum 1. animal skin; **2.** overalls; jump suit; **3.** MUS bagpipe; **4.** tube (*for toothpaste, etc.*); **~ gibi 1.** swollen all over; **2.** as fat as a pig; **~ peyniri** cheese encased in a skin.

tulumba [. x .] pump; **~ tatlısı** a syrup-soaked pastry.

tulumbacı 1. maker *or* seller of pumps; **2.** HIST member of a fire brigade.

tuman long underpants, drawers.

tumba [x .] **1.** NAUT turning upside down; **2.** tumbling into bed; **~ etm.** NAUT to upend (*a boat*).

tumturak *lit.* bombast, fustian.

tumturaklı bombastic, pompous.

Tuna [x .] *pr. n.* **1.** the Danube; **2.** *mf.*

tunç, -cu 1. bronze; **2.** ♀ *mf.*

tungsten CHEM tungsten.

Tunus *pr. n.* Tunisia.

Tunuslu *pr. n.* Tunisian.

tur 1. tour; **2.** round (*of voting*), ballot; **3.** round (*in a contest*); **4.** spin; **5.** *sports:* lap; **~ atmak 1.** to take a stroll around, to have a walk round (*a place*); **2.** to have (*or* take) a spin; **~ bindirmek** to lap (*in a race*).

tura 1. *s.* **tuğra; 2.** skein, coil; **3.** knotted handkerchief used in a game.

turaç zoo francolin.

turba [x .] peat, turf.

turbalık [x . .] peat bog.

turfa 1. not kosher; **2.** curiosity; **~ olm.**

fig. to fall into disgrace.

turfanda 1. early (*fruit, vegetables*); **2.** out-of-season.

turfandalık garden for growing early fruit, *etc.*

turgor [x .] BIOL turgor.

turing, -gi touring.

turist, -ti tourist.

turistik touristic(al).

turizm tourism.

turkuaz turquoise.

turna [x .] zoo crane; **~ katarı** flock of people; **~ olm.** *sl.* to lose (*while playing a card game*); **-yı gözünden vurmak** *fig.* to hit the jackpot.

turnabalığı, -nı zoo pike.

turne THEAT tour; **-ye çıkmak** to go on tour.

turnike turnstile.

turnusol, -lü CHEM turnsole.

turnuva tournament, tourney.

turp, -pu BOT radish; **~ gibi** hale and hearty, in the pink.

turşu 1. pickle; **2.** *sl.* pickled, blotto, soused; **~ gibi** very tired, pooped, bushed; **~ kurmak** to pickle; to make pickles; **~ olm. 1.** to go sour; **2.** *fig.* to be exhausted (*or* pooped *or* bushed); **~ suratlı** *fig.* sour-faced; **-su çıkmak 1.** (*for fruit, etc.*) to be crushed to a pulp; **2.** *fig.* to get tired, to be pooped (*or* bushed).

turşucu pickleman.

turta [x .] pie, tart.

turuncu orange.

turunç, -cu BOT Seville orange, bitter orange.

turunçgiller citrus fruits.

tuş 1. key (*of a piano, typewriter, etc.*); **2.** *wrestling:* fall; **3.** PAINT touch; **4.** FENC touch(é); **-a getirmek** to throw (*one's opponent*).

tutacak potholder.

tutaç 1. potholder; **2.** tongs.

tutak 1. handle; **2.** potholder; **3.** hostage.

tutam 1. pinch; **2.** wisp; **bir ~ saç** a wisp of hair.

tutamaç handle.

tutamak 1. handle; **2.** evidence, proof.

tutanak 1. minutes, record; **2.** official report.

tutar total, sum; number.

tutarak, tutarık 1. fit, seizure; **2.** epilepsy.

tutarlı consistent; coherent.

tutarlık, tutarlılık consistency; coherence.

tutarsız inconsistent, incongruous; incoherent.

tutarsızlık inconsistency, incongruity; incoherence.

tutkal glue; size; **~ gibi** importunate, obtrusive (*person*).

tutkallamak to glue; to size.

tutkallı glued; sized.

tutku passion.

tutkulu passionate.

tutkun 1. in love (*-e* with); **2.** lover (*-e* of), admirer (*-e* of).

tutma 1. *vn. of* **tutmak; 2.** farm hand.

tutmak, (-ar) 1. to hold; to take hold of; to grip, to grab; **2.** to hunt (*birds*); **3.** to restrain, to hold back; **4.** to arrest; to nab; **5.** to detain, to hold up; **6.** MIL to capture, to occupy; **7.** to watch over, to look after; **8.** to take up (*space*); **9.** to cover (*a place*); **10.** to reserve (*a place*); **11.** (*for cloth*) to show (*a stain, dust, etc.*); **12.** to patrol; **13.** to support, to back; **14.** to keep (*one's promise, etc.*); **15.** to approve, to like; **16.** to be accepted, to win general approval, to take on; **17.** to hire, to rent; **18.** to hire, to employ, to take on; **19.** (*for s.o.'s curse*) to be realized, to come true, to come to pass; **20.** to grasp, to understand; **21.** to reach, to arrive at, to come to (*a place*); **22.** to accord with, to agree with, to jibe with; **23.** to take up, to embark on (*a job*); **24.** P (*for a man*) to be married to; **25.** to be seized with (*the hiccups*); **26.** to total, to come to, to amount to; **27.** (*for milk*) to form (*cream*); **28.** to serve, to offer (*a guest*); **29.** (*for a graft or vaccination*) to take; **30.** (*for paint*) to stick, to adhere; **31.** to assume that ..., to suppose that ...; **tutalım ki** let's suppose that ...; **tuttu gitti** he upped and left; **tuttuğu dal elinde kalmak** *fig.* to turn out to be a dud; **tuttuğunu koparmak** *fig.* to know how to get what one wants.

tutsak prisoner of war, captive.

tutsaklık captivity.

tutturmak 1. *caus. of* **tutmak; 2.** to fasten together; to sew together; **3.** to maintain, to carry on, to keep s.th. going; **4.** to get started (*doing s.th.*); **5.** to hit (*a mark, a target*); **6.** *fig.* to run his mind on.

tutturmalık fastener.

tutucu conservative.

tutuculuk conservatism.

tutuk 1. stuttering; tongue-tied; **2.** shy, reserved; **3.** stopped-up, blocked.

tutukevi, -ni gaol, *Am.* jail.

tutuklamak to arrest.

tutuklu prisoner; under arrest.

tutukluk 1. difficulty in talking; **2.** shyness, timidity; **3.** blockage.

tutukluluk arrest.

tutulan popular.

tutulma 1. *vn. of* **tutulmak; 2.** AST eclipse.

tutulmak 1. *pass. of* **tutmak; 2.** to become popular, to catch on, to take on; **3.** to become tongue-tied, to freeze up; **4.** (*for a part of one's body*) to get stiff; **5.** to fall in love (*-e* with), to fall for.

tutum 1. attitude, manner, conduct; **2.** economy, thrift.

tutumlu thrifty, economical.

tutumluluk thriftiness.

tutumsuz thriftless, spendthrift, wasteful, extravagant.

tutumsuzluk thriftlessness, extravagance.

tutunmak 1. to grab hold of; **2.** to hold on (*-e* to), to hang on (*-e* to); to cling (*-e* to); **3.** to apply (*leeches*) to o.s.

tutuşkan (in)flammable; combustible.

tutuşma *vn. of* **tutuşmak; ~ noktası** CHEM ignition point.

tutuşmak 1. to catch fire, to ignite, to kindle; **2.** to start, to begin; **3.** to hold (*hands*).

tutuşturmak 1. *caus. of* **tutuşmak; 2.** to set on fire, to ignite, to kindle; **3.** to fasten together; **4.** (*eline*) to thrust into (*s.o.'s hands*).

tutya CHEM zinc.

tuval, -li PAINT canvas.

tuvalet, -ti 1. toilet, water closet, lavatory; **2.** toilet; **3.** evening dress (*or* gown); **4.** toilette, dress, outfit; **~ ispirtosu** rubbing alcohol; **~ kâğıdı** toilet paper; **~ masası** dressing (*or* toilet) table, vanity.

tuz salt; **~ biber ekmek** (*bşe*) *fig.* to make *s.th.* worse, to rub salt into the wound; **~ buz olm.** to be smashed to smithereens; **~ ekmek** to salt, to add salt (*-e* to); **-la buz etm.** to smash to smithereens; **-u kuru** well off, in easy circumstances; **o, partinin tuzu biberiydi** he was the life and soul of the party.

tuzak trap; snare; **~ kurmak** (*b-ne*) to

set (*or* lay) a trap for *s.o.*; **tuzağa düş-mek** to fall into a trap; **tuzağa düşür-mek** to trap.

tuzla [x .] saltpan.

tuzlama 1. *vn. of* **tuzlamak**; **2.** a tripe soup; **3.** salted, salt.

tuzlamak to salt; to brine; **tuzlayayım da kokma!** F what you're saying is nothing but a lot of tripe!

tuzlu 1. salty; **2.** *fig.* expensive, pricy, high; ~ **su** salt water; **-ya mal olm.** (*or* **oturmak**) (*b-ne*) to cost *s.o.* a bundle, to cost *s.o.* an arm and a leg.

tuzluk saltshaker, saltcellar.

tuzluluk salinity.

tuzruhu, -nu CHEM hydrochloric acid.

tuzsuz saltless; unsalted.

tü [-] *s.* **tüh.**

tüberküloz MED tuberculosis.

tüccar [ā] merchant; ~ **gemisi** trading vessel; ~ **malı** merchandise.

tüf GEOL tufa.

tüfek rifle, gun; ~ **atmak** to fire a rifle; ~ **çatmak** to stack arms; ~ **dipçiği** butt of a rifle; ~ **namlusu** rifle barrel.

tüfekçi 1. gunsmith; **2.** seller of guns.

tüfekhane armo(u)ry.

tüfeklik 1. armo(u)ry; gun-stand; **2.** gun case.

tüh whew!, ouf!; ~ **sana!** shame on you!

tükenmek 1. to be used up (*or* exhausted), to give out, to run out; **2.** to become exhausted, to give out.

tükenmez 1. inexhaustible; **2.** ball-point (pen); ~ **kalem** ball-point pen.

tüketici COM consumer.

tüketim COM consumption.

tüketmek 1. to exhaust, to use up, to expend, to spend; **2.** COM to consume.

tükürmek to spit, to expectorate; **tükürdüğünü yalamak** *fig.* to eat humble pie, to eat one's words, to eat crow.

tükürük spit(tle); ~ **bezi** ANAT salivary gland; ~ **tükürüğünü yutmak** *fig.* (*for s.o.'s mouth*) to begin to water; to lick one's chops.

tükürüklemek to moisten with spittle.

tül 1. tulle; **2.** tulle curtain.

tülbent, -di muslin; gauze.

tüm 1. all (of); **2.** whole, entirety; **3.** completely; ~ **cahil** completely ignorant; **-üyle** completely.

tümamiral, -li vice admiral.

tümbek 1. small protuberance; **2.** small drum.

tümce GR sentence.

tümden completely, totally, wholly.

tümdengelim LOG deduction.

tümel LOG, PHLS universal.

tümen 1. large heap (*or* pile); **2.** ten thousand; **3.** MIL division; ~ ~ thousands of …

tümevarım LOG induction.

tümgeneral, -li major general.

tümleç, -ci GR complement.

tümlemek to complete.

tümler MATH complementary; ~ **açı** complementary angle.

tümör MED tumo(u)r.

tümsayı full number.

tümsek 1. small mound (*or* pile); **2.** protuberance; **3.** protuberant.

tümsekli convex.

tümseklik protuberance.

tünaydın! 1. good evening!; **2.** good night!

tünek perch, roost.

tüneklemek to perch, to roost.

tünel tunnel.

tünemek to perch, to roost.

tünik tunic.

tüp, -bü 1. tube; **2.** (test) tube.

tür 1. kind, sort, type; **2.** ZOO, BOT species.

türban turban.

türbe tomb, turbe(h).

türbin PHYS turbine.

türe justice.

türedi upstart, parvenu.

türel judicial, juridical.

türemek 1. to spring up; to appear; **2.** to multiply, to increase, to mushroom; **3.** GR to be derived (*-den* from).

türeti invention.

türetici inventor.

türetmek 1. to produce; to invent; **2.** GR to derive.

türev GR derivative.

Türk, -kü 1. Turk; **2.** Turkish; ~ **ceza kanunu** Turkish penal code; ~ **dili** the Turkish language; ~ **Dil Kurumu** *pr. n.* The Turkish Language Association.

Türkçe [x .] **1.** Turkish, the Turkish language; **2.** (in) Turkish; ~ **öğretmeni** teacher of Turkish; ~ **söylemek 1.** to speak in Turkish; **2.** *fig.* to say bluntly; ~ **sözlük** Turkish dictionary.

Türkçeci [x . .] **1.** supporter of the movement to purify Turkish of foreign words; **2.** teacher of Turkish.

Türkçeleştirmek to translate into Turkish.

Türkçü Turkist.

Türkçülük Turkism.

Türkistan [ā] *pr. n.* Turkistan.

Türkiye *pr. n.* Turkey; ~ *Büyük Millet Meclisi pr. n.* the Grand National Assembly of Turkey; ~ *Cumhuriyeti pr. n.* the Republic of Turkey, the Turkish Republic.

Türkleştirmek to Turkize, to Turkicize.

Türklük 1. Turkishness; **2.** the Turkish community.

Türkmen Turkoman, Turcoman.

Türkmenistan *pr. n.* Turkmenistan.

Türkolog Turcologist.

Türkoloji Turcology.

türkuvaz turquoise.

türkü folk song; ~ *çağırmak* (*or söylemek*) to sing a folk song; ~ *yakmak* to write a folk song; *-sünü çağırmak* (*b-nin*) *fig.* to sing the praises of *s.o.*

türlü 1. kind, sort, variety; **2.** various, diverse; **3.** meat and vegetable stew; ~ ~ all sorts of, various.

türrühat, -tı [ā] nonsense, rubbish.

tüs fuzz, down (*on a person's face*).

tütmek, (-er) 1. to smoke, to fume; **2.** (*for smoke*) to rise.

tütsü 1. incense; **2.** smoke.

tütsülemek 1. to cense; **2.** to smoke (*fish, meat, etc.*).

tütsülü 1. censed; **2.** smoked (*fish, meat, etc.*).

tütsülük censer, incensory.

tüttürmek 1. *caus. of* **tütmek; 2.** to smoke (*cigarette, pipe, etc.*).

tütün tobacco; ~ *içmek* (*or kullanmak*) to smoke (*tobacco*).

tütüncü 1. tobacconist; **2.** tobacco grower.

tüvana [. - -] vigorous.

tüvit tweed.

tüy 1. feather; down; quill; **2.** hair; **3.** fuzz, down; ~ *atmak* (*for a bird*) to mo(u)lt; ~ *dikmek* (*bşin üzerine*) to be the last straw, to be the straw that broke the camel's back; ~ *dökmek* (*for a bird*) to mo(u)lt; ~ *gibi* as light as a feather, featherlight; ~ *kalem* quill (pen); *-ler ürpertici* blood-curdling, spine-chilling, creepy; *-leri diken diken olm.* to get goose bumps, to get goose-flesh, to stand on end (*hair*); *-ü tüsü yok* he's still wet behind the ears; *-ünü düzmek* **1.** (*for a bird*) to preen; **2.** to start to dress well.

tüydöken *sl.* razor, shiv.

tüydürmek *caus. of* **tüymek,** *sl.* **1.** to steal, to pinch; **2.** to make s.o. leave.

tüylenmek 1. (*for a bird*) to grow feathers, to feather out, to fledge; **2.** *fig.* to get rich, to get flush.

tüylü 1. feathered; feathery; downy; **2.** fuzzy; shaggy; hairy.

tüymek *sl.* to slip away, to sneak off.

tüyo hint, tip; ~ *vermek* to drop (*or give*) a hint.

tüysıklet, -ti boxing: featherweight.

tüysüz 1. unfeathered, unfledged; downless; **2.** fuzzless, downless (*plant, fruit*); **3.** hairless (*animal*); **4.** beardless (*youth*).

tüysüzşeftali bot nectarine.

tüze 1. jurisprudence, law; **2.** justice.

tüzel 1. jurisprudential, legal; **2.** judicial.

tüzelkişi jur juristic person.

tüzük regulations, statutes.

TV (*abbr. for television*) *TV*, television.

U

ubudiyet, -ti [. x . .] **1.** devotion to God; **2.** slavery, bondage.

uca coccyx, tailbone.

ucube [. - .] curiosity, monster, prodigy.

ucuz 1. cheap, inexpensive; **2.** *fig.* easy, easily acquired; ~ *atlatmak* (*or kurtulmak*) to get off lightly, to get away cheaply; ~ *etin yahnisi yavan* (*or tatsız*) *olur pro.* you can't make a silk purse out of a sow's ear; *-a düşürmek* to buy s.th. cheaply; *-dur vardır illeti, pahalıdır vardır hikmeti pro.* if s.th. is cheap, it is usually defective, if s.th. is expensive, there is a good reason.

ucuzcu 1. F the cheap real McCoy, s.o. who sells goods cheaply; **2.** s.o. who is always hunting for bargains, bargain hunter.

ucuzlamak 1. to become cheap, to go down in price (*goods*); **2.** *fig.* to become readily available, to become common, to become known by everybody.

ucuzlatmak 1. to reduce in price, to cheapen; **2.** to make readily available, to make s.th. easy.

ucuzluk 1. cheapness, inexpensiveness; **2.** sale.

uç 1. tip, point; **2.** (tree) top; **3.** end; **4.** *obs.* cause, reason; **5.** HIST border territory; **6.** MATH final point; **7.** extremity; **8.** frontier; ~ *uca* end to end; ~ *uca gelmek* to be just enough; ~ *vermek* **1.** to come to a head (*boil, etc.*); **2.** to appear, to turn out; **3.** to sprout, to come up (*plant*); *-u bucağı olmamak* (*or görünmemek*) to be endless; *-u ortası belli olmamak* not to know exactly, not to know how to start setting a job; *-u dokunmak* (*b-ne*) to be prejudicial to s.o., to cause s.o. harm, to bring up a subject; *-unda bir şey olm.* to be some secret purpose behind s.th.; *-unu kaçırmak fig.* to lose the thread, to lose the control of.

uçak aeroplane, airplane, plane; ~ *bileti* air-travel ticket; ~ *faciası* air disaster; ~ *gemisi* aircraft carrier; ~ *kaçırmak* to hijack an airplane; *-la* **1.** by airplane, by air; **2.** by airmail, via airmail.

uçaksavar MIL anti-aircraft gun.

uçandaire flying saucer.

uçantop, -pu volleyball.

uçar 1. flying; **2.** flying bird; **3.** volatile; *-a atmak* to shoot at a flying bird.

uçarı 1. philanderer, casanova; **2.** wild, uncontrollable.

uçkun spark.

uçkur belt, sash, band (*for holding up trousers*); ~ *çözmek* F to have sex with; *-una gevşek olm.* to sleep around, to have sex with, to be hot or horny; *-una sağlam fig.* chaste.

uçlanmak *sl.* to pay up, to fork out, to hand over, to shell out.

uçlu pointed, tipped.

uçmak 1. to fly; **2.** to evaporate (*perfume, etc.*); CHEM to volatilize; **3.** to fade away (*colo(u)r*); **4.** to go downhill; **5.** F to disappear, to vanish; **6.** to get lost; **7.** to explode, to burst; **8.** to be wild with (*joy*); **9.** to go very fast; *uçan kuşa borcu olm.* to be in debt to everybody, to be up to the ears in debt; *uçan kuştan medet ummak* to try every mean in order to get out of trouble.

uçman aviator, airplane pilot.

uçsuz without a point; ~ *bucaksız* endless, vast, boundless.

uçucu 1. flying, able to fly; **2.** CHEM volatile.

uçuçböceği, -ni zoo ladybug.

uçuk 1. faded (*colo(u)r*); pale; **2.** MED cold sore, herpes (labialis); ~ *benizli* pale.

uçuklamak to develop cold sores; to get herpes.

uçurmak *caus. of* **uçmak 1.** to fly (*kite*); **2.** to rise, to ascend (*plane*); **3.** to cut off, to separate (*head*); **4.** to blow up, to blast; **5.** F to kick out (*doors*); **6.** *sl.* to boast, to brag, to show off; **7.** F to lose, to steal, to purloin, to pilfer.

uçurtma kite.

uçurtmak *caus. of* **uçurmak.**

uçurum 1. abyss, chasm; precipice; **2.** *fig.* corruption, misfortune, disaster.

uçuş flight, flying; ~ *hattı* flight route.

uçuşmak to fly about; to fly together.
udi [- -] lute player, lutist.
uf ouf!, oof!, ow!, oh my God!
ufacık very small, tiny, minute; ~ **tefecik** tiny, minute.
ufak 1. small; **2.** very young; **3.** insignificant; **4.** pedantic; **5.** crumb, small; ~ **çapta** small-scale; ~ **para** small change; ~ **tefek** small and thin, small, of no (or small) account; ~ ~ **1.** bit by bit; **2.** in small pieces.
ufaklık 1. smallness, littleness; **2.** small change (money); **3.** sl. vermin, esp. louse.
ufalamak to break up, to crumble, to powder, to pulverize.
ufalanmak 1. pass. of **ufalamak**; **2.** to crumble away.
ufalmak to diminish, to become smaller.
ufarak very small.
ufki horizontal, level.
uflamak to say 'oof'; **uflayıp puflamak** to keep saying 'oof'.
ufuk, -fku 1. horizon; **2.** skyline; **3.** fig. understanding, conception; **ufkunu genişletmek** fig. to broaden one's horizon.
ufunet, -ti [. - .] **1.** bad smell, stench; **2.** MED inflammation and suppuration.
uğrak 1. frequented place or region; **2.** haunt.
uğramak 1. to pass by, to call (on s.o., at a place); **2.** to (make a) halt, to stop, to touch at; **3.** to pass through; **4.** to get stricken (or afflicted) with; **5.** to rush out; **6.** to meet with, to suffer (a difficulty, etc.); **7.** to undergo; **8.** to encounter.
uğraş, uğraşı 1. occupation, work; pastime; **2.** struggle, striving, dispute.
uğraşmak 1. to exert o.s., to struggle, to strive; **2.** (bşle) to busy (or occupy) o.s. with s.th.; to be engaged in s.th., to be busy; **3.** to create, to produce; **4.** fig. to struggle, to battle (ile with).
uğraştırmak caus. of **uğraşmak**; (b-ni) to give s.o. (a great deal of) trouble.
uğratmak caus. of **uğramak**; **1.** to expose s.o. to; **2.** to dismiss s.o. from.
uğru thief.
uğrulamak to steal.
uğrun secretly; ~ ~ secretly.
uğuldamak 1. to hum, to buzz, to growl, to grumble; **2.** to howl, to cry, to hoot, to wail.

uğultu hum, buzz, howl, roar.
uğunmak 1. to faint; **2.** to feel faint.
uğur[1] **-ğru** purpose, aim, goal; **uğrunda** for the sake of, on account of.
uğur[2] good omen, good luck, lucky charm; ~ **getirmek** to bring good luck; ~ **ola** (or **-lar olsun**)! have a good trip!; **-u açık** lucky, fortunate.
uğurböceği, -ni zoo ladybug.
uğurlamak (b-ni) to accompany s.o., to see s.o. off.
uğurlu lucky, auspicious; ~ **kademli olsun!** may this bring you joy!
uğursamak to regard s.th. as a sign of good luck.
uğursuz inauspicious, ill-omened, ominous; unlucky, unfortunate, fatal.
uğursuzluk ill omen; bad luck, hoodoo.
uhde obligation, charge, responsibility, duty, engagement, undertaking; **-sinde etm.** (b-nin) to be s.o.'s duty, to be incumbent on s.o.; **-sinden gelmek** to fulfil(l), to achieve, to manage, to deal with, to handle; **-sine almak** to carry over, to entrust.
uhrevi [. . -] pertaining to the other world.
uhuvvet brotherhood.
ukala [. . -] wiseacre, smart aleck; ~ **dümbeleği** smart aleck, smart ass, know-it-all.
ukalalık [. . - .] know-it-all behavio(u)r.
ukde 1. BOT, PHYS knot; **2.** BIOL ganglion; **3.** fig. pain, ache, torture.
Ukraynalı Ukrainian.
ukubet, -ti [. - .] **1.** punishment; **2.** pain, torture; **3.** P coarse and ugly.
ulaç GR gerund.
Ulah Wallachian, Vlach.
ulak courier, messenger.
ulam 1. group; **2.** category.
ulama 1. vn. of **ulamak**; **2.** adding, appendage; **3.** liaison.
ulamak to join, to attach, to add, to annex (-e to).
ulan sl. hi!, man alive!, hey you!, man!
ulantı addition, supplement.
ulaşım communication, transport(ation).
ulaşmak 1. to arrive (-e at), to get (-e to), to reach; **2.** to attain, to achieve; **3.** to reach, to hand, to pass; **4.** to get into contact with; **5.** to survive until.
ulaştırma transportation, communication; ♀ **Bakanlığı** Ministry of Transport; ~ **sınıfı** MIL Transportation

Corps.

ulaştırmak to cause to reach, to transport (-e to).

ulema [. . -] *isl.* doctors of Muslim theology, ulema.

ulemalık [. . . -] F scholarship.

ulu great, high, elevated, *fig.* exalted.

ululamak to extol, to exalt, to hono(u)r.

ululuk height, elevation, *fig.* loftiness, sublimity.

ulumak to howl.

uluorta rashly, recklessly, without reserve.

ulus nation, people.

ulusal national.

ulusallaştırmak to nationalize.

ulusallık nationality.

ulusçu nationalist.

ulusçuluk nationalism.

uluslararası, -nı international.

ulussever patriot.

ulvi [. -] high, sublime.

umacı bogy man, ogre.

umar remedy, solution.

umde *obs.* principle.

ummadık [x . .] **1.** unexpected, unhoped-for; **2.** unforeseen.

ummak, (-ar) 1. to hope; **2.** to expect, to await, to presume; **ummadığın taş baş yarar** it is the unexpected stone that wounds the head.

umman ocean.

Umman Oman.

umran *s.* **ümran.**

umulmak *pass. of* **ummak.**

umum [. -] **1.** all, general, universal; **2.** the public; **~ müdür** general manager.

umumhane [. . - .] brothel.

umumi [. - -] **1.** general, common, universal; **2.** public; **~ efkâr** public opinion.

umumiyet, -ti [. . . .] generality.

umumiyetle in general, generally.

umur [. -] **1.** affairs, matters, concern; **2.** *obs.* things, belongings; **~ görmek 1.** to be experienced; **2.** to be in important positions (*person*); **~ görmüş** experienced; **-umda değil** I don't care; **-umun teki** what is that to me?, it is nothing to me.

umursamak to be concerned about, to consider important.

umursamazlık indifference, unconcern.

umut, -du hope, expectation, confidence; **~ beslemek** to hope, to ex-

pect; **~ etm.** to hope, to expect; **~ kesmek** to lose hope; **~ vermek** to give hope to; **-a düşmek** to be hopeful; **-unu kırmak** to disappoint.

umutlandırmak to give hope to, to make s.o. hopeful.

umutlanmak to become hopeful.

umutlu hopeful.

umutsuz hopeless, desperate.

umutsuzluk hopelessness.

un flour; **~ ufak etm.** to crumble s.th. finely; **~ ufak olm.** to be broken into pieces; **-unu elemiş, eleğini asmış 1.** he bas done all the useful work in his life; **2.** he is too old.

unlamak to flour, to sprinkle with flour.

unluk 1. suitable for making flour; **2.** flour bin (*in a mill*).

unsur element, component.

unutkan forgetful.

unutkanlık forgetfulness.

unutmabeni BOT forget-me-not.

unutmak 1. to forget; to unlearn; **2.** to forgive.

unvan [. -] **1.** title; **2.** superscription.

upuslu very well-behaved.

upuygun [x . .] very suitable, perfectly appropriate.

upuzun 1. very long *or* tall; **2.** at full length.

ur tumo(u)r, outgrowth, swelling.

urağan METEOR hurricane.

Uranus AST Uranus.

uranyum CHEM uranium.

urba piece of clothing.

Urduca Urdu, the Urdu language.

urgan rope.

uruk clan.

us reason, state of mind, intelligence, intellect; **~ pahası** warning, teaching.

usanç boredom, disgust; **~ getirmek** to get bored, to get tired of; **~ vermek** to bore, to disgust.

usandırıcı boring, disgusting.

usandırmak to bore, to disgust.

usanmak to become bored, to get tired of, to get disgusted.

usare [. - .] sap, juice.

usavurmak to reason, to think through.

usçu PHLS **1.** rationalist; **2.** rationalistic.

usçuluk PHLS rationalism.

usdışı irrational.

uskumru ZOO mackerel.

uskur NAUT screw, propeller.

uskuru MEC screw thread.

uslamlamak s. **usavurmak**.

uslanmak 1. to become sensible, to become well-behaved; **2.** to listen to reason.

uslu 1. well-behaved, sensible, good (*child*); **2.** reasonable, sensible, rational; ~ **durmak** (*or* **oturmak**) to keep quiet, to sit still, to be good.

ussal mental, rational.

usta 1. skil(l)ful, clever (*at*), able; **2.** master craftsman, master workman; **3.** foreman, chief; ~ **elinden çıkmak** to be made by master; ~ **işi** work of a master.

ustabaşı, -nı foreman.

ustaca skil(l)fully.

ustalaşmak to become skilled.

ustalık 1. mastery, craftsman; **2.** proficiency, expertise.

ustalıkla skil(l)fully.

ustunç, -cu MED set of instruments.

ustura [x . .] **1.** (straight) razor; **2.** *sl.* strong (*drink*); **3.** *sl.* lie; ~ **taşı** whetstone; ~ **tutunmak** to get a shave.

usturlap astrolabe.

usturmaça NAUT fender, padding.

usturpa [. x .] a kind of whip.

usturuplu F **1.** properly, right; **2.** masterly, striking, hitting the target.

usul, -lü 1. method, system, manner; **2.** program(me); **3.** MUS time, measure, rhythm; **4.** JUR procedure; ~ **hukuku** JUR law of procedure; ~ **tutmak** MUS to beat time; ~ ~ quietly, slowly and softly.

usulca 1. slowly; **2.** quietly.

usulcacık slowly, gently, quietly.

usulsüz [. - .] **1.** unmethodical; **2.** contrary to regulations, irregular, incorrect.

usulsüzlük 1. lack of method *or* system; **2.** irregularity.

uşak 1. boy, youth, lad; **2.** servant, domestic, assistant; ~ **olm.** to undertake the duty of a servant.

uşakkapan zoo lammergeier.

uşaklık 1. being a manservant; **2.** *fig.* degrading task; ~ **etm.** to be servitude.

ut¹ lute.

ut² shame, modesty; ~ **yeri** private parts, genitals.

utanç shame, modesty, shyness, embarrassment; **-ından yere geçmek** to feel very ashamed, to feel like 30 cents.

utandırmak to make s.o. ashamed, to cause s.o. to blush, to put s.o. to the blush.

utangaç, utangan bashful, shy, timid, embarrassed, confused, shamefaced.

utangaçlık bashfulness, shyness, shamefacedness.

utanmak 1. to be ashamed; **2.** to feel embarrassed; **3.** to be shy *or* bashful; **4.** to be too timid to do, to recoil at.

utanmaz shameless, impudent, impertinent, insolent.

utanmazlık shamelessness, brazenness.

Utarit AST Mercury.

utku victory, triumph.

utlu 1. chaste; **2.** honest.

utmak 1. to defeat; **2.** to win.

utopya utopia.

uvertür 1. MUS overture; **2.** beginning (*poker game*).

uvunmak s. **uğunmak**.

uyak rhyme.

uyaklı rhymed.

uyaksız unrhymed.

uyandırmak *caus. of* **uyanmak 1.** to wake up, to awaken; **2.** *fig.* to awaken, to arouse, to excite, to call forth; **3.** to light, to kindle; **4.** to revive, to stir.

uyanık 1. awake; **2.** *fig.* bright, cunning; **3.** watchful, vigilant, careful, mindful.

uyanıklık wakefulness, alertness, watchfulness.

uyanış awakening.

uyanmak 1. to wake (up); **2.** *fig.* to awake; **3.** to come up (*plant*); **4.** to appear again, to show up again (*pain, etc.*); **5.** to flame up (*fire*); **6.** to become aware of.

uyar conformable, fit, suitable.

uyaran stimulus, incentive, stimulant.

uyarı 1. warning; **2.** stimulus.

uyarıcı 1. warning; **2.** stimulative.

uyarım stimulation.

uyarınca in accordance with, following, according to.

uyarlaç adapter, adaptor.

uyarlamak 1. to accommodate, to adjust (*-e* to); **2.** to fit, to adapt, to modify.

uyarlayıcı adapter, adaptor (*person*).

uyarlık conformity.

uyarmak 1. to warn, to remind; **2.** to stimulate; **3.** to awaken, to arouse.

uyartı 1. warning; **2.** stimulation; **3.** stimulus.

uydu satellite (*a. fig.*); ~ **antenli radyo**

satellite radio.

uydurma 1. *vn. of* **uydurmak**; **2.** fictitious, improvised; **3.** invented, false, made-up.

uydurmak *caus. of* **uymak 1.** to make fit, to adapt, to adjust; **2.** to invent arbitrarily, to fabricate, to cook up; **3.** to patch up; **4.** F to pick up, to get; **5.** F to manage, to engineer, to wangle; **6.** MEC to fit in(to); **7.** to seduce (*girl, woman*).

uydurmasyon *sl.* **1.** invention, fable, bullshit; **2.** made-up, invented.

uyduruk F fabricated, invented, made-up.

uydurukçu F bullshitter, fabricator.

uygar 1. civilized; **2.** educated.

uygarlaşmak to become civilized.

uygarlık civilization.

uygulama *vn. of* **uygulamak** application, practice, carrying out (*plan, law, etc.*).

uygulamak 1. to apply, to carry through practice; **2.** to superimpose s.th. on.

uygun 1. fit, suitable, corresponding, conformable, appropriate; **2.** proper, qualified, apt; **3.** in accord to, fitting; **4.** reasonable (*price*); **5.** favo(u)rable, good; **~ bulmak** (*or* **görmek**) to see fit, to agree to, to approve of; **~ düşmek** to fit, to suit; **~ gelmek** to suit; **~ katmanlaşma** GEOL concordant stratification.

uygunluk appropriateness, suitability.

uygunsuz unsuitable, inappropriate, unfitting, undue; **~ kadın** prostitute, whore.

uygunsuzluk 1. inappropriate behavio(u)r; **2.** unsuitableness, inappropriateness.

Uygur Uighur.

Uygurca the Uighur language, Uighur.

uyku 1. sleep; **2.** *fig.* carelessness, sleepiness; **~ basmak** (*or* **bastırmak**) to feel very sleepy; **~ durak** (*yok or* **~ nedir bilmeden**) (without a) chance to rest; **~ gözünden akmak** to be very sleepy; **~ tulumu** sleeping bag; **~ tutmamak** not to be able to go to sleep; **~ vermek** (*or* **getirmek**) to make s.o. feel sleepy; **-su ağır** heavy sleeper; **-su bölünmek** not to be able to go back to sleep; **-su gelmek** to feel sleepy; **-su hafif** light sleeper; **-su kaçmak 1.** to lose sleep over; **2.** to

be worried; **-sunu almak** to sleep well; **-ya dalmak** to fall asleep; **-ya varmak 1.** to sleep; **2.** to calm down; **-ya yatmak** to lie down to sleep.

uykucu late riser, lie-abed, sleepyhead, fond of sleep.

uykulu sleepy.

uykusuz 1. sleepless; **2.** blear-eyed, fatigued (*from lack of sleep*).

uykusuzluk lack of sleep, insomnia.

uyluk ANAT thigh.

uylukkemiği, -ni thighbone.

uymak, (-ar) 1. to fit to, to conform; **2.** to adapt o.s. to; to adjust to, to follow, to obey, to comply with, to observe, to submit to, to resign o.s. to, to listen to; **3.** to harmonize with, to be homogeneous.

uyruk POL citizen, subject.

uyruklu s.o. who is a citizen of (*a country*).

uyrukluk citizenship.

uysal conciliatory, easy-going, obedient, pliant, supple, compliant, docile, sociable, peaceable.

uysallaşmak to become docile (*or* compliant).

uysallık complaisance, docility.

uyuklamak to doze (off).

uyum 1. harmony, conformity; **2.** MED accommodation (*of the eye*); **3.** GR harmony.

uyumak 1. to sleep, to go to sleep, to fall asleep; **2.** *fig.* to be negligent; **3.** to be unaware of what's going on.

uyumlu harmonious, in accord, well-proposed.

uyumsuz inharmonious.

uyuntu idle, lazy, indolent, sleepyhead.

uyur 1. sleeping; **2.** still (*water*).

uyurgezer sleepwalker, somnambulist.

uyurgezerlik somnambulism, sleepwalking.

uyuşmak[1] **1.** to become numb, to become insensible, to tingle (*hands from cold, etc.*); **2.** to go to sleep; **3.** to relax.

uyuşmak[2] **1.** to come to an agreement (*ile* with), to come to terms (*price*); **2.** to get on (*or* along) with.

uyuşmazlık disagreement, conflict.

uyuşturanbalığı ZOO crampfish.

uyuşturmak[1] to anesthetize, to narcotize, to benumb, to deaden.

uyuşturmak[2] to cause to come to an

agreement.

uyuşturucu narcotic, anesthetic.

uyuşuk numbed, insensible, asleep.

uyuşukluk 1. numbness; **2.** laziness.

uyutmak *caus. of* **uyumak 1.** to lull to sleep, to send to sleep; **2.** *fig.* to calm, to soothe, to ease, to alley, to hold out; **3.** *fig.* to mitigate, to alleviate; **4.** *fig.* to deceive, to fool; **5.** to put off.

uyutucu 1. narcotic, soporific; **2.** hypnotic.

uyuz 1. MED mange, itch; **2.** itchy, scabious, mangy, scabby; **3.** *fig.* miserable, wretched, sissy; ~ *etm.* to bug; ~ *olm.* **1.** to get the itch; **2.** *fig.* to be bugged.

uyuzböceği, -ni ZOO itch mite.

uyuzotu, -nu BOT scabious.

uyuzsineği, -ni ZOO tiger beetle.

uz able, good, clever, skil(l)ful.

uzak 1. distant, far, out-of-the-way, remote; **2.** unsuitable, unfit (for); **3.** improbable, unlikely, inept, irrelevant; **4.** distance, remoteness; **5.** removal; ~ *akraba* distant relative; ~ *durmak* to stay at a distance, not to interfere; to keep (*or* stay) clear of; ~ *düşmek* (*birbirinden*) to be far from one another; **-ı görmek** to be able to see the future; **-tan** from far off; **-tan bakmak** to stay out of, to remain apart from; **-tan kumanda** remote control; **-tan öğrenim** distance learning; **-tan uzağa 1.** casually (*to know*); **2.** from far away; **-tan yakından** it hasn't got the slightest connection.

Uzakdoğu the Far East.

uzaklaşmak 1. to go away, to remove, to retire; to be far away (**-den** from); **2.** to become a stranger to.

uzaklaştırmak 1. to remove, to deport, to take away; **2.** to turn off, to cause to lose interest.

uzaklık distance, remoteness; interval.

uzam largeness, extent.

uzamak 1. to grow long, to extend; **2.** to be prolonged, to drag out (*time*); **3.** to grow longer (*child*).

uzanmak 1. to be down, to stretch o.s. out on; **2.** to go on, to walk on; **3.** to be extended to; **4.** to stretch one's arm to.

uzantı 1. extension; **2.** prolongation,

lengthening.

uzatım prolongation, extension.

uzatma *vn. of* **uzatmak** lengthening, extension, stretch(ing), expansion; ~ *işareti* circumflex (accent).

uzatmak *caus. of* **uzamak 1.** to lengthen; **2.** to extend, to stretch, to expand; **3.** to let (*hair, etc.*) grow long; **4.** to hand (*-ı over*), to pass (*-e to*); **5.** to drag out, to prolong; **uzatmayalım** let's keep it short.

uzay AST, MATH, PHLS space; ~ *geometri* solid geometry; ~ *kapsülü* space capsule; ~ *uçuşu* space flight.

uzayadamı astronaut, spaceman.

uzaygemisi spaceship, spacecraft.

uzgörür far-sighted.

uziletişim telecommunication.

uzlaşma *vn. of* **uzlaşmak** agreement, understanding, settlement, unification.

uzlaşmak to come to an agreement (*or* understanding), to come to terms.

uzlaşmazlık unwillingness to come to an agreement.

uzlaştırıcı conciliatory.

uzlaştırmak to reconcile, to compromise, to conciliate.

uzluk ability, cleverness, expertise, mastery.

uzman expert, specialist.

uzmanlaşmak to become an expert (*or* specialist), to specialize.

uzmanlık expertness, special(i)ty.

uzun 1. long; **2.** tall (*person*); **3.** *contp.* diffuse, length, prolix; ~ *araç* long vehicle; ~ *atlama* long jump; ~ *boylu* **1.** tall (*person*); **2.** *fig.* diffuse, prolix; ~ *etm.* to draw out, to drag out; ~ *hikaye* long story; ~ *lafın kısası* in short, the long and the short of it; ~ *oturmak* to sprawl; ~ *uzadıya* detailed, full(-length), long and broad.

uzunçalar long play, long-playing record, LP.

uzunlamasına lengthwise.

uzunluk 1. length (*a.* MATH); **2.** *contp.* diffuseness, prolixity.

uzuv, -zvu ANAT member, organ; limb.

uzvi [. -] organic.

uzviyet, -ti 1. organism; **2.** MED system.

uzyazım telex.

Ü

ücra remote, out of the way, outermost.

ücret, -ti 1. wage, pay(ment), compensation, stipend, salary; **2.** fee, charge; **3.** price, cost.

ücretli 1. paid, employed for pay; **2.** s.th. done for a fee.

ücretsiz 1. free, free of charge; **2.** gratis.

üç, -çü three; ~ **aşağı beş yukarı** approximately, roughly; ~ **beş** a few; ~ **buçuk atmak** to be very frightened; ~ **günlük ömür** short life.

üçboyutlu three-dimensional.

üçer three each, three apiece.

üçgen MATH triangle; ~ **piramit** trilateral pyramid; ~ **prizma** triangular prism.

üçkağıtçı fig. swindler, crook.

üçlemek 1. to increase to three, to triple, to treble; **2.** to lease the field in exchange for a third of the crop; **3.** to plow the field three times; **4.** to turn threefold (rope, etc.).

üçlü 1. three-figure number; **2.** ternary; **3.** (a) three (poker, dominoes, etc.) **4.** MUS trio.

üçüncü third; ~ **şahıs** GR the third person; ~ **zaman** GEOL the Tertiary (period).

üçüz triplets, triplet.

üçüzlü 1. who has triplets (mother); **2.** threefold; **3.** (consisting) of three parts.

üfleç, -ci PHYS nozzle, blower, blowpipe.

üflemek 1. to blow; **2.** to blow out; **3.** to blow (-e upon, at); **4.** to blow away (dust, etc.); **5.** to sound (flute, shawm, etc.).

üfürmek 1. to blow, to breathe on; **2.** to blow away; **3.** to cure by breathing on.

üfürük exhaled breath.

üfürükçü quack, sorcerer (who claims to cure by breathing on).

üğrüm AST nutation.

üleşmek to share, to divide (ile with).

üleştirmek to distribute, to share out (-e to).

ülfet, -ti 1. familiarity, acquaintance; **2.** intercourse, relation; **3.** friendship.

ülger fuzz, down.

ülke 1. country; **2.** JUR territory.

Ülker AST the Pleiades.

ülkü ideal.

ülkücü idealist.

ülkücülük idealism.

ülser MED ulcer.

ültimatom POL ultimatum.

ültramodern ultramodern.

ültraviyole ultraviolet.

ümit, -di 1. hope, confidence; **2.** expectation, supposition, presumption; ~ **bağlamak** to set (or pin) one's hopes on; ~ **dünyası** one can always hope; ~ **etm.** to hope, to expect; ~ **kapısı** hope, anything that proves hope; ~ **vermek** to raise s.o.'s hopes (of), to hold out a prospect of, to promise; **ümidi suya düşmek** to lose hope; **ümidini kesmek** to give up hope.

ümitlendirmek to make hopeful.

ümitlenmek to become hopeful, to gather fresh hope.

ümitli hopeful, full of hope.

ümitsiz 1. hopeless (a. fig.); **2.** desperate.

ümitsizlik hopelessness, despair.

ümmet, -ti isl. religious community.

ümmi [. -] illiterate.

ümmilik illiteracy.

ümük P throat.

ün 1. F voice, sound; **2.** fame, reputation, esteem; ~ **salmak** (or **kazanmak** or **yapmak**) to become famous.

üniforma [. . x .] uniform.

ünite 1. unity; **2.** unit.

üniversal universal.

üniversite university.

üniversiteli university student.

ünlem 1. GR interjection; **2.** exclamation, cry, shout; ~ **işareti** exclamation mark.

ünlemek P to call out (-e to).

ünlü 1. famous, well-known; **2.** celeb; **3.** GR vowel.

ünsiyet, -ti 1. familiarity; **2.** friendship.

ünsüz 1. unknown; **2.** GR consonant; ~ **uyumu** consonant harmony.

ürat urate.

Ürdünlü Jordanian.

üre urea.

ürem COM interest.

üremek 1. to reproduce; **2.** to multiply, to increase.

üremi MED uremia.

üreteç PHYS generator.

üretici 1. producer; **2.** of production.

üretim 1. production, manufacture; **2.** product.

üretken productive.

üretkenlik productivity.

üretmek *caus. of* **üremek 1.** to breed, to grow, to raise; **2.** to produce.

ürik asit CHEM uric acid.

ürkek 1. shy, timid; **2.** fearful, timorous; ~ ~ timidly, slowly and shyly.

ürkeklik timidity, shyness, bashfulness.

ürkmek (-er) 1. to shy, to balk (*horse*); **2.** to start (*at*), to wince, to be terrified, to be shocked, to fear from, to be frightened of; **3.** to bear no fruit (*tree*).

ürkünç frightening, scary, terrifying.

ürküntü sudden fright, panic, scare.

ürkütmek *caus of* **ürkmek 1.** to startle, to scare, to frighten; **2.** to lop (*tree*).

ürolog MED urologist.

üroloij MED urology.

ürpermek 1. to stand on end, to bristle up (*hair*); **2.** to shudder, to shiver (*with, at*); **3.** to rise, to start (*voice*).

ürperti[1] shudder, shiver.

ürtiker MED nettle-rash.

ürümek to howl, to bark, to bay; *ürüyen köpek ısırmaz* barking dogs never bite.

ürün 1. product, crop, harvest; **2.** dairy product; **3.** *fig.* result; **4.** work (*art*).

üryan naked, bare, nude.

üs , -ssü 1. base, basis, foundation; **2.** MATH exponent; **3.** MIL base.

üsçavuş MIL sergeant.

üslup , -bu manner, form, style.

üst , -tü 1. upper side, top (side), upper surface; **2.** upper part; **3.** outside, surface; **4.** clothing, dress, clothes; **5.** MIL superior; **6.** rest, remaining, residue; **7.** body; **8.** boss, superior; **9.** at *or* about (*time*); **10.** responsibility; ~ *bagaj* MOT roof rack; ~ *baş* clothes; ~ *çıkmak* (*or gelmek*) to win, to surpass, to exceed; ~ *perdeden konuşmak* to talk big, to bluster; ~ *-e* **1.** one after (*or upon*) another, successively; **2.** one on top of the other; **3.** very crowded; *-e çıkmak* to be innocent seemingly; *-ten* superficially; *-ü*

başı dökülmek to be in rags; *-ü kapalı* (*or örtülü*) in an indirect way, indirectly; *-üme iyilik sağlık* (*-üne, -ünüze sağlık, -üne sağlık or -ünüze şifalar*) may God preserve from such an ill luck; *-ünde durmak* to give a subject importance, to emphasize; *-ünde kalmak* to be left to the highest bidder (*auction*); *-ünden atmak* not to take over the duty; to acquit o.s. of; *-ünden geçmek* **1.** (*b-nin*) to violate, to rape; **2.** to pass over (*time*); *-üne almak* **1.** to bind o.s. to do s.th., to lay o.s. under an obligation; **2.** to take offence (*-i at*); *-üne atmak* (*b-nin*) to put the blame for s.th. on *s.o.*; *-üne basmak* to hit the nail on the head; *-üne bir bardak* (**soğuk**) *su içmek* (*bşin*) to lose hope, to kiss *s.th.* goodbye; *-üne düşmek* to be persistent on; *-üne gitmek* to interfere; *-üne koymak* to add; *-üne olmamak* to be unique; *-üne oturmak* to appropriate illegally; *-üne titremek* to love tenderly, to dance attendance (on); *-üne kondurmamak* to overprotect; *-üne tuz biber ekmek* to rub salt in the wound; *-üne -üne gitmek* (*bşin*) to harp on *s.th.*; *-üne varmak* **1.** to urge, to press s.o. hard, to give s.o. a hard time; **2.** to bid higher; **3.** to attack; **4.** to marry *s.o.* while he is already married; *-üne vazife olmamak* (*or değil*) to be none of one's business; *-üne yatmak* to arrogate; to appropriate s.th. for oneself, not to give s.th. back; *-üne yıkmak* **1.** to dump on s.o. (*a hard job*) **2.** to cast the blame on, to impute; *-üne yok* superb, the best; *-üne yürümek* to pretend as if about attack; to march against; *-ünüze afiyet* (*or sağlık*) may you stay in good health.

üstat [. -] master, teacher, instructor.

üstçene ANAT upper jaw.

üstderi ANAT epidermis.

üstdudak ANAT upper lip.

üste further, in addition; *-sinden gelmek* F to bring about, to manage, to realize, to achieve, to wangle.

üsteğmen MIL first lieutenant.

üstelemek 1. to be added to; **2.** to renew incidence, to recur (*illness*); **3.** to insist on, to dominate, to urge; **4.** to renew (*request, etc.*).

üstelik 1. furthermore, besides, in addition; **2.** extra, addition.

üstgeçit overpass, overcrossing.

üstinsan superman.

üstlük overcoat.

üstsubay senior officer.

üstübeç CHEM white lead.

üstün superior (-den to), outstanding, excellent, exceeding, surpassing, victorious; ~ *gelmek* to surpass, to exceed; ~ *tutmak* to prefer s.th. or s.o. to another, to esteem (or appreciate) s.th. or s.o. more than another, to consider superior.

üstünkörü superficial(ly).

üstünlük superiority; supremacy; ~ *derecesi* GR superlative (degree); ~ *kompleksi* superiority complex.

üstüpü tow, (cotton) waste.

üstyapı superstructure.

üşenç laziness, sloth.

üşengeç, üşengen lazy, slothful.

üşengeçlik laziness, sloth.

üşenmek to be slack, to be too lazy to do, to do with reluctance.

üşmek, (-er) to flock (-e to), to crowd.

üşniye BOT algae.

üşümek 1. to feel cold; 2. to catch cold.

üşüntü flocking, crowding.

üşürmek caus. of üşmek.

üşüşmek to flock together, to crowd.

üşütmek 1. to cause to catch cold; 2. to catch cold; 3. sl. to go nuts.

üşütük sl. nutty.

ütmek[1], (-er) 1. to singe; 2. to hold to (or over) the fire; 3. to roast over the fire (corn, etc.).

ütmek[2], (-er) to win (in a game).

ütopik utopian, unrealizable, unattainable.

ütopist utopist, utopian.

ütopya, ütopi utopia.

ütopyacı utopist.

ütü 1. (flat-)iron; 2. crease; 3. ironing, pressing; ~ *bezi* press cloth; ~ *tahtası* ironing board; ~ *yapmak* to iron, to do the ironing.

ütücü ironer, presser.

ütülemek 1. to iron, to press; 2. to singe off.

ütülmek to get beaten (in a game).

ütülü 1. ironed, pressed; 2. singer.

ütüsüz 1. unironed, not ironed; 2. unsinged.

üvendire oxgoad.

üvey, -i, -si step-; ~ *ana* stepmother; ~

baba stepfather; ~ *evlat* stepchild; ~ *evlat gibi tutmak* (or *bakmak*) to treat s.o. unkindly (or unfairly).

üveyik ZOO wood-pigeon.

üveymek to coo (dove, pigeon, etc.).

üvez[1] (ağacı) BOT service tree.

üvez[2] ZOO a kind of stinging fly.

üye 1. member (of a council, etc.); 2. ANAT organ.

üyelik membership.

üzengi stirrup.

üzengikemiği, -ni ANAT stapes.

üzengilemek to spur.

üzengitaşı, -nı ARCH impost.

üzere 1. (in order) to, just about to; 2. on condition that, provided that; 3. as; 4. of (or from) which; 5. at the point of (doing s.th.).

üzeri 1. top; 2. outer surface; 3. clothes; 4. body; 5. the rest, remainder; 6. at or about (time).

üzerinde 1. on, over, above, on top of; 2. with regard to, as to, concerning, in respect of.

üzerlik harmal.

üzgü oppression, cruelty.

üzgün 1. sad (at), sorrowful, grieved (at, about), 2. weak, feeble, invalid.

üzmek, (-er) 1. to hurt the feelings of, to grieve, to sadden, to vex, to annoy; 2. to strain, to break.

üzücü distressing, annoying, tormenting, saddening.

üzülmek 1. pass. of üzmek; 2. to be sorry for, to regret, to be sad (at, about); 3. to be worn out.

üzüm BOT grape; ~ *şekeri* glucose; ~ *-e baka baka kararır* a man is known by the company he keeps; *-ün çöpü armudun sapı var demek* to be hypercritical, to be fussy; *-ünü ye de bağını sorma* don't look a gift horse in the mouth.

üzüm üzüm (used in üzmek and üzülmek) very, terribly, dreadfully.

üzüntü 1. sorrow, anxiety, worry, trouble; 2. annoyance, vexation, chagrin; 3. grief, dejection.

üzüntülü 1. sad, worried, grieved unhappy; 2. tedious, troublesome; 3. annoying, vexatious; 4. anxious.

üzüntüsüz 1. carefree; 2. easy, simple, effortless.

V, W, X

vaat, -dı promise; commitment, assurance; ~ etm. to promise; -te bulunmak to make a promise (-e to), to promise.

vaaz isl. sermon, homily; ~ etm. to give a sermon, to sermonize, to preach.

vacip, -bi 1. obligatory, incumbent; 2. isl. incumbent on a Muslim (duty); ~ olm. to be necessary.

vade 1. term, time; prompt; 2. due date; date of maturity; 3. one's hour of death; -si geçmiş overdue (check, etc.); -si gelmek 1. to fall due; 2. fig. to live one's last hour.

vadeli having a fixed term, time...; hesap (or mevduat) time deposit; ~ satış time sale.

vadesiz having no fixed term, open...; ~ hesap (or mevduat) demand deposit.

vadetmek [ā] [x ..] to promise.

vadi [- -] 1. valley; 2. fig. topic, subject.

vaftiz baptism; ~ anası godmother; ~ babası godfather; ~ etm. to baptize.

vagon railway car; ~ restoran restaurant car, dining car, diner.

vagonet, -ti RAIL car.

vagonli RAIL wagon-lit, sleeping car, sleeper.

vah what a pity!, too bad!

vaha oasis.

vahamet, -ti [. - .] gravity, seriousness (of a situation).

vahdaniyet, -ti [. - . .] the unity of God.

vahdet, -ti 1. unity, oneness; 2. ♀ mf., wf.

vahi [- -] futile; silly.

vahim serious, grave.

vahimleşmek to become serious.

vahit, -di 1. one, single, sole; 2. unique; 3. ♀ mf.

vahiy, -hyi ECCL inspiration, revelation.

vahşet, -ti 1. wildness, savageness; 2. brutality.

vahşi [ī] 1. wild, savage; barbarous; 2. brutal; 3. untamed; 4. virgin (forest).

vahşilik s. vahşet.

vaız, -a'zı isl. sermon.

vait, -a'di s. vaat.

vaiz isl. preacher.

vajina ANAT vagina.

vajinal ANAT vaginal.

vaka event, happening, incident, occurrence (a. MED); ~ yeri scene.

vakaa [- . -] [x . -] although, though.

vakanüvis [. . . .] chronicler.

vakar [. -] gravity, dignity, sedateness.

vakarlı [. - .] sedate, dignified, grave.

vakarsız undignified.

vaketa [. x .] calfskin.

vakfetmek [x ..] 1. to make over to religious or charitable foundation (property); 2. to devote (-e to), to dedicate (-e to).

vakfiye ECCL deed of trust (of a pious foundation).

vakıa [- . .] 1. event, happening; 2. although, though.

vakıf, -kfı foundation, wakf; Vakıflar Genel Müdürlüğü pr. n. Directorate of Wakfs.

vâkıf aware, cognizant; ~ olm. to be aware (or cognizant) (-e of).

vakıfname [. . - .] deed of trust.

vaki [- -] happening, taking place; ~ olm. to happen, to occur, to take place.

vakit, -kti 1. time; 2. when; ~ almak to take time; ~ daralıyor time presses; ~ geçirmek to pass the time, to occupy o.s.; ~ kaybetmeden without losing any time, at once, promptly; ~ kazanmak to gain time; ~ nakittir pro. time is money; ~ öldürmek to kill time; ~ ~ from time to time, at times; -ler hayrolsun! good day!; vakti gelmek (for s.o.'s hour of death) to be at hand; vakti yerinde well-off, well-fixed; vaktini almak (b-nin) to take s.o.'s time; vaktiyle 1. at the proper time, in time; 2. in the past, once, once upon a time.

vakitli timely, opportune; ~ vakitsiz at all sorts of times.

vakitsiz untimely, inopportune, premature.

vaktaki [. - .] [. x .] obs. when.

vakum [x .] MEC vacuum.

vakumlu MEC vacuum-operated.

vakur [ū] sedate, dignified, grave.

vak vak 1. quack, quack!; 2. quacking

(of a duck).

valans CHEM valence.

vale *cards*: jack, knave.

valf valve.

vali [ā] governor *(of a province)*, vali.

valide [ā] mother; ~ **sultan** HIST mother of the reigning sultan.

valilik 1. governorship; **2.** governor's office.

valiz valise, travel(l)ing bag.

vallahi [x - .] by God!, I swear it's true!; ~ **billahi** I swear to God it's true!

vals waltz; ~ **yapmak** to waltz.

vamp, **-pı 1.** vamp; **2.** vampish.

vampir 1. vampire; **2.** ZOO vampire bat.

vana valve.

vandalizm vandalism.

vanilya [. x .] BOT vanilla.

vantilasyon ventilation.

vantilatör fan, ventilator; ~ **kayışı** fan *(or* ventilator) belt.

vantriok, **-ku** ventriloquist.

vantuz 1. MED cupping glass; **2.** ZOO sucker; ~ **çekmek** to cup.

vaporizasyon vaporization.

vaporizatör vaporizer.

vapur 1. steamer, steamship; **2.** *sl.* very drunk person; ~ **seyahati** voyage.

vapurculuk operating a steamship line.

var 1. existing, in existence; **2.** available, at hand; present, in attendance; **3.** there is; there are; **4.** one's all, everything one has; ~ **etm.** to create; ~ **gücüyle** *(or* **kuvvetiyle)** with all his might; ~ **ol!** may you live long!; good for you!; ~ **olm.** to exist; **-ı yoğu** everything one owns.

varagele boat which is propelled by a guess-rope.

varak 1. sheet *(of paper, gold leaf)*; **2.** leaf *(of a book)*.

varaka printed form; certificate.

varakçı 1. gilder; **2.** silverer.

varaklamak 1. to gild; **2.** to silver.

varaklı 1. gilded; **2.** silvered.

varda [x .] NAUT keep clear!, make way!

vardabandıra NAUT signalman.

vardakosta [. . x .] **1.** NAUT coast guard cutter; **2.** *sl.* big and good-looking woman.

vardiya [x . .] **1.** shift *(in a factory)*; **2.** NAUT watch; ~ **şefi** shift boss.

varılmak *pass. of* **varmak**; **oraya üç saatte varılır** it takes three hours to get there.

varış 1. arrival; **2.** *fig.* comprehension,

understanding; **-ına gelişim, tarhana aşına bulgur aşım** *pro.* as you treat others, so will they treat you.

varışlı clever, quick of comprehension.

varidat, **-tı** [- . -] income; revenue.

varil barrel, keg.

varis MED varix, varicosity.

vâris heir, inheritor.

varisli MED varicose.

varit, **-di** likely to happen; possible.

variyet, **-ti** [ā] P wealth, riches.

varlık 1. existence, being; **2.** presence; **3.** creature; **4.** wealth, riches; ~ **göstermek** to make one's presence felt; ~ **içinde yaşamak** to live in easy circumstances; ~ **içinde yokluk** scarcity despite wealth.

varlıklı wealthy, rich, well-to-do.

varlıksal existential.

varma *vn. of* **varmak**; ~ **limanı** port of discharge.

varmak, **(-ır) 1.** to arrive *(-e* at, in), to reach; to get *(-e* to); **2.** *(for a woman)* to marry *(a man)*; **varsın gelmesin!** it doesn't matter whether he comes or not.

varoluş existence.

varoş suburb.

varsayılı hypothetical.

varsayım hypothesis; supposition, assumption.

varsaymak 1. to suppose, to assume; **2.** to hypothesize.

varta great peril, dangerous situation, tight spot; **-yı atlatmak** to turn the corner.

varyans variance.

varyant, **-tı 1.** variant; **2.** diversion, detour.

varyasyon MUS variation.

varyemez miser, pinchpenny.

varyete variety show.

varyos sledge (hammer).

vasat, **-tı 1.** average; mediocre; **2.** environment; **3.** centre, *Am.* center.

vasati [ī] **1.** average, mean; **2.** central; ~ **olarak** on the average.

vasıf, **-sfı 1.** quality, attribute; **2.** GR adjective.

vasıflandırmak to characterize, to describe.

vasıflı qualified, skilled.

vasıl olm. to arrive *(-e* at, in), to reach.

vasıta [- . . .] **1.** means; **2.** vehicle; **3.** intermediary; **4.** instrument, implement; **-sıyla** by means of, through.

vasıtalı [- . . .] **1.** indirect; **2.** indirectly, through an intermediary.

vasıtasız [- . . .] **1.** direct; **2.** directly.

vasi [. -] JUR guardian; executor.

vâsi, -ii broad, wide.

vasilik JUR guardianship, wardship.

vasistas transom (window).

vasiyet, -ti 1. will, testament; **2.** last request (*of a dying person*); **~ etm.** to bequeath.

vasiyetname [. . . - .] will, testament.

vasletmek [x . .] (*bşi bşe*) to unite *s.th.* to *s.th.*

vaşak ZOO lynx.

vaşington BOT navel orange.

vat, -tı ELECT watt; **~ saat** watt-hour.

vatan native country, motherland, fatherland, mother country; **-a ihanet** treason; **-ı kurtarmak** *sl.* to manage the situation.

vatandaş citizen, compatriot; national.

vatandaşlık citizenship; **~ hakları** JUR civil rights.

vatani [î] patriotic; **~ görev** (*or* **vazife**) military service.

vatanperver, vatansever patriotic.

vatanperverlik, vatanseverlik patriotism.

vatansız stateless.

vatka shoulder padding (*in a garment*).

vatman tram-driver, driver of a streetcar.

vatoz (*balığı*) zoo ray, skate.

vaveyla [- . -] shout; **-yı koparmak** to raise a shout.

vay oh!, woe!; **~ başıma!** woe is me!

vazelin vaseline.

vazetmek 1. to impose (*a tax*); **2.** to make (*a law*).

va'zetmek to preach, to sermonize.

vazgeçmek to give up, to abandon, to quit; to renounce, to waive.

vazıh [â] manifest, clear.

vazife [. - .] **1.** duty, responsibility; **2.** homework; **3.** employment, job; **~ aşkı** love of one's job; **senin ne üstüne ~?** what's that to you?

vazifelendirmek to commission, to entrust, to charge.

vazifeli [. - . .] **1.** charged with a duty; **2.** employed; **3.** on duty.

vazifeşinas [. - . . -] dutiful; conscientious (*worker*).

vaziyet, -ti 1. situation, circumstances, plight; **2.** condition, state; **3.** position; **~ almak** MIL to stand at attention; **-e**

bağlı it all depends.

vazo [x .] vase.

ve and; **~ saire** et cetera, etc., and so forth.

veba [â] MED plague, pestilence.

vebal, -li [â] evil consequences (*of an evil action*); **-i boynuna!** on your head be it!, the responsibility is yours!; **-ini çekmek** to suffer the consequences (*of an evil action*).

vebalı [â] plague-stricken.

veca, -aı [â] pain, ache.

vecibe [î] duty, obligation.

vecih, -çhi 1. face; **2.** way, manner; **bu veçhile** thus, in this way; **hiç bir veçhile** in no way.

vecit, -cdi ecstasy, rapture; **vecde gelmek** to become ecstatic.

veciz [î] pithy, meaty, laconic.

vecize [î] epigram, aphorism.

veçhe 1. direction, way, course; **2.** side, aspect.

veda, -aı [â] farewell, good-bye; **~ etm.** to say farewell (*or* good-bye) (*-e* to); **~ partisi** farewell party; **~ ziyareti** farewell visit; **-a gitmek** (*b-ne*) to pay *s.o.* a farewell visit.

vedalaşmak [. - . .] to say farewell (*ile* to), to say good-bye (*ile* to).

vedia [î] **1.** deposit, trust; **2.** ♀ *wf.*

vefa [â] fidelity, loyalty, faithfulness; **~ etm.** (*for one's life*) to last long enough, to suffice.

vefakâr [- - .], **vefalı** [. - .] faithful, loyal.

vefasız [â] unfaithful, disloyal.

vefasızlık [â] unfaithfulness, disloyalty.

vefat, -tı [â] death, decease; **~ etm.** to die, to pass away.

vehim, -hmi groundless fear.

vehmetmek [x . .] to forebode, to fear.

vejetalin vegetable butter.

vekâlet, -ti 1. procuration, attorneyship; proxy; **2.** POL ministry; **~ etm.** to represent, to act for, to deputize; **~ vermek** (*b-ne*) to give *s.o.* the right of representing.

vekâleten [. x . .] by proxy (*or* procuration).

vekâletname [. - . - .] proxy, procuration.

vekil [î] **1.** agent, representative, attorney, deputy, proxy; **2.** POL minister of state.

vekilharç majordomo, butler.

vekillik 1. proxy; attorneyship; **2.** POL ministry.

vektör MATH vector.
velayet, -ti 1. JUR guardianship, wardship; **2.** sainthood.
velense [. x .] a kind of thick blanket.
velespit, -ti velocipede, bicycle.
velet, -di child, kid, brat.
velev, velev ki even if...
velhasıl [x - .] in short.
veli [i] **1.** guardian, protector (*of a child*); **2.** saint, wali; **3.** ♀ *mf.*
veliaht, -dı heir apparent, crown prince, successor to the throne.
veliahtlık heir apparency.
velilik 1. guardianship, wardship; **2.** sainthood.
velinimet, -ti [. - -.] benefactor, patron.
velur velure, velvet.
velvele clamo(u)r, outcry, hubbub; **-ye vermek** to kick up (*or* raise) a row, to cause a tumult.
velveleci clamorous, noisy.
Venedik [x . .] *pr. n.* Venice.
Venüs AST Venus.
veranda veranda, porch.
veraset, -ti inheritance; heredity; **~ hakkı** right of succession; **~ ve intikal vergisi** death duties.
verecek debt, debit.
verecekli debtor.
verem MED tuberculosis; **~ olm.** to get tuberculosis.
veremli tubercular, tuberculous.
veresiye 1. on credit; **2.** *fig.* partially, halfway.
verev bias, diagonal.
vergi 1. tax; **2.** gift, endowment; **~ beyannamesi** tax statement (*or* return); ♀ **İdaresi** IRS (*American income tax department = Internal Revenue Service*); **~ kaçakçılığı** tax evasion; **~ mükellefi** taxpayer; **~ tahsildarı** tax-collector; **-ye tabi** taxable.
vergilemek to tax.
vergilendirmek to tax.
vergili 1. taxable, subject to taxation; **2.** generous.
vergisiz tax-free.
veri datum.
verici transmitter; **~ istasyonu** transmitting station.
verim output, production, yield.
verimli productive, fruitful.
verimlilik productivity, fruitfulness.
verimsiz unproductive, unfruitful.
verimsizlik unproductiveness, unfruitfulness.
veriştirmek 1. *caus. of* **verişmek; 2.**

(*b-ne*) to give *s.o.* a dressing down.
verkaç, -çı *football*: passing and running.
vermek, (-ir) 1. to give; to hand; to deliver; **2.** to leave, to bequeath; **3.** to attribute (-*e* to); **4.** to abandon o.s. (-*e* to), to give o.s. over (-*e* to); **5.** to give in marriage (*one's daughter*); **6.** to yield, to produce; **7.** to hold (*a party, etc.*); to give (*a concert*); **8.** to suffer (*losses*).
vermut, -tu vermouth.
vernik varnish.
verniklemek to varnish.
veryansın etm. to squander; to destroy without mercy.
vesait, -ti vehicles, means of transportation.
vesayet, -ti JUR guardianship, wardship.
vesika 1. document, certificate; **2.** ration card.
vesikalı licensed (*prostitute*).
vesikalık suitable for a document; **~ fotoğraf** passport photograph.
vesile 1. means, cause; **2.** opportunity; **bu -yle** thus, as a result of this.
vesselam [x . -] so that's that!
vestibül vestibule.
vestiyer cloakroom, checkroom, vestiary.
vestiyerci cloakroom attendant.
vesvese apprehension, misgiving.
vesveseli apprehensive.
veteriner veterinarian.
veterinerlik veterinary medicine.
vetire [i] process.
veto [x .] veto; **~ etm.** to veto.
veya, veyahut or.
veyöz night-light.
vezaret, -ti [ā] HIST vizierate, viziership.
vezin, -zni *poet.* metre, *Am.* meter.
vezinli *poet.* metrical.
vezir [i] **1.** HIST vizier; **2.** *chess*: queen.
veziriazam HIST grand vizier.
vezirlik HIST viziership, vizierate.
vezne cashier's desk (*or* window); teller's window; cashier's office.
vezneci *s.* **veznedar 1.**
veznedar [ā] **1.** cashier, teller; **2.** treasurer (*of a firm, etc.*).
vıcık gooey, sticky; **~ ~ etm.** to make gooey (*or* sticky).
vıdı vıdı etm. F to yak, to chatter.
vınlamak to whiz, to buzz, to whir.
vır vır etm. to nag, to grumble.

vırvırcı grumbler.

vız buzz; hum; ~ **gelir tırıs gider** F I don't give a damn (or tinker's cuss); ~ **gelmek** F to be a matter of indifference.

vızıldamak 1. to buzz; to hum; to ping; **2.** to keep on complaining.

vızıltı 1. buzz; hum; **2.** complaint.

vızır vızır constantly, continually.

vızlamak s. **vızıldamak.**

vibrato MUS vibrato.

vibriyon vibrio.

vicdan conscience; ~ **azabı** pangs (or pricks) of conscience, remorse; ~ **hürriyeti** freedom of conscience; **-ı sızlamak** to suffer a pang of conscience.

vicdanen conscientiously.

vicdani of conscience, pertaining to conscience.

vicdanlı [ā] conscientious, just, fair.

vicdansız [ā] unjust, unfair; unscrupulous.

vida MEC screw.

vidala [. x .] calfskin.

vidalamak to screw.

vidalı [x . .] screwed; ~ **kapak** screw cap.

video 1. video; **2.** video player; video recorder.

videokonferans video conference.

vikaye [ā] protection; ~ **etm.** to protect.

vikont, -tu viscount.

vikontes viscountess.

viladi [. - -] inborn, congenital.

vilayet, -ti province, vilayet.

villa villa.

vinç, -çi MEC crane; winch.

viola MUS viola.

vira [x .] continuously; ~ **etm.** to lift; ~ **söylemek** to talk incessantly.

viraj curve, bend; ~ **almak** to go around (or take) a curve.

viran [- -] ruined, in ruins.

virane [- - .] ruin; **-ye çevirmek** to ruin, to destroy.

virgül comma.

virtüöz MUS virtuoso.

virüs [x .] MED & computer virus.

visamiral, -li vice admiral.

viski whisky.

viskonsül vice-consul.

viskoz viscose.

viskozite viscosity.

vişne [x .] BOT morello, sour cherry, amarelle.

vişneçürüğü, -nü purple-brown, ox-ide-brown.

vitamin vitamin(e).

vitaminli vitamined, vitaminized.

vitaminsizlik MED avitaminosis.

vites gear; ~ **değiştirmek** to shift gears; ~ **kolu** gear lever, gearshift; ~ **kutusu** gearbox, transmission; ~ **küçültmek** to change down, to downshift; **-e takmak** to put into gear.

vitrin 1. shopwindow; **2.** china cabinet.

viyadük viaduct.

viyaklamak to cry, to wail.

viyak viyak: ~ **ağlamak** s. **viyaklamak.**

Viyana [. x .] pr. n. Vienna.

viyola [. x .] MUS viola.

viyolist, -ti MUS violist.

viyolon violon, violin.

viyolonist, -ti violinist.

viyolonsel (violon)cello.

vize visa.

vizite [x . .] **1.** visit, house call; **2.** rounds (made by a doctor in a hospital); **3.** doctor's fee.

viziyer visor, peak (of a cap).

vizon ZOO mink.

vizör PHOT view-finder.

vokal, -li vocal; ~ **müzik** vocal music.

vokalist, -ti vocalist.

volan 1. MEC flywheel; **2.** volant, flounce (on a woman's dress).

vole [x .] football, tennis: volley.

voleybol, -lü volleyball.

volfram CHEM wolfram, tungsten.

volkan volcano.

volkanik volcanic.

volt, -tu ELECT volt.

volta 1. NAUT fouling of a cable; **2.** sl. pacing back and forth; pacing up and down; ~ **atmak** to pace back and forth; to pace up and down; **-sını almak** sl. to run away, to beat it.

voltaj ELECT voltage.

voltmetre ELECT voltmeter.

vonoz young mackerel or sardine.

votka vodka.

voyvo [x .] sl. hey!

voyvoda HIST voivode, vaivode.

v.s. (abbr. for ve saire) etc., et cetera.

vual, -li voile.

vualet, -ti veiling made of voile.

vuku, -uu [- -] occurrence; ~ **bulmak** (or **-a gelmek**) to occur, to happen, to take place; **-u halinde** in case (of).

vukuat, -tı [. - -] **1.** events, incidents; **2.** police case, crime.

vukuf [. -] knowledge, knowing.

vukuflu well-informed.

vukufsuz uninformed, ignorant.
vurdumduymaz 1. thick-headed, stupid; **2.** thick-skinned, insensitive, callous.
vurgu GR stress, accent.
vurgulamak 1. to emphasize, to stress; **2.** GR to stress, to accent.
vurgulu GR stressed, accented.
vurgun 1. in love with, sweet on, smitten with; **2.** ill-gotten gain, gravy; **3.** the bends, caisson disease, the chokes; **4.** swindle; **~ vurmak** F to pull a deal, to make a killing; **~ yemek** to be crippled by the bends; to die from the bends.
vurguncu profiteer.
vurgunculuk profiteering.
vurgusuz GR unstressed, unaccented.
vurmak, (-ur) 1. to hit, to strike; **2.** to knock (-e on); to tap (-e on); **3.** to hunt; **4.** to shoot; to stab; **5.** to kill; **6.** to hit (*a target*); **7.** (*for a shadow, light*) to hit, to strike, to fall on; **8.** (*for a clock*) to strike (*the hour*); **9.** to steal; **10.** (*for a shoe*) to chafe, to pinch, to blister; **11.** (*for one's heart or pulse*) to beat; **12.** to strike out along, to head out along (*a road*); to head for; **13.** to give (*an injection*); ***vur dedikse öldür demedik ya!*** fig. I didn't ask you to go that far!; ***vur patlasın çal oynasın*** enjoying o.s. by

whooping it up (*or* by painting the town red).
vurucu: ~ güç striking power (*of an army*); **~ tim** team of sharpshooters.
vurulmak 1. *pass. of* **vurmak**; **2.** (*b-ne*) to fall in love with s.o., to be smitten with s.o.
vuruntu yapmak MOT to knock, to pink.
vuruş 1. blow, stroke; **2.** MUS beat.
vuruşkan combative, belligerent.
vuruşmak to fight each other, to have a fight.
vuslat, -tı union (*with one's beloved*).
vusul, -lü [. -] arrival; **~ bulmak** to arrive (-e at).
vuzuh [. -] clearness, clarity.
vücut, -du [ü] **1.** body; **2.** existence; **~ bulmak** (*or* **vücuda gelmek**) to arise, to come into being; **vücuda getirmek** to create, to produce; **-tan düşmek** to grow thin.
vücutlu heavily built, hulking (*person*).
vüsat, -ti 1. breadth; **2.** MATH volume; **3.** spaciousness.
web F internet; **~ sayfası** webpage; **~ sitesi** website.
www (= **world wide web**) *bir internet adresin başlangıcı*
x ışınları, -nı X rays.

Y

ya¹ [ā] o!, oh!; **~ Rabbi!** o Lord!, oh my God!
ya² either... or...; **~ bu deveyi gütmeli, ya bu diyardan gitmeli** when in Rome, do as the Romans do; **~ sen, ~ ben!** it's either you or me!
yaba wooden pitchfork.
yabalamak to pitchfork.
yaban 1. wild, wilderness; **2.** P stranger; **-a atmak** to disregard, to sneeze at, to sniff at, to brush aside; **-a söylemek** to talk nonsense (*or* rot).
yabanarısı, -nı ZOO wasp; hornet.
yabancı 1. stranger; foreigner, alien; **2.** foreign, alien; **3.** unfamiliar, strange; **~ düşmanlığı** xenophobia; **-sı olm.** (*bşin*) to be unfamiliar with s.th.; **sesi ~ gelmedi ama ismini hatırlayamadım** his voice struck a cord but I

couldn't remember his name.
yabancılaşmak to become strangers to each other.
yabancılık 1. foreignness; **2.** unfamiliarity, strangeness.
yabandomuzu, -nu ZOO wild boar.
yabangülü, -nü BOT dog rose, dogberry.
yabani [- -] **1.** wild; **2.** *fig.* shy, timid; **3.** *fig.* boorish, crude.
yabanilik [. - - .] **1.** wildness; **2.** *fig.* shyness; **3.** *fig.* boorishness.
yabankedisi ZOO wild cat.
yabanlaşmak to go wild.
yabanlık visiting clothes.
yabansı strange, odd.
yabansımak to find strange.
yad 1. strange, foreign; **2.** enemy; **3.** stranger, foreigner; **~ elde** in a foreign

land; away from home; **~ eller** foreign lands.

yâd etm. to mention, to talk about, to remember.

yadımlama BIOL catabolism, dissimilation.

yadımlamak BIOL to catabolize, to dissimilate.

yadırgamak to find strange (or odd).

yadigâr [- . -] keepsake, souvenir, remembrance.

yadsımak to deny; to reject.

yafa (portakalı) BOT Jaffa (orange), Valencia (orange).

yafta [x .] label.

yağ 1. oil; fat; suet; tallow; **2.** butter; margarine; **3.** grease; lard; **~ bağlamak** to get fat, to put on fat; **~ bal olsun!** I hope you'll enjoy it (food); **~ çekmek** to butter up, to flatter, to toady, to apple-polish; **~ çubuğu** MOT dipstick; **~ gibi gitmek** (or kaymak) (for a vehicle) to go like a bird; **~ kutusu** MEC crankcase; **~ süzgeci** MOT oil filter; **~ tulumu** fig. very fat person, tub of lard; **-dan kıl çeker gibi** as easy as taking candy from a baby, as easy as falling off a log.

yağbezi, -ni ANAT sebaceous gland.

yağcı 1. seller of oil, butter, etc.; **2.** lubricator; greaser; oiler; **3.** fig. flatterer, toady.

yağcılık fig. flattery; **~ etm.** to flatter, to butter up.

yağdanlık oilcan; lubricator.

yağdırmak 1. caus. of **yağmak**; **2.** fig. to rain, to shower.

yağdoku ANAT fatty tissue.

yağımsı oily, oleaginous; fatty.

yağır withers (of a horse).

yağış rain; precipitation.

yağışlı rainy, showery.

yağız dark, swarthy.

yağlama vn. of **yağlamak** lubrication.

yağlamak 1. to grease, to oil, to lubricate; **2.** fig. to flatter, to butter up; **yağlayıp ballamak** to praise to the skies.

yağlanmak 1. pass. of **yağlamak**; **2.** to get fat.

yağlayıcı 1. lubricant; **2.** lubricator; grease gun; **3.** lubricatory.

yağlı 1. oily, greasy; fatty; suety; tallowy; lardy; **2.** fat, obese; plump; **3.** fig. rich, well off, in the money; **4.** fig. profitable; **~ ballı olm.** to be on the sweetest of terms with each other;

~ çarık sl. rich; **~ güreş** greased wrestling; **~ kâğıt 1.** oil paper; **2.** tracing paper; **~ kapı** F rich employer; **~ kuyruk** fig. milch cow; **~ lokma** fig. rich windfall; **~ müşteri** profitable customer.

yağlıboya 1. oil paint; **2.** oil...; **3.** gangway!

yağlık napkin; handkerchief.

yağma 1. pillage, sack; **2.** loot, booty; **~ etm.** to loot, to sack, to plunder, to pillage; **~ yok!** nothing doing!, no way!

yağmacı [x . .] looter, sacker, plunderer, pillager.

yağmacılık [x . . .] pillage.

yağmak, (-ar) to rain, to shower.

yağmalamak to loot, to sack, to plunder, to pillage.

yağmur rain; **~ boşanmak** to pour heavily, to come down in buckets; **~ duası** ritual prayer for rain (said by villagers during a drought); **~ mevsimi** rainy season; **~ yağarken küpünü doldurmak** fig. to make hay while the sun shines; **~ yağıyor** it is raining; **~ yemek** to get wet through (in the rain); **-dan kaçarken doluya tutulmak** fig. to jump out of the frying pan into the fire.

yağmurca ZOO chamois.

yağmurkuşağı, -nı rainbow.

yağmurkuşu, -nu ZOO plover.

yağmurlama sistemi sprinkling system.

yağmurlamak 1. to turn into rain, to get rainy; **2.** to sprinkle.

yağmurlu rainy; **~ gün** rainy day; **~ hava** rainy weather.

yağmurluk raincoat, mackintosh; oilskin.

yağsız 1. oilless; greaseless; butterless; nonfat; **2.** lean, fatless (meat), fat-free (milk, yoghurt).

yahey [ā] hurrah!, yippee!

yahni fricassee, ragout.

yahşi 1. good, nice; **2.** pretty; beautiful; handsome.

yahu [ā] [x .] F see here!, look here!; **ne yapıyorsun ~?** what on earth are you doing?

Yahudi 1. Jew; **2.** Jewish; **~ pazarlığı** fig. hard bargaining, haggle.

Yahudice Hebrew.

Yahudilik 1. Jewishness; **2.** Judaism.

yahut [ā] [x .] or.

yaka 1. collar; **2.** edge, bank, shore; **~ bir tarafta, paça bir tarafta** fig. out at elbows, seedy; dishevel(l)ed; ~ *pa-ça* by main force; ~ *paça etm.* to throw out by main force; ~ *silmek* (*b-den*) to get fed up with *s.o.*; *-dan atmak* *fig.* to get rid (*or* shut) of; *-dan geçirmek* to adopt (*a child*); *-sı-na yapışmak* to badger, to hound, to bedevil; *-sını bırakmamak* *fig.* to hound, to badger, to bedevil; *-yı ele vermek* to get caught, to be collared; *-yı kurtarmak* (*or sıyırmak*) to evade, to wriggle (*-den* out of).

yakacak fuel.

yakalamak 1. to catch, to collar, to nab; to grab, to seize, to get hold of; **2.** to notice, to see, to spot, to detect; **3.** to hold responsible.

yakalanmak 1. *pass. of* **yakalamak**; **2.** to catch (*an illness*); **3.** to be caught in (*the rain, a storm*).

yakalı collared.

yakalık collar.

yakamoz phosphorescence (*in the sea*).

yakarış prayer, entreaty.

yakarmak to beg, to implore, to entreat.

yakı plaster; blister; cautery; ~ *vurmak* (*or yapıştırmak*) to plaster; to blister; to cauterize.

yakıcı 1. burning; **2.** biting (*to the taste*); **3.** CHEM caustic.

yakın 1. near (*-e* to), close (*-e* to), nearby; **2.** close (*friend*); **3.** very similar (*-e* to); **4.** nearby place, neighbo(u)rhood; **5.** relative, relation; ~ *akraba* close relative, near relation; ~ *za-manda* **1.** soon, in a short time; **2.** recently; *-da* **1.** nearby, close at hand; **2.** recently; **3.** in the near future, soon; *-dan* at close range; *-dan bilmek* to know well, to be closely acquainted with.

yakınlaşmak 1. to approach, to draw near; **2.** *fig.* to become close (*-e* to), to become a friend of s.o.

yakınlık 1. nearness, closeness proximity; **2.** *fig.* closeness, warmth, rapport, sympathy; ~ *duymak* to feel close (*-e* to); to feel a sympathy (*-e* for); ~ *gös-termek* to show concern (*-e* for), to behave warmly (*-e* toward).

yakınmak to complain.

yakınsak MATH, PHYS convergent.

yakışık almak to be suitable (*or* proper); *senin annenle böyle alay etmen yakışık almaz* it is not fit that you

should mock your mother so.

yakışıklı handsome, good-looking.

yakışıksız unsuitable, improper, unbecoming, unseemly.

yakışmak 1. to be suitable (*or* proper), to befit; **2.** to suit, to go well with.

yakıştırmak 1. *caus. of* **yakışmak**; **2.** (*bşi b-ne*) to regard *s.th.* as suitable for *s.o.*; to think that *s.th.* befits *s.o.*

yakıt, -tı fuel.

yakinen [. x .] for sure, for certain.

yaklaşık approximate.

yaklaşım approach.

yaklaşmak to approach, to draw near (*-e* to); to come close (*-e* to).

yaklaştırmak 1. to bring near, to draw near; **2.** to approximate.

yakmak, (-ar) 1. to light; to ignite; to set on fire, to set fire to; **2.** to burn (up); **3.** to scorch, to sear, to burn; **4.** (*for wool*) to irritate; **5.** to turn on, to light (*electric lights*); **6.** *fig.* to ruin, to cook s.o.'s goose; **7.** *fig.* to inflame with love; **8.** to apply (*henna*); **9.** to compose (*a folk song*); *yakıp yıkmak* to destroy utterly.

yakşi *s.* **yahşi**.

yakut, -tu [ā] ruby.

yalak 1. trough; **2.** basin (*of a fountain*).

yalama 1. *vn. of* **yalamak**; **2.** worn (*by friction*); ~ *olm.* to get worn.

yalamacı *sl.* toady, lickspittle.

yalamak 1. to lick; to lick up; to lap up; **2.** to skim over; to graze.

yalan 1. lie, fib, falsehood, untruth; **2.** false, untrue; ~ *atmak* to lie, to tell lies; ~ *çıkmak* to turn out untrue; ~ *dolan* pack of lies; ~ *dünya* this transitory life; ~ *makinesi* lie detector; ~ *söylemek* to lie, to tell lies; ~ *yanlış* false, erroneous; ~ *yere yemin* JUR perjury; ~ *yere yemin etm.* JUR to perjure o.s.; *-a şerbetli* prone to lying; *-ını çıkarmak* (*b-nin*) to give *s.o.* the lie; *-ını tutmak* (*or yakalamak*) (*b-nin*) to catch *s.o.* in a lie.

yalancı 1. liar; **2.** imitation, false, artificial; ~ *çıkarmak* (*b-ni*) **1.** to prove that *s.o.* is a liar; **2.** to call *s.o.* a liar; ~ *çıkmak* to turn out to be a liar; ~ *şahit* JUR perjurer; *-nın mumu yatsı-ya kadar yanar* *pro.* It doesn't take long for a lie to come to light.

yalancıakasya BOT black locust.

yalancıktan superficially; in pretence; ~ *bayıldı* he pretended to faint.

yalancılık lying.

yalandan superficially, only for appearance; ~ **ağladı** she pretended to cry.

yalanlamak to deny, to contradict.

yalanmak 1. *pass. of* **yalamak; 2.** to lick one's lips (*or* chops).

yalapşap superficially done.

yalaz flame.

yalçın 1. steep; **2.** ♀ *mf.*

yaldız 1. gilding, silvering; **2.** *fig.* veneer, gloss, glitter, gilt.

yaldızcı gilder, silverer.

yaldızlamak 1. to gild, to silver; **2.** *fig.* to give a deceptive glitter; **3.** F to cuckold.

yaldızlı 1. gilded, gilt, silvered; **2.** *fig.* gilded, honeyed.

yale (kilit) Yale lock.

yalelli [- x .]: ~ **gibi** (*or* **Arabın -si gibi**) unending, monotonous.

yalgın P mirage.

yalı 1. shore; bank; beach; **2.** waterside mansion; ~ **boyu** shore, beach; ~ **kazığı** big and tall.

yalıçapkını, -nı zoo kingfisher.

yalın 1. bare, naked; **2.** GR simple; ~ **hal** GR nominative case.

yalınayak barefoot; ~ **başı kabak 1.** bareheaded and barefoot; **2.** *fig.* clothed in rags.

yalınkat, -tı 1. one layer; **2.** *fig.* superficial, shallow.

yalıtım insulation.

yalıtkân PHYS nonconductive; insulative.

yalıtmak to insulate.

yalıyar GEOGR cliff.

yalız ANAT unstriated (*muscle*).

yallah [x .] go!, get going!

yalnız [x .] **1.** alone, by o.s.; **2.** lonely, lonesome; **3.** solitary, isolated, lone; **4.** just, only; **5.** but, however; ~ **başına** alone, by o.s.; ~ **bırakmak** (*b-ni*) to leave *s.o.* alone, to leave *s.o.* on his own.

yalnızca alone, by o.s.

yalnızcılık POL isolationism.

yalnızlaşmak to become isolated.

yalnızlık 1. loneliness, lonesomeness; **2.** isolation, solitude, loneness.

yalpa [x .] NAUT rolling, lurching; ~ **vurmak** to roll, to lurch.

yalpak P friendly.

yalpalamak *s.* **yalpa vurmak.**

yaltak(çı) *contp.* fawning, cringing.

yaltaklanmak to toady (*-e* to), to fawn, to cringe, to lickspittle, to play up (*-e*

to).

yaltakçılık toadying, fawning; ~ **etm.** to toady, to fawn, to lickspittle.

yalvarmak to beg, to entreat, to implore, to plead; **yalvarıp yakarmak** to beg earnestly.

yama 1. patch; **2.** birthmark, nevus; ~ **vurmak** to put a patch (*-e* on), to patch.

yamacı cobbler, shoe repairman.

yamaç, -cı 1. side; **2.** slope (*of a hill*); hillside; side (*of a mountain*).

yamak helper, apprentice.

yamalak *s.* **yarım ~.**

yamalamak to patch.

yamalı patched.

yamamak 1. to patch; **2.** to foist (*-e* on), to palm off (*-e* on).

yaman 1. very clever and capable; **2.** terrible, disastrous; **3.** frightful, extreme; **4.** violently, strongly.

yamanmak 1. *pass. of* **yamamak; 2.** *contp.* to be foisted (*or* palmed off) (*-e* on).

yampiri 1. lopsided; **2.** crabwise; ~ **gitmek** to move crabwise, to crab.

yamrı yumru 1. misshapen; gnarled, uneven and lumpy; **2.** very crooked.

yamuk 1. (a)skew, lopsided, crooked, bent; **2.** MATH trapezoid.

yamuk yumuk very crooked; twisted out of shape.

yamulmak to become bent to one side; to lean to one side.

yamyam cannibal.

yamyamlık cannibalism.

yamyassı [x .] as flat as a pancake.

yamyaş [x .] very damp.

yan 1. side; **2.** flank; **3.** vicinity, neighbo(u)rhood; **4.** direction; **5.** part (*of one's body*); **6.** aspect, side (*of a matter*); **7.** secondary; ~ **bakmak** to look askance (*-e* at); to leer (*-e* at); ~ **basmak** *fg.* to be deceived (*or* taken in); ~ **cümle** GR subordinate clause; ~ **çizmek** to avoid, to shirk, to evade, to dodge; ~ **etki** side effect; ~ **gelmek** (*or* ~ **gelip yatmak**) to take one's ease, to goof off; ~ **gözle** out of the corner of one's eye; ~ **gözle bakmak 1.** to look out of the corner of one's eye; **2.** *fig.* to leer (*-e* at); ~ **hakemi** linesman; ~ **sokak** by-street; ~ **tutmak** to take sides; ~ **ürün** by-product; ~ ~ sideways; ~ ~ **bakmak** to look daggers (*-e* at), to leer (*-e* at); ~ **-a** side by side; ~ **yatmak** to lean to one side; **-a 1.** in favo(u)r of, for, pro; **2.** concerning, as regards; **-dan** sideways, from one side; in profile; **-dan çarklı 1.** paddlewheel boat, paddle-steamer; **2.** F *tea served with the sugar brought in the saucer*; **-ı sıra** right along with, together with; **-ına bırakmamak** (*or* **koymamak**) not to leave unpunished.

yanak cheek; **yanağından kan damlamak** to be rosy-cheeked and healthy; **yanağından öpmek** to kiss s.o. on the cheek.

yanal lateral; **~ yükseklik** MATH apothem; **~ yüzey** MATH lateral surface.

yanardağ volcano.

yanardöner shot (*silk*); chatoyant (*fabric, gem*).

yanaşık drawn up alongside; parked alongside; docked alongside.

yanaşma 1. *vn. of* **yanaşmak**; **2.** farmhand.

yanaşmak 1. to approach, to draw near; to sidle up (-*e* to); **2.** to draw up (*or* pull) alongside; **3.** NAUT to dock; **4.** to accede to (*a request*); to incline, to seem willing; to go along with (*a plan*); **5.** (*b-ne*) to cozy up to *s.o.*

yanaştırmak 1. *caus. of* **yanaşmak**; **2.** to draw (*a vehicle*) up alongside (*a place*).

yandaş supporter, follower, advocate, adherent, partisan.

yandaşlık support, advocacy, adherence, partisanship.

yangaboz, yangabuç F hunchbacked, bent.

yangeçit bypass.

yangı MED inflammation, infection.

yangılanmak MED to become inflamed, to get infected.

yangılı MED **1.** inflamed, infected; **2.** inflammatory.

yangın 1. fire, conflagration; **2.** P fever; **3.** F madly in love, gone on; **~ bombası** fire (*or* incendiary) bomb; **~ çıkarmak** to start a fire; **~ kulesi** fire tower; **~ sigortası** fire insurance; **~ tulumbası** hand fire pump; **~ var!** fire!; **-a körükle gitmek** fig. to add fuel to the flames; **-dan çıkmış gibi** impoverished, destitute.

yanıbaşında right beside, right next to.

yanık 1. burn; scald; **2.** burnt, burned; **3.** (a)lit, alight, lighted; **4.** love-sick; **5.** doleful, touching, piteous; **~ kokusu**

burned smell, smell of burning; **~ tenli** sunburned, sun-tanned.

yanıkara MED charbon, anthrax.

yanılgı mistake, error.

yanılmak 1. to be mistaken; **2.** to make a mistake, to err.

yanılmaz infallible, unfailing.

yanılsama PSYCH illusion.

yanıltıcı misleading.

yanıltmaca sophism.

yanıltmaç tongue twister.

yanıltmak *caus. of* **yanılmak** to mislead.

yanıt, -tı answer, response, reply; **~ vermek** to answer, to reply.

yanıtlamak to answer, to reply.

yani [ā] [x .] that is (to say), I mean; namely.

yankesici pickpocket.

yankesicilik picking pockets.

yankı 1. echo; **2.** repercussion; **~ uyandırmak 1.** to echo; **2.** to have repercussions.

yankıla(n)mak to echo.

Yanki Yankee.

yanlamak to get by (*or* around).

yanlı 1. ... sided; **2.** supporter of, adherent of, advocate of, partisan of.

yanlış 1. mistake, error, blunder; misstep; **2.** wrong, erroneous, incorrect; **~ çıkmak** to turn out to be wrong; **~ doğru cetveli** list of errata; **~ düşmek** TELEPH to get (*or* have) the wrong number; **~ kapı çalmak** to bark up the wrong tree; **~ yere** by mistake; **-ını çıkarmak** (*b-nin*) to find s.o.'s mistake.

yanlışlık mistake, error, blunder.

yanlışlıkla by mistake.

yanmak, (-ar) 1. to burn, to be on fire; to burn down (*or* up); **2.** (*for electricity*) to be on; **3.** to be burned (*or* scorched *or* singed); to get sunburned; **4.** to get tanned (*by the sun*); **5.** to have fever, to be feverish; **6.** *fig.* to be done for, to have had it, to be in the soup; **7.** to expire; to become void; **8.** to be out (*or* eliminated); **9.** to feel great sadness (-*e* at); **10.** (*for a place*) to be blazing hot; **11.** *fig.* to burn (*to do s.th.*); **12.** to be madly in love (-*e* with); to have the hots (-*e* for); **yanıp kül olm.** to burn to ashes; **yanıp tutuşmak** (*biri için*) to be madly in love with s.o.

yansı 1. BIOL reflex; **2.** reflection.

yansıma reflection.

yansımak 1. (*for light*) to be reflected; **2.** (*for sound*) to echo.

yansıtıcı 1. reflector; **2.** reflective.

yansıtmak 1. to reflect (*light*); **2.** to echo (*sound*).

yansız 1. impartial, unbiased; **2.** POL, CHEM, ELECT neutral.

yanşak garrulous, talkative.

yanşaklık garrulity.

yap yap P = **yavaş yavaş.**

yapağı, yapak spring wool.

yapay 1. artificial, imitation; **2.** artificial, affected.

yapayalnız [x . . -] all alone, completely alone; all by himself; all by itself.

yapaylık artificiality.

yapı 1. building, edifice, construction, structure; **2.** physique; frame; construction; structure, build; **3.** make, origin; ~ *iskelesi* scaffolding; ~ *ustası* master builder.

yapıcı 1. builder; constructor; maker; **2.** constructive; creative; helpful.

yapılı 1. made of ..., constructed of ...; **2.** portly (*person*).

yapım 1. construction, building; **2.** manufacture, production; **3.** production (*of a film, etc.*).

yapımcı 1. builder; **2.** manufacturer, maker; **3.** producer (*of a film, etc.*).

yapımevi 1. factory, manufactory; mill; plant; **2.** *cinema*: production company.

yapınmak 1. to make s.th. for o.s.; **2.** to have s.th. made for o.s.; **3.** to try to (*-e inf.*)

yapısal structural.

yapışık 1. stuck (*-e* to, on); adhering (*-e* to); **2.** *fig.* boring, importunate (*person*); ~ *kardeşler* Siamese twins.

yapışkan 1. sticky, adhesive, viscid; **2.** *fig.* importunate, clingy (*person*).

yapışmak 1. to stick (*-e* to), to adhere (*-e* to), to cling (*-e* to); **2.** to set about (*-e ger.*); **3.** *fig.* to cling to s.o. like a leech, to latch onto s.o. like a leech.

yapıştırıcı adhesive.

yapıştırmak *caus. of* **yapışmak 1.** to glue, to paste, to stick, to tape; to adhere; **2.** to land, to deal, to plant (*a blow*); **3.** to say in quick reply.

yapış yapış very sticky.

yapıt, -tı work (of art), opus.

yapıtaşı, -nı building stone.

yapkın 1. rich, wealthy; **2.** drunk.

yapma 1. *vn. of* **yapmak; 2.** artificial, false, imitation; **3.** affected, mock,

feigned; ~ *uydu* artificial satellite.

yapmacık 1. artificiality, affectation, pose, show; **2.** artificial, affected, mock, feigned.

yapmak, (-ar) 1. to make; to build, to construct; to manufacture; to produce; to prepare; to create; **2.** to do; to carry out, to perform, to execute; **3.** to repair, to fix; **4.** to cause, to bring about (*an illness*); **5.** to make, to acquire (*money*); **6.** (*for a vehicle*) to do (*speed*); **7.** to defecate; to urinate, to wet; **8.** to harm, to do harm; **9.** to do, to arrange; **10.** to have sexual intercourse with, to do it to (*a woman*); *Ahmet öğretmenlik yapıyor* Ahmet teaches, Ahmet's a teacher; *geçen kış çok kar yaptı* it snowed a lot last year; *gelmekle iyi yaptın* you did well to come; *Orhan yapmadığını bırakmadı* Orhan's committed every crime in the book; *yapma!* stop it!, cut it out!

yaprak 1. leaf; **2.** page, leaf (*of a book, etc.*); **3.** layer, sheet; **4.** GEOL folium; ~ *aşısı* bud graft; ~ *dolması* (*or sarması*) stuffed grape leaves; ~ *dökümü* autumn. *Am.* fall; ~ *kurmak* to pickle grape leaves; ~ *oynamamak* (*for the air*) to be no wind at all; ~ *sigarası* cigar; ~ *tütün* leaf tobacco; ~ ~ **1.** multilayered; **2.** in layers.

yaprakbiti, -ni ZOO aphid, plant louse.

yapraklanmak to leaf, to come into leaf, to leave (out).

yapraklı leafy; leafed.

yapraksız leafless.

yaptırım JUR sanction.

yapyalnız s. **yapayalnız.**

yar precipice, cliff, abyss; *-dan atmak fig.* to lead into deep trouble.

yâr, -ri 1. beloved, love; lover; **2.** friend; **3.** helper; ~ *olm.* to be a help, to help, to assist; *-dan mı geçersin, serden mi? fig.* I'm-faced with an impossible choice.

yara 1. wound; injury; **2.** gash, rent, tear; **3.** *fig.* pain, sorrow; ~ *açmak* to make a wound (*-de* in), to wound; ~ *bağı* bandage; ~ *bere* cuts and bruises; wounds and bruises; ~ *işlemek* to discharge (*boil*); ~ *izi* scar; ~ *kabuğu* scab, crust (*over a wound*); ~ *kapanmak* (*for a wound*) to heal; *-sı olan gocunur!* if the cap fits wear it!; *-sını deşmek fig.* to touch a sore spot, to open up an old wound; *-ya*

tuz biber ekmek *fig.* to sprinkle salt on the wound.
Yaradan the Creator, the Maker, God; *-a kurban olayım!* oh Lord!, wow!; *-a sığınıp* mustering his strength.
yaradılış 1. nature, temperament, disposition; 2. creation; *-tan* by nature, naturally.
yarak *sl.* penis, cock, dick, prick, pecker, tool.
yaralamak 1. to wound, to injure; 2. to hurt.
yaralanmak *pass. of* yaralamak to be wounded (*or* injured).
yaralı wounded, injured; *~ kuşa kurşun sıkılmaz* *pro.* don't hit (*or* kick) s.o. when he's down.
yaramak 1. to be of use (*-e* to), to be good (*-e* for), to come in handy; to serve, to avail; 2. to be good for s.o.'s health, to be good (*-e* for), to do s.o. good; 3. to befit.
yaramaz 1. useless, good-for-nothing; 2. naughty, mischievous.
yaramazlık naughtiness, mischievousness, misbehavio(u)r; *~ etm.* to get into mischief, to play up, to cut up, to misbehave.
yaranmak to curry favo(u)r (*-e* with), to cozy up (*-e* to).
yarar 1. useful, serviceable; 2. benefit, profit; advantage; *-ına* for the benefit of.
yararlanmak to benefit (*-den* from), to profit (*-den* from), to make good use (*-den* of), to utilize.
yararlı useful; advantageous; worthwhile.
yararlık service, usefulness.
yararlılık usefulness.
yararsız useless, of no use.
yararsızlık uselessness.
yarasa zoo bat.
yaraşık: *~ almak* to be suitable (*or* fitting).
yaraşıklı suitable, becoming.
yaraşıksız unsuitable, unbecoming.
yaraşmak to suit, to become.
yaratan creator, maker.
yaratıcı creative.
yaratıcılık creativity, creativeness.
yaratık creature.
yaratılış creation, genesis.
yaratmak to create.
yarbay MIL lieutenant colonel.
yarda [x .] yard (= *91, 44 cm.*).
yardak *s.* yardakçı.

yardakçı accomplice, henchman.
yardakçılık complicity; *~ etm.* to aid, to be s.o.'s accomplice.
yardım help, assistance, aid; *~ elini uzatmak* (*b-ne*) to give s.o. a hand; *~ etm.* to help, to assist, to aid; *-a muhtaç* needy; *-ına yetişmek* (*b-nin*) to come to s.o.'s aid.
yardımcı 1. helper, assistant; aide; 2. vice-; 3. GR auxiliary; 4. maid, cleaning woman; *~ fiil* GR auxiliary verb.
yardımlaşmak to help one another; to cooperate, to collaborate.
yardımsamak (*b-den*) to ask s.o. for help.
yadımsever philanthropic, helpful.
yaren [ā] friend.
yarenlik [ā] chit-chat; *~ etm.* to chat.
yarga [x .] one-year-old hen.
yargı 1. idea, opinion; 2. JUR judg(e)ment; verdict (*of a jury*); decision (*of a court*); 3. adjudication; 4. PHLS, LOG judg(e)ment; *~ yetkisi* judicial power.
yargıç, *-cı* JUR judge.
yargıçlık JUR judgeship.
yargılamak to try; to judge, to adjudicate; to hear (*a case*).
Yargıtay *pr. n.* Supreme Court.
yarı 1. half; 2. half of, mid-; 3. *sports*: half time; 4. half(way), partially; *~ açık* half open; *~ beline kadar* to the waist; *~ fiyatına* at half price; *~ resmi* semiofficial; *~-ya* 1. half(way); 2. in half, fifty-fifty; *~ yolda bırakmak* (*b-ni*) to leave s.o. in the lurch, to leave s.o. high and dry; *~ yolda kalmak* to be left stranded in the middle of one's journey; *-da bırakmak* to discontinue, to interrupt; *-da kalmak* to be left half finished.
yarıbuçuk F 1. trivial, trifling, piddling; 2. poor, unsatisfactory.
yarıcı 1. chopper, splitter; 2. sharecropper.
yarıçap, *-pı* MATH radius.
yarıfinal, *-li* *sports*: semifinal.
yarıgeçirgen semipermeable.
yarıiletken ELECT semiconductor.
yarık 1. split, cleft, fissure; slit, chink; 2. split, cleft, cloven; slit.
yarıküre GEOGR semisphere.
yarılamak 1. to be halfway through; to complete half of; 2. to be (*or* go) halfway down.
yarım 1. half; 2. half past noon, twelve-thirty; *~ ağızla* *fig.* half-heartedly,

with one's tongue in one's cheek; ~ *daire* MATH half circle, semicircle; ~ *doğru* MATH half line; ~ *elmanın yarısı o. yarısı bu* they're as like as two peas in a pod; ~ *kalmak* to be left half finished, to be left half done; ~ *saat* half an hour; ~ *yamalak* poor, sorry, crummy, two-bit.

yarımada peninsula.

yarımay half-moon.

yarımca MED migraine.

yarımküre hemisphere.

yarımlamak 1. to halve; **2.** to half-finish; **3.** to be half through.

yarımşar a half each (*or* apiece).

yarın [x .] tomorrow; ~ *değil öbür gün* the day after tomorrow; ~ *öbür gün* soon; ~ *sabah* tomorrow morning.

yarınki tomorrow's; ~ *gazete* tomorrow's paper.

yarısaydam semitransparent, translucent.

yarış 1. race; **2.** competition; ~ *alanı* racecourse, racetrack; ~ *atı* racehorse; ~ *etm.* to race; ~ *pisti* **1.** speedway; **2.** (race)track.

yarışçı contester, contender.

yarışma contest, competition.

yarışmacı competitor, contestant, contender.

yarışmak 1. to race; **2.** to compete, to contest, to contend, to vie.

yarma 1. *vn. of* **yarmak; 2.** cut; **3.** MIL breakthrough; **4.** coarsely ground (*wheat, etc.*); **5.** split (*wood*); ~ *gibi* hugely built (*person*); ~ *şeftali* freestone peach.

yarmak, (-ar) to split, to cleave, to rend, to slit.

yarmalamak to split lengthwise.

yarpuz BOT pennyroyal.

yas mourning; ~ *tutmak* to mourn, to be in mourning.

yasa 1. law; **2.** law code, code of laws; ~ *çıkarmak* (*or* *yapmak*) to make laws; ~ *koyucu* lawmaker, legislator.

yasadışı illegal, unlawful.

yasak 1. prohibition; ban; **2.** prohibited, forbidden; ~ *bölge* off-limits area; ~ *etm.* to forbid, to prohibit; to ban; ~ *savmak* to do in a pinch, to serve in case of need, to be better than nothing.

yasakçı 1. prohibitor, prohibiter, forbidder; **2.** HIST kavass.

yasaklamak to forbid, to prohibit; to ban.

yasaklayıcı prohibitive, prohibitory.

yasal legal, lawful, legitimate, licit.

yasalaşmak to become law.

yasalaştırmak to make law.

yasallaşmak to become lawful (*or* legal).

yasallaştırmak to legalize.

yasallık legality, lawfulness, legitimacy.

yasama legislation; ~ *kurulu* legislative body; ~ *meclisi* house, chamber; ~ *yetkisi* legislative power.

yasamak to legislate.

yasamalı legislative.

yasasız illegal, unlawful, illegitimate, illicit.

yasemin [- . -] **1.** BOT jasmine; **2.** ♀ *wf.*

yaslamak to lean, to prop.

yaslanmak 1. to lean (-*e* against), to prop o.s. (-*e* against); **2.** *fig.* to rely (-*e* on), to count (-*e* on).

yaslı in mourning.

yassı flat; ~ *ekran monitör* flat screen monitor.

yassılaşmak to flatten (out).

yassılık flatness.

yastık 1. pillow; cushion; **2.** seedbed (*for plants*); **3.** MEC buffer, cushion; ~ *kılıfı* (*or* *yüzü*) pillowcase, tick.

yaş[1] age; ~ *günü* birthday; ~ *haddi* **1.** age limit; **2.** retirement age; ~ *ı ne, başı ne?* he's still wet behind the ears; ~ *ı tutmamak* to be under age; ~ *ına başına bakmadan* regardless of his age; ~ *ında* one year old; ~ *ını* (*başını*) *almak* to be old; *kaç yaşındasınız?* how old are you?; *yirmi yaşındayım* I am twenty years old.

yaş[2] 1. damp; moist; **2.** fresh (*fruit*); **3.** tears; **4.** *sl.* bad, rough, tough; ~ *akıtmak* (*or* *dökmek*) to shed tears, to weep, to cry; ~ *tahtaya basmak* fig. to be duped (*or* taken in); *-lara boğulmak* to cry one's eyes out, to burst into tears, to cry buckets.

yaşa hurrah!, hurray!

yaşam life; ~ *biçimi* way of life.

yaşamak 1. to live; **2.** to live, to inhabit; **3.** to live well, to enjoy life; to live in clover; **4.** to experience, to have, to enjoy.

yaşamöyküsü, -nü biography.

yaşamsal vital.

yaşantı life.

yaşarmak (*for one's eyes*) to fill with tears, to water.

yaşatmak *caus. of* **yaşamak**, *part.* to

keep alive.

yaşayış way of living, life.

yaşıt, -tı of the same age; contemporary.

yaşlanmak to grow old, to age.

yaşlı[1] teary, tearful.

yaşlı[2] old, aged, elderly; ~ **başlı** elderly.

yaşlık damp(ness), moistness.

yaşlılık old age, senility.

yaşmak yas(h)mak, veil.

yaşmaklı veiled.

yat[1], **-tı** yacht; ~ **kulübü** yacht club; ~ **limanı** marina.

yat[2]: ~ **borusu** MIL taps, tattoo.

yatağan yataghan.

yatak 1. bed; **2.** mattress; **3.** bed (of a river, lake); **4.** den, lair, hide-out, hideaway (of thieves); **5.** bed, seam, vein (of a mineral); **6.** MEC bearing; **7.** chamber (of a gun); ~ **çarşafı** bed sheet; ~ **liman** big harbo(u)r; ~ **odası** bedroom; ~ **örtüsü** bedspread; ~ **takımı** bedding; ~ **yüzü** (bed)tick; **yatağa düşmek** to be bedfast, to be laid up, to take to one's bed (because of illness); **yatağa girmek** to go to bed, to turn in; **yatağını yapmak** (b-nin) to make up s.o.'s bed; to prepare a bed for s.o.; **-lar çekmek** to feel like hitting the sack.

yatakhane [. . - .] dormitory.

yataklı 1. furnished with a bed or beds; **2.** RAIL sleeping car, sleeper; ~ **vagon** RAIL sleeping car, sleeper.

yataklık etm. to receive and conceal (stolen goods); to harbo(u)r (a criminal).

yatalak bedridden, bedfast.

yatay horizontal.

yatı overnight stay; **-ya gelmek** to make an overnight visit, to come for an overnight stay.

yatık 1. leaning to one side; **2.** low-lying; ~ **yaka** turndown collar.

yatılı 1. boarding (school); **2.** boarding student, boarder; ~ **okul** boarding school.

yatır place where a saint is buried.

yatırım COM investment; deposit.

yatırımcı COM investor; depositor.

yatırmak caus. of **yatmak**, part; **1.** to put to bed; **2.** to accommodate, to bed (down) (an overnight guest); **3.** to put s.o. in (hospital); **4.** to lay flat; **5.** to invest, to deposit (money).

yatısız day (school, student).

yatışmak to die down, to subside; to calm down.

yatıştırıcı sedative, tranquilizing.

yatıştırmak to calm, to soothe, to tranquilize, to mollify, to appease, to allay.

yatkı wrinkle, crease.

yatkın susceptible (-e to); predisposed (-e to), inclined (-e to).

yatmak, (-ar) 1. to go to bed, to turn in; **2.** to be lying down, to be in bed; **3.** to keep to one's bed; to be bedridden; **4.** to lie (flat); **5.** to stay (-de in), to remain (-de in); **6.** to enter, to go into (hospital); **7.** to lean to (one side); **8.** (for a ship) to list; **9.** to be in prison; **10.** to have sex, to sleep with; **yatıp kalkmak 1.** to sleep (-de in); **2.** to have sex (ile with), to sleep (ile with).

yatsı time about two hours after sunset; ~ **namazı** isl. the ritual prayer performed two hours after sunset.

yavan 1. tasteless, insipid, flavo(u)rless (food); **2.** dry (bread); **3.** fig. vapid, dull, insipid.

yavanlaşmak to go flat, to lose its savo(u)r.

yavaş 1. slow; **2.** soft, quiet; **3.** gentle, mild; ~ **gel!** slow down!, take it easy!; ~ **tütün** mild tobacco; ~ ~ **1.** slowly; **2.** gradually, bit by bit.

yavaşça [. x .] **1.** slowly; **2.** quietly, softly.

yavaşcacık [. x . .] **1.** rather slowly; **2.** rather quietly.

yavaşlamak to slow down.

yavaşlatmak to slow (down); to slacken; to retard.

yavaşlık 1. slowness; **2.** quietness, softness; **3.** gentleness.

yave [ā] nonsense, rot, bunk.

yaver [ā] **1.** helper, assistant; **2.** MIL aide-de-camp; ~ **gitmek** to go well.

yavru 1. young animal; **2.** child; **3.** sl. chick, bird; ~ **atmak** (for an animal) to abort; **-m!** darling!, dear!, honey!

yavruağzı, -nı pinkish orange.

yavrucak poor little dear (said of a child).

yavrucuk sweet little darling (said of a child).

yavrukurt cub (scout).

yavrulamak to bring forth young.

yavşak nit.

yavuklamak P to give a token of betrothal.

yavuklanmak P to get engaged.

yavuklu P fiancé; fiancée.

yavuz 1. stern, tough; 2. gutsy, tough; 3. ♀ mf.

yay 1. bow; 2. MEC spring; 3. MATH arc, curve; 4. ♀ AST Sagittarius, the Archer.

yaya pedestrian; ~ **bırakmak** (b-ni) fig. to leave s.o. in the lurch; ~ **geçidi** 1. pedestrian (or zebra) crossing, crosswalk; 2. footbridge; ~ **kaldırımı** pavement, Am. sidewalk; ~ **kalmak** fig. to be left in the lurch.

yayan 1. on foot; 2. fig. uninformed; ~ **gitmek** to go on foot; ~ **yapıldak** bare-footed and travel(l)ing on foot.

yaygara howl, clamo(u)r; hullabaloo; -**yı basmak** (or **koparmak**) to make a great to-do about nothing.

yaygaracı noisy person, brawler, cry-baby, roisterer.

yaygı ground cloth.

yaygın widespread; prevalent.

yaygınlaşmak to become widespread.

yayık[1] churn.

yayık[2] spread out; wide, broad; ~ ~ **ko-nuşmak** to drawl.

yayılı spread (out).

yayılmak 1. pass. of **yaymak**; 2. to spread; 3. to sprawl, to stretch out; 4. to widen; 5. to graze, to pasture.

yayım 1. publication; 2. broadcasting.

yayımcı publisher.

yayımcılık publishing.

yayımlamak 1. to publish; 2. to broadcast.

yayın 1. publication; 2. broadcast.

yayın(balığı) zoo sheatfish.

yayınevi, -ni publishing house.

yayla [x .] high plateau, wold.

yaylak mountain pasture.

yaylanmak 1. to spring, to bounce; 2. sl. to go away, to beat it.

yaylı 1. having springs, sprung; 2. MUS played with a bow (instrument); 3. spring-carriage.

yaylım 1. vn. of **yayılmak**; 2. s. **yaylak**; ~ **ateşi** MIL volley (fire), fusillade.

yayma 1. vn. of **yaymak**; 2. small trader's stall.

yaymak, (-ar) 1. to spread; 2. to scatter, to spread; 3. to disseminate, to broadcast, to spread; 4. to spread (disease); 5. to take to pasture (animals).

yayvan broad and shallow; ~ ~ with a drawl (speaking).

yaz summer; ~ **kış** summer and winter, all the year round; ~ **saati** summer time, daylight saving time; ~ **tarifesi** summer time-table.

yazar writer; author.

yazarlık authorship.

yazgı destiny, fate, ordinance, predestination.

yazı[1] 1. writing; 2. article; 3. handwriting; 4. alphabet; 5. fig. destiny, fate, ordinance; ~ **dili** literary language; ~ **makinesi** typewriter; ~ **masası** writing table; ~ **mı, tura mı?** heads or tails?; ~ **tahtası** blackboard; ~ **tura at-mak** to flip up, to toss up; ~ **yazmak** to write; -**ya dokmek** to indite; -**yı çıkar-mak** (or **sökmek**) to be able to decipher s.o.'s handwriting.

yazı[2] plain.

yazıbilim graphology.

yazıcı 1. scribe; copyist, transcriber; 2. cinema: screenwriter, scriptwriter; 3. MEC recorder.

yazıhane [. . . -.] 1. office; 2. office desk.

yazık 1. pity, shame; 2. what a pity!, what a shame!; ~ **etm.** to spoil, to ruin; -**lar olsun!** shame!

yazıklanmak to pity; to be sorry (-e for).

yazıksız P innocent, sinless.

yazılı 1. written; 2. registered, enrolled; 3. fated, destined to happen; 4. written examination; ~ **sınav** written examination.

yazım spelling.

yazın[1] literature.

yazın[2] [x .] in summer, during the summer.

yazıncı literary man, man of letters, writer, author.

yazınsal literary.

yazışmak to correspond, to write to each other.

yazıt, -tı inscription; epitaph.

yazlık 1. summer house (or place); 2. summer ..., estival; **yazlığa gitmek** to go to one's summer house.

yazma 1. vn. of **yazmak**; 2. handwritten manuscript; 3. handwritten; 4. hand-painted; hand-printed (cloth); 5. hand-painted cloth; hand-printed cloth.

yazmak, (-ar) 1. to write; 2. to register, to enroll; **yaz boz tahtası** school slate.

yazman secretary.

yedek 1. spare, reserve; standby; 2. towrope; towline; ~ (or -**te**) **çekmek** to tow; ~ **parça** spare part; ~ **subay** reserve officer; **yedeğe almak** to tow, to take in tow.

yedi seven; ~ **canlı** invincible; ~ **dûvel 1.** the Great Powers; **2.** *fig.* everybody, all and sundry; ~ **kat el** F total stranger; ~ **kubbeli hamam kurmak** *fig.* to build castles in the air; ~ **mahalle** *fig.* everybody and his brother; **-sinden yetmişine kadar** everybody from nine to ninety.

yediemin [. . . . -] JUR sequester, depositary, trustee.

yedigen 1. heptagon; **2.** heptagonal.

yedili *cards*: the seven.

yedinci seventh.

yedirmek 1. *caus. of* **yemek**; **2.** to feed; **3.** to let absorb.

yedişer seven each (*or* apiece); ~ ~ seven at a time.

yediveren BOT everblooming (*plant*).

yedmek, (-er) 1. to tow; **2.** to lead (*an animal*).

yegâne sole, only, single.

yeğ preferable, better; ~ **tutmak** to prefer.

yeğen nephew; niece.

yeğinlik PHYS intensity.

yeğlemek to prefer.

yeis, -e'si despair.

yek, -ki *rare* one.

yekdiğeri, -ni each other, one another.

yeknesak monotonous.

yeknesaklık monotony.

yekpare in one piece; compact.

yeksan [â] level (*ile* with); ~ **etm.** to level to the ground.

yekta [â] **1.** unique, peerless, matchless; **2.** ♀ *mf.*, *wf.*

yekten [x .] all at once; suddenly.

yekûn total, sum; ~ **çekmek** F to finish speaking.

yel 1. wind; **2.** P flatus, wind, gas; **3.** P rheumatic pain; ~ **yeperek yelken kürek** *fig.* in a great hurry; **-e vermek** to throw away.

yeldeğirmeni, -ni windmill.

yele mane.

yelek 1. waistcoat, vest; **2.** wing feather, pinion; **3.** feather (*of an arrow*).

yeleli maned.

yelken NAUT sail; ~ **açmak 1.** to hoist sail; **2.** to set sail; ~ **bezi** sailcloth; ~ **gemisi** sailing ship; **-leri suya indirmek** *fig.* to draw in one's horns.

yelkenlemek 1. to set sail; **2.** *sl.* to vamoose, to make tracks.

yelkenli sailing ship; sailboat.

yelkovan 1. minute-hand (*of a clock*);

2. weather-cock.

yellemek to fan.

yellenmek 1. *pass. of* **yellemek**; **2.** to break wind, to fart.

yelloz hussy, slut.

yellim yelalim P in great haste.

yelmek, (-er) to run in a fluster.

yelpaze [â] fan.

yelpazelemek [â] to fan.

yelpazelenmek [â] **1.** *pass. of* **yelpazelemek**; **2.** to fan *o.s.*

yelpik P asthma.

yeltek fickle; inconstant.

yeltenmek to presume (-*e* to), to dare, to try.

yem 1. feed; fodder; **2.** bait; **3.** primer (*for a gun*); ~ **borusu 1.** MIL bugle call for horse fodder; **2.** *fig.* empty promise; ~ **torbası** nose (*or* feed) bag.

yemek¹ 1. food; meal; **2.** dish; **3.** dinner, supper; banquet; ~ **borusu 1.** ANAT esophagus; **2.** MIL mess call; ~ **çıkarmak** to serve food; ~ **kitabı** cookery-book, *Am.* cookbook; ~ **masası** dining table; ~ **odası** dining room; ~ **pişirmek** to cook; ~ **seçmek** to be choosy in eating; to be a picky eater; ~ **yapmak** to cook; ~ **yemek** to eat.

yemek² 1. to eat; **2.** to spend (*money*); **3.** to bite; **4.** to corrode; to eat; **5.** to consume, to use up; **6.** F to kill, to do in; **ye kürküm ye!** fine feathers make fine birds; **yeme de yanında yat!** *sl.* it's finger-licking good!; **yemeden içmeden** *fig.* without losing any time; **yemeden içmeden kesilmek** to be off one's food, to have no appetite; **yiyecek gibi bakmak** to leer (-*e* at); **yiyip bitirmek 1.** to eat up; **2.** to squander (*money*).

yemekhane [â] dining hall.

yemekli: ~ **vagon** RAIL dining car, diner.

yemeni 1. hand-printed scarf *or* handkerchief; **2.** a kind of light shoe.

yemin [î] oath; ~ **billah etm.** to swear to God; ~ **etm.** to swear; to take an oath; ~ **ettirmek** (*or* **verdirmek**) to administer an oath (-*e* to), to swear.

yeminli [.- .] under oath; sworn in; ~ **tercüman** certified (*or* official) interpreter.

yemiş 1. dried fruit; **2.** nut; **3.** P fig; ~ **vermek** to bear fruit.

yemişçi fruiterer.

yemlemek 1. to feed; **2.** to bait; **3.** to prime (*a gun*).

yemlik 1. nose (or feed) bag; **2.** feedbox, manger; **3.** fig. bribe.
yemyeşil [x . .] very green.
yen 1. cuff; **2.** sleeve; **3.** BOT spathe; **4.** yen (Japanese monetary unit).
yenge [x .] **1.** affinal aunt, uncle's wife; **2.** sister-in-law, brother's wife.
yengeç, -ci 1. ZOO crab; **2.** ♋ AST Cancer.
yengi victory.
yeni 1. new; **2.** recent; **3.** newly; recently; ~ **evliler** newlyweds; ~ **yetişen nesil** the rising generation; **-den** (or ~ **baştan**) over again from the beginning.
yeniay AST new moon.
yenibahar BOT allspice.
yenice fairly new.
yeniçeri HIST **1.** the Janissary corps; **2.** Janissary.
yeniden again; ~ **doğmak** to revive.
yenidünya 1. BOT loquat; **2.** ♋ the New World.
yenik 1. defeated; **2.** moth-eaten hole; **3.** eroded; ~ **düşmek** to be defeated; **kurt yeniği** wormhole.
yenilemek 1. to renew, to renovate, to restore; to replenish; **2.** to renew (a contract); **3.** to repeat, to reiterate.
yenilenebilir renewable (resources).
yenilgi defeat, beating; **-ye uğramak** to suffer defeat, to get a beating.
yenilik 1. newness; **2.** innovation; renewal; novelty; **3.** inexperience, greenness; ~ **korkusu** PSYCH neophobia; ~ **yapmak** to make a change.
yenilikçi innovator.
yenilmek 1. pass. of **yemek²**; **2.** pass. of **yenmek²**; **yenilir yutulur gibi değil** it is not to be stomached.
yenişememek to be unable to defeat each other.
yeniyetme adolescent.
yeniyetmelik adolescence.
yenmek¹ pass. of **yemek**.
yenmek² to overcome, to conquer; to beat.
yepyeni [x . .] brand-new.
yer 1. place, spot; location; position; **2.** space, room; **3.** seat; **4.** place, position (of employment); **5.** fig. importance; **6.** the ground, the earth; **7.** floor; **8.** piece of land (or property); **9.** the earth; **10.** area, region, terrain; ~ **açmak** to make way (-e for); to make room; ~ **almak 1.** to be situated (or located) (-de in); **2.** to take part (-de in),

to be involved (-de in); ~ **belirteci** GR adverb of place; ~ **cücesi** short but cunning; ~ **etm. 1.** to leave a mark (-de on); **2.** to impress itself in; to be branded on (s.o.'s mind); ~ **odası** ground-floor room; ~ **tutmak 1.** to take up space; **2.** to reserve a place; **3.** fig. to be of importance, to have an important place; ~ **vermek 1.** to give s.o. a seat, to vacate one's seat; **2.** to include, to discuss (in a book or speech); ~ **yarılıp içine girmek** to vanish (or disappear or melt) into thin air; ~ **yatağı** bed spread on the floor; pallet; ~~ in places; here and there; ~ **yurt** place to live in, home; ~ **zarfı** s. ~ **belirteci**; **-de** instead of; **-de kalmak** fig. not to be appreciated; (yerden): ~ **bitme** squat, dumpy; ~ **göğe kadar** infinitely, greatly; ~ **yapma** squat, dumpy; ~ **-e çalmak** to throw (or hurl) to the ground; ~ **-e vurmak** (b-ni) fig. to chew s.o. out; (yere): ~ **bakan yürek yakan** butter wouldn't melt in his (or her) mouth, wolf in sheep's clothing; ~ **bakmak** fig. to have one foot in the grave; ~ **göğe koyamamak** fig. to hono(u)r greatly; ~ **sermek** (b-ni) to knock s.o. flying, to knock s.o. to the ground; (yeri): ~ **olm.** to be the right moment or time or place for s.th.; ~ **öpmek** co. to fall to the ground; ~ **soğumadan** fig. shortly after leaving one's place; ~ **yurdu belirsiz** homeless, vagrant; (yerin): ~ **dibine geçmek** to feel like 30 cents, to feel like sinking through the floor; ~ **kulağı var** walls have ears; (yerinde): ~ **saymak** fig. to mark time; ~ **yener esmek** to be gone with the wind, to have vanished; (yerinden): ~ **ayrılmak** to leave one's place; ~ **oynamak 1.** to move from, to budge from, to stir from; **2.** to come (or get) loose; (yerine): ~ **bakmak** (b-nin) to stand in for s.o.; ~ **geçmek** to replace; ~ **getirmek** to carry out, to execute, to perform, to fulfil(l); ~ **koymak** to look on s.o. as, to regard s.o. as; (yerini): ~ **bulmak** to find one's place (or niche); ~ **doldurmak** (b-nin) fig. to fill s.o.'s shoes; ~ **tutmak** to be able to be used in place of another; (yerle): ~ **beraber** (or **bir**) leveled to the ground, razed; ~ **bir etm.** to level to the ground, to raze; ~ **gök bir olsa** no matter what happens, even if the sky should fall; **yer-**

lerde sürünmek to be down-and-out; *yerlere kadar eğilmek* *fig.* to bow and scrape; *yerleri süpürmek* to trail (*or* drag) on the ground (*long skirt, etc.*).

yeraltı, -nı underground; ~ *geçidi* underground passageway, subway; ~ *örgütü* underground; ~ *sığınağı* bunker; ~ *suyu* GEOL subterranean water.

yerbilim geology.

yerbilimci geologist.

yerçekimi, -ni PHYS gravity.

Yerebatan Sarayı *pr. n.* the underground cistern.

yerel local; ~ *seçim* POL local election.

yerelleştirmek to localize.

yerelması, -nı BOT Jerusalem artichoke.

yerfıstığı, -nı BOT groundnut, peanut.

yergi satire.

yergici satirist.

yerici 1. critical, faultfinding; **2.** satirical.

yerinde 1. apt, appropriate; **2.** well--timed, timely; **3.** good, fine; **4.** old enough to be.

yerine 1. instead of, in place of; in lieu of; **2.** on behalf of, for, in the name of.

yerinmek to feel sad (*or* sorry) (*-e* about); to regret.

yerkabuğu, -nu GEOL crust of the earth.

yerküre 1. the earth; **2.** globe.

yerleşik 1. settled, established; sedentary; **2.** endemic.

yerleşim settlement.

yerleşmek 1. to fit in; **2.** to get established in (*one's job*); **3.** to settle *o.s.* in (*a chair, etc.*); to get established in (*a new home*); **4.** to move into, to settle in (*a place*); **5.** to take root, to catch on.

yerleştirmek 1. *caus. of* **yerleşmek; 2.** to place, to set, to put, to fit; **3.** to place, to put, to install s.o. in (*a job*); **4.** to deploy (*a missile*); **5.** to land, to plant (*a blow*).

yerli 1. local; native; indigenous; **2.** domestic; **3.** immovable, built-in (*piece of furniture*); ~ *mal(ı)* local product; ~ *yerinde* in apple-pie order.

yermantarı, -nı BOT truffle.

yermek, (-er) 1. to criticize, to run down, to speak ill of; **2.** to satirize; to deride; **3.** to condemn; to disapprove.

yermeli pejorative (*word*).

yermerkezli geocentric.

yersarsıntısı, -nı earthquake.

yersiz 1. homeless; **2.** irrelevant; **3.** unsuitable, inappropriate.

yersolucanı, -nı ZOO earthworm.

yeryuvarlağı, -nı the earth.

yeryüzü, -nü the world, the face of the earth.

yeşermek 1. to leaf out; **2.** to green, to turn green; **3.** *fig.* to appear, to emerge.

yeşil 1. green; **2.** *sl.* one hundred lira note.

Yeşilay *pr. n.* the Green Crescent.

yeşilaycı F teetotal(l)er.

yeşilimsi, yeşilimtırak greenish.

yeşillenmek 1. to green; **2.** to leaf out.

yeşillik 1. greenness; **2.** meadow; **3.** greens.

yeşim jade, jasper.

yetenek ability, talent, capability, competence, capacity; aptitude; ~ *testi* aptitude test.

yetenekli talented, capable, competent, able.

yeteneksiz untalented, incapable, incompetent; inept.

yeteneksizlik inability, incapability, incompetence.

yeter 1. enough, sufficient; **2.** that's enough!; *-i kadar* **1.** enough, sufficient, adequate; **2.** enough, sufficiently.

yeterince 1. enough, sufficient; **2.** enough, sufficiently.

yeterli enough, sufficient, adequate.

yeterlik adequacy, competence, qualification; sufficiency.

yetersayı quorum.

yetersiz insufficient, inadequate; ~ *beslenme* malnutrition, undernourishment.

yetersizlik insufficiency, inadequacy.

yetim [ī] orphan.

yetimhane [. - - .] orphanage.

yetinmek (*bşle*) to be content with *s.th.*, to be satisfied with *s.th.*

yetişkin adult, grown-up.

yetişmek 1. to catch; **2.** to reach; to attain; to arrive; **3.** to catch up (*-e* with); **4.** to be enough, to suffice; **5.** (*for a plant*) to grow; **6.** (*for a person or animal*) to grow up; **7.** to be educated; *yetiş(in)!* help!

yetişmiş 1. mature, grown-up; **2.** trained; experienced.

yetiştirici producer, raiser, grower.

yetiştirmek 1. *caus. of* **yetişmek; 2.** to

raise, to bring up, to educate; **3.** to train; **4.** to convey (*news*).

yetki authority, authorization, warrant; *askeri valiye tam ~ verildi* the military governor has been invested with full authority.

yetkili 1. authorized; **2.** competent; **3.** authority; *~ merci* JUR competent authority.

yetkin perfect.

yetkisiz 1. unauthorized; **2.** incompetent.

yetmek, (-er) to be enough, to suffice, to do.

yetmiş seventy.

yetmişer seventy each (*or* apiece); *~ ~* seventy at a time.

yetmişinci seventieth.

yetmişlik septuagenarian.

yevmiye daily wage; *~ defteri* COM daybook.

yezit F scamp, devil, dickens.

yığılı heaped, piled, stacked.

yığılışma crowd, throng.

yığılmak 1. *pass. of* **yığmak; 2.** to collapse in a heap; **3.** to crowd around.

yığın 1. heap, pile, stack; **2.** crowd, mass, throng, passel (*of people*); *-la* a heap of, a lot of.

yığınak 1. MIL concentration; **2.** BOT colony.

yığıntı mass; heap, pile.

yığışık massed.

yığışım GEOL conglomerate.

yığışmak to crowd together; to amass, to accumulate.

yığmak, (-ar) 1. to heap (up), to pile (up), to stack (up); **2.** to amass, to accumulate, to concentrate.

yıkamak 1. to wash, to bath(e); to lave; to launder; **2.** PHOT to develop (*film*).

yıkanmak 1. *pass. of* **yıkamak; 2.** to wash o.s., to take a bath, to bath(e).

yıkayıcı 1. washer; **2.** PHOT developer.

yıkıcı 1. destructive; subversive; **2.** wrecker.

yıkık 1. ruined; demolished, destroyed.

yıkılmak 1. *pass. of* **yıkmak; 2.** to collapse; **3.** to collapse in a heap, to fall to the ground; **4.** to wither (*hopes*); **5.** *fig.* to clear out, to leave; *yıkıl karşımdan!* clear out!, get lost!

yıkım 1. ruin, destruction; **2.** disaster; catastrophe.

yıkımlık damage.

yıkıntı ruin(s), debris.

yıkkın about to collapse, in ruins.

yıkmacı wrecker.

yıkmak, (-ar) 1. to demolish, to wreck, to pull down, to destroy, to ruin; **2.** to overthrow; **3.** to topple; to lay s.o. flat; **4.** to tilt; **5.** to put (*the blame*) on s.o.

yıl year; *-lar -ı* for years.

yılan 1. ZOO snake; serpent; viper; **2.** *fig.* snake in the grass, viper; *~ gibi* malevolent and sneaky (*person*); *~ gömleği* slough; *~ sokması* snakebite.

yılanbalığı, -nı ZOO eel.

yılancık 1. small snake; **2.** MED erysipelas.

yılankavi [. . .-] serpentine, winding; *~ akmak* to meander.

yılbaşı, -nı New Year's Day.

yıldırım 1. thunderbolt, lightning; **2.** ♀ *mf;* *~ gibi* like lightning, with lightning speed; *~ savaşı* blitzkrieg; *~ siperi* lightning rod; *~ telgrafı* urgent telegram; *-la vurulmuşa dönmek* to be thunderstruck.

yıldırımkıran, yıldırımlık, yıldırımsavar lightning rod.

yıldırmak 1. *caus. of* **yılmak; 2.** to daunt; to cow; to intimidate; **3.** to terrorize.

yıldız 1. star; **2.** NAUT north; *~ akmak* (*or* **kaymak** *or* **uçmak**) (*for a shooting star*) to fall; *~ anasonu* BOT star aniseed, badian; *~ yılı* AST sidereal year; *-ı dişi* *fig.* popular; *-ı parlak* lucky; *-ları barışmak* to get along well with each other.

yıldızbilim astrology.

yıldızböceği, -ni ZOO firefly.

yıldızçiçeği, -ni BOT dahlia.

yıldızkarayel NAUT **1.** north-northwest wind; **2.** north-northwest.

yıldızlı 1. starry, starlit; **2.** starred.

yıldızpoyraz NAUT **1.** north-northeast wind; **2.** north-northeast.

yıldönümü, -nü anniversary.

yılgı terror.

yılgın 1. daunted; intimidated; **2.** terrorized; terror-struck.

yılışık obtrusive, saucy, importunate, pert, smarmy; *~ ~* smarmily.

yılışmak 1. to grin (*or* smirk) smarmily; **2.** to smarm.

yıllanmak 1. to age, to grow old; **2.** to become a year old.

yıllanmış 1. aged, mellow (*wine*); **2.** old (*thing*).

yıllık 1. yearbook, annual; **2.** yearly salary; yearly fee; **3.** ... years old; **4.** yearly, annual; **5.** for one year.

yılmak, (-ar) to be daunted (-*den* by), to be intimidated (-*den* by).

yılmaz 1. undaunted; **2.** ♀ *mf.*

yıpranmak 1. to get worn-out, to wear out; **2.** to become burned-out (*or* worn-out).

yıpratıcı gruel(l)ing, exhausting, wearing.

yıpratmak to wear out, to burn out.

yırılmak P to split.

yırmak, (-ar) P to tear, to split.

yırtıcı 1. predatory, predacious; **2.** *fig.* blood-thirsty (*person*); **~ hayvan** beast of prey; **~ kuş** bird of prey.

yırtık 1. torn, ripped, rent; **2.** tear, rip, rent; **3.** *fig.* shameless, brazen(faced); **~ pırtık** in rags.

yırtılmak 1. *pass. of* **yırtmak**; **2.** to overcome one's shyness; **3.** *sl.* to fork over (*money*).

yırtınmak 1. to wear o.s. to a frazzle, to run o.s. ragged; **2.** to shout at the top of one's voice.

yırtmaç, -cı slit, vent (*in a garment*).

yırtmaçlı having a slit (*or* vent).

yırtmak, (-ar) 1. to tear, to rip, to rend; **2.** to tear, to lacerate; **3.** to break in (*a colt*).

yısa [x .] hoist away!; **~ beraber!** hoist together!; **~ etm.** (*halatı*) to heave in (*a rope*); **~ ~** at the very most.

yiğit, -di 1. brave, bold, courageous; **2.** young man, young buck.

yiğitlenmek to pluck up courage.

yiğitlik bravery, courage; **yiğitliğe leke sürmemek** to save one's face.

yine 1. (once) again, once more; **2.** nevertheless, still.

yinelemek to repeat.

yirmi twenty; **~ yaş dişi** ANAT wisdom tooth.

yirmilik 1. twenty-lira note; **2.** twenty- -year old.

yirminci twentieth.

yirmişer twenty each (*or* apiece); **~ ~** twenty at a time.

yisa *s.* **yısa.**

yitik lost, missing.

yitim loss.

yitirmek 1. *caus. of* **yitmek**; **2.** to lose.

yitmek, (-er) to be lost (*or* missing); to disappear, to vanish.

yiv 1. groove, chamfer; **2.** MEC thread; **3.** flute (*on a column*).

yivli 1. grooved, chamfered; **2.** MEC

threaded; **3.** fluted (*column*).

yiyecek food, edible, comestible.

yiyici 1. (*animal*) which feeds on (*a specified food*); **2.** *fig.* taker of bribes, bribee.

yiyinti food.

yo [-] no.

yobaz 1. fanatic, bigot; **2.** fogy, moss- back.

yobazlaşmak to become fanatical.

yobazlık 1. fanaticism, bigotry; **2.** fo- gyism.

yoga yoga.

yogi yogi.

yoğalmak to disappear.

yoğaltım consumption.

yoğaltmak to consume, to use up.

yoğun 1. dense, thick; **2.** intensive, in- tense.

yoğunlaşmak 1. to densen, to thicken; **2.** to intensify.

yoğunlaştırmak 1. to densen, to thick- en; **2.** to intensify.

yoğunluk 1. density, thickness; **2.** in- tensity.

yoğurmak to knead.

yoğurt, -du yog(h)urt, yoghourt.

yoğurtçu maker *or* seller of yog(h)urt.

yoğurtotu, -nu BOT bedstraw.

yok, -ku *or* **-ğu 1.** non-existent; **2.** ab- sent; unavailable; **3.** no (*negative re- ply*); **4.** but if not ...; **~ canım!** F **1.** you're kidding?, really?; **2.** I wouldn't think of it!; **3.** unbelievable!; **~ dene- cek kadar az** next to nothing; **~ deve- nin başı!** you're pulling my leg!; **~ etm.** to do away with, to stamp out, to eradicate; **~ oğlu ~** F non-existent; **~ olm.** to disappear, to vanish; to die out; **~ pahasına** for nothing, for a song; **~ yere** without reason; **-tan** from nothing; **müdür yokken işin başında ben olurum** in the absence of the manager I am in charge of the business.

yoklama 1. *vn. of* **yoklamak**; **2.** roll call; **3.** quiz; **~ yapmak** to call the roll, to call over.

yoklamak 1. to search; to inspect; **2.** to feel with the fingers, to finger; **3.** to sound out; **4.** to visit; **5.** (*for an illness, a pain*) to recur, to reappear.

yokluk 1. non-existence; **2.** absence; **3.** poverty.

yoksa [x .] **1.** or; **2.** otherwise, or else, if not; **daha hızlı çalış, ~ patron seni kapı dışarı eder** work faster or else

the boss will give you the sack.
yoksul poor, destitute.
yoksullaşmak to become poor.
yoksullaştırmak to impoverish.
yoksulluk poverty, destitution, impoverishment.
yoksun deprived (*-den* of), bereft (*-den* of); ~ **bırakmak** to deprive (*-den* of), to bereave (*-den* of); ~ **kalmak** to be deprived (*or* bereft) (*-den* of).
yoksunluk deprivation.
yoksunmak to be deprived (*or* bereft) (*-den* of).
yokuş upward slope; hill; rise; ~ **aşağı** downhill; ~ **yukarı** uphill.
yol 1. road, way; path; course; route; passage; **2.** manner, style; **3.** method, system, **4.** way, means; solution; **5.** speed (*of a ship*); **6.** stripe (*in cloth*); **7.** time; ~ **açmak 1.** to open a road; **2.** *fig.* to bring about, to give rise (*-e* to); ~ **almak** to proceed, to move forward; ~ **aramak** to look for a way (*to solve a problem*); ~ **arkadaşı** fellow--travel(l)er; ~ **boyunca 1.** along the road; **2.** during the trip; ~ **halısı** hall rug, runner; ~ **harcı** travel allowance; ~ **vermek 1.** to make way (*-e* for); **2.** (*b-ne*) *fig.* to fire *s.o.*, to give *s.o.* the sack; ~ **yakınken** *fig.* before it's too late; ~ ~ striped (*cloth*); ~ **yordam** manners, behavio(u)r; ~ **yürümek** to walk; (yola): ~ **çıkmak** (*or* **düzülmek** *or* **koyulmak**) to set off (*or* out), to hit the road; ~ **düşmek** to set out for (*a place*); ~ **germek** (*or* **yatmak**) to come round; to see reason; ~ **getirmek** (*or* **yatırmak**) to bring round; to persuade; ~ **gitmek** to take a trip; ~ **vurmak** P to see off; **yolda kalmak** to be delayed on the road; **yoldan çıkmak 1.** to be derailed (*train*); to go off the road (*car*); **2.** *fig.* to go astray; (yolu): ~ **almak** to reach the end of one's journey; ~ **düşmek** to happen to pass, to happen on, to chance on; **yolun(uz) açık olsun!** have a good trip!, bon voyage!; (yoluna): ~ **bakmak** (*b-nin*) to expect *s.o.*, to await *s.o.*'s arrival; ~ **çıkmak** (*b-nin*) **1.** to go to meet *s.o.*; **2.** to meet *s.o.* by chance; ~ **girmek** to come all right; ~ **koymak** to put (*or* set) to rights; (yolunu): ~ **beklemek** (*b-nin*) to await *s.o.*'s arrival; ~ **bulmak** to find the way to do s.th.; ~ **kaybetmek** to lose one's way; ~ **kes-**

mek to stop, to waylay, to hold up; ~ **sapıtmak** *fig.* to go astray; ~ **şaşırmak 1.** to take the wrong road, to lose one's way; **2.** *fig.* to go astray; *-uyle* **1.** by way of, via; **2.** by means of, through.
yolcu 1. travel(l)er; passenger; **2.** baby about to be born; **3.** sick person who is at death's door; ~ **etm.** to see off; ~ **gemisi** liner; ~ **salonu** passenger waiting room; ~ **uçağı** passenger aircraft.
yolculuk journey, trip; voyage; ~ **etm.** to travel; ~ **ne zaman?** when do you set out on your journey?
yoldaş 1. fellow travel(l)er; **2.** friend, companion; **3.** Communist, comrade.
yolgeçen: ~ **hanı** used of a place which is much frequented.
yollamak to send, to dispatch.
yollanmak 1. *pass. of* **yollamak**; **2.** to pick up speed.
yollu 1. having roads; **2.** striped (*cloth*); **3.** fast (*ship, etc.*); **4.** by way of; **5.** loose (*woman*); ~ **yolsuz** unlawful.
yolluk 1. food for a journey, victuals; **2.** hall rug, runner; **3.** travel allowance.
yolmak, (**-ar**) **1.** to pluck; **2.** to pull out, to tear out (*hair*); **3.** *fig.* to fleece, to milk, to bleed.
yolsuz 1. roadless; **2.** stripeless, unstriped (*cloth*); **3.** slow (*ship, etc.*); **4.** loose (*woman*); **5.** improper; unlawful, illegal; **6.** *sl.* flat broke, penniless.
yolsuzluk 1. lack of roads; **2.** irregularity, malpractice; graft; **3.** *sl.* pennilessness.
yoluk plucked (*chicken, etc.*).
yolunmak 1. *pass. of* **yolmak**; **2.** to tear one's hair with grief.
yom good luck; ~ **tutmak** to regard as lucky.
yonca BOT clover, trefoil.
yonda down.
yonga chip, shaving (*of wood*).
yont, -tu unbroken mare.
yontkuşu, -nu zoo yellow wagtail.
yontma 1. *vn. of* **yontmak**; **2.** chiseled; hewn; ~ **taş devri** palaeolithic age.
yontmak, (**-ar**) **1.** to chisel; to hew, to whittle; to dress (*stone*); to sculpt; to chip; **2.** *fig.* to fleece.
yontulmak 1. *pass. of* **yontmak**; **2.** *fig.* to learn manners; **yontulmamış** *fig.* rough, uncouth.
yordam 1. agility; **2.** method, system; **3.** pomposity; swagger.
yorga jogtrot.

yorgan quilt, duvet, *Am.* comforter; ~ *gitti*, *kavga bitti iro.* the dispute is ended; ~ *iğnesi* quilting-needle.

yorgancı quilt-maker.

yorgun tired, weary, worn out; ~ *argın* dead tired, beat; ~ *düşmek* to be tired out; ~ ~ wearily.

yorgunluk tiredness, fatigue, weariness.

yormak[1], (*-ar*) to tire, to fatigue, to weary.

yormak[2], (*-ar*) to interpret.

yortmak P to rove about.

yortu Christian feast.

yorucu tiring, tiresome, wearisome.

yorulmak to get tired, to tire.

yorum interpretation, commentary.

yorumlamak to interpret.

yosma loose woman.

yosun BOT moss; alga.

yosunlanmak to moss, to get mossy.

yosunlu mossy.

yoz 1. uncultivated, virgin (*forest, land*); 2. boorish, uncouth (*person*); 3. degenerate; decadent.

yozlaşmak to degenerate.

yozlaştırmak to degenerate; to debase.

yön 1. direction; 2. aspect, side; ~ *vermek* to give a direction (*-e* to), to direction; *tarihi -den* from the historical point of view.

yönelim inclination, tendency.

yönelmek 1. to head towards, to go towards; 2. to incline towards.

yöneltim orientation.

yöneltmek to direct; to point (*-e* at).

yönerge directive; instructions.

yönetici manager; administrator.

yöneticilik management; administration.

yönetim management; administration; direction; government; ~ *kurulu* administrative committee, board of directors.

yönetmek to manage, to administer, to govern; to direct, to lead, to conduct; to control.

yönetmelik regulations, instructions, statutes.

yönetmen director (*a.* THEAT, *cinema*); manager.

yönlendirmek to direct, to orient, to steer.

yöntem method, system, procedure.

yöntemli methodical, systematic.

yöntemsiz unmethodical, unsystem-

atic.

yöre vicinity, neighbo(u)rhood, region, environs.

yöresel local.

yörünge orbit; *-sine oturmak* to go into orbit.

yudum sip, sup, gulp, swallow.

yudumlamak to sip.

yuf [ü] *int. expressing disgust*; ~ *borusu çalmak* (*or* ~ *çekmek*) to curse, to revile.

yufka 1. thin layer of dough; 2. fragile, weak; ~ *yürekli* tender-hearted.

Yugoslav Yugoslav(ian).

Yugoslavya [.. x .] *pr. n.* Yugoslavia.

yuğmak to wash.

yuh(a) boo!, ugh!, yuk!; ~ *çekmek* (*or* *yuhaya tutmak*) to boo, to jeer.

yuhalamak to boo, to jeer, to give s.o. the bird, to hoot.

yukarı 1. upper part; upstairs; 2. upper; upstairs; 3. up; *-da* above; upstairs; *-da adı geçen* above-mentioned, aforementioned; *-dan* 1. from above, from upstairs; 2. *fig.* from the boss; from the top (brass); *-dan bakmak* to look down (*-e* on); *-dan aşağı süzmek* (*b-ni*) to give s.o. the once-over.

yulaf BOT oat.

yular halter.

yumak[1] *s.* **yıkamak**.

yumak[2] ball (*of wool, etc.*).

yummak, (*-ar*) to shut, to close (*eye*); to clench, to double (*fist*).

yumru 1. lump; knot; gnarl, knob; node; 2. BOT tuber; ~ *kök* BOT tuber.

yumruk 1. fist; 2. blow (*or* punch *or* sock) with the fist; 3. *fig.* iron hand, fist; ~ *atmak* (*or* *indirmek* *or* *vurmak*) to hit (*or* punch *or* sock) with one's fist; ~ *göstermek* *fig.* to threaten; ~ *hakkı* s.th. gained by force; ~ *kadar* pea-sized, pint-sized; ~ *yumruğa gelmek* to come to blows; *yumruğuna güvenmek* to trust one's physical strength.

yumruklamak to hit with one's fist, to punch, to pummel, to sock.

yumruklaşmak to have a fist fight.

yumrukoyunu, *-nu* sports: boxing.

yumrul(an)mak to become knobby; to become nodular.

yumuk shut (*eye*, *mouth*); clenched, doubled (*fist*).

yumulmak 1. *pass. of* **yummak**; 2. (*for one's eyes*) to shut, to close; to narrow; **3.** to hunch over, to hunker; **4.** to attack.

yumurcak brat, scamp, little dickens.

yumurmak to form a lump.

yumurta 1. egg; **2.** testicle, testis; **~ akı** egg white, albumen; **~ kabuğu** egg--shell; **~ kapıya dayanınca** *fig.* when the chips are down; **~ sarısı** yolk; **-dan daha dün çıkmış** *fig.* young and smart-alecky.

yumurtacı seller of eggs.

yumurtacık ovule.

yumurtalık 1. ovary; **2.** eggcup.

yumurtlamak 1. to lay (eggs); **2.** to ovulate; **3.** *fig.* to blurt out, to come out with (*a remark*).

yumuşacık [x . . .] very soft, as soft as down.

yumuşak soft; tender; mild; gentle; **~ ağızlı** that takes the bit easily (*horse*); **~ başlı** docile, mild; tractable; biddable; **~ iniş** soft landing.

yumuşaklık softness; mildness.

yumuşamak 1. to soften; **2.** *fig.* to relent, to soften, to mellow, to unbend.

yumuşatmak to soften; to tenderize.

Yunan Greek, Grecian.

Yunanca [. x .] Greek.

Yunanistan *pr. n.* Greece.

Yunanlı Greek.

yunus(balığı) *zoo* dolphin.

yurdu eye of a needle.

yurt, -du 1. native country, homeland; **2.** home; **3.** student dormitory, hostel; **~ bilgisi** civics; **~ tutmak** to settle in; **yetiştirme yurdu** orphanage.

yurtlandırmak to settle (*people*).

yurtlanmak 1. to find a homeland; **2.** to settle in (*a place*).

yurtluk country estate, domain.

yurtsever 1. patriotic; **2.** patriot.

yurtseverlik patriotism.

yurttaş 1. citizen; **2.** fellow countryman, compatriot.

yurttaşlık citizenship; **~ bilgisi** civics.

yusyumru [x . .] very round; very knobby.

yusyuvarlak [x . . .] as round as a ball (*or* top).

yutak ANAT pharynx.

yutkunmak to swallow, to gulp.

yutmak, (-ar) 1. to swallow, to gulp; **2.** *fig.* to swallow (*an insult*); **3.** to believe, to fall for, to swallow; **4.** to beat, to skunk (*in a game*); **5.** *fig.* to absorb (*knowledge*).

yutturmak 1. *caus. of* **yutmak; 2.** (*b-ne*

bşi) to palm off *s.th.* on *s.o.*

yuva 1. nest; **2.** home; **3.** nursery school; **4.** den, nest (*of criminals*); **5.** MED socket; **~ kurmak** to set up a home; **-sını yapmak** (*b-nin*) *fig.* to teach *s.o.* a lesson, to show *s.o.* a thing or two; **-sını yıkmak** (*b-nin*) *fig.* to break up *s.o.'s* marriage; **-yı dişi kuş yapar** *pro.* men make houses, women make homes.

yuvak 1. cylinder; **2.** stone roller.

yuvalamak to nest.

yuvar BIOL corpuscle.

yuvarlak round, circular; globular, spherical; **~ hesap** round figure; **~ sayı** round number.

yuvarlaklaşmak to become round.

yuvarlaklaştırmak to round.

yuvarlaklık roundness; circularity.

yuvarlamak 1. to roll; **2.** to roll up; **3.** to round; **4.** to put away, to pack away, to polish off (*food*); **5.** F to tell whoppers.

yuvarlanmak 1. *pass. of* **yuvarlamak; 2.** to roll; to turn over and over; **3.** to fall (down); **4.** *fig.* to kick the bucket suddenly, to up and die; **5.** to get the sack (*or* push); **yuvarlanan taş yosun tutmaz** *pro.* a rolling stone gathers no moss; **yuvarlanıp gitmek** to rub along.

yuvar yuvar with a rolling motion.

yuvgu *s.* **yuvak.**

yuvgulamak to roll with a roller.

yüce exalted, high; lofty; eminent; sublime.

yücelik loftiness; eminence; sublimity.

yücelmek to become lofty (*or* exalted).

yüceltmek to exalt.

yük, -kü 1. load, burden; **2.** cargo; freight; lading; **3.** *fig.* burden; encumbrance; incubus; **4.** PHYS charge; **~ asansörü** goods lift, *Am.* freight elevator; **~ gemisi** freighter; **~ hayvanı** beast of burden; **~ olm.** (*b-ne*) *fig.* to be a burden to *s.o.*; **~ treni** goods train, *Am.* freight train; **~ vagonu** goods wagon, *Am.* freight car; **~ vurmak** to load (*an animal*); **-te hafif pahada ağır** light in bulk, high in value; **-ünü tutmak** *fig.* to get rich, to make money.

yükçü porter.

yüklem GR, LOG predicate.

yüklemek 1. IT to upload; **2.** to load, to freight; **3.** to lay (*a task*) on *s.o.*, to burden s.o. with (*a task*); **4.** *fig.* to lay (*or* put) (*the blame*) on s.o.

yüklenmek 1. *pass. of yüklemek*; **yüklenen dosya** ıt upload; **2.** to shoulder, to take on (*a burden, task, responsibility*); **3.** to push, to press, to pressure.

yükleyici stevedore, longshoreman.

yüklü 1. loaded, freighted; **2.** overburdened with work; **3.** pregnant; **4.** *sl.* drunk, loaded; **5.** *sl.* rich, loaded.

yüklük large cupboard (*for bedding*).

yüksek 1. high; lofty; **2.** high; great; big; **3.** noble, lofty; **4.** loud (*voice*); **5.** high, superior; **6.** high place; height; **~ atlama** *sports*: high jump; **~ basınç** high pressure; **~ fiyat** high price; **~ mühendis** graduated engineer; **~ perdeden konuşmak** *fig.* to talk big; ♀ **Seçim Kurulu** Election Commission; **~ sesle** aloud, loudly; **~ tansiyon** high blood pressure, hypertension; **-ten atmak** to talk big; **-ten bakmak** *fig.* to look down one's nose (*-e* at); **-ten uçmak** *fig.* to chase after the impossible.

yükseklik 1. height; highness; **2.** altitude; elevation; **3.** loudness (*of a voice*); **4.** high place, height.

yüksekokul college.

yükseköğretim higher education.

yükselmek 1. to rise, to ascend; **2.** to increase, to rise, to mount, to go up; **3.** to get louder (*voice*); **4.** to advance, to rise; to come up in the world.

yükselteç ELECT amplifier.

yükselti altitude, elevation (*a.* AST).

yükseltmek 1. *caus. of yükselmek*; **2.** to raise, to elevate; to increase; **3.** ELECT to amplify; **4.** to promote.

yüksük 1. thimble; **2.** BOT cupule.

yüksükotu, -nu BOT foxglove.

yüksünmek to regard as burdensome.

yüküm obligation, liability.

yükümlü obliged (*ile* to), obligated (*ile* to), bound (*ile* to).

yükümlülük obligation, liability.

yün 1. wool; **2.** wool, woolen.

yünlü 1. wool, woolen; **2.** woolen.

yüpürmek to run hither and thither.

yürek 1. heart; **2.** *fig.* courage, guts; **3.** *fig.* compassion, pity; **~ çarpıntısı 1.** palpitation of the heart, heartbeat; **2.** *fig.* anxiety; **~ vermek** to give courage, to embolden; **~ yarası** deep sorrow, heartbreak; (yüreği): **~ açık** simple-hearted; sincere; **~ ağzına gelmek** to have one's heart in one's

mouth; **~ bayılmak** to be starving (*or* caving in), **~ çarpmak** (*for one's heart*) to palpitate; **~ dar** impatient; **~ geniş** carefree, happy-go-lucky; **~ kabarmak** to feel nauseated; **~ kararmak** to lose heart; **~ katılmak** to gasp for breath; **~ parçalanmak** (*for one's heart*) to be wrenched; **~ pek 1.** hardhearted; **2.** fearless; **~ sıkılmak** to feel depressed *or* bored; (yüreğine); **~ dert olm.** to take s.th. to heart; **~ inmek 1.** (*for a great sadness*) to kill, to deal a mortal blow; **2.** to die then and there; **~ işlemek** to cut s.o. to the quick; (yüreğini): **~ pek tutmak** to keep up one's courage; **-ler acısı** heartrending, heartbreaking, piteous; **-ten** from one's heart.

yüreklendirmek to give courage, to embolden.

yüreklenmek to take courage (*or* heart).

yürekli brave, courageous, stouthearted.

yüreksiz fainthearted, cowardly.

yürümek 1. to walk; **2.** to march; **3.** to hurry, to make haste; **4.** to go on, to advance, to move forward; **5.** to accumulate (*interest*); **6.** to work, to function, to run (*machine*); **7.** to die, to pass away; **8.** to vanish; to be stolen; **9.** to cross, to walk across; **yürüyen merdiven** moving staircase, *Am.* escalator.

yürürlük validity; operation; **yürürlüğe girmek** to come into force (*or* operation), to get into effect; **-te olm.** to be in operation (*or* force).

yürütmek 1. *caus. of yürümek*; **2.** to perform, to carry out; **3.** to get s.th. accepted; **4.** to put forward (*a thought, etc.*); **5.** to fire, to dismiss; **6.** to put into force; **7.** *sl.* to steal, to lift, to swipe, to nick, to pinch, to nip.

yürüyüş 1. walking; gait; **2.** walk; **3.** march; **~ yapmak 1.** to go on a walk; **2.** to hold a protest march; **-e çıkmak** to go out for a walk.

yüz¹ hundred; one hundred; **-de 1.** one hundred percent; **2.** sure, certain.

yüz² 1. face; **2.** surface; **3.** outer covering, case; **4.** shame; **5.** side; **~ bulmak** to be emboldened; to be presumptuous; **~ bulunca astar ister** s.; **~ verince astar ister**, **~ çevirmek** *fig.* to turn one's back (*-den* on); **~ etm. 1.** to hand over; **2.** to face up (*two things that are* *to be joined together*); ~ **göstermek** to show up; ~ **göz olm.** (*b-le*) to make free with *s.o.*; ~ **kızartıcı** disgraceful, shameful; ~ **tutmak** to begin (*-meğe* to *inf.*); ~ **verince astar ister** give him an inch and he will take a yard (*or* mile); ~ **vermek** to indulge, to be indulgent (*-e* to); ~ **vermemek** (*b-ne*) to give *s.o.* the cold shoulder; ~ *-e* face to face; ~ *-e* **gelmek** to come face to face (*ile* with); (yüze): ~ **çıkmak 1.** to come to the surface; **2.** *fig.* to get insolent; ~ **gülmek** to feign friendship; (yüzü): ~ **ak alnı pak** pure and honest; ~ **asılmak** to pull a long face; ~ **gözü açılmak** *fig.* to learn about the birds and the bees; ~ **gülmek** to be happy; ~ **kızarmak** to flush, to blush; ~ **olmamak** *fig.* not to have the face (*or* cheek) (*-meğe* to *inf.*); ~ **pek** brazenfaced, shameless; ~ **sıcak** attractive; ~ **soğuk** repulsive, repellent; ~ **suyu hürmetine** for the sake of; ~ **tutmamak** not to have the nerve (*-meğe* to *inf.*); ~ **yazılı kalmak** to remain untouched; ~ **yerde** humble; ~ **yere gelmek** to feel ashamed on *s.o.*'s behalf; ~ **yumuşak** too kind to refuse; (yüzünden): ~ **akmak** to be evident from the look on *s.o.*'s face, to be written all over *s.o.*; ~ **düşen bin parça olur** sour-faced; ~ **kan damlamak** to be in the pink of health; ~ **okumak** to read in *s.o.*'s face; (yüzüne): ~ **bakılmaz** very ugly, like the back (end) of a bus; ~ **gozune bulaştırmak** to make a mess (*or* balls *or* hash *or* bungle) of *s.th.*; ~ **kan gelmek** to recover one's health; ~ **karşı** to *s.o.*'s face; ~ **vurmak** to rub it in, to cast *s.th.* in *s.o.*'s teeth; (yüzünü): ~ **ağartmak** (*b-nin*) to do *s.o.* credit, to be a credit to *s.o.*; ~ **buruşturmak** (*or* **ekşitmek**) to make a face; ~ **gören cennetlik** you are a rare bird; you are a sight for sore eyes; ~ **gözünü açmak** (*b-nin*) to teach *s.o.* about the birds and the bees; ~ **güldürmek** (*b-nin*) to make *s.o.* happy; ~ **şeytan görsün!** the devil take him!; ~ **yüzünün akıyle çıkmak** to succeed in doing *s.th.*

yüzakı, -nı hono(u)r, good name.
yüzbaşı MIL. captain.
yüzde 1. percent; percentage; **2.** commission, percentage; ~ **beş** five percent.
yüzdelik commission, percentage.
yüzden superficial.
yüzdürmek 1. *caus. of* **yüzmek; 2.** to float (*a ship*); **3.** *sl.* to fire, to give *s.o.* the sack.
yüzgelen prominent, important (*people*).
yüzer[1] a hundred each (*or* apiece); ~ ~ a hundred at a time.
yüzer[2] floating; ~ **havuz** floating dock.
yüzey 1. surface; **2.** *geom.* plane.
yüzeysel superficial, surface; cursory; shallow.
yüzgeç, -ci 1. zoo fin (*of a fish*); **2.** natatorial (*animal*).
yüzgörümlüğü, -nü, customary present given by a bridegroom to his bride on first seeing her unveiled face.
yüzkarası, -nı disgrace; black sheep.
yüzlemek to rub it in.
yüzleşmece face to face.
yüzleşmek to meet face to face; to be confronted with one another.
yüzleştirmek to confront.
yüzlü 1. … faced; **2.** impudent, insolent.
yüzlük 1. a hundred lira bill; **2.** centenarian.
yüzme vn. *of* **yüzmek;** ~ **havuzu** swimming pool (*or* bath).
yüzmek[1], (*-er*) to skin, to flay.
yüzmek[2], (*-er*) **1.** to swim; **2.** to float; **3.** to be covered with, to be thick with; **4.** to wallow in, to swim in; **para içinde yüzüyor** he is wallowing (*or* rolling) in money.
yüznumara toilet, loo.
yüzölçümü, -nü area.
yüzsuyu: ~ **dökmek** to grovel.
yüzsüz shameless, brazen(faced), cheeky.
yüzsüzlük shamelessness, brazenness, gall.
yüzücü swimmer.
yüzük ring; **yüzüğü geri çevirmek** (*or* **atmak**) to break off an engagement.
yüzükoyun facedown, prone(ly), prostrate, procumbent.
yüzükparmağı, -nı ring finger.
yüzüncü hundredth.
yüzüstü facedown, prone(ly), prostrate, procumbent; ~ **bırakmak** to throw over, to leave s.o. in the lurch; ~ **kalmak** to be left unfinished.
yüzyıl century.

Z

zaaf weakness; infirmity; debility.

zabıt, **-ptı** minutes; proceedings; court record: police report; **~ ceridesi** printed proceedings; **~ kâtibi 1.** keeper of the minutes; **2.** JUR court reporter; **~ tutmak** to take minutes; (*for a policeman*) to write down a report.

zabıta [- . .] police.

zabıtname [. . - .] minutes; proceedings; court record; police report.

zabit, **-ti** MIL officer.

zaç, **-çı** vitriol.

zaçyağı, **-nı** oil of vitriol.

zadegân [- . -] elite; upper crust.

zafer **1.** victory, triumph; **2.** ♀ *mf*.; **~ alayı** triumphal procession; **~ işareti** V-sign; **~ kazanmak** to gain the victory, to carry (*or* win) the day; **~ takı** triumphal arch, arch of triumph.

zafiyet, **-ti** [ā] weakness; infirmity; debility; inanition.

zağ burr.

zağanos zoo an eagle owl.

zağar terrier.

zağara fur collar (*of a coat*).

zahife *obs*. reptile.

zahir **1.** outer appearance; **2.** clear, evident; **3.** apparently; **-de** outwardly; to all appearances.

zahire [ī] **1.** provisions, stores; **2.** stock of grain; **~ ambarı** granary.

zahiren outwardly; to all appearances.

zahiri **1.** external, outward; **2.** feigned, artificial.

zahit, **-di 1.** ascetic; **2.** ♀ *mf*.

zahmet, **-ti** trouble, difficulty, inconvenience; **~ çekmek** to have trouble (*or* difficulty); **~ etm.** to put o.s. out, to inconvenience o.s.; **~ etmeyin(iz)!** don't trouble yourself!; **~ olmazsa** if it doesn't put you to any trouble; **~ vermek** to trouble, to inconvenience, to put out; **-e değmek** to be worth the trouble; **-e girmek** to put o.s. out, to inconvenience o.s.; **-e sokmak** (*b-ni*) to put *s.o.* to trouble, to put *s.o.* out, to trouble *s.o.*, to inconvenience *s.o.*; **bir ~ bana tuzu verir misiniz?** may I trouble you for the salt?

zahmetli troublesome, hard, difficult, laborious, labo(u)red, onerous.

zahmetsiz easy.

zaıf *s*. **zaaf**.

zaika [- . .] MED taste.

zail transitory, transient; evanescent; **~ olm.** to disappear, to pass.

zait, **-di** [ā] **1.** unnecessary; **2.** MATH plus.

zakkum BOT oleander, rosebay.

zalim [ā] **1.** tyrannical; unjust; cruel; **2.** tyrant.

zalimlik [ā] tyranny; injustice; cruelty.

zam, **-mmı 1.** rise, *Am*. raise; **2.** additional charge, surcharge; **~ görmek 1.** to get a rise (*or Am*. raise); **2.** to be increased in price.

zaman [. -] **1.** time; **2.** age, epoch, era; **3.** time, season; **4.** free time; **5.** GR tense; **6.** MUS time; **7.** when; **~ belirteci** GR adverb of time; **~ birimi** unit of time; **~ geçtikçe** as the time goes on; **~ kaybetmeden** without delay, without loss of time; **~ kazanmak** to gain time; **~ kollamak** to bide one's time; **~ öldürmek** to kill time; **~ ~** from time to time, every now and then, occasionally; **~ zarfı** *s*. **belirteci**; **-ı geçmek 1.** to be out of date (*or* outmoded); **2.** to expire; **-ında** at the proper (*or* right) time; **-la** in the course of time; **o -ın başkanı** the then president.

zamanaşımı, **-nı** JUR prescription.

zamane [. - .] today, the present age; with it; **~ çocukları** children of today, modern youth.

zamanlamak to time well.

zamanlı timely.

zamansız untimely.

zamazingo [. . x .] *sl*. mistress, paramour.

zambak BOT lily.

zamir [ī] **1.** GR pronoun; **2.** inner self, heart.

zamk, **-kı 1.** gum; **2.** glue; paste.

zamkinos [x . .] **1.** thingumabob, what--do-you-call-it; **2.** running away; **~ etm.** (*or* **-u çekmek**) *sl*. to run away, to beat it.

zamklamak to glue, to paste.

zamklı **1.** glued; pasted; **2.** gummed.

zammetmek [x . .] to add, to annex.

zampara womanizer, woman (*or* skirt) chaser, lecher.

zamparalık skirt chasing, lechery; ~ **etm.** to chase after women, to womanize.

zan, -nnı 1. supposition, guess, surmise, conjecture; **2.** suspicion, doubt; ~ **altında bulunmak** to be under suspicion; **-ıma göre** in my opinion; **-ında olm.** to be of the opinion that.

zanaat, -tı craft, trade.

zanaatçı craftsman.

zangırdamak 1. to rattle; **2.** to tremble; **3.** to chatter (*teeth*).

zangırtı rattle.

zangır zangır rattlingly; ~ **titremek** to be all of a tremble.

zangoç sexton, verger (*of a church*).

zani [- .] adulterer; fornicator.

zanlı accused; suspect.

zannetmek [x . .] to think, to suppose, to guess, to believe, to reckon; **zannedersem** I think that ...

zapt 1. capturing; **2.** seizure, confiscation; **3.** taking down, recording; **4.** keeping in mind; ~ **etm. 1.** to capture, to conquer; **2.** to restrain; **3.** to seize, to confiscate; **4.** to take down, to record; **5.** to keep in mind; **6.** to grasp, to understand.

zaptetmek *s.* **zapt** *etm.*

zaptiye, HIST **1.** zaptieh, gendarme; **2.** zaptieh, gendarmerie.

zapturapt, -tı 1. discipline; **2.** order.

zar[1] **1.** ANAT, BOT, ZOO membrane, pellicle; **2.** CHEM membrane.

zar[2] die; ~ **atmak** to throw dice; ~ **tutmak** to cheat in throwing dice.

zarafet, -ti [- .-] grace, elegance, refinement; delicacy.

zarar 1. damage, harm, injury, detriment; **2.** COM loss; ~ **etm. 1.** to lose money; to make a loss; **2.** to damage, to harm, to injure; ~ **görmek** to be damaged (*or* harmed *or* injured) (*-den* by); ~ **ve ziyan** damages; ~ **vermek** to damage, to harm, to injure; **-ı yok!** it doesn't matter!, never mind!, that's OK!; **-ına satmak** to sell at a loss (*or* sacrifice), to sacrifice.

zararına 1. at a loss (*or* sacrifice); **2.** (*b-nin*) to s.o.'s disadvantage.

zararlı harmful, injurious, detrimental; ~ **çıkmak** to end up a loser; to come out of s.th. a loser.

zararsız harmless; innocuous; ~ **hale getirmek** to overpower.

zarf 1. envelope; **2.** case, receptacle; **3.** GR adverb; **üç saat -ında** within three hours.

zarflamak to put into an envelope.

zargana [x . .] ZOO needlefish, gar(-fish).

zarif [î] **1.** elegant, graceful; **2.** elegant, gracious, refined (*action, manner*); **3.** ǒ [x .] *wf.*

zariflik [î] elegance, grace; refinement.

zari zari [ā, ā] bitterly.

zarp, -bı 1. severity, violence; **2.** blow; ~ **etm.** to hit, to strike; ~ **musluğu** main valve.

zarta [x .] fart, poop; **-yı çekmek** *sl.* to die, to kick the bucket.

zartçı *sl.* big talker, windbag.

zart zurt bluster; ~ **etm.** to bluster.

zaruret, -ti [ü] **1.** necessity, essentiality, vitalness; indispensability; unavoidability; **2.** poverty, destitution.

zaruri [. - -] necessary, essential, requisite, vital; indispensable; unavoidable; inevitable.

zar zor 1. unwillingly, reluctantly; **2.** by force, forcibly; **3.** with difficulty.

zat, -tı [ā] **1.** person, individual; personality; **2.** essence, core, heart; ~ **işleri şubesi** personnel department; **-a mahsus** private, personal; **zatı âliniz** your Worship.

zaten, zati [ā] [x .] anyway, anyhow, in any case, at any rate.

zatî [- -] personal, private; ~ **eşya** personal effects.

zatülcenp, -bi [ā] [x . .] MED pleurisy.

zatürree [ā] [x . . .] MED pneumonia.

zavahir *s.* **zevahir.**

zavallı [x . .] **1.** poor, miserable, pitiful; **2.** helpless; ~ **adam!** poor man!

zaviye [ā] **1.** corner; nook; **2.** MATH angle; **3.** point of view, viewpoint.

zayıf 1. thin, meager; scrawny; **2.** weak; faint, frail; **3.** slim, small, slender (*possibility*); ~ **almak** to get a failing grade; ~ **düşmek 1.** to get thin; **2.** to get weak.

zayıflamak 1. to get thin; **2.** to lose weight, to slim down; **3.** to get weak.

zayıflık 1. thinness, meagerness; **2.** weakness; faintness, feebleness.

zayi, -li [ā] lost; ~ **etm.** to lose; ~ **olm.** to be lost.

zayiat, -tı [- . -] losses, casualties; ~ **vermek** to suffer losses (*or* casualties).

zayiçe [ā] horoscope; **-sine bakmak** (*b-nin*) to cast s.o.'s horoscope.

zeamet, -ti [ā] HIST fief, fee.

zebani [. - -] **1.** demon of hell; **2.** *fig.* hellhound.

zebanzet, -di commonly used (*or* popular) (*word, etc.*).

zebella [. . -] **1.** ogre; **2.** ogr(e)ish (*person*); **~ gibi** ogr(e)ish (*person*).

zebir *s.* **zebra.**

zebra [x .] ZOO zebra.

zebun [ū] weak, helpless.

zebunküş [ū] cruel.

Zebur [ū] *pr. n.* the Book of Psalms.

zecir, -cri force, compulsion; oppression.

zecren [x .] by force, by compulsion.

zecri forcible, coercive; **~ tedbirler** coercive measures.

zedelemek 1. to bruise; **2.** to harm, to damage, to injure.

zefir¹ [ī] MED exhalation, expiration.

zefir² zephyr.

zehap, -bı [ā] supposition, surmise.

zehir, -hri poison, toxic; venom; **~ gibi 1.** very hot (*or* peppery *or* pungent); **2.** sharp, biting (*cold*); **3.** very clever, crack, crackerjack.

zehirlemek 1. to poison; **2.** *fig.* to poison, to contaminate.

zehirli poisonous, toxic; venomous.

zehretmek [x .] *fig.* to make distasteful, to embitter, to take all the pleasure out of s.th. for s.o.

zekâ intelligence, intellect; **~ testi** intelligence test; **~ yaşı** mental age.

zekât, -tı *isl.* alms.

zekâvet, -ti acumen.

zeker ANAT penis.

zeki [ī] **1.** intelligent; quick-witted, sharp, clever, acute; **2.** ♀ [x .] *mf.*

zeklenmek P = **zevklenmek.**

zelil [ī] despicable.

zelzele earthquake.

zem, -mmi disparagement.

zemberek spring (*of a watch, etc.*); **zem bereği boşalmak** *fig.* to have a fit of laughter.

zembil shopping bag.

zemheri the dead of winter; **~ zürafası** *person who wears light clothes in the dead of winter.*

zemin [. -] **1.** ground, earth; **2.** floor; **3.** ground floor; **4.** basis, ground; **5.** circumstances, conditions; **~ hazırlamak** to lay the groundwork (*-e* for); **~ katı** ground floor.

zeminlik MIL underground shelter.

zemmetmek [x .] to disparage, to

speak ill of.

zemzem 1. Zamzam; **2.** water from Zamzam; **~ kuyusuna işemek** to do s.th. monstrous merely to acquire notoriety; **-le yıkanmış olm.** *fig.* to be an angel compared to s.o. else.

zencefil BOT ginger.

zenci Black, Negro.

zengin 1. rich, wealthy; **2.** productive, fertile, rich; **3.** rich person; **4.** rich in, abounding in.

zenginle(ş)mek to get rich.

zenginlik 1. richness, wealthiness; **2.** riches, wealth.

zenne 1. women's wear; **2.** *man taking a woman's part in the* **ortaoyunu.**

zenneci seller of women's clothes.

zeplin [x .] zeppelin.

zerdali [ā] BOT wild apricot.

zerdeva ZOO pine marten.

Zerdüşt, -tü *pr. n.* Zoroaster.

zeretmek [x . .] *obs.* to sow (*seed*).

zeri, -r'i sowing (*seed*).

zerk, -ki MED injection; **~ etm.** to inject.

zerre 1. mote, atom; **2.** CHEM molecule; **~ kadar** the least bit.

zerrin 1. gold(en) **2.** BOT jonquil.

zerzevat, -tı vegetables; produce.

zerzevatçı vegetable seller.

zevahir [. - .] appearances; **-i kurtarmak** to save face (*or* appearances).

zeval, -li [ā] **1.** disappearance; **2.** decline, wane; **~ bulmak 1.** to disappear; **2.** to decline, to wane; **~ vakti** noon; **-e yüz tutmak** *fig.* to begin to decline; **-i olm.** (*b-ne*) to be harmful to *s.o.*

zevali [. - -] reckoned from noon (*time*).

zevalsiz [ā] permanent, everlasting.

zevat, -tı [ā] *obs. pl. of* **zat.**

zevce *rare* wife.

zevç, -ci *obs.* husband.

zeveban [ā] melting, fusion; **~ etm.** to melt, to fuse; **~ noktası** PHYS melting (*or* fusion) point.

zevk, -ki 1. pleasure, delight, enjoyment, fun; **2.** taste, discrimination; **3.** taste, liking, preference; **4.** sense of taste, gustation; **~ almak** (*or* **duymak**) (*bşden*) to find (*or* take) pleasure in s.th., to enjoy s.th.; **~ için** for fun; **~ vermek** to give pleasure; **-ine düşkün** addicted to pleasure; **-ini çıkarmak** (*bşin*) to enjoy s.th. to the full; **-ler ve renkler tartışılmaz** there is no accounting for tastes; **-ten dört köşe olm.** *fig.* to be as happy as a lark (*or* sandboy), to be as happy as the day is long, to be as happy as Larry.

zevklenmek 1. to take (*or* find) pleasure (*ile* in); **2.** (*b-le*) to make fun of *s.o.*

zevkli 1. pleasurable, delightful, pleasant; **2.** tasteful.

zevksiz 1. tasteless; **2.** boring, dull, tiresome, insipid, tedious, unpleasant.

zevzek long-winded, talkative.

zevzeklik boring chatter; **~ etm.** to rattle on.

zeybek *swashbuckling village lad of southwestern Anatolia.*

zeyil, -yli appendix, addendum.

zeyrek clever, quick-witted.

zeytin olive.

zeytinlik olive grove.

zeytinyağı, -nı olive oil; **~ gibi üste çıkmak** *fig.* to come off best; to get the better of an argument.

zeytuni [. - -] olive-green.

zıbarmak *sl.* **1.** to die, to croak, to peg out, to pop off; **2.** to pass out (*after getting drunk*); **3.** to fall asleep, to hit the sack.

zıbın quilted jacket for a baby.

zıddiyet, -ti opposition, contrariety; contrast.

zıh 1. edging; piping; **2.** border; **3.** mo(u)lding.

zıkkım poison; **~ olsun!** may you choke on it!

zıkkımlanmak to eat, to cram food in one's gob, to stuff o.s. with food.

zılgıt, -tı F severe tongue-lashing; **~ yemek** to get it in the neck, to cop it, to catch it.

zımba [x .] punch, stapler.

zımbalamak 1. to punch, to staple; **2.** *sl.* to stab, to knife; **3.** *sl.* to fuck, to poke.

zımbalı [x . .] punched, stapled.

zımbırdatmak to strum, to thrum, to twang.

zımbırtı 1. discordant, twang; **2.** what-do-you-call-it, thingumabob.

zımnen [x .] **1.** indirectly, by implication; **2.** implicitly.

zımni [î] indirect, implied, veiled; unspoken; implicit.

zımpara [x . .] emery; **~ kâğıdı** sandpaper.

zımparalamak to sand(paper); to emery.

zındık *fig.* atheist, unbeliever.

zıngadak [x . .] suddenly and with a jolt.

zıngıldamak *s.* **zangırdamak.**

zıngıl zıngıl *s.* **zangır zangır.**

zıngırdamak *s.* **zangırdamak.**

zıngır zıngır *s.* **zangır zangır.**

zınk: ~ diye durmak to come to an abrupt stop.

zıp: ~ diye all of a sudden, suddenly.

zıpçıktı upstart, parvenu.

zıpır F screwy, cracked, loony, crackpot.

zıpkın harpoon; (fish)gig.

zıplamak 1. to jump; **2.** to bounce.

zıppadak [x . .] suddenly, all of a sudden.

zıpzıp, -pı marble.

zıp zıp 1. up and down; **2.** with a bounce, bouncingly.

zırdeli [x . .] as mad as a hatter, stark staring mad.

zırh armo(u)r.

zırhlanmak to put on one's armo(u)r.

zırhlı 1. armo(u)red, armo(u)r-plated, armo(u)r-clad; **2.** NAUT battleship, ironclad; **~ otomobil** armo(u)red car; **~ tümen** MIL armo(u)red division.

zırıldamak 1. to yammer, to yak; **2.** to cry, to blubber, to boohoo.

zırıltı 1. racket; **2.** yammer; **3.** squabble, row, quarrel; **4.** F what-do-you-call-it, thingumabob.

zırıl zırıl: ~ ağlamak to cry buckets; **~ terlemek** to sweat buckets.

zırlak 1. zoo cricket; **2.** weepy.

zırlamak *s.* **zırıldamak.**

zırnık 1. arsenic, zarnich; **2.** *fig.* the least little bit; **~ bile vermem!** I won't leave him so much as a penny!

zırtapoz *sl.* crazy, screwy.

zırt pırt F at any time whatsoever.

zırtullahıkermani [. . - · . . - -] *co.* nut, maniac, loon.

zırt zırt *s.* **zırt pırt.**

zırva [x .] **1.** nonsense, rubbish, rot, bunk, hooey; **2.** nonsensical, stupid; **~ tevil götürmez** *pro.* it is no use trying to make sense out of foolish talk.

zırvalamak to talk nonsense (*or* rot), to drivel.

zır zır: ~ ağlamak to blubber, to boohoo.

zırzop *s.* **zirzop.**

zıt, -ddı opposite, contrary; **~ gitmek** (*b-le*) to oppose *s.o.*; **zıddı olm.** (*bş b-nin*) to dislike *s.th.*; **zıddına gitmek** (*b-nin*) to rile *s.o.*

zıtlaşmak (*for people*) to become the

opposite of each other.

zıvana [. x .] **1.** liner; **2.** tenon; **3.** pin; **4.** mortise; **-dan çıkmak** *fig.* to blow his stack, to fly off the handle.

zıya, -aı [ā] loss.

zıykınefes, zıykısadır, -drı MED dyspnea.

zibidi 1. oddly dressed; **2.** crazy, nutty, screwy.

zifaf [ā] entering the bridal chamber; **~ gecesi** wedding night; **~ odası** bridal chamber.

zifir deposit in a pipe stem.

zifiri: ~ karanlık 1. complete darkness; **2.** pitch black, inky (black), as black as pitch (*or* midnight *or* ink).

zifos [x .] **1.** mud; **2.** F nonsensical; **~ atmak** (*b-ne*) to sling mud at *s.o.*

zift, -ti pitch; **-in pekini yesin!** let him starve for all I care!

ziftlemek to pitch.

ziftlenmek 1. *pass. of* **ziftlemek; 2.** F to make a pig of o.s.

ziftli coated with pitch.

zihin, -hni 1. mind, intellect; **2.** memory, mind; **3.** comprehension; **~ açmak** to stimulate the mind; **~ bulanıklığı** MED mental confusion; **~ yormak** to think hard, to rack one's brains; (zihni): **~ açılmak** to feel mentally alert; **~ bulanmak** to get confused (*or* muddled up); **~ dağılmak** (*for one's mind*) to wander; **~ durmak** to be unable to think clearly, to be mentally fatigued; **~ saplanmak** to get hipped on (*a mistaken idea*); **-ni kurcalamak** (*for s.th.*) to keep popping into one's mind, to recur to s.o. repeatedly.

zihnen mentally.

zihni mental, intellectual.

zihniyet, -ti mentality.

zikir, -kri 1. mention; **2.** *isl.* zikr, dhikr (*repeating the word Allah*); **zikri geçmek** to be mentioned.

zikretmek [x . .] **1.** to mention; **2.** *isl.* to repeat the word **Allah.**

zikzak 1. zigzag; **2.** zigzag(gy); **~ yapmak** to zigzag.

zikzaklı zigzag(gy).

zil 1. bell; doorbell; buzzer; **2.** cymbal; **3.** finger cymbal; **4.** jingle (*on a tambourine*); **5.** *sl.* very hungry, peckish; **~ çalıyor** the bell is ringing; **~ takıp oynamak** *fig.* to jump for joy.

zillet, -ti abasement.

zilli 1. provided with a bell; **2.** *sl.* shrew-

ish (*woman*).

zilyet JUR owner, possessor.

zilyetlik JUR ownership, possession; **~ davası** JUR possessory action.

zilzurna: ~ sarhoş as drunk as a Lord, pissed as a newt, corked, blotto.

zimamdar [. - -] administrator, manager.

zimmet, -ti debit; **-ine geçirmek 1.** (*bir hesabı b-nin*) to debit (*an amount of money*) to *s.o.'s* account; **2.** (*bir parayı kendi*) to embezzle, to peculate.

zina [ā] JUR adultery; fornication.

zincifre cinnabar.

zincir 1. chain; **2.** necklace; **3.** chain, series, succession; **-e vurmak** to chain, to put in chains, to fetter.

zincirleme 1. *vn. of* **zincirlemek; 2.** successive; **~ kaza** pileup.

zincirlemek to chain.

zincirli chained.

zindan [ā] prison; dungeon; **~ gibi** pitch-dark.

zindancı [ā] gaoler, jailer.

zinde energetic, alive, active; robust.

zinhar [ā] never!, no way!

zira [- -] [x -] because.

ziraat, -ti [. - .] agriculture.

ziraatçı agriculturist.

ziraatçılık agriculture.

ziral [. - -] agricultural.

zirman *sl.* big, strapping (*man*).

zirve summit, peak, apex; **~ toplantısı** summit meeting; **mesleğinin zirvesinde** at the top of the tree.

zirzop, -pu F crazy, screwy, loony, crackpot.

ziya [ā] **1.** light; **2.** ♀ *mf.*

ziyadar [. - -] bright, luminous.

ziyade [ā] **1.** excess, surplus; **2.** a lot of, much; many; **3.** excessive; **4.** courtyard (*of a mosque*); **5.** rather (*-den* than), more (*-den* than); **~ olsun!** thank you very much! (*said to s.o. after eating s.th. he has offered one*); **-siyle 1.** extremely, exceedingly; **2.** excessively, too; **burası evden ~ müzeye benziyor** this place is more like a museum than a house.

ziyafet, -ti feast, banquet; **~ vermek** (*or* **çekmek**) to give a banquet.

ziyan [ā] loss; damage; harm; **~ etm.** to waste; **~ olm.** to go for nothing, to go to waste; **~ zebil olm.** P to go to waste, to go for naught; **-ı yok!** never mind!

ziyankâr [ā] destructive; wasteful.

ziyankârlık [ā] destructiveness; wastefulness.

ziyansız [ā] harmless.

ziyaret, -ti [ā] **1.** visit, call; **2.** pilgrimage; **~ etm.** to visit, to call on; **-ine gitmek** (*b-nin*) to go to visit *s.o.*

ziyaretçi [ā] visitor, caller.

ziyaretgâh [. - . -] place of pilgrimage.

ziynet, -ti 1. ornament, decoration; **2.** jewel(le)ry; **3.** ♀ *wf.*; **~ eşyası** jewel(le)ry.

zodyak AST zodiac.

zoka [x .] **1.** fishhook; **2.** *sl.* trap, trick; **-yı yutmak** *sl.* to take the bait, to fall for a trick.

zom *sl.* dead drunk, blotto, corked.

zonklamak to throb.

zonk zonk: ~ zonklamak to throb terribly.

zoolog zoologist.

zooloji zoology.

zoolojik zoological.

zor 1. difficult, hard; **2.** difficulty, trouble; **3.** obligation, necessity, compulsion; **4.** coercion, pressure; **5.** barely, just; **~ bela 1.** with great difficulty; **2.** just barely; **~ gelmek** (*b-ne*) to be difficult for *s.o.*; **~ kullanmak** to use force; **-a başvurmak** to resort to force; **-a gelememek** to be unable to endure pressure; **-a koşmak** to make difficulties for s.o.; **-la** by force; **-la güzellik olmaz** it is no use forcing it; **-u -una** with great difficulty; **-un ne?** what's the matter with you?

zoraki [ā] forced; under compulsion.

zorba tyrant; bully; browbeater.

zorbalık tyranny.

zorgulu PSYCH compulsive.

zorlama 1. *vn. of* **zorlamak**; **2.** compulsion; coercion; **3.** strain; **4.** forced; **~ yürüyüş** forced march.

zorlamak 1. to force, to compel, to coerce, to constrain; **2.** to strain; **3.** to put pressure on.

zorlaşmak to get difficult (*or* hard).

zorlaştırmak to make difficult.

zorlayıcı coercive, forcible; **~ nedenler** JUR forces majeures.

zorlu 1. difficult, hard; **2.** powerful, violent; **3.** powerful, influential.

zorluk difficulty; **~ çıkarmak** to make

(*or* raise) difficulties, to make things difficult.

zorunlu 1. necessary, obligatory; indispensable; **2.** compulsory, imperative; **3.** unavoidable, inevitable.

zorunluluk 1. obligation; indispensability; **2.** imperativeness.

zuhur [. -] appearance; **~ etm. 1.** to appear, to come into view; **2.** to take place suddenly, to come about suddenly.

zuhurat, -tı [. - -] unforeseen events, contingencies; **-a bağlı** contingent.

zuhuri [. - -] player in the **ortaoyunu**; **~ kolu** troupe of **ortaoyunu** players.

zula *sl.* hiding place, cache; **~ etm.** *sl.* **1.** to steal; **2.** to hide, to conceal.

zulmet, -ti darkness.

zulmetmek [x . .] to tyrannize.

zulüm, -lmü tyranny, cruelty; injustice; oppression.

zurna MUS a kind of recorder; **~ gibi** tightly fitting (*trousers*).

zurnabalığı, -nı ZOO saury, skipper.

zübde 1. summary; **2.** the best part, the cream.

zücaciye [ā] glassware; china.

züğürt, -dü *co.* broke, penniless, skint; **~ tesellisi** cold comfort.

züğürtleşmek *co.* to become penniless, to go broke.

züğürtlük *co.* pennilessness.

Zühre AST Venus.

zührevi [ī] MED venereal; **~ hastalıklar** venereal diseases.

zünt, -hdü asceticism.

zühul, -lü [ü] inadvertence; slip; slip of the tongue.

zülüf, -lfü sidelock, earlock.

zümre class, group, set (*of people*).

zümrüdi [ī] emerald.

Zümrüdüanka [. x . . .] a mythical bird; **~ gibi** wonderful but imaginary.

zümrüt, -dü emerald; **~ yeşili** emerald(-green).

züppe fop, coxcomb, snob, toff, la-di-da.

züppelik foppishness, coxcombry.

zürafa [. - .] **1.** ZOO giraffe; **2.** *sl.* lesbian.

zürra, -aı [ā] *obs.* farmers.

zürriyet, -ti progeny, offspring.

A

a [ei, ə] *Sesli harfle başlayan sözcükten önce* **an** [æn; ən] *kullanılır. Ad belirteni, harfi tarif:* bir, herhangi bir; her bir, -de, -ne; *twice a week* haftada iki kere.
A1 F ['ei'wʌn] *adj.* birinci kalite.
a.back [ə'bæk] *adv.* geriye, geri tarafa; **taken ~** şaşkın, afallamış.
ab.a.cus ['æbəkəs] *n. pl.* **ab.a.ci** ['_sai] hesap tahtası; ARCH abak, sütun gövdesi; direk bedeni.
a.baft NAUT [ə'bɑːft] *adv. & prep.* geride, kıç tarafta.
a.ban.don [ə'bændən] *v/t.* terketmek, bırakmak, teslim etm., vazgeçmek; kendi haline bırakmak; *spor:* terketmek; **~ o.s. to** hissiyatına kapılmak; *bşe* düşkün olm., *bşin* müptelâsı olm.; **a'bandoned** *adj.* metruk, terkedilmiş; menfur, alçak; **a'ban.don.ment** *n.* terk, bırakma; sadakat, bağlılık.
a.base [ə'beis] *v/t.* alçaltmak, gururunu kırmak; **a'base.ment** *n.* alçaltma, gururunu kırma, tezlil.
a.bash [ə'bæʃ] *v/t.* utandırmak, mahcup etm., yüzünü kızartmak; **a'bash.ment** *n.* mahcubiyet, hayâ, sıkılganlık.
a.bate [ə'beit] *v/t.* azaltmak, kısaltmak, eksiltmek; kısmak; (*ağrı, sızı*) hafifletmek, teskin etm.; (*fiyat, vergi*) indirmek, azaltmak; JUR sona erdirmek; *v/i.* azalmak, çekilmek, hafiflemek; hükümsüz kalmak; (*fiyat*) düşmek; **a'batement** *n.* azaltma, azaltılma; (*fiyat, vergi, resim*) indirim, tenzil, indirilmiş meblağ.
ab.at.tis MIL [ə'bætis] *n.* mâni, mania.
ab.at.toir [æbətwɑː] *n.* mezbaha, salhane.
ab.bess ['æbis] *n.* bir manastırın baş rahibesi, müdürü *veya* müdiresi; **ab.bey** ['æbi] *n.* manastır; manastır kilisesi; **ab.bot** ['æbət] *n.* bir manastırın baş papazı, müdürü.
ab.bre.vi.ate [ə'briːvieit] *v/t.* kısaltmak, F.1 özetlemek; **ab.bre.vi'a.tion** *n.* kısaltma, özetleme; özet.

ABC ['eibiːˈsiː] alfabe; alfabetik tarife veya rehber; **~ weapons** nükleer, bakteriyolojik ve kimyasal silâhlar.
ab.di.cate ['æbdikeit] *v/i.* taç ve tahtını terketmek; *v/t.* (*görevden*) istifa etm., *bşden* vazgeçmek, feragat etm.; *bşi* bırakmak, terketmek; **~ the throne** tahttan feragat etm., saltanattan çekilmek; **ab.di'ca.tion** *n.* vazgeçme, feragat; tahttan çekilme, terki saltanat.
ab.do.men ['æbdəmən; MED æb'dəumən] *n.* karnın alt kısmı, karın, batın; **ab.dom.inal** [æb'dɔminl] *adj.* karna ait.
ab.duct [æb'dʌkt] *v/t.* zorla almak, gasbetmek; (*kadın veya çocuk*) kaçırmak; **ab'duc.tion** *n.* (*kadın veya çocuk*) kaçırma.
a.be.ce.dar.i.an [eibiːsiːˈdɛəriən] **1.** *adj.* çok basit; **2.** *n.* okumayı öğrenen öğrenci.
a.bed [ə'bed] *adv.* yatakta.
ab.er.ra.tion [æbəˈreiʃən] *n.* ayrılma, uzakiaşma, inhiraf; *fig.* delâlet, hata; AST & PHYS sapma.
a.bet [ə'bet] *v/t.* kışkırtmak, tahrik etm.; *mst.* **aid and ~** JUR *b-ne* (*suç işlemesinde*) yardımcı olm.; **a'bet.tor** *n.* suç ortağı; tahrikçi, önayak.
a.bey.ance [ə'beiəns] *n.* muallaklık, askıda oluş; **in ~** JUR karara bağlanmamıs, muallakta, askıda; sahipsiz.
ab.hor [əb'hɔː] *v/t. bşden, b-den* nefret, ikrah etm., tiksinmek; **ab.hor.rence** [əb'hɔrəns] *n.* nefret, tiksinme; **ab'hor.rent.** ☐ nefret verici, tiksindirici; aykırı, zıt, muhalif (**to** -e).
a.bide [ə'baid] (*irr.*) *v/i.* kalmak; **~ by** sebat etm.; kabullenmek; *v/t. bşi* beklemek; dayanmak, tahammül etm.; *I cannot ~ him* ona tahammül edemem; **a'bid.ing** ☐ daimi, devamlı.
a.bil.i.ty [ə'biliti] *n.* iktidar, ehliyet, yetenek; **to the best of one's ~** yapabildiği kadar; *abilities pl.* zihnî kabiliyetler, beceri.
ab.ject ☐ ['æbdʒekt] menfur, alçak, se-

fih; **ab'jec.tion, ab'ject.ness** *n.* al-çaklık, adilik.

ab.jure [əb'ʒuə] *v/t.* tövbe etm., vazgeç-mek; yeminle inkâr etm.

a.blaze [ə'bleiz] *adj. & adv.* alevli; *fig.* hararetli, şevkli.

a.ble □ ['eibl] güçlü, muktedir, yapabi-len, **be ~ to** bşe gücü yetmek, bşi yapa-bilmek; **~ to pay** ödeme güçlü; **~-bod-ied** ['_'bɔdid] *adj.* vücudu sağlam, güç-lü; MIL askerliğe elverişli; **~ seaman** NAUT birinci sınıf tayfa.

ab.lu.tion [ə'bluːʃən] *n.* yıkanma, ap-tes, gusül

ab.ne.gate [æbnigeit] *v/t.* bşi inkâr etm., tanımamak, reddetmek; **ab.ne-'ga.tion** *n. a.* **self-~** feragat, yokluğa katlanma.

ab.nor.mal □ [æb'nɔːməl] anormal, doğal olmayan, usulsüz; **ab.nor'ma.li-ty** *n.* anormallik, usulsüzlük.

a.board [ə'bɔːd] *adv.* NAUT gemide; ge-miye; **all ~!** *Am.* RAIL, AVIA etc. lûtfen yerlerinizi alınız!

a.bode [ə'bəud] **1.** *pret & p.p. of* **abide**; **2.** *n.* oturulan yer, ikametgâh, mesken; kalma.

a.bol.ish [ə'bɔliʃ] *v/t.* kaldırmak, iptal etm., feshetmek; **a'bol.ish.ment, ab-o.lition** [æbəu'liʃən] *n.* kaldırılma, il-ga; **abo'li.tion.ist** *n.* köleliğin kaldırıl-ması taraftarı.

A-bomb ['eibɔm] = **atomic bomb.**

a.bom.i.na.ble □ [ə'bɔminəbl] iğrenç, nefret verici; **a'bom.i.nate** [_neit] *v/t.* bşden, b-den nefret, ikrah etm., tiksin-mek; **a.bom.i'na.tion** *n.* nefret, iğren-me; çok iğrenç veya menfur şey veya hareket.

ab.o.rig.i.nal □ [æbə'ridʒənl] **1.** □ bir ye-rin en eski halkından olan; **2.** *n.* asıl yerli, ilk yerli; **ab.o'rig.i.nes** [_dʒini:z] *n. pl.* asıl yerliler.

a.bort [ə'bɔːt] *vb.* MED çocuk düşür-mek; dumura uğramak; gelişememek; **a'bor.tion** *n.* MED çocuk düşürme; düşük; *fig.* başarısızlık; **a'bor.tive** [_tiv] □ vaktinden evvel doğmuş; bey-hude, boş; başarısız, gelişmeyen.

a.bound [ə'baund] *v/i.* bol olm.; **~ with** (karınca gibi) kayna(ş)mak, bol olm.

a.bout [ə'baut] **1.** *prp.* hakkında, bşe dair; bşin etrafında, civarında, yakının-da; her yerinde; **talk ~ business** işten konuşmak; **send s.o. ~ his business** b-ne yol vermek, b-ni defetmek; **~ the house** evin herhangi bir yerinde;

wander ~ the streets sokaklarda do-laşmak; **what are you ~?** ne yapmak fikrindesiniz?; **I had no money ~ me** üstümde hiç para yoktu; **be ~ to** bşi yapmak üzere olm.; **2.** *adv.* aşağı yu-karı, takriben, hemen hemen; her ta-rafta; etrafa, etrafına; şurada burada; **it must be somewhere~** bu civarda ol-malı; **a long way ~** uzun dolambaçlı yol; **bring ~** husule getirmek, gerçek-leştirmek; becermek, başarmak; **come ~** husule gelmek, tahakkuk etm.; **he is ~ my height** aşağı yukarı benim bo-yumda; **~ ten o'clock** saat 10 sularında; **right ~!** sağa dön!; **~-face** *n.* geriye dö-nüş; fikir veya karar değişişimi; **~ turn!** MIL geriye dön!

a.bove [ə'bʌv] **1.** *prp.* yukarıda; bşin üs-tünde; bşden yukarı, bşden fazla; *fig.* üstünde, fevkinde; **~ 300** 300'den fazla; **~ all her** şeyden önce, bunlardan baş-ka; **it is ~ me** buna aklım ermez, beni aşıyor; **2.** *adv.* daha yukarıda olarak, önce olarak; **over and ~** bşe ilave ola-rak, bundan başka; **3.** *adj.* yukarıdaki; yukarıda zikredilmiş; **a'bove-'board** *adj.* dürüst, hilesiz; **a'bove-'ground** *adj.* yeryüzünde, gömülmemiş.

ab.ra.ca.dab.ra [æbrəkə'dæbrə] *n.* si-hirli kelime, muska; anlamsız söz.

ab.rade [ə'breid] *v/t.* aşındırmak, ye-mek (*esp. deri*).

ab.ra.sion [ə'breiʒən] *n.* aşınma, yen-me; (*deri*) sıyrık, sıyrıntı; **ab'ra.sive** [_siv] **1.** *n.* MEC aşındırıcı veya törpüle-yici madde; **2.** □ aşındırıcı, törpüleyici; rahatsız edici.

a.breast [ə'brest] *adv.* yan yana; aynı hizada; **keep** *veya* **be ~ of the times** devre uygun olm.

a.bridge [ə'bridʒ] *v/t.* kısaltmak, özet-lemek; mahrum etm.; **a'bridg(e).ment** *n.* kısaltma, özet.

a.broad [ə'brɔːd] *adv.* yabancı ülkede, dışarıda; şurada burada, her tarafta; **there is a report ~** rivayet ediliyor; **the thing has got ~** bş duyuldu, şayi oldu; **all ~** şaşırmış.

ab.ro.gate [æbrəugeit] *v/t.* ilga etm., ip-tal etm., feshetmek; **ab.ro'ga.tion** *n.* il-ga, iptal, feshetme.

ab.rupt □ [ə'brʌpt] ani; sert; ters, haşin (*davranış*); çok dik (*yer*); **ab'rupt.ness** *n.* acele; sertlik, terslik.

ab.scess MED ['æbsis] *n.* apse, çıban.

ab.scond [əb'skɔnd] *v/i.* kaçmak, firar etm., kanundan kaçmak.

ab.sence ['æbsəns] *n.* yokluk, bulunmayış; ~ *of mind* dalgınlık.

ab.sent 1. ☐ ['æbsənt] yok, bulunmayan; **2.** [æb'sent] *vb.*:~ *o.s.* gitmek, bulunmamak; **ab.sen.tee** [æbsən'ti:] *n.* (*görevinde vs.*) bulunmayan kimse; başka bir ülkede devamlı kalan; **ab.sen'tee.ism** *n.* iş veya görevde bulunmama alışkanlığı; devamsızlık; **'absent-'mind.ed** ☐ dalgın; **'ab.sent--'mind.ed.ness** *n.* dalgınlık.

ab.sinth(e) ['æbsinθ] *n.* BOT pelin otu, acı pelin.

ab.so.lute ☐ ['æbsəlu:t] katî, kesin; sade, saf; sonsuz, sınırsız; kayıtsız şartsız; GR soyut; ~ *ceiling* AVIA azamî yükseliş haddi; ~ *scale* mutlak ölçü ve terazi; ~ *temperature* mutlak ısı derecesi; **'ab.so.lute.ness** *n.* mutlakiyet; **ab.so'lu.tion** *n.* (*esp. Hıristiyanlık'da*) günahların affı; **'ab.so.lut.ism** *n.* istibdat, mutlakçılık.

ab.solve [əb'zɔlv] *v/t.* beraat ettirmek (*from -den*); (*günah veya cezayı*) affetmek.

ab.sorb [əb'sɔ:b] *v/t.* emmek, içine çekmek; (*bilgi, fikir vs.*) anlamak; zaptetmek; ~*ed* (*in*) *bşe* dalmış; **ab'sorb.ent** *adj. & n.* içe çekici, emici (madde); ~ *cotton wool* hidrofil pamuk; **ab-'sorb.ing** *adj.* çok ilgi çekici.

ab.sorp.tion [əb'sɔ:pʃən] *n.* içe çekme, emme; dalgınlık.

ab.stain [əb'stein] *v/i.* çekinmek, kaçınmak (*from -den*); **ab'stain.er** *mst. total* ~ içkiye tövbeli.

ab.ste.mi.ous ☐[əb'sti:mjəs] (*esp. yemek, içmek, zevk v.b. şeylerden*) azla kanaat eden, perhizkâr.

ab.sten.tion [əb'stenʃən] *n.* çekinme, kaçınma (*from -den*); PARL çekimser kalma.

ab.sti.nence ['æbstinəns] *n.* (*yiyecek, zevk v.b. şeyler*) perhiz, sakınma (*from -den*); *total* ~ (*esp. içki*) kullanmama; **'ab.sti.nent** ☐ perhizkâr.

ab.stract 1. ☐ ['æbstrækt] mücerret, soyut; nazarî, kuramsal; **2.** *n.* özet; *a.* ~ *noun* GR soyut isim; *in the* ~ kuramsal olarak; **3.** [æb'strækt] *v/t.* çıkarmak, ayırmak, tecrit etm.; çalmak, aşırmak; kimyasal usullerle ayırmak; özetlemek; **ab'stract.ed** ☐ dalgın; çıkarılmış; ayrılmış; **ab.strac.tion** [æb'strækʃən] *n.* soyutlama; çıkarma, ayırma; dalgınlık; çalma, aşırma.

ab.struse ☐ [æb'stru:s] anlaşılması güç, çapraşık; **ab'struse.ness** *n.* çapraşıklık, muğlaklık.

ab.surd ☐ [əb'sə:d] gülünç, anlamsız, saçma; imkânsız, olmayacak; **ab-'surd.ity** *n.* gülünçlük, anlamsızlık, saçmalık; maskaralık.

a.bun.dance [ə'bʌndəns] *n.* bolluk, zenginlik, bereket; *in* ~ bol miktarda; **a'bundant** ☐ çok, bol; **a'bun.dant.ly** *adv.* bol bol.

a.buse 1. [ə'bju:s] *n.* suiistimal, kötüye kullanma; küfür; **2.** [~z] *v/t.* suiistimal etm., kötüye kullanmak; *obs. b-ne* kötü muamele etm.; **a'bu.sive** ☐ [~siv] tahkir edici, aşağılayıcı; ağzı bozuk, küfürbaz.

a.but [ə'bʌt] *v/i.* dayanmak, bitişik olm. (*on, upon, against -e*); **a'but.ment** *n.* ARCH mesnet, dayanak; köprü ayağı.

a.bysm [ə'bizəm] *poet.* = *abyss*.

a.bys.mal ☐ [ə'bizməl] dipsiz, derin; kesif, çok; **a.byss** [ə'bis] *n.* uçurum, boşluk; *fig.* derinlik.

Ab.ys.sin.i.an [æbi'sinjən] *adj. & n.* Habeş (istanlı).

a.ca.cia BOT [ə'keiʃə] *n.* akasya.

ac.a.dem.ic [ækə'demik] *adj.* akademik, üniversiteye ait; pratiğe dayanmayan, soyut; **ac.a'dem.i.cal 1.** ☐ = *academic*; **2.** ~*s pl.* akademik kıyafet; **a.cad.e.mici.an** [əkædə'miʃən] *n.* akademisyen, akademi üyesi.

a.cad.e.my [ə'kædəmi] *n.* akademi.

a.can.thus [ə'kænθəs] *n.* BOT ayı pençesi; ARCH Yunan mimarisinde ayı pençesi yaprağı süslemesi.

ac.cede [æk'si:d] *v/i.* ~ *to* bşe razı olm., *bşi* kabul etm.; iş başına geçmek, iktidara gelmek; tahta çıkmak.

ac.cel.er.ate [ək'seləreit] *v/t. & v/i.* hızlan(dır)mak, çabuklaş(tır)mak; *fig.* teşvik etm., canlandırmak; **ac.cel.er'a.tion** *n.* hızlandırma, süratin artması; **ac'celer.a.tor** *n.* MOT gaz pedalı.

ac.cent 1. ['æksənt] *n.* vurgu, aksan; şive, ağız; aksan işareti; **2.** [æk'sent] *v/t.* vurgu koymak; vurgulamak; *fig.* önemle belirtmek, üzerinde ısrarla durmak.

ac.cen.tu.ate [æk'sentjueit] *v/t.* vurgulamak; önemle belirtmek; **ac.cen-tu'a.tion** *n.* aksan koyma, vurgulama.

ac.cept [ək'sept] *v/t. bşi* kabul etm., almak; COM (*poliçe v.b.*) kabul etm.; *bşi* onaylamak; **ac.cept.a'bil.i.ty** *n.* kabul edilebilirlik; **ac'cept.a.ble** ☐ kabul edilebilir; kabule değer; **ac'cept.ance**

n. kabul, *bşe* razı olma; *bşi* onaylama; COM (*poliçe v.b.*) kabul; **ac.cep.ta.tion** [æksep'teiʃən] *n.* kabul; anlam; **ac.cept.ed** □ [ək'septid] kabul edilmiş; **ac'cept.er**, **ac'cept.or** *n.* kabul eden; COM (*poliçe v.b.*) kabul eden taraf.

ac.cess ['ækses] *n.* giriş, yol, geçit; nöbet; MED *easy of* ~ kolay ulaşılabilir; ~ *road* giriş yolu; *have* ~ *to* girebilmek *-e*; **acces.sa.ry** [ək'sesəri] = *accessory*; **ac.cessi.bil.i.ty** [-si'biliti] *n.* erişilebilme, yaklaşılabilme; **ac'ces.si.ble** □ [-səbl] erişilebilir, tırmanılabilir; **ac'ces.sion** *n.* ulaşma; artma, çoğalma; yeni gelen şey (*to -e*); ~ *to the throne* tahta çıkma; *recent* ~*s pl.* yeni tedarik edilen şeyler.

ac.ces.so.ry [ək'sesəri] **1.** □ yardımcı olan; suç ortaklığı eden; **2.** *n. usu. pl.* aksesuar, yardımcı şey; JUR ferî fail, ikinci derecede suç ortağı.

ac.ci.dence GR ['æksidəns] *n.* sarf, morfoloji.

ac.ci.dent ['æksidənt] *n.* tesadüf; kaza, arıza; ~ *insurance* kaza sigortası; *by* ~ tesadüfen; **ac.ci.den.tal** [æksi'dentl] **1.** □ tesadüfî, arızî; ~ *death* kazaî ölüm; **2.** *n.* ikinci derecede önemi olan şey; MUS tesadüfî olarak gelen bemol veya diyez.

ac.claim [ə'kleim] *v/t.* alkışlamak; (*bağırarak*) ilân etm.

ac.cla.ma.tion [æklə'meiʃən] *n. oft.* ~*s pl.* alkışlama, alkış; *by* ~ alkışlarla (*oylama yerine*).

ac.cli.mate *part. Am.* [ə'klaimit] = *acclimatize*.

ac.cli.ma.ti.za.tion [əklaimətai'zeiʃən] *n.* (*bir yerin hava koşullarına*) alış(tır)ma; **ac'cli.ma.tize** *v/t.* alıştırmak.

ac.cliv.i.ty [ə'kliviti] *n.* yokuş, bayır.

ac.com.mo.date [ə'kɔmədeit] *v/t.* uydurmak, intibak ettirmek (*to -e*); yerleştirmek, yer tedarik etm.; *b-ne bşi* sağlamak, temin etm.; **ac'com.mo.dat.ing** □ uysal; yardıma istekli; **ac.com.mo'dation** *n.* uyma, intibak; uysallık; yerleşme; uzlaştırma; yatacak veya kalacak yer (*oda, ev, otel v.b.*); ~ *bill* COM hatır senedi, hatır bonosu; ~ *ladder* NAUT borda iskelesi; *seating* ~ oturacak yer; ~ *train Am.* birçok istasyonda duran yolcu treni.

ac.com.pa.ni.ment [ə'kʌmpənimənt] *n.* refakat eden şey; MUS *b-ne veya bşe* eşlik eden parça; **ac'com.pa.nist**

n. MUS refakat eden, beraber çalan kimse; **ac'com.pa.ny** *v/t.* refakat etm. *-e*; MUS eşlik etm. *-e*.

ac.com.plice [ə'kɔmplis] *n.* suç ortağı.

ac.com.plish [ə'kɔmpliʃ] *v/t. bşi* bitirmek, başarmak; tamamlamak; **ac'com.plished** *adj.* hünerli, usta; başarılmış; **ac'complish.ment** *n.* başarı, yapıp bitirme; başarılmış eser; *mst.* ~*s pl.* yetenekler.

ac.cord [ə'kɔːd] **1.** *n.* uyum, ahenk; uygunluk, anlaşma, uzlaşma; akort; JUR mahkeme dışında uzlaşma; *with one* ~ hep birlikte; *of one's own* ~ kendiliğin den, kendi arzusu ile; **2.** *v/i.* birbirini tutmak, uymak (*with -e*); *v/t.* uzlaştırmak, uyum sağlamak, teslim etm.; **ac'cord.ance** *n.* uygunluk, ahenk; *in* ~ *with -e* göre, *-e* uygun olarak; **ac'cord.ant** □ (*with, to*) uygun gelen *-e*; **ac'cord.ing:** ~ *to e* göre, *-e* nazaran; ~ *as* göre, aynen; **ac'cord.ing.ly** *adv.* bundan dolayı, gereğince, binaen.

ac.cor.di.on MUS [ə'kɔːdjən] *n.* akordeon.

ac.cost [ə'kɔst] *v/t.* (*esp. bir yabancıya*) yaklaşıp konuşmak; sarkıntılık etm.

ac.cou.cheur [æku:'ʃəː] *n.* ebe hekim; lâvta, akuşör; **ac.cou'cheuse** [-z] *n.* ebe.

ac.count [ə'kaunt] **1.** *n.* hesap; rapor; hikâye, açıklama; sebep; önem, kıymet, değer; COM hesap; *current* ~ câri hesap; *payment on* ~ mahsuben ödeme; *statement of* ~ hesap hülâsası; *of no* ~ önemsiz, sayılmaz; *on no* ~ asla, katiyen; *on* ~ *of* sebebiyle, *-den* dolayı; *place to s.o.'s* ~ *b-nin* hesabına geçirmek; *take into* ~, *take* ~ *of* göz önünde tutmak, hesaba katmak *-i*; *leave out of* ~ *bşe* dikkat etmemek; *bşi* ihmal etm.; *turn to* ~ kullanmak, zayi etmemek; *keep* ~*s* hesap tutmak, *bşin* hesabını tutmak; *call to* ~ cevap istemek, hesap sormak; *give veya render an* ~ *of* anlatmak; *bşin* hesabını vermek; *give an* ~ *of o.s.* yaptıklarının hesabını vermek; *make no* ~ *of* saymamak, itibar etmemek; **2.** *v/i.* ~ *for* hesap vermek; *bşden* sorumlu olm.; HUNT avı vurmak; *be much* (*little*) ~*ed of* çok (az) sayılmak, itibar görmek; *v/t.* saymak, itibar etm.; ~ *o.s. happy* kendini mutlu saymak; **ac.count.a'bil.i.ty** *n.* sorumluluk; **ac'count.a.ble** □ sorumlu; anlatılabilir; **ac'count.an.cy** *n.* muhasebecilik; **ac'count.ant** *n.* muhasebeci, muhasip, hesap uzmanı; **char-tered~**, *Am.* **certified public ~** yeminli hesap uzmanı; **ac'count.ing** *n.* muhasebe.

ac.cou.tre.ments MIL [ə'ku:təmənts] *n. pl.* teçhizat, malzeme (*elbise ve silâh dışında*).

ac.cred.it [ə'kredit] *v/t.* tasdik etm.; yetki vermek *-e*; inanmak, güvenmek; itimatname vererek atamak; **~ s.th. to s.o.**, **~ s.o. with s.th.** *b-nin* hesabına geçirmek.

ac.cre.tion [æ'kri:ʃən] *n.* ilâve, ek; gelişme.

ac.crue [ə'kru:] *v/i.* hâsıl olm., gelmek; ziyadeleşmek (*from -den*); hissesine düşmek.

ac.cu.mu.late [ə'kju:mjuleit] *v/t.* artırmak, toplamak, yığmak; *v/i.* artmak, toplanmak, yığılmak; **ac.cu.mu'la-tion** *n.* toplama, yığın; **ac'cu.mu.la-tive** □ [-lətiv] toplayıcı; toplanmış; **ac'cu.mu.lator** ELECT [-leitə] *n.* akümülatör.

ac.cu.ra.cy ['ækjurəsi] *n.* doğruluk, sıhhat; tam vaktinde olma; **ac.cu.rate** □ ['-rit] doğru, tam.

ac.curs.ed □ [ə'kə:sid], **ac.curst** [ə'kə:st] melûn, lânetlenmiş.

ac.cu.sa.tion [ækju:'zeiʃən] *n.* suçlama, itham; **ac.cu.sa.tive** [ə'kju:zətiv] *a.* **~ case** *n.* & *adj.* GR *-i* halinde; *-i* hali; **accuse** [ə'kju:z] *v/t.* suçlamak, itham etm. (**s.o. of s.th.** *b-ni bşle*); **the ~d** sanık, maznun; **ac'cus.er** *n.* JUR davacı, itham eden.

ac.cus.tom [ə'kʌstəm] *v/t.* alıştırmak (**to -e**); **ac'cus.tomed to** alışık, alışkın *-e*.

ace [eis] *n.* (*iskambil*) birli, bey, as; *fig.* çok cesur savaş havacısı; **~ in the hole** *Am.* F yedek koz; **he was within an ~ of dying** ölmesine ramak kaldı.

a.cer.bi.ty [ə'sə:biti] *n.* burukluk; (*söz*) acılık, sertlik, huysuzluk.

ac.e.tate CHEM ['æsitit] *n.* asetik asit tuzu; bir çeşit sentetik kumaş; **a.ce.tic** [ə'si:tik] *adj.* sirke gibi, ekşi; **~ acid** asetik asit, sirke asidi; **a.cet.i.fy** [ə'set-ifai] *v/t.* ekşitmek; *v/i.* ekşimek; **ac.e-tone** ['æsitəun] *n.* aseton; **ac.e.tous** ['-təs] *adj.* ekşi; **a.cet.y.lene** [ɔ'seti-li:n] *n.* asetilen.

ache [eik] **1.** *n.* (*sürekli*) ağrı, sızı, acı; **2.** *v/i.* ağrımak, sızlamak.

a.chieve [ə'tʃi:v] *v/t.* yapmak, icra etm., meydana çıkarmak, elde etm.,

başarmak; **a'chieve.ment** *n.* başarı; başarılmış şey.

ach.ing ['eikiŋ] □ acıyan, ağrıyan, ıstıraplı.

ach.ro.mat.ic [ækrəu'mætik] *adj.* renkleri doğal haliyle gösteren, renksiz

ac.id ['æsid] **1.** *n.* asit; **2.** *adj.* ekşi; **a.cid.i.fy** [ə'sidifai] *v/t.* asit yapmak, ekşitmek; **a'cid.i.ty** *n.* ekşilik, ekşime; **ac.i.do.sis** [æsi'dəusis] *n.* kanın asitli hali; **'ac.id-proof** *adj.* aside dirençli; **a.cid.u.late** [ə'sidjuleit] *v/t.* ekşitmek; (*hamur*) mayalamak; *v/i.* ekşimek; **a.cid.u.lous** [ə'sidjuləs] *adj.* mayhoş, ekşice.

ac.knowl.edge [ək'nɔlidʒ] *v/t.* kabul etm., tanımak; itiraf etm.; COM *bşin* alındığını bildirmek; *bşi* onaylamak; **ac'knowledg(e).ment** *n.* kabul, tasdik; itiraf; COM teslim makbuzu, alındı.

ac.me ['ækmi] *n.* doruk, zirve; kriz.

ac.ne ['ækni] *n.* akne, bir çeşit cilt hastalığı.

ac.o.nite BOT ['ækənait] *n.* kurtboğan.

a.corn BOT ['eikɔ:n] *n.* meşe palamudu.

a.cous.tic, **a.cous.ti.cal** □ [ə'ku:sti-k(əl)] akustiğe ait; **a'cous.tics** *n. mst sg.* akustik.

ac.quaint [ə'kweint] *v/t.* bildirmek, tanıtmak; (**s.o. with** *b-ne bşi*); **be ~ed with** *bşi* bilmek, *-den* haberdar olm.; **ac'quaint.ance** *n.* tanışma; malûmat; tanıdık.

ac.qui.esce [ækwi'es] *v/i.* kabul etm., muvafakat etm., razı olm.; **ac.qui'es-cence** *n.* uysallık, razı olma, kabul etme; **ac.qui'es.cent** □ itaatli, uysal, yumuşak huylu.

ac.quire [ə'kwaiə] *v/t.* elde etm., kazanmak; **~d** *adj.* kazanılmış, müktesep; **ac'quire.ment** *n.* edinme; edinilen bilgi, hüner.

ac.qui.si.tion [ækwi'ziʃən] *n.* edinme, elde edilen şey, kazanç; **ac.quis.i.tive** □ [ə'kwizitiv] haris, açgözlü; elde edilebilen; **ac'quis.i.tive.ness** *n.* kazanç hırsı; tamahkârlık.

ac.quit [ə'kwit] *v/t.* JUR beraat ettirmek (**of -den**); **~ o.s. of** (*görev*) yerine getirmek; **~ o.s. well** (*ill*) görevini iyi (kötü) yapmak; **ac'quit.tal** *n.* beraat; (*görev*) yerine getirme; **ac'quit.tance** *n.* zimmetten kurtulma; ibraname.

a.cre ['eikə] *n.* İngiliz dönümü (*0,404 hektar*)

ac.rid ['ækrid] *adj.* buruk, acı (*a. fig*).

ac.ri.mo.ni.ous ☐ [ækri'məunjəs] *fig.* acı, ters, sert; ac.ri.mo.ny ['ækriməni] *n. fig.* acılık, terslik, sertlik.

ac.ro.bat ['ækrəbæt] *n.* akrobat, cambaz; ac.ro.bat.ic [ækrəu'bætik] *adj.* (~ally) akrobatik; ac.ro'bat.ics *n. pl.* akrobasi; AVIA akrobasi (*uçuşu*)

a.cross [ə'krɔs] 1. *adv.* ortasından, içinden veya üstünden karşı yana geçerek; *come ~* rast gelmek, tesadüf etm.; *saw ~* testere ile ortasından ikiye bölmek; *a lake three miles ~* üç mil genişliğinde göl; *with arms ~* çapraz kavuşturulmuş (*kol*); 2. *prp.* karşıdan karşıya, öbür tarafa; çapraz; *run ~ the road* yolu koşarak geçmek; *come ~*, *run ~* birdenbire *b-ne*, *bşe* rastlamak.

act [ækt] 1. *v/i.* hareket etm., harekete geçmek, davranmak (*on*, *upon -e göre*); THEAT rol oynamak, temsil etm.; *~ (up) on s.o.'s advice b-nin* önerisine göre hareket etm.; *v/t.* rol yapmak (*a. fig*), oynamak; 2. *n.* fiil, hareket, iş, yapılan şey; JUR kanun; THEAT perde; *♀ of God* mücbir sebep, meydana geleceği önceden kestirilemiyen olay; *♀s of the Apostles* havariyun tarihi; *catch s.o. in the ~ b-ni* suçüstü yakalamak; 'act.ing 1. *n.* THEAT temsil, oyun oynama; 2. *adj.* yapan, işleyen; temsil eden; vekâlet eden.

ac.tion ['ækʃən] *n.* fiil, hareket, iş, faaliyet, etki; JUR dava; harekete geçme (*makine*, *at v.b.*); THEAT oyundaki olaylar dizisi; PAINT duruş, poz; *~ radius* menzil, tesir, hareket sahası; *bring an ~ against b-i* aleyhine dava açmak; *killed in ~* savaşta ölmek; *take ~* harekete geçmek; ac.tion.a.ble ['-ʃnəbl] *adj.* dava edilebilir.

ac.tive ☐ ['æktiv] faal, enerjik, canlı, çevik, hareketli; etkin; faaliyette, iş başında, işleyen; COM hareketli; aktif...; COM *~ demand* fiili talep; *~ officer* muvazzaf subay; *~ voice* GR etken çatı, aktif; '~wear *n. hareketli bir hayat* süren kimseler için spor giysiler.

ac'tiv.i.ty *n.* (*oft. pl.*) faaliyet; çeviklik; etki; faal oluş; *part.* COM hareketlilik, faaliyet; *in full ~* tam faaliyette; *intense ~* hummalı faaliyet.

ac.tor ['æktə] *n.* aktör, artist, rol oynayan; ac.tress ['æktrıs] *n.* aktris, kadın oyuncu.

ac.tu.al ☐ ['æktʃuəl] gerçek, hakiki, asıl; şimdiki, halihazırdaki; ac.tu.al.i.ty [-'æliti] *n.* gerçek, hakikat; ac.tu-

al.ly ['æktʃuəli] *adv.* gerçekten, hakikatte; bilfiil.

ac.tu.ar.y ['æktjuəri] *n.* (*sigorta şirketi*) istatistikçi.

ac.tu.ate ['æktjueit] *v/t.* işletmek, harekete getirmek; *fig.* tahrik, teşvik etm.; ac.tu'a.tion *n.* teşvik, tahrik.

a.cu.men [ə'kju:men] *n.* feraset, basiret, zekâ keskinliği.

a.cute ☐ [ə'kju:t] şiddetli, keskin, ince; keskin akıllı; tiz, keskin (*ses*); MED akut; vahim, ağır, şiddetli; a'cute.ness *n.* zekâ, keskinlik.

ad F [æd] = *advertisement*.

ad.age ['ædidʒ] *n.* darbımesel, atasözü, vecize.

ad.a.mant ['ædəmənt] 1. *n.* taş gibi katı, kaskatı şey; 2. ☐ hoşgörüsüz, çok sert, insafsız; ad.a.man.tine ['-mæntain] *adj.* elmas gibi çok sert; *fig.* = *adamant.*

a.dapt [ə'dæpt] *v/t.* uydurmak, tatbik etm. (*to*, *for -e*); *lit.* adapte etm.; a.dapta'bil.i.ty *n.* uyma yeteneği, intibak kabiliyeti; a'dapt.a.ble *adj.* uyabilir; ad.ap.ta.tion [ædæp'teiʃən] *n.* uyma, intibak (*to -e*); *lit.* adaptasyon, uyarlama; a.dap.ter [ə'dæptə] *n.* radyo: adaptör; a'dap.tive *adj.* uyma yeteneğinde.

ADD MED ['eidi:di:] (= *attention deficit disorder*) dikkatini toplayıp verememe hastalığı.

add [æd] *v/t.* katmak, eklemek, ilâve etm.; zammetmek, toplamak; MATH toplamak; *v/i. b-ne* iltihak etm., katılmak; *~ up* toplamak; neticelenmek; anlaşılmak; 'ad.ded *adj.* ilâve edilen, munzam.

ad.den.dum [ə'dendəm] *n.*, *pl.* ad'den.da [-də] (*kitabın veya konuşmanın sonuna*) ek, ilâve.

ad.der ['ædə] *n.* zoo engerek yılanı.

ad.dict 1. [ə'dikt] *v/t. ~ o.s. to bşe* alışmak, kendini vermek, düşkün olm., *bşin* tiryakisi olm.; 2. ['ædikt] *n.* (*opium* etc. *~*) (*afyon vs. ye*) düşkün, müptelâ; ad.dicted [ə'diktid] *to -e* düşkün, *-in* tiryakisi.

ad.di.tion [ə'diʃən] *n.* ilâve, ek, zam; MATH toplama; *in ~ to -den* başka, *-e* ilâveten, ayrıca; ad'di.tion.al ☐ eklenilen, biraz daha.

ad.dle ['ædl] 1. *adj.* çürük, cılk (*yumurta*); *fig.* boş, kof (*kafa, zekâ vs.*); 2. *v/t.* bozmak, şaşırtmak; *v/i.* çürümek, cılk çıkmak.

ad.dress [ə'dres] **1.** v/t. hitap etm.; söylev vermek; -in üstüne adres yazmak; ~ *o.s. to* (*bir işe*) hazırlanmak; ele almak, girişmek; **2.** n. adres; hitabe, söylev; âdabımuaşeret; *give an* ~ hitap etm.; söylev vermek; *pay one's* ~*es to* b-*ne* kur yapmak; **ad.dress.ee** [ædre'si:] n. alacak olan.

ad.duce [ə'dju:s] v/t. (*delil vs.*) getirmek, göstermek.

ad.e.noids MED ['ædinɔidz] n. pl. bezeler.

ad.ept ['ædept] **1.** ☐ usta, mahir (*in -de*); **2.** n. uzman; *be an* ~ *at* usta olm. -*de*.

ad.e.qua.cy ['ædikwəsi] n. kifayet, yeterlilik, ehliyet; **ad.e.quate** ☐ ['-kwit] uygun, münasip, yeterli.

ad.here [əd'hiə] v/i. yapışmak, yapışık kalmak; iltihak etm.; bağlanmak (*to -e*); **ad'her.ence** n. (*to*) yapışma; vefa, bağlılık; **ad'her.ent 1.** adj. yapışık, merbut; **2.** n. taraftar.

ad.he.sion [əd'hi:ʒən] s. *adherence*; *fig.* rıza, muvafakat; PHYS birbirine yapısma.

ad.he.sive [əd'hi:siv] **1.** ☐ yapışkan, yapışıcı; ~ *plaster*, ~ *tape* plaster, band; **2.** n. zamk, tutkal, çiriş.

a.dieu [ə'dju:] **1.** int. Allaha ısmarladık, elveda; **2.** n. veda; *make one's* ~(*s*) b-*le* vedalaşmak.

ad.i.pose ['ædipəus] adj. etin yağına ait; yağlı; n. etin yağlı tarafı; ~ *tissue* yağdokusu.

ad.it ['ædit] n. giriş, methal; MIL lâğım galerisi.

ad.ja.cen.cy [ə'dʒeisənsi] n. yakınlık, bitişik olma; *adjacencies* pl. civar, etraf, çevre, dolay; **ad'ja.cent** ☐ (*to*) bitişik, komşu -*e*.

ad.jec.ti.val ☐ [ædʒek'taivəl] sıfat cinsinden; **ad.jec.tive** ['ædʒiktiv] **1.** n. sıfat; **2.** adj. sıfat türünden.

ad.join [ə'dʒɔin] v/t. bitişik olm. -*e*; **ad'join.ing** adj. bitişik, yan yana.

ad.journ [ə'dʒə:n] v/t. ertelemek, tehir etm.; v/i. oturuma son vermek, dağılmak; **ad'journ.ment** n. erteleme; JUR ara.

ad.judge [ə'dʒʌdʒ] v/t. b-*ne* bşi tanımak, vermek, hükmetmek; JUR karar vermek.

ad.ju.di.cate [əd'ʒu:dikeit] s. *adjudge*; **adju.di'ca.tion** n. hüküm verme, karar verme; mahkeme kararı; kararın tefhimi.

ad.junct ['ædʒʌŋkt] n. ilâve, ek; iş arkadaşı, yardımcı; GR tayini ilâve, başka kelimeleri tanımlamak için kullanılan kelime(ler).

ad.ju.ra.tion [ædʒuə'reiʃən] n. ciddi dilek; yemin; **ad.jure** [ə'dʒuə] v/t. istirham etm., yalvarıp yakarmak.

ad.just [ə'dʒʌst] v/t. doğrultmak, düzeltmek; ayar etm., uydurmak (*to -e*); ~ *o.s. to* fig. intibak etm. -*e*; ~*ing screw* tanzim vidası; **ad'just.a.ble** ☐ ayar edilebilir, uydurulabilir; **ad'just.ment** n. uydurma, ayarlama, düzeltme; tasfiye.

ad.ju.tan.cy MIL ['ædʒutənsi] n. emir subaylığı; 'ad.ju.tant n. emir subayı.

ad.lib F [æd'lib] v/t. (*irticalen*) söz söylemek; piyano çalmak.

ad.man F ['ædmæn] n. reklâm uzmanı.

ad.min.is.ter [əd'ministə] v/t. yönetmek, idare etm.; tatbik etm.; yerine getirmek; yemin ettirmek; ~ *justice*, ~ *the law* hâkimlik etm.; ~ *punishment* cezalandırmak, b-*ni* para cezasına çarpmak; v/i. hizmet etm. (*to -e*); **ad.min.is'tration** n. idare, yönetim; hükümet; *esp.* Am. başkanlık; ~ *of justice* kaza işleri, adliye; **ad'min.is.tra.tive** [-trətiv] ☐ yönetimle ilgili, idarî; **ad'min.is.tra.tor** [-treitə] n. idareci, müdür, yönetmen; JUR kayyım, vasi, tereke idare memuru.

ad.mi.ra.ble ☐ ['ædmərəbl] takdire değer, çok güzel.

ad.mi.ral ['ædmərəl] n. amiral; ♀ *of the Fleet* donanma kumandanı; 'ad.mi.ral.ty n. amirallik; *First Lord of the* ♀ (*İngiltere'de*) Bahriye Nazırı.

ad.mi.ra.tion [ædmə'reiʃən] n. hayranlık, takdir; *she was the* ~ *of all* herkesin takdirini kazandı.

ad.mire [əd'maiə] v/t. çok beğenmek, takdir etm.; zevkle seyretmek; **ad'mir.er** n. hayran olan kimse; âşık.

ad.mis.si.bil.i.ty [ədmisə'biliti] n. kabul olunabilme; **ad'mis.si.ble** ☐ kabul olunabilir; **ad'mis.sion** n. itiraf, kabul (*into*, *to -e*); girme, giriş (*into*, *to -e*); giriş ücreti, duhuliye; ~ *fee* giriş ücreti, duhuliye.

ad.mit [əd'mit] v/t. içeriye almak, kabul etm. (*in*, *into*, *to*), müsaade etm.; itiraf etm.; v/i.: ~ *of* imkân vermek; *it* ~*s of no excuse* affedilemez, mazur görülemez; **ad'mit.tance** n. kabul; giriş; *no.*~*!* girilmez!; **ad'mit.ted.ly** adv. itiraf edildiği gibi; gerçekten.

ad.mix.ture [əd'mikstʃə] *n.* katma, ilâve; katıp karıştırılmış madde.

ad.mon.ish [əd'mɔniʃ] *v/t.* ihtar etm., tenbih etm., azarlamak; **ad.mo.ni.tion** [ædmɔu'niʃən] *n.* ihtar, tembih, öğüt; **admon.i.to.ry** □ [əd'mɔnitəri] ihtar mahiyetinde, nasihat şeklinde.

a.do [ə'du:] *n.* telâş, gürültü, patırtı; **without much ~** ses çıkarmadan, mesele yapmadan.

a.do.be [ə'dəubi] *n.* kerpiç.

ad.o.les.cence [ædəu'lesns] *n.* gençlik, büyüme çağı; **ad.o'les.cent** *adj.* & *n.* delikanlı, genç; büyümekte olan (kimse); çocukça.

a.dopt [ə'dɔpt] *v/t.* benimsemek, kabul etm., edinmek; evlâtlığa kabul etm.; **~ed child** evlât edinilmiş çocuk, evlâtlık; **a'dop.tion** *n.* kabul; evlât edinme; **a'dop.tive** *adj.* evlâtlığa kabul eden veya edilen.

a.dor.a.ble □ [ə'dɔ:rəbl] tapılacak, şayanı hürmet; **ad.o.ra.tion** [ædɔ:-'reiʃən] *n.* tapma; aşk, aşırı sevgi; **a.dore** [ə'dɔ:] *v/t.* tapmak *-e*, aşırı derecede sevmek *-i*; *v/i* tapınmak; **a'dor.er** *adj.* perestişkâr, tapan.

a.dorn [ə'dɔ:n] *v/t.* süslemek, donatmak; **a'dorn.ment** *n.* süs, tezyinat, dekor.

A.dri.at.ic [eidri'ætik] *n.* Adriya Denizi.

a.drift [ə'drift] NAUT *adj.* sularla sürüklenen; başıboş; **turn s.o. ~** *b-ni* ortada bırakmak, kendi haline terketmek.

a.droit □ [ə'drɔit] becerikli, usta; **a'droitness** *n.* hüner, marifet.

ad.u.late ['ædjuleit] *v/t.* dalkavukluk (*veya* müdahene, tabasbus) etm.; **adu-'la.tion** *n.* aşırı övgü, tabasbus, yaltaklanma; **ad'u.la.tor** *n.* pohpohçu, komplimancı, yüze gülen, dalkavuk; **ad.u.lato.ry** *adj.* fazla metheden, pohpohçu.

a.dult ['ædʌlt] *adj.* & *n.* büyük, reşit, ergin, yetişkin; **~ education** yetişkin eğitimi.

a.dul.ter.ant [ə'dʌltərənt] *n.* karıştırılmış madde; **a'dul.ter.ate 1.** [-reit] *v/t.* karıştırmak, bozmak; *fig.* *bşi* yüzüne gözüne bulaştırmak, berbat etmek; **2.** [-rit] *adj.* karışık; **a.dul.t-er.a.tion** [ədʌltə'reiʃən] *n.* karıştırma; **a.dul.ter.er** JUR *n.* zâni, zina işleyen (*erkek*); **a'dul.ter.ess** *n.* zâniye, zina işleyen (*kadın*); **a'dul.ter.ous** □ zina eden; **a'dul.ter.y** *n.* zina.

ad.um.brate ['ædʌmbreit] *v/t.* ima

etm., sezdirmek; taslağını çizmek; **ad-um'bration** *n.* ima, gösterme, işaret.

ad.vance [əd'vɑ:ns] **1.** *v/i.* ilerlemek, ileri gitmek, terfi etm.; yükselmek (*fiyat*); *v/t.* ilerletmek, ileri götürmek; terfi ettirmek; yükseltmek (*fiyat*); avans vermek; söylemek, teklif etm.; **2.** *n.* ilerleme, terakki; terfi; COM avans, peşin; MIL ileri yürüyüş; ileri harekât; yükselme (*fiyat*); **in ~** *adv.* peşin olarak; **be in ~ of s.o.** yaşından daha olgun olm.; **ad'vanced** *adj.* ilerlemiş, ileri; **~ in years** yaşı ilerlemiş, yaşlı; **~ English** ileri düzeyde İngilizce; **ad'vance.ment** *n.* ilerleme; terfi.

ad.van.tage [əd'vɑ:ntidʒ] **1.** *n.* avantaj, yarar, fayda, kâr, kazanç; üstünlük; zaafından istifade; (*tenis*) düsten sonra gelen puan; avantaj; **2.** *vb.* kazan(dır)-mak, ilerletmek; **take ~ of** faydalanmak *-den*; **you have the ~ of me** bilmediklerimi biliyorsun; benden daha kârlısın; **ad.van.ta.geous** □ [ædvən-'teidʒəs] faydalı, yararlı, kârlı.

ad.vent ['ædvənt] *n.* gelme, baş gösterme; ♀ *eccel.* Noel yortusundan önceki dört hafta; Hazreti Isa'nın dünyaya gelişi; **adven.ti.tious** □ [ædven'tiʃəs] arızî, dıştan gelen, tesadüfî.

ad.ven.ture [əd'ventʃə] **1.** *n.* macera, sergüzeşt; COM rizikolu iş; **2.** *vb.* cesaret etm., göze almak; tehlikeye koymak; yapmağa kalkışmak, yeltenmek; **ad-'ven.tur.er** *n.* avantüriye, maceracı; **ad'ven.tur.ess** *n.* dişi maceracı; **ad-'ven.tur.ous** □ maceraya düşkün, cesaretli, tehlikeli.

ad.verb ['ædvə:b] *n.* GR zarf; **ad.ver.bi-al** [əd'və:bjəl] □ zarfa ait; **~ phrase** zarf gibi kullanılan deyim.

ad.ver.sar.y ['ædvəsəri] *n.* düşman, muhalif; **ad.verse** □ ['-və:s] zıt, ters, karşı gelen; **~ balance of trade** bilânçoda açık; **ad.ver.si.ty** [əd'və:siti] *n.* zorluk; güçlük, sıkıntı, talihsizlik.

ad.vert [əd'və:t] *vb.* zikretmek, ima etm., hissettirmek; bahsetmek (**to** *-den*).

ad.ver.tise ['ædvətaiz] *v/t.* ilân etm., bildirmek; reklâmını yapmak; **ad.ver-tisement** [əd'və:tismənt] *n.* ilân, haber, reklâm; **ad.ver.tis.er** ['ædvətaizə] *n.* ilân eden veya reklâm yapan kimse; ilân gazetesi; **'ad.ver.tis.ing** *n.* reklâm, ilân.

ad.vice [əd'vais] *n.* nasihat, öğüt; tavsiye; COM haber, tebliğ, talimat; **letter of**

~ ihbar mektubu; *take medical* ~ doktora sormak.

ad.vis.a.ble ☐ [əd'vaizəbl] tavsiye edilebilir, makul, uygun; **ad'vise** *v/t.* nasihat etm., öğüt vermek; haber vermek; COM haber vermek, teklifde bulunmak; ~ *s.o. of s.th.* b-ni bş hakkında uyarmak; *v/i.* danışmak, akıl sormak; **ad'vis.ed.ly** [‿idli] *adv.* tedbirli olarak, akıllıca; **ad'vis.er** *n.* danışman, müşavir; **ad'vi.so.ry** [‿əri] *adj.* istişari, tavsiye niteliğinde; ♀ *Board* istişare kurulu.

ad.vo.ca.cy ['ædvəkəsi] *n.* avukatlık, müdafaa, savunma; **ad.vo.cate 1.** ['‿kit] *n.* avukat; *fig.* müdafaasını yapan; **2.** ['‿keit] *v/t.* müdafaa etm., savunmak, tavsiye etm..

adze *Am. a.* **adz** MEC [ædz] *n.* keser.

Ae.ge.an Sea [i:'dʒi:ən'si:] Ege Denizi, Adalar Denizi.

ae.gis ['i:dʒis] *n.* kalkan, siper; koruma.

ae.on, eon ['i:ən] *n.* çok uzun müddet, sonsuzluk.

a.er.at.ed ['eiəreitid] *adj.* karbonik, karbonatlı.

a.e.ri.al ['ɛəriəl] **1.** ☐ havaî, havaya ait; havada yapılan; ~ *car* hava hattı arabası; **2.** *n.* (*radyo, TV.*) anten.

a.er.ie ['ɛəri] *n.* kuş yuvası; *fig.* yuva.

a.er.o... ['ɛərəu] *comb.* hava...; **a.er.o-batics** [‿'bætiks] *n.* (*uçakla, havada*) akrobasi; **a.er.o.drome** ['‿-drəum] *n.* hava alanı; **a.er.o.dy.nam'ic** [‿dinæmik] ☐ hareket halinde olan hava veya gaza ait; **a.er.o.gram** ['‿-græm] *n.* telsiz telgraf. **a.er.o.gramme** ['ɛərəu-græem] *n.* zarfsız uçak mektubu; **a.er.o.lite** ['ɛərəulait] *n.* göktaşı; **a.er.o.naut** ['ɛərənɔ:t] *n.* balon kullanan pilot; **a.er.o'nau.tic, a.er.o'nau.t-i.cal** ☐ uçuculuğa ait; **a.er.o'nau.tics** *n. mst sg.* havacılık; '**a.er.o.plane** *n.* uçak. tayyare; **a.er.o.stat** ['ɛərəustæt] *n.* havada sabit durabilen balon; **a.er.o'stat.ics** *n.* hava kanunları ilmi.

aes.thete ['i:sθi:t] *n.* bediiyat, estetik; **aesthet.ic, aes.thet.i.cal** ☐ [i:s'θeti-k(əl)] bedii, estetik; **aes'thet.ics** *n. pl.* estetik.

afaik (= *as far as I know*; *used in text messages*) bildiğim kadarıyla.

a.far [ə'fɑ:] *adv. mst* ~ *off* uzak(ta); *from* ~ uzaktan.

af.fa.bil.i.ty [æfə'biliti] *n.* nezaket, hatırşinaslık.

af.fa.ble ☐ ['æfəbl] nazik, hatırşinas, sokulgan.

af.fair [ə'fɛə] *n.* iş, mesele, olay; ilişki; ~ *of honour* şeref meselesi; *love* ~ aşk macerası.

af.fect [ə'fekt] *v/t.* tesir etm., dokunmak *-e*; etkilemek, değiştirmek, müteessir etm. *-i*; bşi yalancıktan yapmak, taslamak; gibi görünmek; bşden hoşlanmak; ~ *ignorance* tecahül etm., bilmez gibi görünmek; ~ *sickness* temaruz etm., hastalık taslamak; **af.fec.ta-tion** [æfek'teiʃən] *n.* yapmacık, gösteriş, naz; **affect.ed** ☐ [ə'fektid] yapma, yapmacıklı; tutulmuş (*with -e*); meyyal, düşkün (*towards s.o. -e*); **af'fec-tion** *n.* sevgi, aşk (*for, towards -e*); düşkünlük; hastalık; **af'fec.tion.ate** ☐ [‿kʃnit] şevkatli, sevgi gösteren; *yours ~ly* sevgilerle (*mektup sonunda*); **af'fec.tive** ☐ hissi, dokunaklı.

af.fi.ance [ə'faiəns] **1.** *n.* itimat, inanç, güven (*in -e*); nişan; **2.** *v/t.* nişanlamak (*to ile*).

af.fi.da.vit [æfi'deivit] *n.* (*yazılı*) yeminli ifade, beyan.

af.fil.i.ate [ə'filieit] *vb.* üye olmak; kaynaştırmak, birleştirmek, yakın ilişki kurmak (*with, to ile, -e*); JUR babalığı tayin etm.; ~*d company* bağlı şirket; **affil.i'a.tion** *n.* yakın ilişki; il(ti)hak; evlâtlığa kabul.

af.fin.i.ty [ə'finiti] *n.* yakınlık, benzeşme (*between, with* arasında, ile); sıhrî hısımlık; güçlü cazibe (*for, to, between ile, -e, arasında*); CHEM çekme.

af.firm [ə'fə:m] *v/t.* tasdik etm., onaylamak, yeminsiz olarak teyid etm.; **af.fir-ma.tion** [æfə:'meiʃən] *n.* tasdik, teyit, yeminsiz beyan; **af.firm.a.tive** ☐ [ə'fə:mətiv] **1.** müspet, olumlu, tasdik edilen; **2.** *n.*; *answer in the* ~ olumlu cevap vermek.

af.fix 1. [æfiks] *n.* ek, ilâve (*kelimenin başına veya sonuna*); **2.** [ə'fiks] (*to*) *v/t.* bağlamak, takmak, yapıştırmak; (*mühür*) basmak; (*yazı*) eklemek.

af.flict [ə'flikt] *v/t.* vermek *-e*, eziyet etm., müteessir etm., incitmek; ~*ed* tutulmuş (*with -e*); **af'flic.tion** *n.* dert, keder.

af.flu.ence ['æfluəns] *n.* bolluk, refah, servet; '**af.flu.ent 1.** ☐ bol (*akan*); bol; zengin; **2.** *n.* nehir kolu.

af.flux ['æflʌks] *n.* bir yere akış.

af.ford [ə'fɔ:d] *v/t.* meydana getirmek, vermek; bütçesi müsait olm. *-e*; *I can* ~

it onu alabilirim, param yeter.

af.for.est [æ'fɔrist] *v/t.* ağaçlandırmak. orman haline getirmek; **af.for.est'a-tion** *n.* ağaç dikme, ormanlaştırma.

af.fran.chise [ə'fræntʃaiz] *v/t.* azadetmek, muaf tutmak.

af.fray [ə'frei] *n.* kavga, arbede.

af.front ['əfrʌnt] **1.** *v/t.* (*alenen*) hakaret etm., tahkir etm.; **2.** *n.* hakaret, tahkir; ***put an ~ upon***, ***offer an ~ to*** hakaret etm.

a.field [ə'fi:ld] *adv.* (*evden*) uzak; kıra, kırda; ***far ~*** çok uzakta.

a.fire [ə'faiə] *adj.* tutuşmuş, yanan.

a.flame [ə'fleim] *adj.* alevler içinde, tutuşmuş; *fig.* kızgın.

a.float [ə'fləut] *adj. & adv.* su üzerinde dolaşan; denizde; su basmış; ***keep ~*** su üzerinde durmak; ***set ~*** NAUT yüzdürmek; ***the rumour is ~*** şayia dolaşıyor.

a.foot [ə'fut] *adv.* ayakta; hareket halinde, hazırlanmakta.

a.fore NAUT [ə'fɔ:] *s.* *before*; a'fore-men.tioned [‿menʃənd] *adj.*, a'fore-named [‿neimd] a'fore.said evvelce belirtilen, mezkûr; a'fore.thought *n.* kasıt, taammüt.

a.fraid [ə'freid] *adj.* korkmuş, korkan; ***be ~ of*** korkmak *-den*; ***I am ~*** korkarım, korkuyorum; maalesef, yazık ki.

a.fresh [ə'freʃ] *adv.* yeniden, tekrar.

Af.ri.ca ['æfrikə] *n.* Afrika; **Af.ri.can** ['æfrikən] **1.** *adj.* Afrika'ya ait; **2.** *n.* Afrikalı; *part. Am.* zenci; 'Af.ri.can- -A.mer.i.can *adj. & n.* siyah Amerikalı.

Af.ri.kaans [æfri'kɑ:ns] *n.* Güney Afrika'da konuşulan lehçe (*Hollanda diline çok benzeyen*).

aft NAUT [ɑ:ft] *adj. & adv.* kıçda, kıça doğru.

aft.er ['ɑ:ftə] *adv.*, *prp.*, *cj.*, *adj. -den* sonra; *-e* göre; *-e* rağmen; ardında; ardından; bunun üzerine; ertesi; *-e* nazaran; tarzında; NAUT sekiz kürekli skif; ***~ all*** bununla birlikte, buna rağmen, yine de; ***in ~ days*** gelecekte, ileride; ***the day ~ tomorrow*** öbürgün; ***time ~ time*** tekrar tekrar; ***~.birth*** MED *n.* meşime, etene, son; '~care *n.* (*hastalık vs.*) *-den* sonraki bakım: '~.crop *n.* ikinci mahsül; '~'dinner *adj.* yemekten sonza gelen; '~.ef.fect *n.* bşin bilvasıta neticeleri; '~.glow *n.* akşam kızıllığı; '~.hours *n. pl.* mesai saatleri dışında; ~.math *n.* netice, âkıbet, yan tesir; '~'noon *n.* öğleden sonra, ikindi; '~.pains *n. pl.* doğumdan sonraki ağrı-

lar; '~-sea.son *n.* mevsim sonu: '~-taste *n.* ağızda kalan tat: '~-thought *n.* sonradan akla gelen fikir: ~.wards ['‿wədz] *adv.* sonra, sonradan.

a.gain [ə'gen] *adv.* tekrar, gene, bir daha; bundan başka; ***~ and ~ time and ~*** bazen, arasıra; *as much* (*many*) ~ iki misli; *now and ~* arasıra, bazen.

a.gainst [ə'genst] *prep. -e* karşı, *-e* rağmen: *-in* aleyhinde; ***~ the wall*** duvara dayalı; ***~ a background*** bir fon önünde (*veya üstünde*); *over ~* karşı(sında); yüzyüze; karşılık olarak; ***run ~ s.o.*** *b-ne* rastgelmek.

a.gape [ə'geip] *adv. & adj.* ağzı açık, şaşkın, şaşırmış.

ag.ate ['ægət] *n.* akik taşı; bilye, zıpzıp; *Am.* TYP = *ruby*.

a.ga.ve BOT [ə'geivi] *n.* agave.

age [eidʒ] **1.** *n.* yaş; çağ, devir; (*old*) ~ yaşlılık; ***at the ~ of*** yaşında; ***in the ~ of Queen Anne*** Kraliçe Anne devrinde; *of* reşit, ergin; *over ~* yaşı geçkin; *under ~* küçük, reşit olmayan; ***what is his ~?*** kaç yaşında?; ***come of ~***, ***be of ~*** reşit olm.; **2.** *v/i.* yaşlanmak; *v/t.* bşi eskitmek; aged [eidʒd] *adj.* yaşlı, ihtiyar; ***~ twenty*** 20 yaşında; **a.ged** ['‿id] *adj.* yıllanmış, dinlendirilmiş (*içki*); yaşındaki; 'age.less *adj.* eskimez, kocamaz, ihtiyarlamaz; 'age- -lim.it yaş haddi.

age-old ['eidʒəuld] *adj.* çok eski, kadim.

age-worn ['eidʒwɔ:n] *adj.* eli ayağı tutmaz olmuş; takatten düşmüş.

ag.glom.er.ate [ə'glɔməreit] **1.** *vb.* toplamak, bir araya getirmek, yığmak; **2.** *n.* toplama; volkanik parçaların eriyerek bir araya toplanması; **ag.glom.er-** 'a.tion *n.* yığılma, toplanma, yığın.

ag.glu.ti.nate [ə'glu:tineit] *v/t.* bşi başka bş üzerine yapıştırmak; yapıştırarak örtmek; MED, GR bitiştirmek; **ag.glu.ti.nation** [‿'neiʃən] *n.* yapıştırma; GR bitişme; MED aglütinasyon; **ag'glu.ti-na.tive** [‿nətiv] *adj.* yapıştırına işlemine ait; GR bitişken.

ag.gran.dize [ə'grændaiz] *v/t.* büyütmek (*boyut, güç veya rütbe*); ag'grandizement [-dizmənt] *n.* büyütme; *fig.* itibar veya değerini yükseltme.

ag.gra.vate ['ægrəveit] *v/t.* zorlaştırmak, fenalaştırmak; kızdırmak; abartmak; ag.gra'va.tion *n.* zorlaştırma; hiddet.

ag.gre.gate 1. ['ægrigeit] *vb.* toplamak, yığmak, biriktirmek; yekûn tutmak; 2. □ ['-git] toplu, bütün; 3. ['-git] *n.* yığma, kümeleme; kütle: (*betonda*) çakıllı kum: *in the* ~ bir bütün olarak; ag.grega.tion [-'geiʃən] *n.* toplanma; hepsi, bütün.

ag.gres.sion [ə'greʃən] *n.* saldırma, tecavüz; saldırganlık; ag.gres.sive □ [ə'gresiv] saldırgan, mütecaviz; ~ *war* tecavüzî harp; ag'gres.sor *n.* saldıran (*kimse veya ülke*).

ag.grieve [ə'gri:v] *v/t.* incitmek, rencide etm., gücendirmek.

a.ghast [ə'gɑ:st] *adj.* çok korkmuş, donakalmış; *stand* ~ donup kalmak.

ag.ile □ ['ædʒail] çevik, faal, tetik.

a.gil.i.ty [ə'dʒiliti] *n.* çeviklik, tetiklik.

ag.i.o com ['ædʒəu] *n.* aciyo, paranın gerçek ve nominal değeri arasındaki fark; ag.i.o.tage ['ædʒətidʒ] *n.* aciyotaj, borsa oyunu, sarraflık.

ag.i.tate ['ædʒiteit] *v/t.* sallamak, oynatmak; rahatsız etm.; heyecan vermek; *v/i.* propagandasını yapmak (*for bşin*); ag.i'ta.tion *n.* sallama, heyecana getirme; heyecan; tahrik; 'ag.i.ta.tor *n.* propagandacı; tahrikçi, kışkırtıcı; (*sallayıcı veya karıştırıcı*) makine.

a.glow [ə'gləu] *adj.* (*with -den dolayı*) parlak, kor halinde; kızgın, kıpkırmızı; *fig.* şiddetli, hararetli.

a.go [ə'gəu] *adv.* önce, evvel; *a year* ~ bir yıl önce; *a little while* ~ az önce; *long* ~ uzun zaman önce.

a.gog [ə'gɔg] 1. *adj. bşe* düşkün, haris, teşne, istekli; 2. *adv.* heyecanla, can atarak (*for -e*).

ag.o.nize ['ægənaiz] *v/t. b-ne* ıstırap vermek, işkence etm.; *v/i.* can çekişmek, ıstırap çekmek; 'ag.o.niz.ing □ eziyet verici, cefalı, işkenceli.

ag.o.ny ['ægəni] *n.* ıstıraptan kıvranma, şiddetli acı; can çekişme; ~ *of death*, *mortal* ~ can çekişme; ~ *column* şahsî ilânlar sütunu (*gazete*).

a.grar.i.an [ə'grɛəriən] *adj.* ziraî, tarımsal; tarlalara ait.

a.gree [ə'gri:] *v/i.* razı olm., aynı fikirde olm., muvafakat etm., uyuşmak (*up-*

on, on); *bşde* anlaşmaya varmak, mutabık kalmak, uzlaşmak; ~ *to* razı olm. *-e*, kabul etm. *-i*; ~ *with* anlaşmak, bir fikirde olm. *b-le*; ~ *to differ* münakaşayı kesmek; *be* ~*d* mukavafat etm., birlik olm.; ~*d!* kabul!, tamam!; a.greea.ble □ [ə'griəbl] (*to*) uygun *-e*, münasip *-e*; hoş, nazik; a'gree.a.ble.ness *n.* tatlılık, hoşluk; a.greement [ə'gri:mənt] *n.* anlaşma, uyuşma, ittifak; sözleşme, mukavele, akit; *come to an* ~ bir karara varmak, uyuşmak; *make an* ~ anlaşma yapmak.

ag.ri.cul.tur.al [ægri'kʌltʃərəl] *adj.* zirai, tarımsal; ag.ri.cul.ture ['-tʃə] *n.* ziraat, tarım; ag.ri'cul.tur.ist [-tʃərist] *n.* zira atçi, çiftçi.

a.ground NAUT [ə'graund] *adj. & adv.* karaya oturmuş; *run* ~ karaya oturmak; *run a ship* ~ gemiyi karaya oturtmak.

a.gue ['eigju:] *n.* sıtma, malarya; 'a.guish *adj.* sıtmalı, sıtma getiren.

ah [ɑ:] *int.* ah!, ya!, vay!; bak!; hayret!

a.ha [ɑ:'hɑ:] *int.* şimdi anladım!; işte!, görüyorsun ya!

a.head [ə'hed] *adv.* önde, ileride; ileriye; *straight* ~ doğruca; *go* ~ ilerlemek; önden gitmek; *b-nin* önü sıra yürümek; devam etm.; *go* ~*!* yürüyünüz!, devam ediniz!; siz buyurunuz!

a.hoi, a.hoy NAUT [ə'hɔi] *int.* hey!, hu!, yahu!.

aid [eid] 1. *v/t.* yardım etm. *-e*; 2. *n.* yardım, muavenet; *by (with) the* ~ *of* yardımiyle; *-den* bilistifade; *in* ~ *of* yararına; ~*s and appliances* vasıta, çare, medar.

aide-de-camp MIL ['eiddə'kɑ:ŋ] *n.* yaver.

ai.grette ['eigret] *n.* sorguç, tuğ.

ail [eil] *v/i.* hastalıklı, dertli olm.; *v/t.* sıkıntı vermek, rahatsız etm.; *what* ~*s him?* nesi var?

ai.ler.on AVIA ['eilərɔn] *n.* uçak kanadının hareket eden arka kısmı.

ail.ing ['eiliŋ] *adj.* keyifsiz, hasta, rahatsız; 'ail.ment *n.* rahatsızlık, hastalık.

aim [eim] 1. *v/i.* nişan almak (*at bşi, b-ni*); ~ *at fig.* kastetmek *bşi, b-ni*; ~ *to do part. Am.* niyetinde bulunmak, kastetmek, maksat gütmek; *v/t.* (*top, tüfek, söz vs.*) doğrultmak, nişan almak (*at -e*); 2. *n.* emel, hedef, amaç; nişan alma; *take* ~ nişan almak; 'aim.less □ gayesiz, hedefsiz.

ain't F [eint] = *are not*, *am not*, *is not*, *have not*, *has not*.

air¹ [eə] **1.** *n.* hava; hava cereyanı, kuran; *by ~* hava yoluyla; *go by ~* uçmak, uçakla gitmek; *in the open ~* açıkta, açık havada; *castles in the ~* hayal, hülya; *in the ~* havada; belli olmayan, sonuca bağlanmamış; *on the ~* radyoda (dinlenebilir); *go off the ~* yayını kesmek; *take the ~* dışarıya çıkıp dolaşmak, temiz hava almak; AVIA havalanmak; **2.** *v/t.* havalandırmak; (*çamaşır*) kurutmak; açmak (*fikir, şikâyet vs.*); *~ one's views* fikirlerini açmak.

air² [-] *n.* hal, tavır, eda; görünüş; *give o.s. ~s* kibarlık taslamak; *with an ~* vakarla, haşmetle; *~s and graces* F numara yapma, hava atma.

air³ MUS [-] *n.* nağme, melodi; arya.

air...; *'~-base* n. MIL hava üssü; *'~-bath n.* açık hava banyosu; *'~-bed n.* deniz yatağı; *'~blad.der n.* (*balık*) yüzme kesesi; *'~-borne* adj. havadan gelen (*toz, tohum vs.*); havadan nakledilen; uçmakta; MIL hava indirme; *we are ~* uçuyoruz; *~-brake n.* hava freni; *'~-chamber n.* BIOL hava hücresi; *'~-con.di.tioned* adj. otomatik ısıtma ve soğutma tesisatı olan; *'~-con.di.tion.ing n.* klimatizasyon tesisatı; *'~-cooled* adj. hava ile soğutulmuş; *'~.craft n.* uçak; uçaklar; *~ carrier* uçak gemisi; *'~-cush.ion n.* şişirme yastık; *'~-drop n.* düşman gerisindeki personele havadan teçhizat ve malzeme yardımı; *'~-field n.* hava alanı; *'~-force n.* hava kuvvetleri; *'~-gun n.* hava tüfeği; *~ host.ess* hostes.

air.i.ness ['ɛərinis] *n.* havadar olma; hafiflik, kolaylık, sühulet.

air.ing ['ɛəriŋ] *n.* (*elbise, çarşaf vs.*) havalandırma, kurutma; (*oda vs.*) havalandırma; gezinti, hava alma; açığa vurma.

air...; *'~-jack.et n.* yüzme yeleği; *'~.less* adj. havasız, ağır; *'~-lift n.* hava köprüsü; *'~-line n.* hava yolu; *'~-lin.er n.* yolcu uçağı; *'~-mail n.* uçak postası; *'~.man n.* havacı; *'~-me'chan.ic n.* uçak makinisti; *'~-pas.sen.ger n.* hava yolcusu; *'~.pipe n.* MEC hava borusu; *'~.plane n. part. Am.* uçak; *'~.pock.et n.* AVIA hava boşluğu; *'~-port n.* hava alanı; *'~-proof* adj. hava geçmez, hava geçirmez; *'~-pump n.* hava pompası; *'~ rage n. uçakla yolculuk ederken öfkelenip kavga çıkartılması ya da şiddete*

başvurulması; *'~-raid n.* MIL hava hücumu; *~ precautions pl.* hava hücumu önlemleri; *~ shelter* sığınak; *'~-route* hava yolu; *'~.ship n.* hava gemisi, uçak; *'~.sick* adj. hava tutmuş; *'~.strip n.* ufak hava meydanı; *~ sup.ply* hava verme; *'~-ter.minal n.* (*hava yollarının*) şehir bürosu; *'~-tight* adj. hava geçmez; *'~-transport n.* hava ulaşımı; *'~-tube n.* iç lâstik; *~ umbrel.la* MIL havaya karşı korunma şemsiyesi; *'~.ways n.* hava yolları; *'~.wom.an n.* kadın havacı; *'~.worthy* adj. AVIA uçabilir, uçuş güvenliğine sahip.

air.y ☐ ['ɛəri] havalı, havadar; hafif; havaî, sudan.

aisle [ail] *n.* ARCH bir kilişenin yan kısmı; ara yol, geçit (*esp. kilise ve tiyatroda*); *'~-sit.ter n. Am.* F tiyatro eleştirmeni.

aitch [eitʃ] *n.* h harfinin İngilizce adı; *drop one's aitches* li harfini telaffuz et memek.

aitch.bone ['eitʃbəun] *n.* sığır budu.

a.jar [ə'dʒɑː] *adv.* yarı açık, aralık (*kapı*); *fig.* ahenksiz.

a.kim.bo [ə'kimbəu] *adv.*; *with arms ~* el leri kalçasına dayalı.

a.kin [ə'kin] *adj.* akraba, yakın, benzer (*to -e*).

al.a.bas.ter ['æləbɑːstə] *n.* su mermeri, kaymak taşı, albatr.

a.lack obs. [ə'læk] *int.* ah!, eyvah!; *~-a-day!* int. yazık!, eyvah!

a.lac.ri.ty [ə'lækriti] *n.* çeviklik; isteklilik, şevk.

a.larm [ə'lɑːm] **1.** *n.* alarm, tehlike işareti; korku, telâş; *~ pistol* patlangaç; *give* (*raise, ring, sound*) *the ~* tehlikeyi haber vermek; **2.** *v/t.* tehlikeyi bildirmek *-e*; korkutmak *-i*; a'**larm-bell** *n.* alarm çanı; a'**larm-clock** *n.* çalar saat; a'**larm.ist** *n.* etrafı telâşa veren kimse.

a.las [ə'læs] *int.* vay!, yazık!

alb [ælb] *n.* katolik papazların kilisede giydikleri beyaz cübbe.

Al.ba.ni.an [æl'beinjən] *adj. & n.* Arnavutça; Arnavut.

al.ba.tross ['ælbətrɔs] *n.* bir cins deniz kuşu, albatros.

al.be.it [ɔːl'biːit] *cj.* her ne kadar, vakıa, ise de.

al.bi.no BIOL [æl'biːnəu] *n.* derisi, saçları ve kaşları doğuştan beyaz insan veya hayvan.

al.bum ['ælbəm] *n.* albüm.

al.bu.men, al.bu.min CHEM ['ælbjumin] *n.* yumurta akı; albümin; **al.bu-**

mi.nous [æl'bju:minəs] *adj.* albuminli.

al.chem.ic, al.chem.i.cal □ [æl'kemik(əl)] simya ilmine ait; **al.che.mist** [æ'lkimist] *n.* simyager, alşimist; **'al.che.my** *n.* simya, alşimi.

al.co.hol ['ælkəhɔl] *n.* alkol, ispirto; alkollü içki; **al.co'hol.ic** □ & *n.* alkolik, ispirtolu: ayyaş; **'al.co.hol.ism** *n.* alkolizm, içkiye düşkünlük, ayyaşlık; **al.co.hol.ize** ['_-laiz] *v/t.* alkol haline getirmek.

al.cove ['ælkəuv] *n.* yatak köşesi, hücresi; duvarda hücre; (*bahçe*) çardak, gölgelik.

al.der BOT ['ɔ:ldə] *n.* kızılağaç.

al.der.man ['ɔ:ldəmən] *n.* kıdemli belediye meclisi üyesi; **al.der.man.ship** ['_-mənʃip] *n.* belediye meclisi üyeliği.

ale [eil] *n.* bir çeşit bira.

a.lee NAUT [ə'li:] *n.* rüzgâr altında.

a.lem.bic CHEM [ə'lembik] *n.* imbik.

a.lert [ə'lɔ:t] **1.** □ uyanık, dikkatli; **2.** *n.* silâhbaşı hazırlığı; (*hava*) tehlike işareti; **be on the ~** tetikte olm., hazır olm.; **a'lert.ness** *n.* tetiklik.

al.fal.fa BOT [æl'fælfə] *n.* kaba yonca.

al.fres.co [æl'freskəu] *adv.* & *adj.* açık havada; açık hava.

al.ga BOT ['ælgə] *n.*, *pl.* **al.gae** ['ældʒi:] su yosunu.

al.ge.bra MATH ['ældʒibrə] *n.* cebir; **al.gebraic** [_-'breiik] □ cebirsel.

Al.ge.ri.a [ældʒi:riə] *n.* Cezayir.

a.li.as ['eiliæs] **1.** *adv.* namı diğer, diğer ismi; **2.** *n.* namı müstear, takma isim.

al.i.bi ['ælibai] *n.* (*suç işlendiği anda*) başka yerde bulunduğu iddiası; *Am.*, F özür, mazeret.

al.ien ['eiljən] **1.** *adj.* yabancı uyruklu, ecnebi; *fig.* uymamış, intibak etmemiş (**to** -e); **2.** *n.* yabancı, yabancı uyruklu kimse; **'al.ien.a.ble** *adj.* satılabilir, devir ve ferağı kabil; **al.ien.ate** ['_-eit] *v/t.* satmak, devir ve ferağ etm.; *fig.* soğutmak, vazgeçirmek (**from** -den); **al.ien-'ation** *n.* devir ve ferağ; ferağ yetkisi, temlik; *fig.* soğutma, vazgeçirme; ~ **of mind** cinnet; **'al.ien.ist** *n.* akıl hastalıkları uzmanı, akliyeci.

a.light[1] [ə'lait] *adj.* ateş içinde, yanmakta, tutuşmuş.

a.light[2] [_] *v/i.* çıkmak, inmek; AVIA yere inmek, konmak.

a.lign [ə'lain] *v/t.* sıraya koymak, dizmek, hizaya sokmak; sıralamak; ~ **o.s. with** yanaşmak, bağlanmak -e;

a'lign.ment *n.* dizilme, sıraya girme; hiza.

a.like [ə'laik] **1.** *adj.* benzer, aynı; **2.** *adv.* benzer, aynı şekilde, farksız olarak.

al.i.ment ['ælimənt] *n.* yiyecek, gıda; **al.imen.ta.ry** [_-'mentəri] *adj.* besleyici, yiyeceğe dair; ~ **canal** hazım borusu; **al.imen'ta.tion** *n.* beslenme, besleme.

al.i.mo.ny JUR ['ælimoni] *n.* nafaka.

a.line(.ment) [ə'lain(mənt)] = **align** (**-ment**).

al.i.quot MATH [ælikwɔt] *adj.* bir sayıyı tam bölen.

a.live [ə'laiv] *adj.* canlı, yaşayan, sağ, diri, hayatta; pürhayat, faal; heyecanlı; haberdar, farkında; **be ~** hayatta olm., yaşamak; ELECT üzerinde cereyan olan; **man ~!** F be (mübarek) adam!; ulan!; **keep ~** bşi yaşatmak, muhafaza etm.; **look~!** F çabuk ol, sallanma!

al.ka.li CHEM ['ælkəlai] *n.* alkali, kalevi; **alka.line** ['_-lain] *adj.* alkali, kalevi.

all [ɔ:l] **1.** *adj.* bütün, hep; tam; her; ~ **day** (**long**) bütün gün; ~ **kind**(**s**) **of books** her çeşit kitap; *s.* **above**, **after**, **for** ~ **that** bununla beraber, buna rağmen; **2.** *n.* herkes, herşey; **my** ~ herşeyim; ~ **of them** hepsi; **not at** ~ asla, hiç; **for** ~ (**that**) I **know** bana kalırsa; **in** ~ hepsi, tamamı; **3.** *adv.* tamamen, tamamiyle, büs bütün; ~ **at once** hep birden; ~ **the better** daha iyi ya; ~ **but** hemen hemen, aşağı yukarı, az daha; ~ **right** iyi!, pekâlâ, tamam; şöyle böyle.

all-A.mer.i.can [ɔ:lə'merikən] özbeöz Amerikalı.

al.lay [ə'lei] *v/t.* teskin etm., rahatlandırmak, hafifletmek, azaltmak, (*hararet*i) gidermek.

al.le.ga.tion [æli'geiʃən] *n.* iddia, ileri sürme; **al.lege** [ə'ledʒ] *v/t.* ileri sürmek, iddia etm., itham etm.; **al'leged** denen, iddia edilen; sözde, diye.

al.le.giance [ə'li:dʒəns] *n.* (*vatan*, *hükümdar veya bir fikre*) sadakat, bağlılık; (*tebaa*, *vatandaş*) sadakat, bağlılık (**to** -e); **oath of** ~ sadakat (*veya* bağlılık) yemini.

al.le.gor.ic(**al**) □ [æli'gɔrik(əl)] alegorik, kinaye yolu ile, remzî; **al.le.go.rize** ['æligəraiz] *vb.* (*bir oyun*, *resim*, *hikâye vs.*) alegorik yorumlamak; **'al.le.go.ry** *n.* alegori, remzî hikâye.

al.le.lu.ia [æli'lu:jə] *n.*, *int.* sevinç veya teşekkür ifade eden bir kelime (*veya* *şarkı vs.*), elhamdülillâh.

al.ler.gy MED ['ælədʒi] *n.* alerji, aşırı duyu.

al.le.vi.ate [ə'li:vieit] *v/t.* azaltmak, hafifletmek; **al.le.vi'a.tion** *n.* hafifleme, azalma.

al.ley ['æli] *n.* dar sokak, aralık; iki tarafı ağaçlı yol; (*bowling oyunu*) dar yol; *s.* **back~**; geçit; *s.* **blind 1, skittle-~**; **it's up his ~** tam onun işi, biçilmiş kaftan; **'al.ley.way** *n. Am.* dar yol, geçit.

All Fool's Day ['ɔ:l'fu:lzdei] 1 Nisan günü.

al.li.ance [ə'laiəns] *n.* ittifak, birlik; sıhrî hısımlık; **form an~** ittifak yapmak (**with** *ile*).

al.lied [əlaid] *adj.* müttefik, dost; hısım, akraba; COM **~ company** başka bir şirket tarafından idare edilen veya başka bir şirketi idare eden şirket.

al.li.ga.tor ZOO ['æligeitə] *n.* Amerika timsahı.

all-in ['ɔ:l'in] *adj.* her şey dahil.

al.lit.er.ate [ə'litəreit] *v/t.* birbirine yakın iki veya daha çok kelimede aynı sesi tekrar etm.; **al.lit.er'a.tion** *n.* cümle içindeki kelimelerde aynı sesi tekrarlama; **al'lit.er.a.tive** [.rotiv] □ aynı sesin tekrar edildiği parçaya ait.

al.lo.cate ['æləukeit] *v/t.* tahsis etm., dağıtmak; **al.lo'ca.tion** *n.* tahsis etme, dağıtım, tahsisat.

al.lo.cu.tion [æləu'kju:ʃən] *n.* söylev, nutuk, hitabe.

al.lop.a.thist MED [ə'lɔpəθist] *n.* zıt tedavi usulü uygulayan doktor; **al'lop.a.thy** MED *n.* zıt tedavi usulü.

al.lot [ə'lɔt] *v/t.* ayırmak, tahsis etm., bölüştürmek, vermek; **al'lot.ment** *n.* hisselere ayırma, taksim etme; hisse, pay; (*mahalli idarelerce kiraya verilen*) küçük bostan.

all-out ['ɔ:l'aut] *adj.* elinden gelen; bütün, toplam; **~ effort** azamî güç.

al.low [ə'lau] *v/t.* bırakmak, müsaade etm., kabul etm., razı olm. *-e*; vermek *-i*; *v/i.* hesaba katmak (**for**-*i*); **be.~ed to** izni haiz olm., hakka sahip olm.; **~ for** hesabetmek; **it.~s of no excuse** affedilemez, mazur görülemez; **al'low.a.ble** □ kabul edilebilir; caiz, meşru; **al'low.ance 1.** *n.* müsaade, göz yumma; tahsisat, harçlık, gelir (*aylık, yıllık vs.*); iskonto, indirim; itiraf, kabul; MEC tolerans, yedek pay; **2.** *v/t.* nafakasını tayin etm.; (*ekmek vs.*) tayına bağlamak.

al.loy 1. ['ælɔi] *n.* alaşım, halita; *fig.*

karışım; **2.** [.] *v/t.* halita yapmak; *fig.* değerini veya kalitesini bozmak.

all...: '~'**pur.pose** *adj.* her şeye yarayan; '~'**round** *adj.* çok yeteneği olan; çok cepheli; COM götürü.

All Saints' Day ['ɔ:l'seintsdei] *rel.* Azizler yortusu (*1 Kasım*).

All Souls' Day ['ɔ:l'səulzdei] *rel.* Ölüler günü (*2 Kasım*).

al.lude [ə'lu:d] *v/i.* ima etm., kastetmek (**to** -*i*).

al.lure [ə'ljuə] *v/t. k-ne* çekmek, cezbetmek; **al'lure.ment** *n.* çekicilik, cezbetme; **al'lur.ing** □ çekici, cazip.

al.lu.sion [ə'lu:ʒən] *n.* ima, kinaye (**to** -*e*); **al'lu.sive** □ ima yollu, cinaslı, mecazî.

al.lu.vi.al □ [ə'lu:vjəl] suların bıraktığı toprak gibi, alüvyonlu; **al'lu.vi.on** [.vjən] *n.* suların bıraktığı toprak, alüvyon; **al'lu.vi.um** [.vjəm] *n.* suların bıraktığı toprak, lığ, alüvyon.

al.ly 1. [ə'lai] *vb.* birleşmek, ittifak et(tir)mek (**to, with** -*le*); akraba olm.; **al.lied to** *fig.* benzer, uygun, yakın; **2.** ['ælai] *n.* müttefik; dost, arkadaş; **the Allies** *pl.* Müttefikler.

al.ma.nac ['ɔ:lmənæk] *n.* takvim, yıllık, almanak.

al.might.i.ness [ɔ:l'maitinis] *n.* her şeye kadir olma; **al'might.y 1.** □ her şeye kadir, F kudretli, dehşetli, çok büyük; **2.** ♀ Kadiri mutlak, Allah.

al.mond ['ɑ:mənd] *n.* badem; **~-eyed** *adj.* badem gözlü.

al.mon.er ['ɑ:mənə] *n.* (*hastanede hastaların ihtiyaçları ile ilgili*) sosyal görevli.

al.most ['ɔ:lməust] *adv.* hemen hemen, az kaldı; yaklaşık olarak.

alms [ɑ:mz] *n. sg. & pl.* sadaka; '~-**bag** *n.* sadaka kesesi; '~-**house** *n.* fakirler yurdu, darülâceze.

al.oe BOT & PHARM ['æləu] *n.* sarısabır.

a.loft [ə'lɔft] *adv.* yukarıda, yükseklerde; NAUT yukarıda, gemi direğinde.

a.lone [ə'ləun] *adj. & adv.* yalnız, tek başına, yalnız olarak; **let veya leave s.o. ~** *b-ni* kendi haline bırakmak; **let it ~!** karışma!, dokunma!; **let ~ ... ...** şöyle dursun, nerede kaldı ki.

a.long [ə'lɔŋ] *adv. & prep.* boyunca, müddetince, yanı sıra; **all ~** öteden beri; her zaman; **come~!** haydi gel!; **get~ with** geçinmek, anlaşmak *-le*; **get ~ with you!** F haydi git!; amma yaptın ha!, sana inanmıyorum; **a'long.shore**

adj. & adv. sahil boyunca; **a'long'side 1.** NAUT *adv.* borda bordaya; yan yana; **2.** *prep.* yanında, tarafında.

a.loof [ə'lu:f] *adj. & adv.* uzak, uzakta; NAUT alargada; sokulmaz, soğuk; *keep ~ k-ni* uzak(ta) tutmak; **a'loof.ness** *n.* uzaklık, çekingenlik, sokulmayış.

a.loud [ə'laud] *adv.* yüksek sesle.

alp [ælp] *n.* yüksek dağ; **₂s** *pl.* Alpler.

al.pac.a [æl'pækə] *n.* ZOO (*Peru'ya mahsus*) koyuna benzer bir hayvan, alpaka; alpaka yünü; alpaka yününden kumaş.

al.pen.stock ['ælpinstok] *n.* (*dağcılara mahsus*) ucu demirli sopa.

al.pha.bet ['ælfəbit] *n.* alfabe; **al.phabetic**, **al.pha.bet.i.cal** □ [₋'betik(əl)] alfabe sırasına göre.

Al.pine ['ælpain] *adj.* Alp dağlarına ait; yüksek dağlara ait; **al.pin.ist** [' ₋pinist] *n.* dağcı, alpinist.

al.read.y [ɔ:l'redi] *adv.* şimdiden; şimdiye kadar; zaten.

Al.sa.tian [æl'seiʃjən] **1.** *adj.* Alsas'a ait; **2.** *n.* Alsaslı; *a. ~ dog* (*kurda benzer*) iri bir çeşit köpek (*Am.* **German Shepherd**).

al.so ['ɔ:lsəu] *adv.* dahi, da (*de, ta, te*); bir de; ayrıca; *~-ran n.* yarışçılık: dereceye giremiyen at; *fig.* başarısız sporcu veya politikacı.

al.tar ['ɔ:ltə] *n.* (*üzerinde tanrıya sunulan şeylerin bulunduğu*) Hıristiyan kiliselerindeki masa veya yüksek yer; '*~-piece n.* (*mihrabın yakınındaki*) resim veya tablo.

al.ter ['ɔ:ltə] *v/t.* değiştirmek; *Am.* F (*hayvan*) hadımlaştırmak, iğdiş etm.; *v/i.* değişmek; **'al.ter.a.ble** *adj.* değişir, değiştirilebilir; **al.ter'a.tion** *n.* değişiklik (*to -e*).

al.ter.cate ['ɔ:ltəkeit] *v/i.* kavga etm., çekişmek, dalaşmak; **al.ter'ca.tion** *n.* kavga, çekişme.

al.ter.nate 1. ['ɔ:ltəneit] *vb.* nöbetleşe değiş(tir)mek, nöbetle yap(tır)mak; birbiri ardına gelmek; *alternating current* ELECT dalgalı akım; **2.** □ [ɔ:l'tə:nit] nöbetleşe değişen, münavebeli; *on ~ days* gün aşırı; **3.** [ɔ:l'tə:nit] *n. Am.* mümessil, vekil; **al.ter.na.tion** [ɔ:ltə'neiʃən] *n.* değişiklik; münavebe; **al.ter.na.tive** [ɔ:l'tə:nətiv] **1.** □ ikisinden birini seçme imkânı olan, alternatifi olan, başka; MEC alternatif...; **2.** *n.* iki şıktan biri, alternatif, tercih; imkân; *I have no ~* başka çarem yok, yapacak

başka birşey yok; **al.ter.na.tor** *n.* ELECT alternatör.

al.though [ɔ:l'ðəu] *cj.* her ne kadar, -diği halde, bununla birlikte, gerçi.

al.tim.e.ter ['æltimi:tə] *n.* altimetre, yükseltiyi gösteren alet.

al.ti.tude ['æltitju:d] *n.* yükseklik, irtifa; *~ recorder* irtifa kayıtçısı.

al.to MUS ['æltəu] *n.* alto, kadın veya çocuk seslerinin en pesi.

al.to.geth.er [ɔ:ltə'geðə] *adv.* hep birlikte, tamamen, büsbütün; *in the ~* F çıplak, anadan doğma.

al.tru.ism ['æltruizəm] *n.* şahsî menfaatlerine bakmama, diğerkâmlık, fedakârlık; **'al.tru.ist** *n.* diğerkâm, başkalarını düşünen kimse; **al.tru'is.tic** *adj.* (*~ally*) başkalarını düşünen, diğerkâm.

al.um CHEM ['æləm] *n.* şap; **a.lu.mi.na** [ə'lju:minə] *n.* alüminyum oksit; **al.umin.i.um** [ælju'minjəm], *Am.* **al.umi.num** [ə'lu:minəm] *n.* alüminyum; **a.lu.mi.nous** [ə'lju:minəs] *adj.* şaplı.

a.lum.na [ə'lʌmnə] *n., pl.* **a'lum.nae** [₋ni:] *Am.* (*bir okul veya üniversitenin*) eski kız öğrenci; **a'lum.nus** [₋nəs] *n., pl.* **a'lum.ni** [₋nai] *Am.* eski erkek öğrenci.

al.ve.o.lar [æl'viələ] **1.** *adj.* ANAT diş çukuruna ait; **2.** *n.* GR dilin üst damağa teması ile çıkarılan sessiz harf.

al.ways ['ɔ:lweiz] *adv.* daima, her zaman.

am [æm; əm] *vb.* (*irr. be*) *I ~* ben -im.

a.mal.gam [ə'mælgəm] *n.* malgama, cıva ile başka bir maddenin karışımı; **a'malgam.ate** [₋meit] *v/t.* cıva ile başka bir madeni karıştırmak; karıştırmak, birleştirmek; *v/i.* karışmak, birleşmek; **a.mal.gam'a.tion** *n.* karışma; alaşım; COM iki veya daha fazla şirketin birleşmesi, füzyon.

a.man.u.en.sis [əmænju'ensis] *n., pl.* **aman.u'en.ses** [₋si:z] yazıcı, sekreter.

am.a.ranth BOT ['æmərænθ] *n.* tilki kuyruğu.

a.mass [ə'mæs] *v/t.* yığmak, toplamak.

am.a.teur ['æmətə] *n.* amatör, meraklı, hevesli kimse; **am.a'teur.ish** *adj.* acemice, yarımyamalak bilgili.

am.a.tive [æmətiv], **am.a.to.ry** [' ₋təri] *adj.* aşkla ilgili, şehvanî.

a.maze [ə'meiz] *v/t.* hayrette bırakmak, şaşırtmak; **a'mazed** □ çok şaşırmış (*at -e*); **a'maze.ment** *n.* şaşkınlık, hayret; **a'maz.ing** □ şaşırtıcı, hayret verici, acayip.

Am.a.zon ['æməzən] *n.* Amazon Nehri; ♀ erkeksi kadın; savaşçı, yiğit kadın; **Ama.zo.ni.an** [-'zəunjən] *adj.* Amazon Nehrine ait; ♀ erkeksi (*kadın*).

am.bas.sa.dor [æm'bæsədə] *n.* büyükelçi, sefir; **am.bas.sa.do.ri.al** [-'dɔ:riəl] *adj.* büyükelçi ile ilgili, sefareti ilgilendiren; **am'bas.sa.dress** [-dris] *n.* elçi karısı, sefire, kadın elçi.

am.ber ['æmbə] *n.* kehribar; kehribar rengi; **am.ber.gris** ['-gri:s] *n.* amber.

am.bi.dex.trous □ ['æmbi'dekstrəs] iki elini de aynı şekilde kullanabilen; *fig.* iki yüzlü, riyakâr.

am.bi.ent ['æmbiənt] *adj.* dolaşan; kuşatan, çevreleyen.

am.bi.gu.i.ty [æmbi'gju:iti] *n.* iki manalılık, belirsizlik, müphemiyet; **am-'big.uous** [-gjuəs] □ müphem, şüpheli, iki anlamlı.

am.bit ['æmbit] *n.* mıntıka, bölge, çevre, muhit.

am.bi.tion [æm'biʃən] *n.* ihtiras, hırs; büyük istek; **am'bi.tious** □ hırslı, çok istekli (*to -e*).

am.bi.va.lent ['æmbi'veilənt] □ zıt hisler veya fikirler taşıyan, kararsız (*towards, about -e* karşı, için).

am.ble ['æmbl] **1.** *n.* eşkin, rahvan; rahat yürüyüş; **2.** *v/i.* eşkin gitmek; *fig.* yavaş yavaş dolaşmak; **'am.bler** *n.* eşkinli; rahvan yürüyen hayvan.

am.bro.si.a [æm'brəuzjə] *n.* (*eski masallarda*) tanrıların yemekleri; çok lezzetli veya nefis kokulu yiyecek veya içki; **am'bro.si.al** □ nefis veya güzel kokulu; *fig.* mükemmel, enfes.

am.bu.lance ['æmbjuləns] *n.* cankurtaran, ambulans; *attr.* sıhhî yardım...; **~ box** ilk yardım kutusu; **~ station** ilk yardım istasyonu; **'am.bu.lant** *adj.* seyyar, gezici.

am.bu.la.to.ry ['æmbjulətəri] **1.** *adj.* seyyar, gezici; gezilebilir; **2.** *n.* gezinti yeri, kemerli yol, kulvar.

am.bus.cade [æmbəs'keid], **am.bush** ['æmbuʃ] **1.** *n.* pusu, tuzak; *be veya lie in ~ for s.o.* b-ne pusuya yatmak; **2.** *vb.* pusuda beklemek, tuzak kurmak, pusuya düşürmek.

a.mel.io.rate [ə'mi:ljəreit] *vb.* iyileş(-tir) mek, düzel(t)mek; **a.mel.io'ra.tion** *n.* iyileşme, düzelme.

a.men ['ɑ:'men] *int.* âmin.

a.me.na.ble □ [ə'mi:nəbl] tâbi olan (*to -e*), uysal; yükümlü, sorumlu.

a.mend [ə'mend] *v/t.* düzeltmek, ıslah etm.; JUR düzeltmek, tashih etm.; (*kanun*) değiştirmek, tadil etm.; *v/i.* iyileşmek, düzelmek; **a'mend.ment** *n.* düzeltme, tadil; JUR bir kanunu değiştirme; PARL tadilât, değişiklik; **a'mends** *n. pl.* tazminat, zarar ödentisi; *make ~ for* özür dilemek; kusurunu düzeltmek.

a.men.i.ty [ə'mi:niti] *n.* letafet, zerafet, şirinlik; **amenities** *pl.* hayatın zevki, güzel tarafı.

A.mer.i.can [ə'merikən] **1.** *adj.* Amerikalı, Amerikan; **~ cloth** muşamba; **2.** *n.* Amerika kıtalarının yerlisi; Amerika Birleşik Devletleri tebaası; **A'mer.i.can.ism** *n.* Amerikalılara mahsus kelime, deyim, şive vs.; *Am.* Amerika Birleşik Devletleri inanç ve amaçlarına bağlılık; **A.meri.can.i'za.tion** *n.* Amerikalılaştırma; **A'mer.i.can.ize** *v/t.* Amerikalılaştırmak.

am.e.thyst MIN ['æmiθist] *n.* cebellokum, ametist.

a.mi.a.bil.i.ty [eimjə'biliti] *n.* kanı sıcaklık, tatlılık, sevimlilik; **'a.mi.a.ble** □ hoş, sevimli, tatlı.

am.i.ca.ble □ ['æmikəbl] dostça, dostane.

a.mid(st) [ə'mid(st)] *prp.* arasına, arasında, ortasında *-in.*

a.mid.ships NAUT [ə'midʃips] *adv.* geminin ortasında.

a.miss [ə'mis] *adv.* eksik, yanlış; kusurlu; *take ~* gücenmek; fenaya almak, yanlış anlamak *-i; it would not be ~ (for him)* fena olmaz, zararı dokunmaz.

am.i.ty ['æmiti] *n.* dostluk, iyi ilişki, sevgi.

am.me.ter ELECT ['æmitə] *n.* ampermetre.

am.mo.ni.a [ə'məunjə] *n.* amonyak; *liquid ~* nişadır ruhu; **am'mo.ni.ac** [-niæk], **am.mo.ni.a.cal** [æməu'naiəkəl] *adj.* amonyak ile ilgili; *s. sal.*

am.mon.ite ['æmənait] *n.* nesli tükenmiş bir deniz hayvanı kabuğunun fosili.

am.mu.ni.tion MIL [æmju'niʃən] *n.* cephane, mühimmat.

am.ne.sia MED ['æm'ni:zjə] *n.* (*kısmen veya tamamen*) hafıza kaybı, unutkanlık.

am.nes.ty ['æmnisti] **1.** *n.* genel af; **2.** *v/t.* genel af ilân etm., cezasını affetmek.

a.m(o)e.ba ZOO [ə'mi:bə] *n.* amip.

a.mok [ə'mɔk] = **amuck.**

a.mong(st) [ə'mʌŋ(st)] *prp. -in* arasında, arasına; içinde; *from ~ -in* içinden, arasından.

a.mor.al [ei'mɔrəl] *adj.* ahlâk ile ilişiği olmayan.

am.o.rous □ ['æmərəs] âşık, tutkun (*of -e*); aşk...; '**am.o.rous.ness** *n.* âşıklık.

a.mor.phous □ [ə'mɔːfəs] MIN şekilsiz, özelliği olmayan; *fig.* biçimsiz, çirkin.

am.or.ti.za.tion [əmɔːtɪ'zeiʃən] *n.* itfa, herhangi bir borcu taksitle ödeme, amortisman; **am'or.tize** [-taiz] *v/t.* bir borcu taksitlerle ödemek, amortize etm.

a.mount [ə'maunt] **1.** *v/i. ~ to -e* varmak, baliğ olm.; **2.** *n.* miktar, meblağ, tutar, yekûn; *to the ~ of -e* baliğ olan.

a.mour [ə'muə] *n.* aşk, aşk macerası; **~-pro.pre** ['æmuə'prɔpr] *n.* izzetinefis, onur.

am.pere ELECT ['æmpeə] *n.* amper.

am.phib.i.an [æm'fibiən] **1.** *n.* iki yaşayışlı hayvan (*kurbağa gibi*); hem suya hem de karaya inip kalkabilen uçak; hem suda hem de karada gidebilen araç; **2.** = **am'phib.i.ous** □ hem havada hem de suda yaşayabilen.

am.phi.the.a.tre, *Am.* **am.phi.the.a.ter** ['æmfiθiətə] *n.* amfiteatr.

am.ple □ ['æmpl] geniş, bol; kâfi; etraflı.

am.pli.fi.ca.tion [æmplifi'keiʃən] *n.* genişletme, tevsi; RHET geniş açıklama; PHYS amplifikasyon; **am.pli.fi.er** ['-faiə] *n.* radyo: amplifikatör, büyültücü alet; '**ampli.fy** *vb.* genişletmek, büyütmek; sesini kuvvetlendirmek; mübalâğa etm.; **~ing valve** amplifikatör valfı; **am.pli.tude** ['-tjuːd] *n.* genişlik, bolluk; PHYS genlik, amplitüd.

am.poule MED *n.* ['æmpuːl] ampul.

am.pu.tate MED ['æmpjuteit] *v/t.* (*bir uzvu*) kesmek; **am.pu'ta.tion** *n.* bir uzvun kesilmesi.

a.muck [ə'mʌk]: **run ~** kudurmuş gibi etrafa saldırmak; **run ~ at** veya **on** veya **against** *fig.* üzerine atılmak.

am.u.let ['æmjulit] *n.* muska, tılsım.

a.muse [ə'mjuːz] *v/t.* eğlendirmek, güldürmek *b-ni;* a'**muse.ment** *n.* eğlence, zevk; **~ park,** *Am.* **funfair** luna park; a'**mus.ing** □ eğlenceli, güldürücü, tuhaf; *the ~ thing about it* işin tuhafı.

an GR [æn, ən] *ad.* belirteni; *s.* **a.**

a.nach.ro.nism [ə'nækrənizəm] *n.* (*bir olayı*) ait olmadığı tarihte gösterme.

an.a.con.da ZOO [ænə'kɔndə] *n.* boa yılanı.

a.n(a)e.mi.a MED [ə'niːmjə] *n.* kansızlık, anemi; **a'n(a)e.mic** *adj.* kansız, anemik.

an.(a)es.the.si.a MED [ænis'θiːzjə] *n.* anestezi, uyuşturma, narkoz; **an.(-a)es.thet.ic** [-'θetik] **1.** *adj.* (**~ally**) uyuşturucu; **2.** *n.* uyuşturucu madde, narkotik.

an.a.log.ic, an.a.log.i.cal □ [ænə'lɔdʒik(əl)], a.nal.o.gous □ [ə'næləgəs] benzer, kıyas yoluyla olan; -vari; a'**nal.o.gy** [-dʒi] *n.* kıyas, karşılaştırma; benzerlik, benzeşme.

an.a.lyse ['ænəlaiz] *v/t.* tahlil etm., analiz etm.; çözümlemek, incelemek, tetkik etm., GR çözümlemek, analiz etm.; **a.naly.sis** [ə'næləsis] *n., pl.* a'**nal.y.ses** [-siːz] analiz, çözümleme; a'**nal.yst** ['ænəlist] *n.* tahlilci, tahlil eden kimse; psikoanalist.

an.a.lyt.ic, an.a.lyt.i.cal □ [ænə'litik(əl)] çözümsel, tahlilî.

an.ar.chic, an.ar.chi.cal □ [æ'naːkik(əl)] anarşik; kanunsuz, nizamsız; **an.arch.ist** ['ænəkist] anarşist; '**an.arch.y** *n.* anarşi; kargaşalık.

a.nath.e.ma [ə'næθimə] *n.* afaroz; afaroz edilmiş veya lânetlenmiş kimse; nefret edilen şey (*to... için*); a'**nath.e.ma.tize** *v/t.* afaroz etm., lânetlemek.

an.a.tom.i.cal □ [ænə'tɔmikəl] anatomik, anatomi ile ilgili; a.**nat.o.mist** [ə'nætəmist] *n.* teşrihçi, anatom; a'**nat.o.mize** *v/t.* teşrih etm., dikkatle ayırmak; a'**nato.my** *n.* anatomi, (*insan veya hayvan*) vücut yapısı, teşrih; F iskelet.

an.ces.tor ['ænsistə] *n.* ata, cet, dede; **ances.tral** [-'sestrəl] *adj.* atadan kalma, atalara ait, geçmiş zamana ait; '**an.cestry** *n.* ecdat, dedeler.

an.chor NAUT & *fig.* ['æŋkə] **1.** *n.* çapa, gemi demiri; güven veren şey; *at ~* demirli, demir atmış; **2.** *vb.* demirlemek, demir atmak; '**an.chor.age** *n.* geminin demir attığı yer; liman, koy.

an.cho.ret ['æŋkəret; '-rait] *n.* (*Tanrıya ulaşmak için*) bir köşeye çekilmiş olan kimse.

an.chor.man ['æŋkəmæn] *n.* TV: *görevi haberleri okumak ve stüdyo dışındaki muhabirlerle bağlantı kurmak olan erkek sunucu;* an.chor.wo.man *n.* TV: *görevi haberleri okumak ve stüdyo dışındaki muhabirlerle bağlantı kur-*

mak olan kadın sunucu.

an.cho.vy ['æntʃəvi] *n.* hamsi balığı, ançüez.

an.cient ['einʃənt] **1.** *adj.* eski, kadim, eski zarnandan kalma; **2.** *n.* **the ~s** *pl. (eski Yunan ve Roma gibi)* kadim milletler; '**an.cient.ly** eski zamanlarda, evvel zamanda.

an.cil.lar.y [æn'siləri] *adj.* tabi, bağlı, yardımcı (**to** -e); **~ road** yan sokak.

and [ænd, ənd] *cj.* ve, ile; daha; **thousands ~ thousands** binlerce; **~ so on** vesaire.

and.i.ron ['ændaiən] *n.* ocağın madenî ayaklığı.

an.ec.do.tal [ænek'dəutl], **an.ec.dot-i.cal** [˛'dɔtikəl] *adj.* fıkra tarzında; **an-ec.dote** ['ænikdəut] *n.* fıkra, hikâye.

an.e.mom.e.ter [æni'mɔmitə] *n.* rüzgârın şiddetini ölçen alet.

a.nem.o.ne BOT [ə'neməni] *n.* Manisa lâlesi, anemon.

an.er.oid ['ænərɔid] *a.* **~ barometer** madeni barometre, aneroid.

a.new [ə'njuː] *adv.* yeniden, tekrar.

an.gel ['eindʒəl] *n.* melek; melek gibi kimse; **an.gel.ic, an.gel.i.cal** [æn-'dʒelik(əl)] melek gibi; meleklere mahsus.

an.ge.lus ['ændʒiləs] *n. (Katoliklerce)* günde üç defa okunan bir dua; bu duanın zamanını bildiren çan sesi.

an.ger ['æŋgə] **1.** *n.* hiddet, öfke; **2.** *v/t.* kızdırmak, öfkelendirmek.

an.gi.na MED [æn'dʒainə] *n.* anjin, boğak; **~ pectoris** göğüs anjini.

an.gle ['æŋgl] **1.** *n.* köşe açı; *fig.* görüş açısı; noktai nazar; **~-dozer** *n.* bir tip buldozer, yol düzenleme makinesi; **~-iron** köşebent demiri, korniyer; **2.** *v/i. (olta ile)* balık tutmak; **~ for** F ima yoluyla *bşi* elde etmeğe çalışmak; '**an.gler** *n.* olta ile balık avlıyan kimse.

An.gles ['æŋglz] *n. pl.* Anglo'lar.

An.gli.can ['æŋglikən] **1.** *n.* Anglikan, İngiliz kilisesine mensup kimse; **2.** *adj.* İngiliz kilisesine ait.

An.gli.cism ['æŋlisizəm] *n. (başka bir dilde çok kullanılan)* İngilizce kelime veya deyim.

an.gling ['æŋgliŋ] *n.* olta ile balık avlama.

An.glo-Sax.on ['æŋgləu'sæksən] **1.** *n.* Anglosakson; **2.** *adj.* Anglosakson.

an.gry ['æŋgri] □ öfkeli, kızgın; darılmış (**at, about** -den dolayı); gücenmiş (**with** -e); MED kızarmış, ka-

barmış.

an.guish ['æŋgwiʃ] *n.* ıstırap, keder, şiddetli acı.

an.gu.lar □ ['æŋgjulə] köşeli, açısal; sıska, bir deri bir kemik; *fig.* kaba, yontulmamış; **an.gu.lar.i.ty** [˛'læriti] *n.* açılı veya köşeli olma; *fig.* kabalık.

an.i.line CHEM ['ænili:n] *n.* anilin.

an.i.mad.ver.sion ['ænimædvɔːʃən] *n.* tenkit, eleştiri, kınama; **an.i.mad.vert** [˛'vɔːt] *v/i.* tenkit etm., eleştirmek (**on, upon** -i).

an.i.mal ['æniməl] **1.** *n.* hayvan; **2.** *adj.* hayvanlara ait, hayvanî; **~ spirits** *pl.* canlılık, hayatiyet; **an.i.mal.cule** [˛'mælkjuː] *n.* kolayca görülemiyecek kadar küçük hayvancık; **an.i.mal.ism** ['˛məlizəm] *n.* hayvan oluş, şehvanîyet.

an.i.mate **1.** ['ænimeit] *v/t.* canlandırmak, diriltmek, hayat vermek; **2.** ['˛mit] *mst* **an.i.mat.ed** ['˛meitid] *adj.* canlı; neşeli, hayat dolu; *fig.* canlı; **~ cartoon** canlı resimlerden ibaret film.

an.i.ma.tion [æni'meiʃən] *n.* canlılık, heyecan, şevk.

an.i.mos.i.ty [æni'mɔsiti] *a.* **an.i.mus** ['æniməs] *n.* düşmanlık, nefret, kin.

an.ise BOT ['ænis] *n.* anason.

an.kle ['æŋkl] *n.* ayak bileği, aşık kemiği.

an.klet ['æŋklit] *n.* ayak bileğine takılan bilezik; kısa çorap.

an.nals ['ænlz] *n. pl.* tarihî olaylar; vakayiname.

an.neal MEC [ə'niːl] *v/t. (bir madeni)* kızdırdıktan sonra yavaş yavaş soğutarak yumuşatmak, tavlamak; sertleştirmek (*a. fig.*).

an.nex 1. [ə'neks] *v/t.* ilhak etm., eklemek, katmak (**to** -e); **2.** ['æneks] *n.* ek; müştemilât, ek bina; **an.nex'a.tion** *n.* ilhak (*arazi*); müsadere.

an.ni.hi.late [ə'naiəleit] *v/t.* imha etm., yok etm.; = **annul**; **an.ni.hi'la.tion** *n.* imha, yok etme; = **annulment**.

an.ni.ver.sa.ry [æni'vɔːsəri] *n.* yıldönümü; yıldönümü merasimi.

an.no.tate ['ænəuteit] *v/t.* belirli kısımları açıklamak için bir kitaba kısa notlar ilâve etm., şerhetmek; şerhütefsir etm., bir metni açıklamak; **an.no-'ta.tion** *n.* haşiye, not.

an.nounce [ə'nauns] *v/t.* bildirmek, ilân etm., haber vermek; tebliğ etm.; *(radyo, TV vs. de haberleri)* okumak *veya* (*bir şahıs veya eylemi*) sunmak; **an'nounce.ment** *n.* bildiri, ilân, tebliğ, anons; *radyo:* anons, mesaj; **an'nounc.er** *n. radyo:* sözcü, spiker.

an.noy [ə'nɔi] *v/t.* taciz etm., sıkmak, kızdırmak; **an'noy.ance** *n.* canını sıkma, üzüntü, rahatsızlık; **an'noyed** *adj.* dargın, kızgın (*kimse*); **be ~** kızmak; **an'noy.ing** □ can sıkıcı, nâhoş (*şey*).

an.nu.al ['ænjuəl] **1.** □ senelik, yıllık; yıllık...; *part.* BOT bir yıl *veya* mevsimlik (*bitki*); **2.** *n.* yıllık, almanak; bir yıl *veya* mevsimlik bitki.

an.nu.i.tant [ə'nju:itənt] *n.* kendisine ölünceye kadar *veya* belirli bir süre için gelir bağlanan (*veya eşit miktarlarda para ödenen*) kimse.

an.nu.i.ty [ə'nju:iti] *n.* (*yıllık*) taksit, tahsisat; COM **a. ~ bond** irat, gelir senedi; *s.* **life.**

an.nul [ə'nʌl] *v/t.* feshetmek, iptal etm., bozmak.

an.nu.lar □ ['ænjulə] halka şeklinde.

an.nul.ment [ə'nʌlmənt] *n.* iptal, fesih, kaldırma.

an.nun.ci.a.tion [ənʌnsi'eiʃən] *n.* bildirme, tebliğ etme, haber; ♀ İsa'ya hamile olduğunu Meryem'e bildiren haber (*Cebrail vasıtasıyla*); bu haberin kutlandığı yortu (*25 Mart*).

an.ode ELECT ['ænəud] *n.* pozitif kutup, anod.

an.o.dyne ['ænəudain] *n. & adj.* uyuşturucu, yatıştırıcı, müsekkin (*ilâç*).

a.noint [ə'nɔint] *v/t. part.* ECCL yağlamak; takdis etm. (*a. fig.*).

a.nom.a.lous □ [ə'nɔmələs] anormal, kaideye uymayan, kural dışı; **a'nom.a.ly** *n.* anormallik, kural dışı oluş.

a.non [ə'nɔn] *adv.* hemen, biraz sonra; **ever and ~** zaman zaman, arasıra.

an.o.nym.i.ty [ænə'nimiti] *n.* imzasızlık, anonimlik; **a.non.y.mous** □ [ə'nɔniməs] imzasız, anonim.

a.noph.e.les ZOO [ə'nɔfili:z] *n.* sıtma sivrisineği, anofel.

an.oth.er [ə'nʌðə] *adj.* başka, diğer, öbür, ayrı; **in ~ ten years** bundan on sene sonra; **with one ~** birbirini.

an.swer ['ɑ:nsə] **1.** *vb.* cevap vermek *-e*, yanıtlamak *-i*; sorumlu olm. (**for** *-den*); uymak (**to** *-e*); mukabele etm. (**with** *-ile*); ihtiyacı karşılamak; hesap görmek; **~ the bell** *veya* **door** (*zili duyup*) kapıyı açmak; **~ for** sorumluluğunu üzerine almak; garanti etm., *bşi* tekef-

fül etm.; **2.** *n.* cevap, yanıt (**to** *-e*); MATH çözüm; JUR cevap lâyihası; cevap; **'answer.a.ble** □ mesul, sorumlu; cevap verilebilir.

ant [ænt] *n.* karınca.

an't [ɑ:nt] F = **are not**, **am not**; *sl. veya* P = **is not.**

an.tag.o.nism [æn'tægənizəm] *n.* düşmanlık, ziddiyet (**between** *-arasında*); husumet (**to** *-e karşı*); **an'tag.o.nist** *n.* muhalif, düşman; **an.tag.o'nis.tic** □ (**~ally**) muhalif, düşman, zıt (**to** *-e*); **an'tag.onize** *v/t.* düşman etm.; zıtlık yaratmak, kışkırtmak.

ant.arc.tic [ænt'ɑ:ktik] **1.** *adj.* Güney Kutbuna ait; **2.** *n.* Güney Kutbu; **the** ♀ Antarktik; ♀ **Circle** Güney Kutup dairesi.

an.te *Am.* ['ænti] poker oyunu; **1.** *n.* (*oyunu açış için*) ortaya konulan para; **2.** *v/t. mst.* **~ up** para koymak, sürmek; *v/i. fig.* karınca kararınca yardım etm..

an.te.ced.ence [ænti'si:dəns] *n.* evvellik, öncelik, önce olan (*şey*); **an.te'ced.ent 1.** □ önce gelen, evvel, mukaddem; **2.** *n. b-den*, *bşden* evvel gelen; GR zamirin yerini aldığı isim *veya* tümleç; **his ~s** *pl.* geçmişi.

an.te.cham.ber ['æntitʃeimbə] *n.* bekleme odası, (*içinden daha büyük bir odaya geçilen*) küçük oda.

an.te.date ['ænti'deit] *v/t.* daha eski bir tarih koymak; *bşden* önce gitmek, önüne geçmek.

an.te.di.lu.vi.an ['æntidi'lu:vjən] *adj.* Tufan öncesi.

an.te.lope ZOO ['æntiləup] *n.* antilop; ceylan.

an.te me.rid.i.em ['æntimə'ridiəm] *adv.* öğleden evvel.

an.ten.na [æn'tenə] *n.*, *pl.* **an'ten.nae** [-ni:] ZOO duyarga, böcek boynuzu; *radyo, televizyon:* anten.

an.te.ri.or [æn'tiəriə] *adj.* ön, önceki; önde bulunan.

an.te-room ['æntirum] *n.* bekleme odası.

an.them ['ænθəm] *n.* ilâhi, dinî şarkı; **national ~** millî marş.

an.ther BOT ['ænθə] *n.* başçık, haşefe.

ant.hill ['ænthil] *n.* karınca yuvası.

an.thol.o.gy [æn'θɔlədʒi] *n.* antoloji, (*çeşitli kitap ve yazarlardan derlenmiş*) şiir *veya* yazılar.

an.thra.cite MIN ['ænθrəsait] *n.* antrasit; **an.thrax** VET ['ænθræks] *n.* şarbon, antraks.

an.thro.poid ['ænθrəupɔid] **1.** adj. insana benzer; **2.** n. insanımsı maymun; **an.thropol.o.gist** [ænθrə'pɔlədʒist] n. antropoloji bilgini, antropolog; **anthro'pol.o.gy** [-dʒi] n. antropoloji, insanbilim.

an.ti... ['ænti] prefix ...karşı, muhalif, zıt, ters.

an.ti-air.craft ['ænti'ɛəkrɑːft] adj. uçaksavar; ~ **gun** uçaksavar topu.

an.ti.bi.ot.ic MED ['æntibaɪ'ɔtik] n. antibiyotik.

an.ti.bod.y MED ['æntibɔdi] n. vücutta yapılan ve hastalıklara karşı koyan madde, antikor.

an.tic ['æntik] adj. kaba komedi; ~**s** pl. maskaralık, tuhaflık, soytarılık.

An.ti.christ ['æntikraist] n. deccal.

an.tic.i.pate [æn'tisipeit] v/t. önceden görmek, tahmin etm., sezinlemek, beklemek, ummak; **an.tic.i'pa.tion** n. önceden görme, tahmin, bekleme, sezinleme; **payment by** ~ peşinen ödeme; avans; **in** ~ peşinen, önceden, evvelden; an'tic.i.pa.to.ry [-peitəri] adj. önceden yapılan, ilerisini düşünerek yapılan.

an.ti.cli.max RHET & fig. ['ænti'klaimæks] n. heyecan verici bir olayı takibeden tekdüzey şey; iniş.

an.ti.cor.ro.sive a.gent ['æntikə'rəusiv'eidʒənt] n. pasa mâni olan madde.

an.ti.cy.clone METEOR ['ænti'saikləun] n. yüksek basınç alanı.

an.ti.dote ['æntidəut] n. panzehir, çare (**against**, **for**, **to** -e karşı).

an.ti-fas.cist ['ænti'fæʃist] n. & adj. antifaşist.

an.ti-freeze MOT ['æntifriːz] n. antifriz.

an.ti-fric.tion ['ænti'frikʃən] adj. sürtünmeye karşı; attr. kayma...

an.ti-glo.bal.ist ['ænti'gləubəlist] adj. & n. küreselleşme karşıtı.

an.ti-knock MOT ['ænti'nɔk] n. motorun vuruntusuz çalışması için benzine konan kimyevî madde.

an.ti.mo.ny MIN ['æntiməni] n. rastık taşı, antimon.

an.tip.a.thy [æn'tipəθi] n. antipati, sevişmezlik, hoşlanmama (**against**, **to** -e karşı).

an.tip.o.dal □ [æn'tipədl] tam tersi, taban tabana zıddı; zıt; **an.ti.pode** ['-pəud] n., pl. **an.tip.o.des** [-pədiːz] n. birbirine zıt iki kimse veya şey; ♀ pl. Avustralya ve Yeni Zelanda.

antikaya ait; **2.** n. antikacı, antika meraklısı; **an.ti.quar.y** ['-kwəri] n. antikacı, antika meraklısı; **an.ti.quat.ed** ['-kweitid] adj. eskimiş, modası geçmiş.

an.tique [æn'tiːk] **1.** □ eski zamanlara ait, antika; **2.** n. antika; eski sanat eseri; **an.tiq.ui.ty** [-'tikwiti] n. eskilik, antikalık; eski zamana ait şey; eski zamanlar pl.; **antiquities** pl. âsariatika.

an.ti-rust ['ænti'rʌst] n. pasa mâni olan madde.

an.ti-Sem.ite ['ænti'siːmait] n. Yahudi düşmanı; **an.ti-Sem.i.tism** ['-'semitizəm] n. Yahudi düşmanlığı.

an.ti.sep.tic [ænti'septik] n. & adj. antiseptik.

an.ti.so.cial [ænti'səuʃəl] adj. topluma ve toplumsal yararlara karşı; bencil, uyumsuz.

an.ti.tank MIL [ænti'tæŋk] adj. tanksavar...

an.tith.e.sis [æn'tiθisis] n., pl. **an'tith.e.ses** [-θisiːz] antitez, karşı tez; zıtlık; **an.tithet.ic**, **an.ti.thet.i.cal** □ [-'θetik(əl)] karşıt olan.

ant.ler ['æntlə] n. geyik boynuzu; ~**s** geyiğin boynuzları.

an.to.nym ['æntəunim] n. zıt anlama gelen kelime.

A num.ber 1 ['əinʌmbə'wʌn] Am. F s. **A 1**; **anus** ['einəs] n. anus, makat, şerç.

an.vil ['ænvil] n. örs; örs kemiği.

anx.i.e.ty [æŋ'zaiəti] n. endişe, kuruntu, merak; şiddetli arzu; fig. endişe (**for** için); fig. istek (**to** -e); MED sıkıntı; nefes darlığı

anx.ious □ ['æŋkʃəs] meraklı, endişeli, vesveseli, üzüntülü (**about** -den dolayı); mütereddit; arzulu, istekli, hevesli (**for**, **to**, -e); **be** ~ **to** arzu etm. -i. can atmak -e.

an.y ['eni] adj. & adv. & pron. bir, herhangi, her bir; bazı, birkaç, biraz; hiç, hiçbir; **not** ~ hiç; ~ **more** artık; daha fazla; '~**.bod.y**, '~**.one** pron. herhangi bir kimse; **not** ~ hiçbiri, hiçkimse; '~**.how** adv. her nasılsa; her halde; her ne olursa olsun; '~**.thing** pron. her hangi bir şey, her şey; hiçbir şey; ~ **but** olmasın da ne olursa olsun; '~**.way** = **anyhow**; zaten; esasen; '~**.where** adv. her hangi bir yer(d)e; hiçbir yer(d)e.

an.y.wise ['eniwaiz] adv. her nasıl olursa.

a.or.ta MED [ei'ɔːtə] n. kanı yürekten

vücuda taşıyan en büyük damar, aort.

a.pace [ə'peis] *adv.* çabuk, süratle.

a.part [ə'pɑːt] *adv. & adj.* ayrı, bir taraf(t)a; bağımsız olarak; başka (**from** *-den*); **joking ~** şaka bertaraf, şaka bir tarafa; **set ~ for** bir tarafa koymak, ayırmak, tahsis etm..

a.part.heid POL [ə'pɑːtheit] *n.* (*Güney Afrika'da*) ırk ayırımı.

a.part.ment [ə'pɑːtmənt] *n.* büyük oda, salon; *Am.* apartman dairesi; **~s** *pl.* apartman dairesi; **~ house** apartman.

ap.a.thet.ic [æpə'θetik] ☐ (**~ally**) hissiz, ilgisiz; uyuşuk; '**ap.a.thy** *n.* duygusuzluk, ilgisizlik, soğukluk (**to** *-e karşı*).

ape [eip] **1.** *n.* maymun; **2.** *v/t.* taklit etm.

a.peak NAUT [ə'piːk] *adv. & adj.* amudî, şakulî, dikey.

a.pe.ri.ent [ə'piəriənt] **1.** *n.* müshil, amel ilâcı; **2.** *adj.* müleyyin, yumuşatıcı, müshil.

ap.er.ture ['æpətjuə] *n.* aralık, delik, açık.

a.pex ['eipeks] *n.*, *pl.* **ap.i.ces** ['eipisiːz] zirve, tepe, doruk; *mst fig.* en yüce yer, en üst derece.

aph.o.rism ['æfərizəm] *n.* vecize, darbımesel; **aph.o.'ris.tic** ☐ (**~ally**) vecize kabilinden.

a.pi.ar.y ['eipjəri] *n.* arı kovanı; **a.pi.cul.ture** ['eipikʌltʃə] *n.* arıcılık.

a.piece [ə'piːs] *adv.* her biri(ne), adam başına, beher.

ap.ish ☐ ['eipiʃ] maymun gibi, maymunca; taklitçi.

A-plant ['ei'plɑːnt] *n.* nükleer elektrik fabrikası.

a.poc.a.lypse [ə'pɔkəlips] *n.* vahiy.

A.poc.ry.pha [ə'pɔkrifə] *n. pl. İncil:* Mukaddes kitabın metnine dahil edilmeyen kitaplar; **a'poc.ry.phal.adj.** bu kitaplara ait; sonradan uydurulmuş, doğruluğu kabul edilmeyen.

ap.o.gee ['æpəudʒiː] *n.* AST (*bir uzay aracı, gök cismi, ay, güneş vs.nin*) yeryüzünden en uzak noktası; (*güç veya başarının*) en yüksek noktası, doruk.

a.pol.o.get.ic [əpɔlə'dʒetik] ☐ özür dileyen, af talep eden; savunan; **~ letter** mazeret mektubu; **a'pol.o.gist** *n.* bir inanç veya fikri savunan kimse; **a'pol.o.gize** *v/i.* özür dilemek, itizar etm., af dilemek (**for** *-den*); **a'pol.o.gy** *n.* özür dileme, tarziye; savunma; **make an ~** özür dilemek.

ap.o.plec.tic,   ap.o.plec.ti.cal ☐ [æpəu'plektik(əl)] inme veya felce ait; inmeli, mefluc; **ap.o.plex.y** ['ˌ-pleksi] *n.* inme, felç, nüzul.

a.pos.ta.sy [ə'pɔstəsi] *n.* irtidat, dininden dönme; parti değiştirme; inancından dönme; **a'pos.tate** [ˌ-stit] **1.** *n.* dininden veya inancından dönmüş kimse; **2.** *adj.* din değiştiren; **a'pos.ta.tize** [ˌ-stətaiz] *v/i.* ayrılmak (**from** *-den*); irtidat etm., dininden dönmek (**from**) .

a.pos.tle [ə'pɔsl] *n.* havari; **ap.os.tol.ic, apos.tol.i.cal** ☐ [æpəs'tɔlik(əl)] havariyuna veya papaya ait; yalnız İncil'e dayanan.

a.pos.tro.phe [ə'pɔstrəfi] *n.* GR virgül, kesme işareti; RHET hitabe, nutuk.

a.poth.e.car.y *obs.* [ə'pɔθikəri] *n.* eczacı.

a.poth.e.o.sis [əpɔθi'əusis] *n.* ilâhlaştırma, tanrılaştırma, methüsena etme, ayyuka çıkarma.

ap.pal [ə'pɔːl] *v/t.* korkutmak, ürkütmek; **ap.pall.ing** ☐ korkunç, müthiş.

ap.pa.ra.tus [æpə'reitəs] *n.* cihaz, makine, takım, aletler; **~ work** jimnastik aletleri.

ap.par.el [ə'pærəl] **1.** *n.* elbise, üst baş, kıyafet; **2.** *v/t.* giydirmek.

ap.par.ent ☐ [ə'pærənt] açık, belli; görünüşte olan; kolay anlaşılır; kolay görülür; *s.* **heir; ap.pa.ri.tion** [æpə'riʃən] *n.* hayalet; görünüş; olay.

ap.peal [ə'piːl] **1.** *vb.* JUR daha yüksek mahkemeye müracaat etm., istinaf etm. (**to** *-e*); önemle rica etm., yalvarmak (**to s.o. for s.th.** *b-ne bş için*); başvurmak (**to** *-e*); beğenmek *-i*; *b-nin* hoşuna gitmek; *s.* **country**; **2.** *n.* baş vurma, müracaat (**to** *-e*); yalvarma, ısrarla isteme; temyiz; davet, çağrı (**to** *-e*); *fig.* ilân, beyanname; **~ for mercy** af dilekçesi; **ap'pealer** *n.* başvuran; temyiz eden; **ap'peal.ing** ☐ yalvaran; sevimli, cazip.

ap.pear [ə'piə] *v/i.* görünmek, gözükmek, meydana çıkmak, belli olm.; mahkemeye çıkmak; var olm.; **ap'pear.ance** *n.* görünüş; gösteriş; dış görünüş; meydana çıkma, zuhur etme; olay; mahkemeye çıkma; **keep up** *veya* **save ~s** zevahiri kurtarmak, durumu idare etm.; **make one's ~** ortaya (*veya* sahneye, meydana) çıkmak; alenen görünmek; **put in an ~** ispatı vücut etm., görünüp gitmek; **to** *veya* **by all ~s** görünüşe göre.

ap.pease [ə'piːz] *v/t.* yatıştırmak, teskin etm.; (*açlık vs.*) gidermek; (*dert*) azaltmak, hafifletmek; (*kavga, çarpışma vs.*) bastırmak; **ap'pease.ment** *n.* yatıştırma, teslim etme; (*politikada*) düşmana taviz vererek barışın sağlanabileceği düşüncesi.

ap.pel.lant [ə'pelənt] **1.** *adj.* istinaf yoluna giden, temyiz eden; **2.** *n.* istinaf yoluna giden taraf, temyiz eden kimse; **ap'pellate** [-lit] *adj.* dâvaların yeniden görülmesine ait olan; temyizle ilgili; ~ **court** temyiz mahkemesi; **ap.pel.la-tive** GR [ə'pelətiv] **1.** *n.a.* ~ **name** cins ismi; ünvan; **2.** *adj.* cins ismine ait; tanımlayıcı.

ap.pel.lee [æpe'liː] *n.* aleyhine temyiz veya istinaf yoluna başvurulan taraf.

ap.pend [ə'pend] *v/t.* eklemek, ilâve etm., katmak; **ap'pend.age** *n.* ilâve, katkı, ek; **ap.pen.dec.to.my** [-'dektə-mi] *n.* apandis ameliyatı; **ap.pen.di-ci.tis** [-di'saitis] *n.* apandisit; **ap'pen-dix** [-diks] *n.pl.a.* **ap.pen.di.ces** [-di-siːz] ek, zeyil; MED apandis.

ap.per.tain [æpə'tein] *v/i.* ait olm.; bağlı olm. (**to** -e); *fig. b-ne* ait olm., *b-nin* olm.

ap.pe.tence, ap.pe.ten.cy ['æpitəns(i)] *n.* (**for, after, of**) iştiha, şiddetli arzu; insiyak; içgüdü.

ap.pe.tite ['æpitait] *n.* (**for**) iştah; arzu; istek; şehvet; *fig.* arzu.

ap.pe.tiz.er ['æpitaizə] *n.* iştah açan şey, çerez, aperatif; **'ap.pe.tiz.ing** □ iştah açan.

ap.plaud [ə'plɔːd] *vb.* alkışlamak; takdir etm.

ap.plause [ə'plɔːz] *n.* alkış.

ap.ple ['æpl] *n.* elma; **the~ of s.o.'s eye** *fig.* göz bebeği, favori, gözde; **'~-cart** *n.* (*seyyar satıcının*) el arabası; **upset s.o.'s~** F bir işi bozmak, bir çuval inciri berbat etm.; **'~.jack** *n. Am.* elma rakısı; **'~'pie** *n.* elma turtası; **in ~ order** çok düzenli; **'~-pol.ish.er** *sl.* dalkavuk, yağcı; **'~'sauce** *n.* elma püresi; *Am. sl.* zevzeklik, boş laf.

ap.pli.ance [ə'plaiəns] *n.* alet, cihaz.

ap.pli.ca.bil.i.ty [æplikə'biliti] *n.* uygulanabilme; **'ap.pli.ca.ble** *adj.* uygun, münasip, uygulanabilir (**to** -e); **'ap.pli-cant** *n.* istekli, başvuran kimse, aday (**for** -e, *için*); **ap'pli'ca.tion** *n.* uygulama, tatbik (**of** *bşin*); müracaat (**to** -e); dilekçe; ilâç, merhem; dikkat, özen; ~ **form** müracaat formu; **make an ~** di-

lekçe vermek, başvurmak.

ap.ply [ə'plai] *v/t.* (**to**) , yaklaştırmak; tatbik etm., uygulamak; üstüne koymak; atfetmek; tahsis etm., ayırmak -*e*; ~ **o.s. to** kendini bir işe vermek; *v/i.* müracaat etm., başvurmak (**to, for** -*e, için*); ~ **for** müracaat etm.; talep etm.; **applied sciences** *pl.* tatbikî tabii ilimler.

ap.point [ə'pɔint] *v/t.* tayin etm., atamak; görevlendirmek; kararlaştırmak, tayin etm.; donatmak; **well ~ed** iyi döşenmiş; **ap'point.ment** *n.* tayin, memuriyet, iş; randevu; ~*s pl.* donatım, teçhizat; **by ~** sözleşme mucibince.

ap.por.tion [ə'pɔːʃən] *v/t.* paylaştırmak, taksim etm. (**between, among, amongst** ...*arasında*); **ap'por.tion-ment** *n.* pay; paylaştırma.

ap.po.site □ ['æpəuzit] uygun, münasip (**to** -*e*); **'ap.po.site.ness** *n.* uygunluk.

ap.po.si.tion [æpəu'ziʃən] *n.* GR aynı şahıs veya şeyi açıklayan iki kelimenin bir cümlede yan yana konması.

ap.prais.al [ə'preizəl] *n.* değer biçme, tahmin; **ap'praise** *v/t.* değer biçmek, tahmin etm.; **ap'praise.ment** *n.* değer biçme, tahmin; **ap'prais.er** *n.* değer biçen kimse, muhammin.

ap.pre.ci.a.ble □ [ə'priːʃəbl] sezilebilir, tahmin edilebilir; değer biçilebilir; **ap'pre.ci.ate** [-ʃieit] *v/t.* kıymet takdir etm., paha biçmek; beğenmek, takdir ve teşekkür etm.; kıymetini anlamak -*in*; *v/i.* fiyatı yükselmek, değerlenmek; **appre.ci'a.tion** *n.* değerlendirme, kıymet bilme; COM değer artışı; eleştiri; **ap.pre.cia.tive** □ [ə'priːʃjə-tiv], **ap'pre.ci.a.to.ry** takdir eden, kadirşinas; minnettar; **be ~ of** ... *den* anlamak ve zevk duymak.

ap.pre.hend [æpri'hend] *v/t.* yakalamak, tutuklamak; anlamak; korkmak -*den*; **ap.pre.hen.si.ble** □ [-'hensəbl] anlaşılabilir, farkolunabilir; **ap.pre-'hen.sion** *n.* tutuklama; anlama, anlayış, kavrayış; korku, endişe; zihin; **ap.pre'hen.sive** □ çabuk kavrayan; endişe eden, korkan (**of** -*den*).

ap.pren.tice [ə'prentis] **1.** *n.* çırak; stajyer; **2.** *v/t.* çırak olarak vermek; **ap'pren.tice.ship** *n.* çıraklık.

ap.prise [ə'praiz] *v/t.* haber vermek, bilgi vermek (**of** -*den*).

ap.pro COM ['æprəu]: **on~** örnek olarak, muhayyer olarak.

ap.proach [əˈprəutʃ] **1.** *vb.* yaklaşmak, yanaşmak -*e*, yaklaştırmak, yakına getirmek; müracaat etm.; *fig.* yaklaşmak -*e*; **2.** *n.* yaklaşma, yanaşma; müracaat; giriş yolu; yaklaşım; **make ~es to s.o.** birine avans yapmak; **apˈproach.a.ble** *adj.* yaklaşılabilir, ulaşılabilir, varılması mümkün.

ap.pro.ba.tion [æprəuˈbeiʃən] *n.* beğenme; resmî müsaade, tasdik.

ap.pro.pri.ate 1. [əˈprəuprieit] *v*/*t.* tahsis etm., ayırmak; almak, kendine mal etm. (**for** *için*); **2.** □ [-priit] uygun, münasip (**for, to** *için*, -*e*); **ap.pro.pri.a.tion** [-priˈeiʃən] *n.* ayırma, tahsis; ödenek, tahsisat; **≈ Committee** PARL Bütçe Komisyonu.

ap.prov.a.ble [əˈpruːvəbl] *adj.* şayanı takdir, beğenilir; **apˈprov.al.** *n.* tasvip, uygun görme, onama, resmî izin; **on ~** örnek olarak, muhayyer olarak; **apˈprove** *vb. a.* **~ of** beğenmek, uygun görmek, onaylamak, kabul etm.; **apˈproved** □ tasdikli, izinli, onaylı; **~ school** ıslah evi; **apˈprov.er** *n.* JUR başkalarını suç ortaklığı ile suçlayan sanık; suç ortağı.

ap.prox.i.mate 1. [əˈprɔksimeit] *vb.* yaklaşmak, yaklaştırmak; **2.** □ [-mit] yaklaşık olarak, takribi, yakın (**to** -*e*); **approx.i.ma.tion** [-ˈmeiʃən] *n.* yaklaşma, yakın olma; tahmin; **ap.prox.i-ma.tive** □ [-mətiv] takribî, tahminî.

ap.pur.te.nance [əˈpəːtinəns] *n.* *mst* **~s** *pl.* teferruat, müştemilât; JUR irtifak hakları.

a.pri.cot BOT [ˈeiprikɔt] *n.* kayısı, zerdali.

A.pril [ˈeiprəl] *n.* Nisan; **make an ~ fool of s.o.** 1 Nisan'da birisine muziplik yapmak.

a.pron [ˈeiprən] *n.* önlük, prostela; peştamal; AVIA hangarın önündeki beton saha; THEAT sahnenin seyirciye doğru olan çıkıntılı kısmı; **ˈ~-string** *n.* önlük bağı; **be tied to one's wife's (mother's) ~s** aşırı derecede karısına (annesine) bağlı olm.

ap.ro.pos [ˈæprəpəu] *adj. & adv.* (**of, to**) yerinde olan, uygun, münasip; sırası gelmişken, bu münasebetle.

apt □ [æpt] uygun, elverişli, yerinde (*söz, fikir vs.*); zeki, anlayışlı (**at** -*de*); **he is ~ to believe it** ona inanmak eğiliminde; **~ to bşe** mütemayil, taraflı; meyyal; **ap.ti.tude** [ˈ-titjuːd], **ˈapt.ness** *n.* eğilim, temayül (**to** -*e*); yete-

nek, kabiliyet (**for, to** için -*e*).

aq.ua.lung [ˈækwəlʌŋ] *n.* su altında kullanılan oksijen tüpü.

aq.ua.ma.rine MIN [ækwəməˈriːn] *n.* akvamaren, cama benzer mavimsi yeşil bir ziynet taşı; mavimsi yeşil.

aq.ua.plane [ˈækwəplein] *n.* su kayağı.

aq.ua.relle [ækwəˈrel] *n.* sulu boya resim.

a.quar.i.um [əˈkwɛəriəm] *n.* akvaryum.

a.quat.ic [əˈkwætik] **1.** *adj.* suda yapılan, su...; **~ sports** *pl.* su sporları; **2.** *n.* suda yetişen veya yaşayan, sucul bitki.

aq.ue.duct [ˈækwidʌkt] *n.* su kemeri; **aque.ous** □ [ˈeikwiəs] sulu, su gibi, su ile yapılan.

aq.ui.line [ˈækwilain] *adj.* kartal gibi; kartal gagası gibi kıvrık; **~ nose** gaga burunlu.

Ar.ab [ˈærəb] *n.* Arap, Arabistanlı; Arap atı; *street* **≈** sokak çocuğu; **ar.a-besque** [-ˈbesk] **1.** *n.* arabesk, çiçekli ve yapraklı süsleme; **2.** *adj.* arabesk tarzında olan; **A.ra.bi.an** [əˈreibjən] **1.** *adj.* Arabistan'a ait; **The ~ Nights** Binbir Gece Masalları; **2.** *n.* Arap, Arabistanlı; **Ar.a.bic** [ærəbik] **1.** *adj.* Araplara, Arabistan'a ait; **2.** *n.* Arapça.

ar.a.ble [ˈærəbl] **1.** *adj.* sürülebilir, ziraate elverişli; **2.** *n. a.* **~ land** ekilebilir toprak.

ar.bi.ter [ˈɑːbitə] *n.* hakem; söz sahibi; **ar.bi.trage** COM [ɑːbiˈtrɑːʒ] *n.* arbitraj; **ˈarbi.tral triˈbu.nal** hakem mahkemesi; *spor.* hakem komitesi, **arˈbit.ra-ment** *n.* hakem kararı; (*hakem sıfatıyla*) karar verme; **ˈar.bi.trar.i.ness** *n.* keyfî hareket; **ˈar.bi.trar.y** □ keyfî, ihtiyarî; **ar.bi.trate** [ˈ-treit] *vb.* (*hakem sıfatıyla*) karar vermek; (*hakemle*) halletmek; **ar.biˈtra.tion** *n.* hakem kararı; hakem kararıyla halletme, tahkim; **~ of exchange** COM döviz arbitrajı; **ˈar-bi.tra.tor** *n.* JUR hakem; **ˈar.bi.tress** *n.* kadın hakem; söz sahibi kadın.

ar.bor [ˈɑːbə] *n.* MEC mil, dingil; **≈ Day** A.B.D.'de ağaç dikmeye ayrılan bir ilkbahar günü; **ar.bo.re.al** [ɑːˈbɔːriəl], **arˈbore.ous** *adj.* ağaç..., ağaçlı, ağaçlık; ağaç gibi; **arˈbo.res.cent** □ [ɑːbəˈresnt] ağaca benzeyen.

ar.bour [ˈɑːbə] *n.* çardak, gölgelik, kameriye.

ar.bu.tus BOT [ɑːˈbjuːtəs] *n.* kocayemiş.

arc AST, MATH *etc.* [ɑːk] *n.* (ELECT ışık-) kavis; kemer, ark, yay; **ar.cade** [ɑːˈkeid] *n.* bir sıra kemer; kemer altı, pasaj.

ar.ca.num [ɑːˈkeinəm] *pl.* **ar'ca.na** [-nə] *n.* sır, muamma.

arch¹ [ɑːtʃ] **1.** *n. part.* ARCH kemer, tak; ayak kemeri; ~ *support* düztabanlılara mahsus kundura tabanlığı; **2.** *vb.* kubbe, kemer gibi kabartmak; kabarmak, kubbelenmek.

arch² □ [-] (*kadın ve çocukların davranışları için*) şaklaban, soytarı; kurnaz, açıkgöz.

arch³ □ [-] birinci, ilk, baş; baş...

ar.chae.ol.o.gist [ɑːkiˈɔlədʒist] *n.* arkeolog; **ar.chaeo'l.o.gy** *n.* arkeoloji.

ar.cha.ic [ɑːˈkeiik] *adj.* (*~ally*) eskiye ait, eski, kadim; artık kullanılmayan; **'ar.cha.ism** *n.* artık kullanılmayan kelime veya deyim.

arch.an.gel [ˈɑːkeindʒəl] *n.* baş melek.

arch.bish.op [ˈɑːtʃˈbiʃəp] *n.* başpiskopos; **arch'bish.op.ric** [-rik] *n.* başpiskoposluk makamı veya bölgesi.

arch.dea.con [ˈɑːtʃˈdiːkən] *n.* başdiyakoz.

arch.duch.ess [ˈɑːtʃˈdʌtʃis] *n.* arşidüşes; **'arch'duch.y** *n.* arşidükün idaresi altındaki bölge; **'arch'duke** *n.* arşidük.

arch.er [ˈɑːtʃə] *n.* okçu; **'arch.or.y** *n.* okçuluk.

ar.che.type [ˈɑːkitaip] *n.* orijinal fikir veya örnek, ilk örnek.

arch-fiend [ˈɑːtʃˈfiːnd] *n.* baş şeytan, iblis.

ar.chi.e.pis.co.pal [ɑːkiiˈpiskəpəl] *adj.* başpiskoposluğa ait.

ar.chi.pel.a.go [ɑːkiˈpeligəu] *n.* takımadalar, arşipel; üzerinde çok sayıda küçük ada bulunan deniz.

ar.chi.tect [ˈɑːkitekt] *n.* mimar; yaratıcı, eser meydana getiren; **ar.chi.tec.ton.ic** [-ˈtɔnik] *adj.* (*~ally*) mimarlığa ait; **ar.chi.tec.tu.ral** [-tʃərəl] □ mimarî, mimarlığa ait; **'ar.chi.tec.ture** *n.* mimarlık; inşaat, yapı.

ar.chives [ɑːkaivz] *n. pl.* arşiv.

arch.way [ˈɑːtʃwei] *n.* kemeraltı yolu, kemerli geçit.

arc-lamp [ˈɑːklæmp] *n.*, **'arc-light** *n.* ELECT ark lâmbası.

arc.tic [ˈɑːktik] **1.** *adj.* arktik, Kuzey Kutbunda bulunan (*bölge*); çok soğuk; *the* ♀ Kuzey Kutbu; ♀ *Circle* Kuzey Kutup dairesi; ♀ *Ocean* Kuzey Buz Deni-

zi; **2.** *n. Am.* su geçirmez ve sıcak tutan pabuç, lastik, şoson.

ar.den.cy [ˈɑːdənsi] *n.* şevk; ateşlilik; içtenlik, samimiyet; **'ar.dent** □ *mst fig.* ateşli, şevkli, heyecanlı; candan; ~ *spirits pl.* alkollü içkiler.

ar.do(u)r [ˈɑːdə] *n. fig.* ateşlilik, gayret, şevk.

ar.du.ous □ [ˈɑːdjuəs] zahmetli, güç.

are [ɑː] *s.* **be**.

a.re.a [ˈɛəriə] *n.* saha, alan, bölge; yüzölçümü; (*fikir, iş, çalışma*) alan; *danger ~* tehlikeli bölge; *prohibited ~* yasak bölge.

a.re.na [əˈriːnə] *n.* arena, oyun meydanı, anfiteatrın ortasındaki meydan; mücadele alanı (*a. fig.*).

aren't F [ɑːnt] = *are not*.

a.rête MOUNT [æˈreit] *n.* sırt; hattıbalâ; tepeler hattı.

ar.gent [ˈɑːdʒənt] *adj.* gümüş renginde; gümüş.

Ar.gen.tine [ˈɑːdʒəntain] **1.** *adj.* Arjantinli; **2.** *n.* Arjantin; *the ~* Arjantin.

ar.gil [ˈɑːdʒil] *n.* kil, balçık; **ar.gil.la.ceous** [-ˈleiʃəs] *adj.* killi, balçıklı.

ar.gon CHEM [ˈɑːgɔn] *n.* argon.

ar.gu.a.ble [ˈɑːgjuəbl] □ tartışılabilir;

ar.gue [ˈɑːgjuː] *vb.* münakaşa etm., tartışmak; ileri sürmek, ispat etm.; ~ *s.o. into doing s.th. b-ni bşi* yapmağa ikna etm.; ~ *s.o. out of doing s.th. b-ni bşi* yapmaktan caydırmak.

ar.gu.ment [ˈɑːgjumənt] *n.* tartışma, münakaşa; delil, fikir; özet; **ar.gu.men.tation** [-menˈteiʃən] *n.* ispat; tartışma, münakaşa; **ar.gu.men.ta.tive** □ [-ˈmentətiv] tartışmacı, münakaşacı; delil nevinden.

a.ri.a MUS [ˈɑːriə] *n.* arya, şan solosu.

ar.id [ˈærid] □ kurak, çorak; cansıkıcı (*a. fig.*); **a'rid.i.ty** *n.* kuraklık, çoraklık.

a.right [əˈrait] *adv.* doğru olarak.

a.rise [əˈraiz] *irr. v/i.* kalkmak, çıkmak, doğmak (*from -den*); **a.ris.en** [əˈrizn] *p.p. of* **arise**.

ar.is.toc.ra.cy [ærisˈtɔkrəsi] *n.* aristokrasi (*a. fig.*); **a.ris.to.crat** [ˈ-təkræt] *n.* aristokrat; **a.ris.to'crat.ic**, **a.ris.to'c-rat.i.cal** □ aristokrasiye ait; mümtaz, kibar.

a.rith.me.tic [əˈriθmətik] *n.* aritmetik, hesap; **a.rith.met.i.cal** □ [æriθˈmeti-kəl] aritmetikle ilgili.

ark [ɑːk] *n.* tahta sandık; mavna; *Kutsal Kitap*: *Noah's ~* Nuh'un gemisi; ♀ *of the Covenant* On Emir'in yazılı olduğu taşları havi sandık.

arm[1] [ɑːm] *n.* kol; pazu; dal; şube; koy, küçük körfez; güç, otorite; *within ~'s reach* elin yetişeceği uzaklıkta, yakın; *keep s.o. at ~'s length* b-ni yanına yaklaştırmamak, yüz vermemek; *infant in ~s* meme çocuğu, bebek.

arm[2] [.] **1.** *n. mst. ~s pl.* silah; *mst ~s sg.* silahlı kuvvetlerin bir kolu; *~s pl.* arma; *s. coat*; *be (all) up in ~s* ayaklanmak; öfkelenmek, ateş püskürmek, tepesi atmak; *take up ~s* silaha sarılmak; **2.** *vb.* silahlandırmak, donatmak; silahlanmak, silaha sarılmak.

ar.ma.da [ɑːmɑːdə] *n.* donanma; *the* (*Invincible*) ♀ İspanya tarafından 1588 de İngiltere'ye gönderilen ve İngilizere mağlûp olan donanma.

ar.ma.ment ['ɑːməmənt] *n.* teçhizat *pl.*, silahlar; silahlandırma; *mst. pl.* silahlı kuvvetler; *naval ~* deniz kuvvetleri; *~ race* silahlanma yarışı; **ar.ma-ture** ['‿tjuə] *n.* zırh; ARCH, PHYS armatur, mıknatısın iki kutbu arasına yerleştirilen demir parçası, endüvi.

arm.chair ['ɑːm'tʃɛə] *n.* koltuk.

armed [ɑːmd] *adj.* silahlı; *~ forces pl.* silahlı kuvvetler.

...-armed [ɑːmd] *adj.* ...kollu.

Ar.me.ni.an [ɑːˈmiːnjən] *adj. & n.* Ermeni; Ermenice.

arm.ful ['ɑːmful] *n.* kucak dolusu.

ar.mi.stice ['ɑːmistis] *n.* mütareke, ateşkes (*a. fig.*).

arm.let ['ɑːmlit] *n.* pazıbent; haliç, koy.

ar.mo.ri.al [ɑːˈmɔːriəl] *adj.* armaya ait.

ar.mo(u)r ['ɑːmə] **1.** *n.* MIL silah, (*a. fig.*, ZOO) zırh; dalgıç takımı; MIL F zırhlı vasıta; **2.** *vb.* zırh kaplamak, zırhlamak; *~ed car* zırhlı otomobil; *~ed division* zırhlı tümen; *~ed turret* zırhlı taret; '*~-clad*, '*~-plat.ed adj.* zırhlı; zırhlı...; '**ar.mour.er** *n.* zırhçı, silahçı; MIL, NAUT tüfekçi ustası; '**ar.mo(u)r.y** *n.* silah deposu (*a. fig.*); *Am.* silah fabrikası.

arm.pit ['ɑːmpit] *n.* koltuk altı; '**arm-rest** *n.* kol dayanacak yer.

ar.my ['ɑːmi] *n.* kara ordusu; *fig.* ordu, kalabalık, sürü; *~ chaplain* ordu papazı (*veya* imamı); *s.* service; '*~-corps* *n.* kolordu; '*~-list* *n.* MIL ordu subay listesi.

a.ro.ma [əˈrəumə] *n.* güzel koku, rayiha, aroma; **ar.o.mat.ic** [ærəuˈmætik] □ (*~ally*) güzel kokulu, rayihalı.

a.rose [əˈrəuz] *pret. of* **arise**.

a.round [əˈraund] **1.** *adv. -in* etrafın(-d)a, yakında, civarda; civarında, sularında; *Am.* F buralarda; **2.** *prp.* etrafın(d)a; civarında; dört bir yanın(-d)a; orada burada, oraya buraya.

a.rouse [əˈrauz] *v/t.* uyandırmak, canlandırmak; *fig.* b-ni harekete geçirmek; tabrik, teşvik etm.

ar.rack ['ærək] *n.* rakı.

ar.raign [əˈrein] *v/t.* suçlamak, itham etm., mahkemeye vermek; *fig.* azarlamak, paylamak; **ar'raign.ment** *n.* sanığın sorguya çekilmesi, iddianamenin tefhimi ve sorguya çekme muameleleri.

ar.range [əˈreindʒ] *v/t.* tanzim etm., düzenlemek; *part.* MUS aranjman yapmak; (*gün*) kararlaştırmak; (*anlaşmazlık*) arabuluculuk etm., bertaraf etm., bitirmek; hazırlamak; *v/i.* gerekli hazırlıkları yapmak (*for* için); **ar'range.ment** *n.* düzenleme, tanzim; düzen, sıra; hazırlık; anlaşma; düzenlenmiş şey; MUS aranjman; *make one's ~s* tertibatta bulunmak.

ar.rant □ ['ærənt] tamamen, son derece; çok kötü.

ar.ray [əˈrei] **1.** *n.* saf, sıra, düzen; ordu; teşhir; gösterişli kıyafet; **2.** *v/t.* sıraya koymak, düzenlemek; giydirmek, süslemek.

ar.rear [əˈriə] *n.* sürümcemede bırakılan (*iş vs.*); ödenmemiş (*borç vs.*); *~s of rent* ödenmemiş kira borcu; *be in ~s* borcu vaktinde ödeyememek; **ar'rear.age** *n.* vaktinde ödenmemiş borcun bakiyesi.

ar.rest [əˈrest] **1.** *n.* tutuklama, tevkif; durdurma; *under ~* tutuklu; **2.** *v/t.* tutuklamak, tevkif etm.; durdurmak; çekmek, celbetmek (*dikkat*).

ar.riv.al [əˈraivəl] *n.* geliş, varış; gelen kimse; *a new ~* yeni gelen; **ar'rive** *v/i.* varmak, vâsıl olm. (*at -e*), yetişmek; başarmak.

ar.ro.gance [ˈærəugəns] *n.* kibir, gurur; küstahlık, kendini bilmezlik; '**ar-ro.gant** □ kibirli, mağrur; küstah; **ar-ro.gate** ['‿geit] *v/t. mst. ~ to o.s.* (*haksız yere*) benimsemek, kendine maletmek, iddia etm.; *~ s.th. to s.o.* bşi b-ne maletmek.

ar.row ['ærəu] *n.* ok; '*~-head* *n.* ok başı, temren; '*~-root* *n.* BOT ararot.

arse *sl.* [ɑːs] *n.* göt, makat, kıç.

ar.se.nal ['ɑːsinl] *n.* silah ve mühimmat deposu, tophane; tersane.

ar.se.nic ['ɑːsnik] *n.* arsenik, sıçanotu; **ar.sen.i.cal** [ɑː'senikəl] *adj.* arseniğe ait, arsenikli.

ar.son JUR ['ɑːsn] *n.* kundakçılık, kasten yangın çıkarma.

art¹ [ɑːt] *n.* sanat, hüner, marifet, maharet, ustalık; ilim dalı; **~s** *pl.* ilimler; **Master of ~s** (*abbr.* M.A.) edebiyat fakültesi diploması ile doktora arasında bir derece; **fine ~s** *pl.* güzel sanatlar; **Liberal ~s** edebiyat ve beşerî ilimler; **~s and crafts** el işleri; **Faculty of ~s** Edebiyat Fakültesi.

art² *obs.* [-] sen(sin).

ar.te.ri.al [ɑː'tiəriəl] *adj.* atardamara ait; atardamara benzer; temiz kanla ilgili; **~ road** anayol; **ar.te.ri.o.scle.ro-sis** MED [ɑː'tiəriəusklio'rəusis] *n.* damar sertliği, arteriyoskleroz; **ar.ter.y** ['ɑːtəri] *n.* atardamar, arter; *fig.* büyük cadde, anayol.

ar.te.sian well [ɑː'tiːzjən'wel] *n.* artezyen kuyusu.

art.ful [] ['ɑːtful] kurnaz; ustalıklı, maharet isteyen.

art gal.ler.y ['ɑːt'gæləri] sanat galerisi.

ar.thrit.ic MED [ɑː'θritik] *adj.* mafsala ait, mafsal iltihabına ait; **ar.thri.tis** [ɑː'θraitis] *n.* mafsal iltihabı.

ar.ti.choke BOT ['ɑːtitʃəuk] *n.* enginar.

ar.ti.cle ['ɑːtikl] **1.** *n.* makale; madde, fıkra, fasıl; nesne, madde; GR tanım edatı; **~s of apprenticeship** usta ile çırak arasında anlaşma; **~s of associ-ation** şirket mukavelenamesi, statüsü; **2.** *v/t.* b-ni mukavele ile başkasının yanına vermek (*tatbikî eğitim için*); maddeler halinde düzenlemek; **~d clerk** staj gören kâtip.

ar.tic.u.late 1. [ɑː'tikjuleit] *vb.* eklem ile birleştirmek; eklem oluşturmak; ifade etm., açıkça söylemek, dikkatle telâffuz etm.; **2.** [] [-lit] açık, seçkin; düşünce ve hislerini rahatça anlatan; mafsallı, eklemli; **ar'tic.u.lat.ed** [-leitid] *adj.* mafsallı; **ar.tic.u'la.tion** *n.* ses teşkili; telâffuz; mafsal, eklem; bitiştirme.

ar.ti.fact ['ɑːtifækt] *n.* insan eliyle yapılan faydalı şey.

ar.ti.fice ['ɑːtifis] *n.* hile, oyun, kurnazlık; ustalık, marifet; **ar'tif.i.cer** *n.* usta işçi, sanatkâr; eser sahibi; askerî teknisyeni; **ar.ti.fi.cial** [] [-'fiʃəl] yapma, sunî; taklit; sahte, yapmacık; **~ silk** sunî ipek; **~ insemination** sunî ilkah; **~ person** JUR hükmî şahıs, tüzel kişi.

ar.til.ler.y [ɑː'tiləri] *n.* toplar, ağır silahlar; topçuluk; topçu (*sınıfı*); **ar'til.ler.y-man** [-mən] *n.* topçu eri.

ar.ti.san [ɑːti'zæn] *n.* zanaatçı, endüstri işçisi.

art.ist ['ɑːtist] *n.* sanatkâr, *part.* ressam; sahne sanatçısı; *sl.* düzenbaz, numaracı kimse; **ar.tiste** [ɑː'tiːst] *n.* (*profes-yonel*) şarkıcı, oyuncu, dansöz; **ar.tis-tic, ar.tis.ti.cal** [] [ɑː'tistik(əl)] artistik, sanat yönü olan, sanatkârane, güzel sanatlara ait.

art.less [] ['ɑːtlis] sade, saf, hilesiz; işlenmemiş, doğal; kaba; **'art.less-ness** *n.* saflık, hilesiz oluş.

art.y ['ɑːti] *adj.* sanatkârane, gösterişli.

Ar.y.an ['εəriən] **1.** *adj.* Aryen, Hint-Avrupa grubuna veya diline ait; **2.** *n.* Arî, Hint-Avrupalı.

as [æz, əz] *adv. & cj.* gibi, kadar; iken; -*diği gibi*; -*den* dolayı; -*mekle* beraber; çünkü, mademki, nitekim; **~ a rule** genellikle; **~ if, ~ though** sanki, güya; **~ for, ~ to** -*e* gelince, -*e* sorarsanız, hakkında; **so ~ to go** gitmek için; **~ good ~** hemen hemen; gerçekten; **be ~ good ~ one's word** dediğini yapmak, sözünü tutmak; **~ long ~** mademki, ... olması şartıyle, ... dikçe, ...dıkça; olduğu sürece; **I thought ~** much zaten bunu bekliyordum; **~ from** -*den* başlıyarak, itibaren; **~ per** -*e* göre, nazaran; **~ yet** şimdiye kadar; **~ it were** âdeta; sanki, güya; **~ well** de, da, dahi, bile; **~ well ~** gibi, kadar, -*e* ilâveten.

as.bes.tos [æz'bestɔs] *n.* amyant, asbest.

as.cend [ə'send] *vb.* çıkmak, yukarı çıkmak, yükselmek, tırmanmak -*e*; (*nehir*) akıntıya karşı gitmek; (*tahta*) çıkmak; **as'cend.an.cy** *n.* (**over**) üstünlük; nüfuz; **as'cend.ant 1.** *adj.* yükselen; üstün, hâkim (**over** -*e*); **2.** *n.* **ascendancy**; üstünlük; nüfuz, itibar; cet, dede; **be in the ~** *fig.* itibarı artmak, yükselmek; **as'cend.en.cy, as'cend.ent = ascendancy, ascendant.**

as.cen.sion [ə'senʃən] *n.* yükselme, yukarı çıkış (*part.* AST); **~ (Day)** Urucu İsa, İsa'nın göğe çıkışı (*günü*).

as.cent [ə'sent] *n.* çıkış, tırmanma; yokuş, bayır.

as.cer.tain [æsə'tein] *v/t.* soruşturmak, öğrenmek, gerçeği bulmak; **as.cer-'tain.able** [] soruşturulabilir, anlaşılabilir; **ascer'tain.ment** *n.* soruşturma, anlama.

as.cet.ic [ə'setik] **1.** □ (~*ally*) zahit, münzevi, dünyevi zevklerden el çekmiş; **2.** *n.* din uğruna dünyevi zevklerden el çekmiş kimse, sofu kimse, derviş; **as'cet.icism** [‿tisizəm] *n.* aşırı sofuluk, zahitlik; gösterişten uzak bir hayat sürme.

as.cor.bic ac.id [əs'kɔːbik'æsid] *n.* C vitamini

as.crib.a.ble [əs'kraibəbl] *adj.* atfolunabilir, yüklenebilir (*to* -*e*); **as'cribe** *v/t.* (*to*) atfetmek, hamletmek, yüklemek -*e*.

a.sep.tic MED [æ'septik] *adj.* aseptik, mikropsuz.

ash[1] [æʃ] *n.* BOT dişbudak ağacı; dişbudak kerestesi.

ash[2] [‿] *mst.* **ash.es** ['‿ʃiz] *n. pl.* kül; **Ash Wednesday** Paskalyadan evvelki perhizin ilk Çarşambası.

a.shamed [ə'ʃeimd] □ mahcup, utanmış; **be** *veya* **feel** ~ **of** utanmak -*den*.

ash-bin ['æʃbin], *Am.* **ash-can** ['æʃkæn] *n.* çöp tenekesi.

ash.en[1] ['æʃn] *adj.* dişbudaktan yapılmış.

ash.en[2] [‿] *adj.* kül gibi; kül renginde, soluk renkli.

a.shore [ə'ʃɔː] *adv.* karada, karaya, sahil(d)e; **run** ~, **be driven** ~ karaya oturmak.

ash...: '~-**pan** *n.* ocak küllüğü; '~-**tray** *n.* kül tablası.

ash...: '~-**tree** *n.* BOT dişbudak ağacı; '~-**wood** *n.* dişbudak kerestesi.

ash.y ['æʃi] *adj.* küllü, külle kaplı; kül rengi.

A.sia ['eiʃə] *n.* Asya

A.sian-A.mer.i.can [eiʃənə'merikən] *adj. & n.* Asya kökenli Amerikalı.

A.si.at.ic [eiʃi'ætik] **1.** *adj.* Asya kıtasına *veya* halkına ait; **2.** *n.* Asyalı.

a.side [ə'said] **1.** *adv.* bir tarafa, yana, kendi kendine, başka (**from** -*den*); **2.** *n.* THEAT bir oyuncunun sahnede seyirciye alçak sesle söylediği sözler.

as.i.nine ['æsinain] *adj.* eşekçe, eşeğe ait; aptal.

ask [ɑːsk] *v/t. & v/i.* sormak -*e*; davet etm., teklif etm.; istemek; rica etm. -*den*; ~ **for** aramak, sormak -*i*; talep etm., istemek -*i*; ~ **the price** *b*-*şin* fiyatını sormak; ~ (**s.o.**) **a question** (*b*-*ne*) bir soru sormak; ~ (**him**) **his name** *b*-*ne* ismini sormak; ~ **s.th. of s.o.** birisinden *bş* talep etm.; **you are**

~ing too much çok şey istiyorsun; ~ **s.o. for help** (*b*-*den*) yardım istemek; ~ **s.o. to come** *b*-*ni* davet etm.; ~ **s.o. to dinner** *b*-*ni* yemeğe davet etm.; ~ **s.o. in** *b*-*ni* eve (içeriye) davet etm.; **he ~ed for it** *veya* **for trouble** çanak tuttu, kendi istedi; **to be had for the ~ing** istemeniz kâfidir, parasız verilir.

a.skance [əs'kæns], **a'skant, as.kew** [əs'kjuː] *adv.* yan, yan tarafa, göz ucuyla; beğenmeyerek.

a.slant [ə'slɑːnt] **1.** *adj. & adv.* bir yana doğru, eğri, meyilli; **2.** *prp.* üzerinden meyilli olarak.

a.sleep [ə'sliːp] **1.** *adj.* uykuda, uyumuş; uyuşmuş (*uzuv, organ*); **2.** *adv.* uyurken; **be** ~ uyumak, uykuda olm.; **fall** ~ uykuya dalmak; **sound** ~ derin uykuda.

asp[1] ZOO [æsp] *n.* engerek yılanı.

asp[2] BOT [‿] *n.* telli (*a. titrek*) kavak.

as.par.a.gus BOT [əs'pærəgəs] *n.* kuşkonmaz.

as.pect ['æspekt] *n.* görüş, bakış; görünüş; yüz, çehre; safha, durum, hal (*a.* GR); **the house has a southern** ~ ev güneye bakıyor.

as.pen ['æspən] *n.* telli (*a. titrek*) kavak.

as.per.gill, as.per.gil.lum ECCL ['æspədʒil, ‿'dʒiləm] *n.* Katoliklerin (*kilisede*) kutsal su serpmek için kullandıkları küçük fırça.

as.per.i.ty [æs'periti] *n.* kabalık, şiddet; pürüz, sertlik (*a. fig.*); zorluk, güçlük.

as.perse [əs'pəːs] *v/t.* serpmek, atmak; *fig.* lekelemek, çamur atmak, iftira etm.; **as.per.sion** *n.* serpme; *fig.* iftira, leke.

as.phalt ['æsfælt] **1.** *n.* asfalt; **2.** *vb.* asfaltlamak.

as.pho.del BOT ['æsfədel] *n.* çirişotu.

as.phyx.i.a [æs'fiksiə] *n.* asfeksi, boğulma (*havagası vs. ile*); **as'phyx.i-ate** [‿eit] *vb.* boğ(ul)mak; **as.phyx.i-'a.tion** *n.* boğ(ul)ma.

as.pic ['æspik] *n.* dondurulmuş (*veya* jelâtinli) et.

as.pi.dis.tra BOT [æspi'distrə] *n.* aspidistra, yaprakları yeşil benekli bir salon bitkisi.

as.pir.ant [əs'paiərənt] *n.* tâlip, namzet, istekli (**to, after, for.** -*e*); ~ **officer** subay adayı; **as.pi.rate** ['æspərit] **1.** GR *adj.* «h» sesiyle telâffuz edilen; **2.** GR *n.* «h» sesi, «h» harfi; «h» gibi ses çıkarma; **3.** ['-reit] *vb.* GR «h» sesiyle telâffuz etm.; MEC, MED emmek, içine çekmek; **as.pi'ra.tion** *n.* arzu, istek; önemli ve büyük bir işi gaye edinme; «h» harfinin telâffuzu; MEC, MED emme, içine çekme; **as'pire** [əs'paiə] *vb.* şiddetle arzu etm., elde etmeğe çalışmak (*after veya to -i*).

as.pi.rin PHARM ['æspərin] *n.* aspirin.

as.pir.ing □ [əs'paiəriŋ] gözü ileride olan, bir gayesi olan.

ass [æs] *n.* eşek; *make an ~ of o.s.* aptalca davranmak, aptallık etm..

as.sail [ə'seil] *v/t.* saldırmak, hücum etm. *-e* (*a. fig.*); *fig.* tecavüz etm., dil uzatmak (*with ile*); işe girişmek; **as'saila.ble** *adj.* tecavüz edilebilir; **as'sail.ant, as'sail.er** *n.* saldıran kimse, mütecaviz kimse.

as.sas.sin [ə'sæsin] *n.* katil; **as'sas.si.nate** [-neit] *v/t.* (*sinsice*) adam öldürmek; **as.sas.si'na.tion** *n.* suikast, adam öldürme.

as.sault [ə'sɔːlt] **1.** *n.* saldırı, taarruz, hücum, hamle (*a. fig.* **on, upon** *-e*); MIL hücum; JUR şahsa karşı fiili tecavüz, müessir fiil yapmağa teşebbüs; *s.* **battery, indecent; 2.** *v/t.* saldırmak, hücum etm., tecavüz etm. *-e*; JUR müessir fiile teşebbüs etm.; MIL hücum etm., saldırmak (*a. fig.*).

as.say [ə'sei] **1.** *n.* deneme, tecrübe; tahlil; ayar için alınan madde; **2.** *v/t.* tahlil etm., analiz yapmak; denemek; *v/i. Am.* kıymetli maden ihtiva etm..

as.sem.blage [ə'semblidʒ] *n.* toplantı; kalabalık; bir araya topla(n)ma; MEC montaj; **as'sem.ble** *vb.* topla(n)mak, birleş (tir)mek; bir araya gelmek (*veya* getirmek); MEC takmak, kurmak, monte etm.; **as'sem.bly** *n.* toplantı, kongre, meclis; MEC montaj; **~ shop** montaj atelyesi; **~ hall** konferans salonu; montaj atelyesi; **~ line** sürekli iş bandı; **~ man** POL meclis üyesi.

as.sent [ə'sent] **1.** *n.* rıza, muvafakat, onay; **2.** *v/i.* razı olm., muvafakat etm. *-e*.

as.sert [ə'sɔːt] *v/t.* ileri sürmek, iddia etm.; ısrar etm.; *~ o.s.* kendini göstermek, otoritesini kabul ettirmek; **as'sertion** *n.* öne sürme, iddia, teyit; **as'ser.tive** □ iddiacı; kendine fazla güvenir; **as'sertor** *n.* iddiacı kimse.

as.sess [ə'ses] *v/t.* (*vergi vs. için*) mülk değerini veya gelir miktarını hesaplamak, tayin (*takdir*) etm., tarh etm.,

bağlamak (*at -e*); **as'sess.a.ble** □ vergi tayini için değeri takdir olunabilen, takdiri kabil (*vergi*); **as'sess.ment** *n.* vergi takdiri; vergi matrahı; tahakkuk; **as'ses.sor** *n.* vergi tahakkuk memuru; yalnız istişari oya sahip olan mahkeme üyesi; muhammin.

as.set ['æset] *n.* COM aktif; fayda temin eden şey; kâr; **~s** *pl.* aktifler, mevcudat, değer; bir şahıs veya şirketin sahip olduğu menkul ve gayrimenkuller ile alacak haklarının tümü.

as.sev.er.ate [ə'sevəreit] *v/t.* tekrar tekrar beyan ve iddia etm.; **as.sev.er-'a.tion** *n.* iddia, beyan.

as.si.du.i.ty [æsi'djuːiti] *n.* çalışkanlık, gayret, sebat; **as.sid.u.ous** □ [ə'sidjuəs] çalışkan, gayretli, sebatkâr.

as.sign [ə'sain] *v/t.* ayırmak, tahsis etm. (*to -e*); tayin etm., atamak (*to -e*); JUR alacağını temlik etm. veya devretmek; üstüne çevirmek, ferağ etm.; **as'sign.able** □ tayini mümkün, tahsisi mümkün; devredilebilen, temlik edilebilen; **as.signa.tion** [æsig'neiʃən] *n.* randevu (*esp. gizli ve sevgili ile*); *s.* **assignment; assign.ee** [æsi'niː] *n.* devralan, temellük eden; bir yedi adil, yediemin; **~ in bankruptcy** müflisin malı üzerine hâkim tarafından tayin olunan vekil; **as.sign.ment** [ə'sainmənt] *n.* tayin, atama; *part. Am.* vazife, ödev, görev; JUR devir ve temlik; **as.sign.or** [æsi'nɔː] *n.* JUR bir menkul veya gayrımenkulü yahut bir hak veya menfaati başkasına devreden kimse.

as.sim.i.late [ə'simileit] *v/t.* (**to, into, with**) benzetmek, uydurmak *-e*; bağdaştırmak *-le*; *bşi* özümsemek, hazmetmek, emmek; **as.sim.i'la.tion** *n.* benzeyiş, benzeşme; özümseme, hazım, emme.

as.sist [ə'sist] *v/t.* yardım etm. *-e.* desteklemek; *v/i.* hazır bulunmak (*at -de*); **as'sist.ance** *n.* yardım, müzaheret, iane; **as'sist.ant** *n.* yardımcı, muavin, asistan; **as'sist.ed** liv.ing *yaşlı ya da hasta kimselere yemek yemek ve yıkanmak gibi günlük işlerde yardım edilmesi*; **as'sist.ed su.i.cide** *ölümcül bir hastanın başkalarının yardımıyla intihar etmesi.*

as.size JUR [ə'saiz] *n.* bir hakim ve jüri tarafından muhakeme; bu kurulda alınan karar; **~s** *pl.* geçici mahkeme (*İngiltere'de*).

as.so.ci.a.ble [ə'səuʃjəbl] *adj.* birleş

(-tiril) ebilir; uyum sağlıyabilir; bağlantısı olabilen (**with** *ile*); as'**so.ci.ate** **1.** [-ʃieit] *vb.* birleştirmek, ortak etm., arkadaş etm. -*i*; arkadaşlık etm., ortaklık kurmak (**with** *ile*); ortak olm. (**with** -*e*), katılmak -*e*; yakıştırmak, aralarında ilişki kurmak; **2.** [-ʃiit] *n.* arkadaş, dost; üye; COM ortak, şerik, hissedar; **3.** [-ʃiit] *adj.* tam yetki sahibi olmayan, yardımcı; tam üyelik haklarından yararlanamayan; ortak olan; as.**so.ci.a.tion** [-si'eiʃən] *n.* kurul, kurum, cemiyet; birleşme, ortaklık; arkadaşlık, birlik; şirket; tedai, çağrışım; ~ **football** futbol.

as.**so.nance** ['æsəunəns] *n.* ses benzeyişi; yarım kafiye.

as.**sort** [ə'sɔːt] *v/t.* tasnif etm., sınıflandırmak; COM mal çeşidi uydurmak; *v/i.* (**with**) uymak, uygun olm., yakışmak -*e*; ~**ed** *adj.* çeşitli; as'**sort.ment** *n.* tasnif, sınıflandırma; COM çeşit, mal çeşidi.

as.**suage** [ə'sweidʒ] *v/t.* yumuşatmak, yatıştırmak, hafifletmek, teskin etm.; (*açlık vs.*) gidermek.

as.**sume** [ə'sjuːm] *v/t.* (*bir iş veya görevi*) üzerine almak; gerçekmiş gibi kabul etm., farzetmek; (*sahip olmadığı bşi*) var gibi göstermek; as'**sum.ing** □ azametli, kibirli, küstah; as.**sump.tion** [ə'sʌmpʃən] *n.* farz, zan; tavır, poz; üstüne alma; kibir, azamet, kendini satma; ♀ (**Day**) Urucu Meryem, Meryem'in göğe kabulü yortusu; **on the** ~ **that** beanşart ki; as'**sump.tive** □ farzolunan, zannedilen; kibirli.

as.**sur.ance** [ə'ʃuərəns] *n.* temin; güven, itimat; söz, teminat; inanç; kendine güvenme; pişkinlik, yüzsüzlük; (*part. hayat*) sigorta; as'**sure** *v/t.* temin etm.; söz vermek -*e*; sigorta etm. -*i*; ~ **o.s.** bşden emin olm.; as'**sured** **1.** *adj.* (*adv.* as'**sur.ed.ly** [-ridli]) emin, şayanı itimat; müemmen, sağlanmış; *k-den* emin olan; *b.s.* pişkin, küstah, **2.** *n.* sigortalı kimse; as'**sur.er** [-rə] *n.* sigortalı; *a.* = as'**sur.or** [-rə] *n.* sigorta eden, sigortacı.

As.**syr.i.an** [ə'siriən] **1.** *adj.* Asurca; **2.** *n.* Asuri.

as.**ter** BOT ['æstə] *n.* yıldız çiçeği; as'**ter.isk** TYP ['-risk] *n.* yıldız işareti.

a.**stern** NAUT [ə'stəːn] *adv.* geriye, arkaya, arkada, kıç tarafında, kıçında; **fall** ~ (**of**) bir geminin gerisinde kalmak.

as.**ter.oid** AST ['æstərɔid] *n.* küçük ge-

zegen, asteroid.

asth.**ma** ['æsmə] *n.* nefes darlığı, astma; asth.**mat.ic** [-'mætik] **1.** *a.* asth-'**mat.i.cal** □ astma ile ilgili, astmalı; **2.** *n.* astmalı kimse.

as.**tig.mat.ic** OPT [æstig'mætik] *adj.* (~**ally**) astigmatik; a'**stig.ma.tism** [-mətizəm] *n.* astigmatizm.

a.**stir** [ə'stəː] *adj.* harekette, faaliyette; heyecanlı.

as.**ton.ish** [əs'tɔniʃ] *v/t.* şaşırtmak, hayrete düşürmek; **be** ~**ed** şaşmak, hayret etm. (**at** -*e*); as'**ton.ish.ing** □ şaşırtıcı, hayret verici; as'**ton.ish.ment** *n.* şaşkınlık, hayret.

as.**tound** [əstaund] *v/t.* hayretten dondurmak; son derece şaşırtmak.

as.**tra.khan** [æstrə'kæn] *n.* astragan, yeni doğmuş kuzu postu.

a.**stray** [əs'trei] *adj. & adv.* yolunu şaşırmış, doğru yoldan çıkmış, sapıtmış (*a. fig.*); **go** ~ yolunu şaşırmak; yanlış yola sapmak (*a. fig.*).

a.**stride** [əs'traid] *adv.* bacakları ayrılmış, ata biner gibi.

as.**trin.gent** □ MED [əs'trindʒənt] kanı durduran (*ilaç*); kabız, sıkıştırıcı, büzücü.

as.**tro.dome** AVIA ['æstrədəum] *n.* uçağın üst kısmında astronomik gözlem için kullanılan pencere.

as.**trol.o.ger** [əs'trɔlədʒə] *n.* müneccim, astrolog; as.**tro.log.i.cal** □ [æstrə'lɔdʒikəl] astrolojiye ait; as.**trol.o.gy** [əs'trɔlədʒi] *n.* müneccimlik, astroloji.

as.**tro.naut** ['æstrənɔːt] *n.* astronot.

as.**tro.nau.tics** ['æstrəu'nɔːtiks] *n.* uzay araçları yapım ve işletme ilmi.

as.**tron.o.mer** [əs'trɔnəmə] *n.* astronom; as.**tro.nom.i.cal** □ [æstrə'nɔmikəl] **1.** astronomi ile ilgili; **2.** çok fazla, aşırı, astronomik; as'**tron.o.my** [əs-'trɔnəmi] *n.* astronomi, yıldızlar ilmi; as.**tro.phys.ics** [æstrəu'fiziks] *n.* yıldızların ışığını inceleyen ve fizik yapılarını araştıran bilim kolu, gökfiziği, astrofizik.

as.**tute** □ [əs'tjuːt] keskin zekâlı, cin fikirli; as.**tute.ness** *n.* kurnazlık, cin fikirlilik.

a.**sun.der** [ə'sʌndə] *adv.* ayrı, ayrılmış, parçalara ayrılmış.

a.**sy.lum** [ə'sailəm] *n.* melce, sığınacak (*veya* barınacak) yer; himaye, koruma; (**lunatic**) ~ tımarhane.

a.**sym.me.try** [æ'simitri] *n.* oransızlık,

simetrik olmama.

at [æt; ət] *prp.* -da, -de; -a, -e; *-in* üstün (d)e; yanın(d)a; halinde, üzere; **~ the door** kapıda; **~ my expense** masraflar bana ait olmak üzere, benim hesabıma; **run ~ s.o.** saldırmak *-e*; **~ daybreak** şafakta; **~ table** sofrada; **~ a low price** düşük fiyatla; **~ peace** sulhta, barışta; **~ the age of** yaşında; **~ one blow** bir vuruşta; **~ five o'clock** saat beşte; **~ Christmas** Noel'de.

at.a.vism BIOL ['ætəvizəm] *n.* atavizm, atacılık, atalara çekiş.

a.tax.y. MED [ə'tæksi] *n.* beden faaliyetlerinde düzensizlik.

ate [et] *pret. of eat 1.*

a.the.ism ['eiθiizəm] *n.* ateizm, tanrıtanımazlık; **'a.the.ist** *n.* ateist, tanrıyı inkâr eden kimse; **a.the'is.tic, a.the-'is.ti.cal** □ tanrıyı tanımayan, allahsız.

A.the.ni.an [ə'θi:njən] **1.** *adj.* Atina'ya ait, Atinalı; **2.** *n.* Atinalı.

a.thirst [ə'θə:rst] *adj.* istekli, susamış, teşne (*for -e*).

ath.lete ['æθli:t] *n.* atlet, sporcu; **~'s foot** MED mantar; **ath.let.ic** [æθ'letik], **ath'let.i.cal** □ atletik; kuvvetli; **ath-'let.ics** *n. pl.* atletizm.

at-home [ət'houm] *n.* küçük ve samimi ev toplantısı, kabul.

a.thwart [ə'θwɔ:t] **1.** *prp.* bir yandan karşı yana; karşı, zıt; **2.** *adv.* aykırı, karşı; çapraz, NAUT alabandadan alabandaya.

a-tilt [ə'tilt] *adj. & adv.* eğilmiş, çarpık, yana oturmuş.

At.lan.tic [ət'læntik] **1.** *adj.* Atlas Okyanusu ile ilgili; **2.** *n. a.* **~ Ocean** Atlas Okyanusu.

at.las ['ætləs] *n.* atlas (*kitap*).

ATM [eiti:'em] *n.* bankamatik.

at.mos.phere ['ætməsfiə] *n.* havaküre, atmosfer; *fig.* hava, muhit, çevre; **at-mospher.ic, at.mos.pher.i.cal** □ [-'ferik(əl)] havaya ait, atmosferik; **at-mos'pher.ics** *n. pl.* (*radyoda*) parazit.

at.oll GEOGR ['ætɔl] *n.* atol, mercanada.

at.om CHEM, PHYS ['ætəm] *n.* atom, zerre (*a. fig.*); **~ bomb** atom bombası; **a.tom.ic** [ə'tɔmik] *adj.* atomla ilgili, atom...; **~ age** atom çağı; **~ bomb** atom bombası; **~ energy** nükleer enerji; **~ nucleus** atom çekirdeği; **~ number** atomal sayı; **~ pile** atom reaktörü; **~ power** atom enerjisi; **~ research** atom araştırması; **~ weight** atomal ağırlık; **a'tom.ic-powered** *adj.* atom enerjisiy-

le işleyen; **at.om.ize** ['ætəumaiz] *v/t.* atomlara ayırmak; (*sıvı*) püskürtmek; **'at.om.iz.er** *n.* pülvarizatör, püskürgeç; **at.o.my** ['ætəmi] *n. part. fig.* iskelet.

a.tone [ə'təun] *v/i.:* **~ for** bşi telâfi etm., bş için tarziye vermek, gönül onarımında bulunmak; **a'tone.ment** *n.* tarziye, gönül onarımı.

a.ton.ic [æ'tɔnik] *adj.* MED takatsız, zayıf; GR vurgusuz; **at.o.ny** [ætəni] *n.* MED takatsızlık, kuvvetsizlik.

a.top F [ə'tɔp] *adv. & prp.* üstte, üstünde, üzerinde (*of -in*).

a.tro.cious □ [ə'trəuʃəs] vahşî, tüyler ürpertici, menfur; **a.troc.i.ty** [ə'trɔsiti] *n.* gaddarlık, kötülük, canavarlık (*a. fig.*).

at.ro.phy MED ['ætrəfi] **1.** *n.* (*kansızlıktan*) zafiyet; dumur, atrofi; **2.** *vb.* dumura uğramak.

at-seat TV [æt'si:t 'ti:vi:] *taşıt araçlarında v.b. koltuğa takılan küçük televizyon.*

at.tach [ə'tætʃ] *v/t.* (*to*) bağlamak, yapıştırmak, bitiştirmek, takmak *-e*; (*imza*) basmak; JUR haczetmek, müsadere etm.; (*ad*) takmak; önem vermek; **~ o.s. to** iltihak etm., takılmak *-e*; **~ value to** bşe kıymet vermek, kıymet koymak; *v/i.* **~ to** yapışmak *-e*, ittihat etm., birleşmek *-le*; **at.ta.ché** [ə'tæʃei] *n.* ateşe; **~ case** evrak çantası; **at.tached** [ə'tætʃt]: **~ to** bağlı, ait, müteallik *-e*; hissen bağlı, tutkun *-e*; **at'tach.ment** *n.* bağlılık (*to, for -e*); sadakat, sevgi *-e*; ilâve, ek (*to -e*); MEC takılabilir bir parça; JUR tevkif, haciz; hapsen tazyik, icrai haciz.

at.tack [ə'tæk] **1.** *vb.* hücum etm., saldırmak *-e* (*a. fig.*); başına gelmek (*hastalık*); (*işe*) girişmek; *b-nin* aleyhinde söylemek; **2.** *n.* hücum, saldırma (*a. fig.*); MED nöbet, kriz; *b-nin* aleyhinde söyleme; **at'tack.er** *n.* mütecaviz, saldırgan.

at.tain [ə'tein] *v/t.* (*amaç*) ermek *-e*, elde etm. *-i*, kazanmak *-i*; *v/i.* **~ to** varmak, yetişmek, ulaşmak *-e*; **at'tain.a-ble** *adj.* varılması mümkün, ulaşılabilir; **at'tainder** JUR [-də] *n.* medenî ve siyasî haklardan iskat; **at'tain.ment** *n.* elde etme, erişme; hüner, marifet; **~s** *pl.* hüner ve beceriler.

at.tar [ætə] *n.:* **~ of roses** gülyağı.

at.tem.per [ə'tempə] *v/t.* yumuşatmak, sertliğini gidermek; uydurmak, intibak ettirmek (*to -e*).

at.tempt [ə'tempt] **1.** *v/t.* teşebbüs etm. *-e*, kasdetmek *-i*; denemek *-i*; ~ **the life of** *b-nin* hayatına kasdetmek; **2.** *n.* teşebbüs, gayret; suikast (**on** *veya* **upon s.o.'s life** *-e*).

at.tend [ə'tend] *v/t.* hazır bulunmak *-de*, refakat etm. *-e*; (*hasta*) bakmak *-e*, hizmet etm. *-e*; (*konferans vs.*) takibetmek; *v/i.* dikkat etm. (**to** *-e*), dinlemek *-i*; ~ **on** (*hasta*) bakmak, hizmet etm.; ~ **to** hizmet etm. *-e*, meşgul olm. *-le*; **at'tendance** *n.* refakat; hizmet, bakım; devam, gitme (*okul, kurs vs.*) *-e*; hazır bulunanlar (**at** *-de*); **hours of** ~ mesai (*veya* iş) saatleri; **be in** ~ hizmete hazır, emre amade olm.; **dance** ~ **on** F *b-nin* etrafında dört dönmek; **at'tend.ant 1.** *adj.* *b-nin* refakatinde ve hizmetinde bulunan; refakat eden, eşlik eden; mevcut olan, devam eden; **2.** *n.* hizmetçi; eşlik eden kimse; (*mağaza, müze, tiyatro vs. de*) görevli, memur.

at.ten.tion [ə'tenʃən] *n.* dikkat, ihtimam; iltifat, nezaket; ~**!** MIL hazır ol!; *s.* **call, give, pay**; **at'ten.tive** ☐ dikkatli; nazik (**to** *-e*).

at.ten.u.ate [ə'tenjueit] *v/t.* inceltmek, seyrekleştirmek, hafifletmek, azaltmak; *fig.* hafifletmek, gevşetmek.

at.test [ə'test] *vb.* şahadet etm., tasdik etm. (*a. fig.*); açıkça söylemek, iddia etm.; JUR tanıklık yapmak; *part.* MIL *b-ne* yemin ettirmek, yeminle bağlamak; **attes.ta.tion** [ætes'teiʃən] *n.* şahadet, tasdik; *part.* MIL yemin; **at.test.er, attest.or** [ə'testə] *n.* şahit, tanık.

At.tic¹ ['ætik] *adj.* Atinalı, Atina'ya ait; Atina lehçesi.

at.tic² [‿] *n.* damaltı, tavan arası; ~**s** *pl.* tavan arası katı.

at.tire *lit.* [ə'taiə] **1.** *v/t.* giydirmek; **2.** *n.* elbise.

at.ti.tude ['ætitjuːd] *n.* davranış, tavır; vaziyet alma (**to, towards** *-e*); AVIA meyil; **strike an** ~ poz almak, yapmacık tavırlar takınmak; ~ **of mind** zihniyet, ideoloji; **at.ti'tu.di.nize** [‿dinaiz] *v/i.* yapmacık tavır takınmak, vaziyet almak.

at.tor.ney [ə'tɔːni] *n.* vekil, mümessil, dâva vekili; *Am.* avukat; ~ **at law** avukat; **power of** ~ vekâletname; temsil yetkisi; Ω **General** başsavcı; *Am.* adalet bakanı, başsavcı.

at.tract [ə'trækt] *v/t. k-ne* çekmek, cez-

betmek (*a. fig.*); **at'trac.tion** [‿kʃən] *n.* çekme gücü, çekim; *fig.* alımlılık; eğlence programı, atraksiyon; PHYS çekim; **at'trac.tive** ☐ *mst fig.* çekici, alımlı, cazip.

at.trib.ut.a.ble [ə'tribjutəbl] *adj.* isnat olunabilir; atfolunabilir; **at.trib.ute** [ə'tribjuːt] *v/t.* yüklemek, isnat etm., atfetmek (**to** *-e*); **at.tri.bute** ['ætribjuːt] *n.* sıfat, nitelik; remiz, simge; GR yüklem; **at.tri'bu.tion** *n.* atfetme, hamletme, isnat, nitelik, sıfat; özellik; yetki; **at.tribu.tive** GR [ə'tribjutiv] **1.** ☐ niteleyici; **2.** *n.* sıfat.

at.tri.tion [ə'triʃən] *n.* yıpranma, aşınma, sürtüşme; MEC aşınma, eskime; **war of** ~ yıpratma harbi.

at.tune [ə'tjuːn] *v/t.* MUS akort etm.; ~ **to** *fig.* uydurmak, uyum sağlamak *-e*.

au.burn ['ɔːbən] *adj.* kestane rengi.

auc.tion ['ɔːkʃən] **1.** *n.* artırma ile satış, mezat; **sell by** (*Am.* **at**) ~, **put up for** ~ açık artırma ile satma; **2.** *v/t. mst* ~ **off** müzayedeye çıkarmak; **auc.tion.eer** [‿'niə] *n.* tellal, mezatçı.

au.da.cious ☐ [ɔː'deiʃəs] korkusuz, cüretkâr; *b.s.* küstah, arsız; **au.dac.i.ty** [ɔː'dæsiti] *n.* cüret; *b.s.* küstahlık.

au.di.bil.i.ty [ɔːdi'biliti] *n.* işitilebilme, duyulabilme; **au.di.ble** ☐ ['ɔːdəbl] işitilebilir, duyulabilir.

au.di.ence ['ɔːdjəns] *n.* dinleyiciler, seyirciler; huzura kabul, resmî görüşme; **give** ~ **to** huzura kabul etm.

au.di.o-fre.quen.cy ['ɔːdiəu'friːkwənsi] *n. radyo*: ses frekansı, alçak frekans.

au.di.o-vis.u.al ['ɔːdiəu'vizjuəl] **1.** *n.* görsel-işitsel sistem; **2.** *adj.* görsel-işitsel sistemle ilgili.

au.dit ['ɔːdit] **1.** *n.* hesapların resmî kontrolu, murakabe; **2.** *v/t.* hesapları kontrol etm.; **au'di.tion** *n.* işitme hassası, işitme kuvveti; THEAT (*bir şarkıcı, aktör vs.nin sesini sınamak için*) dinleme; **'au.di.tor.** *n.* dinleyici; kontrolör; hesap uzmanı, murakıp, **au.di.to.rium** [‿'tɔːriəm] *n.* konferans salonu; *Am.* festival salonu (*konferans, konser, toplantı vs. için*); **au.di.to.ry** ['‿təri] **1.** *adj.* işitme ile ilgili; **2.** *n.* dinleyiciler *pl.*; = **auditorium**.

au.ger MEC ['ɔːgə] *n.* avger, burgu, matkap.

aught [ɔːt] *n. & pron.* bir şey, herhangi bir şey; hiçbir şey; hiçbir şekilde; **for** ~ **I care** umurumda değil!, bana ne!; **for** ~ **I know** bildiğim kadarıyla.

aug.ment [ɔ:g'ment] *v/t.* büyütmek, artırmak, çoğaltmak; *v/i.* büyümek, artmak, çoğalmak; **aug.men'ta.tion** *n.* art(ır)ma, büyü(t)me, çoğal(t)ma.

au.gur ['ɔ:gə] **1.** *n. (eski Roma'da)* kâhin, falcı; **2.** *vb.* kehanet etm., önceden haber vermek; ~ **well** (*ill*) hayra (kötüye) alâmet olm. (*for* için); **au.gu.ry** ['ɔ:gjuri] *n.* kehanet; alâmet; falcılık.

Au.gust 1. ['ɔ:gəst] *n.* Ağustos ayı; **2.** ♀ □ [ɔ:'gʌst] aziz, yüce; **Augus.tan** [ɔ:'gʌstən] *adj.* Roma İmparatorluğu veya başka bir ülke edebiyatının en güzel çağına ait; klasik nitelikte.

auk ORN [ɔ:k] *n.* soğuk ülkelerde yaşayan bir cins deniz kuşu.

aunt [ɑ:nt] *n.* teyze; hala; yenge (*dayı veya amca karısı*); ♀ **Sally** oyuncuların eğlenmek için üzerine öteberi attıkları tahtadan yapılmış kadın; herkesin takıldığı kimse veya şey; **aunt.ie**, **aunt.y** F ['-ti] *n.* sevgili teyze, teyzecik.

au.ral ['ɔ:rəl] □ kulağa veya işitme duyusuna ait.

au.re.ole ECCL., AST ['ɔ:riəul] *n.* bale, nur.

au.ri.cle ['ɔ:rikl] *n.* kulak kepçesi; (*kalp*) kulakçık; **au.ric.u.la** BOT [ə'rikjulə] *n.* ayı kulağı; **au.ric.u.lar** □ [ɔ:'rikjulə] kulak veya işitme duyusu ile ilgili; ~ **witness** kulak misafiri.

au.rif.er.ous [ɔ:'rifərəs] *adj.* içinde altın bulunan, altınlı...

au.rist ['ɔ:rist] *n.* kulak mütehassısı.

au.rochs ZOO ['ɔ:rɔks] *n.* yaban sığırı, oroks.

au.ro.ra [ɔ:'rɔ:rə] *n.* fecir, şafak; ♀ seher tanrıçası; ~ **borealis** kuzey fecri; **au'ro.ral** *adj.* güneşin doğuşuna ait.

aus.cul.ta.tion MED [ɔ:skəl'teiʃən] *n.* kulaklık ile dinleme.

aus.pice ['ɔ:spis] *n.* kâhinlik, fal; ~*s pl.* himaye, koruma, nezaret; **under the ~ of** *b-nin* himayesinde; **aus.pi.cious** □ [-'piʃəs] uğurlu, hayırlı.

aus.tere □ [ɔs'tiə] sert, çetin; sade, şatafatsız; hoşgörüsüz; **aus.ter.i.ty** [-'teriti] *n.* sertlik, haşinlik; sadelik, süssüzlük; kısıntılı yaşam şekli, imsâk.

aus.tral ['ɔ:strəl] *adj.* güney.

Aus.tra.lian [ɔs'treiljən] **1.** *adj.* Avustralya'ya ait; **2.** *n.* Avustralyalı.

Aus.tri.an ['ɔstriən] **1.** *adj.* Avusturya'ya ait; **2.** *n.* Avusturyalı.

au.tar.ky ['ɔ:tɑ:ki] *n.* otarşi, kendi kendine yeterlik.

au.then.tic [ɔ:'θentik] *adj.* (~*ally*) sahih, güvenilir, doğru; **au'then.ti.cate** [-keit] *v/t.* *bşin* hakiki olduğunu göstermek, tevsik etm.; **au.then.ti'ca.tion** *n. bşin* doğru olduğunu ispatlama, tevsik etme; **au.then'tic.i.ty** [-siti] *n.* güvenilir olma, sıhhat.

au.thor ['ɔ:θə] *n.* yazar, muharrir, yaratıcı, sebep olan; **'au.thor.ess** *n.* kadın yazar; **au.thor.i.tar.i.an** [ɔ:θɔri-'teəriən] **1.** *adj.* otoriter; otorite taraftarı; **2.** *n.* otoriter veya otorite taraftarı kimse; **au'thor.i.ta.tive** □ [-tətiv] otoriter; yetkili; **au'thor.i.ty** *n.* otorite, salâhiyet; kudret, iktidar, yetki (**for, to** -*de*); tesir, nüfuz (**over, with** -*de, üzerinde*); bilirkişi, uzman; güvenilir, şayanı itimat; şahitlik, tanıklık; *mst* ~*s pl.* makam, idare, otorite; **be an ~ on s.th.** bir konuda uzman; olm.; **have s.th. on good ~** *bşi* güvenilir kaynaktan öğrenmek; **be under s.o.'s ~** *b-nin* emrinde olm.; **au.thor.i.zation** [ɔ:θərai'zeiʃən] *n.* yetki verme, yetkilendirme; izin, ruhsat; **'au.thor.ize** *v/t.* yetki vermek -*e*; müsaade etm. -*e*; izin vermek -*e*; *bşi* teyit etm., tasdik etm.; **'au.thor.ship** *n.* yazarlık; asıl.

au.to... ['ɔ:təu] *prefix* kendi kendine, kendiliğinden, oto...

au.to.bi.og.ra.pher [ɔ:təubai'ɔgrəfə] *n.* otobiyograf; **au.to.bi.o.graph.ic**, **au.to.bi.ograph.i.cal** □ ['-əu'græfik(əl)] kendi hayatından bahseden yazarın biyografisine ait; **au.to.bi.og.ra.phy** [-'ɔgrəfi] *n.* otobiyografi, bir yazarın kendi hal tercümesi, hatırat.

au.to.bus ['ɔ:təubʌs] *n.* otobüs.

au.to.cade *Am.* ['ɔ:təukeid] = **motor-cade.**

au.toch.thon [ɔ:'tɔkθən] *n. (bir yerin)* esas yerlisi; **au'toch.tho.nous** *adj.* yerli, kadim.

au.toc.ra.cy [ɔ:'tɔkrəsi] *n.* otokrasi, istibdat; **au.to.crat** ['ɔ:təukræt] *n.* otokrat, diktatör, müstebit kimse; **au.to-'crat.ic**, **au.to'crat.i.cal** □ müstebit, zorba.

au.tog.e.nous weld.ing MEC [ɔ:'tɔdʒə-nəs'weldiŋ] otojen kaynağı.

au.to.gi.ro AVIA ['ɔ:təu'dʒaiərəu] *n.* otojir uçak, dikine yükselip alçalabilen uçak.

au.to.graph ['ɔ:təgrɑ:f] **1.** *n. b-nin* kendi el yazısı veya imzası; **2.** *v/t.* kendi eli ile yazmak, imzasını atmak; **au.to-graphic** [ɔ:təu'græfik] *adj.* (~*ally*) el yazısına ait; **au.tog.ra.phy** [ɔ:'tɔgrəfi] *n.* insanların el yazısını bilme ilmi; el yazısı koleksiyonu.

au.to.mat ['ɔ:təmæt] *n.* yemeğin otomatik makinelerden dağıtıldığı lokanta; **au.tomat.ic** [ɔ:tə'mætik] **1.** *adj.* (**~ally**) otomatik, mekanik, kendi *k-ne* hareket eden; gayriiradî; gayrihtiyarî; **~ machine** otomatik satış makinesi; **2.** *n. Am.* otomatik tabanca; **au'to'ma.tion** *n.* otomasyon, otomatik sistemle çalışma; **au.tom.a.ton** [ɔ:'tɔmətən] *n. pl. mst* **au'tom.a.ta** [-tə] kendi *k-ne* hareket eden şey veya kimse; robot (*a. fig.*).

au.to.mo.bile *part. Am.* ['ɔ:təməubi:l] *n.* oto(mobil); **au.to.mo.tive** [ɔ:tə-'məutiv] **1.** *adj.* otomobillerle ilgili; **2.** *n.* motorlu vasıta.

au.ton.omous [ɔ:'tɔnəməs] □ özerk, muhtar; özerkliğe ait; **au'ton.o.my** *n.* özerklik, muhtariyet, otonomi.

au.top.sy ['ɔ:təpsi] *n.* otopsi.

au.to.type MEC ['ɔ:təutaip] *n.* suret, faksimile.

au.tumn ['ɔ:təm] *n.* sonbahar, güz; **au.tum.nal** □ [ɔ:'tʌmnəl] sonbahara ait, sonbahar...

aux.il.ia.ry [ɔ:g'ziljəri] *n. & adj.* yardımcı, muavin; yedek; **~ verb** GR yardımcı fiil; **auxiliaries** *pl.* MIL yardımcı kuvvet.

a.vail [ə'veil] **1.** *v/t.* faydalı olm., yaramak *-e;* **~ o.s. of** *bşden* istifade etm., *bşi* kullanmak; **2.** *n.* yarar, fayda; **of no ~** boşuna, beyhude; **a.vail.a'bil.i.ty** *n.* hazır bulunma; geçerli olma; **a'vail-a.ble** □ mevcut, elde edilebilir; geçer (-li) (*bilet vs.*); kullanışlı; **make ~** *b-nin* erişme vermek.

av.a.lanche ['ævəlɑːnʃ] *n.* çığ; *fig.* yığın.

av.a.rice [ævəris] *n.* hırs, tamah; **av.a-'ricious** □ haris, tamahkâr.

a.venge [ə'vendʒ] *v/t. -in* intikamını almak, öç almak; **~ o.s.**, **be ~d** intikam almak, öç almak (**on**, **upon** *-den*); **a'venger** *n.* öç (*veya* intikam) alıcı.

av.e.nue ['ævinju:] *n.* cadde, iki tarafı ağaçlı yol; *fig.* bir sonuca ulaştıran yol.

a.ver [ə'və:] *v/t.* kuvvetle söylemek, ispat etm., JUR delil göstermek, iddia etm..

av.er.age ['ævəridʒ] **1.** *n.* orta, ortalama, vasat; NAUT avarya, denizde meydana gelen maddi zarar ve hasar; **general (particular) ~** NAUT umumî veya büyük (küçük veya hususî) avarya;

on an ~ vasati olarak, ortalama; **2.** □ ortalama, vasati; **3.** *vb. -in* ortasını bulmak; *-in* ortalaması olm.

a.ver.ment [ə'və:mənt] *n.* iddia, söz; JUR delil, iddia; delil gösterme.

a.verse □ [ə'və:s] muhalif, karşı (**to**, **from** *-e*); isteksiz; **a'verse.ness**, **a'ver.sion** *n.* antipati, isteksizlik, gönülsüzlük, nefret (**to**, **from**, **for** *-e karşı*); **he is my ~** ondan nefret ediyorum.

a.vert [ə'və:t] *v/t.* çevirmek, yön değiştirmek (*a. fig.*); önlemek.

a.vi.ar.y ['eivjəri] *n.* kuşhane.

a.vi.ate AVIA ['eivieit] *v/i.* uçak kullanmak; **a.vi'a.tion** *n.* havacılık; uçuş; **~ ground** hava meydanı; **~ spirit** uçak benzini; **'a.vi.a.tor** *n.* havacı.

av.id □ ['ævid] haris, hırslı, arzulu (**for** *-e*); **a.vid.i.ty** [ə'viditi] *n.* hırs, istek, arzu.

av.o.ca.tion [ævəu'keiʃən] *n.* meşguliyet, hobi.

a.void [ə'vɔid] *v/t.* sakınmak, çekinmek, uzak durmak, kaçınmak *-den;* JUR feshetmek, iptal etm.; **a'void.a.ble** *adj.* sakınılır, kaçınılır; fesholunur; **a'void.ance** *n.* sakınma; JUR fesih, iptal; **~ of taxation** vergi kaçakçılığı.

av.oir.du.pois COM [ævədə'pɔiz] *n. a.* **~ weight** İngiliz ağırlık ölçüsü sistemi.

a.vouch [ə'vautʃ] *v/t.* onaylamak, teyit ve tasdik etm., iddia etm.; = **avow**.

a.vow [ə'vau] *v/t.* itiraf etm., kabul etm., beyan etm., ikrar etm.; **a'vow.al** *n.* itiraf, beyan, kabul, tasdik; **a'vow-ed.ly** [-idli] *adv.* açıkça, alenen.

a.wait [ə'weit] *v/t. bşi* beklemek, *bşe* intizar etm. (*a. fig.*).

a.wake [ə'weik] **1.** *adj.* uyanık, tetikte; **wide ~** tamamen uyanmış; *fig.* uyanık, açıkgöz; **2.** (*irr.*) *v/t. mst* **a'wak.en** uyandırmak; uyarmak; kışkırtmak; **~ s.o. to s.th.** *b-ne bşi* hissettirmek, *b-ni bş* hakkında uyarmak; *v/i.* uyanmak; harekete geçmek; farkına varmak (**to s.th. -in**).

a.ward [ə'wɔːd] **1.** *n.* hüküm, karar; ödül, mükâfat; **2.** *v/t.* (*mükâfat vs.*) vermek *-e;* hükmetmek, verilmesini istemek.

a.ware [ə'wɛə] *adj.* haberdar, farkında, bilir; **be ~** bilmek (**of -i**), haberdar olm. (**of -den**); **become ~ of** öğrenmek *-i;* farkına varmak *-in;* **a'ware.ness** *n.* farkında olma.

a.wash NAUT [ə'wɔʃ] **1.** *adv.* su seviyesinde; **2.** *adj.* su üzerinde yüzen; dalgalarla yıkanan.

a.way [ə'wei] **1.** *adv.* uzakta; uzağa; bir yana; -den, -dan; **2.** *adj. spor.* değiştirmece, deplasman...; *2 miles* ~ su mil uzakta; *water has boiled* ~ su kaynayıp buhar oldu; *explain* ~ tevil etm., sözü çevirmek; ~ *back in the past* çok uzak bir geçmişte, tâ geçmişte; *right* ~, *straight* ~ hemen, derhal; *out and* ~ fersah fersah.

awe [ɔ:] **1.** *n.* saygıyla karışık korku, sakınma (*of -den*); **2.** *v/t.* korkutmak, dehşete düşürmek; '~**in.spir.ing** *adj.* korku veren, huşu telkin eden;~**some** ['-səm] *adj.* korku veren, huşu ifade eden; '~**struck** *adj.* huşu içinde, hayran olmuş.

aw.ful □ ['ɔ:ful] korkunç, müthiş; berbat, çok kötü; F çok, muazzam; **aw.ful.ly** ['ɔ:fli] *adv.* F pek, çok, son derece; çok fena; *I'm* ~ *sorry* son derece üzgünüm.

a.while [ə'wail] *adv.* biraz, bir süre.

awk.ward □ ['ɔ:kwəd] beceriksiz, biçimsiz, sakar, hantal, münasebetsiz, kaba; sıkıntılı; '**awk.ward.ness** *n.* beceriksizlik, sakarlık, acemilik.

awl [ɔ:l] *n.* biz, kunduracı bizi.

awn BOT [ɔ:n] *n.* başak bıyığı, kılçık.

awn.ing ['ɔ:niŋ] *n.* tente, güneşlik, güneş tentesi; NAUT güneş tentesi.

a.woke [ə'wəuk] *pret. & p.p. of* **awake 2.**

a.wry [ə'rai] *adj. & adv.* eğri, yanlış, ters; *fig.* ters, aksi; *go* ~, *turn* ~ ters gitmek, bozulmak (*iş, olay*).

ax(e) [æks] **1.** *n.* balta; F *give* (*veya get*) *the* ~ aniden işten çıkar(ıl)mak; *have an* ~ *to grind* (*bir işte*) çıkarı olm.; **2.** *v/t.* balta ile budamak; F aniden işten çıkarmak.

ax.i.om ['æksiəm] *n.* mütearife, belit, aksiyon, kabul edilmiş gerçek; **ax.i.o.mat.ic** [-siəu'mætik] *adj.* (~*ally*) gerçek, kendiliğinden belli; aksiyonla ilgili olan.

ax.is ['æksis] *n.*, *pl.* **ax.es** ['-si:z] mihver, eksen.

ax.le MEC ['æksl] *n.* aks, dingil, mil.

ay(e) [ai] **1.** *adv.* daima, hep; evet, hayhay; **2.** *n.* PARL kabul oyu, olumlu oy, evet; *the* ~*s have it* kabul edilmiştir.

a.zal.ea BOT [ə'zeiljə] *n.* açalya, Amerikan hanımeli.

az.i.muth AST ['æzim
əθ] *n.* semt, azimut, gök kürenin herhangi bir noktası ile güney arasındaki açı.

a.zo.ic GEOL [ə'zəuik] **1.** *n.* azoik çağ, hayat olmayan çağ; **2.** *adj.* azoik, hayat olmayan çağa ait.

az.ure ['æʒə] *n. & adj.* açık mavi, gök mavisi.

B

baa [bɑ:] **1.** *v/i.* melemek; **2.** *n.* koyun melemesi.

bab.bitt ['bæbit] *n.* teneke, bakır ve rastık taşı karışımı bir maden; ~ *metal* bebit metali, regül, yatak maden.

bab.ble ['bæbl] **1.** *v/i.* saçmalamak; saçmalayarak ifade etm.; (*sır*) ağzından kaçırmak; (*bebek gibi*) anlamsız sesler çıkarmak; (*nehir vs.*) şarıldamak, çağlamak; **2.** *n.* saçma sapan konuşma; mırıltı; gevezelik; '**bab.bler** *n.* boşboğaz, geveze; mırıldayan kimse; çağlayan (*ırmak vs.*).

babe [beib] *n. poet.* küçük çocuk, bebek; *esp. Am. sl.* kız, bebek.

Ba.bel ['beibəl] *n. Tevrat ve İncil:* Babil; ♀ *fig.* kargaşalık, gürültü patırtı.

ba.boon ZOO [bə'bu:n] *n.* Habeş maymunu.

ba.by ['beibi] **1.** *n.* küçük çocuk, bebek; *bşin*, aile veya bir grubun en küçüğü; bebek gibi davranan kimse; *Am. sl.* kız, bebek; **2.** *adj.* bebek gibi; bebeğe ait; küçük; **3.** *v/t.* bebek muamelesi yapmak; şımartmak; '~**car.riage** *Am. s.* **perambulator**; '~**farm** *n.* (*ücretli*) çocuk bakımevi; ~**grand** MUS kısa kuyruklu piyano; **ba.by.hood** ['-hud] *n.* çocukluk, bebeklik çağı; '**ba.by.ish** □ çocukça, bebekçe, bebek gibi.

Bab.y.lo.ni.an [bæbi'ləunjən] **1.** *adj.* Babil'e ait; **2.** *n.* Babil'de oturan kimse; Babil dili.

ba.by-sit.ter ['beibisitə] (*kısa süreli*) çocuk bakıcısı.

bac.cha.nal ['bækənl] = **bacchant**; '**bac.cha.nals** *pl.*, **bac.cha.na.li.a** [-'neiljə] *pl.* Baküs şenliği, sefih içki âlemi; **bac.cha'na.li.an** *adj.* Baküs şenliğine ait; içki âlemine ait.

bac.chant ['bækənt] *n.* Baküs rahibi; ayyaş kimse; **bac.chante** [bə'kænti] *n.* Baküs rahibesi; içkiye düşkün kadın.

bac.cy F ['bæki] *n.* tütün.

bach.e.lor ['bætʃələ] *n.* bekâr erkek; UNIV fen veya edebiyat fakültesi mezunu; ~ **girl** bekâr kadın; **bach.e.lor.hood** ['-hud] *n.* bekârlık.

bac.il.la.ry [bə'siləri] *adj.* basilli; **ba'cil.lus** [-ləs] *n., pl.* **ba'cil.li** [-lai] basil.

back [bæk] **1.** *n.* arka, sırt, geri; ters taraf; arka yüz; = **full-back**; **behind s.o.'s** ~ *b-nin* arkasından, gıyabında; **put one's** ~ **into s.th.** bir işe kendini tamamen vermek, olanca gücüyle çalışmak; **put** *veya* **get** *veya* **set s.o.'s** ~ **up** *b-ni* hiddetlendirmek, kızdırmak; **break one's** ~ belini kırmak; **break the** ~ **of s.th.** *bşin* çoğunu bitirmek, hakkından gelmek; **be on one's** ~ arka üstü yatmak; hasta yatmak; **have one's** ~ **to the wall** çıkmazda kalmak; **at the** ~ **of** içinde, arkasında, gerisinde; **on the** ~ **of** fazlasiyle; **2.** *adj.* arka, arkadaki; arkaya doğru olan, evvelki; eski; **3.** *adv.* arkada, arkaya; geri(ye); yeniden, tekrar; **4.** *v/t.* geri yürütmek; himaye etm.; desteklemek; para yatırmak, bahse girmek *-e*; COM ciro etm.; ~ **the sails** NAUT yelkenleri faça etm.; ~ **water**, ~ **the oars** NAUT siya etm.; ~ **up** *bşi* geri sürmek; desteklemek; *v/i.* geri gitmek; dönmek, caymak (**out of**-*den*); ~ **down** F teslim olm., vazgeçmek (**from**-*den*); ~ **al.ley** *n. Am.* arka sokak (*esp. şehrin fakir bölgesinde*); ~'**bend** jimnastik; köprü; '~**bite** (*irr.* bite) *v/t. b-ne* iftira etm., *b-nin* arkasından konuşmak; '~**bone** *n.* omurga, belkemiği (*a. fig.*); karakter kuvveti, metanet; **to the** ~ *fig.* tamamen, sapına kadar; '~**break.ing** *adj.* çok yorucu, yıpratıcı; '~**cloth** *n.* THEAT arka perde; '~'**door** *n.* arka kapı; *adj. fig.* el altından yapılan; **back.er** *n.* arka, taraftar, yardım eden kimse; yarışta bir ata para koyan kimse; COM ciranta.

back...: '~'**fire** MOT **1.** *n.* geri tepme (*vakitsiz ateşlemeden dolayı*); **2.** *vb.* geri tepmek (*a. fig.*); ~ **for.ma.tion** GR bir kelimeden geriye gidilerek türetilen yeni kelime; '~'**gam.mon** *n.* tavla oyunu; '~**ground** *n.* arka plan; fon; mevcut şartlar; *fig.* muhit, görgü; '~'**hand**

1. *n. tenis*; röver, bekhent; **2.** *adj.* elin tersi öne doğru olarak yapılan '~-hand.ed *adj.* elinin tersiyle; *fig.* samimi olmayan, sinsice; '~hand.er *n.* elin tersiyle yapılan vuruş.

back.ing ['bækiŋ] *n.* yardım, destek; arkalık, arka.

back...: '~**.lash** *n.* ani ve şiddetli geri itme; MEC diş boşluğu, ölü nokta, salgı; politik veya toplumsal gelişmeye karşı güçlü tepki; '~**.log** *n.* sürüncemede bırakılan işler; yedek şeyler; ~ **number 1.** günü geçmiş gazete, dergi vs.; **2.** modası geçmiş, itibardan düşmüş kimse veya şey; ~ **pay** ödenmesi gecikmiş maaş veya ücret; '~**-ped.al** *v/t.* (*bisiklette*) ayak frenine basmak; sözünü geri almak, değiştirmek; '~**-room boy** F işi önemli fakat gizli bilim adamı; ~ **seat** arka sırada oturacak yer, arka koltuk; '~'**side** *n.* kıç, arka taraf; '~**.sight** *n. gez*; '~'**slide** (*irr.* slide) *v/i.* doğru yoldan tekrar kötüye dönmek; '~'**slid.er** *n.* tekrar kötü yola dönen kimse; '~'**slid.ing** *n.* tekrar hataya düşme; '~'**stairs 1.** *n. pl.* arka merdiven *sg.*; **2.** *adj.* gizlice yapılan, el altından olan; *b-ni* zemmeden; '~**.stitch 1.** *n.* iğneardı; **2.** *v/t.* iğneardı dikiş dikmek; '~**.stop** *n. Am.* beysbol: topun kaçmasını önleyen engel; *poligon*; toprak siper; '~**.stroke** *n.* sırtüstü yüzme; ~ **talk** küstahça konuşma; ~ **to back** arka arkaya, sırt sırta; '~**.track** *vb. Am.* F *fig.* geriye dönüş yapmak, söylediğini değiştirmek.

back.ward ['bækwəd] **1.** ☐ isteksiz, çekingen; geç kavrayan, gelişmemiş; gecikmiş; **2.** *adv. a.* '**back.wards** geri; arkaya doğru; geri geri, tersine; **back-ward'a.tion** COM *n.* geriye hareket; depor, bir çeşit vadeli muamele; '**back-wardness** *n.* gerilik; geç kavrama.

back...: '~**.wa.ter** *n.* bir nehrin akıntısı olmayan küçük kolu; dümen suyu; durgun su; '~**.woods** *n. pl.* şehirlerden uzakta ve sık ağaçlardan arındırılmamış yerler; '~**.woods.man** *n.* dağ adamı; kaba adam, hödük.

ba.con ['beikən] *n.* tuzlanmış veya tütsülenmiş domuz eti, domuz pastırması; **save one's** ~ yakayı kurtarmak; **bring home the** ~ *sl.* başarılı olm. (*esp. evinin ihtiyaçlarını temin konusunda*).

bac.te.ri.al ☐ [bæk'tiəriəl] bakteriye ait; **bac.te.ri.o.log.i.cal** ☐ [-tiəriə'lɔdʒikəl] bakteriyoloji ilmine ait;

bac.teri.ol.o.gist [ˌtiəri'ɔlədʒist] *n.* bakteriyolog; **bac'teri.um** [ˌriəm] *n.*, *pl.* **bac'te.ri.a** [ˌriə] bakteri.

bad ☐ [bæd] fena, kötü, zararlı, kusurlu; yakışıksız (*söz vs.*); geçersiz (*para vs.*); yetersiz (*delil vs.*); bozuk, zararlı; keyifsiz, hasta; şiddetli, sert; çürük; *not (too)* ~, *not so* ~, *not half* ~ F hiç de fena değil, oldukça iyi; *things are not so* ~ mesele pek o kadar kötü değil; *he is* ~*ly off* mali durumu fenadır; ~*ly wounded* ağır yaralı; *want* ~*ly bşi* şiddetle arzu etm.

bade [bæd] *pret. of* **bid 1**.

badge [bædʒ] *n.* nişan, rozet.

badg.er ['bædʒə] **1.** *n.* zoo porsuk; **2.** *v/t.* tâciz etm.; kızdırmak.

bad hair day F [bæd'hɛədeɪ] *n.* *she was clearly having a* ~ *when this picture was taken* belli ki bu resmi saçına çeki düzen vermeyi başaramadığı bir günde çektirmiş; *a. fig.* *be having a* ~ hiçbir şeyin rast gitmediği bir gün geçiriyor olmak.

bad.lands *Am.* ['bædləndz] *n. pl.* verimsiz, çorak arazi.

bad.min.ton ['bædmintən] *n.* tenise benzer bir çeşit oyun, badminton.

bad.ness ['bædnis] *n.* fenalık, kötülük.

bad-tem.pered ['bæd'tempəd] *adj.* aksi, huysuz.

baf.fle ['bæfl] *v/t.* şaşırtmak, bozmak; (*plan vs.*) akamete uğratmak; *it* ~*s description* tarifi imkânsız.

bag [bæg] **1.** *n.* torba, çuval, kese; çanta; kese kâğıdı; ~*s pl. sl.* bol pantolon; *it's in the* ~ F garantili, çantada keklik; ~ *and baggage* tası tarağı toplayarak, her şeyi ile; ~*s of sl.* bol miktarda, çuvalla; **2.** *vb.* torba veya çuvala koymak; F aşırmak, çalmak; hunt yakalamak; şişirmek, germek.

bag.a.telle [bægə'tel] *n.* ufak tefek şey; bir çeşit bilardo oyunu.

bag.gage ['bægidʒ] *n. Am.* bagaj; mıl ordu ağırlığı; hafifmeşrep kadın; ~ *car* rail *Am.* yük vagonu, furgon; '~*check* *n. Am.* bagaj kâğıdı, eşya makbuzu.

bag.ging ['bægiŋ] *n.* çuval bezi.

bag.gy ['bægi] *adj.* çok bol, torba gibi.

bag...: ~*man* ['bægmən] *n.* F seyyar ticarî mümessil; '~*pipe* *n.* gayda; '~*snatch.er n.* yankesici.

bah [bɑː] *int. b-ni* veya *bşi* aşağılayıcı ifade, Tü!

bail¹ [beil] **1.** *n.* kefalet; kefil; teminat akçesi, kefalet; kefaletle salıverme; *be veya go veya stand* ~ *for b-ne* kefil olm., *b-i* için kefalet vermek; **2.** *v/t.* *b-ne* kefalet etm.; ~ *out* kefaletle tahliye ettirmek.

bail² naut [ˌ] *v/t.* (*suyu*) boşaltmak.

bail³ [ˌ] *n.* *kriket*: çubuk.

bail⁴ [ˌ] *n.* (*kova vs.*) sap, kulp.

bail.iff ['beilif] *n.* çiftlik kâhyası; mübaşir; icra memuru; nezaretçi, idareci.

bail.ment jur ['beilmənt] *n.* malları teminat olarak verme, kefalet.

bail.or jur ['beilə] *n.* emaneten tevdi eden kimse, vedia veren.

bairn *Scots* [bɛən] *n.* çocuk.

bait [beit] **1.** *n.* yem (*a. fig.*); çekici ve aldatıcı şey; mola; **2.** *vb.* oltaya veya kapana yem koymak; hunt köpekleri *b-nin* üzerine saldırtmak; *fig.* tâciz etm., rahatsızlandırmak; mola vermek.

baize [beiz] *n.* kaba yünlü kumaş (*mst yeşil*).

bake [beik] *v/t. & v/i.* (*fırında*) piş(ir)-mek; ateşte kurutmak; *fig.* sıcaktan pişmek; '~*house n.* fırın, ekmekçi dükkânı.

ba.ke.lite mec ['beikəlait] *n.* bakalit.

bak.er ['beikə] *n.* ekmekçi, fırıncı; ~*'s dozen on* üç; '**bak.er.y** *n.* fırın, ekmekçi dükkânı; '**bak.ing** *n.* fırında pişirme; '**bak.ing-pow.der** *n.* kabartıcı toz.

bak.sheesh ['bækʃiːʃ] *n.* bahşiş.

bal.a.lai.ka mus [bælə'laikə] *n.* balalayka, bir cins telli müzik aleti.

bal.ance ['bæləns] **1.** *n.* terazi; denge; denklem; com bilanço, bakiye, mizan; kalan; *a.* ~*wheel* cep saati rakkası; *be (hang) in the* ~ muallâkta olm., nazik bir durumda bulunmak; *keep (lose) one's* ~ dengesini sağlamak (kaybetmek); *throw s.o. off his* ~ *fig. b-nin* dengesini kaybettirmek; *turn the* ~ kati etkili olm.; ~ *of payments* ödemeler dengesi; ~ *of power* pol güçler dengesi; ~ *of trade* dış ticaret bilançosu, dengesi; *s. strike 2*; **2.** *v/t. & v/i.* tartmak, dengelemek; dengeli olm.; com bilanço yapmak, denklemek; *k-ni* dengede tutmak; '~*sheet n.* com bilanço.

bal.co.ny ['bælkəni] *n.* balkon (*a.* theat).

bald [bɔːld] *adj.* saçları dökülmüş, dazlak, kel; *fig.* çıplak, çorak.

bal.da.chin ['bɔːldəkin] *n.* gölgelik, çardak.

bal.der.dash ['bɔːldədæʃ] *n.* boş lâf,

bang

gevezelik.

bald…: '**~-head**, '**~-pate** *n.* dazlak kimse, kel; **go ~ into** körükörüne atılmak -*e*; '**bald.ness** *n.* kellik.

bale[1] COM [beil] *n.* denk, balya.

bale[2] NAUT [-] *v/t.* (*suyunu*) boşaltmak.

bale.fire ['beilfaiə] *n.* işaret ateşi.

bale.ful □ ['beilful] meşum, uğursuz.

balk [bɔːk] **1.** *n.* kiriş, hatıl; engel; hata; tarlada sürülmemiş kısım; **2.** *v/t.* (*tarlada*) sürülmemiş yer bırakmak, durdurmak, engel olm. -*e*; kaçırmak -*ı*; *v/i.* imtina etm., direnmek (**at** -*de*, *için*).

Bal.kan ['bɔːlkən] *adj.* Balkan, Balkan ülkeleri veya oturanlarına ait.

ball[1] [bɔːl] **1.** *n.* top; küre; yumak; bilye; top oyunu; *spor*: atış; *Am. beysbol*: hatalı atılan top; MIL gülle; **keep the ~ rolling** lâfı uzatmak, *bşi* devam ettirmek; **start the ~ rolling** *bşi* başlatmak, açmak; **have the ~ at one's feet** eline fırsat geçmek, başarı yolu açılmak; **the ~ is with you** sıra sende; **play ~** *Am.* F katılmak, beraber çalışmak; **2.** *vb.* top, yumak yapmak; top olm.; **~ ed up** *Am. sl.* karmakarışık, karman çorman.

ball[2] [-] *n.* balo; **open the ~** *fig.* dansı (*veya* baloyu) açmak.

bal.lad ['bæləd] *n.* balad, türkü.

ball-and-sock.et ['bɔːlən'sɔkit] *n.*; **~ joint** MEC bilyalı mesnet.

bal.last ['bæləst] **1.** *n.* NAUT denge ağırlığı, safra; RAIL balast, kırma taş; **mental ~** istikrar, metanet; **2.** *v/t.* safra koymak; denge temin etm.; RAIL çakıl döşemek.

ball…: '**~'bear.ing(s** *pl.*) *n.* MEC bilye; bilyeli yatak; '**~-boy** *tenis*: top toplayan çocuk; '**~-car.tridge** *n.* dolu fişek.

bal.let ['bælei] *n.* bale; bale trupu.

bal.lis.tics [bə'listiks] *n. mst sg.* balistik.

bal.loon [bə'luːn] **1.** *n.* balon; CHEM balon şişe; **~ barrage** balon barajı; **~ tire** MOT büyük lastik, balon lastik; **2.** *vb.* balon gibi şişmek; balonla uçmak; **bal'loon.ist** *n.* balon kullanan kimse.

bal.lot ['bælət] **1.** *n.* oy pusulası; gizli oyla seçim; oy kullanma hakkı; **2.** *v/i.* oy vermek; **~ for** kura çekmek, oy vermek (… *için*); '**~-box** *n.* oy sandığı.

ball…: ~(-**point**) pen tükenmez kalem; '**~-room** *n.* balo salonu, dans salonu.

bal.ly.hoo F [bæli'huː] *n.* tamtam, gürültü, velvele; şamatalı propaganda.

balm [bɑːm] *n.* pelesenk, balsam; *fig.* merhem, teselli.

balm.y □ ['bɑːmi] yatıştırıcı, huzur verici (*a. fig.*); yumuşak, ılık (*hava*, *rüzgâr vs.*); F kaçık.

ba.lo.ney *Am. sl.* [bə'ləuni] *n.* saçmasapan söz, zırva.

bal.sam ['bɔːlsəm] *n.* pelesenk; **bal-sam.ic** [-'sæmik] *adj.* (**~ally**) yatıştırıcı.

Bal.tic ['bɔːltik] *adj.* Baltık; **~ Sea** Baltık Denizi.

bal.us.ter ['bæləstə] *n.* tırabzan kolonu.

bal.us.trade [bæləs'treid] *n.* tırabzon parmaklığı.

bam.boo [bæm'buː] **1.** *n.* bambu; **2.** *adj.* bambudan yapılmış.

bam.boo.zle F [bæm'buːzl] *v/t.* (**into** *veya* **out of**) aldatmak, dolandırmak; şaşırtmak.

ban ['bæn] **1.** *n.* yasak; ECCL afaroz; **2.** *v/t.* *bşi* yasaklamak; afaroz etm.

ba.nal [bə'nɑːl] *adj.* adî, bayağı.

ba.nan.a [bə'nɑːnə] *n.* BOT muz; **~ split** *Am.* dondurmalı muz tatlısı.

band [bænd] **1.** *n.* bağ, şerit, kayış; topluluk, güruh; MUS bando, orkestra, mızıka; MEC transmisyon kayışı; sargı; çizgi; **2.** *v/t.* bağlamak; çizgilerle süslemek; *v/i.* toplanmak; **~ together** birleşmek, bir araya gelmek.

band.age ['bændidʒ] **1.** *n.* sargı, bağ; **2.** *v/t.* sarmak, bağlamak.

ban.dan.na [bæn'dɑːnə] *n.* parlak renkli büyük mendil, şal.

band.box ['bændbɔks] *n.* mukavva şapka kutusu; **as if one came out of a ~** iki dirhem bir çekirdek.

ban.dit ['bændit] *n.* haydut, eşkiya; '**bandit.ry** *n.* haydutluk.

band-mas.ter MUS ['bændmɑːstə] *n.* bando şefi.

ban.do.leer ['bændəu'liə] *n.* fişeklik.

bands.man ['bændzmən] *n.* mızıkacı, bando çalgıcısı; '**band-stand** *n.* bandoya mahsus platform (*esp. açık havada*); **band wag.on** *Am.* bandoyu taşıyan araba.

ban.dy ['bændi] **1.** *v/t.* (top *vs.*) öteye beriye vurmak; (*sitem*, *söz vs.*) teati etm.; **2.** *adj.* eğri, çarpık; '**~-leg.ged** *adj.* çarpık bacaklı.

bane [bein] *n.* afet, felâket; zehir; **bane-ful** □ zararlı; öldürücü, zehirli.

bang [bæŋ] **1.** *n.* çat, pat, gürültü, patlama; şevk; (*usu. pl.*) kâkül, perçem; **go over with a ~** *Am.* F çok başarılı olm.; **2.** *v/t. & v/i.* gürültü ile kapa(n)-

mak, vur(ul)mak; saç kesmek (*kâkül veya perçem*); *sl.* fiyatları indirmek; **3.** *adv.* gürültülü bir şekilde, ansızın.

ban.gle ['bæŋgl] *n.* bilezik, halka, halhal.

bang-up *Am. sl.* ['bæŋʌp] *adj.* birinci sınıf, mükemmel.

ban.ish ['bæniʃ] *v/t.* sürgün etm.; uzaklaştırmak; '**ban.ish.ment** *n.* sürgün.

ban.is.ter ['bænistə] *n.* tırabzan kolonu; '**ban.is.ters** *pl.* tırabzan.

ban.jo MUS ['bændʒou] *n.* dört veya daha fazla telli bir müzik aleti.

bank [bæŋk] **1.** *n.* (*nehir, göl*) kenar, kıyı; bayır; yığın, küme; (*sığ bölge*; (*tekne*) kürekçi sırası; (*org veya piyano*) klavye; (*oyun*) banko; COM banka; ~ **of deposit** mevduat bankası; ~ **of issue** Merkez Bankası, ihraç bankası, emisyon bankası; **2.** *v/t.* set, bent ile kapatmak; COM bankaya yatırmak; AVIA bir tarafa yatırmak; *v/i.* banka veya bankacılık görevini yapmak; (*bankada*) para tutmak (**with** -*de*); AVIA bir tarafa yatmak; ~ **on** güvenmek, ümit bağlamak -*e*; ~ **up** yığmak, istif etm.; '**bank.a.ble** *adj.* bankaca muteber; '**bank(ing)-ac.count** *n.* banka hesabı; '**bank-bill** *n.* banknot, kâğıt para; *Am. s.* **bank-note**; '**bank.er** *n.* bankacı; (*şans oyunlarında*) bankocu; '**bank-holiday** *n.* resmî tatil günü; '**bank.ing** *n.* bankacılık; banka muamelesi; AVIA meyilli durum; '**bank.ing-house** *n.* banka binası; banka; '**bank-note** *n.* banknot, kâğıt para; '**bank-rate** *n.* banka iskonto haddi, faiz oranı; **bank.rupt** ['-rʌpt] **1.** *n.* iflâs etmiş kimse, müflis; ~'**s estate** iflâs masası; müflisin malları; **2.** *adj.* müflis, iflâs eden; **go** ~ iflâs etm.; **3.** *v/t.* iflâs ettirmek, mahvetmek; **bankrupt.cy** ['-rəptsi] *n.* iflâs; **declaration of** ~ iflâs ilânı; ~ **petition** iflâs isteği.

ban.ner ['bænə] **1.** *n.* bayrak, sancak; **2.** *adj. Am.* çok iyi, mümtaz; ~ **headline** (*gazete*) manşet.

banns [bænz] *n. pl.* resmî ilân (*esp. evlenme*), askıya alma; **put up the** ~, **publish the** ~ resmen ilân etm., askıya almak.

ban.quet ['bæŋkwit] **1.** *n.* şölen, ziyafet; **2.** *vb.* ziyafet çekmek -*e*; ~ **hall** ziyafet salonu.

ban.shee *Scots, Ir.* [bæn'ʃiː] *n.* ağlaması o evden ölü çıkacağına işaret sayılan ruh.

ban.tam [bæntəm] *n.* küçük cins tavuk, ispenç; *fig.* ufak tefek kimse; ~ **weight** *spor:* horoz siklet.

ban.ter ['bæntə] **1.** *n.* şaka, takılma, alay; **2.** *vb.* şaka etm., takılmak, eğlenmek; '**ban.ter.er** *n.* şaka eden kimse.

bap.tism ['bæptizəm] *n.* vaftiz, vaftiz ayini; ~ **of fire** bir askerin ilk girdiği düşman ateşi; *bşin* hoş olmayan ilk deneyimi; **bap.tis.mal** [-'tizməl] *adj.* vaftize ait.

Bap.tist ['bæptist] *n.* bir hıristiyan tarikatinin mensubu; '**bap.tis.ter.y** *n.* (*kilise*) vaftiz bölünü; **bap.tize** [-'taiz] *vb.* *b-ni* vaftiz etm.; ad koymak -*e*.

bar [baː] **1.** *n.* çubuk, sırık, kol, kol demiri; engel, mania; (*çikolata, sabun v.b.*) kalıp, parça; nehir ağzında kum ve çakıl seti; *fig.* mâni; engel; MIL toka, nişan şeridi; MUS usul, ölçü, mezur; JUR mahkemede dinleyici ve sanıkları diğerlerinden ayıran bölme; bar, içki satılan veya içilen yer, meyhane; JUR men'i muhakeme; JUR sanık kürsüsü; JUR baro; **horizontal** ~ barfiks; **parallel** ~**s** *pl.* barparalel; **be called to the** ~ JUR baroya yazılmak; **prisoner at the** ~ muhakeme edilen kimse, sanık; **behind the** ~**s** hapiste; **2.** *v/t.* kapamak, sürgülemek; *bşi* önlemek, yasak etm.; geniş çizgi veya yollar yapmak; **3.** *prp.* maada, -den başka; ~ **none** istisnasız.

barb [baːb] *n.* (*olta iğnesi, ok vs.*) keskin uç; kanca; kuş tüyünün bir kılı; ZOO sakala benzer kısım; **barbed** *adj.* bir veya daha fazla keskin uçlu, kancalı, dikenli; (*söz*) alaylı ve kırıcı; ~ **wire** dikenli tel.

bar.bar.i.an [baː'bɛəriən] **1.** *adj.* gaddar, zalim, barbar, medenî olmayan; **2.** *n.* barbar, vahşi kimse; vahşi; yabancı; **bar.bar.ic** [-'bærik] *adj.* (~**ally**) barbarca, vahşice; uygar olmayan; **bar.ba.rism** ['-bərizəm] *n.* barbarlık, kabalık; alışılmamış kelime veya deyim; **bar.bar.i.ty** [-'bæriti] *n.* barbarlık, vahşet, kabalık; **bar.ba.rize** ['-bəraiz] *v/t.* vahşileştirmek; '**bar.barous** ☐ barbarca, vahşî, uygar olmayan; yabancı.

bar.be.cue ['baːbikjuː] **1.** *n.* bütün bir hayvanı çeviren ızgara; hayvanın bütün olarak çevrildiği açık hava yemeği; bütün olarak çevrilmiş hayvan; baharlı ve salçalı bir çeşit et yemeği; **2.** *v/t.* bu çeşit ızgarada bütün hayvan çevirmek.

bar.bel ICHTH ['baːbəl] *n.* bir cins bıyıklı balık.

bar.bell ['bɑːbel] *n. spor*: halter.

bar.ber ['bɑːbə] *n.* berber; **~ shop** berber dükkânı.

bard [bɑːd] *n.* saz şairi, şair, ozan.

bare [bɛə] **1.** □ çıplak, açık; boş; sade; yoksul, mahrum (**of** -*den*); mübalâğasız, basit; **2.** *v/t.* açmak, örtüsünü kaldırmak; başını açmak, şapkasını çıkarmak; '**~-back(ed)** *adj.* eyersiz; '**~.faced** □ yüzsüz, utanmaz; '**~.faced.ness** *n.* yüzsüzlük; '**~.foot** *adj. & adv.* yalınayak; '**~'foot.ed** *adj.* yalınayak; '**~.head.ed** *adj.* başı açık, şapkasız; '**bare.ly** *adv.* sadece, ancak; '**bare.ness** *n.* çıplaklık.

bar.gain ['bɑːgin] **1.** *n.* anlaşma, pazarlık; kelepir, elden düşme; **~ price** ucuz fiyat, tenzilâtlı fiyat; **a (dead) ~** yok pahasına, para ile değil; **it's a ~!** uyuştuk!, anlaştık!; **into the ~** üstelik, caba; **make** *veya* **strike a ~** uzlaşmak; **2.** *vb.* pazarlık etm. (**about** *için*/ *hakkında*); anlaşmak, uyuşmak (**for** *için*); **~ for** düşünmek, hesaplamak, tahmin etm.; '**bargain.er** *n.* pazarlık eden kimse.

barge [bɑːdʒ] **1.** *n.* mavuna, salapurya; NAUT tahlisiye sandalı; işkampaviya; **2.** *vb.* F sendelemek, sersem sepet gitmek; **bar'gee, barge.man** ['~mən] *n.* mavnacı.

bar-i.ron ['bɑːaiən] *n.* çubuk halinde demir.

bar.i.tone MUS ['bæritəun] *n.* tenor ile bas arasındaki erkek sesi, bariton.

bar.i.um CHEM ['bɛəriəm] *n.* baryum.

bark¹ [bɑːk] **1.** *n.* ağaç kabuğu; **2.** *v/t.* kabuğunu soymak; tabaklamak.

bark² [~] **1.** *n.* havlama; F öksürük; **2.** *v/i.* havlamak; yüksek sesle konuşmak; *sl.* çığırtkanlık yapmak; F öksürmek.

bark³ [~] *n.* NAUT = **barque**; *poet.* sandal, yelkenli gemi.

bar-keep.er ['bɑːkiːpə] *n.* barmen.

bark.er ['bɑːkə] *n.* havlayan; çığırtkan.

bar.ley ['bɑːli] *n.* arpa.

barm [bɑːm] *n.* bira köpüğü.

bar.maid ['bɑːmeid] *n.* içki tezgâhında çalışan kız.

bar.man ['bɑːmən] *n. s.* **bartender**.

barm.y ['bɑːmi] *adj.* köpüklü; havaî.

barn [bɑːn] *n.* zahire ambarı; samanlık; *part. Am.* ahır, tavla.

bar.na.cle ['bɑːnəkl] *n.* gemi diplerine, kayalara yapışan bir cins midye; *fig.* sırnaşık adam, çam sakızı.

barn.storm *Am.* POL ['bɑːnstɔːm] *vb.*

siyasî konuşmalar yapmak için dolaşmak; '**barn.yard** *n.* ahır ve ambarların çevrelediği avlu.

ba.rom.e.ter [bə'rɔmitə] *n.* barometre; **bar.o.met.ric, bar.o.met.ri.cal** [bærəu'metrik(əl)] barometreye ait.

bar.on ['bærən] *n.* baron; *esp. Am.* önemli ve güçlü iş adamı; **an oil ~** petrol kıralı; '**bar.on.ess** *n.* baronun karısı, kadın baron, barones; **bar.on.et** ['~nit] *n.* barondan bir derece aşağı asalet unvanı, baronet; **bar.on.et.cy** ['~nitsi] *n.* baronet payesi; **ba.ro.ni.al** [bə'rəunjəl] *adj.* barona ait; şaşaalı, debdebeli; **bar.o.ny** ['bærəni] *n.* baronun rütbesi.

ba.roque [bə'rɔk] **1.** *n.* barok; **2.** *adj.* barok üslûbuna ait, barok; çok süslü; şatafatlı.

barque NAUT [bɑːk] *n.* barka.

bar.rack ['bæræk] **1.** *n. mst* **~s** *pl.* kışla; kışla gibi gösterişsiz bina; **2.** *vb. sl.* bağırarak tezahürat yapmak.

bar.rage ['bærɑːʒ] *n.* baraj, bent, set; MIL baraj ateşi; **~ balloon** savunmada kullanılan ve yere bağlı balon.

bar.rel ['bærəl] **1.** *n.* fıçı, varil; (*top, tüfek*) namlu; MEC tambura, kasnak; silindir kovanı; **2.** *v/t.* fıçıya koymak; '**barrel-or.gan** *n.* MUS laterna.

bar.ren □ ['bærən] kısır; kurak, çorak, verimsiz (*toprak*); yavan; budala; faydasız; COM atıl, kullanılmayan (*sermaye*); '**bar.ren.ness** *n.* kısırlık.

bar.ri.cade [bæri'keid] **1.** *n.* barikat, siper, engel; **2.** *v/t.* siper yapmak; barikat kurmak.

bar.ri.er ['bæriə] *n.* mania, engel (*a. fig*); çit, bariyer, parmaklık.

bar.ring ['bɑːriŋ] *prp.* hariç, -den maada, olmadığı takdirde.

bar.ris.ter ['bæristə] *n. a.* **~-at-law** avukat, dava vekili.

bar.row¹ ['bærəu] *s.* **hand-~, wheel-~**; **~-man** ['~mən] *n.* seyyar satıcı.

bar.row² [~] *n.* mezar tümseği, tepe.

bar.tend.er ['bɑːtendə] *n.* meyhanede içki veren kimse, barmen.

bar.ter ['bɑːtə] **1.** *n.* değişme, mübadele, trampa; **2.** *vb.* takas yapmak; mübadele yolu ile alışveriş yapmak, trampa etm. (**for, with** *ile*); *b.s.* yahudi pazarlığı etm., bezirgânlık etm.

bar.y.tone MUS ['bæritəun] *n.* baso ile tenor arası ses, bariton.

ba.salt ['bæsɔːlt] *n.* bazalt, siyah mermer; **ba.sal.tic** [bə'sɔːltik] *adj.* bazalta ait.

base¹ □ [beis] bayağı, alçak; değersiz; sahte, kalp (*para vs.*).

base² [ˍ] **1.** *n.* temel, esas; taban, kaide; MIL üs; CHEM alkali; baz; **2.** *v/t. fig.* kurmak, tesis etm.; istinat ettirmek, dayandırmak (**on**, **upon** *-e*, *üzerine*); ~ **o.s. on** *bşe* dayanmak, istinadetmek (*a. fig.*); **be ~d (up) on** *bşden* ileri gelmek, *bşe* bağlı olm.; *bşe* dayanmak.

base...: '**~.ball** *n.* beysbol; '**~.born** *adj.* soylu aileden gelmeyen; piç; alçak, zalim; '**~.less** *adj.* asılsız, temelsiz; '**~.line** *n.* esas alınan çizgi; (*tenis*) ana çizgi; '**base.ment** *n.* temel; bodrum katı, zemin katı.

base.ness [beisnis] *n.* alçaklık, aşağılık.

bash.ful □ ['bæʃful] utangaç, sıkılgan.

bas.ic ['beisik] *adj.* (**~ally**) esas, temel, esas teşkil eden; CHEM bazal; ♀ **English** (*İngilizce öğretiminde*) basit İngilizce; ~ **slag** fosfatlı bir cins gübre.

basil BOT ['bæzl] *n.* fesleğen, reyhan.

ba.sil.i.ca ARCH [bəˈzilikə] (*eski Roma'da*) dikdörtgen şeklinde ve iki tarafı sütunlu, nihayeti yarım daire şeklinde salondan ibaret kilise vs.; bu üslûpta yapılmış katolik kilisesi; bazilik, bazilika.

bas.i.lisk ['bæzilisk] *n.* MYTH nefes veya bakışında öldürme gücü olduğuna inanılan yılana benzer yaratık; Güney Amerika kertenkelesi.

ba.sin ['beisn] *n.* leğen, çanak, tas; havuz; havza.

ba.sis ['beisis] *n., pl.* **ba.ses** ['ˍsiːz] esas, temel, dayanak; menşe, kaynak; MIL, NAUT üs; **take as** ~ esas olarak kabul etm.; istinat ettirmek.

bask [bɑːsk] *v/i.* güneşlenmek, ısınmak için ateşe veya güneşe karşı oturmak veya uzanmak; tadını çıkarmak (**in** *bşin*).

bas.ket ['bɑːskit] *n.* sepet, küfe, zembil; sepet dolusu; *spor:* sayı, basket; '**~.ball** *n.* basketbol; basketbol topu; ~ **dinner**, ~ **sup.per** *n. Am.* piknik; '**bas.ket.work** *n.* sepet örgüsü.

bass¹ MUS [beis] *n.* basso, bas.

bass² ICHTH [bæs] *n.* levrek.

bas.si.net [bæsiˈnet] *n.* sepet beşik; (*sepet beşiğe benzeyen*) çocuk arabası.

bas.soon MUS [bəˈsuːn] *n.* fagot.

bast [bæst] *n.* lif, elyaf.

bas.tard ['bæstəd] **1.** □ gayrı meşru (*çocuk*); sahte; alışılmışın dışında; **2.**

n. piç; *sl.* rezil herif; '**bas.tar.dy** *n.* piçlik.

baste¹ [beist] *v/t. -in* üzerine erimiş yağ dökmek; F dayak atmak *-e*, pataklamak *-i.*

baste² [ˍ] *v/t.* teyellemek *-i*, çatmak *-i.*

bas.ti.na.do [bæstiˈneidəu] **1.** *n.* falaka; falaka sopası; **2.** *v/t.* falaka çekmek *-e*; dayak atmak *-e.*

bas.tion MIL ['bæstiən] *n.* kale burcu, tabya; müdafaada güçlü nokta.

bat¹ [bæt] *n.* yarasa; **as blind as a** ~ tamamen kör.

bat² [ˍ] *spor:* **1.** *n.* (*beysbol*, *kriket*) sopa, çomak; (*pingpong*, *tenis*) raket; sert sopa; vurucu (*oyuncu*); **off one's own** ~ *fig.* kendiliğinden, yalnız başına; **2.** *vb.* sopa ile vurmak; oynamak; ~ **for** *s.o. b-ne* sahip çıkmak, *b-nin* yardımına koşmak.

batch [bætʃ] *n.* bir ağız (*veya fırın*) ekmek; yığın (*mektup vs.*).

bate [beit] *vb.* azaltmak *-i.* kısaltmak *-i*, eksiltmek *-i*; (*fiyat*) indirmek; (*nefes*, *soluk*) tutmak; **with ~d breath** nefesi kesilerek, soluk soluğa.

bath [bɑːθ] **1.** *n. pl.* banyo, hamam; kaplıca; (*fotoğraf*, *film v.b.*) banyosu; **2.** *v/t.* (*çocuk*) banyo etm., yıkamak; *v/i.* banyo yapmak.

bathe [beið] **1.** *v/i.* (*nehir veya denizde*) yıkanmak; yüzmek; *v/t.* yıkamak *-i*, banyo etm. *-i*; *bşi* ıslatmak, sulamak.

bath.house ['bɑːθhaus] *n.* hamam; soyunma kabini (*plajda*).

bath.ing ['beiðiŋ] *n.* deniz banyosu, yüzme; '**~.cap** *n.* lâstik başlık, bone; '**~.costume**, '**~.dress** *n.* mayo; '**~.hut** *n.* soyunma kabini; '**~.ma'chine** *n.* seyyar soyunma kabini; '**~.suit** *n.* mayo.

ba.thos RHET ['beiθəs] *n.* çok güzel ve asil düşünce veya sözlerdeki ani değişme; beylik veya müptezel konuları işleme.

bath...: '**~.robe** *n. Am.* bornoz; '**~.room** *n.* banyo dairesi; tuvalet; '**~.tow.el** *n.* hamam havlusu; '**~.tub** *n.* banyo küveti.

ba.tik ['bætik] *n.* batik, kumaşı boyama işi.

ba.tiste [bæˈtiːst] *n.* patiska.

bat.man ['bætmən] *n.* emir eri.

ba.ton ['bætən] *n.* asa; değnek, sopa, baston; MUS orkestra şefinin değneği, baton; polis sopası.

bats.man ['bætsmən] *n.* kriket vs.: topa vurma sırası kendisinde olan oyuncu.

bat.tal.ion MIL [bə'tæljən] n. tabur, müfreze.

bat.ten ['bætn] **1.** n. pervaz, tiriz, takoz; **2.** vb. tiriz çekmek; semir(t)mek (**on, upon** -le); ~ **down the hatches** NAUT kaporta ağızlarını kapatmak.

bat.ter ['bætə] **1.** n. kriket; topa vuran oyuncu; mutfak; sulu hamur; **2.** v/t. şiddetle vurmak -e; dövmek; tahrip etm.; fig. durmadan hamle yapmak; MIL bombardıman etm.; '**bat.tered** adj. hırpalanmış, eskimiş; çarpık; '**bat.tering ram** (eski zamanlarda) kale duvarlarını veya kapılarını kırmak için kullanılan ucu demirli kalın kütük; '**batter.y** n. MIL batarya; ELECT pil, akümülatör; beysbol; atıcı ve tutucu; JUR dövme, müessir fiil; dizi, seri; **assault and** ~ **müessir fiil**.

bat.tle ['bætl] **1.** n. muharebe, savaş; dövüş; ~ **royal** korkunç savaş veya mücadele; **2.** vb. mücadele etm., savaşmak (**for** için); muharebe etm., çarpışmak (**against, with** -e karşı, ile); '~**axe** n. cenk baltası; fig. hırçın kadın.

bat.tle.dore ['bætldɔː] n. tüylü mantarla oynanan bir oyun; bu oyuna ait raket.

bat.tle-field ['bætlfiːld], '**bat.tle--ground** n. savaş alanı (a. fig.).

bat.tle.ment ['bætlmənt] n. göğüs siperi; ~**s** pl. siper.

bat.tle-ship MIL ['bætlʃip] n. zırhlı savaş gemisi.

bat.tue [bæ'tuː] n. sürgün avı.

bat.ty sl. ['bæti] adj. deli, kaçık.

bau.ble ['bɔːbl] n. gösterişli fakat değersiz şey, oyun, oyuncak.

baulk [bɔːk] = **balk**.

baux.ite MIN ['bɔːksait] n. boksit.

baw.bee Scots [bɔː'biː] = **halfpenny**.

bawd [bɔːd] n. pezevenk, genelev patronu; '**bawd.y** □ açık saçık, müstehcen.

bawl [bɔːl] vb. bağırmak, haykırmak, feryat etm.; ~ **out** Am. sl. fena azarlamak, haşlamak.

bay¹ [bei] **1.** adj. doru (at), kızıl kahverengi; **2.** n. doru rengi; doru at.

bay² [-] n. küçük körfez, koy; ~ **salt** kaba tuz.

bay³ [-] n. ARCH iki kiriş veya dikme arası; göz, çekme; çıkma, cumba; bölüm, kısım; **sick-**~ NAUT gemi hastanesi.

bay⁴ BOT [-] n. defne ağacı.

bay⁵ [-] v/i. havlamak, ürümek (kö-

pek); ~ **at** havlamak -e; **stand at** ~ ümitsizlik ve yeis içinde mücadeleye girişmek; **bring to** ~, **keep** veya **hold at** ~ sıkıştırmak, yanına kimseyi yaklaştırmamak (a. fig.).

bay.o.net MIL ['beiənit] **1.** n. süngü, kasatura; **2.** v/t. süngülemek; '~**catch** n. MEC süngü kilidi.

bay.ou Am. GEOGR ['baiuː] n. bir nehir veya gölün akıntısı az ve bataklıklı kolu.

bay-win.dow ['bei'windəu] n. cumba; Am. sl. çıkıntı (göbek).

ba.zaar [bə'zɑː] n. pazar, çarşı; kermes.

be [biː, bi] (irr.) vb. **1.** olmak, bulunmak; mevcut olm., var olm.; hazır olm.; **there is** veya **there are** var, bulunur; **here's to you(r health)** ! sıhhatinize!, şerefinize!; **here you are** buyur, al; ha geldin mi?; işte!; **as it were** gibi, sanki, güya; ~ **about ...** üzere olm.; ~ **after s.o.** b-nin peşinde olm., arkasına düşmek; ~ **at** bulunmak, olmak; ~ **off** ayrılmak, terketmek; yanılmak; (mal, bilet vs.) hepsi satılmış olm.; ~ **off with you!** defol!; **2.** v/aux. p. pr. ile etken süreklilik kalıbını meydana getirir; ~ **reading** okumakta olm.; **I am reading** okuyorum; **3.** v/aux. mastar ile zorunluluk, amaç, olabilirlik bildiren durumlarda; **I am to inform you size** bildirmem gerekir; **it is** (**not**) **to be seen** gözükme(me)li; **if he were to die** ölecek olursa; **4.** v/aux. p.p. ile edilgen fiil yapmaya yarar; **I am asked** benden ...-mam isteniyor.

beach [biːtʃ] **1.** n. kumsal, sahil, plâj; **2.** vb. NAUT karaya çekmek; '~**comb.er** n. sahilde yaşayıp düzenli bir işi olmayan kimse; okyanustan sahile vuran büyük dalga; fig. aylak; '~**head** n. MIL köprübaşı.

bea.con ['biːkən] **1.** n. fener; yüksek bir yerde yakılan işaret ateşi; işaret kulesi; NAUT nirengi feneri, şamandıra; yaya geçitlerdeki sarı ışık; fig. yol gösterici kimse veya şey; **2.** vb. yol göstermek; işaret koymak; fig. yol göstermek.

bead [biːd] **1.** n. boncuk, tesbih tanesi; damla, dane; ~**s** pl. tesbih; **2.** v/t. (inci vs. ile) süslemek; dizmek; v/i. (ter vs.) tane tane toplanmak; '**bead.ing** n. boncuklu işleme.

bea.dle ['biːdl] n. bir kilise görevlisi.

beads.man, **beads.wom.an** ['biːdzmən, '-wumən] n. dua okuyucu.

bead.y ['biːdi] adj. boncuk gibi; küçük,

yuvarlak ve parlak (*göz*).
bea.gle ['bi:gl] *n.* tavşan avında kullanılan kısa bacaklı av köpeği.
beak [bi:k] *n.* gaga, bir kabın ağzı; *sl.* kemerli burun; *sl.* hâkim; öğretmen; **beaked** *adj.* gagalı; sivri.
beak.er ['bi:kə] *n.* geniş ağızlı bardak.
beam [bi:m] **1.** *n.* kiriş, direk, mertek, putrel; terazi kolu; NAUT kemere; şua, ışın (*radyo, güneş*); **2.** *v/t.* yaymak, neşretmek; *v/i.* parlamak; yayılmak; sevinç içinde gülümsemek; '~'**ends** *pl.*: *the ship is on her* ~ gemi alabora olurcasına yan yatmış; *on one's* ~ fig. (*malî açıdan*) sıfırı tüketmiş.
bean [bi:n] *n.* fasulye; tane (*kahve v.b.*); *Am. sl.* kafa; *sl.* metelik; *full of* ~*s* F kanlı canlı, hayat dolu; *give s.o.* ~*s* *sl.* dünyanın kaç bucak olduğunu göstermek, marizlemek; '~-feast, **bean.o** *sl.* [bi:nəu] *n.* şenlik.
bear[1] [beə] **1.** *n.* ayı, ayıya benzer hayvan; *fig.* hantal, hoyrat kimse; COM *sl.* spekülatör; **2.** *v/t.* borsa fiyatlarını indirmeğe çalışmak; spekülâsyon yapmak.
bear[2] [_] (*irr.*) *v/t.* taşımak, kaldırmak; tahammül etm., katlanmak -*e*; doğurmak -*i*; (*meyva*) vermek; üstüne almak -*i*; ~ *away* götürmek; meyletmek; ~ *down* bastırmak, yenmek -*i*; ~ *out* desteklemek, teyidetmek -*i*; ~ *up* (*güçlüklere rağmen*) cesareti elden bırakmamak; sabır ve tahammül etm.; *v/i.* sabretmek, tahammül etm., dayanmak; NAUT (*adv. ile*) yönüne dönmek; ~ *down upon* NAUT ...yönüne seyretmek; ~ *to the right* sağa meyletmek; ~ *up* dayanmak, mukavemet etm. (*against* -*e*); ~ *up!* cesaret!; ~ *with* tahammül etm. -*e*, sabırlı olm. -*e karşı*; *bring to* ~ harekete getirmek; yönlendirmek (*on, upon* -*e*).
beard [biəd] **1.** *n.* sakal; BOT püskül, başak dikeni; **2.** *v/t. b-ne* meydan okumak, karşı gelmek; '**beard.ed** *adj.* sakallı; '**beardless** *adj.* sakalsız.
bear.er ['beərə] *n.* taşıyan kimse; *pasaport*; hâmil, taşıyan kimse; *çek*; hâmil; tabut taşıyan kimse; MEC destek.
bear.ing ['beəriŋ] *n.* tavır, davranma; ilgi (*on* -*ile*); etki (*on* -*e*); tahammül; doğurma, hâsıl etme; NAUT yatak; ~*s pl.* yol, yön; MEC yatak; *ball* ~*s pl.* MEC bilyeli yatak; *beyond all* ~ dayanılmaz; *in full* ~ iyi durumda, verimli (*ağaç*); *lose one's* ~*s* şaşırmak, nerede

olduğunu bilmemek; *take one's* ~*s* bulunan yerin yönünü tayin etm..
bear.ish □ ['beəriʃ] ayı gibi kaba, hantal; COM borsada fiyat indirmeye meyilli, fiyatların düşeceğinden ümitli.
bear.skin ['beəskin] *n.* ayı postu; İngiliz ordusunda törenlerde giyilen bir çeşit kalpak.
beast [bi:st] *n.* hayvan (*esp. dört ayaklı*); vahşi hayvan, canavar (*a. fig.*); ~ *of* burden yük hayvanı; ~ *of prey* yırtıcı hayvan; **beast.li.ness** ['~li-nis] *n.* hayvan gibi davranış; '**beast.ly** *adj.* hayvan gibi; F çok fena; *adv.* çok, aşırı derecede.
beat [bi:t] **1.** (*irr.*) *vb.* tekrar tekrar vurmak, çarpmak; dövmek; (*kalp*) atmak; çarpmak; (*davul vs.*) çalmak; yenmek, galip gelmek; (*yumurta vs.*) çalkamak; üstün olm.; *Am.* F bşin önünü almak; yol açmak; HUNT sürmek; önüne katmak; ~ *it!* *Am. sl.* defol!; ~ *the band* *Am.* F fevkalâde olarak; ~ *one's brains* zihnini karıştırmak; kafa yormak; parçalanmak; ~ *a retreat* geri çekilmek, ricat etm.; ~ *time* MUS tempo tutmak; ~ *one's way* k-ne yol açmak; ~ *down* ezmek, çiğnemek; COM pazarlıkta fiyat kırmak; ~ *up* (*yumurta vs.*) çırpmak; F dövmek, galip gelmek; ~ *about* bşi heyecanla ara(ştır)mak; ~ *about the bush* bin dereden su getirmek; **2.** *n.* vuruş, darbe; *fig.* kalp atışı; MUS tempo; (*polis v.b.*) devriye; (*davul vs.*) çalma; *Am. gazete*: büyük yankı yaratan bir haberin yayınlanması; = *beatnik*; **3.** *adj.* F yorgun, yıpranmış; *dead* ~ bitkin; '**beat.en** **1.** *p.p. of beat* **1**; **2.** *adj.* dövülmüş; yenik; çok kullanılmış; '**beat.er** *n.* çırpma makinesi (*aracı*); HUNT hayvanları yerinden çıkarıp süren kimse.
be.at.i.fi.ca.tion ECCL [bi:ætifi'keiʃən] *n.* ölünün ruhunu takdis etme; **be'at.i.fy** *v/t.* mutluluğa ulaştırmak; ECCL ölünün ruhunu takdis etm.
beat.ing ['bi:tiŋ] *n.* dövme, dayak; yenilgi; *give s.o. a good* ~ b-ni iyice dövmek.
be.at.i.tude [bi:'ætitju:d] *n.* büyük mutluluk, mutlak saadet.
beat.nik ['bi:tnik] *n.* (*1950'li yılların sonu 1960'lı yılların başı*) F bitnik, hipi.
beau [bəu] *n.*, *pl.* **beaux** [_z] modaya uyan adam; sevgili, kavalye.
beau.teous *poet.* ['bju:tjəs] □ güzel, zarif.

beau.ti.ful □ ['bju:təful] güzel, hoş, zarif, latif.

beau.ti.fy ['bju:tifai] *v/t.* güzelleştirmek, süslemek.

beau.ty ['bju:ti] *n.* güzellik (*a. güzel kadın*); F mükemmel, nefis şey; *~ parlo(u) r*, *~ shop* güzellik salonu, kuaför salonu; *~ sleep* güzellik uykusu; *~ spot* (*yüzdeki*) ben; güzel manzaralı yer.

bea.ver ['bi:və] *n.* kunduz; kastor (*kürk*); kastor şapka.

be.bop MUS *Am.* ['bi:bɔp] *n.* bir tür caz müziği.

be.calm [bi'ka:m] *v/t.* teskin etm., yatış tırmak; rüzgârsızlıktan kımıldatamamak; *be ~ed* (*yelkenli*) rüzgârsızlıktan kımıldanamamak.

be.came [bi'keim] *pret. of* **become.**

be.cause [bi'kɔz] *cj.* çünkü, zira, diği için, -den dolayı, sebebiyle; *~ of* -den dolayı, sebebiyle, yüzünden.

beck [bek] *n.* işaret; *at one's ~ and call* b-nin emrine amade.

beck.on ['bekən] *v/t.* işaret etm. -e.

be.cloud [bi'klaud] *v/t.* bulutlandırmak, karartmak.

be.come [bi'kʌm] (*irr.*) *v/i.* olmak; *v/t.* yakışmak, gitmek -e; *what has ~ of him* o ne oldu?, o şimdi ne halde?; *be~coming* □ uygun; yakışık.

bed [bed] **1.** *n.* yatak, yatacak yer, karyola; (*nehir vs.*) yatak; (*hayvan*) in; F sevişme; AGR tarh, çiçeklik; (*arazi*) tabakat, kat; *be brought to ~ of* çocuk dünyaya getirmek; *~ and board* yiyecek ve yatacak yer, iaşe ve ibate; *take to one's ~* yatağa düşmek; *as you make your ~ so you must lie on it* kişi yaptıklarına katlanmalı; **2.** *v/t.* yatırmak, yerleştirmek; misafir etm.; *v/i.* yatmak; AGR *~ (out)* dikmek, ekmek.

be.daub [bi'dɔːb] *v/t.* bulaştırmak, sürmek, karalamak.

be.dazzle [bi'dæzl] *v/t.* kamaştırmak -*i.*

bed...: '*~cham.ber* n. yatak odası; '*~-clothes* n. *pl.* yatak takımı (*örtü, battaniye v.b.*).

bed.ding ['bedin] *n.* yatak takımı; hayvan yatağı.

be.deck [bi'dek] *v/t.* süslemek, donatmak (*with ile.*).

be.dev.il [bi'devl] *v/t.* çıldırtmak, çileden çıkarmak; bozmak; berbadetmek; **be'dev.il.ment** *n.* çileden çıkartma.

be.dew [bi'dju:] *v/t.* çiğ taneleri ile ıslatmak; *poet.* ıslatmak, nemlendirmek.

bed.fel.low ['bedfeləu] *n.* yatak arkadaşı; yakın arkadaş.

be.dight *obs.* [bi'dait] *v/t.* süslemek.

be.dim [bi'dim] *v/t.* karartmak, bulutlandırmak.

be.diz.en [bi'daizn] *v/t.* süsleyip püslemek, kabaca süslemek.

bed.lam ['bedləm] *n.* tımarhane; son derece gürültülü yer veya faaliyet, çıfıt çarşısı; **bed.lam.ite** ['~mait] *n.* akıl hastası, kaçık.

bed-lin.en ['bedlinin] *n.* yatak takımları.

Bed.ou.in ['beduin] *n. & adj.* bedevî.

bed-pan ['bedpæn] *n.* yatak lâzımlığı.

be.drag.gle [bi'drægl] *v/t.* (*elbise vs.*) kirletmek, bulaştırmak.

bed...: '*~.rid(.den)* *adj.* yatalak; '*~'rock* *n.* GEOL üstündeki toprağa destek olan asıl kaya; *fig.* temel, esas; '*~.room* *n.* yatak odası; '*~.side* *n.* yatak yanı, başucu; *good ~ manner* doktorun hastaya iyi davranması; *~ lamp* gece lambası; *~ rug* kaliçe, karyola halısı; *~ table* komodin; '*~'sit.ter* F, '*~'sit-ting-room* *n.* hem oturma hem de yatma için kullanılan oda; '*~.sore* *n.* MED uzun zaman yatmaktan ileri gelen yatak yarası; '*~.spread* *n.* yatak örtüsü; '*~-stead* *n.* karyola, kerevet; '*~.tick* *n.* yatak yüzü; '*~.time* *n.* yatma zamanı.

bee [bi:] *n.* arı; *Am.* toplu çalışma toplantısı; arkadaşlar arasında yapılan yarışma; *have a ~ in one's bonnet* F kafasını *bşe* takmak, *bşe* kurmak.

beech BOT [bi:tʃ] *n.* kayın ağacı; '*~.nut* *n.* kayın kozalağı.

beef [bi:f] **1.** *n.* sığır eti; F adele gücü; *sl. şikâyet;* **2.** *Am.* F *vb.* şikâyet etm.; '*~.eat.er* *n.* Londra Kalesi bekçisi; '*~.steak* ['bi:f'steik] *n.* biftek; '*~'tea* *n.* sığır eti suyu; '**beef.y** *adj.* etli butlu, iri yarı.

bee...: '*~.hive* *n.* arı kovanı; '*~-keep.er* *n.* arı yetiştiricisi; '*~-keep.ing* *n.* arıcılık; '*~-line* *n.* en kısa yol; *make a ~ for bşe* en kısa yoldan ulaşmak.

been [bi:n, bin] *p.p. of* **be.**

beer [biə] *n.* bira; *small ~* hafif bira; F önemsiz şey; *he thinks no small ~ of himself* sanki küçük dağları o yarattı; '**beer.y** *adj.* F bira etkisiyle sarhoş olan.

bees.wax ['biːzwæks] **1.** *n.* balmumu; **2.** *v/t.* balmumu ile cilâlamak.

beet BOT [biːt] *n.* pancar; *white* ~ şeker pancarı.

bee.tle¹ ['biːtl] **1.** *n.* şahmerdan, kazık tokmağı; **2.** *v/t.* şahmerdan veya tokmakla kakmak, tokmaklamak.

bee.tle² [-] *n.* kınkanatlılardan herhangi bir böcek.

bee.tle³ [-] **1.** *adj.* üstünden sarkan, taşan; **2.** *v/i.* bşin üstünden sarkmak, taşmak.

beet.root ['biːtruːt] *n.* pancar.

beet-sug.ar ['biːtʃugə] *n.* pancar şekeri.

beeves [biːvz] *pl. of* **beef**.

be.fall [bi'fɔːl] (*irr.* fall) *v/i.* zuhur etm., vuku bulmak; *v/t.* -in başına gelmek.

be.fit [bi'fit] *v/t.* uygun olm. -e, münasip olm. -e, yakışmak -e; **be'fit.ting** ⬜ uygun, münasip.

be.fog [bi'fɔg] *v/t.* sisle kaplamak, dumanlandırmak.

be.fool [bi'fuːl] *v/t.* aldatmak, saptırmak.

be.fore [bi'fɔː] **1.** *adv. yer:* önde, ileride, -in önünde, önüne; *zaman:* önce, evvel, daha önce; **2.** *cj.* -den önce; **3.** *prp.* -in huzurunda, huzuruna, yerine; *be* ~ *one's time* bir önceki çağda olm.; *be* ~ *s.o.* *fig.* gözü önünde bulunmak; ~ *long* çok geçmeden, az zamanda; ~ *now* şimdiye kadar; *the day* ~ *yesterday* evvelki gün; **be'fore.hand** *adv.* önce, önceden.

be.foul [bi'faul] *v/t.* kirletmek, pislemek.

be.friend [bi'frend] *v/t.* dostça hareket etm., yardım etm. -e.

beg [beg] *v/t.* dilemek, istemek, rica etm. (*of* -den); *v/i.* dilenmek (*for s.th. of s.o.* -den bş); (*köpek*) salta durmak; *I* ~ *to inform you* COM saygılarımla bildiririm; *go* ~*ging* *fig.* isteklisi, alıcısı olmamak.

be.gan [bi'gæn] *pret. of* **begin**.

be.get [bi'get] (*irr.*) *v/t.* -in babası olm., doğurmak; sebep olm.; **be'get.ter** *n.* meydana getiren kimse, baba.

beg.gar ['begə] **1.** *n.* dilenci; F adam, biri; çapkın; **2.** *v/t.* dilendirmek, sefalete düşürmek; *fig.* aşmak; *it* ~*s all description* tarif edilemez, kelimeler yetersiz kalır; **beg'gar.ly** *adj.* dilenci gibi; komik derecede az; **beg'gar.y** *n.* aşırı yoksulluk; *reduce to* ~ aşırı yoksulluğa düşmek.

be.gin [bi'gin] (*irr.*) *vb.* başlamak -*e*; meydana gelmek; başlatmak, önayak olm.; *to* ~ *with* ilk olarak, evvelâ; **be'ginner** *n.* yeni başlayan, başlayıcı; **be'ginning** *n.* başlangıç; menşe; baş, esas; *from the* ~ başlangıçtan.

be.gird [bi'gəːd] (*irr.* gird) *v/t.* kuşatmak, çevirmek.

be.gone [bi'gɔn] *int.* defol!, yıkıl!

be.go.ni.a BOT [bi'gəunjə] *n.* begonya.

be.got, be.got.ten [bi'gɔt(n)] *pret. & p.p. of* **beget**.

be.grime [bi'graim] *v/t.* kirletmek, pisletmek.

be.grudge [bi'grʌdʒ] *v/t.* vermek istememek; çok görmek; *bşi* esirgemek -*den*.

be.guile [bi'gail] *v/t.* baştan çıkarmak, aldatmak (*of, out of* -*de*); hoşça vakit geçirmek (*by, with*); ~ *s.o. into* *b-ni* *bşle* kandırmak, aldatmak.

be.gun [bi'gʌn] *p.p. of* **begin**.

be.half [bi'hɑːf]: *on veya in* ~ *of* adına, namına; lehinde.

be.have [bi'heiv] *v/t.* davranmak, hareket etm.; ~ *o.s.* terbiyesini takınmak, iyi hareket etm.; **be'hav.io(u)r** [-jə] *n.* davranış, tavır, muaşeret; *be on one's good veya best* ~ en iyi davranışı ortaya koymağa çalışmak; *be of good* ~ JUR iyi davranış göstermek; **be'hav.io(u)r.ism** *n.* PSYCH davranışçılık kuramı.

be.head [bi'hed] *v/t.* -in başını kesmek; **be'.head.ing** *n.* -in başını kesme.

be.hest *poet.* [bi'hest] *n.* emir, buyruk.

be.hind [bi'haind] **1.** *adv.* geri, geride, geriye, arkada kalan; **2.** *prp.* arkada; -in arkasında, arkasına, -in gerisinde, geri; *s. time*; **be'hind.hand** *adv. & adj.* gecikmiş, geride.

be.hold [bi'həuld] **1.** (*irr.* hold) *v/t.* görmek; bakmak -*e*; **2.** *int.* işte!, bak!; **be'.hold.en** *adj.* borçlu, medyun; **be'.hold.er** *n.* seyirci.

be.hoof [bi'huːf] *n. to* (*for, on*) (*the*) ~ *of* -in menfaatine, çıkarına.

be.hoove *Am.* [bi'huːv] = **behove**.

be.hove [bi'həuv]: *it* ~*s s.o. to inf.* …*için* gereklidir.

beige [beiʒ] **1.** *n.* bej (*kumaş*); **2.** *adj.* bej (*renk*).

be.ing ['biːiŋ] *n.* oluş; varlık; mahlûk, yaratık; *in* ~ *bilfiil* mevcut; *come into* ~ meydana çıkmak, vücut bulmak.

be.la.bo(u)r [bi'leibə] *v/t.* dil uzatmak -*e*; adamakıllı dövmek -*i*.

benefit

be.laid [bi'leid] *pret. & p.p. of belay.*
be.lat.ed □ [bi'leitid] gecikmiş, geç kalmış.
be.lay [bi'lei] **1.** (*irr.*) *v/t.* NAUT (*halat*) bağlamak, volta etm.; MOUNT emniyete almak; **2.** *n.* MOUNT güvenlik çıkıntısı.
belch [beltʃ] **1.** *v/i.* geğirmek; *v/t.* püskürtmek, fırlatmak; **2.** *n.* geğirme; fırlatma, püskürtme.
bel.dam *contp.* ['beldəm] *n.* kocakarı; nine.
be.lea.guer [bi'li:gə] *v/t.* kuşatmak, muhasara etm.
bel.fry ['belfri] *n.* çan kulesi, çan kulesi sahanlığı.
Bel.gian ['beldʒən] **1.** *adj.* Belçika'ya ait; **2.** *n.* Belçikalı.
be.lie [bi'lai] *v/t.* yalancı çıkarmak, yalanlamak.
be.lief [bi'li:f] *n.* inanç, iman, itikat; güven (*in -e*); *past all* ~ inanılmaz; *to the best of my* ~ benim bildiğime göre.
be.liev.a.ble □ [bi'li:vəbl] inanılır.
be.lieve [bi'li:v] *v/t.* inanmak *-e*; zannetmek *-i*; *v/i.* itimat etm., güvenmek, inanmak (*in -e*); ~ *in* iman etm. *-e*, itimat etm. *-e*; be'liev.er *n.* inanan, inançlı, mümin.
be.lit.tle [bi'litl] *v/t. fig.* küçültmek, küçümsemek.
bell¹ [bel] **1.** *n.* zil, çıngırak, çan, kampana; çan şeklinde olan şey; **2.** *v/t.* ~ *the cat* başkalarının yanaşamadığı tehlikeli bir işi başarmak.
bell² [‿] *v/i.* (geyik) bağırmak.
bell.boy *Am.* ['belbɔi] *n.* otellerde oda servisi yapan çocuk, otel oğlanı.
belle [bel] *n.* güzel ve çekici kadın, dilber.
belles-let.tres ['bel'letr] *n. pl.* edebiyat; edebiyatın seçme örnekleri.
bell...: '~-flow.er *n.* çançiçeği; '~-found.er *n.* çan dökümcüsü; '~-glass *n.* cam kılıf; fanus, karpuz; '~.hop *n. Am. sl.* otel oğlanı.
bel.li.cose ['belikəus] *adj.* kavgacı, döğüşken; savaşmayı seven.
bel.lied ['belid] *adj.* göbekli.
bel.lig.er.ent [bi'lidʒərənt] **1.** *adj.* muharip; kavgacı, münakaşacı; harbe meyilli; **2.** *n.* harpte taraflardan biri.
bel.low ['beləu] **1.** *v/i.* böğürmek; bağırmak; **2.** *n.* böğürme, bağırma.
bel.lows ['beləuz] *n. pl.:* (*a pair of*) ~ körük; PHOT körük.
bell...: '~-pull *n.* çan ipi; '~-push *n.* elektrikli zil düğmesi; '~-weth.er *n.* sü-

rünün önünden giderek ona kılavuzluk eden koç ya da teke, kösemen.
bel.ly ['beli] **1.** *n.* karın; vücudun bu kısmı gibi yuvarlak veya şişkin olan şey; ~ *landing* AVIA gövde üstüne iniş; **2.** *vb.* şiş(ir)mek; bel.ly.ful F ['‿ful] *n.* haddinden fazla.
be.long [bi'lɔŋ] *v/i.* ait olm., mensup olm. (*to -e*); be'long.ings *n. pl.* eşya; F pılı pırtı.
be.lov.ed [bi'lʌvd] **1.** *adj.* sevgili, aziz; **2.** [mst. ‿vid] *n.* sevgili.
be.low [bi'ləu] **1.** *adj.* aşağıda, aşağı; *-in* altında; yeryüzünde; **2.** *prp. -den* aşağı.
belt [belt] **1.** *n.* kayış; kuşak, kemer, bel kayışı; MIL kılıç kayışı; palaska; şerit; bölge; MEC transmisyon kayışı; *sl.* çok hızlı araba yolculuğu; *hit below the* ~ kahpece hareket etm.; **2.** *v/t.* kemer bağlamak; kayışla dövmek; ~ *out Am.* F yüksek sesle şarkı söylemek.
be.moan [bi'məun] *v/t.* bş için keder etm., üzüntüsünü belirtmek, *b-nin* yasını tutmak.
bench [bentʃ] *n.* sıra, bank; yargıç kürsüsü; mahkeme; yargıçlar heyeti; tezgâh; *s. treasury*; 'bench.er *n.* baronun idare meclisi üyesi.
bend [bend] **1.** *n.* kavis, dönemeç, viraj; kıvırma, kıvrım; NAUT bağ, düğüm; **2.** (*irr.*) *v/t.* bükmek, eğriltmek, kıvırmak; *b-ni* ikna etm., yola getirmek; NAUT bağlamak; *v/i.* bükülmek, eğilmek, çevrilmek; teslim olm., râm olm.; *s. bent¹* **1.**
be.neath [bi'ni:θ] = *below.*
ben.e.dick ['benidik] *n.* evlenen yaşı ilerlemiş bekâr; yeni evli adam.
Ben.e.dic.tine ['beni'diktin] *n.* Sen Benuva tarikatından rahip; [‿ti:n] bir cins likör.
ben.e.dic.tion ECCL [beni'dikʃən] *n.* takdis, takdis duası.
ben.e.fac.tion [beni'fækʃən] *n.* iyilik, ihsan, hayır; ben.e.fac.tor ['‿tə] *n.* iyilik eden, velinimet; ben.e.fac.tress ['‿tris] *n.* iyilik eden kadın.
ben.e.fice ['benifis] *n.* papazlık maaşı ve makamı; be.nef.i.cence [bi'nefisəns] *n.* iyilik, lütuf, hayır; be'nef.i.cent □ hayır sahibi, lütufkâr.
ben.e.fi.cial □ [beni'fiʃəl] hayırlı; yararlı (*to -e*); ~ *interest* JUR faydalanma hakkı; ben.e'fi.ci.ar.y *n.* lehtar, faydalanan kimse.
ben.e.fit ['benifit] **1.** *n.* yarar, fayda, menfaat, kâr; hayır için verilen konser

vs.; yetki; **for the ~ of** lehine; yararına, menfaatine; **2.** *v/t.* yaramak, faydalı olm. *-e*; *v/i.* istifade etm., faydalanmak (**by, from** *-den*).

be.nev.o.lence [bi'nevələns] *n.* iyilikseverlik; yardım, sadaka; **be'nev.o.lent** □ iyi dilekli, hayırhah; kâr gayesi gütmeyen.

be.night.ed □ [bi'naitid] gece karanlığında kalmış; *fig.* cahil, karanlıkta kalmış.

be.nign □ [bi'nain] yumuşak huylu, iyi kalpli, şefkatli, MED tehlikesiz, selim; **benig.nant** □ [bi'nignənt] iyi huylu, müşfik; **be'nig.ni.ty** *n.* yumuşaklık, iyi kalplilik.

bent[1] [bent] **1.** *pret* & *p.p. of* **bend 2**; **~ on** azmetmek *-e*, çok istemek *-i*; **2.** *n.* eğim; meyil, temayül; **to the top of one's ~** canı istediği kadar.

bent[2] BOT [~] *n.* birkaç tür sert çimen.

be.numb [bi'nʌm] *v/t.* uyuşturmak, hissini iptal etm.

ben.zene CHEM ['benzi:n] *n.* benzol.

ben.zine CHEM ['benzi:n] *n.* benzin.

be.queath [bi'kwi:ð] *v/t.* vasiyet etm., terketmek, vasiyetle bırakmak.

be.quest [bi'kwest] *n.* vasiyetname ile bırakılan şey, menkul vasiyeti.

be.reave [bi'ri:v] (*irr.*) *v/t.* mahrum etm. *-den*, elinden almak (**of** *-i*); **be ~d of** ölüm nedeniyle mahrum kalmak *-den*; **~d** *adj.* geride kalan, ölen kişinin yakını; **be'reave.ment** *n.* elemli kayıp (*ölüm*); mahrumiyet *-den*.

be.reft [bi'reft] *pret.* & *p.p. of* **bereave**.

be.ret ['berei] *n.* bere.

berg [bə:g] = *iceberg*.

ber.ry ['beri] *n.* (*küçük meyva*) tane.

berth [bə:θ] **1.** *n.* (*vapur, tren, uçak*) ranza, yatak; NAUT geminin rıhtımdaki demir yeri; iş, görev; **give s.o. a wide ~** *-den* uzak durmak, *-den* kaçınmak; **2.** *v/t.* gemiye yer vermek; rıhtıma yanaştırmak; yatacak yer vermek.

ber.yl MIN ['beril] *n.* bir tür zümrüt.

be.seech [bi'si:tʃ] (*irr.*) *v/t.* istirham etm., yalvarmak *-e*; **be'seech.ing** □ yalvaran; **be'seech.ing.ly** *adv.* yalvararak.

be.seem [bi'si:m] *v/t.* yakışmak, yaraşmak, uymak; yakışık almak.

be.set [bi'set] (*irr.* **set**) *v/t.* kuşatmak, sarmak; (*savaş*) kuşatıp saldırıya hazır olm.; **~ting** sin insanın yakasını bırakmayan hata veya günah.

be.side [bi'said] **1.** *adv. s.* **besides**; **2.**

prp. -in yanın(d)a, *-in* tarafın(d)a (*a. fig.*); *-e* nazaran, üstelik; *-den* başka, *-in* dışında; **~ o.s.** kendinden geçmiş, çılgın (**with** *-den*, *-den dolayı*); **~ the purpose** amaca uymıyan; **~ the question** konu ile ilgili olmıyan, sadet dışı; **be'sides** [~dz] **1.** *adv.* bundan başka, ayrıca; üstelik; **2.** *prp. -den* başka, *-den* gayrı, *-den* hariç.

be.siege [bi'si:dʒ] *v/t.* kuşatmak, muhasara etm.; *fig.* musallat olm., sıkıntı vermek, baskı altında tutmak; **be'sieg.er** *n.* kuşatan kimse.

be.slob.ber [bi'slɔbə] *v/t.* salya bulaştırmak.

be.smear [bi'smiə] *v/t.* kirletmek, bulaştırmak.

be.smirch [bi'smə:tʃ] *v/t.* lekelemek, şerefine halel getirmek.

be.som ['bi:zəm] *n.* çalı süpürgesi.

be.sot.ted [bi'sɔtid] *adj.* sarhoş (*a. fig.*).

be.sought [bi'sɔ:t] *pret.* & *p.p. of* **beseech**.

be.spat.ter [bi'spætə] *v/t.* çamur sıçratmak, lekelemek; *fig.* iftira etm., çamur atmak.

be.speak [bi'spi:k] (*irr.*) *v/t.* göstermek, *bşe* delâlet etm.; tutmak, rezerve ettirmek.

be.spoke [bi'spəuk] *pret. of* **bespeak**; *adj.*: **~ tailor** ısmarlama elbise yapan terzi; **be'spo.ken** *p.p. of* **bespeak**.

be.sprin.kle [bi'spriŋkl] *v/t.* serpmek, saçmak.

best [best] **1.** *adj.* en iyi, en çok, en uygun; **~ man** sağdıç; **the ~ part of** çoğunluğu; *s.* **seller**; **2.** *adv.* en iyi şekilde; en çok; **3.** *n.* en iyisi; **Sunday ~** pazarlık elbise, yabanlık; **all for the ~** belki de daha iyi; **to the ~ of** son derece, haddinden fazla; **have** veya **get the ~ of** yenmek, alt etm. *-i*; **make the ~ of** mümkün olduğu kadar yararlanmak *-den*; **to the ~ of my knowledge** bildiğime göre; **at ~** olsa olsa, ancak; en çok; **4.** *v/t.* F yenmek, hakkından gelmek.

be.ste(a)d [bi'sted]: **hard ~** müşkül durumda.

bes.tial □ ['bestjəl] hayvan gibi, hayvanca; çok kaba; vahşî; **bes.ti.al.i.ty** [~-ti'æliti] *n.* hayvanlık; vahşîlik.

be.stir [bi'stə:] *v/t.* harekete getirmek, kımıldatmak.

be.stow [bi'stəu] *v/t.* vermek, hediye etm.; bağışlamak (**on, upon** *-e*); yerleştirmek, koymak; **be'stow.al, be'stow-**

ment *n.* verme, ihsan.

be.strew [bi'stru:] (*irr.* **strew**) *v/t.* saçmak; kaplamak (**with** -*le*).

bet [bet] **1.** *n.* bahis, iddia; **2.** (*irr.*) *vb.* bahse girmek, bahis tutuşmak; iddia etm.; *you* ~ F elbette, şüphesiz; *I* ~ *you a shilling* bir şilinine bahse girerim.

be.take [bi'teik] (*irr.* **take**) *v/t.*: ~ *o.s. to* gitmek, müracaat etm.

be.think [bi'θiŋk] (*irr.* **think**) *v/t.*: ~ *o.s.* düşünmek, hatırlamak (**of** -*i*).

be.tide [bi'taid] *vb.* başına gelmek, vuku bulmak, woe ~ *him!* Allah kahretsin!

be.times [bi'taimz] *adv.* erken, erkenden.

be.to.ken [bi'təukən] *v/t.* delâlet etm., göstermek.

be.tray [bi'trei] *v/t.* ihanet etm., ele vermek; ifşa etm., ağzından kaçırmak; göstermek, ortaya koymak; yanlış yola sevketmek; be'tray.al *n.* hıyanet, ele verme, ifşa; ~ *of trust* emniyeti suiistimal, inancı kötüye kullanma; be'tray.er *n.* hain, gammaz.

be.troth [bi'trəuð] *v/t.* nişanlamak (*to ile*); *the* ~*ed* nişanlı; be'troth.al *n.* nişan.

bet.ter¹ ['betə] **1.** *adj.* daha iyi, daha güzel; daha çok; *he is* ~ daha iyi; *get* ~ iyileşmek; **2.** *n.* daha iyisi; ~*s pl.* mafevk, kendinden üstün kimseler; *get the* ~ *of* yenmek -*i*, üstün olm. -*den*; **3.** *adv.* daha iyi bir şekilde, daha çok; *be* ~ *off* daha iyi durumda olm.; *so much the* ~ daha iyi; isabet! *you had* ~ *go* gitsen iyi olacak; *think* ~ *of it* fikrini değiştirmek, vazgeçmek; **4.** *v/t.* iyileştirmek, ıslah etm.; ~ *o.s.* (*ücret vs.*) daha iyi şekle sokmak; *v/i.* iyileşmek, ıslah olunmak.

bet.ter² [-] *n.* bahse giren kimse.

bet.ter.ment ['betəmənt] *n.* ıslah, iyileştirme.

be.tween [bi'twi:n], *poet & prov. a.* be.twixt [bi'twikst] **1.** *adv.* araya, arada, ortaya, ortada; *betwixt and* ~ ikisinin ortası, ne bu ne o; *in* ~ sallantıda; *far* ~ nadir, seyrek; **2.** *prp.* -*in* arasına, arasında, aralarında, ortasına, ortasında; ~ *ourselves* aramızda; be'tween-decks *n.* NAUT ara güverte.

bev.el ['bevəl] **1.** *adj.* mail, eğik, şevli; **2.** *n.* MEC şev, açı, eğim; **3.** *v/t.* şev vermek, eğik olarak kesmek; '~wheel *n.* MEC konik dişli çark.

bev.er.age ['bevərid3] *n.* içecek, meşrubat.

bevy ['bevi] *n.* kuş sürüsü; küme, zümre, takım; *a* ~ *of beauties* bir sürü güzel kadın.

be.wail [bi'weil] *v/t.* ağlamak -*e*; hayıflanmak -*e*; *v/i.* sızlanmak.

be.ware [bi'wɛə] *v/i.* dikkatli olm; sakınmak, korunmak (**of** -*den*); *int.* dikkat!, sakın!

be.wil.der [bi'wildə] *v/t.* şaşırtmak, hayrette bırakmak; sersemletmek; be'wilder.ment *n.* şaşkınlık, hayret.

be.witch F [bi'witʃ] *v/t.* büyülemek, teshir etm.; be'witch.ment *n.* büyü, cazibe.

be.yond [bi'jond] **1.** *adv.* öbür tarafta, öte, öteye, ötede, ileri; **2.** *prp.* -*in* ötesine, ötesinde, karşısında; -*den* ötede; -*in* dışında, üstünde, haricin(d)e; ~ *doubt* şüphesiz; ~ *endurance* tahammülfersa, dayanılmaz; ~ *measure* hadsız, hesapsız; *to* -*in* aşırı derecede; ~ *dispute* malûm, su götürmez, inkâr edilemez; ~ *words* ifade edilemez; *it is* ~ *me* anlamıyorum, buna aklım ermez.

bi... [bai] *prefix* iki kere, ikişer, iki...

bi.as ['baiəs] **1.** *adj. & adv.* meyilli, çapraz; **2.** *n.* meyil, temayül; peşin hüküm; *terzilik;* verev kesme; **3.** *v/t.* meylettirmek; (*aleyhte*) tesir ve nüfuz altında bulundurmak; ~(*s*)*ed adj.* taraf tutan, bitaraf olmıyan.

bib [bib] *n.* mama önlüğü; iş önlüğünün üst kısmı.

Bi.ble [baibl] *n.* Mukaddes Kitap, Tevrat, Zebur ve İncil.

bib.li.cal □ ['biblikəl] Kitabı Mukaddes'e ait.

bib.li.og.ra.pher [bibli'ɔgrəfə] *n.* bibliyografya bilgini *veya* uzmanı; bib.li.o.graphic, bib.li.o.graph.i.cal [-əu'græfik(əl)] *adj.* bibliyografyaya ait; bib.li.og.ra.phy [-'ɔgrəfi] *n.* bibliyografya; bib.li.o.mani.a [-əu'meinjə] *n.* kitap merakı; bib.lio.ma.ni.ac [-əu'meiniæk] *n. & adj.* kitap koleksiyonu yapan; kitap delisi; bib.li.o.phile ['--əufail] *n. kitap* seven kimse.

bib.u.lous □ ['bibjuləs] ayyaş, içkiye düşkün, bekri; suyu çekici.

bi.car.bon.ate CHEM [bai'kɑ:bənit] *n.* bikarbonat; ~ *of soda* bikarbonat de süt, soda.

bi.ceps ['baiseps] *n.* pazı; *fig.* güç, kuvvet.

bick.er ['bikə] *v/i.* kavga etm., çekiş-

mek, dalaşmak; *(alev)* parıldamak; *(akarsu, yağmur)* şırıldamak; 'bick-er.ing(s *pl.*) *n.* çirkin didişme, atışma.
bi.cy.cle ['baisikl] **1.** *n.* bisiklet; *ride a ~* = **2.** *v/i.* bisiklete binmek, bisikletle dolaşmak.
bid [bid] **1.** *(irr.) v/t.* emretmek, hükmetmek; demek, söylemek; davet etm.; *müzayede:* fiyat artırmak; *briç:* deklarasyon yapmak; teklif vermek; *~ fair to int.* ihtimal dahilinde olm., vadetmek; *~ farewell* vedalaşmak *(to ile)*; *~ up* fiyat artırmak; *~ welcome* «Hoş geldin» demek; **2.** *n.* teklif; girişim, teşebbüs *(to inf. -e)*; briç; deklarasyon; davet; *make a ~ for bşi* elde etmeğe çalışmak, girişimde bulunmak; *no ~ iskambil:* pas; 'bid.den *p.p. of bid*; 'bid.der *n.* teklif veren kimse; *s.* **high, low;** 'bidding *n.* artırma; emir; davet; *briç:* deklarasyon serisi.
bide [baid] *vb.:* *~ one's time* uygun zamanı beklemek.
bi.en.ni.al [bai'eniəl] □ iki yılda bir olan.
bier [biə] *n.* cenaze teskeresi.
bi.fur.cate ['baifə:keit] *v/i. (yol, nehir vs.)* iki kola ayrılmak, çatallanmak; bi-fur'ca.tion *n.* iki kola ayrılma.
big [big] *adj.* büyük, kocaman, iri; F önemli, etkili; gebe *(a. fig. with -e)*; ♀ *Ben* İngiliz parlamento binasındaki büyük saat kulesi; *~ business* büyük sermayeli ticaret; *~ shot* F kodaman; *~ stick Am.* gözünü korkutma, gözdağı verme; *~ top* sirk çadırı, sirk *(a. fig.)*; *talk ~* F yüksekten atmak, atıp tutmak.
big.a.mous □ ['bigəməs] iki kadınla evli olan; iki karılılık suçunu işlemiş olan; 'big.a.my *n.* iki kadınla evlilik, iki karılılık.
bight NAUT [bait] *n.* körfez, koy; halat bedeni.
big.ness ['bignis] *n.* büyüklük, irilik.
big.ot ['bigət] *n.* mutaassıp kimse; dar görüşlü kimse; 'big.ot.ed □ mutaassıp; dar görüşlü; 'big.ot.ry *n.* dar kafalılık.
big.wig F *co.* ['bigwig] *n.* kodaman, önemli kimse.
bike F [baik] *n.* bisiklet.
bi.lat.er.al □ [bai'lætərəl] iki taraflı, iki cepheli.
bil.ber.ry BOT ['bilbəri] *n.* yaban mersini.
bile [bail] *n.* safra; huysuzluk, terslik; *~-stone n.* MED safra kesesi taşı.
bilge [bildʒ] *n.* NAUT sintine, sintine suyu, karina; *sl.* saçmalık, herze.

bi.lin.gual [bai'liŋwəl] *n. & adj.* iki dili aynı derecede konuşan, iki dilli.
bil.ious □ ['biljəs] safraya ait; safralı; *fig.* huysuz, aksi.
bilk [bilk] *v/t.* dolandırmak, aldatmak.
bill¹ [bil] **1.** *n.* gaga; sivri uc; **2.** *v/i.* sevişip koklaşmak.
bill² [_] **1.** *n.* hesap pusulası, fatura, kambiyo senedi, poliçe, bono, tahvil; *Am.* banknot, kâğıt para; kanun lâyihası, kanun tasarısı; dilekçe; afiş; basılı program; *~ of exchange* kambiyo senedi, poliçe, tahvil; *~ of fare* yemek listesi, mönü; *~ of health* sağlık belgesi; *~ of lading* konşimento, yükleme evrakı; *~ of sale* satış bordrosu veya senedi; *~ of rights* insan hakları beyannamesi; **2.** *v/t.* faturasını yapmak; ilân etm.; programa almak; *Am.* kaydetmek, tescil etmek.
bill.board *Am.* ['bilbɔːd] *n.* ilân tahtası, afiş tahtası.
bil.let ['bilit] **1.** *n.* MIL konak yeri; konak tezkeresi; iş, görev; *(odun)* kütük; **2.** *v/t.* MIL konaklatmak *(on -de).*
bill.fold *Am.* ['bilfəuld] *n.* cüzdan.
bill.hook AGR ['bilhuk] *n.* bağcı bıçağı.
bil.liard ['biljəd] *comb.* bilardo..., '~-cue *n.* bilardo sopası; 'bil.liards *n. pl. veya sg.* bilardo.
bil.lion ['biljən] *n.* trilyon; *Am.* milyar.
bil.low ['biləu] **1.** *n.* büyük dalga; dalgalar halinde gelen şey *(alev, duman v.b.)*; **2.** *v/i.* dalgalar halinde kabarmak, yükselmek; 'bil.low.y *adj.* dalgalı.
bill-stick.er ['bilstikə] *n.* afiş yapıştıran kimse.
bil.ly *Am.* ['bili] *n.* kalın sopa: cop: '~-can *n.* teneke kap, tencere; '~-ock *n.* F melon şapka; '~-goat F erkek keçi, teke.
bi.met.al.lism COM [bai'metəlizəm] *n.* çift maden sistemi, altın ve gümüş gibi iki ayrı madeni birbirlerine olan oranlarına göre kullanma sistemi.
bi-mo.tored ['baiməutəd] *adj.* iki motorlu.
bin [bin] *n.* kutu, sandık, teneke.
bi.na.ry ['bainəri] *adj.* iki kısımdan meydana gelen, çift.
bind [baind] *(irr.) v/t.* bağlamak, raptetmek; sarmak; ciltlemek; dondurmak; kenarını tutturmak; kabız vermek; mecbur etm.; *b-ne* vecibe yüklemek, bağlamak; *~ over* JUR teminata veya kefalete bağlamak; *be bound up with fig.* bağlı olm. *-e*; *be bound up in fig.*

bağlı, düşkün; *s.* **bound**[1] **2**; *v/i.* (*çimento vs.*) katılaşmak, donmak; (*makine vs.*) sıkışmak; '**bind.er** *n.* ciltçi; biçer bağlar makine; tutkal; cilt, kap; '**binding 1.** *n.* ciltleme; cilt; kenar şeridi; **2.** *adj.* bağlayıcı, tutucu; JUR bağlayıcı, muteber, kesin; '**bind.weed** BOT *n.* boru çiçeği.

binge *sl.* [bindʒ] *n.* içki âlemi, cümbüş.

bin.go ['biŋgəu] *n.* bingo oyunu.

bin.na.cle NAUT ['binəkl] *n.* pusula dolabı.

bin.oc.u.lar 1. [bai'nɔkjulə] *adj.* iki gözle kullanılan; **2.** [bi'nɔkjulə] *n. mst.* ~*s pl.* dürbün.

bi.o.chem.i.cal ['baiəu'kemikəl] *adj.* biyoşimiye ait; '**bi.o'chem.ist** *n.* biyoşimist; '**bi.o'chem.is.try** *n.* biyoşimi, hayatî kimya.

bi.o.de.gra.da.ble [baıəudı'greıdəbəl] *adj.* biyolojik olarak ayrışabilen.

bi.og.ra.pher [bai'ɔgrəfə] *n. b-nin* hayat hikâyesini yazan kimse, biyografi yazarı; **bi.o.graph.ic**, **bi.o.graph.i.cal** □ [‿əu'græfik(əl)] hayat hikâyesine ait, biyografi ile ilgili; **bi.og.ra.phy** [‿'ɔgrəfi] *n.* biyografi, hayat hikâyesi, yaşam öyküsü.

bi.o.log.ic, **bi.o.log.i.cal** □ [baiəu-'lɔdʒik(əl)] biyoloji ilmine ait, biyolojik; **bi.olo.gist** [‿'ɔlədʒist] *n.* biyoloji bilgini, biyolog; **bi'ol.o.gy** *n.* biyoloji, dirimbilim.

bi.o.weap.on ['baiəu'wepən] *n.* biyolojik silah.

bi.par.tite [bai'pɑːtait] *adj.* iki bölümlü; iki partinin paylaştığı.

bi.ped ['baiped] **1.** *adj.* iki ayaklı; **2.** *n.* iki ayaklı yaratık.

bi.plane AVIA ['baiplein] *n.* çift kanatlı uçak.

birch [bəːtʃ] **1.** *n.* BOT huş ağacı; huş ağacı kerestesi; huş ağacından yapılmış değnek; **2.** *v/t.* huş dalı ile dövmek.

bird [bəːd] *n.* kuş; *sl.* herif; *sl.* kadın, bebek; **kill two** ~**s with one stone** F bir taşla iki kuş vurmak; **give the** ~ F ıslıklamak, yuha çekmek; '~**.call** *n.* kuş ıslığı; '~**.fan.ci.er** *n.* kuş meraklısı, kuşbaz; **bird.ie** ['bəːdi] *n.* F kuşcağız.

bird...: '~**-lime** *n.* ökse, tuzak; '~**-seed** *n.* kuş yemi; '**bird's-eye view** kuş bakışı görünüş; '**bird's-nest 1.** *n.* kuş yuvası; **2.** *vb.* kuş yuvalarını aramak; kuş yumurtası çalmak.

birth [bəːθ] *n.* doğum, doğuş; soy; başlangıç, kaynak; meydana çıkma, zuhur; **give** ~ **to** doğurmak *-i*, meydana getirmek *-i*; *fig.* yaratmak; **date of** ~ doğum tarihi; '~**-control** *n.* doğum kontrolü; '~**.day** *n.* doğum günü; '~**-mark** *n.* doğuştan var olan vücut lekesi; '~**-place** *n.* doğum yeri; '~**-rate** *n.* doğum oranı; '~**.right** *n.* doğuştan kazanılan hak.

bis.cuit ['biskit] *n.* bisküvi; fırınlanmış tabak çanak; açık kahverengi.

bi.sect MATH [bai'sekt] *v/t.* iki çeşit parçaya ayırmak; **bi'sec.tion** *n.* ikiye bölme.

bish.op ['biʃəp] *n.* piskopos; *santraç oyunu:* fil; **bish.op.ric** ['‿rik] *n.* piskoposluk; piskoposluk bölgesi.

bis.muth CHEM ['bizməθ] *n.* bizmut.

bi.son ZOO ['baisn] *n.* bizon.

bis.sex.tile [bi'sekstail]: ~ **year** artık yıl.

bit [bit] **1.** *n.* küçük parça, lokmacık; gem; MEC matkap; anahtar dişi; ~ **by** ~ azar azar, yavaş yavaş; **a** ~ bir parça, biraz; **a good** ~ oldukça; **not a** ~ hiç de değil, asla; **take the** ~ **between one's teeth** gemi azıya almak (*a. fig.*) **2.** *v/t.* gemlemek; sınırlamak; **3.** *pret. of* **bite 2**.

bitch [bitʃ] **1.** *n.* dişi köpek; *sl.* kötü kadın; ~ **fox** dişi tilki; ~ **wolf** dişi kurt; **2.** *v/i.* şikâyet etm.

bite [bait] **1.** *n.* ısırım; ısırma; lokma; diş yarası, sokma (*arı, yılan v.b.*); (*balık*) oltaya vurma; keskinlik (*içki, biber, soğuk*); **2.** (*irr.*) *v/t.* ısırmak, dişlemek; sokmak (*arı, yılan v.b.*); acıtmak, yakmak; aşındırmak (*soğuk, biber*): ~ **at** ısırmağa çalışmak *-i*; ~ **one's lips** nefsine hâkim olm.; '**bit.er** *n.* ısırıcı; **the** ~ **bit men** dakka dukka.

bit.ing □ ['baitiŋ] keskin; acı.

bit.ten ['bitn] *p.p. of* **bite 2**; **be** ~ **with** *fig.* çok arzu etm. *-i, bş* için yanıp tutuşmak.

bit.ter ['bitə] **1.** □ acı, keskin; sert; *fig.* kızgın, gazaplı; **2.** *n.* acı bira.

bit.tern ORN ['bitən] *n.* balaban kuşu.

bit.ter.ness ['bitənis] *n.* acılık; sertlik.

bit.ters ['bitəz] *pl.* bir tür içki, amer, bitter.

bi.tu.men ['bitjumin] *n.* zift, katran; **bi.tumi.nous** [bi'tjuːminəs] *adj.* ziftli, zift gibi.

bi.valve ZOO [bai'vælv] *n.* yumuşakçalardan çift kabuklu hayvanlar (*midye, istiridye gibi*).

biv.ou.ac ['bivuæk] **1.** *n.* çadırsız ordugâh; **2.** *v/i.* çadırsız ordugâh kurmak;
açıkta yatmak.

biz F [biz] *n.* iş.

bi.zarre [bi'zɑː] *adj.* tuhaf, garip, biçimsiz.

blab F [blæb] **1.** *n. a.* '**blab.ber** geveze;
boşboğaz; **2.** *v/i.* gevezelik etm.; boşboğazlık etm.

black [blæk] **1.** ☐ siyah, kara; karanlık;
kirli; uğursuz; ~ *cattle* kasaplık sığır; ~
eye siyah göz; berelenmiş göz, mo-
rarmış göz; *s. frost*; ~ *and white* yazı;
basılı şey; siyah beyaz resim veya görüntü; *beat s.o.* ~ *and blue* b-ni kıyasıya dövmek; *be* ~ *in the face* (*hiddet vs.
den*) morarmak; *look* ~ *at s.o. b-ne* surat asmak; **2.** *v/t.* siyahlatmak, siyaha
boyamak; kara listeye almak; ~ *out* karartmak; örtmek; bayılmak, geçici olarak şuurunu kaybetmek; **3.** *n.* kara, siyah (*a. giysi*); zenci.

black...: ~**a.moor** ['-əmuə] *n.* zenci
(*esp. adam*); '~**ball** *v/t.* (*bir kulüpte
üye seçiminde*) karşı oy vermek;
'~**ber.ry** *n.* ʙᴏᴛ böğürtlen; '~**bird** *n.*
karatavuk; '~**board** *n.* yazı tahtası;
'~**coat.ed:** ~ *worker* kâtip, büroda çalışan kimse; '~**cock** *n.* ᴏʀɴ siyah keklik
(*erkek*); '~'**cur.rant** *n.* siyah frenküzümü; '**blacken** *v/t.* karartmak, karalamak; *fig.* lekelemek.

black...: '~**guard** ['blæɡɑːd] **1.** *n.* alçak,
ahlâksız kimse; **2.** *a.* '~**guard.ly** ☐ alçak, rezil; **3.** *v/t.* küfretmek, sövüp saymak; ~**head** ᴍᴇᴅ ['blækhed] *n.* (*yüzde*) siyah benek; '**black.ing** *n.* ayakkabı boyası, siyah boya; '**black.ish** ☐
siyahımsı.

black...: '~**jack** *n. part. Am.* cop; büyük
içki bardağı (*siyah deri kaplı*); ~**lead**
['-'led] **1.** *n.* grafit, kurşun tozu; **2.**
v/t. kurşun tozu ile boyamak; '~**leg**
n. greve katılmayan işçi; '~'**let.ter**
ᴛʏᴘ gotik harfler; '~**list** **1.** *n.* kara liste;
2. *v/t.* kara listeye koymak; '~**mail 1.** *n.*
şantaj; **2.** *v/t.* şantaj yapmak *-e*;
'~**mail.er** *n.* şantajcı; ~ **mar.ket** karaborsa; ~ **market.eer** karaborsacı;
'**black.ness** *n.* siyah oluş; karanlık olma; kötülük.

black...: '~'**out** *n.* karartma; (*elektrik
kesilmesi dolayısıyle*) karanlıkta kalma; ᴛʜᴇᴀᴛ ışıkların sönmesi; geçici olarak şuurunu kaybetme; *bşin* yayınını
engelleme; ~ **pud.ding** hayvan kanı,
yağ ve yulaftan yapılan siyah renkte

bir tür sos; ~ **sheep** *fig.* saygıdeğer
bir grup içinde değersiz kimse;
'~**smith** *n.* demirci, nalbant; '~**thorn**
n. ʙᴏᴛ alıç, yaban eriği.

blad.der ['blædə] *n.* ᴀɴᴀᴛ mesane, sidik
torbası, kavuk; iç lastik (*top v.b.*).

blade [bleid] *n.* bıçak vs. ağzı; (*kürek,
pervane v.b.*) *bşin* yassı ve geniş kısmı;
(*arpa vs.*) ince uzun yaprak; '~**bone** *n.*
kürek kemiği.

blae.ber.ry ['bleibəri] *n.* ʙᴏᴛ yaban
mersini.

blah F [blɑː] *n.* zırva.

blam.a.ble ☐ ['bleiməbl] kötü, kabahatli; tevbihe müstahak.

blame [bleim] **1.** *n.* kabahat, kusur,
ayıplama; sorumluluk; **2.** *v/t.* ayıplamak, suçlamak; sorumlu tutmak; *be
to* ~ *for bşle* suçlu olm.; *bşin* sorumlusu
olm.; *lay the* ~ *on s.o.* kabahati birine
yüklemek.

blame.ful ['bleimful] ☐ kabahatli;
'**blameless** ☐ kabahatsiz, kusursuz;
'**blameless.ness** *n.* kusursuzluk;
'**blame.wor.thy** *adj.* ayıplanmaya
lâyık, sorumlu, kabahatli.

blanch [blɑːntʃ] *v/t.* beyazlatmak,
ağartmak; kabuğunu soyarak beyazlatmak (*badem vs.*); haşlayarak ağartmak (*et*); *v/i.* ağarmak; sararmak, rengi
uçmak, benzi atmak.

blanc.mange [blə'mɒnʒ] *n. mutfak:*
sütlü pelte. paluze.

bland ☐ [blænd] yumuşak, mülâyim;
sert olmıyan; '**blan.dish** *v/t.* okşamak,
tatlı dil kullanmak; '**blan.dish.ment** *n.*
kompliman; çekici davranış.

blank [blæŋk] **1.** ☐ boş, açık, yazısız, beyaz; anlamsız; şaşkın; ~ *cartridge* ᴍɪʟ
manevra fişeği; **2.** *n.* boş ve açık yer;
yazısız kâğıt; (*piyango*) boş kur'a; hedef; manevra fişeği.

blan.ket ['blæŋkit] **1.** *n.* battaniye; kalın
örtü (*kar, karanlık v.b.*); *wet* ~ *fig.* keyif
kaçıran; **2.** *adj.* geniş kapsamlı; **3.** *v/t.*
battaniye ile örtmek; üstünü örtmek
-in; *bşi* örtbas etm.

blank.ness ['blæŋknis] *n.* boşluk; anlamsızlık.

blare [blɛə] *v/i.* cayırdamak, boru gibi
ses çıkarmak.

blar.ney ['blɑːni] **1.** *n.* dil dökme, *sl.* pi-
yazlama, yağcılık; **2.** *vb.* dil dökmek, *sl.*
yağcılık yapmak.

bla.sé ['blɑːzei] *adj.* içi geçmiş, her şeyden bıkmış.

blas.pheme [blæs'fiːm] *vb.* (*din ve mu-*

kaddes şeylere) küfretmek, sövüp say-mak (*against -e*); blas'phem.er *n.* kü-fürbaz kimse; blas.phe.mous □ ['blæsfiməs] imansız, kâfir; 'blas-phe.my *n.* küfür; mukaddes şeylere hürmetsizlik.

blast [blɑ:st] **1.** *n.* şiddetli ve ani rüzgâr esmesi, hava cereyanı; MEC patlama, infilâk; gürültülü boru veya düdük se-si; BOT mildiyu; *at full* ~ tam süratle; *in* ~ işler halde; *out of* ~ hizmet dışı; **2.** *v/t.* berhava etm., yakmak, patlatmak; mahvetmek (*a. fig.*). ~ (*it*) *!* lânet olsun!; 'blast.ed *adj.* (*yıldırımla*) yanmış; tah-rip edilmiş, mahvolmuş (*a. fig.*); Al-lahın belâsı; 'blast-fur.nace *n.* MEC iza-be ocağı, yüksek fırın; 'blast.ing *n.* berhava etme; patlama.

bla.tant □ ['bleitənt] gürültülü, gürül-tücü, şamatalı; *fig.* ayanbeyan, bâriz.

blath.er *Am.* ['blæðə] **1.** *n.* saçma lâf; **2.** *v/i.* saçma sapan konuşmak.

blaze [bleiz] **1.** *n.* büyük alev, ateş; par-laklık (*a. fig.*); yangın; alevlenme; atın alnındaki beyaz işaret, akıtma; ~*s pl.* cehennem; *go to* ~*s!* cehenneme git!, defol!; *like* ~*s* F çılgınca, alabil-diğine; **2.** *v/i.* alevlenmek, parlamak, yanmak, ışık saçmak; ~ *away* durma-dan ateş etm.; F durmadan çalışmak; *v/t.* alevlendirmek, neşretmek (*ışık vs.*); boru gibi çalmak; ilân etm.; (*ağaç*) gövdelerine işaret koymak; ~ *abroad* (*haber*) dört bir tarafa yay-mak; ~ *a trail* yol çizmek, yol açmak; *fig.* çığır açmak; 'blaz.er *n.* spor ceket.

bla.zon ['bleizn] **1.** *n.* arma; armacılık; **2.** *v/t.* arma çizmek, işaret koymak; *fig.* süslemek; ayyuka çıkarmak; bildir-mek, ilân etm.; F yedi mahalleye davul zurna ile duyurmak; 'bla.zon.ry *n.* ar-ma çizimi.

bleach [bli:tʃ] *v/t.* ağartmak, beyazlat-mak; *v/i.* ağarmak, beyazlanmak; 'bleach.er *n.* çamaşır suyu; ~*s pl.* *Am.* spor müsabakalarında: açık tri-bün; 'bleach.ing *n.* beyazlatma, be-yazlanma; 'bleach.ing-pow.der *n.* ağartma tozu.

bleak □ [bli:k] (*hava*) soğuk, tatsız; çıplak, rüzgârın etkisinde, açık; *fig.* ümitsiz, cesaret kırıcı; 'bleak.ness *n.* rüzgâra açık oluş.

blear [bliə] **1.** □ çapaklı, kızarmış (*göz*); **2.** *v/t.* (*göz*) sulandırmak ve kızartmak; kamaştırmak, bulandırmak; ~*eyed* ['bliəraid] *adj.* gözü akan; 'blear.y □

uykulu (*göz*).

bleat [bli:t] **1.** *n.* meleme; **2.** *v/i.* mele-mek.

bleb [bleb] *n.* küçük kabarcık, sivilce.

bled [bled] *pret.* & *p.p. of* **bleed**.

bleed [bli:d] (*irr.*) *v/i.* kanamak, kanı akmak, kan kaybetmek; *fig.* kan ağla-mak, çok kederli olm.; *v/t.* kan almak; *fig.* -*in* parasını sızdırmak; 'bleed.ing **1.** *n.* kanama; kan alma (*verme*); **2.** *adj. sl.* Allahın belâsı, uğursuz, gaddar.

blem.ish ['blemiʃ] **1.** *n.* kusur, hata; le-ke; **2.** *v/t.* güzellik ve kusursuzluğunu bozmak, lekelemek (*a. fig.*).

blench [blentʃ] *v/i.* ürkmek, çekinmek -*den*; benzi atmak; *v/t.* ağartmak.

blend [blend] **1.** *v/t.* (*çay vs.*) harman yapmak, karıştırmak (*together, with ile*); (*şarap vs.*) kupaj yapmak, hafiflet-mek; *v/i.* karışmak, harman olm.; *fig.* (*ses, renk*) uymak (*well, with -e*); bü-tünleşmek (*into -e, ile*); **2.** *n.* harman, karışım, kupaj; alaşım.

blende MIN [blend] *n.* (*çinko*) sülfür.

bless [bles] *v/t.* kutsamak, takdis etm.; hayır dua etm. -*e*; Allahtan dilemek; mutlu kılmak (*with ile*); ~ *me!*, ~ *my soul!* aman ya Rabbi!, Allah Allah!; bless.ed □ [*p.p.* blest; *adj.* 'blesid] mübarek, kutlu; F Allahın cezası; bless.ed.ness ['blesidnis] *n.* kutluluk; *live in single* ~ bekâr yaşamak; 'bless.ing *n.* hayır dua, takdis, nimet; F onay, teşvik.

blest *poet.* [blest] *s.* **blessed**.

bleth.er ['bleðə] *s.* **blather**.

blew [blu:] *pret. of* **blow**[2] & **blow**[3] **1**.

blight [blait] **1.** *n.* BOT mildiyu, küf, mantar; samyeli; **2.** *v/t.* (*güneş, rüzgâr v.b.*) yakmak, kavurmak, soldurmak; 'blighter *n. sl.* herif, mübarek.

Blight.y MIL *sl.* [blaiti] *n.* memleket, ana vatan (*part. İngiltere*); *a* ~ *one* ana va-tana dönmeyi gerektiren yasa.

blind [blaind] **1.** □ kör; gizli, saklı; *fig.* kısa görüşlü; gözü kararmış; anlaşıl-ması güç; çıkmaz (*yol*); ~ *alley* çıkmaz sokak; *fig.* çıkmaz; ~ *flying* AVIA kör uçuş; ~ *drunk sl.* kör kütük sarhoş; *turn one's* ~ *eye to s.th.* göz yummak, *bşi* görmemezlikten gelmek; **2.** *n.* per-de, stor, kepenk; aldatmaca; pusu; **3.** *v/t.* kör etm., körleştirmek; gözünü ka-maştırmak.

blind.fold ['blaindfəuld] **1.** *adj.* gözleri bağlı; körükörüne olan; **2.** *v/t.* gözleri-ni bağlamak; **3.** *n.* gözbağı; 'blind.ly *adv. fig.* körükörüne; **'blind.man's-** **-'buff** *n.* körebe; **'blind.ness** *n.* körlük; **'blind.worm** *n.* zoo köryılan.

blink [bliŋk] **1.** *n.* göz kırpma; bakış; NAUT pırıltı; **2.** *v/i.* göz kırpmak; gözleri yarı kapayarak bakmak; ışıldamak; ~ **the facts** gerçeğe gözlerini yummak; *v/t.* göz kırptırmak; **'blink.er** *n.* flaş lambası; *at:* meşin göz siperi; **'blink-ing** *adj.* F kötü, berbat.

bliss [blis] *n.* saadet, bahtiyarlık, mutluluk.

bliss.ful □ ['blisful] neşe dolu, mutlu; **'bliss.ful.ness** *n.* sonsuz haz, büyük mutluluk.

blis.ter ['blistə] **1.** *n.* kabarcık, su toplama; yakı; **2.** *vb.* kabar(t)mak, su toplamak; yakı koymak.

blithe □ [blaið], **~.some** ['~səm] *mst. poet.* şen, neşeli; memnun.

blith.er.ing *sl.* ['bliðəriŋ] *adj.:* ~ *idiot* zırvalayan.

blitz [blits] **1.** *n.* ani hava saldırısı; *sl.* kampanya; **2.** *v/t.* bombardıman etm.

bliz.zard ['blizəd] *n.* tipi, kar fırtınası.

bloat [bləut] *v/t. & v/i.* şiş(ir)mek; kabar(t)mak; *balık:* tuzlamak ve tütsülemek; **~ed** *adj.* şişkin, kabarık; *fig.* şişirilmiş, abartılmış; **'bloat.er** *n.* tütsülenmiş ringa balığı.

blob [blɔb] *n.* damla, benek.

block [blɔk] **1.** *n.* kütük, kaya parçası; blok; klişe, kalıp; iki kavşak arasındaki mesafe; bitişik bir sıra bina; *Am.* sokak; MEC takoz, makara; engel; **the ~** insanların başını kesmek için kullanılan ortası delik büyük tahta; **2.** *v/t.* tıkamak, kapamak, önünü kesmek, akamete uğratmak; döviz muamelesini kısıtlamak *veya* durdurmak; ~ *in* bşin krokisini yapmak, taslağını çizmek; *mst.* ~ *up* tıkamak; (*liman vs.*) kapatmak; **~ed account** COM bloke hesap.

block.ade [blɔ'keid] **1.** *n.* abluka; *run the~* ablukayı yarmak; **2.** *v/t.* ablukaya almak; etrafını çevirmek; **block'ade-** **-runner** *n.* ablukayı yaran.

block...: '**~.bust.er** *n. sl.* çok büyük ve güçlü uçak bombası; F çok etkili; '**~.head** *n.* dangalak; '**~.house** *n.* gözetleme kulesi, blokhavs; ~ **let.ters** *pl.* kitap yazısı.

blog [blɔg] *n.* blog.

bloke F [bləuk] *n.* ıт herif.

blond(e) [blɔnd] *adj. & n.* açık renk, sarı şın; ipek tül veya dantel.

blood [blʌd] *n.* kan; *fig.* kan, mizaç, huy; nesil, soy, ırk; kan bağı; *in cold* ~ soğukkanlı, tasarlayıp kurarak; *s.* *run 1;* '**~-and-'thun.der** *adj.* gürültülü patırtılı; '**~-cur.dling** *adj.* tüyler ürpertici; ~ **do.nor** kan veren.

blood.ed ['blʌdid] *adj.* cins, saf kan; ...kanlı.

blood...: '**~-guilt.i.ness** *n.* kanlı cinayet; adam öldürme; '**~-heat** *n.* kan ısısı; '**~-horse** *n.* safkan at; '**~-hound** *n.* bir cins av köpeği, zağar; *fig.* dedektif; '**blood.i.ness** *n.* kana susamışlık, kanlı oluş; '**blood.less** □ kansız, solgun; *fig.* renksiz; kan dökmeden olan; ruhsuz.

blood...: '**~-let.ting** *n.* kan alma; '**~-poi-** **son.ing** *n.* MED kan zehirlenmesi; '**~-pressure** *n.* kan basıncı, tansiyon; '**~-re'lation** *n.* kan bağı; '**~.shed** *n.* kan dökme; '**~.shot** *adj.* kanlanmış, kızarmış; '**~.stain** *n.* kan lekesi; '**~-suck.er** *n.* sülük; *fig.* asalak kimse; '**~.thirst.y** *adj.* kana susamış, canavar ruhlu; '**~-ves.sel** *n.* kan damarı; '**blood.y** □ kana bulanmış; kanlı; P kana susamış, gaddar.

bloom [blu:m] **1.** *n.* çiçek, çiçek açma; *fig.* gençlik, tazelik; meyva üzerindeki buğu; *metall.* dökülmüş demir kütük; *be in* ~ çiçek açmak; **2.** *v/i.* çiçek açmak; *fig.* gelişmek.

bloom.er ['blu:mə] *n. sl.* büyük hata, gaf; **~s** *pl.* kadınların giydiği bir cins şalvar; (*şalvar şeklinde*) külot.

bloom.ing □ ['blu:miŋ] çiçek açmış; bereketli, gelişen, serpilen; *sl.* Allahın belâsı, kör olası.

blos.som ['blɔsəm] **1.** *n.* (*ağaç*) bahar çiçeği; **2.** *v/i.* (*ağaç*) çiçek açmak; *fig.* gelişmek; ~ *into* büyümek, gelişip güzelleşmek.

blot [blɔt] **1.** *n.* leke, mürekkep lekesi; *fig.* leke, kusur; **2.** *v/t.* lekelemek (*a. fig.*), kirletmek, karartmak; kurutma kâğıdı ile kurutmak; *v/i.* lekelenmek, kirlenmek; (*kurutma kâğıdı*) emmek; *mst* ~ *out* örtmek, tanınmaz hale getirmek; yok etm., imha etm.

blotch [blɔtʃ] *n.* (*derideki*) leke veya büyük kırmızı kabartı; iri mürekkep lekesi.

blot.ter ['blɔtə] *n.* kurutma kâğıdı tamponu; *Am.* kayıt defteri (*esp. polis karakolunda*).

blot.ting...: '**~-pad** *n.* altlık, sumen; '**~-paper** *n.* kurutma kâğıdı.

blot.to *sl.* ['blɔtəu] *adj.* zil zurna sarhoş.

blouse [blauz] *n.* bluz.

blow¹ [bləu] *n.* vuruş, darbe; şiddetli rüzgâr, sümkürme; saldırı; (*boru vs.*) çalma; **at one** ~ bir hamlede; **come to ~s** kavgaya tutuşmak.

blow² [-] (*irr.*) *v/i.* (*çiçek*) açmak, çiçeklenmek.

blow³ [-] **1.** (*irr.*) *v/i. & v/t.* (*rüzgâr*) esmek, üflemek; hohlamak; uç(ur)mak, atmak; (*toz vs.*) üfleyerek uzaklaştırmak; (*cama*) üfleyerek şekil vermek; (*boru vs.*) çal(ın)mak; solumak; (*elektrik sigortası*) atmak; (*ampul*) yanmak; *sl.* çarçur etm.; *sl.* ortadan kaybolmak, toz olm.; körüklemek; (*sinek*) yumurtlamak; (*sır vs.*) açıklamak; (*balina*) su fışkırtmak; ~ **in** ansızın gelmek; (*ocak vs.*) yakmak; ~ **over** (*fırtına*) dinmek; *fig.* bitmek, geçmek; ~ **up** havaya uç(ur)mak, patla(t)mak; (*fırtına*) patlak vermek; PHOT büyütmek, agrantisman yapmak; *fig.* büyütmek; F aniden kızmak, tepesi atmak; ~ **one's nose** sümkürmek; ~ **one's own horn** övünmek, kendini methetmek; ~ **one's brains out** beynini patlatmak; **I'll be ~ed if I...!** *sl.* ...sam adam değilim!; **2.** *n.* çiçek açma, çiçeklenme; '**blow.er** *n.* üfleyici; esici; MEC kompresör, körük.

blow...: '~**.fly** *n.* et sineği, kurt sineği; '~**-hole** *n.* hava deliği; '~**.lamp** *n.* kaynak lâmbası, pirimüz lâmbası.

blown [bləun] *p.p.* of **blow²** & **blow³ 1.**

blow...: '~**-out** MOT lâstik patlaması; '~**.pipe** *n.* üfleme borusu; MEC şalumo, hamlaç; '~**.torch** *n. s.* **blowlamp**; '**blow.y** *adj.* rüzgârlı.

blowz.y ['blauzi] *adj.* pasaklı, kırmızı yüzlü (*kadın*).

blub.ber ['blʌbə] **1.** *n.* balina yağı; ağlama; **2.** *v/i.* bağıra bağıra ağlamak.

bludg.eon ['blʌdʒən] **1.** *n.* sopa, kalın değnek, matrak; **2.** *v/t.* matrak ile vurmak.

blue [blu:] **1.** □ mavi; F kederli ve ümitsiz; **2.** *n.* mavi renk; çivit; POL muhafazakâr, tutucu; **3.** *v/t.* maviye boyamak; çivitlemek.

blue...: '~**.bell** *n.* BOT çançiçeği; yabanî sümbül; '~**.ber.ry** *n.* BOT yaban mersini; '~**.bird** *n.* ORN Kuzey Amerika'da yaşayan küçük mavi ve güzel sesli kuş türlerinden herhangi biri; '~**-book** *n. Am.* toplumun önemli kişilerinin adreslerinin yazılı olduğu defter; İngiliz hükümetinin yayınladığı resmî rapor;

'~**.bot.tle** *n.* BOT peygamber çiçeği; ZOO mavi sinek; ~ '**chip** *adj. mali açıdan ünü büyük olup güvenilir bir yatırım oluşturan* (*şirket, hisse senedi vb.*); '~**.jack.et** *n.* bahriyeli, gemici; '~**-jay** ORN mavi tüylü alakarga; ~ **jeans** *pl.* blucin; ~ **laws** *pl.* yutucu ve sert kanunlar; '**blue.ness** *n.* mavilik; '**blue- -'pen.cil** *v/t.* sansür etm.; '**blue.print** *n.* mavi kopya; *fig.* tasarı; **blues** *pl.* *fig.* melankoli; MUS bir tür caz müziği; '**blue.stock.ing** *n. fig.* okumuş kadın, entellektüel kadın.

bluff [blʌf] **1.** □ tok sözlü, açık; sarp, dik (*kıyı*); **2.** *n.* blöf; kayalık, uçurum; **3.** *v/t.* blöf yapmak -*e*, *b-ni* yanıltmak.

blu.ish ['blu:iʃ] *adj.* mavimsi.

blun.der ['blʌndə] **1.** *n.* gaf, büyük hata; **2.** *vb.* gaf yapmak, ahmakça hareket etm.; pot kırmak; ~ **out** F damdan düşercesine *bşi* ortaya atmak; **blun. der.buss** HIST ['blʌndəbʌs] *n.* geniş ağızlı eski zaman karabinası; '**blun. der.er**, '**blun.derhead** *n.* ahmakça hareket eden kimse.

blunt [blʌnt] **1.** □ (*bıçak vs.*) kör, kesmez, (*kalem vs.*) küt; *fig.* körleşmiş; lafını sakınmayan, pervasızca konuşan; pervasız (*söz*); **2.** *v/t.* körleştirmek -*i*, körletmek -*i*; duyarlılığını gidermek -*in*; '**blunt.ness** *n.* pervasızlık; keskin olmayış.

blur [blə:] **1.** *n.* leke, bulanıklık (*a. fig.*), net olarak seçilemeyen şey; **2.** *v/t.* bulaştırmak, silmek; bulanıklaştırmak (**with** -*le*); ~**red** *adj. esp.* PHOT bulanık.

blurb [blə:b] *n.* küçük kitap ilânı; yayıncının kitabın içeriği hakkında yazdığı abartmalı kısa yazı.

blurt [blə:t]: ~ **out** *v/t.* ağzından kaçırmak -*i*, düşünmeden söylemek -*i*.

blush [blʌʃ] **1.** *n.* kızarma, utanma; pembelik; **at the first** ~ ilk bakışta; **2.** *v/i.* kızarmak, yüzü kızarmak (**at**, **for**, **with** -*den*); utanmak; (**for** -*den*); pembeleşmek; ~ **to** *bşden* dolayı utanmak, mahcup olm.; '**blush.ing** □ mahcup, utangaç.

blus.ter ['blʌstə] **1.** *n.* yüksekten atma, kabadayılık; sert rüzgâr ve dalga sesi; **2.** *v/i.* (*rüzgâr*) sert ve gürültüyle esmek; yaygara ile tehdit savurmak; patırtı etm.; *v/t. a.* ~ **out** (*küfür, tehdit v.b.*) savurmak; '**blus.ter.er** *n.* gürültücü kimse, övüngen, palavracı.

bo.a ZOO ['bəuə] *n.* boğa yılanı.

boar [bɔ:] *n.* erkek domuz; HUNT erkek

yaban domuzu.

board [bɔːd] **1.** *n.* tahta, levha; mukavva; masa, sofra; yiyecek, içecek; kurul, idare heyeti; NAUT borda; (*satranç v.b.*) oyun tahtası; *the~s pl.* THEAT sahne; *on ~* gemide; *on ~ a train Am.* trende; *go by the ~* NAUT güverteden denize düşmek; *fig.* (*plan organizasyon vs.*) suya düşmek, bir kenara atılmak; *above ~* dürüst, açıkça; *sweep the~* hemen hemen hepsini kazanmak; *~ of governors* idare heyeti, yönetim kurulu; ♀ *of Trade* Ticaret Odası; Ticaret Bakanlığı; *~ and lodging* yiyecek ve yatacak; **2.** *v/t. & v/i.* (*tahta*) döşemek, kaplamak; (*gemiye vs.*) binmek; NAUT (*gemiye*) saldırı sonucu girmek; para karşılığında yiyecek içecek ve kalacak yer temin etm.; pansiyoner olm.; *~ out* pansiyona yerleştirmek; *~ up* tahta ile kapatmak; NAUT borda etm.; **'boarder** *n.* pansiyoner; yatılı öğrenci.

board.ing ['bɔːdiŋ] *n.* tahta kaplama, tahta parmaklık; iaşe, erzak; *'~house* *n.* pansiyon; *'~school* *n.* yatılı okul.

board...: *'~room* *n.* toplantı salonu; *'~.walk* *n. esp. Am.* plâj gezinti yeri (*tahta zeminli*).

boast [bəust] **1.** *n.* övünme; iftihar; **2.** *v/i.* yüksekten atmak, övünmek (*of, about -le*); iftihar etm. (*-le*; **'boast.er** *n.* övünen kimse; **boast.ful** ☐ ['~ful] övüngen, palavracı.

boat [bəut] **1.** *n.* kayık, sandal, gemi; kayık tabak; *burn one's~s* geri dönme şansını *k-ne* bırakmamak; *take to the ~s* filikayla gemiyi terketmek; *be in the same ~* aynı durumda olm. (*esp. kötü*); *s. sauce~*; **2.** *v/i.* kayıkla gezmek; **'boat-hook** *n.* kanca, çengelli sırık; **'boat-house** *n.* kayıkhane; **'boat.ing** *n.* sandal *vs.*'nin eğlence için kullanılması; **'boat-race** *n.* kayık yarışı; **boat.swain** ['bəusn] *n.* porsun, lostromo; **'boat-train** *n.* gemi yolcularını taşıyan tren.

bob [bɔb] **1.** *n.* püskül; pandül, sarkaç; (*saç*) kısa kesilmiş model; kâkül; âni hareket, birdenbire çekme veya sallama; (*at*) kısa kuyruk; küçük kızların reveransı; *sl.* bir şilin; **2.** *v/t. & v/i.* hafifçe hareket ettirmek; (*saç*) kısa kesmek; hafifçe vurmak; oynamak, kımıldamak; mantarlı olta ile balık avalmak; *~ up* yükselmek, ortaya çıkmak.

bob.bin ['bɔbin] *n.* makara, bobin (*a.*

ELECT); ağaç bobin; *'~-lace* *n.* bir tentene türü, kopanaki.

bob.ble *Am.* F ['bɔbl] *n.* hata, yanılma, gaf.

bob.by *sl.* ['bɔbi] *n.* polis memuru; *'~-pin* *n.* saç tokası; *'~-socks* *n. pl.* kısa çorap, soket; *~-sox.er* *Am. sl.* ['~sɔksə] *n.* ondört ile onyedi yaş arasındaki genç kız.

bob.cat ZOO ['bɔbkæt] *n.* vaşak.

bob.o.link ORN ['bɔbəliŋk] *n.* Kuzey Amerika'ya mahsus güzel sesli bir kuş.

bob.sled ['bɔbsled], **bob.sleigh** ['bɔbslei] *n.* bir tür kızak.

bob.tail ['bɔbteil] *n.* (*at veya köpek*) kısa kuyruklu; *the rag-tag and ~* olur olmaz adamlar, sıradan adamlar.

bob.white ORN ['bɔb'wait] *n.* Kuzey Amerika bıldırcını.

bode [bəud] *v/t. & v/i.* işaret olm., delâlet etm.; *~ well (ill)* hayra (uğursuzluğa) alâmet olm.

bod.ice ['bɔdis] *n.* korsaj, korse.

bod.i.ly ['bɔdili] **1.** *adj.* bedenî, bedensel; maddî; *~ injury* yaralama; cismanî zarar; **2.** *adv.* bütün olarak, tamamen.

bod.kin ['bɔdkin] *n.* kalın ve uzun uçsuz iğne, biz.

bod.y ['bɔdi] **1.** *n.* vücut, beden; ceset; gövde; MOT karoser; kurul, heyet, grup; *bşin* ana bölümü; F kişi; cisim; (*içki*) sertlik; MIL birlik; F büyük kısım; *in a ~* birlikte, yekvücut olarak; **2.** *~ forth* *v/t.* şekil vermek; cisimlendirmek, şahıslandırmak; *~ dou.ble* *n.* dublör; *'~.guard* *n.* hassa askeri.

Boer ['bəuə] **1.** *n.* Hollanda asıllı Güney Afrikalı; **2.** *adj.* Hollanda asıllı Güney Afrikalı ile ilgili.

bof.fin *sl.* ['bɔfin] *n.* araştırmacı, bilgin.

bog [bɔg] **1.** *n.* batak, bataklık; bataklık çamuru; **2.** *v/t. & v/i.* batağa bat(ır)-mak; *be veya get ~ged down* bir yere saplanıp kalmak (*a. fig.*).

bog.gle ['bɔgl] *v/i.* çekinmek, ürkmek, korkmak (*at -den*).

bog.gy ['bɔgi] *adj.* bataklık.

bo.gie ['bəugi] *n.* RAIL lokomotif veya vagonun alt kısmında bulunan çift dingilli kısım; *a. = bogy*.

bo.gus ['bəugəs] *adj.* sahte, yapma, yapmacık.

bo.gy ['bəugi] *n.* cin; umacı; *the~* (*man*) umacı, arap.

Bo.he.mi.an [bəu'hiːmjən] **1.** *adj.* Bohemya'ya özgü; **2.** *n.* Bohemyalı; Çek dili; Çingene; *fig.* Bohem, toplum kurallarını dikkate almadan yaşayan kimse, derbeder, kalender.

boil [bɔil] **1.** v/t. & v/i. kayna(t)mak; haşla(n)mak; fig. öfkeden köpürmek; ~ **over** taşmak; ~**ed egg** rafadan yumurta; **hard** ~**ed egg** hazırlop yumurta; **2.** n. çıban; kaynama; '**boil.er** n. kazan; sıcak su deposu; '**boil.ing 1.** adj. kaynar...; **2.** n. kaynama; sl. **the whole** ~ takım taklavat.

bois.ter.ous □ ['bɔistərəs] (kişi veya davranışı) gürültülü, şiddetli; (hava) fırtınalı, sert; '**bois.ter.ous.ness** n. gürültülü olma.

bold □ [bəuld] pervasız, cesur, yürekli, yiğit, atılgan; b.s. arsız, küstah; dik, sarp (sahil, kıyı); çarpıcı, göz alan; TYP siyah; **make (so)** ~ **(as)** to cesaret etm., cüret etm. -e; '**bold.ness** n. cesaret, yüreklilik; b.s. küstahlık.

bole [bəul] n. ağaç gövdesi.

bo.ler.o [bə'lɛərəu] n. bir tür İspanyol dansı; bu dansın müziği; cepken, bolero.

boll BOT [bəul] n. (pamuk, keten) tohum kabuğu veya zarfı.

bol.lard ['bɔləd] n. NAUT iskele babası, duba.

bo.lo.ney sl. [bə'ləuni] n. saçma söz, zırva.

Bol.she.vism ['bɔlʃivizəm] n. Bolşeviklik; '**Bol.she.vist** adj. & n. Bolşevik.

bol.ster ['bəulstə] **1.** n. uzun yastık, minder; MEC yastık, plator; **2.** vb. mst ~ **up** desteklemek -i, destek olm. -e.

bolt [bəult] **1.** n. cıvata, bulon, sürme; kilit dili; kol demiri; (kumaş) top; (kısa ve ağır) ok; yıldırım; fırlama, kaçış; ~ **upright** dimdik; **2.** v/t. & v/i. sürmelemek; cıvata ile bağlamak; fırlamak; ağzından kaçırmak; çiğnemeden yutmak; (kumaş) top veya rulo haline koymak; Am. POL (partisinden) çekilmek; (partisine) destek olmaktan kaçınmak; gemi azıya almak (a. fig.); elemek, süzmek; dikkatle gözden geçirmek.

bolt.hole ['bəulthəul] n. sığınak, barınak.

bomb [bɔm] **1.** n. esp. MIL bomba; **2.** v/t. bombalamak, bombardıman etm.; ~**ed out** bombalanmış.

bom.bard [bɔm'bɑːd] v/t. topa tutmak, bombardıman etm. (a. fig. & PHYS); **bom'bard.ment** n. bombardıman, topa tutma.

bom.bast ['bɔmbæst] n. tumturaklı söz; **bom'bas.tic**, **bom'bas.ti.cal** □ tumturaklı.

bomb-bay ['bɔmbei] n. (uçakta) bombanın taşındığı bölüm.

bomb.er AVIA ['bɔmə] n. bombardıman uçağı.

bomb...: '~**-proof 1.** adj. bomba geçmez; **2.** n. korugan, bunker; '~ **shell** n. fig. büyük sürpriz; '~**-sight** n. MIL bombardıman vizörü.

bo.nan.za Am. F [bəu'nænzə] n. zenginlik kaynağı; kârlı, kazançlı şey.

bon.bon ['bɔnbɔn] n. bonbon, şekerleme.

bond [bɔnd] **1.** n. bağ, rabıta (a. fig.); ip, zincir; kişileri bir araya getiren ilişki; yapışıklık; yapıştırıcı madde; COM bono, senet, tahvilât; sözleşme; kefalet; **in** ~ COM antrepoda, ambarda; **2.** v/t. malları antrepoya koymak; biraraya getirmek, yapıştırmak (**together, to** -i); ~**ed warehouse** gümrük antreposu; '**bond.age** n. esirlik, serflik, kölelik (a. fig.); '**bondhold.er** n. tahvil (senet) hamili; '**bond(s)man** n. erkek köle, serf; '**bond(s).wom.an** n. cariye, halayık.

bone [bəun] **1.** n. kemik; kılçık; kemikten yapılmış şey; ~**s** pl. iskelet, vücut; zar; ~ **of contention** anlaşmazlık nedeni; **feel in one's** ~**s** derinden hissetmek; b:den çok emin olm.; **have a** ~ **to pick with** F paylaşacak kozu olm. -le, çözüm bekleyen işi olm. -le; **make no** ~**s about** F açıkça söylemek; **2.** v/t. & v/i. kemiklerini ayırmak, ayıklamak; a. ~ **up** F durmadan dinlenmeden çalışmak, ineklemek; sl. çalmak, araklamak; **boned** adj. kemikli; '**bone-'dry** adj. kupkuru; '**bone-dust** n. kemik tozu; '**bone-head** n. sl. aptal, mankafa kimse; '**bon.er** n. Am. sl. hata, yanılma, gaf; '**bone-set.ter** n. çıkıkçı, kırıkçı; '**bone-shak.er** n. köhne otomobil veya bisiklet.

bon.fire ['bɔnfaiə] n. şenlik ateşi; (süprüntü yakmak için) açık havada yakılan ateş.

bon.net ['bɔnit] **1.** n. (kadın ve çocukların giydiği) başlık, bere; İskoç beresi; MEC motor kapağı, kaporta; **2.** v/t. başlık giydirmek.

bon.ny part. Scots ['bɔni] □ güzel, zarif; sıhhatli, gürbüz.

bo.nus COM ['bəunəs] n. ikramiye, prim; hissedarlara verilen fevkalâde temettü.

bon.y ['bəuni] *adj.* kemikleri görünen, zayıf; (*yiyecek*) kemikli, kılçıklı.

boo [bu:] **1.** *int.* yuha; **2.** *v/t.* yuhalamak, ıslık çalmak.

boob *Am. sl.* [bu:b] *n.* ahmak herif, eşek kafalı; **~ tube** F televizyon.

boo.by [bu:bi] *n.* hantal, beceriksiz, budala kimse; çeşitli deniz kuşu türlerinden biri; **~ prize** sonuncuya verilen ödül, teselli mükâfatı; '**~trap** *n.* iyi gizlenmiş ufak bomba; iyi gizlenmiş tuzak.

boo.hoo F [bu:'hu:] *v/i.* çocuk gibi ağlamak; hüngür hüngür ağlamak.

book [buk] **1.** *n.* kitap; defter MUS opera metni; cilt, bap; liste, cetvel; (*bilet, pul vs.*) blok; **the** ♀ Kutsal Kitap; **be in s.o.'s good** (**bad**) **~s** *fig. b-nin* gözünde olm. (olmamak); **bring s.o. to ~** *b-ni bşin* hesabını vermeğe zorlamak; *b-ni* sorumlu tutmak; **2.** *vb.* kaydetmek, deftere geçirmek; ismini kaydetmek; (*bilet, yer*) ayırtmak, rezervasyon yapmak; (*bagaj*) yollamak, sevkettirmek; '**~bind.er** *n.* mücellit, ciltçi; '**~case** *n.* kitap dolabı, kitaplık; '**~end** *n.* kitap desteği; **book.ie** ['buki] *n.* F *spor:* yarış acentası; '**book.ing.clerk** *n.* gişe memuru; '**book.ing-of.fice** *n.* bilet gişesi; '**book.ish** □ hayat tecrübesinden fazla kitaplara bağlı olan; kitaplara bağlı, kitabî; '**book-keep.er** *n.* muhasebeci, defter tutan; **book-keep.ing** *n.* defter tutma, muhasebecilik; **book.let** ['_lit] *n.* broşür, küçük kitap.

book...: '**~mak.er** *n.* kitapçı; yarış acentası; '**~mark(.er)** *n.* (*kitapta*) sayfayı belirlemek için kullanılan kâğıt; '**~plate** *n.* kitabın kime ait olduğunu gösteren desenli kâğıt; '**~sell.er** *n.* kitapçı, kitap satan kimse veya firma; '**~shop** *n.* kitabevi; '**~stall** *n.* kitap sergisi; ufak kitabevi; gazeteci köşesi; '**~worm** *n.* kâğıt kurdu, kitap kurdu (*a. fig.*).

boom[1] NAUT [bu:m] *n.* seren, bumba; vinç kolu; kütüklerin akıntıyla gitmesi ve gemilerin giriş çıkışına engel olunması için liman ağzına gerilmiş mania.

boom[2] [_] **1.** COM fiyatların yükselmesi, piyasada canlılık; hamle; reklâmcılık; **2.** *vb.* (*iş vs.*) hızlı bir gelişme kaydetmek; ileri gitmek, ilerlemek; reklâm yapmak; överek tanıtmak.

boom[3] **1.** *vb.* (*top vs.*) gürlemek; (*rüz-*

gâr) uğultu yapmak; (*arı, böcek*) vızıldamak; **2.** *n.* gürleme, uğultu; vızıltı.

boom.e.rang ['bu:məræŋ] *n.* Avustralya yerlilerinin silah olarak kullandığı ve fırlatıldıktan sonra geri gelen eğri değnek; *fig.* geri tepen kötü hareket *veya plan.*

boon[1] [bu:n] *n.* lütuf, nimet, iyilik.

boon[2] [_] *adj.* şen, neşeli; **~ companion** içki arkadaşı; çok yakın arkadaş.

boor *fig.* [buə] *n.* kaba adam.

boor.ish □ ['buərif] kaba, hoyrat; '**boorish.ness** *n.* kabalık.

boost [bu:st] **1.** *n.* destek, yardım; artış; **2.** *v/t. b-ni* arkasından itmek; (*fiyat, vs.*) artırmak; destek olm. *-e;* lehinde konuşarak veya yazarak yardımcı olm. *-e;* (*radyo, elektrik, su v.b.*) gücü *veya* miktarını artırmak; reklâmını yapmak; '**boost.er** *n.* destek veren kimse; MEC, ELECT güç veya basınç artıran alet; MED bir ilacın etkinliğini artıran madde.

boot[1] [bu:t] *n.:* **to ~** üstelik, ilâve olarak.

boot[2] [_] *n.* bot, potin, çizme; (*araba*) bagaj; tekme; **the ~ is on the other leg** durum değişti; **give s.o. the ~** işinden çıkarmak *-i;* yol vermek *-e;* '**~black** *Am.* = **shoeblack;** '**boot.ed** *adj.* çizmeli; **bootee** ['bu:ti:] *n.* kadın botu; patik.

booth [bu:ð] *n.* (*sergi, panayır, fuar*) satış pavyonu; kulübe, baraka; *Am.* telefon hücresi.

boot...: '**~jack** *n.* çizme çekeceği; '**~lace** *n.* ayakkabı bağı; '**~leg 1.** *vb. part. Am.* içki kaçakçılığı yapmak; kaçak içki satmak veya üzerinde bulundurmak; **2.** *n.* kaçak içki; '**~leg.ger** *n.* içki kaçakçısı; kaçakçı.

boot.less *poet.* ['bu:tlis] *adj.* faydasız, beyhude, boş.

boots [bu:ts] *n.* (*otel*) ayakkabı temizleyen ve bavul taşıyan uşak.

boot-tree ['bu:ttri:] *n.* ayakkabı kalıbı.

boo.ty [bu:ti] *n.* ganimet, yağma.

booze *sl.* [bu:z] **1.** *v/i.* kafayı çekmek, içmek; **2.** *n.* alkollü içki; içki âlemi; '**booz.y** □ sarhoş, kafası dumanlı.

bop [bɔp] = **bebop.**

bo-peep [bəu'pi:p] *n.* bir yere saklanıp aniden ortaya çıkarak oynanan bir çocuk oyunu.

bo.rax CHEM ['bɔ:ræks] *n.* boraks.

bor.der ['bɔ:də] **1.** *n.* kenar, pervaz; hudut, sınır; (*resim, yazı*) çevreleyen süs;

2. *v/t. & v/i.* sınırla(ndır)mak; sınırdaş olm., bitişik olm. (**on, upon** -*e*); '**bor.derer** *n.* sınırda oturan kimse; '**bor.der.land** *n. mst fig.* sınır bölgesi; '**bor.der.line 1.** *n.* sınır; **2.** *adj.* şüpheli, güç ayırt edilebilen; belirli standardın altında olan.

bore[1] [bɔː] **1.** *n.* çap, boru kutru; sonda, delgi; can sıkıcı kimse (*veya* olay); **2.** *v/t.* delik açmak, delmek, sondalamak; -*in* canını sıkmak, baş ağrıtmak.

bore[2] [_] *n.* şiddetli met hareketi.

bore[3] [_] *pret. of bear*[2].

bo.re.al ['bɔːriəl] *adj.* poyraza ait, kuzey rüzgârına ait; kuzey…

bore.dom ['bɔːdəm] *n.* can sıkıntısı, sıkıntı.

bor.er ['bɔːrə] *n.* burgu, matkap, delgi.

bo.ric ac.id CHEM ['bɔːrik'æsid] *n.* asitborik.

bor.ing ['bɔːriŋ] **1.** *n.* sondaj, delme; **2.** *adj.* can sıkıcı.

born [bɔːn] *p.p. of bear*[2] doğmuş.

borne [bɔːn] *p.p. of bear*[2] taşınmış, götürülmüş.

bo.ron CHEM ['bɔːrɔn] *n.* bor.

bor.ough ['bʌrə] *n.* belirli yasal haklara sahip kasaba veya şehir.

bor.row ['bɔrəu] *v/t.* ödünç almak, borç almak (**from** -*den*); (*fikir, kelime v.b.*) almak (**from**-*den*); '**bor.row.er** *n.* borç alan, ödünç alan; '**bor.row.ing** *n.* borç alma, istikraz; GR başka bir dilden alınmış kelime veya deyim.

Bor.stal ['bɔːstl] *n.* suçlu çocuklara mahsus ıslâhhane.

bos.cage ['bɔskidʒ] *n.* ağaçlık, koru.

bosh F [bɔʃ] *n.* boş konuşma, zırva.

bos.om ['buzəm] *n.* göğüs, bağır, koyun; *fig.* kucak, bağır; **~-friend** *n.* candan arkadaş, samimi dost.

Bos.p(h)o.rus ['bɔsfərəs] *n.* İstanbul Boğazı; **the~ and its shores** Boğaziçi.

boss[1] [bɔs] **1.** *n.* kambur, çıkıntı, şişkinlik; ARCH kabartma, süs; **2.** *v/t.* kabartmalarla süslemek.

boss[2] [_] **1.** *n.* patron, şef, amir, ustabaşı; (*siyasî partide*) kodaman, nüfuzlu şahsiyet; **2.** *vb.* sevk ve idare etm. -*i*, kontrol etm. -*i*; *sl.* kumanda etm.

boss.y ['bɔsi] *adj.* kabartmalarla süslü; âmirane, sert, mütehakkim, despotça.

bo.tan.ic, bo.tan.i.cal □ [bə'tænik(əl)] botaniğe ait; bitkisel; **bot.a.nist** ['bɔtənist] *n.* botanist, bitkiler bilgini; **bot.-a.nize** ['_naiz] *v/i.* inceleme için bitki örnekleri toplamak; bu iş için -*e* seya-

hat etm.; '**bot.a.ny** *n.* botanik, bitki bilimi.

botch [bɔtʃ] **1.** *n.* kabaca yapılmış yama; kaba iş; **2.** *v/t.* bşi kötü ve kabaca yapmak; beceriksizce yamamak; '**botch.er** *n.* yamacı, tamirci; *fig. contp.* eskici.

both [bəuθ] *pron., adj. & cj.* her iki(si), her ikisi de; ikisi de; **~ … and** hem … hem de; **~ of them** her ikisi.

both.er F ['bɔðə] **1.** *n.* canını sıkma, sıkıntı, üzüntülü iş; **2.** *v/t.* -*in* canını sıkmak, üzmek, rahatsız ıetm.; *v/i.* merak etm., endişelenmek (**from** -*den*); **~ it!** Allah müstehakkını versin!; **both-er'a.tion** *n.* F can sıkıntısı, üzüntü; **~!** Hay melûn şeytan!, Bırak şunu!; **both.er.some** ['_səm] *adj.* can sıkıcı, üzüntülü.

bot.tle ['bɔtl] **1.** *n.* şişe, biberon; **2.** *v/t.* şişeye koymak; şişelere dodurmak; **~ up** MIL sarmak, muhasara etm.; *fig.* (*öfke, hiddet vs.*) susturmak, zaptetmek; **~d beer** şişe birası; '**~-green** *adj.* çok koyu yeşil; '**~-neck** *n.* şişe boğazı; *fig.* dar geçit; engel.

bot.tom ['bɔtəm] **1.** *n.* dip, alt; kıç; temel, esas; dere, vadi; kuvvet, can; NAUT karina, tekne; **at ~** aslında, esasında; **get to the~ of a matter** bir olayın aslını anlamak, içyüzünü öğrenmek; **knock the ~ out of an argument** bir yargıyı ret ve cerhetmek, çürütmek; **2.** *adj.* esaslı, alt, temel…; **3.** *vb.* (*iskemle vs.*) dip koymak; *fig.* bşe dayan(dır)-mak (**upon**); dibine inmek, ulaşmak; '**bot.tom.less** *adj.* dipsiz; çok derin; '**bot.tom line** *n.* **to keep an eye on the ~** kar etmeye özen göstermek; **that's the ~** sonunda önemli olan bu; '**bot.tom.ry** *n.* NAUT gemi rehni.

bou.doir ['buːdwɑː] *n.* bir kadının yatak veya özel oturma odası.

bough [bau] *n.* ağaç; büyük dal.

bought [bɔːt] *pret. & p.p. of buy*.

bouil.lon ['buːjɔːŋ] *n.* et suyu, konserve.

boul.der ['bəuldə] *n.* çakıl; kaya parçası.

bou.le.vard ['buːlvɑː] *n.* bulvar; *Am.* geniş ana cadde.

bounce [bauns] **1.** *n.* sıçrama, sıçrayış; F canlılık, hayatiyet; F övünme, yüksekten atma; **2.** *v/t. & v/i.* sıçra(t)mak; fırla(t)mak; sek(tir)mek; F (*çek*) iade etm.; F işten atmak, yol vermek; **~ in (out)** hızla girmek (çıkmak); **~ s.o. in-**

to doing s.th. *b-ni* sıkboğaz ederek *bşi* yaptırmak; **'bounc.er** *n.* sıçrayan şey *veya* kimse; F iriyarı adam; *Am. sl.* (*bar, gece kulübü v.b.*) fedai; **'bouncing** *adj.* F gürbüz, neşeli (*çocuk*).

bound¹ [baund] **1.** *pret. & p.p. of* **bind**; **2.** *adj.* bağlı, kayıtlı; ~ **to** *inf. -meğe* mecbur.

bound² [-] *adj.* yolda, gitmek üzere olan (for *-e.*).

bound³ [-] **1.** *n.* hudut, sınır; **keep** within ~s sınırı aşmamak; ölçülü olm., haddini aşmamak; **out of** ~s yasak bölge; **2.** *v/t. & v/i.* sınırla(ndır)mak, tahdit etm.; bitişik olm.

bound⁴ [-] **1.** *n.* sıçrayış, fırlayış, zıplama; **2.** *v/t. & v/i.* sek(tir)mek, sıçra(t)mak, atlamak.

bound.a.ry ['baundəri] *n.* hudut, sınır; ~ **line** hudut hattı.

boun.den ['baundən] *adj.*: **my** ~ **duty** yapmakla zorunlu olduğum görevim, vecibelerim.

bound.less ☐ ['baundlis] sınırsız, sonsuz, tükenmeyen.

boun.te.ous ['bauntiəs] cömert, eli açık; bol; **boun.ti.ful** ☐ ['-tiful] cömert; bol.

boun.ty ['baunti] *n.* cömertlik; cömertçe verilen şey; COM ikramiye, prim.

bou.quet [bu:'kei] *n.* buket, demet; (*şarap*) koku.

bour.geois ['buəʒwa:] **1.** *n.* burjuva, orta sınıf; **2.** *adj.* orta sınıfa mensup.

bour.geoi.sie [buəʒwa:'zi:] *n.* burjuvazi, orta sınıf.

bourn(e) *poet.* [buən] *n.* hudut, sınır; hedef; ülke.

bout [baut] *n.* devre; maç, gösteri; *dans:* yarış, müsabaka; *hastalık*; nöbet.

bou.tique [bu:'ti:k] *n.* butik.

bo.vine ['bəuvain] *adj.* inek ve öküz gibi; ağır, durgun, sıkıcı.

bov.ril ['bɔvril] *n.* etsuyu hülâsası.

bow¹ [bau] **1.** *n.* baş eğerek selâmlama, reverans; **2.** *v/t. & v/i.* reverans yapmak; eğmek; başını eğdirmek; başını eğerek yol göstermek; *fig.* boyun eğmek; ~ **s.o. in** (**out**) *b-ni* saygıyla içeri almak (yolcu etm.).

bow² NAUT [-] *n.* baş, pruva.

bow³ [bəu] **1.** *n.* yay, kavis; ilmek; fiyonk; **2.** *vb.* MUS yay ile çalmak.

bowd.ler.ize ['baudləraiz] *vb.* bir eserden müstehcen görülen kısımları çıkarmak.

bow.els ['bauəlz] *n. pl.* barsaklar; iç

kısımlar.

bow.er ['bauə] *n.* çardak, kameriye; *poet.* bahçe köşkü; NAUT pruvada iki çapadan biri.

bow.ie-knife ['bəuinaif] *n.* av bıçağı.

bow.ing MUS ['bəuiŋ] *n.* yay kullanma.

bowl¹ [bəul] *n.* kâse, tas, çanak; pipo ağzı.

bowl² [-] **1.** *n.* tahta top, yuvarlak; ~**s** *pl.* tahta toplarla oynanan bir tür oyun; **2.** *v/t.* (*top vs.*) yuvarlamak, atmak; ~ **out** *kriket:* *b-ni* oyun harici yapmak; *fig. b-ni* kapı dışarı etm.; ~ **over** devirmek, düşürmek; *fig.* şaşkına çevirmek; *v/i.* yuvarlanmak; **'bowl.er** *n.* *kriket*; topu atan oyuncu; *a.* ~ **hat** melon şapka.

bow.line NAUT ['bəulin] *n.* borina; bir tür düğüm, izbarço bağı.

bowl.ing ['bəuliŋ] *n.* ağır topla oynanan bir tür oyun; ~ **green** bu oyunun oynandığı yeşil alan.

bow...: ~**man** ['bəumən] *n.* okçu, ok atan kimse; '~**sprit** *n.* NAUT civadra; '~**string** *n.* ok kirişi.

bow-wow! ['bau'wau] *int.* havhav!

box¹ [bɔks] **1.** *n.* kutu, sandık; arabacı yeri; kulübe; THEAT loca; MEC yuva, mil yatağı; bir kutu dolusu; at tavlası; *mahkeme*; sanık veya tanık yeri; **2.** *v/t.* kutuya veya sandığa koymak; *a.* ~ **up** ambalaj yapmak.

box² [-] **1.** *v/i.* boks yapmak; ~ **s.o.'s ear** *b-ne* tokat atmak; **2.** *n.* ~ **on the ear** tokat, samar; '**box.er** *n.* boksör.

Box.ing-Day ['bɔksiŋdei] Noeli takip eden gün (*26 Aralık*).

box...: '~**-keep.er** *n.* THEAT localara bakan kimse; '~**-num.ber** *n.* posta kutusu numarası; '~**-of.fice** *n.* (*sinema, tiyatro v.b.*) gişe.

boy [bɔi] *n.* erkek çocuk, oğlan; delikanlı; genç uşak; ~**-friend** *n.* erkek arkadaş; ~ **scout** erkek izci.

boy.cott ['bɔikət] **1.** *v/t.* boykot etm.; **2.** *n.* boykot.

boy.hood ['bɔihud] *n.* çocukluk çağı.

boy.ish ☐ ['bɔiiʃ] erkek çocuk gibi, oğlanlara yakışır.

bra F [bra:] = **brassière**.

brace [breis] **1.** *n.* MEC matkap kolu, köşebent, payanda; kuşak; MED destek; HUNT çift; NAUT prasya; (*dişleri düzeltmeğe yarayan*) tel; (*satırları bağlıyan*) işaret; pantolon askısı; **2.** *v/t.* sağlamlaştırmak, destek olm.; birbirine tutturmak; NAUT prasya etm.

brace.let ['breislit] *n.* bilezik.

brac.ing ['breisiŋ] *adj.* canlandırıcı, kuvvet verici (*hava vs.*).

brack.en BOT ['brækən] *n.* eğreltiotu.

brack.et ['brækit] **1.** *n.* ARCH kol, destek, dirsek; raf; TYP ayraç, parantez; **2.** *v/t.* birleştirmek, birbirine bağlamak; parantez içine almak; *fig.* benzetmek, bir tutmak.

brack.ish ['brækiʃ] *adj.* tuzlumsu, acı.

bract BOT [brækt] *n.* çiçek yaprağı.

brad [bræd] *n.* tel çivi.

brae *Scots* [brei] *n.* bayır, yamaç.

brag [bræg] **1.** *n.* övünme, yüksekten atma; **2.** *v/i.* övünmek, yüksekten atmak, böbürlenmek (*of*, *about -le*).

brag.gart ['brægət] **1.** *n.* övüngen kimse, palavracı kimse, farfara; **2.** □ övüngen, palavracı.

Brahm.an ['brɑ:mən], *mst* **Brah.min** ['-min] *n.* Brahma rahibi, Brehmen.

braid [breid] **1.** *n.* örgü, saç örgüsü; kurdele, örgülü şerit; **2.** *v/t.* örmek; kurdele takmak *-e.*

brail NAUT [breil] *n.* yelken ipi.

braille [breil] *n.* körlere mahsus kabartma yazı.

brain [brein] **1.** *n.* beyin, dimağ; **~s** *pl.* *fig.* kavrayış, zekâ, kafa; **have s.th. on the ~** bşi aklından çıkarmamak; **pick** *veya* **suck s.o.'s ~** F bilgisinden yararlanmak; **turn s.o.'s ~** b-nin başını döndürmek, ne oldum delisi etm.; **2.** *v/t.* kafasını yarmak, beynini patlatmak; **~ drain** beyin göçü; **brained** *comb.* ...beyinli.

brain...: '**~-fag** *n.* beyin yorgunluğu; '**~-fe.ver** *n.* beyin humması; '**~.less** *adj.* akılsız; *fig.* kuş beyinli; '**~-pan** *n.* kafatası; '**~-storm** *n.* anî gelen cinnet; F müthiş ilham; **brain(s) trust** *Am.* bir grup danışman.

brain...: '**~-wash.ing** *n.* beyin yıkama; '**~-wave** *n.* F birdenbire akla gelen fikir; '**brain.y** *adj.* zeki, F kafalı.

braise [breiz] *v/t. mutfak:* kapalı kapta ve ağır ateşte pişirmek.

brake¹ [breik] *n.* eğreltiotu; çalılık.

brake² [-] **1.** *n.* MEC fren (*a. fig.*); gezinti yapılan büyük yolcu arabası; **~ pedal** fren pedalı; **2.** *v/i.* fren yapmak; *v/t.* frenlemek; **brake(s).man** RAIL ['-(s)mən] *n.* frenci.

bram.ble BOT ['bræmbl] *n.* böğürtlen çalısı.

bran [bræn] *n.* kepek.

branch [brɑ:ntʃ] **1.** *n.* dal; kol; şube, bölüm; *local* **~** şube; *chief of* **~** şube âmi-

ri; **2.** *v/i. a.* **~ out** dallanmak, yayılmak, kollara ayrılmak; *a.* **~ off** ikiye ayrılmak.

brand [brænd] **1.** *n.* marka, alâmet, alâmeti farika, cins; kızgın demir, dağ, damga; yanan odun; BOT buğdaypası; *poet.* kılıç; **2.** *v/t.* dağlamak; damgalamak; lekelemek.

bran.dish ['brændiʃ] *v/t.* sallamak, savurmak.

bran(d).new ['bræn(d)'nju:] *adj.* yepyeni.

bran.dy ['brændi] *n.* kanyak, brendi.

brant ORN [brænt] *n.* birkaç tür küçük kaz.

brass [brɑ:s] *n.* pirinç; pirinçten yapılmış eşya; küstahlık, yüzsüzlük; *the* **~** MUS pirinçten yapılmış müzik aletleri; bando; **~ band** bando, mızıka; **~ hat** MIL *sl.* yüksek rütbeli subay; **~ knuckles** *pl. Am.* pirinç muşta; **~ tacks** *pl. sl.*: **get down to ~ tacks** asıl meseleye gelmek, sadede gelmek.

bras.sard ['bræsɑːd] *n.* kol askısı, pazıbent.

bras.se.rie ['brɑːsə'riː] *n.* (*bira satılan*) lokanta.

bras.sière ['bræsiə] *n.* sütyen.

bras.sy ['brɑːsi] *adj.* pirinç kaplama; pirinç renginde; pirinçten yapılmış nefesli saz aleti gibi ses veren; *fig.* (*esp. kadın*) yüzsüz, arsız, cırtlak.

brat F [bræt] *n. contp.* arsız çocuk, yumurcak, piç kurusu.

bra.va.do [brə'vɑːdəu] *n. pl.* **~(e) s** kabadayılık, kuru sıkı atma.

brave [breiv] **1.** □ cesur, yiğit; güzel, muhteşem; **2.** *v/t.* göğüs germek *-e.* karşı gelmek *-e*; **3.** *n.* Kızılderili savaşçı; 'brav.er.y *n.* kahramanlık; ihtişam, tantana.

bra.vo ['brɑː'vəu] *int.* Aferin!, Bravo!

brawl [brɔːl] **1.** *n.* kavga, gürültü, ağız dalaşı; **2.** *v/i.* kavga etm., ağız dalaşı yapmak; 'brawl.er *n.* kavgacı, yaygaracı.

brawn [brɔːn] *n.* (*insan*) kaba et, adale; *fig.* adale kuvveti; jelatinli domuz eti; 'brawn.i.ness *n.* kuvvetlilik, adaleli oluş; 'brawn.y *adj.* adaleli, kuvvetli.

bray¹ [brei] **1.** *n.* anırma, kulakları tırmalayan ses, çınlama; **2.** *v/i.* anırmak; gürültülü ses çıkarmak, çınlamak.

bray² [-] *v/t.* ezmek, rendelemek, dibekte dövmek.

braze MEC [breiz] *v/t.* pirinç ile lehimle-

mek, pirinç kaynağı yapmak.
bra.zen □ ['breizn] pirinçten, tunçtan;
fig. a. **~-faced** yüzsüz, arsız.
bra.zier ['breizjə] *n.* mangal; pirinç
işleri yapan kimse.
Bra.zil.ian [brə'ziljən] **1.** *adj.* Brezilya
ile ilgili; **2.** *n.* Brezilyalı.
Bra.zil-nut [brə'zil'nʌt] *n.* Brezilya kestanesi.
breach [briːtʃ] **1.** *n.* delik, kırık; bozulma; ihlâl; riayetsizlik; MIL gedik,
rahne; **~ of contract** sözleşmenin
bozulması; akdin ihlâli; **~ of duty**
hizmet kusuru; **~ of peace** asayişi
ihlâl; **2.** *v/t.* kırmak, bozmak; gedik
açmak.
bread [bred] *n.* ekmek, yiyecek; *fig.* geçim, maişet; **~ and butter** tereyağlı ekmek; F geçim, maişet; **take the ~ out of
s.o.'s mouth** rızkına engel olm., lok-
masını ağzından çalmak; **know which
side one's ~ is buttered** çıkarının nerede olduğunu bilmek; '**~-bas.ket** *n.*
ekmek sepeti; *fig.* tahıl ambarı; *sl.* mide; '**~-crumb** *n.* ekmek kırıntısı;
'**~-fruit** *n.* BOT ekmek ağacı; '**~-line** *n.*
ücretsiz yiyecek almak için fakirlerin
oluşturduğu kuyruk.
breadth [bredθ] *n.* genişlik, en; *fig.* genişlik, şümul.
bread-win.ner ['bredwinə] *n.* evin geçimini sağlayan kimse.
break [breik] **1.** *n.* kırık; ara; açıklık,
fasıla, dinlenme; âni değişiklik; arası
kesilme; TYP fasıla; COM *Am.* (*fiyat*)
düşüş; (*gün*) ağartı; kaçış; *bilardo*: sıra,
dizi; F fırsat, şans; **a bad ~** safdillik;
şanssızlık; **a lucky ~** şans, bahtiyarlık;
2. (*irr.*) *v/t.* kırmak, koparmak, parçalamak; dağıtmak; açmak, yarmak; (*kanun*) ihlâl etm. *-i.* uymamak *-e*; (*söz*)
tutmamak; (*rekor*) kırmak; mahvetmek; alıştırmak; ara vermek *-e*; sona
erdirmek; ELECT cereyanı kesmek; (*para*) bozdurmak; (*sır, şifre*) çözmek; iflâs ettirmek; (*sır, şifre*) çözmek; if-
mak; **~ down** yıkmak; **~ in** bşe alıştırmak; kırıp girmek; **~ up** parçalamak,
kırmak; dağıtmak; sökmek, yıkmak;
v/i. parçalanmak, kırılmak; kuvvetten
düşmek; (*gün*) ağarmak; kesilmek;
anî yön değiştirmek; fırlamak; ilgisi
kesilmek; iflâs etm.; **~ away** ayrılmak;
dağılmak; kaçıp kurtulmak; kopmak; **~
down** bozulmak, işlemez hale gelmek;
başarısızlığa uğramak; morali bozulmak, kontrolünü kaybetmek; dönüş-

mek; kısımlara ayrılmak; '**break.a.ble**
adj. kırılır; kırılacak; '**break.age** *n.*
kır(ıl)ma; kırık yeri; '**break-down** *n.*
bozulma, yıkılma; MOT ârıza, bozukluk; **nervous ~** asap bozulması. çökme; '**break.er** *n.* kıran, parçalayan *vs.*
(*s.* **break 2**); **~s** *pl.* sahile veya kayalara
vurup kırılan dalga.
break...: **~.fast** ['brekfəst] **1.** *n.* kahvaltı; **have ~** = **2.** *v/i.* kahvaltı etm.;
~.neck ['breiknek] *adj.* çok süratli veya tehlikeli; '**~-out** *n.* kaçma, firar; MIL
çemberi yarma; '**~-through** *n.* MIL yarma; *fig.* başarı; '**~-'up** *n.* bozulma,
dağılma, parçalanma; (*hava*) değişme;
'**~.wa.ter** *n.* dalgakıran.
bream ICHTH [briːm] *n.* karagöz, mercan türü balık.
breast [brest] **1.** *n.* göğüs; meme; kalp,
gönül; **make a clean ~ of s.th.** bütün
gerçeği itiraf etm., içini boşaltmak; **2.**
v/t. göğüs germek, karşı durmak;
göğüslemek (*a. fig.*); '**breast.ed** *adj.*
göğüslü.
breast...: '**~-pin** *n.* broş, kravat iğnesi;
'**~.plate** *n.* göğüslük zırh; '**~-stroke** *n.*
yüzme; kurbağalama; '**~.work** *n.* MIL
göğüs siperi.
breath [breθ] *n.* nefes, soluk; hafif rüzgâr; dem, an; buğu; **under** *veya* **below
one's ~** alçak sesle veya fısıldayarak;
out of ~ soluğu kesilmiş, nefes nefese;
waste one's ~ boşuna nefes tüketmek;
breathe [briːð] *v/t. & v/i.* nefes al(dır)-
mak, teneffüs etm.; hafifçe esmek;
yaşamak; fısıldamak; belirtmek; hayat
vermek; '**breath.er** *n.* nefes alan kimse; ara, paydos, nefes alma.
breath.ing ['briːðiŋ] *n.* nefes (alma);
an; söyleme; püfürtü; '**~-space**, '**~-time**
n. nefes alacak zaman, nefes alma
fırsatı.
breath.less □ ['breθlis] nefesi kesilmiş,
nefes nefese; korkutucu; hareketsiz;
'**breath.less.ness** *n.* soluksuzluk.
breath-tak.ing □ ['breθteikiŋ] nefes kesen, çok heyecanlı.
bred [bred] *pret. & p.p. of* **breed 2**.
breech MEC [briːtʃ] *n.* kıç, dip; top kuyruğu, kama; **breech.es** *pl.* pantolon,
külot pantolon; '**breech.es-buoy** *n.*
NAUT cankurtaran varagelesi; **breech-
-load.er** *n.* kuyruktan dolma top veya
tüfek.
breed [briːd] **1.** *n.* soy, ırk, cins; çeşit; **2.**
(*irr.*) *v/t. & v/i.* doğ(ur)mak, yavrula-
mak, üre(t)mek; yetiştirmek, besle-

mek; hâsıl etm., hasıl olm., türemek; **'breed.er** n. yetiştirici; üretici, yavrulayan; PHYS üretici reaktör; **'breed.ing** n. üreme; yetiştirme; terbiye; ~ **ground** üreme yeri.

breeze[1] [bri:z] **1.** n. hafif rüzgâr, meltem, esinti; F münakaşa; **2.** vb. ~ **in** rahatlıkla gelmek.

breeze[2] [bri:z] n. kül ve sönmüş kömür parçaları; ~ **block** (bu madde ve çimento karışımı) hafif yapı bloğu.

breez.y ['bri:zi] adj. hafif rüzgârlı, havadar; canlı, hareketli.

Bren gun MIL ['bren'gʌn] n. hafif makineli tüfek, mitralyöz.

breth.ren ECCL ['breðrin] n. pl. kardeşler.

breve [bri:v] n. sesli harflerin kısa okunması için üzerine konulan kavisli işaret.

bre.vet MIL ['brevit] n. üst rütbeye atama belgesi.

bre.vi.ar.y ECCL ['bri:vjəri] n. Katolik dua kitabı.

brev.i.ty ['breviti] n. kısalık.

brew [bru:] **1.** v/t. yapmak (bira v.b.), hazırlamak, kaynatmak; fig. tertip etmek, hazırlamak (esp. kötü bş); **2.** n. hazırlanmış içki; **'brew.age** n. lit. maya ile yapılmış içkiler; **'brew.er** n. bira yapan kimse, biracı; **'brew.er.y** n. bira fabrikası.

bri.ar ['braiə] = **brier**[1] & **brier**[2].

bribe [braib] **1.** n. rüşvet; **2.** v/t. rüşvet vermek -e; **'brib.er.y** n. rüşvet verme veya alma.

brick [brik] **1.** n. tuğla; tuğla biçiminde şey; sl. mert adam; F **a regular** ~ yaman bir herif, çok iyi çocuk; **drop a** ~ F pot kırmak, çam devirmek; **make** ~**s without straw** parasız pulsuz iş çevirmek; **2.** v/t. tuğla ile döşemek; ~**bat** n. hırsla fırlatılan şey (tuğla v.b.); fig. eleştiri, taş; **'~-kiln** n. tuğla fırını; **'~.lay.er** n. duvarcı; **'~-work** n. tuğla işi; pl. tuğla ocağı.

brid.al ['braidl] **1.** □ geline ait, düğüne ait; gelin...; ~ **procession** gelin alayı; **2.** n. mst poet. düğün, nikâh, evlenme.

bride [braid] n. gelin, yeni evli kadın; **'~.groom** n. güvey, damat; **'brides-maid** n. düğünde geline refakat eden kız; **brides.man** ['-zmən] n. sağdıç.

bride.well ['braidwəl] n. ıslahane.

bridge[1] [bridʒ] **1.** n. köprü; NAUT kaptan köprüsü; MUS köprü; burnun kemikli üst kısmı; gözlüğün burna oturan kısmı; **2.** v/t. köprü kurmak -e; fig. iki ucunu bir araya getirmek.

bridge[2] [-] n. iskambil: briç.

bridge...: '~**-head** n. köprübaşı; '~**-work** n. köprü inşaatı.

bri.dle ['braidl] **1.** n. at başlığı; dizgin; **2.** v/t. gem vurmak, dizgin takmak -e; hareketlerini kontrol altında tutmak; v/i. a. ~ **up** baş kaldırmak, terslenmek; '~**-path**, '~**-road** n. atlılara mahsus yol.

brief [bri:f] **1.** □ kısa, özetli; **2.** n. özet, yazılı belge; JUR dava özeti; (papalık) mühürlü mektubu; MIL. AVIA görev ve yetki talimatı; **hold a** ~ **for** b-ni mahkemede savunmak; **3.** v/t. JUR (avukat, a. MIL) lüzumlu bilgi veya son talimatı vermek; avukat tutmak; '~**-bag**, '~**-case** n. evrak çantası; **'brief.ing** n. bilgi vermek için yapılan kısa toplantı, brifing; **'brief.ness** n. kısalık.

bri.er[1] BOT ['braiə] n. funda, yabanî gül.

bri.er[2] [-] n. a. ~ **pipe** funda kökünden yapılmış pipo.

brig NAUT [brig] n. iki direkli yelkenli, brik; askeri hapishane.

bri.gade ['bri'geid] **1.** n. MIL tugay; ekip; **2.** v/t. birlikleri tugaylara göre düzenlemek; gruplar oluşturmak; **brig.a.dier** [brigə'diə] n. tuğbay.

brig.and ['brigənd] n. eşkiya, haydut; **'brig.and.age** n. eşkiyalık.

bright □ [brait] parlak, berrak, ışıldayan; neşeli, canlı; zeki; muhteşem; **'bright.en** v/t. & v/i. parla(t)mak, neşelen(dir)mek; a. ~ **up** aydınlatmak; aydınlanmak; **'bright.ness** n. parlaklık; uyanıklık.

brill ICHTH [bril] n. çivisiz kalkan balığı.

bril.liance, bril.lian.cy ['briljəns(i)] n. parlaklık, pırıltı; fig. zekâ parlaklığı; **'brilliant 1.** □ çok parlak; çok zeki; **2.** n. pırlanta.

brim [brim] **1.** n. (bardak, kap v.b.) ağız, (şapka) kenar; **2.** vb. ağzına kadar dol(dur)mak; ~ **over** taşmak (a. fig.); '~**-ful**, '~**-full** adj. ağzına kadar dolu.

brim.stone ['brimstən] n. kükürt.

brin.dle(d) ['brindl(d)] n. (esp. inek veya kedi) benekli, lekeli hayvan.

brine [brain] **1.** n. tuzlu su, salamura; poet. deniz suyu; **2.** v/t. salamura etm., tuzlamak.

bring [briŋ] (irr.) v/t. getirmek; bşe vesile olm., sebebiyet vermek; şikâyet etm., dava açmak, ileri sürmek; ~ **about**, ~ **to pass** sebep olm.; beraberinde getirmek; ~ **an action** dava açmak; ~ **along** yanında getirmek; ~ **down** (*fiyat*) indirmek, azaltmak; ~ **down the house** THEAT çok beğenilen gösteri yapmak, çılgınca alkışlanmak; ~ **forth** meydana çıkarmak; doğurmak; ~ **forward** ileri sürmek, ortaya atmak; öne almak; COM (*hesap toplamı*) geçirmek, nakletmek; ~ **home to** gerçeği kabul ettirmek; ~ **in** kazandırmak; arzetmek, takdim etm.; içeri almak; ithal etm.; ~ **in guilty** suçlu olduğuna karar vermek; ~ **off** başarılı olm. *-de*; çıkarmak, kurtarmak *-den*; ~ **on** sebep olm. *-e*; geliştirmek *-i*; yardımcı olm. *-e*; ~ **out** meydana çıkarmak, üretmek, neşretmek, yayımlamak; ~ **round** ayıltmak *-i*; iyileştirmek *-i*; (*gemi v.b.*) döndürmek; ~ **s.o. to do** *b-ne* bşi yaptırmak; ~ **to** NAUT orsa alabanda etm.; ~ **s.o. to himself** *b-ni* tekrar *k-ne* getirmek, ayıltmak; ~ **under** tâbi kılmak, boyunduruk altına almak; ~ **up** yetiştirmek, büyütmek; söz konusu etm.; yaklaştırmak.

bring.er ['brɪŋə] *n.* getiren, hâmil.
brink [brɪŋk] *n.* kenar, kıyı.
brin.y ['braɪnɪ] *adj.* tuzlu.
bri.quette [brɪ'ket] *n.* briket.
brisk [brɪsk] **1.** ☐ faal, canlı, işlek; (*esp. rüzgâr, hava*) sert, kamçılayan; **2.** *v/t.* & *v/i. mst* ~ **up** canlan(dır)mak, diril(t)mek, hareketlen(dir)mek.
bris.ket [brɪskɪt] *n.* (*dört ayaklı hayvan*) göğüs eti, döş.
brisk.ness ['brɪsknɪs] *n.* canlılık, hareketlilik.
bris.tle ['brɪsl] **1.** *n.* sert kıl; **2.** *v/t. a.* ~ **up** tüyleri ürpermek, dimdik olm. (**with** *-den*); ~ **with** *fig.* bşle dolup taşmak; *b-ne*, *bşe* dik dik bakmak; 'bris.tled, 'bristly *adj.* kıllı; anlaşması güç, öfkeli.
Bri.tan.nic [brɪ'tænɪk] *adj.* Britanya'ya ait.
Brit.ish ['brɪtɪʃ] *adj.* Britanya'ya ait; **the** ~ *pl.* Britanyalı, İngiliz; 'Brit.ish.er *n.* *part. Am.* İngiliz.
Brit.on HIST, *poet.* ['brɪtn] *n.* Britanyalı.
brit.tle ['brɪtl] *adj.* kolay kırılır, gevrek; *fig.* zayıf, hassas.
broach [brəʊtʃ] **1.** *n.* kebap şişi; MEC matkap, boşaltma tığı; **2.** *vb.* (*fıçı, varil*) delmek, delerek sıvıyı akıtmak, delik açmak *-e*; (*konu, fikir*) girişmek *-e*, bahis açmak, dermeyan etm.
broad ☐ [brɔːd] geniş, enli; hudutsuz, uçsuz bucaksız; sade, belli, açık (*öğüt, ikaz vs.*); güpe gündüz; genel;

kaba (*espri*); erkinci, liberal; '~-axe *n.* balta; '~.band *n.* geniş bant; '~'brimmed *adj.* geniş kenarlı; '~.cast **1.** *adj.* AGR saçılmış; yayınlanmış; yayına ait; **2.** (*irr. cast*) *vb. radyo:* yayınlamak, neşretmek; yayın yapmak; *fig.* etrafa yaymak (*haber, dedikodu*); AGR saçarak tohum ekmek; ~**ing station** yayın istasyonu; **3.** *n.* radyo yayını; '~.cast.er *n.* spiker; '~.cloth *n.* iyi cins yünden yapılmış kumaş; 'broad.en *v/t.* & *v/i.* genişle(t)mek; 'broad'mind.ed *adj.* açık fikirli; 'broad.ness *n.* genişlik.

broad...: '~.sheet *n.* el ilânı; '~-side *n.* NAUT borda; borda ateşi; şiddetli hücum (*a. fig*); *a.* = *broadsheet*; '~.sword *n.* pala.
bro.cade [brəʊ'keɪd] *n.* brokar; bro-'cad.ed *adj.* kabartmalı, desenli dokunmuş.
broc.co.li BOT ['brɒkəlɪ] *n.* karnabahara benzer bir bitki.
bro.chure [brəʊ'ʃjʊə] *n.* broşür, risale.
brogue [brəʊg] *n.* bir tür kaba ve sağlam ayakkabı.
broi.der [brɔɪdə] = *embroider*.
broil [brɔɪl] **1.** *n.* gürültü, kavga; ızgara (*et*); **2.** *vb.* münakaşa etm.; ızgara yapmak; *fig.* güneşten yanmak; *fig.* pişmek; ~**ing** *adj.* şiddetli sıcak; 'broil.er *n.* ızgara yapan kimse veya alet; ızgaralık piliç.
broke [brəʊk] **1.** *pret. of* **break 2**; **2.** *adj. sl.* meteliksiz.
bro.ken ['brəʊkən] *p.p. of* **break 2**; ~ **health** zayıf düşmüş, yıkılmış; ~ **home** yıkılmış yuva; ~ **stones** *pl.* balas, moloz; ~ **English** bozuk İngilizce; '~'heart.ed *adj.* ümitsizliğe kapılmış, kalbi kırık; 'broken.ly *adv.* ara vererek; kesik kesik hareket ederek; 'broken-'wind.ed VET tıknefes, astmalı.
bro.ker ['brəʊkə] *n.* COM tellâl, simsar; borsa acentesi, komisyoncu; 'bro.ker.age *n.* COM komisyonculuk, simsarlık; komisyon (*ücret*).
bro.mide ['brəʊmaɪd] *n.* CHEM bromür; *sl.* beylik söz *veya* fikir; **bro.mine** ['-miːn] *n.* CHEM brom.
bron.chi.al ANAT ['brɒŋkjəl] *adj.* broşlara ait; **bron.chi.tis** *n.* MED bronşit.
bron.co ['brɒŋkəʊ] *n.* yabanî veya yarı ehlî at; ~**bust.er** ['-bʌstə] *n. sl.* at terbiyecisi.
Bronx cheer *Am.* ['brɒŋks'tʃiə] *n.* yuha, yuha çekme.

bronze [brɔnz] **1.** *n.* tunç, bronz; bronz rengi; tunçtan eşya; **2.** *adj.* tunçtan yapılmış, bronz...; **3.** *v/t.* bronzla kaplatmak; *fig.* güneşte yakmak, esmerleştirmek; ♀ *Age* Tunç Devri.

brooch [brəutʃ] *n.* broş, iğne.

brood [bru:d] **1.** *n.* yumurtadan çıkan hayvancıklar; sürü, güruh; **2.** *v/i.* kuluçkaya yatmak; *fig.* kuruntulariyle *k-ni* yemek, derin düşüncelere dalmak; 'brood.er *n.* kuluçka makinesi; düşünceye dalan kimse.

brook¹ [bruk] *n.* dere, çay, ırmak.

brook² RHET [-] *v/t.* tahammül etm., çekmek; *the matter ~s no delay* meselenin beklemeye tahammülü yoktur.

brook.let ['bruklit] *n.* küçük dere.

broom BOT [bru:m] *n.* katır tırnağı; süpürge; ~.stick ['brumstik] *n.* süpürge sapı.

broth [brɔθ] *n.* etsuyu, etsuyuna çorba.

broth.el ['brɔθl] *n.* genelev.

broth.er ['brʌðə] *n.* erkek kardeş, birader; aynı cemiyette erkek üye; ~.hood ['-hud] *n.* kardeşlik, beraberlik, birlik; bir kuruluşun üyeleri; '~-in-law *n.* kayınbirader, bacanak, enişte; 'broth.er.ly *adj.* kardeşçe.

brougham ['bru:əm] *n.* kupa arabası.

brought [brɔ:t] *pret. & p.p. of* bring.

brow [brau] *n.* kaş, alın; *poet.* çehre, yüz; bayır sırtı; '~.beat (*irr.* beat) *v/t.* sert bakarak korkutmak.

brown [braun] **1.** *adj.* kahverengi, kahve renkli, esmer; güneşten yanmış; ~ *bread* esmer ekmek; ~ *paper* koyu renkli ambalaj kâğıdı; *be in a ~ study* derin bir düşünce içinde olm.; **2.** *n.* kahve rengi **3.** *v/t. & v/i.* karar(t)mak; esmerletmek, esmerleşmek; *be ~ed off sl.* bıkmak; 'brown.ie ['-ni] *n.* masaldaki iyi huylu küçük peri; kız izci (*8-11 yaşları arasında*); 'brown.ish *adj.* esmerimsi; 'brownstone *n.* kumtaşı; ön yüzü bu taştan yapılmış ev.

browse [brauz] **1.** *n.* taze sürgün veya dal; **2.** *v/b.* otlamak, (*yaprak, sürgün*) yemek (*on*); *fig.* kitaplara göz gezdirmek.

bruise [bru:z] **1.** *n.* bere, çürük; **2.** *v/t.* berelemek, çürütmek; dövmek, ezmek; 'bruis.er *n. sl.* boksör, zorba.

brunch ['brʌntʃ] *n.* erken yenen öğle yemeği, geç yenen kahvaltı.

bru.nette [bru:net] **1.** *n.* esmer kız *veya* kadın; **2.** *adj.* esmer.

brunt [brʌnt] *n.* şiddetli darbe, yüklen-

me; *bear the ~* sıkıntısını çekmek, asıl yüke katlanmak.

brush [brʌʃ] **1.** *n.* fırça, fırçalama; tüylü kuyruk, tilki kuyruğu; ELECT fırça; kısa yumuşak temas; *give a ~* fırçalayarak kaldırmak, çıkarmak; *have a ~ with s.o.* yumruk yumruğa gelmek -*le*, kavgaya tutuşmak -*le*; **2.** *v/b.* fırçalamak, süpürmek; hafifçe dokunmak -*e*; ~ *aside*, ~ *away* bertaraf etm., dikkate almamak, önemsememek; ~ *down* üstünü fırçalamak; ~ *off* tozunu almak; başından atmak, atlatmak, savmak; ~ *up* (*bilgi*) tazelemek; '~.wood *n.* çalılık, fundalık; çalı çırpı.

brusque ☐ [brusk] sert, haşin, kaba, ters.

Brus.sels sprouts BOT ['brʌsl-'sprauts] *n.* frenk lahanası.

bru.tal ☐ ['bru:tl] hayvanca, vahşî; zalim, merhametsiz; çok sert, katlanması güç; kaba; bru.tal.i.ty [-'tæliti] *n.* vahşet, canavarlık; bru.tal.ize ['-təlaiz] *v/b.* hayvanlaştırmak, kabalaştırmak; hayvanca davranmak; brute **1.** *adj.* zalim, hayvan gibi; düşüncesiz; **2.** *n.* hayvan; hayvan gibi adam; canavar; 'brut.ish ☐ = *brute 1*; 'brut.ish.ness *n.* hayvanlık, kabalık.

bub.ble ['bʌbl] **1.** *n.* hava kabarcığı; kaynayış, kaynama; *fig.* sabun köpüğü; **2.** *v/i.* köpürmek, kaynamak, fıkırdamak; 'bub.bly **1.** *adj.* kabarcıklı; coşkun, şakrak; **2.** *n. co.* şampanya, köpüklü şarap.

buc.ca.neer [bʌkə'niə] **1.** *n.* korsan, deniz eşkıyası; **2.** *v/b.* korsanlık etm.

buck [bʌk] **1.** *n.* ZOO erkek hayvan (*part. karaca, geyik*); züppe, modaya düşkün adam; *Am. sl.* dolar; *pass the ~* F sorumluluğu üzerinden atmak; **2.** *v/b.* sıçramak (*esp. at*); binicisini üzerinden atmak; *Am.* F muhalefet etm., karşı gelmek; ~ *up* F canlan(dır)mak, geliştirmeye çalışmak.

bucket ['bʌkit] **1.** *n.* kova, gerdel; *a mere drop in the ~ fig.* denizden katra, devede kulak; **2.** *v/b.* (*at*) koşturarak yormak; delice bir süratle hareket et(tir)mek; (*yağmur*) bardaktan boşanırcasına yağmak; ~.ful ['-ful] *n.* bir kova dolusu; ~ *seat* MOT çanak biçiminde ve katlanır koltuk.

buck.le ['bʌkl] **1.** *n.* toka, kopça; **2.** *v/t. & v/i.* tokalamak, kopçalamak; MEC ısı veya basınç ile bük(ül)mek; ~ *on* tokalamak, takmak; ~ *to* girişmek -*e*, çok

çalışmak; '**buck.ler** *n.* kalkan, siper.
buck.ram ['bʌkrəm] *n.* çirişli pamuklu
bez; *fig.* yapay davranış.
buck...: '**ᴗskin** *n.* güderi; '**ᴗwheat** *n.*
ʙoт kara buğday.
bud [bʌd] **1.** *n.* tomurcuk, konca, sürgün; *fig.* gelişmemiş, olgunlaşmamış;
nip in the ᴗ fig. bşin gelişmesine engel
olm.; **2.** *v/t. & v/i.* tomurcuklan(dır)-
mak, konca vermek; (*ağaç*) aşılamak;
ᴗding tomurcuklanan; gelişmekte
olan.
Bud.dhism ['budizəm] *n.* Budizm, Buda dini; '**Bud.dhist** *n.* Budist.
bud.dy *Am.* F ['bʌdi] *n.* arkadaş, ahbap.
budge [bʌdʒ] *v/t. & v/i.* kımılda(t)mak,
hareket et(tir)mek; *fig.* fikrini değiş-
tir(t)mek.
budg.et ['bʌdʒit] **1.** *n.* bütçe, devlet bütçesi; stok, miktar; ucuz, bütçeye uygun;
2. *vb.* bütçe yapmak; '**budg.et.ar.y** *adj.*
bütçeye ait, bütçe…
buff [bʌf] **1.** *n.* (*renk*) deve tüyü; kalın
bir tür deri; *in* (*one's*) **ᴗ** çırılçıplak; **2.**
v/t. boyamak, (*metal*) yumuşak bşle
parlatmak.
buf.fa.lo zoo ['bʌfələu] *pl.* **buf.fa.loes**
['ᴗz] *n.* manda.
buff.er ['bʌfə] *n.* ʀᴀɪʟ tampon; *fig.*
(*saldırı, güçlük v.b.*) hafifletici; *old ᴗ
sl.* beceriksiz moruk; **ᴗ state** tampon
devlet.
buf.fet[1] ['bʌfit] **1.** *n.* tokat, yumruk; **2.**
vb. tokatlamak, yumruk atmak; müca-
dele etm.. savaşmak (*with ile*).
buf.fet[2] ['bufei] *n.* büfe; tezgâh; büfe
şeklinde hazırlanan hafif yemek; **ᴗ
car** ʀᴀɪʟ büfe, büvet.
buf.foon [bə'fu:n] *n.* soytarı, maskara;
buf.foon.er.y *n.* maskaralık.
bug [bʌg] *n.* tahtakurusu; *Am.* böcek;
Am. sl. kusur, bozukluk, ârıza; gizli
dinleme cihazı; *sl. -in* hastası;
ᴗa.boo [ˌᴗəbu:], '**ᴗbear** *n.* korku
uyandıran hayali şey, umacı; '**bug.gy**
1. *adj.* tahtakurusu üşüşmüş; **2.** *n.* tek
atlı hafif araba; çocuk arabası.
bu.gle[1] ['bju:gl] *n.* borazan, boru.
bu.gle[2] [ˌᴗ] *n.* siyah boncuk.
bu.gler ᴍɪʟ ['bju:glə] *n.* boru çalan
kimse.
buhl [bu:l] *n.* kakma süslemeli eşya.
build [bild] **1.** (*irr.*) *vb.* inşa etm., kurmak, yapmak; *fig.* bina etm., dayan-
mak, güvenmek (*on, upon -e*); **ᴗ** in içine inşa etm., sokmak, yerleştirmek; **ᴗ
up** birik(tir)mek; geliş(tir)mek; bina-

larla doldurmak, gelişmiş bir hale getirmek; *fig.* göklere çıkarmak; **2.** *n.*
(*esp. insan vücudu*) yapı, bünye, biçim;
'**build.er** *n.* inşaatçı; inşaat ustası;
'**build.ing** *n.* bina, yapı, ev; inşa etme;
ᴗ contractor inşaat müteahhidi;
inşaatçı; **ᴗ craftsman** inşaat işçisi; **ᴗ
site** şantiye, yapı yeri; **ᴗ society** inşaat
şirketi, yapı kooperatifi; '**build-up** *n.*
kurma, tanzim; kuruluş, organizasyon.
built [bilt] **1.** *pret. & p.p. of build*; **2.** *adj.*
…inşa edilmiş; … şekillendirilmiş;
'**ᴗ'in** *adj.* gömme; yerleşmiş; '**ᴗ'up** ar-
e.a meskûn bölge, yerleşme bölgesi.
bulb [bʌlb] *n.* ʙoт (*kök*) soğan; (*termometre v.b.*) hazne; ᴇʟᴇᴄᴛ ampul; '**bulbous** *n.* ʙoт yumurlu, yumru köklü.
Bul.gar ['bʌlgɑ:] *n.* Bulgar; **Bul.gar.i-
an** [ˌˌ'gɛəriən] **1.** *adj.* Bulgaristan'a
ait; **2.** *n.* Bulgar; Bulgarca.
bulge [bʌldʒ] **1.** *n.* bel verme, şiş, çıkıntı;
ani ve beklenmeyen yükselme; **2.** *v/i.*
bel vermek, kamburlaşmak, çıkıntı
yapmak.
bulk [bʌlk] *n.* hacım, kütle; en büyük
kısım; hantal vücut; ɴᴀᴜᴛ dökme yük,
kargo; *in ᴗ* dökme, ambalajsız; toptan;
'**ᴗ.head** *n.* ɴᴀᴜᴛ bölme; '**bulk.i.ness** *n.*
irilik; '**bulk y** *adj.* hacimli, büyük, cüsseli; ᴘosт havaleli.
bull[1] [bul] **1.** *n.* boğa; (*iri*) erkek hayvan;
sl. esp. Am. polis memuru; boğa gibi,
çok kuvvetli adam; ᴄoᴍ *sl.* spekülâtör,
borsa hava oyuncusu; *a ᴗ in a china
shop* sakar adam, patavatsız adam;
take the ᴗ by the horns güçlükleri kor-
kusuzca göğüslemek; **ᴗ session** *Am.
sl.* erkeklerin bir araya gelerek yaptıkları toplantı; **2.** *v/t.* ᴄoᴍ *sl.* fiyatları yükselterek spekülasyon yapmak.
bull[2] [ˌᴗ] *n.* (*papalık*) ferman.
bull[3] [ˌᴗ] *n.* yanılma, gaf; *Irish ᴗ* boş
lâkırdı, saçmasapan söz, zırva.
bull.dog ['buldɔg] *n.* buldok köpeği;
cesur ve kararlı adam; ᴜɴɪᴠ laboratuvar yardımcısı.
bull.doze *Am.* F ['buldəuz] *v/t.* üstünden buldozer geçirmek -*in*; tedhiş
etm., zor kullanarak kabul ettirmek;
'**bull.doz.er** *n.* buldozer.
bul.let ['bulit] *n.* kurşun, mermi.
bul.le.tin ['bulitin] *n.* günlük haber,
tebliğ, bülten; dergi; **ᴗ board** *Am.* ilân
tahtası.
bull...: '**ᴗfight** *n.* boğa güreşi; '**ᴗfinch** *n.*
ᴏʀɴ şakrakkuşu; çit, çalı; '**ᴗfrog** *n.* zoo
bir tür iri kafalı kurbağa.

bul.lion ['buljən] *n.* altın veya gümüş külçesi.

bull.ock ['bulək] *n.* iğdiş edilmiş boğa, öküz.

bull.pen *Am.* ['bul'pen] *n.* F hapishane; *beysbol:* yedek oyuncuların bekledikleri yer.

bull's-eye [bulzai] *n.* hedefin ortası; tam vuruş; NAUT lomboz; nane şekeri.

bul.ly[1] ['buli] **1.** *n.* kabadayı, zorba, kendinden küçükleri ezen kimse (*esp. çocuk*); **2.** *adj.* palavracı, farfara; *part. Am.* F şık, klâs, iyi, güzel (*a. int.*); **3.** *v/t.* korkutmak, kabadayılık etm..

bul.ly[2] [_] *a.* ~ *beef* konserve sığır eti.

bul.rush BOT ['bulrʌʃ] *n.* hasırotu, saz.

bul.wark ['bulwək] *n.* toprak tabya, siper (*mst. fig.*); NAUT küpeşte.

bum[1] *sl.* [bʌm] *n.* kaba et, kıç.

bum[2] *Am.* F [_] **1.** *n.* serseri, başıboş kimse, sarhoş; *be veya go on the*~ bozulmak, aşınmak; serseri hayatı yaşamak; **2.** *v/t.* başkalarının sırtından geçinmek, *sl.* otlamak; **3.** *adj.* fena, kötü, kıyafetsiz.

bum.ble-bee ['bʌmblbiː] *n.* ZOO hezen arısı.

bum.boat ['bʌmbəut] *n.* erzak sandalı.

bump [bʌmp] **1.** *n.* çarpma, vuruş; şiş, yumru, tümsek; kabiliyet, Allah vergisi; **2.** *vb.* bindirmek, vurmak, çarpmak (*against* -*e*); çarpışmak (*together*) , sars(ıl)mak; *sandal vs. yarışı;* geçmek, geride bırakmak -*i;* ~ *into s.o.* b-*ne* çarpmak, b-*ni* itmek; ~ *off* F öldürmek, mortlatmak.

bump.er ['bʌmpə] *n.* ağzına kadar dolu bardak; F çok dolu veya büyük şey; MOT tampon; ~ *crop* rekor teşkil eden hasat.

bump.kin ['bʌmpkin] *n.* hödük, ahmak.

bump.tious □ F ['bʌmpʃəs] kendini beğenmiş, küstah.

bump.y ['bʌmpi] *adj.* tümsekli, yamrı yumru; *fig.* inişli çıkışlı; AVIA sallantılı.

bun [bʌn] *n.* kuru üzümlü çörek; (*saç*) topuz.

bu.na ['buːnə] *n.* kauçuk.

bunch [bʌntʃ] **1.** *n.* demet, deste, salkım; grup, takım; kütle, yığın; ~ *of flowers* çiçek demeti, buket; ~ *of grapes* üzüm salkımı; **2.** *vb.* bir araya gelmek, demet yapmak.

bun.combe ['bʌŋkəm] *n.* boş laf, palavra.

bun.dle ['bʌndl] **1.** *n.* deste, demet,

bohça, çıkın, paket, bağ; **2.** *v/t. a.* ~ *up* çıkınlamak, sarmalamak; ~ *away*, ~ *off* F kov(ala)mak, defetmek, sepetlemek.

bung [bʌŋ] **1.** *n.* fıçı tapası, tıkaç; **2.** *v/t.* tapa ile tıkamak; F fırlatmak; ~*ed up* tıkalı (*burun*).

bun.ga.low ['bʌŋgələu] *n.* tek katlı ev.

bung-hole ['bʌŋhəul] *n.* fıçı deliği.

bun.gle ['bʌŋgl] **1.** *n.* kötü iş, bozma, acemice iş; **2.** *vb.* bozmak, berbat etm., yüzüne gözüne bulaştırmak; '**bun.gler** *n.* üstünkörü iş gören adam; '**bun.gling 1.** □ beceriksiz, hantal; **2.** *n.* üstünkörü, kötü iş.

bun.ion MED ['bʌnjən] *n.* ayak parmağı üzerinde oluşan şiş.

bunk[1] *sl.* [bʌŋk] *n.* boş lâf, gevezelik.

bunk[2] [_] *n.* yatak yeri, ranza.

bunk.er NAUT ['bʌŋkə] **1.** *n.* kömürlük; **2.** *vb. be* ~*ed fig.* engele rastlamak.

bun.kum ['bʌŋkəm] = *buncombe*.

bun.ny ['bʌni] *n.* tavşan(cık).

bun.sen ['bunsn]: ~ *burner* Bunsen beki, Bunsen gaz lambası.

bunt *Am.* [bʌnt] *n. beysbol:* topa hafifçe vurma.

bun.ting[1] ORN ['bʌntiŋ] *n.* küçük kuş türlerinden biri.

bun.ting[2] [_] *n.* bayrak kumaşı, süs flamaları.

buoy NAUT [bɔi] **1.** *n.* şamandıra; **2.** *v/t.* suyun yüzünde tutmak, yüzdürmek; *mst* ~ *up* yüzdürmek, suyun üzerinde tutmak; *fig.* desteklemek, ümit vermek, cesaret vermek.

buoy.an.cy ['bɔiənsi] *n.* su yüzünde durabilme; *fig.* kudret, takat; AVIA statik taşıma gücü; *fig.* canlılık; neşe; '**buoy.ant** □ yüzebilir, yüzen, batmaz; *fig.* neşeli; COM fiyatların yükselme gücü.

bur BOT [bəː] *n.* dulavrat otu, pıtrak.

Bur.ber.ry ['bəːbəri] *n.* su geçirmez pardesü veya kumaş.

bur.bot ICHTH ['bəːbət] *n.* morina cinsinden bir balık.

bur.den[1] ['bəːdn] **1.** *n.* yük, ağırlık, ağır iş; sorumluluk; JUR mükellefiyet, yükümlülük; NAUT kargo; NAUT tonilato, yük taşıma kapaistesi; **2.** *v/t.* yüklemek (*s.o. with* -*e* -*i*) (*a. fig.*).

bur.den[2] [_] *n.* ana fikir; nakarat.

bur.den.some ['bəːdnsəm] *adj.* külfetli, sıkıntı verici.

bur.dock BOT ['bəːdɔk] *n.* dulavrat otu.

bu.reau ['bjuərəu] *n., pl. a.* **bu.reaux**

['ˌ-z] büro, yazıhane, daire, şube; *Am.*
çekmeceli dolap; **bu.reau.ra.cy**
[ˌ-'rɔkrəsi] *n.* bürokrasi, resmî formaliteler, kırtasiyecilik; **bu.reau.crat**
['bjuərəukræt] *n.* bürokrat, kırtasiyeci; **bu.reau'crat.ic** *adj.* (**~ally**) bürokratik.

bu.rette CHEM [bjuə'ret] *n.* sıvı ölçmeye yarar cam tüp, büret.

burg *Am.* F [bəːg] *n.* kasaba, ufak şehir.

bur.gee NAUT ['bəːdʒiː] *n.* üç köşeli flâma; flândra.

bur.geon *lit.* ['bəːdʒən] **1.** *n.* gonca, tomurcuk; rüşeym, embriyon; **2.** *vb.* tomurcuk ve filiz vermek, sürmek.

bur.gess ['bəːdʒis] *n.* oy verme hakkına sahip şehirli; HIST murahhas, delege, milletvekili.

burgh *Scots* ['bʌrə] *n.* kasaba; **bur.gher**
HIST ['bəːgə] *n.* kasabada oturan kimse.

bur.glar ['bəːglə] *n.* (*ev soyan*) hırsız, gece hırsızı; **bur.glar.i.ous** ☐ hırsızlığa ait; **bur.gla.ry** ['-gləri] *n.* ev soyma, hırsızlık; **'bur.gle** *vb.* ev soymak.

bur.go.mas.ter ['bəːgəumaːstə] *n.*
(*esp. Almanya ve Hollanda'da*) belediye başkanı.

bur.gun.dy ['bəːgəndi] *n.* Burgonya şarabı.

bur.i.al ['beriəl] *n.* gömme, defin; '**~-ground** *n.* mezarlık; **~ serv.ice** cenaze töreni.

bu.rin MEC ['bjuərin] *n.* hakkâk kalemi.

burke [bəːk] *vb.* örtbas etm..

burl [bəːl] *n.* (*kumaş içinde*) düğüm.

bur.lap ['bəːlæp] *n.* çuval bezi.

bur.lesque [bəː'lesk] **1.** *adj.* hicveden, gülünç, komik; **2.** *n.* hiciv, taşlama; **3.** *vb.* hicvetmek *-i*, taklidini yapmak *-in*, alaya almak *-i*.

bur.ly ['bəːli] *adj.* iriyarı, güçlü kuvvetli, sağlam yapılı.

Bur.mese [bəː'miːz] **1.** *adj.* Birmanyalı; **2.** *n.* Birmanya; Birmanya dili.

burn [bəːn] **1.** *n.* yanık, yanık yarası; **2.** (*irr.*) *v/t. & v/i.* yakmak, yanmak, tutuş(tur)mak; parıldamak; ışık saçmak; '**burn.er** *n.* gaz ocağı memesi; yakıcı şey veya kimse; '**burn.ing** ☐ yanan, yanıcı; şiddetli, hararetli.

bur.nish ['bəːniʃ] *v/t.* cilâlamak, perdahlamak, parlatmak (*esp. maden*); '**burnish.er** *n.* cilâcı; perdah taşı.

burnt [bəːnt] *pret. & p.p. of* **burn 2**; **~ offering** bir tanrıya sunmak için yakılan hayvan veya bitki.

burp *Am. sl.* [bəːp] **1.** *n.* geğirme; **2.** *v/t. & v/i.* geğir(t)mek.

burr [bəː] **1.** *n.* vızıltı; R harfinin boğazdan titrek şekilde söylenmesi; kozalak; MEC ince maden parçası, çapak, kalem pürüzü; **2.** *v/i.* R harfini boğazdan söylemek; '**~-drill** *n.* MED matkap, delgi.

bur.ro F ['burəu] *n.* yük eşeği, merkep.

bur.row ['bʌrəu] **1.** *n.* oyuk, in, yuva; **2.** *vb.* oyuk açmak, tünel kazmak, yuva yapmak; kazdığı yerde saklanmak.

bur.sar ['bəːsə] *n.* (*esp. okullarda*) muhasebeci, mutemet.

bur.sa.ry ['bəːsəri] *n.* muhasebe; burs.

burst [bəːst] **1.** *n.* patlama, fırlama, çatlama; ileri atılma; patlak, yarık; *fig.* coşkunluk, feveran; **2.** (*irr.*) *v/t. & v/i.* parla(t)mak (*a. fig.*); yar(ıl)mak, ayrılmak, ileri fırlamak; kırmak (*a. fig.*); ortaya dökülmek, görülür hale gelmek; BOT birdenbire açmak; (*çıban, apse v.b.*) birdenbire çıkmak; (*göz yaşı, kahkaha*) boşanmak; **~ forth**, **~ out** birdenbire söylemek; fışkırmak; **~ into flame** alevlenmek; **~ into tears** ağlamaya başlamak, gözünden yaşlar boşanmak; **~ out laughing** kahkaha koparmak; **~ upon s.o.** *b-ne* birdenbire görünmek.

bur.then NAUT ['bəːðən] = **burden**.

bur.y ['beri] *v/t.* gömmek, defnetmek; gizlemek, saklamak, örtmek; unutmak; '**bur.y.ing-ground** *n.* mezar(lık), kabir.

bus F [bʌs] **1.** *n.* otobüs; **miss the ~** *sl.* fırsatı kaçırmak, geç kalmak; **~ boy** *Am.* (*lokantada*) çırak; **2.** *vb.* otobüsle gitmek; otobüsle taşımak.

bus.by MIL ['bʌzbi] *n.* bir çeşit küçük kürklü şapka.

bush [buʃ] *n.* çalı, çalılık; MEC zıvana, burç; **bush.el** ['buʃl] *n.* İngiliz kilesi (*takriben 36.5 litre*); **hide one's light under a ~** yeteneğini gizlemek; '**bushman** *n.* Güney Afrika yerlisi; '**bush-ranger** *n.* fundalıklarda yaşıyan eşkiya.

bush.y ['buʃi] *adj.* çalılık; (*saç, sakal*) fırça gibi.

busi.ness ['biznis] *n.* iş, görev, meslek; COM alışveriş, ticaret; iş yeri; mesele, problem; **~ of the day** ruzname, gündem; **on ~** iş için, iş hakkında; **no admittance except on ~** işi olmıyan giremez; **have no ~ to** hakkı olmamak *-e*, ilgisi olmamak *-le*; **mind one's own ~** kendi işine bakmak, karışmamak; **send s.o. about his ~** *b-ni* defetmek, kovmak; ~ **end** F *bşin* tehlikeli tarafı; ~ **hours** *pl.* iş saatleri; '~**-like** *adj.* ciddi, düzenli, sistemli; '~**.man** *n.* iş adamı; ~ **tour**, ~ **trip** iş seyahati.

bus.ker ['bʌskə] *n.* sokak çalgıcısı.

bus.kin ['bʌskin] *n.* potin; tragedi.

bus.man ['bʌsmən] *n.* otobüs şoförü; ~**'s holiday** meslekle ilgili çalışmaları sürdürmek için yapılan tatil; '**bus--stop** *n.* otobüs durağı.

bust¹ [bʌst] *n.* büst; göğüs.

bust² *Am.* F [-] *n.* mahvolma, iflâs, fiyasko.

bus.tard ORN ['bʌstəd] *n.* toy kuşu.

bus.tle ['bʌsl] **1.** *n.* faaliyet, telâş, koşuşma; eskiden kadın elbise eteklerine konulan kafes gibi yastık; **2.** *vb.* telâşlanmak, telâşa vermek; acele et(tir)mek; kovalamak (*a. fig.*); '**bus.tler** *n.* faal, işgüzar adam; '**bus.tling** ☐ çalışkan, işgüzar.

bust-up F ['bʌstʌp] *n.* kavga, gümbürtü, yaygara.

bus.y ['bizi] **1.** ☐ faal, iş gören, meşgul (**with** *-le*); hareketli, canlı; TELEPH meşgul; **be** ~ işi olm., meşgul olm.; **2.** *vb.* *mst* ~ **o.s.** meşgul olm., uğraşmak (**with**, **in**, **at**, **about** *-le*); '~**.bod.y** *n.* her işe burnunu sokan kimse, işgüzar; '**bus.y.ness** *n.* gayret, faaliyet; işgüzarlık.

but [bʌt; bət] **1.** *cj.* ama, fakat, lâkin, ancak, halbuki, şu kadar ki; **2.** *prp.* *-den* başka, *-den* hariç; **the next** ~ **one** birinci değil ikinci; ~ **for** sayesinde, …olmasaydı; **3.** *adv.* sadece, yalnız, sırf; ~ **just** demin, demincek, henüz; **all** ~ …*den* gayrı, az kalsın; **nothing** ~ sırf, hepsi; …*den* başka bir şey değil; **I cannot** ~ *inf.* …*memek* mümkün değil, …*mek* zorundayım; **4.** *n.* «fakat» kelimesi, itiraz.

butch.er ['butʃə] **1.** *n.* kasap, celep; *fig.* katil, cani; **2.** *v/t.* (*kasaplık*) hayvan kesmek; *fig.* öldürmek, boğazlamak; '**butch.er.y** *n.* kasaplık (*a. fig.*); mezbaha, salhane; ~ **business** kasaplık.

but.ler ['bʌtlə] *n.* kahyâ; sofracı.

butt¹ [bʌt] **1.** *n.* tos; *a.* ~ **end** *bşin* enli dibi (*ağaç vs.*); izmarit; dipçik; MEC manşet, birleştirme sathı; hedef levhası gerisindeki toprak siper; **the** ~**s** *pl.* atış alanı; *fig.* amaç, gaye; **2.** *vb.* tos vurmak; ~ **in** F karışmak *-e*.

butt² [-] *n.* büyük şarap fıçısı, damacana.

but.ter ['bʌtə] **1.** *n.* tereyağı; F kompli-

man, kur, yağçılık; **as if** ~ **would not melt in his mouth** çok nazik ve masum görünüyor (*öyle olmadığı halde*); **2.** *v/t.* tereyağı sürmek *-e*; *fig.* kompliman yapmak, yağ çekmek; '~**.cup** *n.* BOT düğünçiçeği; '~**-fin.gers** *n.* sakar kimse; '~**.fly** *n.* kelebek; *fig.* kelebek peşinde, havai kimse; '~**.milk** *n.* yayık ayranı; **but.ter.y 1.** *adj.* tereyağ gibi; tereyağlı…; **2.** *n.* kiler.

but.tock ['bʌtək] *n.* *mst* '**but.tocks** *pl.* kalça, kıç, F popo.

but.ton ['bʌtn] **1.** *n.* düğme; BOT konca, tomurcuk, sürgün; ~**s** *sg.* F otel oğlanı; **2.** *v/t. & v/i. oft.* ~ **up** düğmele(n)mek, ilikle(n)mek; '~**.hole** **1.** *n.* ilik; yakaya takılan çiçek; **2.** *v/t.* ilik açmak; yakalayıp zorla dinletmek; '~**-hook** *n.* düğme kancası; '~**.wood** *n.* BOT çınar ağacı.

but.tress ['bʌtris] **1.** *n.* payanda, destek (*a. fig.*); **2.** *v/t.* ~ **up** ayak koymak, payanda koymak; *fig.* desteklemek, takviye etm.

bux.om ['bʌksəm] *adj.* (*kadın*) dolgun, bıldırcın gibi, cazip, çekici, neşeli.

buy [bai] (*irr.*) *v/t.* almak, satın almak (**from** *-den*); *fig.* *bş* karşılığında elde etm. (**with** *-le*); '**buy.er** *n.* alıcı, müşteri; satın alıcı, mübayaacı; '**buy.ing** *comb.* satın alma…; '**buy.out** *n.* bir şirketin satın alınması.

buzz [bʌz] **1.** *n.* vızıltı, gürültü; F telefon konuşması; ~ **saw** *Am.* devvar testere; **2.** *vb.* vızıldamak, fısıldamak; (*kulak*) çınlamak; telefon etm.; AVIA alçaktan ve süratli uçmak.

buz.zard ORN ['bʌzəd] *n.* bir cins şahin.

buzz.er ELECT ['bʌzə] *n.* vızıltılı sinyal veren elektrik zili; siren.

by [bai] **1.** *prp.* *-in* yanında, yakınında, nezdinde; ile, vasıtasiyle; tarafından, …*den*; *-e* göre, *-e* nazaran; yakınından, yanından; *-e* kadar; hakkında; **North** ~ **East** kuzeydoğuya doğru; **side** ~ **side** yan yana; ~ **day** gündüz, gündüzün; ~ **now** şimdiye kadar; ~ **the time** (**that**) kadar, dek, değin; ~ **the dozen** düzine düzine; ~ **far** çok daha fazla, fersah fersah; **30 feet** ~ **15** otuza onbeş ebadında; ~ **o.s.** yalnız, kendi kendine, bir köşede; ~ **land** karadan, yara yolu ile; ~ **rail** trenle; **day** ~ **day** her gün, günden güne; ~ **twos** ikişer ikişer; **2.** *adv.* bir yana, bir tarafa; yakın, yanında; ~ **and** ~ yavaş yavaş, çok geçmeden, birazdan; ~ **the** ~ pek yakında, bu günlerde; yavaş yavaş, tedricen; **close** ~ yakında,

civarda; *go*~ geçip gitmek; ~ *and large*
genellikle; **3.** *adj.* yan…, tali…
bye [bai] *n.* *spor:* yarışmacının tek kalması, otomatik olarak tur atlama.
bye-bye F [bai'bai] *int.* Allaha ısmarladık!; Hoşça kalın!; Güle güle!
by…: '~**e.lec.tion** *n.* ara seçim; '~**gone**
1. *adj.* geçmiş, eski; **2.** *n.* ~**s** *pl.* geçmiş
olan şey; *let*~**s be**~**s** geçmişi unutmak,
geçmişe sünger çekmek; '~**law** *n.* nizamname, statü; '~**line** *n.* *Am.* (*maka-
lede*) yazar adının verildiği satır;
'~**name** *n.* lakap; '~**pass 1.** *n.* dolaştır-
ma; kestirme yol, varyant; ELECT kısa
devre; **2.** *vb.* yanından geçmek, uğra-

mamak; (*trafik*) başka yola vermek;
bertaraf etm.; '~**path** *n.* dolaylı yol, patika; '~**-play** *n.* THEAT asıl oyunun
yanısıra yapılan önemi az hareket;
'~**-prod.uct** *n.* yan ürün.
byre ['baiə] *n.* inek ahırı.
by-road ['bairəud] *n.* yan yol.
by…: '~**stand.er** *n.* seyirci, olaya karış-
madan seyreden kimse; '~**street** *n.*
yan sokak; '~**way** *n.* gizli yol, dolaşık
yol; '~**word** *n.* darbımesel, atalarsözü;
be a ~ *for* timsali olm. *-in*.
By.zan.tine [bi'zæntain] **1.** *adj.* Bizan-
s'a ait; **2.** *n.* Bizanslı.

C

cab [kæb] *n.* kira arabası, taksi; otobüs;
lokomotifin kapalı kısmı, RAIL makinist yeri, (*otobüs*) şoför yeri.
ca.bal [kə'bæl] **1.** *n.* hile, entrika, fitne;
2. *v/i.* bşde hile, dalavere yapmak, entrika çevirmek, desise kurmak.
cab.a.ret ['kæbərei] *n.* çalgılı meyhane,
kabare.
cab.bage ['kæbidʒ] *n.* bir baş lahana; ~
butterfly lahana yapraklarında yaşayan beyaz kelebek; ~ *lettuce* top salata.
cab.ba.lis.tic,   cab.ba.lis.ti.cal   □
[kæbə'listik(əl)] sırları açıklama ilmine ait.
cab.by ['kæbi] *n.* arabacı.
cab.in ['kæbin] **1.** *n.* kulübe; hücre; NAUT
kamara; **2.** *vb.* ağıllandırmak; bir yere
sıkıştırmak, tıkmak; '~**boy** *n.* NAUT kamarot; subay hizmet eri; ~ *class* ikinci
sınıf; ~ *cruis.er* NAUT kamaralı büyük
gemi.
cab.i.net ['kæbinit] *n.* kabine, küçük
oda; çekmeceli, vitrinli dolap; kabine,
bakanlar kurulu; ♀ *Council* vekiller
meclisi; '~**mak.er** *n.* doğramacı, marangoz.
ca.ble [keibl] **1.** *n.* kablo; NAUT palamar;
telgraf; *buried* ~ yeraltı kablosu; **2.** *vb.*
telgraf çekmek; kablo ile bağlamak;
'~**car** *n.* kablo ile işleyen vagon, teleferik; '~**gram** ['-græm] *n.* telgraf.
cab.man ['kæbmən] *n.* arabacı, taksi
şoförü.
ca.boo.dle *sl.* [kə'buːdl]; *the whole* ~
bütün herkes, herşey.

ca.boose [kə'buːs] *n.* NAUT gemi mutfağı; *Am.* RAIL yük treni işçilerine ait
vagon.
cab.ri.o.let *part.* MOT [kæbriə'lei] *n.*
dört tekerlekli atlı araba; iki kapılı
dört kişilik araba; bir vagonun arkasındaki ufak kompartman.
cab-stand ['kæbstænd] *n.* taksi, fayton
durağı.
ca'can.ny MEC ['kɑː'kæni] *n.* işçilerin
işi yavaşlatma eylemi.
ca.ca.o [kə'kɑːəu] *n.* kakao ağacı, kakao.
cache [kæʃ] **1.** *n.* bir şeyi saklamak için
gizli yer, gizli yerde saklanan şey; **2.** *v/t.*
gizli bir yere bş saklamak.
cack.le ['kækl] **1.** *n.* gevezelik; tavuk
gıdaklaması; **2.** *v/i.* gevezelik etm.;
gıdaklamak; '**cack.ler** *n.* gıdaklayan;
fig. geveze.
ca.coph.o.ny [kæ'kɔfəni] *n.* kötü ses,
ahenksizlik.
cac.tus BOT ['kæktəs] *n.* kaktüs.
cad F [kæd] *n.* kaba kimse; alçak adam.
ca.das.tre [kə'dæstə] *n.* tapu sicili, kadastro.
ca.dav.er.ous □ [kə'dævərəs] ölü gibi,
sapsarı.
cad.die ['kædi] *n.* oyun sırasında golf-
çünün sopalarını taşıyan kişi.
cad.dis ZOO ['kædis] *n.* kurtçuk, tırtıl.
cad.dish F □ ['kædiʃ] alçak; kaba.
cad.dy ['kædi] *n.* çay kutusu; = *caddie*.
ca.dence ['keidəns] *n.* MUS ritim,
ahenk; sesin derece derece inmesi.
ca.det [kə'det] *n.* askerî okul öğrencisi;

~ **corps** asker talimi gören yetişkinler taburu.

cadge [kædʒ] v/t. & v/i. yalvarıp yakarmak, dilenmek; seyyar satıcılık etm.; '**cadg.er** n. bedavacı; dilenci; seyyar satıcı.

ca.di ['kɑːdi] n. (bazı İslâm ülkelerinde) kadı, yargıç.

cad.mi.um CHEM ['kædmiəm] n. sembolü «Ca» olan beyaz, yumuşak bir maden, kadmiyum.

cad.re ['kɑːdə] n. çerçeve, plan; kadro; MIL gerektiğinde kullanmak üzere iyi hazırlanmış birlik veya bu grupdan biri.

ca.du.cous BOT & ZOO [kə'djuːkəs] adj. zamansız ve mevsimsiz dökülen.

cae.cum ANAT ['siːkəm] n. kör bağırsak, apandis.

Cae.sar ['siːzə] n. Sezar; **Cae.sar.i.an** [siː'zɛəriən] adj. Sezar'a ait.

cae.su.ra [siːzjuərə] n. bir mısranın okunuşuna hafifçe duraklanacak yer.

ca.fé ['kæfei] n. kahvehane, küçük restoran, lokanta, pastahane.

caf.e.te.ri.a [kæfi'tiəriə] n. kafeterya, garsonsuz lokanta.

caf.e.to.ri.um Am. [kæfi'tɔːriəm] n. kantin ve dinlenme salonu.

caf.fe.ine ['kæfiːn] n. kahve ve çayda bulunan uyarıcı, kafein.

cage [keidʒ] **1.** n. kafes (a. fig.); hapishane; MIN asansör; **2.** v/t. kafese koymak; hapse atmak.

cage.y □ part. Am. ['keidʒi] kurnaz, hilekâr, pişkin.

cairn [kɛən] n. abide veya mezara benzer taş yığını.

cais.son [kə'suːn] n. MIL cephane arabası; hidrolik inşaat: keson.

cai.tiff ['keitif] adj. & n. alçak, ahlâksız.

ca.jole [kə'dʒəul] v/t. & v/i. birisini tatlılıkla kandırmak veya aldatmak; **ca'jol.er** n. dalkavuk, pohpohçu, komplimancı; **ca'jol.er.y** n. kompliman, kur.

cake [keik] **1.** n. kek, pasta, kurabiye, çörek; parça, kısım, tane, kalıp (sabun vs.); ~**s and ale** eğlence; **a piece of** ~ sl. çocuk oyuncağı, çok kolay; **like hot** ~**s** kapış kapışa; **2.** vb. katılaş(tır)mak, kalıplaşmak.

cal.a.bash ['kæləbæʃ] n. sukabağı; sukabağından yapılmış su kabı.

cal.a.mine MIN ['kæləmain] n. tutya taşı.

ca.lam.i.tous □ [kə'læmitəs] felâketli,

belâlı; **ca'lam.i.ty** n. felâket, belâ, musibet, afet; **ca'lam.i.ty-howl.er** n. karamsar, kötümser; **ca'lam.i.ty-howling** n. Am. karamsarlık.

cal.car.e.ous [kæl'kɛəriəs] adj. kalsiyumlu, kireçli.

cal.ce.o.la.ri.a BOT [kælsiə'lɛəriə] n. çanta çiçeği.

cal.ci.fi.ca.tion [kælsifi'keiʃən] n. kireç tuzları ile sertleştirme, taş haline getirme işlemi; **cal.ci.fy** ['-fai] vb. kireçlenmek; kireç haline getirmek; **cal.ci.na.tion** CHEM [kælsi'neiʃən] n. yakma, kavurma, damıtma; **cal.cine** CHEM [kælsain] vb. yakarak toz haline getirmek veya gelmek; '**cal.cite** n. MIN kalsiyum karbonat; **calci.um** CHEM ['-siəm] n. sembolü «Ca» olan eleman, Kalsiyum; **cal.ci.um car.bide** CHEM karpit.

cal.cu.la.ble ['kælkjuləbl] adj. hesap edilebilir; güvenilir; **cal.cu.late** ['-leit] v/t. hesaplamak, hesap ederek bulmak, saymak; ~**d** hesaplanmış; v/i. hesap etm., güvenmek (**on, upon** -e); F Am. tahmin etm.; **calculating machine** hesap makinesi; **cal.cu'la.tion** n. hesap, tahmin; **calcu.lus** ['-ləs] n. MATH entegral hesabı; MED böbrek veya mesane taşı.

cal.dron ['kɔːldrən] n. kazan.

cal.en.dar ['kælində] **1.** n. takvim; liste; **2.** v/t. zaman sırası ile kaydetmek.

cal.en.der MEC [-] **1.** n. perdah makinesi; **2.** v/t. perdahlamak, baskıya koymak.

cal.ends ['kælindz]: **on the Greek** ~ hiçbir zaman, asla, balık kavağa çıkınca.

calf [kɑːf] n., pl. **calves** [kɑːvz] dana, buzağı; fig. beceriksiz genç; a. ~**-leather** vidala; meşin cilt; kayış; ANAT baldır; **in** ~, **with** ~ yüklü; gebe (buzağı); ~ **love** F ilk aşk, ilk göz ağrısı; '~**skin** n. dana postu.

cal.i.brate MEC ['kælibreit] v/t. çap ölçmek; ayar etm.; **cal.i.bre** ['-bə] n. çap; fig. sanat: kabiliyet, yetenek.

cal.i.co COM ['kælikəu] n. pamuk bez, basma, empirme; hasse, kaliko.

Cal.i.for.nian [kæli'fɔːnjən] **1.** adj. Kaliforniya'ya ait; **2.** n. Kaliforniyalı.

ca.liph ['kælif] n. halife; **cal.iph.ate** ['-eit] n. hilâfet, halifelik.

calk [kɔːk] **1.** n. buzmıhı, kayar; **2.** v/t. NAUT kalafat etm.; buzmıhı çakmak; **calkin** ['kælkin] s. **calk 1.**

call [kɔːl] 1. *n.* seslenme, bağırma, içeri çağırma; *fig.* çağrı, davet (*to* -*e*); yoklama; TELEPH arama; THEAT sahneye çağırma; HUNT boru; kısa ziyaret; hak iddiası, talep; uğrama, görüşme; işaret; **~ money** COM vadesiz verilen borç para; **port of ~** gemilerin kısa süreli uğradıkları liman, emir limanı; **on ~** COM vaki talep üzerine; 2. *v/t.* çağırmak, *b-ne* gelsin diye bağırmak, seslenmek; uyandırmak; adlandırmak, demek; davet etm.; çağrıda bulunmak; telefon etm.; uğramak, ziyaret etm.; *iskambil*: istemek; **be ~ed** bşe (*b-ne*) …demek, bşi tavsif etm.; **~ s.o. names** sövmek, sövüp saymak, hakaret etm.; **~ s.o. down** *Am. sl. b-ni* azarlamak; **~ forth** meydan vermek -*e*, yol açmak -*e*; gayrete getirmek; **~ in** (*para*) geri çekmek, toplamak; celbetmek, davet etm., içeri çağırmak; **~ out** bağırmak; (*işçi*) greve çağırmak; **~ up** yukarı çağırmak; MIL silâh altına almak, celbetmek; hatırlamak; TELEPH aramak; *v/i.* bağırmak, çağırmak; *b-ne* uğramak, *b-ni* ziyaret etm.; **~ at a port** limana uğramak; **~ for** *b-ni veya* bşi uğrayıp almak; THEAT *b-ni* sahneye çağırmak, istemek -*i*; icabetmek -*i*; **to be** (**left till**) **~ed for** gelinip alınacak, postrestant; **~ on** ziyaret etm. -*i*, uğramak -*e*; **~ to** …diye seslenmek (*veya* haykırmak) 'call.a.ble *adj.* istenebilen (*para*); 'cal-box *n.* telefon kulübesi; 'call.er *n.* ziyaretçi; TELEPH telefon eden kişi; **~er ID** (*bazı telefonlarda görülebilen*) arayan numara; '**~girl** *n.* fahişe, tele-kız.

cal.li.graph.ic [kæli'græfik] *adj.* (**~ally**) güzel yazı, hattatlığa ait; cal.lig.ra.phy [kə'ligrəfi] *n.* güzel yazı, hattatlık.

call.ing ['kɔːliŋ] *n.* iş, meslek; **~ card** *Am.* kartvizit, vizita kartı.

cal.li.pers ['kælipəz] *n. pl.* çap pergeli, kompas.

cal.lis.then.ics [kælis'θeniks] *adj. mst sg.* özellikle bayanlar tarafından vücut güzelliği için aletsiz yapılan vücut hareketleri.

call-of.fice ['kɔːlɔfis] *n.* telefon dairesi, telefon kulübesi.

cal.los.i.ty [kæ'lɔsiti] *n.* nasır, nasırlanma; *fig.* nasırlaşmış olma, vurdumduymazlık; 'cal.lous □ nasırlı, katı; *fig.* hissiz, duyguları körelmiş.

cal.low ['kæləu] *adj.* uçacak hale gelmemiş, tüysüz (*kuş*); *fig.* tecrübesiz,

toy, acemi çaylak.

call-up ['kɔːlʌp] *n.* davet, çağrı.

calm [kɑːm] 1. □ sakin, durgun; ağırbaşlı (*a. fig.*); 2. *n.* sakinlik, hareketsizlik (*a. fig.*); NAUT rüzgârın kesilmesi; 3. (**~ down**) *v/i.* yatışmak; *v/t. b-ni* teskin etm., yatıştırmak; 'calm.ness *n.* sakinlik, durgunluk.

Cal.or gas ['kælə'gæs] *n.* bütan gazı.

ca.lor.ic PHYS [kə'lɔrik] *n.* ısı; **~engine** sıcak hava veren motor; cal.o.rie PHYS ['kæləri] *n.* kalori, ısı birimi; cal.o.rif.ic [kælə'rifik] *adj.* ısı meydana getiren, ısıtıcı.

cal.trop BOT ['kæltrəp] *n.* boğa dikeni.

ca.lum.ni.ate [kə'lʌmnieit] *v/t. b-ne* iftira etm.; ca.lum.ni'a.tion *n.* iftira; ca'lum.nia.tor *n.* iftiracı; ca'lum.ni.ous □ iftira türünden; cal.um.ny ['kæləmni] *n.* iftira.

Cal.va.ry ['kælvəri] *n.* Hazreti İsa'nın çarmıha gerildiği yer; İsa'nın haçlanmasının anlatımı; ♀ eza, cefa.

calve [kɑːv] *v/i.* buzağı doğurmak; calves [kɑːvz] *n. pl. of* calf.

Cal.vin.ism ['kælvinizəm] *n.* İsviçreli din bilimci Calvin'in doktrinleri, Kalvinizm.

ca.lyp.so [kə'lipsəu] *n.* kalipso, Batı Hintlilerin isteklerini anlatmak için geliştirdikleri şarkı.

ca.lyx BOT & ZOO ['keiliks] *n., pl.* cal.y.ces ['~lisiːz] çiçek zarfı, çanak.

cam MEC [kæm] *n.* kam, mil dirseği; **~ gear** eksantrik dişlisi.

cam.ber MEC ['kæmbə] 1. *n.* kubbe, kemer; hafif kavis; 2. *v/t.* kubbe, kemer gibi kabartmak.

cam.bric ['keimbrik] *n.* ince pamuklu kumaş, patiska.

came [keim] *pret. of* come.

cam.el ['kæməl] *n.* ZOO deve; NAUT tombaz, kayık biçiminde duba.

ca.mel.li.a BOT [kə'miːljə] *n.* kamelya, çin gülü.

cam.e.o ['kæmiəu] *n.* işlemeli akik.

cam.er.a ['kæmərə] *n.* fotoğraf makinesi, kamera; **in ~** JUR yargıcın özel odasında gizli olarak, gizli celsede.

cami-knick.ers ['kæmi'nikəz] *n. pl.* kadın kombinezonu.

cam.i.on ['kæmiən] *n.* kamyon.

cam.o.mile BOT ['kæməumail] *n.* bir tür papatya; **~ tea** papatya çayı.

cam.ou.flage MIL ['kæmuflɑːʒ] 1. *n.* kamuflaj; 2. *v/t.* kamufle etm., gizlemek.

camp [kæmp] 1. *n.* kamp; MIL ordugâh;

~ bed portatif karyola; **~ chair, ~ stool** portatif iskemle; **2.** v/i. ordugâh, kamp kurmak; **~ out** kamp yapmak, çadırda yatmak.

cam.paign [kæm'pein] **1.** n. sefer, savaş; POL & fig. meydan muharebesi, mücadele; kampanya; **election** ~ seçim kampanyası; **2.** v/i. sefere çıkmak; mücadele etm.; kampanyaya katılmak; **cam'paign.er** n. kampanyaya katılan kişi; **old** ~ F tecrübeli kişi.

camp.er ['kæmpə] n. kampçı, kamp yapan kişi; içinde yatılabilen özel döşenmiş kamp arabası.

cam.phor ['kæmfə] n. kâfur; **camphor.ated** ['-reitid] adj. kâfurlu.

camp.ing ['kæmpiŋ] n. kamping, kamp yapma.

cam.pus Am. ['kæmpəs] n. üniversite veya okul arazisi, kampus.

cam.shaft MEC ['kæmʃɑːft] n. kamlı mil.

can[1] [kæn] (irr.) v/alux. -ebilmek.

can[2] [-] **1.** n. kap, kutu; Am. konserve kutusu; **2.** v/t. konserve yapmak, kutuya koymak.

Ca.na.di.an [kə'neidjən] **1.** n. Kanadalı; **2.** adj. Kanada ile ilgili, Kanada…

ca.nal [kə'næl] n. kanal, mecra, suyolu; ANAT vücuttaki sıvıların akıştığı yol; **~-boat** mavuna, salapurya; **ca.nal.i.za-tion** [kænəlai'zeiʃən] n. kanal açma; kanalizasyon tesisatı; **ca.nal.ize** vb. kanalizasyon tesisatı yapmak, kanal açmak.

can.a.pé ['kænəpei] n. ekmek üzerine peynir vs, sürülerek yapılan ordövr, kanepe.

ca.nard [kæ'nɑːd] n. uydurma haber, asılsız havadis.

ca.nar.y [kə'neəri] n. a. **~-bird** kanarya.

can.cel ['kænsəl] v/t. silmek, çizmek; kaldırmak, iptal etm.; **~ out** MATH kısaltmak, götürmek; **be ~led** iptal edilmiş olm.; **can.cel'la.tion** n. silme, bozma, iptal, iade; iptal damgası.

can.cer ['kænsə] n. MED kanser; ♎ AST Yengeç Burcu; **~ screening** kanser tarama; **'can.cer.ous** adj. kanserli, kanser gibi.

can.did □ ['kændid] samimi, candan; yalansız, dürüst.

can.di.da.cy ['kændidəsi] n. namzetlik, adaylık; **can.di.date** ['kændidit] n. talip, aday, namzet (**for** -e); **can.di-da.ture** ['-tʃə] n. namzetlik, adaylık.

can.died ['kændid] adj. şekerle kap-

lanmış, şekerli; fig. göze hoş görünen, gönül okşayıcı; tatlı dilli.

can.dle ['kændl] n. mum, kandil; **~ power** mum (ışık kuvvet birimi); **hold a ~ to** fig. eline su dökmek, tırnağı olm.; **not worth the ~** zahmete değmez, astarı yüzünden pahalı; **burn the ~ at both ends** değişik işler yaparak kuvvetini tüketmek, gece gündüz eğlenmek; **'~.light** n. mum ışığı; **Can-dle.mas** ECCL ['-məs] n. Subat'ın ikisine rastlayan Hazreti Meryem yortusu; **'can.dle.stick** n. şamdan.

can.dour ['kændə] n. açık kalplilik, samimiyet; tarafsızlık, doğruluk.

can.dy ['kændi] **1.** n. şekerleme, şeker, bonbon; **2.** v/i. şekerlenmek; v/t. şekerleme yapmak; şekerleme haline getirmek.

cane [kein] **1.** n. BOT kamış, bambu; baston, değnek; **2.** v/t. b-ni dövmek, b-ne dayak atmak; (mobilya) kamışla tamir etm.; **~ sug.ar** şeker kamışından yapılmış şeker.

ca.nine **1.** ['keinain] adj. köpek gibi, kurt veya köpek ile ilgili; **2.** ['kænain] n. a. **~ tooth** köpekdişi.

can.is.ter ['kænistə] n. (kahve, çay v.b. konulan) teneke kutu.

can.ker ['kæŋkə] **1.** n. MED ağız ve kulakta meydana gelen yara, pamukçuk; BOT buğday pası; fig. çürütücü etki; **2.** vb. kemirmek; çürü(t)mek, mahvolmak; **'cankered** adj. fig. kötü huylu; **'can.ker.ous** adj. yer yer çürümekte olan; yozlaştıran.

canned Am. [kænd] adj. kutulanmış.

can.ner.y Am. ['kænəri] n. konserve imalâthanesi.

can.ni.bal ['kænibəl] **1.** n. yamyam; kendi cinsinin etini yiyen hayvan; **2.** adj. yamyamca, yamyamlıkla ilgili; **'can.nibal.ism** n. yamyamlık; **'can-ni.bal.ize** v/t. değişme için parçalara ayırmak (araba vs.), MEC çıkma parça takmak.

can.non ['kænən] **1.** n. MIL top; bilârdo; karambol; **2.** v/t. karambol yapmak; topa tutmak; çarpmak (fig. **against, with**); **can.non.ade** ['neid] n. top ateşi, topla bombardıman; **'can.non--fod.der** n. harpte araç gibi düşünülüp harcanan askerler.

can.not ['kænɔt] inf. -ememek.

can.ny □ Scots ['kæni] dikkatli, itinalı, tedbirli, düşünceli; hareketsiz, sakin; açıkgöz, cin fikirli.

ca.noe [kə'nu:] **1.** *n.* hafif sandal, kano; **2.** *v/i.* botta kürek çekmek, kano ile geçmek, kano ile yük taşımak.

can.on ['kænən] *n.* kanun, kaide; kilise kanunu; dinî liste; katedralle bağlantı sağlayan rahip; ~ *law* kilise kanunu.

ca.ñon ['kænjən] = *canyon*.

can.on.ess ['kænənis] *n.* katedral veya büyük kiliselerin özel heyetlerinin kadın üyesi; **can.on.i.za.tion** [₋nai-'zeiʃən] *n.* bir azizi kilisenin resmen kabul edip tanıması; '**can.on.ize** *v/t.* (*ölmüş birini*) kilisece aziz diye resmen kabul edip tanımak; '**can.on.ry** *n.* katedral veya büyük kiliselerin özel heyetlerinde üyelik.

ca.noo.dle *sl.* [kə'nu:dl] *vb.* kucaklamak, okşamak.

can.o.py ['kænəpi] **1.** *n.* gölgelik, tente, çardak, sayvan; *fig.* saçak; AVIA uçakların ön tarafındaki siper; **2.** *v/t.* üstünü örtmek.

cant[1] [kænt] **1.** *n.* meyil; eğilme; **2.** *v/t. & v/i.* eğ(il)mek; meylet(tir)mek, yan yat(ır)mak; ~ *over* devirmek, bir yanı üzerine çevirmek.

cant[2] [₋] **1.** *n.* ikiyüzlülük, riyakârlık; argo; *thieves'*~ hırsızların kullandığı dil, argo; **2.** *vb.* riyakârlıkla söylemek.

can't F [kɑ:nt] = *cannot*.

Can.tab F ['kæntæb] *n.* Cambridge ile ilgili (öğrenci).

can.ta.loup(e) BOT ['kæntəlu:p] *n.* bir tür küçük kavun.

can.tan.ker.ous F □ [kən'tæŋkərəs] ters, aksi, huysuz, kavgacı.

can.teen [kæn'ti:n] *n.* MIL matara; kantin (*kışla, fabrika vs.'de*); MIL yemek kabı; sofra takımı (*çatal, bıçak, kaşık*).

can.ter ['kæntə] **1.** *n.* atın eşkin gidişi; **2.** *v/i.* eşkin gitmek; *v/t.* (*atı*) eşkin yürütmek.

can.ter.bur.y ['kæntəbəri] *n.* nota sehpası; **♫** *bell* bir tür çan çiçeği.

can.thar.i.des MED ['kæn'θæridi:z] *n. pl.*, *mst sg.* kunduz böceğinden yapılan bir müstahzar.

can.ti.cle ['kæntikl] *n.* temcit, methiye; ~*s pl.* İncil'den alınan kısa dini şarkı.

can.ti.le.ver ARCH ['kæntili:və] *n.* dirsek, destek;~ *bridge* destekler üzerine kurulmuş köprü.

can.to ['kæntəu] *n.* uzun şiirlerin bölümlerinden biri.

can.ton 1. ['kæntən] *n.* (*özellikle İsviçre'deki*) küçük eyalet, kanton; **2.** MIL [kən'tu:n] *v/t.* konaklatmak, konağa yerleştirmek; '**can.ton.ment** *n.* MIL konak, karargâh, ordugâh.

can.vas ['kænvəs] *n.* keten bezi, kanava, yelken bezi; çadır, tente; yelken; PAINT yağlı boya resim, tablo, tuval.

can.vass [₋] **1.** *n.* sipariş toplama, oy toplama, propaganda; seçim kampanyası; **2.** *vb.* müzakere etm., tartışmak, görüşmek; soruşturmak; dolaşarak oy veya sipariş toplamak; '**can.vass.er** *n.* talip, müracaat eden; oy veya sipariş toplayan kişi.

can.yon ['kænjən] *n.* kanyon, derin ve uçurumlu dar boğaz, dere yatağı.

caou.tchouc ['kautʃuk] *n.* kauçuk, lastik.

cap [kæp] **1.** *n.* kasket, başlık; kapak; UNIV kep, baret; MEC, CHEM *etc.* kapak, başlık, kapsül; ~ *and bells* çıngıraklı soytarı külahı; ~ *and gown* dört köşeli siyah başlık ve uzun siyah cüppeden oluşan üniversiteye ait kıyafet; ~ *in hand fig.* şapkası elinde, mütevazi tavırla; *set one's* ~ *at s.o.* (*bir erkeği*) cezbetmeye çalışmak; **2.** *vb.* başlık giydirmek *-e*; taçlandırmak *-i*; örtmek, kapamak.

ca.pa.bil.i.ty [keipə'biliti] *n.* kabiliyet, yetenek; '**ca.pa.ble** □ muktedir, kabiliyetli, ehliyetli, yetenekli (*of -e*).

ca.pa.cious □ [kə'peiʃəs] geniş, büyük; **ca.pac.i.tate** [kə'pæsiteit] *v/t.* olası kılmak; yetki vermek; **ca'pac.i.ty 1.** *n.* istiap, sığdırma; yetenek, kabiliyet; kapasite; MEC verim; mevki, sıfat; *disposing* (*or legal*) ~ medenî hakları kullanma; *full to* ~ tamamen dolu.

cap-à-pie [kæpə'pi:] *adv.* tepeden tırnağa kadar, her noktada.

ca.par.i.son *lit.* [kə'pærisn] *n.* eyer örtüsü, çaprak, haşe; *fig.* süs, ziynet; moda kıyafet.

cape[1] [keip] *n.* GEOGR burun.

cape[2] [₋] *n.* pelerin, kap, atkı.

caper[1] BOT ['keipə] *n.* kebere.

ca.per[2] [₋] **1.** *n.* sıçrayıp oynama (*a. fig.*), coşma, havada takla atma; *cut* ~*s* = *v/i.* yaramazlık etm., havada takla atmak, coşmak, sıçramak.

ca.pi.as JUR ['keipiæs] *n.*: *writ of* ~ tutuklama emri.

cap.il.lar.i.ty PHYS [kæpi'læriti] *n.* kapilarite, sıvıların kılcal borulara veya damarlara nüfuz etme özelliği; **cap.il.lar.y** [kə'piləri] **1.** *adj.* kılcal damarlara ait; **2.** *n.* ANAT kılcal damar.

cap.i.tal ['kæpitl] **1.** □ sermaye...; sermayeye ait; baş, başlıca, asıl, ana; en büyük, mükemmel; ~ *crime* cezası idam olan suç; ~ *punishment* ölüm cezası; **2.** *n.* başkent, hükümet merkezi; sermaye, kapital; *a.* ~ *letter* TYP majüskül, büyük harf; ARCH direk başlığı; **cap.i.tal.ism** ['‿təlizəm] *n.* kapitalizm, anamalcılık; '**cap.i.tal.ist** *n.* kapitalist, anamalcı; **capi.tal'is.tic** *adj.* kapitalistliğe ait, anamalcılıkla ilgili; **cap.i.tal.i.za.tion** [kəpitəlai'zeiʃən] *n.* sermaye miktarı; sermayelendirme, sermayeye katma; **cap'i.tal.ize** v/t. sermayeye çevirmek; sermaye olarak kullanmak; majüskül ile yazmak.

cap.i.ta.tion [kæpi'teiʃən] *n. a.* ~ *tax* kişi başına vergi; baş vergisi.

Cap.i.tol ['kæpitl] *n.* Eski Roma'da Jupiter'in mabedi; Washington'da A.B.D. Kongresinin toplandığı bina, Amerika devletlerinden herhangi birinin eyalet meclisi binası.

ca.pit.u.late [kə'pitjuleit] v/i. teslim olm.; silahları bırakmak, teslim şartlarını kararlaştırmak; **ca.pit.u'la.tion** *n.* şartlı teslim; kapitülasyonlar, yabancılara özgü imtiyazlar.

ca.pon ['keipən] *n.* semirmesi için kısırlaştırılmış horoz.

ca.price [kə'priːs] *n.* istek, geçici arzu, kapris; MUS kapriçiyo; **ca.pri.cious** □ [kə'priʃəs] kaprisli, maymun iştahlı; **ca'pricious.ness** *n.* maymun iştahlılık, havailik.

Cap.ri.corn AST ['kæprikɔːn] *n.* Oğlak Burcu.

cap.ri.ole ['kæpriəul] *n.* keçi gibi sıçrama; havada takla atma.

cap.size NAUT ['kæpsaiz] v/i. alabora olm., devrilmek; *fig.* altüst olm., v/t. devirmek, alabora etm.

cap.stan NAUT ['kæpstən] *n.* ırgat, bocurgat.

cap.su.lar ['kæpsjulə] *adj.* kapsüle benzer; **cap.sule** BOT & MED ['kæpsjuːl] *n.* kapsül, mahfaza.

cap.tain ['kæptin] *n.* kumandan, şef; *spor:* takım kaptanı; NAUT kaptan, süvari; deniz albayı; MIL yüzbaşı; ~ *of industry* bir ülkenin endüstrisinde söz sahibi olan kişi; **cap.tain.cy, cap.tain.ship** ['‿si, '‿ʃip] *n.* kaptanlık; yüzbaşılık; liderlik.

cap.tion ['kæpʃən] **1.** *n.* başlık, serlevha; ünvan, resmi sıfat; *film;* yazılı tercüme; **2.** v/t. Am. isim, başlık vermek.

cap.tious □ ['kæpʃəs] tenkitçi, safsa-

talı, kılı kırk yaran.

cap.ti.vate *fig.* ['kæptiveit] v/t. cezbetmek; **cap.ti'va.tion** *n.* büyüleme, cezbetme; '**cap.tive 1.** *adj.* esir düşmüş; baskı altında; ~ *balloon* sabit balon, yere iple bağlı balon; **2.** *n.* tutsak, esir (*a. fig.*); **cap.tiv.i.ty** [‿'tiviti] *n.* tutsaklık, esaret.

cap.tor ['kæptə] *n.* esir eden, zapteden, tutan kişi; **cap.ture** ['‿tʃə] **1.** *n.* yakalama, esir alma; NAUT korsanlık etme; ganimet; **2.** *vb.* tutmak, yakalamak, zaptetmek; NAUT korsanlık etm., zaptetmek; *fig.* bşe el koymak.

Cap.u.chin ECCL ['kæpjuʃin] *n.* Fransiskan rahibi, Kapüsen rahibi.

car [kɑː] *n.* otomobil, araba; vagon; balon sepeti; (*asansör*) kabin.

car.a.cole ['kærəkəul] *binicilik:* **1.** *n.* yarım çark hareketi; **2.** *vb.* iki yana yarım çarklar yaparak at sürmek.

ca.rafe [kə'ræf] *n.* sürahi.

car.a.mel ['kærəmel] *n.* kavrulmuş şeker, karamel; karamela.

car.a.pace ZOO ['kærəpeis] *n.* kaplumbağa gibi hayvanların üst kabuğu.

car.at ['kærət] *n.* kırat (*değerli taşların ağırlık ölçü birimi*).

car.a.van ['kærəvæn] *n.* kervan; arabaya bağlı küçük ev, treyler; **car.a'van.se.rai** [‿sərai] *n.* kervansaray, büyük yolcu hanı.

car.a.way BOT ['kærəwei] *n.* kimyon; çöreotu.

car.bide CHEM ['kɑːbaid] *n.* karpit.

car.bine ['kɑːbain] *n.* kısa tüfek, süvari tüfeği, karabina.

car.bo.hy.drate CHEM ['kɑːˈbəu'haidreit] *n.* karbonhidrat.

car.bol.ic ac.id CHEM [kɑːˈbɔlik'æsid] *n.* fenol.

car.bon ['kɑːbən] *n.* CHEM karbon; ELECT kömür; *a.* ~ *paper* karbon, kopya kâğıdı; ~ *copy* kopya, suret; ~ *dioxide* karbon dioksit; ~ *monoxide* karbon monoksit; **car.bo.naceous** ['‿bəu'neiʃəs] *adj.* karbonlu; **carbon.ate** ['‿bənit] *n.* karbonat; **car.bon.ic** ['‿'bɔnik] *adj.* karbonik; ~ *acid* karbonik asit; **car.bon.if.er.ous** GEOL ['‿bənifərəs] *adj.* kömürün oluştuğu jeolojik devre ait; kömürlü; karbonlu; **car.bon.i.zation** ['‿bənai'zeiʃən] *n.* karbonlaş(tır)ma; '**car.bon.ize** v/t. & v/i. karbonlaş(tır)mak; kömürleş(tir)mek.

car.bo.run.dum [kɑːbə'rʌndəm] *n.* karbon ve silikomdan oluşan ve maddeleri cilalamak ve keskinleştirmek için kullanılan madde.

car.boy ['kɑːbɔi] *n.* büyük sepetli şişe, damacana.

car.bun.cle ['kɑːbʌŋkl] *n.* MIN kırmızı ziynet taşları; MED çıban, şirpençe.

car.bu.ret CHEM ['kɑːbjuret] *v/t.* gaz haline getirmek; **'car.bu.ret.ter,** *mst* **'car.bu.rettor** *n.* MOT karbüratör.

car.case, *mst* **car.cass** ['kɑːkəs] *n.* (*hayvan*) ceste, kadavra, iskelet; *kasap dükkânı:* gövde, beden; *fig.* leş, (*gemi v.b.*) enkaz.

card[1] MEC [kɑːd] **1.** *n.* yün tarağı; kaşağı; **2.** *v/t.* (*yün*) taramak.

card[2] [-] *n.* kart, posta kartı; kartvizit; karton; oyun kâğıdı; *house of ~s* (*çocuk oyunu*) iskambilden ev; *queer ~* F antika, tuhaf; *have a ~ up one's sleeve* gizli kozu olm.

car.dan MEC ['kɑːdən]: **~ joint** kardan mafsalı, üniversal mafsal; **~ shaft** kardan şaftı.

card...: **'~.board** *n.* karton. mukavva.

car.di.ac MED ['kɑːdiæk] **1.** *adj.* kalple ilgili, kalp...; **2.** *n.* kalp ilâcı.

car.di.gan ['kɑːdigən] *n.* örme yün ceket, hırka.

car.di.nal ['kɑːdinl] **1.** □ baş, esaslı, önemli, ana; koyu parlak kırmızı; **~ number** asıl sayı; **2.** *n.* kardinal; ORN erkeği parlak kırmızı tüylü bir tür kuş (*Kuzey Amerika'da*); **car.di.nal.ate** ['-nəleit] *n.* kardinallik; kardinaller heyeti.

card...: **'~-in.dex** *n.* klasör, fişler *pl.*; **'~-sharp.er** *n.* iskambil oyununda hile yapan kimse.

care [kɛə] **1.** *n.* dikkat, bakım, koruma, ilgi; merak, üzüntü; *medical ~* tıbbi bakım; **~ of the mouth** ağız bakımı; **~ of the nails** tırnak bakımı; **~ of** (*abbr. c/o*) evinde, vasıtasiyle, eliyle; *take ~ (of o.s.)* *k-ne* bakmak, dikkat etm.; *take ~ of* muhafaza etm. *-i;* bakmak *-e,* dikkat etm. *-e;* *with ~* dikkatle; **2.** *vb.* yapmak hevesinde olm. (*to -i*); **~ for** ilgilenmek *-le;* bakmak *-e;* beğenmek *-i;* endişe etm. *-den;* *I don't ~ (if I do)!* F umurumda değil, bence aynı şey, Bana ne?; *I don't ~ what he said* ne söylerse söylesin (umurumda değil); **well ~d-for** iyi bakılmış, bakımlı.

ca.reen NAUT [kə'riːn] *v/t.* (*gemiyi*) yan yatırmak; *v/i.* yan yatmak.

ca.reer [kə'riə] **1.** *n.* meslek hayatı, kariyer; **~ diplomat** meslekten yetişme diplomat; **2.** *v/i.* hızla gitmek, koşmak; **ca'reer.ist** *n.* mesleğinde herşeye rağmen ilerlemeye meraklı kimse, ikbalperest.

care.free ['kɛəfriː] *adj.* kaygısız, kayıtsız, dertsiz.

care.ful □ ['kɛəful] dikkatli, ihtimamlı, itinalı, ihtiyatlı, ölçülü; *be ~ to inf.* dikkat etm. *-e;* **'care.ful.ness** *n.* dikkat, dikkatli olma.

care.less □ ['kɛəlis] dikkatsiz, ihmalci, kayıtsız; düşüncesiz, pervasız (*of*); **'careless.ness** *n.* dikkatsizlik, ihmal; düşüncesizlik.

ca.ress [kə'res] **1.** *n.* okşama, öpüş; **2.** *v/t.* sevmek, öpmek; *fig.* okşamak.

care.tak.er ['kɛəteikə] *n.* kapıcı; bina yöneticisi; **~ government** geçici hükümet.

care-worn ['kɛəwɔːn] *adj.* kederden bitkin.

car.fare *Am.* ['kɑːfɛə] *n.* yolcu bilet parası.

car.go NAUT [kɑːgəu] *n.* yük, hamule; *mixed veya general ~* karışık yük.

car.i.bou ZOO ['kæribuː] *n.* Kuzey Amerika'ya ait ren geyiği.

car.i.ca.ture [kærikə'tjuə] **1.** *n.* karikatür; kötü taklit; **2.** *v/t.* karikatürünü yapmak, karikatürleştirmek; **car.i.ca-'tur.ist** *n.* karikatürist.

car.i.es BOT ['kɛəriiːz] *n.* diş ve kemik çürümesi.

car.il.lon [kæ'riljən] *n.* çeşitli tonlarda sesler veren çan takımı.

car.i.ous ['kɛəriəs] *adj.* (*dişleri veya kemikleri*) çürümüş.

car.jack.ing ['kɑːdʒækıŋ] *n.* silah zoruyla araç kaçırma.

car.load ['kɑːləud] *n.* araba veya vagon yükü; F araba dolusu şey.

car.man ['kɑːmən] *n.* arabacı.

car.mine ['kɑːmain] *n.* kızıl, kırmızı.

car.nage ['kɑːnidʒ] *n.* katliam, kan dökme, halkı kılıçtan geçirme; **'car.nal** □ cinsî, şehvanî; dünyevî; **car.nal.i.ty** [-'næliti] *n.* maddiyat, cismaniyet; şehvet; **car.na.tion** [-'neiʃən] **1.** *n.* pembe veya açık kırmızı; BOT karanfil; **2.** *adj.* açık kırmızı.

car.ni.val ['kɑːnivəl] *n.* karnaval, cümbüş, âlem.

car.ni.vore ['kɑːnivɔː] *n.* et yiyen hayvan, etobur; **car.niv.o.rous** [-'nivərəs] *adj.* et yiyen, et yiyen hayvanlara ait.

car.ol ['kærəl] **1.** *n.* neşeli şarkı, dini

şarkı; **2.** *vb.* neşeyle şarkı söylemek; dini şarkı söylemek; şarkıyla methetmek.
ca.rot.id ANAT [kə'rɔtid] *n. a.* ~ **artery** karotis arteri; şahdamar.
ca.rouse [kə'rauz] **1.** *n. a.* **ca'rous.al** ziyafet, içki âlemi; **2.** *v/i.* içmek, içki âlemi yapmak.
carp¹ [kɑ:p] *n.* sazan balığı.
carp² [-] *v/i.* kusur bulmak, beğenmemek; ~ **at** tutturmak, tenkit etm., mızmızlanmak.
car.pen.ter ['kɑ:pintə] **1.** *n.* marangoz, dülger, doğramacı; **2.** *vb.* marangozluk etm., yontmak, doğramak; **'car.pen.try** *n.* doğramacılık, marangozluk, dülgerlik.
car.pet ['kɑ:pit] **1.** *n.* kilim, halı (*a. fig.*); **bring on the** ~ *bşin* lafını etm., *bşi* dermeyan etm., müzakere mevkiine koymak; **2.** *v/i.* halı döşemek; F *b-den* hesap sormak, haşlamak; **'~-bag** *n.* yol çantası, heybe; **'~-bag.ger** *n.* Amerikan sivil savaşından sonra çıkarı için Güneye yerleşen Kuzeyli; prensipsiz politikacı; **'car.pet.ing** *n.* döşemelik halı.
car.pet...: '~-**knight** *n.* salon kahramanı; **'~-sweep.er** *n.* halı sürpürgesi.
car.pool ['kɑ:pu:l] *n.* (*tasarruf amacıyla*) otomobilleri sıra ile kullanma anlaşması; *v/i.* birlikte aynı arabayla işe, okula *v.b.* gitmek.
car.riage ['kærɪdʒ] *n.* araba, vagon; taşıma, nakil; nakliye ücreti; davranış; MIL kundak; ~ **free,** ~ **paid** nakliyesiz, navlun satıcıya ait; **'car.riage.a.ble** *adj.* üzerinden araba geçebilir (*yol*).
car.riage...: '~-**drive** *n.* park yolu; '~-**way** *n.* araba yolu; **dual** ~ iki taraflı yol.
car.ri.er ['kærɪə] *n.* nakliyeci; taşıyan; taşıyıcı (*a.* MED = portör); '~-**pi.geon** *n.* posta güvercini.
car.ri.on ['kærɪən] **1.** *n.* leş; **2.** *adj.* leş gibi; leş yiyen.
car.rot ['kærət] *n.* havuç; **'car.rot.y** *adj.* F havuç renginde (*esp. saç*).
car.ry ['kæri] **1.** *vb.* taşımak, götürmek, nakletmek; çekmek (*yük*); beslemek, desteklemek; üzerinde bulundurmak; *k-ni* idare etm.; (*hastalık, mikrop*) yayılmak; (*silah*) atıcı gücü olm.; satışa arzetmek; hamile olm. *-e*; MATH geçirmek; yayınlamak; (*alkollü içki*) dayanmak *-e*, tahammül etm. *-e*; kapsamak *-i*; desteğini kazanmak; (*parlemento-*

da) kabul edilmek; MIL (*kale vs.*) ele geçirmek, zaptetmek; (*faiz*) getirmek; (*ses*) ...den işitilmek; ~ **the day** başarılı olm.; ~ **away** taşımak, alıp götürmek (*a. fig.*); ~ **every thing before one** her direnişi kırmak, tam bir zafer kazanmak; ~ **forward** *veya* **over** COM yeni sayfaya nakletmek; yekûn nakletmek; ~ **on** devam et(tir)mek; ~ **out,** ~ **through** bitirmek; başarmak, yerine getirmek; ~ **out** JUR (*para cezasını vb.*) icra etm., tenfiz etm.; **~ing capac.ity** taşıma kapasitesi; **2.** *n.* menzil, atış menzili; nakil, taşıma.
cart [kɑ:t] **1.** *n.* iki tekerlekli yük arabası; el arabası; ~ **grease** araba dingil yağı; **put the** ~ **before the horse** *fig.* bir işi tersinden yapmak; **in the** ~ *sl.* hapı yutmuş, güç durumda; **2.** *v/t.* araba ile taşımak; **'cart.age** *n.* araba ile taşıma; nakliye ücreti.
car.tel [kɑ:'tel] *n.* kartel, fabrikalar arasındaki anlaşma; MIL mübadele, değişim, trampa.
cart.er ['kɑ:tə] *n.* arabacı, yük arabasını kullanan kimse.
car.ti.lage ['kɑ:tilidʒ] *n.* kıkırdak; **car.tilag.i.nous** [-'lædʒinəs] *adj.* kıkırdaklı; kıkırdağa benzer.
cart-load ['kɑ:tləud] *n.* araba dolusu yük.
car.tog.ra.pher [kɑ:'tɔgrəfə] *n.* harita mütehassısı, haritacı; **car'tog.ra.phy** *n.* haritacılık.
car.ton ['kɑ:tən] *n.* karton, mukavva kutu.
car.toon [kɑ:'tu:n] **1.** *n.* PAINT karikatür; MEC resim taslağı; **2.** *vb.* karikatürize etm., karikatürleştirmek; **car'toon.ist** *n.* karikatürcü, karikatürist.
car.touche ARCH [kɑ:'tu:ʃ] *n.* kralın ismini gösteren kabartma resim, şekil; fişeklik.
car.tridge ['kɑ:tridʒ] *n.* hartuç, fişek; PHOT kartuş, kaset; '~-**pa.per** *n.* kalın, kaba beyaz kâğıt.
cart-wheel ['kɑ:twi:l] *n.* araba tekerleği; *Am.* gümüş dolar; **turn ~s** elleri üzerinde takla atmak.
cart.wright ['kɑ:trait] *n.* araba imalâtçısı.
carve [kɑ:v] *v/t.* oymak, hakketmek; (*esp. sofrada*) et kesmek; (*yolu*) düzleştirmek (*a. fig.*); **'carv.er** *n.* oymacı, hakkâk; **'carv.ing** *n.* oyulmuş sanat eseri; oymacılık; sofrada et kesme.
cas.cade [kæs'keid] *n.* çağlayan, şela-

le.

case[1] [keis] **1.** *n.* kutu, kasa, göz, çekme, mahfaza, kılıf; *(fişek)* kovan; TYP hurufat kasası; **2.** *v/t.* kaplamak, örtmek; kutuya koymak.

case[2] [-] *n.* hal, husus, hâdise, olay *(a.* MED, JUR); MED hasta; *Am.* F garip herif; JUR hukukî sebep, dava; GR ismin hallerinden biri; *make out one's ~* kuvvetli deliller ileri sürmek; *as the ~ may be* hal ve şartlara göre, gereğince, icabında; *in ~* eğer, şayet; *in any ~ her* halde, mutlaka.

case-hard.en MEC ['keishɑːdn] *v/t.* dış yüzünü sertleştirmek, kalınlaştırmak; *~ed adj. fig.* nasırlaşmış.

case his.to.ry ['keishistəri] *n.* evveliyat, hasta veya güçlük içinde bulunan kişinin geçmisi ile ilgili bilgiler.

ca.se.in CHEM ['keisiːin] *n.* peynir özü, kazein.

case.mate MIL ['keismeit] *n.* top yuvası, kazamat.

case.ment ['keismənt] *n.* pencere kanadı; *~ window* kanatlı pencere.

cash [kæʃ] **1.** *n.* para, nakit; peşin para; *~ down, for ~* peşin para; *in ~* peşin olarak, nakit alarak; *be in (out of)* ~ üstünde parası ol(ma)mak; *~ and carry adj.* peşin para ile alınan; *~ payment* peşin ödeme; *~ on delivery* ödemeli; *~ price* peşin fiyat; *~ register* otomatik kasa; **2.** *v/t.* paraya çevirmek, para bozmak; '*~book* *n.* kasa defteri; '*~cheque* *n.* çizgili olmayan çek; '*~cow* *n. bol nakit para getiren bir kaynak;* **cash.ier** **1.** [kæˈʃiə] *n.* veznedar, kasiyer; **2.** [kəˈʃiə] *v/t.* MIL ordudan tard etm.; **cashless** ['kæʃlis] *adj.* nakden olmayıp havale, çek vs. ile yapılan ödeme.

cash.mere ['kæʃmiə] *n.* kaşmir yünü; ince yün kumaş.

cas.ing ['keisiŋ] *n.* kaplama; çerçeve; ARCH zarf, sandık; *~ paper* ambalaj kâğıdı.

ca.si.no [kəˈsiːnəu] *n.* gazino.

cask [kɑːsk] *n.* fıçı, varil; bir fıçı dolusu.

cas.ket ['kɑːskit] *n.* değerli eşya kutusu; *Am.* tabut.

Cas.pi.an Sea ['kæspiənsiː] *n.* Hazar Denizi.

casque ['kæsk] *n.* zırhlı başlık, miğfer.

cas.sa.tion [kæˈseiʃən] *n.* davayı temyiz, kararı bozma.

cas.sa.va BOT [kəˈsɑːvə] *n.* manyok kökünden çıkartılan nişasta.

cas.se.role ['kæsərəul] *n.* saplı tence-

re, güveç; bu tencerede pişirilen yemek.

cas.si.a BOT ['kæsiə] *n.* Çin tarçını.

cas.sock ['kæsək] *n.* papaz cübbesi.

cas.so.war.y ORN ['kæsəweəri] *n.* devekuşu cinsinden büyük kuş; *New Holland* ~ Avustralya'ya mahsus iri devekuşu.

cast [kɑːst] **1.** *n.* atma, atış, fırlatma; MEC döküm, dökme, kalıp; *(tiyatro oyunu veya filmde)* oynayanlar; rol dağıtımı; alçı; dış görünüş; renk tonu; tip, kalite; NAUT ağ atma, voli; **2.** *v/t.* atmak, saçmak; olta atmak, ağ sermek; *(diş, kıl vs.)* dökmek; *(oy)* vermek; THEAT rol dağıtmak; rol vermek *-e; (döküm)* dökmek; *(hayvan)* doğurmak; *a.* ~ *up* sayıları toplamak; *be* ~ *in a lawsuit* JUR dava kaybetmek; ~ *lots (for) bş* için kura çekmek; ~ *in one's lot with s.o. b-i-le herşeyi pay laşmak;* ~ *one's skin* derisi soyulmak; ~ *s.th. in s.o.'s teeth b-ni bş den* dolayı muaheze etm., yüzüne vurmak; işe yaramaz diye atmak; *be ~ away* NAUT *(gemi)* kazaya uğramak; ~ *down* aşağı atmak, indirmek; *be ~ down* yüreği kararmak, neşesiz ve kederli olm.; ~ *up* kusmak, kayyetmek; ~ *up (accounts)* COM *bşin* hesabını yapmak; *v/i.* eğrilmek; MEC kalıp lanmak; ~ *about for* çare aramak, düşünüp taşınmak; ~ *off* NAUT alarga etm.

cas.ta.net [kæstəˈnet] *n.* kastanyet, çengi zili.

cast.a.way ['kɑːstəwei] **1.** *n.* reddedilmiş kişi, şey; NAUT kazazede; **2.** *adj.* reddedilmiş; kazazede.

caste [kɑːst] *n.* kast, birbirine karşı kapalı sınıf *(a. fig)*; ~ *feeling* zümre zihniyeti.

cas.tel.lan ['kæstələn] *n.* kale kumandanı, şato kâhyası; **cas.tel.lat.ed** ['kæsteleitid] *adj.* duvarları mazgallı, kuleli olan.

cas.ter ['kɑːstə] = *castor*[2]

cas.ti.gate ['kæstigeit] *v/t.* tenkit etm., cezalandırmak, kırbaçlamak; *fig.* teşhir etm.; **cas.ti'ga.tion** *n.* cezalandırma, paylama.

cast.ing ['kɑːstiŋ] **1.** *adj.* kati, kesin *(oy)*; **2.** *n.* atma, atış, fırlatma; döküm, dökme; hesap etme; rol dağıtımı; *~s pl.* döküm kaplar.

cast i.ron ['kɑːstˈaiən] *n.* dökme demir; '*cast-i.ron* *adj.* dökme demirden yapılmış; *fig.* sağlam, dayanıklı, demir gibi.

cas.tle ['kɑːsl] **1.** *n.* hisar, kale; şato; *satranç*; kale; **~s in the air, ~s in Spain** hayal, hülya; **2.** *vb. satranç*: kaleyi şahın yanına koymak, rok yapmak.

cast-off ['kɑːst'ɔf] *n.* (*esp. giysi*) istenilmeyen veya atılmış şey.

cas.tor¹ PHARM ['kɑːstə] *n.*: **~ oil** Hintyağı.

cas.tor² [-] *n.* koltuk vs. tekerleği; tuztuk, biberlik; **~ sugar** pudra şekeri.

cas.trate [kæs'treit] *v/t.* hadımlaştırmak, iğdiş etm.; **cas'tra.tion** hadım etme, iğdiş etme.

cast steel ['kɑːst'stiːl] *n.* dökme çelik; **'cast-'steel** *adj.* dökme çelikten yapılmış.

cas.u.al □ ['kæʒjuəl] tesadüfî, rastgele; F gevşek, üşengeç, heyecansız, tembel, lâubali; sıradan, ciddi olmayan; gündelik (*elbise vs.*) **~ labourer** geçici işçi; **'cas.u.al.ty** *n.* kaza; kayıp; **casualties** *pl.* MIL zayiat.

cas.u.ist ['kæzjuist] *n.* ahlâk konularında doğru ile yanlışı isteği doğrultusunda yorumlayan kişi; safsatacı; **'cas.u.ist.ry** *n.* safsata, gerçeği aksettirmeyen kalıba ustaca yapılmış yorum.

cat [kæt] **1.** *n.* kedi; *Am. sl.* caz meraklısı; **wait for the ~ to jump, see which way the ~ jumps** işlerin nasıl geliştiğini görmek, diğerlerinin tutumunu görünceye kadar işe karışmamak; **not room to swing a ~** çok dar yer; **~ burglar** duvardan tırmanarak içeri giren hırsız; **2.** *v/i.* P kusmak.

cat.a.clysm ['kætəklizəm] *n.* tufan, afet; felâket, musibet.

cat.a.comb ['kætəkuːm] *n.* yer altında dehliz gibi mezarlık.

cat.a.logue, *Am. a.* **cat.a.log** ['kætəlɔg] **1.** *n.* katalog, liste; **2.** *v/t.* bşin kataloğunu yapmak.

cat.a.pult ['kætəpʌlt] *n.* mancınık; sapan; AVIA katapült.

cat.a.ract ['kætərækt] *n.* şelâle, büyük çağlayan; MED katarakt, perde.

ca.tarrh [kə'tɑː] *n.* akıntı, F nezle; **catarrh.al** [kə'tɑːrəl] *adj.* nezleye ait.

ca.tas.tro.phe [kə'tæstrəfi] *n.* facia, felâket; **cat.a.stroph.ic** [kætə'strɔfik] *adj.* (**~ally**) dehşetli, korkunç, felâket getiren.

ca.taw.ba *Am.* BOT [kə'tɔːbə] *n.* üzüm ve şarap.

cat.bird ZOO ['kætbəːd] *n.* ardıç kuşu.

cat.call ['kætkɔːl] **1.** *n.* THEAT *etc.* hoş-

nutsuzluk belirtmek için çalınan ıslık veya çıkarılan ses; **2.** *v/i.* ıslıklamak, yuhalamak.

catch [kætʃ] **1.** *n.* yakala(n)ma, tut(ul)ma; av, şikâr; tuzak, bityeniği; *fig.* kâr, kazanç, fayda; MEC kilit dili, çengel, kanca (*a. fig.*); parola; slogan *s.* **~word**; **2.** (*irr.*) *v/t. & v/i.* kapmak, tutmak, yakalamak, elde etm., ele geçirmek; cezbetmek, çekmek; (*tren vs.*) yetişmek *-e*; (*hastalık*) yakalanmak *-e*, duçar olm. *-e*; (*ateş*) tutuşmak, ateş almak; (*nefes, soluk*) tutmak; (*tokat, darbe*) aşketmek, indirmek; *fig.* anlamak, kavramak; **~ at** tutmağa çalışmak *-i*; **~ it** F azar işitmek; **~ in the act** suçüstü yakalamak; **~ me!** (**doing such a thing**) bunu yapmak mı? ne münasebet!; **~ (a) cold** soğuk almak, nezle olm., üşütmek; **~ on** tutulmak, moda olm.; *Am.* kavramak, anlamak; **~ s.o.'s eye** *b-nin* dikkatini çekmek; **~ the Speaker's eye** (*İngiltere parlamentosunda*) söz almayı başarmak; **~ up** yetişmek; kesmek, *bşe* ara vermek; **~ up with** yetişmek *-e*; **'~.all** *n. Am.* yer; kap, mahfaza; **'~-as-'catch-'can** *n. spor.* serbest güreş; **'catch.er** *n.* tutan kimse; *beysbol*: topu yakalayan oyuncu; **'catching** *adj.* çekici, cazibeli; MUS giriş; MED sâri, bulaşıcı; **'catch-line** *n.* manşet; **'catchment ba.sin** su haznesi, toplama havuzu.

catch...: **'~.pen.ny** *adj.* COM ucuz satmak için yapılan gösterişli fakat değersiz şey; **'~-phrase** *n.* slogan; **'~.pole** *n.* şerif vekili; **'~.word** *n.* parola; slogan; THEAT, TYP replik; **'catch.y** *adj.* F *fig.* cazibeli; şüpheli.

cat.e.chism [kætikizəm] *n.* soru cevaplı öğretme; **cat.e.chize** ['~.kaiz] *v/t.* (*dini konuları*) soru cevap usulü ile öğretmek; **cat.e.chu.men** ['~.kjuː.men] *n.* Kateşizm öğrencisi.

cat.e.gor.i.cal □ [kæti'gɔrikəl] kategorik, kesin, kati; **cat.e.go.ry** ['~.gəri] *n.* kategori, sınıf, cins, zümre.

ca.ter ['keitə] *v/i.* **~ for** hazırlamak *-i*, temin etm. *-i*; *fig. bşi* bulmak, temin etm.; **'ca.ter.er** *n.* yiyecek temin eden, vekilharç; **'ca.ter.ing** *n.* yemek tedariki, ikram.

cat.er.pil.lar ['kætəpilə] *n.* tırtıl, kurt.

cat.er.waul ['kætəwɔːl] **1.** *n.* kedi sesi; **2.** *v/i.* kedi gibi miyavlamak.

cat.fish ['kætfiʃ] *n.* kedi balığı.

cat.gut ['kætgʌt] *n.* kiriş; MED katgüt.

ca.thar.sis [kə'θɑːsis] *n.* MED ishal, amel; **ca'thar.tic** [_tik] **1.** *n.* müshil ilâcı; **2.** *adj.* müshil, bağırsakları temizleyici.

ca.the.dral [kə'θiːdrəl] *n.* katedral, piskoposluk kilisesi.

Cath.er.ine-wheel ['kæθərinwiːl] *n.* ARCH gül şeklinde yapılmış renkli pencere; rozas; döner hava fişeği, çarkıfelek.

cath.ode ELECT ['kæθəud] *n.* katot, negatif elektrot; ~ **ray** katot ışınları.

cath.o.lic ['kæθəlik] **1.** *adj.* (*~ally*) Katolik kilisesine bağlı olan; **2.** *n.* Katolik; **cathol.i.cism** [kə'θɔlisizəm] *n.* Katoliklik.

cat.kin BOT ['kætkin] *n.* söğüt vs. gibi ağaçların çiçeği.

cat.like ['kætlaik] *adj.* kedi gibi; sessiz, sinsi; '**cat.nip** *n.* BOT kedi nanesi.

cat-o'-nine-tails [kætə'nainteilz] *n.* dayak atmak için kullanılan uçları dokuz düğümlü ipten yapılmış kamçı.

CAT scan ['kætskæn] *n.* tıbbi amaçlarla bilgisayarla yapılan tarama; **CAT scan.ner** *n.* tıbbi amaçlarla kullanılan tarama makinesi.

cat's-paw *fig.* ['kætspɔː] *n.* başkası tarafından alet olarak kullanılan kişi, maşa.

cat.tish *fig.* ['kætiʃ] *adj.* kurnaz, şeytan, kinci, hain.

cat.tle ['kætl] *n.* sığır, davar; '~-**breeding** *n.* hayvan yetiştirme, sığırcılık; **~.man** ['_mən] *n.* hayvan yetiştiricisi; hayvan güden kimse; '~-**plague** *n.* bulaşıcı sığır hastalığı; '~-**rus.tler** *n. Am.* davar *veya* **at** hırsızı; '~-**show** *n.* tarım sergisi; sığır sergisi.

cat.ty ['kæti] = *cattish*.

Cau.ca.sian [kɔː'keizjən] **1.** *adj.* Kafkasya'ya ait; Kafkas diliyle ilgili; **2.** *n.* Kafkasyalı; Kafkas dili.

cau.cus ['kɔːkəs] *n.* parti kurulu toplantısı; *contp.* klik; *Am.* POL siyasi parti liderlerinin toplantısı.

cau.dal ['kɔːdl] *adj.* kuyruklu; kuyruğa ait; kuyruğa yakın; **cau.date** ['_deit] *adj.* hem karada hem de denizde yaşayan ve kuyruklu olan.

caught [kɔːt] *pret. & p.p. of* **catch 2.**

caul.dron ['kɔːldrən] *n.* kazan.

cau.li.flow.er BOT ['kɔliflauə] *n.* karnabahar.

caulk NAUT [kɔːk] *v/t.* kalafatlamak; '**caulker** *n.* kalafatçı.

caus.al □ ['kɔːzəl] sebep belirten; sebebe ait, nedensel; **cau.sal.i.ty** [_'zæliti] *n.* sebebiyet, nedensellik; '**caus.a.tive** *adj.* sebep olan (*of -e*); **cause 1.** *n.* sebep, neden; vesile; hedef, amaç; JUR dava; büyük mesele; taraftarlık; *make common ~ with* işbirliği yapmak *-le*; tarafını tutmak *-in*; **2.** *v/t. bşe* sebep olm.; sebebiyet vermek *-e*, meydan vermek *-e*; '**causeless** □ sebepsiz, nedensiz, asılsız.

cause.way ['kɔːzweil], *a.* **cau.sey** ['_zei] *n.* yayalar için yapılan geçici yol, geçit; şose.

caus.tic ['kɔːstik] **1.** *n.* yakıcı (*veya* aşındırıcı, dağlayıcı) madde; kostik, kezzap; **2.** *adj.* (*~ally*) aşındırıcı; *fig.* dokunaklı, iğneli (*söz*), müstehzi.

cau.ter.i.za.tion MED [kɔːtərai'zeiʃən] *n.* dağlama; '**cau.ter.ize** *v/t.* yakmak, dağlamak; '**cau.ter.y** *n.* yakış, dağlayış; dağlama aleti.

cau.tion ['kɔːʃən] **1.** *n.* dikkat; ihtar, uyarma; sakınma; tedbir; JUR kefalet, teminat ~ *money* teminat akçesi, depozito, kefalet; **2.** *v/t. b-ne bşi* ihtar etm., uyarmak (*against -e karşı*); *b-ne bş-den* sakınmasını ihtar etm.; **cau.tion.ar.y** ['_ʃnəri] *adj.* ihtar cinsinden, uyarıcı.

cau.tious □ ['kɔːʃəs] ihtiyatlı, tedbirli, çekingen; '**cau.tious.ness** *n.* dikkat, ihtimam, itina, tedbirlilik.

cav.al.cade [kævəl'keid] *n.* süvari alayı; atlı ve arabalıların geçidi.

cav.a.lier [kævə'liə] **1.** *n.* kavalye; centilmen; suvari, atlı; **2.** □ kibirli, gururlu.

cav.al.ry MIL ['kævəlri] atlı asker, süvari sınıfı.

cave [keiv] **1.** *n.* mağara, *in*; **2.** ~ **in** *v/i.* çökmek, yıkılmak; teslim olm., razı olm.; *v/t.* ⊦ oymak, (*mağara*) açmak.

ca.ve.at JUR ['keiviæt] *n.* işlemlerin durdurulması için yapılan başvurma, ihtar, ikaz.

cave-dweller ['keivdwelə], **cave-man** ['_mən] *n.* taş devri mağara adamı; ⊦ kaba adam.

cav.en.dish ['kævəndiʃ] *n.* kalıplanmış bir cins tütün.

cav.ern ['kævən] *n.* mağara, *in*; '**cav.ernous** *adj.* mağaraları olan; *fig.* boş, kof, mağara gibi.

cav.i.ar(e) ['kæviɑː] *n.* havyar.

cav.il ['kævil] **1.** *n.* anlamsız itiraz, bahane; **2.** *v/i.* bahane aramak, bahane bulmak, itiraz etm. (*at, about -de,*

-e); 'cavil.ler n. itirazcı kimse.
cav.i.ty ['kæviti] n. oyuk, çukur, boşluk.
ca.vort Am. F [kəvɔːt] v/i. şahlanmak, coşmak, oynamak.
caw [kɔː] 1. n. karga sesi, gak; 2. v/i. karga gibi gaklamak.
cay.enne [kei'en] n. a. ~ pepper ['keien] çok acı kırmızı biber.
cay.man zoo ['keimən] n. Güney Amerika'ya ait bir cins timsah.
CD [siː'diː] n. CD; '~ play.er n. CD-çalar; ~-ROM [_'rɔm] n. CD-ROM.
cease [siːs] v/i. (from) bitmek, sona ermek, durmak; v/t. bitirmek; (MIL ateş) kesmek; '~-'fire n. MIL silahların geçici olarak bırakılması, ateşkes; 'cease-less □ durmadan, sürekli, fasılasız.
ce.dar BOT ['siːdə] n. sedir ağacı.
cede [siːd] v/t. bırakmak, terketmek.
ce.dil.la [si'dilə] n. Ç ve Ş harflerinin altındaki işaret, çengel.
ceil [siːl] v/t. tavan yapmak; 'ceil.ing n. tavan; tavan yapma; AVIA uçağın azamî yüksekliği; fig. azamî had; ~ lighting tavan aydınlatma düzeni; ~ price azamî fiyat, tavan fiyat.
cel.an.dine BOT ['selandain] n. kırlangıç otu.
cel.a.nese [selə'niːz] n. bir çeşit suni ipek.
ce.leb F [sə'leb] n. ünlü (kimse).
cel.e.brate ['selibreit] vb. kutlamak; şöhretini yaymak, övmek; ECCL ayin yapmak; 'cel.e.brat.ed adj. meşhur, ünlü (for -le); 'cel.e'bra.tion n. kutlama; ECCL dini ayin yapma; 'cel.e.bra-tor n. kutlayan kimse.
ce.leb.ri.ty [si'lebriti] n. şöhret; ünlü kişi.
ce.ler.i.ty [si'leriti] n. sürat, çabukluk.
cel.er.y BOT ['seləri] n. kereviz.
ce.les.tial □ [si'lestjəl] göğe ait, semavi; kutsal, ilâhi; göklerde oturan, melek.
cel.i.ba.cy ['selibəsi] n. bekârlık; cel.i.bate ['_bit] 1. adj. bekâr, evlenmemiş (esp. dinsel nedenlerle); 2. n. bekâr.
cell [sel] n. hücre; ELECT pil.
cel.lar ['selə] 1. n. kiler, bodrum; şarap mahzeni; 2. v/t. mahzene koymak; 'cellar.age n. mahzenlik yer; mahzen kirası; cel.lar.et [_'ret] n. içki dolabı; ...celled [seld] comb. ...hücreli.
cel.list MUS ['tʃelist] n. viyolonsel çalan; cel.lo ['_ləu] n. viyolonsel.
cel.lo.phane ['seləufein] n. selofon,

şeffaf kâğıt.
cell.phone TELEPH Am. ['selfəun] n. cep telefonu.
cel.lu.lar ['sɘljulə] adj. hücreye ait; hücreleri olan, hücreli, göz göz olan; cel.lule ['_juːl] n. küçük hücre, gözcük; cel.lulose ['_juləus] n. selüloz.
Celt [kelt] n. Kelt, eski orta veya batı Avrupalı kişi; 'Celt.ic n. Keltlere ait; Keltçe.
ce.ment [si'ment] 1. n. çimento; tutkal (a. fig.); 2. v/t. çimentolamak; yapıştırmak; ce.men.ta.tion [siːmen'teiʃən] n. çimentolama.
cem.e.ter.y ['semitri] n. mezarlık.
cen.o.taph ['senəutɑːf] n. b-nin hatırasını anmak için dikilen abide.
cense [sens] v/t. tütsülemek, buhur yakmak; 'cen.ser n. buhurdanlık.
cen.sor ['sensə] 1. n. kontrol memuru, sansör; mümeyyiz; 2. v/t. sansür etm.; yasak etm.; sansürcülük görevi yapmak; cen.so.ri.ous □ [sen'sɔːriəs] kusur bulan, tenkit eden; cen.sorship ['_səʃip] n. sansür, sansür idaresi.
cen.sur.a.ble □ ['senʃərəbl] kötü, cezayı haketmiş; 'cen.sure 1. n. azar(lama); tenkit, kınama; 2. v/t. azarlamak, tenkit etm., kınamak.
cen.sus ['sensəs] n. sayım, nüfus sayımı; '~-pa.per n. sayım formu.
cent [sent] n. Am. sent, 1/100 dolar; per ~ yüzde.
cen.taur ['sentɔː] n. insan başlı at.
cen.tau.ry BOT ['sentɔːri] n. kantaron.
cen.te.nar.i.an [senti'nɛəriən] 1. adj. yüz yıllık, yüz yaşında; 2. n. yüz yaşındaki kişi; cen.te.nar.y [sen'tiːnəri] s. centennial.
cen.ten.ni.al [sen'tenjəl] adj. & n. yüz yılı tamamlayan, yüz yıllık; yüzüncü yıl dönümü.
cen.tes.i.mal □ [sen'tesiməl] yüzüncü, yüzde bir, yüzde birine ait.
cen.ti...['senti]: '~-grade adj. santigrat, yüz dereceye bölünmüş; ~ thermome-ter yüz dereceli termometre, santigrat termometre; '~-gramme n. santigram, gramın yüzde biri; '~-me.tre n. santimetre, metrenin yüzde biri; '~-pede zoo ['_piːd] n. kırkayak.
cen.tral ['sentrəl] 1. □ orta, merkezî; ana, en önemli; ~ heating merkezî ısıtma, kalorifer; 2 Powers pl. HIST Merkezî Güçler (Almanya ve Avusturya-Macaristan); ~ office, ELECT ~ sta-tion n. merkez, santral; 2. n. teleph, te-

lefon santralı; **cen.tral.i.za.tion** [ˌlai-zeiʃən] *n.* merkezileştirme; **'cen.tral.ize** *v/t.* merkezileştirmek.

cen.tre, *Am.* **cen.ter** ['sentə] **1.** *n.* orta; (*a.* MIL, POL) merkez; ~ *forward futbol:* santrfor; ~ *half* santrhaf; ~ *of gravity* ağırlık merkezi; **2.** *adj.* orta, merkezî; **3.** *v/t.* ortaya koymak, merkeze toplamak, santralize etm.; '~-**bit** MEC *n.* matkap; '~-**board** *n.* kontra omurga(lı tekne).

cen.tric, **cen.tri.cal** □ ['sentrik(əl)] merkezî, merkeze ait; **cen.trif.u.gal** □ [sen'trifjugəl] merkezden çıkan; santrifuj, merkezkaç; **'cen'trip.e.tal** □ [ˌ-pitl] merkeze doğru, merkezcil.

cen.tu.ple ['sentjupl] **1.** □ yüz misli; **2.** *v/t.* yüzle çarpmak, yüz katına çıkarmak.

cen.tu.ri.on ['sen'tjuəriən] *n.* eski Roma yüzbaşısı.

cen.tu.ry ['sentʃəri] *n.* yüzyıl, asır.

CEO COM [siːiːˈəu] *n.* (= *chief executive officer*) Genel Müdür.

ce.ram.ic [si'ræmik] *adj.* seramik; porselen, çini vb.'den yapılmış eşya ile ilgili; **ce'ram.ics** *n. pl.* çinicilik; seramik; seramik eşya, çanak çömlek.

ce.re.al ['siəriəl] **1.** *n.* tahıl, hububat, zahire; *mst* ~*s pl.* buğdaysı bitki; *part. Am.* hububattan hazırlanmış kahvaltı yemeği; **2.** *adj.* hububat türünden.

cer.e.bral ANAT ['seribrəl] *adj.* beyne ait.

cere.cloth ['siəkləθ] *n.* kefenlik olarak kullanılan mumlu bez.

cer.e.mo.ni.al [seri'məunjəl] **1.** □ *a.* **cere'mo.ni.ous** □ törensel, resmî; **2.** *n.* ayin, tören; **cer.e.mo.ny** ['seriməni] *n.* tören; ayin; POL protokol, teşrifat; *Master of Ceremonies* töreni yöneten kişi; *stand on* ~ davranışlara dikkat etm.; resmî davranmak; *without* ~ teklifsizce.

cert *sl.* [səːt] *n. bşe* kesin olmuş gözü ile bakma.

cer.tain □ ['səːtn] muhakkak, kesin; emin; belirli, kararlaşmış; güvenilir; bazı; *for* ~ muhakkak, şüphesiz; *make* ~ *bş* hakkında emin olm.; **'cer.tain.ly** *adv.* elbette, tabii; **'cer.tain.ty** *n.* kesinlik, katiyet.

cer.tes *obs.* ['səːtiz] *adv.* elbette, tabii.

cer.tif.i.cate 1. [sə'tifikit] *n.* tasdikname, sertifika; diploma; ruhsat; belge; ilmühaber; ~ *of birth* nüfus (*veya* doğum) kâğıdı; ~ *of death* ölüm belge-

si; ~ *of marriage* evlenme cüzdanı; ~ *of employment* iş kâğıdı, çalışma belgesi; ~ *of origin* COM menşe şahadetnamesi; *medical* ~ sağlık belgesi; **2.** [sə'tifikeit] *v/t.* tasdik etm., onaylamak; belgelerle ispat etm., belgelemek, belge vermek; ~ *d adj.* onaylı; belgelenmiş, onaylanmış; **cer.ti.fi.ca.tion** [səːtifi'keiʃən] *n.* belgeleme, onay, ruhsat; **cer.ti.fy** ['ˌ-fai] *v/t. bşi* onaylamak, tasdik etm.; vesika vermek; doğrulamak; *certified cheque* karşılığı olduğu onaylanan çek, vizeli çek; *s. accountant*; **cer.ti.tude** ['ˌ-tjuːd] *n.* katiyet, kesinlik.

ce.ru.le.an [si'ruːljən] *adj.* gök mavisi.

cer.vi.cal [səːˈvaikəl] *adj.* boyna ait, boyun…

ces.sa.tion [se'seiʃən] *n.* kesilme, durma, ara.

ces.sion ['seʃən] *n.* vazgeçme, terk; devir.

cess.pit ['sespit], **cess.pool** ['sespuːl] *n.* lağım çukuru.

ce.ta.cean [si'teiʃən] **1.** *n.* memeli deniz hayvanı; **2.** *adj. a.* **ce'ta.ceous** memeli deniz hayvanları ile ilgili.

CFO COM [siːefˈəu] *n.* (= *chief financial officer*) Mali İşler Müdürü.

chafe [tʃeif] *v/t.* sürtmek, sürterek berelemek; yıpratmak; ovarak ısıtmak; *v/i. bşe* sürtünmek; sinirlenmek, kızmak.

chaff [tʃɑːf] **1.** *n.* saman tozu, çöp, atlara yem için kesilmiş ot, saman; F saçma söz; **2.** *v/t.* ufak ufak kesmek; F alay etm., *b-ne* takılmak; '~-**cut.ter** *n.* ot, saman kesme makinesi.

chaf.fer ['tʃæfə] *v/t. & v/i.* sıkı pazarlık etm., çekişmek; alışverişte bulunmak.

chaf.finch ZOO ['tʃæfintʃ] *n.* ispinoz.

chaf.ing-dish ['tʃeifiŋdiʃ] *n.* sofrada yemek ısıtmaya veya pişirmeye yarayan kap.

cha.grin ['ʃægrin] **1.** *n.* iç sıkıntısı, keder; **2.** *v/t. b-nin* canını sıkmak, kederlendirmek.

chain [tʃein] **1.** *n.* zincir, kelepçe; (*dağ*) silsile; *fig.* (*olay, mağaza vs.*) zincir; **2.** *v/t.* zincirle bağlamak, zincirlemek; *fig.* kayıt altına almak, zincirlemek; ~ **re-ac.tion** PHYS zincirleme reaksiyonu; '~-**smoker** *n.* peş peşe sigara içen; '~-**store** *n.* büyük bir mağazanın şubesi.

chair [tʃɛə] **1.** *n.* iskemle, sandalye; *Am. a.* elektrikli sandalye; başkanlık makamı; kürsü; *a.* **professorial** ~ kürsü; **be in the** ~, **take the** ~ başkanlık makamında olm.; başkanlık etm.; **2.** *v/t.* toplantıya başkanlık etm.; kürsüye eturtmak; omuzlarında taşımak; '~-**lift** *n.* telesiyej; ~.**man** ['-mən] *n.* başkan, reis; '~.**manship** *n.* başkanlık, riyaset; '~.**wom.an** *n.* kadın başkan.

chaise [ʃeiz] *n.* hafif gezinti arabası.

chal.ice ['tʃælis] *n.* tas, ayinde kullanılan kadeh.

chalk [tʃɔːk] **1.** *n.* tebeşir; **red** ~ kırmızı tebeşir; **by a long** ~ F fersah fersah; **2.** *vb.* beyazlatmak, tebeşir katmak, tebeşirle yazmak, resim yapmak; *mst* ~ **up** tebeşirle yazmak; hesabına katmak, sayı kaydetmek; ~ **out** tebeşirle taslak çizmek; *fig.* karalamak; '**chalk.y** *adj.* kireçli; tebeşir gibi.

chal.lenge ['tʃælindʒ] **1.** *n.* meydan okuma, davet; MIL düelloya davet; *part.* JUR reddi hâkim; ~ **prize** *spor:* çalenç; **2.** *v/t.* çağırmak; meydan okumak; düelloya davet etm.; MIL parola veya kimlik sormak; JUR hâkim veya jüriyi reddetmek; *bşin* doğruluğundan şüphelenmek; '**challeng.er** *n.* meydan okuyan, mücadeleye davet eden kişi.

cha.lyb.e.ate [kə'libiit] *adj.* demirli, demir tadı olan.

cham.ber ['tʃeimbə] *n.* oda, yatak odası, özel oda; salon; MEC fişek yatağı; bölme, hücre; PARL meclis; ~**s** *pl.* yazıhane, büro, hâkimin özel odası; ≗ **of Commerce** ticaret odası; **cham.ber-lain** ['-lin] *n.* mabeyinci, teşrifatçı; kâhya; '**cham.bermaid** *n.* oda hizmetçisi; '**cham.ber-mu.sic** *n.* oda müziği; '**cham.ber-pot** *n.* lâzımlık, oturak.

cham.bray *Am.* ['ʃæmbrei] *n.* ince elbiselik kumaş.

cha.me.le.on ZOO [kə'miːljən] *n.* bukalemun.

cham.fer ARCH ['tʃæmfə] **1.** *n.* küçük oluk, şev (açmaya yarayan alet); **2.** *vb.* oluk açmak, şev yapmak.

cham.ois ['ʃæmwɑː] **1.** *n.* ZOO dağ keçisi; *a.* ~ **leather** keçi derisi, güderi; **2.** *adj.* açık sarı renkli.

champ[1] [tʃæmp] *v/t. & v/i.* ısırmak, çiğnemek; *fig.* sinirden dişlerini sıkmak, sabırsızlanmak.

champ[2] F [-] *s.* **champion** *1.*

cham.pagne [ʃæm'pein] *n.* şampanya.

cham.paign ['tʃæmpein] *n.* ova, kır.

cham.pi.on ['tʃæmpjən] **1.** kahraman, savunucu kimse; *spor:* şampiyon; **2.** *v/t.*

b-ni müdafaa etm., korumak; **3.** *adj.* galip; muhteşem, mükemmel; '**cham-pion.ship** *n.* sampiyonluk; şampiyona.

chance [tʃɑːns] **1.** *n.* şans, talih; tesadüf; fırsat; ihtimal; **by** ~ tesadüfen; **take a** ~, **take one's** ~ işi şansa bırakmak, şans denemek; **2.** *adj.* şans eseri olan, tesadüfî; **3.** *v/t. & v/i.* bir kere denemek; göze almak; tesadüfen olm.; tesadüfe bırakmak; *I* ~*d to be there* tesadüfen oradaydım; ~ **upon** rastlamak *-e*; şans eseri bulmak *-i*.

chan.cel ARCH ['tʃɑːnsəl] *n.* kilisede mihrabın etrafında rahip ve koronun durduğu yer; '**chan.cel.ler.y** *n.* kançılarya, rektörlük (*makamı*, *bürosu*); '**chan.cel.lor** *n.* rektör; yüksek rütbeli devlet memuru; saray kâtibi; (*Almanya'da*) başbakan, şansölye.

chan.cer.y ['tʃɑːnsəri] *n.* (*İngiltere'de*) en yüksek mahkeme; (*Amerika'da*) tenyiz mahkemesi; **in** ~ temyiz mahkemesindeki dava; *fig.* müşkül durumda.

chanc.y F ['tʃɑːnsi] *adj.* tehlikeli, rizikolu.

chan.de.lier ['tʃændi'liə] *n.* avize.

chan.dler ['tʃɑːndlə] *n.* mum yapan veya satan kişi; '**chan.dler.y** *n.* hırdavatçı dükkânı.

change [tʃeindʒ] **1.** *n.* değiş(tir)me, değişiklik; sapma; yenilik; paranın üstü; bozukluk; **for a** ~ değişiklik olsun diye; **2.** *v/t.* değiştirmek; boz(dur)mak; *tren:* aktarma yapmak; (*üstünü*) değiştirmek; ~ **over** endüstri *vs.:* yöntem değiştirmek; *I've* ~*d my mind* fikrimi değiştirdim; *v/i.* başkalaşmak, değişmek; ~ **into second gear** MOT ikinci vitese geçmek; *a.* ~ **trains** (*trende*) aktarma yapmak; **change.a'bili.ty** *n.* değişebilirlik; '**change.a.ble** değişebilir; kararsız, dönek; '**change-gear** *n.* MEC sürat değiştirme düzeni; '**change.less** □ değişmez, sabit; **changeling** ['-liŋ] *n.* bebekken değiştirilmiş çocuk; cin veya perilerin lohusa yatağına koyduğu bozuk şekilli çocuk; '**change-'o.ver** *n.* yöntem değiştirme.

chan.nel ['tʃænl] **1.** *n.* kanal, boğaz; nehir yatağı; yol (*a. fig.*); **by the official** ~**s** resmî yoldan; **2.** *v/t.* kanal açmak; oymak; kanala dökmek; *fig.* yönlendirmek.

chant [tʃɑːnt] **1.** *n.* şarkı, dinî şarkı; monoton bir melodi, monoton ses tonu;

fig. can sıkıcı şarkı; **2.** *v/t.* şarkı söylemek, türkü çağırmak; teganni etm.; **chan.ticleer** *poet.* [tʃænti'kliə] *n.* evcil horoz; **chan.try** ECCL ['tʃɑːntri] *n.* (*kilise*) dua okunan bölüm; dua okutma parası; **chan.ty** ['_ti] *n.* gemici şarkısı, heyamola.

cha.os ['keiɔs] *n.* karışıklık; kaos; **cha-'ot.ic** *adj.* (*~ally*) karmakarışık, altüst olmuş, düzensiz.

chap[1] [tʃæp] **1.** *n.* yırtık, yarık, çatlak (*esp. deride*); **2.** *v/t.* & *v/i.* (*cildi*) çatla(t)mak; yar(ıl)mak; kızar(t)mak.

chap[2] [_] *n.* çenenin etli kısmı (*esp. hayvanlarda*).

chap[3] [_] *n.* oğlan, delikanlı, genç adam, arkadaş; '~-**book** *n.* küçük, ucuz kitap.

chap.el ['tʃæpəl] *n.* küçük kilise, mabet; (*okul v.b. yerlerde*) ibadete ayrılmış bölüm; TYP matbaa bürosu, matbaacılar birliği.

chap.er.on ['ʃæpərəun] **1.** *n.* bir genç kıza refakat eden yaşlıca kadın, yenge kadın, şaperon; **2.** *v/t.* şaperon olarak refakat etm.

chap-fall.en ['tʃæpfɔːlən] *adj.* kederli, mahzun.

chap.lain ['tʃæplin] *n.* papaz; '**chap-lain.cy** *n.* papazlık (*makam, bina veya bürosu*).

chap.let ['tʃæplit] *n.* (*başa takılan*) çelenk; ECCL tesbih.

chap.man ['tʃæpmən] *n.* seyyar satıcı.

chap.py ◻ ['tʃæpi] çatlamış, yarılmış, çatlak, yarık.

chap.ter ['tʃæptə] *n.* bölüm, kısım; bahis; katedrale bağlı rahipler.

char[1] ICHTH [tʃɑː] *n.* bir tür alabalık.

char[2] [_] *v/t.* & *v/i.* kömürleş(tir)mek; karbonlaş(tır)mak.

char[3] [_] **1.** *v/i.* gündelikle ev, ofis temizlemek; **2.** = **charwoman**.

char-à-banc ['ʃærəbæŋ] *n.* açık omnibüs, gezinti otobüsü.

char.ac.ter ['kæriktə] *n.* karakter, seciye; şöhret; vasıf, nitelik; özellik; işaret, harf, yazı; F orijinal *b-i*; THEAT, *roman*: canlandırılan kişi; sanatçının oynadığı rol, karakter; **char.ac.ter'is.tic 1.** *adj.* (*~ally*) karakteristik, kendine özgü, tipik; **2.** *n.* karakter özelliği, vasıf; **char-ac.ter.i.za.tion** [_rai'zeiʃən] *n.* tasvir, tarif, tanımlama; '**char.ac.ter.ize** *v/t.* tanımlamak; vasıflandırmak, karakterize etm.

cha.rade [ʃə'rɑːd] *n.* hece bilmecesi.

char.coal ['tʃɑːkəul] *n.* mangal kömürü; '~-**burn.er** *n.* kömürcü.

chard BOT ['tʃɑːd] *n.* pazı.

chare [tʃɛə] **1.** *vb.* temizlemek, yıkamak; **2.** *n. mst ~s pl.* ev işleri.

charge [tʃɑːdʒ] **1.** *n.* yük, hamule; şarj; MIL hamle, saldırı; sorumluluk; görev, memuriyet; masraf, fiyat; vergi, rüsum; bedel, ücret; JUR, ECCL suçlama, suç isnadı, itham; MIN bir cihazdaki elektrik miktarı, yükleme, şarj; *~s pl.* masraflar; *be in ~ of bş* ile görevli olm., *bşden* sorumlu olm.; *be in the ~ of s.o.* birisinden sorumlu olm.; *take~ of bşi* yüklenmek, sorumluluğunu üstüne almak; *free of ~* karşılıksız, ücretsiz; **2.** *v/t.* & *v/i.* yüklemek, doldurmak; suçlamak (*with ile*); hesabına geçirmek (*on, upon -in*); hücum etm. *-e*; ELECT şarj etm.; istemek (*fiyat*); hesabına kaydetmek, geçirmek; görev vermek; önermek, emretmek; *~ s.o. with the duty of b-ni bş* ile görevlendirmek; '**charge.a-ble** ◻ itham edilebilir, suçlanabilir (*with ile*); hesaba geçirilebilir; ödenebilir (*to -e*).

char.gé d'af.faires POL ['ʃɑːʒeidæ'fɛə] *n.* maslahatgüzar, işgüder.

charg.er *poet.*, MIL ['tʃɑːdʒə] *n.* savaş atı.

char.i.ot *poet.*, HIST ['tʃæriət] *n.* hafif iki tekerlekli araba, savaş arabası; **char-iot.eer** [_tiə] *n.* savaş arabasını süren arabacı.

char.i.ta.ble ◻ ['tʃæritəbl] cömert, hayırsever, yardımsever, fukara babası; *~ society* yardımsevenler derneği; '**chari.ta.ble.ness** *n.* cömertlik, hayırseverlik; merhamet, hoşgörülük.

char.i.ty ['tʃæriti] *n.* hayırseverlik; şefkat, merhamet; hayır, sadaka; *sister of ~* fakire yardım eden rahibe; *~ begins at home* şefkat insanın ev halkına yardım etmesi ile başlar; '~'**child** *n.* yetimler yurdunda yetişen çocuk; '~'**school** *n.* yetimler yurdu.

cha.ri.va.ri ['ʃɑːri'vɑːri] *n.* alay etm. için tencereye vurularak yapılan gürültü.

char.la.tan ['ʃɑːlətən] *n.* şarlatan, yalandan beceri sahibi olduğunu iddia eden kişi; '**char.la.tan.ry** *n.* şarlatanlık.

char.lock BOT ['tʃɑːlɔk] *n.* çalgıcıotu, yabani hardal.

char.lotte ['ʃɑːlət] *n.* bir tür puding.

charm [tʃɑːm] **1.** *n.* sihir, büyü, muska; *fig.* cazibe, çekicilik; **2.** *v/t.* büyülemek,

sihirlemek; *fig.* teshir etm.; meftun
etm.; ~ *away etc.* büyü ile etkileyerek
bşi ortadan kaldırmak, yoketmek;
'**charm.er** *n.* sihirbaz kadın, büyücü;
fig. teshir eden, etkileyen kadın veya
erkek; '**charming** □ çekici, cazip, cana
yakın.
char.nel-house ['tʃɑːnlhaus] *n.* ölü
kemiklerinin toplandığı mahzen.
chart [tʃɑːt] **1.** *n.* NAUT deniz haritası;
plan, çizelge, kroki; **2.** *v/t.* haritasını
yapmak, haritada göstermek; grafiğini
çıkarmak.
char.ter ['tʃɑːtə] **1.** *n.* berat, imtiyaz,
patent; NAUT gemi kira kontratı; *mst*
~-*party* gemi kira kontratı, navlun mukavelesi; **2.** *v/t.* berat, imtiyaz veya patent vermek; (*uçak, gemi*) kiralamak;
s. accountant.
char.wom.an ['tʃɑːwumən] *n.* temizleyici, gündelikçi (*kadın*).
char.y □ ['tʃɛəri] (*of*) dikkatli, itinalı;
düşünceli; tutumlu, pinti.
chase[1] [tʃeis] **1.** *n.* av, takip, kovalama;
kovalanan şey veya kişi; *give ~ to*
peşinde(n) koşmak *-in;* **2.** *vb.* kovalamak, takip etm.; avlamak; *fig.* acele
etm., koşmak.
chase[2] [_] *v/t.* çizmek, oymak, hakketmek; kabartma işleri yapmak (*maden,
tahta üzerine*).
chase[3] TYP [_] *n.* harfler için kullanılan
demir çerçeve.
chas.er ['tʃeisə] *n.* avcı, kovalayan; sert
içkinin üzerine alınan hafif içki veya
su; AVIA avcı uçağı.
chasm ['kæzəm] *n.* yarık, uçurum (*a.
fig.*); kanyon, dar boğaz.
chas.sis MOT ['ʃæsi] *n. pl.* **chas.sis**
['ʃæsiz] (*top, uçak, otomobil*) alt iskelet, şasi.
chaste □ [tʃeist] temiz, iffetli, nezih;
basit, sade, gösterişsiz, tantanasız (*üslup, stil*).
chas.ten ['tʃeisn] *v/t.* terbiyesini vermek *-in,* uslandırmak *-i,* yola getirmek
-i.
chas.tise [tʃæs'taiz] *v/t.* dövmek, cezalandırmak; **chas.tise.ment** ['_tiz-
mənt] *n.* dayak, kötek, ceza.
chas.ti.ty ['tʃæstiti] *n.* iffet, saffet, temizlik.
chas.u.ble ECCL ['tʃæzjubl] *n.* ayinde
papazın giydiği kolsuz kıyafet.
chat [tʃæt] **1.** *n.* konuşma, çene çalma,
sohbet; **2.** *v/i.* sohbet etm., konuşmak,
çene çalmak.

châ.teau ['ʃætəu] *n.* şato, büyük köşk
(*Fransa'da*).
chat line IT ['tʃætlain] *n. cinsel nitelikli
konuşmalar için aranan ücretli telefon
hattı;* **chat room** IT ['tʃætruːm] *n.* chat
odası.
chat.tels ['tʃætlz] *n. pl. mst goods and
~ her* türlü taşınır mal.
chat.ter ['tʃætə] **1.** *n.* gevezelik, boş lâf;
diş çatırdaması; **2.** *v/i.* çene çalmak;
(*diş*) çatırdamak; '~.**box** *n.* F boşboğaz,
geveze; '**chat.ter.er** *n.* geveze, farfa-
racı.
chat.ty ['tʃæti] *adj.* sohbet meraklısı,
geveze.
chauf.feur ['ʃəufə] *n.* şoför, araba sürücüsü; **chauf.feuse** [_'fəːz] *n.* kadın
şoför.
chau.vin.ism ['ʃəuvinizəm] *n.* aşırı
milliyetçilik, şovenlik, şovenizm;
'**chau.vinist** *n.* şoven; **chau.vin'is.tic**
adj. (~*ally*) şovenistliğe ait.
chaw *sl.* [tʃɔː] *v/t.* çiğnemek; ~ *up Am.
sl. mst fig.* mahvetmek, imha etm., yok
etm.; '~'**ba.con** *n.* budala, aptal.
cheap □ [tʃiːp] ucuz; değersiz (*a. fig.*);
bayağı, adî; *feel ~* F keyifsiz olm.; *mahcup* olm.; *hold ~ bşe* önem vermemek;
on the ~ F ucuza, ucuz olarak; *make
o.s. ~ k-ni* küçük düşürmek; ♀ *Jack*
seyyar satıcı; '**cheap.en** *v/t.* ucuzlatmak; *fig.* küçük düşürmek; *v/i.* ucuzlamak; '**cheapskate** *n. Am. sl.* cimri,
avantacı kişi.
cheat ['tʃiːt] **1.** *n.* hile, düzen; hileci, *sl.*
üçkağıtçı; **2.** *v/t.* aldatmak, dolandırmak, *bşi* hile ile birinin elinden almak
(*out of s.th.*); '**cheat.ing** *n.* aldatma,
dolandırma.
check [tʃek] **1.** *n.* engel, durdurma;
kontrol, teftiş; fiş, marka; MIL yenilgi,
hezimet; *Am.* kontrol işareti; *Am.*
eşya makbuzu; *Am.* COM = *cheque; Am.*
tranç: şah; *Am.* (*lokantada*) hesap pusulası; ~ *pattern* ekoseli kumaş; *pass
veya hand in one's ~s Am.* F ölmek;
keep s.o. in ~ b-ni kontrol etm., gözetmek; **2.** *v/t. & v/i.* önlemek, durdurmak; karşılaştırmak, kontrol etm.;
Am. defterine işaret koymak; *satranç:*
şah çekmek; ~ *in Am.* otel defterine
kaydolmak; ~ *one's baggage Am.*
b-nin bavullarını kontrol etm.; ~ *out*
otelden parasını ödeyip ayrılmak; ~
up kontrol etm.; ~ *up on* soruşturmak,
araştırmak; **checked** *adj.* kareli, ekose; '**check.er** *n.* gözcü, müfettiş; dama,

kare, ekose desen; ~s pl. Am. dama
oyunu; = *chequer*; 'check.ered *adj*.
kareli, damalı; 'check.ing *n*. kontrol;
'check-mate 1. *n. satranç*: mat; yenilgi;
2. *v/t. satranç*: mat etm., yenmek (*a.
fig*); 'check-point *n*. kontrol noktası;
'check-room *n. Am.* vestiyer;
'check-up *n. Am.* tıbbî kontrol.

Ched.dar ['tʃedə] *n*. bir çeşit krem peynir, çedar peyniri.

cheek [tʃiːk] 1. *n*. yanak; F arsızlık, yüzsüzlük; MEC fren takozu; *s. jowl*; 2. *v/t.* F
küstahlık etmek -*e*; 'cheek-bone *n*. elmacık kemiği; 'cheek.y *adj.* F yüzsüz,
küstah.

cheep [tʃiːp] *v/i.* cıvıldamak, kuş gibi
cik cik etm.

cheer [tʃiə] 1. *n.* alkış, «yaşa!» sesi;
neşe; *be of good ~* yüreğini ferah tutmak; *three ~s!* üç defa «yaşa!, yaşa!,
yaşa!»; 2. *v/t.* alkışlamak, neşelendirmek; *a. ~ up b-ni* teselli etm, avutmak;
a. ~ on teşvik etm, alkışla cesaret vermek; *v/i.* sevinçle bağırmak, sevinç sesleri çıkarmak; *a. ~ up* cesaretlenmek;
keyiflenmek; sevinmek; 'cheer.ful □
neşeli, şen; 'cheer.ful.ness, 'cheer.i-
ness *n.* neşelilik, neşe; 'cheer.ing *n.*
alkış, cesaret verme; 'cheer.i.o
['_ri'əu] *int.* F Allaha ısmarladık!; merhaba!; 'cheer.less □ neşesiz, kederli;
kasvetli; 'cheer.y □ neşeli, şen.

cheese ['tʃiːz] *n.* peynir; *sl.* mükemmel;
~burg.er *n.* peynirli köfte; '~-cake *n.*
peynirli kek; *sl.* duvara yapıştırılan güzel kadın posteri; '~-cloth *n.* tülbent;
'~-monger *n.* peynirci; '~-par.ing 1.
adj. cimri, pinti; hesabî; 2. *n.* değersiz
şey; hesabîlik.

chees.y ['tʃiːziː] *adj.* peynirli, peynir
gibi.

chee.tah ZOO ['tʃiːtə] *n.* avda kullanılan parsa benzer bir hayvan.

chef [ʃef] *n.* şef, ahçıbaşı.

chem.i.cal ['kemikəl] 1. □ kimyevî,
kimyasal; 2. 'chem.i.cals *n. pl.* kimyevî
maddeler.

che.mise [ʃə'miːz] *n.* (*kadın*) iç gömleği.

chem.ist ['kemist] *n.* kimyager; eczacı;
~'s shop eczane; 'chem.is.try *n.* kimya.

chem.o.ther.a.py MED [keməu'θerəpi]
n. kemoterapi, kimyevî maddelerle tedavi.

cheque COM [tʃek] *n.* çek; *not negotia-
ble* ~, *crossed* ~ çizgili çek; '~-book *n.*

çek defteri.

chequer ['tʃekə] 1. *n. mst ~s pl.* dama
oyunu; 2. *v/t.* damalı yapmak, ekose
desen ile kaplamak; 'cheq.uered *adj.*
kareli, satrançlı; *fig.* karışık, değişik.

cher.ish ['tʃeriʃ] *v/t.* beslemek; gütmek; *b-ni* aziz ve el üstünde tutmak.

che.root [ʃə'ruːt] *n.* bir çeşit yaprak sigara, puro.

cher.ry ['tʃeri] 1. *n.* kiraz; kiraz ağacı; 2.
adj. parlak kırmızı.

cher.ub ['tʃerəb] *n.* melek; nur yüzlü
kimse; nur topu gibi çocuk; che.ru.bic
[_'ruːbik] *adj.* melek gibi.

cher.vil BOT ['tʃəːvil] *n.* frenk maydano-
zu.

chess [tʃes] *n.* satranç oyunu; '~-board
n. satranç tahtası; '~-man *n.* satranç
taşı.

chest [tʃest] *n.* sandık, kutu, kasa; ANAT
göğüs; ~ *of drawers* konsol, çekmeceli
dolap; *get s.th. off one's* ~ *b-ne* içini
dökmek; 'chest.ed *comb.* ...göğüslü.

ches.ter.field ['tʃestəfiːld] *n.* uzun palto; kabarık kanepe.

chest.nut ['tʃesnʌt] 1. *n.* kestane; kestane ağacı; F bayat espri; 2. *adj.* kestane rengi, maron.

che.val-glass [ʃə'vælglɑːs] *n.* boy aynası.

chev.a.lier [ʃevə'liə] *n.* şövalye, silahşör; cesur ve mert kimse.

chev.i.ot ['tʃeviət] *n.* bir çeşit İskoç ko-
yunu; bu koyunun yününden yapılan
kumaş, şevyot.

chev.ron MIL ['ʃevrən] *n.* çavuş ve onbaşı rütbelerine ait kol şeridi.

chev.y F ['tʃevi] 1. *n.* av (narası); 2. *v/t.
& v/i.* avla(n)mak.

chew [tʃuː] *v/t. & v/i.* çiğnemek; derin
düşüncelere dalmak (*on, upon, over*);
~ *the fat veya rag sl.* çene çalmak, laklak etm.; 'chew.ing-gum *n.* çiklet.

chi.cane [ʃi'kein] 1. *n.* hile, şike; 2. *v/t.
& v/i.* hile yapmak; chi'can.er.y *n.* hilekârlık; *fig.* dalavere.

chick [tʃik] *s. chicken.*

chick.a.dee Am. ORN ['tʃikədiː] *n.* iskete kuşu.

chick.a.ree Am. ZOO ['tʃikəriː] *n.*
kırmızı Amerikan sincabı.

chick.en ['tʃikin] *n.* piliç, civciv; tavuk
eti; *sl.* korkak; '~-feed *n. Am.* tavuk yemi; *sl.* bozuk para, az para; '~-heart.ed
adj. korkak; '~-pox *n.* MED suçiçeği;
'chick-pea *n.* BOT nohut; 'chick.weed
n. BOT kuş out.

chic.o.ry ['tʃikəri] *n.* hindiba.

chid [tʃid] *pret. & p.p.*, '**chid.den** *p.p.*
of *chide*.

chide *lit.* [tʃaid] *(irr.) vb. b-ni* azarlamak, ayıplamak; *b-ne* çıkışmak, söylenmek.

chief [tʃiːf] **1.** □ büyük, en önemli,
baş…, ana…, belli başlı; ~ *clerk* daire
şefi, kalem amiri; **2.** *n.* baş, reis, şef,
âmir, **chieftain** ['tʃən] *n.* kabile reisi.

chif.fon ['ʃifɔn] *n.* şifon; **chif.fo.nier**
[ʃifə'niə] *n.* aynalı, çekmeceli dolap,
şifoniyer.

chil.blain ['tʃilblein] *n.* MED soğuk
şişliği.

child [tʃaild] *n., pl.* **chil.dren** ['tʃildrən]
çocuk; *be a good ~!* uslu dur!, iyi ço-
cuk ol!; *from a ~* küçükten beri; *with ~*
hamile; *~'s play fig.* çocuk oyuncağı,
kolay, basit iş; '~**bed** *n.* lohusa yatağı;
'~**birth** *n.* doğum; '**child.hood** *n.* çocukluk; *second ~* bunaklık; '**child.ish**
□ çocukça; *b.s.* aptal, budala; '**child-
ish.ness** *n.* çocuksuluk, çocukçalık;
b.s. dar düşüncelilik; '**child.less** *n.* çocuksuz; '**childlike** *adj. fig.* çocuk gibi,
çocuk ruhlu; **chil.dren** ['tʃildrən] *pl.*
of *child*.

chil.i *Am.* BOT ['tʃili] *n.* kırmızı biber
cinsi.

chill [tʃil] **1.** *adj. lit.* buz gibi soğuk; **2.** *n.*
soğuk; titreme, üşüme; *fig.* soğuk dav-
ranış; soğuk algınlığı; *take the ~ off a
liquid* sıvıyı hafifçe ısıtmak; **3.** *v/t.*
soğutmak; üşütmek; *metall.* soğutmak,
su vermek; *~ed meat* dondurulmuş et;
v/i. soğumak; soğuktan titremek, donmak; *~ out* F dinlenmek, rahatlamak;
'**chill.ness**, '**chill.i.ness** *n.* soğuk;
soğuk davranış; '**chill.y** *adj.* soğuk, serin; hep üşüyen.

chime [tʃaim] **1.** *n.* ahenkli çan sesi; *fig.*
ahenk; **2.** *v/t. & v/i.* çan çal(ın)mak; *fig.*
hepbir ahenk olm.; *~ in* uymak (*with
-e*).

chi.me.ra [kai'miərə] *n.* hayalî canavar,
ejderha; korkunç hayal; **chi.mer.i.cal**
□ [~'merikəl] hayalî; imkânsız.

chim.ney ['tʃimni] *n.* baca; lamba şişesi; yanardağ ağzı (*a.* MOUNT); '~**-piece**
n. şömine üstü, ocak rafı; '~**-pot** *n.*
ocak külâhı; F *fig.* silindir şapka;
'~**-stalk** *n.* baca tepesi; fabrika bacası;
'~**-sweep(.er)** *n.* baca temizleyicisi.

chim.pan.zee ZOO [tʃimpən'ziː] *n.*
şempanze.

chin ¹ [tʃin] *n.* çene; *keep one's ~ up* F

güçlüğe korkmadan göğüs germek;
wag one's ~ konuşmak, çene çalmak.

chin ² *sl.* [~] *v/i.* yarenlik etm., çene çalmak.

chi.na ['tʃainə] *n.* porselen; '**2.man** *n.*
Çinli.

chine [tʃain] *n.* belkemiği, sırt; sırttan
çıkarılan et.

Chi.nese ['tʃai'niːz] **1.** *n.* Çince; Çinli;
2. *adj.* Çin'e ait, Çince'ye ve Çinlilere
ait.

chink ¹ [tʃiŋk] *n.* yarık, çatlak.

chink ² [~] **1.** *n.* şıkırtı; çınlama; **2.** *v/t. &
v/i.* şıngırda(t)mak, tıngırda(t)mak.

chintz [tʃints] *n.* basma, perdelik pamuklu ve desenli kumaş.

chip [tʃip] **1.** *n.* çentik; yonga; küçük
parça; kırıntı; kuşun «çip» sesi;
kızarmış patates; fiş, marka; *have a
~ on one's shoulder* meydan okumak,
kavgaya hazır olm.; **2.** *v/t.* yontmak,
çentmek; *v/i.* (*kuş*) çip sesi çıkarmak;
~ in F bşe iştirak etm., para koymak;
Am. F aniden konuşmaya girmek, sözünü kesmek; **chip.muck** ['~mʌk],
chip.munk ['~mʌŋk] *n.* derisi çizgili
ufak sincap; '**chip.py** *adj.* kurak, verimsiz, zayıf; F sarhoşluktan sonra
olan mide bulantısı.

chirp [tʃəːp] **1.** *n.* cıvıltı; **2.** *v/t. & v/i.*
cıvıldamak, cırcır ötmek; '**chirp.y**
adj. F neşeli, şen.

chirr [tʃəː] *v/i.* (*çekirge v.b.*) sesi çıkarmak.

chir.rup ['tʃirəp] **1.** *v/i.* neşe ile cıvıldamak; **2.** *n.* cıvıltı.

chis.el ['tʃizl] **1.** *n.* çelik kalem, kalem
keski; **2.** *v/t.* kalemle oymak, yontmak;
F dolandırmak; '**chis.el.er** *n.* oymacı;
F dolandırıcı, üçkâğıtçı.

chit [tʃit] *n.* çocuk, yavrucuk; *a ~ of a
girl* delişmen kız.

chit-chat ['tʃittʃæt] *n.* lâf, sohbet.

chiv.al.rous □ ['ʃivəlrəs] mert, kibar,
şövalye gibi; '**chiv.al.ry** *n.* şövalyelik,
kahramanlık, cömertlik, mertlik;
şövalyeler.

chive BOT [tʃaiv] *n.* bir tür taze soğan.

chiv.(v)y F ['tʃivi] = *chevy*.

chlo.ral CHEM ['klɔːrəl] *n.* kloralhidrat;
chloride ['~aid] *n.* klorid; *~ of lime*

kalsiyum klorid; **chlo.rin.ate** ['ˌineit] *v/t.* (*suyu*) sterilize etm., klorlamak; **chlo.rine** ['ˌiːn] *n.* klor; **chlo.ro.form** ['klɔrəfɔːm] **1.** *n.* kloroform; **2.** *v/t.* kloroformla bayıltmak; **chlor.o.phyll** ['ˌɔfil] *n.* bitkilere yeşillik veren madde, klorofil.

choc-ice ['tʃɔkais] *n.* dışı çikolata ile kaplı dondurma.

chock MEC [tʃɔk] **1.** *n.* odun parçası, takoz, kama; difizör; **2.** *v/t.* tıkamak, takozlamak, destek koymak; '~-a-'**block** hıncahınç, tıkabasa (**with** *ile*); '~-'**full** *adj.* dopdolu.

choc.o.late ['tʃɔkəlit] *n.* çikolata; ~ **cream** çikolatalı şekerleme; fondan.

choice [tʃɔis] **1.** *n.* seçme, tercih; tercih hakkı; seçenek, seçilen şey; **have one's** ~ *b-nin* seçme hakkı olm.; **make** *veya* **take one's** ~ kendi tercihini yapmak, almak; **multiple** ~ çok seçenekli (*soru şekli*); **2.** □ seçkin, seçme, güzide, titiz; ~ **fruit** dikkatlice seçilmiş meyva.

choir ['kwaiə] *n.* koro; (*kilisede*) koro yeri.

choke [tʃəuk] **1.** *v/t. & v/i.* tıka(n)mak, boğ(ul)mak (*a. fig.*); MEC boğmak; ELECT kısmak; *mst* ~ **down** zorla yutmak; ~ **off** F durdurmak; vazgeçirmek, menetmek (*from -den*); *mst* ~ **up** tıkanmak; **2.** *n.* boğma, tıkama; MEC daraltma; MOT jigle; ~ **coil** ELECT kısma bobini; '~-**bore** *n.* MEC namlu çapının yavaş yavaş azalması; '~-**damp** *n.* MIN patlamadan sonra madendeki karbondioksit gazı, boğucu gaz; '**chok.er** *n. co.* boğan şey *veya* kimse; madeni gerdanlık; dik yaka; '**chok.y 1.** *adj.* boğazı tıkayan, boğucu; **2.** *n. sl.* hapishane.

chol.er.a MED ['kɔlərə] *n.* kolera; '**chol.er.ic** *adj.* canıtez; öfkesi burnunda.

choose [tʃuːz] (*irr.*) *v/t.* seçmek, tercih etm.; ~ **to** *inf.* *bşi* üstün tutmak, öne almak; '**choos.y** *adj.* titiz, zor beğenen.

chop¹ [tʃɔp] **1.** *n.* darbe, kesme; çırpıntı; parça; pirzola; ~*s pl.* çene, hayvan ağzı; MEC marangoz mengenesi; ~*s and changes pl.* devamlı değişmeler; **2.** *v/t.* balta ile kesmek, yarmak; *usu.* ~ **up** *bşi* kıymak, doğramak; *v/i.* değişmek; ~ **about** (*rüzgâr*) değişmek, dönmek (*a. fig.*); ~ **and change** ne yapacağını bilmemek, bir dakikası bir dakikasına uymamak.

chop² COM [-] *n.* nişan, alamet, marka;

first ~ birinci sınıf, en üstün kalite.

chop-chop *sl.* ['tʃɔp'tʃɔp] *adv.* süratle, gecikmeksizin.

chop-house ['tʃɔphaus] *n.* kebapçı, lokanta; '**chop.per** *n.* el baltası, kasap satırı; F helikopter; '**chop.ping** *n.* kesiş, vuruş; '**chop.py** *adj.* değişken, yön değiştiren (*rüzgâr*); çırpıntılı (*deniz*); = **chappy**; '**chop.stick** *n.* Çinlilerin yemek yerken kullandıkları çubuk; **chop-su.ey** [-'suːi] *n.* Çin lokantalarına ait et suyu veya balıkla pişirilen pirinçli yemek.

cho.ral ['kɔːrəl] koro ile ilgili; koro için yapılmış; **cho.ral(e)** MUS [kɔ'raːl] *n.* kilise ilâhisi, koral.

chord [kɔːd] *n.* MUS, *poet.* kiriş, tel; *fig.* his, duygu; MATH veter, kiriş; MUS akort.

chore *part. Am.* [tʃɔː] = **chare 2**.

chor.ine ['kɔːriːn] *s.* **chorus-girl**.

chor.is.ter ['kɔristə] *n.* koro üyesi, korodaki çocuk; *Am. a.* koro şefi.

cho.rus ['kɔːrəs] **1.** *n.* koro, koro parçası; nakarat, şarkının koro kısmı; **2.** *v/t.* koroda şarkı söylemek; '~-**girl** revüde şarkı söyleyip dans eden kız.

chose [tʃouz] *pret.*, '**cho.sen** *p.p. of* **choose**.

chough ORN [tʃʌf] *n.* küçük karga.

chouse F [tʃaus] **1.** *n.* hile, oyun; **2.** *v/t.* aldatmak, dolandırmak, hile yapmak.

chow *Am. sl.* [tʃau] *n.* yemek, yiyecek.

chow.der *Am.* ['tʃaudə] *n.* bir çeşit balık türlüsü.

chrism ['krizəm] *n.* kutsal mesh yağı.

Christ [kraist] *n.* Hazreti İsa.

chris.ten ['krisn] *v/t.* vaftiz etm., isimlendirmek; **Chris.ten.dom** ['ˌdəm] *n.* Hıristiyan âlemi; '**chris.ten.ing** *n.* vaftiz; vaftiz etme, isimlendirme.

Chris.tian ['kristjən] **1.** □ Hıristiyan, İsa'ya inanan kişi; ~ **name** vaftizde verilen isim; ~ **Science** İsa'nın prensipleri ile kötülük ve fenalıkların yok olabileceğine inanan mezhep; **2.** *n.* Hıristiyan; **Chris.ti.an.i.ty** [-ti'æniti] *n.* Hıristiyanlık; **Chris.tian.ize** ['ˌtjənaiz] *v/t.* Hıristiyanlaştırmak.

Christ.mas ['krisməs] *n.* **Noel**, İsa'nın doğum yortusu; ~ **Day** Noel (*25 Aralık günü*); ~ **Eve** Noel arifesi; '~-**box** *n.* **No.el** hediyeleri ile dolu kutu; '~-**tree** *n.* **Noel** ağacı.

chro.mat.ic PHYS, MUS [krəu'mætik] *adj.* (~*ally*) renklere ait; seslerin yarımşar ton ara ile birbirini takip etmesine ait, kromatik; **chro'mat.ics** *n. pl. &*

sg. renkler ilmi.

chrome CHEM [krəum] *n.* krom; krom boyası; **chro.mi.um** ['‿jəm] *n.* krom (*metal*); '**chro.mi.um-**'**plat.ed** krome, kromlu; **chromo.lith.o.graph** ['‿əu-'liθəugrɑ:f] *n.* renkli taş basma.

chron.ic ['krɔnik] *adj.* (**‿ally**) sürekli, süreğen, müzmin, kronik (*mst* MED); P tiksindirici; iğrenç, nefret uyandırıcı; **chron.i.cle** ['‿l] **1.** *n.* tarih, vakayiname; **2.** *v/t.* tarih sırası ile yazmak; '**chron.i.cler** *n.* tarihçi, tarihe kaydeden kimse.

chron.o.log.i.cal □ [krɔnə'lɔdʒikəl] kronolojik, tarih sırası ile düzenlenmiş; **‿ly** *adv.* tarih sırasına göre; **chro-nol.o.gy** [krə'nɔlədʒi] *n.* kronoloji; olayların tarih sırası ile hazırlanmış listesi.

chro.nom.e.ter [krə'nɔmitə] *n.* vakti inceden inceye ölçen alet, kronometre.

chrys.a.lis ['krisəlis] *n.* böceğin kelebek olmadan koza içindeki hali, krizalit.

chrys.an.the.mum BOT [kri'sænθə-məm] *n.* kasımpatı, krizantem.

chub ICHTH [tʃʌb] *n.* kefal, sazan balığı cinsinden tatlı su balığı; '**chub-by** *adj.* F tombul, hantal (*a. fig.*).

chuck¹ [tʃʌk] **1.** *vb.* gurklamak; *my* **‿!** şekerim!, yavrum!, kuzum!; **2.** *n.* gurklama; **3. ‿! ‿!** bili! bili! (*tavuk çağırmak için*).

chuck² F [‿] **1.** *v/t.* atmak, fırlatmak; **‿** *out* atmak, çöpe atmak; kapı dışarı etm.; **‿** *under the chin* çenesini okşamak; **‿** *it! sl.* bırak!; durdur!; **2.** *n.* atma, fırlatma.

chuck³ MEC [‿] *n.* torna bağlama aynası.

chuck.le ['tʃʌkl] *v/i.* kendi kendine gülmek, kıkır kıkır gülmek.

chug [tʃʌg] *n.* çalışırken çıkan ses (*motor vs.*).

chum F [tʃʌm] **1.** *n.* yakın arkadaş; *be great* **‿s** yakın arkadaş olm.; **2.** *v/i.* arkadaşlık etm., beraber oturmak.

chump F [tʃʌmp] *n.* odun parçası, kütük, takoz; sersem, budala, odun kafalı; *off one's* **‿** ahmak.

chunk F [tʃʌŋk] *n.* kısa kalın parça; kısa boylu tıknaz adam; '**chunk.y** *adj.* kısa ve kalın, tıknaz; topak topak.

church [tʃə:tʃ] **1.** *n.* kilise, dini örgüt; din adamlığı; ♀ *of England* Anglikan kilisesi; **‿** *service* ayini ruhanî; **2.** *vb.*

be **‿ed** kilisede şükran duası etm. (*doğumdan sonra kadınlar*); '**‿-go.er** *n.* devamlı kiliseye giden kişi; '**church.ing** *n.* (*doğum yapan kadının*) kilisedeki şükran duası, ibadet; '**church.man** *n.* papaz, kiliseye mensup kimse; '**church'ward.en** *n.* kilise mütevellisi; kilise işlerini idare eden fahri görevli; '**church'yard** *n.* kilise avlusu; mezarlık.

churl [tʃə:l] *n.* köylü, herif; kaba adam; pinti; '**churl.ish** □ vahşi, kaba; ters; paraya önem veren.

churn [tʃə:n] **1.** *n.* yayık; süt kabı; **2.** *v/t.* yayıkta çalkalamak, köpürtmek; *v/i.* yayık dövmek; çalkalanmak.

chute [ʃu:t] *n.* çağlayan, şelale, su oluğu; paraşüt.

chut.ney ['tʃʌtni] *n.* baharlı bir çeşit salça.

chyle [kail] *n.* barsaklarda bulunan beyaz bir sıvı, kilüs.

chyme [kaim] *n.* midede yarı hazmedilmiş gıda, kimus.

ci.ca.da ZOO [si'kɑ:də] *n.* ağustosböceği.

cic.a.trice ['sikətris] *n.* yara kapatan zar, yara izi; **cic.a.tri.za.tion** [‿trai-'zeiʃən] *n.* (*yaranın*) zar *veya* deri bağlayarak iyileşmesi; '**cic.a.trize** *v/t.* & *v/i.* kapatmak; iyileşmek, kabuk bağlamak (*yara*).

ci.ce.ro.ne [tʃitʃə'rəuni] *n.* turist gezdiren rehber, tercüman.

Cic.e.ro.ni.an [sisə'rəunjən] *adj.* Çiçero gibi; belâgat sahibi.

ci.der ['saidə] *n.* elma suyu, elma şarabı.

ci.gar [si'gɑ:] *n.* yaprak sigarası; puro; **ci'gar-case** *n.* puro tabakası.

cig.a.rette [sigə'ret] *n.* sigara; **cig.a-'rette-case** *n.* tabaka, sigaralık.

ci.gar-hold.er [si'gɑ:həuldə] *n.* ağızlık.

cil.i.a ['siliə] *n. pl.* kirpikler; **cil.i.ar.y** ['siliəri] *adj.* kirpiksi.

cinch *Am. sl.* [sintʃ] *n.* çok kolay şey, çantada keklik.

cin.cho.na BOT [siŋ'kəunə] *n.* kınakına ağacı.

cinc.ture ['siŋktʃə] *n.* kuşak, kemer.

cin.der ['sində] *n.* dışık, cüruf, maden artığı; köz, kor; **‿s** *pl.* kül; **Cin.der.el.la** [‿'relə] *n.* (*ünlü hikâyedeki gibi*) yeteneği ve güzelliği takdir edilmemiş kız, Sinderella; *fig.* ihmal edilmiş şey *veya* kimse; '**cin.der-track** *n.* spor: atletizm pisti.

cin.e-cam.er.a ['sinikæmərə] *n.* **film** çekme makinesi.

cin.e.ma ['sinəmə] *n.* sinema; sinema dünyası; **cin.e.mat.o.graph** [ˌ'mætəgrɑ:f] *n.* sinema makinesi, *film* çekme makinesi; **cin.e.mat.o.graph.ic** [ˌ-mætə'græfik] *adj.* (*~ally*) sinema makinesiyle ilgili.

cin.er.ar.y ['sinərəri] *adj.* kül ile ilgili.

cin.na.bar ['sinəbɑ:] *n.* zincifre.

cin.na.mon ['sinəmən] *n.* tarçın.

cinque [siŋk] *n. iskambil:* beşli; *zar:* beş (*penç*); *~ foil* BOT beşparmak otu.

ci.pher ['saifə] **1.** *n.* şifre; sıfır; *fig.* solda sıfır, hiç; *in ~* şifreli; **2.** *vb.* şifre ile yazmak, şifrelemek; hesap yapmak.

cir.ca ['sə:kə] *adv.* takriben, yaklaşık olarak.

cir.cle ['sə:kl] **1.** *n.* daire, halka, çevre; grup; devir; *ring*; meydan; THEAT balkon; **2.** *vb.* devretmek, dönmek; çevirmek, kuşatmak; **cir.clet** ['ˌklit] *n.* halkacık, küçük daire.

circs F [sə:ks] = *circumstances.*

cir.cuit ['sə:kit] *n.* daire, dolaşım; ELECT devre; JUR (*İngiltere'de*) seyyar mahkeme; AVIA uçakla tur atma; *short ~* ELECT kısa devre, kontak; *~ breaker* ELECT devre kapatan anahtar; *make a ~ of bşin* etrafını dolaşmak; **cir.cu.i.tous** □ [sə:'kju:itəs] dolaşık, dolambaçlı; *~ route* dolmabaçlı yol.

cir.cu.lar ['sə:kjulə] **1.** □ dairevî, dairesel; dolaylı; dolambaçlı; *~ letter* sirküler; *~ note* COM tamim, kredi mektubu; *~ saw* daire testere; *~ skirt* kloş etek; **2.** *n.* tamim, genelge, sirküler; '**cir.cu.lar.ize** *v/t.* sirküler yollamak.

cir.cu.late ['sə:kjuleit] *v/t. & v/i.* deveran etm.; dağıtmak; dolaş(tır)mak; dön(dür)mek; COM tedavül (et(tir)-mek; yay(ıl)mak); '**cir.cu.lat.ing**: *~ decimal* devirli ondalık kesir; *~ library* dışarıya ödünç kitap veren kütüphane; *~ medium* değişim aracı, para; **cir.cu-'la.tion** *n.* dolaşma; deveran; dağıtım miktarı, tiraj; piyasadaki para miktarı.

cir.cum... ['sə:kəm] *prefix* takriben, ...kadar; **cir.cum.cise** MED, eccl. [ˌ'saiz] *v/t.* sünnet etm.; **cir.cum.ci-sion** [ˌ'siʒən] *n.* sünnet; **cir.cum.fer-ence** [sə'kʌmfərəns] *n.* daire çevresi, çember; **cir.cum.flex** ['sə:kəmfleks] *n.* GR uzatma işareti; **circum.ja.cent** [ˌ'dʒəisənt] *adj.* dört taraftan bitişik, efraftaki; **cir.cum.lo.cu.tion** [ˌ-lə'kju:-ʃən] *n.* dolambaçlı söz; **cir.cumloc.u-**

tory [ˌ'lɔkjutəri] *adj.* dolambaçlı, uzun uzadıya; **cir.cum'nav.i.gate** *v/t.* gemi ile etrafını dolaşmak; **cir.cum-'nav.iga.tor** *n.* gemi ile dünyanın etrafını dolaşan kişi; **cir.cum.scribe** MATH ['ˌskraib] *v/t.* bir şeklin etrafına başka bir şekil çizmek, daire içine almak *-i*; sınırlamak *-i* (*a. fig.*); **cir.cum-scrip.tion** MATH [ˌ'skripʃən] *n.* etrafını çizme, kuşatma sınırlama; sınır çizgisi; **cir.cum.spect** □ ['ˌspekt] dikkatli, ihtiyatlı; **cir.cum.spection** [ˌ'spekʃən] *n.* dikkat, özen, dikkatlilik; **cir.cum-stance** ['ˌtəns] *n.* hal, durum, keyfiyet; olay; ayrıntı; *~s pl.* durum, ahval; malî durum; *in veya under the ~s* bu şartlar altında; '**cir.cumstanced** *comb.* ...bir halde bulunan; *poorly ~* kötü, fakir durumda olan kişi; **cir.cum.stan.tial** [ˌ'stænʃəl] □ tafsilatlı, ayrıntılı, uzun uzadıya; tâli, ikinci derecede önemi olan; *~ evidence* JUR emare, ikinci derecede delil; **cir.cum-vent** [ˌ'vent] *v/t.* aldatmak, hile ile galip gelmek.

cir.cus ['sə:kəs] *n.* sirk; meydan.

cir.rus ['sirəs] *n., pl.* **cir.ri** ['ˌrai] saçak bulut, sirrus.

cis.sy ['sisi] = *sissy.*

cis.tern ['sistən] *n.* sarnıç, su deposu.

cit.a.del ['sitədl] *n.* hisar, kale.

ci.ta.tion [sai'teiʃən] *n.* mahkemeye davet, celp; başka eserden alınan metin parçası; (*iyi hal veya kahramanlığı belirten*) resmî bildiri; **cite** *v/t.* celbetmek, mahkemeye davet etm.; beyan etm.; zikretmek, anmak; (*iyi hal veya kahramanlığı*) resmî bildiri ile açıklamak.

cit.i.zen ['sitizn] *n.* hemşeri; vatandaş; MIL sivil; **cit.i.zen.ship** ['ˌʃip] *n.* vatandaşlık, tabiiyet.

cit.ric ac.id ['sitrik'æsid] *n.* sitrik asit; **citron.** ['ˌrən] *n.* ağaçkavunu; ağaçkavunu kabuğu şekerlemesi; **cit.rus** ['ˌrəs] *adj.* turunçgillere ait.

cit.y ['siti] **1.** *n.* şehir, kent; site; *the ♀* Londra'nın iş merkezi; **2.** *adj.* şehir veya belediyeye ait; *~ editor Am.* yöresel haberler yazım sorumlusu; *~ hall Am.* belediye; belediye dairesi; *~ manager Am.* belediye başkanı; *~ state site kent,* şehir devleti.

civ.ic ['sivik] *adj.* şehre ait, belediye ile ilgili; yurttaşlık ile ilgili; madenî; sivil; *~ rights pl.* vatandaşlık hakları; '**civ-ics** *n. sg.* yurttaşlık bilgisi.

civ.il □ ['sivl] *vatandaşlarla ilgili; sivil; nazik; uygar, medenî; iç, dahilî; JUR medenî hukukla ilgili; ~ *ceremony* medeni nikah; ~ *defence* pasif korunma, sivil savunma; ~ *war* iç savaş; ≈ *Servant* devlet memuru; ≈ *Service* devlet hizmeti; **ci.vil.ian** MIL [si'viljən] *n.* sivil şahıs; ~ *population* sivil halk, siviller; **ci'vil.i.ty** *n.* nezaket; **civ.i.li.za.tion** [ˌlai'zeiʃən] *n.* medeniyet, uygarlık; **'civ.i.lize** *v/t.* medenileştirmek, uygar düzeye çıkarmak; ~*d nation* uygar, medenî millet.

civ.vies *sl.* ['siviz] *n. pl.* sivil kıyafet; **'civvy street** *sl.* başıbozuk hayat.

clack [klæk] **1.** *n.* tıkırtı, çıtırtı; *fig.* zevzeklik; MEC klape, subap; **2.** *v/i.* takırdamak; *fig.* laklak etm., boşboğazlık etm.

clad *lit.* [klæd] *pret. & p.p. of **clothe***; *hills* ~ *in verdure poet.* yamaçlar yeşillendi.

claim [kleim] **1.** *n.* istek, talep; JUR iddia; MIN paylaştırılan arazi; *lay* ~ *to* sahip çıkmak -*e*; **2.** *vb.* iddia etm.; istemek; sahip çıkmak; ~ *to be* ... olduğunu iddia etm.; **'claim.a.ble** *adj.* talep edilebilir; **'claim.ant** *n.* iddialı; JUR davacı, alacaklı, hak talep eden.

clair.voy.ance [klɛə'vɔiəns] *n.* geleceği görme yeteneği (*a. fig.*); **clair-'voy.ant(e)** *n.* görünmez şeyleri gören, gaipten haber veren kişi.

clam ZOO [klæm] *n.* bir tür istiridye, tarak.

cla.mant *lit.* ['klemənt] *adj.* gürültülü; ısrarlı.

clam.ber ['klæmbə] *v/i.* (güçlükle) tırmanmak.

clam.mi.ness ['klæminis] *n.* yapışkanlık; **'clam.my** □ soğuk ve ıslak, nemli, yapışkan.

clam.or.ous □ ['klæmərəs] gürültülü, şamatalı; **'clam.our 1.** *n.* gürültü, patırtı; **2.** *vb.* gürültü etm.; yaygara koparmak (*for* için).

clamp[1] MEC [klæmp] **1.** *n.* kenet, köşebent; **2.** *v/t.* bşi bağlamak, raptetmek, tesbit etm.

clamp[2] [ˌ] *n.* yeraltı stoğu (*patates vs.*).

clan [klæn] *n.* kabile, klan; takım, zümre; *fig.* geniş aile.

clan.des.tine □ [klæn'destin] gizli, el altından.

clang [klæŋ] **1.** *n.* şakırtı, takırtı, çınlama; **2.** *v/t. & v/i.* yüksek sesle çal(dır)mak; **clang.or.ous** [ˈˌgərəs] *adj.* gü-

rültülü ses çıkaran; **'clang.o.(u)r** = *clang.*

clank [klæŋk] **1.** *n.* maden sesi, tınlama, çınlama; **2.** *v/t. & v/i.* madenî ses çıkart(tır)mak.

clan.nish ['klæniʃ] *adj.* klana, kabileye ait; (*bir grup insan*) yalnız birbirini destekleyen ve yabancıları sevmeyen.

clap [klæp] **1.** *n.* gürleme, patlama; tokat; vuruş, el çırpma; **2.** *vb.* tokat atmak, el çırpmak, alkışlamak; ~ *eyes on s.o.* *b-ne* gözü ilişmek; **'~.board** *n.* ince tahta, padavra; **'clap.per** *n.* çan tokmağı; alkışlayan kişi; **'clap.trap** *n.* palavra, sahte iltifat, yağcılık.

clar.et ['klærət] *n.* kırmızı şarap; *sl.* kan.

clar.i.fi.ca.tion [klærifi'keiʃən] *n.* aydınlatma, açıklama; **clar.i.fy** ['ˌfai] *v/t.* tasfiye etm.; *fig.* aydınlatmak; *v/i.* açılmak, berraklaşmak.

clar.i.net [klæri'net], **clar.i.o.net** [ˌˌə'net] *n.* klarnet.

clar.i.on ['klæriən] *n.* berrak ve tiz ses.

clar.i.ty ['klæriti] *n.* açıklık, berraklık.

clash [klæʃ] **1.** *n.* şakırtı, çarpışma (sesi); *fig.* çatışma; **2.** *vb.* şakırdamak, takırdamak; çarpışmak; uyuşmamak; çatışmak (*with ile*).

clasp [klɑːsp] **1.** *n.* toka, çengelli iğne, kopça; el sıkma, kucaklama; *fig. b-ne* sarılma; **2.** *v/t.* toka ile tutturmak, bağlamak; (*el*) sıkmak, kavramak, yakalamak; ~ *s.o.'s hand* elleri kavuşturmak; *v/i.* sıkı tutmak; **'~-knife** *n.* sustalı çakı.

class [klɑːs] **1.** *n.* sınıf, tabaka; kategori; (*tren. vapur v.b.*) mevki; *Am.* UNIV aynı yıl okulu bitirenler; ders; *attr.* F kibarlık, üstünlük, şıklık; **2.** *v/t.* sınıflara ayırmak, tasnif etm.; F düşünmek, saymak; ~ *with* bşle kıyas etm.; benzetme yapmak; **'~'con.scious** *adj.* sınıf farkı gözeten; **'~.fel.low** *n.* sınıf arkadaşı.

clas.sic ['klæsik] **1.** *n.* klasik yazar; ~*s pl.* eski Yunan ve Latin edebiyatı eserleri; **2.** = **'clas.si.cal** □ klasik; mükemmel, birinci derece.

clas.si.fi.ca.tion [klæsifi'keiʃən] *n.* tasnif, sınıflandırma; **clas.si.fy** ['ˌfai] *v/t.* sınıflandırmak, tasnif etm.

class...: **'~-mate** *s.* **class-fellow**; **'~-room** *n.* sınıf, derslik; **'~-war.fare** *n.* sınıflar arası mücadele.

clat.ter ['klætə] **1.** *n.* takırtı; **2.** *v/t. & v/i.* takırda(t)mak.

clause [klɔːz] *n.* madde, şart; (*kanun, kontrat v.b.*) bent, fıkra; GR cümlecik; *subordinate* ~ yan cümlecik.

claustral 548

claus.tral ['klɔ:strəl] *adj.* manastıra ait.
clav.i.cle ['klævikl] *n.* köprücük kemiği.
claw [klɔ:] **1.** *n.* hayvan pençesi; pençe tırnağı; (*a.* MEC) tırnak, kavrama, kurtağzı; **2.** *vb.* pençe atmak, yırtmak, tırmalamak; **clawed** *adj.* pençeli, tırnaklı.
clay [klei] *n.* balçık, kil; *fig.* toprak, yerküre; insan vücudu; ~ **pigeon**, ~ **bird** makine ile havaya atılan balçık hedef; **clayey** ['kleii] *adj.* balçıklı, killi.
clean [kli:n] **1.** *adj.* temiz, pak; açık; masum; *fig.* hatasız, kusursuz; **2.** *-adv.* tamamen, iyice; temiz olarak; **3.** *v/t.* & *v/i.* temizle(n)mek, yıkamak, ayıklamak; *be ~ed out* F meteliksiz kalmak; ~ *up* iyice temizlemek; bitirmek; düzenlemek; '**clean.er** *n.* temizlikçi; silgi; temizleyici ilâç; *mst ~s pl.* kuru temizleyici; *send to the ~s* temizleyiciye göndermek; '**clean.ing** *n.* temizleme; ~ *woman* temizlikçi kadın; **clean.li.ness** *n.* temizlik; **cleanse** [klenz] *v/t.* temizlemek, arıtmak.
clean-up ['kli:nʌp] *n.* temizleme; POL temizleme, tasfiye işlemi; *Am.sl.* avanta.
clear [kliə] **1.** ☐ açık, berrak, parlak; sarih, aşikâr; boş, serbest; kesin; *fig.* saf, lekesiz; COM *net*, ~ *of* ...den uzak, ...den arınmış; *as ~ as day* gün gibi aşikâr; *get ~ of bşden* kurtulmak; **2.** *in the ~* ARCH içten içe ölçümde; **3.** *v/t. a.* ~ *up* halletmek; aydınlatmak; açmak, açık hale getirmek; *fig.* aydınlatmak, tenvir etm.; kurtarmak, temizlemek (*of, from -den*); temize çıkarmak (*of -den*); (*at vs.*) engeli aşmak; *a.* ~ *away*, ~ *off* toparlayıp kaldırmak, ortadan kaldırmak; (*hesap, fatura*) ödemek, yoluna koymak; COM *s.* ~ *off*, COM gümrükten çıkarmak; JUR *b-ni* herhangi bir taahhüdünden kurtarmak, muaf tutmak (*from -den*); COM net kâr elde etm.; ~ *off* boşaltmak, tahliye etm., tasfiye etm.; ~ *a port* limanı boşaltmak; ~ *a ship for action* gemiyi savaş için hazırlamak; F bir iş için hazırlanmak; ~ *one's throat* öksürerek boğazını temizlemek; *v/i. a.* ~ *up* (*hava*) açılmak; anlaşılmak; (*dert, hastalık*) iyiye gitmek; *a.* ~ *off* (*bulut vs.*) dağılmak; sıvışmak; ~ *out* ortadan kaybolmak, sıvışmak; ~ *through* geçip gitmek; '**clear.ance** *n.* temizleme; COM kliringten çekleri geçirme; NAUT, COM geminin

gümrük işlemlerini bitirme; MEC makinenin iki kısmı arasındaki boşluk; ~ *sale* tasfiye astışı, likidasyon; '**clear-** -'**cut** düzgün, biçimli; açık, vazıh; - '**clear.ing** *n.* açma; temizleme *etc. s.* **clear³**; açıklık, meydan; COM takas, kliring; ~ *agreement* kliring anlaşması; ~ *bank* ciro bankası; ~ *house* kliring odası, takas odası; ~-*hospital* seyyar hastane; '**clear.ness** *n.* berraklık, açıklık.
cleat [kli:t] *n.* NAUT koç boynuzu; mesnet takozu.
cleav.age ['kl:vidʒ] *n.* yarılma, ayrılma, ayrılık (*a. fig.*); MIN parçalayarak elde edilen maden.
cleave¹ [kli:v] (*irr.*) *v/t.* yarmak; *be in a cleft stick* çıkmaza girmek; *cleft palate* MED yarık damak; *show the cloven hoof* şeytan ruhunu göstermek, ne mal olduğunu göstermek.
cleave² [-] *v/i.* çatlamak; yapışmak; *fig.* sevgi ile bağlanmak (*to -e*); ~ *together* bir arada tutulmak.
cleav.er ['kli:və] *n.* balta, kasap satırı.
cleek [kli:k] *n.* demir topuzlu golf sopası.
clef MUS [klef] *n.* nota anahtarı.
cleft [kleft] **1.** *n.* yarık, çatlak; **2.** *pret.* & *p.p.* *of cleave¹*.
clem.a.tis BOT ['klemətis] *n.* orman asması, filbahar, klemetis.
clem.en.cy ['klemənsi] *n.* şefkat, yumuşaklık; '**clem.ent** ☐ merhametli, şefkatli; (*esp. hava*) mülayim, yumuşak.
clench [klentʃ] *v/t.* (*diş, yumruk vs.*) sıkmak; kavramak; = *clinch*.
clere.sto.ry ARCH ['kliəstəri] *n.* binanın pencereli üst kısmı.
cler.gy ['klə:dʒi] *n.* rahipler sınıfı; '~.**man**, **cler.ic** ['klerik] *n.* papaz, rahip.
cler.i.cal ['klerikəl] **1.** ☐ kâtibe ait; daire işiyle ilgili; rahiplere ait; kilisenin siyasete karışmasını isteyen; ~ *error* yazı hatası, sürçü kalem; ~ *work* büro işi; **2.** *n.* rahip, papaz; POL dinci, ümmetçi.
clerk [klɑ:k] *n.* (*büroda*) kâtip, sekreter; COM satıcı; *part. Am.* tezgâhtar; ECCL rahip.
clev.er ☐ ['klevə] akıllı, becerikli, marifetli; zarif; '**clev.er.ness** *n.* zekâ, akıllılık.
clew [klu:] *n.* yumak, topak; *s. clue*.
cli.ché ['kli:ʃei] *n.* klişe, basmakalıp söz; TYP klişe.

click [klik] **1.** *n.* şıkırtı; çatırtı; *(dil)* şaklama; MEC kilit çengeli; **2.** *v/i.* şıkırdamak, «klik» sesi çıkarmak; *sl.* başarmak, şansı olm.; *sl.* uyuşmak, birbirinden hoşlanmak.

cli.ent ['klaiənt] *n.* müşteri; müvekkil; **cli.en.tèle** [kli:ä:n'teil] *n.* müşterilerin, müvekkillerin hepsi.

cliff [klif] *n.* kayalık, uçurum.

cli.mate ['klaimit] *n.* iklim; **cli.mat.ic** [‚-'mætik] *adj.* (**~ally**) iklime ait.

cli.max ['klaimæks] **1.** *n.* zirve, doruk; dönüm noktası; düğüm noktası; doyum; **2.** *v/i.* en yüksek dereceye gelmek; *v/t.* en yüksek dereceye getirmek.

climb [klaim] **1.** *n.* tırmanma; **2.** *v/t. & v/i.* tırmanmak *-e;* **'climb.er** *n.* tırmanan, dağcı; *fig.* ikbalperest, yükselmek; isteyen kimse; BOT sarmaşık; **'climb.ing** *n.* tırmanma; **'climb.ing--i.ron** *n.* tırmanma demiri, krampon.

clinch [klintʃ] **1.** *n.* MEC perçinleme; *fig.* kucaklama; *boks:* girift olma; **2.** *v/t.* bağlamak, perçinlemek; hüküm vermek; *s.* **clench;** *v/i.* girift olm.; **'clinch.er** *n.* MEC kenet, perçinleme; F koz, düğüm noktası.

cling [kliŋ] *(irr.) v/i.* sıkı sarılmak, yapışmak **(to -e);** vazgeçmemek; **'cling.ing** *adj.* *(elbise)* sıkı, dar; *fig.* başkasına fazla bağımlı, yapışkan.

clin.ic ['klinik] *n.* klinik, muayenehane; **'clin.i.cal** □ kliniğe ait; **~ thermometer** doktor termometresi, derece.

clink¹ *sl.* [kliŋk] *n.* hapishane, kodes.

clink² [‚-] **1.** *n.* şakırtı, şıngırtı; **2.** *v/i.* şakırdamak, şıngırdamak; *v/t.* şakırdatmak, şıngırdatmak, tokuşturmak; **'clinker** *n.* maden kömürü cürufu; *sl.* fiyasko; **'clin.ker-built** *adj.* NAUT üstüste bindirilmiş kaplama parçaları ile yapılmış *(gemi);* **'clink.ing** *sl.* efsanevî; F yaman, fevkalâde, mümtaz.

clip¹ [klip] **1.** *n.* kırpma, kırkım; *at one* ~ *Am.* F ansızın, hep birden; **2.** *v/t.* makasla kesmek, kırpmak, kırkmak; *(hece)* kısaltmak; yutmak; *(bilet)* zımbalamak; **~ s.o.'s wings** *sl.* kısıtlamak, engel olm.

clip² [‚-] **1.** *n.* raptiye, mandal, klips, pens; **2.** *v/t.* kenetlemek; mandallamak.

clip.per ['klipə] *n.* kırpma makası; hızlı giden at; NAUT çok yollu bir tür yelkenli; süratli giden şey; *sl.* yaman şey; *(a. pair of)* **~s** *pl.* saç kesme makinesi; **'clippings** *n. pl.* Am. gazete kupürü;

pl. kırpıntı, talaş.

clique [kli:k] *n.* takım, komite, hizip, klik.

cloak [kləuk] **1.** *n.* manto, palto, pelerin; *fig.* perde, bahane; **2.** *v/t. fig.* örtbas etm., örtmek, gizlemek; **'~-room** *n.* gardrop, vestiyer, helâ, tuvalet; RAIL bagaj gişesi.

clock [klɔk] **1.** *n.* masa saati; duvar saati; *spor. sl.* kronometre; **put the** ~ **back** *fig.* eskiye dönmek; **2.** *v/t. spor. sl.* saat tutmak; *v/i.* ~ **in (out)** *(fabrikada işe gelme, işten çıkma saatlerinde)* kart basmak; **'~.wise** *adj. & adv.* saat yelkovanlarının döndüğü yönde; **'~-work** *n.* saati çalıştıran makine; **like** ~ saat gibi, muntazam.

clod [klɔd] *n.* toprak parçası, kesek; *a.* **~-hopper** *n.* köylü, kaba adam, hödük.

clog [klɔg] **1.** *n.* kütük; *fig.* engel; **2.** *v/i.* tıkanmak, sıkılmak; *v/t. fig.* b-ne engel olm.; sıkıntı vermek; *-e;* **'clog.gy** *adj.* toptop olan şey, düğümlü.

clois.ter ['klɔistə] **1.** *n.* manastır; dehliz; **2.** *v/t.* manastıra kapamak.

clone [kləun] **1.** *n.* klon; **2.** *v/t.* klonlamak.

clon.ing ['kləuniŋ] *n.* klonlama.

close **1.** [kləuz] *n.* son, sonuç, nihayet; avlu, kilise avlusu; **2.** [kləuz] *v/t.* kapamak, kapatmak; son vermek, bitirmek; ~ **down** *(işletme)* kapamak; ~ **one's eyes to** göz yummak, görmezlikten gelmek; *v/i.* sona ermek, kapanmak (**with** *ile*); ~ **in (on** *b)şin* etrafını çevirmek; ~ **up** MIL safları sıklaştırmak; **closing time** *(ticarethane vs.)* kapatma saati; **3.** □ yakın, bitişik; dikkatli; sıkı, sıkı, dar; samimî, yakın; kapalı, havasız, ağır; ağzı sıkı; cimri; ~ **by,** ~ **to** yanıbaşında, yanında; ~ **fight,** ~ **combat,** ~ **quarters** *pl.* göğüs göğüse çarpışma; ~ **prisoner** sıkı göz altında olan mahkûm; ~ **season,** ~ **time** HUNT avlanmanın yasak olduğu mevsim; **sail** ~ **to the wind** NAUT rüzgâra karşı yol almak, orsa gitmek; *fig.* kanun ve ahlâk kurallarına uymamak; **a** ~ **shave** *fig.* kazadan ucuz kurtulma; **'~-'cropped,** '~-**'cut** *adj.* kısa kesilmiş *(saç, çimen vs.).*

closed [kləuzd] *adj.* kapalı; ~ **book** *fig.* az bilinen konu; ~ **circuit** kapalı devre; **~circuit television** kapalı devre televizyon; ~ **shop** yalnız sendika üyesi olanların çalıştığı fabrika vs.

close...: '~-'fist.ed *adj.* cimri; '~-'fit-

ting *adj.* dar, iyi oturan (*elbise*); '~'**grained** *adj.* çizgileri sık (*kereste, deri v.b.*); '~'**hauled** *adj.* NAUT orsa giden; '**close.ness** *n.* kapalılık *vs.* (*s. close 3.*).

clos.et ['klɔzit] **1.** *n. part.* Am. küçük oda; dolap; tuvalet, helâ; *s. water-~;* **2.** *vb.: be ~ed with* b-*le* odaya kapanmak.

clos.ing ['kləuziŋ]: ~ *date* kapanma tarihi.

close-up ['kləusʌp] *n. film*: çok yakından çekilen fotoğraf.

clo.sure ['kləuʒə] **1.** *n.* kapa(n)ma; son verme; PARL mecliste müzakereyi bitirip oylamaya koyma; *apply the ~* müzakerelerin yeterliliğine karar vermek; **2.** *v/t.* (*tartışma vs.*) bitirip oylamaya koymak.

clot [klɔt] **1.** *n.* pıhtı; **2.** *v/t. & v/i.* pıhtılaş(tır)mak; kesilmek (*süt*).

cloth [klɔθ] *n.* kumaş, bez, masa örtüsü; *the ~* F rahiplik; ~ *lay the ~* sofrayı kurmak; ~ *binding* bez cilt.

clothe [kləuð] (*irr.*) *v/t.* giydirmek, örtmek.

clothes [kləuðz] *n. pl.* elbise(ler), giysi; üniforma; çamaşır; '~-**bas.ket** *n.* çamaşır sepeti; '~-**line** *n.* çamaşır ipi; '~-**peg** *n.* çamaşır mandalı; '~-**pin** *n. part.* Am. çamaşır mandalı; '~-**press** *n.* elbise dolabı.

cloth.ier ['kləuðiə] *n.* kumaş, elbise satıcısı.

cloth.ing ['kləuðiŋ] *n.* giyim, elbise.

cloud [klaud] **1.** *n.* bulut; leke; *fig.* bulut gibi toplanmış kalabalık; *be under a ~* şüphe altında olm.; *in the ~s* dalgın, hayal aleminde olma; **2.** *v/t.* bulutla örtmek; lekelemek; bulandırmak (*a. fig.*); *v/i.* bulutlanmak; bulanmak; '~-**burst** *n.* ani sağanak yağışı; '**cloud-less** □ bulutsuz, açık; '**cloud.y** □ bulutlu; bulanık; dumanlı; açık olmayan, müphem.

clough [klʌf] *n.* boğaz, dağ geçidi.

clout [klaut] **1.** *v/t.* F tokat atmak -*e;* **2.** *n.* tokat, darbe; bulaşık bezi; kumaş parçası, bez; yama; F etki, nüfuz.

clove[1] [kləuv] *n.* karanfil (*bahar*).

clove[2] [-] *n.* diş sarmısak.

clove[3] [-] *pret. of cleave*[1]; '**cloven 1.** *p.p. of cleave*[1]; **2.** *adj.* yarık, çatlak, ayrık.

clo.ver BOT ['kləuvə] *n.* yonca, tirfil; *live veya be in ~* refah içinde yaşamak, hali vakti yerinde olm.; '~-**leaf** *n.* otoyol:

yonca yaprağı.

clown [klaun] *n.* palyaço, soytarı; *lit.* kaba adam, hödük; '**clown.ish** □ kaba saba, yontulmamış; budala.

cloy [klɔi] *v/t.* gına getirmek, kanıksatmak, içini bayıltmak.

club [klʌb] **1.** *n.* çomak, tokmak; kulüp; cemiyet; ~*s pl. oyun kartı:* ispati, sinek, trefli; **2.** *v/t.* sopa ile vurmak; ~ *together (para)* yatırmak; *v/i. mst ~ together* masrafa ortak olm.; '**club.(b)a.ble** *adj.* kulüp...; kulüp üyeliğine lâyık; girişken; '**club-'foot** *n.* yumru ayak; '**club-'house** *n.* spor kulübü binası; '**club-'law** *n.* yumruk hakkı, zorbalık.

cluck [klʌk] *v/i.* gıdaklamak (*tavuk*).

clue *fig.* [klu:] *n.* işaret, delâlet, ipucu.

clump [klʌmp] **1.** *n.* yığın, küme; *mst ~ sole* çifte taban; **2.** *vb.* ağır adımlarla yürümek; yığmak, kümelemek.

clum.si.ness ['klʌmzinis] *n.* hantallık, becerisizlik; '**clum.sy** □ hantal, beceriksiz, acemi.

clung [klʌŋ] *pret. & p.p. of cling.*

clus.ter ['klʌstə] **1.** *n.* BOT salkım; demet; küme (*yıldız*); oğul (*arı*); grup; **2.** *v/i.* toplanmak, demet haline gelmek.

clutch[1] [klʌtʃ] **1.** *n.* tutma; MEC kavrama, ambreyaj; *in his ~es ...* in pençesinde; ~ *pedal* MOT debriyaj; **2.** *v/t.* yakalamak, tutmak, kavramak (*at* -*i*).

clutch[2] [-] *n.* kuluçka; kuluçkadan çıkan civcivler.

clut.ter ['klʌtə] **1.** *n.* karmakarışıklık, hercümerç, dağınıklık; **2.** *v/t.* ~ *up* darmadağınık etm., altüst etm.; tıka basa doldurmak.

clys.ter ['klistə] *n.* tenkiye, lavman.

co... [kəu] *prefix bazı sözcüklerin başına gelerek* beraber, müşterek, ortak *anlamını verir.*

coach [kəutʃ] **1.** *n.* araba; RAIL vagon; gezinti arabası; *spor*: hoca, antrenör; **2.** *v/t.* alıştırmak, hazırlamak (*for* -*e*); *v/i.* özel öğretim yapmak; '~-**man** *n.* arabacı.

co.ad.ju.tor *esp.* ECCL [kəu'ædʒutə] *n.* yardımcı (*piskopos*).

co.ag.u.late [kəu'ægjuleit] *v/t. & v/i.* koyulaş(tır)mak, pıhtılaş(tır)mak; **co.agu.la.tion** *n.* pıhtılaşma.

coal [kəul] **1.** *n.* kömür, maden kömürü; F kor; *carry ~ to Newcastle* denize su taşımak, tereciye tere satmak; *haul veya call s.o. over the ~s fig.* b-*ni* azarlamak, tehditle korkutmak, yıldırmak;

2. NAUT *v/i.* kömür almak; *v/t.* kömür vermek; kömür haline gelinceye kadar yakmak; **~ing station** kömür ikmal limanı veya iskelesi; '~'**dust** *n.* kömür tozu.

co.a.lesce [kǝuǝ'les] *v/i.* birleşmek, birlik oluşturmak, yekvücut olm.; **co-a'les.cence** *n.* birlik, beraberlik, birleşme.

coal...: '~**field** *n.* maden kömürü havzası; '~**gas** *n.* havagazı.

co.a.li.tion [kǝuǝ'liʃǝn] *n.* birleşme; POL koalisyon.

coal...: '~**mine**, '~**pit** *n.* kömür ocağı; '~**scut.tle** *n.* kömür kovası.

coarse □ [kɔ:s] kaba, bayağı, adî; *fig.* yontulmamış, terbiyesiz, dangıl dungul; pişmemiş (*yiyecek*); pürüzlü (*yüzey*); '**coarse.ness** *n.* kabalık, terbiyesizlik.

coast [kǝust] **1.** *n.* kıyı, sahil; *esp. Am.* kızak kayma yolu (*yokuş*); yokuş aşağı güç harcamadan inme (*kızak, bisiklet, oto* vs.); **2.** *v/i.* sahil boyunca gitmek; yokuş aşağı güç harcamadan inmek (*bisiklet, kızak, oto* vs.); '**coast.al** *adj.* sahile ait; kıyı... sahil...

coast.er ['kǝustǝ] *n. Am.* el kızağı; NAUT sahil boyunca işleyen ticaret gemisi; altlık (*bardak, şişe*); **~ brake** *Am.* bisiklette fren pedalı.

coast-guard ['kǝustgɑ:d] *n.* sahil muhafızı; '**coast.ing** *n.* kıyı seyri, kabotaj; kızakla kayma; **~ trade** sahil ticareti, kabotaj; '**coast-line** *n.* sahil boyu, kıyı şeridi.

coat [kǝut] **1.** *n.* ceket, palto, manto; kat, tabaka; hayvan postu; **~ of mail** *n.* zırh elbise; **~ of arms** arma; **cut the ~ according to the cloth** ayağını yorganına göre uzat; **turn one's ~** parti *vs.* değiştirmek, başka tarafa geçmek; **2.** *v/t.* kaplamak, örtmek; '~**hang.er** *n.* elbise askısı; '**coating** *n.* kaplama; boya tabakası.

coax [kǝuks] *v/t.* kandırmak, gönlünü yapmak (**into, to**); **~ s.o. out of s.th.** tatlı sözlerle kandırarak *b-den bşi* elde etm.

cob [kɔb] *n.* mısır koçanı; erkek kuğu; kısa bacaklı bir tür binek atı; = **~nut.**

co.balt *min* [kǝu'bɔ:lt] *n.* kobalt.

cob.ble ['kɔbl] **1.** *n.* arnavut kaldırım taşı; **~s** *pl.* = **cob coal; 2.** *v/t.* kaldırım taşı döşemek; ayakkabı tamir etm., pençe vurmak; '**cob.bler** *n.* ayakkabı tamircisi; acemi çaylak, yaptığı işi yü-

züne gözüne bulaştıran kimse; buzlu karışık bir tür içki; '**cob.ble-stone** *n.* parke taşı.

cob...: '~**coal** *n.* parke taşı iriliğinde kömür parçası; '~**.loaf** *n.* yuvarlak sandviç ekmeği; '~**nut** *n.* iri fındık.

co.bra ZOO ['kǝubrǝ] *n.* kobra yılanı.

cob.web ['kɔbweb] *n.* örümcek ağı.

co.caine PHARM [kǝ'kein] *n.* kokain.

coch.i.neal ['kɔtʃini:] *n.* kırmız.

cock [kɔk] **1.** *n.* horoz; erkek kuş; MEC horoz (*silah*); valf, musluk; önder; kumandan; rüzgârgülü; *sl.* penis; **2.** *usu.* **~ up** *v/t. & v/i.* dik(il)mek; kulak kabartmak; (*silah horozunu*) ateşe hazır duruma getirmek; kurmak (*fotoğraf makinesi*); yana yatırmak (*baş, şapka*); **~ one's eye** (**at s.o.** *-e*) göz kırpmak.

cock.ade [kɔ'keid] *n.* şapkaya takılan rozet *veya* şerit, kokart.

cock-a-doo.dle-doo ['kɔkǝdu:dl'du:] *n.* horoz ötmesi, kukuriku.

cock-a-hoop ['kɔkǝ'hu:p] *adj.* neşeli, memnun; *Am.* darmadağınık.

Cock.aigne [kɔ'kein] *n.* hayali bir tembellik ve lüks ülkesi.

cock-and-bull story ['kɔkǝnd'bulstɔ:ri] *n.* gerçekmiş gibi anlatılan aptalca, inanılması zor hikâye; yalan olduğu aşikâr mazeret.

cock.a.too [kɔkǝ'tu:] *n.* ibikli ve rengârenk tüylü birkaç tür papağan.

cock.a.trice ['kɔkǝtrais] *n.* horoz yumurtasından varolduğu varsayılan efsanevî bir yılan.

cock.boat NAUT ['kɔkbǝut] *n.* küçük **sandal.**

cock.chaf.er ['kɔktʃeifǝ] *n.* mayısböceği.

cock-crow(.ing) ['kɔkkrǝu(iŋ)] *n.* tan, şafak.

cocked hat ['kɔkt'hæt] *n.* eskiden giyilen kenarları kıvrık üç köşeli bir tür şapka; **knock into a ~** *sl.* eze eze yenmek.

cock.er[1] ['kɔkǝ]: **~ up** *v/t.* özenli yetiştirmek, yüz vermek, şımartmak.

cock.er[2] HUNT [-] *n.* bir tür spanyel köpeği.

cock...: '~**eyed** *adj. sl.* aptal, budala, saçma; *Am.* sarhoş, küfelik; '~**fight**(**ing**) *n.* horoz dövüşü; '~**horse** *n.* tahta oyuncak at.

cock.le[1] BOT ['kɔkl] *n.* buğdaygiller arasında yetişen zararlı bir ot.

cock.le[2] [-] **1.** *n.* ZOO midye türünden bir deniz hayvanı; kıvrım, kırışık, pli;

warm *veya* **delight the** ~**s of one's heart** *b-ni* mutlu etm.; **2.** *v/t. & v/i.* buruş(tur)mak.

cock.ney ['kɔkni] *n.* Londralı adam, Londra aksanı ile konuşan kimse; '**cock.neyism** *n.* Londra aksanı veya özelliklerinden biri.

cock.pit ['kɔkpit] *n.* horoz dövüş alanı (*a. fig.*); NAUT alçak güverte; AVIA pilot yeri, uçağın baş tarafı.

cock.roach ZOO ['kɔkrəutʃ] *n.* hamamböceği.

cocks.comb ['kɔkskəum] *n.* horoz ibiği (*a.* BOT); '**cock-'sure** F kendinden fazla emin; '**cock.tail** *n.* kokteyl; '**cock.y** □ F kendini beğenmiş, kibirli.

co.co ['kəukəu] *n.* hindistancevizi ağacı.

co.coa ['kəukəu] *n.* kakao.

co.co.nut ['kəukənʌt] *n.* hindistancevizi.

co.coon [kə'ku:n] *n.* (*ipek böceği*) koza.

cod ICHTH [kɔd] *n.* morina balığı; **dried** ~ kurutulmuş tuzsuz balık (*morina*).

cod.dle ['kɔdl] *v/t.* şımartmak *-i*, yüz vermek *-e*; hafif ateşte kaynatmak (*yumurta vs.*).

code [kəud] **1.** *n.* kanun; düstur; şifre, şifre anahtarı; **2.** TEL *v/t.* şifre ile yazmak.

co.de.ine CHEM [kəudi:n] *n.* kodein.

co.dex ['kəudeks] *n., pl.* **co.di.ces** ['-disi:z] eski el yazısı veya el yazması kutsal kitap.

cod.fish ['kɔdfiʃ] = **cod.**

codg.er F ['kɔdʒə] *n.* yaşlı antika adam.

co.di.ces ['kəudisi:z] *pl. of* **codex.**

cod.i.cil ['kɔdisil] *n.* ek vasiyetname; **codi.fi'ca.tion** *n.* kanun halinde toplama; **cod.i.fy** ['-fai] *v/t.* bir sisteme bağlamak, kanun halinde toplamak.

cod.ling ['kɔdliŋ] *n.* BOT pişirmekte kullanılan bir tür ham elma; ICHTH yavru morina balığı.

cod-liv.er oil ['kɔdlivər'ɔil] *n.* balıkyağı.

co-ed *Am.* F ['kəu'ed] *n.* karma yüksek okullarda kız öğrenci.

co-ed.u.ca.tion ['kəuedju:'keiʃən] *n.* karma öğretim.

co.ef.fi.cient [kəui'fiʃənt] **1.** *adj.* işbirliği yapan; **2.** *n.* katsayı.

co.erce [kəu'ə:s] *v/t.* zorlamak, zorla yaptırmak, mecbur etm.; **co'er.ci.ble** *adj.* zorunlu, mecburi; **co'er.cion** [-ʃən] *n.* baskı, zorlama; **under** ~ baskı

altında, zorunlu; **co'er.cive** [-siv] □ zorunlu, mecburi...

co.e.val □ [kəu'i:vəl] yaşıt, akran, çağdaş.

co.ex.ist ['kəuig'zist] *v/i.* bir arada var olm.; '**co.ex'ist.ence** *n.* bir arada var oluş; '**co.ex'ist.ent** *adj.* bir arada var olan.

cof.fee ['kɔfi] *n.* kahve; '~**-bean** *n.* kahve çekirdeği; '~**-grounds** *n. pl.* kahve telvesi; '~**-house** *n.* çayevi, kahvehane; '~**-pot** *n.* kahve ibriği, cezve; '~**-room** *n.* (*otel*) yemek salonu; '~**-set** *n.* kahve servis takımı.

cof.fer ['kɔfə] *n.* sandık, kasa, kutu (*para, mücevher*); ARCH *n.* girintili ve tahta tavan panosu; ~**s** *n. pl.* hazine, sandıkta birikmiş para; *a.* ~**-dam** *n.* batardo, koferdam, batan gemileri kurtarmakta kullanılan duba.

cof.fin ['kɔfin] **1.** *n.* tabut; **2.** *v/t.* tabuta koymak.

cog MEC [kɔg] *n.* çark dişi.

co.gen.cy ['kəudʒənsi] *n.* inandırıcılık, ikna etme yeteneği; '**co.gent** □ inandırıcı, ikna edici.

cogged MEC [kɔgd] *comb.* dişli...

cog.i.tate ['kɔdʒiteit] *v/i.* düşünmek, tasarlamak (*about, on, upon*); *v/t.* icat etm., bulmak, planlamak; **cog.i'ta.tion** *n.* düşünme, tasarlama.

co.gnac ['kɔnjæk] *n.* kanyak.

cog.nate ['kɔgneit] **1.** *adj.* aynı kökten gelen (*dil, sözcük*); akraba, hısım; **2.** *n.* kandaş, aynı soydan veya türden olan şey.

cog.ni.tion [kɔg'niʃən] *n.* anlayış, idrak, kavrama.

cog.ni.za.ble ['kɔgnizəbl] *adj.* tanınabilir, idrak olunur; JUR mahkemenin yetki kapsamına giren; '**cog.ni.zance** *n.* bilgi, malûmat; idrak; anlayış; JUR karar, hüküm; (*görev ve*) yetki; işaret, alâmet; '**cogni.zant** *adj.* haberdar, farkında olan, bilen (*of -den, -in -i*).

cog.no.men [kɔg'nəumen] *n.* soyadı; lâkap.

cog-wheel MEC ['kɔgwi:l] *n.* dişli çark.

co.hab.it [kəu'hæbit] *v/i.* karı koca gibi bir arada yaşamak (*gayrimeşru*); **co.hab.i'ta.tion** *n.* nikâhsız bir arada yaşama.

co.heir ['kəu'εə] *n.* ortak mirasçı; **co.heiress** ['kəu'εəris] *n.* ortak mirasçı (*kadın*).

co.here [kəu'hiə] *v/i.* yapışmak, tutmak; tutarlı olm.; **co'her.ence, co-**

'her.en.cy *n.* tutarlık, uygunluk; yapışma; co'her.ent☐yapışık; uygun, birbirini tutan; co'her.er *n. radyo*: eski tip
dalga almaçı.
co.he.sion [kəu'hi:ʒən] *n.* yapışma,
birleşme, kavuşma; co'he.sive [-siv]
adj. yapışık, bağlı.
co.hort ['kəuhɔ:t] *n. eski* Romalılarda
bir lejyonun onda biri.
coif [kɔif] *n.* takke, bone, kulâh; saç tuvaleti.
coif.feur [kwɑ:'fə:] *n.* kuaför, kadın
berberi; coif.fure [-'fjuə] *n.* saç biçimi, saç tuvaleti; **2.** *v/t. b-nin* saçını tarayıp düzeltmek.
coign of van.tage [kɔinəv'vɑ:ntidʒ] *n.*
bir iş veya gözlem için uygun nokta,
yer.
coil [kɔil] **1.** *part.* ~ **up** *v/t.* sarkmak; *v/i.*
kıvrılmak, burulmak; **2.** *n.* kangal, ro-
da, halka; ELECT bobin; MEC halka şeklinde kıvrılmış saç.
coin [kɔin] **1.** *n.* madeni para, sikke; *pay*
s.o. back in his own ~ *b-ne* aynı şekilde karşılık vermek; **2.** *v/t.* madeni para
bas(tır)mak; uydurmak (*a. fig.*); *be*
~*ing* money para kırıyor olm.; 'coin-
age *n.* para basma; para sistemi; yeni
bir sözcük uydurma, icat etme;
'coin-box tel.e.phone *n.* kasalı telefon, ankesör.
co.in.cide [kəuin'said] *v/i.* tesadüf
etm., uymak (*with* -e); *fig.* bir olm., birbirini tutmak; co.in.ci.dence [kəu'in-
sidəns] *n.* tesadüf, rastlantı; *fig.* bir olma, mutabakat; *mere* ~ tamamen rastlantı; co'in.ci.dent ☐ tesadüfî, rastlantı sonucu olan; uygun gelen.
coin.er ['kɔinə] *n.* para basan kimse,
esp. kalp para basan, kalpazan.
coir ['kɔiə] *n.* hindistancevizi lifi.
coke [kəuk] **1.** *n.* kok kömürü (*a. sl.* =
cocaine); *Am.* F Coca-Cola; **2.** *v/t.*
kok kömürü yapmak.
co.ker.nut ['kəukənʌt] = *coconut.*
col.an.der ['kʌləndə] *n.* mutfak; süzgeç; kevgir.
cold [kəuld] **1.** ☐ soğuk (*a. fig.*); donuk
(*renk*); *throw* ~ *water on* pişmiş aşa su
katmak, *b-nin* hevesini kursağında
bırakmak; *give s.o. the* ~ *shoulder*,
= ~*-shoulder*, ~ *feet* F cesaretsizlik,
korkaklık, cayma; **2.** *n.* soğuk(luk);
soğuk algınlığı; *usu.* ~ açıkta veya yarı yol-
le; *be left in the* ~ açıkta veya yarı yolda bırakılmak; '~-'blood.ed *adj.*
soğukkanlı, duygusuz (*a. fig.*); '~-'-

-heart.ed *adj.* acımasız, duygusuz;
'cold.ness *n.* soğukluk.
cold...: '~-shoul.der *b-ne* omuz çevirme, yüz vermeyiş; ~ steel kesici ve dür-
tücü silah; '~-'stor.age *n.* soğuk havada depo etme; *attr.* soğuk hava (deposu)...; '~-'store *vb.* soğuk havada depolamak; ~ war soğuk harp.
cole BOT [kəul] *mst in compound*
word(s) n. lahana.
cole-seed BOT ['kəulsi:d] *n.* turp lahanası, şalgam.
cole-slaw *Am.* ['kəulslɔ:] *n.* lahana salatası.
col.ic MED ['kɔlik] *n.* sancı, kolik.
col.lab.o.rate [kə'læbəreit] *v/i.* işbirliği
yapmak, birlikte çalışmak (*with*, *on*
ile, -*le*, -*de*); col.lab.o'ra.tion *n.* işbirliği; *in* ~ *with* ortaklaşa, ...ile beraber;
col.labo'ra.tion.ist *n.* POL işgal edilmiş
ülkenin düşman ile işbirliği yapan va-
tandaşı, işbirlikçi; col'lab.o.ra.tor *n.*
beraber çalışan kimse, iş arkadaşı.
col.lapse [kə'læps] **1.** *v/t. & v/i.* çö-
k(ert)mek, yık(ıl)mak; katlayıp bükmek, açılır kapanır olm. (*masa v.b.*);
MED çökmek, yığılmak; ciğerlere hava
gitmemek; düşmek; sönmek (*balon*);
suya düşmek (*plan vs.*); **2.** *n.* çökme,
yıkılma, göçme, ani düşüş; col'laps.i-
ble *adj.* açılır kapanir, katlanır (*masa,*
sandalye v.b.); ~ *boat* sökülüp takılabilen kayık.
col.lar ['kɔlə] **1.** *n.* yaka; gerdanlık; tasma; MEC yatak mesnet, yüksük, burç,
manşon; **2.** *v/t.* yakalamak -*i*, yakasına
yapışmak -*in*; *sl.* izinsiz almak, ele geçirmek; *et*; pişirmek için sarmak;
'~-bone *n.* ANAT köprücük kemiği;
'~-stud *n.* yaka düğmesi.
col.late [kɔ'leit] *v/t. metin*: karşılaştırmak, karşılaştırarak okumak; TYP (*say-*
faları) sıraya koymak, harman yapmak.
col.lat.er.al [kɔ'lætərəl] **1.** ☐ yan yana,
paralel, aynı eğilimde olan; ikincil, tali; tamamlayıcı, vasıtalı; aynı soydan
gelen; **2.** *n.* maddî teminat; soydaş;
col'lat.er.al 'dam.age *n.* MIL *bir askeri*
harekat sırasında sivil halka verilen za-
rar.
col.la.tion [kɔ'leiʃən] *n. metin*: karşılaştırma; soğuk hafif yemek.
col.league ['kɔli:g] *n.* meslekdaş, mesai arkadaşı.
col.lect **1.** ['kɔlekt] *n.* kilisede okunan
kısa dua; **2.** [kə'lekt] *v/t.* toplamak;

bir araya getirmek (*fikir*); tahsil etm. (*para*); kafasını toplamak, kendine gelmek; koleksiyon yapmak, biriktirmek; *b-ni* veya *bşi* uğrayıp almak; ~ **one's wits** kendini toplamak; ~**ing business** para, vergi tahsil etme; *v/i.* birikmek, toplanmak; col'lect.ed □ *fig.* aklı başında, sakin; col'lect.ed.ness *n. fig.* sükûnet, itidal; col'lec.tion *n.* topla(n)ma; koleksiyon; toplanmış şeyler, yığın; kilisede toplanan para; *forcible* ~ cebrî icra, takip; col'lec.tive *adj.* toplu, müşterek, ortak, toplanan...; kolektif...; ~ *bargaining* (*işveren ve işçi temsilcileri arasındaki*) toplu görüşme ve pazarlık; col'lec.tive.ly *adv.* topyekûn, birlikte; col'lec.tiv.ism *n.* POL kolektivizm, ortaklaşacılık; col-'lectiv.ize *vb.* (*sanayi, tarım vs.*'*yi*) devletleştirmek, (*sanayi, tarım vs. de*) devletleşmek; col'lector *n.* toplayan, koleksiyon sahibi; tahsildar; RAIL biletçi; ELECT cereyan toplayıcı, kollektör.

col.leen *Ir.* [kɔ'liːn] *n.* kız.

col.lege ['kɔlidʒ] *n.* kolej; yüksek okul, üniversite, akademi; **col.le.gi.an** [kə-'liːdʒjən] *n.* üniversite öğrencisi veya mensubu; **col'le.giate** [_dʒiit] *adj.* üniversiteye ait; üniversite öğrencilerine özgü.

col.lide [kə'laid] *v/i.* çarpmak (**with** -*e*); çarpışmak (*ile*); *fig. bşe* karşı olm., muhalif olm.

col.lie ['kɔli] *n.* iskoç çoban köpeği.

col.lier ['kɔliə] *n.* maden işçisi; NAUT kömür gemisi; **col.lier.y** ['kɔljəri] *n.* kömür ocağı.

col.li.sion [kə'liʒən] *n.* çarp(ış)ma; *fig.* fikir ayrılığı.

col.lo.ca.tion [kɔləu'keifən] *n.* sıraya koyma, düzenleme, sözdizimi.

col.lo.di.on [kə'ləudjən] *n.* kolodyum.

col.logue [kə'ləug] *v/i.* gizli konuşmak, entrika hazırlamak.

col.lo.qui.al □ [kə'ləukwiəl] konuşma diline ait, teklifsiz konuşma ile ilgili; **col'loqui.al.ism** *n.* konuşma dili üslubu; konuşma dilinde kullanılan deyim.

col.lo.quy ['kɔləkwi] *n.* karşılıklı konuşma, diyalog; sohbet.

col.lude [kə'luːd] *v/i. b-le* gizlice anlaşmak; dolap çevirmek; **col'lu.sion** [_ʒən] *n.* gizli anlaşma, tuzak; JUR sahte gizli anlaşma (*boşanma için*).

co.lon ['kəulən] *n.* TYP iki nokta üst üste; ANAT kolon, kalın bağırsak.

colo.nel MIL ['kɔːnl] *n.* albay; 'colo-

nel.cy *n.* albaylık.

co.lo.ni.al [kə'ləunjəl] *adj.* koloniye ait, sömürgelere ait; co'lo.ni.al.ism *n.* POL sömürgecilik; col.o.nist ['kɔlənist] *n.* sömürgede yerleşen insan; col-o.ni.za.tion [kɔlənai'zeifən] *n.* sömürge kurma; bir yere ahali yerleştirme; 'col.o.nize *v/t. & v/i.* sömürge kurmak -*de*; yerleş(tir)mek -*e*.

col.on.nade [kɔlə'neid] *n.* sıra sütunlar, kemeraltı.

col.o.ny ['kɔləni] *n.* sömürge, koloni.

col.o.pho.ny [kɔ'lɔfəni] *n.* reçine, çamsakızı, kolofan.

Col.o.ra.do bee.tle [kɔlə'raːdəu'biːtl] *n.* Kolorado böceği.

co.los.sal □ [kə'lɔsl] muazzam, olağanüstü büyük; co'los.sus [_səs] *n.* dev heykel; dev gibi şey.

col.our, *Am.* **col.or** ['kʌlə] **1.** *n.* renk, boya; ten, cilt rengi; *fig.* sözü çevirme, tevil, tandans; görünüş; canlılık; ~*s pl.* MIL bayrak, bandıra; *local* ~ yöresel özellikler; **2.** *v/t.* boyamak, renklerle süslemek; *fig.* olduğundan başka göstermek; *v/i.* renklenmek; rengi değişmek, kızarmak; 'col.o.(u)r.a.ble □ aldatıcı, yanıltıcı, göz boyayıcı, su götürür; col.o(u)r'ation *n.* renk verme, renklendirme.

col.o.(u)r...: '~*bar* *n.* ırk ayırımı; '~*blind* *adj.* renkkörü; 'colo(u)red *adj.* renkli; zenci, beyaz ırka mensup olmayan; ~ *film* renkli film; ~ *pencil* renkli kurşun kalemi; ~ (*wo*)*man* zenci kadın (erkek); 'col.o(u)r.ful *adj.* renkli, canlı; 'col.o(u)ring *n.* renk; boya; *bşe* renk verme, boyama; renklendirme; nüans; *fig.* sahte görünüş; mazur gösterme; 'colo(u)r.ist *n.* renkleri ustalıkla kullanan sanatçı; 'col.o.(u)r.less □ renksiz (*a. fig.*); 'col.o(u)r scheme renk düzenlemesi; 'col.o(u)r wash renkli badana.

colt [kəult] *n.* ZOO tay, sıpa; *fig.* acemi, tecrübesiz kimse; 'colts.foot *n.* BOT öksürük otu.

col.um.bine BOT ['kɔləmbain] *n.* haseki küpesi.

col.umn ['kɔləm] *n.* sütun, direk; TYP gazete sütunu; MIL kol (*nizamı*), kafile; **colum.nar** [kə'lʌmnə] *adj.* sütunlar halinde olan, sütun veya direk şeklinde; col.umnist ['kɔləmnist] *n. Am.* fıkra yazarı, gazetede belirli bir köşesi olan yazar.

col.za BOT ['kɔlzə] *n.* kolza, lahana türü

sebzeler veya bunların tohumu.

co.ma ['kəumə] *n.* MED koma, derin baygınlık; BOT püskül.

comb [kəum] **1.** *n.* tarak; horoz ibiği; dağ sırtı (*a. dalga*); MEC kenevir tarağı; *s.* **curry~.**; *s.* **honey~.**; **2.** *v/t.* taramak (*a. fig.*); taraklamak, taraktan geçirmek (*keten*); **~ out** *fig.* taramak, ayırmak, elemek; *v/i.* taranmak; tümselip kırılmak (*dalga*).

com.bat ['kɔmbət] **1.** *n.* dövüş, savaş, çarpışma; **single ~** düello; **2.** *v/t. & v/i.* karşı durmak, dövüşmek, çarpışmak, boğuşmak; '**com.bat.ant** *n.* savaşçı; '**combat.ive** □ cengâver, kavgacı.

comb.er ['kəumə] *n.* MEC yün, keten vs. tarayan kimse ya da makine; NAUT *n.* uzun ve tümsekli dalga.

com.bin.a.ble [kəm'bainəbl] *adj.* birleş(tiril)ebilir; **com.bi.na.tion** [kɔmbi'neiʃən] *n.* birleş(tir)me, bağla(n)ma; bileşim, terkip (*esp.* CHEM); birlik; kilit şifresi (*rakam veya harf*); **~s** *pl.* külot ve gömleği tek parça olan kadın iç çamaşırı; yan arabalı motosiklet; **~ lock** şifreli kilit; **com.bine 1.** [kəm'bain] *v/t. & v/i.* birleş(tir)mek, kombine etm., uyuş(tur)mak; **2.** ['kɔmbain] *n.* COM kartel, tröst, çıkar birliği; *a.* **~ harvester** biçer-döğer makinesi.

com.bus.ti.ble [kəm'bʌstəbl] **1.** *adj.* tutuşabilir, yanabilir; **2.** **~s** *n. pl.* yakacak, yakıt; MOT akaryakıt; **com.bustion** [-'bʌstʃən] *n.* yanma; **~ engine** yanmalı, ihtiraklı motor.

come [kʌm] (*irr.*) *vb.* gelmek, ulaşmak, vasıl olm. (*to -e*); F orgazma ulaşmak; **to ~** önümüzdeki, gelecek, müstakbel; **how ~?** F nasıl oluyor da?; **~ about** olmak, vaki olm., husule gelmek; **~ across** rast gelmek -*e*, karşılaşmak -*le*; **~ along** ilerlemek; acele etm.; birlikte gelmek; **~ at** varmak -*e*; uğraşmak *ile*; saldırmak -*e*; **~ by** yakınından geçmek, uğramak; elde etm., edinmek; **~ down** inmek, düşmek (*a. fig.*); intikal etm., geçmek; **~ down upon s.o.** *b-ne* haddini bildirmek, terbiyesini vermek; **~ down upon s.o.** for £ 10 10 £ borcunu istemek, talep etm. -*den*; **~ down with** kesenin ağzını açmak, paraları sökülmek; *Am.* F hastalanmak; **~ for** alıp götürmek -*i*; üstüne yürümek; **~ in** girmek; katılmak; NAUT limana girmek; yaygın olm.; moda olm.; iktidara gelmek; gelir olarak almak (*para*);

yükselmek (*deniz*); çıkmak (*meyva*); **~ in!** giriniz!; **~ in for** hak olarak almak, elde etm.; **~ off** kaçıp kurtulmak, yakasını kurtarmak; olmak; kopmak (*düğme v.b.*); dökülmek (*saç*); başarıyla sonuçlanmak; **~ on** yaklaşmak; gelişmek, ilerlemek; baş göstermek; sahneye çıkmak; **~ on!** Haydi gel!, Çabuk ol!; Yok canım!; **~ out** yerinden çıkmak; yayınlanmak, neşredilmek; açmak (*çiçek*); meydana çıkmak; açıklığa kavuşmak; çıkmak (*fotoğraf[-ta]*); sosyeteye takdim edilmek (*genç kız*); çıkmak (*yıldız, kir*); çalışmayı reddetmek; sonuçlanmak; **~ out right** doğru çıkmak (*hesap*); **~ round** *b-ne* uğramak, *b-ni* ziyaret etm.; dönmek, yinelenmek; tekrar *k-ne* gelmek, ayılmak; *fig.* razı olm., başka perdeden konuşmak (*b-ni* teskin etm. için); **~ to** *adv.* = **~ to o.s.**; NAUT orsa etm., demirlemek; bulmak, erişmek, yekûn tutmak; ilgilendirmek; **~ to o.s.** *veya* **to one's senses** tekrar *k-ne* gelmek, ayılmak; **~ to anchor** demir atmak; **~ to know** *b-le* tanışmak; *bşi* öğrenmek; **~ up** olmak; yükselmek; yaklaşmak; seçilmek; meydana çıkmak; yukarı gelmek; çimlenmek; **~ up against** *fig.* karşılaşmak -*le*, çatmak -*e*; **~ up to** uymak, tekabül etm.; eşit olm.; aynı başarıyı elde etm.; aynı ölçü, durum vs. ye erişmek; **~ up with** yetişmek, ulaşmak; telafi etm.; öne sürmek, ortaya atmak; **~ upon** rast gelmek -*e*; baskına uğramak, gafil avlamak; **~'at.a.ble** F *adj.* erişilebilir, varılması mümkün; '**~back** *n.* THEAT sahneye dönüş; eski duruma dönüş; *Am. sl.* hazırcevap karşılık.

co.me.di.an [kə'mi:djən] *n.* komik aktör, komedyen; komedi yazarı.

com.e.dy ['kɔmidi] *n.* komedi, komedya, güldürücü piyes veya film.

come.li.ness ['kʌmlinis] *n.* zerafet, şirinlik; '**come.ly** *adj.* lâtif, zarif, hoş, sevimli, güzel, yakışıklı, uygun, yakışan.

com.er ['kʌmə] *n.* gelen kimse; katılan kimse.

co.mes.ti.ble [kə'mestibl] *mst* **~s** *n. pl.* yiyecek şey, gıda maddesi.

com.et ['kɔmit] *n. astr.* kuyruklu yıldız.

com.fort ['kʌmfət] **1.** *n.* konfor, rahat(lık), refah, teselli, avuntu; *fig.* yardım, himaye; serinletici (*ferahlatıcı*) şey; **2.** *v/t.* teselli etm; rahat ettirmek; yatıştırmak; 'com.fort.a.ble □ rahat, konforlu, ferahlatıcı; teselli edici, avutucu; 'com.fort.er *n*. rahatlatıcı şey; teselli eden kimse; yün boyun atkısı; emzik; *Am*. yorgan; 'com.fortless □ huzursuz, rahatsız, konforsuz; can sıkıcı, kasvetli; 'com.fort sta.tion *Am*. umumî helâ.

com.frey BOT ['kʌmfri] *n*. karakafes otu.

com.fy □ F ['kʌmfi] = *comfortable*.

com.ic ['kɔmik] *adj*. (*~ally*) komik, garip, tuhaf, orijinal; komedi...; *fig. mst* 'comi.cal □ keyifli, neşeli; güldürücü, eğlendirici; gülünç, tuhaf; *~ journal, ~ paper* gülmece dergisi; 'com.ics, comic strips *n. pl.* karikatür şeklinde hikâye serisi.

com.ing ['kɔmiŋ] 1. *adj*. gelen; gelecek, yaklaşan; *fig.* gelecek vaat eden; *~, Sir!* hemen geliyorum efendim!; 2. *n.* geliş, yaklaşma, varış.

com.i.ty ['kɔmiti]: *n. ~ of nations* uluslararası dostluk.

com.ma ['kɔmə] *n.* GR virgül.

com.mand [kə'mɑːnd] 1. *n.* emir; otorite, yetki; hakimiyet; MIL kumanda, komut; *at veya by ~ of* emri ile; *have ~ of* hakim olm., iyi bilmek, vakıf olm.; *be (have) at ~ b-nin* emrine hazır olm., emrine amade olm.; *be in ~ of* MIL kumanda altında olm.; 2. *v/t. & v/i.* emretmek, hâkim olm. *-e*; *kafile, gemi vs.*: kumanda etm. *-e*, MIL komuta etm. *-e*; *bş* üzerinde kullanım yetkisi olm.; MIL ateş altına alıp taramak; bakmak, görmek *-e, -i* (*manzara*); com.man.dant MIL [kɔmən'dænt] *n.* kumandan, komutan; kaptan, süvari (*gemi*); com.man.deer [_-'diə] *v/t.* MIL askerî bizmete zorunlu kılmak; zaptetmek, müsadere etm.; com.mand.er MIL [kə'mɑːndə] *n.* komutan, kumandan; NAUT binbaşı; com'mand.er-in-'chief *n.* başkumandan; com'manding *adj.* emreden, hükmeden; etkili; hâkim; *fig.* mükemmel, birinci kalitede; *~ point* stratejik nokta; com'mand.ment *n.* emir; *rel.* Allahın emri; com'man.do MIL [_-dəu] *n.* komando (birliği); com'mand per.form.ance THEAT devlet başkanının emriyle yapılan tiyatro veya müzik gösterisi.

com.mem.o.rate [kə'meməreit] *v/t.* kutlamak *-i*, hatırasını anmak *-in*; com.memo'ra.tion *n.* kutlama, anma; com'mem.ora.tive □ *b-nin, bşin* anısına (*of*), hatıra..., yadigâr...

com.mence [kə'mens] *v/t.* başlamak *-e*; JUR başlamak (*dava*); com'mencement *n.* başlangıç; diploma töreni.

com.mend [kə'mend] *v/t.* övmek, salık vermek; emanet etm. (*to -e*); *~ me to ...* F ... e saygılarımı ilet; com'mend.able □ övgüye değer, salık verilir; commen.dation [kɔmen'deiʃən] *n.* övme; salık verme; com'mend.a.to.ry [_-dətəri] *adj.* öven; salık veren.

com.men.su.ra.ble □ [kə'menʃərəbl] aynı birim ile ölçülebilen, orantılı (*with, to -le, -e*); com'men.su.rate □ [_-rit] (*with, to -le, -e*) orantılı, aynı değerde, eşit, uygun.

com.ment ['kɔmənt] 1. *n.* tefsir, yorum; açıklama; düşünce, fikir (*on*); eleştiri, kritik; 2. *v/i.* (*upon -i*) tefsir etm., yorumlamak; detaylarıyla anlatmak; eleştirmek; 'com.men.tar.y *n.* tefsir, şerh, yorum, izah; com.men.ta.tor ['_-teitə] *n.* yorumcu, eleştirmeci, tefsirci; *radyo*: muhabir.

com.merce ['kɔmɔːs] *n.* ticaret, alım satım; toplumsal ilişkiler; cinsel ilişki; *Chamber of ♀* ticaret odası; com.mercial □ [kə'mɔːʃəl] 1. ticarî, ticaret...; meslekî; *~ traveller* gezici ticarî mümessil; 2. P = *~ traveller, esp. Am.* radyo, TV: reklâm, ilân, ticarî yayın; com'mer.cialism *n.* ticarî anlayış, tutum; ticarî deyim; com'mer.cial.ize *v/t.* ticarileştirmek.

com.mie F ['kɔmi] *n.* komünist.

com.min.gle [kɔ'miŋgl] *vb.* karış(tır)mak, kaynaş(tır)mak.

com.mis.er.ate [kə'mizəreit] *v/t. b-ne* acımak, merhamet etm., kederini paylaşmak (*with -in*); com.mis.er.a.tion [_-'reiʃən] *n.* acıma, teselli (*for*).

com.mis.sar POL [kɔmi'sɑː] *n.* komiser, eskiden Sovyetler Birliğinde herhangi bir idarî örgütün başı.

com.mis.sar.i.at [kɔmi'sɛəriət] *n.* eskiden Sovyetler Birliğinde siyasî örgüt; MIL levazım sınıfı; com.mis.sar.y ['_-səri] *n.* vekil, yardımcı delege; MIL levazım subayı; levazımat mağazası ve kantin.

com.mis.sion [kə'miʃən] 1. *n.* görev, vazife, iş; eylem; işleme; komisyon, yüzde; salahiyetname, yetki belgesi; komisyon, kurul; emir, sipariş; NAUT sefere hazır gemi; *~ sale* komisyonlu satış, yüzde hesabı satış; *on ~* yüzde ile, komisyon ile; 2. *v/t.* yetki vermek

-e, tayin etm., atamak *-e*, görevlendirmek, vazifelendirmek, memur etm.; hizmete koymak *-i*; MIL terfi ettirmek; NAUT sefere hazırlamak (*gemi*); **com.mis.sion.aire** [-'nɛə] *n*. üniformalı uşak; **com'mis.sion.er** *n*. komisyon üyesi, delege, vekil; görevli memur; komiser.

com.mit [kə'mit] *v/t*. işlemek, yapmak; teslim etm., tevdi etm., emanet etm. (**to** *-e*); söz vermek, vaat etm. (**to** *-e*); ~ (**o.s.** *k-ni*) adamak, hasretmek *-e*; taahhüt altına girmek; ~ (**to prison**) hapsetmek; ~ **for trial** daha sonra yargılanmak üzere hapsetmek; **com-'mit.ment** *n*. taahhüt, vaat, söz; bağlılık; sorumluluk; (*suç*) işleme; teslim etme; **com'mit.tal** = **commitment**; (*suç*) işleme; **com'mittee** [-ti] *n*. komite, kurul, komisyon.

com.mode [kə'məud] *n*. konsol, komodin; lâzımlık, oturak; **com'mo.di-ous** □ [-djəs] geniş, ferah, rahat, kullanışlı; **com.mod.i.ty** [kə'məditi] *n*. mal, ticaret eşyası, emtia; ~ **value** hakiki kıymet.

com.mo.dore NAUT ['kɔmədɔ:] *n*. komodor; yat kulübü yöneticisi.

com.mon ['kɔmən] **1.** □ ortak, müşterek; genel, yaygın, umumî; bayağı, adi, kaba; alışılmış, çoğu yerde bulunan, mutat; **of ~ gender** GR hem eril hem dişil; ~ **noun** cins isim; ♀ **Council** Belediye Meclisi; **Book of** ♀ **Prayer** Anglikan kilisesi dua kitabı; ~ **weal** kamu yararı, toplum refahı; **in ~** ortaklaşa, müşterek (**with** *ile*); **in ~ with** *fig*. *-ile* aynı, …gibi; **2.** *n*. umumî otlak, halkın malı olan yer; **com.mon.al.ty** ['-nlti] *n*. halk tabakası, avam; **'com.mon.er** *n*. halk tabakasından olan kimse, burjuva.

com.mon…: ~ **law** örf ve âdete dayanan hukuk; ♀ **Mar.ket** Ortak Pazar; '~**.place 1.** *n*. alışılmış herhangi *bş*, basmakalıp iş; beylik lâf, klişe; **2.** *adj*. adî, sıradan, olağan; *fig*. beylik.

com.mons ['kɔmənz] *n. pl*. halk tabakası, avam; herkesin paylaştığı erzak; **short** ~ yiyecek kıtlığı; *mst* **House of** ♀ Avam Kamarası.

com.mon…; ~ **sense** sağduyu; '~**.wealth** *n*. devlet, ulus; *part*. cumhuriyet; **the British** ♀ İngiliz Milletler Topluluğu; **the** ♀ **of Australia** Avustralya Devletler Konfederasyonu.

com.mo.tion [kə'məuʃən] *n*. heyecan, ayaklanma; karışıklık, gürültü velvele.

com.mu.nal □ ['kɔmjunl] toplumsal…, halk…; umumî…, ortak…, müşterek…; **com.mu.nal.ize** ['-nəlaiz] *v/t*. toplumsallaştırmak; yöresel idare altına sokmak.

com.mune 1. [kə'mju:n] *v/i*. sohbet etm., söyleşmek, senli benli konuşmak; **2.** ['kɔmju:n] *n*. komün; yöresel idare; avam.

com.mu.ni.ca.bil.i.ty [kəmju:nikə'biliti] *n*. bulaşıcılık (*hastalık*); **com'mu-ni.ca.ble** □ bulaşıcı, sâri (*hastalık*); söylenebilir, ifade edilebilir (*fikir*); **com'mu.nicant** *n*. bilgi veren kimse, ele veren kimse; komünyon ayinine katılan kimse; **com'mu.ni.cate** [-keit] *v/t*. bildirmek; ifade etm., anlatmak; geçirmek, nakletmek; bulaştırmak; *v/i*. haberleşmek (**with** *ile*); bitişik olm. (**with** *ile*); **commu.ni'ca.tion** *n*. haberleşme; bulaşma; tebliğ, haber; ulaşım; bağlantı, irtibat, ulaştırma; **be in ~ with** *b-le* temasta olm.; ~ **cord** RAIL imdat freni; **com'mu.ni.cative** □ [-kətiv] konuşkan, lakırdıcı, geveze; hislerini açıklamaktan hoşlanan; **com'mu.ni.ca.tor** [-keitə] *n*. konuşkan kimse; TEL sinyal veren alet; RAIL imdat freni.

com.mun.ion [kəm'ju:njən] *n*. cemaat, birlik, mezhep; paylaşma; katılma; ECCL şarap içme ve yemek yeme ayini.

com.mu.ni.qué [kə'mju:nikei] *n*. resmi tebliğ, bildiri.

com.mu.nism ['kɔmjunizəm] *n*. komünizm; '**com.mu.nist 1.** *n*. komünist; **2.** = **commu'nis.tic** *adj*. (~**ally**) komünist…; komünizm…

com.mu.nity [kə'mju:niti] *n*. topluluk, cemiyet, cemaat; müşterek olma, paylaşma; **the** ~ ahali, halk, toplum; ~ **ownership** ortak mülkiyet; ~ **service** kamu hizmeti; ~ **of interests** çıkar grubu, tröst; ~ **chest** *Am*. fakirlere yardım fonu.

com.mut.a.ble [kə'mju:təbl] *adj*. değiştirilebilir, dönüştürülebilir (**into**, **for** *-e*); **com.mu.ta.tion** [kɔmju:'teiʃən] *n*. değiştirme, değiş (**into**, **for** *-e*); cezanın hafifletilmesi; ~ **ticket** *Am*. abone bilet *veya* kartı; **com.mu.ta.tive** [kə'mju:tətiv] *adj*. değiştirilebilen…; değişme ile ilgili; **com.mu.ta.tor** ELECT ['kɔmju:teitə] *n*. çevirgeç, komütatör; **com.mute** [kə'mju:t] *v/t*.

(*for*, *into*) değiştirmek, değiş tokuş etm., takas etm.; hafifletmek (*ceza*); *v/i.* telafi etm.; toptan ödemek; *Am.* her gün iş ile ev arasında gidip gelmek; **com'mut.er** *n. Am.* her gün işi ile evi arasında gidip gelen kimse.

com.pact **1.** ['kɔmpækt] *n.* sözleşme, mukavele, kontrat, anlaşma; pudralık; *Am.* küçük otomobil; **2.** [kəm'pækt] *adj.* sıkı, kesif, yoğun; kısa, öz; **3.** [_] *vb.* sıkılaştırmak, yoğunlaştırmak, basınçla sıkıştırmak; anlaşma yapmak; **'com.pact disc** compact disk, CD; **com'pact.ness** *n.* yoğunluk, kesiflik, sıkılık; özet.

com.pan.ion [kəm'pænjən] *n.* arkadaş, yoldaş, dost; eş; çift olan şeylerin teki (*eldiven vs.*); refakatçı, bakıcı; el kitabı, rehber; COM ortak; NAUT kamara görevlisi; ~ *in arms* askerlik arkadaşı; **com'pan.ion.a.ble** ☐ arkadaş canlısı, samimi, girgin; **com'pan.ion.ate** [_-nit]: ~ *marriage* anlaşmalı evlilik; **com'pan.ionship** *n.* arkadaşlık, dostluk; eşlik, refakat; ortaklık.

com.pa.ny ['kʌmpəni] *n.* arkadaşlık, beraberlik, eşlik, refakat; misafirler, ziyaretçi grubu; arkadaşlar; COM kumpanya, ortaklık, şirket; MIL bölük; NAUT mürettebat, tayfa; THEAT grup, oyuncu topluluğu; *be good* (*bad*) ~ iyi (kötü) arkadaş olm.; *bear s.o.* ~ *b-ne* eşlik etm., refakat etm., arkadaş olm.; *have* ~ misafirleri olm.; *keep* ~ *with b-ne* eşlik etm., arkadaşlık etm., refakat etm.

com.pa.ra.ble ☐ ['kɔmpərəbl] karşılaştırılabilir, karşılaştırılması mümkün; **compar.a.tive** [kəm'pærətiv] **1.** ☐ orantılı, mukayeseli, karşılaştırmalı; ~ *degree* = **2.** GR üstünlük derecesi; **com'par.a.tive.ly** *adv.* orantılı olarak, karşılaştırmalı olarak; **com.pare** [_-'pɛə] **1.** *n. beyond* ~, *without* ~, *past* ~ fevkalâde, eşsiz, üstün, tartışmasız; **2.** *v/t.* karşılaştırmak, mukayese etm. (*with ile*); benzetmek (*to* -*e*); GR üstünlük derecesini göstermek; (*as*) ~*d with* -*e* nisbetle, -*e* oranla; *v/i.* benzemek (*to* -*e*), karşılaştırılmak, mukayese kabul etm.; **com.par.i.son** [_-'pærisn] *n.* karşılaştırma, mukayese; münasebet, ilişki, benzerlik; GR sıfat *veya* zarfın üstünlük *veya* enüstünlük derecesini gösteren çekim şekli; *in* ~ *with* -*e* nispeten, -*e* oranla.

com.part.ment [kəm'pɑ:tmənt] *n.* bö-

lüm, şube, kısım; ARCH bölme, göz; RAIL kompartıman.

com.pass ['kʌmpəs] **1.** *n.* pusula; çevre; sınır, hacim; saha, alan, menzil; MUS genişlik, kapsam; (*usu. pair of*) ~*es pl.* pergel; **2.** *vb.* çevirmek, sarmak, kuşatmak; içine almak, kapsamak; etrafını dolaşmak; başarmak; elde etm., almak; kavramak, anlamak; gizli plan kurmak.

com.pas.sion [kəm'pæʃən] *n.* merhamet, acıma, şefkat; *have* ~ *on* -*e* acımak; **com'pas.sion.ate** ☐ [_-nit] şefkatli, merhametli, sevecen; *on* ~ *ground* acıdığından -*e*.

com.pat.i.bil.i.ty [kəmpætə'biliti] *n.* uygunluk, uyma, uygun düşme; **com'pat.i.ble** ☐ uygun, münasip, tutarlı (*with ile*).

com.pa.tri.ot [kəm'pætriət] *n.* vatandaş, yurttaş.

com.peer [kɔm'piə] *n.* akran, eş, arkadaş.

com.pel [kəm'pel] *v/t.* zorlamak, mecbur etm. (*a. fig.*).

com.pen.di.ous ☐ [kəm'pendiəs] kısa, öz, özet halinde; **com'pen.di.ous.ness** *n.* kısalık, özlük.

com.pen.di.um [kəm'pendiəm] *n.* özet.

com.pen.sate ['kɔmpenseit] *v/t.* tazmin etm., telâfi etm., karşılamak, bedelini ödemek (*for için*; *with ile*; *by ile*); MEC denkleştirmek, denklemek, eşitlemek; *v/i.* ~ *for* -*in* yerini tutmak; **com.pen'sation** *n.* tazmin, telâfi; bedel, karşılık; *Am.* maaş, ücret; MEC dengeleme; **com'pen.sa.tive** [_-sətiv], **com'pen.sa.to.ry** *adj.* telâfi edici.

com.père ['kɔmpɛə] **1.** *n.* eğlence programı sunucusu; **2.** *vb.* sunuculuk yapmak.

com.pete [kəm'pi:t] *vb.* boy ölçüşmek, müsabakaya girmek, yarışmak (*for için*); rekabet etm., mücadele etm. (*with ile*); ~ *with s.o. b-le* rekabet etm.; yarışmak, aşık atmak.

com.pe.tence, com.pe.ten.cy ['kɔmpitəns(i)] *n.* yeterlik, kifayet; kabiliyet, yetenek, güç; gelir, yetki, salâhiyet; **'com.pe.tent** ☐ yeterli, işinin ehli, kabiliyetli, kompetan; yetkili, salâhiyetli.

com.pe.ti.tion [kɔmpi'tiʃən] *n.* yarışma, müsabaka; COM rekabet; *rifle* ~ atıcılık müsabakası; **com.pet.i.tive** ☐ [kəm'petitiv] rekabet edilebilir; rakip olan; rekabet ile ilgili; yarışma türün-

de; **com'pet.i.tor** *n.* rakip, yarışmacı.
com.pi.la.tion [kɔmpi'leiʃən] *n.* derleme; derleme eser; **com.pile** [kəm'pail] *v/t.* derlemek, toplamak (*from -den*).
com.pla.cence, **com.pla.cen.cy** [kəm'pleisns(i)] *n.* kendi halinden memnun olma; memnuniyet, gönül rahatlığı; **com'pla.cent** ☐ kendini beğenmiş, ukalâ; halinden memnun, rahat.
com.plain [kəm'plein] *v/i.* şikâyet etm., yakınmak (*about, of -den*; *that -ki*; *to -e*); suçlamak; **com'plain.ant** *n.* davacı, şikâyetçi; **com'plain.er** *n.* şikâyetçi; **com'plaint** *n.* şikâyet, yakınma, dert; MED hastalık, rahatsızlık.
com.plai.sance [kəm'pleizəns] *n.* hoşgörü, müsamaha, göz yumma, tolerans; **com'plai.sant** ☐ hoşgörülü, müsamahakâr.
com.ple.ment ['kɔmplimənt] **1.** *n.* tamamlayıcı herhangi bir şey, tümleç (*a.* GR); tüm, bütün; MATH bütünler açı; **com.ple'men.tal**, **com.ple'men.ta.ry** *adj.* tamamlayan, tamamlayıcı, tümleyici (*to -e*).
com.plete [kəm'pli:t] **1.** ☐ tam, tamam, bütün, eksiksiz; bitmiş, tamamlanmış; mükemmel, dört başı mamur; **2.** *v/t.* tamamlamak, bitirmek, bütünleştirmek; **com'plete.ness** *n.* bütünlük, tam olma hali; **com'ple.tion** *n.* tamamlama, bitirme; sona erme; yerine getirme.
com.plex ['kɔmpleks] **1.** ☐ karmaşık, çapraşık, anlaşılması güç; *fig.* karışık; bileşik; **~ sentence** GR girişik cümle; **2.** *n.* karmaşa; karışık *veya* bileşik herhangi birşey; kompleks; **com.plex.ion** [kəm'plekʃən] *n.* cilt, ten; genel görünüm, yön, gidişat; **com'plex.i.ty** *n.* güçlük, zorluk; karmaşa.
com.pli.ance [kəm'plaiəns] *n.* rıza; uyma, itaat, baş eğme, uysallık (*with -e*); **in ~ with** *-e* uygun olarak; **com'pli.ant** ☐ uysal, yumuşak başlı, itaatkâr.
com.pli.cate ['kɔmplikeit] *v/t.* karıştırmak, güçleştirmek, zorlaştırmak; **'compli.cat.ed** *adj.* karmaşık, çapraşık, anlaşılması güç; **com.pli'ca.tion** *n.* karmaşıklık, güçlük, zorluk, engel; MED ihtilât, hastalığın başka bir hastalıkla karışması.
com.plic.i.ty [kəm'plisiti] *n.* suç ortaklığı (*in -de*).
com.pli.ment 1. ['kɔmplimənt] *n.* iltifat, kompliman; **2.** ['–ment] *v/t.* (**on**)

kompliman yapmak *-e*, övmek *-i*. iltifat etm. *-e*; **com.pli'men.ta.ry** *adj.* övücü...; parasız..., ücretsiz...; **~ dinner** ziyafet; **~ ticket** parasız bilet.
com.ply [kəm'plai] *vb.* razı olm., uymak, itaat etm. (**with** *-e*); **~ with the rules** kurallara uymak.
com.po.nent [kəm'pəunənt] **1.** *n.* parçaunsur, eleman; **2.** *adj.* tamamlayıcı, birleştirici; **~ part =** **~** **1.**
com.port [kəm'pɔ:t] *vb.* uymak, uygun olm. (**with** *-e*); **~ o.s.** davranmak, hareket etm.
com.pose [kəm'pəuz] *v/t.* meydana getirmek, oluşturmak; bestelemek (*şarkı*); yazmak (*şiir*); TYP dizmek, tertip etm.; sakinleştirmek, kontrol altına almak; **com'posed** *adj.* kendi halinde, sakin; ibaret (**of** *-den*); **com'pos.ed.ly** [–zidli] *adv.* sakince, sakin sakin; **com'pos.er** *n.* bestekâr, besteci, kompozitör; **com'posing 1.** *adj.* rahatlatıcı, yatıştırıcı, sakinleştirici; **2.** *n.* tertip, dizgi; besteleme; **~ machine** dizgi makinesi; **~ room** dizgi evi; **com.pos.ite** ['kɔmpəzit] **1.** *adj.* bileşik, karma, karışık; **2.** *n.* alaşım, bileşim; BOT bileşikgillerden herhangi bir bitki; **com.po'si.tion** *n.* kompozisyon; MUS beste, eser; CHEM bileşim, terkip; PAINT kompozisyon; COM uzlaşma, anlaşma; derleme, biraraya getirme; nitelik, yapı; **com.pos.i.tor** [kəm'pɔzitə] *n.* TYP dizgici, dizici; **com.post** ['kɔmpɔst] **1.** *n.* çürümüş organik maddeli gübre; **2.** *vb.* gübrelemek; **com.po.sure** [kəm'pəuʒə] *n.* sakinlik, huzur, sükunet.
com.pote ['kɔmpɔt] *n.* komposto.
com.pound[1] **1.** ['kɔmpaund] *adj.* bileşik; **~ fracture** MED açık kırık; **~ interest** bileşik faiz; **2.** [–] *n.* bileşim, alaşım, terkip; *a.* **~ word** GR bileşik kelime; **3.** [kəm'paund] *v/t.* birleştirmek, terkip etm., bütün haline getirmek; çoğaltmak, arttırmak, şiddetlendirmek; *v/i.* birleşmek; COM anlaşmak, uzlaşmak (**for** *hususunda*).
com.pound[2] ['kɔmpaund] *n.* içinde binalar bulunan etrafı çevrili arazi.
com.pre.hend [kɔmpri'hend] *v/t.* anlamak, kavramak, idrak etm.; içine almak, kapsamak.
com.pre.hen.si.ble ☐ [kɔmpri'hensəbl] anlaşılır, makul; **com.pre'hen.sion** *n.* anlayış, idrak; kapsam; **com.pre'hen.sive** ☐ geniş, etraflı, şumüllü;

idrakli, anlama yeteneği olan; ~ *school* bir tür sanat okulu; com.pre-'hen.sive.ness *n.* büyüklük, genişlik; anlayışlılık.

com.press 1. [kəm'pres] *v/t.* sık(ıştır)mak, bas(tır)mak, tazyik etm., basınç yapmak; özetlemek, kısaltmak; **2.** ['kɔmpres] *n.* MED kompres; **com.pressed** [kəm'prest] *adj.* sıkıştırılmış, basınçlı; ~ *air* sıkıştırılmış hava, basınçlı hava; com'press.i.ble *adj.* sıkıştırılabilir; compres.sion [.'reʃən] *n.* özetleme, kısaltma; PHYS basınç, tazyik, sıkıştırma; MEC kompresyon; com'pres.sor [.sə] *n.* MEC kompresör.

com.prise [kəm'praiz] *v/t.* kapsamak, içine almak, ihtiva etm.

com.pro.mise ['kɔmprəmaiz] **1.** *n.* uzlaşma, uyuşma, anlaşma; **2.** *v/t.* uzlaştırmak, aralarını bulmak; *-in* şerefini tehlikeye atmak, *bşi* tehlikeye atmak; *v/i.* uzlaşmak, anlaşmak, uyuşmak (*on konusunda*).

comp.trol.ler [kən'trəulə] *n.* hesap kontrol memuru, kontrolör, denetçi.

com.pul.sion [kəm'pʌlʃən] *n.* zorla(n)ma, mecburiyet, yüküm; com'pul.so.ry [.səri] *adj.* mecburî, zorunlu; ~ *military service* mecburî askerlik; ~ *subject* zorunlu ders.

com.punc.tion [kəm'pʌŋkʃən] *n.* vicdan azabı; pişmanlık, esef.

com.put.a.ble [kəm'pju:təbl] *adj.* hesaplanabilir; **com.pu.ta.tion** [kɔmpju:'teiʃən] *n.* hesap, hesaplama; com.pu'ta.tor = *computer*; com.pute [kəm'pju:t] *v/t.* hesaplamak, hesap etm. (*at olarak*); com'put.er *n.* kompütür, bilgisayar.

com.rade ['kɔmrid] *n.* arkadaş, dost; yoldaş; 'com.rade.ship *n.* arkadaşlık.

con¹ [kɔn] *vb.* incelemek, tetkik etm., dikkatle okumak.

con² NAUT [.] *vb.* dümen kullanmak.

con³ [.] *adv. abbr.* = **contra** aleyhte, karşı; *pro and* ~ lehte ve aleyhte; *the pros and* ~*s* lehte ve aleyhte olan tartışmalar.

con⁴ *Am. sl.* [.] **1.** *s.* *confidence man*; **2.** *vb.* dolandırmak, kandırmak, aldatmak, yutturmak.

con.cat.e.nate [kɔn'kætineit] *vb.* mst *fig.* birbirine bağlamak; con.cat.e'na.tion *n.* birbirine bağlama (*a. fig.*).

con.cave ['kɔn'keiv] içbükey..., konkav...; con.cav.i.ty [.'kæviti] *n.* içbü-

keylik; içbükey yüzey.

con.ceal [kən'si:l] *v/t.* gizlemek, saklamak, saklı tutmak, örtbas etm. (*from s.o. b-den*); con'ceal.ment *n.* gizle(n)-me, sakla(n)ma; *a. place of* ~ gizlenme yeri.

con.cede [kən'si:d] *vb.* kabul etm., kabullenmek; vermek, bahşetmek; müsaade etm.; con'ced.ed.ly *adv.* kabullenerek.

con.ceit [kən'si:t] *n.* kendini beğenmişlik, ukalâlık, kibir, gurur; *out of* ~ *with* -den artık memnun olmayan; con-'ceit.ed □ kibirli, gururlu, kendini beğenmiş, ukalâ; con'ceit.ed.ness *n.* kendini beğenmişlik, gurur, kibir.

con.ceiv.a.ble □ [kən'si:vəbl] akla uygun, düşünülebilir, inanılabilir; con-'ceive *v/i.* hamile kalmak, gebe kalmak *-den*; anlamak, kavramak (*of -i*); *v/t.* ortaya atmak, yaratmak, çıkarmak; anlamak, anlam vermek; fikrinde olm.; hayal etm., zannetmek, tahmin etm.; ~*d in* ...fikrinde olan.

con.cen.trate ['kɔnsəntreit] **1.** *v/t. & v/i.* bir yere topla(n)mak; *fig.* kendini vermek *-e*, zihnini bir noktaya toplamak; CHEM koyulaştırmak; **2.** *n.* koyu madde; **concen'tra.tion** *n.* topla(n)-ma; kendini verme, dikkat; CHEM koyulaş(tır)ma, konsantrasyon; ~ *camp* toplama kampı; con'cen.tre, con-'cen.ter [.tə] *vb.* merkezileş(tir)mek, merkeze topla(n)mak; con'cen.tric *adj.* (~*ally*) ortak merkezli..., merkezleri aynı olan...

con.cept ['kɔnsept] *n.* kavram, görüş, fikir; con.cep.tion [kən'sepʃən] *n.* fikir, görüş, düşünce, kavram; BIOL gebe olma, hamile kalma.

con.cern [kən'sə:n] **1.** *n.* ilgi, alâka (*in -de, for için*); münasebet, irtibat, bağlantı (*with ile*); COM ticarethane, kuruluş; pay, hisse; tasa, kaygı, merak; F şey, nesne; **2.** *v/t.* ilgilendirmek, alâkadar etm.; ilişkisi olm., karışmak, bulaşmak; endişeye düşürmek, üzmek, canını sıkmak; ~ *o.s. with* karışmak, müdahale etm.; *be* ~*ed* endişeli olm., kaygı duymak; ilgi duymak, meşgul olm.; *bşe* bulaşmak, karışmış olm.; *be* ~*ed that* ... *-den* kaygı duymak; *I am* ~*ed to inf.* -*mekle* meşgulüm; *be* ~*ed with* ... ile meşgul olm., uğraşmak; con-'cerned □ ilgili, alâkalı, meşgul (*in ile*); endişeli, kaygılı (*at, about, for -de, hususunda*); *those* ~ ilişkisi olanlar; con'cern.ing *prp*. hakkında, hususunda, -*e* dair, ... ile ilgili olarak.

con.cert 1. ['kɔnsət] *n*. konser; ['-sə:t] *n*. uyum, ahenk; birleşme; 2. [kən'sə:t] *vb*. planlamak, beraberce karar vermek, anlaşmak; con'cert.ed *adj*. kararlaştırılmış, planlı, birlikte yapılmış...; MUS bölüm bölüm düzenlenmiş; con.cer.ti.na MUS [kɔnsə-'ti:nə] *n*. akordeon, körüklü armonika; con.cer.to MUS [kən'tʃə:təu] *n*. konçerto.

con.ces.sion [kən'seʃən] *n*. kabul, teslim, tasdik; bağış, ihsan, teberru; imtiyaz, ayrıcalık; hizmete karşılık devletçe verilen arazi; con.ces.sion.aire [-'neə] *n*. imtiyazlı kimse, ayrıcalık sahibi.

con.ces.sive □ [kən'sesiv] teslim *veya* kabul niteliğinde olan.

conch [kɔŋk] *n*. helezonî sedef kabuk.

con.cil.i.ate [kən'silieit] *v*/*t*. uzlaştırmak, barıştırmak, aralarını bulmak; sakinleştirmek, yatıştırmak; gönlünü almak; con.cil.i'a.tion *n*. uzlaştırma, barıştırma; yatıştırma, sakinleştirme; con'cil.i.a.tor *n*. uzlaştıran kimse, barıştıran kimse; con'cil.i.a.to.ry [-ətəri] *adj*. gönül alıcı; barıştırıcı, uzlaştırıcı; ~ *proposal* anlaşma önergesi.

con.cin.ni.ty [kən'siniti] *n*. ahenk, uyum; tutarlık.

con.cise □ [kən'sais] öz, kısa, özlü, muhtasar; con'cise.ness *n*. kısa ve öz olma.

con.clave ['kɔnkleiv] *n*. özel *veya* gizli toplantı.

con.clude [kən'klu:d] *v*/*t*. & *v*/*i*. bit(ir)mek, sona er(dir)mek, sonuçlan(dır)mak, neticelen(dir)mek; netice çıkarmak; karar vermek (to *inf*. -*meğe*); *to be ~d in our next* sonu gelecek sayıda; con'clud.ing *adj*. son..., bitiş...

con.clu.sion [kən'klu:ʒən] *n*. son, nihayet netice, karar, sonuç; akdetme; netice çıkarma; *in ~* son söz olarak, sözü bitirirken, son olarak; *try ~s with s.o.* b-le yarışmak, boy ölçüşmek; con'clu.sive [-siv] □ son, nihaî; katî, kesin.

con.coct [kən'kɔkt] *vb*. birbirine karıştırarak hazırlamak, yapmak; *fig*. uydurmak; con'coc.tion *n*. karışım, tertip; karıştırma; *fig*. uydurma.

con.com.i.tance, con.com.i.tan.cy [kən'kɔmitəns(i)] *n*. eşlik eden şey, birlikte olan şey; con'com.i.tant 1. □

eşlik eden, beraberinde olan; 2. *n*. eşlik eden şey, birlikte olan şey.

con.cord ['kɔŋkɔ:d] *n*. uygunluk, bağdaşma, ahenk, uyum (*a*. GR); barış, antlaşma; MUS uyum, harmoni, armoni; con'cordance [kən'kɔ:dəns] *n*. uyum, ahenk, uygunluk, uyuşma; ECCL bir kitaptaki önemli kelimelerin alfabetik sırası; con'cord.ant □ uyumlu, uygun; MUS alıenkli; con'cor.dat ECCL [-dæt] *n*. antlaşma; kilise ile devlet arasındaki anlaşma.

con.course ['kɔŋkɔ:s] *n*. toplanma, biraraya gelme; kalabalık, izdiham; *Am*. tren istasyonundaki geniş bina.

con.crete 1. □ ['kɔnkri:t] somut, maddî; belirli, kesin; betondan yapılmış, beton...; 2. [-] *n*. beton; PHLS, GR somut varlık; *in the ~* somut olarak; 3. [kən-'kri:t] *vb*. katılaş(tır)mak; bütünleş(-tir)mek; sertleş(tir)mek; somutlaş(tır)mak; ['kɔnkri:t] beton dökmek, betonla kaplamak (*yol*); ~ **noun** GR somut isim; con.cre.tion [kən'kri:ʃən] *n*. kat(ıl)(dur)ma, katılaş(tır)ma; donmuş madde.

con.cu.bi.nage [kən'kju:binidʒ] *n*. gayri meşru olarak birarada yaşama, metres hayatı; con.cu.bine ['kɔŋkjubain] *n*. kapatma, cariye, odalık, metres.

con.cu.pis.cence [kən'kju:pisəns] *n*. şehvet, cinsel arzu; con'cu.pis.cent *adj*. şehvetli.

con.cur [kən'kə:] *vb*. uymak, razı olm., uyuşmak, aynı fikirde olm., mutabık olm. (*with ile*; *in -de*); beraber olm., aynı anda olm. (*to -mek için*); con-cur.rence [-'kʌrəns] *n*. uyum, anlaşma, fikir birliği, mutabakat; aynı anda olma; *in ~ with* müştereken, beraberce, birlikte; con'cur.rent □ uygun, mutabık; aynı anda olan, beraber bulunan (*s. concur*); işbirliği yapan.

con.cus.sion [kən'kʌʃən] *n*.: ~ *of the brain* beyin sarsıntısı.

con.demn [kən'dem] *v*/*t*. kınamak, ayıplamak; suçlamak; çarptırmak, mahkûm etm. (*a*. *fig*.) (*to -e*); istimlâk etm., kamulaştırmak, elinden almak; ele vermek; *his looks ~ him* bakışları onun suçlu olduğunu gösteriyor; ~*ed cell* ölüm hücresi; con'dem.na.ble [-nəbl] *adj*. mahkûm edilebilir; kınanmaya lâyık; istimlâk edilebilir; con-dem.na.tion [kɔndem'neiʃən] *n*. kınama, ayıplama; suçlu çıkarma; mahkûmiyet; istimlâk; **con.dem.na.to.ry** □ [kən'demnətəri] kınayıcı.

con.den.sa.ble [kən'densəbl] *adj.* yoğunlaştırılabilir; kısaltılabilir, özetlenebilir; **con.den.sa.tion** [kɔnden-'seiʃən] *n.* kısaltma, özet; yoğunlaş(tır)ma, koyulaş(tır)ma; **con.dense** [kən'dens] *v/t. & v/i.* koyulaş(tır)mak, yoğunlaş(tır)mak; MEC sıvılaştırmak; özetlemek, kısaltmak; **con'dens.er** *n.* ELECT, MEC kondansatör.

con.de.scend [kɔndi'send] *vb.* tenezzülde bulunmak, lütfetmek; **con.de-'scend.ing** □ tenezzül eden; **con.de-'scen.sion** *n.* tenezzül, alçak gönüllülük gösterme.

con.dign □ [kən'dain] lâyık, müstahak, hak etmiş (*cezayı*).

con.di.ment ['kɔndimənt] *n.* yemeğe çeşni veren şey.

con.di.tion [kən'diʃən] **1.** *n.* koşul, şart, kayıt; durum, hal, vaziyet; medenî hal; sağlık; **~s** *pl.* şartlar; **on ~ that...** şartı ile; **out of ~** sağlık yönünden iyi durumda olmayan, bedenen uygun olmayan; **2.** *vb.* ayarlamak, uygun bir hale getirmek, eğitmek; düzenlemek; şart koşmak, kayıt altına sokmak; havalandırmak; **con'di.tion.al** □ şartlı, şarta bağlı, şart..., bağlı (**on, upon** -*e*); **~ (mood)** GR şart kipi; **con.di.tion.al.i.ty** [-'næliti] *n.* şarta bağlılık; **con'di.tion.al.ly** [-əli] *adv.* şartlı olarak; **con-'di.tioned** *adj.* şarta bağlı; uygun durumda olan; **con'ditioned re.flex** PSYCH şartlı refleks, şartlı davranış.

con.dole [kən'dəul] *vb.* taziyede bulunmak, (*üzüntüye*) ortak olm., başsağlığı dilemek (**with** -*e*); **con'do.lence** *n.* taziye, başsağlığı.

con'do.min.i.um ['kɔndə'miniəm] *n.* bir ülke üzerinde birkaç devletin ortak hâkimiyeti; *Am.* kat mülkiyeti.

con.do.na.tion [kɔndəu'neiʃən] *n.* göz yumma, görmezden gelme; telâfi, yerini doldurma; **con.done** [kən'dəun] *v/t.* göz yummak, affetmek, görmezden gelmek; karşılamak, telâfi etm.

con.dor ORN ['kɔndɔː] *n.* büyük akbaba.

con.duce [kən'djuːs] *vb.* yardım etm., katkıda bulunmak, sebep olm., vesile olm. (**to** -*e*); **con'du.cive** *adj.* yardım eden, sebep *veya* vesile olan (**to** -*e*).

con.duct 1. ['kɔndʌkt] *n.* davranış, tavır, hareket; idare, yönetim; **2.** [kən-'dʌkt] *vb.* yol göstermek, önderlik

etm., rehberlik etm.; idare etm., yürütmek, yönetmek; PHYS nakletmek, geçirmek, iletmek; davranmak, hareket etm.; MUS orkestra idare etm.; **~ o.s.** davranmak, hareket etm.; para toplamak (*yolcudan*); **con.duct.i.bil.i.ty** [kəndʌkti'biliti] *n.* PHYS iletkenlik; **con'duct.i.ble** [-təbl] *adj.* PHYS ...iletebilen, ...geçirebilen; **conduct.ing** *adj.* iletken...; **con'duc.tion** *n.* iletme, geçirme, nakletme; **con'duc.tive** □ [-tiv] PHYS iletken..., ...geçirici; **con-duc.tiv.i.ty** [kɔndʌk'tiviti] *n.* PHYS iletkenlik; **con.duc.tor** [kən'dʌktə] *n.* biletçi, kondüktör; MUS orkestra şefi; ELECT iletken madde; rehber, kılavuz; **con-'duc.tress** *n.* kadın biletçi.

con.duit ['kɔndit] *n.* oluk, su yolu, kanal; ['-djuit] ELECT elektrik borusu.

cone [kəun] *n.* koni, mahrut; BOT kozalak.

co.ney ['kəuni] *n.* tavşan; tavşan kürkü.

con.fab F ['kɔnfæb] **1.** = **con.fab.u.late** [kən'fæbjuleit] *v/i.* sohbet etm., çene çalmak; **2.** = **con.fab.u'la.tion** *n.* sohbet, hoşbeş.

con.fec.tion [kən'fekʃən] *n.* şekerleme, bonbon; hazırlama, imalât; konfeksiyon, hazır giyim; **con.fec.tion.er** [-'fekʃnə] *n.* şekerci, pastacı; **con'fec.tion.er.y** *n.* şekerlemeler; *part. Am.* şekerci dükkânı, pastane.

con.fed.er.a.cy [kən'fedərəsi] *n.* birlik, konfederasyon; **the** ♀ *Am.* 1860-1861 yıllarında onbir Güney Eyaletin oluşturduğu konfederasyon; **con'fed.er.ate 1.** [-rit] *adj.* müttefik, birleşmiş; **2.** [-rit] *n.* müttefik kimse *veya* devlet; suç ortağı; **3.** [-reit] *v/t. & v/i.* birleş(tir)mek, ittifak et(tir)mek; **con.fed-er'a.tion** *n.* birlik, konfederasyon.

con.fer [kən'fəː] *v/t.* vermek, bahşetmek (**on** -*e*); *v/i.* danışmak, görüşmek (**with** *ile*; **about, upon** *hususunda*); **con.fer.ence** ['kɔnfərəns] *n.* müzakere, konferans, toplantı.

con.fess [kən'fes] *vb.* itiraf etm., ikrar etm.; doğrulamak; **~ to** ECCL günah çıkar(t)mak; **con'fess.ed.ly** [-sidli] *adv.* itiraf edildiği gibi, kendi itirafı ile; **con'fes.sion** [-ʃən] *n.* itiraf, ikrar, doğrulama; ECCL günah çıkar(t)ma; **con'fession.al** [-ʃənl] **1.** *adj.* itiraf *veya* günah çıkar(t)ma ile ilgili, itiraf...; **2.** *n.* günah çıkar(t)ma hücresi; **con-'fes.sor** [-sə] *n.* itiraf eden kimse; ECCL günah çıkartan papaz.

con.fet.ti [kən'feti:] *n. pl.* konfeti.

con.fi.dant [kɔnfi'dænt] *n.* sırdaş, dert ortağı; **con.fi'dante** [_] *n.* kadın dert ortağı.

con.fide [kən'faid] *v/t.* emanet etm., teslim etm., sır vermek, gizlice söylemek (**to s.o.** *b-ne*); güvenmek, itimat etm. (**in** *-e*).

con.fi.dence ['kɔnfidəns] *n.* güven, emniyet, itimat (**in** *-e*); gizlilik, mahremiyet; ~ **game** = **confidence trick**; ~ **man** dolandırıcı, üçkâğıtçı; ~ **trick** dolandırıcılık, üçkâğıtçılık; '**con.fi.dent** □ emin, güvenli (**of** *-den*); **con.fi.dential** □ [_ 'denʃəl] gizli, mahrem; güvenilir; güvenen, inanan; ~ **clerk** özel kâtip.

con.fig.u.ra.tion [kənfigju'reiʃən] *n.* şekil, suret, görünüş; gruplaşma.

con.fine 1. ['kɔnfain] *n. mst* ~**s** *pl.* sınır, hudut; **2.** [kən'fain] *v/t.* sınırlamak, sınırlar içinde tutmak, toplamak, hasretmek (**to** *-e*); hapsetmek, evde *veya* yatakta tutmak; **be** ~**d to bed** yatakta yatmak; lohusa olm.; **be** ~**d (of)** doğurmak; **con'fine.ment** *n.* hapsedilme, kapalı tutulma; lohusalık.

con.firm [kən'fə:m] *v/t.* teyit etm., saptamak, sağlama bağlamak, kuvvetlendirmek, tasdik etm., onaylamak; **confirma.tion** [kɔnfə'meiʃən] *n.* tasdik, teyit, doğrulama, belgeleme; **confirm.a.tive** □ [kən'fə:mətiv], **con'firm.a.to.ry** [_ təri] teyit edici, doğrulayıcı, sağlamlaştırıcı; **con'firmed** *adj.* kökleşmiş, yerleşmiş, müzmin (*part.* MED); düşkün, müptela, tiryaki; COM teyitli, onaylı.

con.fis.cate ['kɔnfiskeit] *v/t.* müsadere etm., haczetmek, el koymak *-e*; istimlâk etm., kamulaştırmak; **con.fis'ca.tion** *n.* müsadere, haciz, el koyma; istimlâk, kamulaştırma; **con'fis.cato.ry** [_ kətəri] *adj.* müsadereye ait, hacze ait.

con.fla.gra.tion [kɔnflə'greiʃən] *n.* büyük yangın.

con.flict 1. ['kɔnflikt] *n.* kavga, çekişme, mücadele, çarpışma, zıtlaşma, çatışma; *fig.* ayrılık, fikir ayrılığı, ihtilâf, anlaşmazlık; **2.** [kən'flikt] *v/i.* (**with**) zıtlaşmak *-le*, ihtilafa düşmek *-le*, çekişmek *-le*, mücadele etm. *-le*, muhalif olm. *-e*.

con.flu.ence ['kɔnfluəns], **con.flux** ['_flʌks] *n.* iki akarsuyun birleştiği

nokta, kavşak; birlikte akma; **con.fluent** ['_fluənt] **1.** *adj.* birlikte akarak birleşen; bir araya birikip karışmış; **2.** *n.* bir ırmağa karışan akarsu.

con.form [kən'fɔ:m] *v/t.* uydurmak *-e*, ayarlamak *-e*, alıştırmak *-e*; *v/i.* ~ **to** uymak *-e*, itaat etm. *-e*, boyun eğmek *-e*; ~ **with** uymak *-e*, uyum içinde olm. *ile*; **con'form.a.ble** □ (**to**) uygun *-e*, yerinde, uyumlu; itaatkâr, uysal, boyun eğen; **con.for.ma.tion** [kɔnfɔ:'meiʃən] *n.* şekil, yapı, çatı; oluşma; uyma, adaptasyon, uygunluk; **con.form.ist** [kən'fɔ:mist] *n.* toplum kurallarına uyan kimse; uyumlu kimse, uysal kimse; **con'form.i.ty** *n.* uygunluk, benzeyiş; **in** ~ **with** uyarak *-e*, uygun olarak *-e*, mucibince.

con.found [kən'faund] *v/t.* şaşırtmak, zihnini karıştırmak, kafasını allak bullak etm., karman çorman etm.; yenmek, mağlûp etm., yıkmak; ~ **it!** F Allahın cezası!; ~ **you!** F Allah belânı versin senin!; **con'found.ed** □ F Allahın cezası, baş belâsı; şaşırmış, zihni karışmış.

con.fra.ter.ni.ty [kɔnfrə'tə:niti] *n.* hayır kurumu, kardeşlik cemiyeti.

con.front [kən'frʌnt] *v/t.* karşılaştırmak, yüzleştirmek (**with** *ile*); karşı durmak, göğüs germek, karşısına çıkmak; karşısında olm. *-in*, bakmak *-e* (*evin cephesi*); **find o.s.** ~**ed with** *k-ni* bşle karşı karşıya bulmak; **confron.ta.tion** [kɔnfrʌn'teiʃən] *n.* yüzleş(tir)me; mücadele, kavga, ihtilâf; karşılaştırma, mukayese.

con.fuse [kən'fju:z] *v/t.* karıştırmak, karmakarışık etm.; şaşırtmak; ayırt edememek; zihnini allak bullak etm.; **con'fused** □ kafası karışmış, zihni allak bullak, şaşkın; ayırt edilemez, seçilemez; şaşırmış, karman çorman; **con'fusion** [_ʒən] *n.* karışıklık, düzensizlik; şaşkınlık.

con.fut.a.ble [kən'fju:təbl] *adj.* çürütülebilir (*iddia*); **con.fu.ta.tion** [kɔnfju:'teiʃən] *n.* tekzip, çürütme (*iddia*, *fikir*); **con.fute** [kən'fju:t] *vb.* tekzip etm., çürütmek (*iddia, fikir*), yalanlamak, aksini ispat etm.

congé ['kɔ:nʒei] *n.* ayrılma izni; yol verme, sepetleme, kovma; referans; **give s.o. his** ~ *b-nin* gitmesine izin vermek.

con.geal [kən'dʒi:l] *v/t. & v/i.* don(dur)mak (*a. fig.*); pıhtılaş(tır)mak;

con'geal.a.ble *adj.* donabilir, pıhtılaşabilir.

con.ge.la.tion [kɔndʒi'leiʃən] *n.* donma; pıhtılaşma.

con.gen.ial □ [kən'dʒi:njəl] uygun, cana yakın (*with ile*); benzer (*to -e*); hoş; con.ge.ni.al.i.ty [ˌ-ni'æliti] *n.* uygunluk, benzerlik, yakınlık.

con.gen.i.tal [kɔn'dʒenitl] *adj.* doğuştan olan, fıtrî, Tanrı vergisi; con'gen-i.tal.ly [ˌ-təli] *adv.* doğuştan.

con.ger (eel) ICHTH ['kɔŋɡə(r'i:l)] *n.* büyük yılanbalığı.

con.gest [kən'dʒest] *v/t. & v/i.* topla(n)mak; yığ(ıl)mak; tıka(n)mak (*damar, trafik*); con'ges.tion *n.* kan birikmesi; tıkanıklık; izdiham, kalabalık; ~ *of population* fazla nüfus yoğunluğu; *traffic* ~ trafik tıkanıklığı.

con.glom.er.ate 1. [kən'glɔmərit] *adj.* küme halinde toplanmış, yığılmış; 2. [ˌ-] *n.* küme, yığın; COM holding; 3. [ˌ-reit] *vb.* bir araya toplamak, yığmak, kümelemek; COM holdingleşmek; con-glom.er'ation *n.* yığın, küme; yığ(ıl)ma.

con.grat.u.late [kən'ɡrætjuleit] *v/t.* tebrik etm., kutlamak (*s.o. on veya upon s.th. b-ni bşden dolayı*); con-grat.u'la.tion *n.* tebrik, kutlama; con-'grat.u.la.tor *n.* tebrik eden, kutlayan; con.grat.u.la.to.ry *adj.* tebrik…, kutlama…

con.gre.gate ['kɔŋɡrigeit] *vb.* topla(n)mak, birleş(tir)mek, biraraya gelmek, biraraya getirmek; con.gre'ga-tion *n.* ECCL cemaat; toplantı, topla(n)-ma; congre'ga.tion.al [ˌ-ʃənl] *adj.* cemaate ait.

con.gress ['kɔŋɡres] *n.* kongre, toplantı; ♀ *Am.* POL Millet Meclisi (*Senato ve Temsilciler Meclisi*); con.gres-sion.al [ˌ-'ɡreʃənl] *adj.* Meclise ait, Meclis…; 'Congress.man, 'Con-gress.wom.an *n. Am.* POL Millet Meclisi üyesi, senatör.

con.gru.ence, con.gru.en.cy ['kɔŋ-gruəns(i)] *n.* = *congruity*; MATH benzeşim; 'congru.ent *adj.* = *congruous*; MATH benzer; con.gru.i.ty [ˌ-'gru:iti] *n.* uygunluk, uyum; con.gru.ous □ ['ˌ-gruəs] uygun, münasip (*to -e*); uyumlu, ahenkli (*to, mst with ile*).

con.ic, con.i.cal □ ['kɔnik(əl)] koni şeklinde, konik…; ~ *section* MATH konik kesit eğrisi.

co.ni.fer ['kəunifə] *n.* kozalaklı ağaç;

co'nif.er.ous *adj.* kozalaklı, kozalak veren.

con.jec.tur.al □ [kən'dʒektʃərəl] tahminî, farazi, varsayılı; con'jec.ture 1. *n.* zan, sanı, tahmin, varsayı, farz; 2. *v/t.* tahmin etm., farzetmek, tasavvur etm., zannetmek, sanmak.

con.join [kən'dʒɔin] *vb.* birleş(tir)mek, bitiş(tir)mek, bağlamak; con.joint ['kɔndʒɔint] *adj.* birleşmiş, ortak; 'con.joint.ly *adv.* birleşmiş olarak.

con.ju.gal □ ['kɔndʒuɡəl] evlilikle ilgili, karıkocalığa ait, evlilik…; con.ju-gate 1. ['ˌ-geit] *v/t.* çekmek (*fiil*); *v/i.* BIOL birleşmek; 2. ['ˌ-git] *adj.* BOT birleşmiş; conju.ga.tion [ˌ-'geiʃən] *n.* fiil çekimi; birleşme.

con.junct □ [kən'dʒʌŋkt] birleşmiş, bitişik, ortak, müşterek; con.junc.tion *n.* birleşme; AST konjonksiyon; GR bağlaç; rastlantı, tesadüf, aynı zamanda olma (*olaylar*); con.junc.ti.va ANAT [kɔndʒʌŋk'taivə] *n.* konjonktiv; con-junc.tive [kən'dʒʌŋktiv] *adj.* birleştiren, bitiştiren; ~ *mood* şart kipi; con-'junc.tive.ly *adv.* birleştirerek, bitiştirerek, bağlayarak; conjunc.ti.vi.tis MED [ˌ-'vaitis] *n.* konjonktivit; con-'junc.ture [ˌ-tʃə] *n.* çeşitli olay *veya* durumların biraraya gelmesi, hal ve şartlar; COM konjonktür.

con.ju.ra.tion [kɔndʒuə'reiʃən] *n.* büyü, sihir; sihirbazlık; ruh çağırma; con.jure [kən'dʒuə] *v/t.* yalvarmak -e, rica etm. -e; ['kʌndʒə] *vb.* el çabukluğu ile yapmak; ruh çağırmak; hokkabazlık yapmak, el çabukluğu ile marifet yapmak; ~ *up* büyü yoluyla çağırmak; 'con.jur.er, con.jur.or *n.* hokkabaz, sihirbaz, büyücü; 'con.jur.ing-trick *n.* hokkabazlık, el çabukluğu.

conk F [kɔŋk] *vb.* işlememek, çalışmamak, durmak; grev yapmak; bayılmak, ölmek, uyumak; başına vurmak.

con.nate ['kɔneit] *adj.* doğuştan olan, fıtrî; akraba olan, benzer; BOT & ANAT bitişik; con.nat.u.ral [kə'nætʃrəl] *adj.* doğuştan, fıtrî, tabii; aynı tabiatta olan.

con.nect [kə'nekt] *v/t. & v/i.* bağla(n)-mak, bitiş(tir)mek, birleş(tir)mek; aralarında ilgi kurmak; ELECT cereyana bağlamak, devreyi açmak; con'nect-ed □ bağlı, bitişik; anlamca ilgili; *be* ~ *with* irtibatta olm. -*le*; bağlı olm. -*le*; akraba olm. -*le*; *be well* ~ iyi bir çevreden gelmek, yüksek tabakadan olm.; con'necting *adj.* bağlayıcı, bağ-

lantı…, bağlama…, irtibat…; **~ rod** bi-
yel, krank kolu, bağlama çubuğu;
con'**nec.tion** s. **connexion**; con'**nec-
tive** □ bağlayıcı, birleştirici; **~ tissue**
ANAT katılgan doku.

con.nex.ion [kə'nekʃən] n. bağlantı, irtibat, ilgi, alâka, ilişki, münasebet;
ELECT bağlama vasıtası, ekleme; süreklilik, devamlılık; akrabalık, hısımlık;
COM müşteriler; ticarî ilişki; iş, görev;
sınıf, mezhep, grup, parti.

conn.ing-tow.er NAUT ['kɔniŋtauə] n.
harp gemilerinde kumanda kulesi.

con.niv.ance [kə'naivəns] n. göz yumma, suç ortaklığı (**at, in, with** -e); con-
'**nive** vb.; **~ at** göz yummak -e, suç ortağı olm. -e. görmezlikten gelmek -i.

con.nois.seur [kɔnə'səː] n. (**of** veya **in
wine** etc. şarapta vs.) erbap, ehil, mütehassıs, uzman, bir işten iyi anlayan
kimse.

con.no.ta.tion [kɔnəu'teiʃən] n.
çağrışım, diğer anlam, asıl anlamından
başka kavram; con'**note** vb. akla getirmek, anlamına gelmek, demeye gelmek, ifade etm.

con.nu.bi.al □ [kə'njuːbjəl] evliliğe
ait, evlilik…, karı koca…

con.quer ['kɔŋkə] v/t. fethetmek, zaptetmek, galip gelmek; fig. yenmek
(korku); '**con.quer.or** n. fatih, galip;
F final maçı.

con.quest ['kɔŋkwest] n. fetih, zapt;
zafer, başarı.

con.san.guin.e.ous [kɔnsæŋ'gwin-
iəs] adj. aynı soydan, aynı ırktan, akraba; con**san'quin.i.ty** n. kan akrabalığı,
aynı soydan gelme.

con.science ['kɔnʃəns] n. vicdan; **in all
~** F doğrusu, vicdanen; mutlaka, elbette; **have the ~ to do** bşi yapmaya vicdanı elvermek; **~ money** vicdanı rahatlatmak için verilen para; '**con.scien-
ce.less** adj. vicdansız.

con.sci.en.tious □ [kɔnʃi'enʃəs] vicdanının sesini dinleyen, vicdan sahibi;
temiz iş yapan, dürüst, insaflı; **~ objector** askerlik hizmetini reddeden kimse;
con.sci'en.tious.ness n. vicdan, vic-
danlılık; dürüstlük.

con.scious □ ['kɔnʃəs] bilinçli, şuurlu,
farkında olan; ayık; **be ~ of** -in farkında
olm., bilincinde olm.; '**con.scious-
ness** n. bilinç, şuur, idrak, anlayış,
akıl, his.

con.script MIL **1.** [kən'skript] vb. askere çağırmak, askere almak; **2.** ['kɔn-

skript] adj. askere alınmış; **3.** [-] n. askere alınmış nefer, kur'a neferi, acemi
asker; **con.scrip.tion** MIL [kən'skrip-
ʃən] n. askere çağırma; mecburi askerlik; savaş zamanında alınan mecburi
vergi; **industrial ~** bedenen çalışma
yükümlülüğü.

con.se.crate ['kɔnsikreit] v/t. takdis
etm.; Tanrıya adamak, tahsis etm., vakfetmek; con.**se'cra.tion** n. takdis merasimi; adama, vakfetme, takdis, ithaf;
'**con.secra.tor** n. kendini adamış kimse; bş bağışlayan kimse.

con.sec.u.tive [kən'sekjutiv] adj. arka
arkaya, birbirini takibeden, art arta
gelen; GR ardıl; con'**sec.u.tive.ly** adv.
birbirini takip ederek, art arta gelerek.

con.sen.sus [kən'sensəs] n. umumun
fikri, fikir birliği, oy birliği, ittifak.

con.sent [kən'sent] **1.** n. (**to** -e) müsaade, izin, rıza, muvafakat; oy birliği, ittifak; **age of ~** erginlik yaşı; **with one ~**
oy birliği ile, tam ittifakla; **2.** vb. razı
olm., muvafakat etm., rıza göstermek
(**to, in** -e); **con.sen.tient** [-'senʃənt]
adj. razı, muvafık, kabul eden.

con.se.quence ['kɔnsikwəns] n. sonuç, netice, akıbet; eser, semere;
ehemmiyet, önem; **in ~ of** neticesinde,
sonucu olarak, sebebiyle; '**con.se-
quent 1.** adj. neticesi olan, sonucu
olan, bağlı; **2.** n. netice, sonuç; con-
se.quen.tial □ [-'kwenʃəl] neticesi
olan, bağlı olan (**on, upon** -e); con.**se-
quent.ly** ['-kwəntli] adv. netice olarak, bu sebeple, sonuç olarak, binaenaleyh.

con.ser.va.tion [kɔnsə:vei'ʃən] n. koruma, muhafaza, himaye; doğal kaynakları koruma; **con.serv.a.tism**
[kən'sə:vətizəm] n. muhafazakârlık,
tutuculuk; con'**serv.ative 1.** □ ihtiyatlı, tedbirli, ılımlı, mutedil (**of**); POL
muhafazakâr, tutucu; **2.** n. tutucu kimse, muhafazakâr kimse; tedbirli kimse;
con'**ser.va.toire** [-twaː] n. MUS konservatuvar; con'**ser.va.tor** n. koruyucu, himaye eden kimse, koruma görevlisi; con'**serv.a.to.ry** [-tri] n. limonluk, ser; MUS konservatuvar; con-
'**serve** v/t. muhafaza etm., korumak;
şeker ile muhafaza etm., konserve yapmak.

con.sid.er [kən'sidə] v/t. düşünmek,
göz önünde tutmak; hesaba katmak,
dikkate almak; addetmek, saymak,
farzetmek, sanmak; hürmet etm.; in-

celemek, mütalâa etm.; *v/i.* tefekkür etm., durup düşünmek; *all things ~ed* enine boyuna düşünülürse, herşey göz önünde tutulursa; **con'sid.er.a.ble** ☐ hayli; çok, epey; büyük; önemli, hatırı sayılır; **con'sid.er.ably** *adv.* epeyce, oldukça; **con'sid.er.ate** [-rit] ☐ saygılı, nazik, düşünceli, hürmetkâr; **con.sid.er.a.tion** [-'reiʃən] *n.* göz önüne alma; saygı, itibar, nezaket, hürmet; düşünce; faktör, husus; karşılık, bedel, ödül; önem, ehemmiyet; COM pey akçesi; *be under ~* görüşülmekte olm., tetkik edilmekte olm., gözden geçirilmekte olm.; *take into ~* göz önüne almak, hesaba katmak; *money is no ~* para önemli değil; *on no ~* hiç bir surette, asla; **con'sid.er.ing 1.** *prp.* -*e* göre, -*e* nazaran; -*i* göz önünde tutulursa; yine de, rağmen; **2.** *adv.* F şartlar göz önünde tutulursa.

con.sign [kən'sain] *v/t.* göndermek, yollamak; teslim etm., vermek, tahsis etm., adamak; COM mal göndermek; **con.sig.nation** [kɔnsai'neiʃən], **con.sign.ment** [kən'sainmənt] *n.* gönderme, sevk, teslim, sevkiyat; COM gönderilen mallar; **con.signee** [kɔnsai'niː] *n.* kendisine mal gönderilen kimse, alıcı; **con.sign.er, con.signor** [kən-'sainə] *n.* mal gönderen kimse.

con.sist [kən'sist] *v/i.* ibaret olm., mürekkep olm., meydana gelmek, oluşmak (*of* -*den*); dayanmak, bağlı olm. (*in* -*e*); uygun olm., uymak (*with ile*); **con'sist.ence, con'sist.en.cy** *n.* birbirini tutma, tutarlık, uyum, ahenk; yoğunluk, kesafet, kıvam, koyuluk; **con'sist.ent** ☐ birbirini tutan, tutarlı; uygun, aralarında bağ olan (*with ile*); *~ly* her zaman, devamlı olarak, mütemadiyen; **con'sis.to.ry** *n.* ECCL kilise idare heyeti, kilise yönetim kurulu.

con.sol.a.ble [kən'səuləbl] *adj.* tesellisi mümkün, avutulabilir; **con.so.la.tion** [kɔnsə'leiʃən] *n.* teselli, avunç.

con.sole 1. [kən'səul] *v/t.* teselli etm., avutmak, avundurmak; **2.** ['kɔnsəul] *n.* konsol, radyo *veya* televizyon kasası; org klavyesi; ARCH dirsek; *~ table* konsol.

con.sol.er [kən'səulə] *n.* teselli eden kimse.

con.sol.i.date [kən'sɔlideit] *v/t. & v/i.* sağlamlaş(tır)mak, pekiş(tir)mek; *fig.* birleş(tir)mek; konsolide etm., vadesini uzatmak; *~d annuities = consols*;

consol.i'da.tion *n.* birleş(tir)me, sağlamlaştırma, takviye; borçları birleştirme.

con.sols [kən'sɔlz] *n. pl.* konsolide borçlar; Duyunu Umumiye'de kayıtlı uzun vadeli borç.

con.so.nance ['kɔnsənəns] *n.* uygunluk, uyum, ahenk, ses uygunluğu; **'con.sonant 1.** ☐ MUS ahenkli, uyumlu, aynı seslere sahip olan (*with, to* -*le*); **2.** *n.* GR konsonant, sessiz harf.

con.sort 1. ['kɔnsɔːt] *n.* eş, karı, koca; NAUT yoldaş gemi; **2.** [kən'sɔːt] (*with*) *vb.* arkadaşlık etm. -*le*, vakit geçirmek -*le*; uymak -*e*, uygun olm. -*e*.

con.spec.tus [kən'spektəs] *n.* taslak, genel plan, özet.

con.spic.u.ous ☐ [kən'spikjuəs] göze çarpan, farkedilir, bariz, dikkati çeken, açık seçik; *fig.* çarpıcı, mükemmel, cazip; *be ~ by one's absence* yokluğunda aranmak, değeri yokluğunda belli olm.; *make o.s. ~* dikkat çekmek.

con.spir.a.cy [kən'spirəsi] *n.* fesat dolu gizli anlaşma, suikast; **con'spir.a.tor** [-tə] *n.* suikastçı; **con'spir.a.tress** *n.* kadın suikastçı; **con.spire** [kən'spaiə] *vb.* fesat maksadı ile anlaşmak, suikast hazırlamak, entrika çevirmek; elbirliği ile çalışmak.

con.sta.ble ['kʌnstəbl] *n.* polis memuru; kraliyet ailesinin valisi *veya* muhafızı; **con.stab.u.lar.y** [kən'stæbjuləri] *n.* polis teşkilâtı; jandarma.

con.stan.cy ['kɔnstənsi] *n.* değişmezlik, sabitlik; tahammül, dayanıklılık; sadakat, bağlılık; **'con.stant 1.** ☐ devamlı, sürekli, daimî; sabit, değişmez; sadık, bağlı; **2.** *n.* MATH konstant, sabite.

con.stel.la.tion AST [kɔnstə'leiʃən] *n.* takımyıldız, burç.

con.ster.na.tion [kɔnstə'neiʃən] *n.* donup kalma, korku, dehşet, hayret, şaşkınlık.

con.sti.pate MED ['kɔnstipeit] *vb.* kabızlığa sebep olm., sıkmak; **con.sti'pa.tion** *n.* MED kabızlık, peklik.

con.stit.u.en.cy [kən'stitjuənsi] *n.* seçim çevresi, seçim bölgesi; F seçmenler; **con'stit.u.ent 1.** *adj.* anayasayı değiştirme yetkisi olan; seçme hakkı olan; bir bütünü oluşturan; **2.** *n.* seçmen; öğe, unsur.

con.sti.tute [kɔnstitjuːt] *v/t.* teşkil etm., oluşturmak, meydana getirmek; tayin etm., atamak; kurmak, tesis etm., kanunî yetki vermek; *~ s.o.*

judge *b-ni* hakim olarak atamak; **con.sti'tu.tion** *n.* anayasa; bünye, beden yapısı; terkip, bileşim; **con.sti'tu.tion.al** [-ʃənl] **1.** □ anayasal, anayasaya uygun; bünyesel, bünyevî, sıhhî, yapısal; **~ law** anayasa; **2.** *n.* F sağlık için yapılan kısa yürüyüş; **consti'tu.tion.al.ist** [-ʃnəlist] *n.* meşrutiyetçi, anayasa taraftarı; **con.sti.tu.tive** □ ['kɔnstitjuːtiv] yapıcı, kurucu, teşkil eden; temelli, köklü, esaslı.

con.strain [kən'strein] *v/t.* zorlamak, mecbur etm., zorla yaptırmak; **con.straint** [-'streint] *n.* zorlama, mecbur etme, sınırlama, tahdit; yapmacıklık, sunilik; JUR tehdit, hürriyetin sınırlanması, manevî zorlama.

con.strict [kən'strikt]   *vb.* sık(ıştır)mak; büzmek; daraltmak; kısaltmak; **con'stric.tion** *n.* sıkma, büzme, kasılma, kısalma; **con'stric.tor** *n.* ANAT büzgen, sıkıcı adale; ZOO *a.* **boa ~** boa yılanı.

con.strin.gent [kən'strindʒənt] *adj.* büzen, kısaltan.

con.struct [kən'strʌkt] *v/t.* inşa etm., yapmak, kurmak; *fig.* düzenlemek, tertip etm.; **con'struc.tion** *n.* yapı, bina, inşaat; yorum, mana; **under ~** inşa halinde; **con'struc.tive** *adj.* yapıcı, olumlu, yapısal; **con'struc.tor** *n.* kurucu, yapıcı, inşaatçı.

con.strue [kən'struː] *vb.* GR tercüme etm., mana vermek, yorumlamak; cümleyi tahlil etm.; gramatik olarak cümle kurmak.

con.sue.tu.di.nar.y [kɔnswi'tjuːdinəri] *adj.* alışılagelen, alışılmış…

con.sul ['kɔnsəl] *n.* konsolos; **~ general** başkonsolos; **con.su.lar** ['kɔnsjulə] *adj.* konsolosa ait, konsolos…, konsolosluk…; **con.su.late** ['-lit] *n.* konsolosluk, konsoloshane; **~ general** başkonsolosluk; **consul.ship** ['kɔnsəlʃip] *n.* konsolosluk.

con.sult [kən'sʌlt] *v/t.* baş vurmak -e, müracaat etmek -e, danışmak -e, sormak -e; göz önünde bulundurmak, hesaba katmak, düşünmek; **~ing engineer** danışman mühendis; **~ing physician** danışman doktor; *v/i.* istişare etm., görüşme yapmak; danışmanlık yapmak; **con'sultant** *n.* müşavir, danışman; **con.sul.ta.tion** [kɔnsəl'teiʃən] *n.* başvurma, danışma, müzakere; konsültasyon; **~ hour** muayene saati; **con.sult.a.tive** [kən'sʌltətiv]

adj. danışmanlıkla ilgili, damşma…

con.sum.a.ble [kən'sjuːməbl] *adj.* tüketilir, sarfolunur, kullanılır; **con'sume** *v/t.* yiyip bitirmek, tüketmek, israf etm., ziyan etm., sarfetmek, yoğaltmak; yakıp kül etm.; *fig.* k-*ni* yemek; deliye dönmek; *v/i.* tükenmek, uçmak, ziyan edilmek, yok olm.; **con'sum.er** *n.* tüketici, yoğaltıcı; **~ goods** *pl.* tüketim maddeleri.

con.sum.mate 1. □ [kən'sʌmit] tam, mükemmel, şahane; **2.** ['kɔnsəmeit] *v/t.* tamamlamak; mükemmelleştirmek; **consum.ma.tion** [-'meiʃən] *n.* tamamlama, yerine getirme; *fig.* son, sonuç.

con.sump.tion [kən'sʌmpʃən] *n.* tüketim, yoğaltım; MED verem; **con.sump.tive** □ tüketilecek…; veremli.

con.tact 1. ['kɔntækt] *n.* temas, dokunma, değme, sürtünme; ilişki, münasebet; haberleşme; bulaşıcı hastalık geçirebilecek kimse; ELECT bağlantı; **make (break) ~** teması temin etm. (kesmek); elektrik devresini bağlamak (kesmek); **2.** [kən'tækt] *v/t.* temasa geçmek -*le*, temas kurmak -*le*, konuşmak -*le*; **~ lens.es** ['kɔntækt'lensiz] *n. pl.* kontakt lensler, mercekler.

con.ta.gion MED [kən'teidʒən] *n.* bulaşma, geçme (*hastalık*); bulaşıcı hastalık; *fig.* kötü tesir; **con'ta.gious** □ bulaşıcı, sâri; yayılan.

con.tain [kən'tein] *v/t.* ihtiva etm., içine almak, kapsamak; eşit olm. -*e*; sınırlamak; kontrol altına almak; tam bölünmek (*sayı*); MIL tutuklamak; *fig.* k-*ni* tutmak; **~ o.s.** k-*ni* tutmak, geri durmak; **con'tain.er** *n.* kap; konteyner; **con'tainment** *n.* alıkoyma, kontrol etme; POL bir devletin etki alanını genişletmesini önleme politikası.

con.tam.i.nate [kən'tæmineit] *v/t.* kirletmek, pisletmek, lekelemek; bulaştırmak, geçirmek (*hastalık, mikrop*); *fig.* bozmak (*ahlâkını*); **con.tam.i'na.tion** *n.* bulaştırma; kirletme, pisletme; pislik.

con.temn *lit.* [kən'tem] *vb.* hor görmek, küçük görmek, adam yerine koymamak.

con.tem.plate ['kɔntempleit] *vb. fig.* seyretmek; düşünmek, tasarlamak, niyetinde olm.; düşünceye dalmak; **con'tem'pla.tion** *n.* derin düşünce; niyet, maksat; umut, bekleme; düşünme, tasarlama; **have in ~** niyetinde olm.;

'con.templa.tive ☐ düşünceli, dalgın.
con.tem.po.ra.ne.ous ☐ [kəntempə-
'reinjəs] aynı zamanda olan; ~ **performance** JUR aynı anda olan icraat;
con'tem.porar.y 1. *adj.* çağdaş, modern; aynı anda olan; aynı yaşta olan,
2. *n. b-le* akran olan kimse, aynı yaşta
olan kimse.
con.tempt [kən'tempt] *n.* nefret, küçük
görme, yukarıdan bakma; hürmetsizlik, saygısızlık; kurallara karşı gelme;
~ *of court* mahkemeye itaatsizlik; *hold
in* ~ hor görmek, hakir görmek; *in* ~ *of*
önemsemeyerek; karşı gelerek; con-
'tempt.i.ble ☐ alçak, rezil, aşağılık,
adî; con'temptu.ous ☐ [-tjuəs] kibirli, küçük gören, hor gören (*of -i*).
con.tend [kən'tend] *v/i.* çarpışmak,
mücadele etm., müsabakaya girmek,
çekişmek (*for için*); *v/t.* iddia etm., ileri
sürmek, tartışmak, münakaşa etm.
con.tent [kən'tent] 1. *adj.* memnun,
hoşnut, razı; *not* ~ memnun değil; 2.
v/t. memnun etm., hoşnut etm.; ~
o.s. yetinmek, idare etm. (*with ile*);
3. *n.* rahatlık; *to one's heart's* ~ canı
istediği kadar, doya doya; ['kontent]
n. hacim, istiap, kapasite; öz, esas, içerik, muhteva, gerçek anlam; ~*s pl.* içindekiler; *table of* ~*s* fihrist, endeks;
con.tent.ed ☐ [kən'tentid] memnun,
hoşnut, rahat, halinden memnun.
con.ten.tion [kən'tenʃən] *n.* kavga, çekişme, mücadele, münakaşa, iddia;
con'ten.tious ☐ kavgacı, münakaşacı;
ihtilâflı.
con.tent.ment [kən'tentmənt] *n.*
memnuniyet, rahatlık, gönül huzuru.
con.test 1. ['kontest] *n.* yarışma, müsabaka, mücadele, çekişme; tartışma,
münakaşa; iddia, bahis; 2. [kən'test]
v/t. itiraz etm. *-e*, karşı koymak *-e*, muhalefet etm. *-e*; ~ *s.o.'s right to do s.th.*
b-nin bş yapma hakkına itiraz etm.; *v/i.*
müsabakaya girmek, mücadele etm.,
çekişmek; ~ *a borough* bir ilçede seçilmek için mücadele etm.; con'test.a-
ble *adj.* itiraz kaldırır, tartışma götürür, münakaşa edilebilir; con'test.ant
n. yarışmacı; bir karar *veya* ödüle itiraz
eden kimse; con'test.ed *adj.* münakaşalı, ihtilâflı.
con.text ['kontekst] *n.* sözün gelişi, münasebet; şartlar ve çevre; con.tex.tu.al
☐ [kən'tekstjuəl] sözün gelişine göre;
con'tex.ture [-tʃə] *n.* yapı, bünye; düzen, tertip; sözün gelişi.

con.ti.gu.i.ty [konti'gju:iti] *n.* yakınlık,
komşuluk, hemhudutluk; con.tig.u-
ous ☐ [kən'tigjuəs] yakın, komşu, bitişik, hemhudut, sınırdaş (*to -e*).
con.ti.nence ['kontinəns] *n.* kendini
tutma, ölçülülük, kendine hâkim olma;
'con.ti.nent 1. ☐ kendine hâkim, ölçülü; 2. *n.* kıta, anakara; con.ti.nen.tal
[-'nentl] 1. ☐ kıtaya ait, kıtasal, karasal
(*iklim*); Avrupa kıtasına ait; 2. *n.* Avrupa kıtasında yaşayan kimse.
con.tin.gen.cy [kən'tindʒənsi] *n.* ihtimal; beklenmedik olay; con'tin.gen-
cies *n. pl.* rastlantı sonucu olan olaylar,
kazara olan olaylar; con'tin.gent 1. ☐
kesin olmayan, şüpheli, olması başka
şeye bağlı olan, kazara olan, rastlantı
eseri olan, tesadüfî; ~ *on* bağlı *-e*, dayalı *-e*; 2. *n.* MIL asker grubu, grup.
con.tin.u.al ☐ [kən'tinjuəl] devamlı,
sürekli, daimî, ardı arkası kesilmez,
mütemadî; sık sık; con'tin.u.ance *n.*
devam, süreklilik, sürdürme; süre,
müddet; erteleme; arta kalan şey;
con.tin.u'a.tion *n.* devam (etme), sürme, sürüp gitme; uzantı; COM uzatma,
temdit, zeyil; ~ *school* (*boş zamanları
değerlendirmek için gidilen*) akşam
okulu; con'tin.ue [-nju:] *v/t.* devam
etm. *-e*; uzatmak, sürdürmek; görevde
tutmak; ertelemek, tehir etm.; ~ *reading* okumaya devam etm.; *to be* ~*d* arkası var, devamı var; *v/i.* sürmek, devam etm.; dayanmak; kalmak; yeniden
başlamak; ~ (*in*) *a business* bir işe devam etm., bir işte kalmak; con.tinu.i-
ty [konti'nju:iti] *n.* devamlılık, süreklilik, ardı arkası kesilmeyiş; *film*: detaylı
senaryo; *radyo*: program metni; con-
tin.u.ous ☐ [kən'tinjuəs] devamlı, sürekli, fasılasız, aralıksız; ~ *current*
ELECT devamlı cereyan, doğru akım.
con.tort [kən'tort] *v/t.* burmak, bükmek, eğmek, çarpıtmak; con'tor.tion
n. bur(ul)ma, bük(ül)me, eğ(il)me;
con'tortion.ist [-ʃnist] *n.* vücudunu
türlü şekillere sokan akrobat, vücuda
lastik gibi olan akrobat.
con.tour ['kontuə] *n.* dış hatlar, çevre;
şekil; düzey çizgisi; ~ *line surv.* eşyük-
selti çizgisi; ~ *map* düzey haritası.
con.tra ['kontrə] *pref.* karşı, zıt, aksi;
per ~ COM öbür taraftan.
con.tra.band ['kontrəbænd] 1. *adj.* kaçak...; 2. *n.* kaçak eşya, kaçak mal.
con.tra.cep.tion [kontrə'sepʃən] *n.* ge-
belikten korunma; con.tra'cep.tive

adj. & n. gebeliği önleyici (hap *veya* alet).

con.tract 1. [kən'trækt] *v/t.* daraltmak, kısaltmak; büzmek, kasmak; buruşturmak; *hastalık:* tutulmak; çatmak (*kaş*); anlaşma yaparak üstlenmek; girmek (*borca*); *v/i.* mukavele yapmak, anlasma yapmak; kasılmak, daralmak, büzülmek, buruşmak; **~ for** ...için mukavele yapmak; **~ing parties** âkit taraflar, sözleşme aktedenler; **2.** ['kontrækt] *n.* sözleşme, anlaşma, mukavele, akit kontrat; **by ~** sözleşmeye dayanan, mukavele ile; **under ~** mukaveleli, sözleşmeli; **con.tract.ed** □ [kən-'træktid] kasılmıs, büzülmüş, kısaltılmış; *fig.* az, kıt, mahdut; **~ form** GR kaynaştırılmış şekil; **con.tract.i-'bil.i.ty** *n.* kısaltılabilirlik; **con'tract.i-ble** *adj.* kısaltılabilir; **con'trac.tile** [_tail] *adj.* toplanabilen, kısal(tıl)abilen; **con'trac.tion** *n.* büzülme, kasılma; GR kaynaştırma; **con'trac.tor** *n.* müteahhit, akdi yapan taraf, mukaveleli kimse *veya* firma; ANAT doğum anında gerilen rahim adeleleri, büzgen; **con'tractu.al** [_tjuəl] *adj.* akitten doğan, mukaveleden doğan, mukavele...

con.tra.dict [kontrə'dikt] *v/t.* yalanlamak, *-in* aksini söylemek, ...ile ters düşmek, ...ile tezat teşkil etm.; **con·tra'dic.tion** *n.* yalanlama; çelişme, aykırılık, tezat; **con.tra'dic.tious** □ aykırı, zıt, aksi, ters; **con.tra'dic.to.ry** [_-təri] □ aykırı, zıt, aksi, ters.

con.tra.dis.tinc.tion [kontrədis'tiŋk-ʃən] *n.* fark, zıt, aksi, tezat; **con.tra·dis'tin.guish** [_gwiʃ] *vb.* zıddı ile ayırmak, ayırt etm.

con.trap.tion *sl.* [kən'træpʃən] *n.* garip alet, cihaz.

con.tra.ri.e.ty [kontrə'raiəti] *n.* zıtlık, tezat, terslik, aksilik; **con.tra.ri.ly** ['_trəlili] *adv.* aksine, bilâkis; '**con.tra.ri.ness** *n.* terslik, zıtlık, aksilik, inatçılık; **con.tra.riwise** ['_waiz] *adv.* aksine, bilâkis; ters yönde, aksi yönde; zıt giderek; '**con.trary 1.** *adj.* ters, zıt, aksi, muhalif, karşı, aykırı; F [kən-'treəri] dik kafalı, aksi, inatçı, asi; **~ to** *prp.* *-e* aykırı, *-e* ters; **2.** *n.* aksi, zıt, ters, karşıt; **on the ~** aksine, bilakis, tersine; **by the ~** aksi yönde, olumsuz yönde, ...rağmen.

con.trast 1. ['kontrɑːst] *n.* tezat, zıtlık, fark, ayrılık; *fotoğraf:* açık ve koyu kısımlar arasındaki fark; **in ~ to** *-e* zıt olarak, *-in* aksine, *-e* ters olarak; **by ~** aksine; **2.** [kən'trɑːst] *v/t.* karşılaştırmak, mukayese etm. (**with** *ile*); *v/i.* ters düşmek, tezat teşkil etm., zıt olm. (**with** *ile*).

con.tra.vene [kontrə'viːn] *vb.* karşı gelmek *-e*, muhalefet etm. *-e*; itiraz etm. *-e*; ihtilâfa düşmek *-le*, zıtlaşmak *-le*, uyumsuz olm. *-le*; **con.tra.ven.tion** [_-'venʃən] *n.* karşı gelme, ihlâl (**of** *-e*, *-i*).

con.trib.u.te [kən'tribjuːt] *v/t.* bağışlamak *-e*, katkıda bulunmak *-e*, iane vermek *-e*; *v/i.* yazı vermek (**to** *-e*); **con·tri.bu.tion** [kontri'bjuːʃən] *n.* yardım, bağış, iane, teberru; makale, yazı; vergi; aidat, prim; MIL işgal kuvvetlerinin elkoyması; **con.trib.u.tor** [kən'trib-jutə] *n.* yardım eden kimse, bağış yapan kimse; yazı yazan kimse (**to a newspaper** *bir gazeteye*); **con'trib.u-to.ry** *adj.* yardımcı, sebep olan (**to** *-e*).

con.trite □ ['kontrait] pişman, tövbekâr; **con.tri.tion** [kən'triʃən] *n.* pişmanlık.

con.triv.ance [kən'traivəns] *n.* buluş, icat; hüner; tertibat, cihaz; gizli plan, entrika; **con'trive** *v/t.* icat etm., bulmak; başarmak, becermek; *v/i.* plan yapmak (**to** *inf. -mek için*); **con'triv.er** *n.* çekip çeviren kimse (*part. ev kadını*); **she is a good ~** iyi bir ev kadınıdır.

con.trol [kən'trəul] **1.** *n.* kontrol, denetleme; idare, hâkimiyet, egemenlik; JUR tasarruf; *attr.* kontrol...; **~ surfaces** *pl.* AVIA kumanda sathı, uçak dümen tertibatı; **remote** *veya* **distant ~** uzaktan kontrol; **~ board** MEC kontrol paneli; **~ column** AVIA kumanda kolonu, volanlı lövye; **~ knob** ayar düğmesi, kontrol düğmesi; **~ valve** radyo: ayar supapı; **be in ~** yöneticiyi durumda olm., kontrolü elinde bulundurmak, yönetmek (**of** *-i*); **put s.o. in ~** *b-ni* yönetici yapmak, başa geçirmek; **2.** *v/t.* kontrol etm., denetlemek, tetkik etm.; idare etm., hâkim olm.; düzenlemek; MEC ayar etm.; AVIA uçak kullanmak; **con·'trolla.ble** *adj.* idare edilebilir, yönetilebilir; **con'trol.ler** *n.* murakıp, denetleyici, muhasebeci, kontrolör; regulatör.

con.tro.ver.sial □ [kontrə'vəːʃəl] çekişmeli, ihtilâflı, **con.tro.ver.sy** ['_vəːsi] *n.* çekişme, münakaşa, tartış-

ma, ihtilâf, mücadele; **con.tro.vert**
['ˌvɔːt] *vb*. yalanlamak, inkâr etm.; itiraz etm.; **con.tro'vert.i.ble** ☐ itiraz
edilebilir, inkâr edilebilir.

con.tu.ma.cious ☐ [kɔntjuˈmeiʃəs]
inatçı, asi, dik başlı, isyankâr; JUR itaatsiz; **contu.ma.cy** ['kɔntjuməsi] *n*. inat,
inatçılık, asilik; JUR itaatsizlik, mahkeme emrine uymama.

con.tu.me.li.ous ☐ [kɔntjuːˈmiːljəs]
terbiyesiz, arsız, küstah; utandırıcı,
yüz kızartıcı; **con.tu.me.ly** ['kɔn-
tjuːmli] *n*. küfür, hakaret, tahkir.

con.tuse MED [kənˈtjuːz] *v/t*. berelemek, çürütmek, ezmek, yaralamak;
con'tu.sion [ˌʒən] *n*. bere, çürük,
ezik.

co.nun.drum [kəˈnʌndrəm] *n*. şaşırtıcı
soru, bilmece.

con.ur.ba.tion [kɔnəːˈbeiʃən] *n*. şehir-
lerin genişleyip birleşmesi.

con.va.lesce [kɔnvəˈles] *vb*. iyileşmek;
con.va'les.cence *n*. iyileşme, nekahet; **con.va.les.cent 1.** ☐ nekahet devresi ile ilgili, iyileşme...; **2.** *n*. iyileşen,
şifa bulan kimse.

con.vec.tion PHYS [kənˈvekʃən] *n*. ısı
nakletme; **con'vec.tor** *n*. konvektör.

con.vene [kənˈviːn] *vb*. topla(n)mak,
biraraya getirmek, toplantı yapmak,
biraraya gelmek; JUR dava açmak,
mahkemeye celbetmek.

con.ven.ience [kənˈviːnjəns] *n*. uygunluk, rahatlık, kolaylık, elverişlilik;
konfor; tuvalet, helâ; **at your earliest**
~ sizce mümkün olan en kısa zamanda;
make a ~ of s.o. *b-nin* iyi niyetini suiistimal etm.; **marriage of ~** maddiyat evliliği, menfaate dayanan evlilik; **con-
'ven.ient** ☐ uygun, elverişli, münasip,
rahat, müsait (**to, for** -*e*).

con.vent ['kɔnvənt] *n*. (*part. rahibele-
rin olduğu*) manastır; **con.ven.ti.cle**
[kənˈventikl] *n*. gizli dinî toplantı, gizli
dinî toplantının yapıldığı bina; **con-
'ven.tion** *n*. toplantı, kongre; anlaşma,
mukavele; âdet, gelenek; **con'ven-
tion.al** [ˌʃənl] *adj*. göreneksel, geleneksel, âdetlere uygun; ~ **weapons**
pl. nükleer silahlar dışındaki silahlar;
con'ven.tion.al.ism [ˌʃnəlizəm] *n*.
âdetlere bağlılık; **conven.tion.al.i.ty**
[ˌʃəˈnæliti] *n*. toplum geleneklerine
bağlılık; **con'ven.tu.al** [ˌtjuəl] ☐ manastır ile ilgili, manastır...

con.verge [kənˈvɔːdʒ] *vb*. bir noktada
birleşmek; MATH birbirine yaklaşmak

(*doğrular*); **con'ver.gence, con'ver-
gen.cy** *n*. birleşme; birbirine yaklaşma; **con'vergent, con'verg.ing** *adj*.
birleşen; birbirine yaklaşan.

con.vers.a.ble [kənˈvɔːsəbl] *adj*.
hakkında konuşulabilir; sohbeti tatlı;
con'ver.sant (**with**) *adj*. iyi bilen, bilgisi olan, erbap; **con.ver.sa.tion** [ˌvə-
ˈseiʃən] *n*. konuşma, sohbet; **con.ver-
'sa.tion.al** [ˌʃənl] *adj*. konuşma..., konuşulabilir..., konuşma diline ait;
con.verse 1. ☐ ['kɔnvɔːs] zıt, aksi,
ters; **2.** [ˌ] *n*. ters fikir, ters ifade; MATH,
PHLS evirtim, akis; **3.** [kənˈvɔːs] *vb*. konuşmak, görüşmek, sohbet etm. (**with**
ile); **con'ver.sion** *n*. değiş(tir)me; MEC,
ELECT çevirme; PHLS evirme, evirtim;
ECCL ihtida, din değiştirme; POL başka
bir görüşü benimseme; COM borçların
tahvili, tahvil.

con.vert 1. ['kɔnvɔːt] *n*. dönme, muhte-
di, din değiştiren kimse; **2.** ['kɔnˈvɔːt]
vb. değiştirmek, tahvil etm., döndürmek, çevirmek; MEC, ELECT şeklini
değiştirmek; ECCL *b-nin* inançlarını
değiştirmek (**to** -*e*); COM paraya çevirmek; **con'vert.er** *n*. değiştiren şey;
MEC, ELECT konvertör, çevirgeç; **con-
vert.i.bil.i.ty** [ˌˈbiliti] *n*. değiştirilebil-
me; COM konvertibilite, çevrilebilme;
con'vert.i.ble 1. ☐ değiştirilebilir;
COM tahvili mümkün, çevrilebilir; **2.**
n. MOT üstü açılıp kapanabilen spor
araba; değiştirilebilen şey.

con.vex ☐ ['kɔnˈveks] dışbükey, konveks; **con'vex.i.ty** *n*. dışbükeylik.

con.vey [kənˈvei] *v/t*. taşımak, götürmek, nakletmek; ifade etm.; PHYS nakletmek, iletmek; JUR devretmek; **con-
'vey.ance** *n*. taşıma, nakil, taşıt; JUR feragatname, terk, temlik, ferağ; ELECT
geçirme, iletme, transmisyon; **public**
~ toplu taşıma aracı; **con'vey.anc.er**
n. JUR temlik ve ferağ muamelelerini
hazırlayan avukat; **convey.or** MEC *a*.
~ **belt** taşıma bandı.

con.vict 1. ['kɔnvikt] *n*. mahkûm, suçlu;
2. [kənˈvikt] *v/t*. ikna etm., inandırmak
(**of** -*e*); suçlandırmak, suçlamak, mahkûm etm. (**of** *ile*); **con'vic.tion** *n*. JUR
suçlandırma, mahkûmiyet, hükümlü-
lük; inanç, katiyet, kesinlik, kanaat
(**of** -*e*); **previous** ~ sabıka.

con.vince [kənˈvins] *v/t*. inandırmak,
ikna etm. (**of** -*e*); **con'vinc.ing** *adj*.
inandırıcı, ikna edici.

con.viv.i.al [kənˈviviəl] *adj*. neşeli...,

şen...; eğlenceye düşkün...; **con.viv.i-ali.ty** [-'æliti] *n.* neşe, eğlence, şamata.

con.vo.ca.tion [kɔnvəu'keiʃən] *n.* toplantı, meclis; kilise temsilcileri meclisi.

con.voke [kɔn'vəuk] *v/t.* toplantıya çağırmak.

con.vo.lu.tion [kɔnvə'luːʃən] *n.* büklüm, kıvrım; sarılma, dürülme.

con.vol.vu.lus BOT [kən'vɔlvjuləs] *n.* kahkahaçiçeği.

con.voy ['kɔnvɔi] 1. *n.* konvoy; koruma, himaye; 2. *v/t.* rehberlik etm., korumak.

con.vulse *fig.* [kən'vʌls] *vb.* sarsmak, sıkıntı vermek, rahatsız etm., kıvrandırmak; **be ~d with laughter** gülmekten katılmak; **con'vul.sion** *n.* ihtilâç, kıvranma, çırpınma, katılma; **~s of laughter** gülmekten katılma; **con'vul.sive** □ ihtilâç gibi, çırpınma...

co.ny ['kəuni] *n.* tavşan; tavşan kürkü.

coo [kuː] *vb.* ötmek (*kumru*); kumru gibi ses çıkarmak; incil danmak.

cook [kuk] 1. *n.* aşçı; 2. *v/t. & v/i.* piş(ir)-mek; *fig.* uydurmak (*hikâye*); F üzerinde oynamak (*hesaplar*); **'~.book** *n. Am.* yemek kitabı; **'cook.er** *n.* soba, ocak; F uydurukçu; **'cook.er.y** *n.* aşçılık, mutfak işleri; **~ book** yemek kitabı; **'cook-house** *n.* dışarıda olan mutfak; NAUT gemi mutfağı; **cook.ie** *Am.* ['-i] *n.* kurabiye, çörek, bisküvi; *Am. sl.* şahıs; *Am. sl.* güzel kadın; **'cook.ing** *n.* pişirme (sanatı); **cook.y** ['-i] = *cookie.*

cool [kuːl] 1. □ serin, soğuk; *fig.* soğukkanlı, sakin, kayıtsız, kendine hâkim; *b.s.* yüzsüz, küstah; *sl.* hoş, güzel, iyi, mükemmel; **~ a thousand pounds** F abartmasız bin pound; 2. *n.* serinlik; serin hava *veya* yer; sükûnet, soğukkanlılık; 3. *v/t. & v/i.* soğu(t)mak, serinle(t)mek; yatışmak, geçmek (*sinir*); **let him ~ his heels** bırak beklesin; **'cool.er** *n.* soğutma cihazı, soğutucu; *sl.* hapishane, kodes; **'cool-'head.ed** *adj.* soğukkanlı, serinkanlı.

coo.lie ['kuːli] *n.* hamal.

cool.ing MEC ['kuːliŋ] *n.* soğutma; *attr.* soğutucu...; **'cool.ness** *n.* serinlik; *fig.* soğukkanlılık.

coomb [kuːm] *n.* derin vadi.

coon *Am.* F [kuːn] *n.* zoo ayıya benzer bir hayvan türü; zenci; **a gone ~** ümitsiz durumda olan kimse; **~ song** zenci şarkısı.

coop [kuːp] 1. *n.* kümes; 2. *vb.* **~ up** *veya* **in** kümese sokmak; tıkmak, sokmak.

co-op F ['kəuɔp] *n.* = *co-operative* (*store*) kooperatif.

coop.er ['kuːpə] *n.* fıçıcı; **'coop.er.age** *n.* fıçıcılık; fıçı imalathanesi.

co-op.er.ate [kəu'ɔpəreit] *v/i.* işbirliği yapmak, beraber çalışmak; **co-op.er-'ation** *n.* işbirliği; **co-'op.er.a.tive** [-rətiv] 1. *adj.* işbirliği yapan, işbirliğine ait; **~ society** tüketim kooperatifi; **~ store** kooperatif; 2. = **~ store**; **co-'op.er.a.tor** [-reitə] *n.* iş arkadaşı.

co-opt [kəu'ɔpt] *vb.* oy ile seçmek, atamak, tayin etm.; **co-op'ta.tion** *n.* oy ile seçme, atama.

co-or.di.nate 1. □ [kəu'ɔːdinit] eşit, aynı derecede; 2. [-neit] *v/t.* ayarlamak, ahenk kazandırmak, alıştırmak, düzeltmek; **co-or.di'na.tion** *n.* tanzim, ayarlama, düzenleme, tertip, koordinasyon.

coot [kuːt] *n.* su tavuğu, sakarmeki; F zararsız kimse, beceriksiz kimse; **coo-tie** MIL *sl.* ['-i] *n.* bit.

cop *sl.* [kɔp] 1. *vb.* yakalamak, kapmak; çalmak, aşırmak; **~ it** cezalandırılmak, dövülmek; 2. *n.* polis memuru, aynasız.

co.pal ['kəupəl] *n.* bir reçine türü, kopal.

co.part.ner ['kəu'pɑːtnə] *n.* ortak; **'co'part.ner.ship** *n.* ortaklık.

cope[1] [kəup] 1. *n.* papaz cüppesi; *fig.* örtü; 2. *vb.* örtmek.

cope[2] [-] *vb.*: **~ with** başa çıkmak, uğraşmak.

Co.per.ni.can [kəu'pɔːnikən] *adj.* Kopernik'e ait, Kopernik...

cope.stone ['kəupstəun] *n. mst. fig.* taç, süsleme.

co-pi.lot [kəu'pailət] *n.* ikinci pilot.

cop.ing ARCH ['kəupiŋ] *n.* duvar tepeliği *veya* üstlüğü '**~-stone** *n. fig.* taç, süsleme.

co.pi.ous □ ['kəupjəs] bol, çok, mebzul, bereketli; '**co.pi.ous.ness** *n.* bolluk, bereket.

cop.per[1] ['kɔpə] 1. *n.* bakır; bakır para; kazan; 2. *adj.* bakıra benzer; bakır...; 3. *vb.* bakır kaplamak.

cop.per[2] *sl.* [-] *n.* polis memuru, aynasız.

cop.per.as CHEM ['kɔpərəs] *n.* demir sulfat, zaç.

cop.per...: **~ beech** BOT kızıl kayın

ağacı; '**~.plate** *n.* işlemeli bakır tabak; bir tür ince el yazısı; '**~-smith** *n.* bakırcı.

cop.pice ['kɔpis], **copse** [kɔps] *n.* küçük koru, ağaçlık, çalılık.

cop.u.late zoo ['kɔpjuleit] *vb.* çiftleşmek (*hayvanlar*); **cop.u'la.tion** *n.* çiftleşme; **cop.u.la.tive** ['-lətiv] **1.** *adj.* birleştiren, bağlayıcı; **2.** *n.* GR bağlaç.

cop.y ['kɔpi] **1.** *n.* kopya, nüsha, suret, numune, örnek; müsvedde; metin, yazı; *fair veya* **clean ~** temiz kopya; *rough veya* **foul ~** müsvedde, karalama, eskiz; **2.** *v/t.* kopya etm., *-in* suretini çıkarmak; taklit etm.; kopya çekmek (*imtihanda*); **~ fair** temiz kopyasını çıkarmak; **~ing stand** PHOT kopya masası; '**~-book** *n.* defter; '**~-hold** *n.* zeamet, tımar; '**cop.y.ing-ink** *n.* kopya çıkarma mürekkebi; '**cop.y.ing-press** *n.* kopya presi; '**cop.y.ist** *n.* kopya eden, taklitçi; '**cop.y.right** *n.* telif hakkı; *attr.* telif hakkı saklı olan.

co.quet [kɔ'ket] *vb.* cilve yapmak, flört etm.; **co.quet.ry** ['-kitri] *n.* işve, cilve, işvebazlık; **co.quette** [-'ket] *n.* cilveli kadın, oynak kadın, koket, yosma; **co-'quet.tish** ❑ cilveli, oynak, şuh.

cor.a.cle ['kɔrəkl] *n.* bez *veya* deri kaplı bir çeşit kayık.

cor.al ['kɔrəl] **1.** *n.* mercan; **2.** *adj. a.* **coral.line** ['-lain] mercana benzer, mercan...

cor.bel ARCH ['kɔ:bəl] *n.* dirsek.

cord [kɔ:d] **1.** *n.* ip, sicim, kaytan, şerit, tel; *fig.* manevî bağ; ANAT ribat, veter, kiriş; = **corduroy**; **2.** *v/t.* iple bağlamak; iple süslemek; yığmak (*kütükleri*); '**cord.ed** *adj.* iple bağlı; gergin (*adale*); kabarık çizgili; '**cord.age** *n.* geminin halat takımı.

cor.dial ['kɔ:djəl] **1.** ❑ samimi, candan, yürekten, içten; **2.** *n.* likör; **cor.dial.i.ty** [-di'æliti] *n.* samimiyet, içtenlik.

cord-mak.er ['kɔ:dmeikə] *n.* ipçi, urgancı, halatçı.

cor.don ['kɔ:dn] **1.** *n.* ARCH kordon; MIL süslü bant, kordon; (*asker, polis araç vs.*) kordon; **2.** *vb.* **~ off** kordon oluşturarak uzak tutmak.

cor.do.van ['kɔ:dəvən] *n.* bir çeşit ince deri.

cor.du.roy ['kɔ:dərɔi] *n.* fitilli kadife; **~s** *pl.* kadife pantolon; **~ road** bataklık üzerindeki kütüklerden yapılmış yol.

core [kɔ:] **1.** *n.* BOT göbek, meyvaların çekirdek kısmı; *fig.* iç, öz, esas, nüve;

2. *vb.* içini çıkarmak (*meyvanın*); '**cor-er** *n.* oyma bıçağı.

co-re.li.gion.ist ['kəuri'lidʒənist] *n.* dindaş, aynı dinden olan kimse.

Co.rin.thi.an [kə'rinθiən] *adj.* Korint üslûbu.

cork [kɔ:k] **1.** *n.* mantar, tapa, tıpa; **2.** *v/t.* mantarla kapamak, tıpalamak; *fig. a.* **~ up** saklamak (*duygularını*); '**corkage** *n.* lokantada müşterilerin beraberinde getirdiği şarap için verilen açma ve servis ücreti; '**corked** *adj.* mantar kokusuyla bozulmuş (*şarap*) *sl.* körkütük sarhoş; '**cork.er** *n. sl.* olağanüstü şey, muazzam şey; tıpalayan kimse *veya* şey; '**cork.ing** *adj. Am.* F fevkalâde, mükemmel, nefis.

cork...: '**~-jack.et** *n.* can kurtaran yeleği; '**~.screw** **1.** *n.* tirbuşon, tıpa burgusu; **2.** *adj.* helezonî; **3.** *vb.* vidalamak, dön(dür)mek; '**~-tree** *n.* BOT mantar meşesi; -

'**cork.y** *adj.* mantara benzer, mantar gibi; F hayat dolu, canlı.

cor.mo.rant ORN ['kɔ:mərənt] *n.* karabatak kuşu.

corn[1] [kɔ:n] **1.** *n.* hububat, buğday, tahıl; *a.* **Indian ~** mısır; *Am.* **~ bread** mısır ekmeği; **2.** *v/t.* tuzlayıp kurutmak; **~ed beef** konserve sığır eti.

corn[2] MED [-] *n.* nasır.

corn...: '**~-chan.dler** *n.* mısırcı, tohumcu; '**~-cob** *n. Am.* mısır koçanı.

cor.ne.a ANAT ['kɔ:niə] *n.* kornea, gözün dış tabakası.

cor.nel BOT ['kɔ:nəl] *n.* karaniya.

cor.nel.ian MIN [kɔ:'ni:ljən] *n.* akik taşı.

cor.ne.ous ['kɔ:niəs] *adj.* boynuzdan yapılmış, boynuz gibi.

cor.ner ['kɔ:nə] **1.** *n.* köşe, köşebaşı; gizli yer; bölge, bucak; *fig.* sıkıntı, çıkmaz; COM piyasayı ele geçirme; **~ kick** köşe vuruşu, korner atışı; **2.** *v/t.* çıkmaza sokmak, köşeye sıkıştırmak (*a. fig.*); COM ele geçirmek (*piyasayı*); '**cor-nered** *comb.* ... köşeli.

corner...: '**~-house** *n.* köşebaşı evi; '**~-stone** *n.* temel taşı; *fig.* temel, esas.

cor.net ['kɔ:nit] *n.* MUS kornet; kağıt külâh.

corn...: '**~-ex.change** *n.* tahıl borsası; '**~.field** *n.* buğday tarlası; *Am.* mısır tarlası; **~ flakes** *n. pl.* mısır gevreği; '**~-flour** = **corn-starch**; '**~-flow.er** *n.* peygamberçiçeği.

cor.nice ['kɔ:nis] *n.* ARCH korniş, geniş

573 **corrugate**

silme.
Cor.nish ['kɔːniʃ] *adj.* Kelt diline ait.
corn...: '~-juice *n. Am. sl.* mısır viskisi;
~ **pone** *Am.* kızartılmış mısır ekmeği;
'~-pop.py *n.* BOT gelincik çiçeği;
'~-stalk *n.* buğday sapı; *Am.* mısır sapı;
'~-starch *n. Am.* mısır nişastası.
cor.nu.co.pi.a *poet.* [kɔːnjuˈkəupjə] *n.*
sanatçılar tarafından bolluk sembolü
olarak kullanılan ve içinden meyva, çiçek ve tahıl taşan boynuz şeklinde süslü kap.
corn.y ['kɔːni] *adj.* eskimiş, basmakalıp; *sl.* adî, bayağı; *part. Am.* MUS
çok duyulan *veya* tekrarlanan.
co.rol.la BOT [kəˈrɔlə] *n.* taçyapraklar,
korol; **cor'ol.la.ry** *n.* sonuç, netice;
fig. akıbet.
co.ro.na [kəˈrəunə] *n., pl.* **co'ro.nae**
[-niː] AST hale, ağıl, ayla; ARCH damlık,
sıçan oluğu; **co'ro.nal** *adj.* ANAT kafatasının üst düzeyine ait; **cor.o.na.tion**
[kɔrəˈneiʃən] *n.* taç giyme töreni;
'cor.o.ner *n.* şüpheli ölüm vakalarını
tahkik eden memur; **cor.o.net** ['-nit]
n. asillerin giydiği küçük taç.
cor.po.ral ['kɔːpərəl] **1.** □ bedenî, cismanî, gövdesel; **2.** *n.* MIL onbaşı; **cor-
po.rate** ['-rit] □ anonim şirkete ait, or-
taklığa ait; birlik olmuş, toplu; ~ **body**
birlik, özel hukuk tüzel kişisi; **cor.po-
ra.tion** [-ˈreiʃən] *n.* birlik; tüzel kişi;
Am. anonim ortaklık; F şiş göbek; ~
tax kurumlar vergisi; **cor.po.ra.tive**
['-rətiv] *adj.* anonim ortaklık...; kor-
poratif...; **cor.pore.al** [-ˈpɔːriəl] bedenî, maddî, cismanî; **cor.po.re.i.ty**
[-pəˈriːiti] *n.* bedenen var oluş, mevcudiyet.
corps [kɔː] *n., pl.* **corps** [kɔːz] kolordu,
müfreze, kıta; topluluk, heyet; *Diplomatic* ♀ kordiplomatik.
corpse [kɔːps] *n.* ceset, ölü.
cor.pu.lence, cor.pu.len.cy ['kɔːpju-
ləns(i)] *n.* şişmanlık; **'cor.pu.lent** *adj.*
şişman, etli butlu.
cor.pus ['kɔːpəs] *n., pl.* **cor.po.ra**
['-pərə] bir yazarın tüm eserlerini içeren yapıt, külliyat; esas; ana para, sermaye; ♀ *Christi* ['kristi] bir katolik yortusu; **corpus.cle** ['kɔːpʌsl] *n.* hücre,
yuvar, kan küreciği.
cor.ral *part. Am.* [kɔːˈrɑːl] **1.** *n.* ağıl; **2.**
vb. ağıla kapamak; *fig.* yakalamak.
cor.rect [kəˈrekt] **1.** □ doğru, sahih,
yanlışsız, tam; dürüst; münasip, uygun;
be ~ doğru, dürüst olm.; **2.** *v/t.* düzelt-

mek, ayarlamak, doğrultmak; cezalandırmak; CHEM yumuşatmak; **cor-
'rec.tion** *n.* düzeltme, tashih, ıslah,
ayarlama; cezalandırma; CHEM yu-
muşatma; *house of* ~ ıslahhane; hapishane; *I speak under* ~ yanlışlarım olduğunu bilerek konuşuyorum; **cor-
'rect.i.tude** [-ˈtitjuːd] *n.* doğruluk, dürüstlük; **cor'rec.tive 1.** *adj.* düzeltici,
ıslah edici; CHEM yumuşatıcı; **2.** *n.* ıslah
eden *veya* düzelten şey, çare; **cor'rector** *n.* düzeltici, düzeltmen; CHEM yumuşatıcı.
cor.re.late ['kɔrileit] **1.** *vb.* karşılıklı
ilişkisi olm.; aralarında uygunluk sağlamak; aralarında ilişki kurmak; **2.** *n.*
aralarında ilişki olan şeylerden her biri; **cor.re'la.tion** *n.* karşılıklı ilişki; bağlantı; **cor.rel.a.tive** [-ˈrelətiv]
karşılıklı; bağlantılı, ilişkili.
cor.re.spond [kɔrisˈpɔnd] *vb.* (*with*, *to*
-*e*, *ile*) uymak, uygun gelmek, benzemek, aynı olm.; mektuplaşmak (*with*
ile); **corre'spond.ence** *n.* uygunluk,
benzerlik; mektuplaşma, yazışma, muhabere; **corre'spond.ent 1.** □
karşılıklı, uygun; **2.** *n.* mektup arkadaşı; muhabir; *my* ~**s** mektup arkadaş-
larım; **cor.re'spond.ing** *adj.* uyan, yerini tutan, aynısı; mektuplaşan, muhabere eden.
cor.ri.dor ['kɔridɔː] *n.* koridor, geçit,
dehliz; ~ **train** bir vagondan diğerine
geçilebilen tren, koridorlu tren.
cor.ri.gi.ble [ˈkɔridʒəbl] düzeltilebilir; ıslah edilebilir (*kimse*).
cor.rob.o.rant [kəˈrɔbərənt] **1.** *adj.*
kuvvetlendirici, destekleyici; **2.** *n.* kuvvetlendirici şey; **cor'rob.o.rate** [-reit]
v/t. doğrulamak, teyit etm., desteklemek (*fikir*); **cor.rob.o'ra.tion** *n.* doğrulama, onaylama, destekleme; **cor-
'rob.o.ra.tive** [-rətiv] *adj.* doğrulayan,
destekleyen.
cor.rode [kəˈrəud] *v/t. & v/i.* aşın(dır)-
mak, çürü(t)mek, paslan(dır)mak;
cor'ro.dent 1. *adj.* aşındırıcı, çürütücü,
paslandırıcı; **2.** *n.* aşındırıcı madde,
paslandırıcı madde; **cor'ro.sion**
[-ʒən] *n.* paslanma, aşınma, çürüme;
MEC asitlenme, korozyon; **cor'ro.sive**
[-siv] **1.** □ çürütücü, aşındırıcı, kemirici; *fig.* yıpratıcı; **2.** *n.* çürütücü madde; **cor'ro.sive.ness** *n.* çürütücülük,
aşındırıcılık.
cor.ru.gate ['kɔrugeit] *vb.* kırıştırmak,
buruşturmak; MEC yiv açmak, oluk aç-

mak; **~d cardboard** oluklu mukavva; **~d iron** oluklu demir levha.

cor.rupt [kə'rʌpt] **1.** □ namussuz, fırsatçı, rüşvet almaya alışkın; kötü, pis; bozuk, çürük; **~ practices** pl. POL rüşvet alma *veya* verme; **2.** v/t. & v/i. boz(ul)mak, çürü(t)mek; ahlâkını bozmak, ayartmak, baştan çıkartmak; rüşvet vermek; **cor'rupt.er** n. rüşvet yiyen kimse; **cor.rupt.i.bil.i.ty** [.tə'biliti] n. rüşvet yeme; **cor'rupt.i.ble** □ rüşvet yiyen; **cor'rup.tion** n. çürü(t)me; rüşvet yeme; ahlâk bozukluğu, fesat; **cor'rup.tive** □ çürütücü.

cor.sage [kɔː'sɑːʒ] n. kadın elbisesinin üst kısmı, korsaj; Am. göğse takılan çiçek buketi.

cor.sair ['kɔːsɛə] n. korsan; korsan gemisi.

corse [kɔːs] poet. = **corpse**.

cors(e).let ['kɔːslit] n. zırh (*yalnız gövdeyi örten*).

cor.set ['kɔːsit] n. korse; **'cor.set.ed** adj. korseli.

cor.tège [kɔː'teiʒ] n. kortej, merasim alayı; maiyet.

cor.tex BOT, ZOO, ANAT ['kɔːteks] n., pl. **corti.ces** ['.tisiːz] kabuk, korteks, kışır.

cor.ti.cal ['kɔːtikəl] adj. kabuk...; fig. harici, dış.

co.run.dum MIN [kə'rʌndəm] n. korindon; zımpara.

cor.us.cate ['kɔrəskeit] vb. parıldamak, ışıldamak (a. fig.).

cor.vette NAUT [kɔː'vet] n. korvet, ufak torpido muhribi; kadırga.

cor.vine ['kɔːvain] adj. karga gibi, karga...

cosh sl. [kɔʃ] **1.** n. cop; **2.** vb. cop ile vurmak; '**~-boy** n. sl. genç haydut.

cosh.er ['kɔʃə] vb. şımartmak, pohpohlamak.

co-sig.na.to.ry ['kəu'signətəri] **1.** adj. birlikte imzalayan; **2.** n. müşterek imza atan kimse.

co.sine MATH ['kəusain] n. kosinüs.

co.si.ness ['kəuzinis] n. rahatlık, konfor.

cos.met.ic [kɔz'metik] **1.** adj. makyaja ait, kozmetik..., güzelleştirici; **2.** n. makyaj malzemesi; **cos.me.ti.cian** [kɔzme'tiʃən] n. güzellik uzmanı.

cos.mic, cos.mi.cal □ ['kɔzmik(əl)] evrensel, kâinata ait, kozmik; **cosmic rays** pl. kozmik ışınlar.

cos.mo.naut ['kɔzmənɔːt] n. kozmonot.

cos.mo.pol.i.tan [kɔzməu'pɔlitən], **cos.mopo.lite** [.'mɔpəlait] **1.** adj. kozmopolit; **2.** n. kozmopolit kimse.

cos.mos ['kɔzmɔs] n. acun, evren, kâinat, kozmos; düzen, sistem.

Cos.sack ['kɔsæk] n. Kazak.

cos.set ['kɔsit] **1.** n. evde beslenen kuzu; **2.** vb. şımartmak, çok iyi davranmak.

cost [kɔst] **1.** n. fiyat, değer, paha, kıymet; zarar, ziyan; masraf, bedel; **~s** pl. mahkeme harcı, dava masrafları; **~ first** *veya* **prime ~** maliyet fiyatı; **~ of living** hayat pahalılığı, geçim masrafı; **at all ~s** ne pahasına olursa olsun; **to my ~** benim zararıma; **as I know to my ~** başıma geldiği için bilirim; **2.** (irr.) vb. mal olm., para tutmak; çok tutmak (*zaman*); COM -in fiyatı olm., mal olm.; hesap etm.; **~ dearly** pahalıya mal olm.

cos.ter F ['kɔstə] n. = '**~.mon.ger** seyyar satıcı.

cost.ing ['kɔstiŋ] n. fiyat tesbiti.

cos.tive □ ['kɔstiv] kabız.

cost.li.ness ['kɔstlinis] n. değer, kıymet, paha; '**cost.ly** adj. değerli, pahalı, kıymetli; fig. pahalıya malolan.

cost-price COM ['kɔstprais] n. maliyet fiyatı.

cos.tume ['kɔstjuːm] n. kostüm, elbise, kıyafet, giysi; **cos'tum.i.er** [.miə] n. kostümleri hazırlayan kimse.

co.sy ['kəuzi] **1.** □ rahat, konforlu, sıcacık, keyifli; **2.** = **tea-cosy**.

cot [kɔt] n. çocuk karyolası; NAUT gemi ranzası; portatif karyola.

cote [kəut] n. kulübe, sığınacak yer (*hayvanlar için*).

co.te.rie ['kəutəri] n. zümre, grup, heyet.

cot.tage ['kɔtidʒ] n. küçük ev, kulübe; yazlık ev, sayfiye evi; **~ cheese** Am. süzme peynir; **~ piano** küçük piyano; '**cot.tag.er** n. rençper; Am. sayfiye evinde oturan kimse.

cot.ter MEC ['kɔtə] n. anahtar, kama.

cot.ton ['kɔtn] **1.** n. pamuk, pamuk bezi, pamuk ipliği; **2.** adj. pamuklu...; **~ wool** ham pamuk, hidrofil pamuk; **3.** vb. F yaltaklanmak, yağcılık yapmak (**to s.o.** b-ne); **~ to s.th** bşi anlamak, çakmak; **~ up** geçinmek, anlaşmak (**with, to** ile); '**~-grass** n. pamuk otu; '**~-seed** n. BOT çiğit; '**~-wood** n. BOT bir nevi kavak ağacı; '**cot.ton.y** adj. pa-

muk gibi, pamuklu, pamuk...
cot.y.le.don BOT [kɔtiˈliːdən] *n.* tohumdan çıkan ilk yaprak, katiledon.
couch [kautʃ] **1.** *n.* yatak, divan, sedir, kanepe; **2.** *v/t.* yatırmak; indirmek; ifade etm., arz etm.; *v/i.* yatmak; çömelmek; pusuya yatmak; '**~-grass** *n.* BOT ayrıkotu; '**~ po.ta.to** *n.* F *oturduğu yerden kalkmayan miskin kimse.*
cou.gar ZOO [ˈkuːgə] *n.* puma.
cough [kɔf] **1.** *n.* öksürük; **2.** *v/i.* öksürmek; **~ down** öksürerek duyulmasını önlemek; **~ up** öksürerek çıkarmak; *sl.* nazlanarak söylemek, zorla vermek.
could [kud] *pret. of* **can**.
couldn't [ˈkundt] = **could not**.
coul.ter [ˈkəultə] *n.* sapan demiri.
coun.cil [ˈkaunsl] *n.* meclis, divan, konsey, encümen, şura, danışma kurulu; **coun.ci(l).lor** [ˈ_-silə] *n.* meclis üyesi, encümen üyesi.
coun.sel [ˈkaunsəl] **1.** *n.* danışma, fikir, düşünce, öğüt, nasihat; COM avukat, dava vekili; **~ for the defence** savunma avukatı; **~ for the prosecution** iddia makamı, dava avukatı; **keep one's (own)** ~ fikirlerini kendine saklamak; **take ~ with** -e başvurmak, danışmak; **2.** *v/t.* öğüt vermek -e, akıl vermek -e; **counse(l).lor** [ˈ_-slə] *n.* müşavir, danışman, müsteşar; avukat, dava vekili; *s.* **counci(l) lor.**
count¹ [kaunt] **1.** *n.* sayma, hesap; JUR şikâyet fıkrası, madde; *boks:* birden ona kadar sayma; *a.* **~-out** PARL yeterli üye olmadığından meclisin başka bir tarihe erteleme; **lose ~** hesabı şaşırmak, sayısını unutmak (*of -in*); **take no ~ of what s.o. says** *b-nin* söylediklerine kulak asmamak; **2.** *v/t.* saymak, hesap etm.; hesaba katmak, göz önünde tutmak; *fig.* addetmek, ... gözü ile bakmak; **be ~ed out** *boks:* nakavt olm.; *v/i.* sayılmak; güvenmek, itimat etm. (**on, upon** -e); değeri olm. (**for little** *az*).
count² [_-] *n.* kont.
count.a.ble [ˈkauntəbl] *adj.* sayılabilen.
count-down [ˈkauntdaun] *n.* hazırlık devresi; geriye doğru sayma.
coun.te.nance [ˈkauntinəns] **1.** *n.* yüz, çehre, sima, görünüş, ifade; destek, onay; **put s.o. out of** ~ *b-ni* utandırmak, mahcup etm.; **2.** *vb.* desteklemek, tasvip etm.

count.er¹ [ˈkauntə] *n.* tezgâh; sayaç; marka, fiş.
coun.ter² [_] **1.** *adv.* (**to** -e) karşı, aykırı, zıt, ters; **2.** *n.* karşıt şey; karşılık (**to** -e); **3.** *v/t.* karşılamak, önlemek; karşı koymak; *boks:* bertaraf etm. (*yumruk*).
coun.ter.act [kauntəˈrækt] *v/t.* karşılamak, önlemek, karşı koymak, tesirsiz hale getirmek; **coun.ter'ac.tion** *n.* karşı hareket.
coun.ter-at.tack [ˈkauntərətæk] *n.* karşı hücum, kontra atak.
coun.ter.bal.ance 1. [ˈkauntəbæləns] *n.* karşılık, eş ağırlık; **2.** [_-ˈbæləns] *v/t.* eşit kuvvetle karşı koymak; COM denkleştirmek.
coun.ter.blast [ˈkauntəblɑːst] *n.* sert cevap.
coun.ter.charge [ˈkauntətʃɑːdʒ] *n.* karşı suçlama.
coun.ter.check [ˈkauntətʃek] *n.* engel, mani, zorluk.
coun.ter-claim JUR [ˈkauntəkleim] *n.* karşı dava.
coun.ter-clock.wise [ˈkauntəˈklɔkwaiz] *adv.* saat yelkovanının ters yönünde, sola doğru.
coun.ter-cur.rent [ˈkauntəˈkʌrənt] *n.* anafor, ters akıntı.
coun.ter-es.pi.o.nage [ˈkauntərespiəˈnɑːʒ] *n.* karşı casusluk.
coun.ter.feit [ˈkauntəfit] **1.** □ sahte, kalp; **2.** *n.* taklit; **3.** *v/t.* taklit etm.; sahte para basmak; '**coun.ter.feit.er** *n.* kalpazan.
coun.ter.foil [ˈkauntəfɔil] *n.* makbuz koçanı.
coun.ter.fort ARCH [ˈkauntəfɔːt] *n.* payanda.
coun.ter-ir.ri.tant MED [kauntərˈiritənt] *n.* panzehir.
coun.ter.mand [kauntəˈmɑːnd] **1.** *n.* iptal emri; **2.** *vb.* yeni bir emir ile eski emri iptal etm.; siparişi iptal etm.
coun.ter.march [ˈkauntəmɑːtʃ] **1.** *n.* geri yürüyüş; **2.** *vb.* geri yürümek.
coun.ter.mark [ˈkauntəmɑːk] *n.* karşı marka.
coun.ter.mine 1. [ˈkauntəmain] *n.* savunma mayını; **2.** [_-main] *vb.* savunma mayını ile durdurmak; savunma mayını dökmek; *fig.* karşı tedbir almak.
coun.ter-move [ˈkauntəmuːv] *n.* *fig.* karşı hareket; tedbir.
coun.ter-or.der [ˈkauntərɔːdə] *n.* karşı emir.

coun.ter.pane ['kauntəpein] *n.* yatak örtüsü.

coun.ter.part ['kauntəpɑːt] *n.* akran, emsal; karşılık; kopya, suret, ikinci suret.

coun.ter.point MUS ['kauntəpɔint] *n.* kontrpuan, polifoni.

coun.ter.poise ['kauntəpɔiz] **1.** *n.* mukabil ağırlık; denge; **2.** *vb.* dengede tutmak, denkleştirmek (*a. fig.*).

coun.ter-rev.o.lu.tion ['kauntərevəluːʃən] *n.* karşı devrim.

coun.ter.scarp MIL ['kauntəskɑːp] *n.* karşı siper.

coun.ter.shaft MEC ['kauntəʃɑːft] *n.* ara mili, transmisyon mili.

coun.ter.sign ['kauntəsain] **1.** *n.* ikinci imza; MIL parola; **2.** *vb.* ikinci olarak imzalamak.

coun.ter.sink MEC ['kauntəsiŋk] *vb.* havşa açmak.

coun.ter-stroke ['kauntəstrəuk] *n.* karşı darbe.

coun.ter-ten.or MUS ['kauntə'nə] *n.* kontrtenor.

coun.ter.vail ['kauntəveil] *vb.* eşit kuvvetle karşı koymak; karşılamak, denkleştirmek.

coun.ter.weight ['kauntəweit] *n.* eş ağırlık, karşılık (**to** *-e*).

count.ess ['kauntis] *n.* kontes.

count.ing-house ['kauntiŋhaus] *n.* muhasebe dairesi.

count.less ['kauntlis] *adj.* sayısız, hesapsız, pek çok.

coun.tri.fied ['kʌntrifaid] *adj.* kırsal, köye ait, köylümsü; basit, sade.

coun.try ['kʌntri] **1.** *n.* memleket, yurt, vatan, milet, ulus; taşra, kır, sayfiye, şehir dışı; jüri; taşrada oturanlar; seçmenler; *appeal* veya *go to the* ~ seçime gitmek; **2.** *adj.* taşra..., sayfiye...; ülke...; ~ **club** şehir dışındaki spor kulübü; '~**-dance** *n.* eşlerin karşılıklı sıralandıkları İngiliz köy dansı; ~ **gen.tle.man** sayfiyede oturan zengin; '~'**house** *n.* yazlık, sayfiye evi; '~**.man** *n.* yurttaş, vatandaş; taşralı; '~**-side** *n.* kır, kırlık, kırsal alan; sayfiye; '~**.wom.an** *n.* vatandaş, yurttaş, taşralı kadın.

coun.ty ['kaunti] *n.* kontluk; vilayet, il; *Am.* ilçe, kaza; ~ **coun.cil** il komisyonu; ~ **seat** *Am.* = ~ **town** ilçe merkezi.

coup [kuː] *n.* askeri darbe, darbe, hükümet darbesi. ~ **d'état** hükümet darbesi.

cou.pé ['kuːpei] *n.* MOT iki kapılı dört kişilik otomobil, kupa arabası.

cou.ple ['kʌpl] **1.** *n.* çift, eş, karı koca; *a* ~ **of** iki, F bir iki, bir kaç; **2.** *v/t. & v/i.* birleş(tir)mek, bitiş(tir)mek, eklemek, ilave etm.; çiftleş(tir)mek; cinsi münasebette bulunmak; MEC bağlamak; *radyo*: devreye sokmak; '**cou.pler** *n.* *radyo*: bağlama kolu; devreye sokup çıkarma kolu; '**cou.ple-skat.ing** *n.* *spor*: çiftli buz pateni; **cou.plet** ['kʌplit] *n.* beyit, çift mısra.

cou.pling MEC ['kʌpliŋ] *n.* kavrama; *radyo*: bağlama; *attr.* bağlama..., ekleme...

cou.pon ['kuːpɔn] *n.* kupon; faiz koçanı; müracaat kuponu.

cour.age ['kʌridʒ] *n.* cesaret, mertlik, yiğitlik, yüreklilik; *take* veya *muster up* veya *pluck up* ~ cesur olm., yiğit olm., cesaretini toplamak; **cou.ra.geous** □ [kə'reidʒəs] cesur, yiğit, yürekli, mert.

cour.i.er ['kuriə] *n.* haberci, kurye; turist rehberi.

course [kɔːs] **1.** *n.* yön, cihet, istikamet; NAUT rota, yol, pist; saha, alan; rayiç; UNIV ders. kurs; kap, tabak, servis; COM vade, zaman; *in due* ~ zamanı gelince, sırası gelince, vadesi gelince; *of* ~ tabii, elbette; *matter of* ~ tabiilik, doğal oluş; ~ *of exchange* kambiyo rayici; *stay the* ~ sonuna kadar devam etm., vaz geçmemek; **2.** *v/t.* kovalamak (*av*); *v/i.* hızla akmak (*kan, gözyaşı*).

cours.er *poet.* ['kɔːsə] *n.* süvari atı.

cours.ing ['kɔːsiŋ] *n.* tazıyla tavşan kovalama.

court [kɔːt] **1.** *n.* avlu, iç bahçe, saha, meydan, kort; mahkeme; hükümet sarayı, saray; kralın maiyeti; kur; *at* ~ mahkemede; *pay* (*one's*) ~ *b-ne* kur yapmak; **2.** *v/t.* aramak, davet etm. (*hastalık*); kur yapmak *-e*; flört etm. *ile*; yol açmak *-e* (*hastalığa, tehlikeye*); '~**-card** *n.* resimli iskambil kâğıdı (*kız, vale* veya *papaz*); ~ **cir.cu.lar** saray genelgesi; '~**-day** *n.* duruşma günü; **cour.te.ous** □ ['kɔːtjəs] nazik, kibar, saygılı, ince; **cour.te.san**, *a.* **cour.te.zan** [kɔːti'zæn] *n.* zenginlerle düşüp kalkan fahişe, orospu; **cour.te.sy** ['kəːtisi] *n.* nezaket, saygı, kibarlık, incelik, hürmet; **court-guide** ['kɔːtgaid] *n.* liste, cetvel, katalog; **court-house** ['kɔːthaus] *n.* adliye sarayı, mahkeme salonu; *Am. a.* ilçe hükümet binası; **cour.ti.er** ['kɔːtjə] *n.* saraylı, padişahın nedimi; 'court.li.ness *n.* nezaket, saygı, kibarlık; 'court.ly *adj.* nazik, kibar.

court...; '~'mar.tial MIL **1.** *n.* askerî mahkeme; **2.** *vb.* askerî mahkemede yargılamak; '~'plas.ter *n.* yapışkan bant; '~.room *n.* mahkeme salonu; '~.ship *n.* kur yapma; '~.yard *n.* avlu, iç bahçe.

cous.in ['kʌzn] *n.* kuzen, kuzin, amca (*veya* dayı, hala, teyze) çocuğu; *first* ~, ~ *german* amca *veya* teyze çocuğu; cousin.hood ['‿hud], 'cous.in.ship *n.* kuzenlik; 'cous.in.ly *adj.* kuzene yakışır..., kuzen...

cove¹ ['kəuv] **1.** *n.* koy, küçük körfez; *fig.* sığınak, barınak; ARCH kemer; **2.** *vb.* üstünü kubbe ile örtmek.

cove² P [‿] *n.* herif, adam.

cov.e.nant ['kʌvənənt] **1.** *n.* JUR sözleşme, anlaşma, mukavele, akit, ahit, söz; **2.** *v/t.* vadetmek, söz vermek, ahdetmek; *v/i.* anlaşmak, uyuşmak, uzlaşmak (*with s.o. for s.th.* *b-le* bş için).

Cov.en.try ['kɔvəntri]: *send s.o. to* ~ *b-le* arkadaşlığı kesmek, *b-nin* yüzüne bakmamak.

cov.er ['kʌvə] **1.** *n.* kap, kapak, örtü, kılıf; cilt; zarf; sığınak, barınak, siper; çalılık, ağaçlık; sofra takımı; COM karşılık, kuvertür; sigorta; ~ *charge* (*lokantada*) giriş ücreti, duhuliye; *under separate* ~ ayrı bir zarfta (*veya* pakette); **2.** *v/t.* kaplamak, kapamak, örtmek (*with ile*); korumak, müdafaa etm.; (*yol*) almak, katetmek; hâkim olm.; silah ile tehdit etm.; COM karşılamak, kâfi olm.; *fig.* kapsamak, içine almak; saklamak, gizlemek; yazmak; ~*ed button* kapalı düğme; ~*ed court* tenis: üstü kapalı kort; ~*ed wire* sarılı tel; 'cov.er.age *n.* olayın takip edilip yazılması (*of*); 'cover girl kapak kızı; 'cov.er.ing *n.* kaplama, muhafaza, örtü, perde; kat, tabaka; *floor* ~ taban döşemesi, taban halısı; cov.er.let ['‿lit] *n.* yatak örtüsü.

co.v.ert **1.** ['kʌvət] ☐ gizli, saklı, örtülü; JUR kocanın himayesi altında; **2.** ['kʌvə] *n.* hayvan barınağı, sığınak; kuşların kanat örtü tüyleri.

cov.et ['kʌvit] *vb.* şiddetle arzu etm., gıpta etm., imrenmek, göz dikmek; 'cov.etous ☐ hırslı, açgözlü (*of*); 'cov.et.ousness *n.* açgözlülük.

cov.ey ['kʌvi] *n.* aynı kuluçkadan çıkan yavruların hepsi; keklik *veya* bıldırcın sürüsü.

cov.ing ARCH ['kəuviŋ] *n.* sundurma.

cow¹ [kau] *n.* inek; dişi manda, dişi fil, dişi balina.

cow² [‿] *vb.* korkutmak, gözünü korkutmak, yıldırmak.

cow.ard ['kauəd] **1.** ☐ korkak, yüreksiz, ödlek; **2.** *n.* korkak kimse, ödlek kimse; cow.ard.ice ['‿dis], 'cow.ard.li.ness *n.* korkaklık, alçaklık, namertlik; 'cow.ardly *adj.* korkak, ödlek, yüreksiz; korkakça..., alçakça...

cow.boy ['kaubɔi] *n.* kovboy, sığırtmaç; 'cow-catch.er *n.* RAIL Am. lokomotif mahmuzu.

cow.er ['kauə] *v/i.* çömelmek, korkudan yere çökmek, korkup çekilmek, büzülüp saklanmak, sinmek (*from den*).

cow.herd ['kauhə:d] *n.* kovboy, çoban, sığırtmaç; 'cow.hide **1.** *n.* sığır derisi, inek derisi; **2.** *vb.* kamçılamak, kamçı ile dövmek; 'cow-house *n.* ahır.

cowl [kaul] *n.* başlıklı rahip cüppesi; kukuleta, başlık; baca şapkası.

cow...: '~.man *n.* sığırtmaç; Am. hayvan yetiştiricisi, çiftlik sahibi; '~-pox *n.* ineklerde çiçek hastalığı; '~-punch-er *n.* Am. F kovboy, sığırtmaç.

cow.rie ['kauri] *n.* eskiden para yerine geçen küçük tropikal deniz hayvanı kabuğu.

cow...: '~-shed *n.* ahır; '~.slip *n.* BOT çuhaçiçeği.

cox F [kɔks] **1.** = *coxswain*; **2.** *vb.* dümen kullanmak.

cox.comb ['kɔkskəum] *n.* züppe adam, hoppa kimse; cox'comb.i.cal ☐ züppe, hoppa.

cox.swain ['kɔkswein, NAUT 'kɔksn] *n.* dümenci, filika *veya* kik serdümeni.

coy [kɔi] ☐ çekingen, ürkek, utangaç, mahçup; cilveli, nazlı; 'coy.ness *n.* mahcubiyet, çekingenlik; cilve, naz.

coy.ote zoo ['kɔiəut] *n.* kır kurdu.

coy.pu zoo ['kɔipu:] *n.* kürkü için beslenen bir çeşit kemirgen hayvan.

coz.en *lit.* ['kʌzn] *vb.* aldatmak, dolandırmak, kandırmak; 'coz.en.age *n.* dolandırıcılık, hilekârlık.

co.zy ['kəuzi] = *cosy*.

crab¹ [kræb] *n.* yengeç, pavurya; AST yengeç burcu; MEC vinç, palan, kriko; *catch a* ~ kürek çekerken sandalın dengesini bozmak.

crab² [‿] **1.** *n.* BOT yaban elma ağacı; bu ağacın meyvası; F şikâyet, homurdanma, tenkit; **2.** *vb.* homurdanmak, şikâ yet etm., tenkit etm.; bozmak, mahvetmek; yengeç avlamak; **'crab.bed** □ ters, aksi, huysuz, sert; okunması *veya* anlaşılması güç (*yazı*).

crab-louse ['kræblaus] *n.* kasık biti.

crack [kræk] **1.** *n.* çatlak, yarık; çatırtı, şaklama, keskin ses; F kuvvetli darbe; *spor: sl.* top; kurnazca cevap; deneme, teşebbüs, girişim; F *tütün gibi yakılıp içilmek üzere kristal haline getirilmiş kokain*; **have a ~ at s.th.** zor olan bşi yapmayı denemek; **2.** *adj.* F birinci sınıf, en iyi kalite; usta; **3.** *int.* çatır!; **4.** *v/t. & v/i.* kır(ıl)mak, çatla(t)mak, yar(ıl)mak; şakla(t)mak; çatırda(t)mak; çatallaşmak (*ses*); açmak (*kasa*); CHEM ayrıştırmak (*petrol*); **~ a bottle** bir şişe içkiyi içip bitirmek; **~ a crib** *sl.* zorla eve girmek (*hırsız*); **~ a joke** şaka yapmak, takılmak; **~ down on** *sl.* sıkı tedbirler almak; **~ up** F elden ayaktan düşmek, bunamak; **get ~ing** ...ile meşgul olm.; **'~-brained** *adj.* saçma, aptalca, acayip; kaçık; **'~-down** *n. sl.* sıkı tedbir; **'cracked** *adj.* çatlak, çatlamış; F kaçık, deli; **'crack.er** *n.* patlangaç; fındık *veya* ceviz kıracağı; *Am.* gevrek bisküvit, kraker; **'crack.er-bar.rel** *Am.* F *attr.* samimi...; **'cracker-jack** *adj. Am.* F mükemmel, kabiliyetli; **'crack.ers** *adj.* F deli, çatlak; **'crack-jaw** *n.* şaşırtmaca; **crack.le** ['krækl] *v/i.* çatırdamak, hışırdamak; **'crack.ling** *n.* çıtırtı, çatırdama, hışırtı; jambon rostosunun kızarmış kısmı; **crack.nel** ['~nl] *n.* gevrek bisküvi; **'cracks.man** *n. sl.* hırsız; **'crack-up** *n.* sinir krizi, şok; AVIA feci uçak kazası; **'crack.y = cracked.**

cra.dle ['kreidl] **1.** *n.* beşik (*a. fig.*); TELEPH ahize yatağı; NAUT gemi kızağı; **2.** *v/t.* beşiğe yatırmak, ihtimamla tutmak; yerine koymak.

craft [krɑːft] *n.* hüner, el sanatı, zanaat; tekne, gemi; F gemiler; esnaf; hile, şeytanlık, üçkâğıtçılık, kurnazlık; **the gentle ~** olta ile balık avlama; **'craftiness** *n.* kurnazlık, şeytanlık; **'craftsman** *n.* sanat erbabı, sanatkâr, usta, zanaatçı; **'crafts.man.ship** *n.* hünerli iş, ince iş; **'craft.y** □ kurnaz, şeytan, hilekâr.

crag [kræg] *n.* sarp kayalık, uçurum; **'crag.gy** *adj.* sarp; **'crags.man** *n.* sarp kayalıklara tırmanmakta usta kimse.

crake ORN [kreik] *n.* su yelvesi.

cram [kræm] **1.** *v/t.* doldurmak, tıkmak; çiğnemeden yutmak, alelacele yemek; imtihana hazırlamak (*öğrenciyi*); *v/i.* tıkabasa yemek yemek, tıkınmak; imtihana çalışmak; **2.** *n.* kalabalık, izdiham; **'~'full** *adj.* dopdolu, ağzına kadar dolu; **'cram.mer** *n.* öğrencileri imtihana hazırlayan okul, öğretmen *veya* kitap; imtihana hazırlanan öğrenci.

cramp [kræmp] **1.** *n.* kramp, adale kasılması; şidetli karın ağrısı; MEC mengene, kenet, krampon; *fig.* engel, mani; **2.** *v/t.* MEC kenetlemek; adale kasılmasına sebep vermek, krampa neden olm.; *fig.* engel olm., mani olm., kısıtlamak; **'cramped** *adj.* okunması zor (*yazı*); kasılmış; **'cramp-frame** *n.* MEC vida mengenesi, işkence; **'cramp-i.ron** *n.* mengene, mandal, kopça.

cram.pon ['kræmpən] *n.* krampon, mengene, kanca, kenet, perşin çivisi.

cran.ber.ry BOT ['krænbəri] *n.* kırmızı yaban mersini.

crane [krein] **1.** *n.* turna kuşu; MEC maçuna, vinç; **2.** *v/t.* uzatmak (*boynunu*); MEC vinç ile kaldırmak; **~ at** tereddüt etm., bir türlü karar verememek; **'crane.fly** *n.* ZOO sivrisinek; **'crane's-bill** *n.* BOT sardunya çiçeği, turna gagası.

cra.ni.um ANAT ['kreinjəm] *n.* kafatası, kafa kemiği.

crank [kræŋk] **1.** *adj.* MEC gevşek, burkulmuş; NAUT kolayca yan yatabilen; neşeli, şen; kendini beğenmiş, kendine güvenen; **2.** *n.* manivela, krank, dirsek, kol; garip huylu *veya* sabit fikirli b-i; **starting ~** MOT krank kolu; **fresh air ~** temiz hava hastası *b-i*; **3.** *v/t.* **~ off** krankla hareket ettirmek; **~ up** MOT harekete getirmek, çalıştırmak; krankla hareket etm. (*a. v/i.*); **'~-case** *n.* motor karteri, krank karteri; **'crank.i.ness** *n.* gariplik, tuhaflık; delilik, kaçıklık; **'crank-shaft** *n.* MEC krank mili; **'crank.y** *adj.* garip, acayip, tuhaf; budala, aptal, bön; güvenilmez (*makine*); çok virajlı (*yol*).

cran.nied ['krænid] *adj.* yarık..., çatlak...; **'cran.ny** *n.* yarık, çatlak.

crape [kreip] **1.** *n.* krepon, krep; yas tutarken giyilen siyah tül; **2.** *vb.* siyah tül ile örtmek.

craps *Am.* [kræps] *n. pl.* çift zarla oynanan bir oyun.

crap.u.lence ['kræpjuləns] *n.* sarhoşluk, mide fesadı; içkiye aşırı düşkünlük; F sarhoşluktan gelen mahmurluk, akşamdan kalmış olma.

crash[1] [kræʃ] **1.** *n.* çatırtı, gürültü, şangırtı, şiddetli ses; COM düşme (*hisse*); iflâs, topu atma; AVIA kaza; **2.** *v/t. & v/i.* parçala(n)mak; kır(ıl)mak; çökmek, yıkılmak; çarpmak, bindirmek, AVIA düşüp parçalanmak, kaza geçirmek; bir yere davetsiz olarak girmek; geceyi bir yerde geçirmek; **3.** *adj. Am.* F şimşek gibi, çok süratli.

crash[2] [-] *n.* havlu yapımında kullanılan kaba bez.

crash...: '~**-dive** NAUT **1.** *n.* birden dalma, ani dalış (*denizaltı*); **2.** *vb.* aniden dalmak; '~**-hel.met** *n.* motosikletçi miğferi, kask; '~**-land** *vb.* AVIA mecburî iniş yapmak; '~**-land.ing** *n.* AVIA mecburi iniş.

crass *lit.* [kræs] *adj.* hissiz, duygusuz; dangalak, bön, aptal; çok aşırı.

crate [kreit] *n.* kafesli sandık, küfe, kasa; *sl.* külüstür araba.

cra.ter ['kreitə] *n.* krater; huni şeklinde çukur, bombanın açtığı çukur.

cra.vat [krə'væt] *n.* fular, kravat, boyunbağı.

crave [kreiv] *v/t.* yalvarmak, rica etm., çok ihtiyacı olm.; *v/i.* şiddetle arzu etm. (**for** -*i*).

cra.ven ['kreivən] **1.** *adj.* korkak, namert; **2.** *n.* korkak kimse.

crav.ing ['kreiviŋ] *n.* şiddetli arzu, özlem.

craw [krɔː] *n.* kursak, hayvan midesi.

craw.fish [krɔːfiʃ] **1.** *n.* kerevides, karavide, istakoza benzer bir deniz hayvanı; **2.** *vb. Am.* F geri çekilmek; tutmamak (*sözünü*), caymak.

crawl [krɔːl] **1.** *n.* sürünme, çok yavaş ilerleme.; **2.** *vb.* sürünmek; çok yavaş ilerlemek; emeklemek; kaynıyor olm. (**with** *ile*) (*göl balık kaynıyordu*); tüyleri ürpermek; krol yüzmek; *it makes one's flesh* ~ insanın tüylerini ürpertiyor; '**crawl.er** *n. fig.* dalkavuk, yağcı; ~*s pl.* bebe kulumu.

cray.fish ['kreifiʃ] *n.* kerevides, istakoza benzer bir deniz hayvanı.

cray.on ['kreiən] **1.** *n.* renkli kalem, mum boya, kreyon; *blue* ~, *red* ~ mavi, kırmızı boya kalemi; **2.** *vb.* mum boya ile resim yapmak.

craze [kreiz] *n.* geçici moda, geçici heves; delilik, çılgınlık (*for* -*için*); *be the* ~ moda olm.; '**crazed** *adj.* çılgın, kaçık, çıldırmış (*with* -*den*); '**cra.zi.ness** *n.* delilik, çılgınlık; '**cra.zy** □ çılgın, deli;

deli olan, düşkün; âşık (*for, about* -*e*); çökecek gibi, emniyetsiz (*yapı*); gelişigüzel.

creak [kriːk] **1.** *n.* gıcırtı; **2.** *vb.* gıcırdamak; '**creak.y** □ gıcırtılı.

cream [kriːm] **1.** *n.* krema, kaymak; krem; *fig.* kalbur üstü, en iyisi; krem rengi; *cold* ~ yağlı krem; ~ *of tartar* krem tartar; **2.** ~-*in* kaymağını almak; kaymak bağlamak; krema haline getirmek; *fig.* kaymağını yemek, en iyi kısmını almak; '**cream.er.y** *n.* sütçü dükkânı; yağ ve peynir imalâthanesi; '**cream.y** *adj.* kaymaklı, kaymak gibi.

crease [kriːs] **1.** *n.* kırma, pli, kat; çizgi; buruşuk; ütü çizgisi, kat yeri; *kriket*: sahadaki beyaz çizgi; **2.** *v/t. & v/i.* buruş(tur)mak, katla(n)mak.

cre.ate [kriː'eit] *v/t.* yaratmak, meydana getirmek; THEAT yaratmak; bırakmak, uyandırmak (*izlenim*); atamak, tayin etm., paye vermek; **cre'a.tion** *n.* yaradılış, yaratma; atama, tayin; evren, acun, kozmos, âlem; **cre'a.tive** *adj.* yaratıcı; **cre'a.tor** *n.* yaratıcı kimse, mucit, meydana getiren kimse; **cre'a.tress** *n.* kadın mucit; **crea.ture** ['-tʃə] *n.* yaratık, varlık, mahlûk; insan; kul, köle, kukla; ~ *comforts pl.* yiyecek, içecek gibi maddî ihtiyaçlar.

crèche [kreiʃ] *n.* kreş, çocuk yuvası.

cre.dence ['kriːdəns] *n.* güven, itimat; *give* ~ *to* inanmak, güvenmek -*e*; *letter of* ~ tavsiyename, bonservis; **cre.den.tials** [kri'denʃəlz] *n. pl.* itimatname.

cred.i.bil.i.ty [kredi'biliti] *n.* güvenirlik; **cred.i.ble** □ ['kredəbl] inanılabilir, güvenilir, itimada şayan.

cred.it ['kredit] **1.** *n.* güven, itimat, emniyet; itibar, şeref, ün; COM kredi; COM borç; *Am. school:* ders kredisi; ~ *note* COM kredi bildirim belgesi; *do s.o.* ~ ününü arttırmak, ününe ün katmak; *get* ~ *for s.th.* -*den* dolayı şeref kazanmak; *give s.o.* ~ *for s.th.* b-ni... sanmak; *letter of* ~ COM akreditif; *on* ~ veresiye; *put veya place veya pass to s.o.'s* ~ b-nin matlubuna geçirmek, alacağına kaydetmek **2.** *v/t.* inanmak -*e*, itimat etm. -*e*; COM matluba geçirmek -*i*; ~ *s.o. with s.th.* b-ni ...sanmak; '**cred.it.a.ble** □ şerefli, beğenilen, takdir edilen, şeref kazandıran (*to* -*e*); '**cred.i.tor** *n.* alacaklı.

cred.it...: ~ *squeeze* COM kredi darlığı; ~ *titles pl.* filmde oynayan ve yönetenlerin isimleri.

cre.du.li.ty [kri'dju:liti] *n.* herşeye inanma, saflık; **cred.u.lous** □ ['kredjuləs] herşeye inanan, saf.

creed [kri:d] *n.* iman, itikat, dinî inanç.

creek [kri:kl] *n.* koy; *Am.* çay, dere.

creel [kri:l] *n.* balık sepeti.

creep [kri:p] **1.** (*irr.*) *vb.* sürünmek, emeklemek, yavaşça hareket etm.; nüfuz etm., sokulmak, yavaş yavaş etkilemek; sarılmak, dal sürmek; ürpermek; *it makes my flesh ~* tüylerimi ürpertiyor; **2.** *n.* sevilmeyen, yaramaz adam; *~s pl.* tüyleri diken diken olma, ürperme; *it gave me the ~s* tüylerimi diken diken yaptı; '**creep.er** *n.* sürüngen; BOT sürüngen bitki; '**creep.y** *adj.* tüyler ürpertici.

creese [kri:s] *n.* kama, hançer, bıçak.

cre.mate [kri'meit] *v/t.* (*ölüyü*) yakmak; **cre'ma.tion** *n.* ölüyü yakma; **crem.a.tori.um** [kremə'tɔ:riəm], *part. Am.* **cre.mato.ry** ['_təri] *n.* ölülerin yakıldığı yer, krematoryum.

cren.el.(l)at.ed ['krenileitid] *adj.* mazgallı.

cre.ole [kri:əul] **1.** *n.* Fransız asıllı kimse; **2.** *adj.* bunların konuştuğu dile ait.

cre.o.sote CHEM ['kriəsəut] *n.* kreozot, katran ruhu.

crêpe [kreip] *n.* krep; *~ pa.per* krepon kâğıdı; *~ rub.ber* krepsol, tırtıklı taban lâstiği.

crep.i.tate ['krepiteit] *vb.* çatırdamak; **crep.i'ta.tion** *n.* çatırdama.

crept [krept] *pret. and p.p. of* **creep.**

cre.pus.cu.lar [kri'pʌskjulə] *adj.* alaca karanlığa ait, alaca karanlık...

cres.cen.do MUS [kri'ʃendəu] *n.* kreşendo; *fig.* zirveye doğru yükselme.

cres.cent ['kresnt] **1.** *adj.* hilâl şeklinde; büyüyen, gelişen; **2.** *n.* hilâl, dilim ay, ayça; ♀ *City Am.* New Orleans kenti.

cress BOT [kres] *n.* tere.

cres.set ['kresit] *n.* demir kandil, meşale, fener.

crest [krest] *n.* ibik, taç; tepe; miğfer püskülü; tepe, zirve, doruk; *family ~* aile arması; '**crest.ed** *adj.* armalı; tepeli, ibikli; *~ lark* tepeli toygar; *~ note-paper* armalı kağıt; '**crest.fall.en** *adj.* üzgün, yılgın, başı önünde.

cre.ta.ceous [kri'teiʃəs] *adj.* tebeşirli.

cre.tin ['kretin] *n.* kreten; '**cre.tin.ous** *adj.* kretenli.

cre.tonne [kre'tɔn] *n.* üstü desenli pamuklu kumaş, kreton.

cre.vasse [kri'væs] *n.* buzul yarığı; *Am.* su bendi.

crev.ice ['krevis] *n.* çatlak, yarık.

crew[1] [kru:] *n.* takım, grup, kitle; NAUT, AVIA tayfa, mürettebat.

crew[2] [_] *pret. of* **crow 2.**

crew.el COM ['kru:il] *n.* gevşek bükülmüs iplik.

crib [krib] **1.** *n.* yemlik, ambar; kulübe, odacık; ahır; kopya malzemesi; anahtar kitap; F kopya; *part. Am.* çocuk karyolası; *crack a ~ sl.* zorla içeri girmek; **2.** *vb.* kapamak, bir yere tıkmak; F kopya çekmek; F çalmak, aşırmak; '**crib.bage** *n.* bir tür iskambil oyunu; **crib.ble** ['_bl] *n.* iri delikli kalbur.

crick [krik] **1.** *n.* adale kasılması, boyun tutulması; *~ in the neck* boyun tutulması; **2.** *vb.* adalesi kasılmak, boynu tutulmak.

crick.et[1] ZOO ['krikit] *n.* cırcır böceği, küçük çekirge.

crick.et[2] [_] **1.** *n.* kriket oyunu; *not ~* F adil olmayan, sportmenliğe aykırı, oyun kurallarına aykırı; **2.** *vb.* kriket oynamak; '**crick.et.er** *n.* kriket oyuncusu.

cri.er ['kraiə] *n.* ağlayan kimse; tellâl; mübaşir.

crime [kraim] *n.* cinayet, suç, cürüm; günah, ayıp.

Cri.me.an War [krai'miən'wɔ:] *n.* Kırım savaşı.

crim.i.nal ['kriminl] **1.** *adj.* ağır cezalarla ilgili, kanuna karşı gelen..., cinayet...; **2.** *n.* suçlu, cani; **crim.i.nal.i.ty** [_'næliti] *n.* suç, kabahat; suçluluk; **crim.i.nate** *lit.* ['_neit] *vb.* suçlamak, itham etm.; **crimi'na.tion** *n. lit.* suçlama, itham.

crimp[1] NAUT, MIL [krimp] **1.** *n.* zorla *veya* kandırarak asker *veya* denizci toplayan kimse; **2.** *vb.* zorla askere almak.

crimp[2] [_] **1.** *vb.* kıvırmak, kıvırcık yapmak (*saçı*); **2.** *n. ~ cut* dalgalı, kıvırcık saç.

crim.son ['krimzn] **1.** *adj.* koyu kırmızı, fes rengi; **2.** *n.* koyu kırmızı renk; **3.** *v/t. & v/i.* kırmızılaş(tır)mak, koyu kırmızıya boyamak; kıpkırmızı olm.

cringe [krindʒ] **1.** *v/i.* korkuyla çömelmek, sinmek; *fig.* yaltaklanmak, köpeklenmek (*to -e*); **2.** *n.* çömelme, sinme; *fig.* yaltaklanma.

crin.kle ['kriŋkl] **1.** *n.* kırışık, buruşuk; **2.** *vb.* buruş(tur)mak, kırış(tır)mak.

crin.o.line ['krinəli:n] *n.* kaba bir kumaş; eskiden kadınların eteklerinin içine geçirdikleri çember.

crip.ple ['kripl] **1.** *n.* sakat, topal, kötürüm; **2.** *v/t.* sakatlamak; *fig.* hasar vermek, bozmak.

cri.sis ['kraisis] *n.*, *pl.* **cri.ses** ['‿si:z] buhran, kriz; dönüm noktası.

crisp [krisp] **1.** *adj.* gevrek; serin, kuru (*hava*); kıvırcık (*saç*); kesin, katî, kararlı; kırışık, buruşuk; temiz, bakımlı; **2.** *vb.* gevre(t)mek; kıvırcıklan(dır)-mak; **3.** *n. a.* **potato‿s** *pl.* cips, patates kızartması.

criss.cross ['kriskrɔs] **1.** *n.* birbirini kesen çapraz doğrular; **2.** *adj.* çapraz, çaprazvari; **3.** *vb.* çapraz doğrular çizmek; çaprazvarî hareket et(tir)mek.

cri.te.ri.on [krai'tiəriən] *n.*, *pl.* **cri'te-ri.a** [‿ə] ölçüt, kriter, değer birimi, mikyas.

crit.ic ['kritik] *n.* eleştirmen; tenkitçi kimse, kusur bulan kimse; '**crit.i.cal** ☐ tehlikeli, kritik, vahim, nazik; tenkitçi, eleştiren; **be ‿ of** -*i* eleştirmek, tenkit etm.; **crit.i.cism** ['‿sizəm] *n.* tenkit, eleştiri; yerme, kınama (**of** -*i*); **crit.i.cize** ['‿saiz] *v/t.* eleştirmek, tenkit etm.; yermek, kınamak, kusur bulmak -*de*; **cri.tique** [kri'ti:k] *n.* eleştiri yazısı, tenkit yazısı.

croak [krəuk] **1.** *vb.* vak vak diye bağırmak, kurbağa gibi bağırmak; F ölmek, nalları dikmek; **2.** *n.* boğuk ses; vaklama; '**croak.er** *n. fig.* herşeyden şikâyet eden kimse; '**croak.y** ☐ boğuk sesli.

Cro.at ['krəuət] *n.* Hırvat.

cro.chet ['krəuʃei] **1.** *n.* tığla işlenen dantel, kroşe; **2.** *vb.* tığ ile işlemek, kroşe yapmak.

crock [krɔk] **1.** *n.* çanak, çömlek, toprak tencere; F yaşlı at; F âciz *veya* beceriksiz kimse; F külüstür araç; **2.** *vb. mst.* **‿ up** *sl.* kuvvetten düş(ür)mek; '**crock-er.y** *n.* çanak çömlek.

croc.o.dile ['krɔkədail] *n.* zoo timsah; F törende ikişer ikişer yürüyen öğrenciler; **‿ tears** *pl. fig.* yalancıktan ağlama, sahte gözyaşları.

cro.cus BOT ['krəukəs] *n.* çiğdem.

Croe.sus *fig.* ['kri:səs] *n.* çok zengin adam, para babası kimse.

croft ['krɔft] *n.* etrafı çevrili küçük tarla, küçük çiftlik; '**croft.er** *n.* bir tarlayı kiralayan ve işleten kimse, tarla sahibi.

crom.lech ['krɔmlek] *n.* dolmen.

crone F [krəun] *n.* kocakarı, ihtiyar kadın.

cro.ny F ['krəuni] *n.* yakın arkadaş, samimi dost, kafadar.

crook [kruk] **1.** *n.* kanca; değnek, sopa, asa; dönemeç, dirsek, viraj; *sl.* dolandırıcı, hırsız, sahtekâr; **on the ‿** namussuzca, dolandırıcılıkla, üçkâğıtla; **2.** *vb.* bükmek, kıvırmak, eğmek; **crook.ed** [‿kt] *adj.* eğri, çarpık; ['‿kid] ☐ *fig.* namussuz, alçak, dolandırıcı, sahtekâr.

croon [kru:n] *vb.* mırıldanmak, alçak sesle şarkı söylemek; '**croon.er** *n.* duygulu şarkılar söyleyen popüler şarkıcı.

crop [krɔp] **1.** *n.* ekin, ürün, mahsul, rekolte; kursak; kırbaç sapı; çok kısa saç; *fig.* hasılat, kazanç, kâr; **2.** *v/t.* kesmek, biçmek, kırpmak, kırkmak, kesip kısaltmak (*saç*); ekmek, dikmek; *v/i.* ürün vermek; **‿ up** meydana çıkmak, doğmak (*sorun*); '**‿dust.ing** *n.* uçakla ekini ilâçlama; '**‿eared** *adj.* kesik kulaklı; çok kısa saçlı; '**crop.per** *n.* kırkma aleti *veya* makinesi; mahsul veren bitki; F bozgun, yıkım, sukut; *Am. sl.* kiracı olup ekine ortak olan tarımcı; **come a ‿** F bozguna uğramak, yıkılmak; *fig.* başarısızlığa uğramak.

cro.quet ['krəukei] **1.** *n.* tahta topla oynanan bir oyun, kroke; **2.** *vb.* kroke oynamak.

cro.quette [krɔ'ket] *n.* bir tür köfte, kroket.

cro.sier ['krəuʒə] *n.* piskopos âsası.

cross [krɔs] **1.** *n.* çapraz işareti; çarmıh; ıstavroz; haç, salip, put; keder, gam, elem, cefa, dert; dörtyol ağzı, kavşak; melez; *sl.* alçak kimse, hilekâr kimse; **2.** ☐ karşıdan gelen (*rüzgâr*); F huysuz, ters, aksi, öfkeli, kızgın (**with**, **at** -*e*); çapraz...; karşılıklı..., mütekabil...; melez...; namussuz..., alçak...; **3.** *v/t.* geçmek, aşmak; üstüne çizgi çekmek, iptal etm., çıkarmak; karıştırmak; üst üste atmak (*bacak*); kavuşturmak (*kollarını*); *fig.* karşı durmak, engellemek, isini bozmak; *fig.* aldatmak; boydan boya geçmek; ulaşmak, varmak; çapraz kovmak; melez olarak yetiştirmek; **‿ o.s.** ıstavroz çıkarmak; **‿ out** çizmek, silmek, çıkarmak; **keep one's fingers ‿ed** şans dilemek; *v/i.* karşıdan karşıya geçmek; birbirine çapraz olm.; karşılaşmak; melez elde etm.; karışmak; '**‿bar** *n. futbol:* kalenin üst direği; '**‿beam** *n.* kiriş; '**‿bench** *n.* PARL Avam Kamarasında bağımsızlara ait koltuk; '**‿bones** *n. pl.*

tehlike işareti olan *veya* korsan bayraklarında bulunan çapraz kemikler; **~bow** ['krɔsbəu] *n.* tatar yayı, arbalet, yaylı tüfek; '**~breed** *n.* melez; '**~'country** *adj.* ülkeyi baştan başa geçen...; ülke çapında...; **~ running** kır koşusu; '**~cut saw** *n.* testere, ince dişli bıçkı; '**~ex.ami'na.tion** *n.* sorgu; '**~ex'amine** *vb.* sorguya çekmek; '**~eyed** *adj.* şaşı; **~ fire** yaylım ateşi, çaprazlama ateş; *fig.* soru yağmuru; '**~grained** *adj.* damarları ters olan (*tahta*); *fig.* ters, huysuz, aksi; '**crossing** *n.* geçiş; geçit, geçiş yeri; '**cross-legged** *adv.* bacak bacak üstüne atarak; *adj.* bacak bacak üstüne atmış; '**cross.ness** *n.* hırçınlık, aksilik, terslik.

cross...: '**~-patch** *n.* F ters ve huysuz kimse; **~ pur.pos.es** *pl.* birbirini yanlış anlama, ayrı gaye; **be at ~** birbirini yanlış anlamak, amaçları ayrı olm.; **~ refer.ence** kitapta bakılması gereken yeri gösteren not; '**~-road** *n.* yan yol, ara yol; '**~-roads** *n. pl. veya sg.* dörtyol ağzı, kavşak; *fig.* dönüm noktası; '**~'sec.tion** *n.* enin e kesit; '**~-stitch** *n.* kanaviçe işi; '**~wise** *adv.* çapraz, birbirini keserek; '**~-word puz.zle** *n.* çapraz bilmece.

crotch [krɔtʃ] *n.* çatal, gövde ile dalın birleştiği yer; **crotch.et** ['~it] *n.* garip fikir, akıl almaz düşünce; *mus* dörtlük; '**crotch.et.y** *adj.* F garip fikirli; aksi, ters, huysuz.

cro.ton *bot* ['krəutən] *n.* kroton.

crouch [krautʃ] **1.** *vb.* çömelmek, yere çökmek, eğilmek, sinmek; **2.** *n.* çömelme vaziyeti.

croup[1] [kru:p] *n.* hayvanın but kısmı.

croup[2] *med* [~] *n.* krup hastalığı.

crou.pi.er ['kru:piə] *n.* krupiye, kumar masasını idare eden kimse.

crow [krəu] **1.** *n.* karga; horoz ötüşü; **eat ~ Am.** F küçük düşürücü bş yapmak zorunda olm., yaltaklanmak; **have a ~ to pick with** *b-le* paylaşılacak kozu olm.; **in a ~ line, as the ~ flies** kuş uçuşu; **2.** (*irr.*) *v/i.* horoz gibi ötmek; *fig.* sevinmek, havalara uçmak (**over** -*e*; -*den dolayı*); '**~bar** *n.* kaldıraç, manivela.

crowd [kraud] **1.** *n.* kalabalık, izdiham; kitle, yığın; halk; F arkadaş grubu; bir sürü şey, yığın; **2.** *v/t.* doldurmak (**with** *ile*), sıkıştırmak; *v/i.* toplanmak, birikmek; **~ out** *b-ni* bir yerden atmak,

çıkarmak; **~ on sail** *naut* bütün yelkenleri açmak; '**crowd.ed** *adj.* kalabalık..., dolu..., tıkış tıkış...

crow.foot *bot* ['krəufut] *n.* düğünçiçeği, kazayağı.

crown [kraun] **1.** *n. mst* taç; hükümdarlık; hükümdar; başa takılan çiçek demeti; kuron; beş şilinlik eski İngiliz parası; baş, tepe; dişin görünen kısmı; taça benzer süs; **2.** *v/t.* taç giydirmek -*e*; ödüllendirmek; tepesinde olm.; süslemek, tamamlamak; (*dişe*) kron takmak; **to ~ all** üstelik, bu da yetmiyormuş gibi; '**crown.ing** *adj. fig.* tamamlayıcı..., en son...; '**crown-jew.els** *n. pl.* saray mücevherleri.

crow's... [krəuz]: '**~-feet** *n. pl.* göz kenarlarındaki kırışıklıklar; '**~-nest** *n. naut* direk üstündeki gözcü yeri.

cru.cial □ ['kru:ʃəl] kesin, önemli, kritik, can alıcı; **cru.ci.ble** ['kru:sibl] *n.* pota, maden eritme kabı; *fig.* zorlu deneme; **cru.ci.fix** ['~fiks] *n.* üzerinde İsa'nın resmi olan haç *veya* heykel; **cru.cifix.ion** ['~fikʃən] *n.* çarmıha ger(il)me; '**cru.ci.form** *adj.* haç şeklinde; **cru.ci.fy** ['~fai] *v/t.* çarmıha germek; *fig.* azap çektirmek.

crude □ [kru:d] ham, rafine edilmemiş (*petrol*); kaba; yarım yamalak, tamamlanmamış; '**crude.ness**, **cru.di.ty** ['~diti] *n.* hamlık; *fig.* kabalık, terbiyesizlik.

cru.el □ ['kruəl] zalim, gaddar, insafsız, merhametsiz, acımasız; *fig.* dayanılmaz, çetin, müşkül; '**cru.el.ty** *n.* zulüm, gaddarlık.

cru.et ['kru:it] *n.* küçük şişe, küçük sirke *veya* yağ şişesi; '**~-stand** *n.* şişelik, şişelerin konulduğu kap.

cruise *naut* [kru:z] **1.** *n.* deniz gezintisi; **2.** *v/i.* gemi ile gezmek; seyrüsefer etm.; **cruising speed** normal sürat, ekonomik sürat; '**cruis.er** *n. naut* kruvazör; *Am.* telsizli devriye arabası; **~ weight** *boks:* yarı ağır siklet.

crumb [krʌm] **1.** *n.* ekmek kırıntısı, parça, zerre; *fig.* biraz, azıcık; ekmek içi; *sl.* değersiz kimse; **2.** *v/t.* sofradan kırıntıları temizlemek; = **crumble** ['~bl] *v/t. & v/i.* ufala(n)mak, parçala(n)mak; *fig.* harap olmak, çökmek; suya düşmek (*ümit*); '**crumbling**, '**crumbly** *adj.* kolayca ufalanan; **crumb.y** ['krʌmi] *adj.* ufalanabilen.

crump *sl.* [krʌmp] *n.* çatırtı, ses; *mıl* bomba, patlama sesi; mermi kovanı.

crum.pet ['krʌmpit] *n.* bir nevi pasta; *sl.* kafa, baş; *sl.* seksi kız *veya* kadın; **be off one's** ~ aklı başında olmamak.

crum.ple ['krʌmpl] *v/t. & v/i.* buruş(tur)mak; *fig.* çökmek, düşmek.

crunch [krʌntʃ] *vb.* çiğnemek, çatır çutur yemek, ezmek; çatırdatmak.

crup.per ['krʌpə] *n.* at sağrısı; kuskun, eyer kayışı.

cru.ral ANAT ['kruərəl] *adj.* bacağa ait, bacak...

cru.sade [kru:'seid] **1.** *n.* Haçlı seferi; *fig.* kampanya, mücadele; **2.** *vb.* mücadeleye katılmak; **cru'sad.er** *n.* Haçlı; mücadeleye katılan kimse.

crush [krʌʃ] **1.** *n.* kalabalık; izdiham; ezme, baskı; sıkma meyva suyu; F geçici aşk, tutku; **have a** ~ *sl.* tutulmak, aşık olm. (**on** -*e*); **2.** *v/t. & v/i.* ez(il)-mek; tık(ıştır)mak; *fig.* yenmek, mahvetmek; kırışmak; kalabalığı yararak ilerlemek; sarılmak, kucaklamak; *Am. sl.* flört etm.; ~ **out** *fig.* suyunu çıkarmak, ezmek; ~ **bar.ri.er** izdihamı önlemek için kurulan barikat; '**crush.er** *n.* sıkma makinesi; F darbe, vuruş; '**crushroom** *n.* THEAT fuaye.

crust [krʌst] **1.** *n.* ekmek kabuğu; kabuk, dış tabaka; şarap tortusu; *Am. sl.* yüzsüzlük, arsızlık; **2.** *v/t. & v/i.* kabukla kapla(n)mak, kabuklanmak, kabuk bağlamak.

crus.ta.cean ZOO [krʌs'teiʃən] *n.* kabuklular sınıfından bir hayvan.

crust.ed ['krʌstid] *adj.* kabuklu; yaşlı, saygıdeğer, muhterem; sabit, içine işlemiş; ~ **snow** buz tutmuş kar; '**crust.y** ☐ kabuklu; kabuk gibi; huysuz, aksi, ters.

crutch [krʌtʃ] *n.* koltuk değneği; manevî destek; çatal; **crutched** *adj.* koltuk değnekli...

crux [krʌks] *n. fig.* çözülmesi zor mesele, pürüzlü nokta, zor kısım; püf noktası; çetin ceviz.

cry [krai] **1.** *n.* ağlama; bağırma, feryat; ses, nida; nara, avaz; rica, yalvarma; parola; genel düşünce, istek; uzaklık, mesafe; kovalama, takip; **a far** ~ **from... to** ...den çok uzak; *fig.* ...den çok farklı; **within** ~ (**of**) duyulabilecek uzaklıkta; **2.** *v/i.* ağlamak; feryat etm.; bağırmak; *v/t.* yalvarmak, rica etm.; reklamını yapmak, bağırarak bildirmek; ~ **for** istemek, arzu etm. -*i*; ~ **off** vazgeçmek, caymak; ~ **out** haykırmak, bağırmak (**against** -*e*); ~ **up** gök-

lere çıkarmak, çok övmek; '~**ba.by** *n.* mızmız çocuk; '**cry.ing** *adj. fig.* dikkat gerektiren; acele, ivedi, mübrem; iğrenç.

crypt [kript] *n.* yeraltı kemeri *veya* türbesi; '**cryp.tic** *adj.* gizli, örtülü, kapalı; gizli anlamlı; **cryp.to-** ['-təu] *prefix* gizli-, saklı-, kapalı-.

crys.tal ['kristl] **1.** *n.* kristal, billûr; *part. Am.* kol saati camı; **2.** *adj.* billûr, şeffaf, berrak, kristale benzer; '~**gaz.ing** *n.* billûr küre ile fal bakma; **crys.tal.line** ['-təlain] *adj.* kristal gibi, parlak, temiz, şeffaf; kristal...; **crys.tal.li'za-tion** *n.* billûrlaşma; '**crys.tal.lize** *v/t. & v/i.* billûrlaş(tır)mak; kesinleş(tir)-mek (*fikir*); şekerle kaplamak; ~**d** şekerlenmiş, şekerli (*meyve*).

cu IT ['si:ju:] (= **see you**) (*kısa mesajda*) görüşmek üzere.

cub [kʌb] **1.** *n.* hayvan yavrusu; genç kimse; tecrübesiz kimse, çırak; **2.** *vb.* yavrulamak; '**cub.bing** *n.* av.

cu.bage ['kju:bidʒ] *n.* kübik hacim.

cub.by-hole ['kʌbihəul] *n.* kapalı ufak yer; rahat yer; masa gözü.

cube MATH [kju:b] **1.** *n.* küp; **2.** *vb.* küp çıkarmak; sayıyı kendiyle iki kere çarpmak; ~ **root** küp kök; '**cub.ic**, '**cub.i.cal** ☐ küp şeklinde, kübik.

cu.bi.cle ['kju:bikl] *n.* odacık, kabin.

cu.bit ['kju:bit] *n.* 45-56 cm. arası eski bir uzunluk ölçüsü.

cub.hood ['kʌbhud] *n. pl.* büyüme çağı.

cuck.old ['kʌkəuld] **1.** *n.* boynuzlanan erkek, karısı tarafından aldatılan adam; **2.** *vb.* kocayı aldatmak, boynuz taktırmak.

cuck.oo ['kuku:] **1.** *n.* guguk kuşu; guguk kuşunun ötüşü; **2.** *adj. sl.* kafadan çatlak, kaçık.

cu.cum.ber ['kju:kʌmbə] *n.* hıyar, salatalık; **as cool as a** ~ *fig.* kendine hâkim, soğukkanlı.

cu.cur.bit [kju'kə:bit] *n.* kabakgillerden bir bitki.

cud [kʌd] *n.* geviş; **chew the** ~ geviş getirmek; *fig.* derin derin düşünmek.

cud.dle ['kʌdl] **1.** *n.* F kucaklama, sarılma; **2.** *v/t.* kucaklamak, bağrına basmak, sarılmak; *v/i.* sarılıp yatmak.

cudg.el ['kʌdʒəl] **1.** *n.* sopa, değnek, çomak; **take up the** ~**s** ...in tarafını tutmak, savunmak, müdafaa etm.; **2.** *v/t.* sopa ile dövmek, dayak atmak; ~ **one's brains** kafa patlatmak, hatırlamaya çalışmak (*about -e*; *for -i*).

cue [kjuː] *n*. isteka, bilardo sopası; *part*. THEAT aktörün sözü arkadaşına bırakmadan önceki son sözü; işaret, üstü kapalı söz, ima; *take the ~ from s.o. b-ni k-ne* örnek almak.

cuff¹ [kʌf] **1.** *n*. sille, tokat, yumruk; **2.** *vb*. tokat atmak.

cuff² [ˌ] *n*. kolluk, yen, kol ağzı, manşet; '*~-links* *n*. *pl*. kol düğmesi.

cui.rass [kwiˈræs] *n*. göğüs zırhı.

cui.sine [kwiːˈziːn] *n*. yemek pişirme usulü, mutfak.

cul-de-sac ['kuldəˈsæk] *n*. çıkmaz sokak.

cu.li.nar.y ['kʌlinəri] *adj*. yemek pişirme ile ilgili, mutfağa uygun.

cull *lit*. [kʌl] *vb*. koparmak, devşirmek (*çiçek*); seçmek, ayırmak.

cul.len.der ['kʌlində] = *colander*.

culm [kʌlm] *n*. kömür tozu.

cul.mi.nate ['kʌlmineit] *vb*. AST neticelenmek, sonuçlanmak, sona ermek, bitmek; *fig*. zirvesine ermek, doruğuna yükselmek; **cul.mi'na.tion** *n*. AST netice, son, bitme; *fig*. zirve, doruk.

cul.pa.bil.i.ty [kʌlpəˈbiliti] *n*. suç, kabahat, kusur; '**cul.pa.ble** □ kusurlu, kabahatli.

cul.prit ['kʌlprit] *n*. suçlu, sanık, mücrim.

cult [kʌlt] *n*. ibadet, tapınma, inanç; mezhep, çığır.

cul.ti.va.ble ['kʌltivəbl] *adj*. ekilebilir; *ARG* ziraate elverişli.

cul.ti.vate ['kʌltiveit] *v/t*. işlemek, sürüp ekmek, yetiştirmek; *fig*. terbiye etm.; *b-ni* kendine bağlamaya çalışmak; '**culti.vat.ed** *adj*. ekili; *fig*. görgülü, terbiyeli, kültürlü, münevver; '**cul.ti.va.tion** *n*. tarım; toprağı işleme; yetiştirme; '**cul.tiva.tor** *n*. çiftçi, ekici, yetiştirici; tırmık makinesi.

cul.tur.al □ ['kʌltʃərəl] kültürel...; uygarlığa ait.

cul.ture ['kʌltʃə] *n*. kültür; terbiye, irfan; medeniyet, uygarlık; yetiştiricilik; MED kültür; '**cul.tured** *adj*. kültürlü, görgülü, kibar, münevver; '**cul.ture-me.di.um** *n*. BIOL kültür maddesi; '**cul.ture-pearl** *n*. üretilmiş inci, kültüve inci.

cul.vert ['kʌlvət] *n*. yeraltı kanalizasyonu, su yolu, ark; (*yolun altında elektrik kablolarının geçtiği*) tünel.

cum.ber ['kʌmbə] *vb*. engel olm., mâni olm.; yükle(n)mek, yük olm., ağırlık

vermek; *~.some* ['ˌsəm], **cum.brous** □ ['ˌbrəs] hantal, ağır; külfetli, sıkıntı verici; POST havaleli.

cum.in BOT ['kʌmin] *n*. kimyon.

cu.mu.la.tive □ ['kjuːmjulətiv] biriken..., birikmiş..., birikerek çoğalan...; **cu.mu.lus** ['ˌləs] *n*., *pl*. **cu.mu.li** ['ˌlai] yığın, bulut yığını; höyük.

cu.ne.i.form ['kjuːniifɔːm] *adj*. çivi şeklinde..., kama şeklinde..., çivi yazısı...

cun.ning ['kʌniŋ] **1.** □ kurnaz, açıkgöz, şeytan, hilekâr; *Am*. sevimli, şirin, cazibeli; **2.** *n*. kurnazlık; şeytanlık; marifet, hüner.

cup [kʌp] **1.** *n*. fincan, kâse, bardak, kadeh; *spor*: kupa; deneyim, tecrübe; BOT çanak; **2.** *vb*. fincan şekline sokmak; şişe çekmek, vantuz çekmek; *~.board* ['kʌbəd] *n*. dolap, yüklük; *~ love fig*. bir çıkar uğruna gösterilen sevgi; *~ful* ['ˌful] *n*. fincan dolusu ölçek.

Cu.pid ['kjuːpid] *n*. eski Roma'da aşk tanrısı.

cu.pid.i.ty [kjuːˈpiditi] *n*. açgözlülük, hırs.

cu.po.la ['kjuːpələ] *n*. küçük kubbe; kubbe tavanı; MIL, NAUT zırhlı kule.

cup.ping-glass MED ['kʌpiŋglɑːs] *n*. şişe, vantuz.

cu.pre.ous MIN ['kjuːpriəs] *adj*. bakırlı, bakır gibi; **cu.pric** ['ˌprik] *adj*. içinde bakır bulunan, bakır...

cur [kəː] *n*. sokak köpeği, azgın köpek; alçak adam, it.

cur.a.bil.i.ty [kjuərəˈbiliti] *n*. tedavi edilebilme, iyileştirilebilme; '**cur.a.ble** *adj*. tedavisi mümkün.

cur.a.cao [kjuərəˈsəu] *n*. portakal likörü.

cu.ra.cy ['kjuərəsi] *n*. papazlık; **cu.rate** ['ˌrit] *n*. papaz; **cu.ra.tor** ['ˌreitə] *n*. müze *veya* kütüphane müdürü.

curb [kəːb] **1.** *n*. atın suluk zinciri; *fig*. engel, mâni, fren; kaldırım taşı (*a. ~stone*); **2.** *vb*. atı kontrol altına almak; *fig*. hâkim olm., yenmek, tutmak, durdurmak; '*~'mar.ket* *n*. *Am. borsa*: tahvil borsası; '*~-roof* *n*. tavanarası çatısı.

curd [kəːd] **1.** *n*. kesilmiş süt, lor peyniri; **2.** *mst* **cur.dle** ['ˌdl] *v/t*. & *v/i*. kes(il)mek (*süt*); pıhtılaş(tır)mak.

cure [kjuə] **1.** *n*. tedavi, çare, derman, şifa, ilaç, kür; *~ of souls* papazlık, imamlık; **2.** *vb*. tedavi etm., iyi etm., çare bulmak, şifa vermek; tuzlamak; tütsülemek.

cur.few ['kə:fju:] *n.* eskiden gece ışıkları mecburî söndürme zamanı; POL sokağa çıkma yasağı.

cu.ri.o ['kjuəriəu] *n.* nadir ve pahalı sanat eseri; **cu.ri.os.i.ty** [-'ɔsiti] *n.* merak, tecessüs; az bulunan *veya* tuhaf şey; **'cu.ri.ous** □ meraklı, mütecessis; garip, tuhaf, acayip; dikkati çeken.

curl [kə:l] **1.** *n.* büklüm, bukle, kıvrım, saç lülesi, kıvırcık saç; **2.** *v/t.* kıvırmak, bukle yapmak, lüle lüle yapmak, bükmek; *v/i.* kıvrılmak, bükülmek.

cur.lew ORN ['kə:lju:] *n.* çulluk.

curl.ing ['kə:liŋ] *n. spor:* buz üzerinde ağır taşlarla oynanan bir İskoç kış oyunu; **'~i.ron,** **'~tongs** *n. pl.* saç maşası; **'curl.y** *adj.* kıvırcık..., kıvrımlı...

cur.mudg.eon [kə:'mʌdʒən] *n.* huysuz adam, aksi kimse; tamahkâr kimse.

cur.rant ['kʌrənt] *n.* frenk üzümü; *a.* **dried ~** kuşüzümü.

cur.ren.cy ['kʌrənsi] *n.* revaç, geçerlik; COM nakit para; *fig.* değer, önem; **'current 1.** □ bugünkü, geçerli, hali hazırdaki; COM tedavülde olan, cari; **~ events** *pl.* günlük olaylar, aktüalite; **~ account** COM cari hesap; **2.** *n.* akım, cereyan (*a.* ELECT); akıntı; *fig.* gidişat (*olayların*); **~ impulse** ELECT akımın ani artışı; **~ junction** elektrik bağlantısı.

cur.ric.u.lum [kə'rikjuləm] *n.*, *pl.* **cur-'ric.u.la** [-lə] müfredat programı; **~ vitae** ['vaiti:] *n.* hal tercümesi, özgeçmiş.

cur.ri.er ['kʌriə] *n.* deriyi işleyen kimse, sepici.

cur.rish □ ['kʌriʃ] *fig.* it gibi, serseri.

cur.ry¹ ['kʌri] **1.** *n.* baharatlı yemek türü; **~powder** *n.* Hint mutfağında kullanılan baharat; **2.** *vb.* baharatlı yemek yapmak.

cur.ry² [-] *vb.* tabaklamak, sepilemek, işlemek (*deri*); tımar etm., kaşağılamak (*at*); dövmek, dayak atmak, pataklamak; **~ favour with** *b-ne* yaltaklanmak, *b-nin* gözüne girmeye çalışmak; **'~comb** *n.* kaşağı.

curse [kə:s] **1.** *n.* lânet, beddua, küfür; belâ, felâket; **2.** *vb.* lânetlemek, beddua etm., sövmek, küfretmek; belâ getirmek, cezalandırmak (**with** *ile*); **curs.ed** □ ['kə:sid] lânetli, Allahın cezası, başbelâsı.

cur.sive ['kə:siv] *adj.* el yazısı...

cur.so.ry □ ['kə:səri] gelişigüzel, aceleyle yapılan, itinasız, üstünkörü,

yarımyamalak.

curt □ [kə:t] kısa, sert (*söz veya davranış*).

cur.tail [kə:'teil] *v/t.* kısaltmak, azaltmak, kısmak (*a. fig.*); *fig.* kısıtlamak, sınırlamak (**of** *-i*); **cur'tail.ment** *n.* kısal(t)ma, azal(t)ma.

cur.tain ['kə:tn] **1.** *n.* perde; tiyatro perdesi; *fig.* maske, örtü; MIL siper, koruma; **draw a ~ over s.th.** *fig.* konuyu bırakmak, artık konuşmamak; **2.** *vb.* perde takmak, perdelemek; **~ off** perdeyle ayırmak; **'~call** *n.* THEAT alkışlayarak sanatçıyı tekrar sahneye çağırma; **'~fire** *n.* MIL baraj ateşi; **'~lecture** *n.* F yalnızken kadının kocasını haşlaması; **'~raiser** *n.* THEAT & *fig.* asıl piyesten önce oynanan kısa oyun.

curt.s(e)y ['kə:tsi] **1.** *n.* reverans, diz bükerek selâmlama; **drop a ~** reverans yapmak; **2.** *vb.* reverans yapmak (**to** *-e*).

cur.va.ture ['kə:vətʃə] *n.* eğilme, bükülme, kavislenme, eğrilik; **~ of the spine** MED belkemiği kayması.

curve [kə:v] **1.** *n.* kavis, eğri, kıvrım; viraj, dönemeç; *Am. beysbol:* topun vurulduktan sonra havada eğri çizmesi; **2.** *v/t.* & *v/i.* eğ(il)mek, bük(ül)mek, kavis oluşturmak.

cush.ion ['kuʃən] **1.** *n.* yastık, minder; bilardo masasının lastikli iç kenarı; **2.** *v/t.* kıtıkla doldurmak, minderlemek; minderle hızını kesmek; *fig.* korumak, etkisini azaltmak; MEC beslemek, doldurmak.

cush.y *sl.* ['kuʃi] *adj.* rahat, kolay, hafif (*iş*).

cusp [kʌsp] *n.* sivri uç; uç nokta; zirve; dilim.

cus.pi.dor *Am.* ['kʌspidɔ:] *n.* tükürük hokkası.

cuss *Am.* F [kʌs] **1.** *n.* küfür; lânet; *co.* herif; **2.** *vb.* küfretmek, sövmek, lânetlemek; **cuss.ed** □ ['kʌsid] *adj.* inatçı, dik kafalı, ters.

cus.tard ['kʌstəd] *n.* süt ve yumurtadan yapılan bir çeşit tatlı; **'~pow.der** *n.* muhallebi tozu.

cus.to.di.an [kʌs'təudjən] *n.* muhafız, koruyucu, nezaret eden kimse; kapıcı; **custo.dy** ['-tədi] *n.* muhafaza, koruma, himaye, nezaret, hapis.

cus.tom ['kʌstəm] *n.* âdet, örf, görenek, gelenek, anane; alışkanlık; COM alışveriş, müşterisi olma; JUR gelenek hukuku; **~s** *pl.* gümrük; **'cus.tom.ar.y**

□ alışılmış, âdet olan, geleneksel;
'**cus.tom.er** *n.* müşteri; '**cus.tom-**
-house *n.* gümrük dairesi; ~ *officer*
gümrük memuru; '**cus.tom-'made**
adj. Am. ısmarlama yapılmış, ısmaria-
ma...; '**cus.toms clear.ance** gümrük
muayene belgesi.
cut [kʌt] **1.** *n.* kesim, kesme, kesiş; kesit;
tenzilât, iskonto, kesinti; kesik kısım;
parça, dilim, bölüm; ELECT elektrik ke-
sintisi; sert vuruş; biçki; *fig.* incitici söz,
taş; *iro.* küçük parça, parçacık; TYP
klişe; oyulmuş geçit; *oyun kağıdı:* kesme; *short-cut* kestirme yol; *cold ~ s pl.*
soğuk et yemekleri; *give s.o. the ~ (di-*
rect) F *b-ni* görmezden gelmek; **2.** (*irr.*)
v/t. kesmek, bicmek, kısaltmak; kam
vermemek; dilimlemek; sansür etm.
(*film*); azaltmak, kesintiye uğratmak;
acmak (*yol. kanal*); F asmak (*okul,*
ders); kesmek (*doğru, çizgi*); kenarına
vurmak (*topun*); durdurmak (*film çe-*
kimini); ~ *one's finger* parmağını kesmek; ~ *teeth* diş çıkarmak (*çocuk*); ~ *a*
figure F şekil vermek; ~ *and come*
again bol bol, çokça almak; ~ *it fine*
F ucu ucuna yetişmek; ~ *short* kısa kesmek; lafını yarıda kesmek; *to ~ a long*
story short uzun lafın kısası; ~ *and run*
F sıvışmak, tüymek; ~ *back* budamak;
azaltmak; ~ *down* kesmek (*ağaç*); öldürmek, yaralamak; azaltmak; fiyatını
indirmek; kısaltmak (*elbise*); ~ *off* kesmek, kesip koparmak; TELEPH kesilmek (*hat*); mahrum etm. (*from*
-den); *Am.* ayırmak, ayıklamak; ELECT
tecrit etm.; *radyo:* kapamak; ~ *out* kesip çıkarmak; *fig.* sıyrı açmak *-e*; F bırakmak (*içki, sigara v.b.*); kesmek (*konuş-*
ma vs.); sürüden ayırmak; *be ~ out for*
istenilen nitelikte olm.; *have one's*
work ~ out (for one) F yapılacak dünya
kadar işi olm.; ~ *it out!* *sl.* bırakın kav-
gayı!, kesin artık!; ~ *up* doğramak; tahrip etm.; çok etkilemek, sarsmak; *fig.*
şiddetle eleştirmek, taş atmak; *v/i.* ~
in arabanın önüne dalmak; dahil
etm.; lafını kesmek; **3.** *adj.* kesik, kesilmiş, biçilmiş; *sl.* sarhoş; ~ *flowers pl.*
kesilmiş çiçekler; ~ *glass* billûr, kristal; ~ *and dry veya dried* sabit, yerleşmiş (*fikir vs.*); önceden hazırlanmış.
cu.ta.ne.ous [kjuːˈteinjəs] *adj.* deriye
ait, deri..., cilt...
cut-a.way [ˈkʌtəwei] *a.* ~ *coat* n. frak,
bonjur.
cut-back [ˈkʌtbæk] *n. film:* tekrar oy-

natma.
cute □ F [kjuːt] zeki, kurnaz, açıkgöz;
Am. F zarif, hoş, sevimli, şirin.
cu.ti.cle ANAT, BOT [ˈkjuːtikl] *n.* epider-
ma, üst deri, tırnakları çevreleyen ölü
deri; ~ *scissors pl.* tırnak makası, et
makası.
cut-in [ˈkʌtin] *n. film:* kesilen parça.
cut.lass [ˈkʌtləs] *n.* NAUT bahriye kılıcı;
kesici alet, pala.
cut.ler [ˈkʌtlə] *n.* bıçakçı; '**cut.ler.y** *n.*
sofra takımı, çatal bıçak takımı;
bıçakçılık.
cut.let [ˈkʌtlit] *n.* pirzola, kotlet.
cut...: '~**-off** *n. Am.* kestirme yol; kesici
alet; kesilen herhangi birşey; *bşin* sona
erme tarihi; '~**-out** *n.* MOT arıza; ELECT
devre kesici; *Am.* mahrumiyet, yoksunluk; '~**-purse** *n.* yankesici; '**cut.ter**
n. kesici; NAUT tek direkli gemi; filika;
kotra; *film:* montajcı; MIN çukur açan
alet; MEC kesici alet, bıçak, freze;
Am. hafif kızak; '**cut-throat 1.** *n.* katil,
cani; **2.** *adj.* zalim, acımasız; amansız,
kıyasıya (*mücadele*); '**cut.ting 1.** □
iğneleyici, acı (*söz*); MEC kesici..., keskin...; dondurucu (*soğuk*); bıçak gibi,
müthiş (*ağrı*); ~ *edge* keskin kenar; ~
nippers pl. kesici kıskaç, kerpeten;
2. *n.* kesme; gazete küpürü; BOT daldırma, çelik; kesim, kayıt; RAIL yol, pasaj;
MEC kesme.
cut.tle ICHTH [ˈkʌtl] = ~**-fish**; '~**-bone** *n.*
mürekkep balığının cilacılıkta kullanı-
lan kabuğu; '~**-fish** *n.* mürekkep balığı.
cy.a.nide CHEM [ˈsaiənaid] *n.* siyanür; ~
of potassium potasyum siyanür.
cy.ber... [ˈsaibə] siber...
cy.ber.net.ics [saibəˈnetiks] *n. sg.*
ayarlama-yönleme bilgisi, sibernetik.
cyc.la.men BOT [ˈsikləmən] *n.* siklamen, tavşankulağı, buhurumeryem çiçeği.
cy.cle [ˈsaikl] **1.** *n.* devre, dönem; MEC
devir, dönme, dönüş; bisiklet, motosiklet; COM dalgalanma, konjonktür;
four-~ engine MOT dört zamanlı motor; **2.** *v/i.* bisikletle gitmek, bisiklete
binmek; '**cy.clic**, '**cy.cli.cal** □ devirli;
COM devresel...; *cycling* [ˈsaikliŋ] **1.**
n. bisiklete binme; **2.** *adj.* devreden...,
dönen...; '**cy.clist** *n.* bisikletçi.
cy.clone [ˈsaikləun] *n.* siklon, kiklon;
kasırga; **cy.clon.ic** [~ˈklɔnik] *adj.* siklon..., kiklon...
cy.clo.pae.di.a [saikləuˈpiːdjə] *n.* ansiklopedi.

damask

Cy.clo.pean [sai'kləupjən] *adj.* dev gibi, muazzam, büyük; heybetli; eski Yunan mitolojilerindeki deve ait.

cy.clo.style ['saikləustail] *n.* teksir makinesi; cy.clo.tron PHYS ['saiklətrən] *n.* siklotron.

cyg.net ['signit] *n.* kuğu yavrusu.

cyl.in.der ['silində] *n.* silindir; cy'lin.dric, cy'lin.dri.cal □ [_drik(əl)] silindir şeklinde.

cym.bal MUS ['simbl] *n.* büyük zil.

cyn.ic ['sinik] 1. *a.* 'cyn.i.cal □ toplum törelerini hor gören, kötü gözle gören, kinik, sinik; alaycı; 2. *n.* toplum törelerini hor gören kimse; alaycı kimse; cyn.icism ['_sizəm] *n.* toplum törele-

rini hor görme, kinizm.

cy.no.sure *fig.* ['sinəzjuə] *n.* dikkati çeken şey *veya* kimse.

cy.press BOT ['saipris] *n.* servi.

Cyp.rian ['sipriən], Cyp.ri.ot ['sipriət] 1. *n.* Kıbrıslı kimse; 2. *adj.* Kıbrıs'a ait, Kıbrıslı..., Kıbrıs...

cyst [sist] *n.* MED kist; 'cyst.ic *adj.* kiste ait, kist...; cys.ti.tis MED [sis'taitis] *n.* sidik torbası iltihabı, sistit.

czar [zɑː] *n.* Rus çarı, çar.

Czech [tʃek] 1. *n.* Çek; 2. *adj.* Çek'lere ait; Çek diline ait.

Czech.os.lo.vak ['tʃekəu'sləuvæk] 1. *adj.* Çekoslavakyalı; 2. *n.* Çek; Çek dili.

D

dab [dæb] 1. *n.* hafif vuruş, *bşe* temas, *bşe* değme; ICHTH bir tür yassı balık; **be a ~ (hand) at s.th.** *bşin* ustası olm.; 2. *v/t.* hafifçe vurmak -*e*, dokunmak -*e*; (*boya*) hafifçe sürmek.

dab.ble ['dæbl] *v/t. & v/i.* hafifçe ıslatmak, su serpmek; (*amatörce*) meşgul olm., uğraşmak (**in**, *at ile*); 'dab.bler *n.* amotör, üstünkörü iş gören adam; şarlatan.

dace ICHTH [deis] *n.* bir tür tatlısu balığı.

dac.tyl *poet.* ['dæktil] *n.* bir açık ve iki kapalı heceden oluşan mısra.

dad F [dæd], dad.dy F [_di] *n.* baba, babacık.

dad.dy-long.legs F zoo ['dædi'lɔŋlegz] *n.* tipula sineği.

daf.fo.dil BOT ['dæfədil] *n.* nergis, zerrin, fulya.

daft □ F [dɑːft] kaçık, ahmak, saçmasapan.

dag.ger ['dægə] *n.* hançer, kama; **be at ~s drawn** kanlı bıçaklı olm. (**with** *ile*).

dag.gle ['dægl] *v/t. & v/i.* çamura sür(ün)mek, çamurlamak.

da.go *Am. sl.* ['deigəu] *n. contp.* İspanyol *veya* İtalyan asıllı kimse.

dahl.ia BOT ['deiljə] *n.* dalya, yıldızçiçeği.

Dail Eir.eann [dail'eərən] *n.* İrlanda millet meclisi.

dai.ly ['deili] 1. *adj.* gündelik, günlük; 2. *adv.* her gün; 3. *n.* gündelik gazete; gündelikçi (*hizmetçi*).

dain.ti.ness ['deintinis] *n.* zarafet, incelik; titizlik; 'dain.ty 1. □ narin, zarif, ince, sevimli; titiz; 2. *n.* (*yemek*) nefis şey, leziz şey.

dair.y ['dɛəri] *n.* süthane, mandıra; süt-çü dükkânı; ~ cat.tle süt veren hayvan; '~farm *n.* süt üretilen çiftlik, mandıra; '~maid *n.* sütçü kız; '~man *n.* sütçü.

da.is ['deiis] *n.* kürsü, salonun baş tarafında yükseltilmiş zemin.

dai.sy ['deizi] 1. *n.* paratya; 2. F *adj.* hoş, sevimli.

dale [deil] *n.* vadi, dere.

dal.li.ance ['dæliəns] *n.* tembellik, üşeniklik; oynaşma, cilveleşme; 'dal.ly ['_li] *vb.* cilveleşmek, oynaşmak (**with** *ile*); boşuna vakit geçirmek, oyalanmak (**about**, **over** *ile*).

dam¹ [dæm] *n.* ana hayvan.

dam² [_] 1. *n.* set, baraj, su bendi; 2. *v/t.* set yapmak, bentle durdurmak; *fig.* durdurmak, engellemek, kepatmak, geri tutmak (**in**, **up** *bşi*).

dam.age ['dæmidʒ] 1. *n.* zarar, hasar; ~s *pl.* JUR tazminat; 2. *v/t.* zarar vermek -*e*, bozmak -*i*; dam.age.a.ble *adj.* bozulabilir, hasara uğrayabilir.

dam.a.scene ['dæmə:si:n] 1. *adj.* damas ko ile ilgili, kakma işi ile ilgili; 2. *v/t. bşi* kakma işi ile süslemek; dam.ask ['dæməsk] 1. *n.* (*kumaş*) damasko; koyu pembe renk; 2. *adj.* Şam işi; damasko; gül rengi, pembe; 3. *v/t.* (*çelik*) kakma ile süslemek; (*kumaş*) damasko ile döşemek;

gül rengi vermek.
dame [deim] *n.* hanım, bayan (*a. unvan*); *sl.* kadın.
damn [dæm] **1.** *v/t.* lânetlemek, beddua etm.; mahkûm etm.; THEAT reddetmek; kınamak; ~ *it!* kahrolası!; Allah belâsı nı versin!; **2.** *n.* lânet, beddua; *fig.* değersiz şey; *I don't care a ~!* umurumda değil!; **dam.na.ble** [ˈdæmnəbl] melûn, lânetlenmeyi hak eden; **dam-ˈna.tion** *n.* lânet, kargıma, belâ, mahkûm etme; **dam.na.to.ry** □ [ˈ-nətəri] lânete (*veya* bedduaya) neden olan; **damned** [dæmd] *adj. veya adv.* lânetli, melûn (*a.* = *ziya de, çok fazla*); **damning** [ˈdæmiŋ] *adj.* şiddetle karşı olan.
Dam.o.cles [ˈdæməkliːz] *n.:* **sword of ~** Demoklesin kılıcı, insanı her an bekle yen tehlike.
damp [dæmp] **1.** □ rutubetli, nemli; **2.** *n.* rutubet, nem; *fig.* cesaretini kırma, ak satma; MIN madenlerde oluşan tehlikeli bir gaz; **3.** *a.* ˈ**damp.en** *v/t. & v/i.* ıslatmak, ıslanmak, nemlen(dir)mek; (*ateş. şevk*) bastırmak, azaltmak; *fig.* neşesini kaçırmak; ˈ**damp.er** *n.* MUS yastık; pedal; soba borusu kapağı; *fig.* sevinci, heyecanı vs. yi azaltma; MOT ses titreşimini azaltan araç, damper; ˈ**damp.ish** *adj.* rutubetli, nemli; ˈ**damp-proof** *n.* nem geçirmeyen şey.
dam.sel *obs.* [ˈdæmzəl] *n.* genç kız, küçük hanım.
dam.son BOT [ˈdæmzən] *n.* mürdümeriği; ~ *cheese* erik reçeli.
dance [dɑːns] **1.** *n.* dans; balo; *lead s.o. a ~ b-ni* üzmek, *b-ne* eziyet etm.; **2.** *v/t. & v/i.* dans et(tir)mek, oyna(t)mak; ˈ**~band** *n.* dans orkestrası; ˈ**~hall** *n.* dans salonu; ˈ**~hos.tess** *n.* beraber dansetmek için ücretle tutulan kız; ˈ**danc.er** *n.* danseden; dansöz.
dancing [ˈdɑːnsiŋ] *n.* dans etme; dans; ~**girl** *n.* danseden, dansöz; ˈ**~les.son** *n.* dans dersi; ˈ**~room** *n.* dans salonu.
dan.de.li.on BOT [ˈdændilaiən] *n.* kara hindiba.
dan.der *sl.* [ˈdændə] *n.* öfke, hiddet; *get s.o.'s ~ up b-ni* kızdırmak, öfkelendirmek.
dan.dle [ˈdændl] *v/t.* (*çocuk*) kolda veya dizde hoplatmak.
dan.druff [ˈdændrʌf] *n. pl.* (*saçta*) kepek, konak.
dan.dy [ˈdændi] **1.** *n.* züppe, bobstil; F şık; **2.** *part. adj.* F klâs, şık, en iyi nitelikte; **dan.dy.ish** [ˈ-diiʃ] *adj.* züppece;

ˈ**dan.dy.ism** *n.* züppelik.
Dane [dein] *n.* Danimarkalı.
dan.ger [ˈdeindʒə] *n.* tehlike; ˈ**~list:** *be on the ~* F ölüm tehlikesi içinde olm.; ~ **mon.ey** tehlikeli iş için ödenen ek para; ˈ**dan.ger.ous** □ tehlikeli; **danger-~sig.nal** RAIL *n.* tehlike işareti.
dan.gle [ˈdæŋgl] *v/t. & v/i.* ası(lı)p salla(n)mak; *fig.* sallanmak, sendelemek; ~ *about, after, round s.o. b-nin, bşin* peşinden koşmak; ˈ**dan.gler** *n.* çapkın, hovarda.
Dan.ish [ˈdeiniʃ] **1.** *n.* Danimarka dili; **2.** *adj.* Danimarkalı.
dank [ˈdæŋk] *adj.* nemli, ıslak.
Da.nu.bi.an [dæˈnjuːbjən] *adj.* Tuna nehri'ne ait.
daph.ne [ˈdæfni] *n.* BOT defne ağacı.
dap.per □ F [ˈdæpə] minyon, zarif; atik, çevik.
dap.ple [ˈdæpl] *v/t. & v/i.* benekle(n)mek; ˈ**dap.pled** *adj.* benekli, lekeli; ˈ**dap.ple-ˈgrey** *adj. & n.* bakla kırı rengi (at).
dare [dɛə] *v/i.* cesaret etm.; kalkışmak -*e*; *I ~ say* diyebilirim ki, sanırım herhalde; *v/t.* cesaretli olm.; meydan okumak *b-ne*; ˈ**~dev.il** *n. & adj.* gözüpek, yiğit, atılgan; ˈ**dar.ing** □ **1.** cüretkâr, pervasız; cesur; **2.** *n.* cesaret, yiğitlik.
dark [dɑːk] **1.** □ *mst* karanlık, koyu; esmer; anlaşılmsı güç olan; esrarlı; üzüntülü; **2.** *n.* karanlık; *before (after)* ~ güneş batmadan önce (sonra); *leap in the ~* körü körüne veya bilmeden bir işe atılma, cüretli iş; ~ *A.ges pl.* ortaçağın ilk yarısı; ˈ**dark.en** *v/t. & v/i.* kara(t)mak; *fig.* karanlıklaş(tır)mak; karıştırmak; *never ~ s.o.'s door b-nin* eşiğine bir daha ayak basmamak; **dark horse** *n.* favori olmayan yarış atı; *fig.* sürpriz aday; ˈ**dark.ish** *adj.* siyahımsı; karanlıkça; **dark.ling** [ˈ-liŋ] *adj.* karanlık; ˈ**dark.ness** *n.* karanlık; koyuluk; ˈ**~room** *n.* karanlık oda; **dark.some** [ˈ-səm] *poet.* = *dark 1;* ˈ**darky** *n.* F zenci.
dar.ling [ˈdɑːliŋ] **1.** *n.* sevgili, şirin; **2.** *adj.* sevgili, gözde; sevilen.
darn[1] [dɑːn] = **damn.**
darn[2] [~] **1.** *n.* gizli yama örgüsü; **2.** *v/t. & v/i.* örerek tamir etm., yamamak; ˈ**darn.er** *n.* örgü yumurtası.
darn.ing [ˈdɑːniŋ] *n.* örülmesi gereken şeyler; ˈ**~cot.ton** *n.* örme ipliği; ˈ**~needle** *n.* örme iğnesi.
dart [dɑːt] **1.** *n.* kargı, cirit, kısa mızrak;

sıçrayış, hamle, fırlayış; **~s** *pl.* küçük okları numaralı, daire şeklindebir hedefe atarak oynanan bir oyun; **2.** *v/t.* fırlatmak; atmak; *v/i.* *fig.* fırlamak, atılmak; hızla atılmak (**at, on** -*e*).

Dar.win.ism ['dɑːwinizəm] *n.* Darwin kuramı, Darvincilik.

dash [dæʃ] **1.** *n.* kısa mesafe koşusu; canlılık, enerji; gösteriş; darbe, vuruş; *fig.* hamle, atılış, saldırma, hızla atılma (**for** -*e*, *için*); *fig.* az miktar; bir tutam (*tuz vs.*); bir yudum (*içki vs.*); çizgi, tire, hat (*a.* MUS, TEL); TYP uzun çizgi; **cut a ~** caka yapmak, çalım satmak; **at a ~** çabuk, seri; **2.** *v/t.* fırlatmak, atmak, savurmak; *mst* **~ to pieces** paramparça etm.; kırmak (*ümit*); üstüne su vs. sıçratmak; karıştırmak; dolaştırmak; **~ down**, **~ off** karalamak, çiziktirmek (*mektup vs.*); **~ it!** *sl.* Allah belâsını versin!; *v/i.* çarpmak; atılmak, fırlamak (**at** -*e*); seğirtmek; küplere binmek, çılgınlık etm.; **~ off** süratle uzaklaşmak, fırlamak, acele gitmek; çiziktirmek; **~ through** yarmak, delmek, (*su vs.*) içinden yürümek; **~ up** acele gelmek; '**~board** *n.* MOT kontrol paneli; tekerlek çamurluğu (*at arabasında*); '**dash.er** *n.* F şık, modaya uygun giyimli; '**dash.ing** □ cesur, atılgan; F atik; şık.

das.tard ['dæstəd] *n.* korkak, zorba, kötü niyetli kimse; '**das.tard.ly** *adj.* korkak, hain, alçak.

da.ta ['deitə] *n. pl.*, *Am. a. sg.* bilgi, haber; veriler; ayrıntılar; **personal ~** kişiye ait bilgi; **~ pro.cess.ing** *komputer*: bilgi toplayıp aktarma işlemi.

date¹ [deit] *n.* hurma.

date² [-] **1.** *n.* tarih; zaman; randevu; flört edilen kimse; JUR, COM vade, önel, mühlet, mehil; *esp. Am.* F randevulaşma, sözleşme; **make a ~** randevu tayin etm., sözleşmek; **out of ~** modası geçmiş, eski; **to ~** şimdiye kadar; **up to ~** modern, modaya uygun; **2.** *v/t.* tarih koymak -*e*; *esp. Am.* F randevulaşmak (**with** *ile*); **~ back to**, **~ from** *bşden* ileri gelmek, sebebi … olm.; **that is ~d** modası geçmiş; '**~block** *n.* yapraklı takvim; '**~less** *adj.* tarihsiz; '**~line** *n.* gün değişim meridyeni (*Greenwich'in 180° karşısındaki*); '**~stamp** *n.* postalanma tarihi, posta damga tarihi.

da.tive ['deitiv] *adj. & n. a.* **~ case** GR -*e* hali, datif.

da.tum ['deitəm] *n.* haber; ayrıntı; veri,

bilinen.

daub [dɔːb] **1.** *n.* harç, çamur; acemice yapılmış resim, karalama; üstünkörü görülen iş; **2.** *v/t.* bulaştırmak, kirletmek; PAINT karalamak; **daub.(st)er** ['-(st)ə] *n.* boyacı; acemi ressam.

daugh.ter ['dɔːtə] *n.* kız evlât; **~-in-law** ['dɔːtərinlɔː] *n.* gelin; '**daugh.ter.ly** *adj.* kız evlâda yakışır.

daunt [dɔːnt] *v/t.* cesaretini kırmak, yıldırmak; **nothing ~ed** *adj.* korkmamış, pervasız; '**~less** □ cesur, korkusuz, yürekli.

dau.phin ['dɔːfin] *n.* eski Fransa krallığında veliaht.

dav.en.port ['dævnpɔːt] *n.* dolaplı yazı masası; sedir, divan.

dav.it NAUT ['dævit] *n.* matafora.

da.vy¹ MIN ['deivi] *a.* **~-lamp** *n.* bir tür emniyetli madenci feneri.

da.vy² *sl.* [-] *n.* yemin, ant; **take one's ~** yemin etm., andiçmek.

daw ORN [dɔː] *n.* küçük karga.

daw.dle F ['dɔːdl] *v/i.* tembellikle vaktini harcamak; dolaşmak, oyalanmak; '**daw.dler** *n.* F haylaz, avare; *fig.* uykucu, üsengeç, miskin, tembel.

dawn [dɔːn] **1.** *n.* şafak, gün ağarması, tan; *fig.* başlangıç, uyanma; **2.** *v/i.* şafak sökmek, gün ağarmak; **it ~ed upon (on) him** nihayet anladı he.

day [dei] *n.* gün; gündüz; zaman, devir; *usu.* **~s** *pl.* (*esp. yaşam*) zaman, süre; **~ off** boş gün; **carry** *veya* **win the ~** *b-ne* galebe çalmak, kazanmak; **the other ~** geçenlerde; **this ~ week** gelecek hafta bugün; bundan bir hafta evvel; **let's call it a ~** bu günlük bu kadar iş yeter; **pass the time of ~ with s.o.** *b-le* günaydınlaşmak; '**~book** *n.* COM yevmiye defteri; '**~boy** *n.* yatısız (*veya* gündüzcü) öğrenci; '**~break** *n.* şafak, tan; '**~dream 1.** *n.* hülya, hayal; **2.** *v/i.* hayal kurmak, dalmak; '**~fly** *n.* günü birliğine uçakla yolculuk; '**~la.bo(u)r.er** *n.* gündelikçi; '**~light** *n.* gün ışığı, aydınlık; **~-saving time** *n.* yazın saatleri ileri alarak kazanılan zaman, yaz saati; '**~long** *adj. & adv.* gün boyu; '**~nur.se.ry** *n.* ana okulu; '**~ spa** [-spɑː] (*büyük otellerde v.b.*) bir günlüğüne kullanılabilen sağlık ve güzellik merkezi; '**~star** *n.* sabah yıldızı; '**~time** *n.* gündüz; '**~to-'day** her günkü, sürekli; '**~ trad.ing** menkul değerleri bir günden fazla tutmadan o gün içindeki artışlarından para kazanmaya

daze 590

çalışmak (*borsada*).

daze [deiz] *v/t.* kamaştırmak; sersemletmek; **dazed** *adj.* uyuşuk, sersem,
şaskın

daz.zle ['dæzl] *v/t. -in* gözünü kamaştırmak (*a. fig.*); NAUT gizlemek, kamuflaj
yapmak.

D-Day ['di:dei] *n.* İkinci Dünya Savaşı
sırasında İngiliz ve Amerikan askerle-
rinin kuzey Fransa'ya çıktıkları gün (*6
Haziran 1944*).

dea.con ['di:kən] *n.* diyakoz, hasta ve
fakirleri gözeten papaz; **'dea.con.ess**
n. hastabakıcı hemşire; **'dea.con.ry**
n. diyakozluk.

dead [ded] **1.** *adj.* ölü, ölmüş; duygusuz
(**to** *-e*); ıssız; sakin, durgun (*su*, COM);
mat, soluk (*renk*); sönük (*ateş vs.*);
tatsız, tuzsuz (*içecek*); derin (*uyku*);
işlemeyen, ölü (*para, kapital vs.*);
ELECT tamamiye, büsbütün; ani; **~ bargain** çok ucuz mal, eşya; **at a ~ bargain**
çok ucuz fiyata; **~ calm** *fig.* ölüm sessizliği, ıssızlık; **~ centre, ~ point** ölü
nokta; **~ heat** birden fazla kişinin aynı
anda bitirdiği yarış; **~ letter** *fig.* uygulamaya konmamış yasa; sahibi buluna-
mayıp postanede kalan mektup; **~ load**
boş, kendi ağırlığı; **~ loss** tam kayıp,
zarar; **~ march** cenaze marşı; **~ set** kararlı; karşıt olma, ters davranma
(**against** *-e*); **a ~ shot** keskin nişancı;
~ wall ses geçirmez duvar; **~ water** durgun su; dümen suyu; **~ weight** net
ağırlık; *fig.* külfet, ağır gelen yük; **~
wood** çalı çırpı; *Am.* eski püskü şey,
pılıpırtı; **2.** *adv.* büsbütün; tamamen;
harfi harfine; katî; **~ against** tamamen
karşısında; **~ asleep** derin uykuda; **~
drunk** körkütük sarhoş; **~ sure** hiç kus-
kusuz; **~ tired** bitkin, yorgun argın; **3.
the ~** ölüler; ıssızlık, sessizlik; **in the
~ of winter** karakışta; **in the ~ of night**
gecenin ortasında; **'~a'live** *adj.* ölü gibi, yarı ölü; can sıkıcı, monoton;
'~'beat 1. *adj.* bitkin, perişan; **2.** *n.
Am. sl.* avantacı, otlakçı, bedavacı (*beleşçi*) kimse; **'dead.en** *v/t.* körletmek,
azaltmak, hafifletmek; *fig.* öldürmek;
zayıflatmak, *bşe* gem vurmak; MEC par-
laklığını gidermek.

dead...: **~ end** çıkmaz sokak; *fig.*
çıkmaz; **'~-end** *n.* çıkmaz yol; *fig.*
umutsuz; **~ kids** *pl.* sokak çocuğu; **~
street** çıkmaz yol; **'~-head** *n.* kaçak
yolcu; serbest giriş kartı sahibi; **'~-line**
n. Am. yasak bölge sınırı (*hapishane*);

son teslim tarihi; **'~.lock** *n.* durgunluk;
tıkanıklık, çıkmaz; *fig.* olduğu yerde
sayma; **'dead.ly** *adj.* öldürücü; ölüm
derecesinde; ölüm gibi; **~ pale** sapsarı;
~ enemy can düşmanı; **~ sin** büyük günah; **'deadness** *n.* uyuşukluk; du-
yarsızlık (*duygusuzluk*); durgunluk;
bitkinlik; NAUT rüzgârın kesilmesi.

dead...: **'~'net.tle** BOT *n.* ballıbaba;
'~'pan *Am. sl. adj. & n.* sönük, cansız
(*yüz, çehre*).

deaf □ [def] sağır; **~ and dumb** sağırdil-
siz; **turn a ~ ear** işitmemezlikten gelmek (**to** *-i*); **'deaf.en** *v/t.* sağır etm.,
sağırlaştırmak; **'deaf-'mute** *n.* sağır-
-dilsiz; **'deaf.ness** *n.* sağırlık.

deal[1] [di:l] *n.* çam tahtası; laden ağacı.

deal[2] [~] **1.** *n.* parça, kısım; miktar; oyun
kağıdını dağıtma; F alış veriş; iş, meşguliyet; *Am. mst* uzlaşma, anlaşma; **a
good ~** çok; **a great ~** bir hayli, oldukça
çok; **give a square ~ to** *b-ne* dürüst
davranmak; **2.** (*irr.*) *v/t.* paylaşmak;
oyun kağıdını dağıtmak; dayak atmak,
tokat aşketmek (**at s.o.** *b-ne*); *v/i.* alış
veriş etm., ticaret yapmak; davranmak;
~ with uğraşmak, meşgul olm. *ile*, iştigal etm. *ile*; muamele etm. *-e*; **have ~t
with s.o.** *b-le* artık hiç bir alâkası kalmamak; **'deal.er** *n.* satıcı, tüccar; oyun
kağıdını dağıtan; **plain** **~** samimi, doğru; **sharp** **~** kurnaz, hilekâr, pişkin;
'deal.ing *n. mst* deal.ings *pl.* ilişkiler,
muamele, usul; (*esp. ticaret*) alış veriş.

dealt [delt] *pret. & p.p. of* **deal**[2] **2.**

dean [di:n] *n.* dekan; **'dean.er.y** *n.* dekanlık.

dear [diə] **1.** □ pahalı; aziz, sevgili,
kıymetli; **2.** *n.* sevgili, gözde; sevimli,
hoş; **3.** F o(**h**) **~!..~ me!** aman tanrım!;
süphanallah!; vah vah, yazık!; **'dear-
ness** *n.* pahalılık, kıymet; sevgi, muhabbet; **dearth** [də:θ] *n.* pahalılık; yokluk, kıtlık; **dear.y** F ['diəri] *n.* sevgili,
favori; sevgilim, nonoşum, kuzum.

death [deθ] *n.* ölüm, vefat; **~s** *pl.* ölüm
hali, vefat; **~ penalty** ölüm cezası; **tired
to ~** yorgun argın, bitkin; **'~-bed** *n.*
ölüm döşeği; **'~-blow** *n.* öldürücü darbe; **'~-du.ty** *n.* veraset vergisi; **'~.less** □
ölümsüz; **'~.like** *adj.* ölüm gibi; öldürücü; **'death.ly** *adj.* öldürücü; **'death-
-rate** *n.* ölüm oranı; **'death-roll** MIL *n.*
şehit düşenler listesi; **'death's-head**
n. kuru kafa; **'death-trap** *n.* ölüm tu-
zağı (*a. fig.*); **'death-war.rant** *n.* idam
kararı; *fig.* ölüm fermanı.

dé.bâ.cle [dei'bɑːkl] *n.* felâket, musibet, yıkım, çökme, mağlûbiyet.

de.bar [di'bɑː] *v/t.* yoksun bırakmak, mahrum etm. (*from -den*); men etm. (*from -den*).

de.bar.ka.tion [diːbɑː'keiʃən] *n.* gemiden karaya çık(ar)ma.

de.base [di'beis] *v/t.* itibarına halel getirmek, alçaltmak, indirmek; *bşin* içine başka bir şey katarak değerini, kalitesini düşürmek; **de'base.ment** *n.* değerini düşürme, kötüleştirme.

de.bat.a.ble □ [di'beitəbl] tartışma götürür; ihtilâflı; **de'bate 1.** *n.* tartışma, müzakere; **2.** *v/t.* tartışmak; danışmak; *bsi* düşünüp taşınmak (**on s.th., with s.o.** *ile*); **de'bat.er** *n.* tartışmacı; becerikli, eli çabuk.

de.bauch [di'bɔːtʃ] **1.** *n.* sefahat, ayyaşlık, ahlâksızlık; **2.** *v/t.* ahlâkını bozmak; ayartmak, baştan çıkarmak; **de-b.au.chee** [debɔː'tʃiː] *n.* zevk ve eğlenceye düşkün, ahlâksız, ayyaş; **de.bauch.er.y** [di'bɔːtʃəri] *n.* sefahat, ayyaşlık.

de.ben.ture [di'bentʃə] *n.* tahvil, borç senedi.

de.bil.i.tate [di'biliteit] *v/t. b-ni* kuvvetten düşürmek, zayıflatmak; **de.bil-i'tation** *n.* zayıflatma; **de'bil.i.ty** *n.* zayıflık, kuvvetsizlik.

deb.it COM ['debit] **1.** *n.* borç, zimmet, açık; **to one's ~** *b-nin* hesabına; **2.** *v/t. -in* zimmetine geçirmek; *b-nin* borç hanesine yazmak (**against** *veya* **to s.o.**); '**~ card** *yapılan harcamaların doğrudan banka hesabına borç kaydedilmesini sağlayan kart;* ATM kartı.

deb.o.nair [debə'neə] *adj.* neşeli, güler yüzlü, nazik.

de.bouch [di'bautʃ] *v/t. & v/i.* dar bir yerden açığa çık(ar)mak; dökülmek, akmak, üzerine yayılmak.

de.bris ['deibriː] *n.* yıkıntı, enkaz, moloz, süprüntü.

debt [det] *n.* borç; **active ~** ödenmemis alacak; **owe s.o. a ~ of gratitude** şükran borcu olm. *-e;* **pay the ~ of nature,** **pay one's ~ to nature** ölmek; '**debt.or** *n.* borçlu.

de.bunk F ['diː'bʌŋk] *v/t. fig.* (*yüceltilmiş*) bir kişi, düşünce *veya* kuruluş hakkındaki yanlış kanıları, inanışları kaldırmak, gerçeği göstermek.

de.bus [diː'bʌs] *v/t.* yük boşaltmak (*kamyon vs.'den*); *v/i.* inmek (*kamyon vs.'den*).

dé.but ['deibuː] *n.* ilk ortaya çıkış, görünüş (*esp. bir genç kızın ilk olarak parti vs.'de görünmesi; sanatçıların ilk sahneye çıkışları*); **dé.butan.te** ['debjuːtɑːnt] *n.* sosyeteye ilk kez takdim olunan genç kız.

dec.ade ['dekeid] *n.* onluk; on yıl.

de.ca.dence ['dekədəns] *n.* düşkünlük, çöküş, gerileme; '**de.ca.dent** *adj.* düşkün, çökmüş, yozlaşmış.

Dec.a.log(ue) ['dekələg] *n.* Musa peygambere bildirilen (*veya* inen) on emir, evamiri aşere.

de.camp [di'kæmp] *v/i.* kampı bozup çekilmek; kaçmak, sıvışmak; **de-'campment** *n.* yola koyulma, hareket.

de.cant [di'kænt] *v/t.* kaptan kaba boşaltmak (*şarap*); **de'cant.er** *n.* sürahi.

de.cap [diː'kæp] *v/t.* (*bomba vs.*) etkisiz hale getirmek.

de.cap.i.tate [di'kæpiteit] *v/t. -in* başını kesmek, boynunu vurmak; *Am.* işten çıkarmak, azletmek; **de-cap.i'ta.tion** *n.* başını kesme, boynunu vurma.

de.car.bon.ize MOT [diː'kɑːbənaiz] *v/t.* karbonu temizlemek.

de.car.tel.i.za.tion [diːkɑːtəlai'zaiʃən] *n.* kartelleşmeyi önleme.

de.cath.lon [di'kæθlɔn] *n. spor:* dekatlon.

de.cay [di'kei] **1.** *n.* çökme, gerileme, çürüme, bozulma, zeval bulma; **2.** *v/i.* çürümek, bozulmak, zeval bulmak; *fig.* azalmak, eksilmek, zayıflamak; **~ed with age** eli ayağı tutmaz olmuş, takatton düsmüş.

de.cease *esp.* JUR [di'siːs] **1.** *n.* ölüm, vefat; **2.** *v/i.* ölmek, vefat etm.; **the ~ed** *adj.* ölmüş, merhum.

de.ceit [di'siːt] *n.* hile, yalan; aldatma, hilekârlık; **de'ceit.ful** □ hilekâr; yalancı, aldatıcı; **de'ceitful.ness** *n.* hilekârlık, yalancılık.

de.ceiv.a.ble [di'siːvəbl] *adj.* kolay aldanan, saf, kanan; **de'ceive** *v/t.* aldatmak; yalan söylemek *-e;* **be ~d** aldanmak; yanılmak; **de'ceiv.er** *n.* hilekâr, dubaracı.

de.cel.er.ate [diː'seləreit] *v/t. & v/i.* yavaşla(t)mak.

De.cem.ber [di'sembə] *n.* aralık ayı.

de.cen.cy ['diːsnsi] *n.* terbiye, iffet; '**decen.cies** *pl.* âdabı muaşeret, davranış töresi.

de.cen.ni.al [di'senjəl] *adj.* on yıllık,

on yılda bir olan; **de'cen.ni.um** [ˌ jəm] *n.* on yıllık süre.

de.cent ☐ ['diːsnt] edepli, terbiyeli, kibar; F makûl, kabul edilebilir.

de.cen.tral.i.za.tion [diːsentrəlai'zeiʃən] *n.* bir merkezden idare edilmeyiş, ademi merkeziyet sistemi; **de'cen.tral.ize** *v/t.* bir merkezden idare etmemek, ademi merkeziyetleştirmek.

de.cep.tion [di'sepʃən] *n.* aldatma, hile; aldanış; **de'cep.ti.ve** ☐ aldatıcı.

dec.i.bel PHYS ['desibel] *n.* desibel, ses yüksekliğini ölçme birimi.

de.cide [di'said] *v/t.* kararlaştırmak (**in favour of, on, upon**); karar vermek (*hakkında*); bitirmek, *bşe* son vermek; karar almak; **de'cid.ed** ☐ kesin, kararlaştırılmış; tereddütsüz; kesin fikirli, inatçı; **de'cid.er** *n. spor.* final, son maç.

de.cid.u.ous BOT, ZOO ☐ [di'sidjuəs] (*her sene*) dökülen, düşen; **~ tree** yapraklı ağaç.

dec.i.mal ['desiməl] *n. &* ☐ ondalık, ondalık...; **~ point** ondalık nokta (*ondalık kesirde*); **~ system** ondalık sistem; **go ~** ondalık sisteme girmek; **dec.i.mate** ['ˌmeit] *v/t.* onda birini *veya* daha büyük bir kısmını öldürmek *veya* ortadan kaldırmak; *fig.* tırpan atmak; **dec.i'ma.tion** *n.* öldürme, yok etme, imha.

de.ci.pher [di'saifə] *v/t. -in* şifresini çözmek; **de'ci.pher.a.ble** [ˌrəbl] *adj.* deşifre edilebilir; **de'ci.pher.ment** *n.* deşifre etme.

de.ci.sion [di'siʒən] *n.* karar, hüküm; JUR ilâm, emir; sebat; **take a ~** *bşi* karara bağlamak; bir karar vermek; **de.ci.sive** ☐ [di'saisiv] katî, kesin; azimkâr.

deck [dek] **1.** *n.* NAUT güverte; *esp. Am.* bir deste oyun kâğıdı; **on ~** güvertede; *Am.* F hazır, âmade, tetikte, müteyakkız; **2.** *lit. v/t.* süslemek, güzelleştirmek; NAUT güverte kaplamak; '**~-chair** *n.* şezlong; '**~-hand** NAUT *n.* tayfa, deniz eri.

deck.le-edged ['dekl'edʒd] *adj.* kenarları kesilip düzlenmemiş (*kâğıt*).

de.claim [di'kleim] *v/t. & v/i.* bir koşuk *veya* edebî parçayı yüksek sesle ve etkileyici üslupla okumak; sövüp saymak (**against** *-e*).

dec.la.ma.tion [deklə'meiʃən] *n.* söz söyleme sanatı; resmî nutuk; **de.clam.a.tory** [di'klæmətəri] *adj.* coşturucu, şatafatlı; hitabete ait.

de.clar.a.ble [di'klɛərəbl] *adj.* gümrük vergisine tabi; **dec.la.ra.tion** [deklə'reiʃən] *n.* beyanname; bildiri; **make a ~** demeç vermek; **de.clar.a.to.ry** [di'klɛərətəri] *adj.* açıklayıcı; sarih, katî; **de'clare** *v/t.* bildirmek, ilân etm.; (*gümrükte*) beyan etm., deklare etm.; **~ o.s.** iddia etm., savunmak; **~ off** geri almak; feshetmek; bozmak; *v/i. bş* hakkında fikir beyan etm.; *b-nin* lehinde söz söylemek; *bşi* önermek; **well, I ~!** F (*şaşkınlık ifadesi*) yapma yahu!; ey!; **de'clared** ☐ katî, belirgin.

de.class.i.fy ['diː'klæsifai] *v/t.* (*artık gizliliği kalmayan askerî veya politik bir sırrı*) açıklamak, ilân etm.

de.clen.sion [di'klenʃən] *n.* meyil, iniş; çöküş; GR isim çekimi.

de.clin.a.ble [di'kainəbl] *adj.* çekilebilir; **dec.li.na.tion** [dekli'neiʃən] *n.* meyil, eğim; AST, PHYS açılım, sapma; **de.cline** [di'klain] **1.** *n.* azalma; *fig.* çöküş, gerileme; MED zayıflama, kuvvetten düşme; **2.** *v/t.* eğmek, eğriltmek; GR çekmek; reddetmek, kabul etmemek; *v/i.* eğilmek; çökmek, gerilemek; azalmak, kuvvetten düşmek.

de.cliv.i.ty [di'kliviti] *n.* iniş, meyil; **de'cliv.i.tous** *adj.* meyilli, inişli.

de.clutch MOT ['diː'klʌtʃ] *v/i.* debriyaj yapmak.

de.coct [di'kɔkt] *v/t.* kaynatmak; **de'coction** *n.* kaynatma; *esp.* PHARM kaynatarak hazırlanan öz.

de.code TEL ['diː'kəud] *v/t. bşin* şifresini çözmek.

dé.colle.té(e) [dei'kɔltei] *adj.* dekolte.

de.col.o(u)r.ize [diːˈkʌləraiz] *v/t.* rengini gidermek, ağartmak.

de.com.pose [diːkəm'pəuz] *v/t.* parçalara ayırmak; ayrıştırmak; *v/i.* çürümek, bozulmak; **de.com.po.si.tion** [diːkɔmpə'ziʃən] *n.* ayrışma; çürüme.

de.con.tam.i.nate ['diːkən'tæmineit] *v/t. bşi veya* bir yeri zararlı maddelerden arıtmak, dezenfekte etm.

de.con.trol ['diːkənt'trəul] **1.** *v/t.* alış verişte kontrolu kaldırmak, ticareti serbest bırakmak; **2.** *n.* kontrolu kaldırma.

dé.cor THEAT ['deikɔː] *n.* sahne dekoru, mizansen.

dec.o.rate ['dekəreit] *v/t.* süslemek, donatmak; nişan vermek; **dec.o'ra.tion** *n.* süs; nişan, madalya; ♀ **Day** *Am.* Birleşik Amerika'da harpte ölenlerin anıldığı gün (*30 Mayıs*); **dec.o-**

ra.tive ['dəkərətiv] *n.* süsleyici, süs; ziynet; **dec.o.ra.tor** ['‿reitə] *n.* süsleyen, dekoratör.

dec.o.rous □ [dekərəs] terbiyeli; uygun.

de.cor.ti.cate ['di'kɔːtikeit] *v/t.* kabuğunu soymak.

de.co.rum [di'kɔːrəm] *n.* edebe uygun olma; uygun davranış.

de.coy [di'kɔi] **1.** *n.* tuzak, yem; *a.* ~ **bird**, ~ **duck** çığırtkan, pırlak, avcı kuş, tuzakçı (*a. fig.*); **2.** *v/t.* tuzağa düşürmek, hile ile cezbetmek.

de.crease 1. ['diːkriːs] *n.* azalma, eksilme; **on the** ~ azalmakta olan; **2.** [diːˈkriːs] *v/t. & v/i.* azal(t)mak.

de.cree [di'kriː] **1.** *n.* kararname; emir; tâmim; JUR hüküm, karar; takdiri ilâhî; **2.** *v/t.* karara bağlamak; emretmek; ~ **ni.si** [‿-'naisai] *n.* belirli bir süre geçtikten sonra kesin hüküm haline gelen geçici boşanma hükmü.

dec.re.ment ['dekrimənt] *n.* eksilme, azalma; kayıp.

de.crep.it [di'krepit] *adj.* dermansız, zayıf; **de'crep.i.tude** [‿tjuːd] *n.* dermansızlık, çökmüşlük.

de.cres.cent [di'kresnt] *adj.* küçülen; azalan.

de.cry [di'krai] *v/t. b-ni* rezil rüsva etm.; *b-ni* haşlamak; yermek.

dec.u.ple ['dekjupl] **1.** *adj.* on misli; on kat; **2.** *n.* on kez tekrarlanan rakam; **3.** *v/t.* on misli yapmak, onla çarpmak.

ded.i.cate ['dedikeit] *v/t.* vakfetmek, adamak, ithaf etm. (**to** -*e*); **ded.i'ca.tion** *n.* tahsis, ithaf; feda etme; açılış töreni; **'ded.i.ca.tor** *n.* vakfeden, adayan, tahsis eden; **ded.i.ca.to.ry** ['‿-kətəri] *adj.* ithaf kabilinden.

de.duce [di'djuːs] *v/t.* anlamak; sonuç çıkarmak (**from** -*den*); **de'duc.i.ble** *adj.* anlaşılabilir.

de.duct [di'dʌkt] *v/t.* hesaptan çıkarmak; sonuç çıkarmak; **de'duc.tion** *n.* çıkarılan miktar; sonuç; COM iskonto; çıkarma; **de'duc.tive** *adj.* tümdengelimli, istidlâli.

deed [diːd] **1.** *n.* iş, eylem; kahramanlık; hareket; belge; senet; **2.** *v/t. Am.* senetle devretmek (**to** -*e*).

deem [diːm] *vb.* zannetmek; saymak; düşünmek; fikrinde olm.; hüküm vermek (**of** ...*hakkında*).

deep [diːp] **1.** □ derin; detaylı; kurnaz; zekî; samimî; dalgın; tok (*ses*); koyu (*a. fig.*); gizli; ~ **hit** *boks*; favullü vuruş; **in**

~ **water(s)** *fig.* zor durumda; **2.** *n.* derinlik; *poet.* deniz; '~'**breathing** *n.* nefes egzersizi; '**deep.en** *v/t. & v/i.* derinleş(tir)mek; koyulaş(tır)mak; art(ır)mak.

deep...: '~'**freeze 1.** *v/t.* (*yiyecek*) dondurmak; **2.** *n.* dipfriz, dondurucu; '~'**laid** *adj.* özenle ve gizlice plânlanmış; '**deepness** *n.* derinlik; tokluk (*ses*).

deep...: '~'**root.ed** *adj.* köklü; '~**sea** *n.* açık deniz; '~'**seat.ed** *adj.* kök salmış, yerleşmiş; '~**set** *adj.* çukur (*göz*).

deer [diə] *n.* geyik, karaca; '~**lick** *n.* geyiğin su içtiği tuzlu su kaynağı; '~**shot** *n.* saçma, dum dum kurşunu; '~**skin** *n.* güderi; '~**stalk.er** *n.* geyik avcısı; '~**stalk.ing** *n.* geyik avcılığı.

de.face [di'feis] *v/t.* şeklini bozmak, silmek, çirkinleştirmek; **de'face.ment** *n.* bozma; silme; silinti, kazıntı.

de.fac.to [diːˈfæktəu] *adj. & adv.* bilfiil, gerçekte, fiilen.

de.fal.ca.tion [diːfælˈkeiʃən] *n.* zimmete geçirme; para asırma, suiistimal.

def.a.ma.tion [defəˈmeiʃən] *n.* iftira; lekeleme; **de.fam.a.to.ry** [diˈfæmətəri] *adj.* iftira kabilinden; iftiralı; **de.fame** [di'feim] *v/t.* iftira etm. -*e*; *b-nin* şeref ve haysiyetine leke sürmek; *b-nin* adını kötüye çıkarmak; **de'fam.er** *n.* iftiracı.

de.fault [di'fɔːlt] **1.** *n.* bulunmama (*duruşmada*); ihmal; gecikme; gıyab; **judgement by** ~ JUR gıyabî hüküm; **in** ~ **of which** hazır bulunmadığı için; aksi halde; **2.** *v/t.* görevini, sözünü yerine getirmemek; ihmal etm.; JUR gıyabında hüküm vermek; **de'fault.er** *n.* ihmalkâr; töhmetli; MIL suçlu er; borçlarını ödemeyen kimse; JUR gaip, hazır bulunmayan.

de.fea.sance [di'fiːzəns] *n.* iptal, fesih, lağvetme.

de.feat [di'fiːt] **1.** *n.* yenilgi, bozgun, hüsran; **2.** *v/t.* MIL yenmek, yok etm., başarısızlığa uğratmak; PARL düşürmek; **de'feat.ist** *n.* bozguncu.

de.fect [di'fekt] *n.* kusur, eksiklik, hata; **de'fec.tion** *n.* ayrılma (**from** -*den*); ihanet; **de'fec.tive** □ kusurlu, eksik; GR bazı cekim sekilleri kullanılmayan.

de.fence, *Am.* **de.fense** [di'fens] *n.* müdafaa, savunma; **witness for the** ~ savunma sahidi; **de'fense.less** *adj.* himayeden yoksun, desteksiz; MIL savunmasız.

de.fend [di'fend] *v/t.* müdafaa etm.; savunmak (**against** *-e karşı*); korumak (**from** *-den*); **de'fen.dant** JUR *n.* davalı; **de'fend.er** *n.* savunucu; koruyucu.

de.fen.si.ble [di'fensəbl] *adj.* savunulabilir; **de'fen.sive 1.** □ korumada olan, savunan; **2.** *n.* savunma; **be on the** ~ savunmada olm.; **act** *veya* **stand on the** ~ savunmada kalmak.

de.fer¹ [di'fəː] *v/t.* ertelemek; *Am.* MIL tecil etm.; **payment on** ~ **red terms** taksitle ödeme.

de.fer² [~] (**to**) *v/i.* itaat etm., hürmet etm. *-e*; **def.er.ence** ['defərəns] *n.* uyma, itaat; hürmet; **in** ~ **to**, **out of** ~ **to** hürmeten *-e*, uyarak *-e*; **def.er.en.tial** □ [~'renʃəl] saygılı, hürmetkâr.

de.fer.ment [di'fəːmənt] *n.* önel, vade, erteleme; *Am.* MIL tecil etme.

de.fi.ance [di'faiəns] *n.* meydan okuma; karşı koyma; **bid** ~ **to** *b-ne* karşı durmak; meydan okumak; **in** ~ **of** *b-ne* nispet için, göze alarak; **de'fi.ant** □ meydan okuyan, karşı gelen; serkeş.

de.fi.cien.cy [di'fiʃənsi] *n.* eksiklik, noksan; açık; **de'fi.cient** □ eksik, noksan; **be** ~ **in** *bşde* eksik olm.

def.i.cit ['defisit] *n.* (*bütçe*, *hesap*) açık; noksan; dezavantaj.

de.fi.er [di'faiə] *n.* meydan okuyan; hakir gören.

de.file¹ **1.** ['diːfail] *n.* geçit, boğaz; **2.** [di'fail] *v/i.* birerli kolda yürümek; resmi geçit yapmak.

de.file² [di'fail] *v/t.* kirletmek, pisletmek; ırzına geçmek; bir yerin kutsallığını bozmak; **de'file.ment** *n.* kirletme; pislik.

de.fin.a.ble [di'fainəbl] *adj.* tanımlanabilir; **de'fine** *v/t.* tanımlamak; açıklamak; sınırlamak; **def.i.nite** ['definit] □ kesin; açık; belirli; sınırlı; **def.i'ni.tion** *n.* tanım; açıklama; OPT netlik; **de'fin.i.tive** □ [di'finitiv] kesin; son; sınırlandıran.

de.flate [di'fleit] *v/t.* havasını boşaltmak *-in*; enflasyonu ortadan kaldırmak; gururunu kırmak; **de'fla.tion** *n.* boşaltma; deflasyon; fiyatların düşmesi; **de'flation.a.ry** *adj.* deflasyonal, deflasyon doğurucu.

de.flect [di'flekt] *v/t.* saptırmak, çevirmek; **de.flec.tion**, *mst* **de.flex.ion** *n.* sapma, dönme.

de.flow.er [diː'flauə] *v/t.* çiçeklerini koparmak; bekâretini bozmak; *fig.* ırzına geçmek.

de.form [di'fɔːm] *v/t.* şeklini bozmak, çirkinleştirmek; deforme etm.; ~**ed** *adj.* çirkin, biçimsiz, şekli bozulmuş; sakat; **de.for.ma.tion** [diːfɔː'meiʃən] *n.* çirkinleştirme, şeklini bozma; sakatlık; **deform.i.ty** [di'fɔːmiti] *n.* biçimsizlik, sakatlık; fazlalık (*a. fig. vücutta ur vs.*); hilkat garibesi.

de.fraud [di'frɔːd] *v/t. b-ni* dolandırmak (**of**); aldatmak.

de.fray [di'frei] *v/t.* masrafı *b-ne* ait olm.; karşılamak, ödemek.

de.freez.er MOT [diː'friːzə] *n.* anti-friz perde.

de.frost [diː'frɔst] *v/t.* buzlarını çözmek *-in*; **de.frost.er** MOT [diː'frɔstə] *n.* (*otomobil camı, buzdolabı vs. de*) buzları eritme düzeni.

deft □ [deft] çevik, eli çabuk, becerikli.

de.funct [di'fʌŋkt] **1.** *adj.* ölmüş, merhum; *fig.* eskimiş, modası geçmiş; **2.** *n.* ölü.

de.fy [di'fai] *v/t. b-ne* meydan okumak, kafa tutmak, karşı koymak; *bşi* hiçe saymak; aldırış etmemek *-e*; alnını karışlamak *-in*; dayanmak *-e*.

de.gen.er.a.cy [di'dʒenərəsi] *n.* soysuzluk, ahlâk bozukluğu; yozlaşma, dejenere olma; **de'gen.er.ate 1.** [~reit] *v/t.* yozlaşmak; soysuzlaşmak; **2.** □ [~rit] yozlaşmış, soysuzlaşmış, dejenere; **de.gen.er.ation** [~'reiʃən] *n.* yozlaşma, soysuzlaşma, bozulma; **de'gen.er.a.tive** [~rətiv] *adj.* yozlaş(tır)an; soysuzlaş(tır)an.

deg.ra.da.tion [degrə'deiʃən] *n.* indirme; alçal(t)ma; azletme; **de.grade** [di'greid] *v/t.* alçaltmak; *-in* rütbesini indirmek; aşağılamak; *fig.* azaltmak, kısaltmak; *v/t.* gerilemek; düşmek, derecede alçalmak; bozulmak.

de.gree [di'griː] *n.* derece (*a.* GEOGR, GR, MATH, PHYS, UNIV); akrabalık derecesi; *fig.* basamak, adım (**to** *-e*); rütbe; seviye; **by** ~**s** gittikçe, aşama aşama; **in no** ~ katiyen; **to a** ~ bir dereceye kadar; **take one's** ~ bir üniversiteden mezun olm.

de.hu.man.ize [diː'hjuːmənaiz] *v/t.* insanlıktan çıkarmak, canavarlaştırmak.

de.hy.drat.ed [diː'haidreitid] *n.* susuz, kurumuş şey; ~ **eggs** *pl.* yumurta tozu; ~ **potatoes** *pl.* kurutulmuş patates; ~ **vegetables** kurutulmuş sebze.

de-ice AVIA ['diː'ais] *v/t.* buzlanmayı önlemek, buzu eritmek; **de'-ic.er** *n.* buzlanmayı önleyen *veya* buzu eriten aygıt *veya* madde.

de.í.fi.ca.tion [di:fi'keiʃən] *n.* tanrılaş(tır)ma; **de.i.fy** ['di:ifai] *v/t.* tanrılaştırmak; tapmak.

deign [dein] *vb.* tenezzül etm. (*to -e*); alçak gönüllü olm.

de.ism ['di:izəm] *n.* yaradancılık, bir dine bağlı olmadan tanrıya inanma; **'deist** *n.* yaradancı, tanrıya inanan; **de'istic, de'is.ti.cal** □ bu inanışa ait.

de.i.ty ['di:iti] *n.* tanrı(ça); tanrılık.

de.ject [di'dʒekt] *v/t.* cesaretini kırmak, keyfini kaçırmak, karamsar kılmak; **de'ject.ed** □ kederli, karamsar; **de'ject.edness, de'jec.tion** *n.* keder, umutsuzluk, neşesizlik.

de jure [di:'dʒuəri] *adj. & adv.* haklı olarak; yasal…

de.lay [di'lei] **1.** *n.* gecikme, tehir, erteleme; **2.** *v/t.* geciktirmek, ertelemek; *b-ni* oyalamak; *v/i.* gecikmek; tereddüt etm; zaman kaybetmek.

de.le TYP ['di:li:] **1.** *n.* silme işareti; **2.** *v/t.* silmek.

de.lec.ta.ble *usu. iro.* □ [di'lektəbl] hoş, nefis, leziz; **de.lec.ta.tion** [di:lek-'teiʃən] *n.* zevk, eğlence, haz.

del.e.ga.cy ['deligəsi] *n.* delegasyon; üyelik; **del.e.gate 1.** ['‿geit] *v/t.* üye atamak *veya* göndermek; yetki vermek, devretmek (*to s.o. -e*); **2.** ['‿git] *n.* temsilci, mümessil, elçi, delege, raportör; **del.e.gation** [‿'geiʃən] *n.* delegasyon; *Am.* PARL kongre üyesi; atama.

de.lete [di'li:t] *v/t.* çizmek, silmek, kazımak; **del.e.te.ri.ous** □ [deli'tiəriəs] zararlı, bozucu, sıhhate dokunur; **de.le.tion** [di'li:ʃən] *n.* silip çıkarma; kazıma, bozma.

delf(t) [delf(t)] *n.* Hollanda porseleni.

de.lib.er.ate 1. [di'libəreit] *v/t.* düşünmek, tartmak; *v/i.* düşünüp taşınmak; danışmak, istişare etm. (on); **2.** □ [‿rit] tedbirli, dikkatli; iyi düşünülmüş; kasti, kasıtlı; **de'lib.er.ate.ness** *n.* dikkatlilik, tedbirli olma; **de.lib.er.a.tion** □ *n.* düşünüp taşınma; tartışma, görüşme; tedbirli olma; **de'lib.er.a.tive** □ [‿rətiv] düşünceli, ihtiyatlı; üzerinde düşünülmüş.

del.i.ca.cy ['delikəsi] *n.* lezzetli şey; nefaset; zarafet, hassasiyet, kibarlık, incelik, nezaket; **del.i.cate** □ ['‿kit] nazik, narin, ince (*a. fig.*); hassas, nefis, titiz; **del.i.ca.tes.sen** [delikə'tesn] *n.* mezeci dükkânı; meze, hazır yemekler.

de.li.cious □ [di'liʃəs] nefis, hoş, leziz, lezzetli.

de.light [di'lait] **1.** *n.* zevk, sevinç, haz; *take ‿ in -den* zevk almak; eğlenmek; **2.** *v/t.* sevindirmek, zevk vermek *-e*; *v/i.* sevinmek, zevk almak (*in*); *‿ to bşden* hoşlanmak; **de'light.ful** □ [‿ful] hoş, zevkli.

de.lim.it [di:'limit], **de.lim.i.tate** [di-'limiteit] *v/t.* sınırlandırmak; tahdit etm.; **de.lim.i'ta.tion** *n.* sınırlandırma.

de.lin.e.ate [di'linieit] *v/t.* taslak çizmek; tarif etm., tasvir etm., betimlemek; **de.lin.e'a.tion** *n.* resim, kroki, tasarı; tarif, betim.

de.lin.quen.cy [di'liŋkwənsi] *n.* kusur, kabahat, hata; suçluluk; **de'lin.quent 1.** *adj.* kabahatli, suçlu, savsakçı; **2.** *n.* kabahatli kimse, suçlu kimse.

del.i.quesce [deli'kwes] *v/i.* (*havadan rutubet kapıp*) sıvı hale gelmek, erimek.

de.lir.i.ous □ [di'liriəs] sayıklayan; şaşkın, cinnet getirmiş, çılgına dönmüş (*with -den, ile*); **de'lir.i.ous.ness** *n.* cinnet, çılgınlık, delilik; **de'lir.i.um** [‿əm] *n.* sayıklama, hezeyan; çılgınlık, taşkınlık; *‿ tremens* [‿əm'tri:menz] içki alışkanlığından ileri gelen hezeyan.

de.liv.er [di'livə] *v/t.* kurtarmak (*from -den*); *a. ‿ up* teslim etm., haber iletmek; bildirmek; konferans vermek; MED doğurtmak (*of a child -i*); teslim etm. (*eşya vs.*); POST vermek, dağıtmak; tokat atmak; fırlatmak (*top vs.*); **de'liv.er.a.ble** *adj.* dağıtılabilir, teslim edilebilir; **de'liv.er.ance** *n.* kurtarış; kurtuluş; ileri sürme; **de'liv.er.er** *n.* kurtaran; dağıtan; **de'liv.er.y** MED doğurma; teslim; POST dağıtım; konferans; fırlatma (*top vs.*); *special ‿* ekspres, özel postacı ile; *on ‿ of* tesliminde; **de'liv.er.y-note** *n.* teslim kâğıdı; **de'liv.er.y-truck, de'liv.er.y-van** *n.* dağıtım arabası.

dell [del] *n.* küçük vadi, dere.

de.louse ['di:'laus] *v/t. b-ni* bitlemek, bitten temizlemek; **de'lous.ing centre** bitleri temizlemeye mahsus buğuevi.

del.ta ['deltə] *n.* Yunan alfabesinin dördüncü harfi; delta.

de.lude [di'lu:d] *v/t.* aldatmak; ayartmak (*into*) .

del.uge ['delju:dʒ] **1.** *n.* tufan, sel, su

baskını; **2.** *v/t.* (**with**) su basmak, tufana boğmak (*a. fig.*).

de.lu.sion [di'luʒən] *n.* aldatma, aldanma; vehim; **de'lu.sive** [‿siv] □, **de'lu.so.ry** [‿səri] aldatıcı, hayalî.

delve [delv] *vb.* kazmak; araştırmak.

dem.a.gog.ic, dem.a.gog.i.cal [dem-ə'gɔgik(əl)] *adj.* demagojiye dayanan; **dem.a.gogue** ['‿gɔg] *n.* demagog, halk avcısı; '**dem.a.gog.y** *n.* demagogluk, demagoji.

de.mand [di'mɑːnd] **1.** *n.* talep, istem, istek (**on**); gereksinim (**for**); COM talep, rağbet; JUR talep, dava, hak iddiası (**on**); **in ~** çok aranılan, rağbet gören; **on ~** talep vukuunda; **2.** *v/t.* istemek, talep etm. (**of**); gerektirmek; JUR hak talep etm.; *b-den* (*veya b-ne*) *bşi* sormak; **~ note** ödeme talebi.

de.mar.ca.tion [diːmɑː'keiʃən] *n.* sınır saptama, ayırma; *mst **line of ~*** sınır çizgisi.

dé.marche POL ['deimɑːʃ] *n.* diplomatik girişim.

de.mean¹ [di'miːn] *v/t. mst **~ o.s.*** kendini alçaltmak, küçültmek.

de.mean² [‿] *v/t.:* **~ o.s.** davranmak, hareket etm.; **de'mean.o(u)r** *n.* davranış, tavır.

de.ment.ed [di'mentid] □ deli, çılgın.

de.mer.it [diː'merit] *n.* kusur, hata; sakınca.

de.mesne [di'mein] *n.* mülk; arazi; toprak; malikâne.

demi... ['demi] *prefix* yarım, buçuk, yarı...

dem.i.god ['demigɔd] *n.* yarı tanrı yarı insan; '**dem.i.john** *n.* damacana, hasırlı büyük şişe.

de.mil.i.ta.ri.za.tion ['diːmilitərai'zeiʃən] *n.* askerden arındırma; '**de-'mil.i.ta.rize** *v/t.* askerden arındırmak.

dem.i.mon.daine ['demimɔn'dein] *n.* yüksek sosyeteye zengin birini bularak girmeye çalışan kadın; **dem.i.monde** ['‿mɔːnd] *n.* dömimond.

de.mise [di'maiz] **1.** *n.* ölüm; devir; ferağ; kiralama; kira haddi; **2.** *v/t.* geçirmek, *bşi* vasiyetle devretmek, icar etm.

de.mist MOT [diː'mist] *v/t.* buğulanmayı önlemek; **de'mist.er** *n.* buğulanmayı önleyen aygıt.

demo F ['deməu] *n.* ispat; göster(il)me; gösteri.

de.mob *sl.* [diː'mɔb] = ***demobilize***; **de-mo.bi.li.za.tion** ['diːməublai'zeiʃən] *n.* seferberliğin sona ermesi; terhis;

de'mobi.lize MIL *v/t.* terhis etm.

de.moc.ra.cy [di'mɔkrəsi] *n.* demokrasi; **dem.o.crat** ['deməkræt] *n.* demokrat, demokrasi yanlısı; **dem.o'crat.ic, dem.o'crat.i.caí** □ demokratik, halkçı; **de.mocra.tize** [di'mɔkretaiz] *vb.* demokratlaş(tır)mak.

dé.mo.dé [dei'məudei] *adj.* modası geçmiş, demode.

de.mog.ra.phy [diː'mɔgrəfi] *n.* demografi, sayısal nüfus bilgisi (*doğum, ölüm vs. oranı*).

de.mol.ish [di'mɔliʃ] *v/t.* yıkmak; *fig.* yok etm.; çekip indirmek; F silip süpürmek (*yemek*); **dem.o.li.tion** [deməˈliʃən] *n.* tahrip, yık(ıl)ma; yok olma.

de.mon ['diːmən] *n.* şeytan, iblis, cin; ***he is a ~ for work*** F kendini işe kaptırır, deli gibi çalışır; **de.mo.ni.ac** [di'məuniæk] **1.** *a.* **de.mo.ni.a.cal** [diːməu-'naiəkəl] şeytanî, çılgın; **2.** *n.* çılgın kimse, cinli kimse; **de.mon.ic** [diː-'mɔnik] *adj.* doğaüstü; cin *veya* şeytanlara ait.

de.mon.stra.ble □ ['demənstrəbl] gösterilebilir, kanıtlanabilir; **dem.on-strate** ['‿streit] *v/t.* kanıtlamak, göstermek; *v/i.* gösteri yapmak; **dem.on-'stra.tion** *n.* kanıt, ispat, göster(il)me; nümayiş, gösteri; POL gösteri, tezahürat; MIL manevra, tatbikat; **dem.on-stra.tive** [di'mɔnstrətiv] **1.** □ açıkça gösteren, *bşi* işaret eden (**of**); inandırıcı; gösteri şeklinde; GR bir noktaya işaret eden; anlamlı; göze çarpan; coşkun; **2.** *n.* GR işaret zamiri; **dem.on-stra.tor** ['demənstreitə] *n.* ispat eden, anlatan; ANAT laboratuvar asistanı; POL gösteri yapan, nümayişçi.

de.mor.al.i.za.tion [dimərəlai'zeiʃən] *n.* karamsarlık; ahlâk bozulması; **de-'mor.alize** *v/t.* ahlâkını bozmak *-in*; karamsar kılmak.

de.mote *Am.* [diː'məut] *v/t.* rütbesini indirmek; *okul:* bir aşağı sınıfa indirmek; **de'mo.tion** *n.* indirme vs.

de.mur [di'məː] **1.** *n.* itiraz; **2.** *v/i.* karşı koymak, itiraz etm. (**to, at** *-e*).

de.mure □ [di'mjuə] ciddî, temkinli; hassas; uslu, ağır başlı; **de'mure.ness** *n.* ciddiyet; duyarlılık, alçak gönüllülük.

de.mur.rage NAUT, RAIL [di'mʌridʒ] *n.* süristarya, istarya müddeti, yükleme süresini geçirme ve bu süre için ödenen para; **de'mur.rer** *n.* JUR itiraz.

den [den] *n.* in, mağara; *sl.* küçük özel

oda.

de.na.tion.al.ize [diːnæʃnəlaiz] *v/t.* devlet tekelinden çıkarmak, serbest bırakmak; ulusal haklarından yoksun kılmak -*i*.

de.na.ture CHEM [diːˈneitʃə] *v/t.* özelliklerini değiştirmek, doğal halinden çıkarmak.

de.ni.a.ble [diˈnaiəbl] *adj.* yadsınabilir, inkâr olunabilir; **deˈni.al** *n.* inkâr, yadsıma, yalanlama; ret.

de.ni.er[1] [diˈnaiə] *n.* yadsıyan, yalanlayan; reddeden.

de.nier[2] [ˈdeniə] *n.* ipek, naylon vs. ipliğinin kalitesini ölçmekte kullanılan eski bir Fransız ölçü birimi.

den.i.grate [ˈdənigreit] *v/t.* iftira etm. -*e*; kara çalmak.

den.im [ˈdenim] *n.* kaba pamuklu kumaş.

den.i.zen [ˈdenizn] *n.* sakin, oturan, ora ahalisindén, yerleşmiş.

de.nom.i.nate [diˈnɔmineit] *v/t.* ad vermek (**to** -*e*); tefrik etm., ayırmak, belirtmek; **de.nom.iˈna.tion** *n.* ad(landırma); sınıf, derece; mezhep; nominal değer; **de.nomi.na.tion.al** [ˈˈneiʃənl] *adj.* bir mezhebe bağlı; ~ **school** mezhep okulu; **deˈnomi.na.tive** [ˈnətiv] *adj.* ad veren, ad gibi kullanılan; **deˈnom.i.nator** MATH [ˈneitə] *n.* payda; **common** ~ ortak payda.

de.no.ta.tion [diːˈnəuˈteiʃən] *n.* işaret; anlam; **de.no.ta.tive** [diˈnəutətiv] *adj.* karakteristik, ayırt eden; önemli (**of**); **deˈnote** *v/i.* göstermek, delâlet etm., nitelendirmek.

de.nounce [diˈnauns] *v/t.* bildirmek, ihbar etm.; suçlamak; (*anlaşmanın*) sona erdiğini bildirmek; **deˈnounce·ment** *n.* açıklama, ihbar.

dense □ [dens] sık, yoğun, kalabalık; anlayışı kıt; **ˈdense.ness** *n.* sıklık, yoğunluk, kalınlık, yakınlık; *fig.* darlık, sıkışıklık; **ˈden.si.ty** *n.* yoğunluk, sıklık, koyuluk; PHYS yoğunluk, sıklık.

dent [dent] **1.** *n.* çentik, basınç *veya* darbe sonucu olan çökük; **2.** *v/t.* çentmek, göçürmek.

den.tal [ˈdentl] **1.** *adj.* diş ya da dişçiliğe ait; ~ **surgeon** diş doktoru; **2.** *n.* dişsel ünsüz; **den.tate** [ˈteit] *adj.* BOT kenarı dişli, tarak şeklinde; **den.ti.frice** [ˈtifris] *n.* diş temizleme tozu *veya* macunu; **ˈdentist** *n.* diş doktoru, dişçi; **ˈden.tist.ry** *n.* dişçilik; **denˈti.tion**

[ˈtʃə] *n.* diş çıkarma; diş yapısı; **denture** *n.* takma dişler.

den.u.da.tion [diːnjuːdeiʃən] *n.* soyulma, açma, çıplak etme; GEOL aşındırma, erözyon; **de.nude** [diˈnjuːd] *v/t.* (**of**) açmak, çıplak hale koymak; *fig.* soymak.

de.nun.ci.a.tion [dinʌnsiˈeiʃən] *n.* ihbar, ifşa, itham, uyarma; feshetme; **deˈnunci.a.tor** muhbir, ithamcı; **deˈnun.ci.a.to.ry** [ˈətəri] *adj.* suçlayıcı, itham edici; gammazlayıcı; küçük düşürücü.

de.ny [diˈnai] *v/t.* yadsımak, inkâr etm.; reddetmek; esirgemek; yalanlamak, tanımamak; ~ **o.s. s.th.** *k-ni bşeden* yoksun bırakmak; ~ **o.s.** (**to a visitor**) evde iken yok dedirtmek.

de.o.dor.ant [diˈəudərənt] *n.* hoş olmayan kokuları gideren madde, deodoran; **deˈo.dor.ize** *v/t.* kokusunu gidermek; **deˈodor.iz.er** *n.* koku giderici şey.

de.part [diˈpɑːt] *vb.* ayrılmak, gitmek; hareket etm. (**for**-*e*); ᴴ ayrılmak (**from**); uzakta durmak, uzaklaşmak, sapmak, ayrılmak (**from** -*den*); vefat etm.; **the ~ed** merhum, vefat edenler; ~ **this life** bu düynadan göçmek; **deˈpart.ment** *n.* kısım, bölüm, şube, daire; COM branş, şube; *Am.* bakanlık; **State**⍏ Dış İşleri Bakanlığı; ~ **store** büyük mağaza; **de.part.men.tal** [diːpɑːtˈmentl] *adj.* bir şube *veya* daireye ilişkin; **de.par.ture** [diˈpɑːtʃə] *n.* gidiş, RAIL, NAUT hareket, kalkış (**from** -*den*); **a new** ~ yeni bir akım, yenilik; ~ **platform** hareket peronu.

de.pend [diˈpend] *v/i.* bağlı olm., tabi olm.; *b-nin* elinde olm. (**on, upon**); *b-ne, bşe* güvenmek (**on, upon**); JUR karar bağlanmamış olm.; **it** ~**s** ᴴ belli olmaz, duruma göre; **deˈpend.a.ble** *adj.* güvenilir, emin; **deˈpend.ant** *n.* bağlı (**on, upon** -*e*); hizmetçi, uşak; taraftar; aile bireylerinden olan; **deˈpend.ence** *n.* bağlılık (**upon** -*e*); sınırlı olma (**on**); güven, inanç (**on**); **deˈpend.en.cy** *n.* bağımlılık; sömürge, müstemleke; ek bina; **deˈpend.ent 1.** □ bağımlı (**on**); muhtaç; güvenen; **2.** *s.* **dependant**.

de.pict [diˈpikt] *v/t.* göstermek, betimlemek, anlatmak; resmetmek, çizmek.

de.pil.a.to.ry [deˈpilətəri] **1.** *adj.* kıl dökücü; **2.** *n.* kıl döken ilaç.

de.plane [diːˈplein] *v/i.* uçaktan inmek.

de.plete [di'pli:t] *v/t.* azaltmak, boşaltmak, dökmek; *fig.* tüketmek; **de'ple-tion** *n.* tüketme, azaltma, boşalt(ıl)ma; **de'ple.tive** *adj.* bosaltıcı.

de.plor.a.ble □ [di'plɔ:rǝbl] acınacak, acıklı, perişan; **de'plore** *v/t.* acımak -*e;* beğenmemek.

de.ploy MIL [di'plɔi] *vb.* açmak, yaymak, yanaşık düzenden dağınık düzene geçmek; **de'ploy.ment** *n.* açılma, yayılma.

de.po.nent [di'pǝunǝnt] *n.* JUR yazılı ifade veren şahit, tanık; GR kipi pasif, anlamı aktif olan fiil.

de.pop.u.late [di:'pɔpjuleit] *v/t.* nüfusunu azaltmak; **de.pop.u'la.tion** *n.* nüfusunu azaltma.

de.port [di'pɔ:t] *v/t.* yurt dışı etm., sürgün etm.; **~ o.s.** davranmak, hareket etm.; **de.por.ta.tion** [di:pɔ:'teiʃǝn] *n.* yurt dışı etme; **de.port'ee** *n.* sürgün, hudut harici edilen kimse; **de.port-ment** [di'pɔ:tmǝnt] *n.* davranış, hareket.

de.pos.a.ble [di'pǝuzǝbl] *adj.* azledilebilir; **de'pose** *v/t.* azletmek; JUR yeminle yazılı ifade vermek (**to s.th.**, **that**).

de.pos.it [di'pɔzit] **1.** *n.* GEOL çöküntü (*a.* MED); maden yatağı; CHEM tortu; COM depo, ambar; mevduat, teminat akçesi; rehin; COM pey, avans; *attr.* depozito; **2.** *v/t.* yatırmak, tevdi etm.; depo etm.; çökeltmek; **de'pos.i.ta.ry** *n.* depo, emanetçi; **dep.o.si.tion** [depǝ'ziʃǝn] *n.* çöküntü; şahidin ifadesi, delil; azil (**from** -*den*); **depos.i.tor** [di-'pɔzitǝ] *n.* mudi, para yatıran; emanet eden; **de'pos.i.to.ry** *n.* depo; *fig.* zengin kaynak, depo.

de.pot ['depǝu] *n.* depo, ambar, antrepo; toplanma yeri; *Am.* tren istasyonu.

dep.ra.va.tion [deprǝ'veiʃǝn] *n.* = **de-pravity**; **de.prave** [di'preiv] *v/t.* ayartmak, ahlâkını bozmak; **de'praved** *adj.* ahlâkı bozuk; **de.prav.i.ty** [di'præviti] *n.* ahlâk bozukluğu; fesat.

dep.re.cate ['diprikeit] *v/t.* onaylamamak, hoş görmemek, reddetmek; **dep-re'ca.tion** *n.* ayıplama, hoşnutsuzluk, beğenmeyiş, ret; **dep.re.ca.to.ry** ['ˌkǝtǝri] *adj.* küçümseyen, beğenmeyen; olumsuz.

de.pre.ci.ate [di'pri:ʃieit] *v/t.* değerini düşürmek, azaltmak, fiyatını kırmak, ucuzlatmak; *fig. b-ne*, *bşe* hor bakmak; *v/i.* değer kaybetmek; **de.pre.ci'a.tion**

n. alçaltma, kötüleme; indirim; COM değerin azalması; aşınma payı, amortisman; **de'pre.ci.a.to.ry** [ˌʃjǝtǝri] *adj.* değerini düşürücü, küçümseyici.

dep.re.da.tion [depri'deiʃǝn] *n.* yağmalama; tahribat; **~s** *pl.* yıkıp bozma; **'depre.da.tor** *n.* yağmacı, çapulcu; **dep.re.dato.ry** *adj.* yağmacılık türünden; F müthiş, korkunç, feci.

de.press [di'pres] *v/t.* indirmek, alçaltmak (*fiyat*, *ses*); basmak -*e;* *fig.* sıkıştırmak, eziyet vermek; **de-'pressed** *fig. adj.* kederli, karamsar; **de.pres.sion** [di'preʃǝn] *n.* çökme, depresyon; keder; indir(il)me; COM durgunluk, ekonomik kriz; MED yorgunluk, kuvvetten düşme; MEC, PHYS, AST düşme, alçalma; GEOGR arazi çöküntüsü, çukur; METEOR alçak basınç bölgesi.

dep.ri.va.tion [depri'veiʃǝn] *n.* yoksunluk, mahrumiyet; kayıp; **dep.ri.ve** [di'praiv] *v/t.* yoksun bırakmak (**of** -*den*); **~ s.o. of s.th.** elinden *bşi* almak; *b-ni bşden* yoksun bırakmak; *bşe* katılmamak.

depth [depθ] *n.* derinlik (*a. fig.*); derin yer; **~ bomb**, **~ charge** su altı bombası; **~ of focus** PHOT odak derinliği; **go beyond one's ~** (*suda*) ayağı yerden kesilmek; **be out of one's ~** *fig.* bilgisinin ötesinde.

dep.u.ta.tion [depju'teiʃǝn] *n.* murahhas heyet, delegasyon; delegelik; **de-pute** [di'pju:t] *v/t.* atamak (*temsilci*), göndermek (*delege*); çıkarmak (*milletvekili*); **dep.u.tize** ['depjutaiz] *v/t.* delege tayin etm.; **~ for** *v/i. b-ne* vekalet etm.; **'dep.u.ty** *n.* vekil; milletvekili; delege; JUR temsilci; yardımcı, muavin.

de.rac.i.nate [di'ræsineit] *v/t.* kökünden çıkarmak, ayırmak (*a. fig.*).

de.rail RAIL ['direil] *v/t.* & *v/i.* raydan çık(ar)mak; **de'rail.ment** *n.* raydan çıkma.

de.range [di'reindʒ] *v/t.* karıştırmak, *bşi* bozmak; (**mentally**) **~d** aklı bozuk; **de'range.ment** *n.* düzensizlik; geçimsizlik; çılgınlık, aklî dengesizlik.

de.rate [di:'reit] *v/t.* (*yerel vergileri*) hafifletmek.

Der.by ['dɑ:bi] *spor:* İngiltere'de geleneksel at yarışı; **'der.by** *Am.* melon şapka.

der.e.lict ['derilikt] **1.** *adj.* terkedilmiş, sahipsiz; *esp. Am.* savsak, kayıtsız; **2.** *n.* sahipsiz mal; gemi enkazı; **der.e'lic-**

tion *n.* terketme; savsaklama; **~ of duty** kayıtsız kalma, görevin ihmali.

de.ride [di'raid] *v/t. b-le, bşle* alay etm.; **de'rid.er** *n.* alaycı.

de ri.gueur [dəri'gəː] *adj.* mutlaka gerekli.

de.ri.sion [di'riʒən] *n.* alay, hor görme; **de.ri.sive** □ [di'raisiv], **de'ri.so.ry** [‑səri] alaylı, istihza kabilinden; gülünç; önemsiz.

de.riv.a.ble □ [di'raivəbl] çıkarılabilir, türetilebilir; **der.i.va.tion** [deri'veiʃən] *n.* türetme; başka tarafa çevirme; kaynak, asıl; **de.riv.a.tive** [di'rivətiv] **1.** □ türetilmiş; **2.** *n.* türetme (*sözcük vs.*); ikincil, tali; **de.rive** [di'raiv] *v/t.* çıkarmak, türetmek (**from** *-den*); **~ from, be ~d from** *b-nin* neslinden olm., gelmek.

der.ma.tol.o.gist [dəːmə'tɔlədʒist] *n.* cilt doktoru, dermatolog; **der'ma.tolo.gy** *n.* cildiye, dermatoloji, cilt hastalıkları ilmi.

der.o.gate ['derəugeit] *v/i.* zarar vermek; saygınlığını bozmak (**from**); küçültmek; değerinden düşürmek (**from**); **der.o'gation** *n.* küçültme (**from**); ket vurma; **derog.a.to.ry** □ [di'rɔgətəri] zararlı (**to** *-e*); ket vurucu.

der.rick ['derik] *n.* MEC döner vinç; NAUT vinç kolu; MIN petrol sondaj kulesi.

der.ring-do ['deriŋ'duː] *n.* atılganlık, cüret, gözüpeklik.

derv [dəːv] *n.* dizel motor yakıtı.

der.vish ['dəːviʃ] *n.* derviş.

de.scale ['diː'skeil] *v/t.* (*kaplarda oluşan kireç taşını*) çıkarmak.

des.cant [dis'kænt] *v/t.* bir konu üzerinde uzunca bir söylev vermek (**upon**); daha yüksek sesle çalmak *veya* söylemek.

de.scend [di'send] *v/i.* inmek, alçalmak; *k-ni* küçültmek, düşmek; MIN maden ocağına inmek; AVIA yere inmek; **~** (**up**)**on** üzerine atılmak, sökün etm., çullanmak; **~ to** miras kalmak; *bşe* yanaşmak; **~ from, be ~d from** *b-nin* soyundan gelmek, nesebi olm.; **de'scend.ant** *n.* torun, oğul.

de.scent [di'sent] *n.* iniş; yokuş; soy, nesil; baskın, istilâ; MIN iniş, geçit; alçalma, düşme; meyilli yüzey; karaya çıkma; JUR miras kalması, tevarüs.

de.scrib.a.ble [dis'kraibəbl] *adj.* tanımlanabilir; **de'scribe** *v/t.* tanımlamak, nitelendirmek; anlatmak.

de.scrip.tion [di'skripʃən] *n.* tanımla

ma, tarif; F cins, çeşit; **de'scrip.tive** □ tanımlayıcı, açıklayıcı.

de.scry [dis'krai] *v/t.* görmek, seçmek, keşfetmek.

des.e.crate ['desikreit] *v/t.* bir yerin kutsallığını bozmak; **des.e'cra.tion** *n.* kutsallığa saygısızlık, kirletme.

de.seg.re.gate *Am.* ['diː'segrigeit] *v/t. & v/i.* ırk ayırımını kaldırmak; **'desegre'ga.tion** *n.* ırk ayırımına son vermek.

des.ert[1] ['dezət] **1.** *adj.* ıssız, boş; **2.** *n.* çöl.

de.sert[2] [di'zəːt] *v/t.* bırakmak, terketmek; *v/i.* askerlikten kaçmak; sıvışmak.

de.sert[3] [di'zəːt] *mst ~s n. pl.* eder, ücret; hakedilen ceza.

de.sert.er [di'zəːtə] *n.* firarî, asker kaçağı; **de'ser.tion** *n.* terketme; firar; JUR terk; askerden kaçma; ıssızlık.

de.serve [di'zəːv] *v/t.* hakkı olm.; *bşe* lâyık olm. (**of**); **de'ser.ved.ly** [‑vidli] *adv.* haklı olarak; **de'serv.ing** *adj.* lâyık (**of**), değerli.

des.ha.bille ['dezæbiːl] = **dishabille**.

des.ic.cate ['desikeit] *vb.* kuru(t)mak; **des.ic'ca.tion** *n.* kuru(t)ma; kuruluk; **'des.ic.ca.tor** *n.* kurutucu aygıt.

de.sid.er.ate [di'zidəreit] *v/t.* arzu etm., istemek; eksikliğini duymak; **de.sid.era.tum** [‑'reitəm] *n.* gereksinim, koşul.

de.sign [di'zain] **1.** *n.* plan, resim, proje, taslak, model; tasarım, niyet; *b.s.* entrika; maksat, kasıt; MEC resmini yapma; desen, şekil; **by ~** kasıtlı olarak; **with the ~ of** amacıyla; **protection of ~s, copyright in ~s** alâmeti farikaların korunması; **2.** *vb.* keşfetmek; taslak çizmek; tasarlamak, hazırlamak; çizmek; amaçlamak; kastetmek.

des.ig.nate 1. ['dezigneit] *v/t.* belirtmek, işaretlemek (**as**); seçmek, atamak (**for**); **2.** ['‑nit] *adj.* geçici olarak atanmış; **des.ig.na.tion** [‑'neiʃən] *n.* atama, tayin, tahsis; isim, ünvan, sıfat.

de.sign.ed.ly [di'zainidli] *adv.* kasıtlı olarak; **de'sign.er** *n.* düzenleyen kimse; modelist, teknik ressam; *fig.* dalavereci; **de'sign.ing** *adj.* düzenci, entrikacı.

de.sir.a.bil.i.ty [dizaiərə'biliti] *n.* arzu edilir olma, hoşa gitme; **de'sir.a.ble** □ istenilir; makbul; hoş; sempatik; beğenilir; **de.sire** [di'zaiə] **1.** *n.* arzu, istek (**for, to** için, *-e*), emel; **at s.o.'s ~**

b-nin arzusu üzerine; **2.** *vb.* arzulamak; arzu etm., istemek; *what do you ~ me to do?* ne yapmamı arzu edersiniz?; **de.sir.ous** □ [di'zaiərəs] istekli (*of, to do*).

de.sist [di'zist] *v/i.* vazgeçmek, çekilmek (*from -den*).

desk [desk] *n.* kürsü, yazı masası; okul sırası.

des.o.late 1. ['desəleit] *v/t.* boş bırakmak; perişan etm., tahrip etm., harabeye döndürmek; **2.** □ ['‿lit] tenha, ıssız; harap, perişan; **des.o.la.tion** [‿'leiʃən] *n.* harap etme; ıssızlık; viranlık, perişanlık.

de.spair [dis'pɛə] **1.** *n.* ümitsizlik, üzüntü, keder; **2.** *v/i.* ümidi kesmek (*of -den*); **de'spair.ing** □ ümitsiz, çaresiz.

des.patch [dis'pætʃ] = *dispatch*.

des.per.a.do [despə'rɑːdəu] *n.* gözü dönmüş haydut.

des.per.ate □ ['despərit] *adj. & adv.* ümitsiz, dönmüş; F çok; müthiş; aşırı; **des.per.a.tion** [‿'reiʃən] *n.* ümitsizlik, çaresizlik; her şeyi göze alma.

des.pi.ca.ble □ ['despikəbl] alçak, aşağılık; küçümsenen.

de.spise [dis'paiz] *v/t.* hor görmek, küçümsemek, yukarıdan bakmak; nefret etm.

de.spite [dis'pait] **1.** *n.* kin, kötülük, nefret; *in ~ of -e* rağmen; ile beraber; **2.** *prp. a. ~ of -e* rağmen; **de'spite.ful** □ *poet.* [‿ful] garazkâr, kinci, fena, kötü.

de.spoil [dis'pɔil] *v/t.* soymak, yağmalamak (*of*); **de'spoil.ment** *n.* soygun, çapulculuk.

de.spond [dis'pɔnd] *v/i.* ümitsizliğe kapılmak, cesaretini kaybetmek; *bşden* ümidini kesmek (*of*); **de'spond.en.cy** *n.* ümitsizlik; **de'spondent** □, **de'spond.ing** □ ümitsiz, cesaretsiz.

des.pot ['despɔt] *n.* despot, zorba hükümdar; **des'pot.ic** *adj.* (*~ally*) despotlukla, zorbalıkla; **des.pot.ism** *n.* despotluk, zorbalık, istibdat.

des.qua.ma.tion [deskwə'meiʃən] *n.* derinin pul pul dökülmesi, soyulması.

des.sert [di'zɔːt] *n.* yemek sonunda yenen tatlı, yemiş vs.; *Am.* tatlı; *~ powder* tatlı kabartma tozu; **des'sert-spoon** *n.* tatlı kaşığı.

des.ti.na.tion [desti'neiʃən] *n.* amaç, hedef; gidilecek yer; **des.tine** ['‿tin] *v/t.* ayırmak, tahsis etm. (*to, for -e*);

be ~d to do alın yazısı olm.; '**des.ti.ny** *n.* kader, yazgı; şans, talih.

des.ti.tute □ ['destitjuːt] yoksul, mahrum; *bşden* yoksun (*of*); **des'ti.tu.tion** *n.* yoksulluk.

de.stroy [dis'trɔi] *v/t.* yıkmak, ortadan kaldırmak; öldürmek; **de'stroy.er** *n.* yok edici; NAUT destroyer, muhrip.

de.struct.i.bil.i.ty [distrʌkti'biliti] *n.* bozulma niteliği; **de'struct.i.ble** [‿təbl] *adj.* yok edilebilir; **de'struction** *n.* yıkım, imha, tahrip; âfet; **de'struc.tive** □ yıkıcı, tahrip edici (*of, to*); zararlı, öldürücü; **de'struc.tive.ness** *n.* yıkıcılık; **de'structor** *n.* yakma fırını; yok eden.

des.ue.tude [di'sjuːitjuːd] *n.* kullanılmama durumu; *fall into ~* yürürlükten kalkmak, kullanılamamak.

des.ul.to.ri.ness ['desəltərinis] *n.* düzensiz olma, tutarsızlık; maymun iştahlılık; '**des.ul.to.ry** □ düzensiz, daldan dala atlayan.

de.tach [di'tætʃ] *v/t.* ayırmak, çıkarmak, çözmek, sökmek; MIL bir göreve atamak; **de'tach.a.ble** *adj.* yerinden sökülebilir, ayrılabilir; **de'tached** *adj.* ayrı, bağımsız, tarafsız; **de'tach.ment** *n.* ayırma; MIL müfreze, kol; tarafsızlık, bağımsız olma.

de.tail [di:teil] **1.** *n.* teferruat, ayrıntı, ayrıntılı plan; MIL müfreze, komando birliği; *~s pl.* ayrıntılar; *in ~* ayrıntılı; *go into ~s* ayrıntılara girmek; **2.** *v/t.* ayrıntılarıyle anlatmak; MIL bir göreve atanmak; '**de.tailed** *adj.* mufassal, ayrıntılı.

de.tain [di'tein] *v/t.* alıkoymak; geciktirmek; JUR *b-ni bşden* yoksun bırakmak; hapsetmek, gözaltına almak; **de'tain.ee** *n.* gözaltına alınmış, hapsedilmiş; **de'tain.er** *n.* alıkoyma; JUR tutukluluk süresini uzatma emri.

de.tect [di'tekt] *v/t.* ortaya çıkarmak, keşfetmek; **de'tect.a.ble** *adj.* ortaya çıkarılabilir; **de'tec.tion** *n.* keşif, bulma, ortaya çıkarma; **de'tec.tive** *n.* gizli polis, hafiye, sivil polis, dedektif; *~ force* cinayet masası görevlileri; *~ story, ~ novel* polis romanı; **de'tec.tor** *n.* ortaya çıkaran; *radyo:* dedektör.

de.tent MEC [di'tent] *n.* çalar saat vs.'de tutma mandalı.

dé.tente POL [dei'tãːt] *n.* yumuşama.

de.ten.tion [di'tenʃən] *n.* alıkoyma; tutuklama; (*okulda:*) izinsizlik, cezaya kalma.

de.ter [di'tə:] *v/t.* caydırmak, vazgeçirmek (**from** -*den*).

de.ter.gent [di'tə:dʒənt] **1.** *adj.* temizleyici; **2.** *n.* temizleme maddesi, deterjan.

de.te.ri.o.rate [di'tiəriəreit] *v/t. & v/i.* fenalaş(tır)mak; kötüleş(tir)mek; **de.te.rio'ra.tion** *n.* fenalaşma, bozulma; soysuzlaşma.

de.ter.ment [di'tə:mənt] *n.* korkutma vasıtası.

de.ter.mi.na.ble □ [di'tə:minəbl] saptanabilir; **de'ter.mi.nant 1.** *adj.* belirleyici; **2.** *n.* belirleyici etken; **de'ter.mi.nate** □ [-nit] sınırlı, belirli, kesin; **de.ter.mi.nation** [-'neiʃən] *n.* saptama; tesbit, sınırlama; azim; hüküm, yargı, karar; **de'ter.mi.na.tive** [-nətiv] *adj. & n.* niteleyici, sınırlayıcı; **de'ter.mine** [-min] *vb.* sınırlamak, belirtmek; azmetmek; saptamak; özendirmek (**to** -*e*); *esp.* JUR karara bağlamak; **be ~d** kararlı olm.; kararlaştırmak; tasarlamak (**on**, **to**); **de'ter.mined** *adj.* azimli, kararlı; kesin.

de.ter.rent [di'terənt] **1.** *adj.* caydırıcı; **2.** *n.* caydıran, vazgeçiren; **nuclear ~** POL nükleer caydırıcı.

de.test [di'test] *v/t.* nefret etm., iğrenmek -*den*; **de'test.a.ble** □ iğrenç, berbat; **de.tes.ta.tion** [di:tes'teiʃən] *n.* nefret, tiksinme (**of** -*den*).

de.throne [di'θrəun] *v/t.* tahttan indirmek (*a. fig.*); **de'throne.ment** *n.* düşürülme, tahttan indirilme.

det.o.nate ['detəuneit] *vb.* patla(t)mak; infilâk et(tir)mek; **'det.o.nat.ing** *n.* patlama, ateş alma; **~ cap** kapsol; **det.o'nation** *n.* patlama, infilâk; **'det.o.na.tor** *n.* RAIL sis işareti; MIL kav, kapsol, fitil, funya.

de.tour [di'tuə], **dé.tour** ['deituə] *n.* dolambaçlı yol, sapak; **make a ~** dolambaçlı yoldan gitmek.

de.tract [di'trækt] *vb.* **~ from s.th.** azaltmak, eksiltmek; yermek; **de-'trac.tion** *n.* eksiltme; yerme; **de'trac.tive** *adj.* yerici; iftiralı; **de'trac.tor** *n.* yeren, kara çalan.

de.train [di'trein] *vb.* trene bin(dir)mek *ya da* in(dir)mek.

de.trib.al.i.za.tion [di:traibəlai'zeiʃən] *n.* eritme; dağıtım; arıtma; **de-'trib.al.ize** *v/t.* aşiret üyesi olarak saymamak.

det.ri.ment ['detrimənt] *n.* zarar, ziyan, hasar (**to**); **det.ri.men.tal** □ [-'mentl]

zarar veren, zararlı (**to** -*e*).

de.tri.tus GEOL [di'traitəs] *n.* hayşat, döküntü taş, kum vs.

de.tune [di'tju:n] *v/t.* radyo: yayın metresini bozmak.

deuce [dju:s] *n.* ikili (*kart, zar vs.*); *tenis;* düs, berabere; F kör talih; **the ~!** şeytan!; Allah belâsını versin; **deu.ced** F [dju:st] □ berbat, Allahın belâsı.

de.val.u.a.tion [di:vælju'eiʃən] *n.* devalüasyon, para değerinin düşürülmesi; **deval.ue** [di:'vælju:] *v/t.* -*in* değerini düşürmek.

dev.as.tate ['devəsteit] *v/t.* harap etm., mahvetmek; **dev.as'ta.tion** *n.* yakıp yıkma.

de.vel.op [di'veləp] *vb.* geliş(tir)mek; genişle(t)mek; PHOT develope etm., banyo etm.; işlenecek hale getirmek; *Am.* görünmek, meydana çıkmak; meşhur olm.; **de'vel.op.er** *n.* PHOT revelâtôr, develope eden ilaç; **de'vel.op.ing** *n.* PHOT develope etme; **de'vel.op.ment** *n.* gelişme; genisletme; meydana çıkma; PHOT developman.

de.vi.ate ['di:vieit] *v/i.* sapmak, yoldan çıkmak (*a. fig.*) (**from** -*den*); **de.vi'a.tion** *n.* sapma; NAUT pusulanın sapması; **de.vi'a.tion.ism** *n.* POL partiden ayrılma; **devi'a.tion.ist** *n.* POL partiden ayrılan, politik düşüncelerinde sapma olan kimse.

de.vice [di'vais] *n.* buluş; alet, aygıt; hile, oyun; arma, nişan; slogan; **leave s.o. to his own ~s** b-*nin* işine karışmamak, kendi haline bırakmak.

dev.il ['devl] **1.** *n.* şeytan, iblis (*a. fig.*); şeytan herif; JUR avukat yardımcısı; *fig.* yamak; MEC lehimci ocağı; **the ~!** Allah belâsını versin!; **between the ~ and the deep sea** aşağı tükürsen sakal, yukarı tükürsen bıyık; **2.** *v/t.* bol baharatla kızartmak; MEC bez, kâğıt vs. 'yi paçavra etm.; rahatsız etm., canını sıkmak; *v/i.* yamak olarak çalışmak; **'dev.il.ish** □ şeytanca; F müthiş; kahrolası; **'dev.il-may-'care** *adj.* pervasız, kayıtsız; **'devil.ment** *n.* şeytanlık, muziplik; **'dev.il(t)ry** *n.* şeytanlık; kötülük; yaramazlık.

de.vi.ous □ ['di:vjəs] dolaşık, sapa, eğri büğrü; hatalı (*a. fig.*); dürüst olmıyan; **~ step** yanlış adım.

de.vis.a.ble [di'vaizəbl] *adj.* tasavvur edilebilir; vasiyet olunabilir; **de'vise 1.** JUR *n.* bşi vasiyetle bırakma, vasiyet; **2.** *v/t.* tasarlamak; icat etm.; JUR vasiyet etm.; **dev.i.see** JUR [devi'ziː] *n.* mirasçı, varis; **de.vis.er** [di'vaizə] *n.* mucit; **de.vi.sor** JUR [devi'zɔː] *n.* vasiyet eden.

de.vi.tal.ize [diː'vaitəlaiz] *v/t.* cansızlastırmak, şevkini kırmak.

de.void [di'vɔid] *adj.* **(of)** boş, hali; ...siz; ...sız, *-den* yoksun.

dev.o.lu.tion [diːvə'luːʃən] *n.* JUR miras kalması; havale; PARL görevi devretme; BIOL gerileme; **de.volve** [di'vɔlv] **(upon, to)** *v/t. b-ne* devretmek; yuvarlamak; *v/i. b-ne, bşe* geçmek, hissesine düşmek, kalmak.

de.vote [di'vəut] *v/t.* vakfetmek, adamak **(to** *-e***)**; **de'vot.ed** □ sadık, bağlı **(to** *-e***)**; **dev.o.tee** [devəu'tiː] *n.* düşkün, hayran; sofu; **de.vo.tion** [di'vəuʃən] *n.* derinden bağlılık **(to s.o.** *-e***)**, fedakârlık, özveri; adayış, tapma; **~s** *pl.* ibadet, dua; **de'vo.tion.al** □ [-ʃənl] ibadete ilişkin, dindar.

de.vour [di'vauə] *v/t.* tıkınmak, yutmak **(***a. fig.***)**; yok etm., bitirmek; **~ed with** hırs ve istekli; **de'vour.ing** □ yiyip bitiren, son derece üzücü, içini kemiren.

de.vout □ [di'vaut] dindar; sadık; samimi; **de'vout.ness** *n.* dindarlık.

dew [djuː] **1.** *n.* çiy, şebnem; **2.** *v/t.* çiyle ıslatmak, nemlendirmek; **~drop** *n.* çiy damlası; **'~lap** *n.* (*öküz vs.*) boynun altında sarkan deri; **'dew-pond** *n.* çiyden oluşmuş ufak ve sığ göl; **'dew.y** *adj.* çiyle kaplı.

dex.ter ['dekstə] *adj.* sağ, sağa ilişkin, sağda olma.

dex.ter.i.ty [deks'teriti] *n.* beceri, ustalık; **dex.ter.ous** □ ['-tərəs] becerikli, usta.

di.a.be.tes [daiə'biːtiːz] *n.* şeker hastalığı, diyabet.

di.a.bol.ic, di.a.bol.i.cal □ [daiə'bɔlik(el)] şeytanca.

di.a.dem ['daiədem] *n.* taç; (*çiçek veya yapraklardan*) başlık.

di.ag.nose ['daiəgnəuz] *v/t.* teşhis etm.; **di.ag'no.sis** [-sis] *n.*, *pl.* **di.ag'no.ses** [-siːz] *n.* teşhis, tanılama.

di.ag.o.nal [dai'ægənl] **1.** □ çapraz, diyagonal; **2.** *n.* köşegen, çapraz örgü.

di.a.gram ['daiəgræm] *n.* diyagram, değişimi gösteren grafik; şema, plân; **dia.gram.mat.ic** [daiəgrə'mætik] *adj.* **(~ally)** şematik, grafiksel.

di.al ['daiəl] **1.** *n.* kadran; güneş saati; taksimatlı daire; TELEPH diks, kurs; *radyo:* dereceli disk; **~ light** kurs lâm-

bası; **2.** *v/t.* TELEPH numaraları çevirmek.

di.a.lect ['daiəlekt] *n.* lehçe, şive, ağız; **di.a'lec.tic, di.a'lec.ti.cal** □ lehçeye ait; mantık ve münazaraya ait; **di.a'lec.tic(s)** *sg n.* diyalektik, eytişim; mantıksal konuşmaları yürütme sanatı.

di.a.logue *Am. a.* **di.a.log** ['daiəlɔg] *n.* diyalog, biriyle konuşma; **~ track** *film:* ses şeridi.

di.al...: '~-sys.tem TELEPH *n.* otomatik telefon sistemi; **'~-tone** TELEPH çevir sesi.

di.am.e.ter [dai'æmitə] *n.* çap.

di.a.met.ri.cal □ [daiə'metrikəl] çapla ilgili.

di.a.mond ['daiəmənd] **1.** *n.* elmas; eşkenar dörtgen şekil; *Am. beysbol:* oyun sahası; oyun kartı; karo; **~ cut ~** dinsizin hakkından imansız gelir; **he is a rough ~** kaba fakat iyi kalpli kimse; **2.** *adj.* kareli, baklava şeklinde; **'~cutter** *n.* elmastraş; **~ wed.ding** evliliğin altmışıncı yıldönümü.

di.a.pa.son MUS [daiə'peisn] *n.* uyum, armoni; ölçü; orgun ana sesleri, sekizinciden itibaren boruları; diyapazon.

di.a.per ['daiəpə] **1.** *n.* baklava desenli keten bezi, *Am.* kundak bezi; **2.** *v/t.* baklava şeklinde desenlemek; *Am.* bebeğin bezini değiştirmek.

di.aph.a.nous [dai'æfənəs] *adj.* şeffaf.

di.a.phragm ['daiəfræm] *n.* ANAT diyafram; MEC bölme, ara duvarı; OPT mercek perdesi; TELEPH diyafram.

di.a.rist ['daiərist] *n.* günlük tutan; **'di.arize** *vb.* günlük tutmak.

di.ar.rhoe.a MED [daiə'riə] *n.* ishal, amel.

di.a.ry ['daiəri] *n.* hatıra defteri, günlük, takvimli defter (*ajanda*).

Di.as.po.ra [dai'æspərə] *n.* Yahudilerin sürgünden sonra dünyanın her yanına dağılmaları.

di.a.ther.my MED ['daiəθəːmi] *n.* elektrikle vücuda ısı vererek tedavi.

di.a.tribe ['daiətraib] *n.* hiciv, hakaret.

dib.ble ['dibl] **1.** *n.* fide kazığı; **2.** *v/t.* fide dikmek; fide kazığı ile çukur açmak.

dibs *sl.* [dibz] *n. pl.* mangır, mangiz.

dice [dais] **1.** *n. pl.* oyun zarları; **2.** *vb.* zar oynamak, zar atmak (*for için*); zar şeklinde parçalara kesip ayırmak; **'~-box** *n.* zar atmaya yarar meşin kap; **'dic.er** *n.* zar oyuncusu.

dick[1] *Am. sl.* [dik] *n.* dedektif, hafiye,

sivil polis.

dick² *sl.* [-] *n.* açıklama; *take one's* ~ yemin etm.

dick.ens F ['dikinz] *n.* şeytan.

dick.er *Am.* ['dikə] *v/i.* pazarlık etm. (*with*, *for b-le*, için).

dick.(e)y ['diki] **1.** *sl. adj.* kötü, adî, çürük, zayıf; **2.** *n.* F araba arkasında uşak yeri; takma gömlek yakası; *a.* ~*bird n.* (*çocuk dilinde*) kuş.

dic.ta.phone ['diktəfoun] *n.* diktafon.

dic.tate 1. ['dikteit] *n.* dikte; emir; **2.** [dik'teit] *vb.* yazdırmak; dikte etm.; *fig.* zorla kabul ettirmek; emretmek; **dic'tation** *n.* emir; dikte; dikte etme; **dic'tator** *n.* diktatör; **dic.ta.to.ri.al** □ [diktə'tɔːriəl] diktatörce, zorbaca, otokratik; **dic.ta.tor.ship** [dik'teitə-ʃip] *n.* diktatörlük, zorbalık.

dic.tion ['dikʃən] *n.* anlatım şekli, diksiyon; **dic.tion.ar.y** ['-ri] *n.* sözlük, lügat.

dict.um ['diktəm], *pl.* **dic.ta** ['-tə] *n.* yetkili söz; özdeyiş; JUR mütalâa.

did [did] *pret. of* **do**.

di.dac.tic [di'dæktik] *adj.* (~*ally*) öğretici, didaktik, öğretsel.

did.dle *sl.* ['didl] *v/t.* aldatmak, dolandırmak, kandırmak.

didn't ['didnt] = **did not**; *s.* **do**.

die¹ [dai] *v/i.* ölmek, vefat etm. (*of*, *from* -*den*); mahvolmak; yavaş yavaş ölmek; F özlemini duymak, şiddetle arzu etm. (*for s.th.*, *to inf. -i*); ~ *away* yavaş yavaş ölmek, kesilmek (*rüzgâr*); yavaş yavaş sönmek (*ses*); yavaş yavaş uçmak (*renk*); sönmek (*ışık*, *ateş*); ~ *down* kaybolmak, küçülmek, sönmek; ~ *off* yavaş yavaş ölmek, kurumak; ~ *out* nesli tükenmek, ortadan kalkmak; ~ *hard* direnmek, (*eski inanç*, *âdet vs.*) ortadan kalkması çok zaman almak; *never say* ~*!* umudunu yitirme!; cesaretini kaybetme!

die² [-], *n. pl.* **dice** [dais] zar; *pl.* **dies** [daiz] *sl.* MEC kalıp; mühür; *lower* ~ matris, harf kalıbı; *upper* ~ zımba; *as straight as a* ~ dimdik; *the* ~ *is cast* ok yaydan çıktı.

die...: '~*a'way adj.* azalıp kaybolan, zayıf, süzgün; uzaklaşan (*ses vs.*); '~*casting n.* MEC basınçlı döküm; '~*hard n.* inatçı, gerici, eski kafalı, tutucu kimse.

di.e.lec.tric [daii'lektrik] *adj.* elektrik geçirmez, izolatör, yalıtkan.

Die.sel en.gine ['diːzl'endʒin] *n.* dizel

motoru.

die-sink.er ['daisiŋkə] *n.* pafta kalıpçısı.

die-stock MEC ['daistɔk] *n. el.* paftası.

di.et ['daiət] **1.** *n.* perhiz, rejim; gıda, yiyecek; ulusal meclis, diyet; **2.** *v/t. & v/i.* perhiz et(tir)mek; rejim yap(tır)mak; '**di.e.tar.y 1.** *n.* beslenme rejimi; perhiz kuralları; **2.** *adj.* perhize ait; **di.e.tet.ics** [daii'tetiks] *n.* diyet bilimi; **di.e.ti.cian**, **di.e.ti.tian** [-'tiʃən] *n.* diyet uzmanı.

dif.fer ['difə] *v/i.* farklı olm., ayrılmak (*with*, *from* -*den*); uygun bulmamak, anlaşamamak (*about*, *on*, *over* -*de*); *they agreed to* ~ anlaşamadıklarını kabul ettiler; **dif.fer.ence** ['difrəns] *n.* ayrılık, fark; ihtilâf, anlaşmazlık; MATH & COM fark; *split the* ~ farkı paylaşmak; '**dif.fer.ent** □ farklı (*from*, *to* -*den*), ayrı, başka; çeşitli; değişik; **dif.fer.en.ti.a** [difə'renʃiə] *n.* alâmeti farika, karakteristik; **dif.fer'en.tial** [-əl] **1.** *adj.* farklı, farklılık gösteren; ~ *calculus* diferensiyel hesap; **2.** MOT *n.* diferansiyel dişlisi; **dif.fer'en.ti.ate** [-ʃieit] *vb.* ayırt etm.; değişiklik göstermek; farklılaşmak; **dif.fer.en.ti'a.tion** *n.* ayırma, ayırt etme, fark.

dif.fi.cult □ ['difikəlt] zor, güç; titiz; inatçı; '**dif.fi.cul.ty** *n.* zorluk, güçlük; *be in difficulties* parasız kalmak, sıkıntıda olm.

dif.fi.dence ['difidəns] *n.* çekingenlik, utangaçlık; '**dif.fi.dent** □ çekingen, utangaç.

dif.frac.tion PHYS [di'frækʃən] *n.* elektromanyetik dalgaların *ya da* ışınların kırılarak ışık tayfını (*gökkuşağını*) oluşturması.

dif.fuse 1. [di'fjuːz] *fig. v/t. & v/i.* yay(ıl)mak, dağıtmak; değişmek; CHEM *bşe* nüfuz etm.; **2.** □ [-s] ayrıntılı; yayılmış, yaygın, dağılmış, geniş; **dif'fused** [-zd] *adj.* yayılmış (*ışık*); **dif'fu.sion** [-ʒən] *n.* yayılma; CHEM dağılma; **dif'fu.sive** □ [-siv] yayılmış, fazla açıklamalı, uzun uzadıya.

dig [dig] **1.** *vb.* kazmak; kazı yapmak; kafa yormak; *bşi* deşelemek (*in*); F itip kakmak; dürtmek; ~ *for* eşeleyerek aramak; ~ *in* gömmek; MIL siper kazmak; ~ *into* kazıp delmek; yemeğe girişmek, yumulmak; ~ *up* kazıp çıkarmak; ortaya çıkarmak; **2.** *n.* kazı, hafriyat; F dürtme, kinaye; ~*s pl.* F oda, pansiyon.

di.gest 1. [di'dʒəst] *v/t. & v/i.* düzenlemek; hazmetmek, sindir(il)mek (*a. fig.*); **2.** ['daidʒest] *n.* özet, derleme, seçme; JUR yasalar toplamı; **di.gest.i-bili.ty** [didʒestə'biliti] *n.* sindirebilme; **di'gest.i.ble** *adj.* hazmı kolay, sindirilebilir; **di'ges.tion** *n.* hazım, sindirim; **di'gestive 1.** *n.* sindirici ilâç; **2.** *adj.* hazmettirici, midevi.

dig.ger ['digə] (*esp. altın*) *n.* kazıcı, arayıcı; toprak kazan kimse; *sl.* Birinci Dünya Savaşı'nda Avustralyalı ya da Yeni Zelandalı asker; **dig.gings** ['.-giŋz] *pl.* pansiyon; *Am.* altın madeni.

dig.it ['didʒit] *n.* parmak; MATH rakam; bir parmak genişliği; **'dig.it.al** *adj.* parmağa ait, dijital; ~ *cable* dijital kablo; ~ *camera* dijital fotoğraf makinesi; ~ *photo* dijital fotoğraf; ~ *projector* dijital gösterici; ~ *watch* dijital saat; **dig.it'ize** *v/t. dijital hale getirmek.*

dig.ni.fied ['dignifaid] *adj.* ağırbaşlı, vakur; **dig.ni.fy** ['.-fai] *v/t.* değer vermek, yükseltmek, şeref vermek; *fig.* asilleştirmek.

dig.ni.tar.y *esp. eccl* ['dignitəri] *n.* yüksek rütbeli kimse, ruhani; **'dig.ni.ty** *n.* ağırbaşlılık, vakar, değer; *stand* (*up-*) *on one's* ~ kendisine saygılı davranılmasında ısrar etm.

di.graph GR ['daigrɑːf] *n.* tek sesi temsil eden iki harf (*örneğin* «*heat*» *sözcüğündeki* «*ea*»).

di.gress [dai'gres] *v/i.* konunun dışına çıkmak, ayrılmak (*from*-*den*); **di'gres.sion** *n.* konudan ayrılma, sapma; **di'gressive** □ yersiz, gereksiz, konu dışı.

dike [daik] **1.** *n.* set, bent; hendek; **2.** *v/b.* bentle kapatmak; hendek açmak, kazmak.

di.lap.i.date [di'læpideit] *v/t.* harap etm.; *v/i.* harap olm.; **di'lap.i.dat.ed** *adj.* harap, yıkılmaya yüz tutan; **di'lap.i'da.tion** *n.* harap olma; viranlık.

di.lat.a.bil.i.ty PHYS [daileitə'biliti] *n.* genleşme yeteneği; **di'lat.a.ble** *adj.* genişliyebilir, uzayabilir; **dil.a'ta.tion** *n.* genleşme, genişleme, yayılma; **di'late** *v/t. & v/i.* genişle(t)mek; ~ *upon* ayrıntılara girmek; **di'la.tion** = *dilatation*; **dil.ato.ri.ness** ['dilətərinis] *n.* tembellik, işini sonraya bırakma; **'dil.a.to.ry** □ tembel, ağırdan alan, yavaş, *b-ni* oyalayıcı.

di.lem.ma [di'lemə] *n.* dilem, ikilem; *fig.* kötü durum, sıkıntı.

dil.et.tan.te *pl.* **dil.et.tan.ti** [dili'tænti, *pl.* .-'tænti:] *n.* güzel sanatlara meraklı; amatör; *adj.* yüzeysel merakı olan.

dil.i.gence ['dilidʒəns] *n.* gayret, çalışkanlık; **'dil.i.gent** □ gayretli, çalışkan.

dill BOT [dil] *n.* dereotu.

dil.ly-dal.ly F ['dilidæli] *v/i.* boş vakit geçirmek, oyalanmak, *bşi* yapmağa üşenmek.

dil.u.ent ['diljuənt] **1.** *n.* sulandırıcı madde; **2.** *adj.* sulandırıcı, çözücü; **di-lute** [dai'ljuːt] **1.** *v/t.* sulandırmak; *fig.* ruhsuzlaştırmak; **2.** *adj.* sulandırılmış; *fig.* ruhsuz; **di'lu.tion** *n.* sulandırma, çözme; *fig.* ruhsuzlaşma, heyecanını yitirme.

di.lu.vi.al [dai'luːvjəl], **di'lu.vi.an** *adj.* GEOL sel sonucu oluşmuş.

dim [dim] **1.** □ bulanık, donuk; loş; F anlayışsız; **2.** *v/t. & v/i.* bulan(dır)mak; karar(t)mak (*ışık*); MOT, *film*: donuklaş(tır)mak.

dime *Am.* [daim] *n.* on sentlik para; ~ *novel* ucuz roman; ~ *store* tek fiyatla ucuz satış yapan mağaza.

di.men.sion [di'menʃən] *n.* boyut, ebat; ~*s pl.* buut; uzaklık.

di.min.ish [di'miniʃ] *v/t. & v/i.* azal(t)mak; küçül(t)mek; eksil(t)mek; **dim.i-nu.tion** [dimi'njuːʃən] *n.* azal(t)ma; eksil(t)me; ARCH küçül(t)me; **di'minu.tive** [.-njutiv] **1.** □ GR küçültme eki; ufak; **2.** *n.* küçültme eki almış sözcük.

dim.ness ['dimnis] *n.* donukluk, matlık.

dim.ple ['dimpl] **1.** *n.* çene *veya* yanak çukuru, gamze; **2.** *v/t. & v/i.* çukur oluş(tur)mak; **'dim.pled** *adj.* gamzeli.

din [din] **1.** *n.* gürültü, patırdı, şamata; **2.** *v/t. & v/i.* gürültü ile sersemletmek; gürültü etm.; ~ *s.th. into s.o.*('*s ears*) tekrar tekrar söyleyerek *bşi b-nin* kafasına sokmak, hatırlatmak.

dine [dain] *v/i.* akşam yemeğini yemek; *v/t.* ağırlamak; yedirip içirmek, ziyafet vermek -*e*; ~ *out* akşam yemeğini dışarda yemek; **'din.er** *n.* akşam yemeği yiyen; akşam yemeğine gelen misafir; RAIL *esp. Am.* vagon restoran, vagon restoran şeklinde düzenlenmiş lokanta; **'diner-'out** *n.* dışarıda akşam yemeğine çok davet edilen kimse; **di-nette** [dai'net] *n.* mutfağa açılan küçük yemek odası.

ding [diŋ] *v/i.* tınlamak, çınlamak; ~**dong** ['.-'dɔŋ] **1.** *n.* çan, zil vs. sesi,

dan dan; **2.** *adj.* çekişmeli bir oyun veya mücadelede önce bir tarafın sonra öteki tarafın üstün gelmesi şeklinde.
din.gey, **din.ghy** ['diŋgi] *n.* küçük sandal, bot; ***rubber ~*** lastik sandal.
din.gle ['diŋgl] *n.* ağaçlık küçük vadi.
din.gus *Am. sl.* ['diŋgəs] *n.* şey.
din.gy □ ['dindʒi] bulanık, rengi solmuş, kirli görünen.
din.ing... ['dainiŋ]: '**~-'al.cove** *n.* duvarda yemek koymak için girinti; '**~-car** *n.* RAIL vagon restoran; '**~-room** *n.* yemek odası.
dink.ey *Am.* ['diŋki] *n.* küçük manevra lokomotifi.
dink.y F ['diŋki] *adj.* küçük ve zarif, sevimli, cici bici.
din.ner ['dinə] *n.* (*öğleyin veya akşam yenen*) esas yemek; akşam yemeği; ziyafet; '**~-jack.et** *n.* smokin; '**~-pail** *n.* *Am.* sefertası; '**~-par.ty** *n.* yemek davetleri; '**~-serv.ice**, '**~-set** *n.* sofra takımı.
di.no.saur ZOO ['dainəusɔː] *n.* çok büyük ve nesli tükenmiş sürüngen, dinazor.
dint [dint] **1.** *n.* çizgi, iz, ufak oyuk; bere; ***by ~ of*** vasıtasiyle, *-den* ötürü, kuvvetiyle; **2.** *v/t.* berelemek, yamrı yumru etm.
di.o.ce.san ECCL [dai'ɔsisən] **1.** *adj.* piskoposluğa ait; **2.** *n.* piskopos; **di.o.cese** ['daiəsis] *n.* piskoposluk ruhanî dairesi.
di.op.tric OPT [dai'ɔptrik] **1.** *adj.* ışınları kırıcı; **2.** *n.* ışık kırılması ile ilgili bilim dalı.
di.ox.ide CHEM [dai'ɔksaid] *n.* molekülde bir diğer elemente bağlanan iki oksijen atomlu oksit, dioksit.
dip [dip] **1.** *v/t.* daldırmak, batırmak; NAUT selâm amacıyla sancağı yarıya indirmek; (*kumaş*) boyamak; su çekmek (***out of***, ***from*** *-den*); MOT farları kısmak; (*bir hayvanı*) antiesptik suya batırmak; *v/i.* dalmak, batmak; eğilmek; GEOL meyletmek; çökmek; ***~ into*** göz gezdirmek; **2.** *n.* dal(dır)ma; bat(ır)ma; dezenfektan banyo (*hayvanlar için*); F deniz banyosu; yokuş, iniş; bayrak gibi bir şeyi indirip kaldırma.
diph.the.ri.a [dif'θiəriə] *n.* difteri.
diph.thong ['difθɔŋ] *n.* iki ünlünün bir hece oluşturması, diftong.
di.plo.ma [di'pləumə] *n.* diploma; **di'ploma.cy** *n.* diplomasi, diplomatlık; görüşmelerde ustalık, incelik; **dip.lo.mat** ['dipləmæt] *n.* diplomat, Dışişleri Bakanlığı memuru; görüşmelerde incelik gösteren kimse; **dip.lo'mati.cal** □ diplomatik, uluslararası siyasete ait; ilişkilerinde usta, siyasî; **dip.lo'mat.ics** *n. sg.* eski resmî belgeleri çözme ve gerçekliğini saptama ilmi; **di'ploma.tist** *n.* diplomat, siyaset adamı.
dip.per ['dipə] *n.* kepçe, maşrapa; *Am.* ***Big*** ♀ AST Büyükayı; '**dip.py** *sl. adj.* deli.
dip.so.ma.ni.a [dipsəu'meinjə] *n.* içki tutkunluğu, ayyaşlık; **dip.so'ma.ni.ac** [₋niæk] *n.* alkolik, ayyaş.
dip-stick ['dipstik] *n.* (*esp. mot*) daldırma çubuk ölçek.
dire ['daiə] *adj.* korkunç, müthiş, dehşetli; uğursuz.
di.rect [di'rekt] **1.** □ doğru, vasıtasız; açık, belirgin; içten, samimi, dürüst; tam; ***~ current*** doğru akım; ***~ hit*** tam isabet; ***~ speech*** konuşmacının gerçek sözleri, dolaysız söz; ***~ tax*** vasıtasız vergi; ***~ train*** aktarmasız tren; **2.** *adv.* doğrudan doğruya; hemen, derhal; açıkça; = ***~ly 1***; **3.** *v/t.* doğrultmak, yöneltmek (***to***, ***towards***, ***at*** *-e*); yol göstermek, idare etm.; düzenlemek; emretmek (***to*** *-i*); zarfa adres yazmak; ***~ to*** ulaştırmak; **di'rec.tion** *n.* yön, cihet, taraf; emir; düzenleme; idare, nezaret; **di'rec.tion.al** [₋ʃənl] *adj. radyo*: yön saptamaya ait; **di'rec.tion-find.er** *n.* *radyo*: yön bulucu alet; sinyal alıcı alet; **di'rec.tion-find.ing** *n. radyo*: yön, sinyal bulma; ***~ set*** yön bulma aleti; **di'rec.tion in.di.ca.tor** MOT yol, yön göstergesi; AVIA rota göstergesi; **directions** *n. pl.* tarifname, kullanış tarzı; **di'rec.tive** *adj.* idare edici, yönlendirici; **di'rect.ly 1.** *adv.* doğrudan doğruya; **2.** *cj.* yapar yapmaz; **di'rect.ness** *n.* doğru gidiş; *fig.* doğruluk, dürüstlük.
di.rec.tor [di'rektə] *n.* direktör, müdür; *film*: rejisör; idare kurulu üyesi; ***board of ~s*** idare kurulu; **di'rec.to.rate** [₋rit] *n.* idare kurulu; müdürlük; *a.* **di'rectorship** müdürlük, direktörlük; **di'rec.to.ry** *n.* adres defteri; ***telephone ~*** telefon rehberi.
di.rec.tress [di'rektris] *n.* müdire, kadın direktör.
dire.ful □ ['daiəful] korkunç, dehşet veren.
dirge [dəːdʒ] *n.* ağıt, mersiye.
dir.i.gi.ble ['diridʒəbl] **1.** *adj.* yönlendirilebilir; **2.** *n.* güdümlü balon *veya* hava

gemisi.

dirk [dəːk] **1.** *n.* bir çeşit kama; **2.** *v/t.* hançerlemek.

dirt [dəːt] *n.* kir, pislik, çamur (*a. fig.*); **treat s.o. like ~** *b-ni* hiçe saymak, hor görmek; **fling** *veya* **throw ~ at s.o.** *b-ni* çamura bulamak, iftira atmak; **'~'cheap** F *adj.* sudan ucuz, bedava; **'~'track** *n. spor:* yarış yapılan toprak yol; **'dirt.y 1.** □ kirli (*a. fig.*) pis, bulanık; iğrenç, alçak; **2.** *v/t.* kirletmek, pisletmek, lekelemek.

dis.a.bil.i.ty [disə'biliti] *n.* kuvvetsizlik, yetersizlik; sakatlık; yetkisizlik.

dis.a.ble [dis'eibl] *v/t.* (*esp. savaşta*) sakatlamak, kuvvetten düşürmek, kullanılmaz hale getirmek; **dis'a.bled** *adj.* sakat, malul; **dis'able.ment** *n.* sakatlık; yetkisizlik.

dis.a.buse [disə'bjuːz] *v/t.* yanlış düşünceyi düzeltmek, *b-nin* gözünü açmak, aklını başına getirmek (**of**).

dis.ac.cord [disə'kɔːd] *v/i.* anlaşmazlık halinde olm. (**with** *ile*); *n.* anlaşmazlık, ihtilâf.

dis.ac.cus.tom ['disə'kʌstəm]: **~ s.o. to s.th.** *v/t.* bir alışkanlıktan vazgeçirmek.

dis.ad.van.tage [disəd'vɑːntidʒ] *n.* mahzur, sakınca, aleyhte oluş; **sell to ~** zararına satış; **dis.ad.van.ta.geous** □ [disædvɑːn'teidʒəs] sakıncalı, mahzurlu, zararlı; elverişsiz.

dis.af.fect.ed □ [disə'fektid] (**to, towards** *-e*) muhalif, aykırı, hoşnutsuz; **dis.af'fection** *n.* antipati, isteksizlik, hoşnutsuzluk.

dis.af.firm JUR [disə'fəːm] *v/t.* reddetmek, bozmak.

dis.af.for.est [disə'fɔrist] *v/t.* ormanları tahrip etm. ormansız bırakmak.

dis.a.gree [disə'griː] *v/i.* uyuşamamak, anlaşamamak (**with** *ile*); araları açık olm. (**on**); uygun gelmemek (**with** *-e*); (*yiyecek*) dokunmak; **dis.a.gree.a.ble** □ [-'griəbl] nahoş, cansıkıcı, hoş olmayan (*a. fig.*); **dis.a.gree.ment** *n.* anlaşmazlık, uyuşmazlık, çekişme.

dis.al.low ['disə'lau] *v/t.* müsaade etmemek, engel olm.; reddetmek.

dis.ap.pear [disə'piə] *v/i.* gözden kaybolmak; yok olmak; **dis.ap.pear.ance** [-'piərəns] *n.* gözden kaybolma; yok olma.

dis.ap.point [disə'pɔint] *v/t.* hayal kırıklığına uğratmak; ümidini boşa çıkarmak, yarı yolda bırakmak;

dis.ap'pointment *n.* hayal kırıklığı, hüsran; **~ in love** karşılık görmeyen aşk.

dis.ap.pro.ba.tion [disæprəu'beiʃən] *n.* beğenmeyiş, uygun görmeyiş, onaylamama.

dis.ap.prov.al [disə'pruːvl] *n.* beğenmeyiş, ayıplama, onaylamama; **dis.ap'prove** *v/t.* beğenmemek, uygun görmemek (**of** *-i*).

dis.arm [dis'ɑːm] *v/t.* silahsızlandırmak; zararsız hale getirmek (*a. fig.*); *v/i.* silahları bırakmak, azaltmak; **dis'ar.mament** *n.* silahsızlanma, silahların sınırlandırılması, silahları bırakma.

dis.ar.range ['disə'reindʒ] *v/t.* karıştırmak, *-in* düzenini bozmak; **disar'rangement** *n.* karışıklık, düzensizlik.

dis.ar.ray ['disə'rei] **1.** *n.* karışıklık; düzensiz kıyafet; **2.** *v/t.* karıştırmak.

dis.as.sem.bly MEC [disə'sembli] *n.* sökme, parçalara ayırma; dağılma.

dis.as.ter [di'zɑːstə] *n.* felâket, belâ, facia; **dis'as.trous** □ felâket getiren, uğursuz, talihsiz, feci, dehşetli, korkunç.

dis.a.vow ['disə'vau] *v/t.* inkâr etm., onaylamamak, tanımamak, tekzip etm., yalanlamak; **dis.a'vow.al** *n.* inkâr, tanımama, onaylamama, tekzip.

dis.band [dis'bænd] *v/t.* terhis etm., dağıtmak; *v/i.* dağılmak; **dis'bandment** *n.* dağılma; terhis.

dis.bar [dis'bɑː] *v/t.* barodan ihraç etm.

dis.be.lief ['disbi'liːf] *n.* imansızlık; güvensizlik; şüphe (**in**); **dis.be.lieve** ['disbi'liːv] *v/t.* inanmamak *-e*; şüphe etm.; **dis.be'liev.er** *n.* inanmayan kimse, şüpheci.

dis.bud [dis'bʌd] *v/t.* meyve ağaçlarının tomurcuklarını seyreltmek.

dis.bur.den [dis'bəːdn] *v/t.* *b-nin* yükünü hafifletmek; kurtarmak (**of**); kalp ferahlatmak (*a. fig.*).

dis.burse [dis'bəːs] *v/t.* ödemek; *b-nin* hesabına para vermek; **dis'bursement** *n.* ödeme; harcama; ödenen para.

disc [disk] = **disk.**

dis.card 1. [dis'kɑːd] *v/t.* atmak, ihraç etm., azletmek; ıskartaya çıkarmak; *kâğıt oyunu;* boş kâğıt atmak; **2.** ['diskɑːd] *n.* oyun kâğıdı; ıskarta, boş kâğıt; *esp. Am.* çöp.

dis.cern [di'səːn] *v/t.* ayırt etm., *bşin* farkına varmak, anlamak, kavramak;

dis'cern.i.ble □ farkedilebilir, görülebilir; **dis'cern.ing 1.** □ anlayışlı, zeki; **2.** *n.* anlama, kavrama; **dis'cern.ment** *n.* idrak, kavrama, muhakeme; görüş, seziş.

dis.charge [dis'tʃɑ:dʒ] **1.** *v/t.* boşaltmak, tahliye etm.; terhis etm.; NAUT yük boşaltmak; ELECT cereyanı boşaltmak; *bşden* affetmek; ateş etm.; ödemek (*borç*); yerine getirmek (*görev*); işten çıkarmak; öfkesini *b-den* çıkarmak; *v/i.* boşalmak, dökülmek; akmak (*in*); **2.** *n.* boşaltma (*a.* ELECT); NAUT yük indirme; salıverme; terhis; işten çıkarılma; ateş etme; ödeme, ifa; makbuz; görev; cerahat; **dis'charg.er** *n.* boşaltma işini yapan kişi *ya da* alet.

dis.ci.ple [di'saipl] *n.* öğrenci, mürit; İsa paygamberin öğütlerini yaymakla görevlendirdiği oniki çömezi, havari; **dis'ciple.ship** *n.* öğrencilik; havarilik.

dis.ci.pli.nar.i.an [disipli'nɛəriən] *n.* sert amir, disiplini sağlayan kimse; *he is a poor ~* disiplini sağlayamayan kimsedir; **'dis.ci.pli.nar.y** *adj.* disipline ait, eğitimsel; **'dis.ci.pline 1.** *n.* disiplin, terbiye; eğitim; cezalandırma; bilim dalı; **2.** *v/t.* disiplin altına almak, terbiye etm.; cezalandırmak.

dis.claim [dis'kleim] *v/t.* inkâr etm.; vazgeçmek *-den*; **dis'claim.er** *n.* vazgeçme, feragat; tekzip, yalanlama.

dis.close [dis'kləuz] *v/t.* ifşa etm., açmak; açığa çıkarmak; **dis'clo.sure** [-ʒə] *n.* ifşa, açma.

dis.col.o(u)r [dis'kʌlə] *v/t. -in* rengini bozmak, soldurmak, rengini değiştirmek; **dis.col.o(u)r'a.tion** *n.* rengini bozma, soldurma, solma.

dis.com.fit [dis'kʌmfit] *v/t.* yenmek, mağlûp etm.; sinirlendirmek; bozmak; **dis'com.fi.ture** [-tʃə] *n.* yenilgi; şaşkınlık; bozgun.

dis.com.fort [dis'kʌmfət] **1.** *n.* rahatsızlık, sıkıntı, huzursuzluk; **2.** *v/t.* rahatsız etm., sıkıntı vermek, üzmek.

dis.com.pose [diskəm'pəuz] *v/t.* şaşırtmak, rahatını bozmak, düzenini bozmak; **dis.com'po.sure** [-ʒə] *n.* rahatsızlık, kaygı, telaş.

dis.con.cert [diskən'sə:t] *v/t.* şaşırtmak; karıştırmak, telaşlandırmak.

dis.con.nect [diskə'nekt] *v/t.* ayırmak, bağlantısını kesmek (*from*, *with* *-den*, *-le*); MEC durdurmak; birbirinden ayırmak; ELECT fişi çekmek; **'dis.con-'nect.ed** □ bağlantısız; **'dis.con'nec-**

tion *n.* ayrılma; MEC bağlantının kesilmesi.

dis.con.so.late □ [diskɔnsəlit] teselli kabul etmez, çok kederli.

dis.con.tent ['diskən'tent] **1.** *rare* = *~ed*; **2.** *n.* hoşnutsuzluk; **'dis.con-'tent.ed** □ hoşnutsuz.

dis.con.tin.u.ance [diskən'tinjuəns] *n.* ara, duraklama, kesilme; vazgeçme; **'dis.con'tin.ue** [-nju:] *v/t.* kesmek, devam etmemek *-e*; vazgeçmek *-den*; *gazete*; aboneyi kesmek; **'dis.con'ti-n.u-**

ous □ [-njuəs] düzensiz, fasılalı, aralıklı, ayrılmış.

dis.cord ['diskɔ:d], **dis'cord.ance** *n.* anlaşmazlık, uyuşmazlık; MUS ahenksizlik; **dis'cord.ant** □ uyumsuz; farklı (*to*, *from*, *with*); aralarında anlaşmazlık bulunan; MUS ahenksiz.

dis.count ['diskaunt] **1.** *n.* COM iskonto, tenzilât; *at a ~* iskonto ile, değerinden ucuza; **2.** *v/t.* iskonto etm., hesaptan indirmek; çıkarmak (*a.* *fig.*); kır(dır)mak (*senet*, *bono*); **dis'count-a.ble** *adj.* iskonto edilebilir; **dis'coun-te.nance** [-tinəns] *v/t.* utandırmak; onaylamamak; cesaretini kırmak.

dis.cour.age [dis'kʌridʒ] *v/t. -in* cesaretini kırmak, gözdağı vermek, yıldırmak, vazgeçirmek (*from -den*); **dis'cour.agement** *n.* cesaretsizlik, hevesin kırılması; güçlük, zorluk.

dis.course [dis'kɔ:s] **1.** *n.* söylev, nutuk; karşılıklı konuşma; bilimsel araştırma; **2.** *v/t.* (*on*, *upon*, *about*) *bş.* hakkında konuşmak, söylev vermek, konferans vermek; *bşle* ilgili görüşmek.

dis.cour.te.ous □ [dis'kə:tjəs] saygısız, kaba; **dis'cour.te.sy** [-tisi] *n.* saygısızlık, kabalık.

dis.cov.er [dis'kʌvə] *v/t.* keşfetmek, bulmak, ortaya çıkarmak; **dis'cov.er-a.ble** □ keşfedilebilir, ortaya çıkarılabilir; **dis'cov.er.er** *n.* bulucu, kâşif, ortaya çıkaran; **dis'cov.er.y** *n.* keşif, buluş, ortaya çıkarma; keşfedilen şey, bulgu.

dis.cred.it [dis'kredit] **1.** *n.* güvensizlik; şüphe; saygınsızlık, itibarsızlık; **2.** *v/t.* kötülemek, itibardan düşürmek, güvenini sarsmak, şüpheye düşürmek; **dis-'credit.a.ble** □ ayıplanacak, onur kırıcı, küçük düşürücü.

dis.creet □ [dis'kri:t] ketum, ağzı sıkı, sır saklayan; tedbirli, akıllı, denli.

dis.crep.an.cy [dis'krepənsi] *n.* ayrılık, anlaşmazlık, zıtlık.

dis.crete ☐ [dis'kri:t] ayrı, farklı, ayrılmış.

dis.cre.tion [dis'kreʃən] *n.* ağzı sıkılık, ketumluk; akıllılık; naziklik; yetki; *banker's ~* bankanın hesabı gizli tutması; *at one's ~* isteği doğrultusunda, istediği kadar, isteğe bağlı; *age veya years of ~* cezaî ehliyet, aklın hakim olduğu yaşlar; *surrender at ~* koşulsuz teslim; dis'cre.tion.ar.y [-ʃnəri] *adj.* isteğe bağlı, ihtiyarî.

dis.crim.i.nate [dis'krimineit] *vb.* ayırmak, ayırt etm.; ayırım yapmak, ayrı tutmak, fark gözetmek; *~ against* farklı davranmak -*e*, daha kötü davranmak -*e*; dis'crim.i.nat.ing ☐ ayırt eden; zevk sahibi olan, en iyiyi seçen, görüş sahibi olan; temyiz hakkı olan; dis.crim.i'na.tion *n.* aleyhte davranma, ayırım, fark gözetme, temyiz; dis'crim.i.na.tive [-nətiv] ☐ ayırt edici, fark gözeten; dis'crim.i.nato.ry law olağanüstü hal yasası.

dis.cur.sive ☐ [dis'kə:siv] konudan konuya geçen, tutarsız; F daldan dala konan; PHLS içeren, sonuca varan.

dis.cus ['diskəs] *n. spor:* disk; disk atma oyunu.

dis.cuss [dis'kʌs] *v/t.* görüşmek, müzakere etm., tartışmak; F (*yemek veya içki*) tadına bakmak; dis'cuss.i.ble *adj.* tartışılabilir, müzakere edilebilir; dis'cussion *n.* görüşme, müzakere, tartışma.

dis.dain [dis'dein] **1.** *n.* hakaret, küçük görme; **2.** *v/t.* aşağısamak, hafifsemek, hor görmek; dis'dain.ful ☐ [-ful] hafifseyen, hor gören (*of*), küçümseyen, mağrur.

dis.ease [di'zi:z] *n.* hastalık, rahatsızlık, illet, maraz; dis'eased *adj.* hasta.

dis.em.bark [disim'ba:k] *v/t. & v/i.* gemiden karaya çık(ar)mak; dis.em.bar.kation [disəmba:'keiʃən] *n.* karaya çık(ar)ma.

dis.em.bar.rass ['disim'bærəs] *v/t.* rahatlatmak; mahcubiyetten kurtarmak (*of*).

dis.em.bod.y [disim'bɔdi] *v/t.* bedenden ayırmak; MIL terhis etm.

dis.em.bogue [disim'bəug] *v/t. & v/i.* (*nehir*) denize dök(ül)mek; ak(ıt)mak.

dis.em.bow.el [disim'bauəl] *v/t.* bağır-

saklarını çıkarmak.

dis.em.broil [disim'brɔil] *v/t.* karışık ve zor durumdan kurtarmak.

dis.en.chant ['disin't ʃɑ:nt] *v/t.* büyüden kurtarmak; ayıltmak, aklını başına getirmek.

dis.en.cum.ber ['disin'kʌmbə] *v/t. b-ni* yük *veya* sıkıntıdan kurtarmak (*of*, *from*).

dis.en.gage ['disin'geidʒ] *v/t.* ayırmak; çözmek; MEC kavramayı gevşetmek; MOT debriyaj yapmak; dis.en'gaged *adj.* serbest, boş; 'dis.en'gage.ment *n.* ilgiyi kesme; salıverme, serbest bırakma.

dis.en.tan.gle ['disin'tæŋgl] *v/t. & v/i.* çıkarmak, çöz(ül)mek, kurtulmak (*from* -*den*); *fig.* serbest bırakmak (*from* -*den*); 'dis.en'tan.gle.ment *n.* çözülme, serbest kalma.

dis.en.tomb [disin'tu:m] *v/t.* kazmak, hafriyat yapmak, mezardan kazıp çıkarmak.

dis.e.qui.lib.ri.um ['disekwi'libriəm] *n.* dengesizlik, denksizlik.

dis.es.tab.lish [disis'tæbliʃ] *v/t.* (*kilise*) devletten ayırmak, ilişkisini kesmek; dis.es'tab.lish.ment *n.* devletle olan ilişkisini kesme.

dis.fa.vo(u)r ['dis'feivə] **1.** *n.* gözden düşme; *b-nin* hoşuna gitmeme; isteksizlik; **2.** *v/t.* gözden düşürmek, istememek; hoşlanmamak; onaylamamak.

dis.fig.ure [dis'figə] *v/t.* çirkinleştirmek, şeklini bozmak; dis'fig.ure.ment *n.* çirkinleştirme, şekilsizlik.

dis.fran.chise ['dis'fræntʃaiz] *v/t.* oy verme *veya* vatandaşlık hakkından yoksun bırakmak; dis.fran.chisement [dis'fræntʃizmənt] *n.* vatandaşlık haklarından yok'sun etme, oy verme hakkını elinden alma.

dis.frock [dis'frɔk] *v/t.* papazlık hakkını elinden almak.

dis.gorge [dis'gɔːdʒ] *v/t.* kusmak; boşaltmak; çalınan *bşi* geri vermek.

dis.grace [dis'greis] **1.** *n.* gözden düşme; yüz karası, utanç; **2.** *v/t.* gözden düşürmek; rezil etm.; *be ~d* rezil olm.; dis'grace.ful ☐ [-ful] ayıp, yüz kızartıcı, rezil.

dis.grun.tled [dis'grʌntld] *adj.* üzgün, canı sıkılmış.

dis.guise [dis'gaiz] **1.** *v/t. & v/i.* kıyafet değiştirmek; ses *vs.* tanınmaz hale getirmek; gizle(n)mek, sakla(n)mak; **2.** *n.* kıyafet değiştirme, gizlenme; *bless-*

ing in ~ gizli ama gerçek.

dis.gust [dis'gʌst] **1.** *n.* nefret, tiksinme, iğrenme (*at, for -den*); **2.** *v/t.* tiksindirmek, bıktırmak; *be ~ed with* nefret etm., kızmak, bıkmak *-den*; dis-'gust.ing □ iğrenç, tiksindirici, nefret uyandırıcı.

dish [diʃ] **1.** *n.* tabak, çanak; yemek; *sl.* güzel kız; *the ~es pl.* sofra takımı (*tabak, çatal, kaşık vs.*); *standing ~ fig.* hep güncel olan konu, temcid pilavı; **2.** *v/t.* tabağa koymak; *mst ~ up* sofraya koymak; sunmak için hazırlamak (*a. fig.*); *sl.* aldatmak; berbat etm.

dis.ha.bille [disæ'bi:l] *n.* sabahlık, ev elbisesi; yarı giyinik olma.

dish-cloth ['diʃklɔθ] *n.* tabak yıkama *veya* durulama bezi.

dis.heart.en [dis'hɑːtn] *v/t.* cesaretini kırmak, ümidini kırmak.

di.shev.el(l)ed [di'ʃeʌəld] *adj.* (*saç, giyim*) darmadağınık, düzensiz; *fig.* pasaklı.

dis.hon.est □ [dis'ɔnist] namussuz, haysiyetsiz, şerefsiz; dis'hon.est.y *n.* namussuzluk, sahtekârlık.

dis.hon.o(u)r [dis'ɔnə] **1.** *n.* namussuzluk, yüzkarası, leke, ayıp, alçaklık; **2.** *v/t. -in* namusuna leke sürmek; *-in* ırzına geçmek; *poliçe:* kabul etmemek, ödememek; dis'hon.o(u)r.a.ble □ namussuz, haysiyetsiz.

dish...: **'~-pan** *n. Am.* bulaşık kabı; **'~.rag** *Am.* = **dish-cloth**; **'~-wash.er** bulaşıkçı, bulaşık yıkama makinesi; **'~-wa.ter** *n.* bulaşık suyu.

dis.il.lu.sion [disi'luːʒən] **1.** *n.* hayal kırıklığı, gözünü açma; **2.** *v/t.* hayal kırıklığına uğratmak, gerçekleri göstermek; *fig.* aklını başına getirmek; dis.il'lu.sionment = **disillusion 1.**

dis.in.cen.tive [disin'sentiv] *n.* yıldırma, gözünü korkutma.

dis.in.cli.na.tion [disinkli'neiʃən] *n.* isteksizlik, gönülsüzlük (*for, to -e*); dis.in.cline ['-'klain] *v/t. bşden, b-den* soğutmak, caydırmak; 'dis.in-'clined *adj.* isteksiz (*for, to -e*).

dis.in.fect [disin'fekt] *v/t.* dezenfekte etm.; dis.in'fect.ant *n.* antiseptik ilaç, dezenfektan; dis.in'fec.tion *n.* dezenfekte etme.

dis.in.fla.tion [disin'fleiʃən] *n.* enflasyondan fiyat ve ücretlerin çok değişmediği duruma geçme, paranın satın alma gücünün yükseltilmesi.

dis.in.gen.u.ous □ [disin'dʒenjuəs]

samimi olmayan, iki yüzlü.

dis.in.her.it ['disin'herit] *v/t.* mirastan yoksun bırakmak, reddetmek; dis.in-'herit.ance *n.* mirastan yoksunluk.

dis.in.te.grate [dis'intigreit] *v/t.* parçalara ayırmak, ayrıştırmak; *v/i.* parçalanmak, ayrışmak; dis.in.te'gra.tion *n.* ayrılıp dağılma.

dis.in.ter ['disin'təː] *v/t.* kazıp çıkarmak, eşmek.

dis.in.ter.est.ed □ [dis'intristid] tarafsız, önyargısız, çıkar gözetmeyen.

dis.join [dis'dʒɔin] *v/t.* ayırmak; dis-joint [-'dʒɔint] *v/t.* düzenini bozmak; ayırmak; sökmek; dis'joint.ed *adj.* ayrılmış; düzensiz, tutarsız (*söz*).

dis.junc.tion [dis'dʒʌŋkʃən] *n.* ayrılma; dis'junc.tive □ [-tiv] ayıran; GR bağlaç.

disk [disk] *n.* yuvarlak levha, disk, kurs; plâk; ~ **brake** MOT fren diski; ~ **clutch** MOT kavrama diski, debriyaj diski; '~ **drive** IT *n.* disk sürücü; '~-**har.row** *n.* keskin çarklarla işleyen tırmık; ~ **jock.ey** plâk sunucusu, diskcokey.

dis.like [dis'laik] **1.** *n.* beğenmeyiş, antipati (*for, of, to -e*); **2.** *v/t.* beğenmemek, sevmemek; *bşden, b-den* hoşlanmamak; **~d** *adj.* sevilmeyen.

dis.lo.cate ['disləukeit] *v/t.* yerinden çıkarmak, yerinden oynatmak; *fig.* altüst etm., şaşırtmak; dis.lo'ca.tion *n.* MED çıkık; yer değiştirme (*esp.* MIL); GEOL yeryüzü tabakasını delip açma; *fig.* şaşırtma.

dis.lodge [dis'lɔdʒ] *v/t.* yerinden çıkarmak; defetmek; siperden çıkarmak; evden taşınmak.

dis.loy.al □ ['dis'lɔiəl] sadık olmayan, vefasız; 'dis'loy.al.ty *n.* sadakatsizlik, vefasızlık, hıyanet.

dis.mal ['dizməl] **1.** □ *fig.* kederli, sıkıntılı, kasvetli, sönük; **2.** *the ~s pl.* F melankoli, kuruntu.

dis.man.tle [dis'mæntl] *v/t.* sökmek; (*kale*) yerle bir etm.; NAUT armasını soymak; (*ev*) eşyasını boşaltmak; MEC parçalara ayırmak; MEC makinaları sökmek; dis'man.tling *n.* sökme; boşaltma; parçalara ayırma.

dis.mast NAUT [dis'mɑːst] *v/t.* gemi direğini çıkarmak.

dis.may [dis'mei] **1.** *n.* korku, dehşet, şaşkınlık, endişe; **2.** *v/t.* korkutmak, ürkütmek, yıldırmak.

dis.mem.ber [dis'membə] *v/t.* parçalamak; uzuvları gövdeden ayırmak; dis-

'mem.ber.ment *n.* parçala(n)ma.

dis.miss [dis'mis] *v/t.* işten çıkarmak, yol vermek *-e*; reddetmek; gitmesine izin vermek; (*konu, fikir*) vazgeçmek; JUR davayı reddetmek; *be ~ed the service* işten atılmak; *v/t.* MIL saftan çıkmak; dis'missal *n.* yol verme, azledilme; izin; JUR davanın reddi.

dis.mount ['dis'maunt] *v/t.* (*bisiklet veya attan*) indirmek; MEC parçalara ayırmak; sökmek; *v/i.* attan inmek.

dis.o.be.di.ence [disə'biːdjəns] *n.* itaatsizlik; dis.o'be.di.ent □ itaatsiz (*to -e*); 'diso'bey *v/t.* itaat etmemek *-e*; söz dinlememek.

dis.o.blige ['disə'blaidʒ] *v/t.* hatırını kırmak, ricasını kabul etmemek, gücendirmek; 'dis.o'blig.ing □ nezaketsiz, hatır kıran, aksi; 'dis.o'blig.ing.ness *n.* nezaketsizlik, kabalık.

dis.or.der [dis'ɔːdə] 1. *n.* karışıklık; rahatsızlık; MED hastalık; *mental ~* aklî dengesizlik; 2. *v/t.* düzenini bozmak, rahatsız etm.; dis'or.dered □ düzensiz, karışık; bozuk (*mide*); dis'or.der.ly *adj.* düzensiz; itaatsiz; çapaçul; rahatsız.

dis.or.gan.i.za.tion [disɔːgənai'zeiʃən] *n.* düzensizlik, karışıklık; dis'organ.ize *v/t.* düzenini bozmak *-in*; karıştırmak *-i*.

dis.or.i.en.tate [dis'ɔːrienteit] *v/t.* *b-nin* yolunu şaşırtmak, zihnini karıştırmak; *he was ~d* yönünü şaşırdı.

dis.own [dis'əun] *v/t.* inkâr etm., yadsımak, tanımamak, reddetmek.

dis.par.age [dis'pæridʒ] *v/t.* kötülemek *-i*, hor görmek *-i*, *b-nin* şeref ve onuruna leke sürmek, küçük düşürmek *-i*; dis'parage.ment *n.* kötüleme, aşağılama; dis'par.ag.ing □ aşağılayıcı, hor gören.

dis.pa.rate ['dispərit] 1. □ eşit olmayan, farklı; 2. *~s n. pl.* kıyaslanamayacak ölcüde farklı şeyler; dis.par.i.ty [dis'pæriti] *n.* eşitsizlik, farklılık.

dis.part [dis'paːt] *v/t.* ikiye ayırmak; *v/i.* ikiye ayrılmak; MEC çapını ayar etm.

dis.pas.sion.ate □ [dis'pæʃnit] tarafsız, soğukkanlı, sakin.

dis.patch [dis'pætʃ] 1. *n.* acele; gönderme; rapor, haber; telgraf; öldürme, idam etme; *mentioned in ~es* savaştaki kahramanlığı raporda belirtilmiş; *happy ~* harakiri; 2. *v/t.* süratle tamamlamak (*a. = öldürmek*); gönder-

mek; dis'patch-box *n.* resmî evrak çantası; dis'patch-goods *n. pl.* ekspresle gönderilen eşya; dis'patch-rider *n.* MIL haberci.

dis.pel [dis'pel] *v/t.* defetmek, uzaklaştırmak, dağıtmak (*a. fig.*).

dis.pen.sa.ble [dis'pensəbl] *adj.* vazgeçilebilir, zorunlu olmayan; dis'pen.sa.ry *n.* dispanser; eczane; dis.pen.sa.tion [dispen'seiʃən] *n.* dağıtma, bölme; takdiri ilahî; dışında bırakma.

dis.pense [dis'pens] *v/t.* dağıtmak; hazırlamak (*ilâç reçetesi*); üstesinden gelmek; *~ from* muaf tutmak, *bşden* affetmek; *b-ne* işten el çektirmek; *v/i. ~ with* vazgeçmek *-den*; *bşe* muhtaç olmamak; dis'pens.er *n.* ilâç hazırlayan kimse; dağıtıcı.

dis.per.sal [dis'pəːsəl] = *dispersion*; dis'perse *v/t.* dağıtmak, yaymak; *v/i.* ayrılmak, dağılmak; dis'per.sion *n.* dağıtma (*a.* OPT), dağılma, dağıtım, yayılma.

dis.pir.it [di'spirit] *v/t.* cesaretini kırmak, keyfini kaçırmak; dis'pir.it.ed □ cesaretsiz, yüreksiz, keyifsiz.

dis.place [dis'pleis] *v/t.* yerinden çıkarmak, götürmek; yerine başka *bşi* (*b-ni*) geçirmek; *b-ni* azletmek; *~d person* ülkesini terketmeye zorlanan kimse; dis'place.ment *n.* yerinden çıkar(ıl)ma; bir geminin boşalttığı suyun ağırlığı; yer değişme.

dis.play [dis'plei] 1. *n.* gösteriş, nümayiş, teşhir; 2. *v/t.* göstermek, teşhir etm., göz önüne sermek, vurgulamak.

dis.please [dis'pliːz] *v/t.* *b-nin* hoşuna gitmemek; *fig.* gücendirmek; dis'pleased □ dargın, kızgın (*at, with -e*); dis'pleasing □ can sıkıcı, hoş olmayan; dis.pleasure [-'pleʒə] *n.* gücenme, hoşnutsuzluk, can sıkıntısı (*at, over*).

dis.port [dis'pɔːt] *vb.*: *~ o.s.* neşe içinde koşuşturmak; eğlenmek, oyna(ş)mak.

dis.pos.a.ble [dis'pəuzəbl] *adj.* elde hazır bulunan; gerektiğinde kullanılabilen; bir kez kullanılıp atılan; dis'pos.al *n.* tertip, düzen; bertaraf etme, tasarruf hakkı (*of*); satma, satış, başkasına verme, elden çıkarma; *at one's ~ b-nin* emrine âmade, hizmetinde; dis'pose *vb.* düzenlemek, dağıtmak; idare etm.; *bşe* sebep olm. (*for, to*); *~ of -in* tasarrufunda olm.; kullanmak *-i*; bertaraf etm. *-i*; satmak *-i*; *k-ni* yiyip bitirmek; dis'posed □ hazır (*to, for*

-e); **well** (*ill*) ~ **towards s.o.** *b-ne* arkadaşça (düşmanca) davranış, yaklaşım; **dis.po.si.tion** [-pə'zifən] *n.* düzen; eğilim; tabiat, huy; tasarruf hakkı (**of**). **dis.pos.sess** ['dispə'zes] (**of**) *v/t.* malına mülküne el koymak, yoksun bırakmak; evden çıkarmak; *fig.* bir alışkanlıktan vazgeçmek; **dis.pos.session** [-'sefən] *n.* mal ve mülke el konulması; evden çıkar(ıl)ma.

dis.praise [dis'preiz] **1.** *n.* kötüleme, azarlama, ayıplama; **2.** *v/t.* kötülemek, azarlamak; *b-ne, bşe* hor bakmak.

dis.proof ['dis'pru:f] *n.* aksini kanıtlama; ret.

dis.pro.por.tion [disprə'pɔ:fən] *n.* oransızlık; **dis.pro'por.tion.ate** □ [-fnit] oransız, gereğinden fazla, aşırı; **dis.pro'portion.ate.ness** *n.* oransızlık; **'dis.pro'portioned** [-fənd] = **disproportionate**.

dis.prove [dis'pru:v] *v/t.* yanlış olduğunu göstermek, aksini kanıtlamak.

dis.pu.ta.ble [dis'pju:təbl] *adj.* yadsınabilir, inkâr edilebilir, tartışılır; **dis'pu.tant** *n.* tartışmacı; **dis.pu'ta.tion** *n.* tartışma, münakaşa; **dis.pu'ta.tious** □ münakaşacı, kavgacı; **dis'pute 1.** *n.* münakaşa, kavga, tartışma; **in** ~ münakaşalı, ihtilâflı; **beyond** (**all**) ~, **past** ~ tartışma götürmez, apaçık; **2.** *v/t.* tartışmak, kabul etmemek; *v/i.* münakaşa etm., kavga etm. (**about**).

dis.qual.i.fi.ca.tion [diskwɔlifi'keifən] *n.* yetkisizlik, ehliyetsizlik; *spor:* oyundan çıkarma cezası; engel; **dis'qual.i.fy** [-fai] *v/t.* yetkisiz kılmak (**for**); *spor:* oyundan atmak, diskalifiye etm.

dis.qui.et [dis'kwaiət] **1.** *n.* merak, endişe; **2.** *v/t.* huzurunu kaçırmak, endişe vermek, üzmek; **dis.qui.e.tude** [-'kwaiitju:d] *n.* rahatsızlık, üzüntü.

dis.qui.si.tion [diskwi'zifən] *n.* araştırma, tetkik; nutuk, söylev (**on**).

dis.re.gard ['disri'gɑ:d] **1.** *n.* ihmal, kayıtsızlık, saymayış; **2.** *v/t.* ihmal etm., saymamak, aldırmamak, önemsememek.

dis.rel.ish [dis'relif] **1.** *n.* tiksinme, beğenmeyiş, nefret (**for**); **2.** *v/t.* hoşlanmamak, tiksinmek.

dis.re.pair ['disri'pɛə] *n.* tamire muhtaç olma, viranlık, bakımsızlık; **fall into** ~ bakıma muhtaç hale gelmek.

dis.rep.u.ta.ble □ [dis'repjutəbl] rezil; itibarsız; **dis.re.pute** ['-ri'pju:t] *n.* kö-

tü şöhret, itibarsızlık.

dis.re.spect ['disris'pekt] *n.* saygısızlık, kabalık; **dis.re'spect.ful** [-ful] □ saygısız, kaba, hürmetsiz.

dis.robe ['dis'rəub] *v/t. & v/i.* soy(un)-mak; elbisesini çıkarmak.

dis.root [dis'ru:t] *v/t.* kökünden sökmek.

dis.rupt [dis'rʌpt] *v/t.* yarmak, ayırmak; **dis'rup.tion** *n.* parçalama, kırılma, ayrılma, engel olma.

dis.sat.is.fac.tion ['dissætis'fækfən] *n.* hoşnutsuzluk, tatminsizlik; **dis.sat.is.fac.tory** ['-'fæktəri] *adj.* uygun olmayan, hoşnutsuz kılan, tatmin etmeyen; **'dis'sat.isfied** [-faid] *adj.* hoşnutsuz, memnun olmayan; **'dis'sat.is.fy** [-fai] *v/t.* memnun etmemek, tatmin etmemek, *b-nin* hoşuna gitmemek.

dis.sect [di'sekt] *vb.* parçalara ayırmak; ANAT kadavrada çalışmak; *fig.* bir konuyu en ince ayrıntılariyle anlatmak, açımlamak; **dis'sec.tion** *n.* parçalama; ANAT otopsi; *fig.* analiz, tahlil.

dis.sem.ble [di'sembl] *v/t.* gizlemek, saklamak; görmezlikten gelmek; *v/i.* *b-ne* karşı sahte tavır takınmak, iki yüzlülük etm.

dis.sem.i.nate [di'semineit] *v/t.* saçmak, yaymak; **dis.sem.i'na.tion** *n.* saç(ıl)ma; yay(ıl)ma.

dis.sen.sion [di'senfən] *n.* ihtilâf, çekişme.

dis.sent [di'sent] **1.** *n.* ihtilâf, ayrılık, reddetme; **2.** *v/i.* bir konuda ayrılmak (**from** *-den*); aynı görüşte olmamak (**with** *-le*); Anglikan kilisesinden ayrılmak; **dis'senter** *n.* muhalif; kiliseden ayrılan; **dis'sentient** [-fiənt] **1.** *adj.* muhalif olan; **2.** *n.* muhalif.

dis.ser.ta.tion [disə'teifən] *n.* bilimsel araştırma; nutuk, söylev (**on**).

dis.serv.ice ['dis'sə:vis] *n.* (**to**) kötülük, zarar.

dis.sev.er [dis'sevə] *v/t.* tamamen ayırmak, kesip ayırmak; **dis'sev.er.ance**, **dis'sev.er.ment** *n.* ayrılık, ayrılma.

dis.si.dence ['disidəns] *n.* fikir ayrılığı, karşı koyma, muhalefet; **'dis.si.dent 1.** *adj.* muhalif, karşı koyan; **2.** *n.* muhalif, karşı gelen kimse.

dis.sim.i.lar □ ['di'similə] farklı (**to**, **from** *-den*); **dis.sim.i.lar.i.ty** [-'læriti] *n.* başkalık, farklılık, benzemeyiş (**to**).

dis.sim.u.late [di'simjuleit] = **dissemble**; **dis.sim.u'lation** *n.* iki yüzlülük, sahte tavır.

dis.si.pate ['disipeit] *v/t.* dağıtmak; is-raf etm., har vurup harman savurmak; *v/i.* dağılmak; müsrif olm.; harcanmak; 'dis.si.pat.ed *adj.* müsrif; sefih; hovar-da; dis.si'pa.tion *n.* zevk ve eğlenceye düşkünlük, sefahat.

dis.so.ci.ate [di'souʃieit] *v/t.* ayırmak; ~ *o.s.* bşden ilgisini kesmek, ayrı tutmak ayrılmak (*from* -den); dis.so.ci-ation [-si'eiʃən] *n.* ayırma, ayrılma; PSYCH düşüncelerin duygulardan ayrıldığı anda ortaya çıkan müdafaa mekanizması, şahsiyetin çözülmesi.

dis.sol.u.bil.i.ty [disəlju'biliti] *n.* çözü-lebilirlik, ayrılabilirlik; dis'sol.u.ble [-jubl] *adj.* erir, eritilebilir; çözülür; feshedilebilir.

dis.so.lute ☐ ['disəlu:t] ahlâksız, sefih, çapkın; dis.so'lu.tion *n.* eri(t)me; sona erme; ölüm.

dis.solv.a.ble [di'zɔlvəbl] *adj.* erir, eri-tilebilir; çözülebilir; feshedilebilir; dis'solve 1. *v/t.* eritmek; feshetmek; çözmek, halletmek (*a. fig.*); *v/i.* eri-mek; *fig.* eriyip gitmek; 2. *n. Am. film:* resmi yeni bir resim ile yavaş yavaş ortadan kaldırma; dis'solv.ent 1. *adj.* eritici, çözücü; 2. *n.* eritici madde.

dis.so.nance ['disənəns] *n.* MUS ahenk-sizlik, uyumsuzluk; akortsuzluk; 'dis-so.nant *adj.* MUS ahenksiz; akortsuz; *fig.* farklı olan (*from* -den).

dis.suade [di'sweid] *v/t.* vazgeçirmek, caydırmak (*from* -den); dis'sua.sion [-ʒən] *n.* vazgeçirme; dis'sua.sive [-siv] ☐ caydırıcı.

dis.taff ['distɑ:f] *n.* öreke, yün eğirmek-te kullanılan bir ucu çatal değnek; *fig.* kadın işi; ~ *side* ailenin kadın tarafı.

dis.tance ['distəns] 1. *n.* mesafe; uzaklık; ara; menzil; *at a* ~ uzakta; belirli bir mesafede; *in the* ~ uzakta; *a great* ~ *away* oldukça uzak; *striking* ~ vurulabilecek uzaklık; tesir sahası; *keep one's* ~ mesafe bırakmak, sokulmamak; *keep s.o. at a* ~ fazla samimi olmamak; 2. *v/t.* geride bırakmak (*a. fig.*); '~ *learn.ing n.* uzaktan öğrenim; 'dis.tant ☐ uzak, ırak; soğuk, mesafeli; ~ *control* uzaktan kontrol.

dis.taste ['dis'teist] *n.* tiksinme, nefret (*for*); hoşlanmayış; *fig.* antipati (*for*); dis'taste.ful ☐ iğrenç, nahoş, antipatik.

dis.tem.per¹ [dis'tempə] 1. *n.* su ile in-celtilebilen bir tür boya; 2. *v/t.* bu boya ile boyamak.

dis.tem.per² [-] *n.* bir tür köpek has-talığı; POL rahatsızlık; dis'tem.pered *adj.* çılgın, hasta, deli.

dis.tend [dis'tend] *v/t. & v/i.* şiş(ir)-mek; yay(ıl)mak; ger(il)mek; dis'ten-sion *n.* şişme, yayılma, gerilme.

dis.tich ['distik] *n.* beyit, iki mısra.

dis.til(l) ['dis'til] *vb.* imbikten çek(il)-mek; CHEM damıtmak; *fig.* sızdırmak; damla damla ak(ıt)mak; (*kitap, fikir, konu*) özünü çıkarmak *veya* almak; dis.til.late ['-lit] *n.* damıtılmış sıvı, öz; dis.til.lation [-'leiʃən] *n.* damıtma, öz; dis'till.er *n.* viski, rakı gibi alkollü içki imal eden kimse; dis'till.er.y *n.* içki imal edilen yer.

dis.tinct ☐ [dis'tiŋkt] ayrı, farklı; belli, açık; dis'tinc.tion *n.* ayırma, ayırt etme, temayüz, üstünlük; nişan; *draw a* ~ *between* arasında farklılık yaratmak; *have the* ~ *of* üstünlük *veya* farklılığa sahip olm.; dis'tinc.tive ☐ ayıran, özellik belirten, orijinal, karakteristik (*of*); dis'tinct.ness *n.* fark, çeşitlilik; açıklık.

dis.tin.guish [dis'tiŋgwiʃ] *v/t.* ayır-mak, ayırt etm.; anlamak; sivrilmek, temayüz etm.; dis'tin.guish.a.ble *adj.* ayırt edilebilir, farkedilebilir; dis-'tin.guished *adj.* seçkin, mümtaz, kibar, meşhur.

dis.tort [dis'tɔ:t] *v/t.* bükmek, burk-mak; *fig.* yanlış anlam vermek, saptır-mak; bozmak, tahrif etm.; ~*ing mirror* eğlence aynası, dev aynası; dis'tor.tion (*söz*) ters anlam verme; çarpıklık, bo-zukluk.

dis.tract [dis'trækt] *v/t.* (*kişi veya aklını*) başka yöne çekmek; rahatsız etm.; şaşırtmak; deli etm.; dis'tract.ed ☐ şaşırmış, deli, çılgın; *k-den* geçmiş (*with ile*); dis'tract.ing ☐ deli eden, çıldırtan; dis'trac.tion *n.* karışıklık; eğlence; çılgınlık; dikkati başka yöne çekme.

dis.train [dis'trein] *v/i.* haczetmek (*on, upon*); dis'train.a.ble *adj.* haczoluna-bilir; dis.traint [-'treint] *n.* haciz, el koyma.

dis.traught [dis'trɔ:t] *adj.* aklı başın-dan gitmiş, çılgın.

dis.tress [dis'tres] 1. *n.* sıkıntı, zaruret, dert, ıstırap; tehlike; = *distraint*; ~ *rocket* NAUT tehlike işareti; 2. *v/t.* sıkıntıya sokmak, rahatsız etm., canını sıkmak, ıstırap çektirmek; dis'tressed *adj.* endişeli; sıkıntı çeken (*for* için); ~

area işsizliğin yoğun olduğu bölge; **dis'tressful** □ [_-ful] *lit.* ıstıraplı, keder verici, acıklı; **dis'tress.ing** □ eziyetli; acıklı.

dis.trib.ut.a.ble [dis'tribjutəbl] *adj.* dağıtılabilir, yayılabilir; **dis'trib.ute** [_-ju:t] *v/t.* dağıtmak, yaymak (**among**, **to**); bölüştürmek, taksim etm. (*mal*); TYP yazı harflerini yerlerine dağıtmak; **dis.tri'bu.tion** *n.* dağıtım; yayılma; taksim etme; **dis'trib.u.tive** *adj.* dağıtan, yayan; GR «her», «her bir» gibi sıfatların anlamını ifade eden **dis-'trib.u.tor** *n.* dağıtan; MED distribütör; COM satıcı, dağıtım yeri.

dis.trict ['distrikt] *n.* bölge; ilçe, kaza, mahalle.

dis.trust [dis'trʌst] **1.** *n.* güvensizlik, şüphe (*of*); **2.** *v/t.* inanmamak, güvenmemek (*-e*); **dis'trust.ful** □ [_-ful] şüpheci, kuşkulu; **~** (*of o.s.*) çekingen, utangaç.

dis.turb [dis'tə:b] *v/t.* karıştırmak, düzenini bozmak; rahatsız etm.; **dis-'turb.ance** *n.* karışıklık; rahatsızlık; **~** *of the peace* JUR *b-nin* hak ve hukukuna saldırı, güvenliğin bozulması; **dis-'turb.er** *n.* huzuru bozan.

dis.un.ion ['dis'ju:njən] *n.* ayrılma; anlaşmazlık, ara bozukluğu; **dis.u.nite** ['_-'nait] *vb.* ayrılmak; aralarını bozmak, ayırmak.

dis.use 1. ['dis'ju:s] *n.* kullanılmayış; ***fall into* ~** kullanılmaz olm.; **2.** ['dis-'ju:z] *v/t. bşi* artık kullanmamak; **dis-used** *adj.* eski, vaktini doldurmuş.

di.syl.lab.ic ['disi'læbik] *adj.* (**~ally**) iki heceli; **di.syl.la.ble** [di'siləbl] *n.* iki heceli sözcük.

ditch [ditʃ] **1.** *n.* hendek; ***die in the last* ~** sonuna kadar dayanmak; **2.** *v/t.* hendeğe yuvarlamak; *v/i.* hendeke açmak; hendekle çevirmek; *Am. sl.* kurtulmak, kaçmak *-den*; **'ditch.er** *n.* hendek açan kimse *ya da* makine.

dith.er ['diðə] *v/i.* titremek; şaşırıp kalmak.

dith.y.ramb ['diθiræmb] *n.* coşkulu ve duygulu bir deyişle yazılmış yazı, şiir.

dit.to ['ditəu] *adj.* yukarıdaki gibi; aynen; *adv.* keza, aynı veçhile, gibi; (*suit of*) **~s** aynı tip elbise, üniforma.

dit.ty ['diti] *n.* şarkı sözü.

di.ur.nal □ [dai'ə:nl] günlük; gündüze ait, gündüz olan.

di.va.ga.tion [daivə'geiʃən] *n.* sapma, ayrılma, konu dışına çıkma.

di.van [di'væn] *n.* sedir, divan; **~bed** ['daivænbed] *n.* divan, yatak.

di.var.i.cate [dai'værikeit] *v/i.* çatallaşmak; BIOL kollara, şubelere ayrılmak.

dive [daiv] **1.** *v/i.* dalmak (*into -e*); AVIA pike yapmak; F başını eğmek, sinmek; **~** *into* elini daldırmak; **2.** *n.* yüzme: dalış, balıkhana dalma (*a. fig.*); batakhane; pike uçuşu, baş aşağı dalış; *Am.* F *boks*: rakibin kasıtlı olarak yenmesini sağlama; **'~bomb** *v/t.* dalış yaparak bombalamak; **'div.er** *n.* dalgıç.

di.verge [dai'və:dʒ] *v/i.* birbirinden ayrılmak, farklı olm.; **di'ver.gence**; **di'vergen.cy** *n.* ayrılma, uzaklaşma; **di'vergent** □ birbirine karşı, muhalif, farklı.

di.vers ['daivə:z] *adj.* muhtelif, çeşitli.

di.verse □ [dai'və:s] çeşitli, değişik; **di-ver.si.fi.ca.tion** [_-fi'keiʃən] *n.* çeşitlilik, değişkenlik; **di'ver.si.fy** [_-fai] *v/t.* çeşitli ve değişik şekle sokmak; **di-ver.sion** [dai'və:ʃən] *n.* başka tarafa çevirme, saptırma; eğlence; **di'version.a.ry** *n.* MIL şaşırtma hareketi, taktikler; **di'ver.si.ty** [_-siti] *n.* fark, başkalık, çeşit, tür.

di.vert [dai'və:t] *v/t.* saptırmak; (*trafik*) başka yöne çevirmek; eğlendirmek.

di.vest [dai'vest] *v/t.* soymak, çıkarmak; mahrum etm.; **~** *o.s. of bşden* özveride bulunmak, *k-ni* yoksun bırakmak; **di'vest.ment** *n.* soy(ul)ma; yoksun ol(un)ma.

di.vide [di'vaid] **1.** *v/t. usu.* **~** *up* bölmek, ayırmak, taksim etm. (**among**); dağıtmak; aralarını açmak; MATH bölmek (**by**); **~** *the house* PARL *bşi* oya koymak; *v/i.* ayrılmak, bölünmek; MATH bölünmek (**by**); kesirsiz bölünmek (*into*); PARL oy vermek; **2.** *n.* su bölümü çizgisi; **div.i.dend** ['dividend] *n.* COM kâr hissesi; temettü; MATH bölünen; **'div.i.dend-war.rant** COM kupon (*esham ve tahvilat*); **di.vi.ders** [di'vai-dəz] *n. pl.* pergel; **di'vid.ing** bölen...; **~** *ridge* su bölüm çizgisi; çatı sırtı.

div.i.na.tion [divi'neiʃən] *n.* fal açma, kehanette bulunma; **di.vine** [di'vain] **1.** □ ilahi (*a. fig.*), kutsal; **~** *service* ibadet; **2.** *n.* imam, papaz; **3.** *vb.* sezmek, hissetmek; fala bakarak kehanette bulunmak; **di'vin.er** *n.* falcı, önceden haber veren kimse; değnekle su *veya* maden damarı arayan kimse.

div.ing ['daiviŋ] *n. yüzme:* tramplenden atlama; *attr.* dalgıç...; **'~bell** *n.*

dalgıç fanusu, haznesi; '~board n. tramplen; '~dress, '~suit n. dalgıç elbisesi.

di.vin.ing-rod [di'vainiŋrɔd] n. yeraltında su ya da maden damarı aramakta kullanılan çatal şeklinde çubuk; di.vin.i.ty [di'viniti] n. tanrılık niteliği; ilâhiyat.

di.vis.i.bil.i.ty [divizi'biliti] n. bölünebilme; di'vis.i.ble □ [-zəbl] bölünebilir; di'vision [-ʒən] n. böl(ün)me, taksim; ayırma; bölüm; ayrılma; kısım, daire; bölge; kaza, nahiye; MIL tümen; MATH bölme; PARL oylamada ikiye ayrılma; ~ of labo(u)r işbölümü; di'vi.sion.al [-zənl] adj. bölme veya bölünme ile ilgili; MIL kıta...; birlik...; di.vi.sive [di'vaisiv] adj. bölen; anlaşmazlık çıkaran; di'vi.sor MATH [-zə] n. bölen.

di.vorce [di'vɔːs] 1. n. boşanma; fig. ayrılış, ayrılma; 2. v/t. & v/i. boşa(n)mak; ayrılmak; ilgisini kesmek; di-'vor.cee [di:vɔ'siː] n. boşanmış kadın; di.vorc.er [di'vɔːsə] n. boşanmaya neden olan.

di.vulge [dai'vʌldʒ] v/t. ifşa etm., açığa vurmak, söylemek, yaymak.

dix.ie MIL sl. ['diksi] n. karavana; ♀ Am. pl. Amerika Birleşik Devletleri'nin güney eyaletleri; ♀ crat Am. POL bu eyaletlerdeki muhalefet; demokrat partililer.

DIY [diːai'wai] (= do-it-yourself) kişinin bir işi, uzmanına başvurmak yerine, kendisinin yapması.

diz.zi.ness ['diziniz] n. baş dönmesi, sersemlik; 'diz.zy 1. □ (kişi) baş döndürücü; (nesne) baş döndüren; 2. v/t. baş döndürmek, sersemletmek.

do [duː] (irr.) (s. a. done) 1. v/t. yapmak; etmek; hazırlanmak; bitirmek; mesafe katetmek; pişirmek; (rol) oynamak; F dolandırmak, kafese koymak; uygun gelmek, yakışmak; ~ London F Londra'yı gezmek; ~ s.o. F b-ne bakmak, beslemek; what is to be done? yapılacak ne var?; ~ the polite etc. nezaket taslamak; have done reading okumayı bitirmiş olm.; ~ a room odayı toplamak; ~ (over) again bir kere daha yapmak; ~ down üstesinden gelmek, alt etm.; ~ in F öldürmek; ~ into tercüme etm.; ~ out süpürmek temizlemek; ~ over (boya vs.) üzerine sürmek; ~ up tamir etm., yenileştirmek; ambalaj yapmak; bağlamak, iliklemek; güzelleştirmek -i; F benzetmek, sakatlamak;

2. v/i. davranmak; bulunmak, olmak; kâfi gelmek, yetmek; elverisli olm., uymak; that will ~ yeter, yetişir; that won't ~ yetmez; how ~ you ~? nasılsınız?; ~ well işi iyi gitmek, iyi para kazanmak; ~ badly işini becerememek; have done! yetişir!, sus!; ~ away with feshetmek, kaldırmak; öldürmek; ~ for b-ne bakmak; ~ with bşde rolü olm.; ...le ilgili olm.; ihtiyacı olm. -e; I could ~ with ... ...olsa fena olmaz; have done with bitirmek, son vermek; ~ without muhtaç olmamak -e; 3. v/aux. soru: ~ you know him? onu tanıyormusunuz?; olumsuz: I ~ not know him onu tanımıyorum; vurgulama: I ~ feel better kendimi gerçekten iyi hissediyorum; ~ come and see me ne olur gel ve beni gör; ~ be quick acele etsene; bir önceki fiilin yerine: you like London? — I do. Londra'yı severmisiniz? — Evet; you write better than I ~ benden daha iyi yazıyorsunuz; I take a bath every day. — So ~ I her gün banyo yaparım. — Ben de; 4. I n. dalavere; büyük olay; şenlik; ziyafet, parti.

doc F [dɔk] = doctor.

doc.ile ['dəusail] adj. uslu, uysal, yumuşak başlı; do.cil.i.ty [-'siliti] n. usluluk, uysallık, yumuşak başlılık.

dock[1] [dɔk] v/t. (kuyruk vs.) kısaltmak, kırpmak; (ücret) azaltmak (off).

dock[2] BOT [-] n. kuzukulağı tu.

dock[3] [-] 1. n. NAUT havuz, dok; esp. Am. rıhtım; JUR sanık yeri; dry ~, graving ~ kuru havuz; floating ~ yüzer havuz; wet ~ su bentli havuz; 2. vb. NAUT havuza çekmek; rıhtıma yanaşmak; '~dues n. pl. havuz veya rıhtım ücreti; 'dock.er n. liman işçisi.

dock.et ['dɔkit] 1. n. yafta, yapılacak işler listesi; gündem; sipariş listesi; etiket; adres etiketi; JUR bekleyen davalar listesi; 2. v/t. listeye kaydetmek, özetlemek; etiketlemek.

dock.yard ['dɔkjaːd] n. tersane.

doc.tor ['dɔktə] 1. n. doktor, hekim; 2. vb. F b-ni tedavi etm.; tamir etm.; tahrif etm., üzerinde değişiklik yapmak, hile karıştırmak; doc.tor.ate ['-rit] n. doktora.

doc.tri.naire [dɔkri'nɛə] 1. n. kuramcı, nazariyeci, doktriner; 2. adj. kuramsal, nazari; doc.tri.nal □ [-'trainl] kuram veya doktrine ait; doc.trine ['-trin] n. doktrin, öğreti.

doc.u.ment 1. ['dɔkjumənt] *n.* belge, vesika, senet, delil; **2.** ['_ment] *v/t.* belgelerle kanıtlamak, belgelemek; **doc-u'menta.ry 1.** ☐ dökümanter, belgelere dayanan, yazılı, belgesel; ~ *film* = **2.** *n.* belgesel film; **doc.u'men.ta.tion** *n.* belgeleme, belgelerle kanıtlama.

dod.der ['dɔdə] **1.** *n.* BOT küsküt; **2.** *v/i.* yaşlılık nedeniyle titremek, sallanmak, sendelemek.

dodge [dɔdʒ] **1.** *n.* oyun, kurnazlık; kurtulma, yana kaçış; **2.** *v/t.* atlatmak; bertaraf etm.; *v/i.* kaçamak bulmak, kenara sıçramak; kaçınmak *-den*; *fig.* dolambaçlı yoldan gitmek, ağız yapmak; *bşden* sıyrılmak; **dod.gem** F ['dɔd-ʒəm] *n.* (*esp. pl.*) çarpışan otomobil; **'dodg.er** *n.* hilekâr kimse, madrabaz, vurguncu; *Am.* küçük el ilânı; *Am.* mısır unundan yapılan bir tür kek.

do-do ORN ['dəudəu] *n.* nesli tükenmiş ve güvercin cinsinden uçmayan bir tür kuş.

doe [dəu] *n.* ZOO dişi geyik *veya* tavşan.

do.er ['duːə] *n.* yapan, eden kimse, fail.

does [dʌz] (*he, she, it*) yapmak (*s. do*).

doe.skin ['dəuskin] *n.* dişi geyik *veya* karaca derisi.

doesn't F ['dʌznt] = **does not** (*s. do*).

dog [dɔg] **1.** *n.* köpek, it; kurt; MEC mandal; sac ayağı; maşa, raptiye; kanca; MIN kömür vagonu; F herif; *Am.* F fazla naz, tafra; **go to the ~s** sefalete düşmek, mahvolmak; **2.** *v/t. b-nin* peşine takılmak, izini araştırmak; **'~bis.cuit** *n.* köpek bisküviti; **'~cart** *n.* arka arkaya iki kişilik oturacak yeri olan tek atlı araba, büyük bir köpek tarafından çekilen hafif araba; **'~cheap** *adj.* sudan ucuz; **'~days** *n. pl.* yılın en sıcak günleri.

doge [dəudʒ] *n.* eski Venedik ve Cenova Dükası.

dog...: **'~eared** = **dog's-eared**; **'~fight** *n.* F hava savaşı; **'~fish** *n.* ZOO bir kaç tür küçük köpek balığı.

dog.ged ☐ ['dɔgid] *n.* inatçı, bildiğinden şaşmaz.

dog.ger.el ['dɔgərəl] *n. a.* ~ *rhymes pl.* edebî değeri olmayan şiir.

dog.gish ['dɔgiʃ] *adj.* köpek gibi; homurdanan; huysuz, ters; **dog.go** *sl.* ['dɔgəu] *adv.:* **lie** ~ sessizce ve hareket etmeden saklandığı yerde durmak; **'dog.gy 1.** *n.* (*çocuk dilinde*) köpek; **2.** *adj.* köpeksever, köpeğe düşkün; köpeğe ait; **'dog-'Lat.in** *n.* kötü ve yanlış

Latince; **'~like** *adj.* köpek gibi sadık.

do.gie *Am.* ['dəugi] *n.* annesiz buzağı.

dog.ma ['dɔgmə] *n.* dogma, inak, doktrin; akide; **dog.mat.ic, dog.mat.i.cal** ☐ [_'mætik(əl)] dogmatik, kesin; iman ve itikada ait; öğretici; kestirip atan, başına buyruk; **dog'mat.ics** *n. sg.* dini dogmaların sistematik olarak incelenmesi; **dog.ma.tism** ['_mətizəm] *n.* dogmatizm, inakçılık; fikir açıklamada kesinlik; **'dog.ma.tist** *n.* dogmatik kimse, kesin fikir beyan eden kimse; **dog.ma.tize** ['_mətaiz] *v/i.* kesin olarak fikrini söylemek, kestirip atmak.

dog's-bod.y *sl.* ['dɔgzbɔdi] *n.* köle gibi çalışan; rençber, hamal; **'dog's-ear** *n.* (*kitap*) sayfanın kıvrılan köşesi; **'dog's-eared** *adj.* köşesi kıvrık (*sayfa*).

dog...: '~**tired** *adj.* çok yorgun, bitkin; '~**tooth** *n.* (*kumaş*) kareli desen (*ekose*), ARCH taş oymacılığında küçük piramit şeklinde süsleme; '~**trot** *n.* yavaş koşma; '~**watch** NAUT akşam üzeri 4-6 ya da 6-8 nöbeti; '~**wood** BOT *n.* kızılcığa benzer bir tür ağaç.

doi.ly ['dɔili] *n.* tabak *ya da* süs eşyası altına konan dantel *veya* işlemeli küçük örtü.

do.ing ['duːiŋ] **1.** *p. pr. of* **do 1.** *vb.* **nothing** ~ ağzınla kuş tutsan bile nafile; COM iş güç yok; **2.** *n.* eylem, hareket, iş; ~**s** *pl.* yapılan işler, olan şeyler; davranış.

doit [dɔit] *n.* metelik, mangır; eski Avusturya kronunun yüzde biri.

dol.drums ['dɔldrəmz] *n. pl.* ümitsizlik, kasvet, durgunluk, cam sıkkın olma; NAUT okyanusun rüzgârsız olan ekvatora yakın kısımları.

dole [dəul] **1.** *n.* teberru, sadaka, muhtaç kimselere yiyecek, giyecek vs. dağıtımı; F işsizlere verilen haftalık hükümet yardımı; **be** *veya* **go on the** ~ hükümetten işsizlik parası almak; **2.** *v/t. mst* ~ **out** azar azar dağıtmak (**to** -*e*).

dole.ful ☐ ['dəulful] üzüntülü, mahzun, melânkolik; **'dole.ful.ness** *n.* hüzün, üzüntü, keder, gam.

doll [dɔl] **1.** *n.* bebek, kukla (*a. fig.*); **2.** *vb.* ~ **up** F süsle(n)mek, şık giyinmek, giydirmek.

dol.lar ['dɔlə] *n.* dolar, 100 sent karşılığı olan Amerikan para birimi.

dol.lop F ['dɔləp] *n.* topak, toparlak parça, bir miktar.

doll.y ['dɔli] *n.* (*çocuk dilinde*) bebek; iki tekerlekli yük taşıyıcısı; film *veya* televizyon kamerasını taşıyan tekerlekli araç.

dol.o.mite MIN ['dɔləmait] *n.* kalsiyum, magnezyum ve karbonattan ibaret bir tür beyaz mermer, dolomi.

dol.o(u)r *mst poet.*, *co.* ['dəulə] *n.* keder, elem, dert, azap; **dol.o.rous** ['dɔlərəs] *adj.* kederli, elemli, üzüntülü.

dol.phin ICHTH ['dɔlfin] *n.* yunusbalığı.

dolt [dəult] *n.* ahmak, budala, kalın kafalı kimse; **'dolt.ish** ☐ kafasız, budala, ahmak.

do.main [dəu'mein] *n.* mülk, arazi, alan; IT etki alanı (*internette*); *fig.* nüfuz sahası, çevre, muhit.

dome [dəum] *n.* kubbe; MEC kapak, dosya gömleği, kitap kabı; **domed** *adj.* kubbeli, kemerli.

Domes.day Book ['du:mzdei'buk] *n.* 1086'da İngiltere'de Kral I. William'ın emri ile hazırlanan tapu sicili.

do.mes.tic [dəu'mestik] **1.** *adj.* (**~ally**) eve ait, ehlî, evcil; yerli; **~ animal** evcil hayvan; **~ coal** ev için kullanılan kömür; **~ science** ev idaresi bilimi; **2.** *n. a.* **~ servant** hizmetçi kız; **~s** *pl.* evde kullanılan eşyalar; **do'mes.ti.cate** [-keit] *v/t.* evcilleştirmek, ehlileştirmek, alıştırmak; **do.mes.ti'ca.tion** *n.* alıştırma, evcilleş(tir)me; **do.mes.tic.i.ty** [-'tisiti] *n.* aile hayatı; evcimenlik.

dom.i.cile ['dɔmisail] **1.** *n. esp.* JUR daimî ikametgah yeri, mesken, oturma yeri, konut; **2.** *vb.* COM (*kambiyo*) tediye etm., ödemek; oturmak, ikamet etm., yerleş(tir)mek; **'dom.i.ciled** *adj.* yerleşmiş, mukim, sakin; **dom.i.cil.i.ar.y** [-'siljəri] *adj.* eve ait; **~ visit** arama, ev araştırması; MED hasta ziyareti, vizita.

dom.i.nance ['dɔminəns] *n.* hâkimiyet, selâhiyet, tahakküm, üstünlük; **'dom.i.nant 1.** *adj.* hâkim, üstün; **2.** *n.* MUS dominant, sol notasına ait; **dom.i.nate** ['-neit] *v/t. & v/i.* idaresi altına almak, hakim olm. *-e*; üstün olm. *-e*; **dom.i'na.tion** *n.* egemenlik, hükmetme; **'dom.i.na.tor** *n.* hükümdar; **dom.i.neer** [dɔmi'niə] *v/t.* tahakküm altında tutmak; zorbalık etm.; **~ over** *b-ne* zulmetmek, gaddarlık etm.; **domi'neer.ing** ☐ otoriter, despotça davranan, zalim.

do.min.i.cal [də'minikəl] *adj.* pazar (*veya* Rab [İsa]) gününe ait; **~ prayer**

Hıristiyanların fatihaya benzetilebilen duası.

Do.min.i.can [də'minikən] *n.* Sen Dominik papazı.

do.min.ion [də'minjən] *n.* hüküm, hakimiyet, dominyon; *usu.* **~s** *pl.* arazi, ülke; nüfuz sahası (*a. fig.*); ☙ POL dominyon, müstemleke (*İngiliz milletler topluluğu içinde*).

dom.i.no ['dɔminəu] *n.* domino taşı; maskeli kostüm; **dom.i.noes** ['-z] *n. pl.* domino oyunu.

don[1] UNIV [dɔn] *n.* öğretim görevlisi.

don[2] [-] *v/t.* giydirmek.

do.nate *Am.* [dəu'neit] *v/t.* bağışlamak *-e*, hediye etm. *-e*, iane vermek *-e*; **do'nation**, **don.a.tive** ['-nətiv] *n.* bağış, iane, hibe.

done [dʌn] **1.** *p.p. of* **do**; **be ~** *usu.* yapılmak; bitkin olm.; **2.** *adj.* tamamlanmış, bitmiş; *a.* **~ up** bitkin; hazır; **well ~** (*yemek*) iyi pişmiş; **he is ~ for** mahvolmuş, bitkin; **3.** *int.* tamam!, kabul!.

do.nee JUR [dəu'ni:] *n.* bağışta bulunan kimse *veya* kurum.

don.jon ['dɔndʒən] *n.* eski zaman şatolarındaki muazzam kule, burç.

don.key ['dɔŋki] *n.* eşek; eşek adam, inatçı kimse; *attr.* yardımcı...; **'~-engine** *n.* yardımcı motor, palamar çekmek için kullanılan küçük yardımcı makine.

don.na ['dɔnə] *n.* hanım.

do.nor ['dəunə] *n.* veren; (*kan, böbrek vs.*) verici.

do-noth.ing F ['du:nʌθiŋ] **1.** *n.* tembel, haylaz kimse; **2.** *adj.* tembel.

don't [dəunt] **1.** = **do not**; **~!** Yapma!; **2.** *n.* yasak, memnuiyet.

doom [du:m] **1.** *n. mst b.s.* kötü kader, kötü talih; kıyamet; **2.** *v/t.* mahkûm etm. (**to** *-e*); hüküm giydirmek; **dooms.day** ['du:mzdei] *rel. n.* kıyamet günü.

door [dɔ:] *n.* kapı; **next ~** (**to**) kapı komşu; *fig.* yakın, iki adımlık yer; **two ~s off** iki ev ötede; (**with**) **in ~s** içerde, evde; **out of ~s** dışarda, açık havada; **show s.o. the ~** *b-ni* kovmak, kapıyı göstermek; **turn out of the ~s** *b-ni* kapı dışarı etm.; **lay s.th. to** *veya* **at s.o.'s ~** *b-ne* kabahat yüklemek; **'~-bell** *n.* kapı zili; **'~-case**, **'~-frame** *n.* kapı çerçevesi; **'~-han.dle** *n.* kapı mandalı; **'~-keep.er**, **'~.man** *n.* kapıcı; **'~-mat** *n.* paspas; **'~-nail** *n.* eskiden kullanılan iri başlı kapı çivisi; **dead as a ~**

ölmüş gitmiş; ~plate *n.* isim yazılı kapı tabelâsı; ~post *n.* kapı pervazı; '~step *n.* eşik; '~way *n.* kapı yeri, giriş; '~yard *n. Am.* ev avlusu.

dope [dəup] **1.** *n.* yağlı ve yapışkan madde; *esp.* AVIA vernik, cilâ; sinir uyarıcı, uyuşturucu madde, esrar, afyon; *Am. sl.* haber, malumat; budala; baş dönmesi; **2.** *v/t.* cilâlamak, verniklemek; ilaçla sersemletmek; *spor:* doping yapmak, uyarıcı ilaç vermek; *Am. sl.* halletmek; 'dope.y *adj. Am. sl.* budala, uyuşuk.

Dor.ic ['dɔrik] *adj.* Dorlara ait; ~ *order* en eski ve basit Yunan mimari tarzı.

dorm F [dɔːm] = *dormitory.*

dor.mant ['dɔːmənt] *adj. mst fig.* uyuyan, uyuşuk, cansız, uykuda gibi hareketsiz; ~ *partner* özel ortak, komanditer.

dor.mer(-win.dow) ['dɔːmə('windəu)] *n.* çatı penceresi.

dor.mi.to.ry ['dɔːmitri] *n.* yatakhane, koğuş; *esp. Am.* öğrenci yurdu.

dor.mouse ['dɔːmaus] *n., pl.* dormice ['dɔːmais] sincaba benzer bir tür küçük orman faresi.

dor.sal □ ['dɔːsəl] sırta ait; arkada, arka tarafa ait.

do.ry NAUT ['dɔːri] *n.* bir tür yassı kayık; bir tür büyük deniz balığı.

dose [dəus] **1.** *n.* doz; **2.** *v/t. a.* ~ *with* belirli miktarda ilaç vermek; (*şarap vs.*) su katmak *-e.*

doss-house *sl.* ['dɔshaus] *n.* ucuz kalacak yer (*han*).

dos.si.er ['dɔsiei] *n.* evrak dosyası.

dost *obs.* [dʌst, dəst] *you do* (*s.* do).

dot [dɔt] **1.** *n.* nokta, benek, ufak leke; *on the* ~ tam vaktinde; **2.** *v/t.* noktalamak, benek benek yapmak; *a.* ~ *about fig.* dağıtmak, oraya buraya saçmak; ~ted *adj.* noktalı, benekli.

dot.age ['dəutidʒ] *n.* bunaklık, ikinci çocukluk; aşırı düşkünlük, iptilâ; **do-tard** ['-təd] *n.* bunak kimse; **dote** [dəut] *v/t. & v/i.* bunamak; düşkün olm., aşırı sevmek, çılgınca sevdalanmak (*on, upon -e*).

doth *obs.* [dʌθ, dəθ] = does (*s.* do).

dot.ing ['dəutiŋ] □ çılgınca seven (*on -i*).

dot.ty *sl.* [dɔti] *n.* sarsak, aptal, budala.

dou.ble ['dʌbl] **1.** □ çift, iki misli, iki kat; bükülmüş, katlı; iki kişilik. **2.** *n.* iki kat, çift; aynı, eş; dublör, tam benzeri; hile, oyun, MIL koşar adım; **3.** *v/t.*

ikilemek, iki kat etm., duble etm.; *a.* ~ *up* eğmek, kıvırmak, iki büklüm etm., (*bilek*) bükmek; ~*d up adj.* eğilmiş, iki büklüm olmuş; *be ~d up with* eğilmek, iki büklüm olm.; *v/i.* iki misli olm.; *a.* ~ *back* aynı yoldan geri dönmek; MIL koşar adım ilerlemek; *kâğıt oyunu:* duble etm., kontr etm.; ~ *up* bükülmek, ikiye katlanmak; '~bar.relled *adj.* çift namlulu; *fig.* iki anlamlı, şüpheli (*söz*); ~ *name* iki addan oluşan soyadı; '~'bass MUS *n.* kontrbas; '~bed.ded *n.* çift yataklı; '~'breasted *adj.* çift düğmeli, kruvaze (*ceket*); '~'click *bilgisayar v/i.* çift tıklamak; '~'cross *sl. v/t.* (ortak) kazık atmak, al datmak; '-'deal.er *n.* iki yüzlü kimse, dolandırıcı; '~'deal.ing *n.* iki yüzlülük, dolandırıcılık; '~'deck.er *n.* iki katlı (*yatak, tekne, otobüs, sandviç*); '~'dyed *adj. fig.* ıslah olmaz, kaşarlanmış (*hırsız, yalancı*); '~'edged *adj.* iki taraflı (*a. fig.*); '~'en.try NAUT *n.* muzaaf kayıt, muhasebede çift defter tutma usulü; '~faced *adj.* iki yüzlü, iki taraflı; '~'fea.ture *n. Am.* iki film birden (*sinema*); '~'head.er *n. Am.* beysbol: iki takım arasında üst üste yapılan iki, karşılaşma; '~'line RAIL *n.* çift ray; 'dou.ble.ness *n.* çift olma durumu; *fig.* iki anlamlılık; 'dou.ble-park *vb.* kaldırıma paralel park etmiş bir arabanın yanına park etm.; 'double-'quick MIL *n.* hızlı yürüyüş.

dou.blet ['dʌblit] *n.* eş, çift, aynısı; HIST ceket; ~s *pl.* çift gelen zarlar.

dou.ble…: '~'talk *n.* lastikli söz; '~time *sl. v/t.* dolandırmak, kafese koymak; '~'track *n.* çift hat.

doub.ling ['dʌbliŋ] *n.* ikileme, duble etme; katlama; geminin burnu dolaşması; 'doub.ly *adv.* çifte, iki kat.

doubt [daut] **1.** *v/i.* kuşkulanmak, şüphelenmek (*about -den*); *v/t.* şüphe etm.; tereddüt etm.; **2.** *n.* şüphe, tereddüt, endişe; güvensizlik; *no* ~ hiç şüphesiz, elbette; 'doubt.er *n.* şüpheci, septik; doubtful □ ['-ful] şüpheli, kararsız, karanlık, muğlak, belirsiz; *be* ~ kestirememek, bir türlü bilememek; 'doubt.ful.ness *n.* şüpheli durum, tereddüt; 'doubt.less *adv.* şüphesiz, muhakkak.

douche [duːʃ] **1.** *n.* duş; MED şırınga; **2.** *vb.* dus yapmak, sudan geçirmek; şırınga etm.

dough [dəu] *n.* hamur; *sl.* para; '~boy

n. Am. F piyade; '**~.nut** *n.* çörek.

dough.ty *co.* ['dauti] *adj.* yiğit, cesaret-li.

dough.y ['dəui] *adj.* hamurumsu, iyice pişmemiş.

dour *Scots.* ['duə] *adj.* asık suratlı, ters, aksi, haşin.

douse [daus] *s.* **dowse**.

dove [dʌv] *n.* güvercin, kumru; *fig.* barış taraftarı kimse, masum ve iyi huylu kimse; '**~col.o(u)red** *adj.* pembemsi kurşuni; **~cot(e)** ['~kɔt] *n.* güvercinlik; '**~tail 1.** *n.* MEC lambalı erkek tahta; **2.** *v/t.* bu tahta ile birleştirmek; *v/i. fig.* iki şeyi uydurmak, telif etm.

dow.a.ger ['dauədʒə] *n.* ölen kocasından *k-ne* ünvan ve mal mülk kalan dul kadın.

dow.dy F ['daudi] **1.** *adj.* derbeder, üstü başı dökülen, kılıksız; **2.** *n.* pasaklı kadın.

dow.el MEC ['dauəl] *n.* ağaç çivi, takoz, kama.

dow.er ['dauə] **1.** *n.* kadının ölen kocasının terekesi üzerindeki kanuni hissesi; *fig.* drahoma; **2.** *v/t.* çeyiz *veya* ağırlık vermek.

down[1] [daun] *n.* ince kuş tüyü, pufla; ayva tüyü, hav.

dow[2][_] = **dune**; **~s** ağaçsız tepeler, dağ sırtları, eksibe, kumul.

down[3] [_] **1.** *adv.* aşağı(ya); aşağıda; **~ and out** *fig.* bitkin, argın, hayatta yenilgiye uğramış; **be ~** (*fiyat*) düşmek, azalmak; **be ~ upon** F *b-ne* acımasız davranmak; **~ in the country** şehir dışında, köyde, taşrada; **~ under** F Avustralya *veya* Yeni Zelanda'da; **2.** *prp.* aşağı(ya); **~ the river** ırmağın aşağısına doğru; **~ (the) wind** rüzgâr yönünde; **3.** *int.* alçak!; **4.** *adj.* **~ train** Londra'dan kalkan tren; **5.** F *v/t.* indirmek; yenmek -*i*; **~ tools** grev yapmak; **6.** *s.* **up 4**; '**~cast** *adj.* üzgün; '**~'draft**, '**~'draught** *n.* aşağı doğru giden hava akımı; **~'East.er** *n. Am.* New England'dan olan (*esp. Maine'den*); '**~fall** *n.* düşüş, yıkılış, gerileme; düşüşün nedeni olan şey *veya* kişi; (*yağmur*) boşanma; '**~grade** *v/t.* alçaltmak, derecesini indirmek; '**~'heart.ed** *adj.* cesareti kırılmış, kederli; '**~'hill 1.** *adv.* yokuş aşağı; **2.** *adj.* inişli, meyilli; '**~load** rr **1.** *v/t.* indirmek; **2.** *n.* indirilen dosya; '**~.mar.ket** *adj.* kalitesiz (*lokanta, ürün*); '**~pour** *n.* şiddetli yağmur, sağanak; '**~right 1.**

adv. tamamiyle, büsbütün, kesin olarak; **2.** *adj.* tamam; kesin, katı; çok; '**~.right.ness** *n.* açıklık, samimiyet, doğruluk, dürüstlük; '**~scale** *adj. Am.* kalitesiz (*lokanta, ürün*); *Brit.* = **downmarket**; '**~.size** *v/t.* küçültmek; '**~.siz.ing** *n.* küçültme; '**~'stairs 1.** *adv.* aşağıda, aşağıya; **2.** *adj.* aşağıda olan, aşağı, alt; '**~'stream** *adv.* akıntı yönünde; '**~stroke** *n.* alt çizgi; MEC pistonun inişi; '**~'town** *n. esp. Am.* şehrin merkezi; '**~.trod.den** *adj.* haksızlığa uğramış, ezilmiş; **~.ward** ['~wəd] **1.** *adj.* aşağı doğru olan; *fig.* kötüye doğru olan; **2.** *adv. a.* **~s** aşağı(ya) doğru; '**~.wash** *n.* AVIA hava akımının aşağı sapması.

down.y ['dauni] *adj.* ince tüylü, havlı; *fig.* kurnaz, şeytana külahını ters giydiren; pişkin.

dow.ry ['dauəri] *n.* çeyiz, drahoma; *fig.* Allah vergisi, yetenek.

dowse ['dauz] **1.** *v/t.* sulamak; söndürmek; **2.** *v/i.* değnekle yeraltında su *veya* maden damarı aramak; '**dows.er** *n.* değnekle su *veya* maden damarı araştıran; '**dows.ing-rod** *n.* yeraltında su aramak için kullanılan ucu çatal şeklinde değnek.

doze [dəuz] **1.** *v/i.* uyuklamak, (**~away**) dalmak; **2.** *n.* hafif uyku, şekerleme.

doz.en ['dʌzn] *n.* düzine; *talk nineteen to the~* hiç durmadan konuşmak, çene çalmak.

drab [dræb] **1.** *adj.* sarımtrak kurşuni; *fig.* monoton, usandırıcı; **2.** *n.* bu renk kumaş; fahişe, orospu; *fig.* monotonluk.

drachm [dræm] *n.* dirhem; = **drach.ma** ['drækmə] *n.* Yunan drahmisi.

draff [dræf] *n.* tortu, posa.

draft [drɑːft] **1.** *n.* tasarı, taslak, müsvedde, kroki; COM poliçe, çek; MIL mecburi askerliğe alma; = **draught**; **~ agreement** mukavele taslağı; **2.** *v/t.* tasarlamak, çizmek; MIL ifraz etm., bir işe ayırmak; *Am.* askere almak, silah altına çağırmak; **draft'ee** *n.* MIL *Am.* askere çağrılan; '**drafts.man** *n.* teknik ressam.

drag [dræg] **1.** *n.* sürükleme; sürüklenen şey; tırmık; takoz, engel (*a. fig.*); tomruk vagonu; hava direnci; *sl.* sıkıcı şey *veya* kimse; **2.** *v/t.* sürüklemek, çekmek; AGR tırmıklamak; (*tekerlek*) durdurmak; = **dredge 2**; **~ along** sürüklemek; **~ out** *bşi* uzatmak; *bir yere* sürüklemek; ~ *one's feet* kasıtlı olarak yavaş hareket etm. *veya* çalışmak; ~ *up a child* gelişi güzel yetiştirmek, terbiye etmemek; *v/i.* sürüklenmek, sürünmek; ağla suyun dibini taramak **(for)**; COM durgun gitmek.

drag.gle ['drægl] *v/t. & v/i.* çamur içinde sürükleyerek ıslatıp kirletmek *veya* kirlenmek; bulaş(tır)mak; '~-tail *n.* pasaklı kadın.

drag.o.man ['drægəmən] *n.* Orta Doğu'da tercüman, rehber.

drag.on ['drægən] *n.* ejderha; '~-fly *n.* zoo yusufçuk.

dra.goon [drə'guːn] *1. n.* ağır süvari; *fig.* vahşi, hayvani; *2. v/t.* zorlamak, mecbur etm. (*into -e*).

drain [drein] **1.** *n.* lağım, su yolu, kanalizasyon, kanal; F yudum, damla; alıp götürme **(on)**; ~s *pl.* kanalizasyon şebekesi; **2.** *v/t.* akıtmak, kurutmak, akaçlamak, drenaj yapmak; (*şişe*) boşaltmak; *a.* ~ *off* içip bitirmek, tüketmek; süzmek; *v/i.* süzülmek, suyu süzülmek; '**drain.age** *n.* akaçlama, drenaj; kanalizasyon; çekilen su; '**drain.ing** *n.* boşaltma, süzme, drenaj; ~s *pl.* kanalizasyon şebekesi; '**draining-board** *n.* yıkanmış bulaşıkların süzüldüğü oluklu kab; '**drain-pipe** *n.* suyu ve artıkları dışarı akıtan boru, oluk.

drake [dreik] *n.* erkek ördek.

dram [dræm] *n.* dirhem; yudum; sert içki.

dra.ma ['drɑːmə] *n.* dram, tiyatro eseri, oyun; tiyatro edebiyatı; **dra.mat.ic** [drə'mætik] *adj.* (*~ally*) dramatik; heyecanlı; tiyatro ile lgili; **dra'mat.ics** *n. mst sg.* tiyatro, sahne faaliyeti; **dram.a.tist** ['dræmətist] *n.* oyun yazarı, piyes yazarı; **dram.a.tis per.so.nae** ['drɑːmətispə'səunai] *n. pl.* oyundaki karakterler, oyuncu listesi; **dram.a.tise** ['dræmətaiz] *v/t. & v/i.* dram şekline sokmak, tiyatro oyunu şeklinde ifade etm.; **dram.atur.gy** ['_təːdʒi] *n.* tiyatro eseri yazma sanatı.

drank [dræŋk] *pret. of* **drink 2**.

drape [dreip] *v/t.* kumaşla kaplamak; -in kıvrımlarını düzeltmek; asarak süslemek *veya* donatmak; '**drap.er** *n.* kumaşçı; '**dra.per.y** *n.* çuhacılık, kumaşçılık; perdelik kumaş, manifatura; kıvrımların düzeltilmesi.

dras.tic ['dræstik] *adj.* (*~ally*) şiddetli; açık, kesin.

draught [drɑːft] *Am.* **draft** *n.* çekme,

içme, yudum; hava cereyanı; NAUT su çekimi; büyük kabtan verilen (*bira vb.*); ~s *pl.* dama oyunu; *s.* **draft**; ~ *beer* fıçı birası; *at a* ~ bir yudumda; '~-board *n.* dama tahtası; '~-horse *n.* koşum atı; '**draughts.man** *n.* teknik ressam; = **draftsman**; '**draught.y** *adj.* cereyanlı.

draw [drɔː] **1.** (*irr.*) *v/t.* çekmek; uzatmak; çekip çıkarmak; sürüklemek, celbetmek, cezbetmek; (*silah*) çekmek; (*para*) bankadan çekmek; (*eşya vs.*) taşımak; (*kümes hayvanı*) içini temizlemek; (*faiz*) getirmek; çizmek, taslağını çizmek -*in*; (*belge, evrak*) ele geçirmek; berabere kalmak; su çekmek; (*hava, sıvı*) emmek, çekmek; germek; (*perde*) kapamak; ~ *away v/t. & v/i.* çekilmek, kendini çekmek (*from -den*); ~ *down v/t.* indirmek; ~ *forth v/t.* çekip çıkarmak; ~ *near v/i.* sokulmak, yaklaşmak; ~ *on v/t.* bşe sebep olm.; ~ *out v/t.* uzatmak; taslağını çizmek; ~ *up v/t.* tasarlamak, hazırlamak; dimdik durmak; *v/i.* yaklaşıp durmak; yerini almak; ~ (*up*)*on* COM (*senet, plan*) düzenlemek, çekmek, keşide etm.; *fig.* talebetmek, istemek; **2.** *n.* çekme; (*kur'a, piyango*) çekiliş; *spor:* berabere biten oyun; F cazibe, çok rağbetli şey; F para sızdırma; '~-back *n.* engel, sakınca; bilinmeyen tarafı -*in*; COM reddi rüsum; vergi iadesi, ihraç primi; *Am.* tazminat; '~-bridge *n.* iner kalkar köprü;

draw'ee *n.* COM poliçe keşidesinde ödeyecek olan, muhatap kişi; '**draw.er** *n.* ressam; [*mst* drɔː] çekmece, göz; COM keşideci, çeken kimse; (*pair of*) ~s *pl.* don, külot; *mst* **chest of** ~s konsol, şifoniyer.

draw.ing ['drɔːiŋ] *n.* resim; çizim; kroki, plan; piyango, çekiliş; COM keşide; *out of* ~ kötü çizilmiş; ~ *instruments pl.* çizim takımı, pergel takımı; '~-account *n.* açık hesap, vadesiz hesap ve mevduat; '~-board *n.* resim tahtası, plançete; '~-pen *n.* cetvel kalemi; '~-pin *n.* raptiye, pünez; '~-room *n.* misafir odası, salon, kabul resmi salonu.

drawl [drɔːl] **1.** *vb. a.* ~ *out* ağır ağır söylemek, konuşmak; **2.** *n.* ağır ağır konuşma.

drawn [drɔːn] **1.** *p.p. of* **draw 1**; **2.** *adj.* berabere; karara bağlanmamış; (*çehre*) süzük, gergin.

draw-well ['drɔːwel] *n.* kuyu.

dray [drei] *n. a.* ~-**cart** yük arabası,

drayman 620

kızak; '~.man *n.* arabacı.
dread [dred] **1.** *n.* korku, dehşet; çekinme; **2.** *v/t.* korkmak *-den*, endişe duymak *-den*; dread.ful □ ['_ful] **1.** korkunç, dehşetli, tüyler ürpertici; **2. penny** ~ ucuz korku romanı; dreadnought ['_nɔːt] *n.* kalın yünlü palto; NAUT eskiden kullanılan bir tür zırhlı.
dream [driːm] **1.** *n.* rüya; hülya; rüya görme; hedef, amaç; F mükemmel (*rüya gibi*) şey *veya* kişi; **2.** (*irr.*) *vb.* rüya görmek (**of**), *bşi* rüyasında görmek; ~ **away** vaktini hayal kurarak geçirmek; 'dream.er *n.* rüya gören kimse; hayalperest kimse; 'dream-land *n.* rüyalar ülkesi; 'dream-like *adj.* rüya gibi; 'dream-read.er *n.* rüya yorumcusu; dreamt [dremt] *pret. & p.p. of dream* **2.**; 'dreamy □ dalgın; hayalperest; rüya gibi; belirsiz, müphem; yatıştırıcı.
drear *poet.* [driə] = *dreary.*
drear.i.ness ['driərinis] *n.* hüzün, üzüntü, keder, melânkoli; 'drear.y □ mahzun, üzüntülü, melânkolik; can sıkıcı, ıssız.
dredge¹ [dredʒ] **1.** *n.* tarak makinesi; ağlı kepçe, ekskavatör; **2.** *v/t. a.* ~ **out** deniz dibini taramak, tarakla temizlemek (*liman, nehir*).
dredge² [_] *v/t.* üzerine serpmek (*un, kum, şeker vs.*) (**over**); bulamak (**with** *-e*).
dredg.er¹ ['dredʒə] *n.* tarak dubası; tarak makinesi.
dredg.er² [_] *n.* (*un, şeker, tuz, biber, kum vs.*) serpmeğe yarayan kap, tuzluk, şekerlik vs.
dregs [dregz] *n. pl.* tortu, telve, posa, cüruf; **drink** *veya* **drain to the** ~ **son** damlasına kadar içmek.
drench [drentʃ] **1.** *n.* sağanak; hayvanlara zorla içirilen ilaç, posyon; **2.** *v/t.* ıslatmak, sırılsıklam etm.; hayvana ilaç içirmek; *fig.* iliklerine kadar ıslatmak; 'drench.er *n.* F fena ıslatan sağanak; hayvanlara ilaç içirilen alet.
dress [dres] **1.** *n.* kadın elbisesi, giysi, kıyafet, *fig. üstbaş; full* ~ frak, tören elbisesi; **2.** *vb.* giydirmek, giyinmek; MIL hizaya getirmek, sıralamak; hazırlamak; düzenlemek; süslemek, donatmak, tezyin etm.; (*yara*) sarmak; (*kütük*) biçmek, yontmak; *b-nin* saçını tarayıp düzeltmek; AGR ekip biçmek, gübrelemek; ~ **s.o. down** *b-ni* paylamak, sövüp saymak, pataklamak; ~ **it** THEAT kostümlü prova yapmak; ~ **up** gi-

yinip süslenmek; (*çocuklar*) büyüklerin kıyafetini giymek; '~'cir.cle *n.* THEAT protokol yeri; '~'coat *n.* frak; 'dress.er *n.* giydiren kimse, *b-nin* giyinmesine yardım eden kimse; dekoratör; asistan doktor; pansumancı; dresuvar; *Am.* tuvalet masası; mutfak dolabı.
dress.ing ['dresiŋ] *n.* giy(in)me; giydirme; pansuman, sargı; apre; mutfak harcı (*esp. salata ve hindi dolması için sirke, salça, mayonez vs.*); AGR gübre; temiz bir dayak; ~**s** *pl.* sargı malzemesi; ~ **down** şiddetli azarlama; '~-case *n.* makyaj çantası; ilk yardım çantası; '~-cubic.le *n.* soyunma kabinesi; '~-glass *n.* tuvalet aynası; '~-gown *n.* sabahlık; '~-jack.et *n.* ropdöşambr, sabahlık; ~ **room** giyinme odası, gardırop; '~-ta.ble *n.* tuvalet masası.
dress...: '~.mak.er *n.* kadın terzisi; '~-parade *n.* defile; MIL üniformalı geçit töreni; ~ re.hears.al THEAT kostümlü prova; '~-shield *n.* subra, koltukluk; '~'shirt *n.* frak gömleği; '~'suit *n.* frak takımı; 'dress.y *adj.* F giyimine özen gösteren, şık, gösterişli giyinen.
drew [druː] *pret. of draw* **1.**
drib.ble ['dribl] *vb.* damla damla ak(ıt)mak, damla(t)mak; salyası akmak; *futbol:* topu zıplatarak ileri götürmek.
drib.let ['driblit] *n.* ufak tefek şey; nebze; damla(cık).
dried [draid] *adj.* kurutulmuş...; kuru...; ~ *fruit* kuru meyve.
dri.er ['draiə] *n.* kurutan kimse; kurutucu makine; çabuk kuruması için boyaya katılan madde.
drift [drift] **1.** *n.* sürüklenme, kar; kum vs. yığıntısı; hedef; NAUT geminin akıntı ve rüzgâr ile sürüklenmesi; *fig.* eğilim, tandans; GEOL birikinti, moren; MIN kanal, geçit; **2.** *v/t. & v/i.* sürükle(n)mek; yığ(ı)lmak, birik(tir)mek; '~-ice *n.* yüzer buz kütleleri, aysberk; '~-net *n.* balık tutmada kullanılan büyük ağ; '~-wood *n.* su üstünde sürüklenen odun parçaları.
drill¹ [dril] **1.** *n.* delgi, matkap; sapan izi; tohum dizisi; AGR mibzer, tohum ekme makinesi; MIL talim (*a. fig.*); alıştırma; ~ **ground** talim alanı; **2.** *v/t. & v/i.* delmek; MIL talim et(tir)mek (*a. fig.*); alıştırma yap(tır)mak; AGR tohum ekmek.
drill², drill.ing [dril, '_iŋ] *n.* çuval bezi.

drink [driŋk] **1.** *n.* içki, içecek; içme; *sl.* deniz; *in ~* sarhoş; **2.** (*irr.*) *vb.* içmek; *~ s.o.'s health b-nin* sıhhatine içmek; *~ away* varını yoğunu îçkide bitirmek; *~ in* zevk duyarak doya doya seyretmek *veya* dinlemek; *~ to b-nin* şerefine kadehini kaldırıp içmek; *~ off veya out veya up* içip bitirmek; '**drink.a.ble** *adj.* içilebilir; '**drink.er** *n.* içki içen kimse; sarhoş, ayyaş, bekri.

drink.ing ['driŋkiŋ] *n.* içme; içki içme alışkanlığı; '**~-bout** *n.* içki alemi; '**~-foun.tain** *n.* su içilen fıskiye; '**~-song** *n.* içki âlemlerinde söylenen şarkı; '**~-water** *n.* içecek su.

drip [drip] **1.** *n.* damlama, su sızma; **2.** *v/t. & v/i.* damla(t)mak, damla damla akmak; *~ ping wet* sırsıklam; '**~-'dry shirt** *n.* buruşmaz, ütü gerektirmeyen gömlek; '**drip.ping** *n.* kızartılan etten damlayan yağ, erimiş yağ; *~s pl.* damlayan şey; *~ pan* damlayan su *veya* yağı toplamaya yarayan kap.

drive [draiv] **1.** *n.* gezinti, araba gezintiti; araba yolu; *tenis vs.*: topa vuruş; MOT işletme mekanizması; *fig.* canlılık, neşe; işleme; teşebbüs, gayret; hamle; dürtü; (*hayvan*) gütme; sürgün avı; **2.** (*irr.*) *v/t.* sürmek; kullanmak; götürmek; sevketmek; zorlamak (**to, into** *-e*); *usu. ~ away* sürüp götürmek; kovmak; *v/i.* sürülmek (*a.* NAUT *&* HUNT); araba ile gitmek, araba kullanmak; acele etm.; *~ at s.th.* amaçlamak, demek istemek; *~ on* gitmeğe devam etm.; *~ out* kovmak, çıkarmak; *~ up* arabasiyle *b-nin* kapısı önüne gelmek.

drive-by shoot.ing ['draivbaiʃuːtiŋ] geçmekte olan bir araçtan ateş ederek yaralama ya da öldürme.

drive-in Am. ['draivin] **1.** *adj. mst attr.* müşterilerine araba içinde servis yapan...; *~ cinema* bu tür sinema; **2.** *n.* seyircilerin arabada oturarak film seyret tikleri açık hava sineması; müşterilere araba içinde servis yapılan lokanta.

driv.el ['drivl] **1.** *v/t. & v/i.* ağzından salya ak(ıt)mak; saçmasapan söylemek, saçmalamak; **2.** *n.* salya; saçmasapan söz.

driv.en ['drivn] *p.p. of drive 2.*

driv.er ['draivə] *n.* şoför, sürücü, RAIL makinist; *obs.* arabacı; MEC işletme (*hareket*) kasnağı, çarkı; '**drive-thru** Am. *n.* araçla bir ucundan girilip yemek alındıktan sonra öbür ucundan çıkılan *restoran*; '**drive.way** *n.* Am. bahçe kapısından eve kadar olan özel oto yolu.

driv.ing ['draiviŋ] **1.** *n.* sürme, kullanma; araba gezintisi; **2.** *adj.* hareket ettiren, çeviren; enerjik, canlı, şiddetli; '**~-belt** *n.* çark kayışı; transmisyon kayışı; '**~-gear** *n.* makine tertibatı; *~ li-cence* şoförlük ehliyetnamesi; *~ mir-ror* dikiz aynası; *~ school* şoförlük okulu; '**~-wheel** *n.* işletme dişlisi, ana çark.

driz.zle ['drizl] **1.** *n.* çiseleme; **2.** *v/i.* çiselemek, ince ince yağmak, serpiştirmek (*yağmur*); '**drizz.ly** *adj.* çiseleyen.

droll [drəul] *adj.* (*adv. drolly*) tuhaf, gülünç; '**droll.er.y** *n.* mizah; tuhaf kimse, maskara, soytarı.

drom.e.dar.y zoo ['drʌmədəri] *n.* hecin devesi, tek hörgüçlü binek devesi.

drone[1] [drəun] **1.** *n.* zoo erkek arı; *fig.* tembel, asalak kimse; uzaktan kumandalı uçak *veya* gemi; **2.** *vb.* tembellik, haylazlık etm.

drone[2] [~] **1.** *n.* vızıltı, çınlama; MUS telli ve nefesli çalgıların pes tonu; **2.** *vb.* vızıldamak; monoton, pes bir ses tonuyla konuşmak.

drool [druːl] **1.** *v/i.* ağzı sulanmak, ağzının suyu akmak; **2.** *n.* Am. F boş laf.

droop [druːp] *v/t. & v/i.* indirmek; sark(ıt)mak; bükülmek; halsiz olm., süngüsü düşük olm., cesareti kırılmak; solmak, tazeliğini kaybetmek; '**droop.ing** □ sarkık; yorgun, bitkin; soluk; ümitsiz.

drop [drɔp] **1.** *n.* damla; düşme, sukut; bonbon şekeri, draje; tavanda *veya* yerde bulunan kapak şeklinde kapı; THEAT perde; düşüş uzaklığı; paraşütle atılan şey; (*mektup vs.*) bırakıldığı yer; *get veya have the ~ on* Am. atik davranarak birinden önce silah çekmek; *~ light* asma lamba; *in ~s, ~ by ~* damla damla (*a. fig.*); **2.** *v/t.* düşürmek, atmak; damlatmak; (*mektup*) posta kutusuna atmak; (*bomba*) atmak; (*gözyaşı*) akıtmak; (*söz, mevzu*) sarfetmek; (*yolcu*) indirmek; (*ses*) alçaltmak; (*surat*) asmak; (*reverans*) yapmak; *~ s.o. a few lines b-ne* birkaç satır mektup yazmak; *~ it!* F yapma!, bırak bunu!; *v/i.* damlamak, sızmak (*fıçı*); düşmek; inmek; azalmak; düşüp ölmek; *~ behind* geri kalmak; *~ in* uğramak (*at, on, upon* *-e*); *~ off* yavaş

yavaş azalmak; uykuya dalmak; düş-mek; ~ **out** ayrılmak (*üyelikten*); okulu bitirmeden ayrılmak; çıkmak; '**drop-ping** *n*. damlama; düşme; ~**s** *pl*. gübre, hayvan tersi; '**drop scene** *n*. THEAT son perde.

drop.si.cal □ ['drɔpsikəl] su toplan-ması ile ilgili; '**drop.sy** *n*. deri altında *veya* organlarda çeşitli hastalıklar yü-zünden su toplanması, hidropizi.

dross [drɔs] *n*. cüruf, tortu, maden po-sası.

drought [draut], **drouth** [drauθ] *n*. ku-raklık, susuzluk; kıtlık; '**drought.y**, '**drouth.y** *adj*. kurak, susuz; kıt.

drove [drəuv] **1.** *n*. sürü, sığır sürüsü, *fig*. kalabalık; **2.** *pret. of* **drive 2**; '**dro-ver** *n*. davar sürücüsü, çoban, celep.

drown [draun] *v/t*. suda boğmak; bir ye-ri su basmak; *fig*. susturmak, sesiyle bastırmak, boğmak; **be** ~**ed** boğulmak; *v/i*. suda boğulmak.

drowse [drauz] *v/i*. uyuklamak, pinek-lemek; '**drow.si.ness** *n*. uykulu olma, uyuşukluk; '**drow.sy** *adj*. uykusu basmış, uyku gözünden akan; uyuşuk; uyutucu.

drub [drʌb] *v/t. b-ne* sopa çekmek, da-yak atmak; adamakıllı yenmek -*i*; *v/i*. parmakların ucuyla tıkırdatmak (*ma-sayı*); '**drub.bing** *n*. dayak, kötek.

drudge [drʌdʒ] **1.** *n. fig*. esir, köle, yük eşeği, hamal, ağır ve kötü işlerde çal-ışan kimse; **2.** *v/i*. ağır işler yapmak; '**drudg.er.y** *n*. ağır ve sıkıcı iş.

drug [drʌg] **1.** *n*. ilaç, tıbbî ecza; uyuştu-rucu madde; esrar; ~ **on the market** satılmayan mal; **2.** *v/t*. ilaçla uyutmak; ilaç vermek, uyusturucu vermek; *v/i*. uyuşturucu almak; '**drug.gist** *n*. ecza-cı; bakkal; '**drug.store** *n*. *Am*. bak-kaliye; eczane.

dru.id HIST ['drui:d] *n*. Hıristiyanlıktan önce İngiltere, İrlanda ve Fransa'da Kelt rahibi.

drum [drʌm] **1.** *n*. davul, trampete, dar-buka; MEC tambura, kasnak; ANAT ku-lak zarı; **2.** *vb*. davul çalmak; davul sesi çıkarmak; davul çalarak biraraya top-lamak, çağırmak; '~**fire** *n*. MIL aralıksız şiddetli ateş; '~**head** *n*. MIL davul derisi; ~ **court-martial** MIL harp divanı; '~'**ma.jor** *n*. MIL bando şefi; '**drum-mer** *n*. davulcu, trampeteci, batarist; *esp. Am*. F gezgin satıcı; '**drum.stick** *n*. davul tokmağı, trampet sopası, ba-get; (*kümes hayvanı*) budun alt kemiği.

drunk [drʌŋk] **1.** *p.p. of* **drink 2.**; **2.** *adj*. sarhoş; **get** ~ sarhoş olm.; **drunk.ard** ['-əd] *n*. ayyaş, sarhoş; **drunk.en** *adj. attr*. sarhoş, ayyaş; '**drunk.en.ness** *n*. sarhoşluk; içki tutkunluğu.

drupe BOT [dru:p] *n*. tek çekirdekli ve etli meyve.

dry [drai] **1.** □ kuru, kurak; susuz; ya-van, can sıkıcı; ince ve düşündürücü (*mizah*); sek (*içki*); süt vermez (*inek*); F susamış; F içki yasağı uygulanan; ~ **cell** kuru pil; ~ **goods** *pl*. F *Am*. tuha-fiye, manifatura; **2.** *n. Am*. F içki yasağı yanlısı; **3.** *v/t*. kurutmak, kurulamak; *v/i*. kurumak; ~ **up** tamamen kuru(t)-mak; ~ **up** F kes sesini!

dry.ad ['draiəd] *n. myth*. orman perisi.

dry...: ~ **bat.ter.y** kuru pil; ~ **bulb ther-mom.e.ter** atmosferdeki nemi ölçmek-te kullanılan biri ıslak biri kuru olan iki termometreden biri; '~'**clean** *v/t*. (*elbise vs.'yi*) su yerine benzen, triklo-retilen vs. kullanarak temizlemek; '~'**clean.ing** *n*. kuru temizleme.

dry.er ['draiə] = **drier**.

dry...: '~'**nurse 1.** *n*. çocuğu emzirme-yen dadı; **2.** *v/i. b-ne* dadılık etm., can-dan bakmak; '~'**rot** *n*. kerestenin için-deki «ev süngeri» denilen toz gibi çü-rüklük; *fig*. yozlaşma; '~'**shod** *adv*. ayaklarını ıslatmadan; '~'**wall.ing** *n*. harçsız duvar örme.

du.al □ ['dju:əl] iki kat, iki misli, çifte; çift...; '**du.al.ism** *n*. ikilik, dualizm.

dub [dʌb] *v/t. b-nin* omuzuna kılıçla do-kunarak şövalye yapmak; *b-ne* yeni bir isim *veya* unvan vermek; dublaj yap-mak; (*kösele*) yağlayıp yumuşatmak; '**dub.bing** *n*. vidala yağı.

du.bi.e.ty [dju:'baiəti] *n*. şüpheli olma; şüpheli şey *veya* durum.

du.bi.ous □ ['dju:bjəs] şüpheli, belir-siz, müphem; **be** ~ kestirememek, şüp-he etm., bir türlü bilememek (**of**, **about**, **over** -*i*, -*den*, -*i*); '**du.bi.ous-ness** *n*. şüphe, belirsizlik.

du.cal ['dju:kəl] *adj*. düke ait.

duc.at ['dʌkət] *n*. Avrupa'da eskiden bazı ülkelerde kullanılan değişik değerlerde altın para.

duch.ess ['dʌtʃis] *n*. düşes.

duch.y ['dʌtʃi] *n*. dükalık.

duck[1] [dʌk] *n*. ördek; ördek eti; *Am. sl*. herifin biri, adam.

duck[2] [-] **1.** *n*. başını eğme, eğilme; sin-me; dalış; **2.** *v/t. & v/i*. dal(dır)mak; başını eğmek, sinmek (*a. fig*.); *b-den*, *bş*den sakınmak için yana çekilmek, gizlenmek; *Am.* *b-le* karşılaşmamağa çalışmak; F sıvışmak.

duck³ F [_] *n.* sevgili, yavru.

duck⁴ [_] *n.* (*yelken*) keten bezi.

duck...: '~-bill *n.* zoo Avustralya'ya mahsus perde ayaklı, gagalı, vücudu kunduza benzeyen bir hayvan; '~-boards *n. pl.* lata, ızgara.

duck.ling ['dʌkliŋ] *n.* yavru ördek.

duck.weed bot ['dʌkwi:d] *n.* su mercimeği.

duck.y F ['dʌki] 1. = *duck*³; 2. *adj.* sevgili, güzel, zarif.

duct [dʌkt] *n.* guddelerden sıvı maddeleri, salgıları akıtan kanal, boru, tüp, damar (*bitki*).

duc.tile □ ['dʌktail] (*metal*) genişleyebilir, uzayabilir; (*çamur*) şekil verilebilir; *fig.* uysal, yumuşak; **duc.til.i.ty** [_ 'tiliti] *n.* uzayıp genişelebilme özelliği; uysallık.

dud *sl.* [dʌd] 1. *n.* patlamayan mermi *veya* bomba; *fig.* kendisinden bekleneni yapamayan, başarıya ulaşamayan kimse *veya* şey; ~s *pl.* kişisel eşya; 2. *adj.* sahte, kalp; yararsız.

dude *Am.* [dju:d] *n.* züppe, giyimine aşırı düşkün erkek; ~ *ranch* tatil köyü olarak düzenlenmiş çiftlik.

dudg.eon ['dʌdʒən] *n.* öfke, hiddet; *in high* ~ çok öfkeli, çok gücenmiş.

due [dju:] 1. *adj.* gerekli; ödenmesi gerekli; uygun; süresi dolan; *bş*e layık; *in* ~ *time* tam vaktinde, zamanı gelince; *the train is* ~ *at...* trenin saat ...te gelmesi bekleniyor; *in* ~ *course* zamanı gelince; zamanında; *be* ~ *to* yüzünden, *-den* dolayı; *be* ~ *to inf.* zorunda olm.; yapması istenilmek; *Am.* ...mak üzere olm.; *fall* ~ com vadesi gelmek; ~ *date* ödeme günü, vade bitimi; 2. *adj.* naut doğru; ~ *east* tam doğuya doğru; 3. *n.* hak; alacak, istihkak; *mst* ~s *pl.* vergi, resim; üye aidatı.

du.el ['dju:əl] 1. *n.* düello; 2. *v/i.* düello etm.; 'du.el.list *n.* düellocu.

du.et(.to) [dju:'et(əu)] *n.* mus düet, iki kişi tarafından söylenen şarkı.

duf.fel ['dʌfəl] *n.* kalın havlı ve kaba bir tür yünlü kumaş; ~ *coat* bir tür kapşonlu (*başlıklı*) kaban.

duff.er F ['dʌfə] *n.* ahmak herif, eşek kafalı.

dug [dʌg] 1. *pret. & p.p. of dig*; 2. *n.* inek memesi, emcik; '~-out *n.* mıl sığınak; *sl.* göreve çağırılan emekli su-

bay; *Am.* *beysbol*: üzerinde oyuncuların oturduğu üstü kapalı sıra *veya* yer.

duke [dju:k] *n.* dük, düka; **duke.dom** *n.* dükalık.

dul.cet ['dʌlsit] *adj.* tatlı, hoş, lâtif, ahenkli; 'dul.ci.mer mus [' _ simə] *n.* simbalom, santur.

dull [dʌl] 1. □ aptal, budala, kalın kafalı; ağır, hantal; (*göz*, *renk*) donuk, sönük; (*ses*) cansız; can sıkıcı; hissiz, alâkasız; kör, kesmez; (*ağrı*, *sızı*) belirsiz, pek hissedilmeyen; (*hava*) kapalı, kasvetli; (*ticaret*) durgun, kesat; naut sakin, sütliman; 2. *v/t. & v/i.* körleş(tir)-mek, *fig.* duygusuzlaş(tır)mak, hayvanlaş(tır)mak; donuklaş(tır)mak; sersemle(t)mek; **dull.ard** [' _ əd] *n.* ahmak kimse; 'dull.ness *n.* ahmaklık, hantallık; donukluk, matlık; sıkıcılık; monotonluk; ilgisizlik, lâkaytlık; dert, keder, sıkıntı; durgunluk.

du.ly ['dju:li] *adv. s. due*; uygun olarak, gereğince; tam zamanında.

dumb □ [dʌm] dilsiz; dili tutulmuş, sessiz, konuşmayan; *Am.* F aptal, budala, *deaf and* ~ sağır ve dilsiz; *s. show 2*; *strike* ~ hayretten dondurmak, şaşırtmak; '~-bell *n.* jimnastik güllesi; *Am. sl.* aptal adam; ~'found *v/t.* F sustur-mak, serseme çevirmek; ~'founded *adj.* hayretler içinde; 'dumb.ness *n.* dilsizlik; dili tutulma; 'dumb-'wait.er *n.* seyyar masa; *Am.* mutfak asansörü.

dum.my ['dʌmi] *n.* aldatmaca; *fig.* kulis; *fig.* kukla adam, figüran; manken (*elbise*); emzik; *attr.* taklit...; uydurma...; ~ *whist* üç kişi ve hayali bir dördüncü ile oynanan bir iskambil oyunu.

dump [dʌmp] 1. *vb.* boşaltmak, atmak (*moloz*, *süprüntü*); *bş*den kurtulmak (*a. fig.*); (*mal*) ucuza ihraç etm., damping yapmak, fiyatları düşürmek, düşmek; 2. *n.* çöp, moloz vs. yığını; çöplük, mezbele; mıl cephanelik; = ~ing; 'dump.ing com *n.* ucuza ihraç etme, damping, ucuzluk, fiyat indirme; 'dump.ing-ground *n.* çöplük, mezbele; 'dump.ling bir tür meyvalı hamur tatlısı; F kısa boylu ve tombul kimse; 'dumps *n.* F *pl.*: (*down*) *in the* ~ keyifsiz, ümitsiz; 'dump.y *adj.* tıknaz, bodur.

dun¹ [dʌn] 1. *adj.* boz, kurşunî; 2. *n.* boz at.

dun² [_] 1. *n.* sıkıştıran alacaklı; 2. *v/t.* borçluyu sıkıştırmak; ~*ning letter n.*

ihbarname.

dunce [dʌns], **dun.der.head** ['dʌn-dəhed] *n.* aptal kimse.

dune [dju:n] *n.* kumul, eksibe.

dung [dʌŋ] **1.** hayvan tersi, gübre; **2.** *v/t.* gübrelemek.

dun.ga.rees [dʌŋgə'ri:z] *n. pl.* kaba pamuklu kumaştan dikilmiş tulum.

dun.geon ['dʌndʒən] *n.* zindan.

dung.hill ['dʌŋhil] *n.* gübre yığını.

dunk ['dʌŋk] *vb.* suya dal(dır)mak; *(çay, çorba vs.'ye)* batırmak, banmak.

du.o ['dju:əu] *n.* düet; çift, eş.

du.o.dec.i.mal [dju:əu'desiməl] *adj.* on iki veya on ikinciye ait; on ikişer on ikişer; *n.* on ikide bir kısım; **du.o-'dec.i.mo** [_məu] *n.* TYP bir kitap boyu, oniki yapraklı forma; *fig.* bücür, bacaksız.

du.o.de.nal ANAT [dju:əu'di:nl] *adj.* onikiparmak bağırsağı...; **du.o'de-num** [_nəm] *n.* onikiparmak bağırsağı.

dupe [dju:p] **1.** *n.* kolayca aldatılabilen, ahmak kimse; **2.** *v/t.* aldatmak, dolandırmak; **'dup.er.y** *n.* aldatma, hile, işletme.

du.plex ['dju:pleks] **1.** *adj.* çift..., dubleks...; TEL karşılıklı aynı anda iki gönderme sistemi olan; **2.** *n. Am.* iki katlı apartman dairesi.

du.pli.cate **1.** ['dju:plikit] *adj.* çift, eş, aynı, kopya; **2.** ['_kit] *n.* eş, kopya, ikinci nüsha, suret; *in ~* iki nüsha olarak; **3.** ['_keit] *v/t. -in* suretini çıkarmak, ikilemek; iki misline çıkarmak; **du.pli'ca-tion** *n.* teksir etme, teksir suret; **du.pli-ca.tor** *n.* teksir makinesi; **du.plic.i.ty** [dju:'plisiti] *n.* iki yüzlülük, düzenbazlık, hile.

du.ra.bil.i.ty [djuərə'biliti] *n.* dayanıklılık, sağlamlık; sürekli oluş; **'du-ra.ble** □ dayanıklı, sağlam, devamlı; **'dur.ance** *n. obs.* tutukluluk, mahpusluk; **du.ra.tion** [_'reifən] *n.* devam, süre, süreklilik.

du.ress JUR ['djuə'res] *n.* cebir, ikrah, tehdit, şantaj; zorlama, baskı.

du.ring ['djuəriŋ] *prp.* esnasında, müddetince, zarfında.

durst [də:st] *pret. of* **dare**.

dusk [dʌsk] *n.* akşam karanlığı, alacakaranlık; **'dusk.y** □ oldukça karanlık *(a. fig.)*; koyu esmer, siyahımsı.

dust [dʌst] **1.** *n.* toz; çiçek tozu; toprak; çöp; küçültücü durum; **2.** *v/t. -in* tozunu silkmek, tozunu almak; *v/i.* toz serpmek, tozlanmak; **'~-bin** *n.* çöp te-

nekesi; **'~-bowl** *n. Am.* A.B.D.'nin batısında kum fırtınaları etkisinde olan bölge; **'~-cart** *n.* çöp kamyonu; **'~-cloak,** **'~-coat** *n.* elbiseyi tozdan korumak için giydirilen örtü, kaşpusiyer; **'dust.er** *n.* toz bezi, toz alan şey, kuş tüyü; *Am.* kaşpusiyer; **'dust.i.ness** *n.* tozluluk, toz; **'dust.ing** *n. sl.* bir iki dayak; **'dust-'jack.et** *n.* kitap cildini tozdan koruyan kitap kabı; **'~.man** *n.* çöpçü; **'~.pan** *n.* faraş; **'dust-'up** *n.* patırtı, şamata; **'dust.y** □ tozlu, toz gibi.

Dutch [dʌtʃ] **1.** *adj.* Hollandalı, Felemenkli; HIST & *Am. sl.* Almanyalı; *~* **treat** *Am.* F yemekte hesabı paylaşma, eşit ödeme *(Alman usulü)*; **2.** *n.* Felemenkçe, Hollanda dili; **the ~** *pl.* Hollanda halkı; **double ~** çetrefil lisan; **auc.tion** *(mezat)* fiyat indirimi; *~* **courage** çakır keyifliliğin verdiği cesaret; **'~.man** *n.* Hollandalı; HIST & *Am. sl.* Alman, **'~.woman** *n.* Hollandalı kadın.

du.te.ous ['dju:tjəs] = **dutiful;** **du.ti-a.ble** ['_tjəbl] *adj.* gümrüğe tabi, **du-ti.ful** □ ['_tiful] görevini bilen, vazifeşinas; itaatli, saygılı.

du.ty ['dju:ti] *n.* ödev, görev, hizmet, sorumluluk, vazife *(to)*; gümrük resmi, vergi; **on ~** hizmette, vazife başında; **off ~** izinli, serbest; *~* **call** resmî ziyaret, nezaket ziyareti; **in ~ bound** vazifesine uygun olarak; **do ~ for** b*şin, b-nin* yerini almak, işlevini görmek; *fig.* b*-nin* yanında çalışmak, hizmetçilik etm.; **'~-'free** *adj.* gümrüksüz, gümrük resmi ödemeden.

DVD [di:vi:'di] *n.* DVD; **~-ROM** DVD--ROM.

dwarf [dwɔ:f] **1.** *n.* cüce, bodur *(insan, ağaç, hayvan)* **2.** *v/t.* büyümesini önlemek, cüceleştirmek; kıyaslayarak küçük göstermek, gölgede bırakmak; **~ed** *adj.* dumura uğramış, körelmiş; **'dwarfish** □ cüceyi andıran, bodurca; **'dwarfish.ness** *n.* cücelik.

dwell [dwel] *(irr.)* *v/i.* oturmak, durmak *(on, upon* üzerinde*)*; *~* **up(on)** bir konu üzerinde durmak, ısrar etm.; **'dwell.er** *n.* oturan, mukim, sakin, ora ahalisinden; **'dwell.ing** *n.* ev, mesken, oturma yeri; **'dwell.ing-house** *n.* ev, mesken, konut; **'dwell.ing-place** *n.* ikametgâh, konut.

dwelt [dwelt] *pret. & p.p. of* **dwell**.

dwin.dle ['dwindl] *v/i.* yavaş yavaş azalmak *veya* küçülmek *veya* ufalmak;

'dwin.dling *n.* azalma, ufalma, küçül-me.

dye [dai] **1.** *n.* boya; *of deepest ~ fig.* en kötü şekilde; **2.** *v/t. & v/i.* boya(n)mak; 'dy.er *n.* boyacı; 'dye-stuff *n.* boya ilacı; 'dye-works *n. pl.* boyahane.

dy.ing □ ['daiiŋ] (*s. die¹*) **1.** *adj.* ölmekte olan; ölen…; *lie ~* can çekişmek; **2.** *n.* ölüm, ölme.

dyke [daik] = *dike*.

dy.nam.ic [dai'næmik] **1.** *a.* dy'nam.i-cal □ dinamik, kuvvetli, faal, enerjik; **2.** *n.* devitken güç, muharrik kuvvet; dy'namics *mst sg.* dinamik birimi;

dy.na.mite ['dainəmait] **1.** *n.* dinamit; **2.** *v/t.* dinamitle havaya uçurmak; 'dy-na.mit.er *n.* dinamitle uçuran kimse; dy.na.mo ['-məu] *n.* dinamo.

dy.nas.tic [di'næstik] *adj.* (~*ally*) hane-dana ait; dy.nas.ty ['dinəsti] *n.* hane-dan, soy.

dyne PHYS [dain] *n.* din (*güç birimi*).

dys.en.ter.y MED ['disntri] *n.* dizanteri, kanlı basur.

dys.pep.sia MED [dis'pepsiə] *n.* hazımsızlık, dipepsi; dys'pep.tic [-tik] **1.** *adj.* (~*ally*) hazımsızlığa ait; **2.** *n.* hazımsızlık çeken kimse.

E

each [i:tʃ] *adj.* her, beher, her bir; *adv.* her biri, tanesi; *~ other* birbiri(ni); *they cost a shilling ~* tanesi bir şilin.

ea.ger □ ['i:gə] hevesli; istekli (*about, after, for*), sabırsız; *fig.* gayretli; şevkli, hararetli; 'eager.ness *n.* istek, gayret, şevk.

ea.gle ['i:gl] *n.* kartal, karakuş; on do-larlık madeni para; '~-'eyed *adj.* kes-kin gözlü; ea.glet ['-lit] *n.* kartal yav-rusu.

ea.gre ['eigə] *n.* şiddetli met hareketi.

ear¹ [iə] *n.* başak.

ear²[-] *n.* kulak; işitim; müziğin inceliklerini sezebilme yeteneği; kulp, sap; kulak verme, dikkat; *be all ~s* can kulağı ile dinlemek; *keep an ~ to the ground esp. Am.* yeni haberleri almak *veya* gelişmeleri bil-dirmek; *up to the ~s fig.* fazla meşgul (*çalışma*); *set by the ~s* birbirine karşı kışkırtmak; ~-ache ['iəreik] *n.* kulak ağrısı; ~-deafen.ing ['-defniŋ] *adj.* ku-lakları sağır edecek kadar gürültülü; '~-drum *n.* kulak zarı.

earl [ə:l] *n.* (*İngiliz*) kont; ♀ *Marshal n.* protokol başkanı; 'earl.dom *n.* kont-luk.

ear.li.ness ['ə:linis] *n.* erken olma.

ear.ly ['ə:li] *adj. & adv.* erken(den), er-ken…; başlangıçta…; eski; ilk; yakın-da; *~ life* gençlik (zamanı); *as ~ as* …kadar erken; *earlier on* evvelce, es-kiden.

ear-mark ['iəmɑ:k] **1.** *n.* hayvanların kulağına takılan marka, işaret; *fig.* alâ-met, karakteristik; **2.** *v/t.* kulağa işaret

koymak; *fig.* karakterize etm.; belirli bir amaç için kenara koymak (*para vs.*).

earn [ə:n] *v/t.* kazanmak, hak etm.; *~ed income* hak edilmiş, çalışarak ka-zanılmış gelir.

ear.nest¹ [ə:nist] *a.* ~*money n.* pey ak-çesi, kaparo, pey, avans; temiant; *fig.* tadımlık, ilk tat; delil.

ear.nest² [-] **1.** □ ciddi, ağırbaşlı; istek-li, samimi; gerçek, hakiki; **2.** *n.* ciddi-yet; *be in ~* ciddi olarak, samimiyetle; 'ear.nest.ness *n.* ciddiyet; istekli ol-ma.

earn.ings ['ə:niŋz] *n. pl.* kazanç, kâr, gelir.

ear…: '~-phones *n. pl. radyo, teyp vs.*: kulaklık; '~.piece *n.* TELEPH işitme ci-hazı; '~-pierc.ing *adj.* kulakları sağır edici (*ses*); '~-ring *n.* küpe; '~.shot *n.* kulak erimi, kulak menzili; '~-split-ting *adj.* kulakları sağır edici.

earth [ə:θ] **1.** *n.* dünya; toprak; kara; yer-yüzü; (*tilki vs.*) in; *a.* ~*-connection n. radyo*: toprak bağlantı; **2.** *v/t.* ELECT toprağa bağlamak; *~ up* toprak ile ört-mek; 'earth.en *adj.* topraktan yapılmış; 'earthen.ware **1.** *n.* çanak çömlek; **2.** *adj.* toprak işi; 'earth.ing *n.* ELECT toprak bağlantı; earth.li.ness *n.* dünyevî oluş, maddilik; 'earth.ly *adj.* dünyaya ait, dünyevî; F düşünüle-bilir, olası; *no ~* … hiç bir …yoktu; 'earth.quake *n.* deprem; 'earth.worm *n.* zoo yer solucanı; *fig.* yaltakçı *b-i*; 'earth.y *adj.* dünyevî, madde ile ilgili; topraklı, toprağa benzer; *fig.* zevk düşkünü, ruhsuz, kaba.

ear...: '**~-trum.pet** *n.* eskiden ağır işiten kimselerin kullandığı kulak borusu; '**~-wax** *n.* kulak kiri; '**~.wig** *n.* zoo kulağakaçan.

ease [i:z] **1.** *n.* rahat, konfor, huzur, refah; kolaylık; *at ~* rahat, hoş; teklifsiz; *be veya feel at ~* içi rahat olm.; *ill at ~* huzursuz, endişeli; *stand at ~!* MIL yerinde rahat!, rahat!; *take one's ~* rahat etm., dinlenmek, yangelmek; *with ~* kolayıkla; *live at ~* rahat koşullarda yaşamak; **2.** *v/t.* hafifletmek; (*ağrı*) yatıştırmak; *b-nin* rahat ve huzurunu sağlamak; (*halat vs.*) gevşetmek; kurtarmak (*of -den*); gerginliğini kaybetmek (*koşullar*); *~ nature* hacet görmek, tuvalete gitmek; hafiflemek; **ease.ful** □ ['-ful] rahat, hoş; sakin.

ea.sel ['i:zl] *n.* ressam sehpası, şövale.

eas.i.ly ['i:zili] *adv.* kolaylıkla, kolayca; rahat rahat; şüphesiz; '**eas.i.ness** *n.* kolaylık, rahatlık, doğal davranma, tabiilik; *~ of belief* saffdilik, kolay aldatılma.

east [i:st] **1.** *n.* doğu, şark; *the ♀ Am.* A.B.D.'de doğu eyaletleri; **2.** *adj.* doğu..., doğu ile ilgili; **3.** *adv.* doğuya doğru.

East.er ['i:stə] *n. rel.* Paskalya yortusu; *~ egg* paskalya yumurtası.

east.er.ly ['i:stəli] *adj. & adv.* doğuda; doğu...; doğuya doğru, doğudan; **eastern** ['-tən] = *easterly*; doğu(da); doğululara ait, oryantal; '**east.ern.er** *n.* doğulu *b-i*; ♀ *Am.* A.B.D.'de doğu eyaletlerinden olan *b-i*; **east.ern.most** ['-məust] *adj.* en uzak doğu.

east.ing NAUT ['i:stiŋ] *n.* doğu yönünde hareket; doğuya doğru giderek katedilen mesafe.

east.ward(s) ['i:stwəd(z)] *adj. & adv.* doğuya doğru (olan).

eas.y ['i:zi] **1.** □ kolay, rahat, sıkıntısız; sakin; uysal; doğal davranışları olan; rahat (*elbise*); COM durgun; *in ~ circumstances* hali vakti yerinde, varlıklı; *on ~ street* iyi koşullarda; *on ~ terms* COM uygun koşullarda, uygun taksitlerle; *make o.s. ~* rahatına bakmak; *take it ~ k-ni* fazla yormamak; yangelmek; *take it ~!* acele etmeyiniz!, telaşlanmayınız!, darılmayınız!; **2.** *n.* kısa mola; '**~'chair** *n.* koltuk; '**~-go-ing** *adj. fig.* kayıtsız, kaygısız.

eat [i:t] **1.** (*irr.*) *v/t.* yemek; aşındırmak (*away -i*); *~ up* hepsini yemek, silip sü-

pürmek, yiyip bitirmek (*a. fig.*); *v/i.* yemek yemek; lezzetli olm.; aşındırmak (*into, through*); biriktirileni yemeğe başlamak; **2.** *~s n. pl. Am. sl.* yemek, yiyecek(ler); '**eat.a.ble** *adj.* yenilebilir; '**eata.bles** *n. pl.* yiyecek, gıda; '**eat.en** *p.p. of eat 1*; '**eat.er** *n.* yiyen *b-i*; *be a great (poor) ~* çok (az) yiyen *b-i* olm.; '**eat.ing** *n.* yemek yeme; '**eat-ing-house** *n.* aşevi, lokanta.

eau-de-Co.logne ['əudəkə'ləun] *n.* kolonya.

eaves [i:vz] *n. pl.* çıkıntı, saçak; '**~-drop** *v/i.* kulak kabartmak, gizlice dinlemek; '**~-drop.per** *n.* kulak misafiri, gizlice dinleyen *b-i*.

ebb [eb] **1.** *n.* cezir, deniz sularının çekilmesi; *fig.* bozulma, düşüş, başarısızlık; *at a low ~* harap, perişan, zor durumda; **2.** *v/i.* çekilmek (*deniz*); *fig.* bozulmak; azalmak; zor durumda olm.; '**~-'tide** *n.* cezir, inik deniz; *fig.* suyunu çekme.

eb.on *poet.* ['ebən] *adj.* abanozdan yapılmıs; abanoz gibi siyah; **eb.on.ite** ['-nait] *n.* ebonit, bir tür siyah sert kauçuk; '**ebon.y** *n.* abanoz (ağacı).

e-book IT ['i:buk] *n.* e-kitap.

e.bri.e.ty [i:'braiəti] *n.* sarhoşluk.

e.bul.li.ent [i'bʌljənt] *n.* taşkın, coşkun, içi içine sığmayan; *fig.* fıkır fıkır (*with*); **eb.ul.li.tion** [ebə'liʃən] *n.* taşkınlık, coşkunluk; kaynama.

e-card ['i:ka:d] *n.* e-kart.

ec.cen.tric [ik'sentrik] **1.** *a.* ec'cen.tri-cal □ eksantrik; *fig.* garip, tuhaf; delişmen, kaçık; **2.** *n.* MEC dışmerkezli, eksantrik; kendi bildiğini okuyan kimse; **eccen.tric.i.ty** [eksen'trisiti] *n.* tuhaflık; dışmerkezlilik; *fig.* delişmenlik, eksantrik olma.

ec.cle.si.as.tic [ikli:zi'æstik] *n.* papaz, rahip; **ec.cle.si'as.ti.cal** □ kiliseye ait, dinî.

ECG [i:si:'dʒi:] *n.* elektrocardiyogram.

ech.e.lon MIL ['eʃələn] **1.** *n.* kademe, mevzi; **2.** *v/t. & v/i.* kademelen(dir)-mek.

e.chi.nus ZOO [e'kainəs] *n.* deniz kestanesi.

ech.o ['ekəu] **1.** *n.* yankı, aksiseda; **2.** *v/t. & v/i.* yansı(t)mak; (*ses*) akset(tir)-mek; *fig.* taklit etm., tekrarlamak; '**~-sound.er** *n.* NAUT sesli iskandil.

e.clat ['eiklɑ:] *n.* büyük başarı, herkesin övgüsünü kazanan mükemmel sonuç.

ec.lec.tic [ek'lektik] **1.** *adj.* (*insan, yöntem, fikir*) bir sistem *ya da* düşünceye

                       educe

bağlanmayan fakat hepsinden yararlanan; seçme şeylerden oluşmuş, derlenmiş; **2.** *n.* felsefe ve sanatta belirli bir düşünceye değil fakat çeşitli düşünce ve yöntemlerden *k-ne* uygun olanı seçen kimse; **ec'lec.ti.cism** [-sizəm] *n.* seçip toplama eğilimi.

e.clipse [i'klips] **1.** *n.* ay tutulması, güneş tutulması; *fig.* şöhretini kaybetme; **2.** *v/t.* karartmak; gölgede bırakmak (*a. fig.*); *b-nin* yıldızını söndürmek; **e'cliptic** AST [-tik] *n.* ekliptik, güneşin sabit yıldızlara göre bir yılda takip ettiği dairesel yol.

ec.logue ['eklɔg] *n.* karşılıklı konuşma şeklinde pestoral şiir.

e.co.friend.ly ['i:kəυfrendli] *adj.* çevre dostu.

e.col.o.gy [i:'kɔlədʒi] *n.* çevrebilim, canlıların çevreleriyle olan ilişkilerini inceleyen biyoloji dalı.

e-com.merce ['i:kɒmɜːs] *n.* e-ticaret.

e.co.nom.ic [i:kə'nɔmik], **e.co'nom.i-cal** ☐ iktisadî, ekonomik; idareli, tutumlu; iktisat…; **e.co'nom.ics** *n. sg.* iktisat bilimi; **e.con.o.mist** [i:'kɔnə-mist] *n.* iktisatçı, ekonomist; **e'con.o-mize** *vb.* idareli kullanmak (**in**, **on**, **with** -*i*), *bşden* tasarruf etm.; **e'con.o-my** *n.* iktisat, ekonomi; tutum, idare; ekonomik sistem; *economies pl.* tasarruf, tutum; ekonomik önlem; *polit-ical* ~ ekonomi politik, iktisat bilimi.

ec.sta.size ['ekstəsaiz] *v/t. & v/i.* coş(tur)mak, kendinden geç(ir)mek; hayran bırakmak, hayran olm.; **'ec.sta.sy** *n.* coşkunluk, kendinden geçme, vecit, esrime; **go into** ~ coşkuyla övmek; **ec-stat.ic** [eks'tætik] *adj.* (~*ally*) coş(tur)an, vecde düşmüş; ~ **fit** coşkunluk hali, ulu *bş* karşısında heyecan duyma.

ec.ze.ma MED ['eksimə] *n.* egzama, mayasıl.

e.da.cious [i'deiʃəs] *adj.* obur, açgözlü, pisboğaz.

ed.dy ['edi] **1.** *n.* girdap, anafor; **2.** *v/t. & v/i.* şiddetle dön(dür)mek; *fig.* velveleye getirmek.

e.den.tate ZOO [i'denteit] *adj.* dişsiz; dişsiz memeli hayvanlara ait.

edge [edʒ] **1.** *n.* kenar, sırt; uç; bıçak ağzı; kıyı, sınır; (*kitap*) kenar; (*dağ*) sırt; şiddet, sertlik; *be on* ~ sinirli olm.; *have the* ~ *on s.o.* sl. *b-den* üstün olm.; *put on* ~ *on* bilemek, keskinleştirmek, zağlamak; *lay on* ~ yanlamasına koymak (*alanı geniş, ince şeyler*

için: *madenî para vs. gibi*); *set s.o.'s teeth on* ~ *b-ni* sinirlendirmek; dişbilemek; **2.** *vb.* bilemek, keskinleştirmek; kenar geçirmek, teyellemek, kenarını süslemek (*with ile*); yan yan ve yavaşça ilerle(t)mek, sokulmak, sürmek, çekmek, **edged** *adj.* keskin; … kenarlı.

edge…: '~.less *adj.* kör, keskin olmayan; *fig.* yavan; '~-tool *n.* kesici alet; '~.ways, ~.wise ['-waiz] *adv.* yandan, kenardan; dolaylı olarak; yana doğru; *get a word in* ~ fırsat bulup konuşabilmek.

edg.ing ['edʒiŋ] *n.* kenarlık, şerit, dantelâ; bordür; '~-shears *n. pl.* çim biçme makası.

edg.y ['edʒi] *adj.* keskin kenarlı; F sinirli.

ed.i.ble ['edibl] *adj.* yenir, yenilebilir; **'ed.i.bles** *n. pl.* yiyecek(ler).

e.dict ['i:dikt] *n.* emir, ferman, buyrultu, kararname.

ed.i.fi.ca.tion *fig.* [edifi'keiʃən] *n.* yüksek duygulara ulaşma, karakter ve düşünce gelişimi; **ed.i.fice** ['-fis] *n.* büyük bina, yapı; bünye, yapılış (*a. fig.*); **ed.i.fy** *fig.* ['-fai] *v/t.* yüksek duygular ilham etm.; öğretmek; doğru yolu göstermek; duyguca yüceltmek; **'ed.i.fy.ing** ☐ yüksek duygulara ulaştıran; iyi bir örnek olan.

ed.it ['edit] *v/t.* (*metin, konu*) yayımlamak, baskasının yazdığı bir yazıyı basılmak için hazırlamak, telif etm.; (*gazete*) idare etm.; **ed.i.tion** [i'diʃən] *n.* baskı, (*kitap*) yayım; **ed.i.tor** ['editə] *n.* yayımlayan; yazı işleri müdürü; **ed-i.to.rial** [-'tɔ:riəl] **1.** *adj.* yazı işleri müdürlüğüne ait; **2.** *n.* başyazı; **ed.i.tor-ship** ['-təʃip] *n.* yazı işleri müdürlüğü, editörlük; redaksiyon.

ed.u.cate ['edju:keit] *v/t.* eğitmek, yetiştirmek, *bşi* öğretmek; ~*d adj.* okumuş, aydın; **ed.u'ca.tion** *n.* eğitim, öğretim, maarif; *Ministry of* ♀ Milli Eğitim Bakanlığı; **ed.u.ca.tion.al** ☐ ['-keiʃənl], **ed.u.ca.tive** ['-kətiv] *adj.* eğitimsel, pedagojik; eğitim…; eğitici; *educational film* öğretici film; **ed.u-ca.tion(.al)ist** [-'keiʃn(əl)ist] *n.* pedagog, eğitimci; **ed.u.ca.tor** *n.* eğitmen, öğretmen.

e.duce [i:'dju:s] *v/t.* sonuca varmak, tümevarım; *fig.* hedefinden çevirmek, CHEM bir karışımdan bir elemanı ayırmak.

e.duc.tion [i'dʌkʃən] *n.* (*anlam, sonuç*) çıkarma, çıkan şey; MEC egzos; istim salıverme; **e'duc.tion-pipe** *n.* istim borusu, egzos borusu.

eel [iːl] *n.* yılanbalığı.

e'en [iːn] = *even.*

e'er [ɛə] = *ever.*

ee.rie, ee.ry ['iəri] *adj.* tekin olmayan, endişe verici, korkutucu, tüyler ürpertici.

ef.face [i'feis] *v/t.* silmek, bozmak (*yüzey*), üstünden sünger geçirmek; *fig.* yok etm., imha etm.; *fig.* unutturmak; ~ *o.s.* bir köşeye çekilmek; **ef'face.a-ble** *adj.* silinebilir; **ef'face.ment** *n.* silme, yok etme; sinme.

ef.fect [i'fekt] **1.** *n.* etki, sonuç; gösteriş; JUR meriyet, yürürlük; MEC randıman, verim; ~*s pl.* menkul kıymetler, taşınır mallar, eşya; COM alacak, matlup; *bring to ~*, *carry into ~* gerçekleştirmek, realize etm.; tahakkuk ettirmek; *take ~*, *be of ~* yürürlüğe girmek; işlemek; *of no ~* etkisiz, faydasız, tesirsiz; *in ~* hakikaten, gerçekten, aslında; halen yürürlükte; *to the ~* genel olarak, anlamında; *to this ~* bu anlamda; **2.** *v/t.* etkilemek; başarmak; *be ~ed* etkili olm.; **ef'fective 1.** ☐ etkili, tesirli; JUR yürürlükte, geçerli; MIL, NAUT muhareebeye elverişli, hizmete hazır; MEC verimli, randımanlı; ~ *capacity* MEC verimli kapasite; ~ *date* geçerli tarih, yürürlüğe girdiği tarih; ~ *range* etkili top menzili; ~ *use* kullan(ıl)ma; **2.** *n.* MIL *mst* ~*s pl.* hazır güç; COM efektif, nakit para; **ef'fec.tive.ness** *n.* etki, geçerlilik, itibar; **ef'fec.tu.al** [_tʃuəl] *adj.* (*davranış*) etkili, sonuç veren, geçerli; **ef'fectu.ate** [_t jueit] *v/t.* yapmak, yerine getirmek, sonuçlandırmak, becermek, başarmak.

ef.fem.i.na.cy [i'feminəsi] *n.* kadınca davranış, erkekçe olmayan durum; **ef-'femi.nate** [_nit] ☐ kadınımsı, kadın tavırlı, yumuşak.

ef.fer.vesce [efə'ves] *v/i.* (*sıvı*) köpürmek, kabarmak; *fig.* coşmak, taşmak, neşelenmek; **ef.fer'ves.cence** *n.* köpürme, kabarma; coşma; **ef.fer'vescent** *adj.* köpüren, kabaran; coşkun; ~ *powder* kabartma tozu.

ef.fete [e'fiːt] *adj.* bitkin, yıpranmış, güçsüz; kısır, verimsiz.

ef.fi.ca.cious ☐ [efi'keiʃəs] etkili, tesirli (*esp. ilaç, tedavi*); **ef.fi.ca.cy** ['_kə-si] *n.* etki, yarar, fayda.

ef.fi.cien.cy [i'fiʃənsi] *n.* kifayet, yeterlik, uzluk, etki; MEC verim, randıman; ~ *expert* rasyonalizasyon uzmanı; **ef'fi-cient** ☐ etkili, yeterli, uz, ehliyetli; verimli.

ef.fi.gy ['efidʒi] *n.* resim, tasvir, şekil, portre; *burn s.o. in ~* (*halkın nefret ifadesi olarak b-nin*) resim *veya* modelini yakmak.

ef.flo.resce [eflɔː'res] *v/i.* BOT çiçek açmak; *fig.* çiçek gibi açılmak; CHEM su kaybederek toz haline gelmek; **ef.flo-'res.cent** *adj.* çiçeklenen; hava ile temas edince tozlanan.

ef.flu.ence ['efluəns] *n.* (*sıvı, gaz, ışık*) dışarı akma, dökülme; **'ef.flu.ent 1.** *adj.* dışarı akan, akıp giden; **2.** *n.* akıntı, dökülme; fabrika vs. den dökülen artık sıvı *vs.*

ef.flux ['eflʌks] *n.* dışarı akış, akıntı.

ef.fort ['efət] *n.* gayret, çaba, uğraş (*at*); F elde edilen başarı; **'ef.fort.less** ☐ zahmetsiz, çaba sarfetmeyen; kolay.

ef.fron.ter.y [i'frʌntəri] *n.* küstahlık, yüzsüzlük, hayasızlık.

ef.ful.gence [e'fʌldʒəns] *n.* parlaklık, parıltı; debdebe, görkem, şaşaa, ihtişam; **ef'ful.gent** ☐ parlak, ışıyan; şaşaalı, görkemli.

ef.fuse [e'fjuːz] *v/t.* dışarı akıtmak, dökmek, sızdırmak; **ef.fu.sion** [i'fjuː-ʒən] *n.* dökme, içini boşaltma (*a. fig.*); akma; dökülen, akan *veya* sızan sıvı *veya* gaz; **ef'fu.sive** ☐ [_siv] taşkın, taşan, bol, coşkun; **ef'fu.sive.ness** *n.* taşkınlık, coşkunluk, bolluk.

eft ZOO [eft] *n.* ufak semender *veya* kertenkele.

egg¹ [eg] *mst* ~ *on v/t.* b-ni bşi yapması için sıkıştırmak, tahrik etm., gayrete getirmek.

egg² [_] *n.* yumurta, tohum; *in the ~* ilk aşamada, başlangıç devresinde; *bad ~* F ciğeri beş para etmez adam; *put all one's ~ in one basket* varını yoğunu tek bir şeye bağlayarak tehlikeye atmak, tüm sermayesini bir işe yatırmak; *as sure as ~s is ~s* F hiç şüphesiz, kaçınılması olanaksız; '~*-cup* *n.* yumurta kabı; '~*-flip* *n.* yumurtalı içki; '~*.head* *n. Am. sl.* entellektüel, aydın *b-i*; '~*-nog* = *egg-flip*; '~*-plant* *n.* BOT patlıcan; '~*-shell* *n.* yumurta kabuğu; '~*-whisk* *n.* yumurta çırpma teli.

eg.lan.tine BOT ['eglıntain] *n.* bir tür kokulu gül, yaban gülü.

e.go ['egəu] *n.* benlik, mevcudiyet,

varlıkı, varoluş, ben, ego; 'e.go.ism n.
bencilik, egoizm, yalnız kendi öz
varlığını düşünme ve sevme, hodbinlik; 'e.goist n. egoist, bencil, hodbin,
yalnız kendi çıkarını düşünen b-i;
e.go'is.tic, e.go'is.ti.cal □ egoist,
bencil, kendi çıkarını düşünen, hodkâm, menfaatperest; e.go.tism ['.-
tizəm] n. kendini beğenme, hodpe-
sentlik; 'ego.tist n. kendinden çok
bahseden kimse, benbenci; k-ni
beğenmiş b-i; e.go'tis.tic, e.go'tis.ti-
cal □ k-ni beğenmiş, k-ni dev aynasında gören.
e.gre.gious iro. □ [i'gri:dʒəs] fevkalâde kötü, çok kötü, işitilmemiş.
e.gress ['i:gres] n. çıkış, çıkılacak yer;
fig. çıkar yol, çare.
e.gret ['i:gret] n. ORN bir tür küçük beyaz balıkçıl; sorguç, kuş tepeliği.
E.gyp.tian [i'dʒipʃən] 1. adj. Mısır'a
ait; 2. n. Mısırlı.
eh [ei] int. nasıl?; ya?; Vay!; Ey!
ei.der ['aidə] n. a. ~-duck ORN pufla, kuzey kutbuna yakın yerlerde yaşayan bir
tür ördek; ~ down pufla tüyünden
yapılan yastık, yorgan vs.
eight [eit] 1. adj. sekiz; 2. n. sekiz rakamı; NAUT sekiz kişilik skif; behind
the ~ ball Am. sıkıntıda, zor durumda;
eighteen ['ei'ti:n] n. & adj. onsekiz;
'eight'eenth [-θ] n. & adj. onsekizinci;
eightfold adj. & adv. sekiz misli;
eighth [eitθ] 1. adj. sekizinci; 2. n. sekizde bir; 'eighthly adv. sekizinci olarak; eight-'hour day sekiz saatlik
çalışma günü; eight.i.eth ['-iiθ] adj.
sekseninci; 'eight.some [-səm] n. (8
dansçı ile yapılan) bir İskoç dansı;
'eight.y n. & adj. seksen.
eis.tedd.fod [ais'teðvɔd] n. Gal ülkesinde müzisyenler, edebiyatçılar ve
saz şairlerinin yıllık yarışması.
ei.ther ['aiðə] 1. adj. & pron. ikisinden
biri, ya o ya bu, her iki; 2. cj. ~ ... or
...ya ...yahut...
e.jac.u.late [i'dʒækjuleit] vb. birdenbire söyleyivermek; atmak, fışkırtmak;
e.jacu'la.tion n. ünlem, nida; dışarı atma, fışkırtma.
e.ject [i:dʒekt] v/t. dışarı atmak, kovmak (from -den), çıkarmak,
fışkırtmak; (görev) azletmek; e'jec-
tion n. çıkarma, kovma, azil; fışkıran
şey; e'ject.ment n. JUR boşaltma, tahliye, çıkarma; e'jec.tor n. MEC tırnak,
tüfekten boş kovanları atan mekaniz-

ma; ~-seat n. AVIA fırlatma koltuğu.
eke [i:k]: ~ out v/t. tamamlamak, ikmal
etm. (with, by ile), (maaş) katkı sağlamak, idareli kullanmak, idare etmek; ~
out a miserable existence kıt kanaat
geçinmek.
EKG ['i:keidʒi:] n. Am. elektrokardiyogram.
el Am. F [el] = elevated railroad.
e.lab.o.rate 1. □ [i'læbərit] dikkatle
işlenmiş, özenilmiş, kusursuz; komplike, detaylı; 2. [-reit] vb. incelikle işlemek, ayrıntılı olarak hazırlamak;
e'lab.o.rateness [-ritnis] n. e.lab.o.ra-
tion [-'reiʃən] n. özenli işleme; detay.
e.lapse [i'læps] v/i. (zaman) geçmek,
akmak.
e.las.tic [i'læstik] 1. adj. (~ally) elâstiki,
esnek (a. fig.), eski şeklini alan; hoşgörü
sahibi, kendini çabuk toparlayan; 2. n.
lastik bant; e.las.tic.i.ty [elæs'tisiti] n.
elastikiyet, esneklik; fig. takat, kudret.
e.late [i'leit] v/t. sevindirmek, mutlu
etm., gurur vermek; e'lated adj. sevinçli, mutlu, gururlu (at, with); e'la-
tion n. sevinç, kıvanç, gurur.
el.bow ['elbəu] 1. n. dirsek; kavis, dönemeç, viraj; MEC dirsek, açı; at one's ~
elinin altında yardıma hazır; out at
~s kılıksız, pejmürde; fig. sefil, perişan; 2. v/t. dirsekle dürtmek; ~ one's
way through ite kaka k-ne yol açmak;
~ out b-ni bir yerden atmak, defetmek;
'~'chair n. koltuk; '~-grease n. F (parlatma, temizleme) el emeği; '~-room n.
hareket serbestliği olan yer.
eld.er¹ ['eldə] 1. adj. daha yaşlı, büyük;
2. n. ihtiyar; kilise mütevelli heyeti
üyesi; my ~s ailedeki büyüklerim.
eld.er² BOT [-] n. mürver ağacı.
eld.er.ly ['eldəli] adj. yaşlı(ca), geçkin.
eld.est ['eldist] adj. en yaşlı, en büyük;
the ~ born ilk doğan çocuk.
e.lect [i'lekt] 1. adj. seçilmiş, seçimi kazanmış; ECCL cennete gidecek; bride ~
nişanlı; 2. vb. seçilmek; karar vermek
(to do); 3. n. pl. ECCL the ~s cennete
gidecek olanlar; e'lec.tion n. seçim;
e.lection.eer [-ʃə'niə] v/i. seçim pro-
pogandası yapmak; e.lec.tion'eer.ing
n. seçim propagandası; e'lec.tive 1.
□ seçimle getirilen; seçme yetkisi
olan; seçim...; Am. isteğe bağlı, ihtiyarî; 2. n. Am. seçmeli ders; e'lec.tive.ly
adv. seçimle, seçim yoluyla; e'lec.tor
n. seçmen, seçme yetkisi olan b-i; HIST
kutsal Roma imparatorunu seçen altı

seçiciden *b-i*; e'**lec.tor.al** *adj.* seçim...; seçmen...; seçimle ilgili; **~ address** seçim nutku; **~ college** *Am.* seçmenler kurulu; **~ roll** seçmen listesi; e'**lec.tor.ate** [ˌtərit] *n.* seçmenler; e'**lectress** *n.* ʜɪsᴛ kutsal Roma imparatorunu seçen altı seçiciden kadın olanı; kadın seçmen.

e.**lec.tric** [i'lektrik], e'**lec.tri.cal** □ elektrik(li); elektro...; *fig.* elektriklen(dir)ilmiş; e'**lec.tri.cal en.gi.neer** elektrik muhendisi.

e.**lec.tric...**; **~ blue** çelik mavisi; **~ chair** elektrikli sandalye.

e.**lec.tri.cian** [ilek'triʃən] *n.* elektrik teknisyeni, elektrikçi; e.lec'**tric.i.ty** [ˌsiti] *n.* elektrik; elektrik akımı; e.**lec.tri.fi'cation** *n.* elektrikle(n)me; e'**lec.tri.fy** [ˌfai], e'**lec.trize** *v/t.* elektrikle(ndir)mek (*a. fig.*); elektrikleştirmek; heyecana getirmek, coşturmak.

e.**lec.tro** [i'lektrəu] *prefix* elektrikle işleyen, elektro...; e'**lec.tro.cute** [ˌtrəkju:t] *v/t.* elektrikli sandalyede idam etm., elektrik akımı vererek öldürmek; e.**lectro'cu.tion** *n.* elektrikle idam *veya* ölüm; e'**lec.trode** [ˌtrəud] *n.* elektrot; e'**lec.tro-dy'nam.ics** *n. mst sg.* elektrodinamik; e.**lec.tro.lier** [ˌ'liə] *n.* elektrikli avize; e'**lec.tro.lyse** [ˌlaiz] *v/t.* elektrikle ayrıştırmak; e.**lec.trol.y.sis** [ilek'trəlisis] *n.* elektroliz; e.**lec.tro.lyte** [i'lektrəulait] *n.* elektrolit; e'**lec.tro.lyt.ic** [ˌ'litik] *adj.* elektrolitik; e'**lec.tro'mag.net** *n.* elektrikli mıknatıs; e'**lec.tro'met.al.lur.gy** *n.* madenleri alaşımlarından ayırmada kullanılan elektrikli yöntem bilimi; e'**lec.tro'mo.tive** *adj.* elektrik akımının geçmesini sağlayan; e'**lec.tro'mo.tor** *n.* elektromotor.

e.**lec.tron** [i'lektrɔn] *n.* elektron; *attr.* elektron...; e.lec'**tron.ic** *adj.* elektronik...; e.**lec'tron.ics** *n. sg.* elektronik bilimi.

e.**lectro.plate** [i'lektrəupleit] **1.** *v/t.* elektroliz usulü ile kaplamak; **2.** *n.* bu şekilde kaplanmış esya; e'**lec.tro.type** *n.* galvanize klişe, elektrikle yapılmış klişe.

el.**ee.mos.y.nar.y** [elii:'məsinəri] *adj.* sadaka olarak verilmiş.

el.**e.gance** ['eligəns] *n.* zarafet, şıklık, incelik; '**el.e.gant** □ zarif, şık, ince, kibar, nazik, *Am.* birinci sınıf.

el.**e.gi.ac** [eli'dʒaiək] **1.** *adj.* hüzünlü, elemli, hazin, mersiye tarzında; **2.** *n.*

mersiye tarzında yazılmış şiir.

el.**e.gy** ['elidʒi] *n.* ağıt, mersiye, eleji.

el.**e.ment** ['elimənt] *n.* öğe, unsur, eleman; cüz, esas (*hava, ateş, toprak, su gibi*) dört ana unsurdan her biri; ᴇʟᴇᴄᴛ pil; ᴄʜᴇᴍ element; **~s** *pl.* esaslar, elementer bilgiler; kötü hava şartları; el.**e.men.tal** [ˌment] □ temel, ilkel, basit, elemanter, esas(lı); doğaya ait; el.**e.'men.ta.ry** □ basit, öz, başlangıç; ilk...; **~ school** ilkokul; **elementaries** *pl.* esaslar, unsurlar.

el.**e.phant** ['elifənt] *n.* ᴢᴏᴏ fil; **white ~** değerli fakat işe yaramayan mal, mülk; el.**e.phan.tine** [ˌ'fæntain] *adj.* fil gibi..., hantal, kaba.

el.**e.vate** ['eliveit] *v/t.* yükseltmek; *fig.* sesini yükseltmek, yaygara koparmak; '**el.e.vat.ed 1.** *adj.* yüksek, yüce, ulu; F çakırkeyf; **~ railroad = 2.** *n. Am.* F şehir içinde yapılmış sütunlar üzerinden geçen demiryolu; el.**e'va.tion** *n.* yükseltme, yüceltme; yükseklik, yücelik, irtifa, rakım, altıtüt; yüksek yer, tepe; ᴀsᴛ yıldızların yükseliği; ᴍᴇᴄ dikey kesit; '**ele.va.tor** *n.* ᴍᴇᴄ kaldırma mekanizması; *Am.* asansör; ᴀᴠɪᴀ irtifa dümeni; (**grain**) **~** *Am.* tahıl ambarı; **bucket ~** ᴍᴇᴄ tahılı üst katlara nakleden makine.

e.**lev.en** [i'levn] **1.** *adj.* onbir; **2.** *n.* onbir rakkamı; **~'plus** ex.am.i.na.tion *n.* İngiltere'de 11 yaşına gelen çocuğun girdiği ortaokul giriş sınavı; e'**lev.enth** [ˌθ] *adj.* onbirinci; **at the ~ hour** son dakika, son anda.

elf [elf] *n., pl.* **elves** [elvs] peri, cin; cüce; **elf.in** [ˌ'in] *adj.* cin gibi, ele avuca sığmaz; '**elf.ish** *adj.* yaramaz, şirret.

e.**lic.it** [i'lisit] *v/t.* (*bilgi vs.*) sağlamak; (*gerçek*) aydınlığa kavuşturmak.

e.**lide** ɢʀ [i'laid] *v/t.* hızlı konuşurken atlamak, telaffuz etmemek (*harf, hece*).

el.**i.gi.bil.i.ty** [elidʒə'biliti] *n.* uygunluk, tercih; '**el.i.gi.ble** □ seçilebilir, uygun, elverişli; evlilik için uygun (*koca*).

e.**lim.i.nate** [i'limineit] *v/t.* ayırmak, bertaraf etm.; ortadan kaldırmak, çıkarmak (*esp.* ᴄʜᴇᴍ, ᴍᴀᴛʜ, ᴍᴇᴅ); e.**lim.i'na.tion** *n.* çıkarma, ayırma.

e.**li.sion** ɢʀ [i'liʒən] *n.* çıkarma, şiirde özellikle sözcük sonundaki harf *ya da* hecenin okunmaması.

elite [ei'li:t] *n.* seçkin kimseler, elit tabaka.

e.**lix.ir** [i'liksə] *n.* iksir.

E.**liz.a.be.than** [ilizə'bi:θən] **1.** *adj.*

İngiltere'de kraliçe I. Elizabeth devrine ait; **2.** *n.* o devirde yaşamış kimse.

elk ZOO [elk] *n.* iri boynuzlu bir geyik türü.

ell HIST [el] *n.* endaze, arşın.

el.lipse MATH [i'lips] *n.* elips; **el'lipsis** [-sis] *n., pl.* **el'lipses** GR [-si:z] bir tümcenin anlamı bozulmaksızın öğelerinden birinin atılması; **el'lip.tic, el-'lip.ti.cal**□[-tik(əl)] oval, eliptik, beyzi; anlatılmak isteneni tam açıklamayan, dolambaçlı (*söz*).

elm BOT [elm] *n.* karaağaç.

el.o.cu.tion [elə'kju:ʃən] *n.* söz söyleme sanatı, hitabet; **el.o'cu.tion.ar.y** [-ʃnəri] *adj.* hitabete ait; **el.o'cu.tion-ist** *n.* hatip, belagat sahibi *b-i.*

e.lon.gate ['i:lɔŋgeit] *v/t.* gerip uzatmak; **e.lon'ga.tion** *n.* uza(t)ma, uza(n)mış kısım; AST bir gezegenin güneş *ya da* uydusu arasındaki açı farkı.

e.lope [i'ləup] *v/i.* aşığı ile kaçmak, evlenmek için evden kaçmak; **e'lope-ment** *n. b-le* kaçma.

el.o.quence ['eləukwəns] *n.* belâgat, güzel söz söyleme sanatı; **'el.o.quent** □ beliğ, dokunaklı, belâgatli.

else [els] *adj. & adv.* yoksa; başka, daha; başka yer, başka zaman, başka şekilde; *all* ~ başka herşey; *anyone* ~ başka herhangi *b-i; what* ~? bundan başka ne var?; *or* ~ yoksa, aksi halde; **else'where** başka yer(de).

e.lu.ci.date [i'lu:sideit] *v/t.* açıklamak, izah etm., (*güçlük, sır*) aydınlatmak; **e.lu.ci'da.tion** *n.* açıklama, izah; **e'lu-cida.to.ry** *adj.* aydınlatıcı, açıklayıcı.

e.lude [i'lu:d] *v/t.* sakınmak, sıyrılmak, paçayı kurtarmak *-den.*

e.lu.sion [i'lu:ʒən] *n.* kaçıp kurtulma, sıyrılma, sakınma; kaçamaklı söz; **e'lu.sive** [-siv] *adj.* tutulmaz, ele geçmez; **e'lusive.ness** *n.* yakalanmayış, sakınma, kaçamak; **e'lu.so.ry** *adj.* aldatıcı, yanıltıcı.

elves [elvz] *pl. of* **elf.**

E.lys.ian [i'lizion] *adj.* cennete ait, cennet gibi; semavî, ilahî; **E'lys.ium** [-iəm] *n.* cennet, mutluluk bahçesi.

em [em] *n.* TYP katrat, harfler arasına konan yazısız maden parçası.

e.ma.ci.ate [i'meiʃieit] *v/t.* cok zayıflatmak, bir deri bir kemik bırakmak; **e.ma.ci.a.tion** [imeisi'eiʃən] *n.* çok zavuflatma.

e-mail ['i:meil] **1.** *n.* e-posta; **2.** *v/t.* e--posta göndermek; ~ *address* *n.* e-pos-

ta adresi.

em.a.nate ['emэneit] *vb.* cıkmak, yavılmak (*from -den*); **em.a'na.tion** *n.* çıkma, yavılma.

e.man.ci.pate [i'mænsipeit] *v/t.* serbest bırakmak, özgür kılmak; **e.manci'pation** *n.* serbest bırakma, eşit hakları verme; **e'man.ci.pa.tor** *n.* serbest bırakan, azat eden *b-i.*

e.mas.cu.late 1. [i'mæskjuleit] *v/t.* hadım etm., iğdiş etm.; kuvvetten düşürmek; (*metin*) sansür ederek hafifletmek; **2.** [-lit] *adj.* kuvvetten düşmüş; efemine, kadın tavırlı; **e.mas-cu.la.tion**[-'leiʃən] *n.* hadım etme *veya* edilme; kuvvetten düş(ür)me; (*metin*) sansür etme.

em.balm [im'bɑ:m] *v/t.* mumyalamak, tahnit etm.; anmak, anısını yaşatmak; *be* ~*ed* unutulmamak; **em'balm.ment** *n.* mumyalama, tahnit.

em.bank [im'bæŋk] *vb.* (*toprak, taş vs. ile*) etrafına set yapmak; **em'bankment** *n.* set, bent; nehir vs. set yapma.

em.bar.go [em'bɑ:gəu] **1.** *n.* ambargo, ticareti sınırlama, yasaklama; **2.** *vb.* ambargo koymak, müsadere etm.

em.bark [im'bɑ:k] *v/t. & v/i.* gemiye bin(dir)mek (*for*); (*para*) yatırmak; *bşe* girişmek, yanaşmak (*in, on, upon*); **em.barka.tion** [embɑ:'keiʃən] *n.* gemiye bin(dir)me; girişim.

em.bar.rass [im'bærəs] *v/t.* şaşırtmak, utandırmak, mahcup etm., sıkmak; engellemek, mani olm.; ~*ed* *adj.* mahcup, sıkılgan, çekingen, şaşkın; (*para*) sıkıntıda; **em'bar.rass.ing** □ utandırıcı; nahoş, sıkıntılı; **em'bar-rass.ment**.*n.* (*para*) sıkıntı; sıkılganlık, utanma, şaşkınlık.

em.bas.sy ['embəsi] *n.* büyük *veya* orta elçilik; sefarethane.

em.bat.tle [im'bætl] *vb.* meydan savaşına hazırlamak; harp düzeninde mevzilemek; mazgal yapmak.

em.bed [im'bed] *v/t.* gömmek, yerleştirmek.

em.bel.lish [im'beliʃ] *v/t.* süslemek, güzelleştirmek; (*hikâye*) gerçek olmayan ayrıntılar ekleyerek ilginç hale sokmak; **em'bel.lish.ment**.*n.* süsleme, güzelleştirme, süs.

em.ber-days ['embədeiz] *n. pl.* bazı hıristiyan kiliselerinde dua ederek *ve* oruç tutarak (*et yemeyerek*) geçirilen üçer günlük dört mevsim perhizi.

em.bers ['embəz] *n. pl.* sönmekte olan

ateş, kor, köz; *fig.* kıvılcım.

em.bez.zle [im'bezl] *vb.* zimmetine geçirmek; **em'bez.zle.ment** *n.* zimmetine geçirme; **em'bez.zler** *n.* zimmetine para geçiren *b-i.*

em.bit.ter [im'bitə] *v/t.* acılaştırmak; gücendirmek, öfkelendirmek.

em.bla.zon [im'bleizən] *vb.* aileye ait armalarla süslemek; *fig.* ayyuka çıkarmak; **em'bla.zon.ry** *n.* arma ressamlığı; süsleme.

em.blem ['embləm] *n.* sembol, simge, amblem, işaret; **em.blem.at.ic**, **emblemat.i.cal** □ [embli'mætik(əl)] sembolik.

em.bod.i.ment [im'bɔdimənt] *n.* cisimlenme, şekil alma; düzenleme; **embod.y** *v/t.* cisimlendirmek, temsil etm., ifade etm., belirtmek; içermek; düzenlemek; (*ülke*) ilhak etm.

em.bold.en [im'bəuldən] *vb.* cesaret vermek, teşvik etm.

em.bo.lism MED [embəlizəm] *n.* amboli, damar tıkanması.

em.bos.om [im'buzəm] *v/t.* kucaklamak, bağrına basmak; **~ed with** etrafı ... ile çevrili.

em.boss [im'bɔs] *vb.* kabartma işleri yapmak, kakmak, çekiçle dövmek; **em'bossed** *adj.* kabartmalı; **~ note-paper** kabartma simgeli kağıt.

em.bow.el [im'bəuləl] *vb.* (*ölen hayvanın*) bağırsaklarını çıkarmak.

em.brace [im'breis] **1.** *v/t. & v/i.* kucakla(ş)mak, kolları arasına almak; (meslek) seçmek, tutmak; kabul etm., benimsemek; **2.** *n.* kucakla(ş)ma, sarılma.

em.bra.sure [im'breiʒə] *n.* bir kapı *veya* pencerenin meyilli pervazı, mazgal eğimi.

em.bro.cate ['embrəukeit] *v/t.* ovmak, friksiyon yapmak; **em.bro'ca.tion** *n.* ovuşturma, friksiyon.

em.broi.der [im'brɔidə] *v/t. -in* üzerine nakış işlemek; *fig.* abartmak, ballandırmak; **em'broi.der.y** *n.* nakış işleme; *fig.* abartı, mübalâğa.

em.broil [im'brɔil] *vb.* ara bozmak, karmakarışık etm., dallandırıp budaklandırmak, karıştırmak; **em'broilment** *n.* karışıklık, anlaşmazlık.

em.bry.o ['embriəu] *n.* cenin, dölüt; *in*~ gelişmemiş halde, tasarı halinde; **embry.on.ic** [_'ɔnik] *adj.* cenine ait; gelişmemiş, ilkel (*a. fig.*).

em.bus [im'bʌs] *vb.* (motorlu araca)

bin(dir)mek.

e.mend [i:mend] *v/t.* (metin) düzeltmek, tashih etm.; **e.men'da.tion** *n.* tashih, düzeltme; '**e.men.da.tor** *n.* (*metin*) tashihçi, düzelten; **e'mend.a.to.ry** [_-dətəri] *adj.* düzeltme kabilinden, tashihî.

em.er.ald ['emərəld] **1.** *n.* zümrüt; **2.** *adj.* zümrüt yeşili rengi.

e.merge [i'mə:dʒ] *v/i.* ortaya çıkmak (*from, out of -den*); *fig.* sökün etm.; görünmek, doğmak, gözükmek; hasıl olm.; **e'mer.gence** *n.* çıkma, zuhur.

e.mer.gen.cy [i'mə:dʒənsi] *n.* olağanüstü durum, tehlike; **~ brake** imdat freni; **~ call** istimdat, imdat isteme; **~ decree** geçici yasa, kararname; **~ ex.it** ihtiyat, imdat kapısı; **~ land.ing** AVIA zorunlu iniş; **~ man** *spor*: yedek oyuncu.

e.mer.gent [i'mə:dʒənt] *adj.* çıkan, zuhur eden; **~ countries** *pl.* fakir ve bağımlı durumdan zengin ve bağımsız duruma geçen devletler.

e.mer.sion [i'mə:ʃən] *n.* yeniden görünme; AST bir gök cisminin tam *veya* yarım tutulmadan sonra yeniden görünmesi.

em.er.y ['eməri] *n.* zımpara; '**~-cloth** *n.* zımpara bezi; '**~-pa.per** *n.* zımpara kağıdı.

e.met.ic [i'metik] **1.** *adj.* kusturucu; **2.** *n.* kusturucu ilaç.

em.i.grant ['emigrənt] **1.** *adj.* göç eden; **2.** *n.* göçmen; **em.i.grate** ['_greit] *v/i.* göçmek, göç etm.; **em.i'gra.tion** *n.* göç, hicret; **em.i.gra.to.ry** ['_greitəri] *adj.* göçmen...

em.i.nence ['eminəns] *n.* yükseklik; yüksek yer, tepe; yüksek rütbe, itibar; '**emi.nent** □ *fig.* seçkin, yüksek, mümtaz, güzide (*in, for*); '**em.i.nent.ly** *adv.* pek, gayet, fevkalade.

e.mir [e'miə] *n.* emir; **e.mir.ate** [e'miərit] *n.* emirlik.

em.is.sar.y *n.* kurye, özel bir görevle gönderilen memur, gizli ajan; **e.mission** [i'miʃən] *n.* yayma, çıkarma, neşretme; çıkarılan şey; PHYS yayılma; *fig.* sonuç, tesir; COM tahvil çıkarma.

e.mit [i'mit] *v/t.* çıkarmak, neşretmek, dışarı vermek, fışkırtmak, yaymak; COM tedavüle çıkarmak; *fig.* söylemek.

e.mol.u.ment [i'mɔljumənt] *n.* ücret, bir hizmet karşılığı alınan para; **~s** *pl.* gelir, irat, varidat.

e.mo.tion [i'məuʃən] *n.* heyecan, duy-

gu, his; **e'mo.tion.al** [-ʃənl] □ duygulu, heyecanlı, hassas, duygusal, dokunaklı, hislerine kolay kapılan; **e.mo-
tion.al.i.ty** [-ʃə'næliti] *n.* duygunluk,
hassasiyet, duyarlık; **e'mo.tion.less**
adj. hissiz, duyarsız, soğuk neva;
e'mo.tive *adj.* duygusal, hissî.
em.pan.el [im'pænl] *vb.* (*jüri heyeti*)
adını listeye yazmak.
em.pa.thy PSYCH ['empəθi] *n.* duyarlık,
b-nin duygularını seziş inceliği.
em.per.or ['empərə] *n.* imparator.
em.pha.sis ['emfəsis] *n.*, *pl.* **em-
pha.ses** ['-siːz] şiddet, vurgu, kuvvet;
önem; **em.pha.size** ['-saiz] *v/t.* önem
vermek *-e*; vurgulamak *-i*; **em.phat.ic**
[im'fætik] *adj.* (**~ally**) etkili; vurgulu,
önemli; **be ~ that** kesinlikle …ki.
em.pire ['empaiə] *n.* imparatorluk; **the
British** ♀ Büyük Britanya İmparator-
luğu.
em.pir.ic [em'pirik] **1.** *n.* bilginin kitap-
lardan değil, deneyle edinileceğine
inanan *b-i*; şarlatan; **em'pir.i.cal** □
edinilen deneyimlere göre, deneysel,
ampirik; **em'pir.i.cism** [-sizəm] *n.* bilginin esasının deneye dayandığını ileri
süren felsefi görüş, görgücülük; şarlatanlık; **em'pir.i.cist** *n.* bu görüşe inanan *b-i*; şarlatan.
em.place.ment MIL [im'pleismənt] *n.*
top mevzii, tabya.
em.plane [im'plein] *v/t.* & *v/i.* uçağa
bin(dir)mek.
em.ploy [im'plɔi] **1.** *v/t.* kullanmak, istihdam etm., çalıştırmak *-i*, iş vermek
-e; (*vakit, enerji*) sarfetmek, vermek; **2.**
n. görev, hizmet; **in the ~ of** hizmetinde; **em.ploy.é, em.ploy.ée** [ɔm'plɔiei],
employ.ee [emplɔi'iː] *n.* işçi, müstahdem, işalan; **em.ploy.er** [im'plɔiə] *n.*
işveren, patron; **em'ploy.ment** *n.* iş
verme, memuriyet, istihdam; **~ agency** iş ve işçi bulma kurumu; **place of
~** işyeri; ♀ **Exchange** iş ve işçi bulma
bürosu.
em.po.ri.um [em'pɔːriəm] *n.* alışveriş
merkezi, dükkân, bonmarşe, ticaret
merkezi.
em.pow.er [im'pauə] *v/t.* yetki vermek
e, ehil kılmak *-i*.
em.press ['empris] *n.* imparatoriçe.
emp.ti.ness ['emptinis] *n.* boşluk;
'**emp.ty 1.** □ boş; anlamsız; *fig.* kof;
F aç; **2.** *vb.* boşal(t)mak, dökmek, akıtmak, tahliye etm.; **3.** *n.* içi boş şey;
empties *pl.* COM bos (*sandıklar, şişeler*

vs.).
em.pur.ple [im'pəːpl] *v/t.* mor renge
boyamak, morartmak.
e.mu ORN ['iːmjuː] *n.* Avustralya'da ya-
sayan devekuşuna benzer bir tür kuş.
em.u.late ['emjuleit] *v/t.* rekabet halinde bulunmak, yarışmak, *b-ni k-ne* örnek almak, aynı başarıları elde etm.;
em.u'lat.ion *n.* rekabet, yarışma gayreti; **em.ula.tive** ['-lətiv] *adj.* rekabet
edici (**of**); **em.u.la.tor** ['-leitə] *n. b-ni
k-ne* örnek alan *b-i*; **'em.u.lous** □
(**of**) *b-ne* benzemeye çalışan, gıpta
eden, *b-ni* kıskanan.
e.mul.sion CHEM [i'mʌlʃən] *n.* emulsi-
yon, sübye, mustahlep.
en.a.ble ['ineibl] *v/t.* muktedir kılmak,
kuvvet vermek *-e*, yetki vermek, imkân vermek *-e*; izin vermek.
en.act [i'nækt] *v/i.* kararlaştırmak, hükmetmek; (*yasa*) çıkarmak; THEAT temsil etm., oynamak; **be ~ed** oynana oynana aşınmak; **en'act.ment** *n.* yasa-
laştırma; yasa, kararname.
en.am.el [i'næməl] **1.** *n.* emay, (*diş*) mine, sır; **2.** *vb.* mine ile kaplamak, sırlamak; *poet.* süslemek.
en.am.o(u)r [i'næmə] *v/t.* aşık etm.; **be
~ed of** aşık, tutkun *-e*.
en.cage [in'keidʒ] *v/t.* kafese koymak,
kafese kapamak.
en.camp MIL [in'kæmp] *v/i.* ordugâh
kurmak, kamp kurmak; **en'campment** *n.* ordugâh, karargâh, kamp.
en.case [in'keis] *v/t.* kılıflamak, örtmek; **en'case.ment** *n.* kılıf, mahfaza,
örtü.
en.cash.ment COM [in'kæʃmənt] *n.*
tahsil etme, paraya çevirme, ahzu
kabz.
en.caus.tic [en'kɔːstik] **1.** *adj.* renkli
mumlar ısıtılarak boyanmış (*kiremit,
çini vs.*); **2.** *n.* renkli mumları bir yüzeye sürüp ısı ile sabitleştirerek yapılan
bir boyama metodu.
en.ceph.a.li.tis MED [enkefə'laitis] *n.*
beyin iltihabı, ansefalit.
en.chain [in'tʃəin] *v/t.* zincirlemek,
zincire vurmak (**in, with, by**); *k-ne*
bağlamak, celbetmek.
en.chant [in'tʃɑːnt] *v/t.* büyülemek,
k-ne bağlamak; *fig.* aklını başından almak, çıldırtmak; **en'chant.er** *n.* büyüleyen kimse, büyücü; **en'chant.ment**
n. büyü, sihir, cazibe; **en'chant.ress**
n. büyücü kadın; büyüleyen kadın, dilber.

en.chase [in'tʃeis] *vb.* kalemle kazımak (*çizmek*, *oymak*); (*kıymetli taş*) yerleştirmek, oturtmak; *fig.* süslemek.

en.cir.cle [in'sə:kl] *v/t.* (**by, with, in**) kuşatmak, etrafını çevirmek, sarmak; **en'cir.cle.ment** *n.* kuşatma, ihata; POL kuşatma politikası.

en.close [in'kləuz] *v/t.* (**by, in**) çitle etrafını çevirmek, kuşatmak, katmak, ilâve etm.; ilişikte göndermek; **en'clo.sure** [-ʒə] *n.* çit; çit *veya* duvarla çevrili arazi; ilişik kağıt, ilişikte gönderilen şey.

en.co.mi.ast [en'kəumiæst] *n.* methiye yazan kimse, kaside yazarı; **en'co.mi.um** [-mjəm] *n.* methiye, övücü nutuk.

en.com.pass [in'kʌmpəs] *v/t.* -*in* etrafını çevirmek, kusatmak.

en.core [ɔŋ'kɔ:] **1.** *int.* bir daha!, tekrar!; **2.** *v/i.* gelsin diye bağırmak; *v/t.* bir şarkı vs.'nin tekrarlanmasını istemek; **3.** *n.* tekrar etme; program dışı parçası, bis.

en.coun.ter [in'kauntə] **1.** *n.* karşılaşma, rastlantı, tesadüf, karşı karşıya gelme; çarpışma; **2.** *v/t.* karşılamak; *b-ne, bşe* birdenbire rastlamak, karşı karşıya gelmek; çarpışmak.

en.cour.age [in'kʌridʒ] *v/t.* teşvik etm., cesaret vermek -*e*; **en'cour.age.ment** *n.* teşvik, cesaret verme; **en'cour.ag.er** *n.* teşvik eden, cesaret veren *b-i*.

en.croach [in'krəutʃ] *v/i.* tecavüz etm., el uzatmak (**on, upon** -*e*); sokulmak, nüfuz etm.; halel getirmek -*e*; ~ *upon s.o.'s kindness b-nin* iyiliğini suistimal etm.; **en'croach.ment** *n.* tecavüz, müdahale, karışma (**on, upon, in** -*e*).

en.crust [in'krʌst] *vb.* kabuk bağlamak, sert bir tabaka oluşturmak (**with** *ile*); MEC üstüne katıca bir kabuk çekmek.

en.cum.ber [in'kʌmbə] *v/t.* yüklemek; tıkabasa doldurmak; mani olm., engel olm. -*e*; tıkamak (*yol*); **en'cum.brance** *n.* yük; *fig.* engel, mani; ipotek, borçlar yükü; **without** ~ çocuksuz; ipoteksiz.

en.cyc.li.cal ECCL [en'siklikəl] *n.* Papanın Katolik piskoposlara gönderdiği mektup, tamim.

en.cy.clo.p(a)e.di.a [ensaiklə u'pi:djə] *n.* ansiklopedi; **en.cy.clo'p(a)e.dic** *adj.* ansiklopedik.

end [end] **1.** *n.* son; amaç, gaye; sonuç, âkıbet; **be at an** ~ bitmiş tükenmiş olm.; **no** ~ **of** sonsuz, pek çok, sayısız; **have s.th. at one's finger's** ~**s** hük-

metmek; **in the** ~ sonunda; **on** ~ dik, ayakta; aralıksız, arka arkaya, biteviye; **stand on** ~ (*tüyleri*) ürpermek; dikine koymak; **to the** ~ **that** …amacı ile, böylece, bu suretle; **to no** ~ nafile, boşuna; **to this** ~ bu amaçla; **come to an** ~ son bulmak, bitmek; **go off the deep** ~ *fig.* kontrolunu kaybetmek, öfkelenmek; **make an** ~ **of, put an** ~ **to** son vermek, bitirmek; **make both** ~**s meet** (*para*) geçinebilmek, iki yakasını bir araya getirmek; **2.** *v/t. & v/i.* bit(ir)mek, son vermek, son bulmak.

en.dan.ger [in'deindʒə] *v/t.* tehlikeye düşürmek.

en.dear [in'diə] *v/t.* sevdirmek (**to** -*e*); **en'dear.ing** *adj.* cazip, çekici, alımlı, edalı; şefkatli, müşfik; **en'dear.ment** *n.* okşama; sevgi dolu söz *ya da* davranış.

en.deav.o(u)r [in'devə] **1.** *n.* emek, çaba, gayret; **2.** *vb.* çalışmak, çabalamak, gayret etm., *bşi* elde etmeğe çalışmak (**after**).

en.dem.ic MED [en'demik] **1.** *a.* en'dem.i.cal □ bir bölge *veya* zümreye ait, yöresel; **2.** *n.* yöresel hastalık.

end.ing ['endiŋ] *n.* son, nihayet; GR sonek.

en.dive BOT ['endiv] *n.* hindiba, andilya.

end.less □ ['endlis] sonsuz, ebedî; MEC (*kayış, zincir vs.*) uçları birleştirilmiş, dairevi.

en.dorse [in'dɔ:s] *v/t.* COM ciro etm.; kloz koymak; onaylamak; *endorsing ink* ıstampa mürekkebi; **en.dor.see** [endɔ:si:] *n. k-ne* ciro edilen kimse; lehdar; **endorse.ment** [in'dɔ:smənt] *n.* onay; COM ciro; **en'dors.er** *n.* ciro eden kimse, ciranta.

en.do.sperm BOT ['endəuspə:m] *n.* besidoku, endosperm, tohumun içindeki besleyici doku.

en.dow [in'dau] *v/t.* donatmak; bahşetmek, (*bir hayır kurumu vs.'ye*) bağış yapmak; **en'dow.ment** *n.* bağış, teberru; vakıf, tahsisat; yetenek; Allah vergisi.

en.due *mst fig.* [in'dju:] *vb.* giy(dir)mek; *b-ni bşle* donatmak, teçhiz etm. (**with**); bahş ve ihsan etm., nasip etm.

en.dur.a.ble [in'djuərəbl] *adj.* dayanılabilir, tahammül edilebilir; **en'dur.ance** *n.* tahammül, sabır, metanet; *past* ~ tahammül edilmez, çekilemez; ~ *flight* havada kalış süresi; ~ *run* mukavemet koşusu; **en'dure** *v/t.* taham-

mül etm., dayanmak *-e*; **en'dur.ing**
adj. sürekli; sabırlı; dayanıklı.

end.way(s) ['endwei(z)], **end.wise**
['‿waiz] *adv.* dik, dikine; uzunluğuna.

en.e.ma MED ['enimə] *n.* lavman, tenkiye, şırınga.

en.e.my ['enimi] **1.** *n.* düşman, hasım;
the ♀ şeytan, iblis; **2.** *adj.* düşmanca,
hasmane.

en.er.get.ic [enə'dʒetik] *adj.* (*‿ally*)
enerjik, faal; etkili; **'en.er.gize** *vb.*
ELECT enerji, güç vermek; harekete
geçmek; **'en.er.gy** *n.* enerji, güç, erke,
kuvvet (*a.* PHYS), gayret, azim; faaliyet,
hareket.

en.er.vate ['enə:veit] *v/t.* kuvvetten
düşürmek, zayıflatmak; **en.er'va.tion**
n. kuvvetten düsürme, zayıflatma.

en.fee.ble [in'fi:bl] *v/t.* kuvvetten
düşürmek; **en'fee.ble.ment** *n.* kuvvetten düşürme; zayıflatma.

en.feoff [in'fef] *vb.* tımar *veya* zeamet
şeklinde vermek; **en'feoff.ment** *n.*
tımar *veya* zeamet fermanı.

en.fi.lade MIL [enfi'leid] **1.** *n.* yan ateşi;
2. *vb.* yan ateşi ile taramak.

en.fold [in'fəuld] *v/t.* sarmak, katlamak; bağrına basmak, kucaklamak.

en.force [in'fɔ:s] *vb.* zorlamak, zorla
yaptırmak; zorla kabul ettirmek (*upon s.o. -e*), sözünü geçirmek (*upon
s.o.-e*); ısrar etm.; yasaları uygulamak,
icra etm., yürütmek; **en'force.a.ble**
adj. uygulanabilir; **en'force.ment** *n.*
uygulama, tatbik.

en.fran.chise [in'fræntʃaiz] *vb.* POL seçim hakkı vermek *-e*; (*köle*) özgür
kılmak, azat etm.; **en'fran.chise.ment**
[-ʃizmənt] *n.* oy verme hakkı, vatandaşlık haklarının tanınması; özgür
kılma, azat etme.

en.gage [in'geidʒ] *v/t.* hizmete almak,
tutmak, işe koymak, angaje etm.; işgal
etm.; ilgi çekmek; MIL saldırmak, taarruz etm.; **be ‿d** nişanlı olm. (*to ile*);
meşgul olm. (*in ile*); dolu olm.; **‿ the
clutch** tutturmak, kavramak; *v/i.* meşgul olm. (*to ile*); söz vermek, garanti
etm.; meşgul olm. (*in ile*); MIL çarpışmak; MEC birbirine geçmek; **en'gage-
ment** *n.* söz, vaat; angajman, hizmete
alma; nişanlanma; randevu; MIL
çarpışma; MEC (*dişli, çark vs.*) birbirine
geçme; **en.gage.ment ring** nişan yüzüğü.

en.gag.ing *fig.* □ [in'geidʒiŋ] cazip,
alımlı, sempatik.

en.gen.der *fig.* [in'dʒendə] *v/t.* meydana getirmek, oluşturmak, yaratmak,
sebep olm.

en.gine ['endʒin] *n.* makine, motor;
RAIL lokomotif; yangın tulumbası;
fig. vasıta, çıkar yol; alet edevat;
...'**en.gined** ...motorlu; **'en.gine-
-driv.er** *n.* makinist.

en.gi.neer [endʒi'niə] **1.** *n.* mühendis;
makinist; makineci; MIL istihkamcı;
NAUT çarkçı; *Am.* makinist; **2.** *vb.* mühendislik yapmak, inşa etm.; F becermek, başarmak; idare etm.; **en.gi-
'neer.ing** *n.* mühendislik, makinistlik;
F hünerle kullanma; *attr.* teknik.

en.gine...: '**‿fit.ter** *n.* tesviyeci; '**‿man**
n. makinist.

en.gird [in'gə:d] (*irr. gird*) *v/t.* kemer
gibi sarmak; *fig.* kuşatmak.

Eng.lish ['iŋgliʃ] **1.** *adj.* İngiliz, İngiliz-
ce; **2.** *n.* İngilizce; **the ‿** *pl.* İngilizler,
İngiltere halkı; İngilizce tercüme; **in
plain ‿** *fig.* sözünü esirgemeden, dobra
dobra; **the Queen's (King's) ‿** temiz
İngilizce; '**‿man** *n.* İngiliz erkeği;
'**‿wom.an** *n.* İngiliz kadını.

en.gorge [in'gɔ:dʒ] *vb.* oburca yemek,
tıka basa doldurmak.

en.graft [in'grɑ:ft] *v/t.* aşılamak (**into,
on, onto** *-e*); *fig. b-nin* hafızasına iyice
yerleştirmek (**in**); dikmek (**on** *-e*).

en.grain [in'grein] *v/b.* boyayı iyice emdirmek; *fig.* (*alışkanlık, zevk*) aşılamak; **en'grained** *adj.* ıslah olmaz, akıllanmaz; kök salmış, iyice yerleşmiş.

en.grave [in'greiv] *v/t.* hakketmek, oymak; *fig. b-nin* kafasına iyice yerleştirmek; **en'grav.er** *n.* hakkâk, oymacı; **‿
on copper** bakır hakkâkı; **en'grav.ing**
n. hakkâk işi, ksilografi.

en.gross [in'grəus] *v/t.* zaptetmek,
meşgul etm., işgal etm.; (*yazı*) temize
çekmek; **‿ed in** ...(*bir şey*)e dalgın; meşgul; **‿ing** *adj.* ilginç, cezbedici (*kitap
vs.*); **‿ing hand** büro yazısı; **en'gross-
ment** *n.* yığma, stok (*mal*); *bşle* meşgul
olma (**of, with**); temize çekilmiş yazı.

en.gulf [in'gʌlf] *fig. vb.* yutmak, içinde
kaybolmak; girdap içine çekip yut-
mak.

en.hance [in'hɑ:ns] *v/t.* artırmak, yükseltmek, ziyadeleştirmek, çoğaltmak
(*değer, güç, güzellik*); **en'hance.ment**
n. artma, çoğalma; artırma.

e.nig.ma ['inigmə] *n.* bilmece, muamma; **en.ig.mat.ic, e.nig.mat.i.cal** □
[enig'mætik(əl)] akıl ermez, muam-

malı, anlaşılmaz.

en.join [in'dʒɔin] *v/t.* emretmek, tembih etm. (*on, upon s.o. -e*); yasaklamak, menetmek (*from, -den*).

en.joy [in'dʒɔi] *v/t.* sevmek, hoşlanmak *-den*, *bşden* dolayı sevinmek, *bşden* zevk, lezzet almak; *did you ~ it?* hoşunuza gitti mi?; *~ o.s.* zevk almak, hoşça vakit geçirmek; **en'joy.a.ble** *adj.* zevkli, enfes, eğlenceli, hoş, tatlı; **en'joy.ment** *n.* eğlence, zevk, haz.

en.kin.dle [in'kindl] *v/t.* tutuşturmak, alevlendirmek; uyandırmak, tahrik etm. (*a. fig.*).

en.lace [in'leis] *v/t.* sarmak, dolamak.

en.large [in'lɑːdʒ] *v/t. & v/i.* büyü(lt)-mek, genişle(t)mek (*a.* PHOT); *fig.* yayılmak (*on, upon*); **en'large.ment** *n.* büyü(lt)me; agrandisman; **en.larg-er** *n.* PHOT agrandisör.

en.light.en [in'laitn] *v/t. fig.* aydınlatmak, bilgi vermek; *~ed adj.* aydın; **en-'lighten.ment** *n.* aydınlatma, aydınlanma; açıklama.

en.list [in'list] *v/t.* askere almak, kaydetmek; bir yardım sağlamak (*in*); *~ed man* MIL asker; *v/i.* asker olm., gönüllü olm.; *~ in bir* işe sahip çıkmak, kayırmak; **en'list.ment** *n.* MIL kaydetme, kaydedilme; *fig.* kazanma.

en.liv.en [in'laivn] *v/t.* canlandırmak, gayrete getirmek, teşvik etm.

en.mesh [in'meʃ] *v/t.* ağa düşürmek, *b-ni* kendi tuzağına düşürmek.

en.mi.ty ['enmiti] *n.* düşmanlık.

en.no.ble [i'nəubl] *v/t.* asilleştirmek (*a. fig.*), yükseltmek, kıymetlendirmek.

e.nor.mi.ty [i'nɔːmiti] *n.* alçaklık, büyük kötülük; büyüklük, e'nor.mous ☐ kocaman, iri, muazzam.

e.nough [i'nʌf] **1.** *adj.* yetişir, elverir; **2.** *int.* yeter!, kâfi!; **3.** *n.* yeterince, gerekli miktar; **4.** *adv.* kâfi derecede; *sure~* elbette!, şüphesiz!; *well ~* fena değil, oldukça iyi; *be kind ~ to inf.* ...mek lûtfunda bulunmak.

en.plane [in'plein] = *emplane*.

en.quire [in'kwaiə] = *inquire*.

en.rage [in'reidʒ] *v/t.* kızdırmak *-i*, öfkelendirmek *-i*; **en'raged** *adj.* kızgın, öfkeli (*at, by*).

en.rap.ture [in'ræptʃə] *v/t.* kendinden geçirmek, sonsuz hazlara boğmak *-i*.

en.rich [in'ritʃ] *v/t.* zenginleştirmek, zengin etm.; süslemek (*by, with ile*); **en'richment** *n.* zenginleş(tir)me; süs, dekor.

en.rol(l) [in'rəul] *vb. b-ni veya k-ni* kaydetmek (*liste*); MIL askere almak, yazmak; asker olm.; üyeliğe kaydetmek (*dernek*); sicile kaydetmek; *~ (o.s.)* yazılmak, kaydedilmek; askere yazılmak; **en'rol(l).ment** *n.* kaydolma; kaydedilenlerin sayısı.

en.san.guined [in'sæŋgwind] *adj.* kana bulanmış, kan lekeli.

en.sconce [in'skɔns] *v/t.* yerleştirmek; yataklık etm.; *mst ~ o.s.* F rahat bir şekilde oturmak, koltuğa gömülmek.

en.sem.ble [ãːn'sãːmbl] *n.* genel tesir, izlenim, parçaların tümünün bir arada algılanması; THEAT topluluk; MUS küçük topluluk; küçük orkestra için yazılmış eser; koro (*opera*); piyesteki oyuncuların tümü; bir müzik topluluğunun birlik, denge ve başarı derecesi; takım (*elbise*), döpiyes, iki *veya* daha fazla parçadan ibaret kadın kostümü.

en.shrine [in'ʃrain] *v/t.* mabede koymak; kutsal olarak kabul etm.

en.shroud [in'ʃraud] *v/t.* kefenlemek; örtmek, gizlemek.

en.sign ['ensain] *n.* bayrak, sancak, bandıra, alem; alâmet, nişan; NAUT *Am.* ['ensn] teğmen.

en.si.lage ['ensilidʒ] **1.** *n.* siloya doldurma (*yem*); **2.** = **en.sile** [in'sail] *v/t.* siloya depolamak (*yem*).

en.slave [in'sleiv] *v/t.* köle yapmak, esir etm. (*to -e*), *k-ne* kul etm.; **en'slave-ment** *n.* köleleş(tir)me, esaret, kölelik; **en'slaver** *n. k-ne* köle eden, boyunduruk altına alan *b-i*.

en.snare [in'snɛə] *v/t.* (*by, in, into*) tuzağa düşürmek; *fig.* baştan çıkarmak, ayartmak *-i*.

en.sue [in'sjuː] *v/i.* ardından gelmek; hasıl olm., gelmek, meydana çıkmak (*from, on -den*).

en.sure [in'ʃuə] *v/t.* sağlamak, temin etm., sağlama almak, garanti etm., korumak (*against, from -den*).

en.tab.la.ture ARCH [en'tæblətʃə] *n.* saçaklık, direk üstü tabanı, sütun pervazı.

en.tail [in'teil] **1.** *v/t. bşe* neden olm., gerektirmek; *b-ne* bir mülkü başkasına devredilmemek üzere miras bırakmak; **2.** *n.* devredilemez mülk.

en.tan.gle [in'tæŋgl] *v/t.* dolaştırmak, karıştırmak; *fig. b-ni* bir işe karıştırmak, *b-nin* başını derde sokmak; **en-'tan.glement** *n.* karışıklık, dolaşıklık;

MIL engel, mania (*dikenli tel*).

en.tente [ā:n'tā:nt] *n.* anlaşma, ittifak, uyuşma, itilâf.

en.ter ['entə] *v/t.* girmek; dahil olm., yazılmak, katılmak; ayak basmak; *bşe* girişmek (*iş*); sokulmak, zorla girmek; söze karışmak; yazmak, kaydetmek; COM deftere geçirmek; (*itiraz*) koymak; *b-ne bşi* bildirmek; *hayvan*, *motor*: alıştırmak, hazırlamak (*koşum, yarış*); *it ~ed his head* kafasına girdi, anladı; *~ s.o. at school* b-ni okula kaydettirmek; *~ up* COM hesap defterine geçirmek; *v/i.* girmek (*into -e*); girişmek *-e*; ismini yazmak; *spor*: müsabakaya girmek, yazılmak (*for*); işe koyulmak; *~ Macbeth* THEAT Makbet sahneye girer; *~ into* unsuru olm. *-in*; söze karışmak; *fig.* incelemek (*teklif*); *fig.* taahhüt altına girmek (*anlaşma*); eşelemek (*konu*); *~ (up)on bşe* başlamak, girişmek (*konu, iş*); JUR mirasa konmak.

en.ter.ic MED [en'terik] *adj.* bağırsaklarla ilgili, bağırsak...; **en.ter.i.tis** [.tə'raitis] bağırsak iltihabı, anterit.

en.ter.prise ['entəpraiz] *n.* girişim, teşebbüs, iş, yatırım; girişkenlik; **en.ter.prising** □ müteşebbis, girişken, uyanık, açıkgöz; pervasız, cesur.

en.ter.tain [entə'tein] *vb.* eğlendirmek, ağırlamak, misafirliğe kabul etm.; göz önünde bulundurmak; hatırda tutmak; *they ~ a great deal* misafirleri eksik olmaz (*sık sık parti verirler*); *~ s.o. to supper* b-ni akşam yemeğine davet etm.; **en.ter'tain.er** *n.* prezantatör, eğlendiren aktör (*veya aktris*); davet veren kimse; **en.ter'tain.ing** □ eğlenceli, hoşsohbet, eğlendiren; **en.ter-'tain.ment** *n.* eğlence; ağırlama, davet; *~ tax* eğlence vergisi.

en.thral(l) [in'θrɔ:l] *v/t. fig.* büyülemek, cezbetmek, hayran bırakmak.

en.throne [in'θrəun] *v/t.* tahta çıkarmak; *b-ni* gönlünde yüceltmek, yüksek yer vermek; **en'throne.ment, en.thron.i.za.tion** [enθrəunai'zeiʃən] *n.* tahta oturtma; tahta çıkma; cülûs (*hükümdar*).

en.thuse F [in'θju:z] *vb.*: *~ over bşe* bayılmak, *b-ne* hayran kalmak, coşmak.

en.thu.si.asm [in'θju:ziæzəm] *n.* coşkunluk; can atma, heves, istek; **en-'thu.si.ast** [.æst] *n. bşin* hayranı, aşırı taraftar (*for, of*); şevkli kimse; **en-**

thu.si'as.tic *adj.* (*~ally*) heyecanlı, coşkun, hislerine kapılan, şevkli, hevesli (*at, about*).

en.tice [in'tais] *v/t.* ayartmak, vaatlerle baştan çıkarmak *-i*; **en'tice.ment** *n.* ayartma, kandırma, baştan çıkarma; cazibe, alımlılık; **en'tic.er** *n.* ayartan, baştan çıkaran, iğfal eden *b-i*; **en'ticing** □ ayartıcı, kandırıcı, cazip, çekici; işveli, fettan.

en.tire □ [in'taiə] tam, bütün, tamam, eksiksiz, bölünmemiş; iğdiş edilmemiş (*hayvan*); **en'tire.ly** *adv.* büsbütün, tamamen; **en'tire.ness** *n.* bütünlük, tamamlık, yekparelik; **en'tire.ty** *n.* bütünlük, mükemmellik, tamamiyet.

en.ti.tle [in'taitl] *v/t.* yetki vermek *-e*, hak kazandırmak (*to -e*); ad vermek; *be ~d to* hakkı, yetkisi olm.

en.ti.ty ['entiti] *n.* varlık, mevcudiyet; *legal ~* tüzelkişi, hukuki varlık.

en.tomb [in'tu:m] *v/t.* gömmek, defnetmek; mezar olm.; **en'tomb.ment** *n.* defin töreni, mezara koyma.

en.to.mol.o.gy zoo [entə'mɔlədʒi] *n.* entomoloji, böcek ilmi.

entr'acte THEAT ['ɔntrækt] *n.* perde arası, antrakt.

en.trails ['entreilz] *n. pl.* bağırsaklar, iç uzuvlar (*hayvan*).

en.trance¹ ['entrəns] *n.* giriş, duhul, girme; giriş yeri, antre, giriş kapısı; vazifeye giriş (*into veya upon office*); THEAT sahneye çıkış, sahneye giriş; (*liman*) boğaz, ağız.

en.trance² [in'trɑ:ns] *v/t.* kendinden geçirmek *-i*, coşturmak *-i*, büyülemek *-i*, hayran bırakmak *-i*.

en.trance... ['entrəns]: *~ ex.am.i.na.tion* giriş sınavı; *~ fee, ~ mon.ey* girmelik, duhuliye, giriş ücreti.

en.trant ['entrənt] *n.* giren, başlayan *b-i*; *spor*: müsabık, yarışmacı.

en.trap [in'træp] *v/t.* tuzağa düşürmek, avlamak, yakalamak; ayartmak (*into, to -e*).

en.treat [in'tri:t] *v/t.* ısrarla rica etm. *-den*, yalvarmak, dilemek (*of*); **en-'treat.y** *n.* yalvarma, rica, dilek, niyaz.

en.trée ['ɔntrei] *n.* giriş, giriş izni, giriş hakkı; ziyafetlerde balık ile asıl yemek arasında verilen yemek.

en.trench [in'trentʃ] *vb.* MIL hendek *veya* siper kazmak, istihkâma yerleştirmek; *fig.* kök salmak; *fig. bşin* arkasına gizlenmek; **en'trench.ment** *n.* istihkâma yerleşme; istihkâm, siper.

en.tre.pre.neur [ˈɔntrəprəˈnɔː] *n.* müteahhit, müteşebbis; müzikaller hazırlayan kimse, emprezaryo.

en.trust [inˈtrʌst] *v/t.* emniyet etm., emanet etm. (*s.th. to s.o. b-ne bşi*).

en.try [ˈentri] *n.* girme, giriş, girilecek yer, antre, methal; JUR mülke giriş (*on, upon -e*); kayıt, not; gümrüğe giriş kaydı yaptırma; (*para*) tahsil, alınma; *spor:* iştirak için kaydolunma, müsabakaya katılma; **~ permit** giriş müsaadesi; **make an ~ of s.th.** hesap defterine geçirmek, giriş yapmak (*tahsilat*); **book-keeping by double (single) ~** çifte (tek taraflı) defter tutma yöntemi.

en.twine [inˈtwain], **en.twist** [inˈtwist] *v/t.* etrafını *bşle* çevirmek, sarmak, birbirine geçirmek, bükmek, dolaştırmak.

e.nu.mer.ate [iˈnjuːməreit] *v/t.* birer birer saymak, sıralamak; **e.nu.merˈa-tion** *n.* sayma, sayım, tadat.

e.nun.ci.ate [iˈnʌnsieit] *vb.* bildirmek, ilan etm.; (*dogma, dava*) ileri sürmek, iddia etm.; (*akıcı ve kesin*) telâffuz etm.; **e.nunciˈa.tion** *n.* telaffuz; bildirme; ileri sürme, ifade ve beyan tarzı.

en.vel.op [inˈveləp] *v/t. bşi bşe* sarmak, örtmek; MIL kuşatmak; **en.ve.lope** [ˈenvələup], *Am. a.* **en.vel.op** [inˈveləp] *n.* zarf; BOT örtü; kılıf (*balon*); **en-vel.op.ment** [inˈveləpmənt] *n.* örtü; sarma, kuşatma.

en.ven.om [inˈvenəm] *v/t.* zehirlemek, zehir katmak *-e*; *fig. a.* şiddetlendirmek, kin aşılamak.

en.vi.a.ble □ [ˈenviəbl] gıpta edilir, mesut, talihli, başarılı, fevkalâde iyi; **ˈenvi.er** *n.* gıpta eden *b-i*, kıskanan *b-i*; **ˈenvi.ous** □ kıskanç, hasut, gıpta eden (*of -e*).

en.vi.ron [inˈvaiərən] *vb.* etrafını çevirmek, kuşatmak, içine almak; **enˈvi-ronment** *n.* muhit, çevre, etraf; **en.vi-ronˈment.al** *adj.* çevresel, etrafındaki çevre…; **en.vi.ronˈment.al pollution** çevre kirlenmesi; **en.vi.ronˈment.ally friend.ly** çevre dostu; **en.vi.rons** [ˈen-virənz] *n. pl.* civar, havali, etraf, dolay.

en.vis.age [inˈvizidʒ] *v/t.* hiçe saymak, göze almak (*tehlike*); planlamak (*amaç*); tasavvur etm., düşünmek, …gibi telâkki etm.

en.voy[1] [ˈenvɔi] *n.* (orta) elçi, delege, murahhas.

en.voy[2] [ˌ] *n.* düzyazı *veya* şiirde yazar *veya* şairin özellikle ithaf şeklindeki ve parçanın ana fikrini açıklayan son sözü.

en.vy [ˈenvi] **1.** *n.* kıskançlık, haset, gıpta, imrenme (*of s.o. b-ne*; *of veya at s.th. bşe*); **his car is the ~ of his friends** arabası arkadaşlarını kıskandırıyor.; **2.** *v/t.* kıskanmak, gıpta etm.; imrenmek *-e*, haset etm., çekememek (*s.o. s.th. b-ni, bşi*).

en.wrap [inˈræp] *v/t.* sarmak, örtmek.

en.zyme BIOL [ˈenzaim] *n.* enzim, ferment, organizmada kimyasal reaksiyonları hızlandıran madde.

e.on [ˈiːən] = *aeon.*

ep.au.let(te) [ˈepəulet] *n.* apolet.

e.pergne [iˈpəːn] *n.* yemek masası ortasına çiçek, meyve vs. koymak için konan süs tabak *veya* kâse.

e.phem.er.a ZOO [iˈfemərə] *n.,* **eˈphem.er.on** [ˌ-rɔn] *pl. a.* **eˈphem.er.a** [ˌ-rə] kısa ömürlü böcekler sınıfı; **eˈphem.er.al** *adj.* kısa ömürlü, bir gün yaşayan, geçici, süresiz.

ep.ic [ˈepik] **1.** □ destan tarzında, destan gibi; **2.** *n.* destan, epope.

ep.i.cure [ˈepikjuə] *n.* düşkün, zevk, lezzet alan *b-i* (*yemek, içki*); **ep.i.cu-re.an** [ˌ-ˈriːən] **1.** *adj.* zevk ve sefaya düşkün; **2.** = *epicure.*

ep.i.dem.ic [epiˈdemik] **1.** *adj.* (**~ally**) salgın, yaygın, genel; **~ disease** = **2.** *n.* salgın (*hastalık*), epidemi.

ep.i.der.mis ANAT [epiˈdəːmis] *n.* üst deri, dış zar.

ep.i.gram [ˈepigræm] *n.* nükteli kısa şiir, hicivli söz, nükte; **ep.i.gram.mat-ic, ep.igram.mat.i.cal** □ [ˌ-grəˈmæt-ik(əl)] nükteli, hicivli, vecizeli.

ep.i.lep.sy MED [ˈepilepsi] *n.* sara, tutarak, yilbik, peri hastalığı; **ep.iˈlep.tic** MED **1.** *adj.* sara ile ilgili; **2.** *n.* saralı *b-i.*

ep.i.logue [ˈepilɔg] *n.* sonsöz, hatime.

E.piph.a.ny [iˈpifəni] *n.* Mecusilerin Hazreti İsa'yı görmek için Bethlehem'e gelmelerini kutlayan yortu (*6 Ocak*).

e.pis.co.pa.cy [iˈpiskəpəsi] *n.* kiliseyi piskoposlar vasıtasıyla idare yöntemi; piskoposluk; **eˈpis.co.pal** *adj. rel.* piskoposa ait; piskoposlarca idare edilen; **e.pis.copa.li.an** [ˌ-kəuˈpəiljən] **1.** *n.* piskoposlarca yönetilen kilise hükümeti taraftarı *b-i*; **2.** *adj.* piskoposlarca yönetilen kilise hükümeti ile ilgili; **eˈpis.co.pate** [ˌ-kəupit] *n.* piskoposluk; piskoposlar sınıfı.

ep.i.sode [ˈepisəud] *n.* olay, hadise, vaka; fıkra, bölüm, parça (*roman*, *hikâye vs.*); **ep.i.sod.ic**, **ep.i.sod.i.cal** □ [ˌ‑'sɔdik(əl)] hadise kabilinden; bölümler halinde olan.

e.pis.tle *n.* çok uzun ve önemli mektup, name, risale; sirküler, tamim; **e'pis.to.lar.y** [ˌ‑tələri] *adj.* mektup (yazma) ile ilgili; mekⁿuplaşma ile yürütülen; mektup türünde.

ep.i.taph ['epitɑːf] *n.* mezar kitabesi.

ep.i.thet ['epiθet] *n.* sıfat, lâkap, vasıf; hakaret *veya* hoşnutsuzluk belirten söz.

e.pit.o.me [i'pitəmi] *n.* özet, öz, hülâsa; örnek, tüm özellikleri gösteren *b-i veya bş*; **e'pit.o.mize** *v/t.* özetlemek, hülâsa etm.; örnek teşkil etm.

ep.och ['iːpɔk] *n.* devir, çağ, çığır; '~-making *adj.* çok önemli, çığır açan.

Epsom salts ['epsəm'sɔːlts] *n. pl.* müshil olarak kullanılan magnezyum sülfat, İngiliz tuzu.

eq.ua.bil.i.ty [ekwə'biliti] *n.* ılımlılık, yeknecaklık, soğukkanlılık, yumuşaklık; '**equa.ble** □ yeknesak, düzenli, ılımlı, sakin; *fig.* istifini bozmayan, soğukkanlılığını yitirmeyen.

e.qual ['iːkwəl] **1.** □ eşit, denk, aynı; eşdeğerli; dengeli, düzenli, düzgün; aynı baklara sahip olan; yeterli; ~ *to* emsal -*e*; yeterli -*e*; *b-nin*, *bşin* üstesinden gelmek, yeterli olm.; *n.* eş, emsal; *my~s pl.* yaşıtlarım; **3.** *v/t.* eşit olm. -*e*, eşdeğerde olm.; *not to be ~led* eşi emsali (*veya* misli menendi) olmamak; **e.qual.i.ty** [iː'kwɔliti] *n.* eşitlik, aynılık; akranlık; **e.qual.i.za.tion** [iːkwəlai'zeiʃən] *n.* eşitle(n)me, aynı olma, uyuşma; **'e.qual.ize** *v/t.* eşitlemek (*to*, *with* -*e*, *ile*); *v/i. spor*: beraberliği sağlamak.

e.qua.nim.i.ty [ekwə'nimiti] *n.* ılım, vakar, soğukkanlılık.

e.quate [i'kweit] *v/t.* eşitlemek; eşit saymak, kıyaslamak (*to*, *with* -*e*, *ile*); **e'quation** *n.* eşitleme; MATH denklem; **e'qua.tor** *n. gco.* ekvator; **e.qua.to.ri.al** □ [ekwə'tɔːriəl] ekvator ile ilgili, ekvatoral.

eq.uer.ry [i'kwəri] *n.* imrahor, ahır bakıcısı; İngiliz Kraliyet ailesinden birinin özel hizmetinde bulunan kimse.

e.ques.tri.an [i'kwestriən] **1.** *adj.* biniciliğe ait; atlı; **2.** *n.* süvari, atlı; at cambazı.

e.qui.dis.tant [iːkwi'distənt] *adj.* eşit uzaklıkta olan.

e.qui.lat.er.al □ ['iːkwi'lætərəl] eşkenar (üçgen).

e.qui.li.brate [iːkwi'laibreit] *v/t.* denge sağlamak, denk kılmak (*ağırlık*, *güç vs.*); *v/i.* dengede olm., denk olm.; **e.quil.i.brist** [iːkwilibrist] *n.* akrobat, ip cambazı; **e.qui'lib.ri.um** [ˌ‑əm] *n.* denge, muvazene.

e.quine ZOO ['iːkwain] *adj.* at ile ilgili, ata benzer; at gibi…

e.qui.noc.tial [iːkwi'nɔkʃəl] *adj.* gece ile gündüzün eşit olduğu zamanla ilgili; **equi.nox** ['ˌ‑nɔks] *n.* gündönümü, gün-tün eşitliği.

e.quip [i'kwip] *v/t.* donatmak, teçhiz etm.; silahlandırmak; **eq.ui.page** ['ekwipidʒ] *n.* harp levazımatı; konak arabası (*atlı*); **e.quip.ment** [i'kwipmənt] *n.* teçhizat, donatım, levazım; *fig.* bir amaca ulaşmak için gerekli olan araçlar.

e.qui.poise ['ekwipɔiz] **1.** *n.* muvazene, denge; karşıt ağırlık; **2.** *vb.* muvazene sağlamak, dengeyi korumak.

eq.ui.ta.ble □ ['ekwitəbl] âdil, insaflı, tarafsız; **'eq.ui.ty** *n.* insaf, adalet; JUR (*esp. İngiliz dilinin konuşulduğu ülkelerde*) örf ve âdet hukukundan ayrı olarak gelişen ve farklı prensiplere dayanan hakkanlyet hukuku; *equities pl.* hisse senedi.

e.quiv.a.lence ['ikwivələns] *n.* eşitlik, eşdeğerlik, denk olma; **e'quiv.a.lent 1.** *adj.* muadil, eşit (*to* -*e*); **2.** *n.* bedel, karşılık, eşit miktar.

e.quiv.o.cal □ [i'kwivəkəl] iki anlamlı, iki anlama gelebilen (*sözcük*); şüpheli, belirsiz, müphem (*davranış*, *olay*); **e'quivo.cal.ness** *n.* şüpheli olma, belirsizlik, iki anlamlılık; **e'quiv.o.cate** [ˌ‑keit] *v/i.* kaçamaklı dil kullanmak, iki anlama gelecek söz söylemek; **e.quiv.o'ca.tion** *n.* kaçamak, iki anlamlı sözle aldatma, müphem davranma.

eq.ui.voque, **eq.ui.voke** ['ekwivəuk] *n.* kelime oyunu; belirsizlik, çift anlam, kaçamak.

e.ra ['iərə] *n.* devir, çağ; tarih.

e.rad.i.cate [i'rædikeit] *v/t.* yok etm., kökünü kurutmak (*hastalık*, *suç*, *kötü alışkanlık vs.*); **e.rad.i'ca.tion** *n.* yok etme, imha.

e.rase [i'reiz] *v/t.* silmek, çizmek, bozmak, kazımak; *fig.* yok etm., öldürmek; **e'ras.er** *n.* lastik, silgi, yazı kazımağa mahsus çakı; **e'ra.sure** [ˌ‑ʒə] *n.*

silme, bozma; silinen yerde kalan iz, silinti.

ere *poet.* [ɛə] *cj. & prp.* evvel, önce, -den önce; ~ **this** evvelce, bundan önce; ~ **long** yakında, neredeyse, birazdan; ~ **now** bundan önce, vaktiyle.

e.rect [i'rekt] **1.** □ dik, doğru, dik duran, dikili, dikilmiş (*saç*); **2.** *v/t.* kurmak, inşa etm., dikmek (*anıt vs.*); **e'rec.tion** *n.* dikme, kurma; yapı, bina; kalkma, dikilme, penis dokusunun kan dolması ile sertleşmesi, ereksiyon; **e'rect.ness** *n.* doğruluk, dik duruş; **e'rec.tor** *n.* kaldıran, diken *veya* inşa eden *b-i veya* *bş.*

er.e.mite ['erimait] *n.* inzivaya çekilmiş kimse, keşiş; **er.e.mit.ic** [ˌ'mitik] *adj.* bir köşeye çekilmiş, insandan kaçan, inziva kabilinden.

erg PHYS [ə:g] *n.* erg, enerji birimi.

er.got BOT ['ə:gət] *n.* çavdar mahmuzu (*çavdar başağı üzerinde türeyen bir tür asklı mantar*).

er.mine ['ə:min] *n.* ZOO kakım, as; kakım kürkü; *fig.* hakim edasıyla.

e.rode [i'rəud] *v/t. & v/i.* azar azar yiyerek kemir(il)mek, aşın(dır)mak.

e.ro.sion [i'rəuʒən] *n.* aşın(dırma); GEOL erozyon; **e'ro.sive** [ˌsiv] *adj.* aşındırıcı, kemirici.

e.rot.ic [i'rɔtik] **1.** *adj.* aşka ait, şehvanî; cinsel arzu uyandıran, erotik, şehvetli; **2.** *n.* âşıkane şiir, erotik şiir; şehevî *b-i;* **e'rot.i.cism** [ˌ-sizəm] *n.* şehvet, erosallık, şehvetperestlik.

err [ə:] *v/i.* yanılmak, yanlış yapmak; günah işlemek.

er.rand ['erənd] *n.* iş, sipariş; habercilik; *fool's* ~ yararsız çaba, boşuna gayret; *go* (*on*) ~*s* bir haber götürmek *veya* bir iş için bir yere gitmek; '~*boy* *n.* ayak işlerine koşulan çocuk, çırak.

er.rant □ ['erənt] maceraperest, doğru yoldan sapan, serseri, delâlete düşen; *s. knight*~; '**er.rant.ry** *n.* serserilik, avarelik, maceraperestlik (*şövalye*).

er.rat.ic [i'rætik] *adj.* (~*ally*) seyyar, dolaşan; düzensiz; sebatsız, ne yapacağı belirsiz, *sl.* osuruğu cinli; ~ *fever* belirli aralıklarla gelen ateş; **er.ra.tum** [e'rɑːtəm] *n., pl.* **er'ra.ta** [ˌtə] dizgi hatası, sehiv.

er.ro.ne.ous □ [i'rəunjəs] hatalı, yanlış.

er.ror ['erə] *n.* hata, yanlışlık; ~ *of judgement* muhakemede usul hatası; ~*s excepted* (*hesap*) olası yanlışlar

müstesna, hatalar kabul edilir.

Erse [ə:s] **1.** *adj.* İrlanda diline ait; **2.** *n.* İrlanda dili.

erst.while ['ə:stwail] *adj.* eski, sabık, evvelce olan.

e.ruc.ta.tion [iːrʌk'teiʃən] *n.* geğirme.

er.u.dite □ ['eruːdait] çok bilgili, âlim, bilgin; **er.u.di.tion** [ˌ-'diʃən] *n.* âlimlik, bilginlik.

e.rupt [i'rʌpt] *v/i.* indifa etm. (*volkan*), fışkırmak, püskürmek; çıkmak (*diş*); **e'rup.tion** *n.* indifa (*volkan*), fışkırma, püskürme, patlama (*a. fig.*); MED isilik, kızartı; diş çıkması; **e'rup.tive** *adj.* patlayan, indifa eden, püsküren, fışkıran; kızartı ile ilgili.

er.y.sip.e.las MED [eri'sipiləs] *n.* yılancık.

es.ca.la.tion POL [eskə'leiʃən] *n.* kızışma, gerginlik, artış, yükseliş.

es.ca.la.tor ['eskəleitə] *n.* yürüyen merdiven.

es.ca.pade [eskə'peid] *n.* haylazlık, yaramazlık, gençlik çılgınlığı; *fig.* hoppalık, yoldan çıkma; **es.cape** [is'keip] **1.** *v/t.* -den çıkmak (*ses, sözcük*); gözünden kaçmak, hatırından çıkmak (*olay vs.*); -den kaçmak, kurtulmak, *bş*den sakınmak; *v/i.* kaçmak, kurtulmak (*from, out of* -*den*); (*gaz*) sızmak (*from* -*den*); **2.** *n.* kaçma, kurtuluş; akma, sızma, sızıntı; *have a narrow* ~ güçbelâ kurtulmak; **es.ca.pee** [eskei-'piː] *n.* firarî, kaçak; **es.cape.ment** MEC [is'keipmənt] *n.* saat çarklarının çalışmasını sağlayan maşa; **es'cap.ism** *n.* hoş olmayan hayatın gerçeklerinden kaçma; hayal kurma; **es'cap.ist 1.** *adj.* gerçeklerden kaçan, hayal kuran; **2.** *n.* gerçeklerden kaçan kimse.

es.carp [is'kɑːp] **1.** *a.* **es'carp.ment** *n.* azmeyilli yüzey, şev, bayır; **2.** *v/t.* meyillendirmek, şev şekilni vermek.

es.cheat JUR [is'tʃiːt] **1.** *n.* mirasçısız ölen kimsenin mülkünün devlete geçişi; **2.** *v/i.* devlete kalmak (*mülk*); *v/t.* müsadere etm., zoralımına çarptırmak.

es.chew [is'tʃuː] *v/t. bş*den kaçınmak, vazgeçmek, sakınmak.

es.cort 1. ['eskɔːt] *n.* muhafız; maiyet; kavalye; refakatçi; **2.** [is'kɔːt] *v/t.* refakat etm. -*e.*

es.cri.toire [eskri:twɑː] *n.* yazı masası, yazıhane.

es.cu.lent ['eskjulənt] **1.** *adj.* yenilebilir; **2.** *n.* gıda maddeleri, yiyecekler.

es.cutch.eon [is'kʌtʃən] *n.* arma, armalı levha, ad tabelası; anahtar deliği çevresindeki süslü madenî çerçeve.

Es.ki.mo ['eskiməu] *n.* Eskimo; Eskimo dili.

e.soph.a.gus [iːˈsɔfəgəs] = *oesophagus*.

es.o.ter.ic [esəu'terik] *adj.* gizli, anlaşılması güç; belirli bir grup tarafından anlaşılan.

es.pal.ier AGR [is'pæljə] *n.* meyve ağacı dallarının bir duvar vs. boyunca gelişmesini sağlayan çerçeve; böyle yetişmiş ağaçlar sırası.

es.pe.cial [is'peʃəl] *adj.* özel, mahsus, hususî; fevkalâde; seçkin; **es'pe.cial.ly** *adv.* özellikle, bilhassa

Es.per.an.to [espə'ræntəu] *n.* Esperanto dili.

es.pi.al [is'paiəl] *n.* gözetleme, keşfetme.

es.pi.o.nage [espiə'nɑːʒ] *n.* casusluk.

es.pla.nade [esplə'neid] *n.* gezinti yeri, deniz kenarında piyasa yapılan yer, kordonboyu.

es.pous.al [is'pauzəl] *n.* benimseme, bir düşünceyi destekleme **(of)**, kabullenme; evlenme *veya* evlenme sözü, nişan; **es'pouse** *v/t.* *b-le* evlenmek; *bşi* benimsemek, desteklemek.

es.pres.so [es'presəu] *n.* İtalyan usulü kahve, espreso kahve; ~ **bar**, ~ **ca.fé** bu tür kahve içilen yer.

es.py [is'pai] *v/t.* uzaktan görmek, gözüne ilişmek.

es.quire [is'kwaiə] *n.* mülk sahibi; *(mektup)* kısaltılmış şekilde ad ve soyadından sonra yazılan ve beyefendi, bay anlamına gelen unvan; *John Smith, Esq.* Bay John Smith.

es.say 1. [e'sei] *v/t.* denemek, tecrübe etm., prova etm.; **2.** ['esei] *n.* makale, yazı; deneme, tecrübe **(at)**; **'es.say.ist** *n.* deneme yazarı.

es.sence ['esns] *n.* öz, esas, cevher, asıl, öz varlık, nitelik; CHEM esans; **es.sen.tial** [i'senʃəl] **1.** □ *(to)* esaslı, karakteristik, önemli; elzem, gerekli; ~ **likeness** özü, esası bir olma; ~ *oil* uçucu yağ; **2.** *n.* esas özellik; esas mesele; gerekli olan şey, esas; **es'sen.tial.ly** *adv.* esasen, esas itibariyle, aslında.

es.tab.lish [is'tæbliʃ] *v/t.* kurmak, tesis etm.; saptamak; atamak *(memur vs.)*; *b-ne* iş bulmak, *b-ni* işe yerleştirmek; tanıtmak; ~ *o.s.* yerleşmek; ϱ*ed Church* resmi *(veya* ulusal) kilise; es-

'**tab.lish.ment** *n.* kurma, kurum, tesis, müessese, teşkilat; egemen çevreler, ileri gelenler, kodamanlar; MIL, NAUT erler, mürettebat; *military* ~ sürekli ordu.

es.tate [is'teit] *n.* mal, mülk, arsa, gayrımenkul; çiftlik, yalı; miras, tereke; durum, hal; tabaka, sınıf, mevki; itibar, yüksek mertebe; *personal* ~ taşınabilir, menkul mallar; *real* ~ taşınamaz, gayrımenkul mallar; *housing* ~ iskân bölgesi, bahçeli evler; *industrial* ~ endüstri bölgesi; ~ **a.gen.cy** emlâk bürosu; ~ **agent** emlâk simsarı, emlâk komisyoncusu; ~ **car** pikap; ~ **du.ty** intikal vergisi, veraset vergisi.

es.teem [is'tiːm] **1.** *n.* saygı, takdir, itibar **(with)**; **2.** *v/t.* takdir etm. *-i*; hürmet etm. *-e*; zannetmek, telâkki etm., sanmak.

es.ter CHEM ['estə] *n.* ester, asitlerin alkollere etkisiyle elde edilen organik bileşik.

es.thet.ic [iːsˈθetik] = *aesthetic.*

Es.t(h)o.ni.an [es'təunjən] **1.** *n.* Estonyalı; Estonya dili; **2.** *adj.* Estonya'ya özgü.

es.ti.ma.ble ['estiməbl] *adj.* saygıdeğer, itibarlı, değerli, hürmete lâyık, takdire değer.

es.ti.mate 1. ['estimeit] *vb.* takdir etm., tahmin etm., değer biçmek **(at)**; **2.** *n.* hesap; tahmin, takdir, değer biçme *the* ϱ*s pl.* PARL bütçe; **es.ti.ma.tion** [˷'meiʃən] *n.* hesap etme; itibar, hürmet; fikir, tahmin, görüş, rey; '**es.ti.ma.tor** *n.* değer biçen, maliyet hesabını yapan *b-i.*

es.trange [is'treindʒ] *v/t.* soğutmak, uzaklaştırmak **(from s.o.** *-den)*, yabancılaştırmak; **es'trange.ment** *n.* yabancılaş(tır)ma, soğu(t)ma, bozuşma.

es.tu.ar.y ['estjuəri] *n.* GEOL nehir ağzı, haliç.

et.cet.er.as [it'setrəz] *n. pl.* ufak tefek çeşitli şeyler.

etch [etʃ] *vb.* kezzapla hakkatmek, madeni bir levhayı asitle yakarak resim kalıbı çıkarmak.

e.ter.nal □ [iːtəːnl] ebedî, sonsuz; ezelî, öncesiz; **e'ter.nal.ize** [˷nəlaiz] *v/t.* ebedîleştirmek; **e'ter.ni.ty** *n.* ebediyet, sonsuzluk, ezeliyet; ölümsüzlük; **e'ter.nize** [˷naiz] *v/t.* ebedileştirmek, ölümsüzleştirmek.

e.ther ['iːθə] *n.* esir, evreni ve atomlar arasındaki boşluğu dolduran ve ağırlığı olmayan bir töz, değişmeden kalan varlık; CHEM eter, lokman ruhu; **e.the.re.al** ☐ [i:'θəriəl] dünyevî olmayan aydınlık ve hassayiyet; ruh gibi, peri gibi; **'e.ther.ize** v/t. eterle bayıltmak, sersemletmek, uyuşturmak.

eth.i.cal ☐ ['eθikəl] ahlâki, manevî, törel; **'eth.ics** n. mst sg. ahlâk (ilmî).

E.thi.o.pi.an [i:θi'əupjən] **1.** adj. Habeşistan'a ait, Habeş...; **2.** n. Habeşistanlı, Habeş.

eth.nic ['eθnik] adj. etnik, ırka ait, ırksal.

eth.nog.ra.phy [eθ'nɔgrəfi] n. etnografya, budunbetim, kavimler ilmi; **eth-'nol.o.gy** [-lədʒi] n. etnoloji, (kıyaslamalı) budunbilim.

eth.yl ['eθil; CHEM 'i:θail] n. etil; (arabada motor sesini azaltmak için) benzine konulan kurşunlu bir bileşim; **eth.yl-ene** ['eθili:n] n. etilen (gazı), hidrokarbon.

e-tick.et ['i:tikit] n. e-bilet.

e.ti.o.late ['i:tiəuleit] v/t. ışıksızlıktan soldurmak (bitki); fig. zayıflatmak, kuvvetten düşürmek.

e.ti.ol.o.gy MED [i:ti'ɔlədʒi] n. hastalıkların nedenlerini araştırma ilmi.

et.i.quette ['etiket] n. görgü kuralları, adabımuaşeret, topluluk töresi, protokol.

E.ton crop ['i:tn'krɔp] n. alagarson saç, erkek saçı gibi kısa kesilmiş saç (kadın).

E.trus.can [i'trʌskən] **1.** adj. eski İtalya'da Etrurya'ya ait; **2.** n. Etrurya'lı; Etrurya dili.

et.y.mo.log.i.cal ☐ [etimə'lɔdʒikl] etimolojik, iştikaka ait, türeme ile ilgili; **et.ymol.o.gy** [-'mɔlədʒi] n. etimoloji, iştikak, sözcük türetme; sözcük kökü bilgisi.

eu.ca.lyp.tus BOT [ju:kə'liptəs] n. okaliptüs, sıtma ağacı.

Eu.cha.rist ['ju:kərist] n. Hıristiyan kilisesine ait Aşai Rabbanî (şarap ve ekmek yeme) ayinî; bu ayin için kutsanan şaarp ve ekmek.

Eu.clid MATH ['ju:klid] n. Öklit geometri.

eu.gen.ic [ju:dʒenik] adj. (**~ally**) insan ırkının soyaçekim yoluyla mükemmelleştirilmesine ait; gelecek nesillerin ıslahına ait; **eu'gen.ics** n. pl. insan ırkının soyaçekim yoluyla ıslahına çalışan bilim dalı.

eu.lo.gist ['ju:lədʒist] n. methiye yazan ve söyleyen kimse, kaside yazarı; **eu.lo.gize** ['-dʒaiz] v/t. övmek, methetmek, sitayişle bahsetmek; **eu.lo.gy** ['-dʒi] n. methiye, kaside, senakâr nutuk.

eu.nuch ['ju:nək] n. hadım, harem ağası.

eu.phe.mism ['ju:fimizəm] n. kaba sayılan sözcükler kullanmayıp kavramı üstü örtülü olarak anlatan başka sözcükler kullanma; **eu.phe'mis.tic**, **eu.phe'mis.ti.cal** ☐ bu tür sözcükler içeren, bu tür sözcüklerle ilgili.

eu.phon.ic, **eu.phon.i.cal** ☐ [ju:'fɔnik(əl)] ahenkli, armonik, öfonik, kulağa hoş gelen; **eu.pho.ny** ['ju:fəni] n. ahenk, armoni, öfoni.

eu.phor.ia [ju:'fɔ:riə] n. öfori, k-ni aşırı derecede mutlu ve zinde hissetme hali.

eu.phu.ism ['ju:fju:izəm] n. yapmacık, zor ve tumturaklı edebî dil (16 yy.'da İngiltere'de).

Eur.a.sian [juə'reiʒjən] **1.** n. bir Avrupalı ile bir Asyalı'nın evlenmesinden doğan çocuk; **2.** adj. Avrupa ile Asya'ya ait.

eu.re.ka [juə'ri:kə] int. buldum!

Eu.ro.pe.an [juərə'pi:ən] **1.** adj. Avrupa ile ilgili; **2.** n. Avrupalı.

eu.tha.na.si.a [ju:θə'neizjə] n. acısız ölüm; ümitsiz durumda veya çok yaşlı olan hastaların acılarını dindirmek için hayatlarına son verme.

e.vac.u.ate [i'vækjueit] v/t. boşaltmak, dökmek, tahliye etm., terketmek (toprak); MED ishal, amel vermek, vücuttan çıkarmak; **e.vac.u'a.tion** n. boşaltma, tahliye; **e.vac.u'ee** n. tehlike yerinden uzaklaştırılan b-i.

e.vade [i'veid] v/t. sakınmak -den, kaçınmak -den, bşden çekinmek, kaçamaklı yol aramak.

e.val.u.ate esp. MATH [i'væljueit] v/t. değerini veya derecesini hesap etm. -in, değerlendirmek -i, sayısını tahmin etm. -in; **e.val.u'a.tion** n. değerlendirme, paha biçme.

ev.a.nesce [i:və'nes] v/i. ortadan kaybolmak, yok olm., yavaş yavaş gözden kaybolmak, unutulmak; **ev.a'nescence** n. yok olma, gözden kaybolma; **ev.a'nescent** ☐ yok olan, gözden kaybolan, unutulan.

e.van.gel.ic, **e.van.gel.i.cal** ☐ [i:væn'dʒelik(əl)] protestan; dört İncil'de yazılanlara göre İsa'yı tanıtma ve öğretme ile ilgili; **e.van.ge.list**

[i'vændʒilist] *n.* gezici vaiz; dört İncili yazanlardan biri; **e'van.ge.lize** *v/t. & v/i.* İncil'i va'zetmek, Hıristiyanlığa sevketmek.

e.vap.o.rate [i'væpəreit] *v/t. & v/i.* buharlaş(tır)mak, uç(ur)mak; *fig.* uçup gitmek, yok olm.; **~d milk** kondanse süt, kısmen suyu alınmış süt; **e.vap·o'ra.tion** *n.* buharlaş(tır)ma, buğulan(dır)ma.

e.va.sion [i'veiʒən] *n.* kaçınma, sakınma; kaçamak, bahane; **e'va.sive** ☐ [~siv] kaçamaklı (**of**), baştan savma; **be ~** *fig.* yan çizmek.

eve [i:v] *n.* arife; arife gecesi; *poet.* gece; **on the ~ of** arifesinde *-in.*

e.ven[1] ['i:vən] **1.** *adj.* ☐ düz, pürüzsüz, müstevi, düzlem; eşit, müsavî; düzgün, muntazam, düzenli; çift, tam (*sayı*); paralel, denk, aynı seviyede; tarafsız; **make ~ with the ground** yerle bir etm., yıkıp yok etm.; **be ~ with s.o.** *b-le* alacağı vereceği kalmamak, ödeşmek; **get~ with s.o.** *b-le* hesaplaşmak, *b-den* bşin acısını çıkarmak, intikam almak; **odd or ~** tek mi çift mi; **of ~ date** COM aynı tarihte; **break~** F kârsız *veya* zararsız kapamak (*hesap*), ancak masrafını karşılamak; **2.** *adv.* hatta, bile, dahi; tamamiyle, tıpkı; **not ~** hatta …bile değil; **~ though,** **~ if** her ne kadar… ise de, olsa bile, (olmasına) rağmen; **3.** *v/t.* düzlemek, düzeltmek, tesviye etm.; kıyas etm. (**to** *-e*), benzetmek.

even[2] *poet.* [~] *n.* akşam.

e.ven-hand.ed ['i:vən'hændid] *adj.* tarafsız, bitaraf.

eve.ning ['i:vniŋ] *n.* akşam; suvare; **~ dress** gece elbisesi, tuvalet, smokin *veya* frak.

e.ven.ness ['i:vənnis] *n.* doğruluk, dürüstlük, tarafsızlık; eşitlik, düz oluş; kalp huzuru; sükûnet.

e.ven.song ['i:vənsɔŋ] *n.* akşam duası.

e.vent [i'vent] *n.* olay, hadise, vaka; hal; *fig.* sonuç, âkıbet; müsabaka, maç, turnuva (*sportif*); numara (*program*); **athletic ~s** *pl.* atletizm yarışmaları; **table of ~s** festival (*şenlik, ziyafet*) programı; **at all ~s** mutlaka, behemehal, her halde, ne olursa olsun; **in any ~** zaten, esasen, haddizatında; **in the ~ of** şayet, …olduğu takdirde.

e.ven-tem.pered ['i:vəntempəd] *adj.* sakin, soğukkanlı.

e.vent.ful [i'ventful] *adj.* olaylarla dolu.

e.ven.tide *poet.* ['i:vəntaid] *n.* akşam, akşam vakti.

e.ven.tu.al ☐ [i'ventʃuəl] muhtemel, olası; nihaî, sonuncu, sonraki; **~ly** sonunda, nihayet, ilerde **e.ven.tu.al.i.ty** [~tʃu'æliti] *n.* ihtimal, olasılık; **e'ven.tu.ate** [~tʃueit] *v/t.* sonuçlanmak; çıkmak, oluşmak.

ev.er ['evə] *adv.* herhangi bir zamanda; hiç, asla; daima, her zaman, tekrar tekrar; **~ so** pek, çok; **as soon as ~ I can** elimden geldiğince çabuk; **~ after,** *-den* beri; **~ and anon** arada sırada; **for ~, for ~ and ~, for ~ and a day** ilelebet, daima, ebediyete kadar; **liberty for ~** sonsuza dek özgürlük; **so much** pek çok; **I wonder who ~** kim olabilir, kim olduğunu merak ediyorum; **the best ~** F en iyisi; **yours ~** daima senin… (*mektup sonunda*); **'~glade** *n. Am.* bataklık alan; **'~green 1.** *adj.* yaprağını dökmeyen; **2.** *n.* yaprağını dökmeyen ağaç; **'~lasting 1.** ☐ sonsuz; devamlı; ölümsüz; **2.** *n.* ebediyet, sonsuzluk; ВОТ kuruduğu zaman rengini ve şeklini koruyan bir tür çiçek; **'~more** *adv.* daima, ebediyen, sürekli.

ev.er.y ['evri] *adj.* her, her bir, her biri; **~ bit as much** tam onun kadar; **~ now and then** arasıra; **~ one of them** istisnasız hepsi; **~ other day** iki günde bir, gün aşırı; **~ twenty years** her yirmi yılda bir; **her ~** movement her hareketi; **'~bod.y** *pron.* herkes; **'~day** *adj.* her günkü, günlük, olağan; **'~one** *pron.* herkes; **'~thing** *pron.* herşey; **'~way** *adv.* her bakımdan; **'~where** *adv.* her yer(d)e.

e.vict [i'vikt] *v/t.* kapı dışarı etm., tahliye et(tir)mek; **e'vic.tion** *n.* tahliye etme *veya* edilme, geri al(ın)ma.

ev.i.dence ['evidəns] **1.** *n.* delil, ispat, tanıt, tutanak; JUR şahitlik, şahadet, tanıklık; şahit, tanık; **be in~** göze çarpmak, kendini göstermek; **furnish~ of, be~ of** kanıtlamak, ispat etm., göstermek, belirtmek, açığa vurmak; **give~, bear~** tanıklık etm., şahadet etm. (**of, for, against** *-e*); **2.** *v/t.* kanıtlamak, göstermek, belirtmek, *-e* delâ; et etm.; **'ev.ident** ☐ aşikâr, belli, açık, sarih; **ev.iden.tial** ☐ [~'denʃəl] delile dayanan, kanıt *veya* tanık türünden.

e.vil ['i:vl] **1.** ☐ fena, kötü, kem; **the ~ eye** kem göz, nazar değme; **the ♀**

One Şeytan, İblis; **2.** *n.* fenalık, kötülük, bela, dert; **'~·'do.er** *n.* muzur, şerir, kötülük eden *b-i*; **'~·'mind.ed** *adj.* kötü niyetli, suiniyet sahibi, kötü yürekli, kötücül.

e.vince [i'vins] *v/t.* ortaya koymak, göstermek, izhar etm., açığa vurmak, kanıtlamak.

e.vis.cer.ate [i'visəreit] *v/t.* (*vurulan hayvanın*) karnını yarıp temizlemek, bağırsaklarını çıkarmak.

ev.o.ca.tion [evəu'keiʃən] *n.* aklına getirme *-i*, zihinde canlandırma *-i*; **e.voc.ative** [i'vɔkətiv] *adj.* hatırlatan, andıran, uyandıran.

e.voke [i'vəuk] *v/t.* uyandırmak, mucip olm., davet etm., hissettirmek, neden olm., doğurmak.

ev.o.lu.tion [i:və'lu:ʃən] *n.* gelişme, inkişaf, evrim; MATH kök alma; MIL manevra, tatbikat; **ev.o'lu.tion.a.ry** [.ʃnəri] *adj.* evrimsel, gelişme ile ilgili.

e.volve [i'vɔlv] *v/t. & v/i.* aç(ıl)mak, yay(ıl)mak, geliş(tir)mek, evrim geçirmek.

ewe [ju:] *n.* ZOO dişi koyun.

ew.er ['ju:ə] *n.* ibrik.

ex [eks] *prefix* COM -de teslim; -den dışarı (*fabrika, liman vs.*); (*borsa*) -siz, olmadan; sabık, eski, önceki; **ex- -minister** *n.* sabık bakan.

ex.ac.er.bate [eks'sæsə:beit] *v/t.* kötüleştirmek, vahimleştirmek, şiddetlendirmek, kızdırmak, öfkelendirmek.

ex.act [ig'zækt] **1.** □ tam, doğru; kati, kesin; fiilî, hakiki; tamamen; aynen; dakikası dakikasına; **2.** *v/t.* tahsil etm., talep etm., ödeme zorunda bırakmak; icbar etm.; **ex'act.ing** *adj.* titiz, müşkülpesent, kibirli, hoşgörüsüz; fazla dikkat ve güç gerektiren; **ex'action** *n.* zorla alma, haraç kesme; zorla yaptırılan iş *veya* alınan para; **ex'act.itude** [.titju:d] *n.* sıhhat, doğruluk, hatasızlık, tam ve doğru olma; **ex'act.ly** *adv.* (*cevap*) tamamen, aynen; **not ~** tam olarak değil, tamamen öyle değil; **ex'actness = exactitude**.

ex.ag.ger.ate [ig'zædʒəreit] *v/b.* mübalağa etm., abartmak; **ex.ag.ger'a.tion** *n.* mübalağa, abartma, aşırılık.

ex.alt [ig'zɔ:lt] *v/t.* yükseltmek, yüceltmek; övmek, göklere çıkarmak; **ex.al- ta.tion** [egzɔ:l'teiʃən] *n.* heyecan, aşka gelme, coşkunluk, esrime; yüksel(t)me; yükseklik, ululuk; **ex.alt.ed** [ig'zɔ:ltid] *adj.* yüce, ulu, yüksek, ulvî;

coşkun.

ex.am *okul: sl.* [ig'zæm] *n.* sınav, imtihan.

ex.am.i.na.tion [igzæmi'neiʃən] *n.* sınav, imtihan; muayene, yoklama, teftiş, tetkik; **ex'am.ine** *v/t.* sınava tabi tutmak, imtihan etm.; yoklamak, muayene etm., teftiş etm., tetkik etm. (*a. ~ into s.th.*); sorguya çekmek; **ex'am.i- 'nee** *n.* sınava giren *b-i*; **ex'am.in.er** *n.* sınav yapan *b-i*, ayırtman; muayene eden *b-i*; sorgu hâkimi; müfettiş.

ex.am.ple [ig'zɑ:mpl] *n.* örnek, misal, numune; **beyond ~** emsalsiz, eşsiz; **for ~** örneğin, meselâ; **make an ~ of** başkalarına ders olsun diye *b-ni* cezalandırmak; **set an ~** örnek olm.

ex.as.per.ate [ig'zɑ:spəreit] *v/t.* kızdırmak, sinirlendirmek, çileden çıkarmak, şiddetlendirmek; **ex.as- per'a.tion** *n.* öfke, hiddet, sinirlenme, dargınlık (**of**).

ex.ca.vate ['ekskəveit] *v/t.* kazmak, hafriyat yapmak, kazıp açmak; **ex.ca- 'vation** *n.* kazı, hafriyat, çukur; **'ex.ca- vator** *n.* ekskavator, kazma makinesi; toprak işçisi.

ex.ceed [ik'si:d] *vb.* aşmak, geçmek; *b-ne* üstün gelmek (**in**); aşırıya kaçmak, ileri gitmek; **ex'ceed.ing** *adj.* aşırı, müfrit, ölçüsüz; **ex'ceed.ing.ly** *adv.* son derece, fazlasıyla, gayet fevkalâde.

ex.cel [ik'sel] *vb.* geçmek, üstün olm. *-den*; *k-ni* göstermek, temayüz etm., sivrilmek (**in, at**); **ex.cel.lence** ['eksələns] *n.* üstünlük, seçkin oluş, mükemmel oluş, fazilet; **'Ex.cel.len.cy** *n.* ekselans (*ünvan*); **'ex.cel.lent** □ mükemmel, çok iyi, kusursuz, mümtaz, üstün.

ex.cept [ik'sept] **1.** *vb.* hariç tutmak, müstesna kılmak, ayrı tutmak; itiraz etm., karşı çıkmak; present **company ~ed** sizden iyi olmasın; hatırınız kalmasın; **2.** *cj.* haricinde, meğer ki, olmadıkça; **3.** *prp.* -den başka, -den maada; **~ for** bir yana, hariç; olmasaydı; **ex'cept.ing** *prp.* -den başka, in dışında, müstesna, hariç (olmak üzere); **ex'cep.tion** *n.* istisna; itiraz (**to** *-e*); **take ~ to** *b-şi* sakıncalı bulmak, hoş görmemek, itiraz etm.; **ex'cep- tion.a.ble** [.ʃnəbl] *adj.* itiraz olunabilir, yakışıksız, ahlâka aykırı; **ex'cep- tion.al** *adj.* müstesna; olağan üstü, fevkalâde, harikulâde; **ex'cep.tion.al.ly** *adv.* müstena olarak, fevkalâde olarak bir defaya mahsus olmak üzere.

ex.cerpt 1. [ek'sə:pt] *vb.* aktarmak, iktibas etm., almak (*from -den*) (*yazı, kitap vs.*); 2. ['eksə:pt] *n.* seçme parça, pasaj, alıntı (*from -den*).

ex.cess [ik'ses] *n.* ifrat, aşırılık, fazlalık, taşkınlık, ölçüsüzlük; *attr.* fazla...; *in ~ of* -den daha çok, -i geçen; *carry to ~* ifrat dereceye vardırmak; *~ fare* bilet ücretine yapılan zam, ücret farkı; *~ luggage* fazla bagaj; *~ postage* taksa, pulsuz gönderilen mektup için alıcının ödediği posta ücreti; *~ profit* fazla kazanç; ex'ces.sive □ aşırı, fazla müfrit.

ex.change [iks'tʃeindʒ] 1. *vb.* değiştirmek, mübadele etm., trampa etm. (*for*), bozmak (*para*); 2. *n.* değişme, trampa; kambiyo; *a. bill of ~* ticaret senedi, poliçe; *a.* ♀ borsa; telefon santralı; *a. foreign ~s pl.* döviz; *in ~ for* -e bedel olarak; *~ control* döviz kontrolu, kambiyo denetimi; *~ list* kur cetveli; *par of ~* kambiyo paritesi, borsa değeri; (*rate of*) *~* döviz kuru, kambiyo rayici; ex'change.a.ble *adj.* değiştirilebilir, mübadele edilebilir (*for*); *~ val-ue* mübadele değeri.

ex.cheq.uer [iks'tʃekə] *n.* POL devlet hazinesi; bir kimsenin kişisel gelirinin tümü; *Chancellor of the* ♀ (*İngiltere*) Maliye Bakanı; *~ bond* hazine bonosu.

ex.cise¹ [ek'saiz] 1. *n.* vasıtalı vergi, ülkede üretilip kullanılan mallardan alınan vergi; 2. *vb.* vergi koymak.

ex.cise² [‿] *v/t.* kesip almak, kesip çıkarmak; oymak, temizlemek (*ur*); budamak; ex.ci.sion [ek'siʒən] *n.* kesip alma, kesip çıkarma; kesip alınan, çıkarılan şey.

ex.cit.a.bil.i.ty [iksaitə'biliti] *n.* kolay heyecanlanma, telaşlanma; ex'cit.a-ble *adj.* kolay heyecanlanır, aşırı derecede hassas, çabuk kızan; ex.cit.ant ['eksitənt] *adj.* uyarıcı, uyandırıcı; ex-ci.ta.tion [‿'teiʃən] *n.* heyecanlandırma, tahrik, uyarma; ex.cite [ik'sait] *v/t.* b-ni bşe kışkırtmak, tahrik etm.; heyecanlandırmak; uyandırmak, uyarmak; *~d adj.* heyecanlı; *get ~d* heyecanlanmak, sinirlenmek; ex'cite.ment *n.* heyecan; telaş; tahrik, uyarı; ex'cit-er *n.* MED uyarıcı, münebbih; ELECT dinamonun sabit sarmalarına akım veren yardımcı dinamo; ex'cit.ing *adj.* heyecanlı, meraklı, ilginç, enteresan.

ex.claim [iks'kleim] *vb.* bağırmak, hayret ifade etm., haykırmak, çağırmak;

sövüp saymak (*against -e*).

ex.cla.ma.tion [eksklə'meiʃən] *n.* ünlem, nida, ani olarak söylenen söz; bağırış, çığlık; *~s pl.* yaygara, şamata, GR ünlem işareti; ex.clam.a.to.ry □ [‿'klæmətəri] sevinç, hayret *veya* keder belirten.

ex.clude [iks'klu:d] *v/t.* hariç tutmak (*from -den*), dahil etmemek, engel olm.; kabul etmemek; yoksun bırakmak.

ex.clu.sion [iks'klu:ʒən] *n.* hariç tutma; *spor.* diskalifikasyon *veya* boykot; ret, ihraç, tart; *to the ~ of* -i hariç tutarak, dışında bırakarak; ex'clu.sive □ [‿siv] has, özgü; tek, yalnız, hariç tutan; özel, sırf; *~ of* -siz, -den hariç, müstesna.

ex.cog.i.tate [eks'kɔdʒiteit] *v/t.* düşünüp bulmak, tasar(ım)lamak, icat etm. (*plan, fikir, vs.*); ex.cog.i'ta.tion *n.* düşünme, tasarım, icat, buluş.

ex.com.mu.ni.cate [ekskə'mju:ni-keit] *v/t.* kiliseden aforoz etm.; 'ex-com.mu.ni'cation *n.* aforoz.

ex.co.ri.ate [eks'kɔ:rieit] *v/t.* sıyırmak, yüzmek (*deri*); *fig.* şiddetle eleştirmek, suçlamak.

ex.cre.ment ['ekskrimənt] *n.* dışkı, pislik, ters.

ex.cres.cence [iks'kresns] *n.* ur, şiş, yumru gibi cisim, fazlalık (*bitki, hayvan vs.'de*); ex'cres.cent *adj.* normalden fazla büyüyen, gereğinden fazla, gereksiz.

ex.crete [eks'kri:t] *vb.* ifraz etm., salgılamak, çıkarmak (*vücuttan*); ex'cre-tion *n.* ifrazat, salgı; ifraz etme, boşaltım; ex'cre.tive, ex'cre.to.ry [‿təri] *adj.* ifraz eden, salgı çıkaran, salgı...

ex.cru.ci.ate [iks'kru:ʃieit] *v/t.* azap vermek, eziyet etm., ıstırap vermek, işkence etm., cefa çektirmek; ex'cru-ci.at.ing □ ıstıraplı, eziyetli, cefalı, işkenceli, dayanılmaz.

ex.cul.pate ['eksʌlpeit] *v/t.* mazur göstermek, haklı çıkarmak, aklamak, beraatine karar vermek (*from*); ex.cul-'pa.tion *n.* beraat, aklanma, af.

ex.cur.sion [iks'kə:ʃən] *n.* gezinti, kısa süreli seyahat; *~ train* özel indirimli tren; ex'cur.sion.ist [‿ʃnist] *n.* gezinti yapan b-i.

ex.cur.sive □ [eks'kə:siv] belirli bir çizgi izlemeyen, dolaşan, kararsız.

ex.cus.a.ble □ [iks'kjuːzəbl] affedile-bilir, affolunacak, mazur; **ex'cuse 1.** *v/t.* affetmek, mazur görmek; **~ s.o. s.th.** *b-ni bşden* affetmek, muaf tut-mak; **be ~d from s.th.** *bşden* muaf tu-tulmak, affedilmek; **~ me** affedersiniz, kusuruma bakmayın; **2.** [iks'kjuːs] *n.* özür, mazeret; bahane.

ex.e.at ['eksiæt] *n. okul vs.*: izin.

ex.e.cra.ble □ ['eksikrəbl] iğrenç, menfur, tiksindirici, berbat, kötü, lâ-net, melun; **ex.e.crate** ['-kreit] *v/t.* lâ-net etm., tel'in etm., beddua etm., belâ okumak; *bşden, b-den* nefret, ikrah etm.; **ex.e'cration** *n.* nefret, istikrah, tiksinme, lânet, beddua.

ex.e.cu.tant MUS [ig'zekjutənt] *n.* icra eden *b-i*; resital veren *b-i*; **ex.e.cute** ['eksikjuːt] *v/t.* icra etm., tatbik etm., yerine getirmek, yapmak; idam etm.; MUS resital vermek; JUR hükmü infaz etm.; yürürlüğe koymak, geçerli kılmak; (*vasiyet*) icra, tenfiz etm.; **ex-e'cu.tion** *n.* icra, ifa, tatbik, yapma; in-faz, idam; (*belge*) verme, tevdi; (*vasi-yet*) cebrî icra, zorlayışlı yerine getir-me; MUS resital; teknik, yapış tarzı; **a man of ~** azimkâr kimse; **take out an ~ against**, *b-nin* malına haciz koymak, malını haczetmek; **do ~** tesir etm.; **put veya carry a plan into ~** bir planı ger-çekleştirmek; **ex.e.cu.tion.er** [-'kjuːʃnə] *n.* cellat, idam hükmünü yerine getiren kimse; **ex.ec.u.tive** [ig'zekjutiv] **1.** □ icra eden, idare eden; yetki sahibi; **~ assistant** üst dü-zey bir yöneticinin yardımcılığını ya da sekreterliğini yapan kimse; **~ commit-tee** idare heyeti; **~ editor** başyazar; **2.** *n.* yetkili kimse, idareci; icra gücü; yü-rütme organı; *Am.* devlet başkanı; COM sevk ve idare eden kimse, müdür; **ex-'ec.u.tor** *n.* vasiyeti tenfiz memuru, ye-rine getiren kimse; **ex'ec.u.to.ry** *adj.* icraî; idarî...; JUR bir süre sonra *veya* beklenmedik bir olayda geçerli olması planlanan; müeccel, ertelenen **ex'ec-u.trix** [-triks] *n.* vasiyet hükümlerini yerine getiren kadın.

ex.e.ge.sis [eksi'dʒːsis] *n.* yorum, tef-sir, şerh (*esp. kutsal kitap*).

ex.em.plar [ig'zemplə] *n.* örnek, nu-mune, model; **ex'em.pla.ri.ness** *n.* ör-nek olma, kusursuzluk; **ex'em.pla.ry** *adj.* örnek verici, numune olarak; ibret verici.

ex.em.pli.fi.ca.tion [igzemplifi'kei-ʃən] *n.* örnek, misal; örnekleme, açık-lama; izah; JUR onaylı kopya, resmî su-ret; **ex'em.pli.fy** [-fai] *v/t.* örnek ola-rak vermek; izah etm., anlatmak; can-landırmak; JUR onaylı kopyasını çıkar-mak.

ex.empt [ig'zempt] **1.** *adj.* muaf, bağışık, ayrı tutulan (*from -den*); imti-yazlı; **2.** *v/t.* muaf tutmak, hariç tut-mak, müstesna kılmak (*from -den*); **ex'emp.tion** *n.* muafiyet, bağışıklık (*from -den*).

ex.e.quies ['eksikwiz] *n. pl.* cenaze alayı, merasimi.

ex.er.cise ['eksəsaiz] **1.** *n.* uygulama, tatbik, yerine getirme, kullanma; ta-lim, idman, jimnastik, beden eğitimi; egzersiz, alıştırma; **take ~** talim, spor yapmak; **~s** *pl. Am.* merasim, tören; MIL manevra; **2.** *v/t.* (*beden*) talim ve terbiye etm.; (*güç vs.*) kullanmak; an-trene etm.; talim yaptırmak; sinirlen-dirmek, rahatsız etm. *-i*; *v/i.* idman yap-mak, talim, spor yapmak.

ex.ert [ig'zəːt] *v/t.* sarfetmek, kullan-mak (*güç, hak, nüfuz vs.*); **~ o.s.** çaba-lamak, uğraşmak; zahmete girmek, yo-rulmak; **ex'er.tion** *n.* kullanma, sarfet-me; çaba, gayret, zahmet, çabalama, uğraşma.

ex.e.unt THEAT ['eksiʌnt] *vb.* sahneden çıkarlar.

ex.fo.li.ate [eks'fəulieit] *v/t.* yaprakları yolmak, koparmak; *v/i.* yaprak dök-mek.

ex.ha.la.tion [ekshə'leiʃən] *n.* koku (*buhar, ter vs.*) çıkarma, nefes verme; çıkış; çıkan buhar, koku vs.; **ex.hale** [-'heil] *v/t. & v/i.* koku vs. çık(ar)mak, nefes vermek; can vermek; ölmek; (*duygu*) açığa vurmak.

ex.haust [ig'zɔːst] **1.** *v/t.* tüketmek, bi-tirmek (*a. fig.*); bitap düşürmek, yor-mak; boşaltmak, dökmek (*of*); (*hava*) tulumba ile çekmek, boşaltmak; **2.** *n.* MEC çürük gaz, çürük istim; egzoz, eg-zoz borusu; **~ box** susturucu; **~ pipe** eg-zoz borusu; **ex'haust.ed** *adj.* bitkin, yorgun; tükenmiş (*a. fig.*); satılıp bit-miş (*kitap vs.*); **ex'haust.i.ble** *adj.* tü-kenir, biter; **ex'haust.ing** □ yorucu, zahmetli; MEC boşaltıcı...; **ex'haus-tion** [-tʃən] *n.* bitkinlik; MEC boşaltma; **ex'haus.tive** □ = **exhausting**; ayrıntılı, detaylı, etraflı.

ex.hib.it [ig'zibit] **1.** *vb.* teşhir etm., ser-mek, göstermek; JUR ibraz etm., arzet-

647

mek; **2.** *n.* JUR delil olarak ibraz edilen şey; sergilenen şey; **ex.hi.bi.tion** [eksi-'biʃən] *n.* sergi; gösterme, teşhir; burs; **make an ~ of o.s.** elâleme gülünç olm.; **on ~** sergilenmekte; **ex.hi'bi-tion.er** [-ʃnə] *n.* burslu öğrenci; **ex.hi-'bi.tionism** *n.* PSYCH *k-ni* teşhir merakı, teşhir hastalığı; **ex.hi'bi.tion.ist** *n. k-ni* teşhir eden kimse, teşhir meraklısı.

ex.hil.a.rate [ig'ziləreit] *v/t. b-ni* neşelendirmek, keyiflendirmek, canlandırmak; **ex.hil.a'ra.tion** *n.* neşe, canlılık; keyiflenme.

ex.hort [ig'zɔːt] *v/t. bşe* teşvik etm.; *b-ni* bşi yapması için uyarmak, ihtar etm.; **ex.hor.ta.tion** [egzɔː'teiʃən] *n.* teşvik, nasihat, öğüt; uyarı.

ex.hu.ma.tion [ekshjuː'meiʃən] *n.* mezardan çıkarma; **ex'hume** *v/t.* mezardan çıkarmak (*ceset*).

ex.i.gence, **ex.i.gen.cy** ['eksidʒəns(i)] *n.* ivedi gereksinim, ihtiyaç; ivedi önlem almayı gerektiren endişe verici durum; koşul, zaruret; lüzum; **ex.i-gent** *adj.* ivedi, acele, gecikme kabul etmez; zorunlu, elzem; zorlayıcı; **be ~ of** gerektirmek, icabetmek, istemek.

ex.ile ['eksail] **1.** *n.* sürgün, sürülme; **2.** *v/t.* sürmek, sürgüne göndermek.

ex.ist [ig'zist] *v/i.* var olm., mevcut olm.; bulunmak, olmak; yaşamak, geçinmek; **ex'ist.ence** *n.* varlık, mevcudiyet; vücut, oluş, hayat; **be in ~** var olm.; **in ~** = **ex'ist.ent** *adj.* mevcut, bulunan, var olan; **ex.is.ten.tial.ism** PHLS [egzis'tenʃəlizəm] *n.* varoluşluk, egzistansializm.

ex.it ['eksit] **1.** *n.* çıkış; çıkış yeri, çıkış kapısı; sahneden çıkış; ölüm; **make one's ~** sahneden çıkmak; **~ permit** çıkış izni; **~ visa** çıkış vizesi; **2.** THEAT sahneden çıkar.

ex.o.dus ['eksədəs] *n.* çıkış, özellikle Musa peygamber zamanında Musevilerin Mısır'dan çıkışları; *fig.* toplu çıkış, panik; ♀ Eski Ahit'te ikinci İncil'in adı.

ex of.fi.ci.o [eksə'fiʃiəu] *adj. & adv.* resmî, resmen; memuriyeti nedeniyle.

ex.on.er.ate [ig'zɔnəreit] *v/t. fig. b-nin* yükünü hafifletmek, *b-ne* yardım etm.; *bşden* affetmek, muaf tutmak (*from -den*); suçsuzluğunu kanıtlamak, temize çıkarmak; **ex.on.er'a.tion** *n.* beraat, temize çıkarma; muafiyet, azadoluş.

ex.or.bi.tance, **ex.or.bi.tan.cy** [ig'zɔː-bitəns(i)] *n.* aşırılık, fazlalık; **ex'or.bi-tant** ☐ aşırı, müfrit, ölçüsüz, fahiş (*fiyat*).

ex.or.cism ['eksɔːsizəm] *n.* dualarla cin, şeytan, kötü ruh vs.'yi defetme; **ex.orcist** *n.* cinci hoca, böyle dua okuyan kimse; **ex.or.cize** ['ːsaiz] *v/t.* efsunla ruhları defetmek, cinleri defetmek (*from -den*); kurtulmak (*of*).

ex.ot.ic [ig'zɔtik] *adj.* dışardan gelen, yabancı; yabancı iklimden gelen, egzotik; garip, alışılmamış.

ex.pand [iks'pænd] *v/t. & v/i.* genişle(t)mek, yay(ıl)mak, aç(ıl)mak (*into -e*); büyü(t)mek; kısaltmadan tam olarak yazmak (samimi, konuşkan) güleryüzlü olm.; **ex'pand.er** *n.* yayılan, genişleyen şey; **ex.panse** [iks'pæns] *n.* genişlet(il)me, yay(ıl)ma; genişlik, en, enginlik; geniş yüzey; **ex.pan.si-bil.i.ty** [-sə'biliti] *n.* genişleyebilirlik, yayılabilirlik; **ex'pan.si.ble** *adj.* yayılabilir, genişleyebilir, uzatılabilir; **ex-'pan.sion** *n.* yayılma, genişleme, genleşme, uzama; genişlik, uzam; POL yayılma, genişleme; **ex'pan.sive** ☐ geniş, engin; yay(ıl)ıp genişle(t)meye uygun; *fig.* duygu ve düşüncelerini belli etmekten hoşlanan, konuşkan; **ex-'pan.sive.ness** *n.* yayılma, genişleme; konuşkanlık; coşma.

ex.pa.ti.ate [eks'peiʃieit] *v/t.* detaylı olarak anlatmak *veya* yazmak (**on**); **ex.pati'a.tion** *n.* detaylı olarak görüşme, anlatma; boş lâkırdı, gevezelik.

ex.pa.tri.ate [eks'pætrieit] **1.** *v/t.* vatandaşlıktan çıkarmak, memleket dışına sürmek; **~ o.s.** göç etm., göçmek; **2.** *n.* ülkesini terkedip başka ülkeye yerleşen *b-i;* **ex.pa.tri'a.tion** *n.* vatandaşlıktan çıkarılma; başka ülkeye yerleşme.

ex.pect [iks'pekt] *v/t.* beklemek (**of**, **from**); F sanmak, farzetmek, düşünmek; ummak, ümit etm.; **ex'pect.an-cy** *n.* bekleyiş, ümit; adaylık; JUR beklenen haklar; **ex'pect.ant 1.** *adj.* bekleyen, sabırsızlanan, uman; **be ~** bebek bekliyor olmak; **~ mother** hamile kadın; **2.** *n.* aday, namzet, bekleyen *b-i;* **ex.pec.ta.tion** [ekspek'teiʃən] *n.* bekleme, umma, ümit, olasılık, şans; **contrary to ~** umulanın aksine; **be-yond ~** umulanın ötesinde; **on** *veya* **in ~ of** olasılığına karşı; **~ of life** yaşanılacağı ümit edilen süre; **ex'pect.ing** = **expectant.**

ex.pec.to.rate [eks'pektəreit] *vb.* öksürerek balgam, tükürük vs.'yi çıkıarmak, atmak; ex.pec.to'ra.tion *n.* tükürme; balgam, tükürük.

ex.pe.di.ence, ex.pe.di.en.cy [iks-'pi:djəns(i)] *n.* amaca uygunluk, yararlılık; kişisel çıkar; ex'pe.di.ent **1.** ☐ yararlı, uygun; her davranışında kendi çıkarlarını düşünen; **2.** *n.* çare, tedbir, önlem, vasıta; ex.pe.dite ['ekspidait] *v/t.* çabuklaştırmak, hızlandırmak, kolaylaştırmak; ex.pe.di.tion [‿'difən] *n.* acele, çabukluk, sürat; MIL sefer (*keşif*); gezi; sevkiyat; sefer, hareket; ex.pe'di.tion.ar.y [‿ʃnəri] *adj.* sürat *veya* gezi vs. ile ilgili, gönderilen, sevkedilen; ex.pe'ditious ☐ süratli, çabuk, seri, eli çabuk, işbilir; acelesi olan.

ex.pel [iks'pel] *v/t.* kovmak, çıkarmak, defetmek (*from -den*); ~ *from school b-ni* okuldan tardetmek, kovmak.

ex.pend [iks'pend] *v/t.* sarfetmek (*para*), harcamak (**on, in** *-e*) (*zaman, emek*); ex'pend.a.ble *adj.* harcanabilen, sarfedilebilir...; ex'pend.i.ture [‿ditʃə] *n.* harcama, masraf, sarfiyat (**of**); masraflar; ex.pense [iks'pens] *n.* masraf, gider, harcamalar; harcanan şey (*para, zaman, emek vs.*); ~**s** *pl.* masraflar; **at my** ~ kendi hesabıma; **at the** ~ **of** *-in* zararına, pahasına; **at great** ~ çok masraflı; **go to the** ~ **of** masrafa girmek, para sarfetmek; **put s.o. to great** ~ *b-ni* masrafa sokmak; ex'pense ac.count masraf (*veya* gider) hesabı; ex'pen.sive ☐ masraflı, pahalı.

ex.pe.ri.ence [iks'piəriəns] **1.** *n.* tecrübe, deneme, görgü; **2.** *v/t. bşi* görmek, geçirmek, tatmak; *bşe* maruz kalmak, uğramak, tecrübe etm., denemek; (*kayıp, zayiat v.b.*) vermek; ex'pe.ri.enced *adj.* tecrübeli, deneyimli, görgülü, görmüş geçirmiş.

ex.per.i.ment **1.** [iks'perimənt] *n.* tecrübe, deney, deneme; **2.** [‿ment] *vb.* tecrübe etm., denemek; deney yapmak (**on, with**); ex.pe.ri.men.tal ☐ deneysel..., tecrübeye dayanan, ampirik, görgül; ex.per.i.men'ta.tion *n.* deney yapma; deneme, deneyim, tecrübe; ex.per.i.ment.er [iks'perimentə] *n.* deney yapan, deneyen, tecrübe eden *b-i.*

ex.pert ['ekspə:t] **1.** ☐ [*pred.* eks'pə:t] usta, mahir, becerikli (**at, in** *-de*); uz-

man, ihtisas..., bilirkişi...; ~ *opinion* (*report*) ekspertiz; **2.** *n.* uzman, eksper, mütehassıs (**at, in**), bilirkişi; ex.per.tise [‿'ti:z] *n.* bilirkişi raporu, ekspertiz; ihtisas, ehliyet, eksperlik; 'ex.pert.ness *n.* ustalık, mahir olma, uzmanlık.

ex.pi.a.ble ['ekspiəbl] *adj.* kefaret edilebilir, cezası çekilebilir; ex.pi.ate ['‿pieit] *v/t.* kefaret etm., cezasını çekmek, gönül onarımında bulunmak; ex.pi'a.tion *n.* kefaret, tarziye, gönül onarımı; ex.pi.a.to.ry ['‿piətəri] *adj.* kefaret olarak.

ex.pi.ra.tion [ekspaiə'reiʃən] *n.* nefes verme; son, hitam, nihayet; *at the time of* ~ COM vade bitiminde; ex.pir.a.to.ry [iks'paiərətəri] *adj.* nefes vermekle ilgili; ex'pire *v/i.* nefes vermek, ölmek; son bulmak (*zaman, mukavele vs.*); COM vadesi gelmek; sönmek, bitmek (*ateş, dava vs.*); ex'pi.ry *n.* vade bitimi, sona erme; ölüm.

ex.plain [iks'plein] *v/t. & v/i.* açıklamak *-i*, anlatmak *-i*, izah etm. *-i*; beyan etm., belirtmek; ~ *away* örtbas etm., tevil etm., sözü çevirmek; ex'plain.a.ble *adj.* açıklanabilir, izah edilebilir.

ex.pla.na.tion [eksplə'neiʃən] *n.* izah, açıklama, beyanat; ex.plan.a.to.ry ☐ [iks'plænətəri] izahlı, açıklayıcı, izahat olarak.

ex.ple.tive [eks'pli:tiv] **1.** ☐ dolduran, tamamlayıcı, yazımla ilgili; **2.** *n.* tamamlayıcı, anlamı kuvvetlendirici söz; heyecan ifade eden söz, küfür.

ex.pli.ca.ble ['eksplikəbl] *adj.* anlatılabilir; anlaşılabilir; ex.pli.cate ['‿keit] *v/t.* yorumlamak, detaylı olarak açıklamak; (*fikir*) açıklamak.

ex.plic.it ☐ [iks'plisit] açık, kesin, kat'î, sarih; *fig.* alenî.

ex.plode [iks'pləud] *v/t. & v/i.* patla(t)mak, infilâk et(tir)mek; patlamak (**in, with**) (*kızgınlık, gözyaşı, kahkaha vs.*); (*kuram*) çürütmek, yanlışlığını kanıtlamak; devirmek, altüst etm.; açığa vurmak, ortaya çıkarmak; ex'plod.ed view MEC parçaları ayrı ayrı fakat birbiriyle ilişkisini anlatan grafik *veya* model.

ex.ploit **1.** [iks'plɔit] *v/t.* sömürmek, istismar etm., kullanmak, işletmek, *k--den* yana yontmak; **2.** ['eksplɔit] *n.* kahramanlık, yiğitlik; macera; ex.ploi'ta.tion *n.* sömürü, istismar, kendi çıkarına kullanma; işletme, kullanım.

ex.plo.ra.tion [eksplɔ:'reiʃən] *n.*

araştırma, keşif, inceleme; **ex'plor.a-to.ry** [ˌ-rətəri] adj. araştırma ile ilgili, araştırma...; **ex.plore** [iks'plɔ:] v/t. araştırmak, keşfetmek, incelemek, tetkik etm., yoklamak; **ex'plor.er** n. kâşif, bulucu; araştırmacı kimse.

ex.plo.sion [iks'plɔuʒən] n. patlama, infilâk; galeyan, feveran, parlama, hiddetlenme; **ex'plo.sive** [ˌ-siv] **1.** □ patlayıcı...; **2.** n. patlayıcı madde; GR patlama sesi.

ex.po.nent [eks'pəunənt] n. MATH üs; açıklayan, destekleyen kimse; temsil eden kimse; örnek, misal.

ex.port 1. [eks'pɔ:t] vb. ihraç etm., yurt dışına mal satmak, ihracat yapmak; **2.** ['ekspɔ:t] n. COM ihraç malı; ihracat, dışsatım **~s** pl. ihraç edilen mallar; **ex'porta.ble** adj. ihraç edilebilir; **ex.por'ta.tion** n. ihraç, ihracat, dışsatım; **export.er** n. ihracatçı, yurt dışına mal satan kimse.

ex.po.sé [eks'pəuzei] n. suçu ortaya koyma, gizli bir şeyi açığa vurma; (esp. utanç verici gerçekleri açıklayan) makale veya kitapçık.

ex.pose [iks'pəuz] v/t. açığa vurmak, ifşa etm.; meydana koymak, teşhir etm.; PHOT film üzerine çıkarmak, almak; poz vermek; maruz bırakmak; karşı karşıya getirmek; terk etm., bırakmak (çocuk); fig. maskesini düşürmek, foyasını ortaya çıkarmak; **ex.po.si.tion** [ekspəu'ziʃən] n. sergi, fuar; açıklama, ortaya koyma (fikir); **ex'pos.i.tor** n. yorumlayan, açıklayan b-i.

ex.pos.tu.late [iks'pɔstjuleit] v/i. bşi protesto etm., bşe itiraz etm. (**with, about, on**); **~ with s.o.** b-ne sitem etm., b-ne serzeniş ve ihtarda bulunmak; **ex.pos.tu'la.tion** n. sitem, ihtar, ikaz, uyarma; **ex'pos.tu.la.to.ry** [ˌ-lətəri] adj. tenkit, ihtar olarak.

ex.po.sure [iks'pəuʒə] n. maruz olma, açık olma; açığa vurma; keşfetme, açma; teşhir; PHOT poz; cephe (ev); **~ meter** PHOT ışıkölçer, pozometre; **death from ~** soğuktan ölme.

ex.pound [iks'paund] v/t. açıklamak, izah etm., yorumlamak.

ex.press [iks'pres] **1.** □ açık, sarih, belli, kesin; özel, mahsus; süratli, hızlı, ekspres...; **~ company** Am. nakliye şirketi; **~ highway** ekspres yol; **2.** n. ekspres; sürat postası; a. **~ train** ekspres, sürat postası; **by ~** = **3.** adv. eks-

presle, sürat postası ile; **4.** v/t. (fikir vs.) ifade etm., beyan etm., anlatmak, söylemek, göstermek; sıkarak çıkarmak (suyunu vs.); **be ~ed** ifade edilmek; **ex'press.i.ble** adj. ifade edilebilir; **ex.pression** [ˌ-'preʃən] n. ifade, deyim (lisan, yüz, MUS, boya, MATH); **ex'pres.sion.ism** n. sanat: ekspresyonizm, dışavurumculuk; **ex'pres.sion.less** adj. sönük, cansız; ifadesiz, anlamsız; **ex'pres.sive** □ açık, sarih; anlamlı (**of**); etkileyici; canlı; **ex'press.ly** adv. açık açık, kesinlikle; özellikle; **ex'press.way** n. Am. otoyol.

ex.pro.pri.ate [eks'prəuprieit] v/t. kamulaştırmak, istimlâk etm., elinden almak (**s.th.** bşi; **s.o.** b-nin; **s.o. from s.th.** bşi b-nin) **ex.pro.pri'a.tion** n. kamulaştırma, istimlâk.

ex.pul.sion [iks'pʌlʃən] n. kov(ul)ma, çıkar(ıl)ma, ihraç; **ex'pul.sive** adj. ihraç edici, defedici.

ex.punge [eks'pʌndʒ] v/t. çıkarmak, silmek (**from** -den); fig. üstünden sünger geçirmek.

ex.pur.gate ['ekspə:geit] vb. (kitap vs.) sansürden geçirmek, silip çıkarmak; temizlemek, arıtmak; **ex.pur'ga.tion** n. temizleme, arıtma, tasfiye, ıslah; **ex'purga.to.ry** [ˌ-gətəri] adj. ıslah edici, ıslah kabilinden.

ex.qui.site □ ['ekskwizit] ince, seçkin, zarif, enfes, mükemmel; şiddetli, sert, keskin (soğuk, acı vs.); '**ex.qui.site.ness** n. mükemmellik, zariflik, incelik, kibarlık, duyarlılık; sertlik, keskinlik.

ex-serv.ice.man MIL ['eks'sə:vismən] n. terhis edilmiş asker.

ex.tant [eks'tænt] adj. hâlâ mevcut, günümüze dek gelen.

ex.tem.po.ra.ne.ous □ [ekstempə'reinjəs], **ex.tem.po.ra.ry** [iks'tempərəri], **ex.tempo.re** [eks'tempəri] düşünülmeden, hazırlıksız, irticalen, doğaçtan, ani olarak yapılan veya söylenen; **ex.tem.po.rize** [iks'tempəraiz] v/i. düşünmeden, hazırlıksız söy söylemek, irticalen söylemek; **ex'tem.po.riz.er** n. hazırlıksız söyleyen, çalan, yazan veya bşi yapan kimse.

ex.tend [iks'tend] v/t. yaymak, büyütmek, uzatmak (el. vs.); genişletmek (arazi vs.); uzatmak, temdit etm. (süre); çekmek (çizgi, tel vs.); bşe devam etm.; steno: detaylı yazmak; göstermek (lütuf); (yardım) el uzatmak; sunmak (*yardım, dostluk vs.*); MIL avcı hattına yayılmak; *spor*. tüm gücünü kullanmak; **~ed order** avcı hattı, açılma düzeni; *v/i.* uzanmak, genişlemek, büyümek, sürmek (**to** *-e*); **ex'tend.ed** *adj.* uzatılan, uzayan, genişletilmiş, büyütülmüş.

ex.ten.si.bil.i.ty [ikstensə'biliti] *n.* uza(tıl)ma kabiliyeti; **ex'ten.si.ble** *adj.* uzatılabilir; **ex'ten.sion** *n.* uzatma; uzanma; yay(ıl)ma, genişle(t)me (*a.* GR); büyütme, yetiştirme; TELEPH tâli hat, munzam telefon, dahilî numara; COM vadenin uzatılması; **~ cord** ELECT uzatma kordonu; *University* ♀ üniversite derslerinin devam edemeyenlere verilmesi, öğretilmesi; **ex'ten.sive** □ geniş, yaygın; şumüllü; uzatılmış; **ex-'ten.sive.ness** *n.* genişlik; şumul.

ex.tent [iks'tent] *n.* derece, had, ölçü, nisbet; büyüklük, saha; mesafe, uzunluk, boy; kapsam, şümul; **to the ~ of** derecede; **to a certain ~** bir dereceye kadar; **to a great ~** büyük ölçüde; **to some ~** kısmen, oldukça, bir ölçüde; **to that ~** o derecede; **grant ~ for** süre vermek *-e*.

ex.ten.u.ate [eks'tenjueit] *v/t.* hafifletmek, gevşetmek, yumuşatmak, mazur göstermek, ayıbını örtmek; hafiften almak; **ex.ten.u'a.tion** *n.* hafifletme, azaltma; hafiften alma.

ex.te.ri.or [eks'tiəriə] **1.** □ dış, haricî, zahirî; dışardan gelen, yabancı; **2.** *n.* dış taraf, dış, hariç; görünüş; *film*: açık havada çekilen resim.

ex.ter.mi.nate [iks'təmineit] *v/t.* imha etm., yok etm., kökünü kurutmak; **ex.ter.mi'na.tion** *n.* imha, izale; **ex'ter.mi.nator** *n.* imha eden ilâç *veya* kimse.

ex.ter.nal [eks'tə:nl] **1.** □ dış, zahirî, harcî; gözle görülen; dıştan gelen, haricî; yabancı ülkelerle ilgili, dış…; haricen kullanılan (*ilâç*); **2.** *n.* **~s** *pl.* dış görünüş, dışta kalan olaylar, durumlar; *fig.* formalite(ler).

ex.ter.ri.to.ri.al ['eksteri'tɔːriəl] *adj.* bulunduğu ülkenin yasalarına bağlı olmayan.

ex.tinct [iks'tiŋkt] *adj.* sönmüş, sönük; nesli tükenmiş, yok olmuş (*a. fig.*); **ex-'tinc.tion** *n.* sön(dür)me (*a. fig.*); bir neslin tükenmesi.

ex.tin.guish [iks'tiŋgwiʃ] *v/t.* söndürmek (*a. fig.*), bastırmak, yok etm., imha etm., kökünü kurutmak; (*görev, iş*) lağvetmek, feshetmek; (*kusur*) silmek;

(*düşman*) susturmak, bertaraf etm.; **ex'tinguish.er** = *fire-~*.

ex.tir.pate ['ekstəːpeit] *v/t.* imha etm., yok etm., kökünü kurutmak; MED kesip almak; **ex.tir'pa.tion** *n.* imha, yok etme; MED kesip alma.

ex.tol [iks'təul] *v/t.* övmek, yüceltmek; **~ s.o. to the skies** *fig.* b-ni överek göklere çıkarmak.

ex.tort [iks'tɔːt] *v/t.* zorla almak, şantajla almak (**from** *-den*), gaspetmek; **ex'tortion** *n.* zorla alma, gasp; **ex'tortion.ate** [-ʃnit] *adj.* zorbalığa ait; şantaj; **ex'tor.tion.er** *n.* zorba *b-i*, görevini kötüye kullanan *b-i*.

ex.tra ['ekstrə] **1.** *adj.* fazla, gereksiz, ziyade, zait; ekstra, alâ, fevkalâde…, seçkin, ayrı…; **~ pay** ücret zammı, fazla ödeme; **2.** *adv.* -den başka, ilâveten, ek olarak, ayrıca, bir de; **3.** *n.* ilâve, ek, zam, katma; fevkalâde nüsha, ikinci, üçüncü vs. baskı (*gazete*); THEAT, *film*: figüran (*kız veya kadın*).

ex.tract 1. ['ekstrækt] *n.* özet, hülâsa (*a.* CHEM); ruh, esans; kupür (*gazete*); COM ekstre, hesap hülâsası; **2.** [iks'trækt] *v/t.* çıkarmak, zorla çıkarmak; (*metin*, CHEM) özetini *veya* özünü çıkarmak; MATH (*kök*) almak, çıkarmak; itiraf ettirmek; seçmek; koparmak; **ex'traction** *n.* çıkarma, çekme (*diş vs.*); nesil, soy, sülâle; öz, hülâsa, özet.

ex.tra.dit.a.ble ['ekstrədaitəbl] *adj.* iade edilebilir (*suçlu*); **'ex.tra.dite** *v/t.* (*suçlu*) iade et(tir)mek; **ex.tra.di.tion** [-'diʃən] *n.* suçluları iade.

ex.tra…: '~.ju'di.cial *adj.* mahkeme dışı, yasaların dışında; **'~'mu.ral** *adj.* şehir *veya* okul duvarları dışında, okullararası (*karşılaşma*); **~ student** misafir öğrenci.

ex.tra.ne.ous [eks'treinjəs] *adj.* ikincil, talî (**to** *-e*); konu dışı; dıştan gelen, yabancı.

ex.traor.di.nar.y [iks'trɔːdnri] *adj.* olağanüstü, fevkalâde, müstesna, garip, seçkin; **envoy ~** yetkili temsilci, murahhas.

ex.tra.sen.so.ry per.cep.tion PSYCH ['ekstrə'sensəri pə'sepʃən] altıncı his.

ex.tra.ter.ri.to.ri.al ['ekstrəteri'tɔːriəl] = *exterritorial*.

ex.trav.a.gance [iks'trævigəns] *n.* israf; aşırılık, ifrat, taşkınlık, delibozukluk; **ex'trav.a.gant** □ tutumsuz, müsrif; delibozuk; aşırı, müfrit, bol bol; **ex.trav.agan.za** THEAT [ekstrævə'gænzə] *n.* zengin dekorlu piyes, büyük mizansenli piyes, fantezi.

ex.treme [iks'tri:m] **1.** □ son derece, fevkalâde; aşırı, müfrit; en uçta *veya* en kenarda olan; son; ~ unction ECCL Katolik kilisesi geleneğine göre ölüm halindeki kişiye mukaddes yağ sürülmesi; **2.** *n.* sınır, uç; ifrat; **go to ~s** aşırıya kaçmak; **in the ~** aşırı derecede; **ex-'trem.ist** *n.* aşırı giden *b-i;* **ex.trem.i.ty** [ˌ-'tremiti] *n.* uç; sınır; had; son; aşırı tehlike; son çare; ıstırap; **ex'trem.i.ties** [ˌ-z] *n. pl.* ANAT eller ve ayaklar.

ex.tri.cate ['ekstrikeit] *v/t.* kurtarmak, çıkarmak; açmak, ayırmak; CHEM ayrıştırmak; **ex.tri'ca.tion** *n.* kurtarma, kurtulma, çıkarma, ayırma.

ex.trin.sic [eks'trinsik] *adj.* (*~ally*) haricî, dıştan gelen (*to -e*).

ex.tro.vert ['ekstrəuvə:t] *n.* dışa dönük karakter, kendi düşünce ve duygularıyla ilgilenmek yerine vaktini başkaları ile geçiren kimse.

ex.trude [eks'tru:d] *v/t.* çıkarmak, ihraç etm., dışarı çıkarmak, sıkıp çıkarmak; *b-ni* bir yerden atmak.

ex.u.ber.ance [ig'zju:bərəns] *n.* coşkunluk, taşkınlık; bolluk; **ex'u.ber.ant** *adj.* coşkun, heyecanlı, taşkın; aşırı; bol, bereketli.

ex.u.da.tion [eksju:'deiʃən] *n.* sızıntı, sızan şey, ifrazat, ter; **ex.ude** [ig'zju:d] *vb.* sızıntı yapmak, sızdırmak, ifraz etm.

ex.ult [ig'zʌlt] *vb.* çok sevinmek (*at veya* **in s.th** bşe), (*bir zafer sonucu*) coşmak, övünmek, hakkından gelip sevinmek (*over s.o. b-nin*); **ex'ult.ant** *adj.* sevinçli, coşkun, neşeli; **ex.ul.ta-**

tion [egzʌl'teiʃən] *n.* sevinç, coşku; övünme.

eye [ai] **1.** *n.* göz (*a. fig.* & BOT); bakış, nazar; delik, iğne deliği (*veya* gözü, kulağı), ilik, dişi kopça; budak; **have an ~ for** bşin iyisini seçebilmek, bşden iyi anlamak; **my ~s!** *sl.* vay iki gözüm benim!, yok canım!; **it's all my ~!** *sl.* zırva, boş lâkırdı; **make ~s at s.o.** *b-ne* aşıkâne bakmak, *b-ne* sevgiyle bakmak, F *b-ne* kaş göz etm.; **up to the ~s in work** başını kaşıyacak vakti yok, işi başından aşkın, çok meşgul; **mind your ~!** dikkatli ol!, gözünü aç; **with an ~ to** göz önünde tutarak, hesaba katarak; **2.** *v/t.* göz atmak *-e*, gözden geçirmek (*şaşkınlıkla*), incelemek, bakmak; **'~.ball** *n.* göz küresi; **'~.brow** *n.* kaş; **'~-catch.er** *n.* göz alan, dikkati çeken şey; **eyed** [aid] *comb.* …gözlü.

eye…: **'~.glass** *n.* tek gözlük, oküler; (**pair of**) **~es** *pl.* gözlük; **'~.hole** *n.* gözçukuru; gözetleme deliği; **'~.lash** *n.* kirpik; **eyelet** [ˌ-'lit] *n.* küçük delik, göz deliği; teknelere açılan küçük delik, matafyon; kopça iliği.

eye…: **'~.lid** *n.* gözkapağı; **'~-o.pen.er** *n.* aydınlatan *veya* şaşırtan haber *veya* olay; sürpriz olay; insanın gözünü açan şey; sabahları mahmurluk gideren ilk içki; **'~-piece** *n.* OPT dürbün *vs.*'nin göz camı, oküler; **'~.shot** *n.* görüş mesafesi; **'~.sight** *n.* görme kuvveti, görüm; **'~.sore** *n.* göze çirkin görünen şey; **'~.tooth** *n.* köpekdişi, gözdişi; **'~.wash** *n. sl.* göz boyama, aldatma; **'~'wit.ness** *n.* JUR görgü tanığı, şahit.

ey.rie, ey.ry ['aiəri] = **aerie**.

F

Fa.bian ['feibjən] **1.** *adj.* ihtiyatlı, tedbirli, işi ağırdan alan, sürüncemede
bırakan, ağır (*kimse*); ~ **policy** işi ağırdan alma politikası, sürüncemede
bırakma politikası; **2.** *n.* (*İngiltere'de*)
ılımlı sosyalist bir derneğe mensup
kişi.

fa.ble ['feibl] *n.* masal, özellikle hayvanları anlatan hikâye, fabl, efsane,
mit; yalan, sahte.

fab.ric ['fæbrik] *n.* kumaş, bez, dokuma; bünye, yapı; **fab.ri.cate** ['˷keit]
v/t. imal etm., yapmak, biraraya getirmek; *fig.* yalan söylemek, uydurmak,
sahtesini yapmak; **fab.ri'ca.tion** *n.*
imal etme, yapma, biraraya getirme;
fig. yalan, uydurma, sahte; **'fab.ri.ca-
tor** *n.* imalatçı; uydurukçu.

fab.u.list ['fæbjulist] *n.* hayal ürünü hi-
kâyeler yazan kimse; yalancı, uydurukçu; **'fab.u.lous** □ hayal mahsulü, uydurma, efsanevî; inanılmaz, olması imkânsız, abartılmış; F harika, şahane,
müthiş, mükemmel, fevkalâde.

fa.cade ARCH [fə'sɑːd] *n.* binanın ön yüzü, cephe; *fig.* dış görünüş, sahte görünüş.

face [feis] **1.** *n.* yüz, çehre, surat, sima;
görünüş, ifade; yüzey, satıh, (*binanın*)
cephesi; yüzsüzlük; **in (the) ~ of**
karşısında, rağmen; ~ **to ~ with** yüz yüze ile; **save one's ~** onurunu kurtarmak, kabahatini örtbas etm.; **lose ~** itibarını kaybetmek, saygınlığını yitirmek; **on the ~ of it** görünüşe bakılırsa,
görünüş itibariyle; **set one's ~ against**
karşı çıkmak *-e*, engel olm. *-e*; **2.** *v/t. &*
v/i. yüzüne bakmak, bakmak, yönel-
mek, cesaretle karşılamak; *-in*
karşısında olm.; *-in* kenarını çevirmek;
kaplamak, astarlamak; **be ~d with**
karşısında olm.; karşı çıkmak *-e*; ~
about ters yöne dönmek; **left~!** MIL sola dön!; **about ~!** geriye dön!; ~ **card**
iskambil: resimli iskambil kağıdı (*papaz, kız veya vale*); **'~-cloth** *n.* yüz havlusu; **faced** *comb.* ... yüzlü, yüzü olan;
'face-lift.ing *n.* MED yüzü ameliyatla
gerdirme, yüz estetik ameliyatı; **'fac.er**
n. aniden karşılaşılan ciddi zorluk,
beklenmedik engel.

fac.et MEC ['fæsit] *n.* kıymetli taşın bir
yüzeyi, faseta; *fig.* yön, görünüş; **'faceted** *adj.* yüzlü, fasetalı.

fa.ce.tious □ [fə'siːʃəs] uygunsuz şaka
yapan, alaycı, nükteli, esprili, şakacı.

face val.ue ['feis'væljuː] *n.* COM itibarî
kıymet, üzerindeki değer, nominal
değer; *fig.* dış görünüşündeki değer *veya* önem; **take s.th. at its ~** bşi dış görünüşüne göre değerlendirmek.

fa.ci.a ['feiʃə] = **fascia.**

fa.cial ['feiʃəl] **1.** □ yüz ile ilgili, yüze
ait; **2.** *n.* yüz masajı.

fac.ile ['fæsail] □ kolay, basit; herşeyi
kolayca yapan (*kimse*), becerikli; kolay
yapılan; uysal; **fa.cil.i.tate** [fə'siliteit]
v/t. kolaylaştırmak; **fa.cil.i'ta.tion** *n.*
kolaylaştırma; **fa'cil.i.ty** *n.* kolaylık, rahatlık; *pl.* vasıta, imkânlar, bina, tesis.

fac.ing ['feisiŋ] *n.* MEC kaplama, astar;
MIL dönüş; **~s** *pl.* volan, süs.

fac.sim.i.le [fæk'simili] *n.* faksimile,
kopya, suret, aynısı, tıpkısı; resim *veya*
yazının radyo *veya* telgrafla gönderilmesi.

fact [fækt] *n.* gerçek, hakikat; durum;
~s *pl.* (**of the case**) olayın unsurları; **after the ~** suç işlendikten sonra; **before
the ~** suç işlenmeden önce; **in (point
of) ~**, **as a matter of ~** gerçekten, hakikatte, işin doğrusu; **know for a ~** kesinlikle bilmek, adı gibi bilmek;
'~-find.ing *n.* gerçekleri ortaya çıkarma.

fac.tion ['fækʃən] *n.* grup, bölünme, çekişme, hizip, ihtilâf, ayrılık; **'fac.tion-
ist** *n.* ihtilafçı, partizan, arabozucu, bölücü, fitneci.

fac.tious □ ['fækʃəs] ihtilafçı, partizan,
arabozucu, fitneci; **'fac.tious.ness** *n.*
fitnecilik, ihtilafçılık, hizipçilik.

fac.ti.tious □ [fæk'tiʃəs] yapmacık, suni, tabii olmayan.

fac.tor ['fæktə] *n.* MATH çarpılanlardan
biri; âmil, sebeplerden biri, faktör; COM
komisyonla satış yapan kimse; **'fac.to-
ry** *n.* fabrika, atölye, imalathane.

fac.to.tum [fæk'təutəm] *n.* kâhya,
uşak, hizmetçi.

fac.tu.al ['fæktʃuəl] *adj.* gerçeklere dayalı, olaylarla ilgili.

fac.ul.ty ['fækəlti] *n.* yetenek, kabiliyet; güç, iktidar; JUR öncelik hakkı, ayrıcalık, imtiyaz; UNIV fakülte, üniversite dalı, branş.

fad F [fæd] *n.* geçici merak, heves, ilgi; 'fad.dish, 'fad.dy *adj.* geçici heves kabilinden; 'fad.dist *n.* geçici hevesleri olan kimse.

fade [feid] *vb.* rengini soldurmak, solmak, sararıp solmak, canlılığını kaybetmek; gözden kaybolmak, hafızadan silinmek; *radyo*: şiddetini artırmak *veya* azaltmak, şiddeti artmak *veya* azalmak; ~ *away*, ~ *out* gözden kaybolmak, duyulmamak; ~ *in* sesi yavaş yavaş yükseltmek; ~ *out* sesi yavaş yavaş azaltmak; 'fade.less *adj.* solmaz; 'fad.ing □ geçici, süreksiz, fanî; *radyo*: zayıflama, kaybolma, feding.

fae.ces PHYSIOL ['fi:si:z] *n. pl.* tortu, posa, pislik, dışkı.

faer.ie, faer.y ['feiəri] *n. obs.* periler ülkesi; *attr.* hayalî.

fag F [fæg] **1.** *n.* yorucu iş; (*İngiltere'de*) üst sınıftaki öğrenciye hizmet eden öğrenci; *sl.* sigara; homoseksüel erkek; **2.** *v/t. & v/i.* didinmek, çalışıp yor(ul)-mak, uşak gibi çalış(tır)mak; '~'end *n.* işe yaramaz kısım, artık; izmarit.

fag.ot, fag.got ['fægət] *n.* ince odun demeti, çubuk demeti; MEC demir çubuk demeti; *Am.* F homoseksüel erkek.

Fahr.en.heit ['færənhait] *n.* fahrenhayt; ~ *thermometer* fahrenhayt termometresi.

fail [feil] **1.** *v/t. & v/i.* başaramamak (*in -i*), başarısız olm., kalmak (*sınavda*), boşa çıkmak; bırakmak (*sınavda*); yetersiz olm., bitmek, zayıflamak; ihmal etm., iflâs etm.; yoksun olm. (*in -den*); *he ~ed to do veya in doing* ... yapmayı başaramadı; *he cannot ~ to inf.* ...yapmadan bırakmaz; *his heart ~ed him* cesareti kırıldı, cesaret edemedi; **2.** *n. without ~* elbette, mutlaka, şüphesiz; 'fail.ing **1.** *n.* kusur, zayıflık, zaaf; **2.** *prp.* yokluğunda, olmadığı takdirde; ~ *which* olmadığı takdirde; fail-ure ['-jə] *n.* başarısızlık; başarısız kimse; başarısızlıkla sonuçlanan şey *veya* teşebbüs; bitme, tükenme; iflâs; ihmal, yetersizlik.

fain *poet.* [fein] *adv.* seve seve, isteyerek, memnuniyetle.

faint [feint] **1.** □ zayıf, cılız (*ses*), silik, belirsiz, başı dönmüş, baygın; **2.** *v/i.* bayılmak; solmak; gevşemek, zayıflamak; **3.** *n.* baygınlık, bayılma; '~'heart.ed □ yüreksiz, korkak; çekingen, mahcup; '~'heart.ed.ness *n.* korkaklık, çekingenlik; 'faint.ness *n.* baygınlık, halsizlik, zayıflık.

fair¹ [feə] **1.** *adj.* dürüst, adil, doğru, haklı; orta, vasat, iyi; açık (*hava*); elverişli (*rüzgâr*); tatminkâr, bol, çok; sarışın, kumral; hoş, güzel; iyi seçilmiş (*kelime*); temiz, açık, lekesiz; ~ *copy* temiz kopya; ~ *name* iyi nam, şöhret; ~ *play* temiz oyun, tarafsızlık; *the ~ sex* kadınlar, cinsi lâtif; **2.** *adv.* dürüstce, adilane, tam, temiz olarak; *write s.th out ~* hatasız yazmak.

fair² [~] *n.* pazar, panayır, fuar, sergi.

fair-haired ['feə'heəd] *adj.* sarışın.

fair.ly ['feəli] *adv.* dürüstçe, adilane; tamamen; âdeta; oldukça; 'fair.ness *n.* doğruluk, dürüstlük, güzellik; 'fair--'spoken *adj.* nazik, tatlı dilli; 'fair.way *n.* NAUT serhest geçit, gemilerin seyredebildiği geçit; 'fair-weath.er friend iyi gün dostu.

fair.y ['feəri] **1.** *n.* peri; *sl.* homoseksüel erkek; **2.** *adj.* peri gibi, perilere ait; 'Fairy.land *n.* periler ülkesi, büyülü yer, güzel yer; 'fair.y.like *adj.* peri gibi; 'fair.y-tale *n.* peri masalı; yalan, uydurma hikâye.

faith [feiθ] *n.* inanç, itikat, iman; itimat, güven; din; söz, vaat; sadakat, vefa; *have ~ in s.th.* itimadı, güveni, inancı olm. *-e*; *in good ~* iyi niyetle, samimiyetle, dürüstlükle; '~-cure = *faith--healing*; faith.ful □ ['-ful] iman sahibi; sadık, vefakâr, güvenilir, doğru; *the ~ pl.* müminler, inananlar; *yours ~ly* saygılarımla, saygılarımızla; faith.ful.ness *n.* sadakat, iman; 'faith-heal.ing *n.* itikatla iyileşme, şifa bulma; 'faith.less □ güvenilmez, sadakatsiz, hain; imansız, dinsiz; 'faith.less.ness *n.* güvensizlik; imansızlık.

fake *sl.* [feik] **1.** *n.* sahte, yapma; uydurma; sahtekâr, şarlatan; *Am. a.* 'fak.er *n.* sahtekâr, dolandırıcı; **2.** *a.* ~ *up v/t.* sahtesini yapmak, uydurmak.

fal.con ['fɔːlkən] *n.* şahin, doğan; 'fal-coner *n.* şahin *veya* doğanla avlanan avcı, şahinci, doğancı; 'fal.con.ry *n.* doğancılık, başçuluk.

fall [fɔːl] **1.** *n.* düşme, düşüş, çöküş, çökme; yağış; şelâle, çağlayan; *Am.* sonbahar, güz; yıkılma; düşüş mesafesi; ucuzlama; dökülme; (*güreşte*) düşüş;

elbise fırfırı; *the* ♀ *(of Man)* Hz. Adem ve Havva'nın işlediği günah ve sonuçları; *have a ~* düşmek; **2.** *v/i.* düşmek, yağmak, dökülmek; doğmak *(hayvan)*; inmek; uzanmak; azalmak, kesilmek *(rüzgâr)*; vaki olm.; çökmek, düşmek *(kale)*; meyletmek *(toprak)*; rastlamak *(tarih)*; *his countenance fell* suratı asıldı; *~ asleep* uykuya dalmak; *~ away* terketmek, çekilmek, ortadan kaybolmak; *~ back* geri çekilmek; *~ back (up)on* yeniden müracaat etm., başvurmak *(güvenilen bşe)*; *~ behind* geri kalmak, yetişememek; *~ between two stools* iki cami arasında beynamaz olm., iki seçenek arasında tereddütten dolayı bir fırsatı kaçırmak; *~ down* düşmek; çökmek, yıkılmak; *~ due* vadesi dolmak; *~ for* F çok beğenmek, bayılmak, kesilmek; aldatılmak, tongaya basmak; *~ from* düşmek *-den*; *~ ill veya sick* hastalanmak; *~ in* çökmek, yıkılmak; MIL sıraya girmek, dizilmek; *~ in with* uymak, kabul etm.; rast gelmek; *~ in love with* aşık olm. *-e*; *~ into* başlamak; bölünmek, ayrılmak; *~ into line with* diğerlerinin yaptığına uymak; *~ off* eksilmek, azalmak; düşmek *(a. fig.)* *(from -den)*, düşüş göstermek; *~ on* saldırmak, hücum etm.; gelmek düşmek; *~ out* MIL sıradan çıkmak; vaki olm., meydana gelmek; kavga etm., bozuşmak, bırakmak; *~ short* kısa düşmek, ulaşamamak *(of -e)*; *~ short of* umduğu gibi çıkmamak, yetersiz olm.; *~ to* başlamak, girişmek; *~ under* altına düşmek, altında toplanmak, altında sınıflandırmak.

fal.la.cious □ [fə'leiʃəs] yanıltıcı, aldatıcı, yanlış, hatalı, boş.

fal.la.cy ['fæləsi] *n.* yanlış fikir, aldatıcı kavram; aldatma, hile, yanlışlık.

fall.en ['fɔːlən] *p.p. of fall 2.*

fall guy *Am. sl.* ['fɔːl'gai] *n.* kolayca aldatılan kimse, keriz, başkalarının cezasını ve sorumluluğunu yüklenen kimse.

fal.li.bil.i.ty [fæli'biliti] *n.* yanılma payı; **fal.li.ble** □ ['fæləbl] yanılabilir, hataya düşebilir, yanlış olabilir.

fall.ing ['fɔːliŋ] *n.* düşüş, çöküş; *~ off* azalma, eksilme; *~ sick.ness* sara, epilepsi; *~ star* göktaşı.

fal.low ['fæləu] **1.** *adj.* açık sarı, deve tüyü; AGR ekilmemiş, nadasa bırakılan; **2.** *n.* nadasa bırakılan arazi, nadas; nadas

etme; *~-deer* *n.* ZOO geyik; **'fal.low.ness** *n.* nadasa bırakma.

false □ [fɔːls] sahte, yanlış, yapma, taklit, hatalı, yalan, takma *(saç, diş)*, sözde; *~ imprisonment* haksız yere hapis, sözde mahkûmiyet; *~ key* maymuncuk; *play s.o. ~* ihanet etm., aldatmak; **falsehood** ['ˌhud] *n.* yalan; **'false.ness** *n.* yalan, sahtelik.

fal.set.to MUS [fɔːl'setəu] *n.* çok ince ses *(erkekte)*; bu sesle şarkı söyleyen kimse, kontrtenor.

fal.si.fi.ca.tion ['fɔːlsifi'keiʃən] *n.* tahrif, taklit, sahtesini yapma, uydurma; **falsi.fi.er** ['ˌfaiə] *n.* yalancı, düzenbaz, tahrifçi, kalpazan; **fal.si.fy** ['ˌfai] *v/t.* tahrif etm., bozmak; taklit etm.; yalan olduğunu söylemek; **fal.si.ty** ['ˌti] *n.* yalan; yanlışlık, hata; hainlik.

fal.ter ['fɔːltə] *v/t. & v/i.* sendelemek, yalpalamak; kekelemek, tutuk konuşmak, titremek *(ses)*, duraklamak, tereddüt içinde söylemek, kısık sesle söylemek.

fame [feim] *n.* şöhret, ün, şan, nam; **famed** *adj.* ünlü, meşhur.

fa.mil.iar [fə'miljə] **1.** □ bilen *-i*, malûmatı olan, haberdar olan, bilinen, her zaman görülen *veya* duyulan, alışılmış; lâubali, senli benli; alışkın *(with -e)*; *be ~ with* bilmek, tanımak; samimi, yakın, teklifsiz olm.; **2.** *n.* samimi arkadaş; **fa.mil.i.ar.i.ty** [ˌli'æriti] *n.* iyi bilme, aşinalık, teklifsizlik, alışkanlık; *pl.* lâubalilik, serbestlik, teklifsizlik; **fa.mil.iar.i.za.tion** [ˌljərai'zeiʃən] *n.* tanıtma, alıştırma, tanıma; **fa'mil.iar.ize** *v/t.* tanıtmak, alıştırmak; ilişki kurmak.

fam.i.ly ['fæmili] *n.* aile, çoluk çocuk, ecdat, akraba; soy, cins; BOT familya; *in the ~ way* F hamile, gebe; *~ allowance* çocuk zammı; *~ doctor* aile doktoru; *~ man* aile babası; *~ planning* aile planlaması; *~ tree* soy ağacı, şecere.

fam.ine ['fæmin] *n.* kıtlık, açlık.

fam.ish ['fæmiʃ] *v/t. & v/i.* çok acıkmak, açlıktan öl(dür)mek, aç bırakmak, aç kalmak.

fa.mous □ ['feiməs] ünlü, meşhur, tanınmış; F mükemmel, çok iyi, tatminkâr.

fan¹ [fæn] **1.** *n.* yelpaze, vantilatör, yelpaze kanadına benzeyen şey; NAUT pervane; **2.** *v/t.* yelpazelemek, hava vermek, körüklemek serinletmek; *~ out* MIL yelpaze gibi açılmak, yayılmak.

fan² [ˌ] *n.* spor, *etc.*: bşin hayranı, meraklısı, delisi, hastası, tiryakisi.

fa.nat.ic [fə'nætik] **1.** *a.* fa'nat.i.cal □ mutaassıp, fanatik, aşırı meraklı, çok düşkün, aşırı fikirli; **fa'nat.i.cism** [-sizəm] *n.* tutuculuk, aşırılık, taassup.

fan.ci.er ['fænsiə] *n.* meraklısı, düşkünü, seven *b-i.*

fan.ci.ful □ ['fænsiful] hayalperest, gerçeklerden uzak, kaprisli; **'fan.ci.ful.ness** *n.* hayalî olma.

fan.cy ['fænsi] **1.** *n.* hayal, düş, kapris, geçici arzu, beğeni, düşkünlük, merak, kuruntu; **take a ~ to** beğenmek, hoşlanmak, sevmek; **2.** □ süslü, parlak renkli; aşırı; iyi kalite (*mal*); hayale dayalı; **~ apron** aşırı bağ; **~ dress** karnaval kıyafeti, maskeli balo kıyafeti; **~-dress ball** maskeli balo; **~ fair** yardım pazarı; **~ goods** fantezi eşya, iyi kalite mallar; **~ man** sevgili; *sl.* pezevenk; **~ price** fahiş fiyat; **3.** *v/t.* hayal etm., tasavvur etm., zannetmek, sanmak; istemek, arzu etm., beğenmek, sevmek; **just ~!** hayret doğrusu!; **'~-work** *n.* ince el işi.

fane *poet.* [fein] *n.* mabet, kilise.

fan.fare ['fænfɛə] *n.* MUS merasim borusu, nefesli çalgıların çaldığı parça, fanfar; **fan.fa.ron.ade** [-færə'na:d] *n.* yüksekten atma, palavra, martaval, övünme.

fang [fæŋ] *n.* azı dişi (*köpek veya kurtların*); yılanın zehirli dişi; MEC pençe, tırnak.

fan.ner MEC ['fænə] *n.* vantilatör, havalandırma tertibatı, üfleç, hamlaç.

fan.tail ZOO ['fænteil] *n.* bir çeşit evcil güvercin; yelpaze şeklinde kuyruk.

fan.ta.sia MUS [fæn'teizjə] *n.* fantezi; **fantas.tic** [-'tæstik] *adj.* hayali; garip, acayip, tuhaf, saçma, F harika, şahane, fevkalâde; **fan.ta.sy** ['-təsi] *n.* hayal, garip fikir; MUS fantezi.

fan.zine ['fænzi:n] *n.* fan dergisi.

far [fɑ:] *adj.* uzak, uzun; daha uzak; ilericmiş; *adv.* uzağa, uzakta, daha, oldukça, epeyce, çok; **~ better** çok daha iyi; **~ the best** en iyisi; **as ~ as** *-e* kadar, *-e* kalırsa; **by ~** hatırı sayılır derecede, büyük farkla; **~ from** hiç, hiç mi hiç, ...bir yana; **in so ~ as** bir dereceye kadar, *-den* dolayı, olduğuna göre; **~ and near, ~ and wide** her yerde; **~-a.way** ['fɑ:rəwei] *adj.* uzak, uzakta; dalgın (*bakış*).

farce THEAT [fɑ:s] *n.* komik tiyatro oyunu, fars; saçma, yararsız şey; **far.ci.cal**

□ ['-sikəl] tuhaf, komik, gülünç.

fare [fɛə] **1.** *n.* yol parası, bilet ücreti; yolcu; yiyecek; **2.** *v/i.* olmak, yaşamak; başından geçmek, gitmek, gelişme göstermek; **how did you ~?** nasıl gitti?; **~ well!** güle güle!; **~ stage** kıta, iki durak arası; **'~-well** *int.* uğurlar olsun, güle güle!; **2.** *n.* ayrılma, gitme, veda, uğurlama; **3.** *adj.* veda, son; **~ party** veda partisi.

far... [fɑ:]: **'~-'fetched** *adj. fig.* zoraki, **'~-'flung** *adj.* çok yaygın; *fig.* uzak; **~ gone** F çok ilerlemiş (*hastalık, delilik, sarhoşluk, borç v.b.*).

far.i.na.ceous [færi'neiʃəs] *adj.* nişastalı, un gibi.

farm [fɑ:m] **1.** *n.* çiftlik; **chicken ~** tavuk çiftliği; **2.** *vb.* ekip biçmek, çiftçilik yapmak; işletmek; *a.* **~ out** kiraya vermek, ekip biçmek; çocuğun bakımı için anlaşmak; işi başkasına devretmek; **'farm.er** *n.* çiftçi; çiftlik sahibi; **'farm.hand** *n.* Am. rençber; **'farm--house** *n.* çiftlik evi; **'farm.ing** *n.* çiftçilik; **farmstead** ['-sted] *n.* çiftlik ve içindeki binalar; **'farm.yard** *n.* çiftlik avlusu.

far.o ['fɛərəu] *n.* kağıdı dağıtana karşı oynanan kumar oyunu.

far-off ['fɑ:r'ɔ:f] *adj.* uzak.

far.ra.go [fə'rɑ:gəu] *n.* karışım, karmakarışık şey.

far-reach.ing ['fɑ:'ri:tʃiŋ] *adj.* geniş kapsamlı.

far.ri.er ['færiə] *n.* nalbant.

far.row ['færəu] **1.** *n.* bir batında doğan domuz yavruları; **2.** *v/i.* yavrulamak (*domuz*).

far-see.ing ['fɑ:'si:iŋ], **'far-'sight.ed** *adj. fig.* uzağı gören, basiretli.

far.ther ['fɑ:ðə], **far.thest** ['-ðist] *comp. & sup. of* **far.**

far.thing ['fɑ:ðiŋ] *n.* çeyrek peni; **not worth a ~** beş para etmez.

fas.ci.a MOT ['feiʃə] *n.* arabada kontrol paneli; uzun tabelâ.

fas.ci.nate ['fæsineit] *v/t.* büyülemek, cezbetmek, teshir etm., hayran bırakmak; **fas.ci.na.tion** *n.* cazibe, çekicilik, büyüleme, teshir.

fas.cine [fæ'si:n] *n.* çalı demeti.

Fas.cism POL ['fæʃizəm] *n.* faşizm; **'fascist** *n.* faşist; **fa'scis.tic** *adj.* (**~ally**) faşistliğe ait.

fash.ion ['fæʃən] **1.** *n.* moda, şekil; tarz, usül; **rank and ~** yüksek zümre; **in (out of) ~** moda ol(may)an; **set the ~** modada öncülük etm.; **2.** *v/t.* yapmak; şekil vermek; **'fash.ion.a.ble** □ ['fæʃnəbl] modaya uygun, şık; zenginler arasında tutulan; **'fash.ion.a.ble.ness** *n.* modaya uygunluk, şıklık; **fash.ion-'is.ta** ['fæʃən'istə] *n.* moda hastası. **'fash.ion-pa'rade** *n.* defile; **'fash-ion-plate** *n.* elbise modeli; son modayı izleyen kimse.

fast[1] [faːst] **1.** *adj.* çabuk, tez, hızlı, süratli; seri; ileri (*saat*); sıkı, sabit; solmaz (*renk*); sadık, yakın (*arkadaş*); zevke düşkün; ahlâksız (*kadın*); ~ **to light** ışığa dayanıklı; ~ **train** süratli tren, ekspres; **my watch is** ~ saatim ileri gitmiş; **2.** *adv.* çabuk, süratle; sıkıca; derin bir şekilde; ~ **asleep** derin uykuda.

fast[2] [~] **1.** *v/i.* oruç tutmak, perhiz etm.; **2.** *n.* oruç; **'~day** *n.* oruç günü, perhiz günü.

fas.ten ['faːsn] *v/t.* & *v/i.* bağlamak, tut(tur)mak, sürmelemek; dikmek, ayırmamak; birleştirmek; ~ (**up)on** dikmek, ayırmamak (*gözünü*); ~ **upon** kavramak, iyice anlamak; **'fas.ten.er** *n.* tutacak, bağ, bağlayan şey, toka kıskacı, çıtçıt; **'fas.ten.ing** *n.* sürgü, toka.

fas.tid.i.ous □ [fəs'tidiəs] titiz, müşkülpesent, memnun edilmesi güç; **fas-'tid.i.ousness** *n.* titizlik.

fast.ness ['faːstnis] *n.* sağlamlık; sürat; solmazlık, solmama (*renk*); **MIL** kale, istihkâm.

fat [fæt] **1.** □ şişman, semiz, yağlı, kalın, dolu; bereketli, verimli (*toprak*); **2.** *n.* yağ; **live on the** ~ **of the land** herşeyin iyisiyle geçinmek; **the** ~ **is in the fire** kıyamet kopacak, iş patlak verecek; **3.** *v/t.* semirtmek, beslemek.

fa.tal □ ['feitl] öldürücü, mahvedici, yok edici; mukadder, alında yazılı; ~ **accident** öldürücü kaza; **fa.tal.ism** ['~təlizm] *n.* herşeyi kadere bağlama inancı, kadercilik, fatalizm; **'fa.tal.ist** *n.* herşeyi kadere bağlayan kimse, fatalist; **fa.tal.i.ty** [fə'tæliti] *n.* felâket, talihsizlik, akıbet, belâ, afet.

fate [feit] *n.* kader, kısmet, talih; ecel; akıbet; **the ₂s** *pl.* üç Yunan kader tanrıçası; **'fat.ed** *adj.* kadere bağlı; **fate.ful** □ ['~ful] kaderi tayin eden, önemli; tarihi önem taşıyan (*karar*); mukadder.

fat-free [fæt~] yağsız.

fa.ther ['faːðə] **1.** *n.* baba; *pl.* ata, soy; kurucu; tanrı; papaz; **2.** *v/t.* icat etm.,

yaratıcısı olm., babası olm.; **to** ~ **an article on s.o.** bir yazıyı birine atfetmek; **fa.ther.hood** ['~hud] *n.* babalık; **'fa-ther-in-law** *n.* kayınpeder; **'fa.ther-land** *n.* anavatan; **'fa.ther.less** *adj.* babasız, yetim; **'fa.ther.ly** *adj.* baba gibi, babacan, babaya ait.

fath.om ['fæðəm] **1.** *n.* anlama, kavrama; NAUT kulaç; **2.** *v/t.* NAUT iskandil etm., derinliğini bulmak, derinliğine inmek; *fig.* -*in* içyüzünü anlamak, kavramak; **'fath.om.less** *adj.* çok derin, dibine erişilemeyen; anlaşılmaz.

fa.tigue [fə'tiːg] **1.** *n.* yorgunluk, bitkinlik; MIL kışla hizmeti; ~**s** *pl.* MIL kışla hizmeti sırasında askerlerin giydiği üniforma; **2.** *v/t.* yormak, yorgunluk vermek; **fa'tigue-par.ty** *n.* MIL kışla hizmeti verilen askerler.

fat.ling ['fætliŋ] *n.* kesim için beslenen genç hayvan; **'fat.ness** *n.* şişmanlık, semizlik; **'fat.ten** *v/t.* & *v/i.* şişmanla(t)mak, semir(t)mek; gübrelemek; **'fat.ty 1.** *adj.* yağlı, şişman, semiz; gübreli; ~ **degeneration** yağ dejenerasyonu, aşırı şişmanlık; **2.** *n.* F şişko, dobiş.

fa.tu.i.ty [fə'tjuːiti] *n.* anlamsızlık, ahmaklık, budalalık; **fat.u.ous** □ ['fætjuəs] aptal, budala, salak, ahmak.

fau.cet *part. Am.* ['fɔːsit] *n.* musluk.

faugh [fɔː] *int.* püf!, pöf!, ne kötü!

fault [fɔːlt] *n.* faul, hata (*a. tennis*); MED hata, yanlış, kusur; MEC hata, bozukluk; GEOL fay, çatlak; **find** ~ **with** kusur bulmak -*de*; **be at** ~ yanılmış olm., şaşırmış olm.; kabahatli olm.; **to a** ~ *fig.* aşırı derecede; **'~find.er** *n.* tenkitçi, kusur bulan kimse; **'~find.ing** *n.* tenkit, eleştiri; **'fault.i.ness** *n.* kusurlu olma, bozukluk; **'fault.less** □ kusursuz, mükemmel; **'faults.man** *n.* TELEPH tamirci; **'fault.y** □ hatalı, kusurlu, bozuk.

faun [fɔːn] *n.* MYTH yarısı keçi yarısı insan olan ilâh.

faun.a ['fɔːnə] *n.* fauna, direy, bir bölgeye *veya* çağa ait tüm hayvanlar.

fa.vo(u)r ['feivə] **1.** *n.* dostça bakış, teveccüh, güleryüz; yardım, destek, kayırma, iltimas, iyilik, rica, lütuf, nişan; **in** ~ **of** -*in* lehinde, -*in* taraftarı; COM lehine, emrine (*çek*); **I am (not) in** ~ **of** it onun lehindeyim (değilim); **un-der** ~ **of night** gecenin karanlığından yararlanarak; **do s.o. a** ~ *b-ne* bir iyilikte bulunmak; **2.** *v/t.* kayırmak -*i*; iltimas geçmek -*e*, tercih etm. -*i*, destek olm. *-e*, lütuf göstermek *-e*, *-in* tarafını tutmak; müsaade etm. (*hava*); **fa-vo(u)r.a.ble** □ ['ˌvərəbl] taraf tutan, öven; olumlu, memnuniyet verici, uygun, elverişli, müsait, münasip; 'fa-vo(u)r.a.ble.ness *n.* taraf tutma, övme, elverişli olma; fa.vo(u)red ['ˌvəd] *adj.* avantajlı, belli bir özelliği olan, iltimas geçilen; **most-~ nation clause** COM bir ülkenin en düşük ithalat vergisini ödeyeceğini belirten özel hüküm; fa.vo(u)r.ite ['ˌvərit] **1.** *adj.* daha çok sevilen, gözde; **2.** *n.* kayırılan kimse; *spor*: favori, kazanması beklenen; 'fa.vo(u)r.it.ism *n.* taraf tutma, adam kayırma.

fawn¹ [fɔːn] **1.** *n.* ZOO geyik *veya* karaca yavrusu; açık kahverengi; **2.** *vb.* doğurmak, yavrulamak (*geyik*).

fawn² [ˌ] *v/i.* kuyruk sallamak (*köpek*); *fig.* yaltaklanmak, dalkavukluk etm. (*upon -e*); 'fawn.er *n.* yağcı, yaltakçı, dalkavuk; 'fawn.ing *n.* dalkavukluk, yağcılık, yaltaklanma.

fay *poet.* [fei] *n.* peri.

faze *part. Am.* F [feiz] *v/t.* telaşa düşürmek, sıkıntı vermek, iki ayağını bir pabuca sokmak.

fe.al.ty ['fiːəlti] *n.* sadakat.

fear [fiə] **1.** *n.* korku, dehşet; endişe, kuruntu; **through** *veya* **from ~ of** korkusuyla, korkusundan; **for ~ of doing** yapma korkusuyla, korkusundan, endişesiyle; **in ~ of one's life** hayatından endişe ederek, ölüm tehlikesiyle; **2.** *vb.* korkmak *-den*, çekinmek *-den*, endişe etm. *-den*, korkuyla bakmak *-e*; **fear.ful** □ ['ˌful] korkunç, dehşetli; berbat, can sıkıcı; korkan, endişeli; **be ~ that** korkmak, endişelenmek *-den*; 'fear.ful.ness *n.* korkaklık; 'fear.less □ korkusuz, gözü pek; 'fear.less.ness *n.* korkusuzluk.

fea.si.bil.i.ty [fiːzə'biliti] *n.* tatbik edilebilme, uygulanabilme, mümkün olma; 'fea.si.ble *adj.* yapılabilir, mümkün, tatbik edilebilir, makûl, münasip.

feast [fiːst] **1.** *n.* bayram, festival, yıldönümü, yortu; ziyafet; **2.** *v/t. & v/i.* (**on, upon**) ziyafete katılmak; ziyafet vermek, ziyafette vakit geçirmek; yiyip içmek; hissi zevk vermek; **~ one's eyes on** doya doya bakmak *-e*.

feat [fiːt] *n.* yapılması beceri, güç *veya* cesaret isteyen şey; başarı.

feath.er ['feðə] **1.** *n.* tüy; *a.* **~s** *pl.* kuşun tüyleri; **show the white ~** F korkaklık

göstermek; **that is a ~ in his cap** gurur duyabileceği bir başarıdır; **in high ~** neşesi yerinde; **2.** *vb.* tüy takmak *-e*; tüylenmek, tüyleri bitmek; NAUT pala çevirmek (*kürek*); **~ one's nest** küpünü doldurmak, zenginleşmek, *k-ne* emanet edilen seyden pay çıkarmak; '~-bed **1.** *n.* kuştüyü yatak; **2.** *v/t.* (*bir gurup insana*) cömertçe avantaj sağlamak; '~-brained, '~-head.ed *adj.* kuş beyinli, aptal; 'feathered *adj.* tüylü; 'feath.er-edge *n.* MEC kolayca kırılan *veya* bükülen çok ince uç; 'feath.er-ing *n.* tüy; 'feath.er.stitch *n.* terzilik: zikzak, civankaşı dikiş; 'feath.er-weight *n.* boks: tüysiklet; 'feath.er.y *adj.* tüylü; tüy gibi hafif ve yumuşak.

fea.ture ['fiːtʃə] **1.** *n.* yüz organlarından biri; *pl.* yüz, surat, çehre; özellik, hususiyet; makale; asıl film; **2.** *vb.* özelliği olm.; önem vermek; baş rolde oynamak; **a film featuring N.N.** N.N.'nin başrolde oynadığı film; **~ film** asıl film; 'fea.tureless *adj.* hiç bir özelliği olmayan, çekici olmayan.

feb.ri.fuge ['febrifjuːdʒ] *n.* MED ateş düşürücü ilaç.

fe.brile ['fiːbrail] *adj.* ateşli, hummalı.

Feb.ru.ar.y ['februəri] *n.* şubat.

feck.less ['feklis] *adj.* bir işe yaramayan, yetersiz, beceriksiz, zayıf, sorumsuz.

fe.cun.date ['fiːkəndeit] *v/t.* gebe bırakmak, döllemek; bereketlendirmek; fecun'da.tion *n.* dölleme; bereketlendirme; fe.cun.di.ty [fi'kʌnditi] *n.* verimlilik; doğurganlık, üreyebilme.

fed [fed] *pret. & p.p. of* **feed** 2.

fed.er.al ['fedərəl] *adj.* federal, federasyona ait, federe; 'fed.er.al.ism *n.* federalizm; 'fed.er.al.ist *n.* federalist, federal sistem taraftarı; 'fed.er.al.ize *v/t.* devletleri birleştirmek, federal sistem altında toplamak; fed.er.ate **1.** ['ˌreit] *v/t. & v/i.* federasyon halinde birleş(tir)mek; **2.** [ˌ'rit] birleşik, müttefik; fed.er.a.tion [ˌ'reiʃən] *n.* federasyon, birlik; 'fed.er.a.tive ['ˌrətiv] *adj.* federasyon esasına dayalı, federatif.

fee [fiː] **1.** *n.* ücret; giriş ücreti; vizite; JUR mülk; **~ simple** mülk, şartsız veraset; **2.** *v/t.* ücretini ödemek, ücretle tutmak.

fee.ble □ ['fiːbl] zayıf, kuvvetsiz, dermansız, takatsiz, cılız; '~'mind.ed *adj.* geri zekâlı, aptal, iradesiz, kararsız; 'fee.ble.ness *n.* zayıflık, kuvvetsizlik.

feed [fi:d] **1.** *n.* yemek, yiyecek, gıda, yem; MEC malzemeyi makineye veren boru; MEC makineye verilen malzeme; MIL yük; **2.** *v/t. & v/i.* beslemek **(on, with** *-le***),** yemlemek, yiyeceğini vermek; ihtiyacını temin etm.; desteklemek; otlamak, yemlenmek; yemek yemek; **~ o.s.** yemek yemek; **~ off** *veya* **down** besini bir yerden almak; **~ up** fazla yiyecek vermek, besleyici yiyecek vermek, semirtmek; **be fed up with** *sl.* bıkmak, usanmak, bezmek *-den*; **well fed** iyi beslenmiş; '**~.back** *n.* radyo: geri itilim; eleştiri; '**feed.er** *n.* besleyici; beslenen; biberon; mama önlüğü; ana yola bağlı hat; MEC elektrik taşıyan hat; radyo vericisinden antene giden hat; '**feed.er line** RAIL ana demiryoluna bağlı hat; '**feed.er road** besleme hattı; '**feed.ing** *n.* besleme, yiyecek verme, yemleme; MEC besleme; **high~** lüks hayat, zevk ve sefa hayatı; '**feeding-bottle** *n.* biberon; '**feeding-stuff** *n.* yem, yiyecek maddesi.

feel [fi:l] **1.** *(irr.) v/t. & v/i.* hissetmek, duymak, dokunmak, elle yoklamak; anlamak, kavramak; fikrinde olm.; MIL keşif yapmak, araştırma yapmak; **~ bad about s.th.** acımak *-e*; **~ cold** üşümek; **~ like doing** canı yapmak istemek; **~ for** acımak *-e*; *-in* üzüntüsünü paylaşmak; **2.** *n.* his, duygu; temas, dokunarak anlama; '**feel.er** *n.* dokunan şey; hisseden kimse; ZOO anten (*a. fig.*); dokunaç; MIL gözleyici, casus; '**feel.ing** *n.* his, duygu, duyu, dokunma; dokunma hissi; his dünyası; merhamet, hassasiyet; **good ~** nezaket, iltifat, teveccüh.

feet [fi:t] *pl. of* **foot.**

feign [fein] *v/t.* yapar gibi görünmek, taklit etm., uydurmak; **~ illness** hasta numarası yapmak; **~ to do** yapar gibi görünmek; **~ o.s. mad** deli numarası yapmak; '**feigned** *adj.* sahte, yapmacık; **feign.ed.ly** ['~idli] *adv.* sahte olarak, yapmacıklı.

feint [feint] **1.** *n.* sahte, yapmacık; bahane, hileli söz; gösteriş, çaka, fiyaka; MIL savaş hilesi; **2.** *v/i.* sahte taarruzda bulunmak, yanıltıcı harekette bulunmak.

feld.spar MIN ['feldspa:] *n.* feldispat.

fe.lic.i.tate [fi'lisiteit] *v/t. bşi* kutlamak, tebrik etm. (**on**); **fe.lic.i'ta.tion** *n.* kutlama, tebrik; **fe'lic.i.tous** □ mutlu; münasip, iyi seçilmiş, yerinde (*keli-*

me); **fe'lici.ty** *n.* mutluluk, saadet; etkileyici yazı *veya* konuşma; iyi seçilmiş deyim.

fe.line ['fi:lain] *adj.* kedi gibi, kedilere ait.

fell[1] [fel] **1.** *pret. of* **fall** *2*; **2.** *v/t.* yere düşürmek, devirmek, kesmek (*ağaç*).

fell[2] *poet.* [~] *adj.* vahşî, korkunç, zalim; öldürücü.

fell[3] [~] *n.* hayvan derisi *veya* postu.

fel.loe ['feləu] *n.* ispit, jant.

fel.low ['feləu] *n.* adam, kişi, herif; arkadaş, dost, hemcins, akran; UNIV hoca; akademi üyesi; dernek üyesi; bir çift şeyin teki (*ayakkabı vs.*); **old ~** F eski dost; **the ~ of a glove** eldivenin teki; **be~s** arkadaş olm.; **he has not his ~** akranı, arkadaşı yok; '**~-'be.ings** *pl.* aynı türden insanlar; '**~-'cit.i.zen,** '**~-'coun.try.man** *n.* vatandaş, yurttaş; '**~-'crea.ture** *n.* hemcins, aynı türden yaratık; '**~-'feel.ing** *n.* ortak duygu, halden anlama; '**~-'pas.sen.ger** *n.* yol arkadaşı; '**~.ship** *n.* arkadaşlık, dostluk; cemiyet, dernek; üyelik; **~ sol.dier** askerlik arkadaşı; '**~-'stu.dent** *n.* okul arkadaşı; '**~-'trav.el.ler** *n.* yol arkadaşı, yoldaş; POL Komünist parti sempatizanı.

fel.ly ['feli] *n.* ispit, jant.

fel.on ['felən] *n.* JUR mücrim, suçlu; MED tırnak etrafında oluşan yara; **fe.lo.ni.ous** □ JUR [fi'ləunjəs] caniyane, suç unsuru olan; **fel.o.ny** JUR ['feləni] *n.* cinayet, silahlı soygun, kundakçılık gibi ağır suç.

fel.spar ['felspa:] = **feldspar.**

felt[1] [felt] *pret. & p.p. of* **feel** *2*.

felt[2] [~] **1.** *n.* keçe; fötr; **2.** *vb.* keçeyle kaplamak; keçe yapmak; keçelenmek.

fe.male ['fi:meil] **1.** *adj.* dişi, dişil, kadın cinsine ait; **~ child** kız çocuk; **~ screw** dişi vida; **2.** *n.* kadın; dişi hayvan *veya* bitki.

fem.i.nine □ ['feminin] *adj.* kadın gibi, kadınımsı, kadına ait; GR dişil; **fem.i-'nin.i.ty** *n.* kadınlık; '**fem.i.nism** *n.* kadın haklarını tanıtma mücadelesi, feminizm; '**femi.nist** *n.* kadın hakları savunucusu, feminist; **fem.i.nize** ['~naiz] *v/t. & v/i.* kadınlaş(tır)mak, kadın gibi olm.

fe.mur ANAT ['fi:mə] *n.* kalça kemiği, uyluk kemiği.

fen [fen] *n.* bataklık.

fence [fens] **1.** *n.* parmaklık, çit, tahta

perde; *sl.* çalıntı malların satıldığı yer; çalıntı mal alıp satan kimse; **sit on the** ~ kararsız olm., tarafsız olm.; **2.** *v/t. a.* ~ **in** *-in* etrafını çitle çevirmek; korumak (**from** *-den*); *v/i.* eskrim yapmak; *fig.* kaçamaklı konuşmak, direk cevap vermekten kaçınmak; *sl.* çalıntı mal almak; '**fence.less** *adj.* kararsız; korunmasız.

fenc.ing ['fensiŋ] *n.* eskrim; çit *veya* parmaklık malzemesi; çit, parmaklık; '~-**foil** *n.* eskrim kılıcı; '~-**mas.ter** *n.* eskrim antrenörü.

fend [fend] *vb.*: ~ **off** kendini korumak *-den*; uzak tutmak, defetmek; ~ **for** geçindirmek *-i*; '**fend.er** *n.* şömine önündeki paravana; araba çamurluğu; koruyucu herhangi bir şey; lokomotif mahmuzu; NAUT çarpışmanın şiddetini azaltan iki gemi arasındaki lastik, usturmaça.

Fe.ni.an ['fi:njən] *n.* **M.S. 2.** ve **3.** yüzyıllarda İrlanda'yı savunan savaşçılar; İrlanda'daki İngiliz yönetiminin yıkılmasına kendilerini adamış **19.** yüzyıl İrlanda ve İrlanda-Amerikan gizli örgüt üyesi.

fen.nel BOT ['fenl] *n.* rezene.

fen.ny ['feni] *adj.* bataklıklı; bataklık gibi.

feoff [fef] *n.* tımar, fief; feodal emlâk; **feoff.ee** [fe'fi:] *n.* tımar sahibi, zaim; '**feoff.ment** *n.* arazi bağışlama; **feoff.or** [fe'fɔː] *n.* arazi bağışlayan kimse.

fer.ment 1. ['fə:mənt] *n.* maya; mayalanma; *fig.* telaş, galeyan, heyecan; **2.** [fə:'ment] *v/t. & v/i.* mayalan(dır)mak; *fig.* heyecanlan(dır)mak, galeyana getirmek; **fer'ment.a.ble** *adj.* mayalanabilir, maya tutabilen; **fer.men'ta.tion** *n.* mayalanma, fermantasyon; *fig.* heyecan, galeyan; **fer'ment.a.tive** [ˌtətiv] *adj.* mayalanan; mayalayan.

fern BOT [fə:n] *n.* eğreltiotu.

fe.ro.cious □ [fə'rouʃəs] vahşi, yırtıcı, zalim, yabanî, canavar ruhlu; **fe.roc.i.ty** [fə'rɔsiti] *n.* vahşilik, vahşet, saldırganlık, zalimlik, canilik.

fer.ret ['ferit] **1.** *n.* ZOO tavşan ve sıçan tutmakta kullanılan kır sansarı, mustela; *fig.* araştırmacı; **2.** *v/i.* bu hayvanlarla avlanmak; ~ **out** araştırıp bulmak, araştırmak.

fer.ric CHEM ['ferik] *adj.* demirli, içinde demir olan, demire ait; **fer.rif.er.ous** [fe'rifərəs] *adj.* demirli; **fer.ru.gi.nous** [fe'ru:dʒinəs] *adj.* demirli, pas rengin-

de; **fer.ro-con.crete** MEC ['ferəu'kɔŋkri:t] *n.* betonarme; **fer.rous** CHEM ['ferəs] *adj.* demirli.

fer.rule ['feru:l] *n.* demir halka, yüzük.

fer.ry ['feri] **1.** *n.* feribot; **2.** *vb.* vapurla karşı tarafa geçirmek; *fig.* götürüp getirmek; '~-**boat** *n.* feribot; '**fer.ry.man** *n.* feribot kullanan kimse.

fer.tile □ ['fə:tail] verimli, bereketli; *fig.* yaratıcı (*kimse veya zekâ*); **fer.til.i.ty** [fə:tiliti] *n.* verimlilik, bereket; *fig.* yaratıcılık; **fer.ti.li.za.tion** [ˌlai-'zeiʃən] *n.* gübreleme, verimini artırma; '**fer.ti.lize** *v/t.* gübrelemek; BIOL döllemek, tohumlamak; verimini artırmak; '**fer.ti.liz.er** *n.* (kimyevî) gübre.

fer.ule ['feru:l] *n.* öğrencinin eline vurmaya yarayan sopa.

fer.ven.cy ['fə:vənsi] *n. mst. fig.* tutku, aşk, aşırı heves, şevk; '**fer.vent** □ sıcak, hararetli; *fig.* deli gibi seven, kara sevdalı, şiddetli, ateşli.

fer.vid □ ['fə:vid] = **fervent**.

fer.vo(u)r ['fə:və] *n.* şiddetli arzu, şevk, gayret, istek.

fes.tal □ ['festl] bayrama ait, festivalle ilgili; şen, eğlenceli.

fes.ter ['festə] **1.** *v/i.* iltihaplanmak, azmak; *fig.* kuruntu etm.; **2.** *n.* iltihap.

fes.ti.val ['festəvəl] *n.* bayram, yortu, festival, şenlik, eğlence; **fes.tive** ['ˌtiv] festivale ait, bayramla ilgili; neşeli; **fes'tiv.i.ty** *n.* şenlik, eğlence; *pl.* bayram, yortu, festival.

fes.toon [fes'tu:n] **1.** *n.* çiçek, yaprak *veya* kurdeladan yapılmış kordon; **2.** *v/t.* çiçek *veya* kurdelayla süslemek.

fetch [fetʃ] *v/t. & v/i.* gidip getirmek, alıp getirmek; çıkarmak (*inilti*); çekmek (*iç*); F para getirmek, para kazandırmak; F vurmak (*tokat, yumruk*); ~ **and carry for s.o.** *b-ne* hizmet etm., onun için koşuşturmak; ~ **up** dur(dur)mak; varmak; kusturmak; '**fetch.ing** F □ çekici, alımlı, cazibeli.

fête [feit] **1.** *n.* açık hava eğlencesi; ~-**day** bir azizin yortusu; **2.** *v/t.* ziyafet vermek *-e*, ağırlamak *-i*, saygı göstermek *-e*.

fet.id □ ['fetid] pis kokan, kokmuş, kokuşmuş.

fe.tish ['fi:tiʃ] *n.* tılsım, putperestlerin taptığı şey, fetiş (*a. fig.*).

fet.lock ['fetlɔk] *n.* atın topuk kılları; topuk mafsalı.

fet.ter ['fetə] **1.** *n.* pranga, zincir, köstek,

bukağı; *pl. fig.* engel, mani, ayak bağı; **2.** *v/t.* ayağını zincire vurmak; *fig.* engel olm., mani olm., ayak bağı olm.

fet.tle [fetl] *n.* durum, şart, şekil; *in fine* ~ iyi durumda, neşesi yerinde.

feud [fjuːd] *n.* kavga, kan davası, çekişme; **feu.dal** □ ['ːdl] derebeyliğe ait; feodal; **feu.dal.ism** ['ːdəlizəm] *n.* derebeylik; **feu.dal.i.ty** [ːdæliti] *n.* derebeylik; **feu.da.to.ry** ['ːdətəri] **1.** *adj.* hizmet borcu olan; **2.** *n.* hizmetli, köle, vasal.

fe.ver ['fiːvə] *n.* ateş, humma, hararet, sıcaklık; *fig.* heyecan, sinirlilik; **'fe.vered** *adj. part. fig.* ateşli, heyecanlı; **'fe.verish** □ ateşli, hummalı, hararetli; *fig.* heyecanlı, telaşlı.

few [fjuː] *adj.* az; *a* ~ birkaç; *quite a* ~, *a good* ~ birçok, pek çok; *the* ~ azınlık.

fez [fez] *n.* fes.

fi.an.cé(e) [fi'ãːnsei] *n.* nişanlı.

fi.as.co [fi'æskəu] *n.* başarısızlık, hezimet, bozgun, fiyasko.

fi.at ['faiæt] *n.* emir, karar; ~ *money Am.* hükümetin kararına dayanarak çıkarılan kağıt para, karşılıksız para.

fib F [fib] **1.** *n.* yalan, palavra; **2.** *v/i.* yalan söylemek, uydurmak, atmak; **'fib.ber** *n.* yalancı, palavracı.

fi.bre ['faibə] *n.* lif, tel; iplik; yapı; karakter; '~.board *n.* liften yapılmış tahta; '~.glass *n.* cam elyafı, fiberglas; **fi.brin** ['ːbrin] *n.* fibrin; **'fi.brous** □ lifli, telli; ~ *material* dokuma maddesi.

fib.u.la ANAT ['fibjulə] *n.* kamış kemik, fibula.

fick.le ['fikl] *adj.* değişken, dönek, kararsız; **'fick.le.ness** *n.* döneklik, kararsızlık.

fic.tion ['fikʃən] *n.* roman; roman ve hikâye edebiyatı; hayal; uydurma; yalan; JUR varsayım; **fic.tion.al** □ ['ːʃənl] roman edebiyatına ait; hayalî.

fic.ti.tious □ ['fik'tiʃəs] hayalî, uydurma; **'fic.tive** *adj.* hayalî, uydurma, sahte.

fid.dle ['fidl] **1.** *n.* keman; **2.** *v/i.* keman çalmak; *v/t. sl.* dalavere yapmak, tevil etm.; ~ *away* israf etm., boşa harcamak; **fid.dle.de.dee** ['ːdi'diː] *int.* saçma!, zırva!; **fid.dle.fad.dle** F ['ːfædl] **1.** *n.* saçma söz; ~*!* saçma!; **2.** *vb.* tembellikle vaktini israf etm.; **'fid.dler** *n.* kemancı; *sl.* vergi kaçakçısı; **'fid.dle.stick** *n.* keman yayı; ~*s!* saçma!; **'fid.dling** *adj.* önemsiz, değersiz.

fi.del.i.ty [fi'deliti] *n.* vefa, sadakat (*to* ~*e*); doğruluk.

fidg.et F ['fidʒit] **1.** *n. oft.* ~*s pl.* huzursuzluk, rahatsızlık, sinirlilik; yerinde duramayan kimse; *have the* ~*s* yerinde duramamak; **2.** *v/t.* rahat oturamamak, yerinde duramamak; **'fidg.et.y** *adj.* yerinde duramayan, kıpır kıpır.

fi.du.ci.ar.y [fi'djuːʃjəri] **1.** *adj.* güvene dayanan, itimat kabilinden; COM itibarî; **2.** *n.* emin, kendisine güvenilen kimse, mutemet.

fie [fai] *int.* ayıp!, yuh!

fief [fiːf] *n.* zeamet, tımar.

field [fiːld] **1.** *n.* çayır, kır, otlak, mera, tarla; meydan, alan; *spor:* saha; *pl.* bir yarışmaya katılanlar; *hold the* ~ yerini muhafaza etm.; *take the* ~ sefere çıkmak; **2.** *vb.* kriket; topu yakalamak *veya* durdurmak; '~-*day* *n.* MIL askeri harekât ve manevraların yapıldığı gün; *fig.* önemli gün; *Am.* spor bayramı; *Am.* beklenmedik başarı; **'field.er** *n.* kriket; dış meydan oyuncusu.

field...: ~ *e.vents* *pl.* atlama ve atma yarışları; '~.fare *n.* ardıçkuşu; '~-glass.es *n. pl.* çifte dürbün; '~-gun *n.* MIL hafif top; '~'hos.pi.tal *n.* MIL sahra hastanesi; '~'mar.shal *n.* mareşal; '~-of.fi.cer *n.* binbaşı *veya* albay; '~-sports *n. pl.* açık hava sporları.

fiend [fiːnd] *n.* iblis, şeytan, canavar, zalim; *fig.* tiryaki; **'fiend.ish** □ şeytanî, vahşi, zalim, gaddar.

fierce □ [fiəs] vahşi, azgın, şiddetli, sert; öfkeli, hiddetli, hararetli; **'fierce.ness** *n.* şiddet, sertlik, vahşet.

fi.er.i.ness ['faiərinis] *n.* hararet, şiddetli sıcaklık; hiddet; **'fi.er.y** □ hararetli; ateşli, alevli, kızgın.

fife [faif] **1.** *n.* fifre, küçük flavta; **2.** *vb.* düdük çalmak; **'fif.er** *n.* düdük çalan kimse.

fif.teen ['fif'tiːn] *n. & adj.* on beş; **'fif.teenth** [ːθ] *n. & adj.* on beşinci; **fifth** [fifθ] **1.** *adj.* beşinci; **2.** *n.* beşte bir; **fifth col.umn** POL beşinci kol; **'fifth.ly** *adv.* beşinci olarak, beşinci sırada; **fif.ti.eth** ['ːtiiθ] **1.** *adj.* ellinci; **2.** *n.* ellide bir; **fif.ty** *n.* elli; **'fif.ty-'fif.ty** F yarı yarıya; *go* ~ yarı yarıya bölüşmek.

fig[1] [fig] *n.* incir; *a* ~ *for...!* ... Allah belâsını versin!; *I don't care a* ~ *for him* Allah onun belâsını versin, o hiç umurumda bile değil.

fig[2] [ː] **1.** *n.* F donanım; hal; *in full* ~ giyimli, tam teçhizatlı; **2.** *vb.* ~ *out* F telleyip pullamak.

fight [fait] **1.** *n.* dövüş, kavga, savaş, mücadele; *make a ~ for* …için mücadele etm.; *put up a good ~* cesaret ve azimle mücadele etm.; *show ~* mücadeleye hazır olm.; **2.** *v/t. & v/i.* mücadele etm., dövüşmek, kavga etm.; defetmek, yapmak, uğraşmak; MIL savaşmak; *~ off* püskürtmek, defetmek, mücadele etm.; *~ one's way* mücadele ederek ilerlemek; *~ against s.th.* bşle mücadele etm.; *~ back* püskürtmek; *~ shy of* kaçınmak *-den*, uzak durmak *-den*, karışmamak *-e*; ʹ**fight.er** *n.* savaşçı; MIL avcı uçağı; *~ pilot* avcı uçağı pilotu; ʹ**fight.ing** *n.* kavga, mücadele, savaş; *~ chance* büyük çabalar sonucunda kazanılabilecek başarı şansı.

fig.ment [ʹfigmənt] *n.* icat, hayal, uydurma.

fig-tree [ʹfigtriː] *n.* incir ağacı.

fig.u.rant(e) [ʹfigjurənt; (ˌ-ʹrãːnt)] *n.* balede figüran; figüran.

fig.u.ra.tion [figjuʹreiʃən] *n.* şekil verme, şekle sokma; şekil, tasvir; **fig.ura.tive** □ [ʹ-rətiv] mecazî, sembolik, simgesel; süslü.

fig.ure [ʹfigə] **1.** *n.* rakam, şekil (*a.* MATH); endam, boy bos, vücut yapısı; şahsiyet, şahıs; mecaz; *dans*; figür; fiyat; *~ of speech* mecaz, istiare, kinaye; *what's the ~?* kaç para?; *at a high ~* pahalı, yüksek fiyata; *be good at ~s* matematiği kuvvetli olm.; **2.** *v/t. & v/i.* temsil etm.; desenlerle süslemek, tasavvur etm., hayal etm., resmetmek, zihinde canlandırmak; *a. ~ to o.s.* hayal etm.; *~ on* güvenmek *-e*, hesaba katmak *-i*; *~ up veya out* hesaplamak; anlamak; *~ out at* …miktarına erişmek; ʹ**~-head** *n.* NAUT gemi pruvasındaki şekil; *fig.* gerçek yetkisi olmayan kimse, mostralık, kukla; ʹ**~-skat.ing** *n.* figür yaparak paten kayma.

fig.u.rine [ʹfigjuriːn] *n.* heykelcik.

fil.a.ment [ʹfiləmənt] *n.* tel, lif; BOT ercik sapı; ELECT lamba teli.

fil.a.ture [ʹfilətʃə] *n.* iplik fabrikası.

fil.bert BOT [ʹfilbəːt] *n.* fındık.

filch [filtʃ] *v/t.* çalmak, aşırmak, yürütmek (*from -den*).

file[1] [fail] **1.** *n.* dosya dolabı; dosya, klasör; MIL dizi, küme; *on ~* dosyalanmış; **2.** *v/t. & v/i.* dosyalamak, dosyaya koymak, tasnif etm.; vermek (*dilekçe vs.*); MIL sırayla yürümek; *~ in (out)* sırayla, arka arkaya yürümek.

file[2] [ˌ-] **1.** *n.* eğe, törpü; **2.** *v/t.* eğelemek, törpülemek.

fil.i.al □ [ʹfiljəl] evlâda ait, evlâda yakışır; **fil.i.a.tion** [fili'eiʃən] *n.* birinin evlâdı olma, aynı soydan gelme, menşe, nesep.

fil.i.bus.ter [ʹfilibʌstə] **1.** *n. Am.* uzun uzun konuşarak bir kanunun kabulünü engelleme; engelleyici konuşma; isyana teşvik eden kimse; **2.** *vb. Am.* engellemek.

fil.i.gree [ʹfiligriː] *n.* telkâri iş; filigran.

fil.ings [ʹfailiŋz] *n. pl.* eğe talaşı.

fill [fil] **1.** *v/t. & v/i.* dol(dur)mak; doyurmak; kabarmak; işgal etm.; şişirmek; tatmin etm.; *Am.* yapmak, icra etm., tamamlamak; *~ in* doldurmak (*eksiklik, form, çek vs.*); *~ out* büyü(t)mek; şiş(ir)mek; doldurmak (*fiş vs.*); *~ up* tamamen dol(dur)mak; **2.** *n.* doyumluk, dolumluk, dolduracak miktar; *eat (drink) one's ~* doyana kadar yemek (içmek), doymak (*of -e*), gına gelmek (*of -den*).

fill.er [ʹfilə] *n.* astar verniği; huni; dolgu maddesi.

fil.let [ʹfilit] **1.** *n.* fileto, dilim; saça takılan bant; pervaz, silme, tiriz (*part.* ARCH); kitap kapağına basılan süs çizgisi; **2.** *v/t.* dilimlemek, (fileto) çıkarmak.

fill.ing [ʹfiliŋ] *n.* doldurma, dolgu; *~ station Am.* benzin istasyonu.

fil.lip [filip] **1.** *n.* fiske; **2.** *v/t.* fiske vurmak; teşvik etm.

fil.ly [ʹfili] *n.* kısrak; *fig.* genç kız.

film [film] **1.** *n.* zar, ince tabaka; film; *take veya shoot a ~* film çekmek, çevirmek; **2.** *v/t. & v/i.* film çevirmek, filme geçirmek; ince örtüyle kaplanmak, zarla kaplamak; ʹ**film.y** □ zarlı, ince tabaka ile kaplı; puslu, dumanlı, bulanık.

fil.ter [ʹfiltə] **1.** *n.* filtre, süzgeç; **2.** *v/t. & v/i.* süzgeçten geç(ir)mek, süz(ül)mek; sızmak, duyulmak; *~ in* MOT trafik kırmızı ışıkta durduğunda sola dönmek; ʹ**fil.ter.ing** *n.* süzme; ʹ**fil.ter tip** sigara filtresi; filtreli sigara.

filth [filθ] *n.* kir, pislik (*part. fig.*) ʹ**filth.y** □ pis, kirli; iğrenç, çirkin.

fil.trate [ʹfiltreit] *v/t. & v/i.* süz(ül)mek; **fil'tra.tion** *n.* süzme.

fin [fin] *n.* zoo yüzgeç, yüzgece benzeyen şey; AVIA kanatçık; MOT kanatçık, kulak, pancur.

fi.nal [ʹfainl] **1.** □ son, nihaî; kesin, ka-

2. *n.* **~s** *pl.* sömestr sonu sınavı; *spor*:
fi.nal ['fainl] **1.** □ son, nihaî; kesin, katî;
final, son yarış; *gazete*: son baskı; **fi.na-
le** [fi'nɑ:li] *n.* MUS final, bitiş; **fi.nal.ist**
['fainəlist] *n. spor*: finale kalan yarışmacı, finalist; **fi.nal.i.ty** [‿'næliti] *n.*
kelinlik, katiyet; son olma.
fi.nance [fai'næns] **1.** *n.* maliye; **~s** *pl.*
malî durum, gelir; **2.** *v/t. & v/i. -in* masraflarını karşılamak, finanse etm. *-i*;
malî işleri idare etm.; **fi'nan.cial** □
[‿ʃəl] malî; **fin'an.cier** [‿siə] *n.* maliyeci; sermayedar.
finch ORN [fintʃ] *n.* ispinoz.
find [faind] **1.** (*irr.*) *v/t.* bulmak, keşfetmek; ulaşmak; rastlamak *-e*; öğren-
mek; tedarik etm., sağlamak; JUR karar
vermek, hüküm vermek, hükmüne
varmak; **~ o.s.** kabiliyetlerini keşfetmek, kendini bulmak; kendine gelmek; *all found* ücretsiz yemek ve kalacak yer; **~ out** öğrenmek; keşfetmek,
ortaya çıkarmak; *I cannot ~ it in my
heart* gönlüm elvermiyor, bu kadar zalim olamam; **2.** *n.* bulunmuş şey; keşif,
buluş; bulgu; **'find.er** *n.* bulucu, bulan;
OPT vizör; **'finding.** *n.* bulgu, bulunan
şey; *a.* **~s** *pl.* sonuç, netice; JUR karar.
fine¹ [fain] **1.** □ ince; güzel, zarif; hoş,
nazik; açık (*hava*); hassas; halis, saf;
şatafatlı (*konuşma veya yazı*); sağlıklı;
you are a ~ fellow! iro. sen yaramaz
adamsın!; **~ arts** *pl.* güzel sanatlar; **2.**
adv. çok iyi, güzel, hoş; *cut* ucu ucuna
hesabetmek (*para, zaman*); **3.** *n.*
METEOR güzel hava; **4.** *vb.* berrak-
laş(tır)mak; **~ away, ~ down, ~ off** in-
cel(t)mek, saflaş(tır)mak; azalmak.
fine² [‿] **1.** *n.* para cezası; *in ~* kısaca,
özetle; **2.** *v/t.* para cezasına çarptırmak;
~ s.o. 5 sh. ceza olarak 5 şilin almak.
fine-draw [fain'drɔ:] *v/t.* inceltmek.
fine.ness ['fainnis] *n.* incelik, zarafet,
güzellik; saflık.
fin.er.y ['fainəri] *n.* gösteriş, süslü giyim, şıklık; şık elbiseler.
fi.nesse [fi'nes] *n.* incelik, ustalık; *iskambil*: fines; kurnazlık, hile.
fin.ger ['fiŋgə] **1.** *n.* parmak; *have a ~ in
the pie* işe karışmak, bir işte parmağı
olm.; *s. end 1*; **2.** *v/t.* parmakla dokunmak; belirtmek, teşhis etm.; göstermek; MUS parmakla çalmak; '**~al-
pha.bet** *n.* işaretlerle anlaşma;
'**~board** *n.* MUS çalgı aletinin sapı;
'**~bowl** *n.* eltası; '**fin.gered** *comb.*
...parmaklı; '**fin.ger.ing** *n.* parmakla

dokunma; MUS parmakları kullanma
usulü.
fin.ger...: '**~lan.guage** *n.* işaret dili;
'**~mark** *n.* parmak izi; '**~nail** *n.* tırnak;
'**~plate** *n.* kilit aynası, parmak izini
önlemek için kapıya takılan plaka;
'**~post** *n.* işaret direği, yön gösteren
levha; '**~print 1.** *n.* parmak izi; **2.** *v/t.
-in* parmak izini almak; '**~stall** *n.* sargı.
fin.i.cal □ ['finikəl], **fin.ick.ing** □,
fin.i.kin ['‿kin] titiz, müşkülpesent,
kılı kırk yaran.
fin.ish ['finiʃ] **1.** *v/t. & v/i.* bit(ir)mek,
tamamlamak; sona er(dir)mek; cilâla-
mak; *a.* **~ off, ~ up** bitirmek; MEC apre
yapmak; **~ed goods** *pl.* fabrika ürünü,
mamûl eşya; **~ing touch** son cilâ, rötuş;
have ~ed bitmiş olm.; **2.** *n.* son; son iş;
cilâ, rötuş; MEC apre; '**fin.ish.er** *n.* bitiren, tamamlayan; MEC apre yapan.
fi.nite □ ['fainait] sınırlı, mahdut;
ölümlü; **~ verb** GR çekimli fiil; '**fi.nite-
ness** *n.* fanilik.
fink *Am. sl.* [fiŋk] *n.* ihbar eden işçi, grevi bozan işçi; sevilmeyen kimse.
Finn [fin] *n.* Finlandiyalı, Finli.
Finn.ish ['finiʃ] **1.** *adj.* Finlandiya'ya
ait; **2.** *n.* Fin dili.
fin.ny ['fini] *adj.* yüzgeçleri olan, yüz-
geçli; yüzgeçlerle ilgili.
fiord [fjɔːd] *n.* fiyord.
fir [fəː] *n.* çam ağacı, köknar; *Scotch ~*
sarı çam; '**~cone** *n.* köknar kozalağı.
fire ['faiə] **1.** *n.* ateş; yangın; soba, ocak;
şevk, ihtiras; cehennem, cehennem
azabı; *on ~* tutuşmuş, yanan, alevler
içinde; *lay a ~* ateş yakmak; *set ~ to*
ateşe vermek, tutuşturmak; **2.** *v/t. &
v/i.* tutuş(tur)mak, yakmak, ateşe vermek; patlatmak, ateş etm.; pişirmek,
fırınlamak; *fig.* tahrik *veya* teşvik
etm.; *a.* **~ off** ateşlemek, ateş etm.; *F*
işinden çıkarmak, koymak; **~ up** sinirlenmek, parlamak; ateş etm. (*at, upon
-e*); **~ away!** *F* haydi başla!; '**~a.larm** *n.*
yangın işareti (*veya* alarmı); '**~arms** *n.
pl.* ateşli silahlar; '**~ball** *n.* atom bom-
basının merkezi; akanyıldız; '**~bomb**
n. yangın bombası; '**~box** *n.* MEC lokomotifin yakıt bölümü; '**~brand** *n.* alevli odun parçası; *fig.* tahrikçi, fesatçı;
'**~break** *n.* ağaçsız orman yolu, yangın
duvarı; '**~brick** *n.* ateş tuğlası; '**~bri-
gade** *n.* itfaiye; '**~bug** *n. Am. F* kundakçı; '**~clay** *n.* ateş tuğlası yapımında
kullanılan kil, çamur; '**~con.trol** *n.* MIL
top ateşini idare sistemi; '**~cracker**.

kağıt fişeği; '~-damp *n.* MIN grizu; '~-de.part.ment *n. Am.* itfaiye; '~-dog *n.* ocağın demir ayaklığı; '~-eat.er *n.* ateş yutan hokkabaz; çabuk sinirlenen kimse, kavgacı kimse; '~-en.gine *n.* MEC yangın tulumbası, itfaiye arabası; '~-es.cape *n.* yangın merdiveni; '~-ex.tin.guish.er *n.* yangın söndürme aleti; '~-fly *n.* ateşböceği; '~-guard *n.* şömine pervazı; '~-in.sur.ance *n.* yangın sigortası; '~-irons *n. pl.* şömine takımı; '~-light-er *n.* ateş yakmak için çalı çırpı; '~.man *n.* itfaiyeci; ateşçi; '~-of.fice *n.* yangın sigortası bürosu; '~-place *n.* ocak, şömine; '~-pow.er *n.* MIL ateş gücü; '~-plug *n.* yangın musluğu; '~.proof *adj.* ateşe dayanır, yanmaz; '~-screen *n.* ateş siperi; '~-side *n.* ocak başı; ev (hayatı), yurt; '~-sta.tion *n.* yangın istasyonu, itfaiye merkezi; '~.wood *n.* odun; '~.works *n. pl.* donanma fişekleri; *fig.* çıngar.

fir.ing ['faiəriŋ] *n.* yakma, ateşleme; MIL ateş etme; '~-line *n.* MIL ateş hattı; '~-party, ~ squad *n.* MIL idam mangası; cenazede saygı gösterisi olarak ateş eden bölük.

fir.kin ['fə:kin] *n.* ufak fıçı.

firm [fə:m] **1.** □ sabit, metin, bükülmez, katı, sıkı, sert; kararlı; **2.** *n.* firma.

fir.ma.ment ['fə:məmənt] *n.* sema, gökkubbe, asuman.

firm.ness ['fə:mnis] *n.* sağlamlık, metanet.

first [fə:st] **1.** *adj.* birinci, ilk; temel; *at ~ hand* doğrudan doğruya, aracısız; *at ~ sight* ilk görüşte, ilk bakışta; **2.** *adv.* önce, başta, evvelâ, ilk kez, öncelikle; tercihen; *at ~* ilk önce, evvelâ; *~ of all* herşeyden önce; *~ and last* genelde; **3.** *n.* başlangıç; birinci; birincilik; *~ of exchange* NAUT ilk poliçe; *from the ~* baştan itibaren; *go ~* önce gitmek, önde gitmek; için birinci mevkiyle seyahat etm.; '~-'aid post *n.* ilk yardım istasyonu; '~-born **1.** *adj.* ilk doğan; **2.** *n.* ilk çocuk; ~ class birinci mevki; '~-'class *adj.* birinci sınıfa ait, mükemmel; '~-fruits *n. pl.* ilk sonuç, ilk hasılat; '~-'hand *adj. & adv.* dolaysız, vasıtasız, direk olarak, doğrudan doğruya; 'first.ly *adv.* evvelâ, ilkin, ilk olarak, en başta.

first...: ~ name isim, ad; ~ pa.pers *pl. Am.* vatandaşlığa kabul için yapılan

ilk müracaat; '~'rate *adj.* birinci sınıf, en iyi cinsten; = *first-class.*

firth [fə:θ] *n.* haliç, dar körfez.

fis.cal ['fiskəl] *adj.* malî.

fish [fiʃ] **1.** *n.* balık; balık eti; RAIL sağlamlaştırma tahtası; F adam, herif; *odd ~* garip herif; *have other ~ to fry* daha önemli bir işi olm.; *a pretty kettle of ~* karmaşık durum; **2.** *v/t. & v/i.* balık tutmak, balık avlamak; ağız aramak *(for)*; RAIL sağlamlaştırmak; *~ out* çekip çıkartmak; *~ in troubled waters fig.* bulanık suda balık avlamak, karışık bir durumdan çıkar sağlamaya çalışmak; '~-bone *n.* kılçık.

fish.er ['fiʃə], fish.er.man ['~mən] *n.* balıkçı; 'fish.er.y *n.* balıkçılık; balık tarlası.

fish-hatch.er.y ['fiʃhætʃəri] *n.* balık yetiştirme *(veya* üretme).

fish-hook ['fiʃhuk] *n.* olta.

fish.ing ['fiʃiŋ] *n.* balık avı, balıkçılık; '~-boat *n.* balıkçı kayığı *veya* gemisi; '~-line *n.* olta (ipi); '~-rod *n.* olta kamışı; '~-tack.le *n.* balıkçı takımı.

fish...: '~-liv.er oil *n.* balıkyağı; '~-mon-ger *n.* balıkçı, balık satan kimse; '~-wife *n.* balıkçı kadın; küfürbaz kadın; 'fish.y *adj.* balık gibi; F şüpheli, inanılmaz.

fis.sion ['fiʃən] *n.* ortadan ikiye bölünme; *s. atomic*; fis.sure ['fiʃə] **1.** *n.* yarık, çatlak; **2.** *v/t. & v/i.* çatla(t)mak, yarmak, ayrılmak.

fist [fist] *n.* yumruk; F el yazısı; fist.i-cuffs ['~ikʌfs] *n. pl.* yumruk yumruğa kavga.

fis.tu.la MED ['fistjulə] *n.* fistül.

fit¹ [fit] **1.** □ uygun, yaraşır, münasip; lâyık; hazır; doğru; zinde, sıhhatli; *it is not ~* yakışık almaz, uygun değildir; *~ as a fiddle* çok iyi, zinde, sağlıklı, turp gibi; **2.** *v/t. & v/i.* uymak, yakışmak; yerleştirmek; donatmak; üstüne olm. *(elbise);* takmak; prova etm.; uygun hale getirmek *(for, to -e);* MEC *~ in* takmak; *~ on* prova etm.; takmak, uydurmak, uymak *(with -e); ~ out* donatmak; *~ up* kurmak, hazırlamak; **3.** *n.* biçim, vücuda uyma; *it is a bad ~* iyi oturmuyor *(elbise).*

fit² [~] *n.* tutarak, hastalık nöbeti, sara; hal, ruh durumu; *by ~s and starts* arasıra, düzensiz olarak, kısa aralıklarla; *give s.o. a ~* b-ni şaşırtmak, kızdırmak.

fitch.ew ZOO ['fitʃuː] *n.* kokarca.

fit.ful □ ['fitful] düzensiz, kesik kesik; *fig.* kararsız, daldan dala konan; **'fit- ment** *n.* mobilya parçası; **~s** *pl.* takım (*mobilya*); **'fit.ness** *n.* uygunluk, sağlık; **'fit-out** *n.* teçhizat; mobilya; **'fit.ter** *n.* boru işlerine bakan kimse, te- sisatçı, montajcı; **'fit.ting 1.** □ uygun, münasip, yerinde; **2.** *n.* prova; takma, montaj; **~s** *pl.* tertibat; bağlantı parça- ları; eşya, mobilya; **'fit-up** *n.* F geçici, kısa süreli tiyatro; *a.* **~ company** seyyar tiyatro.

five [faiv] **1.** *adj.* beş; **2.** *n.* beş sayısı; **~s** *sg.* bir çeşit top oyunu; **'five.fold** *adj.* beş misli, beş kat; **fiv.er** F ['~və] *n.* beş dolar *veya* pound.

fix [fiks] **1.** *v/t. & v/i.* takmak; yerleş(tir)- mek; otur(t)mak; sabitleştirmek; ka- rarlaştırmak; hazırlamak; tamir etm.; çekmek (*dikkat*); hile *veya* rüşvete başvurarak satın almak; hakkından gelmek; *part. Am.* F düzene sokmak, tamir etm.; hazırlamak; рнот tesbit banyosu yapmak; gözlerini dikmek (**on** *-e*); **~ o.s.** *k-ni* bir yere yerleştir- mek; **~ up** kurmak, düzeltmek, ayarla- mak; tedarik etm.; **~ on** seçmek, karar vermek **2.** *n.* F güç durum, çıkmaz; yön bulma; **fix'ation** *n.* tesbit; sabit fikir, gelişmemiş ve anormal bağlılık; **fix.a- tive** ['~ətiv], **fix.ature** ['~ətʃə] *n.* koru- ma maddesi, tesbit maddesi; **fixed** *adj.* sabit, bağlı (*a.* снем); **fixed i.de.a** рsyсн sabit fikir; **fix.ed.ly** ['fiksidli] *adv.* değişmeden; gözlerini dikerek; **'fix.ed.ness** *n.* sabitlik, hareketsizlik (*a. fig.*); **fixed star** durağan yıldız; **'fix- er** *n.* рнот fiksatif, tesbit maddesi; **'fix- ing** *n.* bağlama, sağlamlaştırma, tesbit; **~s** *pl. Am.* tertibat, teçhizat; garnitür; **'fix.i.ty** *n.* sabitlik, karar, sebat; **fix.ture** ['~tʃə] *n.* sabit *bş*, demirbaş (*a. fig. per- son*); *spor.* fikstür; **~s** *pl.* teçhizat; **lighting ~** elektrik teçhizatı.

fizz [fiz] **1.** *v/i.* fışırdamak, fıslamak; **2.** *n.* fışırtı, tıslama, vızıltı; F köpüklü içki; **fiz.zle** ['fizl] **1.** *v/i.* vızlamak, cızırda- mak; *mst* **~ out** vızlayıp sönmek; başarısızlığa uğramak; **2.** *n.* vızıltı; fışırtı; başarısızlık, fiyasko.

flab.ber.gast F ['flæbəga:st] *v/t.* şaşırt- mak; **be ~ed** şaşırmak, hayrete düş- mek.

flab.by □ ['flæbi] gevşek, yumuşak, sarkık; zayıf, iradesiz.

flac.cid □ ['flæksid] gevşek, yu- muşamış, sarkmış.

flag¹ [flæg] **1.** *n.* bayrak, sancak, bandı- ra, flama; **black ~** korsan bayrağı; **2.** *v/t.* bayraklarla donatmak; bayrakla işaret vermek.

flag² [~] **1.** *n.* kaldırım taşı; **2.** *v/t.* bu taş- larla döşemek.

flag³ вот [~] *n.* zambak, süsen.

flag⁴ [~] *v/i.* sarkmak, bükülmek, eğil- mek; kuvvetten düşmek, canlılığını kaybetmek.

flag-cap.tain NAUT ['flæg'kæptin] *n.* amiral gemisi süvarisi.

flag-day ['flægdei] *n.* yardım toplama günü; *Am.* **Flag Day** Amerikan bay- rağının 1777'de resmen kabulünün yıldönümü (*14 Haziran*).

flag.el.lant ['flædʒilənt] *n. -ki* kırbaç- layan kimse; **flag.el.late** ['~dʒəleit] *v/t.* kırbaçlamak; **flag.el'la.tion** *n.* kırbaç- lama; dövünme.

flag.eo.let мus [flædʒəu'let] *n.* küçük flüt.

fla.gi.tious □ [flə'dʒiʃəs] alçakça, kö- tü, iğrenç; cinaî.

flag.on ['flægən] *n.* büyük şişe, bir çeşit sürahi.

flag post ['flægpəust] *n.* bayrak direği, gönder.

fla.grant □ ['fleigrənt] iğrenç, çirkin, rezalet kabilinden; bariz, göze batan.

flag...; **'~.ship** *n.* amiral gemisi; **'~-staff** *n.* bayrak direği, gönder; **'~-stone** *n.* kaldırım taşı.

flail AGR [fleil] *n.* harman döveni.

flair [flɛə] *n.* yetenek, kabiliyet, Allah vergisi; seziş, anlayış.

flake [fleik] **1.** *n.* kuşbaşı, lapa; ince ta- baka; **2.** *v/i.* tabaka tabaka ayrılmak; lapa lapa yağmak; **'flak.y** *adj.* lapa la- pa, kat kat.

flam F [flæm] *n.* yalan, hile, saçma, mar- taval.

flam.beau [flæmbəu] *n.* fener.

flame [fleim] **1.** *n.* alev, ateş, yalaz; *fig.* hiddet, hırs; aşk ateşi; **2.** *v/i.* alevlen- mek, alev alev yanmak; parlamak (*a. fig.*); **~ out**, **~ up** alevlenmek, tutuş- mak; **'flam.ing** *adj.* yanmakta, tutuş- muş, alevler içinde; çok sıcak, ateşli (*a. fig.*).

fla.min.go ORN [flə'miŋgəu] *n.* flamin- go.

flan [flæn] *n.* meyvalı pasta, kek.

flange MEC [flændʒ] *n.* yanak, halka, ke- nar, yaka, kulak, flanş.

flank [flæŋk] **1.** *n.* böğür; yan, yan taraf, kanat; **2.** *v/t.* bitişik olm. *-e*, yan tarafında olm.; kanadı geçmek; kanada hücum etm.; yandan kuşatmak.

flan.nel ['flænl] *n*. fanila, pazen; sabunlama bezi, mutfak bezi; **flan.nel.ette** [_-'et] *n*. fanilaya benzer pamuklu kumaş, pazen; **'flan.nels** *n. pl.* fanila, fanila pantolon, fanila ceket.

flap [flæp] **1.** *n*. sarkık parça, kapak; kanat; vuruş; aşırı heyecan; **2.** *v/t. & v/i.* hafifçe vurmak -*e*, çarp(tır)mak, çırpmak; **'flap.jack** *n*. bir tür börek, gözleme; **'flap.per** *n*. sineklik, balığın geniş yüzgeci; *sl*. (1920'lerde) son moda giyinen genç kız.

flare [flɛə] **1.** *v/t. & v/i.* alevlen(dir)mek; ~ **up** birden alevlenmek, parlamak; *fig*. öfkelenmek, parlamak; **2.** *n*. ışık, parlaklık; işaret fişeği; '~'**up** *n*. alevlenme, parlama; *fig*. ani öfke, parlama, hiddet.

flash [flæʃ] **1.** *adj*. gösterişli fakat sahte, göz boyayan; **2.** *n*. ışıltı, parıltı; *fig*. an; ani alev; gösteriş, fiyaka, hava; *part*. *Am*. bülten; *in a* ~ hemen, derhal, kısa sürede; ~ *of wit* aniden akla esen fikir; ~ *in the pan* kısa sürede neticesiz kalan teşebbüs; **3.** *vb*. parlamak; birden gelmek; birden parıldamak; radyo *ve-ya* TV ile haber yayınlamak; *it* ~*ed on me* birden aklıma geldi; '~**-back** *n*. *film*: geri dönme; '~**-light** *n*. PHOT flaş; el feneri, fener; '~**-point** *n*. yanma ısısı; **'flash.y** □ parıltılı, alevli; gösterişli, frapan, göze çarpan.

flask [flɑːsk] *n*. küçük şişe; matara; termos; CHEM duyumlu imbik.

flat [flæt] **1.** □ düz, yassı; tatsız, yavan; inik *veya* patlak; sıkıcı, monoton; kesin; mat; zayıflamış (*akü*); yüzüstü, sırtüstü; COM durgun, kesat; MUS bemol; ~ *price* tek fiyat; *fall* ~ başarısızlığa uğramak, sonuç vermemek; *sing* ~ MUS bemolden okumak; **2.** *n*. apartman dairesi; yüzey; NAUT sığlık kumsal; MUS bemol; F basit; MOT patlak lastik; '~**-boat** *n*. NAUT altı düz gemi; '~**-foot** *n*. düztaban; *Am. sl.* polis; denizci; '~'**foot.ed** *adj*. düztaban; *Am*. F açık açık, dobra dobra, kesin; '~.**i.ron** *n*. ütü; **'flat.ness** *n*. düzlük, yassılık; tatsızlık, yavanlık; COM durgunluk, kesatlık; '~'**screen 'mon.i.tor** *n*. yassı ekran monitör; **'flat.ten** *v/t. & v/i.* yassılatmak, yassılaşmak, düzleş(tir)mek; ~ *out* düzleş(tir)mek, açmak yassılaş(tır)mak; dalıştan sonra uçağı yerle paralel duruma getirmek.

flat.ter ['flætə] *v/t*. pohpohlamak, göklere çıkarmak, yağ çekmek; **'flat.ter.er** *n*. dalkavuk, yağcı; **'flat.ter.ing** *n*. pohpohlama, yağ çekme; **'flat.ter.y** *n*. dalkavukluk, yağcılık, övgü.

flat.u.lence, flat.u.len.cy ['flætjuləns(i)] *n*. gaz, şişkinlik; **'flat.u.lent** □ midede gaz yapan; gaza ait; şişkin.

flaunt [flɔːnt] *vb*. gösteriş yapmak, hava atmak, kibirle göstermek; dalgalanmak (*bayrak*).

fla.vo(u)r ['fleivə] **1.** *n*. tat, lezzet, çeşni, koku; **2.** *v/t*. tat *veya* lezzet vermek -*e*; **'fla.vo(u)red** *comb*. ...lezzetinde; '**fla-vo(u)ring** *n*. baharat, tat veren *bş*; '**fla-vo(u)rless** *adj*. tatsız, lezzetsiz.

flaw [flɔː] **1.** *n*. çatlak, yarık; noksan, kusur (JUR, MEC), defo; NAUT kısa süreli şiddetli rüzgâr; **2.** *v/t. & v/i.* çatla(t)-mak; defolu olm.; kusurlu olm.; *fig*. hasara uğratmak; zarara sokmak; **'flaw-less** □ kusursuz.

flax BOT [flæks] *n*. keten; **'flax.en, 'flax.y** *adj*. keten; ketene benzer; soluk sarı.

flay [flei] *v/t*. derisini yüzmek; *fig*. azarlamak, haşlamak; **'flay.er** *n*. hayvan derisi yüzen.

flea [fliː] *n*. pire; '~.**bane** *n*. BOT pireotu; '~.**bite** *n*. pire ısırması; *fig*. hafif rahatsızlık.

fleck [flek] **1.** *n*. nokta, benek, leke, zerre; **2.** *v/t*. beneklemek; lekelemek.

flec.tion ['flekʃən] *s*. *flexion*.

fled [fled] *pret. and p.p. of flee*.

fledge [fledʒ] *v/t. & v/i.* tüylenmek; tüy takmak; tüyleninceye kadar beslemek; **fledg(e).ling** ['-liŋ] *n*. yeni tüylenmiş yavru kuş; *fig*. acemi çaylak.

flee [fliː] (*irr.*) *v/t. & v/i.* kaçmak, tüymek, firar etm. (*from -den*); *a*. ~ *from* sakınmak, kaçınmak -*den*.

fleece [fliːs] **1.** *n*. yapak, yünlü, koyun postu; **2.** *v/t*. kırkmak (*koyun*); *b-ni* soymak, çok parasını almak, kazıklamak, yolmak; **'fleec.y** *adj*. yün gibi.

fleer [fliə] **1.** *n*. alay, eğlenme, dalga geçme; **2.** *v/i*. alay etm., dalga geçmek (*at*).

fleet [fliːt] **1.** □ *poet*. çevik, süratli, hızlı, çabuk, atik; **2.** *n*. donanma, filo; ♀ *Street* basın, Londra basını; **3.** *v/t. & v/i.* çabuk geçmek; yok olm.; hızla uçmak; hareket etm.; yerini değiştirmek; **'fleet.ing** □ çabuk geçen, kısa süren, ömürsüz.

Flem.ing ['flemiŋ] *n*. Flaman; **'Flem-ish 1.** *adj*. Flamanlar bölgesine ait; **2.**

n. Flaman dili.

flesh [fleʃ] **1.** *n.* et; vücut, ten; meyvenin etli kısmı; beden; *fig.* şehvet duygusu; **make s.o.'s ~ creep** tüylerini ürpertmek, tüylerini diken diken yapmak; **2.** *v/t. & v/i.* kan dökmek (*a. fig.*); eti sıyırmak; etle beslemek; etle kaplamak; şişmanlamak; '**~brush** *n.* masaj fırçası; '**flesh.ings** *n. pl.* ten renginde külotlu çorap; '**flesh.ly** *adj.* etli, şişman; vücuda ait, bedene ait; '**flesh.y** *adj.* şişman, etli butlu; ete ait.

flew [fluː] *pret. of fly¹ 2.*

flex ELECT [fleks] *n.* esnek kablo; **flex-i.bil.i.ty** [-ə'biliti] *n.* esneklik, elastikiyet; *fig.* uysallık, yumuşak başlılık; '**flex.i.ble** □ bükülebilir, esnek; uysal; **flex.ion** ['flekʃən] *n.* bükülme, esneme; GR çekim; dirsek; **flex.or** ['-ksə] *n.* fleksör kas; **flex.ure** ['flekʃə] *n.* bükülme, katlanma; dirsek.

flib.ber.ti.gib.bet ['flibəti'dʒibit] *n.* dedikocu kimse.

flick [flik] **1.** *v/t.* hafifçe vurmak, fiske vurmak (*at -e*); **2.** *n.* hafif vuruş, fiske; **~s** *n. pl. sl.* sinema.

flick.er ['flikə] **1.** *v/i.* titremek, oynamak, titrek yanmak; ileri geri oynamak; **2.** *n.* titrek ışık; *Am.* ağaçkakan.

flick-knife ['fliknaif] *n.* sustalı bıçak.

fli.er ['flaiə] *s.* **flyer**.

flight [flait] *n.* uçuş, uçma; uçak yolculuğu; çabuk geçme; yükselme; sıra; *a.* **~ of stairs** bir kat merdiven; AVIA, MIL hava filosu; firar, kaçış; **put to ~** kaçırtmak; **take (to) ~** kaçmak, *sl.* tüymek; '**~com'mand.er** *n.* uçuş pilotu; '**~deck** *n.* NAUT (*uçak gemisi*) uçuş güvertesi; pilot mahalli; '**~-lieu'ten.ant** *n.* pilot yüzbaşı; '**flight.y** □ dönek, kararsız; hafifmeşrep, havaî; sorumsuz; budala.

flim.sy [flimzi] **1.** *adj.* ince, gevşek, seyrek; sudan (*bahane*); kolayca yırtılabilen; **2.** *n.* pelür, kopya kâğıdı; *sl.* kâğıt para; telgraf.

flinch [flintʃ] *v/i.* sakınmak, kaçınmak, ürkmek, çekinmek (*from -den*).

fling [fliŋ] **1.** *n.* fırlatma, atma, atış; fırlayış; *fig.* taş, iğneli söz; hareketli dans; **have one's ~** dilediğince eğlenmek, kurtlarını dökmek; **have a ~ at** teşebbüs etm., denemek; **2.** (*irr.*) *v/t. & v/i.* at(ıl)mak, fırlatmak, savurmak (*küfür*); sallamak; hışımla çıkmak; *a.* **~ out** *fig.* kıyameti koparmak; gürültü yapmak; **~ o.s.** hızla atılmak; **~ away**

kaldırıp atmak; **~ forth** atmak, savurmak; **~ open** hızla açmak.

flint [flint] *n.* çakmaktaşı; '**flint.y** *adj.* çok sert; *fig.* katı yürekli, haşin.

flip [flip] **1.** *n.* fiske, hafif vuruş; AVIA *sl.* uçakla zevk için yapılan kısa gezinti; takla; bir içki çeşidi; **2.** *vb.* fiske vurmak; parmakla havaya fırlatmak; öbür yüzünü çevirmek (*plak vs.*); sinirlenmek.

flip-flap ['flipflæp] *n.* takla, perende.

flip.pan.cy ['flipənsi] *n.* küstahlık, düşüncesizlik; '**flip.pant** □ küstah, kendini bilmez.

flip.per ['flipə] *n.* balık kanadı; palet.

flirt [fləːt] **1.** *n.* flört eden; işvebaz *b-i*; ani hareket; **2.** *v/i.* flört etm.; fırlamak; **flir'ta.tion** *n.* flört; **flir'ta.tious** *adj.* flörtçü, işvebaz, F fındıkçı.

flit [flit] *v/i.* geçmek; çırpınmak; oradan oraya dolaşmak.

flitch [flitʃ] *n.* domuz döşü.

flit.ter ['flitə] *v/i.* kanat çırpmak, çırpınmak.

fliv.ver *Am.* F ['flivə] **1.** *n.* külüstür otomobil; **2.** *vb.* başarısızlığa uğramak.

float [fləut] **1.** *n.* olta mantarı; şamandıra, duba; MEC flotör; NAUT pervane tahtası; THEAT ön sahne ışıkları; geçit resminde kullanılan araba; meyvalı gazoz; **2.** *v/t. & v/i.* yüz(dür)mek; suyun yüzünde durmak; hava akımına kapılıp sürüklenmek; *fig.* başlatmak, harekete geçirmek; kurmak; COM satışa arzetmek (*hisse senedi, tahvil*); yaymak; '**float.a.ble** *adj.* yüzebilen, su üstünde durabilen; '**float.age** *n.* yüzen şey; **float'a.tion** *s.* **flotation**; '**float.ing** *adj.* yüzen, değişen, seyyar; **~ bridge** tombaz köprü, dubalı köprü; **~ capital** döner sermaye; **~ ice** suda yüzen buz kütlesi; **~ kidney** yer değiştiren böbrek; **~ light** fener dubası, fenerli şamandıra; '**float-plane** *n.* deniz uçağı.

flock¹ [flɔk] **1.** *n.* sürü; küme; kalabalık, yığın; cemaat; **2.** *v/i.* toplanmak, başına üşüşmek.

flock² [-] *n.* (*part. yün*) yumak, saç yumağı; yün artığı.

floe [fləu] *n.* buz kitlesi.

flog [flɔg] *v/t.* kamçılamak, dövmek; **~ a dead horse** boşuna çaba sarfetmek; '**flog.ging** *n.* dayak, kamçılama.

flood [flʌd] **1.** *n. a.* **~tide** sel, seylap, taşkın; tufan; met, kabarma; **the ~** Nuh tufanı; **2.** *v/t. & v/i.* coşmak, taşmak, su basmak, sel basmak; istilâ etm.; '~-**disas.ter** *n.* sel felâketi; '~-**gate** *n.* set, bent kapağı; '~**light 1.** *n.* projektör; **2.** *v/t.* projektörle aydınlatmak.

floor [flɔː] **1.** *n.* döşeme, zemin; kat; dip; asgarî ücret; AGR harman yeri; PARL meclis salonunun üyelere ayrılmış kısmı; mecliste konuşma hakkı; *sl.* borsa binası; ~ **leader** *Am.* (*yasama meclisi*) grup başkanı; ~ **price** asgarî ücret, taban ücret; ~ **show** eğlence programı; **hold the** ~ PARL mecliste konuşma yapmak; **be kept on the** ~ ortaya atılmak, ileri sürülmek; **take the** ~ mecliste söz almak; **2.** *v/t.* tahta *veya* parke döşemek *-e*; yere yıkmak *-i*; şaşırtmak *-i*; yenmek *-i*; '~-**cloth** *n.* tahta bezi; '**floor.er** *n.* döşemeci; '**floor.ing** *n.* döşemelik; '**floor-lamp** *n.* ayaklı abajur; '**floor-walk.er** *n. Am.* mağazada müşterilere yardım eden görevli; '**floor-wax** *n.* döşeme cilası.

flop F [flɔp] **1.** *v/t. & v/i.* çırpınmak; çöküvermek; düşürmek; devrilmek; *sl.* başarısızlığa uğramak, tutmamak (*kitap, piyes*); **2.** *n.* çarpma; çarpma sesi; başarısız teşebbüs; başarısızlık; çökme; ~ **house** *Am. sl.* ucuz otel; '**flop.py** *adj.* yumuşak; gevşek; başarısız.

flo.ra ['flɔːrə] *n.* flora, bitey, bir bölgede yetişen bitkilerin tümü; '**flo.ral** *adj.* çiçeklere ait; ~ **design** çiçek deseni.

flo.res.cence [flɔːˈresns] *n.* çiçek açma, çiçeklenme devresi.

flor.id □ ['flɔrid] çok süslü; kırmızı (*yüz*); yüzüne ateş basmış; '**flor.idness** *n.* süslülük; kırmızılık; canlılık.

flor.in ['flɔrin] *n.* iki şilin kıymetinde İngiliz parası; Hollanda florini.

flo.rist ['flɔrist] *n.* çiçekçi.

floss [flɔs] *n.* bükülmemiş ham ipek, floş; kısa ipek telleri; ~ **silk** ham ibrişim; '**floss.y** *adj.* ince tüylü; ipeğe ait; süslü.

flo.ta.tion [fləuˈteiʃən] *n.* yüzme; su üzerinde durma; COM sermaye temini, mali destek temini.

flo.til.la NAUT [fləuˈtilə] *n.* küçük filo, flotilla.

flot.sam JUR ['flɔtsəm] *n.* gemi enkazı.

flounce[1] [flauns] **1.** *n.* fırfır, volan; **2.** *v/t.* fırfırla süslemek, volan koymak.

flounce[2] [-] *v/i.* yerinden fırlayıp yürümek; fırlamak; sabırsızlıkla hareket etm.

floun.der[1] ICHTH ['flaundə] *n.* pisibalığı.

floun.der[2] [-] *v/i.* boşuna çabalamak; zorluk çekmek; bata çıka yürümek.

flour ['flauə] **1.** *n.* un; **2.** *v/t.* una bulamak, un serpmek.

flour.ish ['flʌriʃ] **1.** *n.* gösterişli hareket; paraf, gösteriş, süs; sallama, savurma; MUS coşkulu parça, fanfar; **2.** *v/t. & v/i.* sallamak, savurmak; gelişmek; bayındır olm.; sağlıklı olm.; gözde olm.; ortaya çıkmak.

flout [flaut] *v/t. & v/i.* karşı koymak, itaat etmemek; alay etm., eğlenmek; küçümsemek.

flow [fləu] **1.** *n.* cereyan, akıntı; met, kabarma; ~ **of spirits** neşe; neşe dolu; **2.** *v/i.* akmak; dalgalanmak; sallanmak; sarkmak; kabarmak; ~ **from** *-in* sebebi olm., *-den* gelmek.

flow.er ['flauə] **1.** *n.* çiçek; *fig.* seçkin ve güzide *bş*; olgunlaşmış *bş*; en iyi kısım; **say it with** ~**s** süslü bir şekilde söylemek; **2.** *v/i.* çiçeklenmek, çiçek açmak; **flow.er.et** ['-rit] *n.* küçük çiçek; '**floweri.ness** *n.* gösteriş (*a. fig.*); '**flow.er-pot** *n.* saksı; '**flow.er.y** *adj.* çiçekli; süslü, gösterişli.

flown [fləun] *p.p.* of **fly**[1] **2.**

flu F [fluː] = **influenza.**

flub.dub *Am. sl.* ['flʌbdʌb] *n.* boş laf, palavra, saçmalık, saftasa.

fluc.tu.ate ['flʌktjueit] *v/i.* değişmek, düzensiz olm., dalgalanmak; **fluc.tu'a.tion** *n.* değişme, dalgalanma.

flue [fluː] *n.* baca, boru.

flu.en.cy ['fluːənsi] *n.* akıcılık, ifade düzgünlüğü; '**flu.ent** □ akıcı (*söz*); düzgün, pürüzsüz.

fluff [flʌf] **1.** *n.* tüy, hav; kuştüyü; kırpıntı; yumuşak kürk; *fig.* acemice yapılan atılım; **2.** *v/t.* silkinip tüylerini kabartmak; sallamak, kabartmak *veya* yaymak; söyleyeceği sözü unutmak *veya* yanlış söylemek; '**fluff.y** *adj.* tüy gibi yumuşak, yumuşacık; kabarık.

flu.id ['fluːid] **1.** *adj.* akıcı, sıvı, akışan; *fig.* sabit olmayan (*fikir*); **2.** *n.* sıvı madde; **flu'id.i.ty** *n.* akıcılık.

fluke [fluːk] *n.* gemi demirinin tırnağı; *şans*, rastlantı, tesadüf.

flume [fluːm] *n.* suni kanal.

flum.mer.y ['flʌməri] *n.* bir çeşit yemek; bir tatlı çeşidi; boş laf.

flum.mox F ['flʌməks] *v/t.* şaşırtmak.

flung [flʌŋ] *pret. & p.p.* of **fling 2.**

flunk *Am.* F [flʌŋk] *v/t. & v/i.* başaramamak, çakmak, kalmak (*sınavda*); sınavda bırakmak.

flunk.(e)y ['flʌŋki] *n.* üniformalı uşak, hizmetçi; dalkavuk, yağcı; 'flunk.ey-ism *n.* uşaklık.

flu.o.res.cence PHYS [fluə'resns] *n.* fluoresans, flüorışı; **flu.or'es.cent** *adj.* fluoresans, flüorışıl; ~ *lamp* fluoresan lambası.

flur.ry ['flʌri] **1.** *n.* ani rüzgâr; sağanak; telaş; heyecan; acele; **2.** *v/t.* telaşlandırmak, telaşa sokmak, sinirlendirmek.

flush [flʌʃ] **1.** *adj.* MEC bir seviyede, düz; bol parası olan; *fig.* bol, dopdolu, çok; **2.** *n.* kızarma; taşkınlık; galeyan; akıtma; *iskambil:* floş; **3.** *v/t.* & *v/i.* birden akmak; yüzü kızar(t)mak; cesaretlendirmek; bol suyla yıkamak; taşmak; kanatlanıp uçmak; ürkütüp kaçırmak; düzlemek, bir seviyeye getirmek.

flus.ter ['flʌstə] **1.** *n.* telaş, şaşkınlık; **2.** *v/t.* telâşa düşürmek, şaşırtmak; *v/i.* şaşırmak, telaşa etm.

flute [flu:t] **1.** *n.* MUS flavta, flüt; ARCH yiv, oluk; **2.** *v/t.* & *v/i.* flüt çalmak; *fig.* ötmek; oluk *veya* yiv açmak; 'flut-ist *n.* flütçü.

flut.ter ['flʌtə] **1.** *n.* çırpınma; telaş, heyecan; kanat sarsıntısı; F bahis; *have a* ~ *bahse girmek;* **2.** *v/t.* & *v/i.* çırpınmak; kanat çırpmak; telaşa düşürmek; telaşlanmak; düzensiz hareket etm.

flux [flʌks] *n.* *fig.* akış; akıntı; değişme; eritici madde; MED akıntı; ~ *and reflux* gelgit, meddücezir.

fly[1] [flai] **1.** *n.* sinek; uçuş; fermuar; pantolonun düğmeli ön kısmı; çadırdaki bez kapı; bayrak ucu; *Am.* beysbol: havaya atılan top; *flies pl.* THEAT sahne yukarısındaki dekor değiştirme teçhizatı; **2.** *(irr.) v/t.* & *v/i.* uçmak; uçakla gitmek; uçakla taşımak; çabuk gitmek; fırlamak; atılmak; uçurmak; dalgalandırmak; *-den* kaçmak; ~ *high* hırslı olm.; ~ *at* üstüne saldırmak; ~ *in the face of* açıkça karşı gelmek; ~ *into a passion* veya *rage* öfkelenmek, sinirlenmek; ~ *off* uçup gitmek; ~ *blind* veya *on instruments* körükçe yapmak, sadece aletler yardımıyla uçmak; ~ *out at* karşı çıkmak; ~ *open* hızla açılmak; *send s.o.* ~*ing* vurup düşürmek, kaçırtmak.

fly[2] *sl.* [_] *adj.* uyanık, kurnaz, haberdar, aldatması güç.

fly...: '~-blow **1.** *n.* sinek yumurtası; sinek kurdu istilası; **2.** *v/t. -e* yumurta bırakmak; *fig.* kirletmek; bozmak; '~-blown *adj.* bozulmuş, kurtlanmış;

fig. kötü durumda; '~-catch.er *n.* sinekcil; sinek kapanı.

fly.er ['flaiə] *n.* hızlı giden *bş,* (*part.* AVIA), pilot, havacı; *take a* ~ *Am.* F riskli bir işe girmek; ~*s pl.* ARCH dış merdiven.

fly-flap ['flaiflæp] *n.* sinek raketi.

fly.ing ['flaiiŋ] **1.** *n.* uçma, havacılık, uçuş; **2.** *adj.* uçan; havacılıkla ilgili; ~ *boat* deniz uçağı; ~ *buttress* ARCH duvar dirseği; ~ *deck* uçuş güvertesi; ~ *field* havaalanı; ~ *jump* koşarak atlama; ~ *machine* uçak, tayyare; ~ *school* uçuş okulu; ~ *squad* hızlı polis ekibi; ~ *start* hızlı başlangıç; ~ *visit* kısa ziyaret, kapıdan uğrama; '~-of.fi.cer *n.* üsteğmen.

fly...: '~-leaf *n.* TYP bir kitabın başında ve sonundaki boş sayfa; '~-o.ver *n.* üstgeçit; AVIA = '~-past *n.* hava geçit resmi; '~-weight *n.* boks: sineksıklet; '~-wheel *n.* volan, düzenteker.

foal [fəul] **1.** *n.* tay, sıpa; *in* ~, *with* ~ gebe (*kısrak*); **2.** *v/i.* tay doğurmak.

foam [fəum] **1.** *n.* köpük; **2.** *v/i.* köpürmek (*a. fig.*); '~-rub.ber *n.* sünger; 'foam.y *adj.* köpüklü.

fob[1] [fɔb] *n.* saat cebi; saat kösteği.

fob[2] [_] *vb.:* ~ *off fig.* hile yapmak, kazık atmak, aldatmak.

fo.cal ['fəukəl] *adj.* odaksal; ~ *length,* ~ *distance* PHOT odak uzaklığı; ~*-plane shutter* PHOT yarıklı diyafram.

fo'c'sle ['fəuksl] = *forecastle.*

fo.cus ['fəukəs] **1.** *n. pl. a.* fo.ci ['fəusai] odak, mihrak; *fig. a.* merkez; **2.** *v/t.* & *v/i.* bir noktaya getirmek; biraraya gelmek; ayar etm.; dikkatini toplamak; konsantre olm.; 'fo.cus.(s)ing screen PHOT buzlu cam.

fod.der ['fɔdə] **1.** *n.* yem; **2.** *v/t.* yemlemek, beslemek.

foe *poet.* [fəu] *n.* düşman; '~-man *n. obs.* düşman.

foe.tus MED ['fi:təs] *n.* cenin, dölüt.

fog [fɔg] **1.** *n.* sis; *fig.* bunaklık, zihin karışıklığı; PHOT donukluk; **2.** *vb. mst fig.* şaşırtmak; PHOT bulanıklaşmak, donuklaşmak; '~-bank *n.* kalın sis tabakası; '~-bound *adj.* NAUT sise yakalanmış; sis yüzünden hareket edemeyen.

fo.gey F ['fəugi] *n.: old* ~ geri kafalı kimse.

fog.gy □ ['fɔgi] sisli; *fig.* bulanık, belirsiz; 'fog-horn *n.* sis düdüğü; 'fog-sig-nal *n.* RAIL sis işareti.

fo.gy *Am.* [ˈfəugi] = **fogey**.

foi.ble *fig.* [ˈfɔibl] *n.* kusur, zaaf.

foil[1] [fɔil] *n.* ince yaprak, foya, yaldız kâğıdı; ayna sırı; *fig.* engel.

foil[2] [_] **1.** *v/t.* engellemek, işini bozmak, boşa çıkarmak; **2.** *n.* FENC kılıç.

foist [fɔist] *vb.*: ~ **s.th. (off) on s.o.** hile ile kabul ettirmek, yutturmak.

fold[1] [fəuld] **1.** *n.* ağıl; sürü; *fig.* cemaat; **2.** *v/t.* ağıla kapamak.

fold[2] [_] **1.** *n.* kat, kıvrım, büklüm; **2.** *v/t. & v/i.* bükmek; katla(n)mak; karıştırmak; (*elleri*) kavuşturmak; *a.* ~ *up* sarmak; ~ *down* bükmek, katlamak, kıvırmak; ~ *in one's arms* kollarını kavuşturmak; ~ *up* F çökmek, sona ermek; 'fold.er *n.* dosya, klasör; broşür; kutu, kap.

fold.ing [ˈfəuldiŋ] *adj.* katlama; katlanabilir; kırma; '~-bed *n.* katlanır karyola; '~-boat *n.* sökülüp takılabilen kayık; '~-door(s *pl.*) katlanır kapı; '~-screen *n.* katlanır paravana; '~-seat *n.* katlanır sandalye.

fo.li.age [ˈfəuliidʒ] *n.* ağaç yaprakları.

fo.li.o [ˈfəuliəu] *n.* kitap yaprağı; sayfa numarası; hesap defterindeki karşılıklı iki sayfa; iki yapraklık kâğıt tabakası; büyük boy kitap, cilt.

folk [fəuk] *n. pl.* halk, insanlar, ahali; ~*s pl.* F ev halkı; aile; akrabalar; '~-dance *n.* halk oyunu; ~.lore [ˈ_lɔː] *n.* folklor; '~-song *n.* halk şarkısı, türkü.

fol.low [ˈfɔləu] *v/t. & v/i.* takip etm., izlemek; anlamak; mesleğinde çalışmak; riayet etm., uymak; örnek almak; sonucu çıkmak; *to* ~ arkadan, geriden; *it* ~*s that* ...sonucu çıkıyor, ...demektir; ~ *out* sonuna kadar götürmek; ~ *the sea* denizci olm.; ~ *up* kovalamak; 'fol.low.er *n.* taraftar, F hayran; 'fol.low.ing **1.** *n.* taraftarlar, tabi olanlar; *the* ~ şunlar, aşağıdakiler; **2.** *adj.* izleyen; ertesi, müteakip; ~ *wind* arkadan esen rüzgâr.

fol.ly [ˈfɔli] *n.* aptallık, ahmaklık; aptalca şey.

fo.ment [fəuˈment] *v/t.* MED pansuman yapmak; *fig.* kışkırtmak; **fo.men'tation** *n.* pansuman; pansuman için kullanılan şey; tahrik, kışkırtma; **fo'ment.er** *n. fig.* kışkırtıcı, tahrikçi.

fond □ [fɔnd] seven (*of* -*i*); düşkün -*e*; *be* ~ *of* düşkün olm, -*e*, hoşlanmak -*den*; *be* ~ *of dancing* dansa düşkün olm.

fon.dant [ˈfɔndənt] *n.* bir çeşit tatlı, fondan.

fon.dle [ˈfɔndl] *v/t.* okşamak, sevmek.

fond.ness [ˈfɔndnis] *n.* sevgi, düşkünlük.

font ECCL [fɔnt] *n.* vaftiz kurnası.

food [fuːd] *n.* yiyecek, besin, yemek, gıda; yem; 'food.ie F *n.* yemek düşkünü; '~-stuff *n.* gıda maddesi.

fool[1] [fuːl] **1.** *n.* budala, enayi, aptal, ahmak, alık kimse; *make a* ~ *of s.o.* enayi yerine koymak, küçük düşürmek; *make a* ~ *of o.s.* rezil olm., kepaze olm.; ~ *'s paradise* geçici mutluluk, aylaklık; **2.** *adj. Am.* F sersem, şaşkın; **3.** *v/t. & v/i.* aldatmak; boşuna vakit geçirmek; aptalca davranmak; ~ *about* aptalca davranıp durmak; ~ *(a)round part. Am.* aylak aylak dolaşmak, boşuna vakit geçirmek; ~ *away* F tembellikle vakit geçirmek, israf etm.

fool[2] [_] *n.* kremalı meyve.

fool.er.y [ˈfuːləri] *n.* aptalca hareket, budalalık, ahmaklık; 'fool.hard.y □ delice cesur; 'fool.ish □ aptal, akılsız, budalaca; 'fool.ish.ness *n.* enayilik, akılsızlık; 'fool-proof *adj.* MEC emniyetli, sağlam; kusursuz; **fool.scap** [ˈfuːlskæp] *n.* kâğıt ölçüsü.

foot [fut] **1.** *n. pl.* **feet** [fiːt] ayak; kadem (*30.48 cm*); adım; dip, (*dağ*) etek; en alçak kısım; temel, esas; MIL piyade; *poet.* vezin tef'ilesi; *on* ~ yaya, yürüyerek; *be on one's feet* ayakta olm.; *fig.* hastalıktan sonra ayağa kalkmak, iyileşmek; *put one's* ~ *down* ayak diremek, kararlı olm., karşı çıkmak; *I have put my* ~ *into it* F pot kırdım, çam devirdim; *set on* ~ başlatmak, yürütmek; *set* ~ *on* ayak basmak; **2.** *v/t. & v/i.* ayak kısmını örmek; dansetmek; yaya gitmek; seyretmek (*gemi*); ödemek; yekûnunu çıkarmak; *mst* ~ *up* toplamak, yekûn çıkarmak; ~ *it* yaya gitmek; ~ *the bill* hesabı ödemek; 'foot.age *n.* uzunluk.

foot...: '~-and-'mouth dis.ease bir sığır hastalığı; '~.ball *n.* futbol; '~.board *n.* ayakları dayayacak tahta; '~.boy *n.* belboy, (*otelde*) uşak; '~-brake *n.* ayak freni; '~-bridge *n.* yaya köprüsü, köprü geçit.

foot.ed [ˈfutid] *comb.* ...ayaklı; 'foot.er *n.* F futbol.

foot...: '~.fall *n.* ayak sesi; '~-gear *n.* ayak giyecekleri; ♀ **Guards** *pl.* MIL piyade muhafız alayı; '~-hills *n. pl.* dağ eteklerindeki tepeler; '~.hold *n.* ayak

footing 670

basacak yer; *fig.* sağlam yer.
foot.ing ['futiŋ] *n.* ayak basacak yer; mevki; ilişki; MIL hal, durum, vaziyet; *be on a friendly ~ with s.o.* ...ile arası iyi olm.; *upon the same ~ as* ... ile aynı durumda; *get a ~* yer edinmek; *lose one's ~* ayağı kaymak, tökezlemek.
foo.tle F ['fu:tl] 1. *vb.* boşuna vakit geçirmek, maskaralık etm., aptalca konuşmak *veya* hareket etm.; 2. *n.* ahmaklık, budalalık.
foot.lights THEAT ['futlaits] *n. pl.* sahne önündeki bir sıra ışık; sahne hayatı.
foot.ling ['fu:tliŋ] *adj.* önemsiz, değersiz, ufak tefek.
foot...: '~**.man** *n.* üniformalı uşak; '~**.mark** *n.* ayak izi; '~**.note** 1. *n.* dipnot; 2. *vb.* dipnot koymak; '~**.pad** *n.* eşkiya, haydut; '~**.pas.sen.ger** *n.* yaya; '~**.path** *n.* keçi yolu, patika; '~**.print** *n.* ayak izi; '~**.race** *n.* koşu; '~**.rule** *n.* (*tahta veya madenî*) metre; '~**.slog** *v/i. sl.* bata çıka yürümek, zorlukla yürümek; '~**.sore** *adj.* yürümekten ayakları şişmiş; '~**.stalk** *n.* BOT çiçek sapı, yaprak sapı; '~**.step** *n.* adım; ayak sesi; ayak izi; '~**.stool** *n.* ayak taburesi; '~**.wear** = *foot-gear*; '~**.work** *n. spor:* ayak hakimiyeti.
fop [fɔp] *n.* züppe; '**fop.per.y** *n.* züppelik; '**fop.pish** □ züppece.
for [fɔː; fə; f] 1. *prp. mst* için; hususunda; amacıyla; *-e* karşı; *-e* göre; yerine; adına; lehinde, taraftarı; *-den* dolayı; sebebiyle; sonucu olarak; *-e* rağmen; zarfında; *-den* beri; *come ~ dinner* yemeğe gelmek; *the train ~ London* Londra'ya gidecek tren; *it is ~ you to decide* karar vermek size kalmış; *were it not ~* that o olmasaydı; *he is a fool ~ doing that* onu yaptığı için aptaldır; *~ three days* üç gündür, üç günden beri; *I walked ~ a mile* bir mil yürüdüm; *I ~ one* kendi hesabıma; ben de; *~ sure!* şüphesiz!, elbette!; *it is good ~ us to be here* burada olmamız iyi olur; *the snow was too deep ~ them to go on* kar devam edemeyecekleri kadar kalındı; 2. *cj. -den* dolayı, *-diği* için, çünkü, zira.
for.age ['fɔridʒ] 1. *n.* ot, saman, hayvan yemi, arpa; 2. *v/i.* yiyecek peşinde koşmak, yiyecek aramak.
for.as.much [fərəz'mʌtʃ] *cj.:* ~ *as* madem ki, *-den* dolayı, sebebiyle.
for.ay ['fɔrei] 1. *n.* çapul, akın, yağma; 2. *v/i.* yağma etm.

for.bade [fə'bæd] *pret. of* **forbid.**
for.bear[1] ['fɔːbɛə] *n.* ata, cet.
for.bear[2] [fɔː'bɛə] (*irr.*) *v/t. & v/i.* kaçınmak, sakınmak, çekinmek (*from -den*); sabretmek; **for'bear.ance** *n.* sabır, tahammül; sakınma, kaçınma.
for.bid [fə'bid] (*irr.*) *v/t.* yasak etm., yasaklamak, menetmek; *God ~!* Allah esirgesin!; **for'bid.den** *p.p. of* **forbid;** *~ fruit* yasak meyve, ahlak dışı zevk; **for'bidding** □ sert, haşin, ürkütücü, nahoş.
for.bore, for.borne [fɔː'bɔː(n)] *pret. & p.p. of* **forbear**[2].
force [fɔːs] 1. *n. mst* güç, kuvvet, kudret; şiddet, zor, baskı, tazyik; otorite, nüfuz; *the ~* polis; *armed ~s pl.* silahlı kuvvetler; *by ~* zorla; *come (put) in ~* yürürlüğe girmek (koymak); 2. *v/t.* zorlamak, mecbur etm.; sıkıştırmak; zorla almak; kırıp açmak; turfanda sebze ve meyve yetiştirmek; zorla yapmak; *~ back* geri sürmek, püskürtmek; *~ down* AVIA inişe zorlamak; *~ s.o.'s hand* b-ne istemiyerek *bş* yaptırmak, bir işi yapmaya zorlamak; *~ on* harekete geçirmek; kışkırtmak; *~ open* kırıp açmak; **forced** (*adv.* **forc.ed.ly** ['ِ-idli]) mecburî; *~ loan* mecburî borçlanma; *~ landing* mecburî iniş; *~ march* mecburî yürüyüş; *~ sale* mecburî satış; **force.ful** □ ['ِ-ful] güçlü, etkili, tesirli, kuvvetli; **'force.meat** *n.* baharatlı kıyma.
for.ceps MED ['fɔːseps] *n. sg. & pl.* pens, kıskaç, forseps.
force-pump ['fɔːspʌmp] *n.* tazyik pompası.
forc.er MEC ['fɔːsə] *n.* piston.
for.ci.ble □ ['fɔːsəbl] zora dayanan, mecburî; etkili; ikna edici.
forc.ing-house ['fɔːsiŋhaus] *n.* limonluk, ser.
ford [fɔːd] 1. *n.* nehir geçidi, sığ geçit; 2. *v/t.* (*nehir vs.*) sığ yerden geçmek; '**ford.a.ble** *adj.* yürüyerek geçilebilir.
fore [fɔː] 1. *adv.* ön tarafta, baş tarafta, önde; *~ and aft* NAUT baş taraf kıça kadar; 2. *n.* ön; baş taraf, pruva; *to the ~* elde mevcut, hazır bulunan; önemli; *come (bring) to the ~* başa geç(ir)mek, öne geç(ir)mek; 3. *adj.* ön taraftaki, öndeki; ilk; '~**.arm**[1] *n.* önkol; ~'**arm**[2] *v/t.* önceden silahlandırmak; ~'**bode** *v/t.* işareti olm.; önceden haber vermek; önceden hissetmek; ~'**bod.ing** *n.* önsezi; '~**.cast** 1. *n.* hava tahmini, tahmin; 2. (*irr.* **cast**) *v/t.* önceden söylemek; ön-

ceden tahmin etm.; '~.cas.tle NAUT ['fəuksl] *n.* baş kasarası; ~.close [fɔː-'kləuz] *v/t.* & *v/i.* engel olm.; ipotekli malı sahibinin elinden almak; ~'clo-sure [-ʒə] *n.* ipotekli malı sahibinin elinden alma; '~.court *n.* ön avlu, ön bahçe; ~'date *v/t.* önceden tarih koymak; ~'doom *v/t.* önceden hüküm vermek; önceden belli etm.; '~.fa.ther *n.* ata, cet; '~.fin.ger *n.* işaret parmağı; '~.foot *n.* önayak; '~.front *n.* en ileri taraf; en ileri yer; ~'go (*irr.* **go**) *v/t.* & *v/i.* önce gitmek; ~*ing* daha önce belirtilen; ~'gone *adj.* geçmiş, bitmiş, önceki; ~ *conclusion* kaçınılmaz sonuç; '~.ground *n.* ön plan; '~.hand **1.** *n. tenis*; sağ vuruş; **2.** *adj.* evvelki, önceden yapılan; ~.head ['fɔrid] *n.* alın.

for.eign ['fɔrən] *adj.* yabancı, ecnebi; dış; ilgisi olmayan; ~ *body* yabancı cisim; ~*-born* yabancı ülkede doğmuş; 'for.eigner *n.* yabancı, ecnebi; 'for.eign.ness yabancılık, ecnebilik.

for.eign...: ♀ *Of.fice* Dışişleri Bakanlığı; ~ *pol.i.cy* dış politika; ~ *trade* dış ticaret.

fore...: ~'judge *v/t.* önceden hüküm vermek; ~'know (*irr.* **know**) *v/t.* önceden bilmek; '~'knowl.edge *n.* önceden bilme; ~.land ['fɔːlənd] *n.* burun, çıkıntı; '~.leg *n.* ön ayak; '~.lock *n.* kâkül, perçem; **take time by the** ~ fırsatı kaçırmamak, fırsatı hemen kullanmak; '~.man *n.* JUR jüri başkanı; MIN ustabaşı; '~.mast *n.* NAUT baş direği, pruva direği; '~.most **1.** *adj.* başta gelen; ana, en tanınmış; **2.** *adv.* başta, ilkönce; '~.name *n.* birinci isim; '~.noon *n.* öğleden önceki zaman, sabah.

fo.ren.sic [fə'rensik] *adj.* mahkemeye ait, adlî, kazai.

fore...: '~.or'dain *v/t.* önceden takdir etm.; önceden tayin etm.; '~.paw *n.* ön ayağın pençesi; '~.run.ner *n.* haberci, müjdeci; öncü; ~.sail ['~seil; NAUT '~sl] *n.* trinketa yelkeni; ~'see (*irr.* **see**) *v/t.* önceden görmek, ileriyi görmek, önceden bilmek; ~'see.a.ble *adj.* önceden bilinebilen; ~'shad.ow *v/t.* önceden belirtmek, önceden haber vermek; ~.shore *n.* deniz kıyısı, sahil; ~'short.en *v/t.* orantılı olarak küçültmek; '~.sight *n.* basiret, önceden görme; '~.skin *n.* sünnet derisi.

for.est ['fɔrist] **1.** *n.* orman (*a. fig.*); **2.** *v/t.* ağaçlandırmak.

fore.stall [fɔːstɔːl] *v/t.* önüne geçmek;

önce davranıp önlemek; önce davranmak.

for.est.er ['fɔristə] *n.* ormancı; 'for.est.ry *n.* ormancılık; orman.

fore...: '~.taste *n.* önceden tadına varma; önceden alınan tat; ~'tell (*irr.* **tell**) *v/t.* önceden haber vermek, kehanette bulunmak; '~.thought *n.* basiret; önceden düşünme.

for.ev.er [fə'revə] *adv.* devamlı olarak, edebiyen, daima; durmadan.

fore...: ~'warn *v/t.* önceden uyarmak; '~.wom.an *n.* kadın ustabaşı; '~.word *n.* önsöz.

for.feit ['fɔːfit] **1.** *adj.* ceza olarak kaybedilen; **2.** *n.* ceza, *bşin* ceza olarak kaybedilmesi; COM & *spor:* cayma, vazgeçme; ~*s pl.* bir oyun çeşidi; 'for.feit-a.ble *adj.* kaybedilebilir; for.fei.ture ['~.tʃə] *n.* kaybetme, hakkın kaybedilmesi.

for.gath.er [fɔː'gæðə] *v/i.* toplanmak, biraraya gelmek, içtima etm.; rastlamak.

for.gave [fə'geiv] *pret. of* **forgive**.

forge¹ [fɔːdʒ] **1.** *n.* demirhane, demirci ocağı; **2.** *v/t.* demiri kızdırıp işlemek, dövmek; *fig.* kurmak; sahtesini yapmak, uydurmak.

forge² [~] *mst* ~ **ahead** *v/i.* ilerlemek, öne geçmek.

for.ger ['fɔːdʒə] *n.* sahtekâr; demirci; 'for.ger.y *n.* sahte *bş*; kalpazanlık; sahtekârlık, sahte imza atma.

for.get [fə'get] (*irr.*) *v/t.* unutmak; ihmal etm.; *I* ~ F unuttum; for'get.ful □ [-ful] unutkan, ihmalci; for'get.ful-ness *n.* unutkanlık, ihmal; for'get--me-not *n.* BOT unutmabeni.

for.give [fə'giv] (*irr.*) *v/t.* affetmek, bağışlamak; for'giv.en *p.p. of* **forgive**; for'give.ness *n.* af, bağışla(n)ma; for-'giving □ affeden, bağışlayan, merhametli.

for.go [fɔː'gəu] (*irr.* **go**) *v/t.* vazgeçmek.

for.got [fə'gɔt], for'got.ten [-tn] *pret.* & *p.p. of* **forget**.

fork [fɔːk] **1.** *n.* çatal; bel; **2.** *vb.* çatallaş(tır)mak; ayrılmak; çatalla kaldırmak; bellemek; forked *adj.* çatallı; 'fork-lift *n.* çatallı kaldırıcı.

for.lorn [fə'lɔːn] *adj.* kimsesiz, terkedilmiş, sahipsiz; ümitsiz; ~ *hope* boş ümit; ümitsiz bir girişim; MIL fedailer takımı.

form [fɔːm] **1.** *n.* şekil, biçim, suret; hal; üslup, tarz; TYP forma; formül, kâğıt;

formal

okul: sınıf; *in (good)* ~ *spor:* formda; **good (bad)** ~ iyi (kötü) durum, davranış; **2.** *v/t.* teşkil etm., kurmak; şekil vermek *-e;* geliştirmek; düzenlemek; MIL tertiplemek; *v/i.* şekil almak, oluşmak.

for.mal □ ['fɔːməl] resmî, usule uygun; biçimsel, şeklî; 'for.mal.ism *n.* şekilcilik, biçimselcilik; dış görünüşüne önem verme; 'for.mal.ist *n.* biçimci kimse; resmiyet taraftarı; for.mal.i.ty [fɔː'mæliti] *n.* usul, formalite; resmiyet; for.mal.ize ['fɔːməlaiz] *v/t.* şekillendirmek; resmileştirmek.

for.mat ['fɔːmæt] *n.* kitabın genel düzeni, kitabın şekli ve boyutları; düzenleme, tertip.

for.ma.tion [fɔː'meiʃən] *n.* teşkil, kurma; şekillendirme; oluşum, formasyon; *esp.* MIL & GEOL düzen, tertip, oluşum; ~ *flying* AVIA filo uçuşu; **form.a.tive** ['fɔːmətiv] *adj.* şekil vere(bile)n; geliştirici, öğretici; ~ *years pl.* gelişme yılları.

form.er¹ MEC ['fɔːmə] kalıp; şablon; bobin şablonu; *fig.* biçimlendirici şey *veya* kimse.

for.mer² [_] *adj.* önceki, eski, sabık; ilk bahsedilen; 'for.mer.ly *adv.* eskiden.

for.mic ['fɔːmik] *adj.*: ~ *acid* karınca asidi, formik asid.

for.mi.da.ble □ ['fɔːmidəbl] heybetli, korkulur; müthiş, çok zor; çok büyük.

form.less □ ['fɔːmlis] şekilsiz, biçimsiz.

For.mo.san [fɔː'məusən] *n.* Formaza'lı kimse.

for.mu.la ['fɔːmjulə] *n. pl. mst* for.mu.lae ['_liː] formül; usul, kaide; MED reçete, tertip; for.mu.lar.y ['_ləri] *n.* formüler; kodeks; for.mu.late ['_leit] *v/t.* hazırlamak (*plan, öneri vs.*); açıkça belirtmek; formu'la.tion *n.* formülleştirme; kesin ve açık ifade.

for.ni.ca.tion [fɔːni'keiʃən] *n.* evlilik dışı cinsel ilişki.

for.rad.er F ['fɔrədə] *adv.* daha ileriye.

for.sake [fə'seik] (*irr.*) *v/t.* terketmek, bırakmak; vazgeçmek *-den;* for'sak.en *p.p. of forsake;* for.sook [_'suk] *pret. of forsake.*

for.sooth *iro.* [fə'suːθ] *adv.* gerçekten, hakikaten.

for.swear [fɔː'swɛə] (*irr. swear*) *v/t.* yeminle bırakmak, vazgeçmek *-den;* ~ *o.s.* yalan yere yemin etm.; for'sworn *adj.* yalan yere yemin etmiş.

fort MIL [fɔːt] *n.* kale, hisar; istihkâm.

forte *fig.* [fɔːt] *n.* özel yetenek, bir kimsenin asıl hüneri.

forth [fɔːθ] *adv.* ileri, dışarı, açığa; sonra; *from this day* ~ bugünden itibaren; ~'com.ing *adj.* gelecek, çıkacak; hazır, mevcut; F kolaylık gösteren, yardımsever; *be* ~ kolaylık göstermek; güleryüz göstermek; '~.right *adj.* açık, doğru sözlü, içten; '~'with *adv.* derhal, hemen, vakit kaybetmeden.

for.ti.eth ['fɔːtiiθ] **1.** *adj.* kırkıncı; **2.** *n.* kırkta bir.

for.ti.fi.ca.tion [fɔːtifi'keiʃən] *n.* tahkim, kuvvetlendirme; MIL istihkâm; **for.ti.fy** [_'fai] *v/t.* MIL takviye etm., kuvvetlendirmek; *fig.* canlandırmak, zindelik vermek; **for.ti.tude** ['_tjuːd] *n.* metanet, sabır, tahammül.

fort.night ['fɔːtnait] *n.* iki hafta; *this day* ~ iki hafta sonra bugün; *this* ~ bu iki hafta; 'fort.night.ly *adj. & adv.* iki haftada bir.

for.tress ['fɔːtris] *n.* kale, hisar, istihkâm.

for.tu.i.tous □ [fɔː'tjuːitəs] rastlantı sonucu olan, tesadüfî; for'tu.i.tous.ness, for'tu.i.ty *n.* tesadüf, rastlantı.

for.tu.nate ['fɔːtʃnit] *adj.* talihli, şanslı; 'for.tu.nate.ly *adv.* iyi ki, çok şükür, Allahtan, bereket versin, hamdolsun.

for.tune ['fɔːtʃən] *n.* baht, talih, şans; kader, kısmet; servet; uğur; *good* ~ iyi şans; *bad* ~, *ill* ~ kötü talih; *marry a* ~ zengin bir kadınla evlenmek; *tell* ~*s* fal bakmak; '~-hunt.er *n.* servet avcısı; '~-tel.ler *n.* falcı.

for.ty ['fɔːti] **1.** *adj.* kırk; ~*-niner* Am. F 1849'da Kaliforniya'ya altın aramaya giden kimse; ~ *winks pl.* kısa uyku, şekerleme, kestirme; **2.** *n.* kırk; *the forties* 40 ile 49 yılları arası.

fo.rum ['fɔːrəm] *n.* Eski Roma'da meydan, forum.

for.ward ['fɔːwəd] **1.** *adj.* öndeki, ilerideki, önde olan; gelişmiş; küstah; aşırı; COM ilerideki...; ~ *planning* ilerisi için planlama; **2.** *adv.* ileri, ileri doğru; *from this time* ~ bundan böyle; **3.** *n.* futbol: forvet; **4.** *v/t.* sevketmek, göndermek (*to -e*); yeni adrese göndermek; ilerlemesine yardımcı olm.; *please* ~ POST lütfen yeni adrese gönderin; 'for.ward.er *n.* nakliyeci, seykiyatçı.

for.ward.ing ['fɔːwədiŋ] *n.* gönderme, sevkiyat, nakliye; ~ *a.gent* sevkiyat acentesi.

for.ward.ness ['fɔːwədnis] *n.* ilerleme; düşüncesizlik, küstahlık, cüret; **forwards** ['fɔːwədz] *adv.* ileriye doğru, ileri; itibaren.

fosse [fɔs] *n.* MIL hendek; ANAT çukur.

fos.sil ['fɔsl] **1.** *adj.* fosilleşmiş, taşlaşmış; *fig.* eski kafalı, zamana uymayan; **2.** *n.* fosil, taşıl; eski kafalı kimse.

fos.ter ['fɔstə] **1.** *v/t. fig.* beslemek, bakıp büyütmek; bakmak; teşvik etm.; ~ *up* büyütmek, yetiştirmek; **2.** *adj.* süt..., evlatlık...; '**fos.ter.age** *n.* evlatlık büyütme; bakım, besleme, teşvik; '**fos.ter-child** *n.* evlâtlık, evlât gibi büyütülmüş çocuk; **fos.ter.ling** ['ˌliŋ] *n.* evlâtlık, manevi evlât.

fought [fɔːt] *pret. & p.p. of* **fight 2.**

foul [faul] **1.** □ pis, kirli; bozuk; iğrenç; *fig.* çirkin, ayıp, bayağı, kaba, kötü, fırtınalı (*hava*); müstehcen, açık saçık; dolaşmış, karışmış; tıkalı, tıkanık; NAUT bozuk, arızalı, çaparız; **~tongue** kötü lisan, küfürlü konuşma; **fall ~ of** başı derde girmek; NAUT çarpmak, çarpışmak; **2.** *n.* çarpışma, bindirme (*gemi*); *spor.* faul; **through fair and ~** iyi veya kötü zamanlarda; **3.** *v/t. & v/i.* kirletmek, kirlenmek, pisletmek; rezil etm.; dolaş(tır)mak, karışmak; faul yapmak; ~**-mouthed** ['ˌmauðd], '~**-spo.ken** *adj.* ağzı bozuk, küfürbaz.

found[1] [faund] *pret. & p.p. of* **find 1.**

found[2] [ˌ] *v/t.* kurmak, temelini atmak, tesis etm. (*a. fig.*).

found[3] MEC [ˌ] *v/t.* kalıba dökmek, eritmek.

foun.da.tion [faun'deiʃən] *n.* kurma, tesis; vakıf, kuruluş; temel, esas, dayanak (*a. fig.*); ~ **cream** makyaj kremi; ~ **gar.ment** korse; ~**stone** *n.* temel taşı.

found.er[1] ['faundə] *n.* kurucu.

found.er[2] MEC [ˌ] *n.* dökmeci.

found.er[3] [ˌ] *v/i.* NAUT su dolup batmak; *fig.* batmak, iflas etm.; sakatlanmak; tökezlenmek; çökmek; olmamak, suya düşmek; *v/t.* suyla doldurup batırmak; yıkmak.

found.ling ['faundliŋ] *n.* sokakta bulunmuş çocuk, buluntu; ~ **hos.pi.tal** kimsesiz çocuklar yurdu.

found.ress ['faundris] *n.* kadın kurucu.

found.ry MEC ['faundri] *n.* dökümhane.

fount [faunt] *n. poet.* pınar, kaynak, memba; TYP [*a.* fɔnt] baskı harfleri takımı, hurufat takımı.

foun.tain ['fauntin] *n.* çeşme, pınar, kaynak, memba; fıskiye; MEC döküm kanalı; '~**head** *n.* kaynak (*a. fig.*); '~**pen** *n.* dolmakalem.

four [fɔː] **1.** *adj.* dört; **2.** *n.* dört rakamı; *spor.* dört kişilik takım; '~**flush.er** *n. Am. sl.* blöfçü, blöf yapan kimse; '~**fold** *adj. & adv.* dört kat, dört kez.

401k [fɔːˈhʌndrədˈandwʌn'kei] *emeklilik maaşları ile ilgili;* ~ **plan** *n.* emeklilik planı.

'**four-in-'hand** *n.* dört katlı araba; kravat; '~**part** *adj.* MUS dört sesli; '~**pence** *n.* dört penilik madeni para; '~**ply** *adj.* dört katlı, dörtkat; '~**post.er** *n.* dört direkli karyola; '~**score** *adj. & n.* seksen; ~**some** ['fɔːsəm] *n. golf:* dörtlü grup oyunu; '~**square** *adj.* dört köşe, kare; *fig.* metin, sağlam; '~**stroke** *adj.* MOT dört zamanlı...

four.teen ['fɔːˈtiːn] *adj. & n.* on dört; '**four'teenth** [ˌθ] **1.** *adj.* on dördüncü; **2.** *n.* on dörtte bir; **fourth** [fɔːθ] **1.** *adj.* dördüncü; **2.** *n.* dörtte bir; '**fourth.ly** *adv.* dördüncü olarak; '**four-'wheel.er** *n.* dört tekerlekli atlı araba.

fowl [faul] **1.** *n.* kuş, tavuk; kümes hayvanı; bu hayvanların eti; **2.** *vb.* yabanî kuş avlamak; '**fowl.er** *n.* yabani kuş avcısı.

fowl.ing ['fauliŋ] *n.* yabanî kuş avı; '~**piece** *n.* av tüfeği.

fowl-run ['faulrʌn] *n.* kümes.

fox [fɔks] **1.** *n.* tilki; tilki kürkü; kurnaz adam; **2.** *vb.* aldatmak, şaşırtmak, zihnini karıştırmak; '~**brush** *n.* tilki kuyruğu; '~**earth** *n.* tilki ini; **foxed** *adj.* lekeli, sararmış.

fox...: '~**glove** *n.* BOT yüksükotu; '~**hole** *n.* MIL askerin sığınacağı çukur; '~**hound** *n.* tilki avında kullanılan köpek; '~**hunt** *n.* tilki avı; '~**ter.ri.er** *n.* zoo tilki teriyeri; '~**trot** *n.* fokstrot, bir dans müziği; '**fox.y** *adj.* kurnaz, şeytani görünüşlü; cazibeli, çekici; tilki renginde.

foy.er THEAT ['fɔiei] *n.* fuaye, giriş salonu.

fra.cas ['frækɑː] *n, pl.* ~ ['ˌz] gürültü, kavga, velvele.

frac.tion ['frækʃən] *n.* MATH kesir; parça; kır(ıl)ma; oran; ~ **line** kesir çizgisi; **frac.tion.al** ['ˌʃənl] □ kesri, cüzi, az, azıcık.

frac.tious ['frækʃəs] *adj.* ters, aksi,

huysuz, kavgacı.

frac.ture ['fræktʃə] **1.** *n.* (*esp. kemik*) kırık; kır(ıl)ma; **2.** *v/t. & v/i.* kır(ıl)mak; çatla(t)mak.

frag.ile ['frædʒail] *adj.* kolay kırılır, kolay bozulur; kolay yok olan; *fig.* zayıf, nazik; **fra.gil.i.ty** [‿'dʒiliti] *n.* kolay kırılma, narinlik.

frag.ment ['frægmənt] *n.* kırılmış parça, kısım, eksik parça; '**frag.men.tar.y** □ eksik kalmış, parça parça, kısım kısım, tamamlanmamış.

fra.grance ['freigrəns] *n.* güzel koku; '**fra.grant**□ güzel kokulu, mis kokulu.

frail[1] [freil] *n.* küfe, sepet.

frail[2]□ [‿] zayıf, narin, kolay kırılır, kolay bozulan; (*esp. ahlakı*) zayıf; '**frail.ty** *n. fig.* zayıflık, manevi zaaf; hata.

frag.ment ['frægmənt] *n.* kırılış parça, kı-

frame[freim] **1.** *n.* çerçeve, gergef; beden, vücut; yapı; kafes; düzen; NAUT, AVIA kaburga, gövde; PHOT poz; AGR limonluk, sera; ~ *of mind* mizaç, hal, ruhsal durum; **2.** *vb.* şekil vermek -*e*, uydurmak -*i*; çerçevelemek -*i*; düzenlemek, tertip etm.; *a.*~ *up sl.* yalan yere suçlamak; ~ **aer.i.al** çerçeve anten; ~ **house**ahşap ev; '**fram.ern.** çerçeveleme sistemi; '**frame-up**n. *esp. Am.* F hileli düzen, iftira, yalan yere suçlama; '**frame.work**n. MEC şasi; ARCH çatı, iskelet; *fig.* yapı, bünye.

franc[fræŋk] *n.* (*Fransa, Belçika, İsviçre*) frank.

fran.chiseJUR ['fræntʃaiz] *n.* oy verme hakkı; *esp. Am.* imtiyaz, özel hak.

Fran.cis.can ECCL [fræn'siskən] *n.* Fransiskan mezhebine mensup rahip.

Fran.co-['fræŋkəu] *prefix* Fransız.

fran.gi.ble['frændʒibl] *adj.* kırılabilir.

Frank[1] [fræŋk] *n.* Ortaçağda German kavimlerinden birine mensup kimse; Frenk.

frank[2] [‿] **1.** □ açık sözlü, samimi, içi dışı bir, dobra; **2.** *v/t.* posta ücretinin ödendiğini göstermek için mektuba damga vurmak.

frank.furt.er['fræŋkfə:tə] *n.* bir tür baharatlı sosis.

frank.in.cense ['fræŋkinsens] *n.* günlük, buhur, tütsü.

frank.ing-ma.chine ['fræŋkiŋməʃi:n] *n.* pul yapıştırma makinesi, damgalama makinesi.

frank.ness['fræŋknis] *n.* açık sözlülük, samimiyet.

fran.tic ['fræntik] *adj.* (~*ally*) çılgınca heyecanlanmış, çılgın, çileden çıkmış.

fra.ter.nal □ [frə'tə:nl] kardeşçe; fra-'**terni.ty** *n.* kardeşlik; kardeşlik cemiyeti; UNIV *Am.* erkek öğrenci birliği; '**frat-erni.za.tion**[frætənai'zeiʃən] *n.* arkadaşlık; '**frat.er.nize** *v/i.* arkadaş olm., kardeş gibi olm.

frat.ri.cide['freitrisaid] *n.* kardeş katili; kendi kardeşini öldürme.

fraud [frɔːd] *n.* hile; F dolandırıcılık, sahtekârlık; F hilekâr, sahtekâr, dolandırıcı kimse; **fraud.u.lence** ['‿juləns] *n.* hilekârlık; '**fraud.u.lent**□ hilekâr, sahtekâr, dolandırıcı; hile ile kazanılan.

fraught *poet.* [frɔːt] *adj.* dolu, yüklü (**with** *ile*).

fray[1] [frei] *v/t.* yıpratmak; *v/i.* yıpranmak (*kumaş vs.*).

fray[2][‿] *n.* kavga, karışıklık, mücadele, çekişme.

fraz.zle*esp. Am.* F ['fræzl] **1.** *n.* tamamen yıpranma; yorulma; *beat to a* ~ bitkin, çok yıpranmış; **2.** *v/t.* yıpratmak, eskitmek; *v/i.* yıpranmak, eskimek.

freak[fri:k] *n.* acayiplik, kapris; hilkat garibesi, eksantrik kimse; ~ *of nature* şeklen anormal olan insan, hayvan *veya* bitki; '**freak.ish** □ acayip, garip, anormal, kaprisli.

freck.le['frekl] **1.** *n.* çil; leke, benek; *fig.* kusur; **2.** *v/i.* çillenmek, çil basmak; **freck.led**['‿ld] *adj.* çilli.

free[fri:] **1.** □ *com.* serbest; özgür, hür, azat, kurtulmuş (*from, of -den*); bağımsız; açık; bedava, parasız; CHEM terkipsiz; muaf; ...sız, ...meyerek; *b*şin dışında; boş; eli açık, cömert; teklifsiz, rahat; ~ *of debt* borçtan kurtulmuş; *he is* ~ *to inf.* ....mekte serbesttir; ~ *and easy* teklifsiz, laubali, gayrı resmî; *have a* ~ *hand* hareketlerinde bağımsız olm.; *give veya allow s.o. a* ~ *hand* istediğini yapmakta serbest bırakmak; *have one's hands*~ *fig.* serbest olm., istediğini yapmak; *make* ~ *with* laubali olm., yüzgöz olm.; kendi malı gibi kullanmak; *make*~ *of* ayrıcalığa ortak olmak hakkını vermek; *make s.o.* ~ *of the city* fahri hemşeri sıfatını vermek; *set* ~ serbest bırakmak, azat etm. **2.** *v/t.* serbest bırakmak, kurtarmak (*from, of -den*); tahliye etm.; ~.**boot.er** ['‿bu:tə] *n.* korsan, haydut;

'**free.dom** *n.* özgürlük, hürriyet, serbestlik (*from* -*den*); açık sözlülük; aşırı samimiyet, laubalilik; ~ *of the city* şehrin fahrî hemşerilik sıfatı; ~ *of movement* davranış özgürlüğü; ~ *of speech* konuşma özgürlüğü.

free..; ~ **en.ter.prise** serbest teşebbüs; ~ **fight** serbest dövüş; '~**-for-all** *n.* herkese açık yarış, tartışma *veya* kavga; = *free fight*; '~'**hand.ed** *adj.* cömert, eli açık; '~**.hold** *n.* JUR mülkiyet, mülk, sahiplik hakkı; '~.**hold.er** *n.* mülk sahibi; ~ **kick** *spor*: serbest vuruş, frikik; ~ **labo(u)r** sendikaya bağlı olmayan işçiler; '~'**lance 1.** *n.* serbest çalışan yazar, gazeteci *vs.*; **2.** *v/i.* serbest çalışmak; '~'**list** *n.* gümrüksüz giren eşya listesi; bir yere parasız girenlerin listesi; ~ **liver** herşeyden bol bol yiyip içen kimse, boğazına düşkün, zevkperest; '~.**man** *n.* hür kimse, fahri hemşeri; '~.**ma.son** *n.* mason; '~.**ma.son.ry** *n.* masonluk; ~ **port** serbest liman; ~ **speech** serbest konuşma hakkı; '~'**spo.ken** *adj.* açık sözlü, düşündüğünü söyleyen, sözünü esirgemeyen; ~ **state** bağımsız devlet; '~**-stone** *n.* kolay yontulan taş, kumtaşı, kireçtaşı; '~**-think.er** *n.* serbest düşünür; '~'**thinking** ~**-thought 1.** *n.* serbest düşünce; **2.** *adj.* serbest düşünceli; ~ **trade** serbest ticaret; '~'**trad.er** *n.* serbest ticaret taraftarı; '~'**wheel 1.** *n.* pedal çevirmeden gitme; **2.** *v/i.* pedal çevirmeden gitmek.

freeze [fri:z] **1.** (*irr.*) *v/i.* donmak, buz kesmek, buz tutmak; çok üşümek; ~ *to death* donarak ölmek; soğuktan ölmek; *v/t.* dondurmak; fiyatları dondurmak; ~ *out sl.* işten *veya* toplumdan uzaklaştırmak, iş *veya* toplumun dışına itmek; **2.** *n.* donma, don; **wage** ~ ücretleri dondurma; '**freez.er** *n.* dondurucu; dondurma makinesi; RAIL soğuk hava vagonu; '**freez.ing** ☐ dondurucu, donmakta; çok soğuk; ~ **mixture** PHYS soğutucu karışım, dondurucu karışım; ~ **point** donma noktası.

freight [freit] **1.** *n.* navlun, nakliye ücreti; hamule, yük; *attr. Am.* yük...; ~ *out* (*home*) dönüş yükü (*veya* hamulesi); **2.** *v/t.* yüklemek; nakletmek, göndermek, taşımak; '**freight.age** = freight 1.; '**freight-car** *n.* RAIL *Am.* yük vagonu; **freight.er** *n.* NAUT şilep, yük vapuru; AVIA nakliye uçağı; **freight train** *Am.* yük treni, marşandiz.

French [frentʃ] **1.** *adj.* Fransa'ya *veya* Fransızlara ait; ~ *beans pl.* taze fasulye; ~ *fried potatoes pl.* yağda kızarmış patates; **take** ~ **leave** izinsiz sıvışmak, izin almadan çekip gitmek; ~ **window** balkona *vs.* giden camlı kapı; **2.** *n.* Fransızca; **the** ~ *pl.* Fransızlar, Fransız halkı; ~ **horn** MUS Fransız kornosu; '~.**man** *n.* Fransız (*erkek*); '~.**wom.an** *n.* Fransız (*kadın*).

fren.zied ['frenzid] *adj.* çılgın; '**fren.zy** *n.* çılgınlık, taşkınlık.

fre.quen.cy ['fri'kwənsi] *n.* sık sık olma, çok meydana gelme; ELECT frekans; ~ **modu.la.tion** ELECT frekans modülasyonu; **frequent 1.** ☐ ['.kwənt] sık sık olan, alışılmış, daimi; **2.** [fri-'kwent] *v/t.* sık sık gitmek *-e*, çok uğramak *-e*; **fre.quen.tation** *n.* bir yere sık gitme; **fre.quent.er** [fri'kwentə] *n.* devamlı müşteri, müdavim.

fres.co ['freskəu] *n.*, *pl.* **fres.co(e)s** ['.-z] fresk, yaş sıva üzerine yapılan duvar resmi.

fresh [freʃ] **1.** ☐ *com.* taze, yeni; dinç; acemi; yeni toplanmış (*çiçek*); yeni gelmiş; yeni büyümüş; yeni ayrılmış; tatlı (*su*); temiz, serin (*hava*); parlak, canlı (*renk*); *Am. sl.* küstah, yüzsüz; **break** ~ **ground** *fig.* bir şeye yeni başlamak; yeni gerçekler bulmak; yepyeni *bşe* başlamak; ~ **water** tatlı su; **2.** *n.* serinlik; taşma, kabarma; '**fresh.en** *v/t.* & *v/i.* canlan(dır)mak; tazelemek (*içki*); sertleşmek (*rüzgâr*); serinle(t)-mek; **fresh.et** ['.it] *n. fig.* kabarma, taşma, seyelân; '**fresh.man** *n.* UNIV birinci sınıf öğrencisi; '**fresh.ness** *n.* tazelik; acemilik; '**fresh-wa.ter** *adj.* tatlı suya ait, tatlı su...; ~ **college** *Am. sl.* ufak kolej.

fret [fret] **1.** *n.* üzüntü, sıkıntı, öfke; **2.** *v/t.* & *v/i.* üz(ül)mek; sık(ıl)mak; aşın(dır)mak; ye(n)mek; sinirlen(dir)-mek; rahatsız etm.; kız(dır)mak; ~ **away**, ~ **out** yıpratmak, aşındırmak, yenmek.

fret [.] **1.** *n.* ARCH kabartma, oyma; **2.** *v/t.* kabartma yapmak, oymak.

fret [.] *n.* MUS telli sazlarda perde.

fret.ful ☐ ['fretful] sinirli, huysuz, aksi, ters.

fret-saw ['fretsɔ:] *n.* kıl testere.

fret.work ['fretwə:k] *n.* oyma işi.

fri.a.bil.i.ty [fraiə'biliti] *n.* gevreklik, çabuk ufalanma; '**fri.a.ble** *adj.* kolay ufalanabilir, gevrek.

fri.ar [fraiə] *n*. bazı katolik örgütlerinde rahip, keşiş; 'fri.ar.y *n*. manastır.

frib.ble ['fribl] **1.** *vb*. eğlenmek, oynamak; tembel davranmak; boşa harcamak; **2.** *n*. uçarı, hoppa, hafifmeşrep.

fric.as.see [frikə'si.] **1.** *n*. yahni; **2.** *v/t*. *-in* yahnisini yapmak.

fric.tion ['frikʃən] *n*. sürtme, sürtünme, friksiyon; sürtüşme (*a. fig*.); *attr*. = fric.tion.al ['-ʃənl] *adj*. sürtünme…

fridge F [fridʒ] *n*. buzdolabı.

Fri.day ['fraidi] *n*. cuma.

friend [frend] *n*. dost, arkadaş, ahbap; yardımcı; ♀ Kuveykır mezhebine mensup kimse; **make ~s with** *b-le* arkadaş olm.; *b-le* tanışmak; 'friend.less *adj*. dostu olmayan; 'friend.li.ness *n*. dostça duygu ve hareket; 'friend.ly *adj*. dostça, samimi, arkadaşça, dostane; ♀ **Society** yardımlaşma cemiyeti; 'friend.ship *n*. dostluk, arkadaşlık.

frieze [fri:z] *n*. duvar süsü (*kumaş veya* ARCH).

frig.ate NAUT ['frigit] *n*. savaş gemisi, firkateyn.

frig(e) F [fridʒ] = **fridge**.

fright [frait] *n*. dehşet, korku; *fig*. çirkin kılıklı kimse *veya* şey; 'fright.en *v/t*. korkutmak, ürkütmek, korkutup kaçırmak, dehşete düşürmek; **be ~ed of** F *bşden* korkmak, ürkmek; 'frightful □ ['-ful] korkunç, müthiş, berbat; 'fright.ful.ness *n*. korkunçluk, dehşet.

frig.id □ ['fridʒid] soğuk; buz gibi (*a. fig*.); PSYCH cinsel bakımdan soğuk (*kadın*); fri'gid.i.ty *n*. soğukluk (*a. PSYCH*); duygusuzluk.

frill [frill] **1.** *n*. fırfır, volan; farbala; **put on ~s** F *fig*. aşırı süslemek; **2.** *vb*. farbala yapmak, kıvırmak.

fringe [frindʒ] **1.** *n*. saçak; kenar; kâkül; *a. ~s pl*. yele, püskül; **2.** *v/t*. saçak *veya* kenar takmak; çevrelemek, sınır oluşturmak.

frip.per.y ['fripəri] **1.** *n*. elbisede gereksiz süs, cicili bicili şeyler, değersiz süs; **2.** *adj*. kıymetsiz, değersiz…

frisk [frisk] **1.** *n*. sıçrama; oyun, neşe; üstünü arama, silah arama; **2.** *v/t*. & *v/i*. sıçramak, oynamak; üstünü aramak, üstünde silah aramak; 'frisk.i.ness *n*. neşe, canlılık; 'frisk.y □ neşeli, oynak.

frith [friθ] = **firth**.

frit.ter ['fritə] **1.** *n*. gözlemeye benzer börek; **2.** *vb*. **~away** boşuna sarfetmek, ziyan etm., israf etm.

fri.vol ['frivəl] *vb*. sarfetmek, vakit öl-

dürmek, israf etm.; fri.vol.i.ty [-'vɔliti] *n*. hoppalık, hafifmeşreplik; saçmalık, manasızlık; friv.o.lous □ ['-vələs] önemsiz, ehemmiyetsiz, anlamsız; uçarı, zevk düşkünü.

frizz [friz] *v/t*. kıvırmak, bukle yapmak; friz.zle ['-l] *a*. **~ up** *v/t*. & *v/i*. kıvırmak, kıvrılmak, kıvrım kıvrım olm., bukle yapmak; 'friz.z(l)y *adj*. kıvır kıvır, kıvırcık, bukle bukle.

fro [frou] *adv*.: **to and ~** öteye beriye, ileri geri.

frock [frɔk] *n*. kadın elbisesi, rop; rahip cüppesi; cüppe; iş elbisesi; '~'coat *n*. redingot.

frog [frɔg] *n*. kurbağa; RAIL makas göbeği; MIL kılıç kayışı; '~.man *n*. kurbağa adam, balıkadam; '~-march *v/t*. el ve ayaklarını tutarak (mahkûmu) yüzükoyun taşımak.

frol.ic ['frɔlik] **1.** *n*. neşe, eğlence, coşma; **2.** *v/t*. oynamak, gülüp eğlenmek; frol.ic.some □ ['-səm] eğlenceyi seven, şen, neşeli.

from [frɔm, frəm] *prep*. -den, -dan; -den itibaren; -den dolayı; **defend ~** *-den* korumak; **draw ~ nature** doğaya bakarak çizmek; **hide ~** *-den* saklamak; **~ above** yukarıdan, tepeden; **~ amidst** arasından; **~ before** *-den* evvel.

frond BOT [frɔnd] *n*. eğreltiotu yaprağı; hurma ağacı yaprağı.

front [frʌnt] **1.** *n*. ön, yüz; ön taraf; ön saf; MIL cephe; yol kenarı; birleşik hareket, cephe; paravan kişi *veya* kurum; *poet*. alın, yüz; **in ~** önde; **in ~ of** *-in* önünde; **come to the ~** *fig*. göze çarpmak, tanınmak, meşhur olm.; **2.** *adj*. öndeki…; **3.** *vb*. *a*. **~ on**, **~ towards** *-e* bakmak; 'front.age *n*. ARCH bina cephesi, cephe; 'fron.tal **1.** *adj*. alna ait; ön…; **2.** *n*. ARCH cephe; front door sokak kapısı, ön kapı; fron.tier ['-tiə] *n*. sınır, hudut; yerleşilmemiş bölge, boş bölge; 'fron.tiersman *n*. sınırda oturan adam; *fig*. öncü; fron.tis.piece ['-tispi:s] *n*. ARCH binanın yüzü; TYP kitabın başındaki resimli sayfa; front.let ['frʌntlit] *n*. alın bağı; front.man *fig*. gizli maksatları örtmek için kullanılan kimse; 'front-page *n*. baş sayfa; 'front-'wheel drive MOT önden çekişli.

frost [frɔst] **1.** *n*. don, ayaz, *a*. **hoar ~**, **white ~** kırağı; F başarısızlık; **black ~** don; **2.** *v/t*. & *v/i*. don(dur)mak; kırağı tutmak; buz tutmak; şekerle kaplamak; **~ed glass** buzlucam; '~-bite *n*.

soğuk ısırması, soğuğun yakması; **'frost.bit.ten** adj. donmuş; **'frost--bound** adj. buz tutmuş, donmuş; **'frost.i.ness** n. soğuk, don; **'frost.ing** n. pastaya sürülen şekerli karışını; **'frost.y** ☐ ayazlı; buz tutmuş; soğuk (a. fig.).

froth [frɔθ] **1.** n. köpük; fig. boş laf, saçmalık; **2.** v/i. köpürmek; **'froth.i.ness** n. köpük; fig. boş laf, saçmalık; **'froth.y** ☐ köpüklü; fig. yavan, tatsız.

fro.ward obs. ['frəuəd] adj. ters, aksi, inatçı, asi, serkeş.

frown ['fraun] **1.** n. kaş çatma, hiddetli bakış; **2.** vb. kaşlarını çatmak; hiddetle bakmak; ~ **at**, ~ **(up)on** uygun görmemek, tasvip etmemek, hoş görmemek.

frowst F [fraust] n. küf kokusu, küflülük, havasızlık; **'frowst.y** ☐, **frowz.y** ['frauzi] küf kokulu, havasız; dağınık, pasaklı, şapşal.

froze [frəuz] pret. of **freeze 1**; **'fro.zen 1.** p.p. of **freeze 1**; **2.** adj. donmuş, buz kesilmiş; buz gibi, soğuk davranışlı; com donmuş (kıymetler); ~ **meat** dondurulmuş et.

fruc.ti.fi.ca.tion [frʌktifi'keiʃən] n. verimlilik, bereket; **fruc.ti.fy** ['ˍfai] v/t. meyve verir hale getirmek, verimli hale getirmek; v/i. meyve vermek, verimli olm., bereketli olm. (a. fig.).

fru.gal ☐ ['fru:gəl] tutumlu, idareli, ekonomik; ucuz; **fru.gal.i.ty** [ˍ'gæliti] n. tutumluluk, idareli olma.

fruit [fru:t] **1.** n. meyve, yemiş; fig. verim, sonuç; semere; **2.** v/i. meyve vermek; **'fruit.age** n. meyve verme; meyve; sonuç, netice; **frui.ta.ri.an** [fru:-'tɛəriən] n. meyve ile beslenen kimse; **'fruit-cake** n. meyveli pasta, kek; **'fruit.er** n. meyve veren ağaç; meyve taşıyan gemi; **'fruit.er.er** n. manav, yemişçi; **fruitful** ☐ ['ˍful] meyve veren, yemiş veren, verimli (a. fig.); **'fruitful.ness** n. verim, bereket (a. fig.); **fru.i.tion** [fru:'iʃən] n. gerçekleşme, muradına erme, istediğini elde etme; **fruit knife** meyve bıçağı; **fruitless** ☐ meyvesiz; fig. verimsiz; faydasız, nafile; **'fruit-ma.chine** n. F kumar makinesi; **fruit sal.ad** meyve salatası; **'fruity** adj. meyve lezzetinde; meyveli; F çatlak; dolgun, yumuşak (ses), süslü.

frump [frʌmp] n. fig. derbeder kılıklı kimse, üstü başı dökülen kimse; **'frump.ish**, **'frump.y** adj. derbeder kılıklı, üstü başı dökük, demode, rü-

küş.

frus.trate [frʌs'treit] v/t. önlemek, engel olm., işini bozmak; hüsrana uğratmak, hayal kırıklığına uğratmak; **frus'tra.tion** n. önleme, engel olma; psych hüsran, hayal kırıklığı.

fry [frai] **1.** n. kızartma; yeni doğmuş balık; **small** ~ F çocuklar, çoluk çocuk; önemsiz kimse; **2.** v/t. & v/i. kızar(t)-mak; **fried potatoes** pl. kızarmış patates; **'fry.ing-pan** n. tava; **get out of the** ~ **into the fire** yağmurdan kaçıp doluya tutulmak.

fuch.sia bot ['fju:ʃə] n. küpeçiçeği.

fud.dle ['fʌdl] **1.** v/t. şaşırtmak, sersemletmek, sarhoş etm.; **2.** n. sersemlik, şaşkınlık, sarhoşluk.

fudge F [fʌdʒ] **1.** vb. ileri gitmek; umulduğu gibi başaramamak; tahrif etm., uydurmak; abartmak, yalan söylemek, aldatmak; **2.** n. yumuşak bir şekerleme; saçma, boş laf; ~**!** saçma!.

fu.el ['fjuəl] **1.** n. yakacak, yakıt, akaryakıt; мот benzin; ~ **oil** mazot, akaryakıt; **2.** vb. yakıt sağlamak, yakıt yüklemek; desteklemek, teşvik etm.; мот benzin almak.

fug [fʌg] **1.** n. havasızlık; **2.** v/i. havasız bir yerde dolaşmak; v/t. havasını kirletmek.

fu.ga.cious [fju:'geiʃəs] adj. çabuk uçan, uçucu; kısa süreli, geçici.

fu.gi.tive ['fju:dʒitiv] **1.** adj. geçici, muvakkat, kısa süreli, fani (a. fig.); **2.** n. kaçak, firarî; mülteci.

fu.gle.man ['fju:glmæn] n. talimli asker; şef.

fugue mus [fju:g] n. füg, çok sesli müzikte beste.

ful.crum ['fʌlkrəm] n. mec dayanak noktası, dayanma noktası, manivela dayanağı.

ful.fil(l) [ful'fil] v/t. yerine getirmek, yapmak, icra etm.; tamamlamak, bitirmek; **ful'fil.er** n. yerine getiren, yapan, icra eden, görevini tamamlayan b-i; **ful'fil(l)ment** n. icra, yapma, yerine getirme, tamamlama.

ful.gent poet. ['fʌldʒənt] adj. göz kamaştıracak derecede parlak.

full¹ [ful] **1.** ☐ com. dolu; dolgun, tombul; bol, geniş, meşgul; tam; bütün; tok; olgun; **at** ~ **length** etraflıca, tafsilatıyla, uzun uzadıya; tam boy (resim); **of** ~ **age** reşit, ergin; ~ **stop** gr nokta; ~ **up** tamamen dolu, dopdolu; ~ **house** theat her yerin dolu olması; **2.** adv.

tam, tamamen; fazlasıyla, pek çok;
doğru; **3.** *n.* son had, aşırı derece doluluk; *in ~* tam olarak, eksiksiz; *pay in ~*
tamamen ödemek; *to the ~* tamamiyle,
son haddine kadar.

full² MEC [-] *v/t.* büzüp kalınlaştırmak;
bollaştırmak, genişletmek.

full..; '~'**back** *n. futbol:* bek, defans
oyuncusu; '~'**blood.ed** *adj.* safkan;
kuvvetli, dinç; '~'**blown**adj. tamamen
açmış (çiçek); '~'**bod.ied**adj. cüsseli,
kapı gibi; önemli; kuvvetli derecede
(içki); *~* **dress** resmi elbise, merasim
elbisesi; '~'**dress** *adj.* ayrıntılı; *~ debate* geniş kapsamlı müzakere, tartışma; *~ rehearsal* THEAT kostümlerle
yapılan prova, genel prova.

full.erMEC ['fulə] *n.* çırpıcı; demirci çekici.

full..; '~'**fledged** *adj.* ORN kanatları
olan, uçabilen; '~'**grown** *adj.* olgun,
kemale ermiş, reşit, ergin.

full-ing-mill MEC ['fuliŋmil] *n.* çırpıcı
dibeği.

full-length ['ful'leŋθ] *adj.* tam boy
(*portre*); standart uzunlukta.

ful(l).ness ['fulnis] *n.* dolgunluk; bolluk, çokluk; şişmanlık; olgunluk, kemal; bütünlük.

full..; '~'**page**adj. tam sayfa; '~'**scale**
adj. orijinal boyutta; tam; eldeki bütün
kaynakları kullanarak yapılan;
'~'**time**adj. bütün günlük.

ful.ly ['fuli] *adv.* tamamen, bütünüyle;
en azından, hiç olmazsa; *~ two hours*
en azından iki saat; '~'**fash.ioned**adj.
vücuda tam uyacak şekilde yapılmış
(*kadın çorabı vs.*).

ful.marORN ['fulmə] *n.* martıya benzer
bir tür deniz kuşu.

ful.mi.nate *fig.* ['fʌlmineit] *v/i.* ateş
püskürmek, karşı çıkmak; patlamak,
gürlemek (*against -e*); **ful.mi'na.tion**
n. patlama, ateş püskürme, lânet okuma.

ful.some□ ['fulsəm] aşırı, fazla; samimiyetsiz, yalancı, dalkavukça.

fum.ble['fʌmbl] *v/i.* el yordamıyla aramak (*for -i*), elleri beceriksizce kullanmak; *v/t.* tutamamak; becerememek;
(oyunda topu) düşürmek; '**fum.bler**
n. beceriksiz kimse.

fume[fju:m] **1.** *n.* duman, buhar, pis kokulu duman; öfke, hiddet; *in a ~* hiddetle, öfkeyle; **2.** *v/t.* tütsülemek; *v/i.*
kızmak, öfkelenmek; duman çıkar-
mak.

fu.mi.gate['fju:migeit] *v/t.* buharla dezenfekte etm.; **fu.mi'ga.tion**n. buharla
dezenfekte etme.

fum.ing □ ['fju:miŋ] hiddetli, kızgın;
duman çıkaran.

fun[fʌn] *n.* eğlence; şaka, lâtife, alay;
make ~ of ile alay etm., eğlenmek.

func.tion['fʌŋkʃən] **1.** *n.* görev, vazife,
iş; tören, merasim; *physiol*, MATH fonksiyon; **2.** *v/i.* iş görmek, işlemek, çalışmak, görevini yapmak; **func.tion.al**□
['-ʃənl] görevsel, vazifeye ait; işlevsel;
vücut organlarının görevine ait; MATH
fonksiyonel; pratik; **func.tion.ar.y**
['-ʃnəri] *n.* görevli memur.

fund[fʌnd] **1.** *n.* stok; sermaye, kapital;
fon; *~s* pl. para, sermaye, fon; *in ~s* eldeki para; **2.** *vb.* sermaye bulmak, para
temin etm.; kısa vadeli bir borcu uzun
vadeli borca çevirmek.

fun.da.men.tal [fʌndə'mentl] **1.** □
esaslı, önemli, mühim, temele ait, temel...; **2.** *n. ~s* pl. kurallar, prensipler.

fu.ner.al['fju:nərəl] **1.** *n.* cenaze töreni,
cenaze alayı, gömme merasimi, def-
netme; **2.** *adj.* cenaze törenine ait, cenaze...; *~ pile* üzerinde cesetlerin
yakıldığı odun yığını; **fu.ne.re.al** □
[-'niəriəl] cenaze...; kasvetli, sıkıcı,
hazin.

fun.fair['fʌnfɛə] *n.* lunapark.

fun.gous ['fʌŋgəs] *adj.* mantara benzer, mantara ait, mantardan oluşan;
fun.gus ['-gəs] *n., pl. mst* **fun.gi**
['-gai] BOT mantar; MED yara etrafındaki mantar, ur.

fu.nic.u.lar[fju:'nikjulə] **1.** *adj.* kablolu...; **2.** *n. a. ~ railway* kablolu demiryolu, funiküler.

funkF [fʌŋk] **1.** *n.* korku, dehşet; korkak
kimse; **2.** *v/t. & v/i.* çok korkmak; korkup kaçmak; '**funk.y**adj. F duygulu ve
ritmik (*müzik*); korkak.

fun.nel['fʌnl] *n.* huni; boru; NAUT, RAIL
baca.

fun.nies Am. ['fʌniz] *pl. = comics.*

fun.ny□ ['fʌni] eğlenceli, komik, gülünç; garip, acayip, tuhaf; '~'**bone** *n.*
dirsekteki çok duyarlı bir sinirin geçtiği yer.

fur[fə:] **1.** *n.* kürk, post; kürk manto;
pas, kir; *~s* pl. kürklü giyecekler; *make
the ~ fly* ortalığı birbirine katmak, olay
çıkarmak; **2.** *v/t.* kürkle kaplamak;
kürkle süslemek; *v/i.* paslanmak, kirlenmek; *~red* paslı (*dil*).

fur.be.low['fə:biləu] *n.* elbisede gerek-

fuzzy

siz süs, fırfır, farbala.

fur.bish['fə:biʃ] v/t. parlatmak, yeni gibi yapmak; tazelemek.

fur.ca.tion[fə:'keiʃən] n. çatallanma, dallanma.

fu.ri.ous □ ['fjuəriəs] öfkeli, kızgın, küplere binmiş, tepesi atmış; şiddetli, sert.

furl [fə:l] v/t. & v/i. sar(ıl)mak, katla(n)mak.

fur.long['fə:lɔŋ] n. bir milin sekizde biri, 201 metrelik mesafe.

fur.lough['fə:ləu] 1. n. sıla (izni); 2. v/t. sıla izni vermek (part. MIL).

fur.nace ['fə:nis] n. ocak, kalorifer ocağı.

fur.nish['fə:niʃ] v/t. döşemek; tedarik etm., sağlamak, teçhiz etm., vermek (**with** ile); '**fur.nish.er** n. mobilyacı; '**furnish.ings** n. pl. mobilya, eşya, takım, teçhizat.

fur.ni.ture['fə:nitʃə] n. mobilya, eşya, malzeme; MEC matbaa yazılarının arasını doldurmak için kullanılan parçalar.

fu.ro.re[fjuə'rɔ:ri] n. taşkınlık, heyecan, kızgınlık, velvele.

fur.ri.er['fʌrəu] 1. n. kürkçü; '**fur.ri.er.y** n. kürkçülük.

fur.row['fʌrəu] 1. n. saban izi, tekerlek izi; yüz ve alındaki kırışıklık; 2. vb. saban izi yapmak; yüzde kırışıklık oluşturmak.

fur.ry['fə:ri] adj. kürk kaplı, kürke benzer; kürk...

fur.ther['fə:ðə] 1. adj. & adv. daha fazla, daha öteye, daha ileriye; ayrıca, bundan başka; daha çok; 2. v/t. ilerletmek, ilerlemesine yardımcı olm.; '**further.ance** n. ilerleme; yardım; '**further.er**n. ilerleten; yardım eden; '**further'more**adv. ayrıca, bundan başka, ilaveten; '**fur.thermost**adj. en ilerideki.

fur.thest ['fə:ðist] s. **furthermost**; **at** (**the**) ~ en fazla; en ileride; en son.

fur.tive□ ['fə:tiv] gizli, sinsi.

fu.ry['fjuəri] n. kızgınlık, öfke, hiddet; şiddet; sinirli kadın veya kız, şirret kadın.

furzeBOT [fə:z] n. katırtırnağına benzer bir bitki.

fuse[fju:z] 1. v/t. & v/i. eri(t)mek; eriyip kaynaşmak; eritip kaynatmak; sigorta atmak; sigorta takmak; birleştirmek; MIL tapa koymak; 2. n. ELECT sigorta; MIL tapa; patlama cihazı; **time-~** saniyeli tapa.

fu.se.lage['fju:zilɑ:ʒ] n. uçak gövdesi, gövde.

fu.si.bil.i.ty[fju:zə'biliti] n. erime kabiliyeti; **fu.si.ble**['fju:zəbl] adj. eritilebilir.

fu.sil.ierMIL [fju:zi'liə] n. (Bazı İngiliz alaylarında) eski tip tüfekli asker.

fu.sil.lade[fju:zi'leid] n. yaylım ateşi.

fu.sion ['fju:ʒən] n. eri(t)me; birleş(tir)me; ~ **bomb** MIL hidrojen bombası.

fuss F [fʌs] 1. n. telaş, yaygara, karışıklık; itiraz, şikâyet; tartışma; aşırı övgü; **make a** ~ **about**mesele yapmak; **make a** ~ **of s.o.** b-ne aşırı itina göstermek; 2. v/t. & v/i. titiz davranmak, aşırı itina göstermek; ufak ayrıntılarla uğraşmak; yakınmak; sinirlen(dir)mek; telaşa vermek; '**fuss.y** □ F titiz, kılı kırk yaran, telaşçı, sinirli, huysuz; çok süslü, cicili bicili.

fus.tianCOM ['fʌstiən] n. kalın ve kaba yünlü kumaş, dimi; fig. laf bolluğu, saçma konuşma.

fust.i.ness['fʌstinis] n. küflülük, kokmuşluk, çürük kokma; demodelik, geri kafalılık; '**fust.y** □ küflü, kokmuş; fig. modası geçmiş, demode, eski kafalı.

fu.tile □ ['fju:tail] beyhude, boş, sonuçsuz, nafile; değersiz; **fu.til.i.ty** [-'tiliti] n. yararsızlık, faydasızlık, sonuç vermeyiş, abes oluş.

fu.ture['fju:tʃə] 1. adj. gelecekteki, istikbalde olan, müstakbel; ~ **tense** GR gelecek zaman; 2. n. gelecek, istikbal; ~**s** pl. COM vadeli alım satım; '**fu.tur.ism** n. PAINT fütürizm; **fu.tu.ri.ty** [fju:'tjuəriti]n. istikbal, gelecek; ileride olacak olay.

fuzz[fʌz] 1. n. tüy, hav; kabarık veya kıvırcık saç; 2. v/i. tüylenmek; v/t. tüylerle kaplamak; bulanıklaştırmak; '**fuzzy**□ tüy gibi; bulanık, donuk, belirsiz; kabarık (saç).

G

gab F [gæb] *n.* gevezelik, boş laf, konuşma; *the gift of the ~* konuşkanlık, konuşma yeteneği, çenebazlık.

gab.ar.dine ['gæbədi:n] *n.* gabardin.

gab.ble ['gæbl] **1.** *n.* gevezelik, boş laf, anlamsız söz, anlaşılmaz konuşma; **2.** *vb.* çok hızlı konuşmak; gevezelik etm.; anlamsız şeyler söylemek; 'gab**bler** *n.* geveze, boşboğaz, lakırdıcı; 'gab.by *adj.* F konuşkan, geveze, boşboğaz, çenebaz.

gab.er.dine ['gæbədi:n] *n.* palto, aba; iş elbisesi; Ortaçağda Musevilerce giyilen kaba ve bol cüppe; = *gabardine.*

ga.ble ['geibl] *n.* çatı altındaki üç köşeli duvar; 'ga.bled *adj.* böyle duvarı olan.

ga.by ['geibi] *n.* ahmak *veya* budala kimse.

gad F [gæd]: *~ about* v/i. başıboş dolaşmak, aylak aylak gezmek; BOT üremek, türemek; 'gad.a.bout *n.* F avare kimse, başıboş kimse.

gad.fly ZOO ['gædflai] *n.* atsineği.

gadg.et *sl.* ['gædʒit] *n.* küçük alet, hünerli alet, cihaz.

Gael.ic ['geilik] *n.* İskoçya Keltlerinin dili; Gal dili.

gaff [gæf] *n.* balıkçı zıpkını; döğüş horozunun ayağına geçirilen madenî mahmuz; NAUT randa yelkeninin üst sereni; *sl.* hile, oyun, dolap; *blow the ~ sl.* sırrı söylemek, gizli planı açıklamak.

gaffe F [gæf] *n.* gaf (yapma), pot kırma, çam devirme.

gaf.fer F ['gæfə] *n.* yaşlı adam, ihtiyar, taşralı yaşlı kimse; ustabaşı.

gag [gæg] **1.** *n.* ağız tıkacı (*a. fig.*); PARL mecliste serbest konuşmayı engelleme; THEAT sahnede oyuncu tarafından eklenen söz *veya* hareketler; şaka, latife; **2.** *vb.* ağzını tıkamak, susturmak; THEAT oyuna söz *veya* hareketler eklemek; *fig.* serbest konuşmasını önlemek, *b-nin* ağzını tıkamak.

ga.ga *sl.* ['gɑːgɑː] *adj.* bunak, deli, kaçık.

gage¹ [geidʒ] **1.** *n.* rehin; pey; düelloya davet için yere atılan eldiven; **2.** *vb.* *bşi* rehin vermek, pey vermek.

gage² [-] = *gauge.*

gag.gle ['gægl] *n.* kaz sürüsü; *fig.* çenebaz kadınlar grubu.

gai.e.ty ['geiəti] *n.* neşe, şenlik, eğlence; parlak görünüş, gösteriş.

gai.ly ['geili] *adv. of gay.*

gain [gein] **1.** *n.* kâr, kazanç, gelir; yarar; artma, artış (*part.* COM *~s pl.*); **2.** *vb.* kazanmak, elde etm., arttırmak, eklemek, kâr etm.; ileri gitmek (*saat*); varmak *-e; ~ in* kilo almak, şişmanlamak; *~ on* yaklaşmak, aradaki mesafeyi kapatmak; 'gain.er *n.* kazanan kimse *veya* şey; **gain.ful** □ ['-ful] kazançlı, kârlı; *~ employment* para karşılığı yapılan iş, kazançlı iş; *~ly occupied* para ile tutulmuş *b-i,* meslek sahibi; 'gain.ings *n. pl.* kazanç, kâr, gelir.

gain.say *lit.* [gein'sei] (*irr.* **say**) v/t. inkâr etm., reddetmek.

gainst *poet.* [geinst] = *against.*

gait ['geit] *n.* yürüyüş, gidiş, yürüme *veya* koşma şekli.

gai.ter ['geitə] *n.* tozluk, getir.

gal *Am. sl.* [gæl] *n.* kız.

ga.la ['gɑːlə] *n.* gala, bayram, şenlik.

ga.lac.tic AST [gə'læktik] *adj.* gökadaya ait, gökada...

gal.an.tine ['gælənti:n] *n.* galantin, haşlanmış söğüş et.

gal.ax.y ['gæləksi] *n.* AST gökada; samanyolu; *fig.* seçkin kimseler topluluğu.

gale [geil] *n.* bora, fırtına; *fig.* kahkaha tufanı.

ga.le.na MIN [gə'li:nə] *n.* kükürt kurşunu, galen.

gall¹ [gɔ:l] *n.* safra, öd; *fig.* acı duygu; *part. Am. sl.* yüzsüzlük, arsızlık, terbiyesizlik.

gall² BOT [-] *n.* mazı, ağaç uru.

gall³ [-] **1.** *n.* yara, acı veren şişkinlik, sürtünmekten açılmış yer; *fig.* duygularını incitme, utandırma; **2.** v/t. sürterek yara etm.; üzmek, incitmek.

gal.lant ['gælənt] **1.** □ cesur; gösterişli; nazik, kibar; **2.** *n.* çapkın adam; kadınlara karşı hep nazik olan delikanlı; centilmen delikanlı; moda budalası kimse; **3.** *vb.* kadınlara kur yapmak; *fig.* kadınlara nezaket göstermek; modaya uygun giyinmek; 'gal.lant.ry *n.* cesaret, kahramanlık, yiğitlik; kadınlara karşı neza-

gap

ket; âşıkane söz *veya* davranış.

gal.leon NAUT ['gæliən] *n.* kalyon.

gal.ler.y ['gæləri] *n.* galeri; tiyatroda en ucuz yerlere oturan kimseler; üstü kapalı balkon; dehliz, koridor, tünel; MIN galeri; *play to the* ~ halkın sempatisini kazanmaya çalışmak.

gal.ley ['gæli] *n.* NAUT kadırga; NAUT gemi mutfağı; TYP dizilmiş harflerin konulduğu tekne, gale; ~ **proof** ilk düzeltme; '~-**slave** *n.* kürek mahkûmu, forsa.

Gal.lic ['gælik] *adj.* Galya ile ilgili; *co.* Fransa'ya ait; **Gal.li.can** ['-kən] *adj.* Galya *veya* Fransa'ya ait; **Gal.li.cism** ['-sizəm] *n.* Fransızca'dan alınmış terim.

gal.li.vant [gæli'vænt] *v/i.* başıboş dolaşmak, aylak aylak gezmek, gezip tozmak, zevk peşinde koşmak, gününü gün etmeye bakmak.

gall-nut ['gɔːlnʌt] *n.* mazı, yumru.

gal.lon ['gælən] *n.* galon (*4,54 litre, Am. 3,78 litre*).

gal.lop ['gæləp] **1.** *n.* dörtnala gidiş; **2.** *vb.* dörtnala gitmek; koşuşturmak; acele etm.; hızla gelişmek.

gal.lows ['gæləuz] *n. sg.* darağacı; '~-**bird** *n.* asılmaya layık herif, ip kaçkını.

Gal.lup poll ['gæləp'pəul] *n.* kamuoyu yoklaması.

ga.lore [gə'lɔː] *adv.* bol bol, bol miktarda.

ga.losh [gə'lɔʃ] *n.* kaloş, şoson, yağmurlu havada giyilen lastik.

ga.lumph [gə'lʌmf] *v/i.* çalım atarak yürümek, fiyakalı biçimde yürümek.

gal.van.ic [gæl'vænik] *adj.* (~**ally**) galvanik, galvanizme ait; **gal.va.nism** ['gælvənizəm] *n.* galvanizm, kimyasal güçle üretilen elektrik; '**gal.va.nize** *v/t.* galvanizlemek, galvanizle kaplamak; harekete geçirmek (*into -e*); **gal.va.no.plas.tic** ['-nəu'plæstik] *adj.* galvanoplastik.

gam.bit ['gæmbit] *n.* satranç: gambit, daha iyi bir mevki kazanmak için taş feda etme; *fig.* ilk hareket, başlangıç, ilk söz, açış.

gam.ble ['gæmbl] **1.** *v/i.* kumar oynamak (*a. fig.*); **2.** *n.* F kumar, riskli iş (*mst fig.*); '**gam.bler** *n.* kumarbaz; '**gam.bling-den**, '**gam.bling-house** *n.* kumarhane.

gam.boge [gæm'buːʒ] *n.* sanatçıların kullandığı turuncu madde, Hint zamkı, gomagota.

gam.bol ['gæmbəl] **1.** *n.* sıçrama, zıplama, hoplama; **2.** *v/i.* sıçrayıp oynamak, hoplayıp zıplamak.

game[1] [geim] **1.** *n.* oyun, eğlence; oyun aleti; spor; atletizm yarışmaları; oyun partisi; plan, tertip, hile; av; av eti; parti; *beat s.o. at his own* ~ *b-ni* kendi oyunuyle yenmek; *play the* ~ usule uygun oynamak, kurallara uymak; *fig.* açık sözlü ve dürüst olm.; *be off one's* ~ formda olmamak, oynayacak durumda olmamak; *make* ~ *of s.o. b-le* alay etm.; *b-ni* küçük düşürmek; **2.** *adj.* F cesur, yiğit, gözüpek; *die* ~ ölesiye dayanmak, sebat etm.; **3.** *vb.* kumar oynamak.

game[2] [-] *adj.* topal, sakat, kötürüm.

game...: '~-**cock** *n.* dövüş horozu; '~-**keeper** *n.* avlak bekçisi; '~-**laws** *n. pl.* av hukuku, avlanma kuralları; '~-**licence** *n.* avcı tezkeresi; '**games-master** *n.* beden eğitimi öğretmeni; **game.ster** ['-stə] *n.* kumarbaz; '**gaming-house** *n.* kumarhane.

gam.ma rays PHYS ['gæmə'reiz] *n. pl.* gamma ışınları.

gam.mon ['gæmən] *n.* tütsülenmiş jambon; F zırva, saçma, boş laf.

gamp *co.* [gæmp] *n.* büyük şemsiye.

gam.ut ['gæmət] *n.* MUS gam; *fig. bşin* tümü.

gam.y ['geimi] *adj.* cesur, yiğit, gözüpek; av eti kokulu.

gan.der ['gændə] *n.* erkek kaz.

gang [gæŋ] **1.** *n.* takım, ekip, güruh; *b.s.* çete; **2.** *vb.* ~ *up* karşı gelmek, saldırmak (*against, on -e*); '~-**board** *n.* NAUT iskele tahtası; **gang.er** ['gæŋə] *n.* işçi ekibinin başı.

gan.gli.on ['gæŋliən] *n.* ANAT sinir düğümü, ganglion, lenfa bezi; *fig.* kavuşma noktası, ilgi merkezi.

gang-plank NAUT ['gæŋplæŋk] *n.* iskele tahtası.

gan.grene MED ['gæŋgriːn] *n.* kangren.

gang.ster *Am.* ['gæŋstə] *n.* gangster.

gang.way ['gæŋwei] *n.* geçit, yol, pasaj; NAUT borda iskelesi; NAUT iskele tahtası.

gan.net ORN ['gænit] *n.* bir tür deniz kuşu.

gan.try ['gæntri] *n.* RAIL sinyal köprüsü; NAUT yükleme iskelesi.

gaol [dʒeil], '~-**bird**, '**gaol.er** *s. jail* etc.

gap [gæp] *n.* yarık, çatlak, boşluk, aralık, açıklık; eksiklik; geçit; *fig.* ayrılık (*fikir*).

gape [geip] **1.** *v/i.* açık olm., açılmak, yarılmak; ~ **at** esnemek; ağzını açmak; hayretten ağzı açık kalmak; ağzı açık bir şekilde bakakalmak; **2.** *n. the* **~s** *pl.* kümes hayvanlarının ölünceye kadar gagalarının açık kaldığı bir hastalık; esneme nöbeti.

ga.rage ['gærɑːʒ] **1.** *n.* garaj; *Am.* benzin istasyonu; **2.** *v/t.* (*oto*) garaja koymak, garaja sokmak.

garb [gɑːb] **1.** *n.* kıyafet, kılık, üst baş; **2.** *v/t.* giydirmek.

gar.bage ['gɑːbidʒ] *n.* çöp, süprüntü; ~ **can** *Am.*, ~ **pail** çöp kutusu.

gar.ble ['gɑːbl] *v/t.* tahrif etm., bozmak, bazı parçaları seçip kötü bir maksada alet etm.

gar.den ['gɑːdn] **1.** *n.* bahçe; ~*s pl.* park; bostan; **lead s.o. up the** ~ **path** *b-ni* kötü yola sevketmek; **2.** *v/i.* bahçıvanlık etm., bahçe işiyle uğraşmak; '**gar.den.er** *n.* bahçıvan.

gar.de.nia BOT [gɑː'diːnjə] *n.* gardenya.

gar.den.ing ['gɑːdniŋ] *n.* bahçıvanlık; '**gar.den-par.ty** *n.* garden parti, bahçede verilen parti.

gar.gle ['gɑːgl] **1.** *v/t.* gargara etm.; **2.** *n.* gargara.

gar.goyle ARCH ['gɑːgɔil] *n.* çirkin insan *veya* hayvan şeklindeki oluk ağzı.

gar.ish □ ['gɛəriʃ] aşırı parlak, çok süslü, rengârenk, cafcaflı, gösterişli.

gar.land ['gɑːlənd] **1.** *n.* çelenk; **2.** *v/t.* çelenkle süslemek.

gar.lic BOT ['gɑːlik] *n.* sarmısak.

gar.ment ['gɑːmənt] *n.* elbise, giysi.

gar.ner ['gɑːnə] **1.** *n.* tahıl ambarı; *fig.* biriktirilen şey; **2.** *v/t.* toplamak, biriktirmek.

gar.net MIN ['gɑːnit] *n.* lâl taşı, grena, kıymetli bir kırmızı taş.

gar.nish ['gɑːniʃ] *vb.* süslemek, donatmak; yemeği süslemek; garnitür katmak; '**gar.nish.ing** *n.* süsleme, garnitür.

gar.ret ['gærit] *n.* çatı arası, tavan arasındaki oda.

gar.ri.son MIL ['gærisn] **1.** *n.* garnizon; **2.** *vb.* garnizon kurmak; bir yere asker yerleştirmek.

gar.ru.li.ty [gæ'ruːliti] *n.* gevezelik, boşboğazlık; **gar.ru.lous** □ ['gæruləs] geveze, boşboğaz.

gar.ter ['gɑːtə] *n.* çorap bağı; *Am.* jartiyer; **Order of the** ♀ dizbağı nişanı.

gas [gæs] **1.** *n.* gaz, havagazı; F boş laf, anlamsız konuşma, övünme; *Am.* =

gasoline; **step on the** ~ gaza basmak, süratlendirmek; **2.** *vb.* gazla zehirlemek; F saçmalamak, boş boş konuşmak; '~**-bag** *n.* AVIA gaz zarfı, uçakta gaz tutmaya yarayan torba; F laf ebesi, geveze; '~**-brack.et** *n.* gaz kolu; '~**-burn.er** *n.* bek, havagazı memesi; '~**-cham.ber** *n.* gaz odası; '~**-en.gine** *n.* gaz motoru, gazla işleyen makine; **gas.e.ous** ['geizjəs] *adj.* gazlı, gaz gibi, gaz...

gas...: '~**-fire** *n.* gaz ocağı; '~**-fit.ter** *n.* havagazı tesisatçısı; '~**-fit.tings** *n. pl.* havagazı aletleri.

gash [gæʃ] **1.** *n.* uzun ve derin yara, kesik; **2.** *vb.* yaralamak, derin yara açmak.

gas.ket ['gæskit] *n.* NAUT kalçeta, sarılı yelkeni serene bağlamaya yarayan küçük ipler, salmastra; MEC conta.

gas...: '~**-light** *n.* gaz ışığı; '~**-mask** *n.* gaz maskesi; '~**-me.ter** *n.* gaz saati, gaz sayacı; **gas.o.lene, gas.o.line** *Am.* MOT ['gæsəuliːn] *n.* benzin; **gas-om.e.ter** [gæ'sɔmitə] *n.* gazometre; '**gas-oven** *n.* havagazı fırını.

gasp [gɑːsp] **1.** *n.* soluma, nefes; **2.** *v/i.* solumak; soluyarak konuşmak; *a.* ~ **for breath** nefes nefese kalmak, nefesi kesilmek.

gas-pok.er ['gæs'pəukə] *n.* ocak demiri; '**gas-'proof** *adj.* gaz geçirmez; '~**-range** *n.* havagazı ocağı; '**gas-ring** *n.* bek; **gassed** *adj.* gazlanmış, gazlı; gazdan zehirlenmiş; '**gas-stove** *n.* gaz ocağı, fırın; '**gas.sy** *adj.* gaz..., gaz gibi, gazla dolu; '**gas-tar** *n.* kömür katranı.

gas.tric MED ['gæstrik] *adj.* mideye ait, midevî, mide...; **gas.tri.tis** [gæs'traitis] *n.* mide iltihabı, gastrit.

gas.tron.o.my [gæs'trɔnəmi] *n.* iyi yemek seçme, pişirme ve yeme sanatı.

gas-works ['gæswəːks] *n. mst sg.* havagazı üretilen yer, gazhane.

gat *Am. sl* [gæt] *n.* tabanca.

gate [geit] *n.* kapı, giriş, kanal kapağı, su yolu kapağı; dağ geçidi, patika; *spor:* seyirci sayısı; = '~**-money**; '~**-crash.er** *n. sl.* parasız *veya* davetiyesiz giren kimse; '~**-house** *n.* kapıcı odası, bekçi kulübesi; '~**-leg(ged) ta.ble** açılır kapanır ayaklı kanatları olan masa; '~**.man** *n.* AVIA geçit bekçisi; '~**-mon.ey** *n. spor:* hâsilat; '~**-post** *n.* kapı direği; **between you and me and the** ~ laf aramızda, aramızda kalsın; '~**.way** *n.*

giriş yeri, kapı, geçit; *fig.* geçiş; **~ drug** kendisi bağımlılık yaratmayan ama daha ağır uyuşturucuların kullanılmasına yol açabilecek uyuşturucu madde.

gath.er['gæðə] **1.** *v/t.* toplamak, biraraya getirmek; devşirmek, seçmek; yavaş yavaş kazanmak; anlamak, kavramak, sonuç çıkarmak (**from** *-den*); büzmek; **~ speed** hızlanmak; *v/i.* toplanmak, çoğalmak, biraraya gelmek; cerahat toplamak; *a.* **~ to a head** MED iltihaplanıp şişmek; **2.** *n.* **~s** *pl.* kıvrım, büzük; **'gather.ing** *n.* toplantı, toplanma; MED cerahat, apse, iltiyap.

gauche [gəuʃ] *adj.* beceriksiz, acemi; kaba; patavatsız; savruk; **gau.che.rie** ['-əri:] *n.* beceriksizlik; kabalık, münasebetsizlik.

gaud.y ['gɔ:di] **1.** □ zevksizce süslenmiş, aşırı süslü, cicili bicili; **2.** *n.* UNIV yıllık ziyafet.

gauge [geidʒ] **1.** *n.* ölçü, mikyas, ayar, miktar; kalibre; geyç, ölçme aleti; RAIL raylar arasındaki açıklık; MEC enine kesit, çap; COM dokunmuş kumaşın inceliği; **2.** *v/t.* ayar etm., ölçüsünü bulmak, ölçmek; *fig.* tahmin etm.; **'gaug.er** *n.* ölçü aleti, ayar aleti.

Gaul [gɔ:l] *n.* Gal; Galya; Gal'li; *co.* Fransız.

gaunt □ [gɔ:nt] zayıf, ince, kuru, cılız, gıdasızlıktan kurumuş, bir deri bir kemik; tenha, ıssız, korkunç, kasvetli.

gaunt.let[1] [gɔ:ntlit] *n.* zırh eldiveni; uzun eldiven, kolçak; *fig.* meydan okuma; **throw down** (**pick up**, **take up**) **the~** meydan okumak (düelloyu kabul etm., meydan okumayı kabul etm.).

gaunt.let[2][-] : **run the ~** sıra dayağı yemek; *fig.* şiddetli eleştirilere maruz kalmak.

gauze[gɔ:z] *n.* tül, gazlı bez; tül kafes; pus, duman; **silk ~** ipek tül; **'gauz.y** *adj.* tül gibi, hafif, şeffaf.

gave[geiv] *pret. of* **give 1 & 2.**

gav.el *Am.* ['gævl] *n.* açık arttırmacı *veya* hakimlerce kullanılan çekiç, tokmak.

gawkF [gɔ:k] *n.* beceriksiz *veya* utangaç kimse; ahmak kimse, budala kimse, hantal kimse; **'gawk.y***adj.* beceriksiz; utangaç, ahmak; hantal.

gay□ [gei] neşeli, şen, keyifli, neşe dolu, mutlu, neşe saçan; zevk düşkünü; parlak, canlı (*renk*); *Am. sl.* homoseksüel; **~ marriage** eşcinsel evlilik; gay-

e.ty ['geiəti] = **gaiety.**

gaze[geiz] **1.** *n.* dik bakış; **2.** *v/i.* dik dik bakmak, gözünü dikip bakmak (**at** *-e*); **'gaz.er** *n.* dik dik bakan kimse.

ga.zelleZOO [gə'zel] *n.* ceylan, ahu, gazal.

ga.zette[gə'zet] **1.** *n.* (resmi) gazete; **2.** *v/t.* resmi gazetede ilan etm.; **gaz.et-teer**[gæzi'tiə] *n.* coğrafi isimler indeksi.

gear [giə] **1.** *n.* MEC dişli (takımı); MOT şanjman, vites; donanım, tertibat, teçhizat; elbise, eşya, giyim; **in ~** viteste; **out of ~** boşta; **landing~** AVIA iniş takımı; **steering~** NAUT dümen makinesi; MOT direksiyon dişli mekanizması; **hunting~** av malzemesi; **2.** *vb.* vitese takmak; MEC birbirine geçmek; *fig.* uydurmak (**to** *-e*); **~ up** (**down**) vites büyültmek (küçültmek); **'~box***n.* dişli kutusu, vites kutusu; **'gear.ing***n.* şanjman, mekanizma, dişli takımı; **'gear-le.ver** *n.*, *part. Am.* **'gear-shift** vites kolu.

gee[dʒi:] **1.** *n.* g harfi; **2.** *int.* deh!; *Am.* vay canına!, Allah Allah!, ya!, öyle mi?

geese[gi:s] *pl. of* **goose.**

Gei.ger['gaigə]: **~ counter** radyoaktivite ölçme aracı, geyger sayacı.

gei.sha['geiʃə] *n.* geyşa.

gel.a.tin(e)[dʒelə'ti:n] *n.* jelatin; **ge-lat.inize**[dʒi'lætinaiz] *vb.* jelatin yapmak, jelatinle kaplamak; **ge'lat.i-nous***adj.* jelatinli, jelatin gibi.

geld [geld] (*irr.*) *v/t.* hadım etm., kısırlaştırmak, iğdiş etm.; **'geld.ing** *n.* kısırlaştırılmış hayvan (*mst at*).

gel.ig.nite['dʒelignait] *n.* gelignit, jelatinli dinamit.

gelt[gelt] *pret. & p.p. of* **geld.**

gem [dʒem] **1.** *n.* kıymetli taş, cevher, mücevher; *fig.* kıymetli şey, pahalı şey; **2.** *v/t.* kıymetli taşlarla süslemek, donatmak.

Gem.i.ni[dʒenimai] *n.* İkizler burcu.

gen.darme['ʒɑ:ndɑ:m] *n.* jandarma.

gen.derGR ['dʒendə] *n.* cins, ismin cinsi.

geneBIOL [dʒi:n] *n.* gen; **~ therapy** gen tedavisi.

gen.e.a.log.i.cal □ [dʒi:njə'lɔdʒikəl] soy *veya* şecereye ait, soy...; **~ tree** şecere, soy ağacı; **gen.e.al.o.gy**[dʒi:n-i'ælədʒi] *n.* nesep, şecere, soy, silsile.

gen.er.a['dʒenərə] *pl. of* **genus.**

gen.er.al['dʒenərəl] **1.** □ genel, umumî, genel...; şef, amir, reis; ~ *election* genel seçim; *as a ~ rule*, *in* ~ genellikle, ekseriya; ~ *knowledge* genel bilgi; **2.** *n.* MIL general; F *a.* ~ *servant* hizmetçi kız; **gen.er.al.i.ty** [~'ræliti] *n.* genel kural, genellik, umumiyet; şüpheli söz; **gen.er.ali.za.tion** [~rəlai'zeiʃən] *n.* genelleştirme, umumileştirme, genellik, umumilik; genel bir sonuç çıkarma; **'gen.er.al.ize** *vb.* genelleştirmek, umumileştirmek, genel bir sonuç çıkarmak, genel olarak ifade etm.; **'gen.er.al.ly** *adv.* genellikle, ekseriya, geniş ölçüde; detaylara inmeden, genel olarak; **'gen.er.al.ship** *n.* generallik; liderlik, başkanlık, önderlik, müdürlük, şeflik.

gen.er.ate ['dʒenəreit] *v/t.* husule getirmek, doğurmak, üretmek, meydana getirmek, oluşturmak (*a. fig.*); '**gen.er.ating sta.tion** elektrik santralı; **gen.er'ation** *n.* meydana getirme, üretme; nesil, döl, soy; ortalama olarak insan nesli sayılan otuz yıl; batın; **gen.er.a.tive** ['-rətiv] *adj.* üretken; doğuşa ait; üreme kabiliyeti olan; **gen.er.a.tor** ['-reitə] *n.* üreten kimse, doğuran kimse, meydana getiren kimse; MEC jeneratör; *part.* Am. MOT dinamo.

ge.ner.ic [dʒi'nerik] *adj.* cinse ait; genel, umumî; geniş kapsamlı.

gen.er.os.i.ty [dʒenə'rɔsiti] *n.* cömertlik, eli açıklık; gönlü yücelik; '**gen.er.ous** □ cömert, eliaçık; yüce gönüllü, asil; bol, bereketli, verimli.

gen.e.sis ['dʒenisis] *n.* başlangıç, başlama noktası, menşe, yaradılış; ≈ *İncil ve Tevrat*: İlk kitap.

ge.net.ic [dʒi'netik] *adj.* (~*ally*) bir şeyin aslına ait; genetiğe ait, genetik...; ~ *code* genetik kod; ~ *engineering* genetik mühendisliği; ~ *fingerprinting* suçluların bulunması ya da hastalıkların önlenmesi için bir kimsenin genetik kimliğinin saptanması; **ge'net.i.cal.ly en.gin.eered** genetik mühendisliği yoluyla elde edilmiş; **ge'net.i.cal.ly mod.i.fied** genetik olarak değiştirilmiş; *abbr.* GM; **ge'net.ics** *mt. pl.* genetik, soyaçekim olaylarını inceleyen biyoloji dalı.

gen.ial □ ['dʒi:njəl] güler yüzlü, hoş, sempatik, arkadaş canlısı; elverişli, müsait, uygun (*iklim*); **ge.ni.al.i.ty** [-ni'æliti] *n.* sempatiklik, sevimlilik, nezaket, güler yüzlülük.

ge.nie ['dʒi:ni] *n.* cin, peri (*Arap hikâyelerinde*).

ge.ni.i ['dʒi:niai] *pl. of* **genius**.

gen.i.tals ['dʒenitlz] *n. pl.* tenasül (*veya* üreme) organları.

gen.i.tive GR ['dʒenitiv] *n. a.* ~ *case* -in hali.

gen.ius ['dʒi:njəs] *n.*, *pl.* **ge.ni.i** ['-niai] deha; üstün kabiliyet, istidat, yetenek; dâhi; cin, ruh, iblis, peri, doğaüstü yaratık; **gen.ius.es** ['-njəsiz] *n.* deha, dâhilik.

gen.o.cide ['dʒenəsaid] *n.* soykırım, katliam.

Gen.o.ese [dʒenəu'i:z] **1.** *n.* Cenovalı kimse; **2.** *adj.* Cenovalı, Cenevizli.

genre [ʒɑ:ŋr] *n.* tarz, tür, nevi; ~*painting* günlük hayatı anlatan üslup.

gent F [dʒent] *n.* kibar adam, beyefendi, centilmen.

gen.teel □ *sl. veya iro.* [dʒen'ti:l] soylu, kibar, nazik, terbiyeli; yüksek tabakaya mensup.

gen.tian BOT ['dʒenʃiən] *n.* yılanotu.

gen.tile ['dʒentail] **1.** *adj.* Musevî olmayan; **2.** *n.* Musevi olmayan kimse.

gen.til.i.ty *mst iro.* [dʒen'tiliti] *n.* kibarlık, asalet, soyluluk.

gen.tle □ ['dʒentl] nazik, kibar; yumuşak; tatlı; ılımlı, mutedil; dikkatli; soylu, asil; '~*folk(s pl.*) soylu kişiler, yüksek tabaka; '~*man n.* centilmen, kibar adam, beyefendi; *gentlemen!* baylar! efendiler!; '~*man.like*, '~*man.ly adj.* centilmence, beyefendiye yakışır şekilde; '~*man's a.gree.ment* centilmen anlaşması, söz anlaşması, kontratsız anlaşma; '**gen.tle.ness** *n.* kibarlık, nezaket; '**gen.tle.wom.an** *n.* hanımefendi, kibar kadın.

gen.try ['dʒentri] *n.* küçültücü soyluluk; *contp.* orta sınıf.

gen.u.flec.tion, **gen.u.flex.ion** [dʒenju:'flekʃən] *n.* diz çökme (*ibadet ederken*).

gen.u.ine □ ['dʒenjuin] hakiki, gerçek, taklit olmayan; içten, samimi.

ge.nus ['dʒi:nəs] *n.*, *pl.* **gen.er.a** ['dʒenərə] cins, nevi, çeşit, tür, sınıf.

ge.o.cen.tric [dʒi:əu'sentrik] *adj.* yeryüzünün merkezine ait.

ge.od.e.sy [dʒi:'ɔdisi] *n.* yeryüzü düzlemini ölçme bilgisi, jeodezi.

ge.og.ra.pher [dʒi'ɔgrəfə] *n.* coğrafyacı, coğrafya uzmanı; **ge.o.graph.ic**, **ge.ograph.i.cal** □ [-ə'græfik(əl)] coğrafî, coğrafyaya ait; **ge.og.ra.phy**

[ˌ'ɔgrəfi] *n.* coğrafya; coğrafya konusunda bilimsel inceleme.

ge.o.log.ic, ge.o.log.i.cal □ [dʒiə'lɔdʒik(əl)] jeolojiye ait, jeolojik; **ge.ol.o-gist** [ˌ'ɔlədʒist] *n.* jeolog; **ge'ol.o.gy** *n.* jeoloji, yerbilim.

ge.om.e.ter [dʒi'ɔmitə] *n.* geometri uzmanı; bir tür tırtıl; **ge.o.met.ric, ge.o-met.rical** □ [dʒiə'metrik(əl)] geometrik; **geometrical progression** geometrik artma *veya* eksilme; **ge.om.e-try** [ˌ'ɔmitri] *n.* geometri.

ge.o.phys.ics [dʒiːəu'fiziks] *n. sg.* jeofizik.

ge.o.pol.i.tics [dʒiːəu'pɔlitiks] *n. sg.* jeopolitik; siyasi ve iktisadi coğrafya.

geor.gette [dʒɔː'dʒet] *n.* ince ipekli kumaş, jorjet.

ge.ra.ni.um BOT [dʒi'reinjəm] *n.* ıtır, sardunya çiçeği.

ger.i.at.rics MED [dʒeri'ætriks] *n. pl.* yaşlıların tıbbi bakımı, yaşlılarla ilgili tıp ihtisası.

germ [dʒəːm] **1.** *n.* mikrop; tohum; başlangıç, başlama noktası (*bir fikrin*); **2.** *vb.* çimlenmek, topraktan fışkırmak, filiz vermek (*a. fig.*).

Ger.man¹ ['dʒəːmən] **1.** *adj.* Almanya *veya* Almanlara ait; **2.** *n.* Alman(ca).

ger.man² [ˌ]: **brother** *etc.* ~ öz kardeş *vs.*; **ger.mane** [dʒəː'mein] *adj.* (*to*) *b-le* ilgili, alâkalı, ilişkili.

Ger.man.ic [dʒəː'mænik] *adj.* Almanya, Almanca *veya* Almlanlarla ilgili; German dil ailesine ait; **Ger.man.ism** ['dʒəːmənizəm] *n.* Alman dili (özelliği); Almanya *veya* Alman geleneklerine karşı özel sevgi.

germ-car.ri.er ['dʒəːmkæriə] *n.* portör, mikrop taşıyıcı *b-i.*

ger.mi.cide ['dʒəːmisaid] *n.* mikrop öldürücü madde, antiseptik dezenfektan.

ger.mi.nal ['dʒəːminl] *adj.* oluşum safhasında; mikrop...; **ger.mi.nate** ['ˌneit] *v/t. & v/i.* filizlen(dir)mek; **ger.mi'na.tion** *n.* filizlenme, sürme, filiz verme.

germ...: '~**proof** *adj.* mikrop geçirmez; ~**war.fare** MIL savaşta mikrop kullanılması.

ger.on.tol.o.gy MED [dʒerən'tɔlədʒi] *n.* yaşlılıkla ilgili bilim dalı.

ger.ry.man.der POL ['dʒerimændə] *n.* seçim bölgesini bir siyasî partinin çıkarına göre ayarlama.

ger.und GR ['dʒerənd] *n.* fiilimsi, ey-

lemsi, ulaç, isim-fiil.

ges.ta.tion [dʒes'teiʃən] *n.* gebelik (süresi); hamilelik (süresi).

ges.tic.u.late [dʒes'tikjuleit] *v/i.* konuşurken el hareketleri yapmak; el hareketleri yaparak konuşmak, jestler yapmak; **ges.tic.u'la.tion** *n.* konuşurken el hareketleri yapma; konuşurken yapılan el hareketi.

ges.ture ['dʒestʃə] *n.* hareket, jest.

get [get] (*irr.*) **1.** *v/t.* almak, elde etm., ele geçirmek; olmak; sağlamak, hazırlamak, tedarik etm.; başlamak; yaptırmak; ikna etm.; sebep olm.; kazanmak; yakalanmak (*hastalığa*); ceza yemek, hapse mahkûm edilmek; anlamak, kavramak; şaşırtmak; *b-ni* sıkıştırmak; başarmak; *-mek* fırsatı bulmak, *-mek* fırsatına erişmek; **have got** sahip olm., ...si olm.; **you have got to obey** F itaat etmeye mecbursun, itaat etmelisin, itaat etmen gerekir, itaat etmek zorundasın; ~ **one's hair cut** saçını kestirmek; ~ **me the book!** kitabı bana getir!; ~ **by heart** ezberlemek; ~ **with child** hamile bırakmak, gebe bırakmak; ~ **away** kaçmak, kurtulmak; ~ **down** masadan kalkmak; canını sıkmak, moralini bozmak; yutmak; yazmak, not etm.; aşağı inmek; ~ **in** varmak; içeri girmek; seçilmek; toplamak; tedarik etm.; kaldırmak (*ürün*); ~ **s.o. in** *b-ni* eve çağırmak; ~ **off** inmek (*araçtan*); başlamak; göndermek; cezadan kurtarmak; çıkarmak; ~ **on** binmek (*araca*); uyuşmak, anlaşmak, geçinmek; ~ **out** dışarı çıkmak; açığa çıkmak, ortaya çıkmak (*sır*); güçlükle söylemek; yayınlamak; dağıtmak; kaç(ın)mak; yavaş yavaş bırakmak (*kötü alışkanlık*); çıkarmak; ~ **over** unutmak; üzerinden atmak (*öfke, şok*); yenmek anlaşılmasını sağlamak; ~ **through** geçmek (*imtihanı*); bitirmek; anlamasını sağlamak; geçirmek (*imtihanda öğrenciyi, tasarıyı, kanunu*); ~ **up** binmek; yataktan kaldırmak; düzenlemek; ~ **up steam** kuvvetini toplamak; heyecanlanmak *veya* öfkelenmek; hızlanmak, istim kaldırmak; **2.** *v/i.* gelmek; varmak; ulaşmak; ~ **ready** hazırla(n)mak; ~ **about** dolaşmak, ayağa kalkmak (*hastalıktan sonra*); yayılmak (*söylenti*); ~ **abroad** yurt dışına çıkmak; ~ **ahead** geçmek, geride bırakmak, üstün olm.; ilerlemek; ~ **along** geçinmek; idare etm.; başar-

mak, ilerleme kaydetmek; ~ **along
with** *b-le* geçinmek, anlaşmak, uyuşmak, araları iyi olm.; ~ **around to
s.th.** *bşi* geç yapmak, *bşe* eli geç değmek; ~ **at** ulaşmak, yanına varmak; rüşvet vermek; azarlamak; açığa çıkarmak, ortaya çıkarmak (*gerçekleri*); ~
away kurtulmak, kaçmak; ~ **away with**
alıp kaçmak, yakayı ele vermemek,
şüphe uyandırmadan atlatmak; ~ **by**
geçmek; geçinmek; yaşamak; ~ **down
to** uğraşmak, kendini vermek; F işe koyulmak; ~ **in** içeri girmek; varmak; seçilmek; binmek; ~ **into** giymek; girmek; edinmek, sahip olm.; ~ **off** yakayı
kurtarmak, paçayı kurtarmak, kaçmak, sıvışmak; NAUT yola çıkmak; ~
off with s.o. *b-le* tanışmak; hissi *veya*
cinsel ilişkiye girmek; ~ **on** ilerlemek,
gelişme kaydetmek; geçmek (*zaman*);
~ **over** atlatmak (*hastalık*); ~ **through**
temas kurmak; çıkarmak (*telefonda*); ~
to hear *veya* **know** *veya* **learn** duymak
veya bilmek, tanımak *veya* öğrenmek;
~ **up** yataktan kalkmak; ayağa kalkmak; yükselmek, yukarı çıkmak; sertleşmek (*hava*); **get-at-a.ble** [get'æt-
əbl] *adj.* yanına girilebilir, ulaşılabilir;
get-a.way ['getəwei] *n.* spor: start;
kaçış, kaçıp kurtulma; kaçan şey;
make one's ~ kaçmak; **'get.ter** *n.* alan,
kazanan, elde eden *b-i*; gaz giderici
şey; **'get.ting** *n.* elde etme, kazanma,
geçim, kazanç; **'get-up** *n.* tertip, düzen;
Am. F garip kıyafet.

gew.gaw ['gju:gɔ:] *n.* süslü değersiz
şey, biblo, kıymetsiz şey, oyuncak; ~ *s
pl.* süs müs, cici bici, değersiz şeyler.

gey.ser ['gaizə] *n.* GEOGR gayzer, aralıklarla sıcak su fışkırtan kaynak; ['gi:zə]
şofben.

ghast.li.ness ['gɑ:stlinis] *n.* ölü gibi olma, soluk olma; korku, dehşet;
'ghast.ly *adj.* ölü gibi, sapsarı, solgun,
beti benzi atmış; korkunç, dehşetli.

gher.kin ['gə:kin] *n.* turşuluk salatalık,
ufak hıyar.

ghet.to ['getəu] *n.* eskiden bazı ülkeler-
deki Musevi mahallesi; azınlık mahallesi.

ghost [gəust] *n.* hayalet, hortlak; cin; iz,
gölge; ruh; = ~ **writer**, **'ghost.like** *adj.*
hortlak gibi; **'ghost.ly** *adj.* hayalet gibi;
manevî; **ghost writ.er** başkasının adına çalışan yazar.

ghoul [gu:l] *n.* gulyabani; mezar hırsızı;
fig. korkunç zevk ve alışkanlıkları olan

kimse, canavar ruhlu kimse.

gi.ant ['dʒaiənt] **1.** *adj.* dev gibi, iri, kocaman, muazzam; **2.** *n.* dev; anormal
ölçüde insan, hayvan *veya* bitki; olağanüstü yetenekli kimse; **'gi.ant.ess** *n.*
dişi dev, dev gibi kadın.

gib.ber ['dʒibə] *v/i.* çok hızlı ve anlaşılmaz biçimde konuşmak; **gib.ber.ish**
['-riʃ] *n.* anlaşılmaz söz, karışık söz.

gib.bet [dʒibit] **1.** *n.* darağacı; MEC maçuna kolu; **2.** *v/t.* asmak, idam etm., darağacına asmak; *fig.* rezil etm., teşhir
etm.

gib.bon ZOO ['gibən] *n.* uzun kollu bir
maymun cinsi.

gib.bos.i.ty [gi'bɔsiti] *n.* dışbükeylik;
kamburluk; **gib.bous** *adj.* dışbükey;
kambur.

gibe [dʒaib] **1.** *v/i.* alay etm., eğlenmek,
dalga geçmek (*a.* **at s.o.** *b-le*); **2.** *n.* alay,
pis şaka, eşek şakası.

gib.lets ['dʒiblits] *n. pl.* tavuğun yenebilen iç kısımları, tavuk sakatatı.

gid.di.ness ['gidinis] *n.* baş dönmesi,
sersemleme; *fig.* hoppalık, uçarılık,
havaîlik; **'gid.dy**□ baş döndürücü, sersemletici; başı dönen, başı dönmüş; *fig.*
hoppa, uçarı, havaî.

gift [gift] **1.** *n.* hediye, armağan; Allah
vergisi, doğuştan kabiliyet, hüner; verme hakkı, hibe; ~ **card** hediye çeki; ~
shop hediyelik eşya satan dükkân; *s.*
horse; **2.** *vb.* hediye vermek, hibe
etm.; **'gift.ed** *adj.* hünerli, kabiliyetli.

gig [gig] *n.* iki tekerlekli tek katlı hafif
araba; NAUT kık, hafif filika.

gi.gan.tic [dʒai'gæntik] *adj.* (~**ally**) kocaman, dev gibi, aşırı ölçüde.

gig.gle ['gigl] **1.** *vb.* kıkır kıkır gülmek;
kıkırdayarak belirtmek; **2.** *n.* kıkırdama, kıkır kıkır gülme.

gig.o.lo ['ʒigələu] *n.* jigolo, tokmakçı.

gild [gild] (*irr.*) *v/t.* yaldızlamak, altın
rengine boyamak, süslemek, parlak
göstermek, altın kaplamak; ~ **the pill**
fig. göz boyamak; ~**ed youth** zengin
ve moda düşkünü gençlik; **'gild.er** *n.*
yaldızcı; **'gild.ing** *n.* yaldız, altın kaplama.

gill [dʒil] *n.* litrenin sekizde biri kadar
bir sıvı ölçü birimi.

gill [gil] *n.* ICHTH solungaç; *fig.* insan-
larda çene altındaki kısım; BOT ince
yaprak.

gill [dʒil] *n.* kız, sevgili.

gil.lie ['gili] *n.* avcı *veya* balıkçı
yardımcısı.

gilt [gilt] **1.** *pret. & p.p. of gild*; **2.** *n.* yaldız; '**~-edged** *adj.* kenarı yaldızlı; COM emin, sağlam, çok güvenilir; COM *sl.* en iyi kalite, birinci sınıf, mükemmel.

gim.bal ['dʒimbəl] *n. mst* **~s** *pl.* pusula yalpalıkları, yalpa çemberleri.

gim.crack ['dʒimkræk] **1.** *n.* işe yaramaz süs, değersiz süs, süslü adi şey; **2.** *adj.* değersiz, adi, kıymeti olmayan, kötü yapılmış.

gim.let MEC ['gimlit] *n.* burgu, delgi, matkap.

gim.mick *Am. sl.* ['gimik] *n.* hile, tertip, dalavere; hileli alet; bit yeniği.

gin[1] [dʒin] *n.* cin, ardıç rakısı.

gin[2] [_] **1.** *n.* tuzak, kapan; MEC çiğidi pamuktan ayıran makine, çırçır; **2.** *vb.* tuzağa düşürüp yakalamak; MEC pamuk çekirdeklerini çıkarmak.

gin.ger ['dʒindʒə] **1.** *n.* zencefil (kökü); canlılık, enerji; **2.** *vb.* **~ up** canlandırmak, hareketlendirmek; **3.** *adj.* koyu kahverengi, kızılımsı; **~ ale ~ beer** zencefilli alkolsüz içki, gazoz; '**~.bread** *n.* zencefilli çörek *veya* bisküvi; '**gin.ger.ly** *adj. & adv.* ihtiyatlı, tedbirli; yavaşça, ihtiyatla, dikkatle; '**gin.ger-nut** *n.* zencefilli bisküvi.

ging.ham ['giŋəm] *n.* çizgili *veya* kareli pamuklu kumaş.

gip.sy ['dʒipsi] *n.* çingene.

gi.raffe ZOO [dʒi'rɑːf] *n.* zürafa.

gird[1] [gəːd] **1.** *n.* iğneli söz, alaycı söz; **2.** *v/t.* alay etm.; küçümsemek (*at* -*i*).

gird[2] [_] (*irr.*) *vb.* kayışla bağlamak; kuşak sarmak; bağlamak; sarmak, kuşatmak, çevrelemek; hazırlanmak; giydirmek, teçhiz etm.

gird.er MEC ['gəːdə] *n.* kiriş, direk.

gir.dle ['gəːdl] **1.** *n.* kemer, kuşak; korsa; kuşak gibi saran herhangi birşey; **2.** *vb.* çevrelemek, sarmak, kuşatmak; kabuğunu soyarak ağacı kurutmak.

girl [gəːl] *n.* kız; kız evlât; genç kadın; sevgili; hizmetçi kız; '**~-friend** kız arkadaş, sevgili; ♀ **Guide** kız izci; **girl.hood** ['_hud] *n.* kızlık (çağı); **girl.ie** ['_i] *adj.* açık saçık kızları gösteren; '**girl.ish** □ kızlara ait, kız gibi, kıza yakışır; '**girl-ish.ness** *n.* genç kızlık hali; '**girl.y** *adj. Am.* F açık saçık kızları gösteren (*dergi, program*).

girt [gəːt] **1.** *pret. & p.p. of gird*[2]; **2.** *n.* MEC çevre, daire çevresi; genişlik.

girth [gəːθ] *n.* kolan, çevre; kuşak.

gist [dʒist] *n.* ana fikir, meselenin esası,

özet, öz, sadet.

git *sl.* [git] = **get**.

give [giv] **1.** (*irr.*) *v/t.* vermek; emanet etm., teslim etm.; hak vermek; sağlamak, temin etm.; kaynağı olm.; geçirmek, bulaştırmak (*hastalık*); bağışlamak, hibe etm., adamak; **~ attention to** dikkat etm.; **~ battle** savaş vermek, savaşmak; **~ birth to** doğurmak; **~ chase to** kovalamak; **~ credit to** kredi açmak; **~ ear to** kulak vermek, dinlemek; **~ one's mind to** dikkatini vermek; **~ it to s.o.** *b-ni* cezalandırmak, azarlamak, haşlamak; **~ away** feda etm.; hediye etm.; vermek; dağıtmak; F ele vermek, belli etm., sırrını açığa vurmak; **~ away the bride** düğünde gelini damada teslim etm.; **~ back** geri vermek, geri göndermek; geri çekilmek; **~ forth** dışarı vermek, çıkartmak, yaymak, salmak (*koku, duman*); **~ in** vermek, teslim etm.; **~ out** dağıtmak, göndermek; **~ over** vazgeçmek, kesmek, bırakmak; teslim etm.; ayrılmak; **~ up** vazgeçmek; pes etm.; ümidi kesmek; terketmek, bırakmak; **~ o.s. up** teslim olm.; **2.** *v/i. mst* **~ in** vazgeçmek, teslim olm., boyun eğmek, kabul etm.; **~ into**, **~ (up)on** bakmak -*e*; *bşi* küçümsemek, hor görmek; **~ out** bitmek, tükenmek; kuvveti kesilmek; **~ over** durmak, vazgeçmek, kesmek; **3.** *n.* elastikiyet, esneklik; kabullenme; **~ and take** ['givən'teik] *n.* karşılıklı fedakârlık; çalışma, uyuşma; elbirliği; **~-a.way** ['_əwei] *n.* hediye, armağan; açığa vurma, belli etme, istemeyerek ağzından kaçırma; **~ show**, **~ program** radyo, TV: hediyeli, ödüllü yarışma, program; '**given** *p.p. of give 1 & 2*; **~ to** *bşe* düşkün, müptelâ, meyilli; '**giv.er** *n.* veren, hediye eden kimse; saçan kimse (*neşe*); **~ of a bill** keşideci.

giz.zard ORN ['gizəd] *n.* taşlık, boğaz, kursak; **it sticks in my ~** çok gücüme gidiyor, hazmedemiyorum, bana ağır geliyor.

gla.ci.al □ ['gleisjəl] buza ait, buzlu; buz devrine ait; buz gibi; buz...; **~ era** buzul devri; **gla.ci.a.tion** GEOL [glæsi'eiʃən] *n.* buzul ile kaplanma; **gla.cier** ['glæsjə] *n.* buzul; **gla.cis** ['glæsis] *n.* hafif meyilli; kaleden inen bayır; tampon devlet, tampon bölge.

glad □ [glæd] memnun, mutlu, sevinçli (*of, at* -*den*); mutluluk veren; güzel...; **give s.o. the ~ eye** F *b-ne* âşikane bak-

mak, göz etm.; ~ *rags* pl. sl. bayramlık
giysi, en süslü elbise; **glad.den** ['-dn]
v/t. memnun etm., sevindirmek.
glade [gleid] n. ormanda açıklık yer;
Am. bataklık bölgesi.
glad.i.a.tor ['glædieitə] n. gladyatör.
glad.i.o.lus BOT [glædi'əuləs] n. kılıççi-
çeği, glayol, kuzgunkılıcı, kuzgunotu,
keklik çiğdemi.
glad.ly ['glædli] adv. memnuniyetle, seve seve; **glad.ness** n. memnunluk, sevinç; **glad.some** ['-səm] adj. memnun,
sevinçli, neşeli, şen.
Glad.stone ['glædstən] n. a. ~ *bag* bir
çeşit seyahat çantası, bavul, valiz.
glair [gleə] **1.** n. yumurta akı; yumurta
akına benzer yapışkan madde; **2.** vb.
böyle bir madde sürmek.
glam.or.ous ['glæmərəs] adj. göz alıcı,
cazibeli, çekici, cazip, büyüleyici;
glam.our ['-mə] **1.** n. parlaklık, cazibe,
çekicilik, göz alıcılık; ~ *girl* cazibeli kız,
çekici kız, seksî kız; **2.** vb. büyülemek,
cezbetmek.
glance [glɑːns] **1.** n. bakış; göz atma;
parıltı; **2.** vb. göz gezdirmek (*over*
-e); ~ *at* göz atmak -e, bakmak -e; parlamak; *mst* ~ *off* sıyırmak, sıyırıp geçmek; ~ *over* göz gezdirmek -e.
gland ANAT, BOT [glænd] n. bez, gudde,
salgı hücresi, salgı bezi; **glan.dered** VET
['-dəd] adj. ruamlı, sakağı hastalığına
tutulmuş; **glan.ders** VET ['-dəz] n. sg.
bir çeşit at hastalığı, sakağı, ruam;
glan.du.lar ['-djulə] adj. gudde gibi,
guddeye ait, gudde...
glare [gleə] **1.** n. göz kamaştırıcı ışık,
parıltı; dargın bakış, öfkeli bakış, sabit
bakış; **2.** v/i. parıldamak, göz kamaştıracak şekilde parlamak; ters ters bakmak, yiyecekmiş gibi bakmak (*at* -e);
glar.ing ['-riŋ] göz kamaştırıcı,
çok parlak; hemen göze çarpan,
apaçık, bariz; aşırı parlak (*renk*); fig.
kızgın, hiddetli, öfkeli.
glass [glɑːs] **1.** n. cam; bardak; camdan
yapılmış herhangi bş; bir bardak dolusu; ayna; teleskop; barometre; pl. dürbün; (*a pair of*) ~es pl. gözlük; mercek;
cam eşya; **2.** adj. camdan yapılmış
cam...; **3.** v/t. camla kaplamak; cam
takmak; cam kaba koymak; cam gibi
yapmak; v/i. cam gibi olm.; '~-blow.er
n. üfleyerek cam ve şişe yapan kimse;
'~-case n. küçük vitrin, cam dolap;
'~-cut.ter n. cam kesen kimse; camcı
elması; **glass.ful** ['-ful] n. bir bardak

(dolusu); '**glass-house** n. limonluk,
ser; MIL sl. askeri hapishane; '**glass.i-
ness** n. cam gibi olma; çarşaf gibi olma
(*deniz*); donukluk, anlamsızlık;
'**glass.ware** n. züccaciye; '**glass.y**
adj. cam gibi; dümdüz, çarşaf gibi (*deniz*); donuk, anlamsız, dalgın (*bakış*).
glau.co.ma MED [glɔː'kəumə] n. bir göz
hastalığı, gözde karasu hastalığı, glo-
kom; '**glau.cous** adj. mat grimsi yeşil
veya mavi; üstü toza benzer beyaz
bir maddeyle kaplı (*yaprak*, *üzüm*).
glaze [gleiz] **1.** n. cam gibi sır, cila, perdah; **2.** v/t. cilalamak; cam geçirmek -e,
cam takmak; sırlamak; cam gibi bir tabakayla kaplamak; ~*d paper* parlak
kâğıt, cilalı kâğıt; ~*d(-in) veranda*
camlı taraça; v/i. donuklaşmak, an-
lamsızlaşmak, dalmak; **gla.zier** ['-jə]
n. camcı; '**glaz.ing** n. cam takma;
camcılık; sır, mine, cila, emaye; '**glaz.y**
adj. cam gibi, cama benzer; donuk,
dalgın.
gleam [gliːm] **1.** n. parıltı; ışın, şua, hafif
ve geçici ışık; **2.** v/i. parıldamak, ışın
saçmak.
glean [gliːn] v/t. hasattan sonra toplamak; azar azar toplamak (*bilgi*); ortaya çıkarmak; v/i. hasattan sonra ekin
toplamak; azar azar bilgi toplamak;
'**glean.er** n. ekinci; fig. bilgi toplayan
kimse; '**glean.ings** n. pl. çeşitli kay-
naklardan toplanmış bilgi.
glebe [gliːb] n. vakıf arazisi, papazlığa
ait arazi; poet. yer, toprak.
glee [gliː] n. neşe; birkaç sesle söylenen
şarkı; ~ *club* koro kulübü, koro birliği;
glee.ful □ ['-ful] şen, neşeli, sevinçli.
glen [glen] n. küçük vadi, dere.
glib □ [glib] fig. süratli konuşan; içten
olmasa da kolayca söylenen; kayıtsız;
çevik; üstün körü; yarım yamalak;
'**glib.ness** n. çabuk konuşma, akıcılık;
kayıtsızlık, hareketlerde serbestlik.
glide [glaid] **1.** n. kayma; AVIA havada süzülme; GR sesin yavaş değişmesi; **2.** v/i.
kaymak, kayıp gitmek, akmak, süzülmek; motoru işletmeden inmek; '**glid-
er** n. planör; ~ *pilot* planörcü; '**glid.ing**
n. planörcülük; kayma, süzülme, akış.
glim.mer ['glimə] **1.** n. parıltı, hafif ışık,
cılız ışık, donuk ışık; nebze, zerre,
azıcık olan şey; MIN mika; **2.** v/i. parıldamak, hafif ışık vermek, sönük sönük
parıldamak.
glimpse [glimps] **1.** n. kısa bakış, bir an
için görme, gözüne ilişme; **2.** v/t. bir an

için görmek, gözüne ilişmek; v/i. parlayıp sönmek; ~ **at** bir an için bakmak.

glint [glint] 1. v/i. parlamak, parıldamak; 2. n. parıltı, parlaklık.

glis.sade MOUNT [gli'sɑːd] 1. v/i. kaymak; buzlu dağ eteğinde kaymak; 2. n. kayma.

glis.ten ['glisn], **glis.ter** obs. ['glistə], **glitter** ['glitə] v/i. parlamak, parıldamak, pırıldamak; '**glit.ter.ing** adj. parlak, cezbedici, göz alıcı, şaşaalı; ~ **personality** mükemmel kişilik.

gloam.ing ['gloumiŋ] n. akşam karanlığı, alaca karanlık.

gloat [glout]: ~ **(up)on**, ~ **over** v/i. şeytanca bir zevk duymak, şeytani bir zevkle seyretmek; başkalarının başarısızlığını zevkle seyretmek.

glob.al ['gloubəl] adj. tüm dünyayı kapsayan; küresel; dünya çapında; ~ **navigation system** küresel seyir sistemi; ~ **warming** küresel ısınma; **glob.al.i.za.tion** [gloubəlai'zeiʃən] n. küreselleşme; **glob.al.ize** ['gloubəlaiz] v/t. küreselleştirmek (ticareti); **globe** n. küre, top, yuvarlak; dünya; dünya küresi modeli; lamba karpuzu; '**globe-fish** n. ICHTH kirpibalığı; '**globe-trot.ter** n. durmadan dünyayı dolaşan kimse; **glo.bose** ['-bəus], **glob.u.lar** □ ['globjulə] küre şeklinde, küresel; küreciklerden meydana gelen; **glo.bos.i.ty** [gləu'bositi] n. küresellik, yuvarlak olma; **glob.ule** ['globjuːl] n. kürecik, küçük yuvarlak; küçük damla.

gloom [gluːm] 1. n. (yarı) karanlık; belirsizlik, çapraşıklık; üzgünlük, hüzün, kasvet; ümitsizlik; 2. v/i. ümitsiz veya hüzünlü bakmak veya davranmak; surat asmak; kararmak; uzakta hayal gibi gözükmek; v/t. canını sıkmak; kasvetlendirmek; karartmak; '**gloom.i.ness** n. karanlık, kasvet; sıkıcılık; ümitsizlik; mahzunluk, hüzün; '**gloom.y** □ karanlık, kapanık; kederli, endişeli; üzüntülü; kasvetli, sıkıcı; ümitsiz.

glo.ri.fi.ca.tion [gloːrifi'keiʃən] n. övme, ululama, yüceltme; tapma; fazlasıyla büyültme; **glo.ri.fy** ['-fai] v/t. yüceltmek, methetmek, göklere çıkarmak, büyültmek, yükseltmek; tapmak; ululamak, şereflendirmek; F güzelleştirmek, olduğundan daha muhteşem göstermek; '**glo.ri.ous** □ şanlı, şerefli, parlak, muhteşem, mükemmel, fevkalâde; eğlenceli.

glo.ry ['gloːri] 1. n. şan, şeref, ihtişam; övgü, medih; tapınma; şaşaa; 2. v/i. iftihar etm., övünmek, şeref duymak, gururlanmak (in ile).

gloss[1] [glos] 1. n. açıklama (dipnot veya kitap sonundaki), yorum; 2. v/t. açıklamak; açıklayıcı yazı eklemek; yorumlamak; açımlamak.

gloss[2] [-] 1. n. cilâ, perdah; parlaklık; parlak ve düzgün yüzey; aldatıcı görünüş, dış güzellik; 2. v/t. parlatmak, cilâlamak; ~ **over** sahte bir biçimde gizlemek, kusurlarını örtmek, hatalarını örtbas etm.

glos.sa.ry ['glosəri] n. ek sözlük, özel kelimelerin açıklamaları.

gloss.i.ness ['glosinis] n. parlaklık; '**glossy** □ parlak, cilâlı; ~ **periodical** iyi kalite parlak kâğıda basılmış mecmua, part. moda mecmuası.

glot.tis ANAT ['glotis] n. nefes borusunun ağzı, glotis.

glove [glʌv] n. eldiven; s. **hand** 1; '**glov.er** n. eldivenci.

glow [glou] 1. n. kızıllık, kızartı, parlaklık; hararet, ısı; şevk ve gayret; 2. v/i. parıldamak; ısı vermek; kızarmak; yanakları al al olm.; kor haline gelmek, kızıllaşmak; yüzü kızarmak; coşmak, şevklenmek.

glow.er ['glauə] v/i. dik dik bakmak, öfkeyle bakmak, yiyecekmiş gibi bakmak.

glow-worm ['glouwəːm] n. ateşböceği.

gloze [glouz]: ~ **over** v/t. örtbas etm.

glu.cose [gluːkəus] n. glikoz.

glue [gluː] 1. n. tutkal, yapışkan; 2. v/t. tutkallamak, yapıştırmak; fig. iyice yaklaştırmak, gözünü dikmek (**to** -e); '**glue.y** adj. tutkal gibi, yapışkan, yapış yapış.

glum □ [glʌm] asık suratlı, somurtkan; hüzünlü, üzgün; kasvetli.

glut [glʌt] 1. n. bolluk, tokluk; 2. v/t. piyasaya fazla sürmek (mal); tıka basa doyurmak; ağzına kadar doldurmak; tam manasıyla memnun etm.

glu.ten ['gluːtən] n. glüten, nişasta çıkarıldıktan sonra geri kalan albuminli madde; **glu.ti.nous** □ ['-tinəs] yapışkan, yapış yapış; yapışkan gibi, tutkal cinsinden.

glut.ton ['glʌtn] n. obur, boğazına düşkün kimse, pisboğaz, açgözlü kimse (**of, for, at**); ZOO kutup porsuğu; '**glut.ton.ous** □ obur, açgözlü, pisboğaz; '**glut.ton.y** n. oburluk, pisboğazlık, açgözlülük.

glyc.er.in ['glisərin], **glyc.er.ine** [.'ri:n] *n.* gliserin.

G-man *Am.* F ['dʒi:mæn] *n.* Federal soruşturma Bürosu (FBI) memuru.

gnarl [nɑ:l] *n.* budak, yumru, boğum; **gnarled**, *a.* '**gnarl.y** *adj.* budaklı, boğumlu, boğum boğum; yıpranmış, şekli bozuk (*el, parmak*).

gnash [næʃ] *v/t.* gıcırdatmak (*diş*).

gnat [næt] *n.* tatarcık, sivrisinek.

gnaw [nɔ:] *vb.* kemirmek; azap çektirmek, eziyet vermek; aşındırmak; '**gnawer** *n.* kemirgen hayvan, kemiren hayvan *veya* insan.

gnome [nəum] *n.* yeraltındaki hazinelerin bekçileri farzolunan yaşlı cüce; ['nəumi:] vecize, atasözü; **gnom.ish** ['nəumiʃ] *adj.* cüce gibi.

go [gəu] **1.** (*irr.*) *vb. com.* gitmek (*s.a.* **going**, **gone**); ayrılmak; hareket etm., kalkmak; yeri olm.; sığmak; ulaşmak, uzanmak, erişmek; olmak; işlemek, çalışmak; ilerlemek, gelişmek; mevcut olm.; satılmak; harcanmak; elden gitmek, kaybolmak; devam etm.; çökmek, düşmek, kırılmak; iflas etm.; ölmek; sonuçlanmak; uymak; ses çıkarmak; bahse girmek; başlamak; çıkmak; gezmek; ~ *bad* kötüye gitmek; bozulmak, çürümek; *s. mad*; *s. sick*; *the dog must ~* köpeğin gitmesi lâzım, köpeği satmalıyız; *the story ~es* deniliyor ki..., söylendiğine göre; *here ~es!* sl. hadi! yürü! başla!; ~ *it* sl. bir işe koyulmak; ~ *it!* sl. atıl! durma yürü!; *as men*, *etc.* ~ diğer kişilere göre, diğerleri gözönüne alınırsa; *let* ~ bırakmak, salmak; ~ *shares* bölüşmek, paylaşmak; ~ *to see*, ~ *and see* görmeye gitmek, gidip görmek; *just* ~ *and try!* bir denesenize!, bir deneyiverin!; ~ *about* gezmek; dolaşmak (*söylenti*); tiramola etm.; ~ *abroad* yurt dışına çıkmak; ~ *ahead* ilerlemek, gelişmek, ileri gitmek; başlamak; ~ *at* saldırmak; üzerinde çalışmak, *bşi* ele almak; ~ *back* geri dönmek; eskiye uzanmak; ~ *back from*, F *on* vazgeçmek, caymak (*sözünden*); ~ *behind* aslını araştırmak; ~ *between* araya girmek, aralarını bulmak; ~ *by* geçmek; -*e* göre davranmak; ~ *by the name of ...* ...ismiyle tanınmak, ...ismini kullanmak; ~ *down* batmak; yutulmak; üniversiteden mezun olm.; sakinleşmek, durulmak, kesilmek (*deniz, rüzgâr*);

ucuzlamak, azalmak, düşmek (*fiyat*); yenilmek (*before tarafından*); geçmek (*tarihe*); yazılı, kayıtlı olm.; kabul edilmek, beğenilmek, benimsenmek (*with tarafından*); ~ *for* almaya gitmek, gidip getirmek; saldırmak; sayılmak, geçerli olm.; beğenmek; kabul etm.; ~ *for a walk* yürüyüşe çıkmak; ~ *in* girmek, sığmak; bulutlarca engellenmek (*güneş*); *kriket*: vuruş yapmak; katılmak (*yarışmaya*); ~ *in for* girmek, katılmak (*imtihana, yarışmaya*); meraklısı olm., ilgi duymak; ~ *in for an examination* imtihana girmek; ~ *into* girmek; araştırmak, soruşturmak, incelemek; tutulmak (*hastalık*); ~ *off* patlamak, ateş almak; bozulmak, kalitesi düşmek; ekşimek; uyumak; fenalaşmak, bayılmak; satılmak; elden çıkmak; iyi gitmek; çıkmak (*sahneden*); ~ *on* geçmek (*zaman*); devam etm; olmak; sahneye çıkmak; *kriket*: topu savurmak; ~ *on!* devam et!; sana inanacağım sanma!; ~ *out* dışarı çıkmak; gezip tozmak, sosyal faaliyetlere katılmak; sönmek; modası geçmek; görevden ayrılmak; iktidardan çekilmek (*hükümet*); grev yapmak; bitmek, sona ermek (*yıl*); ~ *over* başarı kazanmak, tutmak (*oyun*); etkilemek; tetkik etm., incelemek; prova etm., gözden geçirmek; karşı tarafa geçmek, partisini değiştirmek; ~ *through* kabul edilmek (*tasarı*); neticelenmek, sonuca bağlanmak; gözden geçirmek, incelemek; aramak, araştırmak, yoklamak; yapmak; atlatmak (*zorluk*); geçirmek (*hastalık, tecrübe*); satılmak; harcamak, sarfatmek, yiyip bitirmek; ~ *through with* bşi sonuca bağlamak, bitirmek, tamamlamak, yarım bırakmamak; ~ *to* katkıda bulunmak; ~ *up* yükselmek, çıkmak, artmak; havaya uçmak, patlamak, infilâk etm.; üniversiteye girmek; şehre inmek; tırmanmak; ~ *with* eşlik etm., beraber gitmek; aynı görüşte olm.; uymak, yakışmak; flört etm.; ~ *without* -siz olm., mahrum kalmak, yoksun olm.; **2.** *n.* F gitme, gidiş, hareket; moda; olay, vaka; gayret, enerji; başarı; sefer, sıra; hamle, teşebbüs; izin, müsaade, başlama işareti; MED nöbet, tutulma; *little* ~ UNIV *sl.* ilk imtihan; *great* ~ ana imtihan; *on the* ~ meşgul, aktif, faal, hareket halinde; *it is no* ~ olacak iş değil, hayret edilecek şey; faydasız; *in one* ~ bir seferde; *have a* ~ *at* *s.th.* bşe teşebbüs etm., *bşi* denemek.

goad [gəud] **1.** *n.* üvendire, davarı dürtmeye yarayan değnek; *fig.* b-ni harekete geçiren şey; **2.** *v/t. fig.* dürtmek, harekete geçirmek, kışkırtmak, isteklendirmek, teşvik etm.

go-a.head F ['gəuəhed] **1.** *adj.* ilerleyen, gelişen, gelişmekte olan; gelişme ümidi gösteren; başlama…; **2.** *n. part. Am.* F enerji, canlılık; izin, müsaade; izni olan kimse; başlama işareti.

goal [gəul] *n.* hedef, amaç, gaye; *futbol:* gol; kale; '**~-keep.er** *n. futbol:* kaleci.

goat [gəut] *n.* zoo keçi, teke; Oğlak burcu; zampara adam, çapkın kimse; başkalarının günah ve sorumluluğunu yüklenen kimse; *get s.o.'s ~* b-ni kızdırmak, sinirlendirmek, b-nin sinirine dokunmak; *separate the sheep from the ~s fig.* iyileri kötülerden ayırmak; *play the giddy ~* kaba ve budalaca davranmak, aptal aptal hareket etm.; **goat'ee** *n.* keçi sakalı, sivri sakal; '**goat.ish** *adj.* keçi gibi; kaba, pis; '**goat.skin** *n.* keçi derisi, keçi postu.

gob [gɔb] *n. sl.* büyük miktar, çok; parça, küme; ağız; *Am.* F denizci, deniz eri; **gob.bet** ['gɔbit] *n.* parça, külçe, küme.

gob.ble ['gɔbl] *v/i.* hindi gibi ses çıkarmak, glu glu etm.; *v/t.* çabuk çabuk yemek, oburca yutmak; kapmak; hızlı hızlı okumak; **gob.ble.dy.gook** *Am. sl.* ['gɔbldiguk] *n.* karışık ve anlamsız söz; '**gob.bler** *n.* baba hindi, erkek hindi.

go-be.tween ['gəubitwi:n] *n.* aracı, arabulucu; simsar, tellal.

gob.let ['gɔblit] *n.* kadeh.

gob.lin ['gɔblin] *n.* gulyabani, cin.

go-by ['gəubai] *n.:* *give s.o. the ~* b-ni görmezden gelmek, tanımazlıktan gelmek, b-ne yüz vermemek.

go-cart ['gəuka:t] *n.* hafif el arabası; çocuğu yürümeye alıştırmakta kullanılan tekerlekli sandalye; portatif bebek arabası; hafif araba, motorlu küçük yarış arabası.

god, ECCL ♀ [gɔd] *n.* Tanrı, Allah, Cenabı Hak; ilâh; put, sanem; *fig.* çok sevilen kimse, herkesin hayran olduğu kimse; çok nüfuzlu kimse; çok önem verilen şey; *the gods pl.* THEAT balkonda oturan seyirciler; '**god.child** *n.* vaftiz evlâdı; '**god.dess** *n.* tanrıça, ilâhe; çok cazip kadın; '**god.fa.ther** *n.* vaftiz babası, manevi baba; '**god.fear.ing**

adj. dindar; '**godhead** *n.* Allah, Tanrı, mabut; '**god.less** *adj.* Allahı tanımayan, Allahsız, dinsiz; günahkâr; '**god.like** *adj.* Allah gibi; tanrısal; '**god.li.ness** *n.* dindarlık; '**god.ly** *adj.* dindar; Allaha saygı duyan; '**godmoth.er** *n.* vaftiz anası; '**god.send** *n.* beklenmedik anda gelen ve ihtiyaç duyulan şey, Hızır gibi gelen yardım; '**god. 'speed:** *bid veya wish s.o. ~* b-ne iyi yolculuklar dilemek, 'yolun açık olsun' demek, 'Tanrıya emanet ol' demek, 'uğurlar olsun' demek.

go.er ['gəuə] *n.* giden kimse.

gof.fer ['gəufə] *v/t.* kırma yapmak, kırmak, kıvırmak.

go-get.ter *Am.* F ['gəu'getə] *n.* girişken kimse, uyanık kimse, açıkgöz kimse, çok faal kimse.

gog.gle ['gɔgl] **1.** *v/i.* şaşı bakmak, gözlerini devirmek; gözlerini faltaşı gibi açarak bakmak; **2.** *n. ~s pl.* gözlük (*pilot, motosiklet yarışçısı, balıkadam*); '**~-eyed** *adj.* patlak gözlü.

go.ing ['gəuiŋ] **1.** *adj.* işleyen, hareket eden; yaşayan, hayattaki; şu anki; *be ~ to inf.* -mek üzere olm., … yapacak olm; *keep ~* devam etm., durmadan yürümek; *set ~* kurmak (*saat*); *a ~ concern* başarılı iş; *~, ~, gone!* satıyorum, satıyorum, sattım! (*açık arttırmada*); **2.** *n.* gidiş, ayrılış; yol durumu; gidişat; gidiş hızı, sürat; '**go.ings-'on** *n. pl.* F olup bitenler; gidişat; hal ve hareket.

goi.tre MED ['gɔitə] *n.* guatr; **goi.trous** ['gɔitrəs] *adj.* guatrı olan; guatra ait, guatr…

go-kart MOT ['gəuka:t] *n.* motorlu küçük yarış arabası.

gold [gəuld] **1.** *n.* altın; servet, zenginlik; altın rengi, sarı renk; değerli herhangi bş; **2.** *adj.* altın, sırmalı, yaldızlı; altından yapılmış; '**~-bear.ing** *adj.* altınlı, altın madeni ihtiva eden; '**~.brick 1.** *n. fig.* kıymetli görünen değersiz şey; görevden kaçınan kimse; **2.** *v/t.* aldatmak; *v/i.* görevden kaçınmak, işten kaçınmak; '**~.dig.ger** *n. Am.* altın arayıcısı; *sl.* erkeklerden para sızdırmaya çalışan kadın, fındıkçı; '**gold.en** *adj. mst fig.* altın gibi; altından yapılmış; altın renkli; çok kıymetli; şahane, fevkalade; önemli; '**gold-en.rod** *n.* BOT uzun saplı sarı bir çiçek.

gold…: '**~.finch** *n.* ORN saka kuşu; '**~.fish** *n.* ICHTH havuz balığı, kırmızı balık; '~.mine *n.* altın madeni; *fig.* servet kaynağı; ~ **plate** altın kaplama eşya; '~-rush *n.* altına hücum; '~.smith *n.* kuyumcu.

golf [gɔlf] **1.** *n.* golf oyunu; **2.** *vb.* golf oynamak; '~-course = **golf-links**; '**golf.er** *n.* golf oyuncusu; '**golf-links** *n. pl.* golf alanı.

gol.li.wog(g) ['gɔliwɔg] *n.* siyah yüzlü acayip oyuncak bebek, zenci oyuncak bebek; *fig.* garip kimse, umacı.

go.losh [gə'lɔʃ] *n.* kaloş, şoson, yağmurlu havada giyilen lastik.

gon.do.la ['gɔndələ] *n.* NAUT gondol; altı düz mavna; üstü açık yük vagonu; AVIA uçağın alt kısmına takılan ek kısım; **gon.dolier** [‿'liə] *n.* gondolcu.

gone [gɔn] **1.** *p.p. of* **go**; **2.** *adj.* geçmiş; ilerlemiş (*hastalık*); âşık olmuş, sevdalanmış; hamile; ölmüş; F mahvolmuş; kaybolmuş; F ümitsiz; büyük, çok iyi, fevkalade; **be ~!, get you ~!** kaybol gözümden!, gözüm görmesin seni!; ~ **on s.o.** *sl. b-ne* abayı yakmış, âşık olmuş; '**gon.er** *n. sl.* hayatından ümit kesilmiş kimse, yolcu, mahvolmuş kimse, bedbaht kimse.

gong [gɔŋ] *n.* gong; *sl.* madalya.

good [gud] **1.** *adj. com.* iyi, güzel, âla, hoş; uygun, münasip, yerinde; faydalı, sağlığa yararlı; yetenekli, kompetan; memnuniyet verici; nazik, kibar, hayır sahibi; kuvvetli, sağlıklı, sağlam; eğlenceli, komik; taze, bozulmamış; güvenilir, sağlam, emin; COM döneme kabiliyeti olan, ticari yönden sağlam; uslu, edepli, iyi huylu; faziletli, kerim; çok, hayli, fazla; tam; **the ~ Samaritan** merhametli kimse, hayır sahibi, yardıma muhtaçlara yardım eden kimse; ~ **at** *bşde* becerikli, başarılı; **in ~ earnest** çok ciddi olarak, gayet samimiyetle; **2.** *n.* iyilik; fayda, yarar; doğruluk; iyi ve hayırlı şey; kâr; ~**s** *pl.* eşya, mallar, emtia; *pl.* (*the ile kullanıldığında*) iyi insanlar; *pl.* suçun kanıtları; **that's no** ~ yararı yok, faydalı değildir; **it is no** ~ **talking** konuşmanın yararı yok; **for** ~ temelli olarak, daimi olarak; **piece of** ~**s** F kadın, parça; ~**s in process** işleme konulmuş mallar, yarı mamûl; ~**-bye,** *Am. a.* ~**-by 1.** ['gud'bai] *n.* veda; **2.** ['gud'bai] *int.* Allahaısmarladık!, hoşça kal!, güle güle!, selâmetle!; '~**-for-'noth.ing 1.** *adj.* bir işe yaramaz; **2.** *n.* hiç bir işe yaramayan kimse, serseri; ♀ **Fri.day** Paskalyadan önceki Cu-

ma; '~'hu.mo(u)red *adj.* şakacı, şen, hoş, sevimli; '**goodli.ness** *n.* iyilik, iyi huyluluk; '**good-looking** *adj.* yakışıklı, güzel; '**good.ly** *adj.* güzel, hoş görünüşlü; *fig.* büyük, çok; '**good-'na.tured** *adj.* iyi huylu, yumuşak huylu, halim, nazik, kibar; '**good.ness 1.** *n.* iyilik, erdem, fazilet; faydalı kısım; **2.** *int.* Allah!, Tanrım!, Yarabbim!; *s.* **gracious**; **goods train** yük treni, marşandiz; '**good.wife** *n.* ev kadını, karı, eş; '**good'will** *n.* iyi niyet, hüsnüniyet, hayırhahlık, dostça duygu (**towards** -*e karşı*); COM prestij; COM firma itibarı ve değeri.

good.y¹ ['gudi] *n.* şekerleme, bonbon.

good.y² [‿], *a.* '**good.y-'good.y 1.** *adj.* aşırı iyi, melek gibi, yapmacık iyilik gösteren; **2.** *n.* aşırı iyi görünen kimse, yapmacık iyilik yapan kimse.

goof.y *sl.* ['gu:fi] *adj.* aptal, ahmak, budala, akılsız.

goon *Am. sl.* [gu:n] *n.* ahmak kimse, budala kimse, beecriksiz kimse; *part.* grev; işverenin grevcilere karşı şiddet kullanan adamı.

goose [gu:s] *n.*, *pl.* **geese** [gi:s] kaz (*a. fig.*); **cook s.o.'s** ~ *b-nin* işini bozmak; *pl.* '**goos.er** *n.* terzi ütüsü; *sl.* parmaklama, parmak atma.

goose.ber.ry ['guzbəri] *n.* bektaşi üzümü; **play** ~ F iki sevgiliye eşlik etm.

goose...: '~-**flesh** *n.* tüyleri ürpermiş deri; '~.**herd** *n.* kaz çobanı; ~'**pim.ples** *pl. Am.* = **goose-flesh**; '~-**step** *n.* kaz adımı, dizleri kırmadan atılan adım; '**goos.ey, 'goos.ie** *n.* F kaz kafalı kimse.

go.pher *part. Am.* ['gəufə] *n.* Kuzey Amerika'da yaşayan sıçana benzer bir hayvan.

Gor.di.an ['gɔ:djən]: ~ **knot** kördüğüm; zor iş.

gore¹ [gɔ:] *n.* pıhtılaşmış kan.

gore² [‿] **1.** *n.* peş, apışlık; **2.** *vb.* kumaşı üç köşeli kesmek, apışlık koymak.

gorge [gɔ:dʒ] **1.** *n.* boğaz, dar geçit, koyak, vadi; gırtlak; mide içindeki şeyler; tiksinti; **my ~ rises** midem bulanıyor, tiksiniyorum; **2.** *vb.* oburcasına yemek yemek; tıka basa doldurmak, yutmak, tıka basa yemek; ağzına kadar doldurmak.

gor.geous □ ['gɔ:dʒəs] parlak, tantanalı, muhteşem, harikulâde, debdebeli, göz kamaştırıcı; zevk veren, güzel; '**gorgeous.ness** *n.* ihtişam, parlaklık.

go.rilla ZOO [gə'rilə] *n.* goril.

gor.mand.ize ['gɔːməndaiz] *vb.* oburca yemek, çok yemek, yiyip yutmak, mideye indirmek.

gorse BOT [gɔːs] *n.* katırtırnağına benzer bir bitki.

gor.y □ ['gɔːri] kanlı; kan dondurucu, korkunç, ürpertici.

gosh P [gɔʃ] *int.* aman Yarabbi!, hay Allah!

gos.hawk ORN ['gɔshɔːk] *n.* atmaca.

gos.ling ['gɔzliŋ] *n.* kaz yavrusu, kaz palazı.

gos.pel ['gɔspəl] *n.* İncil; *fig.* doğru söz, hakikat; '**gos.pel.(l)er** *n.* İncil okuyan kimse.

gos.sa.mer ['gɔsəmə] *n.* havada uçan ince örümcek ağı; yumuşak, hafif, ince kumaş.

gos.sip ['gɔsip] **1.** *n.* dedikodu; gevezelik, çene çalma, boş laf; dedikoducu kimse; **2.** *v/i.* dedikodu etm.; gevezelik etm., çene çalmak.

got [gɔt] *pret. & p.p. of* **get**.

Goth [gɔθ] *n.* HIST Got, Got kavminden biri; *fig.* kaba adam, barbar kimse; '**Goth.ic** *adj.* Got'lara ait, Gotik; Gotik tarzına ait; Gotik diline ait; Gotik yazıya ait; *fig.* barbarlık, yıkıcılık.

got.ten *Am.* ['gɔtn] *p.p. of* **get**.

gouge [gaudʒ] **1.** *n.* MEC oluklu keski, marangoz kalemi, heykeltıraş kalemi; **2.** *vb. mst ~ out* kalemle işlemek, kesmek, şekil vermek; gözünü oymak; *Am.* F kazıklamak, fazla para almak.

gou.lash ['guːlæʃ] *n.* tas kebabı, biberli haşlanmış et ve sebze.

gourd BOT [guəd] *n.* sukabağı, kabak.

gour.mand ['guəmənd] **1.** *adj.* obur, pisboğaz, boğazına düşkün; **2.** *n.* obur kimse, boğazına düşkün kimse.

gout MED [gaut] *n.* gut, nıkris; '**gout.y** □ gut hastalığına tutulmuş.

gov.ern ['gʌvən] *v/t.* yönetmek, idare etm.; hâkim olm. *-e* (*a. fig.*); kontrol etm.; kontrol altında tutmak; almak, *ile* kullanılmak; *v/i.* hükümet sürmek; hüküm sürmek; **~ing body** idare, yönetim, hükümet; '**gov.ern.ess** *n.* mürebbiye; '**gov.ern.ment** *n.* hükümet; idare, yönetim, hüküm; yönetme, hükümet sürme; **gov.ern.men.tal** [~'mentl] *adj.* devlet..., devletle ilgili; '**gov.er.nor** *n.* vali, eyalet reisi; yönetim kurulu üyesi; F patron, şef, baba; MEC düzengeç, regülatör; **gover.nor gen.er.al** genel vali; '**gov.er.norship**

n. valilik; idarecilik, yöneticilik.

gown [gaun] **1.** *n.* rop; cüppe; kadın elbisesi, kadın geceliği; resmi elbise; **2.** *v/t.* elbise giydirmek; '**gowns.man** *n.* cüppe giyme hakkı olan kimse; üniversiteli; MIL sivil.

grab F [græb] **1.** *v/t.* kapmak, ele geçirmek, zorla almak, gaspetmek; çabucak yakalamak; **2.** *n.* kapma, kapış, gasp, el koyma; MEC eşya kaldırmaya mahsus kıskaçlı alet; **~-bag** *Am.* eşya piyangosu torbası; '**grab.ber** *n.* herşeyi kapmak isteyen kimse, aç gözlü kimse, hayatta tek amacı servet yapmak olan kimse.

grace [greis] **1.** *n.* zarafet; lütuf; fazilet, erdem, iyi niyet; sofrada şükran duası; rahmet, kerem, merhamet; borç ertelemesi, mühlet, vade; MUS asıl notaların yanına eklenen ufak nota; **~s** *pl.* cazibe; **2s** *pl.* MYTH çeşitli güzellikleri temsil eden üç ilahe; **act of ~** genel af; **with (a) good (bad) ~** isteyerek (istemeyerek, nazlanarak); **Your 2** Yüce Başpiskoposum; Yüce Düküm *veya* Düşesim; **good ~s** *pl.* iltimas, teveccüh; tasvip, beğeni; **period of ~** bekleme müddeti, borcun vadesinden sonra tanınan süre; *s.* **say 1**; **2.** *v/t.* süslemek; lütuf göstermek; şeref vermek; **grace-ful** □ ['~ful] zarif, lâtif, nazik; '**graceful.ness** *n.* zarafet, incelik, nezaket; '**grace.less** □ kötü, nahoş, hoşa gitmeyen, ahlâksız.

gra.cious □ ['greiʃəs] cana yakın, şirin; merhametli; nazik, kibar, ince; cömert; **good ~!**, **goodness ~!**, **~ me!** Allah Allah!, olacak iş değil!, yok canım!; '**gracious.ness** *n.* zarafet; sıcakkanlılık, cana yakınlık; merhamet.

grack.le ORN ['grækl] *n.* sığırcık *veya* ona benzer kuş.

gra.da.tion [grə'deiʃən] *n.* derece, basamak, sıralama; bir durumdan diğerine yavaş yavaş geçiş; yavaş değişim; GR sesli harfi yavaş yavaş değiştirme.

grade [greid] **1.** *n.* derece; rütbe; mertebe; sınıf; basamak; cins; *part. Am.* = **gradient**; sınıf. *Am. okul:* sınıf, dönem; not; **make the ~** *Am.* F başarmak, muvaffak olm.; **~ crossing** *Am.* hemzemin geçit; **~ (d) school** *Am.* ilkokul; **2.** *v/t.* sınıflandırmak, tasnif etm.; derecelere ayırmak; tesviye etm., aynı seviyeye getirmek (*yol*); neslini ıslah etm. (*at, davar*); RAIL *etc.* düzleştirmek, aynı seviyeye getirmek.

gra.di.ent ['greidjənt] *n.* RAIL *etc.* yokuş, meyil, irtifa.

grad.u.al □ ['grædʒuəl] derece derece, tedricî, kademeli, yavaş yavaş olan; '**grad.u.al.ly** *adv.* derece derece, tedricen, yavaş yavaş; **grad.u.ate** **1.** ['‿djueit] *v/i.* mezun olm., diploma almak; derecelere ayrılmak; *v/t.* derecelere ayırmak *-i;* sınıflarına göre ayırmak *-i;* mezun etm., diploma vermek *-e;* **2.** ['‿dʒuit] *n.* mezun, diplomalı (*üniversiteden etc.*); **grad.u.a.tion** [‿dju'eiʃən] *n.* mezuniyet, mezun olma, diploma alma; diploma töreni; ölçü bardağındaki derece işareti.

graft[1] [grɑːft] **1.** *n.* AGR ağaç aşısı; **2.** *v/t. & v/i.* aşıla(n)mak (**in, upon**); MED ameliyatla doku yerleştirmek, transplante etm.

graft[2] *Am.* [‿] **1.** *n.* rüşvet; para yeme; yolsuzluk, suiistimal; **2.** *v/i.* F rüşvet almak, para yemek; '**graft.er** *n.* F *part.* POL menfaatçi kimse, rüşvetçi.

Gra.haim ['greiəm]: **~ bread** buğday ekmeği.

Grail [greil] *n.* son akşam yemeğinde Hz. İsa'nın kullandığı farzolunan sahan *veya* kâse.

grain [grein] *n.* tane, habbe, tohum, zerre; damar, doku; hububat; 0,065 gram; *fig.* huy, mizaç; **in ~** esaslı, inceden inceye, natürel; **dyed in the ~** iyice boyanmış; **against the ~** *fig.* tabiatına zıt, hoşuna gitmeyen; **grained** *adj.* taneli, damarlı.

gram [græm] = **gramme.**

gra.mer.cy *obs.* [grə'məːsi] *int.* çok teşekkür!, sağolun!, minnettarım!; Allah Allah!, nasıl olur!

gram.i.na.ceous [greimi'neiʃəs], **gra-mine.ous** [grei'miniəs] *adj.* ota benzer, ot gibi, ot…

gram.ma.logue ['græməlɔg] *n. stenografi:* kısaltma, özet.

gram.mar ['græmə] *n.* gramer, dilbilgisi; gramer kitabı; gramatik kurallara göre hazırlanmış konuşma *veya* yazı; **grammar.i.an** [grə'mɛəriən] *n.* gramer uzmanı, dilbilgisi kitabı yazarı, gramerci; '**gram.mar-school** *n.* İngiltere'de üniversiteye hazırlık okulu; *Am. a.* ilk ve orta okul; **gram.mat.i.cal** □ [grə'mætikəl] gramatik, gramere ait, dilbilgisi kurallarına uygun.

gramme [græm] *n.* gram.

gram.o.phone ['græməfəun] *n.* gramofon; **~ record** gramofon plağı.

gran.a.ry ['grænəri] *n.* tahıl ambarı; çok tahıl yetiştiren bölge.

grand [grænd] **1.** □ *fig.* muhteşem, fevkalade, enfes, mükemmel, depdebeli, saltanatlı; heybetli, muazzam; büyük, ulu, baş; tam; ♀ **Duchess** grandüşes; ♀ **Duke** grandük; ♀ **Old Party** *Am.* Cumhuriyetçi parti; **~ stand** tribün; **2.** *n. a.* **~ piano** MUS kuyruklu piyano; *Am. sl.* bin dolar; **miniature ~** kısa kuyruklu piyano; **grandad** F ['grændæd] *n.* büyükbaba, dede; **gran.dam(e)** ['‿dæm] *n.* nüfuzlu yaşlı kadın; '**grand.child** *n.* torun; '**grand.daughter** *n.* kız torun; **gran.dee** [græn'diː] *n.* ekâbir, itibarlı kimse; İspanyol *veya* Portekiz soylusu; **gran.deur** ['grændʒə] *n.* büyüklük, azamet, ihtişam, güzellik; '**grand.fa.ther** *n.* büyükbaba, dede; **~ clock** sarkaçlı büyük dolap saati.

gran.dil.o.quence [græn'diləkwəns] *n.* tantanalı, süslü kelimeler kullanma; tumturak; **gran'dil.o.quent** □ süslü, tantanalı, tumturaklı.

gran.di.ose □ ['grændiəus] heybetli, muhteşem, göz alıcı, tantanalı, gösterişli.

grand.moth.er ['grænmʌðə], F **grand.ma** ['grænmɑː] *n.* anneanne, babaanne, nine; '**grand.ness** = **gran-deur.**

grand…: '~.pa ['grænpɑː] = **grandfather,** '~-par.ents *n. pl.* büyükanne ve büyükbaba, dede ve nine **~.sire** ['‿saiə] *n. obs.* büyükbaba, dede; yaşlı adam; '**~.son** *n.* erkek torun.

grange [greindʒ] *n.* binalarıyla birlikte çiftlik; *Am.* çiftçi birliği; '**grang.er** *n.* çiftçi; çiftçi birliği üyesi.

gran.ite ['grænit] *n.* granit; **gra.nit.ic** [‿'nitik] *adj.* granit cinsinden, granit…

gran.ny F ['græni] *n.* babaanne, anneanne, nine; titiz kadın; ebe.

grant [grɑːnt] **1.** *n.* bağış, teberru; tahsisat; bahşedilen arazi *veya* para; JUR ferağ, terk, hibe; **2.** *v/t.* vermek, ihsan etm., bahşetmek; kabul etm., onaylamak, tasdik etm., farzetmek; JUR devretmek, ferağ etm., hibe etm.; **take for ~ed** doğru olarak kabul etm., muhakkak olacak gözüyle bakmak, olmuş gibi kabul etm.; **~ing this (to) be so** bunun böyle olduğunu farzederek; **God ~ …!** inşallah…!; **gran'tee** *n.* JUR kendisine birşey hibe edilen kimse; **grant-**

in-aid ['grɑːntin'eid] n. para yardımı, iane, tahsisat; grant.or JUR [ˈtɔː] n. devreden, temlik eden, hibe eden kimse.

gran.u.lar ['grænjulə] adj. taneli, tane tane olan, granüle; gran.u.late [ˈleit] v/t. & v/i. tanele(n)mek; 'gran.u.lat.ed adj. taneli; ~ sugar tozşeker; gran.u-'la.tion n. taneleme; gran.ule [ˈjuːl] n. tanecik, zerre, habbe; gran.u.lous [ˈjuləs] adj. üstü taneli, granüle.

grape [greip] n. üzüm; asma; '~.fruit n. BOT greyfrut; '~-shot n. MIL top mermisi; '~-sug.ar n. glikoz, desktroz, levüloz, üzüm şekeri; '~-vine n. asma; dedikodu yoluyla haber alma; a. ~ tele-graph ağızdan duyma, dedikodu yoluyla duyma.

graph [græf] n. grafik; 'graph.ic, 'graph.ical □ resim veya yazıya ait, şeklî, çizgili; tam tasvir edilmiş, canlı; graphic arts pl. grafik sanatlar; graph.ite MIN [ˈfait] n. grafit; graph-ol.o.gy [ˈfɔlədʒi] n. grafoloji; graph pa.per çizgili kâğıt.

grap.nel NAUT ['græpnəl] n. filika demiri; dört tırnaklı demir; borda kancası.

grap.ple ['græpl] 1. n. NAUT borda kancası, filika demiri; yakalama, sıkıca sarılma; göğüs göğüse savaşma; MEC kanca, tırnaklı demir; 2. vb. yakalamak, kavramak, sıkıca tutmak; göğüs göğüse mücadele etm.; kanca ile tutmak; uğraşmak; ~ with sıkıca tutmak, kavramak, yakalamak.

grasp [grɑːsp] 1. n. tutma, yakalama, yakalayış, kavrama, kavrayış; anlama, idrak; 2. vb. tutmak, kavramak, yakalamak; kavramak, idrak etm.; yakalamayı denemek, istekle kabul etm. (at -i); 'grasp.ing □ haris, açgözlü, cimri, pinti.

grass [grɑːs] 1. n. ot, çimen, çim, yeşillik; çayır, otlak; sl. haşiş; at ~ otlamakta (hayvan); fig. izinli; emekliye ayrılmış; send to ~ = 2. v/t. & v/i. otla(t)mak; otla kaplamak; sl. ispiyon etm. (on -i); '~.hop.per n. çekirge; '~-plot n. çimenlik; ~ roots pl. Am. taşra halkı veya seçmenleri; yüzeye yakın toprak; '~-wid.ow(.er) n. eşinden bir süre ayrı kalmış kadın (veya erkek); 'grass.y adj. otlu, çimenli, yeşillikli.

grate¹ [greit] n. demir parmaklık, ızgara; fig. hapishane, kodes.

grate² [ˈ] v/t. rendelemek; gıcırdatmak, sürterek ses çıkarmak; v/i. sürtünerek ses çıkarmak; ~ (up)on fig. sinirine dokunmak, sinirlendirmek; gıcırdamak.

grate.ful □ ['greitful] minnettar, müteşekkir; hoş, güzel, rahatlatıcı.

grat.er ['greitə] n. rende.

grat.i.fi.ca.tion [grætifi'keiʃən] n. memnuniyet, haz, zevk; grat.i.fy ['~fai] v/t. memnun etm., hoşnut etm.; tatmin etm.; 'grat.i.fy.ing adj. memnuniyet verici, hoş, güzel; tatminkâr.

grat.ing ['greitiŋ] 1. □ tiz, cırlak, kulakları tırmalayan; 2. n. demir parmaklık, pencere kafesi; ızgara.

gra.tis ['greitis] adv. & adj. bedava, parasız, ücretsiz.

grat.i.tude ['grætitjuːd] n. minnettarlık, şükran.

gra.tu.i.tous □ [grə'tjuːitəs] bedava, parasız, ücretsiz; sebepsiz; gra'tu.i.ty n. hediye, teberru; bahşiş.

gra.va.men JUR [grə'veimen] n. suçun esasını oluşturan şey, suçlamanın ağırlık merkezi.

grave¹ □ [greiv] ciddi, ağır, vahim, önemli; ~ accent GR sesli harf üzerindeki aksan işareti.

grave² [ˈ] 1. n. mezar, kabir; 2. (irr.) v/t. mst fig. oymak, hakketmek, işlemek (hafızaya); '~-dig.ger n. mezarcı.

grav.el ['grævəl] 1. n. çakıl; MED kum, idrar taşı; 2. v/t. çakıl döşemek; F şaşırtmak, aklını karıştırmak; grav.el.ly ['grævəli] adj. çakıllı; kalın ve kaba ses.

grav.en ['greivən] p.p. of grave² 2.

grav.er MEC ['greivə] n. hakkâk, oymacı (kalemi).

grave...: '~-side at his ~ bir ayağı çukurda; '~-stone n. mezar taşı; '~-yard n. mezarlık, kabristan.

grav.ing dock NAUT ['greiviŋ'dɔk] n. kalafat havuzu, kuru havuz.

grav.i.tate ['græviteit] vb. çekilmek, yer çekimi ile hareket etm.; cezbedilmek, meyletmek (towards -e doğru); grav.i'tation n. yerçekimi; fig. cazibe; grav.i'tation.al pull [ˈʃənl'pul] yerçekimi kuvveti.

grav.i.ty ['græviti] n. yerçekimi; ağırlık; önem, ciddiyet, ehemmiyet; centre of ~ ağırlık merkezi; specific ~ özgül ağırlık.

gra.vy ['greivi] n. etsuyu, sos, salça; kolay kazanılan para; '~-boat n. sosluk.

gray part. Am. [grei] adj. gri, kurşuni, boz, kır (saç); gri giysili; F neşesiz, kasvetli; **gray.ish** *part. Am.* ['-iʃ] *adj.* grimsi, grimtrak.

graze [greiz] **1.** *v/t. & v/i.* otla(t)mak; sıyırmak, sıyırıp geçmek; **2.** *n.* sıyrık, bere.

gra.zier ['greizjə] *n.* çoban.

grease 1. [gri:z] *v/t.* yağlamak, yağ sürmek; ~ *s.o.'s palm* *fig. b-ne* rüşvet vermek; **2.** [gri:s] *n.* yağ, et yağı, kuyruk yağı; makine yağı; '~-cup *n.* MEC gres kabı, yağlama kutusu, yağdanlık; '~-gun *n.* MOT gres pompası; '~-proof *adj.* yağ geçirmez; **greas.er** ['gri:zə] *n. Am. sl.* Meksikalı; gemide makine yağcısı.

greas.y ☐ ['gri:zi] yağlı, yağlanmış.

great ☐ [greit] **1.** *adj. com.* büyük, kocaman, iri, heybetli, cüsseli, azametli; *fig.* kabiliyetli, yetenekli, usta, mahir; F mükemmel şahane, harikulâde, fevkalâde; önemli; meşhur; yüksek; çok iyi; *s.* **deal²** *1*, **many**; **2.** ~ *the* ~ *pl.* kodamanlar, büyükler; ~*s pl.* gözde kimseler, önemli kişiler; '~.coat *n.* palto; '~'grand.child *n.* evlâdının torunu; '~'grand.fa.ther *n.* büyük dede; 'great.ly *adv.* çokça, pek çok; 'great.ness *n.* büyüklük; şöhret; önem.

Gre.cian ['gri:ʃən] *adj.* Yunan...

greed [gri:d], 'greed.i.ness *n.* açgözlülük, oburluk, hırs; 'greed.y ☐ obur, açgözlü; hırslı, haris; hevesli, arzulu.

Greek [gri:k] **1.** *adj.* Yunanistan, Yunanlı *veya* Yunanca'ya ait; **2.** *n.* Yunanlı, Grek, Rum; Yunanca; *that is* ~ *to me* hiç birşey anlayamıyorum, anlıyorsam arap olayım.

green [gri:n] **1.** ☐ yeşil; ham, olmamış; yaş, taze; F tecrübesiz, toy, acemi, cahil; **2.** *n.* yeşil renk; ~*s pl.* yeşil yapraklı sebzeler; yeşillik, çimen, çayır; ortak arazi; meşra; golf oyununda hedef deliğinin etrafındaki çimen; '~.back *n. Am.* arkası yeşil banknot; **green.er.y** ['-nəri] *n.* yeşillik, çimen, botanik.

green...: ~ **fin.gers** *pl.* bahçıvanlıktan anlama; '~.gage *n.* BOT frenkeriği, bardakeriği; '~.gro.cer *n.* manav, yemişçi; '~.gro.cer.y *n.* manavlık; '~.horn *n.* acemi *veya* toy kimse; '~.house *n.* limonluk, ser; 'green.ish *adj.* yeşilimsi, yeşilimtrak.

Green.land.er ['gri:nləndə] *n.* Grönland Adası'nda yaşayan kimse.

green light ['gri:n'lait] *n.* yeşil ışık (F *fig. = izin, salâhiyet, yetki*); 'green.ness *n.* yeşillik.

green...: '~-room *n.* THEAT oyuncuların dinlenme odası; '~.sick.ness *n.* MED kloroz, genç kızlarda demir eksikliğinden oluşan hastalık; ~.sward ['-swɔ:d] *n.* çimen.

Green.wich ['grinidʒ]: ~ *time* Greenwich saat ayarı.

green.wood ['gri:nwud] *n.* yemyeşil orman.

greet [gri:t] *v/t.* selâmlamak, selâm vermek; karşılamak; 'greet.ing *n.* selâm.

gre.gar.i.ous ['gri'gɛəriəs] *adj.* toplu halde yaşayan, topluluğu seven.

gre.nade MIL ['gri'neid] *n.* el bombası; **gren.a.dier** [grenə'diə] *n.* eskiden el bombası atan asker; İngiliz piyade alayında er.

grew [gru:] *pret. of* **grow**.

grey [grei] **1.** ☐ gri, kurşunî, kül rengi, kır, boz, ağarmış (*saç*); ☒ *Friar* Fransiskan mezhebine ait rahip; **2.** *n.* gri renk, kurşuni renk; **3.** *v/t. & v/i.* ağar(t)mak; '~.beard *n.* yaşlı adam, ak sakallı adam; **grey.cing** ['-siŋ] *n.* tazı yarışı.

grey...: '~'head.ed *adj. fig.* eski; yaşlı; '~.hound *n.* tazı; 'grey.ish *adj.* grimsi, grimtrak; **grey mat.ter** ANAT gri madde; *fig.* beyin, akıl.

grid [grid] *n. part. radyo:* valfta kontrol voltajı taşıyan ızgara; şebeke; haritada kesişen dikey ve yatay hatlar sistemi; ray şebekesi; *Am. futbol:* saha.

grid.dle ['gridl] *n.* (alçak kenarlı) tava.

grid.i.ron ['gridaiən] *n.* ızgara; *Am. futbol:* saha.

grief [gri:f] *n.* keder, acı, ıstırap, dert, elem; felâket, belâ.

griev.ance ['gri:vəns] *n.* keder verici şey, dert; **grieve** *v/t. & v/i.* kederlen(dir)mek, üz(ül)mek, eseflen(dir)mek; 'griev.ous ☐ kederli, acıklı, üzücü, keder verici, elem verici; şiddetli; 'grievous.ness *n.* acıklı durum, dert, keder; şiddet, tehlike.

grif.fin ['grifin] *n.* yarısı aslan yarısı kartal farzolunan garip yaratık.

grig [grig] *n.* hayat dolu kimse, neşeli kimse, şen şakrak kimse.

grill [gril] **1.** *v/t. & v/i.* ızgarada pişir(il)mek, çok ısıtmak, çok sıcağa maruz bırakmak; *sl.* soru yağmuruna tutmak, sorguya çekmek; **2.** *n.* ızgara, tava; ızgarada pişmiş et; *a.* ~-**room** otel *veya* lokantada ızgaraların pişirildiği yer.

grim ☐ [grim] haşin, vahşi, gaddar, zalim, merhametsiz, korkunç, çetin; ~

facts *pl.* acı gerçekler; **~ humour** uğursuz, meşum neşe.

gri.mace [gri'meis] **1.** *n.* yüz buruşturma, surat ekşitme; **2.** *v/i.* yüz buruşturmak, surat ekşitmek.

grime [graim] **1.** *n.* kir, pislik, pasak; **2.** *v/t.* kirletmek, pisletmek; **'grim.y** □ kirli, pis.

grin [grin] **1.** *n.* sırıtma, sırıtış; **2.** *v/i.* sırıtmak, dişlerini göstererek gülmek; *v/t.* sırıtarak belirtmek.

grind [graind] **1.** *(irr.) v/t.* öğütmek, ufalamak; bilemek; ezmek; sürterek parlatmak; gıcırdatmak (*diş*); *fig.* eziyet vermek; *sl.* ineklemek, hafızlamak (*ders*); döndürerek çalıştırmak; **~ out** durmadan üretmek (*esp. yazı veya müzik*); *v/i.* öğütülmek; sürtünmeden dolayı parlamak; gıcırdamak; *sl.* dersini ineklemek, hafızlamak; seksi biçimde kalçalarını kıvırmak (*striptizci*); **2.** *n.* bitip tükenmek bilmeyen iş, uzun ve monoton iş, sıkıcı iş; öğütme, ezme; *sl.* inek, hafız (*öğrenci*); kalça kıvırma; **'grind.er** *n.* öğütücü, bileyici; **~s** *pl.* dişler; büyük sandviç; *sl.* inek, hafız; **'grind.ing** *n.* öğütme, çekme (*kahve*); bileme; parlatma, cilalama; **'grindstone** *n.* bileği taşı; **keep s.o.'s nose to the ~** *b-ni* durmadan çalıştırmak, köle gibi çalıştırmak.

grip [grip] **1.** *v/t.* sıkı tutmak, sarılmak, kavramak (*a. fig.*), yakalamak; etkilemek, *-in* dikkatini çekmek, tesir etm.; **2.** *n.* sıkı tutma, kavrama; kabza, sap; MEC kıskaç, kenet; *Am.* = **gripsack**; **get to ~s with** *bşle* uğraşmak.

gripe [graip] **1.** *n.* tutma, yakalama; kontrol, yönetme; şikâyet, sızlanma; sap, kabza; tutan alet (*fren*); **~s** *pl.* F sancı, karın ağrısı; *part. Am.* sıkıntı, dert; **2.** *v/t.* tutmak, yakalamak; keder vermek, ıstırap çektirmek, sıkıntı vermek; kızdırmak, sinirlendirmek; sancı vermek (*karın*); *v/i. part. Am.* F mızmızlanmak, sızlanmak.

grip.sack *Am.* ['gripsæk] *n.* yolcu çantası.

gris.ly ['grizli] *adj.* korkunç, dehşetli, tüyler ürpertici.

grist [grist] *n.* öğütülecek zahire, hububat; **bring ~ to the mill** *fig.* ele geçen her şeyden yararlanmak; **all is ~ that comes to his mill** eline geçen her şeyden istifade eder.

gris.tle ['grisl] *n.* ANAT kıkırdak; **gris.tly** *adj.* kıkırdaklı, kıkırdaktan ibaret.

grit [grit] **1.** *n.* çakıl, iri taneli kum; *fig.* metanet, cesaret, yiğitlik; **2.** *v/t.* çakıl döşemek, kum döşemek; gıcırdatmak (*diş*); cesaret göstermek; **'grit.ty** *adj.* kumlu; cesur, yiğit.

griz.zle F ['grizl] *v/i.* sızlanmak, homurdanmak, halinden şikâyet etm.; **'grizzled = grizzly 1**; **'griz.zly 1.** *adj.* gri, kurşuni, boz; **~ bear = 2.** *n.* boz ayı.

groan [grəun] **1.** *n.* inilti, figan; **2.** *v/i.* inlemek, ah etm., figan etm.; *v/t. bşi* inleyerek belirtmek, inleyerek söylemek, üzülerek anlatmak.

groat [grəut] *n.*: **not worth a ~** beş para etmez.

groats [grəuts] *n. pl.* (*part. yulaf*) dövülmüş hububat.

gro.cer ['grəusə] *n.* bakkal; **gro.cer.ies** ['~riz] *n. pl.* bakkaliye, bakkalın sattığı şeyler; **'gro.cer.y** *n.* bakkal dükkânı.

grog [grɔg] *n.* su katışmış içki; **'grog.gy** *adj.* sallanan, düşecek gibi, sersemlemiş.

groin [grɔin] **1.** *n.* ANAT kasık; ARCH iki kemerin birleştiği kenar; **2.** *v/t.* böyle kenarlarla donatmak.

groom [grum] **1.** *n.* seyis; güvey; = **bridegroom**; **2.** *v/t.* tımar etm.; çekidüzen vermek; bir işe hazırlamak; *Am.* POL aday göstermek; **well ~ed** iyi giyimli, şık; **grooms.man** ['~zmən] *n.* sağdıç.

groove [gru:v] **1.** *n.* oluk, yiv, saban izi; *fig.* alışkanlık, âdet; **in the ~** *fig.* keyfi yerinde, neşeli; **2.** *v/t.* oluk açmak; F *bşe* kendini vermek; **'groov.y** *adj. Am.* son modaya uygun, şık, mükemmel.

grope [grəup] *v/t. & v/i.* el yordamıyla aramak; körü körüne araştırmak; **~ one's way** el yordamıyla yürümek, yolunu bulmak.

gross [grəus] **1.** □ kaba, çirkin, kötü; iğrenç, tiksindirici, adi; hantal, şişko; göze batan, bariz; bereketli; bol; toptan; COM brüt...; **2.** *n.* on iki düzine; **in the ~** toptan, bütünüyle; genel olarak; **'grossness** *n.* kabalık; toptancılık; hantallık, iri yarılık.

gro.tesque □ [grəu'tesk] acayip, tuhaf, garip; kaba.

grot.to ['grɔtəu] *n., pl.* **'grot.to(e)s** mağara; yapay yeraltı odası.

grouch *Am.* F [grautʃ] **1.** *v/i.* şikâyet etm., homurdanmak, söylenmek, mırıldanmak; **2.** *n.* suratsızlık, homurdanma; söylenme, şikâyet; suratı asık kimse, memnun olmamış kimse, şikâyetçi kimse; 'grouch.y *adj.* suratsız, asık suratlı, somurtkan.

ground¹ [graund] *pret. & p.p. of grind 1*; ~ *glass* kristal cam; PHOT buzlucam.

ground² [_] 1. *n. mst* yer, zemin; toprak, arsa; yeryüzü; meydan, saha, alan; ELECT toprak; PAINT astar boya, üstüne desen çizilen düz satıh; ~s *pl.* bahçe; dip, denizin dibi; kahve telvesi, dibe çöken kısım, tortu; neden, sebep; *on the ~(s) of* sebebiyle, *-den* dolayı, ...yüzünden; *fall to the ~* düş(ür)mek; *fig.* suya düşmek (*plan*); *give ~* geri çekilmek; avantajını koruyamamak; *stand veya hold veya keep one's ~* ayak diremek, boyun eğmemek, davasından vazgeçmemek; 2. *v/t.* yere oturtmak, kurmak; esaslı olarak öğretmek; bir esasa dayandırmak; ELECT toprağa bağlamak; AVIA kalkışa izin vermemek; NAUT karaya oturtmak; MEC zemin boyası sürmek; *v/i.* temeli olm.; karaya oturmak; topa vurmak; *well ~ed* temeli iyi; sağlam temeller üzerine kurulmuş; 'ground.age *n.* COM demirleme için ödenen ücret, liman resmi.

ground...: '~con.nex.ion*n.* ELECT toprak hattı; ~ *crew = ground-staff*; ~ *floor* zemin katı; '~'hog *n.* ZOO *part. Am.* dağsıçanı; '~less☐ temelsiz, yersiz, sebepsiz, asılsız; ground.ling ['_liŋ] *n.* THEAT ayakta duran seyirci; basit zevkleri olan kimse; toprağa yakın çalışan *veya* yaşıyan bitki *veya* hayvan.

ground...: '~nut *n.* yerfıstığı; '~'plan *n.* binanın zemin planı; '~rent *n.* arsa kirası.

ground.sel BOT ['graunsl] *n.* kanaryaotu.

ground...; ~ *speed* AVIA yer sürati; '~staff *n.* AVIA hava meydanı ekibi, yer mürettebatı; ~ *swell* soluğan, uzakta esen rüzgârdan oluşan ölü dalga; '~wire *n.* ELECT toprak teli; '~work *n.* temel, esas.

group [gru:p] 1. *n.* grup, küme, öbek; heyet, topluluk; 2. *v/i.* gruplaşmak, grup halinde toplanmak; bir gruba ait olm.; *v/t.* toplamak; gruplara ayırmak.

grouse¹ ORN [graus] *n.* ormantavuğu.
grouse² F [_] *v/i.* homurdanmak, söylenmek, sızlanmak, şikâyet etm.

grove [grəuv] *n.* koru, ormancık, ağaçlık.

grov.el ['grɔvl] *v/i. mst fig.* yerde sürünmek; ayaklarına kapanmak; kendini alçaltmak; yaltaklanmak; 'grov.el.(-l)er *n.* alçalmış kimse, hor görülen kimse; dalkavuk; 'grov.el.(l)ing 1. *adj.* dalkavuk, alçalmış, rezil; 2. *n.* dalkavukluk, kendini küçük düşürme.

grow [grəu] (*irr.*) *v/i.* büyümek, gelişmek; olmak; serpilmek; çoğalmak, artmak, genişlemek; kökleşmek, yerleşmek (*alışkanlık*); çekici olm.; ~ *out of* çok büyük gelmek; içine sığmamak (*elbise*); bırakmak (*kötü alışkanlık*); ~ *(up)on s.o.* b-nin içine yerleşmiş olm.; ~ *up* büyümek, olgunlaşmak; gelişmek; *v/t.* büyütmek, yetiştirmek, üretmek; geliştirmek; 'grow.er *n.* yetiştirici, üretici; belirli şartlarla büyüyen bitki.

growl [graul] 1. *n.* homurtu, homurdanma, hırlama; 2. *v/i.* hırlamak, homurdanmak; guruldamak (*mide*); gümbürdemek (*şimşek*); *v/i.* homurdanarak söylemek; 'growl.er *n. fig.* homurdanan kimse; *Am. sl.* bira kabı; küçük buzul.

grown [grəun] 1. *p.p. of grow*; 2. *adj.* büyümüş, yetişkin, olgun; '~up 1. *adj.* yetişkin, olgun, büyümüş; 2. *n.* yetişkin kimse, olgun kimse; growth [grəuθ] *n.* büyüme, gelişme; artma, yükselme, çoğalma; mahsul, ürün; hastalıklı durum; *of one's own* ~ kendi eliyle yetiştirmiş.

groyne [grɔin] *n.* set, erozyonu önlemek için yapılmış duvar.

grub [grʌb] 1. *n.* tırtıl, kurtçuk; *sl.* yiyecek; *contp.* meşe odunu; köle gibi çalışan kimse; 2. *v/t.* kazmak, eşelemek, kökünden sökmek, kökünden sökerek temizlemek; *sl.* yedirmek (*yemek*); ~ *up* kökünden sökmek; *mst* ~ *out* yuvasından çıkarmak; *v/i.* toprağı kazmak (*for için*); didinmek, çalışıp yorulmak (*for için*); 'grub.by *adj.* pis, kirli, yıkanmamış; kurtlu.

grudge [grʌdʒ] 1. *n.* kin, garez, diş bileme; 2. *v/t.* isteksizce vermek, çok görmek, kıskanmak, gözü kalmak, vermek istememek; diş bilemek; ~ *no pains* özen göstermek, itina etm., hiçbir zahmetten kaçınmamak; 'grudg.er *n.* kıskanç, *bşde* gözü kalan kimse; 'grudg.ing.ly *adv.* istemeye istemeye, istemeyerek, isteksizce.

gru.el ['gruəl] *n.* pişirilmiş yulaf ezmesi;

get *veya* **have one's** ~ *sl*. cezasını bulmak, hak ettiğini bulmak; **'gru.el.(-l)ing** *adj*. çok yorucu, bitap düşürücü; şiddetli.

grue.some □ ['gru:səm] korkunç, dehşetli, ürkütücü; iğrenç.

gruff [grʌf], **'gruff.y** *adj*. kaba, ters, aksi; sert; boğuk (*ses*); boğuk sesli.

grum.ble [grʌmbl] *v/i*. mırıldanmak; şikâyet etm. (*at -den*); homurdanmak; guruldamak; gürlemek; *v/t*. mırıldanarak söylemek, homurdanarak söylemek; **'grum.bler** *n*. *fig*. homurdanan kimse, halinden şikâyetçi kimse.

grump.y □ F ['grʌmpi] aksi, ters, kaba, kötü huylu.

Grun.dy.ism ['grʌndiizəm] *n*. iffet taslama, dar görüşlülük.

grunt [grʌnt] **1.** *n*. homurtu, hırıltı; **2.** *vb*. domuz gibi hırıldamak; homurdanmak; homurdanarak söylemek; **'grunt.er** *n*. domuz.

guar.an.tee [gærən'ti:] **1.** *n*. garanti, kefalet, teminat; kefil; = **guaranty**; **2.** *v/t*. garanti etm.; kefil olm.; **guar.an.tor** [‿tɔ:] *n*. kefil; **'guar.an.ty** *n*. garanti, kefalet.

guard [gɑ:d] **1.** *n*. koruma, muhafaza, himaye, müdafaa; gardiyan; koruyucu alet; MIL nöbet; nöbetçi; muhafız; RAIL tren memuru, frenci; ⚥s *pl*. MIL muhafız alayı; **be on (off) ones** ~ hazırlıklı (hazırlıksız) olm., dikkatli olm., (gafil avlanmak); **mount** ~ MIL nöbet tutmak; **relieve** ~ MIL nöbet değiştirmek, nöbeti devralmak; **2.** *v/t*. korumak, muhafza etm., himaye etm. (*from -den*; **against** *-e karşı*); beklemek; göz altına almak; *v/i*. uyanık bulunmak; nöbet tutmak; korunmak (*against -e karşı*); **'~boat** *n*. NAUT karakol gemisi; **'guard.ed** □ uyanık, tetikte; korunan, muhafazalı; tedbirli; **'guard.house** *n*. askerî karakol; **'guard.i.an** *n*. koruyucu, muhafız, gardiyan; JUR vasi, veli; ~ **angel** koruyucu melek; ~ **of the poor** fakirlerin koruyucusu, fakir babası; **'guard.i.an.ship** *n*. muhafızlık; vasilik, velilik; **guards-man** MIL ['gɑ:dzmən] *n*. muhafız askeri.

gudg.eon ['gʌdʒən] *n*. ICHTH yem için kullanılan ufak tatlı su balığı; *fig*. saf kimse, bön kimse; MEC mil, pin, menteşe kovanı, çengel, kanca.

guer.don *lit*. ['gə:dən] **1.** *n*. ödül, mükâfat; **2.** *v/t*. ödüllendirmek, mükâfat ver-mek.

guer(r).ril.la [gə'rilə] *n*. gerilla, çeteci; ~ **war** çete harbi, gerilla savaşı.

guess [ges] **1.** *n*. tahmin, zan; **at a** ~ tahminen; **2.** *v/t*. tahmin etm., sanmak, zannetmek, farzetmek; inanmak; *v/i* tahminde bulunmak (**at** *-e hakkında*); *part*. *Am*. zannetmek, farzetmek, sanmak; **'guess.work** *n*. tahmin, varsayı.

guest [gest] *n*. misafir, davetli, konuk, otel *veya* pansiyon müşterisi; **paying** ~ pansiyoner; **'~house** *n*. pansiyon; **'~room** *n*. misafir yatak odası.

guf.faw [gʌ'fɔ:] **1.** *n*. kaba gülüş, kahkaha **2.** *v/i*. kabaca kahkaha atmak.

guid.a.ble ['gaidəbl] *adj*. yönetilebilir, idare edilebilir; **guid.ance** ['‿dəns] *n*. rehberlik, yol gösterme, liderlik; yönetme; eğitim sırasında çocuğa verilen öğüt.

guide [gaid] **1.** *n*. rehbet, kılavuz; yönetmelik; *s*. ~-**book**; MEC yatak, kızak, ray; **2.** *v/t*. yol göstermek *-e*; sevketmek, idare etm. *-i*; ~**d missile** MIL güdümlü roket; **'~book** *n*. seyahat rehberi; ~ **dog** körlere yol gösteren köpek; **'~post** *n*. yol işareti; **'~rope** *n*. AVIA kılavuz ipi.

gui.don MIL ['gaidən] *n*. tabur sancağı, flama; sancak taşıyan er.

guild [gild] *n*. esnaf birliği, lonca, hayır kurumu; **'guild.er** *n*. Hollanda para birimi; **'Guild'hall** *n*. esnaf birliği merkez binası; Londra belediye dairesi.

guile [gail] *n*. aldatma, hile, kurnazlık, şeytanlık; **guile.ful** □ ['‿ful] hilebaz, düzenbaz, şeytan gibi, kurnaz; **'guileless** □ saf, bön, samimi, temiz kalpli; **'guileless.ness** *n*. samimiyet, saflık.

guil.lo.tine [gilə'ti:n] **1.** *n*. giyotin; MEC kağıt bıçağı; POL tartışma sınırlaması; **2.** *v/t*. giyotinle idam etm.

guilt [gilt] *n*. suç, kabahat; **'guilt.i.ness** *n*. suçluluk; **'guilt.less** □ masum, suçsuz (**of** *-den*); **'guilt.y** □ suçlu, kabahatli; **plead** ~ suçu kabul etm.

guin.ea ['gini] *n*. 21 şilin değerindeki eski İngiliz parası; **'~fowl** *n*. Afrika tavuğu, beç tavuğu; **'~pig** *n*. kobay; *fig*. üzerinde deney yapılan insan.

guise [gaiz] *n*. elbise; aldatıcı görünüş, maske, kisve.

gui.tar MUS [gi'tɑ:] *n*. gitar.

gulch *Am*. [gʌlʃ] *n*. küçük ve derin dere.

gulf [gʌlf] *n*. körfez; uçurum, derin yarık; *fig*. ayrılık (*fikir*).

gull¹ ORN [gʌl] *n.* martı.

gull² [-] **1.** *n.* hile, oyun, aldatma; kolay aldatılan kimse, saf kimse; **2.** *v/t.* aldatmak, dolandırmak, hile yoluyla almak.

gul.let [ˈgʌlit] *n.* boğaz, gırtlak.

gul.li.bil.i.ty [gʌliˈbiliti] *n.* kolay aldanma, saflık, bönlük; **gul.li.ble** □ [ˈ-ləbl] kolay aldanır, saf, ahmak, bön.

gul.ly [ˈgʌli] *n.* sel ve yağmur suyunun oluşturduğu dere; su kanalı.

gulp [gʌlp] **1.** *n.* yudum, yutma; **2.** *v/t.* yutmak, yutuvermek.

gum¹ [gʌm] *n. a.* ~**s** *pl.* dişeti.

gum² [-] **1.** *n.* zamk; sakız, çiklet; jelatinli şekerleme; sakız ağacı; ~**s** *pl. Am.* lastik ayakkabı; **2.** *v/t.* zamklamak, yapıştırmak.

gum.boil MED [ˈgʌmbɔil] *n.* dişeti iltihabı.

gum.my [ˈgʌmi] *adj.* yapışkan, sakız gibi, yapış yapış.

gump.tion F [ˈgʌmpʃən] *n.* girişkenlik, cesaret, beceriklilik.

gun [gʌn] **1.** *n.* top, tüfek, silâh; *part. Am.* tabanca, revolver; **big** *veya* **great** ~ F kodaman, nüfuzlu kimse; **stick to one's** ~ ayak diremek, davasından vazgeçmemek; **2.** *vb. Am.* tüfekle ateş etm.; tüfekle avlanmak; '~**.boat** *n.* NAUT gambot; '~**-car.riage** *n.* MIL top arabası; '~**-cot.ton** *n.* pamuk barutu; '~**-li.cence** *n.* silah taşıma ruhsatı; '~**.man** *n. part. Am.* silahlı kimse, silahlı gangster, silahlı soyguncu; '~**-met.al** *n.* top dökümü, kızıl döküm; '**gun.ner** *n.* MIL, NAUT topçu (subayı); '**gunner.y** *n.* MIL topçuluk (tekniği).

gun.ny [ˈgʌni] *n.* çuval bezi, çul.

gun…; '~**.pow.der** *n.* barut; ♀ *Plot* HIST 5 Kasım 1605'te Parlamento binasını havaya uçurmayı amaçlayan suikast; '~**-room** *n.* NAUT subaylara ait oda; '~**-running** *n.* silah kaçakçılığı; '~**.shot** *n.* silah atışı; top menzili; '~**-shy** *adj.* silah sesinden ürken (*esp. köpek, at*); '~**.smith** *n.* silahçı, tüfekçi; '~**-tur.ret** *n.* taret, zırhlı kule.

gun.wale NAUT [ˈgʌnl] *n.* filika küpeştesi, borda tirizi.

gur.gle [ˈgɔːgl] **1.** *n.* çağıltı, gurultu, fokurtu; **2.** *v/i.* çağıldamak, guruldamak, fokurdamak; çağıltı gibi ses çıkarmak.

gush [gʌʃ] **1.** *n.* fışkırma, taşma; *fig.* coşku, taşkınlık; **2.** *v/i.* fışkırmak (**from** *-den*); *fig. b-ne* hayran kalmak, bayılmak; '**gush.er** *n. fig.* hayran olmuş kimse; petrol kuyusu; '**gush.ing**

□ coşkun, taşkın, heyecanlı.

gus.set [gʌsit] *n.* elbiseleri bollaştırmak için yanlarına eklenen kumaş parçası, üç köşeli peş.

gust [gʌst] *n.* ani rüzgâr, bora; coşku.

gus.ta.to.ry [ˈgʌstətəri] *adj.* tatma duyusuyla ilgili, tatma…

gus.to [ˈgʌstəu] *n.* zevk alma, haz, kişisel arzu, istek (**for** *-e*).

gus.ty [ˈgʌsti] rüzgârlı, fırtınalı.

gut [gʌt] **1.** *n.* bağırsak; MUS bağırsaktan yapılan çalgı teli; ~**s** *pl.* bağırsaklar; *sl.* cesaret, azim, kararlılık; **2.** *v/t.* bağırsaklarını dışarı çıkarmak (*ölü hayvanın*); içini tamamen tahrip etm., yağma etm.

gut.ta-per.cha [ˈgʌtəˈpəːtʃə] *n.* gutaperka, Malezya'da bazı ağaçlardan elde edilen kauçuğa benzer bir madde.

gut.ter [ˈgʌtə] **1.** *n.* oluk, suyolu, hendek; *fig.* bayağılık, sefalet; **2.** *v/t.* hendek açmak, oluk açmak, su yolu kazmak; *v/i.* oluk gibi akmak; eriyip akmak (*mum*); ~ **press** müstehcen hikâyelere veya skandallara daha çok yer veren gazeteler; '~**-snipe** *n.* sokak çocuğu, köprüaltı çocuğu, kenar mahalle çocuğu.

gut.tur.al [ˈgʌtərəl] **1.** □ gırtlağa ait, gırtlak…; **2.** *n.* GR gırtlaktan çıkarılan ses.

guy¹ [gai] **1.** *n.* F acayip kılıklı herif; *part. Am.* F herif, adam; **2.** *v/t.* alay etm., dalga geçmek.

guy² [-] *n. bşi* yerinde tutan halat *veya* zincir; NAUT gemi direklerini yerinde tutan halat.

guz.zle [ˈgʌzl] *vb.* obur gibi yemek, çok ve hızlı içmek.

gym F [dʒim] = *gymnasium, gymnastics.*

gym.kha.na [dʒimˈkɑːnə] *n.* atletizm yarışması; araba yarışı.

gym.na.si.um [dʒimˈneizjəm] *n.* spor salonu; **gym.nast** [ˈ-næst] *n.* beden eğitimi öğretmeni *veya* uzmanı; **gym-'nas.tic 1.** *adj.* (~**ally**) beden eğitimine ait, atletizm…; ~ **competition** jimnastik müsabakası; **2.** ~**s** *n. pl.* jimnastik, idman, beden eğitimi; '**gym-shoes** *n. pl.* F beden ayakkabısı, jimnastik ayakkabısı.

gyn.ae.col.o.gist [gainiˈkɔlədʒist] *n.* jinekolog, kadın-doğum hastalıkları mütehassısı; **gyn.ae'col.o.gy** *n.* jinekoloji, kadındoğum hastalıkları bilgisi.

gyp [dʒip] *n.* (*Cambridge Üniversite-*

si'nde) öğrencilere hizmet eden erkek hizmetçi; hilebaz, dolandırıcı; **give s.o. ~ b-ni** acımasızca azarlamak *veya* cezalandırmak, dövmek.

gyp.se.ous ['dʒipsiəs] *adj.* alçı gibi; alçılı.

gyp.sum MIN ['dʒipsəm] *n.* alçıtaşı.

gyp.sy *part. Am.* ['dʒipsi] = **gipsy**.

gy.rate [dʒaiə'reit] *v/i.* dönmek, deveran etm., devretmek; **gy'ra.tion** *n.* dönüş, dönme, deveran; **gy.ra.to.ry** ['-rə-təri] *adj.* dönen..., devreden...

gy.ro-com.pass PHYS ['dʒaiərəu-'kʌmpəs] *n.* giroskoplu pusula, topaç pusulası; **gyro.scope** ['gaiərəskəup] *n.* giroskop, topaç; **gy.ro.scop.ic sta-bi.liz.er** [gaiərəs'kɔpik'steibilaizə], **gy.ro'sta.bi.liz.er** *n.* giroskopik stabilizatör.

gyve *poet.* [dʒaiv] **1.** *n.* ~s *pl.* ayak zinciri, pranga; **2.** *v/t.* prangaya vurmak.

H

h [eitʃ]: **drop one's h's** h harfini söylememek.

ha [ha:] *int.* ha!, vay!, ya!, oh!

ha.be.as cor.pus JUR ['heibjəs'kɔ:pəs] *n. a.* **writ of ~** bir suçluyu hakim huzuruna çıkarma emri, ihzar emri.

hab.er.dash.er ['hæbədæʃə] *n.* tuhafiyeci; *Am.* erkek giyimi satan mağaza; 'haber.dash.er.y *n.* tuhafiye dükkânı; tuhafiye (eşyası); *Am.* erkek giyim eşyası.

ha.bil.i.ments [hə'bilimənts] *n. pl.* elbise, kıyafet, kılık; teçhizat, tertibat.

hab.it ['hæbit] **1.** *n.* âdet, alışkanlık, huy, tabiat; iptilâ, düşkünlük; zihni yapı; yaradılış; din adamlarının giydiği özel kıyafet; **fall** *veya* **get into bad ~s** kötü huylar edinmek; **get out of a ~** bir alışkanlıktan kurtulmak, bir alışkanlığı bırakmak; **get into the ~ of smoking** sigara içmeye alışmak, sigara içmeyi alışkanlık haline getirmek; **be in the ~ of** ...alışkanlığında olm., alışmak -e; **2.** *vb.* giydirmek; 'hab.it.a.ble *adj.* oturmaya elverişli, oturulabilir; **hab.i.tat** BOT, ZOO ['-tæt] *n.* bir hayvan *veya* bitkinin büyüdüğü yer; **hab.i'ta.tion** *n.* ikamet, oturma; ikametgâh, mesken, ev.

ha.bit.u.al □ [hə'bitjuəl] âdet olmuş, alışılmış; daimî...; **ha'bit.u.ate** [-eit] *vb.* alıştırmak (**to** -e); **hab.i.tude** ['hæbitju:d] *n.* âdet, alışkanlık; eğilim, istidat; **habit.u.é** [hə'bitjuei] *n.* müdavim, daimî ziyaretçi, gedikli müşteri.

hack¹ [hæk] **1.** *n.* vuruş, darbe; madenci kazması; kesici alet, çentik aleti; çentik, kertik, diş; kuru öksürük; *futbol:* tekme yarası; **2.** *v/t.* çentmek, yarmak, yontmak; kıymak, doğramak; keserek

temizlemek; becermek; *futbol:* tekme atmak; **~ing cough** kuru öksürük.

hack² [-] **1.** *n.* kira beygiri; yaşlı at; kiralık at arabası; taksi; taksi şoförü; *a.* ~ **writer** değersiz yazılar yazan kalitesiz yazar **2.** *adj.* kiralık...; *fig.* âdi, bayağı, basmakalıp; bayatlamış; **3.** *vb.* yıpratmak, eskitmek, âdileştirmek; rahvan yürüyüşle ata binmek; araba kullanmak; taksi şoförlüğü yapmak.

hack.le ['hækl] **1.** *n.* MEC kendir *veya* keten tarağı; ORN horozun boynundaki uzun tüyler; **get s.o.'s ~ up** *fig.* b-ni kızdırmak, öfkelendirmek; **2.** *vb.* keten tarağı ile taramak; olta ucuna sunî sinek yemi takmak; yarmak, yontmak, çentmek, parçalamak.

hack.ney ['hækni] *n.* binek *veya* koşum atı; ~ **car.riage**, ~ **coach** kiralık at arabası; 'hack.neyed *adj. fig.* adi, bayağı; eskimiş, yıpranmış; basmakalıp; kaşarlanmış.

hack-saw MEC ['hæksɔ:] *n.* demir testeresi.

had [hæd, həd] *pret. & p.p. of* **have**.

had.dock ICHTH ['hædək] *n.* mez(g)it balığı.

Ha.des ['heidi:z] *n.* ölülerin ruhlarının bulunduğu yer, ölüler diyarı.

h(a)e.mal ['hi:məl] *adj.* kanla *veya* damarlarla ilgili, kan...

h(a)em.a.tite MIN ['hemətait] *n.* hematit.

h(a)e.mo... ['hi:məu] *prefix* kan...

h(a)e.mo.glo.bin MED [hi:məu'gləubin] *n.* hemoglobin; **h(a)e.mo.phil.i.a** [-'filiə] *n.* hemofili, kanın pıhtılaşmaması.

h(a)em.or.rhage ['heməridʒ] *n.* kanama; **h(a)em.or.rhoids** ['-rɔidz] *n. pl.*

basur, emeroit.

haft [hɑːft] *n.* balta *veya* bıçak sapı, kılıç kabzası.

hag [hæg] *n. mst fig.* acuze, cadı, çirkin kadın, kocakarı, büyücü kadın.

hag.gard □ ['hægəd] bitkin görünüşlü, çökmüş, çelimsiz, bir deri bir kemik.

hag.gle ['hægl] *vb.* sıkı pazarlık etm.; çekişmek, münakaşa etm.; doğramak, parçalamak.

hag.i.ol.o.gy [hægi'ɔlədʒi] *n.* azizlerin hayatı ile ilgili edebiyat.

hag.rid.den ['hægridn] *adj.* bitkin, yorgun, usanmış.

hah [hɑː] *int.* ha!, vay!, ya!, oh!

ha-ha [hɑː'hɑː] *n.* alçak çit.

hail¹ [heil] **1.** *n.* dolu; dolu gibi yağan şey; **2.** *vb.* dolu yağmak; yağdırmak (*küfür*); hızlı ve şiddetli gelmek (*yumruk*).

hail² [-] **1.** *vb.* çağırmak; demek; alkışlarla karşılamak, selâmlamak; ~ *from* ...limanından kalkmak; ...li olm.; **2.** *n.* selâmlama, seslenme; ~*! selâm!; within* ~ duyulacak mesafede, yakın; *be~fellow-well-met with* b-*le* samimi dost olm., yakın arkadaş olm, canciğer olm.

hail.stone ['heilstəun] *n.* dolu tanesi; '**hailstorm** *n.* dolu fırtınası; *fig.* yağmur (*soru, küfür, mermi*).

hair [hɛə] *n.* saç, kıl, tüy; kıl payı mesafe; *keep your ~ on! sl.* sakin ol!; *not turn a* ~ kılını kıpırdatmamak; ~*'s breadth* = '~**breadth** *n.* kıl payı mesafe, ucuz kurtulma; *by veya within* ~ az kaldı, ramak kaldı; '~*cut n.* saç kesme, saç traşı; saç kesilme biçimi; '~*do n. Am.* saç tuvaleti; '~*dress.er n.* (*part. kadın*) ku(v)aför, berber; '~*dri.er n.* saç kurutma makinesi; **haired** *comb.* ...saçlı; '**hairi.ness** *n.* tüylülük, kıllılık; tehlike, risk.

hair...: '~*less adj.* saçsız, kel, saçlara dökülmüş; '~*pin n.* firkete, saç tokası; ~ *bend* keskin viraj; '~*rais.ing adj.* tüyler ürpertici, korkunç; '~*shirt n.* sert hayvan kılından yapılmış gömlek; '~*split.ting n.* kılı kırk yarma; '~*spring n. mec* saat içindeki kıl yay; '**hair.y** *adj.* kıllı, tüylü; kıldan yapılmış; kıl gibi; *sl.* tehlikeli, riskli.

ha.la.tion PHOT [hə'leiʃən] *n.* resmin sürekspoze kısmı.

hal.berd MIL ['hælbəːd] *n.* Ortaçağda kullanılan baltalı kargı.

hal.cy.on ['hælsiən] **1.** *n.* yalıçapkını, is-

kelekuşu, emircik; **2.** *adj.* durgun, sakin, dingin.

hale [heil] *adj.* sağlam, dinç, zinde; ~ *and hearty* dinç ve canlı.

half [hɑːf] **1.** *adj.* yarımbuçuk; ~ *a crown* iki buçuk şilin değerindeki eski İngiliz parası; *a pound and a* ~ bir buçuk pound; *not~ sl.* hem de nasıl; çok fazla; adamakıllı; **2.** *n. pl.* **halves** [hɑːvz] yarı; eş; yarım saat; *okul:* sömestr, dönem; yarım dolar; *s.* ~*back; too clever by* ~ gereğinden fazla akıllı; *by halves* yarımyamalak, tamamlanmamış; *go halves* yarı yarıya bölüşmek *-i*; '~*back n. futbol:* hafbek; '~*baked adj. fig.* acemi, deneyimsiz, toy; aptalca, iyi düşünülmemiş; iyi pişmemiş; '~*bind.ing n.* arkası ve köşeleri daha iyi kalite bezle kaplı cilt; '~*blood n.* melez, yarım kan; '~*bound adj.* arkası ve köşeleri daha iyi kalite bez kaplı; '~*bred adj.* melez...; '~*breed n.* melez; '~*calf n.* kitabın arkasını ve köşelerini kaplama derisi; '~*caste n.* melez; '~*crown n.* iki buçuk şilin değerindeki eski İngiliz parası; '~*'heart.ed* □ isteksiz, gayretsiz; '~*'hol.i.day n.* yarım günlük tatil; '~*'hour* **1.** *n.* yarım saat; **2.** *adj.* yarım saatlik; '~*hour.ly adj. & adv.* yarım saatte bir; '~*'length n.* vücudun yukarı kısmını gösteren resim; '~*life* (**pe.ri.od**) *n.* PHYS yarıla(n)ma süresi; '~*'mast:* (*at*) ~ yarıya indirilmiş (*bayrak*); '~*'moon n.* yarımay; '~*mourning n.* yarı matem elbisesi; '~*'pay n.* yarım maaş; açıkta bekleme maaşı; ~*pen.ny* ['heipni] *n.* yarım peni; ~*seas-o.ver* F ['hɑːfsiːz'əuvə] *adj.* çakırkeyf; '~*time n. spor:* haftaym, yarı devre; '~*tone proc.ess* MEC resmi hafif noktalarla gösterme işlemi; '~*track n.* yarısı paletli askeri araç; '~*way adj.* yarı yolda; yetersiz; ~ *house* yarı yolda bulunan otel *veya* han; *fig.* akıl hastası *veya* uyuşturucu madde kullananları toplum hayatına alıştıran yer; '~*'wit n.* aptal (*veya* ahmak, budala) kimse; '~*'wit.ted adj.* aptal, ahmak, budala.

hal.i.but ICHTH ['hælibət] *n.* kalkana benzer yassı bir balık.

hall [hɔːl] *n.* salon; resmi bina; hol; koridor; UNIV yemek salonu; ~ *of residence* yurt, lojman.

hal.le.lu.jah [hæli'luːjə] *n.* Tanrıya şükretme.

hall...: '~-mark **1.** *n.* altın *veya* gümüşte ayar damgası; *fig.* kalite işareti; **2.** *vb.* ayar damgası basmak; '~'stand *n.* portmanto.

hal.lo(a) [hə'ləu] *int.* alo!, hey!, yok ya!, bana bak!.

hal.loo [hə'lu:] **1.** *int.* hadi yavrum! (*köpeklere*); **2.** *n.* avda köpekleri saldırtma ünlemi; **3.** *v/i.* 'saldır' diye bağırmak; *v/t.* saldırtmak, tahrik etm.

hal.low ['hæləu] *vb.* kutsallaştırmak; kutsamak, takdis etm.; **Hal.low.mas** ['ˌmæs] *n.* Azizler yortusu.

hal.lu.ci.na.tion [həlu:si'neiʃən] *n.* varsanı, sanrı, kuruntu, vehim.

hall.way ['hɔːlwei] *n.* koridor; hol.

ha.lo ['heiləu] *n.* AST ağıl, hale, ışık halkası.

halt [hɔːlt] **1.** *n.* duruş; durma, duraklama; mola; RAIL ara istasyon; **2.** *v/t. & v/i.* dur(dur)mak; *mst fig.* tereddüt etm., duraksamak, duraklamak; **3.** *adj.* topal, aksak.

hal.ter ['hɔːltə] *n.* yular; idam ipi.

halve [hɑːv] *v/t.* yarıya bölmek; yarıya indirmek; **halves** [ˌz] *pl. of* **half 2**.

hal.yard NAUT ['hæljəd] *n.* bayrak *veya* seren ipi, kandilisa, abli.

ham [hæm] *n.* jambon, domuz budu; *sl.* amatör radyocu; amatör; *a.* ~ **actor** *sl.* amatör oyuncu.

ham.burg.er *Am.* ['hæmbəːgə] *n.* hamburger, köfteli sandviç; sığır kıyması; köfte.

ham-hand.ed ['hæmhændid] *adj.* eli ağır, beceriksiz.

ham.let ['hæmlit] *n.* küçük köy.

ham.mer ['hæmə] **1.** *n.* çekiç, tokmak; çekiç kemiği; tüfek horozu; ~ **and tongs** F büyük gürültü ve gayretle; **2.** *v/t.* çekiçle işlemek, çekiçle vurmak, çekiçle çakmak, çekiçlemek; yumruklamak; ~ **at** didinmek, uğraşıp durmak, durmadan çalışmak; ~ **out** düzeltmek, şekil vermek, plan yapmak.

ham.mock ['hæmək] *n.* hamak; ~ **chair** şezlong.

ham.per ['hæmpə] **1.** *n.* büyük sepet, sandık, çamaşır sepeti; **2.** *v/t.* engel olm. -*e*, mâni olm. -*e*.

ham.ster ZOO ['hæmstə] *n.* sıçan türünde bir hayvan.

ham.string ['hæmstriŋ] **1.** *n.* ANAT diz arkasındaki iki büyük kirişten biri; **2.** (*irr.* **string**) *vb.* bu kirişleri kesmek, kötürümleştirmek, sakatlamak; *fig.* gücünü kesmek, etkinliğini azaltmak,

kolunu kanadını kırmak.

hand [hænd] **1.** *n.* el; kuvvet, etki; elleri kullanmadaki hüner; ZOO ön ayak; işçi, amele; gemi tayfası; işe karışma, parmak; akrep, ibre; F adam, herif, biri; el yazısı; imza; *iskambil*: el, oyun; *pl.* sorumluluk, yetki, salahiyet; sahip olma; alkış; *at* ~ yakında, yakın, yanında; *be at* ~ yakın olm., yakında olm.; *at first* ~ doğrudan doğruya, ilk elden; *at s.o.'s* ~**s** ...den; *a good (poor)* ~ *at* ...de becerikli (beceriksiz); ~ *and glove* el ele, yardımlaşarak; *bear a* ~ yardım etm. -*e*; *by* ~ el ile; elden (*mektup*); *change* ~**s** el değiştirmek; sahip değiştirmek; *have a* ~ *in* ...de parmağı olm.; *in* ~ elde, mevcut, hazırda; bitirilmek üzere; COM nakit para; *lay* ~**s** *on* el atmak -*e*; şiddet kullanmak -*e*; bulmak -*i*; kutsamak, takdis etm. -*i*; *lend a* ~ yardım etm. -*e*; *off* ~ derhal, hemen, doğrudan doğruya; ~**s** *off!* elini sürme!, dokunma!; *on* ~ elde; COM mevcut, stokta; part. Am. hazır, rezerve edilmiş; *on one's* ~**s** ...nin elinde; *on all* ~**s** her tarafta, her yerde; *on the one* ~ bir taraftan; *on the other* ~ diğer taraftan; *out of* ~ derhal, hemen, gecikmeksizin; bitirilmiş; kontrolden çıkmış, çığrından çıkmış, elden çıkmış; ~ *over fist* süratle ve başarıyla; *take a* ~ *at* (*oyun v.b.*) katılmak -*e*; *to* (*one's*) ~ ...nin eline, ...nin elinde, eline geçmiş; ~ *to* ~ göğüs göğüse, yumruk yumruğa; *come to* ~ var mak, ele geçmek; *you can feed him out of your* ~ *fig.* onu kendine kul köle yapabilirsin; ona kendi fikirlerini kabul ettirebilirsin; *get the upper* ~ *of* ...in kontrolünü ele geçirmek, üstünlük sağlamak; *put one's* ~ *to* el koymak -*e*; *he can turn his* ~ *to anything* on parmağında on marifet var; ~**s** *up!* eller yukarı!; *s.* **high 1**; **2.** *v/t.* el ile vermek, uzatmak; yardım etm.; teslim etm.; ~ *down* nesilden nesile devretmek; ~ *in* teslim etm.; ~ *out* dağıtmak; sadaka olarak vermek; ~ *over* vermek, teslim etm., devretmek (*to* -*e*); '~-bag *n.* kadınların el çantası; para cüzdanı; '~-bar.row *n.* el arabası; '~-bill *n.* el ilanı; '~-book *n.* el kitabı, rehber; '~-brake *n.* MEC el freni; '~-cart *n.* el arabası, çekçek; '~-clap *n.* alkış; '~-cuff **1.** *n.* kelepçe; **2.** *v/t.* kelepçe vurmak; '**hand.ed** *comb.* ...elli; **hand.ful** ['ˌful] *n.* avuç dolusu; F avuç kadar miktar, çok az miktar; F ele avuca sığmayan kimse; '**hand-glass** *n*. saplı küçük ayna; '**hand.held** IT *n*. avuçiçi bilgisayar.

hand.i.cap ['hændikæp] **1.** *n*. engel, mâni, sekte, ket (*a. fig.*); handikap, elverişsiz durum; engelli koşu; **2.** *v/t*. sakatlamak engel olm. -*e*. mâni olm. -*e*; *fig. a*. ket vurmak -*e*, sekte vurmak -*e*.

hand.i.craft ['hændikrɑːft] *n*. el sanatı, el hüneri; '**hand.i.crafts.man** *n*. zanaatçı, küçük esnaf; '**hand.i.ness** *n*. beceri, maharet, ustalık; '**hand.i.work** *n*. iş, elişi.

hand.ker.chief ['hæŋkətʃif] *n*. mendil.

han.dle ['hændl] **1.** *n*. sap, kulp, tokmak, kabza, tutamaç, tutamak; *fig*. vasıta, imkân, bahane; F ünvan, paye, rütbe; *fly off the* ~ F tepesi atmak, küplere binmek; **2.** *v/t*. ellemek, ele almak, el sürmek, dokunmak, kullanmak; idare etm., muamele etm., davranmak; alıp satmak; '~-bar *n*. gidon (*bisiklette*).

hand...: '~.loom *n*. el dokuma tezgâhı; '~-lug.gage *n*. elde taşınabilir bagaj; '~-'made *adj*. elişi, el yapımı; '~-maid(.en) *n*. *fig*. hizmetçi kız, besleme, kız evlâtlık; '~-me-downs *n*. *Am*. F *pl*. kullalanılmış herhangi bş (*part. elbise*); '~-organ *n*. latarna, kollu çalgı aleti; '~-out *n*. F sadaka; bildiri; '~-rail *n*. trabzan, merdiven parmaklığı; '~.saw *n*. el testeresi; **hand.sel** ['hænsəl] *n*. uğur getirsin diye verilen hediye; siftah; pey; ilk taksit; '**hands-free** *adj*. hands-free (*araba telefonu, alet*); **hand.shake** ['hændʃeik] *n*. el sıkma; **hand.some** □ ['hænsəm] yakışıklı, güzel; cömert; iyi; bol.

hand...: '~.work *n*. elişi, el yapımı; '~.writing *n*. el yazısı; '**hand.y** □ yakın, el altında; eli işe yatkın, becerikli, usta, mahir; kullanışlı, elverişli, faydalı; ~ *man* elinden her iş gelen kimse.

hang [hæŋ] **1.** (*irr.*) *v/t*. asmak; asarak idam etm. (*pret. & p.p. mst* ~*ed*); takmak; yapıştırmak; sarkıtmak; eğmek (*baş*); galeride sergilemek (*resim*); *I'll be* ~*ed if* ... F ...irsem kahrolayım; ~ *it!* F lânet olsun!; ~ *fire* zamanında ateş almamak; yavaşlamak, gecikmek; ~ *out* asmak (*çamaşır*); sarkıtmak; *sl*. yaşamak, oturmak; ~ *up* kapamak (*telefonu*); asmak; *fig*. ertelemek, tehir etm., geri bırakmak; *v/i*. asılı olm. (*on -de*); asılmak, sallanmak; üstünde

dolaşmak; sallantıda olm., muallakta olm.; sarkmak; ~ *about* aylak aylak dolaşmak, başıboş gezerek beklemek, avare dolaşmak; ~ *back* tereddüt etm., çekinmek; ~ *on* sıkı tutmak, yapışmak; *fig*. peşini bırakmamak, azimle devam etm., bağlı olm. -*e*; ~ *by a hair*, ~ *by a single thread fig*. pamuk ipliğine bağlı olm.; *let things go* ~ F olayları gidişatına bırakmak, hiç aldırış etmemek; **2.** *n*. duruş (*elbise, perde*); F anlam, mana, kullanış şekli; *get the* ~ *of s.th.* F bşin nasıl çalıştığını öğrenmek, anlamını kavramak; *I don't care a* ~ *sl*. vız gelir tıris gider, hiç umurumda değil, iplemem.

hang.ar ['hæŋə] *n*. hangar.

hang.dog ['hæŋdɔg] **1.** *n*. sinsi adam, alçak adam; **2.** *adj*. sinsi, kurnaz, alçak, adi...

hang.er ['hæŋə] *n*. askı, kanca, çengel; '~.on *n*. *contp. fig*. beleşçi, çanak yalayıcı, asalak.

hang.ing ['hæŋiŋ] *adj*. asılı..., sarkan...; idama layık; ~ *committee* PAINT asılacak tablo seçimi yapan jüri; '**hang.ings** *n*. *pl*. oda duvarlarına asılan kumaş.

hang.man ['hæŋmən] *n*. cellat.

hang-nail MED ['hæŋneil] *n*. şeytantırnağı.

hang.out F ['hæŋ'aut] *n*. ev, mesken, sık gidilen yer.

hang-over ['hæŋəuvə] *n*. *sl*. içkiden gelen baş ağrısı, içkinin verdiği mahmurluk; *Am*. eski zamandan kalmış şey, kalıntı.

hank [hæŋk] *n*. çile; kangal.

han.ker ['hæŋkə] *vb*. arzulamak, özlemek, istemek (*after, for -i*); '**han.ker-ing** *n*. özlem, istek, arzu.

han.kie, han.ky F ['hæŋki] *n*. mendil.

han.ky-pan.ky F ['hæŋki' pæŋki] *n*. hilekârlık, üçkâğıtçılık, dümen, dolap.

Han.sard ['hænsɑːd] *n*. parlamento tutanağı (*İngiltere'de*).

Hanse [hæns] *n*. *the* ~ HIST tüccar loncası.

han.sel ['hænsəl] = *handsel*.

han.som ['hænsəm] *n. a*. ~-*cab* iki tekerlekli ve tek atlı araba.

hap *rare* [hæp] *n*. şans, talih; **hap'hazard 1.** *n*. şans, rastlantı; *at* ~ rasgele, şansa, gelişigüzel; **2.** *adj*. rasgele, gelişigüzel; '**hap.less** □ şanssız, talihsiz, bahtsız; '**hap.ly** *adv. obs*. şansa, belki, muhtemelen.

ha'p'orth F ['heipəθ] = *halfpenny-*

worth.

hap.pen ['hæpən] *vb.* olmak, vuku bulmak, meydana gelmek, vaki olm.; *he ~ed to be at home* bereket versin ki evdeydi, Allahtan evdeydi; **~ on, ~ upon** rast gelmek *-e,* şans eseri bulmak *-i;* **~ in** *Am.* F pat diye çıkıp gelmek; **~ to** *inf.* rasgele olm.; **'hap.pen.ing** *n.* olay, vaka, hadise.

hap.pi.ly ['hæpili] *adv.* mutlulukla, sevinçle.

hap.pi.ness ['hæpinis] *n.* mutluluk, saadet, bahtiyarlık.

hap.py □ ['hæpi] *com.* mutlu, mesut, bahtiyar, memnun, sevinçli, neşeli; şanslı, talihli; yerinde, uygun, münasip; **'~-go-'luck.y** *adj.* F kaygısız, gamsız, bir şeye aldırmaz, vurdumduymaz.

ha.rangue [hə'ræŋ] **1.** *n.* uzun konuşma, tirad, nutuk; **2.** *v/t.* nutuk çekmek *-e; v/i.* uzun uzun konuşmak, tirad söylemek.

har.ass ['hærəs] *v/t.* taciz etm. *-i,* tedirgin etm. *-i,* üzmek *-i,* rahat vermemek *e,* canını sıkmak; aralıksız saldırmak *-e.*

har.bin.ger ['ha:bindʒə] **1.** *n.* haberci, müjdeci; **2.** *vb.* olacağını önceden söylemek, haber vermek, müjdelemek.

har.bo(u)r ['ha:bə] **1.** *n.* liman; sığınak, barınak; **2.** *v/t. & v/i.* barın(dır)mak, korumak, saklamak, gizlemek; beslemek; akılda tutmak; sığınmak; yaşamak, oturmak; **'har.bo(u)r.age** *n.* barınak, sığınak; **har.bo(u)r dues** NAUT *pl.* liman ücreti.

hard [ha:d] **1.** *adj. com.* sert, katı; zor, güç, ağır, müşkül; çetin; kötü, acı; merhametsiz, acımasız, gaddar, kalpsiz; kuvvetli ve adaleli; GR kalın sesli (*harf*); *part. Am.* sert (*içki*), alkol derecesi yüksek; *the ~ facts pl.* kesin deliller; **~ of hearing** kulağı ağır işiten; *~ to deal with* uğraşması zor; *be ~ (up-) on s.o.* b-ne haşin davranmak, acımasızca muamele etm.; **2.** *adv.* sıkıca, zorla, kuvvetle, kuvvetlice, hızla; güçlükle, zorlukla, acıyla, mücadeleyle; katı, sıkı; **~ by** pek yakın, yanıbaşında; **~ up** parasız, eli dar, muhtaç (*for -e*); *be ~ put to it* büyük güçlükle karşılaşmak, zor durumda olm.; *ride ~* atı çatlatırcasına sürmek; **3.** *n.* F çalışma yükümlülüğü; **~ and fast** değişmez, kati (*kanun*); **'~-back** *n.* ciltli kitap; **'~-'bitten** *adj.* inatçı, bildiğini okuyan;

'~-'boiled *adj.* lop, katı (*yumurta*); *part. Am.* sert, katı; eski kurt, pişkin; **~ cash** madeni para; nakit para; **'~-cov.er = hard-back; ~ curren.cy** sağlam döviz, sağlam para; **'harden** *v/t. & v/i.* katılaş(tır)mak, sertleş(tir)mek, pekiş(tir)mek, kuvvetlen(dir)mek, don(dur)mak; *fig.* hissizleştirmek; COM yükselmek (*fiyat*).

hard...: '~-'fea.tured *adj.* sert ifadeli; '~-'fist.ed *adj.* eli sıkı, cimri, pinti; bileği kuvvetli; '~-head.ed *adj.* makûl düşünen, gerçekçi; inatçı, dik kafalı; '~-'heart.ed □ taş yürekli, kalpsiz, vicdansız, acımasız.

har.di.hood ['ha:dihud] *n.* yiğitlik, cesaret; cüret; arsızlık, küstahlık; **'har.di.ness** *n.* dayanıklılık, mukavemet, tahammül; *rare* cesaret, yiğitlik.

hard.ly ['ha:dli] *adv.* hemen hiç; ancak; güçlükle, güçbelâ; az bir ihtimalle; **'hard-'mouthed** *adj.* inatçı, dik kafalı; azimkâr, azimli; **'hard.ness** güçlük, zorluk; sertlik (*a. fig.*); terslik, aksilik.

hard...: '~.pan *n. Am.* sert toprak, killi toprak; *fig.* sağlam temeller, temel ilkeler; '~-'set *adj.* donmuş (*çimento vs.*); sert, katı, sabit; acıkmış; '~.shell *adj.* sert kabuklu; *fig.* sabit fikirli; **'hard.ship** *n.* sıkıntı, güçlük, zorluk, meşakkat, cefa; **'hard.ware** *n.* madeni eşya, hırdavat; silah; *bilgisayar:* mekanik aksam; **'hardwood** *n.* sert tahtalı ağaç (*kerestesi*); **'hard-working** *adj.* çok çalışkan.

har.dy □ ['ha:di] dayanıklı, tahammüllü, mukavim; cesur, yiğit, gözüpek; küstah, arsız, yüzsüz; soğuğa dayanıklı (*bitki*).

hare [hɛə] *n.* tavşan; ~ **and hounds** yola kâğıt parçaları saçarak oynanan tavşantazı oyunu; '~.bell *n.* çançiçeği, yaban sümbülü; '~-brained *adj.* aptal, kuş beyinli, kafasız; '~.lip *n.* MED tavşandudağı, yarık dudak.

ha.rem ['hɛərəm] *n.* harem (dairesi).

har.i.cot ['hærikəu] *n.* fasulye; *a.* **~ bean** kuru fasulye.

hark [ha:k] *v/i.* dinlemek (*to -i*); **~!** dinle!, kulağını aç!; **~ back** HUNT geri çağırmak (*tazı*); *fig.* sadede gelmek, aynı konuya değinmek (*to*); **'hark.en = hearken.**

har.lot ['ha:lət] *n.* fahişe, orospu; **'har.lot.ry** *n.* fahişelik, orospuluk.

harm [ha:m] **1.** *n.* zarar, ziyan, hasar; kötülük; felâket; *out of ~'s way* emin

yerde, emniyette, kötülükten uzak; **2.**
v/t. zarar vermek *-e*, kötülük etm. *-e*;
harm.ful □ ['-ful] zararlı, kötü, fena;
'**harm.less**□ zararsız, masum, suçsuz.
har.mon.ic [hɑː'mɔnik] *adj.* (**~***ally*)
uyumlu, ahenkli; harmonik, kulağa
hoş gelen; **har'mon.i.ca** MUS [-kə] *n.*
armonika, ağız mızıkası; **har.mo.ni-
ous**□ [hɑː'məunjəs] ahenkli, uyumlu
(*a. fig.*); düzenli, muntazam; iyi geçinen; tatlı sesli, hoş sesli; **har.monize**
['hɑːmənaiz] *v/t.* akord etm., harmoni-
sini yapmak, düzen vermek; *v/i.* ahenkli çalmak *veya* şarkı söylemek; uymak
-e, uyum sağlamak *-e*; '**har.mo.ny** *n.*
uyum, ahenk; harmoni, ses uyumu.
har.ness ['hɑːnis] **1.** *n.* koşum; iş donanımı; işbaşı; zırh; *die in* ~ iş başında
ölmek, çalışırken ölmek; **2.** *v/t.* koşmak
(*atı*), koşum takımını vurmak; boyunduruk vurmak; kullanmak, yararlanmak; istifade etm.
harp MUS [hɑːp] **1.** *n.* harp; **2.** *vb.* harp
çalmak; ~ (*up*)*on* *bşin* üzerinde çok
durmak, *bşi* defalarca anlatmak; *be always* ~*ing on the same string* hep
aynı telden çalmak; '**harp.e**r, '**harp.ist**
n. harpçı.
har.poon [hɑː'puːn] **1.** *n.* zıpkın; **2.** *v/t.*
zıpkınlamak, zıpkınla öldürmek.
harp.si.chordMUS ['hɑːpsikɔːd] *n.* eski
tip piyano, harpsikord.
har.py['hɑːpi] *n.* MYTH yüzü kadına, kanatları kuşa benzeyen vahşi yaratık;
fig. zalim kadın, merhametsiz kadın.
har.ri.dan ['hæridən] *n.* huysuz kocakarı.
har.ri.er['hæriə] *n.* HUNT tavşan tazısı;
kros koşucusu.
har.rowAGR ['hærəu] **1.** *n.* sürgü, tapan,
tırmık; **2.** *vb.* sürgü geçirmek *-e*, tırmık
çekmek *-e*, kesek kırmak; *fig.* sinirlendirmek *-i*, keder vermek *-e*; ~*ing* üzücü.
har.ry ['hæri] *vb.* yağma etm., talan
etm., soymak; saldırmak; üzmek,
canını sıkmak, rahat vermemek.
harsh□ [hɑːʃ] sert, haşin, merhametsiz, gaddar, ters, huysuz; kalın, kaba,
kulağı tırmalayan (*ses*); '**harsh.ness**
n. kabalık, haşinlik, terslik, gaddarlık.
hartZOO [hɑːt] *n.* erkek karaca; **hartshorn** CHEM ['hɑːtshɔːn] *n.* amonyum
karbonatı, nişadır kaymağı.
har.um-scar.um F ['hɛərəm'skɛərəm]
1. *adj.* patavatsız, pervasız, kayıtsız,
dünyayı umursamayan; **2.** *n.* düşünce-

sizce hareket eden kimse, delidolu
kimse.
har.vest ['hɑːvist] **1.** *n.* hasat (mevsimi); ürün, mahsül, rekolte; *fig.* semere,
sonuç, netice; ~ *festival*, ~ *thanksgiv-
ing* hasattan sonra yapılan şenlik; **2.**
v/t. toplamak (*ürün*); biçmek *-i*, hasat
etm. *-i*; '**har.vest.er**n. orakçı, hasatçı;
orak makinesi, biçerdöver; '**har.vest-
-'home**n. harman sonunda verilen ziyafet.
has[hæz, həz] *s. have*; '~**-been**n. F eski
özelliği kalmamış şey *veya* kimse, modası geçmiş şey *veya* kimse.
hash[hæʃ] **1.** *n.* kıymalı yemek; *Am.* F
haşiş; *fig.* karmakarışık şey, karman
çorman şey; *make a* ~ *of* F *bşi* karman
çorman etm., yüzüne gözüne bulaştırmak; *settle s.o.'s* ~ F *b-nin* defterini
dürmek; **2.** *v/t.* doğramak *-i*, kıymak *-i*.
hasp[hɑːsp] **1.** *n.* asma kilit köprüsü,
kenet; **2.** *vb.* kenetlemek, kopçalamak.
has.sock ['hæsək] *n.* diz dayayacak
minder; ECCL kilisede üstünde diz çö-
külüp dua edilen minder.
hastobs. [hæst] *2nd sg. of* **have**.
haste[heist] *n.* acele, hız, sürat, telaş,
ivedilik; *make* ~ acele etm.; çabuk davranmak; *more* ~ *less speed*, *make* ~
slowly acele işe şeytan karışır; **has.ten**
['heisn] *v/t. & v/i.* acele et(tir)mek,
hızlan(dır)mak, sıkış(tır)mak; **hast.i-
ness** ['heistinis] *n.* acelecilik, telaş;
'**hast.y** □ acele, çabuk, ivedi, süratli,
tez; üstünkörü.
hat[hæt] *n.* şapka; *my* ~*!* sl. hayret doğrusu!, vay canına!; *hang up one's* ~
devam etmemek, noktalamak; *talk
through one's* ~ aptal aptal konuşmak, palavra atmak.
hatch[1] [hætʃ] **1.** *n.* kuluçka, civciler;
yumurtadan çıkan hayvancıklar; NAUT,
AVIA ambar ağzı, ambar kapağı, kaporta; üstü açık kapı; *under* ~*es* güverte
altında; **2.** *v/t. & v/i.* yumurtadan
çık(ar)mak; *fig.* kurmak (*plan*), tasarlamak (*entrika*).
hatch[2] [-] *vb.* ince çizgilerle süslemek
-i, paralel çizgiler çekmek *-e*.
hatch.er.y['hætʃəri] *n.* üretme çiftliği
(*esp. balık*).
hatch.et['hætʃit] *n.* küçük balta; *bury
the* ~ barışmak, dost olm.; '~**-face**n. ince yüz.
hatch.way NAUT ['hætʃwei] *n.* lombar
ağzı, ambar ağzı.
hate[heit] **1.** *n. poet.* nefret, kin, garez,

düşmanlık (**to**, **towards** -e karşı); **2.** v/t. nefret etm. -den; kin beslemek -e karşı; F üzülmek -e, pişman olm. -e; **hate.ful**□ ['-ful] nefret verici, iğrenç, kötü;   'hat.er n. kinci kimse.

ha.tred ['heitrid] n. kin, nefret, düşmanlık (**of** -e karşı).

hat.ter['hætə] n. şapkacı; **as mad as a** ~ zırdeli.

haugh.ti.ness ['hɔ:tinis] n. gurur, kurum, kibir, kendini beğenmişlik;   'haugh.ty □ kibirli, mağrur, kendini beğenmiş.

haul [hɔ:l] **1.** n. çekme, çekiş; bir ağda çıkarılan balık miktarı, foroz; Am. taşıma mesafesi; çalınmış mal; çekici alet; yük; **2.** vb. çekmek (**at** -i); NAUT geminin yönünü değiştirmek; MIN çıkarmak, taşımak; NAUT çekerek taşımak; ~ **down one's flag** bayrağını indirmek; fig. teslim olm.;   'haul.age n. taşıma, nakliye; nakliye ücreti; MIN çıkarma, çekme; haul.ier['-jə] n. nakliye şirketi; nakliyeci.

haulm [hɔ:m] n. ekin sapı, saman; bitki sapı.

haunch [hɔ:ntʃ] n. kalça, but; sağrı.

haunt [hɔ:nt] **1.** n. uğrak, sık sık gidilen yer; **2.** v/t. sık sık uğramak -e; sık görünmek -de, sık sık ziyaret etm. -i (hortlak olarak); akıldan çıkmamak, devamlı aklına gelmek; **the house is** ~**ed** ev perilidir; ~**ed house** perili (veya tekin olmayan) ev; 'haunt.er n. devamlı müşteri, müdavim.

haut.boy MUS ['əubɔi] n. obua.

hau.teur [əu'tə:] n. kibir, gurur, azamet.

Ha.van.a[hə'vænə] n. a. ~ **cigar** Havana purosu.

have[hæv, həv] **1.** (irr.) v/t. malik olm., sahip olm. -e; olmak; fikir taşımak, fikri olm.; izin vermek -e; ettirmek; almak, elinde tutmak; yemek; çekmek, katlanmak -e, geçirmek; aldatmak, üc kağıda getirmek; yenmek, alt etm., mat etm. -i; yaptırmak -i; ~ **to** inf. -meğe mecbur olm.; **I** ~ **my hair cut** saçımı kestiririm; **he had his leg broken** ayağı kırıldı, düşüp bacağını kırdı; **I would** ~ **you know** bilmeni isterim ki, şunu bilesin ki; **he will** ~ **it that...** ...diğini iddia ediyor, iddia ediyor ki; **I had better** (**best**) **go** gitsem iyi olur (en iyisi ben gideyim); **I had rather go** gitmeyi tercih ederim; **let s.o.** ~ **it**

b-ni cezalandırmak, dövmek; ~ **about one** üzerinde bulundurmak (para vs.); ~ **at him!** saldır ona!; ~ **on** taşımak, üzerinde giyiyor olm.; fig. kastetmek, niyetinde olm.; kandırmak, oyun oynamak; ~ **it out with** b-le bşi tartışarak veya kavga ederek çözümlemek; ~ **s.o. up** F b-ni misafir olarak ağırlamak; ~ mahkemeye çıkarmak (**for** için); **2.** v/aux. (yardımcı fiil olarak bileşik fiil şekillerine katılır) **I** ~ **come** geldim; **3.** n. F dolandırıcılık, dalavere, yalan dolan, düzen, hile.

ha.ven['heivn] n. liman; sığınak, barınak (a. fig.).

have-not['hævnɔt] n. fakir kimse, yoksul kimse.

haven't['hævnt] = **have not**.

hav.er.sack ['hævəsæk] n. MIL asker çantası, kumanya torbası.

hav.ing ['hæviŋ] n. ~**s** pl. mal, mülk, servet, zenginlik.

hav.oc ['hævək] n. zarar, ziyan, hasar, tahribat; **make** ~ **of**, **play** ~ **with** veya **among** harabeye çevirmek -i, çok zarar vermek -e, tahrip etm. -i, yerle bir etm. -i.

haw[1] BOT [hɔ:] n. alıç.

haw[2][_] **1.** vb. 'hım' demek, kaçamaklı konuşmak; kekelemek; hafifçe öksürmek; **2.** n. kekeleme, kaçamaklı konuşma, hafifçe öksürme.

Ha.wai.ian[hɑː'waiiən] **1.** adj. Hawaii'ye ait, Hawaii...; **2.** n. Hawaii'li kimse.

haw.finch ORN ['hɔ:fintʃ] n. flurcun.

haw-haw['hɔː'hɔː] vb. şiddetli kahkaha atmak.

hawk[1][hɔ:k] **1.** n. ORN şahin, doğan, atmaca; **2.** vb. doğan şahin veya atmacayla avlamak (**at** -i).

hawk[2][_] vb. 'öhö öhö' diye öksürmek; balgam çıkarmak.

hawk[3][_] vb. seyyar satıcılık yapmak, işportacılık yapmak, sokak sokak dolaşıp öteberi satmak; **hawk.er** n. seyyar satıcı, işportacı.

hawk-eyed ['hɔ:kaid] adj. keskin bakışlı;   'hawk.ing n. doğancılık, doğanla avlanma.

hawse NAUT [hɔ:z] n. a. ~**-hole** loça deliği.

haw ser NAUT ['hɔ:zə] n. palamar, yoma, kablo.

haw.thorn BOT ['hɔ:θɔːn] n. yabani akdiken, alıç.

hay[hei] **1.** n. kuru ot, saman; **make**~ **of** karmakarışık etm. -i; **2.** vb. kuru ot biç-

mek; samanla beslemek *-i*, saman yedirmek *-e*; '**~box** *n. a.* ~ **cooker** yemek
pişirme kutusu; '**~.cock** *n.* ot yığını;
tınaz; '**~.fe.ver** *n.* MED saman nezlesi;
'**~.loft** *n.* otluk, samanlık; '**~.mak.er**
n. sl. kuvvetli darbe, oturaklı yumruk;
'**~.rick** = **haycock**; '**~.seed** *n. part. Am.*
F hödük kimse, budala kimse, ahmak
kimse; '**~.stack** = **haycock**; '**~.wire**:
go ~ sapıtmak, kafayı üşütmek.
haz.ard ['hæzəd] **1.** *n.* riziko, tehlike; talih, baht, şans; **run a** ~ tehlikeye atılmak, riske girmek; **2.** *v/t.* talihe bırakmak *-i*, şansa bırakmak *-i*; tehlikeye atmak *-i*; '**haz.ard.ous** □ tehlikeli, rizikolu; şansa bağlı.
haze[1] [heiz] *n.* hafif sis, pus; *fig.* belirsizlik, çapraşıklık, şüphe.
haze[2] NAUT & *Am.* [-] *vb.* zulmetmek *-e*,
fazla çalıştırarak yormak *-i*; eşek
şakaşı yaparak üzmek *-i*.
ha.zel ['heizl] **1.** *n.* BOT fındık (ağacı); **2.**
adj. elâ (*göz*); '**~-nut** *n.* fındık.
ha.zy □ ['heizi] sisli, dumanlı, puslu;
fig. belirsiz, şüpheli, bulanık, kararsız;
be ~ kararsız olm., şüpheli olm.
H-bomb MIL ['eitʃbɔm] *n.* hidrojen
bombası.
he [hi:; hi] **1.** *pron.* o, kendisi, kimse (*erkek*); ~ **who o** ki; **2.** *prefix* erkek…
head [hed] **1.** *n. com.* baş, kafa, kelle;
fig. akıl, zihin, zekâ; tura, madeni paranın resimli yüzü; kişi, adam başı;
üst kısım; baş taraf, ön taraf; zirve, doruk; ekin başı, başak; (*pl. değişmez*)
baş, adet, tane (= *elli baş sığır*); başkan, şef, amir, reis, yönetici; GEOGR burun; suyun düşme yüksekliği; birikmiş
basınç; başlık, manşet, konu; bira köpüğü; ~ **and shoulders above the rest**
diğerlerinden üstün; **bring to a** ~ sonuçlandırmak, karar noktasına getirmek; **come to a** ~ bitmek, sona ermek,
doruğa ulaşmak; baş vermek (*sivilce*,
çıban); **gather** ~ yayılmak, çoğalmak;
get it into one's ~ **that…** …kafasına
koymak, …sanmak; **keep one's** ~
soğukkanlılığını korumak, kendine hâkim olm.; ~**(s) or tail(s)?** yazı mı tura
mı?; ~ **over heels** havada perende atma; adamakıllı, tamamen; **over** ~ **and
ears** aklının almadığı *veya* duymadığı;
I can't make ~ **or tail of it** hiçbir şey anlayamıyorum, anlıyorsam Arap
olayım; **take the** ~ idareyi eline almak,
yönetmek, başa geçmek; **2.** *adj.* başa
ait; başta olan; baş…; şef…; **3.** *v/t.*

başında olm. *-in*, önünde olm. *-in*, birinci sırasında gelmek *-in*; başını kesmek *-in*, budamak *-i*; baş takmak *-e*;
baş olm. *-e*; başına geçmek *-in*, lider
olm. *-e*; önüne geçmek *-in* (*yarışta*);
başa koymak *-i* (*listede*); başını çevirmek (*geminin*); *futbol*: kafa vurmak
(*topa*); **be ~ed** gidiyor olm. *-e*; ~ **off** yolunu kesmek *-in*; *v/i.* baş vermek (*lahana*, *turp*); NAUT başı bir yöne doğru
olm., gitmek, yönelmek (**for** *-e doğru*);
meydana çıkmak, olmak; *Am. futbol*:
topa kafa atmak; '**head.ache** *n.* baş
ağrısı; *fig.* dert, sorun; '**head.ach.y**
adj. başı ağrıyan; '**headband** *n.* saç
bantı; '**head-boy** *n.* okul temsilcisi erkek; '**head-dress** *n.* başlık; saçın ta-
ranış şekli; '**head.ed** *comb.* …başlı,
…kafalı; '**head.er** *n.* ARCH bağlantı
taşı; F balıklama (suya dalış); *futbol*:
kafa vuruşu; '**head-gear** *n.* başlık, şapka, baş örtüsü; dizgin, yular; '**head-girl**
n. okul temsilcisi kız; '**head-hunt.er** *n.*
kelle avcısı; F teknik eleman avcısı;
COM *bir kuruluş için gerekli önemli ele-
manları bulup transfer eden kimse*;
'**head.i.ness** *n.* sabırsızlık, acelecilik,
düşüncesizlik; haşinlik, sertlik, zorbalık, dikkafalılık; baş döndürücülük,
çarpıcılık (*içki*); '**head.ing** *n.* serlevha,
başlık; *spor*: kafa atma; '**head.land** *n.*
burun, çıkıntı; '**headless** *adj.* kafasız
(*a. fig.*); başkansız, amirsiz.
head…: '**~.light** *n.* MOT ön ışık, far;
'**~.line** *n.* başlık, serlevha; ~**s** *pl. radyo*:
haberlerden özetler; **he hits the ~s** F
afişte ismi baştadır; '**~.long 1.** *adj.*
düşüncesiz, kayıtsız, aceleci; **2.** *adv.*
düşüncesizce, aceleyle, paldır küldür,
önünü ardını düşünmeden; başı önde
olarak; '**~.man** *n.* kabile reisi; muhtar;
cellat; idareci, ustabaşı; '**~.mas.ter** *n.*
okul müdürü; '**~.mis.tress** *n.* okul müdiresi; '**~.most** *adj.* en ilerideki, en baştaki; '**~.on** *adj.* baştan, önden, kafadan; ~ **collision** kafadan çarpışma;
'**~.phone** *n. radyo*: kulaklık; '**~.piece**
n. baş zırhı, miğfer; F akıl, kafa, zekâ;
TYP bölüm başlarına konan süs;
'**~.quar.ters** *n. pl.* MIL karargâh; merkez büro; '**~.room** *n.* araç üzerinde
bırakılan güvenlik boşluğu, boş yer;
'**~.set** *n. radyo*: kulaklık; '**head.ship**
n. müdürlük, başkanlık, reislik, amirlik; '**heads.man** *n.* cellat.
head…: '**~.stone** *n.* mezar taşı;
'**~.strong** *adj.* dikkafalı, inatçı, ka-

fasının dikine giden, bildiğini okuyan; '~.wa.ters *n. pl.* ırmağı besleyen kaynak; '~.way *n.* gelişme, ilerleme; *make* ~ gelişmek, ilerlemek; '~.wind *n.* karşıdan esen rüzgâr; '~ word *n.* (*sözlükte*) madde başı sözcük; '~.work *n.* kafa işi; 'head.y □ inatçı, dik başlı; sert, çarpıcı (*içki*).

heal [hi:l] *v/t. & v/i.* iyileş(tir)mek, kapanmak (*yara*); tedavi etm. (*of -i*), şifa vermek *-e*; bitirmek, sonuçlandırmak, sona erdirmek; ~ *up* kapanmak (*yara*); '~-all *n.* her derde deva; 'heal.er *n.* iyileştiren kimse *veya* şey, doktor; *time is a great* ~ zaman en iyi tedavi yoludur; 'heal.ing 1. □ iyileştirici…, tedavi edici, faydalı; 2. *n.* iyileşme, şifa.

health [helθ] *n.* sağlık, sıhhat; *Ministry of* ♀ Sağlık ve Sosyal Yardım Bakanlığı; health.ful □ ['‿ful] sıhhat için faydalı, sıhhî, sağlıklı; 'health.i.ness *n.* sıhhat, sağlık; 'health-re.sort *n.* ılıca; 'health.y □ sağlıklı, sıhhatli, sağlam; sıhhî, sıhhate yarar.

heap [hi:p] 1. *n.* yığın, küme, öbek; F çok miktar, kalabalık, izdiham; *all of a* ~ darmadağınık; *struck veya knocked all of a* ~ şaşırmış, sersemlemiş; 2. *v/t. a.* ~ *up* yığmak *-i*, kümelemek *-i*.

hear [hiə] (*irr.*) *v/t.* işitmek, duymak, dinlemek, kulak vermek; mektup almak (*from -den*); haber almak (*of -den*); öğrenmek (*about -i*); ~ *s.o. out* b-ni sonuna kadar dinlemek; heard [hə:d] *pret. & p.p. of hear*, hear.er ['hiərə] *n.* dinleyici; 'hear.ing *n.* işitme (duyusu), işitim, dinleme; JUR celse, duruşma, oturum, sorgu; ses erimi; heark.en ['hɑ:kən] *vb.* dinlemek (*to -i*); hear.say ['hiəsei] *n.* söylenti, dedikodu.

hearse [hə:s] *n.* cenaze arabası.

heart [hɑ:t] *n. com.* kalp, yürek, gönül, sevgi, can; göğüs; vicdan; merkez, can damarı, orta yer; verimlilik; *iskambil*: kupa; cesaret; sevilen kimse; *a. dear* ~ sevgili; ~ *and soul* tamamen, canı gönülden, seve seve; *at* ~ içten; hakikatte, aslında, içyüzünde; *I have a matter at* ~ çok ilgilendiğim bir konu var; *by* ~ ezbere, ezberden; *for one's* ~ kendi canı için; *in good* ~ iyi durumda; *in his* ~ (*of* ~*s*) kalbinin derinliklerinde; *out of* ~ kötü durumda, verimsiz; *speak from one's* ~ samimi olarak konuşmak; *cut to the* ~ yüreğine inmek;

with all my ~ tüm kalbimle; *lose* ~ cesaretini yitirmek, cesareti kırılmak; *take* ~ cesaretlenmek; *take veya lay to* ~ içine işlemek, çok etkilenmek; '~.ache *n.* ıstırap, keder, kalp ağrısı; '~-beat *n.* kalp atışı; '~-break *n.* keder, büyük acı, kalp kırıklığı; '~-break.ing □ son derece keder verici; '~-bro-ken *adj.* kalbi kırık, acılı, kederli; '~.burn *n.* mide ekşimesi; '~-burning *n.* kıskançlık, imrenme, kin; '~-com-plaint, '~-dis.ease *n.* kalp hastalığı; 'heart.ed *comb.* …kalpli; 'heart.en *v/t.* yüreklendirmek, cesaretlendirmek, canlandırmak, memnun etm., neşelendirmek; 'heart-fail.ure *n.* kalp yetmezliği; 'heart.felt *adj.* samimi, içten, yürekten, candan.

heart [hɑ:θ] *n.* ocak (*a. fig.*), şömine; aile ocağı, yurt; '~-rug *n.* ocağın önüne yayılan halı; '~-stone *n.* ocak taşı; ocak, yuva, yurt.

heart.i.ness ['hɑ:tinis] *n.* içtenlik, samimiyet; dinçlik, sıhhatlilik (*s. hearty*); 'heart.less □ kalpsiz, merhametsiz, acımasız, zalim, vicdansız; 'heart.rend.ing *adj.* yürekler acısı, yürek parçalayıcı, çok acıklı.

heart…: '~.s.ease *n.* BOT viola; '~-sick *adj. fig.* kederli, üzgün, acı dolu; '~-strings *n. pl. fig.* kalbin en kuvvetleri hisleri; ~ trans.plant kalp nakli; '~-whole *adj.* âşık olmayan, kalbi boş; samimi, içten; 'heart.y 1. □ içten, samimi, yürekten, candan; sağlam, sıhhatli, dinç; bol, çok; ~ *eater* obur, çok yemek yiyen kimse, iştahı açık kimse; 2. *n.* NAUT denizci; UNIV sporcu.

heat [hi:t] *n. com.* hararet, sıcaklık, ısı, vücut ısısı; sıcak yer; tav, ısıtma; cinsi heyecan (*dişi hayvanlarda*); yarışın tek ayağı; eleme yarışı, final koşusu; *sl.* baskının artması; *sl.* polis; baskı; *dead* ~ iki *veya* daha çok atletin aynı anda ipi göğüslediği yarış; 2. *v/t.* ısıtmak *-i*; kızdırmak *-i*; *fig.* heyecanlandırmak *-i*; *v/i.* ısınmak, kızmak; 'heated □ heyecanlı, hararetli, öfkeli, kan beynine sıçramış; 'heat.er *n.* MEC ısıtıcı, soba, ocak, radyatör; 'heat-flash *n.* radyasyon.

heath [hi:θ] *n.* çalılık, fundalık; BOT funda, süpürgeotu.

hea.then ['hi:ðən] 1. *n.* dinsiz kimse, kâfir kimse, putperest kimse; 2. *adj.* dinsiz, kâfir, putperest; 'hea.then-dom *n.* putperestler ülkesi; 'hea-

then.ish☐ *mst fig.* barbar; '**hea.then-
ism** *n.* putperestlik, dinsizlik.
heath.er вот ['heðə] *n.* süpürgeotuna
benzer bir çalı; '**~-bell** *n.* kara süpürgeotu.
heat.ing['hi:tiŋ] *n.* ısıtma; *attr.* ısıtıcı...;
~ *battery* ısıtma batarya; ~ *pad* elektrik yastığı.
heat..: ~ *light.ning* *Am.* gök gürlemesi
olmadan çakan şimşek; '**~-stroke** *n.*
güneş çarpması, sıcak çarpması;
'**~-val.ue** *n.* ısı değeri; '**~-wave** *n.* sıcak
dalgası.
heave [hi:v] **1.** *n.* kaldırma; fırlatma,
kaldırıp atma; **2.** *(irr.)* *v/t.* kaldırmak,
çekmek; atmak, fırlatmak; güçlükle
çıkarmak *(inilti)*; yükseltmek, kabartmak, şişirmek; ~ *the anchor* demir almak; ~ *down* naut karina etm.; ~ *out*
atmak, fırlatmak; *v/i.* yükselmek, ka-
barıp inmek, şişmek; solumak; öğürmek; vira etm.; ~ *for breath* nefes nefese kalmak; ~ *in sight* naut aniden görünmek; ~ *to* naut dur(dur)mak *(gemi).*
heav.en['hevn] *n.* cennet; gök, sema; ♀
Tanrı, Cenabı Hak; mutluluk, saadet;
~*s* *pl.* gök kubbe, asuman; *move ~
and earth* elinden geleni yapmak,
mümkün olan herşeyi yapmak; '**heav-
en.ly** *adj.* göksel..., tanrısal...; *fig.* çok
güzel, nefis; **heav.en.ward(s)**
['~wəd(z)] *adj. & adv.* cennete doğru
(giden).
heav.er['hi:və] *n.* manivela, kaldıraç.
heav.i.ness['hevinis] *n.* ağırlık, siklet;
fig. yavaşlık; sıkıcılık.
heav.y☐ ['hevi] *com.* ağır; güç, zor *(iş)*;
şiddetli, kuvvetli *(yağmur)*; kederli,
üzgün; sert *(toprak)*; berbat *(yol)*; bulutlu, kapalı *(hava)*; dalgalı *(deniz)*;
hazmı güç *(yemek)*; ciddi, önemli;
uyuşuk, tembel, mıymıntı; kasvetli,
sıkıcı; uyku basmış, ağırlaşmış *(göz)*;
sıkışık *(trafik)*; kalın, kaba *(kumaş, elbise)*; ağır *(koku)*; dik, sarp; vurgulu;
mil tepeden tırnağa silahlı; ~ **cur.rent**
elect kuvvetli akım; '**~-'hand.ed** *adj.*
eli ağır, beceriksiz, sakar; '**~-'heart.ed**
adj. kederli, üzgün; '**~-'lad.en** *adj.* ağır
yüklü; *fig.* kalbi kırık, kederli;
'**~-weight** *n. boks:* ağır siklet.
heb.dom.a.dal ☐ [heb'dɔmədl] haftalık, haftada bir olan.
He.bra.ic [hi'breiik] *adj. (~ally)* İbra-
ni...; İbranice...
He.brew['hi:bru:] **1.** *adj.* İbranilere ait,

İbrani...; İbraniceye ait, İbranice...;
Musevi...; **2.** *n.* İbrani; Yahudi; İbrani-
ce.
hec.a.tomb['hekətu:m] *n.* katliam; 100
öküzlük kurban.
heck.le ['hekl] *vb.* sözünü kesip soru
sormak, soru yağmuruna tutmak,
sıkıştırmak; '**heck.ler** *n.* konuşmacının
sözünü kesip soru soran kimse.
hec.tic med ['hektik] **1.** *adj.* veremli,
hummalı; *sl.* heyecanlı, telaşlı; **2.** *n.* verem kızartısı; *mst* ~ *fever* humma.
hec.tor['hektə] *v/t.* gözünü korkutmak,
yıldırmak, sindirmek; *v/i.* kabadayılık
etm., zorbalık etm.
hedge [hedʒ] **1.** *n.* çit, çalı; *fig.* mânia,
engel; tedbir; **2.** *v/t.* çit ile çevirmek,
kuşatmak, sarmak; engel olm., önlemek; ~ *off* etrafını çit ile çevirmek; ~
up önlemek, engel olm.; ~ *a bet* iki taraf için bahse girişmek; *v/i.* etrafına
çalı dikmek; dolaylı konuşmak; önlem
almak, tedbir almak; '**~.hog** *n.* zoo kirpi; *Am.* oklu kirpi; '**~-hop** *v/i. sl.* avıa
alçaktan uçmak; '**~.row** *n.* çit; '**~-spar-
row** *n.* orn çit serçesi.
heed[hi:d] **1.** *n.* dikkat, özen, ihtimam;
take ~ of, give veya pay ~ to -*e* dikkat
etm., kulak asmak, önemsemek; **2.** *v/t.*
dikkat etm., kulak vermek -*e*, önemsemek -*i*; **heed.ful** ☐ ['-ful] dikkatli,
önem veren *(of -e)*; '**heed.less** ☐ dikkatsiz, düşüncesiz, önem vermeyen *(of
-e).*
hee-haw ['hi:'hɔ:] **1.** *n.* eşek anırması;
fig. kaba kahkaha; **2.** *v/i.* anırmak;
fig. kabaca gülmek.
heel[1] naut [hi:l] *v/t. & v/i.* bir yana
yat(ır)mak *(gemi).*
heel[2][-] **1.** *n.* topuk, ökçe; *part. Am. sl.*
alçak herif, namussuz kimse, aşağılık
adam; *at veya on veya upon s.o.'s
~s* hemen ardında, peşi sıra; *down at
~* topukları çok eskimiş; *fig.* perişan
kılıklı, hırpani, pejmürde; *take to
one's ~s, show a clean pair of ~s* kaçmak, tüymek, sıvışmak, tabanları yağlamak; *lay s.o. by the ~s* b-ni hapsetmek, kodese tıkmak; *come to ~*
çağrılınca gelmek *(köpek)*; uslanmak;
2. *vb.* ökçe takmak; dizinin dibinden
ayrılmamak *(köpek)*; *a.* ~ *out* futbol:
topukla geri pası vermek; **heeled**
adj. Am. ⊢ ensesi kalın, para babası;
'**heel.er** *n. Am. sl.* pol bir politikacının
adamı.
heel-tap ['hi:ltæp] *n.* içki artığı; *no* ~*!*

artık bırakmak yok! (*içki*).
heft [heft] **1.** *n.* ağırlık, siklet; *Am.* F
önem, etki, tesir; **2.** *v/t.* kaldırmak;
kaldırarak ağırlığını bulmak; **'heft.y**
adj. F güçlü, kuvvetli, tesirli.
he.gem.o.nyPOL [hi:'gemǝni] *n.* üstünlük, egemenlik, hakimiyet, hegemonya.
he.goat ['hi:gǝut] teke, erkeç.
heif.er ['hefǝ] *n.* düve, doğurmamış
genç inek.
heigh [hei] *int.* hey!, bana bak!; **~ho**
['ˏ'hǝu] *int.* a!, ya!, yazık!, tüh be!
height [hait] *n.* yükseklik, irtifa, yükselti; tepe, dağ; doruk, zirve, en yüksek
nokta; *what is your* **~?** boyunuz kaç?;
'height.en *v/t.* & *v/i.* yüksel(t)mek,
art(tır)mak, çoğal(t)mak.
hei.nous □ ['heinǝs] iğrenç, kötü, berbat, çirkin, tiksindirici; **'hei.nous-
ness** *n.* iğrençlik, tiksindiricilik.
heir[εǝ] *n.* vâris, mirasçı; *be* **~** *to* -e vâris
olm.; **~ apparent**, **~ at law** kanuni vâris;
~ presumptive muhtemel vâris; **'heir-
dom** *n.* vârislik, mirasçılık; miras;
'heir.ess *n.* kadın vâris; **'heir.less**
adj. vârissiz, mirasçısı olmayan; **heirloom** ['ˏluːm] *n.* evlâdiyelik, nesilden
nesile intikal eden değerli şey.
held [held] *pret.* & *p.p. of* **hold 2.**
hel.i.bus *Am.* F ['helibʌs] *n.* helikopter.
hel.i.cal ['helikǝl] *adj.* helezonî, spiral,
sarmal.
hel.i.cop.ter ['helikɔptǝ] *n.* helikopter.
he.li.o... ['hiːliǝu] *prefix* güneş...; **he-
lio.graph** ['ˏǝugrɑːf] *n.* güneş ışığı
yansıtılarak sinyal gönderen alet, helyosta, pırıldak; **he.li.o.trope** ['heljǝ-
trǝup] *n.* BOT güneş çiçeği.
he.li.um CHEM ['hiːljǝm] *n.* helyum.
he.lix ['hiːliks] *n.*, *pl. mst* **hel.i.ces**
['helisiːz] helis; ZOO sümüklüböcek,
salyangoz; ARCH sarmal eğri; ANAT
dışkulak kıvrımı.
hell [hel] *n.* cehennem; *attr.* cehennem...; *like* **~**, çok, son derecede, müthiş; hiç; *oh* **~!** Allah kahretsin!; *go to* **~!**
canın cehenneme!; *what the* **~ ...?** F
Allahaşkına ne...?; *a* **~** *of a noise*
çok fazla gürültü; *raise* **~** kıyameti koparmak; *ride* **~** *for leather* mümkün olduğu kadar hızlı at sürmek, dolu dizgin gitmek; **'~-'bent**adj. *Am. sl.* istekli,
şevkli, azimli; **'~-cat**n. *fig.* öfkeli kimse; cadı; şirret kadın.
hel.le.bore BOT ['helibɔ:] *n.* çöpleme.

Hel.lene ['heliːn] *n.* Helen, Yunanlı;
Hel'len.ic [he'liːnik] *adj.* Helen, Yunanlı; Yunan...
hell.ish □ ['heliʃ] korkunç, dehşetli,
şeytani; cehennemi.
hel.lo [he'lǝu] *int.* merhaba!, selâm!,
günaydın!; alo!
helm NAUT [helm] *n.* dümen; *fig.* idare.
hel.met ['helmit] *n.* miğfer, tolga; kask;
'hel.met.ed *adj.* miğferli; kasklı.
helms.man NAUT ['helmzmǝn] *n.* dümenci.
hel.ot HIST ['helǝt] *n.* esir, köle; *fig.* kul,
köle.
help [help] **1.** *n. com.* yardım, imdat; çare, çözüm; yardımcı, hizmetçi, uşak;
by the **~** *of* -*in* yardımı ile; **2.** *v/t.* yardım
etm. -*e*; rahatlatmak, ferahlaştırmak;
kurtarmak, imdadına yetişmek, çare
bulmak; faydası olm. -*e*, yararı dokunmak *e*-; kendini tutmak, kendini almak -*den*; önlemek, önüne geçmek; ikram etm. (*yemek*); **~** *o.s.* kendi kendine servis yapmak, yemeğe buyurmak;
~ *o.s. to s.th.* bşden almak, bşe buyurmak (*yemek*); *I could not* **~** *laughing*
gülmemek elimde değildi, gülmekten
kendimi alamadım; *that cannot be*
~ed ne yapalım, elden bir şey gelmez;
v/i. bşe faydası dokunmak, işe yaramak; **'help.er** *n.* yardımcı, muavin,
çırak; hizmetçi, uşak; **help.ful** □
['ˏful] yardımsever; yardımcı, faydalı,
yararlı, işe yarar; **'help.ing**n. porsiyon
(*yemek*); **'help.less** □ âciz, çaresiz,
kendini idare edemeyen, beceriksiz,
kabiliyetsiz, gücü yetmez; **'helplessness** n. âcizlik, beceriksizlik, güçsüzlük; **'help.mate**, **help.meet** ['ˏmiːt]
n. arkadaş, eş, yardımcı; karı *veya* koca.
helter-skel.ter ['heltǝ'skeltǝ] *adv.* aceleyle, telâşla, alelacele, apar topar.
helve [helv] *n.* sap, tutamak.
Hel.ve.tian [hel'viːʃjǝn] **1.** *adj.* İsviçre-
li...; İsviçre...; **2.** *n.* İsviçreli (*kimse*).
hem[1] [hem] **1.** *n.* kenar (*elbise*), baskı;
2. *v/t.* -*in* kenarı kıvırıp dikmek,
bastırmak; **~** *in* kuşatmak, etrafını içeri almak, içine almak.
hem[2][ˏ] **1.** *v/i.* hafifçe öksürmek; 'hım'
demek; tereddütlü konuşmak; **2.** *int.*
hım!
he-man *sl.* ['hiːmæn] *n.* erkek adam,
yiğit adam, güçlü kuvvetli erkek.
hem.i.sphere ['hemisfiǝ] *n.* yarımküre.

hem-line ['hemlain] *n.* etek ucu (*elbise*); *lower* (*raise*) *the* ~ elbisenin boyunu uzatmak (kısaltmak).

hem.lock BOT ['hemlɔk] *n.* köknara benzer bir çam ağacı.

he.mo... ['hi:məu] *s. haemo...*

hemp [hemp] *n.* kenevir, kendir; '**hemp.en** *adj.* kendir gibi, kendirden yapılmış, kendir...

hem.stitch ['hemstitʃ] **1.** *n.* ajur, antika, gözenek; **2.** *vb.* kenarına ajur yapmak.

hen [hen] *n.* tavuk; dişi kuş; ~'*s egg* tavuk yumurtası.

hen.bane BOT ['henbein] *n.* banotu.

hence [hens] *adv. usu.* *from* ~ buradan, bundan, bu zamandan itibaren; bu sebeple, bundan dolayı; ~*!* defol!, yıkıl karşımdan!; *a year* ~ bundan bir yıl sonra; '~'**forth**, '~'**for.ward** *adv.* bundan böyle, şu andan itibaren, gelecekte.

hench.man POL ['hentʃmən] *n.* kendi çıkarı için taraf tutan kimse; bir kimsenin sağ kolu, hizmetkâr.

hen...: '~-**coop** *n.* tavuk kümesi; '~-**par.ty** *n.* F kadınlar toplantısı; '~.**pecked** *adj.* kılıbık (*koca*); '~-**roost** *n.* tavuk tüneği.

hep *Am. sl.* [hep]: *be* ~ *to* -in farkında olm., -den haberi olm.

he.pat.ic ANAT [hi'pætik] *adj.* karaciğere ait, karaciğer...

hep.cat *Am. sl.* ['hepkæt] *n.* caz hastası (*veya* delisi).

hep.ta... ['heptə] *adj.* yedi...; **hep.ta.gon** ['~gən] *n.* yedigen, yedi kenarlı çokgen.

her [hə:, hə] *adv. & adj.* (*dişil*) onun; ona, onu.

her.ald ['herəld] **1.** *n.* haberci, müjdeci; **2.** *v/t.* ilân etm., haber vermek, müjdelemek; selâmlamak; ~ *in* tanıtmak, takdim etm.; **he.ral.dic** [he'rældik] *adj.* (~*ally*) hanedan armacılığına ait; **her.ald.ry** ['herəldri] *n.* hanedan armacılığı.

herb [hə:b] *n.* ot, bitki; **her.ba.ceous** [~'beiʃəs] *adj.* ot cinsinden; '**herb.age** *n.* yeşillik, ot; JUR başkasının merasında hayvan otlatma hakkı; '**herb.al 1.** *adj.* otlara ait, ot..., bitkisel...; **2.** *n.* şifalı bitkiler kitabı; '**herb.al.ist** *n.* şifalı bitki satan kimse; **her.bar.i.um** [~'bɛəriəm] *n.* kurutulmuş bitki koleksiyonu; kurutulmuş bitki koleksiyonu saklanan yer; **her.bivo.rous** [~'bivə-rəs] *adj.* otçul (*hayvan*); **her.bo.rize**

['~bəraiz] *vb.* bitki yetiştirmek.

Her.cu.le.an [hə:kju'li:ən] *adj.* Herkül'e ait, Herkül...; çok güçlü, çok zor...

herd [hə:d] **1.** *n.* sürü, davar sürüsü; *fig.* avam, ayak takımı; **2.** *v/t. & v/i.* sürü gibi biraraya topla(n)mak; sürüyü gütmek; sürüye kat(ıl)mak; ~ *together* biraraya topla(n)mak; '**herd.er**, '**herds-man** *n.* çoban, sığırtmaç.

here [hiə] **1.** *adv.* buraya; burada; şu anda, şimdi; bu noktada; bu dünyada, bu hayatta; **2.** *int.* ~*!* bana bak! baksana!, dur!; ~'*s to...!* ... -in şerefine!

here.a.bout(s) ['hiərəbaut(s)] *adv.* buralarda, bu yakınlarda, bu civarda; **hereaft.er** [hiər'ɑ:ftə] **1.** *adv.* ileride, gelecekte, bundan sonra; **2.** *n.* gelecek; öbür dünya, ahiret; '**here'by** *adv.* bu vesile ile, bundan dolayı.

he.red.i.ta.ble [hi'reditəbl] *adj.* kalıtsal, irsî; **her.e.dit.a.ment** JUR [heri-'ditəmənt] *n.* miras yoluyla kalan mal; **he.red.i.tar.y** [hi'reditəri] *adj.* kalıtsal, irsî, miras yoluyla kalan...; **he'red.i.ty** *n.* kalıtım, irsiyet, soyaçekim.

here.in ['hiər'in] *adv.* bunda, bunun içinde; **here.of** [hiər'ɔv] *adv.* bununla ilgili olarak.

her.e.sy ['herəsi] *n.* bir akideye aykırı mezhep.

her.e.tic ['herətik] **1.** *n.* kabul olunmuş doktrinlere karşı olan kimse; **2.** = **he-ret.i.cal** □ [hi'retikəl] kabul olunmuş doktrinlere karşı olan.

here.to.fore ['hiətu'fɔ:] *adv.* şimdiye dek, bundan önce; **here.up.on** ['hiər-ə'pɔn] *adv.* bunun üzerine; '**here'with** *adv.* bununla, ilişikte, beraberce.

her.it.a.ble ['heritəbl] *adj.* miras yoluyla intikali mümkün; '**her.it.age** *n.* miras, tereke.

her.maph.ro.dite [hə:'mæfrədait] *n.* çift cinsiyetli bitki *veya* hayvan.

her.met.ic, **her.met.i.cal** □ [hə:'met-ik(əl)] hava geçirmez, sımsıkı kapalı.

her.mit ['hə:mit] *n.* yalnız kalmayı seven kimse, münzevi; '**her.mit.age** *n.* yalnız kalmayı seven kişi *veya* kişilerin hücresi, inziva yeri.

her.ni.a MED ['hə:njə] *n.* fıtık, kasık yarığı, kavlıç; '**her.ni.al** *adj.* fıtıklı, fıtık...

he.ro ['hiərəu] *n., pl.* **he.roes** ['~rəuz] kahraman, yiğit; baş karakter; **he.ro.ic** [hi'rəuik], **he'ro.i.cal** *adj.* kahramanca, cesur; gerçek boyutundan büyük (*heykel*); kahramanlıklar anlatan, destansı, epik (*şiir*); abartmalı sözlere ait.

her.o.in PHARM ['herəuin] *n.* eroin.

her.o.ine ['herəuin] *n.* kadın kahraman; '**her.o.ism** *n.* kahramanlık, cesaret.

her.on ORN ['herən] *n.* balıkçıl; '**her-on.ry** *n.* balıkçılların yumurtladığı yer.

her.ring ICHTH ['heriŋ] *n.* ringa; '**her-ring-bone** *n.* ringa kemiğine benzer dikiş, çapraz dikiş.

hers [hɜːz] *pron.* onun(ki) (*dişil*).

her.self [hɜː'self] *pron.* kendisi (*dişil*).

Hertz.i.an ELECT ['hɜːtsiən] *n.*: **~ waves** elektromanyetik dalgalar, radyo dalgaları.

he's ['hiːz] = *he is*; *he has*.

hes.i.tance, hes.i.tan.cy ['hezitəns(i)] *n.* tereddüt, duraksama; **hes.i.tate** ['‿teit] *v/i.* tereddüt etm., duraksamak (*about, over -de*); kem küm etm., kekelemek (*to inf. -mekte*); **hes.i'ta.tion** *n.* tereddüt, duraksama, şüphe; kekeleme.

Hes.sian ['hesiən] **1.** *adj.* Almanya'nın Hesse eyaletine ait; Hesse'li; **2.** *n.* Hesse'li kimse; ♀ çuval bezi.

het.er.o.dox ['hetərəudɔks] *adj.* kabul edilmiş dini esaslara aykırı olan; '**het-er.odox.y** *n.* kabul edilmiş doktrinlere karşı çıkma; **het.er.o.dyne** ['‿dain] *adj. radyo*: gelen sinyali devamlı bir frekansa karıştıran...; **het.er.o.ge.ne-i.ty** [‿dʒi'niːiti] *n.* farklı oluş; **het.er.o-ge.ne.ous** □ ['‿rəu'dʒiːnjəs] heterojen, ayrı cinsten.

hew [hjuː] (*irr.*) *vb.* yontmak, yarmak, kesmek, çentmek; MEC yontarak şekil vermek; '**hew.er** *n.* baltacı, oduncu; MIN kömür madencisi; **hewn** [hjuːn] *p.p. of* **hew**.

hex.a... ['heksə] *prefix* altı...; **hex.a-gon** ['‿gən] *n.* altıgen; **hex.ag.o.nal** □ [hek'sægənl] altıgen, altı kenarlı; **hex.am.eter** [hek'sæmitə] *n.* altı ayaklı mısra.

hey [hei] *int.* hey!, haydi!, a!

hey.day ['heidei] **1.** *int.* yaşasın!, yok ya!; **2.** *n. fig.* en enerjik çağ, altın çağ.

hi [hai] *int.* hey!; selam!, merhaba!

hi.a.tus [hai'eitəs] *n.* aralık, açıklık, boşluk; GR hemze.

hi.ber.nate ['haibəneit] *v/i.* kış uykusuna yatmak; **hi.ber'na.tion** *n.* kış uykusu.

hi.bis.cus BOT [hi'biskəs] *n.* amberçiçeği.

hic.cup, hic.cough ['hikʌp] **1.** *n.* hıçkırık; **2.** *v/i.* hıçkırmak, hıçkırık tutmak.

hick F [hik] *n.* taşralı, kaba köylü; *attr.* taşralı...

hick.o.ry ['hikəri] *n.* Kuzey Amerika'da bulunan bir tür ceviz ağacı.

hid [hid] *pret. of* **hide²**; **hid.den** ['hidn] *p.p. of* **hide²**.

hide¹ [haid] **1.** *n.* hayvan derisi, post; F insan derisi, cilt; **2.** *v/t.* F pataklamak, dayak atmak.

hide² [‿] (*irr.*) *v/t.* & *v/i.* sakla(n)mak, gizle(n)mek (*from s.o. b-den*); örtbas etm.; '**hide-and'-seek** *n.* saklambaç oyunu; *play (at)* **~** saklambaç oynamak.

hide.bound *fig.* ['haidbaund] *adj.* dar görüşlü, geri kafalı.

hid.e.ous □ ['hidiəs] çirkin, iğrenç, korkunç; '**hid.e.ous.ness** *n.* iğrençlik, çirkinlik, korkunçluk.

hid.ing¹ F ['haidiŋ] *n.* dayak, kötek.

hid.ing² [‿] *n.* sakla(n)ma, gizle(n)me; *in* **~** saklı, gizli; '**~-place** *n.* gizlenecek (*veya* saklanacak) yer.

hie *poet.* [hai] *vb.* (*p. pr.* **hying**) çabucak gidivermek.

hi.er.arch.y ['haiərɑːki] *n.* hiyerarşi.

hi.er.o.glyph ['haiərəuglif] *n.* hiyeroglif, resimlerden oluşan yazı; **hi.er.o-'glyph.ic,** *a.* **hi.er.o'glyph.i.cal** □ hiyerogliflere ait, hiyeroglif...; **hi.er.o-'glyph.ics** *n. pl.* hiyeroglif.

hi-fi *Am.* ['hai'fai] = **high fidelity**.

hig.gle.dy-pig.gle.dy ['higldi'pigldi] *adj. & adv.* karmakarışık, karman çorman, altüst.

high [hai] **1.** *adj.* □ (*s. a.* **~ly**) *com.* yüksek, yukarı; önemli (*mevki*), yüce, baş; tiz, cırlak (*ses*); aşırı, şiddetli; fahiş (*fiyat*); kibirli, kendini beğenmiş; kızgın, öfkeli; coşkun, taşkın (*neşe*); lüks; asil, soylu; kokmuş (*et, yemek*); sarhoş, kafayı bulmuş; esrarın etkisinde; dolgun; **~ and dry** karaya oturmuş (*gemi*); suyun dışında; çaresiz, terkedilmiş; *be on one's* **~** *horse, ride the* **~** *horse* kendini beğenmiş olm., kibirli olm., yukarıdan bakmak; *with a* **~** *hand* kibirle, küstahça; *in* **~** *spirits* neşeli, keyfi yerinde; *a* **~** *Tory* aşırı tutucu kimse; **~ colo(ur),** **~ complexion** koyu kırmızı renk; **~ life** sosyete hayatı; **~ words** *pl.* ağır sözler, öfkeli sözler; **~ time** tam vakit; **2.** *n.* METEOR yüksek basınç bölgesi; *Am.* F = **high school**; **~ and low** toplumun her kesimi, zengin fakir; her yerde; **on ~** yüksekte, gökte; hızla, süratle; **3.** *adv.* yükseğe, yüksekte; pahalı olarak; lüks içinde; '**~-ball**n. *Am.* sodalı viski; '**~-born** *ajd.* soylu olarak doğmuş; '**~-bred** *adj.* asil, soylu; '**~-brow**F **1.** *n.* entelektüel kimse, fikir adamı; **2.** *adj.* entelektüel; '**~-class**adj. birinci sınıf, kaliteli, '**~-'colo(u)red** *adj.* parlak renkli..., kırmızı...; ○ **Com.mis.sion.er**büyükelçi ayarındaki temsilci; '**~-ex'plo.sive**n. kuvvetli patlayıcı madde; **~-fa.lu.tin(g)** ['-fə-'lu:tin, '-fə'lu:tin] **1.** *n.* şatafat, gereksiz süs; **2.** *adj.* şatafatlı, aşırı süslü; '**~-fi'del.i.ty**adj. sesi çok tabii şekilde veren... Hi-Fi; '**~.flier** = *highflyer*; '**~-flown**adj. şatafatlı, çok süslü (*söz, yazı*); '**~.fly.er**n. hırslı kimse, ihtiraslı kimse; '**~-grade** *adj.* üstün kaliteli; '**~'hand.ed**adj. amirlik taslayan, küstah; '**~'hat**s/. **1.** *n.* züppe kimse; **2.** *adj.* züppe; '**~'heeled** *adj.* yüksek ökçeli; '**~.land.er**n. dağlı kimse; '**~.lands**n. *pl.* dağlık bölge; '**~'lev.el**adj. yüksek seviyeli (*konferans*); '**~.light**v/t. dikkati çekmek -*e*; önem vermek -*e*; '**~-lights**n. *pl. fig.* ilgi çekici olay; ~ **liv-ing**lüks hayat; '**high.ly**adv. yüksek derecede, çok, fazlasıyla; *speak ~ of s.o.* b-den övgüyle bahsetmek; **~ de-scended** asil, soylu; '**high-'mind.ed** *adj.* âlicenap, yüce gönüllü; '**high--'necked**adj. balıkçı yakalı, dik yakalı; '**high.ness**n. yükseklik; *fig.* yücelik; *His veya Your* ♀ Ekselansları.

high..; '**~-'pitched**adj. çok tiz (*ses*); dik (*çatı*); '**~-'pow.er ~ station** yüksek güçlü santral; **~ radio station** güçlü radyo istasyonu; '**~-'pow.ered**adj. güçlü, dinamik, enerjik (*kimse*); '**~-'priced**adj. pahalı; ~ **road**anayol; ~ **school**lise; '**~-'spir.it.ed**adj. neşeli, şen; oynak, yerinde duramayan (*at*); '**~-'strung**adj. çok sinirli, sinir küpü.

hightpoet. veya co. [hait] adj. isminde, adında, denilen.

high..; ~ **tea**ikindi kahvaltısı; '**~-'toned** *adj.* kaliteli, sosyetik; ~ **wa.ter**taşkın, kabarma; '**~.way**n. anayol, karayolu; *fig.* en kolay ve kısa yol; ~ **code** karayolları nizamnamesi; '**~.way.man** *n.* eşkiya, soyguncu.

hi.jack['haidʒæk] v/t. kuvvet zoru ile çalmak, kaçırmak; '**hi.jack.er**n. uçak korsanı; yol kesici.

hikeF [haik] **1.** v/i. yürümek, yürüyüşe

çıkmak; **2.** *n.* uzun yürüyüş; *part. Am.* F artış, yükselme; '**hik.er**n. uzun yürüyüşe çıkan kimse.

hi.lar.i.ous□ [hi'lɛəriəs] çok şamatalı, neşeli ve gürültülü.

hi.lar.i.ty[hi'læriti] *n.* neşe, kahkaha.

Hil.a.ry['hiləri]: ~ *term* JUR, UNIV ocak ayında başlayan devre.

hill [hil] *n.* tepe; bayır, yokuş; küme, yığın; **~.bil.ly**Am. F ['-bili] *n.* çiftçi, orman köylüsü; ~ **climb** MOT tırmanma yarışı; **hill.ock**['hilək] *n.* tepecik, tümsek; '**hill.side**n. yamaç, dağ eteği; '**hill--top**n. tepe doruğu; '**hill.y**adj. tepelik.

hilt[hilt] *n.* kabza; *up to the* ~ *fig.* tamamiyle, tamamen.

him[him] *pron.* onu, ona (*eril*).

him.self[him'self] *pron.* kendi(si), bizzat (*eril*); *of* ~ kendinden; *by* ~ yalnız başına; kendisi, kimsenin yardımı olmaksızın.

hind[haind] *n.* dişi geyik.

hind[_] *adj.* arkadaki, geride olan, arka...; ~ *leg*arka bacak; ~ *wheels* *pl.* arka tekerlekler.

hind.er['haində] *adj.* arkadaki, gerideki, arka...

hin.der[_] v/t. engellemek, mâni olm. -*e*, alıkoymak (*from -den*).

hind.most['haindməust] *adj.* en arkadaki, en gerideki.

hin.drance['hindrəns] *n.* engel, mâni (*to -e*).

Hin.du *a.* **Hin.doo**['hin'du:] *n.* Hintli, Hindu.

Hin.du.sta.ni [hindu'stɑːni] *adj.* Hindistan'a ait, Hindistan...; Hintli...

hinge[hindʒ] **1.** *n.* menteşe, reze; *fig.* dayanak noktası, esas; *off the* ~**s** *fig.* dayanağı olmayan; **2.** v/b. ~ *upon fig.* dayanmak, bağlı olm.

hin.ny['hini] *n.* (*at ile dişi eşekten hasıl olan*) katır.

hint [hint] **1.** *n.* ima, üstü kapalı söz, çıtlatma; **2.** v/i. ima etm., çıtlatmak, dokundurmak (*at -i*).

hin.ter.land['hintəlænd] *n.* iç bölge, arka bölge, hinterland.

hip[hip] *n.* kalça, kaba et; *attr.* kalça...

hip[_]²BOT [_] *n.* kuşburnu.

hip[_]³[_] *int.:* ~, ~, *hurra(h) !* şa! şa! şa!

hip..; '**~-bath**n. yarım banyo (*küvet*); '**~-flask** *n.* cebe konan küçük yassı şişe.

hip-hopMUS ['hiphɔp] *n.* hip-hop (*müzik*).

hip.poF ['hipəu] = *hippopotamus.*

hock

hip-pock.et['hippɔkit] *n.* arka cep.
hip.po.pot.a.mus [hipə'pɔtəməs] *n.*,
pl. a. hip.po'pot.a.mi[_mai] suaygını.
hip.py['hipi] *n. a.* hippiehipi.
hip-roof ARCH ['hipru:f] *n.* ortası kabarık çatı.
hip-shot['hipʃɔt] *adj.* çıkık kalçalı.
hire['haiə] **1.** *n.* kira, ücret; kiralama;
on ~ kiralık; **2.** *vb.* kiralamak, ücretle
tutmak; ücretle çalışmak; *~ out* kiraya
vermek; hire.ling*contp.*['_liŋ] **1.** *n.* ücretli adam, uşak; **2.** *adj.* kiralık; 'hire-
-'pur.chase*n.* taksit; *by ~* taksitle.
hir.sute ['hɔːsjuːt] *adj.* kıllı, tüylü,
saçlı.
his[hiz] *adj. & pron.* onun(ki) (*eril*).
hiss[his] **1.** *n.* tıslama, yılan sesi; ıslıklama; **2.** *vb.* tıslamak; ıslık çalmak; *a. ~
off* ıslık çalarak yuhalamak, ıslıklamak.
hist[sːt] *int.* hişt!, dur!, sus!
his.to.ri.an[his'tɔːriən] *n.* tarihçi, tarih
bilgini; **his.tor.iç** **his.tor.i.cal** □
[_'tɔrik(əl)] tarihî, tarihsel; önemli,
mühim; histo.ri.og.ra.pher [_tɔːri-
'ɔgrəfə] *n.* tarihçi, tarih yazarı; his.to-
ry['_təri] *n.* tarih, tarihi olaylar; *make
~* tarihe geçmek.
his.tri.on.ic[histri'ɔnik] *adj.* sahneye
ait, oyuna ait, sahne..., tiyatro...,
oyunculuk...; dramatik..., yapmacık,
suni, sahte.
hit [hit] **1.** *n.* vuruş, vurma, darbe;
başarı; şans, talih; isabet; *fig.* iğneli
söz, taş; THEAT, MUS başarı kazanmış
eser; **2.** (*irr.*) *vb.* vurmak, çarpmak
-e; isabet et(tir)mek *-e*; tesir etm. *-e*;
Am. F ulaşmak, varmak, erişmek *-e*;
gitmek *-e*; bulmak *-i*; uymak *-e*; çok içmek (*içki*); yumruk atmak; olmak, vuku bulmak; uygun olm.; *~ s.o. a blow
b-ne* yumruk atmak; *~ at* vurmak; *~ or
miss* rasgele, şansa, tesadüfî; gayesiz,
amaçsız; *~ off* F kısaca tarif etm.; süratle yapmak; *~ it off with* F *ile* uyuşmak,
anlaşmak, geçinmek; *~ out* yumruklamak, saldırmak; *~ (up)on* rastgele bulmak *-i*; *he ~ his head against a tree*
başını bir ağaca çarptı; '~-and-'run
driv.er*MOT* çarpıp kaçan şoför.
hitch[hitʃ] **1.** *n.* ani çekme *veya* itme,
çekiş; NAUT adi düğüm; *fig.* engel, arıza, mâni, pürüz; **2.** *v/t. & v/i.* çek(iştir)-
mek; bağla(n)mak, iliştir(il)mek,
tak(ıl)mak (*on -e*); topallamak, aksamak; evlen(dir)mek; otostop yapmak;
~ up yukarı çekmek (*pantolon*);

'~-hike*v/i.* F otostop yapmak.
hith.er*lit.* ['hiðə] *adv.* buraya, buraya
doğru; hith.er.to['_'tuː] *adv.* şimdiye
kadar, bu zamana kadar; hith.er-
ward(s)['_wəd(z)] = *hither.*
hive[haiv] **1.** *n.* kovan; kovandaki arı
kümesi; *fig.* çok hareketli yer, arı kovanı gibi kaynaşan yer; *~s pl.* MED kurdeşen, ürtiker; **2.** *v/t.* kovana doldurmak, kovanda biriktirmek, toplamak;
~ up toplamak, biriktirmek; *v/i.* kovana girmek; birarada oturmak.
ho[həu] *int.* ya!, yok ya!, hadi canım!
hoar[hɔː] *adj.* kır, ak, ağarmış (*saç*); kır
saçlı.
hoard[hɔːd] **1.** *n.* saklanan stok, biriktirilmiş şey; **2.** *v/t.* *a. ~ up* saklamak,
biriktirmek, istif etm.; 'hoard.er*n.* istifçi, biriktirip saklayan kimse.
hoard.ing['hɔːdiŋ] *n.* geçici tahta perde; ilan tahtası.
hoar.frost['hɔːˈfrɔst] *n.* kırağı.
hoar.i.ness['hɔːrinis] *n.* ak saç, kırlık.
hoarse □ [hɔːs] boğuk, kısık (*ses*);
boğuk sesli; 'hoarse.ness*n.* boğukluk, boğuk seslilik.
hoar.y['hɔːri] *adj.* kır, ak, ağarmış, ak
düşmüş; eski.
hoax[həuks] **1.** *n.* şaka, muziplik; hile,
oyun; **2.** *v/t.* aldatmak, oyun etm., işletmek, gırgır geçmek.
hob¹[hɔb] *n.* şömine pervazı.
hob²[_] = *hobgoblin*; *raise ~ part.* *Am.*
F yaramazlık yapmak.
hob.ble['hɔbl] **1.** *n.* topallama, aksama;
F engel, mâni, köstek; **2.** *v/i.* topallamak, aksamak (*a. fig.*); *v/t.* kösteklemek; topal etm.; bukağı vurmak
(*ata*); engel olm., mâni olm.
hob.ble.de.hoyF['hɔbldi'hɔi] *n.* beceriksiz delikanlı.
hob.byfig. ['hɔbi] *n.* merak, özel zevk,
hobi; '~-horse*n.* sallanan oyuncak at;
atlıkarınca atı; çocuğun at diye bindiği
değnek; bir kimsenin hoşlandığı konu.
hob.gob.lin['hɔbgɔblin] *n.* gulyabani,
ifrit.
hob.nail['hɔbneil] *n.* iri başlı kısa çivi,
ayakkabıların altına vurulan çivi, kabara.
hob.nob['hɔbnɔb] *v/i.* arkadaşlık etm.,
sıkıfıkı olm., araları iyi olm.
ho.bo*Am. sl.* ['həubəu] *n.* serseri, aylak, boş gezenin boş kalfası.
Hob.son's choice*fig.* ['hɔbsnz'tʃɔis]
n. tek çözüm yolu, yapılacak tek şey.
hock¹[hɔk] **1.** *n.* zoo hayvanların içdizi;

2. *v/t.* topal etm. (*at*).

hock² [_] *n.* Ren şarabı, beyaz Alman şarabı.

hock³ [_] **1.** *n.* rehin; **2.** *v/t.* rehine koymak; '~-shop *n.* rehinci dükkânı.

hock.ey ['hɔki] *n. spor:* hokey oyunu.

ho.cus ['həukəs] *v/t.* aldatmak, kandırmak; uyuşturucu vererek sersemletmek; ~-**po.cus** ['ˌ-'pəukəs] *n.* hokus pokus; hokkabazlık, hile; sihirbazın sözleri; aldatıcı hareketler.

hod [hɔd] *n.* harç *veya* tuğla teknesi.

hodge-podge ['hɔdʒpɔdʒ] = **hotch-potch**.

hod.man ['hɔdmən] *n.* yamak, el ulağı.

hoe AGR [həu] **1.** *n.* çapa; **2.** *vb.* çapalamak, çapa kullanmak.

hog [hɔg] **1.** *n.* domuz; *fig.* obur ve pis kimse; *go the whole ~ sl.* bir işi tam yapmak; **2.** *v/t.* açgözlülükle kapmak; hakkından fazlasını almak; *v/i.* MOT yolun ortasında gitmek; **hogged** *adj.* açgözlü; 'hog.gish ☐ açgözlü ve bencil; 'hog.gishness *n.* açgözlülük, bencillik.

hog.ma.nay *Scots* ['hɔgmənei] *n.* yılbaşı arifesi.

hogs.head ['hɔgzhed] *n.* büyük fıçı; 240 litrelik sıvı ölçü birimi; 'hog.skin *n.* domuz derisi; 'hog.wash *n.* çerçöp, artık şey; F saçma şey, atmasyon.

hoi(c)k [hɔik] *v/t.* birden çekmek, aniden yukarıya doğru döndürmek (*uçak*).

hoi pol.loi [hɔi'pɔlɔi] *n. pl.* halk yığını, ayak takımı, avam.

hoist [hɔist] **1.** *n.* kaldıraç; yük asansörü; itme *veya* çekme; **2.** *v/t.* yükseltmek, kaldırmak; çekmek (*bayrak*).

hoi.ty-toi.ty F ['hɔiti'tɔiti] **1.** *adj.* kibirli, kendini beğenmiş; **2.** *int.* yok yahu!, deme!

ho.kum *Am. sl.* ['həukəm] *n.* boş laf, palavra; seyircinin ilgisini çekmek için başvurulan oyunlar.

hold [həuld] **1.** *n.* tutma, tutuş; nüfuz, hüküm, otorite; dayanak, destek; tutunacak yer; kale, istihkam; hapis; hapishane, kodes; kavrama, anlama, idrak; MUS uzatma işareti; NAUT gemi ambarı; *catch, get, lay, take, seize ~ of* yakalamak, tutmak, kavramak; *have a ~ of veya on* ...üzerinde etkisi olm., otoritesi olm.; *keep ~ of -i* kontrol altına almak; **2.** (*irr.*) *v/t. com.* tutmak; kavramak; dayanmak *e*; malik olm. *-e*, sahip olm. *-e*, elinde tutmak *-i*; zapt etm.,

işgal etm., ele geçirmek *-i*; kontrol atına almak, hükmetmek *-e*; alıkoymak, salıvermemek, durdurmak *-i*; kanunen bağlamak, mecbur etm.; germek (*kas*); çekmek, tartmak, tasımak (*ağırlık*); hapsetmek, gözaltına almak *-i*; içine almak, kapsamak *-i*; stok etm. *-i*; desteklemek (*teori*); düzenlemek (*toplantı*); çevirmek, yöneltmek, doğrultmak (*silah*); JUR hüküm vermek, kara ra bağlamak; ~ *a job down* F bir işi yürütmek; ~ *one's ground, ~ one's own* ayak diremek, yerini korumak, dayanmak, durumunu muhafaza etm.; ~ *the line* TELEPH telefonu açık tutmak, telefonda beklemek, kapatmamak; ~ *water* su kaldırmak; *fig.* makul olm., mantıklı olm., geçerli olm.; ~ *off* uzak tutmak, uzaklaştırmak; AVIA rotasında gitmek; ~ *on* devam etm., dayanmak; beklemek; yerinde tutmak; ~ *out* dayanmak, karşı koymak; yetmek; tutmak; ileri sürmek; ~ *over* ertelemek, tehir etm.; *-i* silah olarak kullanmak; ~ *up* geciktirmek, durdurmak, engel olm., tutmak; **3.** (*irr.*) *v/i.* durumunu korumak, dayanmak, karşı koymak; sürmek, devam -etm.; bağlı olm.; geçerli olm.; doğru gitmek, ilerlemek; durmak, ara vermek; uyuşturucu maddesi olm.; ~ *forth* nutuk atmak, gururla konuşmak; ileri sürmek, teklif etm.; ~ *good veya true* geçerli olm.; ~ *hard!* F sıkı tut!; ~ *in* tutmak, zapt etm., kontrol altına almak; ~ *off* uzakta kalmak, uzak durmak; ~ *on* devam etm.; TELEPH durmak, beklemek; ~ *on!* F dur!, bekle!; ~ *to* devam etm.; sadık kalmak, tutmak; yönelmek; ~ *up* yolunu kesip soymak; 'hold-all *n.* valiz, çanta, bavul; 'hold.er *n.* COM sahip, hamil; kulp, tutacak, tutamak, sap; ~ *of shares* hisse senedi sahibi; 'hold.fast *n.* kenet, mandal, çengel, kanca; 'hold.ing *n.* holding; mülk; mal; arazi; tutma; *small* ~ ekilip biçilen küçük arazi; ~ *company* holding; 'hold.o.ver *n. Am.* artık, posa; bakiye, geriye kalan kısım; 'hold-up *n.* gecikme; yol kesme, soygun.

hole [həul] **1.** *n.* delik, çukur, boşluk, oyuk, gedik; F *fig.* güç durum, çıkmaz; hayvan ini, barınağı, yuvası; pis yer; golf çukuru; *pick ~s in* kusur bulmak, ince eleyip sık dokumak; **2.** *vb.* delik açmak; *golf:* topu deliğe sokmak; 'hole-and-'cor.ner *adj.* gizli, el altından.

hol.i.day ['hɔlədi] *n.* tatil günü; bayram günü; **~s** *pl.* tatil; '**~-mak.er** *n.* tatile çıkmış kişi.

ho.li.ness ['həulinis] *n.* kutsallık, kutsiyet.

hol.la ['hɔlə] **1.** *int.* haydi! (*köpeklere*); **2.** *vb.* bağırmak, seslenmek (*köpeğe*).

hol.land ['hɔlənd] *n. a.* **brown~** ağartılmamış keten bezi; **~s** *sg.* ardıç suyu, cin.

hol.ler *Am.* F ['hɔlə] **1.** *vb.* bağırmak, haykırmak; **2.** *n.* bağırış, haykırış.

hol.lo(a) ['hɔləu] = **holla.**

hol.low ['hɔləu] **1.** □ içi boş, oyuk; derin, boşluktan gelen (*ses*); yalan, sahte, aldatıcı; çökük, çukurlaşmış; **2.** F *adv a.* **all ~** tamamen, büsbütün; sahte, aldatıcı; çökük; çukurlaşmış; **3.** *n.* çukur, boşluk; küçük dere; MEC oyuk, yiv; **4.** *vb.* oy(ul)mak, çukurlatmak, içini oymak; '**hol.low.ness** *n.* boşluk, oyukluk; *fig.* sahtelik, aldatıcılık.

hol.ly BOT ['hɔli] *n.* çobanpüskülü.

hol.ly.hock BOT ['hɔlihɔk] *n.* gülhatmi.

holm [həum] *n. a.* '**~'oak** BOT pırnal.

hol.o.caust ['hɔlɔkɔːst] *n.* tahribat, büyük yıkım, yangın felâketi.

hol.ster ['həulstə] *n.* deri tabanca kılıfı.

ho.ly ['həuli] **1.** *adj.* kutsal, mukaddes, kutsî mübarek; **♀ Week** paskalyadan önceki hafta; **2.** *n.* **~ of holies** İncil: en kutsal yer; Musevi tapınağının en iç kısmı; '**~.stone** *n.* NAUT maltataşı.

hom.age ['hɔmidʒ] *n.* hürmet, saygı; biat, *b-nin* egemenliğini tanıma; **do ve~ya pay veya render ~** saygı göstermek, hürmet etm. (**to** *-e*).

home [həum] **1.** *n.* ev, yuva, aile ocağı, mesken; vatan, yurt, memleket; bazı oyunlarda hedef; **at ~** evde; memleketinde; *spor:* kendi sahasında; **make o.s. at ~** rahatına bakmak, kendi evindeymiş gibi davranmak; **be at ~** evde bulunmak; *b-ni* evinde kabul etm.; **2.** *adj.* eve ait; memleketine ait; yerli; **♀ Office** İçişleri Bakanlığı; **♀ Rule** muhtariyet, özerklik; **♀ Secretary** İçişleri Bakanı; **~ trade** iç ticaret; **3.** *adv.* evde, eve; kendi ülkesine, ülkesinde; tam yerine; **be ~** evde olm.; **bring veya drive s.th. ~ to s.o.** *bşi b-nin* kafasına sokmak, *bşi* iyice anlamasını sağlamak; **come ~ veya come ~ to s.o.** *fig.* tamamiyle farkına varmak; *b-ni* çok etkilemek; **that comes ~ to you** onu iyice anlıyorsunuz; **hit veya strike**

~ fig. tam yerine vurmak; **4.** *v/i.* eve gitmek *veya* dönmek; yuvasına dönmek (*hayvan*); dikkatini bir yöne çevirmek; evi olm.; '**~'brewed** *adj.* evde yapılma (*içki*); '**~-com.ing** *n.* eve *veya* yurda dönüş; mezunlar günü; **♀ Coun.ties** *pl.* kontluklar; **~ e.co'nom.ics** *mst sg. Am.* ev idaresi bilgisi, ev ekonomisi; '**~-felt** *adj.* kendini evindeymiş gibi hisseden; '**~'grown** *adj.* ülkede yetişen; '**home.less** *adj.* evsiz barksız, yurtsuz; '**home.like** *adj.* ev gibi, rahat; '**home.liness** *n.* basitlik, sadelik, gösterişsizlik; *Am.* cazibesizlik, çirkinlik; '**home.ly** □ *fig.* basit, sade, gösterişsiz, süssüz; ev gibi, evi andıran; *Am.* cazibesiz, çirkin.

home...: '**~'made** *adj.* evde yapılmış; '**~.mak.er** *n.* ev kadını; '**~.sick: be ~** yurt hasreti çekmek, sıla hasreti çekmek; '**~.sick.ness** *n.* sıla hasreti; '**~.spun 1.** *adj.* evde dokunmuş; temiz, saf; **2.** *n.* evde dokunmuş kumaş; '**~.stead** *n.* ev ve eklentileri; çiftlik evi; **~ team** *spor:* ev sahibi takım; **~ward(s)** ['~wəd(z)] *adj. & adv.* eve doğru (giden); '**~.work** *n.* ev ödevi.

hom.i.cide ['hɔmisaid] *n.* adam öldürme; adam öldüren kimse, katil.

hom.i.ly ['hɔmili] *n.* vaız, uzun ve sıkıcı konuşma.

hom.ing ['həumiŋ] *adj.* salıverildiğinde tekrar yuvaya dönebilen (*güvercin*); **~ instinct** tekrar yuvayı bulabilme içgüdüsü; **~ pigeon** posta güvercini.

hom.i.ny ['hɔmini] *n.* mısır lapası.

ho.m(o)e.o.path ['həumjəupæθ] *n.* hastalığı benzeri ile tedavi eden doktor; **hom(o)e.o'path.ic** *adj.* (**~ally**) benzeri ile tedavi olunan hastalığa ait; **ho.m(o)e.op.athist** [~mi'ɔpəθist] *n.* hastalığı benzeri ile tedavi eden doktor; **ho.m(o)e'op.a.thy** *n.* hastalığı benzeri ile tedavi etme usulü.

ho.mo.ge.ne.i.ty [hɔməudʒe'niːiti] *n.* aynı cinsten olma, cinsdeşlik, türdeşlik; **homo.ge.ne.ous** □ [~'dʒiːnjəs] aynı cinsten olan, cinsdeş, türdeş, homojen; **hom.ograph** ['hɔməugrɑːf] *n.* yazılışı aynı fakat anlam *veya* telaffuzu farklı olan kelime; **ho.mol.o.gous** [hɔ'mɔləgəs] *adj.* birbirine benzer *veya ya* eşit; **ho'mol.o.gy** [~dʒi] *n.* benzeşim, benzeyiş; eşitlik; **hom.o.nym** ['hɔmənim] *n.* eşsesli, anlamları farklı fakat telaffuzu aynı olan kelime; **hom.o.phone** ['~fəun] = **homonym;**

ho.mo.sex.u.al ['həuməu'seksjuəl] *adj.* homoseksüel, eşcinsel.

hom.y F ['həumi] = *homelike.*

hone MEC [həun] **1.** *n.* bileğitaşı; **2.** *v/t.* bilemek.

hon.est □ ['ɔnist] doğru, dürüst, namuslu, güvenilir, doğru sözlü, açık kalpli; '**hon.es.ty** *n.* namusluluk, dürüstlük, doğruluk, iffet.

hon.ey ['hʌni] *n.* bal; F tatlılık; sevgili; canım; '**hon.ey-bee** *n.* bal arısı; '**honeycomb 1.** *n.* bal peteği; **2.** *v/t.* delikler açmak; **hon.eyed** ['hʌnid] *adj.* tatlı (*söz*); '**hon.ey.moon 1.** *n.* balayı; **2.** *vb.* balayı geçirmek; '**hon.ey.suck.le** *n.* BOT hanımeli.

honk MOT [hɔŋk] **1.** *n.* klakson sesi; **2.** *v/i.* klakson çalmak.

honk.y-tonk *Am. sl.* ['hɔŋkitɔŋk] *n.* ucuz gece kulübü batakhane.

hon.o.rar.i.um [ɔnə'reəriəm] *n.* ücret; **honor.ar.y** ['ɔnərəri] *adj.* onursal, fahrî; ücretsiz.

hon.o(u)r ['ɔnə] **1.** *n.* şeref, onur, namus, itibar, saygıdeğerlik; şöhret, nam; ün; şeref kaynağı, yüz akı; yargıçlara verilen ünvan; ayrıcalık; imtiyaz; iskambilde en yüksek kart; ~s *pl.* üstün başarılı ünversite öğrencilerine verilen şeref payesi; *Your* ♀ Sayın Yargıç; *in* ~ *of s.o. b-nin* şerefine; *do the* ~s *of the house* ev sahipliği yapmak, misafir ağırlamak; **2.** *v/t.* şereflendirmek, şeref vermek, saygı göstermek; COM *-in* karşılığını ödemek.

hon.o(u)r.a.ble □ ['ɔnərəbl] şerefli, namuslu, itibarlı; muhterem, sayın; *Right* ♀ pek muhterem, çok saygıdeğer (*markizin altındaki kişilere söylenir*); '**hon.o(u)r.a.ble.ness** *n.* şeref, itibar, namus.

hooch *sl.* [huːtʃ] *n.* içki.

hood [hud] *n.* kukuleta, başlık, kapşon; kukuletaya benzer herhangi bir şey; MOT arabanın üst kısmı; *Am.* motor kapağı; MEC kapak; UNIV rütbe göstermek için cüppelere takılan başlık şeklindeki parça; gangster, azılı katil, serseri; '**hooded** *adj.* başlıklı, kukuletalı, kapşonlu.

hood.lum *Am.* F ['huːdləm] *n.* serseri, kabadayı, gangster, azılı katil.

hoo.doo *part. Am.* ['huːduː] **1.** *n.* uğursuz kimse *veya* şey; **2.** *v/t.* uğursuzluk getirmek.

hood.wink ['hudwiŋk] *v/t.* aldatmak, hile yapmak, oyuna getir-mek.

hoo.ey *Am. sl.* ['huːi] *n.* saçma şey, zırva, saçmalık; martaval, dü-men.

hoof [huːf] *n., pl.* **hoofs** *veya* **hooves** [huːvz] *at. vs.* tırnağı, toynak; '~**-beat** *n.* toynak sesi; **hoofed** [huːft] *adj.* toy-naklı.

hook [huk] **1.** *n.* çengel, kanca, kopça; orak; *boks:* kroşe; ~s **and eyes** erkek ve dişi kopçalar; *by* ~ *or by crook* şu veya bu şekilde; ~, *line, and sinker* F tamamen tümüyle; **2.** *v/t.* kıvırmak, bükmek, eğmek; kancayla yakalamak, tutmak, çekmek, bağlamak; *sl.* çalmak, araklamak, aşırmak; ~ *it sl.* kaç-mak, tüymek; ~ *up* birleştirmek, bağla-mak; *v/i. a.* ~ *on* kanca şeklini almak; takılmak, asılmak.

hook.a(h) ['hukə] *n.* nargile.

hooked [hukt] *adj.* çengelli; çengel şek-linde; tığ ile örülmüş; müptelâ, düş-kün; '**hook.er** *n.* NAUT tek direkli balıkçı gemisi; eski ve hantal gemi; fa-hişe, orospu; '**hook.ey** = *hooky;* '**hook-up** *n.* birleşme, bağlantı; birkaç elektrik devresinin birbirine bağlan-ması; *radyo:* birkaç radyo istasyonunu birleştirme; '**hook.y** *n.* okul kaçağı; *play* ~ *Am. sl.* okulu asmak, okulu kırmak.

hoo.li.gan ['huːligən] *n.* serseri, kül-hanbeyi, kabadayı.

hoop [huːp] **1.** *n.* kasnak, çember; kadınların eteklerinin içine geçirilen çember; MEC tasma kelepçe; **2.** *v/t.* çemberlemek, çemberle bağlamak; '**hoop.er** *n.* fıçıcı, varilci.

hoo.poe ORN ['huːpuː] *n.* çavuşkuşu, ibibik, hüthüt.

hoot [huːt] **1.** *n.* baykuş sesi; klakson se-si; vapur düdüğü; bağırma, azarlama; yuhalama; **2.** *v/i.* yuhalamak, yuha çek-mek; bağırmak, azarlamak; baykuş gi-bi ötmek; ötmek (*baykuş*); MOT klak-son çalmak; *v/t. a.* ~ *at*, ~ *out*, ~ *away* ıslıklamak, yuhalamak; '**hoot.er** *n.* fabrika düdüğü, siren; MOT klakson.

Hoov.er ['huːvə] **1.** *n.* elektrik süpürge-si; **2.** *v/t.* elektrik süpürgesiyle temizle-mek.

hop [hɔp] **1.** *n.* BOT şerbetçiotu; ~s *pl.* şerbetçiotu (*biraya katılan ve ona lez-zet veren*); ~**-picker** şerbetçiotu topla-yan kimse *veya* makine; **2.** *v/t.* yetiştir-mek (*şerbetçiotu*); *v/i.* şerbetçiotu top-lamak.

hop²[-] **1.** *n.* sekme, sıçrama, zıplama; AVIA uçak seferi; F dans partisi; **2.** *vb.* sıçramak, sekmek, zıplamak, seke seke yürümek; uçakla seyahat etm.; ~ *it sl.* yaylanmak, gidivermek; ~ *off* AVIA havalanmak, kalkmak.

hope[həup] **1.** *n.* umut, ümit (*of -den*); umut kaynağı; *of great* ~*s* umut veren; **2.** *vb.* ummak, ümit etm., beklemek (*for -i*); ümitle aramak; umutla beklemek; ~ *in* güvenmek, itimat etm. *-e;* ~ *against* ~ ümidini kesmeyerek beklemek; **hopeful**□ ['-ful] ümitli, ümit verici; *be* ~ *that* bşden ümitli olm.; 'hope.less□ ümitsiz.

hop-o'-my-thumb ['hɔpəmi'θʌm] *n.* cüce.

hop.per['hɔpə] *n.* MEC besleme hunisi; tahıl ambarı; büyük kova; sıçrayan herhangi bir böcek.

horde [hɔːd] *n.* göçebe aşiret; kalabalık, izdiham; çokluk, fazlalık.

ho.ri.zon [hə'raizn] *n.* ufak, çevren; **hori.zon.tal**□ [hɔri'zɔntl] yatay, ufkî, ufka paralel.

hor.mone['hɔːməun] *n.* hormon.

horn [hɔːn] *n.* MUS boru; ZOO boynuz; MOT korna, klakson; boynuz şeklindeki herhangi bş; *draw in one's* ~*s fig.* korkup geri çekilmek, yelkenleri suya indirmek; (*stag's*) ~*s pl.* geyik boynuzları; ~ *of plenty* bolluk (sembolü); '~.beam *n.* BOT gürgen; ~.blende ['-blend] *n.* MIN hornblent; **horned** ['-id] *adj.* boynuzlu.

hor.net ZOO ['hɔːnit] *n.* eşekarısı, büyük sarı arı.

horn.less ['hɔːnlis] *adj.* boynuzsuz, boynuzları olmayan; 'horn.pipe *n. a.* *sailor's* ~ gemici dansı; bu dansın müziği; 'horn-rimmed ~ *spectacles pl.* bağa gözlük, boynuzdan yapılma gözlük; **horn.swoggle** *Am. sl.* ['-swɔgl] *v/t.* faka bastırmak, aldatmak, dolandırmak, işletmek; 'horn.y□ boynuzlu; boynuzdan yapılmış; sert, nasırlaşmış, nasır tutmuş (*el*); şehvetli, tahrik olmuş.

ho.rol.o.gy[hɔ'rɔlədʒi] *n.* vakit ölçme ilmi; saatçilik; **hor.o.scope** ['hɔrəskəup] *n.* zayice, yıldız falı; *cast a* ~ yıldız falına bakmak.

hor.ri.ble□ ['hɔrəbl] dehşetli, korkunç, müthiş, iğrenç; kötü, berbat; **hor.rid**□ ['hɔrid] korkunç, dehşetli, iğrenç; kötü; berbat; **hor.rif.ic**[hɔ'rifik] *adj.* dehşetli, korkunç; **hor.ri.fy** ['-fai] *v/t.*

korkutmak, dehşete düşürmek; **hor.ror**['hɔrə] *n.* dehşet, korku, yılgı; nefret, tiksinme (*of -den*); *chamber of* ~*s* mumyalar müzesi; ~ *fiction* (*film*) korku romanı (filmi); 'hor.ror-strick.en *adj.* korkudan donakalmış.

horse[hɔːs] **1.** *n.* at, beygir; aygır; F süvari birliği; MEC sehpa, kasa; *look a gift* ~ *in the mouth fig.* bahşiş atın dişine bakmak, bir armağanı beğenmeyip kusur bulmak; *a* ~ *of another colo(u)r* tamamiyle farklı bir konu, apayrı bir mesele; (*straight*) *from the* ~*'s mouth* asıl kaynağından öğrenilmiş *veya* alınmış; **2.** *vb.* ata bin(dir)mek, at koşmak; hayvan gücüyle hareket ettirmek; *sl.* eşek şakası yapmak; '~.back *on* ~ ata binmiş at üstünde; atla; *go on* ~ atla gitmek; '~-bean *n.* BOT bakla; '~-box*n.* at taşımak için kullanılan kapalı araç; '~-break.er*n.* at terbiyecisi; ~ *chest.nut*n. BOT atkestanesi; '~-collar*n.* hamut; '~-deal.er*n.* at satıcısı; '~-flesh *n.* at eti; F atlar, at sınıfı; '~-fly*n.* ZOO atsineği; ♀ Guards*n. pl.* atlı muhafız bölüğü; '~.hair*n.* at kılı; '~-laugh *n.* F kaba kahkaha; '~.man *n.* binici, süvari; '~.man.ship*n.* binicilik; ~ *op.er.a*Am. kovboy filmi; '~-play *n.* eşek şakası; '~-pond*n.* at sulama *veya* yıkama havuzu; '~.pow.er*n.* beygir gücü; '~-rad.ish *n.* BOT yabanturbu, acırga; '~-sense *n.* sağduyu; '~.shoe *n.* at nalı; '~.whip *n.* kamçı, kırbaç; '~.wom.an*n.* kadın binici.

hors.y['hɔːsi] *adj.* ata ait, at…; at yarışları…; ata benzeyen…; binici…

hor.ta.tive □ ['hɔːtətiv], **hor.ta.to.ry** ['-təri] teşvik edici, gayret verici, yüreklendirici; nasihat verici, öğütleyici.

hor.ti.cul.tur.al [hɔːti'kʌltʃərəl] *adj.* bahçvanlığa ait, bahçvanlık…; 'horti.culture *n.* bahçvanlık, bahçecilik, çiçekçilik; **hor.ti'cul.tur.ist** *n.* bahçvan, bahçecilik uzmanı.

ho.san.na [həu'zænə] *n.* şükretme (*Tanrıya*)

hose[həuz] **1.** *n.* hortum; F çorap; **2.** *v/t.* hortumla sulamak *veya* yıkamak.

ho.sier ['həuziə] *n.* çorapçı ve iç çamaşırcı; 'ho.sier.y*n.* çorap ve iç çamaşırı, mensucat.

hos.pice['hɔspis] *n.* misafirhane; darülaceze, düşkünler evi.

hos.pi.ta.ble □ ['hɔspitəbl] misafirperver, konuksever; açık (*to -e*).

hos.pi.tal['hɔspitl] *n.* hastane; MIL askeri hastane; **hos.pi.tal.i.ty** [_'tæliti] *n.* konukseverlik, misafirperverlik; **hos.pi.tal.ize** ['_təlaiz] *v/t.* hastaneye yatırmak; **'hospi.tal-train** *n.* MIL askeri hastane treni.

host¹ [həust] *n.* ev sahibi (*erkek*), mihmandar; otelci, hancı; ZOO, BOT bir asalağı besleyen organizma; *reckon without one's ~* güçlükleri düşünmeden plan yapmak; ilgili kişilere danışmadan hesap yapmak.

host² [_] *n. fig.* kalabalık, çokluk; ordu; *Lord of ~s Incil:* ordulara zafer veren Allah; *he is a ~ in himself* bir çok adama bedeldir.

Host³ ECCL [_] *n.* okunmuş ekmek, takdis edilen fodla.

hos.tage ['həstidʒ] *n.* rehine, tutak.

hos.tel ['həstəl] *n.* han; UNIV talebe yurdu; **'hos.tel.(l)er** *n.* handa kalan kimse; **'hos.tel.ry** ['_ri] *n.* han, otel.

host.ess ['həustis] *n.* ev sahibesi; hancı kadın; konsomatris; hostes.

hos.tile ['həstail] *adj.* düşmanca; saldırgan; düşmana ait, düşman...; **hos.til.i.ty** [_'tiliti] *n.* düşmanlık (*to -e*); **~s** *pl.* savaş, çarpışmalar.

hos.tler ['əslə] *n.* seyis.

hot [hɔt] **1.** □ sıcak, kızgın; acı, yakıcı, biberli; hiddetli, öfkeli; yeni, taze (*iz, haber*); ritmik, hareketli (*müzik*); *Am. sl.* elden çıkarması güç (*çalıntı mal*); şiddetli, sert, hararetli; şehvetli; istekli; şevkli; inanılmaz, imkânsız; yüksek gerilim taşıyan (*tel*); radyoaktif; çalıntı (*mal*); polisçe aranan; hızlı, süratli (*araç*); *~ air* F boş laf, atmasyon, martaval; *go like ~ cakes* kapışa kapışa satın alınmak, çok hızlı gitmek; *~ stuff sl.* birinci sınıf şey; değerli kimse; *get into ~ water* başını belâya sokmak; **2.** *v/t. & v/i. mst ~ up* F ısıtmak; heyecanlan(dır)mak; ısınmak; **'hot.bed** *n.* camlık, ısıtılmış gübreli toprak; *fig.* huzursuzluk (*veya* kötülük) kaynağı, yuvası, yatağı; **'hot-'blood.ed** *adj.* hiddetli, kan beynine sıçramak üzere olan.

hotch.potch F ['hɔtʃpɔtʃ] *n.* karmakarışık şey, karman çorman şey; düzensizlik, intizamsızlık; türlü (*yemek*).

hot dog F ['hɔt'dɔg] *n.* sosis, sıcak sosisli sandviç.

ho.tel [həu'tel] *n.* otel.

hot...: '~**foot 1.** *adv.* aceleyle, telaşla; **2.** *vb.* aceleyle gitmek; '~**head** *n.* öfkeli (*veya* çabuk kızan, ateşli) kimse; '~**house** *n.* limonluk, ser, camlık;

'**hotness** *n.* sıcaklık, hararet; heyecan; hiddet, öfke; acılık, yakıcılık.

hot...: '~**plate** *n.* küçük elektrik ocağı; '~**pot** *n.* güveç; '~**press** *vb.* sıcak saç ütüsüyle ütülemek (*kağıt, kumaş*); ~ **rod** MOT *Am. sl.* takviyeli külüstür araba; '~**spur** *n.* çabuk öfkelenen adam; ~**water bot.tle** sıcak su torbası.

hough [hɔk] = *hock¹.*

hound [haund] **1.** *n.* av köpeği, tazı; *fig.* it herif, adi adam, aşağılık herif; **2.** *v/t.* tazı ile avlamak (*veya* kovalamak); peşini bırakmamak, izlemek, takip etm.

hour ['auə] *n.* saat (*60 dakika*); vakit, zaman; ~**s** *pl.* belirli süre; mesai (*veya* iş) saatleri; ECCL dua vakti; *s. eleventh;* '~**glass** *n.* kum saati; '~**hand** *n.* akrep (*saatteki*); '**hour.ly 1.** *adv.* saatte bir, saat başı; herhangi bir saatte; **2.** *adj.* her saat başı olan; devamlı, sürekli.

house 1. [haus] *n., pl.* **hous.es** ['hauziz] *com.* ev, mesken, hane; PARL hükümet meclis binası; COM ticarethane, müessese; PARL meclis; ev halkı, aile; soy; hanedan; tiyatro; THEAT seyirciler; *the ♀* borsa; Avam Kamarası, Lordlar Kamarası; ~ *and home* ev barkı; *keep ~* ev idare etm., ev işlerini görmek; *on the ~* masrafı patrona *veya* şirkete ait; **2.** [hauz] *v/t.* barındırmak, evinde misafir etm.; yerleştirmek, yığmak; eve koymak; korumak, muhafaza etm.; *v/i.* evde oturmak, barınmak; ~**a.gent** ['hauseidʒənt] *n.* ev komisyoncusu; ~ **ar.rest** evde göz hapsi; '~**boat** *n.* yüzen ev; '~**break.er** *n.* ev hırsızı; '~**flag** *n.* NAUT gemi bayrağı; '~**fly** *n.* karasinek; '~**hold** *n.* ev halkı, aile; *attr.* eve ait, ev...; *King's ~* Kral'ın saray hayatı; ~ *troops pl.* hassa askeri; ~ *word* hergün kullanılan kelime; '~**holder** *n.* ev sahibi; aile reisi; '~**keep.er** *n.* kâhya kadın, evi idare eden kadın; '~**keep.ing 1.** *n.* ev idaresi; **2.** *adj.* ev..., aile...; '~**less** *adj.* evsiz barksız, evi olmayan; '~**maid** *n.* orta hizmetçisi; '~**mas.ter** *n.* yatılı okulda bir binayı idare eden öğretmen; ~ *of cards* çocuğun iskambil kağıtlarından yaptığı ev; *fig.* sallantılı iş; ♀ *of God* tapınak, kilise; ~ *of ill fame* genelev; '~**paint.er** *n.* badanacı, boyacı; '~**phy.si.cian** *n.* revir doktoru; '~**room** *n.* bir evde barınacak yer, bir evdeki boş yer; *give s.o. ~ b-ni* evine kabul etm., *b-ne* evinde oda vermek; '~-to-'house *adj.* kapı kapı; ~ **collection** kapı kapı dolaşarak toplama; '~-top *n.* dam; **proclaim from the**~**s** herkese ilan etm., *fig.* davul çalmak, sağır sultana bile duyurmak; '~-train.ed *adj.* evcil, ehli, uysal (*hayvan*); '~-warm.ing *n.* yeni eve taşınanların verdikleri ziyafet; ~**wife** ['.waif] *n.* ev kadını; ['hʌzif] *n.* dikiş kutusu; ~**wife.ly** ['hauswaifli] *adj.* ev kadınına ait, ev kadınının...; ~**wif.er.y** ['.wifəri] *n.* ev kadınlığı; '~**work** *n.* ev işi; '~**wreck.er** *n. Am.* ev yıkıcısı.

hous.ing[1] ['hauziŋ] *n.* iskân; evler; barınacak yer; ~ **conditions** *pl.* yaşam şartları; ~ **shortage** evsizlik sorunu.

hous.ing[2] [.] *n.* eyer bellemesi, süslü koşum takımı.

hove [həuv] *pret. & p.p. of* **heave 2**.

hov.el ['həvəl] *n.* açık ağıl; harap kulübe.

hov.er ['həvə] *v/i.* havada durmak (*helikopter*); etrafında dolaşıp durmak (*kuş*); dolaşmak, sallanmak; *fig.* tereddüt etm., arada kalmak; ~**ing accent** şüpheli konuşma; '~.**craft** *n.* basınçlı hava üzerinde gidebilen taşıt, hoverkraft.

how [hau] *adv.* nasıl, ne, kadar; ne derecede, ne durumda; ~ **do you do?** nasılsınız?; ~ **large a room!** ne geniş bir oda!; ~ **about... ?...** ne dersin?; ~.**be.it** *obs.* F ['.'bi:it] *cj.* bununla beraber, yine de; ~**d'ye-do** *sl.* ['.djə'du:] *n.* sıkıntılı, durum; ~'**ev.er**, a. howe'er [.'ɛə] *adv. & cj.* ne kadar... olursa olsun; F nasıl oldu da...?; mamafih, bununla beraber.

how.itz.er MIL ['hauitsə] *n.* havan topu, obüs.

howl [haul] **1.** *v/i.* ulumak; inlemek, feryat etm.; kahkaha atmak; uğuldamak (*rüzgâr*); *v/t.* bağırmak -*e*, yuhalayarak susturmak; **2.** *n.* uluma; inleme, inilti, feryat, bağırma; uğultu; *radyo*: vınlama; '**howl.er** *n.* uluyan hayvan; bağıran kimse; *sl.* gülünç hata, budalaca yanlışlık; '**howl.ing 1.** *adj.* uluyan; uğuldayan; ıssız, tenha, vahşi (*yer*); F çok büyük, göz kamaştırıcı; **2.** *n.* uluma; feryat, inleme.

how.so.ev.er ['hausəu'evə] *adv.* her nasıl olursa olsun, her ne kadar olursa olsun, her ne derecede olursa olsun.

hoy [hɔi] **1.** *int.* hey! (*dikkat çekmek için*); ho! (*hayvanları uzaklaştırmak*

için); **2.** *n.* NAUT direksiz *veya* tek direkli mavna *veya* duba.

hoy.den ['hɔidn] *n.* kaba ve arsız kız, erkek Fatma.

hub [hʌb] *n.* tekerlek poyrası, tekerlek göbeği; *fig.* merkezi yer.

hub.ble-bub.ble ['hʌblbʌbl] *n.* nargile.

hub.bub ['hʌbʌb] *n.* gürültü, velvele.

hub(.**by**) F ['hʌb(i)] *n.* koca.

hub.ris ['hju:bris] *n.* kibir, gururlanma, kasılma.

huck.a.back ['hʌkəbæk] *n.* havluluk bir çeşit kumaş.

huck.le ['hʌkl] *n.* kalça, but; '~.**ber.ry** *n.* BOT Kuzey Amerika'da yetişen bir cins ufak ve siyah meyve; '~-**bone** *n.* kalça kemiği.

huck.ster ['hʌkstə] **1.** *n.* seyyar satıcı, işportacı; reklamcı; **2.** *vb.* sıkı pazarlık etm.; *bşi* dolaşa dolaşa satmak.

hud.dle ['hʌdl] **1.** *v/t. & v/i. a.* ~ **together** sıkı halde topla(n)mak, biraraya sıkış(tır)mak, karmakarışık tık(ıştır)mak; ~ (**o.s.**) **up** *b-ne* sokulup sarılmak; **2.** *n.* karışıklık, düzensizlik, yığın; **go into a** ~ F *baş* başa verip konuşmak.

hue[1] [hju:] *n.* renk (tonu).

hue[2] [.] *n.:* ~ **and cry** çığlık, bağrışma; protesto, karşı çıkma.

huff [hʌf] **1.** *n.* huysuzluk, surat asma, dargınlık, içerleme; **2.** *vb.* şişirmek; kabadayılık etm.; zulmetmek; öfkelendirmek, kızdırmak; solumak; püfür püfür esmek; tehdit etm., göz dağı vermek; kızmak, öfkelenmek; '**huff.ish** □ çabuk kızan; öfkeli, darılmış, gücenmiş, içerlemiş; '**huff.i.ness**, '**huff.ish.ness** *n.* öfke, kızgınlık, dargınlık; '**huff.y** □ çabuk kızan, parlamaya hazır; öfkeli, sinirli, dargın, gücenmiş, içerlemiş.

hug [hʌg] **1.** *n.* kucaklama, sarılma; **2.** *v/t.* kucaklamak, sarılmak -*e*; bağrına basmak -*i*; *fig.* benimsemek -*i*, bağlı olm. -*e*; ~ **o.s.** *k-ni* kutlamak, tebrik etm., kendi halinden memnun olm. (**on** -*den dolayı*).

huge □ [hju:dʒ] pek büyük, kocaman, cüsseli, heybetli, muazzam; '**huge-ness** *n.* irilik, kocamanlık, büyüklük, muazzamlık.

hug.ger-mug.ger F ['hʌgəmʌgə] **1.** *adj.* gizli; karışık, düzensiz; **2.** *v/t.* gizli tutmak, örtbas etm., sır olarak saklamak; *v/i.* gizlice, sinsice, çaktırmadan hareket etm. *veya* görüşmek; **3.** *n.* gizlilik; düzensizlik, karışıklık; ağzı sıkılık.

Hu.gue.not HIST ['hju:gənɔt] *n.* (*16 ve 17. yüzyıllarda*) Fransız Protestan.

hu.la ['huːlə] *n.* Hawaii dansı.

hulk NAUT [hʌlk] *n.* kullanılmaz hale gelmiş gemi teknesi, hurda gemi, eskiden hapishane olarak kullanılan gemi; *fig.* büyük ve kaba gemi; iri ve hantal kimse *veya* şey; **'hulk.ing** *adj.* hantal, eli ağır, beceriksiz, sakar.

hull [hʌl] **1.** *n.* BOT kabuk; çanak; NAUT tekne, gövde; **~ down** yalnız direk, yelken ve bacası görünecek kadar uzakta; **2.** *v/t.* *-in* kabuğunu soymak; NAUT geminin teknesine gülle isabet ettirmek.

hul.la.ba.loo [hʌləbə'luː] *n.* gürültü, velvele, yaygara.

hul.lo ['hʌ'ləu] *int.* merhaba!, selam!; hey!; hadi canım!; alo!

hum [hʌm] **1.** *n.* vızıltı; mırıltı; uğultu; **2.** *int.* hım!, ya!, öyle mi?; **3.** *vb.* mırıldanmak; vınlamak, vızıldamak; faaliyette olm., harıl harıl çalışmak; *sl.* kötü kokmak, kokuşmak; mırıldanarak söylemek (*şarkı*); mırıldanarak belirtmek *veya* etkilemek; **~ and haw** kemküm etm., mırın kırın etm.; **make things ~** F faaliyete geçirmek, harıl harıl çalıştırmak.

hu.man ['hjuːmən] **1.** □ insana ait, insanî, beşerî; **~ly** insanca, insanın yapabileceği kadar, insanın yeteneği dahilinde; **~ly possible** insanın elinden geldiği kadar; **~ly speaking** beşeri bakımdan; **2.** *n.* F insan; **hu.mane** □ [hjuː'mein] insancıl, merhametli, şefkatli, müşfik; uygarlaştırıcı; **~ killer** hayvanları acı vermeden öldürmeye yarayan alet; **~ learning** beşeriyet kültürü; **human.ism** ['hjuːmənizəm] *n.* insanlık çıkarlarına bağlılık, hümanizm; genel kültür; **'human.ist** *n.* insan tabiatı *veya* toplumsal olay dalında okuyan öğrenci; Hümanizm görüş ve felsefesini tutan kimse (*veya* düşünce, davranış), hümanist kimse; **human.i.tar.i.an** [hjuːmæni'tɛəriən] **1.** *n.* yardımsever kimse; **2.** *adj.* hayırsever, yardımsever, insancıl, insaniyetperver; **hu'man.i.ty** *n.* beşeriyet, insanlık; insan, beşer; merhamet, şefkat; **the humanities** *pl.* klasik Yunan ve Latin edebiyatı üzerine çalışma; konusu insan olan bilimler, hümaniter bilimler; **hu.man.i.za.tion** [hjuːmənai'zeiʃən] *n.* insanlaştırma;

insanileştirme; **'hu.man.ize** *v/t.* & *v/i.* insanlaş(tır)mak; insanileş(tir)mek; **hu.mankind** ['hjuːmən'kaind] *n.* insanoğlu, beşeriyet.

hum.ble ['hʌmbl] **1.** □ alçak gönüllü, mütevazi; önemsiz; fakir, yoksul; vasat, orta; saygılı, hürmetkâr; *my ~ self* bendeniz, kulunuz; *your ~ servant* âciz kulunuz; *eat ~ pie* kibri kırılmak, burnu sürtülmek, kabahatini kabul edip özür dilemek, tükürdüğünü yalamak; **2.** *v/t.* kibrini kırmak, burnunu sürtmek, aşağılamak, boyun eğdirmek.

hum.ble-bee ['hʌmblbiː] *n.* bir çeşit iri gövdeli arı.

hum.ble.ness ['hʌmblnis] *n.* alçak gönüllülük, tevazu.

hum.bug ['hʌmbʌg] **1.** *n.* şarlatanlık, yalan, hile, dolap, dümen, martaval; yalancı kimse; üçkağıtçı kimse; **2.** *v/t.* aldatmak, kazıklamak, hile yapmak.

hum.ding.er *Am.* *sl.* [hʌm'diŋə] *n.* olağanüstü şey *veya* kimse.

hum.drum ['hʌmdrʌm] **1.** *adj.* can sıkıcı, tekdüzen, monoton, yavan; âdi, bayağı, değersiz, sıradan; **2.** *n.* can sıkıcı şey *veya* kimse; monoton şey; boş ve sıkıcı söz.

hu.mer.al ANAT ['hjuːmərəl] *adj.* kol kemiği *veya* omuza ait, kol kemiği..., pazı kemiği...;

hu.mid ['hjuːmid] *adj.* rutubetli, nemli, yaş; **hu'mid.i.ty** *n.* rutubet, nem.

hu.mil.i.ate [hjuː'milieit] *v/t.* küçültmek, *-in* kibrini kırmak, aşağılamak, utandırmak, rezil etm.; **hu.mil.i'a.tion** *n.* küçültme, kibrini kırma, aşağılama, rezil etme, utandırma.

hu.mil.i.ty [hjuː'militi] *n.* alçak gönüllülük, tevazu; boyun eğme.

hum.mer ['hʌmə] *n.* cızırtı yapan alet (*part.* TELEPH); *sl.* harıl harıl çalışan kimse.

hum.ming F ['hʌmiŋ] *adj.* vızıldayan, uğuldayan, mırıldanan; **'~-bird** *n.* ORN sinekkuşu; **'~-top** *n.* Alman topacı.

hum.mock ['hʌmək] *n.* yuvarlak tepe, tümsek yer, tepecik.

hu.mor.ist ['hjuːmərist] *n.* şakacı kimse, nüktedan kimse; mizahçı, güldürü yazarı.

hu.mor.ous □ ['hjuːmərəs] komik, gülünç, mizahî; **'hu.mor.ous.ness** *n.* komiklik, gülünçlük; şakacılık.

hu.mo(u)r ['hjuːmə] **1.** *n.* güldürü, mizah, komiklik, nükte; huy, mizaç, tabiat; **out of** ~ canı sıkkın, keyfsiz; **2.** *v/t.* memnun etm., hoşnut etm., kaprisine boyun eğmek; 'hu.mo(u)r.less *adj.* keyifsiz, canı sıkkın; hu.mo(u)r-some ☐ ['~səm] somurtkan, huysuz, ters, kaprisli.

hump [hʌmp] **1.** *n.* hörgüç; kambur; tümsek, tepe; *sl.* huzursuzluk, iç sıkıntısı; **give s.o. the** ~ *b-nin* canını sıkmak, içini karartmak; **2.** *vb.* kamburlaştırmak; ~ **o.s.** *Am. sl.* gayret sarfetmek, çabalamak, uğraşmak; 'hump.back, 'humpbacked *s.* **hunch-back**.

humph [mm; hʌmf] *int.* hım! (*şüphe veya tereddüt belirtmek için dudakları hareket ettirmeden çıkarılan ses*).

hump.ty-dump.ty F ['hʌmpti'dʌmpti] *n.* düşüp kırılınca tamir edilemeyen şey.

hump.y ['hʌmpi] *adj.* kambur, girintili çıkıntılı.

hu.mus ['hju:məs] *n.* humus.

hunch [hʌntʃ] **1.** *s.* **hump**; iri parça; *Am.* F önsezi; **2.** *v/t. a.* ~ **out**, ~ **up** kamburlaştırmak; eğmek, bükmek; omuzlamak, itmek, dürtmek; 'hunch.back *n.* kambur kimse; 'hunch.backed *adj.* kambur.

hun.dred ['hʌndrəd] **1.** *adj.* yüz; **2.** *n.* yüz sayısı, yüz rakamı; hun.dred.fold ['~fəuld] *adv.* yüz misli, yüz kat; hun-dredth ['~θ] **1.** *adj.* yüzüncü; **2.** *n.* yüzde bir; 'hun.dred.weight *n.* 50.8 kilo, *Am.* 45.4 kilo.

hung [hʌŋ] **1.** *pret. & p.p. of* **hang 1.**; **2.** *adj.* asılmış, asılı.

Hun.gar.i.an [hʌŋˈgɛəriən] **1.** *adj.* Macar, Macaristan halkından; **2.** *n.* Macar; Macar dili, Macarca.

hun.ger ['hʌŋgə] **1.** *n.* açlık; *fig.* arzu, özlem, kuvvetli istek (**for** *-e*); **2.** *v/i.* acıkmak; şiddetle arzulamak (**for, after** *-i*); *v/t.* aç bırakmak.

hun.gry ☐ ['hʌŋgri] aç, karnı acıkmış; pek istekli, arzulu (**for** *-e*); kıraç, verimsiz (*toprak*); ~ **work** zahmetli iş, acıktıran iş.

hunk F [hʌŋk] *n.* iri parça; 'hun.kers *n. pl.* kalça, popo.

hunks F [hʌŋks] *n.* cimri (*veya* pinti) kimse.

hunt [hʌnt] **1.** *n.* av, avlanma, avcılık, avcı grubu; avlanma bölgesi; *fig.* arama; **2.** *v/t.* avlamak; kovalamak; peşine düşmek, aramak; ~ **out** *veya* **up** ara-mak, arayıp bulmak; *v/i.* avlanmak; bulmaya çalışmak (**for, after** *-i*); 'hunt.er *n.* avcı; av atı; 'hunt.ing **1.** *n.* avcılık; **2.** *adj.* avcı...; 'hunt.ing--box *n.* avcı kulübesi; 'hunt.ing--ground *n.* avlanma bölgesi; 'hunt.ress *n.* kadın avcı; 'hunts.man *n.* avcı; av köpekleri bakıcısı.

hur.dle ['həːdl] *n.* çit, engel (*a. fig.*); 'hur.dler *n.* çit yapan kimse; engelli yarış koşucusu; 'hur.dle-race *n.* engelli koşu.

hur.dy-gur.dy ['həːdigəːdi] *n.* latarna, kolu çevrilerek çalınan müzik sandığı.

hurl [həːl] **1.** *n.* fırlatma, savurma; **2.** *v/t.* hızla atmak, fırlatmak, savurmak.

hurl.y-burl.y ['həːlibəːli] *n.* gürültü, karışıklık, velvele.

hur.ra(h) [hu'rɑː], **hur.ray** [~'rei] *int.* yaşa!, hura!

hur.ri.cane ['hʌrikən] *n.* kasırga, bora; ~ **lamp** gemici feneri, rüzgâr feneri.

hur.ried ☐ ['hʌrid] aceleyle gelen, acele ile yapılmış, telaşlı.

hur.ry ['hʌri] **1.** *n.* acele, telaş; **in a** ~ acele ile, telâşla; isteyerek; kolayca, kolay kolay; **be in a** ~ acelesi olm.; **is there any** ~? aceleye gerek var mı?, telaşa lüzum var mı?; **2.** *v/t.* aceleleştirmek, çabuklaştırmak, hızlandırmak; acele ile göndermek; dürtmek, tahrik etm., sıkıştırmak; ~ **on**, ~ **up** acele ettirmek; *v/i.* acele etm., acele ile gitmek; *a.* ~ **up** acele etm., çabuk olm.; ~ **over s.th.** *b-şi* acele ile yapmak; '~'scur.ry **1.** *n.* karışıklık, koşuşturma, telâş; **2.** *adv.* telâşla, acele ile.

hurt [həːt] **1.** *n.* yara, bere; zarar, hasar; acı, sızı, ağrı; **2.** (*irr.*) *v/t.* (*a. fig.*) yaralamak, incitmek, acıtmak; zarar vermek, hasara uğratmak; engel olm.; *v/i.* ağrımak, acımak; F incinmek; hurt.ful ☐ ['~ful] zararlı (**to** *-e*).

hur.tle ['həːtl] *v/i.* fırlamak, uçup gitmek; *v/t.* savurmak, fırlatıp atmak.

hus.band ['hʌzbənd] **1.** *n.* koca, eş; **2.** *v/t.* idareli kullanmak; 'hus.band.man *n.* çiftçi; 'hus.band.ry *n.* ziraat, tarım, çiftçilik; idarecilik; **good** *etc.* ~ iyi *vs.* ev idaresi.

hush [hʌʃ] **1.** *adj.* durgun, sessiz; **2.** *n.* susma, sessizlik, sükût; **3.** *v/t. & v/i.* sus(tur)mak; yatış(tır)mak, sakinleş(tir)mek; ~ **up** örtbas etm., gizli tutmak; '~'hush *adj.* gizli, örtülü, gizli kapaklı; '~-mon.ey *n.* sus payı.

husk [hʌsk] **1.** *n.* BOT kabuk; kılıf; *fig.* işe yaramayan dış kısım; **2.** *v/t. -in* kabuğunu soymak; '**husk.i.ness** *n.* boğukluk, kısıklık (*ses*).

husk.y¹ ['hʌski] **1.** ☐ kabuklu; kabuk gibi (*kuru*); boğuk, kısık (*ses*); F dinç, gürbüz, sağlıklı, kuvvetli, dayanıklı; **2.** *n.* F dinç (*veya* gürbüz) kimse.

hus.ky² [-] *n.* Eskimo köpeği; Eskimo.

hus.sar MIL [hu'zɑː] *n.* süvari eri.

hus.sy ['hʌsi] *n.* adı çıkmış kadın; şirret kız.

hus.tings ['hʌstiŋz] *n. pl.* seçim hazırlığı.

hus.tle ['hʌsl] **1.** *v/t.* itip kakmak; acele ettirmek; hile ile satmak *veya* almak; *v/i.* itişip kakışmak, itişmek; acele etm.; fahişelik yapmak; **2.** *n.* itişip kakışma, acele, telaş; **~ and bustle** telaş, koşuşma; '**hus.tler** *n.* eline çabuk kimse, çok faal kimse; fahişe.

hut [hʌt] **1.** *n.* kulübe, baraka; MIL asker barakası; **2.** *v/t.* barakaya yerleştirmek *veya* koymak.

hutch [hʌtʃ] *n.* tavşan kafesi; dolap; kümes; kulübe, baraka.

hut.ment MIL ['hʌtmənt] *n. a.* **~ camp** karargâh, ordugâh.

huz.za [hu'zɑː] *int.* yaşa!, varol!

huz.zy ['hʌzi] = **hussy**.

hy.a.cinth BOT ['haiəsinθ] *n.* sümbül.

hy.ae.na ZOO [hai'iːnə] *n.* sırtlan.

hy.brid ['haibrid] **1.** *n.* melez hayvan *veya* bitki; iki ayrı dilden alınmış kelimelerden oluşan bileşik kelime; **2.** *adj.* melez...; karışık...; '**hy.brid.ism** *n.* melezlik; **hy'brid.i.ty** *n.* melezlik; '**hy.brid.ize** *v/t. & v/i.* melez olarak yetiş(tir)mek.

hy.dra ['haidrə] *n.* Herkül tarafından öldürülen çok başlı yılan.

hy.dran.gea BOT [hai'dreindʒə] *n.* ortanca.

hy.drant ['haidrənt] *n.* yangın musluğu.

hy.drate CHEM ['haidreit] **1.** *n.* hidrat; **2.** *vb.* su ile karıştırmak; su ile karıştırarak bileşik meydana getirmek.

hy.drau.lic [hai'drɔːlik] **1.** *adj.* (**~ally**) hidrolik, su kuvvetiyle işleyen; su altında sertleşen; **2.** *n.* **~s** *sg.* hidrolik bilmi.

hy.dro ['haidrəu] *n.* ılıca, kaplıca.

hy.dro... ['haidrəu] *prefix* su.... hidro-; '**~car.bon** *n.* hidrokarbon; '**~chlo.ric ac.id** hidroklorik asit, tuzruhu; '**~dy.'nam.ics** *n. sg.* hidrodinamik; '**~e'lec.tric** *adj.* hidroelektrik; **~ generating station** hidroelektrik santralı; **hy.dro-**

gen CHEM ['haidridʒən] *n.* hidrojen; **hy.dro.gen.ated** [hai'drɔdʒineitid] *adj.* hidrojenle birleştirilmiş; '**hy.dro.gen bomb** hidrojen bombası; **hy.drog.e.nous** [hai'drɔdʒinəs] *adj.* hidrojenli; **hy'drog.ra.phy** [-grəfi] *n.* hidrografi; **hy.dro.path.ic** ['haidrəu'pæθ-ik] **1.** *adj.* hidropatik, su kürü ile yapılan; **2.** *n. a.* **~ establishment** hidroterapi müessesesi; **hy.drop.a.thy** [hai'drɔpəθi] *n.* hidropati, su kürü.

hy.dro...: **~.pho.bi.a** ['haidrəu'fəubjə] *n.* kuduz; sudan korkma hastalığı; '**~.plane** *n.* deniz uçağı, suya inebilen uçak; **~.ponics** *n. sg.* ilaçlı suda bitki yetiştirme bilimi; **~'stat.ic 1.** *adj.* hidrostatik...; **~ press** hidrostatik basınç; **2.** *n.* **~s** *sg.* hidrostatik.

hy.e.na ZOO [hai'iːnə] *n.* sırtlan.

hy.giene ['haidʒiːn] *n.* sağlık bilgisi, hıfzısıhha; **hy'gien.ic** *adj.* (**~ally**) sağlıkla ilgili; **~s** *sg.* = **hygiene**.

hy.grom.e.ter [hai'grɔmitə] *n.* higrometre.

Hy.men ['haimen] *n.* evlilik tanrısı; kızlık zarı; **hy.me.ne.al** [-'niːəl] *adj.* evlenme (*veya* düğün) ile ilgili, evlilik..., düğün....

hymn [him] **1.** *n.* ilahi; **2.** *v/t.* ilahi okuyarak kutlamak *veya* ifade etm.; **hym.nal** ['-nəl] **1.** *adj.* ilahi ile ilgili; **2.** *n. a.* '**hymn-book** ilahi kitabı.

hy.per.bo.la MATH [hai'pɔːbələ] *n.* hiperbol; **hy'per.bo.le** RHET [-bəli] *n.* abartma, büyütme, mübalağa; **hy.per.bol.ic** MATH [-'bɔlik] *adj.* hiperbolik; **hy.per'bol.i.cal** ☐ RHET çok abartılmış; **hy.per.crit.i.cal** ☐ ['-'kritikəl] aşırı eleştiri niteliğinde; **hyper'mar.ket** *n.* büyük süpermarket; **hy'per.tro.phy** [-trəufi] *n.* bir organın anormal irileşmesi.

hy.phen ['haifən] **1.** *n.* tire, çizgi; **2.** *v/t.* tire ile birleştirmek; **hy.phen.at.ed** ['-eitid] *adj.* tire ile birleştirilmiş; **~ Americans** *pl.* yarı Amerikalılar.

hyp.no.sis [hip'nəusis] *n.*, *pl.* **hyp'no.ses** [-siːz] ipnoz, suni uyutma.

hyp.not.ic [hip'nɔtik] **1.** *adj.* (**~ally**) uyutucu; **2.** *n.* uyuşturucu madde; **hyp.no.tism** ['-nətizəm] *n.* hipnotizma, suni uyutma; '**hyp.no.tist** *n.* hipnotizmacı; **hyp.no.tize** ['-taiz] *v/t.* hipnotize etm., uyutmak.

hy.po PHOT ['haipəu] *n.* fotoğrafçılıkta kullanılan sabitleştirici ilaç.

hy.po.chon.dri.a [haipəu'kɔndriə] *n.*

hastalık kuruntusu; **hy.po'chon.dri-ac** [_driæk] **1.** *adj.* kuruntulu...; **2.** *n.* kuruntulu kimse; **hy.poc.ri.sy** [hi'pɔkrəsi] *n.* ikiyüzlülük, riyakârlık; **hyp.o-crite** ['hipəkrit] *n.* ikiyüzlü kimse; **hyp.o.crit.i.cal** □ [hipəu'kritikəl] ikiyüzlü; **hy.po.der.mic** MED [haipəu'dəːmik] **1.** *adj.* deri altına ait; **~ injection =** **2.** *n.* şırınga, iğne; **hy.pote.nuse** MATH [hai'pɔtinjuːz] *n.* hipotenüs; **hy'poth.e.cate** [_θikeit] *v/t.* ipotek etm.; rehin olarak vermek; **hy'poth.e.sis** [_θisis]

n., pl. **hy'poth.e.ses** [_θisiːz] varsayım, hipotez, kuram, faraziye; **hy-pothet.ic**, **hy.po.thet.i.cal** □ [haipəu-'θetik(əl)] kuramsal, nazari.

hys.sop BOT ['hisəp] *n.* zufa out, çördük.

hys.te.ri.a MED [his'tiəriə] *n.* isteri, peri hastalığı; **hys.ter.ic**, *mst* **hys.ter.i.cal** □ [his'terik(əl)] isterik, isteriye ait; **hys'ter.ics** *n. pl.* isteri nöbeti; **go into ~** isterikleşmek, sinir buhranına girmek.

I

I [ai] *pron.* ben.

i.am.bic [ai'æmbik] **1.** *adj.* bir kısa bir uzun vezinle yazılmış...; **2.** *n. a.* **i'am-bus** [_bəs] bir kısa bir uzun vezin.

i.bex ZOO ['aibeks] *n.* kıvrık boynuzlu dağ keçisi.

i.bi.dem [i'baidem] *adv.* evvelce bahsedilen yerde, aynı kitapta.

ice [ais] **1.** *n.* buz; meyveli dondurma; dondurma; buza benzeyen şey; pırlanta, mücevher; **cut no ~** F önemi *veya* etkisi olmamak; **2.** *v/t.* buz ile kaplamak, soğutmak, dondurmak, buz gibi yapmak; krema ile kaplamak (*pasta*); *v/i.* buzlanmak; *a.* **~ up** buzla kaplamak, buz tutmak; buz gibi soğumak; '~-age *n.* buzul devri; '~-axe *n.* dağcıların kullandıkları buz baltası; **~ bag** MED buz torbası; **iceberg** ['_bəːg] *n.* aysberk, buz adası, buzdağı (*a. fig.*).

ice...: '~-boat *n.* yelkenli kızak; '~-bound *adj.* her tarafı donmuş (*liman*); etrafı buzla çevrilmiş (*gemi*); '~-box *n.* buzluk; *Am. a.* buzdolabı; '~-break.er *n.* NAUT buzkıran; '~-cap *n.* buzul; '~-cream *n.* dondurma; '~-fall *n.* donmuş şelâle; '~-field *n.* büyük buz kitlesi, buzul; '~-floe *n.* buzul, denizde yüzen geniş buz kitlesi; '~-free *adj.* buzsuz; '~-hock.ey *n.* buz hokeyi; '~-house *n.* buz deposu, buzhane.

Ice.land.er ['aisləndə] *n.* İzlandalı; **Ice-lan.dic** [_'lændik] *n.* İzlanda dili.

ich.thy.ol.o.gy [ikθi'ɔlədʒi] *n.* zoolojinin balıklar bölümü; balıklar üzerine tez.

i.ci.cle ['aisikl] *n.* buz parçası, buz saçağı, buz salkımı. **i.ci.ness** ['aisinis] *n.* soğukluk, buz gibi

olma, çok soğuk olma.

ic.ing ['aisiŋ] *n.* şekerli krema.

i.con ['aikɔn] *n.* Ortodoks kiliselerinde azizlerin resmi, ikon.

i.con.o.clast [ai'kɔnəuklæst] *n.* yerleşmiş gelenekleri hiçe sayan kimse; putkıran, azizlerin resimlerini parçalayan kimse.

i.cy □ ['aisi] buz gibi soğuk (*a. fig.*); buzlu, buz kaplı.

I'd [aid] = **I had**; **I would**.

i.de.a [ai'diə] *n.* fikir, düşünce; sanı, tahmin; plan, tasarı; kavram, idrak, anlayış; düşünme şekli, kafa, akıl; **form an ~ of** *-in* hakkında kafada bir fikir oluşturmak; **i'de.al 1.** □ ideal; ülküsel; istenilen...; hayali...; mükemmel; şahane...; **2.** *n.* ülkü, ideal; örnek alınacak kimse; amaç, gaye, erek; **i'de.al.ism** *n.* idealizm, ülkücülük; **i'de.al-ist** *n.* idealist, ülkücü; **i.de.al'is.tic** *adj.* (**~ally**) ülkücü..., idealizme ait; kamu yararına çalışan...; **i'de.al.ize** [_laiz] *vb.* idealleştirmek, mükemmel olarak görmek.

i.den.ti.cal □ [ai'dentikəl] aynı, bir, tıpkı, özdeş; **i'den.ti.cal.ness = identi-ty**; **i.denti.fi'ca.tion** *n.* hüviyet, kimlik tesbiti; **~ card = identity card**; **~ mark** MOT marka, alâmeti farika; **i'den.ti.fy** [_fai] *vb.* *-in* hüviyetini göstermek, teşhis etm., ispatlamak (*hüviyetini*); bir tutmak, fark gözetmemek (**with** *ile*); desteklemek; **i'denti.ty** *n.* aynılık, özdeşlik; hüviyet, kimlik; **~ card** kimlik cüzdanı, hüviyet kartı; **~ disk** MIL üzerinde askerlerin kimliği yazılı olan madalyon.

id.e.o.gram ['idiəugræm], **'id.e.o-**

graph ['ˌgrɑːf] *n.* GR ideogram, bir fikri ifade etmek için harf yerine kullanılan şekil.

id.e.o.log.i.cal □ [aidiə'lɔdʒikl] ideolojik; **id.e.ol.o.gy** [ˌ-'ɔlədʒi] *n.* ideoloji.

ides [aidz] *n. pl.* eski Roma takviminde mart, mayıs, temmuz, ekim'in 15'i *veya* diğer ayların 13'ü.

id.i.o.cy ['idiəsi] *n.* ahmaklık, bönlük, aptallık; aptalca hareket.

id.i.om ['idiəm] *n.* şive, lehçe; deyim, tabir; **id.i.o.mat.ic** [ˌ-'mætik] *adj.* (**~ally**) deyimsel; dilin anlatım özelliklerini belirten.

id.i.o.syn.cra.sy [idiə'siŋkrəsi] *n.* kişisel özellik, hususiyet; mizaç, huy.

id.i.ot ['idiət] *n.* anadan doğma deli, geri zekâlı kimse; aptal, salak, bön kimse; **id.i.ot.ic** [idi'ɔtik] *adj.* (**~ally**) ahmak, bön, aptal, salak.

i.dle ['aidl] **1.** □ aylak, işsiz güçsüz, başıboş; tembel; işlemeyen; boş; aslı esası olmayan, değersiz, işe yaramaz; faydasız, yararsız, nafile; **~ hours** *pl.* boşa geçen zaman; **2.** *v/t. mst* **~ away** boşa harcamak (*zaman*); sarfetmek; *v/i.* oyalanmak, boş şeylerle meşgul olm.; boş gezmek; boşa zaman harcamak; MEC boşta çalışmak; **'i.dle.ness** *n.* tembellik, işsizlik, aylaklık; **'i.dler** *n.* boş gezen kimse, başıboş kimse, tembel kimse, aylak kimse.

i.dol ['aidl] *n.* put, sanem, mabut; *fig.* tapılan kimse, çok sevilen kimse *veya* şey; **i.dol.a.ter** [ai'dɔlətə] *n.* putperest kimse; taparcasına seven kimse, hayran; **i'dola.tress** *n.* putperest kadın; **i'dol.a.trous** □ putperestlik...; **i'dol.a.try** *n.* putperestlik; çılgınca sevgi; hayranlık; **i.dol.ize** ['aidəlaiz] *v/t.* tapınmak *-e*, aşırı derecede sevmek *-i*; putlaştırmak *-i*.

i.dyll ['idil] *n.* idil, pastoral şiir *veya* düz yazı; **i.dyl.lic** [ai'dilik] *adj.* (**~ally**) pastoral; saf ve sevimli.

if [if] **1.** *cj.* eğer, şayet, ise, rağmen; **2.** *n.* şart, madde; **'if.fy** *adj. Am.* F şüpheli.

ig.loo ['igluː] *n.* Eskimo evi.

ig.ne.ous ['igniəs] *adj.* volkanik; ateş gibi, kızgın; ateş...

ig.nit.a.ble [ig'naitəbl] *adj.* kolay tutuşan; **ig'nite** *v/t. & v/i.* tutuş(tur)mak, ateşlemek, yakmak; ateş almak, yanmak; CHEM ısıtmak; **ig.ni.tion** [ig'niʃən] *n.* ateşleme, tutuş(tur)ma, ateş alma, yakma; MOT marş; CHEM ısıtma.

ig.no.ble □ [ig'nəubl] alçak, âdi, şerefsiz, haysiyetsiz; utanç verici, çirkin, yüzkarası.

ig.no.min.i.ous □ [ignəu'miniəs] alçakça, namussuzca, şerefsizce, haysiyetsizce; **ig.no.min.y** ['ignəmini] *n.* rezalet, kepazelik; alçaklık, şerefsizlik; namussuzca davranış.

ig.no.ra.mus F [ignə'reiməs] *n.* cahil kimse; **'ig.no.rance** *n.* cahillik, cehalet; **'igno.rant** *adj.* cahil, bilgisiz, bilmez; habersiz (**of** *-den*); **ig.nore** [ig'nɔː] *vb.* önem vermemek *-e*, bilmezlikten gelmek, anlamazlıktan gelmek; JUR reddetmek, kabul etmemek, tanımamak.

i.gua.na ZOO [i'gwɑːnə] *n.* büyük kertenkele.

i.kon ['aikɔn] = *icon*.

i.lex BOT ['aileks] *n.* çobanpüskülü.

Il.i.ad ['iliəd] *n.* Homer'in 'İlyada' adlı destanı.

ill [il] **1.** *adj.* hasta, rahatsız, keyifsiz; fena, kötü; uğursuz; ahlâka aykırı, ahlâksız, edepsiz; zor, güç; düşmanca; haşin, sert, zalim, gaddar; **2.** *adv.* düşmanca; keyifsizce; haşince; sertçe; aleyhinde; güç belâ, zar zor; uğursuzca; **fall ~, be taken ~** hastalanmak, yatağa düşmek; *s.* **ease**; **3.** *n.* fenalık, kötülük, zarar; uğursuzluk; acı, belâ, dert, sıkıntı; hastalık, rahatsızlık.

I'll [ail] = **I will** *veya* **I shall**.

ill...: **'~-ad'vised** *adj.* tedbirsiz, ihtiyatsız; **'~-af'fect.ed** *adj.* kötü niyetli (**to** *-e*, *-e karşı*); **'~-bred** *adj.* terbiyesiz, kaba; **~ breed.ing** kötü davranışlar; **'~-con'ditioned** *adj.* kötü durumda; **'~-dis'posed** *adj.* kötü niyetli; karşı (**to** *-e*).

il.le.gal □ [i'liːgəl] kanuna aykırı, kanunsuz, yolsuz; **il.le.gal.i.ty** [iliː'gæliti] *n.* kanunsuzluk, kanuna aykırılık, yolsuzluk.

il.leg.i.ble □ [i'ledʒəbl] okunmaz, okunaksız (*yazı*).

il.le.git.i.ma.cy [ili'dʒitiməsi] *n.* gayrı meşruluk, yolsuzluk; kanuna aykırılık; piçlik; mantıksızlık; **il.le'git.i.mate** □ [ˌ-mit] kanuna aykırı; gayrı meşru, evlilik dışı doğan; mantıki olmayan, saçma.

ill...: **'~-'fat.ed** *adj.* talihsiz, bahtsız; uğursuz, nahoş; **'~-'fa.vo(u)red** *adj.* çirkin; **'~-'got.ten** *adj.* kötülükle *veya* kanunsuzlukla elde edilmiş; **'~-'humo(u)red** *adj.* aksi, huysuz, fena huylu, sinirli, alıngan.

il.lib.er.al □ [i'libərəl] cimri, pinti, eli sıkı, hasis; dar görüşlü; hoşgörüsüz; kültürsüz, bilgisiz; il.lib.er.al.i.ty [-'ræliti] n. cimrilik; dar görüşlülük; hoş görmeme; bilgisizlik.

il.lic.it □ [i'lisit] kanuna aykırı, caiz olmayan, yasaklanmış; ~ trade karaborsa, kanunsuz ticaret.

il.lim.it.a.ble □ [i'limitəbl] hudutsuz, sınırsız, limitsiz, sınır tanımayan, sonsuz.

il.lit.er.a.cy [i'litərəsi] n. cehalet, okumamışlık, cahillik, okuma yazma bilmeme, kara cahillik; il'lit.er.ate [-rit] 1. adj. okumamış, kara cahil, okuma yazma bilmeyen; 2. n. kara cahil kimse, okumamış kimse.

ill..: '~'judged adj. tedbirsiz, düşüncesiz; '~'man.nered adj. terbiyesiz, kaba; '~'na.tured □ huysuz, ters, serkeş.

ill.ness ['ilnis] n. hastalık, rahatsızlık, keyifsizlik.

il.log.i.cal □ [i'lɔʒikəl] mantıksız, mantığa aykırı.

ill..: ~-o.mened ['il'əumend] adj. uğursuz; '~'starred adj. bahtı kara, talihsiz, şanssız; '~'tem.pered adj. huysuz; '~'timed adj. vakitsiz, zamansız; '~'treatv/t. kötü davranmak, kötü muamele etm. -e.

il.lume poet. [i'lju:m] v/t. aydınlatmak (a. fig.).

il.lu.mi.nant [i'lju:minənt] 1. adj. parlak; 2. n. aydınlatıcı alet veya madde, lamba; il'lu.mi.nate [-neit] v/t. aydınlatmak (a. fig.); ışıklarla donatmak, süslemek; renkli resim ve harflerle süslemek; anlatmak, açıklamak, izah etm.; ~d advertising ışıklı reklam; il-'lu.mi.nat.ing adj. aydınlatıcı; fig. açıklayıcı; il.lumi'na.tion n. aydınlatma, tenvir; kitaptaki süslemeler; il'lu-mi.na.tive [-nətiv] adj. aydınlatıcı; il-'lu.mi.na.torn. aydınlatıcı kimse veya şey; kitap yaldızcısı; il'lu.mine = illuminate.

ill-use ['il'ju:z] v/t. kötü muamele etm., kötü davranmak -e.

il.lu.sion [i'lu:ʒən] n. hayal, kuruntu, aldanma, hulya; yanlış görüş, hata; il-'lusive □ [-siv], il'lu.so.ry □ [-səri] aldatıcı, yanıltıcı, asılsız.

il.lus.trate v/t. tasvir etm., anlatmak, tanımlamak, izah etm., açıklamak, tarif etm.; resimlerle süslemek, resimlemek; il.lus'tra.tion n. re-

sim, şema, diyagram, çizelge; izah, açıklama; örnek, misal; 'il.lus.tra.tive □ tarif eden, tanımlayan, tasvir edici; be ~ of izah etm., açıklamak -i; 'il.lus-tra.tor n. tasvir eden kimse veya şey; kitap veya dergilere resim çizen kimse.

il.lus.tri.ous □ [i'lʌstriəs] ünlü, meşhur, şöhretli; şanlı, şerefli.

ill will ['il'wil] n. kötü niyet, düşmanlık, garez, kin.

I'm [aim] = I am.

im.age ['imidʒ] 1. n. şekil, suret, tasvir, heykel; fikir, hayal; teşbih, mecaz; yansıma, akis; 2. vb. tasvirini yapmak, tanımlamak, tarif etm.; yansıtmak, aksettirmek; hayal etm., zihinde canlandırmak; 'im.age.ry n. betim, betimleme, tasvir, tanımlama; düş, imge, hayal.

im.ag.i.na.ble □ [i'mædʒinəbl] hayal edilebilir, göz önüne getirilebilir; im-'ag.inar.y adj. hayali, hayal mahsulü; im.agi.na.tion [-'neiʃən] n. hayal gücü, yaratıcılık, yaratma kabiliyeti; hayal, kuruntu; im'ag.i.na.tive [-nətiv] yaratıcı, hayal gücü kuvvetli...; im'ag.ine v/t. hayal etm., tasavvur etm., tasarımlamak; düşünmek, sanmak, farzetmek.

im.bal.ance [im'bæləns] n. dengesizlik; oransızlık.

im.be.cile ['imbisi:l] 1. □ ahmak, budala, bön, aptal; 2. n. ahmak kimse, aptal kimse; im.be.cil.i.ty [-'siliti] n. ahmaklık, aptallık, budalalık.

im.bed [im'bed] = embed.

im.bibe [im'baib] vb. içmek, içine çekmek; emmek; fig. öğrenmek, kapmak.

im.bro.glio [im'brəuliəu] n. karmakarışık küme; karışık durum, dolambaçlı mesele; ciddi anlaşmazlık.

im.brue [im'bru:] vb. ıslatmak, sırılsıklam etm., batırmak (sıvıya) (in, with ile).

im.bue [im'bju:] vb. boyamak, iyice ıslatmak, emdirmek; fig. doldurmak (his, fikir vs. ile).

im.i.ta.ble ['imitəbl] adj. taklit edilebilir; im.i.tate ['-teit] v/t. taklit etm., benzetmek, taklidini yapmak; b-ni örnek almak MEC taklidini yapmak, kopya etm.; im.i'tation n. taklit, sahte şey; taklit etme, benzetme; MEC yapma; attr. taklit..., suni..., yapma...; ~ leather suni deri; im.i.ta.tive □ ['-tətiv] taklit eden, örnek alan (of -i); ~ word sesi taklit eden sözcük; **im.ita.tor** [' ̣teitə] *n.* taklitçi.

im.mac.u.late □ [i'mækjulit] saf, tertemiz, lekesiz, pak; kusursuz.

im.ma.nent ['imənənt] *adj.* her yerde mevcut, hazır ve nazır; içinde olan, tabiatında olan.

im.ma.te.ri.al □ [imə'tiəriəl] önemsiz, ehemmiyetsiz (*to için*); maddî olmayan, manevi, cisimsiz, tinsel.

im.ma.ture [imə'tjuə] *adj.* olgunlaşmamış, ham, olmamış; kemale ermemiş, toy, gelişmemiş, pişmemiş; **imma'tu.ri.ty** *n.* hamlık; toyluk.

im.meas.ur.a.ble □ [i'meʒərəbl] ölçülemez; sınırsız, hudutsuz, çok geniş.

im.me.di.ate □ [i'mi:djət] doğrudan doğruya, vasıtasız, en yakın; şimdiki, hazır, derhal olan, elde mevcut; **im-'me.di.ate.ly 1.** *adv.* derhal, hemen, doğrudan doğruya; **2.** *cj.* …ir …irmez.

im.me.mo.ri.al □ [imi'mɔːriəl] hatırlanamayacak kadar çok eski; *from time* ~ çok eskiden beri, ezelden beri.

im.mense □ [i'mens] çok büyük, engin, geniş, hudutsuz; *sl.* harika, şahane, fevkalade; **im'men.si.ty** *n.* genişlik, enginlik, uçsuz bucaksız olma; çok büyük şey.

im.merse [i'məːs] *v/t.* daldırmak, sokmak, suya batırmak; ~ *o.s.* in *fig.* dalmak -*e*; ~*d in* -*e* dalmış; **im'mer.sion** *n.* daldırma; bat(ırıl)ma; bütün vücudu suya daldırarak vaftiz etme; *fig.* dalma; ~ *heater* elektrikli su ısıtıcısı, daldırma ısıtıcı.

im.mi.grant ['imigrənt] *n.* göçmen, muhacir; **im.mi.grate** [' ̣greit] *v/i.* göç etm., hicret etm.; *v/t.* göçmen olarak yerleştirmek (*into* -*e*); **im.mi'gra.tion** *n.* göç, hicret; göçmenlik.

im.mi.nence ['iminəns] *n.* yakında olabilecek durum, tehdit eden şey; **'im-mi.nent** □ yakında olan, hemen olacak olan, yakın.

im.mit.i.ga.ble □ [i'mitigəbl] hafifletilemez, yatıştırılamaz, bastırılamaz.

im.mo.bile [i'məubail] *adj.* hareketsiz; kımılda(tıl)a)maz; **im.mo.bil.i.ty** [̣ 'biliti] *n.* hareketsizlik, yerinden kımıldamama; **im'mo.bi.lize** [̣bilaiz] *v/t.* hareketsizleştirmek, yerinde tutmak, tesbit etm., kımıldamaz hale getirmek; askeri kuvvetleri savaşamaz hale getirmek; piyasadaki parayı tedavülden çekmek.

im.mod.er.ate □ [i'mɔdərit] ölçüsüz,

ifrata kaçan, aşırı, çok fazla; **im'moder.ateness** *n.* aşırılık, ölçüsüzlük, ifrat.

im.mod.est □ [i'mɔdist] açık saçık, utanmaz, arsız, yüzsüz; haddini bilmez, terbiyesiz, küstah; **im'mod.es.ty** *n.* küstahlık, haddini bilmezlik; utanmazlık, arsızlık.

im.mo.late ['iməleit] *v/t.* kurban etm., kurban olarak kesmek; **im.mo'la.tion** *n.* kurban etme, kesme.

im.mor.al □ [i'mɔrəl] ahlâkı bozuk, ahlâksız, terbiyesiz, edepsiz; **im.mo.ral-i.ty** [imə'ræliti] *n.* ahlâksızlık, edepsizlik.

im.mor.tal [i'mɔːtl] **1.** □ ölümsüz, ölmez, ebedî, sonsuz, baki; **2.** *n.* ölümsüz varlık, ebedî varlık, unutulmayan şey; **immor.tal.i.ty** [̣'tæliti] *n.* ölmezlik, ölümsüzlük, ebedilik; **im'mor.tal.ize** [̣təlaiz] *v/t.* ebedileştirmek, ölümsüzleştirmek.

im.mov.a.ble [i'muːvəbl] **1.** □ kımıldamaz, yerinden oynamaz, sabit; değişmez, dönmez; **2.** *n.* ~*s pl.* gayrımenkul, taşınmaz mallar.

im.mune [i'mjuːn] *adj.* MED & *fig.* bağışık; muaf (*from -den*); **im'mu.ni.ty** *n.* muafiyet (*from -den*); bağışıklık (*from -e karşı*); dokunulmazlık; **im-mu.nize** [' ̣naiz] *v/t.* muaf kılmak; bağışık kılmak.

im.mure [i'mjuə] *v/t.* hapsetmek; kendini vermek; duvara gömmek.

im.mu.ta.bil.i.ty [imjuːtə'biliti] *n.* değişmezlik; **im'mu.ta.ble** □ değişmez, sabit.

imp [imp] *n.* küçük şeytan; şeytanın çocuğu; afacan (*veya* haşarı, yaramaz) çocuk.

im.pact ['impækt] *n.* vuruş, vur(uş)ma, çarpışma; etki, tesir.

im.pair [im'pɛə] *v/t.* bozmak, zayıflatmak; eksiltmek, azaltmak.

im.pale [im'peil] *v/t.* kazığa sokarak öldürmek.

im.pal.pa.ble □ [im'pælpəbl] dokunulunca hissedilemeyen; *fig.* kolayca kavranılmayan.

im.pan.el [im'pænl] = *empanel*.

im.part [im'pɑːt] *v/t.* vermek; bildirmek, söylemek.

im.par.tial □ [im'pɑːʃəl] tarafsız, bitaraf; **im.par.ti.al.i.ty** [̣'ʃiæliti] *n.* tarafsızlık.

im.pass.a.ble □ [im'pɑːsəbl] geçil(e)mez, aşılamaz, geçit vermez.

im.passe [æm'pɑːs] *n.* çıkmaz (*a. fig.*);

fig. içinden çıkılmaz durum, kördüğüm.

im.pas.si.ble ☐ [im'pæsibl] hissiz, duygusuz (*to -e karşı*); ağrı duymaz, acı çekmeyen.

im.pas.sion [im'pæʃən] *v/t.* hırslandırmak, kızdırmak, çileden çıkarmak; heyecanlandırmak; **im'pas.sioned** *adj.* ateşli, hararetli, heyecanlı.

im.pas.sive ☐ [im'pæsiv] duygusuz, hissiz, vurdumduymaz, kayıtsız, soğuk; **im'pas.sive.ness** *n.* vurdumduymazlık, kayıtsızlık.

im.pa.tience [im'peiʃəns] *n.* sabırsızlık, tahammülsüzlük; **im'pa.tient** ☐ hoşgörüsüz, müsamaha etmeyen (*at, of -e*); **be ~ of s.th.** *bşe* anlayış göstermemek, müsamaha etmemek; **~ for** çok arzu eden *-i*; sabırsız, tahammülsüz.

im.peach [im'piːtʃ] *v/t.* suçlamak (*of, with ile*); şüphe etm. *-den*; mahkemeye sevketmek (*devlet memurunu*); **im'peach.a.ble** *adj.* suçlanabilir; **im'peachment** *n.* suçlama; devlet memuruna karşı dava açma.

im.pec.ca.bil.i.ty [impekə'biliti] *n.* hatasızlık, kusursuzluk; **im'pec.ca.ble** ☐ hatasız, kusursuz; günahsız.

im.pe.cu.ni.ous [impi'kjuːnjəs] *adj.* parasız, züğürt, fakir.

im.pede [im'piːd] *v/t.* engellemek, mâni olm.

im.ped.i.ment [im'pedimənt] *n.* mania, engel (*to -e*); **~ in one's speech** pelteklik; **im.ped.i.men.ta** MIL [-'mentə] *n. pl.* levazım.

im.pel [im'pel] *v/t.* sevketmek, tahrik etm., harekete geçirmek, zorlamak, sürmek, mecbur etm.; **im'pel.lent 1.** *adj.* sevkeden, harekete geçiren; **2.** *n.* tahrik edici unsur.

im.pend [im'pend] *v/i.* asılı olm., dolaşmak (*over üzerinde*); olmasına az kalmak, meydana gelmesi yakın olm.; tehdit etm.; **im'pend.ence** *n.* asılı olma; vukuu yakın olma; **im'pend.ent**, **im'pend.ing** *adj.* olması yakın.

im.pen.e.tra.bil.i.ty [impenitrə'biliti] *n.* içine girilememe, nüfuz edilememe; *fig.* anlaşılamama; **im'pen.e.tra.ble** ☐ nüfuz edilemez, delinmez, içine girilemez, geçilemez (*to, by -e*); *fig.* anlaşılmaz, kestirilemez; idrak edilemez; *fig.* kabul edilemez, uygun düşmez (*to -e*).

im.pen.i.tence [im'penitəns] *n.* pişmanlık duymama, pişman olmama;

im'pen.i.tent ☐ pişman olmayan, pişmanlık duymayan.

im.per.a.tive [im'perətiv] **1.** ☐ mecburi, zorunlu, zaruri; gerekli, lüzumlu, âcil; emredici, buyurucu; GR emir belirten; **~ mood** = **2.** *n.* GR emir kipi.

im.per.cep.ti.ble ☐ [impə'septəbl] hissolunamaz, görülemez, seçilemez, farkedilemez, algılanamaz.

im.per.fect [im'pəːfikt] **1.** ☐ eksik, kusurlu, tamam olmayan, noksan, bitmemiş; **~ tense** = **2.** *n.* GR bitmemiş bir eylemi gösteren zaman; **im.per.fec.tion** [-pə'fekʃən] *n.* kusur, eksiklik, noksan, hata.

im.pe.ri.al [im'piəriəl] **1.** ☐ imparator(luğ)a ait; şahane, görkemli, haşmetli, muhteşem; İngiliz ölçü standartlarına uygun; **2.** *n.* keçi sakalı; çok büyük şey; görkemli şey; imparator; **im'pe.ri.al.ism** *n.* emperyalizm, sömürgecilik; imparatorluk sistemi; **im'pe.ri.al.ist** *n.* emperyalist, sömürgecilik taraftarı; imparator(luk) taraftarı; **im.pe.ri.al.'is.tic** *adj.* emperyalizme ait, sömürgeci.

im.per.il [im'peril] *v/t.* tehlikeye düşürmek, tehlikeye atmak.

im.pe.ri.ous ☐ [im'piəriəs] zorba, zalim, hükmeden; kibirli, küstah; zaruri, mecburi; âcil.

im.per.ish.a.ble ☐ [im'periʃəbl] ölümsüz, yok olmaz; bozulmaz, çürümez.

im.per.ma.nent [im'pəːmənənt] *adj.* sürekli olmayan, devam etmeyen.

im.per.me.a.ble ☐ [im'pəːmjəbl] (*su veya hava*) geçirmez; nüfuz edilemez.

im.per.son.al ☐ [im'pəːsnl] kişisel olmayan, şahsî olmayan; GR yalnız üçüncü tekil şahsı kullanılan (*fiil*); **im.per.sonal.i.ty** [-sə'næliti] *n.* kişisel olmama, şahsi olmama.

im.per.son.ate [im'pəːsoneit] *v/t.* kişilik kazandırmak; THEAT temsil etm.; taklit etm.; **im.per.son'a.tion** *n.* şahıslandırma, kişilik kazandırma; THEAT temsil etme, oynama; taklit etme.

im.per.ti.nence [im'pəːtinəns] *n.* küstahlık, arsızlık, saygısızlık, münasebetsizlik, laubalilik, sululuk; **im'per.tinent** ☐ terbiyesiz, arsız, saygısız, küstah, münasebetsiz, laubali, sulu, sırnaşık; JUR konuyla ilgisi olmayan, tali, ikincil.

im.per.turb.a.bil.i.ty ['impəːtəːbə'liti] *n.* ağırbaşlılık, soğukkanlılık, sakinlik; **imper'turb.a.ble** ☐ ağırbaşlı, soğukkanlı, sakin, nefsine hakim.

im.per.vi.ous □ [im'pəːvjəs] (*su veya hava*) geçirmez, dayanıklı (*to* -e) (*a. fig.*); nüfuz edilemeyen, kapalı.

im.pe.ti.go MED [impi'taigəu] *n.* impetigo, bir çeşit deri hastalığı.

im.pet.u.os.i.ty [impetju'ɔsiti] *n.* tez canlılık, atılganlık, acelecilik, coşkunluk; **im'pet.u.ous** □ coşkun, atılgan, aceleci, düşünmeden hareket eden; zorlu, sert, şiddetli; **im.pe.tus** ['impitəs] *n.* hız, güç, zor, şiddet; güdü, hızlandırıcı güç, dürtü.

im.pi.e.ty [im'paiəti] *n.* saygısızlık, hürmetsizlik (*esp. dinsel*); saygısız söz *veya* davranış.

im.pinge [im'pindʒ] *v/i.* çarpmak (**on, upon, against** -e); **~ on** tecavüz etm. (*b-nin hakkına*); **im'pinge.ment** *n.* çarpma (**on, upon** -e); *fig.* tecavüz etme (*b-nin hakkına*).

im.pi.ous □ ['impiəs] kâfir, Allahın varlığını tanımayan, dine karşı hürmetsiz.

imp.ish □ ['impiʃ] cin gibi, şeytan gibi, afacan, yaramaz.

im.pla.ca.bil.i.ty [implækə'biliti] *n.* amansızlık, affetmezlik; **im'pla.ca.ble** □ yatıştırılamaz, bastırılamaz, teskin edilemez, amansız, affetmez.

im.plant [im'plɑːnt] *v/t. mst fig.* aşılamak (**in** -e), aklına sokmak; dikmek, ekmek.

im.plau.si.ble [im'plɔːzəbl] *adj.* inanılmaz, inanılması güç, makul olmayan.

im.ple.ment 1. ['implimənt] *n.* alet, araç; **2.** ['-ment] *v/t.* yerine getirmek, tamamlamak, yürütmek; **im.ple.men'ta.tion** [-men'teiʃən] *n.* yürütme, yerine getirme.

im.pli.cate ['implikeit] *v/t.* sokmak, karıştırmak, bulaştırmak (**in** -e); dokundurmak, ima etm.; **im.pli'ca.tion** *n.* bulaştırma, karıştırma (*suç*); ima, üstü kapalı söyleme; **what are the ~s?** anlatılmak istenilen nedir?

im.plic.it □ [im'plisit] ima edilen, zımnî, altık; aslında olan; tam, kesin, katî; **im'plic.it.ly** *adv.* zımnen, dolayısıyla, üstü kapalı olarak; tamamiyle, kesinlikle.

im.plied □ [im'plaid] ima edilen, demek istenen, kastedilen.

im.plore [im'plɔː] *v/t.* yalvarmak, istirham etm., dilemek, rica etm. -*e*; **im'ploring** □ [-riŋ] yalvaran, yakaran, rica eden.

im.ply [im'plai] *v/t.* ima etm., demek, belirtmek, ifade etm.; içine almak, kapsamak; **do you ~ that...?** ...mi demek istiyorsunuz?

im.po.lite □ [impə'lait] nezaketsiz, terbiyesiz, kaba.

im.pol.i.tic □ [im'pɔlitik] siyasete aykırı, politik olmayan; uygun olmayan, uygunsuz, isabetsiz, münasip olmayan.

im.pon.der.a.ble [im'pɔndərəbl] **1.** *adj.* tartılamayan...; ölçülemeyen...; **2.** *n.* **~s** *pl.* önceden etkisi ölçülemeyen şeyler.

im.port 1. ['impɔːt] *n.* anlam, mana; önem, ehemmiyet; COM ithal, ithalat, dışsatım; **~s** *pl.* ithal malları; **2.** [im'pɔːt] *vb.* ithal etm.; belirtmek, ifade etm., ima etm., demek istemek; önemi olm., hüküm olm.; **im'por.tance** *n.* önem, ehemmiyet; etki, tesir, nüfuz, itibar; **im'por.tant** □ önemli, ehemmiyetli, mühim; etkili, nüfuzlu, itibarlı; **im.por.ta.tion** [-'teiʃən] *n.* ithal (*malı*), ithalat, dışsatım; **im'port.er** *n.* ithalatçı.

im.por.tu.nate □ [im'pɔːtjunit] ısrarla isteyen, defalarca talep eden; acil; **im'portune** [-tjuːn] *vb.* sıkıştırmak, ısrarla istemek, tekrar tekrar istemek; **im.por'tuni.ty** *n.* usandırıcı ısrar, tekrar tekrar isteme, sıkıştırma.

im.pose [im'pəuz] *v/t.* koymak, yüklemek (*vergi*) (**on** -e); zorla kabul ettirmek (**on, upon** -e); dizilmiş sayfaları sıraya koymak, düzenlemek; hile ile kabul ettirmek; *v/i.* **~ upon** -*den* yararlanmak, istifade etm.; aldatmak -*i*, kazıklamak -*i*; **im'pos.ing** □ heybetli, muhteşem, görkemli; **im.po.si.tion** [impə'ziʃən] *n.* üzerine koyma, yükleme; vergi; yük; ceza; istenmeyen misafir; hile, aldatma.

im.pos.si.bil.i.ty [impəsə'biliti] *n.* olanaksızlık, imkânsızlık; **im'pos.si.ble** □ imkânsız, olanaksız; çekilmez, dayanılmaz.

im.post ['impəust] *n.* vergi, gümrük resmi; **im.pos.tor** [im'pɔstə] *n.* sahtekâr (*veya* hilekâr) kimse, dolandırıcı; **im'posture** [-tʃə] *n.* hile, sahtekârlık, dolandırıcılık.

im.po.tence [im'impətəns] *n.* güçsüzlük, etkisizlik, tesirsizlik; PHYSIOL iktidarsızlık; **im.po.tent** *adj.* kudretsiz, âciz, zayıf, etkisiz; iktidarsız.

im.pound [im'paund] *v/t.* haczetmek, kanunen el koymak; ağıla kapamak.

im.pov.er.ish [im'pɔvəriʃ] *v/t.* fakirleştirmek, yoksullaştırmak; kuvvetini kesmek, tüketmek, bitirmek.

im.prac.ti.ca.bil.i.ty [impræktikə'biliti] *n.* elverişsizlik, pratik olmama, kullanışsızlık; **im'prac.ti.ca.ble** ☐ yapılamaz, uygulanamaz; kullanışsız, elverişsiz, pratik olmayan; geçilmez, geçit vermez (*yol*).

im.prac.ti.cal [im'præktikəl] *adj.* elverişsiz, kullanışsız, pratik olmayan.

im.pre.cate ['imprikeit] *v/t.* lânet okumak, beddua etm. (**upon** *-e*); **im.pre-'ca.tion** *n.* lânet, beddua; **im.pre.ca.to.ry** ['-keitəri] *adj.* lânet..., beddua...; lânet kabilinden.

im.preg.na.bil.i.ty [impregnə'biliti] *n.* zaptedilememe, ele geçirilememe; **im'pregna.ble** ☐ zaptedilemez, ele geçirilemez, dayanıklı; **im.preg.nate** **1.** ['-neit] *v/t.* hamile bırakmak, gebe bırakmak; вот döllemek; снем emdirmek, doyurmak (*a. fig.*); *fig.* zihnini doldurmak; мес emprenye etm.; **2.** [im'pregnit] *adj.* gebe, hamile; dolu; doymuş; **im.preg.na.tion** [-'neiʃən] *n.* dölleme, hamile bırakma; doyurma, emdirme; emprenye etme.

im.pre.sa.ri.o [impre'saːriəu] *n.* tiyatro temsillerini düzenleyip yöneten kimse, impresario.

im.pre.scrip.ti.ble [impris'kriptəbl] *adj.* hükmü geçmez; sürekli, daimi.

im.press 1. ['impres] *n.* damga, basma, nişan, iz, eser, işaret; *fig.* etkileme; **2.** [im'pres] *v/t.* basmak (**on s.th.** *veya* **s.th. with** *-e*); etkilemek, aklına sokmak (**on, upon** *-i*); izlenim bırakmak, yer etm. (**on** *-de*); **~ s.o. with s.th.** *b-ni* *bşle* etkilemek; NAUT çalışmaya zorlamak; sıkıştırmak; **im'press.i.ble** *adj.* etkilenebilir, hassas; **im'pres.sion** [-ʃən] *n.* basma; baskı; tabetme; damga; *fig.* izlenim, intiba, tesir, etki; турсmopya, nüsha; **be under the ~ that** ...izleniminde olm., ...zannetmek, ...gibi gelmek; **im'pres.sion.a.ble** [-ʃnəbl] *adj.* aşırı duygulu, çok hassas; kolay etkilenen; kolay kalıplanır; **im'pres.sionism** *n.* empresyonizm, izlenimcilik; **im'pres.sion.ist** *n.* empresyonist, izlenimci; **im'pres.sion.is.tic** *adj.* empresyonistik, izlenimciliğe ait; **im'pres.sive** ☐ [-siv] etkili, tesirli, müessir; **im'press.ment** *n.* NAUT

sıkıştırma.

im.print 1. [im'print] *v/t.* basmak (*damga, mühür*) (**on** *-e*); *fig.* etkilemek, tesir etm., zihnine sokmak (**on, in**); **2.** ['imprint] *n.* damga; baskı; турр bir kitaptaki yayınevi ve basımevinin adları; *fig.* etki, tesir, izlenim, intiba.

im.pris.on [im'prizn] *v/t.* hapsetmek, zındana kapamak, içeri atmak; **im-'pris.onment** *n.* hapis, tutukluluk, mahpusluk.

im.prob.a.bil.i.ty [imprɔbə'biliti] *n.* ihtimal dahilinde olmama, olasılığı olmama; ihtimal dahilinde olmayan şey; **im'prob.able** ☐ ihtimal dahilinde olmayan.

im.pro.bi.ty [im'prəubiti] *n.* şerefsizlik, iffetsizlik, haysiyetsizlik.

im.promp.tu [im'prɔmptjuː] **1.** *n.* мus empromptü, küçük parça; **2.** *adj.* hazırlıksız; **3.** *adv.* hazırlıksız olarak.

im.prop.er ☐ [im'prɔpə] yersiz, yakışıksız, uygunsuz, münasebetsiz, yakışık almaz, çirkin; yanlış, hatalı; **~ fraction** матн payı paydasından büyük olan kesir; **impro.pri.e.ty** [imprə-'praiəti] *n.* uygunsuzluk, yersizlik, münasebetsizlik; yanlışlık; uygunsuz söz *veya* hareket.

im.prov.a.ble ☐ [im'pruːvəbl] düzeltilmesi mümkün, ıslah edilebilir, yoluna girebilir; tarıma elverişli (*toprak*).

im.prove [im'pruːv] *v/t. & v/i.* düzel(t)-mek; geliş(tir)mek; değerlen(dir)mek, kıymeti(ni) art(tır)mak; yoluna koymak; ıslah etm.; yola girmek; ıslah olm.; **~ upon** mükemmelleştirmek; **im'prove.ment** düzelme, ıslah; gelişme, ilerleme (**on, upon** *-de*); **im'prov-er** *n.* ıslahatçı, reformcu.

im.prov.i.dence [im'prɔvidəns] *n.* tedbirsizlik, ihtiyatsızlık; israf, ziyankârlık; **im'prov.i.dent** ☐ tedbirsiz, ihtiyatsız; savurgan, müsrif.

im.pro.vi.sa.tion [imprəvai'zeiʃən] *n.* önceden düşünmeden şiir söyleme *veya* şarkı besteleme; o anda uydurma; **im.provise** ['-vaiz] *vb.* doğaçtan söylemek *veya* yapmak, önceden düşünmeden söylemek *veya* bestelemek; o anda uydurmak; **im.pro.vised** *adj.* uydurma, eğreti.

im.pru.dence [im'pruːdəns] *n.* tedbirsizlik, ihtiyatsızlık, düşüncesizlik; **im-'pru.dent** ☐ tedbirsiz, ihtiyatsız, düşüncesiz, sağgörüsüz.

im.pu.dence ['impjudəns] *n.* yüzsüzlük, arsızlık, küstahlık, terbiyesizlik; **'im.pu.dent** □ arsız, edepsiz, saygısız, terbiyesiz, yüzsüz, küstah.

im.pugn [im'pjuːn] *v/t.* dil uzatmak, aksini iddia etm., aleyhinde olm., yalanlamak, yalancı çıkarmak; **im-'pugn.a.ble** *adj.* inkâr edilebilir, yalanlanabilir.

im.pulse ['impʌls], **im'pul.sion** *n.* dürtme, itme, dürtü, itici kuvvet, sevk, tahrik; *fig.* içtepi, güdü; **im'pul.sive** □ tahrik edici, itici; *fig.* atılgan, düşüncesizce hareket eden; **im'pul.sive.ness** *n.* düşünmeden hareket etme.

im.pu.ni.ty [im'pjuːniti] *n.* cezadan muaf olma; **with ~** cezasız.

im.pure □ [im'pjuə] pis, kirli (*a. fig.*); karışık, katışık; **im'pu.ri.ty** [_riti] *n.* pislik, kirlilik; pis (*veya* kirli) şey.

im.put.a.ble [im'pjuːtəbl] *adj.* başkasının üstüne atılabilir; başkasına yüklenebilir; **im.pu.ta.tion** [_'teiʃən] *n.* suçlama; başkasına yükleme, başkasının üstüne atma; **im'pute** *v/t.* itham etm., suçlamak (**to** *ile*), üstüne yıkmak, yüklemek.

in [in] **1.** *prp.* içinde, içine, dahilinde, -de, -e, -(y)e; esnasında, sürecinde, zarfında; giy(in)miş, kılığında, bürünmüş; düzenlenmiş; vasıtasıyla; olarak; bakımından, yönünden; ile meşgul; -den yapılmış; halinde, durumunda, vaktinde, mevsiminde; **~ 1983** 1983'de; **there is nothing ~ it** temelsiz, asılsız, boş; F önemsiz; **it is not ~ her** içinde yok; **he hasn't it ~ him** o yaradılışta değil; **~ that...** ...den dolayı, ...yüzünden, ...için; **2.** *adv.* içeriye, içeride, içine; evde; varmakta; hasat edilmekte; mevsimi gelmiş; moda; iktidarda, seçilmiş; yanmakta; **be ~** evde olm.; varmak; hasat edilmek, toplanmak (*ürün*); mevsimi olm. (*yiyecek*); moda olm.; iktidarda olm.; görevde olm.; yanıyor olm.; **be ~ for** başına gelecek olm., bşle karşı karşıya olm.; -e katılmayı kabul etmiş olm.; **be well ~ with** F *b-le* araları iyi olm., arkadaş olm.; **3.** *adj.* dahilî, iç; görevdeki; iktidardaki; yürürlükteki; içeri doğru gelen; yanmakta olan; son derece moda olan...; **4.** *n. su.*: **the ~s** *pl.* PARL iktidardaki parti; **the ~s and outs** *pl.* bir işin bütün ayrıntıları, gizli çıktısı.

in.a.bil.i.ty [inə'biliti] *n.* yetersizlik, kifayetsizlik, iktidarsızlık, beceriksizlik, âcizlik.

in.ac.ces.si.bil.i.ty ['inæksesə'biliti] *n.* erişilmezlik, yanına varılamama; **in-ac'cessi.ble** □ erişilemez, yanına varılamaz.

in.ac.cu.ra.cy [in'ækjurəsi] *n.* yanlışlık, hatalı olma; kusur, hata, yanlış; **in'accu.rate** □ [_rit] yanlış, kusurlu, hatalı.

in.ac.tion [in'ækʃən] *n.* hareketsizlik, faaliyetsizlik; tembellik, avarelik.

in.ac.tive □ [in'æktiv] hareketsiz; tembel, üşengeç; COM durgun, atıl, kesat; CHEM tesirsiz, etkisiz; **in.ac'tiv.i.ty** *n.* hareketsizlik; tembellik; durgunluk; tesirsizlik.

in.ad.e.qua.cy [in'ædikwəsi] *n.* yetersizlik, kifayetsizlik, yetmezlik, eksiklik, noksanlık; **in'ad.e.quate** □ [_kwit] yetersiz, kifayetsiz, eksik, noksan.

in.ad.mis.si.bil.i.ty ['inədmisə'biliti] *n.* kabul olunmama, uygun görülmeme; **inad'mis.si.ble** □ kabul olunmaz, uygun görülmez.

in.ad.vert.ence, **in.ad.vert.en.cy** [in-əd'vəːtəns(i)] *n.* dikkatsizlik; kasıtsızlık; **in.ad'vert.ent** □ dikkatsiz; kasıtsız; **~ly** istemeyerek, kasıtsız olarak.

in.ad.vis.a.ble □ [inəd'vaizəbl] tavsiye edilmez; akla yakın olmayan, makul olmayan.

in.al.ien.a.ble □ [in'eiljənəbl] geri verilemez, devrolunamaz, satılamaz.

in.al.ter.a.ble □ [in'ɔːltərəbl] değiş(tirile)mez.

in.am.o.ra.ta [inæmə'rɑːtə] *n.* sevgili, sevilen kadın, âşık olunan kadın; **in-amo'ra.to** [_təu] *n.* âşık kadın.

in.ane □ [i'nein] *mst fig.* boş, anlamsız, aptalca; budala, ahmak.

in.an.i.mate □ [in'ænimit] cansız, ruhsuz, ölü; *fig.* donuk, sönük, sıkıcı.

in.a.ni.tion MED [inə'niʃən] *n.* zafiyet; boşluk.

in.an.i.ty [i'næniti] *n.* anlamsızlık; boş laf, anlamsız söz (*s.* **inane**).

in.ap.pli.ca.bil.i.ty ['inæplikə'biliti] *n.* uygun olmama, tatbik edilememe; **in-'ap.plica.ble** *adj.* uymaz, tatbik edilemez (**to** -*e*); ilgisiz, alâkasız.

in.ap.po.site □ [in'æpəzit] uygunsuz, münasebetsiz.

in.ap.pre.ci.a.ble □ [inə'priːʃəbl] takdir edilemez; azıcık, cüzi.

in.ap.pre.hen.si.ble □ [inæpri'hensəbl] anlaşılmaz, idrak edilemez.

in.ap.proach.a.ble [inə'prəutʃəbl] *adj.*

yaklaşılamaz, erişilemez.

in.ap.pro.pri.ate □ [inə'prəupriit] münasebetsiz, uygunsuz, yakışmaz.

in.apt □ [in'æpt] beceriksiz, yeteneksiz, hünersiz; uygunsuz, yakışıksız; **in'apt.itude** [-titjuːd], **in'apt.ness** n. yeteneksizlik, kabiliyetsizlik; uygunsuzluk.

in.ar.tic.u.late □ [inaːˈtikjulit] anlaşılmaz, açık seçik olmayan, belirsiz; iyi birleşmemiş; derdini anlatmaktan âciz; mafsalsız, oynak yeri olmayan; açıkça konuşmayan; **in.ar'tic.u.late-ness** n. derdini anlatamama; anlaşılmazlık, belirsizlik.

in.as.much [inəzˈmʌtʃ]: ~ **as** madem ki, çünkü, -i göz önünde bulundurarak.

in.at.ten.tion [inəˈtenʃən] n. dikkatsizlik, ihmal; **in.at'ten.tive** □ [-tiv] dikkatsiz, ihmalkâr, dikkat etmeyen (**to** -e).

in.au.di.ble □ [in'ɔːdəbl] işitilemez, duyulamaz.

in.au.gu.ral [i'nɔːgjurəl] **1.** adj. açılışa ait, açılış…; ~ **lecture** açılış konuşması; **2.** n. açılış konuşması; açılış töreni; **in'augu.rate** [-reit] v/t. açmak; törenle göreve getirmek; törenle başlamak -e; başlatmak; **in.au.gu'ra.tion** n. resmen göreve başlama; açılış (töreni); ♀ **Day** Am. Amerika Cumhurbaşkanı'nın resmen göreve başladığı gün.

in.aus.pi.cious □ [inɔːsˈpiʃəs] uğursuz.

in.board NAUT [ˈinbɔːd] **1.** adj. geminin içindeki; **2.** adv. geminin içinde, bordalarında.

in.born [ˈinbɔːn] adj. doğuştan, fıtrî, tabii, yaradılıştan.

in.bred [ˈinˈbred] adj. tabii, yaradılıştan, fıtrî, doğuştan, tanrı vergisi; aynı soydan gelen hayvanların dölünden elde edilmiş.

in.breed.ing [ˈinˈbriːdiŋ] n. aynı soy ve cinsten hayvan ve bitkilerin çiftleştirilmesi.

in.cal.cul.a.ble □ [inˈkælkjuləbl] hesap edilemez, hesaplanamaz, hesap edilemeyecek kadar; belirsiz, kararsız, dönek, değişken.

in.can.des.cence [ˈinkænˈdesns] n. akkorluk; **in.can'des.cent** adj. akkor; ~ **light** akkor ışık; ~ **mantle** akkor gaz fitili.

in.can.ta.tion [inkænˈteiʃən] n. büyü, sihir; sihirli söz.

in.ca.pa.bil.i.ty [inkeipəˈbiliti] n. güçsüzlük, yetersizlik, âcizlik, ehliyetsizlik; kabiliyetsizlik, iktidarsızlık; **in'ca-pa.ble** □ güçsüz, yeteneksiz, kabiliyetsiz, kudretsiz, iktidarsız, ehliyetsiz, âciz (**of** -den); **in.ca.pac.i.tate** [inkə-ˈpæsiteit] v/t. kudretsizleştirmek, kuvvetten düşürmek, zayıflatmak (for, from -de); **in-ca'pac.i.ty** n. kabiliyetsizlik, güçsüzlük, yetkisizlik, ehliyetsizlik, salahiyetsizlik (**for** için, -de).

in.car.cer.ate [in'kaːsəreit] v/t. hapsetmek, kapatmak; **in.car.cer'a.tion** n. hapsetme, hapsedilme.

in.car.nate 1. [in'kaːnit] adj. vücudu olan, vücutlu, vücut bulmuş, insan şekline girmiş; fig. şahıslanmış, cisimlenmiş; **2.** [ˈinkaːneit] v/t. vücut kazandırmak, canlandırmak; fig. cisimlendirmek; **in.car'na.tion** n. belirme, canlanma, vücut bulma; fig. cisimlenme.

in.case [in'keis] = **encase.**

in.cau.tious □ [in'kɔːʃəs] düşüncesiz, tedbirsiz, dikkatsiz, ihtiyatsız; **in'cau-tiousness** n. düşüncesizlik, tedbirsizlik, dikkatsizlik.

in.cen.di.ar.y [in'sendjəri] **1.** adj. yangın çıkarıcı, kasten yangın çıkaran; çok ısı meydana getirebilen; fig. tahrik edici, ortalığı karıştırıcı; ~ (**bomb**) yangın bombası; **2.** n. kundakçı; ortalığı karıştıran kimse.

in.cense[1] ['insens] **1.** n. tütsü, buhur, günlük; **2.** v/t. tütsülemek; günlük yakmak.

in.cense[2] [in'sens] v/t. öfkelendirmek, kızdırmak, darıltmak (**with** hususunda).

in.cen.tive [in'sentiv] **1.** adj. teşvik edici; harekete geçirici; **2.** n. dürtü, saik, güdü.

in.cep.tion [in'sepʃən] n. başlama, başlangıç; **in'cep.tive** [-tiv] adj. başlayan…, başlayıcı…; GR bir hareketin başladığını gösteren (fiil).

in.cer.ti.tude [in'səːtitjuːd] n. belirsizlik, kararsızlık; şüphe, tereddüt.

in.ces.sant □ [in'sesnt] sürekli, devamlı, daimî, ardı arkası kesilmeyen.

in.cest ['insest] n. akraba arasında cinsi temas, akraba ile zina; **in.ces.tu.ous** □ [in'sestjuəs] akrabası ile cinsi temasta buiunmuş; akraba ile zina kabilinden.

inch [intʃ] n. pus (2,54 cm), inç; fig. az miktar; ~**es** pl. boy; **by** ~**es** yavaş yavaş, ağır ağır, azar azar, kıl payı; **every**

~ tepeden tırnağa, tamamiyle, tam manasıyla; **inched** *comb.* …inçlik.

in.cho.a.tive ['inkəueitiv] *adj.* başlayan, başlayıcı; GR bir hareketin başladığını gösteren (*zaman, kip*).

in.ci.dence ['insidəns] *n.* isabet, tesadüf etme; tekrar oranı; oluş derecesi; **angle of** ~ geliş açısı; **'in.ci.dent 1.** *adj.* bağlı, tabi (*to* -e); **2.** *n.* olay, vaka, hadise; önemsiz olay; THEAT perde; **in.ci.den.tal** ☐ [-'dentl] tesadüfi…, rastlantıya bağlı…; küçük ve önemsiz; doğal olarak takip eden…; **be** ~ **to** -e bağlı olm., ait olm.; ~**ly** tesadüfen, şans eseri, şansa; aklıma gelmişken.

in.cin.er.ate [in'sinəreit] *v/t.* yakıp kül etm.; **in.cin.er'a.tion** *n.* yakıp kül etme; **in'cin.er.a.tor** *n.* (*işe yaramaz maddelerin yakıldığı*) fırın, ocak.

in.cip.i.en.cy [in'sipiənsi] *n.* başlangıç; **in'cip.i.ent** *adj.* başlangıç halinde, yeni başlayan…

in.cise [in'saiz] *v/t.* oymak, hakketmek; **in.ci.sion** [-'siʒən] *n.* yarma, deşme, kesme; MED ensizyon, yarık; **in.ci.sive** ☐ [-'saisiv] sivri, keskin; zeki, açıkgöz; açık seçik; **in.ci.sor** [-'saizə] *n.* ön diş, kesici diş.

in.ci.ta.tion [insai'teiʃən] = **incitement**; **in'cite** *v/t.* teşvik etm., tahrik etm., kışkırtmak; **in'cite.ment** *n.* teşvik, tahrik, kışkırtma.

in.ci.vil.i.ty [insi'viliti] *n.* kabalık, nezaketsizlik; kaba davranış *veya* söz.

in.clem.en.cy [in'klemənsi] *n.* fırtınalı, (*veya* sert, şiddetli, soğuk) hava; **in'clement** *adj.* sert, fırtınalı, şiddetli, soğuk (*hava*).

in.cli.na.tion [inkli'neiʃən] *n.* meyil, eğilim, yatma; bayır, yokuş, eğiklik; *fig.* istek, rağbet, heves; **in.cline** [-'klain] **1.** *v/t. & v/i.* eğ(il)mek, meylet(tir)mek, yat(ır)mak; ~**d plane** eğri yüzey; ~ **to** *fig.* -e meyletmek, eğilim göstermek; **2.** *n.* eğri yüzey; yokuş, meyil, eğilme.

in.close [in'kləuz], **in'clos.ure** [-ʒə] = **enclose**, **enclosure**.

in.clude [in'kluːd] *v/t.* içine almak, dahil etm., kapsamak, ihtiva etm., hesaba katmak.

in.clu.sion [in'kluːʒən] *n.* dahil olma, dahil etme, kapsama, hesaba kat(ıl)ma; **in'clu.sive** [-siv] *adj.* kapsayan, dahil, ihtiva eden, içine alan; **be** ~ **of** dahil olm., katılmış olm.; ~ **terms** *pl.* herşey dahil olan fiyatlar.

in.cog F [in'kɔg], **in'cog.ni.to** [-nitəu] **1.** *adv.* takma adla; kıyafet değiştirerek; **2.** *n.* takma ad.

in.co.her.ence, **in.co.her.en.cy** [inkəu'hiərəns(i)] *n.* anlaşılmazlık, manasızlık, tutarsızlık; **in.co'her.ent** ☐ anlaşılmaz, manasız, tutarsız, abuk sabuk.

in.com.bus.ti.ble ☐ [inkəm'bʌstəbl] yanmaz, ateş almaz, tutuşmaz.

in.come ['inkʌm] *n.* gelir, irat, kazanç; **'in.com.er** *n.* yeni gelen; muhacir; JUR yerine geçen, halef, ardıl; **in.come-tax** ['inkəmtæks] *n.* gelir vergisi.

in.com.ing ['inkʌmiŋ] **1.** *n.* girme, geliş, varış; ~**s** *pl.* gelir, kazanç; **2.** *adj.* gelen, varan; yeni gelen; göreve yeni başlayan.

in.com.men.su.ra.bil.i.ty ['inkəmenʃərə'biliti] *n.* nisbetsizlik, kıyas kabul etmezlik, ölçülemezlik, karşılaştırılamaz olma; **in.com'men.su.ra.ble** ☐ oransız, nisbetsiz, kıyaslanamaz, ölçülemez, oranlı kabul etmez; **in.com'men.su.rate** [-rit] *adj.* orantısız, nisbetsiz, kıyaslanamaz (**with. to** *ile*); = **incommensurable**.

in.com.mode [inkə'məud] *v/t.* rahatsız etm., zahmet vermek, tedirgin etm.; **in.com'mo.di.ous** ☐ [-djəs] rahatsız, kullanışsız; zahmetli, işe yaramaz.

in.com.mu.ni.ca.ble [inkə'mjuːnikəbl] ☐ ifade edilemez, söylenilemez; nakledilemez; **in.com.mu.ni.ca.do** *part.* Am. [-'kaːdəu] *adj.* kimseyle görüştürülmeyen (*hapiste*); **in.com'mu.ni.ca.tive** ☐ [-kətiv] fikrini başkasına açıklamayan, ağzı sıkı, ağzı pek.

in.com.mut.a.ble ☐ [inkə'mjuːtəbl] değiş(tirile)mez.

in.com.pa.ra.ble ☐ [in'kɔmpərəbl] emsalsiz, eşsiz; kıyas kabul etmez, karşılaştırılamaz.

in.com.pat.i.bil.i.ty ['inkəmpætə'biliti] *n.* uygunsuzluk, birbirine uymama, tutarsızlık; **in.com'pat.i.ble** ☐ birbirine uymayan, birbirine zıt, tutarsız, bir diğerine uymayan.

in.com.pe.tence, **in.com.pe.ten.cy** [in'kɔmpitəns(i)] *n.* ehliyetsizlik, yetersizlik, işinin ehli olmama; **in'com.pe.tent** ☐ ehliyetsiz, yetersiz, kifayetsiz, işinin ehli olmayan.

in.com.plete ☐ [inkəm'pliːt] tam olmayan, eksik, noksan, bitmemiş, kusurlu.

in.com.pre.hen.si.bil.i.ty [inkɔmprihensə'biliti] *n.* anlaşılmazlık; **in.com-pre'hensible** □ anlaşılamaz, kavranmaz, akıl ermez; **in.com.pre'hen.sion** *n.* anlayışsızlık, akıl erdirememe, kavrayamama.

in.com.press.i.ble   [inkəm'presəbl] *adj.* sıkıştırılamaz; sert ve dayanıklı.

in.con.ceiv.a.ble □ [inkən'si:vəbl] tasavvur olunamaz, anlaşılamaz, inanılmaz; idrak edilemez, kavranamaz.

in.con.clu.sive □ [inkən'klu:siv] sonuçsuz, neticesiz, bir sonuca varmayan, ikna edici olmayan, kifayetsiz, yetersiz; **in.con'clu.sive.ness** *n.* sonuçsuzluk, neticesizlik, bir sonuca varmama.

in.con.gru.i.ty [inkɔŋ'gru:iti] *n.* uyuşmazlık, uyumsuzluk; uyuşmayan şey; **in'con.gru.ous** □ [ˍgruəs] uymayan, uyuşmaz, bağdaşmaz, uyumsuz, aykırı (**with** *ile*); uygunsuz, yersiz, münasebetsiz.

in.con.se.quence [in'kɔnsikwəns] *n.* mantıksızlık; irtibatsızlık, birbirini tutmama; **in'con.se.quent** □ mantıksız, birbirini tutmaz, irtibatsız; **in.con.se.quen.tial** [ˍ'kwenʃəl] *adj.* önemsiz; = **inconsequent**.

in.con.sid.er.a.ble □ [inkən'sidərəbl] önemsiz, ehemmiyetsiz, düşünmeye değmez; ufak, küçük, az; **in.con'sid.er.ate** [ˍrit] düşüncesiz, saygısız, terbiyesiz (**towards** *-e karşı*); tedbirsiz, ihtiyatsız; **in.con'sid.er.ate.ness** *n.* düşüncesizlik, saygısızlık, tedbirsizlik.

in.con.sist.en.cy [inkən'sistənsi] *n.* tutarsızlık, uyuşmazlık, uyumsuzluk; zıtlık, tezatlık; **in.con'sist.ent** □ kararsız, sebatsız; uyuşmaz, uyumsuz, aykırı, tutarsız.

in.con.sol.a.ble □ [inkən'səuləbl] teselli edilemez, avutulamaz.

in.con.spic.u.ous □ [inkən'spikjuəs] önemsiz, ehemmiyetsiz; göze çarpmayan, farkedilemeyen.

in.con.stan.cy [in'kɔnstənsi] *n.* kararsızlık, değişkenlik, döneklik; vefasızlık; **in'constant** □ kararsız, dönek, değişken; vefasız.

in.con.test.a.ble □ [inkən'testəbl] malûm, bilinen, su götürmez, inkâr edilemez, muhakkak, itiraz kaldırmaz.

in.con.ti.nence [in'kɔntinəns] *n.* kendini tutamama, nefsine hâkim olamama; ~ **of urine** MED idrarını tutamama; **in'con.ti.nent** □ kendini tutamayan,

nefsine hâkim olamayan; iradesiz; idrarını tutamayan; ~**ly** kendini tutamayarak; hemen, derhal.

in.con.tro.vert.i.ble □ ['inkəntrə'və:təbl] itiraz kabul etmez, tartışma götürmez, su götürmez, muhakkak.

in.con.ven.ience [inkən'vi:njəns] **1.** *n.* zahmet, rahatsızlık, güçlük, zorluk; uygunsuzluk, münasebetsizlik; **2.** *v/t.* zahmet vermek, rahatsız etm.; **in.con'ven.ient** □ zahmetli, müşkül, güç, zor, çetin; uygunsuz, elverişsiz, münasebetsiz (**to** *için, -e*).

in.con.vert.i.bil.i.ty ['inkənvə:tə'biliti] *n.* değiştirilemezlik; COM altına çevrilemez olma; **in.con'vert.i.ble** □ değiştirilemez; COM altına çevrilemez (*para*).

in.con.vin.ci.ble □ [inkən'vinsəbl] inandırılamaz, kandırılamaz, ikna edilemez.

in.cor.po.rate 1. [in'kɔ:pəreit] *v/t. & v/i.* birleş(tir)mek (**into** *-e*); JUR anonim şirket haline getirmek; biraraya getirmek; biraraya gelmek; **2.** [in'kɔ:pərit] *adj.* anonim...; birleşik, birleşmiş...; **in'corpo.rat.ed** [ˍreitid] *adj.* anonim; **in.corpo'ra.tion** *n.* birleş(tir)me; şirket, tüzel kişi.

in.cor.po.re.al □ [inkɔ:'pɔ:riəl] tinsel, manevî, ruhanî, cisimsiz.

in.cor.rect □ [inkə'rekt] yanlış, hatalı, kusurlu; uygunsuz, yakışıksız, yakışmaz, münasebetsiz; **in.cor'rect.ness** *n.* hata, kusur, yanlış.

in.cor.ri.gi.bil.i.ty [inkɔridʒə'biliti] *n.* yola getirilemez olma, ıslah edilememe, düzeltilememe; **in'cor.ri.gi.ble** □ düzelmez, ıslah edilemez, değiştirilemez, yerleşmiş.

in.cor.rupt.i.bil.i.ty ['inkərʌptə'biliti] *n.* dürüstlük, rüşvet yememe; bozulmazlık, çürümezlik; **in.cor'rupt.i.ble** □ dürüst, rüşvet yemeyen; bozulmaz, çürümez, kokuşmaz.

in.crease 1. [in'kri:s] *v/t. & v/i.* art(tır)-mak, çoğal(t)mak, büyü(t)mek, geliş-(tir)mek, verimlen(dir)mek; **2.** ['in-kri:s] *n.* çoğalma, artma, büyüme; üreme, yavrulama, döl; **in'creas.ing.ly** *adv.* gittikçe artarak; ~ **difficult** gittikçe zorlaşan.

in.cred.i.bil.i.ty [inkredi'biliti] *n.* inanılmazlık, inanılmaz hal; **in'cred.i.ble** □ [ˍdəbl] inanılmaz.

in.cre.du.li.ty [inkri'dju:liti] *n.* inanılmazlık, kuşku, şüphecilik; **in.cred.u-**

lous □ [in'kredjuləs] inanmaz; güvenmez, kuşkulu, kuşkusu olan.

in.cre.ment ['inkrimənt] *n.* artma, çoğalma, kâr, fazlalık.

in.crim.i.nate [in'krimineit] *v/t.* suçlamak, suç yüklemek *-e;* **in'crim.i.na.to.ry** [_nətəri] *adj.* suçlayıcı.

in.crust [in'krʌst] = **encrust; in.crus-'tation** *n.* üstü kabuk bağlama, kabuk tutma, kabuklanma; MEC kaplama.

in.cu.bate ['inkjubeit] *v/t.* üstüne oturarak *veya* suni ısı ile çıkarmak (*civ-civ*); uygun şartlarda geliştirmek (*bakteri*); *v/i.* kuluçkaya yatmak; **in.cu'ba.tion** *n.* kuluçkaya yatma; BIOL, MED bir hastalığın vücuda girmesiyle ilk belirtilerinin ortaya çıkması arasındaki zamanda mikropların gelişmesi; **'in.cu.ba.tor** *n.* kuluçka makinesi; kuvöz; **in.cu.bus** ['iŋkjubəs] *n.* kâbus, karabasan, ağırlık basması; kâbus gibi şey.

in.cul.cate ['inkʌlkeit] *v/t.* iyice kafasına sokmak, telkin etm., aşılamak (*upon*); **in.cul'ca.tion** *n.* telkin.

in.cul.pate ['inkʌlpeit] *v/t.* suçlamak, suç yüklemek; **in.cul'pa.tion** *n.* suçlama, itham; **in'cul.pa.to.ry** [_pətəri] *adj.* suçlayıcı.

in.cum.ben.cy [in'kʌmbənsi] *n.* görev, vazife, ödev; görev süresi; **in'cum.bent 1.** *adj.* zorunlu, mecburi, yükümlü, görevli; *be ~ on s.o. b-ne* düşmek, *b-nin* vazifesi olm.; **2.** *n.* ECCL görevli kimse, memur.

in.cu.nab.u.la [inkju:'næbjulə] *n. pl.* 1501 yılından önce basılmış kitaplar; eskiden kalma sanat eserleri.

in.cur [in'kə:] *v/t.* uğramak *-e,* girmek *-e,* yakalanmak *-e,* tutulmak *-e,* maruz kalmak *-e.*

in.cur.a.bil.i.ty [inkjuərə'biliti] *n.* tedavi edilemezlik, çaresizlik, şifa bulmazlık; **in'cur.a.ble 1.** □ şifa bulmaz, devasız, tedavi edilemez, iyileşmez; **2.** *n.* şifasız hasta, tedavi edilemeyen hasta.

in.cu.ri.ous □ [in'kjuəriəs] meraksız, meraklı olmayan; kayıtsız, lâkayt, ilgisiz, dikkatsiz.

in.cur.sion [in'kə:ʃən] *n.* akın, hücum, baskın, saldırı; *fig.* tecavüz, el atma.

in.cur.va.tion [inkə:'veiʃən] *n.* eğme, bükme; **in'curve** *v/t.* eğmek; bükmek.

in.debt.ed [in'detid] *adj.* borçlu (*to -e*); *fig.* minnettar, müteşekkir (*to -e*); **in-'debt.ed.ness** *n.* borçluluk; borç mik-

tarı.

in.de.cen.cy [in'di:snsi] *n.* ahlâksızlık; **in'de.cent** □ utanmaz, yüzsüz; edepsiz, ahlâksız, çirkin, kaba; JUR toplum töresine aykırı.

in.de.ci.pher.a.ble [indi'saifərəbl] *adj.* okunmaz, çözülmez, sökülmez, anlaşılmaz, karışık.

in.de.ci.sion [indi'siʒən] *n.* kararsızlık; tereddüt, duraksama; **in.de.ci.sive** □ [_'saisiv] kararsız; kesin olmayan.

in.de.clin.a.ble GR [indi'klainəbl] *adj.* çekilmez, kipsiz.

in.dec.o.rous □ [in'dekərəs] edebe aykırı, ayıp, yakışmaz, çirkin, utandırıcı, uygunsuz, yakışık almaz; **in'dec.o.rousness** = **in.de.co.rum** [indi'kɔ:rəm] *n.* edebe aykırı hareket, uygunsuz davranış, terbiyesizlik.

in.deed [in'di:d] **1.** *adv.* gerçekten, hakikaten, doğrusu; **2.** *int.* öyle mi?

in.de.fat.i.ga.ble □ [indi'fætigəbl] yorulmaz, yorulmaz bilmez.

in.de.fea.si.ble □ [indi'fi:zəbl] feshedilemez, iptal edilemez (*hak*).

in.de.fect.i.ble □ [indi'fektəbl] çürümez, bozulmaz; hatasız, kusursuz.

in.de.fen.si.ble □ [indi'fensəbl] savunulamaz, savunmasız, müdafaasız; affedilemez, mazur görülemez.

in.de.fin.a.ble □ [indi'fainəbl] tarif edilemez, tanımlanamaz, anlatılamaz.

in.def.i.nite □ [in'definit] belirsiz, bellisiz, şüpheli, bulanık; GR belgisiz.

in.del.i.ble □ [in'delibl] silinmez, çıkmaz; *~ ink* silinmez mürekkep; *~ pencil* kopya kalemi.

in.del.i.ca.cy [in'delikəsi] *n.* kabalık, uygunsuzluk; kaba davranış *veya* söz; **in'del.i.cate** □ [_kit] kaba, nezaketsiz, terbiyesiz.

in.dem.ni.fi.ca.tion [indemnifi'keiʃən] *n.* tazminat; **in'dem.ni.fy** [_fai] *v/t. -in* zararını ödemek (*from, against -e karşı*); geri ödemek, tazmin etm.; **in'dem.ni.ty** *n.* tazminat; kefalet, teminat, güvence.

in.dent 1. [in'dent] *v/t. -in* kenarını oymak, diş diş oymak; çentmek, kertmek; içerden başlamak, içerlek yazmak (*satır*); JUR senede bağlamak; COM ısmarlamak, sipariş etm. (*upon s.o. b-ne bş*); *~ed coastline* girintili çıkıntılı sahil; *v/i.* anlaşma yapmak; çentik açmak; **2.** ['indent] *n.* çentik, kertik, bere; COM yabancı ülkeden alınan sipariş; MIL resmi emir; içerlek

yazma; = *indenture*; inden'ta.tion *n.*
çentik, kertik, diş; çentme, kertme;
içerlek yazma; girinti, oyuntu; in'den-
tion *n.* TYP içerlek yazma; in'denture
[-tʃə] **1.** *n.* sözleşme, senet, mukavele,
iki taraflı kontrat; **2.** *v/t.* sözleşmeye
bağlamak.

in.de.pend.ence, in.de.pend.en.cy
[indi'pendəns(i)] *n.* bağımsızlık, hürriyet, istiklâl; *Independence Day* Am.
Birleşik Amerika'da Bağımsızlık Günü (*4 Temmuz*); in.de'pend.ent **1.** □
bağımsız, hür, özgür (*of -den*); başlı
başına, ayrı, serbest; ~ *means* özel imkânlar; **2.** *n.* POL bağımsız (*veya* parti
üyesi olmayan) kimse.

in.de.scrib.a.ble □ [indis'kraibəbl]
tanımlanamaz, anlatılmaz, nitelendi-
rilemez.

in.de.struct.i.ble □ [indis'trʌktəbl]
yıkılmaz, tahrip edilemez, yok edilemez, bozulmaz, çok dayanıklı.

in.de.ter.mi.na.ble □ [indi'tə:minəbl]
çözümlenemez, halledilemez, karara
bağlanamayan, kararlaştırılamaz; inde'termi.nate □ [-nit] belirsiz, bellisiz, bilinmeyen, şüpheli, belli olmayan;
in.de'termi.nate.ness, in.de.ter.mi-
na.tion ['-'neiʃən] *n.* belirsizlik, bilin-
mezlik.

In.dex ['indeks] **1.** *n., pl. a.* in.di.ces
['indisi:z] indeks, fihrist; gösterge, işaret, ibre; işaret parmağı; ECCL okunması yasak kitaplar listesi; MATH üs;
a. ~ *number* indeks sayı; **2.** *v/t. -in* in-
deksini yapmak, indeks içine koymak.

In.di.a.man *n.* ['indjəmən] *n.* NAUT eskiden Hindistan ile yapılan ticarette kullanılan gemi.

In.di.an ['indjən] **1.** *adj.* Hindistan'a ait,
Hindistan...; Amerika kızılderilisine
ait; **2.** *n.* Hintli, Hint; Amerikan
kızılderilisi; *a. Red* ~ kızılderili; ~ *club*
lobut; ~ *corn* mısır; ~ *file: in* ~ tek sıra
(*yürüyüş*); ~ *ink* çini mürekkebi; ~
pud.ding Am. mısır muhallebisi; ~
sum.mer pastırma yazı.

India...: ~ *paper* ince Çin kağıdı, pelür
kağıdı; '℥rub.ber kauçuk, lastik.

in.di.cate ['indikeit] *v/t.* göstermek,
işaret etm., belirtmek; in.di'ca.tion
n. belirti, delil, kanıt; bildirme, belirtme, gösterme, işaret etme; in.dic.a-
tive □ [in'dikətiv] belirten, gösteren,
bildiren (*of -i*); ~ *mood* GR bildirme kipi; in.di.ca.tor ['-keitə] *n.* gösteren şey
veya kimse, işaret eden şey, delil, be-

lirti; MEC müşir, ibre, gösterge; TEL
kayıt ibresi; in'di.cato.ry [-kətəri]
adj. gösteren (*of -i*); belirtici..., işaret
edici.

in.di.ces ['indisi:z] *pl. of. index.*

in.dict [in'dait] *v/t.* suçlamak (*for, on
charge of -den*); in'dict.a.ble *adj.* suçlanabilir; in'dict.er *n.* şikâyetçi, davacı; in'dict.ment *n.* suçlama; iddianame.

in.dif.fer.ence [in'difrəns] *n.* aldırmazlık, kayıtsızlık, tasasızlık; hissizlik,
duygusuzluk (*to, towards -e, -e karşı*);
in'differ.ent □ kayıtsız, tasasız, aldırmaz, lakayt, umursamaz (*to -e*); şöyle
böyle, orta derecede, vasat.

in.di.gence [in'didʒəns] *n.* fakirlik,
yoksulluk, züğürtlük.

in.di.gene ['indidʒi:n] *n.* yerli insan,
hayvan *veya* bitki; in'dig.e.nous
[-dʒinəs] *adj.* yerli; doğuştan ait (*to
-e*).

in.di.gent □ ['indidʒənt] yoksul, fakir,
züğürt.

in.di.gest.ed [indi'dʒestid] *adj.* iyice
düşünülmemiş; düzensiz, biçimsiz, intizamsız; sindirilmemiş, hazmolun-
mamış; indi'gest.i.ble □ sindirileme-
yen, hazmı güç, hazmolunmaz; in.di-
'ges.tion *n.* hazımsızlık, mide fesadı.

in.dig.nant □ [in'dignənt] dargın, öfkeli, kızgın, hiddetlenmiş (*at -e*); in-
dig'nation *n.* dargınlık, öfke,
kızgınlık, hiddet (*with hususunda*); ~
meeting bir haksızlığı protesto için
yapılan toplantı; in'digni.ty [-niti] *n.*
hürmetsizlik, saygısızlık, hakaret; kaba muamele *veya* söz.

in.di.go ['indigəu] *n.* çivit; ~ *blue* çivit
mavisi.

in.di.rect □ [indi'rekt] dolaşık, dolambaçlı, dolaylı, dolayısıyla olan; GR *a.*
dolaylı.

in.dis.cern.i.ble [indi'sə:nəbl] *adj.*
ayırt edilemez, seçilemez, farkına varılamaz.

in.dis.ci.pline [in'disiplin] *n.* disiplin-
sizlik, itaatsizlik.

in.dis.creet □ [indis'kri:t] boşboğaz,
patavatsız, geveze, ağzı gevşek, düşüncesiz, sağgörüsüz; in.dis.cre.tion
[-'kreʃən] *n.* boşboğazlık, pata-
vatsızlık, düşüncesizlik; düşüncesiz
söz *veya* davranış.

in.dis.crim.i.nate □ [indis'kriminit]
gelişigüzel, rastgele, tesadüfi; karışık,
karmaşık, karman çorman; = in.dis-

'crim.inat.ing ☐ [-neitiŋ], in.dis-'crim.i.na.tive [-nətiv] farkı göremeyen, ayırt edemeyen, ayıramayan; *fig.* kör; in.dis.crim.ina.tion ['-'neiʃən] *n.* ayırt edememe, farkı görememe, birbirinden ayıramama.

in.dis.pen.sa.ble ☐ [indis'pensəbl] zaruri, zorunlu, elzem, mecburi, kaçınılmaz.

in.dis.pose [indis'pəuz] *v/t.* soğutmak, caydırmak, hevesini kırmak (*towards*, *from* -e karşı, -den); elverişsizleştirmek (*for s.th. to* *inf.* bş için, -mek için); indis'posed *adj.* rahatsız, keyifsiz; isteksiz (*to* -e karşı); in.dis.po.si.tion [indispə'ziʃən] *n.* rahatsızlık, keyifsizlik; isteksizlik, gönülsüzlük (*to* -e karşı).

in.dis.pu.ta.ble ☐ ['indis'pju:təbl] söz götürmez, su götürmez, tartışma götürmez, şüphe götürmez, muhakkak.

in.dis.so.lu.bil.i.ty ['indisɔlju'biliti] *n.* erimezlik; çözülmezlik; *fig.* bozulmazlık, ayrılmazlık, daimilik, süreklilik; in.dis.solu.ble ☐ [-'sɔljubl] erimez, çözülmez; *fig.* bozulmaz, ayrılmaz, sabit, sürekli, daimi.

in.dis.tinct ☐ [indis'tiŋkt] iyice görülmez, seçilmez, ayırt edilmez, bulanık, belirsiz, sönük; in.dis'tinct.ness *n.* belirsizlik, bulanıklık.

in.dis.tin.guish.a.ble ☐ [indis-'tiŋgwiʃəbl] ayırt edilemez, seçilemez, fark edilemez.

in.dite [in'dait] *v/t.* kaleme almak, yazıya dökmek, yazmak; bestelemek.

in.di.vid.u.al [indi'vidjuəl] **1.** ☐ bireysel, ferdî; tek, yalnız; ayrı, başlı başına, kendine özgü; **2.** *n.* birey, fert, kimse, şahıs; in.di'vid.u.al.ism *n.* ferdiyetçilik, bireycilik; bencillik, kendini beğenmişlik, egoizm; in.di'vid.u.al.ist *n.* bireyci, ferdiyetçi, erkinci, liberal; in.di.vid.u.ali.ty [-'æliti] *n.* ferdiyet, hususiyet, kendine özgülük; erkinlik; in.di'vid.u.al.ize [-əlaiz] *v/t.* bireyleştirmek, ferdileştirmek; tek tek ele almak.

in.di.vis.i.bil.i.ty ['indivizi'biliti] *n.* bölünmezlik; in.di'vis.i.ble ☐ bölünmez, taksim olunmaz.

In.do... ['indəu] *prefix* Hintli, Hint...

in.doc.ile [in'dəusail] *adj.* yola gelmez, adam olmaz, inatçı, serkeş; in.doc.il.i.ty [-'siliti] *n.* kolay yola getirilememe, adam edilememe.

in.doc.tri.nate [in'dɔktrineit] *v/t.* aşıla-

mak (*fikir*), telkin etm., kafasını doldurmak (*with ile*).

In.do-Eu.ro.pe.an ['indəujuərə'pi:ən] *n.* Hint-Avrupa dillerinden birini konuşan kimse.

in.do.lence ['indələns] *n.* tembellik, üşengeçlik; 'in.do.lent ☐ tembel, üşengeç; MED ağrısız, acısız.

in.dom.i.ta.ble ☐ [in'dɔmitəbl] boyun eğmez, itaat etmez, direngen, inatçı, ayak direyici.

in.door ['indɔ:] *adj.* ev içinde olan, ev içinde yapılan; *spor:* ev içinde oynanan...; ~ *aerial* oda anteni; ~ *game* ev içinde oynanan oyun; ~ *swimming-bath* ev içindeki yüzme havuzu; 'in'doors *adv.* ev içinde, evde; ev içine, eve.

in.dorse [in'dɔ:s], in'dorse.ment, *etc* = **endorse**, *etc.*

in.du.bi.ta.ble ☐ [in'dju:bitəbl] şüphe edilmez, kuşku duyulmaz, kati, kesin.

in.duce [in'dju:s] *vb.* teşvik etm., kandırıp yaptırmak, ikna etm.; sebep olm. -e, meydana getirmek, oluşturmak; ELECT indüklemek; ~d *current* ELECT indüksiyon cereyanı; in'duce.ment *n.* neden, sebep, vesile, dürtü, güdü; ikna, teşvik, tahrik.

in.duct [in'dʌkt] *v/t.* ECCL resmen göreve getirmek; üye olarak kabul etm.; askere almak; in'duct.ance *n.* ELECT indüktans; ~ *coil* indüktans bobini; in-'duc.tion *n.* göreve getirme; başlama; askere alma; PHYS tümevarım; PHYS indüksiyon; in'duc.tive *n.* PHLS tümevarımsal, tümevarımlı...; PHYS indüksiyon yapan, indüksiyon...

in.due [in'dju:] = **endue**.

in.dulge [in'dʌldʒ] *v/t.* müsamaha etm. -e, anlayış göstermek -e, hoşnut etm.; boyun eğmek -e (*istek*, *kapris*); şefkatle muamele etm. -e; *v/i.* düşkün olm., müptelâ olm., kapılmak (*in* -e); ~ *with* bşle sevindirmek, memnun etm.; ~ (*o.s.*) *in s.th.* -e kapılmak, -in müptelâsı olm.; in'dul.gence *n.* müsamaha, hoşgörü, göz yumma; düşkünlük, iptilâ (*of*, *in* -e); ECCL kilise tarafından cezanın affedilmesi; in'dul.gent ☐ müsamahakâr, hoşgörülü.

in.du.rate ['indjuəreit] *v/t. & v/i.* katılaş(tır)mak, sertleş(tir)mek; sağlamlaş(tır)mak; in.du'ra.tion *n.* katılaş(tır)ma, sertleş(tir)me; sağlamlaş(tır)ma.

in.dus.tri.al [in'dʌstriəl] **1.** ☐ sınai, endüstriyel, endüstri ile ilgili...; ~ **area** endüstri alanı, sanayi sahası; ~ **estate** endüstri bölgesi; ~ **school** teknik okul; çocuk suçlular için sanayi okulu; **2.** = in'dus.tri.al.ist *n.* sanayici, fabrikatör; in'dus.tri.al.ize [-laiz] *v/t. & v/i.* sanayileş(tir)mek; in'dus.tri.ous □ çalışkan, gayretli.

in.dus.try ['indəstri] *n.* sanayi, endüstri; çalışkanlık, gayret; **heavy industries** *pl.* ağır sanayi.

in.dwell ['in'dwel] (*irr.* **dwell**) *vb.* oturmak, ikamet etm.; *fig.* içinde olm.

in.e.bri.ate **1.** [i'ni:brieit] *v/t.* sarhoş etm., mest etm., kafayı buldurmak; **2.** [-briit] *adj.* sarhoş, mest; **3.** [-briit] *n.* sarhoş kimse; in.e.bri'a.tion, in.e-bri.e.ty [-'braiəti] *n.* sarhoşluk, ayyaşlık.

in.ed.i.ble [in'edibl] *adj.* yenmez.

in.ed.it.ed [in'editid] *adj.* yayınlanmamış.

in.ef.fa.ble □ [in'efəbl] tarif olunamaz, anlatılamaz; söylenemez, ağıza alınmaz.

in.ef.face.a.ble □ [ini'feisəbl] silinemez.

in.ef.fec.tive [ini'fektiv], in.ef'fec.tu.al □ [-tʃuəl] etkisiz, tesirsiz; başarısız; (*part.* MIL) kabiliyetsiz, beceriksiz, âciz.

in.ef.fi.ca.cious □ [inefi'keiʃəs] etkisiz, tesirsiz, yetersiz; in'ef.fi.ca.cy [-kəsi] *n.* tesirsizlik, etkisizlik, yetersizlik.

in.ef.fi.cien.cy [ini'fiʃənsi] *n.* etkisizlik, tesirsizlik, verimsizlik; randımansızlık; inef'fi.cient □ etkisiz, tesirsiz, verimsiz, randımansız.

in.el.e.gance [in'eligəns] *n.* zarafetsizlik, çirkinlik, incelikten yoksunluk; in'el.egant □ zarafetsiz, çirkin, incelikten yoksun.

in.el.i.gi.bil.i.ty [inelidʒə'biliti] *n.* uygun olmama, münasip olmama, yeterli niteliği olmama; in'el.i.gi.ble □ uygun olmayan, yeterli niteliği olmayan; *part.* MIL hizmete yaramaz, çürük.

in.e.luc.ta.ble [ini'lʌktəbl] *adj.* kaçınılamaz.

in.ept □ [i'nept] yersiz, uygunsuz, aptalca; hünersiz, beceriksiz, toy; in'ept.i.tude [-'titju:d], in'ept.ness *n.* beceriksizlik; yersizlik; yersiz söz *veya* davranış.

in.e.qual.i.ty [ini:'kwɔliti] *n.* eşitsizlik, farklılık; düzensizlik; intizamsızlık.

in.eq.ui.ta.ble □ [in'ekwitəbl] insafsız, haksız, adaletsiz; in'eq.ui.ty *n.* insafsızlık, haksızlık, adaletsizlik.

in.e.rad.i.ca.ble □ [ini'rædikəbl] sökülemez, kökünden çıkarılamaz, giderilmesi olanaksız.

in.ert [i'nə:t] □ hareketsiz, süreduran; tembel, uyuşuk, ağır; tesirsiz; in.er.tia [i'nə:ʃiə], in'ert.ness *n.* atalet, süredurum; tembellik, uyuşukluk.

in.es.cap.a.ble [inis'keipəbl] *adj.* kaçınılamaz.

in.es.sen.tial ['ini'senʃəl] *adj.* gereksiz, lüzumsuz (**to** -*e*).

in.es.ti.ma.ble □ [in'estiməbl] hesaplanamaz, hesaba sığmaz; çok kıymetli, paha biçilmez.

in.ev.i.ta.ble □ [in'evitəbl] kaçınılamaz, sakınılamaz, çaresiz; in'ev.i.ta.ble.ness *n.* kaçınılmazlık; in'ev.i.ta.bly *adv.* kaçınılmaz surette.

in.ex.act □ [inig'zækt] doğru olmayan, yanlış, hatalı; in.ex'act.i.tude [-ti-tju:d], in.ex'act.ness *n.* tam doğru olmama, yanlışlık, hata.

in.ex.cus.a.ble □ [iniks'kju:zəbl] affedilemez, bağışlanamaz, mazur görülemez.

in.ex.haust.i.bil.i.ty ['inigzɔ:stə'biliti] *n.* yorulmazlık; bitmeme, tükenmeme; in.ex'haust.i.ble □ tükenmez, bitmez; yorulmaz.

in.ex.o.ra.bil.i.ty [ineksərə'biliti] *n.* merhametsizlik, amansızlık, insafsızlık; boyun eğmezlik, direngenlik; in'ex.o.ra.ble □ merhametsiz, insafsız; boyun eğmez, direngen.

in.ex.pe.di.en.cy [iniks'pi:djənsi] *n.* uygunsuzluk, münasebetsizlik; in.ex-'pe.di.ent □ uygunsuz, münasebetsiz.

in.ex.pen.sive □ [iniks'pensiv] ucuz, masrafı az.

in.ex.pe.ri.ence [ineks'piəriəns] *n.* tecrübesizlik, deneyimsizlik, acemilik; in.ex'pe.ri.enced *adj.* tecrübesiz, deneyimsiz, acemi.

in.ex.pert □ [in'ekspə:t] acemi, tecrübesiz, deneyimsiz.

in.ex.pi.a.ble □ [in'ekspiəbl] kefaretle ödenemez (*suç*); yatıştırılamaz, bastırılamaz (*öfke*).

in.ex.pli.ca.ble □ [in'eksplikəbl] izah edilemez, açıklanamaz.

in.ex.press.i.ble □ [iniks'presəbl] ifade edilemez, anlatılamaz, tarif edilemez.

in.ex.pres.sive □ [iniks'presiv] anlatımsız, ifade etmeyen; **in.ex'pres-sive.ness** *n.* anlatımsızlık.

in.ex.tin.guish.able □ [iniks'tiŋgwiʃ-əbl] söndürülemez; bastırılamaz, yatıştırılamaz (*öfke*).

in.ex.tri.ca.ble [in'ekstrikəbl] sökülemez, içinden çıkılmaz, çözümlenemez; kaçınılmaz; karmaşık, karman çorman.

in.fal.li.bil.i.ty [infælə'biliti] *n.* yanılmazlık; şaşmazlık; **in'fal.li.ble** □ yanılmaz, şaşmaz.

in.fa.mous □ ['infəməs] ahlâkı bozuk, rezil, kepaze, adı çıkmış; utanç verici, ayıp; '**in.fa.my** *n.* rezalet, kepazelik; utanç verici davranış.

in.fan.cy ['infənsi] *n.* çocukluk, bebeklik, küçüklük; JUR ergin olmama, reşit olmama; başlangıç; *in its ~* başlangıcında; **in.fant** ['infənt] **1.** *n.* küçük çocuk, bebek; JUR ergin (*veya* reşit) olmayan kimse; *~ school* anaokulu, çocuk yuvası; **2.** *adj.* çocuksu, çocuk...; başlangıç safhasında olan.

in.fan.ta [in'fæntə] *n.* Portekiz *veya* İspanya prensesi; **in'fan.te** [_ti] Portekiz *veya* İspanya prensi.

in.fan.ti.cide [in'fæntisaid] *n.* çocuk öldürme; istenmeyen yeni çocukları öldürme; çocuk katili; **in.fan.tile** ['infəntail] *adj.* çocuğa ait, çocukça, çocuk...; *~ paralysis* çocuk felci; **in.fan.tine** ['_tain] = *infantile*.

in.fan.try MIL ['infəntri] *n.* piyade, yaya asker; '**in.fan.try.man** *n.* piyade, yaya er.

in.fat.u.ate [in'fætjueit] *v/t.* çıldırtmak, aklını çelmek, kara sevdaya düşürmek; *~d* meftun, deli gibi âşık (*with -e*); **in.fat.u'a.tion** *n.* delicesine sevdalanma, kara sevdaya düşme (*for* için).

in.fect [in'fekt] *v/t.* bulaştırmak, geçirmek (*a. fig.*); *become~ed* yakalanmak (*hastalık*); **in'fec.tion** *n.* bulaş(tır)ma, geç(ir)me; **in'fec.tious** □, **in'fec.tive** [_tiv] bulaşıcı, bulaşık...; başkalarına hemen geçen (*gülme, neşe*).

in.fe.lic.i.tous [infi'lisitəs] *adj.* açıklaması zor, anlaşılması güç, beceriksizce yapılmış, münasebetsiz; **in.fe'lic.i.ty** *n.* uygunsuz söz *veya* davranış, talihsizlik, hoşnutsuzluk.

in.fer [in'fəː] *v/t.* anlamak, çıkarmak, sonuca varmak (*from -den*); **in'fer.a-ble** *adj.* anlaşılır; **in.fer.ence** ['infər-əns] *n.* sonuç çıkarma; netice, sonuç; **in.fer.en.tial** □ [_'renʃəl] sonuç olarak

çıkarılabilir; **infer'en.tial.ly** *adv.* dolayısıyle anlayarak, sonuca vararak.

in.fe.ri.or [in'fiəriə] **1.** *adj.* aşağı, alt; ikinci derecede, adi, bayağı; ast; önemi az; **2.** *n.* aşağı derecede olan kimse *veya* şey; **in.fe.ri.or.i.ty** [_ri'ɔriti] *n.* aşağılık, adilik, bayağılık; *~ complex* aşağılık duygusu.

in.fer.nal □ [in'fəːnl] cehenneme ait, cehennemi...; şeytanca..., şeytani...; F iğrenç, berbat; *~ machine* suikast bombası; **in'fer.no** [_nəu] *n.* cehennem; cehennem gibi yer.

in.fer.tile [in'fəːtail] *adj.* verimsiz, kısır, kıraç, çorak; **in.fer.til.i.ty** [_'tiliti] *n.* verimsizlik; kıraçlık.

in.fest [in'fest] *v/t.* zarar vermek *-e*; *fig.* sarmak, istilâ etm. (*bit, kurt, fare*); **in-fes'ta.tion** *n.* istilâ (*bit, kurt, fare*).

in.fi.del ['infidəl] **1.** *adj.* kâfir, imansız; **2.** *n.* kâfir kimse; **in.fi.del.i.ty** [_'deliti] *n.* sadakatsizlik, hıyanet (*to -e*); zina; imansızlık, kâfirlik.

in.field ['infiːld] *n.* kriket, beysbol: dört esas çizgi dahilindeki saha; bu saha oyuncuları.

in.fight.ing ['infaitiŋ] *n. boks:* yakın dövüş.

in.fil.trate ['infiltreit] *v/t. & v/i.* süz(ül)mek; girmek; içeri süzülmek, nüfuz etm.; **in.fil'tra.tion** *n.* süz(ül)me.

in.fi.nite □ ['infinit] sonsuz, nihayetsiz, hudutsuz, bitmez, tükenmez, pek çok, sayısız; **in.fin.i.tes.i.mal** [_'tesiməl] *adj.* bölünemeyecek kadar küçük, parçalara ayrılamayan; **in'fin.i.tive** *n.* GR *a. ~ mood* mastar; **in'fin.i.tude** [_tjuːd], **in'fin.i.ty** *n.* sonsuzluk, nihayetsizlik.

in.firm □ [in'fəːm] zayıf, kuvvetsiz, halsiz; hastalıklı; *~ of purpose* amaçsız; kararsız; **in'fir.ma.ry** *n.* hastane; revir; **in'fir.mi.ty** *n.* zayıflık, hastalık, sakatlık; *fig.* kusur, hata, zaaf.

in.fix [in'fiks] *v/t.* tutturmak, bağlamak (*in -e*); kelimenin ortasına yerleştirmek; *fig.* telkin etm., aşılamak.

in.flame [in'fleim] *v/t. & v/i.* tutuş(tur)-mak, alevlen(dir)mek; *fig.* kızdırmak, öfkelen(dir)mek; MED iltihaplan(dır)-mak.

in.flam.ma.bil.i.ty [inflæmə'biliti] *n.* tutuşabilme; **in'flam.ma.ble 1.** □ tutuşur, yanar, alev alır; parlar, çabuk parlar; **2.** *n.* *~s pl.* yanabilen maddeler; **in.flam.ma-tion** [inflə'meiʃən] *n.* iltihap(lanma), yangı, kızarıklık; alevlenme, tutuşma; **in.flam.ma.to.ry** [in'flæmətəri] *adj.*

tahrik edici; iltihaplı…
in.flate [in'fleit] *v/t*. şişirmek; piyasaya çok sürmek (*para*); suni olarak yükseltmek (*fiyat*); *fig*. gururlandırmak; in'**flat.ed** *adj*. şiş(iril)miş; abartmalı, süslü; in'**fla.tion** *n*. şişkinlik; şiş(iril)-me; COM enflasyon; *fig*. kendini beğenmişlik; in'**fla.tion.ar.y** COM [-ʃnəri] *adj*. enflasyon…, enflasyona neden olan; ~ **spiral** enflasyon sonucu ücretlerin artması.
in.flect [in'flekt] *v/t*. değiştirmek (*ses tonu*); kıvırmak, eğmek; GR çekmek; in'**flec.tion** = **inflexion**.
in.flex.i.bil.i.ty [infleksə'biliti] *n*. eğilmezlik; *fig*. azim, kararlılık; in'**flex.i-ble** □ eğilmez, bükülmez; sarsılmaz; *fig*. azimli, kararlı; in'**flex.ion** [-ʃən] *n*. bükülme, eğilme, eğrilik; GR çekim.
in.flict [in'flikt] *v/t*. getirmek, uğratmak, vermek (*ağrı, ceza*), atmak (*yumruk*) (**on, upon** *s.o. b-ne*); *fig*. yüklemek, yamamak (**on** *-e*); in'**flic-tion** *n*. ceza; sıkıntı, eziyet.
in.flo.res.cence BOT [inflɔ:'resns] *n*. çiçeklenme; çiçeklerin sapları üzerindeki duruşu.
in.flow [infləu] = **influx**.
in.flu.ence ['influəns] **1.** *n*. nüfuz, etki, tesir (**with, on, upon** *-e*); baskı, hüküm (**on, upon** *-e*); **2.** *v/t*. etkilemek, tesir etm, sözünü geçirmek; in'**flu.en.tial** □ [-'enʃəl] sözü geçer, nüfuzlu.
in.flu.en.za MED [influ'enzə] *n*. grip, enflüanza.
in.flux ['inflʌks] *n*. içeriye akma; *fig*. akın (*turist vs.*).
in.fold [in'fəuld] = **enfold**.
in.fo.mer.cial ['infəumɜ:ʃl] *n*. TV'de bilgi vermek amacıyla yapılan kısa yayın.
in.form [in'fɔ:m] *v/t*. haber vermek *-e*, bilgi vermek *-e* (**of, about** hakkında); bildirmek *-i*, söylemek *-i*; haberdar etm. (**s.o. of s.th.** *b-ni bşden*); şekil vermek *-e*, şekillendirmek *-i*; canlandırmak *-i*; **well ~ed** bilgili; herşeyden haberi olan; **keep s.o. ~ed** *b-ni* haberdar etm., *b-ne* bilgi vermek; *v/i*. ihbar etm., şikâyet etm. (**against** *s.o. b-ni*); in'**for.mal** □ resmi olmayan, gayri resmi, teklifsiz, merasimsiz, formalitesiz; in.for.mal.i.ty [-'mæliti] *n*. teklifsizlik, resmiyetsizlik; in'**form.ant** [-mənt] *n*. bilgi veren kimse, ihbarcı; = **informer**, in.for.ma.tion [infə'mei-ʃən] *n*. bilgi, haber, malûmat; danışma;

JUR iddia; **gather** ~ bilgi toplamak (**about** hakkında); in.form.a.tive [in-'fɔ:mətiv] *adj*. aydınlatıcı, bilgi verici, eğitici; in'**form.er** *a*. **common** ~ muhbir, jurnalcı, ele veren kimse.
in.fra ['infrə] *adv*. aşağıda, altta; **see** ~ aşağıya bakınız (*kitap*).
in.frac.tion [in'frækʃən] *n*. suç, kuralı bozma, kanuna karşı gelme.
in.fra…: ~ **dig** F ['infə'dig] *adj*. şanına yakışmaz; '~'**red** *adj*. PHYS kızılötesi.
in.fre.quen.cy [in'fri:kwənsi] *n*. seyreklik; in'**fre.quent** □ seyrek, nadir, az bulunur.
in.fringe [in'frindʒ] *vb*. *a*. ~ **upon** tecavüz etm. (*hak*); bozmak, ihlâl etm., çiğnemek (*kanun, kural, yemin*); in'**fringement** *n*. tecavüz (*hak*); bozma, ihlâl, çiğneme (*kanun, kural, yemin*).
in.fu.ri.ate [in'fjuərieit] *v/t*. çıldırtmak, çileden çıkartmak, küplere bindirtmek.
in.fuse [in'fju:z] *v/t*. aşılamak, telkin etm. (**into** *-e*); CHEM, PHARM suya batırmak; demlendirmek (*çay*); in'**fu.sion** [-ʒən] *n*. suya batır(ıl)ma; demlendirme; demlenmiş *veya* kaynamış sıvı (*çay, ilâç*); karıştırma, katma; *fig*. telkin, aşılama; infu.so.ri.a ZOO [-'zɔ:riə] *n. pl*. haşlamlılar; in.fu'**so.ri.al** *adj*. haşlamlı…
in.gath.er.ing ['ingæðəriŋ] *n*. hasat (*veya* ürün) toplama.
in.gen.ious [in'dʒi:njəs] hünerli, marifetli, becerikli; usta; zeki; yaratıcı; ustaca yapılmış; in.ge.nu.i.ty [indʒi-'nju:iti] *n*. hüner, marifet, maharet, yaratıcılık; in.gen.u.ous □ [in'dʒenjuəs] açık, samimi, candan; masum, saf; doğal, tabii.
in.gle ['ingl] *n*. alev, ateş; şömine; köşe; '~.**nook** *n*. baca kenarı, ocak başı.
in.glo.ri.ous □ [in'glɔ:riəs] utanç verici, yüz kızartıcı; alçakça, şerefsiz; tanınmamış, belirsiz.
in.go.ing ['ingəuiŋ] **1.** *n*. içeri girme; başlama; **2.** *adj*. içeri giren; başlayan.
in.got ['ingət] *n*. külçe; '~.**steel** *n*. akma çelik.
in.grain ['in'grein] *adj*. kökleşmiş; ham iken boyanmış; *fig*. *a*. ~**ed** kökleşmiş; yerleşmiş, tam.
in.gra.ti.ate [in'greiʃieit]: ~ **o.s.** *v/t*. çıkarı için yaltaklanmak, yağcılık yaparcasına sokulmak (**with** *-e*); in.grat-i.tude [in'grætitju:d] *n*. nankörlük.
in.gre.di.ent [in'gri:djənt] *n*. cüz, par-

ça, harç; *fig.* unsur.

in.gress ['ingres] *n.* giriş, girme; girme yetkisi.

in.grow.ing ['ingrəuiŋ] *adj.* içe doğru büyüyen.

in.gui.nal ANAT ['iŋgwinl] *adj.* kasığa ait; kasık…

in.gur.gi.tate [in'gə:dʒiteit] *v/t.* oburcasına yutmak.

in.hab.it [in'hæbit] *v/t.* oturmak, ikamet etm., sakin olm. -*de*; **in'hab.it.a.ble** *adj.* oturulabilir, oturmaya elverişli; **in'habit.an.cy** *n.* oturma, ikamet, sakin olma; **in'hab.it.ant** *n.* oturan, sakin, ikamet eden kimse.

in.ha.la.tion [inhə'leiʃən] *n.* nefes alma, solukla içeri çekme, teneffüs, enhalâsyon; MED solukla içeri çekilen ilâç; **in.hale** [in'heil] *v/t.* MED içine çekmek; *v/i.* nefes almak, teneffüs etm., solumak; **in'hal.er** *n.* MED enhalâsyon aleti.

in.har.mo.ni.ous □ [inhɑ:'məunjəs] uyumsuz, ahenksiz.

in.here [in'hiə] *v/i.* içinde. olm., tabiatında olm. (*in* -*in*); **in'her.ence**, **in'her.en.cy** [-rəns(i)] *n.* içinde olma, tabiatında olma; **in'her.ent** □ içinde olan, tabiatında olan (*in* -*in*).

in.her.it [in'herit] *v/t.* miras almak, kalıt almak; vâris olm. -*e*; **in'her.it.a.ble** □ miras kalması mümkün olan; irsî, kalıtsal; **in'her.it.ance** *n.* miras, kalıt; veraset; BIOL kalıtım, irsiyet, soyaçekim; **in'her.i.tor** *n.* vâris, mirasçı; **in-'her.i.tress**, **in'her.i.trix** [-triks] *n.* kadın vâris.

in.hib.it [in'hibit] *v/t.* engel olm. -*e*, mâni olm. -*e*; bırakmamak, geri tutmak, alıkoymak (**s.o. from s.th.** *b-ni bşden*); **in.hibi.tion** [-'biʃən] *n.* yasak; alıkoyma, engelleme durdurma; **in'hib.i.to.ry** [-təri] *adj.* yasaklayıcı; engelleyici…

in.hos.pi.ta.ble □ [in'hɔspitəbl] misafir sevmez; barınılmaz (*yer*); **in.hospi.tal.ity** ['-'tæliti] *n.* misafir sevmezlik, soğuk muamele.

in.hu.man □ [in'hju:mən] gaddar, kıyıcı, zalim, şefkatsiz, merhametsiz, insanlık dışı; **in.hu.man.i.ty** [-'mæniti] *n.* insaniyetsizlik; zalim davranış.

in.hu.ma.tion [inhju:'meiʃən] *n.* ölüyü gömme, defin.

in.hume [in'hju:m] *v/t.* gömmek, defnetmek.

in.im.i.cal □ [i'nimikəl] düşman, zarar

verici; zıt, karşı, ters, aksi.

in.im.i.ta.ble □ [i'nimitəbl] emsalsiz, eşsiz; taklit edilemez, aynı yapılamaz.

in.iq.ui.tous □ [i'nikwitəs] günahkâr; kötü; haksız, kanunsuz, adaletsiz; **in-'iq.uity** *n.* günah; kötülük; haksızlık, adaletsizlik.

in.i.tial [i'niʃəl] **1.** □ ilk baştaki, birinci; evvelki; **2.** *n.* ilk harf; büyük harf; **3.** *v/t.* adının baş harfleriyle imzalamak, parafe etm.; **in.i.ti.ate** **1.** [i'niʃiit] *n.* yeni üye (*in* -*de*); **2.** [-ʃieit] *v/t.* başlatmak -*i*; başlamak -*e*; POL sunmak, teklif etm.; kabul etm. (*into* -*e*); göstermek, bilgi vermek, alıştırmak; **ini.ti'a.tion** *n.* başla(t)ma; üyeliğe kabul (töreni); *part. Am.* **~ fee** kayıt ücreti; **in'i.ti.a.tive** [-ətiv] **1.** *adj.* başlatan, ilk, ön; **2.** *n.* öncecilik, inisiyatif; ilk adım, ilk hareket; girişim, kişisel teşebbüs; *on* *one's own* **~** kendi kararıyla, kimseden emir almadan; *take the* **~** ilk adımı atmak; **in'i.ti.a.tor** [-eitə] *n.* önayak olan kimse; **in'i.ti.a.to.ry** [-ətəri] *adj.* tanıtıcı, başlatan, başlangıç türünden.

in.ject [in'dʒekt] *v/t.* şırınga etm., enjeksiyon yapmak, iğne yapmak (*into* -*e*); iğne ile içine sokmak, zerk etmek (*with* -*e*); **in'jec.tion** *n.* içeri atma; içeri atılan şey; MED enjeksiyon, iğne yapma, zerk.

in.ju.di.cious □ [indʒu:'diʃəs] akılsız, tedbirsiz, düşüncesiz, basiretsiz.

in.junc.tion [in'dʒʌŋkʃən] *n.* uyarı, ihtar, nasihat, öğüt; yasaklama; mahkeme emri.

in.jure ['indʒə] *v/t.* incitmek -*i*, zarar vermek -*e*, dokunmak -*e*; bozmak -*i*, ihlâl etm. -*i*; rencide etm. -*i*, haksızlık etm. -*e*; **in.ju.ri.ous** □ [in'dʒuəriəs] zararlı, zarar verici, dokunur; yerici, aşağılayıcı, onur kırıcı (*söz*); rencide edici, haksız; **in.ju.ry** ['indʒəri] *n.* zarar ziyan, hasar; haksızlık, adaletsizlik; yara, bere.

in.jus.tice [in'dʒʌstis] *n.* haksızlık, adaletsizlik; haksız davranış.

ink [iŋk] **1.** *n.* mürekkep; mürekkep balığının çıkardığı sıvı; *mst* **printer's** **~** matba mürekkebi; *attr.* mürekkep…; **2.** *v/t.* mürekkep bulaştırmak, üzerinden mürekkeple geçmek; **~ in** *veya* *over* -*i* mürekkeplemek.

ink.ling ['iŋkliŋ] *n.* ima, işaret, iz, ipucu; seziş, kuşku.

ink…: **'~pad** *n.* ıstampa; **'~pen.cil** *n.* mürekkepli kalem; **'~pot** *n.* mürekkep hokkası; '~.stand *n.* yazı takımı; 'ink.y *adj.* mürekkepli, mürekkep gibi, simsiyah, zifiri (*karanlık*).

in.laid ['inleid] *adj.* kakma, işlemeli...; ~ *floor* parke döşeme.

in.land 1. ['inlənd] *adj.* iç, dahili, ülkenin iç kısmında olan; ♀ *Revenue* vergilerden elde edilen devlet geliri; 2. [‿] *n.* ülke içi, dahil; 3. [in'lænd] *adv.* içeriye doğru, içerilerde, denizden uzakta; in.lander ['inləndə] *n.* ülkenin iç kısmında oturan kimse.

in.lay 1. ['in'lei] (*irr. lay*) *v/t.* kakma ile süslemek, kakma işlemek, içini kakmak; 2. ['inlei] *n.* kakmacılık; kakmacılık malzemesi; kakma deseni; dolgu (*diş*).

in.let ['inlet] *n.* giriş yolu; koy; MEC giriş, giriş deliği.

in.mate ['inmeit] *n.* oturan, sakin; başkası ile aynı yerde oturan kimse (*esp. hastane, hapishane*).

in.most ['inməust] *adj.* en içerideki, dahili; çok özel *veya* gizli.

inn [in] *n.* otel, han; ♀s *pl. of Court* Londra Barosu.

in.nards F [inədz] *n. pl.* iç organlar; mide ve bağırsaklar; iç kısımlar (*makine*).

in.nate □ ['i'neit] fıtrî, doğuştan olan, Tanrı vergisi; tabii, yaradılıştan olan.

in.ner ['inə] *adj.* iç, içerideki, dahilî; manevî, ruhanî; ~ *tube* iç lastik; *the* ~ *man* insan ruhu *veya* aklı; *co.* mide, iştah; in.ner.most ['‿məust] *adj.* en içerideki, en içtekı.

in.ner.vate ['inə:veit] *v/t.* kuvvetlendirmek (*sinir*); canlandırmak; cesaret vermek.

in.nings ['iniŋz] *n. sg. spor.* bir oyuncu *veya* takımın atış yaptığı zaman; iktidar devresi; *have one's* ~ atış yapmak; *fig.* uzun ve mutlu yaşamak; uzun süre iktidarda kalmak.

inn.keep.er ['inki:pə] *n.* otelci, hancı.

in.no.cence ['inəsns] *n.* suçsuzluk, masumiyet; saflık; in.no.cent ['‿snt] 1. □ suçsuz, masum, günahsız (*of-den*); zararsız; saf, aklı ermez; ~ *of* F -sız, -siz, -sızın; 2. *n.* masum kimse *veya* çocuk; saf kimse, aptal kimse.

in.noc.u.ous □ [i'nɔkjuəs] zararsız (*esp. hakaret. söz vs.*).

in.nom.i.nate [i'nɔminit] *adj.* adsız, isimsiz.

in.no.vate ['inəuveit] *v/t.* yenilik yapmak, değişiklik yapmak; in.no'va.tion

n. yenilik, icat, buluş; 'in.no.va.tor [‿tə] *n.* yenilikçi.

in.nox.ious □ [i'nɔkʃəs] zararsız.

in.nu.en.do [inju:'endəu] *n.* ima, kinaye; imleme, dolayısıyla söyleme.

in.nu.mer.a.ble □ [i'nju:mərəbl] sayısız, pek çok, bir sürü.

in.nu.tri.tious [inju:'triʃəs] *adj.* gıdasız, yeterli beslenmeyen.

in.ob.serv.ance [inəb'zə:vəns] *n.* (*of*) dikkatsizlik; yerine getirememe.

in.oc.cu.pa.tion ['inɔkju'peiʃən] *n.* işsizlik.

in.oc.u.late [i'nɔkjuleit] *v/t.* MED & *fig.* aşılamak (*with ile, for -e karşı*); AGR aşı yapmak (*ağaç*); in.oc.u'la.tion *n.* aşı(-lama).

in.o.dor.ous [in'əudərəs] *adj.* kokusuz.

in.of.fen.sive □ [inə'fensiv] zararsız, incitmez, dokunmaz; in.of'fen.sive.ness *n.* zararsızlık.

in.of.fi.cial [inə'fiʃəl] *adj.* resmi olmayan, gayri resmi.

in.op.er.a.ble [in'ɔpərəbl] *adj.* MED ameliyat edilemez (*ur*); işlemez, çalışmaz.

in.op.er.a.tive [in'ɔpərətiv] *adj.* tesirsiz, etkisiz; işlemeyen; boş, hükümsüz, geçersiz.

in.op.por.tune □ [in'ɔpətju:n] vakitsiz, zamansız, uygunsuz, sırasız, münasebetsiz, mevsimsiz.

in.or.di.nate □ [i'nɔ:dinit] aşırı, haddinden fazla; düzensiz, intizamsız.

in.or.gan.ic [inɔ:'gænik] *adj.* cansız, inorganik.

in-pa.tient ['inpeiʃənt] *n.* hastanede yatan hasta.

in.put ['input] *n.* MEC *part.* ELECT giriş, besleme; emiş gücü; elektronik beyne verilen bilgi; COM girdi.

in.quest JUR ['inkwest] *n.* resmi soruşturma (*on hakkında*); *coroner's* ~ nedeni bilinmeyen ölümlerle ilgili resmi soruşturma.

in.qui.e.tude [in'kwaiitju:d] *n.* endişe, kaygı, tasa.

in.quire [in'kwaiə] *v/t.* & *v/i.* ara(ştır)-mak, tahkikat yapmak, sor(uştur)mak (*about, after, for -i; of -e*); ~ *into* araştırmak, soruşturmak *-i*; in'quir.er *n.* soruşturan kimse, araştıran kimse; in'quiring □ soruşturan, araştıran, meraklı; in'quir.y *n.* sorgu, soruşturma, araştırma; *make inquiries* soruşturma yapmak (*of -i hakkında; on, about hakkında*); in'quir.y-'of.fice *n.*

soruşturma bürosu.

in.qui.si.tion [inkwi'ziʃən] *n.* soruşturma, araştırma, tahkikat; sorgu, sorguya çekme (*a.* JUR); ♀ HIST Engizisyon mahkemesi; **in'quis.i.tive** ☐ [_tiv] çok sual soran; meraklı; **in'quis.i.tive.ness** *n.* meraklılık; **in'quis.i.tor** *n.* soruşturmacı, tahkikat yapan kimse; HIST Engizisyon mahkemesi üyesi; **in.quis.i.to.ri.al** ☐ [_'tɔːriəl] soruşturma…, araştırma…; Engizisyona ait, Engizisyon…

in.road ['inrəud] *n.* akın, baskın, saldırı (*in, on* -*e*).

in.rush ['inrʌʃ] *n.* içeriye hücum, akın. baskın.

in.sa.lu.bri.ous [insə'luːbriəs] *adj.* sağlığa zararlı, sıhhate dokunur.

in.sane ☐ [in'sein] deli, çıldırmış; delice, manasız, anlamsız; **~ asylum** tımarhane, akıl hastanesi; **in.san.i.tar.y** ☐ [in'sænitəri] sağlığa zararlı, pis; **in'san.i.ty** *n.* akıl hastalığı, delilik, cinnet.

in.sa.ti.a.bil.i.ty [inseiʃjə'biliti] *n.* doymazlık, açgözlülük; **in'sa.ti.a.ble** ☐, **in'sa.tiate** [_ʃiit] çok obur, doymak bilmez, hiç kanmaz (*of* -*e*).

in.scribe [in'skraib] *v/t.* kaydetmek, yazmak (*with* -*i*); hakketmek; COM tescil etm.; MATH içine çizmek; *fig.* iz bırakmak (*in, on* -*de*); ithaf etm. (*to* -*e*); **~d stock** *pl.* müseccel hisse senedi.

in.scrip.tion [in'skripʃən] *n.* kayıt; yazıt, kitabe, yazı; ithaf; COM tescil.

in.scru.ta.bil.i.ty [inskruːtə'biliti] *n.* anlaşılmazlık; esrarengizlik; **in'scru.ta.ble** ☐ anlaşılmaz, esrarengiz (*insan veya davranışlar*).

in.sect ['insekt] *n.* böcek, haşere; **in'secti.cide** [_tisaid] *n.* haşarat ilâcı; **in'sectiv.o.rous** [_'tivərəs] *adj.* böcek yiyen, böcekçil.

in.se.cure ☐ [insi'kjuə] emniyetsiz, sağlam olmayan, garantisiz, güvenilmez; endişeli; korumasız; **in.se'cu.ri.ty** [_riti] *n.* emniyetsizlik, güvenilmezlik.

in.sem.i.nate BIOL [in'semineit] *v/t.* tohum ekmek, tohumlamak; döllemek; *fig.* aşılamak (*fikir*); **in.sem.i'na.tion** *n.* dölleme.

in.sen.sate [in'senseit] *adj.* hissiz, duygusuz; insafsız, merhametsiz; cansız; **insen.si.bil.i.ty** [_sə'biliti] *n.* duygusuzluk, hissizlik; aldırmazlık, ilgisizlik (*of, to* -*e* karşı); **in'sen.si.ble** ☐ hissiz,

duygusuz (*of, to* -*e* karşı); baygın, şuursuz, kendinden geçmiş; farkına varılamaz, hissedilemez; aldırış etmeyen, ilgisiz, lâkayt, kayıtsız; farkında olmayan; yavaş, az; anlamsız; **~ of veya to s.th.** bşin farkında olmayan; **in'sen.si.tive** [_sitiv] *adj.* duygusuz, hissiz (*to* -*e* karşı).

in.sen.ti.ent [in'senʃənt] *adj.* cansız; duygusuz, hissiz; farkında olmayan.

in.sep.a.ra.bil.i.ty [insepərə'biliti] *n.* ayrılmazlık; **in'sep.a.ra.ble** ☐ ayrılmaz.

in.sert 1. [in'səːt] *v/t.* sokmak, sıkıştırmak, arasına koymak; vermek (*ilân*); **2.** ['insəːt] *n.* ortaya eklenen şey; kitap ortasına eklene sayfalar; **in'ser.tion** *n.* ekleme; eklenen şey; ilân.

in.set ['inset] *n.* ilâve, ek; kitabın ortasına konan ilâve sayfalar.

in.shore NAUT ['in'ʃɔː] *adj.* kıyıya yakın, kıyı…, sahil…

in.side ['in'said] **1.** *n.* iç, iç taraf, dahil, iç yüz; F mide, karın; **turn ~ out** ters yüz etm., içini dışına çevirmek; altüst etm.; **2.** *adj.* iç…, içteki, dahilî; **~ information** içeriden sızan haberler; **~ left** *futbol:* solaçık; **~ right** sağaçık; **3.** *adv.* içerde, içeriye; **~ of** F icinde, süresinde, zarfında; **4.** *prp.* -*in* içerisinde, içerisine; **'in'sid.er** *n.* bilgi elde edebilecek durumda olan kimse, içerideki kimse.

in.sid.i.ous ☐ [in'sidiəs] sinsi, gizlice zarar veren, görünmez; hain, hilekâr.

in.sight ['insait] *n.* bilgi, iyice anlama, öğrenme; **~ into** idrak, anlayış, kavrama -*i.*

in.sig.ni.a [in'signiə] *n. pl.* nişanlar; rütbe işaretleri.

in.sig.nif.i.cance, *a.* **in.sig.nif.i.can.cy** [insig'nifikəns(i)] *n.* önemsizlik; anlamsızlık, manasızlık; **in.sig'nif.i.cant** *adj.* önemsiz, ehemmiyetsiz; anlamsız, manasız; değersiz, değmez; cüzî, pek az.

in.sin.cere ☐ [insin'siə] ikiyüzlü, riyakâr, samimiyetsiz, vefasız, sadakatsiz; **in.sincer.i.ty** [_'seriti] *n.* samimiyetsizlik, vefasızlık, ikiyüzlülük.

in.sin.u.ate [in'sinjueit] *v/t.* ima etm., üstü kapalı söylemek, çıtlatmak; yavaş yavaş girmek; **~ o.s. into** sokulmak, yavaş yavaş girmek -*e*; **in.sin.u.at.ing** ☐ üstü kapalı, imalı; **in.sin.u'a.tion** *n.* ima, üstü kapalı itham, çıtlatma; göze girmeye yöneltilmiş söz *veya* hareket.

in.sip.id ☐ [in'sipid] yavan, lezzetsiz,

tatsız; sönük, cansız; **in.si'pid.i.ty** *n*. yavanlık, tatsızlık; sönüklük, cansızlık.

in.sist [in'sist]: ~ *on*, ~ *upon* v/i. üzerinde ısrar etm., diretmek, direnmek; ~ *that* …konusunda ısrar etm.; **in'sist.ence** *n*. ısrar (*on*, *upon* üzerinde); *at his* ~ ısrarı üzerine; **in'sist.ent** ☐ ısrarlı, inatçı, direngen (*on*, *upon* -*de*); zorlayıcı, âcil.

in.so.bri.e.ty [insəu'braiəti] *n*. sarhoşluk, içkiye düşkünlük, ayyaşlık.

in.so.la.tion [insəu'leiʃən] *n*. güneşe bırakma, güneşlendirme; güneş çarpması.

in.sole ['insəul] *n*. ayakkabının iç tabanı; taban astarı, keçe.

in.so.lence ['insələns] *n*. küstahlık, terbiyesizlik, arsızlık; '**in.so.lent** ☐ küstah, terbiyesiz, arsız.

in.sol.u.bil.i.ty [insɔlju'biliti] *n*. erimezlik (*sıvı*); çözülemezlik (*problem*); **in'sol.uble** ☐ [-jubl] erimez (*sıvı*); çözülemez, halledilemez, açıklanamaz (*problem*, *sorun*).

in.sol.ven.cy [in'sɔlvənsi] *n*. iflâs; **in'solvent 1.** *adj*. iflâs etmiş, borcunu ödeyemez; **2.** *n*. müflis.

in.som.ni.a [in'sɔmniə] *n*. uykusuzluk, uyumama.

in.so.much [insəu'mʌtʃ] *adv*.: ~ *that* o kadar ki.

in.spect [in'spekt] v/t. teftiş etm., denetlemek; muayene etm., yoklamak, bakmak; **in'spec.tion** *n*. teftiş, denetleme, yoklama, muayene; *for* ~ com örnek olarak, denenmek üzere; **in'spec.tor** *n*. müfettiş, tetkik memuru, enspektör; kontrol memuru; **in'spec.tor.ate** [-tərit] *n*. müfettişlik.

in.spi.ra.tion [inspə'reiʃən] *n*. ilham, esin; ilham kaynağı; parlak fikir; vahiy; nefes alma; **in.spire** [in'spaiə] v/t. ilham etm., esinlemek; içine çekmek (*nefes*); sevketmek; etkilemek; sebep olm., vesile olm.; yaymak (*dedikodu*); fig. telkin etm., aklına sokmak (*s.th. in s.o.*, *s.o. with s.th.* bşi b-ne, b-nin); v/i. nefes almak; **in.spir.it** [in'spirit] v/t. canlandırmak, şevklendirmek, neşelendirmek.

in.spis.sate [in'spiseit] v/t. kalınlaştırmak, koyulaştırmak, yoğunlaştırmak.

in.sta.bil.i.ty [instə'biliti] *n*. dayanıksızlık; *part. fig.* kararsızlık, sebatsızlık.

in.stall [in'stɔːl] v/t. yerleştirmek (*in* -*e*); makamına getirmek; MEC kurmak,

tesis etm., takmak; **in.stal.la.tion** [instə'leiʃən] *n*. yerleştirme; MEC tesisat, tertibat, donanım; ELECT kurma, montaj; askeri üs.

in.stal(l).ment [in'stɔːlmənt] *n*. taksit; kısım, bölüm; *by* ~*s* taksitle, taksit taksit; *payment by* ~*s* taksitle ödeme; ~ *plan* taksit usulü.

in.stance ['instəns] **1.** *n*. misal, örnek; rica, istek; defa, kere, sefer; JUR dava; aşama, basamak, durum; *for* ~ örneğin, meselâ; *in the first* ~ ilk olarak, öncelikle; *at the* ~ *of* -*in* isteği üzerine; **2.** v/t. örnek olarak göstermek; örnek ile belirtmek.

in.stant ['instənt] **1.** ☐ hemen olan, derhal olan; âcil; şimdiki, şu anki; cari, içinde bulunulan ayda olan; çabuk ve kolay hazırlanabilen (*yiyecek, içecek*); ~ *coffee* sıcak su *veya* süt katılarak yapılan toz kahve; ~ *message* IT anında görülen e-posta mesajı; *on the 10th* ~ bu ayın onunda; **2.** *n*. an, dakika; *the* ~ *you call* sen telefon eder etmez; **in-stan.ta.ne.ous** ☐ [-'teinjəs] ani, bir anlık, bir anda olan…; **in.stant.ly** *adv*. hemen, derhal.

in.state [in'steit] v/t. yerleştirmek, koymak (*in* -*e*); yatırmak, vermek (*para*); bağışlamak, hediye etm.

in.stead [in'sted] *adv*. yerine, karşılık olarak, yerinde ~ *of* -*in* yerine; ~ *of going* gitmek yerine.

in.step ['instep] *n*. ayağın üst kısmı; ayakkabı *veya* çorabın üst kısmı; *be high in the* ~ F burnu havada olm.

in.sti.gate ['instigeit] v/t. kışkırtmak, tahrik etm., teşvik etm., ayartmak; **in-sti'ga.tion** *n*. kışkırtma, tahrik, teşvik, ayartma; *at the* ~ *of* -*in* teşvikiyle; '**in-sti.ga.tor** *n*. kışkırtıcı.

in.stil(l) [in'stil] v/t. damla damla akıtmak (*ilâç*); *fig.* aşılamak (*fikir*) (*into* -*e*); **in.stil'la.tion**, **in'stil(l).ment** *n*. damla damla akıtma; fikir aşılama.

in.stinct 1. ['instiŋkt] *n*. içgüdü, insiyak; sezgi, içe doğma; **2.** [in'stiŋkt] *adj*. dolu; ~ *with life* hayat dolu; **in-'stinc.tive** ☐ içgüdülü, içgüdüsel.

in.sti.tute ['institjuːt] **1.** *n*. enstitü, okul, kuruluş, müessese; kurum, cemiyet; **2.** v/t. kurmak, tesis etm.; atamak, tayin etm. (*to into* -*e*); **in.sti'tu.tion** *n*. kuruluş, müessese, kurum, tesis; yerleşmiş gelenek *veya* kanun; kurma, yerleştirme; atama, tayin etme; **in.sti-'tu.tion.al** [-ʃənl] *adj*. kuruluş…, kurum...; geleneksel...; *care* ~ huzurevi, yetimhane, ıslahane *vs.* bakımı; in.sti-'tu.tion.al.ize [-ʃnəlaiz] *v/t.* müesseseleştirmek, kurum haline getirmek; gelenekselleştirmek, âdet haline getirmek; F düşkünler evine yatırmak.

in.struct [in'strʌkt] *v/t.* eğitmek, öğretmek, okutmak, ders vermek; talimat vermek *-e*, emir vermek *-e*, direktif vermek *-e*; bilgi vermek *-e*; in'struc.tion *n.* eğitim, talim, öğrenim, öğretim; bilgi verme; ~*s pl.* emir, talimat, direktif; in'struc.tion.al [-ʃənl] *adj.* eğiticici..., öğretici...; ~ *film* eğitici film; in-'struc.tive □ öğretici, eğitici; in'struc.tor *n.* eğitmen, okutman, öğretmen; *Am.* UNIV doçent; in'struc.tress *n.* kadın okutman, öğretmen.

in.stru.ment ['instrumənt] *n.* alet; MUS enstruman, saz, çalgı; *fig.* maşa, alet; JUR belge; ~ *board* MOT, AVIA dağıtım (*veya* kontrol) tablosu; *fly on* ~*s* AVIA aletler yardımıyla uçmak, kör uçuş yapmak; in.stru'men.tal □ [instru-'mentl] yardımcı, aracı olan; MUS enstrumental; faydalı, yararlı, tesirli, etkili; *be* ~ *to -e* yardımcı olm.; *be* ~ *in -de* aracı olm.; in.stru'men.tal.ist MUS [-təlist] *n.* çalgıcı; in.stru.men.tal.i.ty [-'tæliti] *n.* vasıta, araç.

in.sub.or.di.nate [insə'bɔːdnit] *adj.* itaatsiz, asi, baş kaldıran, kafa tutan, isyankâr; in.sub.or.di.na.tion ['-di-'neiʃən] *n.* itaatsizlik, baş kaldırma, asilik.

in.sub.stan.tial [insəb'stænʃəl] *adj.* gerçek olmayan, hayalî; zayıf, temelsiz, esassız, asılsız.

in.suf.fer.a.ble □ [in'sʌfərəbl] tahammül olunamaz, çekilmez, katlanılmaz; çok gururlu, fazla kibirli.

in.suf.fi.cien.cy [insə'fiʃənsi] *n.* yetersizlik, yetmezlik, eksiklik, kifayetsizlik; insuf'fi.cient □ eksik, yetersiz, kifayetsiz.

in.su.lar □ ['insjulə] adaya özgü, ada..., adada yaşayan; *fig.* dar görüşlü; in.su.lar.i.ty [-'læriti] *n.* adalı olma; *fig.* dar görüşlülük; in.su.late ['-leit] *v/t.* ayırmak, izole etm., yalıtmak, tecrit etm. (*a.* ELECT); 'in.su.lat.ing *adj.* izole eden, izole...; ~ *tape* izole bant; in.su-'la.tion *n.* tecrit, izolasyon, yalıtım (*a.* PHYS); 'insu.la.tor *n.* ELECT izolatör, fincan.

in.su.lin MED ['insjulin] *n.* insülin.

in.sult 1. ['insʌlt] *n.* hakaret, onur

kırma, aşağılama, hor görme; 2. [in-'sʌlt] *v/t.* hakaret etm., hor görmek, aşağılamak, şerefini kırmak.

in.su.per.a.bil.i.ty [insju:pərə'biliti] *n.* başa çıkılmazlık, yenilemezlik, geçilemezlik, aşılmazlık; in'su.per.a.ble □ başa çıkılmaz, yenilemez; geçilemez, aşılamaz.

in.sup.port.a.ble □ [insə'pɔːtəbl] çekilmez, dayanılmaz, tahammül edilemez; haksız, yersiz.

in.sup.press.i.ble [insə'presəbl] *adj.* bastırılamaz, söndürülemez, önlenemez.

in.sur.ance [in'ʃuərəns] *n.* sigorta, sigorta etme; sigorta parası, sigorta taksidi; sigorta poliçesi; *attr.* sigorta...; ~ *pol.icy* sigorta poliçesi; in'sur.ant *n.* sigorta primi ödeyen kimse; in'sure *v/t.* sigorta etm.; temin etm., sağlamak; *v/i.* sigorta olm.; in'sured *n.* sigortalı kimse; in'sur.er *n.* sigorta şirketi; sigortacı.

in.sur.gent [in'sɜːdʒənt] 1. *adj.* asi, baş kaldıran, kafa tutan; 2. *n.* ihtilâlci, asi kimse.

in.sur.mount.a.ble □ [insə'mauntəbl] yenilemez, başa çıkılmaz, üstesinden gelinemez, seçilemez.

in.sur.rec.tion [insə'rekʃən] *n.* isyan, ayaklanma, ihtilâl; in'sur'rec.tion.al [-ʃənl] *adj.* isyan kabilinden; in.sur-'rec.tion.ist [-ʃnist] *n.* asi kimse, isyan taraftarı, ihtilâlci.

in.sus.cep.ti.ble [insə'septəbl] *adj.* duygusuz, hissiz, vurdumduymaz (*of, to -e karşı*).

in.tact [in'tækt] *adj.* bozulmamış, dokunulmamış, el sürülmemiş, tam, eksiksiz.

in.take ['inteik] *n.* giriş, ağız; içeri giren miktar, alınan miktar; tarıma uygun hale getirilen arazi.

in.tan.gi.bil.i.ty [intændʒə'biliti] *n.* tutulamazlık, dokunulamazlık; kavranamazlık; in'tan.gi.ble □ tutulamaz, dokunulamaz; *fig.* kavranamaz, idrak edilemez; manevî (*değer*).

in.te.ger ['intidʒə] *n.* MATH tam sayı; bütünlük, tam mevcudiyet; in.te.gral ['-grəl] 1. □ gerekli, lüzumlu; tam, bütün, yekpare; MATH tam sayılardan oluşan, tam sayı...; 2. *n.* MATH integral; in.te.grant ['-grənt] *adj.* bir bütünü oluşturan, bütünleyici; in.te.grate ['-greit] *v/t.* tamamlamak, bütünlemek; katmak, ilâve etm., eklemek (*in-*

to, **in** -e); kaldırmak (*ırk ayırımını*); in.te'gra.tion *n. mst* POL ırk ayırımını kaldırma; bütünleme, tamamlama; in.teg.ri.ty [in'tegriti] *n.* bütünlük; dürüstlük, doğruluk.

in.teg.u.ment [in'tegjumənt] *n.* deri, zar, kabuk, gömlek (*a.* BOT, ANAT).

in.tel.lect ['intilekt] *n.* akıl, zihin, idrak; anlık; in.tel'lec.tu.al [‿tjuəl] **1.** ☐ akla ait, aklî, zihnî; bilgili, akıllı, zekâ sahibi, okumuş, âlim, münevver; **2.** *n.* entelektüel (*veya* münevver) kimse; in-
tellec.tu.al.i.ty ['‿tju'æliti] *n.* münevverlik, zihnî kabiliyet.

in.tel.li.gence [in'telidʒəns] *n.* akıl, zekâ, anlayış; haber, bilgi, malûmat; ~ **department** istihbarat bölümü; in'tel.li.genc.er *n.* casus, gizli ajan; muhbir, muhabir.

in.tel.li.gent ☐ [in'telidʒənt] akıllı, zeki, anlayışlı; becerikli, maharetli, kabiliyetli, usta; in.tel.li.gent.si.a [‿'dʒentsiə] *n.* aydınlar sınıfı, münevver sınıf; in.tel.ligi.bil.i.ty [‿dʒə'biliti] *n.* anlaşılabilme, açıklık; in'tel.li.gi.ble ☐ anlaşılır, açık (**to** için).

in.tem.per.ance [in'tempərəns] *n.* aşırılık, taşkınlık; düşkünlük, ayyaşlık; in'temper.ate ☐ [‿rit] taşkın, aşırı; şiddetli, sert, bozuk, fırtınalı (*hava*); ayyaş.

in.tend [in'tend] *v/t.* niyet etm., niyetlenmek, tasarlamak, zihninde kurmak; kastetmek, demek istemek (**by** *ile*); ~ **for** -e, için niyet etm.; in'tend.ant *n.* idare memuru; in'tend.ed **1.** *adj.* tasarlanmış, amaçlı; müstakbel; ~ **husband** müstakbel koca; **2.** *n.* F nişanlı kimse.

in.tense ☐ [in'tens] şiddetli, kuvvetli, hararetli, ateşli, gergin; in'tense.ness *n.* şiddet, kuvvet, hararet, gerginlik.

in.ten.si.fi.ca.tion [intensifi'keiʃən] *n.* kuvvetlendirme, koyulaştırma (*a.* PHOT); in'ten.si.fy [‿fai] *v/t. & v/i.* şiddetlen(dir)mek; -*in* şiddetini arttırmak, koyulaştırmak.

in.ten.sion [in'tenʃən] *n.* keskinlik, şiddet; koyuluk, yoğunluk; in'ten.si.ty = **intenseness**; in'ten.sive ☐ = *intense*; şiddetli, kuvvetli.

in.tent [in'tent] **1.** ☐ gayretli, şevkli, istekli, arzulu (**on** -*e*); meşgul, niyetli, dalmış, kendini vermiş (**on** *ile*, -*e*); **2.** *n.* niyet, maksat, amaç, gaye, kasıt, meram; **to all** ~ **s and purposes** esas iti-

bariyle, her bakımdan, tamamiyle; **with** ~ **to kill** öldürmek amacıyla; in-'ten.tion *n.* niyet, maksat, amaç; meram, kasıt; evlenme niyeti; önem, ehemmiyet; yaranın kapanması; in-'ten.tion.al ☐ [‿ʃənl] kasıtlı, maksatlı, mahsus; in'ten.tioned *comb.* ...niyetli; **well-**~ iyi niyetli; in'tent.ness *n.* büyük dikkat, gayret, şevk, istek, arzu.

in.ter [in'tə:] *v/t.* gömmek, defnetmek, toprağa vermek.

in.ter... ['intə] *prefix* arasında, ortasında; karşılıklı, birbiriyle.

in.ter.act **1.** ['intərækt] *n.* THEAT perde arası, antrakt; **2.** [‿'ækt] *v/i.* birbirini etkilemek; in.ter'ac.tion *n.* birbirini etkileme.

in.ter.breed ['intəbri:d] (*irr.* **breed**) *v/i.* melez elde etm.; *v/t.* melezleştirmek.

in.ter.ca.lar.y [in'tə:kələri] *adj.* takvime eklenen (*ay, gün*); ilâve edilmiş ay *veya* günü olan (*yıl*); in'ter.ca.late [‿leit] *v/t.* araya eklemek (*gün*); ortasına ilâve etm.; in.ter.ca'la.tion *n.* araya ekleme; ortaya ilâve etme.

in.ter.cede [intə'si:d] *v/i.* aracılık etm., arasına girmek (**with** *ile*); in.ter'ced.er *n.* aracı.

in.ter.cept [intə'sept] *v/t.* durdurmak, engellemek; -*in* yolunu kesmek, yolda iken yakalamak; in.ter'cep.tion *n.* durdurma, yolunu kesme, engelleme; in.ter'cep.tor *n.* yol kesen kimse *veya* şey; MIL süratli avcı uçağı.

in.ter.ces.sion [intə'seʃən] *n.* iltimas, şefaat; başkaları için yalvarma, rica; inter'ces.sor [‿'sesə] *n.* iltimasçı kimse, başkaları için yalvaran kimse; in-ter'cesso.ry *adj.* başkaları için yardım isteyen.

in.ter.change **1.** [intə'tʃeindʒ] *v/t. & v/i.* değiş(tir)mek, mübadele etm., değiş tokuş etm.; **2.** ['‿tʃeindʒ] *n.* mübadele, değiştirme, değiş tokuş etme; in.ter'change.a.ble *adj.* birbiriyle değiştirilebilir.

in.ter.com.mu.ni.cate [intəkə'mju:nikeit] telefon sistemi.

in.ter.com.mu.ni.cate [intəkə'mju:nikeit] *v/i.* birbiriyle haberleşmek; 'in-ter.commu.ni'ca.tion *n.* birbirle haberleşme; ~ **system** = *intercom*; in-ter.com'mun.ion [‿njən] *n.* karşılıklı münasebet.

in.ter.con.nect ['intə'kə'nekt] *v/t.* birbiriyle birleştirmek.

in.ter.con.ti.nen.tal ['intəkɔnti'nentl]

adj. kıtalararası.

in.ter.course ['intəkɔːs] *n.* münasebet, ilişki; ticaret, iş, alışveriş; cinsi münasebet.

in.ter.de.pend.ence [intədi'pendəns] *n.* karşılıklı dayanışma; **in.ter.de'pend.ent** *adj.* birbirine bağlı olan, birbirine muhtaç.

in.ter.dict 1. [intə'dikt] *v/t.* yasak etm., yasaklamak, menetmek (**s.th. to s.o.** *bşi b-ne*; **s.o. from doing** *b-ni bş yapmaktan*); kilise ayinlerinden menetmek; **2.** ['intədikt], **in.ter'dic.tion** *n.* yasak(lama).

in.ter.est ['intrist] **1.** *n.* ilgi, merak; alâka, hobi, özel zevk; hisse, pay; COM faiz; ~**s** *pl.* kâr, kazanç; menfaat, çıkar; ~**s** *pl.* iktisadi hayatta hâkim grup; **in the ~ of** *-in* menfaatine, çıkarı için; **be of ~ to** *-in* çıkarına olm.; **take an ~ in** *-e* ilgi duymak, merak duymak; **return a blow with ~** daha kuvvetli bir yumrukla karşılık vermek; **banking ~s** *pl.* banka faizleri; **2.** *v/t. com.* ilgilendirmek, alâkadar etm.; merakını uyandırmak (**for s.o.** *b-nin*); **be ~ed in** *ile* ilgilenmek, ilgili olm.; *-e* merak duymak, meraklı olm.; ~ **o.s. in** *ile* ilgilenmek; '**in.ter.est.ed** □ ilgili, alâkalı (**in** *ile*); meraklı *-e*; '**in.ter.est.ing** □ ilgi çekici, ilginç, enteresan.

in.ter.face ['intəfeis] *n.* ortak yüzey.

in.ter.fere [intə'fiə] *vb.* karıştırmak, kurcalamak (**with** *-i*); karışmak, müdahale etm., burnunu sokmak (**in** *-e*); mâni olm., engel olm. (**with** *-e*); **in.ter'fer.ence** *n.* karışma, müdahale; parazit; PHYS girişim, karışım; engel, mâni; *spor:* obstrüksiyon.

in.ter.flow [intə'flou] (*irr.* **flow**) *vb.* içine akmak.

in.ter.fuse [intə'fjuːz] *v/t.* karıştırmak, katmak; kaplamak, istilâ etm., nüfuz etm.

in.ter.im ['intərim] **1.** *n.* aralık, fasıla; **in the ~** arada, aradaki zamanda; **2.** *adj.* geçici, muvakkat...; ~ **report** geçici rapor.

in.te.ri.or [in'tiəriə] **1.** □ içerdeki, içe ait, dahili, kıyıdan *veya* sınırdan uzak; manevî; ~ **decorator** iç dekoratör; **2.** *n.* iç, dahil; iç kısımlar; POL içişleri; **Department of the ♀** *Am.* İçişleri Bakanlığı.

in.ter.ja.cent [intə'dʒeisənt] *adj.* ortasında bulunan.

in.ter.ject [intə'dʒekt] *vb.* arasına kat-

mak (*söz*); **in.ter'jec.tion** *n.* ünlem, nida; söz arasına koyma; **in.ter'jec.tion.al** □ [~ʃənl] araya konulan (*söz*); ünlem şeklinde.

in.ter.lace [intə'leis] *v/t. & v/i.* birbiriyle ör(ül)mek, beraber doku(n)mak, karış(tır)mak.

in.ter.lard [intə'lɑːd] *v/t. fig.* doldurmak (*süslü sözlerle*); içine karıştırmak (*yabancı kelime*).

in.ter.leave [intə'liːv] *v/t.* kitabın yaprakları arasına eklemek (*boş sayfa*).

in.ter.line [intə'lain] *v/t.* orta astarı koymak (*elbiseye*); TYP yazının satırları arasına koymak (*başka yazı*); **in.ter.line.ar** [~'liniə] *adj.* satır aralarına yazılmış; **in.ter.lin.e.a.tion** ['~lini'ei-ʃən] *n.* satır aralarına yazılan yazı.

in.ter.link [intə'liŋk] *v/t. & v/i.* birleş-(tir)mek, birbirine bağla(n)mak.

in.ter.lock [intə'lɔk] *v/t. & v/i.* birbirine bağla(n)mak, kenetle(n)mek.

in.ter.lo.cu.tion [intələu'kjuːʃən] *n.* konuşma; **in.ter.loc.u.tor** [~'lɔkjutə] *n.* konuşan kimse, konuşmacı (*tartışmada*); **in.ter'loc.u.to.ry** *adj.* konuşmaya ait, konuşma...; JUR geçici...

in.ter.lope [intə'ləup] *v/i.* başkasının işine burnunu sokmak; COM başkalarının hakkına tecavüz etm.; '**in.ter.lop.er** *n.* başkasının işine burnunu sokan kimse; COM başkasının hakkına tecavüz eden kimse.

in.ter.lude ['intəluːd] *n.* ara faslı; perde arası, antrakt; ara, fasıla; ~**s of bright weather** geçici güzel hava.

in.ter.mar.riage [intə'mæridʒ] *n.* değişik aile, kabile, millet *vs.* arasında evlenme; **in.ter'mar.ry** *v/i.* değişik aileden, kabileden, milletten *vs.* birisi ile evlenmek.

in.ter.med.dle [intə'medl] *v/i.* karışmak, müdahale etm. (**with, in** *-e*); **in.ter'meddler** *n.* herşeye burnunu sokan kimse.

in.ter.me.di.ar.y [intə'miːdjəri] **1.** *adj.* aracılık eden, vasıta olan, arada bulunan; **2.** *n.* vasıta; ortada olan şey; COM aracı; **in.ter.me.di.ate** □ [~'miːdjət] ortadaki, aradaki; orta..., ara...; ~ **landing** AVIA ara iniş; ~**-range ballistic missile** orta menzilli roket; ~ **school** *Am.* ortaokul; ~ **stage** orta kademe, ara safha; ~ **trade** komisyonculuk.

in.ter.ment [in'təːmənt] *n.* ölüyü gömme, defnetme; defin.

in.ter.mez.zo [intə'metsəu] *n.* küçük

fasıl, aranağme.

in.ter.mi.na.ble □ [in'tə:minəbl] sonsuz, nihayetsiz, bitmez, tükenmez, sonu gelmez.

in.ter.min.gle [intə'miŋgl] v/t. & v/i. birbirine karış(tır)mak.

in.ter.mis.sion [intə'miʃən] n. aralık, fasıla, ara; antrakt; mola.

in.ter.mit [intə'mit] v/t. & v/i. dur(dur)-mak; ara vermek, tatil etm.; tatil olm.; **in.ter'mit.tent 1.** □ arada kesilen, aralıklı, kesik kesik; ~ **fever = 2.** n. MED sıtma; **in.ter'mit.tent.ly** adv. ara ara, kesik kesik, zaman zaman durarak, aralıklı.

in.ter.mix [intə'miks] v/t. & v/i. birbirine karış(tır)mak; **in.ter'mix.ture** [-tʃə] n. birbirine karış(tır)ma; karışım, karışmış şey; alaşım.

in.tern[1] [in'tə:n] v/t. enterne etm., gözaltına almak, hapsetmek, alıkoymak.

in.tern[2] ['intə:n] n. stajyer doktor, stajını yapan tıp öğrencisi.

in.ter.nal □ [in'tə:nl] iç, içe ait, dahilî, içinde bulunan; içilir (ilâç); bir ülkenin içişlerine ait; ~**com'bus.tion en.gine** içten yanmalı motor.

in.ter.na.tion.al [intə'næʃənl] **1.** □ uluslararası, milletlerarası, beynelmilel, enternasyonal; ~ **law** milletlerarası hukuk; **2.** n. POL ♀ uluslararası 4 sol kanat kurumundan herhangi biri; **in.ter.na.tion.al.ity** [-'næliti] n. beynelmilellik, enternasyonellik; **in.ter'na.tion.al.ize** [-nəlaiz] v/t. beynelmilel kılmak, milletlerarası kontrole sokmak, enternasyonelleştirmek.

in.terne ['intə:n] = **intern**[2].

in.ter.ne.cine war [intə'ni:sain'wɔ:] n. iki tarafa da büyük kayıplar verdiren savaş.

in.tern.ee [intə:'ni:] n. gözaltındaki (veya enterne edilmiş) kimse; tutuklu.

In.ter.net ['intənet] n. internet.

in.tern.ment [in'tə:nmənt] n. enterne edilme, gözaltına alınma, hapsedilme; ~ **camp** toplama kampı.

in.ter.pel.late [in'tə:pəleit] v/t. gensoru açmak; **in.ter.pel'la.tion** n. gensoru.

in.ter.phone ['intəfəun] n. AVIA Am. dahili telefon.

in.ter.plan.e.ta.ry [intə'plænitri] adj. gezegenlerarası.

in.ter.play ['intə'plei] n. karşılıklı etkileme.

in.ter.po.late ['intə:pəleit] v/t. katmak, ilâve etm., eklemek (metne); **in.ter-**

po'lation n. ekleme, ilâve etme, metni değiştirme.

in.ter.pose [intə'pəuz] v/t. arasına koymak, araya sokmak; ortaya atmak; v/i. araya girmek, karışmak, müdahale etm.; arabuluculuk yapmak; **in.ter-po.si.tion** [intəpə'ziʃən] n. araya girme, karışma, müdahale.

in.ter.pret [in'tə:prit] v/t. -in anlamını açıklamak, izah etm.; yorumlamak; tercüme etm.; v/i. tercümanlık yapmak; **inter.pre'ta.tion** n. yorum, tefsir, izah, açıklama, mana; **in'ter.pre.ta.tive** [-tətiv] adj. açıklayıcı, yorumlayıcı (of-i); **in'ter.pret.er** n. tercüman, çevirmen.

in.ter.ra.cial [intə'reiʃəl] adj. ırklararası.

in.ter.reg.num [intə'regnəm] n. hükümetin kanunen çalışmadığı devre; ara, fasıla.

in.ter.re.la.tion ['intəri'leiʃən] n. karşılıklı münasebet.

in.ter.ro.gate [in'terəgeit] v/t. sorguya çekmek; **in.ter.ro'ga.tion** n. sorgu, sorguya çekme; **note** veya **mark** veya **point of**~ soru işareti; **in.ter.rog.a.tive** [intə'rɔgətiv] **1.** □ sorulu..., soru sorar gibi, soru ifade eden..., soru...; **2.** n. GR soru kelimesi; **in.ter'rog.a.to.ry** [-təri] **1.** adj. soru belirten, soru türünden; **2.** n. yazılı olarak bildirilen resmi soru.

in.ter.rupt [intə'rʌpt] vb. kesmek, ara vermek -e, durdurmak, engellemek; b-nin sözünü kesmek; **in.ter'rupt.ed.ly** adv. aralıklarla; **in.ter'rupt.er** n. ELECT devre kesici, şalter; **in.ter'rup.tion** n. ara, fasıla, kesilme, engelleme.

in.ter.sect [intə'sekt] v/t. & v/i. kes(iş)-mek, ikiye bölmek; **in.ter'sec.tion** n. kes(iş)me, kavşak; RAIL kesişme hattı.

in.ter.space ['intə'speis] n. ara, aralık, fasıla.

in.ter.sperse [intə'spə:s] v/t. arasına serpmek, serpiştirmek; değişik hale sokmak (**with** ile).

in.ter.state Am. ['intə'steit] adj. eyaletlerarası.

in.ter.stice [in'tə:stis] n. yarık, çatlak, küçük aralık; **in.ter.sti.tial** [-'stiʃəl] çatlağa ait, çatlak..., yarık...

in.ter.tri.bal [intə'traibəl] adj. kabilelerarası.

in.ter.twine [intə'twain], **in.ter.twist** [-'twist] v/t. & v/i. birbiriyle ör(ül)-mek, birbirine sar(ıl)mak.

in.ter.ur.ban [intər'ə:bən] adj. şehirlerarası.

in.ter.val ['intəvəl] *n.* ara, fasıla, aralık; müddet, zaman; MUS es, enterval, aralık.

in.ter.vene [intə'vi:n] *v/i.* araya girmek, karışmak, müdahale etm.; arada bulunmak; diğer olaylar arasında olm.; **in.terven.tion** [ˌ'venʃən] *n.* araya girme, müdahale, karışma; aracılık.

in.ter.view ['intəvju:] **1.** *n.* görüşme, mülâkat; röportaj; **2.** *v/t.* görüşmek, röportaj yapmak '**in.ter.view.er** *n.* röportajcı, mülâkat yapan kimse.

in.ter.weave [intə'wi:v] (*irr.* **weave**) *v/t.* beraber dokumak, birbirine dokumak, birbirine karıştırmak (*a. fig.*).

in.tes.ta.cy JUR [in'testəsi] *n.* vasiyetsiz ölme; **in'tes.tate** JUR [ˌ'-tit] **1.** *adj.* vasiyetname bırakmadan ölmüş; **2.** *n.* vasiyetname bırakmadan ölmüş kimse.

in.tes.ti.nal ANAT [in'testinl] *adj.* bağırsaklara ait, bağırsak...; **in'tes.tine 1.** *adj.* iç..., içe ait; **2.** *n.* bağırsak; **~s** *pl.* bağırsaklar.

in.ti.ma.cy ['intiməsi] *n.* samimiyet, yakın dostluk, sıkı dostluk, içlidışlı olma, teklifsizlik; **in.ti.mate 1.** [ˌ'-meit] *v/t.* ima etm., üstü kapalı anlatmak, dolayısiyle anlatmak; açıklamak, ilan etm., bildirmek; **2.** ☐ [ˌ'-mit] sıkı fıkı, içten, candan, samimi, içlidışlı; gizli, mahrem; **3.** [ˌ'-mit] *n.* yakın dost, samimi arkadaş; **in.ti.ma.tion** [ˌ'meiʃən] *n.* ima, dolayısiyle anlatma; bildirme, haber verme; teklif, öneri.

in.tim.i.date [in'timideit] *v/t.* korkutmak, sindirmek, yıldırmak, gözdağı vermek; **in.tim.i'da.tion** *n.* gözdağı verme, yıldırma, korkutma.

in.to ['intu] *prp.* -e, -ye, içeri, -in içerisine.

in.tol.er.a.ble ☐ [in'tolərəbl] tahammül olunmaz, çekilmez, dayanılmaz; **in'tol.erance** *n.* hoş görmeme, taassup; **in'tol.erant** ☐ hoşgörüsüz, müsamahasız; tahammülsüz.

in.to.na.tion [intə'neiʃən] *n.* düz bir sesle okuma; MUS doğru ses perdesi, seslem, tonötüm; GR ses tonunun yükselip alçalma şekli, tonlama; **in.to.nate** ['ˌ-neit], **in'tone** *vb.* monoton bir makamla okumak; monoton bir sesle konuşmak.

in.tox.i.cant [in'tɔksikənt] **1.** *adj.* sarhoş edici; **2.** *n.* sarhoş edici içki; **in'tox.i.cate** [ˌ-keit] *vb.* sarhoş etm., mest etm. (*a. fig.*); **in.tox.i'ca.tion** *n.* sarhoş-

luk, mest olma (*a. fig.*).

in.trac.ta.bil.i.ty [intræktə'biliti] *n.* kolayca yola getirilememe, kolay kontrol edilememe; **in'trac.ta.ble** ☐ kolay yola getirilemeyen, kolay kontrol edilemeyen, ele avuca sığmaz.

in.tra.mu.ral ['intrə'mjuərəl] *adj.* bir bina içinde olan *veya* yapılan; okul içinde olan *veya* yapılan.

in.tran.si.gent [in'trænsidʒənt] *adj.* uzlaşmaz, uzlaşması olanaksız.

in.tran.si.tive [in'trænsitiv] ☐ GR geçişsiz, nesnesiz (*fiil*).

in.tra.state *Am.* [intrə'steit] *adj.* eyaletlerarası.

in.trench [in'trentʃ], **in'trench.ment** = **entrench** *etc.*

in.tre.pid ☐ [in'trepid] yılmaz, korkusuz, cesur, yiğit, gözüpek; **in.tre.pid.i.ty** *n.* yiğitlik, korkusuzluk, cesurluk, gözüpeklik.

in.tri.ca.cy ['intrikəsi] *n.* karışıklık, anlaşılmazlık; şaşırtıcılık; **in.tri.cate** ☐ ['ˌ-kit] karışık, anlaşılması zor, çapraşık; şaşırtıcı.

in.trigue [in'tri:g] **1.** *n.* entrika, hile, dolap, desise, dalavere; gizli aşk macerası; **2.** *v/i.* entrika çevirmek, dalavere yapmak, dolap çevirmek; *v/t.* merakını uyandırmak, ilgisini çekmek; **in'tri.guer** *n.* hilekâr (*veya* dalavereci, entrikacı, düzenbaz) kimse.

in.trin.sic, **in.trin.si.cal** ☐ [in'trinsik(əl)] aslında olan, esasi, asıl, hakiki; yaradılıştan.

in.tro.duce [intrə'dju:s] *v/t.* teklif etm., sunmak, öne sürmek, tanıştırmak, tanıtmak, takdim etm. (**to** -*e*); ortaya çıkarmak, ortaya koymak, getirmek (*yeni fikir*); öğretmek; sokmak, arasına koymak; **in.tro.duc.tion** [ˌ'dʌkʃən] *n.* takdim, tanıştırma; önsöz; başlangıç, giriş; *letter of ~* tavsiye mektubu; **in.tro'duc.tory** [ˌ-təri] *adj.* tanıtıcı, tanıtma maksadiyle yapılan.

in.tro.spect [intrə'spekt] *vb.* kendi düşünce ve hislerini tahlil etm.; **in.tro'spection** *n.* kendi düşünce ve hislerini tahlil etme; iç gözlem; **in.tro'spec.tive** ☐ [ˌ-tiv] kendi kendini tetkik kabilinden.

in.tro.vert 1. [intrə'və:t] *v/t.* içeri doğru çevirmek, kendi üzerine çevirmek (*düşünce*); **2.** ['intrəvə:t] *n.* içine kapanık (*veya* içedönük) kimse.

in.trude [in'tru:d] *v/t.* & *v/i.* zorla sok(ul)mak (**into** -*e*); davetsiz olarak girmek, izinsiz dalmak; kendini zorla kabul ettirmek (*upon s.o. b-ne*); ihlâl etm., bozmak (*upon -i*); in'trud.er *n.* davetsiz misafir; zorla sokulan kimse *veya* şey; *a.* ~ *aircraft* düşman uçağı.

in.tru.sion [in'tru:ʒən] *n.* içeri sokulma, zorla içeri girme; davetsiz olarak girme.

in.tru.sive □ [in'tru:siv] zorla içeri giren, izinsiz içeri giren; davetsiz olarak giren.

in.trust [in'trʌst] = *entrust*.

in.tu.i.tion [intju:'iʃən] *n.* sezgi, içine doğma, sezi; in'tu.i.tive □ [-tiv] sezgi yolu ile öğrenilen; sezgili.

in.un.date ['inʌndeit] *v/t.* sel basmak, su ile kaplamak; garketmek, boğmak; inun'da.tion *n.* sel, tufan; garketme, boğma.

in.ure [i'njuə] *v/t.* alıştırmak (*to -e*); in-'ure.ment *n.* alıştırma.

in.u.til.i.ty [inju:'tiliti] *n.* faydasızlık, lüzumsuzluk, yararsızlık.

in.vade [in'veid] *vb.* saldırmak, hücum etm. *-e*, istilâ etm. *-i*; *fig.* tecavüz etm. (*hak*); ihlâl etm. *-i*; in'vad.er *n.* saldırgan; istilâcı.

in.val.id¹ [in'vɑli:d] 1. *adj.* hasta, sakat, yatalak, zayıf; 2. *n.* hasta kimse; MIL, NAUT sakat (*veya* malûl) kimse; 3. *v/t.* MIL, NAUT çürüğe çıkarmak, hastaneye göndermek; hasta diye memleketine göndermek.

in.val.id² [in'vælid] *adj.* hükümsüz, geçersiz; in.val.i.date *v/t.* zayıflatmak, kuvvetten düşürmek; JUR hükümsüz kılmak, geçersiz saymak; in.val.i'da.tion *n.* hükümsüz kılma, geçersiz sayma; in.va.lidi.ty [invə'liditi] *n.* hükümsüzlük, geçersizlik.

in.val.u.a.ble □ [in'væljuəbl] paha biçilmez, çok kıymetli.

in.var.i.a.ble □ [in'veəriəbl] değişmez, sabit, daimi, sürekli, devamlı; in'var.i-a.bly *adv.* değişmeyerek, aynı şekilde, mütemadiyen, devamlı, her zaman.

in.va.sion [in'veiʒən] *n.* akın, saldırı, hücum, istilâ; JUR ihlâl, tecavüz (*of -i, -e*); MED nöbet, kriz; in'va.sive [-siv] *adj.* saldıran...; ihlâl eden, bozan (*of -i*); yayılan.

in.vec.tive [in'vektiv] *n.* küfür, sövüp sayma, hakaret, aşağılama.

in.veigh [in'vei] *vb.* çatmak, çıkışmak, sözle saldırmak (*against -e*).

in.vei.gle [in'vi:gl] *vb.* kandırmak, ayartmak, baştan çıkarmak, aldatmak,

cezbetmek, çekmek (*into -mesi için, -e*); in'vei.gle.ment *n.* aldatma, kandırma, baştan çıkarma.

in.vent [in'vent] *v/t.* icat etm., bulmak, keşfetmek; uydurmak, düzmek, atmak; in'ven.tion *n.* icat, buluş, keşif; uydurma, atma, yalan; in'ven.tive □ [-tiv] yaratıcı; in'ven.tive.ness *n.* yaratıcılık; in'ven.tor *n.* mucit, türeten kimse, yaratıcı kimse; in.ven.to.ry ['invəntri] 1. *n.* envanter, mal stoku, mevcut; mal sayımını gösteren defter *veya* liste, envanter defteri; 2. *v/t.* envanterini çıkarmak.

in.verse □ ['in'və:s] ters, ters çevrilmiş, tersyüz edilmiş; in'ver.sion *n.* ters dönme, altüst olma; ters çevirme; tersine dönmüş şey; değişim, değişme; homoseksüellik; GR cümledeki kelime sırasının değişmesi.

in.vert 1. [in'və:t] *v/t.* tersine çevirmek, tersyüz etm.; sırasını değiştirmek; ~ed commas *pl.* tırnak işareti; ~ed flight AVIA sırtüstü (*veya* ters) uçuş; 2. ['in-və:t] *n.* homoseksüel, sevici.

in.ver.te.brate [in'və:tibrit] 1. *adj.* omurgasız, vertebrasız; *fig.* zayıf iradeli, dayanıksız, kuvvetsiz; 2. *n.* omurgasız hayvan; *fig.* kuvvetsiz kimse.

in.vest [in'vest] *v/t.* yatırmak (*para*) (*in -e*); sarfetmek (*para, güç, zaman*); giydirmek; süslemek, donatmak (*with ile*); vermek (*yetki*); kaplamak, sarmak (*with ile*); MIL kuşatmak *-i*, çevirmek *-i*; *v/i.* ~ *in* F satın almak *-i*.

in.ves.ti.gate [in'vestigeit] *vb.* araştırmak, incelemek, tetkik etm., gözden geçirmek, teftiş etm., tahkik etm.; in-ves.ti'ga.tion *n.* araştırma, tetkik, inceleme, tahkik, teftiş; in'ves.ti.ga.tor [-geitə] *n.* araştırmacı.

in.ves.ti.ture [in'vestitʃə] *n.* resmen görevine getirme, tayin; in'vest.ment *n.* yatırma, para koyma, yatırım; resmen göreve getirme; yatırılan sermaye; MIL kuşatma, muhasara, çevirme; in'vest.or *n.* sermayedar, yatırım yapan kimse.

in.vet.er.a.cy [in'vetərəsi] *n.* yerleşme, kökleşme (*alışkanlık, duygu*); tiryakilik; in'vet.er.ate □ [-rit] kökleşmiş, yerleşmiş (*alışkanlık, duygu*); tiryaki, düşkün, müptelâ.

in.vid.i.ous □ [in'vidiəs] kıskandırıcı; kıskanç; iğrenç, tiksindirici, çirkin.

in.vig.i.late [in'vidʒileit] *vb.* gözcülük etm., nezaret etm.; in'vig.i.la.tor *n.*

gözcü, nezaretçi.

in.vig.or.ate [in'vigəreit] *v/t.* kuvvet vermek, kuvvetlendirmek, cesaret vermek, cesaretlendirmek, canlandırmak, zindelik vermek; **in.vig.or'a.tion** *n.* kuvvetlendirme, canlandırma.

in.vin.ci.bil.i.ty [invinsi'biliti] *n.* yenilmezlik, yılmazlık; **in'vin.ci.ble** □ yenilmez, yılmaz.

in.vi.o.la.bil.i.ty [invaiələ'biliti] *n.* dokunulmazlık; bozulmazlık; **in'vi.o.la.ble** □ dokunulmaz; bozulamaz, ihlâl edilemez; **in'vi.o.late** [‿lit] *adj.* şeref ve haysiyetine dokunulmamış; bozulmamış, ihlâl edilmemiş; kutsal sayılmış.

in.vis.i.bil.i.ty [invizə'biliti] *n.* görülmezlik; **in'vis.i.ble** □ görülmez, görünmez; ~ *mending* dokuma kumaşları gözle farkedilemeyecek kadar iyi onarma.

in.vi.ta.tion [invi'teiʃən] *n.* davet, çağrı, çağırma; davetiye; **in.vite** [in'vait] *v/t.* davet etm., çağırmak; istemek; cezbetmek, celbetmek; **in'vit.ing** *adj.* çekici, davetkâr, cezbedici.

in.vo.ca.tion [invə'keiʃən] *n.* dua, niyaz, Tanrı'ya yakarış; **in.voc.a.to.ry** [in'vɔkətəri] *adj.* dua kabilinden.

in.voice COM ['invɔis] **1.** *n.* fatura; gönderilen mal; **2.** *v/t.* faturasını çıkarmak, fatura etm.

in.voke [in'vəuk] *v/t.* yalvarmak -*e*, yakarmak -*e*, dua etm., -*e*; çağırmak -*i*, davet etm. -*i*; istemek -*i*, rica etm. -*i*; yerine getirmek -*i*, yürütmek -*i*; sebep olm. -*e*.

in.vol.un.tar.y □ [in'vɔləntəri] tasarlanmamış, istenilmeden yapılan; bilinçsizce yapılan.

in.vo.lute ['invəlu:t] *adj.* dolaşık, karışık, karmaşık, çapraşık, girift, girişik; girintili çıkıntılı (*dişli*); helezonî kıvrılmış; **in.vo'lu.tion** *n.* kıvırma, sarma; kıvrılmış şey; karışıklık, dolaşıklık, karmaşıklık; karışık herhangi bir şey; eski haline dönme.

in.volve [in'vɔlv] *v/t.* sarmak, kuşatmak; içine almak, ihtiva etm., kapsamak; sokmak, karıştırmak, bulaştırmak (*in* -*e*); gerektirmek, icap ettirmek; etkilemek, tesir etm.; **in'volved** *adj.* karmaşık, karışık, çapraşık, anlaşılması güç; **in'volvement** *n.* ilgi, alâka, bağlılık; sarılma; karıştırılma, bulaştırılma.

in.vul.ner.a.bil.i.ty [invʌlnərə'biliti] *n.*

yaralanamazlık, incitilemezlik; zaptedilemezlik; **in'vul.ner.a.ble** □ yaralanamaz, incitilemez; zaptedilemez, fethedilemez; *fig.* sağlam (*mevki*).

in.ward ['inwəd] **1.** *adj.* içerde olan, iç, dahilî (*a. fig.*); manevî, ruhsal; içe kıvrık; **2.** *adv.* = *inwards*; **3.** *n. fig.* maneviyat; ~*s pl.* iç organlar; **'in.ward.ly** *adv.* içte, içeride; akıl yoluyla, manen (*a. fig.*); **'in.ward.ness** *n.* içyüz, gerçek durum; maneviyat; **in.wards** ['‿z] *adv.* içe doğru; ruhun derinliğine doğru.

i.od.ic CHEM [ai'ɔdik] *adj.* iyot…, iyotlu…; **i.o.dide** ['aiədait] *n.* iyodür; **i.o.dine** ['‿di:n] *n.* iyot.

i.o.do.form CHEM [ai'ɔdəfɔːm] *n.* iyodoform.

i.on PHYS ['aiən] *n.* iyon.

I.o.ni.an [ai'əunjən] **1.** *adj.* İyonya *veya* İyonyalılara ait; **2.** *n.* İyonyalı.

I.on.ic [ai'ɔnik] *adj.* İyonik; İyonya'ya ait.

i.oni.c PHYS ['‿] *adj.* iyon…; **i.on.ize** PHYS ['aiənaiz] *v/t. & v/i.* iyonlaş(tır)mak.

i.o.ta [ai'əutə] *n.* Yunan alfabesinin dokuzuncu harfi, yota; çok küçük herhang bir şey.

I O U ['aiəu'juː] (= *I owe you*) size olan borcum; borç senedi.

ip.so fac.to ['ipsəu'fæktəu] *adv.* yalnız bu sebeple.

I.ra.ni.an [i'reiniən] **1.** *adj.* İran'a ait; **2.** *n.* İranlı.

i.ras.ci.bil.i.ty [iræsi'biliti] *n.* kızgınlık, huysuzluk, çabuk parlama; **i'ras.ci.ble** □ ['‿sibl] çabuk öfkelenir, sinirli, huysuz, çabuk parlar.

i.rate [ai'reit] *adj.* öfkeli, kızgın, hiddetli.

ire *poet.* ['aiə] *n.* öfke, hiddet, kızgınlık.

ire.ful □ ['aiəful] öfkeli, kızgın, tepesi atmış.

ir.i.des.cence [iri'desns] *n.* yanardönerlik; **ir.i'des.cent** *adj.* yanardöner, oynadıkça renk değiştiren, gökkuşağı gibi renkleri olan.

i.rid.i.um [i'ridiəm] *n.* iridyum.

i.ris ['aiəris] *n.* ANAT iris tabakası; BOT iris; ~ *diaphragm* PHOT iris diyaframı, ayarlı diyafram.

I.rish ['aiəriʃ] **1.** *adj.* İrlanda'ya ait; İrlanda diline ait; **2.** *n.* İrlandalı; İrlanda dili, İrlanda şivesiyle konuşulan İngilizce; *the* ~ *pl.* İrlanda halkı, İrlandalılar; **'I.rish.ism** *n.* İrlandalılara özgü kelime, deyim *veya* ifade; **'I.rish-**

man *n.* İrlandalı erkek; '**l.rish.wom.an** *n.* İrlandalı kadın.

irk [əːk] *v/t.* bıktırmak, usandırmak, canını sıkmak, bezdirmek.

irk.some ☐ ['əːksəm] bıktırıcı, usandırıcı, sıkıcı, bezdirici.

i.ron ['aiən] **1.** *n.* demir; *fig.* kuvvet, dayanıklılık; *a.* **flat-~** ütü; **~s** *pl.* pranga, zincir; **strike while the~ is hot** *fig.* demir tavında dövülür; **2.** *adj.* demirden yapılmış; demir gibi; *fig.* sağlıklı, dinç, sapasağlam; değişmez, sabit; merhametsiz, zalim, katı yürekli, taş kalpli; **3.** *v/t. & v/i.* ütüle(n)mek; demir kaplamak; zincirle bağlamak, prangaya vurmak; '**~bound** *adj.* engebeli, girintili çıkıntılı (*kıyı*); katı (*gelenek*); sert, haşin, şiddetli, kuvvetli; sabit; demirle takviye edilmiş; '**~clad 1.** *adj.* demir kaplı, zırhlı; kuvvetli, bozulmaz (*yemin, söz*); katı (*kural*); **2.** *n.* zırhlı gemi; **~ cur.tain** POL demirperde '**i.ron.er** *n.* ütücü; '**i.ron-found.ry** *n.* dökümhane, demirhane; '**iron-'heart.ed** *adj. fig.* taş kalpli, zalim, insafsız.

i.ron.ic, i.ron.i.cal ☐ [ai'rɔnik(əl)] alay eden, alaylı, cinaslı.

i.ron.ing ['aiəniŋ] **1.** *n.* ütüleme, ütü işi; ütülenen *veya* ütülenecek elbiseler; **2.** *adj.* ütü...; **~board** ütü tahtası.

i.ron...: **~ lung** MED susun akciğer; '**~mas.ter** *n.* demirci ustası; '**~mon.ger** *n.* demirci, hırdavatçı, nalbur; '**~mon.ger.y** *n.* demircilik, hırdavatçılık, nalburluk; demir eşya; '**~mould** *n.* pas lekesi; '**~.sides** *n. pl.* Cromwell'in süvari askerleri; '**~work** *n.* demir eşya; '**~works** *n.* MEC *mst sg.* demirhane, dökümhane.

i.ro.ny¹ ['aiəni] *adj.* demirden yapılmış, demire benzer.

i.ro.ny² ['aiərəni] *n.* alay, istihza; kötü tesadüf, cilve (*kaderin*).

ir.ra.di.ance, ir.ra.di.an.cy [i'reidjəns(i)] *n.* parlaklık, aydınlık; *fig.* şaşaa; **ir'ra.diant** *adj.* ışık saçan, ışıldayan, parlayan (**with** *ile*).

ir.ra.di.ate [i'reidieit] *v/t.* MED röntgen ışınlarına tutmak; aydınlatmak, parlatmak (**with** *ile*); *fig.* aydınlığa kavuşturmak (*bir konu*); **ir.ra.di'a.tion** *n.* aydınlatma, parlaklık; PHYS röntgen ışınlarına tutma; *fig.* aydınlığa kavuşturma.

ir.ra.tion.al ☐ [i'ræʃənl] akla uymaz, akılsız, mantıksız; yersiz, sebepsiz, münasebetsiz, saçma; MATH yadrasyo-

nel; **ir.ration.al.i.ty** [ˌ-'næliti] *n.* mantıksızlık, saçmalık, yersizlik.

ir.re.claim.a.ble ☐ [iri'kleiməbl] ıslah olmaz, akıllanmaz, yola gelmez.

ir.rec.og.niz.a.ble ☐ [i'rekəgnaizəbl] tanınamaz.

ir.rec.on.cil.a.ble ☐ [i'rekənsailəbl] uzlaştırılamaz, barıştırılamaz; uyuşmaz (*fikir, tutum*).

ir.re.cov.er.a.ble ☐ [iri'kʌvərəbl] geri alınamaz, telâfi edilemez; düzeltilemez; tahsili mümkün olmayan, tahsil edilemeyen.

ir.re.deem.a.ble ☐ [iri'diːməbl] ıslah olunamaz, çaresiz, düzeltilemez; nakde tahvil olunamaz; bedeli ödenerek kurtarılamaz.

ir.re.duc.i.ble [iri'djuːsəbl] *adj.* azaltılamaz, küçültülemez, ufaltılamaz (**in.to, to** *-e*).

ir.ref.ra.ga.bil.i.ty [irefrəgə'biliti] *n.* aksi iddia edilmezlik, inkâr edilemezlik; değişmezlik, sabitlik; kırılmazlık; **ir'ref.raga.ble** ☐ aksi iddia edilemez, inkâr edilemez, itiraz kabul etmez; değişmez, sabit (*kural*); kırılmaz, sert.

ir.ref.u.ta.ble ☐ [i'refjutəbl] inkâr edilemez, reddedilemez, itiraz kaldırmaz, su götürmez.

ir.reg.u.lar [i'regjulə] **1.** ☐ düzensiz, kuralsızı, nizamsız, intizamsız; usule aykırı, yolsuz, usulsüz; GR kural dışı; çarpık, düz olmayan, eğri; başıbozuk (*asker*); **2.** *n.* **~s** *pl.* başıbozuk asker, çeteci; **ir.reg.u.lar.i.ty** [ˌ-'læriti] *n.* düzensizlik, intizamsızlık, karışıklık, yolsuzluk, aykırılık.

ir.rel.a.tive [i'relətiv] *adj.* ilgisi olmayan, ilgisiz, alâkasız, konu dışı (**to** *ile*).

ir.rel.e.vance, ir.rel.e.van.cy [i'relivəns(i)] *n.* konu dışı olma; konu dışı olan şey; **ir'rel.e.vant** ☐ konu dışı, ilgisiz, alâkasız (**to** *ile*).

ir.re.li.gion [iri'lidʒən] *n.* dinsizlik; din aleyhtarlığı; **ir.re'li.gious** ☐ dinsiz, dine karşı olan.

ir.re.me.di.a.ble ☐ [iri'miːdjəbl] çaresiz, telâfi olunamaz, düzeltilemez; tedavisi mümkün olmayan.

ir.re.mis.si.ble ☐ [iri'misəbl] affolunamaz, bağışlanamaz; zorunlu, mecburi, kaçınılmaz.

ir.re.mov.a.ble ☐ [iri'muːvəbl] sabit, oynamaz; yerinden atılamaz, azlonulamaz.

ir.rep.a.ra.ble ☐ [i'repərəbl] tamir olunamaz, çaresiz, düzeltilemez, telâfisi imkânsız.

ir.re.place.a.ble [iri'pleisəbl] *adj.* yeri doldurulamaz; yenisi tedarik edilemez.

ir.re.press.i.ble □ [iri'presəbl] söndürülemez, bastırılamaz, baskıya gelmez; önüne geçilemez; kontrol edilemez, ele avuca sığmaz, zaptolunamaz.

ir.re.proach.a.ble □ [iri'prəutʃəbl] hatasız, kusursuz; **ir.re'proach.a.ble.ness** *n.* kusursuzluk, hatasızlık.

ir.re.sist.i.bil.i.ty ['irizistə'biliti] *n.* karşı konulamazlık; **ir.re'sist.i.ble** □ karşı konulamaz, dayanılmaz, çok çekici, pek cazip.

ir.res.o.lute [i'rezəluːt] *adj.* kararsız, mütereddit, zayıf; **ir'res.o.lute.ness**, **ir.reso'lu.tion** *n.* kararsızlık, tereddüt, zayıflık.

ir.re.solv.a.ble [iri'zɔlvəbl] *adj.* çözümlenemez, tahlil edilemez, analiz edilemez.

ir.re.spec.tive □ [iri'spektiv] **(of)** -e bakmaksızın; -i düşünmeden, -i hesaba katmayan, -i göz önünde bulundurmadan.

ir.re.spon.si.bil.i.ty ['irispɔnsə'biliti] *n.* sorumsuzluk, güvenilmezlik; **ir.re-'spon.sible** □ sorumsuz, mesuliyetsiz, güvenilmez.

ir.re.triev.a.ble □ [iri'triːvəbl] telâfi edilemez, bir daha ele geçmez, yeri doldurulamaz, karşılanamaz.

ir.rev.er.ence [i'revərəns] *n.* saygısızlık, hürmetsizlik; **ir'rev.er.ent** □ saygısız, hürmetsiz.

ir.re.vers.i.ble □ [iri'vəːsəbl] ters çevrilemez; değiştirilemez, geri döndürülemez, geri alınamaz, kesin, katî (*karar*).

ir.rev.o.ca.bil.i.ty [irevəkə'biliti] *n.* geri alınamazlık, değiştirilemezlik, feshedilemezlik; **ir'rev.o.ca.ble** □ değiş(tirile)mez, geri alınamaz, feshedilemez, gayri kabili rücu.

ir.ri.gate ['irigeit] *v/t.* sulamak; tazelendirmek; MED antiseptik su ile yıkamak (*yara*); **ir.ri'ga.tion** *n.* sulama.

ir.ri.ta.bil.i.ty [iritə'biliti] *n.* alınganlık, titizlik, havadan nem kapma, çabuk öfkelenme; **ir.ri.ta.ble** □ çabuk kızan, alıngan, titiz, sinirli; **ir.ri.tant 1.** *adj.* sinirlendirici, öfkelendirici; tahrik edici; tahriş edici; **2.** *n.* tahriş edici madde; sinirlendirici herhangi bir şey; **ir.ri.tate** ['ːteit] *v/t.* gücendirmek, kızdırmak,

sinirlendirmek; tahrik etm.; tahriş etm.; **'ir.ri.tat.ing** □ sinirlendirici, sinir bozucu, kızdırıcı; tahrik edici; tahriş edici; **ir.ri'ta.tion** *n.* sinirlilik, dargınlık, öfke, hiddet.

ir.rup.tion [i'rʌpʃən] *n.* içeriye baskın, hücum, akın, istilâ; **ir'rup.tive** [ːtiv] *adj.* baskın kabilinden.

IRS *Am.* ['aiɑːes] *n.* (= **Internal Revenue Service**) Vergi İdaresi.

is [iz] -dir, -dır, -tir, -tur (*s.* **be**).

i.sin.glass ['aiziŋglɑːs] *n.* balık tutkalı; mika.

Is.lam ['izlɑːm] *n.* İslâm; İslâm âlemi; İslâmiyet, Müslümanlık.

Is.land ['ailənd] *n.* ada, ada gibi yer; refüj; **'is.land.er** *n.* adalı (*veya* adada oturan) kimse.

isle [ail] *n. poet.* ada; **is.let** ['ailit] *n.* adacık.

ism *mst contp.* ['izəm] *n.* özel bir doktrin *veya* meslek.

isn't ['iznt] = **is not**.

i.so... ['aisəu] *prefix* aynı..., eşit...

i.so.bar METEOR ['aisəbɑː] *n.* izobar, eşbası.

i.so.late ['aisəleit] *v/t.* ayırmak, tecrit etm., yalıtmak, izole etm.; karantinaya almak; **'i.so.lat.ed** *adj.* tek, ayrı, ayrılmış, kendi başına olan, tecrit edilmiş, ücra, yalıtılmış; **i.so'la.tion** *n.* ayırma, tecrit, yalıtma, izole etme; karantinaya alma; **~ ward** karantina odası; **i.so'lation.ist** *Am.* POL [ːʃnist] *n.* tecrit politikası taraftarı, kendi memleketinin diğerlerinden ayrı hareket etmesi taraftarı.

i.sos.ce.les MATH [ai'sɔsiliːz] *adj.* ikizkenar...

i.so.therm METEOR ['aisəθəːm] *n.* eşsıcak, izoterm, eşsıcağı gösteren çizgi.

i.so.tope CHEM ['aisətəup] *n.* izotop.

i.so.type ['aisəutaip] *n.* (= diyagram, grafik.

Is.ra.el.ite ['izriəlait] *n.* İsrail kavminden bir kimse; **'Is.ra.el.it.ish** *adj.* İsrail kavmine ait.

is.sue ['iʃuː] **1.** *n.* boşalma, çıkış, gidiş; çıkış kapısı, boşalma yeri, yol, ağız, delik; JUR füru, çocuklar, torunlar, nesil, soy, döl; *fig.* sonuç, netice, son, nihayet, akıbet; JUR dava konusu olan ihtilâf, münakaşalı mesele, tartışma konusu, sorun; boşalma, akıntı, akış, cerahat; COM ihraç, emisyon, tedavüle çıkarma (*papa*); yayınlama, yayın, basım; sayı (*dergi*); dağıtım, tevzi, donatma; **~ of**

fact asıl sorun; ~ **of law** kanun konusu, hukuk meselesi; **force an** ~ zorla karar ver(dir)mek; **join (the)** ~ tartışmak, münakaşa etm. (**on** *konusunda*); **join ~ with s.o.** *b-le* tartışmak, münakaşa etm.; **be at** ~ tartışma konusu olm., üzerinde konuşulmak; **point at** ~ tartışma konusu, bahis konusu; **2.** *v/i.* çıkmak, dışarı akmak (**from** *-den*); meydana gelmek, ortaya çıkmak, doğmak, hâsıl olm.; basılıp yayınlanmak; hak olarak hissesine düşmek; sonuç vermek, sonuçlanmak, neticeye varmak, bitmek (**in** *içinde*); *v/t.* çıkarmak, dağıtmak; yayınlamak; vermek, ihraç etm.; com tedavüle çıkarmak (*para*); dağıtmak, tevzi etm. (**with** *-i*); **'is.sue-less** *adj.* çocuksuz, torunsuz.

isth.mus ['ismǝs] *n.* kıstak, berzah.

it [it] **1.** *pron.* o, onu, ona (*cinssiz*); *edattan sonra*: onun… (= **by it** onun ile; **for it** onun için); **how is ~ with…?** …nasıl?, …den ne haber?; *s.* **lord 2, foot 2, go** ~ F cesaret etm., yapmağa kalkmak, yeltenmek; **go ~!** hadi!, yürü!, atıl!; **we had a very good time of ~** doya doya tadını çıkardık; **2.** *n.* oyun: ebe; *sl.* önemli nokta.

I.tal.ian [i'tæljǝn] **1.** *adj.* İtalya, İtalyanlar ve İtalyanca ile ilgili; **2.** *n.* İtalyan; İtalyanca.

i.tal.ics TYP [i'tæliks] *n. pl.* italik; **i'tal-icize** [-saiz] *vb.* italik harflerle basmak.

itch [itʃ] **1.** *n.* MED kaşıntı, kaşınma; uyuz hastalığı; şiddetli arzu, özlem (**for** *için*, *-e*; **to** *inf.* *-meye*); **2.** *vb.* kaşınmak; *fig.* şiddetle arzu etm., özlem duymak, can atmak; **be ~ing to** *inf.* *-meye* can atmak; **have an ~ing palm** paraya düşkün olm., para canlısı olm.; **'itch.ing** *n.* kaşıntı, kaşınma; *fig.* şiddetli arzu, özlem; **'itch.y** *adj.* kaşıntılı, kaşınan.

i.tem ['aitǝm] **1.** *adv.* keza, dahi; **2.** *n.* parça, kalem, adet; bent, madde, fıkra; **3.** *vb.* not etm., kaydetmek; **it.em.ize** ['-maiz] *vb.* ayrıntıları ile yazmak.

it.er.ate ['itǝreit] *vb.* tekrarlamak, tekrar tekrar söylemek; **it.er'a.tion** *n.* tekrarla(n)ma, tekerrür; **it.er.a.tive** ['itǝrǝtiv] mükerrer, tekrarlanmış, yinelemeli.

i.tin.er.ant □ [i'tinǝrǝnt] dolaşan, gezgin, seyyar…; **i.tin.er.ar.y** [ai'tinǝrǝri] **1.** *n.* yol; yolcu rehberi; seyahat kitabı, seyahatname; seyahat programı; **2.** *adj.* yola (*veya* seyahate) ait, yol…, seyahat…; **i.tin.er.ate** [i'tinǝreit] *vb.* yolculuk etm., seyahat etm.; gezici vaizlik etm.

its [its] *adv.* onun(ki) (*cinssiz*).

it's F [its] = **it is, it has.**

it.self [it'self] *adv.* bizzat, kendi(si); **of ~** kendi kendine, kendiliğinden; **in ~** haddi zatında, aslında, başlı başına; **by ~** kendi kendine, otomatikman; yalnız başına, tek başına.

I've F [aiv] = **I have.**

i.vied ['aivid] *adj.* sarmaşık kaplı, sarmaşıklarla örtülü.

i.vo.ry ['aivǝri] **1.** *n.* fildişi; fildişi rengi; fildişinden yapılmış eşya; **2.** *adj.* fildişi…; fildişi renginde…

i.vy BOT ['aivi] *n.* sarmaşık.

J

jab F [dʒæb] **1.** *v/t.* dürtmek, itmek; ucu keskin bir şeyle dürtmek; **2.** *n.* dürtme, itme; *boks*: direk; F şırınga, iğne, enjeksiyon.

jab.ber ['dʒæbə] **1.** *vb.* hızlı konuşmak, çabuk çabuk konuşmak; anlaşılmaz şekilde söylemek; **2.** *n.* hızlı konuşma; anlamsız söz.

jab.ot ['ʒæbəu] *n.* kadın elbisesinin önüne takılan süslü fırfır.

Jack¹ [dʒæk] *n.* 'John' ismi; ~ Frost Ayaz Paşa, şiddetli ayaz; *before one could say ~ Robinson* çok hızlı *veya* ani, apansız.

jack² [~] **1.** *n.* kriko; adam, herif; denizci, gemici; hizmetçi, uşak, işçi; bocurgat, kaldıraç; erkek hayvan (*eşek*); NAUT cıyadra sancağı; beş taş oyunu; *iskambil*: vale, bacak; pot, ortada biriken para; *sl.* para, mangır; *sl.* polis memuru, aynasız; priz; elma rakısı; çakı; **2.** *v/t. a.* ~ *up* bocurgat ile kaldırmak, kriko ile kaldırmak.

jack.al ['dʒækɔːl] *n.* zoo çakal; *fig.* başkasının hesabına karanlık işler gören kimse.

jack.a.napes ['dʒækəneips] *n.* kendini beğenmiş kimse; yaramaz çocuk; 'jack.ass *n.* erkek eşek; *fig.* eşek herif, ahmak adam; 'jack.boots *n. pl.* eskiden süvarilerin giydiği dizi aşan çizme; 'jack.daw *n.* ORN küçük karga.

jack.et ['dʒækit] *n.* ceket; MEC kaplama, kılıf, gömlek, silindir ceketi; kitap zarfı, ciltli kitabın üstüne geçirilen kağıt kap; *dust s.o.'s ~* F *b-ni* dövmek, pataklamak; *potatoes in their ~s* kabuğu soyulmamış patates.

jack...: '~-in-of.fice *n.* kılı kırk yaran ukalâ memur; '~-in-the-box *n.* kutu açılınca içinden fırlayan yaylı kukla; ♀ Ketch cellât; '~-knife *n.* büyük çakı; '~-of-'all-trades *n.* elinden her iş gelen kimse, becerikli kimse, *on* parmağında on marifet olan kimse; ~-o'-lan.tern ['dʒækəulæntən] *n.* bataklık yakamozu; içi oyulmuş ve bir tarafına insan çehresi şekli verilmiş kabaktan oyuncak fener; '~-plane *n.* kaba planya, marangoz rendesi; '~-pot *n. poker*; pot, ortada biriken para; *hit the ~* Am. F tur-

nayı gözünden vurmak, büyük başarı kazanmak; ~ pudding maskara, soytarı, palyaço; ~ tar gemici, denizci; '~-tow.el *n.* el havlusu.

Jac.o.bin HIST ['dʒækəubin] *n.* Fransız ihtilâli sırasında örgütlenen ihtilâlci grupların üyesi; Jac.o.bite HIST ['~bait] *n.* 1685-1688 yılları arasında hüküm süren II. James yanlısı kimse.

jade¹ [dʒeid] **1.** *n.* yaşlı ve işe yaramaz beygir; *contp.* adı kötüye çıkmış kadın, cilveli kız; **2.** *v/t. & v/i.* çok yor(ul)mak, bitkin düş(ür)mek, ağır işler vererek yormak.

jade² MIN [~] *n.* yeşim, yeşil renkte değerli bir taş.

jag [dʒæg] **1.** *n.* diş, sivri uç, ok ucu, kanca; *sl.* sarhoşluk, ayyaşlık; içki âlemi; **2.** *vb.* diş diş etm., çentmek; 'jag.ged □, 'jag.gy dişli, çentikli, kertikli; *part. Am. sl. jagged* sarhoş, ayyaş.

jag.uar zoo ['dʒægjuə] *n.* jaguar.

jail [dʒeil] **1.** *n.* cezaevi, tutuevi, hapishane, kodes; **2.** *v/t.* hapsetmek, tutuklamak, hapse atmak; '~-bird *n.* hapishane gediklisi, mahkûm; ip kaçkını; pranga kaçağı.

jail.er ['dʒeilə] *n.* gardiyan.

ja.lop.(p)y *part. Am.* F MOT, AVIA [dʒə-'lɔpi] *n.* külüstür otomobil *veya* uçak.

jam¹ [dʒæm] *n.* reçel, marmelat.

jam² [~] **1.** *n.* sıkış(tırıl)ma; MEC kasılma, tekleme, kilitlenme; *radyo*: yayına karışan parazit; kalabalık, izdiham, sıkışıklık; zor durum, çıkmaz; *traffic ~* trafik sıkışıklığı; *be in a ~* *sl.* zor durumda olm., hapı yutmak, ayyayı yemek; ~ *session* caz müzisyenlerinin toplanarak müzik yapmaları; **2.** *v/t. & v/i.* sıkış(tır)mak; tık(ıştır)mak; *radyo*: parazit yapmak; MEC kasılmak, sıkışıp durmak, kenetlenmek; bloke etm., ~ *the brakes* frenleri kenetlemek, kasmak, kilitlemek.

Ja.mai.ca [dʒə'meikə] *n. a.* ~ *rum* Jamaika romu.

jamb [dʒæm] *n.* kapı *veya* pencere pervazı.

jam.bo.ree [dʒæmbə'riː] *n.* (*part. izcilerin yaptığı*) toplantı; *sl.* eğlenti, cümbüş, âlem, şamata, gırgır.

jam-jar ['dʒæmdʒɑː] n. reçel kavanozu.
jan.gle ['dʒæŋgl] **1.** vb. kavga etm., çekişmek, ağız münakaşası etm.; ahenksiz ses çıkarmak; ahenksiz bir şekilde söylemek; **2.** n. gürültü; ahenksiz ses; **'jangling** adj. tiz, cırlak, kulakları tırmalayan (ses).
jan.i.tor ['dʒænitə] n. kapıcı, odacı; Am. hademe.
Jan.u.ar.y ['dʒænjuəri] n. ocak (ayı).
Jap F [dʒæp] n. Japon.
Ja.pan [dʒə'pæn] **1.** n. laka, parlak ve sert cila, Japon verniği; **2.** v/t. Japon lakası ile cilalamak.
Jap.a.nese [dʒæpə'niːz] **1.** adj. Japonya'ya ait; **2.** n. Japon(yalı); Japonca; **the ~** pl. Japon halkı.
ja.pan.ner [dʒə'pænə] n. cilacı, vernikçi, lakacı.
jar¹ [dʒɑː] n. kavanoz.
jar² [_] **1.** n. sarsıntı, titreşim; şok; çatlak ses, bozuk ses; **2.** v/t. & v/i. sars(ıl)mak, titre(t)mek, salla(n)mak; çatlak ses çıkarmak, ahenksiz ses vermek; sinirlendirmek (upon -i); dokunmak (sinirine); tırmalamak (kulak); **~ with** ile uyuşmamak, -e uymamak.
jar.gon ['dʒɑːgən] n. anlaşılmaz dil veya söz; teknik lisan.
jas.min(e) BOT ['dʒæsmin] n. yasemin.
jas.per MIN ['dʒæspə] n. yeşime benzer bir taş.
jaun.dice ['dʒɔːndis] n. MED sarılık hastalığı; fig. sağduyuyu bozan hissi durum, kıskançlık, haset, gıpta; **'jaundiced** adj. sarılık olmuş; fig. kıskanç.
jaunt [dʒɔːnt] **1.** n. gezinti; **2.** v/i. gezmek; **'jaun.ti.ness** n. neşe; kibarlık; şıklık; **'jaunt.ing-car** n. iki tekerlekli hafif at arabası; **'jaun.ty** ☐ soylu, kibar; şık, gösterişli, fiyakalı; neşeli, canlı.
Jav.a.nese [dʒɑːvəˈniːz] **1.** adj. Cava'ya veya Cava diline özgü; **2.** n. Cava halkı veya dili; **the~** pl. Cava halkı, Cavalılar.
jave.lin ['dʒævlin] n. kargı, mızrak; spor: cirit; **throwing the ~** cirit atma.
jaw [dʒɔː] **1.** n. çene; **~s** pl. ağız; dar geçit, boğaz; MEC sap, çene; F konuşkanlık, gevezelik; sıkıcı konuşma; **2.** v/i. çene çalmak, gevezelik etm., laklak etm.; v/t. P verip veriştirmek, çıkışmak, dırlanmak; **'~-bone** n. çene kemiği; **'~-breaker** n. F telaffuzu zor kelime.
jay [dʒəi] n. ORN alakarga, kestane kar-

gası; F geveze kimse, lakırdıcı; **'~.walker** n. bir caddeyi trafik kurallarını çiğneyerek geçen kimse.
jazz [dʒæz] **1.** n. caz; caz müziği parçası; yalan, martaval, dümen; şey, zımbırtı, falan filan; **2.** adj. F göz kamaştırıcı, fiyakalı; **3.** v/t. caz türünde çalmak veya düzenlemek (şarkı); **~ up** canlandırmak, hareketlendirmek; **'~-band** n. cazbant, caz orkestrası; **'jaz.zy = jazz 2.**
jeal.ous ☐ ['dʒeləs] kıskanç, kıskanan (of -i); aşırı titiz, dikkatli; şüpheci; **'jealous.y** n. kıskançlık, haset.
jean [dʒiːn] n. bir çeşit kaba pamuklu bez; **~s** pl. blucin pantolon.
jeep [dʒiːp] n. cip.
jeer [dʒiə] **1.** n. alay, alaylı söz, taş, yuha; **2.** v/i. alay etm., eğlenmek, dalga geçmek (at ile); v/t. alaya almak, küçümsemek; **'jeer.er** n. alaycı kimse; **'jeering** ☐ alaylı, iğneli, taşlı.
je.june ☐ [dʒi'dʒuːn] yavan, anlamsız, manasız, kuru, sıkıcı, esp. Am. çocukça.
jell F [dʒel] v/t. & v/i. pelteleş(tir)mek, pelte gibi donmak; fig. şekillenmek, şekil almak.
jel.ly ['dʒeli] **1.** n. pelte, meyve özünden yapılmış jelatinli marmelat; jelatin; **2.** v/t. & v/i. pelteleş(tir)mek, pelte gibi donmak; **'~-fish** n. ZOO denizanası, medüz.
jem.my ['dʒemi] n. kısa demir çubuk, levye.
jen.ny MEC ['dʒeni] n. pamuk eğirme makinesi, çıkrık; **= spinning-~**.
jeop.ard.ize ['dʒepədaiz] v/t. tehlikeye atmak, tehlikeye koymak; **'jeop.ard.y** n. tehlike.
jer.bo.a ZOO [dʒɔː'bəuə] n. Asya ve Kuzey Afrika'da yaşayan tarla faresi.
jer.e.mi.ad [dʒeri'maiəd] n. yakınma, figan, feryat, dert yanma, can sıkıcı şikâyet.
jerk [dʒɔːk] **1.** n. ani çekiş, itme, başlama, duruş, bükme, kaldırma veya fırlatma; silk(in)me; büzülme, burkulma, gerilme; sl. aptal, ayı; **by~s** hamle ile; **physical ~s** pl. F jimnastik hareketleri, idman, beden eğitimi; **2.** vb. atmak, fırlatmak; kesik kesik söylemek; uzun parçalar halinde kesip güneşte kurutmak (et); birdenbire çekmek.
jer.kin ['dʒɔːkin] n. dar deri yelek.
jerk.wa.ter Am. ['dʒɔːkwɔːtə] **1.** n. banliyö treni; **2.** adj. F taşra...; küçük,

önemsiz; 'jerk.y 1. □ sarsıntılı; *sl.* aptal, salak, ahmak; 2. *n. Am.* güneşte kurutulmuş sığır eti.

jer.ry *sl.* ['dʒeri] *n.* MIL ♀ Alman askeri; lâzımlık, oturak; '~-build.er *n.* kötü malzeme kullanan inşaatçı; '~-build-ing *n.* kötü malzeme kullanarak inşa etme; '~-built *adj.* kötü malzeme kullanılarak yapılmış; ~ house kötü malzeme ile yapılmış (*veya* derme çatma) ev; '~.can *n.* benzin *veya* yağ bidonu.

jer.sey ['dʒəːzi] *n.* jarse; yün kazak; ♀ *n.* ZOO Jersey adasında bulunan sütü çok yağlı bir cins inek.

jes.sa.mine BOT ['dʒesəmin] *n.* yasemin.

jest [dʒest] 1. *n.* şaka, lâtife, alay; 2. *vb.* şakaya almak; hafife almak, yabana atmak; alaya almak; şaka söylemek; şaka etm.; alaylı konuşmak; 'jest.er *n.* şakacı, dalkavuk, soytarı.

Jes.u.it ['dʒezjuit] *n.* Cizvit; Jes.u'it.ic, Jes.u'it.i.cal □ Cizvit gibi.

jet[1] MIN [dʒet] *n.* siyah kehribar, kara amber, Erzurum taşı; simsiyah renk.

jet[2] [-] 1. *n.* fışkırma, püskürme; tepki; jet uçağı; jet motoru; MEC meme; ~ pro-pulsion jetle tepki, jetle çalıştırma; ~ set jet sosyete; 2. *v/t. & v/i.* fışkır(t)mak, püskür(t)mek; jet uçağı ile seyahat etm.

jet-black ['dʒet'blæk] *adj.* simsiyah, kapkara.

jet...: ~ en.gine jet motoru; '~ lag *n.* uçakla kısa bir süre içinde birçok saat dilimi geçmiş olmaktan kaynaklanan yorgunluk ve benzeri belirtiler; '~-plane *n.* jet uçağı, tepkili uçak; '~-pow.ered *adj.* tepki ile çalışan, tepkili.

jet.sam ['dʒetsəm] *n.* tehlike anında gemiyi hafifletmek için denize atılan mal; bu şekilde atıldıktan sonra karaya vuran eşya; flotsam and ~ denizin attığı enkaz; *fig.* serseriler, ayaktakımı.

jet.ti.son ['dʒetisn] 1. *n.* tehlike anında gemiyi hafifletmek için eşyayı denize atma; bu suretle denize atılan mal; 2. *v/t.* tehlike anında gemiyi hafifletmek için denize atmak (*eşya*); *fig.* feda etm.; 'jet.ti.son.a.ble *adj.* atılabilir türden, atılabilir...

jet.ty NAUT ['dʒeti] *n.* dalgakıran, set, mendirek; iskele, rıhtım.

Jew [dʒuː] *n.* Yahudi; *attr.* Yahudi...

jew.el ['dʒuːəl] 1. *n.* kıymetli taş, mücevher, cevher (*a. fig.*); 2. *v/t.* kıymetli taşlarla süslemek; 'jew.el(l)er *n.* kuyumcu; 'jew.el.ry, 'jew.el.ler.y *n.* kuyumculuk; *pl.* mücevherat.

Jew.ess ['dʒuːis] *n.* Yahudi kadın; 'Jewish *adj.* Musevi..., Yahudi...; Jew.ry ['dʒuəri] *n.* Musevi halkı; Yahudilik.

jib [dʒib] 1. *n.* NAUT flok yelkeni; MEC vinç kolu; the cut of his~ dış görünüşü; 2. *v/i.* aniden durmak (*at*); inat edip ileri gitmemek (*at*); *fig.* ayak diremek, dayatmak; ~ at -e isteksizlik göstermek, -i istememek, beğenmemek; 'jib.ber *n.* inat edip ileri gitmeyen at; 'jib'boom *n.* NAUT bumba, gemi bastonu.

jibe [dʒaib] *vb. Am.* F uy(uş)mak; = gibe.

jif.fy F ['dʒifi] *n.* an; in a ~ hemen, derhal, göz açıp kapayıncaya kadar.

jig [dʒig] 1. *n.* oynak ve hızlı bir dans, cig dansı; bu dansın müziği; MEC delme cihazı, cig; 2. *v/t. & v/i.* cig dansı yap(tır)mak; iki yana salla(n)mak; bir aşağı bir yukarı zıpla(t)mak.

jig.ger ['dʒigə] *n.* pire; kene, sakırga; *Am.* kokteyller için ölçü olarak kullanılan ufak cam bardak.

jig.gered F ['dʒigəd] *adj.: I'm ~ if ...* ...irse hayret doğrusu.

jig.gle ['dʒigl] *v/t. & v/i.* salla(n)mak.

jig-saw ['dʒigsɔː] *n.* makineli oyma testeresi; ~ puz.zle oyma testeresi ile kesilmiş tahta parçalarından ibaret bilmece.

jill [dʒil] = gill[3].

jilt [dʒilt] 1. *n.* sevgilisini reddeden kız; 2. *v/t.* reddetmek, yüzüstü bırakmak (*sevgili*).

Jim *Am. sl.* [dʒim] *n.:* ~ Crow zenci.

jim-jams *sl.* ['dʒimdʒæmz] *n. pl.* aşırı sinirlilik.

jim.my ['dʒimi] *n.* hırsızların kullandıkları demir çubuk.

jin.gle ['dʒiŋgl] 1. *n.* çıngırtı, şıngırtı; tekerleme gibi kelimeler; 2. *v/t. & v/i.* çıngırda(t)mak, şıngırda(t)mak; alliterasyon ve kafiyelerle dolu olm. (*mısra*).

jin.go ['dʒiŋgəu] *n.* şoven, savaş taraftarı; by~! *sl.* ya!, öyle mi!, vallahi!; 'jin-go.ism *n.* aşırı milliyetçilik.

jinks [dʒiŋks] *n. pl.: mst high~* eğlence, şamata, gırgır, cümbüş, tantana.

jinn [dʒin] = genie.

jinx *sl.* ['dʒiŋks] *n.* uğursuz şey *veya* kimse.

joker

jit.ney *Am. sl.* ['dʒitni] *n.* beş sentlik para; minibüs, dolmuş.

jit.ter F ['dʒitə] **1.** *v/i.* sinirli olm.; sinirli davranmak; **2.** *n.* **~s** *pl. sl.* aşırı sinirlilik; **have the ~s** heyheyleri üstünde olm.; **~.bug** ['-bʌg] **1.** *n. fig.* heyheyleri üstünde (*veya* şaşalamış, şaşkın) kimse; 1940'lı yılların hareketli ve popüler bir dansı; caz müziği delisi; **2.** *v/i.* deli gibi caz dansı yapmak; **'jit.ter.y** *adj. sl.* çok sinirli, heyheyleri üstünde; korkmuş.

jiu-jit.su [dʒuː'dʒitsuː] *n.* silahsız dövüş sanatı.

jive *Am. sl.* [dʒaiv] *n.* caz müziği; caz müziği argosu; yanıltıcı *veya* aptalca konuşma, gevezelik.

Job[1] [dʒəub] *n.*: **~'s comforter** sözde teselli etmeye çalışarak bir kimsenin sıkıntısını arttıran kimse.

job[2] [dʒɔb] **1.** *n.* iş, görev, vazife, memuriyet; hizmet; soygun; dalavere, hileli iş; COM parti malı; **by the ~** götürü usulü; **make a good ~ of it** *bşi* başarmak, üstesinden gelmek; **a bad ~** ümitsiz (*veya* kötü) şey *veya* durum; **~ lot** satın alınan çeşitli eşya; **~ printer** küçük matbaacı; **~ work** götürü iş; **2.** *v/t.* götürü usulü çalıştırmak; kira ile tutmak; aldatmak, dolandırmak; COM kâr amacıyla alıp satmak; kötüye kullanmak, suiistimal etm.; *v/i.* götürü iş yapmak; kişisel çıkarı için resmi işe girmek; komisyonculuk yapmak.

job.ber ['dʒɔbə] *n.* komisyoncu, simsar, tellal; götürü usulü çalışan kimse; resmi görevini suiistimal eden kimse; toptancı; **'job.ber.y** *n.* resmi işlerde dalaverecilik; **'job.bing** *n.* komisyonculuk; götürü usulü çalışma; *s.* **jobbery**.

jock.ey ['dʒɔki] **1.** *n.* cokey; **2.** *vb.* aldatmak, dolandırmak; cokey sıfatıyla binmek (*at*); işletmek, çalıştırmak; yerini değiştirmek.

jo.cose □ [dʒəu'kəus] şakacı, latifeci; komik, gülünç; şen, neşeli; **jo'cose.ness** *n.* şakacılık, latifecilik; komiklik.

joc.u.lar ['dʒɔkjulə] *adj.* şaka yollu, şaka türünden, şakalı; **joc.u.lar.i.ty** [-'læriti] *n.* şakacılık.

joc.und □ ['dʒɔkənd] neşeli, şen, hoş, keyifli, canlı.

Jodh.purs ['dʒɔdpuəz] *n. pl.* ata binerken giyilen pantolon, potur.

Joe [dʒəu]: **~ Miller** bayat espri.

jog [dʒɔg] **1.** *n.* sarsma, hafifçe itme, dürtme; tırıs yürüyüş; girinti *veya* çıkıntı; keskin viraj; **2.** *v/t.* sarsmak, itmek, dürtmek; canlandırmak (*hafıza*); tırıs yürütmek (*at*); *v/i. mst* **~ along, ~ on** yavaş yavaş gezinmek, bir tempoda ilerlemek; yavaş yavaş koşmak; **jog.ging** *n.* yavaş yavaş koşma, ağır ağır ilerleme.

jog.gle ['dʒɔgl] **1.** *v/t. & v/i.* hafifçe sars(ıl)mak, yavaşça salla(n)mak, MEC dişlemek, çentik açmak; **2.** *n.* sarsma, sallama; MEC geçme, dişli yiv.

jog-trot ['dʒɔg'trɔt] *n.* tırıs yürüyüş, yavaş yürüyüş; *fig.* lakaytlik, işi oluruna bırakma.

John [dʒɔːn]: **~ Bull** İngiliz milleti; tipik İngiliz; **~ Hancock** *Am.* bir kimsenin kendi el yazısı ile imzası.

join [dʒɔin] **1.** *v/t. & v/i.* birleş(tir)mek, bağlanmak, bitiş(tir)mek, kavuş(tur)-mak (**to -e**); MEC raptetmek; katılmak *-e* (*kulüp, parti, ordu*); evlendirmek **~ battle** savaşa girmek; **~ company** gruba katılmak (**with**); **~ hands** el ele tutuşmak; *fig.* birlik olm.; **~ in** katılmak *-e*; **~ up** askere yazılmak, orduya katılmak; üye kaydolunmak; **I ~ with you** ben senden tarafayım, sana katılıyorum; **2.** *n.* bitişim noktası; birleşme, bitişme.

join.er ['dʒɔinə] *n.* doğramacı, marangoz; **'join.er.y** *n.* doğramacılık, marangozluk.

joint [dʒɔint] **1.** *n.* ek; ek yeri; et parçası; batakhane; ANAT eklem, mafsal; BOT nod, düğüm, boğum; *Am. sl.* esrarlı sigara; **put out of ~** yerinden oynatmak, burkmak, çıkarmak (*kol, bacak*); **out of ~** çıkık; *fig.* çığrından çıkmış; **2.** □ birleşik, ortaklaşa, müşterek...; **~ heir** müşterek vâris; **3.** *v/t.* bitiştirmek, birleştirmek, eklemek; MEC raptetmek; **'joint.ed** *adj.* birleştirilmiş, bitiştirilmiş; mafsallı; **~ doll** parçalardan yapılmış oyuncak bebek; **joint stock** ana sermaye; **'joint-stock com.pa.ny** anonim şirket; **joint.ture** JUR ['-tʃə] *n.* bir kadına kocasının ölümünden sonra kalmak şartıyla bağlanan gelir.

joist [dʒɔist] *n.* kiriş.

joke [dʒəuk] **1.** *n.* şaka, latife, nükte; şaka konusu; **practical ~** eşek şakası; **2.** *v/i.* şaka yapmak, latife etm.; *v/t.* takılmak, şakadan aldatmak, alaya almak, eğlenmek (*about -e, -i, ile*); **jok.er** *n. iskambil:* koz, joker; şakacı kimse; *Am.* bir kanun tasarısına gizlice eklenen ve anlamını değiştiren madde;

herif, adam; 'jok.(e)y □ komik, gülünç, eğlendirici.

jol.li.fi.ca.tion F [dʒɔlifi'keiʃən] n. eğlence, gırgır, şamata, cümbüş, âlem; 'jol.li.ness, 'jol.li.ty n. neşe, zevk.

jol.ly ['dʒɔli] 1. □ şen, neşeli, keyifli, neşe dolu, sevinçli, memnun, mutlu; F hoş, güzel, sevimli, zarif, cazip; çakır-keyf; 2. adv. F çok, pek çok, fazlasıyla; 3. vb. F b-nin gönlünü yapmak, b-ni tatlı sözle kandırmak; eğlenmek, alay etm., takılmak.

jol.ly-boat NAUT ['dʒɔlibəut] n. küçük filika.

jolt [dʒəult] 1. v/t. & v/i. sars(ıl)mak; 2. n. sarsıntı, sarsma; sürpriz, şok; 'jolt.y adj. sarsıntılı.

Jon.a.than ['dʒɔnəθən]: Brother ~ Amerikalı.

jon.quil BOT ['dʒɔŋkwil] n. fulya, zerrin.

jo.rum ['dʒɔːrəm] n. büyük içki kabı; bu kabın içindeki içki (esp. punç).

josh Am. sl. [dʒɔʃ] 1. n. şaka, takılma; 2. v/t. alay etm., takılmak; v/i. şaka yapmak.

joss [dʒɔs] n. Çin tanrısı; '~-house n. Çin mabedi, Çin tapınağı.

jos.tle ['dʒɔsl] 1. vb. itip kakmak, it-(tir)mek, dürtüklemek; 2. n. itip kakma, iteleme.

jot [dʒɔt] 1. n. zerre, pek az şey, az miktar; 2. v/t. ~ down yazıvermek, not almak; 'jot.ter n. not defteri; 'jot.tings n. pl. alınan notlar.

jour.nal ['dʒɔːnl] n. gazete, dergi; COM yevmiye defteri; NAUT seyir defteri; günlük, muhtıra; meclis zabıt defteri; MEC mil ucu, mihver mili; jour.nal.ese F ['_nəˈliːz] n. gazeteci üslubu, gazeteci ağzı; 'journal.ism n. gazetecilik; 'jour.nal.ist n. gazeteci; jour.nal'is.tic adj. (~ally) gazeteciliğe ait, gazeteci-lik...; 'jour.nal.ize vb. COM yevmiye defterine geçirmek; COM yevmiye defteri tutmak; günlük tutmak; gazeteci-lik yapmak.

jour.ney ['dʒɔːni] 1. n. yolculuk, seyahat, gezi, sefer, yol; 2. v/i. yolculuk etm.; '~.man n. usta, kalfa; '~work n. usta işi.

joust [dʒaust] 1. n. at üstünde yapılan mızrak dövüşü; 2. v/i. at üstünde mızrak dövüşü yapmak; polemiğe girmek.

Jove [dʒəuv] n. Jupiter, baş tanrı; by ~! Allah Allah!, yok ya!

jo.vi.al □ ['dʒəuvjəl] şen, neşeli, keyifli;

jo.vi.al.i.ty [_vi'æliti] n. şenlik, neşe, keyif.

jowl [dʒaul] n. çene; gıdık; gerdan; cheek by ~ sıkı fıkı; yana yana.

joy [dʒɔi] n. sevinç, neşe, keyif, haz, memnuniyet; joy.ful □ ['_ful] neşeli, sevinçli, keyifli, neşe dolu, memnun; 'joy.fulness n. neşelilik, sevinçlilik, keyiflilik; 'joy.less □ neşesiz, keyifsiz, kederli, üzgün, tasalı; 'joy.ous □ sevinçli, keyifli, neşeli; 'joy-ride n. sl. çalıntı araba ile zevk için yapılan gezinti; 'joy-stick n. AVIA sl. manevra kolu, kumanda levyesi.

jpeg ['dʒeipeg] n. Jpeg (bir tür grafik dokümanı).

ju.bi.lant ['dʒuːbilənt] adj. büyük neşe içinde, çok memnun, sevinçli, coşkulu; zafer sarhoşu; ju.bi.late ['_leit] v/i. coşmak, çok sevinmek; ju.bi'la.tion n. çok sevinme, coşma; ju.bi.lee ['_liː] n. yıldönümü şenliği; ellinci yıldönümü; neşeli kutlama, jübile.

Ju.da.ism ['dʒuːdeiizəm] n. Yahudilik.

Ju.das ['dʒuːdəs] n. fig. hain, asi; a. 2--hole gözetleme deliği.

judge [dʒʌdʒ] 1. n. hâkim, yargıç; hakem; bilirkişi; Yahudilerde krallardan önce geçici hükümdarlık yetkisi verilen hâkim; 2. vb. bş hakkında fikir edinmek; bir davayı çözmek; hâkimlik yapmak; bir hükme varmak (from, by -den; of hakkında); yargılamak, muhakeme etm.; hüküm vermek (by -den); eleştirmek, tenkit etm.; karar vermek (hakkında).

judg(e).ment ['dʒʌdʒmənt] n. hüküm, yargı, karar; mahkeme kararı, bildiri, tebligat; muhakeme, yargılama; fikir, düşünce; Allah tarafından verilen ceza; in my ~ bence, bana kalırsa, kanımca; pronounce ~ kararı bildirmek; sit in ~ duruşma yapmak; come to ~ kararavarmak; Day of 2, 2-Day kıyamet günü, hüküm günü.

judge.ship ['dʒʌdʒʃip] n. hâkimlik, yargıçlık.

ju.di.ca.ture ['dʒuːdikətʃə] n. yargılama; hâkimler kurulu; mahkeme; yargılama işlemi.

ju.di.cial □ [dʒuː'diʃəl] mahkemeye ait, adlî, hukukî; hâkime ait; şer'î; ~ murder mahkeme kararı ile fakat haksız yere ölüm cezası; ~ system hukuk sistemi.

ju.di.ci.a.ry [dʒuː'diʃiəri] adj. adlî, hukukî.

ju.di.cious ☐ [dʒuː'diʃəs] akıllı, tedbr-
li; sağgörülü; **ju'di.cious.ness** *n.* sağ-
görülülük, basiretlilik.
ju.do ['dʒuːdəu] *n. spor.* judo.
jug [dʒʌg] **1.** *n.* testi, çömlek; *sl.* hapishane, kodes; **2.** *v/t.* çömlekte haşlamak; *sl.* kodese tıkmak; **~ged hare**
haşlanmış tavşan.
Jug.ger.naut *fig.* ['dʒʌgənɔːt] *n.* put,
sanem; insanın kendisini körü körüne
feda etmesini gerektiren inanç.
jug.gins F ['dʒʌginz] *n.* pısırık (*veya*
sünepe, sümsük) kimse.
jug.gle ['dʒʌgl] **1.** *n.* hokkabazlık; hile,
aldatmaca; **2.** *vb.* hokkabazlık yapmak; hile yapmak; aldatmak; *fig.*
carpıtmak, olduğundan değişik göstermek; mahrum etm. (**out of** *-den*); 'juggler *n.* hokkabaz, jonglör; hilekâr kimse, dolandırıcı; 'juggler.y *n.* hokkabazlık; hile.
Ju.go.slav ['juːgəu'slaːv] **1.** *n.* Yugos-
lav(yalı); **2.** *adj.* Yugoslav…
jug.u.lar ANAT ['dʒʌgjulə] *adj.* boyna
ait, boyun…; **~ vein** şahdamarı; ju.gu-
late *fig.* ['_leit] *v/t.* durdurmak, önüne
geçmek, önlemek.
juice [dʒuːs] *n.* özsu, usare; sebze, meyve *veya* et suyu; insan vücudunun sıvı
kısımları; MOT *sl.* benzin; ELECT *sl.* elektrik, cereyan; kuvvet, güç; 'juic.i.ness
n. özlülük, sululuk; 'juic.y ☐ özlü, sulu; F ilginç, enteresan, merak
uyandırıcı.
ju.jube ['dʒuːdʒuːb] *n.* BOT hünnap;
PHARM hünnap şekerlemesi.
ju-jut.su [dʒuː'dʒutsuː] *n.* silahsız dövüş sanatı.
juke-box *Am.* F ['dʒuːkbɔks] *n.* para ile
çalışan müzik dolabı, otomatik pikap.
ju.lep ['dʒuːlep] *n.* ilâca karıştırılan
tatlı bir sıvı; *part. Am.* buzlu ve naneli
içki.
Ju.ly [dʒuː'lai] *n.* temmuz.
jum.ble ['dʒʌmbl] **1.** *n.* karmaşa,
karışıklık, karmakarışık iş; **2.** *vb. a.* **~
up** karmakarışık etm.; karmakarışık
olm.; '**~-sale** *n.* eski *veya* elden düşme
malların birarada satışı (*yardım için*).
jump [dʒʌmp] **1.** *n.* atlama, sıçrama,
zıplama; irkilme; fırlama, yükselme,
artış (*fiyat*); **~s** *pl.* sinirlilik; **high
(long)** **~** yüksek (uzun) atlama; **get
(have) the ~ on** *Am.* F *-den* önce davranmak; **give a ~** korkutmak, ürkütmek; **2.** *v/t. & v/i.* atla(t)mak, sıçra(t)-
mak, zıpla(t)mak, fırla(t)mak, üzerin-

den atla(t)mak; içine atlamak, binmek (*tren, taksi*); geçivermek (*konudan konuya*); küt küt atmak (*kalp*);
fig. aniden fırlamak (*fiyat*); **~ at** hemen
kabul etm., *-e* dünden razı olm.; **~ to
conclusions** acele hüküm vermek,
hemen karara varmak; **~ on**, **~ upon**
saldırmak; azarlamak, çatmak, paylamak; **~ the queue** *bşi* haksız yere elde
etm., başkasının sırasını kapmak;
'jump.er *n.* atlayıcı, sıçrayan kimse,
hayvan *veya* böcek; kazak; çocuk önlüğü, göğüslük; 'jump.ing-'off *n.* başlangıç; 'jump.y *adj.* sinirli, diken üstünde.
junc.tion ['dʒʌŋkʃən] *n.* birleşme, bitişme; birleşme yeri, kavşak; RAIL makas, iki demiryolunun birleştiği yer; **~
box** ELECT bağlantı kutusu, buat;
junc.ture ['_tʃə] *n.* birleşme yeri; bitişme, bağlantı; nazik zaman, önemli an;
at this ~ bu kritik durumda.
June [dʒuːn] *n.* haziran.
jun.gle ['dʒʌŋgl] *n.* orman, cengel.
jun.ior ['dʒuːnjə] **1.** *adj.* yaşça küçük;
ast; küçük (*babasıyla aynı ismi taşı-
yanın ismine eklenir*); *Am.* UNIV üçüncü sınıfa ait; **~ high school** *Am.* ortaokul (*7.8. ve 9. sınıfları kapsayan*); **~
partner** ikinci derecede ortak; **2.** *n.*
yaş, mevki *veya* kıdemce küçük kimse;
Am. lise *veya* üniversitede üçüncü
sınıf öğrencisi; erkek evlât, oğul; F küçük boy (*elbise vs.*); **he is my ~ by four
years, he is four years my ~** benden
dört yaş küçüktür; **jun.ior.i.ty** [dʒuːn-
i'ɔriti] *n.* yaşça küçüklük; astlık.
ju.ni.per BOT ['dʒuːnipə] *n.* ardıç.
junk¹ NAUT [dʒʌŋk] *n.* altı düz ve yelkenli Çin gemisi.
junk² [_] *n.* pılı pırtı, çöp; hurda.
jun.ket ['dʒʌŋkit] **1.** *n.* kesilmiş sütten
yapılmış bir çeşit kaymak; *Am.* ziyafet;
piknik; **2.** *vb.* ziyafet vermek; ziyafete
katılmak.
junk food P ['dʒʌŋkfuːd] *n.* gıdasal
değeri az abur cubur.
jun.ta ['dʒʌntə] *n.* cunta; **jun.to** ['_təu]
n. amaçları ortak olan grup, klik.
ju.rid.i.cal ☐ [dʒuə'ridikəl] *adli*, hukukî, kanunî…
ju.ris.dic.tion [dʒuəris'dikʃən] *n.*
yargılama hakkı; yetki, salâhiyet; nüfuz dairesi, kaza dairesi; **ju.ris.pru-
dence** ['_pruːdəns] *n.* hukuk ilmi; '**ju-
ris.pru.dent** *n.* hukuk uzmanı, hukukçu.

ju.rist ['dʒuərist] *n.* hukuk uzmanı, hukukçu.

ju.ror JUR ['dʒuərə] *n.* jüri üyesi.

ju.ry JUR ['dʒuəri] *n.* jüri; '**ju.ry-box** *n.* mahkemede jürinin oturduğu yer; '**ju.ry.man** *n.* jüri üyesi.

ju.ry-mast NAUT ['dʒuərimɑːst] *n.* yedek (*veya* geçici) direk.

just [dʒʌst] **1.** *adj.* ☐ âdil, haklı, insaflı, haktanır, doğru; akla yakın, makûl, mantıkî; **2.** *adv.* sadece, yalnız; tam, tam tamına, kesin olarak; hemen; şimdi, biarz önce, az evvel; neredeyse; güçbelâ, darı darına; çok, epey; ~ **now** hemen şimdi; az evvel, biraz önce; ~ **over** (*below*) hemen yukarıda (aşağıda); ~ **let me see!** bir bakayım!; **it's ~ splendid!** harika!

jus.tice ['dʒʌstis] *n.* adalet, hak, insaf; hâkim, yargıç; doğruluk, dürüstlük; ♀ **of the Peace** sulh hâkimi; **court of ~** sulh mahkemesi; **do ~ to s.o.** *b-nin* hakkını gözetmek, *b-ne* âdil davranmak; **do o.s. ~** elinden geleni yapmak; '**jus.tice.ship** *n.* hâkimlik.

jus.ti.fi.a.bil.i.ty [dʒʌstifaiə'biliti] *n.* haklı olma; '**jus.ti.fi.a.ble**☐ doğruluğu ispatlanabilir, haklı çıkarılabilir, savunulabilir.

jus.ti.fi.ca.tion [dʒʌstifi'keiʃən] *n.*

haklı çık(ar)ma; mazur gösterme; mazeret, sebep; **jus.ti.fi.ca.to.ry** ['~təri] *adj.* haklı çıkaran, mazur gösteren.

jus.ti.fi.er TYP ['dʒʌstifaiə] *n.* satır düzenleyici; '**jus.ti.fy** *v/t.* haklı çıkarmak, doğrulamak; temize çıkarmak; TYP düz olarak ayarlamak (*yazının sağ kenarını*).

just.ly ['dʒʌstli] *adv.* haklı olarak.

just.ness ['dʒʌstnis] *n.* hak; haklılık, adalet; doğruluk, dürüstlük (*s. just 1*).

jut [dʒʌt] **1.** *v/i. a.* ~ **out** dışarı çıkmış olm.; çıkıntı yapmak; **2.** *n.* çıkıntı.

Jute¹ [dʒuːt] *n.* beşinci yüzyılda İngiltere'yi istilâ eden bir Germen kabilesinden olan kimse.

jute² BOT [~] *n.* hintkeneviri; bu bitkiden çıkarılan elyaf.

ju.ve.nes.cence [dʒuːvi'nesns] *n.* gençleşme; **ju.ve'nes.cent** *adj.* gençleşen; gençleştirici; **ju.ve.nile** ['~nail] **1.** *adj.* genç; gençlikle ilgili, gençliğe özgü; ♀ **Court** çocuk mahkemesi; ~ **delinquency** çocuğun suç işlemesi; **2.** *n.* genç kimse, çocuk; **ju.ve.nil.i.ty** [~'niliti] *n.* gençlik, gençler; olgunlaşmamış birinin davranışı.

jux.ta.po.si.tion [dʒʌkstəpə'ziʃən] *n.* yanyana koyma; bitişiklik, bitişme.

K

Ka(f).fir ['kæfə] *n.* Afganistan'da Kâfiristan halkından biri; Güney Afrika'da Bantu kabilesinden olan kimse; ~**s** *pl.* COM *sl.* Güney Afrika'ya ait altın madeni hisseleri.

kale [keil] *n.* bir çeşit kıvırcık yapraklı lahana; *Am. sl.* para, mangır.

ka.lei.do.scope OPT [kə'leidəskəup] *n.* çiçek dürbünü, kaleydoskop.

kal.ends ['kælendz] = **calends**.

kan.ga.roo ZOO [kæŋɡə'ruː] *n.* kanguru.

ka.o.lin MIN ['keiəlin] *n.* arıkil, kaolin.

ka.pok ['keipɔk] *n.* sıcak memleketlere özgü yumuşak pamuksu lif.

ka.put *sl.* [kæ'puːt] *adj.* mahvolmuş; harap olmuş.

ka.yak ['kaiæk] *n.* Eskimo balıkçı kayığı; küçük kano.

keck [kek] *vb.* öğürmek; iğrenmek, tiksinmek (**at** *-den*).

kedge NAUT [kedʒ] **1.** *n.* tonoz çapası; **2.** *vb.* tonoz çapasına bağlı yoma ile yürütmek (*gemi*).

ked.ge.ree [kedʒə'riː] *n.* balık, yumurta *vs.* ile pişirilen pilav.

keel NAUT [kiːl] **1.** *n.* gemi omurgası; **on an even** ~ dengede (*gemi*); *fig.* muntazam, düzenli; **2.** *v/i.* ~ **over** alabora olm.; *v/t.* devirmek, yana yatırmak (*gemi*); '**keelage** *n.* NAUT liman resmi; **keel-haul** NAUT ['~hɔːl] *v/t. b-ni* ceza olarak geminin altından geçirmek; şiddetle azarlamak, haşlamak; **keel.son** NAUT ['kelsn] *n.* geminin iç omurgası.

keen¹ ☐ [kiːn] keskin, sivri; şiddetli, sert; zeki, akıllı; kuvvetli, canlı, yoğun; hassas; şahane; ~ **on** F düşkün, meraklı, hevesli -*e*; **be** ~ **on hunting** avcılığa meraklı olm.

keen² *Ir.* [~] *n.* ağıt.

keen-edged ['kiːnedʒd] *adj.* keskin kenar -*lı*; '**keen.ness** *n.* keskinlik; düş-künlük; akıllılık.

keep [ki:p] **1.** *n.* geçim; HIST kale, hisar; zindan, hapishane; himaye; *for*~*s* F temelli olarak, her zaman için, ebediyen; **2.** (*irr.*) *v/t. com.* tutmak, korumak, himaye etm., saklamak, muhafaza etm.; yerine getirmek; sürdürmek, devam ettirmek; yönetmek, işletmek; beslemek, bakmak, geçindirmek; ücretle tutmak; geri tutmak, alıkoymak; biriktirmek, bir kenara ayırmak; elde tutmak; ~ *s.o. company b-ne* refakat etm.; ~ *company with ile* arkadaşlık etm.; ~ *silence* susmak; ~ *one's temper k-ne* hâkim olm.; ~ *time* doğru işlemek, doğru gitmek (*saat*); MUS tempo tutmak; MIL aynı adımlarla yürümek; ~ *s.o. waiting b-ni* bekletmek; ~ *away* uzak tutmak; ~ *down* baskı yapmak; kontrol altına almak; kısıtlamak, sınırlamak; ~ *s.o. from b-ni -den* alıkoymak; ~ *s.th. from s.o. bşi b-den* saklamak; ~ *in* yanmaya devam etm. (*ates*); içeride tutmak, alıkoymak, saklamak; ~ *in money* parayı idare etm.; ~ *in view* gözönünde bulundurmak; ~ *off* uzak tutmak (*from -den*); ~ *on* çıkarmamak (*elbise*); söndürmemek; devam etm.; ~ *out* yaklaştırmamak, uzak tutmak, çıkarmak; ~ *up* korumak; devam ettirmek; sürdürmek; *b-ni* ayakta tutmak; toplamak (*cesaret*); ~ *it up* dayanmak; **3.** (*irr.*) *v/i.* F oturmak, yaşamak; devam etm., sürüp gitmek; kalmak, durmak; açık olm. (*okul*); geri durmak, *k-ni* alıkoymak; ~ *doing* yapmaya devam etm.; ~ *away* uzak durmak; ~ *clear of -den* uzak durmak, kaçınmak, sakınmak; ~ *from -den* uzak durmak; ~ *in with ile* iyi geçinmek, dost kalmak; ~ *off* uzak kalmak; ~ *on* devam etm.; ~ *on talking* konuşmaya devam etm., konuşmayı sürdürmek; ~ *on at s.o. b-ni* sıkboğaz etm.; ~ *to -e* sadık olm., -*e* bağlı kalmak; ~ *up* ayakta durmak; ~ *up with* -*de* geri kalmamak, -*e* ayak uydurmak; ~ *up with the Joneses* komşularıyla rekabet etm.; toplumsal değişmelere ayak uydurmak.

keep.er ['ki:pə] *n.* bakıcı; bekçi; gardiyan; '**keep.ing** *n.* koruma, tutma, muhafaza etme, bakım; geçim; *be in* (*out of*) ~ *with* -*e* uygun ol(ma)mak; **keep.sake** ['~seik] *n.* hatıra, andaç, yadigâr.

keg [keg] *n.* küçük fıçı, varil.

kelp BOT [kelp] *n.* büyük deniz yosunu, varek.

kel.son NAUT ['kelsn] = *keelson*.

ken [ken] *n.* bilgi alanı, görüş açısı, görüş sahası.

ken.nel[1] ['kenl] *n.* su kanalı, oluk.

ken.nel[2] [~] *n.* köpek kulübesi; köpek yetiştirilen yer; köpek sürüsü.

kept [kept] *pret. and. p.p. of keep 2.*

kerb [kə:b], '~*.stone* = *curb etc.*

ker.chief ['kə:tʃif] *n.* başörtüsü, eşarp; boyun atkısı, fular; mendil; '**ker-chiefed** *adj.* başörtülü, eşarplı.

kerf [kə:f] *n.* çentik; yarık; kesilmiş parça.

ker.nel ['kə:nl] *n.* tahıl tanesi; iç; çekirdek; *fig.* öz, cevher, esas, ruh.

ker.o.sene ['kerəsi:n] *n.* gazyağı, gaz.

kes.trel ORN ['kestrəl] *n.* kerkenez.

ketch NAUT [ketʃ] *n.* iki direkli bir çeşit yat, kotra.

ketch.up ['ketʃəp] *n.* keçap, domates sosu.

ket.tle ['ketl] *n.* çaydanlık; kazan; güğüm; tencere; '~*.drum n.* MUS tembal, bir çeşit davul, dümbelek.

key [ki:] **1.** *n.* anahtar; *fig.* çözüm yolu; MEC kama, dil; cevap cetveli, şifre cetveli; tercüme, çeviri; ELECT düğme, buton; MUS tuş, anahtar (işareti), ses perdesi; *fig.* ton, tel; telgraf maniplesi; **2.** *v/t.* ~ *up* MUS perdesini yükseltmek; *fig.* heyecanlandırmak, coşturmak; '~*.board n.* klavye; '~*.bu.gle n.* MUS boru, korno; '~*.hole n.* anahtar deliği; ~ *in.dus.try* temel endüstri; '~*.man n.* kilit adam; '~*.mon.ey n.* hava (*veya* anahtar) parası; '~*.note n.* esas perde, ana nota; *fig.* temel, ilke, anafikir; '~*.stone n.* anahtar taşı, kilit taşı; *fig.* temel, ilke, esas madde; '~*.word* IT *n.* anahtar sözcük.

khak.i ['ka:ki] **1.** *adj.* hâki; toprak rengi; **2.** *n.* bu renk kumaş; bu kumaştan üniforma.

khan[1] [ka:n] *n.* han, emir, kağan.

khan[2] [~] *n.* kervansaray, han.

kibe [kaib] *n.* el ve ayakta soğuktan oluşan çatlak, yarık.

kib.itz.er *Am.* F ['kibitsə] *n.* iskambil oynayanların arkasında durup ellerini gören seyirci; istenmeyen öğüt veren kimse.

ki.bosh *sl.* ['kaibɔʃ] *n.* zırva, saçma; *put the* ~ *on* son vermek -*e*, altüst etm. -*i.*

kick [kik] **1.** *n.* tekme, tepme; F heyecan, zevk, haz; *fig.* kuvvet, enerji, canlılık; silahın geri tepmesi; karşı gelme, yakınma, şikâyet; kuvvet, sertlik (*içki*); merak, heves; topa vurma; **more ~s than halfpence** takdirden çok eleştiri; **get a ~ out of** F *bşin* tadını çıkarmak, *-den* zevk duymak; **2.** *v/t.* tekmelemek, çiftelemek; *sl. -den* yakasını kurtarmak, bırakmak (*uyuşturucu madde*); F baştan savmak, atlatmak; *futbol*: atmak (*gol*); **~ the bucket** *sl.* nalları dikmek, ölmek, gebermek; **~ one's heels** F çok beklemek, ağaç olm.; **~ out** F kovmak, defetmek; **~ up a row** *veya* **fuss** *veya* **dust** F kavga çıkarmak, ortalığı birbirine katmak; *v/i.* tekme atmak, çifte atmak; topa vurmak; geri tepmek (*silah*); karşı durmak (**against, at** *-e*); **~ in with** *Am. sl.* para yardımında bulunmak; **~ off** *futbol*: oyuna başlamak; 'kick.back *n. part. Am.* F kârdan hisse, komisyon; 'kick.er *n.* vuran şey *veya* kimse; vurucu; futbolcu; 'kick-'off *n. futbol*: başlama (vuruşu); 'kick.shaw *n.* çerez türünden yiyecek, abur cubur; değersiz şey, ıvır zıvır; 'kick-start.er *n.* ayakla basılan marş; 'kick-'up *n. sl.* kavga, gürültü, patırtı.

kid [kid] **1.** *n.* oğlak, keçi yavrusu; oğlak eti; oğlak derisi; *sl.* çocuk; **2.** *vb. sl.* takılmak *-e*, gırgır geçmek *ile*, işletmek *-i*; şaka yapmak; oğlak doğurmak; 'kid.dy *n. sl.* çocukcağız, yavrucak; **kid glove** oğlak derisinden eldiven; *fig.* yumuşaklık; 'kid-glove *adj.* yumuşak, nazik.

kid.nap ['kidnæp] *v/t.* zorla kaçırmak (*part. çocuk*); 'kid.nap.(p)er *n.* zorla insan kaçıran kimse.

kid.ney ['kidni] *n.* ANAT böbrek; F soy, tip, huy, karakter; **~ bean** BOT fasulye.

kike *Am. sl. contp.* [kaik] *n.* Yahudi.

kill [kil] **1.** *v/t.* öldürmek, katletmek; *fig.* yok etm., mahvetmek; bitirmek, sona erdirmek; PARL veto etm., reddetmek; *fig.* yenmek, mağlûp etm., durdurmak; geçirmek, boşa harcamak, öldürmek (*zaman*); çok yormak; hepsini bitirmek (*içki*); tesirini yok etm.; çok etkilemek; **~ off** hepsini öldürmek, kırıp geçirmek; **~ time** vakit öldürmek; **2.** *n.* öldürme; avda öldürülen hayvan, av; 'kill.er *n.* adam öldüren kimse, katil, cani; 'killing **1.** □ öldürücü; çok yorucu; F komik, gülünç; **2.** *n. Am.* F vurgun, büyük kazanç; 'kill-joy *n.* neşe bozan kimse.

kiln [kiln, MEC kil] *n.* tuğla *veya* kireç ocağı, fırın; '~-dry *v/t.* ocakta kurutmak, fırınlamak.

kil.o.cy.cle PHYS ['kiləusaikl] *n.* kilosikl, kilo elektron volt; **kil.o.gram, kil.o.gramme** ['-græm] *n.* kilo(gram); **kil.o.me.ter, kilo.me.tre** ['kiləumi:tə] *n.* kilometre; **ki.lowatt** ELECT ['kiləuwɔt] *n.* kilovat.

kilt [kilt] **1.** *n.* İskoç erkeklerinin giydiği eteklik; **2.** *v/t.* pli yapmak; etek giydirmek; *v/i.* çevik davranmak.

ki.mo.no [ki'məunəu] *n.* uzun Japon entarisi, kimono.

kin [kin] **1.** *n.* akraba, hısım; soy, nesep; akrabalık; **the next of ~** yakın akraba; **2.** *adj.* akraba olan (**to** *-e*).

kind [kaind] **1.** □ müşfik, iyi kalpli, nazik, iyi, iyi huylu, sevimli; insancı(l); uysal, yumuşak başlı (**to** *-e, -e karşı*); **2.** *n.* cins, çeşit, tür, nevi; huy, karakter, mizaç, tabiat; **people of all ~s** her türden insan; **different in ~** başka çeşitten; **pay in ~** eşya ile borç ödemek, aynıyla ödemek; *fig.* aynen karşılık vermek; **I ~ of expected it** F biraz da bunu bekliyordum.

kin.der.gar.ten ['kindəga:tn] *n.* anaokulu.

kind.heart.ed ['kaind'ha:tid] *adj.* iyi kalpli.

kin.dle ['kindl] *v/t. & v/i.* tutuş(tur)mak, alevlen(dir)mek; aydınlatmak, yakmak; yanmak; *fig.* parlamak, uyan(dır)mak, çekmek (*ilgi*).

kind.li.ness ['kaindlinis] *n.* şefkat, insancıllık, sevecenlik, yumuşaklık.

kin.dling ['kindliŋ] *n. a. ~s pl.* çalı çırpı.

kind.ly ['kaindli] **1.** *adj.* müşfik, şefkatli, dostça; **2.** *adv.* doğal olarak; içten, gönülden; şefkatle; nazikçe, kibarca.

kind.ness ['kaindnis] *n.* şefkat, yumuşaklık.

kin.dred ['kindrəd] **1.** *adj.* akraba olan; birbirine benzer; **2.** *n.* akraba, hısım; akrabalık; soy, sülâle.

kine *obs.* [kain] *pl. of* **cow¹**.

ki.ne.ma ['kinimə] = **cinema**.

kin.e.mat.o.graph [kaini'mætəugra:f] = **cinematograph**.

ki.net.ic [ki'netik] *adj.* devimsel, kinetik; ki'net.ics *n. sg.* kinetik bilimi.

king [kiŋ] *n.* kral (*a. fig.*); satranç: şah; başta olan kimse; *iskambil*: papaz; dama olan taş; **~'s evil** MED sıraca hastalığı; **turn ~'s evidence** suç ortağı aleyhinde ifade vermek; 'king.bird *n.*

ORN kral kuşu; 'king.craft n. krallık hüneri; 'king.cup n. BOT düğünçiçeği; altıntabak; 'king.dom n. krallık, kraliyet, hükümdarlık; hükümet; saltanat; part. BOT, ZOO âlem; ~ come F öteki dünya, ahret; 'king.fish.er n. yalıçapkını, iskelekuşu, emircik; king.let ['-lit] n. küçük kral; 'king.like adj. kral gibi, krala yaraşır; haşmetli, muhteşem, mükellef; 'king.li.ness n. haşmet; 'king.ly adj. krala ait; krala yaraşır; haşmetli, muhteşem, şahane; 'king.pin n. dingil başı pimi, göbek mili; fig. çok gerekli kimse veya şey, baş, elebaşı; 'king.post n. ARCH baba, çatının orta direği; 'king.ship n. krallık, hükümdarlık; 'king-size adj. F normalden büyük, büyük boy.

kink [kiŋk] 1. n. halat, tel veya ipin dolaşması; fig. kaçıklık, üşütüklük; acayiplik, tuhaflık; Am. kapris, garip fikir; have a ~ F tahtası eksik olm.; 2. v/t. & v/i. halat gibi dolaş(tır)mak.

kins.folk ['kinzfəuk] n. pl. akraba, hısım; 'kin.ship n. akrabalık, hısımlık; benzerlik; 'kins.man n. erkek akraba; 'kinswom.an n. kadın akraba.

ki.osk ['kiːɔsk] n. küçük kulübe; telefon kulübesi; köşk, sayfiye.

kip.per ['kipə] 1. n. tuzlanmış isli ringa balığı, çiroz; sl. delikanlı, adam; 2. v/t. tuzlayıp tütsülemek veya kurutmak (balık).

kirk [kəːk] n. kilise.

kir.tle obs. ['kəːtl] n. kadın fistanı; erkek ceketi veya paltosu.

kiss [kis] 1. n. öpüş, öpücük, buse; fig. hafif temas; 2. vb. öpmek; hafifçe dokunmak; ~ the book kutsal kitabı öperek ant içmek, kitaba el basmak; ~ the dust boyun eğmek, mağlûp olm.; vurulup ölmek, öldürülmek; '~-proof adj. silinmez.

kit [kit] n. avadanlık, alet takımı; takım, malzeme (a. MIL & spor); takım çantası; do-it-yourself~ monte edilmemiş takım; '~-bag n. MIL asker hurcu, sırt çantası; NAUT denizci çantası.

kitch.en ['kitʃin] n. mutfak; 'kitch.en.er n. mutfak ocağı; kitch.en.ette [-'net] n. ufak mutfak.

kitch.en...: '~'gar.den n. sebze bahçesi; '~maid n. aşçı yamağı kız; '~range n. ocak, fırın.

kite [kait] n. ORN çaylak; uçurtma; fig. balon; COM sl. sahte bono; ~ balloon MIL yere bağlı sabit balon; fly a~ uçurt-

ma uçurmak; fig. balon uçurmak, nabız yoklamak.

kith [kiθ] n.: ~ and kin dostlar ve akrabalar, hısım akraba.

kit.ten ['kitn] 1. n. yavru kedi; 2. v/i. yavrulamak (kedi); kit.ten.ish ['kitniʃ] adj. kedi yavrusu gibi; oynamayı seven.

kit.tle fig. ['kitl] adj. nazik, tehlikeli, korkulur.

kit.ty¹ ['kiti] n. yavru kedi, kedicik.

kit.ty² [-] n. iskambil: kasa.

ki.wi ORN ['kiːwiː] n. Yeni Zeland'a ait bir kuş, kivi.

Klan Am. [klæn] n. Birleşik Amerika'da iç savaştan sonra güney eyaletlerinde zencilerin siyasi hakları olması aleyhinde kurulan gizli bir cemiyet; Klansman ['klænzmən] n. bu cemiyetin üyesi.

klax.on MOT ['klæksn] n. otomobil kornası, klakson.

klep.to.ma.ni.a [kleptəu'meinjə] n. hırsızlık hastalığı, kleptomani; klepto'ma.ni.ac [-niæk] n. hırsızlık hastası, kleptoman.

knack [næk] n. ustalık, marifet, hüner.

knack.er ['nækə] n. sakat at alıp kesen ve hayvan maması olarak satan kimse; malzemesi için eski ev veya gemi alan kimse; 'knack.er.y n. sakat atları kesip satma; malzemesi için eski ev veya gemi alma.

knag [næg] n. budak.

knap.sack ['næpsæk] n. sırt çantası.

knar [nɑː] n. budak.

knave [neiv] n. herif, düzenbaz kimse, üçkağıtçı; iskambil: bacak; 'knav.er.y n. hilekârlık, düzenbazlık; 'knav.ish □ hilekâr, dolandırıcı.

knead [niːd] v/t. yoğurmak; masaj yapmak.

knee [niː] 1. n. diz; diz yeri; dize benzer şey; MEC dirsek, mafsal; bring s.o. to his ~s b-ni yola getirmek, dize getirmek; on the ~s of the gods Allaha kalmış, henüz belli olmayan; 2. v/t. diz ile vurmak; '~-breech.es n. pl. kısa pantolon; '~-cap n. dizkapağı; '~-deep adj. diz boyu derinliğinde; '~-joint n. diz mafsalı; kneel [niːl] (irr.) v/i. diz çökmek (to -in önünde); diz üstü oturmak; 'kneel.er n. diz çökmüş kimse; 'knee-pan n. dizkapağı.

knell [nel] n. matem çanı sesi; salâ; ölüm haberi, kara haber.

knelt [nelt] pret. & p.p. of kneel.

knew [nju:] *pret. of* ***know 1***.

knick.er.bockers ['nikəbɔkəz] *n. pl.*
diz altından büzgülü bol pantolon, golf
pantolonu; '**knick.ers** *n. pl.* F dizde bü-
zülen kadın donu; = ***knickerbockers***.

knick.knack ['niknæk] *n.* ufak süs
eşyası, biblo; *~s pl.* süs müs, cici bici.

knife [naif] **1.** *n.*, *pl.* **knives** [naivz]
bıçak, çakı; makine bıçağı; ***get one's
~ into s.o.*** *fig. b-ne* karşı kötü niyetler
beslemek, diş bilemek; **2.** *v/t.* bıçaklamak; bıçakla kesmek; arkadan vur-
mak; '*~-grind.er n.* bıçak bileyici.

knight [nait] **1.** *n.* silahşör, şövalye; asılzade, soylu kimse; *satranç:* at; *k-ni bşe*
adayan kimse; **2.** *v/t. b-ne* şövalyelik
payesi vermek; **knight-er.rant**
['-'erənt] *n.* kahramanlık göstermek
için dolaşan seyyar silahşör; **knight-
hood** ['-hud] *n.* silahşörlük payesi,
şövalyelik; şövalyeler; '**knight.li.ness**
n. şövalyeye yakışırlık; '**knight.ly** *adj.*
şövalyeye ait; şövalyeye yakışır; şövalye gibi.

knit [nit] *(irr.) vb.* örmek; birleştirmek;
kavuşturmak; kaynatmak *(kemik)*;
çatmak *(kaş)*; birbirine yapışmak; kay-
na(ş)mak *(kemik)*; *~ the brows* kaşlarını çatmak; '**knit.ter** *n.* örgü ören
kimse; = ***knitting-machine***; '**knit.ting
1.** *n.* örme; örgü; **2.** *adj.* örgü...; '**knit-
ting-ma.chine** *n.* örgü makinesi;
'**knit.ting-nee.dle** *n.* örgü şişi; '**knit-
wear** *n.* trikotaj eşyası, örme.

knives [naivz] *pl. of* ***knife***.

knob [nɔb] *n.* top, yumru; topuz, tokmak; pürtük; tepecik, yuvarlak tepe;
'**knobbed**, '**knob.by** *adj.* yumrulu; tokmak gibi; '**knob-stick** *n.* topuzlu sopa;
grev bozan *(veya* kırıcı) kimse.

knock [nɔk] **1.** *n.* vuruş, vurma, darbe;
çalma, kapı çalınması; мот vuruntu;
2. *v/i.* vurmak, çalmak *(at* -*e*, -*i)*; çarpışmak; koşuşmak; gezip tozmak; vurun-
tu yapmak *(motor)*; tenkitçilik yapmak; *~ about* F oradan oraya dolaşmak; *~ off sl.* yüzüstü bırakıp gitmek;
~ under meydana çıkmak; *v/t.* vurmak;
çarpmak *e*-; çarpıştırmak; *Am. sl.* kusur bulmak, tenkit etm.; *~ about* tekrar
tekrar vurmak; şiddetle sarsmak; *~
down* vurup yere devirmek, yere sermek, yıkmak; açık arttırma: son fiyatı
verenin üstüne bırakmak; kazanmak,
kırmak *(para)*; мес sökmek, parçalara
ayırmak; *~ off* aceleyle yapmak; tatil
etm., işi bırakmak; indirmek *(fiyat)*;

öldürmek; soymak; *~ out boks:* nakavt
etm.; *~ up* kapıya vurup uyandırmak;
yormak; hamile bırakmak; *~.a.bout*
['-əbaut] **1.** *adj.* kaba ve dayanıklı
(eşya); gürültülü; тнеат güldürücü,
komik; **2.** *n.* komedi oyuncusu; kaba
ve dayanıklı şey; '*~-down adj.* yıkıcı,
yere serici, mat edici; portatif, sökülür
takılır; düşük, indirimli *(fiyat)*;
'**knock.er** *n.* kapı tokmağı; çalan *veya*
vuran şey *veya* kimse; *Am. sl.* tenkitçi;
'**knock-'kneed** *adj.* çarpık bacaklı; *fig.*
topal, aksak; '*~-out n. boks:* nakavt;
oyun dışı etme; *sl.* çekici kimse *veya*
şey.

knoll[1] [nəul] *n.* tepecik.

knoll[2] [-] *vb.* matem çanı ile ilân *veya*
davet etm.; ağır ağır çalmak *(çan)*.

knot [nɔt] **1.** *n.* düğüm, bağ; güç durum,
zorluk; naut deniz mili; halat cevizi;
вот nod; küme; **2.** *v/t. & v/i.* düğüm-
le(n)mek, bağla(n)mak *(a. fig.)*;
düğüm olm.; '**knot.hole** *n.* budak deliği; '**knot.ti.ness** *n.* karışıklık, zorluk;
'**knot.ty** *adj.* düğümlü; budaklı; *fig.*
karışık, güç, zor; '**knot.work** *n.* düğüm
işi.

knout [naut] **1.** *n.* kamçı; **2.** *v/t.* kamçılamak.

know [nəu] **1.** *(irr.) vb.* bilmek; tanımak;
seçmek, ayırmak, farketmek; tecrü-
beyle bilmek; haberdar olm., farkında
olm.; *~ French* Fransızca bilmek;
come to ~ öğrenmek, haber almak;
get to ~ bilmek, tanımak; *~ one's business*, *~ the ropes*, *~ a thing or two*, *~
what's what* usulünü bilmek, çaresini
bilmek, işini bilmek, dünyadan haberi
olm.; ***do you ~ how to play chess?*** satranç oynamayı biliyor musunuz?; ***you
ought to ~ better than to do that*** o işi
yapmayacak kadar akıllı olmalısınız; ***I
don't ~ one from the other*** birini diğe-
rinden ayıramıyorum; ***you ~*** biliyorsu-
nuz ki; **2.** *n.* ***be in the ~*** F haberdar olm.
(of -den); '**know.a.ble** *adj.* bilinmesi
mümkün, bilinir; '**know-all 1.** *adj.* herşeyi bilen; **2.** *n.* herşeyi bilen *veya* bildiğini iddia eden kimse; '**know-how** *n.*
yaratıcılık; teknik ustalık, maharet,
hüner, kabiliyet; '**know.ing 1.** □ bilgisi
olan; akıllı, zeki, kurnaz; fikir sahibi,
düşünceli; F şeytan, kurnaz, açıkgöz;
2. *n.* bilgi, malumat; '**know.ing.ly**
adv. bilerek, bile bile, kasten; **knowledge** ['nɔlidʒ] *n.* bilgi, malumat; anlayış; ***to my ~*** bildiğime göre, bildiğim

kadarıyla; **'knowl.edge.a.ble** *adj.* F
bilgili, zeki; **known** [nəun] *p.p. of*
know †; come to be ~ tanınmak, meşhur olm.; **make ~** *b-ni b-le* tanıştırmak;
make o.s. ~ *k-ni* tanıtmak.

knuck.le ['nʌkl] **1.** *n. a.* '**~-bone** parmak
orta eklemi, aşık kemiği; **2.** *v/i.* **~
down**, **~ under** boyun eğmek, pes demek, teslim olm.; işe koyulmak;
'**~-dust.er** *n.* muşta.

ko.a.la zoo [kəu'ɑːlə] *n.* keseli ayı.

ko.dak PHOT ['kəudæk] *n.* küçük fotoğraf makinesi.

Ko.ran [kɔ'rɑːn] *n.* Kur'an.

Ko.re.an [kə'riən] **1.** *n.* Koreli; Korece;
2. *adj.* Kore'ye ait.

kosh.er ['kəuʃə] *n.* Musevi şeriatına
göre temiz sayılan et, kaşer.

ko.tow ['kəu'tau] **1.** *n.* Çinlilerde diz çö-
küp alnı yere vurarak yapılan ibadet
veya hürmet; **2.** *vb.* bu şekilde ibadet
veya hürmet etm.; *fig.* yaltaklanmak
(to *-e*).

Krem.lin ['kremlin] *n.* Kremlin, Moskova'da yüksek duvarlı kale.

ku.dos *co.* ['kjuːdɔs] *n.* şöhret, şan,
şeref, itibar.

Ku-Klux-Klan *Am.* ['kjuː'klʌks'klæn]
*n. Bir leşik Amerika'da iç savaştan
sonra Güney eyaletlerinde zencilerin
siyasi haklara sahip olması aleyhinde
kurulan gizli cemiyet.

Kurd [kəːd] *n.* Kürt.

Kurdish [kəːdiʃ] *adj. & n.* Kürt(çe).

L

la MUS [lɑː] *n.* la notası.

lab F [læb] = **laboratory.**

la.bel ['leibl] **1.** *n.* etiket, yafta; *fig.* sıfat,
ünvan; JUR sınıf; ARCH saçak, pervaz; **2.**
v/t. etiketlemek; COM üzerine fiyatını
yazmak; *fig.* …damgasını vurmak
(as).

la.bi.al ['leibjəl] **1.** *adj.* dudaklarla ilgili;
dudaksıl…; **2.** *n.* dudak ünsüzü, dudaksıl ses.

lab.o.ra.to.ry [lə'bɔrətri] *n.* laboratuvar; **~ assistant** laborant, deneme
hazırlayıcısı.

la.bo.ri.ous □ [lə'bɔːriəs] çalışkan,
işgüzar; yorucu, zahmetli.

la.bo(u)r ['leibə] **1.** *n.* iş, çalışma; emek;
işçi sınıfı; MED doğum ağrıları; zahmet,
sıkıntı, zorluk; **Ministry of ♀** Çalışma
Bakanlığı; **hard ~** çalışma yükümlülüğü, ağır iş cezası; **2.** *adj.* iş…, çalışma…; **3.** *v/i.* çalışmak, uğraşmak, çabalamak; emek vermek, sıkıntı çekmek; zorlukla ilerlemek; **~ under**
sıkıntı çekmek, zorluk altında olm.,
-in kurbanı olm.; *v/t.* emekle meydana
getirmek; işlemek **(toprak)**; sıkıntı vermek, yüklenmek; detayına girmek; **~
camp** çalışma kampı; '**la.bo(u)red**
adj. zorlu, zahmetli; şaşaalı, şatafatlı;
'**la.bo(u)r.er** *n.* işçi, emekçi, rençber;
La.bo(u)r Ex.change İş ve İşçi Bulma
Kurumu; '**la.bo(u)r.ing** *adj.* zorlu; yorucu…; **~ breath** tıknefes; **la.bo(u)rite**
['~rait] *n.* İşçi Partisi üyesi *veya* yandaşı; **La.bour Par.ty** POL İşçi Partisi;
'**la.bo(u)r-sav.ing** *adj.* işi kolaylaştıran; **la.bor un.ion** *Am.* işçi sendikası.

Lab.ra.dor ['læbrədɔː] *n.:* **~ dog** zoo
Labrador cinsi köpek.

la.bur.num BOT [lə'bəːnəm] *n.* sarı-
salkım.

lab.y.rinth ['læbərinθ] *n.* labirent, dolambaçlı ve çok karışık yer *veya* iş;
lab.y'rin.thi.an [-θiən], *mıst* **lab.y-
'rin.thine** [-θain] *adj.* çapraşık, karmaşık.

lac [læk] *n.* reçineli sıvı, laka; **a ~ of
rupees** yüz bin rupi.

lace [leis] **1.** *n.* bağ **(ayakkabı)**, şerit;
dantel(a); kaytan; kordon; **2.** *v/t. &
v/i.* bağla(n)mak **(ayakkabı bağı vs.)**;
dantel ile süslemek; karıştırmak **(with
ile)**; **~ (into) s.o.** *b-ni* pataklamak, paylamak.

lac.er.ate **1.** ['læsəreit] *v/t.* yırtmak, yaralamak; *fig.* kırmak **(kalp)**, incitmek
(his); **2.** ['-rit] *adj.* yaralı, yırtık, parça-
lanmış, ezilmiş; **lac.er.a.tion** [-'reiʃən]
n. yırtma, yaralama, incitme.

lach.es JUR ['leitʃiz] *n.* hakkını aramakta ihmal.

lach.ry.mal ['lækriməl] *adj.* gözyaşına
ait, gözyaşı…; **lach.ry.mose** ['-məus]
adj. sulu gözlü; göz yaşartıcı.

lack [læk] **1.** *n.* noksan, eksiklik, kusur;
ihtiyaç, gereksinme; yoksunluk; **2.** *v/t.*
muhtaç olm. *-e*; ihtiyacı olm. *-e*; yoksun olm. *-den*; **he ~s money** paraya ih-

tiyacı var, para sıkıntısı çekiyor; *v/i.* eksik olm., yetmemek; *be ~ing* eksikliği olm., mevcut olmamak, bulunmamak; *he is ~ing in courage* yeteri kadar cesur değil, o kim cesur olmak kim.

lack.a.dai.si.cal □ [lækə'deizikəl] canından bezmiş gibi; ilgisiz, uyuşuk.

lack.ey ['læki] **1.** *n.* uşak, erkek hizmetçi; *fig.* dalkavuk; **2.** *vb.* uşaklık etm.

lack.ing ['lækiŋ] *s. lack 1.*

lack.land ['læklænd] *adj.* topraksız, arazisiz; **lack.lus.tre**, *Am.* **lack.lus.ter** ['_lʌstə] *adj.* cansız, donuk, sönük.

la.con.ic [lə'kɔnik] *adj.* (*~ally*) az ve öz, özlü, veciz; az konuşur.

lac.quer ['lækə] **1.** *n.* vernik; **2.** *v/t.* vernik ile kaplamak, verniklemek; *~ed* vernikli...

lac.quey ['læki] = *lackey.*

la.crosse [lə'krɔs] *n. spor.* raketle oynanan bir top oyunu.

lac.ta.tion [læk'teiʃən] *n.* süt salgılama; emzirme.

lac.tic ['læktik] *adj.* süte ait, süt...; *~ acid* süt asidi, laktik asit.

la.cu.na [lə'kjuːnə] *n.* boşluk, aralık, eksiklik.

lac.y ['leisi] *adj.* dantel gibi; dantelli...

lad [læd] *n.* genç erkek, delikanlı.

lad.der ['lædə] **1.** *n.* el merdiveni; *fig.* basamak; çorap kaçığı; NAUT ip merdiven; **2.** *v/i.* kaçmak (*çorap*); '*~-proof* *adj.* kaçmaz (*çorap*).

lad.die ['lædi] *n.* genç erkek, delikanlı.

lade [leid] (*irr.*) = *load;* 'lad.en **1.** *p.p. of lade;* **2.** *adj.* yüklü.

la-di-da ['lɑːdi'dɑː] **1.** *n.* gösterişçi kimse; **2.** *adj.* gösterişçi.

la.ding ['leidiŋ] *n.* hamule, yük, kargo; yükleme.

la.dle ['leidl] **1.** *n.* kepçe; MEC büyük kepçe, pota; **2.** *v/t.* *~ out* kepçe ile servis yapmak; *fig.* bahşetmek, bol keseden vermek.

la.dy ['leidi] *n.* bayan, hanım(efendi); asilzade kadın, leydi; *Ladies sg.* kadınlar tuvaleti; *Ladies and Gentlemen!* bayanlar baylar!; ♀ *Day* 25 Martta kutlanan bir kilise yortusu; *~ doctor* kadın doktor; *~'s maid* bir hanımın oda hizmetçisi; *~'s veya ladies' man* kadınlara karşı nazik ve onların hoşlandığı adam, kadın düşkünü, kadıncıl; '*~-bird* *n.* gelinböceği; '*~-in-'wait.ing* *n.* kraliçe nedimesi; '*~-kill.er* *n.* kadın avcısı, çapkın; '*~-like* *adj.* hanıma yakışır, hanım hanımcık; *contp.* kadınsı (*er-*

kek); '*~-love* *n.* sevgili, metres; *~ of the* **bedcham.ber** kraliçe nedimesi; '*~.ship* *n.* hanımefendilik; *her veya your ~* hanımefendi.

lag¹ [læg] **1.** *v/i.* oyalanmak; *a. ~ behind* geri kalmak; **2.** *n.* geri kalma, gecikme.

lag² *sl.* [_] **1.** *n.* suçlu, mahkûm; **2.** *v/t.* tutuklamak; hapse atmak.

lag³ [_] *v/t.* kaplamak (*su boruları, kazan vs.*); tecrit (*veya izole*) etm.

la.ger (beer) ['lɑːgə('biə)] *n.* Alman birası.

lag.gard ['lægəd] *n.* uyuşuk kimse; geri kalan şey *veya* kimse.

la.goon [lə'guːn] *n.* denizkulağı.

la.ic ['leiik] **1.** *a.* 'la.i.cal □ layik; **2.** *n.* layik kimse; **la.i.cize** ['_saiz] *v/t.* layikleştirmek.

laid [leid] *pret. & p.p. of lay⁴ 2;* *~ up* biriktirilmiş; yatağa düşmüş (*with -den*).

lain [lein] *p.p. of lie² 2.*

lair [lɛə] *n.* in, yatak (*a. fig.*).

laird *Scots* [lɛəd] *n.* mülk sahibi.

la.i.ty ['leiiti] *n.* ruhbandan olmayanlar; meslekten olmayanlar.

lake¹ [leik] *n.* göl.

lake² [_] *n.* morumsu kırmızı boya.

lake-dwel.lings ['leikdweliŋz] *n. pl.* göl kıyısındaki kazık temelli evler.

lam *sl.* [læm] *v/t.* dövmek, sopa çekmek, pataklamak; *v/i.* tüymek, sıvışmak; *~ into s.o.* *b-ni* adamakıllı dövmek, *b-ne* çıkışmak.

la.ma ['lɑːmə] *n.* Lama, Tibet'li Buda rahibi; 'la.ma.se.ry ['_səri] *n.* lama manastırı.

lamb [læm] **1.** *n.* kuzu (eti); *fig.* kuzu gibi kimse; *like a ~* *fig.* kuzu gibi; **2.** *v/i.* kuzulamak.

lam.baste *sl.* [læm'beist] *v/t.* dövmek, pataklamak; haşlamak, paylamak.

lam.bent ['læmbənt] *adj.* yalayarak yayılan (*alev*); hafifçe parlayan (*göz, gök*).

lamb.kin ['læmkin] *n.* kuzucuk; 'lamb-like *adj.* kuzu gibi; 'lamb.skin *n.* kuzu derisi.

lame [leim] **1.** □ topal, ayağı sakat, aksak (*a. fig.*); *fig.* eksik, kusurlu, sudan (*sebep*); *Am. sl.* dünyadan habersiz; **2.** *v/t.* topal etm.; *v/i.* topallamak; 'lame.ness *n.* topallık.

la.ment [lə'ment] **1.** *n.* inilti, feryat, figan, keder; **2.** *v/t. & v/i.* inlemek; ağlamak, figan etm., matem tutmak (*for için*); **lam.en.ta.ble** □ ['læməntəbl] acınacak, içler acısı; matemli, kederli;

lam.en'ta.tion *n.* ağlayış, inleme, feryat, figan.

lam.i.na ['læminə] *n., pl.* **lam.i.nae** ['‿niː] ince levha; ELECT, BOT varak, tabaka; '**lam.inar** *adj.* levha şeklinde; **lam.i.nate** ['‿neit] *v/t.* ince tabakalara ayırmak; **‿d glass** katmerli cam.

lamp [læmp] *n.* lamba, ışık (*a. fig.*); '**‿.black** *n.* kandil isi; '**‿chim.ney** *n.* lamba şişesi; '**‿.light** *n.* lamba ışığı; '**‿.lighter** *n.* fenerleri yakan adam, fenerci; '**‿.oil** *n.* gazyağı.

lam.poon [læm'puːn] **1.** *n.* taşlama, yergi, hicviye; **2.** *v/t.* yermek, taşlamak, hicvetmek.

lamp-post ['læmppəust] *n.* sokak feneri direği, elektrik direği.

lam.prey ICHTH ['læmpri] *n.* yılanbalığına benzer su hayvanı.

lamp.shade ['læmpʃeid] *n.* abajur.

lance [lɑːns] **1.** *n.* mızrak; **2.** *v/t.* neşterle yarmak, deşmek (*a.* MED); '**‿'cor.po.ral** *n.* MIL geçici onbaşı; **lan.ce.o.late** BOT ['lænsiəlit] *adj.* mızraksı, lanseolat; **lanc.er** MIL ['lɑːnsə] *n.* mızraklı süvari; **‿s** *pl.* dörtlü kadril dansı.

lan.cet ['lɑːnsit] *n.* neşter; **‿** arch ARCH sivri kavislı dar kemer; **‿** win.dow sivri kavisli pencere.

land [lænd] **1.** *n.* toprak, kara; ülke; memleket; arsa, yer; *by* **‿** karadan, kara yolu ile; **‿s** *pl.* emlâk, arazi; *see how the* **‿** *lies* nabzını yoklamak, gidişata bakmak; **2.** *v/t. & v/i.* karaya çık(ar)-mak, yere in(dir)mek; elde etm., kazanmak; vurmak, indirmek (*yumruk vs.*); NAUT boşaltmak; yakalamak (*balık*); **‿** *on one's feet* dört ayak üstüne düşmek; **‿** *up in prison* hapsi boylamak; '**‿-a.gent** *n.* emlâkci, emlâk komisyoncusu.

lan.dau ['lændɔː] *n.* landon, dört tekerlekli ve çift körüklü binek arabası.

land.ed ['lændid] *adj.* arazi sahibi; gayrimenkul…

land…: '**‿.fall** *n.* NAUT karanın ilk görünmesi; '**‿-forc.es** *n. pl.* kara kuvvetleri; '**‿-grab.ber** *n.* hile ile başkasının arazisine tecavüz eden kimse; '**‿.hold.er** *n.* mülk sahibi.

land.ing ['lændiŋ] *n.* iniş; karaya çık(ar)ma; iskele; sahanlık; '**‿-craft** *n.* NAUT, MIL çıkartma gemisi; '**‿-field** *n.* AVIA havaalanı; '**‿-gear** *n.* AVIA iniş takımı; '**‿-net** *n.* ağ kepçe; '**‿-par.ty** *n.* MIL çıkartma birliği; '**‿-stage** *n.* NAUT iskele; '**‿-strip** = *landing-field.*

land.la.dy ['lændleidi] *n.* pansiyoncu kadın; ev sahibesi.

land.less ['lændlis] *adj.* arazisiz.

land…: '**‿.locked** *adj.* kara ile çevrilmiş; '**‿.lop.er** *n.* serseri, derbeder; **‿.lord** ['lændlɔːd] *n.* mal sahibi; hancı, otelci, pansiyoncu; **‿-lub.ber** NAUT *contp.* ['lændlʌbə] *n.* deniz ve gemiden anlayan kimse; '**‿.mark** *n. part.* NAUT uzaktan görülebilen işaret; sınır taşı; *fig.* dönüm noktası; '**‿-own.er** *n.* arazi sahibi; **‿.scape** ['lændskeip] *n.* manzara, peyzaj; **‿.slide** ['lændslaid] *n.* toprak kayması, kayşa, heyelân; POL büyük çoğunluğun kazanılması; *a Democratic* **‿** Demokratik partinin zaferi; '**‿.slip** *n.* kayşa, heyelân, toprak kayması; **‿.s.man** NAUT ['‿zmən] *n.* denizci olmayan kimse; '**‿-sur.vey.or** *n.* mesahacı, yüzölçümü memuru; '**‿-tax** *n.* arazi vergisi; **‿.ward** ['‿wəd] *adj.* karaya doğru uzanan.

lane [lein] *n.* dar sokak, dar yol, dar geçit; kulvar; MOT şerit.

lang syne Scots ['læŋ'sain] *n. & adv.* eski zaman(da), geçmiş(te).

lan.guage ['læŋgwidʒ] *n.* dil, lisan; konuşma yeteneği; *bad* **‿** küfür; *strong* **‿** sert dil, ağır söz.

lan.guid ☐ ['læŋgwid] gevşek, cansız, sönük, yavaş, ağır; isteksiz, gayretsiz; COM durgun, kesat; '**lan.guid.ness** *n.* cansızlık, yavaşlık; durgunluk.

lan.guish ['læŋgwiʃ] *v/i.* gevşemek, zayıf düşmek, kuvveti kesilmek; isteği kalmamak (*for -e karşı*); COM kesat gitmek; '**lan.guish.ing** ☐ kuvvetsiz, zayıf; COM kesat, durgun.

lan.guor ['læŋgə] *n.* gevşeklik, cansızlık, ağırlık, bitkinlik, isteksizlik, halsizlik; '**lan.guor.ous** ☐ bitkinlik veren, halsiz düşüren.

lank ☐ [læŋk] uzun ve zayıf, boylu, ince; düz (*saç*); '**lank.y** ☐ uzun boylu ve zayıf, sırık gibi.

lan.o.lin ['lænəuliːn] *n.* lanolin.

lan.tern ['læntən] *n.* fener (*a.* ARCH); *dark* **‿** hırsız feneri; '**‿-jawed** *adj.* uzun çeneli; '**‿-slide** *n.* hayalci feneri, diyapozitif; **‿** *lecture* projeksiyonlu konferans.

lan.yard NAUT ['lænjəd] *n.* kordon, ince ip, savla.

lap[1] [læp] **1.** *n.* kucak; diz üstü; etek; MEC örtü, kat, bindirme dikişi; *spor:* tur; **2.** *v/t. & v/i.* üst üste bin(dir)mek, katla(n)mak, sar(ıl)mak; kuşatmak,

çevirmek, örtmek; *spor*: tur bindirmek.
lap² [ˌ] **1.** *n.* yalayarak içme; dalga sesi; **2.** *v/t.* yalayarak içmek; can kulağı ile dinlemek; *v/i.* hafif hafif çarpmak (*dalga*).
lap-dog ['læpdɔg] *n.* küçük ev köpeği.
la.pel [lə'pel] *n.* klapa.
lap.i.dar.y ['læpidəri] **1.** *adj.* yazıta elverişli…; taşlara ait, taş…; *fig.* özlü; **2.** *n.* oymacı, hakkâk, kıymetli taş kesicisi.
lap.is laz.u.li [læpis'læzjulai] *n.* lacivert taş; bu taşın rengi.
lapse [læps] **1.** *n.* kusur, yanlış, hata; kayma; ara; geçme, mürur, geçiş, düşme (*into -e*); *jur* sukut; **2.** *v/i.* geçmek; başkasına intikal etm.; gömülmek, sapmak, düşmek, dalmak (*into -e*); *jur* hükmü kalmamak; yanılmak, hata etm.
lap.top ['læptɔp] *n.* dizüstü bilgisayar.
lap.wing orn ['læpwiŋ] *n.* kızkuşu.
lar.ce.ny jur ['lɑːsəni] *n.* hırsızlık.
larch bot [lɑːtʃ] *n.* karaçam.
lard [lɑːd] **1.** *n.* domuz yağı; **2.** *v/t.* domuz yağı ile yağlamak; *fig.* süslemek (*yazı veya söz*); **'lard.er** *n.* kiler; **'larding-needle**, **'lard.ing-pin** *n.* yağlama şişi.
large □ [lɑːdʒ] büyük, geniş, iri; bol, çok; serbest; cömert; sınırsız (*yetki*); kaba (*dil*); elverişli (*rüzgâr*); abartmalı, övüngen; *at ~* kontroldan çıkmış, serbest; ayrıntılı olarak, detaylı; genellikle; rasgele; *talk at ~* ayrıntılı olarak konuşmak; *in ~* büyük ölçüde; **'large.ly** *adv.* büyük ölçüde; başlıca; cömertçe, bol bol, çok; **'large.ness** *n.* büyüklük (*a. fig.*), genişlik; **'large-'mind.ed** *adj.* geniş fikirli, serbest düşünüşlü; **'large-'scale** *adj.* büyük çapta; **'large-'sized** *adj.* büyük boy.
lar.gess(e) *obs.* [lɑː'dʒes] *n.* cömertlik; bağış.
lar.go mus ['lɑːgəu] **1.** *n.* yavaş çalınan parça; **2.** *adv.* largo.
lar.i.at *Am.* ['læriət] *n.* kement.
lark¹ orn [lɑːk] *n.* tarlakuşu.
lark² [ˌ] **1.** *n.* şaka, eğlence, cümbüş, şamata; **2.** *v/i.* cümbüş yapmak, şamata yapmak, eğlenmek; **lark.some** ['-səm] = *larky*.
lark.spur bot ['lɑːkspəː] *n.* hezaren çiçeği.
lark.y F ['lɑːki] *adj.* şamatacı, gırgır.
lar.va zoo ['lɑːvə] *n.*, *pl.* **lar.vae** ['-viː] tırtıl, kurtçuk, sürfe; **lar.val** ['-vəl] *adj.*

tırtıla ait, tırtıl…; tırtıl şeklinde.
lar.yn.gi.tis med [lærin'dʒaitis] *n.* larenjit; **lar.ynx** ['læriŋks] *n.* gırtlak, boğaz, hançere.
las.civ.ious □ [lə'siviəs] şehvetli.
la.ser phys ['leizə] *n.* lazer; '~ sur.ge.ry med *n.* lazerle ameliyat.
lash [læʃ] **1.** *n.* kamçı (darbesi); vuruş, vurma; kirpik; acı hiciv, zem; *the ~* kamçılama, dövme; **2.** *vb.* kamçılamak, dövmek, çarpmak, vurmak; *fig.* yermek, eleştirmek; sıkıca bağlamak; kışkırtmak, galeyana getirmek; *~ out* saldırmak; çifte atmak; *fig.* çatmak, çıkışmak; **'lash.ing** *n.* ip, halat; kamçılama, dövme; azarlama; *~s pl.* çok miktar, bolluk.
lass [læs] *n.* kız; sevgili, kız arkadaş; **las.sie** ['læsi] *n.* kızcağız.
las.si.tude ['læsitjuːd] *n.* yorgunluk, bitkinlik; ilgisizlik.
las.so ['læsəu] **1.** *n.* kement; **2.** *v/t.* kementle yakalamak.
last¹ [lɑːst] **1.** *adj.* son(uncu), en sonraki, en gerideki; geçen, evvelki; eski, sabık; son derece, gayet; *~ but one* sondan bir evvelki; *~ night* dün gece; **2.** *n.* son, nihayet; *my ~* sonuncu (*çocuğum, mektubum vs.*); *at ~* sonunda, nihayet; *at long ~* en sonunda; *breathe one's ~* son nefesini vermek, ölmek; **3.** *adv.* en sonra, son olarak, nihayet; *~, but not least* özellikle, son fakat önemli.
last² [ˌ] *v/i.* devam etm., sürmek; dayanmak, bitmemek, tükenmemek, yetmek.
last³ [ˌ] *n.* kundura kalıbı; *stick to one's ~* üstesinden gelemediği şeyi yapmaya kalkışmamak; çizmeden yukarı çıkmamak.
last.ing ['lɑːstiŋ] **1.** □ sürekli, devamlı, uzun süreli, dayanıklı; **2.** *n.* dayanma, sürme.
last.ly ['lɑːstli] *adv.* son olarak, nihayet.
latch [lætʃ] **1.** *n.* mandal, sürgü; kilit dili; *on the ~* sürgülü, mandallanmış; **2.** *v/t. & v/i.* mandalla(n)mak; '~*key* *n.* kapı anahtarı.
late [leit] *adj.* geç; gecikmiş, geri kalmış; sabık, geçmiş; ölü, rahmetli, merhum; yakında olmuş, yeni; *at (the) ~st* en geç; *as ~ as yesterday* ancak dün; *of ~* son zamanlarda, yakınlarda; *of ~ years* son yıllarda; *~r on* daha sonra; *be ~* geç kalmak, gecikmek; rail rötar yapmak; *keep ~ hours* gece geç saatlere kadar yatmamak; eve geç gelmek;

'**~-com.er** *n.* geç gelen *veya* kalan kimse.

la.teen NAUT [lə'tiːn] *adj.*: **~ sail** latin yelkeni.

late.ly ['leitli] *adv.* geçenlerde, yakınlarda, bu günlerde.

la.ten.cy ['leitənsi] *n.* gelişmemişlik, gözükmezlik, gizli olarak varolma.

late.ness ['leitnis] *n.* gecikme, geçlik.

la.tent □ ['leitənt] gelişmemiş, gözükmez; gizli kalmış.

lat.er.al □ ['lætərəl] yana ait, yan...; yanal, yandan gelen; yana doğru olan.

la.tex BOT ['leiteks] *n.* lateks; kauçuk hammaddesi.

lath [lɑːθ] **1.** *n.* lata, tiriz; **2.** *v/t.* lata ile kaplamak.

lathe [leið] *n.* torna tezgâhı; çömlekçi çarkı.

lath.er ['lɑːðə, 'læðə] **1.** *n.* sabun köpüğü; atın köpüklü teri; **2.** *v/t. & v/i.* köpür(t)mek; sabunlamak; pataklamak, sopa çekmek.

Lat.in ['lætin] **1.** *adj.* Latin(ce)...; **2.** *n.* Latince; **~ A.mer.i.ca** Latin Amerika; '**Lat.in.ism** *n.* Latin dili özelliği; '**Lat.in.ize** *v/t.* Latinceye çevirmek.

lat.i.tude ['lætitjuːd] *n.* enlem, arz; *fig.* serbestlik, hoşgörü; genişlik; **~s** *pl.* bölge, mıntıka; **lat.i'tu.di.nal** [_-dinl] *adj.* enine...; **lat.i.tu.di.nar.i.an** ['_-di-'nɛəriən] **1.** *adj.* serbest fikirli, hoşgörülü; **2.** *n.* serbest fikirli kimse.

la.trine [lə'triːn] *n.* helâ çukuru.

lat.ter ['lætə] *adj.* son(raki)..., *poet.* daha sonraki...; **~ end** son; ölüm; '**~-day** *adj.* çağa uygun, modern..., çağdaş...; '**lat.ter.ly** *adv.* bu yakınlarda, son zamanlarda.

lat.tice ['lætis] **1.** *n. a.* **~-work** kafes; **2.** *v/t.* kafesle çevirmek.

Lat.vi.an ['lætviən] **1.** *adj.* Letonya...; **2.** *n.* Letonyalı; Letonya dili.

laud [lɔːd] *v/t.* övmek, methetmek, yüceltmek; '**laud.a.ble** □ övgüye değer; **lau'da.tion** *n.* övme; **laud.a.to.ry** □ ['_-dətəri] övücü, öven (**of** -*i*).

laugh [lɑːf] **1.** *n.* gülme, gülüş, hande; **have a ~** gülmek; **raise a ~** güldürmek; **2.** *vb.* gülmek (**at** -*e*); **~ at s.o.** b-*le* alay etm.; **~ off** gülerek geçiştirmek, gülüp geçmek; **~ out of** gülerek meseleyi kapatmak; **you will ~ on the wrong side** *veya* **on the other side of your mouth** *veya* **face** bu kadar gülme pişman olursun; **he ~s best who ~s last** son gülen iyi güler; *s.* **sleeve**; '**laugh.a.ble** □ gü-

lünç, komik; '**laugh.er** *n.* gülen kimse; '**laugh.ing 1.** *n.* gülme, gülüş; **2.** □ gül(dür)en; *it is no ~ matter* işin şaka götürür yanı yok; '**laugh.ing-gas** *n.* güldürücü gaz; '**laugh.ing-stock** *n.* alay konusu kimse *veya* şey; **laugh.ter** ['_-tə] *n.* gülüş, gülme, kahkaha.

launch [lɔːntʃ] **1.** *n.* NAUT kızaktan suya indirme; işkampaviye; roketi fezaya fırlatma; **2.** *v/t.* kızaktan suya indirmek (*gemi*); fırlatmak (*roket*); atmak, fırlatmak, savurmak (*a. fig.*); *fig.* başlatmak; *v/i.* **~ out** başlamak, girişmek; **~ (out) into** -*e* girişmek, -*e* başlamak; '**launch.ing-pad** *n.* fırlatma (*veya* atış) rampası.

laun.der ['lɔːndə] *v/t. & v/i.* yıka(n)mak, yıkayıp ütül(en)mek; **laun.der.ette** [lɔːndə'ret] *n.* çamaşırhane.

laun.dress ['lɔːndris] *n.* çamaşırcı kadın; '**laun.dry** *n.* çamaşır(hane); çamaşırcılık; '**laun.dry-man** *n.* çamaşırcı.

lau.re.ate ['lɔːriit] **1.** *adj.* defne dallarından çelenk giymiş; **2.** *n.* the ♀, *the Poet* ♀ saray şairi.

lau.rel BOT ['lɔrəl] *n.* defne ağacı; **win ~s** *fig.* şöhret kazanmak; '**lau.relled** *adj.* defne dallarından çelenk giymiş; şan, şeref kazanmış.

lav F [læv] *n.* helâ, kenef.

la.va ['lɑːvə] *n.* lav.

lav.a.to.ry ['lævətri] *n.* helâ, tuvalet; lavabo; yıkanma yeri; *public ~* umumî helâ.

lave *mst poet.* [leiv] *v/t. & v/i.* yıka(n)mak; banyo yapmak; yanısıra akıvermek (*nehir*).

lav.en.der BOT ['lævində] *n.* lavanta.

lav.ish ['læviʃ] **1.** □ savurgan, müsrif, tutumsuz; çok, bol, aşırı; **2.** *v/t.* bol bol harcamak, çarçur etm.; aşırı... göstermek; '**lav.ish.ness** *n.* savurganlık.

law [lɔː] *n.* kanun, yasa; kaide, kural; nizam; JUR kanunlar; tabiat kanunu; usül, töre; *at* **~** kanunî, meşru; *be a ~ unto o.s.* bildiğini okumak; *go to ~* mahkemeye başvurmak; dava etm.; *have the ~ of s.o.* b-*ni* dava etm.; *...-in-law* kayın...; *necessity knows no ~* ihtiyaç kanun tanımaz; *lay down the ~* dediği dedik olm...; *practise ~* avukatlık (*veya* hukukçuluk) etm.; '**~-a.bid.ing** *adj.* JUR kanuna uyan; '**~-break.er** *n.* kanunu çiğneyen kimse; '**~-court** *n.* mahkeme; **law.ful** □ ['_-ful] kanuna uygun, meşru, kanunî; '**law-**

giv.er *n*. kanun yapan kimse; 'law.less ☐ kanuna aykırı, kanun tanımaz; kanunsuz; vahşi, azılı; 'law.mak.er *n*. kanun koyucu; meclis üyesi.

lawn¹ [lɔːn] *n*. patiska.

lawn²[-] *n*. çimen(lik), çayır; '~-mow.er *n*. çim biçme makinesi; '~-sprin.kler *n*. çim sulama aleti; '~-'ten.nis *n*. çim tenisi.

law.suit ['lɔːsjuːt] *n*. dava; law.yer ['-jə] *n*. avukat, dava vekili.

lax ☐ [læks] gevşek (*a. fig.*); ihmalci, kayıtsız, savsak, lâkayt; lax.a.tive ['-ətiv] 1. *adj*. ishal edici (*ilâç*); 2. *n*. sürgün ilâcı, müshil; 'lax.i.ty, lax.ness *n*. gevşeklik; kayıtsızlık.

lay¹ [lei] *pret. of* lie² 2.

lay² [-] *n*. türkü, balad; *poet.* şiir, gazel.

lay³ [-] *adj*. layik; işin ehli olmayan...

lay⁴ [-] 1. *n*. durum, duruş, yatış, mevki; *sl.* iş güç, meşgale; 2. (*irr.*) *v/t.* koymak, yatırmak, yaymak, sermek; kurmak (*masa*); gömmek; yumurtlamak; yatıştırmak; koymak (*vergi*); yüklemek (*suç*); hazırlamak (*plan vs.*); dayamak, yaslamak; *sl. ile* cinsî münasebette bulunmak; ~ aside bir tarafa koymak; biriktirmek (*para*); terketmek, bırakmak, vazgeçmek; ~ bare açmak; ortaya çıkarmak (*sır vs.*); ~ before s.o. b-ne sunmak, takdim etm., *b-ne* göstermek; ~ by yığmak, biriktirmek (*para*); ~ down bırakmak; feda etm.; planlamak; yapmak, inşa etm.; yatırmak; saklamak, depo etm.; emretmek; ~ s.o. (*fast*) by the heels *b-ni* yakalamak, tutuklayıp hapsetmek; ~ in biriktirmek, stoklamak; ~ low yere sermek; yatağa düşürmek; ~ off geçici olarak işten çıkarmak; *Am. sl.* bırakmak, vazgeçmek, kesmek; ~ on sağlamak, temin etm.; saldırmak, yüklenmek; ~ it on (*thick*) *fig*. abartmak; pohpohlamak, göklere çıkarmak; ~ open ortaya çıkarmak; kesmek, yarmak; ~ (*o.s.*) open to s.th. *k-ni* ...ile karşı karşıya bırakmak; ~ out yaymak, sermek; sergilemek; tasarlamak; düzenlemek; tertiplemek; gömülmeye hazırlamak, kefenlemek (*ölü*); harcamak, sarfetmek (*para*); yere sermek *b-ni*; ~ *o.s.* out *k-ni* paralamak, paralanmak (*for için*); ~ s.o. under an obligation *veya* a necessity *b-ni* mecbur bırakmak; ~ up biriktirmek, saklamak; NAUT kızağa çekmek; be laid up yatağa düşmek; ~ with ...ile yatmak; *v/i.* yumurtlamak; *a.* ~

a wager bahse girmek; ~ about saldırmak, sağına soluna vurmak; çıkışmak; ~ into s.o. *sl. b-ne* girişmek, *b-ni* pataklamak; *b-ne* verip veriştirmek; ~ (*it*) on F saldırmak, yüklenmek, veriştirmek.

lay.a.bout *sl.* ['leiəbaut] *n*. aylak (*veya* serseri) kimse; 'lay-by *n*. yol kenarındaki park yeri.

lay.er *n*. ['leiə] *n*. kat, tabaka; tavuk; daldırma; 2. AGR ['lɛə] *v/t.* daldırmak.

lay.ette [lei'et] *n*. yeni doğmuş bebeğin çamaşır ve elbise takımı.

lay-fig.ure ['lei'figə] *n*. manken.

lay.man ['leimən] *n*. meslek sahibi olmayan kimse.

lay...: '~-off *n*. işçilerin geçici olarak işten çıkartılması; '~-out *n*. düzen, tertip; mizanpaj.

laz.a.ret, *mst* laz.a.ret.to [læzə'ret(əu)] *n*. karantina merkezi; NAUT erzak ambarı.

laze F [leiz] *v/i.* ense yapmak; *v/t.* aylak aylak geçirmek (*zaman*); 'laz.i.ness *n*. tembellik, uyuşukluk, aylaklık; 'la.zy *adj*. tembel, miskin, uyuşuk, aylak, hantal, ağır; 'la.zy-bones *n*. tembel kimse.

lea *poet.* [liː] *n*. çimenlik, çayırlık, mera.

leach [liːtʃ] *vb*. damıtmak, süzmek.

lead¹ [led] 1. *n*. kurşun; NAUT iskandil; TYP anterlin; grafit; ~s *pl.* kurşun levha; ~ pencil kurşunkalem; swing the ~ *sl.* temaruz etm., hasta numarası yaparak işten kaçmak; 2. *v/t.* kurşunlamak; TYP anterlin ile açmak (*satır araları*).

lead² [liːd] 1. *n*. kılavuzluk, öncülük, rehberlik; tasma kayışı; THEAT başrol (*oyuncusu*); ELECT ana tel; başa geçme; *iskambil*: ilk oynama hakkı; ilk oynayacak kimse; *it's my* ~ *iskambil*: sıra bende; take the ~ başa geçmek; örnek olm.; 2. (*irr.*) *v/t.* yol göstermek *-e*, rehberlik etm. *-e*, götürmek *-i*; kumanda etm. *-i*; idare etm. *-i*, yönetmek *-i*; elinden tutarak götürmek *-i*; sürmek (*hayat*); önde götürmek (*yarış vs.*); etkilemek *-i*; ikna etm. *-i*; sebep olm. (*to -e*); *iskambil*: ...ile oyun açmak; ~ on ayartmak, kandırıp yaptırmak; *v/i.* gitmek, çıkmak (*yol*); başta olm.; ~ off başlamak; *spor*: oyuna başlamak; ~ up to *-e* getirmek, *-e* sebep olm.

lead.en ['ledn] *adj*. kurşun(dan); kurşun renginde, kurşunî; *fig*. ağır, kasvetli, sıkıcı; hüzünlü.

lead.er ['liːdə] *n*. önder, lider, kumandan, baş, önayak; kılavuz, rehber; solo kemancı; orkestra şefi; JUR (çok avukatlı davada) kıdemli avukat; gazete: başmakale; BOT filiz, sürgün; ANAT kiriş, veter; **lead.er.ette** [-'ret] n. (baş makaleden sonra gelen) kısa makale; '**lead.ership** n. önderlik, liderlik, öncülük.

lead-in ELECT ['li:din] n. anten iniş teli.

lead.ing ['li:diŋ] **1.** adj. önde olan, baş(lıca), ana, en önemli; yol gösteren; yöneten; ~ **article** başmakale; COM çok tutulan mal; ~ **case** JUR emsal karar; ~ **man** THEAT baş aktör; ~ **lady** baş aktris; ~ **question** istenilen cevaba götüren soru; **2.** n. yol gösterme, rehberlik, öncülük; '~**strings** n. pl. çocuk yürütme kayışları; **keep in** ~ b-nin başına kâhya kesilmek.

lead... [led]: ~ **poi.son.ing** kurşun zehirlenmesi; '~**works** n. mst sg. kurşun dökümhanesi.

leaf [li:f] n., pl. **leaves** [li:vz] yaprak; kanat (kapı, masa); **in** ~ yapraklanmış, yeşermiş; **come into** ~ yapraklanmak; '**leaf.age** n. yapraklar; '**leaf-bud** n. yaprak tomurcuğu; '**leaf.less** adj. yapraksız; **leaf.let** ['-lit] n. yaprakçık; ufak risale, broşür; '**leaf.y** adj. yapraklı.

league[1] [li:g] **1.** n. birleşme, ittifak; birlik, cemiyet; spor: lig; ♀ **of Nations** Milletler Cemiyeti; **2.** v/t. & v/i. birleş(tir)mek.

league[2] mst poet. [-] n. fersah (4,8 km.).

leak [li:k] **1.** n. delik, akıntı, sızıntı (a. fig.); **2.** v/t. & v/i. sız(dır)mak; ~ **out** fig. sız(dır)mak (haber); '**leak.age** n. sızıntı, sızma (a. fig.); COM fire; '**leak.y** adj. sızıntılı, delik.

lean[1] [li:n] **1.** adj. zayıf, cılız; yağsız (yemek); verimsiz, kıraç; **2.** n. yağsız et.

lean[2] [-] **1.** (irr.) v/t. & v/i. daya(n)mak yasla(n)mak (**against** -e); güvenmek (**on, upon** -e); yana yat(ır)mak, eğilmek; meyletmek (**to, towards** -e); **2.** n. (fig. a. '**lean.ing**) eğilim, meyil.

lean.ness ['li:nnis] n. zayıflık; yağsızlık.

leant [lent] pret. & p.p. of **lean**[2] 1.

lean-to ['li:ntu:] n. sundurma.

leap [li:p] **1.** n. atlama, sıçrayış; atlanılan mesafe; ani artış; **by** ~**s** (**and bounds**) büyük hızla, çok hızlı; **2.** (irr.) v/t. & v/i. atla(t)mak, sıçra(t)mak, fırla(t)mak; **he** ~**t at the opportunity** fırsatı kaçırmadı, fırsatı ganimet bildi; '~**frog 1.** n. birdirbir oyunu; **2.** v/i. birdirbir oynamak; **leapt** [lept]

pret. & p.p. of **leap 2**; '**leap-year** n. artıkyıl.

learn [lə:n] (irr.) vb. öğrenmek; işitmek, haber almak; ezberlemek; sl. sormak, göstermek; ~ **from** -den haber almak; **learn.ed** □ ['-nid] âlim, bilgili; üstünde çok çalışılmış; '**learn.er** n. bşi öğrenen kimse, yeni başlayan; '**learn.ing** n. bilgi, öğrenme, ilim; **learnt** [lə:nt] pret. & p.p. of **learn**.

lease [li:s] **1.** n. kira(lama); kira kontratı; **let (out) on** ~ kiraya vermek; **a new** ~ **of life** yeniden doğma; **2.** v/t. kiralamak; kiraya vermek; '~**.hold 1.** n. kiralanmış mal; **2.** adj. kiralanmış...; '~**.holder** n. kiracı.

leash [li:ʃ] **1.** n. tasma sırımı (veya kayışı); **hold in** ~ fig. yuları elden bırakmamak; **strain at the** ~ fig. serbest kalmağa can atmak; **2.** v/t. iple bağlamak.

least [li:st] **1.** adj. en az, en ufak, en küçük, asgarî; **2.** adv. a. ~ **of all** hiç, zerre kadar; **at (the)** ~ hiç olmazsa, en azından, bari; **at the very** ~ en az, en aşağı; **not in the** ~ hiç; **to say the** ~ en azından, hiç olmazsa.

leath.er ['leðə] **1.** n. deri, kösele, meşin; F meşin top; ~**s** pl. deri ürünleri; **2.** adj. deriden mamul, deri...; **3.** v/t. deri ile kaplamak; kayışla dövmek; **leath.erette** [-'ret] n. suni deri; '**leath.ern** ['leðən] adj. deriden yapılmış; '**leather.neck** n. MIL Am. sl. bahriyeli; '**leather.y** adj. kösele gibi (a. fig.).

leave [li:v] **1.** n. müsaade; a. ~ **of absence** izin; veda, ayrılma; izin süresi; **by your** ~ izninizle, müsaadenizle; **take one's** ~ veda etm., ayrılmak; **take** ~ **of** ile vedalaşmak; -den ayrılmak; **take** ~ **of one's senses** kafayı üşütmek, aklını kaçırmak; **2.** (irr.) v/t. bırakmak, terketmek; ayrılmak -den; geçmek -i; ardında bırakmak; miras olarak bırakmak; vazgeçmek; **be left** (arta) kalmak; ~ **it at that** burada bırakmak, burada kesmek, üstelememek; s. **call**; ~ **behind** geride bırakmak; unutmak; ~ **off** bırakmak, vazgeçmek; giymemek; takmamak; ~ **s.o. to himself** veya **to his own devices** b-ni kendi haline bırakmak; ~ **s.o.** veya **s.th. alone** b-ne veya bşe karışmamak, dokunmamak; **be (nicely) left** F üçkâğıda getirilmek, şapa oturtulmak; çıkmazda olm.; v/i. gitmek, yola çıkmak (**for** -e).

leav.en ['levn] **1.** *n.* maya (*a. fig.*); **2.** *v/t.* mayalamak; *fig.* bozmak, değiştirmek; etkilemek; '**leav.en.ing** *n.* mayalama; bozma.

leaves [li:vz] *pl. of* **leaf**.

leav.ings ['li:viŋz] *n. pl.* artık.

lech.er ['letʃə] *n.* zampara, çapkın erkek, şehvet düşkünü adam; '**lech.er.ous** *adj.* şehvet düşkünü, çapkın; '**lech.er.y** *n.* şehvet (düşkünlüğü), çapkınlık.

lec.tern ECCL ['lektən] *n.* kürsü.

lec.ture ['lektʃə] **1.** *n.* konferans; umumî ders; azarlama, paylama; *s.* **curtain**; **read s.o. a ~** *b-ni* azarlamak, paylamak; **~ room** konferans salonu; **2.** *v/i.* konferans vermek, ders vermek (**on** *üzerine, hakkında*); *v/t.* azarlamak, paylamak; '**lectur.er** *n.* konferansçı; UNIV doçent; ECCL vaiz; '**lec.ture.ship** *n.* doçentlik.

led [led] *pret. & p.p. of* **lead²** *2*.

ledge [ledʒ] *n.* düz çıkıntı; kaya tabakası.

ledg.er ['ledʒə] *n.* COM defteri kebir; MEC travers; *a.* **~ line** MUS yardımcı çizgi.

lee NAUT [li:] *n.* rüzgâr altı, boca.

leech [li:tʃ] *n.* ZOO sülük (*a. fig.*); **stick like a ~** *fig.* sülük gibi yapışmak.

leek BOT [li:k] *n.* pırasa.

leer [liə] **1.** *n.* yan gözle bakma; **2.** *v/i.* kötü niyetle bakmak, yan gözle bakmak (**at** *-e*); '**leer.y** ☐ *sl.* kuşkulu (**of** *-den*).

lees [li:z] *n. pl.* tortu, posa.

lee.ward NAUT ['li:wəd] *adj. & adv.* boca(ya doğru).

lee.way NAUT ['li:wei] *n.* rüzgâr altına düşme; **make ~** bocalamak; *fig.* geri kalmak; **make up ~** *fig.* kaybolan zamanı telâfi etm., açığı kapatmak.

left¹ [left] *pret. & p.p. of* **leave** *2*.

left² [-] **1.** *adj.* sola ait, sol(daki)...; **2.** *adv.* sola doğru; **3.** *n.* sol taraf; sol kanat; '**~-hand** *adj.* sol koldaki..., soldaki...; sol elle yapılan; '**~-'hand.ed** ☐ solak; solaklar için yapılmış; *fig.* sakar, beceriksiz, salak; içten olmayan (*iltifat*); MEC sağdan sola.

left...: '**~-'lug.gage of.fice** eşya dairesi, emanet; '**~.o.vers** *n. pl.* artık yemek.

left-wing ['left'wiŋ] *adj.* POL sol kanat.

leg [leg] *n.* bacak; mobilya ayağı; but; pantolon bacağı; MATH pergel ayağı; **give s.o. a ~ up** binmesine *veya* tırmanmasına yardım etm.; *fig. b-ne* kara gününde yardım etm.; **be on one's last ~s** F ayaklarına kara su inmek; ölüm döşeğinde olm.; **pull s.o.'s ~** *b-ne* takılmak; **not have a ~ to stand on** *fig.* fikrini savunamamak, tutunacak dalı kalmamak.

leg.a.cy ['legəsi] *n.* miras, kalıt; '**~-hunt.er** *n.* miras avcısı.

le.gal ☐ ['li:gəl] kanunî, meşru, kanuna uygun; hukukî; **~ capacity** medeni hakları kullanma ehliyeti; **~ entity** tüzel kişi, hükmî şahıs; **~ remedy** kanunî çözüm; **~ status** hukuki durum; *s.* **tender**; **le.gal.i.ty** [li:'gæliti] *n.* kanunilik, kanuna uygunluk; **le.gal.i.za.tion** [li:gəlai'zeiʃən] *n.* tasdik, onaylama, kanunlaştırma; '**legal.ize** *v/t.* kanunlaştırmak, meşru kılmak.

leg.ate ['legit] *n.* Papa elçisi; elçi, sefir.

leg.a.tee JUR [legə'ti:] *n.* vâris, mirasçı, kalıtçı.

le.ga.tion [li'geiʃən] *n.* orta elçilik (dairesi).

leg-bail ['leg'beil] *n.*: **give ~** tabanları yağlamak, sıvışmak.

leg.end ['ledʒənd] *n.* masal, hikâye, efsane; yazı; '**leg.end.ar.y** *adj.* efsanevî.

leg.er.de.main ['ledʒədə'mein] *n.* el çabukluğu, hokkabazlık.

legged [legd] *adj.* ...bacaklı; '**leg.gings** *n. pl.* tozluk; '**leg.gy** *adj.* uzun bacaklı.

leg.horn [le'gɔ:n] *n.* legorn, bir çeşit tavuk.

leg.i.bil.i.ty [ledʒi'biliti] *n.* okunaklılık; **leg.i.ble** ['ledʒəbl] ☐ okunaklı (*yazı*).

le.gion ['li:dʒən] *n.* eski Roma alayı; *fig.* kalabalık; birçok; '**le.gion.ar.y 1.** *adj.* alaya ait, alay...; **2.** *n.* alay eri.

leg.is.late ['ledʒisleit] *v/i.* kanun yapmak; **leg.is'la.tion** *n.* yasama; yasa, kanunlar; **leg.is.la.tive** ☐ ['_lətiv] yasamalı; **leg.is.la.tor** ['_leitə] *n.* kanun yapan kimse; **leg.is.la.ture** ['_leitʃə] *n.* yasama kurulu.

le.git.i.ma.cy [li'dʒitiməsi] *n.* kanuna uygunluk, kanuni olma, yasallık; **le-'git.imate 1.** ☐ [_mit] kanuna uygun, kanunî, meşru; mantıklı, akla yatkın, makûl; meşru doğmuş; **2.** [_meit] *v/t.* kanuna uygun kılmak; onaylamak; **le.git.i'ma.tion** *n.* kanunî kılma; '**le'git.i.ma.tize** [_mətaiz], **le'git.i.mize** = **le.gitimate** *2*.

leg.ume ['legju:m] *n.* baklagillerden herhangi bir bitki; **le'gu.mi.nous** [_minəs] *adj.* baklagillere ait, baklagiller...

lei.sure ['leʒə] **1.** *n.* boş vakit; serbestlik; *be at* ~ serbest olm., boş vakti olm.; acelesi olmamak; *at your* ~ boş vaktinizde, vaktiniz olduğunda; **2.** *adj.* boş..., serbest...; **'lei.sured** *adj.* boş vakti olan; *the* ~ *classes* aristokrat sınıfı; **'lei.sure.ly 1.** *adj.* acelesiz iş yapan; acelesiz yapılan; **2.** *adv.* rahatça, acelesiz, yavaş yavaş.

lem.on ['lemən] *n.* limon (ağacı); limon sarısı renk; **lem.on.ade** [-'neid] *n.* limonata; **'lem.on-'squash** *n.* limon suyu; **'lem.on-squeez.er** *n.* limonluk.

lend [lend] (*irr.*) *v/t.* ödünç vermek, borç vermek; vermek; ~ *a hand* yardım elini uzatmak; ~ *o.s. to* -*e* yanaşmak; -*e* elverişli olm.; ~*ing library* ödünç kitap veren kütüphane; **'lend.er** *n.* ödünç veren kimse; **'Lend-'Lease Act** ödünç verme *veya* kiralama sistemi kanunu (*Am. 1941*).

length [leŋθ] *n.* uzunluk; boy; süre, müddet; mesafe; *at* ~ nihayet, sonunda; baştan sona kadar; *at* (*great*) ~ ayrıntılarıyle, uzun uzadıya; *go all* ~*s* sonuna kadar gitmek, her çareye başvurmak; *go* (*to*) *great* ~*s* ...için çok uğraşmak, her çareye başvurmak; *he goes the* ~ *of saying* ...diyecek kadar ileri gider; **'length.en** *v/t.* & *v/i.* uza(t)-mak; **'length.ways, 'length.wise** *adv.* uzunluğuna, uzunlamasına; **'length.y** □ upuzun.

le.ni.ence, le.ni.en.cy ['liːnjəns(i)] = *lenity;* **'le.ni.ent** □ yumuşak huylu, merhametli; kibar; **'len.i.tive** MED **1.** *adj.* yatıştırıcı; **2.** *n.* yatıştırıcı ilâç; **len.i.ty** ['leniti] *n.* yumuşaklık; merhamet; kibarlık.

lens [lenz] *n.* mercek, adese, pertavsız; PHOT objektif; ~ *system* PHOT mercek sistemi.

lent[1] [lent] *pret.* & *p.p.* of *lend.*

Lent[2] [-] *n.* büyük perhiz.

Lent.en ['lentən] *adj.* büyük perhize ait, büyük perhiz...

len.tic.u.lar □ [len'tikjulə] merceğe ait, mercek...; mercekli...

len.til BOT ['lentil] *n.* mercimek.

leop.ard ['lepəd] *n.* pars, panter.

lep.er ['lepə] *n.* cüzamlı kimse.

lep.re.chaun *Ir.* ['leprəkɔːn] *n.* cin.

lep.ro.sy MED ['leprəsi] *n.* cüzam, miskin hastalığı; **'lep.rous** *adj.* cüzamlı; cüzama ait, cüzam...

les.bian ['lezbiən] *n.* sevici (*kadın*); **'lesbian.ism** *n.* sevicilik.

lese-maj.es.ty JUR ['liːz'mædʒisti] *n.* hıyanet, hainlik.

le.sion ['liːʒən] *n.* yara, bere.

less [les] **1.** *adj.* & *adv.* daha az, daha küçük; **2.** *prp.* MATH eksi; COM indirimli, çıkarılmak üzere; *no* ~ *than* en azından; *no* ~ *a person than* ... kadar önemli; *none the* ~ yine de, bununla birlikte, hal böyle iken.

...less [lis] *suffix* ...sız, ...siz.

les.see [le'siː] *n.* kiracı.

less.en ['lesn] *v/t.* & *v/i.* küçül(t)mek, azal(t)mak, eksil(t)mek; *fig.* küçümsemek.

less.er ['lesə] *adj.* daha az, daha küçük.

les.son ['lesn] *n.* ders; ibret (*a.* ECCL); ~*s pl.* dersler, öğretim; *teach s.o. a* ~ *b-ne* ders vermek; *b-ne* ders olm.

les.sor [le'sɔː] *n.* kiraya veren kimse.

lest [lest] *cj.* olmasın diye, ...mesin diye; korkusu ile, belki, olmaya ki.

let[1] [let] (*irr.*) *v/t.* müsaade etm. -*mesine,* izin vermek -*mesine;* bırakmak; kiraya vermek; ~ *alone* el sürmemek, dokunmamak; *adv.* ...saymazsak, ...bırak, ...şöyle dursun; ~ *be* dokunmamak, kendi haline bırakmak; ~ *down* indirmek; kısaltmak; düşürmek; hayal kırıklığına uğratmak, boşa çıkarmak; ~ *s.o. down gently b-ni* hafifçe cezalandırmak, *b-ni* alıştıra alıştıra hayal kırıklığına uğratmak; ~ *drive at s.o. b-ne* girişmek; ~ *fly* savurmak, fırlatmak, atmak; *fig.* bağırıp çağırmak; ~ *go* elinden bırakmak, koyvermek, salıvermek; ~ *it go at that* konuyu burada kesmek; ~ *into* -*e* ortak etm., -*e* sırdaş etm.; -*e* açmak (*pencere vs.*); ~ *loose* salıvermek, serbest bırakmak; ~ *off* cezasını affetmek, cezasını hafifletmek; patlatmak, ateşlemek; *s.* *steam;* ~ *out* boşaltmak; genişletmek, bollaştırmak (*elbise*); ağzından kaçırmak (*sır*); salıvermek; kiraya vermek; ~ *the cat out of the bag* ağzından kaçırmak; *v/i.* kiralanmak (*at, for* -*e*); ~ *on* F ağzından kaçırmak; ~ *out at* -*e* saldırmak, -*e* çifte atmak; *fig.* -*e* çıkışmak; ~ *up* durmak, dinmek (*yağmur*).

let[2] [-] *n. a.* ~ *ball tenis:* net; *without* ~ *or hindrance* hiç bir engelle karşılaşmadan.

le.thal □ ['liːθəl] öldürücü.

le.thar.gic, le.thar.gi.cal □ [le'θɑː-dʒik(əl)] uyuşuk (*a. fig.*); **leth.ar.gy** ['leθədʒi] *n.* bitkinlik; *fig.* uyuşukluk.

Le.the ['li:θi:] *n.* MYTH suyundan içenlere geçmişi unutturan nehir.

let.ter ['letə] **1.** *n.* mektup; harf; **~s** *pl.* edebiyat, ilim; **by ~** mektupla; **man of ~s** edebiyatçı, ilim adamı; **to the ~** harfi harfine, harfiyen; **2.** *v/t.* kitap harfiyle yazmak; '**~-bal.ance** *n.* mektup terazisi; '**~-box** *n.* mektup kutusu; '**~-card** *n.* katlanınca zarf olan mektup kağıdı; '**~-carri.er** *n. Am.* postacı; '**~-case** *n.* mektup mahfazası, portföy; '**~-cov.er** *n.* mektup zarfı; '**let.tered** *adj.* okumuş, bilgili, tahsilli; '**let.ter-file** *n.* mektup dosyası; '**letter-found.er** *n.* harf dökümcüsü; **let.tergram** ['~græm] *n.* indirimli telgraf; '**letter-head** *n.* mektup başlığı; başlıklı kağıt; '**let.ter.ing** *n.* harflerle yazma, harf sıralama; harfler.

let.ter...; '**~.less** *adj.* kültürsüz; '**~.o.pen.er** *n.* mektup açacağı; '**~'per.fect** *adj.* THEAT rolünü harfi harfine ezberlemiş; '**~.press** *n.* TYP kitabın yazılı kısmı; **~ printing** tipo baskısı; '**~-press** *n.* linotip; '**~-weight** *n.* kağıdın uçmasını önlemek için üstüne konulan ağırlık, prespapye.

let.tuce BOT ['letis] *n.* salata, marul.

leu.ko... ['lju:kəu] *prefix* renksiz, beyaz; **leu.ko.cyte** ['~.sait] *n.* akyuvar, lökosit; **leu.k(a)e.mi.a** MED [lju:'ki:miə] *n.* lösemi, kan kanseri.

Le.vant¹ [li'vænt] *v/i.* kaçmak (*esp. alacaklılardan*).

Le.vant² [~] *n.* Akdeniz'in doğusu ve buradaki ülkeler; **Le.vant.ine** ['levəntain] **1.** *n.* Yakın Doğulu kimse, Levanten; **2.** *adj.* Yakın Doğu'da ticaret yapan; Yakın Doğu'ya ait.

lev.ee¹ HIST ['levi] *n.* kabul merasimi.

lev.ee² *Am.* [~] *n.* set; rıhtım.

lev.el ['levl] **1.** *adj.* düz, düzlem; ufkî, yatay, bir hizada; dengeli, ölçülü; **my ~ best** elimden ne gelirse; **~ crossing** RAIL hemzemin geçit; **~ stress** GR serbest vurgu; **2.** *n.* seviye, hiza, derece; düzlük, düz yer, yüzey; tesviye aleti; *fig.* sosyal norm; **~ of the sea** deniz seviyesi; **on a ~ with** ile aynı seviyede (*a. fig*); **dead ~** dümdüz yüzey; *fig.* tekdüzelik, monotonluk; **on the ~** F dürüst, doğru sözlü; **3.** *v/t.* düzlemek, tesviye etm.; *surv.* tesviye aletleriyle ölçmek; *fig.* alıştırmak, uydurmak; doğrultmak (*silah*) (**at** *-e*); **~ with the ground** yerle bir seviyeye getirmek; **~ down** alçaltarak eşitlemek; **~ up** yükselterek eşitle-

mek; *v/i.* **~ at**, **~ against** *-i* suçlamak, *-e* suç yüklemek; **~ off** AVIA havalandıktan sonra yatay olarak uçmak; '**~'head.ed** *adj.* sağgörülü, mantıklı; '**lev.el.(l)er** *n. surv.* düzlemci; *fig.* sınıf farklarını yok etmek isteyen kimse; '**lev.el.(l)ing** *adj.* tesviye etme... düzeltme...

le.ver ['li:və] **1.** *n.* manivela (kolu); **2.** *v/t.* manivela ile kaldırmak; '**le.ver.age** *n.* manivela gücü; *sl.* piston.

lev.er.et ['levərit] *n.* tavşan yavrusu.

le.vi.a.than [li'vaiəθən] *n.* büyük su hayvanı.

le.vis ['li:vaiz] *n. pl.* blucin.

lev.i.tate ['leviteit] *v/t.* havaya kaldırmak; *v/i.* havaya kalkmak.

Le.vite ['li:vait] *n. İncil*: Levi kabilesinden biri.

lev.i.ty ['leviti] *n.* hoppalık; ciddiyetsizlik; hafife alma.

lev.y ['levi] **1.** *n.* toplama, tarh; MIL zorla asker toplama; toplanan asker; *capital* **~** varlık (*veya* sermaye) vergisi; **2.** *v/t.* tarh etm., toplamak (*vergi* vs.); zorla toplamak; haczetmek, el koymak; açmak (*savaş*) (**on**, **against** *-e* karşı).

lewd □ [lu:d] şehvet düşkünü; müstehcen, açık saçık; '**lewd.ness** *n.* şehvet düşkünlüğü; müstehcenlik.

lex.i.cal □ ['leksikəl] sözlüğe ait, kelimelere ait, kelime...

lex.i.cog.ra.pher [leksi'kɔgrəfə] *n.* sözlük düzenleyen kimse, sözlükçü; **lex.i.cograph.i.cal** □ [~.kəu'græfikəl] sözlüğe ait, sözlük...; **lex.i.cog.ra.phy** [~'kɔgrəfi] *n.* sözlük düzenleme, sözlükçülük; **lex.i.con** ['~.kən] *n.* sözlük.

li.a.bil.i.ty [laiə'biliti] *n.* sorumluluk, mesuliyet; JUR mükellefiyet; *fig.* engel, ayak bağı; *liabilities pl.* borç; COM pasif.

li.a.ble □ ['laiəbl] sorumlu (**for** *-den*); JUR mükellef; maruz (**to** *-e*); ıstırap çeken (**to** *-den*); meyilli (**to** *inf. -meğe*); **be ~ to** *-e* maruz olm.; **~ to duty** gümrüğe tabi; **~ to punishment** cezalandırılabilir, cezaya tabi.

li.ai.son [li'eizn] *n.* bağlantı, birleş(tir)-me; gizli ilişki (*cinsel*); MIL irtibat; **~ officer** irtibat subayı.

li.ar ['laiə] *n.* yalancı.

li.ba.tion [lai'beifən] *n.* fanrı'nın şerefine içilen içkinin yere dökülmesi; içki, işret.

li.bel ['laibəl] **1.** *n.* hakaret (**on** *-e*); JUR iftira; dava dilekçesi; **2.** *v/t. -e* iftira etm., *-e* leke sürmek; JUR dilekçe vererek dava etm.; '**li.bel.(l)ous**□ iftira kabilinden; iftiracı, lekeleyici...

lib.er.al ['libərəl] **1.** □ serbest düşünceli, açık fikirli; POL liberal; cömert, eli açık; bol, pek çok; yüksek (*tahsil*); serbest; **2.** *n.* liberal; '**lib.er.al.ism** *n.* liberalizm, serbest fikirlilik; **lib.er.al.i.ty** [‿'ræliti] *n.* cömertlik; serbest fikirlilik, liberallik.

lib.er.ate ['libəreit] *v/t.* kurtarmak, özgür kılmak (**from** -*den*); salıvermek, azat etm., serbest bırakmak; **lib.er.a-tion** *n.* kurtuluş; serbest bırakma, kurtarma; '**lib.er.a.tor** *n.* kurtarıcı.

lib.er.tine ['libəti:n] **1.** *n.* şehvet düşkünü kimse, ahlâksız adam; **2.** *adj.* şehvet düşkünü, ahlâksız, hovarda, çapkın; **liber.tin.ism** ['libətinizəm] *n.* çapkınlık, hovardalık.

lib.er.ty ['libəti] *n.* hürriyet, serbestlik, özgürlük; ayrıcalık, hak; **take liberties** küstahlık etm., terbiyesizlik etm.; **be at ‿** serbest olm., özgür olm.; **be at ‿ to do** *bş* yapmaya hakkı olm.; **‿ of conscience** vicdan hürriyeti; **‿ of speech** konuşma özgürlüğü; **‿ of the press** basın özgürlüğü.

li.bid.i.nous □ [li'bidinəs] şehvet düşkünü.

li.brar.i.an [lai'beəriən] *n.* kütüphane memuru, kütüphaneci; **li.brar.y** ['laibrəri] *n.* kütüphane, kitaplık; kitaplar serisi.

li.bret.to MUS [li'bretəu] *n.* opera güftesi, opera kitabı.

lice [lais] *pl. of* **louse**.

li.cence ['laisəns] *n.* ruhsat(name), izin (tezkeresi); müsaade, lisans; çapkınlık, serbestlik, riayetsizlik; **driving ‿** ehliyet.

li.cense [‿] **1.** = **licence**; **2.** *v/t.* ruhsat *veya* yetki vermek -*e*; izin vermek -*e*; **licensing hours** *pl.* meyhanelerde içki içilebilen saatler; **li.cen.see** [‿'si:] *n.* ruhsat sahibi.

li.cen.ti.ate UNIV [lai'senʃiit] *n.* resmen izinli kimse.

li.cen.tious □ [lai'senʃəs] şehvet düşkünü, ahlâksız.

li.chen BOT & MED ['laikən] *n.* liken.

lich.gate ['litʃgeit] = **lychgate**.

lick [lik] **1.** *n.* yalama, yalayış; *Am.* hayvanların tuz yaladığı yer; *sl.* darbe, tokat, sille; F sürat, hız, tempo; **2.** *v/t.* yalamak; F dayak atmak -*e*, pataklamak; yenmek, üstesinden gelmek; *v/i.* hızla gitmek; **‿ the dust** yenilmek; öldürül-

mek; yeri öpmek; **‿ into shape** hazırlamak; adam etm.; '**lick.er.ish** *adj.* ahlâksız, hovarda; pisboğaz, obur, açgözlü; '**lick.ing** *n.* yalama, yalayış; F dayak, kötek; F yenilgi; '**lick.spit.tle** *n.* dalkavuk, yaltakçı kimse, çanak yalayıcı.

lic.o.rice BOT ['likəris] *n.* meyan(kökü).

lid [lid] *n.* kapak; göz kapağı; *sl.* şapka; **put the ‿ on it** F üzerine tüy dikmek, bardağı taşıran son damla olm.; sonu olm.

li.do ['li:dəu] *n.* havuz; plaj.

lie¹ [lai] **1.** *n.* yalan, palavra; **give s.o. the ‿** *b-ni* yalancılıkla suçlamak; **tell a ‿** yalan söylemek; **white ‿** zararsız yalan; **2.** *v/i.* yalan söylemek.

lie² [‿] **1.** *n.* yatış; yer, mevki; **the ‿ of the land** bir arazinin doğal özellikleri; durum, gidişat; **2.** (*irr.*) *v/i.* yatmak, uzanmak; durmak, kalmak, olmak; JUR kanunen uygun olm.; **‿ by** istifade edilmemek; istirahat etm., sakin olm.; **‿ down** yatmak, uzanmak; **take it lying down** alttan almak, sineye çekmek, ister istemez katlanmak; **as far as in me ‿s** elimden geldiğince; **‿ in** geç saatlere kadar yatmak; loğusa olm.; **‿ in wait for** pusuya yatmak; **‿ over** COM sonraya bırakılmak, ertelenmek; **‿ to** NAUT rüzgâra karşı giderken (neredeyse) durmak; **‿ under** -*e* bağlı olm.; **‿ up** çok yatmak; gizlenmek, saklanmak; **it ‿s with you** o sizin işiniz, o size kalmış; **let sleeping dogs ‿** *fig.* uyuyan yılanın kuyruğuna basma.

lie-a.bed ['laiəbed] *n.* uykucu kimse; **lie-'down** *n.* kestirme, şekerleme.

lief *lit.* [li:f] *adv.* seve seve, memnuniyetle; '**lief.er** *adv.* daha çok, tercihan.

liege HIST [li:dʒ] **1.** *adj.* işini kullarına gördüren; **2.** *n. a.* **‿man** derebeyi kölesi; *a.* **‿ lord** derebeylik lordu.

lie-in [lai'in] *n.* **have a ‿** sabahleyin geç vakte kadar yatmak.

li.en JUR ['liən] *n.* ipotek.

lieu [lju:] *n.*: **in ‿ of** -*in* yerine.

lieu.ten.an.cy [lef'tenənsi, NAUT le'tenənsi] *n.* teğmenlik; NAUT yüzbaşılık.

lieu.ten.ant [lef'tenənt, NAUT le'tenənt] *n.* teğmen; NAUT yüzbaşı; vekil, yardımcı; '**‿colo.nel** *n.* yarbay; '**‿com'mand.er** *n.* kıdemli yüzbaşı; '**‿gen.er.al** *n.* korgeneral; '**‿gov.er.nor** *n.* vali muavini.

life [laif] *n., pl.* **lives** [laivz] hayat, yaşam, ömür; can(lılık); biyografi,

yaşam öyküsü; yaşam tarzı; ~ *and limb*
hayat; *for* ~ hayat boyu; *for one's* ~, *for*
dear ~ bütün gücü ile, canla başla; *to*
the ~ tıpatıp, aynen; ~ *sentence* müebbet (*veya* ömür boyu) hapis cezası;
have the time of one's ~ dilediğince
eğlenmek, kurtlarını dökmek; '~an-
nu.i.ty *n.* ömür boyu gelir; '~as.sur.
ance *n.* hayat sigortası; '~belt *n.* cankurtaran kemeri; '~blood *n.* yaşam
için gerekli olan kan (*a. fig.*); '~boat
n. cankurtaran sandalı, filika; '~buoy
n. cankurtaran simidi; '~giv.ing *adj.*
canlandırıcı, hayat verici; '~guard *n.*
cankurtaran yüzücüsü; '~'in.ter.est
n. kaydı hayat şartıyla intifa, yaşadığı
sürece mülk hakkı (*in -de*); '~jack.et
n. NAUT cankurtaran yeleği; '~less ☐
cansız (*a. fig.*); ölü (gibi); '~less.ness
n. cansızlık; '~like *adj.* canlı gibi görünen; '~line *n.* cankurtaran halatı;
'~long *adj.* ömür boyu süren; '~pre-
serv.er *n. Am.* cankurtaran yeleği; topuzlu baston, lobut.
lif.er *sl.* ['laifə] *n.* ömür boyu hapse
mahkûm kimse.
life...: '~sav.er *n.* cankurtaran kimse
veya şey; '~'size(d) *adj.* doğal büyük-
lükte (*resim, heykel vs.*); '~sup.port *n.*
ağır hasta bir kimsenin hayatta kal-
masını sağlayan tıbbi aygıt ya da maki-
ne, yaşam destek (*ünitesi/makinesi*);
'~strings *n. pl.* hayat bağları; '~time
n. hayat süresi, ömür; '~'work *n.*
tüm hayatın verildiği (*veya* ömür boyu)
iş.
lift [lift] 1. *n.* kaldırma, kaldırış, yük-
sel(t)me; MEC sia; PHYS, AVIA kaldırma
gücü; asansör; *fig.* neşe, canlılık; *give*
s.o. a ~ *b-ni* arabasına almak; 2. *v/t.*
& v/i. kaldırmak (*a. fig.*), yüksel(t)-
mek; *oft.* ~ *up* kaldırmak (*masa vs.*);
yükseltmek (*ses*); dikmek (*kulak-*
larını); kökünden sökmek (*bitki*); *sl.*
aşırmak, yürütmek, araklamak; '~at-
tend.ant, '~boy *n.* asansör görevlisi;
'lift.er *n.* vinç, kaldırıcı; hırsız, yankesici; 'lift.ing *adj.* MEC kaldırıcı, kaldırma...; ~ *power* AVIA kaldırma kuvveti;
'lift-off *n.* kalkış, yükselme (*roket vs.*).
lig.a.ment ANAT ['ligəmənt] *n.* bağ.
lig.a.ture ['ligətʃə] 1. *n.* bağ(lama); MED
kanı durduran bağ; MUS, TYP bağ; 2. *v/t.*
tel ile bağlamak.
light¹ [lait] 1. *n.* ışık (*a. fig.*), aydınlık;
ateş; bilgi kaynağı; *fig.* parlaklık,
canlılık; gün ışığı, gündüz; görüş; ~s

pl. yetenekler, cevher; örnek alınacak
kimse; pencere, aydınlık; PAINT resmin
aydınlık kısmı; *in the* ~ *of -in* ışığında,
-e göre; *come* (*bring*) *to* ~ açığa
çık(ar)mak, ortaya çık(ar)mak; *will*
you give me a ~ ateşinizi rica edebilir
miyim?, sigaramı yakar mısınız?; *put a*
~ *to* yakmak *-i*, tutuşturmak *-i*; *see the*
~ doğmak, dünyaya gelmek; ortaya
çıkmak, meydana gelmek; *fig.* sonunda anlamak; 2. *adj.* aydınlık; soluk, solgun; açık (*renk*); 3. (*irr.*) *v/t. & v/i. oft.* ~
up yakmak, tutuş(tur)mak; aydınlat-
mak; neşelen(dir)mek, gül(dür)mek;
canlan(dır)mak; yanmak, alev almak;
parıldamak; ~ *out Am. sl.* yola koyulmak (*veya* düzülmek).
light² [-] 1. ☐ hafif; eksik; hazmı kolay
(*yemek*); vurgusuz (*hece*); önemsiz;
hafifmeşrep, mal (*kadın*); neşeli; endişesiz; başı dönmüş, sersemlemiş; çevik; az, küçük; ~ *current* ELECT zayıf
akım; *make* ~ *of* hafife almak -*i*, önemsememek -*i*; 2. *n. su.* = *lights*; 3. *vb.*
~*on*, ~ *upon* rastlamak, tesadüfen bulmak.
light-col.o(u)red ['laitkʌləd] *adj.* açık
renk (*elbise vs.*).
light.en¹ ['laitn] *v/t.* aydınlatmak (*a.*
fig.); *v/i.* aydınlanmak; şimşek çakmak.
light.en² [-] *v/t. & v/i.* hafifle(t)mek,
yükü(nü) azal(t)mak; neşelen(dir)-
mek.
light.er¹ ['laitə] *n.* yakıcı alet; çakmak.
light.er² NAUT [-] *n.* mavna, salapurya.
light...: '~fin.gered *adj.* hırsızlığa
yatkın, eli uzun; eli yatkın; '~hand.ed
adj. eli hafif; *fig.* becerikli; '~hand-
ed.ness *n.* becekliklik, eli hafiflik;
'~head.ed *adj.* başı dönen, sersemlemiş; düşüncesiz; kuş beyinli; '~heart-
ed ☐ neşeli, şen şakrak, mutlu;
'~house *n.* fener kulesi.
light.ing ['laitiŋ] *n.* aydınlatma; yakma;
ışıklandırma sistemi; ~ *up* ışıklandırma.
light.ly ['laitli] *adv.* hafifçe, az; kolayca;
iyice düşünmeden; çevikçe; canlılıkla,
neşeyle; 'light'mind.ed *adj.* hafif, cid-
diyetten yoksun, düşüncesiz; 'lightness *n.* hafiflik.
light.ning ['laitniŋ] *n.* şimşek, yıldırım;
like ~, *with* ~ *speed* şimşek (*veya*
yıldırım) gibi, çok çabuk; '~ar'rest.er
n. elektrik aletlerini yıldırımdan koruyan aygıt; ~ *bug Am.* ateşböceği;
'~con.duc.tor, '~rod *n.* paratoner,

yıldırımsavar, yıldırımkıran.
lights [laits] n. pl. hayvan akciğeri.
light.ship ['laitʃip] n. fener gemisi (*veya* dubası).
light.some ['laitsəm] adj. neşeli, şen şakrak; kaygısız, endişesiz; parlak, ışıklı.
light-weight ['laitweit] **1.** n. spor: tüysüklet; **2.** adj. hafif; önemsiz; karaktersiz.
lig.ne.ous ['ligniəs] adj. odunsu..., oduna benzer; **lig.nite** ['lignait] n. linyit.
lik.a.ble ['laikəbl] adj. sevimli, hoş; çekici.
like [laik] **1.** adj. & prp. gibi, benzer -e; eşit -e; **~ a man** adama yakışır(casına), adam gibi; **such ~** böylesi, benzeri, gibi; **feel ~** F hoşlanmak, canı istemek, arzulamak -i; s. **look**; **something ~** ... ...gibi bir şey, takriben; **~ that** öyle, böyle, onun gibi; **what is he ~?** neye benziyor, nasıl biridir?; **that's more ~** it bu daha iyi, kulağa daha hoş geliyor; **2.** n. benzeri, eşit; **~s** pl. sevilen şeyler, tercihler; **his ~** emsali, eşi, benzeri; **the ~** gibi, aynı; **the ~(s) of** F ...gibi, -in benzeri; **3.** v/t. sevmek -i, beğenmek, hoşlanmak -den; istemek, arzu etm. -i; **~ best** en çok sevmek; **how do you ~ London?** Londra'yı nasıl buluyorsunuz?; **I should ~ to know** bilmek istiyorum.
like.a.ble ['laikəbl] = **likable**.
like.li.hood ['laiklihud] n. ihtimal, olasılık; **'like.ly 1.** adj. muhtemel, olası; ...cek gibi; uygun, yerinde; sevimli, çekici; inanılır, güvenilir; **2.** adv. muhtemelen, belki de, galiba; **as ~ as not** olabilir ki, büyük bir olasılıkla; **he is ~ to die** galiba ölecek.
like-mind.ed ['laik'maindid] adj. hemfikir, aynı görüşte; **'lik.en** v/t. benzetmek (**to** -e); **'like.ness** n. benzerlik; görünüş; resim, tasvir; **have one's ~ taken** fotoğrafını çektirmek, resmini yaptırmak; **'likewise** adv. aynı şekilde, aynen, aynısı, dahi, keza; ayrıca, bundan başka.
lik.ing ['laikiŋ] n. (**for**) beğenme, meyil, beğeni, düşkünlük; sevme; **to s.o.'s ~** b-nin istediği gibi, zevkine göre.
li.lac ['lailək] **1.** adj. açık mor; **2.** n. BOT leylâk (rengi); açık mor.
Lil.li.pu.tian [lili'pju:ʃən] **1.** n. 'Guliver'in Seyahatleri adlı kitaptaki adada yaşayan kimse; **2.** adj. küçücük, min-

nacık.
lilt [lilt] **1.** v/i. kıvrak şarkı söylemek; **2.** n. kıvrak şarkı.
lil.y BOT ['lili] n. zambak; **~ of the valley** inciçiçeği; **'~ 'liv.ered** adj. ödlek, yüreksiz; **'~-white** adj. bembeyaz.
limb¹ [lim] n. uzuv, örgen; BOT dal; F haylaz çocuk; **out on a ~** F desteksiz.
limb² AST, BOT [-] n. kenar.
limbed [limd] suffix ...uzuvlu.
lim.ber¹ ['limbə] **1.** n. MIL toparlak; **2.** vb. mst **~ up** top arabasına koşum parçasını bağlamak.
lim.ber² [-] **1.** adj. gevşek, oynak, bükülebilir, esnek; **2.** v/t. & v/i. **~ up** esne(t)-mek, ger(il)mek, ısın(dır)mak (adale).
lim.bo ['limbəu] n. vaftiz edilmeden ölenlerle İsa'dan önce yaşayanların ruhlarının olduğu yer; sl. kodes; fig. şüphe, tereddüt.
lime¹ [laim] **1.** n. kireç; **2.** v/t. kireçlemek.
lime² BOT [-] n. ıhlamur.
lime³ BOT [-] n. misket limonu; **'~-juice** n. misket limonu suvu.
lime...: '**~-kiln** n. kireç ocağı; '**~.light** n. kireç lambası; **in the ~** fig. göz önünde, halkın dilinde.
lim.er.ick ['limərik] n. beş mısralı nükteli şiir.
lime...: '**~.stone** n. kireçtaşı; '**~-tree** n. BOT ıhlamur ağacı; '**~.twig** n. ökse çubuğu.
lim.it ['limit] **1.** n. had, sınır, uç, son, hudut; limit; **in (off) ~s** serbest (yasak) bölge (**to** için); **that is the ~!** F bu kadarı da fazla!, yetti be!; **go the ~** Am. F sınıra dayanmak; her şeyi göze almak; **2.** v/t. sınırlamak, kısıtlamak; hasretmek, vermek, ayırmak (**to** e); **lim.i'ta-tion** n. sınırlama, tahdit, kısıtlama (a. fig.); JUR sınırlandırma, hudutlandırma; kayıtlama; '**lim.it.ed 1.** adj. mahdut sayılı, sınırlı, az, kısıtlı (**to** -e); sınırlı sorumlu, limited; **~ (liability) company** sınırlı sorumlu (*veya* limited) şirket; **~ in time** zamanı kısıtlı; **2.** n. ekspres; '**limit.less** □ sınırsız, sayısız, sonsuz, uçsuz bucaksız.
limn obs. [lim] v/t. resmetmek; tasvir etm
lim.ou.sine ['liməzi:n] n. (*bölmeli şoför mahalli olan*) lüks otomobil.
limp¹ [limp] **1.** v/i. topallamak, aksamak; **2.** n. topallama.
limp² [-] adj. gevşek, yumuşak; zayıf, kuvvetsiz.

lim.pet ['limpit] *n.* zoo denizminaresi; *fig.* sülük gibi kimse.

lim.pid □ ['limpid] berrak, şeffaf; '**lim- pid.ness** *n.* berraklık, şeffaflık.

lim.y ['laimi] *adj.* kireçli; kireç gibi.

lin.age ['lainidʒ] *n.* satır sayısı.

linch.pin ['lintʃpin] *n.* dingil çivisi.

lin.den вот ['lindən] *n.* ıhlamur ağacı.

line[1] [lain] **1.** *n.* sıra, dizi, seri; çizgi, yol, hat; ip, olta, sicim; теlерн hat; *fig.* yol, metod; satır, mısra; plan, desen; сом mal; мıl saf, sıra; pusula, not; hiza; **~s** *pl.* çevre, şekil, anahat; тнеат rol; silsile, sıra; soy; çığır, devir; meslek, iş; sınır, hudut; kuyruk; demiryolu hattı; ekvator çizgisi; **~ of battle** savaş hattı; **~ of business** meslek, branş; **~ of conduct** hayat (*veya* hareket) tarzı; **ship of the ~** savaş gemisi; **hard ~s** şanssızlık, kötü talih; **all down the ~** tamamen, her yönden; **in ~ with** uygun -*e*; aynı hizada *ile*; **that is not in my ~** bu benim işim değil; **stand in ~** sıraya girmek, kuyrukta beklemek; **fall into ~ with s.o.** *b-ne* uymak, *b-le* hemfikir olm., *b-ne* katılmak; **draw the ~** *fig. bşi* reddetmek, geri çevirmek; **party ~** POL parti siyaseti; **party ~, shared ~** теlерн birkaç abonenin birden bağlandığı telefon sistemi; **toe the ~** POL kanun *veya* kurala uymak; denilen'i yapmak; **hold the ~** теlерн telefonu kapatmamak; **2.** *v/t.* dizmek, sıralamak; çizgilerle göstermek; *fig.* kırıştırmak (*yüz vs.*); **~ the streets** caddelere dizilmek; **~ out** taslağını çizmek; **~ through** çizmek, karalamak; **~ up** sıraya dizmek; *v/i.* **~ up** sıraya girmek.

line[2] [_] *v/t.* astarlamak; kaplamak; doldurmak.

lin.e.age ['liniidʒ] *n.* soy, nesil; **lin.e.al** □ ['_-əl] babadan oğula geçen; **lin.e.a.ment** ['_-əmənt] *n.* yüz hattı; **lin.e.ar** ['_-ə] *adj.* doğrusal, çizgisel.

line.man ['lainmən] *n.* demiryolu *veya* telgraf hat memuru, monoton; *Am.* = **linesman**.

lin.en ['linin] **1.** *n.* keten bezi; iç çamaşır; masa örtüleri ve yatak çarşafları; **wash one's dirty ~ in public** *fig. b-nin* kirli çamaşırlarını ortaya dökmek; **2.** *adj.* keten...; '**~-clos.et**, '**~-cup.board** *n.* çamaşır dolabı; '**~-drap.er** *n.* bez satıcısı.

lin.er ['lainə] *n.* transatlantik; yolcu uçağı; makyaj kalemi; astar; **lines.man**

['lainzmən] *n.* spor: yan hakem; '**line- -up** *n.* sıraya girme; sıra; program; *spor:* oyuncuların yerini alması, diziliş.

ling[1] ICHTH [liŋ] *n.* morinaya benzer bir balık.

ling[2] вот [_] *n.* süpürgeotu.

lin.ger ['liŋgə] *v/i.* gecikmek, ayrılamamak, oyalanmak (**over, upon** *başında*); ölüm döşeğinde kalmak; kolayca geçmemek (*ağrı vs.*); **~ at, ~ about** oyalanarak gitmek.

lin.ge.rie ['lænʒəri:] *n.* kadın iç çamaşırı.

lin.ger.ing □ ['liŋgəriŋ] uzun süre geçmeyen.

lin.go ['liŋgəu] *n.* (yabancı) dil, lisan; anlaşılması güç deyimlerle dolu konuşma.

lin.gua fran.ca ['liŋgwə'fræŋkə] *n.* ortak dil.

lin.gual ['liŋgwəl] *adj.* dile ait, dil...

lin.guist ['liŋgwist] *n.* dil uzmanı, dilci; çok dil bilen kimse; **lin'guis.tic** *adj.* (**~ally**) dile at, dil...; dilbilime ait, dilbilim...; **lin'guis.tics** *n. sg.* dilbilim, lengüistik.

lin.i.ment MED ['linimənt] *n.* liniment, merhem.

lin.ing ['lainiŋ] *n.* astar(lama); **every cloud has a silver ~** her işte bir hayır vardır.

link[1] [liŋk] **1.** *n.* zincir halkası; *fig. & bilgisayar* bağ(lantı), ilişki; **~s** *pl.* kol düğmesi; **2.** *v/t. & v/i.* bağla(n)mak, birleş(tir)mek; zincirlemek.

link[2] HIST [_] *n.* meşale, fener.

link.man ['liŋkmən] *n.* fenerci.

links [liŋks] *n. pl.* kumullar; *a.* **golf-~** golf oyunu alanı.

lin.net ORN {'linit] *n.* ketenkuşuna benzer bir kuş.

li.no ['lainəu] = **linoleum**; '**~-cut** *n.* linolyum gravürü.

li.no.leum [li'nəuljəm] *n.* linolyum, mantarlı taban muşambası.

lin.o.type TYP ['lainəutaip] *n.* linotip.

lin.seed ['linsi:d] *n.* ketentohumu; **~ oil** beziryağı, ketentohumu yağı.

lin.sey-wool.sey ['linzi'wulzi] *n.* yarı keten kumaş.

lint MED [lint] *n.* keten tiftiği.

lin.tel ARCH ['lintl] *n.* üst eşik, lento.

li.on ['laiən] *n.* aslan (*a.* AST & *fig.*); *fig.* tanımış şahsiyet, şöhretli kimse; **place** *veya* **put one's head in the ~'s mouth** tehlikeye atılmak, kellesini koltuğuna almak; **the ~'s share** aslan payı; '**li.on-**

ess n. dişi aslan; **'lion-heart.ed** adj. aslan yürekli; **'.~hunt.er** n. fig. ünlü kişi avcısı; **'li.on.ize** v/t. b-ni el üstünde tutmak.

lip [lip] n. dudak (a. BOT); kenar, uç; sl. küstahlık, yüzsüzlük; **curl one's ~** dudak bükmek; **none of your ~!** yüzsüzlüğün lüzumu yok!, gevezelik istemez!

lip.o.suc.tion ['lipəusʌkʃən] n. liposuction.

'lip-ser.vice n. sözde bağlılık; **'lip.stick** n. ruj.

liq.ue.fac.tion [likwi'fækʃən] n. sıvılaş(tır)ma, eri(t)me; **'liq.ue.fi.able** ['ˌfaiəbl] adj. eritilebilir; **'liq.ue.fy** v/t. & v/i. sıvılaş(tır)mak, eri(t)mek; **'liq.ues.cent** [li'kwesnt] adj. eriyebilir, eriyen.

li.queur [li'kjuə] n. likör; alkollü içki.

liq.uid ['likwid] **1.** □ SIVI..., akıcı..., akışkan...; sulu, ıslak; berrak, şeffaf; net, tatlı (ses); COM likit, kolayca paraya çevrilebilen; **2.** n. sıvı, mayi; GR yarım sesli harf.

liq.ui.date ['likwideit] v/t. COM tasfiye etm., likide etm.; ortadan kaldırmak; gebertmek, temizlemek; **liq.ui'da.tion** n. tasfiye, likidasyon; **'liq.ui.da.tor** n. tasfiye memuru.

liq.uor ['likə] **1.** n. alkollü içki, sert içki; sıvı madde; et suyu; **in ~, the worse for ~** çakırkeyf, sarhoş; **2.** v/t. & v/i. a. **~ up** sl. içki iç(ir)mek, kafayı çekmek.

liq.uo.rice BOT ['likəris] n. meyan(kökü).

li.ra ['liərə] n., pl. **li.re** ['ˌri] lira; liret.

lisp [lisp] **1.** n. peltek konuşma; **2.** v/i. peltek konuşmak.

lis.som(e) ['lisəm] adj. kıvrak, çevik, atik.

list[1] [list] **1.** n. liste, cetvel, dizin, fihrist; **2.** v/t. listeye yazmak, kaydetmek; -in listesini yapmak; v/i. askere yazılmak.

list[2] NAUT [ˌ] **1.** n. yan yatma; **2.** v/i. yan yatmak.

list.en ['lisn] **(to)** dinlemek -i, kulak vermek -e; **~ in** TELEPH, radyo; gizlice dinlemek; **~ in to** radyo: dinlemek -i; **'listen.er** n. dinleyici.

lis.ten.ing ['lisniŋ] adj. dinleme...; **~ apparatus** dinleme aleti; **'~post** n. dinleme noktası.

list.less □ ['listlis] halsiz, bitkin; kayıtsız, kaygısız; **'list.less.ness** n. halsizlik; kayıtsızlık.

lists [lists] n. pl. dövüş meydanı; **enter the ~** fig. mücadeleye girişmek, yarışa katılmak.

lit [lit] **1.** pret & p.p. of **light**[1] **3**; **2.** adj. **~ up** sl. küfelik, sarhoş.

lit.a.ny ECCL ['litəni] n. münacaat; tekrar, nakarat.

li.ter Am. ['liːtə] = **litre**.

lit.er.a.cy ['litərəsi] n. okuryazarlık; **'lit.eral 1.** □ harfi harfine, kelimesi kelimesine; kelime ile ilgili, kelime...; kesin, doğru, gerçek; fig. alelade, bayağı; kuru fikirli; **2.** n. a. **~ error** basım hatası; **'liter.al.ism**, **'lit.er.al.ness** n. harfiyen uyma; gerçekçilik.

lit.er.ar.y □ ['litərəri] edebiyatla (veya yazınla) ilgili, edebî...; **~ man** edip, yazıncı, edebiyatçı; edebiyat meraklısı; **lit.er.ate** ['ˌrit] **1.** adj. okuryazar; kültürlü, çok okumuş; **2.** n. okuryazar kimse; **lit.e.ra.ti** [litə'raːtiː] n. pl. edebiyatçılar, yazıncılar; **lit.e'ra.tim** [ˌtim] adv. kelimesi kelimesine; **lit.er.a.ture** ['litəritʃə] n. edebiyat, yazın; edebî eserler; broşür.

lithe(.some) ['laið(səm)] adj. elâstikî, esnek, kıvrak.

lith.o.graph ['liθəugraːf] **1.** n. taşbasması resim, litograf; **2.** v/t. & v/i. taşbasması ile (resim) yapmak; **li.thog.ra.pher** [li'θɔgrəfə] n. litografyacı; **lith.o.graphic** [liθəu'græfik] adj. **(~al.ly)** litografiye ait, litografi...; **li.thog.ra.phy** [li'θɔgrəfi] n. taşbasması, litografi, litografya.

Lith.u.a.ni.an [liθjuː'einjən] **1.** adj. Lituanya diline ve halkına ait; **2.** n. Lituanyalı; Lituanya dili.

lit.i.gant JUR ['litigənt] **1.** adj. davacı...; **2.** n. davacı; **lit.i.gate** ['ˌgeit] v/i. mahkemeye başvurmak; dava açmak; v/t. mahkemeye sunmak; **lit.i'ga.tion** n. dava (etme); **li.ti.gious** □ [li'tidʒəs] dava seven; JUR davaya ait, dava...; çekişmeli, kavgalı.

lit.mus CHEM ['litməs] n. turnusol; **'~pa.per** n. turnusol kâğıdı.

li.to.tes RHET ['laitəutiːz] n. bir fikri olumsuz şekilde ifade etme.

li.tre ['liːtə] n. litre.

lit.ter ['litə] **1.** n. çöp, süprüntü, çerçöp; düzensizlik, karışıklık; tahtırevan; sedye, teskere; ZOO bir batında doğan yavrular; hayvanlar için yataklık saman; **2.** v/t. karman çorman etm., karmakarışık etm., saçmak, dağıtmak; doğurmak; **~ down** altına yataklık saman sermek; **~ up** altüst etm., karmakarışık etm.; **'~bas.ket**, **'~bin** n. çöp kutusu.

lit.tle ['litl] **1.** *adj.* küçük, ufak; önemsiz, değersiz; kısa, az, biraz; *a ~ one* ufaklık, çocuk; *a ~ house* küçük bir ev; *my ~ Mary* F midem; *his ~ ways* onun garip usulleri, şeytanlıkları; ~ *people* periler; **2.** *adv.* az miktarda, birazcık, hemen hiç, nadiren, seyrek olarak; *a ~ red* hafif kırmızı; **3.** *n.* ufak miktar; az zaman; ~ *by* ~, *by ~ and* ~ azar azar, yavaş yavaş; *for a ~* kısa bir süre; *not a ~* çok; '~-go *n.* F UNIV ön imtihan; 'lit.tle.ness *n.* küçüklük.

lit.to.ral ['litərəl] **1.** *adj.* sahile yakın...; **2.** *n.* sahil boyu.

lit.ur.gy ECCL ['litə:dʒi] *n.* dua usulü.

liv.a.ble ['livəbl] *adj.* F içinde yaşanabilir; yaşamaya değer; çekilir, tahammül edilir; *mst ~-with* F geçimli (*kimse*).

live 1. [liv] *v/t. & v/i. com.* yaşamak; oturmak, ikamet etm.; geçirmek, sürmek (*hayat*); geçinmek (*on ile*); ~ *to see* bşi görecek kadar yaşamak; ~ *s.th. down* bşi unutturmak; üstesinden gelmek; ~ *in* (*out*) çalıştığı yerde (çalıştığı yer dışında) yatıp kalkmak; ~ *through* güçlüklere rağmen yaşamaya devam etm., geçmek; ~ *up to* ulaşmak *-e*, bşi doğrulayacak şekilde yaşamak; ~ *and learn* yaşadıkça öğrenmek; ~ *and let* ~ hoşgörülü olm.; **2.** [laiv] *adj.* diri, canlı, zinde; hayat dolu; gerçek; yanan (*kömür*); sönmemiş (*kor*); direkt, doğrudan; MIL patlamamış (*bomba*); ELECT akımlı, cereyanlı (*tel*); *radyo*: canlı (*yayın*); ~ *wire* fig. enerjik kimse; ~ *broadcast* canlı yayın; live.a.ble ['livəbl] *s.* **livable**; lived *comb.* ...ömürlü; live.li.hood ['laivlihud] *n.* geçim, geçinme; rızk; 'live.liness *n.* canlılık, zindelik; parlaklık; live.long ['livlɔŋ] *adj.*: *the ~ day* poet. bütün gün; live.ly ['laivli] *adj.* canlı, neşeli, şen, keyifli; hayat dolu; parlak (*renk*); zıplayan (*top*); gerçekmiş gibi; *make things ~ for s.o.* b-nin başına iş açmak, başını derde sokmak.

liv.en ['laivn] *v/t. & v/i. mst ~ up* F canlan(dır)mak, neşelen(dir)mek.

liv.er¹ ['livə] *n.* yaşayan kimse; *fast ~* hızlı yaşayan, hovarda; *good ~* zevkperest, iyi yaşamayı seven.

liv.er² [~] *n.* karaciğer; 'liv.er.ish *adj.* F karaciğerinden rahatsız, hasta.

liv.er.y¹ ['livəri] *= liverish.*

liv.er.y² [~] *n.* hizmetçi üniforması; özel üniforma; *fig.* kılık, kıyafet; *= ~-stable*;

~ **com.pa.ny** Londra'da bulunan özel üniformalı loncalardan biri; '~.man *n.* Londra'da lonca üyesi; '~-sta.ble *n.* kiralık at ahırı.

lives [laivz] *pl. of life*; 'live-stock *n.* çiftlik hayvanları; 'live-weight *n.* ücrete tabi yük (*uçak vs.'de*).

liv.id ['livid] *adj.* mavimsi, morumsu; solgun, soluk; kanı beynine sıçramış, tepesi atmış; li'vid.i.ty *n.* kurşun rengi; solgunluk.

liv.ing ['liviŋ] **1.** □ hayacta, canlı, yaşayan, diri, sağ; tıpkı; zinde, kuvvetli; *the ~ image of -in* tıpkısı, hık demiş burnundan düşmüş; *the ~ theatre* tiyatro; *the ~ pl.* yaşayanlar; *in ~ memory* yaşayanların hafızalarında; **2.** *n.* yaşayış; yaşama, geçim, geçinme; gelir; meslek; ECCL maaşlı papazlık makamı; '~-room *n.* oturma odası; '~-space *n.* hayat sahası.

liz.ard ['lizəd] *n.* ZOO kertenkele.

Liz.zie *Am. co.* ['lizi] *n.* T model Ford otomobil.

lla.ma ['lɑːmə] *n.* lama.

Lloyd's [lɔidz] *n.* Lloyd sigorta şirketi.

lo *obs.* [ləu] *int.* bak!, işte!

loach ICHTH [ləutʃ] *n.* çoprabalığı.

load [ləud] **1.** *n.* yük (*a. fig.*), hamule; ELECT şarj; endişe, üzüntü; ağırlık; MEC mukavemet; ~*s of* F dünya kadar, kucak dolusu; **2.** *v/t. & v/i.* yükle(n)-mek, yükletmek; doldurmak (*silah*); yığmak; makineye koymak (*film*); tıka basa doldurmak (*mide*); *fig.* gark etm., boğmak (*with -e*); ~ *test* dayanıklılık deneyi; ~*ed* yüklü, dolu; *sl.* küfelik, sarhoş; şaşırtıcı (*soru*); F ensesi kalın; ~*ed dice pl.* hileli zar; ~ *the dice against s.o.* fig. b-nin şansını azaltmak; b-nin aleyhine bş yapmak; 'load.er *n.* yükleyici; 'loading **1.** *adj.* yükleme...; yük...; **2.** *n.* yükleme; yük; 'load-line *n.* NAUT geminin yükleme sınırını gösteren çizgi; 'load.stone *n.* mıknatıs taşı.

loaf¹ [ləuf] *n.*, *pl.* **loaves** [ləuvz] bütün bir ekmek, somun; *sl.* kafa, kelle; *use your ~* kafanı kullan.

loaf² [~] *v/i.* vaktini boş geçirmek, aylak aylak vakit geçirmek; 'loaf.er *n.* haylaz (*veya* aylak) kimse.

loaf-sug.ar ['ləufʃugə] *n.* kesmeşeker.

loam [ləum] *n.* balçık, lüleci çamuru; verimli toprak; 'loam.y *adj.* balçık gibi; balçığa ait, balçık...

loan [ləun] **1.** *n.* ödünç verme; ödünç alma, borçlanma; ödünç verilen şey; *on*

~ **ödünç** olarak; *ask for the* ~ *of s.th.* *bşi* ödünç istemek; *put out to* ~ ödünç vermek; **2.** *v/t. part. Am.* ödünç vermek.

loath [ləuθ] *adj.* isteksiz; *be* ~ *for s.o. to do s.th.* *b-nin bş* yapmasına karşı isteksiz olm.; *nothing* ~ isteyerek, seve seve.

loathe [ləuð] *v/t.* iğrenmek, nefret etm., tiksinmek *-den*; '**loath.ing** *n.* nefret; **loath.some** □ ['-səm] iğrenç, nefret verici, tiksindirici; '**loath.some.ness** *n.* iğrençlik.

loaves [ləuvz] *pl. of loaf¹.*

lob [lɔb] *tenis:* **1.** *n.* havaya vurulan top; **2.** *v/t.* havaya vurmak *(top).*

lob.by ['lɔbi] **1.** *n.* koridor; antre; PARL kulis faaliyeti; THEAT fuaye; PARL kulis yapanlar; bekleme salonu, lobi; **2.** *v/i.* PARL meclis üyelerini etkilemek; kulis yapmak; *v/t.* kulis yaparak geçirtmek *veya* reddettirmek *(tasan);* '**lob.by.ist** *n.* PARL kulis yapan kimse.

lobe ANAT, BOT [ləub] *n.* kulak memesi; lop; ~ *of the ear* kulak memesi.

lob.ster ['lɔbstə] *n.* ıstakoz.

lo.cal ['ləukəl] **1.** □ mahalli, yöresel, yerel, bölgesel, lokal; kısmi; *s. branch*; ~ *call* TELEPH şehiriçi telefon konuşması; ~ *colour* yöresel özellikler; ~ *government* mahalli idare; **2.** *n. gazete:* yerel haber; *a.* ~ *train* RAIL banliyö treni; F semt meyhanesi; ~*s pl.* semt sakinleri; **lo.cale** [ləu'kɑːl] *n.* mahal, yer, yöre, olayın geçtiği yer; **lo.cal.ism** ['-kəlizəm] *n.* belirli bir yere duyulan ilgi; yöresel şive *veya* töre; **lo.cal.i.ty** ['-kæliti] *n.* yer, yöre, mevki; semt, mahalle; **lo.cal.ize** ['-kəlaiz] *v/t.* sınırlamak; yerini bulmak.

lo.cate [ləu'keit] *v/t.* yerleştirmek; bulmak; *Am.* yerini tayin etm., *be* ~*d* bulunmak, yerleştirilmek; *v/i.* oturmak; **lo'ca.tion** *n.* yerleş(tir)me; yer, mahal; JUR kiraya verme; *film:* stüdyo dışındaki çekim yeri; *on* ~ stüdyo dışında film çekme.

loch *Scots* [lɔk] *n.* göl, haliç, körfez.

lock¹ [lɔk] **1.** *n.* kilit; yükseltme havuzu; MEC kilitlenme; tekerlek turu; silah çakmağı; ~, *stock and barrel* tamamen, ne var ne yok hepsi; **2.** *v/t. & v/i.* kilitle(n)mek, kapa(n)mak, kenetle(n)mek; MEC bloke etm.; ~ *s.th. away* *bşi* kitleyip kaldırmak; ~ *s.o. in* *b-nin* üzerine kapıyı kilitlemek; ~ *s.o. out* *b-ni* dışarda bırakmak; lokavt yapmak;

~ *up* kilitleyip kaldırmak, kilit altında saklamak; kapıları kilitlemek; hapsetmek; yatırmak, bağlamak *(para).*

lock² [-] *n.* bukle, lüle; ~*s pl. co.* saç.

lock.age ['lɔkidʒ] *n.* gemiyi kanal havuzundan geçirme; havuzdan geçme parası; '**lock.er** *n.* dolap; *go to Davy Jones's* ~ denizin dibini boylamak, boğulmak; **lock.et** ['lɔkit] *n.* madalyon.

lock...: '~*gates* *n. pl.* kanal kapıları; '~*jaw* *n.* tetanos; '~*keep.er* *n.* kanal görevlisi; '~*nut* *n.* MEC kilit somunu; '~*out* *n.* lokavt; '~*smith* *n.* çilingir; '~*stitch* *n.* mekik dikişi; '~*up* **1.** *n.* tutukevi; COM sermayenin dondurulması; **2.** *adj.* kilitlenebilen.

lo.co *Am. sl.* ['ləukəu] *adj.* deli, kaçık.

lo.co.mo.tion [ləukə'məuʃən] *n.* hareket; **lo.co.mo.tive** ['-tiv] **1.** *adj.* harekete ait, hareket...; hareket edebilen; **2.** *n. a.* ~ *engine* lokomotif.

lo.cust ['ləukəst] *n.* çekirge; *a.* ~*tree* BOT salkım *(veya* akasya) ağacı.

lo.cu.tion [ləu'kjuːʃən] *n.* konuşma şekli, tabir, terim.

lode MIN [ləud] *n.* maden damarı; '~*star* *n.* Çobanyıldızı, Kutupyıldızı; *fig.* yol gösterici ilke; '~*stone* *n.* mıknatıs taşı.

lodge [lɔdʒ] **1.** *n.* kulübe; in; masonlar *veya* toplanma yeri, loca; küçük ev; kapıcı odası; **2.** *v/t. & v/i.* yerleş(tir)mek, barın(dır)mak; misafir etm.; emaneten vermek; sunmak; arzetmek; kirada oturmak; misafir olm.; '**lodge.ment** *s.* **lodgment**; '**lodg.er** *n.* misafir, kiracı; '**lodg.ing** *n.* kiralık oda; geçici konut; ~*s pl.* pansiyon; '**lodg.ing--house** *n.* pansiyon; '**lodg.ment** *n.* JUR arzetme, sunma, emaneten verme; sığınak, barınak; ikamet etme, yerleşme.

lo.ess ['ləuis] *n.* lös, verimli sarımtırak toprak.

loft [lɔft] *n.* çatı arası (odası), tavan arası; samanlık; kilise balkonu; '**loft.i.ness** *n.* yükseklik; *fig.* yücelik; kibirlilik; '**loft.y** □ yüksek; yüce, asil; üstün; mükemmel; gururlu, kibirli, çalımlı.

log [lɔg] *n.* kütük; NAUT parakete, geminin süratini ölçme aleti; = *log-book*; *sleep like a* ~ kütçe gibi uyumak.

lo.gan.ber.ry BOT ['ləugənbəri] *n.* yarı böğürtlen yarı ağaççileği türünden bir çeşit meyve.

log.a.rithm MATH ['lɔgəriθm] *n.* logaritma.

log...: '**~book** *n*. NAUT rota (*veya* seyir) defteri; gemi jurnalı; MOT ruhsatname; AVIA rota defteri; **~ cab.in** kütüklerden yapılmış kulübe; **logged** *adj*. ağırlaşmış (*su ile*); **log.ger.head** ['lɔgəhed] *n*.: **be at ~s** kavgalı olm. (**with** *ile*).

log.gia ['lɔdʒə] *n*. kemeraltı, sundurma, kenarı açık sıra kemerler.

log.ging ['lɔgiŋ] *n*. kerestecilik; **log house**, **log hut** kütüklerden yapılmış kulübe.

log.ic ['lɔdʒik] *n*. mantık, eseme; '**log-i.cal** □ mantıkî, makûl, uygun, mantıklı, esemeli; **lo.gi.cian** [ləu'dʒi-ʃən] *n*. mantıkçı, mantık ilmi uzmanı.

log in IT [lɔg'in] *v/i*. oturum açmak.

lo.gis.tics MIL [ləu'dʒistiks] *n. oft. sg.* lojistik.

log on IT [lɔg'ɔn] *v/i*. oturum açmak.

log out IT [lɔg'aut] *v/i*. oturum kapamak.

log.roll *part*. POL ['lɔgrəul] *v/i*. karşılıklı birbirini desteklemek.

log.wood ['lɔgwud] *n*. bakkam ağacı.

loin [lɔin] *n*. bel; fileto; **gird up one's ~s** harekete geçmeye hazırlanmak; '**~cloth** *n*. peştamal, kuşak.

loi.ter ['lɔitə] *v/i*. gezmek, yolda sık sık durarak gitmek, aylak aylak dolaşmak; **~ away** *v/t*. boşa geçirmek (*zaman*); '**loi.ter.er** *n*. aylak (*veya* avare) kimse.

loll [lɔl] *v/i*. sallanmak; aylaklık etm.; **~ about** avare dolaşmak; **~ out** dışarı sark(ıt)mak (*dil*).

lol.li.pop F ['lɔlipɔp] *n*. lolipop, şekerleme.

lol.lop F ['lɔləp] *v/i*. ayağını sürüyerek yürümek.

Lom.bard ['lɔmbəd] *n*.: **~ Street** Londra para piyasası.

Lon.don.er ['lʌndənə] *n*. Londralı.

lone [ləun] *adj*. yalnız, kimsesiz; ıssız, tenha; **lone.li.ness** ['~linis] *n*. yalnızlık, kimsesizlik; '**lone.ly**, **lonesome** □ ['~səm] yalnız, kimsesiz; ıssız, tenha; sıkıcı, kasvetli.

long¹ [lɔŋ] **1.** *n*. uzun zaman; uzun hece; **before ~** çok geçmeden, yakında; **for ~** uzun süre; **take ~** uzun sürmek; **the ~ and the short of it** uzun lâfın kısası, doğrusu; **2.** *adj*. uzun; yorucu; uzak (*tarih*); **at ~ date** COM uzun vadeli; **in the ~ run** eninde sonunda; zamanla, uzun vadede; **be ~** uzun sürmek; **take the ~ view** ileriyi görmek; **3.** *adv*. çok, pek; süresince, boyunca; çoktan; geç;

as ~ ago as 1960 1960'dan beri; **so ~!** Allaha ısmarladık!, hoşça kal!; **~er** daha uzun; daha çok; **no ~er ago than** ...den çok önce değil.

long² [~] *v/i*. can atmak (**for** -*e*), özlemek (**for** -*i*), özlemini çekmek (**to** -*in*), çok istemek (**to** *inf. -meği*).

long...: '**~boat** *n*. NAUT yelkenli geminin en büyük sandalı; **~bow** ['~bəu] *n*. HIST uzun yay; **draw the ~** *fig.* atıp tutmak, tıraş etm., palavra atmak; '**~dated** *adj*. uzun vadeli (*veya* süreli); '**~dis.tance** *adj*. şehirlerarası; uzun mesafe...; **~ flight** uzun mesafe uçuşu; **~ race** uzun mesafe yarışı; '**~drawn--'out**, *a*. '**~drawn** *adj*. uzun süren; **lon-gev.i.ty** [lɔn'dʒeviti] *n*. uzun ömür(lük); **long firm** dolandırıcılar, dolandırıcı takımı; '**long.hair** *n*. F profesör tipli kimse; hippi; klasik müzik düşkünü; '**long.haired** *adj*. F münevver, bilgili, entelektüel; hippi; uzun saçlı; '**long.hand** *n*. el yazısı; '**long-'head.ed** *adj. fig.* ileriyi gören; zeki, akıllı.

long.ing ['lɔŋiŋ] **1.** □ özlem dolu, arzulu; **2.** *n*. özlem, hasret, iştiyak.

long.ish ['lɔŋiʃ] *adj*. uzunca, upuzun.

lon.gi.tude GEOGR ['lɔndʒitjuːd] *n*. boylam, tul; **lon.gi'tu.di.nal** □ [~dinl] uzunlamasına...; boylama ait.

long...: '**~lived** *adj*. uzun ömürlü; '**~range** *adj*. uzun vadeli; MIL uzun menzilli...; AVIA büyük hareket sahası olan...; '**~shore-man** *n*. dok işçisi; '**~shot** *n. film*: telefotografi; '**~sight.ed** *adj*. presbit, uzağı iyi gören; *fig.* ileriyi görebilen, basiretli, sağgörülü; '**~stand.ing** *adj*. eskisi gibi, uzun süren; '**~suf.fering 1.** *adj*. cefakâr, cefakeş, sabırlı; **2.** *n*. cefa, sabır, tahammül; '**~term** *adj*. uzun vadeli; **~ waves** *pl*. ELECT uzun dalga; '**~ways** *adv*. uzunlamasına; '**~wind.ed** □ sözü bitmez, kafa ütüleyen.

loo¹ [luː] *n*. bir çeşit iskambil oyunu, lû.

loo² F [~] *n*. tuvalet.

loo.fah BOT ['luːfɑː] *n*. lif kabağı.

look [luk] **1.** *n*. bakış, nazar, bakma; *oft.* **~s** *pl*. görünüş, güzellik, yüz ifadesi; **new ~** yeni çehre (*veya* moda); **have a ~ at s.th.** bşi gözden geçirmek, bşe göz atmak; **I don't like the ~ of it** onu beğenmiyorum, onu gözüm tutmadı; **2.** *v/i*. bakmak (**at**, **on** -*e*), görmek; görünmek, gözükmek, benzemek; **it ~s like rain** yağmur yağacağa benziyor; *he ~s like winning* kazanacağa benziyor; *~ about* bakınmak, araştırmak, kollamak, aramak *(for -i)*; *~ after* bakmak *-e*, gözetmek *-i*; *~ at* seyretmek *-i*, bakmak *-e*; göz önüne almak *-i*, düşünmek *-i*; kontrol etm. *-i*; *not much to ~ at* yüzüne bakılmaz, görünüşü kötü; *~ down on* tepeden bakmak *-e*, küçük görmek *-i*; *~ for* aramak *-i*; beklemek *-i*; *~ forward to* beklemek, ummak *-i*, iple çekmek *-i*, dört gözle beklemek *-i*; *~ in* uğramak (on *-e*); *~ into* araştırmak *-i*, soruşturmak *-i*, incelemek *-i*; içine bakmak *-in*; *~ on* seyretmek, bakıp durmak; bakmak *-e* (*as gözüyle*); *~ on to* bakmak *-e*; *my bedroom ~s to the garden* yatak odam bahçeye bakıyor; *~ out* dikkat etm., sakınmak; seçmek, çıkarmak; *~ out for* aranmak, bakınmak *-e*; *~ over s.th.* bşi gözden geçirmek, incelemek, yoklamak, *bşe* gözgezdirmek; *~ round* iyi düşünmek, enine boyuna düşünmek; kafasını çevirip bakmak; gezmek, dolaşmak; *~ through* gözden geçirmek *-i*, incelemek *-i*; *~ to* dikkat etm. *-e*, önem vermek *-e*, bakmak *-e*; *~ to s.o. to* inf. *b-nin* …ceğine güvenmek; *~ up* yukarıya bakmak, başını kaldırıp bakmak; gelişmek, düzelmek, iyileşmek; bulup ziyaret etm.; *~ up to s.o. b-ne* saygı göstermek, *b-ni* saymak; *~ (up)on* fig. bakmak *-e* (*as gözüyle*); *v/t. ~ s.o. in the face* (sıkılmadan) *b-nin* gözünün içine bakmak; *~ one's age* yaşını göstermek; *~ disdain* tepeden bakmak, hor görmek; *~ over* gözden geçirmek *-i*, incelemek *-i*, yoklamak *-i*; *~ up* sözlükte aramak; ziyaret etm. *-i*, uğramak *-e*, arayıp sormak *-i*.

look.er-on ['lukər'ɔn] *n.* seyirci.

look-in ['luk'in] *n.* kısa bakış; kısa ziyaret, uğrama; F kazanma şansı.

look.ing-glass ['lukiŋɡlɑːs] *n.* ayna.

look-out ['luk'aut] *n.* gözetleme (yeri); olasılık, ümit; gözleyici; *be on the ~* gözetlemek, araştırmak, tetikte olm.; *that is my ~* o benim bileceğim iş; 'look-o.ver *n.* gözden geçirme, tetkik; *give s.th. a ~ bşi* gözden geçirmek.

loom¹ [luːm] *n.* dokuma tezgâhı.

loom² [_] *v/i.* karaltı gibi görünmek, uzakta hayal gibi görünmek, belirmek; *~ large* fig. kafasını kurcalamak, gözünde büyümek.

loon¹ *Scots* [luːn] *n.* işe yaramaz (*veya* serseri) kimse.

loon² ORN [_] *n.* gerdanlı dalgıç.

loop [luːp] **1.** *n.* ilmik, düğüm, ilmek; kıvrık sap; doğum kontrolü için kullanılan cihaz, spiral; *~ aerial* radyo: çerçeve anten; **2.** *v/t.* ilmiklemek, düğümlemek; *~ up* iğne ile tutturmak (*elbise*); firkete ile toplamak (*saç*); *~ the ~* AVIA takla atmak; *v/i.* ilmik yapmak; ilmik olm., ilmikle tutulmak; '~-hole *n.* gözetleme deliği; *fig.* kaçamak, açık (*kapı*); MIL mazgal; '~-line *n.* RAIL & TEL ana hattan ayrılıp tekrar birleşen hat, şube hattı.

loose [luːs] **1.** □ *com.* çözük, gevşek; sallantılı; boş, serbest; hafifmeşrep, başıboş; bol, dökümlü (*elbise*); şüpheli; seyrek, dağınık; dikkatsiz; *~ connection* ELECT gevşek bağlantı; *at a ~ end* yapacak işi olmayan, boşta; *play fast and ~ with* aldatmak, kandırmak; **2.** *v/t.* gevşetmek, çözmek, açmak; *a. ~ off* salıvermek, serbest bırakmak (*esir*); atmak, fırlatmak (*ok*); ateşlemek (*silah*); *~ one's hold on s.th. bşi* serbest bırakmak, *bş* üzerindeki baskıyı kaldırmak, gevşek bırakmak; *v/i.* ateş etm.; atış yapmak; **3.** *n. give (a) ~ to* gevşetmek, salıvermek; '~-leaf *adj.* sayfaları çıkarılıp yeniden takılabilen; *~ book*, *~ ledger* sayfaları çıkarılıp takılabilen defter; **loos.en** ['luːsn] *v/t.* & *v/i.* gevşe(t)mek, çöz(ül)mek; **'looseness** *n.* gevşeklik; düzensizlik; kararsızlık; MED ishal.

loot [luːt] **1.** *v/i.* yağma etm.; **2.** *n.* yağma, ganimet, çapul.

lop¹ [lɔp] *v/t.* budamak, kesmek (*ağaç*); *mst ~ away*, *~ off* budamak; kaldırmak, durdurmak.

lop² [_] *v/i.* sarkmak.

lope [ləup] **1.** *v/i.* seke seke koşmak; **2.** *n.* sekme, koşuş.

lop…: '~-ears *n. pl.* sarkık kulaklar; '~-'sid.ed *adj.* bir tarafa yatkın; dengesiz, orantısız.

lo.qua.cious [ləu'kweiʃəs] *adj.* konuşkan, çenebaz, dilli, geveze; **lo.quac.i-ty** [ləu'kwæsiti] *n.* konuşkanlık, çenebazlık.

lo.ran AVIA, NAUT ['lɔːrən] *n.* radyo sinyalleri ile uçağın *veya* geminin yerini tesbit eden sistem.

lord [lɔːd] **1.** *n.* sahip, efendi; mal sahibi; lord; hükümdar; *co.* koca; nüfuzlu kimse; *the ♀* Allah, Tanrı; Hazreti İsa; *my ~* efendim, lord hazretleri; *the ♀'s Prayer* İsa'nın öğrettiği dua;

the ♀'s *Supper* Aşai Rabbanî ayini, kudas, liturya; *as drunk as a* ~ kör kütük sarhoş; *live like a* ~ krallar gibi yaşamak; **2.** *vb.* ~ *it* amirlik taslamak (*over s.o. b-ne*); **'lord.li.ness** *n.* haşmet, heybet, görkem; *b.s.* gurur, kibir; **'lord.ling** *n.* değersiz lord, küçük lord; **'lord.ly** *adj.* lorda yaraşır; görkemli, haşmetli; gururlu, kibirli; **'lord.ship** *n.* lordluk; üstünlük, egemenlik.

lore [lɔː] *n.* bilgi, ilim, bilim.

lor.gnette [lɔːˈnjet] *n.* saplı gözlük.

lor.ry [ˈlɔri] *n.* üstü açık yük arabası; kamyon; RAIL furgon, dekovil vagonu.

lose [luːz] (*irr.*) *v/t. & v/i.* kaybet(tir)mek, yitirmek, kaçırmak; geri kalmak (*saat*); şaşırmak; kaybolmak; yenilmek; ~ *o.s.* kendini kaybetmek, kendinden geçmek; yolunu kaybetmek; dalmak, kendini vermek (*in -e*); ~ *sight of* gözden kaybetmek *-i*; dikkate almamak *-i*, unutmak *-i*; **'los.er** *n.* kaybeden (*veya* yenik) kimse; *come off a* ~ yenik düşmek; **'los.ing 1.** *adj.* kazançlı olmayan, zarar gören...; yenilen; **2.** *n.* ~*s pl.* kayıplar, zaiat.

loss [lɔs] *n.* kayıp; zarar, ziyan, hasar; *at a* ~ şaşırmış, afallamış; zararına (*satış*); *be at a* ~ *for words* söyleyecek kelime bulamamak; *be at a* ~ *what to say* ne diyeceğini bilememek; **'~-lead.er** *n.* COM müşteri çekmek için zararına satılan mal.

lost [lɔst] *pret. & p.p. of lose*; *be* ~ kaybolmak; *fig.* kendini kaptırmak, dalmak (*in -e*); *this won't be* ~ *on me* o beni etkilemez, o bana vız gelir; *be* ~ *upon s.o. b-nin* gözünde bir hiç olm; **'~'prop.er.ty of.fice** kayıp eşya bürosu.

lot [lɔt] **1.** *n.* kur'a, adçekme; hisse, pay; arazi parçası, yer; *fig.* şans, talih, kısmet, kader; COM parti (*mal*), kısım, parça; nevi, tip, cins; F çok miktar, çokluk; *Am. film:* film stüdyosu; *a* ~ *of people* F pek çok (*veya* bir sürü) kimse; *draw* ~*s* kur'a çekmek, adçekmek (*for için*); *fall to s.o.'s* ~ *b-nin* payına düşmek; *throw in one's* ~ *with* ile şansını denemek, *ile* alın yazısı birleştirmek; *he is feeling a* ~ *better* F kendini çok daha iyi hissediyor; **2.** *v/t.* bölüştürmek, taksim etm., paylaştırmak.

loth [ləʊθ] = *loath*.

lo.tion [ˈləʊʃən] *n.* losyon.

lot.ter.y [ˈlɔtəri] *n.* piyango, lotarya; talih, kader.

lo.tus BOT [ˈləʊtəs] *n.* nilüfer çiçeği; **'~-eater** *n.* hayal âleminde yaşayan kimse.

loud [laʊd] **1.** ☐ yüksek (*ses*); gürültülü, patırtılı; çiğ (*renk*); kaba; **2.** *adv.* yüksek sesle, gürültü ile; **'~-'hail.er** *n.* NAUT megafon; **'loud.ness** *n.* gürültü; *radyo:* ses şiddeti; **'loud-'speak.er** *n.* hoparlör.

lough *Ir.* [lɔk] *n.* göl, haliç.

lounge [laʊndʒ] **1.** *v/i.* tembelce uzanmak, yayılıp oturmak; avare dolaşmak; **2.** *n.* dinlenme salonu, hol; bekleme salonu; şezlong; avarelik; THEAT fuaye; **'~-'chair** *n.* şezlong; **'~-liz.ard** *n. sl.* jigolo, salon züppesi; **'loung.er** *n.* avare (*veya* aylak) kimse; **'lounge-'suit** *n.* günlük (takım) elbise.

lour [ˈlaʊə] *v/i.* surat asmak, kaşlarını çatmak, kötü kötü bakmak; kararmak (*hava*); **lour.ing** ☐ [ˈ-riŋ] somurtkan; kapalı (*hava*).

louse 1. [laʊs] *n., pl. lice* [laɪs] bit, kehle; *sl.* ciğeri bes para etmez adam; **2.** [laʊz] *v/t.* *-in* bitlerini ayıklamak; **lousy** [ˈlaʊzi] *adj.* bitli; alçak; berbat, rezalet; *he is* ~ *with money sl.* denizde kum onda para.

lout [laʊt] *n.* kaba adam, *sl.* eşek; **lout-ish** *adj.* kaba..., maskara...

lov.a.ble ☐ [ˈlʌvəbl] sevimli, cana yakın, hoş, çekici.

love [lʌv] **1.** *n.* sevgi (*of, a. for, to, to-wards -e karşı*); aşk; sevgili; F sevimli kimse *veya* şey, şeker kimse *veya* şey; ♀ aşk tanrısı, Küpid; *spor:* sıfır; *attr.* aşk...; *for the* ~ *of God* Allah aşkı için; *play for* ~ zevk için oynamak; *four* (*to*) ~ sıfıra karşı dört; *give* ~ *veya send one's* ~ *to s.o. b-ne* selâm yollamak (*veya* söylemek); *in* ~ *with -e* âşık; *fall in* ~ *with* aşık olm. *-e*, vurulmak *-e*; *make* ~ sevişmek; *make* ~ *to* kur yapmak *-e*; *neither for* ~ *nor money* hiç bir surette; **2.** *vb.* sevmek, âşık olm. *-e*; tapmak *-e*; düşkün olm. *-e*; ~ *to do* yapmayı sevmek; **'~-af.fair** *n.* aşk macerası; **'~-bird** *n.* muhabbetkuşu; **'~-child** *n.* aşk meyvesi, piç; **'love.less** *adj.* sevgisiz, aşksız, sevgiden yoksun; sevilmeyen; **'love-let.ter** *n.* aşk mektubu; **'loveli.ness** *n.* güzellik, sevimlilik; **'love.lock** *n.* kâkül, zülüf, lüle; **love-lorn** [ˈ-lɔːn] *adj.* aşk acısı çeken, sevgilisi dönmemiş; **'love.ly** *adj.* sevimli, güzel, hoş, çekici; eğlenceli; **'love-mak-ing** *n.* sevişme; aşk dolu kelimeler;

'love-match *n.* aşk evliliği; 'love-phil-tre, 'love-po.tion *n.* aşk iksiri; 'lov.er *n.* sevgili, dost, metres, yâr, âşık (*a. fig.*); *a ~ of art* sanat âşığı; *~s pl.* sevgililer; *pair of ~s* sevişen çift; 'love set *n. spor:* sıfıra karşı alınan set; 'love.sick *adj.* sevdalı; 'love-to.ken *n.* aşk hatırası.

lov.ing □ ['lʌviŋ] seven, sevgi gösteren, sevgi dolu; '~'kind.ness *n.* şefkat, merhamet, iyilik.

low[1] [ləu] **1.** (□ *rare*) aşağı, alçak; bayağı, adi, ucuz; düşük (MED *nabız vs.*); yavaş, zayıf (*ses*); kuvvetsiz, halsiz; neşesiz, üzgün; *fig.* karamsar; gelişmemiş; basit; alçak gönüllü; ufka yakın; kısa, bodur; *~est bid* en düşük teklif; *be brought ~* burnu sürtülmek; mahvolmak; *lay ~* yıkmak, mahvetmek; burnunu sürtmek; *lie ~* saklanmak; susup beklemek; **2.** *n.* METEOR düşük basınç bölgesi; *part. Am.* düşük şey (*fiyat, seviye vs.*).

low[2] [~] **1.** *v/i.* böğürmek; **2.** *n.* böğürme.

low...: '~'born *adj.* aşağı tabakadan; '~'bred *adj.* soysuz, kaba, terbiyesiz; '~brow **1.** *adj.* kültürsüz, basit; **2.** *n.* kültürsüz (*veya* basit) kimse; lo(w) carb [ləu'kɑːb] *adj.* düşük karbonhidratlı (*yiyecek*); ~ co.me.di.an *mst fig.* maskara, soytarı; ~ com.e.dy konusu hafif güldürü; fars; ~ coun.try ova, düz arazi; '~-down **1.** *adj.* F alçak(ca), âdi(ce); **2.** *n. sl.* gerçek, bşin içyüzü.

low.er[1] ['ləuə] **1.** *adj.* daha aşağı, daha alçak (*s. low[1]*); *~ case* TYP küçük harf, minüskül; **2.** *v/t. & v/i.* in(dir)mek, alçal(t)mak, düş(ür)mek, azal(t)mak, eksil(t)mek; küçük düşürmek, rezil etm.; zayıflatmak; *~ one's voice* sesini alçaltmak.

low.er[2] ['lauə] *s. lour.*

low.er.most ['ləuəməust] *adj.* en düşük, en alçak, en aşağı; '~-fat □ az yağlı (*margarin, peynir*); 'low.land *n.* ova, düz arazi; 'low.land.er *n.* ovalı kimse; 'low.li.ness *n.* alçak gönüllülük; 'low.ly *adj. & adv.* ikinci derecede, aşağı; alçak gönüllü; 'low-'necked *adj.* dekolte (*elbise*); 'low.ness *n.* düşüklük, alçaklık; MUS peslik; ~ of spirits üzgünlük, ümitsizlik, neşesizlik; 'low pres.sure *adj.* alçak basınçlı; 'low-'spir.it.ed *adj.* kederli, üzgün, neşesiz, mutsuz; low wa.ter cezir, inik deniz; *in ~ fig.* züğürt, cebi delik.

loy.al □ ['lɔiəl] sadık, vefalı; 'loy.al.ist

n. krala sadık kalan kimse; 'loy.al.ty *n.* sadakat, bağlılık, vefa.

loz.enge ['lɔzindʒ] *n.* eşkenar dörtgen; PHARM pastil.

£.s.d F ['eles'diː] *n.* para.

lub.ber ['lʌbə] *n.* acemi kimse; 'lub-ber.ly *adj.* acemi, bön.

lu.bri.cant ['luːbrikənt] *n.* yağ(layıcı madde); lu.bri.cate ['~keit] *v/t.* yağlamak; lu.bri'ca.tion *n.* MEC yağlama; 'lu.bri.ca.tor *n.* MEC yağdanlık; yağcı; lu'bric.i.ty [~siti] *n.* MEC kayganlık, yağlılık; *fig.* kaypaklık; zamparalık, şehvete düşkünlük.

lu.cern(e) BOT [luː'sɜːn] *n.* kabayonca.

lu.cid □ ['luːsid] *mst poet.* açık, kolay anlaşılır, berrak, vazıh, şeffaf, parlak; ~ interval MED hastanın aklı başına geldiği ara; lu'cid.i.ty, 'lu.cid.ness *n.* açıklık, berraklık, şeffaflık, sağduyu.

Lu.ci.fer ['luːsifə] *n.* şeytan, İblis; Venüs, sabah yıldızı.

luck [lʌk] *n.* şans, talih, baht, uğur; good ~ iyi şans; bad ~, hard ~, ill ~ aksilik, talihsizlik, fena talih, kötü şans; be down on one's ~ F şansı yaver gitmemek; worse~ maalesef, ne yazık ki; 'luck.i.ly *adv.* Allahtan, bereket versin ki, iyi ki; 'lucki.ness *n.* şanslılık; 'luck.less *adj.* şanssız, talihsiz, bahtsız; 'luck.y □ şanslı, talihli, uğurlu; be ~ şanslı olm.; 'luck.y-bag, 'luck.y-dip *n.* piyango torbası.

lu.cra.tive □ ['luːkrətiv] kazançlı, kârlı; lu.cre ['luːkə] *n.* para, servet, kazanç.

lu.cu.bra.tion [luːkjuː'breiʃən] *n.* emekle ortaya çıkarılmış eser; *mst ~s pl.* emek isteyen işler.

lu.di.crous □ ['luːdikrəs] gülünç, komik; saçma, aptalca.

luff NAUT [lʌf] **1.** *n.* orsa seyiri; **2.** *v/i. a. ~ up* orsa etm.

lug[1] [lʌg] **1.** *v/t.* çekmek, sürüklemek; ~ in *fig.* b-ni saçlarından sürüklemek; **2.** *n.* kulp, sap; kulak (memesi).

lug[2] [~] = lugsail.

luge [luːʒ] **1.** *n.* kızak; **2.** *v/i.* kızakla kaymak.

lug.gage ['lʌgidʒ] *n.* bagaj; '~-car.ri.er *n.* portbagaj; '~-of.fice *n.* RAIL eşya bürosu; '~-rack *n.* bagaj filesi; üst bagaj; '~-ticket *n.* bagaj bileti; '~-van *n.* RAIL furgon, eşya vagonu.

lug.ger NAUT ['lʌgə] *n.* bir *veya* daha çok aşırmalı yelkenli küçük gemi.

lug.sail NAUT ['lʌgseil, 'lʌgsl] *n.* aşırmalı (*veya* hasır) yelken.

lu.gu.bri.ous □ [luːˈguːbriəs] dokunaklı, hazin, acıklı, kederli.

luke.warm [ˈluːkwɔːm] *adj.* ılık; *fig.* kayıtsız, ilgisiz; 'luke.warm.ness *n.* ılıklık; kayıtsızlık.

lull [lʌl] 1. *v/t. & v/i.* uyuş(tur)mak, sakinleş(tir)mek, yatış(tır)mak; uyutmak (*bebek*); 2. *n.* ara, fasıla; geçici sükûnet, dinginlik.

lull.a.by [ˈlʌləbai] *n.* ninni.

lum.ba.go MED [lʌmˈbeigəu] *n.* lumbago, bel ağrısı.

lum.ber [ˈlʌmbə] 1. *n.* lüzumsuz eşya, ıvır zıvır; kereste; 2. *v/t. a.* ~ **up** lüzumsuz eşya ile (*veya* ıvır zıvırla) doldurmak; *v/i.* kereste kesmek; hantal hantal yürümek, ağır ağır ilerlemek; 'lumber.er, 'lum.ber.man *n.* keresteci, bıçkıcı; 'lumber.ing *adj.* hantal; gürültülü; 'lum.berjack *n.* ormanda ağaç kesen kimse, keresteci; 'lum.ber-mill *n.* hızarhane, bıçkıhane; 'lum.ber-room *n.* sandık odası; 'lum.ber-yard *n.* kereste deposu.

lu.mi.nar.y [ˈluːminəri] *n.* ışık veren cisim (*yıldız, ay veya güneş*); *fig.* aydın kimse; lu.mi.nos.i.ty [ˌ'nɔsiti] *n.* parlaklık; açıklık; 'lu.mi.nous □ parlak, aydınlık; *fig.* açık, anlaşılır, berrak; ~ **dial** ışıklı kadran; ~ **paint** fosforlu boya.

lump [lʌmp] 1. *n.* toprak, yumru, küme; öbek; şiş(kinlik); *fig.* ahmak kimse; **in the** ~ toptan, hep birden; ~ **sugar** kesmeşeker; ~ **sum** toptan ödenen para, götürü; **have a** ~ **in the throat** *fig.* boğazı düğümlenmek; 2. *v/t.* yığmak (**into, in** -*e*); bir araya toplamak; *fig.* tahammül etm., katlanmak; **if you don't like it you can** ~ **it** istesen de istemesen de; ~ **together** bir araya getirmek; *v/i.* yığılmak; hantal hantal dolaşmak; 'lump.ish *adj.* sakar; aptal, kalın kafalı; mıymıntı, tembel; 'lump.y □ yumru yumru, topak topak; şapşal; çırpıntılı (*su*).

lu.na.cy [ˈluːnəsi] *n.* delilik, cinnet, kaçıklık; **lunacies** *pl.* deli deli hareketler.

lu.nar [ˈluːnə] *adj.* aya ait, ay...; ~ **caustic** CHEM cehennemtaşı, gümüş nitrat; ~ **module** ay modülü.

lu.na.tic [ˈluːnətik] 1. *adj.* deli..., akıl hastası...; saçma sapan; delice...; 2. *n.* deli kimse, akıl hastası; ~ **a.sy.lum** tımarhane, akıl hastanesi; ~ **fringe** ga-

rip fikirli taşkın kimseler topluluğu.

lunch [lʌntʃ] 1. *n.* öğle yemeği; 2. *v/t. & v/i.* öğle yemeği ye(dir)mek; **luncheon** [ˈ-tʃən] = **lunch** 1; 'lunch-hour *n.* öğle tatili.

lu.nettes [luːˈnets] *n. pl.* dalgıç (*veya* sualtı) gözlüğü.

lung [lʌŋ] *n.* akciğerlerin her biri; **the**~**s** *pl.* akciğer.

lunge [lʌndʒ] 1. *n.* FENC hamle, saldırış; 2. *v/i.* ileri atılmak, hamle etm., saldırmak (**at** -*e*); *v/t.* itmek, kakmak.

lung.er *sl.* [ˈlʌŋə] *n.* ciğerlerinden rahatsız kimse, veremli; 'lung-pow.er *n.* ses gücü.

lu.pin(e) BOT [ˈluːpin] *n.* acı bakla.

lurch[1] [ləːtʃ] 1. *n.* NAUT birden sallanma *veya* silkinme; *fig.* sendeleme; 2. *v/i.* NAUT sallanmak, silkinmek; *fig.* sendelemek, sendeleyerek yürümek.

lurch[2] [ˌ] *n.:* **leave in the** ~ yüzüstü bırakmak.

lurch.er [ˈləːtʃə] *n.* zağar, kopoy, bir cins melez av köpeği.

lure [ljuə] 1. *n.* yem; *fig.* cazibe, tuzak; 2. *v/t.* cezbetmek, çekmek.

lu.rid [ˈljuərid] *adj.* parlak, pırıl pırıl; dehşetli, korkunç, tüyler ürpertici.

lurk [ləːk] *v/i.* gizlenmek, saklanmak, gizli gizli dolaşmak, kol gezmek (*tehlike*); 'lurk.ing-place *n.* pusu yeri.

lus.cious [ˈlʌʃəs] pek tatlı, nefis, bal gibi; çekici, güzel; olgun (*meyva*); süslü; *b.s.* yapmacık; 'lus.cious.ness *n.* lezzetlilik, pek tatlılık.

lush [lʌʃ] 1. *adj.* bereketli, verimli, bol; lezzetli, leziz; çok sulu; şatafatlı, konforlu; 2. *n.* Am. *sl.* ayyaş kimse.

lust *lit.* [lʌst] 1. *n.* şehvet; *fig.* hırs, arzu; 2. *v/t.* şehvetle arzu etm. (**after, for** -*i*); **lust.ful** □ [ˈ-ful] şehvetli.

lust.i.ness [ˈlʌstinis] *n.* dinçlik, kuvvet, canlılık.

lus.tre [ˈlʌstə] *n.* parlaklık, parıltı; perdah, cilâ; görkem, ihtişam; avize; şöhret, ün; 'lus.tre.less *adj.* donuk, mat; parıltısız.

lus.trous □ [ˈlʌstrəs] pırıl pırıl, parlak.

lust.y □ [ˈlʌsti] dinç, kuvvetli, gürbüz; *fig.* canlı; şehvetli.

lu.ta.nist [ˈluːtənist] *n.* udî, kopuzcu.

lute[1] MUS [luːt] *n.* ut, lavta, kopuz.

lute[2] [ˌ] 1. *n.* macun; 2. *v/t.* macunlamak, sıvamak.

Lu.ther.an [ˈluːθərən] 1. *adj.* Martin Luther'e ait; 2. *n.* Lüteriyen, Martin Luther taraftarı; 'Lu.ther.an.ism *n.*

Martin Luther taraftarlığı, Luther doktrini.

lut.ist ['luːtist] = *lutanist*.

lux.ate ['lʌkseit] *v/t.* MED mafsaldan çıkarmak, burkmak.

lux.u.ri.ance [lʌg'zjuəriəns] *n.* bolluk; **lux'u.ri.ant** □ bol, bereketli; şatafatlı; **lux'u.ri.ate** [‿rieit] *v/t.* büyük bir zevk almak (*in* -*den*), tadını çıkarmak -*in*; *v/i.* lüks içinde yaşamak; **lux'u.ri.ous** □ lüks, konforlu; pahalı; zevk verici; F süslü, tantanalı; **lux'u.ri.ous.ness** *n.* rahatlık, konfor; **lux.u.ry** ['lʌkʃəri] *n.* lüks, konfor; süs.

ly.ce.um [lai'siəm] *n. part.* Am. konferans salonu; lise.

lych.gate ['litʃgeit] *n.* üstü damlı kilise kapısı.

lye [lai] *n.* kül (*veya* boğada) suyu.

ly.ing ['laiiŋ] **1.** *p.pr. of lie¹ 2 & lie² 2*; **2.** *adj.* yalancı...: yanıltıcı...; '‿'in *n.* loğusalık; ~ *hospital* doğumevi.

lymph [limf] *n.* MED lenfa, akkan; *poet.* pınar, kaynak; **lym.phat.ic** [‿'fætik] **1.** *adj* (**~ally**) lenfatik...; lenfe ait, lenf...; *fig.* mıymıntı, tembel; **2.** *n.* lenf damarı.

lynch [lintʃ] *v/t.* linç etm.; '~-law *n.* linç kanunu.

lynx ZOO [liŋks] *n.* vaşak, karakulak; '~-eyed *adj. fig.* keskin gözlü.

lyre [laiə] *n.* çenk, harp; '~-bird *n.* ORN kuyruğu çenk şeklinde bir cins kuş.

lyr.ic ['lirik] **1.** *adj.* lirik; **2.** *n.* lirik şiir; ~*s* *pl.* güfte; '**lyr.i.cal** □ liriğe ait, lirik...; heyecanlı, hevesli, gayretli.

ly.sol PHARM ['laisɔl] *n.* lizol.

M

ma F [mɑː] *n.* anne.

ma'am [mæm] *n.* majeste; [məm] F *s.* **madam**.

mac F [mæk] = *mackintosh*.

ma.ca.bre [mə'kɑːbr] *adj.* ölümü hatırlatan, dehşetli, meş'um; *danse* ~ ölüm dansı.

mac.ad.am [mə'kædəm] *n.* şose, makadam; kırma taş, balast; **mac'ad.am.ize** *vb.* yol yüzeyini makadam ile kaplamak; şose yapmak.

mac.a.ro.ni [mækə'rəuni] *n.* (düdüklü) makarna.

mac.a.roon [mækə'ruːn] *n.* bademli kurabiye.

mace¹ [meis] *n.* HIST gürz, topuz; süslü tören asası.

mace² [‿] *n.* kurutulmuş küçük hindistancevizi kabuğundan yapılan baharat.

Mac.e.do.ni.an [mæsi'dəunjən] **1.** *n.* Makedonyalı; Makedonya dili; **2.** *adj.* Makedonya ile ilgili.

mac.er.ate ['mæsəreit] *vb.* katı maddeyi sıvıda yatırarak yumuşatmak; zayıfla(t)mak; **mac.er'a.tion** *n.* yumuşama; zayıflama.

Mach PHYS [mæk] *n.*: ~ *number* Mah sayısı; ~ *two* ses hızının iki katı.

ma.che.te [mə'tʃeiti] *n.* Latin Amerika'da kullanılan bir çeşit mala.

Mach.i.a.vel.li.an [mækiə'veliən] *adj.* Makyavelce.

mach.i.na.tion [mæki'neiʃən] *n.* entrika, kumpas kurma; ~*s* *pl.* düzen, dolap; **mach.i.na.tor** ['‿tə] *n.* düzenbaz kimse; **ma.chine** [mə'ʃiːn] **1.** *n.* makine; alet; bisiklet; motorlu araç, araba; parti kontrol organizasyonu; mekanizma (*a. fig.*); **2.** *vb.* şekil vermek *veya* makine ile imal etm.; **ma'chine-gun** *n.* MIL makineli tüfek, mitralyöz; **ma-'chine-made** *adj.* makine yapımı; **ma-'chin.er.y** *n.* mekanizma (*a. fig.*); makinenin işleyen bölümleri; makineler; **ma'chine-shop** *n.* torna, makine atölyesi; **ma'chine-tool** *n.* torna, planya makinesi; imalat aleti; **ma'chin.ist** *n.* makinist; makine yapımcısı.

mack F [mæk] = *mackintosh*.

mack.er.el ICHTH ['mækrəl] *n.* uskumru.

mack.i.naw Am. ['mækinɔː] *n.* yünlü kısa kruvaze palto, kaban.

mac(k).in.tosh ['mækintɔʃ] *n.* yağmurluk.

mac.ro... ['mækrəu] *prefix* büyük..., uzun...; ~.**cosm** ['‿kɔzəm] *n.* kâinat, evren.

mad □ [mæd] deli, çılgın, çıldırmış; kuduz; öfkeli, çok kızmış, kudurmuş (*with*, *at* -*den*, -*den dolayı*); deli, çok düşkün (*about*, *for* -*e*); *go* ~ çılgına dönmek; *drive* ~ *b-ni* çileden çıkar(t)-

mak, çıldırtmak.

mad.am ['mædəm] *n.* madam, bayan, hanımefendi.

mad.cap ['mædkæp] **1.** *adj.* vahşi, tehlikeli, zıpır; **2.** *n.* delişmen (*veya* kudurgan) kimse; **mad.den** ['mædn] *vb. b-ni* çıldırtmak, sinirlendirmek.

mad.der BOT, MEC ['mædə] *n.* boya kökü; parlak kırmızı boya; kökboyası.

made [meid] *pret. & p.p. of* **make 1.**

made-up ['meid'ʌp] *adj.* uydurma; makyajlı, yüzü boyalı; tamamlanmış; zararı ödenmiş; ~ *clothes pl.* konfeksiyon; ~ *of -den* teşekkül etmiş, *-den* yapılmış.

mad.house ['mædhaus] *n.* akıl hastanesi; '**mad.man** *n.* deli (*veya* mecnun) kimse; '**mad.ness** *n.* delilik, çılgınlık; VET kuduz hastalığı; *Am.* kızgınlık (*at -e*).

Ma.don.na [mə'dɔnə] *n.* Meryem Ana, Hazreti Meryem; Meryem Ana resmi *veya* heykeli; ~ **li.ly** BOT beyaz zambak.

mad.ri.gal MUS ['mædrigəl] *n.* çalgı eşliği olmadan söylenen çok sesli yarı şarkı.

mad.wom.an ['mædwumən] *n.* deli, çılgın, mecnun (*kadın*).

maelstrom ['meilstrəum] *n.* girdap.

ma.es.tro ['maistrəu] *n.* usta, üstat (*esp. virtüöz, mayestro, orkestra şefi*).

maf.fick ['mæfik] *v/i.* çılgınca eğlenmek.

mag.a.zine [mægə'ziːn] *n.* dergi, mecmua; ambar, depo, kiler; MIL cephanelik; şarjör.

mag.da.len ['mægdəlin] *n.* tövbekâr kimse.

ma.gen.ta CHEM [mə'dʒentə] *n.* parlak koyu kırmızı boya.

mag.got ['mægət] *n.* kurt, sürfe; *fig.* kuruntu; '**mag.got.y** *adj.* kurtlu; kaprisli, şımarık.

Ma.gi ['meidʒai] *n. pl.* gördükleri yıldız aracılığı ile Hazreti İsa'yı ziyaret eden ve ona hediye sunan üç müneccim.

mag.ic ['mædʒik] **1.** *a.* '**mag.i.cal** □ sihirli, büyülü..., cazip; **2.** *n.* sihirbazlık, büyücülük; *fig.* sihir, büyü; **ma.gi.cian** [mə'dʒiʃən] *n.* sihirbaz, büyücü; **mag.ic lan.tern** projektör.

mag.is.te.ri.al □ [mædʒis'triəriəl] hükümeti ilgilendiren; devletçe, hükümetçe, resmî; yetkili, otoriter; *b.s.* âmirane, sert; **mag.is.tra.cy** ['ˌtrəsi] *n.* hâkimlik, yargıçlık; yargıçlar; **mag.istrate** ['ˌtreit] *n.* sulh yargıcı.

mag.na.nim.i.ty [mægnə'nimiti] *n.* yüce gönüllülük; **mag.nan.i.mous** □ ['ˌnæniməs] yüce gönüllü, âlicenap.

mag.nate ['mægneit] *n.* patron, sermayedar, kodaman.

mag.ne.sia CHEM [mæg'niːʃə] *n.* magnezyum oksit, manyezi; **mag'ne.si.um** CHEM [ˌzjəm] *n.* magnezyum.

mag.net ['mægnit] *n.* mıknatıs; **magnetic** [ˌ'netik] *adj.* (*~ally*) manyetik, mıknatısla çekilen; ~ *tape* teyp bandı; **magnet.ism** ['ˌnitizəm] *n.* manyetizma; **magnet.i.za.tion** [ˌnitai'zeiʃən] *n.* mıknatıslama; '**mag.net.ize** *v/t.* manyetize etm., mıknatıslamak; *fig.* cezbetmek, çekmek; '**mag.net.iz.er** *n.* manyetizmacı; **mag.neto** [mæg'niːtəu] *n.* MOT manyeto.

mag.nif.i.cat ECCL [mæg'nifikæt] *n.* Meryem Ana'nın Tanrı'ya övgü sunma ilâhisi; *fig.* methiye, övgü.

mag.nif.i.cence [mæg'nifisns] *n.* azamet, ihtişam, görkem; **mag'nif.i.cent** *adj.* muhteşem, görkemli; fevkalâde, harika; **mag.ni.fi.er** ['ˌfaiə] *n.* büyük gösteren şey, büyüteç; '**mag.ni.fy** *v/t.* büyütmek (*a. fig.*); ~*ing glass* büyüteç, pertavsız; **mag.nil.o.quence** [mæg'niləukwəns] *n.* tantanalı söz söyleme; **mag'nil.o.quent** *adj.* şatafatlı, abartmalı (*söz*); **mag.nitude** ['ˌtjuːd] *n.* büyüklük; önem, ehemmiyet; *star of the first* ~ birinci kadirden olan yıldız.

mag.no.lia BOT [mæg'nəuljə] *n.* manolya.

mag.pie ORN ['mægpai] *n.* saksağan; *fig.* geveze kimse.

Magyar ['mægjuː] *n. & adj.* Macar; Macarca.

mahl.stick PAINT ['mɔːlstik] *n.* ressamın çalışırken fırçayı tutan elini dayadığı değnek.

ma.hog.a.ny [mə'hɔgəni] *n.* mahun, maun; kırmızımsı kahverengi.

maid [meid] *n. lit.* kız; *obs.* kız oğlan kız, bakire; kadın hizmetçi; *old* ~ gençliği geçmiş kız, kız kurusu; ~ *of hono(u)r* kraliçe *veya* prenses nedimesi; bir tür küçük kek.

maid.en ['meidn] **1.** *prov. veya co.* = *maid*; **2.** *adj.* evlenmemiş; el değmemiş, bakir; *fig.* ilk...; ~ *name* kızlık adı, evli kadının bekârlık soyadı; ~ *speech* (*milletvekili tarafından parlamentoda yapılan*) ilk konuşma; '~**.hair** *n.* BOT baldırıkara; '~**.head** *n.* bikir;

'~.hood *n.* kızlık, bakirelik, erdenlik; '~.like, 'maid.en.ly *adj.* genç kız gibi; mahçup, iffetli.

maid-of-all-work ['meidəv'ɔ:lwə:k] *n.* her işe bakan hizmetçi kız; 'maid-serv.ant *n.* kız hizmetçi.

mail¹ HIST [meil] *n.* zırh.

mail² [_] 1. *n.* posta arabası; posta; 2. *v/t. part. Am.* postaya vermek, posta ile göndermek; 'mail.a.ble *adj. Am.* posta ile gönderilebilir.

mail...: '~-bag *n.* posta torbası; '~-box *n. part. Am.* mektup kutusu; ~ car.ri.er *Am.* postacı; '~.man *n. part. Am.* postacı; '~-or.der firm, *part. Am.* '~-or.der house posta ile sipariş alan mağaza; '~-train *n.* posta treni.

maim [meim] *v/t.* sakatlamak, sakat etm. *-i.*

main [mein] 1. *adj.* asıl, esas, başlıca..., ana...; ~ chance kişisel çıkar; ~ sta-tion TELEPH esas irtibat hattı, santral; by ~ force var gücüyle, kuvvetle; ~ plane unit AVIA ana uçak ünitesi, uçak kanadı; 2. *n.* güç, kuvvet; ana su boru hattı; *poet.* derya, açık deniz; ~s *pl.* ELECT şebeke; ~s aerial ışık ağlı anten; in the ~ çoğu, ekseriyetle; *s.* might 1; '~.land *n.* (ana)kara; 'main.ly *adv.* başlıca, esasen.

main...: '~.mast ['-mɑ:st, NAUT '-məst] *n.* ana gemi direği; ~.sail ['-seil, NAUT '-sl] *n.* mayistra yelkeni; '~.spring *n.* ana yay, büyük zemberek; *fig.* asıl neden; '~.stay *n.* NAUT grandi çanaklarını pruva direğinin altına bağlayan payanda; *fig.* direk, başlıca dayanak; ♀Street *Am.* kasabanın çarşısındaki cadde; taşra gelenekleri.

main.tain [mein'tein] *v/t.* sürdürmek; korumak, muhafaza etm.; bakmak, beslemek, geçindirmek; iddia etm.; ~ that öyle olduğunu iddia etm.; main-'tain.a.ble *adj.* tutulabilir; müdafaası mümkün; main'tain.er *n.* gözeten (*ve-ya* koruyan, destekleyen) kimse.

main.te.nance ['meintənəns] *n.* bakım; müdafaa; muhafaza; iddia; na-faka.

main.top NAUT ['meintɔp] *n.* grandi ça-naklığı.

mai.son.(n)ette [meizə'net] *n.* küçük daire *veya* ev; dubleks daire.

maize BOT [meiz] *n.* mısır, darı.

ma.jes.tic [mə'dʒestik] *adj.* (~ally) muhteşem, heybetli, şahane; maj.es-ty ['mædʒisti] *n.* heybet, haşmet, aza-

met.

ma.jor ['meidʒə] 1. *adj.* daha büyük, da-ha önemli; iri; başlıca, asıl; MUS majör; A ~ Do majör; ~ third tiyers majör; ~ key majör perdesi; ~ league *Am. beys-bol:* en büyük iki ligden biri; 2. *n.* bin-başı; reşit olan kimse; PHLS büyük te-rim, önerme; *Am.* UNIV ana ders; 3. *v/i. Am.* üniversite öğrenimini belirli bir konuda yoğunlaştırmak, belirli bir ko-nuyu izlemek; '~-'gen.er.al *n.* tümge-neral; ma.jori.ty [mə'dʒɔriti] *n.* çoğun-luk, ekseriyet; erginlik, reşitlik; join the ~ çoğunluğa katılmak; 'ma.jor road anayol.

make [meik] 1. (*irr.*) *v/t. com.* yapmak, yaratmak, meydana getirmek; teşkil etm.; sağlamak; kazanmak, elde etm.; yazmak (*şiir*); inşa etm.; hazırla-mak, düzeltmek; karıştırmak (*oyun kâğıdı*); etmek, çıkarmak; atamak; ye-rine getirmek; koymak (*fiyat*); kapat-mak (*devre*); zorlamak, yaptırmak; ulaşmak, varmak; olmak; girmek (*takıma*); dahil etm., içine almak; ya-kalamak, yetişmek; anlamak, kavra-mak; göstermek; katetmek, almak (*yol*); ~ believe that gibi görünmek, taklit etm.; ~ the best of it bşden en iyi biçimde yararlanmak; ~ capital out of bşden istifade etm., bşi istismar etm., kendi çıkarına kullanmak, kötü-ye kullanmak; ~ do with yetinmek *ile*, idare etm. *ile*; ~ good başarılı olm.; te-lâfi etm, karşılamak; refaha erişmek; ~ it F başarmak, kazanmak; zamanında varmak; ~ (the) land NAUT karayı gör-mek; ~ or mar s.o. b-ni ya yüceltmek ya da batırmak; do you ~ one of us? bize katılır mısınız?; ~ port NAUT lima-na uğramak; ~ shift idare etm., yetin-mek (*with ile*); ~ way ilerlemek; ~ way for yol vermek *-e.*; ~ into dönüştürmek *-e*, çevirmek *-e*; ~ out yazmak; doldur-mak; anlamak, çözmek, sökmek; gö-rebilmek; iddia etm.; ~ over çevirmek, dönüştürmek, değiştirmek; devret-mek; ~ up uydurmak; teşkil etm., hazırlamak; telâfi etm., tamamlamak (*for -i*); COM ödemek (*borç*); kapat-mak, örtmek; dikmek (*elbise vs.*); top-lamak, bir araya getirmek; düzenle-mek; hazırlamak, meydana getirmek, oluşturmak; yapmak (*yatak vs.*); ~ up one's mind karar vermek (*to inf. -meğe*); 2. (*irr.*) *v/i.* davranmak, hare-ket etm.; yola koyulmak; yükselmek, kabarmak (*met*); ~ *as if* yapar gibi görünmek, …miş gibi davranmak; ~ *after* peşinden gitmek -*in*, kovalamak -*i*; ~ *against* zarar vermek -*e*, zararı dokunmak -*e*; ~ *at* üstüne yürümek -*in*, atılmak; ~ *away* F tüymek, sıvışmak; ~ *away with* F öldürmek; yok etm.; çalmak, yürütmek; ~ *for* gitmek -*e*, yolunu tutmak -*in*; koşmak -*e*, üşüşmek -*e*, saldırmak -*e*; sağlamak -*i*, katkıda bulunmak -*e*; ~ *off* sıvışmak, tüymek; ~ *up* barışmak; makyaj yapmak; ~ *up to s.o. b-nin* gözüne girmeye çalışmak; **3.** *n.* şekil; yapı, biçim; marka; verim, randıman; ELECT devrenin kapanması; *of poor* ~ düşük kaliteli; *on the* ~ *sl.* çıkarı peşinde; cinsî münasebet peşinde; '~-be.lieve **1.** *n.* yalandan yapma, taklit; hile, bahane; **2.** *adj.* sahte, samimiyetsiz; 'mak.er *n.* yapan, fabrikatör; ♀ Allah, Tanrı.

make…: '~.shift **1.** *n.* eğreti tedbir, geçici çare; **2.** *adj.* eğreti, geçici…; '~-up *n.* mizanpaj, tertip; makyaj; *fig.* mizaç, tabiat; '~.weight *n.* tartı tam gelsin diye eklenen ağırlık; *fig.* bir açığı dolduran önemsiz kimse *veya* şey.

mak.ing ['meikiŋ] *n.* başarı nedeni; yapma, etme; ~*s pl.* F nitelikler; *in the* ~ yapılırken; yapılmakta; *that was the* ~ *of him* başarılı olmasının nedeni o oldu; *have the* ~*s of* …olmak için gerekli niteliklere sahip olm.

mal.a.chite MIN ['mæləkait] *n.* bakırtaşı, malakit.

mal.ad.just.ed PSYCH ['mælə'dʒʌstid] *adj. k-ni* çevreye, topluma uyduramayan, uyumsuz; 'mal.ad'just.ment *n.* uyumsuzluk.

mal.ad.min.is.tra.tion ['mælədminis'treiʃən] *n.* kötü yönetim, idare.

mal.a.droit ['mælə'drɔit] *adj.* beceriksiz, sakar.

mal.a.dy ['mælədi] *n.* hastalık, dert.

ma.laise [mæ'leiz] *n.* huzursuzluk, rahatsızlık.

mal.a.prop.ism ['mæləprɒpizəm] *n.* sözcükleri yanlış yerde kullanma; mal.a.pro.pos ['_-'æprəpəu] **1.** *adj.* uygunsuz, münasebetsiz; **2.** *adv.* uygunsuzca, münasebetsizce; **3.** *n.* münasebetsizlik, yakışıksızlık, yersizlik, vakitsizlik.

ma.lar.i.a MED [mə'lɛəriə] *n.* sıtma; ma'lar.ial *adj.* sıtmalı, malarya…

Ma.lay [mə'lei] **1.** *n.* Malaya dili; Malayalı; **2.** *adj.* Malaya'ya *veya* halkına ait.

mal.con.tent ['mælkəntent] **1.** *adj.* memnun olmayan, hoşnutsuz; **2.** *n.* tatmin olmayan kimse.

male [meil] **1.** *adj.* erkek, erkekçe; ~ *child* erkek çocuk; ~ *screw* vida; **2.** *n.* erkek.

mal.e.dic.tion [mæli'dikʃən] *n.* lânet, kargış, beddua; iftira.

mal.e.fac.tor ['mælifæktə] *n.* suçlu (*veya* kötülük eden) kimse.

ma.lev.o.lence [mə'levələns] *n.* kötülük; ma'lev.o.lent □ kötü niyetli, hain.

mal.for.ma.tion ['mælfɔː'meiʃən] *n.* sakatlık, kusurlu oluşum.

mal.ice ['mælis] *n.* garaz, kötü niyet; muziplik; JUR suiniyet, suç işleme kastı.

ma.li.cious □ [mə'liʃəs] kötü niyetli, garazkâr; muzip; JUR kasten, taammüden; ma'li.cious.ness *n.* kötü niyetlilik, kötülük.

ma.lign [mə'lain] **1.** □ zararlı; MED habis, kötü, ağır; **2.** *v/t.* iftira etm.; ma.lig.nan.cy [mə'lignənsi] *n.* habislik; MED habis tümör; ma'lig.nant **1.** □ kötü yürekli, garazkâr, kötücül; MED habis (*tümör*); **2.** *n.* kötü niyet; ma'lig.ni.ty *n.* kötülükçülük; şiddetli nefret; *part.* MED habaset, kötülük.

ma.lin.ger [mə'liŋgə] *v/i.* hasta pozu yapmak, *k-ni* hasta gibi göstermek; ma'linger.er *n.* hasta pozu yaparak görevden kaçan kimse.

mall [mɔːl] *n.* gezinti yolu.

mal.lard ORN ['mæləd] *n.* bir tür yaban ördeği.

mal.le.a.ble ['mæliəbl] *adj.* dövülür (*metal*); *fig.* uysal, yumuşak huylu.

mal.let ['mælit] *n.* lastik *veya* tahta başlı çekiç; *spor*; (*kriket*, *polo*) sopa.

mal.low BOT ['mæləu] *n.* ebegümeci.

malm.sey ['mɑːmzi] *n.* tatlı şarap.

mal.nu.tri.tion ['mælnjuː'triʃən] *n.* gıdasızlık, yetersiz *veya* kötü beslenme.

mal.o.dor.ous □ [mæ'ləudərəs] kötü kokulu.

mal.prac.tice ['mæl'præktis] *n.* yolsuzluk; MED yanlış tedavi; JUR görevi kötüye kullanma, görevde ihmal *veya* suiistimal.

malt [mɔːlt] **1.** *n.* bira yapılan çimlendirilmiş arpa, malt; ~ *liquor* malttan mayalanma ile yapılan içki, *part.* bira; **2.**

mangy

vb. arpa *veya* başka tahıldan malt yapmak.
Mal.tese ['mɔːl'tiːz] **1.** *adj.* Maltız; Malta dili; **2.** *n.* Maltalı, Maltız.
mal.treat [mæl'triːt] *v/t.* kötü davranmak *-e,* eziyet etm. *-e;* **mal'treat.ment** *n.* kötü davranma.
malt.ster ['mɔːltstə] *n.* malt imalâtçısı.
mal.ver.sa.tion [mælvə'seiʃən] *n.* rüşvet yeme, suiistimal, zimmete para geçirme.
ma.ma, mam.ma [mə'mɑː] *n.* anne.
mam.mal ['mæməl] *n.* memeli hayvan; **mam.ma.li.an** [mə'meiljən] *adj.* memeli hayvanla ilgili, memeli hayvan...
mam.mon ['mæmən] *n.* hırs ve ihtirasın esiri olan servet.
mam.moth ['mæməθ] **1.** *n.* ZOO mamut; **2.** *adj.* dev gibi, iri.
mam.my F ['mæmi] *n.* anne; *Am.* zenci sütnine, Arap dadı.
man [mæn, mən] **1.** *n., pl.* **men** [men] erkek, adam; er, asker; insan; uşak; erkek işçi; koca; satranç *veya* dama taşı; şahıs, kişi; **to a ~, to the last ~** son kişiye kadar, hepsi birden; **~ on leave** MIL izinli er; **be one's own ~** dilediğince hareket edebilmek, özgür olm.; **2.** *vb.* MIL, NAUT *(kadro, kuvvet, tayfa)* koymak *-e;* **~ o.s.** cesaretlenmek.
man.a.cle ['mænəkl] **1.** *n.* kelepçe; **2.** *v/t.* kelepçelemek, kelepçe takmak.
man.age ['mænidʒ] *v/t.* kullanmak; becermek; yönetmek, idare etm., çekip çevirmek *(ticarethane vs.);* terbiye etm. *(hayvan); -in* yolunu bulmak; **~ to inf.** *-meği* başarmak; *v/i.* müdür olm.; *bşle* geçinmek, yet(iş)mek; işini uydurmak, işin içinden sıyrılmak; **'man.age.a.ble** □ idare edilebilir; kullanışlı; **'man.age.ment** *n.* idare, yönetim; müdürlük; yönetim kurulu; **'man.age.er** *n.* müdür, direktör, yönetmen, idareci, yönetici; **good (bad) ~** iyi (kötü) yönetici, idareci; **'man.ag.eress** *n.* müdire, kadın direktör, kadın yönetici; **man.a.ge.ri.al** □ [̩ə'dʒiəriəl] yönetimsel, idarî...
man.ag.ing ['mænidʒiŋ] *adj.* idareci, yöneten; sevk..., idarî...; **~ clerk** büro şefi.
man-at-arms ['mænət'ɑːmz] *n. obs.* asker, zırhlı süvari neferi.
Man.ches.ter ['mæntʃistə] *n.:* **~ goods** *pl.* pamuklu mensucat.
Man.chu [mæn'tʃuː], **Man.chu.ri.an** [̩ 'tʃuəriən] **1.** *adj.* Mançulara *veya* dillerine ait; **2.** *n.* Mançuryalı, Mançu; Mançurya dili.
man.da.mus JUR [mæn'deiməs] *n.* daha yüksek bir mahkemeden alt mahkemeye verilen yazılı emir.
man.da.rin ['mændərin] *n.* mandalina likörü; mandalina rengi; F tutucu ve eyyamcı politikacı; *a.* **'man.da.rine** *n.* BOT mandalina.
man.da.tar.y JUR ['mændətəri] *n.* vekil, temsilci; **man.date** [' ̩deit] **1.** *n.* manda, bir ulusun diğer bir ulus üzerindeki egemenliği; ferman, emir; vekillik; **2.** *v/t.* egemenlik altına almak *-i;* **man-'da.tor** *n.* müvekkil; **man.da.to.ry** [' ̩dətəri] **1.** *adj.* emredici; *Am.* zorunlu, gerekli; **2.** *n.* vekil; mandater.
man.di.ble ANAT ['mændibl] *n.* çene kemiği, alt çene.
man.do.lin MUS ['mændəlin] *n.* mandolin.
man.drag.o.ra [mæn'drægərə], **man-drake** BOT [' ̩dreik] *n.* muhabbetotu, kankurutan, adamotu.
man.drel MEC ['mændril] *n.* toka dili, mil, mandrel.
man.drill ZOO [̩] *n.* bir tür iri ve yırtıcı maymun.
mane [mein] *n.* yele; **maned** *adj.* yeleli.
man-eat.er ['mæniːtə] *n.* yamyam; insan eti yiyen hayvan.
ma.nes ['mɑːneiz] *n. pl.* ölmüş kişilerin ruhları.
ma.neu.ver [mə'nuːvə] *= manoeuvre.*
man.ful □ ['mænful] erkekçe, mert; **'manful.ness** *n.* mertlik, yiğitlik.
man.ga.nese CHEM [mæŋgə'niːz] *n.* manganez; **man.gan.ic** [̩'gænik] *adj.* manganez...; manganez türünden.
mange VET [meindʒ] *n.* uyuz hastalığı.
man.ger ['meindʒə] *n.* yemlik; **dog in the ~** *k-ne* yararı olmayan *bşden* başkasının yararlanmasını istemeyen kimse.
man.gle [1] ['mæŋgl] **1.** *n.* sıkma makinesi; ütü cenderesi; **2.** *v/t.* cendereden geçirmek, silindirli makine ile ütülemek.
man.gle [2] [̩] *v/t.* vurarak ezmek, parçalamak, yırtmak; *fig.* sakatlamak; **'mangler** *n.* iki silindirli ütü makinesi.
man.go BOT ['mæŋgəu] *n.* Hint kirazı, mango.
man.grove BOT ['mæŋgrəuv] *n.* tropikal bölgelerde yetişen bir bitki türü.
man.gy ['meindʒi] *adj.* uyuz; yırtık pırtık; âdi, bayağı.

man...: '**~-han.dle** *v/t.* *bşi* insan gücüyle hareket ettirmek; kabaca itmek; *sl.* itip kakmak; '**~-hat.er** *n.* insanlardan kaçan kimse; '**~-hole** *n.* MEC baca, yeraltında boru, kablo yapmak için caddelerdeki üstü kapaklı delik; '**~-hood** *n.* erkeklik; mertlik; insanlık; '**~-'hour** *n.* bir saatlik çalışma.

ma.ni.a ['meinjə] *n.* tutku, mani, manya; delilik, cinnet, çılgınlık; **ma.ni.ac** ['-niæk] **1.** *n.* manyak, çılgın; **2.** *a.* **ma.ni.a.cal** □ [mə'naiəkəl] çılgın, deli.

man.i.cure ['mænikjuə] **1.** *n.* el ve tırnak tuvaleti, manikür; **2.** *v/t.* manikür yapmak; '**~-case** *n.* manikür kutusu; **man.i.cur.ist** ['-rist] *n.* manikürcü.

man.i.fest ['mænifest] **1.** □ belli, açık, anlaşılır; **2.** *n.* NAUT manifesto, gümrük beyannamesi; **3.** *v/t.* açıkça göstermek, belirtmek, ortaya koymak; işaret etm.; eliyle *b-ni*, *bşi* göstermek; beyan etm., bildirmek; *v/i. k-ni* göstermek, belli etm.; **man.i.fes'ta.tion** *n.* gösteri, izhar; **mani'fes.to** [-təu] *n.* bildiri, beyanname.

mani.fold ['mænifəuld] **1.** □ türlü türlü, çok; **2.** *v/t.* teksir etm., çoğaltmak; **3.** *n.* MEC birçok giriş ve çıkışı olan ana boru, kollektör; *intake* **~** MOT ana emme borusu; **~** writ.er teksir makinesi.

man.i.kin ['mænikin] *n.* ufak adam, cüce; manken; insan şekli.

Ma.nil.(l)a [mə'nilə] *n. a.* **~** *cheroot* Manila purosu; *a.* **~** *hemp* kenevir muzu; Manila kenevir; **~** *paper* Manila kenevirinden yapılan bir cins ambalaj kağıdı.

ma.nip.u.late [mə'nipjuleit] *v/t.* becermek; beceriyle kullanmak, idare etm.; hünerle kullanmak; el ile idare etm., işletmek; *bşe* hile karıştırmak; *b-ni*, *k-nin* çıkarı için kullanmak, dalavere yapmak; **ma.nip.u'la.tion** *n.* el ile işletme, beceriyle kullanma; suiistimal, hile, dalavere; **ma'nip.u.la.tive** [-lətiv] *adj.* el ile işletilebilir; dalavereci; **ma-'nip.u.la.tor** [-leitə] *n.* yöneten kimse; PHYS manipülatör; maniple.

man.kind [mæn'kaind] *n.* insanlık, beşeriyet; ['-] erkekler; *man.like = manly*; *mannish*; '**man.li.ness** *n.* mertlik, yiğitlik; '**man.ly** *adj.* mert, yiğit, erkeğe.

man.na ['mænə] *n.* kudret helvası.

manned [mænd] *adj.* içinde insan bulunan, insanlı...

man.ne.quin ['mænikin] *n.* manken; **~**

parade defile.

man.ner ['mænə] *n.* tavır, yol, usül (*a. lit.*); PAINT çeşit, stil; **~** *s pl.* terbiye, görgü; üslûp; *no* **~** *of doubt* hiç şüphe yok; *in a* **~** belli bir düzeyde, bir bakıma, bir anlamda; *in such a* **~** *that o* derece ki, şöyle ki; '**man.nered** *adj.* yapma tavırlı, ... '**man.ner.ism** *n.* yapmacık; (*sanatçıya ait*) özellik; '**man.ner.li.ness** *n.* görgülülük, nezaket; '**man.ner.ly 1.** *adj.* terbiyeli; **2.** *adv.* nazikçe.

man.nish ['mæniʃ] *adj.* erkeksi, erkek gibi (*esp. -kadın*); erkeğe yakışır.

ma.noeu.vra.ble, *Am. a.* **ma.neu.ver.a.ble** [mə'nuːvrəbl] *adj.* manevralı, manevra yeteneği olan; **ma'noeu.vre**, *Am. a.* **ma'neu.ver** [-və] **1.** *n.* manevra (*a. fig.*); **~** *s pl.* F *fig.* bahane, kaçamaklı söz, ağız yapma, hile, dolap; **2.** *vb.* manevra yapmak; sokmak (*into* -e); tedbir almak; dolap çevirmek.

man-of-war ['mænəv'wɔː] *n.* savaş gemisi.

ma.nom.e.ter PHYS, MEC [mə'nɔmitə] *n.* manometre, basıölçer.

man.or ['mænə] *n.* tımar; malikâne; *lord of the* **~** derebeyi; malikâne sahibi; '**~-house** *n.* şato; **ma.no.ri.al** [mə-'nɔːriəl] *adj.* malikâneye ait, malikâne...

man.pow.er ['mænpauə] *n.* el emeği, insan gücü; işçi sayısı, personel; işgücü.

manse *Scots* [mæns] *n.* papaz konutu.

man.serv.ant ['mænsə:vənt] *n.* erkek hizmetçi, uşak.

man.sion ['mænʃən] *n.* konak, büyük ve güzel ev; **~** *s pl.* evler bloku.

man.slaugh.ter ['mænslɔːtə] *n.* tasarlamadan adam öldürme, kasıtsız adam öldürme.

man.tel.piece ['mæntlpiːs], '**man.tel.shelf** *n.* şömine rafı.

man.til.la [mæn'tilə] *n.* şal.

man.tle ['mæntl] **1.** *n.* kolsuz üstlük, harmani, pelerin; örtü (*a.* ARCH, ANAT, ZOO); *fig.* perde, örtü; *a. incandescent* **~** (*lamba*) lüks gömleği; **2.** *v/t.* üstünü örtmek; *fig.* örtbas etm., gizlemek; **~** *on* üstüne *bşi* örtmek, yaymak; *v/i.* kızarmak (*yüz*); **~** *with bşle* kapla(n)-mak.

man.trap ['mæntræp] *n.* tuzak.

man.u.al ['mænjuəl] **1.** □ ele ait, el ile yapılan...; **~** *exercises pl.* MIL tüfek talimi; **~** *training* elişi eğitimi; **2.** *n.* elkitabı, talimname; (*org*) klavye, tuş düzeni.

man.u.fac.to.ry [mænju'fæktəri] *n.* fabrika, yapımevi.

man.u.fac.ture [mænju'fæktʃə] **1.** *n.* imal, yapım; yapılmış şeyler, mamulât; **2.** *v/t.* imal etm., yapmak; *fig.* uydurmak; **~d goods** *pl.* fabrika mamulâtı; **man.u'factur.er** *n.* fabrikatör; **man.u-'fac.tur.ing** *n.* imalât; *attr.* imalât…

ma.nure [mə'njuə] **1.** *n.* gübre; **2.** *v/t.* gübrelemek.

man.u.script ['mænjuskript] **1.** *n.* el yazması; müsvedde; yazma; **2.** *adj.* elle yazılı.

Manx [mæŋks] **1.** *adj.* Man adasına mensup; **2.** *n.* Man adası halkı.

man.y ['meni] **1.** *adj.* çok, birçok; **~ a** sayıca çok; **~ a one** birçoğu; **as ~ as** …kadar çok; **one too ~** gereğinden bir fazla; lüzumundan fazla, fuzuli; **be one too ~ for s.o.** *b-den* daha kurnazca davranmak; *b-ni* yenecek kadar akıllı olm.; **2.** *n.* bir çoğu; **a great ~, a good ~** hayli, pek çok, büyük sayıda; **'~'sid.ed** *adj.* çok taraflı, çok cepheli.

map [mæp] **1.** *n.* harita; **off the ~** F ortadan kaybolmuş; **on the ~** F önemli; **2.** *v/t. bşin* haritasını yapmak; not etm., kaydetmek, geçirmek; **~ out** ayrıntılarıyle planlamak, düzenlemek.

ma.ple BOT ['meipl] *n.* akçaağaç.

map.per ['mæpə] *n.* harita ve plan yapan *veya* çizen kimse, haritacı.

ma.quis ['mæki:] *n. II.* Dünya savaşında Nazilere direnen Fransız örgütü.

mar [mɑ:] *v/t.* zarar vermek, halel getirmek, bozmak, ihlâl etm.

mar.a.bou ORN ['mærəbu:] *n.* büyük Güney Afrika leyleği.

mar.a.schi.no [mærə'ski:nəu] *n.* siyah kirazdan yapılan tatlı likör.

mar.a.thon ['mærəθən] *n. a.* **~ race** uzun yol koşusu, maraton.

ma.raud [mə'rɔ:d] *vb.* çapulculuk etm.; **ma'raud.er** *n.* yağmacı, çapulcu.

mar.ble ['mɑ:bl] **1.** *n.* mermer; mermerden yapılmış eser; bilya, zıpzıp; **2.** *adj.* mermerden yapılı; *fig.* katı yürekli, hissiz, merhametsiz; **3.** *v/t.* ebrulamak, harelemek.

mar.cel [mɑ:'sel] **1.** *n. a.* **~ wave** perma (*saç*); **2.** *v/t.* perma yapmak (*saç*).

March¹ [mɑ:tʃ] *n.* mart.

march² [_] **1.** *n.* yürüyüş; marş; ilerleme, terakki; MUS marş; **~ past** MIL geçit töreni; **steal a ~ on s.o.** daha çabuk davranarak *b-ne* karşı üstünlük kazan-

mak; **2.** *vb.* yürümek, yürüyüş yapmak; zorla yürütmek; *fig.* ilerlemek; **~ off** MIL götürmek, posta etm.; **~ past** önünden yürüyüp geçmek.

march³ [_] **1.** *n. mst.* **~es** *pl.* HIST hudut, sınır, hudut bölgesi; **2.** *vb.* hemhudut (*veya* sınırdaş) olm. (**with** *ile*).

march.ing ['mɑ:tʃiŋ]: **~ order** askeri araçların dizilişi; **~ orders** *pl.* askere verilen yürüyüşe başlama emri, yürüyüş emri; **in heavy ~ order** seferî.

mar.chion.ess ['mɑ:ʃənis] *n.* markiz.

march.pane ['mɑ:tʃpein] *n.* acıbadem kurabiyesi.

mare [mɛə] *n.* kısrak; **~'s nest** *fig.* uydurma haber, değersiz *veya* uydurma buluş.

mar.ga.rine [mɑ:dʒə'ri:n] *n.*, F a. **marge** [mɑ:dʒ] margarin.

mar.gin ['mɑ:dʒin] *n.* kenar, ara, marj, sınır, hudut; hareket serbestliği; *a.* **~ of profit** kâr marjı; **~ of safety** güvenlik payı; '**mar.gin.al** □ kenarda olan; kenarda bulunan…, marjinal; **~ note** çıkma, derkenar, haşiye.

mar.grave ['mɑ:greiv] *n.* Roma İmparatorluğunda prenslere verilen bir ünvan; **mar.gra.vine** ['_grəvi:n] *n.* Roma İmparatorluğunda prens eşi.

mar.gue.rite BOT [mɑ:gə'ri:t] *n.* çayır papatyası, margrit.

Ma.ri.a [mə'raiə] *n.:* **Black ~** F cezaevi arabası.

mar.i.gold BOT ['mærigəuld] *n.* kadife çiçeği.

mar.i.jua.na [mæri'hwɑ:nə] *n.* haşiş.

mar.i.nade [mæri'neid] **1.** *n.* şarap, sirke, yağ ve baharat karışımı salamura; salamuraya yatırılmış et *veya* balık; **2.** = **ma.ri.nate** ['_'neit] *v/t.* salamuraya yatırmak.

ma.rine [mə'ri:n] **1.** *adj.* denize ait, deniz…, okyanus…; deniz kuvvetlerine ait, bahriye…; gemi…; **2.** *n.* silahendaz; deniz kuvvetleri; denizcilik, bahriye; PAINT deniz tablosu; **tell that to the ~s!** külahıma anlat!; **mar.i.ner** *poet. veya* JUR ['mærinə] *n.* gemici, denizci, bahriyeli.

mar.i.o.nette [mæriə'net] *n.* kukla.

mar.i.tal □ ['mæritl] evliliğe ait; **~ status** medeni hal.

mar.i.time ['mæritaim] *adj.* deniz(ciliğ)e ait; denize yakın; deniz…, sahil…; gemicilik…; **~ power** donanması olan devlet.

mar.jo.ram BOT ['mɑ:dʒərəm] *n.* mercankőşk.

mark¹ [mɑːk] *n.* Alman parası, mark.

mark² [-] **1.** *n.* nişan, alâmet, marka, işaret; COM etiketleme, damga; yara izi; yer, nokta, benek; şöhret; iz, eser, delil, emare; numune, örnek, norm, standart; *okul:* not, derece, numara; *spor:* başlama çizgisi; nişan, hedef; VET damga; *a man of ~* meşhur *(veya* önemli) adam; *up to the ~ fig.* istenilen düzeyde, derecede; *hit the ~* hedefi bulmak, nişanı vurmak; *miss the ~* hedefe isabet ettirememek; *fig.* konu dışı olm.; *beside the ~, wide of the ~* doğru olmayan, yanlış; **2.** *v/t.* işaretlemek, markalamak, etiketlemek, nişan koymak, damgalamak; etiketlere yazmak *(fiyat);* not vermek *-e;* beyan etm.; nazarı dikkate almak *-i,* hesaba katmak *-i,* dikkat etm. *-e; bşi* zihinde tutmak; *~ down* fiyat indirmek, azaltmak; *bşi* not etm., kaydetmek, yazmak; *~ off* ayırmak, tecrit etm., hudutlarını çizmek *ile;* *~ out* işaretlemek, *-in* sınırlarını çizmek; seçip ayırmak; *~ time* MIL yerinde saymak *(a. fig.);* **3.** *v/i. bşe* dikkat etm.; *~! dikkat!; **marked** adj.* işaretlenmiş; göze çarpan; hissolunabilecek; belli, aşikâr, meydanda; **mark.ed.ly** [ˈmɑːkidli] *adv.* belirgin bir şekilde; **ˈmark.er** *n. bilardo: esp.* sayıları işaret eden *b-i;* işaretleyen *veya* belli eden *bş.*

mar.ket [ˈmɑːkit] **1.** *n.* pazar (yeri), çarşı (meydanı); alışveriş, ticaret; piyasa; sürüm, revaç; *in the ~* piyasada; satın almaya hazır; *come into the ~* piyasada satışa çıkmak; *play the ~ Am. sl.* borsada alışveriş yaparak para kazanmak; **2.** *v/t.* satışa çıkarmak, çarşıda *veya* piyasada satmak; *v/i.* alışveriş etm., satın almak; **ˈmar.ket.a.ble** ☐ COM satılabilir, revaçlı, sürümlü; satılık; **mar.keteer** [-ˈtiə] *n.;* *black ~* karaborsacı, karapazarcı; **ˈmar.ket-gar.den** *n.* bahçe, bostan; **ˈmar.ket.ing** *n.* pazarlama; alışveriş etme; **ˈmar.ket-place** *n.* çarşı (meydanı); **ˈmar.ket-town** *n.* pazarı olan kasaba; **ˈmar.ket-value** *n.* piyasa rayici *(veya* değeri).

mark.ing [ˈmɑːkiŋ] *n.* işaret, marka, etiket; nişan; *ˈ~ink n. (çamaşırlarda markayı belirtmeye yarayan)* mürekkep.

marks.man [ˈmɑːksmən] *n.* nişancı, atıcı; **ˈmarks.man.ship** *n.* atıcılık, nişancılık.

marl [mɑːl] **1.** *n.* MIN marn, pekmez toprağı, kireçli toprak; **2.** *v/t.* AGR kireçli toprakla gübrelemek.

mar.ma.lade [ˈmɑːməleid] *n.* portakal marmelatı, reçel.

mar.mo.re.al ☐ *poet. &* RHET [mɑːˈmɔːriəl] mermer gibi beyaz, soğuk ve cilalı; mermerden yapılmış.

mar.mot ZOO [ˈmɑːmət] *n.* marmot, dağ sıçanı.

ma.roon¹ [məˈruːn] *adj.* kestane renginde.

ma.roon² [-] *v/t.* terketmek, *b-ni* ıssız bir kıyıya çıkarıp bırakmak.

ma.roon³ [-] *n.* uyarı sinyali niteliğinde kullanılan patlayıcı fişek.

mar.plot [ˈmɑːplɔt] *n.* meclisbozan.

mar.quee [mɑːˈkiː] *n.* büyük çadır, otağ.

mar.quess, *mst* **mar.quis** [ˈmɑːkwis] *n.* marki.

mar.que.try [ˈmɑːkitri] *n.* mobilyacılıkta kakma işi, marketri.

mar.riage [ˈmæridʒ] *n.* evlenme, izdivaç, nikâh, evlilik; evlilik hali; *civil ~* medenî nikâh; *by ~* evlenme suretiyle elde edilmiş; *related by ~* sıhrî hısım; *take in ~* evlenmek, almak; *ˈmar.riage.a.ble adj.* evlenmeye ehil, gelinlik, evlenecek çağda.

mar.riage...: *~ ar.ti.cles n. pl.* evlenme sözleşmesi; *~ lines pl.* evlenme kâğıdı *(veya* cüzdanı); *~ por.tion* drahoma, çeyiz.

mar.ried [ˈmærid] *adj.* evliliğe ait; evli, evlilik...; *~ couple* karıkoca.

mar.row [ˈmærəu] *n.* ilik; *fig.* öz, esas, asıl; *vegetable ~* BOT sakızkabağı; *ˈ~.bone n.* ilikli kemik; *~s pl. co.* çapraz iki kemik; *ˈmar.row.y adj.* ilik gibi, ilik dolu; özlü, kuvvetli.

mar.ry [ˈmæri] *v/t. & v/i.* evlenmek *(a. fig.)* *(s.o. ile);* evlendirmek *(s.o. to -i ile),* nikâh kıymak; birleş(tir)mek; *get married* evlenmek.

marsh [mɑːʃ] *n.* batak(lık); *attr.* bataklık...; *~ fever* bataklık humması, sıtma, malarya; *~ gas* bataklıkta oluşan metan gazı.

mar.shal [ˈmɑːʃəl] **1.** *n.* mareşal, müşür; HIST saray nazırı; protokol sorumlusu, şenlik görevlisi; *Am.* polis müdürü; **2.** *v/t.* sıralamak, tertip etm., tanzim etm., dizmek; sevketmek, yerleştirmek; **ˈmarshal.ling-yard** [-ˈʃliŋjɑːd] *n.* RAIL manevra istasyonu.

marsh mal.low [ˈmɑːʃmæləu] *n.* BOT hatmi; hafif yuvarlak şekerleme;

marsh mar.igold sarı çuhaçiçeği; 'marsh.y adj. bataklığa ait, bataklık gibi.

mar.su.pi.al zoo [mɑːˈsjuːpjəl] 1. adj. keseli...; 2. n. keseli hayvan.

mart[mɑːt] n. pazar(yeri); çarşı; ticaret merkezi.

mar.ten zoo [ˈmɑːtin] n. zerdeva.

mar.tial □ [ˈmɑːʃəl] harbe ait, savaşa özgü; askerî; savaşkan, savaşçı; ~ law örfî idare, sıkıyönetim; state of ~ law sıkıyönetim hali; ~ music askeri mızıka.

Mar.tian[ˈmɑːʃjən]1.n. Merihli; 2. adj. Mars..., Merih...

mar.tin¹[ˈmɑːtin] n. kırlangıç.

Mar.tin²[_]n.: St.~'s summer pastırma yazı.

mar.ti.net [mɑːtiˈnet] n. eziyetçi; katı (veya sert) kimse.

mar.ti.ni [mɑːˈtiːni] n. martini, cin ve vermut karışımı bir içki.

Mar.tin.mas [ˈmɑːtinməs] n. 11 Kasım'da yapılan St. Martin günü.

mar.tyr [ˈmɑːtə] 1. n. şehit, bir amaç uğrunda ölen kimse; 2. v/t. şehit etm.; işkence etm.; 'mar.tyr.dom n. şehitlik; 'martyr.ize vb. eziyet veya işkence etm.; şehit etm.; şehit olm.

mar.vel [ˈmɑːvəl] 1. n. mucize, harika; şaşkınlık; 2. vb. hayret etm., şaşmak (at -e).

mar.vel.(l)ous □ [ˈmɑːvələs] hayret verici; şaşılacak nitelikte; fevkalâde; 'marvel.(l)ous.ness n. acayiplik, gariplik.

Marx.ian [ˈmɑːksjən] 1. n. Marksizm taraftarı; 2. adj. Marks'ın kuramına ait; 'Marx.ism n. Marksizm; 'Marx.ist = Marxian.

mar.zi.pan [mɑːziˈpæn] n. acıbadem kurabiyesi.

mas.ca.ra[mæsˈkɑːrə]n. kirpikleri koyulaştırmak için kullanılan madde, rimel, maskara.

mas.cot [ˈmæskət] n. tılsım, muska, maskot, uğur bebeği.

mas.cu.line [ˈmæskjulin] 1. □ erkeğe ait; erkeksi; 2. n. GR eril, müzekker.

mash [mæʃ] 1. n. lapa, karışım; biracılıkta kullanılan arpa eziği ile su karışımı; ARG ezme; 2. v/t. ezmek; püre yapmak; ezilmiş arpayı su ile karıştırmak; sl. baştan çıkarmak, teshir etm.; ~ed potatoes pl. patates ezmesi, patates püresi; be~ed on sl. b-ne asılmak; 'mash.er n. ezen b-i veya bş;

sl. çapkın erkek; sahte âşık.

mask[mɑːsk] 1. n. maske; yüz kalıbı; s. masque; 2. vb. maske ile örtmek, maskelemek (a. fig.), gizlemek; maske takınmak, kılık değiştirmek; masked adj. gizli, belli olmayan; maskeli...; ~ ball maskeli balo; 'mask.er n. maske takan kimse.

ma.so.chism PSYCH [ˈmæzəukizəm] n. mazoşizm.

ma.son [ˈmeisn] n. taşçı, duvarcı; ♀ (far)mason; Ma.son.ic [məˈsɔnik] adj. mason veya farmasonluğa özgü; ma.son.ry[ˈmeisnri]n.duvarcılık; duvarcı işi; masonluk.

masque[mɑːsk]n. 16 ve 17. yüzyıllarda İngiltere'de maske giyilerek oynanan konuşmasız dram türünde yapıt; mas.querade [mæskəˈreid] 1. n. maskeli balo; maskeli balo giyisi; 2. v/i. fig. maskelenmek, olduğundan değişik görünmek.

mass¹ ECCL [mæs] n. kuddas âyini; High ♀ (Katoliklerde) kuddas; Low ♀ kuddas âyininin basit düzeni.

mass² [_] 1. n. kütle, küme, yığın; çokluk; the ~es pl. halk kütlesi, avam takımı; in the ~ bütün olarak; 2. vb. yığın olarak topla(n)mak.

mas.sa.cre [ˈmæsəkə] 1. n. katliam, kırım; 2. v/t. katletmek, kırıp geçirmek.

mas.sage [ˈmæsɑːʒ] 1. n. masaj, ovma; 2. v/t. masaj yapmak, ovmak.

mass com.mu.ni.ca.tions [ˈmæskəmjuːniˈkeiʃənz] n. pl. = mass media.

mas.seur [mæˈsəː] n. masajcı, masör; mas.seuse[mæˈsəːz]n.kadınmasajcı.

mas.sif [ˈmæsiːf] n. dağ kitlesi.

mas.sive□ [ˈmæsiv] som, masif, kütle halinde; ağır; esaslı, derin; kuvvetli, kudretli; 'mas.sive.ness n. irilik, ağırlık.

mass...: ~ me.di.a pl. kitle iletişim; ~ meeting halka açık toplantı; '~pro-duce vb. seri halde üretmek; ~ pro-duc.tion seri üretim.

mas.sy [ˈmæsi] adj. cüsseli, iri yapılı; ağır; sağlam, dayanıklı.

mast¹ NAUT [mɑːst] 1. n. gemi direği; 2. v/t. direk dikmek.

mast² [_] n. (domuzlar için) palamut, kayın kozalağı, kestane gibi ağaç yemişi.

mas.ter [ˈmɑːstə] 1. n. üstat, usta (a. fig.); efendi (a. fig.); sahip, patron, âmir; erkek öğretmen; kaptan, süvari; dinî lider; UNIV rektör; ♀ *of Arts* üniversite mezuniyeti ile doktora arasında bir derece; ♀ *of Ceremonies* teşrifatçı, protokol görevlisi; *be one's own ~* başına buyruk olm.; **2.** *adj. fig.* mümtaz, ileri gelen; baş, esas, temel, asıl; **3.** *v/t.* yenmek, hakkından gelmek; hükmetmek, idare etm.

mas.ter-at-arms NAUT ['mɑ:stərət-'ɑ:mz] *n.* güvenlik görevlisi; **mas.ter build.er** kalfa; mimar; **mas.ter.ful** □ ['-ful] zorba, gaddar; üstatça; '**mas-ter-key** *n.* ana anahtar; '**mas.ter.less** *adj.* sahipsiz; yönetimsiz; '**mas.ter.ly** *adj.* ustaca, hünerli.

mas.ter…: '**~piece** *n.* şaheser; harika; '**~ship** *n.* ustalık, üstatlık; şampiyonluk; yöneticilik, yönetim; *okul:* müdürlük; '**~stroke** *n.* maharetli iş, çok ustalıklı iş; '**mas.ter.y** *n.* hüküm, hakimiyet, hükümdarlık, saltanat, otorite; üstünlük; üstün gelme; ustalık, üstatlık, şampiyonluk; maharet, hüner.

mast-head ['mɑ:sthed] *n.* çanaklık, direk ucu.

mas.tic ['mæstik] *n.* macun; sakız rakısı, mastika.

mas.ti.cate ['mæstikeit] *vb.* çiğnemek; **mas.ti'ca.tion** *n.* çiğneme.

mas.tiff ['mæstif] *n.* avcılıkta ve gözetlemede kullanılan köpek, mastı.

mas.to.don ZOO ['mæstədɔn] *n.* mamuta benzer fil.

mas.toid MED ['mæstɔid] *n.* kulak arkası kemiği.

mat¹ [mæt] **1.** *n.* hasır; minder; paspas; altlık; **2.** *vb.* hasır ile örtmek; keçeleş-(tir)mek; birbirine dolaşmak.

mat² MEC [-] *adj.* donuk, mat.

match¹ [mætʃ] *n.* kibrit.

match² [-] **1.** *n.* oyun, maç, müsabaka, turnuva; evlenme, izdivaç; eş, benzer, denk *bş*; *be a ~ for* …e denk olm., eş olm., ayak uydurabilmek; *meet one's ~* rakibi ile karşılaşmak, üstesinden gelebileceği *b-ni* bulmak; **2.** *v/t.* uydurmak, intibak ettirmek; mukayese etm., kıyaslamak, karşılaştırmak (*with ile*); uymak, benzemek, denk olm. *-e*; *well ~ed* uygun, münasip, yerinde; *v/i.* uymak; *~ with* birbirine yakışmak, birbirini tutmak.

match-box ['mætʃbɔks] *n.* kibrit kutusu.

match.et ['mætʃet] = *machete*.

match.less □ ['mætʃlis] eşsiz, emsal-siz, rakipsiz; '**match.mak.er** *n.* çöpçatan.

match.wood ['mætʃwud] *n.* kibritlik odun, kıymık.

mate¹ [meit] *vb. satranç:* mat etm.

mate² [-] **1.** *n.* arkadaş, dost; koca, eş, karı, zevce; çiftin erkek *veya* dişisi (*hayvan*); yardımcı, muavin; NAUT ikinci kaptan; **2.** *v/t. & v/i.* evlen(dir)mek, çiftleş(tir)mek; eşlemek; '**mate.less** *adj.* yalnız, tek.

ma.ter *sl.* ['meitə] *n.* anne.

ma.te.ri.al [mə'tiəriəl] **1.** □ maddi, cismanî; bedenî, bedensel; esaslı, mühim, önemli, etkili (*to için*); **2.** *n.* malzeme, levazım, harç, materyel, madde, cevher, unsur; dokuma, kumaş; F *veya ~s pl.* levazım, malzeme; bileşik unsur; *working ~* iptidaî madde; *writing ~s pl.* yazı malzemesi; **ma'te.ri.al.ism** *n.* materyalizm, maddecilik; **ma'te.ri.al.ist** *n.* materyalist, maddeci; **ma.te.ri-al'is.tic** *adj.* (*~ally*) materyalist, maddeci; **ma.te.ri.al.i.za.tion** [-riəlai'zeiʃən] *n.* maddileş(tir)me, cisimlenme; **ma'te.ri.al.ize** *v/t. & v/i.* maddileş(tir)mek, gerçekleşmek; realize etm.

ma.ter.nal □ [mə'tə:nl] anaya mahsus, anneye yakışır; ana…, anne…, valide…; ana tarafından; **ma'ter.ni.ty** [-niti] *n.* analık; annelik; *mst ~ hospital* doğumevi; *~ dress* hamile elbisesi.

mat.ey ['meiti] *adj.* teklifsiz, samimi, senli benli, arkadaşça.

math.e.mat.i.cal □ [mæθi'mætikəl] matematiksel; **math.e.ma.ti.cian** [-mə'tiʃən] *n.* matematikçi; **math.e-mat.ics** [-'mætiks] *n. mst sg.* matematik.

maths F [mæθs] = *mathematics*.

mat.ie ['meiti] *n.* ringa balığının küçüğü.

mat.in ['mætin] **1.** *adj. poet.* sabah…, sabahleyin; **2.** *n. ~s pl.* ECCL sabaha karşı yapılan ibadet; *poet.* (*kuşların*) sabah şarkısı.

mat.i.née ['mætinei] *n.* matine.

ma.tri.arch ['meitriɑ:k] *n.* aile (*veya* kabile) reisi (*kadın*); '**ma.tri.ar.chy** *n.* anaerki; **ma.tri.cide** [-'said] *n.* anasını öldürme; anasını öldüren kimse, ana katili.

ma.tric.u.late [mə'trikjuleit] *v/t. & v/i.* üniversiteye öğrenci olarak kaydedilmek; kaydetmek; **ma.tric.u'la.tion** *n.* öğrenci kaydı.

mat.ri.mo.ni.al □ [mætri'məunjəl] ev-

liliğe ait, evlilik...; **mat.ri.mo.ny**
['ˌməni] *n.* evlilik hali, evlilik.

ma.trix ['meitriks] *n. fig. bşe* şekil veren
veya onu geliştiren canlı kısım; GEOL
fosilin bulunduğu kaya parçası; MEC
a. ['mætriks] matris, hurufat kalıbı.

ma.tron ['meitrən] *n.* ağırbaşlı orta
yaşlı evli kadın; ana kadın; amir kadın,
başhemşire; '**ma.tron.ize** *v/t. b-ne*
analık etm.; '**ma.tron.ly** *adj.* ana gibi;
toplu, etine dolgun; *fig.* temkinli, ağırbaşlı, ciddi (*kadın*).

mat.ter ['mætə] **1.** *n.* madde, cevher,
unsur; MED cerahat, irin; şey; konu;
içindekiler, muhteviyat; illet, neden;
iş, mesele, meşguliyet; TYP dizilecek
metin, müsvedde; ~*s pl.* hal, ahval,
şartlar, vaziyet, durum; *postal* ~ posta
ile gönderilen her şey; *printed* ~ basma, matbua; *in the* ~ *of* ... bakımından, ...in hususunda, *-e* gelince;
what's the ~? ne var?; *what's the* ~
with you? neyiniz var?; *no* ~ mühim
değil, zararı yok; *no* ~ *who* her kim
olursa olsun; ~ *of course* kendiliğinden anlaşılan *bş*, doğal *bş*., işin tabii gidişi; *as a* ~ *of course* doğal olarak; *for
that* ~, *for the* ~ *of that* ona gelince,
hatta; ~ *of fact* hakikat, realite, gerçek;
as a ~ *of fact* işin doğrusu, gerçekte,
zaten; ~ *in hand* söz konusu mevzu;
that is a hanging ~ cezasırn kellen
ile ödeyebilirsin, hayatına malolur;
no laughing ~ şakaya gelmez; **2.** *v/i.*
ehemmiyeti olm., önemi olm. (*to için*);
cerahatlenmek; *it does not* ~ önemi
yok, farketmez; '~-*of*-'course *adj.*
doğal; '~-*of*-'fact *adj.* fiilî, hakiki, gerçek; soğukkanlı, sakin, heyecansız.

mat.ting ['mætiŋ] *n.* hasır (örme).

mat.tock ['mætək] *n.* kazma.

mat.tress ['mætris] *n.* döşek, şilte.

ma.ture [mə'tjuə] **1.** ☐ olgun, ergin;
reşit; dikkatli, ölçüp biçen; COM vadesi
gelmiş; **2.** *v/t. & v/i.* olgunlaş(tır)mak,
kemale er(dir)mek; erginleşmek; COM
vadesi gelmek;**ma'tu.ri.ty** *n.* olgunluk,
erginlik; COM vade.

ma.tu.ti.nal ☐ [mætju:'tainl] sabaha
ait, sabah...; erken.

maud.lin ☐ ['mɔːdlin] aşırı duygusal,
aşırı duygulanan.

maul [mɔːl] *v/t.* dövmek, berelemek,
ezmek, hırpalamak; *fig. b-ni* fena halde hırpalamak.

maul.stick PAINT ['mɔːlstik] *n.* resim çi-
zerken dayanılan değnek.

maun.der ['mɔːndə] *v/i.* anlaşılmaz
şekilde konuşmak, mırıldanarak söylenmek; düzensiz hareket etm.

Maun.dy Thurs.day ['mɔːndi'θəːzdi]
n. Paskalya öncesi Perşembe günü.

mau.so.le.um [mɔːsə'liəm] *n.* türbe,
mozole.

mauve [məuv] *n. & adj.* leylâk rengi.

mav.er.ick *Am.* ['mævərik] *n.* damgalanmamış dana; POL *& fig.* disipline uymayan, tek başına hareket eden kimse.

maw [mɔː] *n.* (*hayvanlarda*) kursak,
mide; ağız.

mawk.ish ☐ ['mɔːkiʃ] tiksindirici;
'**mawkish.ness** *n.* tiksindiricilik.

maw.worm ['mɔːwəːm] *n.* bağırsak
kurdu.

max.il.lar.y [mæk'siləri] *adj.* çene kemiğine ait, çene kemiği...

max.im ['mæksim] *n.* vecize, ata(lar)
sözü; kural; **max.i.mum** ['ˌməm] **1.**
n. en yüksek derece, maksimum; **2.**
adj. azami..., en çok...; ~ *wages pl.*
en yüksek ücret, tavan ücreti.

May[1] [mei] *n.* mayıs (ayı); ⚶ BOT yabani
akdiken.

may[2] [ˌ] *v/aux. (irr.)* -ebilmek, muhtemel olm., -meğe izinli olm.

may.be ['meibiː] *adv.* belki, olabilir.

may-bee.tle ZOO ['meibiːtl] *n.* '**may-
-bug** mayısböceği.

May Day ['meidei] *n.* bahar bayramı ve
işçi bayramı olarak kutlanan gün.

may.fly ZOO ['meiflai] *n.* mayıssineği.

may.hap *obs.* ['meihæp] *adv.* belki, ihtimal ki.

may.on.naise [meiə'neiz] *n.* mayonez.

may.or [mɛə] *n.* belediye reisi (*veya*
başkanı); '**may.or.al** *adj.* belediye baş-
kan(lığ)ına ait; '**may.or.al.ty** *n.* belediye başkanlığı; '**may.or.ess** *n.* belediye
başkanının eşi; kadın belediye başkanı.

may.pole ['meipəul] *n.* bahar bayra-
mında etrafında dans edilen çiçek-
lerle süslü direk.

maze [meiz] *n.* labirent; *fig. a.*
karışıklık; *be* ~*d*, *be in a* ~ şaşkına dönmek, şaşkınlık içinde olm.; '**ma.zy** ☐
dolaşık, darmadağın, karmakarışık,
muğlak.

Mc.Coy *Am. sl.* [mə'kɔi] *n.: the real* ~
gerçeği.

me [miː, mi] *pron.* beni; bana; F ben.

mead[1] [miːd] *n.* mayalı bal ve sudan
yapılan bir içki.

mead[2] *poet.* [ˌ] = **meadow**.

mead.ow ['medəu] *n.* çayır, çimen;
'~'saf.fron *n.* BOT güzçiğdemi;
'mead.ow.y *adj.* çimenli.

mea.ger, mea.gre □ ['mi:gə] zayıf, yavan, cılız, çelimsiz, sıska, kuru (*a. fig.*);
noksan, eksik, az, kıt, kifayetsiz;
'mea.gerness, 'mea.gre.ness *n.*
zayıflık, cılızlık, sıskalık, çelimsizlik;
kuruluk; noksanlık, eksiklik, azlık,
kıtlık, kifayetsizlik.

meal¹ [mi:l] *n.* yemek, öğün.

meal²[.] *n.* un; **meal.ies**['.iz] *n. pl. Güney Afrika*: mısır (buğdayı).

meal.time ['mi:ltaim] *n.* yemek vakti.

meal.y ['mi:li] *adj.* un gibi, unlu;
'~-mouthed *adj.* sinsi, samimiyetsiz.

mean¹□[mi:n] bayağı, alçak, pis, kaba,
adi, aşağı; acınacak, zavallı; çirkin; lime lime olmuş, yırtık pırtık; cimri, pinti, hasis; dar kafalı.

mean² [.] **1.** *adj.* orta, alelade; ortalama, vasati; *in the* ~ *time* = *~time*; **2.**
n. orta, vasat; alelade; ılımlılık; MATH
ortalama, nicelik; *~s pl.* para, sermaye,
gelir, servet, mali vaziyet, mali durum;
imkân, olanak; vasıta, araç; *by all ~s*
kuşkusuz, şüphesiz; *by no ~s* hiçbir suretle, asla, katiyen; *by this ~s* bunun
üzerine, sonradan; *by ~s of* vasıtasiyle,
yardımıyla; *by some ~s or other* herhangi bir suretle, herhangi bir usulde,
herhangi bir tarzda, ne yapıp yapıp.

mean³[.] (*irr.*) *v/t.* söylemek, demek istemek; yapmak niyetinde olm.; ifade
etm., mana vermek, kastetmek, amaç
gütmek, tasarlamak; uygun olm. (*for*
-*e*); arzuladığını söylemek, istediğini
söylemek, niyetinde olduğunu söylemek (*by ile*); ...manasına gelmek, demek; ~ *well* (*ill*) niyeti iyi (kötü) olm.
(*by, a. to ile*).

me.an.der [mi'ændə] **1.** *n.* dolambaç,
dirsek; *~s pl.* kıvrım, menderes; **2.**
v/i. kıvrılmak, yılankavi akmak (*nehir,
dere*); avare dolaşmak *veya* konuşmak.

mean.ing ['mi:niŋ] **1.** □ *bşe* delâlet
eden, anlamlı; *well* ~ hüsnüniyet sahibi, iyi kalpli; **2.** *n.* mana, anlam; *rare* niyet, maksat, hedef, fikir, kasıt; 'mean-
ing.less *adj.* ehemmiyetsiz, önemsiz;
anlamsız; sönük, cansız.

mean.ness ['mi:nnis] *n.* alçaklık, adilik, aşağılık, kabalık.

meant [ment] *pret. & p.p. of* **mean**³.

mean.time ['mi:n'taim], **mean.while**
['mi:n'wail] *adv.* bu aralık, bu sırada,
aynı zamanda.

mea.sles ['mi:zlz] *n. pl.* MED kızamık;
VET uyuz; *German* ~ kızamıkçık;
'mea.sly *adj.* kızamıklı; benekli; *sl.*
acınacak, adi, değersiz, zavallı.

meas.ur.a.ble □ ['meʒərəbl] ölçülebilir.

meas.ure ['meʒə] **1.** *n.* ölçü; MUS usül,
ölçü, mezür; tedbir, önlem; ölçüm, ölçme; ~ *of capacity* istiap ölçüsü; *beyond* ~ son derece, haddinden fazla;
in some ~ bir dereceye kadar, kısmen;
in a great ~ ekserisi, en büyük kısmı;
made to ~ ısmarlama yapılmış; *for
good* ~ fazladan, ek olarak; *set ~s to*
sınırla(ndır)mak; *take s.o.'s* ~ *b-nin*
karakter ve yeteneklerini sınamak;
take ~s önlem almak, hazırlıklı bulunmak; **2.** *vb.* ölçmek, kıymet biçmek,
tartmak (*a. fig.*); ölçüsü ...kadar
olm.; ~ *up Am.* yeterli nitelikte olduğunu göstermek (*to -e*); 'mea.sure.less
□ ölçüsüz, sınırsız; 'meas.ure.ment
n. ölçü, ölçme, tartı, ölçüm; NAUT tonaj.

meat [mi:t] *n.* (*yenecek*) et; *obs. veya
prov.* yiyecek (*şey*); *fig.* büyük zevk;
butcher's ~ kasaplık et; *fresh* ~ taze
et; *preserved* ~ konserve et; *roast* ~
kızartma et, rosto; '~-fly *n.* ZOO etsineği, kurtsineği; ~ *pie* kıymalı börek;
'~-safe *n.* yemek dolabı; 'meat.y *adj.*
etli; *fig.* özlü, değerli fikirlerle dolu.

Mec.ca.no [mi'kɑ:nəu] *n.* bir çeşit
oyuncak.

me.chan.ic [mi'kænik] *n.* makinist,
makine ustası; MOT tamirci; me'chan-
i.cal □ makineye ait, mekanik, makine...; ~ *engineering* makine mühendisliği; **mecha.ni.cian** [mekə'niʃən]
n. makinist, mekanisyen; me.chan.ics
[mi'kæniks] *n. mst sg.* mekanik, makine ilmi.

mech.a.nism ['mekənizəm] *n.* mekanizma; 'mech.a.nize *v/t.* makineleştirmek; MIL motörleştirmek, mekanize
hale getirmek.

med.al ['medl] *n.* nişan, (*hatıra*) madal-
ya(sı); 'med.al(l)ed *adj.* madalyalı;
me.dallion [mi'dæljən] *n.* madalyon;
süslü şekil. **med.al.(l)ist** ['medəlist]
n. madalya kazanan (*veya* yapan) kimse.

med.dle ['medl] *v/i.* karışmak, müdahale etm., burnunu sokmak (*in, with -e*);
'med.dler *n.* başkalarının işine burnunu sokan kimse; **med.dle.some**
['.səm] □ sırnaşık, usandıran, sıkıcı;
herşeye burnunu sokan.

me.di.a ['mi:djə] *n. pl. of* **medium**.

me.di.ae.val [medi'i:vəl] = **medieval**.

me.di.al □ ['mi:djəl], '**me.di.an** orta(-lama), vasat(i), avaraj.

me.di.ate 1. □ ['mi:diit] bilvasita, vasıtalı, endirek(t), dolayısıyla olan; **2.** ['mi:dieit] *vb.* aracılık etm., vasıta olm.; aralarını bulmak; **me.di'a.tion** *n.* tavassut, aracılık; '**me.di.a.tor** *n.* aracı; ECCL arabulucu, şefaatçi; **me.di-a.to.ri.al** □ [-ə'tɔːriəl], **me.di.a.to.ry** ['-ətəri] uzlaştırma ile ilgili, uzlaştırıcı; arabulucu...; **me.di.a.trix** ['-eitriks] *n.* aracı kadın.

med.i.cal □ ['medikəl] tedaviye ait, tıbbî; iyileştirici; ~ **board** sağlık kurulu, sağlık heyeti; ~ **certificate** doktor raporu; ~ **evidence** tıbbî delil; ~ **jurisprudence** adlî tıp; ~ **man** doktor, hekim, tabip; ~ **officer** devlet kademesinde tıp sorumluluğu olan kimse; ~ **specialist** uzman doktor; ~ **student** tıp öğrencisi; ☿ **Superintendent** baştabip, başhekim; **me'dic.ament** *n.* ilâç.

med.i.cate ['medikeit] *v/t.* ilâç ile tedavi etm.; bşin içine ilâç katmak; **med.i-'cation** *n.* ilâçla tedavi; bşin içine ilâç katma; ilâç (*esp.* yatıştırıcı); **med.i.ca-tive** ['-kətiv] *adj.* ilâçla tedavi kabilinden.

me.dic.i.nal □ [me'disinl] tıbbî, iyileştirici, tedavi (*veya* teskin) edici, şifalı.

med.i.cine ['medsin] *n.* tıp, hekimlik; ilâç, deva; '~-**ball** *n. spor:* ağır top, sağlık topu; ~-**chest** *n.* ev ecza dolabı; '~-**man** *n.* sihirbaz hekim.

med.i.co F *co.* ['medikəu] *n.* doktor.

me.di.e.val □ [medi'i:vəl] ortaçağa ait.

me.di.o.cre [mi:di'əukə] *adj.* orta derecede, olağan; **me.di.oc.ri.ty** [-'ɔkriti] *n.* orta, vasat olma; ne iyi ne kötü zekâsı olan (*veya* alelade) kimse.

med.i.tate ['mediteit] *v/t. & v/i.* düşünüp taşınmak, düşünceye dalmak (**on** üzerinde); bşi düşünmek, ölçüp biçmek; tasarlamak, planlamak, proje yapmak; **medi'ta.tion** *n.* düşünüp taşınma, düşünceye dalma; dalgınlık; **med.i.ta.tive** □ ['-tətiv] derin düşüncelere dalmış, düşünceli.

Med.i.ter.ra.ne.an [meditə'reinjən] *n.* Akdeniz.

me.di.um ['mi:djəm] *n., pl. a.* **me.di.a** ['-djə] **1.** orta; çevre, ortam; araç, vasıta; PHYS & *ispiritizma:* medyum; BIOL mikrop üretilebilir madde; **2.** *adj.* orta(lama), vasat(i); '~-'**sized** *adj.* orta

boylu.

med.lar BOT ['medlə] *n.* muşmula, beşbıyık, döngel (ağacı).

med.ley ['medli] *n.* karmakarışıklık; *contp.* karışık insanlar *veya* şeyler; MUS potpuri.

me.dul.la [me'dʌlə] *n.* ilik; **med'ul-lar.y** *adj.* ilikli, ilik...; özlü, kuvvetli.

me.du.sa ZOO [mi'dju:zə] *n.* denizanası, medüz.

meed *poet.* [mi:d] *n.* mükâfat, ödül.

meek □ [mi:k] uysal, yumuşak huylu; mütevazı, alçakgönüllü; '**meek.ness** *n.* alçakgönüllülük; uysallık.

meer.schaum ['miəʃəm] *n.* eskişehirtaşı, lületaşı.

meet[1] [mi:t] *adj.* uygun, münasip, yerinde, yakışık alır.

meet[2] [-] **1.** (*irr.*) *v/t.* rast gelmek, rastlamak -*e*; karşılamak -*i*; tanışmak, görüşmek (**s.o.** *ile*); tediye etm., ödemek -*i*; bitişmek, kavuşmak; tatmin etm., cevap vermek (*ihtiyaca*); ~ **one's death** kaza sonucu ölmek; ~ **the ear** kulağa gelmek; ~ **the eye** göze ilişmek; ~ **s.o.'s eye** b-ne gözlerini dikmek; *v/i.* rastlamak -*e*; görüşmek, buluşmak; kavuşmak, bitişmek; toplanmak; uğramak (**with** -*e*); birdenbire b-ne, bşe rastlamak, karşılaşmak -*le*; toplantı yapmak -*le*; ~ **with an accident** kazaya uğramak; **make both ends** ~ geçinebilmek, ipin iki ucunu biraraya getirebilmek; **2.** *n. spor:* karşılaşma, yarışma.

meet.ing ['mi:tiŋ] *n.* toplantı, miting; heyet, meclis, cemaat; birleşme; '~-**house** *n.* toplantı evi; kilise; '~-**place** *n.* toplanma yeri.

meg.a.cy.cle ELECT ['megəsaikl] *n.* megasikl, bir milyon sikl; **meg.a.lith** ['-liθ] *n.* megalit, büyük taş anıt; **meg-a.lo.ma.ni.a** ['-ləu'meinjə] *n.* megalomani; **meg.aphone** ['-fəun] *n.* megafon, ses nakil borusu; **meg.a.ton** ['-tʌn] *n.* büyükton, megaton.

me.grim ['mi:grim] *n.* yarım baş ağrısı, migren, yarımca; ~**s** *pl.* melankoli, karasevda, bunalım.

mel.an.chol.ic [melən'kɔlik] *adj.* hüzünlü, karasevdalı, melankolik; **mel-an.chol.y** ['-kəli] **1.** *n.* karasevda, melankoli; **2.** *adj.* melankolik, karasevdalı; hüzünlü, mahzun.

mé.lange [mei'lã:nʒ] *n.* karışık şey.

mê.lée ['melei] *n.* saç saça baş başa dövüşme; kalabalık, izdiham.

mel.io.rate ['mi:ljəreit] *v/t. & v/i.* iyileş(tir)mek; düzel(t)mek.

mel.lif.lu.ent [me'lifluənt], *mst* **mel-** '**lif.luous** *adj.* bal gibi (tatlı).

mel.low ['meləu] **1.** □ olgun, olmuş, kemale ermiş; *fig.* görmüş geçirmiş; yıllanmış (*şarap*); tatlı (*ses, renk*); yumuşak; *fig.* nazik, ince; *sl.* çakırkeyf; **2.** *vb.* olgunlaş(tır)mak; yumuşa(t)mak; '**mel.low.ness** *n.* olgunluk, kemal; yumuşaklık; incelik, zayıflık.

me.lo.di.ous □ [mi'ləudjəs] melodik, ahenkli, armonik, hoş sesli; **me'lo.di-ousness** *n.* ahenk(lilik), armoni **mel-o.dist** ['melədist] *n.* kompozitör, şarkıcı; '**mel.odize** *vb.* ahenk vermek; bestelemek, kompoze etm.; **mel.o-dra.ma** ['melǝudrɑ:mǝ] *n.* melodram, heyecanlı dram; **me.lo.dra'mat.ic** *adj.* melodrama uygun; aşırı duygusal; **mel.o.dy** ['melədi] *n.* nağme, hava, ezgi, melodi.

mel.on BOT ['melən] *n.* kavun.

melt [melt] *v/t. & v/i.* eri(t)mek; *fig.* erimek; yumuşa(t)mak (*a. fig.*); **~ away** eriyip kaybolmak (*a. fig.*); **~ down** (*hammadde olarak kullanılmak üzere*) eritmek; **~ into tears** göz yaşlarına boğulmak.

melt.ing □ ['melting] (*esp. ses*) yumuşak, hoş; '**~-point** *n.* erime noktası; '**~-pot** *n.* pota (*a. fig.*).

mem.ber ['membə] *n.* aza, üye, PARL mebus, milletvekili; organ, uzuv; '**mem.bership** *n.* azalık, üyelik; üye sayısı, üyeler; **~ fee** üye aidatı.

mem.brane ['membrein] *n.* (ince) zar, gışa; **mem'bra.nous, mem'bra.ne-ous** [-jəs] *adj.* zarımsı, zardan ibaret.

me.men.to [mi'mentəu] *n.* hatıra, yadigâr.

mem.o ['meməu] = *memorandum.*

mem.oir ['memwɑ:] *n.* biyografi; inceleme yazısı; **~s** *pl.* hatırat, anılar; tutanaklar.

mem.o.ra.ble □ ['memərəbl] anmağa değer.

mem.o.ran.dum [memə'rændəm] *n.* not, muhtıra, memorandum; POL nota.

me.mo.ri.al [mi'mɔ:riəl] **1.** *adj.* hatırlatıcı; **2.** *n.* abide, anıt; muhtıra, dilekçe, önerge; **me'mo.ri.al.ist** *n.* dilekçe sahibi; **me'mo.ri.al.ize** *v/t.* anmak *-i,* hatırasını yad etm. *-in.*

mem.o.rize ['meməraiz] *v/t.* ezberlemek.

mem.o.ry ['meməri] *n.* hatıra, andaç; hafıza, zihin, hatır; *commit to ~* ezber-

lemek; *within living ~* olayları hatırlanan zaman içinde; *in ~ of* hatırasına, anısına *-in.*

men [men] *n. pl. of* **man.**

men.ace ['menəs] **1.** *v/t.* tehdit etm., gözünü korkutmak, yıldırmak; **2.** *n.* tehlike; tehdit.

me.nag.er.ie [mi'nædʒəri] *n.* gösteri için kafeslerde tutulan vahşi hayvan koleksiyonu; bu hayvanların sergilendiği yer, hayvanat bahçesi.

mend [mend] **1.** *v/t.* ıslah etm.; onarmak, tamir etm., yamamak; daha iyi yapmak; **~ the fire** ateşe daha fazla yakıt atmak; **~ one's ways** davranışlarına dikkat etm.; *v/i.* iyileşmek, ıslah olunmak, düzelmek, şifa bulmak; **2.** *n.* tamir, onarım; tamir olunmuş yer, yama; *on the ~* iyileşmekte, gelişen, düzelen.

men.da.cious □ [men'deiʃəs] yalan; yalancı, yalana şerbetli; **men.dac.i.ty** [-'dæsiti] *n.* yalancılık; yanlışlık; yalan.

mend.er ['mendə] *n.* tamirci.

men.di.can.cy ['mendikənsi] *n.* dilencilik; '**men.di.cant 1.** *adj.* dilenen, dilencilik eden; **2.** *n.* dilenci; **men'dic.i.ty** [-siti] *n.* dilencilik.

men.folk F ['menfəuk] *n.* erkekler, erkek kısmı (*veya* milleti).

men.hir ['menhiə] *n.* abide, büyük taş anıt.

me.ni.al *contp.* ['mi:njəl] **1.** □ hizmetçiye ait; süfli, bayağı; **2.** *n.* uşak, hizmetçi.

men.in.gi.tis MED [menin'dʒaitis] *n.* beyin zarı iltihabı, menenjit.

men.ses ['mensi:z] *n. pl.* âdet, aybaşı (*s. menstruation*); **men.stru.al** ['-struəl] *adj.* âdetle ilgili; âdet (görme)…, aybaşı…; **men.stru'a.tion** *n.* âdet (görme), aybaşı.

men.su.ra.ble ['menʃurəbl] *adj.* ölçülebilir; **men.su.ra.tion** [-sjuə'reiʃən] *n.* ölçme.

men.tal □ ['mentl] akılla ilgili, zihne ait, zihnî…; **~ arithmetic** akıldan yapılmış hesap; **~ institution** tımarhane, asabiye hastanesi, akıl hastanesi; **~ly ill** akıl hastası; **men.tal.i.ty** [-'tæliti] *n.* zihniyet, düşünme tarzı.

men.thol PHARM ['menθol] *n.* mantol, nane ruhu.

men.tion ['menʃən] **1.** *n.* anma, ima, ifade, zikir; **2.** *v/t.* anmak, zikretmek, ima etm.; *don't ~ it!* estağfurullah!, birşey

değil efendim!; **not to ~ ...**, **without
~ing ...** ...den başka, üstelik; **men-
tion.a.ble** ['-ʃnəbl] *adj.* kayda değer,
anılabilir, söylenebilir.

men.tor ['mentɔ:] *n.* akıllı ve güvenilir
danışman, akıl hocası.

men.u ['menju:] *n.* yemek listesi, mönü.

Meph.is.to.phe.le.an [mefistə'fi:ljən]
adj. şeytanca, haince.

mer.can.tile ['mə:kəntail] *adj.* ticarete
ait, ticari, ticaret...; **~ marine** ticaret filosu.

mer.ce.nar.y ['mə:sinəri] **1.** □ ücretli;
yalnız çıkar gözeten, kazanç düşkünü,
para canlısı; **2.** *n.* MIL ücretli asker.

mer.cer ['mə:sə] *n.* kumaş satıcısı, kumaşçı; **'mer.cer.y** *n.* kumaş, dokuma,
manifatura.

mer.cer.ize ['mə:səraiz] *v/t.* ipeğe ben-
zeyecek şekilde işlemek (*pamuklu kumaş*).

mer.chan.dise ['mə:tʃəndaiz] *n.* ticaret eşyası, emtia, mal.

mer.chant ['mə:tʃənt] **1.** *n.* tacir, tüccar; *Am.* perakendeci, satıcı; **2.** *adj.* ticarete ait, ticari, ticaret...; **law ~** ticaret kanunu; **'mer.chant.a.ble** *adj.* satılabilir,
satışı kolay; sürümlü; **'mer.chant-
man, mer.chant ship** *n.* ticaret gemisi.

mer.ci.ful □ ['mə:siful] merhametli,
sevecen; şefkatli; **'mer.ci.ful.ness** *n.*
rahmet, merhametlilik.

mer.ci.less □ ['mə:silis] acımasız,
merhametsiz, amansız; **'mer.ci.less-
ness** *n.* merhametsizlik.

mer.cu.ri.al [mə:'kjuəriəl] *adj.*
cıvalı...; CHEM cıva...; *fig.* bir türlü yerinde durmaz, cıva gibi; değişken.

Mer.cu.ry ['mə:kjuri] *n.* Merkür, Utarit; *fig.* haberci, mesajcı, kurye; ♀ CHEM
cıva.

mer.cy ['mə:si] *n.* merhamet, şefkat; af,
rahmet, bereket; **be at s.o.'s ~** *b-nin* in-
safına kalmış olm., *b-nin* elinde olm.;
at the ~ of the waves dalgalara karşı
güçsüz, dalgaların keyfine bağlı; **have
~ upon** *b-ne* acımak, merhamet etm.; **it
is a ~ that...** iyi ki...; **~ killing** ıstırapsız
(*veya* rahat) ölüm.

mere[1] [miə] *n.* küçük göl.

mere[2] [-] *adj.* halis, saf, sade, hakiki,
karışıksız, katıksız; önemsiz; **~(st)
nonsense** son derece saçma; **~ words**
pl. sırf laf, boş söz; **'mere.ly** *adv.* sadece, ancak, yalnız.

mer.e.tri.cious □ [meri'triʃəs] cicili bi-

cili; *fig.* sırnaşık, usandırıcı, cıvık, lâubali, küstah.

merge [mə:dʒ] *v/t.* & *v/i.* (**in**) kay-
naş(tır)mak, birleş(tir)mek; içinde
kaybolmak; **'merg.er** *n.* COM birleşme,
füzyon.

me.rid.i.an [mə'ridiən] **1.** *adj.* öğleye
ait, öğle...; *fig.* en yüksek; **2.** *n.* GEOGR
meridyen, boylam dairesi; öğle vakti;
fig. tepe, zirve, doruk; **me'rid.i.o.nal**
□ boylam dairesine ait; güneye ait; güneyde olan.

me.ringue [mə'ræŋ] *n.* yumurta akın-
dan yapılan bir tür krema; bir tür kremalı pasta, beze.

me.ri.no [mə'ri:nəu] *n.* merinos koyu-
nu; merinos yünü; merinos yününden
yapılmış kumaş.

mer.it ['merit] **1.** *n.* liyakat; değer; fazilet; **~s** *pl. part.* JUR esas, gerçek değer,
kıymet; **on the ~s of the case** davanın
esasına göre; **on its (own) ~s** değerine
göre; **make a ~ of** övgüye değer dav-
ranışta bulunmak; **2.** *v/t. fig.* hak
etm. *-i*, lâyık olm. *-e*; **mer.i.to.ri.ous**
□ [-'tɔ:riəs] değerli, methedilmeye
değer, hürmete lâyık.

mer.maid ['mə:meid] *n.* denizkızı;
merman ['-mæn] *n.* belinden aşağısı
balık şeklinde olan deniz adamı.

mer.ri.ment ['merimənt] *n.* keyif, neşe,
şenlik, cümbüş.

mer.ry □ ['meri] keyifli, neşeli, şen, sevinçli; neşe verici, eğlenceli, güldürücü, eğlendirici; çakırkeyf; **make ~** cümbüş (*veya* âlem) yapmak; **~an.drew**
['-ændru:] *n.* maskara, soytarı, paskal, palyaço; **~go-round** *n.* atlıkarınca; **~mak.ing** *n.* eğlence, şenlik, bayram, cümbüş; **~thought** *n.* lades kemiği.

me.sa GEOGR ['meisə] *n.* küçük plato.

mé.sal.li.ance [me'zæliəns] *n.* daha
düşük seviyeden *b-i* ile olan evlilik.

me.seems *obs.* [mi'si:mz] *vb.* bana öyle görünüyor.

mesh [meʃ] **1.** *n.* ağ gözü, file ilmiği; *fig.
oft.* **~s** *pl.* tuzak; **be in ~** MEC birbirine
geçmek; **2.** *vb.* ağla yakalamak; uygun
düşmek (*nitelik, fikir vs.*); MEC birbirine geçmek; **meshed** *adj.* ...gözlü, ...il-
mikli; **'mesh-work** *n.* ağ örgüsü.

mes.mer.ism ['mezmərizəm] *n.* ipnoz;
'mes.mer.ize *v/t.* ipnotize etm.; hay-

rette bırakmak.

mess¹ [mes] **1.** *n.* karmakarışıklık, düzensizlik; kaos, karışık durum; kirlilik, pislik; sofra arkadaşları; sofra arkadaşlarıyla yenen yemek; F sıkıntı, darlık; **make a ~ of** bozmak, berbat etm. *-i;* **2.** *v/t. a.* **~ up** yüzüne gözüne bulaştırmak, bozmak, karıştırmak, berbat etm.; *v/i.* **~ about** düzensiz, plansız iş yapmak; tembellik etm.

mess² [-] **1.** *n.* porsiyon, tabak; MIL subaylara mahsus yemek ve dinlenme salonu; **2.** *vb.* birlikte yemek yemek.

mes.sage ['mesidʒ] *n.* haber, mesaj; **~ board** IT ilan tahtası.

mes.sen.ger ['mesindʒə] *n.* haberci, ulak; kurye; **~ boy** özel haber vs. götüren çocuk.

Mes.sieurs, *mst* **Messrs.** ['mesəz] *n.* baylar, efendiler (*özellikle firmalar için kullanılır*).

mess...: '**~-jacket** *n.* MIL kısa üniforma ceket; '**~-mate** *n.* MIL. NAUT sofra arkadaşı; '**~-room** *n.* orduevi; '**~-tin** *n.* aş kabı.

mes.suage JUR ['meswidʒ] *n.* mesken, müştemilâtlı ev.

met [met] *pret. & p.p. of* **meet²** 1.

met.a.bol.ic [metə'bɔlik] *adj.* metabolik; **me.tab.o.lism** PHYSIOL ['me'tæbəlizəm] *n.* metabolizma.

met.age ['mi:tidʒ] *n.* ölçme ücreti.

met.al ['metl] **1.** *n.* maden, metal; çakıl, kırma taş; camın soğumadan önceki sıvı hali; **~s** pl. F ray, yol; **2.** *v/t.* çakılla kaplamak; **me.tal.lic** [mi'tælik] *adj.* (**~ally**) madenî, maden..., metal...; **metal.lif.er.ous** [metə'lifərəs] *adj.* madenli; **met.al.line** ['-lain] *adj.* madenî; '**met.allize** *v/t.* madene dönüştürmek, maden özelliği vermek; **met.al.log.ra.phy** [-'lɔgrəfi] *n.* metalografi; **met.al.loid** ['-lɔid] **1.** *adj.* madene benzer; **2.** *n.* metal olmayan cisim; **met.al.lur.gic, met.allur.gi.cal** [-'lə:dʒik(ə)l] metalurjiye ait; **met.al.lur.gy** [mi'tælədʒi] *n.* metalurji.

met.a.mor.phose [metə'mɔ:fəuz] *v/t. & v/i.* başkalaş(tır)mak; **met.a'mor.pho.sis** [-fəsis] *n.*, *pl.* **met.a'mor.pho.ses** [-fəsi:z] metamorfoz, istihale, şekil değişimi, başkalaşım.

met.a.phor ['metəfə] *n.* mecaz; **met.a.phoric,** *mst* **met.a.phor.i.cal** [-'fɔrik(ə)l] mecazî.

met.a.phys.ic [metə'fizik] **1.** *mst* **met.a'phys.i.cal** metafiziğe (*veya* fiziköte-

tesine) ait; **2.** **met.a'phys.ics** *n. oft. sg.* metafizik, fizikötesi.

mete [mi:t] *v/t.* ölçmek; *mst* **~ out** hissesini ölçmek; paylaştırmak.

me.te.or ['mi:tjə] *n.* akanyıldız, meteor(taşı); **me.te.or.ic** [mi:ti'ɔrik] *adj.* meteortaşına benzer, meteortaşı...; *fig.* parlak, göz kamaştırıcı; **me.te.or.ite** ['mi:tjərait] *n.* yere düşen meteortaşı; **me.teor.o.log.i.cal** □ [mi:tjərə-'lɔdʒikəl] meteorolojik; **me.te.or.ol.o.gist** [-'rɔlədʒist] *n.* meteorolog, meteoroloji bilgini; **me.teor'ol.o.gy** □ *n.* meteoroloji.

me.ter ['mi:tə] *n.* saat, sayaç, ölçü aleti.

me.thinks *obs.* [mi'θiŋks] *vb.* (*pret.* **methought**) sanırım, galiba.

meth.od ['meθəd] *n.* usul, metod, yöntem; düzen; sistem; **me.thod.ic,** *mst* **me.thod.i.cal** □ [mi'θɔdik(ə)l] yöntemli, düzenli, metodik, metotlu; **Meth.od.ism** ECCL ['meθədizəm] *n.* Hıristiyanlıkta ibadet öğretimi ve düzeni; '**Meth.od.ist** *n.* ECCL metodist, Protestan mezhebi üyesi; '**meth.od.ize** *v/t.* düzene sokmak, usule uydurmak.

me.thought *obs.* [mi'θɔ:t] *pret. of* **me.thinks.**

meth.yl CHEM ['meθil] *n.* metil; **meth.y.l.at.ed** spir.it ['meθileitid'spirit] *n.* ısıtma ve ışıklandırma için kullanılan alkol; **methyl.ene** ['meθili:n] *n.* metilen.

me.tic.u.lous □ [mi'tikjuləs] titiz, çok dikkatli.

me.tre ['mi:tə] *n.* metre; vezin.

met.ric ['metrik] *adj.* (**~ally**) metre sistemini kullanan, metrik; **~ system** metre sistemi; '**met.ri.cal** □ metrik; şiir vezniğe ait, ölçülü.

met.ro F ['metrəu] *n.* metro, şehir çevresinde işleyen demiryolu, tünel; '**~-land** *n.* F banliyö, dış mahalle.

me.trop.o.lis [mi'trɔpəlis] *n.* başkent, başşehir; büyük şehir; **met.ro.pol.i.tan** [metrə'pɔlitən] **1.** *adj.* başşehre ait; ♀ **Railway** şehir çevresinde işleyen demiryolu; **2.** *n.* başpiskopos, metropolit; başkentte oturan kimse.

met.tle ['metl] *n.* cesaret, yiğitlik, yüreklilik, hararetli gayret; **be on one's ~** elinden gelenin en iyisini yapmaya hazır olm.; **put s.o. on his ~** en iyisini yapmaya teşvik etm.; '**met.tled, met.tle.some** ['-səm] *adj.* canlı, ateşli.

mew¹ ORN [mju:] *n.* martı.

mew² [-] **1.** *n.* miyavlama; **2.** *vb.* miyavlamak.

mew³ [.] *v/t. mst ~ up* kilitlemek, kapa(t)mak.

mewl [mju:l] *vb.* inlemek, sızla(n)mak.

mews [mju:z] *n.* HIST dar sokak.

Mex.i.can ['meksikən] **1.** *adj.* Meksikalıya ait, Meksikalı...; **2.** *n.* Meksikalı.

mez.za.nine ['metsəni:n] *n.* asma kat; *Am.* THEAT birinci balkon.

mi.aow [mi:'au] **1.** *n.* miyavlama; **2.** *v/i.* miyavlamak.

mi.as.ma [mi'æzmə] *n., pl. a.* **mi'as-ma.ta** [.tə] pis ve zehirli sis; **mi'as.mal** □ zehirli, tehlikeli, mikroplu.

miaul [mi'ɔ:l] *v/i.* miyavlamak.

mi.ca MIN ['maikə] *n.* mika; **mi.ca-ce.ous** [.'keiʃəs] *adj.* mıkalı; mikaya ait; mikamsı.

mice [mais] *n. pl. of **mouse**.*

Mich.ael.mas ['miklməs] *n.* 29 Eylül'-de kutlanan St. Mişel festivali.

mi.cro... ['maikrəu] *prefix* küçük..., ufak..., mikro...

mi.crobe ['maikrəub] *n.* mikrop, bakteri; **mi'cro.bi.al** [.bjəl] *adj.* mikrobik.

mi.cro.chip ['maikrəutʃip] *n.* mikroçip; **mi.cro.cosm** ['.kɔzəm] *n.* küçük dünya; insan (*evreni temsil eden*); **mi.cro fi.ber** ['.faibə] *n.* mikrolif; **mi-cro.film** ['.film] **1.** *n.* mikrofilm; **2.** *v/t.* mikrofilm üzerine film çekmek.

mi.crom.e.ter [mai'krɔmitə] *n.* mikrometre; **mi.cro.phone** ['maikrəfəun] *n.* mikrofon; **mi.cro.scope** ['.skəup] *n.* mikroskop; **mi.cro.scop.ic, mi.cro-scop.i.cal** □ [.s'kɔpik(əl)] mikroskobik; pek ufak; **mi.cro.wave** ELECT ['maikrəuweiv] *n.* bir çeşit elektromanyetik dalga.

mid [mid] *s. **middle** 2, poet. = **amid*** arasında, ortasında; *in ~ air* havada; *in ~ winter* kış ortasında; '~**.day 1.** *n.* öğle vakti; **2.** *adj.* öğle.

mid.den ['midn] *n.* gübre (*veya* çöp) yığını.

mid.dle ['midl] **1.** *n.* merkez, orta (yer); bel; ~*s pl.* COM orta kalite; **2.** *adj.* orta, vasat; aradaki, ortadaki; **♀ Ages** *pl.* Ortaçağ; **~ class(es** *pl.*) ortahalliler sınıfı, orta sınıf, burjuva; '~**'aged** *adj.* orta yaşlı; '~**'class** *adj.* orta sınıfa ait, orta...; ~ **dis.tance** PAINT arka ve ön görüntü arasındaki kısım; ~ **King-dom** *lit.* Çin; '~**.man** *n.* arabulucu; COM mutavassıt tüccar, komisyoncu;

'~**.most** *adj.* en ortadaki; ~ **name** göbek adı; '~**-of-the-'road** *adj.* POL ılımlı; '~**'sized** *adj.* orta boy; '~**weight** *n. boks:* orta sıklet.

mid.dling ['midliŋ] **1.** *adj.* orta, alelade; oldukça iyi; şöyle böyle; **2.** *adv. a.* ~*ly* orta halde, şöyle böyle; **3.** *n.* ~*s pl.* COM orta kalite mahsül.

mid.dy F ['midi] = **midshipman**.

midge [midʒ] *n.* tatarcık; **midg.et** ['midʒit] *n.* cüce.

mid.land ['midlənd] **1.** *adj.* ülkenin iç bölgelerinde bulunan; **2.** *n. the ♀s pl.* İngiltere'nin iç bölgeleri; '**mid-'morn-ing break** öğleden evvelki büyük ara; '**mid.most** *adj.* tam ortadaki; '**mid-night 1.** *n.* geceyarısı; **2.** *adj.* gece yarısı olan, geceyarısı...; **mid.riff** ['.rif] *n.* ANAT diyafram; '**mid.ship.man** *n.* deniz okulu öğrencisi; deniz yarsubayı; *Am.* (*denizci*) asteğmen; '**mid.ships** *adv.* NAUT geminin ortasın(d)a; **midst** [midst] **1.** *n.* orta, merkez; *in the ~ of-in* ortasında; *in our ~* aramızda, bizim ile; **2.** *prp. poet. s. amidst* arasında, ortasında; '**mid.stream 1.** *n.* nehrin orta yeri; **2.** *adv.* nehrin orta yerinde; '**mid.sum.mer** *n.* yaz ortası; yaz dönümü; **♀ Day** 24 Haziran; '**mid'way 1.** *n.* yarı yol; *Am.* eğlence yeri, lunapark; **2.** *adj.* yarı yolda olan; **3.** *adv.* yarı yolda; '**mid.wife** *n.* ebe; **mid.wife.ry** ['.wifə-ri] *n.* ebelik; '**mid'win.ter** *n.* karakış, kış ortası.

mien *lit.* [mi:n] *n.* çehre, surat; eda, hal, tavır.

miff F [mif] *n.* dargınlık, bozuşma.

might [mait] **1.** *n.* kuvvet, kudret, güç, iktidar, takat; *with ~ and main* var kuvveti ile, elden geldiğince; **2.** *pret. of may*; **might.i.ness** ['.tinis] *n.* güçlülük; **mighty 1.** *adj.* güçlü, kuvvetli; F muazzam, pek büyük; **2.** F *adv.* pek çok, fazla, ziyade, son derecede.

mi.gnon.ette BOT [minjə'net] *n.* muhabbetçiçeği.

mi.graine ['mi:grein] *n.* migren, yarım başağrısı.

mi.grant ['maigrənt] **1.** = **migratory**; **2.** *n. a.* ~ **bird** göçmen kuş.

mi.grate [mai'greit] *v/i.* göç etm., hicret etm.; **mi'gra.tion** *n.* göç; **mi.gra.to.ry** ['.grətəri] *adj.* göçebe; göçle ilgili; göçmen.

mike *sl.* [maik] *n.* mikrofon.

mil [mil] *n.* bin; 1/1000 pus.

mil.age ['mailidʒ] = **mileage**.

Mil.an.ese [milə'niːz] **1.** *adj.* Milano'ya ait; **2.** *n.* Milanolu.

milch [miltʃ] *adj.* süt veren, sağmal; ~ *cow* süt ineği, sağmal inek.

mild □ [maild] yumuşak, zarif; hafif; ılımlı; nazik; *to put it ~ly* en azından, en hafif deyimiyle.

mil.dew ['mildjuː] **1.** *n.* mildiyu; küf; **2.** *v/t. & v/i.* küflen(dir)mek.

mild.ness ['maildnis] *n.* yumuşaklık; hafiflik; nezaket; ılımlılık.

mile [mail] *n.* mil (*1609,33 metre*).

mile.age ['mailidʒ] *n.* mil hesabıyla uzaklık; mil başına ödenen ücret.

mil.er ['mailə] *n. spor:* bir millik koşuya katılan koşucu *veya* yarış atı.

mile.stone ['mailstəun] *n.* kilometre taşı; *fig.* dönüm noktası.

mil.foil BOT ['milfɔil] *n.* civanperçemi.

mi.lieu ['miːljə:] *n.* çevre, muhit.

mil.i.tan.cy ['militənsi] *n.* saldırganlık; **'mil.i.tant** □ militan, saldırgan; faal; kavgacı; **mil.i.ta.rism** ['-tərizəm] *n.* militarizm, savaşçı politika; askerlik ruhu; **'mil.i.ta.rist** *n.* militarizm yandaşı; **'mil.itar.y 1.** □ askerî; askerliğe *veya* savaşa ait; harp...; ~ *college* harp okulu, harbiye (mektebi); ♀ *Government* askerî hükümet; ~ *map* kurmay haritası; **2.** *n.* asker, ordu; **mil.i.tate** ['-teit] *v/t.:* ~ *in favour of* (*against*) lehine (aleyhine) etkilemek; **mi.li.tia** [mi'liʃə] *n.* milis; yedek askerler; **mi'li.tia.man** *n.* yedek er.

milk [milk] **1.** *n.* süt; *the ~ of human kindness* insanın yapısında olan şefkati; *it's no use crying over spilt ~* olan oldu, iş işten geçti, üzülmek için çok geç; **2.** *vb.* süt sağmak; süt vermek (*inek, koyun vs.*); almak, çekmek *-den*; *fig.* sağmak *-i*; faydalanmak *-den*, kötüye kullanmak *-i*; **'milk-and-'wa.ter** *adj.* yavan, değersiz, tatsız (*bş veya b-i*); **'milk-bar** *n.* süt barı (*süt ve sütlü maddelerin satılıp içildiği ve yendiği dükkân*); **'milk-churn** *n.* süt kabı (*veya* güğümü); **'milk.er** *n.* süt sağan kimse; sağmal inek; **'milk.ing-ma'chine** *n.* süt sağma makinesi.

milk...: '~.maid *n.* süt sağıcı kız; **'~.man** *n.* sütçü; **'~-pow.der** *n.* süttozu; **'~-'shake** *n.* dondurma ile karıştırılan süt; **'~.sop** *n.* çıtkırıldım, dandini bebek, mahalleli çocuğu; **'~.weed** *n.* BOT sütleğenotu; **'~-white** *adj.* süt gibi beyaz; **'milk.y** *adj.* süt gibi; sütlü; süt...; *fig.* yumuşak, nazik, uysal, ince;

♀ *Way* samanyolu.

mill[1] [mil] **1.** *n.* değirmen; fabrika, imalâthane; iplikhane; öğütme makinesi; *sl.* dövüşme; *go through the ~ fig.* (*zorluklar sonucu*) deneyim kazanmak; **2.** *vb.* öğütmek, çekmek; MEC frezelemek; kenarını diş diş yapmak (*para*); çalkalamak.

mill[2] *Am.* [-] *n.* doların binde biri (= *1/10 cent*).

mill.board ['milbɔːd] *n.* kalın karton; **'mill.dam** *n.* değirmen barajı.

mil.le.nar.i.an [mili'nɛəriən], **mil.len.ni.al** [mi'leniəl] *adj.* bininci; bin yıllık devreye ait; **mil.le.nar.y** ['-nəri] **1.** *adj.* bin yıla ait; bin yıllık devreye ait; **2.** *n.* bin yıllık devre; bu devre inanan kimse; **mil'len.ni.um** [-niəm] *n.* bin yıllık devre; herkes için mutluluk içinde geçeceği düşünülen bin yıllık devre; mutluluk devresi.

mil.le.pede ZOO ['milipiːd] *n.* kırkayak.

mill.er ['milə] *n.* değirmenci; MEC freze tezgâhı.

mil.les.i.mal [mi'lesiməl] *n.* binde bir.

mil.let BOT ['milit] *n.* darı.

milli...: '~-girl *n. part.* iplikçi (*kız*); **'~-hand** *n.* fabrika işçisi.

mil.li.ard ['miljɑːd] *n.* milyar.

mil.li.gram ['miligræm] *n.* miligram.

mil.li.me.tre ['milimiːtə] *n.* milimetre.

mil.li.ner ['milinə] *n.* kadın şapkacısı; **'mil.li.ner.y** *n.* kadın şapkacılığı; kadın şapkaları.

mill.ing ['miliŋ] *n.* değirmencilik; ~ *cutter* MEC freze çakısı; ~ *machine* freze makinesi.

mil.lion ['miljən] *n.* milyon; **mil.lion.aire** [-'nɛə] *n.* milyoner; **mil.lionth** ['miljənθ] **1.** *adj.* milyonuncu; **2.** *n.* milyonda bir.

mill...: '~-pond *n.* değirmen havuzu; **'~-race** *n.* değirmen deresi; **'~.stone** *n.* değirmentaşı; *fig.* engel, yük; *see through a ~* F ukalâ dümbeleği olm.; **'~-wheel** *n.* değirmen dolabı, değirmen çarkı; **'~.wright** *n.* değirmenci, değirmen yapan ve tamir eden adam.

mi.lord [mi'lɔːd] *n.* lord; zengin, asılzade.

milt[1] [milt] *n.* balık menisi.

milt[2] *rare* [-] *n.* dalak.

milt.er ICHTH ['miltə] *n.* erkek ringa balığı.

mime [maim] **1.** *n.* pandomima; pandomimci; **2.** *vb.* taklidini yapmak; mimiklerle rol oynamak.

mim.e.o.graph ['mimiəgrɑ:f] **1.** *n.* teksir makinesi; **2.** *v/t.* teksir etm.

mi.met.ic [mi'metik] *adj.* taklide ait.

mim.ic ['mimik] **1.** *adj.* taklit eden; yanıltıcı; **2.** *n.* taklitçi; taklit; **3.** *v/t.* taklit etm., kopya etm; taklidini yapmak; '**mim.ic.ry** *n.* taklitçilik; zoo benzetme, tatbik.

mi.mo.sa вот [mi'məuzə] *n.* mimoza, küstümotu.

min.a.ret ['minəret] *n.* minare.

min.a.to.ry ['minətəri] *adj.* tehdit edici, korkutucu.

mince [mins] **1.** *vb.* kıymak; ufaltmak; aşırı nezaketle konuşmak; kırıtarak yürümek; *he does not ~ matters* dobra dobra konuşur; *~ one's words* açıkça söylemek; **2.** *n. a. ~d meat* kıyma; '*~.meat* *n.* tatlı ve etli börek dolgusu; *make~ of* hezimete uğratmak *-i*, parça parça etm. *-i*; '*~'pie* *n.* (*mincemeat dolgusu ile*) börek, poğaça; '**minc.er** *n.* et kıyma makinesi.

minc.ing □ ['minsiŋ] işveli, nazlı; yapmacık, sahte tavırlı; '*~-ma.chine* = *mincer.*

mind [maind] **1.** *n.* his, duygu; zihin, akıl, beyin; zekâ; düşünce, fikir, kanaat; niyet, maksat, hedef, kasıt; arzu, istek, heves; hafıza; dikkat, itina; *to my ~* benim düşünceme göre; *~'s eye* düş, hayal; *out of one's ~, not in one's right ~* deli, kaçık; *since time out of ~* ezelden beri, oldum olası; *change one's ~* fikrini değiştirmek, caymak; *bear s.th. in ~* bşi hatırda tutmak, unutmamak; *have (half) a ~ to* bş yapmaya eğilim göstermek, niyet etm.; *have s.th. on one's ~* zihnini işgal eden bşi olmak; *have in ~* tasavvur etm., düşünmek; *(not) know one's own ~* ne istediğini bil(me)mek; *make up one's ~* karar vermek; *make up one's ~ to s.th.* kabullenmek *-i*, sonucuna razı olm. *-in*; *put s.o. in ~ of* b-ne bşi hatırlatmak; *speak one's ~* düşündüğünü açıkça söylemek; **2.** *vb.* bakmak, dikkat etm. *-e*; endişe etm., kaygı duymak; saymak; dikkatli olm.; önem vermek *-e*; karşı çıkmak *-e*; *~! dikkat!*; *never ~! önemi yok!, zararı yok!; ~ the step!* önüne bak!, düşme!; *I don't ~ (it)* aldırmam; zararı yok; *do you ~ if I smoke?* sigara içmemde sakınca var mı?; *would you ~ taking off your hat?* lütfen şapkanızı çıkarır mısınız?; *~ your own business!* kendi işine

bak!, başkaşının işine karışma!; '**mind.ed** *adj.* niyetli; gönlü yatmış; '**mind.er** *n.* bşe bakmakla görevli kimse; **mind.ful** ['~.ful] *adj.* unutmaz, dikkatli (*of -e*); '**mind.ful.ness** *n.* dikkat, itina; '**mind.less** □ akılsızca yapılan, aptalca; aldırışsız, lâkayt, pervasız (*of -e*).

mine[1] [main] *pron.* benim(ki); benimkiler.

mine[2] [~] **1.** *n.* maden ocağı; lağım; *fig.* zengin kaynak, hazine; мıı. mayın; **2.** *vb.* lağımlamak; kazmak; мın kazıp çıkarmak; мıı. mayın dökmek; мıı. tünel kazmak; '*~.field* *n.* мıı. mayın tarlası; мın maden alanı; '*~.lay.er* *n.* NAUT, мıı. mayın döken gemi; '**min.er** *n.* madenci, maden işçisi; *part.* мıı. tünel kazan *veya* mayın döken kimse; NAUT mayın dökme gemisi.

min.er.al ['minərəl] **1.** *n.* mineral, maden; madensel madde; *~s pl.*, *~ water* madensuyu; **2.** *adj.* mineral, madensel; '**miner.al.ize** *v/t.* mineralleştirmek; taşlaştırmak; **min.er.al.o.gist** [~'rælədʒist] *n.* madenler ilmi uzmanı; **min.er'al.o.gy** *n.* madenler ilmi, mineroloji.

mine.sweep.er NAUT ['mainswi:pə] *n.* mayın temizleme (*veya* tarama) gemisi.

min.gle ['miŋgl] *v/t. & v/i.* karış(tır)-mak (*in -e*); kat(ıl)mak (*with -e*).

min.gy F ['mindʒi] *adj.* cimri.

min.i.a.ture ['minjətʃə] **1.** *n.* minyatür; **2.** *adj.* küçük, çok ufak...; çok ufak yapılmış; *~ camera* 35 mm'lik *veya* daha dar film kullanılan fotoğraf makinesi.

min.i.kin ['minikin] **1.** *adj.* pek ufak, cüzi; yapmacık, yapay, sahte tavırlı; **2.** *n.* bücür, cüce, bodur, bacaksız.

min.im ['minim] *n.* мus yarım nota; damla; '**min.i.mize** *v/t.* en aza indirgemek; *fig.* önemsememek; **min.i.mum** ['~məm] **1.** *n.* en az miktar; **2.** *adj.* minimum, asgari, en az..., en küçük...

min.ing ['mainiŋ] *n.* maden kazma; COM madencilik, maden işletmeciliği; мıı, NAUT mayın dökme.

min.ion ['minjən] *n.* efendisinin dediklerini körü körüne yapan hizmetçi; *fig.* köle, peyk; TYP yedi puntoluk matbaa harfi; *~s of the law* polis, zabıta memurları, gardiyan *vs.*

min.is.ter ['ministə] **1.** *n.* papaz; *fig.* alet ve edevat; POL bakan; devlet vekili; ortaelçi; **2.** *vb.* bakmak, yardım etm., hizmet sunmak **(to** *-e)*; **min.is-te.ri.al** □ [-'tiəriəl] POL bakanlığa ait; elçiliğe ait; ECCL ruhanî.

min.is.trant ['ministrənt] **1.** *adj.* hizmet eden; **2.** *n.* ECCL destekleyen *veya* yardım eden kimse; **min.is'tra.tion** *n.* hizmet; yardım, servis *(part.* ECCL.]; '**min.is.try** *n.* dinsel hizmet, papazlık; POL bakanlık, vekâlet; yardım.

min.i.ver ['minivə] *n.* (*süs*) beyaz kürk.

mink ZOO [miŋk] *n.* vizon.

min.now ICHTH ['minəu] *n.* golyan balığı.

mi.nor ['mainə] **1.** *adj.* daha küçük, önemi az, ikinci derecede olan; rüştünü ispat etmemiş; MUS minör...; **A ~** minör; **~ key** minör anahtarı; **2.** *n.* rüştünü kanıtlamamış kimse; PHLS küçük önerme; **Am.** UNIV ikinci branş; *spor: Am.* ikinci lig; **mi.nor.i.ty** [mai'nɔriti] *n.* azınlık; reşit olmama.

min.ster ['minstə] *n.* büyük kilise, katedral.

min.strel ['minstrəl] *n. obs.* saz şairi; **~s** *pl.* yüzü siyaha boyanmış şarkıcı; **min-strelsy** ['-si] *n.* saz şairliği; lirik şiir ve baladlar.

mint[1] BOT [mint] *n.* nane; **~ sauce** naneli sos.

mint[2] [-] **1.** *n.* darphane; *fig.* zengin kaynak; **a ~ of money** büyük miktar para; **2.** *adj.* yeni, kirlenmemiş, iyi durumda (*madalya, kitap pul v.b.*); **3.** *v/t.* basmak (*madenî para*); yaratmak, uydurmak (*kelime, deyim vs.*); '**mint.age** *n.* para basma ücreti; basılan para; paraya basılan damga.

min.u.et MUS [minju'et] *n.* menuetto, mönüe, gruplar halindeki çiftlerin yaptığı yavaş dans.

mi.nus ['mainəs] **1.** *prp.* eksi; F -sız, -siz; **2.** *adj.* eksi; sıfır, hiç; **3.** *n.* eksi işareti; sıfırdan eksik miktar.

mi.nute[1] [mai'nju:t] □ çok ufak; dikkatli, titiz.

min.ute[2] ['minit] **1.** *n.* dakika; *fig.* an; **~s** *pl.* tutanak; **in a ~** yakında, şimdi; **to the ~** tam zamanında; dakikası dakikasına; **the ~** (*that*) olur olmaz, yapar yapmaz; **2.** *v/t.* not tutmak; tutanak hazırlamak; '**min.ute-hand** *n.* saat yelkovanı.

min.ute.ly[1] ['minitli] *adv.* dikkatle, inceden inceye.

mi.nute.ly[2] [mai'nju:tli] *adj.* sürekli; **mi'nute.ness** *n.* küçük olma.

mi.nu.ti.a [mai'nju:ʃiə] *n., pl.* **mi'nu.ti-ae** [-ʃii:] önemsiz ayrıntılar.

minx [miŋks] *n.* lâubali kız, haspa.

mir.a.cle ['mirəkl] *n.* mucize, harika; **to a ~** son derece güzel, enfes; **~ play** Hazreti İsa ve havarilerini konu alan dinsel piyes; **mi.rac.u.lous** □ [mi'rækjuləs] mucize gibi, hayret verici, harikulâde; doğa yasalarına aykırı, doğaüstü; **mi-'racu.lous.ness** *n.* mucize kabilinden oluş.

mi.rage ['mirɑ:ʒ] *n.* ılgım, serap (*a. fig.*).

mire ['maiə] **1.** *n.* çamur, batak; pislik; **be in the ~** güçlük içinde olm.; **drag s.o. through the ~** b-ni rezil etm., ipliğini pazara çıkarmak; **2.** *v/t. & v/i.* çamur ile kirletmek; çamura bat(ır)mak (*a. fig.*); **his car was ~d** arabası çamurlanmıştı.

mir.ror ['mirə] **1.** *n.* ayna (*a. fig.*); **2.** *v/t.* yansıtmak (*a. fig.*).

mirth [mə:θ] *n.* neşe, şenlik, cümbüş; **mirth.ful** □ ['-ful] neşeli, şen; '**mirth-less** □ neşesiz.

mir.y ['maiəri] *adj.* çamurlu, pis.

mis... [mis] *prefix* yanlış, kötü, hatalı.

mis.ad.ven.ture ['misəd'ventʃə] *n.* talihsizlik, felâket, kaza.

mis.al.li.ance ['misə'laiəns] *n.* yanlış evlilik.

mis.an.thrope ['mizənθrəup] *n.* insanlardan nefret eden kimse; **mis.an-throp.ic, mis.an.throp.i.cal** □ [-'θrɔp-ik(əl)] insanlardan nefret eden; **mis-an.thro.pist** [mi'zænθrəpist] *n.* merdümgiriz kimse, mizantrop; **mis'an-thro.py** *n.* insanlardan nefret etme *veya* kaçma.

mis.ap.pli.ca.tion ['misæpli'keiʃən] *n.* yanlış uygulama; **mis.ap.ply** ['-ə'plai] *v/t.* yerinde kullanmamak, yanlış uygulamak.

mis.ap.pre.hend ['misæpri'hend] *v/t.* yanlış anlamak; '**mis.ap.pre'hen.sion** *n.* yanlış anlama.

mis.ap.pro.pri.ate ['misə'prəuprieit] *v/t.* haksız kullanmak, emanete hıyanet etm.; '**mis.ap.pro.pri'a.tion** *n.* emanete hıyanet.

mis.be.come ['misbi'kʌm] *vb.* uygun olmamak, uymamak; '**mis.be'com-ing** *adj.* uygunsuz.

mis.be.got(.ten) ['misbigɔt(n)] *adj.* gayet çirkin, iğrenç; piç.

mis.be.have ['misbi'heiv] *vb.* kötü davranmak; '**mis.be'hav.io(u)r** [-ʒə]

mishap

n. kötü davranış, yaramazlık.

mis.be.lief ['misbi'li:f] *n.* imansızlık, inançsızlık; **mis.be.lieve** ['ˌ-'li:v] *vb.* inanmamak; **'mis.be'liev.er** *n.* imansız (*veya* inançsız) kimse, kâfir.

mis.cal.cu.late ['mis'kælkjuleit] *vb.* yanlış hesap etm.; **'mis.cal.cu'la.tion** *n.* yanlış hesap(lama).

mis.call ['mis'kɔːl] *v/t.* yanlış isim vermek.

mis.car.riage [mis'kæridʒ] *n.* başarısızlık; yanlış sevkiyat; çocuk düşürme; ~ **of justice** adlî hata; **mis-'car.ry** *v/i.* başaramamak; doğru adrese ulaşamamak (*mektup v.b.*); çocuk düşürmek.

mis.cast THEAT [mis'kɑːst] (*irr.* **cast**) *v/t.* yanlış rol vermek.

mis.ce.ge.na.tion [misidʒi'neiʃən] *n.* ırk karışımı, değişik ırklardan kişilerin evlenmesi.

mis.cel.la.ne.ous □ [misi'leinjəs] türlü türlü, çeşitli, muhtelif; **mis.cel'la.ne.ousness** *n.* çeşitlilik.

mis.cel.la.ny [mi'seləni] *n.* derleme; **mis'cel.la.nies** *n. pl.* edebî derlemeler.

mis.chance [mis'tʃɑːns] talihsizlik, şanssızlık, kaza.

mis.chief ['mistʃif] *n.* zarar, ziyan, hasar, telef; yaramazlık, haylazlık; fesat; F şeytan, haylaz kimse; **make ~ between** aralarını bozmak -*in*; **get into** ~ yaramazlık etm.; **'~-mak.er** *n.* kavga çıkaran *veya* fitnecilik eden kimse.

mis.chie.vous □ ['mistʃivəs] zararlı; arabozucu; yaramaz; **'mis.chie.vousness** *n.* arabozuculuk; yaramazlık.

mis.con.ceive ['miskən'si:v] *vb.* yanlış anlamak; **mis.con.cep.tion** ['ˌ-'sepʃən] *n.* yanlış anlama, hata.

mis.con.duct 1. [mis'kɔndʌkt] *n.* kötü davranış; kötü yönetim; zina; suiistimal; **2.** ['ˌ-kən'dʌkt] *v/i.* kötü yönetmek; ~ **o.s.** kötü (*veya* ahlâksızca) davranmak.

mis.con.struc.tion ['miskən'strʌkʃən] *n.* yanlış yorumlama *veya* anlama; **mis.construe** ['ˌ-'stru:] *v/t.* yanlış yorumlamak, yanlış anlamak.

mis.count ['mis'kaunt] **1.** *vb.* yanlış saymak, yanlış hesap etm.; **2.** *n.* yanlış sayma.

mis.cre.ant ['miskriənt] **1.** *n.* alçak (*veya* kötülükçü) kimse; **2.** *adj.* zalim, gaddar, merhametsiz.

mis.cre.a.ted ['miskri'eitid] *adj.* bi-

çimsiz, çirkin.

mis.date [mis'deit] **1.** *n.* yanlış tarih koyma; **2.** *v/t.* yanlış tarih koymak.

mis.deal ['mis'di:l] (*irr.* **deal**) *vb.* iskambil; yanlış dağıtmak.

mis.deed ['mis'di:d] *n.* kötülük, ahlâksızca hareket.

mis.de.mean.ant JUR [misdi'mi:nənt] *n.* kabahat türünden bir suçtan dolayı suçlanan kimse; **mis.de'mean.o(u)r** JUR [ˌ-nə] *n.* hafif suç, cürum, kabahat.

mis.di.rect ['misdi'rekt] *v/t.* yanlış yere göndermek; yanıltmak; **'mis.di'rection** *n.* yanlış yere gönderme; yanıltma.

mis.do.ing ['mis'du:iŋ] *n. mst* ~**s** *pl.* kötü davranma.

mise-en-scène THEAT ['mi:zɑ:n'sein] *n.* mizansen.

mi.ser ['maizə] *n.* hasis (*veya* cimri, pinti) kimse.

mis.er.a.ble □ ['mizərəbl] mutsuz, dertli; sefil; hasta; pek kötü; utanmaz; **'miser.a.ble.ness** *n.* yoksulluk, sefalet.

mi.ser.ly ['maizəli] *adj.* hasis, pinti, cimri.

mis.er.y ['mızəri] *n.* yoksulluk, sefalet; bedbahtlık; F yoksulluk çeken *veya* yakınan kimse.

mis.fea.sance JUR [mis'fi:zəns] *n.* yolsuzluk, kanunsuzluk.

mis.fire ['mis'faiə] **1.** *n.* ateş almama (*tabanca*); MOT ateşlememe, iştial bozukluğu; **2.** *v/i.* ateş almamak; *fig.* anlaşılmamak (*espri*); hedefine ulaşamamak (*plan*).

mis.fit ['misfit] *n.* iyi uymayan şey, oturmayan elbise; *fig.* pozisyonuna *veya* çevresine uymayan (*veya* uyumsuz) kimse.

mis.for.tune [mis'fɔ:tʃən] *n.* talihsizlik; şanssız kaza *veya* olay.

mis.give [mis'giv] (*irr.* **give**) *v/t.* şüpheye düşürmek; **my heart misgave me** şüpheye düştüm; **mis'giv.ing** *n.* şüphe, kuşku, endişe, güvensizlik.

mis.gov.ern ['mis'gʌvən] *v/t.* kötü yönetmek; **mis'gov.ern.ment** *n.* kötü yönetim.

mis.guide ['mis'gaid] *v/t.* yanlış bilgi *veya* yön vermek; **'mis'guid.ed** *adj.* yanlış yola yönlendirilmiş; yanlış değerlendirilmiş.

mis.han.dle ['mis'hændl] *v/t.* kötü kullanmak; kötü yönetmek.

mis.hap ['mishæp] *n.* talihsizlik, kaza,

aksilik.

mish.mash ['miʃmæʃ] *n.* karma-karışıklık.

mis.in.form ['misin'fɔːm] *v/t.* yanlış bilgi vermek *-e*; **'mis.in.for'ma.tion** *n.* yanlış bilgi.

mis.in.ter.pret ['misin'təːprit] *v/t.* yanlış yorumlamak, yanlış anlamak *-i*; **'mis.inter.pre'ta.tion** *n.* yanlış yorum.

mis.judge ['mis'dʒʌdʒ] *vb.* yanlış hüküm vermek; yanlış kanaat oluşturmak; **'mis'judg(e).ment** *n.* yanlış yargı.

mis.lay [mis'lei] (*irr.* **lay**) *v/t.* bşi yanlış bir yere koymak, kaybetmek.

mis.lead [mis'liːd] (*irr.* **lead**) *v/t.* yanlış yönlendirmek; yanlış yapmaya neden olm.; aldatmak, yanlış fikir vermek; **mis'lead.ing** *adj.* yanlış etki *veya* izlenim veren, yanıltıcı.

mis.man.age ['mis'mænidʒ] *v/t.* kötü *veya* yanlış yönetmek; **'mis'man.age.ment** *n.* kötü (*veya* yanlış) yönetim.

mis.name ['mis'neim] *v/t.* yanlış isim ile çağırmak.

mis.no.mer ['mis'nəumə] *n.* isim *veya* sözcüğün yanlış kullanımı.

mi.sog.a.mist [mi'sɔgəmist] *n.* evlilikten nefret eden kimse.

mi.sog.y.nist [mai'sɔdʒinist] *n.* kadın düşmanı, kadınlardan nefret eden kimse; **mi'sog.y.ny** *n.* kadınlardan nefret etme.

mis.place ['mis'pleis] *v/t.* yanlış yere koymak; istismar etm.

mis.print 1. [mis'print] *v/t.* yanlış basmak; **2.** ['mis'print] *n.* baskı hatası.

mis.pro.nounce ['misprə'nauns] *v/t.* yanlış telaffuz etm.; **mis.pro.nun.ci.a.tion** ['-prənʌnsi'eiʃən] *n.* yanlış telaffuz.

mis.quo.ta.tion ['miskwəu'teiʃən] yanlış aktarma; **'mis'quote** *v/t.* yanlış aktarmak.

mis.read ['mis'riːd] (*irr.* **read**) *v/t.* yanlış okumak; yanlış yorumlamak.

mis.rep.re.sent ['misrepri'zent] *v/t.* kötü temsil etm.; yanlış anlatmak; **'mis.repre.sen'ta.tion** *n.* kötü temsil etme; yalan.

mis.rule ['mis'ruːl] **1.** *n.* kötü yönetim; karışıklık; kanunsuzluk; **2.** *v/t.* kötü yönetmek.

miss¹ [mis] *n. mst* ♀ bekâr bayan, genç kız; Bayan.

miss² [-] **1.** *n.* başarısızlık; isabet ettireme, boşa gitme; **2.** *vb.* vuramamak, isabet et(tire)memek; bulamamak, kaçırmak, yetişememek; göreceği gelmek, özlemek, hasret çekmek; eksik olm.; ~ *fire* ateş alamamak; ~ *one's footing* (ayağı) kaymak, sürçmek; ~ *out* atlamak, gözden kaçırmak; kaçırmak, bulunmamak (*şans*).

mis.sal ECCL ['misəl] *n.* Aşaî Rabbanî ayini kitabı.

mis.shap.en ['mis'ʃeipən] *adj.* deforme olmuş, biçimsiz.

mis.sile ['misail] *n.* mermi; ok; atılan madde; füze.

miss.ing ['misiŋ] *adj.* hazır bulunmayan eksik, nâmevcut; *part.* MIL kayıp, âkıbeti meçhul kalan; *be* ~ yokluğu çok hissedilmek, onsuz yapılamamak.

mis.sion ['miʃən] *n.* görev, misyon, hizmet; görevle bir yere gönderilen kimseler; ECCL dinî propaganda; misyon; POL delegasyon; sefarethane, elçilik; hedef, amaç; **mis.sion.ar.y** ['miʃənri] **1.** *n.* misyoner; **2.** *adj.* dinsel görev ile ilgili.

mis.sis F ['misiz] *n.* eş, hanım.

mis.sive ['misiv] *n.* uzun mektup.

mis.spell ['mis'spel] (*irr.* **spell**) *v/t.* yanlış hecelemek (*veya* yazmak).

mis.spend ['mis'spend] (*irr.* **spend**) *v/t.* israf etm., heba etm., saçıp savurmak, boş yere sarfetmek.

mis.state ['mis'steit] *v/t.* yanlış ifade etm.; **'mis'state.ment** *n.* yanlış ifade.

mis.sus F ['misəz] *n.* eş, hanım.

miss.y F ['misi] *n.* genç kız.

mist [mist] **1.** *n.* sis, duman; *fig.* karartı, bulanıklık; *in a* ~ yolunu şaşırmış, şaşkın; **2.** *vb.* sis ile kapla(n)mak.

mis.tak.a.ble [mis'teikəbl] *adj.* yanlış anlaşılabilir; **mis'take 1.** (*irr.* **take**) *v/t.* tanımamak, teşhis etmemek; benzetmek (*for -e*); kazı koz anlamak, yanlış anlamak, karıştırmak (*with*); *be* ~ *n* yanılmak; *v/i. rare* yanılmak, hata etm.; **2.** *n.* yanlış(lık), hata, yanılma; *by* ~ yanlışlıkla; *and no* ~ F kesinlikle; **mis'tak.en** □ hatalı, yanlış.

mis.ter ['mistə] *n.* (*abbr.* **Mr.**) Bay, Efendi.

mis.time ['mis'taim] *v/t.* zamansız söylemek, zamansız yapmak, vaktini yanlış hesaplamak; **'mis'timed** *adj.* vakitsiz, zamansız, yersiz.

mist.i.ness ['mistinis] *n.* sis, pus, duman; *fig.* karanlık.

mis.tle.toe BOT ['misltəu] *n.* ökseotu.

mis.trans.late ['mistræns'leit] *v/t.* yanlış tercüme etm., yanlış çevirmek; 'mistrans'la.tion *n.* yanlış tercüme (*veya* çeviri).

mis.tress ['mistris] *n.* evin hanımı; (*kadın*) öğretmen; bilgili kadın; metres, dost.

mis.tri.al JUR ['mis'traiəl] *n.* geçersiz duruşma.

mis.trust ['mis'trʌst] **1.** *v/t.* güvenmemek, itimat etmemek *-e;* **2.** *n.* güvensizlik, itimatsızlık; 'mis'trust.ful ☐ [-ful] kuşkulu, güvensiz, şüpheli.

mist.y ☐ ['misti] sisli, puslu, dumanlı; *fig.* bulanık, müphem, karanlık.

mis.un.der.stand ['misʌndə'stænd] (*irr.* **stand**) *vb.* yanlış anlamak, ters anlamak, kazı koz anlamak; 'mis.under'stand.ing *n.* yanlış anlama.

mis.us.age [mis'ju:zidʒ] *n.* yanlış kullanılış; kötü davranma.

mis.use 1. ['mis'ju:z] *v/t.* yanlış kullanmak, suiistimal etm.; kötü davranmak; **2.** ['-'ju:s] *n.* yanlış kullanma, suiistimal.

mite¹ ZOO [mait] *n.* kene, peynir kurdu, uyuz böceği.

mite² [-] *n.* çok ufak *bş;* **a ~** (*of a child*) yavrucak.

mit.i.gate ['mitigeit] *v/t.* teskin etm., yatıştırmak (*a. fig.*); azaltmak, hafifletmek; **mit.i'ga.tion** *n.* yatıştırma; azaltma.

mi.tre, mi.ter ['maitə] **1.** *n.* piskoposluk tacı; MEC gönye; **2.** *vb.* piskoposluk tacı giymek; MEC gönye ile ölçmek; 'mi.tre-wheel *n.* MEC konik dişli çark.

mitt [mit] *n.* beysbol, *boks:* eldiven; = **mitten.**

mit.ten ['mitn] *n.* kolçak, parmaksız eldiven; **get the~** F ret cevabı almak, kovulmak.

mix [miks] **1.** *v/t. & v/i.* karış(tır)mak; karmak; katmak; birleşmek; kaynaşmak, uyuşmak, bağdaşmak; **~ in society** toplum hayatına katılmak; **~ed** karışık, karmaşık (*a. fig.*); karma; **~ed marriage** değişik din ve ırklardan kimselerin evlenmesi; **~ed pickles** *pl.* karışık turşu; **~ up** (zihnini) karıştırmak; **be ~ed up with** karışmak *-e,* bulaşmak *-e,* atılmak *-e;* **~ with** uyum sağlamak *ile,* geçinmek *ile;* **2.** *n.* karış(tır)ma; karışım; 'mix.er *n.* karıştırıcı kimse *veya* şey; mikser (*a. radyo*); **good** (**bad**) **~** girişken (olmayan) kimse; **mix.ture** ['-tʃə] *n.* karışım; karış(tır)-

ma; kaynaşma (*a. fig.*); 'mix-'up *n.* karışıklık, anlaşmazlık.

miz.en, miz.zen NAUT ['mizn] *n.* mizana direği (*veya* yelkeni); *attr.* mizana...

miz.zle F ['mizl] *v/i.* serpiştirmek, çiselemek (*yağmur*).

mne.mon.ic [ni:'mɔnik] **1.** *adj.* (**~ally**) hafızaya yardımcı olan; **2.** *n.* mne'mon.ics *pl.* hafızayı kuvvetlendirme sanatı.

mo *co. veya sl.* [mou] = **moment.**

moan [moun] **1.** *n.* inilti, figan; uğultu (*rüzgâr*); şikâyet; **2.** *v/i.* inlemek, figan etm.; uğuldamak (*rüzgâr*); şikâyet etm., sızlanmak.

moat [mout] *n.* kale hendeği; 'moat.ed *adj.* hendekli.

mob [mɔb] **1.** *n.* ayaktakımı, avam; izdiham, kalabalık; gangster çetesi; **2.** *v/t.* etrafını sarmak; saldırmak, hücum etm.; doluşmak; 'mob.bish *adj.* kaba, âmiyane.

mob-cap ['mɔbkæp] *n.* kadın başlığı.

mo.bile ['moubail] **1.** *adj.* oynak, yer değiştirebilen, devingen, hareketli, değişken; MIL seyyar (*ordu*); **2.** *n.* ince tellere bağlı parçaları hava akımı ile hareket eden bir tür süs eşyası *veya* sanat eseri; **mo.bil.i.ty** [-'biliti] *n.* hareketlilik; değişkenlik; **mo.bi.li.za.tion** MIL [-bilai'zeiʃən] *n.* seferberlik; 'mobi.lize *v/t.* MIL seferber etm., silah altına almak.

mob-law ['mɔblɔ:] *n.* linç kanunu.

mob.oc.ra.cy [mɔ'bɔkrəsi] *n.* avamtakımı yönetimi; **mob.ster** ['mɔbstə] *n.* gangster.

moc.ca.sin ['mɔkəsin] *n.* mokasen.

mo.cha ['mɔkə] *n.* Yemen kahvesi.

mock [mɔk] **1.** *n.* alay, dalga geçme; **2.** *adj.* sahte, taklit, yapmacık...; **~ fight** yalandan kavga; **3.** *v/t. & v/i.* taklit etm., taklidini yapmak; karşı koymak *-e;* alay etm., dalga geçmek, eğlenmek (*at ile*); 'mock.er *n.* alaycı (*veya* dalgacı) kimse; 'mock.er.y *n.* alay, dalga geçme; taklit; alaya alınan şey; 'mock-he'ro.ic *adj.* destansı taşlama türünden; 'mock.ing **1.** *n.* alay etme, dalga geçme; **2.** ☐ alaycı..., dalgacı...; 'mock.ing-bird *n.* alaycı kuş.

mock...: '~king *n.* kral müsveddesi, sözde kral; '~'tur.tle soup kaplumbağa çorbası tadında et çorbası; '~up *n.* model, kalıp.

mod.al ☐ ['moudl] *part.* GR kipe ait, kip... **mo.dal.i.ty** [-'dæliti] *n.* usül, şekil, tarz.

mode [məud] *n*. tarz, usül, üslup, şekil, moda; GR kip.

mod.el ['mɔdl] **1.** *n*. örnek, numune, model; şekil, kalıp; plan, resim; manken; *fig*. örnek alınacak kimse; *attr*. örnek…; model…; *act as a* ~ modellik yapmak (*to -e*); ~ *aircraft* model uçak; **2.** *v/i*. *-in* modelini yapmak; örneğine göre yapmak; *v/i*. mankenlik (*veya* modellik) yapmak; *fig*. kendine örnek almak (*after, on, upon -i*); **mod.el.(l)er** ['mɔdlə] *n*. modelci.

mod.er.ate 1. □ ['mɔdərit] ılımlı; orta; makûl; **2.** ['-reit] *v/t. & v/i.* hafifle(t)-mek, azal(t)mak, yatış(tır)mak, yumuşa(t)mak; başkanlık etm.; **mod.er.ateness** ['mɔdəritnis] *n*. ılımlılık; **mod.er.ation** ['-reiʃən] *n*. itidal, ölçülülük, ılımlılık; *in* ~ ölçülü olarak, aşırıya kaçmadan, kararında; ~*s pl.* UNIV Oxford Üniversitesinde edebiyat fakültesi diploması için ilk genel imtihan; 'mod.er.a.tor *n*. toplantı başkanı; UNIV imtihan gözcüsü; PHYS yavaşlatıcı madde.

mod.ern ['mɔdən] **1.** *adj*. yeni, modern, çağdaş, çağcıl; ~ *languages pl*. çağdaş diller; **2.** *n*. *the* ~*s pl*. çağdaş kimseler; modern görüşlü kimseler; 'mod.ern.ism *n*. çağdaşlık, modernlik; yenilik; 'modern.ist *n*. yenilikçi kimse; mod.ern'is.tic *adj*. yenilikçi; mo.der.ni.ty [mə'də:niti] *n*. yenilik, çağdaşlık; mod.ern.ize ['mɔdənaiz] *v/t. & v/i.* modernleş(tir)mek, yenileş(tir)mek.

mod.est □ ['mɔdist] alçak gönüllü, mütevazı; gösterişsiz; tutarlı, ılımlı; 'mod.esty *n*. tevazu, alçak gönüllülük; tutarlılık.

mod.i.cum ['mɔdikəm] *n*. azıcık miktar, nebze.

mod.i.fi.a.ble ['mɔdifaiəbl] *adj*. değiştirilebilir; mod.i.fi.ca.tion [-fi'keiʃən] *n*. değişiklik; değiştirme; mod.i.fy ['-fai] *v/t*. değiştirmek; azaltmak, hafifletmek; GR nitelemek, tamamlamak.

mod.ish ['məudiʃ] *adj*. modaya uygun, son model.

mo.diste [məu'di:st] *n*. kadın şapkacısı *veya* terzisi.

mod.u.late ['mɔdjuleit] *v/t*. ayarlamak; tatlılaştırmak, yumuşatmak, hafifleştirmek (*ses*): radyo: modüle etm.; **modu'la.tion** *n*. hafifle(t)me; modülasyon, geçiş; 'mod.u.la.tor *n*. modülatör; ~ *of tonality film*: ses modülatörü;

mod.ule ['-dju:l] *n*. sabit değer; çap, mikyas (*a. ARCH*); *s. lunar* ~; mod.u.lus PHYS ['-djuləs] *n*. modül.

Mo.gul [məu'gʌl]: *the Great veya Grand* ~ Timur hanedanından Hindistan imparatoru.

mo.hair ['məuhɛə] *n*. moher, tiftik yünü; moherden yapılan kumaş.

Mo.ham.med.an [məu'hæmidən] **1.** *n*. Müslüman kimse; **2.** *adj*. Müslüman.

moi.e.ty ['mɔiəti] *n*. yarı(m); kısım, pay.

moil [mɔil] *v/i*. çok çalışmak, didinmek.

moi.ré ['mwɑ:rei] *n*. hareli (ipek) kumaş.

moist [mɔist] *adj*. nemli, rutubetli; ıslak; yaşlı (*göz*); **mois.ten** ['mɔisn] *v/t*. ıslatmak; *v/i*. ıslanmak, nemlenmek, yaşarmak (*göz*); **moist.ness** ['mɔistnis], **moisture** ['-tʃə] *n*. nem, rutubet, ıslaklık.

moke *sl*. [məuk] *n*. eşek.

mo.lar ['məulə] *n*. *a*. ~ *tooth* azıdişi.

mo.las.ses [məu'læsiz] *n*. melas.

mold [məuld], 'mold.board *etc. s.* **mould** *etc.*

mole[1] ZOO [məul] *n*. köstebek.

mole[2] [-] *n*. ben, leke.

mole[3] [-] *n*. dalgakıran, mendirek.

mo.lec.u.lar [mə'lekjulə] *adj*. moleküle ait, moleküllü; **mol.e.cule** PHYS ['mɔlikju:l] *n*. molekül, zerre, tozan.

mole.hill ['məulhil] *n*. köstebek tepesi; *make a mountain out of a* ~ pireyi deve yapmak; 'mole-skin *n*. köstebek derisi; köstebek derisine benzer kumaş.

mo.lest [mə'lest] *v/t*. rahatsız etm.; tecavüz etm., sarkıntılık etm.; **mo.les.ta.tion** [-'teiʃən] *n*. rahatsız etme; tecavüz, sarkıntılık.

moll F [mɔl] *n*. gangsterin sevgilisi; fahişe, orospu.

mol.li.fy ['mɔlifai] *v/t*. yumuşatmak, yatıştırmak, sakinleştirmek.

mol.lusc ZOO ['mɔləsk] *n*. yumuşakçalar sınıfından bir hayvan; 'mol.lusk = *mollusc*.

mol.ly.cod.dle ['mɔlikɔdl] **1.** *n*. muhallebi çocuğu, hanım evlâdı; **2.** *v/t*. üstüne titremek.

Mo.loch ['məulɔk] *n*. üstü dikenli Avustralya kertenkelesi.

mol.ten ['məultən] *adj*. erimiş; dökme.

mo.lyb.den.um CHEM [mə'libdinəm] *n*. molibden.

mo.ment ['məumənt] *n*. an; önem; kuvvet; unsur; = ~*um*; *at veya for the* ~ şimdi, şu anda; *to the* ~ dakikası dakikasına; 'mo.men.tar.y □ anî, bir anlık...; geçici; 'mo.ment.ly *adv.* her an; bir anlık; mo.men.tous □ [məu'mentəs] önemli, mühim, ciddî; mo'mentum PHYS [-təm] *n.* moment; *fig.* hız, sürat.

mon.a.chism ['mɔnekizəm] *n.* manastır hayatı.

mon.ad PHLS ['mɔnæd] *n.* monad.

mon.arch ['mɔnək] *n.* kral, hükümdar; mo.nar.chic, mo.nar.chi.cal □ [mɔ-'nɑːkik(əl)] monarşiye ait, monarşik; 'mon.archism ['mɔnəkizəm] *n.* kraliyetçilik; 'monarch.ist *n.* kraliyetçi; 'mon.arch.y *n.* krallık, monarşi, tekerklik.

mon.as.ter.y ['mɔnəstəri] *n.* manastır; monas.tic, mo.nas.ti.cal □ [mə'næstik(əl)] manastıra ait, manastır...; mo'nas.ticism [-sizəm] *n.* manastır hayatı (*veya* sistemi).

mon.au.ral [mɔn'ɔːrəl] *adj.* tek kulaklı; tek kulakla duymaya ait; mono...

Mon.day ['mʌndi] *n.* pazartesi.

mon.e.tar.y ['mʌnitəri] *adj.* paraya ait, parasal; ~ *reform* para reformu.

mon.ey ['mʌni] *n.* para, nakit; *ready* ~ nakit, peşin para; *out of* ~ parasız; ~ *down* peşin; *get one's* ~*'s worth* parasının karşılığını almak; *marry* ~ zengin biriyle evlenmek; *make* ~ para kazanmak; '~box *n.* kumbara; '~chang.er *n.* sarraf; mon.eyed ['mʌnid] *adj.* paralı, para babası. mon.ey...: '~grub.ber *n.* para canlısı kimse; '~lend.er *n.* tefeci, faizci; '~mar.ket *n.* para piyasası, borsa; '~or.der *n.* para havalesi; '~spin.ner *n.* F iyi para getiren şey.

mon.ger ['mʌngə] *suffix* ...satıcısı; ...yapan.

Mon.gol ['mɔŋgɔl], Mon.go.lian [-'gəuljən] **1.** *adj.* Moğol ırkına *veya* Moğolcaya ait; **2.** *n.* Moğol(ca).

mon.grel ['mʌŋgrəl] **1.** *n.* melez köpek, bitki *veya* insan; **2.** *adj.* karışık soylu, melez...

mo.ni.tion [məu'niʃən] *n.* ikaz, ihtar; moni.tor ['mɔnitə] *n.* sınıf başkanı; NAUT ağır toplu savaş gemisi; *radyo*: dinleme servisi görevlisi; monitör; 'mon.i.to.ry *adj.* uyarıcı, ikaz edici, öğüt veren.

monk [mʌŋk] *n.* rahip, keşiş; 'monk.er.y *n. part. contp.* manastır (hayatı).

mon.key ['mʌŋki] **1.** *n.* maymun (*a. fig.*); MEC şahmerdan başı; *sl.* 500 pound *veya* dolar; *put s.o.'s* ~ *up* F

b-nin tepesini attırmak; ~ *business* Am. *sl.* düzenbazlık; aşk ilişkisi; **2.** *v/i.* F oynamak; ~ *about with* kurcalamak *-i*, oynayıp durmak *ile*; '~-en.gine *n.* şahmerdan motoru; '~-jack.et *n.* NAUT gemici ceketi; '~-nut *n.* BOT yerfıstığı; '~-puz.zle *n.* BOT bir tür çam ağacı; '~-wrench *n.* MEC İngiliz anahtarı; *throw a* ~ *in s.th.* Am. *sl.* bşi bozmak, bşe çomak sokmak.

monk.hood ['mʌŋkhud] *n.* keşişlik, rahiplik; 'monk.ish *adj. mst contp.* keşiş gibi.

mono... ['mɔnəu] *prefix* tek, bir, mono...; mo.no.chrome PAINT ['mɔnəkrəum] **1.** *adj.* tek renkli; **2.** *n.* tek renkli resim; mon.o.cle ['mɔnɔkl] *n.* tek gözlük, monokl; mo.no.cot.y.le.don BOT ['mɔnəukɔti'liːdən] *n.* tek çenekli bir bitki, monoko tiledon; mo.noc.u.lar [mɔ'nɔkjulə] *adj.* tek gözlük; mo'nog.a.my [-gəmi] *n.* tekeşlilik, monogami; mon.o.gram ['mɔnəgræm] *n.* monogram, bir ismin baş harflerinden oluşan desen; mon.o.graph ['-grɑːf] *n.* monografi, tekyazım; mono.lith ['mɔnəuliθ] *n.* yekpare taştan abide; mon.o.logue ['mɔnəlɔg] *n.* monolog; mon.o.ma.ni.a ['mɔnəu'meinjə] *n.* sabit fikir, saplantı; 'mon.o'ma.ni.ac [-niæk] *n.* saplantılı kimse; mono.plane AVIA ['mɔnəuplein] *n.* tek kanatlı uçak; mo.nop.o.list [mə'nɔpəlist] *n.* tekelci; mo'nop.o.lize [-laiz] *v/t.* tekeline almak (*a. fig.*); mo'nop.o.ly *n.* tekel (*maddesi*); mon.o.syl.lab.ic ['mɔnəusi'læbik] *adj.* (~*ally*) tek heceli; mon.o.syl.la.ble ['mɔnəsiləbl] *n.* tek heceli kelime; mono.the.ism ['mɔnəuθiːzəm] *n.* tektanrıcılık, monoteizm; mon.o.tone ['mɔnətəun] **1.** *n.* düz ses; *in* ~ yeknesak, monoton, düz sesle; **2.** *v/t.* tekdüze konuşmak (*veya* okumak *veya* şarkı söylemek); monot.o.nous □ [mə'nɔtnəs] monoton, tekdüze, sıkıcı, yeknesak; mo'not.o.ny *n.* monotonluk, tekdüzelik, yeknesaklık; mon.o.type TYP ['mɔnəutaip] *n.* monotip; mon.ox.ide CHEM [mɔ'nɔksaid] *n.* monoksit.

mon.sieur [mə'sjəː] *n.* bay, bey, efendi, mösyö.

mon.soon [mɔn'suːn] *n.* muson.

mon.ster ['mɔnstə] *n.* canavar, dev (*a. fig.*); *attr.* koskocaman..., dev gibi...

mon.strance ECCL ['mɔnstrəns] *n.* içinde okunmuş ekmek olan kap.

monstrosity

814

mon.stros.i.ty [mɔns'trɔsiti] *n.* canavar(lık); çirkin şey; **'mon.strous** □ canavar gibi; anormal; koskocaman; ürkünç, korkunç, inanılmaz, hayret verici; saçma sapan.

mon.tage [mɔn'tɑːʒ] *n.* fotomontaj.

month [mʌnθ] *n.* ay; **this day ~** önümüzdeki ay bugün; **'month.ly 1.** *adj. & adv.* aylık, ayda bir (olan); **~ season ticket** aylık bilet; **2.** *n.* aylık dergi.

mon.u.ment ['mɔnjumənt] *n.* anıt, abide; eser; tarihî yapı; **mon.u.men.tal** □ [-'mentl] anıtsal, abidevî...; muazzam, şahane; koskocaman.

moo [muː] **1.** *v/i.* böğürmek; **2.** *n.* böğürme.

mooch F [muːtʃ] *v/i.:* **~ about** aylak aylak dolaşmak.

mood[1] GR [muːd] *n.* kip.

mood[2] [-] *n.* mizaç, ruh haleti (*veya* durumu).

mood.i.ness ['muːdinis] *n.* karamsarlık; **'mood.y** □ dargın, küskün; karamsar, umutsuz; sinirli, huysuz, aksi.

moon [muːn] **1.** *n.* ay, kamer; uydu; mehtap; **once in a blue ~** F kırk yılda bir; **2.** *v/i. mst* **~ about** dalgın dalgın gezinmek; *v/t.* **~ away** boşa geçirmek (*zaman*); **'moon.beam** *n.* ay ışını; **'moon.less** *adj.* aysız, mehtapsız; **'moon.light** *n.* mehtap; **'moon.lit** *adj.* mehtaplı.

moon...: **'~.shine** *n.* mehtap; saçmalık; *Am.* kaçak içki; **'~.shin.er** *n. Am.* F içki kaçakçısı; **'~.struck** *adj.* aysar, deli; **'moon.y** □ aya ait, ay...; hayali şeklinde; F hayalperest, dalgın, düşünceli; *sl.* aylak.

Moor[1] [muə] *n.* Mağribî; Faslı.

moor[2] [-] *n.* kır, *part.* avlak; *obs. veya prov.* bataklık.

moor[3] NAUT [-] *v/t. & v/i.* palamarla bağla(n)mak; **moor.age** ['muəridʒ] *n.* demir atma; gemi bağlama yeri.

moor.fowl ['muəfaul], **'moor.game** ['-geim] *n.* ormantavuğu.

moor.ing-mast ['muəriŋmɑːst] *n.* balon bağlama direği.

moo.rings ['muəriŋz] *n. pl.* NAUT palamar takımı; gemi bağlama yeri; ahlakî değerler.

Moor.ish ['muəriʃ] *adj.* Mağribî; Fas'a ait, Fas...

moor.land ['muələnd] *n.* (boz)kır.

moose ZOO [muːs] *n. a.* **~-deer** bir çeşit geyik.

moot [muːt] **1.** *n.* **~ case, ~ point** şüpheli (*veya* tartışmalı) mesele; **2.** *v/t.* tartış-

mak.

mop [mɔp] **1.** *n.* silme bezi; dağınık saç; **2.** *v/t.* silip süpürmek, temizlemek; **~ up** silmek; *sl.* silip süpürmek; *sl.* işini bitirmek; **~ the floor with s.o.** *b-ni* alt etm., ezip geçmek, mat etm.

mope [məup] **1.** *n.* sıkıcı kimse; üzüntü; **the ~s** *pl.* sıkıntı, bunaltı, hüzün; **2.** *v/i.* hüzünlü (*veya* keyifsiz) olm.

mo.ped ['məuped] *n.* moped, motorlu bisiklet.

mop.ing □ ['məupiŋ], **'mop.ish** hüzünlü, kasvetli.

mo.raine GEOL [mɔ'rein] *n.* buzultaş, moren.

mor.al ['mɔrəl] **1.** □ ahlâki..., törel...; erdemli, faziletli; manevî; doğru, dürüst; **2.** *n.* ahlâk dersi; **~s** *pl.* ahlâk; **mo.rale** [mɔ'rɑːl] *n. part.* MIL maneviyat, manevî güç, moral; **mor.al.ist** ['mɔrəlist] *n.* ahlâkçı; **mo.ral.i.ty** [mɔ'ræliti] *n.* ahlâk (dersi); HIST THEAT karakterlerin erdem ve kötülük gibi ahlâki değerleri simgelediği bir dram türü; **mor.al.ize** ['mɔrəlaiz] *v/i.* ahlâk dersi vermek (**upon** hususunda); *v/t.* ahlâki yönden değerlendirmek.

mo.rass [mə'ræs] *n.* batak(lık); engel, güçlük.

mor.bid □ ['mɔːbid] hastalıklı; bozuk, çarpık (*fikir*); **mor'bid.i.ty**, **'mor.bid.ness** *n.* marazi konulara aşırı ilgi duyma; hastalık oranı, morbidite.

mor.dant ['mɔːdənt] **1.** *adj.* iğneleyici, sert, keskin; **2.** *n.* renkleri sabitleştiren madde, mordan.

more [mɔː] **1.** *adj.* daha çok; daha fazla; biraz daha; **2.** *adv.* daha; bir daha; **once ~** bir (kez) daha; **two ~** iki tane daha; **so much ~, all the ~** haydi haydi; **no ~** artık ...değil; **~ and ~** gittikçe; **3.** *n.* fazlalık, çokluk.

mo.rel BOT [mɔ'rel] *n.* siyah mantar.

mo.rel.lo BOT [mə'reləu] *n. a.* **~ cherry** vişne.

more.o.ver [mɔː'rəuvə] *adv.* bundan başka, ayrıca, üstelik.

Mo.resque [mɔ'resk] **1.** *adj.* Fas mimarisi türünde; **2.** *n.* Fas mimarisinde süs, arabesk.

mor.ga.nat.ic [mɔːgə'nætik] *adj.* (**~ally**) yukarı ve aşağı tabakadan kişilerce yapılan (*evlilik*).

morgue [mɔːg] *n.* morg.

mor.i.bund ['mɔribʌnd] *adj.* ölüm döşeğinde, can çekişmekte (*a. fig.*); sonu gelmiş.

motion

Mor.mon ['mɔːmən] *n.* Mormon.

morn *poet.* [mɔːn] *n.* sabah.

morn.ing ['mɔːnin] **1.** *n.* sabah, seher; *fig.* başlangıç; *good* ~*!* günaydın!, iyi sabahlar!; *in the* ~*, during the* ~ sabahleyin; *this* ~ bu sabah; *tomorrow* ~ yarın sabah; **2.** *adj.* sabaha mahsus, sabah …; ~ *coat* jaketatay; ~ *dress* frak, resmî sabah kıyafeti; '~'glo.ry *n.* BOT gündüzsefası, kahkahaçiçeği; ~ *performance* matine, gündüz seansı.

Mo.roc.can [mə'rɔkən] *adj.* Fas'a ait, Fas…; Faslı…

mo.roc.co [mə'rɔkəu] *n. a.* ~ *leather* maroken.

mo.ron ['mɔːrɔn] *n.* doğuştan geri zekâlı kimse; F kuş beyinli kimse.

mo.rose □ [mə'rəus] somurtkan, suratsız, asık suratlı; mo'rose.ness *n.* suratsızlık.

mor.phi.a ['mɔːfjə], mor.phine ['mɔːfiːn] *n.* morfin.

mor.pho.lo.gy BIOL, GR [mɔː'fɔlədʒi] *n.* şekilbilim, morfoloji.

mor.row ['mɔrəu] *n. mst poet.* sabah; yarın, ertesi gün; *the* ~ *of* -*in* ertesi günü.

Morse [mɔːs] *n. a.* ~ *code* Mors alfabesi.

mor.sel ['mɔːsəl] *n.* lokma, parça.

mor.tal ['mɔːtl] **1.** □ ölümlü, fani, geçici; öldürücü, amansız; ölene dek süren; kin dolu; çok uzun (*süre*); F çok büyük, aşırı; F olası, mümkün; **2.** *n.* insan(oğlu); mor.tal.i.ty [mɔː'tæliti] *n.* ölümlülük, fanilik; ölüm oranı; ölü sayısı, can kaybı.

mor.tar ['mɔːtə] **1.** *n.* harç; havan; MIL havan topu; **2.** *v/t.* harç ile sıvamak; '~board *n.* harç tahtası; UNIV kep.

mort.gage ['mɔːgidʒ] **1.** *n.* ipotek; *a.* ~-*deed* ipotekli borç senedi; **2.** *v/t.* rehine koymak; ipotek etm.; mort.ga.gee [mɔːgə'dʒiː] *n.* ipotekli alacak sahibi; mort.ga.gor [~'dʒɔː] *n.* ipotek yapan borçlu.

mor.tice ['mɔːtis] = *mortise*.

mor.ti.cian *Am.* [mɔː'tifən] *n.* cenaze işleri görevlisi.

mor.ti.fi.ca.tion [mɔːtifi'keifən] *n.* MED kangren; küçük düşme, rezil olma.

mor.ti.fy ['mɔːtifai] *v/t.* alçaltmak, rezil etm., küçük düşürmek; *v/i.* MED kangren olm.

mor.tise MEC ['mɔːtis] **1.** *n.* zıvana, yuva; **2.** *v/t.* zıvana ile birleştirmek; -*e* zıvana açmak.

mor.tu.ar.y ['mɔːtjuəri] **1.** *adj.* ölüme ait, ölüm…; cenazeye ait, cenaze…; **2.** *n.* morg.

mo.sa.ic[1] [məu'zeiik] *n.* mozaik.

Mo.sa.ic[2] [~] *adj.* Musa'ya ait.

mo.selle [məu'zel] *n.* beyaz Alman şarabı.

Mos.lem ['mɔzləm] **1.** *adj.* Müslüman; **2.** *n.* Müslüman, Müslim.

mosque [mɔsk] *n.* cami.

mos.qui.to zoo [məs'kiːtəu] *n., pl.* mos.qui.toes [~z] sivrisinek; mos'qui.to-craft *n.* NAUT küçük savaş gemileri; mos'qui.to-net *n.* cibinlik.

moss [mɔs] *n.* BOT yosun; *a rolling stone gathers no* ~ yuvarlanan taş yosun tutmaz; 'moss.i.ness *n.* yosunlu olma; 'mossy *adj.* yosunlu, yosunumsu.

most [məust] **1.** □ en çok, en fazla; *for the* ~ *part* genellikle, çoğunlukla, tamamen; başlıca; **2.** *adv.* pek, en çok, son derecede; en çoğu; **3.** *n.* çoğunluk, çokluk, en çok miktar; *at (the)* ~ en fazla, olsa olsa; *make the* ~ *of* -*den* sonuna kadar yararlanmak.

…most [məust, məst] *suffix* en…

most.ly ['məustli] *adv.* ekseriya, çoğunlukla çoğu kez.

mote [məut] *n.* zerre; *the* ~ *in another's eye* kendi yaptıklarına oranla önemsiz bir hata.

mo.tel [məu'tel] *n.* motel.

mo.tet MUS [məu'tet] *n.* çok sesli kilise ilâhisi.

moth [mɔθ] *n.* güve; pervane; '~-ball *n.* yuvarlak naftalin; *in* ~*s fig.* bir kenara kaldırılmış; '~-eat.en *adj.* güve yemiş.

moth.er ['mʌðə] **1.** *n.* anne, ana, valide; **2.** *v/t.* bakmak, annelik etm.; doğurmak; himaye etm.; ~ *coun.try* anayurt, anavatan; moth.er.hood ['~hud] *n.* analık, annelik; 'moth.er-in-law *n.* kaynana, kayınvalide; 'moth.er.less *adj.* anasız, öksüz; 'moth.er.li.ness *n.* anaya yakışırlık; 'moth.er.ly *adj.* ana gibi; anaya yakışır.

moth.er…: '~-of-'pearl *n.* sedef; ~ *ship* (*diğer gemilerin her türlü ihtiyacını sağlayan*) ana gemi; ~ *tongue* anadili.

moth-proof ['mɔθpruːf] **1.** *adj.* güve yemez; **2.** *v/t.* güve yemez hale getirmek; 'moth.y *adj.* güve dolu.

mo.tif [məu'tiːf] *n.* motif.

mo.tion ['məuʃən] **1.** *n.* hareket, devinim (*a.* MEC); PARL teklif, talep, önerge;

MED dışkılama; **bring forward a ~** teklif sunmak; **agree upon a ~** önergeyi kabul etm.; **go through the ~s** bşi yapar görünmek, baştan savma yapmak; **set in ~** harekete getirmek, çalıştırmak; **2.** v/t. el ile işaret etm. -e; '**motion.less** adj. hareketsiz; **motion picture** sinema filmi.

mo.ti.vate ['məutiveit] v/t. sevketmek, harekete geçirmek; **mo.ti'va.tion** n. sevketme; saik, güdü, dürtü.

mo.tive ['məutiv] **1.** adj. hareket yaratan, itici...; devindirici...; güdüsel; **power** itici güç; **2.** n. saik, güdü, dürtü; sebep, neden; motif; **3.** v/t. harekete getirmek; '**mo.tive.less** adj. sebepsiz, nedensiz.

mo.tiv.i.ty [məu'tiviti] n. hareket kuvveti.

mot.ley ['mɔtli] adj. rengârenk, alaca; ayrı cinsten.

mo.tor ['məutə] **1.** n. motor; makine; otomobil, araba; MED adele, kas; **2.** adj. motorlu; devindirici; makine...; motor...; araba...; hareket kaslarına ait; **~ nerve** motor sinir; **3.** v/i. otomobille gitmek; '**~as.sist.ed** adj. motor takviyeli; '**~bicy.cle**, '**~bike = motor-cycle**; '**~boat** n. deniz motoru, motorbot; '**~'bus** n. otobüs; **~cade** Am. ['_keid] n. araba korteji, konvoy; '**~car** n. otomobil; '**~coach** n. otobüs; '**~cy.cle** n. motosiklet; '**~cyclist** n. motosiklet sürücüsü; **mo.to.ri.al** [məu'tɔːriəl] adj. hareket ettiren, işleten; **mo.tor.ing** ['məutəriŋ] n. otomobilcilik; araba kullanma; '**mo.tor.ist** n. sürücü, otomobil kullanan; **mo.tor.i.za.tion** [_rai'zeiʃən] n. motorize etme; '**mo.torize** v/t. motorla donatmak, motörleştirmek, motorize etm.; '**mo.tor-launch** n. motorbot, çok küçük vapur; '**mo.tor.less** adj. motorsuz.

mo.tor...: '**~man** n. makinist; sürücü; vatman; '**~plough** n. motorlu saban; '**~road**, '**~way** n. karayolu, otoyolu.

mot.tle [mɔtl] v/t. beneklemek; '**mot-tled** adj. benekli.

mot.to ['mɔtəu] n., pl. **mot.toes** ['_z] vecize; parola, ilke.

mo(u)ld¹ [məuld] n. bahçıvan toprağı; gübreli toprak; küf.

mo(u)ld² [_] **1.** n. kalıp; fig. yapı, karakter; **2.** v/t. kalıba dökmek; şekillendirmek, şekil vermek (**on, upon** -e).

mo(u)ld-board ['məuldbɔːd] n. saban kulağı.

mo(u)ld.er¹ ['məuldə] n. kalıpçı, dökmeci.

mo(u)lder² [_] v/i. a. **~ away** çürümek, çürüyüp gitmek.

mo(u)ld.i.ness ['məuldinis] n. küflülük.

mo(u)ld.ing ['məuldiŋ] n. kalıplama; ARCH tiriz, silme, korniş, pervaz; attr. kalıplama...

mo(u)ld.y ['məuldi] adj. küflü.

moult [məult] **1.** n. tüy dökme; **2.** v/i. tüylerini dökmek.

mound [maund] n. höyük; tepecik, tümsek; **burial~** mezar tümseği.

mount [maunt] **1.** n. dağ, tepe; binek; dayanak; top arabası; **2.** v/t. & v/i. ata bin(dir)mek; çıkmak -e, tırmanmak -e; asmak; takmak; üzerine koymak, oturtmak; MEC kurmak, monte etm. -i; üzerine yapıştırmak, çerçeveye geçirmek; girişmek -e; THEAT sahneye koymak; mst **~ up** yükselmek, artmak, çoğalmak; çiftleşmek (hayvan); **~ed** atlı; binmiş; takılı, hazır; kakma; s. **guard 1**.

moun.tain ['mauntin] n. dağ, tepe; **~s** pl. dağ silsilesi; attr. dağ...; **~ ash** BOT üvez; **~ chain** dağ silsilesi; **~ dew** F İskoç viskisi; **mou.tain.eer** [_ti'niə] n. dağlı; dağcı; **moun.tain'eer.ing** n. dağcılık; **mountain'ous** adj. dağlık; dağ gibi; **mountain sick.ness** dağ hastalığı.

moun.te.bank ['mauntibæŋk] n. şarlatan kimse.

mount.ing MEC ['mauntiŋ] n. montaj; dayanak, destek.

mourn [mɔːn] v/i. yas tutmak; v/t. -in matemini tutmak; '**mourn.er** n. yaslı kimse; **~'s bench** Am. = **anxious bench**; **mourn.ful** ☐ ['_ful] yaslı, matemli; kederli, üzgün; acıklı; '**mourn.ful.ness** n. yaslılık; üzgünlük.

mourn.ing ['mɔːniŋ] **1.** ☐ yas..., matem...; **2.** n. matem, yas; kederlenme, ağıt; **~s** pl. matem elbiseleri; '**~band** n. matem bandı; '**~bor.der**, '**~edge** n. siyah kenar; '**~pa.per** n. siyah kenarlı mektup kâğıdı.

mouse [maus] **1.** n., pl. **mice** [mais] fare, sıçan; **2.** [mauz] vb. fare yakalamak; **mous.er** ['mauzə] n. fare yakalayan kedi; '**mouse-trap** n. fare kapanı.

mousse [muːs] n. bir çeşit dondurma.

mous.tache [məs'tɑːʃ] n. bıyık.

mouth 1. [mauθ] n., pl. **mouths** [mauðz] ağız; haliç, boğaz; **down in**

the ~ keyifsiz, karamsar; *laugh on the wrong side of one's* ~ gülerken ağlamak, hüsrana uğramak; **2.** [mauð] *v/t. & v/i.* mırıldanmak, ağzında gevelemek (*laf*); söylemek; savurmak (*küfür*); ağıza almak, yemek; ağızla dokunmak; geme alıştırmak (*at*); surat burusturmak; atıp tutmak; **mouth.ful** ['mauθful] *n.* ağız dolusu; lokma.

mouth...: '~-or.gan *n.* ağız mızıkası, armonika; '~.piece *n.* ağızlık; MEC zıvana; *fig.* sözcü; '~-wash *n.* gargara, ağız çalkalamada kullanılan antiseptik sıvı.

mov(e).a.ble ['mu:vəbl] **1.** *adj.* taşınabilir; kımıldayabilir; JUR menkul; **2.** *n.* ~*s pl.* menkul eşya; 'mov(e).a.ble.ness *n.* hareketlilik, devingenlik.

move [mu:v] **1.** *v/t. & v/i. com.* hareket et(tir)mek, kımılda(t)mak, oyna(t)mak, harekete getirmek, yürütmek; tahrik etm.; önermek, teklif etm.; teşvik etm., gayretlendirmek; tesir etm., etkilemek; MED işletmek (*bağırsak*); ilerlemek; *a.* ~ *house* taşınmak; yürümek, gitmek; ~ *for s.th* bşi için öneride bulunmak; ~ *heaven and earth* her çareye baş vurmak; ~ *in* eve taşınmak; ~ *on* ileri gitmek, ilerlemek, yürümek; değiştirmek; ~ *out* evden çıkmak, taşınmak; **2.** *n.* hareket, kımıldama; göç, nakil, taşınma; *fig.* tedbir; *satranç:* taş sürme, hamle; *on the* ~ hareket halinde, ilerlemekte; *get a* ~ *on* F acele etm., çabuk olm., işe girişmek; *make a* ~ gitmek; harekete geçmek; 'move.ment *n.* hareket, kımıldanma; MUS tempo, usül, ölçü; MEC mekanizma; MED bağırsakların işlemesi; MIL manevra; 'mover *n.* hareket eden kimse; teklif sunan kimse; nakliyeci.

mov.ie F ['mu:vi] *n.* film; ~*s pl.* sinema.

mov.ing □ ['mu:viŋ] oynar, hareketli; *fig.* dokunaklı, acıklı; ~ *staircase* yürüyen merdiven.

mow¹ [mau] *n.* ekin (*veya* ot) yığını.

mow² [məu] (*irr.*) *v/t.* biçmek; 'mow.er *n.* biçen kimse *veya* alet; 'mow.ing *n.* biçme; 'mow.ing-ma.chine *n.* ekin biçme makinesi; mown *p.p. of mow²*.

much [mʌtʃ] *adj. & adv.* çok(ça), fazla(ca), hayli(ce); *as* ~ *more, as* ~ *again* bu kadar daha, bir misli daha; *as* ~ *as* ...ile aynı, ...kadar; *not so* ~ *as* ...bile değil, hatta; *nothing* ~ hiçbir şey; ~ *less* ...bırak, ...şöyle dursun; ~ *as I would like* sevmeme rağmen; *I*

thought as ~ bunu bekliyordum, aklıma gelmedi de değil; *make* ~ *of* anlamak *-i*; önem vermek *-e*; *I am not* ~ *of a dancer* iyi bir dansöz değilimdir, ben kim dansöz olmak kim; (*not*) *up to* ~ iyi (değil); *this veya that* ~ bu *veya* şu kadar; 'much.ness *n.* F çokluk; *much of a* ~ hemen hemen aynı.

mu.ci.lage ['mju:silidʒ] *n.* zamk, yapışkan; **mu.ci.lag.i.nous** [~'lædʒinəs] *adj.* zamklı.

muck [mʌk] **1.** *n.* gübre; F pislik (*a. fig.*); *make a* ~ *of s.th* bşi kirletmek; *bşi* bozmak; **2.** *v/t.* gübrelemek; *mst* ~ *up* kirletmek, pisletmek; bozmak; ~ *s.th. up* bşi kirletmek; *bşi* berbat etm., bozmak; ~ *about sl.* dalga geçmek; aylaklık etm.; 'muck.er *n. sl.* ayaktakımı, it; *come veya go a* ~ *part. fig.* batmak, başarısızlığa uğramak; **muck-rake** ['~reik] **1.** *n.* gübre yabası; = ~*r*, **2.** *vb.* çamur atmak, karalamak; 'muck-rak.er *n. Am.* skandal yaratan kimse *veya* şey; kötücül kimse; 'muck.y *adj.* kirli, pis.

mu.cous PHYSIOL ['mju:kəs] *adj.* sümüklü; sümüksü; sümük (*veya* balgam) salgılayan; ~ *membrane* mukoza, salgılı zar.

mu.cus ['mju:kəs] *n.* sümük; balgam.

mud [mʌd] *n.* çamur; *throw* ~ *at s.o.* b-ne çamur atmak; 'mud-bath *n.* çamur banyosu; 'mud.di.ness *n.* çamurluluk; **muddle** ['mʌdl] **1.** *v/t.* karıştırmak; *a.* ~ *up*, ~ *together* birbirine karıştırmak, karman çorman etm., birbirinden ayıramamak; F yüzüne gözüne bulaştırmak; *v/i.* kafası karışmak; ~ *through* F işin içinden başarıyla sıyrılmak; **2.** *n.* karışıklık; şaşkınlık; F arapsaçı; *get into a* ~ belâya çatmak, işleri karışmak; 'mud.dle-headed *adj.* sersem, kalın kafalı; 'mud.dy **1.** □ çamurlu; çamur gibi, bulanık; karışık; **2.** *v/t.* çamurlamak, çamura bulamak.

mud...: '~.guard *n.* çamurluk; '~.lark *n.* F sokak çocuğu, afacan; '~-sling.ing *n.* F çamur atma, karalama.

muff¹ [mʌf] **1.** *n.* F beceriksizlik; beceriksiz kimse; **2.** *v/t.* yüzüne gözüne bulaştırmak; yakalayamamak (*top*).

muff² [_] *n.* manşon; MEC boru bileziği.

muf.fin ['mʌfin] *n.* yassı pide; **muf.fin.eer** [_'niə] *n.* tuzluk, şekerlik.

muf.fle ['mʌfl] **1.** *n.* MEC mufla; **2.** *v/t. oft.* ~ *up* sar(ın)mak; boğmak (*ses*);

'**muffler** *n.* boyun atkısı, fular; MUS piyano yastığı; MOT susturucu.

muf.ti ['mʌfti] *n.* sivil elbise (*part.* MIL); **in** ~ sivil elbiseli.

mug [mʌg] **1.** *n.* maşrapa, bardak; ağız; *sl.* yüz, surat; budala, (*veya* avanak) kimse; gangster, eşkiya; kimlik fotoğrafı; **a** ~'s **game** boş iş; **2.** *v/t.* saldırıp soymak; ~ **up** iyi bilmek; ineklemek.

mug.gy ['mʌgi] *adj.* kapalı, sıkıntılı, sıcak ve rutubetli (*hava*).

mug.wort BOT ['mʌgwəːt] *n.* pelin.

mug.wump *Am. iro.* ['mʌgwʌmp] *n.* kendini beğenmiş kimse; POL bağımsız kimse.

mu.lat.to [mjuːˈlætəu] *n.* beyaz ile zenci melezi kimse.

mul.ber.ry ['mʌlbəri] *n.* dut.

mulch [mʌltʃ] **1.** *n.* bitki köklerini koruyucu tabaka; **2.** *v/t.* böyle tabakayla örtmek.

mulct [mʌlkt] **1.** *n. rare* para cezası; **2.** *v/t.* para cezasına çarptırmak; dolandırmak.

mule [mjuːl] *n.* katır; F katır gibi inatçı kimse; şıpıdık, arkalıksız terlik; **as stubborn** *veya* **obstinate as a** ~ katır gibi inatçı; =ʹ~**jenny** *n.* çıkrık makinesi; **mu.le.teer** [ˌliˈtiə] *n.* katırcı; '**mule-track** *n.* katır yolu, patika.

mul.ish ☐ [ˈmjuːliʃ] katır gibi inatçı.

mull[1] COM [mʌl] *n.* ince müslin kumaş.

mull[2] F [ˌ] *v/t.:* ~ **over** düşünüp taşınmak.

mulled [mʌld] *adj.:* ~ **ale** sıcak bira; ~ **wine** şekerli ve baharatlı sıcak şarap.

mul.le(i)n BOT ['mʌlin] *n.* sığırkuyruğu.

mul.let ICHTH ['mʌlit] *n.* dubar; **red** ~ barbunya.

mul.li.gan *Am.* F ['mʌligən] *n.* türlü, güveç; **mul.li.ga.taw.ny** [mʌligəˈtɔːni] *n. a.* ~ **soup** etli ve baharatlı çorba.

mul.li.grubs *sl.* ['mʌligrʌbz] *n. pl.* karın ağrısı.

mul.lion ARCH ['mʌliən] **1.** *n.* pencere çerçevesinin dikey bölme tirizlerinden biri; **2.** *v/t.* tirizlerle ayırmak.

mul.ti.cul.tu.ral ☐ [mʌltiˈkʌltʃərəl] *birden fazla kültür grubu barındıran (toplum),* çok kültürlü; **mul.ti.fa.ri.ous** ☐ [ˌˈfɛəriəs] çeşitli, çeşit çeşit; **mul.ti.form** [ˈˌfɔːm] *adj.* çok şekilli; **mul.ti.lat.er.al** ☐ [ˌˈlætərəl] çok yanlı, çok taraflı; **mul.ti.mil.lion.aire** [ˈˌmiljəˈnɛə] *n.* mültimilyoner.

mul.ti.ple ['mʌltipl] **1.** *adj.* katmerli, çeşitli, çok yönlü, çok kısımlı; ~ **choice** çok seçenekli; ~ **firm,** ~ **shop** firma (*veya* mağaza) şubesi; ~ **switchboard** ELECT çok hatlı santral; **2.** *n.* ELECT çok safhalı akım; MATH katsayı.

mul.ti.plex ['mʌltipleks] **1.** *adj.* çok kısımlı, kat kat, katmerli; **2.** *n.* multipleks (*sinema*).

mul.ti.pli.cand MATH [mʌltipliˈkænd] *n.* çarpılan; **mul.ti.pli.ca.tion** [ˌpliˈkeiʃən] *n.* çoğal(t)ma; MATH çarpma; **compound** (**simple**) ~ bileşik (âdi) çarpım; ~ **table** çarpım tablosu; **mul.ti.plici.ty** [ˌˈplisiti] *n.* çokluk, fazlalık; çeşitlilik; **mul.ti.pli.er** [ˌˈplaiə] *n.* çarpan; **mul.ti.ply** [ˈˌplai] *v/t. & v/i.* çoğal(t)mak; art(tır)mak; çarpmak; üremek.

mul.ti.task.ing [mʌltiˈtɑːskiŋ] *adj. birden fazla görevi aynı anda yerine getirebilen (bilgisayar, kişi).*

mul.ti.tude ['mʌltitjuːd] *n.* kalabalık, izdiham; çokluk; avam; **mul.ti.tu.di.nous** [ˌˈtjuːdinəs]☐ (pek) çok, bir sürü.

mum[1] [mʌm] **1.** *n.* sessizlik; **2.** *int.* sus!; **3.** *v/i.* kılık değiştirip eğlenceye katılmak.

mum[2] F [ˌ] *n.* anne.

mum.ble ['mʌmbl] *v/t. & v/i.* mırılda(n)mak, ağzında gevelemek (*laf*); kemirmek.

Mum.bo Jum.bo ['mʌmbəu'dʒʌmbəu] *n.* anlaşılmaz söz *veya* büyü.

mum.mer *contp.* ['mʌmə] *n.* maskeli aktör; '**mum.mer.y** *n. contp.* maskeli gösteri; anlamsız ayin.

mum.mied ['mʌmid] *adj.* mumyalı.

mum.mi.fi.ca.tion [mʌmifiˈkeiʃən] *n.* mumyalama; **mum.mi.fy** ['ˌfai] *v/t.* mumyalamak; kupkuru yapmak.

mum.my[1] ['mʌmi] *n.* mumya; **beat to a** ~ F eşek sudan gelinceye kadar dövmek, pestilini çıkarmak.

mum.my[2] F [ˌ] *n.* anneciğim.

mump [mʌmp] *v/i.* dilenmek; '**mump.ish** *adj.* asık suratlı, somurtkan; **mumps** [mʌmps] *n. sg.* MED kabakulak.

munch [mʌntʃ] *v/t.* kıtır kıtır (*veya* katır kutur, şapır şupur, hapır hupur) yemek.

mun.dane ☐ ['mʌndein] günlük, olağan, dünyevî...; sıradan...

mu.nic.i.pal ☐ [mjuːˈnisipl] belediyeye ait, belediye...; şehre ait, şehir...; **mu.nic.ipal.i.ty** [ˌˈpæliti] *n.* belediye.

mu.nif.i.cence [mjuːˈnifisns] *n.* cömertlik; **mu'nif.i.cent** ☐ cömert, eli açık.

mu.ni.ments ['mjuːnimənts] *n. pl.* senet, belgit.

mu.ni.tions [mjuːˈniʃənz] *n. pl.* savaş gereçleri, cephane.

mu.ral ['mjuərəl] **1.** *adj.* duvara ait, duvar...; duvar gibi; duvara asılan; **2.** *n.* fresk, duvara yapılan resim.

mur.der ['məːdə] **1.** *n.* katil, adam öldürme, cinayet; **2.** *v/t.* öldürmek, katletmek (*a. fig.*); *fig.* berbat etm., rezil etm.; '**mur.der.er** *n.* katil, cani; '**mur.der.ess** *n.* kadın katil; '**mur.der.ous** □ öldürücü; kanlı; *fig.* sert, şiddetli.

mure [mjuə] *v/t. mst ~ up* hapsetmek.

mu.ri.at.ic ac.id CHEM [mjuəriˈætik-ˈæsid] *n.* tuzruhu.

murk.y □ ['məːki] karanlık, kasvetli; yoğun (*sis*); utanç verici.

mur.mur ['məːmə] **1.** *n.* mırıltı, mırıldanma; söylenme; uğultu; **2.** *vb.* mırılda(n)mak; homurdanmak, söylenmek (*against, at -e karşı*); çağıldamak, uğuldamak; '**mur.mur.ous** □ mırıltılı, homurtulu.

mur.phy *sl.* ['məːfi] *n.* patates.

mur.rain ['mʌrin] *n.* hayvanlara özgü bulaşıcı bir hastalık.

mus.ca.dine ['mʌskədin], **mus.cat** ['ˌkət], **mus.ca.tel** [ˌkəˈtel] *n.* misket üzümü *veya* şarabı.

mus.cle ['mʌsl] **1.** *n.* adale, kas; **2.** *v/i. ~ in* Am. *sl.* kaba kuvvet kullanmak; '**~-bound** *adj.* adaleli; kas tutukluğu olan; **mus.cu.lar** □ ['ˌkjulə] adaleye ait, adale...; adaleli; kuvvetli.

Muse[1] [mjuːz] *n.* Müzlerden biri.

muse[2] [ˌ] *v/i.* düşünceye dalmak, dalıp gitmek (*on, upon -e*); '**mus.er** *n.* dalgın kimse.

mu.se.um [mjuːˈziəm] *n.* müze.

mush [mʌʃ] *n.* mısır unu lapası.

mush.room ['mʌʃrum] **1.** *n.* mantar; *fig.* türedi şey *veya* kimse; **2.** *adj.* mantarımsı...; *fig.* türedi...; *fig.* hızlı...; **3.** *v/i.* mantar gibi yerden bitmek, artmak, çoğalmak; **~ out** hızla yayılmak; **~ up** göklere yükselmek; *go ~ing* mantar toplamak.

mu.sic ['mjuːzik] *n.* müzik, musiki; makam, nota; **set to ~** bestelemek; **face the ~** F güçlüklere *veya* eleştirilere göğüs germek; '**mu.si.cal 1.** □ müziğe ait, müzik...; müzikal; ahenkli, uyumlu; müziksever; **~ box** müzik kutusu; **~ clock** müzikli saat; **~ instrument** müzik aleti (*veya* enstrumanı);

2. *n. a.* **~ comedy** müzikal komedi.

mu.sic...; '**~-book** *n.* nota kitabı; '**~-box** *n. Am.* müzik kutusu; '**~-hall** *n.* müzikhol; varyete.

mu.si.cian [mjuːˈziʃən] *n.* çalgıcı; müzisyen, bestekâr.

mu.sic...; '**~-pa.per** *n.* nota kâğıdı; '**~-stand** *n.* nota sehpası; '**~-stool** *n.* piyano taburesi.

musk [mʌsk] *n.* misk (kokusu); BOT amberçiçeği, miskotu; = '**~'deer** *n.* ZOO misk geyiği.

mus.ket ['mʌskit] *n.* asker tüfeği; **musket.eer** [ˌtiə] *n.* tüfekli asker, silahşör; **mus.ket.ry** MIL ['ˌri] *n.* tüfek atışı; tüfekler.

musk...; '**~-rat** *n.* ZOO misk sıçanı; '**~-rose** *n.* BOT misk gülü; '**musk.y** *adj.* misk kokulu.

Mus.lim ['mʌslim] *s.* **Moslem**.

mus.lin COM ['mʌzlin] *n.* muslin.

mus.quash ['mʌskwɔʃ] *n.* misk sıçanı kürkü.

muss *part. Am.* F [mʌs] **1.** *n.* karışıklık, arapsaçı; **2.** *v/t.* bozmak, dağıtmak, arapçasına çevirmek.

mus.sel ['mʌsl] *n.* midye.

Mus.sul.man ['mʌslmən] **1.** *n.* Müslüman; **2.** *adj.* Müslüman...

must[1] [mʌst, məst] **1.** *v/aux.* (*irr.*) -meli, -malı; *I ~ not* ...mamalıyım, izinli değilim; **2.** *n.* zorunluluk, şart, gereklilik; *this book is a ~* bu kitap mutlaka okunmalıdır.

must[2] [mʌst] *n.* şıra.

must[3] [ˌ] *n.* küf (kokusu).

mus.tache Am. [məsˈtɑːʃ], **mus.ta.chio** Am. [məsˈtɑːʃiːəu] *s.* **moustache**.

mus.tang ['mʌstæŋ] *n.* yabani at.

mus.tard ['mʌstəd] *n.* hardal (bitkisi); **~ gas** MIL iperit; **~ plas.ter** MED hardal yakısı.

mus.ter ['mʌstə] **1.** *n.* MIL içtima, bir araya toplanma; yoklama; toplanan kimseler *veya* sayıları; *mst ~ roll* MIL yoklama defteri; *pass ~ fig.* yeterli (*veya* tatminkâr) olm., kabul olunmak; **2.** *v/t. & v/i.* MIL topla(n)mak; **~ in** askere kaydetmek; *mst ~ up fig.* toplamak (*cesaret*).

mus.ti.ness ['mʌstinis] *n.* küflülük; '**musty** *adj.* küflü, küf kokulu; *fig.* demode, bayat, eski.

mu.ta.bil.i.ty [mjuːtəˈbiliti] *n.* değişebilirlik; '**mu.ta.ble** □ değişebilir, değişken; **mu.ta.tion** [ˌˈteiʃən] *n.* değişme, dönüşme; GR bir ünlü *veya*

ünsüzün değişmesi.
mute [mjuːt] **1.** □ sessiz, suskun; dilsiz;
GR okunmaz (*harf*); **2.** *n.* dilsiz kimse;
MUS surdin; GR sağır ses, okunmayan
harf; **3.** *v/t. part.* MUS sesini kısmak.
mu.ti.late ['mjuːtileit] *v/t.* kötürüm
etm. (*a. fig.*); *fig.* bozmak, katletmek;
muti'la.tion *n.* kötürüm etme; bozma.
mu.ti.neer [mjuːti'niə] *n.* isyan eden
asker, isyancı, asi; **'mu.ti.nous** □ isyankâr, asi; **'mu.ti.ny 1.** *n.* isyan, ayaklanma; **2.** *v/i.* ayaklanmak, isyan etm.
(*against* -*e* karşı).
mutt *sl.* [mʌt] *n.* kuş beyinli kimse.
mut.ter ['mʌtə] **1.** *n.* mırıltı; **2.** *v/i.*
mırıldanmak, homurdanmak, söylen-
mek.
mut.ton ['mʌtn] *n.* koyun eti; **leg of** ~
koyun budu; '~'**chop** *n.* koyun pirzolası.
mu.tu.al □ ['mjuːtʃuəl] karşılıklı; ortak, müşterek; ~ **fund** menkul kıymetler yatırım fonu; ~ **insurance** karşılıklı
sigorta; **mu.tu.al.i.ty** [‿tju'æliti] *n.*
karşılıklı olma.
muz.zle ['mʌzl] **1.** *n.* hayvan burnu; burunsalık; top *veya* tüfek ağzı; **2.** *v/t.* burunsalık takmak -*e*; *fig.* susturmak;
'~-**load.er** *n.* MIL ağızdan dolma top *ve-*
ya tüfek.
muz.zy □ ['mʌzi] kafası karışmış; keyifsiz; sersem; bulanık.
my [mai] *pron.* benim.
my.al.gi.a MED [mai'ældʒiə] *n.* kasınç,
kas ağrısı.
my.col.o.gy [mai'kɔlədʒi] *n.* mantar-

ları inceleyen bilim dalı.
my.ope MED ['maiəup] *n.* miyop kimse;
myo.pi.a [mai'əupjə] *n.* miyopluk;
my.op.ic [‿'ɔpik] *adj.* (~**ally**) miyop.
myr.i.ad ['miriəd] **1.** *n.* çok sayı; **2.** *adj.*
çok, sayısız.
myr.mi.don ['məːmidən] *n. contp.* körü
körüne itaat eden kimse.
myrrh BOT [məː] *n.* mür(rüsafî).
myr.tle BOT ['məːtl] *n.* mersin.
my.self [mai'self] *pron.* ben, kendim,
bizzat.
mys.te.ri.ous □ [mis'tiəriəs] esrarengiz, gizemli, garip; **mys'te.ri.ous.ness**
n. esrarengizlik, gizemlilik.
mys.ter.y ['mistəri] *n.* gizem, sır; anlaşılmaz şey; *a.* ~ **play** HIST dinî piyes;
'~-**ship** *n.* MIL tuzak gemi.
mys.tic ['mistik] **1.** *a.* '**mys.ti.cal** □ mistik, tasavvufa ait; gizemli; gizli; gizli
anlamlı, esrarlı; **2.** *n.* gizemci, mutasavvıf; **mys.ti.cism** ['‿sizəm] *n.* gizemcilik, mistisizm, tasavvuf; **mys.ti.fi.ca-**
tion [‿fi'keiʃən] *n.* şaşırtma; **mys.ti.fy**
['‿fai] *v/t.* şaşırtmak, hayrette bırakmak.
mys.tique [mis'tiːk] *n.* yetenek, marifet, gizli güç; özellikler.
myth [miθ] *n.* efsane, mit; hayalî kimse
veya şey; **myth.ic, myth.i.cal** □
['‿ik(əl)] efsanevî, esatirî; hayalî.
myth.o.log.ic, myth.o.log.i.cal □
[miθə'lɔdʒik(əl)] mitolojik, esatirî;
my.thol.ogy [mi'θɔlədʒi] *n.* mitoloji.
myx.o.ma.to.sis [miksəumə'təusis] *n.*
öldürücü bir tavşan hastalığı.

N

nab *sl.* [næb] *v/t.* yakalamak, enselemek, tutuklamak; almak.

na.bob ['neibɔb] *n.* ensesi kalın (*veya* çok varlıklı) kimse.

na.celle AVIA [næ'sel] *n.* motor yeri.

na.cre ['neikə] *n.* sedef; **na.cre.ous** ['‿kriəs] *adj.* sedefli.

na.dir ['neidiə] *n.* AST ayakucu; *fig.* en düşük nokta.

nag¹ F [næg] *n.* yaşlı at.

nag² [‿] *v/i.* dırlanmak, dırdır etm., söylenip durmak; **~ at** *-in* başının etini yemek.

Nai.ad ['naiæd] *n.* su perisi.

nail [neil] **1.** *n.* çivi, mıh; ANAT & ZOO tırnak; **fight tooth and ~** çok şiddetli dövüşmek; dişe diş kavga etm.; **on the ~** derhal, hemen; **hit the (right) ~ on the head** tam üstüne basmak, taşı gediğine koymak; **as hard as ~s** acımasız, sert; turp gibi; **2.** *v/t.* çivilemek, mıhlamak (**to** *-e*); F tutmak, yakalamak, esir almak; dikmek (*göz*); **~ down** çivilemek; F garantiye almak; **~ s.o. down to** *fig. b-ni* zorla konuşturmak; **~ to the counter** teşhir etm., yalancı çıkarmak, yalanlamak; **'~brush** *n.* tırnak fırçası; **'nail.ing** *adj. sl. oft.* **~ good** şahane, emsalsiz; **'nail-scissors** *n. pl.* tırnak makası; **'nail-var.nish** *n.* tırnak cilâsı, oje.

nain.sook ['neinsuk] *n.* nansuk, bir tür ince ve sık dokunmuş patiska.

na.i.ve □ [naːˈiːv] **na.ive** [neiv] saf, bön; deneyimsiz, toy; **na.ive.té** [naːˈiːvtei], **na.ive.ty** ['neivti] *n.* saflık, bönlük; toyluk.

na.ked □ ['neikid] çıplak; *fig.* yalın, açık; örtüsüz; silahsız; *poet.* korumasız, himayesiz; sade; salt (*gerçek*); **'na.ked.ness** *n.* çıplaklık.

nam.by-pam.by ['næmbi'pæmbi] **1.** *adj.* budalaca duygusal; kararsız; **2.** *n.* budalaca duygusal (*veya* sıkılgan) kimse.

name [neim] **1.** *n.* isim, ad; nam, şöhret, ün; ünvan; meşhur kimse; **of** *veya* **by the ~ of...** ...isminde, ...adında; **call s.o. ~s** *b-ne* sövüp saymak; **not have a penny to one's ~** meteliğe kurşun atmak, cebi delik olm.; **know s.o. by ~**

b-ni ismen tanımak; **2.** *v/t.* adlandırmak, isim koymak *-e*; söylemek; vermek (*fiyat*); tayin etm., atamak; **'~-day** *n.* ECCL isim günü; **'name.less** □ isimsiz, adsız; bilinmeyen; bahsedilmeye değmez; tarifi olanaksız; **'name.ly** *adv.* yani, şöyle ki; **'name-part** *n.* başrol; **'name-plate** *n.* tabela; **'name-sake** *n.* adaş.

nan.cy *sl.* ['nænsi] *n.* çıtkırıldım, hanım evlâdı; homoseksüel.

nan.keen [næŋ'kiːn] *n.* pamuklu kumaş; **~s** *pl.* pamuklu kumaştan elbise.

nan.ny ['næni] *n.* dadı; **'~-goat** *n.* dişi keçi.

nap¹ [næp] *n.* tüylü yüz, hav.

nap² [‿] **1.** *n.* şekerleme, kestirme, kısa uyku; **have** *veya* **take a ~** şekerleme yapmak, kestirmek; **2.** *v/i.* şekerleme yapmak, kestirmek; **catch s.o. ~ping** *b-ni* gafil avlamak.

nap³ [‿] *n.:* **go ~** *fig.* tek bir darbe ile başarıyı elde etmeğe çalışmak.

na.palm ['neipaːm] *n.:* **~ bomb** MIL napalm bombası.

nape [neip] *n. mst.* **~ of the neck** ense.

naph.tha CHEM ['næfθə] *n.* neftyağı.

nap.kin ['næpkin] *n.* peçete; kundak bezi; **'~-ring** *n.* peçete halkası.

Na.po.le.on.ic [nəpəuli'ɔnik] *adj.* Napolyon'a ait.

nap.py F ['næpi] *n.* çocuk bezi.

nar.cis.sism PSYCH [naːˈsisizm] *n.* narkislik, narkisizm, kendi kendine aşık olma; **nar.ciss.us** BOT [‿ˈsisəs] *n.* nergis, zerrin, fulya.

nar.co.sis MED [naːˈkəusis] *n.* narkoz.

nar.cot.ic [naːˈkɔtik] **1.** *adj.* (**~ally**) narkotik, uyuşturucu; **2.** *n.* uyuşturucu ilâç, narkotik; uyuşturucu düşkünü kimse; **nar.co.tize** ['naːkətaiz] *v/t.* ilâç ile uyuşturmak *veya* uyutmak.

nard [naːd] *n.* hintsümbülü.

nark¹ *sl.* [naːk] *n.* ajan; narkotik ajanı.

nark² F [‿] *v/t.* canını sıkmak, tepesini attırmak; *v/i.* sızlanmak, yakınmak.

nar.rate [nə'reit] *v/t.* anlatmak, nakletmek; **nar'ra.tion** *n.* anlatma, anlatım; hikâye; **nar.ra.tive** ['nærətiv] **1.** □ hikâye türünde; hikâye anlatmaya ait; **2.** *n.* rivayet, hikâye, anlatı (sanatı);

nar.ra.tor [nə'reitə] *n.* hikâyeci; anlatan kimse.

nar.row ['nærəu] **1.** □ dar, ensiz; kısıtlı; kesin; darlık içinde; dar fikirli; cimri, pinti; *s.* **escape**; **2.** *n.* ~**s** *pl.* dar boğaz; **3.** *v/t. & v/i.* daral(t)mak; kısmak (*göz*); kısıtlamak; '~'**chest.ed** *adj.* dar göğüslü; '~**gauge** *n.* RAIL dekovil; '~'**mind.ed** □ dar fikirli (*veya* görüşlü); '**nar.rowness** *n.* darlık (*a. fig.*).

nar.whal ZOO ['nɑːwəl] *n.* denizgergedanı.

nar.y *Am.* ['nɛəri] *adj.* hiç bir.

na.sal ['neizəl] **1.** □ buruna ait, burun…; genzel; **2.** *n.* genzel ses; **na.sal.i.ty** [ˌ'zæliti] *n.* genzellik; **na.sal.ize** ['ˌzəlaiz] *v/i.* genizden konuşmak; *v/t.* GR genizden çıkarmak (*ses*).

nas.cent ['næsnt] *adj.* oluşmaya (*veya* gelişmeye) başlayan, filizlenen.

nas.ti.ness ['nɑːstinis] *n.* iğrençlik; çirkinlik.

nas.tur.tium BOT [nəs'təːʃəm] *n.* lâtinçiçeği.

nas.ty ['nɑːsti] □ pis, kirli, fena kokulu, iğrenç, berbat, tiksindirici, kötü, çirkin; yaramaz; ayıp, terbiyesiz, edepsiz, açık saçık, ahlâksız; tehlikeli, korkutucu, ürkütücü, şiddetli.

na.tal ['neitl] *adj.* doğuşa ait, doğum…; **na.tal.i.ty** [nə'tæliti] *n.* doğum oranı.

na.ta.tion [nə'teiʃən] *n.* yüzme (sanatı); **na.ta.to.ri.al** [nætə'tɔːriəl] *adj.* yüzmeye ait, yüzme…

na.tion ['neiʃən] *n.* millet, ulus; budun.

na.tion.al ['næʃənl] **1.** □ millete ait, ulusal…, millî…; **2.** *n.* vatandaş, yurttaş; **na.tion.al.ism** ['næʃnəlizəm] *n.* ulusçuluk, milliyetçilik; '**na.tion.al.ist 1.** *n.* milliyetçi; **2.** *adj.* = **na.tion.al'is.tic** milliyetçiliğe ait, milliyetçilik…; **na.tion.al.i.ty** [næʃə'næliti] *n.* milliyet; millet; vatandaşlık; uyrukluk, tabiiyet; **na.tion.al.i.za.tion** [næʃnəlai'zeiʃən] *n.* millîleştirme; '**nation.al.ize** *v/t.* millîleştirmek, kamulaştırmak, devletleştirmek.

na.tion-wide ['neiʃənwaid] *adj.* millet (*veya* ülke) çapında.

na.tive ['neitiv] **1.** □ yerli, doğal; doğma; doğuştan; özgü (**to**-*e*); Tanrı vergisi (*yetenek*); saf(i) (*maden*); ~ **land** anavatan, anayurt; ~ **language** anadili; **2.** *n.* yerli, yerli mal *veya* hayvan; **a** ~ **of Ireland** İrlanda'nın yerlisi; ♀ **A.mer.i.can** *adj. & n.* Amerikan yerlisi; '~**born** *adj.* yerli, doğma büyüme.

na.tiv.i.ty [nə'tiviti] *n.* doğuş, doğum; ♀ **Play** Hz. İsa'nın doğumunu anlatan oyun.

na.tron CHEM ['neitrən] *n.* tabiî sodyum karbonat.

nat.ter F ['nætə] *v/i.* çene çalmak, laklak etm.

nat.ty □ ['næti] şık, zarif.

na.tu.ral ['nætʃrəl] **1.** □ tabiî, doğal; doğuştan; sunî olmayan, normal; MUS natürel; gayri meşru (*çocuk*); ~ **history** tabiat bilgisi; ~ **note** MUS tabiî nota; ~ **philosopher** tabiat bilgini; ~ **philosophy** tabiat bilgisi; ~ **science** tabiat bilgisi; **2.** *n. obs.* doğuştan geri zekâlı kimse; MUS bekar; piyanonun beyaz tuşu; *bşe* tam uygun kimse *veya* şey; '**nat.u.ral.ism** *n.* doğacılık, natüralizm; '**nat.u.ral.ist** *n.* natüralist, doğacı; tabiat bilgisi uzmanı; **natu.ral.i.za.tion** [ˌlai'zeiʃən] *n.* vatandaşlığa kabul etme; '**nat.u.ral.ize** *v/t.* vatandaşlığa kabul etm.; lisana almak (*yabancı kelime*); BOT, ZOO yerlileştirmek; tabiîleştirme; *v/i.* yerlisi gibi olm.; '**natu.ral.ness** *n.* tabiîlik; **na.tu.ral se.lec.tion** BIOL doğal ayıklanma.

na.ture ['neitʃə] *n.* tabiat, doğa; mizaç, yaradılış, yapı; çeşit, tür, tip; kâinat, dünya, evren; '**na.tured** *comb.* …mizaçlı, …huylu.

naught [nɔːt] *n.* sıfır; *obs.* hiç; **come (bring) to** ~ boşa çık(ar)mak, suya düş(ür)mek; **set at** ~ aldırmamak, önemsememek; **naugh.ti.ness** ['ˌtinis] *n.* yaramazlık, haylazlık; '**naughty** □ yaramaz, haylaz, haşarı; kötü; ahlâksız, açık saçık; münasebetsiz.

nau.se.a ['nɔːsjə] *n.* mide bulantısı; deniz tutması; *fig.* iğrenme, tiksinme; **nause.ate** ['nɔːsieit] *v/t. & v/i.* midesi(ni)bulan(dır)mak, iğren(dir)mek, tiksin(dir)mek; **be** ~**d** midesi bulanmak; iğrenmek; **nau.seous** □ ['nɔːsjəs] mide bulandırıcı, iğrenç.

nau.ti.cal ['nɔːtikəl] gemiciliğe ait, gemicilik…, deniz(s)el…; ~ **mile** deniz mili.

naut.i.lus ZOO ['nɔːtiləs] *n.* sedefli deniz helezonu.

na.val □ ['neivəl] bahriye ile ilgili, deniz(s)el; savaş gemilerine ait; ~ **base** deniz üssü; ~ **staff** deniz kurmay subayları.

nave[1] ARCH [neiv] *n.* kilisede halkın oturduğu orta kısım.

nave[2] [ˌ] *n.* dingil başlığı, tekerlek poyrası.

na.vel ['neivəl] *n.* göbek; *fig.* merkez; ~ **or.ange** bir tür göbekli ve çekirdeksiz portakal.

nav.i.ga.ble □ ['nævigəbl] gidiş gelişe elverişli; dümen kullanılabilir (*gemi*); **nav.i.gate** ['_geit] *v/i.* gemi ile gezmek, gemi kullanmak, seyretmek; kaptanlık (*veya* kılavuzluk) etm.; *v/t.* kullanmak (*gemi*, *uçak*); **nav.i'ga.tion** *n.* denizcilik; dümencilik; gemicilik; **'nav.i.ga.tor** *n.* denizci, gemici, dümenci, NAUT seyir subayı; AVIA kaptan pilot.

nav.vy ['nævi] *n.* işçi, amele.

na.vy ['neivi] *n.* deniz kuvvetleri, donanma; deniz filosu; **'~-'blue** *adj.* lâcivert, koyu mavi.

nay [nei] **1.** *adv. obs. veya prov.* hayır, yok; hem de, hatta; **2.** *n.* ret oyu (veren kimse).

Naz.a.rene [næzə'ri:n] *n.* Nasıralı; Nasranî.

naze [neiz] *n.* burun, sahil çıkıntısı.

Na.zi ['nɑ:tsi] **1.** *n.* Nazi; **2.** *adj.* Nazi...

neap [ni:p] *n. a.* **~-tide** alçalma ile yükselmenin en az olduğu gelgit; **'neaped** *adj.*: *be ~* NAUT (*gelgit nedeniyle*) kara üzerinde kalmak (*gemi*).

Ne.a.pol.i.tan [niə'pɔlitən] **1.** *adj.* Napoli'ye ait, Napoli'ye özgü; **2.** *n.* Napolili.

near [niə] **1.** *adj.* yakın; bitişik; samimi, içlidışlı; soldaki; cimri, eli sıkı; ~ *at hand* el altında, yakın; *a ~ thing* ucu ucuna kazanma; darı darına (*veya* ucuz*) kurtulma; **2.** *adv.* yakın(da); hemen hemen, az daha, neredeyse; aşağı yukarı; **3.** *prp.* bitişik, yakın; **4.** *v/i.* yaklaşmak -*e*; **near.by** ['_bai] *adj.* & *adv.* yakın(da); **'near.ly** *adv.* hemen hemen, âdeta, neredeyse; yakından; *not ~* hiç te, katiyen; **'near.ness** *n.* yakınlık; **'near-'sight.ed** *adj.* miyop.

neat[1] □ [ni:t] temiz, düzenli, düzgün, zarif, zevkli; nefis, enfes; zekice, akıllıca; su katılmamış, saf, katışıksız (*içki*).

neat[2] *rare* [_] *n.* büyükbaş hayvanlar.

neat.ness ['ni:tnis] *n.* temizlik, düzgünlük.

neat...: **'~'s-foot oil** sığır paçası yağı; **'~'s-leath.er** *n.* sığır derisi; **'~'s--tongue** *n.* sığır dili.

neb.u.la AST ['nebjulə] *n.* nebula; **'neb.ular** *adj.* nebulaya ait, nebula...; **neb.u.losi.ty** [_'lɔsiti] *n.* bulutluluk; **'neb.u.lous** □ bulutlu, dumanlı, bu-

lanık (*a. fig.*).

ne.ces.sa.ri.ly ['nesisərili] *adv.* mutlaka, muhakkak, illâ(ki); **'nec.es.sar.y 1.** □ gerekli, zorunlu, lüzumlu, zarurî, lâzım; kaçınılmaz; **2.** *n.* *mst* **necessaries** *pl.* gerekli şey; levazım; **ne.cessi.tate** [ni'sesiteit] *v/t.* gerektirmek, zorunlu kılmak; **ne'ces.si.tous** *adj.* fakir, yoksul, muhtaç; elzem; **ne'ces.si.ty** *n.* lüzum, zaruret, ihtiyaç, gerekseme, gereksinme; *mst* **necessities** *pl.* gerekli şey; *of ~* zorunlu olarak, mutlaka.

neck [nek] **1.** *n.* boyun, gerdan; şişe boğazı; kıstak, boğaz, dil; elbise yakası; keman sapı; *break the ~ of a task* bir işin hakkından gelmek; ~ *and ~* başa baş, at başı beraber; ~ *and crop* F tamamen; paldır küldür; pılı pırtıyı toplayarak; ~ *or nothing* F herşeyi göze alarak, ya hep ya hiç; *get it in the ~ sl.* zılgıt yemek, azar işitmek, canına okunmak; **2.** *v/i. sl.* öpüşmek, cinsî münasebette bulunmadan sevişmek; **'~.band** *n.* dik elbise yakası; **'~.cloth** *n.* fular; **neck.erchief** ['nekətʃif] *n.* boyun atkısı; **necklace** ['_lis],**neck.let** ['_lit] *n.* kolye, gerdanlık; **'neck.tie** *n.* kravat; **'neckwear** *n.* COM boyuna takılan şeyler.

ne.crol.o.gy [ne'krɔlədʒi] *n.* ölenlerin isim listesi; bir ölü hakkında yazılmış yazı; **nec.ro.man.cy** ['nekrəumænsi] *n.* ruh çağırma; büyücülük.

nec.tar ['nektə] *n.* nektar, abıhayat; **nectar.ine** ['_rin] *n.* tüysüz şeftali, durakı.

née [nei] *adj.* kızlık soyadıyle.

need [ni:d] **1.** *n.* ihtiyaç, lüzum, gereklik, zorunluluk, gereksinme, gerekseme (*for* için); fakirlik, darlık, yokluk; *one's own ~s pl.* b-nin gereksinmeleri; *if ~ be* gerekirse; *be veya stand in ~ of* -*e* muhtaç olm., gereksinme duymak; **2.** *v/t.* ihtiyacı olm. -*e*, gereksemek -*i*, gereksinmek -*e*, istemek -*i*; gerektirmek -*i*; **needful** ['_ful] **1.** □ gerekli, lâzım; **2.** *n.* F ihtiyaç (*part. para*); **'need.i.ness** *n.* fakirlik, yoksulluk.

nee.dle ['ni:dl] **1.** *n.* iğne; ibre; örgü şişi; tığ; dikilitaş; **2.** *v/t.* iğne ile dikmek, tutturmak, delmek; *part. Am.* kızdırmak; F artırmak (*alkol derecesini*); ~ *one's way through* yol bulup geçmek, arasından sıyrılmak; **'~-case** *n.* iğne kutusu; **'~-gun** *n.* iğneli tüfek.

need.less □ ['ni:dlis] gereksiz, lüzumsuz; '**need.less.ly** *adv.* gereksizce, lüzumsuzca; '**need.less.ness** *n.* gereksizlik, lüzumsuzluk.

nee.dle...: '~.**wom.an** *n.* dikişçi kadın; '~.**work** *n.* iğne işi, işleme.

needs [niːdʒ] *adv.* ister istemez, mutlaka; '**need.y** □ muhtaç, fakir, yoksul.

ne'er [nɛə] = *never;* ~-**do-well** ['‿duːwel] *n.* bir işe yaramaz kimse.

ne.far.i.ous □ [ni'fɛəriəs] kötü, şeytansı; kanunlara *veya* ahlâk prensiplerine aykırı.

ne.gate [ni'geit] *v/t.* inkâr etm., reddetmek; etkisini yok etm.; **ne'ga.tion** *n.* inkâr, ret; eksiklik; **neg.a.tive** ['negətiv] **1.** □ olumsuz; negatif; aksi, ters; **2.** *n.* olumsuz söz *veya* yanıt; ret yanıtı; PHOT negatif; **3.** *v/t. a.* **answer in the** ~ olumsuz yanıt vermek; inkâr etm.; hükümsüz kılmak; çürütmek; tesirini yok etm.; menetmek.

neg.lect [ni'glekt] **1.** *n.* ihmal; **2.** *v/t.* ihmal etm., savsaklamak; bakmamak, yapmamak; **neg'lect.ful** □ [‿ful] ihmalci, savsak, kayıtsız (**of** -*e karşı*).

nég.li.gé, neg.li.gee ['negliːʒei] *n.* süslü gecelik.

neg.li.gence ['neglidʒəns] *n.* dikkatsizlik, kayıtsızlık; JUR ihmal; '**neg.li.gent** □ kayıtsız, ihmalci, savsak (**of** -*e karşı*).

neg.li.gi.ble ['neglidʒəbl] *adj.* önemsemeye değmez, az.

ne.go.ti.a.bil.i.ty [nigəuʃjə'biliti] *n.* satılabilme; akdolunma olanağı; ne'**go.ti.a.ble** □ tartışılabilir; akdolunabilir; tedavülü kolay, ciro edilebilir; devredilebilir; aşılabilir (*yol vs.*); **not** ~ geçerli değildir, takas (*veya* ciro) edilemez; **ne'go.ti.ate** [‿ʃieit] *v/t.* müzakere etm.; ciro etm. (*çek, bono*); akdetmek; aşabilmek, geçebilmek; başarmak; tamamlamak; *v/i.* görüşme yapmak; **ne.go.ti'a.tion** *n.* müzakere, görüşme; tamamlama; ciro etme; **under** ~ görüşülmekte, halledilmekte; ne'**go.ti.a.tor** *n.* delege; arabulucu.

ne.gress ['niːgris] *n.* zenci kadın; **ne.gro** ['niːgrəu] *n., pl.* **ne.groes** ['‿z] zenci; **negroid** ['niːgrɔid] *adj.* zencilere ait, zenci...; zenciye benzer.

ne.gus ['niːgəs] *n.* baharatlı ve şekerli sıcak şarap.

neigh [nei] **1.** *n.* kişneme; **2.** *v/i.* kişnemek.

neigh.bo(u)r ['neibə] **1.** *n.* komşu; **2.** *v/t. & v/i.* yaklaş(tır)mak; komşu olm.;

yakın olm.; **neigh.bo(u)r.hood** ['‿hud] *n.* komşuluk, yakınlık; komşular; civar, semt, mahalle; **in the** ~ **of** -*in* havalisinde, -*in* civarında (*a. fig.* F); '**neigh.bo(u)ring** *adj.* yakın, civar; komşu, bitişik; '**neigh.bo(u)r.li.ness** *n.* komşuya yaraşır davranış; '**neigh.bo(u)r.ly** *adj.* dostça, arkadaşça, komşuya yaraşır; komşuluğa ait, komşuluk...

nei.ther ['naiðə] **1.** *adj. & pron.* hiç biri, ne bu ne öteki; ve ne de; **2.** *adv.:* ~ ...**nor** ne... ne de...; **not...** ~ bile değil.

nem.e.sis ['nemisis] *n.* hak edilen ceza; kuvvetli rakip *veya* düşman.

ne.o.lith.ic [niːəu'liθik] *adj.* ikinci taş devrine ait, neolitik.

ne.ol.o.gism [niː'ɔlədʒizəm] *n.* yeni kelimeler bulma *veya* kullanma; yeni kelime.

ne.on ['niːɔn] *n.* neon; ~ **light** neon ışığı; ~ **sign** ışıklı reklam.

neph.ew ['nevjuː] *n.* erkek yeğen.

ne.phri.tis MED [ne'fraitis] *n.* böbrek iltihabı, nefrit.

nep.o.tism ['nepətizəm] *n.* akraba kayırma.

Nep.tune ['neptjuːn] *n.* Neptün gezegeni.

Ne.re.id ['niəriid] *n.* su perisi.

nerve [nəːv] **1.** *n.* sinir, asap; cesaret, soğukkanlılık; ~**s** *pl.* duyarlık; BOT damar; küstahlık, yüzsüzlük; **get on s.o.'s** ~**s** *b-nin* sinirine dokunmak; **2.** *v/t.* cesaret vermek -*e* (**for** *için*); '~-**cell** *n.* sinir hücresi; '~-**cen.tre** *n.,* Am. '~-**cen.ter** sinir merkezi; **nerved** *adj.* BOT damarlı; '**nerveless** □ zayıf, cansız, güçsüz, dermansız; cesaretsiz; soğukkanlı; **nerve-rack.ing** *adj.* sinir bozucu.

nerv.ine MED ['nəːviːn] **1.** *adj.* sinirleri yatıştırıcı; **2.** *n.* sinirleri yatıştırıcı ilâç.

nerv.ous □ ['nəːvəs] sinirli, asabî; çekingen, ürkek; sinirsel; '**nerv.ous.ness** *n.* sinirlilik.

nerv.y *sl.* ['nəːvi] *adj.* yüzsüz, küstah; sinirli.

nes.ci.ence ['nesiəns] *n.* bilgisizlik, cehalet; '**nes.ci.ent** *adj.* cahil, bilgisiz, habersiz (**of** -*den*).

ness [nes] *n.* burun, çıkıntı.

nest [nest] **1.** *n.* yuva (*a. fig.*); haydut yatağı; **2.** *v/t. & v/i.* iç içe yerleş(tir)mek; yuva yapmak; '**nest.ed** *adj.* iç içe; '**nest-egg** *n.* fol; *fig.* ilerisi için biriktirilen para, ihtiyat akçesi; '**nest.er** *n.*

yuva yapan kuş; **'nes.tle** ['nesl] *v/i.* sokulmak (**to** -e); gömülmek; *v/t.* barındırmak, sığındırmak; yaslamak; bağrına basmak; **nest.ling** ['nestliŋ] *n.* yavru kuş.

net[1] [net] **1.** *n.* ağ, tuzak; şebeke; hile; F internet; **2.** *v/t.* ağ ile tutmak; ağ ile örtmek; *fig.* avlamak.

net[2] [_] **1.** *adj.* net, kesintisiz; halis, safi, katışıksız; **2.** *v/t.* kazanmak, kâr etm.

net.ball ['netbɔːl] *n.* voleybol türünde bir oyun.

neth.er ['neðə] *adj.* alt(taki); '**~most** *adj.* en alttaki.

net.ting ['netiŋ] *n.* ağ (örme); örgü.

net.tle ['netl] **1.** *n.* BOT ısırgan; **2.** *v/t. rare* ısırganla yakmak; *fig.* kızdırmak, öfkelendirmek; '**~rash** *n.* MED kurdeşen, ürtiker.

net.work ['netwɔːk] *n.* şebeke; ağ örgüsü; *radyo:* yayın istasyonları şebekesi; **net.work.ing** ['netwɔːkıŋ] *n. sosyal amaçlı bir toplantıda iş alanında yararlı olacak ilişkiler geliştirmek.*

neu.ral MED ['njuərəl] *adj.* sinirlere ait, sinirsel.

neu.ral.gia MED [njuə'rældʒə] *n.* nevralji; **neu.ras.the.ni.a** MED [njuərəs-'θiːnjə] *n.* nevrasteni; **neu.ras.then.ic** [_'θenik] **1.** *adj.* nevrasteniye ait, nevrasteni...; **2.** *n.* sinir hastası, nevrastenik kimse; **neu.ritis** MED [njuə'raitis] *n.* sinir iltihabı; **neurol.o.gist** [_'rɔlədʒist] *n.* asabiyeci; **neu'rol.o.gy** *n.* nevroloji, sinirbilim; **neuro.path.ic** MED [_rəu'pæθik] **1.** *adj.* nevropatik; **2.** *n.* nevropat kimse; **neu.ro.sis** MED [_'rəusis] *n.* nevroz; **neu.rot.ic** [_'rɔtik] **1.** *adj.* nevrozlu, sinir hastalığı olan; evhamlı; **2.** *n.* nevrozlu kimse.

neu.ter ['njuːtə] **1.** *adj.* BOT, ZOO cinsiyetsiz; GR cinssiz; geçişsiz (*fiil*); **2.** *n.* cinsiyetsiz hayvan *veya* bitki; GR cinsiyet belirtmeyen kelime.

neu.tral ['njuːtrəl] **1.** ☐ yansız, tarafsız; CHEM nötr; belirli bir özelliği olmayan; rengi belirsiz; tarafsız ülkeye ait; MOT boşta (*vites*); **2.** *n.* tarafsız kimse *veya* ülke; boş vites; CHEM nötr; **neu.tral.i.ty** [_'træliti] *n.* tarafsızlık; **neu.tral.i.za.tion** [_trəlai'zeiʃən] *n.* yansız kılma; CHEM nötrleme; '**neu.tral.ize** *v/t.* etkisiz bırakmak; yansız kılmak; CHEM nötrlemek.

neu.tron PHYS ['njuːtrɔn] *n.* nötron.

né.vé MOUNT ['nevei] *n.* kar; karlı alan.

nev.er ['nevə] *adv.* asla, hiç bir zaman, hiç, katiyen; **~ so** hiç de öyle değil; **on**

the **~** *sl.* taksitle; *the* ☐-☐ (*Land*) hayal beldesi; '**nev.er'more** *adv.* asla, artık hiç, bundan böyle; **nev.er.the.less** [_ðə'les] *adv.* bununla beraber, mamafih, yine de.

new [njuː] *adj.* yeni; taze; acemi; yeni keşfedilmiş; görülmemiş, alışılmamış; '**~born 1.** *adj.* yeni doğmuş; **2.** *n.* yeni doğmuş bebek; '**new'com.er** *n.* yeni gelmiş kimse; **New Eng.land.er** kuzey Amerikalı; **new.fan.gled** ['_fæŋgld] *adj.* yeni çıkmış, yeni model; **new look** yeni moda; '**new.ly** *adv.* geçenlerde, yakınlarda, yeni; yeni bir şekilde; '**newly-weds** *n. pl.* yeni evliler; '**new.ness** *n.* yenilik.

news [njuːz] *n.* haber, havadis; *what's the* **~**? ne haber?, ne var ne yok?; *he is much in the* **~** F herkesin diline düştü; '**~a.gen.cy** *n.* haber ajansı; '**~a.gent** *n.* gazeteci; '**~boy** *n.* gazeteci çocuk; '**~butch.er** *Am. sl.* seyyar gazeteci; '**~cast** *n. radyo:* haber yayını; **~ cin.e.ma** aktualite filmleri gösteren sinema; '**~letter** *n.* sirküler, genelge; '**~monger** *n.* dedikoducu kimse; '**~pa.per** *n.* gazete; *attr.* gazete...; '**~print** *n.* gazete kâğıdı; '**~reel** *n.* film; aktualite filmi; '**~room** *n.* gazete bayii; *Am. gazete:* haber alma ve derleme bürosu; '**~stall**, *Am.* '**~stand** *n.* gazete tezgâhı; '**~vendor** *n.* gazete satıcısı, gazeteci; **news.y** ['njuːzi] *adj.* F haber (*veya* havadis) dolu (*mektup vs.*).

newt ZOO [njuːt] *n.* semender, su keleri.

New World ['njuː'wɔːld] *n.* Yeni dünya, Amerika.

new year ['njuː'jəː] *n.* yılbaşı; **~'s day** yılbaşı günü; **~'s eve** yılbaşı arifesi; **~'s gift** yılbaşı hediyesi.

next [nekst] **1.** *adj.* en yakın, yanı başındaki; bir sonraki; gelecek, önümüzdeki, ertesi; **~ but one** bir evvelki; **~ door** bitişik ev(deki); **~ door to** *fig.* hemen hemen, neredeyse; *the* **~** *of kin* en yakın akraba; **~ to** -e bitişik, -*in* yanın(d)a, -*den* sonra; F sıkı fıkı, içlidışlı; **~ to nothing** hemen hemen hiç; *what* **~**? başka?; **2.** *adv.* (ondan) sonra, daha sonra.

nib [nib] *n.* kalem ucu.

nib.ble ['nibl] *v/t. & v/i.* azar azar ısırmak; *a.* **~ at** kemirmek -*i*; *fig.* ilgi göstermek -*e*, iyice düşünmek -*i*.

nib.lick ['niblik] *n.* golf sopası.

nice ☐ [nais] güzel, hoş, sevimli; cazip; ince; iyi; kibar, nazik; titiz; *iro.* zor,

güç, kötü; ~ **and warm** sıcacık, oldukça
sıcak; '**nice.ly** adv. F iyi bir şekilde, çok
iyi, incelikle; '**nice.ness** n. incelik;
hoşluk, güzellik; **nice.ty** ['-siti] n. incelik, titizlik; doğruluk, kesinlik; güzellik, hoşluk; **to a** ~ tamı tamamına,
tam karar; **stand upon niceties**
ayrıntılar üzerinde durmak.

niche [nitʃ] n. duvarda hücre (veya
oyuk); fig. uygun yer.

Nick[1] [nik] n.: **Old** ~ şeytan.

nick[2] [-] **1.** n. çentik, kertik, diş; sl.
durum, sağlık; **in the (very)** ~ **of time**
tam zamanında; **2.** v/t. çentmek; kesmek; sl. aşırmak, yürütmek; sl. enselemek.

nick.el ['nikl] **1.** n. MIN nikel; Am. beş
sent; ~**-in-the-slot machine** Am. otomatik tevzi makinesi; **2.** v/t. nikel ile
kaplamak.

nick.el.o.de.on Am. [nikl'əudjən] n.
eskiden beş sente film gösterilen sinema; eskiden para ile çalınan otomatik
pikap.

nick-nack ['niknæk] = **knickknack**.

nick.name ['nikneim] **1.** n. takma isim,
lakap, takılmış ad; **2.** v/t. lakap takmak
-e.

nic.o.tine ['nikəti:n] n. nikotin.

nid-nod ['nidnɔd] v/i. başını
eğmek.

niece [ni:s] n. kız yeğen.

niff sl. [nif] n. leş gibi koku.

niff.y sl. ['nifi] adj. leş gibi kokan.

nif.ty Am. ['nifti] **1.** adj. şık; hoş; oturaklı (darbe); **2.** sl. kokmuş, leş gibi kokan; **2.** n. şık bş.

nig.gard ['nigəd] **1.** n. cimri (veya eli
sıkı) kimse; **2.** □ tamahkâr, cimri;
'**nig.gardli.ness** n. cimrilik; '**nig-
gard.ly** adj. & adv. cimri(ce), tamah-
kâr(ca).

nig.gle ['nigl] v/i. lüzumsuz ayrıntılarla zaman geçirmek, önemsiz şeylerle uğraşmak; '**nig.gling** adj. can
sıkıcı; dikkat isteyen (iş); gereksiz
ayrıntılı.

nigh obs. veya prov. [nai] = **near**.

night [nait] n. gece; akşam; **by** ~, **in the**
~, **at** ~ geceleyin; ~ **out** izinli gece;
make a ~ **of it** eğlenceli bir gece geçirmek; '~**-bell** n. gece kullanılan kapı zili;
'~**-bird** n. gece kuşu (a. fig.); '~**.cap** n.
yatarken giyilen bere; yatmadan önce
içilen alkollü içki; '~**-club** n. gece kulübü; '~**-dress** n. gecelik; '~**.fall** n. akşam
vakti; '~**-gown** = **night-dress**; **night-**

in.gale ORN ['-ıŋgeil] n. bülbül;
'**night.ly** adv. & adj. geceleyin (olan),
her gece (olan).

night...: '~**.mare** n. karabasan, kâbus;
'~**-school** n. gece okulu; '~**.shade** n.
BOT itüzümü, köpeküzümü; **deadly** ~
güzelavratotu, belladon; '~**-shirt** n. erkeklerin giydiği gecelik entarisi;
'~**.spot** n. Am. gece kulübü; '~**.stop**
n. geceleme, gece molası; '~**-stop** vb.
gecelemek; '~**-time** n. gece vakti;
'~**-walk.er** n. gece dolaşan kimse, uyurgezer; '~**-watch** n. gece nöbeti; gece
bekçisi; '~**.watch.man** n. gece bekçisi
(veya nöbetçisi); '~**.work** n. gece işi;
'**night.y** n. F gecelik.

ni.hil.ism ['naiilizəm] n. hiçlik, nihilizm; '**ni.hil.ist** n. nihilizm yanlısı.

nil [nıl] n. part. spor: sıfır, hiç.

nim.ble □ ['nimbl] çevik, tez, atik; keskin (zekâ); '**nim.ble.ness** n. çeviklik,
çabukluk.

nim.bus ['nimbəs] n. ayla, hale; yağmur
bulutu.

nim.i.ny-pim.i.ny ['nimini'pimini] adj.
titiz, kılı kırk yaran; çıtkırıldım; fazla
resmî.

Nim.rod ['nimrɔd] n. Nemrud; usta
avcı.

nin.com.poop F ['ninkəmpu:p] n. geri
zekâlı (veya ahmak) kimse.

nine [nain] **1.** adj. dokuz; ~ **day's wonder** kısa süre ilgi çekip sonra unutulan
şey; **2.** n. dokuz sayısı; **dressed up to
the** ~**s** F iki dirhem bir çekirdek;
'~**.fold** adj. & adv. dokuz misli; '~**.pins**
n. pl. kiy oyunu; **nine.teen** ['-'ti:n] adj.
on dokuz; **talk** ~ **to the dozen** car car
konuşmak; '**nine'teenth** adj. on dokuzuncu; on dokuzda bir; **nine.tieth**
['-tii0] **1.** adj. doksanıncı; doksanda
bir; **2.** n. doksanda bir kısım; '**nine.ty**
adj. doksan.

nin.ny F ['nini] n. ahmak (veya budala)
kimse.

ninth [nain0] **1.** adj. dokuzuncu; dokuzda bir; **2.** n. dokuzda bir kısım; '**ninth-
ly** adv. dokuzuncu olarak.

nip[1] [nip] **1.** n. çimdik; BOT ayaz; **2.** v/t.
çimdiklemek, kıstırmak; kesmek, bu-
damak; dondurmak, sızlatmak
(soğuk); zarar vermek -e; sl. aşırmak,
yürütmek; ~ **in the bud** dal budak sal-
madan yok etm., başlarken bastırmak;
suya düşürmek -i (plan vs.); v/i. hızlı
gitmek.

nip[2] [-] **1.** n. azıcık içki; **2.** v/t. azıcık içmek, yudumlamak (*içki*).

nip.per ['nipə] *n.* F kırpan *veya* kesen kimse *veya* şey; (**a pair of**) **~s** *pl.* kıskaç; F küçük çocuk (*part. erkek*).

nip.ple ['nipl] *n.* meme başı; şişe emziği; MEC nipel, emzik.

nip.py F ['nipi] *adj.* çevik, atik, çabuk; yakıcı, soğuk, dondurucu.

nir.va.na [niə'vɑːnə] *n.* *Budizm*: aşırı istek *ve* tutkulardan kurtularak erişilen mutluluk hali.

Ni.sei *Am.* ['ni'sei] *n.* (*a. pl.*) Amerika'-da doğup büyüyen Japon asıllı kimse.

Nis.sen hut ['nisn'hʌt] *n.* çelikten yapılmış yarım silindir biçiminde bina, baraka.

nit [nit] *n.* bit yumurtası, sirke.

ni.trate CHEM ['naitreit] *n.* nitrat.

ni.tre, ni.ter CHEM ['naitə] *n.* güherçile.

ni.tric ac.id CHEM ['naitrik'æsid] *n.* nitrik asit, kezzap.

ni.tro-chalk ['naitrəu'tʃɔːk] *n.* çim gübresi.

ni.tro.gen CHEM ['naitrədʒən] *n.* nitrojen, azot; **ni.trog.e.nous** [˳'trɒdʒinəs] *adj.* nitrojene ait, nitrojen…; azotlu.

ni.tro.glyc.er.in(e) CHEM ['naitrəu-glisə'riːn] *n.* nitrogliserin.

ni.trous CHEM ['naitrəs] *adj.* azota ait, azot gibi; azotlu.

nit.wit F ['nitwit] *n.* kuş, beyinli kimse; '**nit.wit.ted** *adj.* F kuş beyinli.

nix [nıks] *n.* küçük su perisi; **nix.ie** ['˳i] *n.* dişi su perisi.

no [nəu] **1.** *adj.* hiç (bir); **in ~ time** çarçabuk, derhal, hemencecik; **~ man's land** iki cephe arasındaki sahipsiz arazi; **~ one** hiç kimse; **2.** *adv.* hayır, yok, olmaz, öyle değil; **3.** *n.* yok yanıtı, hayır kelimesi; **noes** *pl.* bşe karşı çıkanlar.

nob[1] *sl.* [nɒb] *n.* baş, kafa; MEC topuz, tokmak.

nob[2] *sl.* [˳] *n.* asılzade, soylu.

nob.ble *sl.* ['nɒbl] *v/t.* kazanmasını önlemek (*yarış atı*); *-in* dikkatini çekmek; hile ile kazanmak.

nob.by *sl.* ['nɒbi] *adj.* fiyakalı, afili.

no.bil.i.ar.y [nəu'biliəri] *adj.* asılzadelere ait.

no.bil.i.ty [nəu'biliti] *n.* asalet, soyluluk, asılzadelik; asılzadeler sınıfı.

no.ble ['nəubl] **1.** ☐ asil, soylu; yüce gönüllü; heybetli, muhteşem, ulu, yüce; kimyasal değişiklik göstermeyen (*maden*); **2.** *n.* asılzade, soylu kimse; '**~.man** *n.* asılzade; '**~'mind.ed** *adj.* asil fikirli; '**no.ble.ness** *n.* asalet, soy-

luluk; '**no.blewom.an** *n.* soylu kadın.

no.bod.y ['nəubədi] **1.** *pron.* hiç kimse; **2.** *n.* bir hiç olan kimse.

no-brain.er F [nəu'breinə] *n.* çok kolay, apaçık bir şey; *the math test was a no-brainer* matematik sınavı çok kolaydı.

nock [nɒk] *n.* okun arka ucundaki kertik.

noc.tur.nal [nɒk'tɔːnl] *adj.* geceye ait, gece…; geceleyin olan; geceleyin yapılan; geceleri gezen.

noc.turne ['nɒktəːn] *n.* PAINT gece manzarası; MUS tatlı ve duygulu parça.

nod [nɒd] **1.** *v/i.* başını sallamak (*kabul ifade etmek için*); uyuklamak; hata yapmak; sallanmak; **~ding acquaintance** az tanıma (*veya* bilme), tanıdık(lık); pek tanımadık (*veya* sadece selamlaşılan) kimse; **~ off** uyuklamak; *v/t.* başını sallayarak belirtmek; **~ out** dışarıyı işaret etm.; **2.** *n.* baş sallama.

nod.dle F ['nɒdl] *n.* baş, kafa.

node [nəud] *n.* düğüm (*a.* BOT & AST); MED yumru, şiş.

nod.u.lar ['nɒdjulə] *adj.* yumru *veya* düğüme ait; yumrulu, düğümlü.

nod.ule ['nɒdjuːl] *n.* yumru, düğüm, boğum; şiş, bezecik.

No.el [nəu'el] *n.* Noel.

nog [nɒg] *n.* (içinde yumurta bulunan) alkollü içki; kuvvetli bira; takoz; **nog-gin** ['nɒgin] *n.* kafa, baş; ufak bir içki ölçüsü; '**nog.ging** *n.* ARCH duvar örme.

no.how F ['nəuhau] *adv.* asla, hiç bir suretle.

noil [nɒil] *n.* *dokumacılık*: tarak döküntüsü.

noise [nɒiz] **1.** *n.* gürültü, patırtı, ses, şamata, yaygara, velvele; parazit; **big ~** *part. Am.* F kodaman, önemli şahıs; **2.** *v/t.* **~ abroad** yaymak, duyurmak, söylemek.

noise.less ☐ ['nɒizlis] sessiz, gürültüsüz; '**noise.less.ness** *n.* sessizlik.

nois.i.ness ['nɒizinis] *n.* gürültü.

noi.some ['nɒisəm] *adj.* iğrenç, berbat; can sıkıcı; zararlı; '**noi.some.ness** *n.* iğrençlik; zararlılık.

nois.y ☐ ['nɒizi] gürültülü, sesli; gürültücü, yaygaracı.

no.mad ['nəumæd] *n.* göçebe kimse; **nomad.ic** [˳'mædik] *adj.* (**~ally**) göçebeye ait, göçebe…; göçebe gibi, yersiz yurtsuz; **no.mad.ize** ['˳mədaiz] *v/i.* göçebelik etm.

nom de plume

nom de plume [ˈnɔːmdəˈpluːm] *n.* yazarın takma adı.

no.men.cla.ture [nəuˈmenklətʃə] *n.* terminoloji.

nom.i.nal □ [ˈnɔminl] sözde; itibarî, saymaca; önemsiz; değersiz; çok düşük *(fiyat)*; GR isimle ilgili; nominal; ~ **val-ue** itibarî kıymet, nominal değer; **nom.i.nate** [ˈ_neit] *v/t.* atamak, görevlendirmek; aday göstermek; **nom.i-ˈna.tion** *n.* aday gösterme; atama, tayin; **in** ~ aday olarak; **nom.i.na.tive** GR [ˈ_nətiv] *n. a.* ~ **case** yalın hal; **no-m.i-na.tor** [ˈ_neitə] *n.* atayan kimse; **nom-i.nee** [_ˈniː] *n.* aday, namzet.

non [nɔn] *prefix* -siz, -sız, gayri-.

non-ac.cept.ance [ˈnɔnəkˈseptəns] *n.* ret, kabul etmeme.

non.age [ˈnəunidʒ] *n.* küçüklük, çocukluk, rüşte ermemiş olma.

non.a.ge.nar.i.an [nəunədʒiˈnɛəriən] *n.* doksanlık kimse.

non-ag.gres.sion [ˈnɔnəˈɡreʃən] *n.:* ~ **pact** saldırmazlık antlaşması.

non-al.co.hol.ic [ˈnɔnælkəˈhɔlik] *adj.* alkolsüz.

non-a.lign.ment POL [nɔnəˈlainmənt] *n.* müttefik olmama.

non-ap.pear.ance JUR [ˈnɔnəˈpiərəns] *n.* hazır bulunmama, gıyap.

non-at.tend.ance JUR [ˈnɔnəˈtendəns] *n.* katılmama, gıyap.

nonce [nɔns] *n.:* **for the** ~ şimdilik.

non.cha.lance [ˈnɔnʃələns] *n.* ilgisizlik, soğukkanlılık; **ˈnon.cha.lant** □ ilgisiz, soğuk, kayıtsız; soğukkanlı, sakin.

non.com MIL F [nɔnˈkɔm] *n.* erbaş.

non-com.mis.sioned [ˈnɔnkəˈmiʃ-ənd] *adj.* resmen görevli olmayan; asteğmenden aşağı rütbesi olan; ~ **offi-cer** MIL erbaş.

non-com.mit.tal [ˈnɔnkəˈmitl] *adj.* tarafsız, yansız; fikrini söylemeyen.

non-com.pli.ance [ˈnɔnkəmˈplaiəns] *n.* itaatsizlik *(with* -*e).*

non com.pos men.tis JUR [nɔnˈkɔm-pɔsˈmentis] *adj.* aklî dengesi bozuk, mümeyyiz olmayan.

non-con.duc.tor ELECT [ˈnɔnkən-dʌktə] *n.* yalıtkan madde.

non.con.form.ist [ˈnɔnkənˈfɔːmist] *n.* topluma uymayan kimse; Anglikan kilisesine bağlı olmayan kimse; **non-conˈform.ity** *n.* uymama, ayak uydurmama; ECCL kiliseye uymama.

non-de.liv.er.y [ˈnɔndiˈlivəri] *n.* ademiteslim, teslim etmeme.

non-de.nom.i.na.tion.al school [ˈnɔndinəmiˈneiʃənlˈskuːl] *n.* mezhep farkı gözetmeyen okul.

non.de.script [ˈnɔndiskript] **1.** *adj.* kolay tanımlanamaz, alelade; **2.** *n.* tanımlanamayan *(veya* alelade, sıradan) kimse.

none [nʌn] **1.** *pron.* hiç biri, hiç kimse; **2.** *adv.* hiç, asla, hiç bir suretle; ~ **the less** yine de, bununla birlikte.

non.en.ti.ty [nɔˈnentiti] *n.* önemsiz kimse; var olmayan *(veya* hayalî) şey; *fig.* hiçlik, yokluk.

non-es.sen.tial [ˈnɔniˈsenʃəl] **1.** *adj.* gereksiz, önemsiz; **2.** *n.* gereksizlik.

non-ex.ist.ence [ˈnɔniɡˈzistəns] *n.* yokluk, varolmayış; **ˈnon.exˈist.ent** *adj.* varolmayan.

non-fic.tion [ˈnɔnˈfikʃən] *n.* kurgusal olmayan düzyazı.

non-in.ter.fer.ence [ˈnɔnintəˈfiərəns], **non-in.ter.ven.tion** [ˈnɔnintəˈvenʃən] *n.* başka devletlerin işine karışmama politikası.

non-lad.der.ing [ˈnɔnˈlædəriŋ] *adj.* kaçmaz *(çorap).*

non-mem.ber [ˈnɔnˈmembə] *n.* üye olmayan kimse.

non-ob.serv.ance [ˈnɔnəbˈzəːvəns] *n.* uymama, çiğneme *(kural vs.).*

non.pa.reil [nɔnpəˈrel] *n.* eşsiz *(veya* emsalsiz) kimse *veya* şey; TYP altı puntoluk harf.

non-par.ti.san [nɔnˈpɑːtizæn] *adj.* partizan olmayan; tarafsız.

non-par.ty POL [ˈnɔnˈpɑːti] *adj.* partisiz.

non-pay.ment [ˈnɔnˈpeimənt] *n.* ödememe.

non-per.form.ance JUR [ˈnɔnpəˈfɔːm-əns] *n.* yerine getirmeme, yapmama.

non.plus [ˈnɔnˈplʌs] **1.** *n.* şaşkınlık, hayret; **at a** ~ şaşkınlık içinde; **2.** *v/t.* şaşırtmak; ~**sed** apışıp kalmış, şaşkın.

non-pro.lif.er.a.tion [ˈnɔnprəulifə-ˈreiʃən] *n.* nükleer silahların artması ve yayılmasını önleme; istenmeyen şeylerin yayılmasını önleme.

non-res.i.dent [ˈnɔnˈrezidənt] *adj.* görevli olduğu yerde oturmayan.

non.sense [ˈnɔnsəns] *n.* saçma, boş laf; aptalca davranış; **non.sen.si.cal** □ [_ˈsensikəl] saçma, abuk sabuk, ipe sapa gelmez.

non-skid [ˈnɔnˈskid] *adj.* kaymaz *(las-*

notable

tik).

non-smok.er ['nɔn'sməukə] *n.* sigara içmeyen kimse; sigara içilmeyen kompartıman.

non-stop ['nɔn'stɔp] *adj.* RAIL, AVIA doğru giden, aktarmasız, direkt; aralıksız.

non(e).such ['nʌnsʌtʃ] *n.* eşsiz (*veya* emsalsiz) kimse *veya* şey.

non.suit JUR ['nɔn'sjuːt] *n.* davanın reddi; davanın düşmesi.

non-U F ['nɔnjuː] *adj.* üst tabakaya ait olmayan.

non-un.ion [nɔn'juːnjən] *adj.* sendikaya ait olmayan, sendikasız; sendika kurallarına uymayan; sendikaları tanımayan.

noo.dle[1] F ['nuːdl] *n.* ahmak (*veya* sersem) kimse.

noo.dle[2] [ˍ] *n.* şehriye.

nook [nuk] *n.* bucak, köşe.

noon [nuːn] **1.** *n.* öğle (vakti); **2.** *adj.* öğle vaktinde olan, öğle...; '~.day, '~.tide = noon.

noose [nuːs] **1.** *n.* ilmik; **2.** *v/t.* ilmikle tutmak; ilmiklemek.

nope *Am.* F [nəup] *int.* yok!, hayır!, olmaz!

nor [nɔː] *cj.* ne de, ne; ~ do I ben de (*olumsuz anlamda*).

Nor.folk jack.et ['nɔːfək'dʒækit] *n.* bir çeşit kuşaklı erkek ceketi.

norm [nɔːm] *n.* kural, norm, örnek; ortalama; 'nor.mal **1.** □ normal; düzgün, doğal, uygun; düzgülü; MATH dikey; ~ school öğretmen okulu; **2.** *n.* normal, standart; MATH dikey; 'nor.mal.ize *v/t.* & *v/i.* normalleş(tir)mek, normale dön(dür)mek.

Nor.man ['nɔːmən] **1.** *n.* Normandiyalı kimse; Normandiyalıların konuştuğu Fransızca lehçe; **2.** *adj.* Normandiya *veya* Normandiyalılara ait.

Norse [nɔːs] **1.** *adj.* İskandinavya'ya *veya* İskandinavya dillerine ait; **2.** *n.* İskandinavya dili; Norveç dili; 'Norse.man *n.* İskandinavyalı; Norveçli.

north [nɔːθ] **1.** *n.* kuzey; **2.** *adj.* kuzey...; kuzeye bakan; kuzeyden gelen *veya* esen; '~'east **1.** *n.* kuzeydoğu; **2.** *adj. a.* ~'east.ern kuzeydoğuda olan; kuzeydoğudan gelen; north.er.ly ['ˍðəli] *adj.* & *adv.* kuzeye doğru (olan); kuzeyden (esen) kuzeydeki; north.ern ['ˍðən] *adj.* kuzeye ait, kuzey...; kuzeyde olan, kuzeyli; 'north.ern.er *n.*

kuzeyli kimse; ♀ *Am.* kuzey eyaletlerinde oturan kimse; 'north.ern.most *adj.* en kuzeydeki; 'northing ['ˍθiŋ] *n.* NAUT kuzey rotası; AST kuzeye doğru katedilen mesafe; 'North.man *n.* İskandinavyalı; north.ward(.ly) ['ˍwəd(li)] *adj.* & *adv.*, north.wards ['ˍwədz] *adv.* kuzeye doğru (olan), kuzeyden (esen).

north...: '~'west **1.** *n.* kuzeybatı; **2.** *adj. a.* '~'west.ern, '~'west.er.ly kuzeye ait, kuzey...; kuzeyden gelen; karayel yönünden.

Nor.we.gian [nɔː'wiːdʒən] **1.** *adj.* Norveçli, Norveç'e ait; **2.** *n.* Norveçli; Norveç dili.

nose [nəuz] **1.** *n.* burun; koklama duyusu; uç; NAUT pruva; *cut off one's ~ to spite one's face* nispet olsun diye kendi çıkarını zedelemek, gâvura kızıp oruç bozmak; *pay through the ~* avuç dolusu para ödemek, ateş pahasına almak; *poke veya push veya thrust one's ~ into s.th.* bşe burnunu sokmak; *turn one's ~ up at -i* hor görmek, -e burun kıvırmak; *put s.o.'s ~ out of joint* b-nin pabucunu dama atmak; *b-nin* ayağını kaydırmak; **2.** *v/t. a.* ~ out koklayarak bulmak, arayıp bulmak -i; -in kokusunu almak; burunla itmek; kıl payı kazanmak; ~ one's way dikkatle ilerlemek; *v/t.* koklamak (*after, for -i*); '~-bag *n.* atın yem torbası; '~-band *n.* yuların atın burnu üzerinden geçen kısmı; nosed *comb.* ...burunlu.

nose...: '~-dive *n.* AVIA pike; '~-gay *n.* çiçek demeti; '~-heav.y *adj.* AVIA pike yapmaya çalışan; '~-o.ver *n.* AVIA burun üstüne çakılma; '~-ring *n.* burun halkası.

nos.ing ARCH ['nəuziŋ] *n.* basamak çıkıntısı.

nos.tal.gi.a [nɔs'tældʒiə] *n.* özlem; vatan (*veya* sıla) hasreti; nos'tal.gic [ˍdʒik] *adj.* sıla hasreti kabilinden.

nos.tril ['nɔstril] *n.* burun deliği.

nos.trum ['nɔstrəm] *n.* kocakarı ilâcı; her derde deva.

nos.y ['nəuzi] **1.** *adj.* meraklı; *b.s.* başkasının işine burnunu sokan; ♀ *Parker* = **2.** *n.* başkasının işine burnunu sokan kimse.

not [nɔt] *adv.* değil, olmayan; ~ at all asla, hiç; birşey değil, rica ederim.

no.ta.bil.i.ty [nəutə'biliti] *n.* şöhret; şöhretli kimse; 'no.ta.ble **1.** □ dikkate değer; tanınmış, meşhur; göze çarpan; **2.** *n.* tanınmış (*veya* meşhur) kimse; **'nota.bly** *adv.* dikkate değer şekilde; özellikle.

no.tar.i.al ☐ [nəu'tɛəriəl] notere ait, noter…; **no.ta.ry** ['nəutəri] *n. oft. public ~** noter.

no.ta.tion [nəu'teiʃən] *n.* not; MATH rakamlar ve işaretler sistemi; MUS notalar ile işaretler sistemi; kayıt.

notch [nɔtʃ] **1.** *n.* çentik, kertik; MEC diş, yiv; *Am.* dar dağ geçidi; derece, basamak; **2.** *v/t.* çentmek, kertmek; **~ up** kazanmak, kırmak (*rekor vs.*).

note [nəut] **1.** *n.* not, işaret; MUS, POL nota; COM senet, pusula; önem; şöhret, itibar; dikkat; banknot; **take ~** -*e* dikkat etm., önem vermek; **strike the right ~** lafı gediğine oturtmak; **strike** *veya* **sound a false ~** *k-ni* gözden düşürecek *bş* yapmak *veya* söylemek; **2.** *v/t.* kaydetmek; *a.* **~ down** deftere yazmak, not almak; dikkat etm., önem vermek; **'~.book** *n.* not defteri, defter; **'not.ed** *adj.* ünlü, meşhur, tanınmış (*for ile*, **as** *olarak*); **~ly** özellikle, bilhassa; **'note-pa.per** *n.* mektup kâğıdı; **'note-wor.thy** *adj.* önemli, dikkate değer.

noth.ing ['nʌθiŋ] **1.** *n.* hiç bir şey; sıfır; önemsiz kimse *veya* şey; hiçlik, yokluk; **for ~** ücretsiz, parasız, bedava; boş yere; **good for ~** hayırsız, hiç bir işe yaramaz; **come** (**bring**) **to ~** boşa çık(ar)mak, suya düş(ür)mek; **go for ~** boşa gitmek; **make ~ of** -*i* önemsememek; *-i* anlayamamak; **I can make ~ of it** anlıyorsam arap olayım; **say ~ of** bile değil, şöyle dursun; **think ~ of** -*i* önemsememek; **2.** *adv.* hiç (bir suretle), asla, katiyen; **'noth.ing.ness** *n.* yokluk, hiçlik; boşluk, anlamsızlık, önemsizlik.

no.tice ['nəutis] **1.** *n.* haber; ilân, ihbarname; uyarı, ikaz, ihtar; önemseme, dikkat; eleştiri; saygı; **at short ~** kısa ihbar süreli, kısa mühletli; **give ~** *bş* önceden haber vermek; **give a week's ~** bir hafta önceden bildirmek; **take ~ of** -*i* dikkate almak, -*e* aldırış etm.; **until further ~** yeni bir habere kadar; **without ~** haber (*veya* mühlet) vermeden, müddetsiz; **2.** *v/t.* farkına varmak -*in*, farketmek -*i*, görmek -*i*; dikkat etm. -*e*; önem vermek -*e*; saygı göstermek -*e*; eleştirmek (*kitap*); **'no.tice.a.ble** ☐ görülebilir, farkedilir; önemsenmeye değer; **'no.tice-board** *n.* ilân tah-

tası.

no.ti.fi.a.ble ['nəutifaiəbl] *adj.* bildirilmesi zorunlu; **no.ti.fi.ca.tion** [˳-fi'keiʃən] *n.* bildirme; ihbar.

no.ti.fy ['nəutifai] *v/t.* ilân etm.; bildirmek.

no.tion ['nəuʃən] *n.* sanı, zan; fikir, düşünce, bilgi; inanç; **~s** *pl. Am.* tuhafiye; **have no ~ of** …hakkında bir fikri olmamak; **'no.tion.al** ☐ hayalî, soyut, kuramsal; itibarî (*değer*).

no.to.ri.e.ty [nəutə'raiəti] *n.* kötü şöhret; adı çıkmışlık; **no.to.ri.ous** ☐ [˳-'tɔːriəs] adı çıkmış, dile düşmüş (*for -den dolayı, için*).

not.with.stand.ing [nɔtwið'stændiŋ] **1.** *prp.* -*e* rağmen, yine de; **2.** *adv.* gerçi, her ne kadar, buna rağmen; **3.** *cj.* **~ that** …rağmen, …ise de.

nou.gat ['nuːgɑː] *n.* koz helvası.

nought *part.* MATH [nɔːt] *n.* sıfır; hiç.

noun GR [naun] *n.* isim, ad.

nour.ish ['nʌriʃ] *v/t.* beslemek (*a. fig.*), yedirmek; gübrelemek (*toprak*); *fig.* desteklemek; **'nour.ish.ing** *adj.* besleyici; **'nour.ish.ment** *n.* yemek, gıda; besle(n)me.

nous [naus] *n.* akıl, zekâ; sebep; sağduyu; idrak, anlayış.

nov.el ['nɔvəl] **1.** *adj.* yeni, tuhaf, acayip, alışılmamış; **2.** *n.* roman; **short ~** = **novel.ette** [nɔvə'let] *n.* kısa roman; **'nov.el.ist** *n.* romancı, roman yazarı; **nov.el.ty** ['nɔvəlti] *n.* yenilik; yeni *bş.*

No.vem.ber [nəu'vembə] *n.* kasım (ayı).

nov.ice ['nɔvis] *n.* çırak; acemi kimse; ECCL rahip *veya* rahibe adayı.

no.vi.ci.ate, no.vi.ti.ate [nəu'viʃiit] *n.* çıraklık (*veya* acemilik) devresi; papaz adaylığı devresi.

now [nau] **1.** *adv.* şimdi, bu anda; işte; **by ~** şimdiye dek; **just ~** demin(cek), hemen şimdi; **before ~** bundan önce; **~ and again, ~ and then** arasıra, bazen, zaman zaman; **2.** *cj. a.* **~ that** mademki, artık; **3.** *n.* şu an, şimdiki zaman.

now.a.day ['nauədei] *adj.* bugünkü, şimdiki; **now.a.days** ['˳-z] *adv.* bugünlerde, şimdi, günümüzde.

no.way(s) F ['nəuwei(z)] *adv.* hiç su retle, asla, olmaz.

no.where ['nəuwɛə] *adv.* hiçbir yer(-d)e.

no.wise ['nəuwaiz] *adv.* hiç su surette, asla.

nox.ious ☐ ['nɔkʃəs] zararlı.

noz.zle ['nɔzl] *n.* MEC ağızlık, meme, burun; hortum başı.

nu.ance [nju:'ã:ns] *n.* nüans, ince fark.

nub [nʌb] *n.* yumru, topak; *Am.* F öz, püf noktası.

nu.bile ['nju:bail] *adj.* evlenecek yaşa gelmiş, gelinlik (*kız*).

nu.cle.ar ['nju:kliə] *adj.* nükleer...; ~ *disintegration* çekirdek dağılması; ~ *physics* sg. nükleer fizik; ~ *pile* atom reaktörü; ~ *power plant* nükleer elektrik santralı; ~ *research* nükleer araştırma; ~ *station* nükleer elektrik santralı; **nucle.on** PHYS ['-kliɔn] *n.* nükleon; **nu.cleus** ['-kliəs] *n., pl. a.* **nu.cle.i** ['-kliai] çekirdek, cevher, öz.

nude [nju:d] **1.** *adj.* çıplak; **2.** *n.* çıplak insan vücudu; PAINT nüd; *study from the* ~ çıplak modelle çalışma.

nudge F [nʌdʒ] **1.** *v/t.* dirsek ile dürtmek; **2.** *n.* dürtme.

nud.ism ['nju:dizəm] *n.* çıplak dolaşma; '**nud.ist** *n.* çıplak kimse; *attr.* çıplaklar... (*kampı*); '**nu.di.ty** *n.* çıplaklık.

nu.ga.to.ry ['nju:gətəri] *adj.* önemsiz, değersiz, ufak tefek, boş; geçersiz.

nug.get ['nʌgit] *n.* (*part. altın*) külçe.

nui.sance ['nju:sns] *n.* sıkıcı şey *veya* kimse; sıkıntı, baş belâsı, dert; *fig.* yük, külfet; *what a* ~*!* tüh be!, işe bak!, hay Allah!; *commit no* ~*!* çöp dökmeyiniz!, işemek (*veya* pislemek) yasaktır!; *make o.s. veya be a* ~ can sıkıcı olm.

null [nʌl] *adj.* JUR & *fig.* etkisiz, değersiz; ~ *and void* hükümsüz, geçersiz; **nul.li.fica.tion** [nʌlifi'keiʃən] *n.* hükümsüz kılma; **nul.li.fy** ['-fai] *v/t.* hükümsüz kılmak; etkisiz bırakmak; '**nul.li.ty** *n.* hükümsüzlük; iptal; *fig.* hiç.

numb [nʌm] **1.** *adj.* uyuşuk, uyuşmuş (*with -den*); duygusuz, hissiz; **2.** *v/t.* uyuşturmak; azaltmak (*acı*); ~*ed* uyuşmuş.

num.ber ['nʌmbə] **1.** *n.* sayı, adet, numara, rakam; miktar; nüsha, sayı; ~*s* *pl.* MATH aritmetik; ~*s* *pl. poet.* şiir; MUS parça; *your* ~ *is up* işin bitik, suyun kaynadı, hapı yuttun, ayvayı yedin; *without* ~ sayısız, hesapsız; *in* ~ sayıca; **2.** *v/t.* saymak; numara koymak *-e*, numaralamak; hesaplamak; kapsamak, katmak; ~ *among*, ~ *in*, ~ *with* katmak, saymak; '**num.ber.less** *adj.* sayısız, pek çok; **number one** F insanın

kendi çıkarı; bir numaralı kimse; en önemli; *look after* ~ kendi çıkarını düşünmek; '**num.ber-plate** *n.* MOT plaka.

numb.ness ['nʌmnis] *n.* uyuşukluk, duygusuzluk.

nu.mer.a.ble ['nju:mərəbl] *adj.* sayılabilir; '**nu.mer.al 1.** *adj.* sayıya ait, sayı...; sayı yerini tutan; **2.** *n.* sayı, rakam, adet; **nu.mer'a.tion** *n.* numaralama, sayma; '**nu.mer.a.tor** *n.* MATH pay; sayıcı.

nu.mer.i.cal ☐ [nju:'merikəl] sayıya ait, sayı...

nu.mer.ous ☐ ['nju:mərəs] birçok, sayısız, dünya kadar, bir hayli; '**nu-mer.ousness** *n.* çokluk.

nu.mis.mat.ic [nju:miz'mætik] *adj.* (~*ally*) paraya ait, para...; **nu.mis-'mat.ics** *n.* mst sg. para ve madalya ilmi; **nu'mis.ma.tist** [-mətist] *n.* para uzmanı.

num.skull F ['nʌmskʌl] *n.* kalın kafalı (*veya* mankafa) kimse.

nun [nʌn] *n.* rahibe; ORN mavi iskete kuşu.

nun.ci.a.ture ECCL ['nʌnʃjətʃə] *n.* papalık elçisinin görev süresi; **nun.ci.o** ECCL ['-ʃiəu] *n.* papalık elçisi.

nun.ner.y ['nʌnəri] *n.* rahibe manastırı.

nup.tial ['nʌpʃəl] **1.** *adj.* evlenmeye *veya* düğüne ait; **2.** *n.* ~*s* *pl.* düğün, nikâh.

nurse [nə:s] **1.** *n.* hemşire, hastabakıcı; *a.* *wet* ~ sütnine; dadı; *at* ~ bakılmakta; *put out to* ~ bakmak; emzirmek; **2.** *v/t.* & *v/i.* emzirmek; beslemek; bakmak *-e*; iyileştirmek; hastabakıcılık yapmak; ~ *a cold* soğukalgınlığını tedavi etm.; '~*-maid* *n.* dadı.

nurs.er.y ['nə:sri] *n.* çocuk odası; AGR fidanlık; ~ *school* anaokulu; '~*.man* *n.* fidanlık bahçıvanı; '~*-rhymes* *n. pl.* çocuk şiirleri *veya* şarkıları; ~ *slopes* *pl. kayak:* yeni öğrenenler için yamaçlar.

nurs.ing ['nə:siŋ] *n.* hastabakıcılık, hemşirelik; '~*-bot.tle* *n.* biberon; '~*-home* *n.* özel sağlık yurdu.

nurs.ling ['nə:sliŋ] *n.* süt çocuğu.

nur.ture ['nə:tʃə] **1.** *n.* büyütme; terbiye; eğitim; **2.** *v/t. a.* ~ *up* büyütmek, yetiştirmek; *fig.* eğitmek, geliştirmek.

nut [nʌt] **1.** *n.* fındık, ceviz; MEC vida somunu; *sl.* baş, kafa; *sl.* F *pl.* deli, çılgın, kaçık; *that is* ~*s* *to veya* for him *sl.* onun için deli olur; *be* ~*s on* *sl.* -*e* abayı yakmak, -*in* delisi olm.; *drive* ~*s* *sl.*

çıldırtmak; **go ~s** sl. keçileri kaçırmak;
2. v/i. **go ~ting** fındık veya ceviz toplamak.
nu.ta.tion AST [nju:'teiʃən] n. nütasyon,
üğrüm.
nut.crack.er ['nʌtkrækə] n., mst (**a pair
of**) **~s** pl. fındıkkıran; '**nut-gall** n. meşe
mazısı; '**nut-house** n. sl. tımarhane;
nut.meg ['-meg] n. ufak hindistancevizi ağacı.
nu.tri.a ['nju:triə] n. kunduz (kürkü).
nu.tri.ent ['nju:triənt] **1.** adj. besleyici...; gıdalı...; **2.** n. besin, gıda; '**nu.tri-
ment** n. gıda, besin, yemek.
nu.tri.tion [nju:'triʃən] n. besle(n)me;

yiyecek, gıda; **nu'tri.tious** □ besinli,
besleyici...; **nu'tri.tious.ness** n. besle-
yicilik.
nu.tri.tive □ ['nju:tritiv] = **nutritious.**
nut.shell ['nʌtʃel] n. fındık kabuğu; **in a
~** kısaca, bir iki kelime ile; '**nut.ting** s.
nut 2.; **nut.ty** ['nʌti] adj. fındık veya
ceviz tadında; cevizli veya fındıklı; sl.
çatlak, kaçık, deli.
nuz.zle ['nʌzl] vb. burun ile itmek veya
dokunmak, burun sürtmek; a. **~ o.s.**
sokulmak.
ny.lon ['nailən] n. naylon; **~s** pl. naylon
çorap.
nymph [nimf] n. peri.

O

o [əu] **1.** int. o!, ya!; **2.** n. TELEPH sıfır.
oaf [əuf] n. budala (veya ahmak) kimse,
kaba adam; '**oaf.ish** adj. kaba, sersem,
budala.
oak [əuk] **1.** n. meşe ağacı; meşe odunu;
s. **sport**; **2.** adj. meşe...; '**~ap.ple,
'~gall** n. meşe mazı; '**oak.en** adj. meşe-
den yapılmış, meşe...
oa.kum ['əukəm] n. üstüpü.
oar [ɔ:] **1.** n. kürek; F kürekçi; **pull a
good ~** iyi bir kürekçi olm.; **put in
one's ~** F burnunu sokmak; **rest on
one's ~s** işleri yavaşlatmak, bir süre
dinlenmek; **2.** vb. kürek çekmek;
oared [ɔ:d] adj. kürekli...; **oars.man**
['ɔ:zmən] n. kürekçi; '**oars.man.ship**
n. kürekçilik; '**oars.woman** n. kadın
kürekçi.
o.a.sis [əu'eisis] n., pl. **o'a.ses** [-si:z]
vaha.
oast [əust] n. şerbetçiotu kurutma
fırını.
oat [əut] n. mst **~s** pl. yulaf (tanesi); **feel
one's ~s** Am. F k-ni zinde hissetmek;
k-ni beğenmek; **sow one's wild ~s**
gençlikte çılgınlık yapmak; '**oat.en**
adj. yulaftan yapılmış, yulaf...
oath [əuθ] n., pl. **oaths** [əuðz] yemin,
ant; b.s. küfür, lânet; **administer** veya
tender an ~ to s.o., **put s.o. to** veya on
his ~ b-ne yemin ettirmek, ant içirmek;
bind by ~ yeminle bağlamak; **on ~** yeminli, yemin etmiş; **take** veya **make** veya **swear an ~** yemin etm., ant içmek
(**on, to** üzerine).
oat.meal ['əutmi:l] n. yulaf ezmesi, yu-

laf unu.
ob.du.ra.cy ['ɔbdjurəsi] n. inatçılık,
sertlik; **ob.du.rate** □ ['-rit] inatçı, katı
kalpli; sert, kırıcı.
o.be.di.ence [ə'bi:djəns] n. itaat (etme), söz dinleme, boyun eğme; **in ~
to** -e itaat ederek; **o'be.di.ent** □ itaatli,
söz dinleyen, yumuşak başlı, uysal.
o.bei.sance [əu'beisəns] n. hürmetle
eğilme; hürmet, saygı; **do** veya **make**
veya **pay ~** hürmet etm., saygı göstermek.
ob.e.lisk ['ɔbilisk] n. dikilitaş, abide;
TYP başvurma işareti.
o.bese □ [əu'bi:s] çok şişman, şişko;
o'bese.ness, o'bes.i.ty n. şişmanlık.
o.bey [ə'bei] v/t. itaat etm. -e, boyun
eğmek -e; yerine getirmek; v/i. denileni
yapmak, söz dinlemek.
ob.fus.cate fig. ['ɔbfʌskeit] v/t. şaşırtmak; karartmak.
o.bit.u.ar.y [ə'bitjuəri] **1.** n. ölüm ilânı;
anma yazısı; **2.** adj. b-nin ölümüne ait,
ölüm...; **~ notice** ölüm ilânı.
ob.ject 1. ['ɔbdʒikt] n. şey, madde, nesne, obje; fig. amaç, hedef, gaye; GR nesne; komik veya acayip kimse veya şey;
what an ~ you look! ne komik görünü-
yorsun!; **salary no ~** ücret söz konusu
değildir; **2.** [əb'dʒekt] v/t. itiraz etm.
(**to** -e); v/i. razı olmamak, itiraz etm.
(**to** -e), karşı gelmek (**to** -e); **~-glass**
OPT ['ɔbdʒiktglɑ:s] n. objektif.
ob.jec.tion [əb'dʒekʃən] n. itiraz; kusur, mahzur; **there is no ~ (to it)**
(ona) itiraz yok; **ob'jec.tion.a.ble** □

[-ʃnəbl] itiraz edilebilir; hoşa gitmeyen, tatsız (*söz*).

ob.jec.tive [əb'dʒektiv] **1.** □ objektif;
gerçek; tarafsız; nesnel; **2.** *n.* amaç, gaye, hedef (*a.* MIL.); OPT mercek, objektif; *a.* ~ *case* GR ismin -i hali; **ob'jec-
tive.ness**, **ob.jec'tiv.i.ty** *n.* tarafsızlık.

ob.ject...: '~**-lens** *n.* OPT objektif, mercek; '~**.less** □ gayesiz, amaçsız;
'~**-les.son** *n.* uygulamalı ders; *fig.* ibret, ders; '~**.teach.ing** *n.* uygulamalı
öğretim; **ob.jector** [əb'dʒektə] *n.* itirazcı, aleyhtar, muhalif; *s.* ***conscientious.***

ob.jur.gate ['ɔbdʒɜːgeit] *v/t.* azarlamak, paylamak, haşlamak; **ob.jur'ga-
tion** *n.* azarlama, paylama, haşlama;
ob'jur.gato.ry [-gətəri] *adj.* azarlayıcı, paylayıcı.

ob.late □ ['ɔbleit] MATH kutupları yassı-
laşmış; '**ob.late.ness** *n.* yassılık.

ob.la.tion [əu'bleiʃən] *n.* adak.

ob.li.gate □ *fig.* ['ɔbligeit] *v/t.* zorlamak, mecbur etm., zorunda bırakmak;
ob.li'ga.tion *n.* mecburiyet, zorunluluk, yüküm, ödev, görev, vazife; senet,
borç; ***be under (an)~ to s.o.*** *b-ne* minnettar olm., müteşekkir olm.; ***be un-
der~ to*** *inf. -meğe* yükümlü olm.; **ob-
lig.a.to.ry** □ ['-gətəri] mecburî, gerekli, zorunlu (***on** için*).

o.blige [ə'blaidʒ] *v/t.* zorunlu kılmak,
zorlamak, mecbur etm.; minnettar
kılmak; memnun etm.; ~ ***s.o.*** *b-ni*
memnun etm., *b-ne* iyilikte bulunmak;
~ ***the company with*** beraberindekile-
rin eğlencesine ...ile katkıda bulunmak; ***be~d*** minnettar olm., müteşekkir olm.; mecbur olm., zorunlu olm.
(***to*** *inf. -meğe*); ***much~d*** çok minnettar, müteşekkir; *v/i.* ~ ***with a song*** F
eğlenceye bir şarkı ile katkısı olm.;
please~ with an early reply erken ve-
receğiniz cevap bizi minnettar kıla-
caktır; **ob.li.gee** [ɔbli'dʒiː] *n.* alacaklı;
o.blig.ing □ [ə'blaidʒiŋ] nazik,
yardımsever, hoş, sevimli, tatlı;
o'blig.ing.ness *n.* yardımseverlik, nezaket; **ob.li.gor** [ɔbli'gɔː] *n.* borçlu.

ob.lique □ [ə'bliːk] eğri, eğik, meyilli;
dolaylı, ima yollu; GR hal; ~ ***case*** ismin
hitap ve yalın halinden başka herhangi
bir hali; **ob'lique.ness**, **ob.liq.ui.ty**
[ə'blikwiti] *n.* meyil, eğilim, eğiklik;
ahlâksızlık, yoldan çıkma.

ob.lit.er.ate [ə'blitəreit] *v/t.* silmek,
yok etm., bozmak, gidermek; *fig.* tah-

rip etm., mahvetmek, harap etm.; **ob-
lit.er'a.tion** *n.* yok etme, silme; mah-
vetme.

ob.liv.i.on [ə'bliviən] *n.* unut(ul)ma;
POL af; bilinçsizlik, farkında olmama;
ob'livi.ous □ unutkan; bilinçsiz, habersiz; ***be~ of*** *-i* unutmak; *-den* haberi
olmamak; ***be~ to*** *-i* önemsememek,
nazarı dikkate almamak.

ob.long ['ɔblɔŋ] **1.** *adj.* dikdörtgen şeklinde, boyu eninden fazla; **2.** *n.* dikdörtgen.

ob.lo.quy ['ɔbləkwi] *n.* kötüleme, kınama, iftira etme, yerme, küfretme.

ob.nox.ious □ [əb'nɔkʃəs] iğrenç, tiksindirici; **ob'nox.ious.ness** *n.* iğrençlik, çirkinlik, tiksindiricilik.

o.boe MUS ['əubəu] *n.* obua.

ob.scene □ [əb'siːn] açık saçık, müstehcen; tiksindirici, iğrenç; ağıza alınmaz (*söz*); **ob'scen.i.ty** [-niti] *n.* açık
saçıklık, müstehcenlik; açık saçık söz.

ob.scu.ra.tion [əbskjuə'reiʃən] *n.* ka-
rar(t)ma; **ob.scure** [əb'skjuə] **1.** □
çapraşık; *fig.* belirsiz, şüpheli, anlaşılmaz; karanlık, bulutlu; saklı, gizli;
tanınmamış, bilinmeyen; **2.** *v/t.* karartmak; örtmek, saklamak, gizlemek;
ob'scu.ri.ty *n.* çapraşıklık; *fig.* belirsizlik.

ob.se.quies ['ɔbsikwiz] *n. pl.* cenaze
törenleri.

ob.se.qui.ous □ [əb'siːkwiəs] dalkavukluk eden, yağcılık eden, aşırı itaatli
(***to** -e*); **ob'se.qui.ous.ness** *n.* dalkavukluk.

ob.serv.a.ble □ [əb'zɜːvəbl] görünür,
farkedilir; ölçülür; izlenebilir; izlen-
meye değer, incelenmeye değer; **ob-
'serv.ance** *n.* yerine getirme, yapma;
görenek; âdet; tören, usul; **ob'serv.ant**
□ dikkatli, dikkat eden (***of** -e*); itaatli,
uyan, riayetkâr (***of** -e*); ***be~ of the
rules*** kurallara uymak; **ob.ser.va.tion**
[ɔbzə'veiʃən] *n.* gözetleme; dikkatli
bakma, inceleme; gözlem, rasat; fikir,
yorum; *attr.* gözetleme...; inceleme...;
~ ***car*** RAIL geniş pencereli vagon; ~
post topçu gözleme yeri; **ob.serv.a-
to.ry** [əb'zɜːvətri] *n.* rasathane, gözlemevi; **ob'serve** *v/t.* gözlemek; *fig.* yerine getirmek, uymak, itaat etm. (*kural*); incelemek; kutlamak; ileri sürmek, belirtmek; *v/i.* dikkat etm.; gözlem yapmak; fikrini söylemek (***on**
hakkında*); **ob'serv.er** *n.* gözleyen
kimse, gözlemci, itaat eden kimse;

toplantıya gözlemci olarak katılan temsilci.

ob.sess [əb'ses] *v/t*. musallat olm. *-e*, tedirgin etm. *-i*; meşgul etm. (*zihin*); **~ed by** *veya* **with** musallat *-e*; tedirgin *-den*, endişeli *-den*, kafayı takmış *-e*; **ob.session** [əb'seʃən] *n*. kafayı meşgul eden düşünce; sürekli endişe; sabit fikir; musallat fikir.

ob.sid.i.an MIN [əb'sidiən] *n*. koyu renkli volkanik cam.

ob.so.les.cence [əbsə'lesns] *n*. eskime, demode olma, kullanılmama; **obso'lescent** *adj*. eskiyen, demode olan, modası geçmekte olan, az kullanılan.

ob.so.lete ['əbsəliːt] *adj*. eskimiş, kullanılmayan, modası geçmiş, demode; BIOL eskilerine oranla az gelişmiş.

ob.sta.cle ['əbstəkl] *n*. engel, mâni; **~ race** engelli yarış.

ob.stet.ric [əb'stetrik], **ob'stet.ri.cal** *adj*. MED doğum *veya* gebeliğe ait, çocuk doğum...; gebelik...; **ob.ste.tri.cian** [‿'triʃən] *n*. doğum mütehassısı; **ob'stet.rics** [‿triks] *n. mst sg*. gebelik *veya* doğumla uğraşan tıp dalı.

ob.sti.na.cy ['əbstinəsi] *n*. inatçılık, dik başlılık; **ob.sti.nate** □ ['‿nit] inatçı, dik kafalı, söz dinlemez; yenmesi güç, direnci kırılmaz (*fig. hastalık*).

ob.strep.er.ous □ [əb'strepərəs] gürültücü, şamatacı, yaygaracı; ele avuca sığmaz, haylaz.

ob.struct [əb'strʌkt] *v/t*. tıkamak, kapamak *-i*; engel olm., mâni olm. *-e*; zorlaştırmak *-i*; **ob'struc.tion** *n*. engel, mâni(a), set; blokaj; PARL engelleme; **ob'struc.tive** □ [‿tiv] engelleyici (**of** *-i*).

ob.tain [əb'tein] *v/t*. bulmak, almak, ele geçirmek, elde etm.; *v/i*. geçerli olm., süregelmek, yerleşmiş olm. (*gelenek*); **ob'tain.a.ble** *adj*. bulunabilir, elde edilebilir; COM satın alınabilir; **ob'tainment** *n*. elde etme, bulma, alma.

ob.trude [əb'truːd] *v/t*. zorla kabul ettirmek (**on** *-i*); *v/i*. k-ni zorla kabul ettirmek; **ob'tru.sion** [‿ʒən] *n*. k-ni zorla kabul ettirme; **ob'tru.sive** □ [‿siv] k-ni zorla kabul ettiren, sokulup sıkıntı veren, yılışık.

ob.tu.rate ['əbtjuəreit] *v/t*. engellemek, mâni olm., kapamak, tıkamak; **'ob.tu.rator** *n*. engelleyen kimse *veya* şey, tıkayıcı şey.

ob.tuse □ [əb'tjuːs] keskin olmayan,

kör, küt; MATH geniş (*açı*); *fig*. kalın kafalı, aptal, bön; duygusuz; **ob'tuseness** *n*. duygusuzluk; *fig*. bönlük, aptallık.

ob.verse ['əbvəːs] *n*. paranın yüz kısmı, tura; herhangi bir şeyin yüz tarafı; *fig*. eş, karşılık; ters önerme.

ob.vi.ate *fig*. ['əbvieit] *v/t*. önlemek, gidermek, ortadan kaldırmak.

ob.vi.ous □ ['əbviəs] (bes)belli, (ap)açık, aşikâr; **'ob.vi.ous.ness** *n*. aşikârlık, açıklık, meydanda olma.

oc.ca.sion [ə'keiʒən] **1.** *n*. fırsat, münasebet, vesile, durum, hal; sebep, neden, gereklilik, lüzum; F olay, hadise; iş; kutlama; **on ~** ara sıra, fırsat düştükçe; gerektiğinde; **on the ~ of** dolayısıyla, vesilesiyle; **2.** *v/t*. vesile olm., sebep olm. *-e*; **oc'ca.sion.al** □ [‿ʒənl] ara sıra olan, fırsat düştükçe yapılan; **oc'ca.sion.al.ly** [‿ʒnəli] *adv*. ara sıra, bazen.

oc.ci.dent *poet. & rhet* ['əksidənt] *n*. batı, batı yarıküresi; **oc.ci.den.tal** □ [‿'dentl] batılı, batıya ait, batısal, batı...

oc.cult □ [ə'kʌlt] gizli, saklı, bilinmez, anlaşılmaz; doğaüstü, büyülü, esrarlı, sihirli; **oc.cul'ta.tion** *n*. AST karartma, gizleme; **oc.cult.ism** ['əkəltizəm] *n*. gizli güçlere inanma; **'oc.cult.ist** *n*. gizli güçlere inanan kimse; **oc.cult.ness** [ə'kʌltnis] *n*. gizlilik.

oc.cu.pan.cy ['əkjupənsi] *n*. işgal (**of** *-i*); **'oc.cu.pant** *n*. işgal eden kimse; **oc.cu'pation** *n*. meslek, iş, sanat, meşguliyet; MIL işgal; **oc.cu'pa.tion.al** [‿ʃənl] *adj*. iş (*veya* meslek) ile ilgili, iş..., meslek...; işgal kuvvetleri; **~ therapy** meşguliyetle tedavi, rehabilitasyon; **oc.cu.pi.er** ['əkjupaiə] *s*. **occupant**; **oc.cu.py** ['‿pai] *v/t*. ...de oturmak, ...de yaşamak; MIL işgal etm., zaptetmek; meşgul etm., doldurmak (*süre*); bulunmak (*görev*); **~ o.s.** *veya* **be occupied with** *veya* **in** ile meşgul olm.

oc.cur [ə'kəː] *v/i*. olmak, meydana gelmek, yer bulmak; hatıra gelmek, akla gelmek; bulunmak, mevcut olm.; **it ~red to me** aklıma geldi; **oc.cur.rence** [ə'kʌrəns] *n*. olay, hadise, vaka; olma, meydana çıkma.

o.cean ['əuʃən] *n*. okyanus, derya, deniz; **~ liner** okyanus gemisi; **~s of time** F dünya kadar vakit; **'~-go.ing** *adj*. okyanus..., okyanuslarda işleyen...;

o.ce.an.ic [əuʃi'ænik] *adj.* okyanusa ait, okyanus…; okyanusta bulunan…

o.chre MIN ['əukə] *n.* toprak boya, aşı boyası; koyu sarı renk.

o'clock [ə'klɔk] *adv.* saate göre; **five ~** saat beş.

oc.ta.gon ['ɔktəgən] *n.* sekizgen; **oc-tag.onal** [ɔk'tægənl] *adj.* sekiz kenarlı.

oc.tane CHEM ['ɔktein] *n.* oktan; **~ rating** MOT oktan sayısı.

oc.tave MUS ['ɔktiv] *n.* oktav; sekiz notalık ara; bir sonenin sekiz mısraı; sekiz mısralı şiir; **oc.ta.vo** [ɔk'teivəu] *n.* yarım fasiküllük kâğıt tabakası *veya* kitap; **octet(te)** [ɔk'tet] *n.* MUS sekiz kişi tarafından söylenen *veya* çalınan müzik parçası.

Oc.to.ber [ɔk'təubə] *n.* ekim (ayı).

oc.to.ge.nar.i.an [ɔktəudʒi'nɛəriən] **1.** *adj.* seksen yaşında, seksenlik, sekseninde; **2.** *n.* seksenlik kimse.

oc.to.pus ZOO ['ɔktəpəs] *n.* ahtapot; *fig.* yaygın ve yıkıcı örgüt.

oc.to.roon [ɔktə'ruːn] *n.* zenci karışımı beyaz kimse.

oc.u.lar □ ['ɔkjulə] göze ait, göz…; gözle görülür; **~ demonstration, ~ proof** kesin delil; **'oc.u.list** *n.* göz mütehassısı, göz doktoru.

odd □ [ɔd] tek, ikiye bölünemeyen (*sayı*); tek (*ayakkabı, eldiven vs.*); geriye kalan, küsur; düzensiz, seyrek, ara sıra olan; tuhaf, acayip, garip; **50 ~** 50 küsur; **14 pounds ~** 14 küsur pound; **~ jobs** *pl.* düzensiz işler, geçici işler; **at ~ times** boş vakitlerde, vakit buldukça; **~ man out** garip adam, acayip herif; *s.* **odds**; **'odd.i.ty** *n.* tuhaflık, acayiplik, gariplik; F garip kimse; **'odd.ments** *n. pl.* ufak tefek şeyler, artık şeyler; COM döküntüler, kırıntılar; **odds** [ɔdz] *n. pl. oft. sg.* eşitsizlik, fark, üstünlük; ihtimal (*veya* olabilirlik) oranı; **the ~ are against you** ihtimaller aleyhinizdedir; **the ~ are that** ihtimali var ki, muhtemeldir ki; **be at ~ with s.o.** b-le arası açık olm.; **~ and ends** *pl.* ufak tefek şeyler, eften püften şeyler; **it makes no ~** zararı yok, farketmez; **what's the ~?** ne çıkar?, ne önemi var?

ode [əud] *n.* gazel; övgü, kaside.

o.di.ous □ ['əudjəs] tiksindirici, iğrenç, çirkin, nefret verici; **o.di.um** ['əudjəm] *n.* nefret, kin; yüz karası, ayıp; iğrençlik.

o.dom.e.ter MOT [ɔ'dɔmitə] *n.* kilome-tre sayacı, mesafe kaydedici, odometre.

o.don.to.lo.gy MED [ɔdɔn'tɔlədʒi] *n.* diş, diş gelişimi ve diş hastalıkları ile uğraşan ilim.

o.dor.if.er.ous □ [əudə'rifərəs] hoş kokulu, güzel koku yayan; **'o.dor.ous** □ (hoş) kokulu.

o.do(u)r ['əudə] *n.* koku; *fig.* şöhret, itibar; **'o.do(u)r.less** *adj.* kokusuz.

O.dys.sey ['ɔdisi] *n.* Odise destanı; *fig.* maceralı uzun yolculuk.

oe.col.o.gy [iː'kɔlədʒi] *s.* **ecology**.

oec.u.men.i.cal ECCL □ [iːkjuː'menikəl] kiliselerin birleşmesine ait; bütün Hıristiyanlarca kabul edilen.

oe.de.ma MED [iː'diːmə] *n.* ödem, vücutta su toplanması.

o'er [əuə] = **over.**

oe.soph.a.gus ANAT [iː'sɔfəgəs] *n.* yemek borusu.

of [ɔv, əv, v] *prp. com.* -(n)in (*the works of Shakespeare: Shakespear'in eserleri*); -den (*proud / ashamed / afraid / glad/ tired of: -den gurur duyan / utanan/ korkan/ memnun olan/ bıkan*); -den yapılmış (*a table of wood: tahtadan yapılmış bir masa*); -li (*a man ~ honour: şerefli bir adam*); **~ o.s.** kendiliğinden, kendi teşebbüsüyle; kendi hakkında; **this world ~ ours** bizim bu dünyamız; **~ an evening** F akşamları.

off [ɔːf, ɔf] **1.** *adv.* uzakta, ileride, ötede; uzağa, ileriye, öteye (*3 miles ~; 3 mil ötede*); bitmiş, bozulmuş (*their engagement is ~: nişanları bozuldu*); kesik (*the water/electricity is ~: su/elektrik kesik*); görev dışında, izinli (*the manager gave the staff a day ~: müdür personele bir günlük izin verdi*); kopuk; **~ and on** arasıra, bazen; **be ~** ayrılmak, terketmek, gitmek; **be ~ with s.o.** b-den ayrı kalmak; **right ~, straight ~** derhal, hemen; **well etc. ~** hali vakti yerinde, zengin *vs.*; **2.** *prp.* -den, -dan (*fall ~ a ladder/ a tree/ a horse: merdivenden/ ağaçtan/ attan düşmek*); -den uzak (*a house ~ the main road: ana yoldan uzak bir ev*); NAUT açıklarında (*a ship anchored ~ the harbour entrance: liman girişi açıklarında demirlemiş gemi*); bırakmış (*she's ~ smoking: sigarayı bıraktı*); **a street ~ the Strand** Strand'den ayrılan sokak; **be ~ duty** izinli olm.; **be ~ smoking** sigarayı bırakmak; **~ the point** konudan uzak, konu dışı: **be ~ one's feed** sl. hiç iştahı olmamak; **~ one's head** sl. kafayı üşütmüş; **3.** adj. sağdaki (the **~** front wheel: sağ ön tekerlek); uzak; NAUT denize doğru açılan; bitmiş, ertenlemiş; çalışmayan, işlemeyen; yanlış, hatalı; normalden aşağı, âdi; izinli, görev dışında; cansız, hareketsiz, ölü (mevsim, sezon); solmuş, soluk; bitmiş, tükenmiş; **~ chance** zayıf bir ihtimal; **~ shade** COM rengi kaçmış, solmuş; **4.** int. defol!, çek arabanı!, yaylan!

of.fal ['ɔfəl] n. çerçöp, süprüntü; **~s** pl. hayvanın yenemeyen iç kısımları; sakatat.

off-beat F ['ɔf'biːt] adj. olağandışı, alışılmamış, tuhaf.

of.fence [ə'fens] n. suç, kabahat, kusur; hakaret, incitme, gücendirme; hücum, tecavüz, saldırı; **no ~!** gücenmeyin!, darılmayın!; **give ~** gücendirmek, darıltmak; **take ~** gücenmek, darılmak (**at** -e).

of.fend [ə'fend] v/t. gücendirmek, darıltmak, hatırını kırmak; ihlâl etm., bozmak; kızdırmak; v/i. suç işlemek, kabahat işlemek (**against** -e karşı); **of'fender** n. suçlu; **first ~** ilk kez suç işlemis kimse.

of.fense [ə'fens] = **offence**.

of.fen.sive [ə'fensiv] **1.** □ çirkin, iğrenç; yakışmaz; kötü...; saldırı..., hücum...; **2.** n. taarruz, saldırı, hücum.

of.fer ['ɔfə] **1.** n. teklif; sunu; **~ of marriage** evlenme teklifi; **on ~** satışa sunulmuş; **2.** v/t. teklif etm.; vermek (fiyat); takdim etm., arzetmek, sunmak; göstermek; v/i. meydana çıkmak, gözükmek, görünmek; 'of.fer.ing n. teklif; sunu; kurban.

of.fer.to.ry ECCL ['ɔfətəri] n. kilisede ayin esnasında para toplama; para toplanırken çalınan müzik.

off-hand ['ɔːf'hænd] adj. düşünmeden yapılmış, rasgele yapılmış, hazırlıksız yapılmış; ters (hareket, söz).

of.fice ['ɔfis] n. büro, yazıhane, ofis; daire; bakanlık; hizmet, iş, memuriyet, vazife, görev; iktidar; **~s** pl. yardım; **booking ~**, THEAT **box ~** bilet gişesi; **Divine ♀** ibadet; dinî ayin; '**~bear.er** n. memur, görevli; '**~block** n. iş hanı; '**~boy** n. yazıhanede ayak işlerine bakan çocuk.

of.fi.cer ['ɔfisə] n. memur; polis memuru; MIL subay; 'of.fi.cered: **~ by** -in kumandası altında.

of.fi.cial [ə'fiʃəl] **1.** □ resmî; memuriyete ait; memura yakışır; MED = **officinal**; **2.** n. memur; of'fi.cial.dom n. memur sınıfı, memurlar; of.fi.cial.ese [~'liːz] n. resmî yazı üslubu; of'fi.cial.ism = **officialdom**.

of.fi.ci.ate [ə'fiʃieit] v/i. resmî bir görevi yerine getirmek.

of.fic.i.nal [ɔfi'sainl] adj. hazır (ilâç); iyileştirici, tedavi edici.

of.fi.cious □ [ə'fiʃəs] her şeye karışan, el sokan, işgüzar, gereksiz yere yardım etmek isteyen.

off.ing NAUT ['ɔfiŋ] n. sahilden görülen açık deniz; **in the ~** fig. olması yakın; 'off.ish adj. F uzak duran, soğuk (davranış).

off...: '**~li.cence** n. içki satma ruhsatı; içki satılan dükkân; '**~print** n. ayrı baskı; '**~scour.ings** pl., '**~scum** n. çerçöp, süprüntü, pislik; '**~set 1.** n. ARCH düz çıkıntı; MEC dirsek; TYP ofset; s. **offshoot**. s. **set-off**. **2.** v/t. dengelemek, denkleştirmek; ofset usulü basmak; '**~shoot** n. dal (a. fig.); '**~shore** adj. kıyıdan uzak; kıyıdan esen (rüzgâr); '**~'side** adj. spor. ofsayt; '**~spring** n. döl, evlât; ürün; '**~the-'rec.ord** adj. kayda geçmeyecek, yayınlanmayacak, gizli; '**~time** n. boş vakit.

oft poet. [ɔft] adv. çok kere, sık sık.

of.ten ['ɔfn] adv. çok defa, çoğu kez, sık sık; **as ~ as** her ne zaman, her; **as ~ as not**, **more ~ than not** ekseriya, çok sık; **every so ~** arasıra, bazen; 'of.ten.times, 'oft-times adv. obs. sık sık.

o.gee ARCH ['oudʒiː] n. S şeklinde korniş veya köşebent, deve boynu.

o.gi.val [əu'dʒaivəl] adj. sivri kemer..., beyzî kemer...; 'o.give n. ARCH sivri tepeli kemer; grafikte bir eğri çeşidi.

o.gle ['ougl] vb. âşıkane bakmak, göz süzerek bakmak; âşıkane süzmek.

o.gre ['ougə] n. insan yiyen dev; o.gress ['əugris] n. insan yiyen dişi dev.

oh [əu] int. ya!, sahi!, öyle mi?

ohm ELECT [əum] n. om, elektrik direnç birimi.

o.ho [əu'həu] int. ha!, çaktım!, anladım!, tamam!

oil [ɔil] **1.** n. yağ; petrol; zeytinyağı; yağlıboya (resim); F pohpohlama, yağ çekme; **burn the midnight ~** geç vakte kadar çalışmak, gecesini gündüzüne katmak; **smell of ~** gece geç vakte kadar çalıştığı belli olm.; **pour ~ on the**

flame(s) kızıştırmak, yangına körükle gitmek; **pour ~ on the (troubled) waters** yatıştırmak; **strike ~** petrol bulmak; *fig.* köşeyi dönmek; **paint in ~s** yağlıboya resim yapmak; **2.** *v/t.* yağlamak; *fig. b-ne* rüşvet vermek; yağ çekmek; **~ s.o.'s palm** *b-ne* rüşvet vermek; **'~-burn.er** *n.* yağ brülörü, yağ memesi; **'~-cake** *n.* yağ küspesi; **'~-can** *n.* yağdanlık; **'~.cloth** *n.* muşamba; **'~-col-o(u)r** *n.* yağlıboya; **'oil.er** = **oil-can**; **oil tanker**, **'oil-field** *n.* petrol sahası; **'oil.i.ness** *n.* yağlılık; *fig.* kaypaklık, yağcılık, dalkavukluk; **'oil-man** *n.* yağ *veya* yağlı boya üreticisi *veya* satıcısı; makine yağcısı; **'oil-paint.ing** *n.* yağlıboya resim; **'oil-pa.per** *n.* yağlı kâğıt; **'oil-skin** *n.* çok ince muşamba; **~s** *pl.* bu muşambadan yapılmış elbiseler; **'oil-tank.er** *n.* tanker; **'oil-well** *n.* petrol kuyusu; **'oil.y** □ yağlı (*a. fig.*); *fig.* yağcı, dalkavuk.

oint.ment ['ɔintmənt] *n.* merhem.

O.K., o.kay ['əu'kei] **1.** *adj. & adv.* peki; doğru; geçer; iyi, makbul; **2.** *v/t.* onaylamak, tasdik etm.

old [əuld] *adj.* eski, köhne, eskimiş, aşınmış; ihtiyar, yaşlı; sabık, önceki; tecrübeli, deneyimli, pişkin; F sevgili (*dost*); *sl.* çok; harika, fevkalâde; **the ~** yaşlılar, ihtiyarlar; **young and ~** herkes; **~ age** yaşlılık, ihtiyarlık; **the ~ man** koca; baba; gemi kaptanı; **~ man** yaşlı adam; **the ~ woman** karı, eş; **the ~ country** göçmenin eski vatanı; **an ~ boy** eski öğrenci; **a high ~ time** *sl.* eski güzel günler; **the ~ one**, **the ~ gentleman**, **~ Harry** *veya* **Scratch** şeytan; **days of ~** geçmiş günler, mazi; **'~-age** *adj.* yaşlılık...; **'~-'clothes.man** *n.* eskici; **'old.en** *adj. obs. veya poet.* eski; **in the ~ days** eskiden, eski günlerde.

old...: **'~-'fash.ioned 1.** *adj.* modası geçmiş, demode; eski kafalı; sitemkâr (*bakış*); **2.** *n. Am.* viski ile yapılan bir çeşit kokteyl; **'~-'fo.g(e)y.ish** *adj.* eski kafalı; ♀ **Glo.ry** A.B.D.'nin bayrağı; **'old.ish** *adj.* oldukça yaşlı *veya* eski; **'old-'maid.ish** *adj.* titiz, düzenli, tertipli; **old.ster** ['-stə] *n.* yaşlı adam; **'old-time** *adj.* eski; yaşlı; **'old-'tim.er** *n.* kıdemli kimse; *esp. Am.* yaşlı adam; **'old-'wom.an.ish** *adj.* titiz, müşkülpesent, kılı kırk yaran; **'old-world** *adj.* eski, modası geçmiş.

o.le.ag.i.nous [əuli'ædʒinəs] *adj.*

yağlı; yağ çıkaran; şişman; yağlı...

o.le.an.der BOT [əuli'ændə] *n.* zakkum, ağıağacı, gül defnesi.

ol.fac.to.ry ANAT [ɔl'fæktəri] *adj.* koklamaya ait, koklama..., koku ...

ol.i.garch.y ['ɔligɑːki] *n.* oligarşi.

ol.ive ['ɔliv] *n.* BOT zeytin; zeytin ağacı; zeytin dalı *veya* çelengi; **'~-branch** *n.* barış sembolü olan zeytin dalı; **'~-tree** *n.* zeytin ağacı.

O.lym.pi.ad [əu'limpiæd] *n.* olimpiyat; **O'lym.pi.an** [-piən] *adj.* tanrısal; harika, şahane; **O'lym.pic games** *pl.* olimpiyat oyunları.

om.e.let, **om.e.lette** ['ɔmlit] *n.* omlet, kaygana.

o.men ['əumen] *n.* kehanet.

om.i.nous □ ['ɔminəs] uğursuz; korkutucu; **~ of disaster** uğursuz felâket.

o.mis.si.ble [əu'misibl] *adj.* atlanabilir, yapılmayabilir; **o.mis.sion** [ə'miʃən] *n.* atlama, bırakma, yapmama; ihmal; **sin of ~** ihmal suçu.

o.mit [ə'mit] *v/t.* bırakmak, atlamak, ihmal etm. (*a. to inf. -meği*).

om.ni.bus ['ɔmnibəs] **1.** *n. obs.* otobüs; antoloji; **2.** *adj.* çok maddeli...; çok maksatlı...; **~ volume** içinde birçok konu olan cilt.

om.nip.o.tence [ɔm'nipətəns] *n.* herşeye gücü yetme; sonsuz güç; **om-'nip.o.tent** □ her şeye kadir.

om.ni.pres.ence ['ɔmni'prezəns] *n.* her yerde bulunma; **'om.ni'pres.ent** □ her yerde ve her zaman hazır, her yerde hazır ve nazır.

om.nis.cience [ɔm'nisiəns] *n.* her şeyi bilme; sonsuz bilgi; **om'nis.cient** □ her şeyi bilen, âlim.

om.niv.o.rous [ɔm'nivərəs] *adj.* her şeyi yiyen; *fig.* her çeşit kitabı okuyan.

on [ɔn] **1.** *prp. mst* üzerinde, üstünde (**~ the wall:** duvarın üzerinde); esnasında, zarfında, sürecinde; hakkında, konusunda, hususunda (*talk ~ a subject:* bir konu hakkında konuşmak); -e doğru (*march ~ London:* Londra'ya doğru yürümek); -e yakın; kenarında (*a house ~ the main road:* ana yolun kenarında bir ev); halinde; **get ~ a train** *part. Am.* trene binmek; **turn one's back ~ s.o.** *b-ne* sırt çevirmek; **~ these conditions** bu şartlarda; **~ this model** bu modele göre; **~ hearing it** onu duyması üzerine; **2.** *adv.* üzerinde, üstünde; ileriye, ileride; aralıksız, durmadan; olmakta; **~ and ~** durmaksızın, ara vermeden, biteviye; **~ to...** ...(y)e; **from that day ~** o günden itibaren; **be ~** olmak, vuku bulmak; THEAT oynamak; **what is ~ tonight?** bu gece ne oynuyor?; **be a bit ~** sl. çakırkeyf olm., kafayı bulmak; **3.** int. haydi!

once [wʌns] **1.** adv. bir defa, bir kez, bir kere; bir zamanlar, eskiden; hemen, derhal: **at ~** derhal, hemen; aynı anda; **all at ~** aniden, birden(bire); **~ again** bir kez daha; **~ for all** (ilk ve) son olarak; **for ~** bu seferlik, bir kerelik; **~ in a while** arasıra, bazen; **this ~** bu sefer; **~ more** tekrar, bir kez daha; **~ upon a time there was ...** evvel zaman içinde bir ... varmış; **2.** cj. a. **~ that** ...ir ...irmez.

once-o.ver Am. F ['wʌnsəuvə] n. hemen bakma, inceleme, tetkik.

on-com.ing ['ɔnkʌmiŋ] **1.** adj. yaklaşmakta olan, yaklaşan, ilerleyen; **2.** n. yaklaşma.

one [wʌn] **1.** adj. & pron. bir, tek; biri(si); herhangi biri(si); **his ~ care** onun tek endişesi, üzüntüsü; **~ day** bir gün, günün birinde; **~ of these days** bu günlerde; **~ Mr. Miller** Mr. Miller isminde bir zat; s. any, every, no; take **~'s walk** yürüyerek gezmek; **a large dog and a little ~** büyük bir köpek ve bir de küçük bir tane; **for ~ thing** sebeplerden biri, çünkü; **~ and the same** tıpkısı, aynı; **2.** n. bir tane; biri(si); adam, kimse, kişi; bir rakamı; **the little ~s** pl. küçük çocuklar; **~ another** birbir(ler)ini, birbir(ler)ine; **at ~** beraber, birleşmiş, uyuşmuş; **~ by ~**, **~ after another** birer birer, birbiri ardına; **it is all ~ (to me)** (benim için) hava hoş, farketmez; **I for ~** bana kalırsa, bence; **~ with another** ortalama olarak; **'~-armed** adj. tek kollu; **~ bandit** para ile çalışan oyun makinesi; **'~-eyed** adj. tek gözlü; fig. kısıtlı, az; **'~'horse** adj. tek atlı; fig. sl. ikinci derecede, adi; **~ town** küçük ve can sıkıcı kasaba; **'~-i'dea'd** adj. sabit fikirli; **'one.ness** n. birlik, bir olma.

on.er.ous □ ['ɔnərəs] ağır, zor, külfetli, sıkıntılı.

one...: **~'self** pron. kendisi, bizzat, kendi kendine; **by ~** kendi kendine; **'~-'sid.ed** □ tek taraflı; **'~-time** adj. sabık, eski; **have a ~ mind** tek bir şey düşünmek, ak '**~-'track** adj. tek yollu; ısrarcı, şaşmaz; lında bir tek şey olm.; **'~-way:** **~ street** tek yönlü sokak;

~ ticket gidiş bileti.

on.fall ['ɔnfɔːl] n. hücum, taarruz.

on.go.ings ['ɔngəuiŋz] n. pl. olay, hadise, vaka.

on.ion ['ʌnjən] n. soğan; **off one's ~** sl. kafayı üşütmüş.

online ['ɔnlain] adj. & adv. online; **~ banking** online bankacılık; **~ dating** karşı cinsten kimselerle online olarak tanışıp arkadaşlık kurmak; **~ shopping** online alışveriş.

on.look.er ['ɔnlukə] n. seyirci.

on.ly ['əunli] **1.** adj. (bir) tek, biricik, eşsiz; yegâne; **2.** adv. yalnız, ancak, sadece, yalnızca, başlı başına; **~ yesterday** sadece dün; **~ just** ancak, henüz; hemen hemen hiç; **~ think!** düşün bir kere!; **3.** cj. **~ (that)** ne var ki, ...mezse.

on.o.mat.o.poe.ia [ɔnəumætəu'piːə] n. doğal sesleri yansılayan kelimeleri kullanma.

on.rush ['ɔnrʌʃ] n. üşüşme, saldırma.

on.set ['ɔnset], **on.slaught** ['ɔnslɔːt] n. başlama, başlangıç; part. fig. şiddetli saldırı, hücum.

on.to ['ɔntu, 'ɔntə] prep. -in üstün(d)e.

on.tol.o.gy PHLS [ɔn'tɔlədʒi] n. ontoloji.

o.nus fig. ['əunəs] n. yük, görev, sorumluluk, külfet.

on.ward ['ɔnwəd] **1.** adj. ileriye doğru giden, ilerleyen; **2.** a. **~s** adv. ileri, ileriye doğru, ileride.

on.yx MIN ['ɔniks] n. damarlı akik.

oo.dles sl. ['uːdlz] n. pl. büyük miktar (of).

oof sl. [uːf] n. mangır, mangiz.

oomph sl. [umf] n. azim, şevk, gayret; cinsî cazibe.

ooze [uːz] **1.** n. çamur, balçık; MEC sızıntı; **2.** v/t. & v/i. sız(dır)mak; dışarı sızmak, duyulmak (sır, haber); dışarı vermek, çıkarmak; **~ away** azalmak, eksilmek.

oo.zy □ ['uːzi] sızıntılı; sızdıran; sulu çamur gibi.

o.pac.i.ty [əu'pæsiti] n. donukluk, şeffaf olmama; fig. ahmaklık, mankafalık.

o.pal min. ['əupəl] n. opal, panzehirtaşı.

o.pal.es.cent [-'lesnt] adj. yanardöner, şanjan.

o.paque □ [əu'peik] donuk, şeffaf olmayan, ışık geçirmez, kesif; fig. ahmak, mankafa.

ope poet. [əup] = **open**.

o.pen ['əupən] **1.** □ com. açık, içine girilir, serbest; üstü açık; açık (hava);

açmış (*çiçek*); aşikâr, meydanda, gizli olmayan; herkese açık, umumî; karar verilmemiş, halledilmemiş (*mesele*); korumasız, sipersiz; ödenmemiş (*borç*); kapanmamış (*hesap*); açık fikirli (*to -e*); **with ~ arms** samimiyetle; **with ~ hands** cömertçe; **the ~ door** serbest ticaret; **keep ~ house** evinin kapısı herkese açık olm.; **lay o.s. ~ to** -*e* maruz kalmak; **~ letter** açık mektup; **~ season** HUNT serbest sezon; **2.** *n.* **in the ~** (*air*) açık havada; açıkta; **come out into the ~** *fig.* açığa çıkmak; **3.** *v/t.* & *v/i.* aç(ıl)mak; umuma açmak; başla(t)mak -*e*; kesip açmak, yar(ıl)mak, deşmek; gevşe(t)mek; çöz(ül)mek; yay(ıl)mak, ser(il)mek; göz önüne çıkarmak; çatla(t)mak; göstermek, bildirmek; **~ into** içeri doğru açılmak; **~ on to** -*e* açılmak; **~ out** yaymak; sermek; açılmak; **~ up** açmak; başlamak; geliştirmek; **'~-'air** *adj.* açık hava...; '**~-armed** *adj.* candan, içten, samimi

o.pen.er ['əupnə] *n.* açacak; '**o.pen-'eyed** *adj.* açıkgöz, dikkatli; şaşkın, afallamış; '**o.pen-'hand.ed** *adj.* eli açık, cömert; '**o.pen-'heart.ed** *adj.* açık kalpli, samimi; **o.pen.ing** ['əupniŋ] **1.** *n.* açıklık, delik; başlangıç; açılış, açılma; fırsat; münhal görev; **2.** *adj.* ilk..., birinci...; '**o.pen-'mind.ed** *adj.* *fig.* açık fikirli; '**o.pen-'mouthed** *adj.* ağzı açık kalmış (*hayretten*); açgözlü, obur; **o.pen.ness** ['əupnnis] *n.* açıklık.

open...: **~ or.der** MIL dağınık savaş düzeni; **~ shop** sendikalı *veya* sendikasız herkesi çalıştıran kuruluş; **~ vow.el** açık sesli harf; **~ work** kafes halinde işlemeli süs.

op.er.a ['ɔpərə] *n.* opera; opera müziği; opera binası; '**~-cloak** *n.* bayanların tuvalette birlikte giydikleri pelerin; '**~-glass**(**es** *pl.*) *n.* opera dürbünü; '**~-hat** *n.* katlanabilen silindir erkek şapkası; '**~-house** *n.* opera binası.

op.er.ate ['ɔpəreit] *v/t.* & *v/i.* işle(t)mek, çalış(tır)mak, kullanmak; iş görmek; etkilemek; COM borsada alışveriş yapmak; MED ameliyat etm.; MIL tatbikat yapmak; MEC işletmek, çalıştırmak; **be operating** işler olm.; **op.er.at.ic** [~'rætik] *adj.* operaya ait, opera...; **~ singer** opera şarkıcısı; **op.er.at.ing** ['ɔpəreitiŋ] *adj.* ameliyat...; işletme...; **~ expenses** *pl.* işletme masrafları; **~ instructions** *pl.* işletme tali-

matı; **~ theatre** ameliyat odası; **op.er-'a.tion** *n.* işle(t)me, çalışma (tarzı); iş, fiil; etki, hüküm; COM borsada alışveriş; MED ameliyat; MIL harekât; **be in ~** yürürlükte olm.; **come into ~** yürürlüğe girmek; **op.er'a.tion.al** [~ʃənl] *adj.* işletme...; kullanıma hazır...; **op.er.a.tive** ['ɔpərətiv] **1.** ☐ işleyen, faal, çalışan; etkin, etkili; geçerli, yürürlükte olan; MED ameliyata ait, ameliyat edilebilir; **2.** *n.* usta işçi, teknisyen; **op.er.a.tor** ['~reitə] *n.* MED cerrah, operatör; *film*: gösterici; santral memuru; MEC operatör, teknisyen; COM spekülatör.

op.er.et.ta [ɔpə'retə] *n.* operet.

oph.thal.mi.a MED [ɔf'θælmiə] *n.* göz iltihabı; **oph'thal.mic** *adj.* göze ait, göz...; **~ hospital** göz hastalıkları hastanesi.

o.pi.ate PHARM ['əupiit] **1.** *n.* afyonlu ilâç; **2.** *adj.* afyonlu...; uyuşturucu..., sersemletici...

o.pine [əu'pain] *v/t.* yürütmek (*fikir*) zannetmek, düşünmek, farzetmek; **o.pin.ion** [ə'pinjən] *n.* fikir, düşünce; zan, tahmin, kanı, görüş; **the** (**public**) **~** kamuoyu; **I am of the ~ that** ...fikrindeyim, görüşündeyim; **in my ~** bence, kanımca, fikrimce, kanaatimce; **o'pin.ion.at.ed** [~eitid] *adj.* inatçı, fikrinden dönmeyen, dik kafalı.

o.pi.um PHARM ['əupjəm] *n.* afyon.

o.pos.sum ZOO [ə'pɔsəm] *n.* opossum, keselisıçangillerden Amerika'ya mahsus memeli bir hayvan.

op.po.nent [ə'pəunənt] **1.** *n.* hasım, düşman, rakip, muhalif; **2.** *adj.* karşı(ki); karşıt, zıt.

op.por.tune ☐ ['ɔpətjuːn] elverişli, uygun, münasip; tam vaktinde yapılan; '**op.portun.ism** *n.* fırsatçılık; '**op.portun.ist** *n.* fırsatçı kimse; **op.por'tu.ni.ty** *n.* fırsat, uygun zaman, elverişli durum.

op.pose [ə'pəuz] *v/t.* direnmek, engel olm., mâni olm., karşı koymak, karşı çıkmak -*e*; karşıla(ştır)mak -*i*; **op'posed** *adj.* karşı; karşısında; zıt, aksi; **be ~ to** -*e* karşı olm.; **op.po.site** ['ɔpəzit] **1.** ☐ karşı, ([**to**] *s.th. bşe*); karşıdaki, karşıki; zıt, aksi, karşıt, ters; **~ number** karşı taraftaki meslektaş, iş arkadaşı; **2.** *prp.* & *adv.* karşı sıra; karşılıklı; karşıda; karşıya; **3.** *n.* zıt kelime *veya* şey; **oppo'si.tion** *n.* zıtlık, karşıtlık; muhalefet (**to** -*e*); mücadele;

karşı durma, karşı koyma; COM rekabet; PARL muhalif parti; AST birbirinden
180° uzaklıktaki iki gökcisminin durumu.
op.press [ə'pres] *v/t.* sık(ıştır)mak,
baskı yapmak; zulmetmek *-e*, canını
yakmak; canını sıkmak, üzerine yüklenmek; **op.pres.sion** [ə'preʃən] *n.*
baskı, zulüm, cefa; zulmetme; sıkıntı,
güçlük; **op'pressive** □ [ˌ-siv] ezici, zul-
medici; sıkıcı, bunaltıcı; **op'pres.sive-
ness** *n.* gaddarlık; sıkıcılık; **op'pres-
sor** *n.* zalim (*veya* acımasız) kimse.
op.pro.bri.ous □ [ə'prəubriəs] hakaret
dolu, aşağılayıcı; utandırıcı, yüz
kızartıcı; **op'pro.bri.um** [ˌ-briəm] *n.*
hakaret, aşağılama; rezalet, ayıp.
op.pugn [ɔ'pjuːn] *v/t.* karşı koymak *-e*,
karşı olm. *-e*.
opt [ɔpt] *vb.* seçmek; karar vermek (*for
-e*); **op.ta.tive** GR ['ɔptətiv] *n.* istek kipi, dilek kipi.
op.tic ['ɔptik] *adj.* görme duyusuna ait,
göz...; = **'op.ti.cal** □ optikle ilgili; **op-
'tician** [ˌ-ʃən] *n.* gözlükçü; **'op.tics** *n.
sg.* optik.
op.ti.mism ['ɔptimizəm] *n.* iyimserlik;
'opti.mist *n.* iyimser kimse; **op.ti'mis-
tic** *adj.* (**~ally**) iyimser.
op.ti.mum ['ɔptiməm] **1.** *n.* en uygun
durum..., en elverişli ortam; **2.** *adj.* en
uygun..., en elverişli..., en ideal...
op.tion ['ɔpʃən] *n.* seçme (hakkı), tercih (hakkı); seçme yetkisi; seçilen
şey, şık, seçenek; COM satma *veya* satın
alma hakkı; **op.tion.al** □ ['ɔpʃənl] isteğe bağlı, zorunlu olmayan, ihtiyarî,
seçmeli.
op.u.lence ['ɔpjuləns] *n.* servet, zenginlik; bolluk, bereket; **'op.u.lent** □
zengin; bol, bereketli.
o.pus ['əupəs] *n.* müzik parçası, opus;
magnum ~ edebiyat *veya* sanatta
şaheser.
or [ɔː] *cj.* veya, yahut; yoksa; ya; **either
... ~** ya ... ya da...; **~ else** yoksa, aksi
takdirde; **two ~ three** iki veya üç; **~
so** aşağı yukarı, tahminen, takriben.
or.a.cle ['ɔrəkl] *n.* kehanet; eski Yunanistan'da gaipten haber veren kâhin;
kehanette bulunulan kutsal yer; vahiy,
ilham; **work the ~** F başarı için kulis
yapmak, torpil işletmek; **o.rac.u.lar**
[ɔ'rækjulə] *adj.* kehanetle ilgili, kehanet...; *fig.* gizli anlamlı.
o.ral □ ['ɔːrəl] sözlü, ağızdan söylenen;
ağızdan alınan...; ağız...

o.rang ['ɔːræŋ] = *orang-outang.*
or.ange ['ɔrindʒ] **1.** *n.* portakal; portakal rengi, turuncu; **2.** *adj.* portakal ren-
gindeki; **or.ange.ade** ['ˌ-'eid] *n.* portakal şurubu; **or.ange.ry** ['ˌ-əri] *n.* iklimi
soğuk olan yerlerde portakal yetiştirilen kapalı yer, limonluk.
o.rang-ou.tang, **o.rang-u.tan** ZOO
['ɔːræŋ 'uːtæŋ] *n.* orangutan.
o.ra.tion [ɔː'reiʃən] *n.* nutuk, söylev, hitabe; **or.a.tor** ['ɔrətə] *n.* hatip, söyleyi-
ci, güzel konuşan kimse; **or.a.tor.i.cal**
□ [ˌ-'tɔrikəl] hatipliğe ait, hitap...;
hatibe yakışır; **or.a.to.ri.o** MUS [ˌ-'tɔː-
riəu] *n.* oratoryo; **or.a.to.ry** ['ˌ-təri] *n.*
hatiplik, hitabet, güzel konuşma sa-
natı; ECCL küçük mabet, özel tapınak.
orb [ɔːb] *n.* küre; daire; *fig.* gökcismi;
poet. göz; **or.bic.u.lar** □ [ɔː'bikjulə]
küre şeklinde, küresel, yuvarlak, dai-
remsi; **or.bit** ['ɔːbit] **1.** *n.* yörünge; çember; göz çukuru; **2.** *v/t. & v/i. -in*
etrafında dön(dür)mek; yörüngeye
sokmak; bir yörüngede dönmek.
or.chard ['ɔːtʃəd] *n.* meyve bahçesi.
or.ches.tra MUS ['ɔːkistrə] *n.* orkestra;
~ pit THEAT orkestranın bulunduğu
yer, parter; **or.ches.tral** [ɔː'kestrəl]
adj. orkestraya ait, orkestra...; **or-
ches.trate** MUS ['ɔːkistreit] *v/t.* orkestra için bestelemek.
or.chid BOT ['ɔːkid] *n.* orkide, salep; **or-
chis** BOT ['ɔːkis] *n.* salepotu.
or.dain [ɔː'dein] *v/t.* papazlığa atamak,
papaz yapmak; mukadder kılmak, (ka-
derini) tayin etm.
or.deal [ɔː'diːl] *n.* işkence yaparak
yargılama usulü; *fig.* büyük sıkıntı.
or.der ['ɔːdə] **1.** *n.* düzen, nizam, intizam; sıra, dizi; usül, yol, kural; emir;
COM sipariş, ısmarlama; havale; niyet,
amaç, gaye; tabaka, sınıf; tarikat, mezhep; şeref rütbesi; mimarî tarz; çeşit,
cins, tür; **by~** emre göre, emir gereğince; **~ of the day** gündem; MIL günlük
emir; **take (holy) ~s** papaz olm.; **put
in ~** düzene koymak; **in ~ to... -mek**
için; **in ~ that ...** diye; **on the ~s of**
-in emrinde; **on~** COM ısmarlama, sipariş üzerine; **make to ~** sipariş üzerine
yapmak, ısmarlama yapmak; **standing
~s** *pl.* PARL geçerliği süren emirler; **2.**
v/t. emretmek, buyurmak; COM ısmarlamak, sipariş etm.; düzenlemek, inti-
zama sokmak; **~ arms!** tüfek çıkar!; **~
about** emir yağdırmak; **~ down (up)**
getirmesini emretmek; **'~-book** *n.*

COM sipariş defteri; 'or.dered adj. muntazam, tertipli, derli toplu; 'order.li.ness n. intizam, düzenlilik, derli topluluk; 'or.der.ly 1. adj. düzgün, düzenli, intizamlı, derli toplu; itaatkâr, uysal, uslu; MIL emre ait, emir…; ~ officer nöbetçi subayı; ~ room yazıhane, büro; 2. n. MIL emir eri; hastane hademesi.

or.di.nal ['ɔːdinl] 1. adj. sıra veya derece gösteren…; 2. n. a. ~ number sıra sayısı.

or.di.nance ['ɔːdinəns] n. emir; düzen, kural; kanun; alın yazısı, yazgı.

or.di.nar.y ['ɔːdənri] 1. □ adi, bayağı, alışılmış, alelade; ~ debts pl. COM adi borçlar; ~ seaman acemi denizci, gemici; s. share; 2. n. alışılmış şey; in ~ devamlı olarak, sürekli.

or.di.nate MATH ['ɔːdnit] n. ordinat.

or.di.na.tion [ɔːdi'neiʃən] n. papaz atama töreni; papazlığa atama.

ord.nance MIL, NAUT ['ɔːdnəns] n. savaş gereçleri; ~ map kurmay haritası; ~ survey bir ülkenin resmî haritası; ~-survey map (1:25000) ölçekli harita.

or.dure ['ɔːdjuə] n. pislik, gübre, dışkı.

ore [ɔː] n. maden cevheri; poet. maden, metal.

or.gan ['ɔːgən] n. MUS org, erganun; organ, örgen, uzuv; araç, vasıta, alet; haber organı.

or.gan.die, or.gan.dy ['ɔːgəndi] n. ince ve yarı şeffaf muslin; organze.

or.gan-grind.er ['ɔːgəngraində] n. latarna çalan kimse; or.gan.ic [ɔː'gænik] adj. (~ally) organik, örgensel; yaşayan, canlı; yapısal; or.gan.ism ['ɔːgənizəm] n. organizma, örgenlik; oluşum; 'or.gan.ist n. org çalan kimse; or.gan.i.za.tion [ˌnai'zeiʃən] n. teşkilât, örgüt, kurum, teşekkül, dernek; düzen(leme); organizma, yapı; 'or.gan.ize v/t. düzenlemek, örgütlemek, kurmak, tertip etm., teşkil etm., teşkilâtlandırmak; 'or.gan.iz.er n. düzenleyici, organizatör.

or.gy ['ɔːdʒi] n. çılgınca eğlenme; içki âlemi; aşırı miktar.

o.ri.el ARCH ['ɔːriəl] n. cumba, çıkma.

o.ri.ent 1. ['ɔːriənt] adj. doğuya özgü, doğu…; yükselen, doğan (güneş); 2. [-] n. doğu, şark; doğu memleketleri; 3. ['-ent] v/t. doğuya yöneltmek; o.ri.en.tal [-'entl] 1. □ doğu ile ilgili, doğuya özgü, doğusal; 2. n. doğulu

kimse; o.ri.en.tate ['ɔːrienteit] v/t. doğuya yöneltmek; alıştırmak; o.ri.en'ta.tion n. yönel(t)me; çevreye uy(dur)ma, alış(tır)ma.

or.i.fice ['ɔrifis] n. delik, ağız.

or.i.gin ['ɔridʒin] n. asıl, köken, kaynak, başlangıç; nesil, soy, doğuş.

o.rig.i.nal [ə'ridʒənl] 1. □ aslî, esasa ait, ilk, birinci; yeni, orijinal, yeni icat olunmuş; yaratıcı (kimse, zekâ); COM menşe…; s. share; ~ capital ilk sermaye, kuruluş sermayesi; ~ sin yaradılıştan olan günah; 2. n. asıl nüsha; asıl kaynak, köken, menşe; garip kimse; o.rig.i.nal.i.ty [ˌ'næliti] n. yaratıcılık; orijinallik, özgünlük; o.rig.i.nal.ly [ə'ridʒnəli] adv. aslen, esasında, aslında; orijinal bir biçimde.

o.rig.i.nate [ə'ridʒineit] v/t. meydana getirmek, sebep olm., çıkarmak, yaratmak, türetmek, icat etm.; v/i. meydana gelmek, çıkmak (from, in s.th. bşden; with, from s.o. b-den); o.rig.i'na.tion n. icat etme, icat edilme, meydana gelme; o'rig.i.na.tive □ [-tiv] yaratıcı; o'rig.i.nator n. yaratıcı kimse.

o.ri.ole ORN ['ɔːriəul] n. sarı asma kuşu, sarıcık.

o.ri.son ['ɔrizən] n. dua, yakarış.

or.mo.lu ['ɔːməuluː] n. yaldızlı bronz, altın taklidi pirinç.

or.na.ment 1. ['ɔːnəmənt] n. süs, ziynet; süsle(n)me; fig. şan, şeref; 2. ['-ment] v/t. süslemek, donatmak; or.na'men.tal □ süs kabilinden; or.na.men'ta.tion n. süs, ziynet; süsle(n)me.

or.nate □ [ɔː'neit] çok süslü, şatafatlı, gösterişli; dili süslü (yazı).

or.ni.tho.log.i.cal □ [ɔːniθə'lɔdʒikl] kuşlar bilgisine ait, ornitolojik; or.ni.thol.o.gist [ˌ'θɔlədʒist] n. kuş uzmanı, ornitolog; or.ni'thol.o.gy n. zoolojinin kuşlarla ilgili bölümü, ornitoloji.

o.ro.tund ['ɔrəutʌnd] adj. heybetli, muhteşem; dolgun sesli; süslü, tumturaklı.

or.phan ['ɔːfən] 1. n. öksüz, yetim, kimsesiz b-i; 2. adj. a. ~ed öksüz, yetim, kimsesiz; or.phan.age n. öksüzler yurdu, yetimhane.

or.rer.y ['ɔrəri] n. planetaryum, güneş ve gezegenlerin hareketlerini gösteren aygıt.

or.tho.dox □ ['ɔːθədɔks] ortodoks; dinsel inançlarına sadık; geleneksel, göreneksel; 'or.tho.dox.y n. ortodoks-

luk; inanç sağlamlığı.
or.tho.graph.ic, or.tho.graph.i.cal □
[ɔ:θəu'græfik(əl)] imlâya ait, imlâ...;
or.thogra.phy [ɔ:'θɔɡrəfi] *n.* imlâ
(usulü).
or.tho.p(a)e.dic [ɔ:θəu'pi:dik] *adj.*
(**~ally**) ortopedik; **or.tho'p(a)e.dist** *n.*
ortopedi uzmanı, ortopedist; '**or.tho**-
p(a)e.dy *n.* ortopedi.
or.to.lan ORN ['ɔ:tələn] *n.* kirazkuşu.
Os.car ['ɔskə] *n.* Oskar ödülü (*Amerikan sinemasında*).
os.cil.late ['ɔsileit] *v/t.* sallanmak,
sarsılmak; *fig.* tereddüt etm.; **os.cil'la-
tion** *n.* sallanma, salınma, titreşim; **os-
cil.la.tory** ['~lətəri] *adj.* sallanan, salınan; **oscil.lo.graph** [ɔ'siləuɡrɑ:f] *n.*
osilograf, elektrik akımlarındaki ti-
treşimi kaydeden alet.
os.cu.late *co.* ['ɔskjuleit] *v/t.* öpmek.
o.sier BOT ['əuʒə] *n.* sepetçi söğüdü.
os.mo.sis PHYS [ɔz'məusis] *n.* geçişme,
osmos.
os.prey ['ɔspri] *n.* balık kartalı, deniz
tavşancılı; COM şapka tüyü.
os.se.ous ['ɔsiəs] *adj.* kemikli...; kemik gibi; iskeleti olan; **os.si.fi.ca.tion**
[ɔsifi'keiʃən] *n.* kemikleşme; **os.si.fy**
['~fai] *v/t. & v/i.* kemikleş(tir)mek; kemik gibi sertleş(tir)mek; katılaş(tır)-
mak; **ossu.ar.y** ['ɔsjuəri] *n.* kemikha-
ne, kemik saklanan yer.
os.ten.si.ble □ [ɔs'tensəbl] görünüşte-
ki, görünen.
os.ten.ta.tion [ɔsten'teiʃən] *n.* gösteriş, fiyaka, caka; **os.ten'ta.tious** □ gösterişli, fiyakalı, afili, cakalı.
os.te.ol.o.gy ANAT [ɔsti'ɔlədʒi] *n.* os-
teoloji, kemikbilimi; **os.te.o.path** ['ɔs-
tiəpæθ] *n.* kemikleri ve kasları düzeltme yoluyla tedavi yapan uzman.
ost.ler ['ɔslə] *n.* seyis.
os.tra.cism ['ɔstrəsizəm] *n.* toplum
dışında bırakma, ilişkiyi kesme; **os-
tra.cize** ['~saiz] *v/t.* toplum dışında
bırakmak, toplum dışına itmek.
os.trich ORN ['ɔstritʃ] *n.* devekuşu.
oth.er ['ʌðə] **1.** *adj.* başka, diğer, gayrı,
sair; **2.** *pron.* başka birisi, başka kimse,
başkası, diğeri; **3.** *adv.* başka şekilde,
başka türlü; *the ~ day* geçen gün; *the
~ morning* geçen sabah; *every ~ day*
gün aşırı; *each ~* birbirini, birbirine;
somebody or ~ herhangi biri, şu veya
bu kimse; '*~wise* *adv.* başka türlü, başka şekilde; yoksa, aksi takdirde; diğer
taraftan.

o.ti.ose □ ['əuʃiəus] faydasız, yararsız,
verimsiz, boş; aylak, tembel, başıboş.
ot.ter ZOO ['ɔtə] *n.* susamuru, sarı samur; samur kürk.
Ot.to.man ['ɔtəmən] *n. & adj.* Osmanlı;
♀ divan.
ought [ɔ:t] **1.** = *aught*; **2.** *v/aux.* (*irr.*)
-meli, -malı; I *~ to do it* onu yap-
malıyım; *you ~ to have done it* onu
yapmalıydın.
ounce[1] [auns] *n.* ons (*28, 35 gram*); *you
wouldn't do that if you had an ~ of
sense* beş paralık aklın olsa bunu yap-
mazsın.
ounce[2] ZOO [.] *n.* tekir, kar parsı.
our ['auə] *adj.* bizim; **ours** ['auəz] *pron.*
bizimki; *pred.* bizim; **our'selves** *pron.*
kendimiz, bizler.
oust [aust] *v/t.* yerinden çıkarmak, defetmek, kovmak, dışarı atmak.
out [aut] **1.** *adv.* dışarı, dışarıda; dışarıya; dışında; yüksek sesle; bütün bütün,
tamamen; meydana, ortaya; sonuna
kadar; *be ~* dışarıda olm.; grevde
olm.; mevcut olmamak; alçalmış olm.
(*gelgit*); iktidarda olmamak (*parti*);
modası geçmiş olm., demode olm.;
sönmek (*yangın*); ortaya çıkmak
(*sır*); açmak (*çiçek*); basılmak (*kitap*);
süresi dolmak (*kontrat*); hatalı olm.,
yanlış yapmak; *be ~ for s.th.* veya *to
do s.th.* *sl.* *bşin* veya *bş* yapmak peşinde olm.; *she is not ~ yet* henüz dışarı
çıkmadı; *be ~ with* dargın olm. *ile*; *~
and ~* tam manasıyla, tamamen, her
yönüyle; *~ and about* kalkmış, iyileş-
miş (*hasta*); *~ and away* pek çok, büyük bir farkla, fersah fersah; *s. elbow*;
have it ~ with s.o. *bşi* *b-le* tartışarak
çözümlemek; *voyage ~* gidiş, çıkış, gemiyle dışarı gitme; *way ~* çıkış yolu;
her day ~ günü boş, serbest; *~ with
him!* dışarı atın onu!, defedin gitsin!;
2. *n.* TYP atlanmış kelime; *Am.* Ç çıkar
yol, çözüm yolu; *the ~s pl.* PARL muhalefet; *spor.*: oyuncuyu çıkarma; çıkarılan oyuncu; **3.** *adj.* dışarıdaki, dış...;
uzakta bulunan; iktidarda olmayan,
muhalif; modası geçmiş; imkânsız, olanaksız; COM zararda olan; **4.** *prp.* *~ of*
-*den* dışarı; -*in* dışında; -*den* başka;
için; -*in* arasından; -*den* yapılmış;
-*siz*, -*sız*; -*in* açığında; *s. date, drawing,
laugh, money*; **5.** *v/t.* F kovmak, kapı
dışarı etm.; *boks*: nakavt etm.
out...: ~and-~ ['autnd'aut] *adj.* tam...,
bütün...; '*~and-'out.er* *n.* *bşde* aşırıya

kaçan kimse; '~.**back 1.** *adj.* (*Avustral-ya'da*) nüfusu seyrek olan yerlere ait; **2.** *n.* nüfusu seyrek olan yerler; ~'**bal-ance** *v/t.* geçmek, daha ağır gelmek (*tartı*); ~'**bid** (*irr.* **bid**) *v/t.* (*açık arttır-mada*) artırmak (*fiyat*); '~.**board** *adj.* takma motorlu..., dıştan motorlu...; ~'**brave** *v/t.* cesaretle karşı gelmek -*e*, karşı koymak -*e*; '~.**break** *n.* feve-ran, patlama, patlak verme; yükselme (*ateş*); fışkırma, çıkma; istilâ (*böcek*); isyan, ayaklanma, ihtilâl; '~.**build.ing** *n.* ek bina; '~.**burst** *n.* feveran, patla-ma, patlak verme, fışkırma, tufan (*kahkaha*); '~.**cast 1.** *adj.* toplumdan atılmış, serseri; **2.** *n.* toplumdan atılmış kimse, serseri kimse; '~.**caste** *n.* (*Hin-distan'da*) kast dışı olan kimse, parya; ~'**class** *v/t. spor:* geçmek -*i*, üstün gel-mek -*e*; *be* ~*ed* geri kalmak, geçilmek; '~.**come** *n.* sonuç; etki; '~.**crop** *n.* pat-lama, patlak verme; GEOL yeryüzüne çıkmış kaya; kayanın yeryüzüne çıkması; '~.**cry** *n.* haykırma, çığlık, fer-yat, bağırma; açık arttırma; protesto; ~'**dated** *adj.* modası geçmiş, demode; ~'**distance** *v/t.* geçmek, arkada bırak-mak; ~'**do** (*irr.* **do**) *v/t.* üstün gelmek -*e*, geçmek -*i*; '~.**door** *n.* dışarıda yapı-lan..., açık hava...; ~ **dress** açık hava giysisi; '~.**doors** *adv.* açık havada, dışarıda.

out.er ['autə] *adj.* dış(taki), dışarıda-ki...; ~ **garments** *pl.* üste giyilen giysi-ler; ~ **space** yıldız ve gezegenlerin bu-lunduğu boşluk; '~.**most** *adj.* en dışta-ki...

out...; ~'**face** *v/t.* karşı durmak -*e*, mey-dan okumak -*e*; bakışlarını kaçırınca-ya kadar birine dik dik bakmak; *b-ni* utandırmak; '~.**fall** *n.* çıkış yeri, nehir ağzı; '~.**fit 1.** *n. pl.* gereçler, araç gereç, takım taklavat; *Am.* askeri birlik; **2.** *v/t.* donatmak; '~.**fit.ter** *n.* giyim eşyası satan kimse; teçhizatçı; ~'**flank** *v/t.* MIL çevirmek (*düşman kanadını*); '~.**flow** *n.* akış, akma; gönderilme; ~'**gen.er.al** *v/t.* (*daha iyi plan yaparak*) yenmek; ~'**go 1.** (*irr.* **go**) *v/t.* geçmek, aşmak; *fig.* yenmek; **2.** [' -] *n. pl.* masraf, gider; ~'**go.ing 1.** *adj.* giden, çıkan, ayrılan; sempatik, arkadaş canlısı; **2.** *n.* gidiş, çıkış, ayrılış; ~*s pl.* masraf, giderler, harcama; ~'**grow** (*irr.* **grow**) *v/t.* -*den* daha çabuk büyümek; *fig.* zamanla bırakmak (*kötü alışkanlık vs.*); sığma-mak (*elbiselerine*); '~.**growth** *n.* büyü-

me, gelişme; sonuç, netice, akıbet; dal; '~.**house** *n.* (*sundurma, baraka, ahır gibi*) küçük ek bina; *Am.* dışarıda olan tuvalet.

out.ing ['autiŋ] *n.* tatil, gezinti.

out...; ~'**land.ish** *adj.* tuhaf, acayip, ga-rip; yabancı, ecnebi; uzak, ırak; ~'**last** *v/t.* -*den* daha çok dayanmak; -*den* da-ha çok sürmek; '~.**law 1.** *n.* kanun dışı adam; kanun kaçağı; **2.** *v/t.* kanun dışı etm.; toplum dışı bırakmak; yasakla-mak, men etm.; '~.**law.ry** *n.* kanuna karşı gelme; kanun dışı bırakma; '~.**lay** *n.* masraf, giderler; harcama, masraf etme; '~.**let** *n.* çıkış (yeri); kapı; yol, ağız, delik; *fig.* açılma fırsatı; COM satış alanı, pazar, mahreç; ELECT çıkış, fiş; '~.**line 1.** *n.* taslak, plan; ~*s pl.* (*re-sim, harita vs.*) ana hat(lar); **2.** *v/t.* -*in* taslağını çizmek; -*in* ana hatlarını gös-termek; ~'**live** *v/t.* -*den* fazla yaşamak; '~.**look** *n.* görünüş (*a. fig.*); manzara; bakış açısı, görüş açısı; POL genel görü-nüş; '~.**ly.ing** *adj.* uzakta bulunan, üc-ra...; ~.**ma'noeu.vre** *v/t.* rakibinden daha etkili hareket etm., manevra yap-mada yenmek; ~'**march** *v/t.* daha hızlı veya daha uzun yürüyerek geçmek -*i*; ~'**match** *v/t.* üstün gelmek -*e*, geçmek -*i*; ~'**mod.ed** *adj.* modası geçmiş, de-mode; '~.**most** *adj.* en dışarıdaki; ~'**num.ber** *v/t.* sayıca üstün gelmek -*e*; '~-*of*-'**door**(s) = **outdoor**(s); '~-*of*--'**pock.et** **ex.pens.es** *makbuz aran-maksızın masraf olarak gösterilebilen küçük harcamalar*; '~-*of*-the-'**way** *adj.* uzak, sapa, ücra, ulaşılması güç; *fig.* garip, acayip; '~-*of*-'**work pay** işsiz-lik tazminatı; ~'**pace** *v/t.* ...den daha çabuk gitmek, geçmek -*i*; '~-**pa.tient** *n.* ayakta tedavi edilen hasta; ~'**play** *v/t.* -*den* daha iyi oynamak, yenmek -*i*; ~'**post** *n.* ileri karakol; '~.**pour.ing** *n.* dökülme, taşma, akma (*a. fig.*); '~.**put** *n.* verim, randıman; güç, enerji; bilgisayardan alınan bilgi.

out.rage ['autreidʒ] **1.** *n.* zorbalık, zu-lüm (*on* -*e*); tecavüz (*on* -*e*); hakaret (*on* -*e*); rezalet; **2.** *v/t.* kötü davranmak -*e*; hakaret etm. -*e*, sövüp saymak -*e*; tecavüz etm. -*e*, bozmak -*i*; **out'ra-geous** □ gaddar, insafsız, zalim; çok çirkin, iğrenç, tiksindirici; terbiyesiz.

out...; ~'**range** *v/t.* -*den* daha iyi menzilli olm.; ~'**rank** *v/t.* -*den* daha yüksek rüt-bede olm.

ou.tré ['u:trei] *adj.* alışılagelmişin

dışında, garip, acayip, tuhaf.

out...: ~'**reach** vb. aşmak -i, geçmek -i, -den fazla gelmek; '~-**re.lief** n. fakirlere evlerinde yapılan yardım; ~'**ride** (irr. *ride*) v/t. -den daha hızlı sürmek; NAUT atlatmak (fırtına); '~.**rid.er** n. bir arabanın yanı sıra giden atlı veya motosiklet sürücüsü; '~.**rig.ger** n. NAUT avara demiri; ~.**right 1.** ['autrait] adj. tam, bütün; açık, belli; karşılıksız; **2.** [aut-'rait] adv. açıkça, açık açık; tamamen, bütün bütün; büsbütün; doğrudan doğruya; bir seferde; ~'**ri.val** v/t. rekabette geçmek -i; ~'**run** (irr. *run*) v/t. -den daha hızlı koşmak; aşmak -i; '~.**run.ner** n. bir arabanın yanı sıra koşan uşak; '~.**set** n. başlangıç; ~'**shine** (irr. *shine*) v/t. -den daha çok parlamak; fig. gölgede bırakmak -i; '~'**side 1.** n. dış (taraf); fig. dış görünüş; **at the** ~ en fazla, taş çatlasa, olsa olsa; **2.** adj. dış...; azamî..., en fazla...; dıştan gelen..., haricî...; ~ **right** spor: sağaçık; ~ **left** solaçık; **3.** adv. dışarıda, dışarıya; ~ **of** = **4.** prp. -in dışında, -den başka; '~'**sid.er** n. bir grubun dışında olan kimse; kazanma ihtimali az olan yarışmacı veya at; '~.**size** n. COM büyük boy; '~.**skirts** n. pl. kenar, civar, varoş, dış mahalleler; etek (dağ); ~'**smart** v/t. Am. F -den daha akıllı olup yenmek; '~.**source** (işi) başkasına devretmek; ~'**spoken** □ sözünü sakınmaz, açık sözlü, dobra dobra konuşan; '~'**spread** adj. açık, açılmış, yayılmış; ~'**stand.ing** adj. göze çarpan, önemli; fig. çıkıntılı, fırlak, kepçe (kulak) kalmış (borç); ~'**stay** v/t. -den fazla kalmak; ~ **one's welcome** ev sahibini bıktırıncaya kadar kalmak; ~'**stretched** = **outspread**; ~'**strip** v/t. yarışta geçmek -i; fig. -den üstün çıkmak; '~.**turn** n. verim, randıman; ~'**vie** v/t. yarışta yenmek -i; ~'**vote** v/t. -den daha çok oy toplamak.

out.ward ['autwəd] **1.** adj. dış, haricî; **2.** adv. mst 'out.**wards** görünüşte; dışarıya doğru; 'out.**ward.ly** adv. görünüşte; dışa doğru; 'out.**ward.ness** n. haricî olma; dışa doğru olma.

out...: ~'**wear** (irr. *wear*) v/t. -den daha uzun dayanmak; yıpratmak; tüketmek; ~'**weigh** v/t. -den daha ağır gelmek; fig. daha ağır basmak; ~'**wit** v/t. -den daha akıllıca davranıp atlatmak, -den daha kurnazca davranmak; '~.**work** n. MIL haricî istihkâm; MEC evlerde yapılmak

üzere verilen fabrika işi; '~.**work.er** n. eve iş getiren kimse; '~.**worn** adj. fazla eskimiş; fig. modası geçmiş, demode.

ou.zel ORN ['uːzl] n. karatavuk.

o.val ['əuvəl] **1.** adj. oval..., beyzî...; **2.** n. oval biçimde herhangi bş.

o.va.ry ['əuvəri] n. ANAT yumurtalık; BOT yumurtalık, ovar.

o.va.tion [əu'veiʃən] n. coşkunca alkış.

ov.en ['ʌvən] n. fırın; '~.**bird** n. ORN Am. bir tür ötleğen.

o.ver ['əuvə] **1.** adv. yukarıda; tamamen, baştan başa; tekrar, yine, gene, yeniden, bir daha; karşı taraf(t)a; fazla, artık; bitmiş; geçmiş (fırtına); ~ **and above** -den başka, -den fazla, -e ilâveten; **(all)** ~ **again** bir daha, tekrar; ~ **against** -in karşısın(d)a, -e karşı; **all** ~ **her** tarafında, büsbütün, tamamiyle; ~ **and** ~ **again** tekrar tekrar, defalarca; **fifty times** ~ elli defa daha; **read** ~ baştan başa okumak; **2.** prp. üzerin(d)e, üstün(d)e, yukarısın(d)a; karşıdan karşıya, karşı tarafa, öbür tarafına; boyunca; başında (yönetim); bütün (zaman); -den fazla; sırasında, esnasında; **all** ~ **the town** tüm şehirde; ~ **night** tüm gece; ~ **a glass of wine** bir kadeh şaraptan fazla; ~ **the way** yolun karşısında, karşı tarafta.

o.ver...: '~'**act** v/t. & v/i. abartmalı bir şekilde oynamak (rol); '~.**all 1.** n. iş elbisesi; ~**s** pl. iş tulumu; **2.** adj. baştan başa olan..., kapsamlı; ~'**arch** v/t. & v/i. (üstünde) kemer oluşturmak; ~'**awe** v/t. çok korkutmak; ~'**bal.ance 1.** n. fazla ağırlık; **2.** v/t. dengesini bozmak, devirmek; -den fazla gelmek; v/i. tartıda ağır gelmek; dengesini kaybetmek; ~'**bear** (irr. *bear*) vb. yenmek, -den üstün gelmek; -den ağır gelmek; fazla ürün vermek; ~'**bear.ing** □ buyurucu, küstah, amirlik taslayıcı; zorba tavırlı; ~'**bid** (irr. *bid*) vb. -den fazla fiyat vermek (açık artırmada); -in değerinden fazla fiyat vermek; briç: deklarasyon yapmak; '~'**blown** adj. tazeliğini kaybetmiş (çiçek); heybetli, cüsseli; abartmalı; ~.**board** adv. NAUT gemiden denize; ~'**brim** v/i. üstünden aşmak, taşmak; ~'**bur.den** v/t. fazla yük yüklemek -e; fazla sıkıntı vermek -e; '~.**cast 1.** adj. bulutlu (hava); fig. kasvetli, sıkıcı; **2.** n. bulutlu hava; ~'**charge 1.** v/t. aşırı fiyat istemek -den, kazıklamak -i; fazla doldurmak -i; abartmak -i; **2.** n. fazla yük; fazla fiyat; ~'**cloud**

vb. bulutlarla kaplamak; *fig.* kederlendirmek, tatsızlaştırmak; '~.coat *n.* palto; ~'come (*irr. come*) *vb.* yenmek, alt etm., hakkından gelmek; çaresini bulmak; '~'con.fi.dent ☐ kendine çok güvenen (*of hususunda*), ~'crowd *v/t.* fazla kalabalık etm.; ~'do (*irr. do*) *v/t.* abartmak, şişirmek; abartarak oynamak (*rol*); fazla özenmek -*e*; fazla pişirmek; çok yormak; ~.done [‿-'dʌn] *adj.* abartmalı; çor yorgun, bitkin; ['‿-'dʌn] çok pişmiş; '~.draft *n.* COM hesaptan çekilen fazla para; hesaptan fazla para çekme; açık itibar; '~'draw (*irr. draw*) *vb.* abartmak; COM (*bankadaki hesabından*) fazla para çekmek; '~'dress *v/t.* aşırı süslü giydirmek; *v/i.* aşırı süslü giyinmek; '~.drive *n.* MOT fazla sürat düzeni; ~'due *adj.* RAIL gecikmiş, rötarlı; COM vadesi geçmiş; '~'eat (*irr. eat*); ~ o.s. *v/i.* aşırı yemekten gına gelmek; ~'es.ti.mate *vb.* -*den* fazla tahmin etm.; '~.ex'pose *v/t.* PHOT fazla poz vermek (*filme*); '~.ex'po-sure *n.* PHOT filme fazla poz verme; '~.fa'tigue 1. *adj.* bitkin, çok yorgun; 2. *n.* bitkinlik, aşırı yorgunluk; '~'feed (*irr. feed*) *v/t.* fazla yem vermek; ~.flow 1. [‿-'fləu] (*irr. flow*) *v/t.* su basmak; *v/i.* taşmak; 2. ['‿-fləu] *n.* taşma; sel; taşkın şey; çok bol şey; '~.freight *n.* fazla yük; '~.ground *adj.* yer üzerinde yükselen; '~'grow (*irr. grow*) *vb.* -*den* daha çok büyümek; hızla büyümek; '~.growth *n.* aşırı büyüme; '~.hand *adj. spor.* yukarıdan aşağıya inen...; ~.hang 1. ['‿-'hæŋ] (*irr. hang*) *vb.* (*üzerine*) sarkmak; *fig.* tehlikesi olm.; 2. ['‿-hæŋ] *n.* çıkıntı; ~'haul *v/t.* elden geçirmek, kontrol etm.; yetişmek -*e*; ~.head 1. [‿-'hed] *adv.* yukarıda, tepede, üstte, üst katta; 2. ['‿-hed] *adj.* COM genel masraflarla ilgili; yukarıdan geçen; ~ *railway* asma demiryolu, havaî demiryolu; ~ *wire* ELECT havaî hat; 3. ['‿-hed] *n.: ~s pl.* COM genel masraflar; ~'hear (*irr. hear*) *v/t.* rastlantılı olarak işitmek, kulak misafiri olm.; '~'heat *v/t.* fazla ısıtmak; *v/i.* fazla ısınmak; '~.is.sue *v/t.* fazla basmak (*para*); ~'joy *v/t.* çok sevindirmek; '~.land 1. *adj.* kara yolu ile yapılan...; 2. *adv.* karada(n); ~'lap *v/t. & v/i.* üst üste kapla(n)mak; üst üste getirmek *veya* gelmek; ~.lay 1. [‿-'lei] (*irr. lay*) *v/t.* kaplamak; MEC katlamak; 2. ['‿-lei] *n.* kaplama; kaplayan şey; ~

mattress katlama yatak; '~'leaf *adv.* sayfanın öbür tarafında; '~'leap (*irr. leap*) *v/t.* -*in* üstünden atlamak; ~ o.s. *fig.* haddini aşmak, ileri gitmek; ~.load 1. ['‿-'ləud] *v/t.* fazla yüklemek *veya* doldurmak; 2. ['‿-ləud] *n.* fazla yük; ~'look *v/t.* gözden kaçırmak, dikkate almamak; göz yummak; muayene *veya* teftiş etm.; yukarıdan bakmak -*e*; '~.lord *n.* lordlar lordu; derebeyi; '~.man.tel *n.* ocak davlumbazı; ~'mas.ter *v/t.* boyun eğdirmek, hakkından gelmek; ~'match *v/t.* yenmek; '~'much *adj. & adv.* pek çok, aşırı, gereğinden fazla; '~'night 1. *adv.* gece sırasında, geceleyin, bir gecede; dün gece; 2. *adj.* geceleyin olan...; bir gece için, bir gecelik...; '~.pass *n.* üst geçit; '~'pay (*irr. pay*) *v/t.* fazla ödemek; ~'peo.pled *adj.* aşırı kalabalık; ~.plus *n.* fazlalık; ~'pow.er *v/t.* zararsız hale getirmek, yenmek; '~'print *vb.* -*in* üstüne yeniden basmak; '~.pro'duc.tion *n.* fazla üretim; '~'rate *v/t.* fazla önem vermek -*e*, çok önemsemek -*i*; ~'reach *v/t.* aldatmak, dolandırmak; yetişip geçmek; ~ o.s. kendi çıkarını gözetmek; ~'ride (*irr. ride*) *v/t. fig.* önem vermemek -*e*; ~'rid.ing *adj.* ağır basan; ~'rule *v/t.* yönetmek, etkili olm.; JUR geçersiz kılmak, bozmak, nakzetmek; ~'run (*irr. run*) *v/t.* kaplamak, istilâ etm.; geçmek -*i*, aşmak -*i*; TYP yeniden dizmek; '~'sea 1. *adj. a.* ~s denizaşırı; 2. *adv.* ~s denizaşırı; yurt dışında; '~'see (*irr. see*) *v/t.* yönetmek, idare etm.; '~.se.er *n.* ustabaşı; müfettiş, yönetici, denetçi, idareci; ~'set (*irr. set*) *v/t.* devirmek; *fig.* perişan etm., sarsmak; '~.sew (*irr. sew*) *v/t.* teyellemek; ~'shad.ow *v/t.* gölgelemek, gölge düşürmek, küçültmek; '~.shoe *n.* şoson, lastik, kaloş; '~'shoot (*irr. shoot*) *vb.* ötesine atmak, aşırmak; ~ o.s. aşırılığa kaçmak; '~'shot *adj.* suyu üstten alan...; '~.sight *n.* kusur, yanlış; gözetim; '~.simplifi'ca.tion *n.* anlamını yitirecek derecede basitleştirme; '~'sleep (*irr. sleep*) *v/i. a.* ~ o.s. uyuya kalıp gecikmek, çok uyumak; '~.sleeve *n.* kolluk; '~.spill *n.* (*part. nüfus*) fazlalık; '~'state *v/t.* abartmak; '~'state.ment *n.* abartma, abartı; '~'step *v/t.* aşmak, geçmek; '~'stock *vb.* (*fazla mal ile*) doldurmak; ~.strain 1. ['‿-'strein] *v/t.* fazla yormak; *fig.*

aşırıya kaçırmak; **2.** ['‿strein] *n.* fazla
yorma; **~.strung** ['‿'strʌŋ] *adj.* çok sinirli; ['‿strʌŋ] telleri üst üste gerilmiş
(*piyano*); '**~.sub**'**scribe** *v/t.* gereğinden fazlasını taahhüt etm.; '**~.sup**'**ply**
n. talep fazlası.

o.vert ['əuvə:t] *adj.* açıkça yapılan.

over...: '**~**'**take** (*irr.* **take**) *v/t.* yetişmek
-e, yakalamak *-i*; '**~**'**tax** *v/t.* ağır vergi
koymak; *fig.* aşırı yüklenmek *-e*;
~.throw 1. [‿'θrəu] (*irr.* **throw**) *v/t.* devirmek, yıkmak (*a. fig.*); bozmak, yen-
mek; harap etm.; **2.** ['‿θrəu] *n.* devirme, yıkma; MIL bozgun, yenilgi; '**~.time**
n. fazla çalışma süresi, mesai; '**~.tire**
v/t. çok yormak; '**~.tone** *n.* MUS armonik seslerden biri; '**~**'**top** *v/t.* -*in* tepesini aşmak; üstün gelmek; '**~.trump** *vb.*
-*den* daha yüksek koz oynamak.

over.ture ['əuvətjuə] *n.* MUS uvertür;
teklif, öneri.

o.ver...: **~.turn 1.** ['‿tə:n] *n.* devirme;
devrilme; **2.** [‿'tə:n] *v/t.* devirmek, altüst etm., bozmak; *v/i.* devrilmek;
'**~**'**val.ue** *v/t.* fazla kıymet takdir
etm.; **~**'**ween.ing** *adj.* kendinden çok
emin, gururlu, kibirli; **~.weight 1.**
['‿weit] *n.* fazla ağırlık; **2.** ['‿'weit]
v/t. fazla yük koymak *-e*; **~.whelm** *v/t.*
yenmek, alt etm.; *fig.* bunaltmak, garketmek, boğmak; '**~**'**wise** □ ukalâ;
~.work 1. ['‿wə:k] *n.* fazla çalışma; **2.**
[‿'wə:k] (*irr.* **work**) *v/t.* & *v/i.* fazla
çalış(tır)mak; '**~**'**wrought** *adj.* sinirleri
bozuk; çok heyecanlı; aşırı süslü, cicili
bicili.

o.vi.duct MED ['əuvidʌkt] *n.* dölyatağı
borusu; **o.vi.form** ['‿fɔ:m] *adj.* oval,
yumurta şeklindeki; **o**'**vip.a.rous** ZOO
[‿pərəs] *adj.* yumurtlayan; **o.vule** BIOL
['əuvju:l] *n.* yumurtacık; **o.vum** BIOL
['əuvəm] *n.*, *pl.* **o.va** ['əuvə] yumur-
ta(cık).

owe [əu] *vb.* borcu olm., borçlu olm.
(*s.o. s.th. -e -den dolayı*); etkisinde
olm.; minnettarı olm.; *spor.* avans vermek; **~** *s.o.* **a grudge** *b-ne* kin beslemek.

ow.ing ['əuiŋ] *adj.* borç olan; **~** *to* sebebiyle, yüzünden, ...den dolayı; *be* **~** *to*
...den dolayı olm.

owl ORN [aul] *n.* baykuş, puhu; **owl.et**
['aulit] *n.* baykuş yavrusu; '**owl.ish** □
baykuşa benzeyen, baykuş gibi...

own [əun] **1.** *adj.* kendi(nin), özel, kendine özgü; öz; *my* **~** *self* bizzat ben; **~**
brother to s.o. b-nin öz kardeşi; *she
makes her* **~** *clothes* kendi elbiselerini
kendi diker; **2.** *my* **~** kendi malım, benim; *a house of one's* **~** *b-nin* kendi
evi; *come into one's* **~** lâyık olduğu yere erişmek, *k-ni* göstermek; *get one's*
~ *back* F öcünü almak; *hold one's* **~**
dayanmak, karşı koymak, yerini korumak; *on one's* **~** F yalnız, tek başına;
kendi hesabına, kendi başına; üstüne
olmayan, bir eşi daha olmayan; **3.** *v/t.*
sahip olm., malik olm. *-e*; kabul etm.,
tanımak, itiraf etm., doğrulamak *-i*; **~**
up (*to*) F açıkça itiraf etm.

own.er ['əunə] *n.* sahip, mal sahibi;
'**~**'**driv.er** *n.* kendi aracını kullanan
şoför; '**~.less** *adj.* sahipsiz; '**~**'**oc.cu-
pied** *adj.* sahibinin oturduğu (*ev*);
'**own.er.ship** *n.* mülkiyet, sahiplik.

ox [ɔks] *n.*, *pl.* **ox.en** ['ɔksən] öküz,
sığır.

ox.al.ic ac.id CHEM [ɔk'sælik'æsid] *n.*
oksalik asit.

Ox.bridge ['ɔksbridʒ] *n.* Oxford *ve(ya)*
Cambridge üniversitesi.

ox-cart ['ɔkskɑ:t] *n.* kağnı, öküz arabası; **ox.en** ['ɔksən] *n. pl. of ox*; '**ox-
-eye** *n.* BOT sarı papatya.

Ox.ford shoes ['ɔksfəd'ʃu:z] *n. pl.*
bağlı erkek ayakkabısı.

ox.i.da.tion [ɔksi'deiʃən] *n.* oksitlenme, oksidasyon; **ox.ide** ['ɔksaid]
n. oksit; **ox.i.dize** ['ɔksidaiz] *v/t. & v/i.*
oksijen ile birleş(tir)mek; oksitle(n)-
mek.

ox.lip BOT ['ɔkslip] *n.* çuhaçiçeği.

Ox.o.ni.an [ɔk'səunjən] **1.** *adj.* Oxford
Üniversitesi...; **2.** *n.* Oxford üniversitesi *veya* öğretim görevlisi.

ox.y.gen CHEM ['ɔksidʒən] *n.* oksijen;
ox.ygen.ate [ɔk'sidʒineit] *v/t.* oksijen
ile karıştırmak.

ox.y.hy.dro.gen CHEM ['ɔksi'haidrid-
ʒən] *n.* oksihidrojen gazı.

o.yer JUR ['ɔiə] *n.* sorguya çekme, sorgu.

o.yez [əu'jes] *int.* dinleyin!

oys.ter ['ɔistə] *n.* istiridye; *attr.* istiridye...; '**~.bed** *n.* istiridye yatağı.

o.zone CHEM ['əuzəun] *n.* ozon;
o.zon.ic [əu'zɔnik] *adj.* ozona ait,
ozon...

P

P [piː]: *mind one's* Ps and Qs hareketlerine dikkat etm.

pa F [pɑː] *n.* baba.

pab.u.lum ['pæbjuləm] *n.* yiyecek, gıda.

pace [peis] **1.** *n.* adım, yürüyüş (hızı); gidiş; rahvan yürüyüş (*at*); *fig.* gelişme, ilerleme hızı; *keep ~ with* ayak uydurmak *-e*; *put s.o. through his ~s* b-nin yeteneğini ölçmek; *set the ~* sürati tayin etm., tempoyu ayarlamak; **2.** *v/t.* adımlamak; ayarlamak; *spor.* tayin etm. (*sürat*); *v/i.* yürümek, gezinmek; eşkin gitmek, rahvan gitmek (*at*); **paced** *adj.* adımlanmış…; rahvan yürüyüşlü…; 'pace-mak.er *n. spor.* yarışta sürati ayarlayan binici *veya* koşucu; 'pac.er *n.* yaya yürüyen (*veya* ölçülü adımlarla giden) kimse; = *pace-maker.*

pach.y.derm zoo ['pækidəːm] *n.* kalın derili ve dört ayaklı bir hayvan (*fil, suaygırı, gergedan v.b.*).

pa.cif.ic [pə'sifik] **1.** *adj.* (*~ally*) barışçı, barışsever, sulhçu, sulhperver; sakin; *the ♀ Ocean* = **2.** *n. the ♀* Büyük Okyanus, Pasifik Okyanusu; **pac.i.fi.ca-tion** [pæsifi'keiʃən] *n.* barış(tır)ma, uzlaş(tır)ma; barış anlaşması.

pac.i.fi.er ['pæsifaiə] *n.* barıştıran kimse; *Am.* emzik; 'pac.i.fism *n.* barışseverlik, sulhperverlik; 'pac.i.fist *n.* barışçı kimse.

pac.i.fy ['pæsifai] *v/t.* yatıştırmak, sakinleştirmek; barıştırmak, uzlaştırmak; boyun eğdirmek, baskı altında tutmak (*ülke*).

pack [pæk] **1.** *n.* bohça, çıkın; sürü; takım; köpek sürüsü; *iskambil:* deste; *Am.* paket (*sigara*); balya; denk; MED kompres, buz torbası; *a. ~ice* buz kütlesi; *a ~ of nonsense* bir sürü saçmalık; **2.** *v/t.* bohçalamak; denk etm.; ambalajlamak, paketlemek, sarmak (*a.* MED); istif etm.; tıkıştırmak, sıkıştırmak, tıka basa doldurmak; hazırlamak, toplamak (*bavul*); denk, sandık *veya* kutuya koymak; *a. ~ off* defetmek, kovmak, postalamak; *Am.* F taşımak, nakletmek, götürmek; MEC kalafatlamak; *v/i. a. ~ up* gitmek,

defolmak; birleşmek, bir araya gelmek, sıkışmak; *send s.o. ~ing* pılıyı pırtıyı toplatıp defetmek; *~ up* F durmak; 'pack.age *n.* ambalaj; bohça; *part. Am.* paket; balya; koli; 'packaged tour grup turu; 'pack-an.i.mal *n.* yük hayvanı; 'pack.er *n.* ambalajcı, paket yapan kimse *veya* alet; pack.et ['pækit] *n.* paket, çıkın, bohça, deste; *sl.* dünya kadar para; *a. ~-boat* posta gemisi; *catch a ~ sl.* ağır yaralı olm.; 'pack-horse *n.* yük beygiri.

pack.ing ['pækiŋ] *n.* bağlama, paketleme, ambalaj; MEC salmastıra, tıkaç, conta, tampon; *attr.* paket…; '~-box *n.* RAIL eşya sandığı; ~ house *Am.* büyük mezbaha.

pack.thread ['pækθred] *n.* sicim, kınnap.

pact [pækt] *n.* antlaşma, sözleşme, pakt.

pad¹ *sl.* [pæd] *vb. a. ~ it, ~ along* yayan gitmek, taban tepmek.

pad² [.] **1.** *n.* yastık; kâğıt destesi; *spor.* tekmelik; ıstampa; MEC rampa; bazı hayvanların yumuşak tabanı; *sl.* yatak, oda, apartman dairesi; **2.** *v/t. -in* içini doldurmak; takviye etm.; şişirmek (*konuşma, yazı vs.*); ~ *out fig.* şişirmek (*konuşma, yazı vs.*); *~ded cell* duvarları takviyeli hücre; 'pad.ding *n.* vatka; kıtık; *fig.* abartma.

pad.dle ['pædl] **1.** *n.* tokaç; nehir vapurunun yan çarkı; NAUT kısa kürek, pala; **2.** *v/t. & v/i.* kısa kürekle yürü(t)mek; yavaş yavaş kürek çekmek; tokmakla dövmek (*çamaşır*); el ve ayakları suda oynatmak; sendeleyerek yürümek; suda oynamak; *paddling pool* sığ havuz; *~ one's own canoe* kendi işini kendi görmek; '~-box *n.* NAUT davlumbaz, yandan çark mahfazası; '~-steam.er *n.* NAUT yandan çarklı gemi; '~-wheel *n.* geminin yan çarkı.

pad.dock ['pædək] *n.* çayırlık, otlak; *spor.* pist; eyerleri tartma yeri; pözaj.

pad.dy¹ COM ['pædi] *n.* kabuklu pirinç, çeltik; pirinç tarlası.

pad.dy² F [.] *n.* öfke, hiddet, köpürme.

pad.lock ['pædlɔk] **1.** *n.* asma kilit; **2.** *vb.* asma kilitle kilitlemek, asma kilit vurmak.

pad.re F MIL ['pɑːdrei] *n.* papaz, rahip, vaiz.

pae.an ['piːən] *n.* şükran *veya* zafer şarkısı.

p(a)ed.er.as.ty ['pedəræsti] *n.* oğlancılık, ibnelik, kulamparalık.

p(a)e.di.a.tri.cian [piːdiə'triʃən] *n.* çocuk doktoru; **p(a)e.di.at.rics** [-'ætriks] *n. sg.* çocuk bakımı *veya* tedavisi ilmi.

pa.gan ['peigən] **1.** *adj.* dinsiz, putperest, kâfir; **2.** *n.* putperest kimse; 'pa-gan.ism *n.* putperestlik.

page¹ [peidʒ] **1.** *n.* otel garsonu; iç oğlanı; *Am.* ulak, uşak; **2.** *v/t. Am.* hoparlör ile çağırmak.

page² [-] **1.** *n.* sayfa; *fig.* kayda değer olay; **2.** *v/t.* -*in* sayfalarını numaralamak (*gazete, kitap vs.*).

pag.eant ['pædʒənt] *n.* tarihi oyun; alay, tören; gösteri, temsil; 'pag.eant-ry *n.* görkemli temsil (*veya* gösteri).

pag.i.nate ['pædʒineit] *s.* **page²** 2; **pag.i'nation** *n.* kitap sayfalarını numaralama.

pa.go.da [pə'gəudə] *n.* pagoda, Uzak Doğu'da tapınak.

paid [peid] *pret. & p.p. of* **pay 2**.

pail [peil] *n.* kova.

pail.lasse ['pæliæs] *n.* ot minder.

pain [pein] **1.** *n.* ağrı, sızı, acı; dert, keder, elem, ıstırap, azap; **~s** *pl.* özen, itina, zahmet; doğum sancıları; **on** *veya* **under ~ of death** aksi takdirde cezası ölüm; **be in ~** acı çekmek; bir yeri ağrımak; **be at ~s, take ~s** özen göstermek, özenmek, zahmete girmek; **2.** *v/t.* acı vermek -*e*, ağrı vermek -*e*; üzmek -*i*, eziyet etm. -*e*; **pain.ful** [-'ful] acı veren, ıstırap çektiren; zahmetli, güç; üzücü; 'pain-kill.er *n.* ağrı kesici ilâç; 'painless □ acısız, ağrısız; 'pains.tak-ing **1.** □ özenli, dikkatli; hamarat, çalışkan; **2.** *n.* özenme, itina etme.

paint [peint] **1.** *n.* boya; kozmetik; makyaj; **wet ~!** yeni boyanmıştır!; **2.** *v/t.* boyamak; boyayarak süslemek; boya ile resim yapmak; *fig.* tasvir etm., resmetmek; **~ out** üzerine boya sürerek kapatmak (*veya* gidermek); *v/i.* yağlıboya resim yapmak; makyaj yapmak; '~box *n.* boya kutusu; '~brush *n.* boya fırçası.

paint.er¹ ['peintə] *n.* ressam; boyacı.

paint.er² NAUT [-] *n.* pruva halatı.

paint.ing ['peintiŋ] *n.* ressamlık; resim, tablo.

pair [pɛə] **1.** *n.* çift, iki adet; karı koca; karşı cinsten iki hayvan; **a ~ of scis-sors** makas; **in ~s** ikişer ikişer, çifter çifter; **2.** *v/t. & v/i.* çiftleş(tir)mek; *a.* **~ off** çiftlere ayırmak *veya* ayrılmak; **~ off with** F evlenmek.

pa.ja.mas [pə'dʒɑːməz] = **pyjamas**.

Pa.kis.ta.ni [pɑːkis'tɑːni] *n. & adj.* Pakistanlı.

pal *sl.* [pæl] **1.** *n.* arkadaş, dost, ahbap; **2.** *v/i.* **~ up with s.o.** *b-le* arkadaş (*veya* kafadar) olm.

pal.ace ['pælis] *n.* saray; saray gibi bina; lüks eğlence yeri.

pal.ae.o- ['pæliəu] *comb.* eski zaman...; **pal.ae.o.lith.ic** [-əu'liθik] *adj.* taş devrine ait; **pal.ae.on.tol.o.gy** [-ɔn'tɔlədʒi] *n.* paleontoloji.

pal.at.a.ble □ ['pælətəbl] lezzetli, leziz; *fig.* makûl, akla yatkın; 'pal.at.a.ble-ness *n.* lezizlik.

pal.a.tal ['pælətl] **1.** *adj.* damağa ait; dilin damağa dokunmasıyla çıkarılan (*ses*); **2.** *n.* GR dilin damağa dokunmasıyla çıkarılan ses, damak sessizi.

pal.ate ['pælit] *n.* damak; *fig.* ağız tadı, zevk, haz.

pa.la.tial □ [pə'leiʃəl] saray gibi, görkemli.

pa.lat.i.nate [pə'lætinit] *n.* palatinlik, kont *veya* dük'ün yönettiği ülke; **the** ♀ Palatina.

pal.a.tine ['pælətain] *adj.* Palatinalı, Palatinliğe ait, Palatina...; **Count**♀ Palatinlik kontu.

pa.lav.er [pə'lɑːvə] **1.** *n.* görüşme, konuşma; *sl.* boş laf, palavra; **2.** *v/i.* boş laf etm., palavra atmak, atıp tutmak.

pale¹ [peil] **1.** □ soluk, solgun, renksiz, mat, donuk; **~ ale** beyaz bira; **2.** *v/t. & v/i.* sarar(t)mak, sol(dur)mak, donuklaş(tır)mak, beti benzi atmak.

pale² [-] *n.* kazık; etrafı çevrili yer.

pale-face ['peilfeis] *n.* soluk benizli.

pale.ness ['peilnis] *n.* solgunluk, renksizlik, matlık.

pa.le.o- ['pæliəu] *s.* **palaeo-**.

pal.ette PAINT ['pælit] *n.* palet; '~knife *n.* boya malası.

pal.frey ['pɔːlfri] *n.* binek atı.

pal.imp.sest ['pælimpsest] *n.* önceden yazılan silinerek üzerine yeniden başka yazı yazılmış parşömen.

pal.ing ['peiliŋ] *n.* kazıklardan yapılmış çit.

pal.i.sade [pæli'seid] **1.** *n.* parmaklık, çit; **~s** *pl. Am.* kayalık uçurum; **2.** *v/t.*

kazıklarla çevirmek *veya* sağlamlaştırmak.

pall¹ [pɔːl] *n.* tabut örtüsü; *fig.* kasvetli hava.

pall² [-] *vb.* yavanlaşmak, tatsızlaşmak, tadı kaçmak; usandırmak, bıktırmak, gına getirmek (*upon s.o. b-ni*).

pal.la.di.um [pə'leidjəm] *n.* himaye, koruma; koruyucu şey, güverinlik unsuru.

pal.let ['pælit] *n.* ot minder.

pal.liasse ['pæliæs] = *paillasse*.

pal.li.ate ['pælieit] *v/t.* hafifletmek (*ağrı, hastalık*), yatıştırmak; örtbas etm., mazur göstermek (*suç*); **pal.li'a-tion** *n.* hafifletme, yatıştırma; özür; **pal.li.a.tive** ['-ətiv] *adj. & n.* hafifletici (*şey*); *fig.* örtbas etme; geçici önlem.

pal.lid □ ['pælid] solgun, sararmış, beti benzi atmış, renksiz; '**pal.lid.ness**, **pal.lor** ['pælə] *n.* solgunluk.

palm [pɑːm] **1.** *n.* avuç içi, el ayası; BOT hurma ağacı; palmiye; *have an itching* ~ anaforcu olm., para canlısı olm.; **2.** *v/t.* avuç içinde saklamak; avuç içi ile dokunmak *veya* vurmak; ~ *s.th. off upon s.o. b-ne bşi* yutturmak, sokuşturmak; **pal.mer** ['pɑːmə] *n.* Kudüs'-ten hurma dalı ile dönen hacı; '**palm-ist** *n.* el falına bakan kimse; '**palm.is-try** *n.* el falı; '**palm-oil** *n.* hurma yağı; *co.* rüşvet; '**palm-tree** *n.* hurma ağacı; '**palm.y** *adj.* muhteşem, görkemli, refah içindeki.

pal.pa.ble ['pælpəbl] □ hissedilebilir, dokunulabilir; *fig.* açık (seçik), belli, belirgin, bariz.

pal.pi.tate ['pælpiteit] *v/i.* küt küt atmak (*kalp*); heyecandan titremek; **pal.pi'tation** *n.* çarpıntı, küt küt atma (*kalp*).

pal.sy ['pɔːlzi] **1.** *n.* felç, inme; *fig.* aciz, kuvvetsizlik; **2.** *v/t. fig.* felce uğratmak, aksatmak.

pal.ter ['pɔːltə] *vb.* küçümsemek, yabana atmak, önemsememek (*with -i*).

pal.tri.ness ['pɔːltrinis] *n.* değersizlik, önemsizlik; '**pal.try** □ değersiz, önemsiz.

pam.pas ['pæmpəz] *n. pl.* Güney Amerika'daki ağaçsız geniş ovalar.

pam.per ['pæmpə] *v/t.* şımartmak, pohpohlamak, üstüne çok düşmek.

pam.phlet ['pæmflit] *n.* broşür, kitapçık, risale; **pam.phlet.eer** [-'tiə] *n.* broşür yazarı.

pan [pæn] **1.** *n.* tava; kefe, terazi gözü; eski tüfeklerde falya tavası; *sl.* yüz, surat; sert eleştiri; **2.** *v/t. & v/i.* toprağı yıkayarak çıkarmak (*altın*); tavada yıkamak; tavaya koymak; *Am.* F şiddetle eleştirmek; bir yandan öbür yana çevirmek (*kamera*); maden cevherini yıkamak; ~ *out* başarıya ulaşmak; sonuç vermek, değmek.

pan... [-] *prefix* bütün..., tüm...

pan.a.ce.a [pænə'siə] *n.* her derde deva.

pan.cake ['pænkeik] *n.* gözleme; ~ *landing* AVIA uçağın yere yatay durumda çarparak inişi.

pan.cre.as MED ['pæŋkriəs] *n.* pankreas.

pan.de.mo.ni.um *fig.* [pændi'məunjəm] *n.* karışıklık, kargaşa, şamata, kıyamet; cehennem.

pan.der ['pændə] **1.** *vb.* hoşnut etm. (*to -i*); pezevenklik etm.; **2.** *n.* pezevenk.

pane [pein] *n.* pencere camı; MEC levha, tabaka.

pan.e.gyr.ic [pæni'dʒirik] *n.* övgü, methiye, kaside; **pan.e'gyr.ist** *n.* kaside yazarı, methiyeci.

pan.el ['pænl] **1.** *n.* ARCH kapı aynası; pano; PAINT resim tahtası; elbise eteğine konulan parça; JUR jüri heyeti (isim listesi); panel, açık oturum; heyet; **2.** *v/t.* tahta ile kaplamak; '~*-doc.tor* *n.* sigorta doktoru; '**pan.el.ist** *n.* açık oturumda konuşmacı; '**pan.el.(l)ing** *n.* tahta kaplama.

pang [pæŋ] *n.* anî ağrı, sancı; *fig.* ıstırap, sıkıntı.

pan.han.dle ['pænhændl] **1.** *n.* tava sapı; *Am.* ileri doğru uzanan dar kara parçası; **2.** *v/i. Am.* F dilenmek, avuç açmak; '**pan.han.dler** *n. Am.* F dilenci.

pan.ic ['pænik] **1.** *adj.* yersiz, sebepsiz (*korku*); **2.** *n.* panik, korku; **3.** *v/t. & v/i. pret. & p.p.* '**pan.icked** paniğe uğratmak; korkmak, paniğe kapılmak; *sl.* coşturmak, kahkahadan kırıp geçirmek; '**panick.y** *adj.* paniğe kapılmış; '**pan.ic-monger** *n.* panik yaratan kimse; '**pan.ic-strick.en** *adj.* paniğe kapılmış, panik içinde.

pan.nier ['pæniə] *n.* küfe, sepet.

pan.ni.kin ['pænikin] *n.* küçük madeni kap.

pan.o.ply ['pænəpli] *n.* zırh takımı.

pan.o.ra.ma [pænə'rɑːmə] *n.* panorama, manzara; *fig.* devamlı değişen şey; toplu bakış; **pan.o.ram.ic** [-'ræmik] *adj.* (~*ally*) panoramik.

pan.sy ['pænzi] *n.* BOT alaca menekşe, hercai menekşe; *a.* **~-boy** homoseksüel erkek.

pant [pænt] *v/i.* solumak, kalmak (*for breath* nefes nefese); nefesi kesilmek; özlem duymak (*for, after* -e); *v/t.* **~ out** nefes nefese söylemek.

pan.ta.loon [pæntə'lu:n] *n.* maskara, soytarı, palyaço; **~s** *pl. co. veya Am.* pantolon.

pan.tech.ni.con [pæn'teknikən] *n. a.* **~ van** eşya kamyonu.

pan.the.ism ['pænθiizm] *n.* panteizm, kamutanrıcılık; **pan.the'is.tic** *adj.* (**~ally**) panteizme ait, kamutanrısal.

pan.ther ZOO ['pænθə] *n.* pars, panter, puma.

pant.ies F ['pæntiz] *n. pl.* kadın külotu; kısa çocuk pantolonu.

pan.tile ['pæntail] *n.* kiremit.

pan.to F [pæntəu] = *pantomime.*

pan.to.graph MEC ['pæntəugra:f] *n.* pantograf.

pan.to.mime ['pæntəmaim] *n.* pandomima; **pan.to.mim.ic** [..'mimik] *adj.* (**~ally**) pandomima kabilinden.

pan.try ['pæntri] *n.* kiler; sofra takımının muhafaza edildiği yer; (*otel, gemi vs.*) soğuk yemeklerin hazırlandığı yer.

pants [pænts] *n. pl.* pantolon; COM don, külot.

pant.y [pænti] **hose** *n.* külotlu çorap.

pap [pæp] *n.* lapa *veya* sulu yemek (*çocuklar veya hastalar için*).

pa.pa [pə'pa:] *n.* baba (*çocuk dilinde*).

pa.pa.cy ['peipəsi] *n.* papalık (sistemi).

pa.pal □ ['peipəl] papa *veya* papalığa ait.

pap.a.raz.zi [pæpə'rærsi] *n. pl.* paparazziler *pl.*

pa.per ['peipə] **1.** *n.* kâğıt; gazete; *a.* **~ money** kâğıt para, banknot; *sl.* paso; hüviyet kartı, kimlik belgesi; imtihan soruları; makale, yazı; duvar kâğıdı; **~s** *pl.* evrak; *send in one's* **~s** istifa etm.; **2.** *v/t.* duvar kâğıdı ile kaplamak, kâğıtlamak; '**~back** *n.* karton kapaklı kitap; **~bag** kesekâğıdı; '**~chase** *n.* tavşan tazı oyunu; '**~clip** *n.* raptiye; **~cred.it** COM vadeli senet; '**~fast.en.er** *n.* tel raptiye, ataş; '**~hang.er** *n.* duvar kâğıdı yapıştıran kimse; '**~hang.ings** *n. pl.* duvar kâğıdı yapıştırma; '**~mill** *n.* kâğıt fabrikası; '**~weight** *n.* uçmasını önlemek için kâğıt üzerine konan ağırlık, prespapye; '**pa.per.y** *adj.*

kâğıt gibi, ince.

pa.pier-mâ.ché ['pæpjei'ma:ʃei] *n.* kartonpiyer.

pa.pist *contp.* ['peipist] *n.* katolik.

pap.py ['pæpi] *n.* baba.

pap.ri.ka ['pæprikə] *n.* kırmızı biber.

pa.py.rus [pə'paiərəs] *n.* papirüs; papirüs üzerine yazılmış yazı.

par [pa:] *n.* COM itibarî kıymet, nominal değer; eşitlik, parite; *above* (*below*) **~** itibarî kıymetten (*veya* pariteden) fazla (düşük); *at* **~** paritede, başabaş; *be on a* **~** *with* ...ile eşit derece *veya* kıymette olm.

par.a.ble ['pærəbl] *n.* mesel, ibret alınacak öykü.

pa.rab.o.la MATH [pə'ræbələ] *n.* parabol; **para.bol.ic, par.a.bol.i.cal** □ [pærə'bɔlik(əl)] benzetme *veya* kıyas yoluyla ifade edilen; MATH parabolik.

par.a.chute ['pærəʃu:t] *n.* paraşüt; '**par.achut.ist** *n.* paraşütçü.

pa.rade [pə'reid] **1.** *n.* MIL geçit resmi, tören; gösteri, nümayiş; tören alanı; mesire yeri; ECCL dinî alay; *make a* **~** *of s.th.* bşle hava atmak; **2.** *v/t. & v/i.* MIL sıraya diz(il)mek; MIL saflar halinde yürü(t)mek; gösteriş yapmak; kibirle göstermek; **pa'rade-ground** *n.* MIL tören alanı.

par.a.digm GR ['pærədaim] *n.* çekim listesi.

par.a.dise ['pærədais] *n.* cennet; cennet bahçesi; cennet gibi yer; büyük mutluluk.

par.a.dis.i.ac [pærə'disiæk] *adj.* cennete ait, cennet gibi, cennet...

par.a.dox ['pærədɔks] *n.* paradoks, kökleşmiş düşüncelere aykırı olarak ileri sürülen düşünce; **par.a'dox.i.cal** □ mantığa aykırı görünen.

par.af.fin CHEM ['pærəfin] *n.* mum, parafin; gazyağı.

par.a.gon [pærəgən] *n.* fazilet örneği.

par.a.graph ['pærəgra:f] *n.* satırbaşı; paragraf, bent, fıkra; paragraf işareti.

par.a.keet ORN ['pærəki:t] *n.* muhabbetkuşu, bir çeşit ufak papağan.

par.al.lel ['pærəlel] **1.** *adj.* paralel, koşut; *fig.* aynı, benzer; **2.** *n.* paralel doğru; *fig.* benzerlik; karşılaştırma, mukayese; ELECT paralel bağlantı; *without* (*a*) **~** emsalsiz, eşsiz; **3.** *v/t.* kıyaslamak, karşılaştırmak; paralel olm. -e; benzer olm. -e; **~ bars** *pl. spor:* barfiks; '**par.al.lel.ism** *n.* paralellik; benzerlik; **par.al'lel.o.gram** MATH

[ˌləugræm] *n.* paralelkenar, paralelogram.

par.a.lyse ['pærəlaiz] *v/t.* felce uğratmak; *fig.* etkisiz bırakmak; **pa.ral.ysis** MED [pəˈrælisis] *n.* felç, inme; **para.lyt.ic** [pærəˈlitik] **1.** *adj.* (**∼ally**) felçli, inmeli, kötürüm; **2.** *n.* felçli kimse.

par.a.mil.i.tar.y ['pærəˈmilitəri] *adj.* yarı askerî.

par.a.mount ['pærəmaunt] *adj.* üstün, en önemli, fevkalâde.

par.a.mour RHET ['pærəmuə] *n.* gayri meşru karı *veya* koca, metres.

par.a.pet ['pærəpit] *n.* MIL siper; korkuluk duvarı.

par.a.pher.na.li.a [pærəfəˈneiljə] *n. pl.* özel eşya; F teçhizat, takım taklavat.

par.a.phrase ['pærəfreiz] **1.** *n.* başka kelimelerle açıklama; **2.** *v/t.* başka kelimelerle açıklamak.

par.a.site ['pærəsait] *n.* parazit, asalak (*a. fig.*); **par.a.sit.ic, par.a.sit.i.cal** □ [ˌ-ˈsitik(əl)] asalak olarak yaşayan, parazit…, asalak…

par.a.sol [pærəˈsɔl] *n.* güneş şemsiyesi, güneşlik.

par.a.troop.er ['pærətruːpə] *n.* MIL paraşütçü; '**par.a.troops** *n. pl.* paraşütçü kıtası.

par.a.ty.phoid MED ['pærəˈtaifɔid] *n.* paratifo.

par.boil ['pɑːbɔil] *v/t.* yarı kaynatmak; *fig.* kavurmak.

par.cel ['pɑːsl] **1.** *n.* paket, koli, bohça, çıkın; COM parça, kısım, parsel; *contp.* küme, yığın; **2.** *v/t.* ∼ *out* bölmek, taksim etm.; parsellemek (*arazi*); ∼ *post* paket postası.

parch [pɑːtʃ] *v/t. & v/i.* kavurup kurutmak, kavurmak, yakmak (*güneş*); kavrulmak, kurumak; ∼*ing heat* kavurucu sıcak

parch.ment ['pɑːtʃmənt] *n.* parşömen (*kâğıdı*), tirşe.

pard *sl.* [pɑːd] *n.* arkadaş, dost.

par.don ['pɑːdn] **1.** *n.* af, bağışlama; JUR özel af; ECCL günah çıkarma; *I beg your* ∼*!* affedersiniz!; **2.** *v/t.* affetmek, bağışlamak (*s.o. b-ni*; *s.th.* bş için); '**par.don.a.ble** □ affolunabilir, bağışlanabilir; '**par.don.er** *n.* HIST Orta Çağda günahların affını satmaya yetkili kimse.

pare [pɛə] *v/t.* yontmak; *-in* kabuğunu soymak; ∼ *away*, ∼ *down fig.* azaltmak, kısmak (*masraf*).

par.ent ['pɛərənt] *n.* baba; anne; ata,

cet; *fig.* sebep, neden, kaynak; ∼*s pl.* ana baba, ebeveyn; *attr. fig.* anne…; asıl…; '**par.en.tage** *n.* soy, nesil, ebeveynlik; **paren.tal** □ [pəˈrentl] ana babaya ait, ana baba…

pa.ren.the.sis [pəˈrenθisis] *n.*, *pl.* **pa'renthe.ses** [ˌ-siːz] parantez, ayraç; parantez cümlesi; TYP parantez işareti; **paren.the.tic, par.en.thet.i.cal** □ [pærənˈθətik(əl)] parantez gibi; parantez…

par.ent.hood ['pɛərənthud] *n.* analık *veya* babalık; '**par.ent.less** *adj.* anasız babasız.

pa.ri.ah ['pæriə] *n.* parya; *fig.* toplum dışı bırakılmış kimse.

pa.ri.e.tal [pəˈraiitl] *adj.* parietal…; ∼ *bone* ANAT kafatasının yan kemiği.

par.ing ['pɛəriŋ] *n.* kabuğunu soyma; soyulmuş kabuk; ∼*s pl.* kabuk parçaları, kırpıntı; '∼*-knife* *n.* MEC soyma bıçağı.

par.ish ['pæriʃ] *n.* cemaat; bir papazın idaresindeki bölge; *go on the* ∼ kilise yardımıyla geçinmek; *attr.* kilise…; papaz…; ∼ *clerk* kilise kâtibi; papaz muavini; ∼ *council* kilise meclisi; ∼ *register* kilise defteri; **pa.rish.ion.er** [pəˈriʃənə] *n.* kilise cemiyeti üyesi.

Pa.ri.sian [pəˈrizjən] **1.** *adj.* Paris'e ait, Paris…; **2.** *n.* Parisli.

par.i.ty ['pæriti] *n.* eşitlik; *borsa:* fiyat birliği, değer eşitliği, parite.

park [pɑːk] **1.** *n.* park; MIL savaş gereçlerinin saklandığı yer; *mst car*∼ otopark; **2.** *v/t.* MOT park etm.; F koymak, yerleştirmek.

par.ka ['pɑːkə] *n.* parka, anorak.

park.ing MOT ['pɑːkiŋ] *n.* park yapma; ∼ *lot* araba park yeri; ∼ *me.ter* otopark sayacı.

par.ky *sl.* ['pɑːki] *adj.* soğuk, buz gibi (*hava*).

par.lance ['pɑːləns] *n.* konuşma şekli; tabir, deyiş, deyim.

par.ley ['pɑːli] **1.** *n.* (*esp. düşman ile yapılan*) toplantı, görüşme; **2.** *v/i.* barış görüşmeleri yapmak; *v/t.* müzakere etm.

par.lia.ment ['pɑːləmənt] *n.* parlamento, millet meclisi; **par.lia.men.tar.i.an** [ˌ-men'tɛəriən] *n.* parlamenter; **parlia.menta.ry** □ [ˌ-ˈmentəri] parlamentoya ait, parlamento…

par.lo(u)r ['pɑːlə] *n.* oturma odası, salon; makam; *beauty* ∼ *part.* Am. güzellik salonu; ∼ *car* RAIL Am. lüks vagon;

'~maid *n.* sofra hizmetçisi kız.

pa.ro.chi.al □ [pə'rəukjəl] cemaate ait, cemaat...; *fig.* dar, sınırlı; ~ **politics** *pl.* dargörüşlülük siyaseti.

par.o.dist ['pærədist] *n.* hezel (*veya* parodi) yazarı; '**par.o.dy 1.** *n.* parodi, edebi bir eserin gülünç biçimde taklidi; **2.** *v/t.* gülünç biçimde taklit etm.

pa.role [pə'rəul] **1.** *n.* MIL parola, şeref sözü; mahkûmu şartlı olarak serbest bırakma; *put on ~* = *3*; **2.** *adj.* JUR sözlü, şifahî; **3.** *v/t.* JUR *part. Am.* şartlı olarak serbest bırakmak.

par.ox.ysm ['pærəksizəm] *n.* anî kriz *veya* boşalma.

par.quet ['pɑːkei] *n.* parke; *Am.* THEAT orkestranın olduğu yer ile parter arasındaki kısım; **par.quet.ed** ['pɑːkitid] *adj.* parke...; '**par.quet.ry** *n.* parke (döşeme).

par.ri.cide ['pærisaid] *n.* ana baba katili; kendi ana babasını öldürme.

par.rot ['pærət] **1.** *n.* ORN papağan (*a. fig.*); **2.** *v/t.* papağan gibi tekrarla(t)mak.

par.ry FENC ['pæri] **1.** *n.* savuşturma, bertaraf etme (*darbe*); **2.** *v/t.* bertaraf etm. (*darbe*); *fig.* kaçamak cevaplamak.

parse [pɑːz] *v/t.* dilbilgisi yönünden incelemek (*kelime, cümle*).

Par.see [pɑː'siː] *n.* Zerdüşt.

par.si.mo.ni.ous □ [pɑːsi'məunjəs] aşırı tutumlu; *b.s.* cimri, pinti; **par.si-'mo.nious.ness, par.si.mo.ny** ['~mə-ni] *n.* cimrilik, pintilik.

pars.ley BOT ['pɑːsli] *n.* maydanoz.

pars.nip BOT ['pɑːsnip] *n.* yabanî havuç.

par.son ['pɑːsn] *n.* rahip, vaiz, papaz; '**par.son.age** *n.* papaz evi.

part [pɑːt] **1.** *n.* parça, bölüm, kısım; THEAT rol; MUS fasıl, parti; *~s pl.* bölge, semt; görev, vazife; katkı; taraf; pay, hisse; yedek parça; *bşin* esas kısmı; *~ of speech* GR sözbölüğü; *~ and parcel of -in* esas kısmı; *a man of ~s* yetenekli (*veya* çok yönlü) adam; *have neither ~ nor lot in* hiç bir kârı olmamak; *in for-eign ~s* dış ülkelerde; *play a ~ fig.* rol oynamak; *take a ~ in s.th.* katılmak *-e*, iştirak etm. *-e*; *take in good (bad) ~ bşi* iyi (kötü) yönünden almak; *for my (own) ~* bence, bana kalırsa, kanımca; *for the most~* çoğunlukla, ekseriya; *in ~* kısmen; *do one's ~* kendine düşeni yapmak; *on the ~ of* ...nin tarafından; *on my ~* benim tarafımdan; **2.** *adv.*

kısmen; **3.** *v/t.* (parçalara) ayırmak, bölmek, taksim etm.; ~ **company** ayrılmak, bırakmak, terketmek (*with* -*den*, -*i*); *v/i.* ayrılmak (*from* -*den*); ~ **with** bırakmak -*i*, ayrılmak -*den*.

par.take [pɑː'teik] (*irr. take*) *v/i.* katılmak, iştirak etm. (*in veya of s.th. bşe*); ~ **of** ...niteliğinde olm.; yemeğe buyurmak; **par'tak.er** *n.* iştirak eden, katılan kimse (*of -e*).

par.terre [pɑː'tɛə] *n.* çiçek bahçesi; THEAT parter.

Par.thian ['pɑːθjən] *adj.* Partiya'ya *veya* Partlılara ait.

par.tial □ ['pɑːʃl] eksik, tam olmayan; taraflı, taraf tutan; kısmî; düşkün (*to* -*e*); **par.ti.al.i.ty** [pɑːʃi'æliti] *n.* taraf-girlik, taraf tutma; beğenme, düşkünlük (*to, for* -*i*, -*e*).

par.tic.i.pant [pɑː'tisipənt] *n.* katılan kimse, iştirakçi; **par'tic.i.pate** [_peit] *v/i.* katılmak, iştirak etm., ortak olm. (*in* -*e*); **par.tic.i'pa.tion** *n.* katılma, iştirak; **parti.cip.i.al** □ [_'sipiəl] GR ortaç kabilinden; **par.ti.ci.ple** ['_sipl] *n.* GR ortaç, sıfat-fiil.

par.ti.cle ['pɑːtikl] *n.* cüz, zerre, tane-cik; *fig.* azıcık şey; GR edat, takı, ek.

par.ti-col.oured ['pɑːtikʌləd] *adj.* ren-gârenk, alaca.

par.tic.u.lar [pə'tikjulə] **1.** □ *mst* belirli, muayyen; özel, hususî, has, mahsus; şahsî, kişisel; dikkate lâyık; ayrıntılı, etraflı, detaylı; titiz, müşkülpesent (*in, about, as to hususunda*); **2.** *n.* madde, husus; *~s pl.* ayrıntılar, detay; *in ~* özellikle, bilhassa; **par.tic.u.lar.i-ty** [_'læriti] *n.* özellik, hususiyet; titizlik; **par'tic.ular.ize** [_ləraiz] *v/t.* ayrı ayrı söylemek; ayrıntıları ile anlatmak; *v/i.* ayrıntılara girmek; **par'tic.u.lar.ly** *adv.* özellikle, bilhassa.

part.ing ['pɑːtiŋ] **1.** *n.* ayrılma; veda etme; saçı ayırma çizgisi; ~ *of the ways part. fig.* iki şıktan birini seçme; **2.** *adj.* ayıran..., bölen...; ayrılırken yapılan...

par.ti.san [pɑːti'zæn] **1.** *n.* taraftar, partizan; MIL gerillacı, çeteci; **2.** *adj.* parti-zanla ilgili, partizan...; **par.ti'san.ship** *n.* partizanlık, taraftarlık.

par.ti.tion [pɑː'tiʃən] **1.** *n.* taksim; bölme, duvar, tahta perde; bölünme, ayrılma; ~ *wall* bölme duvar; **2.** *v/t.* ~ *off* taksim etm., bölmek, ayırmak.

par.ti.tive □ ['pɑːtitiv] kısımlara ayıran; bir bütünün parçasını belirten (*kelime*).

part.ly ['pɑːtli] *adv.* kısmen, bir dereceye kadar.

part.ner ['pɑːtnə] **1.** *n.* eş, karı *veya* koca; dans (*veya* oyun) arkadaşı; COM ortak; **2.** *v/t.* ortak etm.; *v/i.* ortak gibi davranmak; ortak olm.; 'part.ner.ship *n.* COM ortaklık; **enter into ~ with** ...ile ortak olm.

part...: '~own.er *n.* hissedar; '~payment *n.* kısmen ödeme; taksit; avans; kaparo.

par.tridge ORN ['pɑːtridʒ] *n.* keklik.

part...: '~song *n.* birkaç sesle söylenen şarkı; '~time **1.** *adj.* yarım günlük..., **2.** *adv.* yarım gün olarak.

par.ty ['pɑːti] *n.* grup; parti, toplantı, şölen, ziyafet, eğlence; POL siyasal parti; JUR taraf; MIL birlik; *co.* kimse, şahıs; *s.* **line¹ 1.**

par.ve.nu ['pɑːvənjuː] *n.* sonradan görme kimse, türedi.

pas.chal ['pɑːskəl] *adj.* Musevilerin Fısıh bayramına ait; paskalyaya ait.

pa.sha ['pɑːʃə] *n.* paşa.

pass [pɑːs] **1.** *n.* geçiş, geçme; paso, şebeke; *futbol:* pas; UNIV sınavda geçme; hokkabazların kaybetme oyunu; FENC hamle; boğaz, geçit; *iskambil:* pas; pasaport; hal, durum; *sl.* kur, flört; **free ~** parasız giriş kartı; **hold the ~** *fig.* bir fikri savunmak; **2.** *v/i.* ileri gitmek, ilerlemek; gitmek, ayrılmak; geçmek (*zaman*); dönüşmek; karar vermek, hüküm vermek; intikal etm., miras kalmak; olmak, meydana gelmek; kabul edilmek; FENC hamle yapmak; *futbol:* pas vermek, paslaşmak; *iskambil:* pas demek; bitmek, sona ermek; sayılmak (**as, for** *olarak*); *a.* **~ away** ölmek, vefat etm.; geçmek; **~ for** ...olarak sayılmak, ...gözüyle bakılmak; **~ off** bitmek, sona ermek; geçmek (*ağrı*); meydana gelmek, olmak; **~ out** F bayılmak, kendinden geçmek; **come to ~** olmak, meydana gelmek; **bring to ~** sonuçlandırmak; **3.** *v/t.* geçmek, aşmak; geçirmek, atlatmak; geçirmek (*zaman*); kabul ve tasdik ettirmek; devretmek (*hak*); tedavüle çıkarmak, sürmek (*para*); vermek, uzatmak; gezdirmek, dolaştırmak; bildirmek, söylemek, açıklamak (*fikir, karar*); boşaltmak, dışarı atmak; vurmak (*topa*); **~ s.o. (s.th.) by** *b-ni (bşi)* önememek; **~ off** görmemezlikten gelmek, geçiştirmek, çevirmek (*dikkati-*

ni); **~ o.s. (s.th.) off as** *k-ne* ...süsü vermek, *k-ni* ...diye satmak, ...tavrı takınmak; **~ over** göz yummak, görmezlikten gelmek, ihmal etm.; **it ~es my comprehension** ona benim aklım ermiyor; **~ one's hand across one's forehead** eliyle alnını silmek; **~ water** işemek; **~ one's word** söz vermek; 'pass.a.ble □ geçilebilir, geçit verir (*yol*); oldukça iyi, kabul edilir, geçerli.

pas.sage ['pæsidʒ] *n.* geçme, gitme; yol; geçit, boğaz; yolculuk, seyahat; pasaj; koridor, dehliz; bent, parça, paragraf, fıkra; tasarının kabul edilip kanunlaşması; **~s** *pl.* tanışıklık, karşılıklı güven; MUS geçiş; geçiş hakkı (*veya* ücreti); **~ of** *veya* **at arms** mücadele, kavga, çekişme; **bird of ~** göçmen kuş; '~way *n.* pasaj, geçit; koridor.

pass-book COM ['pɑːsbuk] *n.* hesap cüzdanı.

pas.sé(e) ['pɑːsei] *adj.* geçmiş, eski; modası geçmiş, demode.

pas.sen.ger ['pæsindʒə] *n.* yolcu, seyyah, gezgin.

passe-par.tout ['pæspɑːtuː] *n.* ana anahtar.

pass.er-by, *pl.* **pass.ers-by** ['pɑːsə(z)-'bai] *n.* yoldan gelip geçen kimse.

pas.sim ['pæsim] *adv.* çeşitli yerlerde (*kitapta*); sık sık.

pass.ing ['pɑːsiŋ] **1.** *n.* geçiş, gitme; göçme, ölüm; **in ~** antrparantez, sırası gelmişken; geçerken; **2.** *adj.* geçen, geçici; rastgele, tesadüfi; olup biten; '~bell *n.* matem canı.

pas.sion ['pæʃən] *n.* hırs, ihtiras, tutku; aşk, cinsel istek, şehvet; hiddet, öfke; ıstırap, elem; aşırı heves; ♀ Hz. İsa'nın çarmıha gerilmesinde çektiği acı; **be in a ~** son derece öfkelenmek; **in ~** JUR şiddetli ve ani heyecan anında; ♀ **Week** paskalyadan bir önceki hafta; **pas.sionate** □ ['~ʃənit] heyecanlı, ateşli, şiddetli, hararetli; hiddetli; kara sevdalı; 'passion-flow.er *n.* BOT çarkıfelek; 'pas.sion.less □ soğukkanlı, heyecansız; 'pas.sion-play *n.* Hz. İsa'nın çarmıha gerilmesini canlandıran piyes.

pas.sive □ ['pæsiv] pasif, hareketsiz, ilgisiz, uysal, eylemsiz, faaliyetsiz; GR edilgen; **~ smoking** başkalarının sigara içtiği bir ortamda duman soluyarak dolaylı olarak sigara içmek zorunda kalmak, pasif sigara kullanımı; 'pas.sive.ness, pas'siv.i.ty *n.* pasiflik, ilgisizlik, uysallık; dirençsizlik.

pass-key ['pɑːskiː] *n.* ana anahtar; kapı anahtarı.

Pass.o.ver ['pɑːsəuvə] *n.* Musevilerin Fısıh bayramı.

pass.port ['pɑːspɔːt] *n.* pasaport.

pass.word MIL ['pɑːswɔːd] *n.* parola.

past [pɑːst] **1.** *adj.* geçmiş, geçen, bitmiş, olmuş, sabık; GR geçmiş zaman...; ~ **master** usta kimse, erbap; **for some time** ~ bir süreden beri; **2.** *adv.* geçecek şekilde, -*in* yanından geçerek; **rush** ~ fırlayıp yanından geçmek; **3.** *prp.* -*den* daha ilerde *veya* ileriye; ötesinde; **half** ~ **two** iki buçuk; **it is** ~ **comprehension** akıl almaz; ~ **cure** tedavi edilemez; ~ **endurance** tahammül edilemez, dayanılmaz; ~ **hope** ümitsiz; **4.** *n.* geçmiş zaman; bir kimsenin geçmişi.

paste [peist] **1.** *n.* macun; çiriş, kola; hamur; lapa; elmas taklidi cam; **2.** *v/t.* (kola ile) yapıştırmak; '~**.board** *n.* mukavva; *sl.* kartvizit; iskambil kâğıdı; bilet; *attr.* mukavva...

pas.tel [pæs'tel] *n.* PAINT pastel kalemi (ile yapılmış resim); pastel renk; **pas.tel.(i)ist** ['‿təlist] *n.* pastel resim yapan kimse.

pas.tern VET ['pæstəːn] *n.* atın ayağına bukağı takılan yer.

pas.teur.ize ['pæstʃəraiz] *v/t.* pastörize etm.

pas.tille ['pæstəl] *n.* pastil.

pas.time ['pɑːstaim] *n.* eğlence, oyun, meşgale.

pas.tor ['pɑːstə] *n.* papaz; '**pas.to.ral 1.** ☐ doğa güzelliklerini anlatan, pastoral...; papazlığa ait, papazlık...; ~ **staff** papazlık asası; **2.** *n.* idil; PAINT pastoral resim; ECCL papazın kendi bölgesindeki kilise görevlilerine yazdığı resmi mektup.

pas.try ['peistri] *n.* hamur işi, pasta; '~**-cook** *n.* pastacı.

pas.tur.age ['pɑːstjuridʒ] *n.* ot; otlak; otlatma hakkı.

pas.ture ['pɑːstʃə] **1.** *n.* çayır, otlak, mera; ~ **ground** otlak; **2.** *v/t. & v/i.* çayırda otla(t)mak.

past.y 1. ['peisti] *adj.* hamur gibi; solgun; **2.** ['pæsti] *n.* etli börek.

pat [pæt] **1.** *n.* el ile hafif vuruş; 'pat' sesi; ufak kalıp (*tereyağ*); **2.** *v/t.* hafifçe vurmak -*e*; *v/i.* hafif adımlarla koşmak; **3.** *adv.* hemen, anında, tam vaktinde; **stand** ~ alışkanlığını bozmamak; kararından dönmemek.

patch [pætʃ] **1.** *n.* yama; MED yakı; MED göz sargısı; benek, ben, leke; arazi parçası; **strike a bad** ~ şanssızlığa uğramak; ~ **pocket** yama cep; **2.** *v/t.* yamamak, yamalamak, yama vurmak; ~ **up** tamir etm.; *fig.* halletmek, yoluna koymak.

patch.work ['pætʃwəːk] *n.* yama işi; *fig.* uydurma iş; '**patch.y** *adj.* yamalı; derme çatma yapılmış, uydurma; düzensiz.

pate F [peit] *n.* baş, kafa, kelle; beyin; akıl.

pat.ent ['peitənt] **1.** *adj.* belli, açık, aşikâr, apaçık, meydanda olan...; patent almış, patentli...; **letters** ~ ['pætənt] *pl.* patent; ~ **article** patentli mal, tescilli mal; ~ **leather** güderi; **2.** *n.* patent, imtiyaz; patentli mal; ~ **agent** patent işleri uzmanı; ~ **office** patent dairesi; **3.** *v/t.* -*in* patentini almak; **pat.ent.ee** [peitən'tiː] *n.* patent sahibi.

pa.ter.nal ☐ [pə'təːnl] babaya ait, babaya yakışır, baba...; babadan kalma; **pa'ter.ni.ty** *n.* babalık; kaynak, köken; ~ **leave** *n.* babalık izni (*çocuğu doğan erkeklere verilen izin*).

path [pɑːθ] *n., pl.* **paths** [pɑːðz] keçi yolu, patika; takip edilen yol, davranış; *spor.* pist.

pa.thet.ic [pə'θetik] *adj.* (~**ally**) acıklı, dokunaklı, etkileyici, üzücü.

path.less ['pɑːθlis] *adj.* patikasız, yolsuz.

path.o.log.i.cal ☐ [pæθə'lɔdʒikəl] patolojik; **pa.thol.o.gy** [pə'θɔlədʒi] *n.* patoloji, hastalıklar bilimi.

pa.thos ['peiθɔs] *n.* merhamet ve sempati hissi uyandırma gücü.

path.way ['pɑːθwei] *n.* patika.

path.y *Am.* MED *comb.* ['pæθi] *n.* tedavi.

pa.tience ['peiʃəns] *n.* sabır, tahammül, dayanma, dişini sıkma; tek başına oynanılan iskambil oyunu; **be out of** ~ **with, have no** ~ **with** sabrı tükenmek; '**pa.tient 1.** ☐ sabırlı, tahammüllü, dayanıklı; **be** ~ **of** sabırlı olm. -*e karşı*; *fig.* bşe göz yummak; **2.** *n.* hasta.

pa.ti.o *Am.* ['pætiəu] *n.* avlu, teras, veranda.

pa.tri.arch ['peitriɑːk] *n.* patrik; yaşlı ve saygıdeğer adam; bir aile *veya* kabilenin başı; **pa.tri'ar.chal** ☐ patriğe ait; saygıdeğer.

pa.tri.cian [pə'triʃən] **1.** *adj.* soylulara ait, soylu...; **2.** *n.* soylu kimse, asılzade.

pat.ri.mo.ny ['pætriməni] *n.* babadan

kalan miras; kilise vakfı.

pa.tri.ot ['pætriət] *n.* vatanperver (*veya* yurtsever) kimse; **pa.tri.ot.eer** [ˌ-ə'tiə] *n.* şoven, aşırı milliyetçi kimse; **pa.tri.ot.ic** [ˌ-'ɔtik] *adj.* (**∼ally**) yurtsever, vatanperver; **pa.tri.ot.ism** ['-ətizəm] *n.* yurtseverlik, vatanperverlik.

pa.trol MIL [pə'trəul] **1.** *n.* devriye, karakol; keşif kolu; devriye gezme; **∼ wagon** *Am.* polis devriye arabası; **2.** *v/i.* devriye gezmek; **∼.man** [pə'trəulmən] *n.* (devriye) polis.

pa.tron ['peitrən] *n.* veli, hami; patron, efendi; daimi müşteri, velinimet; **pa.tron.age** ['pætrənidʒ] *n.* himaye, koruma; *b-ni* göreve atama hakkı; müşteriler; hor görme; iş, ticaret; **pa.tron.ess** ['peitrənis] *n.* koruyan azize *vs.* (*s. patron*); **pa.tron.ize** ['pætrənaiz] *v/t.* korumak, himaye etm.; kanatları altına almak; hor görmek; müşterisi olm.; '**patron.iz.er** *n.* koruyucu, hami.

pat.ter ['pætə] **1.** *v/t. & v/i.* hızlı hızlı konuşmak; pıtırdamak; ısya ve süratli adımlarla yürümek; mırıldar gibi söylemek; **2.** *n.* konuşma tarzı; çok hızlı söylenen şarkı; pıtırtı, ses.

pat.tern ['pætən] **1.** *n.* model, örnek (*a. fig.*); numune, mostra; elbiselik kumaş; motif, süs; şablon; döküm kalıbı; elbise patronu; *fig.* şekil, düzen; **by ∼ post** kıymetsiz numune; **2.** *v/t.* örneğe göre yapmak; örnek almak; motiflerle süslemek; '**∼-mak.er** *n.* MEC modelci.

pat.ty ['pæti] *n.* küçük börek.

pau.ci.ty ['pɔːsiti] *n.* azlık, kıtlık, yetersizlik.

Paul.ine ['pɔːlain] *adj.* apostol Paul'e ait.

paunch [pɔːntʃ] *n.* göbek; '**paunch.y** *adj.* göbekli, şişko.

pau.per ['pɔːpə] *n.* sadaka ile geçinen fakir kimse, yoksul; *attr.* fakir…, yoksul…; '**pau.per.ism** *n.* fakirlik, yoksulluk; '**pau.per.ize** *v/t.* sadakaya muhtaç hale getirmek, fakirleştirmek.

pause [pɔːz] **1.** *n.* ara(lık), fasıla, mola, teneffüs; durma; MUS notanın üzerine *veya* altına konan uzatma işareti; **give ∼ to s.o.** *b-ni* düşündürmek, tereddütte bırakmak; **2.** *v/i.* durmak, duraklamak; tereddüt etm., duraksamak (**upon hususunda**).

pave [peiv] *v/t.* kaldırım döşemek; *fig.* yolu açmak; '**pave.ment** *n.* kaldırım; **∼ artist** kaldırım ressamı.

pa.vil.ion [pə'viljən] *n.* büyük çadır;

müzikhol; pavyon; köşk.

pav.ing-stone ['peiviŋstəun] *n.* kaldırım taşı.

paw [pɔː] **1.** *n.* pençe; *co.* el; **2.** *v/t. & v/i.* pençelemek; ön ayaklarıyla eşelemek (*at*); F kabaca ellemek; pençe atmak.

pawn[1] [pɔːn] *n.* satranç: piyon, piyade, paytak; *fig.* maşa, bir işe alet edilen kimse, kukla.

pawn[2] [ˌ-] **1.** *n.* rehin; rehine koyma; **in ∼, at ∼** rehinde; **2.** *v/t.* rehine koymak; *fig.* tehlikeye atmak; '**∼.bro.ker** *n.* rehinci, tefeci; **pawn'ee** *n.* rehinli alacaklı, rehinle borç veren kimse; '**pawn.er** *n.* malını rehine veren kimse; '**pawn.shop** *n.* rehinci dükkânı; '**pawn-tick.et** *n.* rehin makbuzu.

pay [pei] **1.** *n.* maaş, ücret; ödeme; bedel, karşılık; *fig.* mükâfat; **2.** (*irr.*) *v/t.* ödemek, tediye etm.; karşılığını vermek; etmek; yarar sağlamak; getirmek (*kâr*); **∼ attention** *veya* **heed to** dikkat etm. *-e*; **∼ away**, **∼ out** NAUT kaloma etm. (*halat, zincir*); **∼ down** peşin ödemek; **∼ off** tamamen ödemek (*borç*); ücretini verip kovmak; **∼ s.o. out for s.th.** misliyle mukabele etm., *bşin* acısını *b-den* çıkarmak, *bşden* dolayı *b-den* öç almak; **∼ up** tamamını ödemek, kapatmak (*borç*); **∼ one's way** borca girmemek; **put paid to s.th.** F halletmek, yoluna koymak; *v/i.* borcunu ödemek; masrafına *veya* çabasına değmek; **∼ for** *bş* için para vermek; *-in* cezasını çekmek; '**pay.a.ble** *adj.* ödenmesi gereken; ödenebilir; MIN, COM verimli, kârlı; '**pay-as-you-'earn** *n.* gelir vergisinin gelirin kaynağından kesildiği sistem; '**pay-day** *n.* ücretlerin verildiği gün, aybaşı; **pay dirt** *Am.* içinde işletilebilecek kadar maden olan toprak; **pay'ee** *n.* COM alacaklı kimse; '**pay-en.ve.lope** *n.* maaş zarfı; maaş miktarı; '**pay.er** *n.* ödeyen kimse; COM muhatap, borçlu kimse; '**paying** *adj.* kârlı, kazançlı, verimli; **∼ concern** kârlı (*veya* verimli) iş; '**pay-load** *n.* gelir getiren yük; füze içindeki bomba; uzay aracının mürettebatı *veya* teçhizatı; '**pay.mas.ter** *n.* MIL, NAUT maaş kâtibi, mutemet; '**pay.ment** *n.* ödeme, tediye; ücret maaş; *fig.* ödül; ceza; **additional ∼** ek ödeme; **on ∼ of** …ödemek üzere.

pay…: '**∼-off** *n.* hesaplaşma (*a. fig.*); *Am.* F doruk noktası; ödül, kâr; sonuç; netice; '**∼-of.fice** *n.* kasa, gişe, vezne dairesi; '~-**pack.et** *n.* maaş zarfı; '~-**per-view** *seyredilen program başına ücret ödenen kablolu ya da uydu antenli TV sistemi*; '~-**roll** *n.* ücret bordrosu; '~-**station** *n. Am.* umumî telefon.

PDA ıt [pi:di:'ei] (= *personal digital assistant*) avuçiçi bilgisayar.

pea ʙoᴛ [pi:] *n.* bezelye.

peace [pi:s] *n.* barış, sulh; huzur, sükûn(et); asayiş; barış anlaşması; *the* **(King's)** ~ huzur, barış, asayiş; *be at* ~ barış halinde olm., huzur içinde olm.; *break the* ~ huzuru (*veya* asayişi) bozmak; *keep the* ~ barışı korumak, asayişi sağlamak; '**peace.a.ble** □ barışsever; sakin; '**peace-break.er** *n.* huzur bozucu kimse; **peace.ful** □ ['-ful] sakin, yumuşak başlı, uysal; barışsever; '**peace.mak.er** *n.* barıştırıcı kimse, arabulucu.

peach[1] [pi:tʃ] *n.* ʙoᴛ şeftali (ağacı); şeftali rengi; *sl.* çekici kimse *veya* şey.

peach[2] *sl.* [.]: ~ (*up*) *on vb.* ihbar etm., ispiyon etm., ele vermek, gammazlamak; boşboğazlık etm.

pea-chick ['pi:tʃik] *n.* yavru tavus.

peach.y ['pi:tʃi] *adj.* şeftali gibi; *sl.* mükemmel.

pea.cock ['pi:kɔk] *n.* tavus; '**pea.fowl** *n.* tavus; '**pea'hen** *n.* dişi tavus.

pea-jack.et ɴᴀᴜᴛ ['pi:dʒækit] *n.* gemici ceketi.

peak [pi:k] **1.** *n.* zirve, tepe, doruk; kasket siperi; *attr.* zirve…, tepe…; ~ *hour* sıkışık saat (*trafik*); ~ *load* azamî yük; ~ *power etc.* azamî güç *vs.*; **2.** *v/i.* F zayıflamak, süzülmek; doruk noktasına ulaşmak; **peaked** [pi:kt] *adj.* zayıf düşmüş, bitkin durumda; siperli; ~ *cap* siperli şapka; '**peak.y** *adj.* sivri tepeli; bitkin durumda.

peal [pi:l] **1.** *n.* gürültü; gürültülü çan sesi; çan takımı; ~*s pl. of laughter* kahkaha tufanı; **2.** *v/t. & v/i.* gürültülü çal(ın)mak (*çan*); ses vermek.

pea.nut ['pi:nʌt] *n.* Amerikan fıstığı, yerfıstığı; *fig.* önemsiz kimse.

pear ʙoᴛ [pɛə] *n.* armut (ağacı).

pearl [pɜ:l] **1.** *n.* inci (*a. fig.*); inci rengi; sedef; ᴛʏᴘ beş puntoluk harf; *attr.* inci…; **2.** *v/i.* inci avlamak; *v/t.* incilerle süslemek; inciye benzetmek; '**pearl.y** *adj.* inci gibi; incilerle süslenmiş.

pear-tree ['pɛətri] *n.* armut ağacı.

peas.ant ['pezənt] *n.* köylü, rençper; *attr.* köylü…; '**peas.ant.ry** *n.* köylüler, köylü sınıfı.

pease [pi:z] *n. pl.* bezelye.

pea-shoot.er ['pi:ʃu:tə] *n.* üfleyerek bezelye atılan oyuncak boru.

pea soup ['pi:'su:p] *n.* bezelye çorbası; '**pea-'soup.er** *n.* F koyu sis.

peat [pi:t] *n.* turba, çürümüş bitkilerden elde edilen yakacak; '~-**bog** *n.* turbalık.

peb.ble ['pebl] *n.* çakıl taşı; '**peb.bly** *adj.* çakıllı, çakıl döşeli.

pe.can ʙoᴛ ['pi'kæn] *n.* cevize benzer bir ağaç.

pec.ca.ble ['pekəbl] *adj.* günah işleyebilir.

peck[1] [pek] *n.* 9,087 litrelik bir hacim ölçü birimi; *fig.* büyük miktar.

peck[2] [.] *v/t. & v/i.* gaga ile vurmak (*at -e*); az yemek yemek; ~ *at one's food* yemeğini iştahsızca yemek; gagalamak; gagalayarak açmak (*delik*); '**peck.er** *n. sl.* büyük burun; *keep one's* ~ *up* neşesini kaybetmemek; '**peck.ish** *adj.* F karnı aç olan, karnı zil çalan.

pec.tin ['pektin] *n.* pektin.

pec.to.ral ['pektərəl] **1.** *adj.* göğüse ait, göğüs…; göğüse takılan…; **2.** *n.* göğüse takılan süs; göğüs hastalıklarına ait ilâç.

pec.u.late ['pekjuleit] *v/t.* zimmetine geçirmek; **pec.u'la.tion** *n.* zimmetine geçirme; '**pec.u.la.tor** *n.* zimmetine para geçiren kimse.

pe.cul.iar □ [pi'kju:ljə] özel, hususî; acayip, garip, tuhaf, alışılmamış; mahsus, özgü, kendine has; **pe.cu.li.ar.i.ty** [.li'æriti] *n.* özellik, hususiyet; gariplik, acayiplik.

pe.cu.ni.ar.y [pi'kju:njəri] *adj.* parayla ilgili, parasal…, maddî…;

ped.a.gog.ic, ped.a.gog.i.cal □ [pedə'gɔdʒik(əl)] pedagojik; **ped.a'gog.ics** *n. mst sg.* pedagoji ilmi; **ped.a.gogue** ['-gɔg] *n.* pedagog; F ukalâ (*veya* işgüzar) öğretmen; **ped.a.go.gy** ['-gɔdʒi] *n.* pedagoji.

ped.al ['pedl] **1.** *n.* pedal; **2.** *adj.* ayağa ait, ayak…; **3.** *v/t. & v/i.* ayakla işletmek; pedal kullanmak; bisiklete binmek.

ped.ant ['pedənt] *n.* ukalâ kimse; **pedantic** [pi'dæntik] *adj.* (~**ally**) ukalâ, bilgiçlik taslayan; **ped.ant.ry** ['pedəntri] *n.* ukalâlık.

ped.dle ['pedl] *v/t. & v/i.* seyyar satıcılık yapmak; önemsiz şeylerle ilgilenmek; azar azar satmak; '**ped.dling** *adj.*

önemsiz, ufak tefek; 'ped.dler *Am.* = *pedlar.*

ped.es.tal ['pedistl] *n.* heykel *veya* sütun tabanı, kaide; *fig.* esas, temel; pe.destri.an [pi'destriən] **1.** *adj.* yürümeye ait, yürüme…; sıkıcı, ağır; **2.** *n.* yaya; ~ **crossing** yaya geçidi.

ped.i.cab ['pedikæb] *n.* üstü kapalı, üç tekerlekli ve bisiklete benzer bir tür yolcu taşıma aracı.

ped.i.cure ['pedikjuə] *n.* pedikür.

ped.i.gree ['pedigriː] **1.** *n.* soy, nesep, şecere, soy ağacı; **2.** ~d *adj.* soyu sopu belli olan.

ped.i.ment ARCH ['pedimənt] *n.* alınlık.

ped.lar ['pedlə] *n.* seyyar satıcı; 'ped.lar.y *n.* seyyar satıcılık.

pe.dom.e.ter [pi'dɔmitə] *n.* pedometre, adımölçer.

peek [piːk] **1.** *v/i.* gizlice bakmak, dikizlemek; **2.** *n.* gizlice bakma, gözetleme, dikiz; peek.a.boo ['piːkəbuː] *n.* çocuklara «ce» yapılan oyun.

peel [piːl] **1.** *n.* (*meyve veya sebze*) kabuk; **2.** *a.* ~ **off** *v/t.* -*in* kabuğunu soymak; çıkarmak (*elbise*); *v/i.* soyulmak (*kabuk*); *sl.* soyunmak.

peel.er *sl. obs.* ['piːlə] *n.* polis.

peel.ing ['piːliŋ] *n.* soyulmuş kabuk.

peep[1] [piːp] **1.** *n.* civciv gibi ötme; civciv sesi; **2.** *v/i.* civciv gibi ötmek, «cik cik» etm.

peep[2] [_] **1.** *n.* azıcık bakış, kaçamak (*veya* gizli) bakış; **2.** *v/i.* gizlice bakmak (*at* -*e*); röntgencilik etm., dikiz geçmek; *a.* ~ **out** yavaş yavaş ortaya çıkmak (*a. fig.*); ~ *at* gizlice bakmak -*e;* 'peep.er *n.* röntgenci kimse; *sl.* göz; 'peep-hole *n.* gözetleme deliği; 'peep-show *n.* büyüteçle küçük bir delikten seyredilen resim *vs.*

peer[1] [piə] *v/i.* dikkatle bakmak; ~ *at* yakından bakmak -*e.*

peer[2] [_] *n.* eş, akran, emsal; asılzade; 'peer.age *n.* asalet, asılzadelik; 'peer.ess *n.* kadın asılzade; asılzade karısı; 'peerless □ eşsiz, emsalsiz.

peeved F [piːvd] *adj.* sinirli, hırçın, huysuz.

pee.vish □ ['piːviʃ] titiz, huysuz, ters, aksi, hırçın, densiz; 'pee.vish.ness *n.* huysuzluk, aksilik, hırçınlık, densizlik.

pee.wit ['piːwit] = *pewit.*

peg [peg] **1.** *n.* ağaç çivi; askı, kanca; küçük kazık; MUS yaylı çalgılarda akort anahtarı; *fig.* sebep, vesile, bahane; so-

dalı viski *veya* konyak; F tahta bacak; **take s.o. down a** ~ **or two** *b-ni* küçük düşürmek; **be a square** ~ **in a round hole** yeteneklerine uygun işte olmamak, bulunduğu mevkiye yakışmamak; **2.** *vb.* ağaç çivi ile mıhlamak; asmak (*çamaşır*); kısıtlamak, sınırlamak; COM -*de* istikrar sağlamak; *a.* ~ **out** çiviler çakarak işaretlemek; fırlatmak, atmak; *a* ~ **away, along** F istikrarlı bir şekilde çalışmak; koşuşturmak; ~ **out** *sl.* ölmek, gebermek.

peg-top ['pegtɔp] *n.* topaç.

peign.oir ['peinwɑː] *n.* sabahlık.

pe.jo.ra.tive ['piːdʒərətiv, pi'dʒɔrətiv] *adj.* küçük düşürücü, alçaltıcı.

pelf *contp.* [pelf] *n.* para, servet.

pel.i.can ORN ['pelikən] *n.* pelikan, kaşıkçıkuşu.

pel.let ['pelit] *n.* küçük topak; ufak kurşun, saçma; hap.

pel.li.cle ['pelikl] *n.* ince zar.

pell-mell ['pel'mel] **1.** *adv.* paldır küldür, apar topar, alelacele; karman çorman, allak bullak; **2.** *n.* karmakarışıklık.

pel.lu.cid [pe'ljuːsid] *adj.* açık seçik; yarı şeffaf.

Pel.o.pon.ne.sian [peləpə'niːʃən] *adj.* Moralı, Mora'ya ait.

pelt[1] [pelt] *n.* deri, post, kürk; COM işlenmemiş deri.

pelt[2] [_] **1.** *v/t.* & *v/i.* atmak, fırlatmak; taşlamak; boşanmak (*yağmur*); koşuşturmak; **2.** *n.* atma, fırlatma; boşanma (*yağmur*); **at full** ~ son süratle (koşarak).

pelt.ry ['peltri] *n.* hayvan deri *veya* postları.

pel.vis ANAT ['pelvis] *n.* pelvis, leğen, havsala.

pem.mi.can ['pemikən] *n.* dövülüp çöreklere karıştırılan kurutulmuş et.

pen[1] [pen] **1.** *n.* yazı kalemi, tüy kalem; tükenmez kalem; dolmakalem; yazı üslubu; **2.** *v/t.* mürekkepli kalemle yazmak.

pen[2] [_] **1.** *n.* ağıl, kümes, kafes; NAUT denizaltı doku; *a.* **play-**~ çocukların içinde oynadıkları portatif bahçe; **2.** (*irr.*) *oft.* ~ **up,** ~ **in** *v/t.* kapatmak, ağıla koymak.

pe.nal □ ['piːnl] cezaya ait, cezaî, ceza…; ~ **code** ceza kanunu; ~ **servitude** ağır hapis cezası; pe.nal.ize ['piːnəlaiz] *v/t.* cezalandırmak (*a. fig.*); pen.al.ty ['penlti] *n.* ceza; *spor*: penaltı; ~

area *futbol*: ceza sahası; ~ *kick* penaltı atışı; *under* ~ *of* …cezası ile.

pen.ance ['penəns] *n.* ceza; pişmanlık; kefaret.

pen…: '~-and-'ink draw.ing *n.* mürekkepli kalemle çizilmiş resim.

pence [pens] *pl. of penny.*

pen.cil ['pensl] **1.** *n.* kurşunkalem; makyaj kalemi; **2.** *v/t.* kurşunkalem ile yazmak *veya* çizmek; '~-sharp.en.er *n.* kalemtıraş.

pend.ant ['pendənt] *n.* asılı şey; pandantif; avize; flama.

pend.ent [-] *adj.* asılı, sarkık, sarkan; muallâkta olan, karar verilmemiş.

pend.ing ['pendiŋ] **1.** *adj.* JUR henüz karara bağlanmamış, askıda olan; **2.** *prp.* zarfında, esnasında, -*e* kadar.

pen.du.lous ['pendjuləs] *adj.* sarkan, asılı, sallanan; **pen.du.lum** ['-ləm] *n.* rakkas, sarkaç.

pen.e.tra.bil.i.ty [penitrə'biliti] *n.* içine nüfuz edilebilirlik; 'pen.e.tra.ble □ delinebilir, nüfuz edilebilir; anlaşılır; **pen.e.tra.li.a** [-'treiljə] *n. bşin* en iç kısmı; **pen.e.trate** ['-treit] *v/t. & v/i.* delip girmek -*e*, -*in* içine girmek, nüfuz etm.; anlamak, idrak etm.; içeriye sızmak; **pene'tra.tion** *n.* sokulma, nüfuz etme, içine işleme; etki, tesir; anlayış; **pen.e'tra.tive** □ ['-trətiv] delici, nüfuz edici (*a. fig.*); ~ *effect* delme etkisi.

pen-friend ['penfrend] *n.* mektup arkadaşı.

pen.guin ORN ['peŋgwin] *n.* penguen.

pen.hold.er ['penhəuldə] *n.* kalem sapı.

pen.i.cil.lin PHARM [peni'silin] *n.* penisilin.

pen.in.su.la [pi'ninsjulə] *n.* yarımada; **pen'in.su.lar** *adj.* yarımadaya ait, yarımada…

pen.i.tence ['penitəns] *n.* pişmanlık, tövbe; 'pen.i.tent **1.** □ pişman, tövbekâr; **2.** *n.* tövbekâr kimse; **pen.i.ten.tial** □ [-'tenʃəl] pişmanlıkla ilgili; **pen.i.ten.tiary** [-'tenʃəri] *n. Am.* hapishane, cezaevi.

pen.knife ['pennaif] *n.* çakı.

pen.man ['penmən] *n.* yazar; hattat; *he is a poor* ~ kötü bir elyazısı vardır; 'penman.ship *n.* yazı yazma sanatı; hattatlık, el yazısı.

pen-name ['penneim] *n.* yazarın takma adı.

pen.nant ['penənt] *n.* NAUT flama,

flandra; *part. Am.* şampiyonluk forsu; *fig.* şampiyonluk.

pen.ni.less □ ['penilis] (beş) parasız, meteliksiz, cebi delik.

pen.non ['penən] *n.* MIL bayrak, sancak; flama.

pen.ny ['peni] *n.,pl.* **pence** [pens] pens, peni; *Am.* sent; *a pretty* ~ dünya kadar para; *in for a* ~, *in for a pound* ne pahasına olursa olsun bitirilmesi gerekir, battı balık yan gider; *turn an honest* ~ alın teri ile para kazanmak; ~ *wise and pound foolish* ufak şeylerde tutumlu, büyük şeylerde müsrif olan; '~-a-'lin.er *n.* kalitesiz yazar; '~-'dread.ful *n.* ucuz fakat tutulan polisiye roman; '~-weight *n.* 1,56 gr. ağırlığında eczacı tartısı; ~.worth ['penəθ] *n.* bir penilik *bş*; *a* ~ *of tobacco* bir penilik tütün.

pen.sion ['penʃən] **1.** *n.* emekli aylığı; ['pãːŋsiɔː ŋ] pansiyon; **2.** *oft.* ~ *off* *v/t.* emekli aylığı bağlamak; 'pen.sion.ar.y, 'pen.sion.er *n.* emekli (aylığı alan kimse)

pen.sive □ ['pensiv] dalgın, düşünceli, endişeli, kara kara düşünen; 'pensiveness *n.* dalgınlık, kara kara düşünme.

pent [pent] *pret. & p.p. of pen² 2*; '~-'up *adj.* bastırılmış; kapatılmış, hapsedilmiş.

pen.ta.gon ['pentəgən] *n.* beşgen; *the* 2 *Am.* Millî Savunma Bakanlığı (binası); **pen.tag.o.nal** [-'tægənl] *adj.* beş köşeli, beşgen biçiminde.

pent.house ['penthaus] *n.* çatı katı, çekme kat.

pe.num.bra [pi'nʌmbrə] *n.* yarı gölge, yarı karanlık.

pe.nu.ri.ous □ [pi'njuəriəs] fakir, yoksul; cimri, pinti; az, kıt; **pe'nu.ri.ous.ness** *n.* cimrilik, pintilik; fakirlik, yoksulluk.

pen.u.ry ['penjuri] *n.* yoksulluk, fakirlik; eksiklik.

pe.o.ny BOT ['piəni] *n.* şakayık.

peo.ple ['piːpl] **1.** *n. F* halk, ahali; akrabalar; *my* ~ ailem; ulus, millet; ırk, kavim; *the* ~*s pl. of Asia* Asya milletleri; **2.** *v/t.* insanla doldurmak.

pep *sl.* [pep] **1.** *n.* kuvvet, enerji; azim, şevk; **2.** ~ *up* *v/t.* canlandırmak, hareketlendirmek.

pep.per ['pepə] **1.** *n.* biber; kırmızı biber; **2.** *v/t.* biberlemek; *-e* yağdırmak *(taş, soru, mermi);* '**~-box** *n.* biberlik; '**~.corn** *n.* tane biber; '**~.mint** *n.* BOT nane; '**pep.per.y** □ biberli; *fig.* sert huylu, geçimsiz.

per [pɔː, pə] *prp.* vasıtasıyle, eliyle; tarafından.

per.ad.ven.ture RHET [pəːrəd'ventʃə] **1.** *adv.* belki, olabilir, şayet, kazara; **2.** *n.* şüphe, belirsizlik; ihtimal; **beyond ~, without ~** şüphesiz.

per.am.bu.late [pə'ræmbjuleit] *v/t.* (etrafını) gezmek; teftiş etm.; *v/i.* gezinmek, dolaşmak; **per.am.bu'la.tion** *n.* gez(in)me, dolaşma; **per.am.bu.la.tor** ['præmbjuleitə] *n.* çocuk arabası.

per.cale [pə'keil] *n.* ince ve sık dokunmuş pamuklu bez.

per cap.i.ta [pə'kæpitə] *adv.* nüfus başına, kişi başına.

per.ceive [pə'siːv] *v/t.* görmek, anlamak, idrak etm., farkına varmak.

per cent, *a.* **per.cent** [pə'sent] *n.* yüzde; **per'cent.age** *n.* yüzde(lik); oran, nispet; *fig.* hisse, pay, kâr.

per.cep.ti.ble □ ICHTH [pəːtʃʃ] *n.* tatlı su levreği. anlaşılabilir, idrak edilebilir, algılanabilir, duyulur, farkına varılır; **per'cep.tion** *n.* idrak, algı, anlayış, seziş; **per'cep.tive** □ *[-tiv]* idrak edebilen; idrak kabilinden; **per'cep.tive.ness, per.cep'tiv.i.ty** *n.* anlayış, idrak kabiliyeti.

perch[1] ICHTH [pəːtʃ] *n.* tatlı su levreği.

perch[2] *[-]* **1.** *n.* 5,029 metrelik uzunluk ölçüsü; tünek; yüksekçe yer; F *fig.* yüksek mevki; **2.** *vb.* tüne(kle)mek; yüksek bir yere oturmak; yüksekte olm.; *~ed fig.* mevki sahibi.

per.chance [pə'tʃɑːns] *adv.* muhtemelen, belki; şans eseri olarak.

per.cip.i.ent [pə'sipiənt] **1.** *adj.* anlayışlı, idraki keskin; **2.** *n.* anlayışlı kimse, idraki kuvvetli kimse.

per.co.late ['pəːkəleit] *v/t. & v/i.* süz(ül)mek, sızmak, filtreden geçirmek; 'per.cola.tor *n.* süzgeçli kahve ibriği.

per.cus.sion [pə'kʌʃən] *n.* vurma, çarpma (sesi); MED perküsyon; **~ cap** tüfek kapsülü; **~ instruments** *pl.* MUS vurularak çalınan enstrümanlar; **per'cus.sive** *[-siv] adj.* vuruş kabilinden.

per.di.tion [pəː'diʃən] *n.* mahvolma, harap olma; cehennem azabı.

per.e.gri.nate ['perigrineit] *v/t. & v/i.* seyahat etm.; yürümek; katetmek;

aşmak; **per.e.gri'na.tion** *n.* yolculuk, seyahat.

per.emp.to.ri.ness [pə'remtərinis] *n.* katilik, kesinlik, mutlaklık; *b.s.* otoriterlik, despotluk; **per'emp.to.ry** □ katî, kesin, mutlak; *b.s.* otoriter, despot.

per.en.ni.al [pə'renjəl] **1.** □ bir yıl süren; daimî, uzun süren; BOT iki yıldan fazla yaşayan *(bitki);* **2.** *n.* BOT iki yıldan fazla yaşayan bitki.

per.fect 1. ['pəːfikt] □ tam, kusursuz, mükemmel, fevkalâde; iyi öğrenilmiş; oldukça, tamamen; **2.** *[-]* *n. a.* **~ tense** GR geçmiş zaman; **3.** [pə'fekt] *v/t.* tamamlamak, bitirmek; mükemmelleştirmek, geliştirmek; **per'fec.tion** *n.* kusursuzluk, mükemmellik; bitirme, tamamlama, ikmal; *fig.* zirve, doruk.

per.fid.i.ous □ [pə'fidiəs] hain, asî, sadakatsiz **(to** *-e* karşı); **per'fid.i.ous.ness,** 'per.fi.dy *n.* hainlik, hıyanet, sadakatsizlik.

per.fo.rate ['pəːfəreit] *v/t.* delmek; sıra sıra delmek *(pul);* **per.fo'ra.tion** *n.* delme; delik; 'per.fo.ra.tor *n.* delgi, zımba.

per.force [pə'fɔːs] *adv.* mecburen, ister istemez.

per.form [pə'fɔːm] *v/t. & v/i.* yapmak, yerine getirmek; ifa etm.; THEAT oynamak, sunmak *(oyun);* canlandırmak; MUS çalmak, icra etm.; rol yapmak; **per'formance** *n.* yerine getirme, yapma, ifa, icra; THEAT gösteri, temsil, oyun; MEC çalışma, işleme; **per'form.er** *n.* artist, oyuncu; icracı; yerine getiren kimse; **per'form.ing** *adj.* terbiye edilmiş *(hayvan).*

per.fume 1. ['pəːfjuːm] *n.* güzel koku, ıtır; parfüm, esans; **2.** [pə'fjuːm] *v/t.* lavanta sürmek, parfüm sürmek *-e;* **per-'fum.er** *n.* parfüm yapan *veya* satan kimse; **per'fum.er.y** *n.* parfümeri, ıtriyat (dükkânı).

per.func.to.ry □ [pə'fʌŋktəri] baştan savma, dikkatsizce yapılan, yarımyamalak, iş olsun diye yapılan.

per.haps [pə'hæps, præps] *adv.* belki, muhtemelen.

per.i.gee AST ['peridʒiː] *n.* bir gezegenin yeryüzüne en yakın olan noktası.

per.il ['peril] **1.** *n.* tehlike, risk; **at my ~** benim sorumluluğumda; **2.** *v/t.* tehlikeye atmak; 'per.il.ous □ tehlikeli, riskli.

pe.ri.od ['piəriəd] *n.* çağ, devir, devre, dönem, süre, müddet; nokta; GR tam cümle; ~**s** *pl.* MED âdet, aybaşı; ~ *furniture* belli bir çağa ait mobilya; **per.i-od.ic** [_'ɔdik] *adj.* belirli aralıklarla yer bulan, peryodik; **pe.ri'od.i.cal 1.** □ belli zamanlarda çıkan; **2.** *n.* dergi, mecmua.

per.i.pa.tet.ic [peripə'tetik] *adj.* (~*ally*) gezen, gezgin(ci).

pe.riph.er.y [pə'rifəri] *n.* dış sınır çizgisi *veya* yüzeyi.

pe.riph.ra.sis [pə'rifrəsis] *n., pl.* **pe'riph.ra.ses** [_si:z] dolaylı anlatım; **per.iph.ras.tic** [peri'fræstik] *adj.* (~*ally*) dolaylı anlatılmış.

per.i.scope NAUT, MIL ['periskəup] *n.* periskop.

per.ish ['periʃ] *v/t. & v/i.* ölmek; mahvolmak, yok olm.; yok etm.; *be* ~*ed with* -*den* mahvolmak, -*den* helâk olm.; '**perish.a.ble 1.** □ kolay bozulur (*yiyecek*); **2.** *n.* ~*s pl.* kolay bozulabilen gıda maddeleri; '**per.ish.ing** □ mahvedici, yok edici; F çirkin, iğrenç.

per.i.style ['peristail] *n.* bir binayı çevreleyen sıra sütunlar; sütunlarla çevrili yer.

per.i.wig ['periwig] *n.* peruka, takma saç.

per.i.win.kle¹ BOT ['periwiŋkl] *n.* Cezayir menekşesi.

per.i.win.kle² ZOO [_] *n.* bir cins deniz salyangozu.

per.jure ['pə:dʒə] *v/t.*: ~ *o.s.* yalan yere yemin etm.; '**per.jured** *adj.* yalan yere yemin eden; '**per.jur.er** *n.* yalan yere yemin eden kimse; '**per.ju.ry** *n.* yalan yere yemin (etme).

perk¹ F [pə:k] = *percolate*.

perk² F [_] **1.** *mst* ~ *up* *v/t. & v/i.* neşelen(dir)mek, canlan(dır)mak; kaldırmak (*başını*); **2.** = ~*y*; **perk.i.ness** ['_inis] *n.* havailik, hoppalık; canlılık.

perks F [pə:ks] *pl.* = *perquisites*.

perk.y □ ['pə:ki] hoppa, havaî, canlı; kendinden emin.

perm F [pə:m] **1.** *n.* perma(nant); **2.** *v/t.* perma yapmak.

per.ma.nence ['pə:mənəns] *n.* süreklilik, devam, istikrar; '**per.ma.nen.cy** *s.* *permanence*; sürekli *bş*; '**per.ma.nent** □ sürekli, devamlı, daimî; ~ *wave* perma(nant); ~ *way* RAIL demiryolu üst yapısı.

per.me.a.bil.i.ty [pə:mjə'biliti] *n.* geçirgenlik, nüfuz edilme kabiliyeti; '**perme.a.ble** □ geçirgen, nüfuz edilebilen (*to* -*e*); **per.me.ate** ['_mieit] *v/t.*

& *v/i.* -*den* geçmek, sızmak; nüfuz etm. (*into* -*e*); yayılmak, yaygınlaşmak (*among arasında*).

per.mis.si.ble □ [pə'misəbl] izin verilebilir, hoş görülebilir, uygun; **per.mis.sion** [pə'miʃən] *n.* izin, müsaade; ruhsat; **per'mis.sive** □ [_siv] izin veren, müsaade eden; JUR ihtiyarî, istemli, keyfî.

per.mit 1. [pə'mit] *vb. a.* ~ *of* izin vermek, müsaade etm.; fırsat vermek, imkân tanımak, bırakmak; kabul etm.; *weather* ~*ting* müsait hava; **2.** ['pə:mit] *n.* permi, ruhsatname, izin kâğıdı.

per.ni.cious □ [pə'niʃəs] zararlı, tehlikeli; MED öldürücü, habis.

per.nick.et.y F [pə'nikiti] *adj.* kılı kırk yaran, titiz.

per.o.ra.tion [perə'reiʃən] *n.* konuşmanın özeti ve sonu.

per.ox.ide CHEM [pə'rɔksaid] *n.*: ~ *of hydrogen* oksijenli su.

per.pen.dic.u.lar [pə:pən'dikjulə] **1.** □ dik(ey), düşey, amudî, şakulî; ~ *style* ARCH Gotik mimari tarzı; **2.** *n.* dikey çizgi, şakulî hat; dik duruş.

per.pe.trate ['pə:pitreit] *v/t.* işlemek (*suç, hata*); F yapmak (*şaka*); **per.pe-'tra.tion** *n.* işleme (*suş, hata*); yapma (*şaka*); '**per.pe.tra.tor** *n.* fail, suçlu kimse.

per.pet.u.al □ [pə'petʃuəl] sürekli, daimî, ebedî, aralıksız, bitip tükenmez; **per'pet.u.ate** [_eit] *v/t.* ebedîleştirmek, ölümsüzleştirmek, daimî kılmak; **perpet.u'a.tion** *n.* sürdürme, devam (ettirme); **per.pe.tu.i.ty** [pə:pi'tju:iti] *n.* ebediyet, daimîlik; daimî gelir; *in* ~ ebediyen, sonsuza kadar.

per.plex [pə'pleks] *v/t.* şaşırtmak, allak bullak etm. (*zihin*); anlaşılması güç hale getirmek, karıştırmak; **per'plexed** □ zihni karışmış, şaşırmış; karışık; **per-'plex.i.ty** *n.* şaşkınlık; karışıklık; zihni karıştıran şey.

per.qui.sites ['pə:kwizits] *n. pl.* maaştan ayrı gelir.

per.se.cute ['pə:sikju:t] *v/t.* sıkıştırmak, zorlamak, baskı yapmak; zulmetmek -*e*, eziyet etm. -*e*; **per.se-'cu.tion** *n.* zülüm, gaddarlık; zulmetme; ~ *mania* zulmetme hastalığı; **per.se.cu.tor** ['_tə] *n.* gaddar kimse, zalim.

per.se.ver.ance [pə:si'viərəns] *n.* sebat, azim; **per.se.vere** [_viə] *v/i.* sebat göstermek, azimle devam etm. (*at, in, with* -*de*, -*e*); **per.se'ver.ing** □ azimli,

sebat eden.
Per.sian ['pə:ʃən] **1.** *adj.* İranlı, İran'a ait; Farsça'ya ait; **2.** *n.* İranlı; Farsça.
per.sim.mon BOT [pə'simən] *n.* hurma.
per.sist [pə'sist] *v/i.* ısrar etm., üstelemek, sebat etm., inat etm. (*in -de*); kalmak, devam etm.; **per'sist.ence**, **per'sisten.cy** *n.* sebat, ısrar, inat, devam etme; **per'sist.ent** ◻ ısrarlı, inatçı; devamlı.
per.son ['pə:sn] *n.* kimse, adam, kişi, şahıs (*a.* GR), fert; şahsiyet, sıfat; THEAT rol; *in ~* şahsen, bizzat; 'per.son.a.ble *adj.* güzel görünümlü, yakışıklı, cana yakın; 'per.son.age *n.* şahsiyet, zat, önemli kişi; THEAT karakter; 'per.son.al **1.** ◻ özel, hususi, şahsi, zatî; GR üç şahıstan birine ait; bedensel; *~ property veya estate* JUR *s.* personalty; **2.** *n.* belirli bir kişi hakkında çıkmış gazete yazısı; person.al.i.ty [pə:sə'næliti] *n.* şahsiyet, kişilik, ferdiyet; şahıs, zat, kimse; *personalities n. pl.* kaba sözler; per.son.al.ty ['pə:snlti] *n.* JUR şahsî *veya* menkul (*veya* taşınır) mal; per.son.ate ['-səneit] *v/t.* canlandırmak (*karakter*); k-ni ...diye satmak, k-ne ...süsü vermek; per.son'ation *n.* k-ni ...diye satma; canlandırma; per.son.i.fi.ca.tion [pə'sɔnifi'keiʃən] *n.* cisimlendirme; şahıslandırma, canlandırma; per.son.i.fy [pə'sɔnifai] *v/t.* cisimlendirmek; şahıslandırmak, canlandırmak; per.son.nel [pə:sə'nel] *n.* kadro, personel, takım.
per.spec.tive [pə'spektiv] **1.** ◻ perspektife göre çizilmiş; **2.** *n.* perspektif (resim); görüş açısı.
per.spex ['pə:speks] *n.* transparan plastik, mika.
per.spi.ca.cious ◻ [pə:spi'keiʃəs] keskin zekâlı, anlayışlı; per.spi.cac.i.ty ['-'kæsiti] *n.* keskin zekâ, anlayış; per.spi.cu.i.ty [-'kjuiti] *n.* açıklık, anlaşılırlık; per.spicu.ous [pə'spikjuəs] ◻ açık, anlaşılır.
per.spi.ra.tion [pə:spə'reiʃən] *n.* ter(-leme); per.spire [pəs'paiə] *v/i.* terlemek.
per.suade [pə'sweid] *v/t.* kandırmak, ikna etm., razı etm. (*to inf. -meğe, into -e*); inandırmak (*of -e*); per'suad.er *n. sl.* tabanca.
per.sua.sion [pə'sweiʒən] *n.* ikna (kabiliyeti), inandırma, kandırma; inanç, kanaat, itikat; mezhep, din; F *co.* cins,

nevi, tür.
per.sua.sive ◻ [pə'sweisiv] kandırıcı, ikna edici; per'sua.sive.ness *n.* ikna kabiliyeti.
pert ◻ [pə:t] sırnaşık, yılışık, arsız, yüzsüz, küstah, şımarık, lâubali.
per.tain [pə'tein] *v/i.* ait olm.; ilgili olm.; uygun olm. (*to -e*).
per.ti.na.cious ◻ [pə:ti'neiʃəs] azimli, kararlı, sebatkâr; inatçı; per.ti.nac.i.ty [-'næsiti] *n.* azim, kararlılık, sebat, inatçılık.
per.ti.nence, **per.ti.nen.cy** ['pə:tinəns(i)] *n.* ilgi, alâka; uyum; 'per.ti.nent ◻ ilgili, alâkalı; uygun, uyumlu; *be ~* to ilgili olm. *-e*.
pert.ness ['pə:tnis] *n.* arsızlık, küstahlık, lâubalilik.
per.turb [pə'tə:b] *v/t.* altüst etm., rahatsız etm., canını sıkmak; per.tur.ba.tion [pə:tə'beiʃən] *n.* huzursuzluk, rahatsızlık.
pe.ruke [pə'ru:k] *n.* peruka, takma saç.
pe.rus.al [pə'ru:zəl] *n.* dikkatle okuma; pe'ruse *v/t.* dikkatle okumak; *fig.* incelemek, tetkik etm.
Pe.ru.vi.an [pə'ru:vjən] **1.** *adj.* Perulu; Peru'ya özgü; *~ bark* BOT kınakına kabuğu; **2.** *n.* Perulu kimse.
per.vade [pə'veid] *v/t.* kaplamak, istilâ etm.; yayılmak *-e*; per'va.sion [-ʒən] *n.* kaplama; yayılma; per'va.sive [-siv] *adj.* yayılmış, kaplayan, geniş.
per.verse ◻ [pə'və:s] ters, aksi, zıt; ahlâksız, yoldan çıkmış; MED sapık; per'verseness = perversity; per'ver.sion *n.* (cinsel) sapıklık; ayartma, yoldan çıkarma; ters anlam verme; per'ver.si.ty *n.* yoldan çıkma; ahlâksızlık; MED sapıklık; per'ver.sive *adj.* yanıltıcı (*of*).
per.vert 1. [pə'və:t] *v/t.* (doğru yoldan) saptırmak, ayartmak, baştan çıkarmak, çelmek (*aklını*), yanlış yola sürüklemek; yanlış anlam vermek; **2.** ['pə:və:t] *n.* MED cinsî sapık.
per.vi.ous ['pə:vjəs] *adj.* yanına girilebilir, nüfuz edilebilir (*a. fig.*); geçirgen (*toprak vs.*).
pes.ky ◻ *sl.* ['peski] baş belâsı, sıkıntı veren, sinir bozucu.
pes.si.mism ['pesimizəm] *n.* kötümserlik, karamsarlık; 'pes.si.mist *n.* kötümser kimse; pes.si'mis.tic *adj.* (*~ally*) kötümser, karamsar.
pest [pest] *n. fig.* baş belâsı, sıkıcı şey *veya* kimse, zararlı şey *veya* kimse; ve-

ba, taun; 'pes.ter *v/t.* sıkmak, sinirlendirmek, sıkıntı vermek, usandırmak, bıktırmak, baş ağrıtmak.

pest.i.cide ['pestisaid] *n.* böcek zehiri; **pes'tif.er.ous** □ [_fərəs] bulaşıcı; zararlı; ahlâksız; baş belâsı; **pes.ti.lence** ['_ləns] *n.* salgın ve çok tehlikeli hastalık, *part.* veba, taun; 'pes.ti.lent *adj.* bulaşıcı hastalık getiren; tehlikeli; öldürücü; ahlâk bozucu; baş belâsı; **pesti.len.tial** □ [_'lenʃəl] veba getiren; ahlâk bozucu; sıkıcı; tehlikeli.

pes.tle ['pesl] **1.** *n.* havan tokmağı; **2.** *v/t.* havanda dövmek.

pet¹ [pet] *n.* öfke, hiddet, kızgınlık; *in a ~* kızgın.

pet² [_] **1.** *n.* evde beslenen hayvan; çok sevilen kimse *veya* şey, sevgili; **2.** *adj.* evcil...; gözde...; **~ dog** evcil köpek, ev köpeği; **~ name** takma isim; *it is my ~ aversion* ondan nefret ederim, o benim sinirime dokunuyor; **3.** *v/t.* okşamak, sevmek; F sevişmek, öpüşmek.

pet.al BOT ['petl] *n.* çiçek yaprağı, petal.

pe.tard [pe'taːd] *n. obs.* kapı, duvar *vs.* yıkmak için kullanılan bomba.

pe.ter ['piːtə] *v/i.:* **~ out** yavaş yavaş azalmak, tükenmek.

pet.i.ole BOT ['petiəul] *n.* yaprak sapı, petiol.

pet.it ['peti] *adj.* küçük, ufak; **pe.tite** [pə'tiːt] *adj.* küçük, ince, narin.

pe.ti.tion [pi'tiʃən] **1.** *n.* dilekçe; rica, istirham, dilek, talep; **~ in bankruptcy** JUR alacaklı *veya* borçlu tarafından yapılan iflas talebi; **~ for divorce** JUR boşanma talebi; **2.** *vb.* dilekçe vermek *-e (for için; to inf. -mek için)*; rica (*veya* istirham, talep) etm., dilemek (*s.o. b-ne; for için*); **pe'ti.tion.er** [_ʃnə] *n.* dilekçe (*veya* müracaat) sahibi.

pet.rel ORN ['petrəl] *n.* uzun kanatlı bir çeşit deniz kuşu.

pet.ri.fac.tion GEOL [petri'fækʃən] *n.* taşlaşma, taş kesilme (*a. fig.*); fosil.

pet.ri.fy ['petrifai] *v/t. & v/i.* taşlaş(tır)mak; taş haline getirmek; taş haline gelmek; *fig.* aklını başından almak.

pet.rol MOT ['petrəl] *n.* benzin; **~ engine** benzin motoru; **~ station** benzin istasyonu; **~ tank** benzin deposu.

pe.tro.le.um [pi'trəuljəm] *n.* petrol; **~ jelly** vazelin, parafin.

pe.trol.o.gy GEOL [pe'trɔlədʒi] *n.* kaya ilmi.

pet.ti.coat ['petikəut] *n.* iç etekliği, jü-

pon.

pet.ti.fog.ger ['petifɔgə] *n.* madrabaz avukat; kılı kırk yaran kimse; 'pet.ti-fogging *adj.* kılı kırk yaran; gereksiz detaylı (*metod*).

pet.ti.ness ['petinis] *n.* önemsizlik; aşağılık, küçüklük.

pet.tish □ ['petiʃ] hırçın, huysuz; 'pet-tish.ness *n.* hırçınlık, huysuzluk.

pet.ty □ ['peti] küçük; önemsiz, ehemmiyetsiz, adi, ufak tefek; dar kafalı; **~ cash** COM küçük kasa; **~ officer** NAUT assubay, erbaş; **~ sessions** *pl.* JUR adi mahkeme.

pet.u.lance ['petjuləns] *s.* **pettish-ness**; 'petu.lant *s. pettish.**

pew [pjuː] *n. (kilisede)* oturacak sıra.

pe.wit ORN ['piːwit] *n.* kızkuşu.

pew.ter ['pjuːtə] *n.* kurşun ve kalay alaşımı; bu alaşımdan yapılan kap; 'pewter.er *n.* kurşun ve kalay alaşımı dökümcüsü.

pha.e.ton HIST ['feitn] *n.* fayton, payton.

pha.lanx ['fælæŋks] *n.* eski Yunanistan'da asker alayı.

phan.tasm ['fæntæzəm] *n.* hayalet; hayal, aldanış, fantezi; **phan.tas.ma.go-ri.a** [_mə'gɔːriə] *n.* rüyadaki gibi bir seri tutarsız hayal.

phan.tom ['fæntəm] **1.** *n.* hayal(et); aldanış, görüntü; **2.** *adj.* hayalet gibi...

Phar.i.sa.ic, Phar.i.sa.i.cal □ [færi-'seiik(əl)] Ferisîlere ait; ikiyüzlü.

Phar.i.see ['færisiː] *n.* Ferisî; ikiyüzlü kimse.

phar.ma.ceu.ti.cal □ [fɑːmə'sjuːtikəl] eczacılığa ait, eczacılık...; ilâç...; **phar.macist** ['_sist] *n.* eczacı; **phar-ma.col.o.gy** [_'kɔlədʒi] *n.* farmokoloji, eczacılık ilmi; 'phar.ma.cy *n.* eczane; eczacılık.

phar.ynx ANAT ['færiŋks] *n.* farinks, yutak.

phase [feiz] *n.* safha, faz, görünüş; **phased** *adj.* safhalı.

phat *sl.* □ [fæt] çok kaliteli (*şarkı v.b.*).

pheas.ant ORN ['feznt] *n.* sülün (eti).

phe.nom.e.nal □ [fi'nɔminl] algılanabilir; fenomen ile ilgili; olağanüstü, hayret verici; **phe'nom.e.non** [_nən] *n., pl.* **phe'nom.e.na** [_nə] fenomen; *fig.* harika şey, kimse *veya* olay.

phew [fjuː] *int.* öf!, pöf!

phi.al ['faiəl] *n.* ufak şişe.

Phi Be.ta Kap.pa *Am.* ['fai'biːtəkæpə] *n.* çok eski üniversiteliler birliği.

phi.lan.der [fi'lændə] *v/i.* kur yapmak, flört etm.

phil.an.throp.ic [filən'θrɔpik] *adj.* (~**ally**) iyiliksever, yardımsever; insan sevgisine ait; **phi.lan.thro.pist** [fi'lænθrəpist] *n.* hayırsever, yardımsever; insancıl kimse; **phi'lan.thro.py** *n.* insanseverlik, insancıllık, hayırseverlik.

phi.lat.e.list [fi'lætəlist] *n.* pul meraklısı; **phi'lat.e.ly** *n.* pul koleksiyonculuğu.

phi.lip.pic [fi'lipik] *n.* tenkit niteliğinde sert konuşma.

Phi.lis.tine ['filistain] *n.* Filistinli; *fig.* kültürsüz (*veya* estetik anlayıştan yoksun) kimse.

phil.o.log.i.cal ☐ [filə'lɔdʒikəl] filolojik; **phi.lol.o.gist** [fi'lɔlədʒist] *n.* dilbilimci, filoloji uzmanı; **phi'lol.o.gy** *n.* filoloji, dilbilim.

phi.los.o.pher [fi'lɔsəfə] *n.* filozof, felsefeci; kendine hakim (*veya* dengeli, kalender) kimse; ~**s' stone** herhangi bir madeni altına dönüştürdüğü farzolunan tılsımlı taş; **phil.o.soph.ic**, **phil.o.soph.i.cal** [filə'sɔfik(əl)] *adj.* felsefî, filozofça; akıllıca, düşünceli; **phi.los.o.phize** [fi'lɔsəfaiz] *v/i.* filozofça konuşmak *veya* düşünmek; **phi'los.o.phy** *n.* felsefe; ağır başlılık, kalenderlik.

phil.tre, *phil.ter* ['filtə] *n.* aşk iksiri.

phiz F *co.* [fiz] *n.* yüz (ifadesi).

phle.bi.tis MED [fli'baitis] *n.* f(i)lebit.

phlegm [flem] *n.* balgam; kayıtsızlık; kaygısızlık; **phleg.mat.ic** [fleg'mætik] *adj.* (~**ally**) soğukkanlı, sakin.

phoe.be ORN ['fi:bi] *n.* bir çeşit sinekyutan.

Phoe.ni.cian [fi'niʃiən] **1.** *adj.* Fenikeli, Fenike'ye ait; **2.** *n.* Fenike dili; Fenikeli kimse.

phoe.nix MYTH ['fi:niks] *n.* Anka kuşu.

phone¹ F [fəun] **1.** *n.* telefon; **2.** *v/t.* telefon etm. -*e*.

phone² [-] *n.* ses.

phone-card ['fəunka:d] *n.* telefon kartı.

pho.neme ['fəuni:m] *n.* fonem; **pho'nemics** *n.* fonem bilimi; fonem sistemi.

pho.net.ic [fə'netik] *adj.* (~**ally**) fonetik, sesçil; ~ **spelling** fonetik imlâ; ~ **transcription** transkripsiyon fonetik; **pho.neti.cian** [-ni'tiʃən] *n.* fonetik uzmanı, sesbilimci; **pho.net.ics** [-'netiks] *n. sg.* fonetik, sesbilim.

pho.ney *sl.* ['fəuni] *adj.* sahte, düzme, kalp.

pho.no.graph *Am.* ['fəunəgra:f] *n.* pikap, fonograf.

pho.nol.o.gy [fə'nɔlədʒi] *n.* fonoloji.

pho.ny *Am. sl.* ['fəuni] **1.** *n.* sahtekâr kimse; **2.** = **phoney**.

phos.phate CHEM ['fɔsfeit] *n.* fosfat.

phos.pho.resce [fɔsfə'res] *v/i.* fosfor gibi parlamak; **phos.pho'res.cent** *adj.* fosfor, gibi parlayan, fosforlu; **phos.phor.ic** CHEM [-'fɔrik] *adj.* fosforlu...; **phos.pho.rous** CHEM ['-fərəs] *adj.* fosforlu; **phos.pho.rus** CHEM ['-fərəs] *n.* fosfor.

pho.to F ['fəutəu] *n.* fotoğraf; ~**en-'graving** *n.* fotoğraf vasıtasıyla klişe çıkarma işi; '~-**'finish** *n. Am.* fotofiniş; '~-**flash** *n.* flaş; ~**.gen.ic** [fəutəu'dʒenik] *adj.* ışık üreten (*veya* yayan); fotojenik; ~**.gramme.try** [-'græmitri] *n.* fotogrammetri.

pho.to.graph ['fəutəgra:f] **1.** *n.* fotoğraf; *take a* ~ fotoğraf çekmek; **2.** *v/t.* -*in* fotoğrafını çekmek; **pho.tog.ra.pher** [fə'tɔgrəfə] *n.* fotoğrafçı; **pho.to.graph.ic** [fəutə'græfik] *adj.* (~**ally**) fotoğraflarla ilgili; ~ **print** foto baskısı; **pho.tog.raphy** [fə'tɔgrəfi] *n.* fotoğrafçılık.

pho.to.gra.vure [fəutəgrə'vjuə] *n.* fotogravür; **pho.tom.e.ter** [-'tɔmitə] *n.* fotometre, ışıkölçer; **pho.to-play** ['-təplei] *n.* filme alınan piyes; **photostat** ['-təustæt] *n.* fotostat; fotokopi; **pho.to.te.legra.phy** [-təti'legrəfi] *n.* telle resim gönderme usulü; **pho.totype** ['-təutaip] *n.* fotoğraftan yapılan klişe.

phrase [freiz] **1.** *n.* ibare; deyim, tabir; MUS cümle; **2.** *v/t.* kelimelerle ifade etm.; '~-**mon.ger** *n.* süslü konuşan kimse; **phrase.ol.o.gy** [-i'ɔlədʒi] *n.* ifade tarzı, cümle dizimi, üslup; '**phras.ing** *n.* deyim kurma tarzı.

phre.net.ic [fri'netik] *adj.* (~**ally**) coşkun, çok heyecanlı.

phre.nol.o.gy [fri'nɔlədʒi] *n.* frenoloji.

phthis.i.cal MED ['θaisikəl] *adj.* veremli; astımlı; **phthi.sis** ['-sis] *n.* verem.

phut *sl.* [fʌt] *n.:* **go** ~ suya düşmek (*plan*); hapı yutmak.

phys.ic F ['fizik] **1.** *n.* tıp ilmi, hekimlik; ilâç; **2.** *v/t.* amel vermek; iyileştirmek; '**phys.i.cal** ☐ fiziksel, fizikî; maddî; bedene ait, bedensel, cismanî ~ **condi-**

tion sağlık durumu; ~ *culture* vücut bakımı; ~ *education*, ~ *training* beden eğitimi; **phy.si.cian** [fi'ziʃən] *n.* doktor, hekim; **phys.i.cist** ['‿sist] *n.* fizikçi; **phys.ics** ['fiziks] *n. sg.* fizik.

phys.i.og.no.my [fizi'ɔnəmi] *n.* fizyonomi; dış görünüş; **phys.i.o.log.i.cal** [‿ə'lɔdʒikəl] *adj.* fizyolojik, diriksel; **phys.i.ol.ogist** [‿'ɔlədʒist] *n.* fizyolog; **phys.i'ol.ogy** *n.* fizyoloji.

phy.sique [fi'ziːk] *n.* bünye, vücut, fizik, beden yapısı.

pi.an.ist ['piənist] *n.* piyanist.

pi.a.no¹ MUS ['pjɑːnəu] *adj. & adv.* hafif (sesle).

pi.an.o² ['pjænəu] *n. a.* **pi.an.o.for.te** [‿'fɔːti] piyano; *grand piano* kuyruklu piyano.

pi.as.ter [pi'æstə] *n.* kuruş.

pi.az.za [pi'ætsə] *n.* (İtalya'da) şehir meydanı *veya* pazar yeri; *Am.* veranda, taraça.

pi.broch ['piːbrɔk] *n.* gaydalarla çalınan askerî müzik.

pic.a.resque [pikə'resk] *adj.* külhanbeyler *veya* sabıkalılarla ilgili; ~ *novel* külhanbeyleri *veya* sabıkalılarla ilgili roman.

pic.a.yune *Am.* [pikə'juːn] **1.** *n. mst fig.* önemsiz kimse *veya* şey; **2.** *adj.* önemsiz, küçük, değersiz.

pic.ca.nin.ny *co.* ['pikənini] **1.** *n. part.* zenci çocuk; **2.** *adj.* çocukça, çok küçük.

pick [pik] **1.** *n.* seçme; = *pickaxe*; kürdan; sivri uçlu herhangi bir alet; **2.** *v/t. & v/i.* delmek; kazmak; yolmak, koparmak, toplamak (*meyve*, *çiçek*); seçmek; aşırmak, çalmak, soymak; sebep olm.; parmaklarla çalmak (*enstruman*); gagalamak; anahtarsız açmak (*kilit*); azar azar yemek (*yiyecek*); kazma ile çalışmak; hırsızlık yapmak; azar azar yemek yemek; ~ *s.o.'s pocket* b-nin cebinden bş yürütmek; ~ *one's way* k-ne yol açmak; ~ *one's words* ağzından çıkanı kulağı duymak; ~ *at* iştahsızca yemek; *Am.* F rahat vermemek, dır dır etm.; ~ *off* koparmak, yolmak; silahla vurmak; ~ *on* seçmek; ~ *out* seçmek, ayırmak; anlamak; ~ *over* ayıklamak; ~ *up* kazmak; kaldırmak; toplamak; kulaktan öğrenmek (*dil*); hızlanmak; rasgele bulmak; iyileşmek; tanışmak; ayağa kalkmak; beraberinde götürmek; ~ *o.s. up* ayağa kalkmak; ~ *up speed* hızlanmak; ~ *up with* tanış-

mak, ayarlamak; ~*-a-back* [‿'əbæk] *adv.* omuzda, sırtta; '~*-axe* *n.* kazma; '**pick.er** *n.* toplayıcı şey *veya* kimse; pamuk atma makinesi.

pick.er.el ICHTH ['pikərəl] *n.* yavru turnabalığı.

pick.et ['pikit] **1.** *n.* kazık; MIL ileri karakol; grev gözcüsü; **2.** *v/t. & v/i.* kazıklarla etrafını çevirmek; MIL nöbetçi *veya* karakol koymak; kazığa bağlamak (*hayvan*); nöbet beklemek; grev gözcülüğü yapmak.

pick.ing ['pikiŋ] *n.* toplama (*s.* **pick**); *mst* ~*s pl.* aşırma (mallar).

pick.le ['pikl] **1.** *n.* turşu, hıyar turşusu, salamura; F haşarı çocuk; F sıkıntılı durum; *s.* *mix*; **2.** *v/t. -in* turşusunu kurmak; ~*d herring* salamura ringa balığı.

pick...: '~*.lock* *n.* maymuncuk; hırsız; '~*-me-up* *n.* F canlandırıcı içki; '~*.pock.et* *n.* yankecisi; '~*-up* *n.* pikap (kolu); pikap, kamyonet; hızlanma; alıcı cihaz; radyoda mikrofon tertibatı; gelişme; *a.* ~ *in prices* COM borsadaki fiyatların yükselmesi; *sl.* rastgele tanışılan kimse.

pic.nic ['piknik] **1.** *n.* piknik; *fig.* kolay *veya* hoşa giden şey; **2.** *v/i.* piknik yapmak.

pic.to.ri.al [pik'tɔːriəl] **1.** □ resimli...; resimlerle ilgili; ~ *advertising* resimli ilan; **2.** *n.* resimli dergi.

pic.ture ['piktʃə] **1.** *n.* resim, tablo; tasvir, suret, timsal; tanımlama; film; görüntü; ~*s pl.* F sinema; *put s.o. in the* ~ *b-ni bşden* haberdar etm.; **2.** *v/t. -in* resmini yapmak, boyamak; tasavvur etm., hayal etm., canlandırmak; tanımlamak, tasvir etm.; '~*-book* *n.* resim kitabı, resimli kitap; '~*-gal.ler.y* *n.* resim galerisi; '~*-go.er* *n.* sinema tutkunu; ~ *postcard* resimli kartpostal.

pic.tur.esque □ [piktʃə'resk] *adj.* pitoreks, resme elverişli; canlı, kuvvetli; etkili; güzel; **pic.tur'esque.ness** *n.* pitorekslik; güzellik, canlılık.

pidg.in ['pidʒin] *n.:* ~ *English* Uzak Doğu'da konuşulan İngilizceden bozma karışık dil; *that's not my* ~ F bu benim işim değil.

pie¹ [pai] *n.* tart, börek, turta; *s.* *finger 1*.

pie² ORN [‿] *n.* saksağan.

pie.bald ['paibɔːld] *adj.* alaca, benekli (*at*).

piece [piːs] **1.** *n.* parça, bölüm, kısım, tane; piyes, oyun; madenî para; numune, örnek; dama taşı; resim; heykel; silah;

a ~ of advice bir nasihat; *a ~ of news* bir haber; *~ by ~* birer birer, parça parça; *of a ~* aynı, tıpkısı, benzer; *be of a ~ with* uygun olm. *-e*, aynı olm. *ile*; *give s.o. a ~ of one's mind* b-*nin* hakkında ne düşündüğünü açıkça söylemek, *b-ni* paylamak, azarlamak; *take to ~s* parçalara ayırmak, sökmek; **2.** *v/t. a.. ~ up* parçalarını bir araya getirerek tamir etm., parça eklemek, yamamak; *~ together* birleştirmek, bir araya getirmek; *~ out* parça ekleyerek tamamlamak; '*~-goods* n. *pl.* parça mal, metreyle satılan kumaş vs.; '*~-meal* adv. & adj. parça parça (yapılmış); '*~-work* n. parça başı iş.

pied [paid] *adj.* benekli, alaca.
pie.plant *Am.* ['paipla:nt] n. ravent.
pier [piə] n. iskele, rıhtım; kemer *veya* köprü payandası; iki pencere *veya* kapı arasındaki duvar; '**pier.age** n. NAUT rıhtım ücreti.
pierce [piəs] *v/t.* & *v/i.* delmek, delip geçmek, delik açmak; nüfuz etm. *-e*; içine işlemek; etkilemek, tesir etm.; bıçaklamak; zorla girmek; '**pierc.ing** □ keskin, tiz (ses); içe işleyen (soğuk).
pier glass ['piəgla:s] n. boy aynası.
pi.e.tism ['paiətizəm] n. softalık; dindarlık.
pi.e.ty ['paiəti] n. kendini Tanrıya adama; dindarlık.
pif.fle sl. ['pifl] **1.** n. saçma söz; **2.** *v/i.* saçmalamak.
pig [pig] **1.** n. domuz (yavrusu); domuz eti; domuz derisi; domuz gibi herif; *metall.* pik (demiri); kötü yola düşmüş kadın; sl. polis, aynasız; *buy a ~ in a poke* bşi görmeden (*veya* körü körüne) almak; **2.** *v/i.* yavrulamak (domuz); F domuz gibi yaşamak, süfli bir hayat sürmek.
pi.geon ['pidʒin] n. güvercin; sl. kolay aldanan kimse, safdil, aval; '*~'breast-ed* adj. çıkık göğüslü; '*~-hole* **1.** n. (yazı masasında vs.) göz; **2.** *v/t.* göze yerleştirmek; bir yana atmak; hasıraltı etm.; tasnif etm.; '**pi.geon.ry** n. güvercinlik.
pig.ger.y ['pigəri] n. domuz ahırı (*veya* ağılı, çiftliği).
pig.gish □ ['pigiʃ] domuz gibi; pis; obur, pisboğaz.
pig.gy ['pigi] **1.** n. küçük domuz; *~ bank* domuz şeklinde kumbara; **2.** *adj.* obur.
pig.head.ed ['pig'hedid] *adj.* aksi, inatçı.
pig-i.ron ['pigaiən] n. pik demiri.

pig.ment ['pigmənt] n. boya (*veya* renk) maddesi, pigment.
pig.my ['pigmi] = *pygmy*.
pig…: '*~.nut* n. bir çeşit ceviz; '*~.skin* n. domuz derisi; *~.sty* ['-stai] n. domuz ağılı; '*~.tail* n. saç örgüsü; '*~.wash* n. domuza verilen yiyecek artığı.
pike [paik] n. MIL kargı, mızrak; ICHTH turnabalığı; ana yol, asfalt; paralı yol; '**piker** n. Am. sl. az parayla oynayan kumarbaz; *fig.* cimri kimse; '**pike.staff** n.: *as plain as a ~* apaçık, meydanda.
pil.chard ICHTH ['piltʃəd] n. sardalya.
pile[1] [pail] **1.** n. yığın, küme; büyük para; kocaman bina; ELECT pil; *atomic ~* atom reaktörü; **2.** *v/t.* & *v/i. oft. ~ up, ~ on* yığ(ıl)mak, birik(tir)mek; üşüşmek, doluşmak; çarpışmak; istif etm., kümelemek; çatmak (*silah*); doldurmak.
pile[2] [_] n. kazık, direk.
pile[3] [_] n. tüy, hav.
pile-driv.er MEC ['paildraivə] n. kazık varyosu, şahmerdan; '**pile-dwell.ing** n. kazık temelli ev.
piles MED [pailz] n. *pl.* basur memesi, hemoroid.
pil.fer ['pilfə] *v/t.* çalmak, aşırmak, yürütmek.
pil.grim ['pilgrim] n. hacı; yolcu, seyyah; ♀ *Fathers pl.* 1620'de Amerika'ya göç edip «Plymouth» kolonisini kuran İngiliz Püriterleri; '**pil.grim.age** n. hacca gitme, hac(ılık).
pill [pil] n. hap; *the ~* doğum kontrol hapı.
pil.lage ['pilidʒ] **1.** n. yağma, talan, çapulculuk; **2.** *v/t.* yağmalamak, talan etm.
pil.lar ['pilə] n. direk, sütun; dikme (benzeri şey); destek (*a. fig.*); '*~-box* n. posta kutusu; '**pil.lared** adj. sütunlu, destekli.
pil.lion ['piljən] n. binicinin arkasında oturana mahsus minder; MOT motosiklet arkalığı; *ride ~* atın terkisine binmek.
pil.lo.ry ['piləri] **1.** n. teşhir direği; *in the ~* teşhir edilmekte; **2.** *v/t.* teşhir direğine bağlamak; *fig.* elâleme rezil etm., küçük düşürmek *-i*.
pil.low ['piləu] **1.** n. yastık; MEC yatak kovanı; **2.** *v/t.* yastığa yatırmak; '*~-case*, '*~-slip* n. yastık yüzü.
pi.lot ['pailət] **1.** n. NAUT kılavuz; AVIA pilot; *fig.* rehber; *~ instructor* öğretmen pilot; *~ officer* havacı teğmen; *~ pupil*

öğrenci pilot; **2.** *adj.* pilot, deney...; **~ plant** deney tertibatı; **3.** *v/t.* kılavuzluk etm. *-e,* yol göstermek *-e;* kullanmak *(uçak);* 'pi.lot.age *n.* kılavuzluk; kılavuz ücreti; 'pi.lot-bal'loon deney balonu; 'pi.lot-light *n.* gaz lambalarında *veya* şofbende devamlı yanan küçük alev.

pi.men.to [pi'mentəu] *n.* yenibahar.

pimp [pimp] **1.** *n.* pezevenk, kadın simsarı; **2.** *v/i.* pezevenklik etm.

pim.ple ['pimpl] *n.* sivilce; 'pim.pled, 'pimply *adj.* sivilceli.

pin [pin] **1.** *n.* topluiğne; broş, iğne; askı çivisi; mil; lobut; değersiz şey; *MUS* akort anahtarı; **~s** *pl. sl.* bacaklar; **2.** *vb.* iğnelemek, iliştirmek, tutturmak; yüklemek *(sorumluluk);* hareketsiz kılmak; *a.* **~ down** *sl. fig.* içyüzünü araştırmak; **~ one's hopes on** bel bağlamak *-e.*

pin.a.fore ['pinəfɔː] *n.* göğüslük, önlük.

pin.cers ['pinsəz] *n. pl.* (**a pair of~**) kerpeten, kıskaç.

pinch [pintʃ] **1.** *n.* çimdik; tutam; sıkıntı, ihtiyaç; hırsızlık; tutuklama; *at a* **~** gerektiğinde, icabında; **2.** *v/t.* çimdiklemek, kıstırmak, sıkıştırmak; sıkıştırıp acıtmak; sıkıntıya düşürmek; F aşırmak, çalmak, yürütmek; *sl.* enselemek, tutuklamak; *be* **~ed for money** eli darda olm.; *v/i.* cimrilik etm.; ıstırap vermek; vurmak *(ayakkabı);* **pinched** *adj.* az, kıt; *fig.* ince, zayıf.

pinch.beck ['pintʃbek] **1.** *n.* MEC altın taklidi olarak kullanılan bakır ve çinko alaşımı; *fig.* taklit şey; **2.** *adj.* taklit...

pinch-hit *Am.* ['pintʃhit] *(irr. hit) v/i. beysbol:* vuruş yapmak *(for-in yerine).*

pin.cush.ion ['pinkuʃən] *n.* iğne(den)lik.

pine¹ BOT [pain] *n.* çam (ağacı).

pine² [-] *v/i.* zayıflamak, bitkinleşmek; hasret çekmek, özlemek *(for, after -i);* **~ away** eriyip gitmek, sararıp solmak.

pine...: '**~.ap.ple** *n.* BOT ananas; '**~cone** *n.* çam kozalağı; 'pin.er.y *n.* ananas serî; '**~tree = pine¹.**

pin-feath.er ['pinfeðə] *n.* yeni biten kuş tüyü.

ping [piŋ] *v/i.* «vız» diye ses çıkarmak *(kurşun).*

ping-pong ['piŋ pɔŋ] *n.* masa tenisi, pingpong.

pin.ion ['pinjən] **1.** *n.* kanat *(a. poet.); a.* **~feather** kanat tüyü; MEC dişli çark, pinyon; **2.** *v/t.* uçmasını engellemek

için ucunu kesmek *(kanat); fig.* elini koluna bağlamak.

pink¹ [piŋk] **1.** *n.* BOT karanfil; pembe renk; *in the* **~** *sl.* sapasağlam, demir *(veya* turp) gibi; **2.** *adj.* pembe.

pink² [-] *v/t.* bıçaklamak; küçük delikler açmak; deliklerle süslemek.

pink³ MOT [-] *v/i.* vuruntu yapmak.

pink.ish ['piŋkiʃ] *adj.* pembemsi, pembemtirak.

pin.nace NAUT ['pinis] *n.* büyük filika.

pin.na.cle ['pinəkl] *n.* ARCH sivri tepeli kule; *fig.* zirve, tepe, doruk.

pin.nate BOT ['pineit] *adj.* tüysü.

PIN num.ber ['pinʌmbə] *n.* PIN numarası, kart şifresi.

pi.noc(h).le *Am.* ['piːnʌkl] *n.* 48 kâğıtla oynanan bir iskambil oyunu.

pin...: '**~.prick** *n. fig.* iğne, taş, kinaye; '**~stripe** *n.* çok ince çizgi *(kumaşta).*

pint [paint] *n.* galonun sekizde biri *(0,57 l. Am. 0,47 l).*

pin-up ['pinʌp] *n.* duvara asılan seksi kadın resmi.

pi.o.neer [paiə'niə] **1.** *n.* öncü; MIL istihkâm eri; **2.** *v/t. & v/i.* öncülük etm.; açmak *(yol);* göstermek *(yeni metodlar).*

pi.ous □ ['paiəs] dindar.

pip¹ [pip] *n.* VET tavuklarda görülen dilaltı hastalığı, kurbağacık; *sl.* efkâr, öfke, hiddet; *have the* **~** canı sıkılmak, öfkelenmek; *it gives me the* **~ o** benim kafamı bozuyor, tepemi attırıyor, sinirime dokunuyor.

pip² [-] *n.* meyve çekirdeği; zar üzerindeki nokta; MIL teğmenlere takılan yıldız işareti.

pip³ *sl.* [-] *vb.* öl(dür)mek; yenmek; sınavda kalmak, sınavda çak(tır)mak; yumurtadan çıkmak için delmek *(kabuk);* **~ out** ölmek, kuyruğu titretmek.

pip⁴ [-] *n.* radyoda saati belirten vuruşlardan biri.

pipe [paip] **1.** *n.* boru; kaval, düdük; çubuk; pipo; MUS gayda; NAUT silistre; nefes borusu; künk; bir çubukluk tütün; 470 litrelik şarap fıçısı; **2.** *v/t. & v/i.* düdük çalmak; düdük çalarak kumanda vermek; cırlak sesle konuşmak; silistre ile çağırmak; borularla iletmek; borularla donatmak; **~ one's eye** F ağlamak; **~ down** F sesini kesmek, susmak; **~ up** F söze, şarkıya *veya* çalmaya başlamak; '**~.clay** **1.** *n.* kil; **2.** *v/t.* kil ile beyazlatmak *veya* temizlemek; '**~lay.er** *n.* boru döşeyen kimse; *Am.* POL elebaşı, öncü kimse; '**~line** *n.* petrol borusu (*veya* hattı); **'pip.er** *n.* kavalcı; gaydacı; **pay the** ~ F masrafı yüklenmek.

pip.ing ['paipiŋ] **1.** *adj.* düdük gibi ses çıkaran; tiz, cırlak, kulak tırmalayıcı (*ses*); ~ **hot** çok sıcak, buram buram; dumanı üstünde; **2.** *n.* borular; şerit şeklinde süs (*elbisede, pastada*); kaval çalma; kaval sesi.

pip.pin BOT ['pipin] *n.* birkaç çeşit elma.

pip-squeak *sl.* ['pipskwi:k] *n.* ciğeri beş para etmez kimse.

pi.quan.cy ['pi:kənsi] *n.* mayhoşluk; cazibe; **'pi.quant** ☐ mayhoş, iştah açıcı; etkileyici, merak uyandırıcı.

pique [pi:k] **1.** *n.* gurur; incinme, darılma, içerleme; **2.** *v/t.* gururunu kırmak, incitmek, darıltmak; kışkırtmak; ~ **o.s. upon** övünmek *ile.*

pi.ra.cy ['paiərəsi] *n.* korsanlık; izinsiz olarak yayımlama; **pi.rate** ['-rit] **1.** *n.* korsan (gemisi); **wireless** ~, **radio** ~. ~ **listener** kaçak dinleyen kimse; **2.** *vb.* izinsiz yayımlamak (*başkasının eserini*); korsanlık etm.; **pi.rat.i.cal** ☐ [pai'rætikl] korsanca.

pis.ci.cul.ture ['pisikʌltʃə] *n.* balık üretimi.

pish [piʃ] *int.* öf!, püf!

piss *sl.* [pis] **1.** *n.* çiş, sidik; **2.** *vb.* işemek, çiş yapmak; ıslatmak (*altını, yatağı*).

pis.ta.chi.o [pi'stɑːtʃiəu] *n.* şamfıstığı (ağacı); şamfıstığı yeşili.

pis.til BOT ['pistil] *n.* pistil, dişi organ; **pistil.late** ['-lit] *adj.* dişi organı olan.

pis.tol ['pistl] *n.* tabanca, pistol, revolver, piştov.

pis.ton MEC ['pistən] *n.* piston; '~-rod *n.* piston kolu; '~-stroke *n.* piston tulû (*veya* sıası).

pit [pit] **1.** *n.* çukur (*a. MI)N*; ANAT koltuk altı; hendek şeklinde tuzak; çiçek hastalığından sonra vücutta kalan küçük çukur; THEAT parter; parterde oturan seyirciler; *Am. borsa;* bölüm; pilot kabini; etli meyve çekirdeği; **the** ~ cehennem; **2.** *vb.* çukurlaştırmak; çukurcuklarla doldurmak; çekirdeklerini çıkarmak; çukura yerleştirmek *veya* gömmek; yüzde çopur bırakmak; ~ **against** kapıştırmak; **~ted with smallpox** çiçek hastalığından dolayı çukur çukur olmuş (*yüz*).

pit-a-pat ['pitə'pæt] *adv.* küt küt (*kalp*); pat pat (*ayak sesi*).

pitch[1] [pitʃ] **1.** *n.* zift; **2.** *v/t.* ziftlemek; NAUT katranlamak;

pitch[2] [-] **1.** *n.* fırlatma, atış, atım; yükseklik; MUS perde; derece; meyil, eğim, yokuş; NAUT baş kıç vurma; *spor:* saha; işportacının tezgâh yeri; F satıcı ağzı; **2.** *v/t.* kurmak (*çadır*); atmak, fırlatmak; *beysbol:* vurucuya atmak (*top*); MUS tam perdesini vermek; aşağıya meyletmek; düşürmek; **~ed battle** meydan savaşı; *v/i.* MIL ordugâh kurmak; NAUT baş kıç vurmak; düşmek; *beysbol:* atıcı olarak oynamak; ~ **upon** rasgele seçmek; ~ **into** F saldırmak; girişmek.

pitch...: '~-and-'toss *n.* yazı tura atma oyunu; '~'black, '~'dark *adj.* simsiyah, kapkaranlık, zifiri karanlık.

pitch.er ['pitʃə] *n.* testi, sürahi, ibrik; maşrapa.

pitch.fork ['pitʃfɔːk] **1.** *n.* saman tırmığı, diren; MUS diyapazon; **2.** *v/t.* saman tırmığı ile savurmak; zorla getirmek (**into** bir mevkiye).

pitch-pine BOT [pitʃpain] *n.* çıra (lı çam).

pitch.y ['pitʃi] *adj.* ziftli, katranlı; simsiyah.

pit-coal MIN ['pitkəul] *n.* taşkömür, madenkömürü.

pit.e.ous ☐ RHET ['pitiəs] acınacak halde olan, hazin, yürekler acısı.

pit.fall ['pitfɔːl] *n.* tuzak (olarak kazılan çukur), gizli tehlike.

pith [piθ] *n.* yumuşak ve süngerimsi doku; ilik; *fig.* öz, cevher, ruh; güç, kuvvet, enerji.

pith.y ☐ ['piθi] özlü; kuvvetli, etkili, tesirli; anlamlı.

pit.i.a.ble ☐ ['pitiəbl] acınacak halde olan, acıklı.

pit.i.ful ☐ ['pitiful] acınacak halde olan, merhamet uyandıran; *contp.* değersiz, aşağılık; merhametli, şefkatli.

pit.i.less ☐ ['pitilis] merhametsiz, acımasız, kalpsiz.

pit.man ['pitmən] *n.* maden ocağı işçisi.

pit.tance ['pitəns] *n.* çok az ücret, az miktarda gelir.

pi.tu.i.tar.y [pi'tjuːitəri] *adj.* balgam salgılayan...; ~ **gland** hipofiz guddesi.

pit.y ['piti] **1.** *n.* merhamet, acıma, şefkat (**on** -*e*); **for~'s sake!** Allah aşkına!; **it is a** ~ yazık, vah vah, tüh; **it is a thousand pities** aman ne yazık; **2.** *v/t.* acımak, merhamet etm.; **I** ~ **him** ona acıyorum.

piv.ot ['pivət] **1.** *n.* MEC mil, eksen, mih

ver; *fig.* önemli kimse *veya* şey; **2.** *v/i.*
mil *veya* eksen üzerinde dönmek (**on,**
upon); *v/t.* mil üzerine yerleştirmek;
piv.o.tal ['-tl] *adj.* mile ait; asıl, esas,
en önemli.
pix.i.lat.ed *Am.* F ['piksəleitid] *adj.*
kaçık, çatlak, delidolu, bir tahtası eksik.
piz.za [pi:tsə] *n.* pizza.
pla.ca.bil.i.ty [plækə'biliti] *n.* kolay
yatıştırılabilirlik; '**pla.ca.ble** □ kolay
yatışır, hoşgörülü, uysal.
pla.card ['plækɑːd] **1.** *n.* afiş, levha, yafta, duvar ilanı, poster; **2.** *v/t.* afiş ile bildirmek; *-in* üzerine afiş yapıştırmak.
pla.cate [plə'keit] *v/t.* yatıştırmak, teskin etm.
place [pleis] **1.** *n.* yer, mevki, mahal,
mekân, mevzi; semt, şehir, kasaba;
alan, meydan; bina; MATH basamak, hane; memuriyet, görev, vazife; arazi,
toprak; ev, yuva; oturacak yer, koltuk;
~ of delivery teslim yeri; **~ of employment** işyeri; **give ~ to** yer vermek; öncelik tanımak; **in (out of) ~** yerli yerinde (yersiz); *fig.* uygun(suz); **in ~ of** *-in*
yerine; **in his ~** onun yerinde; **in the
first ~** ilk olarak, ilk etapta; **2.** *vb.* koymak, yerleştirmek; atamak, tayin etm.;
bir mevkiye getirmek; yatırmak (*para*); vermek (*sipariş*); MIL mevzilemek;
be ~d *spor:* ilk üç arasında olm.;
'**~name** *n.* yer ismi; '**plac.er** *n.* yerleş-
tiren kimse; derece *veya* yer alan kimse
veya şey; nehir sularının getirdiği kum,
çakıl *vs.* birikintisi.
plac.id □ ['plæsid] sakin, halim, yumuşak, uysal; durgun; **pla'cid.i.ty** *n.*
sükûnet, yumuşak başlılık, uysallık.
plack.et ['plækit] *n.* giyside fermuar yeri; eteklik cebi.
pla.gi.a.rism ['pleidʒjərizəm] *n.* çalıntı
(eser); '**pla.gi.a.rist** *n.* başkasının eserini kendisininmiş gibi yayımlayan
kimse; '**pla.gi.a.rize** *vb.* (*bir başkasının eserini*) kendisininmiş gibi
yayımlamak, aşırmalar yapmak *-den.*
plague [pleig] **1.** *n.* veba; belâ, musibet,
dert; **2.** *v/t.* bezdirmek *-i,* eziyet vermek *-e,* rahatsız etm. *-i,* canını sıkmak
-in, belâsını vermek; '**~spot** *n. mst fig.*
kötülük kaynağı.
pla.gu(e)y ['pleigi] *adj.* F sıkıcı, başa
belâ olan.
plaice *ichth* [pleis] *n.* pisibalığı.
plaid [plæd] *n.* ekose kumaş; ekose desen; İskoçya dağlılarının giydiği ekose

şal.
plain [plein] **1.** □ düz, sade, basit, desen-
siz, süssüz; açık seçik, basit, kolay anlaşılır, net; sıradan, alelade; yavan, baharatsız (*yiyecek*); dobra dobra, dürüst; alımsız, çirkin; **~ fare** orta hallile-
rin yedikleri yemek; **~ knitting** düz örgü; **~ sewing** düz dikiş; **2.** *adv.* açıkça;
tamamen; **3.** *n.* ova, düzlük; *part. Am.
attr.* çayır...; '**~clothes man** sivil polis;
~ deal.ing dürüstlük; dürüst iş; '**plainness** *n.* düzlük; sadelik, basitlik,
açıklık; **plain sail.ing** *fig.* kolay (*veya*
basit) iş.
plains.man ['pleinzmən] *n.* ovalı (*veya*
ovada yaşayan) kimse; *Am.* çayırlıkta
yaşayan kimse.
plaint JUR [pleint] *n.* dava (dilekçesi);
şikâyet, yakınma; feryat, figan; **plaintiff** ['-tif] *n.* JUR davacı; '**plain.tive** □
iniltili, kederli, yakınan, sızlanan.
plait [plæt] **1.** *n.* örgü; = **pleat 1;** **2.** *v/t.*
örmek (*saç vs.*); = **pleat 2.**
plan [plæn] **1.** *n.* plan, taslak, kroki; niyet, maksat, fikir; yol, usül, tarz; **2.** *v/t.*
planını çizmek; tertiplemek, düzenle-
mek; *fig.* niyetlenmek, düşünmek, tasarlamak, planlamak; **~ned economy**
planlı ekonomi; **~ning board** planlama
dairesi.
plane¹ [plein] **1.** *adj.* düz, dümdüz; düzlem; yassı; **2.** *n.* MATH düzlem; düzey,
seviye; AVIA uçak; *fig.* derece, kademe,
basamak, sınıf; MEC planya, rende; **ele-
vating (depressing) ~s** *pl.* AVIA yükselme (alçalma) dümeni; **3.** *v/t. & v/i.* rendelemek, düzeltmek; AVIA uçmak; havada süzülmek.
plane² BOT [-] *n. a.* **~tree** çınar (ağacı).
plan.et AST ['plænit] *n.* gezegen, seyyare.
plane-ta.ble *surv.* ['pleinteibl] *n.* plançete.
plan.e.tar.i.um [plæni'teəriəm] *n.* planetaryum; **plan.e.tar.y** ['-təri] *adj.* ge-
zegenlerle ilgili, gezegen gibi; *fig.* seyyar, gezginci.
pla.nim.e.try MATH [plæ'nimitri] *n.* yüzölçümü ölçme şekli.
plan.ish MEC ['plæniʃ] *v/t.* parlatmak,
perdahlamak.
plank [plæŋk] **1.** *n.* uzun tahta, kalas;
Am. PARL parti programı; ana maddesi;
2. *v/t.* tahta ile kaplamak; **~ down** *veya*
out *sl., Am.* F derhal ödemek; **~ bed**
kerevet; '**plank.ing** *n.* döşeme tahtası;
kaplama.

plank.ton BIOL ['plæŋktɔn] n. plankton.

plant [plɑːnt] **1.** n. bitki, nebat, ot; fabrika, atelye; demirbaş; teçhizat; sl. hile, oyun, dolap; **2.** vb. dikmek, ekmek; kurmak, tesis etm.; fig. tohumlarını atmak (fikir); koymak, yerleştirmek; ∼ **o.s.** dikilmek; sl. yapıştırmak, aşketmek, indirmek (tokat, yumruk); ∼ **s.th. on s.o.** b-ne bşi yüklemek.

plan.tain¹ BOT ['plæntin] n. sinirotu.

plan.tain² BOT [-] n. bir çeşit muz.

plan.ta.tion [plæn'teiʃən] n. koru, fidanlık; büyük çiftlik, geniş tarla; **plant.er** ['plɑːntə] n. ekici, ziraatçı; çiftlik sahibi; tohum serpme makinesi; '**plant-louse** n. yaprakbiti.

plaque [plɑːk] n. levha, plaket.

plash [plæʃ] **1.** n. şıpırtı, su sıçratma sesi; **2.** int. foş!; **3.** vb. su sıçratmak.

plash.y ['plæʃi] adj. çamurlu, ıslak, bataklık.

plas.ma BIOL ['plæzmə] n. (proto)plazma.

plas.ter ['plɑːstə] **1.** n. PHARM yakı; plaster; MEC sıva; mst ∼ **of Paris** alçı; ∼ **cast** alçı; **2.** v/t. sıvamak, sıva vurmak; yakı yapıştırmak -e; '**plas.ter.er** n. sıvacı; '**plas.ter.ing** n. sıva; alçı; F acı yenilgi.

plas.tic ['plæstik] **1.** adj. (∼ally) plastik...; naylon...; şekil verilebilen...; ∼ **arts** plastik sanatlar; **2.** n. plastik; **plas.ti.cine** ['-tisiːn] n. modelci çamuru; **plas.tic.i.ty** [-'tisiti] n. istenilen şekle sokulabilme; '**plas.tics = plastic 2**.

plat [plæt] s. **plait**; s. **plot¹**.

plate [pleit] **1.** n. com. tabak; levha; PHOT fotoğraf camı; TYP klişe; plaka; Am. beysbol: kale işareti olan levha; kupa, şilt; altın veya gümüş sofra takımı; a. **dental** ∼ damak, takma diş, protez; radyo: anot; MEC maden baskı kalıbı; **2.** v/t. madenle kaplamak; MIL, NAUT zırh levhalarla kaplamak.

pla.teau GEOGR ['plætəu] n. plato, yayla.

plate-bas.ket ['pleitbɑːskit] n. sofra takımı sepeti; **plate.ful** ['-ful] n. bir tabak dolusu.

plate...: '∼-**glass** n. dökme cam; '∼-**lay-er** n. RAIL demiryolu işçisi.

plat.en ['plætən] n. TYP daktilo merdanesi.

plat.er ['pleitə] n. MEC kaplamacı; spor: ikinci sınıf yarış atı.

form; GEOGR yayla, plato; RAIL peron; Am. part. kürsü; podyum; POL parti programı; part. Am. POL çalışma programı.

plat.i.num MIN ['plætinəm] n. platin.

plat.i.tude fig. ['plætitjuːd] n. yavan laf; adilik, bayağılık.

pla.toon MIL [plə'tuːn] n. takım, müfreze.

plat.ter ['plætə] n. düz ve büyük tabak.

plau.dit ['plɔːdit] n. mst ∼**s** pl. alkış, takdir, tezahürat.

plau.si.bil.i.ty [plɔːzə'biliti] n. akla yatkınlık, makûl olma; olasılık.

plau.si.ble □ ['plɔːzəbl] akla sığan, makûl, akla yatkın; olası.

play [plei] **1.** n. oyun, eğlence; THEAT piyes; şaka; oynama; kumar; fig. hareket serbestliği; faaliyet (alanı); MEC işleme, çalışma; **fair** (**foul**) ∼ doğru (hileli) oyun; ∼ **on words** kelime oyunu, cinas; **bring into** ∼ kullanmak, harekete geçirmek; **make great** ∼ **with** vurgulamak, ısrar etm.; **2.** v/i. oyun oynamak, eğlenmek; hareket etm., kımıldamak, sallanmak; MUS çalgı çalmak; rol yapmak; kumar oynamak; MEC çalışmak; ∼ **fast and loose with** ikiyüzlü davranmak, oyun etm. -e; ∼ **at cards** iskambil oynamak; ∼ **for time** zaman kazanmaya çalışmak; ∼ **up** gayretle oynamak; yaramazlık yapmak; ∼ **upon** istismar etm. -i; v/t. oyna(t)mak; yapmak (hile); THEAT temsil etm., canlandırmak; çalmak (enstruman); işletmek, kullanmak; ∼ **off** fig. düşürmek (**against each other** birbirine); ∼**ed out** yorgun, bitkin; modası geçmiş; demode; '∼-**act.ing** n. temsil etme; fig. gösteriş çilik; '∼-**bill** n. tiyatro afişi; oyun programı; '∼-**book** n. THEAT libretto; '∼-**boy** n. zevk peşinde koşan zengin delikanlı; '**play.er** n. oyuncu; aktör; çalgıcı; kumarbaz; müzik çalmak için kullanılan alet; '**play.fel.low** n. oyun arkadaşı; '**play.ful** □ ['-ful] oyunbaz, şakacı, eğlenceli, şen; '**play.ful.ness** n. oyunbazlık; şakacılık.

play...: '∼-**go.er** n. tiyatro meraklısı; '∼-**ground** n. oyun sahası; ∼-**house** n. tiyatro; Am. çocukların içinde oynadıkları küçük ev.

play.ing...: '∼-**card** n. iskambil kâğıdı; '∼-**field** n. oyun sahası.

play...: '∼-**mate** s. **playfellow**; '∼-**off** n. spor: rövanş maçı; '∼-**thing** n. oyuncak

(*a. fig.*); '*~*.**wright** *n.* THEAT piyes yazarı.

pla.za ['plɑːzə] *n.* (İspanya'da) meydan,
pazar yeri.

plea [pliː] *n.* JUR müdafaa, savunma; dava; rica, yalvarma; itiraz; bahane, özür,
mazeret; **make a** *~* itirazda bulunmak,
reddetmek; **on the** *~* **of** *veya* **that** ... ba-
hanesiyle.

plead [pliːd] *v/i.* yalvarmak, rica etm.,
istirham etm.; dava açmak; *~* **for** savunmak -*i*; *s.* **guilty**; *v/t.* ileri sürmek, iddia
etm.; savunmak; suçlamak; mazeret
olarak göstermek; '**plead.a.ble** *adj.*
davada cevap, delil *veya* özür olarak
gösterilebilir; '**plead.er** *n.* JUR avukat,
dava vekili; '**plead.ing** *n.* JUR dava açma; *~s pl.* lâyihalar, yazılı savunmalar.

pleas.ant □ ['pleznt] hoş, latif, güzel,
tatlı, cana yakın; '**pleas.ant.ness** *n.*
hoşluk, letafet; '**pleas.ant.ry** *n.*
şaka(cılık), komiklik; neşe, hoşbeş.

please [pliːz] *v/i.* memnun edici olm.; **if
you** *~* *iro.* ister misin...!; lütfen, rica
ederim; isterseniz; *~* **come in!** lütfen
girin!; *v/t.* sevindirmek, hoşnut etm.,
memnun etm., -*in* hoşuna gitmek; *~*
yourself F nasıl isterseniz öyle yapın;
be *~d* **to do** seve seve yapmak, yapmaktan memnun *~* *b-ni* memnun
etm.; **take** *~* **in** ...*den* **pleased** *adj.*
memnun, hoşnut.

pleas.ing □ ['pliːzɪŋ] hoş, sevimli, hoşa
giden, memnuniyet verici, zevk veren.

pleas.ur.a.ble □ ['pleʒərəbl] zevk veren, hoşa giden; tatminkâr.

pleas.ure ['pleʒə] **1.** *n.* zevk, keyif,
memnuniyet, sevinç, sefa, haz, lezzet;
emir, irade, istek, arzu; *attr.* zevk veren...; **at** *~* arzuya göre, istenildiği kadar; **give s.o.** *~* *b-ni* memnun etm.;
take *~* **in** ...*den* zevk almak; **2.** *vb.* zevk
almak; zevk vermek; '*~*-**ground** *n.* lunapark.

pleat [pliːt] **1.** *n.* pli, plise; **2.** *v/t.* pli yapmak.

ple.be.ian [pliˈbiːən] **1.** *adj.* (*eski Roma'da*) aşağı tabakadan olan; adi, bayağı; **2.** *n.* aşağı tabakadan kimse.

pleb.i.scite ['plebisit] *n.* plebisit.

pledge [pledʒ] **1.** *n.* rehin; söz, vaat, yemin, ant; güvence, teminat, taahhüt;
put in *~* rehine koymak; **take out of**
~ rehinden kurtarmak; **2.** *v/t.* rehin olarak vermek, rehine koymak; taahhüt
etm.; söz verdirmek; -*in* şerefine içmek; **he** *~d* **himself** vaat etti; **pledgee**

n. rehinli alacaklı; **pledg.er** *n.* rehinli
borçlu, rehin veren.

Ple.iad ['plaiəd] *n.*, *pl.* **Ple.ia.des**
['ˌdiːz] Süreyya burcu, Ülker.

ple.na.ry ['pliːnəri] *adj.* tam (*yetki*),
sınırsız, sonsuz, bütün; tüm üyelerin
katıldığı (*toplantı*).

plen.i.po.ten.ti.ar.y [plenipəuˈtenʃəri]
1. *adj.* tam yetkili (*elçi vs.*); **2.** *n.* tam
yetkili elçi.

plen.i.tude ['plenitjuːd] *n.* bolluk, çokluk, doluluk, bütünlük.

plen.te.ous □ *poet.* ['plentjəs] çok,
bol, bereketli; '**plen.te.ous.ness** *n.*
bolluk, çokluk, bereket.

plen.ti.ful □ ['plentiful] bol, çok, bereketli, verimli.

plen.ty ['plenti] **1.** *n.* bolluk, çokluk,
zenginlik; *~* **of** çok, bol; **horn of** *~* bolluk (sembolü); **2.** *adj.* F pek çok, bol,
bereketli.

ple.o.nasm ['pliːənæzəm] *n.* kelime
fazlalığı, laf kalabalığı, söz uzatımı.

pleth.o.ra ['pleθərə] *n.* dolgunluk, fazlalık; MED kan fazlalığı; **ple.thor.ic**
[pleˈθɔrik] *adj.* (*~ally*) pletorik; *fig.*
şişman.

pleu.ri.sy MED ['pluərisi] *n.* zatülcenp.

pli.a.bil.i.ty [plaiəˈbiliti] *n.* esneklik,
yumuşaklık; *fig.* uysallık.

pli.a.ble □ ['plaiəbl] bükülür, esnek,
yumuşak; *fig.* uysal.

pli.an.cy ['plaiənsi] *n.* esneklik, bükü-
lebilirlik.

pli.ant □ ['plaiənt] = **pliable**.

pli.ers ['plaiəz] *n. pl.* (**a pair of** bir)
kıskaç, pens(e).

plight[1] [plait] **1.** *v/t.* söz vermek, güvence vermek; **2.** *n.* söz, vaat.

plight[2] [ˌ] *n.* kötü durum, çıkmaz.

plim.solls ['plimsəlz] *n. pl.* tenis ayakkabısı.

plinth ARCH [plinθ] *n.* duvar etekliği,
etek tahtası.

plod [plɔd] *vb. a.* *~* **along,** *~* **on** ağır ağır
yürümek, çalışmak *vs.*; '**plod.ding** □
ağır, hantal.

plop [plɔp] **1.** *int.* cup!; **2.** *n.* 'cup' sesi; **3.**
v/i. 'cup' diye ses çıkarmak; 'cup' diye
düşmek.

plot[1] [plɔt] *n.* arsa, parsel.

plot[2] [ˌ] **1.** *n.* entrika, suikast, fesat, gizli
plan, kumpas, komplo, dolap; romanın
konusu; **2.** *v/t. a.* *~* **down** -*in* haritasını
çıkarmak; plan *veya* haritada göster-
mek; *b.s. -e* karşı entrika çevirmek;
v/i. kumpas kurmak, kötü niyetlerle

plan yapmak; **plot.ter** *n.* entrikacı, suikastçı, fesatçı.

plough [plau] **1.** *n.* saban, pulluk; MEC sabana benzer alet; UNIV *sl.* başarısızlık, çakma, kalma (*sınavda*); **the** ♎ AST Büyükayı; **2.** *v/t.* sabanla işlemek; yarıp geçmek; **~ back** tekrar yatırmak (*para*); **be ~ed** UNIV *sl.* çakmak, kalmak (*sınavda*); *v/i.* saban sürmek; ağır ağır ilerlemek; **'~.man** *n.* saban süren kimse; çiftçi, köylü; **'~.share** *n.* saban demiri, saban kulağı.

plov.er ['plʌvə] *n.* ORN yağmurkuşu.

plow [plau], **plow.man** *part. Am.* = **plough** *etc.*

pluck [plʌk] **1.** *n.* cesaret, yiğitlik; koparma, yolma; çekme; **2.** *v/t.* koparmak, yolmak; çekmek, çekip almak (**from** -*den*); *sl.* soyup soğana çevirmek, yolmak (*kumarda*); parmakla çalmak (*telli saz*); UNIV *sl.* döndürmek, çaktırmak (*sınavda*); **~ at** tutup çekmek, çekiştirmek -*i*; **~ up courage** cesaretini toplamak.

pluck.y □ ['plʌki] cesur, yiğit, yürekli, yılmaz.

plug [plʌg] **1.** *n.* tapa, tıkaç, tampon; ELECT fiş; MOT buji; tütün parçası; *Am. radyo:* durmadan tekrarlanan reklam; F vuruş, vurma; değersiz şey; yaşlı at; yangın musluğu; **~ socket** elektrik prizi; **2.** *v/t.* tıkamak; *sl.* tabanca ile vurmak; yumruklamak; *Am.* F durmadan reklamını yapmak; **~ in** ELECT prize sokmak; *sl.* eşek gibi çalışmak; ateş etm.; **plug-'ug.ly** *n. Am. sl.* gangster, eşkiya, katil.

plum [plʌm] *n.* erik (ağacı); kuru üzüm; arzulanacak şey; F en güzel lokma, kıyak şey; bonbon, şekerleme; *sl.* £ 100.000.

plum.age ['pluːmidʒ] *n.* kuşun tüyleri.

plumb [plʌm] **1.** *adv.* düşey olarak, dimdik; tamamen, kesinlikle; **2.** *n.* şakul, iskandil kurşunu; **3.** *vb.* iskandil etm., şakule vurmak, şakullemek; ölçmek, tartmak; doğrultmak, düzeltmek; kurşunla kaplamak; *fig.* araştırmak, kökenine inmek; F tesisatçılık yapmak; **plum.ba.go** [ˌ'beigəu] *n.* kalem kurşunu, grafit; **plumb.er** *n.* lehimci, muslukçu, su tesisatçısı; **plumbic** ['plʌmbik] *adj.* CHEM kurşun...; **plumb ing** ['.miŋ] *n.* boru tesisatçılığı, muslukçuluk; su tesisatı; **'plumb-line** *n.* MEC şakul (sicimi), çekül; **'plumb--rule** *n.* çekül.

plume [pluːm] **1.** *n.* iri ve gösterişli tüy, sorguç; tüye benzer şey; şeref madalyası; nişan; **2.** *vb.* (gaga ile) düzeltmek (*tüylerini*); tüylerle süslemek; övünmek; **~ o.s. on** ...*ile* övünmek, *k-ni* beğenmek.

plum.met ['plʌmit] *n.* şakul kurşunu, çekül; ağırlık.

plum.my F ['plʌmi] *adj.* iyi, güzel, hoş, çekici, cazip; sahte tavırlı, yapmacık.

plump[1] [plʌmp] **1.** *adj.* dolgun, tombul, tıknaz, şişman, balık etinde; semiz (*hayvan*); **2.** *v/t. & v/i.* şişmanla(t)mak, dolgunlaş(tır)mak.

plump[2] [.] **1.** *v/t. & v/i.* birden düş(ür)-mek; «pat» diye oturmak; PARL oy vermek (**for** -*e*); yardım etm. -*e*; **2.** *n.* ani düşüş; **3.** *adv.* F aniden, birden; açıkça, kabaca; **4.** □ F tam, kesin, direkt.

plump.er ['plʌmpə] *n.* PARL oy; *sl.* yalan.

plump.ness ['plʌmpnis] *n.* dolgunluk, tombulluk; F samimiyet, içtenlik, doğruluk.

plum-pud.ding ['plʌm'pudiŋ] *n.* baharatlı Noel pudingi.

plum.y ['pluːmi] *adj.* tüylü, tüy gibi, tüylerle süslenmiş.

plun.der ['plʌndə] **1.** *n.* yağma(cılık), çapulculuk; **2.** *v/t. & v/i.* yağma etm., soymak, talan etm.; çapulculuk etm.; **'plunder.er** *n.* yağmacı, çapulcu.

plunge [plʌndʒ] **1.** *n.* dalış, dalma; yüzme; F tehlikeli girişim; **make** *veya* **take the ~** tehlikeli bir işe girişmek; **2.** *v/t. & v/i.* dal(dır)mak, sokmak; at(ıl)mak (**into** -*e*); boğmak (*karanlığa*); batırmak (**into** -*e*); gir(iş)mek; ileriye atılmak (*at*); NAUT baş kıç vurmak; büyük kumar oynamak; borca girmek.

plung.er ['plʌndʒə] *n.* piston; dalgıç; *sl.* kumarbaz; vurguncu.

plunk [plʌŋk] *v/t. & v/i.* birden düş(ür)-mek.

plu.per.fect GR ['pluː'pəːfikt] *n.* geçmiş zamanın hikâye şekli.

plu.ral GR ['pluərəl] *n.* çoğul; **plu.ral.i.ty** [ˌ'ræliti] *n.* çokluk, ekseriyet, çoğunluk; **~ of wives** poligami, çokevlilik.

plus [plʌs] **1.** *prp.* fazlasıyle, ilavesiyle; ayrıca, ve; **2.** *adj.* fazla, ilave olan; pozitif; **3.** *n.* artı (işareti); pozitif miktar; fazlalık; **~fours** F [ˌ'fɔːz] *n. pl.* golf pantolonu.

plush [plʌʃ] *n.* pelüş.

plush.y ['plʌʃi] *adj.* pelüş...; *sl.* süslü, gösterişli, lüks.

plu.toc.ra.cy [plu:ˈtɔkrəsi] *n*. plütokra-si, zenginler hâkimiyeti; zenginerki; **plu.tocrat** [ˈ‿təukræt] *n*. plütokrat.

plu.to.ni.um CHEM [plu:təunjəm] *n*. plutonyum.

plu.vi.al [ˈplu:viəl] *adj*., **plu.vi.ous** yağmurlu, yağmurla ilgili; **plu.vi.om-e.ter** [‿ˈɔmitə] *n*. yağmurölçer.

ply [plai] **1**. *n*. kat, katmer, tabaka; *fig*. meyil, eğilim; iplik teli; **2**. *v/t*. işletmek, kullanmak; etmek, yapmak; eğmek; durmadan vermek (*yiyecek, içki*); tut-mak (*soru yağmuruna*); **~ a trade** tica-ret yapmak; *v/i*. çalışmak; düzenli se-ferler yapmak, gidip gelmek.

ply-wood [ˈplaiwud] *n*. kontrplak.

pneu.mat.ic [nju:ˈmætik] **1**. *adj*. (**~ally**) hava basıncı ile ilgili; hava basıncı ile çalışan...; içinde sıkıştırılmış hava olan...; **~ hammer** hava çekici; **~ tire** şişirilmiş otomobil lastiği; **2**. *n*. şişiril-miş otomobil lastiği, iç lastik.

pneu.mo.ni.a MED [nju:ˈməunjə] *n*. za-türree.

poach[1] [pəutʃ] *v/i*. bata çıka yürümek; cıvık cıvık olm. (*toprak*); gizlice avlan-mak, yasak bölgede avlanmak.

poach[2] [‿] *vb. a*. **~ up** kazıp karıştır-mak.

poach[3] [‿]: **~ed eggs** *pl*. sıcak suya kırılıp pişirilmiş yumurtalar.

poach.er [ˈpəutʃə] *n*. ruhsatsız avlanan kimse, yasak bölgede avlanan kimse; yumurta haşlama kabı.

po.chette [pɔˈʃet] *n*. el torbası, poşet.

pock MED [pɔk] *n*. çiçek hastalığı ka-barcığı.

pock.et [ˈpɔkit] **1**. *n*. cep; GEOL çukur, gedik; para, maddi olanak; AVIA hava boşluğu; bölge, semt; **2**. *v/t*. cebe koy-mak, cebine atmak, *sl*. iç etmek; *Am*. POL veto etm.; gizlemek, saklamak, bastırmak; **3**. *adj*. cebe sığan..., cep...; **~ lighter** cep çakmağı; **~ lamp** cep feneri; **'~book** *n*. cep kitabı; cüz-dan; *Am*. kadın cüzdanı *veya* el çanta-sı.

pod [pɔd] **1**. *n*. BOT kabuk, zarf; hayvan sürüsü; **2**. *v/t*. -*in* kabuğunu soymak; *v/i*. tohum zarfı oluşturmak.

po.dag.ra MED [ˈpɔdəgrə] *n*. ayakta gö-rülen gut hastalığı.

podg.y F [ˈpɔdʒi] *adj*. bodur, tıfıl, tıknaz.

po.di.um [ˈpəudiəm] *n*. podyum, plat-form.

po.em [ˈpəuim] *n*. şiir, koşuk, manzu-me.

po.e.sy [ˈpəuizi] *n*. şairlik, şiir sanatı; şiirler.

po.et [ˈpəuit] *n*. şair, ozan; **po.et.as.ter** [‿ˈtæstə] *n*. şair bozuntusu, kalitesiz şair; **'po.et.ess** *n*. kadın şair; **po'et.ic, poet.i.cal** □ [pəuˈetik(əl)] şiire ait, şiir niteliğinde, manzum, şairane; **po'et-ics** *n*. *pl*. vezin tekniği; koşuk kural ve usulü; **poet.ize** [ˈ‿itaiz] *vb*. şiir yaz-mak; **'po.et.ry** *n*. şiir sanatı; F şiirler.

poign.an.cy [ˈpɔinənsi] *n*. keskinlik, acılık; *fig*. ıstırap; **'poign.ant** □ acı, keskin; kuvvetli; tesirli, şiddetli; *fig*. dokunaklı.

point [pɔint] **1**. *n*. nokta (*a. gr*, MATH, PHYS *etc*.); uç, burun; puan; sayı; dere-ce; husus, özel bir durum; NAUT pusula taksimatından biri, kerte; mesele, ana fikir; punto; cihet, bakım; sebep, ne-den; özellik; ELECT priz; etki, tesir; **~s** *pl*. RAIL makaslar; *s*. **~-lace**; **~ of view** görüş noktası, bakış açısı; **the ~ is that...** mesele şu ki...; **there is no ~ in ger**. ...mekte bir yarar yok, ...menin bir anlamı yok; **make a ~ of s.th**. bşe özen göstermek; **make the ~ that** ...dığını göstermek; **stretch a ~** ödün vermek, göz yummak, izin vermek; **in ~ of** hususunda, bakımından; **in ~ of fact** hakikaten, gerçekten; **off** *veya* **beyond the ~** konu dışında; **differ on many ~s** birçok noktada ayrılmak; **he was on the ~ of coming** gelmek üzereydi; **win on ~s** *boks*: sayı ile ka-zanmak; **to the ~** isabetli, uygun; **stick to the ~** konuya bağlı kalmak, konu dışına çıkmamak; **2**. *v/t*. ucunu sivrilt-mek; doğrultmak, yöneltmek; çimento *veya* harç ile doldurmak; noktalamak; virgülle hanelere ayırmak; *oft*. **~ out** göstermek, belirtmek, işaret etm.; **~ at** yöneltmek *-e*, doğrultmak *-e*, çevir-mek *-e*; *v/i*. göstermek; silahın doğ-rultmak *-e*; ferma etm. (*köpek*); yönel-mek; **~ at** göstermek *-i*; **~ to** göstermek *-i*, delâlet etm. *-e*; **'~blank** *adj*. yatay olarak atılan; yakın menzilden yapılan (*atış*); açık, kesin, dolaysız; **~ shot** yakın menzil atışı; **'~du.ty** *n*. belli bir noktada yapılan görev (*part. trafik kontrolü*); **'point.ed** □ sivri uçlu; *fig*. manalı, anlamlı; keskin, tesirli; **'point-ed.ness** *n*. sivri uçluluk; anlamlı olma; **'point.er** *n*. işaret değneği; gösterge, ibre; F anlamlı söz, ima; zağar, bir cins av köpeği; **'point-'lace** *n*. oya işi;

'**point.less** *adj.* uçsuz; anlamsız, manasız; gayesiz, amaçsız; puansız, sayısız (*oyun*); '**point-po'lice.man** *n.* belli bir noktada görev yapan trafik polisi; '**points.man** *n.* RAIL makasçı; '**point-to-'point race** arazide iki nokta arasında yapılan at yarışı.

poise [pɔiz] **1.** *n.* denge; istikrar; kendine güven; kendine hâkim olma; duruş, hal; **2.** *v/t. & v/i.* dengele(n)mek; *-in* dengesini sağlamak; dik tutmak, kaldırmak, havada tutmak; dengeli olm.; asılı olm., sarkmak; havada durmak; *be ~d* dengede durmak.

poi.son ['pɔizn] **1.** *n.* zehir; **2.** *v/t.* zehirlemek (*a. fig.*); '**poi.son.er** *n.* zehirleyici; zehirle adam öldüren kimse; '**poi.sonous** □ zehirli; *fig.* fesat; F iğrenç, tiksindirici.

poke [pəuk] **1.** *n.* itme, dürtme; yumruk atma; **2.** *v/t.* dürtmek; saplamak; atmak, vurmak (*yumruk*); uzatmak, çıkarmak; sokmak; *a.* ~ *up* karıştırmak; ~ *fun at* alay etm., dalga geçmek *ile*; ~ *one's nose into s.th.* bşe burnunu sokmak; *v/i.* dürtüklemek (*at -i*); araştırmak (*into -i*); oyalanmak, aylak aylak dolaşmak; çıkıntı yapmak.

pok.er[1] ['pəukə] *n.* ocak demiri.

po.ker[2] [ˌ] *n.* poker oyunu; ~ *face fig.* ifadesiz yüz.

pok.er-work ['pəukəwəːk] *n.* pirogravür.

pok.y ['pəuki] *adj.* küçük, ufak; sıkıcı, kasvetli, bunaltıcı; çok yavaş.

po.lar ['pəulə] *adj.* kutba ait, kutupsal; tamamen birbirine zıt; ~ *bear* kutup ayısı; **po.lar.i.ty** PHYS [pəu'læriti] *n.* kutbiyet, polarite; **po.lar.i.za.tion** PHYS [ˌ-ləraiˈzeiʃən] *n.* polarma; '**po.lar.ize** *v/t. & v/i.* PHYS polarmak; iki zıt kutba ayırmak (*veya* ayrılmak).

Pole[1] ['pəul] *n.* Polonyalı, Lehli.

pole[2] [ˌ] *n.* kutup (GEOGR, AST, PHYS, *fig.*).

pole[3] [ˌ] **1.** *n.* direk, kazık, sırık; 5,029 metrelik bir uzunluk; olta kamışı; **2.** *v/t. & v/i.* sırıklamak, sırıklarla donatmak; sırıkla desteklemek; sırıkla itmek; sırıkla kayığı yüzdürmek; '~*-ax(e)* *n.* MIL uzun saplı balta; teber; kasap satırı; '~*.cat* *n.* ZOO kokarca; *Am.* sansar; ~ *jump = pole vault.*

po.lem.ic [pɔ'lemik] **1.** *a.* do'lem.i.cal □ tartışmalı, münakaşalı, polemiğe ait; **2.** *n.* tartışma, münakaşa; tartışmacı, münakaşacı; **po'lem.ics** *n. pl.*

tartışma sanatı, polemik.

pole-star ['pəulstaː] *n.* Kutupyıldızı; *fig.* önder, yönetici unsur.

pole-vault ['pəulvɔːlt] *n.* *spor.* sırıkla yüksek atlama.

po.lice [pə'liːs] **1.** *n.* polis (teşkilâtı); *two* ~ iki polis; ~ *dossier* iyi hal belgesi; **2.** *v/t.* polis kuvvetiyle sağlamak (*düzen ve asayişi*); idare etm., kontrol etm.; **po'lice.man** *n.* polis memuru; **po'lice-of.fice** *n.* karakol; **po'lice-of.fi.cer** *n.* polis memuru; **po'lice-sta.tion** *n.* karakol; **po'lice-sur'veil.lance** *n.* polis gözetimi; **po'lice-trap** *n.* hız kontrol bölgesi; **po'licewom.an** *n.* kadın polis.

pol.i.cy[1] ['pɔlisi] *n.* siyaset, politika, idare, yönetim; takip edilen yol, hareket tarzı.

pol.i.cy[2] [ˌ] *n.* poliçe; *Am.* bir çeşit lotarya.

po.li.o(.my.e.li.tis) ['pəuliəu(maiə'laitis)] *n.* çocuk felci; omurilikteki gri maddenin iltihabı.

Pol.ish[1] ['pəuliʃ] *adj.* Leh, Polonya *veya* Polonyalılara ait.

pol.ish[2] ['pɔliʃ] **1.** *n.* cilâ, perdah; boya; cilâlama; *fig.* incelik, zarafet, terbiye, nezaket; **2.** *v/t. & v/i.* cilâla(n)mak, parla(t)mak; *fig.* terbiye etm., süslemek, zarifleştirmek; ~ *off* hemen bitirmek, silip süpürmek (*yemek*); ~ *up* pırıl pırıl yapmak, iyice cilâlamak; '**pol.ish.ing** **1.** *n.* cilâ(lama); **2.** *adj.* cilâlı..., parlak...

po.lite □ [pə'lait] nazik, kibar, terbiyeli, ince; **po'lite.ness** *n.* nezaket, kibarlık, incelik.

pol.i.tic □ ['pɔlitik] siyasî, politik; basiretli, sağgörülü, tedbirli, akıllı; *body* ~ devlet teşekkülü; **po.lit.i.cal** □ [pə'litikəl] siyasî, siyasal, politik; devlet *veya* hükümete ait; **pol.i.ti.cian** [pɔli'tiʃən] *n.* politikacı, siyasetçi; *contp.* kendi çıkarına siyaset ile uğraşan kimse; **pol.i.tics** ['ˌ-tiks] *n. sg.* siyaset, politika; parti entrikaları.

pol.i.ty ['pɔliti] *n.* hükümet *veya* idare şekli; devlet, hükümet.

pol.ka ['pɔlkə] *n.* polka dansı *veya* müziği; ~ *dot Am.* puanlı, benekli (*kumaş*).

poll[1] ['pəul] **1.** *n.* seçim, oy verme; oy (sayısı); seçmen sayısı; seçim bürosu; anket; *co.* baş, kelle, kafa; *go to the* ~*s* oy vermek; **2.** *v/t.* kesmek, kırkmak, kırpmak; toplamak (*oy*); seçim listesine kaydetmek; = **pollard 2**; v/i. oy vermek; ~ **for** oy vermek -e.

poll² [pɔl] n. papağan.

pol.lard ['pɔləd] **1.** n. boynuzsuz hayvan; budanmış ağaç; **2.** v/t. budamak (ağaç); -in boynuzlarını kesmek.

poll-book ['pəulbuk] n. seçmen kütüğü.

pol.len BOT ['pɔlin] n. çiçek tozu; **pol.li.nation** [pɔli'neiʃən] n. tozaklama.

poll.ing...: '~-**booth** n. oy verme hücresi; '~-**dis.trict** n. seçim bölgesi; '~-**place** n. oy atılan yer; '~-**sta.tion** n. oy verme yeri.

poll-tax ['pəultæks] n. kişi başına düşen vergi; baş vergisi; oy kullanmak için ödenen vergi.

pol.lute [pə'lu:t] v/t. pisletmek, kirletmek (a. fig.); **pol'lu.tion** n. pisletme, kirletme; kirlilik.

po.lo ['pəuləu] n. spor: polo, çevgen; **water** ~ sutopu; '~-**neck** adj. balıkçı yaka...

po.lo.ny [pə'ləuni] n. domuz etinden yapılan sosis.

pol.troon [pɔl'tru:n] n. korkak kimse; **pol'troon.er.y** n. korkaklık.

po.lyg.a.my [pɔ'ligəmi] n. çokkarılılık, poligami; **pol.y.glot** ['~glɔt] adj. birçok dilde yazılmış olan; birçok dil bilen; **pol.ygon** ['~gən] n. poligon, çokgen; **po'lyg.onal** [~gənl] adj. çokköşeli, çokgen...; **pol.y.phon.ic** MUS ['~'fɔnik] adj. çok sesli, polifonik; **pol.yp** ZOO ['pɔlip] n., **pol.y.pus** MED ['~pəs] polip; **pol.y.syl.lab.ic** ['~si'læbik] adj. çok heceli; **pol.y.syl.la.ble** ['~siləbl] n. üçten fazla heceli kelime; **pol.y.tech.nic** [~'teknik] n. sanat veya fen öğreten okul; **pol.y.the.ism** ['~θi:izəm] n. çoktanrıcılık.

po.made [pə'mɑːd] n. briyantin, merhem, pomat.

pome.gran.ate BOT ['pɔmigrænit] n. nar.

Pom.er.a.nian [pɔmə'reinjən] **1.** adj. Pomeranya'ya ait; **2.** n. Pomeranyalı; a. ~ **dog** Pomeranya köpeği.

pom.mel ['pʌml] **1.** n. eyer kaşı; kılıç kabzasının başı; **2.** v/t. yumruklamak, yumrukla dövmek.

pomp [pɔmp] n. gösteriş, tantana, ihtişam, azamet, görkem.

pompom ['pɔmpɔm] n. otomatik uçaksavar top.

pom.pos.i.ty [pɔm'pɔsiti] n. tantana, ihtişam, görkem; '**pomp.ous** □ tanta-

nalı, debdebeli, görkemli; azametli, gururlu; süslü.

pon.cho ['pɔntʃəu] n. baştan geçme kepenek, panço.

pond [pɔnd] n. havuz, gölcük.

pon.der ['pɔndə] v/t. zihninde tartmak, düşünmek; v/i. uzun boylu düşünmek (**on, over**-i); **pon.der.a.bil.i.ty** [~rə'biliti] n. ölçülebilirlik, tartılabilirlik; '**pon.der.able** adj. ölçülebilir, tartılabilir; **pon.deros.i.ty** [~'rɔsiti] n. ağırlık, sıklet; '**ponder.ous** □ ağır, hantal, iri, cüsseli; can sıkıcı; '**ponder.ous.ness** = **ponderosity**.

pone [pəun] n. mısır ekmeği.

pon.iard ['pɔnjəd] n. kama, hançer.

pon.tiff ['pɔntif] n. papa, piskopos; **pon'tif.i.cal** □ papaya veya piskoposa ait; gururlu; amirane; **pon'tif.i.cate** [~kit] n. papanın makamı veya görev süresi, papalık.

pon.toon MIL [pɔn'tu:n] n. duba, tombaz; **pon'toon-bridge** n. dubalar üstüne kurulan köprü, tombaz köprüsü.

po.ny ['pəuni] n. ZOO midilli; sl. 25 İngiliz lirası; '~'**en.gine** n. RAIL manevra lokomotifi; '~-**tail** n. at kuyruğu (saç).

pooch Am. sl. [pu:tʃ] n. it, köpek.

poo.dle ['pu:dl] n. kaniş köpeği.

pooh [pu:] int. öf!

pooh-pooh [pu:'pu:] v/t. küçümsemek, alaya almak.

pool¹ [pu:l] n. gölcük, su birikintisi; herhangi bir sıvı birikintisi; havuz; bir nehrin derin ve durgun bölümü.

pool² [~] **1.** n. ortaya konulan para; toto; COM tüccarlar birliği; bir çeşit bilardo oyunu; ~ **room** bilardo salonu; **2.** v/t. COM ortaklaşa toplamak, birleştirmek.

poop NAUT [pu:p] **1.** n. pupa; **2.** v/t. pupadan yemek (dalga).

poor □ [puə] fakir, yoksul, muhtaç; zavallı, biçare; fena, adi, bayağı, naçizane; az, biraz, kıt; zayıf, kuru, kuvvetsiz; **the** ~ yoksullar, fakir fukara; ~ **me!** zavallı ben!; ~ **health** bozuk sıhhat; '~-**box** n. sadaka kutusu; '~-**house** n. darülaceze, düşkünler yurdu; '~-**law** n. JUR fakirleri koruyan kanun; '**poorly 1.** adj. pred. hasta, rahatsız; **2.** adv. kötü bir şekilde, fena, başarısızlıkla; kusurlu olarak; **he is** ~ **off** meteliğe kurşun atıyor; '**poor.ness** n. fakirlik, yoksulluk; '**poor-rate** n. zekât; halktan alınan fakirlere yardım vergisi; '**poor-'spir.it.ed** korkak, ödlek, yüreksiz; çekingen.

pop[1] [pɔp] **1.** *n.* patlama sesi; F gazoz; *in ~ sl.* rehinde; **2.** *v/t. & v/i.* patla(t)mak, 'pat' diye ses çıkarmak; ateş etm.; *sl.* rehine vermek; *Am.* patlatmak (*mısır*); hemen sokuvermek; *~ in* uğramak; birden sokmak; *~ the question to a lady* bir kadına evlenme teklif etm.; *~ up* birden gelmek, çıkıvermek; **3.** *adv.* aniden, birden; **4.** *int.* pat!, çat!

pop[2] F [-] **1.** *adj.* sevilen, tutulan, popüler; **2.** *n.* pop müziği; pop şarkısı.

pop[3] *Am.* F [-] *n.* baba.

pop-corn *part. Am.* ['pɔpkɔːn] *n.* patlamış mısır.

pope [pəup] *n.* papa; 'pope.dom *n.* papalık; 'pop.er.y *n. contp.* papalık sistemi.

pop-eyed ['pɔpaid] *adj.* patlak gözlü.

pop.gun ['pɔpgʌn] *n.* oyuncak mantarlı tüfek, patlangaç.

pop.in.jay ['pɔpindʒei] *n.* züppe kimse.

pop.ish □ ['pəupiʃ] Katolik kiliselerine ait.

pop.lar BOT ['pɔplə] *n.* kavak.

pop.lin ['pɔplin] *n.* poplin.

pop.pet ['pɔpit] *n.* NAUT kızak payandası; MEC başlıklı cıvata; *s. puppet.*

pop.py BOT ['pɔpi] *n.* gelincik; haşhaş, afyon; '~.cock *n. Am.* F saçma, boş laf.

pop.u.lace ['pɔpjuləs] *n.* halk, avam, kitle.

pop.u.lar □ ['pɔpjulə] halka ait; herkesçe anlaşılabilen; halkın kesesine uygun; herkesçe sevilen, popüler, revaçta olan; genel, yaygın; *~ front* faşizm ve gericiliğe karşı olan solcu koalisyonu; **pop.ular.i.ty** [-'læriti] *n.* halk tarafından tutulma, rağbet, popülerlik; **pop.u.lar.ize** ['-lǝraiz] *vb.* halkın beğeneceği şekle sokmak; herkesin anlayacağı şekle sokmak; halka hitap etm.; '**pop.u.lar.ly** *adv.* herkesçe sevilerek; halka hitap eder şekilde.

pop.u.late ['pɔpjuleit] *v/t.* şeneltmek, nüfuslandırmak; bayındırlaştırmak; **popu'la.tion** *n.* nüfus, ahali.

pop.u.lous □ ['pɔpjuləs] nüfusu çok, kalabalık, yoğun nüfuslu.

por.ce.lain ['pɔːslin] *n.* porselen (eşya).

porch [pɔːtʃ] *n.* kapı önünde sundurma; *Am.* veranda, taraça.

por.cu.pine ZOO ['pɔːkjupain] *n.* oklukirpi.

pore[1] [pɔː] *n.* gözenek, mesane.

pore[2] [-] *v/i.* dikkatle bakmak (*over-e*); derin derin düşünmek (*over, on, upon*

-i).

pork [pɔːk] *n.* domuz eti; '~-bar.rel *n. Am. sl.* politik amaçlarla kullanılmak üzere devlet hazinesinden ayrılan para; '~-butch.er *n.* domuz kasabı; 'pork.er *n.* besili domuz; 'pork.y **1.** *adj.* F yağlı, semiz, şişko; **2.** *Am.* F = *porcupine.*

por.nog.ra.phy [pɔː'nɔgrəfi] *n.* pornografi, müstehcen yazı *veya* resimler.

po.ros.i.ty [pɔː'rɔsiti] *n.*, **po.rous.ness** ['pɔːrəsnis] gözenekli olma.

po.rous □ ['pɔːrəs] gözenekli; su *veya* hava geçiren.

por.phy.ry MIN ['pɔːfiri] *n.* somaki, porfir.

por.poise ICHTH ['pɔːpəs] *n.* yunusbalığı.

por.ridge ['pɔridʒ] *n.* yulaf lapası; **por.ringer** ['pɔrindʒə] *n.* çorba *veya* lapa kâsesi.

port[1] [pɔːt] *n.* liman (şehri); *~ of call* uğranılacak (*veya* ara) liman; *~ of destination* gidilecek liman; *~ of trans--shipment* aktarma limanı.

port[2] NAUT [-] *n.* lombar (kapağı).

port[3] [-] **1.** *v/t.* MIL namlusu sol omuza doğru olmak üzere eğri tutmak (*tüfek*); **2.** *n.* tüfek *veya* başka bir silahın omuzdaki duruşu.

port[4] NAUT [-] **1.** *n.* geminin sol *veya* iskele tarafı; **2.** *v/t.* iskeleye kırmak (*dümen*).

port[5] [-] *n.* porto şarabı.

port.a.ble ['pɔːtəbl] *adj.* taşınabilir, portatif; *~ radio set* portatif radyo; *~ type writer* portatif daktilo.

por.tage ['pɔːtidʒ] *n.* taşıma, nakletme; nakliyat yolu; *s. porterage.*

por.tal ['pɔːtl] *n.* görkemli kapı, giriş; 'por.tal-to-'por.tal pay işçinin işyerinde harcadığı zamana göre ödenen para.

port.cul.lis MIL [pɔːt'kʌlis] *n.* kaleye girişi önlemek için indirilen demir parmaklık.

por.tend [pɔː'tend] *v/t.* yakında olacağına alâmet olm. (*kötü bir olay*), delâlet etm. *-e.*

por.tent ['pɔːtent] *n.* kehanet; alâmet, geleceği gösteren işaret; 'por'ten.tous □ [-.təs] uğursuz; harikulâde, fevkalâde; olağanüstü.

por.ter[1] ['pɔːtə] *n.* kapıcı.

por.ter[2] [-] *n.* hamal; yataklı vagon görevlisi; siyah bira; 'por.ter.age *n.* hamallık (ücreti), hamaliye; 'por.ter-

house *n.* birahane; *a.* **~ steak** bir çeşit biftek.

port.fire ['pɔːtfaiə] *n.* barutlu fitil.

port.fo.li.o [pɔːt'fəuljəu] *n.* evrak çantası; bakanlık (görevi); bir kimseye ait tüm tahviller; **minister without ~** sandalyesiz bakan.

port-hole NAUT ['pɔːthəul] = **port²**.

por.ti.co ARCH ['pɔːtikəu] *n.* revak, kemeraltı, sütunlu giriş.

por.tiere ['pɔːtieə] *n.* kapı gibi kullanılan kalın perde.

por.tion ['pɔːʃən] **1.** *n.* hisse, pay; parça, kısım; porsiyon; kısmet, talih, kader; çeyiz; **2.** *v/t.* ayırmak, bölmek, taksim etm.; kızına vermek (*çeyiz*); **'por.tionless** *adj.* çeyizsiz.

port.li.ness ['pɔːtlinis] *n.* şişmanlık, heybet, iriyarılık; **'port.ly** *adj.* iri yapılı, iriyarı, cüsseli, şişman; heybetli, gösterişli.

port.man.teau [pɔːt'mæntəu] *n.* bavul; **~ word** GR birleşik (*veya* uydurma) sözcük, kelime.

por.trait ['pɔːtrit] *n.* portre, resim, tasvir; kelimelerle yapılan tanım; **'por.traitist** *n.* portreci; **por.trai.ture** ['-tʃə] = **portrait**; resim sanatı; tanımlama.

por.tray [pɔː'trei] *v/t.* resmetmek, *-in* resmini yapmak; tanımlamak, tasvir etm.; **por'tray.al** *n.* resmetme; tanımlama, tasvir etme.

Por.tu.guese [pɔːtju'giːz] **1.** *adj.* Portekiz'le ilgili; **2.** *n.* Portekizce; Portekizli.

pose [pəuz] **1.** *n.* poz, duruş, vaziyet; tavır; yapmacık tavır, numara; **2.** *v/t.* & *v/i.* yerleş(tir)mek; poz vermek; poz almak; ortaya atmak (*soru*), yaratmak (*sorun*); tavır takınmak; taslamak (**as** *-i*) **'pos.er** *n.* poz veren kimse; şaşırtıcı soru(n).

posh *sl.* [pɔʃ] *adj.* şık, modaya uygun; lüks, birinci sınıf, en iyi.

po.si.tion [pə'ziʃən] *n.* yer, mevki, mahal (*a. fig.*); durum, vaziyet; MIL mevzi; AST, NAUT duruş, pozisyon; *fig.* sosyal durum; hal, tavır; iş, görev, vazife, memuriyet; fikir, iddia; tutum; **~ light** seyir ışığı, pozisyon ışığı; **be in a ~ to do** *bşi* yapma yetki ve durumunda olm.

pos.i.tive ['pɔzətiv] **1.** ☐ kesin, katî, mutlak; olumlu, müspet; emin; yapıcı; tam, gerçek; esaslı; gerekli; MATH, PHLS, PHYS, PHOT, ELECT pozitif; **2.** *n.* olumlu derece; PHOT pozitif resim; GR belgin

sıfat; kesin şey; **'pos.i.tive.ness** *n.* kesinlik.

pos.se ['pɔsi] *n.* polis müfrezesi; heyet, takım, grup.

pos.sess [pə'zes] *v/t.* malik olm., sahip olm. *-e*; hükmetmek; meşgul etm.; kurcalamak (*zihin*); **~ed** deli, çılgın; düşkün (**with** *-e*); **~ed of** sahip olan *-e*, ...si olan; **~ o.s. of** ele geçirmek *-i*, sahibi olm. *-in*; **pos.ses.sion** [pə'zeʃən] *n.* iyelik, sahiplik, sahip olma; cinnet, delilik; sömürge, koloni; tasarruf, kullanma yetkisi; **~s** *pl.* mal, mülk, servet; **in ~ of** elinde, elde etmiş *-i*; **pos'ses.sive** GR [-siv] **1.** ☐ iyelik gösteren, iyelik...; **~ case** *-in* hali; **2.** *n.* *-in* hali; **pos'ses.sor** *n.* mal sahibi; **pos'ses.so.ry** *adj.* sahipliğe ait.

pos.set ['pɔsit] *n.* bira *veya* şaraplı baharatlı sıcak süt.

pos.si.bil.i.ty [pɔsə'biliti] *n.* imkân, olanak; ihtimal, olabilirlik; **'pos.si.ble 1.** ☐ mümkün, olası, muhtemel, kabil; makûl, akla yatkın; **2.** *n. spor:* rekor; olası *bş*, imkân; **'pos.si.bly** *adv.* belki, ihtimal, mümkündür ki, imkân dahilinde; **if I ~ can** olurda ...bilirsem; **how can I ~ do it?** onu nasıl yapabilirim acaba?; **I cannot ~ do it** onu yapmama imkân yok.

pos.sum F ['pɔsəm] = **opossum**; **play ~** uyur *veya* ölü taklidi yapmak.

post¹ [pəust] **1.** *n.* direk, kazık, destek; **2.** *v/t. mst ~ up** yapıştırmak, asmak (*ilan*).

post² [-] **1.** *n.* MIL ordugâh, kışla, askeri menzil; COM alışveriş merkezi; MIL kol, karakol, devriye; polis noktası; iş, görev, memuriyet; atama, tayin; POST posta (servisi); atlı postacı; posta arabası; posta kutusu; postane; **at one's ~** MIL nöbeti başında; **by ~** posta ile; **2.** *v/t.* yerleştirmek, koymak; görevlendirmek; postaya vermek, postalamak; COM defteri kebire işlemek; *oft.* **~ up** COM yevmiye defterinden defteri kebire geçirmek; bildirmek, bilgi vermek; **keep s.o. ~ed up** *b-ni* haberdar etm.; *v/i.* posta atlarıyle seyahat etm.; acele gitmek.

post³ MIL [-] *n.* sinyal, boru; **last ~** yat borusu.

post.age ['pəustidʒ] *n.* posta ücreti; **~ due** eksik ödenmiş posta ücreti; **~ stamp** posta pulu.

post.al ['pəustəl] **1.** ☐ posta ile ilgili, posta...; **~ order** posta havalesi; ♀ **Un-**

ion milletlerarası posta birliği; **2.** *n. a.* ~
card *Am.* kartpostal.

post.card ['pəustkɑːd] *n.* kartpostal,
posta kartı.

post.date ['pəust'deit] *v/t. -in* üzerine
ileri bir tarih atmak.

post.er ['pəustə] *n.* yafta, afiş, poster;
a. **bill-**~ afiş yapıştıran kimse.

poste res.tante ['pəust 'restɑːnt] *n.*
postrestant.

pos.te.ri.or F [pɔs'tiəriə] **1.** □ sonra gelen, sonraki (**to** *-den*); gerideki; **2.** *n. a.*
~**s** *pl.* kaba etler, insan kıçı.

pos.ter.i.ty [pɔs'teriti] *n.* gelecek nesil-
ler; döl.

pos.tern ['pəustəːn] *n.* yan kapı, yan giriş; arka kapı.

post-free ['pəust'friː] *adj.* posta ücretine tabi olmayan; posta ücreti ödenmiş.

post-grad.u.ate ['pəust'grædjuit] **1.**
adj. üniversite sonrası öğrenime ait;
2. *n.* üniversite mezunu, doktora talebesi.

post-haste ['pəust'heist] *adv.* büyük
bir telaşla, apar topar, alelacele, ivedi-
likle.

post.hu.mous □ ['pɔstjuməs] ölümden sonra olan; yazarın ölümünden
sonra yayınlanan (*eser*); babasının ölümünden sonra doğmuş (*çocuk*).

pos.til.(l)ion [pəs'tiljən] *n.* posta arabasını çeken atlardan birine binerek
sürücülük eden kimse.

post...: '~**man** *n.* postacı; '~**mark 1.** *n.*
posta damgası; **2.** *v/t.* damgalamak;
'~**mas.ter** *n.* postane müdürü; ♀ **General** posta genel müdürü.

post me.rid.i.em ['pəust mə'ridiəm]
adj. öğleden sonraya ait; **post-mor-
tem** ['·'mɔːtem] **1.** *adj.* öldükten sonra
yapılan; **2.** *n. a.* ~ **examination** otopsi.

post...: '~**of.fice** *n., mst* ~ **of.fice** postane; *Am.* öpücük oyunu; **general** ~
merkez postane; ~ **box** posta kutusu;
~ **order** posta havalesi; '~**paid** *adj.*
& adv. posta ücreti ödenmiş (olarak).

post.pone [pəus'pəun] *v/t.* ertelemek,
sonraya bırakmak, tehir etm.; **post-
'ponement** *n.* erteleme, tehir.

post.pran.di.al □ *co.* [pəust'prændiəl]
yemek sonrası.

post.script ['pəusskript] *n.* derkenar,
(dip)not.

pos.tu.lant ['pɔstjulənt] *n.* namzet,
aday; **pos.tu.late 1.** ['·lit] *n.* önerme;
kabulü zorunlu olan esas; **2.** ['·leit]
v/t. istemek, talep etm., dilemek; öneri

olarak kabul etm.; var saymak; **postu'la.tion** *n.* talep, istek, dilek; öneri
olarak kabul etme.

pos.ture ['pɔstʃə] **1.** *n.* duruş, poz, vaziyet; hal, durum, gidişat; davranış, tutum; **2.** *v/t. & v/i.* poz ver(dir)mek;
tavır takınmak.

post-war ['pəust'wɔː] *adj.* savaş sonrası…

po.sy ['pəuzi] *n.* çiçek demeti.

pot [pɔt] **1.** *n.* çömlek, kavanoz, kap;
saksı; F *spor:* gümüş kupa; *Am. sl.*
haşiş; büyük miktar; **a** ~ **of money** F
dünya kadar para; **big** ~ F kodaman;
2. *v/t.* saksıya dikmek; kavanozda konserve etm.; rasgele vurmak, avlamak;
lâzımlığa oturtmak (*bebek*); *bilardo:*
çukura düşürmek (*top*); *v/i.* F rasgele
ateş etm.

po.ta.ble ['pəutəbl] *adj.* içilebilir.

pot.ash CHEM ['pɔtæʃ] *n.* potas, kalya
taşı, potasyum hidrat.

po.tas.si.um CHEM [pə'tæsjəm] *n.* potasyum.

po.ta.tion [pəu'teiʃən] *n. mst* ~**s** *pl.* içki
(içme).

po.ta.to [pə'teitəu] *n., pl.* **po'ta.toes**
[-z] patates; ~ **bee.tle** ZOO patates böceği.

pot...: '~**bel.ly** *n.* göbek; göbekli kimse; '~**boil.er** *n.* sadece para kazanmak
için yazılan kitap *vs.*; '~**boy** *n.* meyhanede içki servisi yapan garson.

po.ten.cy ['pəutənsi] *n.* güç, kuvvet,
kudret; potansiyel; erkeğin cinsel ikti-
darı; '**po.tent** □ kuvvetli, güçlü, kudretli, etkili, tesirli; nüfuzlu; cinsî ikti-
darı olan (*erkek*); **po.ten.tate** ['·teit]
n. nüfuzlu kimse; hükümdar, kral; **po-
ten.tial** [pəu'tenʃəl] **1.** *adj.* kuvvetli;
muhtemel, olası; PHYS potansiyel, gizil;
2. *n. a.* ~ **mood** GR yeterlik kipi; ihtimal, olasılık; güç, iktidar; ELECT potansiyel, gerilim; **po.ten.tial.i.ty** [-ʃi'æli-
ti] *n.* imkân, ihtimal.

poth.er ['pɔðə] **1.** *n.* dert, sıkıntı; gürültü, karışıklık, şamata; **2.** *v/t.* başını
ağrıtmak, üzmek, sinirlendirmek; *v/i.*
gürültü etm.

pot...: '~**herb** *n.* yemeğe çeşni veren
yeşillik; '~**hole** *n.* MOT derin çukur;
GEOL kayalarda suyun açtığı çukur;
'~**hook** *n.* tencereyi ateş üstüne asmaya yarayan S şeklinde çengel; ~**s** *pl.*
yazmayı öğrenenlerin S şeklindeki çizgileri; '~**house** *n.* düşük kaliteli meyhane, birahane.

po.tion ['pəuʃən] *n.* ilâç dozu; iksir.

pot-luck ['pɔt'lʌk] *n.*: *take* ~ Allah ne verdiyse yemek.

pot.tage ['pɔtidʒ] *n.* koyu sebze çorbası.

pot.ter[1] ['pɔtə] *vb.*: ~ *about* oyalanmak; ~ *away* vakit geçirmek.

pot.ter[2] [_] *n.* çömlekçi; ~'s *wheel* çömlekçi çarkı; 'pot.ter.y *n.* çanak çömlek; çömlek imalâthanesi; çömlekçilik.

pot.ty ['pɔti] **1.** *adj. sl.* önemsiz, ufak tefek; çılgın, deli; **2.** *n.* çocuk lâzımlığı.

pouch [pautʃ] **1.** *n.* torba, kese (*a. zo*); göz altlarındaki şişlik; **2.** *vb.* torbaya koymak; torba gibi yapmak; **pouched** *adj.* keseli.

poul.ter.er ['pəultərə] *n.* tavukçu.

poul.tice MED ['pəultis] *n.* yara lapası.

poul.try ['pəultri] *n.* kümes hayvanları.

pounce [pauns] **1.** *n.* saldırma, atılma, hamle; **2.** *v/i.* atılmak (**on**, **upon** -*in üzerine*).

pound[1] [paund] *n.* libre (= *453,6 g*); ~ (**sterling**) sterlin, İngiliz lirası (*abbr.* £ = *100 pence*).

pound[2] [_] **1.** *n.* sahipsiz araç *veya* hayvanların muhafaza edildiği yer; **2.** *v/t.* ağıla kapamak.

pound[3] [_] *v/t.* dövmek, vurmak, ezmek; yumruklamak; *sl. borsa:* indirmek (*fiyat*); *v/i.* küt küt atmak (*kalp*); ~ *away* ağır ağır yürümek.

pound.age ['paundidʒ] *n.* sterlin başına alınan komisyon.

pound.er ['paundə] *n.* ... librelik bş.

pour [pɔ:] *v/t. & v/i.* ak(ıt)mak, dök(ül)mek, boşal(t)mak; koymak (*çay vs.*); akın etm.; bardaktan boşanırcasına yağmak; ~ *out* boşaltmak, koymak; *fig.* içini dökmek; ~ *with rain* bardaktan boşanırcasına yağmak; *it never rains but it ~s fig.* aksilikler üst üste gelir.

pout [paut] **1.** *n.* somurtma, surat asma; **2.** *v/t.* sarkıtmak (*dudaklarını*); *v/i.* somurtmak, surat asmak; 'pout.er *n.* zoo kursağını şişirebilen bir güvercin.

pov.er.ty ['pɔvəti] *n.* yoksulluk, fakirlik; yetersizlik, eksiklik; '~-strick.en *adj.* çok fakir, yoksul, muhtaç.

pow.der ['paudə] **1.** *n.* toz; pudra; barut; **2.** *v/t. & v/i.* toz *veya* pudra sürmek -*e*, pudralamak; pudra kullanmak; '~-box *n.* pudralık, pudriyer; '~-puff *n.* pudra ponponu; 'pow.der.y *adj.* tozlu, toz gibi, toz halinde.

pow.er ['pauə] *n.* kuvvet, kudret, güç (*a.* MEC, ELECT); yetki, salâhiyet; etki, tesir; hâkimiyet, nüfuz, sözü geçerlik; JUR vekâlet(name); etkili kişi, otorite, MATH üs; F çok miktar; yetenek, kabiliyet; devlet, hükümet; merceğin büyütme kabiliyeti; *in* ~ iktidarda; '~-current *n.* yüksek gerilimli akım; '~-dive *n.* AVIA pike; 'pow.er.ful ['_ful] □ kuvvetli, güçlü, kudretli; etkili, tesirli; nüfuzlu, yetkili; 'pow.er-house = *power-station*; 'pow.er.less *adj.* kuvvetsiz, güçsüz, kudretsiz; beceriksiz; pow.er line ELECT elektrik hattı; 'pow.er lunch *n.* önemli iş konularının görüşüldüğü ve büyük kararların verildiği öğle yemeği; pow.er plant = *power-station*; pow.er pol.i.tics *n. sg.* kuvvet politikası; 'pow.er-sta.tion *n.* elektrik santralı.

pow.wow ['pauwau] *n.* toplantı; *Am.* Kızılderililerin yaptığı toplantı; F büyücü hekim.

pox *sl.* [pɔks] *n.* frengi.

pra(a)m NAUT [prɑ:m] *n.* altı düz bir çeşit kayık.

prac.ti.ca.bil.i.ty [præktikə'biliti] *n.* pratiklik, kullanışlılık; 'prac.ti.ca.ble □ yapılabilir; elverişli, kullanışlı; 'prac.ti.cal □ uygulamalı, pratik; kullanışlı, elverişli, uygulanabilir; gerçekçi; tecrübeli, deneyimli; işlek; ~ *joke* eşek şakası; ~ *chemistry* uygulamalı kimya; prac.ti.cal.i.ty [_'kæliti] *n.* uygulanabilme, elverişlilik; prac.ti.cal.ly ['_kəli] *adv.* pratik olarak; hemen hemen, yaklaşık olarak; gerçekte, fiilen.

prac.tice ['præktis] **1.** *n.* uygulama, tatbikat; alışıklık, alışkanlık, âdet; pratik, egzersiz, idman; müşteriler; meslek icrası; doktorluk, avukatlık; işyeri; *out of* ~ körlenmiş, körelmiş; *put into* ~ uygulamaya koymak; *sharp* ~ dalavere; **2.** *Am.* = practise.

prac.tise [_] *v/t. & v/i.* yapmak; uygulamak, tatbik etm.; talim etm., eğitmek; çalışmak; *k-ni* alıştırmak; pratik yapmak, egzersiz yapmak; bir meslekte çalışmak; *spor:* idman (*veya* antrenman) yapmak; MUS pratik yapmak; ~ *upon k-ne* yontmak; istifade etm. -*den*; 'prac.tised *adj.* tecrübeli, deneyimli; alışık, talimli; hünerli.

prac.ti.tion.er [præk'tiʃnə] *n.* pratik yapan kimse; doktor; avukat; *a. general* ~ pratisyen doktor.

prae.tor ['pri:tə] *n.* eski Roma'da hâkim.

prag.mat.ic [præg'mætik] *adj.* (*~ally*) pratik, amelî; pragmatizme ait.

prai.rie *Am.* ['prɛəri] *n.* bozkır, büyük çayırlık; *~ schooner* üstü kapalı atlı araba.

praise [preiz] **1.** *n.* övgü; şükür; tapınma; **2.** *v/t.* övmek, methetmek; şükretmek.

praise.wor.thy ['preizwəːði] ⬜ övülmeye değer, takdire lâyık.

pram F [præm] *n.* çocuk arabası.

prance [prɑːns] *v/i.* fırlamak (*at*); caka satarak yürümek; zıp zıp zıplamak, zıplayan ata binmek; *v/t.* zıplatıp oynatmak (*at*).

pran.di.al ⬜ ['prændiəl] yemekle ilgili, yemek…

prang MIL *sl.* [præŋ] *n.* şiddetli bombardıman.

prank [præŋk] **1.** *n.* kaba şaka, eşek şakası; oyun; **2.** *vb.* *~ out* telleyip pullamak, çok süslemek; caka satmak.

prate [preit] **1.** *n.* gevezelik; **2.** *vb.* gevezelik etm., çok konuşmak, boş laf etm.; '**prat.er** *n.* geveze kimse.

prat.tle ['prætl] = *prate*.

prawn ZOO [prɔːn] *n.* büyük karides, deniz tekesi.

pray [prei] *v/i.* dua etm. (*to -e; for* için); ibadet etm., namaz kılmak; yalvarmak (*to -e*); *v/t.* çok rica etm. (*for -i*); *~ tell me* lütfen bana söyleyin.

prayer [prɛə] *n.* dua, niyaz; duacı, dua eden kimse; ibadet, namaz; *oft. ~s pl.* temenni, rica; *Lord's ~* Hıristiyanların fatihaya benzetebilen duası; *Book of Common* ⚹ dua kitabı; '*~book* *n.* dua kitabı; '*~rug* *n.* seccade.

pre… [priː, pri] *prefix* önce, evvel, ön.

preach [priːtʃ] *v/t.* & *v/i.* va'zetmek, vaız vermek (*to -e*); nasihat etm., öğüt vermek; ileri sürmek; telkin etm.; '**preacher** *n.* vaiz; '**preach.ing** *n.* vaız; öğüt; '**preach.ment** *n.* vaız; va'zetme.

pre.am.ble [priːæmbl] *n.* önsöz, başlangıç.

pre.ar.range [priːə'reindʒ] *v/t.* önceden düzenlemek.

preb.end ECCL ['prebənd] *n.* papaza bağlanan ödenek; '**pre.ben.dar.y** *n.* ödenek alan papaz.

pre.car.i.ous ⬜ [pri'kɛəriəs] kararsız, şüpheli; tehlikeli, rizikolu, nazik; güvenilmez, istikrarsız, asılsız; **pre'car.i.ous.ness** *n.* riziko, tehlikeli durum.

pre.cau.tion [priː'kɔːʃən] *n.* tedbir, önlem, ihtiyat; **pre'cau.tion.ar.y** [*~*ʃnəri] *adj.* önlem olarak, ihtiyati.

pre.cede [priː'siːd] *vb.* *-den* önce gelmek, *-den* önde olm.; *-in* önünden yürümek; *fig. -den* daha önemli (*veya* üstün) olm.; **pre'ced.ence**, **pre'ced.en.cy** *n.* önce gelme, öncelik, üstünlük; kıdem; **prec.e.dent** ['presidənt] *n.* emsal; örnek, numune; **pre.ced.ing** [priː'siːdiŋ] *adj.* önceki, önde olan, takip edilen.

pre.cen.tor ECCL [pri'sentə] *n.* kilisede müziği idare eden kimse.

pre.cept ['priːsept] *n.* emir, hüküm; ilke, ahlâkî kural; talimat, yönerge; JUR mahkeme emri; **pre.cep.tor** [pri'septə] *n.* öğretmen, eğitmen; **pre'cep.tress** [*~*tris] *n.* bayan öğretmen.

pre.cinct ['priːsiŋkt] *n.* mıntıka, bölge, yöre; *part. Am.* seçim bölgesi; *~s pl.* havali, çevre; *pedestrian ~* sadece yayalara mahsus yol.

pre.cious ['preʃəs] **1.** *n.* kıymetli, değerli; çok sevilen, gözde; aşırı titiz, müşkülpesent; kibar, nazik; F kötü, rezil; **2.** *adv.* F pek, çok; '**pre.cious.ness** *n.* değer, kıymet; pahalılık; aşırı kibarlık.

prec.i.pice ['presipis] *n.* uçurum; sarp kayalık; **pre.cip.i.tance**, **pre.cip.i-tan.cy** [pri'sipitəns(i)] *n.* acele(cilik); telaş; **pre'cip.i.tate** **1.** [*~*teit] *n.* & *v/i.* yüksek bir yerden aşağı at(ıl)mak, düş(ür)mek; zamanından önce meydana getirmek; hızlandırmak; CHEM çökel(t)mek; yoğunlaştırmak (*buhar*); yoğunlaşıp yağmur *vs.* şeklinde yağmak; **2.** [*~*tit] ⬜ aceleci; düşüncesiz; acele ile yapılmış; anî; **3.** [*~*tit] *n.* tortu, çökelti; **pre.cip.i.ta.tion** [*~*'teiʃən] *n.* yağış (miktarı); acelecilik; telaş; CHEM çökelme; **pre'cip.i.tous** ⬜ çok dik, sarp, uçurum gibi; aceleci, atılgan; çok hızlı.

pré.cis ['preisiː] *n.* öz(et).

pre.cise ⬜ [pri'sais] tam(am), katî, kesin; titiz, dakik; kusursuz; *~ly!* elbette!; **pre'cise.ness** *n.* kesinlik; dakiklik; açıklık, vuzuh.

pre.ci.sion [pri'siʒən] *n.* dikkat, kesinlik, katîlik; dakiklik; doğruluk; *attr.* dakik; hassas (*alet*).

pre.clude [pri'kluːd] *v/t.* önlemek, engel olm., meydan vermemek; *~ s.o. from* ger. *b-ni bş* yapmaktan alıkoymak.

pre.co.cious ⬜ [pri'kəuʃəs] vaktinden

önce gelişmiş, *fig.* büyümüş de küçülmüş; pre'co.cious.ness, pre.coc.i.ty [pri'kɔsiti] *n.* erken gelişmişlik.

pre.con.ceive ['pri:kən'si:v] *vb.* peşin hüküm vermek, önyargıda bulunmak; ~*d* önyargılı.

pre.con.cep.tion ['pri:kən'sepʃən] *n.* önyargı, peşin hüküm.

pre.con.cert.ed ['pri:kən'sə:tid] *adj.* önceden kararlaştırılmış.

pre.cur.sor [pri:'kə:sə] *n.* haberci, müjdeci; işaret, alâmet; pre'cur.so.ry *adj.* ön, ilk; önceden haber veren.

pre.date ['pri:'deit] *vb.* erken tarih atmak; daha önce gelmek.

pred.a.to.ry ['predətəri] *adj.* yağmacılıkla geçinen, çapulcu, talancı; yırtıcı (*hayvan*).

pre.de.cease ['pri:di'si:s] *v/t. -den* önce ölmek.

pre.de.ces.sor ['pri:disesə] *n.* öncel, selef; ata, cet.

pre.des.ti.nate [pri:'destineit] *v/t.* önceden nasip etm., alnına yazmak *-in*, önceden mukadder kılmak; pre.desti'na.tion *n.* takdir; ECCL yazgı, alın yazısı, kader, nasip, kısmet; pre'destined *adj.* seçkin, güzide.

pre.de.ter.mine ['pri:di'tə:min] *v/t.* önceden tayin etm.; önceden kararlaştırmak.

pred.i.ca.ble ['predikəbl] *adj.* iddia edilebilir.

pre.dic.a.ment [pri'dikəmənt] *n.* PHLS kötü durum, çıkmaz.

pred.i.cate 1. ['predikeit] *v/t.* doğrulamak; belirtmek, ifade etm., göstermek; dayan(dır)mak (*on -e*); 2. ['_-kit] *n.* GR yüklem; pred.i.ca.tion [_-'keiʃən] *n.* hüküm, yükleme; pred.i.ca.tive [pri'dikətiv] □ doğrulayıcı; GR yüklemi oluşturan.

pre.dict [pri'dikt] *v/t.* önceden bildirmek, kehanette bulunmak; pre.dic.tion [_-'dikʃən] *n.* önceden haber verme, kehanet.

pre.di.lec.tion [pri:di'lekʃən] *n.* yeğleme, tercih (*for -i*).

pre.dis.pose ['pri:dis'pəuz] *v/t.* önceden hazırlamak (*to -e*); yetenekli kılmak; pre.dis.po.si.tion ['_-dispə'ziʃən] *n.* yatkınlık, yetenek, kabiliyet; *part.* MED eğilim (*to -e*).

pre.dom.i.nance [pri'dɔminəns] *n.* üstünlük, ağır basma; pre'dom.i.nant □ üstün, ağır basan, hâkim, galip; pre'dom.i.nate [_-neit] *v/i.* hâkim olm.

(*over -e*); üstün olm., galip gelmek.

pre-em.i.nence [pri:'eminəns] *n.* üstünlük, seçkinlik; pre-'em.i.nent □ üstün, seçkin.

pre-emp.tion [pri:'empʃən] *n.* başkalarından önce satın alma (hakkı).

preen [pri:n] *v/t.* gaga ile düzeltmek (*tüy*); *k-ne* çekidüzen vermek; ~ *o.s. on fig.* övünmek *ile*.

pre-en.gage [pri:in'geidʒ] *v/t.* önceden taahhüt etm.; önceden tutmak, peylemek; pre-en'gage.ment *n.* önceden taahhüt etme.

pre-ex.ist ['pri:ig'zist] *v/i.* daha önce var olm. *veya* yaşamak; 'pre-ex'ist-ence *n.* daha önce var olma.; 'pre-ex-'ist.ent *adj.* daha önce var olan.

pre.fab ['pri:fæb] 1. *adj.* prefabrik...; 2. *n.* prefabrik yapı; 'pre'fab.ri.cate [_-rikeit] *v/t.* parçalarını önceden hazırlamak *veya* imal etm.

pref.ace ['prefis] 1. *n.* önsöz, başlangıç; 2. *v/t.* önsöz ile başlamak; *-in* önsözünü yazmak.

pref.a.to.ry □ ['prefətəri] önsözle ilgili, önsöz niteliğinde...

pre.fect ['pri:fekt] *n.* eski Roma'da vali, yüksek rütbeli memur; Paris polis şefi; *okul:* sınıf mümessili (*veya* başkanı).

pre.fer [pri'fə:] *v/t.* tercih etm., yeğlemek (*to -e*); daha çok beğenmek; sunmak, arzetmek; atamak; terfi ettirmek; *s. share 1; I should ~ you not to go* gitmemenizi yeğlerim, bence gitmeseniz daha iyi; pref.er.a.ble □ ['prefərəbl] daha iyi (*to -den*), tercih edilir (*to -e*); 'pref.era.bly *adv.* tercihen; 'pref.er.ence *n.* yeğleme, yeğ tutma, tercih (hakkı); *part.* COM öncelik, üstünlük, rüçhan; *s. share 1;* pref.er.en-tial □ [_-'renʃəl] tercihli; tercih ed(il)en...; pref.er'en.tial.ly *adv.* tercihen; pre.fer.ment [pri'fə:mənt] *n.* terfi, yükselme; öncelik.

pre.fix 1. ['pri:fiks] *n.* önek; ünvan; 2. [pri:'fiks] *v/t.* koymak (*önek*).

preg.nan.cy ['pregnənsi] *n.* gebelik, hamilelik; *fig.* dolgunluk; derinlik; anlam; 'preg.nant □ hamile, gebe; *fig.* anlamlı, manalı; dolu, yüklü; verimli.

pre-heat MEC ['pri:'hi:t] *vb.* önceden ısıt mak.

pre.hen.sile [pri'hensail] *adj.* kavrayabilen, tutabilen.

pre.his.tor.ic ['pri:his'tɔrik] *adj.* tarih öncesine ait, tarihöncesi..., tarihten

önceki...
pre-ig.ni.tion MOT ['pri:ig'niʃən] *n.* erken ateşleme.
pre.judge ['pri:'dʒʌdʒ] *v/t.* önceden hüküm vermek.
prej.u.dice ['predʒudis] **1.** *n.* önyargı, peşin hüküm; haksız hüküm; tarafgirlik; *without ~ to* etki altında kalmadan, zarar vermeksizin *-e*; **2.** *v/t.* haksız hüküm verdirmek *-e* (*against -e karşı*); haksız hüküm *veya* iş ile zarar vermek *-e*; *~d* tarafgir; zarar görmüş.
prej.u.di.cial □ [predʒu'diʃəl] önyargılı; zararlı (*to -e*).
prel.a.cy ['preləsi] *n.* piskoposluk.
prel.ate ['prelit] *n.* piskopos.
pre.lec.tion [pri'lekʃən] *n.* konferans, ders; **pre'lec.tor** *n.* konferansçı.
pre.lim F [pri'lim] *n.* ön sınav, yeterlik sınavı.
pre.lim.i.nar.y [pri'liminəri] **1.** □ hazırlayıcı, ilk, ön, başlangıç niteliğinde; **2.** *n.* ön sınav, yeterlik sınavı; **pre'lim.i-na.ries** [_riz] *n. pl.* ön hazırlık, başlangıç.
prel.ude ['prelju:d] **1.** *n.* MUS peşrev, fasıl, prelüd; başlangıç, giriş; **2.** *vb.* MUS peşrevle açmak; bir başlangıçla açmak; peşrev çalmak.
pre.ma.ture □ [premə'tjuə] *fig.* zamanından evvel olan *veya* gelişen, erken...; erken doğan; vakitsiz, mevsimsiz; *~ delivery* erken doğum; **pre.ma-'ture.ness, prema'tu.ri.ty** [_riti] *n. fig.* zamanından evvel gelişme, mevsimsizlik.
pre.med.i.tate [pri:'mediteit] *v/t.* önceden düşünmek, tasarlamak, amaçlamak; *~d murder* JUR taammüden cinayet; **pre.medi'ta.tion** *n.* tasarlama, kasıt; önceden düşünme.
pre.mi.er ['premjə] **1.** *adj.* baştaki, birinci, ilk, baş, asıl; **2.** *n.* başbakan.
prem.ière ['premiɛə] *n.* gala.
pre.mi.er.ship ['premjəʃip] *n.* başbakanlık.
prem.ise 1. ['premis] *n.* terim, önerme, öncül; *~s pl.* mülk, ev ve müştemilâtı; JUR ana madde; *licensed ~s pl.* meyhane; *on the ~s* yerinde, mahallinde, bina müştemilâtı içinde; **2.** **pre.mise** [pri'maiz] *v/t.* açıklayarak önceden belirtmek.
pre.mi.um ['pri:mjəm] *n.* prim; mükâfat, ödül; değer; ikramiye; hediye; ücret; COM prim, acyo, kâr, temettü; *at a ~* fazla fiyatla; çok rağbette, tutulan.

pre.mo.ni.tion [pri:mə'niʃən] *n.* önsezi; uyarma; **pre.mon.i.to.ry** □ [pri'mɔnitəri] önsezi kabilinden, haber verici, uyarıcı.
pre-na.tal ['pri:'neitl] *adj.* doğum öncesine ait.
pre.oc.cu.pan.cy *fig.* [pri:'ɔkjupənsi] *n.* dalgınlık (*in -e*); **pre.oc.cu.pa.tion** [_'peiʃən] *n.* zihin meşguliyeti (*with ile*); zihni meşgul eden şey, tasa, kaygı; **pre'occu.pied** [_paid] *adj.* zihni meşgul; **pre'oc.cu.py** [_pai] *v/t.* meşgul etm. (*zihin*); başkasından önce ele geçirmek.
pre.or.dain [pri:ɔː'dein] *v/t.* önceden takdir etm., önceden nasip etm.
prep F [prep] = *preparation*, *preparatory school*.
pre.paid ['pri:'peid] *adj.* önceden ödenmiş.
prep.a.ra.tion [prepə'reiʃən] *n.* hazırlama; hazırlık; hazırlanan şey; hazır ilâç; ev ödevi; **pre.par.a.tive** [pri'pærətiv] *n.* hazırlık, hazırlama; **pre'par.a.to.ry** [_təri] □ hazırlayıcı, hazırlık; *~ school* üniversiteye hazırlayan özel okul; *~ to -den* evvel, *-meden* önce.
pre.pare [pri'pɛə] *v/t. & v/i.* hazırla(n)mak; düzenlemek; donatmak; pişirmek; yapmak; **pre'pared** □ hazır; *~ for* hazır *-e*; **pre'pared.ness** *n.* hazırlık, hazır olma (*for -e*).
pre.pay ['pri:'pei] (*irr. pay*) *v/t.* peşin ödemek; **pre'pay.ment** *n.* peşin ödeme.
pre.pense □ [pri'pens] önceden düşünülmüş, tasarlanmış, kasıtlı; *with mal-ice ~* taammüden, kasten, kasıtlı.
pre.pon.der.ance [pri'pɔndərəns] *n.* çoğunluk, üstünlük, fazlalık; **pre'pon.der.ant** □ ağır basan, baskın gelen, hâkim, galip; **pre'pon.der.ate** [_reit] *v/i.* ağır basmak, baskın gelmek, galip gelmek; hâkim olm.; ağır çekmek.
prep.o.si.tion GR [prepə'ziʃən] *n.* edat, ilgeç; **prep.o'si.tion.al** □ [_ʃənl] edat niteliğinde, edat...
pre.pos.sess [pri:pə'zes] *v/t.* lehinde fikir hâsıl ettirmek, gönlünü çelmek, etkilemek; meşgul etm. (*zihin*); **pre-pos'sess.ing** □ cazibeli, çekici, alımlı; **prepos.ses.sion** [_'zeʃən] *n.* tarafgirlik; zihin meşguliyeti.
pre.pos.ter.ous [pri'pɔstərəs] *adj.* akıl almaz, mantıksız, inanılmaz, saçma.
pre.puce ANAT ['pri:pju:s] *n.* sünnet derisi.

pre.req.ui.site ['pri:'rekwizit] *n.* önceden gerekli olan şey.

pre.rog.a.tive [pri'rɔgətiv] *n.* ayrıcalık, yetki hak, imtiyaz.

pres.age ['presidʒ] **1.** *n.* önsezi; geleceği bildiren belirti; **2.** *v/t.* önceden bildirmek *veya* göstermek; kehanet etm.

pres.by.ter ['prezbitə] *n.* kilise ileri gelenlerinden biri; **Pres.by.te.ri.an** [‿'tiəriən] **1.** *adj.* İskoç Protestan kilisesine ait; **2.** *n.* bu kiliseye ait üye; **pres.by.ter.y** ECCL ['‿təri] *n.* kilisede sadece papazlara ait kapalı kısım; Presbiteryen kiliselerinde yönetim kurulu.

pre.sci.ence [presiəns] *n.* geleceği görme, önceden bilme, öngörü; '**pre.sci.ent** *adj.* geleceği gören, önceden bilen, öngörülü.

pre.scribe [pris'kraib] *v/t. & v/i.* emretmek; MED (salık) vermek (*ilâç*), reçete yazmak; nizam koymak (*for* için); JUR zaman aşımına uğramak.

pre.script ['pri:skript] *n.* kanun, emir, yönerge, hüküm; **pre.scrip.tion** [pri'skripʃən] *n.* emir, talimat; MED reçete; JUR zaman aşımına dayanan hak; **pre'scriptive** □ [‿tiv] emreden, buyuran; yetkili; yapılagelen.

pres.ence ['prezns] *n.* huzur, varlık, hazır bulunma; hal, tavır, davranış; hayal, görüntü; **~ of mind** serinkanlılık, soğukkanlılık; '**~-cham.ber** *n.* kabul salonu.

pres.ent¹ ['preznt] **1.** □ bulunan, hazır, mevcut; şimdiki, şu anki; **~ tense** GR şimdiki zaman; **~ company** mevcut topluluk; **~ company excepted** söz meclisten dışarı; **~ value** şu anki değer; **~!** burada!; **2.** *n.* GR *a.* şimdiki zaman; halihazır, şimdiki durum; **by the ~** COM, **by these ~s** JUR bu belge ile, ilişikte; **at ~** şimdi, şu anda; **for the ~** şimdilik, şu anda.

pre.sent² [pri'zent] *v/t.* sunmak, takdim etm., arzetmek; tanıştırmak; göstermek; doğrultmak (*silah*), MIL selâm vaziyetinde tutmak (*tüfek*); sağlamak (**with** -*i*); **~ o.s.** görünmek, meydana çıkmak, hazır bulunmak; **~ one's compliments to s.o.** *b-ne* kompliman yapmak.

pres.ent³ ['preznt] *n.* hediye, armağan; **make s.o. a ~ of s.th.** *b-ne bş* armağan etm.

pre.sent.a.ble [pri'zentəbl] *adj.* sunulabilir; düzgün görünüşlü, prezentabl;

is this suit ~? bu elbise iyi görünüyor mu?

pres.en.ta.tion [prezən'teiʃən] *n.* sunma, takdim; hediye; temsil, oyun; gösterme; COM ibraz; **~ copy** hediyelik kopya (*kitap*).

pres.ent-day ['prezəntdei] *adj.* şimdiki, günümüz...

pre.sen.ti.ment [pri'zentimənt] *n.* önsezi, içe doğuş.

pres.ent.ly ['prezntli] *adv.* derhal, hemen; birazdan, yakında; *Am.* şimdi, şu anda.

pre.sent.ment [pri'zentmənt] *n. s.* **presentation**; JUR büyük jüri raporu; THEAT temsil, oyun.

pres.er.va.tion [prezə'veiʃən] *n.* sakla(n)ma, koru(n)ma, muhafaza; **in good ~** iyi korunmuş; **pre.serv.a.tive** [pri'zə:vətiv] **1.** *adj.* saklayan, koruyan, koruyucu; **2.** *n.* koruyucu madde.

pre.serve [pri'zə:v] **1.** *v/t.* korumak, saklamak, esirgemek (**from** -*den*); -*in* konservesini yapmak; -*in* reçelini yapmak; dayandırmak, sağlam tutmak; **2.** *n.* HUNT *oft.* **~s** *pl.* av hayvanları için ayrılmış koru; *fig.* alan, saha; *mst* **~s** *pl.* reçel; **pre'ser.ver** *n.* koruyucu; konserveci.

pre.side [pri'zaid] *v/i.* başkanlık etm. (**over** -*e*); **~ over an assembly** bir toplantıya başkanlık etm.

pres.i.den.cy ['prezidənsi] *n.* başkanlık (süresi); reislik; '**pres.i.dent** *n.* başkan; baş, reis; rektör; *Am.* (*şirket*, *banka*) müdür; **pres.i.den.tial** [‿'denʃəl] *adj.* başkanlığa ait, başkanlık...

press [pres] **1.** *n.* baskı, sıkıştırma; basın (mensupları); matbaa, basımevi; pres, cendere, mengene; kalabalık, izdiham; elbise dolabı; ütü (*giyside*); *a.* **printing~** matbaa makinesi; *fig.* sıkıntı, baskı; **~ of sail** NAUT yelkenlerin rüzgârın elverdiğince açılması; *the freedom of the ~* basın özgürlüğü; **2.** *v/t.* sık(ıştır)mak (*a.* MIL); basmak; baskı suyunu çıkarmak; *fig.* zorlamak, baskı yapmak, sıkıştırmak; ütülemek; zorla kabul ettirmek (**on** -*e*); ısrar etm., üstelemek; **~ the button** düğmeye basmak (*a. fig.*); **~ the point that** ...konusunda ısrarla durmak; **be ~ed for time** sıkışmak, vakti dar olm., az vakti olm.; *v/i.* kitle halinde ilerlemek; üşüşmek; koşuşturmak; **~ for** ısrarla istemek, sıkıştırmak için; **~ on** zorla kabul ettirmek -*e*; **~ (up) on** baskı yapmak -*e*, zerlamak -i; '~a.gen.cy n. basın sözcülüğü; ~ a.gent basın sözcüsü; '~-button n. çıtçıt; elektrik düğmesi; '~-correc.tor n. TYP matbaa provasını düzelten kimse, düzeltmen; '~-cut.ting n. gazete kupürü; 'press.er n. basımcı, matbaacı; gazeteci; ütücü; 'press.ing 1. □ acele, âcil, ivedili; sık boğaz eden, sıkıcı; ısrarlı...; 2. n. plak; 'press.man n. basımcı, matbaacı; gazeteci; ütücü; 'press-mark n. kütüphanede kitap numarası; pres.sure ['preʃə] n. basınç, tazyik; baskı (a. fig.); pressure cooker n. düdüklü tencere; 'pressure-gauge n. MEC basıölçer, manometre; pres.sur.ize ['-raiz] v/t. basınç altında tutmak; 'press-work n. TYP basım işi, matbaa işi.

pres.ti.dig.i.ta.tion ['prestididʒi'teiʃən] n. el çabukluğu, hokkabazlık.

pres.tige [pres'tiːʒ] n. ün, şöhret; nüfuz, itibar, prestij, saygınlık.

pres.to ['prestəu] adj. & adv. çabuk, hızlı; hızla, çabucak.

pre-stressed ['priː'strest] adj.: ~ concrete öngerilimli beton.

pre.sum.a.ble □ [pri'zjuːməbl] tahmin olunur, farz edilir; pre'sume v/t. & v/i. tahmin etm., farzetmek; ihtimal vermek; cesaret etm. -e; haddini aşmak, cüret etm. (to -e); ~ (up) on istismar etm. -i; pre'sum.ed.ly [-idli] adv. tahminen, galiba; pre'sum.ing □ haddini aşan, cüretkâr, kendini beğenmiş.

pre.sump.tion [pri'zʌmpʃən] n. farz, tahmin, varsayım, ipucu; küstahlık, cüret; pre'sump.tive □ [-tiv] muhtemel, olası; tahminî, varsayılı; pre'sump.tu.ous □ [-tjuəs] küstah, kibirli, kendine fazla güvenen.

pre.sup.pose [priːsə'pəuz] v/t. önceden farzetmek; koşul olarak gerektirmek, belirtmek; pre.sup.po.si.tion [priːsʌpə'ziʃən] n. önceden farzetme; önceden farzedilen şey, tahmin.

pre.tence, Am. pre.tense [pri'tens] n. hile, bahane; iddia; gösteriş; false ~ sahte tavır; make ~ yapar gibi görünmek, yalandan yapmak.

pre.tend [pri'tend] v/t. yalandan yapmak, k-ne ...süsü vermek, taslamak (to inf. -meği); taklit etm., benzetmek; ~ to be ill hasta numarası yapmak; v/i. yapar gibi görünmek; iddia etm. (to -i); pre'tend.ed □ yapmacık, sözde, sahte, yalan; pre'tend.er n. hak iddia eden

kimse.

pre.ten.sion [pri'tenʃən] n. sav, iddia, hak iddiası (to -e); haksız iddia; gösteriş.

pre.ten.tious [pri'tenʃəs] adj. gösterişçi, kurumlu; pre'ten.tious.ness n. gösterişçilik.

pret.er.it(e) GR ['pretərit] n. geçmiş zaman kipi.

pre.ter.mis.sion [priːtə'miʃən] n. ihmal; vaz geçme, cayma.

pre.ter.nat.u.ral □ [priːtə'nætʃrəl] olağandışı; doğaüstü.

pre.text ['priːtekst] n. bahane, sudan sebep, kulp.

pret.ti.fy ['pritifai] v/t. güzelleştirmek.

pret.ti.ness ['pritinis] n. güzellik, sevimlilik.

pret.ty ['priti] 1. □ güzel, sevimli, hoş, latif; iyi, âlâ; F epey büyük, kocaman; a ~ penny F avuç dolusu para; my ~! canım!, tatlım!; 2. adv. oldukça, hayli, epeyce.

pre.vail [pri'veil] v/t. hâkim olm.; yürürlükte olm.; galip gelmek (over, against -e karşı); yaygın olm., âdet olm.; başarmak, etkili olm.; ~ (up) on s.o. to do b-ni bş yapmaya ikna etm.; pre'vail.ing □ en sık esen (rüzgâr); geçerli, yaygın; hâkim olan; galip gelen.

prev.a.lence ['prevələns] n. yaygınlık; hüküm sürme, hâkim (veya egemen) olma.; 'prev.a.lent □ yaygın, olagelen, hüküm süren, etkili.

pre.var.i.cate [pri'værikeit] v/i. yalan söylemek, yalan ifade vermek, kaçamaklı cevap vermek; pre.var.i'ca.tion n. kaçamak söz, yalan.

pre.vent [pri'vent] v/t. önlemek, engellemek, durdurmak, alıkoymak (from ger. -mekten); pre'vent.a.ble adj. önlenebilir, durdurulabilir; pre'vent.a.tive [-tətiv] = preventive; pre'ven.tion n. önleme, engelleme; pre'ven.tive 1. □ önleyici, engelleyici (of); ~ detention tekrar suç işlememeleri için suçluların yargılanıncaya kadar hapsedilmesi; 2. n. önleyici şey veya tedbir.

pre view ['priː'vjuː] n. THEAT. film: gelecek programdan gösterilen parçalar; bir film, sanat eseri vs. nin halka gösterilmeden önce özel olarak gösterilmesi.

pre.vi.ous □ ['priːvjəs] önceki, evvel(ki), eski, sabık; F vaktinden önce, mevsimsiz; ~ conviction sabıka; ~ to -den önce; 'pre.vi.ous.ly *adv.* önce(den), evvelce.

pre.vi.sion [pri:'viʒən] *n.* basiret, sağduyu; önsezi, öngörü.

pre-war ['pri:'wɔ:] *adj.* savaş öncesi...

prey [prei] **1.** *n.* av; *fig.* yem; *beast* (*bird*) *of ~* yırtıcı hayvan (kuş); *be a ~ to* kurbanı olm. -*in*, av olm. -*e*, kapılmış olm. -*e*; **2.** *vb.* beslenmek (*on ile*); ~ *on*, ~ *upon* soymak, yağma etm. -*i*; *fig.* sıkıntı vermek, içine dert olm.

price [prais] **1.** *n.* fiyat, paha, bedel; değer, kıymet; ödül; rüşvet; *at any ~ her* ne pahasına olursa olsun; **2.** *v/t.* fiyat koymak -*e*, paha biçmek -*e*; fiyatını sormak -*in*; 'price.less *adj.* paha biçilmez; gülünç, komik, çok hoş, yaman.

prick [prik] **1.** *n.* iğne *veya* diken batması; iğnele(n)me; diken; *sl.* kalleş; *sl.* penis; **2.** *v/t.* (iğne, diken *vs.*) sokmak, delmek; vicdan azabı vermek; *a.* ~ *out* oymak, açmak (*delik*); ~ *out* AGR toprağa dikmek (*fide*); ~ *up one's ears* (*at*, *köpek*) kulaklarını dikmek; *fig.* kulak kabartmak; *v/i.* batmak; batma acısı duymak; mahmuzla atı dürtmek; ~ *up* dikmek; 'pricker *n.* delen şey *veya* kimse; delgi; prickle ['-l] *n.* diken, sivri uç; karıncalanma; 'prick.ly *adj.* dikenli; kirpi gibi; karıncalanan; huysuz, çabuk öfkelenen; ~ *heat* MED isilik; ~ *pear* BOT hintinciri, frenkinciri, firavuninciri.

pride [praid] **1.** *n.* kibir, gurur, tafra, azamet, övünme, iftihar; küme, sürü; ~ *of place* en üstün mevki; *take* (*a*) ~ *in* gurur duymak -*den*, iftihar etm. *ile*; **2.** *vb.* ~ *o.s.* (*up*)*on* *bşle* övünmek, gurur duymak, iftihar etm.

priest [pri:st] *n.* papaz, rahip; '~.craft *n.* papazlık; 'priest.ess *n.* dinsel tören yöneten kadın; priest.hood ['-hud] *n.* papazlık, rahiplik; 'priest.ly *adj.* papaz gibi; papaza ait, papaza yakışır; 'priest-rid.den *adj.* papaz (*veya* kilise) yönetimindeki...

prig [prig] *n.* kendini beğenmiş (*veya* ukalâ) kimse; 'prig.gish □ kendini beğenmiş, ukalâ(ca).

prim [prim] □ düzgün, düzenli, tertipli; fazla resmî, biçimci, formaliteci, kurallara fazla bağlı.

pri.ma.cy ['praiməsi] *n.* öncelik, üstünlük; başpikoposluk; pri.mal ['praiməl] *adj.* esasî, aslî; baş(lıca)...; pri.ma.ri.ly ['-rili] *adv.* evvela, öncelikle; aslında; 'prima.ry **1.** □ ilk, birinci, asıl, ana;

başlıca, ileri gelen; ilk(s)el; ELECT, MED primer; **2.** *n. a.* ~ *meeting Am.* parti aday seçimi; *s. share*; 'pri.mary school ilkokul; primate ECCL ['-mit] *n.* başpiskopos.

prime [praim] **1.** □ birinci, ilk; baş(lıca), asıl, aslî; asal (*sayı*); en önemli; en iyi, birinci kalite; ~ *cost* maliyet; ♀ *Minister* başbakan; ~ *number* asal sayı; **2.** *n. fig.* en mükemmel devir, her şeyin en iyisi; olgunluk çağı; başlangıç; *in the* ~ *of youth* gençliğin baharında; **3.** *v/t.* kullanıma hazırlamak; talimat vermek, (ne diyeceğini) öğretmek; F içirmek *veya* yedirmek; PAINT astar vurmak.

prim.er[1] ['praimə] *n.* ilk okuma kitabı; TYP ['primə]: *great ~* on sekiz puntoluk harf; *long ~* on puntoluk harf.

prim.er[2] ['praimə] *n.* astar boya; falya barutu.

pri.me.val [prai'mi:vəl] *adj.* ilk(s)el, çok eski...

prim.ing ['praimiŋ] *n.* PAINT astar boya; MIL falya barutu; *attr.* ateşleme...

prim.i.tive ['primitiv] **1.** □ ilkel, iptidaî; basit; kaba; demode; ilk, eski; **2.** *n.* GR kök kelime; 'prim.i.tive.ness *n.* ilkellik; basitlik.

prim.ness ['primnis] *n.* resmiyet; fazla ciddiyet.

pri.mo.gen.i.ture [praiməu'dʒenitʃə] *n.* ilk evlât olma; en büyük erkek evlât önceliği.

pri.mor.di.al □ [prai'mɔ:djəl] başlangıçta var olan, ilk; en eski...

prim.rose BOT ['primrəuz] *n.* çuhaçiçeği; ~ *path veya way fig.* zevk ve sefa yolu; *take the ~ path* zevk ve sefa içinde yaşamak.

prince [prins] *n.* prens; kral, hükümdar, emir; ♀ Con.sort kraliçenin kocası; 'prince.ly *adj.* prense ait; prense yakışır; cömert, asil, kibar; şahane; princess [prin'ses] *n.* prenses.

prin.ci.pal ['prinsəpəl] **1.** □ baş(lıca), en önemli, ana, büyük, asıl; GR ~ *parts* *pl.* İngilizce fiillerin çekim şekilleri; **2.** *n.* müdür, yönetici, başkan; *part. Am.* okul müdürü; COM patron, şef; müvekkil; sermaye, anapara, anamal; asıl sorumlu; prin.ci.pal.i.ty [prinsi'pæliti] *n.* prenslik.

prin.ci.ple ['prinsəpl] *n.* prensip, ilke; kural; temel sebep, köken; dürüstlük, ahlâk; CHEM tamamlayıcı unsur; *in* ~ genel olarak, genelde; *on* ~ prensip olarak, prensip yönünden, ilke olarak.

prink F [priŋk] *vb.* giydirip kuşatmak, süslemek; **~ oneself (up)** süslenip püslenmek.

print [print] **1.** *n.* bası, tabı; basılmış yazı, matbua; damga, kalıp; emprime, basma kumaş; iz; basılı resim; PHOT negatiften yapılmış resim; *Am.* gazete, dergi; **out of ~** baskısı tükenmiş; **in cold ~** yazılmış, basılmış; **2.** *v/t.* basmak, yayımlamak; PHOT negatiften çıkarmak (*resim*); matbaa harfleriyle yazmak; *fig.* nakşetmek (**on** -*e*); **~ed form** çizelge, cetvel; **~ed matter** matbua, basma; *v/i.* matbaacılık yapmak; '**print.er** *n.* basımcı, matbaacı; **~'s devil** matbaacı çırağı; **~'s flower** çiçek modelli süsleme; **~'s ink** matbaa mürekkebi.

print.ing ['printiŋ] *n.* matbaacılık, baskıcılık; PHOT basma, tabetme; '**~.frame** *n.* PHOT kopya şasisî; '**~.ink** *n.* matbaa (*veya* baskı) mürekkebi; '**~.of.fice** *n.* basımevi, matbaa; '**~.press** *n.* matbaa makinesi.

pri.or ['praiə] **1.** *adj.* önce, evvel(ki) (**to** -*den*); sabık; kıdemli; **2.** *adv.* **~ to** -*den* önce, -*den* evvel; **3.** *n.* ECCL manastır başrahibi; '**pri.or.ess** *n.* ECCL başrahibe; **pri.or.i.ty** [-'ɔriti] *n.* öncelik, kıdem; üstünlük hakkı (**to**, **over** -*de*); *s.* **share 1**; **pri.o.ry** ECCL ['-əri] *n.* manastır.

prism ['prizəm] *n.* prizma, biçme; prizmatik şeffaf cisim; **~ binoculars** *pl.* prizmalı dürbün; **pris.mat.ic** [-'mætik] *adj.* (**~ally**) prizma biçiminde, prizmatik, biçmesel; şeffaf prizmadan oluşan (*renk*).

pris.on ['prizn] **1.** *n.* cezaevi, hapishane, tutukevi; **2.** *v/t. poet.* hapsetmek; '**prison.er** *n.* tutuklu, hükümlü, mahkûm; esir; JUR mevkuf, sanık; **be a ~ to** *fig.* esiri olm. -*in-* mahkûm olm. -*e*; **take s.o. ~** *b-ni* esir almak; **~'s bars**, **~'s base** köşe kapmaca oyunu.

pris.sy *Am.* F ['prisi] *adj.* titiz, kılı kırk yaran.

pris.tine ['pristain] *adj.* eski zamana ait, eski...; bozulmamış; taze ve temiz.

prith.ee *obs.* ['priði:] *int.* lütfen, rica ederim.

pri.va.cy ['praivəsi] *n.* özellik; gizlilik, mahremiyet; kişisel dokunulmazlık.

pri.vate ['praivit] **1.** □ özel, hususî, kişisel, şahsî; gizli, mahrem; gözden uzak, yalnız, baş başa; gayri resmi; **~ compa-**

ny özel şirket; **~ member** milletvekili; **~ theatre** özel tiyatro; **~ view** özel açılış; **at ~ sale** el altından; **2.** *n.* MIL nefer, er, asker; **~s** *pl.*, **mst ~ parts** *pl.* edep yerleri; **in ~** gizlice, özel olarak.

pri.va.teer NAUT [praivə'tiə] *n.* özel korsan gemisi (komutanı); **pri.va'teer.ing** *n.* korsanlık yapma; *attr.* korsan...

pri.va.tion [prai'veiʃən] *n.* yoksunluk, sıkıntı, mahrumiyet, ihtiyaç.

pri.va.tive □ ['privətiv] yok eden, mahrum eden, -*den* yoksun bırakan; olumsuz (*a.* GR).

priv.et BOT ['privit] *n.* kurtbağrı, kurt baharı

priv.i.lege ['privilidʒ] **1.** *n.* ayrıcalık, imtiyaz; özel izin, müsaade, ruhsat; hak; **2.** *v/t.* ayrıcalık vermek; **~d** imtiyazlı, ayrıcalıklı.

priv.i.ty JUR ['priviti] *n.* ortak çıkarlara dayanan ilişki; gizli bilgi.

priv.y ['privi] **1.** □ **~ to** sır ortağı olan -*e*; JUR ortak, hissedar; gizli; özel, kişisel; **♀ Council** İngiltere'de kralın danışma meclisi; özel meclis; **♀ Councillor** kralın danışma meclisi üyesi; **~ parts** *pl.* edep yerleri, cinsel organlar; **~ purse** hazineden kralın şahsına ayrılan para; **♀ Seal** resmî devlet mührü; **Lord ♀ Seal** ferman mührü emini; **2.** *n.* JUR ortak (**to** -*e*); tuvalet, helâ, ayakyolu.

prize¹ [praiz] **1.** *n.* ödül, mükâfat, ikramiye; NAUT ganimet; **first ~ piyango:** en büyük ikramiye; **2.** *adj.* ödül olarak verilen; mükâfata lâyık...; ödül kazanan...; mükemmel; NAUT ganimet; **~ competition** ödüllü yarışma; **3.** *v/t.* değer vermek -*e*; paha biçmek -*e*; NAUT zaptetmek, el koymak.

prize² [-] **1.** *v/t. a.* **~ open** zorla (*veya* manivela *vs.* ile) açmak; **2.** *n.* kaldıraç.

prize...: '**~.fight.er** *n.* profesyonel boksör; '**~.list** *n.* ödül listesi, kazananlar listesi; '**~.man** = **prize-winner**; '**~.ring** *n. boks:* ring; '**~.winner** *n.* ödül kazanan (*veya* birinci gelen) kimse.

pro [prəu] **1.** *prp.* için; *s.* **con³**; **2.** *adv.* lehinde, ...taraftarı; **3.** *n.* profesyonel oyuncu.

prob.a.bil.i.ty [prɔbə'biliti] *n.* ihtimal, olasılık; muhtemel şey; '**prob.a.ble** □ muhtemel, olasılı.

pro.bate JUR ['prəubit] *n.* vasiyetnamenin resmen onaylanması; vasiyetnamenin onaylı kopyası.

pro.ba.tion [prə'beiʃən] *n.* deneme süresi; *part.* JUR gözaltında tutma koşuluyle salıverme; JUR vasiyetnamenin onaylanması; ~ *officer* suçluyu gözaltında tutan memur; *on~* denenmekte; JUR gözaltında; **pro'ba.tion.ar.y** *adj.*: ~ *period* JUR gözaltında bulunma süresi; **pro'ba.tion.er** *n.* stajyer hemşire (*veya* doktor *vs.*); deneme devresinde olan kimse; JUR gözaltında olan kişi.

pro.ba.tive JUR ['prəubətiv] *adj.*: ~ *force* ispat kudreti.

probe [prəub] **1.** *n.* MED cerrah mili, sonda; *fig.* araştırma; insansız uzay roketi; *lunar* ~ ay araştırması; **2.** *vb. a.* ~ *into* sonda ile yoklamak *-i,* sondaj yapmak *-e*; derinliğine araştırmak, incelemek; '~**scis.sors** *n. pl.* yara makası.

prob.i.ty ['prəubiti] *n.* doğruluk, dürüstlük.

prob.lem ['prɔbləm] *n.* sorun, mesele; MATH problem; *do a* ~ *problem* çözmek; **problem.at.ic, prob.lem.at.i.cal** □ [₋bli'mætik(əl)] şüpheli, belli olmayan.

pro.bos.cis [prəu'bɔsis] *n.* fil hortumu; böcek hortumu.

pro.ce.dur.al [prə'si:dʒərəl] *adj.* yargılama usulüne ait; **pro'ce.dure** *n.* işlem, muamele; davaya bakma usulü, yargılama yöntemi; iş görme usulü.

pro.ceed [prə'si:d] *v/i.* ilerlemek (*a. fig.*); girişimde bulunmak, başlamak *veya* devam etm. (*with* -*e*); gitmek; dava açmak (*against* -*e karşı*); UNIV doktor ünvanını kazanmak; ~ *from* çıkmak -*den*, doğmak -*den*; ~ *on one's journey* seyahatine devam etm.; ~ *to* başlamak *-e*, geçmek *-e*; **pro'ceed.ing** *n.* usül, yöntem, muamele, işlem; hareket tarzı, tavır, davranış; ~*s pl.* JUR dava işlemleri, yargılama usülleri; ~*s pl.* tutanak, zabıt; *take* ~*s against* dava açmak *-e karşı*; **pro.ceeds** ['prəusi:dz] *n. pl.* kazanç, gelir, hâsılat (*from* -*den*).

proc.ess ['prəuses] **1.** *n.* yöntem, metod, işlem, yol, usül; gidiş, gelişme, ilerleme; JUR dava (muamelesi); çağrı kâğıdı, celpname; CHEM işlem, ANAT, BOT yumru; süreç; *in* ~ yapılmakta; *in* ~ *of construction* inşa halinde; **2.** *v/t.* belli bir işleme tabi tutmak; muamelesini yapmak; MEC işlemek; tebliğ etm.; dava açmak; ~ *into* işlemek; '**pro.cess.ing** *n.* MEC işleme; **proces.sion** [prə'seʃən] *n.* alay, tören alayı; geçit töreni; **pro'ces.sion.ar.y** [₋ʃnəri] *adj.* alay kabilinden, alay...

pro.claim [prə'kleim] *v/t.* ilan etm.; beyan etm.; göstermek, ele vermek, açığa vurmak.

proc.la.ma.tion [prɔklə'meiʃən] *n.* ilan; bildiri, beyanname.

pro.cliv.i.ty [prə'kliviti] *n.* eğilim, meyil (*to* -*e*).

pro.con.sul [prəu'kɔnsəl] *n.* eski Roma'da vali, prokonsül.

pro.cras.ti.nate [prəu'kræstineit] *vb.* süründe bırakmak, geciktirmek, ağırdan almak; ertelemek; **pro.cras.ti'na.tion** *n.* geciktirme; erteleme.

pro.cre.ate ['prəukrieit] *vb.* döllemek; doğurmak, yaratmak; **pro.cre'a.tion** *n.* dölleme; doğurma; '**pro.cre.a.tive** *adj.* dölleyici; doğurgan...

proc.tor ['prɔktə] *n.* JUR dava vekili, hukuk müşaviri; UNIV disiplini sağlayan memur.

pro.cum.bent [prəu'kʌmbənt] *adj.* sürüngen (*sap*); yüzükoyun.

pro.cur.a.ble [prə'kjuərəbl] *adj.* bulunabilir, elde edilebilir.

proc.u.ra.tion [prɔkjuə'reiʃən] *n.* tedarik, elde etme, bulma; COM vekillik, vekâlet(name); pezevenklik; *by~* temsilen, vekâleten; '**proc.u.ra.tor** *n.* vekil.

pro.cure [prə'kjuə] *v/t.* elde etm., tedarik etm., sağlamak (*s.o. s.th., s.th. for s.o. b-ne bş*); edinmek; sebep olm. *-e*, neden olm. *-e*; *v/i.* pezevenklik etm.; **pro'curement** *n.* tedarik, elde etme; **pro'cur.er** *n.* tedarik eden kimse; pezevenk; **pro'curess** *n.* pezevenk kadın.

prod [prɔd] **1.** *n.* üvendire; dürtme, itme; *fig.* tahrik, teşvik; **2.** *v/t.* dürtmek, itmek; *fig.* tahrik etm., kışkırtmak, özendirmek.

prod.i.gal ['prɔdigəl] **1.** □ savurgan, müsrif, tutumsuz, har vurup harman savuran (*of* -*i*); çok bol; *the* ~ *son* mirasyedi (*veya* savurgan) kimse; **2.** *n.* müsrif (*veya* tutumsuz) kimse; **prod.i-gal.i.ty** [₋'gæliti] *n.* bolluk, bereket; müsriflik, savurganlık.

pro.di.gious □ [prə'didʒəs] kocaman, çok büyük; şaşılacak, harika, müthiş; **prodi.gy** ['prɔdidʒi] *n.* olağanüstü şey, mucize, harika; dâhi (*a. fig.*); *oft. infant* ~ harika çocuk.

prod.uce[1] ['prɔdju:s] *n.* ürün, mahsül; sebze, zerzevat.

pro.duce[2] [prə'dju:s] *vb.* üretmek, yapmak, imal etm.; yetiştirmek; meydana getirmek; (ortaya) çıkarmak, göstermek; doğurmak; sebep olm., neden olm., yaratmak; MATH uzatmak (*doğru*); *film*: sahneye koymak; **pro'duc.er** *n.* üretici; *film*: prodükter, yapımcı; THEAT rejisör; *radyo*: yayın direktörü; gaz jeneratörü; **pro'duc.i.ble** *adj.* üretilebilir; sahneye konabilir; **pro'ducing** *adj.* üretim...

prod.uct ['prɔdʌkt] *n.* ürün, mahsül, hâsılat; sonuç, netice; MATH çarpım; **pro.duction** [prə'dʌkʃən] *n.* üretim, imal(ât) ürün; eser, yapıt; THEAT sahneye koyma; ~ **line** sürekli iş şeridi; **pro'duc.tive** □ verimli, bereketli; yaratıcı (*of -i*); **pro'duc.tive.ness**, **produc.tiv.i.ty** [prɔdʌk'tiviti] *n.* verimlilik.

prof *Am.* F [prɔf] *n.* profesör.

prof.a.na.tion [prɔfə'neiʃən] *n.* kutsiyetini bozma, kutsal şeylere karşı saygısızlık; **pro.fane** [prə'fein] **1.** □ dinle ilgisi olmayan, dünyevî, cismanî; kâfir; adî, bayağı; küfürlü; **2.** *v/t.* kutsiyetini bozmak; suiistimal etm.; kirletmek; saygısızca kullanmak; **pro.fan.i.ty** [‿'fæniti] *n.* hürmetsizlik; ağız bozukluğu; küfür.

pro.fess [prə'fes] *v/t. & v/i.* açıkça söylemek, itiraf etm.; ikrar etm. (*inancını*); iddia etm., taslamak; icra etm. (*meslek*), öğretmenlik yapmak; **pro'fessed** □ iddia edilen; açıklanmış, itiraf edilmiş; sözde, güya; **pro'fess.ed.ly** [‿sidli] *adv.* iddiaya göre; sözde, güya.

pro.fes.sion [prə'feʃən] *n.* uğraş, iş, meslek, sanat; iddia, söz; itiraf; beyan, ikrar; **pro'fes.sion.al** [‿ʃənl] **1.** □ mesleğe ait, meslekî; ustalıklı; meslek sahibi; profesyonel; ~ **men** *pl.* üniversite mezunu kimseler (*doktor, avukat vs.*); **2.** *n.* mütehassıs, uzman; *part. spor*: profesyonel kimse; **pro'fes.sion.al.ism** [‿ʃnəlizm] *n. spor*: profesyonellik.

pro.fes.sor [prə'fesə] *n.* profesör; **pro'fessor.ship** *n.* profesörlük.

prof.fer ['prɔfə] **1.** *v/t.* teklif etm., önermek, sunmak, arzetmek; **2.** *n.* teklif, öneri.

pro.fi.cien.cy [prə'fiʃənsi] *n.* ehliyet, beceriklilik, ustalık, maharet; **pro'ficient 1.** □ ehliyetli, usta, mahir, becerikli (*in, at -de*); **2.** *n.* uzman, mütehassıs (*in -de*).

pro.file ['prəufail] *n.* profil, kesit, yanal görünüş (*a.* ARCH); enine kesit; *fig.* kısa biyografi.

prof.it ['prɔfit] **1.** *n.* kâr, kazanç; menfaat, fayda, yarar; **2.** *vb.* kazanç getirmek *-e*, kâr getirmek *-e*; ~ **by** (**from**) yararlanmak *-den*, istifade etm. *-den*; **'profita.ble** □ kazançlı, kârlı; faydalı, yararlı; **'prof.it.a.ble.ness** *n.* kazançlılık, fayda; **prof.it.eer** [‿'tiə] **1.** *v/i.* çok para kazanmak, vurgunculuk yapmak; **2.** *n.* vurguncu (*veya* fırsatçı) kimse; **war** ~ savaş zengini; **prof.it'eer.ing** *n.* vurgunculuk; **'prof.it.less** □ kârsız; faydasız; **prof.it-shar.ing** [‿'ʃɛəriŋ] *n.* kârı bölüşme, kâra katılma.

prof.li.ga.cy ['prɔfligəsi] *n.* ahlâksızlık; müsriflik, savurganlık; utanmazlık; hovardalık; **prof.li.gate** ['‿git] **1.** □ ahlâksız; müsrif, savurgan; utanmaz; hovarda, uçarı; **2.** *n.* ahlâksız (*veya* edepsiz, savurgan) kimse.

pro.found □ [prə'faund] derin; engin; esaslı, adamakıllı, çok büyük; çok bilgili; *fig.* şüpheli; **pro'found.ness**, **pro.fun.di.ty** [‿'fʌnditi] *n.* derinlik (*a. fig.*), genişlik.

pro.fuse □ [prə'fjuːs] çok, bol; savurgan, aşırı bol; cömert; verimli; **pro'fuse.ness**, **pro.fu.sion** [‿'fjuːʒən] *n.* bolluk; *fig.* savurganlık, aşırılık.

prog.*sl.* UNIV [prɔg] *n.* disiplini sağlayan memur.

pro.gen.i.tor [prəu'dʒenitə] *n.* ata, cet, dede; **pro'gen.i.tress** [‿tris] *n.* büyükkanne, nine; **prog.e.ny** ['prɔdʒini] *n.* soy, nesil, torunlar; *fig.* mahsül, ürün.

prog.no.sis MED [prɔg'nəusis] *n., pl.* **prog'noses** [‿siːz] prognoz, tahmin.

prog.nos.tic [prɔg'nɔstik] **1.** *adj.* önceden gösteren (*of -i*); **2.** *n.* belirti, alâmet; kehanet; **prog'nos.ti.cate** [‿keit] *v/t.* önceden haber vermek, kehanette bulunmak; **prog.nos.ti'ca.tion** *n.* önceden haber verme, kehanet, belirti.

pro.gram, *mst* **pro.gramme** ['prəugræm] *n.* program; *radyo*: yayın; düzen.

prog.ress[1] ['prəugres] *n.* gelişme, ilerleme (*a.* MIL), yükselme; **in** ~ yapılmakta, ilerlemekte, gelişmekte.

pro.gress[2] [prə'gres] *v/i.* ilerlemek, ileri gitmek, gelişmek, kalkınmak; iyiye gitmek, düzelmek; devam etm.; **pro'gression** [‿ʃən] *n.* ilerleme, devam; MATH dizi; **pro'gres.sion.ist** [‿ʃnist], **pro'gress.ist** [‿sist] *n.* POL ilerici, erkinci kimse; **pro'gres.sive 1.** □ ilerleyen, gelişen; genişleyen, ar-

tan; POL ilerici, erkinci; ~ *form* GR sürekli zaman şekli; **2.** *n.* POL ilerici, erkinci kimse.
pro.hib.it [prə'hibit] *v/t.* yasaklamak, yasak etm., menetmek (*s.th. bşi; s.o. from ger. b-ni -mekten*); mâni olm. *-e*, engel olm. *-e*; **pro.hi.bi.tion** [prəuhi'biʃən] *n.* yasak (emri); içki yasağı, içkilerin yasak olması; **pro.hi'bi.tion- ist** [-ʃnist] *n. part. Am.* içki yasağı taraftarı; **prohib.i.tive** □ [prə'hibitiv] yasaklayıcı; engelleyici; aşırı, fahiş (*fiyat*); ~ *duty* yasak gümrüğü.
proj.ect ['prɔdʒekt] *n.* plan, proje, tasarı.
pro.ject [prə'dʒekt] *v/t.* tasarlamak, düşünmek, tasavvur etm.; perdede göstermek (*film, resim*); *-in* planını çizmek; yansıtmak (*gerçekleri*); fırlatmak, atmak, savurmak; MATH izdüşürmek; ~ *o.s. into* k-ni götürmek *-e*, k-ni …de farz etm.; *v/i.* çıkık olm., çıkıntı oluşturmak; **projec.tile 1.** ['prɔdʒiktail] *n.* mermi, top güllesi, fırlatılan taş *veya* mermi; **2.** [prəu'dʒektail] *adj.* fırlatıcı…, atıcı…; fırlatılan…; **pro.jec.tion** [prə'dʒekʃən] *n.* projeksiyon; gösterim; fırlatma, atma, atış; çıkıntı; proje, tasarı; MATH, AST, PHOT izdüşüm; ~ *room film:* projeksiyon odası; **pro'jec.tion.ist** [-ʃnist] *n.* film makinisti (*veya* göstericisi); **pro'jec- tor** *n.* proje (*veya* plan) yapan kimse; COM kurucu; OPT sinema makinesi, projektör, ışıldak.
pro.le.tar.i.an [prəuli'tɛəriən] **1.** *adj.* ücretle çalışan sınıftan; **2.** *n.* proleter, emekçi; **pro.le'tar.i.at**, *mst.* **pro.le'tar- i.ate** [-riət] *n.* proletarya, işçi sınıfı.
pro.lif.ic [prəu'lifik] *adj.* (~*ally*) doğurgan; *fig.* bereketli, verimli, semereli (*of, in*).
pro.lix □ ['prəuliks] sözü çok uzatan; yorucu, sıkıcı; uzun, ayrıntılı; **pro'lix- i.ty** *n.* sözü boşuna uzatma, söz uzunluğu.
pro.logue, *Am. a.* **pro.log** ['prəulɔg] *n.* prolog, önsöz, başlangıç, giriş; ~ *to* fig *-in* başlangıcı.
pro.long [prə'lɔŋ] *v/t.* uzatmak, sürdürmek; COM temdit etm.; **pro.lon.ga.tion** [-'geiʃən] *n.* uzatma, sürdürme.
prom F [prɔm] = *promenade concert.*
prom.e.nade [prɔmi'nɑːd] **1.** *n.* gezinti, gezme (yeri), mesire; büyük balo; **2.** *v/t. & v/i.* gez(dir)mek, gezinmek; ~ *concert* ayakta dinlenilen konser.

prom.i.nence ['prɔminəns] *n.* ün, şöhret; önem; göze çarpan şey; çıkıntı; *concr.* tümsek, engebe; **'prom.i.nent** □ çıkık, çıkıntılı, ileri fırlamış; önemli, mühim; meşhur, şöhretli; göze çarpan; *fig.* seçkin, güzide, ileri gelen.
prom.is.cu.i.ty [prɔmis'kjuːiti] *n.* (karma)karışıklık, (darma)dağınıklık; **pro.miscu.ous** □ [prə'miskjuəs] (karma)karışık, (darma)dağınık; farksız; rasgele; rasgele cinsel ilişkide bulunan.
prom.ise ['prɔmis] **1.** *n.* söz, vaat, taahhüt, vaat edilen şey; *fig.* ümit verici şey (*of*); *of great* ~ çok ümit verici; **2.** *vb.* söz vermek *-e*, vaat etm. *-e*; belirtisi olm. *-in*, göstermek; temin etm., garanti etm., ümit vermek; *I ~ you* F sana söz veriyorum; **'prom.is.ing** □ ümit verici, geleceği parlak; **prom.is.so.ry** ['-səri] *adj.* vaat (*veya* taahhüt) içeren; ~ *note* COM bono, emre yazılı senet.
prom.on.to.ry ['prɔməntri] *n.* dağlık burun.
pro.mote [prə'məut] *v/t.* ilerletmek; terfi ettirmek, rütbesini yükseltmek; *part. Am. okul:* sınıf geçirmek; PARL desteklemek; COM kurmak, tesis etm.; *part. Am.* reklâmını yaparak tanıtmak; **pro'mot.er** *n.* destekleyen kimse; COM girişim sahibi, kurucu; organizatör; **pro'mo.tion** *n.* terfi, yüksel(t)me; geçme; COM tesis; reklâm; mevki, rütbe; teşvik.
prompt [prɔmpt] **1.** □ hemen, çabuk, acele, hazır, seri, tez; dakik; **2.** *adv.* tam, dakikası dakikasına; **3.** *vb.* tahrik etm., sevketmek, teşvik etm., harekete getirmek, kışkırtmak; THEAT suflörlük etm.; **4.** *n.* COM vade; THEAT oyuncuya hatırlatılan söz, hatırlatma; '~*box n.* THEAT suflör hücresi; **'prompt.er** *n.* THEAT suflör; **promp.ti.tude** ['-titjuːd] *n.*, **'prompt.ness** sürat, çabukluk; harekete hazır olma.
pro.mul.gate ['prɔmʌlgeit] *v/t.* resmen ilân etm., duyurmak, bildirmek, neşretmek; yaymak (*fikir*); yürürlüğe koymak (*kanun*); **pro.mul'ga.tion** *n.* duyuru; resmen yürürlüğe koyma.
prone □ [prəun] yüzükoyun (yatmış, yere uzanmış); eğilimli, meyilli; ~ *to fig.* eğimli *-e*; **'prone.ness** *n.* eğilim, meyil (*to -e*).
prong [prɔŋ] *n.* çatal dişi; sivri uç(lu alet); boynuz çatalı; **pronged** *adj.* dişli, sivri uçlu.

pro.nom.i.nal ☐ GR [prəu'nɔminl] zamire ait, zamir kabilinden.

pro.noun GR ['prəunaun] *n.* zamir, adıl.

pro.nounce [prə'nauns] *v/t. & v/i.* resmen bildirmek, beyan etm., ilan etm., açıklamak (*karar vs.*); telaffuz etm., söylemek; fikrini söylemek (*on hakkında*); **pro'nounced** ☐ (*adv.* ~*ly*) katî, kesin; belli, belirgin, bariz; **pro'nounce.ment** *n.* bildiri, duyuru, beyan, tebliğ.

pro.nounc.ing [prə'naunsiŋ] *adj.* telaffuz…

pron.to *Am.* F ['prɔntəu] *adv.* hemen, derhal, çabuk.

pro.nun.ci.a.tion [prənʌnsi'eiʃən] *n.* telaffuz, söyleniş, söyleyiş.

proof [pru:f] **1.** *n.* delil, kanıt, tanıt, ispat; imtihan, tecrübe, deneme, test; TYP prova; TYP, PHOT ayar; MATH sağlama; CHEM alkol derecesi; *in* ~ *of -in* delili olarak; **2.** *adj.* dayanıklı, kuvvetli, dirençli (*against*, *to -e karşı*); geçirmez (*kurşun, su, ses vs.*); *fig.* karşı çıkan (*against -e*); **3.** *v/t.* (*su, hava vs.*) geçirmez yapmak; '~**read.er** *n.* TYP düzeltmen; '~**sheet** *n.* TYP prova; '~**spir.it** CHEM standart dereceli alkol.

prop [prɔp] **1.** *n.* destek (*a. fig.*), ayak, payanda; çamaşır sırığı; destek olan kimse; THEAT *sl.* sahne eşyası, dekor; *pit-* ~**s** *pl.* maden ocağı direkleri; **2.** *v/t. a.* ~ *up* desteklemek; dayamak, yaslamak.

prop.a.gan.da [prɔpə'gændə] *n.* propaganda; **prop.a'gan.dist** *n.* propagandacı; **prop.a.gate** ['_geit] *v/t. & v/i.* üre(t)mek, çoğal(t)mak; çiftleştirmek; *fig.* yaymak, dağıtmak; geçirmek, bulaştırmak; nakletmek; yavrulamak, türemek; **prop.a'ga.tion** *n.* üreme, yavrulama; yayım, yay(ıl)ma; 'prop.a.ga.tor *n.* üretici; yayıcı.

pro.pel [prə'pel] *v/t.* sevketmek, itmek, ileri doğru sürmek; **pro'pel.lant** *n.* ileriye sevkedici şey, muharrik kuvvet; kurşun *veya* uzay gemisini iten kuvvet; yakıt; **pro'pel.lent =** *propellant*; **pro'pel.ler** *n.* pervane, uskur; ~ *shaft* kardan mili; **pro'pel.ling** *adj.* itici…; ~ *pencil* sürgülü kurşun kalem.

prop.er ☐ ['prɔpə] uygun, yakışır, münasip, layık (*for -e*); has, hususi, mahsus, ait (*to -e*); F doğru, gerçek, tam; hürmete layık, saygıdeğer; güzel, fevkalâde; F yakışıklı; ~ *name* özel isim; 'prop.er.ty *n.* mal, mülk, emlâk, arazi;

özellik; JUR mülkiyet, sahiplik; *proper-ties pl.* THEAT sahne donanımı; 'prop-er.ty-man *n.* THEAT sahne donanımcısı; 'prop.er.ty-tax *n.* emlâk vergisi.

proph.e.cy ['prɔfisi] *n.* önceden haber verme, kâhinlik, kehanet; **proph.e.sy** ['_sai] *v/t. & v/i.* önceden haber vermek, kehanette bulunmak; peygamberlik etm.; önceden tahmin etm.

proph.et ['prɔfit] *n.* peygamber; kâhin; taraftar; öncü; 'proph.et.ess *n.* kadın peygamber; **pro.phet.ic**, **pro.phet.i-cal** ☐ [prə'fetik(əl)] peygamber *veya* peygamberliğe ait; kehanete ait, kehanet gibi.

pro.phy.lac.tic MED [prɔfi'læktik] *adj.* (~*ally*) hastalıktan koruyan, koruyucu, önleyici.

pro.pin.qui.ty [prə'piŋkwiti] *n.* yakınlık; akrabalık; yapı benzerlik.

pro.pi.ti.ate [prə'piʃieit] *v/t.* yatıştırmak, sakinleştirmek; -*in* gönlünü almak; -*in* teveccühünü kazanmak; **pro-pi.ti'a.tion** *n.* yatıştırma; teveccühünü kazanma, telâfi etme (*suç vs.*); **pro'pi-ti.a.to.ry** [._ʃiətəri] yatıştırıcı; gönül alan…

pro.pi.tious ☐ [prə'piʃəs] uygun, elverişli; bağışlayıcı, şefkatli; yardımsever; uğurlu, hayırlı; **pro'pi.tious.ness** *n.* elverişlilik (*hava*); yardımseverlik; şefkat.

pro.por.tion [prə'pɔ:ʃən] **1.** *n.* oran(tı), nispet; hisse, pay; MATH, CHEM orantı (kuralı); ~*s pl.* ebat, boyutlar; **2.** *v/t.* oranlamak (*to -e*); **pro'por.tion.al 1.** ☐ orantılı; *s. proportionate*; **2.** *n.* MATH orantılı sayı; **pro'por.tion.ate** ☐ [._ʃnit] uygun, orantılı (*to -e*); **pro'por-tioned** *adj.* … orantılı.

pro.pos.al [prə'pəuzəl] *n.* önerme, teklif, öneri; evlenme teklifi; **pro'pose** *v/t.* önermek, teklif etm.; sunmak, arzetmek; niyetlenmek; ~ *to o.s.* bş yapmaya niyetlenmek; ~ *a motion* bir teklifte bulunmak; *v/i.* evlenme teklif etm. (*to -e*); **pro'pos.er** *n.* teklifte bulunan kimse; **propo.si.tion** [prɔpə'ziʃən] *n.* teklif, öneri; mesele, sorun; ifade; PHLS, MATH teorem, sav, tez, dava; *sl.* uygunsuz teklif, sevişme teklifi.

pro.pound [prə'paund] *v/t.* ileri sürmek, ortaya atmak, arzetmek, önermek.

pro.pri.e.tar.y [prə'praiətəri] **1.** *adj.* sicilli, markalı, müseccel; sahipli, hususi; patentli, tescilli; mal sahipliğine ait; ~

name tescilli marka; **2.** *n.* mal sahibi; mal sahipleri; pro'**pri.e.tor** *n.* mal sahibi, sahip; pro'**pri.e.tress** *n.* mal sahibi kadın; pro'**pri.e.ty** *n.* uygunluk, münasebet, yerindelik, mantıklılık; ***the pro-prieties*** *pl.* töre, adap, görgü kuralları.

props F THEAT [prɔps] *n. pl.* sahne donanımı.

pro.pul.sion MEC [prə'pʌlʃən] *n.* itici güç; sevk, tahrik; pro'**pul.sive** [-siv] *adj.* yürütücü, çalıştırıcı, itici...; tahrik edici...

pro.rate *Am.* [prəu'reit] *v/t.* eşit olarak bölüp dağıtmak.

pro.ro.ga.tion PARL [prəurə'geiʃən] *n.* parlementoyu tatil etme; **pro.rogue** PARL [prə'rəug] *v/t.* tatil etm.

pro.sa.ic [prəu'zeiik] *adj.* (**~ally**) *fig.* sıkıcı; adi, bayağı, yavan.

pro.scribe [prəus'kraib] *v/t.* yasaklamak; yasal haklardan yoksun bırakmak.

pro.scrip.tion [prəus'kripʃən] *n.* yasakla(n)ma.

prose [prəuz] **1.** *n.* nesir, düzyazı; **2.** *adj.* nesir...; nesir şeklinde yazılmış; can sıkıcı, yavan **3.** *vb.* nesir yazmak.

pros.e.cute ['prɔsikjuːt] *vb.* devam etm. *-e*, sürdürmek *-i*; JUR kovuşturmak, cezalandırmak, kanunî takibat yapmak (**for** için); **pros.e'cu.tion** *n.* devam, sürme; takibat, kovuşturma; JUR dava(cı); iddia makamı; ***witness for the* ~** sanığın aleyhindeki tanık; 'pros.e.cu.tor *n.* JUR davacı; savcı; ***public*** **~** savcı.

pros.e.lyte ECCL ['prɔsilait] *n.* din değiştiren kimse, dönme; pros.e.lyt-ism['-litizəm]*n.* başkalarını kendi dinine sokmaya çalışma; 'pros.e.lyt.ize *vb.* dininden çevirmek.

pros.er ['prəuzə] *n.* nesir yazarı; sıkıcı yazar *veya* konuşmacı.

pros.o.dy ['prɔsədi] *n.* vezin tekniği, prosodi, aruz.

pros.pect 1. ['prɔspekt] *n.* manzara, görünüş (*a. fig.*); ümit, umut; gelecek; olasılık, ihtimal; COM *part. Am.* muhtemel müşteri; ***have in* ~** ümidi olm.; ***hold out a* ~ *of s.th.*** ümit vermek; **2.** [prəs'pekt] *vb.* MIN araştırmak (**for** *-i*); pro'**spec.tive** □ beklenen, umulan, ümit edilen; müstakbel; muhtemel; ***~ buyer*** muhtemel alıcı; pros-'pec.tor *n.* MIN maden arayıcısı; pro-'spec.tus [-təs] *n.* prospektüs; tarif(nam)e.

pros.per ['prɔspə] *v/i.* başarılı olm.; gelişmek, büyümek; zenginleşmek; *v/t.* başarısına yardımcı olm., korumak; **prosper.i.ty** [-'periti] *n.* başarı; *fig.* refah, saadet, gönenç; **pros.per.ous** □ ['-pərəs] başarılı; bayındır; uygun, elverişli; şanslı, talihli; *fig.* refah içinde.

pros.ti.tute ['prɔstitjuːt] **1.** *n.* fahişe, orospu; **2.** *v/t.* fahişeliğe sevketmek; *fig.* kötüye kullanmak; pros.ti'tu.tion *n.* fahişelik, fuhuş; *fig.* kötüye kullanma.

pros.trate 1. ['prɔstreit] *adj.* yüzükoyun yatmış, yere uzanmış; takati kesilmiş, dermansız; sarsılmış, yıkılmış (*üzüntüden*); **2.** [prɔs'treit] *v/t.* yıkmak, devirmek, yere sermek; *fig.* halsiz bırakmak; sarsmak (*üzüntü*); **pros'tra.tion** *n.* yere atılma, kapanma; *fig.* takatsizlik, dermansızlık, bezginlik.

pros.y □ *fig.* ['prəuzi] sıkıcı, ağır, usandırıcı, yavan.

pro.tag.o.nist [prəu'tægənist] *n.* THEAT başrol oyuncusu, kahraman; *fig.* öncü.

pro.tect [prə'tekt] *v/t.* korumak, muhafaza etm., saklamak (**from** *-den*); COM yabancı mallara gümrük koyarak (yerli malları) korumak; pro'**tec.tion** *n.* koruma, muhafaza, himaye; yabancı mallara gümrük koyarak yerli malları koruma; koruyucu kimse *veya* şey; pro-'tection.ist **1.** *n.* ithalât üzerine vergi koyarak yerli sanayii koruma taraftarı; **2.** *adj.* koruyucu...; pro'**tec.tive** *adj.* koruyucu, himaye edici; koruyucu; ***~ custody*** koruyucu (*veya* ihtiyatî) tevkif; **~ duty** koruyucu gümrük resmi; pro'**tec.tor** *n.* koruyucu, hami; HIST kral vekili; pro'**tec.tor.ate** [-tərit] *n.* başka devletin idaresinde olan küçük devlet; pro'**tec.to.ry** *n.* ıslahevi; pro-'tec.tress *n.* kadın koruyucu.

pro.té.gé [prəuteʒei] *n.* başkasının himayesinde olan kimse.

pro.te.in CHEM ['prəutiːn] *n.* protein.

pro.test 1. [prəutest] *n.* protesto, itiraz (beyannamesi); ***in* ~ *against*** protesto ederek *-i*; ***enter* *veya* *make a* ~** itirazda bulunmak, protesto etm.; **2.** [prə'test] *v/t. & v/i.* karşı çıkmak, itiraz etm. *-e*; iddia etm.; protesto etm. (***against*** *-i*). **Prot.es.tant** ['prɔtistənt] **1.** *adj.* Protestanlara ait; **2.** *n.* Protestan; 'Prot.es-tant.ism *n.* Protestanlık, Protestan mezhebi.

prot.es.ta.tion [prəutes'teiʃən] *n.* pro-

testo etme, itiraz.
pro.to.col ['prəutəkɔl] **1.** *n.* tutanak; pro tokol; **2.** *vb.* protokol yapmak.
pro.ton PHYS ['prəutɔn] *n.* proton.
pro.to.plasm BIOL ['prəutəuplæzəm] *n.* protoplazma.
pro.to.type ['prəutəutaip] *n.* esas model, ilk örnek, prototip.
pro.tract [prə'trækt] *v/t.* uzatmak; **pro'trac.tion** *n.* uzatma; **pro'trac.tor** *n.* MATH iletki, minkale.
pro.trude [prə'truːd] *v/t. & v/i.* dışarı çık(ar)mak, çıkıntı yapmak, pırtlamak; **pro'tru.sion** [-ʒən] *n.* çıkar(ıl)ma; çıkıntı.
pro.tu.ber.ance [prə'tjuːbərəns] *n.* tümsek, şiş(kinlik), çıkıntı, bel verme; **pro'tuber.ant** *adj.* şiş, tümsek, çıkık, bel vermiş, pırtlak, dışarı uğramış.
proud □ [praud] kıvanç duyan, iftihar eden, gurur duyan (**of** *-den*; **to** *inf.* *-mekten*); kibirli, gururlu, mağrur; görkemli, muhteşem; **~ flesh** MED yara etrafındaki şiş; **do s.o. ~** F *b-ne* hürmet göstermek.
prov.a.ble □ ['pruːvəbl] tanıtlanabilir, ispatı mümkün, ispat edilebilir; **prove** *v/t.* tanıtlamak, ispatlamak, ispat etm, göstermek; denemek, sınamak; *v/i.* olmak, çıkmak; **~ true (false)** doğru (yanlış) çıkmak; **he has ~d to be the heir** onun vâris olduğu ortaya çıktı; **the exception ~s the rule** istisnalar kaideyi bozmaz; **proven** ['-vən] *adj.* ispatlanmış, tanıtlanmış; sınanmış, denenmiş.
prov.e.nance ['prɔvinəns] *n.* kaynak, köken, asıl, menşe.
prov.en.der ['prɔvində] *n.* hayvan yemi; F yiyecek.
pro.verb ['prɔvəːb] *n.* atasözü; **be a ~** atasözü olm. *veya b.s.* adı çıkmış olm. (**for** *-den dolayı*); **pro.ver.bi.al** □ [prə'vəːbjəl] atasözüne ait, atasözü gibi; ünlü, herkesçe bilinen.
pro.vide [prə'vaid] *v/t.* tedarik etm., sağlamak, bulmak (**with** *-i*); donatmak; şart koşmak; *v/i.* sağlamak (**for** *-i*); önlem almak, hazırlıklı bulunmak (**against** *-e karşı*; **for** *için*); **~ for** geçimini sağlamak; **~d** (**that**) *-si, -mek* şartıyle, yeter ki.
prov.i.dence ['prɔvidəns] *n.* ilâhî takdir; basiret, sağgörü; ☿ Tanrı; **'prov.i-dent** □ tedbirli, basiretli; **prov.i.den-tial** □ [-'denʃəl] Allahtan, Tanrıdan gelen *veya* olan; talihli, kısmetli.

pro.vid.er [prə'vaidə] *n.* tedarik eden kimse; aile geçindiren kimse.
prov.ince ['prɔvins] *n.* il, vilâyet; taşra; *fig.* yetki alanı.
pro.vin.cial [prə'vinʃəl] **1.** *adj.* eyalete ait; taşraya ait, taşra...; taşralı, kaba, görgüsüz, dar düşünceli; **2.** *n.* taşralı kimse, köylü (*a. contp.*); **pro'vin.cial-ism** *n.* taşralılık, köylülük; taşraya özgü âdet ve ağız.
pro.vi.sion [prə'viʒən] **1.** *n.* tedarik (olunan şey); hazırlama, hazırlık; JUR (kanuni) hüküm; şart, koşul; **~s** *pl.* erzak, zahire; **make ~ for** *bş* için gerekli tedbiri almak; **~ merchant** gıda maddeleri satıcısı; **2.** *v/t. -in* erzağını tedarik etm.; **pro'vi.sion.al** [-ʒənl] □ geçici, muvakkat.
pro.vi.so [prə'vaizəu] *n.* kayıt, şart, koşul; **pro'vi.so.ry** [-zəri] *adj.* şartlı, koşullu.
prov.o.ca.tion [prɔvə'keiʃən] *n.* kızdırma, sinirlendirme, gücendirme; kışkırtma; kızılacak şey; **pro.voc.a-tive** [prə'vɔkətiv] **1.** *adj.* sinirlendirici, kızdırıcı; kışkırtıcı; cazip, çekici; **2.** *n.* tahrik edici kimse *veya* şey.
pro.voke [prə'vəuk] *v/t.* kızdırmak, sinirlendirmek, öfkelendirmek; kışkırtmak, tahrik etm., dürtmek; sebep olm. *-e*, neden olm. *-e*; **pro'vok-ing** □ sinirlendirici, can sıkıcı, sinir bozucu.
prov.ost ['prɔvəst] *n.* bazı üniversitelerde dekan; İskoçya'da belediye başkanı; MIL [prə'vəu] **~ marshal** inzibat amiri, adlî subay.
prow NAUT [prau] *n.* pruva.
prow.ess ['prauis] *n.* yiğitlik, cesaret, mertlik; cesaret isteyen iş.
prowl [praul] **1.** *v/t. & v/i.* gizli gizli gezinmek; etrafı kolaçan etm.; sinsi sinsi dolaşmak; **2.** *n.* sinsi sinsi dolaşma; **~ car** *Am.* polis devriye arabası.
prox.i.mate □ ['prɔksimit] en yakın, hemen yanındaki; yaklaşık, takribi; **prox'im.i.ty** *n.* yakınlık, civar; **prox.i-mo** ['-məu] *adj.* COM gelecek ayın...
prox.y ['prɔksi] *n.* vekil(lik), vekâlet(-name); **by ~** vekâleten, adına.
prude [pruːd] *n.* fazilet taslayıcı.
pru.dence ['pruːdəns] *n.* ihtiyat, basiret, sağgörü; akıl, sağduyu; **'pru.dent** □ ihtiyatlı, tedbirli, basiretli, sağgörülü; tutumlu; **pru.den.tial** □ [-'denʃəl] basiretli, sağgörülü, ihtiyatlı.
prud.er.y ['pruːdəri] *n.* aşırı erdem (*ve-*

ya iffet) taslama; erdem taslayıcı hareket *veya* söz; '**prud.ish** □ aşırı erdem taslayan.

prune[1] [pru:n] *n.* kuru erik, çir.

prune[2] [-] *v/t.* budamak (*a. fig.*); *a.* ~ *away*, ~ *off* fazla kısımları atmak.

prun.ing...: '~-hook, '~-knife *n.* budama bıçağı; '~-saw *n.* budama testeresi.

pru.ri.ence, pru.ri.en.cy ['pruəriəns(i)] *n.* şehvet (düşkünlüğü); '**pru.ri.ent** □ şehvetli; şehvet düşkünü; BOT çok üreyen.

Prus.sian ['prʌʃən] **1.** *adj.* Prusyalı, Prusya'ya ait; ~ *blue* koyu lâcivert; **2.** *n.* Prusyalı; Prusya dili.

prus.sic ac.id CHEM ['prʌsik'æsid] *n.* asit prusik.

pry[1] [prai] **1.** *v/t.* ~ *open* manivela ile açmak; ~ *up* kaldırmak; **2.** *n.* manivela, kaldıraç.

pry[2] [-] *vb.* merakla bakmak, gözetlemek; ~ *into* burnunu sokmak *-e*; '**pry.ing** □ meraklı.

psalm [sɑ:m] *n.* ilâhi; '**psalm.ist** *n.* ilâhi yazarı; **psal.mo.dy** ['sælmədi] *n.* ilâhi okuma; ilâhiler kitabı.

Psal.ter ['sɔ:ltə] *n.* ilâhiler kitabı.

pseu.do... ['psju:dəu] *prefix* sahte..., yalancı..., takma...; **pseu.do.nym** ['-dənim] *n.* takma ad; **pseu.don.y.mous** □ [-'dɔniməs] takma ad altında yazılmış.

pshaw [pʃɔ:] *int.* öf!

pso.ri.a.sis MED [psɔ'raiəsis] *n.* sedef hastalığı.

psy.che ['saiki:] *n.* insan ruhu; can; akıl.

psy.chi.a.trist [sai'kaiətrist] *n.* ruh doktoru, psikiyatr; **psy'chi.a.try** *n.* psikiyatri, ruh hekimliği.

psy.chic, psy.chi.cal □ ['saikik(əl)] ruhsal, ruhî; zihnî; telepati ile ilgili; '**psychics** *n. sg.* psikoloji.

psy.cho-a.nal.y.sis [saikəuə'næləsis] *n.* psikanaliz; **psy.cho-an.a.lyst** [-'ænəlist] *n.* psikanalist, ruhsal çözümleme.

psy.cho.log.i.cal □ [saikə'lɔdʒikəl] psikolojik, ruhbilimsel; ruhî; **psy.chol.o.gist** [sai'kɔlədʒist] *n.* psikolog, ruh bilgini; **psy'chol.o.gy** *n.* psikoloji, ruhbilim.

psy.cho.path ['saikəupæθ] *n.* psikopat, ruh hastası.

psy.cho.sis [sai'kəusis] *n.* psikoz, akıl hastalığı, ruhsal bozukluklar.

psy.cho.ther.a.py ['saikəu'θerəpi] *n.*

psikoterapi, ruhî tedavi.

pto.maine CHEM ['təumein] *n.* bozulan yiyecekte bulunan bir çeşit zehir.

pub F [pʌb] *n.* birahane, meyhane.

pu.ber.ty ['pju:bəti] *n.* ergenlik çağı, buluğ, rüşt, erinlik.

pu.bes.cence [pju:'besns] *n.* erginleşme, buluğa erme; **pu'bes.cent** *adj.* ergin, erin, buluğa ermiş; BOT tüylü.

pub.lic ['pʌblik] **1.** □ halka ait, umuma ait; umumî, genel; açık, alenî; herkese mahsus; devletle ilgili; ~ *address system* hoparlör tertibatı; ~ *man* halktan biri; ~ *spirit* yardımseverlik; *s. utility*; *works*; **2.** *n. sg. & pl.* halk, ahali, umum; seyirciler; *in* ~ açık açık, açıkça, alenen; **pub.li.can** ['-kən] *n.* meyhaneci, birahaneci; HIST vergi tahsildarı; **pub.li.ca.tion** [-'keiʃən] *n.* yayım(lama); yayın; *monthly* ~ aylık mecmua; '**pub.lic house** lokanta, birahane, meyhane; **pub.li.cist** ['-sist] *n.* politika yazarı; reklamcı; **pub'lic.i.ty** [-siti] *n.* aleniyet, alenîlik; şöhret; tanıtma, reklam; ~ *agent* reklamcı; **pub.li.cize** ['-saiz] *v/t.* reklamını yapmak; halka duyurmak.

pub.lic...: ~ **li.bra.ry** halk kütüphanesi; '~'**pri.vate** *adj.* karma (*ekonomi*); ~ **rela.tions** *pl.* halkla ilişkiler; ~ **school** özel okul; *Am.* parasız resmî okul; '~'**spirit.ed** □ yardımsever, umumun yararını düşünen.

pub.lish ['pʌbliʃ] *vb.* yayımlamak, neşretmek; bastırmak; ilan etm., söylemek, açığa vurmak; '**pub.lish.er** *n.* yayınlayıcı, yayımcı; *Am.* yayınevi; '**pub.lish.ing** *n.* yayın, basım; *attr.* yayın...; ~ *house* yayınevi.

puce [pju:s] *n.* koyu mor renk, koyu kahverengi.

puck [pʌk] *n.* folklorda yaramaz peri; *hokey*: lastik disk.

puck.a ['pʌkə] *adj.* gerçek; kaliteli; üstün, lüks, birinci sınıf.

puck.er ['pʌkə] **1.** *n.* kırışık, buruşukluk; **2.** *v/t. & v/i. a.* ~ *up* buruş(tur)mak, kırış(tır)mak, büz(ül)mek.

puck.ish □ ['pʌkiʃ] yaramaz.

pud.ding ['pudiŋ] *n.* puding, muhallebi; *black* ~ kan, yulaf ezmesi *vs.* ile doldurulmuş domuz bağırsağı; '~-**face** *n.* tombul surat.

pud.dle ['pʌdl] **1.** *n.* su birikintisi, gölcük; MEC kumlu harç; **2.** *vb.* MEC ocakta tavlamak (*dökme demir*); sıva haline sokmak (*çamur ve kumu karıştırarak*);

bulamaç yapmak; 'pud.dler *n.* MEC dökme demircisi; 'pud.dling-fur.nace *n.* MEC tavlama fırını.

pu.den.cy ['pju:dənsi] *n.* utangaçlık, sıkılganlık; 'pu.dent *adj.* utangaç, sıkılgan.

pudg.y F ['pʌdʒi] *adj.* tıknaz, bodur, küt.

pueb.lo [pu'ebləu] *n.* kızılderili köyü.

pu.er.ile ☐ ['pjuərail] çocukça, çocuksu, aptalca; önemsiz; pu.er.il.i.ty [‿'ril-iti] *n.* çocukluk; aptallık; çocukça davranış *veya* söz.

puff [pʌf] **1.** *n.* üfleme, püf; üfürük, soluk; hafif yumuşak börek, pufböreği; pudra ponponu; elbisenin büzülmüş ve kabarık yeri; aşırı övgü; yorgan; saç lülesi; abartmalı övgü; **2.** *v/t.* şişirmek; gururlandırmak; abartarak övmek; överek reklamını yapmak; *a.* ~ *at* tüttürmek (*pipo vs.*); *oft.* ~ *out*, ~ *up* üfleyerek söndürmek (*mum vs.*); şişirmek; abartarak övmek; gururlandırmak; ~ *up* çıkmak (*duman vs.*); ~*ed up fig.* kendini beğenmiş, kibirli; ~*ed eyes pl.* şişmiş gözler; ~*ed sleeve* büzgülü kol; *v/i.* üflemek; püflemek; solumak; püfür püfür esmek; '~*box n.* pudra kutusu; 'puff.er *n.* püfleyen şey *veya* kimse; F lokomotif; kirpi balığı; 'puff.er.y *n.* aşırı övgü; 'puff.i-ness *n.* kabartı, şişkinlik; 'puff.ing *n.* aşırı övme; puff paste pufböreği hamuru; 'puff.y *adj.* nefesi kesilmiş; şişkin, kabarık; abartmalı, görkemli; püfür püfür esen (*rüzgâr*).

pug [pʌg] *n.*, '~dog buldoğa benzeyen bir cins köpek.

pu.gil.ism ['pju:dʒilizəm] *n.* boksörlük; 'pu.gil.ist *n.* boksör.

pug.na.cious [pʌg'neiʃəs] *adj.* kavgacı, hırçın, dövüşken; pug.nac.i.ty [‿'næsiti] *n.* kavgacılık, dövüşkenlik.

pug-nose ['pʌgnəuz] *n.* basık burun.

puis.ne JUR ['pju:ni] *adj.* ikinci gelen, küçük…

pu.is.sant ['pju:isnt] *adj.* güçlü, kudretli, nüfuzlu.

puke *sl.* [pju:k] *v/t.* & *v/i.* kus(tur)mak.

pule [pju:l] *v/i.* ağlam(sam)ak.

pull [pul] **1.** *n.* çekme, çekiş; yudum, fırt; TYP prova; cazibe (*of*); *sl.* torpil, iltimas (*with -den*); gayret; tutamaç, sap; ~ *at the bottle sl.* şişeden alınan yudum, fırt; ~ *fastener* fermuar; **2.** *v/t.* çekmek; koparmak; yolmak (*tüy*); sürüklemek; aşırı zorlamak; TYP çıkarmak

(*prova*); NAUT çekmek (*kürek*); soymak; çalmak; çekmek (*diş, silah*); ~ *one's weight* gerekli gayreti göstermek; ~ *about* oraya buraya sürüklemek, çekiştirmek; ~ *down* yıkmak, indirmek; *fig.* çökertmek; ~ *in* içeriye çekmek; durdurmak (*at*); yakalamak, tevkif etm.; F kazanmak (*para*); ~ *off* kenara çekmek (*araç*); çıkarmak, soymak, kazanmak, başarmak; ~ *round* iyileştirmek, kendine getirmek; ~ *through* iyileştirmek; zorluktan kurtarmak; imtihanı kazandırmak; ~ *o.s. together* kendine gelmek, kendine hâkim olm.; ~ *up* durdurmak; azarlamak; *v/i.* gelmek; bir yudum içki içmek; NAUT kürek çekmek; bir nefes çekmek; silah çekmek; tezahürat yapmak (*for -e*); ~ *in* istasyona girmek (*tren*); ~ *out* ayrılmak, çıkmak; ~ *round* iyileşmek, kendine gelmek; ~ *through* iyileşmek, kendine gelmek; başarılı olm.; ~ *together* beraber çalışmak, işbirliği yapmak; ~ *up* durmak; ~ *up with*, ~ *up to* yetişmek *-e*; 'pull.er *n.* çeken şey *veya* kimse, çekici.

pul.let ['pulit] *n.* piliç.

pul.ley MEC ['puli] *n.* makara; kasnak; *a. set of* ~s palanga.

pull-in ['pulin] = *pull-up*.

Pull.man car RAIL ['pulmən'kɑ:] *n.* pulman vagon; yataklı vagon.

pull…: '~-o.ver *n.* kazak, süveter; '~-up *n.* mola yeri.

pul.mo.nar.y ANAT ['pʌlmənəri] *adj.* akciğere ait, akciğer…

pulp [pʌlp] **1.** *n.* meyve *veya* sebze eti; lapa; MEC kâğıt hamuru; *a.* ~ *magazine* Am. ucuz dergi; **2.** *v/t.* & *v/i.* lapalaş(tır)mak; hamurlaş(tır)mak (*kâğıt*).

pul.pit ['pulpit] *n.* mimber, kürsü.

pulp.y ☐ ['pʌlpi] etli, özlü, yumuşak.

pul.sate ['pʌl'seit] *v/t.* & *v/i.* nabız gibi atmak, yürek gibi çarpmak, nabız gibi kımıldamak, titre(t)mek, titreşmek; pulsa.tile MUS ['‿sətail] *adj.* ritmik…; pul.sation [‿'seiʃən] *n.* nabız (atışı).

pulse[1] [pʌls] **1.** *n.* nabız (atışı); **2.** *v/i.* nabız atmak, çarpmak.

pulse[2] [‿] *n.* baklagiller, bakliyat.

pul.ver.i.za.tion [pʌlvərai'zeiʃən] *n.* ezme, toz haline getirme; 'pul.ver.ize *v/t.* ezmek, toz haline getirmek; *fig.* mahvetmek; *v/i.* toz haline gelmek; 'pul.ver.iz.er *n.* toz haline getiren kimse *veya* alet.

pu.ma zoo ['pju:mə] *n.* puma.
pum.ice ['pʌmis] *n.*, *a.* **~-stone** süngertaşı.
pum.mel ['pʌml] *v/t.* yumruklamak, dövmek.
pump¹ [pʌmp] **1.** *n.* tulumba, pompa; *attr.* pompa...; **2.** *v/t.* tulumba ile çekmek; pompa ile şişirmek (*lastik vs.*); pompa ile basmak (*hava*); F ağzını aramak; *sl.* zorla sokmak (*kafasına*); *v/i.* tulumba işletmek.
pump² [-] *n.* iskarpin.
pump.kin BOT ['pʌmpkin] *n.* helvacıkabağı.
pump-room ['pʌmprum] *n.* kaplıcada şifalı suyun bulunduğu oda.
pun [pʌn] **1.** *n.* kelime oyunu, söz oyunu, cinas; **2.** *v/i.* kelime oyunu yapmak.
Punch¹ [pʌntʃ] *n.* bodur ve kambur kukla; **~ and Judy show** ['dʒu:di] İngiltere'de kukla oyunu.
punch² [-] **1.** *n.* MEC zımba, delgi, matkap, ıstampa; **2.** *v/t.* zımbalamak, zımba ile açmak (*delik*), ıstampa ile basmak; biz ile delmek.
punch³ [-] **1.** *n.* yumruk, muşta; F etki, tesir; *fig.* enerji, kuvvet; **2.** *vb.* yumruklamak; *Am.* gütmek (*sığır vs.*).
punch⁴ [-] *n.* meşrubat, punç.
pun.cheon ['pʌntʃən] *n.* çatı direği; zımba; şarap fıçısı; 320 litrelik şarap ölçüsü.
punch.er ['pʌntʃə] *n.* zımba; F kavgacı kimse; *Am.* kovboy; '**punch.ing-ball** *n.* boksörlerin antrenman için kullandıkları torba.
punc.til.i.o [pʌŋk'tiliəu] *n.* titizlik; formalite ve görgü kurallarına düşkünlük; = **punctiliousness**; **punc.til.i.ous** [-'tiliəs] *adj.* merasime (*veya* resmiyete) düşkün, titiz; **punc'til.i.ous.ness** *n.* titizlik.
punc.tu.al ['pʌŋktʃuəl] tam zamanında gelen, dakik; **punc.tu.al.i.ty** [-'eliti] *n.* dakiklik, şaşmazlık.
punc.tu.ate ['pʌŋktʃueit] *v/t.* noktalamak; *fig.* kesmek (*sözünü*); **punc.tu-'a.tion** *n.* noktalama (kuralı).
punc.ture ['pʌŋktʃə] **1.** *n.* delik (delme); MOT lastik patlaması; patlak; **have a ~** lastiği patlamak **2.** *v/t. & v/i.* patla(t)mak, delmek.
pun.dit ['pʌndit] *n.* Hindu dini bilgini; bilgin, âlim, üstat; F bilgiç, ukalâ kimse.
pun.gen.cy ['pʌndʒənsi] *n.* keskinlik, acılık (*a. fig.*); '**pun.gent** *adj.* sert,

acı, keskin, tesirli, iğneleyici (*söz*).
pun.ish ['pʌniʃ] *v/t.* cezalandırmak; kötü dövmek, hırpalamak; yola getirmek; azarlamak; F silip süpürmek (*içki, yemek vs.*); '**pun.ish.a.ble** □ cezalandırılabilir; cezayı hak etmiş; '**pun.ish.er** *n.* cezalandıran kimse; '**pun.ish.ment** *n.* ceza(landırma).
pu.ni.tive ['pju:nitiv] *adj.* cezalandırıcı; ceza...; cezayı gerektirici.
punk¹ *Am.* [pʌŋk] **1.** *n.* çürük tahta; kav; F değersiz şey, boş laf, saçma; *sl.* ciğeri beş para etmez adam; **2.** *adj. sl.* kalitesiz, değersiz; rahatsız, hasta.
punk² [-] *n.* «**punk rock**» hayranı kimse; it, kopuk, serseri; **~ rock** *s.* **pop music**.
pun.ster ['pʌnstə] *n.* kelime oyunu yapan kimse.
punt¹ NAUT [pʌnt] **1.** *n.* altı düz kayık; **2.** *v/t.* sırıkla yüzdürmek; kayık ile taşımak; *v/i.* sandalla gitmek.
punt² [-] *vb.* yere düşmeden vurmak (*topa*).
pu.ny □ ['pju:ni] çelimsiz, zayıf; önemsiz, ufak.
pup [pʌp] **1.** = **puppy**; **2.** *v/i.* yavrulamak (*köpek*).
pu.pa zoo ['pju:pə] *n.* krizalit.
pu.pil ['pju:pl] *n.* ANAT gözbebeği; öğrenci, talebe; **pu.pil.(l)age** ['-pilidʒ] *n.* öğrencilik; küçüklük.
pup.pet ['pʌpit] *n.* kukla (*a. fig.*); '**~-show** *n.* kukla oyunu.
pup.py ['pʌpi] *n.* köpek yavrusu; *fig.* züppe genç.
pur.blind ['pə:blaind] *adj.* yarı kör; *fig.* mankafa, ahmak, gabi.
pur.chase ['pə:tʃəs] **1.** *n.* satın alma, alım; satın alınan şey; sıkı tutma, kavrama; MEC makara; bedel; **make ~s** alışveriş yapmak, öteberi almak; **at twenty years'~** yirmi yıllık gelirine bedel; **his life is not worth an hour's ~** bir saatlik ömrü kaldı; **2.** *v/t.* satın almak; *fig.* gayretle elde etm., kazanmak; MEC manivela ile kaldırmak *veya* çekmek; '**pur.chas.er** *n.* alıcı, müşteri.
pure □ ['pjuə] *com.* saf(i), halis, som, has, temiz; kusursuz, lekesiz; kuramsal, teorik; namuslu, masum; '**~-bred** *adj. Am.* saf kan; **pu.rée** ['pjuərei] *n.* püre, ezme; '**pure.ness** *n.* safilik, temizlik; iffet; nezaket.
pur.ga.tion [pə:'geiʃən] *n.* mst *fig.* temizleme, paklama, arındırma (*günahtan*); MED müshil ile bağırsakların te-

mizlenmesi; **pur.ga.tive** MED ['‑gətiv]
1. *adj.* müshil; **2.** *n.* müshil, sürgün ilâcı;
'**pur.ga.to.ry** *n.* ECCL Araf.

purge [pə:dʒ] **1.** *n.* MED müshil ilâcı; POL
tasfiye; **2.** *n. mst fig.* temizlemek, pak‑
lamak, arındırmak (**of, from** ‑*den*); POL
tasfiye etm.; MED ishal (*veya* amel) ver‑
mek.

pu.ri.fi.ca.tion [pjuərifi'keiʃən] *n.* te‑
mizleme; tasfiye; **pu.ri.fi.er** ['‑faiə]
n. temizleyici (*part. alet*); **pu.ri.fy**
['‑fai] *v/t.* temizlemek, paklamak
(**of, from** ‑*den*); MEC arıtmak; *fig.* ıslah
etm.

Pu.ri.tan ['pjuəritən] **1.** *n.* Püriten, mu‑
taassıp Protestan; **2.** *adj.* sofu, mu‑
taassıp; **pu.ri.tan.ic** [‑'tænik] *adj.*
(**~ally**) sofu; **Pu.ri.tan.ism** ['‑tənizəm]
n. sofuluk.

pu.ri.ty ['pjuəriti] *n.* temizlik, haslık,
saflık (*a. fig.*); iffet; nezaket.

purl[1] [pə:l] *n.* dantela için sırma teli;
yün örgüsünde ters iğne; pli.

purl[2] [‑] **1.** *n.* çağıltı, şırıltı; **2.** *v/i.* çağıl‑
dayarak akmak.

purl.er F ['pə:lə] *n.* şiddetli düşüş;
come a ~ baş aşağı düşmek.

pur.lieus ['pə:lju:z] *n.* dış mahalleler,
etraf, hudut, civar, çevre.

pur.loin [pə:'lɔin] *v/t.* çalmak, aşırmak;
pur'loin.er *n.* hırsız.

pur.ple ['pə:pl] **1.** *adj.* mor, erguvanî; **~**
passage süslü yazı; **2.** *n.* mor, erguva‑
nî, eflatun renk; **3.** *v/t.* mor renge bo‑
yamak; *v/i.* mor rengini almak; '**pur‑**
plish *adj.* morumsu, eflatunî.

pur.port ['pə:pət] **1.** *n.* anlam, mana,
kavram; **2.** *v/t.* …anlamında olm., de‑
lâlet etm. ‑*e*, göstermek; iddia etm.

pur.pose ['pə:pəs] **1.** *n.* maksat, niyet,
meram, murat, amaç; karar; **for the**
~ of …maksadıyle; **on ~** isteyerek, kas‑
ten, mahsus, bile bile; **to the ~** isabetli,
yerinde, asıl konu ile ilgili; **to no ~** fay‑
dasızca, boşuna, boş yere; **2.** *v/t.* niyet
etm., tasarlamak; istemek; **pur.pose‑**
ful [] ['‑ful] maksatlı; önemli; anlamlı,
manalı; '**pur.pose.less** [] manasız;
amaçsız, maksatsız; '**pur.pose.ly** *adv.*
bile bile, kasten, mahsus.

purr [pə:] **1.** *v/i.* mırlamak (*kedi*); *v/t.*
mırıldanmak; **2.** *n.* kedi mırlaması.

purse [pə:s] **1.** *n.* para kesesi; *Am.* el
çantası; yardım parası, fon; hazine;
public ~ devlet hazinesi; **2.** *v/t. oft.* **~**
up büzmek, bükmek (*dudak*); keseye
koymak; '**~proud** *adj.* parasına güve‑

nen; '**purs.er** *n.* NAUT gemi muhasebe‑
cisi *veya* veznedarı; '**purse‑strings** *n.*:
hold the ~ para işini idare etm.; **loosen**
the ~ kesenin ağzını açmak.

pur.si.ness ['pə:sinis] *n.* tıknefeslik;
şişmanlık.

purs.lane BOT ['pə:slin] *n.* semizotu.

pur.su.ance [pə'sju:əns] *n.* takip et‑
me; devam; ifa; tatbik; *in* **~ of** ifa eder‑
ken, yaparken; **pur'su.ant** []: **~ to** uy‑
gun olarak ‑*e*, gereğince.

pur.sue [pə'sju:] *v/t. & v/i.* takip etm.,
izlemek, kovalamak, peşine düşmek;
devam etm. ‑*e*, sürdürmek; aramak;
fig. ‑in peşini bırakmamak (*talihsizlik*
vs.); ardı sıra gitmek; **~ after** takip
etm., izlemek; **pur'su.er** *n.* takip eden
kimse; JUR davacı; **pur.suit** [pə'sju:t]
n. kovalama, takip, izleme, arama
(**of** ‑*i*); *mst.* **~s** *pl.* iş, meşguliyet,
uğraş; **~ plane** avcı uçağı; **pur.sui.vant**
['pə:sivənt] *n.* izleyen kimse; refakat‑
çi, teşrifatçı.

pur.sy[1] ['pə:si] *adj.* şişman; tıknefes.

pur.sy[2] [‑] *adj.* büzülmüş (*dudak vs.*);
buruşuk, kırışık; servetine güvenen.

pu.ru.lent [] ['pjuərulənt] cerahatli,
irinli.

pur.vey [pə:'vei] *v/t.* tedarik etm., sağ‑
lamak, temin etm.; *v/i.* **~ for** erzak te‑
min etm. ‑*e*; **pur'vey.ance** *n.* sağlama,
tedarik etme; **pur'vey.or** *n.* satıcı, te‑
min eden kimse (*part. erzak*).

pur.view ['pə:vju:] *n.* konu; saha; faali‑
yet (alanı).

pus [pʌs] *n.* irin, cerahat.

push [puʃ] **1.** *n.* itiş, kakış, dürtüş; giriş‑
kenlik, teşebbüs; çaba, güç, gayret;
ilerleme, hücum, atak; azim; **at a ~** ge‑
rekirse, gerektiğinde, icabında; **when**
it comes to the ~ sıkışınca, iş esasa bi‑
nince; **get the ~** *sl.* kovulmak, sebep‑
lenmek; **give s.o. the ~** *sl. b‑ne* yol ver‑
mek, kovmak, sepetlemek; **2.** *v/t.* it‑
mek, dürtmek; sürmek, sevketmek;
yürütmek; saldırmak; *fig.* sıkıştırmak;
basmak (*düğmeye vs.*); kanunsuz yol‑
dan satmak (*uyuşturucu madde*); *a.* **~**
through çaba harcayarak kabul ettir‑
mek, geçirmek, (*tasarı vs.*); **~ s.th.**
on s.o. *bşi b‑ne* zorla kabul ettirmek;
~ one's way başarılı olm., yükselmek;
ite kaka ilerlemek; **be ~ed for time**
(**money**) vakti (eli) dar olm.; **she is**
~ing thirty otuza merdiven dayadı;
v/i. itişip kakışmak; hücum etm.;
uğraşmak (**for** için); **~ along, ~ on, ~**

forward devam etm., ileri sürmek; ~ *off* avara etm. (*kayık*); F (çekip) gitmek; '~-ball *n*. bir çeşit top oyunu; '~-bike *n*. bisiklet; '~-but.ton *n*. ELECT pusbuton, elektrik düğmesi; 'push.er *n*. fırsat düşkünü kimse; uyuşturucu madde satan kimse; *Am*. RAIL itici lokomotif; push.ful □ ['.ful], 'push.ing □ girişken, enerjik; *b.s.* sırnaşık, küstah; 'push-off *n*. baş(langıç); '~-o.ver *n*. *part*. *Am*. çok kolay iş, çocuk oyuncağı; kolay aldanır kimse; 'push-up *n*. şınav.

pu.sil.la.nim.i.ty [pju:silə'nimiti] *n*. çekingenlik, ürkeklik, korkaklık; pu-sil.lan.imous □ [.'lænimos] korkak, ürkek, yüreksiz, çekingen, pısırık.

puss [pus] *n*. kedi; *fig*. kız; *sl*. surat; 'puss.y *n*. BOT söğüt tırtılsısı; *a*. ~-*cat* kedi; 'puss.y.foot *Am*. F **1.** *n*. sır küpü (*veya* fikrini belirtmeyen) kimse; **2.** *v/i*. F fikrini belirtmemek; kedi gibi sessizce yürümek; çok tedbirli davranmak.

pus.tule MED ['pʌstju:l] *n*. sivilce, kabarcık, püstül.

put [put] (*irr*.) **1.** *v/t*. koymak, yerleştirmek, sokmak, takmak (**on, to** *-e*); maruz bırakmak; söylemek, öne sürmek; oya koymak; kelimelerle ifade etm.; tercüme etm.; uyarlamak; adamak; sevketmek, zorlamak; tahrik etm., kışkırtmak; yatırmak; tahmin etm. (*at olarak*); yazmak; işaretlemek; avucu yukarı doğru tutarak atmak (*gülle*); ~ *about* yaymak (*dedikodu*); NAUT çevirmek (*geminin başını*); ~ *across sl*. başarı ile yapmak; yutturmak; ~ *away* kaldırmak, yerine koymak; biriktirmek, bir kenara ayırmak (*para*); vazgeçmek; *sl*. öldürmek; F tımarhaneye kapatmak; *sl*. silip süpürmek; ~ *back* NAUT geri dönmek; geri koymak, yerine koymak; geri almak (*saat*); *fig*. geriletmek, sekte vurmak; ~ *by* biriktirmek, bir kenara ayırmak (*para*); ~ *down* indirmek, yere koymak; yerleştirmek; bastırmak (*ayaklanma vs.*); susturmak; yazmak, kaydetmek (*for -e*); geçirmek (*to -e*); yüklemek, vermek (*to -e*); koymak (*as, for yerine*); ~ *forth* ileri sürmek; çıkarmak, yayımlamak; sürmek (*tomurcuk*); ortaya koymak; ~ *forward* ileri sürmek, ortaya atmak; ileri almak (*saat*); ~ *o.s. forward* k-ni öne sürmek, sokulmak; adaylığını koymak; ~ *in* başvurmak (*for için*); sokmak; yerleştirmek; arzetmek, sunmak;

vurmak (*yumruk*); söylemek (*söz*); yapmak; seçmek; F geçirmek (*vakit*); ~ *in an hour's work* bir saatlik iş yapmak; ~ *off* sonraya bırakmak, tehir etm., ertelemek; çıkarmak (*elbise*); engellemek; vazgeçirmek; *fig*. bırakmak, üstünden atmak (*korku, şüphe vs.*); ~ *on* giymek (*elbise*); takınmak (*tavır*); COM eklemek (*to -e*); açmak; artırmak; koymak (*ek sefer vs.*); THEAT sahneye koymak (*oyun*); ileri almak (*saat*); F aldatmak; *he is ~ting it on* abartıyor; ~ *it on thick* abartmak, izam etm.; ~ *on airs* hava atmak, caka satmak; ~ *on weight* kilo almak, şişmanlamak; ~ *out* söndürmek (*ışık, ateş vs.*); çıkarmak; faize vermek (*para*); üretmek; kovmak; yayınlamak (*haber vs.*); sinirlendirmek; şaşırtmak; rahatsız etm.; ~ *out of action* faaliyet dışı bırakmak, işe yaramaz hale sokmak; ~ *over* başarmak; ertelemek, tehir etm.; ~ *o.s. over* etkilemek; ~ *right* düzeltmek, düzene koymak; ~ *through* TELEPH bağlamak (*to -e*); tabi tutmak (*test vs.*); F gerçekleştirmek, yapmak, yürütmek (*iş vs.*); ~ *s.o. through it* F *b-nin* yeteneğini ölçmek; ~ *to* ilâve etm., birleştirmek; sunmak; arzusuna bırakmak; açıklamak; *be* (*hard*) ~ *to it* akla karayı seçmek, çok sıkıntı çekmek; ~ *to expense* masrafa sokmak; ~ *to death* öldürmek; ~ *to the rack veya torture* eziyet etm., işkence etm.; ~ *together* birleştirmek, biraraya getirmek, monte etm.; kafasında toplamak (*fikir, düşünce vs.*); ~ *up* kaldırmak; çekmek (*bayrak vs.*); kurmak (*çadır vs.*); inşa etm.; asmak (*ilan vs.*); artırmak, yükseltmek; ortaya koymak; sağlamak, temin etm. (*para*); kınına sokmak (*kılıç*); salıvermek (*hayvan*); toplamak (*saç*); misafir etm.; aday göstermek (*for için*); ~ *s.o. up to s.th. b-ni bşe* teşvik etm., kışkırtmak; **2.** *v/i*. acele gitmek; NAUT yol almak; ~ *off*, ~ *out*, ~ *to sea* NAUT denize açılmak; ~ *in* NAUT limana girmek; ~ *up at* konaklamak, gecelemek; ~ *up for* adaylığını koymak *-e*; ~ *up with* katlanmak *-e*, çekmek *-i*, tahammül etm. *-e*.

pu.ta.tive ['pju:tətiv] *adj*. farzedilen, varsayılan.

put.log MEC ['pʌtlɔg] *n*. iskele kirişi.

pu.tre.fac.tion [pju:tri'fækʃən] *n*. kokma, çürüme, bozulma; çürümüş şey; pu.tre'fac.tive [.tiv] *adj*. çürütücü.

pu.tre.fy ['pju:trifai] v/t. & v/i. çürü(t)-mek, kok(ut)mak, bozulmak, kokuş-mak.

pu.tres.cence [pju:'tresns] n. çürük-lük, bozukluk; pu'tres.cent adj. çürü-yen, çürümekte olan.

pu.trid □ ['pju:trid] çürük, bozuk, kok-muş; sl. iğrenç; pu'trid.i.ty n. çürüklük; çürük şey.

putt [pʌt] golf: 1. vb. deliğe sokmak için topa hafifçe vurmak; 2. n. topu deliğe sokmak için yapılan hafif vuruş.

put.tee ['pʌti] n. dolak.

putt.er ['pʌtə] n. golf: golf sopası.

put.ty ['pʌti] 1. n. a. glaziers' ~ camcı macunu; a. plasterers' ~ sıva, harç; 2. vb. macunlamak.

put-up job ['put'ʌp'dʒɔb] n. hile(li iş).

puz.zle ['pʌzl] 1. n. bilmece, bulmaca; mesele, sorun; şaşkınlık, hayret; 2. v/t. & v/i. şaşır(t)mak, hayrete düş(ür)mek; düşündürmek; çok düşünmek (over -i); ~ one's brains ka-fa patlatmak, zihnini yormak; ~ out kafa yorarak çözmek; '~-head.ed adj. şaşırmış, kafası bulanık; 'puz.zler n. güç durum, karışık mesele; anlaşıl-maz kişi.

pyg.m(a)e.an [pig'mi:ən] adj. cüce...; pygmy ['pigmi] n. pigme; fig. cüce, bo-dur kimse; attr. cüce...

py.ja.mas [pə'dʒɑːməz] n. pl. pijama.

py.lon ['pailən] n. pilon, çelik telgraf di-reği.

py.lo.rus ANAT [pai'lɔːrəs] n. pilor, mi-de kapısı.

py.or.rh(o)e.a MED [paiə'riə] n. piyore, dişeti iltihabı.

pyr.a.mid ['pirəmid] n. piramit, ehram; py.ram.i.dal □ [pi'ræmidl] piramit şeklinde.

pyre ['paiə] n. odun yığını (part. ölüleri yakmak için).

py.ri.tes [pai'raiti:z] n.: copper ~ bakır sülfid; iron ~ demir sülfid, pirit.

py.ro... ['paiərəu] prefix ateş veya ısı ile ilgili, ateş..., ısı...; py.rog.ra.phy [pai'rɔgrəfi] n. pirogravür; py.ro-tech.nic, py.ro.tech.ni.cal [pairəu-'teknik(əl)] adj. fişeklere veya fişekçi-liğe ait; py.ro'technics n. pl. fişekçilik; fişek eğlenceleri; fig. ortalığı birbirine katan hareket; pyro'tech.nist n. fişek-çi.

Pyr.rhic vic.to.ry ['pirik'viktəri] n. bü-yük kayıp verilerek kazanılan başarı.

Py.thag.o.re.an [paiθægə'ri:ən] 1. adj. Pitagor'a ait; 2. n. Pitagor taraftarı kimse.

Pyth.i.an ['piθiən] adj. Apollon'a ait.

py.thon ['paiθən] n. piton yılanı.

pyx [piks] n. ECCL Katolik kilisesinde kutsal ekmeğin konulduğu kutu.

Q

Q-boat NAUT ['kju:bəut] n. düşman de-nizaltılarını tuzağa düşüren ticaret ve-ya balıkçı gemisi görünümündeki ge-mi.

quack¹ [kwæk] 1. n. ördek sesi, vak vak; 2. v/i. ördek gibi bağırmak, 'vak vak' etm.

quack² [_] 1. n. doktor taslağı, şarlatan, yalancı doktor; 2. adj. şarlatan...; 3. v/i. şarlatanlık etm.; quack.er.y ['_əri] n. şarlatanlık.

quad [kwɔd] = quadrangle, quadrat.

quad.ra.ge.nar.i.an [kwɔdrədʒi'neəri-ən] 1. adj. kırk ile elli yaşları arasında olan (kimse); 2. n. kırk ile elli yaşları arasındaki kimse.

quad.ran.gle ['kwɔdræŋgl] n. dörtgen; avlu, bahçe (okul vs.).

quad.rant ['kwɔdrənt] n. oktant, yük-seklik ölçme aleti; part. MATH çeyrek daire.

quad.rat TYP ['kwɔdræt] n. katrat; quadrat.ic MATH [kwɔ'drætik] 1. adj. dörtgen gibi; MATH ikinci dereceden; 2. n.: ~ equation ikinci dereceden denklem; quad.ra.ture ['kwɔdrətʃə] n. kare yapma; MATH alan hesabı; AST dördün.

quad.ren.ni.al □ [kwɔ'drenjəl] dört senede bir olan; dört sene süren.

quad.ri.lat.er.al MATH [kwɔdri'lætərəl] 1. adj. dört kenarlı; 2. n. dörtgen, dört-kenar.

qua.drille [kwə'dril] n. kadril dansı (müziği).

quad.ri.par.tite [kwɔdri'pɑːtait] adj. dört taraflı, dört kısımlı.

quad.ru.ped ['kwɔdruped] 1. n. dört

ayaklı hayvan; **2.** *adj. a.* **quad.ru.pe-dal** [kwɔ'druːpidl] dört ayaklı (*hayvan*); **quadru.ple** ['kwɔdrupl] **1.** ☐ dört kısımlı; dört kişilik; *a.* ~ **to**, ~ **of** dört misli, dört katı -*in*; **2.** *n. bşin* dört misli; **3.** *v/t. & v/i.* dört misli çoğal(t)mak, art(ır)mak; **quad.ru.plet** ['kwɔdruplit] *n.* dördüzlerden biri; **quadru.pli.cate 1.** [kwɔ'druːplikit] *adj.* dört kat, dört misli; **2.** [-keit] *v/t.* dörtle çarpmak; dört misli çoğaltmak.

quaff [kwɑːf] *vb.* (bir yudumda) içmek; ~ **off** kana kana içmek.

quag [kwæg] = ~**mire**; '**quag.gy** *adj.* bataklık gibi; gevşek, yumuşak; **quag-mire** ['-maiə] *n.* batak(lık).

quail[1] ORN [kweil] *n.* bıldırcın.

quail[2] [-] *v/i.* yılmak, sinmek, ürkmek, korkmak.

quaint ☐ [kweint] tuhaf, acayip, antika, orijinal, garip ve hoş; '**quaint.ness** *n.* tuhaflık, antikalık, garip hoşluk.

quake [kweik] **1.** *v/i.* sallanmak, sarsılmak; titremek (**with**, **for**-*den*); **2.** *n.* sallantı; zelzele, deprem; titreme, ürperme.

Quak.er ['kweikə] *n.* Kuveykır mezhebinin üyesi.

qual.i.fi.ca.tion [kwɔlifi'keiʃən] *n.* nitelik, vasıf, meziyet, ehliyet; şart; kayıt, kısıtlama; GR niteleme; **qual.i.fied** ['-faid] *adj.* ehliyetli, vasıflı, kalifiye; şartlı; kısıtlı, sınırlı; **qual.i.fy** ['-fai] *v/t. & v/i.* hak kazan(dır)mak, ehliyetli kılmak; kısıtlamak, sınırla(ndır)mak; hafifletmek; nitelendirmek; tanımlamak, tasvir etm.; GR nitelemek; ehliyet göstermek; **qualifying examination** eleme sınavı, yeterlilik imtihanı; **qual.i.ta.tive** ☐ ['-tətiv] niteliğe ait, nitel(e-yici); '**qual.i.ty** *n.* kalite; nitelik, vasıf; özellik, hususiyet; üstünlük; çeşit, sınıf, nevi; ~ **time** *başka birisine gerçekten ilgi ve dikkat gösterilerek geçirilen zaman.*

qualm [kwɑːm] *n.* vicdan azabı, pişmanlık; bulantı; şüphe, huzursuzluk, kuruntu, kuşku; '**qualm.ish** ☐ mide bulandırıcı, tiksindirici; midesi çabuk bulanan; vicdanının sesini dinleyen.

quan.da.ry ['kwɔndəri] *n.* şüphe, tereddüt, hayret, şaşkınlık; müşkül durum, ikilem.

quan.ti.ta.tive ☐ ['kwɔntitətiv] nicel, niceliğe ait; '**quan.ti.ty** *n.* nicelik, nicelik (*a.* MATH); miktar; ~**s** *pl.* bolluk, çokluk, çok miktar; ~ **surveyor** yapı

malzeme tahmincisi.

quan.tum ['kwɔntəm] *n.* miktar, meblağ, tutar; pay, hisse; ~ **theory** PHYS kuantum teorisi.

quar.an.tine ['kwɔrəntiːn] **1.** *n.* karantina; **2.** *v/t.* karantina altına almak.

quar.rel ['kwɔrəl] **1.** *n.* kavga, münakaşa, çekişme, bozuşma; **2.** *v/i.* kavga etm., münakaşa etm., çekişmek, bozuşmak; **quar.rel.some** ['-səm] ☐ kavgacı, ters, huysuz.

quar.ry[1] ['kwɔri] **1.** *n.* taş ocağı; *fig.* zengin kaynak, maden; **2.** *vb.* taş ocağından kazıp çıkarmak; araştırmak (**for** -*i*).

quar.ry[2] [-] *n.* av (*a. fig.*).

quar.ry.man ['kwɔrimən] *n.* taş ocağı işçisi.

quart [kwɔːt] *n.* kuart, galonun dörtte biri (*1,136 I, Am. 0,946 I*); FENC [kaːt] bir duruş şekli.

quar.ter ['kwɔːtə] **1.** *n.* dörtte bir, çeyrek; *part.* çeyrek saat; üç aylık süre; *Am.* 25 sent; NAUT kıç; NAUT gemide tayfanın gözere yeri; MIL aman, hayatını bağışlama; *fig.* hoşgörü, müsamaha; *fig.* yön, istikamet; taraf, civar, bölge, havali, semt, mahalle; ~**s** *pl.* MIL kışla, ordugâh, konak; *fig.* kaynak; dördün **live in close** ~**s** yakında oturmak; **at close** ~**s** yan yana, çok yakından; **come to close** ~**s** göğüs göğüse dövüşmek; **2.** *v/t.* dörde ayırmak, bölmek; parçalara ayırmak; MIL yerleştirmek (*asker*); '~**.back** *n. Am. spor.* oyunu idare eden oyuncu; '~**-deck** *n.* kıç güvertesi; savaş gemisi *veya* donanmanın subayları; '**quar.ter.ly 1.** *adj. & adv.* üç aylık, üç ayda bir (olan); **2.** *n.* üç ayda bir çıkan dergi; '**quar.ter.master** *n.* MIL levazım subayı; NAUT serdümen; **quartern** ['-tən] *n.* bir ölçünün dörtte biri; *a.* ~**-loaf** dört librelik ekmek somunu; '**quar.ter.staff** *n.* eskiden silah olarak kullanılan sopa.

quar.tet(te) MUS [kwɔː'tet] *n.* kuartet, dörtlü müzik topluluğu; dört ses *veya* çalgı ile yapılan müzik parçası.

quar.to ['kwɔːtəu] *n.* dört yapraklık forma.

quartz MIN [kwɔːts] *n.* kuvars; **quartzite** ['-ait] *n.* kuvarsit.

quash JUR [kwɔʃ] *v/t.* iptal etm., feshetmek, kaldırmak, bozmak.

qua.si ['kwɑːziː] *prefix* güya, sanki, sözümona.

qua.ter.na.ry [kwə'təːnəri] *adj.* dördüncü; dörtlü; GEOL son zamana ait.

qua.ver ['kweivə] **1.** *n.* titreme; MUS ses titremesi; MUS sekizlik; **2.** *vb.* titremek (*ses*); titrek sesle söylemek (*şarkı vs.*); 'quaver.y *adj.* titrek.

quay [ki:] *n.* rıhtım, iskele; **quay.age** ['ˌ-idʒ] *n.* iskele ücreti.

quea.si.ness ['kwi:zinis] *n.* bulantı, mide bulanması; 'quea.sy □ mide bulandırıcı (*yiyecek*); midesi kolayca bulanan; midesi bulanmış, kusacak durumda; titiz, müşkülpesent; kılı kırk yaran; **I feel ~** midem bulanıyor.

queen [kwi:n] **1.** *n.* kraliçe; *satranç:* vezir; *iskambil:* kız; *sl.* ibne; **~ bee** arı beyi, ana arı; **~'s ware** krem renginde bir tür İngiliz çömleği; **2.** *v/t. satranç:* vezir çıkmak; kraliçe olarak saltanat sürmek; (*bir kadını*) kraliçe yapmak; **~ it** caka satmak, hava atmak (**over** -*e*); 'queen.like, 'queen.ly *adj.* kraliçe gibi; kraliçeye yaraşır; haşmetli, muhteşem.

queer [kwiə] **1.** *adj.* acayip, tuhaf, garip, alışılmamış; şüpheli; F rahatsız, hasta; F deli, kaçık; F sarhoş; F sahte, kalp; F homoseksüel; **2.** *v/t.* bozmak; **~ s.o.'s pitch** *sl. b-nin* planını bozmak, işine engel olm.; **3.** *n.* homoseksüel kimse.

quell RHET [kwel] *v/t.* bastırmak (*ayaklanma vs.*), ezmek, boyun eğdirmek; yatıştırmak.

quench [kwentʃ] *v/t. fig.* gidermek (*susuzluk, hararet*); söndürmek (*ateş, yangın*); son vermek; bastırmak (*ayaklanma vs.*); su ile soğutmak (*çelik*); 'quench.er *n.* F içki; quench.less □ söndürülemeyen (*ateş, alev vs.*); giderilemez.

que.rist ['kwiərist] *n.* soruşturma yapan kimse.

quern [kwə:n] *n.* el değirmeni.

quer.u.lous □ ['kwerʊləs] yakınan, şikâyetçi, titiz, ters, aksi, huysuz.

que.ry ['kwiəri] **1.** *n.* soru (işareti), sual, sorgu; şüphe, kuşku; **2.** *v/t.* sormak -*e*, araştırmak; koymak (*soru işareti*); şüphelenmek, kuşku duymak -*den*.

quest [kwest] **1.** *n.* ara(ştır)ma; soruşturma; macera; **in ~ of** ...aramak için, aramaya, -*in* peşinde; **2.** *vb.* ara(ştır)-mak; av izini aramak (*köpek*).

ques.tion ['kwestʃən] **1.** *n.* soru, sual; mesele, konu, sorun; şüphe, kuşku; teklif, öneri; ihtimal, imkân, şans; sorgu, soruşturma; **~!** PARL konuya gelelim!, konu dışına çıkmayalım!; **be-**

yond (**all**) **~** elbette, şüphesiz; **in ~** söz konusu olan; **come into ~** konu olm., tartışılmak; **call in ~** şüphe etm., itiraz etm.; **beg the ~** söz konusu meseleyi etkin olarak cevaplandırma-mak; **the ~ is** mesele şu ki; **that is out of the ~** bu söz konusu olamaz, imkânsızdır, olanak yok; **there is no ~ of** *veya* **of** ger. söz konusu değil, sözü edilmez; **2.** *v/t.* sual (*veya* soru) sormak -*e*; sorguya çekmek -*i*; şüphe etm. -*den*, kuşku duymak -*den*; 'ques.tion.a.ble □ şüpheli, kuşkulu; kesin olmayan; 'question.a.ble.ness *n.* şüpheli durum; 'question.er *n.* soru soran *veya* sorguya çeken kimse; ques.tion.naire [kwestʃə'nɛə] *n.* anket; soru kâğıdı.

queue [kju:] **1.** *n.* kuyruk, sıra, bekleyen halk *veya* araba dizisi; saç kuyruğu; **2.** *v/i. mst* **~ up** kuyruğa girmek, kuyruk olm.

quib.ble ['kwibl] **1.** *n.* kaçamaklı cevap *veya* söz, yanıltmaca; **2.** *v/i.* kaçamaklı cevap vermek; önemsiz konu üzerinde durmak; 'quib.bler *n.* safsatacı kimse.

quick [kwik] **1.** *adj.* çabuk, hızlı, tez, süratli, seri; keskin, anlayışlı; işlek, faal; akıllı, zeki, titiz, çabuk kızan; canlı, parlak; **~ march** MIL hızlı yürüyüş; **2.** *n.* tırnak altındaki hassas et; can alıcı nokta; **the ~** *pl.* canlılar; **to the ~** tırnak altındaki hassas ete kadar; *fig.* en hassas noktaya kadar; **cut s.o. to the ~** *b-ni* can evinden vurmak, duygularını incitmek; **3.** *s.* **~.ly**; '~-change ac.tor kostüm *veya* görünüşünü sık değiştiren aktör; 'quicken *v/t.* & *v/i.* hızlan(dır)mak, çabuklaş(tır)mak; canlan(dır)mak, diril(t)mek; neşe-len(dir)mek, heveslen(dir)mek; rahimde hayat belirtisi göstermek (*çocuk*); 'quick-fir.ing *adj.* MIL seri ateşli (*top*); quick.ie ['ˌ-i] *n.* çok çabuk yapılan şey; F kısa metrajlı ucuz film; 'quick.lime *n.* sönmemiş kireç; 'quick.ly *adv.* çabuk(ça), hızlı hızlı, acele; 'quick-match *n.* ateşleme fitili; 'quick-mo.tion pic.ture *film:* hızlı çekim film; 'quick.ness *n.* çabukluk, sürat, hız.

quick...: '~.sand *n.* bataklık kumu; '~.set *n.* AGR çit; *a.* **~ hedge** köklü bitkilerden oluşan çit; '~-sight.ed *adj.* keskin gözlü; '~.sil.ver *n.* MIN civa; '~.step *n.* hareketli dans; MIL hızlı askerî yürüyüş; '~-wit.ted *adj.* çabuk anlayan, zeki, hazırcevap.

quid[1] [kwid] *n.* ağızda çiğnenen tütün parçası.

quid[2] *sl.* [-] *n.* bir sterlin.

quid.di.ty PHLS ['kwiditi] *n.* nitelik, öz; önemsiz konu, safsata.

quid pro quo ['kwid prəu 'kwəu] *n.* karşılık, bedel; ödün, taviz.

qui.es.cence [kwai'esns] *n.* sükûn(et), istirahat, hareketsizlik, pasiflik; **qui-'escent** □ hareketsiz, pasif, istirahatte, sakin; *fig.* uyuşuk.

qui.et ['kwaiət] **1.** □ sessiz, sakin, durgun (*deniz vs.*); hareketsiz, rahat; nazik, yumusak huylu, tatlı, uslu (*çocuk*); gösterişsiz, yumuşak (*renk*); **2. on the ~** (*sl.*: **on the q.t.** ['kju:'ti:]) gizlice, çaktırmadan; **3.** *v/i. a.* **~ down** susmak, yatışmak, sakinlesmek; dinmek; *v/t.* susturmak, yatıştırmak, sakinleştirmek; **'qui.et.en** = **quiet 3**; **qui.et.ism** ['kwaiitizəm] *n.* ECCL dünya olaylarından ilgiyi keserek Tanrı düşüncesine dalma felsefesi; **'qui.et.ist** *n.* bu felsefe taraftarı kimse; **qui.et.ness** ['kwaiət-nis] *n.*, **qui.e.tude** ['kwaiitju:d] sessizlik, sakinlik, durgunluk, sükûnet, rahat.

qui.e.tus [kwai'i:təs] *n.* hesabın ödenip kapanması, aklama, ibra; öldürme; susturma, bastırma.

quill [kwil] **1.** *n.* tüy (kalem); kirpi dikeni; tüy sapı; makara; MUS mızrap; **2.** *vb.* makaraya sarmak (*iplik*); fitilli dikmek (*elbise*); '**~driv.er** *n.* yazar; '**quill.ing** *n.* farbala, fırfır; '**quill-pen** *n.* tüy kalem.

quilt [kwilt] **1.** *n.* yorgan; **2.** *vb.* yorgan gibi dikmek; içine pamuk doldurup yorgan yapmak; '**quilt.ing** *n.* yorgancılık; yorgan yapma; yorganlık malzeme.

quince BOT [kwins] *n.* ayva (ağacı).

qui.nine PHARM [kwi'ni:n, *part. Am.* 'kwainain] *n.* kinin.

quin.qua.ge.nar.i.an [kwiŋkwədʒi-'nɛəriən] **1.** *adj.* elli yaşlarında olan; **2.** *n.* elli yaşlarındaki kimse.

quin.quen.ni.al □ [kwiŋ'kweniəl] beş yılda bir; beş yıl süren.

quins F [kwinz] *n. pl.* beşiz.

quin.sy MED ['kwinzi] *n.* anjin.

quin.tal ['kwintl] *n.* 100 kiloluk ağırlık, kental.

quint.es.sence [kwin'tesns] *n.* öz, cevher, hulâsa, esas nokta.

quin.tu.ple ['kwintjupl] **1.** *adj.* beş kat, beş misli; **2.** *v/t. & v/i.* beş misli art(ır)-mak; beş misli yapmak *veya* olm.;

quin.tu.plets ['-plits] *n. pl.* beşiz.

quip [kwip] *n.* alaylı şaka, hazır cevap, iğneli söz, saçma cevap.

quire ['kwaiə] *n.* 24 tabakalık kâğıt destesi.

quirk [kwə:k] *n.* tuhaflık, acayiplik; garip hareket, delilik; ARCH kabartmalı süslemede aralık *veya* girinti.

quis.ling ['kwizliŋ] *n.* istilâcılarla işbirliği yapan vatan haini.

quit [kwit] **1.** *v/t. & v/i.* terketmek, bırakmak, boşaltmak, çıkmak (*ev*); ayrılmak (*iş*); ödemek (*borç*); durmak, kesilmek, dinmek; gitmek; işten çıkmak; vaz geçmek; **2.** *adj.* kurtulmuş, serbest (*of -den*).

quite [kwait] *adv.* tamamen, bütün bütün, tam tamına, tamamiyle, büsbütün, gerçekten, hakikaten; hayli, epey; **~ a lot** epeyce; defalarca; **~ (so)!**, **that!** gerçekten öyle!, ya öyle!; **~ the thing** F moda olmuş, modaya uygun.

quits [kwits] *adj.* ödeşmiş, fit olmuş, berabere, başabaş (**with** *ile*); **cry ~** ye-ter artık demek.

quit.tance ['kwitəns] *n.* borçtan *veya* yükümden kurtuluş (belgesi); karşılık, bedel, ücret.

quit.ter *Am.* F ['kwitə] *n.* işi bırakan kimse; sözünden dönen kimse.

quiv.er[1] ['kwivə] **1.** *n.* titreme; **2.** *v/t. & v/i.* titre(t)mek, titreş(tir)mek.

quiv.er[2] [-] *n.* ok kılıfı, sadak.

quix.ot.ic [kwik'sɔtik] *adj.* donkişotvari, dünyadan haberi olmayan, romaneks.

quiz [kwiz] **1.** *n.* küçük imtihan; sorgu, test; alay, eğlence; eşek şakası; garip kimse; **2.** *v/t.* sorguya çekmek; imtihan etm.; alay etm., takılmak; küstahça bakmak; '**quiz.zi.cal** □ tuhaf, garip, gülünç; şakacı, alaycı.

quod *sl.* [kwɔd] *n.* kodes, cezaevi.

quoin [kɔin] *n.* duvarın dış köşesi; köşe (taşı); TYP harf takozu.

quoit [kɔit] *n.* oyunda atılan çember, halka; **~s** *pl.* halka oyunu.

quon.dam ['kwɔndæm] *adj.* eski, sabık.

Quon.set *Am.* ['kwɔnsit] *n. a.* **~ hut** çelik baraka.

quo.rum PARL ['kwɔ:rəm] *n.* yetersayı, çoğunluk; **have a ~**, **form a ~** yetersayıyı oluşturmak.

quo.ta ['kwəutə] *n.* hisse, pay, kota, kontenjan.

quot.a.ble ['kwəutəbl] *adj.* aktarılabi-

lir, aktararak söylenebilir.
quo.ta.tion [kwəuˈteiʃən] *n.* aktarma; aktarılan söz; COM fiyat, piyasa rayici, kur; *familiar* ~*s pl.* vecizeler; **quoˈta-tion-marks** *n. pl.* tırnaklar, tırnak işareti.
quote [kwəut] *vb.* (aktarma yolu ile) söylemek, aktarmak, tekrarlamak

(*b-nin sözünü*); tekrar yazmak; COM vermek (*fiyat*) (*at olarak*); tırnak işareti içine almak.
quoth *obs.* [kwəuθ] *v/t.*; ~ *I*, ~ *he* dedim, dedi.
quo.tid.i.an [kwɔˈtidiən] *adj.* her gün olan, günlük.
quo.tient MATH [ˈkwəuʃənt] *n.* bölüm.

R

r [ɑː]: *the three R's* (= *reading, writing, arithmetic*) okuma, yazma ve aritmetik.
rab.bet MEC [ˈræbit] **1.** *n.* ek yeri, dişli yiv, lamba, zıvana yuvası; **2.** *v/t.* içiçe geçirmek, içine sokmak; yiv açmak.
rab.bi [ˈræbai] *n.* haham, Musevi dinî lider.
rab.bit [ˈræbit] *n.* ZOO adatavşanı; F acemi oyuncu; '~-**fe.ver** *n.* bir tür veba, tularemi.
rab.ble [ˈræbl] *n.* ayaktakımı, düzensiz kalabalık; '~-**rous.er** *n.* demagog, halk avcısı.
rab.id ☐ [ˈræbid] kudurmuş (*hayvan*); *fig.* aşırı, bağnaz; yabanî, vahşi; hiddetli, gazaplı, öfkeli; '**rab.id.ness** *n.* kudurmuşluk, kuduzluk, cinnet, delilik, çılgınlık, kaçıklık.
ra.bies VET [ˈreibiːz] *n.* kuduz (hastalığı).
rac.coon [rəˈkuːn] = *racoon.*
race[1] [reis] *n.* ırk, soy; nesil, döl, tür, cins; familya, aile.
race[2] [-] **1.** *n.* yarış, koşu (*a. fig.*), koşu yarışması; yaşam süresi; akıntı, cereyan; ~*s pl.* at yarışı; **2.** *v/i.* yarışmak, koşmak, seğirtmek; yıldırım kanunu çıkarmak; MOT hızlı çalışmak; *v/t.* yarıştırmak, koşuya sokmak; '~-**course** *n.* yarış pisti, koşu yolu, parkur.
race-ha.tred [ˈreisˈheitrid] *n.* ırklar arasındaki kin ve nefret duygusu.
race-horse [ˈreishɔːs] *n.* yarış atı.
rac.er [ˈreisə] *n.* yarış atı; yarış kayığı (*veya* teknesi); yarış otomobili; yarışçı, koşucu.
ra.cial [ˈreiʃəl] *adj.* ırka ait, ırksal…; 'ra.cial.ism *n.* ırkçılık, ırklar arasındaki kin ve nefret duygusu.
rac.i.ness [ˈreisinis] *n.* canlılık, neşe, coşkunluk, zindelik; müsehcenlik; ori-

jinallik.
rac.ing [ˈreisiŋ] *n.* yarış(çılık); *attr.* yarış…; ~ *car* yarış otomobili.
rack[1] [ræk] **1.** *n.* parmaklık; raf; portmanto, askılık; eşya filesi (*araba, tren vs.'de*); yemlik; MEC dişli çubuk; işkence sehpası; kerevet; **2.** *v/t.* yormak; germek, (gerip) işkence etm.; *fig.* azap vermek; istismar etm., kendinden yana yontmak; (*fiyat vs.*) yükselterek sıkıntıya sokmak, eziyet etm.; ~ *one's brains* kafa yormak (*veya* patlatmak) -*e*.
rack[2] [-] **1.** *n.* sürüklenen hafif bulut; **2.** *v/i.* rüzgârda sürüklenmek (*bulut*).
rack[3] [-] *n.* haraplık, yıkım; *go to* ~ *and ruin* tamamiyle mahvolmak, harabeye dönmek.
rack[4] [-] *v/t. a.* ~ *off* tortudan bira *veya* şarap çıkarmak, süzmek.
rack.et[1] [ˈrækit] *n. tenis vs.*: raket; ~*s pl.* dört duvarda sektirilerek oynanan bir tür tenis oyunu.
rack.et[2] [-] **1.** *n.* gürültü, patırdı, velvele, şamata; *fig.* hareket, faaliyet, telaş, heyecan; *Am.* F dolandırıcılık, şantaj, haraç(çılık); F iş, meslek; *sl.* rahat iş, beleş; *stand the* ~ sınavda başarılı olm.; suçu, masraf vs.'yi üstlenmek, sorumluluğu almak; **2.** *v/i.* gürültü patırtı etm., eğlenmek, şamata yapmak; **rack-et.eer** *n. esp. Am. sl.* şantajcı, haraççı; **rack.etˈeer.ing** *n. esp. Am. sl.* şantaj yapma, haraç kesme; 'rack.et.y *adj.* haşarı, gürültücü, şamatacı; gürültülü, şamatalı.
rack-rail.way [ˈrækreilwei] *n.* dişli tren.
rack-rent [rækrent] **1.** *n.* fahiş kira; **2.** *vb.* fahiş kira talep etm.
ra.coon ZOO [rəˈkuːn] *n.* Kuzey Amerikada yaşayan et yiyici ve tilkiden büyücek bir tür hayvan, rakun.

rac.y □ ['reisi] canlı, dinç, zinde; çeşnili, baharlı, aromatik; açık saçık, orijinal.

ra.dar ['reidə] n. radar (aygıtı).

rad.dle ['rædl] 1. n. kırmızı tebeşir, aşı-boyası; 2. v/t. kırmızıya boyamak.

ra.di.al □ ['reidjəl] merkezden çevreye doğru düzenlenmiş, yelpazevarî, rad-yal, yayılan ışın şeklinde; MATH yarıça-pa ait; ~ **engine** yıldız motor.

ra.di.ance, **ra.di.an.cy** ['reidjəns(i)] n. parlaklık, aydınlık; '**ra.di.ant** □ parlak, parlayan, aydın; şaşaalı, muhteşem (a. fig.); ısı yayan...; ışın yayan...

ra.di.ate 1. ['reidieit] v/i. ışın yaymak, neşretmek; yelpazevarî yayılmak; v/t. yaymak, saçmak; 2. ['ˍit] adj. bir mer-kezden yayılan, yelpazevarî, ışın...; **ra-di'a.tion** n. yayılma, ışık ve sıcaklık verme, radyasyon; **ra.di.a.tor** ['ˍeitə] n. radyatör, kalorifer; MOT radyatör, soğutucu aygıt.

rad.i.cal ['rædikəl] 1. □ kökten, köke ait, temel...; esaslı, kök salmış, yerleş-miş; radikal (a. POL); köksel; ~ **sign** MATH kök işareti; 2. n. GR kök; CHEM un-sur, eleman, anamadde; part. POL aşırı-lar, müfritler; '**rad.i.cal.ism** n. radika-lizm, köktencilik; radikalizm ilkeleri.

ra.di.o ['reidiəu] 1. n. radyo; telsiz telg-raf; radyogram, telsiz haberi; radyo alıcı veya vericisi, telsiz telgraf aygıtı; ~ **car** telsizli polis arabası; ~ **drama**, ~ **play** radyo tiyatrosu, radyofonik pi-yes; ~ **engineering** radyo (veya telsiz) mühendisliği; ~ **set** radyo makinesi; 2. v/t. & v/i. yayımlamak, telsizle gönder-mek; telsiz veya telgrafla haberleş-mek; '**~'ac.tive** adj. radyoaktif; '**~ac-'tiv.i.ty** n. radyoaktivite; radyo etkin-liği; **ra.di.o.gram** ['ˍgræm] n. radyog-ram, radyo telgraf; = **ra.di.o-gram.o-phone** ['ˍ'græməfəun] n. pikaplı (veya gramofonlu) radyo; **radi.o-graph** ['ˍgrɑːf] 1. n. radyografi; röntgen (fil-mi); 2. v/t. röntgenini almak; radyogra-fisini çıkarmak; **ra.di.o-lo'cation** n. ra-darla yerini saptama; **ra.di.olo.gy** PHYS [reidi'ɔlədʒi] n. radyoloji; **radi.o-tel-e.gram** ['reidiəu'teligræm] n. radyog-ram, telsiz telgraf; '**ra.di.o-'ther.a.py** n. radyoterapi, röntgen ile tedavi.

rad.ish BOT ['rædiʃ] n. bayır turpu; **red ~** kırmızı turp.

ra.di.um ['reidjəm] n. radyum.

ra.di.us ['reidjəs] n., pl. **ra.di.i** ['ˍdiai] yarıçap; ANAT radyus, önkol kemiği; MEC tekerlek parmağı; fig. çevre, mu-

hit, alan.

raff.ish ['ræfiʃ] adj. ihmalkâr; sefape-rest, rezil, hovarda.

raf.fle ['ræfl] 1. n. piyango, kur'a, çeki-liş; 2. v/t. bşi piyangoya koymak, piyan-go çekmek.

raft [rɑːft] 1. n. sal; 2. v/t. salla taşımak; salla karşıya geçmek; sal yapmak -i; v/i. sal kullanmak; '**raft.er** n. MEC çatı ki-rişi, kiriş; '**rafts.man** n. salcı.

rag[1] [ræg] n. paçavra, bez parçası; contp. değersiz gazete, değersiz şey.

rag[2] sl. [ˍ] 1. v/t. & v/i. b-ni kızdırmak, takılmak; muziplik yapmak, kaba şaka yapmak; gürültü ve şamata yapmak, ortalığı velveleye vermek, etrafı gürül-tüye boğmak; 2. n. muziplik, kaba şaka; gürültü patırdı, yaygara, şamata.

rag.a.muf.fin ['rægəmʌfin] n. üstü başı perişan sokak (veya mahalle) çocuğu.

rag...: '**~bag** n. paçavra, ufak tefek bez parçaları torbası; '**~book** n. yırtılmaz resimli kitap.

rage [reidʒ] 1. n. öfke, hiddet, gazap; ih-tiras, hırs, düşkünlük (for -e); heyecan, coşkunluk, cezbe; **it is all the ~** çok rağ-bet görüyor, moda oldu, alıp yürüdü; 2. v/i. hiddetlenmek, kudurmak, azmak, küplere binmek, köpürmek.

rag-fair ['rægfeə] n. bitpazarı.

rag.ged □ ['rægid] pürüzlü, düzgün ol-mayan; düzensiz; yırtık pırtık, lime li-me.

rag.man ['rægmən] n. paçavracı, eskici.

ra.gout ['ræguː] n. yahni.

rag...: '**~tag** n. mst ~ **and bobtail** ayak-takımı, avam, olur olmaz adamlar; '**~time** n. MUS cazda olduğu gibi kesik tempo, kesik tempolu parça.

raid [reid] 1. n. akın, baskın; polis ve gümrük memurları baskını; (hava) akın, taarruz; 2. vb. baskın yapmak -e; yağma etm., çapulculuk etm.; akın etm.; '**raid.er** n. akıncı, baskıncı.

rail[1] [reil] 1. n. a. **~s** pl. parmaklık, kor-kuluk, tırabzan; RAIL ray, fig. demiryo-lu; **off the ~s** yoldan (veya raydan) çıkmış; fig. yoldan (veya çığrından) çıkmış, düzensiz; **by ~** demiryolu ile; 2. v/t. a. ~ **in**, ~ **off** parmaklıkla çevir-mek.

rail[2] [ˍ] v/i. küfretmek, sövüp saymak (**at**, **against** b-ne, bşe).

rail[3] ORN [ˍ] n. sutavuğu.

rail-car [reil'kɑː] n. otomotris.

rail.ing ['reiliŋ] n. a. ~**s** pl. parmaklık, korkuluk, tırabzan, lata ile yapılan çit.

rail.lery ['reiləri] *n.* alay, istihza, şaka(cılık).

rail.road *Am.* ['reilrəud] **1.** *n.* demiryolu; **2.** *v/t.* yıldırım kanunu çıkarmak; demiryolu ile göndermek; aceleye getirmek.

rail.way ['reilwei] *n.* demiryolu; '~.man *n.* demiryolcu.

rai.ment RHET ['reimənt] *n.* elbise, giysi.

rain [rein] **1.** *n.* yağmur; **2.** *v/t. & v/i.* (yağmur) yağmak; yağmur gibi yağdırmak (*bomba, ok vs.*); ~.bow ['‿bəu] *n.* alkım, gökkuşağı; '~.coat *n. Am.* yağmurluk; '~.drop *n.* yağmur damlası; '~.fall *n.* yağış miktarı; sağanak; ~.ga(u)ge ['‿geidʒ] *n.* yağış ölçer, yağmur ölçeği; '~proof **1.** *adj.* su (*veya* yağmur) geçirmez; **2.** *n.* yağmurluk, muşamba; 'rain.y □ yağmurlu, yağmur...; *a.* ~ *day fig.* sıkıntılı (*veya* darda kalınan) zaman, kara gün.

raise [reiz] *v/t. oft.* ~ *up* kaldırmak, yükseltmek; bina etm., dikmek; artırmak, çoğaltmak (*a. fig.*); sağlamak, ödünç almak (*para*); toplamak, mevzilemek (*ordu*); ayağa kaldırmak; yerden kaldırmak; büyütmek, yetiştirmek (*çocuk, hayvan, tahıl*); ses yükseltmek; öldükten sonra diriltmek; ileri sürmek (*soru vs.*); neden olm. *-e*, uyandırmak; teşvik etm., harekete getirmek; son vermek *-e*, kaldırmak (*kuşatma*); 'rais.er *n.* hayvan *veya* bitki yetiştiren *b-i*; kurucu.

rai.sin ['reizn] *n.* kuru üzüm.

ra.ja(h) ['rɑːdʒə] *n.* raca (*Hindistan Prensi*).

rake[1] [reik] **1.** *n.* saplı tarak, tırmık; **2.** *v/t.* taramak, tırmıklamak; *a.* ~ *up, ~ over fig.* köşe bucak aramak, araştırmak, taramak; MIL, NAUT ateşle taramak; kuşbakışı taramak; ~ *off, ~ away* ortadan kaldırmak, toparlayıp kaldırmak; *v/i.* taraklamak, tırmıklamak; ara(ştır)mak (*for*); '~off *n. Am. sl.* anafor, pay komisyon, kârdan hisse.

rake[2] NAUT [‿] **1.** *n.* meyil, baca ve direğin kıça doğru meyli; **2.** *vb.* meyletmek, yan yatmak.

rake[3] [‿] *n.* sefih (*veya* hovarda) adam, safa pezevengi.

rak.ish ['reikiʃ] **1.** *adj.* şık, zarif, modaya uygun; **2.** □ sefih, ahlâksız, çapkın.

ral.ly[1] ['ræli] **1.** *n.* toplama, toplantı, miting; istirahat; *tenis*: karşılıklı arkaya birkaç vuruş; MOT ralli; **2.** *v/i.* dü-

zene girmek; toplanmak; iyileşmek; *v/t.* düzeltmek; toplamak, canlandırmak.

ral.ly[2] [‿] *v/t. b-ne* takılmak, şakalaşmak.

ram [ræm] **1.** *n.* ZOO koç; AST Koç takımyıldızı; MIL HIST mancınık; MEC, NAUT şahmerdan; harp gemisi mahmuzu; su terazisi; **2.** *v/t.* vurmak, vurarak yerleştirmek; NAUT bindirerek batırmak; ~ *up* barikatlamak.

ram.ble ['ræmbl] **1.** *n.* gezinme, gezinti; **2.** *v/i.* boş gezinmek; konuyu dağıtmak; enine boyuna gelişip büyümek (*bitki*); 'ram.bler *n.* yaya gezen, dolaşan kimse; BOT çardak gülü; 'rambling **1.** □ avare, dolaşan; sabit olmayan, değişken, kararsız; dağınık; **2.** *n.* avare (*veya* boş gezinen) kimse.

ram.i.fi.ca.tion [ræmifi'keiʃən] *n.* dallanıp budaklanma; **ram.i.fy** ['‿fai] *v/i.* çatallaşmak, dallanıp budaklanmak; *v/t.* kollara, şubelere ayırmak.

ram.jet ['ræmdʒet] *n. a.* ~ *engine* dinamik basınçlı jet motoru.

ram.mer MEC ['ræmə] *n.* şahmerdan.

ramp[1] *sl.* [ræmp] *n.* dolandırıcılık, kazık atma.

ramp[2] [‿] **1.** *n.* rampa; **2.** *v/i.* şahlanmak, şaha kalkmak, kudurmak; **ram.page** *co.* [ræm'peidʒ] **1.** *v/i.* kudurmak, sağa sola saldırmak; **2.** *be on the* ~ heyheyleri tutmak, çılgınca davranışlarda bulunmak; **ramp.an.cy** ['‿pənsi] *n.* şaha kalkma, şahlanma, azma; 'rampant □ şahlanmış; *fig.* dizginlerini koparmış, azgın, başıboş kalmış; ARCH yukarı çıkan, rampa.

ram.part ['ræmpɑːt] *n.* sur, kale duvarı, siper.

ram.rod ['ræmrɔd] *n.* tüfek harbisi; top tomarı.

ram.shack.le ['ræmʃækl] *adj.* viran, yıkılmaya yüz tutan, harap; cılız, sıska.

ran [ræn] *pret. of* **run 1.**

ranch [rɑːntʃ] *n.* hayvan çiftliği, büyük çiftlik; 'ranch.er, 'ranch.man *n.* çiftlik sahibi, çiftçi; kovboy.

ran.cid □ ['rænsid] acılaşmış, ağırlaşmış, kokmuş, küflü, ekşimiş (*yağlı yemek vs.*); 'ran'cid.i.ty, 'ran.cid.ness *n.* acılık, ekşilik, küflülük.

ran.cor.ous □ ['ræŋkərəs] kinci, garazkâr.

ran.co(u)r ['ræŋkə] *n.* kin, hınç, garaz.

ran.dom ['rændəm] **1.** *at* ~ rasgele, tesadüfî, körükörüne, gelişigüzel; **2.**

adj. rasgele, gelişigüzel, ince eleyip sık dokumaksızın.

rang [ræŋ] *pret. of* **ring²** *2*.

range [reindʒ] **1.** *n.* sıra, dizi, seri, COM seçme mal, koleksiyon; mutfak ocağı; alan, saha; erim, menzil, tesir sahası; hareket serbestliği; uzaklık; atış yeri; *Am.* otlak; **take the ~** mesafeyi tahmin etm.; **2.** *v/t.* dizmek, sıralamak; dolaşmak, gezmek; NAUT ...boyunca seyretmek; otlatmak; sınıflandırmak; menzile ulaşabilmek, menzili ... olm.; *v/i.* bir sırada olm., sıralanmak, dizilmek; dolaşmak, gezinmek (**through**); uzanmak, yetişmek (**over**); **~ along** ...boyunca gitmek; **'~-find.er** *n.* telemetre; **'rang.er** *n.* korucu, orman memuru; MIL komando; **'rang.y** *adj.* dağlık; ince, fidan gibi.

rank¹ [ræŋk] **1.** *n.* sıra, dizi, saf; MIL rütbe, derece, sınıf, paye, aşama, mevki; *satranç:* yatay kareler; **the ~ s** *pl.*, **the ~ and file** erat, erler; üyeler, fertler; *fig.* aşağı tabaka, büyük kitle; **join the ~s** orduya katılmak; **rise from the ~s** erlikten subaylığa yükselmek; **2.** *v/t.* sıralamak, tasnif etm.; saymak, addetmek (**with** *-i*); *v/i.* sıralanmak, dizilmek; katılmak (**among, with** *-e*), addolunmak, sayılmak, dahil olm. *-e*; daha yüksek rütbede olm, rütbece *-den* üstün olmak, derecelenmek (**above**; **next to**); **~ as** sayılmak, addedilmek, telâkki edilmek.

rank² ☐ [~] uzun büyümüş, dolgun üreyen; verimli, mümbit (*toprak*); bozulmuş, kokmuş, bozuk.

rank.er ['ræŋkə] *n.* alaylı, erbaş.

ran.kle *fig.* ['ræŋkl] *v/i.* için için yemek, yiyip bitirmek, kemirmek, acısı unutulmak; kaçırımak (*kız*).

rank.ness ['ræŋknis] *n.* uzun ve dolgun büyüme; verimlilik; kokmuşluk, bozulmuşluk.

ran.sack ['rænsæk] *v/t.* araştırmak, altını üstüne getirmek, üstünü yoklamak; yağma (*veya* talan) etm.

ran.som ['rænsəm] **1.** *n.* fidye, kurtulmalık; ECCL kefaret; kurtuluş; **2.** *v/t.* fidye ile kurtarmak; halâs etm.

rant [rænt] **1.** *n.* lâf kalabalığı (*veya* bolluğu), tumturak, farfaralık, ağız kalabalığı; **2.** *vb.* lâf kalabalığı etm., yüksekten atmak; yüksek sesle ve aktör gibi mimikler yaparak konuşmak, va'zetmek; **'rant.er** *n.* ağız kalabalığı eden, tumturaklı konuşan kimse, pa-

lavracı.

ra.nun.cu.lus BOT [rə'nʌŋkjuləs] *n.* düğünçiçeği.

rap¹ [ræp] **1.** *n.* hafif vuruş *veya* darbe; MUS rap (*müzik*); **2.** *v/t.* hafifçe vurmak, çalmak, çarpmak (**at** *-e*); **~ s.o.'s fingers** *veya* **knuckles** *fig.* *b-nin* parmaklarına vurmak; *b-ne* haddini bildirmek; **~ out** şiddetle söylemek *veya* vurmak; ağızdan kaçırmak.

rap² *fig.* [~] *n.* mangır, metelik.

ra.pa.cious ☐ [rə'peiʃəs] haris, açgözlü, doymak bilmez, tamahkâr; yırtıcı, zorba; **ra.pac.i.ty** [rə'pæsiti] *n.* yırtıcılık hırsı, zorbalık; hırs, açgözlülük.

rape¹ [reip] **1.** *n.* kız kaçırma, dağa kaldırma; JUR zorla ırza geçme; **~ and murder** ırza saldırı ve öldürme; **2.** *v/t. -in* ırzına geçmek; yağma etm., zorla elinden almak; kaçırmak (*kız*).

rape² BOT [~] *n.* kolza, küçük şalgam; **'~-oil** *n.* kolza yağı; **'~.seed** *n.* kolza tohumu.

rap.id ['ræpid] **1.** ☐ çabuk, hızlı, tez, serî, süratli, ani(den); PHOT aydınlık (*nesne*); hassas (*film*); **~ fire** serî ateş eden (*silah*); **2.** *n.* **~s** *pl. geo.* ivinti yeri, şiddetli nehir akıntısı; **ra.pid.i.ty** [rə'piditi] *n.* sürat, hız.

ra.pi.er FENC ['reipjə] *n.* dar ve uzun kılıç, meç.

rap.ine RHET ['ræpain] *n.* yağma(cılık), çapulculuk.

rap.proche.ment POL [ræ'prɔʃmãːŋ] *n.* uzlaşma.

rapt [ræpt] *adj. fig.* dalgın, esri(k) (**in** *-e*); meftun, baygın (**with** *-e*).

rap.ture ['ræptʃə] *n. a.* **~s** *pl.* kendinden geçme, esrilik, vecit, mest olma; **in ~s** etekleri zil çalan, coşku içinde, mest olmuş; **go into ~s** *bşe* delice sevinmek, sevinçten deliye dönmek; **'rap.tur.ous** ☐ *k-den* geçmiş, sevinç içinde, vecit halinde; *k-den* geçiren, çok sevindirici, coşku veren.

rare ☐ [rɛə] seyrek, nadir (*a. fig. harikulâde*); az bulunur, tek tük; PHYS *etc.* az oksijenli, yoğun olmayan (*hava*).

rare.bit [reəbit] *n.:* **Welsh ~** kızarmış ekmeğe sürülen peynir.

rar.e.fac.tion PHYS [reəri'fækʃən] *n.* basıncı azaltma; **rar.e.fy** ['~fai] *v/t. & v/i.* seyrekleş(tir)mek, azal(t)mak; incel(t)mek; **'rare.ness**, **'rar.i.ty** *n.* nadirlik; ender rastlanan şey, kıymetli şey; seyreklik; değerlilik.

ras.cal ['rɑːskəl] *n.* çapkın, serseri; hain, alçak herif, pezevenk, teres; yaramaz, haşarı kimse; **ras.cal.i.ty** [-'kæliti] *n.* alçaklık, hainlik; serserilik, çapkınlık, pezevenklik; **ras.cal.ly** *adj. & adv.* ['-kəli] alçak(ça), hain(ce); yaramaz, müzevir.

rash¹ ☐ [ræʃ] aceleci, sabırsız, düşüncesiz, ihtiyatsız; gözünü budaktan sakınmaz.

rash² MED [-] isilik, egzama.

rash.er ['ræʃə] *n.* ince kesilmiş jambon vs. dilimi.

rash.ness ['ræʃnis] *n.* acelecilik, düşüncesizlik, tedbirsizlik.

rasp [rɑːsp] **1.** *n.* raspa, kaba törpü; **2.** *v/t.* törpülemek, rendelemek; *b-nin* canını acıtmak, ıstırap vermek; *v/i.* cızırdamak, törpü gibi ses çıkarmak.

rasp.ber.ry BOT ['rɑːzbəri] *n.* ahududu.

rasp.er ['rɑːspə] *n.* çamurluk demiri; törpü.

rasp.ing ['rɑːspiŋ] *n.* törpüleme; cızırdayan şey; **~s** *pl.* törpü, rende artığı, yonga, talaş.

rat [ræt] **1.** *n.* ZOO sıçan, iri fare; POL karşı tarafa geçen milletvekili; *sl.* grev bozucu; **smell a ~** ortalıkta bir tehlike sezmek; **~s!** *sl.* boş lâkırdı!, saçmasapan söz!, zırva!; **2.** *v/i.* fare tutmak; POL karşı tarafa geçmek.

rat.a.ble ☐ ['reitəbl] vergiye tabi, vergi ile yükümlü.

ratch MEC [rætʃ] *n.* dişli çark mandalı.

ratch.et MEC ['rætʃit] *n.* tevkif mandalı, dişli çark mandalı, kastanyola; '**~-wheel** *n.* kilit çarkı, mandallı çark.

rate¹ [reit] **1.** *n.* nispet, oran, ölçü; fiyat, paha, eder; belediye vergisi, mülk vergisi; sınıf, çeşit, derece, *part.* NAUT mevki; hız, sürat; ücret; **at the ~ of** oranında, miktarında; hızında; **at a cheap ~** COM ucuza; **at any ~** herhalde, her nasılsa; **~ of exchange** NAUT kambiyo rayici (*veya* sürümdeğeri), döviz kuru; **~ of interest** faiz oranı; **~ of taxation** vergi oranı; **2.** *vb.* tahmin etm., (kıymet) takdir etm. (**at**); vergi koymak.

rate² [-] *v/t.* azarlamak, haşlamak (**for**, **about**); *v/i. b-ni* azarlamak (**at**).

rate-pay.er ['reitpeiə] *n.* vergi mükellefi (*veya* yükümlüsü).

rath.er ['rɑːðə] *adv.* oldukça, bir hayli, epeyce; daha çok, tercihan, *-e* kalırsa, *-den* ziyade; daha doğrusu; tersine, aksine; **~!** [a. 'rɑː'ðəː] *int.* F hem de nasıl!,

sorular mu!; **I had** *veya* **would ~ do** yapmayı yeğlerim; **I ~ expected it** doğrusu bunu umuyordum; **~ than** *-den* ziyade.

rat.i.fi.ca.tion [rætifi'keiʃən] *n.* onay, tasdik; **rat.i.fy** ['-fai] *v/t.* tasdik etm., onaylamak.

rat.ing¹ ['reitiŋ] *n.* değerlendirme, tahmin, takdir; vergi oranı; NAUT rütbe, hizmet derecesi; NAUT deniz eri, tayfa.

rat.ing² [-] *n.* tekdir, azar(lama).

ra.tio ['reiʃiəu] *n.* oran, nispet.

ra.tion ['ræʃən] **1.** *n.* pay, hisse; tayın; miktar; **~ card** (**book**) (*gıda maddeleri*) vesika, karne; **2.** *v/t.* karneye bağlamak; *b-nin* tayın miktarını saptamak.

ra.tion.al ☐ ['ræʃənl] akıl sahibi, akıllı, mantıklı, anlayışlı, rasyonel (*a.* MATH).

ration.al.ism ['ræʃnəlizəm] *n.* usculuk, akılcılık, rasyonalizm; '**ra.tion.al.ist** *n.* rasyonalist, akılcı, uscu; **ra.tion.al.i.ty** [ræʃə'næliti] akıl, us, aklıselim; **ra.tional.i.za.tion** [ræʃnəlai'zeiʃən] *n.* akla uydurma; rasyonalizasyon; modernleşme; '**ra.tion.al.ize** *v/t.* akla uydurmak, mantıklı kılmak; ölçülü şekle sokmak, modernleştirmek.

rat race ['rætreis] *n.* anlamsız mücadele, koşuşturma, hengame.

rat-tat ['ræt'tæt] *n.* kapı çalınma sesi.

rat.ten ['rætn] *v/t.* sabote etm., baltalamak *-i*; *v/i.* sabotaj yapmak; '**rat.ten.ing** *n.* sabotaj, baltalama.

rat.tle ['rætl] **1.** *n.* takırtı, çıtırtı; boş lâf, gevezelik; zırıltı; bebek çıngırağı; hırıltı; can çekişme (*veya* hırıltısı); **2.** *v/i.* takırdamak; gevezelik etm.; hırıldamak; *v/t.* takırdatmak; F sinirlendirmek *-i*; **~ off** *veya* **out** ezbere çabucak okumak *-i*; '**~-brain**, '**~-pate** *n.* zihni darmadağınık, çalçene, geveze kimse; '**~-brained**, '**~-pat.ed** *adj.* çalçene, geveze; '**rat.tier** *n.* geveze, boşboğaz, lâkırdıcı kimse; *sl.* yaman herif, şeytanın art bacağı; *Am.* F = '**rat.tle-snake** *n.* ZOO çıngıraklı yılan; '**rat.tle-trap 1.** *adj.* cılız, mecalsiz; **2.** *n.* kırık dökük hurda şey (*araba vs.*).

rat.tling ☐ ['rætliŋ] tıkırdayan; F canlı, vızır vızır işleyen, çalışan; *adv.* çok, gayet; **at a ~ pace** delice bir süratle.

rat.ty *sl.* ['ræti] *adj.* sinirli, hiddetli, huysuz.

rau.cous ☐ ['rɔːkəs] boğuk, kısık.

rav.age ['rævidʒ] **1.** *n.* tahribat, harap etme; **2.** *v/t.* tahrip etm., harabetmek, kırıp geçirmek, yakıp yıkmak; *v/i.* tah-

ribat yapmak.
rave [reiv] *v/i.* çıldırmak, kudurmak, küplere binmek; hezeyan etm., sayıklamak; bayılmak (**about**, **of** -*e*).
rav.el ['rævəl] *v/t.* dolaştırmak, karıştırmak; *a.* ~ **out** sökmek, ayırmak (*teyelleri*); *v/i. a.* ~ **out** açılmak, çözülmek, tel tel olm., sökülmek.
ra.ven¹ ['reivn] **1.** *n.* zoo kuzgun; **2.** *adj.* kuzgunî (*renk*).
rav.en² ['rævn] **1.** *s.* **ravin**; **2.** *vb.* yağmacılık, çapulculuk etm.; hırslı, açgözlü olm.; oburca yutmak, tıkıştırmak; **raven.ous** □ ['rævənəs] obur, pisboğaz, hasis, doymak bilmez; 'rav.e-n.ous.ness *n.* hırslılık; oburluk, pisboğazlık; şiddetli açlık.
rav.in RHET ['rævin] *n.* yırtıcılık hırsı; yağma; av.
ra.vine [rə'viːn] *n.* boğaz, dağ geçidi, çukur, koyak.
rav.ings ['reiviŋz] *n. pl.* deli saçması söz(ler).
rav.ish ['ræviʃ] *v/t.* esritmek, mest etm., çok sevindirmek, coşturmak; *b-nin* ırzına geçmek; RHET *b-den bşi* gaspetmek, zorla almak; 'rav.ish.er *n.* ırza geçen, alçak kimse; 'rav.ish.ing □ cazip, cazibeli, coşturan, alımlı; 'rav.ish-ment *n.* esrime, kendinden geçme; ırza tecavüz.
raw [rɔː] **1.** çiğ, pişmemiş; ham, işlenmemiş; yaralı, bereli, derisi soyulmuş; seğuk ve yağışlı (*hava*); *fig.* acemi, tecrübesiz; ~ **material** hammadde; **he got o** ~ **deal** *sl.* haksızlığa uğradı; **2.** *n.* yara; hassas nokta, bam teli (*part. fig.*); '~-**boned** *adj.* zayıf, kuru, çelimsiz, bir deri bir kemik, kemikleri sayılan; '~.**hide** *n.* ham deri; '~**raw.ness** *n.* kabalık, hayvanca davranış; çiğlik; acemilik.
ray¹ [rei] **1.** *n.* şua, ışın; *fig.* iz, eser, zerre; **2.** *v/i.* şua (*veya* ışın) salmak, ışımak.
ray² ICHTH [-] *n.* vatoz; tırpana.
ray.less ['reilis] *n.* şuasız, ışınsız.
ray.on ['reiɔn] *n.* sunî ipek.
raze [reiz] *v/t.* temelinden yıkmak (*ev vs.*); ~ **to the ground** yerle bir etm.
ra.zor ['reizə] *n.* ustura; tıraş makinesi; '~-**blade** *n.* ustura ağzı; jilet; '~'**edge** *n. fig.* bıçak ağzı; zor, kritik durum; '~.**strop** *n.* bileği kayışı.
razz *Am. sl.* [ræz] *v/t.* alay etm. *ile.* alaya almak -*i.*
raz.zi.a ['ræziə] *n.* çapul(culuk), yağma(cılık), akın(cılık).

raz.zle-daz.zle *sl.* ['ræzldæzl] *n.* karmakarışıklık, şamata, gürültü patırtı, cümbüş, alem.
re JUR, COM [riː] *prep.* hakkında, dair, -*e* ait.
re… [-] *prefix* geri(ye); yeniden, tekrar.
reach [riːtʃ] **1.** *n.* uzatma; uzanma, yetişme; menzil, erim; ufuk, görüş sahası; alan, bölge; *beyond* ~, *out of* ~ erişilmez, yetişilmez; *within easy* ~ kolay erişilebilir; **2.** *v/t.* & *v/i. a.* ~ *out* uzanmak, erişmek (*to, for* -*e*); uzamak, yetişmek; NAUT rüzgâr yönünde seyretmek; uzatmak, *bşi* elden ele geçirmek, *bşi* almak için elini uzatmak; *oft.* ~ *out bşi* uzatmak; vasıl olm., varmak, gelmek; görüşebilmek, temas kurmak.
reach-me-downs F ['riːtʃmi'daunz] *n. pl.* kalitesiz, ucuz hazır elbise.
re.act [riː'ækt] *v/i.* tepkimek, tepki göstermek, karşılık vermek; etkilemek (*to*), etki etm. (*on, upon* -*e*); isyan etm., ayaklanmak (*against* -*e*).
re.ac.tion [riː'ækʃən] *n.* tepki(me) (*to* -*e*); aksi tesir, reaksiyon (*upon* -*e*); POL gericilik, irtica; re'ac.tion.ar.y *part.* POL [-ʃnəri] **1.** *adj.* gerici; **2.** *n.* gerici, eski kafalı kimse.
re.ac.tive □ [riː'æktiv] tepkisel, aksi tesir yaratan; re'ac.tor *n.* PHYS reaktör; kimyasal reaksiyonda kullanılan kap.
read 1. [riːd] (*irr.*) *v/t.* okumak (*a. fig.*), anlam vermek, yorumlamak; göstermek, işaret etm., kaydetmek (*termometre vs.*): ~ *off* bir yerden (*veya* bir sayfadan) okumak; ~ *out* yüksek sesle okumak; sonuna dek okumak; ~ *to s o. b-ne bşi* okumak; *v/i.* okumak, anlamak; okunmak; *üniv.* bir konu üzerinde çalışmak; ~ *between the lines* gizli anlamını keşfetmek; **2.** [red] *pret.* & *p.p.* of *1*; **3.** [red] *adj.* okumuş, bilgili (*in*).
read.a.ble □ ['riːdəbl] okunaklı; oku(n)mağa değer.
re-ad.dress ['riːə'dres] *v/t.* değişik bir adres yazmak, değişik bir adresle göndermek.
read.er ['riːdə] *n.* okuyucu, okur; TYP düzeltmen, musahhih; *üniv.* doçent (*in*); okuma kitabı; 'read.er.ship *n.* okur sayısı; doçentlik, okutmanlık.
read.i.ly ['redili] *adv.* seve seve, gönüllü olarak; kolayca; 'read.i.ness *n.* hazır olma; rıza, muvafakat; tezlik, çabukluk, sürat; ~ *of mind veya wit* hazırcevaplık, şaşırmazlık.

read.ing ['riːdiŋ] *n.* oku(n)ma (*a.* PARL); göstergenin kaydettiği ölçüm (*termometre vs.*); bilgi, edebi araştırma; kıraat, okuma (tarzı); anlayış, fikir; - '**~-room** *n.* okuma odası.

re.ad.just ['riːə'dʒʌst] *v/t.* & *v/i.* tekrar düzenlemek, yeniden ayarlamak, uydurmak; POL yeni bilgi vermek; '**re-ad'justment** *n.* yeni koşullara alış(tır)ma; yeniden düzenleme, reorganizasyon.

re.ad.mis.sion ['riːəd'miʃən] *n.* yeniden kabul edilme (*üyelik, öğrencilik vs.*).

re.ad.mit ['riːəd'mit] *v/t.* yeniden kabul etm.; '**re.ad'mit.tance** *n.* yeniden kabul edilme.

read.y ['redi] **1.** *adj.* ☐ hazır, amade (**to do s.th.** *-i yapmağa*); istekli, razı; hazır, elde bulunan; *-mak* üzere olan (**to -e**); serî, çabuk, çevik, atik (**at, in** *-de*); kolay, külfetsiz; yakında, hemen alınıverecek; COM nakit (*para*); NAUT hazır; **~ reckoner** hesap cetveli; barem; **~ for action** muharebeye hazır; **~ for take-off** AVIA uçuşa hazır; **~ for use** kullanılmaya hazır; **~ to serve** sofra servisine hazırlanmış; **make** *veya* **get ~** hazırla(n)mak; **~ money** hazır para, nakit; **2.** *adv.* önceden hazır(-lanmış); **3.** *su.* **at the ~** atışa hazır; '**~'made** *adj.* hazır, konfeksiyon...; *fig.* klişeleşmiş, gündelik, hergünkü; '**~-to-'wear** *adj.* konfeksiyon (*elbise*).

re.af.firm ['riːə'fəːm] *v/t.* yeniden onaylamak, teyit etm.

re.a.gent CHEM [riː'eidʒənt] *n.* miyar, belirteç.

re.al ☐ [riəl] gerçek, hakiki; asıl; samimî, içten; **~ es.tate** gayrimenkul (*veya* taşınmaz) mal, mülk.

re.a.lign ['riːə'lain] *v/t.* siyasal reorganizasyon yapmak, yeni gruplar oluşturmak; '**re.a'lign.ment** *n.* siyasal reorganizasyon.

re.a.lism ['riəlizəm] *n.* gerçekçilik, realizm; '**re.al.ist 1.** *n.* gerçekçi, realist kimse; **2.** = re.al'is.tic *adj.* (**~ally**) gerçekçi, realist; gerçeğe uygun; **re.al.i.ty** [riː'æliti] *n.* gerçeklik, realite, hakikat; **~ (TV) show** *n.* (*TV'de*) gerçek kimselerin hayatlarını konu alan program; **re.al.iz.able** ☐ ['riəlaizəbl] gerçekleştirilebilir, realize edilebilir; **re.al.i'za.tion** *n.* gerçekleştirme; farketme, anlama, idrak; BOT paraya çevirme; '**re.al-

ize *v/t.* anlamak, farkına varmak *-in*; gerçekleştirmek *-i*; COM paraya çevirmek, satmak *-i*; kâr etmek; '**re.al.ly** *adv.* gerçekten, sahiden, hakikati halde, aslında.

realm [relm] *n.* kırallık; *fig.* alan, saha, ülke; **Peer of the ~** Lordlar Kamarası üyesi

re.al.tor *Am.* ['rıəltə] *n.* emlâkçı; '**re.al.ty** *n.* JUR gayrimenkul (*veya* taşınmaz) mal, mülk.

ream¹ [riːm] *n.* 480 *veya* 500 tabakalık kâğıt topu.

ream² MEC [-] *v/t.* genişletmek (*çukur*); *mst* **~ out** delik açmak, delmek, burgulamak; '**ream.er** *n.* bıcırgan, rayma; limon sıkacağı.

re.an.i.mate ['riː'ænimeit] *v/t.* yeniden canlandırmak, taze hayat vermek, canlılık kazandırmak; '**re.an.i'ma.tion** *n.* yeniden hayata kazandırma, diriltme.

reap [riːp] *vb.* biçmek, hasat etm., oraklamak, tırpanlamak; *fig.* kazanmak, semeresini almak; '**reap.er** *n.* orakçı, tırpancı; biçerdöver; '**reap.ing** *n.* hasat; '**reap.ing-hook** *n.* orak; '**reap-ing-ma.chine** *n.* biçerdöver.

re.ap.pear ['riːə'piə] *v/i.* tekrar görünmek, ortaya çıkmak; '**re.ap'pear.ance** *n.* yeniden görünme.

re.ap.pli.ca.tion ['riːæpli'keiʃən] *n.* yeniden uygulama, tatbik etme.

re.ap.point ['riːə'pɔint] *v/t.* yeniden tayin etm.

re.ap.prais.al ['riːə'preizəl] *n.* yeniden gözden geçirme, inceleme.

rear¹ [riə] *v/t.* yetiştirmek, büyütmek; RHET dikmek, inşa etm.; *v/i.* yükselmek, şahlanmak.

rear² [-] **1.** *n.* arka, geri (taraf); MOT, NAUT kıç, kupa; MIL artçı, dümdar, arkadan gelen kıta; kıç, popo; **at the ~ of, in (the) ~ of** *-in* arkasın(d)a, gerisinde; **from the ~** geriden, arkadan; **2.** *adj.* arkadaki, en geri, arka... geri...; **~ wheel drive** MOT arkadan itisli; '**~'ad-mi.ral** *n.* NAUT tuğamiral; '**~-guard** *n.* MIL artçı, dümdar; '**~-lamp**, '**~-light** *n.* MOT arka lambası (*veya* feneri).

re-arm ['riː'ɑːm] *v/t.* & *v/i.* yeniden silahlan(dır)mak; '**re-'ar.ma.ment** *n.* yeniden silahlan(dır)ma.

rear.most ['riəməust] *adj.* en arkadaki.

re.ar.range ['riːə'reindʒ] *v/t.* yeniden düzenlemek.

rear.ward ['riəwəd] **1.** *adj.* arkada bulu-

nan; **2.** *adv. a.* **~s** arkaya doğru.
re.as.cend ['ri:ə'send] *v/i.* yeniden yükselmek, çıkmak, tırmanmak.
rea.son ['ri:zn] **1.** *n.* akıl, idrak, muhakeme; sebep, neden, illet; insaf, itidal,
hak; delil, tanıt; **by ~ of** nedeniyle, sebebiyle, *-den* dolayı; **for this ~** bu nedenle, bu sebeple, bundan dolayı; **listen to ~** lâf anlamak; **it stands to ~
that...** aşikârdır ki..., apaçıktır ki...;
2. *v/i.* makûl (*veya* mantıklı) olm., anlamak, sonuç çıkarmak, müzakere
etm.; kandırmağa çalışmak (**with** *-e*);
v/t. a. **~ out** düşünmek; hesabetmek kitabetmek, uslamlamak, muhakeme
etm.; **~ away** münakaşada (*veya* müna-
zarada) bulunmak; **~ s.o. into** (**out of**)
s.th. *b-ne bşi* kanıtlar göstererek
inandırmak, vazgeçirmek; **~ed** *adj.*
üzerinde düşünülmüş, mantıklı, akla
dayanan; '**reason.a.ble** □ akla uygun,
makûl, mantıklı; orta, vasat; '**rea.son-
a.bly** *adv.* oldukça, epeyce; makûlce;
'**rea.son.er** *n.* fikir adamı, mantıklı
kimse; '**rea.son.ing** *n.* muhakeme, us-
lamlama, usa vurma, kıyaslama; *attr.*
düşünme..., muhakeme...
re.as.semble ['ri:ə'sembl] *v/t. & v/i.*
yeniden birleş(tir)mek, topla(n)mak.
re.as.sert ['ri:ə'sə:t] *v/t.* yeniden iddia
etm., ileri sürmek.
re.as.sur.ance [ri:ə'ʃuərəns] *n.* yeniden temin etme, güven ver(il)me; güven veren şey; **re.as'sure** *v/t.* tekrar
güven vermek *-e*, temin etm. *-i*.
re.a.wak.en [ri:ə'weikən] *v/t. & v/i.* yeniden uyan(dır)mak.
re.bap.tize ['ri:bæp'taiz] *v/t.* yeniden
vaftiz etm.
re.bate¹ COM ['ri:beit] *n.* iskonto, tenzilat, indirim.
re.bate² MEC ['ræbit] **1.** *n.* dişili yiv,
oluk; **2.** *v/t.* içiçe geçirmek; yiv açmak.
reb.el 1. ['rebl] *n.* asi, ihtilâlci; **2.** [–] *adj.*
isyan eden, ayaklanan; *fig.* itaatsiz, ser-
keş, marazacı; **3.** [ri'bel] *v/i.* isyan etm.,
ayaklanmak; **re'bel.lion** [-jən] *n.* isyan, ayaklanma; **re'bel.lious = rebel 2**.
re.birth ['ri:'bə:θ] *n.* yeniden doğma,
dünyaya gelme; yeniden uyanış, canlanma, rönesans.
re.bound [ri'baund] **1.** *v/i.* (çarpıp) geri
tepmek, sıçramak; **2.** *n.* geri tepme,
sıçrama.
re.buff [ri'bʌf] **1.** *n.* ret; ters cevap, azarlama; **2.** *v/t.* reddetmek; ters cevap vermek, azarlamak.

re.build ['ri:'bild] (*irr.* **build**) *v/t.* yeniden inşa etm., kurmak.
re.buke [ri'bju:k] **1.** *n.* azar, paylama; **2.**
v/t. azarlamak, paylamak.
re.bus ['ri:bəs] *n.* resimli bilmece, soru-
lan sözcük *ya da* tümcenin kısımlarını
ayrı resim *ya da* harflerle göstererek
oynanan bir tür bulmaca (*örneğin bir
çanak ve bir kale resmi Çanakkale oku-
nacak*).
re.but [ri'bʌt] *v/t.* yanlışlığını kanıtlamak; **re'but.tal** *n.* yanlışlığını kanıtlama *veya* kanıtlayan şey.
re.cal.ci.trant [ri'kælsitrənt] *adj.* serkeş, aksi, dikkafalı.
re.call [ri'kɔ:l] **1.** *n.* geri çağırma; anımsama, hatırlama; geri çağırma işareti
veya emri; **beyond ~, past ~** geri alınamaz, dönülemez; hatırlanamaz; **2.** *v/t.*
geri çağırmak; *fig.* (**to s.o.'s mind**) *bşi
b-nin* hatırına getirmek, hatırlatmak;
gönderilmesini emretmek (*mal*); *bşi*
hatırlamak, anımsamak; uyandırmak
(*duygu, his*); feshetmek, geri almak;
COM geri çekmek (*kapital*); **~ that** *-i*
(*b-ne*) hatırlat ki; **until ~ed** geri çağrı-
lana kadar.
re.cant [ri'kænt] *vb.* sözünden dönmek,
caymak; **re.can.ta.tion** [ri:kæn'teiʃən]
n. sözünden dönme, cayma.
re.cap¹ F ['ri:kæp] = **recapitulate**; **re-
capitulation**.
re.cap² Am. ['ri:'kæp] *v/t.* taban geçirmek, kaplamak (*lastik tekerlek*).
re.ca.pit.u.late [ri:kə'pitjuleit] *vb.*
kısaca yeniden özetlemek; '**re.ca.pit-
u'la.tion** *n.* kısa özet.
re.cap.ture ['ri:'kæptʃə] **1.** *n.* yeniden
ele geçirme (*veya* zaptetme); **2.** *v/t.* yeniden elde etm., geri almak.
re.cast ['ri:'kɑ:st] **1.** (*irr.* **cast**) *v/t.* MEC
eriterek başka bir kalıba dökmek; kap-
tan kaba nakletmek, şeklini değiştirmek; THEAT oyuncuları değiştirmek;
2. *n.* yeni şekil verme *-e*.
re cede [ri:'si:d] *v/i.* geri çekilmek, gerilemek; COM düşmek (*fiyat*); **receding**
adj. basık, içeri kaçık (*alın, çene*).
re.ceipt ['ri:si:t] **1.** *n.* alındı. tesellüm,
makbuz; giriş (*mal*); COM alındı mak-
buzu; reçete; yemek tarifi; **~s** *pl.* gelir;
2. *v/t.* makbuz vermek, alındığına dair
imza etm.
re.ceiv.a.ble [ri'si:vəbl] *adj.* kabul edilebilir, alınabilir, elverişli; COM tahsil
edilecek; **re'ceive** *v/t.* almak (*haber,
mektup vs.*); kabul etm., misafir etm.;

909 reclaimable

maruz kalmak; almak (radyo, TV yayını); teslim almak; v/i. ev sahipliği yapmak; re'ceived adj. teslim alınmış; kabul edilmiş; re'ceiv.er n. alıcı (a. TEL & radyo); TELEPH ahize; a. ~ of stolen goods çalıntı malı bilerek satın alan şahıs; yatakçı; a. official ~ JUR iflâs masası görevlisi; PHYS hava boşaltma tulumbasının cam kavanozu; CHEM distilasyonda toplama kabı; re'ceiv.ership n. JUR davalı malların idaresi; re'ceiv.ing n. kabul, teslim; radyo: alma, ahiz; yataklık; ~ set radyo veya TV alıcısı.

re.cen.cy ['ri:snsi] n. yenilik, yeni vuku bulma.

re.cen.sion [ri'senʃən] n. düzeltme, tashih; düzeltilmiş metin.

re.cent □ ['ri:snt] yeni (olmuş), yakın geçmişte olan; in ~ years son yıllarda; 're.cent.ly adv. son zamanlarda, geçenlerde, yakın zamanda; 're.cent.ness n. yeni vuku bulma.

re.cep.ta.cle [ri'septəkl] n. kap, zarf; depo vs.; a. floral ~ BOT çiçek tablası.

re.cep.tion [ri'sepʃən] n. kabul (a. fig.); al(ın)ma (a. radyo); kabul merasimi; resepsiyon (otel); re'cep.tion.ist n. resepsiyon memuru; re'cep.tion--room n. kabul odası.

re.cep.tive □ [ri'septiv] çabuk kavrayan, anlayışlı (of); alıcı, kabul eden; re.cep'tiv.i.ty n. çabuk kavrayış; alma yeteneği (radyo vs.).

re.cess [ri'ses] 1. n. paydos, fasıla verme, teneffüs, ara; part. PARL tatil; arch. girinti, boşluk (duvarda dolap vs. için); ~es pl. fig. iç taraf; 2. vb. girintiye yerleştirmek; girinti yapmak, oymak; ara vermek, paydos yapmak.

re.ces.sion [ri'seʃən] n. geri çekilme, gerileme; BOT fiyat düşüşü; durgunluk; re'ces.sion.al [-ʃənl] 1. adj. ECCL son...; PARL tatil...; 2. n. ECCL dinî tören sonunda okunan ilâhî; re'ces.sive [-siv] adj. geri çekilme eğiliminde olan; BIOL resesif.

re.chris.ten ['ri:'krisn] v/t. b-nin adını değiştirmek.

re.cid.i.vist [ri'sidivist] n. sabıkalı, tövbesini bozan kimse, mükerrir, mutat suçlu.

rec.ipe ['resipi] n. reçete; yemek tarifi.

re.cip.i.ent [ri'sipiənt] n. alıcı, verilen veya gönderilen bşi alan kimse.

re.cip.ro.cal [ri'siprəkəl] 1. adj. karşılıklı, mütekabil; MATH, GR, PHLS

ortak, karşılıklı; 2. n. MATH karşıt, ortak değer; re'cip.rocate [-keit] v/t. & v/i. bşin acısını çıkarmak, misillemede bulunmak, öcünü almak; bir iyiliğin karşılığını vermek; MEC bir düzlem içinde ileri geri çalışmak (piston vs.); karşılıklı iyi dileklerini iletmek, değişmek, mukabele etm.; reciprocating engine pistonlu motor; re.cip.ro-'ca.tion n. ileri geri çalışma; karşılık, tekabül, değişme, mübadele; karşılıklı etki; rec.i.proc.i.ty [resi'prositi] n. karşılıklı durum, karşılıklık.

re.cit.al [ri'saitl] n. beyan, ifade, birer birer anlatma; hikâye; ezberden okuma; JUR ifade, takrir, gerçekleri sergileme; MUS solist konseri, resital; rec.i-ta.tion [resi'teiʃən] n. ezberden okuma; ezberden okunan parça, bölüm; Am. dersle ilgili soruları yanıtlayarak ders anlatma; rec.i.ta.tive MUS [-tə-'ti:v] 1. adj. resital şeklinde, ezber şeklinde; 2. n. konuşur gibi okunan güfte veya makam; re.cite [ri'sait] v/t. & v/i. ezberden okumak; nakletmek, ileri sürmek; yüksek sesle ve yakışır bir tavırla okumak; Am. ders anlatmak, soruyu yanıtlamak re'cit.er n. ezberden okuyan (veya nakleden, ileri süren) kimse.

reck poet. [rek] vb. önemsemek, ehemmiyet vermek, bşe aldırış etm., bşin önemi olm. (of).

reck.less □ ['reklis] pervasız, dikkatsiz, lâkayt (of), saygısız, düşüncesiz; 'reckless.ness n. pervasızlık, dikkatsizlik, lâkaytlık; saygısızlık.

reck.on ['rekən] v/t. hesap etm., saymak; a. ~ for, ~ as tahmin etm., takdir etm., farzetmek, sanmak; ~ up saymak, bşin hesabını yapmak; v/i. sayı saymak; zannetmek, tahmin etm.; ~ (up)on b-ne, bşe güvenmek, bel bağlamak; ~ with hesaba katmak -i; reck.on.er ['reknə] n. sayan, hesap eden kimse; 'reck.on.ing n. hesap(lama); hesap görme; be out in veya of one's ~ fig. b-nin hesabında yanılmak; tahmininde aldanmak.

re.claim [ri'kleim] v/t. geri istemek, tekrar elde etm.; elverişli hale koymak, iyileştirmek, yoluna koymak; ıslah etm.; ehlileştirmek, alıştırmak (hayvan); medenileştirmek; toprağı temizleyerek tarla haline getirmek; MEC hurdadan yararlanmak; iadesini talep etm., hak iddia etm.; re'claim-

a.ble *adj.* ıslah edilebilir, yararlanılabilir.

rec.la.ma.tion [reklə'meiʃən] *n.* ıslah; geri isteme; tarıma elverişli kılma (*toprak*); hurdadan yararlanma.

re.cline [ri'klain] *vb.* uzanmak (**against, on** *-e*); dayanmak, istinat etm. (**against, on**); ~ **upon** *fig. b-ne* sırtını dayamak; **reclin.ing chair** koltuk.

re.cluse [ri'klu:s] **1.** *adj.* dünyadan elini eteğini çekmiş, münzevi, insanlardan kaçan; **2.** *n.* münzevi kimse; keşiş.

rec.og.ni.tion [rekəg'niʃən] *n.* tanı(n)ma; itiraf, ona(n)ma, kabul, tasdik; **rec.ogniz.a.ble** *adj.* [' -naizəbl] tanınabilir, tanı(n)ması olası, farkedilebilir; **re.cog.nizance** JUR [ri'kɔgnizəns] *n.* taahhütname, kefalet, teminat; tanıma; **rec.og.nize** ['rekəgnaiz] *v/t.* tanımak; onaylamak, kabul etm., teslim ve itiraf etm., itibar etm., takdir etm.; selâm vermek (*sokakta*).

re.coil [ri'kɔil] **1.** *v/i.* geri çekilmek; geri tepmek; **2.** *n.* geri tepme; geri çekilme; iğrenme.

rec.ol.lect[1] [rekə'lekt] *v/t.* hatırlamak *-i.*

re.col.lect[2] ['ri:kə'lekt] *v/t.* yeniden toplamak, yığmak; ~ **o.s.** *k-ni* toplamak.

rec.ol.lec.tion [rekə'lekʃən] *n.* hatıra (**of** *-in*), anı, hatırlanan şey.

re.com.mence ['ri:kə'mens] *v/t.* & *v/i.* yeniden başla(t)mak.

re.com.mend [rekə'mend] *v/t.* tavsiye etm., salık vermek; çekici kılmak; **recom'mend.a.ble** *adj.* tavsiye etmeğe değer, salık verilir; **rec.om.men'da.tion** *n.* tavsiye, salık, referans, bonservis; **recom'mend.a.to.ry** [-dətəri] *adj.* tavsiye kabilinden, tavsiye…

re.com.mis.sion ['ri:kə'miʃən] *v/t.* yeniden yerleştirmek, tekrar hizmete almak.

re.com.mit ['ri:kə'mit] *v/t.* PARL yeniden görüşülmek için *b-ne* havale etm.; ~ **to prison** yeniden tutuklamak.

rec.om.pense ['rekəmpens] **1.** *n.* mükâfat, karşılık, ikramiye, ödül; ceza; misilleme; **2.** *v/t.* mükâfatlandırmak *veya* cezalandırmak *-i*, zarar ve ziyanı ödetmek, telâfi etm., tazminat vermek.

re.com.pose ['ri:kəm'pəuz] *v/t.* yeniden oluşturmak (*veya* düzenlemek).

rec.on.cil.a.ble ['rekənsailəbl] *adj.* uzlaşma sağlanabilir, barıştırılabilir, teklif edilebilir, birleşmeleri sağlanabilir; **'rec.on.cile** *v/t.* barıştırmak, uzlaştırmak; mutabık kılmak, bağdaştırmak, uydurmak (**with, to** *ile*); arabuluculuk etm. (*kavga vs.'de*); ~ **o.s.** *to* razı olm. *-e*; *b-le* barışmak, uzlaşmak; alışmak *-e*; **'rec.on.cil.er** *n.* uzlaştırıcı, ara bulan kimse; **rec.on.cil.i.a.tion** [-sili'eiʃən] *n.* uzlaşma, barışma.

re.con.dite □ *fig.* [ri'kɔndait] derin; muğlak, kapalı, anlaşılmaz (*konu, fikir vs.*).

re.con.di.tion ['ri:kən'diʃən] *v/t.* tamir edip yenilemek; revizyon yapmak; MEC rektifiye etm.

re.con.nais.sance ['ri'kɔnisəns] *n.* MIL keşif, yoklama, istikşaf; *fig.* kavrama, anlayış; ~ **car** MIL zırhlı keşif arabası.

rec.on.noi.ter, rec.on.noi.tre MIL [rekə'nɔitə] *vb.* keşif yapmak, keşfetmek; incelemek, araştırma yapmak.

re.con.quer ['ri:kɔŋkə] *v/t.* yeniden fethetmek, zaptetmek; **'re'con.quest** [-kwest] *n.* yeniden fetih, zapt.

re.con.sid.er ['ri:kən'sidə] *vb.* tekrar düşünmek, muhakeme etm.; **'re.con.sid.er'a.tion** *n.* tekrar düşünme (*veya* tetkik).

re.con.sti.tute ['ri:'kɔnstitju:t] *v/t.* yeniden oluşturmak (*veya* kurmak); eski haline getirmek; **'re.con.sti'tu.tion** *n.* yeniden oluşturma (*veya* kurma).

re.con.struct ['ri:kəns'trʌkt] *v/t.* yeniden inşa etm., kurmak; yinelemek; **'re.con'struc.tion** *n.* tekrar inşa; yeniden kalkınma; **re.con.'struc.tive 'sur.ger.y** *n.* hasar görmüş bir vücut parçasının ameliyatla düzeltilerek eski haline getirilmesi.

re.con.ver.sion ['ri:kən'və:ʃən] *n.* yeniden düzenle(n)me, reorganizasyon (*part. savaş sonrası*); reorganizasyon süreci; **'re.con'vert** *v/t.* yeniden düzenlemek, reorganize etm.

rec.ord[1] ['rekɔ:d] *n.* kayıt, not; JUR zabıt, tutanak, tutulga, mazbata; belge, vesika (*a. fig.*); sicil, dosya; şan, şöhret (*part.* POL); liste, cetvel, katalog; plâk, disk; *spor*: rekor; ~ **time** rekor süresi; **it is on** ~ …gerçekten olmuştur, …dığı vakidir; **place on** ~ kaydetmek; **beat** *veya* **break the** ~ rekoru kırmak; **set up** *veya* **establish a** ~ rekor kırmak (*veya* tesis etm.); ~ **Office** devlet arşivi; **off the** ~ gayriresmî; gizli, yayınlanmamak koşuluyla.

re.cord² ['ri'kɔ:d] *v/t.* kaydetmek, yazmak, not etm.; yazıya dökmek; plağa almak, banda almak, kaydetmek; re'cord.er *n.* kayıt (*veya* sicil) memuru; hâkim, yargıç; kayıt aygıtı, teyp; MUS blokflüt; re'cord.ing *n. radyo:* plak; bant; kayıt, plağa al(ın)ma; 're.cord-play.er *n.* pikap.

re.count¹ ['ri'kaunt] *v/t.* anlatmak, hikâye etm., nakletmek.

re-count² ['ri:'kaunt] **1.** *v/t.* yeniden saymak (*oy vs.*); **2.** *n.* yeniden sayım.

re.coup [ri'ku:p] *v/t. b-nin* zarar ve ziyanını ödemek, telâfi etm., karşılamak.

re.course [ri'kɔ:s] *n.* yardım dileme, başvurma; have ~ to başvurmak -*e*, *b*şden çare aramak.

re.cov.er¹ [ri'kʌvə] *v/t.* yeniden elde etm., ele geçirmek; telâfi etm.; tahsil etm. (*alacak*); be ~ed eski sağlığına kavuşmak; *v/i.* iyileşmek, şifa bulmak; *k-ne* gelmek; *a.* ~ o.s. *k-ni* toplamak, silkinmek, *k-ne* gelmek; JUR (in one's suit) kazanmak (*dava*).

re-cov.er² ['ri:'kʌvə] *v/t.* yeniden kaplamak, döşemesini yenilemek.

re.cov.er.a.ble [ri'kʌvərəbl] *adj.* geri alınabilir; tahsil edilebilir; iyileştirilebilir; re'cov.er.y *n.* geri alma; iyileşme; *k-ne* gelme.

rec.re.ant ['rekriənt] **1.** □ korkak, ödlek; hain, sadakatsiz, sadık olmayan; **2.** *n.* korkak (*veya* sadakatsiz, hain) kimse.

rec.re.ate ['rekrieit] *v/t.* yenilemek, tazelemek (*anı vs.*); canlandırmak, neşelendirmek, dinlendirmek; *v/i. a.* ~ o.s. dinlenmek, istirahat etm.; rec-re'a.tion *n.* dinlenme, istirahat; eğlence, neşelenme; ~ ground spor sahası, oyun sahası; 'recre.a.tive *adj.* canlandırıcı, dinlendirici, neşelendirici, eğlendirici.

re.crim.i.nate [ri'krimineit] *v/t.* şikâyete karşı şikâyet *veya* iftiraya karşı iftirada bulunmak; re.crim.i'na.tion *n.* karşılıklı birbirini suçlama, şikâyet etme.

re.cross ['ri:'krɔs] *v/t.* yeniden geçmek (*nehir vs.*).

re.cru.desce [ri:kru:'des] *v/i.* nüksetmek (*hastalık vs.*); tekrar şiddetlenmek; açılmak (*yara vs.*); re.cru'descence *n.* nüksetme, yenilenme.

re.cruit [ri'kru:t] **1.** *n.* acemi er; *fig.* acemi, deneyimsiz; **2.** *v/t.* toplamak, oluş-

turmak (*grup, asker vs.*); ikmal etm., bütünlemek; iyileştirmek (*hasta*); MIL silah altına çağırmak; *v/i.* iyileşmek; re'cruit.ment *n.* acemi erleri silah altına toplama; iyileş(tir)me.

rec.tan.gle ['rektæŋgl] *n.* dik dörtgen; rec'tan.gu.lar □ [_gjulə] dik dörtgen şeklinde; dik açılı.

rec.ti.fi.a.ble ['rektifaiəbl] *adj.* düzeltilebilir; rec.ti.fi.ca.tion [_fi'keiʃən] *n.* düzelt(il)me, tashih; tasfiye; MATH eğri uzunluğunu ölçme; CHEM sürekli distilasyonla saflaştırma; rec.ti.fi.er ['_faiə] *n.* düzelten *b-i veya* bş; *radyo:* redresör, doğrultmaç; rec.ti.fy ['_fai] *v/t.* düzeltmek, tashih etm., doğrultmak; MATH uzunluğunu ölçmek (*eğri*); CHEM saflaştırmak; ELECT, *radyo:* doğru akıma çevirmek; rec.ti.lin.e.al [rekti'linjəl], rec.ti'lin.e.ar □ [_njə] doğrusal, doğrulu, düz çizgili; rec.ti.tude ['rektitju:d] *n.* doğruluk, düzlük; dürüstlük, samimiyet.

rec.tor ['rektə] *n. papaz;* UNIV rektör; (*okul*) müdür; rec.tor.ate ['_rit], 'rec.tor.ship *n.* rektörlük, müdürlük; 'rec.tory *n.* papaz ikâmetgâhı (*veya* konutu).

rec.tum ANAT ['rektəm] *n.* rektum, kalın barsağın son kısmı.

re.cum.bent □ [ri'kʌmbənt] uzanan, yatan, dayanmış.

re.cu.per.ate [ri'kju:pəreit] *v/i.* iyileşmek, sağlığına kavuşmak; re.cu.per'a.tion *n.* iyileşme; re'cu.per.a.tive [_rətiv] *adj.* sıhhatini yeniden kazandıran.

re.cur [ri'kə:] *v/i.* tekrar dönmek (to -*e*); tekrar olm., tekrarlamak (*olay, hastalık vs.*); ~ to s.o.'s mind *b-nin* hatırına gelmek; ~ring decimal devirli ondalık kesir; re.cur.rence [ri'kʌrəns] *n.* dönüş; tekrarlanma, tekerrür; nüksetme; ~ to tekrar bahis konusu olma; re'cur.rent □ tekrar olan; ANAT tersyöne giden; ~ fever tekrar tekrar gelen nöbet.

re.curve [ri:kə:v] *v/t. & v/i.* geriye *veya* içe doğru eğ(il)mek.

rec.u.sant ['rekjuzənt] *adj.* özellikle kilise kurallarına uymayı redden; dikkafalı, serkeş.

re.cy.cla.ble [ri:'saikləbl] *adj.* geri kazanılabilir (*madde, atık*); re.cy.cle *v/t.* (*kullanılmış maddeyi*) yeniden işlemek, değerlendirmek; re.cy.cling *n.* yeniden işleme.

red [red] **1.** *adj.* kırmızı, kızıl, al; ♀ *Crescent* Kızılay; ♀ *Cross* Kızılhaç; ~ *currant* (*kırmızı veya siyah*) frenküzümü; ~ *deer* kırmızı derili bir tür geyik; ~ *ensign* İngiltere'de ticaret gemileri bayrağı; ~ *heat* tav (*metal*); ~ *herring* ilgiyi başka yöne çekmek için ortaya atılan konu; *draw a ~ herring across the trail* dikkati başka yöne çevirmek, oyalamak; ~ *lead* sülüğen; *paint the town ~ sl.* sarhoş olup ortalığı velveleye vermek, gürültü çıkarmak; **2.** *n.* kırmızı renk; *part.* POL kızıl, komünist; *see ~* birden öfkelenmek; *be in the ~ Am.* F borç içinde olm.

re.dact [ri'dækt] *v/t.* telif etm., kaleme almak, neşretmek; re'dac.tion *n.* redaksiyon, düzeltilmiş ve düzenlenmiş nüsha, metin; yeni bası.

red.breast ['redbrest] *n. a.* robin ~ ZOO kızıl gerdan, nar bülbülü; kızıl göğüslü kuş; 'Red.brick *n.* Londra dışında kurulmuş üniversite(ler); 'red.cap *n.* askerî polis; *Am.* bagaj hamalı; red.den ['redn] *v/t. & v/i.* kırmızılaş(tır)mak, kızıllaş(tır)mak, kızarmak; 'red.dish *adj.* kırmızımtırak, kızılımsı, kızılca; red.dle ['-l] *n.* kırmızı tebeşir (*veya* boya).

re.dec.o.rate ['ri:'dekəreit] *vb.* yenileştirmek, yeniden dekore etm.; 're.dec.o'ration *n.* yeniden dekore etme, redekorasyon.

re.deem [ri'di:m] *v/t.* fidye vererek kurtarmak, rehinden kurtarmak, bedelini verip geri almak; COM amortize etm.; nakit olarak ödemek, tazminat vermek, borçtan kurtarmak; telâfi etm. (*zaman*); korumak (*from -den*); re'deem.able *adj.* COM paraya çevrilir (*senet*); fidye ile kurtarılabiilr; amorti edilebilir; Re'deem.er *n.* Kurtarıcı, Halâskâr; *rel.* Hazreti İsa.

re.de.liv.er ['ri:di'livə] *v/t.* yeniden teslim etm., dağıtmak; yeniden kurtarmak, halâs etm.

re.demp.tion [ri'dempʃən] *n.* halâs, kurtar(ıl)ma; COM amortisman; paraya çevrilme; tazminat; re'demp.tion.er *n.* HIST Amerika göçmeni; re'demp.tive *adj.* kurtarıcı, kurtaran.

re.de.ploy ['ri:di'plɔi] *v/t.* daha etken olacak şekilde yeniden düzenlemek (*asker, işçi vs.*).

red...: '~faced *adj.* kırmızı yüzlü; '~haired *adj.* kızıl saçlı; '~'hand.ed *adj.:* catch s.o. ~ b-ni suçüstü yakalamak; '~.head *n.* kızıl saçlı kimse; '~'head.ed *adj.* kızıl saçlı; '~'hot *adj.* kızgın (*metal*); *fig.* canı tez, kabına sığmayan; kızgın, çok öfkeli; en yeni (*veya* son) (*haber vs.*).

re.dif.fu.sion ['ri:di'fju:ʒən] *n.* merkezî bir alıcı aygıttan diğer umumî yerlerdeki alıcılara yapılan ses ve televizyon yayım sistemi.

Red In.di.an [re'dindjən] *n.* Kızılderili.

red.in.te.grate [re'dintigreit] *v/t.* yeniden eski haline getirmek, iyi hale koymak, yenilemek, tamir etm.; red.in.te'gra.tion *n.* yenileme.

re.di.rect ['ri:di'rekt] *v/t.* düzeltilmiş adresi yazmak (*mektup*); yeni adresine göndermek.

re.dis.count [ri:'diskaunt] **1.** *vb.* reeskont etm., senet kır(dır)mak; **2.** *n.* reeskont.

re.dis.cov.er ['ri:dis'kʌə] *v/t.* yeniden keşfetmek (*veya* bulmak).

re.dis.trib.ute ['ri:dis'tribju:t] *v/t.* yeniden dağıtmak (*veya* hisselere bölmek).

red-let.ter day ['red'letə'dei] *n.* yortu günü; *fig.* önemli gün, mutlu bir gün.

red-light dis.trict ['redlait'distrikt] *n.* genelev mahallesi.

red.ness ['rednis] *n.* kırmızılık, kızıllık.

re.do ['ri:'du] (*irr. do*) *vb.* yeniden yapmak.

red.o.lence ['redəuləns] *n.* güzel koku, ıtır, rayiha; 'red.o.lent *adj.* güzel kokulu (*of*); *be ~ of fig.* hatırlatmak, akla getirmek.

re.dou.ble [ri'dʌbl] *v/t.* tekrarlamak, iki misli yapmak -*i*; *v/i.* iki misli olm.

re.doubt MIL [ri'daut] *n.* tabya, palanka, ağaç ve toprakla yapılıp hendekle çevrilmiş küçük hisar; re'doubt.a.ble *adj.* RHET müthiş, dehşetli.

re.dound [ri'daund] *v/t.:* ~ *to* artırmak, yükseltmek, bahşetmek (*şan, şeref vs.*); ~ (*up*)*on* gözden düşmek, gerilemek (*şeref, şan vs.*).

re.draft ['ri:'drɑ:ft] **1.** *n.* yeni müsveddede; COM protesto olan bir senedin masraflarla beraber yeni şekli; **2.** *vb.* yeni müsvedde yapmak.

re.dress [ri'dres] **1.** *n.* çare, düzeltme, telâfi; JUR tazminat; *legal ~* adlî yardım; **2.** *v/t.* düzeltmek; telâfi etm.

red...: '~.skin *n.* kızılderili; '~.start *n.* ORN kızılkuyruk; ~ *tape*, '~.tap.ism ['-'teipizəm] *n.* kırtasiyecilik, bürokrasi; '~'tapist *n.* bürokrat, kırtasiyeci,

evrak adamı.
re.duce [ri'dju:s] *v/t. fig.* geri getirmek (*to -e*), azaltmak, indirmek, küçültmek (*to -e*); düşürmek (*fiyat*); MIL fethetmek; *fig.* zayıflatmak, kuvvetten düşürmek; zorlamak, mecbur etm. (*to -e*); MATH, CHEM indirgemek, redüklemek; PHOT zayıflatmak; MED (*çıkık, kol vs.*) yerine koymak; COM bakıyeri eşitlemek; F bir deri bir kemik bırakmak; *v/i.* perhiz *vs.* ile zayıflamak; **~ to writing** yaz(dır)mak, kaleme almak, kaydetmek; **re'duc.i.ble** *adj.* indirilir, azaltılabilir (*to -e*); zayıflatılabilir; indirgenebilir; **re.duc.tion** [ri-'dʌkʃən] *n.* azaltma, indirme, küçültme; azaltılmış şey; indirim, tenzilat, ıskonto; küçültülmüş harita, resim *vs.*; zaptetme, galibiyet; MED çıkık kol vs.'yi yerine koyma.
re.dun.dance, re.dun.dan.cy [ri'dʌndəns(i)] *n.* fazlalık, bolluk, çokluk; bol bol mevcut olma; işsizlik (oranı), işten çıkarılma; ağdalı ifade; **re'dundant** ☐ gerekenden fazla, bol bol, kesretli, artakalan; işsiz, işten çıkarılmış; fazla sözle ifade edilmiş, ağdalı, fazla detaylı, uzun uzadıya.
re.du.pli.cate [ri'dju:plikeit] *v/t.* iki kat yapmak, ikilemek, tekrarlamak, duble etm., iki misline çıkarmak; **re.du.pli'cation** *n.* iki misline çık(ar)ma, tekrarlama.
red.wood ['redwud] *n.* kırmızı kereste veren bir tür ağaç; bu ağacın kerestesi.
re.dye ['ri:'dai] *v/t.* yeniden boyamak -*i.
re-ech.o [ri:'ekəu] *vb.* aksiseda vermek, tekrar akset(tir)mek, yankıla(n)mak.
reed [ri:d] *n.* saz, kamış (sapı); sazlık; kamış düdük (*zurna vs.nin ucuna takılan*); **the ~s** *pl.* MUS ağzında bulunan ince maden *veya* kamış vasıtasiyle ses çıkaran müzik aletleri (*obua, klarnet zurna vs.*).
re.ed.it ['ri:'edit] *v/t.* yeniden basmak, yayımlamak.
re-ed.u.ca.tion ['ri:edju'keiʃən] *n.* yeniden eğitme.
reed.y ['ri:di] *adj.* kamış (*veya* saz) dolu; kamış düdük gibi tiz ses çıkaran.
reef¹ [ri:f] *n.* resif, kayalık.
reef² NAUT [_] **1.** *n.* yelkenin bir kat camadanı; yelkeni camadan ile küçültme; **2.** *v/t.* yelken camadanını bağlayarak küçültmek; cıvadıra bastonunu

mayna etm.
reef.er¹ ['ri:fə] *n.* denizci ceketi.
reef.er² *Am. sl.* [_] *n.* esrarlı sigara.
reek [ri:k] **1.** *n.* duman, buhar, sis; fena koku; **2.** *v/i.* duman çıkmak, tütmek; buğulanmak (*with ile*); kokusunu yaymak (*of, with -in*); **'reek.y** *adj.* dumanlı; fena kokulu.
reel [ri:l] **1.** *n.* makara, iplik çıkrığı; bobin, masura; film makarası; bant makarası (*teyp*); olta çubuğunun alt ucuna takılan makara; makaraya sarılmış ip, tel, bant *vs.*; **2.** *v/t.* makaraya sarmak, çile (*veya* tura) yapmak, dolamak; **~ off** çıkrıktan geçirmek; ezberden çabucak söylemek, sayıp dökmek; *v/i.* sendelemek, sallanmak; başı dönmek.
re-e.lect ['ri:i'lekt] *v/t.* POL yeniden seçmek; **'re-e'lec.tion** *n.* yeniden seç(il)me.
re-el.i.gi.ble ['ri:'elidʒəbl] *adj.* yeniden seçilebilir.
re-en.act ['ri:i'nækt] *v/t.* yeniden kararlaştırmak; THEAT yeniden sahneye koymak.
re-en.force ['ri:in'fɔ:s] *etc.* = **reinforce** *etc.*
re-en.gage ['ri:in'geidʒ] *v/t.* yeniden hizmete almak (*veya* tutmak).
re-en.list MIL ['ri:in'list] *v/t.* yeniden askere almak.
re-en.ter ['ri:'entə] *vb.* yeniden girmek -*e* (*veya* kaydetmek, kaydolmak, katılmak); girişmek; **'re-'ent.er.ing, re-entrant** [ri:'entrənt] *adj.* girintili (*köşe*).
re-es.tab.lish ['ri:is'tæbliʃ] *v/t.* yeniden kurmak, tesis etm., eski haline getirmek, iyileştirmek.
reeve¹ NAUT [ri:v] *v/t.* halatın ucunu bir delik *veya* makaradan geçirmek.
reeve² [_] *n.* HIST İngiltere'de vali, idareci, hakim *vs.*
re-ex.am.i.na.tion ['ri:igzæmi'neiʃən] *n.* yenilenen sınav; yeniden değerlendirme; **'re-ex'am.ine** *v/t.* yeniden sorguya çekmek.
re-ex.change ['ri:iks'tʃeindʒ] *n.* yeniden değiştirme, trampa etme; COM protestolu senedi masrafları ekleyerek yenileme; retret.
re.fec.tion [ri'fekʃən] *n.* serinlik; hafif yemek (*veya* kahvaltı); hafif yemek *veya* içki ile ferahla(t)ma, serinle(t)me; **re'fec.to.ry** [_təri] *n.* yemekhane (*okul vs.de*).
re.fer [ri'fə:] *v/t.:* **~ to** göndermek, hava-

le etm. *-e, b-ni b-ne* göndermek; müracaat etm., başvurmak, danışmak; *v/i.* ima etm., zikretmek, işaret etm., göstermek (*to -i*); *bşi* içermek, kapsamak, ilgili olm. *ile*; isnat etm., bir nedene bağlamak; **re'fer.a.ble** *adj.*; **~ to** havale edilebilir *-e*, isnat edilebilir *-e*; başvurulabilir *-e*; **ref.er.ee** [refə'ri:] *n.* hakem; *boks*: ring hakemi; PARL raportör, eksper; bilirkişi; **ref.er.ence** ['refrəns] *n.* referans, tavsiye; başvuruş; ilgi, münasebet; havale etme *veya* olunma; ima, kinaye; isnat etme (*to -e*); bilgi, malûmat (veren *b-i veya bş*); ~ **with ~ to** ...*e* gelince, ...*le* ilgili olarak, ...hakkında, ait, ... e nispetle; *terms pl.* **of ~** direktif, talimat; yetki alanı; **work of ~**, **~ book** başvuru kitabı; **~ library** araştırmada yararlanılan fakat dışarı kitap alınmayan kütüphane; ~ **number** dosya (*veya* evrak) numarası; **make a ~ to** zikretmek *-i;* başvurmak *-e*, bakmak *-e*.

ref.er.en.dum [refə'rendəm] *n.* referandum, halk oyuna başvurma.

re.fill ['ri:fil] **1.** *n.* yedek takım, eksilen, biten maddenin yerine konan yedek; yedek kalem içi; yedek kâğıt; **2.** *v/t.* tekrar doldurmak.

re.fine [ri'fain] *v/t.* tasfiye etm., saflaştırmak, arıtmak; inceltmek (*a.* MEC & *fig.*); MEC rafine etm.; *fig.* ıslah etm.; *v/i.* incelmek, zarifleşmek; saflaşmak, temizlenmek; kılı kırk yarmak, titizlik etm. (**on, upon**); ~ (**up**)**on** arılaştırmak, ıslah etm., geliştirmek (*yöntem, plan vs.*); **re.fine.ment** *n.* arıtma, saflaştırma; saflık; halislik; tasfiye; incelik, kibarlık; nezaket, zariflik; **re'fin.er** *n.* tasfiye eden, arıtan *b-i veya bş*; **re'fin.er.y** *n.* MEC rafineri; şeker fabrikası; *metall.* dökümhane, izabehane.

re.fit NAUT ['ri:'fit] **1.** *v/t.* & *v/i.* yeniden donatmak, yenilemek; yeniden donatılıp sefer için hazır olm.; **2.** *n.* tamir, yeniden donatma.

re.flect [ri'flekt] *v/t.* & *v/i.* aksettirmek (*ısı, ışık, ses vs.*) (*a. fig*); ifade etm., beyan etm., açıklamak; ~ (**up**)**on** düşünmek *-i*, ölçüp biçmek, düşünüp taşınmak *-i*; suçlayarak düşüncesini söylemek; *b-nin, bşin* kötü yanını göstermek, kusurunu göstermek; şeref kazandırmak; **re'flec.tion** *n.* yansıma, aksetme; yansıyan (*veya* akseden) şey; düşünme, düşünce, fikir; ayıplama,

kınama; leke, kusur, şaibe; **re'flec.tive** ☐ yansıtan, aksettiren; yansıyan, akseden; düşünceli, derin düşüncelere dalmış; **re'flec.tor** *n.* yansıtan yüzey; projektör, ışıldak; yansıtaç (*karayolunda*); reflektör; aynalı teleskop.

re.flex ['ri:fleks] **1.** *adj.* yansımalı, geri çevrilmiş, tepkimiş, refleks...; **2.** *n.* refleks, tepke, yansı (*a.* PHYSIOL); akis, yansımış şekil; **re'flex.ion** [ri'flek∫ən] = **reflection**; **re.flex.ive** ☐ [ri'fleksiv] üzerinde tepki yapan; GR dönüşlü (*veya* eylem gösteren).

ref.lu.ent ['refluənt] *adj.* dönüp geri akan.

re.flux ['ri:fl∧ks] *n.* geri(ye) akış, cezir haline geliş.

re.for.est.a.tion ['ri:fɔris'tei∫ən] *n.* yeniden orman haline getirme, ağaçlandırma.

re.form[1] [ri'fɔ:m] **1.** *n.* reform, ıslah(at), düzeltme, yenilik; **2.** *v/t.* ıslah etm., düzeltmek, iyileştirmek, geliştirmek; *v/i.* iyileşmek, düzelmek, ıslah olm.

re-form[2] [ri:'fɔ:m] *vb.* yeniden şekil vermek (*veya* teşkil etm.), düzenle(n)mek; MIL yeniden dizmek, oluşturmak.

ref.or.ma.tion [refə'mei∫ən] *n.* gelişme, yenileşme, nefis ıslahı, ıslahat, ıslah olma *veya* etme; ☺ ECCL Reformasyon, dinsel devrim; **re.form.a.to.ry** [ri'fɔ:mətəri] **1.** *adj.* düzeltici, ıslah edici; ıslahat gerektiren; **2.** *n.* ıslahhane, ıslahevi; **re'formed** *adj.* ıslah edilmiş, ıslah olmuş; ECCL Kalvinist, protestan; **re'form.er** *n.* ıslahatçı, reformcu; **re'formist** *adj.* reform (*veya* ıslahat) taraftarı olan, reformist.

re.found ['ri:'faund] *v/t.* kaptan kaba nakletmek, eriterek başka bir kalıba (*veya* bir daha) dökmek.

re.fract [ri'frækt] *v/t.* kırmak (*ışınları*); **~ing telescope** mercekli teleskop; **re'frac.tion** *n.* kırılma; **re'frac.tive** *adj.* OPT kır(ıl)an...; **re'frac.tor** *n.* OPT mercekli teleskop; **re'frac.to.ri.ness** *n.* inatçılık, dikkafalılık; CHEM ısıya dayanıklılık, kolay ergimezlik; **re'frac.to.ry 1.** ☐ inatçı, dikkafalı, serkeş; MEC ısıya dayanıklı, işlenemez; CHEM erimez; **2.** *n.* MEC ısıya dayanıklı malzeme.

re.frain[1] [ri'frein] *v/i.* çekinmek, sakınmak (**from -den**), yapmaktan vazgeçmek, *k-ni* tutmak (**from -den**).

re.frain[2] [-] *n.* MUS nakarat, şarkı nakaratı.

re.fran.gi.ble PHYS [ri'frænd ʒəbl] *adj.* kırılabilir.

re.fresh [ri'freʃ] *v/t. & v/i.* canlan(dır)-mak, serinlet(t)mek, dinlen(dir)mek; hayat vermek, tazelemek; kuvvetlendirmek (*anı*); **re'fresh.er** *n.* F içki, serinletici (*veya* canlandırıcı) şey; JUR uzayan celse için avukata ödenen ek ücret; ~ *course* eski bilgileri hatırlayıp yenilikleri öğrenmek için yapılan eğitim çalışması; **re'fresh.ment** *n.* canlan(dır)ma; canlandırıcı şey; ~ *room* büfe, büvet (*istasyonda*).

re.frig.er.ant [ri'fridʒərənt] **1.** *adj.* soğutucu, serinletici; **2.** *n.* soğutucu *veya* dondurucu şey (*kimyasal madde*); **re'frig.erate** [_reit] *v/t.* soğutmak, serinletmek, dondurmak; **re'frig.er.at.ing** *adj.* soğutan, buz...; **re.frig.er'a.tion** *n.* soğutma, dondurma, serin tutma; **re'frig.er.a.tor** *n.* buzdolabı, soğutucu; soğuk hava deposu; ~ *lorry* frigorifik kamyon, soğuk hava vagonu.

re.fu.el [riː'fjuəl] *vb.* yakıt almak (*veya* ikmal etm.).

ref.uge ['refjuːdʒ] *n.* sığınak, barınak, melce; çare; *a.* *street*- ~ refüj; MOUNT sığınak, kulübe, barınacak yer; *take* ~ *in* sığınmak, barınacak yer bulmak; **ref.ugee** [_'dʒi] *n.* mülteci, başka ülkeye sığınan kimse, sığınık; ~ *camp* mülteci kampı.

re.ful.gence [ri'fʌldʒəns] *n.* parlaklık, parıltı; **re'ful.gent** ☐ parlak, parlıyan, ışın saçan, ışıl ışıl; görkemli.

re.fund 1. [riː'fʌnd] *v/t.* parayı geri vermek; **2.** ['riːfʌnd] *n.* geri ödeme; geri ödenen meblağ.

re.fur.bish ['riː'fəːbiʃ] *v/t.* yeniden cilâlamak, perdahlamak, parlatmak (*a. fig.*).

re.fur.nish ['riː'fəːniʃ] *v/t.* yeniden döşemek (*veya* tefriş etm.).

re.fus.al [ri'fjuːzəl] *n.* ret, kabul etmeyiş *veya* olunmayış, ret cevabı; kabul *veya* reddetme hakkı.

re.fuse¹ [ri'fjuːz] *v/t. & v/i.* reddetmek, kabul etmemek, istememek; vazgeçmek; ürkmek, hendek *vs.*'den atlamayı istememek (*at*).

ref.use² ['refjuːs] *n.* süprüntü, döküntü, çöp; *fig.* ayaktakımı.

ref.u.ta.ble ☐ ['refjutəbl] çürütülebilir, cerhedilebilir, yalanlanabilir; **ref.uta.tion** [refjuː'teiʃən] *n.* yalanlama, çürütme, tekzip; **re.fute** [ri'fjuːt] *v/t.* yalanlamak, çürütmek, cerhetmek, tek-

zip etm.

re.gain [ri'gein] *v/t.* tekrar ele geçirmek (*veya* kazanmak).

re.gal ☐ ['riːgəl] krala ait, krala yakışır, şahane.

re.gale [ri'geil] *v/t.* ağırlama ve ikramda bulunmak, ağırlamak, yedirip içirmek; eğlendirmek, hoşça vakit geçirtmek; *v/i.* zevk ve safa içinde yaşamak (*on*).

re.ga.li.a [ri'geiljə] *n. pl.* kral tacı ve süsü; nişan ve rütbe alâmetleri.

re.gard [ri'gɑːd] **1.** *n.* bakış, nazar; saygı, hürmet, takdir; itibar, sayma; fikir; dikkat, önem; ilişki; ~*s pl.* selâm; *have*~ *to* bşe riayet etm., nazarı itibara almak *-i*; *with* ~ *to* bakımından, karşısında, nazaran, *-e* gelince; *with kind* ~*s* saygılar, selâmlar; **2.** *vb.* dikkatle bakmak *-e*; nazarı dikkate almak, *-i*, hesaba katmak *-i*; itibar etm. *-e*, saymak *-i*; hürmet etm., riayet etm., uymak; ...nazariyle bakmak, ...gibi telâkki etm.; ait olm.; *as* ~*s* hakkında, hususunda, *-e* gelince; **re'gard.ful** ☐ [_ful] saygılı, hürmet eden, göz önünde bulunduran, düşünüp hatırlayan (*of*); **re'gard.ing** *adj.* hakkında, hususunda, *-e* gelince; **re'gard.less** ☐ pervasız, lâkayt, aldırış etmeyen, dikkatsiz, saygısız; ~ *of* *-e* bakmayarak, ne olursa olsun, aldırmayarak.

re.gat.ta [ri'gætə] *n.* kürek *veya* yelken yarışı.

re.gen.cy ['riːdʒənsi] *n.* hükümdarlık, saltanat (süresi); kral naipliği; naipler kurulu; naiplik süresi.

re.gen.er.ate 1. [ri'dʒenəreit] *v/t. & v/i.* yeniden hayat vermek, yeniden teşkil etm., canlandırmak; ıslah etm. *veya* olm., iyileş(tir)mek; ahlâkî yönden geliş(tir)mek; **2.** *adj.* ahlâk ve davranışları ıslah olmuş; yeniden doğmuş; **re.gen.er.a.tion** [_'reiʃən] *n.* yenileme; *fig.* yeniden hayat verme, doğma; iyileşme, ıslah olma; *part.* BIOL yeniden oluşma; **re'gen.er.a.tive** [_rətiv] *adj.* radyo: reaksiyonu harekete geçirici, reaktif.

re.gent ['riːdʒənt] **1.** *adj.* hükümdarın yokluğu *veya* hastalığında vekillik eden; **2.** *n.* saltanat vekili, kral naibi; **'re.gentship** *n.* hükümdarlık; saltanat vekilliği.

reg.i.cide ['redʒisaid] *n.* hükümdarı öldürme; hükümdar katili.

ré.gime, re.gime [rei'ʒi:m] *n.* rejim, sistem, idare (şekli), hükümet şekli; = **regime**.

reg.i.men ['redʒimen] *n.* perhiz, rejim; GR bir sözcüğün kendisiyle ilgili başka bir sözcüğü biçimsel olarak etkilemesi; = **régime**.

reg.i.ment ['redʒimənt] 1. *n.* MIL alay; *fig.* insan sürüsü, kalabalık; 2. ['.ment] *v/t.* alay oluşturmak; sistematik şekle koymak, organize etm., (*insanları*) kontrol altına almak; reg.i.men.tal [.'mentl] *adj.* MIL alaya ait, alay...; reg.i.men.tal.ly [.'mentəli] *adv.* alay gibi; reg.i'men.tals *n. pl.* MIL askerî üniforma; reg.i.men'tation *n.* sistematik şekle koyma, organize etme, kontrol etme.

re.gion ['ri:dʒən] *n.* bölge, mıntıka, semt, taraf, yer, çevre, havali, saha; *fig.* muhit, çevre; olasılık alanı; re.gion.al ['.dʒənl] 1. □ bölgesel, mıntıkaya ait, mahallî, lokal, yöresel; *radyo*: **~ station** mahalli radyo istasyonu.

reg.is.ter ['redʒistə] 1. *n.* sicil; kayıt, liste, katalog, fihrist, cetvel; kütük, resmî kayıt defteri; MEC valf, subap, sürgü; regülatör; MUS ses perdesi; **cash ~** otomatik yazar kasa; **parish ~** kilise cemaati sicil kütüğü; 2. *v/t.* kaydetmek, deftere geçirmek, tescil etm., kütüğe geçirmek; göstermek (*termometre vs.*); ifade etm. (*yüz ifadesi*); taahhütlü olarak göndermek (*mektup vs.*); *v/i.* kaydolunmak, adını sicil *vs.*'ye geçirtmek; 're.gis.tered *adj.* taahhütlü; kaydolunmuş, kayıtlı; **~ design** kullan(ıl)ma kılavuzu.

reg.is.trar [redʒis'trɑ:] *n.* kayıt tescil memuru, sicil memuru; nüfus memuru; reg.is.tra.tion [.'treiʃən] *n.* kayıt, tescil; **~ fee** kayıt ücreti; 're.gis.try *n.* kayıt, tescil; sicil dairesi, evrak kalemi; **~ office** evlen(dir)me dairesi, nikâh memurluğu; **servants' ~** iş bulma bürosu.

reg.nant ['regnənt] *adj.* hükmeden, tahtta olan, saltanat süren n (*part. kraliçe*).

re.gress ['ri:gres] *n.* geri dönüş, avdet, eskiye dönüş; *fig.* azalma, düşüş; re.gres.sion [ri'greʃən] *n.* dönüş, avdet; PSYCH gerileme; re'gres.sive □ [.siv] geri giden, tersyön, gerileyen, tepki oluşturan.

re.gret [ri'gret] 1. *n.* teessüf (**at**); üzün-

tü, keder (**for**); pişmanlık; 2. *v/t.* teessüf etm., üzülmek -*e*, müteessir olm., kederlenmek; pişman olm. -*e*; özlemini çekmek -*in*, yokluğunu hissetmek -*in*, bşin kaybolduğunu farketmek; re-'gret.ful □ [.ful] kederli, üzüntülü, esef dolu; **~ly** esefle, acınarak, teessüfle; re'gret.ta.ble □ acınacak, şayanı teessüf, üzücü.

reg.u.lar ['regjulə] 1. □ muntazam, düzgün; düzenli, kurallı; aynı zamanda olan; değişken olmayan; MIL muvazzaf; ECCL manastır sistemine bağlı, tarikat...; 2. *n.* ECCL bir tarikat *veya* manastır sistemine bağlı imam *veya* papaz; MIL muvazzaf asker; F müdavim; devamlı (*veya* gedikli) müşteri; reg.u.lar.i.ty [.'læriti] *n.* düzen, intizam, nizam, tertip.

reg.u.late ['regjuleit] *v/t.* düzenlemek; yoluna koymak; kurala bağlamak, düzeltmek; ayar etm., tesviye etm., tanzim etm., uydurmak; 'reg.u.lat.ing *adj.* MEC ayar..., tanzim...; reg.u'la-tion 1. *n.* düzen, intizam, nizam; hüküm, kural, emir, karar; **~s** *pl.* tüzük; kurallar; **contrary to ~s** nizama aykırı; 2. *adj.* talim(at)nameye uygun; MIL askerlik...; reg.u.la.tive □ ['.lətiv] düzenleyici, ayarlayıcı; reg.u.la.tor ['.leitə] *n.* düzenleyici *b-i veya bş*; MEC regülatör, düzengeç; saat rakkası.

re.gur.gi.tate [ri:'gə:dʒiteit] *v/t.* kusturmak, istifrağ ettirmek; geri dökmek, akıtmak, fışkırtmak, çıkartmak; *v/i.* kusmak; geri akmak, fışkırmak (*su, gaz vs.*).

re.ha.bil.i.tate [ri:ə'biliteit] *v/t.* yenileştirmek, tamir etm., onarmak (*ev*); bir hastalıktan, özellikle sıtmadan kurtarmak (*mahalleyi*); yeniden dahil etm., koordine etm. (*meslek*); eski hakları iade etm.; yeniden eğiterek eski yaşantılarına kavuşturmak (*savaş malülleri vs.*); 're.habil.i'ta.tion *n.* eski hakların iadesi; eski hale gelme, eski yaşama kavuşma; yenileme, onarım.

re.hash *fig.* ['ri:'hæʃ] 1. *v/t.* aynı şeyi *veya* konuyu tekrar gündeme getirmek, tekrar açmak, temcit pilavı gibi sunmak; 2. *n.* tekrarlama, aynısını sunma; tekrarlanan konu *veya* şey.

re.hears.al [ri'hə:səl] *n.* THEAT, MUS prova; tekrarlama; re'hearse *vb.* THEAT prova etm.; tekrarlamak; ezberden okumak, sayıp dökmek; alıştırmak (*oyuncu*).

re.heat [riː'hiːt] *v/t.* yeniden ısıtmak.

reign [rein] **1.** *n.* hükümet, hükümdarlık, saltanat (devri); *fig.* nüfuz, otorite; **2.** *v/i.* hüküm sürmek, hâkim olm., hükümet etm.

re.im.burse [riːim'bəːs] *v/t.* masrafı geri ödemek; *b-ne* tazminat vermek; parasını geri vermek; COM masraflarını kapatmak; **re-im'burse.ment** *n.* geri ödeme, masrafını iade; tazmin etme.

rein [rein] **1.** *n.* dizgin; yönetim, idare; *give ~ to* yularını salıvermek, başıboş bırakmak; **2.** *v/t.*; *~ in, ~ up, ~ back* bir atın dizginlerini çekmek; *fig. bşe* gem vurmak, *bşi* frenlemek.

rein.deer ZOO ['reindiə] *n.* rengeyiği.

re.in.force [riːin'fɔːs] **1.** *v/t.* kuvvetlendirmek, takviye etm., sağlamlaştırmak; asker *veya* kuvvet göndererek takviye etm.; *~d concrete* MEC betonarme; **2.** *n.* **re.in'force.ment** *n.* takviye (etme), kuvvetlendirme; tahkim (*beton*); *~s pl.* MIL takviye birliği.

re.in.stall ['riːin'stɔːl] *v/t.* yeniden yerleştirmek, kurmak, eski haline getirmek; '**re.in'stal(l).ment** *n.* yeniden yerleş(tir)me.

re.in.state ['riːin'steit] *v/t.* eski görevine iade etm.; eski haline getirmek; tamir etm., onarmak; '**re.in'state.ment** *n.* eski görevine iade edilme; restore etme, onarım.

re.in.sur.ance ['riːin'ʃuərəns] *n.* reasürans, yinelenmiş (*veya* mükerrer) sigorta; **rein.sure** ['‿-'ʃuə] *v/t.* yeniden sigorta etm.

re.in.vest ['riːin'vest] *v/t.* yeniden yatırmak (*veya* yatırım yapmak).

re.is.sue ['riː'isjuː] **1.** *v/t.* tekrar çıkarmak (*veya* neşretmek, yayımlamak); **2.** *n.* yeni baskı.

re.it.er.ate [riː'təreit] *v/t.* tekrarlamak; **re.it.er'a.tion** *n.* tekrarlama.

re.ject [ri'dʒekt] *v/t.* reddetmek, kabul etmemek, tanımamak; işe yaramaz diye atmak; **re'jec.tion** *n.* ret, reddedilme; seçip atma; *~s pl.* özürlü (*veya* sakat) eşya, mezat malı; **re.jec.tor** *circuit radyo:* kısma devresi.

re.jig ['riː'dʒig] *v/t.* (*fabrika*) yeni makinelerle donatmak.

re.joice [ri'dʒɔis] *v/t.* sevindirmek, hoşlandırmak, memnun etm.; *rejoiced at veya by* memnun, sevinçli, neşeli *-den*; *v/i. bşden* dolayı sevinmek, memnun olm. (*at, in*); **re'joic.ing 1.** □ sevinçli, mutlu; sevindiren; **2.** *n. oft. ~s pl.* se-

vinç, neşe, hoşnutluk; şenlik, eğlence.

re.join¹ ['riː'dʒɔin] *v/t. & v/i.* tekrar kavuş(tur)mak, birleş(tir)mek (*to, with -e, ile*).

re.join² [ri'dʒɔin] *v/t.* cevap vermek *-e,* yanıtlamak *-i,* karşılık vermek *-e;* **re-'join.der** *n.* yanıt, cevap karşılık.

re.ju.ve.nate [ri'dʒuːvineit] *v/t. & v/i.* yeniden gençleş(tir)mek; canlan(dır)-mak; **re.ju.ve'na.tion** *n.* gençleş(tir)-me, canlan(dır)ma.

re.kin.dle ['riː'kindl] *v/t. & v/i.* yeniden tutuş(tur)mak, yakmak, yanmak, alevlen(dir)mek (*a. fig.*).

re.lapse [ri'læps] **1.** *n.* eski hale dönme; nüksetme, yinelenme (*hastalık vs.*); tekerrür; **2.** *v/i.* tekrar fenalaşmak, nüksetmek (*hastalık*); tekrar (*kötü yola*) sapmak (*into -e*), aynı hataya tekrar düşmek.

re.late [ri'leit] *v/t.* anlatmak, hikâye etm., nakletmek, söylemek, bildirmek; ilişki (*veya* bağlantı) kurmak (*to, with -(l)e*); *v/i.* ilgili olm. (*to ile*), ait olm., bağlı olm. (*to -e*); **re'lat.ed** *adj.* akraba olan (*to -in*); ilgili, ilişik, ilgisi olan; anlatılmış; **re'lat.er** *n.* anlatan, hikâye eden kimse.

re.la.tion [ri'leiʃən] *n.* ilişki; ilgi, alâka (*with ile*); nispet, oran (*to -e*); akraba(lık), hısım(lık); hikâye (etme), nakil, anlatma; *in ~ to* hakkında, *-e ilişkin, -e* dair, *-e* gelince; *-e* nispetle; **re-'la.tionship** *n.* akrabalık; ilgi, alâka, ilişki.

rel.a.tive ['relətiv] **1.** □ göreli, nispî, bağıntılı, izafî; bağlı, ait, ilişkin (*to -e*); GR nispî, izafî; **2.** *n.* GR ilgi adılı (*veya* zamiri); akraba, hısım; '**rel.a.tive.ly** *adv.* nispeten, oldukça; **rel.a'tiv.i.ty** *n.* izafyet, görelik, nispilik; mensubiyet, ilişkili olma, görelilik.

re.lax [ri'læks] *v/t. & v/i.* gevşe(t)mek, hafifle(t)mek, rahatla(t)mak, yumu(şat)mak, dinlen(dir)mek, gerginliğini gidermek *veya* kaybetmek; **re-lax'a.tion** *n.* gevşeme, rahatlama, dinlenme, rehavet; **re'laxed** *adj.* gevşek, rahat, dinlenmiş; teklifsiz, lâubali.

re.lay¹ [ri'lei] **1.** *n.* değiştirme atı, nöbetleşe iş gören hayvan *veya* insan(lar) *veya* şey; ELECT düzenleyici, röle; *radyo:* naklen yayın; *~ race spor:* bayrak koşusu; **2.** *v/t. radyo:* nakletmek, yaymak.

re-lay² ['riː'lei] (*irr.* **lay**) *v/t.* (*kablo, halı vs.*) yeniden döşemek (*veya* sermek).

re.lease ['riː'liːs] **1.** *n.* kurtarma, salıverme; *fig.* azadetme, azat olunma; serbest bırak(ıl)ma; *film: oft.* **first ~** ilk temsil, ilk gece, vizyona sokma, gösterme; JUR vazgeçme, feragat; MEC, PHOT deklanşör; ilk basım (*hikâye vs.*); **2.** *v/t.* affetmek, kurtarmak; serbest bırakmak, salıvermek (*from -den*); vazgeçmek, feragat etm., devir ve ferağ etm., ibra etm.; *film:* gösterilmesine izin vermek, ilk kez göstermek; yayınlanmasına izin vermek (*kitap, plak vs.*); MEC harekete geçirmek; PHOT deklanşöre basmak.

rel.e.gate ['religeit] *v/t.* göndermek, sürmek, *b-ni veya bşi* daha aşağı sınıf (*veya* sıraya, yere) indirmek; havale etm. (*to -e*); **rel.e'ga.tion** *n.* sürgün; daha alt seviyeye indirme; havale etme.

re.lent [ri'lent] *v/i.* yumuşamak, acıyıp merhamete gelmek; şiddetini azaltmak (*rüzgâr*); **re'lent.less** □ merhametsiz, acımayan, şefkatsiz, amansız, zalim.

rel.e.vance, rel.e.van.cy ['relivəns(i)] *n.* ilgi, alâka; uygunluk (*to -e*); **'rel.e-vant** *adj.* (amaca) uygun, ilgili, alâkalı (*to -e*).

re.li.a.bil.i.ty [rilaiə'biliti] *n.* güvenilir olma; **re'li.a.ble** □ güvenilir, emin.

re.li.ance [ri'laiəns] *n.* güven, itimat, emniyet, inanç (*on*); *fig.* destek, istinat; **re'li.ant** *adj.* güvenen, inanan, itimat eden, bel bağlayan.

rel.ic ['relik] *n.* kalıntı, bakiye, döküntü, artık; ECCL kutsal emanet; anı, yadigâr; **~s** *pl.* bir azizin kemikleri; **rel.ict** ['rel-ikt] *n.* dul (*kadın*); türü tükenmekte olan bir hayvan *veya* bitki.

re.lief [ri'liːf] *n.* ferahlama, iç rahatlaması; teselli, avuntu; ara verme, fasıla; yardım, imdat, bağış; MIL nöbet değiştirme; MIL kurtarmaya gelen kuvvetler; JUR mağduriyetin giderilmesi, çare, düzeltme; ARCH kabartma (iş), rölyef; **be on ~** yardım almak (*para vs.*); **poor ~** fakirlere yardım (kuruluşu); **~ work** sosyal yardım; **~ works** *pl.* işsizlere iş sağlamak amacıyla yapılan yol, köprü *vs.*; **stand out in ~ against** kontrast teşkil etm., iyice belirmek, göze çarpmak.

re.lieve [ri'liːv] *v/t.* hafifletmek, ferahlatmak, yumuşatmak, teskin etm., yatıştırmak, azaltmak; yardım etm. *-e*; MIL nöbet değiştirmek; MIL imdada yetişerek kuşatmadan kurtarmak; JUR çare bulmak; hariç tutmak, muaf

kılmak (*of -den*), *b-ni bşden* kurtarmak, esirgemek (*of*); çeşni katmak, renklendirmek (*parti vs.*); **~ nature, ~ o.s.** def'i hacet etm., aptes bozmak, dışarı çıkmak.

re.lie.vo [ri'liːvəu] *n.* kabartma, rölyef.

re.li.gion [ri'lidʒən] *n.* din, iman; din duygusu, dindarlık; *fig.* onur meselesi; tapma; ilke edinilen şey.

re.li.gious □ [ri'lidʒəs] dinî, dinsel, din...; dindar; ECCL tarikat..., mezhep...; dikkatli, itinalı, vicdanlı, sadakatli; **re'ligious.ness** *n.* dindarlık.

re.lin.quish [ri'liŋkwiʃ] *v/t.* terketmek, bırakmak; vazgeçmek; *-den.* feragat etm., davasından vazgeçmek; **re'lin-quish.ment** *n.* terk, cayma, vazgeçme, feragat (*of*).

rel.i.quar.y ['relikwəri] *n.* kutsal emanetler mahfazası.

rel.ish ['reliʃ] **1.** *n.* tat, lezzet, çeşni; lezlet veren şey (*hardal, salça, v.b.*); *fig.* tadımlık, örnek, mostra; haz, zevk, sevinç, hoşnutluk; **2.** *v/t. & v/i.* severek, ağız tadıyla yemek; *bşden* hoşlanmak, zevk almak; lezzet vermek, çeşni katmak; beğenmek; lezzetli olm., çeşnisi olm.; *bş* hoşuna gitmek, *bşi* beğenmek (*of*); **did you ~ your dinner?** yemek hoşunuza gitti mi?

re.load ['riː'ləud] *v/t.* yeniden yüklemek, doldurmak.

re.lo.ca.tion ['riːləu'keiʃən] *n.* yeni bir bölgeye yerleştirme (*veya* taşıma, sevketme).

re.luc.tance [ri'lʌktəns] *n.* isteksizlik, gönülsüzlük, rızasızlık; *part.* PHYS manyetik mukavemet (*veya* direnç); **re'luctant** □ gönülsüz (olarak), isteksiz(ce), zoraki, istemeyerek; **be ~ to do** *bşi* yapmak için isteksiz olm., *bşi* yapmayacağım diye dayatmak.

re.ly [ri'lai] *v/t.*; **~ (up)on** *b-ne, bşe* güvenmek, bel bağlamak, itimat etm.

re.main [ri'mein] **1.** *v/i.* kalmak(ta devam etm.); geri kalmak; (arta) kalmak; durmak; **2.** *n.* **~s** *pl.* kalıntılar (*yemek artığı, posa, harabe vs.*); cenaze, ceset; **re'main.der** [-də] *n.* bakiye, artan, geri kalan miktar, kalıntı; *kitapçılık: b-nin* ölümünden sonra basılan eserleri; JUR tekrar intikal.

re.mand [ri'mɑːnd] **1.** *v/t.* (JUR *tutuklu*) tutukevine geri göndermek; iade etm., geri göndermek; **2.** *n.* (*tutukevine*) geri gönderme; **be on ~** tutuklu olm.; **pris-oner on ~** tutuklu; **~ home** tutukevi (*çocuklar için*).

re.mark [ri'mɑːk] **1.** *n.* söz, fikir ve mütalâa beyanı; mülâhaza, düşünce; dikkat (etme), farketme; *pass a ~ b-i veya bş* hakkında fikir beyan etm.; **2.** *v/t.* farkına varmak, farketmek *-i*; söylemek, demek; *v/i.* fikir beyan etm., düşüncesini söylemek (*upon*); **re-'mark.a.ble** ☐ dikkate değer; olağanüstü, harikulâde; **re'mark.a.ble.ness** *n.* fevkalâdelik, olağanüstü olma; tuhaflık.

re.mar.riage ['riːmæridʒ] *n.* yeniden evlenme (*veya izdivaç*); **'re'mar.ry** *v/t. & v/i.* yeniden evlenmek.

re.me.di.able ☐ [ri'miːdjəbl] çaresi bulunur, iyileştirilebilen; **re.me.di.al** ☐ [ri'miːdjəl] iyileştiren; çare kabilinden.

rem.e.dy ['remidi] **1.** *n.* çare, vasıta, düzeltme; ilaç, panzehir; yasal yollar; **2.** *v/t.* düzeltmek; çaresini bulmak *-in*, iyileştirmek.

re.mem.ber [ri'membə] *v/t.* bşi hatırlamak, anımsamak; unutmamak, hatırda tutmak; saygılarını sunmak (*mektupta*); (*bahşiş, hediye vs.*) vermeyi unutmamak; anmak, yâdetmek; *~ me to him!* ona benden selâm söyleyin!, ona saygılarımı iletin!; **re'mem.brance** *n.* hatırlama; andaç, yadigâr, hatıra; *~s pl.* selâm, saygı(lar).

re.mil.i.ta.rize ['riː'militəraiz] *v/t.* yeniden ordu *veya* silahla donatmak (*ulus vs.'yi*).

re.mind [ri'maind] *v/t. b-ne* bşi hatırlatmak (*of*), hatırına getirmek; *~ me to answer that letter* bana o mektubu yanıtlamayı hatırlat; **re'mind.er** *n.* hatırlatma; hatırlatan *b-i veya bş*, tekit, üsteleme.

rem.i.nis.cence [remi'nisns] *n.* anımsama, hatırlama (*geçmişi*); hatıra, hatırlanan şey; **rem.i'nis.cent** ☐ hatırlatan, anımsatan, andıran (*of -i*); hatırlayan; hatıra…; *be ~ of b-ne* bşi hatırlatmak, anımsatmak.

re.miss ☐ [ri'mis] üşengeç, miskin, tembel; ihmalkâr, gevşek, kayıtsız; **re'mis.si.ble** *adj.* affedilebilir; **re'mis.sion** *n.* af, bağışlama (*borç vs.*); günah çıkarma; hafifle(t)me (*humma hastalığı vs.*); cezasını azaltma; *~ of fees* ücretleri eksiltme (*veya azaltma*); **re'miss.ness** *n.* ihmal, kusur, kabahat, özensizlik.

re.mit [ri'mit] *v/t. & v/i.* affetmek,

bağışlamak; *b-nin* borcunu silmek; *b-ni* bir cezadan affetmek; ara vermek, vazgeçmek *-den*; JUR yeniden görüşülmek üzere *b-ne* havale etm., yollamak, göndermek, havale etm. (*para*); azalmak, eksilmek, inmek, dinmek; **re-'mit.tance** *n.* (*part. para*) gönderme, havale etme; gönderilen para; COM poliçe, römiz; **re'mit.tee** *n.* alıcı, adına gönderilen; **re'mit.tent** *adj.* artıp eksilen, azalıp çoğalan; bir iyileşip bir kötüleşen (*humma vs.*); **re'mit.ter** *n.* (*para*) gönderen; affeden *veya* bağışlayan; JUR *b-ni* eski makamına iade etme kararı; COM poliçe eden (*veya* gönderen).

rem.nant ['remnənt] *n.* bakiye, artık, döküntü, kalıntı; kumaş parçası; *~ sale* parça *veya* kilo ile kumaş satışı.

re.mod.el ['riː'mɔdl] *v/t.* değişiklikler yapmak *-de*, şeklini değiştirmek *-in*, yeni şekline koymak *-i*.

re.mon.strance [ri'mɔnstrəns] *n.* itiraz, protesto, çıkış, şikâyet, sitem; **re-'monstrant** *n.* itiraz eden kimse; **re-mon.strate** ['remənstreit] *v/i.* protesto etm. (*against, on, with -i*); *v/t.* itiraz etm. (*that -e*).

re.morse [ri'mɔːs] *n.* vicdan azabı, pişmanlık, nedamet; **re'morse.ful** ☐ [.ful] pişman, tövbeli, nadim; **re-'morse.less** ☐ merhametsiz, katı yürekli; **re'morse.less.ness** *n.* merhametsizlik, katı yüreklilik, gaddar, acımayan.

re.mote ☐ [ri'məut] uzak(ta), ırak; bambaşka, büyük farklılıklar gösteren (*teori vs.*); çok seyrek olan; pek az (*olasılık vs.*); *~ control* uzaktan kontrol (*cihazı*); uzaktan kumanda; **re-'mote.ness** *n.* uzaklık.

re.mount [riː'maunt] *vb.* tekrar binmek (*at vs.*); tırmanmak (*merdiven, tepe vs.*); dinlenmiş at vermek (*b-ne, orduya*); çerçevelemek (*resim vs.*); **2.** ['riːmaunt] *n.* yedek at; MIL yedek süvari atları dairesi.

re.mov.a.ble [ri'muːvəbl] *adj.* kaldırılabilir, uzaklaştırılabilir, nakledilebilir; azledilebilir; temizlenebilir; **re-'mov.al** [.vəl] *n.* kaldır(ıl)ma; taşınma, nakil; yol verme, ihraç etme (*from office görevden*); *~ van* nakliye kamyonu; **re'move 1.** *v/t.* kaldırmak, uzaklaştırmak, ortadan kaldırmak, toparlayıp kaldırmak; yerini değiştirmek, başka yere nakletmek; yol vermek, azletmek (*from office*); temizlemek, izale etm.; *v/i.* taşınmak, başka yere naklolmak, gitmek; **2.** *n.* uzaklaş(tır)ma;

ayrılıp gitme, yer değiştirme; derece, kademe; **get one's~** ara sınıfa alınmak (*İngiltere'de*); re'**mov.er** *n.* leke *vs.* giderici; nakliyeci.

re.**mu.ner.ate** [ri'mju:nəreit] *v/t.* ödüllendirmek, mükâfatını vermek; hakkını vermek, emeğinin karşılığını vermek; re.**mu.ner'a.tion** *n.* ödül, mükâfat; karşılık, hak, ücret; re'**mu.ner-a.tive** ☐ [_.rətiv] kârlı, kazançlı.

Ren.**ais.sance** [ri'neisəns] *n.* Rönesans.

re.**nal** ANAT ['ri:nl] *adj.* böbreklere ait.

re.**name** ['ri:'neim] *v/t.* yeni bir ad vermek *-e*.

re.**nas.cence** [ri'næsns] *n.* yeniden doğma, canlanma, uyanma, yenilenme; **the ♀** Rönesans; re'**nas.cent** *adj.* yeniden doğan, canlanan.

rend [rend] (*irr.*) *v/t.* & *v/i.* yırt(ıl)mak, parçala(n)mak.

ren.**der** ['rendə] *v/t.* kılmak, yapmak, etmek; iade etm., geri vermek; göstermek (*iyi muamele, teveccüh vs.*), şükranlarını sunmak (*esp. Tanrıya*); tercüme etm., çevirmek (*into -e*); teslim etm.; MUS çalmak, icra etm.; anlatmak, anlamını açıklamak; COM tevdi etm., görmek, vermek (*hesap*); eritmek (*yağ*); birinci katını sürmek (*sıva*); '**ren.der.ing** *n.* iade, tediye, ödeme; tercüme, açıklama; MUS icra; *theat.* temsil, oynama.

ren.**dez.vous** ['rɔndivu:] *n.* randevu (yeri), buluşma (yeri).

ren.**di.tion** [ren'diʃən] *n.* tercüme, tefsir; icra, temsil; teslim, ödeme.

ren.**e.gade** ['renigeid] *n.* mürtet, dinden dönen kimse; ülkesinden kaçan kimse, firarî.

re.**new** [ri'nju:] *v/t.* yenile(ştir)mek, yenisi ile değiştirmek; re'**new.able** *adj.* yenilenebilir (*kaynaklar*); re'**new.al** *n.* yenile(n)me; yenilenen şey.

ren.**net** ['renit] *n.* yoğurt (*veya* peynir) mayası.

re.**nom.i.nate** [ri:'nɔmineit] *v/t.* yeniden atamak (*veya* görevlendirmek).

re.**nounce** [ri'nauns] *v/t.* terketmek *-i*; vazgeçmek *-den*, reddetmek *-i*, tanımamak, yadsımak *-i*; *v/i. iskambil:* başka renkten kâğıt atmak.

ren.**o.vate** ['renəuveit] *v/t.* yenileştirmek, tazele(ştir)mek; ren.o'**va.tion** *n.* yenileme, onarım; 'ren.**o.va.tor** *n.* yenileştiren kimse.

re.**nown** [ri'naun] *n.* şöhret, ün; re-

'**nowned** *adj.* ünlü, meşhur.

rent[1] [rent] **1.** *pret.* & *p.p. of* **rend**; **2.** *n.* yırtık, yarık, çatlak; bölünme (*a. fig.*).

rent[2] [_] **1.** *n.* kira (bedeli); **2.** *vb.* kiralamak, kira ile vermek *veya* tutmak; kira getirmek; '**rent.a.ble** *adj.* kiralanabilir; kira getirebilir; 'rent.**al** *n.* kira bedeli; ~ **value** kira değeri (*veya* ederi); '**rent-charge** *n.* kira üzerinden alınan vergi; 'rent.**er** *n.* kiracı; film kiraya veren kimse; '**rent-'free** *adj.* kirasız, bedava.

re.**nun.ci.a.tion** [rinʌnsi'eiʃən] *n.* vazgeçme, feragat, terk (**of**).

re.**o.pen** ['ri:'əupən] *v/t.* & *v/i.* yeniden aç(ıl)mak, yeniden başla(t)mak.

re.**or.ga.ni.za.tion** ['ri:ɔgənai'zeiʃən] *n.* reorganizasyon, yeniden örgütle(n)me (*veya* düzenleme); COM ıslah; 're-'**or.gan.ize** *v/t.* düzenlemek, reorganize etm.; COM ıslah ederek sağlamlaştırmak.

rep[1] [rep] *n.* koltuk, sandalye döşemesinde kullanılan kalın kumaş.

rep[2] *sl.* [_] *n.* hovarda, çapkın; ün, şöhret, nam.

rep[3] F [_] *n.* repertuvarındaki piyesleri birbiri ardına değişik günlerde oynayan tiyatro topluluğu.

re.**pack** ['ri:'pæk] *v/t.* yeniden denk yapmak, ambalajını değiştirmek.

re.**paint** ['ri:'peint] *v/t.* yeniden boyamak, badana etm.

re.**pair**[1] [ri'pɛə] **1.** *n.* tamir, onarma; ~**s** *pl.* tamirat, onarım; ~ **shop** tamir evi; **in good** ~ iyi durumda, iyi halde bulunan; **out of** ~ yıkılmağa yüz tutan, kötü durumda. **2.** *v/t.* tamir etm., onarmak, düzeltmek, restore etm., yenilemek; telâfi etm., tazminat vermek *-e*.

re.**pair**[2] [_] *v/i.*: ~ **to** gitmek, çekilmek.

rep.**a.ra.ble** ['repərəbl] *adj.* tamir edilebilir; rep.a'**ra.tion** *n.* onar(ıl)ma, onarım; özür dileme, tarziye; ~**s** *pl.* POL tazminat; **make** ~**s** POL (*harp*) tazminat vermek.

rep.**ar.tee** [repɑ:'ti:] *n.* hazırcevap sözlerle konuşma, hazırcevaplık; **be good at** ~ hazırcevap olm.

re.**par.ti.tion** ['ri:pɑ:'tiʃən] *n.* yeniden dağıtım (*veya* bölme).

re.**pass** ['ri:pɑ:s] *v/i.* geri gitmek, dönmek; *v/t.* yeniden *b-nin* yanından geçmek.

re.**past** [ri'pɑ:st] *n.* yemek (vakti), öğün.

re.**pa.tri.ate 1.** [ri:'pætrieit] *v/t. b-ni*

kendi vatanına göndermek *veya* getirtmek; **2.** [-it] *n.* evine (*veya* yurduna)
dönen kimse; **re.pa.tri.a.tion** ['-'ei-
ʃən] *n.* kendi vatanına dönme.
re.pay (*irr.* **pay**) [ri:'pei] *v/t.* geri ödemek; *fig.* karşılık vermek, misilleme
yapmak; tazminat vermek; ödüllendirmek, *-in* karşılığını veirmek; **re'pay.a-
ble** *adj.* geri ödenebilir, karşılığı verilir; **re'pay.ment** *n.* geri ödeme, tediye;
karşılık, mukabele.
re.peal [ri'pi:l] **1.** *n.* iptal, ilga, fesih, yürürlükten kaldırma (*yasa*); **2.** *v/t.* yürürlükten kaldırmak, feshetmek, iptal
etm. (*yasa*).
re.peat [ri'pi:t] **1.** *v/t. & v/i.* tekrarlamak, bir daha yapmak; bir daha söyle-
mek, yinelemek; ezberden okumak;
aynını söylemek *veya* yapmak; yasaya
aykırı olarak ikinci kez oy vermek; (*silah*) kesintisiz ateş etm.; tekrarlanmak, yinelenmek; ~ **an order for
s.th.** tekrar ısmarlamak; **2.** *n.* tekrar-
la(n)ma; tekrarlanan şey; *oft.* ~ **an order** tekrar sipariş verme; MUS tekrar
(işareti); **re'peat.ed** □ mükerrer, tekrarlanan; **re'peat.er** *n.* tekrarlayan
b-i veya bş; tekrarlanan ondalık kesir;
makineli tüfek; sabıkalı, bir kaç kez
hapse girip çıkmış *b-i*; TEL bir mesajı
zayıf devreden kuvvetli devreye nakleden otomatik röle; çalar saat.
re.pel [ri'pel] *v/t.* püskürtmek, defetmek; reddetmek; *fig.* tiksindirmek,
nefret ettirmek; **re'pel.lent** *adj.* uzak-
laştırıcı; tiksindirici, iğrenç.
re.pent [ri'pent] *v/t. a.* ~ *of* pişman olm.
-e, tövbe etm. *-e*.
re.pent.ance [ri'pentəns] *n.* pişmanlık,
nedamet, tövbe; **re'pent.ant** *adj.* pişman (olan), nadim, tövbekâr.
re.peo.ple ['ri:'pi:pl] *v/t.* nüfusu artırmak; yeni insanlar yerleştirmek.
re.per.cus.sion [ri:pə:'kʌʃən] *n.* geri
tepme; akis, yankı; *fig.* ters tepki, reaksiyon.
rep.er.toire THEAT etc. ['repətwɑ:] *n.*
repertuvar.
rep.er.to.ry ['repətəri] *n.* THEAT temsile
hazır oyunlar, repertuvar; *fig.* zengin
kaynak.
rep.e.ti.tion [repi'tiʃən] *n.* tekrarla(n)-
ma; ezberden okuma; ezbere okunan
parça; ~ *order* COM tekrar sipariş (etme).
re.pine [ri'pain] *v/i.* yakınmak, hoşnut
olmamak, şikâyet etm. *-den.* homur-

danmak, mırıldanmak, üzülmek (*at
-e*); **re'pin.ing** □ somurtkan, homurdanan, asık suratlı, hoşnutsuz, memnun olmayan.
re.place [ri'pleis] *v/t.* tekrar yerine koymak; *-in* yerini almak; *b-nin* yerine
geçmek; ödemek; **re'place.ment** *n.*
yerine geçen şey *-in*; tekrar yerine koyma; *b-nin* yerine geçen kimse; yedek
kuvvet.
re.plant ['ri:'plɑ:nt] *v/t.* etrafına bitki
(*veya* ağaç vs.) dikmek.
re.plen.ish [ri'pleniʃ] *v/t.* tekrar doldurmak; **re'plen.ish.ment** *n.* tekrar
doldur(ul)ma, ikmal.
re.plete [ri'pli:t] *adj.* dolu, dolmuş
(*with* ile), ikmal edilmiş, depolanmış;
re'pletion *n.* çokluk, bolluk, bol bol
mevcut olma.
rep.li.ca ['replikə] *n.* PAINT etc. kopya,
suret; *fig.* tam benzeri, örnek, numune.
rep.li.ca.tion [repli'keiʃən] *n.* JUR da-
vacının mahkemeye verdiği yanıt;
eko, akis; kopya, suret.
re.ply [ri'plai] **1.** *vb.* cevap vermek,
yanıtlamak (*to -e, -i*); karşılık vermek,
mukabele etm.; **2.** *n.* cevap, yanıt,
karşılık; ~ *postcard* yanıtlı kartpostal.
re.port [ri'pɔ:t] **1.** *n.* rapor (*on*); haber,
gazete haberi; bilgi; bildiri; söylenti, rivayet, şayia; (iyi) ün, şöhret; patlama
(sesi), infilâk (sesi); not karnesi, diploma; **2.** *v/t.* bildirmek, haber vermek;
anlatmak; söylemek; (rapor) vermek
veya yazmak; raportörlük etm. (*on,
upon*); geldiğini haber vermek (*to
-e*); **re'port.er** *n.* muhabir; raportör;
muhbir.
re.pose [ri'pəuz] **1.** *n. com.* rahat, huzur
(*a. fig.*), istirahat, sükûn; ahenk; **2.** *v/t.*
yatırmak, dinlendirmek, rahat (*veya*
huzur) sağlamak; ~ *trust* etc. *in* güvenmek *-e*, itimat etm. *-e*; *v/i. a.* ~ *o.s.* istirahat etm., yatmak, dinlenmek, uyu-
mak; dayanmak (*on -e*); **re.pos.i.to.ry**
[ri'pozitəri] *n.* mahfaza (*kutu, dolap,
oda* vs.), depo, antrepo; *fig.* zengin
kaynak; sırdaş.
rep.re.hend [repri'hend] *v/t.* azarlamak, tekdir etm.; **rep.re'hen.si.ble**
□ [-səbl] azarlanmayı hakeden, kına-
nacak, kötü; **rep.re'hen.sion** *n.* ihtar,
kınama, azar tekdir.
rep.re.sent [repri'zent] *vb.* göstermek;
cisimlendirmek, şahıslandırmak;
THEAT (*piyes*) oynamak, rolünü yap-

mak; anlatmak, tasvir etm.; temsil etm; olduğunu *veya* olacağını söylemek, belirtmek, ifade etm. **(as)**; *b-ni veya bşi* temsil etm., *b-ne* vekâlet etm.; **rep.re·sen'ta.tion** *n.* temsil (edilme); göster(il)me; tasvir, anlatım; THEAT oyun, temsil, piyes; fikir, düşünce; JUR, POL vekillik, vekâlet; önerme; simge, işaret; **rep.re'sent.a.tive** ☐ [-tətiv] **1.** temsil eden, numune olan, örnek..., tipik, karakteristik **(of** *-in*); **~ government** seçimle iş başına gelen (*veya* temsile dayanan, temsilî) hükümet; **2.** *n.* vekil; mümessil, temsilci; milletvekili; **House of ℒs** Am. PARL Temsilciler Meclisi.

re.press [ri'pres] *v/t.* bastırmak, baskı altında tutmak; PSYCH ihtibas etm., bilinçdışına itmek (*duygu, istek vs.*); kontrol altına almak; **re'pres.sion** *n.* bastır(ıl)ma, baskı altında tut(ul)ma; tutma, zaptetme, ihtibas, ket vurma (*duygu*); **re'pres.sive** ☐ bastırıcı, baskı altında tutan, engelleyici, sıkı.

re.prieve [ri'pri:v] **1.** *n.* geçici olarak erteleme, tehir, (ölüm cezasının infazını) geciktirme; **2.** *v/t.* geçici olarak ertelemek, tehir etm., süre tanımak, (ölüm cezasının infazını) geciktirmek.

rep.ri.mand ['reprimɑ:nd] **1.** *n.* azar, paylama, tekdir; **2.** *v/t.* azarlamak, paylamak *-i*; resmen kınamak *-i*.

re.print ['ri:print] **1.** *v/t.* yeni baskısını yapmak, tekrar basmak; **2.** *n.* yeni baskı.

re.pris.al [ri'praizəl] *n.* misilleme, karşılık, zorunlu önlem.

re.proach [ri'prəutʃ] **1.** *n.* ayıp(lama), serzeniş, tekdir, azar; yüz karası (olan *b-i veya bş*); **2.** *v/t.* ayıplamak, serzenişte bulunmak, *b-ni bşden* dolayı kınamak **(with)**; azarlamak **(for** *için, -den dolayı*); **re'proach.ful** ☐ [-ful] sitem dolu, serzenişkâr, ayıplayan; yüz kızartıcı, utanılacak.

rep.ro.bate ['reprəubeit] **1.** *adj.* ahlâkı bozuk, sefih, serseri; **2.** *n.* ahlâkı bozuk (*veya* serseri) kimse; **3.** *v/t.* ayıplamak, uygun görmemek, tel'in etm., lânetlemek; **rep.ro'ba.tion** *n.* ayıplama, lânet(leme); mahkûmiyet, reddolunma.

re.pro.duce [ri:prə'dju:s] *v/t.* yeniden meydana getirmek, yaratmak; çoğaltmak; kopya etm., taklit etm., reprodüksiyon yapmak (*resim vs.*); THEAT (*piyes*) yeniden oynamak; *v/i.* çoğalmak, üremek; **re.pro.duc.tion** [-'dʌkʃən] *n.*

çoğalma, üreme, yayılma (*a.* PHYSIOL); kopya, reprodüksiyon; **re.pro'duc.tive** ☐ üretken, üreyen, çoğalan; kopya etme ile ilgili, reprodüksiyon...

re.proof¹ [ri'pru:f] *n.* azar, paylama, serzeniş.

re.proof² ['ri:'pru:f] *v/t.* yeniden emprenye etm., su geçirmez yapmak (*yağmurluk, çadır vs.*).

re.prov.al [ri'pru:vəl] *n.* azar(lama), sitem, paylama, tekdir; **re'prove** *v/t.* ayıplamak, azarlamak, tekdir etm.

rep.tile ['reptail] **1.** *n.* sürüngen (*yılan, timsah vs.*); *fig.* aşağılık kimse, dalkavuk; **2.** *adj.* sürüngenlerle ilgili, sürünen; *fig.* alçak, sefil.

re.pub.lic [ri'pʌblik] *n.* cumhuriyet; **re'pub.li.can 1.** *adj.* cumhuriyete ait; **2.** *n.* cumhuriyetçi; **re'pub.li.can.ism** *n.* cumhuriyetçilik, cumhuriyet idaresi.

re.pub.li.ca.tion ['ri:pʌbli'keiʃən] *n.* yeniden yayınlama (*veya* basma, neşretme); yeni bası.

re.pub.lish ['ri:'pʌbliʃ] *v/t.* yeniden yayınlamak (*veya* neşretmek).

re.pu.di.ate [ri'pju:dieit] *v/t.* tanımamak, reddetmek, kabul etmemek; yadsımak (*çocuğunu, borcunu vs.*); **re.pu.di'a.tion** *n.* ret, yadsıma, tanımama.

re.pug.nance [ri'pʌgnəns] *n.* nefret, tiksinme, isteksizlik, antipati **(to** *-e*); **re'pug.nant** ☐ iğrenç, çirkin, tiksinti veren, hoş olmayan, can sıkıcı.

re.pulse [ri'pʌls] **1.** *n.* püskürtme, bozguna uğratma; *fig.* ret, kabul etmeme, defetme; **2.** *v/t.* püskürtmek, kovmak; *fig.* reddetmek, defetmek; **re'pul.sion** *n.* PHYS isteleme; *fig.* nefret, tiksinme, tiksinti ve korku **(of** *-den*); **re'pul.sive** ☐ *fig.* iğrenç, tiksindirici, mide bulandıran; PHYS uzaklaştıran, geri itici, defedici.

re.pur.chase [ri'pɔ:tʃəs] **1.** *n.* tekrar satın alma; **2.** *v/t.* geri satın almak.

rep.u.ta.ble ☐ ['repjutəbl] saygıdeğer, muhterem; şerefli, namuslu; **rep.u.ta.tion** [repju'teiʃən] *n.* (*part. iyi*) şöhret, ün, itibar, şeref; **re.pute** [ri'pju:t] **1.** *n.* ün, şöhret, itibar; **by ~** ismen, ününden (*tanımak*); **2.** *v/t.* saymak, kabul etm., farzetmek, itibar etm.; **be ~d to be** *veya* **as** ...sayılmak, farzedilmek, addedilmek; **be well (ill) ~d** iyi (kötü) sanılmak, farzedilmek, bilinmek; **re'put.ed** *adj.* ünlü, namlı, şöhretli; ...sayılan, farzedilen, sözüm ona, denen, diye; re'**put.ed.ly** *adv.* sözde, söylenenlere göre, güya.

re.quest [ri'kwest] **1.** *n.* rica, dilek, istek; COM talep, rağbet; *at s.o.'s ~ b-nin* ricası üzerine; *by ~, on ~* arzu edilirse, istenildiği zaman, rica üzerine; *in (great) ~* (çok) aranılan, rağbet gören; *~ stop* ihtiyarî durak; (*musical*) *~ programme* dinleyici isteklerinden oluşan (müzik) program(ı); **2.** *v/t.* rica etm., dilemek (*from -den*).

re.qui.em ['rekwiem] *n.* ölünün ruhu için okunan dua (*huristiyanlıkta*); bu tören için yazılan dinsel müzik.

re.quire [ri'kwaiə] *v/t.* gerektirmek, istemek, talep etm. (*of -i*); muhtaç olm., gereksinimi olm. (*of -e*); *~ (of) s.o. to b-ne* ...nı emretmek, istemek; **re-'quired** *adj.* gerekli, lüzumlu; **re'-quire-ment** *n.* gereksinim, ihtiyaç; lüzum, koşul; *fig.* talep.

req.ui.site ['rekwizit] **1.** *adj.* gerekli, elzem (*for*); **2.** *n.* gerekli şey, elzem şey; *toilet ~s pl.* tuvalet eşyası; **req.ui'si-tion 1.** *n.* rica, talep, başvuru; MIL elkoyma; **2.** *v/t.* MIL el koymak, zaptetmek (*resmi olarak*); istemek, talep etm.

re.quit.al [ri'kwaitl] *n.* misilleme, karşılık; mukabele, bedel.

re.quite [ri'kwait] *v/t. b-ni* ödüllendirmek, mükâfatlandırmak; *-in* karşılığını vermek, misilleme yapmak; hak edilen ödül *veya* cezayı vermek.

re-read ['ri:'ri:d] (*irr. read*) *v/t.* yeniden okumak.

re.scind [ri'sind] *v/t.* feshetmek, iptal etm.; vazgeçmek.

re.scis.sion [ri'siʒən] *n.* fesih, iptal, ilga, yürürlükten kaldırma.

re.script ['ri:skript] *n.* emir, karar(name), tamim.

res.cue ['reskju:] **1.** *n.* kurtuluş, kurtarış; (JUR yasal gözetimden) kurtulma, kurtarılma; **2.** *v/t.* kurtarmak; (JUR yasal gözetimden) b-ni bağışık kılmak, muaf tutmak; '**res.cu.er** *n.* kurtarıcı, halâskâr.

re.search [ri'sə:tʃ] **1.** *n.* araştırma, tetkik, inceleme; **2.** *v/i.* araştırma yapmak (*into, on -da*); re'**search.er** *n.* araştırıcı, araştırmacı.

re.seat ['ri:'si:t] *v/t.* yeni sandalye koymak, oturacak yeni yer sağlamak; yeniden oturtmak.

re.se.da ['residə] *n.* BOT muhabbetçi-

çeği.

re.sell ['ri:sel] (*irr. sell*) *v/t.* yeniden satmak; **re'sell.er** *n.* yeniden satan.

re.sem.blance [ri'zembləns] *n.* benzeyiş, benzerlik (*to -e*); *bear~ to* ile benzerliği olm.; **re'sem.ble** [_bl] *v/t.* benzemek -*e*, andırmak -*i*.

re.sent [ri'zent] *v/t. bşden* dolayı *b-ne* gücenmek, darılmak, içerlemek; alınmak -*den*; re'**sent.ful** [_ful] gücenik, dargın, alıngan; *~ of* darılmış, gücenmiş -*e*; re'**sent.ment** *n.* gücenme, darılma, içerleme, kızma.

res.er.va.tion [rezə'veiʃən] *n.* JUR ihtiraz kaydı, çekince; *Am.* POL yerlilere ayrılmış bölge; yer ayırtma, rezervasyon; ayrılmış yer (*oda vs.*); kuşku, şüphe.

re.serve [ri'zə:v] **1.** *n.* yedek olarak saklanan şey, stok; BOT fon, karşılık, ihtiyat (*veya* yedek) akçesi; yedek, ihtiyat (*a.* MIL); çekingenlik, ağırbaşlılık, açılamama; ağız sıkılığı; COM ihtiraz kaydı, çekince, rezerv; *spor:* yedek (*oyuncu*); bir amaç için ayrılmış arazi; *in ~* yedek olarak elde mevcut; *with certain ~s* belli koşullarla, belli ihtiraz kaydıyla; **2.** *v/t.* saklamak, tasarruf etm., rezerve etm.; ayırtmak, rezerve ettirmek (*yer vs.*); (*hakkını*) muhafaza etm., sonraya bırakmak -*i*; re'**served** □ *fig.* ağzı sıkı; sesi çıkmaz, çekingen; saklı tutulmuş, mahfuz.

re.serv.ist MIL [ri'zə:vist] *n.* yedek, ihtiyat.

res.er.voir ['rezəvwɑ] *n.* su haznesi, rezervuar; havza; *fig.* hazne.

re.set ['ri:set] (*irr. set*) *v/t.* yeniden yerine koymak, yerleştirmek; bilemek, keskinleştirmek (*testere vs.*); TYP yeniden dizmek; ayarlamak (*saat*).

re.set.tle ['ri:'setl] *v/t. & v/i.* yeni bir ülkeye yerleş(tir)mek, iskân et(tir)mek; re'**set.tle.ment** *n.* yeni bir ülkeye yerleşme, iskân.

re.ship ['ri:'ʃip] *v/t.* yeniden gemi ile nakletmek (*veya* gemiye yüklemek).

re.shuf.fle ['ri:'ʃʌfl] **1.** *v/t. & v/i.* değişiklikler yapmak, değiştirmek; (*oyun kâğıtlarını*) yeniden karıştırmak; **2.** *n.* değişiklikler yapma, yeniden kurma.

re.side [ri'zaid] *v/i.* oturmak, ikamet etm.; *~ in -de* bulunmak; ait olm. -*e* (*güç, hak vs.*); **res.i.dence** ['rezidəns] *n.* ikamet(gâh), ev, mesken; bir yerde oturma; *~ permit* ikamet tezkeresi;

'res.i.dent **1.** *adj.* oturan, yerleşmiş, sakin, mukim; **2.** *n.* bir yerde oturan kimse, yerli; (*sömürgede*) devlet temsilcisi, genel vali; resi.den.tial [‗'denʃəl] *adj.* ikametgâh…; içinde oturulur, oturmaya ayrılmış.

re.sid.u.al [ri'zidjuəl] *adj.* artan, kalan; tortu niteliğinde; re'sid.u.ar.y *adj.* artan, geri kalan; res.i.due ['rezidju:] *n.* artan miktar, artık; JUR ölen *b-nin* borç ve vasiyetinden artan tereke; re.sid.u.um [ri'zidjuəm] *n. part.* CHEM tortu, posa; çöküntü, (*a. fig.*); MATH kalan bakiye.

re.sign [ri'zain] *v/t.* bırakmak, terketmek; vazgeçmek *-den*; (görevden) istifa etm., çekilmek; ~ *o.s. to* baş eğmek *-e*; *bşle* yetinmek; *v/i.* istifa etm., çekilmek; tevekkül göstermek; res.ig.na.tion [rezig'neiʃən] *n.* istifa, çekilme; tevekkül, uysallık; re.signed □ [ri-'zaind] baş eğmiş, uysal, teslimiyet göstermiş, mütevekkil, işi oluruna bırakmış; istifa etmiş.

re.sil.i.ence [ri'ziliəns] *n.* elâstikiyet, esneklik, geri fırlama; *fig.* kabiliyet, kuvvet, iktidar; re'sil.i.ent *adj.* elâstikî, esnek; *k-ni* çabuk toparlayan (*insan*); *fig.* kabiliyetli, kuvvetli, takatlı.

res.in ['rezin] **1.** *n.* sakız, reçine; **2.** *v/t.* reçinelemek *-i*; 'res.in.ous *adj.* reçineli, sakızlı.

re.sist [ri'zist] *v/t.* karşı koymak, direnmek, mukavemet etm. *-e*; dayanmak, tahammül etm. *-e*; re.sist.ance *n.* direniş, mukavemet, karşı koyma, rezistans, direnç (*a.* PHYS, ELECT; *to -e*); *line of least ~ en* kolay yol, çözüm; *attr.* mukavemet…; re'sist.ant *adj.* karşı koyan, direnen, dayanıklı, mukavemetli, dirençli (*to -e*); re'sis.tor *n.* ELECT rezistan(s), direnç.

re.sole ['ri:'səul] *v/t.* yeni pençe (*veya* taban) geçirmek.

res.o.lute □ ['rezolu:t] kararlı, azimli, sebatlı, tereddütsüz; cesur, yiğit; 'res.olute.ness *n.* azim(kârlık), sebat, kararlılık, metanet; cesaret, yiğitlik.

res.o.lu.tion [rezə'lu:ʃən] *n.* PHYS, MATH, MUS ayrışma, çözme, çözüm; kararlılık, azim; PARL önerge; karar; çözüm, açıklama.

re.solv.a.ble [ri'zɔvəbl] *adj.* çözümlenebilir, halledilebilir.

re.solve [ri'zɔlv] **1.** *v/t.* çözmek, ayırmak (*into -e*; *a.* CHEM, MATH, MUS); *fig.* halletmek (*soru*); ortadan kaldır-

mak (*sorun*); kararlaştırmak (*to -i*); ~ *o.s.* (*itself*) *into -e* dönüşmek, halini almak; ayrışmak; *v/i.* *a.* ~ *o.s.* karar vermek, kararlaştırmak, tasarlamak; ~ (*up*)*on* azmetmek, *bşe* kesin karar vermek, karara varmak; **2.** *n.* karar, hüküm, tasarlama; *lit.* azim(kârlık); re-'solved □ azimli, kararlı, tereddütsüz.

res.o.nance ['reznəns] *n.* yankılama, aksiseda, rezonans; 'res.o.nant □ yankılayan, (*sesi*) aksettiren; tanınan; tok sesli.

re.sorp.tion PHYSIOL [ri'sɔ:pʃən] *n.* em(il)me.

re.sort [ri'zɔ:t] **1.** *n.* dinlenme yeri, mesire; sık sık gidilen, uğranılan yer; barınak, sığınacak yer; çare; yardımına başvurulan kişi *veya* şey; *health* ~ kaplıca, ılıcalar; *seaside* ~ plâj (kenti); *summer* ~ sayfiye, yazlık; *in the last* ~ son çare olarak; **2.** *v/i.* ~ *to* sık sık gitmek *-e*, ziyaret etm. *-i* (*yer*); başvurmak *-e*, *bşden* çare aramak.

re.sound [ri'zaund] *v/i.* çınlamak, yankılamak (*with ile*).

re.source [ri'sɔ:s] *n.* (*doğal*) kaynak, zenginlik; çare, yardım kaynağı, vasıta; halletme yeteneği, kafalılık, iş bilme, beceriklilik; oylanan; oyalayan, vakit geçirten şey, dinlendiren meşgale; ~*s pl.* olanaklar, imkânlar; re'source.ful □ [‗.ful] becerikli, hünerli, mahir; zengin kaynaklı; re'source.ful.ness *n.* zenginlik, servet; beceriklilik.

re.spect [ris'pekt] **1.** *n.* saygı, hürmet, itibar (*to, of -e*); münasebet, ilgi, alâka, oran, nispet, husus, cihet; takdir, hürmet (*for -e*); ~*s pl.* selâmlar, saygılar, hürmetler; *with* ~ *to -e* gelince, … hakkında, ait, nispetle, göre; *in* ~ *of* …bakımından, …gözönüne alındığında; *pay one's* ~*s on s.o.* *b-ne* nezaket ziyaretinde bulunmak, saygılarını sunmak; **2.** *v/t.* *b-ne* saygı göstermek, hürmet etm.; *bşe* riayet etm.; *k-ne* özsaygısı olm.; respect.a'bil.i.ty *n.* saygınlık, itibar, saygıdeğer olma; COM ekonomik açıdan güçlü, güvenilir olma; *respectabilities pl.* âdabı muaşeret, görgü kuralları; re'spect.a.ble □ namuslu, iffetli, saygın; epeyce, haylî, kayda değer; *part.* COM ekonomik itibarı sağlam; re'spect.ful □ [‗.ful] saygılı, saygı eden, nazik, terbiyeli; *Yours* ~*ly* derin saygılarını sunarım (*mektupta*); re'spect.ful.ness *n.* saygılı olma, hürmetkârlık; re'specting *prep.* *-e* bakımından, *-e* gelince, *-e* ilişkin; **re'spec.tive** □ ayrı ayrı, her biri *k-nin* olan; **we went to our ~ places** her birimiz kendi evimize gittik; **re-'spec.tive.ly** *adv.* sırası ile, biri birine ve diğeri ötekine ait olmak üzere, biri ... öteki ...

res.pi.ra.tion [respə'reiʃən] *n.* nefes (alma), soluma, teneffüs; soluk.

res.pi.ra.tor ['respəreitə] *n.* gaz maskesi, nefes filtresi, respirator; MED solunum cihazı; **re.spir.a.to.ry** [ri-'spaiərətəri] *adj.* solunumla ilgili, solunum...

re.spire [ris'paiə] *v/i.* teneffüs etm., nefes almak, soluk almak; *fig.* ferahlamak, soluk almak.

res.pite ['respait] **1.** *n.* JUR mühlet, mehil, tecil, vâde, süre, geçici erteleme; pay dos, ara, fasıla; **2.** *v/t.* ertelemek, tehir etm.; mühlet vermek *-e*.

re.splend.ence, re.splend.en.cy [ri-'splendəns(i)] *n.* parlaklık, parıltı; *fig.* şaşaa, ihtişam, debdebe, lüks; **re-'splend.ent** □ parlak, göz alıcı; şaşaalı, ihtişamlı.

re.spond [ri'spɔnd] *v/i.* cevap vermek, karşılık vermek, mukabelede bulunmak (**to** *-e*); **re'spond.ent 1.** *adj.* JUR savunan, dâvalı; **~ to** karşılık veren, cevap veren *-e*; **2.** *n.* JUR savunan, dâvalı kimse.

re.sponse [ris'pɔns] *n.* cevap (verme), yanıt, karşılık; *fig.* tepki, reaksiyon (**to** *-e*).

re.spon.si.bil.i.ty [rispɔnsi'biliti] *n.* sorumluluk (**for, of** *-in*); güvenilirlik; COM ödeme gücü, sağlamlık; **re'spon.si.ble** *adj.* sorumlu, mesul (**for** *-den,* **to** *-e*); güvenilir; COM ödeme gücü olan; **be ~ for** *bşde* suçu olm., kabahati olm., *bşin* nedeni olm., sorumlusu olm.; **re'spon.sive** □ cevap veren, karşılık...; *bş* karşısında duygulu, duyarlı, hassas, uyumlu (**to** *-e*).

rest[1] [rest] **1.** *n.* rahat, huzur, sükûnet, sessizlik; istirahat, dinlenme; uyku; *fig.* ölüm; mesnet, dayanak, destek; MUS es, fasıla, durak işareti; **at ~** hareketsiz; rahatta; ölmüş; **2.** *v/i.* dinlenmek, istirahat etm., mola vermek; uyumak; dayanmak, yaslanmak, istinat etm. (*a. fig.*) (**on, upon** *-e*); **~ (up)on** *fig.* *bşden* ileri gelmek, *bşe* bağlı olm.; **it ~s with you** bu sizin elinizdedir, size bağlıdır; *v/t.* dinlendirmek, dayamak, yaslamak, koymak (**on** *-e*); da-

yandırmak, bir nedene bağlamak (*sav*); (*gözlerini*) bir yöne dikmek, sabit bakmak; durdurmak (*makine vs.*).

rest[2] [_] **1.** *n.* artan, geri kalan miktar, artık, bakiye; diğerleri, ötekileri, devamı; üst yanı; diğer şeyleri; COM ihtiyat akçesi; **for the ~** belirtilenin dışında, zaten, esasen, herşeyin ötesinde; **2.** *v/i.* olmağa devam etm.; kalmak; **~ assured** emin olm., kesinlikle inanmak.

re.state ['riː'steit] *v/t.* yeniden belirtmek, söylemek, sekillendirmek.

re.stau.rant ['restrɔnt] *n.* restoran, lokanta; '**~-car** *n.* yemekli vagon, vagon-restoran

rest-cure MED ['restkjuə] *n.* dinlenme tedavisi.

rest.ful ['restful] *adj.* sakin, rahat (verici), huzurlu, dinlendirici.

res.ting-place ['restiŋpleis] *n.* dinlenme yeri, konak yeri; mezar.

res.ti.tu.tion [resti'tjuːʃən] *n.* çalınan *veya* kaybolan *bşi* sahibine geri verme; zararı ödeme; tazminat; onarma, restore et.me, eski haline getirme; **make ~** tazmin etm., zararı ödemek (**of** *-i*).

res.tive □ ['restiv] inatçı, dikkafalı, aksi, rahat durmaz; '**res.tive.ness** *n.* inatçılık, dikkafalılık.

rest.less ['restlis] *adj.* yerinde durmaz; huzursuz, rahatsız; dalgalı, hareketli (*deniz vs.*); uykusuz; durup dinlenmeyen, kıpır kıpır; tezcanlı, vesveseli; '**rest.less.ness** *n.* huzursuzluk, rahatsızlık; tezcanlılık; yerinde durama-ma.

re.stock ['riː'stɔk] *v/t.* & *v/i.* doldurmak, eksikleri tamamlamak; yeniden stok etm. (**with** *ile*).

res.to.ra.tion [restə'reiʃən] *n.* yenileme, restore etme, eski haline getirme; eski görevini iade etme (**to** *-e*); *bşi* geri verme, iade; *bşin* aslını gösteren model; **restor.a.tive** □ [ris'tɔrətiv] güçlendiren, düzelten, canlandıran; ayıltan (*ilaç vs.*).

re.store [ris'tɔː] *v/t.* yenilemek, eski haline getirmek, restore etm.; iade etm., geri vermek; *bşi* yerine koymak; zarar ve ziyanı ödemek, telâfi etm.; yeniden canlandırmak; **~ s.o. to liberty** *b-ne* özgürlüğünü geri vermek; **~ to health** *veya* **life** iyileştirmek, sağlığına kavuşturmak, hayata döndürmek; **re-'stor.er** *n.* yenileyen, eski haline getiren, restore eden kimse; **hair~** saç gür-

restrain

leştiren ilaç.

re.strain [ris'trein] v/t. geri tutmak, alıkoymak, tutmak (*from* -*den*), zaptetmek; bastırmak, sınırlamak, yasaklamak; re'strained adj. kontrollu, zaptedilmiş; restraint [_'treint] n. k-ni tutma, sinirlerine hâkim olma; sınırlılık, tahdit, engel; zorunluluk; baskı, tazyik; tutukluluk; çekinme, sıkılma.

re.strict [ris'trikt] v/t. kısıtlamak, sınırlamak -i, tahdit koymak -e; re'stric.tion n. sınırlama, kısıtlama, tahdit (*of, on*); koşul, kayıt, sınır; re'stric.tive □ sınırlayıcı, kısıtlayıcı, bağlayıcı.

rest room *Am.* tuvalet, helâ.

re.sult [ri'zʌlt] **1.** n. sonuç, netice; son; **2.** v/i. meydana gelmek, çıkmak (*from* -*den*); ~ *in* bşle sonuçlanmak, son bulmak; re'sult.ant **1.** adj. meydana gelen, çıkan; **2.** n. MEC sonuç, netice.

ré.su.mé ['rezju:mei] n. özet, hulâsa; özgeçmiş.

re.sume [ri'zju:m] vb. yeniden başlamak, kalan yerden devam etm. -e; geri almak, yeniden elde etm. -i; re'sump.tion [ri'zʌmpʃən] n. yeniden başlama, devam etme; geri alma.

re.sur.face ['ri:'sɔ:fis] v/t. yüzeyi yeniden kaplamak (*yol vs.*); v/i. suyun yüzüne çıkmak (*denizaltı*).

re.sur.gence [ri'sə:dʒəns] n. yeniden yükselme, sivrilme, doğma, dirilme, taraftar bulma, canlanma (*fikir, inanış vs.*); re'sur.gent adj. yeniden canlanan, doğan, dirilen, yükselen.

res.ur.rect [rezə'rekt] v/t. yeniden canlandırmak, moda etm., ortaya çıkarmak; F arayıp bulmak, keşfetmek; yeniden kazmak, hafriyat yapmak; yeniden diriltmek, hortlatmak; res.ur-'rec.tion n. yeniden diril(t)me, basübadelmevt; yeniden canlanma, ortaya çıkma; res.ur'rec.tionist [_ʃnist], res.ur'rec.tion-man [_ʃənmən] n. ceset hırsızı.

re.sus.ci.tate [ri'sʌsiteit] v/t. & v/i. yeniden diril(t)mek, canlan(dır)mak; re.susci'ta.tion n. yeniden diril(t)me.

re.tail 1. ['ri:teil] n. perakende satış, perakendecilik; *by* ~ perakende; ~ *price* perakende fiyat(ı); **2.** [_] adj. perakende...; **3.** [_] adv. s. *by* ~; **4.** [ri:'teil] v/t. perakende olarak satmak; ayrıntılarıyle anlatmak; v/i. perakende olarak satılmak (*at* -*e*); re'tail.er n. perakendeci.

re.tain [ri'tein] v/t. alıkoymak, zaptet-

mek; hatırda tutmak, unutmamak; tutmak, elinde bulundurmak; hizmetine almak, ücretle tutmak (*avukat*); re-'tain.er n. HIST hizmetkâr, uşak; *old* ~ yaşlı uşak, kâhya; re'tain.ing fee avans olarak (*avukata*) verilen para.

re.take [ri:'teik] (*irr. take*) v/t. geri almak (*savaşta kaybedilen yeri*); tekrar fotoğrafını çekmek.

re.tal.i.ate [ri'tælieit] v/t. dengiyle karşılamak, misillemek; v/i. öcünü almak, intikam almak (*on, upon* -*den*); re.tal.i'ation n. misilleme, kısas, misliyle karşılık verme; re'tal.i.a.to.ry [_ətəri] adj. misilleme kabilinden, misilleme...

re.tard [ri'tɑ:d] v/t. geciktirmek, sürüncemede bırakmak, tecil, talik etm., alıkoymak; ~*ed ignition* MOT geç ateşleme; *mentally* ~*ed* zihnî gelişmesi yavaş olan, geri zekâlı; re.tar.da.tion [ri:tɑ:-deiʃən] n. gecik(tir)me, alıkoyma; geciktiren şey, engel.

retch [retʃ] v/i. öğürmek, kusmağa çalışmak.

re.tell ['ri:'tel] (*irr. tell*) v/t. tekrar anlatmak, başka bir yol *veya* dilde anlatmak.

re.ten.tion [ri'tenʃən] n. alıkoyma, tutma; hatırda tutma; MED idrar tutulması, vücuttan atılamaması; muhafaza etme (*anane, ahlâk vs.*); re'ten.tive □ alıkoyan, tutan, salıvermeyen; hatırda iyi tutan, hafızası kuvvetli olan.

re.think ['ri:'θiŋk] (*irr. think*) vb. yeniden etraflıca düşünmek, hesabetmek kitabetmek.

ret.i.cence ['retisəns] n. ağız sıkılığı, sır saklama, susma, ketumiyet (*of*); 'ret.i-cent adj. ağzısıkı, ketum, suskun, sesi çıkmaz.

ret.i.cle ['retikl] n. optik cihazlarda göz merceğine yerleştirilen ve görüşü kolaylaştıran çizgiler *veya* küçük bir ağ sistemi.

re.tic.u.late □ [ri'tikjulit], re'tic.u.lat-ed □ [_leitid] ağ gibi, ağ şeklinde, ağ..., şebekeli; ret.i.cule ['retikju:l] n. küçük bayan elçantası; = *reticle*.

ret.i.na ANAT ['retinə] n. ağtabaka, retina.

ret.i.nue ['retinju:] n. maiyet, heyet.

re.tire [ri'taiə] v/t. emekli etm.; emekliye ayırmak; v/i. geri çekilmek (*a. MIL.*); (*bir köşeye*) çekilmek; emekliye ayrılmak; *a.* ~ *to bed* yatağa yatmak; re-'tired □ emekli; münzevî, dünyadan elini eteğini çekmiş; ıssız, uzaklarda (*yer*); ~ **pay** emekli maaşı; **re'tire.ment** *n*. emeklilik; inziva; **re'tir.ing** □ çekingen, sıkılgan, utangaç, mahcup, sesi çıkmaz; ~ **pension** emekli maaşı.

re.tort [ri'tɔːt] **1.** *n*. cevap, karşılık; sert, hazır ve çoğu zaman eğlendirici cevap; CHEM (boynuzlu) imbik; **2.** *v/t. & v/i.* (*hakaret vs.*) karşılık vermek, cevap vermek (**on, upon** -*e*); sert cevap vermek.

re.touch ['riː'tʌtʃ] *v/t.* gözden geçirmek, revizyon yapmak; PHOT rötüş yapmak.

re.trace [ri'treis] *v/t.* (-*in izini*) takip ederek kaynağına gitmek; ~ **one's steps** geldiği yönden geri gitmek.

re.tract [ri'trækt] *v/t. & v/i.* geri çek(il)mek, geri al(ın)mak; MEC içeri *veya* geri çekmek; sözünü geri almak; caymak, sözünden dönmek; **re'tract.a.ble** *adj.* geri çekilebilir, alınabilir (AVIA *tekerlekler*); **re'trac'ta.tion** *n*. cayma, sözünden dönme; sözünü geri alma; **re-'trac.tion** *n*. geri çek(il)me, geri alma; cayma, vazgeçme.

re.trans.late ['riː'trænsˈleit] *v/t.* yeniden tercüme etm.; '**re.transˈla.tion** *n*. yeniden tercüme.

re.tread ['riː'tred] **1.** *v/t.* (*lastik tekerlek*) dışını kaplamak; **2.** *n*. kaplanmış lastik (*tekerlek*).

re.treat [ri'triːt] **1.** *n*. geri çek(il)me; geri çekilme işareti; sığınak, inziva köşesi, emniyette ve huzur içinde olunacak yer, tenha yer; MIL ricat borusu; **beat a ~** *fig.* geri çekilme, hoş olmayan bir durumla karşılaşmamak için kaçmak; **2.** *v/i.* geri çekilmek; *fig.* gerilemek, vazgeçmek.

re.trench [ri'trentʃ] *v/t. & v/i.* azaltmak, kısmak, indirmek, küçültmek; çizmek, iptal etm. (*sözcük vs.*); MIL tahkim etm.; azalmak, küçülmek, masrafları azaltmak; **re'trench.ment** *n*. azaltma, kısma, tasarruf, idare; MIL savunma hattı.

re.tri.al JUR ['riː'traiəl] *n*. yeniden dava açma.

ret.ri.bu.tion [retri'bjuːʃən] *n*. karşılıkta bulunma, misilleme; ceza, günahların bedeli; **re.trib.u.tive** □ [ri'tribjutiv] karşılık olarak, misilleme…, cezalandırıcı, ödüllendirici.

re.triev.a.ble [ri'triːvəbl] *adj.* tekrar ele geçirilebilir, düzeltilebilir, telâfi edilebilir, geri getirilebilir; **re'triev.al** *n*. geri alma, geri getirme, düzeltme, telâfi; **beyond ~, past ~** geri getirilemez, düzeltilemez, telâfi edilemez.

re.trieve [ri'triːv] *vb.* tekrar ele geçirmek; düzeltmek, iyileştirmek, telâfi etm., tazminat vermek; HUNT bulup getirmek; **re'triev.er** *n*. HUNT kapıp getiren av köpeği.

ret.ro… ['retrəu] *prefix* geriye doğru, geri(ye), arkada, arkaya…; ~'**ac.tive** *adj.* geriye dönük, evvelce olanı kapsayan (*part. yasa*); ~'**cede** *v/i.* geri gitmek, çekilmek, dönmek; geri vermek; ~'**cession** *n*. geri çekilme, gerileme; geri verme, iade; ~**gra'da.tion** *n*. AST doğudan batıya doğru geri gitme; gerileme, geri çekilme; *fig.* gerileme, düşüş; '~**grade 1.** *adj.* gerileyen, geri giden, ters yönde giden; giderek kötüleşen; **2.** *v/i.* gerilemek; bozulmak, kötüye gitmek (*a. fig.*).

ret.ro.gres.sion [retrəu'greʃən] *n*. gerileme, geriye gitme; bozulma, yozlaşma; **ret.ro.spect** ['~spekt] *n*. geçmişe bakış; **in ~** geçmişe bakıldığında; **retro'spection** *n*. geçmişe bakış, geçmişi anma; **ret.ro'spec.tive** □ geçmişle ilgili, geçmişi hatırlayan; geriye dönük, önceyi kapsayan; ~ **view** geçmişe bakış.

re.trous.sé [rə'truːsei] *n*.: ~ **nose** yukarı kalkık kısa burun.

re.try JUR ['riː'trai] *v/t.* yeniden yargılamak.

re.turn [ri'təːn] **1.** *n*. (geri) dönüş; PARL seçim; seçim mazbatası; seçilme; *oft.* ~**s** *pl.* kazanç, kâr; MED nüksetme, tekrar olma; iade, geri ver(il)me; ödeme, tediye; misilleme, karşılık, cevap; şükran, teşekkür; resmî rapor, banka raporu; vergi beyanı, beyanname; ARCH bir binanın yan kısmı; F dönüş bileti; ~**s** *pl.* istatistik cetveli; **many happy ~s of the day!** nice muflu-yıllara! (*b--nin isim gününde söylenir*); **election** ~**s** *pl.* seçim mazbataları, seçim sonuçları; **in ~** karşılık olarak; **in ~ for** -*e* karşılık, -*in* karşılığında; **by ~ (of post)** ilk posta ile, hemen, acele; ~ **match** rövanş maçı; ~ **ticket** gidiş dönüş bileti; *Am.* dönüş bileti; ~ **visit** iadei ziyaret; **2.** *vb.* geri dönmek; tekrar olm.; ~ **to** *fig.* bir konuya geri dönmek; eski alışkanlıklarına dönmek; yeniden *b-nin* eline geçmek; geri vermek, iade etm., geri göndermek; cevap vermek, yanıtlamak; geri ödemek; iadei ziyarette bulunmak, şükranlarını sunmak; JUR yargılamak, hüküm vermek; resmî rapor vermek; PARL seçmek; kâr bırakmak; ~ **guilty** JUR suçlu olduğuna karar vermek; re'**turn.a.ble** *adj.* geri verilmesi *veya* gönderilmesi gereken; geri verilebilir *veya* gönderilebilir; re-'**turn.er** *n.* geri ödeyen, geri gönderen; re'**turn.ing-offi.cer** *n.* seçim memuru.

re.u.ni.fi.ca.tion ['riːjuːnifi'keifən] *n.* yeniden birleşme, uzlaşma.

re.un.ion ['riːjuːnjən] *n.* tekrar birleşme, bir araya gelme; **re.u.nite** ['riːjuː-'nait] *v/t. & v/i.* yeniden birleş(tir)mek, bir araya gelmek, getirmek.

rev MOT F [rev] **1.** *n.* devir, dönme; **2.** *v/t. & v/i.* dön(dür)mek; ~ **up** motorun hızını artırmak.

re.val.or.i.za.tion ['riːvælərai'zeifən], **reval.u.a.tion** ['riːvæljuːeifən] *n.* yeniden değerlendirme; re'**val.or.ize** [ˌ-əraiz], **reval.ue** ['riː'væljuː] *v/t.* yeniden değerlendirmek, kıymetlendirmek.

re.vamp MEC ['riː'væmp] *v/t.* tamir etm., yenilemek; *Am.* döşemesini değiştirmek (*koltuk vs.*).

re.veal [ri'viːl] *v/t.* açığa vurmak, ifşa etm.; göstermek, ortaya koymak; re-'**veal.ing** *adj.* anlamlı, manidar; bir kısmını gösteren (*elbise vs.*).

re.veil.le MIL [ri'væli] *n.* kalk borusu.

rev.el ['revl] **1.** *n.* eğlence, şenlik, eğlenti, cümbüş, içki alemi; **2.** *v/i.* eğlenmek, cümbüş yapmak; mest olm. (**in** *-de*); keyiflenmek, zevk almak (**in** *-den*).

rev.e.la.tion [revi'leifən] *n.* açığa vurma, ifşa; *rel.* ilham, vahiy.

rev.el.(l)er ['revlə] *n.* eğlenen, şenlik yapan kimse, sabahçı, sabaha dek eğlenen, akşamcı, eğlence düşkünü kimse; '**revel.ry** *n.* gürültülü eğlenti, cümbüşlü eğlence, sefahat taşkınlıkları, âlem, şenlik.

re.venge [ri'vendʒ] **1.** *n.* öç, intikam, hınç; rövanş (*oyun*); **2.** *v/t.* intikam almak, hıncını çıkarmak (**on, upon** *-den*); ~ **o.s. on, be ~d on** *b-den* intikamını almak, öcünü almak, *b*şin acısını çıkarmak; re'**venge.ful** □ [ˌ-ful] kinci, kin tutan; re'**venge.ful-ness** *n.* intikam hırsı, kincilik; re-'**veng.er** *n.* intikam alıcı kimse.

rev.e.nue ['revinjuː] *n.* gelir, irat, varidat; ~**s** *pl.* devletin vergi gelir(ler)i; ~

board, ~ **office** defterdarlık, maliye tahsilât şubesi; ~ **cutter** gümrük muhafaza gemisi; ~ **officer** gümrük memuru; ~ **stamp** damga pulu, bandırol.

re.ver.ber.ate [ri'vəːbəreit] *v/t. & v/i.* akset(tir)mek, yankıla(n)mak, yansı(t)mak; **re.ver.ber'a.tion** *n.* yankıla(n)ma, akset(tir)me; re'**ver-ber.a.tor** *n.* yansıtaç, ışıldak.

re.vere [ri'viə] *v/t.* saymak, saygı göstermek *-e*, yüceltmek, ululamak *-i*; **re.ver-ence** ['revərəns] **1.** *n.* derin saygı, hürmet; saygı ile eğilme, reverans; **Your** ♀ *obs. veya co.* saygıdeğer efendim; **2.** *v/t.* saygı göstermek *-e*, yüceltmek *-i*; '**rev-er.end** **1.** *adj.* saygıdeğer, muhterem, sayın; **Right** ♀ muhterem, aziz (*papaz*); **2.** *n.* muhterem (*papazın lakabı*).

rev.er.ent □ ['revərənt], **rev.er.en.tial** □ [ˌ-'renfəl] saygılı, hürmetkâr, saygıdan ileri gelen.

rev.er.ie ['revəri] *n.* dalgınlık, sayıklama, derin düşünüş; hayal.

re.ver.sal [ri'vəːsəl] *n.* evirtim, tersine çevirme, aksi, ani değişiklik; JUR iptal, fesih, geri alma; MEC geri dönme. çevirme; re'**verse 1.** *n.* arka, ters taraf, arka yüz; aksi, zıt, ters olan şey; aksilik, başarısızlık; geri tepme; **in** ~ tersine, sondan başa doğru; MIL arkadan hücum; **2.** □ ters, aksi, arka, geriye, gerisin geriye; ~ **gear** MOT geri vites; ~ **side** ters taraf (*kumaşta arka yüz*); **3.** *vb.* ters(ine) çevirmek; tersine dönmek; (*iş*) feshetmek, lağvetmek, kapatmak; MEC geri hareket ettirmek; JUR iptal etm., hükmü değiştirmek; re'**vers.i.ble** *adj.* tersine çevrilebilir; geri çalıştırılabilir, döndürülebilir; iki taraflı, ters yüz edilebilir (*kumaş, pardesü vs.*); re-'**vers.ing** *adj.* MEC geri dönebilen...

re.ver.sion [ri'vəːfən] *n.* eski konu, durum *veya* alışkanlıklarına dönme, dönüş; JUR tekrar intikal, mülkün sahibine geçmesi; veraset hakkı (**of** *-in*); BIOL çok uzun süredir görülmemiş ilkel özelliklerin yeniden belirmesi; re'**ver-sionar.y** JUR [ˌ-fnəri] *adj.* intikal ile ilgili; re'**ver.sion.er** JUR [ˌ-fənə] *n.* aslî zilyet.

re.vert [ri'vəːt] *vb.* eski durumuna (*veya* alışkanlıklarına) dönmek, geri gitmek (**to** *-e*); *fig.* gerilemek, geri kalmak; eski konuya dönmek; JUR intikal etm., mülk sahibine geçmek; çevirmek (*bakış*).

rev.er.y ['revəri] = **reverie**.

re.vet.ment MEC [ri'vetmənt] *n*. kaplama duvarı.

re.view [ri'vjuː] **1.** *n*. gözden geçirme, tetkik, resmî teftiş, inceleme; MIL, NAUT geçit töreni; eleştiri, tenkit; mecmua, dergi; ders tekrarı; *pass s.th. in* ~ geçit töreni yapmak; *year under* ~ denetim yılı; **2.** *v/t*. yeniden incelemek, gözden geçirmek; MIL, NAUT teftiş, denetim yapmak; eleştirmek; *v/i*. eleştiri yazısı yazmak; **re'view.er** *n*. eleştirmen, eleştirici; ~*'s copy* eleştiri yazısı nüshası.

re.vile [ri'vail] *v/t*. küfretmek, hakaret etm., yermek, sövmek (*for -e*).

re.vis.al [ri'vaizl] *n*. yeniden inceleme, tetkik, teftiş, revizyon.

re.vise [ri'vaiz] **1.** *v/t*. tekrar gözden geçirip düzeltmek, provaları tashih etm. (*kitap*); değiştirmek; tekrar çalışmak (*ders*); **2.** *n*. TYP tashih provası, ikinci prova; = *revision*; **re'vis.er** *n*. *bşi* gözden geçirip düzelten, inceleyen kimse; TYP tashih eden, düzeltmen, musahhih.

re.vi.sion [ri'viʒən] *n*. yeniden inceleyip düzeltme, gözden geçirme, tetkik, teftiş; tashih, düzelt(il)me, revizyon.

re.vis.it ['riː'vizit] *v/t*. tekrar ziyaret etm.

re.vi.so.ry [ri'vaizəri] *adj*. düzeltici; tashih...

re.vi.tal.ize ['riː'vaitəlaiz] *v/t*. yeniden canlandırmak, güç katmak, teşvik etm., tazelemek.

re.viv.al [ri'vaivəl] *n*. yeniden canlan(dır)ma, taze hayat bulma, diril(t)-me, revaç bulma; yıllar sonra yeniden oynanma (*piyes vs.*); *fig*. uyanma, uyanış; **re.vive** *v/t*. (yeniden) canlandırmak, ihya etm., diriltmek, taze hayat vermek; yeniden kurmak, tesis etm.; yenilemek; yeniden ilgi gördürmek; yıllar sonra yeniden sahneye koymak (*piyes vs.*); *v/i*. yeniden canlanmak; yeniden ilgi görmek, revaç bulmak; **re'viv.er** *n*. yeniden canlandıran, dirilten, ihya eden kimse; canlandıran, kuvvetlendiren ilaç, serinleten *bş*; **re-viv.i.fy** [riː'vivifai] *v/t*. yeni bir hayat ve sağlık vermek *-e*, canlandırmak.

rev.o.ca.ble □ ['revəkəbl] geri alınabilir, feshedilebilir; BOT kabili rücu, iptal edilebilir; **rev.o.ca.tion** *n*. geri alınma, iptal, fesih, hükümsüz kılma.

re.voke [ri'vəuk] *v/t*. geri almak, iptal etm.; sözünden dönmek; *v/i*. *iskambil*: aynı renkten kâğıt atmamak.

re.volt [ri'vəult] **1.** *n*. isyan, ayaklanma,

ihtilâl, kıyam; **2.** *v/i*. isyan etm., ayaklanmak; *fig*. tiksinmek (*at, against -den*); *v/t. fig*. tiksindirmek, nefret hissi vermek; **re'volt.ing** *adj*. tiksindirici, iğrenç, menfur.

rev.o.lu.tion [revə'luːʃən] *n*. devrim, yeni bir dönem, ihtilâl; devir, dönme; POL devrim, inkılâp; ~*s per minute* MOT dakikada devir sayısı; **rev.o'lu.tion.ary** [-ʃnəri] **1.** *adj*. devrimci; ihtilâlci; **2.** *a*. **rev.o'lu.tion.ist** *n*. devrimci, ihtilâlci kimse; **rev.o'lu.tion.ize** *v/t*. tamamen değiştirmek; ayaklandırmak, isyan ettirmek; devirmek, devrim yapmak.

re.volve [ri'vɔlv] *v/t. & v/i*. dön(dür)-mek (*about, on, round*); *fig*. düşünüp taşınmak *-i*; **re'volv.er** *n*. revolver, altıpatlar, tabanca; **re'volv.ing** *adj*. dönen..., döner...

re.vue THEAT [ri'vjuː] *n*. revü, kabare, dans ve şarkılı sahne gösterisi.

re.vul.sion [ri'vʌlʃən] *n. fig*. nefret, tiksinme, ânî reaksiyon, tiksinti; düşünce *veya* duyguda anî değişiklik; MED başka yöne çevirme; **re'vul.sive** MED [-siv] **1.** □ ters etki yapan; **2.** *n*. ters etki yapan ilaç.

re.ward [ri'wɔːd] **1.** *n*. ödül, ikramiye, mükâfat, karşılık; **2.** *v/t*. ödüllendirmek, mükâfat vermek.

re.word ['riː'wɔːd] *v/t*. yeni sözcüklerle söylemek *veya* yazmak.

re.write ['riː'rait] (*irr. write*) *v/t*. yeniden değişik ve daha uygun şekilde yazmak.

rhap.so.dist ['ræpsədist] *n*. eski Yunan'da profesyonel destan anlatıcı; **'rhap.so.dize** *v/i. bşi* öve öve bitirememek, *bşden* fazla heyecanla bahsetmek; **'rhap.so.dy** *n. fig*. coşkunluk, heyecan, esrime; rapsodi, değişik parçalardan düzenlenmiş eser; heyecanlı konuşma *veya* yazı.

rhe.o.stat ELECT ['riːəustæt] *n*. direnç aygıtı, reosta.

rhet.o.ric ['retərik] *n*. hitabet; beyan ve belâgat sanatı; **rhe.tor.i.cal** □ [ri'tɔri-kəl] retorik, güzel söz söylemeye (*veya* sanatına) ait; **rhet.o.ri.cian** [retə'ri-ʃən] *n*. güzel konuşma ustası, iyi hatip.

rheu.mat.ic MED [ruː'mætik] **1.** *adj*. (*al-ly*) romatizma ile ilgili, romatizmalı; ~ *fever* eklem romatizması; **2.** *n*. romatizmalı kimse; ~*s* F *pl*. = **rheu.ma.tism** MED ['ruːmətizəm] *n*. romatizma.

rhi.no[1] *sl*. ['rainəu] *n*. mangır, mangiz.

rhino 930

rhi.no² F [.] = rhi.noc.er.os ZOO [rai-'nɔsərəs] n. gergedan.

rhomb, rhom.bus MATH ['rɔm(bəs)] n. eşkenar dörtgen, main.

rhu.barb BOT [ruːbɑːb] n. ravent.

rhyme [raim] 1. n. kafiye, uyak (to -e); kafiyeli yazma; beyit, şiir; without ~ or reason mantıksız olarak, anlamsız, saçma, ipsiz sapsız; 2. vb. kafiyeli olarak yazmak; kafiyeli sona ermek; 'rhymeless ☐ kafiyesiz, uyaksız; 'rhym.er,rhyme.ster ['ˌstə]n. şair taslağı (veya bozuntusu).

rhythm ['riðəm] n. ritim, kadans, müzikte ahenk, uyum, düzün, düzenlilik, ahenkli hareket; vezin; rhyth.mic, rhyth.mi.cal ☐ ['riðmik(əl)] ritmik, ahenkli, uyumlu, düzünlü.

Ri.al.to Am. [ri'æltəu] n. tiyatroların çok olduğu bölge.

rib [rib] 1. n. ANAT kaburga (kemiği); pirzola; BOT yaprak damarı; şemsiye teli; gemi iskeleti; 2. v/t. damarlı, yivli desende örnek (çorap vs.); Am. sl. takılmak, alaya almak -i.

rib.ald ['ribəld] 1. adj. ağzı bozuk, kaba, sağa sola sataşan, etrafı rahatsız eden; açık saçık, müstehcen; 2. n. ağzı bozuk, küfürbaz kimse; dedikoducu kimse; 'ribald.ry n. soğuk şaka, küstahça alay etme; kaba dil.

rib.and MEC ['ribənd] n. şerit, seri imalatta kullanılan döner bant.

ribbed [ribd] adj. yivli, girintili, çıkıntılı, çizgili.

rib.bon ['ribən] n. kurdele, şerit, bant; madalya kurdelesi; daktilo şeridi; çizgi, çubuk (kumaş); ~s pl. bez parçası, paçavra; dizgin (at); ~ building, ~ development şehir imarının anayol boyunca şehir dışına doğru gelişmesi.

rice [rais] n. BOT pirinç.

rich ☐ [ritʃ] zengin, servet sahibi; bol, fazla, külliyetli (in -de); mükellef, muhteşem, değerli, kıymetli; verimli; bereketli; gür, tok, dolgun (ses); yağlı, ağır, hazmı güç (yemek); koyu, canlı, parlak (renk); besleyici, vitaminli; F mükemmel, enfes, şahane (şaka, nükte); the ~ pl. zenginler, servet sahipleri; rich.es ['ˌiz] n. pl. zenginlik, servet; 'rich.ness n. zenginlik, bolluk, verim, bereket; yağlılık; gürlük (ses); parlaklık (renk).

rick¹ AGR [rik] 1. n. kuru ot yığını, tınaz; 2. v/t. kuru ot yığını yapmak, yığmak.

rick² [.] = wrick.

rick.ets MED ['rikits] n. sg. veya pl. raşitizm; 'rick.et.y adj. rasitizm hastalığına tutulmus, raşitik; sakat, hastalıklı, sarsık sursuk; çürük, köhne.

rick.shaw ['rikʃɔː] n. bir veya iki kişilik olup insan tarafından çekilen hafif bir Doğu Asya faytonu.

rid [rid] (irr.) v/t. kurtarmak (of -den); get ~ of başından atmak, defetmek, savmak -i; 'rid.dance n. kurtuluş, kurtulma, başından atma; he is a good ~ ondan kurtulduğumuz iyi oldu, iyi ki çekip gitti.

rid.den ['ridn] p.p. of ride 2; comb. ...ile dolu; ... in istilâsına uğramış.

rid.dle¹ ['ridl] 1. n. bilmece, bulmaca, muamma; 2. vb. anlamını çıkarmak; bilmece çözmek, bilmece ile söylemek; ~ me F tahmin etsene!

rid.dle² [.] 1. n. kalbur; 2. v/t. kalburdan geçirmek, elemek; delik deşik etm., kalbura çevirmek.

rid.dling ☐ ['ridliŋ] akıl ermez, muammalı, şaşırtıcı.

ride [raid] 1. n. atla gezinti; gezinti yeri veya yolu, ağaçsız orman yolu; binme, biniş; go for a ~ bir araçla gezmeğe çıkmak, atla gezintiye çıkmak; 2. (irr.) v/i. ata binmek, atla gitmek; ata biner gibi oturmak; part. bisiklet veya araçla gitmek; fig. muallâkta kalmak, sürüklenmek; rahat gitmek (araba); ~ at anchor demirli yatmak (gemi); ~ for a fall fig. körüküörüne bir felâkete sürüklenmek, akılsızca davranmak; v/t. binmek -e, sürmek -i (at, bisiklet vs.); (bir yeri) atla dolaşmak, gezmek; binip gitmek -e; su üstünde gitmek, yüzmek (gemi); bindirmek -e; ~ s.o. down b-ni atla yetişip yakalamak; b-ni atla çiğnemek; ~ (on) a bicycle bisiklete binmek; ~ out NAUT su yüzünde kalmak (fırtınada), kazasız belâsız atlatmak (a. fig.);'rid.er n. atlı, binici, süvari; ek, ilâve, özel hüküm; MEC değişebilen, hareket edebilen ağırlık (veya parça).

rid.ge [ridʒ] 1. n. sırt, bayır, dağ sırtı, dağ sırası; ARCH çatı sırtı; AGR tarla kenarı; 2. v/t. evlek açmak, iz bırakmak; kırıştırmak (alın);'~-pole n. çatının yatay direği.

rid.i.cule ['ridikjuːl] 1. n. alay, istihza, eğlenme, saraka; hold s.o. up to ~ b-ni elâleme rezil etm., herkesin alay konusu etm.; 2. v/t. b-le alay etm., zevklenmek, b-ni alay konusu etm.; ri'dic-

u.lous [-juləs] *adj.* gülünç, gülünecek, alay edilecek, tuhaf, saçma; **ri'dic.u-lous.ness** *n.* maskaralık, soytarılık, gülünçlük, tuhaflık.

rid.ing ['raidiŋ] **1.** *n.* biniş; binicilik; **2.** *adj.* binek...; '**~-breech.es** *n. pl.* süvari pantalonu; '**~-hab.it** *n.* kadın için binici elbisesi.

rife □ [raif] yaygın, bol, sık sık olan; dolu olan (**with** *ile*); **~ with** *ile* dolu.

riff-raff ['rifræf] *n.* ayak takımı, avam, aşağı sınıf.

ri.fle¹ ['raifl] *v/t.* yağma etm., soyup soğana çevirmek.

ri.fle² [-] **1.** *n.* tüfek, karabina; **~s** *pl.* MIL avcı erleri; **2.** *v/t.* yiv açmak; '**~man** *n.* MIL avcı eri; '**~range** *n.* poligon, atış alanı; atış menzili.

ri.fling MEC ['raifliŋ] *n.* yiv helezonu (*tüfek*).

rift [rift] *n.* yarık, açıklık, çatlak.

rig¹ [rig] **1.** *v/t.* (*pazar, piyasa vs.*) hile karıştırmak -*e*, hileli şekilde kurmak; **2.** *n.* (hile)kârlık, dalavere.

rig² [-] **1.** *n.* NAUT donanım, arma; *fig.* süs, şatafat; elbise; **2.** *vb.* donatmak, teçhiz etm., armasını takmak; **~ s.o. out** *b-ne* bşi sağlamak, temin etm.; *b-ni* telleyip pullamak (**with** *ile*), hazırlamak, giydirmek; **~ s.th. up** hemen uydurmak, acele ile geçici olarak bş yapmak; '**rigger** *n.* NAUT armador; AVIA makinist, mekanisyen; '**rig.ging** *n.* NAUT donanım, geminin arması.

right [rait] **1.** □ doğru, dürüst, hatasız, kusursuz; âdil, insaflı; doğru, sahih; sağlam, sıhhatli; en uygun, münasip; haklı; gereken, aranan; sağ (*taraf*); **~ angle** MATH dik açı; **be ~** haklı olm.; **be ~ to** -*mekle* iyi etm.; -*mak* üzere olm.; **all ~!** herşey yolunda!; münasip, uygun, kusursuz; pekalâ, tamam!; peki, hay hay!; **on the ~ side of 30** yaşı otuz yoktur; **get s.th. ~** bşi düzeltmek, yoluna koymak; **put** *veya* **set ~** düzeltmek, ayarlamak, yoluna koymak; **2.** *adv.* sağa doğru; doğru (olarak); hemen; doğruca, dosdoğru; uygun şekilde; tamamiyle; pek, çok, ziyade; **~ away** derhal, hemen; haydi!, yürü!; **~ on** doğruca; **3.** *n.* sağ (*taraf*); hak, selâhiyet, yetki (**to, of** -*e*); PARL sağ kanat; *boks:* sağ; **the ~s of man** insan hakları; **in ~ of his mother** annesinin tarafında, annesini haklı bulan; **in one's own ~** *k-si* hak sahibi olarak; **the ~s and wrongs** doğru ile eğri; haklı ile haksız,

işin doğrusu, gerçeği; **by ~(s)** usulen, yasal olarak; **by ~ of** nedeniyle, hak *veya* yetkisiyle; **set** *veya* **put to ~s** yeniden düzeltmek, yoluna koymak; **on** *veya* **to the ~** sağ taraf(t)a; **4.** *v/t.* düzeltmek; NAUT doğrultmak; ayarlamak; **~an.gled** MATH ['-'æŋgld] *adj.* dik açılı; '**~down** *adj.* uygun, muntazam, tam, sapına kadar; olumlu; **right.eous** □ ['-ʃəs] dürüst, adil, erdemli, namuslu; '**right.eous.ness** *n.* dürüstlük; **right.ful** □ ['-ful] haklı; yasal; gerçek; '**right-hand** *adj.* sağdaki, sağdan; sağ elle yapılan; sağa doğru...; güvenilir; '**right-'hand.ed** *adj.* sağ elini kullanan; sağ elle kullanmak için yapılmış (*makas vs.*); '**right.ly** *adv.* doğru, gerçek olarak; haklı olarak; emin olarak; '**right-'mind.ed** *adj.* dürüst, adil, sağduyu sahibi; '**right.ness** *n.* doğruluk, adalete uygunluk; **right of way** önden geçme hakkı, geçiş hakkı.

rig.id □ ['ridʒid] eğilmez, bükülmez, dimdik, kaskatı; *fig.* sert, haşin, boyun eğmez; **ri'gid.i.ty** *n.* sertlik, bükülmezlik, diklik.

rig.ma.role ['rigmərəul] *n.* boş lâf, gevezelik, saçma konuşma.

rig.or ['rəigɔ:] *n.* sertlik, katılık, eğilmezlik; insafsızlık; MED titreme, ürperme; **~ mortis** ölümden sonra kasların katılaşması; **rig.or.ous** □ ['rigərəs] sert, şiddetli.

rig.o.(u)r ['rigə] *n.* sertlik, şiddet; **~s** kötü koşullar.

rile F [rail] *v/t.* kızdırmak, sinirlendirmek.

rill *poet.* [ril] *n.* küçük dere.

rim [rim] **1.** *n.* kenar; jant, ispit; **2.** *v/t.* kenar çevirmek (*veya* yapmak).

rime¹ [raim] *n.* kafiye, uyak.

rime² *poet.* [-] *n.* kırç, kırağı; '**rim.y** *adj.* kırağı ile örtülü; kırağı gibi.

rind [raind] *n.* kabuk, kışır; herhangi *bşin* dış yüzeyi.

ring¹ [riŋ] **1.** *n.* halka, çember; *boks:* ring; kartel, tröst; daire; yüzük; sirk çadırı vs.; at yarışı acentası (*veya* tezgâhı); **make ~s round s.o.** F *bşi b-den* daha iyi *ve* daha hızlı yapmak; **2.** *vb.* daire (*veya* yuvarlak) içine almak -*i*, halka takmak (*hayvanın burnuna, ayağına vs*); halka atmak (*oyunda*); *mst* **~ in, ~ round, ~ about** sarmak, ortaya almak -*i*.

ring² [-] **1.** *n.* zil sesi, çan sesi, çınlama;

zil çalma; *give s.o. a ~ b-ne* telefon etm.; **2.** (*irr.*) *v/i.* çan, zil, saat çal(ın)mak; çınlamak, tınlamak; *oft.* ~ *out* çınlamak (*with ile*); ~ *again* yankılanmak; ~ *off* TELEPH telefonu kapamak; *the bell ~s* zil çalıyor; *v/t.* çalmak, çınlatmak; *fig.* tesir bırakmak, çalkanmak (*şöhret*); ~ *the bell* zile basmak, çıngırağı çekmek; F başarmak, muvaffak olm.; ~ *a bell* F *b-ne bş* hatırlatmak, çağrışım yapmak; yabancı gelmemek; ~ *s.o. up b-ne* telefon etm.; 'ring.er *n.* çan çalan cihaz; çancı, zangoç; *sl. b-nin* tıpatıp benzeri; 'ring.ing □ çalan, çınlayan; 'ring.lead.er *n.* çete başı, elebaşı; ringlet ['_lit] *n.* saç lülesi; 'ring.worm *n.* MED mantar hastalığı.

rink [rıŋk] *n.* patinaj alanı; buz sahası.

rinse [rins] **1.** *v/t. oft.* ~ *out* çalka(la)mak; **2.** = 'rins.ing *n.* çalkalama, sudan geçirme; ~*s pl.* bulaşık suyu.

ri.ot ['raiət] **1.** *n.* kargaşalık, gürültü, patırtı, velvele; cümbüş, eğlenti; taşkınlık (*a. fig.*); F çok komik ve başarılı kimse *veya bş*; isyan, ayaklanma, baş kaldırma; *run* ~ gemi azıya almak, kontrolden çıkmak, kıyameti koparmak; **2.** *v/i.* kargaşalık yaratmak, gürültü patırtı çıkarmak, azmak, kudurmak; ayaklanmak, isyan etm.; *fig.* mest olm. (*in -de*); 'riot.er *n.* asi, ayaklanan; gürültücü kimse; 'ri.ot.ous □ gürültülü, karışıklık yaratan, gürültücü; sefih, maceraperest.

rip[1] [rip] **1.** *n.* yırtık, yarık; sökük dikiş; **2.** *v/t.* sökmek, teyelleri ayırmak; ~ *up* yırtmak, yarmak, çatlatmak (*kereste vs.*); *v/i.* yırtılmak, yarılmak, dikişleri açılmak; çok hızlı geçip gitmek.

rip[2] F [_] *n.* uçarı, yaramaz, haylaz, çapkın.

rip-cord ['ripkɔ:d] *n.* paraşüt (*veya* balon vs.) ipi.

ripe □ [raip] olgun(laşmış); kemale ermiş, yetişmiş; 'rip.en *v/t. & v/i.* olgunlaş(tır)mak; yetişmek, erginleşmek; 'rip.ness *n.* olgunluk, kemal, erginlik.

ri.poste [ri'pəust] **1.** *n.* FENC karşı darbe, hücum, atak; *fig.* çabuk ve zekice verilen yanıt; **2.** *v/i.* çabuk karşı darbe (*veya* atak) yapmak; çabuk ve zekice yanıt vermek.

rip.per ['ripə] *n.* kesici *b-i veya bş*; *sl.* yaman adam; müstesna bir parça; 'ripping □ *sl.* fevkalâde, harikulâde, yaman, muhteşem.

rip.ple ['ripl] **1.** *n.* ufacık dalga, dalgacık; **2.** *v/t. & v/i.* hafifçe dalgalan(dır)mak, çağıldamak, şırıldamak, kırış(tır)mak.

rise [raiz] **1.** *n.* yükseliş, artış, çıkış, çoğalış (*ses, fiyat, su vs.*); bayır, tepe, yokuş; *fig.* yükselme; *rare* doğma, çıkış (*güneş vs.*); başlangıç noktası, kaynak; *give ~ to bşe* neden olm., sebebiyet vermek; *take (one's) ~* kaynağından çıkmak, ortaya çıkmak, doğmak; **2.** (*irr.*) *v/i.* kalkmak, yükselmek, artmak, çıkmak (*fiyat vs.*); kabarmak, yükselmek (*nehir vs.*); ayağa kalkmak; doğmak, yükselmek (*güneş vs.*); toplantıyı bitirmek; kızmak, sinirlenmek (*against, on -e*); doğmak, ortaya çıkımak, hasıl olm. (*nehir vs.*); ayaklanmak, baş kaldırmak; su yüzüne çıkmak (*balık vs.*); yukarı doğru meyillenmek (*bayır vs.*); ~ *to b-nin veya bşin* hakkından gelmek; ~ *to the bait* yemi ağzıyla kapmaya çalışmak; ris.en ['rizn] *p.p. of. rise 2*; 'ris.er *n.* merdiven basamağının dik olan kısmı; yokuş; *early* ~ sabah erken kalkan.

ris.i.bil.i.ty [rizi'biliti] *n.* gülme eğilimi (*veya* isteği); ris.i.ble □ ['_ibl] gülme..., gülmeye eğilimi olan; gülünç, komik.

ris.ing ['raiziŋ] **1.** *n.* yükselme, yükseliş; kalkma; artma, çoğalma; doğma, çıkış; ayaklanma, isyan; **2.** *adj.* yükselen, artan, çoğalan; yetişen, büyüyen.

risk [risk] **1.** *n.* tehlike, tehlikeli girişim; COM risk, riziko; *at the ~ of* göze alarak, tehlikeye atarak; *run the ~* zararı göze almak, rizikolu bir işe girişmek; **2.** *v/t.* tehlikeye atmak, göze almak; 'risk.y □ tehlikeli, riskli.

ris.sole ['risəul] *n.* (*patates, yumurta vs. ile kızgın yağda pişirilen*) bir tür et *veya* balık yemeği.

ríte [rait] *n. rel.* ayin, tören; rit.u.al ['ritʃuəl] **1.** □ törensel, merasimle yapılan; ayine ait; **2.** *n.* dinî ayin ve merasim (kuralları).

ri.val ['raivəl] **1.** *n.* rakip, müsabık; **2.** *adj.* rekabet eden, çekişen, yarışan *ile*; COM rakip...; **3.** *v/t.* rekabet etm., yarışmak, çekişmek *ile*; 'ri.val.ry *n.* rekabet, rakip olma.

rive [raiv] (*irr.*) *vb.* çatla(t)mak, yar(ıl)mak, yarık açmak.

riv.en ['rivn] *p.p. of rive*.

riv.er ['rivə] *n.* nehir, ırmak, akıntı (*a. fig.*); *sell s.o. down the ~ b-ne* ihanet etm.; '~-horse *n.* suaygırı; '~.side *n.* ırmak (*veya* su) kenarı; *attr.* nehir kıyısı.

riv.et ['rivit] **1.** *n.* MEC perçin; **2.** *v/t.* perçinlemek; *b-nin* ilgisini çekmek; *b-ne* gözünü dikmek (**on, upon**).

riv.u.let ['rivjulit] *n.* dere, çay.

roach *icht.* [rəutʃ] *n.* çamça balığı.

road [rəud] *n.* yol, sokak, cadde, şose; *Am.* = *railroad*; *mst* ~*s pl.* NAUT demirleme sahası, liman ağzı; *take the* ~ yola düzülmek; *main* ~ ana cadde, kalabalık yol; '~.bed *n.* yol yapı temeli; RAIL sürekli (*veya* bozulmayan) hat; '~-block *n.* barikat, yol maniası; '~-hog *n.* MOT süratli, bencil ve dikkatsiz şoför (*veya* sürücü); '~-mend.er *n.* yol amelesi; '~-race *n.* sokak yarışı; '~ rage *n.* araç kullanırken saldırgan davranışlar; '~-sense *n.* MOT trafikte yürür *veya* araba kullanırken kazadan sakınma duyusu; '~.side *n.* yol kenarı; '~.sign trafik işareti; '~.stead *n.* NAUT liman ağzı, demirleme yeri; road.ster ['-stə] *n.* iki kişilik üstü açık araba; 'road.way *n.* araba yolu.

roam [rəum] *v/i.* dolaşmak, gezinmek, başıboş (*veya* amaçsız) gezinmek; *v/t.* gezmek, dolaşmak; 'roam.er *n.* yaya gezen; turist; kaldırımları eskiten kimse, serseri, aylak, boş gezen kimse.

roan [rəun] **1.** *adj.* demir kırı donlu (*at, inek vs.*); **2.** *n.* demir kırı donlu at; MEC güderi, koyun derisi.

roar [rɔː] **1.** *vb.* gürlemek (*a. fig. konuşma, gülme*), gümbürdemek; gök gürlemek; kükremek (*aslan*); kızıp bağırmak; gürleyerek akıp gitmek; **2.** *n.* gürleme, gümbürdeme, kükreme; çatırdama; kahkaha; roar.ing ['-rɪŋ] **1.** = *roar* 2; **2.** □ gürleyen, gümbürdeyen, kükreyen; gittikçe artan; *be in* ~ *health* sıhhati çok yerinde olm.

roast [rəust] **1.** *vb.* kızartmak; kavurmak; *sl. b-ne* takılmak, *b-ni* alaya almak; **2.** *adj.* kızar(tıl)mış; kavrulmuş; ~ *beef* sığır orstosu (*veya* kızartması), rozbif; ~ *meat* kebap, kızartma (*et*); **3.** *n.* kebap kızartma; *rule the* ~ idare etm., dizginleri elinde tutmak; 'roast.er *n.* kızartma fırını (*kahve*) kavurma makinesi; henüz süt emen domuz yavrusu; 'roast.ing-jack *n.* döner yapma cihazı.

rob [rɔb] *vb.* soymak, yağma etm., çalmak, *b-nin* para ve eşyasını alıp soymak; *b-den* bşi gaspetmek; 'rob.ber

n. hırsız; soyguncu haydut, karmanyolacı; 'rob.ber.y *n.* yol kesme, soygun, adam soyma, karmanyolacılık, haydutluk.

robe [rəub] **1.** *n.* rop, cübbe, kisve, biniş; kaftan; *poet.* üstlük giysi, urba; *Am.* penyuvar, ropdöşambr, sabahlık; ~*s pl.* resmî *veya* tören elbisesi; *gentlemen of the* ~ hukukçular; **2.** *v/t.* & *v/i.* giyinmek, giydirmek, kaftan vs. giydirmek; *fig.* süsle(n)mek.

rob.in ORN ['rɔbin] *n.* kızıl gerdan (kuşu).

ro.bot ['rəubɔt] *n.* makine adam, robot (*a. fig.*); otomat; *attr.* otomatik…, mekanik…, robot…

ro.bust □ [rəu'bʌst] dinç, sağlam, güçlü kuvvetli, dayanıklı; ro'bust.ness *n.* sağlamlık, dinçlik, güçlülük, dayanıklılık.

rock¹ [rɔk] *n.* kaya(lık), büyük taş parçası; *sl.* kıymetli taş; naneli çubuk şekeri; *get down to* ~ *bottom* bir konuyu inceden inceye araştırmak; ~ *crystal* necef taşı; ~ *salt* kayatuzu.

rock² [.] *v/t.* & *v/i.* salla(n)mak, tartmak, sars(ıl)mak, silkmek; *fig.* müteessir etm., sarsmak.

rock-bottom F ['rɔk'bɔtəm] *adj.* en düşük (*fiyat*).

rock.er ['rɔkə] *n.* beşik v.s.'nin altındaki kavisli ayak; *Am.* salıncaklı koltuk; *sl.* çatlak (*veya* deli) kimse.

rock.er.y ['rɔkəri] *n.* kayalık bahçe, taş yığınından parçacık, taş çiçeklik.

rock.et¹ ['rɔkit] **1.** *n.* roket, füze; havaî fişek; F azarlama; haşlama; ~ *plane* füze uçağı; ~ *propulsion* roket tahrikî; **2.** *v/i.* F aniden yükselmek, fırlamak (*fiyat*); rüzgâr gibi gitmek.

rock.et² BOT [.] *n.* roka.

rock.et-pow.ered ['rɔkitpauəd] *adj.* roket tahrikli; rock.et.ry ['-ri] *n.* roket kullanma tekniği.

rock…: '~.fall *n.* kaya yığını; '~-gar.den *n.* kayalık bahçe.

rock.ing… ['rɔkiŋ]: '~-chair *n.* salıncaklı koltuk; '~-horse *n.* salıncaklı oyuncak at.

rock.y ['rɔki] *adj.* kayalık; kaya gibi; F sallantılı, titrek.

ro.co.co [rəu'kəukəu] *n.* mimarîde rokoko tarzı.

rod [rɔd] *n.* çubuk, değnek; falaka değneği; baston; olta kamışı; MEC rot; beş metrelik uzunluk ölçüsü (= *5 1/2 yards*); *Am. sl.* revolver, tabanca; *have*

rode 934

a ~ in pickle for s.o. b-le paylaşılacak kozu olm.

rode [rəud] *pret. of ride 2.*

ro.dent ['rəudənt] *n.* kemirgen hayvan.

ro.de.o *Am.* [rəu'deiəu] *n.* rodeo.

rod.o.mon.tade [rɔdəmɔn'teid] *n.* övünme, yüksekten atma.

roe¹ [rəu] *n. a. hard ~* balık yumurtası; *soft ~* balık menisi.

roe² [-] *n.* karaca; '~.buck *n.* erkek karaca.

ro.ga.tion ECCL [rəu'geiʃən] *n.* yakarış, yalvarma; *~ Sunday* Miraçtan önceki pazar.

rogue [rəug] *n.* çapkın (*veya* derbeder, sefil) kimse; dolandırıcı (*veya* düzenbaz) kimse; yaramaz kimse; azgın fil; *~s' gallery* sabıkalıların resimlerinin olduğu koleksiyon; 'ro.guer.y *n.* derbederlik, çapkınlık; düzenbazlık; yaramazlık; 'ro.guish □ çapkın, derbeder; kurnaz; yaramaz; düzenbaz.

roist.er ['rɔistə] *v/i.* şamata (*veya* âlem, cümbüs) yapmak; 'roist.er.er *n.* şamatacı, cümbüşçü.

role, rôle THEAT [rəul] *n.* rol (*a. fig.*).

roll [rəul] **1.** *n.* yuvarla(n)ma; top, rulo; sicil, kayıt, liste, defter; MEC silindir, merdane, makara; tomar; küçük ekmek; NAUT yalpa; gümbürtü, gürleme; **2.** *v/t. & v/i.* yuvarla(n)mak, tekerle(n)mek; sar(ıl)mak; silindirle düzletmek; *sl.* soymak; atmak (*zar*); çevirmek, devirmek (*göz*); kalın sesle söylemek; açmak; dolaşmak, dönmek; inişli yokuşlu uzanıp gitmek; dalgalanmak; gürlemek (*gök*); geçip gitmek (*zaman*); gülmekten katılmak; yalpalamak; NAUT yalpa vurmak; *~ed gold* altın kaplama; *be ~ing in money* para içinde yüzmek; *~ up* tomar yapmak, dürmek, sarmak, sıvamak (*kol*); birikmek, yığılmak; art(tır)mak; gelmek, varmak; durmak (*araç*); '~-call *n.* yoklama (*a.* MIL); 'roll.er *n.* silindir; merdane; büyük dalga; bigudi; *mst ~ bandage* sargı; *~ coaster* Am. (*Lunaparklarda*) keskin viraj ve iniş-çıkışları olan tren; *~ skate* tekerlekli paten; *~ towel* uçları birbirine dikili bir makaraya asılarak kullanılan havlu; 'roll-film *n.* PHOT makaralı film.

rol.lick.ing ['rɔlikiŋ] *adj.* gürültülü, şamatalı, eğlenceli.

roll.ing ['rəuliŋ] **1.** *adj.* inişli yokuşlu (*arazi*); çok zengin, para babası; **2.** *n.* yuvarlanma; *~ mill* MEC haddehane; *~*

press TYP rotatif; '~-stock *n.* RAIL lokomotif ve vagonlar.

roll-on ['rəulɔn] *n. a. ~ belt* korse.

roll-top desk ['rəultɔp'deks] *n.* kapağı kıvrılarak açılıp kapanan yazı masası.

ro.ly-po.ly ['rəuli'pəuli] **1.** *n.* marmelatlı kek; **2.** *adj.* tıknaz, tombul.

Ro.man ['rəumən] **1.** *adj.* Roma'ya *veya* Romalılara ait; Roma mimarîsine ait; **2.** *n.* Romalı; *mst ♀* TYP Latin harfleri.

ro.mance¹ [rəu'mæns] **1.** *n.* macera; aşk macerası; macera romanı; romantiklik; *fig.* martaval, palavra; **2.** *v/i. fig.* atıp tutmak, tıraş etm., palavra atmak.

Ro.mance² [rəu'mæns] *adj.: ~ languages* pl. Latince kökenli diller.

ro.manc.er [rəu'mænsə] *n.* roman yazarı; palavracı kimse.

Ro.man.esque [rəumə'nesk] *n.* 11. ve 12. yüzyıl Roma mimarî tarzı.

Ro.man.ic [rəu'mænik] *adj.* Latince kökenli; *part. ~ people* pl. Latin Milletleri.

ro.man.tic [rəu'mæntik] **1.** *adj.* (*~ally*) roman gibi; hayalperest, romantik; düssel, gerçek dışı, hayalî; **2.** = ro-'man.ticist [-tisist] *n.* romantik kimse; ro'manti.cism *n.* romantizm.

Rom.ish *mst contp.* ['rəumiʃ] *adj.* Katolik.

romp [rɔmp] **1.** *n.* ele avuca sığmaz (*veya* haşarı) çocuk; boğuşma; **2.** *v/i.* gürültü ile oynamak, boğuşmak, azmak, kudurmak (*çocuk*); 'romp.er(s *pl.*) *n.* çocuk tulumu.

ron.do MUS ['rɔndəu] *n.* rondo.

rood [ru:d] *n.* haç; bir uzunluk ölçüsü (*10, 117 ar*); '-loft *n.* ARCH (*kilise*) balkon.

roof [ru:f] **1.** *n.* dam, çatı; *~ of the mouth* damak; **2.** *v/t. a. ~ over* çatı ile örtmek; 'roof.ing **1.** *n.* çatı malzemesi; **2.** *adj.* çatı...; *~ felt* katranlı mukavva, tavan keçesi; 'roof-tree *n.* çatı kirişi.

rook¹ [ruk] **1.** *n.* ORN ekinkargası; *fig.* düzenbaz kimse; **2.** *v/t.* dolandırmak, kazıklamak.

rook² [-] *n.* satranç; kale.

rook.er.y ['rukəri] ekinkargalarının yuvalarının olduğu yer; ayıbalığı *veya* penguen barınağı; *fig.* çok sefil insanların oturduğu kalabalık ev.

rook.ie *sl.* ['ruki] *n.* MIL acemi asker; *fig.* acemi çaylak.

room [rum] *n.* oda; yer, meydan; şans; neden; sebep; *~s* pl. apartman dairesi;

make ~ yer açmak (*for -e*); ...**room.ed**
comb. ...odalı; '**room.er** *n. part. Am.*
pansiyoner; '**room.ing-house** *n. part.*
Am. pansiyon; '**room-mate** *n.* oda arkadaşı; '**room.y** □ geniş, ferah; bol (*elbise*).

roost [ru:st] **1.** *n.* tünek; **2.** *v/i.* tünemek; *fig.* gecelemek, konaklamak; '**roost.er** *n.* horoz.

root[1] [ru:t] **1.** *n.* kök (*a. fig.*, ANAT, MATH, GR); ~ *and branch* kökünden, tamamen; *take veya strike* ~ kök salmak; kökleşmek (*fikir*); ~ *idea* ana fikir; **2.** *v/t. & v/i.* kökleş(tir)mek, tut(tur)mak; ~ *out* kökünden sökmek; kökünü kazımak; '**root.ed** *adj.* mıhlanmış; kökleşmiş, sabit (*fikir*).

root[2] [_] *v/t. a.* ~ *up* karmakarışık (*veya* altüst) etm.; ~ *out veya up* arayıp bulmak; *v/i. bşi* karıştırmak, eşelemek; ~ *for Am. sl.* tezahürat yapmak *-e*, desteklemek *-i*; '**root.er** *n. Am. sl.* koyu taraftar.

root.let ['ru:tlit] *n.* kökçük.

rope [rəup] **1.** *n.* halat; ip; ipe çekme, idam; *on the* ~ birbirine bağlı; *be at the end of one's* ~ F çaresiz kalmak; *know the* ~*s* bir işin yolunu yordamını bilmek; *learn the* ~*s* çalışarak öğrenmek; **2.** *v/t.* halatla bağlamak; kementle yakalamak; *mst* ~ *in*, ~ *off*, ~ *out* ip çevirerek sınırlamak, iple çevirmek; MOUNT iple bağlamak; ~ *down* iple bağlamak; *v/i.* ip haline gelmek; '~**-danc.er** *n.* ip cambazı; '~**-lad.der** *n.* ip merdiven; '~**-mak.er** *n.* ipçi, halatçı, urgancı; '**rop.er.y** *n.* ipçilik, halatçılık, urgancılık; '**rope-walk** *n.* halat bükme yeri; '**rope-way** *n.* asma hat, teleferik.

rop.i.ness ['rəupinis] *n.* kalitesizlik, berbatlık.

rop.y ['rəupi] *adj.* kalitesiz, berbat; ip gibi; yapışkan, cıvık; adaleli, kuvvetli.

ro.sa.ry ['rəuzəri] *n.* ECCL tespih; dua kitabı; tespih ile okunan dualar; gül bahçesi.

rose[1] [rəuz] *n.* BOT gül (rengi); hortum süzgeci.

rose[2] [_] *pret. of* **rise 2**.

rose...: '~**.bud** *n.* gül goncası; *Am.* güzel kız; '~**-col.o(u)red** *adj.* gül renginde; *fig.* ümit verici.

ro.se.ate ['rəuziit] *adj.* gül renginde, kırmızı; ümit verici.

rose.mar.y BOT ['rəuzməri] *n.* biberiye.

ro.se.ry ['rəuzəri] *n.* gül tarhı.

ro.sette [rəu'zet] *n.* gül şeklinde rozet.

rose.wood ['rəuzwud] *n.* koyu kırmızı sert bir odun.

ros.in ['rɔzin] **1.** *n.* reçine; **2.** *v/t.* reçine sürmek *-e*.

ros.ter MIL ['rəustə] *n.* nöbet listesi.

ros.trum ['rɔstrəm] *n.* kürsü.

ros.y □ ['rəuzi] gül gibi; kırmızı, al; *fig.* ümit verici.

rot [rɔt] **1.** *n.* çürüme, bozulma; çürük; çürüme hastalığı; *sl.* saçma(lık), zırva; **2.** *v/t. & v/i.* çürü(t)mek, boz(ul)mak; *sl.* bozmak (*plan vs.*).

ro.ta.ry ['rəutəri] *adj.* dönen, dönel, döner...; ~ *press* TYP rotatif; **ro.tate** [rəu'teit] *v/t. & v/i.* dön(dür)mek; sıra ile çalış(tır)mak; **ro'ta.tion** *n.* dönme, deveran, tur; ~ *of crops* AGR her yıl sıra ile değişik ekinler ekme; **ro.ta.to.ry** ['_.tətəri] *s.* **rotary**; nöbetleşe, sıra ile.

rote [rəut] *n.*; *by* ~ ezbere.

ro.tor ['rəutə] *n.* MEC rotor, döneç; AVIA helikopter pervanesi.

rot.ten □ ['rɔtn] çürük, bozuk; *sl.* berbat, rezalet; '**rot.ten.ness** *n.* çürüklük; berbatlık.

rot.ter *sl.* ['rɔtə] *n.* ciğeri beş para etmez kimse.

ro.tund □ [rəu'tʌnd] yuvarlak, toparlak; dolgun (*ses*); tumturaklı (*söz, yazı*); **ro'tun.da** ARCH [_də] *n.* kubbeli bina *veya* oda; **ro'tun.di.ty** *n.* yuvarlaklık; dolgunluk (*ses*).

rouge [ru:ʒ] **1.** *n.* allık; ruj; **2.** *vb.* allık sürmek.

rough [rʌf] **1.** □ pürüzlü; sert; *fig.* kaba, yontulmamış; engebeli; inişli yokuşlu (*yol*); zor, çetin (*hayat vs.*); kabataslak; fırtınalı (*hava, deniz*); müsveddelik (*kâğıt*); talihsiz, şanssız; tüylü; belâlı (*yer*); yaramaz, haşarı (*çocuk*); ahenksiz (*ses*); ~ *and ready* konforsuz, basit; çetin; *fig.* eğreti, geçici (*yöntem vs.*); şöyle böyle; ~ *copy* taslak, müsvedde; *cut up* ~ F tepesi atmak, sinirlenmek; **2.** *n.* engebeli arazi; pürüzlü yüzey; zorluk, güçlük; nahoşluk; taslak; sokak serserisi, külhanbeyi; kaba herif; **3.** *v/t.* hırpalamak, dövmek, saldırmak; pürüzlendirmek; *-in* taşlağını yapmak; dağıtmak (*saç*); bozmak; ~ *it* sefalet çekmek, sürünmek; '**rough.age** *n.* selülozu bol yiyecek; kaba madde; '**rough-and-'tum.ble 1.** *adj.* düzensiz, kuralsız; şiddetli (*kavga, mücadele*). **2.** *n.* düzensiz durum; '**rough.cast 1.** *n.* ARCH kaba sıva; **2.** *adj.* bitmemiş, ek-

sik; **3.** *v/t.* ARCH kaba sıva vurmak;
'**rough.en** *v/t.* & *v/i.* pürüzlen(dir)-
mek; kabar(t)mak.

rough...: '~'**hewn** *adj.* kabaca kesilmiş;
kaba; '~-**house** *sl.* **1.** *n.* kavga, boğuşma; gürültü patırtı; **2.** *v/i.* boğuşmak;
gürültü patırtı çıkarmak; '~-**neck** *n.*
Am. sl. serseri, külhanbeyi; kaba saba
herif; '**rough.ness** *n.* kabalık, sertlik;
'**rough-rid.er** *n.* at terbiyecisi; azgın
ata binebilen kimse; '**rough-
shod**; *ride* ~ *over* kaba davranmak
-*e*; başkasının hakkını yemek; aldırmamak -*e*, önemsememek -*i*.

rou.lette [ruːˈlet] *n.* rulet.

Rou.ma.nian [ruːˈmeinjən] = *Rumanian*.

round [raund] **1.** □ yuvarlak, toparlak,
küresel, top; tam; dolgun (*ses*); hayli,
çok; yuvarlak (*rakam*); süratli, hızlı,
atik; okkalı (*küfür*); ~ *hand* okunaklı
el yazısı; ~ *table* yuvarlak masa toplantısı; ~ *trip* gidiş dönüş, tur; **2.** *adv.*
etrafa, etrafında, civarında; *a.* ~ *about*
civarda; *all* ~ çepeçevre; *fig.* fark gözet-
meksizin, ayırmaksızın; *all the year* ~
tüm yıl boyunca; *40 inches* ~ çevresi
kırk inç; **3.** *prp.* -*in* etrafın(d)a, -*in* çev-
resin(d)e; *go* ~ *the house* evi gezmek;
~ *about 8 o'clock* saat 8 sularında; **4.** *n.*
yuvarlak, daire; devir, sefer, posta; sıra;
MUS kanon; MIL devriye; *boks:* ravnt;
dönem; parti; MIL tek atış, bir el; *100*
~*s* MIL yüz el atış; **5.** *v/t.* & *v/i.* yuvar-
laklaş(tır)mak, yuvarlak hale getir-
mek; büzmek (*dudak*); dönmek -*den*,
dolaşmak; ~ *off* yuvarlak yapmak
(*sayı*); bitirmek, tamamlamak; ~ *up*
bir araya toplamak; yakalamak (*suçlu*); yuvarlak yapmak (*sayı*).

round.a.bout [ˈraundəbaut] **1.** *adj.* dolambaçlı; dolaylı; **2.** *n.* atlıkarınca, dönme dolap; MOT yuvarlak kavşak, döner
ada.

roun.del [ˈraundl] *n.* daire içinde kabartma *veya* resim gibi süs; askeri
uçağın hangi millete ait olduğunu gösteren yuvarlak levha; **roun.de.lay**
[ˈ_-dilei] *n.* nakaratlı basit ve kısa şarkı.

round.ers [ˈraundəz] *n. pl.* beysbola
benzer bir oyun; '**round.head** *n.* HIST
İngiltere iç savaşında cumhuriyetçi;
'**roundish** *adj.* yuvarlakça; '**roundness** *n.* yuvarlaklık, toparlaklık; dolgunluk; **rounds-man** COM [ˈ_-zmən] *n.*
dağıtıcı; '**round-the-clock** *adj.* gece
gündüz, devamlı, 24 saat; '**round-ta-**

ble con.fer.ence yuvarlak masa kon-
feransı; '**round-up** *n.* bir araya toplama; toparlama.

roup VET [ruːp] *n.* bir çeşit tavuk nezlesi.

rouse [rauz] *v/t.* & *v/i.* uyan(dır)mak;
canlandırmak; tahrik etm., kışkırtmak;
~ *o.s.* bütün gücünü toplamak, canlanmak; '**rous.ing** *adj.* heyecan verici; büyük, eşsiz; faal, canlı.

roust.a.bout *Am.* [ˈraustəˈbaut] *n.* gemi *veya* rıhtım işçisi, iskele hamalı;
vasıfsız işçi.

rout[1] [raut] *n.* ayaktakımı, izdiham,
halk yığını; *obs.* serseri takımı; parti,
eğlence.

rout[2] [_] **1.** *n.* bozgun; *put to* ~ = **2.** *v/t.*
bozguna uğratmak.

rout[3] [_] = *root*[2].

route [ruːt] MIL *a.* raut] *n.* yol; rota; MIL
yüyürüş yolu; *en* ~ yolda; '~-**march** *n.*
adi adım yürüyüş, uzun talim yürüyüşü.

rou.tine [ruːˈtiːn] **1** *n.* usül, iş programı;
2. *adj.* alışılmış, her zamanki; düzenli.

rove [rəuv] *v/t.* dolaşmak, gezinmek;
'**rover** *n.* gezen (*veya* avare) kimse.

row[1] [rəu] *n.* dizi, saf, sıra *a.* (THEAT); *a
hard* ~ *to hoe* güç iş, zorluklarla dolu
hayat.

row[2] [_] **1.** *v/i.* kürek çekmek; *v/t.* kürek
çekerek götürmek; **2.** *n.* kürek çekme;
sandal gezintisi.

row[3] F [rau] **1.** *n.* kavga, patırtı, münakaşa, kargaşa, gürültü; *what's the* ~*?*
ne oluyor yahu*?*; **2.** *vb.* azarlamak, haşlamak; kavga (*veya* münakaşa) etm.
(*with ile*).

row.an BOT [ˈrauən] *n.* üvez.

row-boat [ˈrəubout] *n.* sandal, kayık.

row.dy [ˈraudi] **1.** *n.* külhanbeyi; **2.** *adj.*
zorba, kaba, terbiyesiz.

row.el [ˈrauəl] **1.** *n.* mahmuz; **2.** *v/t.*
mahmuzlamak.

row.er [ˈrəuə] *n.* kürekçi, kayıkçı, san-
dalcı.

row.ing-boat [ˈrəuiŋbəut] *n.* kayık,
sandal.

row.lock [ˈrɔlək] *n.* ıskarmoz.

roy.al [ˈrɔiəl] **1.** □ krala (*veya* krallığa)
ait; krala yaraşır; şahane, muhteşem,
görkemli **2.** *n.* NAUT kontra babafingo;
'**royal.ism** *n.* kralcılık; '**roy.al.ist 1.** *n.*
kralcı; **2.** *adj.* kralcı...; '**roy.al.ty** *n.* hükümdarlık, krallık; saltanat; kâr hisse-
si, işletme payı.

rub [rʌb] **1.** *n.* ovalama, sürt(ün)me; *fig.*
güçlük, engel; *there is the* ~ işin güç

yanı asıl bu, işte sorun da orada; **2.** *v/t.* & *v/i.* sürt(ün)mek, ov(ala)mak; ovarak cilâlamak; ovuşturmak; sürmek; sürtüşmek; ~ *along*, ~ *on*, ~ *through* *fig.* geçinip gitmek; ~ *down* aşındırmak; zımparalayarak düzeltmek; kurulamak; ~ *in* ovarak yedirmek (*krem vs.*); *fig.* üzerinde ısrarla durmak; tekrar tekrar söylemek; ~ *off* çık(ar)mak, dökülmek; sil(in)mek; ~ *out* sili(n)mek, çık(ar)mak; *Am. sl.* gebertmek, temizlemek; ~ *up* ovarak cilâlamak, silip parlatmak; tazelemek (*bilgi*).
rub.ber [ˈrʌbə] *n.* lastik, kauçuk; silgi; MEC sürtünme levhası; ovan kimse *veya* alet; *Am.* prezervatif, kaput; ~*s pl.* lastik ayakkabı; *attr.* lastik..., kauçuk...; ~ *check Am. sl.* karşılıksız (*veya* sahte) çek; ~ *solution* lastik solüsyon; '~.neck *Am. sl.* **1.** *n.* meraklı kimse, herkese *veya* herşeye dönüp dönüp bakan kimse; turla gezen turist; **2.** *v/i.* merakla bakmak, dönüp dönüp bakmak; geziye çıkmak; ~ *stamp* lastik mühür, ıstampa; *Am.* F *fig.* taklitçi (*veya* kişiliksiz) kimse; '~·'stamp *v/t.* düşünmeden onaylamak.
rub.bish [ˈrʌbiʃ] *n.* süprüntü, çöp; *fig.* saçma; 'rub.bish.y *adj. fig.* beş para etmez, tapon.
rub.ble [ˈrʌbl] *n.* moloz (taşı), yapı döküntüsü.
rube *Am. sl.* [ruːb] *n.* yontulmamış (*veya* hödük) kimse.
ru.be.fa.cient MED [ruːbiˈfeiʃjənt] *adj.* deriyi kızartan.
ru.bi.cund [ˈruːbikənd] *adj.* kırmızı, al; yüzünden kan damlayan, sağlıklı.
ru.bric [ˈruːbrik] *n.* kırmızı bölüm başlığı; kural, açıklama, direktif; ECCL dinî bir kitapta bölüm başı; **ru.bri.cate** [ˈ-keit] *v/t.* kırmızı renkle yazmak.
ru.by [ˈruːbi] **1.** *n.* MIN yakut (rengi), lâl; TYP 5 1/2 puntolu harf; **2.** *adj.* kırmızı, al.
ruck [rʌk] *n.:* **the** ~ kalabalık, izdiham, insan yığını; *at yarışı;* geri kalan atların oluşturduğu grup; *the (common)* ~ *fig.* normal yaşam düzeyi.
ruck(.le) [ˈrʌk(l)] *v/t.* & *v/i. a.* ~ *up* buruş(tur)mak, kırış(tır)mak.
ruck.sack [ˈrʌksæk] *n.* sırt çantası.
ruc.tion *sl.* [ˈrʌkʃən] *n.* kargaşa, karışıklık, kıyamet.
rud.der NAUT, AVIA [ˈrʌdə] *n.* dümen.
rud.di.ness [ˈrʌdinis] *n.* kırmızılık; 'ruddy *adj.* kırmızı, al; kırmızı yanaklı;

sl. kahrolası.
rude □ [ruːd] kaba; terbiyesiz; edepsiz; sert, şiddetli; yontulmamış, kaba saba; ilkel; basit; dinç, kuvvetli, gürbüz; işlenmemiş, ham; vahşî; ayıp; 'rude-ness *n.* kabalık; terbiyesizlik.
ru.di.ment BIOL [ˈruːdimənt] *n.* gelişmemiş kısım (*of bir organın; a. fig.*); ~*s pl.* ilke, ilk adım; **ru.di.men.ta.ry** [-ˈmentəri] *adj.* temel; gelişmemiş, eksik.
rue[1] BOT [ruː] *n.* sedefotu.
rue[2] [-] *v/t.* pişmanlık duymak *-den.*
rue.ful □ [ˈruːful] pişman; acıklı; 'rue-ful.ness *n.* pişmanlık.
ruff[1] [rʌf] *n.* kırmalı yakalık.
ruff[2] [-] *iskambil:* **1.** *n.* kozla alma; **2.** *v/t.* kozla almak.
ruf.fi.an [ˈrʌfjən] *n.* kavgacı (*veya* gaddar, zalim) kimse; 'ruf.fi.an.ly *adj.* zalimce, gaddarca, canavarca.
ruf.fle [ˈrʌfl] **1.** *n.* kırma, farbala, fırfır; hafifçe dalgalandırma (*su vs.*); *fig.* kargaşa, patırtı, gürültü; ~ *collar* kırmalı yaka; **2.** *v/t.* & *v/i.* kabartmak (*saç, tüy*); buruşturmak; büzmek, kırma yapmak; *fig.* rahatsız etm.; kız(dır)mak, öfkelen(dir)mek; hafifçe dalgalandırmak, çırpıntılı yapmak (*göl vs.*).
rug [rʌg] *n.* halı, kilim; örtü.
Rug.by [ˈrʌgbi] *n. a.* ~ *football* Amerikan futbolu.
rug.ged □ [ˈrʌgid] engebeli, pürüzlü, arızalı; düzensiz; *fig.* sert, haşin; bakımsız; kaba; terbiyesiz; kırışık, buruşuk; kulak tırmalayıcı; sıhhatli, zinde; sağlam, dayanıklı; fırtınalı; 'rugged.ness *n.* sertlik; kabalık; zindelik.
rug.ger F [ˈrʌgə] = *Rugby.*
ru.in [ˈruːin] **1.** *n.* yıkım, yıkılma, harabiyet; tahrip; perişanlık; iflâs; *mst* ~*s pl.* yıkıntı, kalıntı, harabe; *lay in* ~*s* harap etm., tahrip etm.; **2.** *v/t.* yıkmak, tahrip etm., harap etm., viraneye çevirmek; perişan etm., mahvetmek, altüst etm.; batırmak, iflâs ettirmek; bozmak; **ru.in'ation** *n.* yık(ıl)ma, yıkım, harabiyet; F felâket; 'ru.in.ous □ yıkıcı, felâkete götüren; yıkık, harap, viran.
rule [ruːl] **1.** *n.* yönetim; idare; âdet; alışkanlık; yol, usûl; ECCL kaide, kural; JUR kanun, nizam; *a.* **standing**~ statü, tüzük; MEC cetvel, metre; *as a* ~ genellikle, çoğunlukla; ~*(s) of court* mahkeme hükümleri; ~*(s) of the road* yol nizam-

namesi, trafik kuralları; ~ **of three**
MATH üçlü kuralı; ~ **of thumb** göz kararı, pratik usul; **make it a** ~ alışkanlık
haline getirmek, âdet (*veya* prensip)
edinmek; **work to** ~ kurallara uygun
çalışmak; **2.** *v/t.* idare etm., yönetmek;
a. ~ **over** hükmetmek; (cetvelle) çizmek (*kâğıt vs.*); dizginlemek, hâkim
olm.; buyurmak, emretmek; çok etkilemek; ~ **out** çıkarmak, silmek; bir kenara bırakmak; önlemek, engellemek;
v/i. üstün olm.; hüküm (*veya* saltanat)
sürmek; *obs.* belli bir seviyede olm. (*fiyat*); 'rul.er *n.* cetvel; hükümdar, yönetici; 'rul.ing *n. part.* JUR yargı, hüküm;
çizme; çizgi; yönetim, hükümdarlık; ~
price COM piyasada günlük fiyat, cari
fiyat.
rum[1] [rʌm] *n.* rom; *Am.* alkollü içki.
rum[2] *sl.* □ [-] garip, tuhaf, acayip.
Ru.ma.nian [ruːˈmeɪnjən] **1.** *adj.* Romen; **2.** *n.* Romanyalı; Romen(ce).
rum.ble[1] [ˈrʌmbl] **1.** *n.* gürleme, gümbürtü, gürültü; guruldama, gurultu;
Am. a. ~-**seat** MOT arka koltuk; *Am.*
F dalaş, sokak kavgası; **2.** *v/i.* gümbürdemek, gürlemek (*gök*); guruldamak,
gurlamak (*mide*).
rum.ble[2] *sl.* [-] *v/t. b-nin* içini okumak.
ru.mi.nant [ˈruːmɪnənt] **1.** *adj.* gevişgetiren; **2.** *n.* gevişgetiren hayvan; **ru.mi-
nate** [-ˈneɪt] *v/i.* geviş getirmek; *fig.*
derin derin düşünmek; **ru.mi'na.tion**
n. geviş getirme; derin derin düşünme.
rum.mage [ˈrʌmɪdʒ] **1.** *n.* adamakıllı
arama, araştırma; ~ **sale** fakirlerin yararına yapılan eşya satışı; **2.** *v/t.* araştırmak; didik didik aramak; *v/i.* araştırma
yapmak.
rum.mer [ˈrʌmə] *n.* ayaklı içki bardağı.
rum.my[1] *sl.* □ [ˈrʌmi] = **rum**[2].
rum.my[2] [-] *n.* bir tür iskambil oyunu.
ru.mo(u)r [ˈruːmə] **1.** *n.* söylenti, şayia;
dedikodu; **2.** *v/t.* yaymak, çıkarmak
(*dedikodu*); **it is** ~**ed** söylentiye göre;
'~-mon.ger *n.* dedikoducu kimse.
rump [rʌmp] *n.* ANAT but; ORN kıç; *co.*
popo, kıç; artan parça, bakiye.
rum.ple [ˈrʌmpl] *v/t.* buruşturmak; karmakarışık etm., bozmak.
rump steak [ˈrʌmpsteɪk] *n.* biftek.
rum.pus F [ˈrʌmpəs] *n.* gürültü, şamata; kavga, münakaşa.
rum-run.ner *Am.* [ˈrʌmrʌnə] *n.* içki kaçakçısı.
run [rʌn] **1.** (*irr.*) *v/i. com.* koşmak; akmak, dökülmek (*nehir, su vs.*); gitmek,

uzanmak; işlemek, çalışmak;
adaylığını koymak (**for** *için*); dörtnala
gitmek (*at*); kaçmak, tüymek; arkadaşlık etm. (**with** *ile*); yarışmak; yuvarlanmak; kaçmak (*çorap*); dönmek; göç
etm. (*balık*); erimek; irin akıtmak; yönelmek *-e*; devam etm.; oynanmak (*piyes*); geçmek; yayılmak; ~ **across s.o.**
b-ne rast gelmek, rastlamak; ~ **after** *-in*
peşinden koşmak; ~ **away** kaçmak (*a.
fig.*); akıp gitmek; ~ **down** bitmek; durmak (*saat*); çarpmak *-e*; *fig.* kuvvetten
düşmek; ~ **dry** kurumak; ~ **for** koşmak
-e; PARL adaylığını koymak *-e*; ~ **high**
kabarmak, çok dalgalı olm. (*deniz*);
şiddetli olm. (*his, duygu*); yükselmek,
artmak (*fiyat*); ~ **in** akmak (*su vs.*);
b-ni arabasıyla bırakmak; yarışmak;
that ~**s in the blood (family)** aile içinde kalıtsal olm., aileden gelmek,
kanında olm.; ~ **into** girmek *-e*; karşılaşmak *ile* (*güçlük*); akmak, dökülmek
-e; *b-ni* arabasıyla bırakmak; çarpmak
-e; ulaşmak *-e*; ~ **into s.o.** *b-ne* rast gelmek, rastlamak; ~ **low** azalmak; ~ **mad**
delirmek; ~ **off** kaçmak; gitmek; akmak; kaymak; ~ **on** konuşup durmak;
geçmek (*vakit*); ~ **out** sona ermek (*süre*), bitmek, tükenmek; akmak; uzanmak; **I have** ~ **out of tobacco** tütünüm
bitti; ~ **over** bir koşu gitmek; *b-ni* arabasıyla götürmek; taşmak; geçirmek; ~
short tükenmek, bitmek, kıtlaşmak; ~
through akmak; dolaşmak (*haber vs.*);
~ **to** akmak, dökülmek *-e* (*nehir*); *b-ni*
arabasıyla götürmek; devam etm. *-e
kadar*; uzanmak *-e doğru*; ulaşmak
-e; F kesesi müsaade etm. *-e*; ~ **up** artmak, fırlamak (*fiyat*); birikmek (*borç*);
~ **up to** yanaşmak, yaklaşmak *-e*; ulaşmak *-e*; ~ **(up)on** *ile* meşgul olm. (*zihin*); çarpmak, bindirmek *-e* (*gemi*);
~ **with** yarışmak *ile*; arkadaşlık etm.
ile; **2.** (*irr.*) *v/t.* sürmek, kullanmak;
yarıştırmak; aday göstermek; gütmek
(*davar*); HUNT kovalamak, takip etm.;
yarmak (*abluka*); batırmak, saplamak;
geçirmek; çarpmak; kaçırmak (*mal*);
gezdirmek (*göz*); işletmek, çalıştırmak; yönetmek, idare etm.; doldurmak; dökmek, akıtmak; tasfiye etm.
(*petrol*); girmek (*riske*); çizmek; basmak (*kitap vs.*); taşımak, nakletmek,
götürmek; ~ **the blockade** ablukayı
yarmak; ~ **down** arayıp bulmak; kova-
layıp yakalamak; yormak, bitkin
düşürmek; gezdirmek (*göz vs.*); *fig.*

yermek, kötülemek; *be ~ down* bitkin (*veya* yorgun) olm.; ~ *errands* haber götürmek *veya* bir iş için bir yere gitmek; ~ *hard* sıkıştırmak (*rakip*); ~ *in* MOT alıştırmak, açmak; geçirmek (*iplik vs.*); batırmak, saplamak (*kılıç*); eklemek, katmak; yarıştırmak; F içeri atmak, hapsetmek; ~ *into* batırmak, saplamak (*iğne, kılıç*); sokmak -*e* (*borç vs.*); ~ *off* akıtmak, boşaltmak; kaçırtmak (*davar*); yazıvermek; basmak; ezbere okumak; etkilememek -*i*, tesir etmemek -*e*; ~ *out* uzatmak; salıvermek (*ip vs.*); kovmak, sepetlemek; ~ *over* ezmek, çiğnemek; göz gezdirmek -*e*, gözden geçirmek -*i*; tekrarlamak -*i*, -*in* üzerinden geçmek; ~ *s.o. through* b-ne kılıç saplamak, b-ni süngülemek; ~ *up* çekmek (*bayrak*); artırmak, yükseltmek (*borç vs.*); yapıvermek; toplamak (*sayı*); denemek (*motor*); **3.** *n.* koşma, koşuş; koşu (*part. sporda*); gezi(nti); gidilen mesafe; yol, rota; seri, sıra; oynama (*veya* gösterim) süresi; süre; kümes bahçesi; akış, seyir; gidişat, eğilim; *spor*: sayı; kayma yokuşu; balık sürüsü; COM talep, rağbet (*on, upon* -*e*); *Am,* çay, dere, ırmak; *part. Am.* çorap kaçığı; MUS sesgeçidi, nağmeleme; COM cins, nevi, çeşit, tür; *the common* ~ alışılmış türden, sıradan; *have a* ~ *of 25 nights* THEAT 25 gece oynamak; *have the* ~ *of s.th.* bşi serbestçe kullanabilmek; *be in the* ~ *veya* ~*ing* kazanma şansı olm.; *in the long* ~ eninde sonunda, zamanla; *in the short* ~ kısa vadede; *on the* ~ kaçmakta; telâş içinde, koşuşturmakta.

run.a.bout MOT [ˈrʌnəbaut] *n.* küçük araba.

run.a.way [ˈrʌnəwei] **1.** *n.* kaçak, kaçgın, firarî; **2.** *v/i.* kaçmak; **3.** *adj.* kontrolden çıkmış; kaçak...

rune [ruːn] *n.* eski Germen alfabesinin bir harfi.

rung[1] [rʌŋ] *p.p. of* **ring**[2] **2.**

rung[2] [_] *n.* portatif merdiven basamağı; sandalyenin basamak çubuğu; *fig.* kademe.

run.ic [ˈruːnik] *adj.* eski Germen alfabesi harfleriyle yazılmış.

run-in [ˈrʌnˈin] *n. spor*: hız alma mesafesi; F çatışma, anlaşmazlık.

run.let [ˈrʌnlit], **run.nel** [ˈrʌnl] *n.* çay, dere; su oluğu.

run.ner [ˈrʌnə] *n.* koşucu, atlet; MIL haberci, ulak; kızak ayağı; kaçakçı; BOT

yan filiz; uzun masa örtüsü; yol halısı, yolluk; '~-'*up n. spor*: ikinci gelen yarışmacı *veya* takım.

run.ning [ˈrʌniŋ] **1.** *adj.* koşan; akan; koşarak yapılan; sürekli, devamlı, aralıksız; işlek, bitişik (*elyazısı*); koşuyla ilgili, koşu...; genel; içinde bulunulan (*ay, yıl vs.*); arka arkaya, peş peşe; cerahatli, akıntılı, sızıntılı; *two days* ~ peş peşe iki gün; ~ *hand* bitişik elyazısı; ~ *start spor*: hızlı başlangıç, iyi çıkış; ~ *stitch* düz dikiş; **2.** *n.* koşu; koşma; '~-*board n.* MOT, RAIL *etc.* marşpiye, basamak.

runt [rʌnt] *n.* ZOO çelimsiz hayvan; *fig.* bücür kimse, beberuhi.

run.way [ˈrʌnwei] *n.* AVIA pist; HUNT geçit.

ru.pee [ruːˈpiː] *n.* rupi.

rup.ture [ˈrʌptʃə] **1.** *n.* kopma, kır(ıl)ma; kesilme; MED fıtık; *fig.* dostça ilişkilerin sona ermesi; **2.** *v/t. & v/i.* kop(ar)mak, kır(ıl)mak; ilişkisini kesmek; fıtık olm.

ru.ral □ [ˈruərəl] köye ait, kırsal; tarımsal, ziraî; köy yaşamına ait; 'ru.ral.ize *vb.* köylüleştirmek; köyde yaşamak.

ruse [ruːz] *n.* hile, tuzak, oyun.

rush[1] BOT [rʌʃ] *n.* saz, hasırotu; *fig.* ıvır zıvır, fasa fiso.

rush[2] [_] **1.** *n.* hamle, saldırış, hücum; koş(uştur)ma; telâş; üşüşme; sıkışıklık; hengâme; COM büyük talep (*for* -*e*); ELECT akım artışı; ~ *hour(s pl.*) işin *veya* trafiğin en yoğun olduğu zaman, kalabalık saatler; ~ *order* COM acele sipariş; **2.** *v/i.* koş(uştur)mak, acele etm.; fırlamak; ~ *at* saldırmak -*e*; ~ *into extremes* aşırıya kaçmak; ~ *into print* yayımlamakta acele etm.; *v/t.* acele ettirmek, koşturmak; püskürtmek; MIL & *fig.* hücum etm. -*e*; acele ile yapmak; ~ *s.o. off his feet* b-nin iki ayağını bir pabucca sokmak; ~ *through* PARL acele ile meclisten geçirmek; 'rush.ing □ hararetli.

rusk [rʌsk] *n.* gevrek, peksimet.

rus.set [ˈrʌsit] **1.** *adj.* koyu kırmızı; **2.** *n.* koyu kırımızı renk; kış elması.

Rus.sia (leath.er) [ˈrʌʃə(ˈleðə)] *n.* Rus meşini, sahtiyan; '**Rus.sian 1.** *adj.* Rus, Rusya *veya* Rusçaya ait; **2.** *n.* Rus(yalı); Rusça.

rust [rʌst] **1.** *n.* pas (rengi); BOT pas hastalığı; zehirli mantar; **2.** *v/t. & v/i.* paslan(dır)mak (*a. fig.*).

rus.tic [ˈrʌstik] **1.** *adj.* (~*ally*) köye ait,

kırsal; *fig.* kaba saba, yontulmamış; **2.**
n. köylü; basit ve kaba kimse; **rus.ti-
cate** ['‿keit] *v/t. & v/i.* UNIV geçici
uzaklaştırma cezası vermek; kaba işçi-
likle yapmak; köyde yaşamak; **rus.ti-
'ca.tion** *n.* köyde yaşama; UNIV geçici
olarak uzaklaştırma; **rus.tic.i.ty** [‿'tisi-
ti] *n.* köylülük; köy yaşamı; kabalık.
rus.tle ['rʌsl] **1.** *v/t. & v/i.* hışırda(t)-
mak; hışırtı çıkararak ilerlemek; *Am.*
F davar çalmak; **~ up** bulmak, bulup
buluşturmak; **2.** *n.* davar *veya* at hırsızı.
rust...: '**~.less** *adj.* paslanmaz;
'**~'proof,** '**~re'sist.ant** *adj.* pas tutmaz;
'**rusty** *adj.* paslı, paslanmış (*a. fig.*); *fig.*
unutulmuş, ham, körelmiş; rengi atmış

(*siyah kumaş*).
rut¹ HUNT [rʌt] **1.** *n.* azgınlık dönemi,
kösnüme; **2.** *v/i.* kösnümek.
rut² [‿] *n.* tekerlek izi; *part. fig.* alışkı,
âdet.
ruth.less □ ['ru:θlis] merhametsiz, acımasız, zalim, insafsız; '**ruth.less.ness**
n. acımasızlık, merhametsizlik.
rut.ted ['rʌtid] *adj.* tekerlek izleriyle
dolu (*yol*).
rut.ting HUNT ['rʌtiŋ] *adj.* kösnüme ile
ilgili, kösnüme...; **~ season** kösnüme
mevsimi.
rut.ty ['rʌti] *adj.* tekerlek izleriyle dolu
(*yol*).
rye BOT [rai] *n.* çavdar.

S

Sab.bath ['sæbəθ] *n.* sebt günü, kutsal
dinlenme günü (*Yahudilerin cumartesi, Hıristiyanların pazar günü*).
sab.bat.i.cal □ [sə'bætikəl] sebt gününe ait, tatil...; **~ year** UNIV yedi yılda bir
gelen tatil yılı (*öğretim üyesi için*).
sa.ble ['seibl] **1.** *n.* ZOO samur (kürkü);
samur rengi, siyah renk; **2.** *adj. lit.* siyah, çok koyu.
sab.o.tage ['sæbətɑ:ʒ] **1.** *n.* sabotaj,
baltalama; **2.** *v/t.* baltalamak, sabote
etm.
sa.bre ['seibə] **1.** *n.* kılıç, suvari kılıcı; **2.**
v/t. kılıçtan geçirmek, katletmek.
sac ANAT, *zo* [sæk] *n.* kese, küçük torba.
sac.cha.rin CHEM ['sækərin] *n.* sakarin;
saccha.rine ['‿-rain] *adj.* çok tatlı...,
şeker...; *fig.* şeker gibi, bal gibi; suni,
yapay, yapmacık, doğal olmayan.
sac.er.do.tal □ [sæsə'dəutl] papazlığa
ait, papaz...
sack¹ [sæk] **1.** *n.* çuval, torba, *Am.* kese
kâğıdı; bir çuval (dolusu); bol gelen ceket, kadın ceketi; *give* (*get*) *the* **~** F
işinden çıkar(ıl)mak; kapının önüne
vermek, sepetlemek; **2.** *v/t.* torba vs'ye
koymak; F işinden çıkarmak, atmak,
kovmak.
sack² [‿] **1.** *n.* yağma, çapul; **2.** *v/t.* yağma etm.
sack³ [‿] *n.* Güney Avrupa'ya mahsus
beyaz şarap.
sack.cloth ['sækklɔ:θ], **sack.ing** *n.* çuval bezi, çul.
sac.ra.ment ECCL ['sækrəmənt] *n.*

(*Hıristiyanlıkta*) kutsal ayin; **sac.ra-
men.tal** □ [‿'mentl] dinî ayine ait, ayin
niteliğinde.
sa.cred □ ['seikrid] kutsî, kutsal, mukaddes; dinî, dinsel (*şiir, müzik*); saygıdeğer, aziz, mübarek; '**sa.cred.ness** *n.*
kutsiyet, kutsallık, azizlik.
sac.ri.fice ['sækrifais] **1.** *n.* kurban; fedakârlık, özveri; *at a* **~** COM zararına,
pahasına; **2.** *v/t. & v/i.* kurban etm.; feda etm., gözden çıkarmak; COM zararına satmak.
sac.ri.fi.cial [sækri'fiʃəl] *adj.* kurbanlık, kurbanla ilgili; COM zararına,
çok ucuza...
sac.ri.lege ['sækrilidʒ] *n.* kutsal bir yere *veya* şeye saygısızlık, tecavüz etme;
sac.ri.le.gious □ [‿'lidʒəs] kutsal şeye
saygısız, şerir, günahkâr; tecavüzkâra-
ne.
sa.crist, sac.ris.tan ECCL [sækrist(ən)]
n. zangoç, kilise kayyumu, kilisede hizmet eden kimse.
sac.ris.ty ECCL ['sækristi] *n.* kilisede
kutsal eşyaların muhafaza edildiği
oda.
sad □ [sæd] kederli, üzgün; acıklı; acınacak, endişe verici; donuk, karanlık,
kasvetli (*renk*).
sad.den ['sædn] *v/t. & v/i.* kederlen-
(dir)mek, acınmak, müteessir etm. *veya* olm., üz(ül)mek.
sad.dle ['sædl] **1.** *n.* eyer; sırt; *break to
the* **~** talim ve terbiye etm. (*at*); **2.** *v/t.*
eyerlemek; *fig.* ağırlık vermek, ağır

gelmek, sıkıntı vermek; yüklemek (**up-on**); '**~bag** *n.* heybe, hurç, eyer çantası; '**~cloth** *n.* haşa, çul, teğelti, eyer altına konan çul, '**sad.dler** *n.* saraç; '**sad.dler.y** *n.* saraçhane; saraçlık; saraciye.

sad.ism ['seidizəm] *n.* sadizm.

sad.ness ['sædnis] *n.* keder, üzgünlük, hüzün, üzüntü, mahzunluk, melânkoli, karasevda.

sa.fa.ri [sə'fɑːri] *n.* safari, (*part.* Afrika'da) av partisi.

safe [seif] **1.** ☐ *com.* emin (**from** -*den*), güvenilir, emniyetli, sağlam; tehlikesiz, salim; **to be on the ~ side** ihtiyatlı davranmak, sonuçtan emin olm.; **2.** *n.* kasa; yemek dolabı, teldolap; **~ de-posit** kasa dairesi; '**~blow.er** *n.* kasa hırsızı; **~ con.duct** geçiş izni, himaye *veya* seyahat belgesi (*savaşta*); '**~.guard 1.** *n.* koruma, himaye, koruyucu şey; muhafız; **2.** *v/t.* korumak, emniyet altına almak (**against** -*e karşı*); **~ ing duty** koruyucu gümrük vergisi; '**safe.ness** *n.* emniyet, güvenlik.

safe.ty ['seifti] *n.* güvenlik, asayiş, emniyet; **~ belt** MOT emniyet kemeri; **~ curtain** THEAT yanmaz perde; **~ is.land** trafik adası, refüj; '**~lock** *n.* emniyet kilidi; '**~pin** *n.* çengelli iğne; **~ ra.zor** traş ma kinesi.

saf.fron ['sæfrən] **1.** *n.* BOT safran; bu çiçeğin boya maddesi *veya* baharat olarak kullanılan tohumları; koyu sarı renk; **2.** *adj.* safran renginde, koyu sarı.

sag [sæg] **1.** *v/i.* eğilmek, sarkmak, çökmek; MEC bel vermek; NAUT batmak (*a. fig.*); rüzgâr altına sürüklenmek; düşmek (*fiyat*); kaybolmak, kaçmak (*neşe*, *heves*); **2.** *n.* çöküntü, eğilme; MEC bel verme; düşüş (*fiyat*).

sa.ga ['sɑːgə] *n.* eski İskandinav hikâyesi, saga, efsane; destan.

sa.ga.cious ☐ [sə'geiʃəs] akıllı, sağgörülü, zeki, anlayışlı, keskin görüşlü.

sa.gac.i.ty [sə'gæsiti] *n.* akıllılık, zekâ, anlayış, anlak, sağgörü.

sag.a.more ['sægəmɔː] *n.* kızılderili kabile reisi.

sage[1] [seidʒ] **1.** ☐ akıllı; hikmet sahibi, ağırbaşlı, hakim; **2.** *n.* hikmet sahibi kimse, yaşını başını almış akıllı kimse, filozof, bilge.

sage[2] BOT [_] *n.* adaçayı.

sage.brush BOT ['seidʒbrʌʃ] *n.* A.B.D.'de bir tür kokulu çalı.

sa.go ['seigəu] *n.* sagu, bir kaç tür hurma ağacından alınan bir tür nişasta.

sa.hib ['sɑːhib] *n.* Hindistan'da Avrupalılara verilen ünvan; efendi.

said [sed] *pret. & p.p. of* **say 1**.

sail [seil] **1.** *n.* yelken; deniz yolculuğu; yel değirmeni yelpazesi; yelkenli; **set ~** yelken açıp denize açılmak; **2.** *v/t. & v/i.* yelkenliyle (*veya* gemiyle) gitmek; (gemi ile) yola çıkmak, ayrılmak; üzerinde seyretmek (*veya* gitmek); uç(ur)mak, süzülmek; yönetmek (*yelkenli*); '**~boat** *n.* yelkenli gemi; '**~cloth** *n.* yelken bezi; '**sail.er** *n.* yelkenli gemi; '**sailing-ship**, '**sail.ing-ves.sel** *n.* yelkenli, yelken gemisi; '**sail.or** *n.* gemici, denizci; tayfa, deniz eri; **~'s knot** gemici düğümü; **be a good (bad) ~** *k-ni* deniz tut(ma)mak; '**sail-plane** *n.* planör.

saint [seint] **1.** *n. & adj.* kutsal, aziz, veliya, eren; (*özel ismin önünde: S., St.*) Ermiş. Aziz; **2.** *v/t.* azizler mertebesine çıkarmak; '**saint.ed** *adj.* aziz; aziz mertebesine ulaşmış, cennete giden, merhum; mukaddes, kutsal; '**saint.li-ness** *n.* azizlik, evliyalık; kutsiyet; '**saint.ly** *adj.* evliya gibi, azizlere yakışır, mübarek.

saith *obs. veya poet.* [seθ] *3rd sg. person of* **say**.

sake [seik] *n.*: **for the ~ of** -*in* uğruna, -*in* aşkına, -*in* hatırı için; **for my ~** hatırım için, benim için; **for God's ~** Allah aşkına.

sal CHEM [sæl] *n.* tuz; **~ ammoniac** nişadır; **~ volatile** karbonat amonyum ruhu.

sal.a.ble ['seiləbl] *adj.* satılabilir, geçer.

sa.la.cious ☐ [sə'leiʃəs] şehvani, şehvetli; müstehcen, açık saçık.

sal.ad ['sæləd] *n.* salata.

sal.a.man.der ['sæləmændə] *n.* ZOO semender; ateşte yanmayan efsanevi bir tür hayvan; ocak demiri; salamandra.

sa.la.mi [sə'lɑːmiː] *n.* salam.

sal.a.ried ['sælərid] *adj.* maaşlı, ücretli; maaşlı...; '**sal.a.ry 1.** *n.* maaş, ücret, aylık; **2.** *v/t.* maaş (*veya* aylık, ücret) vermek; '**sal.a.ry earn.er** maaş (*veya* aylık, ücret) alan kimse.

sale [seil] *n.* satış, satım, satma, satılış; mezat; talep, revaç; indirimli satış; **for ~, on ~** satılık; **by private ~** el altından satış; '**sale.a.ble** *adj.* satılabilir.

sales... [seilz]: '**~man** *n.* satıcı, tezgâhtar; '**~man.ship** *n.* satıcılık, satma yeteneği, işin adamı (*veya* eri) olma; **~ re-sist.ance** alıcının isteksizliği *veya* satıcıyı geri çevirebilmesi; **'~wom.an** *n.* satıcı kadın.

sa.li.ence ['seiljəns] *n.* çıkıntı, çıkma, cumba; göze çarpan şey; dikkati çekme; **'sa.li.ent 1.** □ belirgin, çarpıcı, göze çarpan, dikkati çeken; çıkıntılı, çıkık; *fig.* mükemmel, mümtaz, frapan, birinci kalitede; **2.** *n.* çıkıntı, cumba; MIL (*cephe, siper*) dış açı.

sa.line 1. ['seilain] *adj.* tuzlu; tuz gibi, tuz...; **2.** [sə'lain] *n.* madensel tuz; tuzla; MED tuzlu eriyik.

sa.li.va PHYSIOL [sə'laivə] *n.* salya, tükürük; **sal.i.var.y** ['sælivəri] *adj.* salya ile ilgili; tükürük salgılayan; **sal.i'va-tion** *n.* tükürük çıkarma (*veya* salgılama).

sal.low[1] BOT ['sæləu] *n.* bodur söğüt ağacı.

sal.low[2] BOT [~] *adj.* soluk yüzlü, benzi sararmış; **'sal.low.ness** *n.* solgunluk, sarılık, solukluk.

sal.ly ['sæli] **1.** *n.* MIL çıkış, çemberi yarma, huruç hareketi; nükteli çıkış, espri; **2.** *v/i.* MIL *a.* **~ out** dışarı fırlamak, çemberi yarmak; **~ forth, ~ out** yola düzülmek, toplu halde geziye çıkmak.

sal.ma.gun.di [sælmə'gʌndi] *n.* (*kıyılmış et, ançüez, yumurta ve sebze karışımı*) bir tür salata; *fig.* karmakarışık şey.

salm.on ['sæmən] **1.** *n.* som balığı (rengi); **2.** *adj.* som balığı renginde, sarımsı pembe.

sal.on ['sælɔn] *n.* ressam ve yazarlar topluluğu; sergi salonu, galeri; güzel sanatlar sergisi; salon, misafir odası.

sa.loon [sə'lu:n] *n.* büyük salon; birinci mevki salon (*gemide*); bar; *Am.* meyhane; = **sa'loon-car** RAIL *n.* vagon-salon; MOT üstü kapalı 4-7 kişilik otomobil, limozin.

salt [sɔ:lt] **1.** *n.* tuz; *fig.* tat, tat tuz, lezzet, çeşni; tuzluk; **old ~** *fig.* eski deniz kurtlarından; **with a grain of ~** hakları kullanabilme koşuluyla; kuşkuyla, ihtiyatla; **2.** *adj.* tuzlu; tuzlanmış; **3.** *v/t.* tuzlamak -*i*, salamura yapmak -*i*; *fig.* heyecan katmak, ilginç göstermek; **'~-cel.lar** *n.* tuzluk; **'salt.ed** *adj.* tuzlu; *sl.* bağışık, pişkin; **salt.pe.tre** ['~pi:tə] *n.* güherçile; **'salt-wa.ter** *adj.* tuzlu su (-da) ...; **'salt.works** *n. sg.* tuzla, tuz fabrikası; **'salt.y** *adj.* tuzlu; denizi hatırlatan; keskin, nükteli, müstehce-

ne kaçan.

sa.lu.bri.ous □ [sə'lu:briəs] sağlam, salim, sıhhatli, sıhhî; **sa.lu.bri.ty** [sə-'lu:briti], **sal.u.tar.i.ness** ['sæljutərinis] *n.* sıhhatlilik, yararlılık, sıhhî oluş; **sal.u.tar.y** □ ['sæljutəri] = **salu-brious**.

sal.u.ta.tion [sælju:'teifən] *n.* selâm (verme), hatır sorma; hitap, seslenme; **salu.ta.to.ry** [səl'ju:tətɔri] *adj.* selâm niteliğinde; selâm veren; **sa.lute** [sə-'lu:t] **1.** *n.* selâm (verme); *co.* öpücük, buse; MIL selâmlama; **2.** *vb.* selâmlamak, selâm vermek; MIL selâm çakmak; resmî saygı ile bulunmak, karşılamak.

sal.vage ['sælvidʒ] **1.** *n.* tahlisiye (ücreti), kurtarma ve yardım (ücreti); kurtarılan mal; **2.** *v/t.* kurtarmak, çıkarmak, emniyet altına almak (*eşya*).

sal.va.tion [sæl'veifən] *n.* kurtuluş, kurtar(ıl)ma, kurtarış, selâmet; *fig.* kurtuluş; ♀ **Army** selâmet ordusu, fakirler için para toplayan bir Protestan grubu; **sal'va.tion.ist** *n.* selâmet ordusu üyesi.

salve[1] [sælv] *v/t.* (*kaza, deniz veya yangından*) kurtarmak.

salve[2] [sɑ:v] **1.** *n.* merhem, pomat; *fig.* teselli; **2.** *v/t. mst fig.* merhem sürmek; acısını dindirmek, teskin etm.

sal.ver ['sælvə] *n.* tepsi.

sal.vo ['sælvəu] *n., pl.* **sal.voes** ['~z] MIL salvo, yaylım ateşi; selâm topu; *fig.* alkış, kahkaha vs. tufanı; **~ release** AVIA bombardıman; **sal.vor** NAUT ['~və] *n.* kurtarma gemisi.

Sa.mar.i.tan [sə'mæritn] **1.** *adj.* Samariye ile ilgili; **2.** *n.* Samariyeli, Samariye dili.

same [seim] : **the ~** aynı, tıpkı(sı); eşit; adı geçen; **all the ~** bununla beraber, mamafih, yine, hal böyle iken; **it is all the ~ to me** bence hepsi bir, benim için hava hoş; **'same.ness** *n.* ayrılık, monotonluk, tekdüzelik; benzerlik.

samp *Am.* [sæmp] *n.* iri taneli öğütülmüş mısır unu.

sam.ple ['sɑ:mpl] **1.** *n. part.* COM numune, örnek, eşantiyon; mostra; model, tip; **2.** *v/t.* örnek olarak denemek, numune almak; çeşnisine bakmak, kalitesini saptamak; **'sam.pler** *n.* el işi örneği; örnekleri deneyen kimse, çeşnici.

san.a.tive ['sænətiv] *adj.* iyileştiren, şifa verici; sıhhi, yararlı; **san.a.to.ri.um** [~'tɔ:riəm] *n.* (*part. akciğer*) sanator-

yum, sağlık yurdu; temiz havalı yer;
san.a.to.ry ['‿təri] *adj.* şifa verici; yararlı.
sanc.ti.fi.ca.tion [sæŋktifi'keiʃən] *n.*
kutsama, takdis, tasvip; resmen ibadete tahsis; **sanc.ti.fy** ['‿fai] *v/t.* kutsallaştırmak, takdis etm.; tasvip etm.,
onaylamak; günahlardan arındırmak;
sanc.timo.ni.ous □ [-'məunjəs] kaba
sofu, iki yüzlü, riyakâr; **sanc.tion**
['sæŋkʃən] **1.** *n.* onay, tasdik, tasvip;
yaptırım, zorunlu önlem; **2.** *v/t.* uygun
bulmak, onaylamak; **sanc.ti.ty** ['‿titi]
n. kutsallık, mukaddes olma; **sanc.tu-
ar.y** ['‿tjuəri] *n.* kutsal yer; tapınak,
mabet; sığınak; **sanc.tum** ['‿təm] *n.*
kutsal yer; inziva yeri, *b-nin* sessiz ve
yalnız olabileceği yer.
sand [sænd] **1.** kum; **~s** *pl.* kumluk,
kumsal, kum çölü; *his ~s are running
out* ömrünün sonuna geldi, ömrü
kısalıyor; **2.** *v/t.* üstüne kum serpmek,
içine kum atmak, kumla örtmek.
san.dal¹ ['sændl] *n.* çarık, sandal.
san.dal² [‿], '**~.wood** *n.* sandal ağacı,
sandal tahtası.
sand...: '**~.bag** *n.* kum torbası; '**~.bank**
n. kumsal sığlık, kum bankı (*su altın-
da*); '**~.blast** MEC *n.* kum fışkırtma aleti; '**~.boy** *n.*: *as jolly as a ~* çok keyifli;
'**~.glass** *n.* kum saati; '**~.hill** *n.* kumul,
kum tepesi; '**~.pa.per 1.** *n.* zımpara
kâğıdı; **2.** *v/t.* zımparalamak *-i*; '**~.pip-
er** *n.* ORN kum çulluğu; '**~.shoes** *n.* plaj
ayakkabısı, lastik tabanlı bez ayakkabı; '**~.stone** *n.* kumtaşı, gre.
sand.wich ['sænwidʒ] **1.** *n.* sandviç; **2.**
v/t. a. **~ in** *-in* arasına yerleştirmek,
sıkıştırmak; '**~.man** *n.* önünde ve arkasında reklâm yaftaları asılı gezen
adam.
sand.y ['sændi] *adj.* kumlu; kum...;
kumsal; kum renginde, saman sarısı
(*saç*).
sane [sein] *adj.* aklı başında, akıllı; makûl; mantıklı (*cevap vs.*).
San.for.ize ['sænfəraiz] *vb.* çekmesini
önlemek üzere özel bir işleme tabi tutmak (*kumaş*).
sang [sæŋ] *pret. of* **sing**.
san.gui.nary □ ['sæŋgwinəri] kana susamış, kan dökücü, zalim; kanlı; **sanguine** [-'gwin] *adj.* neşeli, kanı sıcak
(*mizaçlı*); iyimser, ümitli, emin; gayretli; kan gibi kırmızı (*cilt*); **san.guin-
e.ous** [-'giwiniəs] *adj.* kan...; = *s. san-
guine*.

san.i.tari.an [sæni'tɛəriən] *n.* sağlık
uzmanı, sıhhıyeci; **san.i.ta.ri.um** [sæn-
i'tɛəriəm] *n.* *Am. of* **sanatorium**;
san.i.tar.y □ ['‿təri] sağlıkla ilgili,
MEC sıhhî...; **~ towel** âdet bezi.
san.i.ta.tion [sæni'teiʃən] *n.* sağlık koruma, hıfızısıhha; sağlık işleri (örgütü); sıhhî tertibat; '**san.i.ty** *n.* akıl
sağlığı, akıllılık, aklı başında olma.
sank [sæŋk] *pret. of* **sink 1**.
sans *lit.* [sænz] *prp.* -siz.
San.skrit [sænskrit] *n.* Sanskrit dili,
Sanskritçe.
San.ta Claus [sæntə'klɔːz] *n.* Noel baba.
sap¹ [sæp] *n.* BOT özsu, usare; *fig.*
canlılık, dirilik, hayatiyet, öz, ruh; *sl.*
alık, öküz aleyhisselâm; pısırık, sünepe.
sap² [‿] **1.** *n.* MIL lağım, siper, hendek,
sıçanyolu; inek, çok çalışan, hafızlayan
kimse; **2.** *v/i.* siper kazmak; *sl.* ineklemek, hafızlamak; *v/t.* altından sıçanyolu kazarak yıkmak *-i*, lağım açmak;
kuvvetten düşürmek *-i*, takatini kesmek *-in*.
sap.id ['sæpid] *adj.* lezzetli, tadı tuzu
yerinde; **sa.pid.i.ty** [sə'piditi] *n.* lezzet, çeşni, tat.
sa.pi.ence *mst iro.* ['seipjəns] *n.* akıl,
hikmet, dirayet; '**sa.pi.ent** *mst iro.* □
akıllı, hikmetli, dirayetli.
sap.less ['sæplis] *adj.* kuvvetsiz, kudretsiz, mecalsiz, takatsiz.
sap.ling ['sæpliŋ] *n.* fidan, körpe ağaç;
fig. delikanlı, genç çocuk.
sap.o.na.ceous CHEM *veya co.* [sæp-
əu'neiʃəs] *adj.* sabunlu, sabun gibi.
sap.per MIL ['sæpə] *n.* istihkâm eri,
sıçanyolu kazan.
sap.phire MIN ['sæfaiə] *n.* safir, gökyakut.
sap.pi.ness ['sæpinis] *n.* canlılık, hayatiyet; özlü oluş; toyluk.
sap.py ['sæpi] *adj.* özlü; canlı; *fig.* dinç,
kuvvetli; *sl.* ahmak, sünepe, alık.
Sar.a.cen ['særəsn] *n.* Haçlı seferleri
zamanında müslümanlara verilen ad.
sar.casm ['sɑːkæzəm] *n.* dokunaklı
alay, acı istihza, saraka; **sar.cas.tic**,
sar.casti.cal □ [sɑː'kæstik(əl)] iğneleyici, istihzalı, alaylı, dokunaklı, müstehzi, tahkiramiz, sarkastik.
sar.coph.a.gus *n.*, *pl.* **sar'coph.a.gi**
[sɑː'kɔfəgəs, gai] lahit, sanduka.
sar.dine ICHTH [sɑː'diːn] *n.* sardalya,
ateşbalığı.

Sar.din.i.an [sɑː'dinjən] **1.** *adj.* Sardinya ile ilgili; **2.** *n.* Sardinyalı.

sar.don.ic [sɑː'dɔnik] *adj.* (**~ally**) alaycı, hor gören, acı, hakaret dolu, sinik, kelbi.

sar.to.ri.al [sɑː'tɔːriəl] *adj.* terzi *veya* terziliğe ait.

sash[1] [sæʃ] *n.* pencere çerçevesi.

sash[2] [_] *n.* geniş kuşak, omuz atkısı.

sash-window ['sæʃwindəu] *n.* sürme pencere.

sas.sa.fras BOT ['sæsəfræs] *n.* kuzey Amerika ve Asya'da yetişen bir tür küçük ağaç.

sat [sæt] *pret. & p.p. of* **sit**.

Sa.tan ['seitən] *n.* ECCL Şeytan, İblis.

sa.tan.ic [sə'tænik] *adj.* (**~ally**) şeytanî, şeytanca, ibliskârane, hınzırca.

satch.el ['sætʃəl] *n.* okul çantası, el çantası.

sate [seit] = **satiate**.

sa.teen [sæ'tiːn] *n.* satene benzer pamuklu kumaş.

sat.el.lite ['sætəlait] *n.* (*a. suni, yapma*) uydu, peyk, satelit, bir gezegenin uydusu; uydu devlet; **~ dish** *n.* çanak anten; **~ radio** uydu antenli radyo.

sa.ti.ate ['seiʃieit] *v/t.* doyurmak, kandırmak, tok hale getirmek, tıka basa yedirmek, *b-nin* açlığını gidermek; **sa.ti'a.tion** *n.* doy(ur)ma; **sa.ti.e.ty** [sə'taiəti] *n.* doymuşluk, usanç, gına, tokluk.

sat.in ['sætin] *n.* saten, atlas; **sat.i-net(te)** [_'net] *n.* ince saten *veya* saten taklidi kumaş.

sat.ire ['sætaiə] *n.* hiciv, yergi, taşlama; **sa.tir.ic, sa.tir.i.cal** □ [sə'tirik(əl)] yergili, hicivli, satirik; **sat.i.rist** ['sætərist] *n.* hicivci, taşlama yazarı; **'sat.i.rize** *v/t.* alay etm., istihza etm. hicvetmek.

sat.is.fac.tion [sætis'fækʃən] *n.* hoşnutluk, memnuniyet; tarziye, hoşnut etme, tatmin; ödeme, tazmin; **sat.is.fac.to.ri.ness** [sætis'fæktərinis] *n.* memnuniyet verici durum, yeterlik; **satis'fac.to.ry** □ memnuniyet verici, hoşnut kılan; doyurucu, tatminkâr, kâfi, yeterli.

sat.is.fied ['sætisfaid] memnun, hoşnut, tatmin olmuş, ikna olmuş, inanmış; **satis.fy** ['_fai] *vb. com.* memnun etm. *-i.* hoşnut etm. *-i;* tazmin etm., zararı ödemek; yetmek, kâfi gelmek; koşulları yerine getirmek; *b-ni* bşe inandırmak, ikna etm. (**of**); doyurmak; ortadan kaldırmak (*şüphe*).

sa.trap ['sætrəp] *n.* eski İran'da vali.

sat.u.rate CHEM & *fig.* ['sætʃəreit] *v/t.* doyurmak, doymuş hale getirmek, içirmek, işba haline getirmek; **sat.u'ra-tion** *n.* doy(ur)ma, işba.

Sat.ur.day ['sætədi] *n.* cumartesi.

Sat.urn ['sætən] *n.* Satürn, zühal; MYTH Satürn, ziraat tanrısı; **sat.ur.nine** ['_nain] *adj.* melânkolik, asık yüzlü, sıkıcı, kasvetli.

sat.yr ['sætə] *n.* yarı insan yarı keçi şeklinde bir yarıtanrı; şehvet düşkünü kimse.

sauce [sɔːs] **1.** *n.* (*oft.* soğuk) salça, sos; *Am.* komposto; *fig.* tat, lezzet, çeşni; F yüzsüzlük, küstahlık; **2.** *v/t.* sos ilave etm., lezzet, çeşni katmak; F *b-nin* tepesine çıkmak, küstahlık etm.; '**~boat** *n.* salçalık; '**~pan** *n.* uzun saplı tencere, kaçarula; '**sauc.er** *n.* fincan tabağı.

sau.ci.ness F ['sɔːsinis] *n.* arsızlık, saygısızlık, küstahlık.

sau.cy □ F ['sɔːsi] küstah, cüretli, arsız, saygısız, yüzsüz, utanmaz, pişkin.

saun.ter ['sɔːntə] **1.** *n.* ağır ağır ve amaçsız yapılan yürüyüş, dolaşma, gezinti, gezme; **2.** *v/i.* yavaş yavaş dolaşmak, gezinmek; '**saun.ter.er** *n.* avare, kaldırım mühendisi.

sau.ri.an ZOO ['sɔːriən] *n.* kertenkele ve timsah türünden eski çağ hayvanı, soryen.

sau.sage ['sɔsidʒ] *n.* sucuk, salam, sosis.

sau.té [sə'utei] *adj.* tavada hafif kızartılmış, sote (*az yağda*).

sav.age ['sævidʒ] **1.** □ vahşi, yabanî, medeniyetsiz; yırtıcı, gaddar, merhametsiz, zalim; işlenmemiş, yontulmamış; F gazaplı, şiddetli, hiddetli; **2.** *n.* vahşî, barbar, zalim kimse; medeniyetsiz kimse; **3.** *v/t.* vahşice saldırmak (*hayvan*); '**sav.age.ness, 'sav.age.ry** *n.* yabanilik, barbarlık, vahşet, gaddarlık, vandalizm.

sa.van.na(h) [sə'vænə] *n.* savana, ağaçsız ova, kır.

sav.ant ['sævənt] *n.* âlim, bilgin, hakim.

save [seiv] **1.** *v/t. & v/i.* kurtarmak; (*gemi vs*) çıkarmak, kurtarmak; korumak, saklamak, muhafaza etm. (**from** *-den*); biriktirmek, tasarruf etm.; sakınmak, esirgemek; kaybını önlemek, kazandırmak; para biriktirmek, tutumlu olm.; **2.** *prp. & cj. a.* **~ that** *-den* başka, maada, müstesna, yalnız.

sav.e.loy ['sævilɔi] *n.* bir tür yağsız pişirilmiş sosis.

sav.er ['seivə] *n.* kurtarıcı; para biriktiren kimse; para ve zaman kazandıran alet.

sav.ing ['seiviŋ] **1.** ☐ tasarrufkâr, tutumlu, idareli; **2.** *n.* kurtarma; **~s** *pl.* biriktirilen paralar, tasarruf, iktisat.

sav.ings... ['seiviŋz]: '**~-bank** *n.* tasarruf sandığı *veya* bankası; '**~-de.pos.it** *n.* tasarruf.

sav.io(u)r ['seivjə] *n.* kurtarıcı, halâskâr, *Saviour* Hazreti İsa.

sa.vo(u)r ['seivə] **1.** *n.* tat, lezzet, çeşni; *fig.* lezzet, tat tuz; **2.** *v/i.* tadı olm., andırmak (*of* -*i*), kokmak; *v/t.* tadına bakmak, kokusunu almak -*in*; tadını (*veya* zevkini) çıkarmak -*in*; **sa.vo(u)r.i.ness** ['-rinis] *n.* lezzetlilik, hoş tat; '**sa.vo(u)rless** *adj.* tatsız (tuzsuz), kokusuz.

sa.vo(u)r.y[1] ☐ ['seivəri] lezzetli, tadı tuzu yerinde, iştah açıcı; güzel kokulu; baharatlı.

sa.vo(u)r.y[2] BOT [-] *n.* kekiğe benzer bir tür kokulu ot.

sa.voy [sə'vɔi] *n.* bir tür kıvırcık kış lahanası.

sav.vy *sl.* ['sævi] **1.** *v/i.* anlamak, idrak etm., kavramak; **2.** *n.* kavrayış, anlayış, anlak, idrak, kafa.

saw[1] [sɔ:] *pret. of* **see**.

saw[2] [-] *n.* vecize, atasözü, özdeyiş, darbımesel.

saw[3] [-] **1.** *n.* testere, bıçkı, hızar; **2.** *vb.* testere ile kesmek, bıçkılamak; '**~.dust** *n.* testere talaşı, bıçkı tozu; '**~-horse** *n.* tahta biçmeye mahsus sehpa; '**~-mill** *n.* kereste fabrikası, hızarhane; **sawn** [sɔ:n] *p.p. of* **saw**[3] **2.**; **saw.yer** ['-jə] *n.* bıçkıcı, hızarcı.

Sax.on [sæksn] **1.** *adj.* Saksonya ile ilgili; Sakson...; Cermen...; **2.** *n.* Saksonyalı.

sax.o.phone MUS ['sæksəfəun] *n.* saksafon.

say [sei] **1.** (*irr.*) *v/t.* söylemek, demek; ezberden söylemek; beyan etm.; bildirmek, haber vermek; **~ grace** yemekten önce ve sonra dua etm.; **~ mass** kuddas ayini yapmak; *that is to* **~** yani, demekki; *do you* **~ so?** sahi mi (diyorsun)?; *you don't* **~ so!** yok canım!, deme!; 1 **~!** (*bir tümce başında dikkati çekmek için kullanılan deyim*) bana bak!, beni dinle!, yaa!; *he is said to be...* onun -*diği* söyleniyor; *no sooner said than done* demesiyle yapması bir

oldu; **2.** *n.* söz, denilen şey, kelam, kelime; söz sırası; *it is my* **~** *now* şimdi söz sırası benim; *let him have his* **~** bırak söyleyeceğini söylesin; *have a veya* **some** (*no*) **~** *in s.th.* bir meselede söz sahibi ol(ma)mak; '**saying** *n.* söz; atasözü, özdeyiş; *it goes without* **~** hiç kuşku yok ki, elbette.

scab [skæb] *n.* yara kabuğu; uyuz illeti; *sl.* grev bozan.

scab.bard ['skæbəd] *n.* (*kılıç vs.*) kın.

scab.by ☐ ['skæbi] yara gibi kabuk kabuk olan, kabuk bağlamış; uyuz, uyuza tutulmuş.

sca.bi.es MED ['skeibii:z] *n.* uyuz illeti.

sca.bi.ous BOT ['skeibjəs] *n.* uyuzotu.

sca.brous ['skeibrəs] *adj.* pul pul, kabuk bağlamış, kepekli, pürtüklü; pürüzlü, çapraşık; açık saçık, edepsizce, yakışıksız.

scaf.fold ['skæfəld] *n.* yapı iskelesi, darağacı platformu; '**scaf.fold.ing** *n.* yapı iskelesi kerestesi.

scald [skɔ:ld] **1.** *n.* haşlama, haşlayıp yakma; kaynar sudan ileri gelen yanık *veya* yara; **2.** *vb.* kaynar su ile haşlamak; *a.* **~ out** iyice kaynatmak; (*süt*) kaynatmak.

scale[1] [skeil] **1.** *n.* balık pulu; kazan çeperine yapışan kefeki (taşı); diş pası, kefeki, pesek; *remove the* **~s from s.o.'s eyes** *b-nin* gözünü açmak, gerçekleri görmesini sağlamak; **2.** *v/t.* pullarını çıkarmak, derisini yüzmek; üst kısmını kazımak; MEC (*kazandaki kefeki taşı*) vurarak düşürmek; (*diş pası*) temizlemek; *v/i. oft.* **~ off** pul pul dökülmek.

scale[2] [-] **1.** *n.* terazi gözü, kefe; (*a pair of*) **~s** *pl.* terazi; **~s** *pl.* AST Mizan, Terazi; **2.** *v/t.* tartmak, ağırlığını ölçmek.

scale[3] [-] **1.** *n.* ölçek; dereceli cetvel; MUS ıskala, gam; derece taksimatı, derece; *fig.* ölçü, mikyas; *on a large* **~** geniş ölçüde (*veya* çapta); **2.** *v/t.* bşe tırmanmak, çıkmak; **~ up (down)** belli oranda büyütmek (küçültmek).

scaled [skeild] *adj.* pullu; kepekli.

scale.less ['skeillis] *adj.* pulsuz; kepeksiz.

scal.ing-lad.der ['skeiliŋlædə] *n.* MIL tırmanma merdiveni; yangın merdiveni.

scal.lion BOT ['skæljən] *n.* yeşil soğan; pırasa.

scal.lop ['skɔləp] **1.** *n.* ZOO tarak; tarak kabuğu şeklinde tabak *veya* tava; tarak kabuğu şeklinde işlenmiş oya, fisto; **2.** *v/t.* tarak kabuuğ şeklinde kesmek *veya* yapmak; yemeğin üstüne sos katarak fırında pişirmek; fisto yapmak.

scalp [skælp] **1.** *n.* kafatasını kaplayan deri; zafer alâmeti; **2.** *v/t. -in* başının derisini yüzmek; karaborsa sinema, tiyatro *vs.* bileti satmak.

scal.pel MED ['skælpǝl] *n.* ufak ve düz bıçak, tesrih bıçağı.

scal.y ['skeili] *adj.* pul pul, pullarla kaplı; kabukları pul pul soyulan.

scamp [skæmp] **1.** *n.* yaramaz (*veya* haylaz, çapkın) kimse; **2.** *v/t.* kötü iş görmek, acele ile yüzüne gözüne bulaştırmak; '**scamp.er 1.** *v/i.* acele ve neşeli koşuşturmak, seyirtmek; **2.** *n. fig.* acele kaçış, tüyme, dört nala kaçış.

scan [skæn] **1.** *v/t.* incelemek, tetkik etm.; gözden geçirmek; *fig.* göz gezdirmek; *televizyon:* bir resmin tüm noktalarından sıra ile geçmek; MED & *bilgisayar:* taramak; *v/i.* vezne göre okumak, vezin analizi yapmak; **2.** *n.* MED & *bilgisayar:* tarama.

scan.dal ['skændl] *n.* rezalet, skandal, ayıp, kepazelik, rüsvaylık; dedikodu, iftira; '**scan.dal.ize** *v/t.* rezalet çıkararak *b-ni* utandırmak; *be ~d at veya by bşi* mahzurlu bulmak, hoş görmemek, '**scan.dal-mon.ger** *n.* geveze (*veya* dedikoducu) kimse; **scan.dal.ous** ☐ ['-dǝlǝs] rezil, iftiralı, dokunaklı, kepaze, ayıp; dedikoducu, boşboğaz; '**scan.dal.ous.ness** *n.* rezalet, kepazelik.

Scan.di.na.vi.an [skændi'neivjǝn] **1.** *adj.* İskandinavyalı; İskandinavya'ya ait; **2.** *n.* İskandinavyalı; İskandinav dili.

scan.ner MED ['skænǝ] *n. bilgisayar:* tarayıcı.

scant *lit.* [skænt] **1.** *adj.* kıt, eksik, az, dar; yetersiz; sınırlı; **2.** *v/t.* cimrilik etm., kısmak, sınırlamak.

scant.i.ness ['skæntinis] *n.* kıtlık, eksiklik, yetmezlik, darlık.

scant.ling ['skæntliŋ] *n.* çatı kirişi; kereste kalınlığı; eşantiyon, numune.

scant.y ☐ ['skænti] az, kıt, noksan, eksik, dar, yetersiz.

scape.goat ['skeipgǝut] *n.* başkalarının suçlarını yüklenen kimse; *fig.* şamar oğlanı.

scape.grace ['skeipgreis] *n.* hiç bir işe yaramayan değersiz ve güvenilmez kimse; hayırsız, yaramaz.

scap.u.lar ['skæpjulǝ] **1.** *adj.* ANAT kürek kemiğine ait; **2.** *n.* ECCL bazı keşişlerin giydiği kolsuz gömlek.

scar[1] [skɑ:] **1.** *n.* yara izi; tırmık, yırtık, yara; *fig.* namus lekesi; leke, kusur, şaibe; tahrip izi; **2.** *v/t. -in* üstünde yara izi bırakmak; hafifçe sıyırmak, tırmıklamak; *v/i.* yara izi oluşmak, kapanmak (*yara*).

scar[2] [ ] *n.* kayalık, çıplak kaya; dik yamaç, sarp yokuş.

scar.ab ZOO ['skærǝb] *n.* bokböceği; eski Mısırlıların kutsal böceği.

scarce [skɛǝs] *adj.* az bulunur, nadir, seyrek; kıt; **make o.s. ~** F ortadan kaybolmak, sıvışmak; '**scarce.ly** *adv.* pek az, hemen hemen hiç; güçlükle; '**scar-ci.ty** *n.* azlık, kıtlık, eksiklik (*of*) pahalılık, fiyat yüksekliği.

scare [skɛǝ] **1.** *v/t.* korkutmak; *a.* **~ away** ürkütmek, kovmak; *be ~d* korkmak, ürkmek (*of -den*); **2.** *n.* panik, bozgun, anî (*veya* sebepsiz) korku; '**~.crow** *n.* bostan korkuluğu; '**~.head** *n. Am.* büyük harf manşet, heyecan yaratıcı başlık (*gazetede*); '**~.mon.ger** *n.* şom ağızlı, bedbin, korkulu söylentiler yayan kimse.

scarf[1] [skɑːf] *n., pl. a.* **scarves** [skɑːvz] boyun atkısı; şal; eşarp, kaşkol; fular, boyunbağı.

scarf[2] MEC [ ] **1.** *n.* geçme ek yeri, oyuk yer, yuva; süyek, cebire; **2.** *v/t.* iki kereste, metal *vs.*'nin ucunu birbirine geçirerek eklemek.

scarf...: '**~.pin** *n.* kravat iğnesi; '**~-skin** *n.* üstderi, epiderm.

scar.i.fi.ca.tion [skɛǝrifi'keiʃǝn] *n.* MED tarama, hacamat; gücendirme (*kırıcı eleştiri*); **scar.i.fy** ['-fai] *v/t.* hacamat etm., deriyi kazımak ve yer yer hafifçe kesmek; AGR taramak, sürgü ile eşmek; gücendirmek; incitmek, şiddetle eleştirmek.

scar.la.ti.na MED [skɑːlǝ'tiːnǝ] *n.* kızıl.

scar.let ['skɑːlit] **1.** *n.* al, kırmızı, erguvanî (renk); **2.** *adj.* al, kırmızı, erguvanî; *~ fever* MED kızıl hastalığı; *~ runner* BOT çalıfasulyesi; *~ woman* fahişe.

scarp [skɑːp] **1.** *vb.* dikine kesmek; *~ed adj. dik, sarp;* **2.** *n.* uçurum, dik yamaçlar silsilesi.

scarred [skɑːd] *adj.* yara izi olan.

scarves [skɑːvz] *pl. of* **scarf**[1]

scar.y F ['skɛǝri] *adj.* korku veren; korkak.

scath.ing *fig.* ['skeiðiŋ] *adj.* sert, kırıcı;

yakıcı.

scat.ter ['skætə] *v/t. & v/i.* saç(ıl)mak, dağıtmak, dağılmak, serpmek, yay(ıl)- mak; **~ed** dağınık, aralıklı, seyrek; **'~-brain** *n.* zihni darmadağınık kimse; **'~-brained** *adj.* şaşırmış, aklı fikri pe- rişan.

scav.enge ['skævindʒ] *v/t. & v/i.* sü- pürmek, temizlemek (*sokak*), çöpçü- lük etm.; çöplükten işe yarar şey ara- mak; silindirden egzos boşaltmak; **'scav.enger** *n.* leş yiyen hayvan; çöp- leri karıştırarak işe yarar şeyleri ara- yan kimse; çöpçü.

sce.nar.i.o [si'nɑːriou] *n. film:* senaryo, bir film *veya* tiyatro eserinin konusu- nun ana hatları; **sce.nar.ist** ['siːnərist] *n.* senaryo yazarı, senarist.

scene [siːn] *n.* sahne; olayın geçtiği yer- ve koşullar; THEAT sahne, tablo; sahne dekoru, mizansen; manzara, peysaj; **~s** *pl.* kulis; *behind the ~s* perde arkasın- dan, gizlice; **'~-paint.er** *n.* sahne deko- ru, ressamı; **scen.er.y** ['~əri] *n.* doğal manzara; THEAT sahne dekoru, dekor.

sce.nic, sce.ni.cal □ ['siːnik(əl)] man- zara ile ilgili, pitoresk, manzara kabi- linden; sahneye (*veya* tiyatroya) ait; *scenic railway* minyatür tren (*veya* demiryolu).

scent [sent] **1.** *n.* güzel koku, rayiha, parfüm, ıtır; HUNT koku alma (has- sası); HUNT iz (kokusu); yol; **2.** *v/t. -in* kokusunu almak, sezmek; koku ile doldurmak *-i;* güzel koku saçmak; koklayarak iz sürmek; **'scent.ed** *adj.* güzel kokulu, ıtırlı; **'scent.less** *adj.* kokusuz.

scep.tic ['skeptik] *n.* şüpheci kimse; **'scep.ti.cal** □ şüpheci, septik (*about*); **scep.ti.cism** ['~sizəm] *n.* kuşkuculuk, şüphecilik.

scep.tre ['septə] *n.* hükümdarlık asası, asa.

sched.ule ['ʃedjuːl, *Am.* 'skedjul] **1.** *n.* liste, program; COM envanter, bilanço; JUR ek, zeyil, ilâve; *part. Am.* hareket cetveli, tarife; *on~* planlandığı zaman- da, dakik; **2.** *v/t. -in* listesini yapmak; kararlaştırmak, program yapmak; ta- rifeye geçirmek *-i;* JUR eklemek, ilâve etm. (*to -e*); **~d for** programlanmış *-e,* tarifeye göre.

scheme [skiːm] **1.** *n.* plân, proje, tasarı; entrika; **2.** *v/t. & v/i.* tasarlamak, plân- lamak; *b.s.* entrika çevirmek (*for, against -e karşı*); plân yapmak;

'schem.er *n.* plân yapan kimse; dolap (*veya* entrika) çeviren kimse.

schism ['sizəm] *n.* hizip(leşme), bölün- tü, bölünme; *fig.* ayrılık, bozuşma; **schismat.ic** [siz'mætik] **1.** *a.* schis- 'mat.i.cal □ hizip yaratan, ayrılık çıka- ran, bölücü; **2.** *n.* hizipçi, ayrılıkçı, bö- lücü.

schist MIN [ʃist] *n.* tabaka halinde kaya, kayağantaş, şist.

schi.zo.phre.nia PSYCH [skitsəu- 'friːnjə] *n.* şizofreni, kişiliğin ikiye bö- lünmesi belirtilerini gösteren hastalık.

schol.ar ['skɔlə] *n.* alim, bilgin; UNIV burslu öğrenci; *obs.* öğrenci; *he is an apt ~* yetenekli bir öğrencidir; **'schol- ar.ly** *adj.* alimce, bilgince; çok bilgili; ilmî; **'scholar.ship** *n.* alimlik, bilgin- lik; bilim; UNIV burs.

scho.las.tic [skə'læstik] **1.** *adj.* (*~ally*) okul ve öğretime ait, eğitimsel; alima- ne; ortaçağda felsefe *veya* din okulları- na ait, iskolastik; kuru, cansız; **2.** *n.* or- taçağda felsefe *veya* dinî konularda ilmi metodlarla çalışan kimse; **scho.lasti.cism** [skə'læsti- zəm] *n.* iskolastik felsefe.

school[1] [skuːl] = *shoal*[1] **1.**

school[2] [~] **1.** *n.* okul, mektep (*a. fig.*); UNIV fakülte, yüksek okul, ilim şubesi; ekol, aynı tarz, üslup ve düşüncede olan kişilerin oluşturduğu grup (*güzel sanatlarda*); okul binası; *at ~* okulda; *put to ~* okula yaz(dır)mak; **2.** *v/t.* alıştırmak, terbiye etm., eğitmek, öğretmek, okutmak; **'~.boy** *n.* erkek öğrenci; **'~.fel.low** *n.* okul arkadaşı; **'~.girl** *n.* kız öğrenci; **'~.house** *n.* okul binası; **'school.ing** *n.* eğitim, öğretim, terbiye; okul ücreti.

school...: '~-leav.ing age zorunlu ola- rak öğrenim görülmesi gereken yaş sınırı; '~.man *n.* ortaçağda bilgin; '~.mate *n.* okul arkadaşı; '~.mis.tress *n.* kadın öğretmen; '~.teach.er *n.* öğretmen.

schoon.er ['skuːnə] *n.* NAUT ıskuna, go- let, iki *veya* üç direkli ve yelkenleri yandan olan gemi; *Am.* büyük bira bardağı; = *prairie~.*

sci.at.i.ca MED [sai'ætikə] *n.* siyatik.

sci.ence ['saiəns] *n.* ilim, bilgi, bilim; fen, teknik.

sci.en.tif.ic [saiən'tifik] *adj.* (*~ally*) il- mî; bilimsel, fennî; spor: profesyonel(- ce).

sci.en.tist ['saiəntist] *n.* ilim adamı;

fen adamı.

scim.i.tar ['simitə] *n.* enli kılıç, pala.

scin.til.late ['sintileit] *v/t. & v/i.* parlamak, pırıldamak, ışıldamak, çıkarmak (*ışık*); saçmak (*kıvılcım*); **scin.til'lation** *n.* parıldama, ışıldama.

sci.on ['saiən] *n.* AGR aşılanacak *veya* daldırılacak filiz, fidan; *fig.* oğul, evlât.

scis.sion ['siʒən] *n.* kes(il)me, biçme; çatlama, böl(ün)me; **scis.sors** ['sizəz] *n. pl.* (**a pair of ~**) makas.

scle.ro.sis MED [skliə'rəusis] *n.* doku sertleşmesi, skleroz.

scoff [skɔf] **1.** *n.* alay, istihza; küçümseme; **2.** *v/i.* alay etm., tahkir etm., eğlenmek, zevklenmek (**at** *ile*); *v/t.* açgözlü gibi çabucak yemek, silip süpürmek; **'scoff.er** *n.* alaycı, müstehzi.

scold [skəuld] **1.** *n.* huysuz (*veya* kavgacı) kadın; **2.** *v/t. b-ni* azarlamak, tekdir etm., ayıplamak, paylamak, *b-ne* çıkışmak; *bşe*, *b-ne* sövüp saymak; **scold.ing** *n.* azar, tekdir, paylama.

scol.lop ['skɔləp] = **scallop**.

sconce[1] [skɔns] *n.* aplik, duvar şamdanı.

sconce[2] UNIV *sl.* [~] *v/t.* cezalandırmak; para cezasına çarpmak.

scone [skɔn] *n.* küçük francala, pötipen.

scoop [sku:p] **1.** *n.* kepçe, kürek, kova; MED spatül; F vurgun, büyük kazanç; *gazete:* atlatma (*haber*); **2.** *vb. mst ~ out* kepçe ile çıkarmak, oymak, kazmak, çukurlaştırmak; *sl.* vurgun vurmak, para kesmek; *gazete:* atlatmak (*haber*).

scoot ['sku:t] *v/i.* F kaçmak, tüymek, fırlamak.

scoot.er ['sku:tə] *n.* trotinet; skuler, küçük motosiklet; süratli motor.

scope [skəup] *n.* saha, alan; faaliyet alanı; konu, mevzu; ufuk, fırsat, olanak; çevre, genişlik; **have free ~** hareket serbestliği olm.

scorch [skɔ:tʃ] *v/t.* kavurmak, yakmak, alazlamak, ütülemek; *v/i.* kavrulmak, yanmak; F küplere binmek, kudurmak; **'scorch.er** *n.* F kavurucu sıcak gün; delice süratle giden şoför.

score [skɔ:] **1.** *n.* çentik, kertik, sıyrık; hesap, masraf, fatura; 20 sayısı; *spor:* puan sayısı; neden, vesile; MUS partisyon; hınç, hesap; *sl.* hazırcevap karşılık; **~s of** pek çok kalabalık; **four ~ seksen**; **run up ~s** borçlanmak; **on the ~ of** -den, -dan dolayı, nedeniyle,

yüzünden, için; **2.** *v/t. & v/i.* çentmek; çetele tutmak, (*puanları*) saymak; hesap etm.; *spor:* (*puan*) kazanmak, sayı yapmak; kazanmak, MUS partisyon yazmak, orkestralamak; *Am.* F *bşi* eleştirmek; kaydetmek, not etm.; başarı kazanmak; *fig.* iyi not almak; *futbol:* gol atmak; *spor:* sayı yapmak, puan kazandırmak; *iskambil:* sayı almak; *sl.* şansı yaver gitmek, şanslı olm.; **~ off s.o.** F *b-ni* baştan savmak, atlatmak; *b-ni* mat etm., yenmek; **'scor.er** *n.* puanları kaydeden kimse; *futbol:* gol atan futbolcu.

sco.ri.a *n., pl.* **sco.ri.ae** MEC ['skɔ:riə, '~rii:] cüruf, dışık.

scorn [skɔ:n] **1.** *n.* küçümseme, hor görme; tahkir; **laugh s.o. to ~** *b-le* alay etm., *b-nin* küçümsenmesine neden olm.; **2.** *v/t.* küçümsemek, *bşe* hor bakarak tenezzül etmemek, reddetmek; **'scorn.er** *n.* alaycı, müstehzi; **scornful** □ ['~ful] tahkir edici, hakaret dolu; hor gören, küçümseyen.

scor.pi.on ZOO ['skɔ:pjən] *n.* akrep.

Scot[1] [skɔt] *n.* İskoçyalı.

scot[2] [~] *n.:* **pay ~ and lot** tamamen ödemek.

Scotch[1] [skɔtʃ] **1.** *adj.* İskoçya ile ilgili; **2.** *n.* İskoçyalı; İskoçyalı lehçesi; İskoç viskisi; **the ~** *pl.* İskoçyalı.

scotch[2] [~] *v/t.* incitmek, hafifçe yaralamak; yalanlamak *-i*, son vermek *-e*.

Scotch.man ['skɔtʃmən] *n.* İskoçyalı.

scot-free ['skɔt'fri:] *adj.* vergiden muaf.

Scots [skɔts] = **Scotch**[1]; **Scots.man** = **Scotchman**.

Scot.tish ['skɔtiʃ] *adj.* İskoçya halkı ve diline ait; İskoçyalı.

scoun.drel ['skaundrəl] *n.* alçak herif, hain, kötü adam, teres; **'scoun.drel.ly** *adj.* alçak, hain.

scour[1] ['skauə] *v/t.* oyalayarak temizlemek, silmek; su yatağı açmak.

scour[2] [~] *v/i.* acele etm., seğirtmek, koşuşturmak; **~ about** *bşin* peşinden koşuşturup aramak; *v/t.* araştırmak, köşe bucak aramak.

scourge [skə:dʒ] **1.** *n.* kırbaç, kamçı; *fig.* felâket, musibet, afet; **2.** *v/t.* kamçılamak, kırbaçlamak; *fig.* teşhir etm., şiddetle eleştirmek.

scout[1] [skaut] *n.* casus, keşif eri, gözcü, öncü; NAUT keşif gemisi; AVIA keşif uçağı; UNIV hademe; (**Boy**) ♀ (erkek) izci; **~ party** MIL keşif kolu; **2.** *vb.* keş-

fetmek, taramak; gözetlemek; keşfe
çıkmak.
scout[2] [_] *vb.* hor görerek reddetmek;
hor görmek.
scout.mas.ter ['skautmɑːstə] *n.* izci-
başı, oymak beyi.
scow NAUT [skau] *n.* salapurya, mav-
nanın küçüğü.
scowl [skaul] **1.** *n.* kaş çatma, tehditkâr
bakış; **2.** *vb.* kaşlarını çatıp bakmak,
sert sert bakmak, surat asmak.
scrab.ble ['skræbl] *vb.* sıyırmak, kazımak; hafifçe kaşımak; acele ile yazmak, kargacık burgacık yazmak, karalamak.
scrag [skræg] **1.** *n. fig.* iskelet, çok zayıf
(*veya* kuru kemikli) kimse; *a.* **~-end (of
mutton)** koyun etinin kemikli gerdan
tarafı; **2.** *v/t. sl.* boğmak, boğarak öldürmek; boğazını sıkmak; '**scrag.gi-
ness** *n.* sıskalık, cılızlık; '**scrag.gy** □
kuru, cılız, zayıf, bir deri bir kemik.
scram *sl.* [skræm] *v/t.* sıvışmak, kaçmak, tüymek.
scram.ble ['skræmbl] **1.** *vb.* tırmanmak
-e; itişip kakışmak (**for** *için*); karıştırmak *-i*; sinyal *veya* dalgayı değiştirmek
(*radyo, telefon vs.*); **~d eggs** *pl.*
karıştırılıp yağda pişirilmiş yumurtalar; **2.** *n.* tırmanış; itişip kakışma, mücadele; motokros yarışı.
scrap [skræp] **1.** *n.* parça, döküntü, hurda, kırıntı, kırpıntı; küpür; **~s** *pl.* artık;
erimiş yağdan arta kalan kıkırdak; tortu; **~ of paper** paçavrası; **2.** *vb.*
hurda olarak kullanmak; hurdaya (*veya* çürüğe, açığa) çıkarmak; parçalamak, kırıntı haline getirmek; '**~-book**
n. albüm, kolleksiyon defteri.
scrape [skreip] **1.** *n.* kazıma, sıyırma;
güçlük, varta, sıkıntı, dert; sürtme; **2.**
vb. kazımak, sıyırmak; raspa etm.;
tırmalamak; sıyırtmak; sürtmek
(*ayak*); güçlükle biriktirmek, çok tutumlu olm.; hafifçe dokunmak, sürtünmek; gıcırda(t)mak; **~ away**, **~ off**
kazıyarak silmek, kazıyıp çıkarmak;
~ together, **~ up** güçlükle biriktirmek,
azar azar toplamak, dişinden tırnağından artırmak; **~ acquaintance with** *-in*
yanına sokulup tanışmaya gayret etm.;
'**scrap.er** *n.* raspa, sistre; demir çamurluk (*kapıda*); kazıma aleti; greyder;
'**scrap.ing** *n.* kazıma, sıyırma; **~s** *pl.*
kazıntılar; *fig.* zar zor bir kenara biriktirilen para.
scrap...: '**~-heap** *n.* hurda, çöp yığını;

'**~-i.ron** *n.* hurda demir; '**scrap.py** □
kırıntı ve parçalardan ibaret, bölük
pörçük, yarım yamalak; kavgacı.
scratch [skrætʃ] **1.** *n.* çizik, sıyrık,
tırmık, çizgi; cızırtı (sesi); *spor:* başlama çizgisi; karalama; **come up to ~**
tam zamanında hazır bulunmak; bek-
lenilen sonucu vermek; formda olm.;
sonuna kadar dayanmak; **up to ~** iyi
durumda; **start from ~** *fig.* bşe sıfırdan
başlamak; **2.** *adj.* yarışçılık: avanssız,
handikapsız; gelişigüzel, rastgele, tesadüfî; **3.** *v/t.* kaşımak, tırmalamak,
tırnaklamak, tahriş etm.; PARL & *spor:*
iptal etm., listeden çıkarmak; **~ out**
kazıyarak çıkarmak; karalamak, çizmek; **~ the surface** *fig.* ilk adımı atmak; *v/i.* kaşınmak; eşelenmek;
cızırdamak; *spor:* yarıştan çekilmek;
'**scratch.y** *adj.* kaşıntı veren, kaşındı-
ran; gıcırtılı, cızırtılı; karalanmış, çok
kötü yazılmış; derme çatma; *spor:*
denk olmayan, uyumsuz.
scrawl [skrɔːl] **1.** *v/t.* acele ile yazmak,
karalamak, kargacık burgacık yazı ile
yazmak; **2.** *n.* dikkatsiz yazı.
scraw.ny *Am.* F ['skrɔːni] *adj.* zayıf,
cılız, kemikleri sayılan.
scream [skriːm] **1.** *n.* feryat, çığlık,
haykırış; **he is a ~** F amma da komik
kimse; **2.** *vb.* feryat etm., haykırmak,
çığlık atmak, bağırmak; '**scream.ing**
□ haykıran, çığlık atan; göze çarpan;
gülmekten kırıp geçiren, çok komik.
scree [skriː] *n.* dağ yamacında yassı
çakıl, kayşak.
screech [skriːtʃ] = **scream.** '**~-owl** *n.*
ORN cüce baykuş.
screed [skriːd] *n.* uzun ve bıktırıcı konuşma *veya* yazı.
screen [skriːn] **1.** *n.* paravana, bölme,
soba paravanı; ARCH perde, örtü; *fig.*
maske; *film:* beyaz perde, ekran, sinema; kalbur, elek; parmaklık, kafes; **2.**
v/t. gizlemek, korumak, saklamak;
elemek, kalburdan geçirmek, seçmek;
MIL örtmek, maskelemek, gizlemek,
kamuflâj yapmak; perdeye aksettirmek (*film*); filme almak; *fig.* araştır-
mayı derinleştirmek; **~ play** senaryo
(*film*); TV filmi.
sceev.er ['skriːvə] *n.* kaldırım ressamı.
screw [skruː] **1.** *n.* vida; NAUT pervane,
uskur; AVIA pervane; F (*tütün vs.*) küçük paket; *sl.* gardiyan; *sl.* maaş, ücret;
yaşlı ve zayıf at; **he has a ~ loose** F tahtası eksik, kaçık; **2.** *vb.* vidalamak,

sıkıştırmak, sıkmak; döndürmek, çevirmek, burmak; tehdit ve hile ile almak, sızdırmak, dolandırmak; *sl.* cinsel ilişkide bulunmak *-le*; **~ round** tamamen çevirmek; **~ up** vidalamak, sıkıştırıp düzeltmek; *sl.* düzensizliğe itmek; **~ up one's courage** cesaretlenmek; '**~.ball** *n. Am. sl.* garip herif, deli, kaçık; '**~.driv.er** *n.* tornavida; '**~.jack** *n.* kriko; '**~-pro'pel.ler** *n.* uskur, gemi pervanesi.

scrib.ble ['skribl] **1.** *n.* dikkatsiz yazı; **2.** *vb.* dikkatsiz yazmak, karalamak, kargacık burgacık yazı ile yazmak; **~ over** çızıktırmak, çizmek; '**scrib.bler** *n.* çalakalem yazan kimse; ikinci sınıf yazar, yazar taslağı.

scribe [skraib] *n.* yazan, yazıcı, kâtip, yazman; kopye eden; *İncil:* İsa öncesinde ve zamanında papaz olmayan dinî öğretmen ve hakim.

scrim [skrim] *n.* hafif keten bezi.

scrim.mage ['skrimid3] *n.* göğüs göğüse çarpışma, saç saça baş başa dövüşme; karışıklık, dağdağa, gürültü; *rugby;* topu ilerletmek için hücum, saldırı.

scrimp [skrimp], '**scrimp.y = skimp** etc.

scrip COM [skrip] *n.* geçici senet.

script [skript] *n.* yazı, yazış; el yazısı, müsvedde; THEAT *& film:* senaryo; **~s** *pl.* sınav kâğıdı; **~-writer** *n.* radyo ve TV oyun yazarı.

Scrip.tur.al ['skript∫ərəl] *adj.* Tevrat ve İncille ilgili; **Scrip.ture** ['-t∫ə] *mst the Holy ~s* Kutsal kitap.

scrof.u.la MED ['skɔfjulə] *n.* sıraca illeti; '**scrof.u.lous** □ sıracalı, sıracası olan.

scroll [skrəul] *n.* tomar (*kâğıt*); liste, cetvel; ARCH helezoni kıvrım (*sütun, kolon*); süslü püslü harf, girift yazı.

scro.tum ANAT ['skrəutəm] *n.* haya torbası, safen.

scrounge F [skraund3] *v/t. & v/i. k-ne* mal etm., gaspetmek, benimsemek, aşırmak, yürütmek.

scrub[1] [skrʌb] *n.* çalılık, fundalık; cüce, bodur bacaksız, beberuhi.

scrub[2] [-] **1.** *v/t.* fırçalayarak yıkamak, temizlemek, silmek; iptal etm.; **2.** *n. spor:* B takımı (oyuncusu).

scrub.bing-brush ['skrʌbiŋbrʌ∫] *n.* tahta fırçası.

scrub.by [skrʌbi] *adj.* dik duran (*saç*); karışık; kaba killi, fırça gibi sert; yırtık pırtık, lime lime; sefil, perişan, acınacak.

scruff [skrʌf] *n.:* **~ of the neck** ense, boyun.

scrum [skrʌm], '**scrum.mage = scrim.mage**.

scrump.tious *sl.* ['skrʌmp∫əs] *adj.* fevkalâde, harikulâde, emsalsiz, yaman, enfes, mükemmel.

scrunch [skrʌnt∫] *v/t.* ezmek, hurdahaş etm., pestilini çıkarmak; *v/i.* gıcırdamak, çatırdamak.

scru.ple ['skru:pl] **1.** *n.* şüphe, tereddüt, kararsızlık; vicdan; endişe; az miktar; 1296 gr.'lık eczane tartısı; *make no ~ to do bşi* yapmakta tereddüt etmemek; **2.** *vb.* tereddüt etm.; vicdan elvermemek; **scru.pu.lous** □ ['-pjuləs] dikkatli, titiz, düşünceli (*about*), vicdanlı, dürüst.

scru.ti.neer [skru:ti'niə] *n.* seçimde oyları sayan *veya* gözcülük eden resmi görevli; '**scru.ti.nize** *v/t.* incelemek, tahkik etm.; '**scru.ti.ny** *n.* tetkik, inceleme; seçimde oyların yeniden sayımı.

scud [skʌd] **1.** *n.* hızla gitme, sürüklenme; kısa süren şiddetli rüzgâr; rüzgârda sürüklenen hafif bulutlar; **2.** *v/i.* hızla sürüklenmek, hızla hareket etm.; NAUT rüzgârın önüne düşüp seyretmek.

scuff [skʌf] *v/t. & v/i.* yürürken (*ayakları*) sürümek; sürüyerek aşındırmak; ayağı sürüyerek yürümek; yürürken aşınmak; şıp şıp yürümek.

scuf.fle ['skʌfl] **1.** *n.* dövüşme, boğuşma, itişme; **2.** *v/i.* itişip kakışmak, saç saça baş başa gelmek, çekişmek, dövüşmek.

scull NAUT [skʌl] **1.** *n.* kısa kürek, boyna küreği; bu kürekle çekilen küçük sandal; **2.** *vb.* kürek çekmek, boyna etm.

scul.ler.y [skʌləri] *n.* (*büyük veya eski evlerde mutfak yanındaki bulaşık kapların yıkanıp muhafaza edildiği*) küçük oda; **~ maid** ortalık hizmetçisi; **scul.lion** obs. ['skʌljən] *n.* bulaşıkçı.

sculp.tor ['skʌlptə] *n.* heykeltıraş.

sculp.ture ['skʌlpt∫ə] **1.** *n.* heykel(tıraşlık), plastik sanat; **2.** *vb.* oymak, hakketmek; şekil vermek; kalıplamak; heykelini yapmak *-in*.

scum [skʌm] *n.* pis köpük; kir tabakası; cürüf; *fig.* ayaktakımı.

scup.per NAUT ['skʌpə] *n.* frengi deliği, geminin güvertesinden suyun denize akmasına mahsus delik.

scurf [skə:f] *n.* kepek, konak (*başta*);

'scurf.y □ kepekli, pullu, kabuklu.

scur.ril.i.ty [skʌ'riliti] *n.* küfür, ağız bozukluğu, kabalık, bayağılık; müstehcenlik; 'scur.ril.ous *adj.* iğrenç, pis, kaba, bayağı, küfürlü; ağzı bozuk, küfürbaz.

scur.ry ['skʌri] 1. *vb.* acele etm., hızlı olm., seğirtmek; kovalamak, takip etm.; 2. *n.* acele kaçış (*veya* gidiş), seğirtme; kısa at yarışı.

scur.vy¹ MED ['skə:vi] *n.* iskorbüt.

scur.vy² [ ] *adj.* alçak, adi, bayağı, iğrenç.

scut [skʌt] *n.* kısa kuyruk (*tavşan v.b.*).

scutch.eon ['skʌtʃən] = escutcheon.

scut.tle¹ ['skʌtl] *n.* kömür kovası.

scut.tle² [ ] 1. *n.* NAUT lomboz, ambar kapağı; 2. *v/t.* (*gemi*) dibini delerek batırmak.

scut.tle³ [ ] 1. *n.* seğirtme, sıvışma, tabanları yağlama; 2. *vb.* seğirtmek, sıvışmak; *fig.* kaçmak (*tehlike, güçlük vs.'den*).

scythe AGR [saið] 1. *n.* tırpan; 2. *vb.* orak *veya* tırpanla biçmek.

sea [si:] *n.* deniz, okyanus, derya (*a. fig.*); yüksek dalga; **at ~** denizde, gemide; *fig.* şaşkın, çaresiz, ne yapacağını bilmeyen; **by the ~** deniz kenarında, **go to ~** denizci olm.; deniz yolculuğuna çıkmak, açılmak; *s.* **put 2.**;'~.board *n.* deniz kıyısı, kıyı (bölgesi); ~ **cap-tain** kaptan, süvari; ~ **coast** deniz kıyısı, sahil;'~.dog *n.* eski gemici, deniz kurdu, deniz kahramanı, büyük denizci; = **seal¹**;'~.far.ing *adj.* denizcilikle uğraşan;~.food *n. Am.* yenebilen deniz ürünü;'~.go.ing *adj.* açık denizlerde kullanmaya elverişli, açık deniz…, okyanus…;'~.gull *n.* zoo martı.

seal¹ zoo [si:l] *n.* fok, ayıbalığı.

seal² [ ] 1. *n.* mühür, damga; teyit, onay, taahhüt, teminat; *great~, broad~* devlet mührü; 2. *v/t.* mühürlemek, damgalamak; *fig.* mühürünü basmak; onaylamak; ~ **off** *fig.* son vermek; kapatmak, kilitlemek, tıkamak; ~ **up** sıkıca kapamak; MEC contalamak.

seal.er ['si:lə] *n.* fok balığı avcısı *veya* av gemisi.

sea-lev.el ['si:levl] *n.* deniz seviyesi.

seal.ing ['si:liŋ] *n.* fok balığı avı.

seal.ing-wax ['si:liŋwæks] *n.* mühür mumu.

seal.skin ['si:lskin] *n.* fok balığı derisi.

seam [si:m] 1. *n.* dikiş (yeri); MEC ek yeri; GEOL tabaka, damar, yatak; yara izi;

MED dikiş yeri; **burst at the ~s** çok dolu, dopdolu (*a. fig.*); 2. *vb.* hafifçe yaralamak, sıyırmak, tırmıklamak; evlek açmak; birbirine dikmek (*kumaş*).

sea.man ['si:mən] *n.* denizci, gemici; bahriyeli, deniz eri; 'sea.man.ship *n.* gemicilik.

sea mew ['si:mju:] *n.* martı.

seam.less □ ['si:mlis] dikişsiz; kaynaksız; eksiz.

seam.stress ['semstris] *n.* dikişçi kadın.

seam.y ['si:mi] *adj.* yara izi, çirkin görünüşlü; dikişli; ~ **side** *fig.* madalyonun tersi.

sea…:'~-piece *n.* PAINT deniz manzaralı tablo; '~.plane *n.* deniz uçağı; '~.port *n.* liman, liman şehir;'~-pow.er *n.* deniz kuvveti, donanma.

sear [siə] 1. *adj.* kurumuş, solgun, solmuş, pörsümüş, kuru; 2. *v/t.* kurutmak; hafifçe yakmak, alazlamak, dağlamak; MED koterize etm.; *fig.* katılaştırmak, sertleştirmek, körletmek.

search [sə:tʃ] 1. *n.* arama, araştırma (**for**), tetkik, sondaj; **in ~ of** ara(ştır)-makta, peşinde; 2. *v/t.* ara(ştır)mak, yoklamak, tetkik etm.; MED sondalamak; gedik açmak (*mermi vs.*); ~ **out** keşfetmek, ortaya çıkarmak, arayıp bulmak; *v/i.* araştırmak, soruşturmak (**for**); ~ **into** iyice incelemek -*i*, içyüzünü araştırmak -*in*; 'search.er *n.* arayan, araştıran, arayıcı, kâşif; 'search-ing □ araştırıcı, inceden inceye araştıran; araştırıcı, sıkı, tetkik edici (*bakış*); 'search-light *n.* ışıldak, projektör; 'search-warrant *n.* JUR arama emri.

sea…:'~-rov.er *n.* deniz haydutu, korsan (gemisi);~.scape ['si:skeip] *n.* deniz manzaralı tablo; '~-ser.pent *n.* deniz yılanı;'~-shore *n.* sahil;'~.sick *adj.* deniz tutmuş; '~.sick.ness *n.* deniz tutması;'~.side *n.* deniz kıyısı, sahil; ~ **place**, ~ **resort** plaj; **go to the ~** deniz kıyısına gitmek.

sea.son ['si:zn] 1. *n.* mevsim; zaman; dönem, devre, sezon; F = ~**-ticket**; **height of the ~** mevsimin en civcivli zamanları; **in** (**good** *veya* **due**) ~ uygun bir zamanda, tam zamanında; **cher-ries are in ~** şimdi kirazın tam mevsimidir (*ucuz, olgun*); **out of ~** vakitli vakitsiz, yersiz; **for a ~** mevsimlik, bir süre; **with the compliments of the ~** yeni yıl (*veya* bayram *vs.*) için en iyi dileklerimle; 2. *v/t. & v/i.* çeşnilendirmek;

yumuşatmak; alış(tır)mak (**to** -*e*); ku-ru(t)mak (*yapı kerestesi v.b.*); **'sea-son.a.ble** □ tam vaktinde olan, uygun, zamana uygun; **season.al** □ mevsim-lik; mevsime uygun; COM mevsimlik, mevsime bağlı; '**sea.son.ing** *n.* çeşni veren şey, bahar(at); '**sea.son-tick.et** *n.* RAIL abone kartı, karne; THEAT abo-ne (bileti).

seat [si:t] **1.** *n.* oturulacak yer, iskemle, sandalye, tabure, peyke, kanepe; ikâ-metgâh, mesken, köşk, yalı, çiftlik; POL koltuk, mevki; kaba et, makat, kıç; sahne, saha, yer, merkez; mahal; THEAT koltuk; **2.** *vb.* oturtmak, yerleş-tirmek (*rütbe veya makama*); mevki sahibi olm.; oturacak yer temin etm.; yerine oturtmak (*makine parçası vs.*); ~ **o.s.** oturmak; **be** ~**ed!** oturunuz!; '~**belt** *n.* AVIA emniyet kemeri; '**seat-ed** *adj.* oturmuş, yerleşmiş; '**seat.er** *comb. part.* MOT, AVIA belirli sayıda otu-racak yeri olan; …kişilik.

sea-ur.chin ['si:'ə:tʃin] *n.* denizkesta-nesi; **sea.ward** ['-wəd] *adj.* denize doğru giden; *adv. a.* **sea.wards** ['-wədz] denize doğru.

sea…; '~**weed** *n.* BOT yosun, deniz sazı; '~**wor.thy** *adj.* denize elverişli (*veya* dayanıklı).

se.ba.ceous PHYSIOL [si'beiʃəs] *adj.* yağlı…, yağ içeren.

se.cant MATH ['si:kənt] **1.** *adj.* birbirini kateden (*veya* kesen); **2.** *n.* sekant.

se.c.a.teur AGR [sekə'tə:] *n. mst* (**a pair of**) ~**s** *pl.* bahçıvan makası.

se.cede [si'si:d] *v/i.* çekilmek, ayrılmak (*örgüt, üyelik vs.'den*); *bşden* vazgeç-mek; **se'ced.er** *n.* sadakatsiz, asî; mür-tet, dininden dönmüş.

se.ces.sion [si'seʃən] *n.* ayrılma, vaz-geçme, bölünme; **se'ces.sion.ist** [-ʃnist] *n.* ayrılma taraftarı.

se.clude [si'klu:d] *v/t.* ayırmak, tecrit etm., uzaklaştırmak; **se'clud.ed** *adj.* tecrit edilmiş; kuytu, tenha, ıssız; dün-yadan el çekmiş; **se'clu.sion** [-ʒən] *n.* inziva, yalnızlık, köşeye çekilme.

sec.ond[1] ['sekənd] **1.** □ ikinci (derece-de), -*den* sonraki, diğer, öteki; **he is** ~ **to none** kimseden aşağı kalmaz, o en iyisidir; **on**~**thoughts** iyice düşündük-ten sonra; **2.** *n.* ikinci kimse *veya* şey; düello şahidi; yardımcı, muavin; sani-ye; ~**s** *pl.* COM ikinci kalite mal, tapon mal; ~ **of exchange** COM poliçenin ikin-ci nüshası; **3.** *v/t. b-ne* yardım etm., *b-ni*

destelemek, *b-nin* lehinde olm.; düel-loda *b-ne* şahitlik etm.

se.cond[2] MIL [si'kɔnd] *v/t.* bir işe, vazi-fefeye tayin etm., atamak (*usu. belirli bir süre için*).

sec.ond.ar.i.ness ['sekəndərinis] *n.* ikincil (*veya* tali) olma; **sec.ond.ar.y** □ ikincil, tali, ikinci derecede; …yanında; ast, alt aşamada bulunan; **sec.ond.ar.y school** orta dereceli okul; '**sec.ond-'best** *adj.* ikinci (kali-te); en iyiden hemen sonra gelen; **come off** ~ F başkası tarafından mağ-lûp edilmek, alt edilmek; '**sec.ond-'class**_adj._ ikinci derece, ikinci kalite(-li); RAIL ikinci mevki; '**sec.ond.er** *n.* destekleyen kimse (*part.* PARL); **sec-ond-hand 1.** ['sekənd'hænd] *adj.* kul-lanılmış, elden düşme; başkasından öğrenilmiş, ikinci elden; ~ **bookseller** sahaf; ~ **bookshop** ikinci elden kitap-ların satıldığı kitapçı; **2.** ['sekənd-hænd] *n.* saat kadranında saniyeleri gösteren ibre; '**second.ly** *adv.* ikinci olarak, saniyen; '**second-'rate** *adj.* ikinci derecede; COM ~ **quality** ikinci kalite.

se.cre.cy ['si:krisi] *n.* sır saklama; giz-lilik, ketumiyet, saklılık; **se.cret** ['si:-krit] **1.** □ gizli, mahrem, saklı; ~ **agent** gizli ajan; **2.** *n.* sır, gizli şey; **in** ~ gizlice; **be in the** ~, **be taken into the** ~ sırra ortak olm.

sec.re.tar.i.at(e) [sekrə'tɛəriət] *n.* ka-lem odası; kâtiplik; müdüriyet (perso-neli).

sec.re.tar.y ['sekrətri] *n.* zabıt kâtibi, sekreter, kâtip, yazman; yazı masası; ♀ **of State** bakan; *Am.* Dışişleri Ba-kanı; '**secre.tar.y.ship** *n.* kâtiplik, sek-reterlik, yazmanlık.

se.crete [si'kri:t] *v/t.* gizlemek, sakla-mak, örtmek; PHYSIOL salgılamak, ifraz etm.; **se'cre.tion** *n.* PHYSIOL salgı, ifra-z(at); **se'cre.tive** *adj. fig.* kapalı kutu, ağzı sıkı; salgılayan.

sect [sekt] *n. rel.* tarikat, mezhep; **sec-tar.i.an** [-'tɛəriən] **1.** *adj.* mezhebe ait; bağnaz, darkafalı; **2.** *n.* mezhep yanlısı; bağnaz yandaş, darkafalı kimse.

sec.tion ['sekʃən] *n.* MED operasyon; kesme, kesiş; kesilmiş şey; MATH kesit; ARCH profil; kısım, parça; TYP paragraf, fıkra, fasıl; *s.* ~ **mark**; grup, dal, kol, şube, daire; bölge, kesim; **shopping (residential)** ~ alış veriş (yerleşim) böl-gesi; **sec.tional** ['-fənl] *adj* bir bölüme ait, bir bölgeye ait, bölgesel, mahalli; kesit, parça halinde; 'sec'tion.al.ism *n.* bölgecilik, grupçuluk; 'sec.tion mark *n.* paragraf işareti.

sec.tor ['sektə] *n.* daire kesmesi, daire dilimi; MIL bölge, mıntıka; sektör, kesim.

sec.u.lar □ ['sekjulə] layik; dünyevî, cismanî; manastır *veya* tarikat sistemine bağlı olmayan; yüz yıllık, yüz yılda bir olan; sec.u.lar.i.ty [‿'læriti] *n.* layiklik; dünyevîlik, cismanîlik; sec.u.lar.ize ['‿ləraiz] *v/t.* layikleştirmek; dünyevileştirmek.

se.cure [si'kjuə] **1.** □ güvenli, emin, emniyetli, sağlam (*of, against, from* -*e* karşı); **2.** *v/t.* sağlamak, temin etm., elde etm.; bağlamak; güven altına almak (*from, against*); saklamak, muhafaza etm.

se.cu.ri.ty [si'kjuəriti] *n.* emniyet, güven(lik); sağlam (*veya* kesin) bilgi; rehin, teminat (akçesi), emanet, kefalet, depozito; se'cu.ri.ties *pl.* kıymetli evrak, tahviller, senetler, menkul kıymetler.

se.dan [si'dæn] *n.* limuzin, kapalı büyük otomobil; *a.* ~*chair n.* sedye; tahtırevan.

se.date □ [si'deit] temkinli, ağırbaşlı, sakin, vakarlı, ciddî, 'se'date.ness *n.* temkin, ağırbaşlılık, sükûn(et), sessizlik.

sed.a.tive *mst* MED ['sedətiv] **1.** *adj.* teskin edici, rahatlatıcı, yatıştırıcı, hafifletici; **2.** *n.* müsekkin, yatıştırıcı ilaç.

sed.en.tar.i.ness ['sedntərinis] *n.* yerleşik, oturgan oluş; 'sed.en.tar.y □ yerleşmiş, mukim, daimi ikametgâhı olan, temelli oturmuş; oturmaya alışmış, evden dışarı çıkmayan; oturularak yapılan.

sedge BOT [sedʒ] *n.* saz, kamış, ayakotu.

sed.i.ment ['sedimənt] *n.* tortu, telve, posa, rüsup; GEOL çöküntü, suyun dibinde biriken şey; sed.i.men.ta.ry [‿'mentəri] *adj.* GEOL tortul, tortudan oluşmuş; tortulu.

se.di.tion [si'diʃən] *n.* ayaklanma(ya teşvik), isyan; kargaşalık; fesat, fitne.

se.di.tious □ [si'diʃəs] fesatkârane; arabozucu; fitneci; ayaklandıran.

se.duce [si'dju:s] *v/t.* baştan çıkarmak, ayartmak; iğfal etm.; se'duc.er *n.* ayartan (*veya* baştan çıkaran) kimse; iğfal eden kimse; se.duc.tion [‿'dʌk-

[ʃən] *n.* baştan çıkarma, ayartma; iğfal; baştan çıkaran şey; se'duc.tive □ ayartıcı, kandırıcı; cazip, çekici.

sed.u.lous □ ['sedjuləs] faal, aktıf, gayretli, sebatlı, çalışkan.

see¹ [si:] (*irr.*) *v/i.* görmek; icabına bakmak; *fig.* anlamak, kavramak; *I* ~ anlıyorum, anladım; ~ *about s.th.* bşe karışmak, bşi düsünmek, bşle meşgul olm., icabına bakmak -*in*; ~ *through s.o. veya s.th.* bnin *veya* bsin içini okumak, arasından *veya* içinden bakmak *veya* görmek; ~ *to* bakmak -*e*, dikkat etm. -*e.* meşgul olm. *ile*; ~ *for o.s.* bşi kendi gözüyle görmek; *v/t.* görmek -*i*, bakmak -*e*; göz(et)mek, anlamak, kavramak; (*hasta*) ziyaret etm., vizita yapmak; ~ *s.th. done* bşin yapılmasını sağlamak; *go to* ~ *s.o.* b-*nin* ziyaretine gitmek; ~ *s.o. home* b-*ni* evine götürmek, eşlik etm.; ~ *off* uğurlamak; ~ *out* kapıya kadar geçirmek; bitirmek; sonuna kadar beklemek; ~ *over s.th.* bşi gözden geçirmek, incelemek; ~ *s.th. through* sonuna kadar sabretmek, dayanmak, muradına ermek, bir işi başarmak; ~ *s.o. through* b-*ne* bşi yapması için sonuna kadar yardım etm.; *live to* ~ yaşayıp görmek.

see² [‿] *n.* piskoposluk; *Holy* ♀ Papalık (makamı).

seed [si:d] **1.** *n.* tohum, tohumluk hububat; (*meyve*) çekirdek; döl, evlât; kaynak, menşe; sperma, meni, bel suyu; *go veya run to* ~ tohuma kaçmak; *fig.* kuvvetten düşmek; **2.** *v/t.* tohum ekmek; (*meyve*) çekirdek çıkarmak; *spor:* (*oyuncu*) b-*ni* b-*nin* yerine geçirmek; *v/i.* filizlenip tohum vermek; '~.bed = *seed-plot*; 'seed.i.ness *n.* tohuma kaçma; F (*sarhoşluktan gelen*) mahmurluk; 'seedless *adj.* çekirdeksiz (*meyve*); 'seed.ling *n.* AGR fide; 'seed-plot *n.* AGR fidelik; *fig.* menba, ocak, kaynak; seeds.man ['‿zmən] *n.* tohumcu, tohum satıcısı; 'seed.y □ *adj.* tohumlu, tohuma kaçmış; havı dökülmüş, lime lime olmuş, yırtık pırtık; F rahatsız, yoksul, sefil.

see.ing ['si:iŋ] **1.** *n.* görme, bakma; ~ *worth* ~ gör(ül)meğe değer; **2.** *cj.* ~ *that* madem(ki), -*dığı* için; ...*e* göre, ...karşısında.

seek [si:k] (*irr.*) *v/t. & v/i. a.* ~ *after,* ~ *for* aramak -*i*; araştırmak; istemek, bşi çok arzu etm., elde etmeğe çalışmak; 'seek.er *n.* arayıcı kimse *veya* şey.

seem [si:m] *v/i.* görünmek, gözükmek, gelmek (*like* gibi), benzemek; '**seem·ing 1.** □ görünüşte, zahirî, gûya, yalandan; **2.** *n.* görünüş, zevahir, dış (*veya* aldatıcı) görünüş; '**seem.li.ness** *n.* uygunluk, yakışık alma, münasebet, edep ve ahlâka uygun olma, terbiye; '**seem·ly** *adj.* yakışık alır, uygun, münasip.

seen [si:n] *p.p. of* **see**[1].

seep [si:p] *v/i.* sızmak, sızıntı yapmak, damlaya damlaya akmak; '**seep.age** *n.* sızıntı.

seer ['si:ə] *n.* seyirci; resul, peygamber; kâhin.

see.saw ['si:sɔ:] **1.** *n.* tahterevalli; ileri geri hareket, iniş çıkış; **2.** *v/i.* ileri geri *veya* aşağı yukarı hareket etm.; tahterevalliye binmek; *fig.* tereddüt etm., ne yapacağını bilmemek, kararsız olm.

seethe [si:ð] *v/t. & v/i.* kayna(t)mak, haşla(n)mak, piş(ir)mek, öfkelenmek, küplere binmek.

seg.ment ['segmənt] *n.* parça, kısım; *part.* MATH daire kesmesi.

seg.re.gate ['segrigeit] *vb.* ayırmak, tecrit etm.; bir bütünden ayrılmak; **seg.re'ga.tion** *n.* ayırım, fark gözetme, ırk ayırımı.

seine [sein] *n.* balıkçılık: iğrip ağı, büyük ağ.

sei.sin JUR ['si:zin] *n.* temellük, tasarruf, mülkiyeti elinde bulundurma.

seis.mo.graph ['saizməgrɑ:f] *n.* depremölçer, sismograf.

seize [si:z] *v/t.* yakalamak, tutmak, kavramak; gaspetmek, zaptetmek, ele geçirmek; haczetmek, el koymak, müsadere etm.; *fikir*: kavramak; etkisi altına almak; NAUT sicim sarıp bağlamak; *v/i.* MEC sıkışıp çalışmamak, takılmak, yapışmak; **∼ upon** b-ni *veya* bşi emri altına almak, hükmü altına almak; '**seiz.ing** *n.* tutma, kavrama, yakalama; *mst* **∼s** *pl.* NAUT halat; **sei.zure** ['-ʒə] *n.* yakalama, zapt; JUR müsadere, el koyma, haciz; MED anî nöbet, tut(ul)ma, felç.

sel.dom ['seldəm] *adv.* nadiren, seyrek.

se.lect [si'lekt] **1.** *v/t.* seçmek, ayırmak, içinden beğenip almak; **2.** *adj.* seçkin, seçilmiş, güzide, elit, seçme, iyi gibi; **se'lec.tion** *n.* seçme (şeyler); seçme, ayırma, beğenme; ZOO, BOT doğal ayıklanma; **∼ musical ∼** seçme parçalar, potpuri; **se'lec.tive** □ ayıran, seçici, seçimli; seçme...; *radyo*: selektif, seçi-

ci, yayını parazitsiz alan; **se.lec'tiv.i.ty** *n.* *radyo*: selektivite, seçicilik, yayını parazitsiz alma; **se'lect.man** *n.* Am. belediye meclisi üyesi; **se'lec.tor** *n.* seçen kimse *veya* aygıt, seçici kimse; *radyo*: selektör, seçici, dalga ayırıcı.

self [self] **1.** *pron.* bizzat, kendi(si), kendi kendine; COM *veya* F **= myself** etc.; **2.** *adj.* şahsî; BOT düz renkli, üni; **3.** *n. pl.* **selves** [selvz] zat, kişi, kendi; karakter, kişilik, şahsiyet, benlik; kişisel çıkar, bencillik; *my poor ∼* âcizleri, âciz kulları; '**∼-a'base.ment** *n.* k-ni alçaltma, aşağılanma, bayağılanma, yalvarıp yakarma; '**∼'act.ing** *adj.* otomatik, mekanik, kendi k-ne hakaret eden; '**∼-cen.tred,** Am. '**∼'cen.tered** *adj.* hodperest, hodpesent, hep k-ni düşünen, bencil; **∼-'col.o(u)red** *adj.* düz renkli, boyanmamış; '**∼-com.mand** *n.* k-ni tutma, nefsini yenme; '**∼con'ceit** *n.* k-ni beğenmişlik, azamet; '**∼-con'ceit.ed** *adj.* kibirli, mağrur, kurumlu, azametli, hodperest; '**∼'con.fidence** *n.* k-ne güven, nefse güven; '**∼-'con.scious** *adj.* utangaç, sıkılgan; ne yaptığını bilen; '**∼'con.scious.ness** *n.* utangaçlık, mahcupluk, sıkılganlık; '**∼-con'tained** *adj.* kendi k-ne yeter; kendi içinde bir bütün oluşturan; az konuşur, çekingen, ağzı sıkı, düşüncelerini başkalarına rahat söyleyemeyen; **∼ country** kendi k-ne yeten ülke; **∼ house** bir ailelik ev, müstakil daire; '**∼-con'trol** *n.* k-ne hakim olma, k-ni yenme, nefsini zaptetme; '**∼-de'fence** *n.* nefis müdafaası, nefsini koruma, k-ni savunma; **in ∼** meşru müdafaa; '**∼-de'ni.al** *n.* feragat, özveri, k-ni tutma; '**∼-de.ter.mi'na.tion** *n.* bir ulusun kendi yönetim şeklini k-nin kararlaştırması, hür irade; '**∼-em'ployed** *adj.* müstakil, bağımsız, serbest çalışan; '**∼'ev.i.dent** *adj.* aşikâr, belli; '**∼'govern.ment** *n.* kendi k-ni yönetme, özerklik, muhtariyet, otonomi; '**∼-in'dul.gent** *adj.* kendi isteklerine düşkün; lâkayt, tembel, istifini bozmayan; '**∼-'in.ter.est** *n.* kişisel çıkar, bencillik, hodbinlik; '**self.ish** □ egoist, bencil, hodbin; '**self.ish.ness** *n.* bencillik, egoizm, hodkâmlık.

self...: '**∼-'made** *adj.* k-ni yetiştirmiş; **∼ man** kendi k-ni yetiştirmiş kişi; '**∼-'pos'ses.sion** *n.* k-ne hâkim olma, itidal, soğukkanlılık, nefsini yenme; '**∼-pre.ser'vation** *n.* nefsini idame, mevcudiyetini koruma; '~-re'gard *n.* k-*ni* önemseme; '~-re'li.ance *n.* k-*ne* güven, öz güven; '~-re'li.ant *adj.* k-*ne* güvenir; '~-re'spect *n.* izzetinefis, onur, öz saygısı;'~-re'spect.ing: *every* ~ *nation* onurlu ve dimdik ayakta olan her ulus; '~-'right.eous *adj.* k-*ni* beğenmiş, hodpesent; '~'sacri.fice *n.* özveri, fedakârlık; '~.same *adj. lit.* tıpkı, aynı; '~'seek.ing *adj.* bencil, menfaatperest, çıkarcı, egoist; '~'ser-vice res.tau.rant selfservis lokanta; '~'start.er *n.* MOT hareket tertibatı, starter, marş; '~-suf'fi.cien.cy *n.* kendi k-*ne* yetme, başkasına muhtaç olma-ma; '~-sup'pli.er *n.* tüketim mallarını k-*si* ürelen; '~-sup'port.ing *adj.* kendi k-*ne.* başkasının yardımı olmadan; (ekonomik açıdan) bağımsız; '~-'will *n.* dikkafalılık, inatçılık; '~-'willed *adj.* inatçı, dikkafalı.

sell [sel] **1.** *(irr.)* v/*t.* satmak *(a. fig.);* Am. F önermek, tavsiye etm., methet-mek, beğendirmek; ~ *(out)* F aldat-mak, kazıklamak; ~ *off* COM hepsini satmak, satıp kurtulmak; ~ *up* b-*nin* malını satmaya zorlamak; v/*i.* ticaret yapmak; alıcı bulmak, satılmak; revaç bulmak *(mal);* ~ *off,* ~ *out* COM bütün stoku satmak, elden çıkarmak; **2.** *n.* F dolandırıcılık, hilekârlık, dalavere; ha-yal kırıklığı, fiyasko; 'sell.er *n.* satıcı, bayi; *good etc.* ~ çok *vs.* satılan mal.

selt.zer ['seltsə] *n. a.* ~ *water* soda, ma-den suyu.

sel.vage, sel.vedge MEC ['selvidʒ] *n.* kumaş kenarı.

selves [selvz] *pl.* of *self 3.*

se.man.tics [si'mæntiks] *n. sg.* seman-tik, anlambilim.

sem.a.phore ['semǝfɔ:] **1.** *n.* semafor, taşıtlara yolun açık olduğunu göster-mek için renkli levha *veya* ışıkla işaret veren dikme *(tren vs.);* MIL işaretçi, fla-macı; RAIL işaret direği; **2.** v/*b.* işaretler-le bildirmek, haberleşmek, semaforla haberleşmek.

sem.blance ['semblǝns] *n.* benzerlik; biçim, dış görünüş.

se.mes.ter UNIV [si'mestǝ] *n.* sömestr, ders yılı yarısı.

sem.i... ['semi] *prefix* yarı, yarım, bu-çuk, yarı...; '~.breve *n.* MUS dörtlük nota, tam nota; '~.cir.cle *n.* yarım dai-re;'~'cir.cu.lar *adj.* yarım daire şeklin-de;'~'co.lon *n.* noktalı virgül; '~-de-'tached house ortak duvarlı iki daire-

yi içeren ev;'~-'fi.nal *n. spor:* yarı final, finalden bir önceki müsabaka; '~.man-u'factured *adj.* yarı mamul; yarıda kalmış.

sem.i.nal ['si:minl] *adj.* sonraki gelişmenin tohumlarını içeren; başkalarına yeniliklerle etki eden, yeni ufuklar açan; sperma ile ilgili, meni içeren, spermalı.

sem.i.nar.y ['seminǝri] *n.* seminer; *fig.* okul; papaz okulu.

sem.i-of.fi.cial ['semiǝ'fiʃǝl] *adj.* yarı resmî.

sem.i.qua.ver MUS ['semikweivǝ] *n.* onaltılık nota.

Sem.ite ['si:mait] *n.* Samî ırkından olan kimse; Se.mit.ic [si'mitik] *adj.* Samî.

sem.i.tone MUS ['semitǝun] *n.* yarım ton.

sem.i.vow.el ['semivauǝl] *n.* yarı ünlü ses.

sem.o.li.na [semǝ'li:nǝ] *n.* irmik.

semp'stress ['sempstris] *n.* dikişçi kadın.

sen [sen] *n.* sen *(Japon madenî parası).*

sen.ate ['senit] *n.* senato.

sen.a.tor ['senǝtǝ] *n.* senatör; sen.a-to.ri.al □ [_'tɔ:riǝl] senatörlük *veya* senatör ile ilgili; senatörlerden oluşan.

send [send] *(irr.)* v*b.* yollamak, gönder-mek; fırlatmak, atmak, savurmak *(top vs.);* atış yapmak *(kurşun vs.); s. pack 2; ~ for* çağırmak -*i;* getirtmek -*i,* ayağı-na davet etm. -*i,* celbetmek; ısmarla-mak; ~ *forth* neşretmek, yaymak, sal-mak *(ışık, koku vs.);* kamuoyuna bil-dirmek; ~ *in* sunmak, arzetmek, tak-dim etm.; ~ *in one's name* b-*nin* gel-diğini haber vermek; ~ *off* göndermek, uğurlamak, yolcu etm.; ~ *up* yukarı göndermek; *fig.* yükseltmek *(fiyat);* ~ *word* haber yollamak; b-*ne bş* hakkın-da bilgi vermek;'send.er *n.* gönderen; TEL radyo istasyonu, verici; 'send-'off *n.* yolcu etme, veda, uğurlama (töre-ni).

sen.e.schal ['seniʃǝl] *n.* ortaçağda asilzadelerin en güvendikleri yardımcısı *(veya* mutemedi *veya* teşri-fatçısı).

se.nile ['si:nail] *adj.* ihtiyarlıkla ilgili; eli ayağı tutmaz olmuş; bunak; se.nil-i.ty [si'niliti] *n.* ihtiyarlık; güçsüzlük; bunaklık.

sen.ior ['si:njǝ] **1.** *adj.* yaşça büyük *(to);* kıdemli; son sınıfa ait; üst...; ~ *partner*

COM patron, baş; **2.** *n.* yaşça büyük kimse; kıdemli kimse; son sınıf öğrencisi; oğula nisbetle baba; *he is my ~ by a year, he is a year my ~* o benden bir yaş büyüktür; **sen.ior.i.ty** [siːniˈɔriti] *n.* yaşça büyüklük; kıdem(lilik).

sen.sa.tion [senˈseiʃən] *n.* his, duygu, izlenim; heyecan, merak; heyecan uyandıran olay, sansasyon; **sen'sation.al** [-ʃənl] duygusal, hissî, sansasyonal, heyecan verici, müthiş, heyecanlı; **sen'sation.al.ism** [-ʃnəlizəm] *n.* göze girmeye çalışma, heyecan uyandırıcı yollara baş vurma, sansasyon hevesi, sansasyonalizm, duyumculuk.

sense [sens] **1.** *n.* duyu, his (*of*); duyum, duyarlık; akıl; zekâ; anlayış; mana, anlam; fikir, düşünce, kanı; *in* (*out of*) *one's ~s* aklı başında (n gitmiş, deli); *bring s.o. to his ~s* b-*nin* aklını başına getirmek; *make~* anlamı olm., akla uygun gelmek; *talk ~* akıllıca konuşmak, saçmalamamak; **2.** *v/t.* hissetmek, duymak, sezmek; anlamak.

sense.less ☐ ['senslis] baygın; duygusuz hissiz, donuk; anlamsız, manasız, abuksabuk, saçma; **'sense.less.ness** *n.* baygınlık, şuursuzluk; hissizlik, duygusuzluk, saçmalık.

sen.si.bil.i.ty [sensiˈbiliti] *n.* duyarlık, duygunluk, duygululuk, hassasiyet (*to, a. of*); seziş inceliği; *sensibilities pl.* anlayış, hassasiyet, nezaket.

sen.si.ble ☐ ['sensəbl] aklı başında, makûl, mantıklı; farkedilir, hissedilir; akla uygun, yerinde; bş karşısında pek hassas, duyarlı (*of*); *be ~ of* bşi iyice bilmek, sezmek -*i*, farkına varmak -*in*; **'sen.si.ble.ness** *n.* akıllılık, makûl olma; şuurlu olma; hassasiyet.

sen.si.tive ☐ ['sensitiv] hassas, içli, duygulu (*to*), alıngan; PHOT ışığa duyarlı; **'sen.si.tive.ness, sen.si.tiv.i.ty** *n.* duyarlık, hassasiyet, hassaslık; alınganlık.

sen.si.tize PHOT ['sensitaiz] *v/t.* ışığa duyarlı hale getirmek (*kâğıt, film*).

sen.so.ri.al [senˈsɔːriəl], *adj.* **sen.so.ry** ['-səri] duygu ile ilgili, duyusal…

sen.su.al ☐ ['sensjuəl] şehvanî, şehvetli; tensel, duyusal; **'sen.su.al.ism** *n.* duyumculuk; şehevilik, şehvet (düşkünlüğü); **'sen.su.al.ist** *n.* şehvet düşkünü (*veya* zevkine düşkün) kimse; **sen.su.al.i.ty** [-'æliti] *n.* şehvet (düşkünlüğü), kösnü; duyarlık.

COM patron, baş; **2.** *n.* yaşça büyük kim-

sen.su.ous ☐ ['sensjuəs] duyumsal, hissi, hislere ait.

sent [sent] *pret. & p.p. of* **send**.

sen.tence ['sentəns] **1.** *n.* JUR hâkim kararı, hüküm, yargı; GR tümce, cümle; *serve one's ~* ceza süresini (hapiste) doldurmak; *s. life*; **2.** *v/t.* mahkûm etm., hüküm giydirmek (*to*).

sen.ten.tious ☐ [senˈtenʃəs] aşırı tatlı dilli, şatafatlı; veciz, anlamlı; anlamlı sözlerle dolu olan.

sen.tient ['senʃənt] *adj.* hisseden, sezgili; duygulu.

sen.ti.ment ['sentimənt] *n.* his, duygu, seziş; düşünce, fikir, kanaat, hüküm; *s. ~ality*; **sen.ti.men.tal** ☐ [-'mentl] hisli, duygusal, yanık, içli, duygulara kapılarak yapılan; **sen.ti.men.tal.ist** [-'mentəlist] *n.* duygularına aşırı kapılan kimse; **sen.ti.men.tal.i.ty** [-men-'tæliti] *n.* aşırı duygusallık (*veya* duyarlık), içlilik.

sen.ti.nel ['sentinl], **sen.try** ['sentri] *n.* MIL nöbetçi, gözcü.

sen.try...: '*~-box* *n.* nöbetçi kulübesi; '*~-go* *n.* nöbet.

se.pal BOT ['sepəl] *n.* çanak yaprağı, sepal.

sep.a.ra.bil.i.ty [sepərəˈbiliti] *n.* ayrılabilir olma; '**sep.a.ra.ble** ☐ ayrılabilir; **sep.arate 1.** ☐ ['seprit] ayrı(lmış), müstakil; *~ property* JUR karı *veya* kocanın şahsî malları; **2.** ['-əreit] *v/t. & v/i.* ayırmak; bölmek; ayrılmak; **sep.a'ra.tion** *n.* ayırma, ayrılma, ayrılış; **sep.a.ra.tist** ['-ərətist] *n.* ECCL tarikat yanlısı; POL partiden ayrılma taraftarı, ayrılık çıkaran; **sep.a.ra.tor** MEC ['-əreitə] *n.* ayırıcı, santrifüjör; krema makinesi (*süt*).

se.pi.a PAINT ['siːpjə] *n.* sepya, mürekkep balığı salgısından yapılan boya *veya* mürekkep; bu rengin hâkim olduğu fotoğraf *veya* resim.

sep.sis MED ['sepsis] *n.* septisemi, kana mikrop ve toksin karışması.

Sep.tem.ber [sep'tembə] *n.* eylül.

sep.ten.ni.al ☐ [sep'tenjəl] yedi yıl süren, yedi senelik, yedi yılda bir olan.

sep.tic MED ['septik] *adj.* bulaşık, mikroplu.

sep.tu.a.ge.nar.i.an [septjuedʒiˈnɛəriən] *n.* yetmişle yetmişdokuz yaşlar arasında olan kimse.

se.pul.chral [si'pʌlkrəl] *adj.* mezara ait; ölü…; *fig.* loş, kasvetli, hüzünlü; **sep.ulchre** ['sepəlkə] **1.** *n.* mezar, kabir; **2.** *v/t.* gömmek, defnetmek; **sep.ul.ture** ['‿tʃə] *n.* gömme, defin.

se.quel ['si:kwəl] *n.* bşin devamı, arkası; son, sonuç, netice; **in the ~** sonradan.

se.quence ['si:kwəns] *n.* art arda gelme, sürüp gitme, ardıllık; sıra; *film*: sahne; **~ of tenses** GR zaman uyumu.

se.ques.ter [si'kwestə] *s.* **sequestrate**; **~ o.s.** geri çekilmek (*from -den*), tenha bir yere çekilmek; **~ed** dünyadan el çekmiş, münzevî, tek başına.

se.ques.trate JUR [si'kwestreit] *v/t.* (*mal, mülk*) el koymak, haczetmek; **se.questra.tion** [si:kwes'treiʃən] *n.* inziva, bir köşeye çekilme; JUR el koyma, müsadere; '**se.ques.tra.tor** JUR yediemin, yasaca güvenilir kimse olarak seçilen kimse.

se.quoi.a BOT [si'kwɔiə] mamut ağacı, sekoya.

se.ragl.io [se'rɑ:liəu] *n.* sultan sarayı; harem dairesi.

ser.aph ['seræf] *n., pl. a.* **ser.a.phim** ['‿fim] melâikeden *b-i*; **se.raph.ic** [se'ræfik] *adj.* (**~ally**) melek gibi, meleğe ait; çok güzel ve masum.

Serb, Ser.bi.an ['sə:b(jən)] **1.** *adj.* sırp, Sırbistan'a ait; **2.** *n.* sırp(lı); Sırp dili, Sırpça.

sere *poet.* [siə] *adj.* kuru, solgun.

ser.e.nade [seri'neid] **1.** *n.* MUS serenat; **2.** *vb. b-nin* penceresi önünde serenat çalmak.

se.rene □ [si'ri:n] açık, berrak, belli, aşikâr; sakin, hareketsiz; **se.ren.i.ty** [si'reniti] *n.* sükunet, sessizlik, durgunluk; huzur.

serf [sə:f] *n.* serf, köle; *fig.* kul, esir; '**serf.age**, '**serf.dom** *n.* kölelik, serflik.

serge [sə:dʒ] *n.* serj, yünlü kumaş.

ser.geant MIL ['sɑ:dʒənt] *n.* çavuş; (*polis*) komiser muavini; '**~'ma.jor** *n.* MIL başçavuş.

se.ri.al □ ['siəriəl] **1.** seri halinde olan, tefrika halinde yayımlanan; sıra takibeden, seri…; **~ly** tefrika halinde, seri olarak; **2.** *n.* tefrika (*roman vs.*).

se.ries ['siəri:z] *n. sg. & pl.* sıra, dizi (*a.* MATH), seri; BIOL grup; **~ in** ELECT seri bağlama.

se.ri.ous □ ['siəriəs] ciddî, ağırbaşlı, vakarlı; önemli; ağır, tehlikeli; gerçek, içten; **be ~** ciddiye almak, ciddi söylemek; '**se.ri.ous.ness** *n.* ciddiyet, ağırbaşlılık, vakar.

ser.jeant PARL ['sɑ:dʒənt] *n.*: **~-at-arms** oturumlarda güvenlik görevlisi.

ser.mon ['sə:mən] *n.* dinsel konuşma, vaiz; *iro.* şiddetli kınama, ihtar, yüzleme; '**ser.mon.ize** *vb.* vazetmek, nasihat etm., uzun ve sıkıcı öğütler vermek; azarlamak, haddini bildirmek.

se.rol.o.gy MED [siə'rɔlədʒi] *n.* seroloji, serom ve etkilerinden bahseden ilim.

se.rous ['siərəs] *adj.* seromla ilgili; ince ve sulu (*sıvı*).

ser.pent ['sə:pənt] *n.* yılan; iblis; hain adam; **ser.pen.tine** ['‿tain] **1.** *adj.* yılankavî, yılan gibi kıvrılan, dolambaçlı; **2.** *n.* MIN yılantaşı.

ser.rate ['serit], **ser.rat.ed** [se'reitid] *adj.* girintili çıkıntılı, testere dişli (*yaprak*), serrat; **ser'ra.tion** *n.* testere gibi dişli oluş.

ser.ried ['serid] *adj.* sıkışık, sıkı sıra halinde.

se.rum ['siərəm] *n.* serom (MED *aşı maddesi*; PHYSIOL *özsu*).

serv.ant ['sə:vənt] *n.* hizmetçi, uşak; *a.* **domestic ~** hizmetçi; '**~-girl** *n.* hizmetçi kız.

serve 1. [sə:v] *v/t.* hizmet etm. *-e*; yardım etm., yardımcı olm. *-e*; servis yapmak, sofraya koymak *-i*; yararı dokunmak, yaramak *-e*; sağlamak, vermek, …olarak kullanılmak (**with**); (*müşteriye*) istediği şeyleri vermek; (*sofraya*) bakmak; *b*ṣden yararlanmak; idare etm, işlerini çevirmek; *a.* **~ up** (*yemek*) sofraya koymak *-i*; amacına uymak *-in*; muamele etm., davranmak *-e*; *tenis*: servis atmak; (*it*) **~s him right!** oh olsun!, bunu hak etti!, yapmasaydı!, söz dinleseydi!; *s.* **sentence 1**; **~ out** dağıtmak, taksim etm.; F hizmetini tamamlamak; **~ a writ on s.o.**, **~ s.o. with a writ** JUR *b-ne* bir mahkeme emrini tebliğ etm.; *v/i.* hizmette bulunmak (*a.* MIL), işini görmek, hizmetçi olm.; yetişmek, elvermek; amaca uymak; yaramak, faydası dokunmak (**as, for** *-e*); **~ at table** sofrada hizmet etm.; **2.** *n.* tenis: servis (*yapma sırası*); '**server** *n.* tenis: servis atan oyuncu; ECCL papaz cömezi; tepsi.

serv.ice ['sə:vis] **1.** *n.* hizmet; servis; askerlik; görev, iş; hizmetçilik; COM müşteriye hizmet; *a.* **divine ~** ibadet, din töreni; yarar, fayda, istifade; servis takımı; NAUT palamar kaplama; JUR tebliğ, tebligat; *tenis*: servis; *be at s.o.'s* ~ *b-nin* hizmetinde olm.; **2.** *vb.* candan bakmak; *b-ne* pervane olm., *b-ne* yardım etm., omuz vermek; MEC *bşe* bakmak, işleyecek hale koymak; **'serv.ice.a.ble** ☐ işe yarar, faydalı, elverişli; dayanıklı, çok kullanılabilen; **'serv.ice.a.ble.ness** *n.* yarar, elverişli olma; dayanıklılık.

serv.ice...: '~**ball** *n. tenis*: servis topu; ~ **flat** hizmetçili apartman dairesi; '~**line** *n. tenis*: servis çizgisi; ~ **pipe** MEC bağlantı borusu; ~ **station** benzin istasyonu.

ser.vile ☐ ['sə:vail] kölelere ait, kölelere özgü; köle gibi, gurursuz, hakir, aşağılık; **ser.vil.i.ty** [~'viliti] *n.* kölelik; aşağılık, gurursuzluk.

serv.ing ['sə:viŋ] *n.* tabak, porsiyon.

ser.vi.tude ['sə:vitju:d] *n.* serflik, esaret, kölelik, kulluk, uşaklık; JUR irtifak hakkı, başkasının mal *veya* mülkünden belirli bir yolla yararlanma hakkı; *s. penal.*

ser.vo-brake MOT ['sə:vəubreik] *n.* servo fren.

ses.a.me BOT ['sesəmi] *n.* susam.

ses.sion ['seʃən] *n.* oturum, celse; toplantı (hali); toplanma süresi, dönem; *be in* ~ toplantı halinde olm.; **session.al** ['seʃənl] *adj.* oturum..., celse..., oturumla ilgili.

set [set] **1.** (*irr.*) *v/t.* koymak, yerleştirmek, yerli yerine koymak; dikmek (*bitki*); kurmak (*çalar saat*); düzeltmek, tanzim etm.; üzerine saldırtmak (*köpek*) (*at, on -e*); bilemek (*bıçak vs.*); yerleştirmek, oturtmak (*mücevher*); tespit etm., kararlaştırmak (*zaman*); katılaştırmak, pıhtılaştırmak; MED yerine koymak, yerleştirmek (*kırık, çıkık*); kuluçkaya yatırmak; ~ *s.o.* laughing *b-ni* güldürmek; ~ *an example* örnek vermek; ~ *the fashion* moda çıkarmak; ~ *sail* rüzgâra yelken açmak; ~ *one's teeth* azmetmek, dişini sıkmak; karar vermek; ~ *against* karşısına koymak, karşı koymak; dayamak *-e*; *s. apart*; ~ *aside* bir kenara koymak, rezerve etm.; lağvetmek, feshetmek; *fig.* reddetmek, tanımamak; ~ *at defiance* *b-ne* karşı durmak, meydan okumak; ~ *at ease* teskin etm., rahatlatmak *-i*; ~ *at liberty* tahliye etm.; ~ *at rest* rahatlatmak *-i*; karara bağlamak (*soru*); ~ *store by* çok değerli saymak; ~ *down* indirmek (*yolcu*); kay-

detmek; tespit etm., koymak (*kural, yöntem*); bir arada yazmak (*to s.o. b-ne*); izah etm.; ~ *off* yola çıkmak; belirtmek; hesaba katmak, göz önüne almak (*against -e karşı*); eşitlemek, denklemek; ~ *on* tahrik etm., teşvik etm., ayartmak; ~ *out* teşhir etm., yaymak, göstermek; anlatmak, izah etm.; daldırmak, dikmek (*bitki*); ~ *up* dikmek, kurmak, tesis etm.; koymak, va'zetmek (*fikir*); çıkarmak (*nida, haykırış*); yoluna koymak; girişmek, teşebbüs etm. (*iş*); ~ *up in type* TYP dizmek, tertip etm.; **2.** (*irr.*) *v/i.* batmak (*güneş vs.*); pıhtılaşmak, koyulaşmak; akmak (*elektrik akımı, seyelan*); HUNT av grubuna başkanlık etm.; vücuda iyi oturtmak, yakışmak (*elbise*); ~ *about s.th.* bir işe koyulmak; ~ *about s.o.* F *b-nin* üzerine atılmak; ~ *forth* açılmak, yola düzülmek; ~ *forward* ilerletmek, yol açmak; ~ *in* başlamak (*kış, hastalık vs.*); ~ *off* yola düzülmek; araba *vs.* ile gitmek (*for*); ~ (*up*)*on* üzerine saldır(t)mak; *fig.* başlamak, azmetmek; ~ *to* başlamak *-e*, girişmek *e-*; ~ *up* bir yere konmak, yerleşmek (*as*); ~ *up for* sarfolunmak (*para*), *k-ne ...* süsü vermek, *k-ni ...* diye tanıtmak; **3.** *adj.* sabit, değişmez, hareketsiz; muayyen, belirli; düzenli; ~ *up(on) bşe* düşkün, haris; azimli; ~ *with* meşgul *ile*; ~ *fair* barometre: sabit, devamlı açık hava; *hard* ~ büyük ihtiyaç (*veya* güçlük *vs.*); ~ *piece* sanat eseri; ~ *speech* klişe nutuk, iyi düşünülüp hazırlanmış konuşma; **4.** *n.* sıra, dizi, seri; grup, zümre, takım; sofra takımı; TV, radyo alıcısı; koleksiyon; şirket; cemaat, topluluk, grup, klik; AGR fide, fidan; *tenis*: set; meyil, eğilim, temayül; heves, istek; yön, yol; kesim, biçim, makas (*elbise*); *poet.* batma, sukut; THEAT dekor, mizansen; (*güneş*) batma, gurup; *sinema*: set; *make a dead* ~ *fig.* üzerine atılmak *-in*, kancayı takmak *-e*, tavlamaya çalışmak *-i*.

set.back ['setbæk] *n. fig.* geri tepme, aksilik; kötüleşme; nüksetme; ARCH belli bir noktadan geride inşa etme; **'set-down** *n.* indirme, azaltma; hiçe sayma, hakir görme; **'set-'off** *n.* kontrast, tezat, ayrılık; süs, dekor; *obs. &* JUR mahsup, karşılık, mukabil talep.

set.tee [se'ti:] *n.* kanepe.

set.ter [setə] *n.* dizici, mürettip; HUNT

seter (*av köpeği*).

set the.o.ry MATH *n.* dizi teorisi.

set.ting ['setiŋ] *n.* yuva (*s. **set 1 & 2***); katılaşma, pıhtılaşma; bir defada kuluçkaya yatırılan yumurtalar; AST batma, gurup; yön, seyir (*rüzgâr*); yerleştirme, oturtma; ortam, çevre, koşullar; THEAT dekor, mizansen; *fig.* kuşatma; MUS beste, kompozisyon; sofra takımı; '~-lo.tion *n.* (*saç*) fiksatif, sprey.

set.tle ['setl] **1.** *n.* tahta kanepe, peyke, sıra; **2.** *v/t.* kararlaştırmak; bakmak (*çocuk*); yerleştirmek, iskân etm.; düzeltmek; halletmek, çözmek; bitirmek, sona erdirmek (*iş*); bir karara bağlamak (*soru*); görmek, ödemek (*hesap*); teskin etm., rahatlatmak; yatıştırmak (*kavga*); maaş bağlamak (*on s.o. b-ne*); insan yerleştirmek, iskân etm.; yerine getirmek; *v/i. oft.* ~ *down, a.* ~ *o.s.* oturmak, yerleşmek; *a.* ~ *in* evini döşeyip yerleşmek; konmak, tünemek; NAUT dibe çökmek, batmak; hafiflemek, inmek, yatışmak (*hiddet vs.*); durulmak (*hava*); azmetmek, kararlı olm. (*on*); yetinmek, kanaat etm. (*with ile*); *it is settling for a frost* don olacak gibi; ~ *down to k-ni b-şe* vakfetmek, adamak.

set.tled ['setld] *adj.* sabit; devamlı, muntazam; muayyen; katî, kesin; sakin, durgun, değişmez (*rüzgâr*); ödenmiş (*hesap*); ~ *in life* evli (barklı), iş güç sahibi; meskûn, şenelmiş.

set.tle.ment ['setlmənt] *n.* yerleş(tir)me, bir yerde oturma; anlaşma, uzlaşma; yeni koloni; JUR ferağ, gelir bağlama; COM hesap görme, tasfiye; halletme; yeni iskân edilmiş yer; mülk (*veya* para, hediye vs.) verme; misyon, sosyal faaliyetlerde bulunan cemiyet; ev, mesken; temelin oturması (*bina*).

set.tler ['setlə] *n.* yeni yerleşen göçmen; *sl.* nihaî darbe, susturucu cevap.

set.tling ['setliŋ] *n.* yerleşme, iskân (*s. **settle 2***); COM hesaplaşma, tasfiye.

set...: '~-'to *n.* kavga, dövüş, çarpışma, tartışma, dalaşma; '~-up *n.* F durum, vaziyet; yapı, organizasyon; F kazanılması plânlanmış maç; F kolay iş; *Am.* F içki için ikram edilen bardak, buz ve soda.

sev.en ['sevn] **1.** *adj.* yedi; **2.** *n.* yedi sayısı; '**sev.en.fold** *adj.* yedi kat, yedi misli; **sev.en.teen** ['~'tiːn] *adj.* on yedi; **seventh** ['sevnθ] **1.** ◻ yedinci; **2.** *n.* yedide bir; MUS yedili; **se.ven.ti.eth**

['~-tiiθ] *adj.* yetmişinci; '**sev.en.ty 1.** *adj.* yetmiş; **2.** *n.* yetmiş sayısı.

sev.er ['sevə] *v/t. & v/i.* ayırmak, ayrılmak, kop(ar)mak; çöz(ül)mek; parçala(n)mak.

sev.er.al ◻ ['sevrəl] birçok, muhtelif, birkaç; çeşitli, bazı; ayrı, başka; *joint and ~* JUR müteselsil, müştereken ve münferiden, zincirleme; '**sev.er.al.ly** *adv.* birer birer, ayrı ayrı, teker teker.

sev.er.ance ['sevərəns] *n.* ayrılma, ayrılık, ilişik kesme; '~ ('pack.age) *n.* kıdem tazminatı.

se.vere ◻ [si'viə] sert, şiddetli, haşin; sert, kasvetli (*hava, kış*); sert, acı (*eleştiri*); ciddî; şiddetli (*ağrı*); keskin, sert (*üslup, güzellik*); kötü, berbat (*kaza, yara*); **se.ver.i.ty** [si'veriti] *n.* sertlik, şiddet; ciddiyet.

sew [səu] (*irr.*) *vb.* dikiş dikmek; dikmek, ciltlemek (*kitap*); ~ *up* dikmek, dikerek kapamak.

sew.age ['sjuːidʒ] *n.* pis su, lağım suyu; ~ *farm* lağım sularıyla sulanan tarla.

sew.er¹ ['səuə] *n.* dikici, dikişçi.

sew.er² ['sjuə] *n.* lağım; '**sew.er.age** *n.* lağım, kanalizasyon.

sew.ing ['səuiŋ] **1.** *n.* dikiş, iğne işi; **2.** *adj.* dikiş...

sewn [səun] *p.p. of* **sew**.

sex [seks] *n.* cins; cinsiyet, seks, eşey; cinsel ilişki; *attr.* cinsî...; ~ *appeal* cinsî cazibe, seksapel; ~ *education* üreme konusunda aydınlatma, seks eğitimi.

sex.a.ge.nar.i.an [seksədʒi'nɛəriən] *n.* altmış ile yetmiş yaşları arasındaki kimse;

sex.en.ni.al ◻ [sek'senjəl] altı senede bir olan, altı sene süren, altı senelik; **sextant** ['sekstənt] *n.* sekstant, gemilerde yıldızlar arasındaki açıyı ölçmeye yarayan alet.

sex.ton ['sekstən] *n.* zangoç, kilise kayyumu.

sex.tu.ple ['sekstjupl] *adj.* altı misli, altı kat.

sex.u.al ◻ ['seksjuəl] cinsî, seksüel, cinsel, eşeysel, cinsî...; ~ *desire* cinsel arzu; ~ *intercourse* cinsel ilişki; **sex-u.al.i.ty** [~'æliti] *n.* cinsiyet, cinsellik.

shab.bi.ness ['ʃæbinis] *n.* kılıksızlık; alçaklık, haksızlık; '**shab.by** ◻ kılıksız, pejmürde, yırtık pırtık, sefil; alçak, adi; cimri, hasis.

shack *part. Am.* ['ʃæk] *n.* baraka, kulübe, salaş.

shack.le ['ʃækl] **1.** *n.* zincir, pranga, boyunduruk (*fig. mst ~s pl.*); engel, mania; NAUT, MEC bağlantı demiri (*veya* zincir baklası), kelepçe; **2.** *v/t.* bağlamak, zincire vurmak, kelepçe takmak; kösteklemek, engel olm.

shad ICHTH [ʃæd] *n.* tirsi balığı (*ringa türü*).

shade [ʃeid] **1.** *n.* gölge; karanlık, zulmet (*a. fig.*); abajur, karpuz (*lamba*); gölgelik (*yer*), siper; *Am.* bir tür perde; *fig.* kolay iş, çocuk oyuncağı; renk tonu; nüans, ayırtı, çok hafif fark; himaye, koruma; hayalet; tayf; **2.** *vb.* ışıktan korumak (*from -den*); gölgelemek (*a. fig.*); örtmek, maskelemek (*ışık*); muhafaza etm.; PAINT resme gölge vermek; ~ **away**, ~ **off** yavaş yavaş değişmek (*renk, durum vs.*) (*into -e*); 'shad.ing PAINT resimde gölgeleme; *fig.* nüans, ayırtı.

shad.ow ['ʃædəu] **1.** *n.* gölge, karanlık (*a. fig.*); hayal, karaltı; eser, iz, alâmet; koruma, himaye; *b-nin* peşinden ayrılmayan (*b-i, köpek*); rahatsız eden duygu; **2.** *v/t.* gölgelemek, karartmak (*a. fig.*); örtmek, gizlemek; *mst* ~ **forth**, ~ **out** ima etm., sezdirmek; sembolize etm.; gizlice gözetlemek, peşini bırakmamak; 'shad.ow.y *adj.* gölgeli, karanlık, loş; müphem, şüpheli; belirsiz, hayal gibi.

shad.y ['ʃeidi] *adj.* gölgeli, karanlık; F şüpheli, kötü, namussuz; **on the ~ side of forty** kırkını aşmış.

shaft [ʃɑːft] *n.* sap, kol; sütun, dayak, payanda, destek (*a. fig.*); *poet.* aydınlık, parıltı, ışın; MEC şaft, mil, araba oku; MIN kuyu; aydınlık, hava bacası.

shag [ʃæg] *n.* ince kıyılmış sert tütün.

shag.gy ['ʃægi] *adj.* kaba tüylü.

sha.green [ʃæ'griːn] *n.* sağrı; köpekbalığı derisi.

Shah [ʃɑː] *n.* İran şahı.

shake [ʃeik] **1.** (*irr.*) *v/t.* silkmek, silkelemek, sallamak, sarsmak, çalka(la)mak; titretmek; ~ **down** sarsarak yere düşürmek; küme halinde yığmak (*buğday*); *sl.* sızdırmak (*para*); ~ **hands** el sıkışmak, tokalaşmak; ~ **up** sallayarak silkerek gevşetmek, sertliğini gidermek (*yatak vs.*); *fig.* sarsarak uyandırmak; *v/i.* titremek, sarsılmak, sallanmak (**with** *ile*); MUS titreşim halinde olm.; ~ **down** arkadaşlık, ahbaplık oluşturmak; **2.** *n.* sarsıntı, titreme; MUS sesi titretme, rulat; çalkalanmış

şey; F an, lâhza; *Am.* F deprem; ~ **of the hand** el sıkma; **no great ~s** F adî, sıradan, söyle böyle, pek o kadar değil; '~'down *n.* yer yatağı; *Am. sl.* şantaj, para sızdırma; *Am.* son deneme, tecrübe; ~ **cruise** NAUT deney seferi; '~-hands *n.* el sıkışma; 'shak.en **1.** *p.p. of* **shake 1**; **2.** *adj.* sarsılmış; müteessir, etkilenmiş; 'shak.er *n.* karıştırıcı, içinde *bş* çalkalanan kap; tuzluk vs.

shake-up F ['ʃeik'ʌp] *n.* yeniden düzenleme, personelde değişiklik yapma.

shak.i.ness ['ʃeikinis] *n.* titreklik, sarsaklık; zayıflık, sakatlık; 's.hak.y' □ *mst* titrek, sarsak, sarsıntılı; zayıf, sakat; şüpheli, sallantıda.

shale GEOL [ʃeil] *n.* tortulu şist.

shall [ʃæl] (*irr.*) *v/aux.* -ecek; -meli.

shal.lot BOT [ʃə'lɔt] *n.* bir tür yabanî sarmısak *veya* ufak soğan.

shal.low ['ʃæləu] **1.** *adj.* sığ, yalpık; *fig.* üstünkörü; **2.** *n.* sığ yer, kumsal; **3.** *v/t. & v/i.* sığlaş(tır)mak, düzle(n)mek; 'shal.low.ness *n.* sığlık, sığ olma; *fig.* yavan (*veya* tatsız) olma.

shalt *obs.* [ʃælt] *v/aux.* -eceksin, *s.* **shall**.

sham [ʃæm] **1.** *adj.* yapma, taklit, sahte, suni, yapay; **2.** *n.* taklit, yalan, hile, dolap, aldat(ıl)ma; dolandırıcı, hilekâr, dubaracı; **3.** *vb.* yalandan yapmak, yapar gibi görünmek; *b-ne* karşı sahte tavır takınmak; sayrımsamak; ~ **ill** *k-ni* yalandan hasta göstermek.

sham.ble ['ʃæmbl] *vb.* badi badi (*veya* paytak paytak) yürümek.

sham.bles *fig.* ['ʃæmblz] *n.* harp yeri; yıkıntı, moloz.

sham.bling ['ʃæmbliŋ] sallanan, oynayan, gevşek, sarsak.

shame [ʃeim] **1.** *n.* utanç, ar; ayıp, rezalet; ~**!**, **for** ~, ~ **on you!** tuu!, ayıp!, pöf!, yazıklar olsun!, utan!; **cry** ~ **upon s.o.** *b-nin* yüzüne «utan!» diye bağırmak; **put to** ~ utandırmak, mahcup etm., rezil etm.; **2.** *vb.* utandırmak *-i*, mahcup etm. *-i*; *b-nin* namusuna tecavüz etm., lekelemek, namussuzluk etm.

shame.faced □ ['ʃeimfeist] mahcup, utangaç, sıkılgan; 'shame.faced.ness *n.* utangaçlık, mahcubiyet.

shame.ful □ ['ʃeimful] utandırıcı, ayıp, yüzkarası, utanç verici; alçak, kepaze; 'shame.ful.ness *n.* utanç verici durum, namussuzluk, alçaklık.

shame.less □ ['ʃeimlis] utanmaz,

arsız, edepsiz; **'shame.less.ness** *n.*
arsızlık, hayâsızlık, edepsizlik.
sham.my ['ʃæmi] *n.* süet, podösüet, güderi.
sham.poo [ʃæm'puː] **1.** *n.* şampuan;
saçı şampuanla yıkama; **2.** *v/t.* şampuanla yıkamak (*saç*).
sham.rock ['ʃæmrɔk] *n.* вот yonca; tirfil yaprağı (*İrlanda'nın ulusal sembolü*).
shang.hai NAUT *sl.* [ʃæŋ'hai] *v/t. b-ni*
sersemletip *veya* sarhoş edip kaçırarak
gemide çalışmaya zorlamak.
shank [ʃæŋk] *n.* incik, baldır; вот sap;
NAUT çapa gövdesi; *go on ♀'s mare veya pony* F tabanvayla gitmek;
shanked *comb.* ... baldırlı.
shan't [ʃɑːnt] = **shall not**.
shan.tung [ʃæn'tʌŋ] *n.* şantug (*bir tür
ipek*).
shan.ty ['ʃænti] *n.* kulübe, baraka; =
chanty.
shape [ʃeip] **1.** *n.* şekil, biçim, tarz, suret, düzen; hal, durum; *in bad ~* kötü
durumda; **2.** *v/t.* şekil vermek *-e*, teşkil
etm. *-i*; düzenlemek *-i*; uydurmak (*to
-e*); *~ one's course for b-nin* geleceği-
ni yönlendirmek; *v/i.* gelişmek, ortaya
çıkmak, şekillenmek; gibi görünmek,
manzara arzetmek; **shaped** *adj.* ...
şeklinde; şekilli, biçimli; **'shape.less**
adj. biçimsiz, şekilsiz; **'shape.ly** *adj.*
biçimli, endamlı, yakışıklı.
share¹ [ʃɛə] *n.* saban demiri.
share² [_] **1.** *n.* pay, hisse, parça, kısım;
kontenjan; COM hisse senedi, aksiyon;
MIN itibarî değeri olmayan madencilik
hisse senedi; *original ~*, *ordinary ~*,
primary ~ COM adî hisse senedi; *preference ~*, *preferred ~*, *priority ~* COM imtiyazlı hisse senedi; *have a ~ in bşe* iştira-
rak etm.; *go ~s* paylaşmak, bölüşmek
(*with s.o.*; *in s.th.*); *~ and ~ alike* eşit
paylarla; **2.** *v/t.* paylaşmak (*among,
with* arasında, *ile*); *bşe* katılmak, *bşe*
iştirak etm.; *v/i. b-ne bşden* pay
çıkmak, hissesi olm.; ortaklaşa kullanmak; *'~.crop.per n. Am.* ortakçı, tarla
kiracısı; *'~.hold.er n.* COM hissedar;
'shar.er n. hissedar.
shark [ʃɑːk] *n.* ICHTH köpekbalığı; *fig.*
hilebaz, dolandırıcı; *Am. sl.* bir işin ehli, otorite.
sharp [ʃɑːp] **1.** □ bilenmiş, keskin (*a.
fig.*); sivri; zeki; sert, şiddetli (*ağrı
vs.*); sek, ekşi, buruk (*şarap vs.*); tiz,
kulakları tırmalayan (*ses*); canı tez,

kabına sığmayan (*mizaç*); tez, acele,
anî; kurnaz, hilekâr, şeytanı şişeye sokan; MUS yarım ton ince, diyez; **2.** *adv.*
MUS yarım ton ince; F dakikası dakikasına, tam; *look ~!* haydi çabuk!; **3.**
n. MUS diyez, yarım ton ince nota; hilebaz, dolandırıcı; **'sharp.en** *vb.* bilemek, keskinleştirmek, sivriltmek,
yontmak; iştah açmak, teşvik etm.,
hırslandırmak; şiddetlendirmek, güçlendirmek; acılaştırmak, ekşileştir-
mek; **'sharp.en.er** *n.* kalemtıraş; biley
taşı, zağ taşı; **'sharp.er** *n.* hilekâr, dolandırıcı; **'sharp.ness** *n.* keskinlik (*a.
fig.*); şiddet, sertlik; *fig.* şiddetli oluş
(*ağrı*); zeki oluş; hilekârlık.
sharp...: *'~'set* *adj.* karnı aç; *bşe* düşkün, haris (*on*); *'~-shoot.er* *n.* keskin
nişancı; *'~'sight.ed* *adj.* keskin
bakışlı, keskin görüşlü; *'~'wit.ted*
adj. zeki.
shat.ter ['ʃætə] *v/t. & v/i.* kır(ıl)mak,
parçala(n)mak, tahrip etm., yok etm.
(*a. fig.*); bozmak (*sinir*), şirazesinden
çıkarmak.
shave [ʃeiv] **1.** (*irr.*) *v/t.* tıraş etm., kazımak; (*part. ağaç*) soymak, yüzmek,
rendelemek; çok yakınından sürtünür
gibi geçmek; *v/i.* tıraş olm.; *~ through*
maharetle bir engelden geçmek, *fig.
bşden* ucuz kurtulmak; **2.** *n.* tıraş; rende; *have a ~* tıraş olm.; *by a ~* az kaldı,
kıl payı; *a close ~*, *a narrow ~* güçbelâ
(*veya* daradar, kılpayı) kurtuluş;
'shav.en *p.p. of shave 1*; *a ~ head* ustura ile kazınmış kafa; **'shav.er** *n.* berber; tıraş makinesi; *young ~* F acemi
çaylak.
shav.ing ['ʃeiviŋ] *n.* tıraş; *~s pl. part.*
(*rende, planya*) yonga, talaş, kırpıntı;
attr. tıraş..., berber...; *'~-brush n.* tıraş
fırçası.
shawl [ʃɔːl] *n.* omuz atkısı, şal.
shawm MUS [ʃɔːm] *n.* çoban kavalı.
shay *obs. veya* F [ʃei] *n.* hafif gezinti
arabası.
she [ʃiː, ʃi] **1.** *pron.* o (*dişil*); **2.** *n.* kadın,
dişi; *she-...* dişi (*hayvanlar için*).
sheaf [ʃiːf] *n., pl.* **sheaves** [ʃiːvz] demet, deste, bağlam.
shear [ʃiə] **1.** (*irr.*) *v/t.* kırkmak, kesmek, makaslamak; F soymak, yolun-
muş tavuğa döndürmek; **2.** *n.* (*a pair
of*) *~s pl.* büyük makas; **'shear.er** *n.*
kesen kimse, orakçı, tırpancı; **'shearing** *n.* kırkım, kırpma, makaslama;
~s pl. yapağı, yün.

sheath [ʃiːθ] *n.*, *pl.* **sheaths** [ʃiːðz] kın, kılıf (*a.* BOT & ANAT); ZOO mahfaza, zarf
sheathe [ʃiːð] *v/t.* içine koymak, sokmak, örtmek; MEC kaplamak, donatmak; '**sheath.ing** *n.* MEC kaplama (malzemesi), zırh, örtü.
sheave MEC [ʃiːv] *n.* makara, bobin; yuvarlak levha, disk.
sheaves [ʃiːvz] *pl. of* **sheaf**.
she.bang *Am. sl.* [ʃəˈbæŋ] *n.* yıkılmak üzere olan, virane baraka; **the whole** ~ hepsi, tümü.
shed[1] [ʃed] (*irr.*) *vb.* dökmek, akıtmak, boşaltmak (*kan, gözyaşı vs.*); yaymak, neşretmek (*ışık, fikir vs.*) (**upon**); dökmek, değiştirmek (*kıl, deri vs.*); çıkarıp atmak, kurtulmak -*den*.
shed[2] [_] *n.* baraka, kulübe; sundurma, odunluk; uçak hangarı.
sheen [ʃiːn] *n.* parlaklık, parıltı (*kumaş*); '**sheen.y** *adj.* parlak.
sheep [ʃiːp] *n.* koyun(lar *pl.*) koyun derisi, meşin; *fig.* safdil, budala kimse; '~**cot** = **sheep-fold**; '~**dog** *n.* çoban köpeği; '~**fold** *n.* koyun ağılı; '**sheepish** □ sıkılgan, utangaç; sersem, budala; koyun gibi; '**sheep.ish.ness** *n.* aptallık, budalalık; mahcubiyet, sıkılganlık.
sheep...: '~**man** *n. Am.* koyun yetiştiren kimse; '~**run** = **sheep-walk**; '~**skin** *n.* pösteki, koyun postu; *Am.* diploma; '~**walk** *n.* koyun otlağı.
sheer[1] [ʃiə] *adj. & adv.* halis, saf, katışıksız, hakiki; (büs)bütün, tam(amiyle); dik, sarp, dikey; doğru(dan), vasıtasız; çok ince, hafif ve şeffaf (*kumaş*).
sheer[2] [_] **1.** *vb.* NAUT rotadan sapmak, yolundan ayrılmak; ~ **off** *fig.* tüymek, sıvışmak; **2.** *n.* NAUT borda kavsi; yoldan sapma.
sheet [ʃiːt] **1.** *n.* yatak çarşafı; yaprak, tabaka (*kâğıt*); levha (*cam, metal vs.*); geniş yüzey (*su vs.*); NAUT ıskota, büyük yelkenleri yönetmek için kullanılan ip; **the rain came down in** ~**s** yağmur sağanak halinde indi; ~ **iron** saç (*demir*); **2.** *v/t.* çarşaf vs. ile örtmek; '~**an.chor** *n.* NAUT ocaklık demiri, çapa; *fig.* kurtuluş ümidi; '**sheet.ing** *n.* çarşaflık keten bezi, '**sheet-light.ning** *n.* ufukta şimşek çakması.
sheik(h) [ʃeik] *n.* şeyh, kabile reisi.
shelf [ʃelf] *n. pl.* **shelves** [ʃelvz] raf, etajer, pervaz; GEOL resif, şelf, sığlık, kum bankı; **on the** ~ *fig.* rafa kaldırılmış, kadro dışı; **get on the** ~ *fig.* dansa davet edilmemek (*kız*).
shell [ʃel] **1.** *n.* kabuk; kaplumbağa kabuğu, bağa; istiridye (*veya* midye) kabuğu; MEC iskelet (*bina*); MIL top mermisi, obüs, bomba; ince uzun yarış kayığı; **2.** *v/t. & v/i.* kabuğunu çıkarmak (*veya* soymak, kırımak); koçandan ayırmak (*mısır*); başaktan ayırmak (*buğday*); MIL borbardıman etm.; kabuktan ayrılmak, sıyrılmak, soyulmak; ~ **out** *sl.* mangizleri sökülmek, hesabı ödemek.
shel.lac [ʃəˈlæk] *n.* gomalaka, şelak, cilâ yapmakta kullanılan bir tür reçine.
shell-cra.ter [ˈʃɔlkreitə] *n.* mermi hunisi; **shelled** [ʃeld] *comb.* ... **shell** kabuklu.
shell...: '~**fire** *n.* top ateşi; '~**fish** *n.* ZOO kabuklu hayvan; '~**proof** *adj.* mermi (*veya* bomba) işlemez; '~**shock** *n.* savaş yorgunluğu, savaşın neden olduğu ruhsal çöküntü.
shel.ter [ˈʃeltə] **1.** *n.* sığınak, barınak, siper, sundurma, saçak; *fig.* himaye, koru(n)ma; **2.** *v/t. & v/i.* barın(dır)mak, koru(n)mak, muhafaza etm.; '**shel.terless** *n.* himayeden yoksun, korunmasız; desteksiz, arkasız.
shelve[1] [ʃelv] *v/t.* (içine) raflar yapmak; rafa koymak; *fig.* rafa kaldırmak, ertelemek, bir kenara koymak; emekliye ayırmak, kadro dışı bırakmak; F *b-ne, bşe* aldırış etmemek.
shelve[2] [_] *v/i.* (yavaş yavaş) meyletmek.
shelves [ʃelvz] *pl. of* **shelf**.
shelv.ing [ˈʃelvɪŋ] **1.** *n.* raf (malzemesi); **2.** *adj.* eğik, meyilli.
she.nan.i.gan *Am.* F [ʃiˈnænɪgən] *n.* açıkgözlük, dolandırıcılık, dalaverecilik, maskaralık.
shep.herd [ˈʃepəd] **1.** *n.* çoban; **2.** *vb.* otlatmak, çobanlık etm.; rehberlik etm., sevk ve idare etm.; '**shep.herdess** *n.* kadın çoban.
sher.bet [ˈʃɔːbət] *n.* şerbet; karbonatlı limonata, gazoz; dondurma.
sher.iff [ˈʃerif] *n.* şerif; (*ilçe veya bucakta*) polis müdürü.
sher.ry [ˈʃeri] *n.* beyaz İspanyol şarabı.
shew *rare* [ʃəu] = **show**.
shib.bo.leth [ˈʃibələθ] *n.* tanıtma işareti, parola; artık fazla anlamı olmayan eski deyim *veya* âdet.
shield [ʃiːld] **1.** *n.* kalkan; siper, koruyucu şey; **2.** *v/t.* korumak, himaye etm. (**from** -*den*); '**shield.less** *adj.* koru-

masız, himayesiz.

shift [ʃift] **1.** *n.* değiş(tir)me; nöbet; geçici çare; önlem; hile, desise; çalışma grubu, iş devresi, vardiya, posta; taşınma; *make ~* çaresini bulmak (*to -e*); işin içinden sıyrılmak (*with; without*); **2.** *v/t.* yerini değiştirmek; NAUT dümen kırmak; bir yerden başka bir yere aktarmak; başka yere nakletmek (*yer, sahne*), yerini değiştirmek; MOT vites değiştirmek; (*işletme*) başka işler için ayarlamak (*to -e*); *v/i.* değişmek, başkalaşmak; (*rüzgâr*) dönmek; NAUT (safra) fazla gelmek; işin içinden sıyrılmak, çare bulmak; *~ for o.s.* başının çaresine bakmak, *k-ni* geçindirmek, kendi işine bakmak; '**shift.ing** ☐ değisken, değisir; *~ sands pl.* bataklık kumu; '**shift.less** ☐ biçare, çaresiz; *fig.* beceriksiz, uyuşuk, sünepe; '**shift.y** ☐ hilekâr, kurnaz, pişkin.

shil.ling [ʃiliŋ] *n.* şilin, eski İngiliz gümüş parası; *cut off with a ~* mirastan yoksun bırakmak.

shil.ly-shal.ly [ʃiliʃæli] *adj.* kararsız, mütereddit.

shim.mer [ʃimə] *v/i.* parıldamak, pırıldamak, hafif ışık salmak.

shin [ʃin] **1.** *a. ~-bone* n. incik kemiği; **2.** *vb. ~ up* tırmanmak.

shin.dy F [ʃindi] *n.* gürültü, patırdı, şamata, arbede, yaygara.

shine [ʃain] **1.** *n.* parlaklık, ışık, ziya; cilâ(lama); *give one's shoes a ~ b-nin* ayakkabılarını boyayıp cilâlamak; *rain of ~* hava nasıl olursa olsun; **2.** *v/i.* parıldamak, ışık vermek; *fig.* parlamak, mükemmel olm.; *v/t.* cilâlamak, parlatmak.

shin.gle[1] [ʃiŋgl] **1.** *n.* çatı padavrası, ince tahta, tahta kiremit; *Am.* F levha, tabela; **2.** *v/t.* çatıyı padavra ile kaplamak; kısa kesmek (*saç*).

shin.gle[2] F [_] *n.* çakıl(lı sahil).

shin.gles MED [ʃiŋglz] *n. pl.* zona (hastalığı).

shin.gly [ʃiŋgli] *adj.* çakıllı, çakıl...

shin.y ☐ [ʃaini] parlak, cilâlı; açık, berrak.

ship [ʃip] **1.** *n.* gemi, vapur; *Am.* F uçak; *~'s company* gemi mürettebatı; **2.** *v/t.* gemiye yüklemek; gemiyle sevketmek, yollamak; yandan su almak (*gemi*); *~ the oars* kürekleri yerine takmak; *~ a sea* dalga yemek (*gemi*); *v/i.* gemi hizmetine yazılmak; gemiye binmek; '**~-board: on ~** NAUT gemide

'**~-brok.er** *n.* gemi simsarı; deniz sigortası acentası; '**~-build.er** *n.* gemi yapıcısı; '**~-build.ing** *n.* gemi yapımı, gemi inşaatı; '**~-ca.nal** *n.* yapay gemi kanalı; '**~-chan.dler** *n.* gemi levazımatı satan kimse; '**~-chandler.y** *n.* gemi levazımatı *veya* kumanyası; '**~.load** *n.* kargo, gemi hamulesi *veya* yükü; '**ship.ment** *n.* gemiye yükleme; yüklenen eşya, yük, kargo, hamule; '**ship-own.er** *n.* armatör, gemi sahibi; '**ship-per** *n.* gemiye yüklenen *veya* yükleten kimse, ihracatçı.

ship.ping [ʃipiŋ] **1.** *n.* gemiye yükleme; filo, donanma; tonaj; gemicilik, gemi trafiği; gemi ile mal taşımacılığı, deniz nakliyesi; **2.** *adj.* gemilere *veya* gemiciliğe ait, gemi...; deniz...; '**~-a.gent** *n.* deniz nakliyecisi, gemicilik şirketi (*veya* temsilciliği); '**~-of.fice** *n.* sevkiyat bürosu, nakliye şirketi, deniz taşımacılığı bürosu.

ship...: '**~.shape** *adj.* temiz ve düzenli; '**~-way** *n.* gemi yapı kızağı; '**~.wreck 1.** *n.* deniz kazası; gemi enkazı; **2.** *v/t.* karaya oturmak; *be ~ed* kazaya uğramak; '**~.wrecked** *adj.* kazazede; batık; '**~.wright** *n.* tersane işçisi; '**~.yard** *n.* tersane.

shire [ʃaiə, *in compound word* ...ʃiə] *n.* kontluk; *~ horse* bir tür İngiliz kadanası.

shirk [ʃəːk] *vb.* kaçınmak *-den*, yan çizmek, kaytarmak, atlatmak; '**shirk.er** *n.* atlatan, yan çizen kimse, kaytarıcı.

shirt [ʃəːt] *n.* gömlek; *a. ~-waist Am.* gömlek şeklinde blûz; *keep one's ~ on sl.* soğukkanlılığını kaybetmemek; '**shirt.ing** *n.* COM gömleklik (*kumaş*); '**shirt-sleeve** *n.* gömlek kolu; **2.** *adj.* kollu; *~ diplomacy part. Am.* açık diplomasi; '**shirt.y** *adj. sl.* hiddetli, şiddetli, kızgın ve kaba.

shiv.er[1] [ʃivə] **1.** *n.* ufak parça, kıymık; *break to ~s* **2.** *v/t. & v/i.* ufak parçalara böl(ün)mek).

shiv.er[2] [_] **1.** *n.* titreme, heyecan; *the ~s pl.* hararet, humma; ürperme; *it gives me the ~s* tüylerimi ürpertiyor; **2.** *v/i.* titremek, (tüyleri) ürpermek; soğuktan titremek; *~ing fit* nöbet titremesi; '**shiv.er.y** *adj.* titrek; tüyler ürpertici.

shoal[1] [ʃəul] **1.** *n.* oğul, küme, kalabalık, sürü (*balık; a. fig.*); **2.** *vb.* bir araya toplanmak, sürü oluşturmak (*balık*).

shoal² [-] **1.** *n.* sığlık yer, resif; **2.** *vb.* sığlaş(tır)mak; **3.** = 'shoal.y *adj.* sığ, kumsal.

shock¹ AGR [ʃɔk] *n.* ekin yığını, dokurcun.

shock² [-] **1.** *n.* sars(ıl)ma, sarsıntı, darbe, vuruş; rezalet, kepazelik, skandal; MED şok, sinir buhranı; elektrik çarpması; **2.** *v/t. & v/i. fig.* kalbi kır(ıl)mak, darıl(t)mak, hatırlı *b-ni* gücendirmek; sars(ıl)mak; iğrendirmek.

shock³ [-] *n.* (*of hair saç*) demet, perçem; kabarık, kıtık gibi saç.

shock...: '~ab.sorb.er *n.* MOT amortisör; '~bri.gade *n.* çarpışma, hücum tugayı; '~proof *adj.* sarsıntıya dayanır; ~thera.py, ~ treat.ment elektroterapi, elektro sokla tedavi.

shock.er *sl.* [ˈʃɔkə] *n.* heyecanlı roman.

shock.ing □ [ˈʃɔkiŋ] korkunç şok etkisi yapan; yakısıksız, müstehcen, iğrenç; kızdırıcı, inciticı, günül kırıcı; tüyler ürpertici.

shod [ʃɔd] *pret. & p.p. of shoe 2.*

shod.dy [ˈʃɔdi] **1.** *n.* kullanılmamış fakat bir kez örülüp sökülerek yeniden örülmüş yün, kumaş tiftiği; *fig.* değersiz seyler, değersiz eser; **2.** *adj.* sahte, taklit, yapay, suni; bavağı, değersiz, fena.

shoe [ʃuː] **1.** *n.* kundura, ayakkabı; nal; tekerlek çarığı; fren balatası; **2.** (*irr.*) *vb.* ayakkabı giydirmek; nallamak, nal çakmak; '~black *n.* lostracı, ayakkabı boyacısı; '~black.ing *n.* boyama, parlatma (*ayakkabı*); '~horn *n.* ayakkabı çekeceği, kerata; '~lace *n.* ayakkabı bağı; '~mak.er *n.* kunduracı, ayakkabıcı; '~string *n.* ayakkabı bağı; **on a** ~ F çok az parayla.

shone [ʃɔn] *pret. & p.p. of shine 2.*

shoo [ʃuː] *vb.* korkutmak, ürkütmek, kışkışlamak (*kuş, çocuk vs.*).

shook [ʃuk] *pret. of shake 1.*

shoot [ʃuːt] **1.** *n. fig.* atım, atış; av (partisi); av alanı; AGR filiz, sürgün; **2.** (*irr.*) *v/t.* ateş etm., atış yapmak, ateşlemek; atmak, fırlatmak; silahla vurmak, öldürmek; *film:* filme almak; (*resim*) çekmek; kurşunla delmek; BOT sürmek, filizlenmek; sürmek (*sürgü, mandal*); boşaltmak, dökmek (*çöp, kamyon*); yuvarlamak (*fıçı vs.*); MED enjekte etm.; *v/i.* ateş etm. (**at** *-e*); zonklamak, sancımak (*uzuv*); bir yerden fırlamak; *a.* ~ **forth** filizlenmek, sürmek; NAUT

fazla gelmek (*safra*); ~ **ahead** ok gibi fırlamak, atılmak; ~ **ahead of** mesafeyi açmak; ~ **down** düşürmek; ~ **up** hızla büyümek, yükselmek; 'shoot.er *n.* nişancı; avcı.

shoot.ing [ˈʃuːtiŋ] **1.** *n.* atış; avcılık (hukuku), düzensiz silah atma; *film:* filme alma; **2.** *adj.* zonklayan (*uzuv*); '~box *n.* avcı kulübesi; '~brake *n.* kaptıkaçtı, pikap (*araba*); '~gal.ler.y *n.* poligon, atış meydanı; (*lunapark*) atış barakası; '~range *n.* poligon; ~ **star** akanyıldız, göktaşı; '~war *n.* sıcak savaş.

shop [ʃɔp] **1.** *n.* dükkân, mağaza; atelye, iş yeri, fabrika; **set up** ~ dükkân açmak, yeni bir iş kurmak; **talk** ~ iş konusunda konuşmak; **2.** *vb. mst go ~ping* alış-veriş yapmak, satın almak; ~a.hol.ic [ˈʃɔpəˈhɒlık] *n.* alışverişçi hastası kimse; '~as.sist.ant *n.* satıcı tezgâhtar; '~keep.er *n.* dükkâncı, mağaza sahibi; '~lift.er *n.* dükkân hırsızı; '~man *n.* tezgâhtar; 'shop.per *n.* alıcı, müşteri; 'shop.ping *n.* alışveriş (etme); ~ **centre** *Am.* ~ **center** alış-veriş merkezi, büyük çarşı.

shop...: '~soiled *adj.* uzun süre dükkânda kalıp ellenmekten hasar görmüş *veya* kirlenmiş *veya* vitrinde bekletilmiş (*mal*); '~'stew.ard *n.* işyeri temsilcisi; '~walk.er *n.* mağazada çalışanlara ve alıcılara yardım eden görevli; '~'window *n.* vitrin.

shore¹ [ʃɔː] *n.* sahil, kıyı, yaka; **on** ~ karada.

shore² [-] **1.** *n.* destek, istinat, payanda; **2.** *vb.:* ~ **up** payanda vurmak, desteklemek.

shore...: '~line *n.* kıyı şeridi; '~ward ['.wəd] *adv.* kıyıya doğru.

shorn [ʃɔːn] *p.p. of shear 1.;* ~ **of** yoksun *-den.*

short [ʃɔːt] **1.** *adj.* kısa; bodur, kısa boylu; az, eksik, yetersiz; iyi pişmiş, gevrek, yumuşak (*çörek, pasta vs.*); çapaklı, karıncalı (*metal*); kaba, nezaketsiz (*cevap*); COM kısa vadeli; *s.* **circuit;** ~ **wave** radyo: kısa dalga; **in** ~ sözün kısası, kısaca; ~ **of** *-si* eksik; **nothing** ~ **of** *-den* başka bir şey değil; sırf, hepsi; doğrudan doğruya; ~ **of London** Londra'ya varmadan az önce; **come** *veya* **fall** ~ **of** yetmemek, erişememek, ulaşamamak; **cut** ~ birden kesmek, bşe ara vermek; kısa kesmek; **fall** *veya* **run** ~ yetmemek, tükenmek, kıtlaşmak; **stop** ~ **of** bşe ara vermek; **2.** *n.*

GR yarı sesli; kısa hece; kısa metrajlı film; ELECT kontak, kısa devre; s. **shorts**; ~ **circuit**, 'short.age n. yokluk, kıtlık, eksiklik.

short…: '~.cake n. üstüne ezilmiş meyve dökülmüş kek; '~'cir.cuit n. ELECT kısa devre; '~'com.ing n. kusur; noksan, eksiklik; ~ cut kestirme yol; '~'dated adj. COM kısa vadeli; 'short-en v/t. & v/i. kısal(t)mak; 'short.en-ing n. unla karıştırılan yağ.

short…: '~.fall n. açık, eksik; '~.hand n. stnenografi; ~ **typist** steno daktilo; '~'hand.ed adj. yardımcısı az; '~'lived adj. kısa ömürlü; 'short.ly adv. kısaca, sözün kısası; birazdan, yakında; 'shortness n. kısalık, eksiklik.

shorts [ʃɔːts] n. pl. şort, kısa pantolon, dizlik, külot, kispet.

short…: '~'sight.ed adj. miyop; fig. kısa görüşlü; '~'tem.pered adj. çabuk kızan, öfkeli; '~-term adj. kısa vadeli; '~-wave adj. radyo: kısa dalga…; '~'wind.ed adj. tık nefes, nefes darlığı olan.

shot[1] [ʃɔt] **1.** pret. & p.p. of **shoot 2**; **2.** adj. şanjan, yanardöner (kumaş).

shot[2] [-] n. atış, atım; gülle, küre, top; erim, menzil; girişim; tahmin; a. **small** ~ av saçması; pl. mst ~ saçma tanesi; nişancı, avcı; spor: vuruş (bilardo); şut; PHOT, film: fotoğraf, resim, film; MED şırınga, iğne; sl. bir yudum içki; sl. cinsel birleşme, boşalma; **have a** ~ **at** bşi bir kez denemek, şansını denemek; **not by a long** ~ F katiyen, hiç; **within (out of)** ~ atış menzili içinde (dışında); **like a** ~ F mermi gibi; **big** ~ F önemli şahıs, kodaman, nüfuzlu kimse, **make a bad** ~ hedefi kaçırmak; fig. yanlış tahmin etm.; '~.gun n. av tüfeği, çifte; ~ **marriage** Am. F zorunlu evlilik; '~-proof adj. mermi işlemez.

shot.ten her.ring [ʃɔtn'heriŋ] n. yumurtlamış ringa balığı.

should [ʃud] pret. of **shall**.

shoul.der ['ʃəuldə] **1.** n. omuz (a. hayvanların); fig. destek; omuza benzer çıkıntı; dağ kolu (veya yamacı); kürek eti; **give s.o. the cold** ~ bne soğuk davranmak; **put one's** ~ **to the wheel** çok çaba göstermek, omuz vermek; **rub** ~s **with** arkadaşlık etm., temas etm. ile; ~ **to** ~ omuz omuza, birlikte; **2.** vb. omuzlamak; MIL omuz vurmak, yüklenmek; ~ **one's way** yol açmak;

'~-blade n. ANAT kürek kemiği; '~-strap n. MIL apolet; omuz askısı (elbise).

shout [ʃaut] **1.** n. bağırma, nida, seslenme, çığlık; **2.** v/t. & v/i. bağırmak, seslenmek, haykırmak, çağırmak, sevinç nidaları çıkarmak, yaygara koparmak.

shove [ʃʌv] **1.** n. itme, kakma, dürtme; **2.** vb. itmek, dürtmek, sürmek, itip kakmak.

shov.el ['ʃʌvl] **1.** n. kürek, faraş; **2.** vb. kürelemek, kürekle alıp atmak; '~-board n. gemide oynanan bir tür oyun.

show [ʃəu] **1.** (irr.) v/t. göstermek; işaret etm.; sergilemek; göstermek (lûtuf, tenezzül); tanıtlamak; kanıtlamak; anlatmak; öğretmek; seyrettirmek; ~ **forth** göstermek, teşhir etm.; ~ **in** içeri sokmak; ~ **out** uğurlamak, kapıya kadar geçirmek; ~ **round** dolaştırmak, gezdirmek; ~ **up** meydana çıkarmak, maskesini düşürmek; v/i. a. ~ **up** görünmek, gözükmek; ~ **off** göstermek; övünmek, palavracılık etm., k-ni … gibi göstermek; **2.** n. gösteriş, gösterme; görünüş; sergi, teşhir; THEAT temsil, oyun, gösteri; sl. iş, konu, girişim; ~ **of hands** el kaldırarak yapılan oylama; **dumb** ~ pandomima; **on** ~ sergilenmekte; **run the** ~ sl. dükkân, iş vs. işletmek, idare etm.; ~ **busi.ness** eğlence sanayii, tiyatroculuk vs.; '~-card n. ticarî ilân, afiş, pankart; '~-case n. küçük vitrin; '~-down n. iskambilde eldeki kâğıtları açma, kozları ortaya koyma (a. fig.); fig. güç denemesi.

show.er ['ʃauə] **1.** n. sağanak; duş; fig. dolgunluk, bolluk, çokluk; **2.** v/i. sağanak halinde yağmak (a. fig.), dökülmek, akmak; v/t. bol vermek, yağdırmak; dökmek, üstünden aşağı akıtmak; '~-bath ['~bɑːθ] n. duş; 'show-er.y adj. yağmurlu; yağmur…

show.i.ness ['ʃəuinis] n. gösteriş, debdebe, tantana saltanat; 'show.man n. oyun, müzikal vs. hazırlayan kimse; şovmen, seyirciyi eğlendiren, oyalayan kimse; sirk, eğlence yeri vs. müdürü; 'showman.ship n. seyircinin ilgisini çekme sanatı; **shown** [ʃəun] p.p. of **show 1**; 'show-place n. görülmeye değer olan yer; 'show-room n. sergi salonu; 'show-window n. vitrin; 'show.y □ gösterişli, mükemmel, göze çarpan, göz alıcı.

shrank [ʃræŋk] *pret. of* **shrink**.

shrap.nel MIL ['ʃræpnl] *n.* şarapnel.

shred [ʃred] **1.** *n.* dilim, ufak kesilmiş *veya* yırtılmış parça, kırpıntı, paçavra (*a. fig.*); **2.** (*irr.*) *v/t.* parçalamak, çekip yırtmak, tarazlamak.

shrew [ʃruː] *n.* kavgacı, şirret kadın; *a.* ~-**mouse** ZOO sivri burunlu fare, soreks.

shrewd □ [ʃruːd] kurnaz, becerikli, zeki; 'shrewd.ness *n.* kurnazlık, açıkgözlük, cin fikirlilik.

shrew.ish □ ['ʃruːiʃ] kavgacı, huysuz, şirret.

shriek [ʃriːk] **1.** *n.* feryat, yaygara, çığlık; **2.** *vb.* çığlık koparmak, cıyaklamak, haykırmak.

shríke ORN [ʃraik] *n.* örümcekkuşu.

shrill [ʃril] **1.** □ keskin sesli, kulakları tırmalayan; **2.** *vb.* acı ve tiz sesle haykırmak.

shrímp ZOO [ʃrimp] *n.* karides, deniz tekesi; *fig.* bücür, cüce, çelimsiz kimse.

shrine [ʃrain] *n.* kutsal emanetler mahfazası; türbe.

shrink [ʃriŋk] (*irr.*) *v/i.* küçülmek, büzülmek, çekmek, daralmak (*kumaş*); geri çekilmek; *a.* ~ **back** ürkerek gerilemek (**from, at** *-den*); *v/t.* daraltmak, büzmek; MEC çektirmek; 'shrink.age *n.* çekme payı, fire, daralma; *fig.* kıymetten düşme, inme, düşüş.

shriv.el ['ʃrivl] *vb. a.* ~ **up** büzülmek, buruşmak, pörsümek; *fig.* içi geçmek; âciz duruma düşmek.

shroud[1] [ʃraud] **1.** *n.* kefen; tabut örtüsü; *fig.* örtü. **2.** *v/t.* kefenlemek, kefene sarmak; *fig.* sarmak, örtmek.

shroud[2] NAUT [-] *n.* çarmık, ana direkleri ve gabya çubuklarını tutan halatlar; *mst* ~**s** *pl.* çarmıklar.

Shrove.tide ['ʃrəuvtaid] *n.* Hıristiyanlarda büyük perhizden önce gelen süre, et kesimi, apukurya; **Shrove Tuesday** büyük perhizin arife günü.

shrub [ʃrʌb] *n.* çalı, küçük ağaç, funda; 'shrub.ber.y *n.* çalılık, fundalık; 'shrub.by *adj.* çalı gibi; çalılık…

shrug [ʃrʌg] **1.** *vb.* omuz silkmek; ~ **s.th. off** bşe aldırmamak, boşvermek; **2.** *n.* omuz silkme.

shrunk [ʃrʌŋk] *p.p. of* **shrink**, 'shrunk.en *adj.* daral(tıl)mış, çekmiş; çökmüş (*yanak*).

shuck *Am.* [ʃʌk] **1.** *n.* kabuk, kılıf, zarf; ~**s!** F boş lâf!, saçma!, zırva!; **2.** *vb.* kabuğunu vs. çıkarmak, soymak.

shud.der ['ʃʌdə] **1.** *v/i.* ürpermek, titremek (*at*); **2.** *n.* titreme, ürperti.

shuf.fle ['ʃʌfl] **1.** *v/t. & v/i.* karıştırmak, karman çorman etm.; karıştırmak, karmak (*oyun kâğıdı*); yer değiştirmek, elden ele dolaştırmak; kaçamaklı cevap vermek, sözü değiştirmek, ağız yapmak; ayak sürümek; başından atmak, defetmek; ~ **away** güçlükle ve acemice ilerlemek; ~ **off** üstünden atmak (*sorumluluk*); ~ **through one's work** kötü iş görmek; **2.** *n.* kırıştırma (*oyun kâğıdı*); ayak sürüme; bu tür bir dans; POL düzenleme (*kabinede*); 'shuffler *n.* karıştıran kimse (*kâğıt*); ağız değiştiren kimse, dubaracı; 'shuf.fling □ kaçamaklı; hilekâr.

shun [ʃʌn] *v/t.* bşden sakınmak, kaçınmak.

shunt [ʃʌnt] **1.** *n.* RAIL manevra; RAIL makas; ELECT paralel devre; **2.** *vb.* RAIL yan yola geçirmek, manevra yapmak, makas değiştirmek, yolunu değiştirmek; ELECT paralel bağlamak, akımın bir kısmını başka kablodan geçirmek; *fig.* b-ni yerinden oynatmak, b-nin yerini değiştirmek; 'shunt.er *n.* RAIL manevracı; 'shunt.ing sta.tion *n.* RAIL manevra istasyonu.

shut [ʃʌt] (*irr.*) *v/t.* kapa(t)mak; ~ **one's eyes** göz yummak, müsamaha etm. *-e*; ~ **down** tatil etm., faaliyeti durdurmak, kapamak (*iş yeri*); ~ **in** kapamak, kilitlemek; sıkıştırmak (*parmak*); ~ **out** dışarıda bırakmak; ~ **up** kapamak, kilitlemek; ~ **up shop** dükkânı kapamak, işten vazgeçmek; *v/i.* kapanmak; ~ **up!** F sus!; kapat çaneni!; '~.**down** *n.* işin tatil olması, faaliyetin durması; '~.**out** *n. spor:* sayı vermeden mağlûp etme; 'shutter *n.* kepenk, panjur; PHOT obtüratör, kapak; **put up the ~s** kepenkleri indirmek, dükkânı kapatmak; **rolling ~** kepenk.

shut.tle ['ʃʌt] **1.** *n.* mekik (*a. dikiş makinesinde*); RAIL kısa mesafede mekik dokuyan tren servisi; ~ **train** karşılıklı sefer yapan tren; **2.** *vb.* mekik dokumak, mekik gibi işlemek; karşılıklı sefer yapmak; '~.**cock** *n.* raketle oynanan ucu tüylü mantar banminton topu *veya* bu topla oynanan oyun.

shy[1] [ʃai] **1.** □ korkak, ürkek, çekingen, mahçup, utangaç; **be** *veya* **fight ~ of** ürkmek, çekinmek *-den veya* sakınmak *-den*; **2.** *v/i.* bşden, bden çekinmek, korkmak, ürkmek (*at*).

shy² F [_] **1.** *v/t.* fırlatmak, atmak; **2.** *n.* atış, fırlatma; **have a ~ at** *bş* üzerinde tecrübe yapmak, bir denemek.

shy.ness ['ʃainis] *n.* çekingenlik, ürkeklik, korkaklık.

shy.ster *part Am. sl.* ['ʃaistə] *n.* iyi şöhreti olmayan avukat, hileli iş yürüten kimse.

Si.a.mese [saiə'miːz] **1.** *adj.* Siyamlı; Siyam diline ait; **2.** *n.* Siyam halkı *veya* dili.

Si.be.ri.an [sai'biəriən] **1.** *adj.* Sibiryalı; **2.** *n.* Sibiryalı kimse.

sib.i.lant ['sibilənt] **1.** □ ıslık gibi, vızıltılı; **2.** *n.* GR ıslık gibi ses veren harf (*s, z, ş, j*).

sib.yl ['sibil] *n.* eski zamanda falcı, kâhin kadın; **sib'yl.line** [_lain] *adj.* fala, kehanete ait.

Si.cil.ian [si'siljən] **1.** *adj.* Sicilyalı; **2.** *n.* Sicilyalı kimse.

sick [sik] *adj.* hasta, keyfisiz (**of, with**); midesi bulanmış; bıkmış, bezmiş (**of** -*den*); **be ~ for** *bşin* hasretini çekmek, *bş* için yanıp tutuşmak; **be ~ of** bıkmak, tiksinmek, usanmak; **go~, report ~** *k-ni* hasta diye bildirmek; '**~bed** *n.* hasta yatağı; '**~ben.e.fit** *n.* hastalık parası; '**sick.en** *v/i.* hastalanmak, hastalıklı (*veya* dertli) olm.; **~ at** *bşden* tiksinmek, nefret etm.; **~ of** bıkıp usanmak, gına gelmek -*den*; *v/t.* hasta etm.; bıktırmak, usandırmak.

sick.le ['sikl] *n.* orak.

sick-leave ['sikliːv] *n.* hastalık izni; '**sickly** *adj.* hastalıklı, dertli; zayıf bünyeli, hassas; solgun; gayrisıhhi (*iklim*); tiksindirici, iğrenç (*koku vs.*); bitkin, yorgun; '**sick.ness** *n.* hastalık; kusma, mide bulantısı.

side [said] **1.** *n. com.* yan, taraf; sahil, kıyı, konar; *spor*: takım, taraf; grup, hizip; yön; **~ by ~** yan yana; *fig.* yanıbaşında; **by one's ~** *b-nin* tarafında; **~ by ~ with** yanında -*in*, ... ile beraber; **at** *veya* **by s.o.'s ~** *b-nin* yanında; **put on ~** F caka satmak, tafra satmak; **2.** *adj.* yan..., ikinci derecede, ... den başka; **3.** *vb.* taraf tutmak, desteklemek (**with, against**); '**~arms** *n. pl.* MIL kasatura, kılıç vs. gibi yana takılan silahlar; '**~board** *n.* büfe; '**~car** *n.* MOT motosiklet yan arabası, sepet; '**sid.ed** *comb.* ... taraflı, cepheli; çevrili. **side...:** '**~face** *n.* yandan görünüş, profil; **~ is.sue** önemsiz, ikincil soru *veya*

konu; '**~light** *n.* borda feneri; yan pencere; sinyal lambaları; *fig.* önemsiz fakat bir konuyu aydınlatan açıklama; '**~line** *n.* RAIL tali hat; ek görev; *spor*: kenar çizgisi; '**~long 1.** *adv.* yan (tarafa), yandan; **2.** *adj.* yan, kenardan, meyilli; *fig.* gizli, saklı.

si.de.re.al AST [sai'diəriəl] *adj.* yıldızlarla ilgili, yıldızlarla hesaplanan.

side...: '**~sad.dle** *n.* kadın eyeri; '**~slip** *v/i.* AVIA yan inişi yapmak; MOT patinaj yapmak; **sides.man** ['_zmən] *n.* Anglikan kilisesinde mütevelli yardımcısı.

side...: '**~split.ting** *adj.* kahkahaya boğan, çok komik; '**~step 1.** *n.* yana atılan adım; kaçınma, yan çizme; **2.** *vb.* yana kaçmak, yan çizmek, sorumluluktan kaçmak; '**~stroke** *n.* yan yüzme; '**~track 1.** *n.* RAIL yan hat; **2.** *v/t.* yan hatta geçirmek; *part. Am. fig.* önemli ve faydalı bir şeyi geri bıraktırıp önemsiz bir şeyle uğraştırmak; '**~walk** *n. part. Am.* yaya kaldırımı; **side.ward** ['_wəd] **1.** *adj.* yana doğru olan, yan; **2.** *adv.* = **side-wards** ['_wədz], '**side.ways**, '**side.wise** yan tarafa, yana doğru.

sid.ing RAIL ['saidiŋ] *n.* yan hat, içtinap durağı.

si.dle ['saidl] *vb.* yan yan gitmek.

SIDS ['esaidiː'es] (= **sudden infant death syndrome**) ani çocuk ölümü sendromu.

siege [siːdʒ] *n.* kuşatma, muhasara; **lay ~ to** kuşatmak, sarmak, ele geçirmeye çalışmak.

si.er.ra ['siərə] *n.* zirveli dağ silsilesi.

sieve [siv] **1.** *n.* kalbur, elek; **2.** *v/t.* elemek, kalburdan geçirmek.

sift [sift] *v/t.* kalburdan geçirmek, elemek; *fig.* incelemek; ayırmak.

sift.er ['siftə] *n.* üstü delikli un, şeker vs. kabı (*tuzluk, şekerlik vs.*).

sigh [sai] **1.** *n.* iç çekme; **2.** *v/i.* iç çekmek; *bş* için yanıp tutuşmak, hasret kalmak (**for, after** -*e*).

sight [sait] **1.** *n.* görme, görüm, görüş; *fig.* bakış, nazar; manzara; görünüş, temaşa; nisangâh; F büyük miktar, birçok; çokluk; **~** *pl.* gezip görülecek yerler; **second ~** gaipten haber verme, kehanet; **at** *veya* **on ~** görür görmez, derhal, görü(lü)nce; MUS notaya bakarak; COM ibrazında, gösterilince; **catch ~ of** görüvermek, gözüne ilişmek; **lose ~ of** gözden kaybetmek, unutmak;

within ~ göz önünde, gözle görünür; **out of** ~ gözden uzak; çok yüksek, fahiş; **take**~ nişan almak; **not by a long** ~ asla, hiç; **know by** ~ yüzünden tanımak, göz aşinalığı olm.; **2.** *vb.* görmek; nişan almak (**along**); 'sight.ed *adj.* görebilen, ... görülen; 'sight.ing-line *n.* nişan hattı; 'sight.less *adj.* kör, göremeyen; 'sight.li.ness *adj.* güzellik, yakışıklılık, göze hitap etme; 'sight.ly *adj.* güzel, yüzüne bakılır, kayda değer.

sight...: '~.see.ing *n.* seyredecek yerleri görmeğe gitme, gezme; '~.se.er *n.* turist; '~-sing.ing *n.* MUS notaya bakarak şarkı söyleme.

sign [sain] **1.** *n.* işaret, ikaz, ima, alâmet; iz, belirti; levha, trafik işaret levhası; AST on iki burçtan biri; **in** ~ **of** ... işareti olarak; **2.** *v/i.* işaret vermek; ~ **on** (**off**) *radyo*: yayına başlamak *veya* yayını bitirmek; *v/t.* imzalamak; işaret etm. *-e*; ~ **on** mukavele ile taahhüt altına al(ın)-mak.

sig.nal ['signl] **1.** *n.* işaret, sinyal; ihtar, ikaz; ~**s** *pl.* MIL parola; **busy** ~ TELEPH meşgul işareti; **2.** □ kayda değer, dikkate değer, fevkalâde, harikulâde; **3.** *vb.* işaretle bildirmek, işaret etm.; *b-ne bşi* bildirmek, haber vermek; '~-box *n.*, RAIL manevra tertibatı *veya* merkezi; **sig.nalize** ['~nəlaiz] *v/t.* dikkati çekerek bildirmek; şöhret kazandırmak, nişan vermek; = **signal 3.**

sig.na.to.ry ['signətəri] **1.** *n.* imza sahibi, imza eden kimse; **2.** *adj.* imzalayan; **powers** ~ **to an agreement** devletler arası anlaşmaları imzalayanlar.

sig.na.ture ['signitʃə] *n.* imza; marka, damga, işaret (*a.* TYP, MUS, COM); ~ **tune** *radyo*: tanıtma müziği.

sign.board ['sainbɔːd] *n.* tabela, afiş, yafta; 'sign.er *n.* imza sahibi.

sig.net ['signit] *n.* mühür, damga; '~-ring *n.* mühür yüzüğü.

sig.nif.i.cance, sig.nif.i.can.cy [sig-'nifikəns(i)] *n.* mana, anlam; önem; **sig'nifi.cant** □ anlamlı, manidar; önemli; karakteristik (**of**); sig.ni.fi-'ca.tion *n.* anlam, mana; **sig'nif.i.ca-tive** [-kətiv] *adj.* anlamlı, karakteristik (**of**), manidar, *bş* anlatan, ifade eden.

sig.ni.fy ['signifai] *vb.* belirtmek, ifade etm., işaretle anlatmak; delâlet etm. *-e*, ... anlamına gelmek; **it does not** ~ önemi yok, farketmez.

si.gnor ['siːnjɔː] *n.* bay, efendi, İtalyanların kullandığı bir ünvan; **si'gnor.a**

[_.rə] *n.* bayan, hanım (*evli*); **si.gno.ri.na** [_'riːnə] *n.* matmazel, bayan, genç kızlara verilen unvan.

sign...: '~-paint.er *n.* tabelacı, levhacı; '~.post *n.* yol gösteren levha, işaret direği.

si.lage ['sailidʒ] *n.* siloda muhafaza olunan hayvan yemi, ot vs.

si.lence ['sailəns] **1.** *n.* sessizlik, sükut, durgunluk, huzur; susma, *bşden* bahsetmeme; ~**!** sus(unuz)!; **put** *veya* **re-duce to** ~ = **2.** *v/t.* susturmak, sesini kesmek; 'si.lenc.er *n.* MEC ses azaltıcı, susturucu; MOT egzoz borusuna takılan susturucu.

si.lent □ ['sailənt] sessiz, sakin; suskun, susan, sesi çıkmaz; sessiz (*harf*); ~ **film** sessiz film; ~ **partner** *part. Am.* COM hususi şerik, komanditer.

Si.le.sian [sai'liːzjən] **1.** *adj.* Silezyalı; **2.** *n.* Silezyalı kimse.

sil.hou.ette [silu:'et] **1.** *n.* siluet, gölge (resim); **2.** **be** ~**d against** iyice belirmek, kontrast teşkil etm.

sil.i.ca CHEM ['silikə] *n.* silis(li toprak); **sil.icat.ed** ['-keitid] *adj.* silisit asitli; **si'liceous** [-ʃəs] *adj.* silisli; **sil.i.con** ['-kən] *n.* silisyum; **sil.i.cone** ['-kəun] *n.* silikon; **sil.i.co.sis** MED [-'kəusis] *n.* silis tozu teneffüs etmekten oluşan bir tür akciğer hastalığı.

silk [silk] **1.** *n.* ipek; JUR ipek cüppe; kral(içe) avukatı; ipeğe benzer mısır püskülü; **take** ~ kral(içe) avukatı olm.; **2.** *adj.* ipekli, ipek...; **silk.en** □ ipekli; *s. silky:* 'silk.i.ness *n.* ipek gibi oluş; yumuşak oluş; 'silk-'stock.ing *n. Am.* kibar, aristokrat, soylu, asil; '~.worm *n.* ipekböceği; 'silk.y □ ipek gibi; yumuşacık.

sill [sil] *n.* eşik, pencere tahtası; denizlik.

sil.li.ness ['silinis] *n.* ahmaklık; saçma şey, herze.

sil.ly □ ['sili] ahmak, budala, aptal, bön; saçma, gülünç; ~ **season** (*gazete*) haber bakımından kısır dönem.

si.lo ['sailəu] *n.* silo.

silt [silt] **1.** *n.* çamur, balçık, mil; **2.** *vb.* *mst* ~ **up** çamur *veya* mille dol(dur)-mak.

sil.ver ['silvə] **1.** *n.* gümüş (*para, sofra takımı vs.*); **2.** *adj.* gümüşten, gümüş kaplı; gümüş gibi; gümüş...; **3.** *vb.* gümüş kaplamak *-e*; gümüş gibi parla(t)-mak; '~'plate *n.* MEC gümüş kaplama; '~.ware *n. Am.* gümüş eşya, gümüş sofra takımı; 'sil.ver.y adj. gümüş gibi, parlak; zoo & вот gümüş gibi parlak...; yumuşak ve berrak (ses).

sim.i.lar □ ['similə] benzer (to -e), gibi, ... vari; sim.i.lar.i.ty [ˌ-'læriti] n. benzerlik, benzeşlik.

sim.i.le ['simili] n. mecaz, teşbih, kıyas, benzetme.

si.mil.i.tude [si'militjuːd] n. benzerlik, benzeşme; tam benzeri; kıyas, teşbih, mecaz, benzetme.

sim.mer ['simə] v/t. & v/i. yavaş yavaş kayna(t)mak; fig. galeyana getirmek veya gelmek (duygu); ~ down yatışmak, sakinleşmek.

Si.mon ['saimən] n. on iki havariden biri; the real ~ Pure F hakikisi; simple ~ F budala, ahmak; si.mo.ny ['ˌ-ni] n. kilise görev veya donatımının alım satımı.

si.moom METEOR [si'muːm] n. samyeli.

sim.per ['simpə] 1. n. aptalca sırıtma; 2. v/i. aptal aptal sırıtmak.

sim.ple □ ['simpl] basit, sade, gösterişsiz, alçak gönüllü; kolay; bölünmeyen, tek; katışıksız, saf; doğal, yapmacıksız; aptal, budala, safdil; önemsiz, basit (rütbe, sınıf); '~'heart.ed, '~'mind-ed adj. safdil, temiz yürekli, kolay kanan; simple.ton ['ˌ-tən] n. ahmak, budala.

sim.plic.i.ty [sim'plisiti] n. sadelik, berraklık, açıklık; saflık, budalalık; temiz yüreklilik, safdillik; sim.pli.fi.ca.tion [ˌ-fi'keiʃən] n. basitleştirme, sadeleştirme; basitleşme; sim.pli.fy ['ˌ-fai] v/t. kolaylaştırmak, sadeleştirmek.

sim.ply ['simpli] adv. basit olarak (s. simple); sadece, sırf, ancak; doğrusu, gerçekten.

sim.u.late ['simjuleit] v/t. yalandan yapmak, ... gibi görünmek; taklit etm., benzetmek; ... taslamak; sim.u-'la.tion n. taklit; sahte tavır, yapmacık; 'sim.u.la.tor n. herhangi bir eğitimde o ortamın koşullarını hissettiren cihaz.

si.mul.ta.ne.i.ty [siməltə'niəti] n. aynı zamanda olma, eşzamanlık.

si.mul.ta.ne.ous □ [siməl'teinjəs] aynı zamanda olan, eşzamanlı; si-mul'ta.ne.ousness n. eşzamanlılık, aynı zamanda olma.

sin [sin] 1. n. günah; suç, kabahat; 2. v/i. günah işlemek.

since [sins] 1. prp. -den beri, -den itibaren, olalı, edeli; 2. adv. o zamandan

beri; önce, evvel; long ~ uzun zamandan beri, çok zaman oluyor; how long ~? ne zamandan beri?; a short time ~ geçenlerde; 3. cj. -diğinden beri, olalı, yapalı; madem ki, çünkü, zira.

sin.cere □ [sin'siə] samimî, içten, yalansız, doğal; Yours ~ly saygılarımla (mektup sonunda); sin.cer.i.ty [ˌ-'ser-iti] n. samimiyet, içtenlik, doğruluk.

sine MATH [sain] n. sinüs.

si.ne.cure ['sainikjuə] n. kolay ve iyi maaşlı iş, arpalık.

sin.ew ['sinjuː] n. kiriş, veter; sinir; mst ~s pl. güç, enerji; güçlü kılan şey; 'sin-ew.y adj. kiriş gibi; fig. güçlü, dinç, kuvvetli.

sin.ful □ ['sinful] günahkâr; utanç verici, çok kötü; şerir, fena; 'sin.ful.ness n. günahkâr olma, günah(kârlık).

sing [siŋ] (irr.) v/i. şarkı söylemek; ötmek, şakımak; uğuldamak (rüzgâr); çınlamak (kulak); v/t. söylemek, okumak; ~ out bağırmak, seslenmek; ~ small, ~ another song veya tune süt dökmüş kedi gibi olm., yelkenleri suya indirmek, aşağıdan almak.

singe [sindʒ] v/t. yakmak, ütülemek, alazlamak.

sing.er ['siŋə] n. şarkıcı.

sing.ing ['siŋiŋ] n. şarkı söyleme, şakıma, ırlama; ~ bird ötücü kuş.

sin.gle [siŋgl] 1. □ tek, bir, yalnız, ayrı; tek kişilik, özel; münferit...; bekâr; sade, basit, saf; ~ bill com bono; ~ com-bat teke tek kavga, düello, vuruşma; bookkeeping by ~ entry basit (veya tek taraflı) defter tutma usulü; ~ file tek sıra, birbiri ardına; 2. n. tenis: tekler; tek kişilik oda; gidiş bileti; 3. ~ out seçmek, ayırmak; '~'breast.ed adj. tek sıra düğmeli (ceket vs.); '~'en-gin.ed adj. AVIA tek motorlu; '~'hand.ed adj. tek başına; '~'heart-ed □, '~'mind.ed □ samimî, içten, doğru dürüst; yolundan şaşmayan, tuttuğunu koparan, azimli; '~'line adj. tek hatlı; 'sin.gle-'seat.er n. tek kişilik (uçak); 'sin.gle.stick n. eskrim değneği; kısa kalın sopa; sin.glet ['siŋglit] n. fanila, iç gömleği; sin.gle.ton ['ˌ-tən] n. iskambil: oyun başında oyuncunun elindeki bir renkten tek kâğıt; 'sin.gle-'track adj. tek yönlü; 'sin.gly adv. yalnız, tek başına; tek tek, birer birer.

sing.song ['siŋsɔŋ] n. aynı tonda ve can sıkıcı şarkı söyleme veya konuşma.

sin.gu.lar ['siŋgjulə] **1.** □ yalnız, tek, ayrı; eşsiz, müstesna, fevkalâde; acayip, garip, tuhaf; GR tekil **2.** *n.* GR *a.* ~ *number* tek sayı; tekil sözcük; **sin.gu.lar.i.ty** [‿'læriti] *n.* özellik, hususiyet; tuhaflık; eşsizlik, görülmemişlik.

Sin.ha.lese [siŋhə'li:z] **1.** *adj.* Sri Lankalı, Sri Lanka diline ait; **2.** *n.* Sri Lankalı kimse; Sri Lanka dili.

sin.is.ter □ ['sinistə] uğursuz, meşum; endişe verici; tekin olmayan (*yer*); fesat, kötü.

sink [siŋk] **1.** (*irr.*) *vb.* batmak (*gemi, güneş vs.*); ağır ağır inmek; çökmek; çukurlaşmak; alçalmak, azalmak; dalmak (*uyku*); düşmek (*fiyat*); kötüleşmek, ölüme yaklaşmak (*hasta*); batırmak; daldırmak, gömmek (*into -e*); MIN kazmak, açmak (*kuyu*); yatırmak (*para*); yavaş yavaş ödemek (*borç*); uzlaşmak, yatıştırmak, unutmak (*kavga*); **2.** *n.* fosseptik, lağım çukuru; musluk taşı, bulaşık oluğu; *fig.* bataklık; '**sink.er** *n.* MIN kuyucu, maden işçisi; iskandil, olta *veya* ağ kurşunu; '**sink.ing** *n.* düşüş, batış; MED dermansızlık, zayıflık, halsizlik; ~ *fund* bir borcu ödemek için oluşturulan fon, itfa fonu, amortisman sandığı.

sin.less ['sinlis] *adj.* günahsız, masum, saf.

sin.ner ['sinə] *n.* günahkâr kimse.

Sinn Fein ['ʃin'fein] *n.* bir İrlanda milliyetçi teşkilâtı.

Sin.o... ['sinəu] *comb.* Çin ile ilgili, Çinli; Çin...

sin.u.os.i.ty [sinju'ɔsiti] *n.* yılankavilik, dolaşıklık, eğilip bükülme; kavis, viraj, dönemeç; '**sin.u.ous** □ yılankavi, dolaşık, eğri, çarpık (*a. fig.*), dolambaçlı.

si.nus ANAT ['sainəs] *n.* sinüs; **si.nus.i.tis** [‿'saitis] *n.* sinüzit, sinüs iltihabı.

Sioux [su:] *n.*, *pl.* ~ [su:z] Siyu (*Kuzey Amerika kızılderilileri*).

sip [sip] **1.** *n.* yudum; yudumlama; **2.** *vb.* yudumlamak, azar azar içmek.

si.phon ['saifən] **1.** *n.* sifon, pipet; **2.** *vb.* sifonla su çekmek (*out*); emmek, içine çekmek.

sir [sə:] *n.* bay; beyefendi; efendim; ♀ sör (*bir asalet ünvanı*).

sire ['saiə] *n. mst poet.* baba, peder; cet, ata; zoo bir at, köpek vs.'nin babası; *obs.* haşmetmeap, efendimiz.

si.ren ['saiərən] *n.* canavar düdüğü, siren.

sir.loin ['sə:lɔin] *n.* sığır filetosu.

sir.rah *contp. obs.* ['sirə] herif, adam.

sir.up ['sirəp] *n.* şurup; melâs.

sis F [sis] *n.* **sister'in** kısaltılmış şekli.

sis.al ['saisəl] *n.* sisal keneviri, dayanıklı bir tür kenevir.

sis.kin ORN ['siskin] *n.* karabaşlı iskete.

sis.sy *Am.* ['sisi] *n.* çıtkırıldım, muhallebi çocuğu, hanım evlâdı.

sis.ter ['sistə] *n.* kızkardeş, hemşire; hastabakıcı, hemşire; rahibe; ~ *of charity veya mercy* hayırsever rahibeler birliği üyesi; **sis.ter.hood** ['‿hud] *n.* kızkardeşlik; rahibeler birliği; '**sis.ter-in-law** *n.* görümce, baldız, yenge, elti; '**sis.ter.ly** *adj.* kızkardeş gibi, kızkardeşe yakışır; müşfik.

sit [sit] (*irr.*) *v/i.* oturmak; toplanmak, toplantı yapmak, müzakerede bulunmak (*meclis*); kuluçkaya yatmak (*tavuk*); ~ *down* (yerine) oturmak; tünemek, konmak; ~ (*up*)*on* araştırmak, incelemek; F susturmak, yola getirmek; ~ *up* dik oturmak; yatmamak; doğrulmak; *make s.o.* ~ *up* b-ni sarsarak uyandırmak; *b-ne* kulak kesilmek, dikkatli dinlemek; *v/t.* oturtmak; (*at vs.'ye*) oturmak, binmek; ~ *a horse well* ata iyi binmek; ~ *s.th. out* bşin sonuna kadar oturmak; ~ *s.o. out* b-ne uzun süre tahammül etm.; ~*-down strike* oturma grevi.

site [sait] **1.** *n.* yer, mahal, mevki, nokta, alan; **2.** *v/t.* yaymak, açmak.

sis.ter ['sistə] *n.* oturan *b-i veya* bş; poz veren kimse; kuluçka; *sl.* kolay av, kolay iş, avanta; '~'*in* **n.** anne ve babası evde yokken ücretle çocuğa bakan kimse.

sit.ting ['sitiŋ] *n.* oturma, oturuş; oturum, toplantı, celse; *at one* ~ bir defada; '~*-room* **n.** oturma odası.

sit.u.ate ['sitjueit] *vb.* başka bir yere koymak, yerleştirmek; yerini tayin etm. -*in*; '**sit.u.at.ed** *adj.* bulunan, olan, vaki; *be* ~ bulunmak (*in -de*); *thus* ~ bu (*veya* şu, o) durumda; **sit.u.'a.tion** *n.* yer, mevki; durum, koşullar.

six [siks] **1.** *adj.* altı; **2.** *n.* altı sayısı; *be at* ~*es and sevens* tam bir karışıklık ve şaşkınlık içinde olm.; '~*.fold* *adj.* altı kat, altı misli; '~*.pack* **n.** altılı paket (*maden suyu*); '~*.pence* **n.** altı peni(lik para); **six.teen** ['‿'ti:n] *adj.* on altı; **sixteenth** ['‿'ti:nθ] **1.** *adj.* on altıncı; **2.** *n.* on altıda bir; **sixth** [‿θ] **1.** *adj.* altıncı; **2.** *n.* altıda bir; **sixth.ly** *adv.*

altıncı olarak; **six.ti.eth** ['ˌtiəθ] *adj.*
altmışıncı; '**six.ty 1.** *adj.* altmış; **2.** *n.*
altmış sayısı.
siz.a.ble ☐ ['saizəbl] oldukça büyük,
büyücek, oylumlu.
size[1] [saiz] **1.** *n.* hacim, oylum; büyüklük, ebat; beden (*elbise*); numara
(*ayakkabı*); **2.** *vb.* büyüklüğüne göre
düzenlemek; ~ **up** F *b-ni veya bşi* tartmak, değerlendirmek, takdir, tahmin
etm.; **sized** *comb.* ... büyüklüğünde,
... genişliğinde, ... ölçüsünde.
size[2] [ˌ] **1.** *n.* çiriş, tutkal; **2.** *adj.* çirişli,
tutkallı.
size.a.ble ☐ ['saizəbl] = *sizable*.
siz.zle ['sizl] *v/i.* tıslamak, cızırdamak,
hışıldamak (*kâğıt, yaprak vs.*), çıtır
çıtır yanmak (*ateş*); *sizzling hot* bunaltıcı sıcak.
skate [skeit] **1.** *n.* paten; *roller*~ tekerlekli paten; **2.** *v/i.* patinaj yapmak, pa-
tenle kaymak; '**skat.er** *n.* patinajcı;
'**skat.ing-rink** *n.* patinuvar, patinaj sahası.
ske.dad.dle F [ski'dædl] *v/i.* sıvışmak,
tüymek, tabanları yağlamak.
skein [skein] *n.* yumak, çile.
skel.e.ton ['skelitn] **1.** *n.* iskelet; insan
kurusu, çok zayıf kimse; çatı, iskelet,
karkas (*bina*); taslak, müsvedde; MIL
kadro, çekirdek birlik; **2.** *adj.* iskelete
benzer; kaba taslak..., iskelet...; MIL
kadro..., esas...; ~ **key** maymuncuk,
her kilidi açan anahtar.
skep.tic ['skeptik] = *sceptic*.
sketch [sketʃ] **1.** *n.* taslak, kroki; küçük
hikâye, skeç; **2.** *vb.* taslak yapmak,
krokisini almak, kabataslak tarif
etm.; *-in* taslağını çizmek; '**sketch.y**
☐ kabataslak; noksan, yarım yamalak,
yüzeysel.
skew [skju:] *adj.* meyilli, inişli; eğri,
çarpık, eğri büğrü.
skew.er ['skuə] **1.** *n.* kebap şişi; şişe
benzer *bş*; **2.** *vb.* kebap şişine geçirmek, şişe dizmek.
ski [ski:] **1.** *n. pl. a.* ~ kayak, ski; **2.** *v/i.*
kayak yapmak.
skid [skid] **1.** *n.* takoz, köstek, fren
çarığı; AVIA kayma kızağı; MOT patinaj;
(yana) kayma; **2.** *vb.* takoz koymak,
kösteklemek; yana kaymak; süzülmek; aşağı kaymak; MOT patinaj yapmak.
ski.er ['ski:ə] *n.* kayakçı.
skiff NAUT [skif] *n.* hafif yelkenli, filika,
kik (*yarış kayığı*).

ski.ing ['ski:iŋ] *n.* kayakçılık, kayak
yapma; '**ski-jump** *n.* kayakçının
yaptığı sıçrama *veya* atlama; atlama
tepesi; '**ski-jump.ing** *n.* kayakla atlama.
skil.ful ☐ ['skilful] hünerli, mahir, becerikli, eli yatkın; '**skil.ful.ness**, skill
[skil] *n.* hüner, ustalık, beceriklilik,
maharet.
skilled [skild] *adj.* deneyimli, usta, hünerli; kalifiye; ~ **worker** kalifiye işçi,
vasıflı işçi.
skil.let ['skilit] *n.* tava.
skill.ful ['skilful] *Am. of skilful*.
skim [skim] **1.** *vb. a.* ~ **off** kaymağını,
yağını almak (*süt*); *bş* üzerinden kaymak, süzülmek, sıyırıp geçmek; *fig.*
göz gezdirmek *-e*; üstünkörü incelemek *-i*; *-den* uçarak geçmek (*uçak*);
su üstünde sektirmek (*taş*); köpüğünü
(*veya* istenmeyen maddeleri) almak
-in; ~ **through** kitabın sayfalarını birer
birer çevirmek, üstünkörü göz gezdirmek; **2.** *n.* ~ **milk** kaymağı alınmış süt;
'**skim.mer** *n.* kevgir, köpük kepçesi.
skimp [skimp] *v/t. & v/i.* cimri davranmak, cimrilik etm., kıt vermek, hesaplı
davranmak; '**skimp.y** ☐ kıt, az, eksik,
yetersiz; yarım yamalak.
skin [skin] **1.** *n.* cilt, deri; post, pösteki;
kabuk; NAUT dış kaplama; (*balon*) kılıf;
(*şarap*) tulum; *by veya* **with the ~ of
one's teeth** güç belâ, daradar, ancak;
have a thick (*thin*) ~ vurdumduymaz
(hassas) olm.; **2.** *v/t.* yüzmek, *-in* kabuğunu soymak; F dolandırmak, so-
yup soğana çevirmek (*of*); ~ **off** F (*çorap vs.*) çıkarmak; *keep one's eyes
~ned* F dikkat etm., gözünü dört açmak; *v/i. a.* ~ **over** kapanmak (*yara
vs.*); '~'**deep** *adj.* sathî, yüzeysel;
'~'**div.ing** *n.* (*aletsiz*) suya dalma spo-
ru; '~'**flint** *n.* cimri kimse; '~'**graft.ing**
n. MED deri transplantasyonu; '**skin-
ner** *n.* derici, kürkçü; '**skin.ny** *adj.*
sıska, çelimsiz, bir deri bir kemik; F
berbat.
skip [skip] **1.** *n.* sekme, zıplama,
sıçrayış; MIN kafes; **2.** *vb.* zıplamak,
sekmek, sıçramak; ip atlamak; *a.* ~
over atlamak, sıçrayarak geçmek *-i*;
'~'**jack** *n.* suyun yüzünde sıçrayan herhangi bir tür balık; ZOO sıçrayan bir tür
böcek.
skip.per[1] ['skipə] *n.* sıçrayan *b-i veya
bş.*
skip.per[2] [ˌ] *n.* NAUT kaptan, süvari; F

spor: takım kaptanı.

skip.ping-rope ['skipiŋrəup] *n.* atlama ipi.

skir.mish MIL ['skə:miʃ] **1.** *n.* çatışma, hafif çarpışma; **2.** *v/i.* çatışmak, çekişmek; '**skir.mish.er** *n.* avcı, gözcü.

skirt [skə:t] **1.** *n.* etek(lik); *oft.* **~s** *pl.* kenar (*kumaş*); kenar, sınır (*bölge*), varoş; *sl.* kız, kadın; **2.** *vb. bşin* kenarından geçmek, bastırmak; ana konuya temas etmemek, kaytarmak; *a.* **~ along** *bşin* kenarı boyunca gitmek *veya* uzanmak; '**skirt.ing-board** *n.* süpürgelik.

skit¹ [skit] *n.* dokunaklı söz, iğneleme, hiciv, kinaye (**on**, **upon**).

skit² [_] *n.* kalabalık, sürü, yığın.

skit.tish □ ['skitiʃ] azgın, serkeş, ürkek (*part. at*); haşarı, şamatacı, muzip.

skit.tle ['skitl] *n.* dokuz kuka, kiy oyunu; **play** (**at**) **~s** kiy oyunu oynamak; '**~al.ley** *n.* kiy oyunu sahası.

skiv.vy F *contp.* ['skivi] *n.* karı, hizmetçi kız.

skul.dug.ger.y *Am.* F [skʌl'dʌgəri] *n.* dalavere, hilekârlık alçaklık.

skulk [skʌlk] *v/i.* sessizce yaklaşmak, gizlice sokulmak; gizlenmek, saklanmak, pusuda beklemek; *b-ne* pusu kurmak; sıvışmak, yan çizmek, kaytarmak; '**skulker** *n.* gizlenen kimse.

skull [skʌl] *n.* kafatası, kafa, beyin; **~ and cross-bones** (*tehlike işareti*) kuru kafa; **have a thick ~** kalın kafalı, aptal olm.

skunk [skʌŋk] *n.* ZOO kokarca (kürkü); F alçak, hain, teres, köpeoğlu köpek kimse.

sky [skai] *oft.* **skies** *n. pl.* gök(yüzü), sema, gök kubbe; **praise to the skies** *fig.* göklere çıkarmak, öve öve bitirememek; '**~'blue** *adj.* gök mavisi; '**~jack** *v/t.* kaçırmak (*uçak*); '**~lark 1.** *n.* ORN tarlakuşu; **2.** *v/i.* cümbüş yapmak, eğlenmek (**about**); '**~light** *n.* dam pencceresi, kaporta, vazistas; '**~line** *n.* ufuk çizgisi; silûet; '**~rock.et** *v/i.* aniden ve dikine yükselmek; kabarmak; '**~'scrap.er** *n.* gökdelen; **sky.ward(s)** ['~wəd(z)] *adv.* göğe dogru; '**sky-writ-ing** *n.* AVIA uçakla havada yazılan yazı.

slab [slæb] *n.* kalın, dilim, tabaka, levha, plâka, tabla; fayans, çini, tuğla; MEC kaplama tahtası.

slack [slæk] **1.** *adj.* gevşek, gerilmemiş, sarkık, kayıtsız, miskin, üşengeç, tembel; COM durgun; **~ water** NAUT durgun su; **2.** *n.* NAUT halat vs.'nin sarkık, çözük kısmı; NAUT durgunluk, kesat; kömür tozu; *s.* **~s**; **3.** *vb.* = **~en**; = **slake**; F tembel davranmak, *bşi* yapmağa üşenmek; '**slack.en** *vb.* tembellik etm., miskin olm.; gevşe(t)mek (*halat vs.*); hafifle(t)mek, şiddetini kaybet(tir)mek; yavaşla(t)mak; '**slack.er** *n.* F tembel, haylaz kimse; '**slack.ness** *n.* gevşeklik; üşengeçlik, tembellik; **slacks** *n. pl.* bol pantolon (*kadın*).

slag [slæg] *n.* cüruf, dışık, mucur; '**slag-gy** *adj.* cüruflu; '**slag-heap** *n.* cüruf yığını.

slain [slein] *p.p. of **slay**.*

slake [sleik] *vb.* gidermek (*susuzluk, hasret vs.*); söndürmek (*kireç*).

sla.lom ['sleiləm] *n. spor*: slalom.

slam [slæm] **1.** *n.* patlama, infilâk sesi; hızla ve gürültülü vurma, çarpma; *is-kambil*: kaput; mars; şilem; **2.** *vb.* kapıyı hızla ve gürültülü çarpıp kapamak; yere vurmak; sözle saldırmak, kalaylamak.

slan.der ['slɑːndə] **1.** *n.* iftira, karacılık; **2.** *v/t. b-ne* iftira etm., karalamak; '**slan.der.ous** □ iftira niteliğinde; karalayıcı havadis yayan.

slang [slæŋ] **1.** *n.* argo, külhanbeyi dili, laubali konuşma dili; **2.** *v/t.* argo konuşmak, sövüp saymak; '**slang.y** □ argo..., bayağı; argo konuşan.

slant [slɑːnt] **1.** *n.* eğim, meyil; meyilli düzey; *Am.* F yan bakış; görüş noktası, tutum; **2.** *v/t.* & *v/i.* eğ(il)mek, meyletmek; '**slant.ing** □ *adj.*, '**slant.wise** *adv.* meyilli (olarak), verev.

slap [slæp] **1.** *n.* şamar, tokat, hafif sille; **~ in the face** hakaret, tokat (*a. fig.*); **2.** *v/t.* avuçla vurmak *-e*, *b-ne* tokat aşketmek, şaklatmak; **3.** *adv.* doğrudan (doğruya), hemen, birdenbire; '**~'bang** *n.* apansızın, pattadak; '**~dash** *adj.* aceleci, atılgan, alelacele yapılmış, baştan savma; *adv. a.* dikkatsizce, düşünmeyerek; '**~jack** *n. Am.* tatlı omlet, krep konfitür; '**~stick** *n.* THEAT güldürü, hokkabaz oyunu; *a.* **~ comedy** kaba komedi, maskara; '**~up** F *adj.* kıyak, iki dirhem bir çekirdek, fevkalâde.

slash [slæʃ] **1.** *n.* uzun yara; yarık; kamçı vuruşu; yırtmaç (*elbise*); **2.** *v/t.* & *v/i.* uzunluğuna açmak, yarmak; kamçılamak; *fig.* teşhir etm., şiddetle eleştirmek; F çok indirmek (*fiyat*); çalakılıç yürümek, yol açmak (**at**);

'**slash.ing** □ keskin, şiddetli, tahripkâr (*eleştiri*).

slat [slæt] *n.* tiriz, lata, ince varak, levha (*pancur için*).

slate [sleit] **1.** *n.* kayağantaş, arduvaz; taş tahta, kara tahta; *part. Am.* aday listesi; *start with a clean ~* yeni bir hayata başlamak; **2.** *v/t.* arduvazla kaplamak; şiddetle eleştirmek, kınamak; *Am.* F bir görev *veya* amaç için tayin etm.; '~'**pencil** *n.* taş kalem; '**slat.er** *n.* arduvaz kaplama; '**slat.ing** *n.* sert eleştiri.

slat.tern ['slætə:n] *n.* pasaklı kadın; '**slattern.ly** *adj.* pasaklı, şapşal, hırpanî, pis.

slat.y □ ['sleiti] aduvazlı *veya* arduvaza benzer.

slaugh.ter ['slɔ:tə] **1.** *n.* kesim (*hayvan*), kan dökme, katliam; *fig.* katil, katletme; **2.** *v/t.* kesmek, boğazlamak, katletmek, kılıçtan geçirmek; '**slaugh.ter.er** *n.* kasap; katil; '**slaugh.ter-house** *n.* mezbaha, salhane, kesimevi; '**slaugh.ter.ous** □ RHET öldürücü, korkunç; katil, kırıp geçiren.

Slav [slɑ:v] **1.** *n.* İslav ırkından kimse; İslav dili; **2.** *adj.* İslav diline ait.

slave [sleiv] **1.** *n.* köle, esir, kul, halayık, cariye; *fig.* köle gibi çalışan kimse; **2.** *v/i.* köle gibi çalışmak, eşek gibi çalışmak (*away*).

slav.er[1] ['sleivə] *n.* esir tüccarı *veya* gemisi.

slav.er[2] ['slævə] **1.** *n.* salya; **2.** *v/i.* salya akıtmak, salyası akmak (*a. fig.*).

slav.er.y ['sleivəri] *n.* kölelik, esirlik, esaret.

slav.ey *sl.* ['slævi] *n.* kâhya, orta hizmetçisi.

Slav.ic ['slɑ:vik] **1.** *adj.* İslav; İslav diline ait; **2.** *n.* İslav ırkından olan kimse.

slav.ish □ ['sleiviʃ] dalkavuk, aşağılık, köle gibi, köpek gibi sadık; '**slav.ishness** *n.* dalkavukluk, körü körüne itaat.

slaw [slɔ:] *n.* lahana salatası.

slay RHET [slei] (*irr.*) *v/t.* öldürmek, katletmek; '**slay.er** *n.* katil.

sled [sled] = *sledge*[1].

sledge[1] [sledʒ] **1.** *n.* kızak, yük kızağı; **2.** *v/i.* kızakla gitmek *veya* yük taşımak.

sledge[2] [_] *n. a.* **~-hammer** balyoz.

sleek [sli:k] **1.** □ düzgün, parlak (*saç vs., a. fig.*); **2.** *v/t.* düzlemek, düzeltmek; '**sleek.ness** *n.* düzgünlük, par-

laklık.

sleep [sli:p] **1.** (*irr.*) *v/i.* uyumak, ayakta (*veya* hareketsiz) durmak (*topaç*); *~ up* (*on*) *veya over* bir işin sonucu için isti hareye yatmak; *bşi* ertesi güne bırakmak (*daha fazla düşünebilmek için*); *v/t. b-ne* yatacak yer sağlamak; *~ away* geç uyanmak; *~ off* uyuyarak geçirmek (*sarhoşluk vs.*); **2.** *n.* uyku; *go to ~* yatağa yatmak; '**sleep.er** *n.* uyuyan kimse; RAIL yataklı vagon; travers; *be a light (fast) ~* uykusu hafif (derin) olm.; '**sleepi.ness** *n.* uykulu olma, uyuklama.

sleep.ing ['sli:piŋ] *adj.* uyuyan, uykuda, uyku...; '~**-bag** *n.* uyku tulumu; ♀ Beauty Uyuyan Güzel; '~**-car**, '~**-car riage** *n.* RAIL yataklı vagon; '~**-draught** *n.* yatmadan önce içilen uyku getirici madde; ~ **partner** COM özel ortak, komanditer; '~'**sickness** *n.* uyku hastalığı.

sleep.less □ ['sli:plis] uykusuz; '**sleepless.ness** *n.* uykusuzluk.

sleep.walk.er ['sli:pwɔ:kə] *n.* uyurgezer.

sleep.y □ ['sli:pi] uykusu gelmiş, uyku basmış, uyku gözünden akan; '~**.head** *n.* F *fig.* uykucu, miskin, üşengeç.

sleet [sli:t] **1.** *n.* sulusepken kar; **2.** *v/i.* sulusepken yağmak; '**sleet.y** *adj.* sulusepken gibi.

sleeve [sli:v] **1.** *n.* yen, elbise kolu; MEC manşon, rakor, kol, bilezik; *have something up one's ~* bir sırrı gelecekte koz olarak kullanmak üzere saklamak; **2.** *vb.* kol takmak; **sleeved** *com.* ...kollu; '**sleeve.less** *adj.* kolsuz, yensiz; '**sleeve-link** *n.* kol düğmesi.

sleigh [slei] **1.** *n.* kızak (*atlı*); **2.** *v/i.* kızakla gitmek.

sleight [slait] *n.:* *~ of hand* elçabukluğu, hokkabazlık, hüner, marifet.

slen.der □ ['slendə] ince (belli), narin, fidan gibi; küçük, ufak, kıt, az; zayıf, dermansız; '**slen.der.ness** *n.* incelik, zayıflık; dermansızlık.

slept [slept] *pret. & p.p. of sleep 1.*

sleuth [slu:θ] *n.* '~**-hound** bir tür av köpeği; *fig.* hafiye.

slew[1] [slu:] *pret. of slay.*

slew[2] [_] *v/t. & v/i. a.* **~ round** dön(dür)mek, çevirmek, devret(tir)mek.

slice [sl is] **1.** *n.* dilim, parça, kısım; hisse; balık bıçağı; **2.** *vb.* dilimlemek; bıçakla kesmek; topu keserek atmak (*golf*).

slick F [slik] **1.** *adj.* düz(gün), parlak,

kaygan; *fig.* yapmacık kibar, kurnaz, hilekâr, şeytan gibi; **2.** *adv.* ustalıkla, kurnazca; **3.** *n. a.* ~ **paper** *Am. sl.* klâs mecmua; '**slick.er** *n.* muşamba yağmurluk; kurnaz, hilekâr kimse.

slid [slid] *pret. & p.p. of* **slide 1**.

slide [slaid] **1.** (*irr.*) *v/t. & v/i.* kay(dır)-mak, süzülmek; sessizce ortadan kaybolmak, savuşmak; **let things** ~ işleri oluruna bırakmak, sermek; **2.** *n.* kayma; MEC sürme, sürgü; diyapozitif slayt; *a.* **land** ~ heyelân, kayşa; '**slid.er** *n.* sürgü, sürme; '**slide-rule** *n.* hesap cetveli.

slid.ing ['slaidiŋ] **1.** *n.* kayma; **2.** *adj.* sürme..., kayıcı; ~ **roof** açılır kapanır tavan; ~ **rule** sürgülü hesap cetveli; ~ **scale** değişebilen değerlendirme oranı; ~ **seat** (*yarış kayığı*) kızaklı kürekçi oturma yeri.

slight [slait] **1.** □ zayıf, ince, narin, hafif; önemsiz, değersiz, cüzi; **2.** *n.* saygısızlık, küçümseme; **3.** *v/t.* önem vermemek -*e*, hesaba katmamak, küçümsemek -*i*; '**slight.ing** □ küçümseyen, hafifseyen; '**slight.ly** *adv.* biraz, bir parça; '**slightness** *n.* zayıflık; önemsizlik.

slim [slim] **1.** □ ince, zayıf, narin, fidan gibi; az, kıt, eksik; *sl.* kurnaz, şeytana çarığı ters giydiren; **2.** *v/i.* incelmek, zayıflamak.

slime [slaim] *n.* sümük, balgam; balçık, çamur.

slim.i.ness ['slaiminis] *n.* kayganlık, yapışkanlık; çamurlu ve sümüksel olma.

slim.ness ['slimnis] *n.* incelik, narinlik.

slim.y □ [slaimi] çamurlu, balçıklı; sümüksü, pis.

sling [sliŋ] **1.** *n.* sapan, mancınık; (*kayış*) askı; COM bocurgat, yük kaldırmakta kullanılan mekanik aygıt; **2.** (*irr.*) *v/t.* sapanla atmak; askı ile kaldırmak; *a.* ~ **up** yukarı kaldırmak.

slink [sliŋk] (*irr.*) *vb.* sinsi sinsi yürümek, gizlice sokulmak; sıvışmak; vakitsiz yavrulamak, (*hayvan*) yavrusunu düşürmek.

slip [slip] **1.** *v/t. & v/i.* kay(dır)mak, ayağı kaymak; kaç(ır)mak; hataya düşmek, yanılmak; salıvermek; (*hayvan*) yavrusunu düşürmek; *oft.* ~ **away** kaçmak, sıvışmak; geçip gitmek (*zaman*); ~ **in** arasına girmek (*lâf*); ~ **into** içine koymak, sokmak, tutuşturmak -*e*; ~ **on** giyivermek, üzerine geçirmek (*elbise*

vs.); **2.** *n.* kayma; yanlış adım (*a. fig.*), hata, kusur; sürçme, söz kaçırma, dikkatsizlik; *a.* ~ **paper** pusula, kâğıt; AGR daldırma, çelik; *fig.* evlât, döl; jüpon, kombinezon; ~**s** *pl. veya* ~ **way** NAUT geminin suya indirildiği *veya* sudan çekildiği kızak; yastık yüzü; ~**s** *pl.* deniz donu; **a** ~ **of a girl** ince, narin bir kız; ~ **of a pen** yazı hatası; **it was a** ~ **of the tongue** dil sürçmesiydi; **give s.o. the** ~ *b-nin* elinden kurtulmak, sıvışmak; '~-**knot** *n.* ilmik, fiyonk; '~-**on** *n.* kolay giyilip çıkarılan (*elbise vs.*); '**slip.per** *n.* terlik; '**slip.per.y** □ kaygan; *fig.* kaypak; '**slip-road** *n.* otoyola çıkan yol; **slip.shod** ['-ʃɔd] *adj.* dikkatsiz, kayıtsız, düzensiz, pasaklı, kötü; **slip.slop** ['-'slɔp] *n.* dil hatası; '**slip-stream** *n.* AVIA motorun arkaya ittiği hava akıntısı; '**slip-up** *n.* F hata, kabahat, sürçme.

slit [slit] **1.** *n.* kesik, yarık, çatlak; **2.** (*irr.*) *v/t.* yarmak, uzunluğuna açmak, kesmek.

slob.ber ['slɔbə] **1.** *n.* salya; **2.** *vb.* salya akıtmak, üzerine salya bulaştırmak; abartmalı söz söylemek, gevezelik etm. (*over*); '**slob.ber.y** *adj.* ıslak, cıvık; salyalı.

sloe BOT [slǝu] *n.* çakaleriği; kara diken.

slog F [slɔg] **1.** *vb.* dövmek, rasgele vurmak; didinmek, ağır ve zahmetli iş görmek, eşek gibi çalışmak; **2.** *n.* vuruş, darbe; uzun gayret.

slo.gan ['slǝugǝn] *n. fig.* parola, slogan.

sloop NAUT [slu:p] *n.* şalopa, büyük sandal.

slop[1] [slɔp] **1.** *n.* sulu çamur, pis su birikintisi; ~**s** *pl.* bulaşık suyu; hasta çorbası, kalitesiz sulu yemek; **2.** *v/t. a.* ~ **over** beceriksizce dökmek; *v/i.* dökülmek, taşmak; *fig.* taşkınlık yapmak.

slop[2] [.] *n.:* ~**s** *pl.* ucuz konfeksiyon elbise; NAUT elbise ve yatak takımı.

slop-ba.sin ['slɔpbeisn] *n.* tabağa dökülen çay *veya* kahveyi dökmek için kullanılan kap.

slope [slǝup] **1.** *n.* bayır, iniş, yokuş; meyilli düzey; **2.** *v/t.* meyillendirmek, meyilli kılmak, eğmek; MEC meyilli, şevli kesmek; ~ **arms!** MIL tüfek omuza!; *v/i.* meyletmek, meyilli olm., eğilmek; ~ **off**, *a.* **do a** ~ *sl.* sıvışmak, tüymek; '**slop.ing** □ eğik, eğri, mail.

slop-pail ['slɔppeil] *n.* çöp kovası, bulaşık kabı; '**slop.py** □ çamurlu, balçıklı, nemli; kirli, pasaklı, pis; sulu, çorba gibi.

slop-shop ['slɔpʃɔp] *n.* ucuz konfeksiyon malları satılan mağaza.

slosh [slɔʃ] *vb.* suda *veya* çamurda yürümek; suda çalkalamak; su sıçratmak; *sl.* dayak atmak *-e.*

slot [slɔt] *n.* HUNT iz, yol; delik, kertik, uzun ensiz yarık (*mektup vs. atmak için*); MEC dişili yiv.

sloth [sləuθ] *n.* tembellik, haylazlık; ZOO Amerika'da ağaçlara tırmanan ve yavaş hareket eden bir kaç tür hayvan; **slothful** □ ['_ful] tembel, yavaştan alan.

slot-ma.chine ['slɔtməʃiːn] *n.* (*mal veya oyun için*) otomatik makine.

slouch [slautʃ] **1.** *v/i.* yorgun, omuzlar düşük, ayakları sürüyerek yürümek; **2.** *n.* yorgun, bitap yürüyüş; tembel, düzensiz kimse; ~ *hat* geniş ve sarkık kenarlı şapka.

slough¹ [slau] *n.* bataklık.

slough² [slʌf] **1.** *n.* ZOO değiştirilip atılan deri (*yılan vs.*); MED kabuk, ruhya; **2.** *v/t. & v/i.* pul pul olm. (*kabuk vs.*), derisi soyulmak, gömlek değiştirmek; dökmek, değiştirmek (*deri*).

slough.y ['slaui] *adj.* batak, çamurlu.

Slo.vak ['sləuvæk] **1.** *n.* Slovakyalı kimse, Slovak; Slovak dili; **2.** = **Slo'va.ki-an** *adj.* Slovakyalı; Slovak diline ait.

slov.en ['slʌvn] *n.* hırpani, şapşal giyinen kimse; **'slov.en.li.ness** *n.* hırpanilik, şapşallık; **'slov.en.ly** *adj.* hırpani, yırtık pırtık, şapşal.

slow [sləu] **1.** □ ağır, yavaş (*of*); vakit alan; geri (kalmış) (*saat*); hantal, üşengeç; yavaş etki eden (*ateş*); can sıkıcı, monoton; aptal, kalın kafalı; *spor:* yorucu; *be ~ to do s.th.* bşi yaparken yavaş davranmak; *my watch is ten minutes* ~ saatim 10 dakika geri kalmış; **2.** *adv.* yavaş yavaş, ağır ağır, tembelce; **3.** *v/t. & v/i. oft.* ~ *down,* ~ *up,* ~ *off* yavaşla(t)mak; yavaş gitmek, ağırlaşmak; '~-*coach* *n.* hareketleri ağır kimse; eski kafalı kimse; '~-*match* *n.* funya, barutlu fitil; '~'mo.tion film yavaşlatılmış, ağır çekim film; 'slow.ness *n.* yavaşlık, ağırlık; 'slow.worm *n.* ZOO köryılan.

sludge [slʌdʒ] *n.* sulu çamur, balçık.

slue [sluː] = *slew*².

slug¹ [slʌg] *n.* işlenmemiş metal parça; TYP linotip makinesinin döktüğü bir satır yazı.

slug² ZOO [_] *n.* kabuksuz sümüklü bö-

cek.

slug³ [_] *Am. of slog*¹.

slug.gard ['slʌgəd] *n.* tembel, haylaz kimse; **'slug.gish** □ tembel, haylaz, cansız.

sluice [sluːs] **1.** *n.* savak, kapaklı su bendi; **2.** *v/t.* (*out, down*) yıkayarak temizlemek, çalkalamak; '~'*gate* *n.* savak kapağı; '~'*way* *n.* savak yatağı.

slum [slʌm] *n. a.* ~*s pl.* teneke mahallesi, şehrin fakir mahallesi, kenar mahalle, fukara yatağı, gecekondu bölgesi.

slum.ber ['slʌmbə] **1.** *n. a.* ~*s pl.* uyku, uyuklama; **2.** *v/i.* uyumak, uyuklamak.

slum.brous, **slum.ber.ous** □ ['slʌmbrəs, '_bərəs] uykusu gelmiş, uyku gözünden akan; uyku getiren.

slump [slʌmp] *borsa:* **1.** *v/i.* düşmek, değer kaybetmek; **2.** *n.* düşme, ekonomik bunalım, durgunluk.

slung [slʌŋ] *pret. & p.p. of sling* 2.

slunk [slʌŋk] *pret. & p.p. of slink*.

slur [sləː] **1.** *n.* leke, ayıp; *fig.* serzeniş, eleştiri; MUS bağ işareti; **2.** *v/t. oft.* ~ *over* dikkate almamak, *b-ne, bşe* itibar etmemek; MUS bağlama işaretini koymak; birbirine bağlayarak telâffuz etm. (*hece vs.*).

slush [slʌʃ] *n.* eriyen kar; çamur, balçık; F değersiz eser; **'slush.y** *adj.* çamurlu, batak; F zevksiz, zevke hitap etmeyen.

slut [slʌt] *n.* pasaklı kadın; **'slut.tish** *adj.* pasaklı, düzensiz, hırpani, ihmalkâr.

sly □ [slai] kurnaz, şeytan gibi, sinsi; *on the* ~ gizli(den), sezdirmeden, sinsice; '~.*boots* *n.* F akıl kumkuması; **'sly.ness** *n.* hile, kurnazlık, sinsilik, şeytanlık.

smack¹ [smæk] **1.** *n.* tat, lezzet, hafif çeşni; tutam (*tuz vs.*); *fig.* zerre, nebze; **2.** *vb.* çeşnisi olm. (*of -in*).

smack² [_] **1.** *n.* şapırtı (*öpücük, ağız*); şaklayış (*kırbaç*); şamar, tokat; **2.** *vb.* şaplatmak, patlatmak; ağzını şapırdatmak; şapır şupur öpmek; *b-ne* tokat aşketmek; **3.** *int.* şaklama, şakırdama.

smack³ NAUT [_] *n.* büyük balıkçı teknesi.

smack.er *Am. sl.* ['smækə] *n.* bir dolar *veya* sterlin; şapırtılı öpücük.

small [smɔːl] **1.** *adj. com.* küçük, ufak; az; önemsiz; *fig.* hasis (ruhlu); alçak, soysuz; ~ *eater* az yiyen, boğazsız; *feel* ~, *look* ~ utanmak, küçük düşmek; *the*

~ hours pl. gece yarısından sonraki saatler; **in a ~ way** mütevazi şekilde, alçak gönüllü; **2.** n. ufak şey; az miktar; **~s** pl. F iç çamaşırı, mendil vs. gibi ufak çamaşırlar; **~ of the back** ANAT sağrı kemiği, kuyruk sokumu; **'~-arms** n. pl. tabanca vs. gibi el silahları; **~ beer** hafif bira; **think no ~ of o.s.** F k-ne toz kondurmamak; **be ~** önemsiz olm.; **~ change** bozuk para; fig. önemsiz söz; **'~'hold.er** n. küçük çiftçi; **'~'holding** n. küçük çiftlik; **'small.ish** adj. küçükçe, ufakça; **'small.ness** n. ufaklık, küçüklük; azlık.

small…: **'~.pox** n. pl. MED çiçek hastalığı; **~ talk** boş lâflar, önemsiz sohbet; havadan sudan konuşma; **'~.time** adj. Am. F önemsiz, ikinci derecede.

smalt MEC [smɔ:lt] n. potas, silis ve kobalt karışımından yapılan mavi cam; bu camdan elde edilen koyu mavi boya maddesi.

smarm.y F ['smɑ:mi] adj. sırnaşık, sulu, dalkavuk.

smart [smɑ:t] **1.** □ şık, zarif, temiz, pak; yakışıklı, gösterişli; yeni, pırıl pırıl; şiddetli, sert (savaş vs.); çevik, canlı; kurnaz; becerikli, eli yatık; **~ aleck** Am. ukalâ dümbeleği; **2.** n. sızı; acı, elem, keder; **3.** vb. ağrımak, sızlamak, sancımak, dert çekmek; **you shall ~ for it** bunun cezasını çekeceksin; **'smart.en** vb. mst **~ up** üstünü başını düzeltmek, canlandırmak, telleyip pullamak; **'smart-mon.ey** n. manevi zarar için tazminat; **'smart.ness** n. şıklık; açıkgözlük; ustalık, beceri.

smash [smæʃ] **1.** v/t. oft. **~ up** ezmek, parçalamak; **~ in** vurup kırmak; fig. yok etm., mahvetmek, tahrip etm.; hiddetle yere atmak; v/i. ezilmek, parçalanmak; fig. kırılmak; düşüp kırılmak; oft. **~ up** iflâs etm., mahvolmak; **2.** n. parçalanma, şangırtı ile kırılma, ezilme; çarpışma, kaza; mahvolma, iflâs; tenis: kut inme; **'~-and -'grab raid** camekânı kırarak teşhir malını çalma; **'smash.er** n. sl. müthiş b-i veya bş; kırıcı eleştiri; **'smash.ing** adj. fig. çok güzel; **'smash-up** n. şiddetli çarpışma; parçalanma.

smat.ter.ing ['smætəriŋ] n. çat pat bilgi, az buçuk bilme.

smear [smiə] **1.** vb. bulandırmak, lekelemek, karalamak (yazı); sürmek, yağlamak (on); fig. karalamak, pislemek; **~(ing) campaign** iftira kampanyası;

2. n. yağlı ve yapışkan madde, pislik, (bulaşık) leke; iftira.

smell [smel] **1.** n. (fena) koku; koklama; ima; **2.** (irr.) v/t. -in kokusunu almak, bşi koklamak; v/i. kokmak (a. **~ at**; **of**); **'smell.ing-salt** n. amonyak ruhu; **'smell.y** adj. (fena) kokulu, pis kokan.

smelt¹ [smelt] pret. & p.p. of **smell 2**.

smelt² ICHTH [‾] n. çamuka.

smelt³ [‾] v/t. eritmek (maden filizi); **'smelt.er** n. dökümcü, dökmeci; **'smelting-'fur.nace** n. izabe fırını, yüksek fırın.

smile [smail] **1.** n. gülümseme, tebessüm; **2.** vb. gülümsemek (at -e); **~ on**, **~ at** b-ne gülümsemek.

smirch RHET [smə:tʃ] v/t. leke sürmek, kirletmek; fig. karalamak.

smirk [smə:k] **1.** v/t. (pişmiş kelle gibi) sırıtmak; **2.** n. budalaca sırıtma, yapmacık gülümşeyiş.

smite [smait] (irr.) vb. poet. veya co. darbe indirmek, vurmak, çarpmak, kırıp geçirmek; belâ kesilmek; çok etkilemek; pişman etm.; üzmek, rahatsız etm. (vicdan); **~ upon** part. fig. (kulağında) şaklamak.

smith [smiθ] n. demirci, nalbant.

smith.er.eens F ['smiðə'ri:nz] n. pl. ufak parçalar; mermi parçaları; paçavra; kıymık; **smash to ~** paramparça etm.

smith.y ['smiði] n. nalbant dükkânı; demirhane.

smit.ten ['smitn] **1.** p.p. of **smite**; **2.** adj. çarpılmış, etkilenmiş, şaşkın; fig. âşık, vurgun (with -e).

smock [smɔk] **1.** v/t. plise yapmak (elbise); **2.** n. a. **~ frock** iş kıyafeti, gömlek, önlük; **'smock.ing** n. bal peteği şeklinde iğne işi.

smog [smɔg] n. dumanlı sis.

smoke [smouk] **1.** n. duman; MIL kamuflaj sisi; F içme (sigara vs.); F tütün, sigara; **have a~** sigara içmek; **2.** v/i. tütmek, duman çıkarmak; v/t. tütsülemek; içmek, kullanmak (sigara vs.); MIL sisle karartmak (hava); **'~-bomb** n. sis bombası; **'~-dried** adj. tütsülenmiş; **'~-free** sigara içilmeyen (bölge, bina); **'smoke.less** □ dumansız; **'smoker** n. tütün içen; RAIL tütün içenlere mahsus vagon; **'smoke-screen** n. MIL sis perdesi; **'smoke-stack** n. RAIL & NAUT baca.

smok.ing ['smoukiŋ] **1.** n. tütün içme; **no ~!** sigara içilmez!; **2.** comb. tüten…;

tütün içen...; '~-com.part.ment *n*.
RAIL tütün içenlere mahsus vagon;
'~-room *n*. tütün içenlere mahsus salon.

smok.y ☐ ['sməuki] dumanlı, tüten;
duman renginde koyu füme.

smol.der *Am*. ['sməuldə] = **smoulder**.

smooth [smuːð] **1.** ☐ düz(gün), pürüzsüz; *fig*. engelsiz; sakin, yumuşak, halim; tatlı dilli, yüze gülen; akıcı, kaygan; sert olmayan (*içki, sigara vs.*); **2.** *v/t. oft*. ~ *out*, ~ *down* düzlemek, düzeltmek; kolaylaştırmak (*a. fig.*); inceltmek, tesviye etm.; *a*. ~ *down* yatıştırmak, teskin etm.; *a*. ~ *over*, ~ *away* ortadan kaldırmak, kurtulmak (*üzüntü, güç durum vs.*); ~ *down* düzlenmek; 'smooth.ing **1.** *n*. düzle(n)me; **2.** *adj*. düz..., düzgün...; ~ *iron* ütü; ~ *plane* plânya; 'smooth.ness *n*. düzlük, pürüzsüzlük; kayganlık; sokulganlık, tatlılık.

smote [sməut] *pret. of* **smite**.

smoth.er ['smʌðə] **1.** *n*. kesif duman; boğucu madde; baskı altında kalma; **2.** *v/t. & v/i. a*. ~ *up* boğ(ul)mak (*a. fig.*).

smoul.der ['sməuldə] *v/i*. dumansız yanmak, için için yanmak.

smudge [smʌdʒ] **1.** *v/t*. kirletmek, pislemek, bulaştırmak; *v/i*. kirlenmek, pislenmek, is bulaşmak; **2.** *n*. leke, kir (*veya* pislik, çamur) lekesi; 'smudg.y ☐ lekeli, isli, kirli, pis.

smug [smʌg] *adj. k-ni* beğenmiş, hodperest, *k-ni* dev aynasında gören; şıklık meraklısı.

smug.gle ['smʌgl] *vb*. kaçırmak (*gümrükten*), yurda kaçak mal sokmak *veya* çıkarmak; 'smug.gler *n*. kaçakçı; 'smuggling *n*. kaçakçılık.

smut [smʌt] **1.** *n*. is, kurum, kir, pislik; pis laf, yakası açılmadık söz; BOT buğday pası, sürme, bir tür buğday mantar hastalığı; **2.** *v/t*. kirletmek, pisletmek, lekelemek; BOT buğday pası ile lekelemek.

smutch [smʌtʃ] **1.** *v/t*. kirletmek, pislemek, lekelemek; **2.** *n*. koyu leke.

smut.ty ☐ ['smʌti] isli, kirli; müstehcen; BOT mantarlı, sürmeli.

snack [snæk] *n*. hafif yemek, kahvaltı, çerez; '~-bar, '~-coun.ter *n*. hafif yemek yenen lokanta vs.

snaf.fle[1] ['snæfl] *n*. bir tür gem.

snaf.fle[2] *sl*. [_] *v/t*. aşırmak, çalmak.

snaf.fle-bit ['snæflbit] *n*. gem ağızlığı.

sna.fu *Am. sl*. MIL [snæ'fuː] **1.** *adj*. karmakarışık, allak bullak, talan olmuş; **2.** *n*. karmakarışıklık, dağınıklık.

snag [snæg] *n*. kırık dal; kırık diş; *fig*. pürüzlü nokta, müşkül taraf; *Am*. ağaç gövdesi (*nehirde*); **snag.ged** ['_gid], 'snag.gy *adj*. budaklı, çıkıntılı.

snail ZOO [sneil] *n*. sümüklüböcek, salyangoz; '~ mail F *n*. *e-postanın aksine, gönderilenleri fiziksel yöntemlerle alıcısına ulaştıran normal posta*.

snake ZOO [sneik] *n*. yılan (*a. fig.*); '~-charm.er *n*. yılan oynatan; '~-weed *n*. BOT yılan kökü, kurt pençesi.

snak.y ☐ ['sneiki] yılankavi, yılan gibi kıvrılan, kıvrak; *fig*. hain, kurnaz.

snap [snæp] **1.** *n*. ısırma, ağızıyla kapma; çatırtı, çatlama, şıkırtı, şaklama; *fig*. hamle, coşkunluk; kopça, çıtçıt; PHOT enstantane; bisküvit, pötibör; *cold* ~ soğuk dalgası; **2.** *v/i*. aniden ısırmak, dişlemek (*at -ı*); kopmak, çatırdayıp kırılmak; birdenbire kapanmak (*kilit*); terslemek, veriştirmek, çıkışmak (*at s.o. -i, -e*); ~ *into it* Am. *sl*. haydi gayret!, çabuk ol!; ~ *out of it* Am. *sl*. kendine gelmek; *v/t*. kırmak; şaklatmak (*kamçı, parmak vs.*); PHOT enstantane fotoğraf çekmek; ~ *one's fingers at s.o. b-ni* umursamamak, hiçe saymak; ~ *out* birdenbire söyleyivermek (*söz*); ~ *up* kapmak, yakalamak; *b-ne* çıkışmak, veriştirmek; *b-nin* sözünü kesmek; **3.** *int*. iki aynı şey görüldüğünde söylenen söz; '~-drag.on *n*. BOT ağlanağzı; '~-fas.ten.er *n*. çıtçıt (*elbisede*); 'snap.pish ☐ huysuz, kavgacı, aksi; alaycı, müstehzi; *k-ni* beğenmiş, laübali; 'snap.pish.ness *n*. huysuzluk, aksilik, *k-ni* beğenmişlik; 'snap.py = **snappish**; F atılgan, yaman, çevik, tez, atik; *make it* ~! elini çabuk tut!, sallanma!; 'snap.shot **1.** *n*. enstantane fotoğraf; **2.** *vb*. enstantane fotoğraf çekmek.

snare [snɛə] **1.** *n*. tuzak, kapan; **2.** *v/t*. tuzağa düşürmek, yakalamak; *fig*. ele geçirmek.

snarl [snɑːl] **1.** *v/i*. hırlamak; homurdanmak, söylenmek; **2.** *n*. hırlama; homurdanma, ters laf.

snatch [snætʃ] **1.** *n*. kapma, kapış, yakalama, anî hareket, birdenbire çekme; an, lahza; *sl*. adam kaçırma; *by* ~**es** kesik kesik hareket ederek, hamle ile; **2.** *v/t*. kapmak, koparmak, yakalamak; *k-ne* doğru çekmek; eline geçirmek; ~ **at** *bşe* el uzatmak, kapmaya çalışmak; ~ **from s.o.** *bşi b-nin* elinden zorla almak.

sneak [sni:k] **1.** *v/i.* sinsi sinsi dolaşmak, gizlice sokulmak; F ihbar etm., ispiyon etm. (*okulda*); *v/t.* F aşırmak, çalmak; **2.** *n.* sır küpü, yere bakan yürek yakan, sinsi kimse; F gammaz, ispiyoncu; '**sneak.ers** *n. pl.* F hafif lastik tenis ayakkabısı; '**sneak.ing** □ sinsi, gizli (*duygu*), şüpheli.

sneer [sniə] **1.** *n.* alay, istihza; hakaret; **2.** *v/i.* küçümsemek (**at** *-i*), zevklenmek, alay etm. **ile**, alaycı gülmek; '**sneer.er** *n.* alaycı, müstehzi kimse; '**sneer.ing** □ alaycı.

sneeze [sni:z] **1.** *v/i.* aksırmak, hapşırmak; **not to be** ~**d at** F hiç de fena değil, yabana atılmaz; **2.** *n.* aksırma, aksırık.

snick.er ['snikə] *v/i.* kıs kıs gülmek; kişnemek (*at*).

sniff [snif] **1.** *v/i.* burnuna hava çekmek; *bşe* burun kıvırmak (**at**); *v/t. bşi* koklamak; **2.** *n.* koklama; burun kıvırma; '**sniff.y** *adj.* F burnu havada, *k-ni* beğenmiş, kibirli; pis kokan, fena kokulu.

snig.ger ['snigə] *v/i.* kıs kıs gülmek, alaylı gülmek (**at** *-e*).

snip [snip] **1.** *n.* kesme, biçme; kesilmiş parça; **2.** *v/t.* makasla kesmek (**off**); zımbalamak (*bilet*).

snipe [snaip] **1.** *n.* ORN çulluk; bekasin, su çulluğu; **2.** *v/i.* MIL pusuya yatarak düşmanı vurmak (*çete savaşı*), pusudan ateş etm.; '**snip.er** *n.* MIL pusuya yatan nişancı; çeteci, partizan.

snip.pets ['snipits] *n. pl.* kısa, küçük parçalar (*yazı, konuşma vs.*); *fig.* parça, fragman.

snitch *sl.* [snitʃ] *v/i.*: ~ **on s.o.** *b-ni* ihbar etm., gammazlamak.

sniv.el ['snivl] *v/i.* burnu akmak; ağlayıp sızlamak, burnunu çekerek ağlamak; '**sniv.el.(l)ing** *adj.* çıtkırıldım, ağlayıp sızlayan, çabuk ağlayan; acınacak durumda; sırılsıklam.

snob [snɔb] *n.* snop, züppe, farfara kimse; '**snob.ber.y** *n.* züppelik; '**snob.bish** □ snop, züppe tavırlı, kibarlık taslayan.

snook.er ['snu:kə] **1.** *n.* yirmi bir topla altı delikli masada oynanan bir tür tür bilardo oyunu; **2.** *v/t.* **be** ~**ed** F sıkıştırılmak, zor duruma sokulmak.

snoop *Am. sl.* [snu:p] **1.** *vb. fig.* burnunu sokmak (**upon** *-e*); **2.** *n.* her işe burnunu sokan kimse; casus, ajan.

snoot.y F ['snu:ti] *adj.* züppe, *k-ni* beğenmiş.

snooze F [snu:z] **1.** *n.* şekerleme, uyuklama; **2.** *v/i.* şekerleme yapmak, kısaca uyumak.

snore [snɔ:] **1.** *n.* horlama, horultu; **2.** *v/i.* horlamak.

snor.kel NAUT ['snɔ:kəl] *n.* şnorkel.

snort [snɔ:t] **1.** *n.* horuldama, öfke ile belirtme, hızlı hızlı nefes alma, soluma; **2.** *v/i.* at gibi horuldamak, burnundan solumak.

snot P [snɔt] *n.* mankafa, alçak herif; sümük; '**snot.ty** *adj.* sümüklü; *fig.* alçak, küstah, kibirli.

snout [snaut] *n.* ZOO hortum, burun.

snow [snəu] **1.** *n.* kar (yağışı); *sl.* kokain; **2.** *v/i.* kar yağmak; **be** ~**ed under with** *fig.* işe boğulmak; ~**ed in** *veya* **up** karla kaplanmak, kardan mahsur kalmak; '~**ball 1.** *n.* kar topu; **2.** *v/i.* çığ gibi büyümek; '~**bound** *adj.* kardan mahsur kalmış; '~**capped**, '~**clad**, '~**covered** *adj.* karla örtülü, karlı; '~**drift** *n.* kar yığıntısı; '~**drop** *n.* BOT kardelen; '~**fall** *n.* kar yağışı; '~**flake** *n.* kar lapası, kar tanesi, kuşbaşı; '~**gog.gles** *n. pl.* (**a pair of**) kar gözlüğü; '~**line** *n.* toktağan (*veya* hiç erimeyen) karların hududu; '~**plough**, *Am.* '~**plow** *n.* kar temizleme makinesi; '~**shoe** *n.* kar ayakkabısı; '~**storm** *n.* kar fırtınası, tipi; '~**white** *adj.* bembeyaz, kar gibi; '**snow.y** □ karlı; kar gibi, beyaz.

snub [snʌb] **1.** *v/t.* hor davranmak, terslemek, küçümsemek, hiçe saymak; **2.** *n.* hiçe sayma, küçümseme; '**snub nose** ucu kalkık kısa burun; '**snub-nosed** *adj.* kısa ve kalkık burunlu.

snuff [snʌf] **1.** *n.* fitilin yanmış yeri (*mum*); enfiye; **up to** ~ F keyfi yerinde; kurnaz, açıkgöz, uyanık; **2.** *vb. a.* **take** ~ enfiye çekmek, buruna çekmek; fitilin yanık ucunu kesmek (*mum*); '~**box** enfiye kutusu; '**snuff.ers** *n. pl.* mum makası; **snuf.fle** ['~fl] *v/i.* burnunu çekmek, solumak; genizden konuşmak; '**snuff.y** *adj.* enfiye gibi, enfiyeli; pis kokan; *fig.* rencide olan, dargın, öfkeli, ters.

snug □ [snʌg] rahat, konforlu; kuytu; emniyetli; iyi oturmuş (*elbise*); '**snug.ger.y** *n.* konforlu yer, sıcak yuva;

'snuggle ['-gl] *v/i. a. ~ up* yerleşmek, sokulmak (*to, in -e*).

so [səu] 1. *adv.* böyle, öyle, şöyle; bu derece, bu kadar; onun için, bu nedenle, bu münasebetle; o derece, ... kadar; çok, pek; pek çok; dahi, de, da; 2. *conj.* şartı ile, -ması için, -sin diye; müddetçe; *int.* ya!, Öyle mi?, Tamam!; demek ki; yeter; 3. *adj.* doğru; *I hope ~* umarım öyledir; *you are tired, ~ am I* yorgunsunuz, ben de; *a mile or ~* bir mil kadar; *~ as to* ...mak için, ...cek şekilde, maksadiyle; *~ far* şimdiye kadar; *~ far as I know* bildiğim kadariyle.

soak [səuk] 1. *v/t.* ıslatmak, suya batırmak, sırsıklam etm.; *sl.* para sızdırmak, kazıklamak; *~ up veya in* emmek, içine çekmek; *v/i.* (suda) ıslanmak, yumuşamak, içine geçmek (*into, in*); F içkiyi fazla kaçırmak; 2. *n.* ıslanma, ıslatma, emme; = 'soak.er F ayyaş kimse.

so-and-so ['səuənsəu] *n.* filanca; *Mr.* ♀ falanca zat.

soap [səup] 1. *n.* sabun; *soft ~* arap sabunu; F dalkavukluk, yağcılık; 2. *v/t.* sabunlamak, sabun sürmek; '~-box *n.* sabun sandığı; *fig.* sokakta nutuk çekenlerin üstüne çıktığı sandık; *~ orator* sokak konuşmacısı, sokakta nutuk atan kimse; *~ race* çocukların kendi yaptığı sandık arabalarla yaptıkları yokuş aşağı yarış; '~-dish *n.* sabun tası; '~-bub.ble *n.* sabun köpüğü; '~-op.er.a *n. Am.* radyo *veya* televizyonda yayınlanan dizi melodram; '~-suds *n. pl., a. sg.* sabun köpüğü; 'soapy ☐ sabunlu, sabun gibi; *fig.* yağcı, boyun eğen.

soar [sɔː] *v/i.* yükselmek, yücelmek, havalanmak (*a. fig.*); AVIA havada süzülmek; aynı yükseklikte uçmak; artmak, fırlamak (*fiyat vs.*).

sob [sɔb] 1. *n.* hıçkırık, hıçkırma; 2. *v/i.* hıçkıra hıçkıra ağlamak, hüngür hüngür ağlamak.

so.ber ['səubə] 1. ☐ ayık; temkinli, kendine hakim; makûl, ölçülü, ılımlı; ciddi, ağırbaşlı; sade, gösterişsiz; 2. *v/t. & v/i. oft. ~ down* ciddileş(tir)mek, aklını başına getirmek, ayıl(t)mak; 'so.ber.ness, so.bri.e.ty [-'braiəti] *n.* ayıklık; ağırbaşlılık, ciddiyet; ılımlılık.

sob-stuff ['sɔbstʌf] *n.* santimantalizm, duygusallık.

so-called ['səu'kɔːld] *adj.* diye anılan, sözde, güya.

soc.cer F ['sɔkə] *n.* futbol (oyunu); '~ mom F *n.* çocuklarına futbol eğitimi veren anne.

so.cia.bil.i.ty [səuʃə'biliti] *n.* hoşsohbetlik, toplumsal olma, girişkenlik; 'so.cia.ble ☐ 1. girgin, arkadaş canlısı; nazik, tatlı dilli, sempatik; 2. *n.* sohbet toplantısı.

so.cial ['səuʃəl] 1. ☐ hoş sohbet, girgin; sosyal, toplumsal, topluma ait; *~ activities pl.* sosyal faaliyetler; *~ insurance* sosyal sigorta; *~ services pl.* sosyal hizmetler; 2. *n.* sohbetli toplantı (meclisi); 'so.cial.ism *n.* sosyalizm, toplumculuk; 'so.cial.ist 1. *n.* sosyalist, toplumcu; 2. *adj. a.* so.cial'is.tic sosyalizme ait, toplumcu; so.cial.ite ['-lait] *n.* tüm modaya uygun partilere katılan; 'so.cial.ize *vb.* kamulaştırmak, topluma mal etm.; sosyalleştirmek.

so.ci.e.ty [sə'saiəti] *n.* kurum, şirket, ortaklık; cemiyet, toplum, topluluk; kulüp, dernek; sosyete; arkadaşlık, dostluk; *secret ~* gizli cemiyet.

so.ci.o.log.i.cal ☐ [sousjə'lɔdʒikəl] sosyolojik, toplumbilimsel, sosyolojiye ait; soci.ol.o.gist [-si'ɔlədʒist] *n.* sosyolog, toplumbilimci; so.ci'ol.o.gy *n.* sosyoloji, toplumbilim.

sock[1] [sɔk] *n.* kısa çorap, şoset; mantar taban.

sock[2] *sl.* [.] 1. *n.* dayak, kötek; *give s.o. ~s* = 2. *v/t. b-ne* dayak atmak, pataklamak.

sock.er F ['sɔkə] = *soccer*.

sock.et ['sɔkit] *n.* sap deliği, yuva, oyuk (*göz, diş*); mafsal oyuğu; ELECT duy, priz.

so.cle ['sɔkl] *n.* kaide, ayaklık, kürsü; temel, destek, taban.

sod [sɔd] 1. *n.* çimen (parçası), çim; 2. *vb.* çimen parçaları ile kaplamak.

so.da CHEM ['səudə] *n.* soda; karbonat, sodyum bikarbonat; '~-foun.tain *n.* sifon; büfe, büvet, dondurma salonu; '~-wa.ter *n.* maden sodası; gazoz.

sod.den ['sɔdn] *adj.* sırsıklam; iyice ıslanmış; hamurumsu (*ekmek*); ayyaş suratlı.

so.di.um CHEM ['səudjəm] *n.* sodyum, sut.

so.ev.er [səu'evə] *adv.* her ne, herhangi, her.

so.fa ['səufə] *n.* kanepe, sedir.

sof.fit ARCH ['sɔfit] *n.* kemer, taban, balkon *veya* merdivenin alt yüzü.

soft [sɔft] **1.** □ *com.* yumuşak; yumuşak başlı, mülayim, uysal; ılık, tatlı (*iklim*); zayıf, gevşek; ince, narin; hafif, kolay, rahat; F aklı kıt, budala; ~ *drink* F alkolsüz içki, içecek; *a* ~ *thing sl.* kolay ve paralı iş; *s. soap 1*; **2.** *adv.* yavaşça; **3.** *n.* yumuşak şey; F ahmak, öküz aleyhisselâm, sünepe; '~'**boiled** *adj.* rafadan (*yumurta*).

soft.en ['sɔfn] *v/t. & v/i.* yumuşa(t)mak (*a. fig.*); yatış(tır)mak, teskin etm.; kısmak (*ses*); sindirmek (*boya*); MEC tavlayıp yavaş yavaş soğutarak sertleştirmek (*metal*); 'soft.en.er *n.* yumuşatıcı (*madde*); soft-head.ed ['sɔft'hedid] *adj.* bunak, budala, ebleh; 'soft-'heart.ed *adj.* yumuşak kalpli, yufka yürekli; 'soft.ness *n.* yumuşaklık, uysallık; 'soft-'ped.al *v/t.* MUS pianoyu pedalla çalmak; *fig.* basitleştirmek, önememek, hafifletmek, gevşetmek; 'soft-'saw.der **1.** *v/i.* tatlı dil dökmek, pohpohlamak; **2.** *n.* tatlı dil, yüze gülüş, pohpohlama; 'soft-'soap *vb.* yağ çekmek, ayartmak, yaltaklanmak; 'soft-ware *n.* kompütere verilen program; 'soft.y *n.* F ahmak, sünepe.

sog.gy ['sɔgi] *adj.* sırsıklam, iyice ıslanmış, yas, ıslak.

so.ho ['səu'həu] *int.* hey!

soil[1] [sɔil] *n.* toprak, yer; arazi, memleket, ülke.

soil[2] [̲] *n.* kir, leke, pislik, çöp; gübre, dışkı; **2.** *v/t.* kirletmek, lekelemek; namusuna leke sürmek; *v/i.* kirlenmek, pislenmek, lekelenmek; 'soil-pipe *n.* künk, boşaltma borusu.

so.journ ['sɔdʒəːn] **1.** *n.* konukluk, misafirlik; **2.** *v/i.* kalmak, konaklamak, misafir olarak kalmak; 'so.journ.er *n.* konuk, misafir.

sol MUS [sɔl] *n.* sol, gamda beşinci nota.

sol.ace ['sɔləs] **1.** *n.* avuntu, teselli; **2.** *v/t.* teselli etm., avutmak.

so.lar ['səulə] *adj.* güneşe ait, güneş...

sold [səuld] *pret. & p.p. of sell 1.*

sol.der MEC ['sɔldə] **1.** *n.* lehim; **2.** *v/t.* lehimlemek (*up*); 'sol.der.ing-i.ron *n.* havya.

sol.dier ['səuldʒə] **1.** *n.* asker, er; **2.** *v/i.* askerlik yapmak; *go ~ing* asker olm.; 'sol.dier.like, 'sol.dier.ly *adj.* askerî, askerce, asker gibi; 'sol.dier.ship *n.* askerlik; 'sol.dier.y *n.* askerler, ordu, asker sınıfı; *contp.* düzensiz asker topluluğu.

sole[1] □ [səul] tek, yalnız, biricik, yegâne; ~ *agent* tek mümessil.

sole[2] [̲] **1.** *n.* taban, pençe; **2.** *v/t.* pençe vurmak -*e.*

sole[3] ICHTH [̲] *n.* dilbalığı.

sol.e.cism ['sɔlisizəm] *n.* dilbilgisi kurallarının dışına çıkma, deyim hatası; aykırı davranış ve tutum.

sol.emn □ ['sɔləm] törenli, merasimle yapılan; ağırbaşlı, vakur; kutsal; heybetli; so.lem.ni.ty [sə'lemniti] *n.* tantanalı tören, kutlama; ağırbaşlılık, vakar; solem.ni.za.tion ['sɔləmnai'zeiʃən] *n.* kutla(n)ma, ayin, tören; 'sol.em.nize *vb.* kutlamak, resmî ayin yapmak.

so.lic.it [sə'lisit] *vb.* istemek, rica etm. (*s.o.; s.th.; s.o. for s.th. veya s.th. of s.o.*), dilemek; rahatsız etm., huzurunu kaçırmak, balta elm.; so.lic.i'ta.tion *n.* rica, talep, müracaat, istek; tahrik, davet; so'lic.i.tor *n.* JUR müşavir avukat, dava vekili; *Am.* acenta, propagandist, reklamcı; ♀ *General* başsavcı, müddei umumi; so'lic.it.ous □ endişeli, meraklı, vesveseli (*about, for için*); ~ *of* istekli, arzulu -*e;* ~ *to* dikkatli, gayretli; so'lic.i.tude [̲tjuːd] *n.* endişe, kaygı, sıkıntı, korku, vesvese; gayret, çaba(lama), ilgi.

sol.id ['sɔlid] **1.** □ katı; sağlam, dayanıklı; som, masif, yekpare; MATH cisimsel; *fig.* güvenilir, emin; *part.* COM ekonomik saygınlığı tam; dayanışık, aralarında dayanışma olan; *a ~ hour* tam bir saat; ~ *geometry* MATH uzay geometri; ~ *leather* köselenin en iyi kısmı; **2.** *n.* katı madde; üç boyutluluk; sol.i.dar.i.ty [̲'dæriti] *n.* dayanışma, omuzdaşlık, tesanüt; so'lid.i.fy [̲difai] *vb.* katılaş(tır)mak, sertleş(tir)mek, kuvvetlendirmek; so'lid.i.ty *n.* katılık; uyuşum, tesanüt; sağlamlık, dayanıklılık; güvenirlik, emniyet.

so.lil.o.quize [sə'liləkwaiz] *vb.* kendi *k-ne* konuşmak; so'lil.o.quy *n.* monolog, kendi *k-ne* konuşma.

sol.i.taire [soli'tɛə] *n.* mücevherde tek taş; tek kişilik kâğıt oyunu. **sol.i.tar.y** □ [' ̲təri] tek, yalnız; tenha, ıssız; tek başına; ~ *confinement* münferit hapis, hücre hapsi; sol.i.tude [' ̲tjuːd] *n.* yalnızlık; ıssızlık, boşluk.

so.lo ['səuləu] *n.* MUS *& iskambil:* solo; iki *veya* üç kişiye karşı tek oynanan oyun; AVIA tek başına uçuş; 'so.lo.ist *n.* solist.

sol.stice ['sɔlstis] *n. astr.* gündönümü.
sol.u.bil.i.ty [sɔlju'biliti] *n.* eriyebilme
yeteneği; sol.u.ble ['.bl] *adj.* eriyebilir, çözülebilir.
so.lu.tion [sə'lu:ʃən] *n.* erime, çözünme; çöz(ül)me, çözüm (*a.* MATH &
CHEM), çare; MEC kauçuk, eriyik.
solv.a.ble ['sɔlvəbl] *adj.* çözülür, halledilir; solve *v/t.* halletmek, çözmek,
yanıt bulmak; sol.ven.cy COM ['.vənsi] *n.* ödeme gücü; 'sol.vent 1. *adj.* COM
borcunu ödeyebilir, ödeme gücü olan;
eritici, çözücü; 2. *n.* eritici sıvı, eritken.
som.bre, *Am.* som.ber □ ['sɔmbə] loş,
karanlık (*a. fig.*); bulanık, mat.
some [sʌm, səm] 1. *pron. & adj.* bazı;
bir, herhangi bir; biraz, bir parça, birkaç, birçok; hayli, epey; bazısı, kimi(-
si); ~ bread bir parça ekmek; ~ few oldukça; ~ 30 miles yaklaşık 30 mil; in ~
degree, to ~ extent kısmen, bir dereceye kadar; this is ~ speech! konuşma
diye buna denir!, öyle bir konuşma ki!;
2. *adv.* yaklaşık (olarak), biraz; *Am.*
klâs, şık; '~.body *pron.* biri(si);
'~.day *adv.* bir gün (*gelecekte*);
'~.one *pron.* biri(si); '~.how *adv.* her
nasılsa, bir yolunu bulup, herhangi
bir şekilde; ~ or other her nasıl olursa
olsun.
som.er.sault ['sʌməsɔːlt] *n.* taklak,
perende; turn a ~ takla atmak.
some...: ~.thing ['sʌmθiŋ] *pron.* bir
şey; ~ like daha çok ... e benzeyen;
yaklaşık; '~.time *n.* günün birinde,
gelecekte; 2. *adj.* eski, sabık; '~.times
adv. bazen, arasıra; '~.what *adv.* bir
dereceye kadar; '~.where *adv.* bir
yer(d)e; '~.while *adv.* bir süre, arasıra
yapılan.
som.nam.bu.lism [sɔm'næmbjulizəm] *n.* uyurgezerlik; som'nam.bu-
list *n.* uyurgezer.
som.nif.er.ous □ [sɔm'nifərəs] uyutucu, uyku getirici; uyuşturucu.
som.no.lence ['sɔmnələns] *n.* uyku
basması, uyuklama, uykulu hal;
'som.no.lent *adj.* uykusu gelmiş, uyku
basmış, uyuklayan.
son [sʌn] *n.* oğul, erkek evlât.
so.na.ta MUS [sə'nɑːtə] *n.* sonat.
song [sɔŋ] *n.* şarkı, türkü, kanto, şan;
şiir, manzume; ötme; for a mere *veya*
an old ~ yok pahasına, çok ucuza;
nothing to make a ~ about F pek o kadar değil, mesele yapmağa değmez;
'~-bird *n.* ötücü kuş; '~-book *n.* şarkı

kitabı; '~-hit *n.* günün şarkısı; song-
ster ['.stə] *n.* şantör, şarkıcı; ötücü
kuş; song.stress ['.stris] *n.* şantöz,
hanende, kantocu.
son.ic ['sɔnik] *adj.* ses hızı *veya* dalgalariyle ilgili; ~ bang ses duvarını aşan
bir uçağın neden olduğu patlama sesi;
~ barri.er ses duvarı.
son-in-law *n.*, *pl.* sons-in-law ['sʌn(z)-
inlɔ:] damat.
son.net ['sɔnit] *n.* sone, on dört dizeli
bir batı koşuk türü.
son.ny ['sʌni] *n.* oğlum, yavrum, evlâdım.
so.no.rous □ [sə'nɔ:rəs] tınlayan,
yankılı, ses çıkaran, sesli; so'no.rous-
ness *n.* ses bolluğu, dolgun seslilik.
soon [su:n] *adv.* birazdan, biraz sonra;
hemen, şimdi, derhal; erken; seve seve,
memnuniyetle; as *veya* so ~ as -ince,
olur olmaz, yapar yapmaz; 'soon.er
adv. daha önce, daha erken; daha
çok (*veya* fazla), tercihan; no ~ ... than
-ir -mez, olur olmaz; no ~ said than
done demesiyle yapması bir oldu.
soot [sut] 1. *n.* is, kurum; 2. *v/t.* is(e) bulaştırmak (up).
sooth [su:θ] *n.*: in ~ gerçekte, hakikatte; soothe [su:ð] *v/t.* yatıştırmak, teskin etm., rahatlatmak; sooth.say.er
['su:θseiə] *n.* falcı (kadın), geleceği
söyleyen, kâhin.
soot.y □ ['suti] isli, kurumlu.
sop [sɔp] 1. *n.* sıvıda yumuşatılmış şey,
tirit; *fig.* yumuşatıcı şey, rüşvet, sus
payı; 2. *v/t.* etsuyuna banmak, batırmak; ıslatarak yumuşatmak; ~ up suyu
emmek; kurulamak, silmek.
soph.ism ['sɔfizəm] *n.* sofizm, bilgicilik, safsata, mantığa uymazlık.
soph.ist ['sɔfist] *n.* safsatacı kimse, sofist; so.phis.tic, so.phis.ti.cal □ [sə-
'fistik(əl)] safsatalı, sofistçe; so'phis-
ti.cate [.keit] *vb.* safsata karıştırmak;
hile ile saflığını bozmak; deneyim kazandırmak; so'phis.ti.cat.ed *adj.* hayata alışmış, kasarlanmış, kurnaz, pişkin; çağdaş, kültürlü, entelektüel;
karışık, komplike; yapmacık; so-
phis.ti'ca.tion *n.* safsata(cılık); çokbilmişlik, kurnazlık; komplike *veya*
karışık olma; soph.ist.ry ['sɔfistri]
n. safsata(cılık), sofistlik.
soph.o.more *Am.* ['sɔfəmɔ:] *n.* kolej
veya üniversitede ikinci sınıf öğrencisi.
so.po.rif.ic [sɔpə'rifik] 1. *adj.* (~ally)
uyutucu; uyuşturucu; 2. *n.* uyutucu

ilaç.

sop.ping ['sɔpiŋ] *adj. a.* ~ **wet** sırsıklam; 'sop.py *adj.* çok ıslanmış, sırsıklam; F aptal; duygusal, sentimental (*hikâye vs.*).

so.pran.o MUS [sə'prɑːnəu] *n.* soprano.

sor.cer.er ['sɔːsərə] *n.* büyücü, sihirbaz; 'sor.cer.ess *n.* büyücü kadın, cadı; 'sorcer.y *n.* büyü(cülük), afsun.

sor.did □ ['sɔːdid] alçak, sefil, adi, bayağı (*a. fig.*); kirli, pis, pasaklı; pinti, hasis, çıkarcı; 'sor.did.ness *n.* alçaklık, sefillik; pintilik, cimrilik.

sore [sɔː] **1.** □ acı veren, azmış (*yara*), ıstırap veren, ağrıyan, sızlayan; iltihaplı, yaralı; şiddetli, sert; *fig.* vahim, endişe verici; kırgın, küskün; ~ **throat** boğaz ağrısı; **2.** *n.* ağrıyan yer; yara (*a. fig.*), bere 'sore.head *n.* Am. F hayal kırıklığına uğramış *veya* asık suratlı, çabuk sinirlenen kimse; 'sore.ly *adv.* şiddetle, pek çok; 'sore.ness *n.* elem, acı(lık).

so.ror.i.ty [sə'rɔriti] *n.* Am. UNIV kız öğrenciler birliği (*veya yurdu*).

sor.rel¹ ['sɔrəl] **1.** *adj.* kırmızımsı kahverengi (*part. at*); **2.** *n.* al don, kızıl doru, kula (at).

sor.rel² BOT [_] *n.* kuzukulağı.

sor.row ['sɔrəu] **1.** *n.* keder, acı, dert, tasa, elem, gam, üzüntü; **2.** *v/i.* kederlenmek, esef etm., kasvet çekmek; **sor.rowful** □ ['sɔrəful] kederli, elemli; keder veren, üzüntülü.

sor.ry □ ['sɔri] üzgün, kederli, gamlı, mahzun; acınacak, pişman; (*I am*) (*so*) ~! üzgünüm!, maalesef!, pardon!, affedersiniz!; *I am* ~ *for him* ona acıyorum, onun için üzülüyorum; *we are* ~ *to say* üzülerek söylemek zorundayız, maalesef söylemek zorundayız.

sort [sɔːt] **1.** *n.* çeşit, nevi, tür; usül, tarz, yol; *what* ~ *of* nasıl bir; *of a* ~, *of* ~*s* sözüm ona, sıradan; *out of* ~*s* F rahatsız, keyifsiz; canı sıkılmış, neşesiz; *a good* ~ çok iyi bir adam; (*a*) ~ *of peace* sözüm ona (*veya* iyi kötü) huzur, barış; **2.** *vb.* sınıflandırmak, ayıklamak; COM tasnif etm.; ~ *out* seçmek, seçip ayırmak, ayıklamak.

sor.tie MIL ['sɔːtiː] *n.* huruç, çıkış hareketi; AVIA bombardıman uçuşu.

sot [sɔt] *n.* ayyaş kimse, bekri.

sot.tish □ ['sɔtiʃ] ayyaş, küfelik.

sou [suː] *n.* eski bir ufak Fransız parası; *fig.* mangır, metelik.

souf.flé ['suːflei] *n.* sufle.

sough [sau] **1.** *n.* vızıltı, uğultu; **2.** *v/i.* uğuldamak, hışıldamak (*part. rüzgâr*).

sought [sɔːt] *pret. & p.p. of* **seek**; '~'after *adj.* revaçta olan, çok rağbet gören.

soul [səul] *n.* ruh, can (*a. fig.*); '~-destroy.ing *adj.* can sıkıcı, monoton; 'soulless □ ruhsuz, cansız, duygusuz.

sound¹ □ [saund] *com.* sağlam, esen, salim (*a. fig.*); mükemmel, inceden inceye, tamamen; akıllı, mantıklı, anlayışlı; derin (*uyku*); şiddetli (*vuruş, darbe*); COM emin, güvenilir; JUR yasal, meşru, muteber, geçerli.

sound² [_] **1.** *n.* ses, sada; ima, anlam; gürültü; ses erimi; **2.** *v/i.* ses çıkarmak, ses vermek, duyulmak, aksetmek; gelmek, görünmek (*like gibi*); *v/t.* (*ses*) çıkartmak, çalmak -*i*, öttürmek -*i*; sesle ilân etm.; açıkça övmek; ~ *the charge* MIL hücum borusu çalmak.

sound³ [_] *n.* GEOL boğaz, balığın yüzme kesesi, solungaç.

sound⁴ [_] **1.** *n.* MED sonda; **2.** *v/t.* MED sondalamak (*a. fig.*); NAUT iskandil etm.; MED kulaklık ile muayene etm.; ~ *s.o. out* b-nin ağzını aramak, düşüncesini öğrenmeğe çalışmak.

sound...: '~-box *n.* gramafon, pikap; diyafram; ~ **broad.cast.ing** sesli radyo yayını; ~ **ef.fects** *pl.* (*radyo, tiyatro*) efekt, konuşmaların dışındaki sesler; '~-film *n.* sesli film.

sound.ing NAUT ['saundiŋ] *n.* iskandil etme; ~*s pl.* iskandil edilen suyun derinliği.

sound.ing-board ['saundiŋbɔːd] *n.* ses yansıtıcısı; rezonans gövdesi (*keman vs.'de*).

sound.less □ ['saundlis] sessiz, sedasız.

sound.ness ['saundnis] *n.* sıhhat, sağ(lam)lık, esenlik; doğruluk; metanet.

sound...: '~-proof, '~-tight *adj.* ses geçirmez; '~-track *n. film:* ses yolu; '~-wave *n.* PHYS ses dalgası.

soup¹ [suːp] *n.* çorba, etsuyu.

soup² Am. sl. [_] **1.** *n.* beygir gücü; **2.** *vb.* ~ *up* (*motor*) gücünü artırmak.

sour ['sauə] **1.** □ ekşi(miş); *fig.* acı, dokunaklı; *fig.* somurtkan, asık suratlı, huysuz; **2.** *v/t.* ekşitmek; asitlendirmek; *fig. b-nin* hayatını zehir etm.; *v/i.* ekşimek, kesilmek (*süt*); *fig.* somurtkan, surat asmak.

source [sɔːs] *n.* kaynak, memba, pınar; menşe, köken; '~ *code* IT *n.* köken kodu.

sour.ish □ ['sauəriʃ] ekşi(ce), mayhoş; '**sour.ness** *n.* ekşilik; *fig.* huysuzluk, somurtkanlık, terslik.

souse [saus] **1.** *v/t.* batırmak, banmak, daldırmak, ıslatmak; tuzlamak, salamura yapmak, turşu yapmak; **2.** *n.* güm diye düşme, gümbürtü, «plof» diye ses çıkararak düşme; salamura; **soused** *adj. sl.* sarhoş, ayyaş.

sou.tane ECCL [su:'tɑːn] *n.* papaz cüppesi.

south [sauθ] **1.** *n.* güney, cenup; *to the* **~** *of* -*in* güneyinde; **2.** *adj.* güney..., cenubî, güneye doğru; güneyden gelen.

south-east ['sauθiːst] **1.** *n.* güney doğu; **2.** *adj. a.* **south-'east.ern** -*in* güney-doğusunda.

south.er.ly ['sʌðəli], **south.ern** ['-ən] *adj.* güneye doğru, güney...; '**south-ern.er** *n. Am.* A.B.D.'nin güneydoğu eyaletlerinden olan kimse, güneyli.

south.ern.most ['sʌðənməust] *adj.* en güneyde olan.

south.ing ['sauðiŋ] *n.* NAUT güneye doğru rota.

south...: '**~.land** *n.* güney bölgesi; '**~.paw** *n. Am. beysbol:* solak oyuncu; ♀ **Pole** Güney Kutbu.

south.ward(s) ['sauθwəd(z)] *adv.* güneye doğru.

south...: '**~'west 1.** *n.* güney batı; **2.** *adj. a.* **~'west.er.ly**, **~'west.ern** güney(d)e; güneyden esen (*rüzgâr*), lodos(tan); **~'west.er** *n.* güney rüzgârı, lodos; = **sou'west.er** NAUT [sau'wəstə] *n.* gemicilerin muşamba başlığı.

sou.ve.nir ['suːvəniə] *n.* hatıra, andaç (**of**).

sov.er.eign ['sɔvriŋ] **1.** □ en yüksek, yüce; mükemmel, şahane; etkili (*ilâç*); mutlak, bağımsız; hükümran; **2.** *n.* hükümdar, kral(içe); eski altın İngiliz lirası; **sov.er.eign.ty** ['-rənti] *n.* hükümranlık, hâkimiyet, egemenlik; bağımsızlık.

so.vi.et ['səuviət] *n.* Sovyet; idare meclisi.

sow¹ [sau] *n.* ZOO dişi domuz; MEC erimiş maden oluğu; bu olukta yapılan maden külçesi.

sow² [səu] (*irr.*) *vb.* ekmek, serpmek, yaymak (*tohum*); yaymak, neşretmek; '**sower** *n.* tohum; tohum ekme makinesi; çiftçi; **sown** [səun] *p.p. of* **sow**².

so.ya BOT ['sɔiə] *n.* soya; **~** *bean* soya fasulyesi.

soz.zled *sl.* ['sɔzld] *adj.* sarhoş, ayyaş.

spa [spɑː] *n.* kaplıca, içmeler, ılıca (*yeri*).

space [speis] **1.** *n.* feza, uzay; alan, yer, mevki; aralık, açıklık, mesafe; müddet, süre; TYP espas, iki sözcük arasını açmak için kullanılan maden parçası; **2.** *vb. a.* **~** *out* aralık koymak, fasıla bırakmak; TYP aralıklı dizmek; '**~-craft**, '**~-ship** *n.* uzay gemisi; '**~-suit** *n.* uzay elbisesi; '**~-'time** *n.* yer-zaman ilintisi.

spa.cious □ ['speiʃəs] geniş, engin, bol, pek büyük; ferah, havadar; '**spa-ciousness** *n.* genişlik, enginlik, açıklık.

spade [speid] **1.** *n.* bahçıvan beli, kazma; *call a* **~** *a* **~** açıkça, isim vererek söylemek; *mst* **~s** *pl. iskambil:* maça, pik; **2.** *vb.* bellemek, bel ile kazmak; '**~-work** *n.* bel işi; bir iş için zahmetli hazırlık.

spa.ghet.ti [spə'geti] *n.* çubuk makarna, spageti.

spake *obs. veya poet.* [speik] *pret. of* *speak*.

spam (mail) IT [spæm] *n.* spam.

span¹ [spæn] **1.** *n.* karış; süre, aralık; ARCH kemer *veya* köprü ayakları arasındaki açıklık; *Am.* çift koşum; **2.** *v/t.* ölçmek, karışlamak; boydan boya uzatmak.

span² [.] *pret. of* *spin* 1.

span.gle ['spæŋgl] **1.** *n.* pul, payet, pul gibi pırıldayan süs; **2.** *v/t.* pullarla süslemek.

Spang.lish ['spæŋglıʃ] *n. İspanyolca- -İngilizce karışımı.*

Span.iard ['spænjəd] *n.* İspanyol.

span.iel ['spænjəl] *n.* uzun tüylü ve uzun sarkık kulaklı bir tür köpek, spanyel.

Span.ish ['spænıʃ] **1.** *adj.* İspanyol, İspanyalı; İspanya *veya* İspanyolca'ya ait; **2.** *n.* İspanyalı; İspanyolca; *the* **~** *pl.* İspanya halkı.

spank F [spæŋk] **1.** *v/t.* -*in* kıçına şaplak vurmak; **~** *along* hızlı gitmek *veya* denizde seyretmek; **2.** *n.* şaplak, hafif vurma; '**spank.er** *n.* NAUT randa yelkeni; '**spanking 1.** □ şiddetli, kuvvetli (*rüzgâr*); tez, çabuk koşan; F inanılmayacak kadar büyük; **2.** *n.* F iyi bir dayak; şaplak atma.

span.ner MEC ['spænə] *n.* somun anahtarı; *throw a* **~** *into the works* *fig.* işe çomak sokmak.

spar¹ [spɑː] *n.* NAUT seren, direk; AVIA kanat ana kirişi.

spar² [ˍ] *v/i.* *boks*: hafif boks yapmak (**with** *ile*); *fig.* ağız kavgası etm. (*at*), horoz gibi dövüşmek; **~ring partner** *boks*: idman arkadaşı.

spar³ MIN [ˍ] *n.* ispat (*bir tür taş*).

spare [speə] **1.** □ az, yetersiz, seyrek, kıt, dar; pinti, eli sıkı; boş, serbest; fazla, artakalan, kullanılmayan; yedek…, ihtiyat; sıska, zayıf; **~ hours** *pl.* boş zaman; **~ room** misafir için yatak odası; **~ time** boş vakit; **2.** *n.* MEC yedek parça; **3.** *v/t.* canını bağışlamak; biriktirmek (*para*); kazanmak (*vakit*); zahmetten kurtulmak; esirgemek; tutumlu kullanmak *-i*; vazgeçmek *-den*; **enough and to ~** yeter de artar; *v/i.* idareli olm., tutumlu olm.; esirgemek; **'spare.ness** *n.* azlık, kıtlık; zayıflık; **spare part** yedek parça; **'sparerib** *n.* az etli domuz pirzolası.

spar.ing □ ['speərɪŋ] tutumlu, idareli (*in, of*); az kullanan; **'spar.ing.ness** *n.* tutum, tasarruf.

spark¹ ['spɑːk] **1.** *n.* kıvılcım (*a. fig.*); **2.** *v/i.* kıvılcım saçmak; *v/t.* **~ s.th. off** bşi harekete geçirmek; *b-ni* teşvik etm., kışkırtmak.

spark² [ˍ] *n.* şık ve yakışıklı delikanlı, kavalye.

spark.ing-plug MOT ['spɑːkɪŋplʌg] *n.* buji.

spar.kle ['spɑːkl] **1.** *n.* kıvılcım; parlayış, parıltı; parıldayan şey; **2.** *v/i.* parıldamak; kıvılcım saçmak (*zekâ*); köpürmek (*şarap*); köpüklenmek; **sparkling wine** köpüklü şarap; **spark.klet** ['ˍklɪt] *n.* küçük kıvılcım, zerre (*a. fig.*).

spark-plug MOT ['spɑːkplʌg] *n.* buji.

spar.row ORN ['spærəu] *n.* serçe; **'~-hawk** *n.* ORN atmaca.

sparse [spɑːs] seyrek, sık olmayan.

Spar.tan ['spɑːtən] **1.** *adj.* Spartalı; Sparta ile ilgili; güçlüklere dayanan, yılmaz; **2.** *n.* Spartalı kimse.

spasm MED ['spæzəm] *n.* kramp, ıspazmoz, sinir kasılması; **spas.mod.ic**, **spas.mod.ical** □ [ˍ'mɔdik(əl)] kasılımlı, ıspazmoz kabilinden; sürekli olmayan, düzensiz; *fig.* daldan dala konan.

spat¹ [spæt] *n.* istiridye yumurtası.

spat² [ˍ] *n.* kısa tozluk, dolak.

spat³ [ˍ] *pret. & p.p. of* **spit²** 2.

spatch-cock ['spætʃkɔk] *vb.* serpiştir-

mek, içine katmak (*konuşma, not*).

spate [speit] *n.* sel, su baskını; *fig.* akın, kütle, kalabalık; **be in ~** sele kapılmak.

spa.tial □ ['speiʃəl] mekân, hacim vs. itibariyle, uzaysal.

spat.ter ['spætə] **1.** *v/t. & v/i.* serpmek, sıçratmak (*su vs.*); damlalar halinde dökülmek; **2.** *n.* kısa süren sağanak, serpinti; serpme, sıçratma (*a. fig.*).

spat.u.la ['spætjulə] *n.* spatüla, macun malası.

spav.in VET [spævin] *n.* at ayağının oynak yerinin şişmesi.

spawn ['spɔːn] **1.** *n.* balık yumurtası; *fig. mst contp.* döl, evlât; **2.** *vb.* yumurta dökmek; üretmek, *fig.* meydana getirmek, yumurtlamak; **'spawn.er** *n.* yumurtlayan (*balık*); **'spawn.ing 1.** *n.* yumurtlama; **2.** *adj.* yumurtlayan…

speak [spiːk] (*irr.*) *v/i.* konuşmak (**to** *ile*); bahsetmek (**about**, **of** *-den*); konuşma yapmak; MUS tınlamak; **~ing!** TELEPH evet!; **Brown ~ing!** ben Bay Brown'ım; **~ out** yüksek sesle söylemek; açıkça söylemek; **~ to** *b-le* konuşmak, *b-ne* söylemek; **~ up** çekinmeden açıkça söylemek; **~ up!** yüksek sesle konuş!; **~ up against** aleyhinde konuşmak, karşısında olm.; **that ~s well for him** bu onun iyi olduğunu kanıtlar; *v/t.* söylemek, beyan etm. (*düşünce*), bildirmek; **'~-eas.y** *n.* *Am. sl.* gizli içki satılan yer; **'speak.er** *n.* konuşan *veya* söyleyen kimse, konuşmacı, sözcü, spiker; **'speak.er phone** TELEPH *n.* hoparlörlü telefon.

speak.ing ['spiːkɪŋ] *adj.* konuşan; canlı; açık ve düzgün (*ifade*); dokunaklı (*tablo, bakış*); **be on ~ terms with** selâm vermekten öteye gitmeyen düzeyde tanışıyor olm.; **'~-trum.pet** *n.* ses nakil borusu; megafon.

spear [spiə] **1.** *n.* mızrak, kargı; **2.** *v/t.* mızrakla vurmak *-e*; saplamak; **'~-head 1.** *n.* mızrak ucu; *fig.* baş, öncü öncüsü; **2.** *v/t.* öncülük etm., önayak olm. *-e.*

spec COM *sl.* [spek] *n.* spekülasyon, vurgun.

spe.cial ['speʃəl] **1.** □ özel, hususi, fevkalâde; *k-ne* mahsus, ayrı; **2.** *n. a.* **~ constable** yardımcı polis; *a.* **~ edition** özel baskı; *a.* **~ train** özel tren; *Am.* özel teklif (*iş*); *Am.* günün özel yemeği (*lokanta*); **'spe.cial.ist** *n.* uzman, mütehassıs; MED mütehassıs hekim; **spe.ci.al.i.ty** [speʃi'æliti] *n.* özellik, hususiyet; COM ihtisas; **spe.cial.i.za.tion** [speʃəlai'zeiʃən] *n.* ihtisas sahibi olma; '**spe.cial.ize** *vb.* ihtisas yapmak; tek bir konu üzerinde çalışmak; ihtisas sahibi olm. (*in -in*), mütehassıs olm.; **spe.cial.ty** ['ˌti] *n. s.* **speciality**; JUR mühürlü sözleşme.

spe.cie ['spi:ʃi:] *n.* madenî para, sikke; '**spe.cies** *n. pl. & sg.* tür, çeşit, cins.

spe.cif.ic [spi'sifik] **1.** *adj.* (**~ally**) özgü, *k-ne* has; özel, spesifik, hususi, mahsus; belirli, muayyen; kati, kesin; **~ gravity** PHYS özgül ağırlık; **2.** *n.* MED belirli tedavide kullanılan ilâç.

spec.i.fi.ca.tion [spesifi'keiʃən] *n.* tayin, belirtme; JUR şartname; **~s** *pl* ayrıntılı tanımlama; (*teknik*) tarifname; **spec.i.fy** ['ˌfai] *v/t.* belirtmek, ayrı ayrı göstermek *veya* söylemek.

spec.i.men ['spesimin] *n.* örnek, numune, model.

spe.cious ☐ ['spi:ʃəs] aldatıcı yanıltıcı (*dış görünüş olarak*), sahte; samimiyetsiz, güvenilmez; '**spe.cious.ness** *n.* dış görünüşün aldatıcı olması.

speck [spek] **1.** *n.* nokta, benek, ufak leke; küçük parça, parçacık; **2.** *vb.* lekelemek; **speck.le** ['ˌkl] **1.** *n.* ufak benek *veya* leke, çil; **2.** *vb. s.* **speck 2**.

specs F [speks] *n. pl.* gözlük.

spec.ta.cle ['spektəkl] *n.* manzara, görülecek şey, görünüş; (*a pair of*); **~s** *pl.* gözlük; '**spec.ta.cled** *adj.* gözlüklü.

spec.tac.u.lar ☐ [spek'tækjulə] **1.** görülmeye değer, göz alıcı, olağanüstü, göze çarpan; **2.** *n. Am.* F hayret verici manzara.

spec.ta.tor [spek'teitə] *n.* seyirci.

spec.tral ☐ ['spektrəl] hayalet kabilinden; hayal gücüne dayanan; hayalî; OPT tayfî, ışık dağılımına ait; **spec.tre** ['ˌtə] *n.* hayal(et); **spec.tro.scope** OPT ['ˌtrəskəup] *n.* spektroskop, ışığı yedi renge ayıran alet; **spec.trum** ['ˌtrəm] *n.* tayf.

spec.u.late ['spekjuleit] *vb.* zihnini kurcalamak, (kuramsal olarak) düşünmek, mütalâa etm. (*on, upon -i*); COM borsada oynamak, spekülasyon yapmak; **specu'la.tion** *n.* kurgu, vehim, işkil; COM spekülasyon; **spec.u.la.tive** ☐ ['ˌlətiv] spekülatif; kuruntulu, vesveseli; kuramsal, nazarî, teorik; COM borsa oyunuyla ilgili, spekülatif; rizikolu, tehlikeli; **spec.u.lator** ['ˌleitə] *n.* COM spekülatör, kapatçı, vurguncu.

spec.u.lum MED, OPT ['spekjuləm] *n.* (*metal*) ayna, spekülom.

sped [sped] *pret. & p.p. of* **speed 2**.

speech [spi:tʃ] *n.* konuşma yeteneği, düzgün ve iyi konuşma yetisi; söz, nutuk, söylev; dil; **make a ~** söylev vermek, konuşma yapmak, nutuk çekmek; '**~-day** *n.* (*okul*) diploma töreni; **speech.i.fy** *contp.* ['ˌifai] *v/i.* fazla konuşmak, nutuk çekmek, kafa şişirmek; '**speech.less** ☐ dili tutulmuş, dilsiz; sessiz; sözle anlatılamaz.

speed [spi:d] **1.** *n.* hız, sürat, çabukluk, acele; MEC devir sayısı; PHOT ışığa karşı duyarlık; **2.** (*irr.*) *v/i.* hızla gitmek, acele etm. çabuk gitmek; **~ up** (*pret. & p.p. ~ed*) hızlanmak; *v/t.* hızlandırmak; uğur getirmek; **~ up** (*pret. & p.p. ~ed*) hızını arttırmak; '**~-boat** *n.* sürat motoru, yarış kayığı; '**~-cop** *n.* motorlu trafik polisi; '**~ dial(.ing** TELEPH *n. telefonda bir numarayı tek bir düğmeye basarak çevirme*; hızlı çağrı; '**~-di.al but.ton** *n.* hızlı çağrı tuşu; '**~-in.di.ca-tor = speedometer**; '**~-lim.it** *n.* azami sürat; **speed.om.e.ter** *n.* MOT hızölçer; '**speed.way** *n.* sürat yolu, hız yolu; '**speed.well** *n.* BOT yavşanotu; '**speed.y** ☐ çabuk, hızlı.

spell¹ [spel] **1.** *n.* nöbet, süre; MEC vardiya, posta; **2.** *vb.* nöbeti devralarak *b-ni* serbest kılmak (*at*), nöbetini almak *-in*.

spell² [ˌ] **1.** *n.* büyü, sihir, tılsım; **2.** (*irr.*) *vb.* büyülemek; bir sözcüğün hecelerini ayrı ayrı söylemek, hecelemek; ifade etm., belirtmek, söylemek; **~ out** heceleyerek okumak *veya* yazmak, deşifre etm.; detaylı açıklamak; '**~.bind.er** *n. Am.* büyüleyici konuşan hatip; '**~.bound** *adj. fig.* büyülenmiş; '**spell.er**: **he is a bad ~** doğru yazamaz.

spell.ing ['speliŋ] *n.* imlâ, yazım; '**~-book** *n.* yazım kılavuzu.

spelt¹ [spelt] *pret. & p.p. of* **spell² 2**.

spelt² BOT [ˌ] *n.* kaplıca buğday.

spel.ter ['speltə] *n.* çinko.

spen.cer ['spensə] *n.* kısa ceket.

spend [spend] (*irr.*) *v/t.* harcamak (*on, upon -e*), sarfetmek (*para*) (*on*); israf etm., havaya savurmak; geçirmek (*zaman*); (*part.* **~ o.s.**) *k-ni* tüketmek; **~ the night** gecelemek, konaklamak; *v/i.* kuvvetini azalmak; sarfolunmak; '**spender** *n.* müsrif, mirasyedi.

spend-thrift ['spendθrift] **1.** *n.* müsrif, mirasyedi kimse; **2.** *adj.* müsrif(ce), mirasyedi.

spent [spent] **1.** *pret. & p.p. of* **spend**; **2.** *adj.* tükenmiş, bitkin, yorgun; harcanmış, sarfedilmiş.

sperm [spəːm] *n.* sperma, belsuyu, meni; **sper.ma.ce.ti** [-məˈseti] *n.* ispermeçet, balinadan çıkarılan bir tür yağ; **sper.mato.zo.on** BIOL [-ətəu-'zəuɔn] *n.* sperma hayvancığı.

spew [spjuː] *vb.* kus(tur)mak, istifrağ et(tir)mek.

sphere [sfiə] *n.* küre, yuvarlak, yerküre, arzküre; *fig.* muhit, çevre; alan, arazi, saha; sınıf, derece; **spher.i.cal** □ ['sferikəl] küresel, yusyuvarlak.

sphinc.ter ANAT ['sfiŋktə] *n.* büzgen kas.

sphinx [sfiŋks] *n.* (i)sfenks; *fig.* anlaşılması güç ve konuşmayan kimse, esrarengiz adam.

spice [spais] **1.** *n.* bahar(at); *fig.* tat, çeşni; **2.** *v/t.* baharat koymak, çeşni vermek -*e*; 'spic.er.y *n.* baharat.

spic.i.ness ['spaisnis] *n.* çeşnili, aromatik oluş; *fig.* açık saçık oluş.

spick and span ['spikən'spæn] *adj.* yeni ve temiz, pırıl pırıl.

spic.y □ ['spaisi] baharatlı, çeşnili; *fig.* açık saçık.

spi.der ZOO ['spaidə] *n.* örümcek; 'spi.der.y *adj.* örümcek gibi; örümcekli; zarif, çok ince.

spiel *Am. sl.* [spiːl] *n.* konuşma, lafazanlık.

spiff.y *sl.* ['spifi] *adj.* güzel, şık.

spig.ot ['spigət] *n.* (fıçı, *varil*) tıpa, tıkaç, musluk.

spike [spaik] **1.** *n.* ince başsız çivi, uçlu demir, sivri uçlu şey; *spor:* ayakkabı altına çakılan çivi parçaları, kabara; MOT ekser, enser; BOT başak; **2.** *v/t.* çivi ile tutturmak, ekserlemek; MIL topu körletmek için falya deliğini çivi ile tıkamak; çivi ile delmek; **spike.nard** ['-naːd] *n.* sümbül yağı; Hint sümbülü; 'spik.y □ sivri uçlu, çivili.

spill¹ [spil] **1.** (*irr.*) *v/t.* dökmek, döküp saçmak; akıtmak (*kan*); F üstünden atmak, düşürmek, fırlatmak (*süvari*); F açığa vurmak, ifşa etm.; *v/i.* dökülmek, saçılmak; **2.** *n.* dökme; F düşüş, düşme (*at vs.'den*).

spill² [-] *n.* lamba, pipo vs. yakmağa yarıyan kâğıt *veya* tahta parçası.

spill.o.ver ['spiləuvə] *n.* taşan şey; nüfus fazlalığı.

spill.way ['spilwei] *n.* taşma savağı.

spilt [spilt] *pret. & p.p. of* **spill¹ 1.**; **cry over ~ milk** boşuna üzülmek, iş işten geçtikten sonra dövünmek.

spin [spin] **1.** (*irr.*) *v/t.* eğirmek, bükmek (*a. fig.*); döndürmek, çevirmek; tasarlayıp uydurmak; ~ **s.th. out** bşi uzatmak; *v/i.* iplik vs.'yi eğirmek; *a.* ~ **round** dönmek; AVIA dikine düşmek, vril yapmak; ~ **along** hızla geçip gitmek; **send s.o.** (**s.th.**) ~**ning** b-ni (bşi) fırlatıp yere atmak; **2.** *n.* (fırıl fırıl) dönme, devir; kısa gezinti; AVIA dikine düşüş.

spin.ach BOT ['spinidʒ] *n.* ıspanak.

spi.nal ['spainl] *adj.* ANAT belkemiğine ait, omurga...; ~ **column** belkemiği, omurga; ~ **cord**, ~ **marrow** omurilik; ~ **curvature** kamburluk, omurga eğriliği.

spin.dle ['spindl] *n.* iğ, eğirmen; mil, dingil; 'spin.dly *adj.* uzun, ince ve zayıf görünüşlü, leylek bacaklı.

spin doc.tor ['spindɔktə] *n.* görevi haberleri, gelişmeleri vb. belli bir siyasi partinin ya da kimsenin çıkarlarına ve imajına yarayacak bir vurguyla sunmak olan kimse.

spin-dri.er ['spindraiə] *n.* santrifüjlü çamaşır kurutma makinesi.

spin-drift ['spindrift] *n.* dalga serpintisi.

spine [spain] *n.* ANAT omurga, belkemiği; diken; sırt (*dağ, kitap*); 'spine.less *adj.* omurgasız (*hayvan*); *fig.* cesaretsiz, yüreksiz.

spin.et MUS ['spi'net] *n.* spinet, bir tür küçük piyano.

spin.na.ker NAUT ['spinəkə] *n.* üç köşe büyük yarış yelkeni.

spin.ner ['spinə] *n.* eğiren, iplikçi kimse; eğirme *veya* bükme makinesi; **spin.neret** ZOO ['spinərət] *n.* örümcek ve ipekböceğinin iplik salan uzvundaki memeciklerden her biri.

spin.ning...: ~**-jenny** MEC ['spiniŋ-'dʒəni] *n.* iplik eğirme makinesi, çıkrık makinesi; '~**-mill** *n.* iplikhane; '~**-wheel** *n.* çıkrık.

spin.ster ['spinstə] *n.* kalık, yaşı geçmiş kız, evde kalmış, evlenmemiş kız.

spin.y ['spaini] *adj.* dikenli, iğneli; güçlüklerle dolu.

spi.ra.cle ['spaiərəkl] *n.* nefes alıp verme deliği.

spi.rae.a BOT [spai'riə] *n.* çayırmelikesi, erkeçsakalı.

spi.ral ['spaiərəl] **1.** □ helozonî, bur-

malı, sarmal; **2.** *n.* helis, helezon; *fig.*
karışıklık, hercümerç; sarmal hareket;
MED spiral; **3.** *vb.* helezon teşkil etm.,
dönmek.

spire ['spaiə] *n.* tepe (*kule, dağ, ağaç*).

spir.it ['spirit] **1.** *n. com.* ruh, can; his,
duyarlık; canlılık; cesaret; peri, cin;
CHEM ispirto; alkol; **~s** *pl.* huy, karakter; alkollü içikler; **~ of wine** şarap ruhu; **in** (**high**) **~s** keyifli, neşeli; **in low
~s** kederli, üzgün; **2.** *vb.* **~ away, ~
off** gizlice götürmek *veya* göndermek,
ortadan yok etm.; **~ up** canlandırmak,
şenlendirmek; cesaretlendirmek.

spir.it.ed □ ['spiritid] cesur, faal, canlı,
esprili, nüktedan; 'spir.it.ed.ness *n.*
canlılık, şevk, cesaret.

spir.it.ism ['spiritizəm] *n.* ispritizma;
'spirit.ist *n.* ispiritizmaya inanan ve
onunla ilgilenen kimse.

spir.it.less □ ['spiritlis] ruhsuz, cansız,
hevessiz, sıkıcı; üzgün, neşesiz; korkak, yüreksiz.

spir.it-lev.el ['spiritlevl] *n.* tesviye ruhu, su terazisi.

spir.it.u.al ['spirituəl] **1.** □ ruhanî, manevî, ruhî, ruhsal; dinî, kutsal; **2.** *n.*
Amerikan zencilerine özgü ilâhi;
'spir.it.u.alism *n.* ispritizma, ruhanilik, ruhlara inanma; spir.it.u.al.i.ty
[-'æliti] *n.* ruhanîlik, manevilik, tinsellik, dua, ibadet vs. gibi dinî şeylere
düşkünlük; spir.it.u.alize ['-əlaiz]
v/t. ruhanileştirmek, manevî değer kazandırmak.

spir.it.u.el(le) [spiritju'el] *adj.* zeki,
akıllı, nüktedan, espri sahibi.

spir.it.u.ous ['spirituəs] *adj.* alkollü,
ispirtolu.

spirt [spə:t] **1.** *v/t. & v/i.* sıçra(t)mak,
fışkır(t)mak (*su*); anî hamle yapmak;
2. *n.* anî hamle; fışkır(t)ma (*su*).

spit[1] [spit] **1.** *n.* kebap şişi; GEOGR dil; **2.**
v/t. şiş saplamak, şişlemek.

spit[2] [-] **1.** *n.* tükürük, salya; **be the very
~ of s.o.** *b-ne* tıpatıp benzemek, hık
deyip burnundan düşmüş olm.; **2.**
(*irr.*) *v/i.* tükürmek (**on** *-e*); tükürük saçarak konuşmak; (*kedi*) tıslamak; çiselemek, serpiştirmek; **~ at** (yüzüne) tükürmek, hakaret etm.; **~ upon** (üstüne) tükürmek; *v/t.* (*mst ~ out*) bşi tükürmek, tükürük gibi saçmak; **~ it
out!** F açıkla!, söyle!

spit[3] [-] *n.* bir bel boyu derinlik (*toprak*).

spite [spait] **1.** *n.* kin, garaz, şer, kötülük; **in ~ of** *-e* rağmen; **2.** *v/t.* kindarlık
etm. *-e*, inadına yapmak *-i*, üzmek;
kahretmek *-i*.

spite.ful □ ['spaitful] garazkâr, kinci;
'spite.ful.ness *n.* kötülük, şer, garazkârlık.

spit.fire ['spitfaiə] *n.* çabuk öfkelenen,
ateş püsküren kimse.

spit.tle ['spitl] *n.* tükürük, salya.

spit.toon [spi'tu:n] *n.* tükürük hokkası.

spiv *sl.* [spiv] *n.* karaborsacı, vurguncu,
adi soyguncu.

splash [splæʃ] **1.** *n.* zifos, sıçratılmış çamur *veya* su; su sıçratma (sesi); **make a
~** F sükse yapmak, sansasyon yaratmak, dikkat çekmek; **2.** *v/t. & v/i.* zifos
atmak, su sıçratmak *-e*; etrafa sıçratarak suya dalmak, suya çarpmak; kötü
resim yapmak; *sl.* reklamını yapmak;
~ one's money about *sl.* parasını saçıp
savurmak; '**~-board** *n.* çamurluk, siper; '**~-down** *n.* denize inme (*uzay gemisi*); 'splash.y □ ıslak, çamurlu, lekeli; F gösterişli.

splay [splei] **1.** *n.* yayvanlık; meyilli
kısım (*kapı, pencere vs.*), eğik kesilmiş
kenar; **2.** *vb.* dışa doğru meyletmek;
yayılmak, genişlemek; **3.** *adj.* geniş
ve yayvan; eğik kesilmiş; '**~-foot** *n.*
düztaban.

spleen [spli:n] *n.* ANAT dalak; huysuzluk, terslik, kızgınlık, öfke, kin;
spleen.ful ['-ful], **spleen.y** *adj.*
kızgın, aksi, ters, huysuz, somurtkan.

splen.did □ ['splendid] parlak, gösterişli; mükemmel, fevkalâde, enfes;
splendif.er.ous F [-'difərəs] = **splendid**; 'splen.do(u)r *n.* parlaklık, parıltı,
şaşaa, ihtişam, debdebe, heybet, tantana.

sple.net.ic [spli'netik] **1.** *a.* **sple'net.i-
cal** □ aksi, ters, kızgın, öfkeli; **2.** *n.* hipokondriyak, titiz, merak hastalığı
olan kimse.

splice [splais] **1.** *n.* iki ucu birbirine ekleme, dikiş; NAUT fazla içki alma; **2.** *vb.*
iki ucu örerek birbirine eklemek; iki
tahtayı birbirine çivileyerek tutturmak; yapıştırarak eklemek (*band,
film*); NAUT fazla içki hakkını vermek;
MEC eklemek; *sl.* evlen(dir)mek.

splint MED [splint] **1.** *n.* cebire, süyek,
kırık tahtası; **2.** *vb.* kırık tahtası ile
çıkık (*veya* kırık) bağlamak; '**~-bone**
n. ANAT incik kemiği.

splin.ter ['splintə] **1.** *n.* kıymık; küçük

parça; **2.** *v/t.* & *v/i.* parçala(n)mak, parça parça olm. *veya* etm. *veya* etm.; yar(ıl)mak;
'**splinter-proof** *adj.* mermi parçalarını
geçirmeyen; çatlamaz, dağılmaz.

split [split] **1.** *n.* yarık, çatlak; *fig.* bölünme, ikiye ayrılma, hizipleşme; **~s** *pl.*
ayaklar ayrıkken elleri yere değdirme
hareketi; **2.** *adj.* yarılmış, çatlamış,
ayrılmış; **3.** *v/t.* yarmak, bölmek; ayırmak, dağıtmak; *v/i.* yarılmak, ayrılmak, çatlamak; **~ hairs** kılı kırk yarmak; **~ one's sides with laughter**
b-nin gülmekten kasıkları çatlamak;
~ up bölünmek, taksim olm.; bölüştürmek; *fig.* araları açılmak, bozuşmak; **~
on** *sl.* ispiyon etm., *b-ni* ele vermek;
'**split.ting** *adj.* şiddetli, keskin; F delice, çılgınca (*sürat*).

splotch [splɔtʃ] *n.* leke, benek.

splurge [splɜːdʒ] *n.* gösteriş, fiyaka; savurganlık.

splut.ter ['splʌtə] *s.* **sputter**, *vb.* AVIA
cızırdamak, boğulmak (*motor*).

spoil [spɔil] **1.** *n. oft.* **~s** *pl.* yağma, çapul, ganimet, karmanyola; *fig.* hasılat;
moloz, süprüntü; **2.** (*irr.*) *v/t.* zorla elinden almak, *b-den* bşi gaspetmek; yağma etm.; bozmak, mahvetmek; yüz
vermek, nazlı alıştırmak (*çocuk*),
şımartmak; *v/i.* bozulmak, çürümek,
telef olm.; **~ing for a fight** kavgacı, kavga arayan; '**spoiler** *n.* eşkiya, haydut,
korsan, karmanyolacı; *bşi* yüzüne gözüne bulaştıran, bozan kimse; **spoilsman** *Am. pol* ['-zmən] *n.* koltuk avcısı;
'**spoil-sport** *n.* oyunbozan, mızıkçı;
spoils system *Am.* POL çıkar sağlamak için kurulan rüşvet verme sistemi.

spoilt [spɔilt] *pret.* & *p.p.* of **spoil 2.**

spoke[1] [spəuk] *pret. of* **speak**.

spoke[2] [-] *n.* tekerlek parmağı, basamak; NAUT dümen dolabı parmaklığı.

spo.ken ['spəukən] *p.p. of* **speak**.

spokes.man ['spəuksmən] *n.* sözcü,
başkası adına konuşan kimse.

spo.li.a.tion [spəuli'eiʃən] *n.* yağma,
çapul, soygun, talan.

spon.dee ['spɔndiː] *n.* iki uzun heceli
sözcük.

sponge [spʌndʒ] **1.** *n.* sünger; **throw up
the ~** *boks* & *fig.* havlu atmak, mücadeleden vazgeçmek; **2.** *v/t.* süngerle silmek *veya* suyunu almak (**away, off**); **~
up** emmek, suyu massetmek; *v/i.* tufeylilik (*veya* otlakçılık) etm. (**on, from**),
başkasının kesesinden geçinmek;
'**~cake** *n.* pandispanya; '**spong.er** *n.*

asalak, tufeyli, *fig.* otlakçı.

spon.gi.ness ['spʌndʒinis] *n.* sünger
gibi oluş; '**spon.gy** *adj.* sünger gibi,
mesameli, gözenekli.

spon.sor ['spɔnsə] **1.** *n.* vaftiz babası;
kefil; hami, koruyucu; reklâm giderlerini üstlenen firma; **2.** *v/t.* desteklemek
-i; kefil olm. *-e*; korumak, himaye etm.
-i; '**spon.sor.ship** *n.* kefalet, kefillik;
destek.

spon.ta.ne.i.ty [spɔntə'niːiti] *n.* kendiliğinden, ihtiyari olarak yapma *veya*
olma, doğrudan doğruya, vasıtasız olma; **sponta.ne.ous** □ [-'teinjəs] kendiliğinden olan, ihtiyarî, içten gelen;
BOT hızlı büyüyen; **~ combustion** içten
yanma, kendiliğinden yanma; **~ generation** cansızdan canlı oluşumu.

spoof *sl.* [spuːf] **1.** *v/t. b-ni* alaya almak,
b-ne yalan yutturmak; **2.** *n.* süprüntü;
saçma; yalan, hilekârlık.

spook [spuːk] *n.* hayalet, hortlak; *Am.
sl.* casus; '**spook.y** *adj.* hayalet gibi; tekin olmayan.

spool [spuːl] **1.** *n.* makara, bobin; **2.** *v/t.*
makaraya sarmak.

spoon [spuːn] **1.** *n.* kaşık, kaşık şeklindeki şey; *sl.* deli divane, vurgun kimse;
be ~s on *sl. b-ne* abayı yakmak; **2.** *vb.*
kaşıklamak; *sl.* zevzeklik etm., oynaşmak *ile*; '**~drift** *n.* rüzgârın denizden
getirdiği su serpintisi; '**spoon.er.ism**
n. ses *veya* heceleri konuşurken şaka
olsun diye *veya* yanlışlıkla karıştırma
(*örnek*; '*gözünü aç*' *yerine* '*açını
göz*'); '**spoon-fed** *adj. fig.* nazlı yetişmiş, şımarık; kaşıkla beslenmiş (*bebek*); **spoon.ful** ['-ful] *adj.* kaşık dolusu; '**spoon-meat** *n.* (*çocuk, hasta için*)
lapa, bulamaç; '**spoon.y** □ F abayı
yakmış (**on**).

spoor HUNT [spuə] *n.* vahşî hayvan izi.

spo.rad.ic [spə'rædik] *adj.* (**~ally**) tektük, münferit, seyrek.

spore BOT [spɔː] *n.* spor.

sport [spɔːt] **1.** *n.* spor; oyun (*a. fig.*);
eğlence, eğlenti; alay, şaka, latife; **~s**
pl. com. atletik sporlar; spor bayramı,
şöleni; *a.* **good ~** iyi bir kimse; **make ~
of** *b-le* alay etm., *b-ni* alaya almak; **2.**
v/i. takılmak (**at, over** *-e*); oynamak;
şaka söylemek; eğlenmek; *v/t.* övünmek *ile*; '**~ one's oak** F rahatsız edilmemek için kapıyı kapamak; '**sport.ing**
□ sporla ilgili. av... spor... sportmence, sportif; **~ chance** kazanma olasılığı
tanıma; '**spor.tive** □ eğlendirici; neşe-

li; oyun oynamayı seven; 'sports-car *n*. MOT spor araba; 'sports-jack.et *n*. spor ceket; 'sports-man *n*. sporcu, sportmen; avcı; profesyonel kumarbaz; 'sports.man.like *adj*. sportmence, sporcuya yakışır; 'sports.man.ship *n*. sportmenlik, sporculuk; 'sports- -wear *n*. spor giysi; 'sportswom.an *n*. sporcu kadın.

spot [spɔt] 1. *n. com*. nokta, benek, leke; kusur, şaibe, ayıp; yer, mevki; insan vücudunda leke, ben; sivilce, ergenlik; ~*s pl*. peşin parayla satılan mallar; ~ *of* F biraz, bir parça; **on the ~** yerinde; derhal, hemen, doğrudan doğruya; **be on the ~** hazır bulunmak; 2. *adj*. peşin; rasgele; 3. *v/t*. lekelemek (*a. fig.*), beneklemek; bulmak, keşfetmek, görmek; *v/i*. lekelenmek, benek benek olm.; F yağmur yağmak; 'spotless ☐ lekesiz, temiz; 'spot.less.ness *n*. lekesizlik, temizlik; 'spot.light *n*. THEAT sahne projektörü; MOT müteharrik projektör; **in the ~** *fig*. ön planda, dikkati çeken; 'spot.ted *adj*. noktalı, lekeli, benekli; ~ *fever* MED lekeli humma, tifüs; 'spot.ter *n*. gözcü, gözetleyici, rasat eden kimse *veya* şey (*özellikle düşman uçaklarını*); *Am*. kontrolör, murakıp, müfettiş; 'spot.ti.ness *n*. lekelilik; 'spot.ty *adj*. lekeli, benekli, noktalı.

spouse [spauz] *n*. eş, koca, karı.

spout [spaut] 1. *n*. bir kabın ağzı, ağız; emzik; jet borusu; ARCH oluk ağzı; fışkıran su; *v/t. & v/i*. fışkır(t)mak; F tumturaklı konuşmak.

sprain [sprein] 1. *n*. burkulma (*mafsal*); 2. *v/t*. burkmak.

sprang [spræŋ] *pret. of* **spring** 2.

sprat ICHTH [spræt] *n*. çaçabalığı.

sprawl [sprɔ:l] *v/i*. yerde uzanmak, *fig*. maça beyi gibi kurulmak, terbiyesizce uzanmak; BOT üremek, azmak, yayılmak; *v/t*. ~ *out* uzatmak, germek.

spray¹ [sprei] *n*. yapraklı ve çiçekli ufak dal (*süs için*).

spray² [-] 1. *n*. (toz halinde) serpinti, sprey; çise, çisinti; püskürgeç; = ~*er*, 2. *vb*. (toz halinde) serpmek, püskürtmek; 'spray.er *n*. püskürteç, vaporizatör, pülverizatör, sprey.

spread [spred] 1. (*irr.*) *v/t. a*. ~ *out* yaymak, sermek, açmak, genişletmek, uzatmak; neşretmek, yaymak (*söylenti, hastalık vs.*); sürmek (*yağ*); ~ *the ta-*

ble sofrayı kurmak; *v/i*. yayılmak (*a. fig.*), genişlemek; 2. *adj*. ~ *eagle* kanat ve ayakları gerilmiş durumda, uçan (*arma kartalı*); 3. *n*. yayılma; genişlik, vüsat, enginlik; saha; kanatların yayılımı; *Am*. örtü, yorgan, çarşaf, sofra örtüsü; F ziyafet; '~-ea.gle *adj*. F gösterişçi; şoven; 'spread.er *n*. yayan *veya* süren kimse *veya* şey; 'spreading *adj*. geniş, yaygın, engin.

spree F [spri:] *n*. eğlence, cümbüş, âlem; **go on a ~** âlem yapmak.

sprig [sprig] 1. *n*. ince dal, fışkın, sürgün; *fig*. delikanlı; MEC başsız çivi; 2. *vb*. başsız çivi ile sağlamlaştırmak; budamak; ince dallarla süslemek; ~*ged adj*. çiçekli, dallı, çiçek işlemeli.

spright.li.ness ['spraitlinis] *n*. canlılık, neşeli olma; 'spright.ly *adj*. canlı, pürhayat, neşeli, şen.

spring [spriŋ] 1. *n*. sıçrayış, hamle, fırlama; helezoni yay; yay elastikiyeti; *tech*. yay, zemberek; kaynak, memba, pınar; *fig*. köken, menşe; (ilk)bahar; 2. (*irr.*) *v/t*. fırlatmak; parçalamak; birdenbire ortaya çıkarmak; av hayvanını yerinden çıkarmak; ~ *a leak* NAUT su etmeğe başlamak; ~ *s.th. on s.o. b-ne* sürpriz yapmak; *v/i*. sıçramak, fırlamak; çıkmak (*from -den*); BOT çimlenmek, filiz sürmek; ~ *up* fırlayıp ayağa kalkmak; doğmak (*fikir*); baş göstermek; ~ *into existence* birdenbire doğmak, çıkmak; '~-'bal.ance *n*. yaylı terazi, kantar; '~-board *n*. tramplen, sıçrama tahtası.

springe HUNT [sprindʒ] *n*. ilmekli tuzak, kuş kapancası.

spring gun ['spriŋgʌn] *n*. kendiliğinden boşanan atım; 'spring.i.ness *n*. elastikiyet, yaylılık; 'spring mat.tress yaylı somya; **spring tide** şiddetli met hareketi; 'spring.tide, 'spring.time *n*. ilkbahar; 'spring.y ☐ yaylı, elastiki, esnek.

sprin.kle ['spriŋkl] *vb*. serpmek, ekmek, saçmak; sulamak; çiselemek (*yağmur*); 'sprin.kler *n*. sulama tesisatı, püskürgeç, pülverizatör; 'sprinkling *n*. az miktar, serpinti, çise; *a ~ of fig*. bir tutam, bir parça.

sprint [sprint] *spor*: 1. *v/i*. (tabana kuvvet) koşmak; 2. *n*. kısa koşu; sürat koşusu; 'sprint.er *n*. kısa mesafe koşucusu.

sprit NAUT [sprit] *n*. yan yelkenin sereni.

sprite [sprait] *n*. hayal(et); peri, cin.

sprit.sail NAUT ['spritsl] *n.* yan yelken serenine açılan yelken.

sprock.et-wheel MEC ['sprɔkitwi:l] *n.* zincir dişlisi.

sprout [spraut] **1.** *v/t. & v/i.* filizlenmek, tomurcuklanmak, bitmek; filiz sürdürmek; **2.** *n.* BOT filiz, fidan, tomurcuk; *a.* **Brussels ~s** Brüksel lahanası.

spruce[1] □ [spru:s] **1.** *adj.* şık, zarif; temiz, pak; **2.** *vb.* **(up)** temiz ve şık giyinmek, çekidüzen vermek, derleyip toplamak.

spruce[2] BOT [-] *n. a. ~ fir* ladin ağacı, alaçam.

sprung [sprʌŋ] *pret. (rare) & p.p. of* **spring 2.**

spry [sprai] *adj.* canlı, çevik, faal.

spud [spʌd] *n.* çapa, tirpidin, bahçe malası; F patates.

spume *lit.* [spju:m] *n.* köpük; '**spumous**, '**spum.y** □ köpüklü.

spun [spʌn] *pret. & p.p. of* **spin 1.**

spunk [spʌŋk] *n.* kav, mantar kavı; alev, kıvılcım; F cesaret, yüreklilik; '**spunk.y** □ cesur, yiğit, mert.

spur [spə:] **1.** *n.* mahmuz (*a.* ZOO); BOT bazı çiçeklerde mahmuz şeklindeki çıkıntı; *fig.* güdü; saik, teşvik eden şey; çıkıntı, çıkma, cumba; dağ kolu; *on the ~ of the moment* anında, derhal, hemen; *put veya set ~s to* mahmuzlamak; *fig.* teşvik etm.; *win one's ~s* liyakatini kanıtlamak; *~ gear* MEC alın dişlisi, düz dişli çark; **2.** *vb. a. ~ on* kışkırtmak (*into -e*); mahmuzlamak, dürtmek (*a. fig.*); *poet.* atını dört nala koşturmak.

spurge BOT [spə:dʒ] *n.* sütleğenotu.

spu.ri.ous □ ['spjuəriəs] sahte, taklit, yapma, suni; '**spu.ri.ous.ness** *n.* taklidi, benzeri olma.

spurn [spə:n] *v/t.* hor bakarak *bşe* tenezzül etmemek, hakaretle reddetmek, hiçe saymak.

spurt [spə:t] **1.** *v/i.* ani hamle yapmak, davranmak; son derece artmak (*satış vs.*); *spor:* finişe kalkmak; *s. spirt*; **2.** *n.* ani hamle, kısa süre için gösterilen gayret; *spor:* finiş, ani hamle; *s. spirt*.

sput.nik ['sputnik] *n.* Sovyetler Birliği'nin uzaya gönderdiği ilk uydunun adı, sputnik.

sput.ter ['spʌtə] **1.** *n.* tükürük saçma; kuru gürültü; **2.** *vb.* tükürük saçmak; tükürük saçarak konuşmak (*at s.o.*); *a. ~ out* alelâcele ve anlaşılmaz söylemek; saçmak.

spy [spai] **1.** *n.* casus, hafiye, ajan; **2.** *v/i.* gözetlemek; casusluk etm.; *~* **(up)on** *s.o. b-ni* gizlice gözetlemek; '**~.glass** *n.* küçük teleskop; '**~.hole** *n.* gözetleme deliği.

squab [skwɔb] *n.* yavru güvercin.

squab.ble ['skwɔbl] **1.** *n.* ağız kavgası, çekişme, hırgür; **2.** *v/i.* kavga etm., çekişmek, dalaşmak; '**squab.bler** *n.* kavgacı.

squad [skwɔd] *n.* takım, ekip, grup; **squad.ron** ['-rən] *n.* MIL suvari bölüğü; AVIA uçak bölüğü, uçak filosu; NAUT filo.

squal.id □ ['skwɔlid] kirli, pis, bakımsız, sefil, perişan.

squall[1] [skwɔ:l] **1.** *n.* yaygara, feryat, haykırış; **~s** *pl.* bağrışma; **2.** *v/i.* yaygara koparmak, bağrışmak, feryat etmek.

squall[2] NAUT [-] *n.* bora, kasırga, az süren şiddetli rüzgâr; '**squall.y** *adj.* NAUT fırtınalı, boralı.

squa.lor ['skwɔlə] *n.* kir, pislik, sefalet, bakımsızlık.

squa.mous ['skweiməs] *adj.* pullu, kepekli, pul pul.

squan.der ['skwɔndə] *v/t.* boş yere harcamak, çarçur etm., israf etm., savurmak; '**~'ma.ni.a** *n.* savurganlık tutkunluğu.

square [skwɛə] **1.** □ dördül, kare şeklinde, dört köşeli; dikey, dik açılı (*to, with -e, ile*); uygun, münasip; düzenli; direkt, kesin, açık; tam, eşit (*with ile*); F namuslu, şerefli, dürüst; özlü, doyurucu; *Am.* F modası geçmiş, eski kafalı; *~ measure* yüzey ölçü birimi; *~ mile* mil kare (*259 hektar*); **(take a)** *~ root* MATH kare kök (almak); *~ sail* NAUT dört köşe seren yelkeni; **2.** *n.* dördül, kare; gönye; MATH bir sayının ikinci kuvveti, kare; F bol ve doyurucu yemek; satranç tahtası; ARCH sütun kaidesi; MIL kale (*veya* kare) nizamı; meydan, alan, saha; *Am.* F darkafalı adam; **3.** *v/t.* dört köşeli yapmak; MATH *-in* karesini almak; doğrultmak, düzlemek (*with ile*); COM ödemek, tediye etm. *-i*; rüşvet vermek, para yedirmek *-e*; *v/i.* (*with*) uymak, muvafık gelmek; '**~'built** *adj.* iri yapılı, kaba saba; *~ dance* dört çiftle yapılan bir tür dans; '**~'rigged** *adj.* NAUT dört köşe seren yelkeni olan, kabasorto; '**~'toed** *adj.* küt burunlu (*ayakkabı*); eskiye düşkün, tutucu.

squash¹ [skwɔʃ] **1.** *n.* ezme; şerbet, meyve suyu; ağır ve yumuşak bir şeyin düşmesi; raketle oynanan bir tür oyun; *mst ~-hat* geniş kenarlı şapka; **2.** *vb.* ezmek, sıkmak, bastırmak, son vermek *-e; fig.* bunaltmak; F *b-nin* ağzını tıkamak, susturmak *-i,* haddini bildirmek *-e.*

squash² BOT [_] *n.* kabak.

squat [skwɔt] **1.** *adj.* çömelmiş; bodur, tıknaz; çok alçak (*bina*); **2.** *v/i.* çömelmek; boş topraklara yerleşmek; **'squatter** *n.* boş bir mülkü işgal eden kimse; sahipsiz bir araziyi işgal eden kimse, gecekonduda oturan kimse; koyun yetiştirici (*Avustralyalı*).

squaw [skwɔ:] *n.* kızılderili kadın.

squawk [skwɔ:k] **1.** *v/i.* cıyaklamak, acı acı bağırmak (*ördek vs.*); **2.** *n.* cıyaklama, yaygara.

squeak [skwi:k] **1.** *v/i.* cırlamak; gıcırdamak (*kapı, yay vs.*); *sl.* ihbar etm., ele vermek; **2.** *n.* cırlama; gıcırtı; *a narrow ~* F paçayı güçbelâ kurtarma; **'squeak.y** □ cızırtılı, gıcırtılı.

squeal [skwi:l] *v/i.* domuz gibi ses çıkarmak; vak vak etm., acı acı feryat etm.; *s.* **squeak**.

squeam.ish □ ['skwi:miʃ] titiz, hassas, çabuk gücenen, müşkülpesent; çabuk tiksinen, midesi hemen bulanan; **'squeamish.ness** *n.* aşırı duyu, tiksinti.

squee.gee ['skwi:'dʒi:] *n.* araba cam sileceğine benzer kısa saplı cam, tahta vs. silicisi; PHOT lastik silindir.

squeez.a.ble ['skwi:zəbl] *adj.* uysal, uslu, munis.

squeeze [skwi:z] **1.** *v/t.* sık(ıştır)mak; *fig.* rahatsız etm., baskı yapmak; **2.** *n.* tazyik, baskı (*a. fig.*), sıkıştırma; kuvvetli el sıkma; kalabalık, izdiham; **'squeez.er** *n.* sıkıştırma aygıtı, pres (*part. meyve*).

squelch F [skweltʃ] *vb.* susturmak, bastırmak, son vermek *-e;* pestilini çıkarmak, hurdahaş etm.

squib [skwib] *n.* fişek, kestane fişeği, maytap; hiciv, yergi.

squid ZOO [skwid] *n.* mürekkepbalığı.

squif.fy *sl.* ['skwifi] *adj.* çakırkeyf.

squill BOT [skwil] *n.* adasoğanı.

squint [skwint] **1.** *v/i.* şaşı bakmak; yan bakmak; gözleri kısarak bakmak; **2.** *n.* şaşılık, şaşı bakma; F yan bakış; **'~-eyed** *adj.* şaşı; *fig.* kötü(cül), şerir.

squire ['skwaiə] **1.** *n.* asılzade; geniş arazi sahibi, bey, köy ağası; *Am.* F avukatlık *veya* yargıçlık ünvanı; HIST silahtar; *co.* kavalye; **2.** *v/t.* (*bir bayana*) refakat etm.

squir(e).arch.y ['skwaiərɑ:ki] *n.* geniş arazi sahiplerinin hükümranlığı.

squirm F [skwə:m] *v/i.* kıvranmak.

squir.rel ZOO ['skwirəl] *n.* sincap.

squirt [skwə:t] **1.** *n.* fışkıran su, fıskiye; fışkır(t)ma; F nanemolla, *k-ni* beğenmiş genç; **2.** *v/t. & v/i.* fışkır(t)mak.

squish F [skwiʃ] *n.* marmelat.

stab [stæb] **1.** *n.* bıçak yarası; bıçakla yaralama; F deneme; *~ in the back fig.* arkadan vurma; **2.** *vb.* bıçaklamak; saplamak (*at*).

sta.bil.i.ty [stə'biliti] *n.* denge; sağlamlık; istikrar, kararlılık, sebat; AVIA dinamik denge.

sta.bi.li.za.tion [steibilai'zeiʃən] *n.* dengede tutma, istikrar, stabilizasyon, sabit kılma *veya* olma; sağlamlaştırma.

sta.bi.lize ['steibilaiz] *v/t.* dengelemek, sağlamlaştırmak, sabit kılmak, istikrar kazandırmak, stabilize etm.; AVIA dengeyi sağlamak; **'sta.bi.liz.er** *n.* AVIA, NAUT dengeyi sağlayan aygıt.

sta.ble¹ □ ['steibl] sağlam, dayanıklı, muhkem; sabit, sarsılmaz, devrilmez, değişmez; sürekli, kalıcı.

sta.ble² [_] **1.** *n.* ahır; *Am.* F ekip; **2.** *v/t.* ahıra bağlamak, ahırda tutmak.

sta.bling ['steibliŋ] *n.* ahır ve ahır malzemesi.

stac.ca.to MUS [stə'kɑ:təu] *adj.* her ses ayrı ve kesik kesik olarak.

stack [stæk] **1.** *n.* AGR saman, ot vs. yığını, tınaz, istif; bacaz; MIL tüfek çatısı; raf (*büyük kütüphanelerde*); *~s pl. part. Am.* kütüphanede kitap deposu; F bolluk, kalabalık, sürü; **2.** *v/t.* yığmak, istif etm.

sta.di.um ['steidjəm] *n. spor.* stadyum, spor sahası, arena.

staff [stɑ:f] **1.** *n.* değnek, asa, sopa; direk, gönder (*bayrak*); destek, dayak, payanda; MIL erkânıharbiye, kurmay; personel, kadro, bir kurumun çalışanları; öğretim kurulu; MUS *pl.* **staves** [steivz] *n.* porte; **2.** *v/t.* personel, kadro *vs.'yi* sağlamak.

stag [stæg] *n. zoo* erkek geyik; F (*bir toplantı vs.'de*) bayansız erkek; COM piyasaya yeni çıkan hisse senetleri üzerine borsa oynayan kimse.

stage [steidʒ] **1.** *n.* sahne, meydan, saha; tiyatro; tiyatro sahnesi; safha, aşama, merhale; yapı iskelesi; konak; **go on the** ~ sahne hayatına atılmak; **2.** *vb.* sahneye koymak; sahneye konmaya elverişli olm.; '~**coach** *n.* posta arabası; '~**craft** *n.* piyes yazma *veya* sahneye koyma sanatı; ~ **di.rec.tion** senaryo; ~ **fright** seyirci önünde korku, heyecan hali; ~ **mana.ger** rejisör, sahne âmiri; '**stag.er:** *old* ~ çok deneyimli kimse; '**stage.y** = **stagy**.

stag.ger ['stægə] **1.** *v/i.* sallanmak, sendelemek, sersemlemek; *fig.* tereddüt etm., kuşkulanmak; *v/t.* şaşırtmak, sersemletmek, hayrete düşürmek; MEC derecelere ayırmak, kademelendirmek; **2.** *n.* sendeleme, sallanma, bocalama, kuşku; MEC derecelendirme, kademe; ~**s** *pl.* VET (*at*) beyin hastalığı.

stag.nan.cy ['stægnənsi] *n.* durgunluk; kesatlık; '**stag.nant** ☐ durgun (*su*); atıl; COM durgun, kesat; **stag.nate** [-'neit] *v/i.* durgunlaşmak, durgun olm., kesat gitmek; **stag.na.tion** *n.* durgunluk.

stag-par.ty F ['stægpu:ti] *n.* yalnız erkeklere mahsus toplantı, eğlence.

stag.y ☐ ['steidʒi] gösterişli, sahte tavırlı; aktör gibi, aktörce.

staid ☐ [steid] sakin, heyecansız, temkinli, ağırbaşlı, ciddi; '**staid.ness** *n.* ağırbaşlılık, ciddiyet, sakin olma.

stain [stein] **1.** *n.* leke (*a. fig.*); boya, vernik; benek; **2.** *v/t.* lekelemek (*a. fig.*), kirletmek, pisletmek; MEC abanoz renginde boyamak, *bşe* renk vermek; *v/i.* kirlenmek, lekelenmek, rengi kararmak; ~**ed glass** renkli cam; '**stain.less** ☐ lekesiz; tertemiz; MEC paslanmaz.

stair [steə] *n.* basamak; ~**s** *pl.* merdiven; '~**car.pet** *n.* merdiven halısı; '~**case** *n.* merdiven, binanın merdiven bölümü; '~**rod** *n.* merdiven halısı çubuğu; '~**way** = **staircase**.

stake [steik] **1.** *n.* kazık, direk; işkence direği; işkence direğinde ölüm cezası; kumarda ortaya konan para; çıkar, menfaat; ~**s** *pl.* (*at yarışı*) ödül; koşu, yarış; **pull up ~s** *Am.* F defolup gitmek; **be at** ~ tehlikede olm.; **place one's** ~ **on** varını yoğunu *bşe* bağlamak; **2.** *v/t.* tehlikeye koymak, riske sokmak; kumarda para koymak; ~ **out**, ~ **off** sınırını kazıklarla işaretlemek.

stal.ac.tite ['stæləktait] *n.* sarkıt, iskalaktit; **stal.ag.mite** ['stæləgmait] *n.* dikit; iskalagmit.

stale[1] ☐ [steil] taze olmayan, dura dura bozulmuş, tatsız, bozuk (*su, haber vs.*), bayat (*ekmek*); bitkin, yorgun, tükenmiş (*güç, hava vs.*); eski, bayat (*espri*).
stale[2] [-] **1.** *v/i.* kaşanmak, işemek (*at*); **2.** *n.* idrar, sidik (*at, sığır*).
stale.mate ['steil'meit] **1.** *n.* satranç: pata; *fig.* açmaz, çıkmaz, kitlenme; **2.** *v/t.* satranç: pata duruma getirmek; *fig.* durdurmak, çıkmaza sokmak.

stalk[1] [stɔːk] *n.* sap, bitki sapı.
stalk[2] [-] **1.** *v/i.* azametle yürümek; HUNT sezdirmeden ava yaklaşmak; *v/t.* sinsice takip etm.; **2.** *n.* HUNT sezdirmeden ava yaklaşma; '**stalk.er** *n.* iz üstündeki avcı; '**stalk.ing-horse** *n. fig.* bahane, ardına gizlenilen şey.

stall [stɔːl] **1.** *n.* ahır (bölmesi); sergi, satış yeri, tezgâh, büfe (*gazete vs.*); soyunma kabini; THEAT koltuk; ECCL kısmen kapalı koro sandalyeleri; **2.** *v/t.* ahıra kapamak; AVIA hızını düşürmek; MOT durdurmak, stop etm.; *v/i.* MOT durmak; AVIA hız kaybedip düşmek; *fig.* oyalamak, ağız yapmak, estek köstek etm.; '~**feed.ing** *n.* ahırda besleme.

stal.lion ['stæljən] *n.* aygır, damızlık at.
stal.wart ['stɔːlwət] **1.** ☐ kuvvetli, iri yapılı; cesur, gözüpek; güvenilir; **2.** *n.* POL sadık, tuttuğu yoldan ayrılmayan kimse, güvenilir taraftar.

sta.men BOT ['steimen] *n.* ercik, stamen, erkeklik uzvu; **stam.i.na** ['stæminə] *n.* dayanıklılık, güç, canlılık, tahammül; **stam.i.nate** BOT ['-nit] *adj.* ercikli, erkeklik uzvu olan *veya* üreten.

stam.mer ['stæmə] **1.** *v/i.* kekelemek, pepelemek; **2.** *n.* kekemelik; '**stammer.er** *n.* kekeme.

stamp [stæmp] **1.** *n.* tepinme, ayağını yere vurma; MEC tokmak, şahmerdan; damga, mühür, alâmeti farika; istampa; zımba; *fig.* alâmet, iz; pul, posta pulu; kabartma şekil; cins, nitelik, tür; **2.** *v/t.* tepinmek, ayağıyle yere vurmak; şekil vermek, kalıba sokmak; zımbalamak; damgalamak, mühürlemek *-i*; pul yapıştırmak *-e*; ~ **on the memory** hafızasına yerleştirmek; ~ **out** ayağıyle ezmek, çiğnemek; *fig.* kökünü kurutmak; *v/i.* ayağıyle yere vurup ses çıkarmak; '~**al.bum** *n.* pul albümü; '~**col.lec.tor** *n.* filatelist, pul koleksiyoncusu; '~**deal.er** *n.* pul satıcısı; '~**du.ty** *n.* damga resmi.

stam.pede [stæm'pi:d] **1.** *n.* panik, bozgun, izdiham; **2.** v/t. & v/i. panik halinde kaç(ır)mak

stamp.er ['stæmpə] n. tokmak, tokaç; damga, mühür, ıstampa, zımba; 'stamp(.ing)-mill n. metall. maden filizi kırma makinesi.

stance [stæns] n. golf: topa vururken bacakların duruş şekli.

stanch [stɑːntʃ] **1.** v/t. durdurmak (kan), alıkoymak; **2.** adj. = staunch 1; **stanchion** ['stɑːnʃən] n. destek, dayak, payanda, kazık.

stand [stænd] **1.** (irr.) v/i. com durmak, olmak, bulunmak, mevcut olm.; sebat etm.; mst ~ still yerinde durmak, kımıldamamak, (ayakta) durmak; ~ against karşı koymak, kafa tutmak -e; ~ aside bir kenara çekilmek; ~ back, ~ clear geri çekilmek, gerilemek; ~ by yanında durmak, hazır beklemek; fig. ilgisiz kalmak, arka çıkmamak; ~ for manası olm.; talip olm., istemek; Am. parl aday olm.; b-ne sahip çıkmak, kayırmak; b-ni temsil etm.; F hoşgörmek, nazını çekmek; ~ in dublörlük yapmak, b-nin yerine iş görmek (for); naut karaya yanaşmak; ~ in with araları iyi olm.; ~ off uzak durmak, gerilemek; naut denize doğru açılmak; ~ off! çekil oradan!; ~ on ısrar etm. -de; ~ out fırlamak; fig. göze çarpmak; iyice belirmek, kontras teşkil etm. (against); k-ni uzak(ta) tutmak; karşı koymak, dayanmak (against); bildiğinden şaşmamak (for); naut denize açılmak; ~ over olduğu yerde hareketsiz kalmak; ertelenmek; ~ pat Am. F dikkafalılık etm., düşüncesinde ısrar etm.; ~ to -in üzerinde ısrar etm.; s. reason; ~ to! mıl tüfek as!; ~ up ayağa kalkmak; fig. yükselmek; ~ up for taraftarı olm. -in. b-ne sahip çıkmak; ~ up to cesaretle karşılamak, dayanmak; ~ upon -in üzerinde ısrar etm.; -in tarafını tutmak; v/t. bir yere koymak, dikmek; dayanmak, tahammül etm., katlanmak -e; s. ground; ~ s.o. a dinner F b-ne yemek ikram etm.; s. treat; **2.** n. durma, duruş; ayaklık, sehpa, askı; satış sergisi; tezgâh; durak; direnme; vaziyet, durum; durma; seyirci tribünü; hatip kürsüsü; part. Am. mahkemede tanık yeri; make a veya one's ~ against dayanmak, mukavemet etm. -e, karşı koymak -e.

stan.dard ['stændəd] **1.** n. sancak, flama, bayrak; standart, model, tekbiçim,

norm(a); mikyas, ölçü; düzey, seviye, derece; (ilkokul) sınıf; para ayarı; direk, çubuk; вот gövdesi ağaç gibi büyüyen bir tür çalı; ~ lamp ayaklı lamba; ~ of living hayat standardı; **2.** adj. standart, genel, herkesçe kabul edilen, normal…, ölçü olarak kabul edilmiş; '~-bear.er n. part. fig. bayraktar, sancaktar; parti vs. lideri; '~-ga(u)ge adj. rail standart ray aralığı (1,435 m); **stand.ardi.za.tion** [_ai'zeifən] n. standartlaştırma, standardizasyon, ayarlama, tek tipe indirme; normalleştirme; 'stand.ard.ize v/t. belirli bir ölçüye uydurmak, standardize etm., tek tipe indirmek, ayarlamak, kararlaştırmak.

stand-by ['stændbai] n. yardım, destek, himaye; yedek, hazır bekleyen b-i veya bş.

stand.ee ['stæn'diː] n. ayakta kalan kimse (yer olmadığı için).

stand.er-by ['stændə'bai] n. yanında duran kimse; seyirci.

stand-in ['stænd'in] n. film: dublör.

stand.ing ['stændiŋ] **1.** □ ayakta (duran); sabit, devamlı, değişmez; dayanıklı; ~ committee pol daimî encümen; ~ jump ayakta sıçrayış, atlama; ~ orders pl. parl iç tüzük; **2.** n. ayakta durma; durum, vaziyet; mevki, şöhret; şan; süreklilik, devam; of long ~ çoktan beri devam eden, eski; '~-room n. ayakta duracak yer.

stand...: '~.off n. Am. karşı kuvvet, etkisiz bırakma; ilgisizlik; erteleme; (oyun) denklik, beraberlik; '~'off.ish adj. ilgisiz; soğukneva; ~'pat.ter n. Am. F pol tutucu, değişikliğe karşı olan kimse; '~-pipe n. dikme boru; yangın musluğu; '~.point n. bakım, görüş (noktası); '~.still n. durma, duraklama; be at a ~ yerinden kımıldanmamak, durgun halde olm.; come to a ~ duraklamak, sekteye uğramak; '~-up adj.: ~ collar dik yaka; ~ fight kurallara uygun mücadele, müsabaka; ~ supper ayakta yenen soğuk yemekler.

stank [stæŋk] pret. of stink 2.

stan.nic chem ['stænik] adj. kalay cinsinden, kalaya ait.

stan.za ['stænzə] n. şiirde stans denilen kıta şekli, kıta, kesim.

sta.ple[1] ['steipl] **1.** n. başlıca ürün; fig. başlıca konu, esas; hammadde; elyaf, lif; **2.** adj. başlıca, esas, temel…

sta.ple[2] [_] n. U şeklindeki kanca; iki

başlı çivi; tel raptiye, zımba.
sta.pler ['steiplə] *n.* zımba.
star [stɑː] **1.** *n.* yıldız; yıldız işareti; *fig.*
talih, kader; THEAT sahne yıldızı; **♀s
and Stripes** *pl. Am.* A.B.D.'nin bayrağı; **2.** *v/t.* yıldızla işaret koymak; *v/i.*
THEAT başrolde oynamak; *fig.* birinci
rolü oynamak; **~** (*it*) parlamak; THEAT
misafir sanatçı olarak oynamak; *~ring*
başrolde...
star.board NAUT ['stɑːbəd] **1.** *n.* sancak,
geminin sancak tarafı; **2.** *adj.* sancak
tarafında olan (*dümen*).
starch [stɑːtʃ] **1.** *n.* nişasta; kola; *fig.*
katılık, sertlik; **~ flour** nişasta; **2.** *v/i.*
kolalamak; *~ed adj. fig.* sert, katı;
'starchi.ness *n.* sertlik, katılık;
'starch.y □ nişastalı; kolalı; sert, katı,
soğuk tavırlı.
stare [stɛə] **1.** *n.* sabit bakış, bakışların
bir noktaya takılıp kalması; **2.** *v/i.* dik
bakmak (**at** *-e*), uzun uzun bakmak,
bakakalmak, hayretle bakmak (**at** *-e*).
star.fish ZOO ['stɑːfiʃ] *n.* denizyıldızı.
star.ing □ ['stɛəriŋ] sabit, hareketsiz
(*bakış*); göze çarpan, göz kamaştırıcı,
çok parlak.
stark [stɑːk] *adj.* sert, kaskatı, dik; bütün bütün, tam; sade; *adv.* büsbütün,
tamamen; **~ naked** çırılçıplak.
star.light ['stɑːlait] *n.* yıldız ışığı.
star.ling[1] ORN ['stɑːliŋ] *n.* sığırcık.
star.ling[2] [-] *n.* buzkıran (*köprü*).
star.lit ['stɑːlit] *adj.* yıldızlarla aydınlanmış.
star.ry ['stɑːri] *adj.* yıldızlı, yıldızlarla
dolu.
star-span.gled ['stɑːspæŋgld] *adj.*
yıldızlarla süslü; *Star-Spangled Banner Am.* A.B.D.'nin bayrağı.
start [stɑːt] **1.** *n.* başlangıç, başlama; anî
hareket; *spor:* start, çıkış; yola koyulma; kalkış; sıçrama; *fig.* avans, avantaj;
get the ~ of s.o. *b-den* önce başlamak;
give a ~ ürküp yerinden fırlamak;
(*yarış*) avans vermek; *s. fit2;* **2.** *v/i.* ürkmek, sıçramak; ani bir hareket yapmak
(**at**); *spor:* start yapmak, çıkmak; hareket etm., yola çıkmak; yola düzülmek
(**for** *-e*); *fig.* (*düşünce vs.*) -den yola
çıkmak, başlamak (**on** *-e*; **doing**
-meğe) **to ~ with** her şeyden önce, ilk
iş olarak; *v/t.* harekete geçirmek,
çalıştırmak *-i*, işletmek (*makine*); *spor:*
başlatmak; vahşi av hayvanını yerinden çıkarmak; *fig.* teşebbüs etm. *-e*;
bşe teşvik etm., sevketmek (**doing**);

kurmak, tesis etm. (*iş*); *ortaya* atmak,
yöneltmek (*soru*).
start.er ['stɑːtə] *n. spor:* starter, çıkış
işareti veren; koşucu, müsabık; MOT
marş.
start.ing-point ['stɑːtiŋpɔint] *n.* başlama noktası, hareket noktası.
star.tle ['stɑːtl] *v/t.* ürkütmek, korkutmak; **'star.tling** □ şaşırtıcı, sansasyonel; ürkütücü.
start-up ['stɑːtʌp] *n.* start-up (*şirket*).
star.va.tion [stɑːˈveiʃən] *n.* açlık(tan
ölme); *starve v/t. & v/i.* açlıktan öl-
(dür)mek; *fig.* mahrum olm., özlemini
çekmek (**for, of** *-den, -in*); **starve.ling**
['-liŋ] **1.** *n.* dilenci, açlıktan ölecek durumda olan *b-i veya bş; fig.* cılız, kavruk kimse; **2.** *adj.* açlıktan ölecek durumda, çok zayıf; *fig.* perişan, yoksul,
sefil.
state [steit] **1.** *n.* hal, durum; görkem,
ihtişam, debdebe; devlet; POL *mst* ♀ hükümet; eyalet; **~ of life** sosyal mevki; **in
~** merasimle yapılan, debdebeli; **get in-
to a ~** F heyecanlanmak, sinirlenmek;
2. *v/t.* beyan etm., belirtmek; tayin
etm., saptamak, tesbit etm.; **~ a.part-
ment** gösterişli salon; **~ coach** büyük
merasim arabası; **'~.craft** *n.* POL devlet
idaresi, devletçilik; ♀ **De.part.ment**
Am. POL Dışişleri Bakanlığı; **'stateless** *adj.* vatansız, tabiyetsiz; **'state.li-
ness** *n.* haşmetli olma; ihtişam, lüks;
'state.ly *adj.* haşmetli, heybetli; görkemli; **'state.ment** *n.* ifade; demeç; rapor; COM (**of account**) hesap raporu,
hesap hülâsası; MEC, COM tarife, cetvel;
'state room *n.* NAUT tek kişilik kamara;
yataklı vagon kompartmanı; merasim
odası; **'state.side** *adj. Am.* F A.B.D'de
olan, A.B.D...; **go ~** (*eve, yurda*) dönmek.
states.man ['steitsmən] *n.* devlet
adamı; **'states man like** *adj.* devlet
adamına yakışır, akıllı ve tedbirli;
'states.man.ship *n.* siyaset, devlet idaresi sanatı.
stat.ic ['stætik] *adj.* PHYS statik, değişmeyen, duruk; sakin...; **'stat.ics** *n.*
pl. veya sg. nesneler arasında dengeyi
sağlayan güçleri inceleyen bilim, statik
ilmi; *radyo:* parazit.
sta.tion ['steiʃən] **1.** *n.* durak; yer, mevki; MIL, RAIL istasyon, gar; radyo,
TV istasyonu; makam, rütbe; sosyal
durum, derece; *rare* meslek, iş; (*TV*)
kanal; MIL, NAUT özel görev yeri, kara-

kol; **2.** *v/t.* yerleştirmek, bir yere tayin etm.; **sta.tionar.y** □ ['-ʃnəri] sabit, hareketsiz; ~ **engine** sabit makine; '**station.er** *n.* kırtasiyeci; **⚇s' Hall** İngiltere'de bir kitabın telif hakkını almak üzere kaydedilen daire; '**sta.tion.er.y** *n.* kırtasiye, yazımalzemesi; **sta.tion-** **-mas.ter** ['-ʃənmɑ:stə] *n.* RAIL istasyon müdürü; **sta.tion wag.on** *Am.* MOT pikap, kaptıkaçtı.

sta.tis.ti.cal □ [stə'tistikəl] istatistikî, istatistikle ilgili, istatistiğe dayanan; **stat.is.ti.cian** [stætis'tiʃən] *n.* istatistik uzmanı; **stat'is.tics** *n. pl.* istatistik (bilimi); **vital** ~ nüfus istatistiği.

stat.u.ar.y ['stætjuəri] **1.** *adj.* heykeltraşlıkla ilgili, heykel...; **2.** *n.* heykeltraşlık; heykeller; heykeltraş; **stat.ue** ['-tʃu:] *n.* heykel; **stat.u.esque** □ [-tju'esk] heykel gibi; **stat.u.ette** [-tju'et] *n.* küçük heykel, heykelcik.

stat.ure ['stætʃə] *n.* boy bos, endam, şekil; kişilik.

sta.tus ['steitəs] *n.* durum, hal, vaziyet; sosyal durum, sınıf; medenî hal.

stat.ute ['stætju:t] *n.* kanun, yasa; kural, nizamname, statü; emir, hüküm; '~**book** *n.* yasalar kitabı, kanunname; ~ **law** yazılı hukuk; ~ **mile** bir mil (*1,609 km.*).

stat.u.to.ry □ ['stætjutəri] yasal, meşru.

staunch [stɔ:ntʃ] **1.** □ sağlam, kuvvetli; güvenilir, sadık; **2.** *v/t.* durdurmak, akmasını önlemek (*part. kan*).

stave [steiv] **1.** *n.* fıçı tahtası; değnek, çubuk; *poet.* kıta, beyit; **2.** (*irr.*) *vb.* *mst* ~ **in** döşeme vs.'yi kırmak, delmek; ~ **off** defetmek, savmak, uzaklaştırmak; geciktirmek.

staves MUS [steivz] *pl. of* **staff 1.**

stay [stei] **1.** *n.* NAUT istralya; *fig.* destek, payanda; kalma, ikamet, kalış, durma; oturma, ziyaret; tehir, erteleme; ~**s** *pl.* *obs.* korse; **2.** *v/t. & v/i.* dur(dur)mak, alıkoymak; tehir etm., ertelemek; kalmak; beklemek; dayanmak, devam etm. -*e*; desteklemek; geçici olarak gidermek, bastırmak (*açlık*); ~ **away** gelmemek; ~ **in** evde kalmak, dışarı çıkmamak; ~ **for** *b-ne* bakmak; ~ **(for) supper** akşam yemeğine kalmak; ~ **put** F yerinden kımıldamamak; ~ **up** yatmamak; ~ **the course** sonuna kadar dayanmak, sabretmek; ~**ing power** dayanma gücü, metanet; '~**at-home** *n.* evinden dışarı çıkmayan kimse, kül

kedisi; '~'**down strike** oturma grevi; '**stay.er** *n.* *spor*: yarışı tamamlayan koşucu *veya* at; **be a good** ~ sonuna kadar dayanmak, yarışı tamamlamak.

stead [sted] *n.* başkasının yeri; yer, mevki; **in his** ~ onun yerine; **stand** **s.o. in good** ~ *b-ne* yararlı olm., *b-ne* faydası dokunmak.

stead.fast □ ['stedfəst] sabit, sarsılmaz, metin; sabırlı; sadık; '**stead.fastness** *n.* sebat.

stead.i.ness ['stedinis] *n.* sebat, metanet.

stead.y ['stedi] **1.** □ devamlı, düzenli, sürekli; sabit, sarsılmaz; sakin, sessiz, ağırbaşlı; COM sağlam, sarsılmaz, güvenilir; **2.** *v/t. & v/i.* sabit kılmak; sağlamlaş(tır)mak; yatış(tır)mak, teskin etm. *veya* olm.; **3.** *n.* *Am.* devamlı çıkılan karşı cinsten arkadaş.

steak [steik] *n.* biftek, fileto, kontrfile.

steal [sti:l] **1.** (*irr.*) *v/t.* çalmak, aşırmak (*a. fig.*); ~ **a march on s.o.** *b-den* önce davranmak; *v/i.* gizlice hareket etm.; ~ **into** sokulmak, gizlice girmek; **2.** *n.* *Am.* çalıntı mal; hırsızlık; *sl.* kelepir.

stealth [stelθ] *n.* gizlilik; gizli iş *veya* girişim; **by** ~ gizlice; '**stealth.i.ness** *n.* gizlilik; sinsilik; '**stealth.y** □ gizli, hırsızlama; sinsi.

steam [sti:m] **1.** *n.* buhar, istim; buğu; F güç, enerji; F öfke, hiddet; **let off** ~ MEC buhar salıvermek, istim boşaltmak; *fig.* içini döküp rahatlamak; **2.** *attr.* buharlı, buhar...; **3.** *v/i.* buhar salıvermek; buharla hareket etm.; ~ **up** buğulanmak (*cam*); *v/t.* buharda pişirmek, buğulamak; '~**.boat** *n.* buharlı vapur; '~'**boil.er** *n.* buhar kazanı; **steamed** *adj.* buğulu (*pencere*); '**steam-en.gine** *n.* buhar makinesi; **steam.er** *n.* NAUT vapur; MEC buharla yemek pişirmeye (*veya veya* yıkamaya) yarayan kap; '**steam.i.ness** *n.* buharlılık.

steam... : '~**roller 1.** *n.* buharlı yol silindiri; *fig.* ezici güç; **2.** *v/t. fig.* zorla elde etm., ezmek; '~**.ship** = **steamboat**; ~ **tug** NAUT şilep, romorkör; '**steam.y** □ buharlı; buğulu, sisli.

ste.a.rin CHEM ['stiərin] *n.* stearin.

steed RHET [sti:d] *n.* at.

steel [sti:l] **1.** *n.* çelik; çelik bileği, masat; büyük güç; **2.** *adj.* çelik gibi sağlam, çelikten; **3.** *v/t.* çelik gibi sertleştirmek, çelik gibi yapmak, katılaştırmak; '~**clad** *adj.* çelik zırh giymiş; ~ **en.grav.ing** *n.* çelik levha üzerine gravür; '~-'plat.ed *adj.* çelik zırhlı; '~-works *n.* çelik fabrikası; 'steel.y *adj. mst fig.* sert, çelik gibi, çelikten; 'steel.yard *n.* kollu el kantarı.

steep¹ [sti:p] **1.** *adj.* dik, sarp, yalçın; F aşırı, yüksek *(fiyat)*; **2.** *n. poet.* dik yokuş.

steep² [-] *vb.* suya batırmak, ıslatmak; *fig.* içine dalmak, *bşin* içine gömülmek *(in)*.

steep.en ['sti:pən] *v/t. & v/i.* dikleş(tir)mek.

stee.ple ['sti:pl] *n.* kilise kulesi, çan kulesi; '~-chase *n.* engelli yarış; '~.jack *n.* kule *veya* baca işçisi.

steep.ness ['sti:pnis] *n.* diklik, sarplık.

steer¹ [stiə] *n.* boğa; öküz.

steer² [-] *v/t.* (dümenle) idare etm., yönetmek; ~ **clear of** *fig.* sakınmak, uzak durmak; 'steer.a.ble *adj.* yönetilebilir, idare edilebilir.

steer.age NAUT ['stiərid3] *n.* dümen kullanma; ara güverte; '~-way *n.* NAUT geminin dümen dinlemesi için gerekli asgari hız.

steer.ing... ['stiəriŋ]: ~ col.umn MOT direksiyon mili; '~-gear *n.* NAUT dümen donanımı; '~-wheel *n.* direksiyon.

steers.man NAUT ['stiəzmən] *n.* dümenci, serdümen.

stein [stain] *n.* büyük bira bardağı *(1 lt. 'lik).*

stel.lar ['stelə] *adj.* yıldızlarla ilgili.

stem¹ [stem] **1.** *n.* ağaç gövdesi; sap, kol; sözcük kökü; pipo sapı; **2.** *vb.* saplarını koparmak; *Am.* gelmek, çıkmak *(from -den), b-nin* neslinden olm.

stem² [-] **1.** *n.* NAUT geminin baş bodoslaması; pruva; **2.** *vb.* karşı durmak, dayanmak, mücadele etm.; *(kayak)* göğüs verip ilerlemek; ~(ming) *turn* eğri duruş.

stem cell ['stemsel] *n.* kök hücre.

stench [stentʃ] *n.* pis koku.

sten.cil ['stensl] **1.** *n.* kalıp, klişe, şablon, model, patron, matris; mumlu kâğıt, stensil; **2.** *vb.* kalıpla örneğini çıkarmak; teksir makinesiyle çoğaltmak.

ste.nog.ra.pher [ste'nɔgrefə] *n.* stenograf; sten.o.graph.ic [-nə'græfik] *adj.* (~ally) stenografik; ste.nog.ra.phy [-nɔgrəfi] *n.* stenografi.

step [step] **1.** *n.* adım; basamak, eşik; *fig.* kısa yol; ayak sesi; ayak izi; kademe, derece; girişim, eylem; *(a pair of)* ~s *pl.* evin dışındaki taş merdiven;

in ~ *with* ayak uydurarak *ile;* **take** ~s *bşe* önlem almak, girişmek, yapmağa kalkmak; **2.** *v/i.* adım atmak, girmek *(into -e),* ayak basmak *(on -e);* ~ *in fig. bşe* karışmak, müdahale etm.; ~ *on it! sl.* çabuk ol!; ~ *out* geniş adımlarla hızlanmak; acele etm.; *v/t.* ~ *out, off* adımla ölçmek, adımlamak; ~ *up* arttırmak, hızlandırmak; *fig.* canlandırmak.

step² [-] *prefix* üvey...; '~.fa.ther *n.* üvey baba; '~.moth.er *n.* üvey ana.

steppe [step] *n.* bozkır, step.

step.ping-stone ['stepiŋstəun] *n.* atlama taşı; *fig.* basamak.

ster.e.o ['stiəriəu] **1.** *n.* TYP klişe; **2.** *adj.* MUS stereo...

ster.e.o... ['stiəriə]:~.phon.ic [-'fɔnik] *adj.* stereofonik, iki ayrı sesli, stereo...; '~.scope *n.* stereoskop; '~.type **1.** *n.* stereotip, sayfa halinde baskı klişesi; *fig.* basmakalıp söz; **2.** *vb.* bir kalıba sokmak; stereotipten basmak; ~*d* stereotip, basmakalıp, klişe.

ster.ile ['sterail] *adj.* kısır, ürün vermeyen; verimsiz; mikropsuz; ste.ril.i.ty [-'riliti] *n.* kısırlık, verimsizlik; ster.i-l.iza.tion [sterilai'zeiʃən] *n.* kısırlaştırma; mikroptan arındırma, sterilize etme; 'ster.i.lize *v/t.* kısırlaştırmak; sterilize etm., mikroptan arındırmak.

ster.ling ['stə:liŋ] *adj.* kıymetli, değerli; halis, gerçek, hakikî, esaslı; COM sterlinle ödenebilen; *pound* ~ İngiliz lirası; sterlin; ~ *a.re.a* İngiliz lirası kullanılan ülkeler bloku.

stern¹ □ [stə:n] ciddî, ağırbaşlı; acımasız, sert, haşin, katı; şiddetli.

stern² NAUT [-] *n.* kıç, pupa.

stern.ness ['stə:nnis] *n.* sertlik, katılık, haşinlik.

stern-post NAUT ['stə:npəust] *n.* kıç bodoslaması.

ster.num ANAT ['stə:nəm] *n.* göğüs kemiği.

steth.o.scope MED ['stəθəskəup] *n.* stetoskop, göğüs dinleme aleti.

ste.ve.dore NAUT ['sti:vidɔ:] *n.* yükleme ve boşaltma işçisi, istifçi.

stew [stju:] **1.** *v/t. & v/i.* hafif ateşte kayna(t)mak; **2.** *n.* güveç, yahni; F heyecan, telaş, üzüntü.

stew.ard ['stjuəd] *n.* kâhya, vekilharç; NAUT kamarot; ambar memuru, idare memuru; stew.ard.ess *n.* NAUT kadın kamarot; AVIA hostes.

stew...: '~-pan, '~-pot *n.* güveç, türlü

tenceresi.

stick¹ [stik] **1.** *n.* değnek, sopa, çubuk; sap (*süpürge vs.*); baston; F çam yarması, hantal, kaba kimse; **~s** *pl.* ufak odun; **the ~s** *pl. Am.* F taşra; **2.** *vb.* AGR (kazığa) saplamak, kazıklamak.

stick² [~] (*irr.*) *v/i.* saplanıp kalmak; yapışmak, takılmak (**to** *-e*); *fig.* ayağını, başını vs.'yi bir yere çarpmak (**at**); **~ at nothing** hiç bşden çekinmemek, korkmamak; **~ out, ~ up** çıkıntılı olm., ucu dışarı çıkmak; F dayanmak, karşı koymak; F ısrar etm. (**for**); **~ to** bş üzerinde ısrar etm., ayrılmamak *-den*; **~ up for s.o.** *b-nin* tarafını tutmak; *v/t.* saplamak; bıçaklamak; iğneyle tutturmak; yapıştırmak; yafta asmak; F tahammül etm., dayanmak *-e*; **~ it on** *sl.* fahiş fiyat istemek; **~ out** dışarı çıkarmak, uzatmak; **~ it out** F dayanmak, katlanmak *-e*; **~ up** *sl.* (*banka vs.*) soymak; yolunu kesmek; '**stick.er** *n.* yapışan etiket; etiket yapıştıran kimse; '**stick.i.ness** *n.* yapışkanlık; '**sticking-plas.ter** *n.* yara bandı; '**stick-in-the-mud 1.** *adj.* tutucu, gerici; uyuşuk; **2.** *n.* gerici, darkafalı adam, mıymıntı. **stick.le** ['stikl] *vb.* titiz davranmak, pürüz çıkarmak, tereddüt etm.; '**stick.le-back** *n.* ICHTH dikence balığı; '**stick.ler** *n.* mutaassıp, titizlenen kimse (**for**). **stick-up** ['stikʌp] *n. a.* **~ collar** F dik yaka; *sl.* yol kesme.

stick.y □ ['stiki] yapışkan; çamurlu, ağdalı, üstüne başına bulanan; zor, berbat; aksi, huysuz; **come to a ~ end** *sl.* kötü akıbete uğramak; **be ~ about doing** F bşi yapmakta gönülsüz, isteksiz olm.

stiff □ [stif] katı, sert; bükülmez, eğilmez; inatçı, serkeş; yorucu, zahmetli, zor; tutulmuş (*adele vs.*); resmî, soğuk (*gülümseme vs.*); sert, alkolü çok (*içki vs.*); **be bored** ~ F uzun sıkıcı konuşmadan bıkmak, bezmek; **keep a ~ upper lip** cesaretini kaybetmemek; '**stiff.en** *v/t. & v/i.* katılaş(tır)mak, sertleş(tir)mek; *fig.* desteklemek, takviye etm.; '**stiff.ener** *n.* sertleştirici parça; destekleyici şey; '**stiff-'necked** *adj.* dikkafalı, serkeş.

sti.fle¹ VET ['staifl] *n.* diz eklemi. **sti.fle**² [~] *v/t. & v/i.* boğ(ul)mak, nefesi tıka(n)mak.

stig.ma ['stigmə] *n.* cilde vurulan kızgın damga; kötülük izi (*veya* eseri), leke, ar; BOT tepecik; MED araz, belirti,

alâmet; **stig.ma.tize** ['~taiz] *v/t. fig.* damga vurmak, leke sürmek.

stile [stil] *n.* çit *veya* duvar basamağı; MEC kenar tahtalarından biri (*kapı, pencere vs.*).

sti.let.to [sti'letəu] *n.* ufak hançer; biz. **still**¹ [stil] **1.** *adj.* sessiz; sakin; durgun, sütliman, hareketsiz; **~ wine** köpüksüz şarap; **2.** *n.* (*sinema filmi tanıtan*) fotoğraf; sessizlik; **3.** *adv.* hâlâ, henüz; yine, her şeye rağmen; daha (da); **4.** *cj.* bununla beraber, mamafih, yine de, (olduğu) halde; **5.** *vb.* durdurmak; yatış(tır)mak, teskin etm.

still² [~] *n.* imbik, damıtma aleti.

still... : '~-**born** *adj.* ölü doğmuş; '~-**hunt** *vb.* sessizce ve gizlenerek avlamak; '~-**hunt.ing** *n.* sessizce ve gizlice avlama; **~ life** natürmort, çiçek ve meyve resmetme; '**still.ness** *n.* durgunluk, sessizlik, huzur.

still-room ['stilrum] *n.* kiler, depo; imbik odası.

still.y *poet.* ['stili] *adj.* sakin, durgun, hareketsiz.

stilt [stilt] *n.* yere basmadan yürümeye yarayan tek basamaklı sırık, ayaklık; '**stilt.ed** *adj.* tumturaklı, tantanalı; sunî, zorlayışlı.

stim.u.lant ['stimjulənt] **1.** *adj.* MED uya(ndı)rıcı; **2.** *n.* MED uya(ndı)rıcı ilaç; F alkollü içki; **stim.u.late** ['~-leit] *v/t.* uyarmak, canlandırmak, teşvik etm., tahrik etm., gayrete getirmek; **stim.u'la.tion** *n.* uyarım, teşvik; **stim.u.la.tive** ['~lətiv] *adj.* uyandırıcı, canlandırıcı, muharrik; **stim.u.lus** ['~ləs] *n.* dürtü (**to** *-e*), uyarıcı şey.

sting [stiŋ] **1.** *n.* iğne (*arı vs.*); sokma, ısırma; *fig.* iğneleyici söz; acı, sızı; yakıp kavurma; **2.** (*irr.*) *v/t.* sokmak, yakmak *-i*, batmak *-e*; *fig.* incitmek, gücendirmek; işkence, eziyet etm.; yakmak, kavurmak; *v/i.* acımak, canı yanmak; yanmak, kavrulmak; **be stung** *sl.* kazıklanmak (**for**); '**sting.er** *n.* F acıtıcı darbe vs.

stin.gi.ness ['stindʒinis] *n.* pintilik, cimrilik.

sting(.ing)-net.tle BOT ['stiŋ(iŋ)netl] *n.* ısırgan.

stin.gy □ ['stindʒi] pinti, cimri; kıt, az.

stink [stiŋk] **1.** *n.* pis koku; **2.** (*irr.*) *v/i.* pis kokmak, kokusunu çıkarmak (**of** *-in*; *sl. a. fig.*); *v/t.* kokutmak.

stint [stint] **1.** *n.* had, sınır, kayıt, limit; belirli bir süre için yapılan görev, iş (*as-*

kerlik vs.); **2.** *vb. bşi* esirgemek, cimrilik etm., *b-ne* az para *veya* yemek vermek; sınırlamak, kayıtlamak, azaltmak, kısmak (*masraf*).

sti.pend ['staipend] *n.* ücret, maaş (*part. papazlara*); **sti'pen.di.ar.y** [ˌ-djərɪ] **1.** *adj.* ücretli, maaşlı; **2.** *n.* ücretli sulh yargıcı.

stip.ple PAINT ['stipl] *vb.* noktalayarak resmetmek.

stip.u.late ['stipjuleit] *vb. a.* ~ *for* şart koymak; kararlaştırmak, anlaşmak *-de*; **stip.u'la.tion** *n.* şart (koyma).

stir[1] [stəː] **1.** *n.* karıştırma; hareket, kımıldanma; canlılık, heyecan, telâş; gürültü, patırtı; **2.** *v/t.* karıştırmak; harekete geçirmek, tahrik etm.; yerini değiştirmek; ~ *up* karıştırmak (*sıvı*); kışkırtmak; *v/i.* kımılda(n)mak, yerinden oynamak.

stir[2] *sl.* [ˌ-] *n.* hapishane, kodes.

stir.ring ['stəːriŋ] *adj.* heyecan verici, canlandırıcı, canlı, heyecanlı.

stir.rup ['stirəp] *n.* üzengi.

stitch [stitʃ] **1.** *n.* dikiş; ilmik; böğür sancısı; *not have a dry* ~ *on one* sırılsıklam, çok ıslanmış olm.; *a* ~ *in time saves nine* vaktinde yapılan küçük bir iş insanı büyük zahmetten kurtarır; **2.** *vb.* dikmek, dikiş dikmek; ciltlemek (*kitap*).

stoat ZOO [stəut] *n.* kakım, as.

stock [stɔk] **1.** *n.* ağaç gövdesi, kütük; sap, kabza, dipçik; soy, nesil, aile; hammadde; çorba malzemesi (*et, sebze vs.*); mevcut mal, stok, depo mevcudu; *a. live* ~ hayvan mevcudu, çiftlik hayvanları; HIST boyunbağı; BOT üzerine aşı yapılan dal; COM esas sermaye, kapital; ~*s pl.* menkul değerler, sermaye hisseleri; hisse senetleri; ~*s pl.* NAUT yapı kızağı; ~*s pl.* HIST tomruk (*ceza*); *in* (*out of*) ~ mevcut (-du tükenmiş); *take* ~ COM mal mevcudunu sayarak kontrol etm.; *take* ~ *of fig.* farkına varmak *-in*, tahmin etm.; **2.** *adj.* stok olarak bulundurulan, stok…; *part.* THEAT devamlı; standart…; basmakalıp, alelâde; ~ *play* repertuvardan seçilen oyun; **3.** *vb.* yığmak, stok etm., mal ile doldurmak; filiz sürmek.

stock.ade [stɔ'keid] **1.** *n.* lata ile yapılan çit, hatıllı çit, şarampol; **2.** *vb.* şarampolla çevirmek, korumak.

stock…: '~**breed.er** *n.* büyükbaş yetiştiren çiftçi; '~**brok.er** *n.* borsacı; '~**car** *n.* hayvan vagonu; ~ **com.pa.ny** THEAT daimî tiyatro grubu; ~ **ex.change** borsa; '~**farm.er** *n.* hayvan yetiştiricisi; '~**holder** *n.* hissedar, hisse senedi sahibi.

stock.i.net [stɔki'net] *n.* triko, jarse.

stock.ing ['stɔkiŋ] *n.* uzun çorap.

stock.ist COM ['stɔkist] *n.* stokçu.

stock…: '~**in-'trade** *n.* mevcut mal, sermaye, malzeme, teçhizat, alet ve edevat; '~**job.ber** *n.* borsa acentası, borsacı; ~ **mar.ket** borsa; '~**pil.ing** *n.* stok etme; '~**still** *adv.* kımıldamadan, hareketsiz; '~**tak.ing** *n.* stok sayımı, envanter yapma.

stock.y ['stɔki] *adj.* bodur, tıknaz.

stock.yard ['stɔkjɑːd] *n.* hayvanın geçici muhafaza edildiği yer, ağıl.

stodge *sl.* [stɔdʒ] *v/t. & v/i.* tıkabasa ye(dir)mek; '**stodg.y** □ hazmı güç olan, ağır; *fig.* hantal, can sıkıcı, monoton.

sto.gy, sto.gie *Am.* ['stəugi] *n.* ucuz, kalitesiz puro.

sto.ic ['stəuik] **1.** *adj.* heyecan, sevinç, üzüntü duygularını göstermeyen, revaki, stoik; **2.** *n.* sevinç, keder duygularını belli etmeyen kimse; '**sto.i.cal** □ *fig.* revaki, stoik, metin; **sto.i.cism** ['ˌ-sizəm] *n.* stoacılık, stoik felsefe; sevinç ve kedere karşı kayıtsızlık, soğukkanlılık.

stoke [stəuk] *vb.* ateşe kömür atmak; ateş yakmak, ısıtmak; '~**hold**, '~**hole** *n.* NAUT külhan ağzı; '**stok.er** *n.* ateşçi.

stole[1] [stəul] *n.* uzun cüppe.

stole[2] [ˌ-] *pret.*, '**sto.len** *p.p. of* **steal 1**.

stol.id □ ['stɔlid] duygusuz, vurdumduymaz, kayıtsız, duygularını belli etmez; **sto'lid.i.ty** *n.* duygusuzluk, vurdumduymazlık.

stom.ach ['stʌmək] **1.** *n.* mide; karın; *fig.* heves, istek (*for -e*); **2.** *v/t.* hazmetmek, sindirmek; *fig.* bşe tahammül etm.; '~**ache** *n.* mide ağrısı; **sto.mach.ic** [stəu'mækik] **1.** *adj.* (~**ally**) mide ile ilgili, mide…, hazmı kolaylaştıran; **2.** *n.* hazmı kolaylaştıran ilaç.

stomp *Am.* [stɔmp] *vb.* tepinmek, ayağını yere vura vura yürümek *veya* dansetmek.

stone [stəun] **1.** *n.* taş; çekirdek (*meyve*); mesane taşı; *a. precious* ~ kıymetli taş, mücevher; 6.35 kg.'lık bir ağırlık ölçüsü; **2.** *adj.* taştan yapılmış, taş…; **3.** *vb.* taşlamak, taş atmak; *-in* çekirdeğini çıkarmak (*meyve*); ♀ *Age* taş devri, '~**blind** *adj.* tamamen kör;

'~-'**cold** *adj.* buz gibi soğuk; '~-**crop** *n.* BOT damkoruğu, kayakoruğu; '~-'**dead** *adj.* ölmüş gitmiş; '~-'**deaf** *adj.* tamamen sağır, duvar gibi sağır; '~-**fruit** *n.* BOT çekirdekli meyve; '~-**ma.son** *n.* taşçı, duvarcı; '~-**pit** *n.* taş ocağı; '~-**wall.ing** *n.* *spor:* kazanmaktansa kaybetmemek için oynama, müdafaa yapma; POL mecliste engelleme ile görüşmeleri yavaşlatma; '~-**ware** *n.* bir tür sert taş içeren topraktan yapılmış çanak çömlek; '~-**work** *n.* taşçı işi.

ston.i.ness ['stəuninis] *n.* sertlik, taş gibi oluş.

ston.y ['stəuni] *adj.* taşlı(k); *fig.* taş gibi, katı; *a.* ~-**broke** *sl.* meteliksiz, beş parasız, tırıl, züğürt.

stood [stud] *pret. & p.p. of* **stand**.

stooge *sl.* [stu:dʒ] **1.** *n.* THEAT ikili komedyenlerden kendisine gülüneni; *fig.* el ulağı, yamak, yardakçı; **2.** *v/i.* sahnede aptal, *k-ne* gülünen kimse olm.; sarsak sursak yürümek.

stool [stu:l] *n.* tabure, arkalıksız iskemle; MED dışkı, büyük aptes; BOT filiz veren kök *veya* kütük; BOT kök sürgünü; '~-**pigeon** *n. part. Am.* çığırtkan güvercin; *sl.* polisin kullandığı muhbir, gammaz.

stoop [stu:p] **1.** *v/i.* eğilmek; alçalmak, tenezzül etm.; ikibüklüm yürümek; *v/t.* eğmek (*baş*); **2.** *n.* kambur duruş; *Am.* veranda.

stop [stɔp] **1.** *v/t.* durdurmak, önlemek, kesmek, engellemek (**from** -*den*); son vermek -*e*; *a.* ~ **up** tıkamak, kapa(t)mak; doldurmak (*diş*); kapa(t)mak, kesmek (*yol*); bloke etm., durdurmak (*çek*); kesmek (*ödeme*); alıkoymak (*ücret, kira vs.*); MUS dokunmak (*ses, tel*); *v/i.* durmak, kesilmek, hareket etmemek; bitmek, sonu olm.; F kısa süre için kalmak; ~ **dead**, ~ **short** aniden durmak; ~ **at home** F evde kalmak; ~ **over** yolculukta mola vermek; ~ **up late** F yatmamak; **2.** *n.* dur(dur)ma; durak, mola, ara; MEC vurma, çarpma; sonuç; durak yeri, istasyon; *mst* **full** ~ GR nokta; MUS org düğmesi; MUS flavta anahtarı, kle; GR patlama sesi; '~-**cock** *n.* MEC valf, vana; '~-**gap** *n.* geçici önlem *veya* çare; '~-**o.ver** *n.* mola, konaklama; AVIA ara iniş; '~-**page** *n.* tıkama, durdurma, kes(il)me; maaşa haciz koyma; stopaj; MEC işletme arızası; tıkanıklık (*trafik*); '**stop.per** **1.** *n.* tıkaç,

tapa; spor: top kesici; ~ **circuit** ELECT kapalı devre; **2.** *vb.* (*tapa, tıkaç vs. ile*) tıkamak; '**stop.ping** *n.* MED dolgu; '**stop-press** *n.* baskı bitmek üzereyken gazeteye eklenen son haber(ler); '**stop-watch** *n.* kronometre, saniye ölçer saat.

stor.age ['stɔːridʒ] *n.* depoya koyma, saklama, depolama; ardiye (ücreti); ~ **battery** akümülatör.

store [stɔː] **1.** *n.* stok, depo mevcudu; *a.* ~**s** *pl. fig.* bolluk; ambar, depo, antrepo; *Am.* dükkân, mağaza; ~**s** *pl.* bonmarşe; ~**s** *pl.* MIL, NAUT mühimmat, savaş gereçleri, levazım, kumanya; *in* ~ elde, mevcut, depoda; *be in* ~ *for* *b-ni, bşi* beklemek; *have in* ~ *for* rezerve etm., temin etmiş olm., hazırlamak -*e*; *set veya put great* ~ *by bşe* çok değer vermek; **2.** *v/t. a.* ~ *up* koymak, yığmak, koymak, istif etm., yerleştirmek, depo etm.; saklamak; biriktirmek; doldurmak (*with ile*); '~-**house** *n.* ambar, depo; *mst fig.* hazine; '~-**keep.er** *n.* ambar memuru; *Am.* mağazacı; '~-**room** *n.* ambar, kiler, depo.

sto.rey(ed) ['stɔːri(d)] *s.* **story²**, **storied²**.

sto.ried¹ ['stɔːrid] *adj.* pek çok hikâyeye konu olma.

sto.ried² [-] *adj.* ...katlı.

stork [stɔːk] *n.* leylek.

storm [stɔːm] **1.** *n.* fırtına, kasırga, bora; MIL hücum; (*alkış vs.*) tufan; şiddetli öfke; *take by* ~ hücum ederek almak; **2.** *v/t.* hücumla zaptetmek (*a.* MIL); *v/i.* fırtına patlamak, fırtınalı geçmek; hiddetlenmek, kudurmak (*at* -*e*); '**storm.y** □ fırtınalı.

sto.ry¹ ['stɔːri] *n.* hikâye, öykü, masal, roman, efsane; tarih; konu, makale; F yalan, palavra; *short* ~ kısa hikâye, fıkra.

sto.ry² [-] *n.* bina katı.

sto.ry-tell.er ['stɔːritelə] *n.* öykü anlatan, masalcı; F yalancı kimse.

stout [staut] **1.** □ sağlam, kuvvetli, sıhhatli; şişman, göbekli; cesur, yiğit; **2.** *n.* sert bira, siyah bira; '~-'**heart.ed** *adj.* yiğit, cesur, yürekli; '**stout.ness** *n.* cesaret, yiğitlik, mertlik; şişmanlık; *spor:* sebat, azim, metanet.

stove [stəuv] **1.** *n.* soba; fırın, ocak; AGR ser, limonluk; **2.** *vb.* kurutmak; dezenfekte etm. (*ısı ile*); **3.** *pret. & p.p. of* **stove 2**; '~-**pipe** *n.* soba borusu; *Am.*

F silindir şapka.

stow [stəu] *v/t.* saklamak, istif etm., paketlemek; **'stow.age** *n.* istifleme, yerleştirme; istif yeri; NAUT istif ücreti; istif olunan şey; **'stow.a.way** *n.* NAUT kaçak yolcu.

stra.bis.mus MED [strə'bizməs] *n.* şaşılık.

strad.dle ['strædl] *v/t. & v/i.* apış(tır)mak, bacaklar açık oturmak, durmak *veya* yürümek, ata biner gibi oturmak; MIL hedefin hem önüne hem arkasına ateş ederek hedefi ayarlamak; *Am. fig.* iki tarafı birden idare etm.; ne yapacağını bilmemek.

strafe [strɑːf] *v/t.* F cezalandırmak; MIL borbardıman etm.; AVIA ağır makineli ile hücum etm.

strag.gle ['strægl] *vb.* yoldan sapmak; sürü *veya* grubun gerisinde kalıp dağınık gitmek, dağınık olm.; dağınık büyümek; *fig.* konu dışına çıkmak; BOT üremek, türemek; **'strag.gler** *n.* arkada kalan; MIL döküntü er(ler); **'strag.gling** ☐ dağınık, seyrek.

straight [streit] **1.** *adj.* doğru, müstakim, (düm)düz; *fig.* dürüst, samimi, namuslu; düz (*saç*); *Am.* saf, halis (*içki*); *Am.* POL sabit yüzdeli; F güvenilir, doğru; ciddî; *put* ~ düzeltmek, yoluna koymak; **2.** *n.* yarışçılık; yarış çizgisi, düz hat; **3.** *adv.* doğrudan doğruya, doğruca, sapmaksızın; derhal, hemen; açıkça, dobra dobra; ~ *away,* ~ *off* hemen, derhal; ~ *out* açıkça, dobra dobra; **'straight.en** *v/t. & v/i.* doğrul(t)mak, düzel(t)mek; ~ *out* yoluna koymak; düzeltmek; **straight'for.ward** ☐ doğru sözlü, dürüst, samimi; **'straight.way** *adv.* derhal, hemen.

strain[1] [strein] **1.** *n.* MEC gerginlik, ger(il)me; aşırı zihinsel ve duygusal gerginlik; zorlama, baskı, tazyik (*on*); MED burkulup incinme, bir veterin fazla gerilmesi; *mst* ~ *spl.* MUS melodi, makam, nağme; soydan gelen nitelik (*of*) (*delilik vs.*); *put a great* ~ *on* yük olmak, yük getirmek; **2.** *v/t.* germek, zorlamak (*a. fig.*); zarar vermek, zayıflatmak (*vücut*); MEC zorlamak; işletmek; MED (zorla, hırpalayarak) çekmek; süzgeçten geçirmek, süzmek; *v/i.* gerilmek, zorlanmak; nefsine eziyet etm. (*after*); çabalamak; süzülmek; çekmek (*at*); burkulup incinmek.

strain[2] [-] *n.* nesil, soy, kan, menşe, nesep, soy sop.

strain.er ['streinə] *n.* süzgeç, filtre; elek, kalbur.

strait [streit] **1.** *n.* GEOGR boğaz (*özel isimlerle* ⅋*s pl.*), dar geçit; ~ *s pl.* sıkıntı, zorluk, darlık; **2.** *adj.* dar, sıkı; ~ *jacket* deli gömleği; **'strait.en** *v/t.* sıkıştırmak, daraltmak; ~ *ed* *adj.* sıkıntıda, darlık içinde, çaresiz (*for*); **strait-laced** ['-leist] *adj.* tutucu, dargörüşlü; **'strait-ness** *n.* darlık, sıkışıklık, eksiklik.

strand[1] [strænd] **1.** *n.* sahil, plaj, deniz kıyısı; **2.** *v/t. & v/i.* karaya otur(t)mak (*gemi*); *fig.* başarısızlığa uğra(t)mak; ~ *ed* *adj.* zor durumda, sıkıntıda; MOT bir yere saplanıp kalmış.

strand[2] [-] *n.* halat bükümü, kablo örgüsü; iplik, tel (*saç*).

strange ☐ [streindʒ] yabancı, elâlem (*a. fig.*); tuhaf, garip, acayip; yeni, acemi; **'strange.ness** *n.* tuhaflık, acayiplik; yabancılık; **'stran.ger** *n.* yabancı, el, tanınmayan kimse; yeni gelen kimse (*to* -*e*).

stran.gle ['stræŋgl] *vb.* boğ(ul)mak, boğazlamak; *fig.* bastırmak, zulmetmek; **'~.hold** *n.* boğazı sıkma vaziyeti.

stran.gu.late MED ['stræŋgjuleit] *vb.* boğ(ul)mak, düğümle(n)mek (*bağırsak vs.*), sıkıştırmak (*damar vs.*); **stran.gu'la.tion** *n.* boğ(ul)ma; MED düğümlenme.

strap [stræp] **1.** *n.* kayış, sırım; şerit, bant, atkı; kayışla döverek cezalandırma; tutunma kayışı (*otobüs, tren vs.'de*); **2.** *v/t.* kayışla bağlamak; kayışla dövmek, kamçılamak; bantlamak; **'~.hang.er** *n.* F ayakta kayışa tutunan yolcu (*otobüste*); **'strap.less** *adj.* atkısız (*bayan elbisesi*); **'strap.ping 1.** *adj.* dolgun (*bayan*); kuvvetli, iriyapılı; **2.** *n.* MED bant, yapışkan şerit, plaster.

stra.ta ['strɑːtə] *pl. of* **stratum.**

strat.a.gem ['strædʒəm] *n.* harp hilesi; desise, kurnazlık.

stra.te.gic [strə'tiːdʒik] *adj.* (~*ally*) stratejik; **strat.e.gist** ['strætidʒist], *n.* stratej, strateji uzmanı; **'strat.e.gy** *n.* strateji, bir amaca varmak için eylem birliği sağlama ve düzenleme sanatı.

strat.i.fy ['strætifai] *vb.* tabakalar halinde düzenlemek.

stra.to.cruis.er AVIA ['strætəukruːzə] *n.* stratosfer uçağı.

strat.o.sphere PHYS ['strætəusfiə] *n.* stratosfer.

stra.tum GEOL ['strɑːtəm] *n., pl.* **stra.ta** ['-tə] kat, tabaka, katman, zümre (*a.*

fig.).

straw [strɔ:] **1.** *n.* saman, saman çöpü; *fig.* önemsiz şey, hiç; *I don't care* ~ bu bana vız gelir; *a man of* ~ *fig.* kukla adam; **2.** *adj.* saman...; ~ *vote Am.* POL genel seçimden önceki nabız yoklaması (*veya* kamuoyu araştırması) '~.ber.ry *n.* çilek; 'straw.y *adj.* samanlı, saman gibi.

stray [strei] **1.** *v/i.* yoldan sapmak, yolunu şaşırmak, sapmak (*from* -*den*; *a.* *fig.*); dolaşmak, gezinmek, avarelik etm.; **2.** *adj. a.* ~*ed* yoldan sapmış; başıboş, dağınık; tesadüfî; **3.** *n.* sürüden ayrılmış hayvan; başıboş kimse; ayrı düşmüş *b-i veya bş*; ~*s pl.* ELECT yıldırım yüzünden oluşan parazitler.

streak [stri:k] **1.** *n.* çizgi, hat; *fig.* damar; iz, eser; kısa süre; ~ *of lightning* yıldırım; **2.** *vb.* çizgilemek, çizgilerle süslemek; acele etm., çok hızlı hareket etm.; çırılçıplak durumda herkesin önünden hızla geçmek; 'streak.y □ çizgili, çubuklu, yollu.

stream [stri:m] **1.** *n.* ırmak; çay, dere; akıntı; akım, cereyan; sel; (*okulda*) başarı derecesi; *go with the* ~ *fig.* ayak uydurmak; -*e*; **2.** *v/i.* (çağlayarak) akmak, sel gibi akmak; dalgalanmak (*saç, bayrak vs*); taşmak; *v/t.* akıtmak; **streamer** *n.* flama, fors; serpantin, renkli kâğıt tekerleği; göğe doğru yükselen ışık sütunu (*kuzey veya güneyde*); *gazete*; manşet; **stream.let** ['~lit] *n.* küçük çay *veya* dere.

stream.line ['stri:mlain] **1.** *n.* aerodinamik şekil düzenli akıntı; **2.** *v/t.* aerodinamik şekil vermek, su *veya* hava içinde kolay hareket edebilir hale koymak; kolay ve elverişli duruma getirmek; *fig.* modernleştirmek.

street [stri:t] *n.* sokak, cadde, yol; *not in the same* ~ *with* F ...ile kıyaslanamaz; '~.car *n. part. Am.* tramvay; '~.walk.er *n.* sokak kadını, fahişe, adi orospu.

strength [streŋθ] *n.* kuvvet, güç (*a. fig.*); MIL, NAUT kadro, askerî güç; *on the* ~ *of* -*e* uyarınca, -*e* dayanarak, güvenerek; 'strength.en *v/t.* kuvvetlendirmek; desteklemek; *v/i.* kuvvetlenmek, güçlenmek.

stren.u.ous □ ['strenjuəs] faal, gayretli, çalışkan, istekli; 'stren.u.ous.ness *n.* gayret, çaba, canlılık, çalışkanlık.

stress [stres] **1.** *n.* baskı, tazyik, şiddet; GR vurgu, aksan; MEC gerilme, zorla-

ma; önem; PSYCH sıkıntı, gerginlik; *lay* ~ (*up*)*on* bşi önemle belirtmek, üzerinde ısrarla durmak -*in*; **2.** *v/t.* üzerinde durmak, vurgulamak; MEC tazyik etm., germek, baskı yapmak, zorlamak; üzerine basmak, vurgu koymak.

stretch [stretʃ] **1.** *v/t.* germek, uzatmak; sermek, yaymak; *mst* ~ *out* uzatmak (*kol vs.*); kurmak (*yay*); *fig.* abartmak, aşırıya kaçırmak; *v/i.* uzanmak, gerilmek, genişlemek (*into* -*e*); *a.* ~ *one's powers* tüm gücünü kullanmak; **2.** *n.* uzanma, gerilme; gerginlik; abartma; geniş yer, yüzey; süre; *at a* ~ aralıksız, hiç durmadan, ara vermeden; *on the* ~ gergin, sıkı; 'stretch.er *n.* sedye, teskere; ayakkabı kalıbı; (*kayık*) yarım oturak; 'stretch.er-bear.er *n.* sedye taşıyan hastabakıcı.

strew [stru:] (*irr.*) *v/t.* serpmek, dağıtmak, yayılarak kaplamak; **strewn** [stru:n] *p.p. of* **strew**.

stri.ate ['straiit], **stri.at.ed** [~'eitid] *adj.* dar çizgili, şeritli.

strick.en ['strikən] *adj.* müteessir, başına gelmiş, uğramış (*with* -*e*); yaralı, yaralanmış; ~ *in age* yaşlı, kocamış.

strict [strikt] *adj.* sıkı, sert, şiddetli; kesin; titiz; tam, harfi harfine olan, mutlak; ~*ly speaking* doğrusunu söylemek gerekirse; 'strict.ness *n.* sıkılık, sertlik, disiplin; kesinlik; **stric.ture** ['~tʃə] *n. oft.* ~*s pl.* kınama, yerme, şiddetli eleştiri; MED kanal daralması.

strid.den ['stridn] *p.p. of* **stride 1**.

stride [straid] **1.** (*irr.*) *v/i.* yürüyerek bir yerden geçmek, bir yeri aşmak; *v/i. a.* ~ *out* geniş adımlar atmak; **2.** *n.* (geniş) adım; *get into one's* ~ harekete gelmek, tam yoluna girmek.

stri.dent □ ['straidənt] gıcırtılı, cıyak cıyak, keskin, tiz (*ses*).

strife *lit.* [straif] *n.* çekişme, didişme, mücadele, ihtilâf.

strike [straik] **1.** *n.* grev; bulma (*maden filizi, petrol vs.*); vurma, çarpma; *fig.* beklenmedik başarı, isabet, büyük vurgun; MIL hava hücumu (*tek hedefe*); *Am. beysbol*: topa vuramama; *be on* ~ grevde olm.; *go on* ~ greve gitmek, grev yapmak; **2.** (*irr.*) *v/t.* vurmak, çarpmak, darbe indirmek; beklenmedik bir anda yapmak; çalmak (*saat, nota vs.*); etkilemek; dehşet salmak; indirmek (*bayrak, yelken vs.*); yıkmak (*çadır vs.*); çınlatmak (*ses*); birden aklına gelmek; bulmak, keşfetmek;

kök salmak; akdetmek, anlaşmak (*pazarlık vs.*); yakmak, tutuşturmak (*ateş, ışık*); *s.* **attitude**; **~ a balance** hesapları dengelemek, hesap bakiyesini saptamak; **~ oil** petrole rastlamak, petrol bulmak; F vurgun vurmak, bahtı açık olm.; **~ off** listeden çıkarmak, çizip silmek; **~ out** *plan*: taslağını çizmek; çıkarmak, silmek *-den*; **~ through** çizmek, karalamak; **~ up** şarkı söylemeğe başlamak; başlatmak (*arkadaşlık*); *v/i.* çarpmak (**at**); NAUT karaya oturmak; NAUT, MIL fors indirmek; grev yapmak; çalmak (*saat*); çakmak (*şimşek*); ateş almak (*kibrit*); kök tutmak; **~ home** etkilemek, tesirli olm.; **~ in** vurup saplamak; lâfa karışmak; **~ into** bşe düşmek; **~ up** çalmaya başlamak (*orkestra*); **~ upon the ear** kulağına çalınmak; '**~-bound** *adj.* grev yüzünden felce uğramış; '**~-break.er** *n.* grev kırıcı işçi; '**~-pay** *n.* grevdeyken işçilere ödenen para; '**strik.er** *n.* grevci; MEC müsademe (*veya* çarpışma) iğnesi, zil çekici.
strik.ing □ ['straikiŋ] çarpıcı, göze çarpan; şaşılacak, şaşırtıcı.
string [striŋ] **1.** *n.* ip, sicim; kordon, şerit, bağ; *Am.* F koşul, şart, pürüz; veter, kiriş; BOT lif, yaprak damarı; MUS tel, kiriş; sıra, dizi, kol; **~s** *pl.* MUS telli çalgı(lar), yaylı sazlar; **harp on the same ~** aynı konuyu tekrarlayıp durmak, diline dolamak; **have two ~s to one's bow** *b-nin* elinde iki olanak bulunmak; **pull the ~s** iltimas yaptırmak; **there are ~s attached to it** F işin altından bir çapanoğlu çıktı; **2.** (*irr.*) *vb.* dizmek, ipe geçirmek; tel takmak *-e* (*keman vs.*); kılçıklarını çıkarmak (*taze fasulye*); *Am. sl.* **~ b-ne** yalan yutturmak; *b-ni* alaya almak; **~ up** F ipe çekmek, asmak; **be strung up** çok heyecanlı, sinirli, endişeli vs. olm; **~ bag** file; **~ band** MUS yaylı sazlar orkestrası; **~ bean** çalı fasulyesi; **stringed** *adj.* MUS telli...; ...telli.
strin.gen.cy ['strindʒənsi] *n.* sıkılık, sertlik, şiddet; COM para darlığı; '**strin.gent** □ sert, şiddetli, zorlu; sıkı; para darlığında olan.
string.y ['striŋi] *adj.* lifli; telli, tel tel olan; kılçıklı.
strip [strip] **1.** *v/t.* soymak (**off**), *fig.* soyup soğana çevirmek, yağma etm. (**off**); sıyırmak, soymak (*kabuk vs.*); MEC sökmek, parçalara ayırmak; NAUT armasını soymak; *a.* **~ off** çıkarmak (*el-*

bise vs.); *v/i.* F soyunmak; **2.** *n.* şerit, uzun ve dar parça; **~ car.toon = com-ics.**
stripe [straip] **1.** *n.* çubuk, kumaş yolu, çizgi; MIL sırma, şerit; **2.** *v/t.* çizgilemek, çizgilerle süslemek; **striped** *adj.* çizgili, yollu.
strip-light.ing ['striplaitiŋ] *n.* neon ışığı ile aydınlatma.
strip.ling ['stripliŋ] *n.* delikanlı, genç adam.
strip mall ['stripmɔːl] *n.* şehir dışında yer alan alışveriş sokağı.
strip-tease ['striptiːz] *n.* striptiz.
strive [straiv] (*irr.*) *vb.* uğraşmak, çalışmak (**for, after** *-meğe*); zahmet etm., yorulmak; mücadele etm. (**against, for** *-e karşı, için*); **striv.en** *p.p. of* **strive 1.**
strode [stroud] *pret. of* **stride 1.**
stroke [strouk] **1.** *n.* vuruş, çarpma, darbe (etkisi); sars(ıl)ma, şok; MED inme, felç; MEC piston siası; fırça darbesi; vuruş sesi (*saat*); hamlacı; yüzme tarzı, kulaç; okşama; **~ of genius** dahiyane bir davranış; **~ of luck** şans, iyi tesadüf; **2.** *v/t.* okşamak; (*kürek*) hareket işareti vermek.
stroll [stroul] **1.** *v/i.* gezinmek, dolaşmak; **2.** *n.* gezme; '**stroll.er** *n.* gezinen kimse, avare; *Am.* acılır kapanır çocuk arabası.
strong □ [strɔŋ] *com.* kuvvetli, güçlü, dinç; *fig.* yetenekli, ehil; enerjik, istekli, gayretli; sağlam, dayanıklı; basa vuran, sert (*icki, koku vs.*); şiddetli; GR mastarın ünlü harfinin değişmesi ile geçmiş zamanlarını oluşturan (*örnek: sing, song, sung*); *s.* **language**; **feel ~(ly) about** bşe sinirlenmek, heyecanlanmak; *bş* hakkında *k-ne* has düşüncesi olm.; **be going.~** F yaşına göre sağlam, güçlü olm.; '**~-box** *n.* çelik kasa; '**~.hold** *n.* kale, müstahkem yer; *fig.* merkez; '**~-'mind.ed** *adj.* azimli, bildiğinden şaşmaz, kararlı; '**~-room** *n.* hazine odası; '**~-'willed** *adj.* inatçı, iradeli, kararlı.
strop [strɔp] **1.** *n.* bileği kayışı, ustra kayışı; NAUT direk sapanı; **2.** *v/t.* kayışa sürterek bilemek (*ustra vs.*).
stro.phe ['stroufi] *n.* (*özellikle eski Yunan'da*) koronun okuduğu kıta, bent.
strove [strouv] *pret. of* **strive.**
struck [strʌk] *pret. & p.p. of* **strike 2.**
struc.tur.al □ ['strʌktʃərəl] bina *veya* yapıya ait, yapı...; organik, yapısal;

structure *n.* bina, yapı; yapılış, bünye; teşekkül, çatı.

strug.gle ['strʌgl] **1.** *v/i.* çabalamak, mücadele etm., uğraşmak **(for**, **against** *ile)*; *k-ni* çok yormak, yapmayacağım diye dayatmak, çırpınmak; **2.** *n.* savaş, mücadele **(for** *için)*; çaba, uğraş, gayret; zorluk, zahmet; **'strug.gler** *n.* savaşan, mücadele eden kimse.

strum [strʌm] **1.** *v/t. & v/i.* tıngırda(t)-mak *(müzik aleti vs.)*; **2.** *n.* yaylı sazları tıngırdatma.

strum.pet *obs.* ['strʌmpit] *n.* fahişe, orospu.

strung [strʌŋ] *pret. & p.p. of* **string 2.**

strut [strʌt] **1.** *v/i.* baba hindi gibi gezmek, azametle yürümek; *v/t.* MEC payanda vurmak, desteklemek; **2.** *n.* azametli yürüyüş; MEC bağlama kirişi, destek, payanda.

strych.nine CHEM ['strikni:n] *n.* striknin, kargabüken özü.

stub [stʌb] **1.** *n.* kütük, kesilmiş ağaç gövdesi; *sigara* izmariti; *Am.* koçan, kontrol kuponu; **2.** *vb. mst ~ up* kökleri temizlemek, köklemek; ayağını bir yere çarpmak; **~ out** söndürmek *(sigara)*.

stub.ble ['stʌbl] *n.* ekin anızı; uzamış tıraş.

stub.bly ['stʌbli] *adj.* anızlı; sert kıllı.

stub.born ['stʌbən] inatçı, dikkafalı, aksi, sert, serkeş; azimli, sebatlı; sıkışmış, oynamayan *(kilit vs.)*; **'stub-born.ness** *n.* dikkafalılık, inatçılık.

stub.by ['stʌbi] *adj.* kısa ve kalın, küt, güdük.

stuc.co ['stʌkəu] **1.** *n.* dış duvar sıvası, alçı vs. **2.** *vb.* karışımla sıvamak, süslemek.

stuck [stʌk] *pret. & p.p. of* **stick²**; **~ on** *Am.* F *b-ne* abayı yakmış, tutkun, âşık; **'~'up** *adj.* F burnu havada, hodpesent.

stud¹ [stʌd] **1.** *n.* duvar çivisi, iri başlı çivi; topuz; yaka düğmesi; saplama; **2.** *v/t.* iri başlı çiviler çakmak, çivilerle donatmak, süslemek.

stud² [_] *n.* hara; damızlık at, aygır; **'~-book** *n.* özellikle yarış atlarının soy defteri.

stud.ding ARCH ['stʌdiŋ] *n.* iskelet, çatı.

stu.dent ['stju:dənt] *n.* öğrenci; araştırıcı, uzman; **'stu.dent.ship** *n.* öğrencilik; burs.

stud.ied □ ['stʌdid] prova edilmiş, hazırlanmış *(rol)*; sahte, yapmacık, zoraki; kasıtlı, maksatlı.

stu.di.o ['stju:diəu] *n.* stüdyo, atelye; yayın odası *(radyo, TV)*.

stu.di.ous □ ['stju:djəs] çalışkan, gayretli; dikkatli **(of)**; çabalayan **(to** *-e)*; kasıtlı, bilerek; **'stu.di.ous.ness** *n.* çalışkanlık, gayret, çaba.

stud.y ['stʌdi] **1.** *n.* tahsil, öğrenim; tetkik, araştırma; çalışma *(odası)*; taslak *(resim vs.)*; **be in a brown ~** çok dalgın, zihni karmakarışık olm.; **2.** *v/i.* incelemek, araştırma yapmak **(for)**; *v/t.* incelemek, araştırmak; öğrenim görmek, tahsil etm.; gayret etm.; hazırlamak.

stuff [stʌf] **1.** *n.* madde; malzeme; kumaş; *obs.* yün(lü kumaş); eşya, şey; ilaç; *fig.* zırva, saçma; **2.** *v/t.* doldurmak, tıkıştırmak **(into** *-e)*; **~ up** kapa(t)mak, tıkamak; **~ed shirt** *Am. sl.* *k-ni* bş sanan kimse, ukalâ; *v/i.* tıkınmak, çok yemek; **'stuff.ing** *n.* dolma *(içi)*; doldurma, şişirme; dolgu; MEC fodra, elbisede kumaşı dik tutan kolalı bez; **'stuffy** □ havasız, küf kokulu; F alıngan, dargın, öfkeli; F kibirli, soğuk; tıkalı.

stul.ti.fi.ca.tion [stʌltifi'keiʃən] *n.* aptallaştırma; ket vurma; **stul.ti.fy** ['_fai] *v/t.* aptallaştırmak; faydasız *veya* aptalca göstermek, maskaraya çevirmek, rezil kepaze etm.

stum.ble ['stʌmbl] **1.** *n.* sürçme, sendeleme, tökezleme; hata, yanılgı; **2.** *v/i.* ayağı dolaşmak, sendelemek, sürçmek; kekelemek, dili sürçmek; **~ across**, **~ upon** rastlamak *-e*; **'stumbling-block** *n. fig.* engel, ket.

stump [stʌmp] **1.** *n.* kütük; kesilen bir şeyin geri kalan parçası; kırık diş kökü; *(sigara)* izmarit; *kriket oyunu*= üç hedef sopasından her biri; F seçim propagandası *veya* propagandanın yapıldığı yer; **~s** *pl.* F bacaklar; **stir one's ~s** F hızlı yürümek, pergelleri açmak; **2.** *v/t.* kriket: hedefi vurarak *b-ni* oyun dışı etm.; F şaşırtmak, afallatmak; *Am.* F *b-ne* meydan okumak; **~ up** *sl.* ödemek; **~ the country** ülkeyi dolaşarak seçim propagandası yapmak; **~ed for** çekingen, mahcup; *v/i.* ağır basarak yürümek, tahta ayaklı gibi yürümek; **'~.or.a.tor** *n.* sokak hatibi, halk hatibi; **'stump.y** □ kısa, bodur, tıknaz; küt; güdük.

stun [stʌn] *v/t.* sersemletmek *(a. fig.)*; **~ned** *fig.* şaşkın, afallamış, sersem, ağzı açık kalmış.

stung [stʌŋ] *pret. & p.p. of* **sting 2.**

stunk [stʌŋk] *pret. & p.p. of stink 2.*

stun.ner F ['stʌnə] *n.* yaman kimse *veya* şey; çok çekici kimse (*part. kadın*); 'stun.ning □ F enfes, fevkalâde.

stunt¹ F [stʌnt] 1. *n.* hüner, ustalık, marifet, dikkati çekmek *veya* reklâm yapmak için yapılan davranış; AVIA akrobasi uçuşu; 2. *vb.* akrobasi uçuşu (*veya* gösterisi) yapmak.

stunt² [-] *v/t.* büyümesini önlemek *-in*, bodur bırakmak *-i*; 'stunt.ed *adj.* bodur kalmış.

stupe MED [stju:p] 1. *n.* sıcak kompres; 2. *vb.* kompres yapmak.

stu.pe.fac.tion [stju:pi'fækʃən] *n.* şaşkınlık, hayret; sersemlik; duyumsuzluk; stu.pe.fy ['-fai] *v/t. fig.* sersemletmek, şaşırtmak, afallatmak; aptallaştırmak.

stu.pen.dous □ [stju:'pendəs] şaşılacak; hayret edilecek, muazzam.

stu.pid □ ['stju:pid] budala, aptal, akılsız, alık; saçma; stu'pid.i.ty *n.* aptallık, budalalık.

stu.por ['stju:pə] *n.* uyuşukluk, sersemlik.

stur.di.ness ['stə:dinis] *n.* sağlamlık, güçlülük, dayanıklılık; metanet; 'sturdy *adj.* kuvvetli, güçlü, dayanıklı; metanetli; azimli, sebatlı.

stur.geon ICHTH ['stə:dʒən] *n.* mersin balığı.

stut.ter [stʌtə] 1. *v/i.* kekelemek, pepelemek; 2. *n.* kekeleme, kekemelik; 'stut.terer *n.* kekeme.

sty¹ [stai] *n.* domuz ahırı.

sty² [-] *n.* (*göz*) arpacık, itdirseği.

style [stail] 1. *n.* taş kalem; BOT pistil, boyuncak; tarz, üslup, usul; çeşit, tip, stil; giyimde moda; takvim usulü; *in* ~ klas, birinci sınıf; *under the* ~ *of...* BOT ...ticaret ünvanı altında; 2. *vb.* ad vermek, demek.

styl.ish □ ['stailiʃ] şık, modaya uygun, zarif; üsluba uygun; 'styl.ish.ness *n.* modaya uygunluk, şıklık.

styl.ist ['stailist] *n.* üslupçu; modacı, desinatör.

sty.lo F ['stailəu], sty.lo.graph ['-grɑ:f] *n.* dolmakalem, stilo.

styp.tic ['stiptik] *adj.* kan durdurucu *veya* dindirici (*ilaç*).

sua.sion ['sweiʒən] *n.* ikna etme, razı etme.

suave □ [swɑ:v] nazik, hoş tavırlı; tatlı (*şarap vs.*); 'suav.i.ty *n.* tatlı dillilik, hoş tavır, nezaket.

sub F [sʌb] *abbr. of subordinate 2*; *subscription*; *substitute 2*; *submarine 2.*

sub... [-] *prefix mst* ast-, alt, aşağı; ikincil; yan; biraz (daha)..., hemen hemen...

sub.ac.id ['sʌb'æsid] *adj.* ekşimtrak, mayhoş, buruk; *fig.* hırçın, kavgacı, sert.

sub.al.tern ['sʌbltən] *n.* ikincil, ast; MIL astsubay.

sub.a.tom.ic ['sʌbə'tɔmik] *adj.* atomdan küçük, atom içindeki.

sub.com.mit.tee ['sʌbkəmiti] *n.* alt komisyon.

sub.con.scious □ ['sʌb'kɔnʃəs] bilinçaltındaki.

sub.con.tract [sʌb'kɔntrækt] *n.* yan mukavele, alt sözleşme.

sub.cu.ta.ne.ous □ ['sʌbkju:teinjəs] deri altındaki, deri altına şırınga edilen.

sub.deb *Am.* F [sʌb'deb] *n.* ondört ile onyedi yaş arasındaki genç kız.

sub.di.vide [sʌbdi'vaid] *v/t. & v/i.* kısımlara ayırmak, parsellemek; sub.di.vi.sion ['-viʒən] *n.* parselleme; parsellenmiş toprak; alt bölüm.

sub.due [səb'dju:] *v/t.* zaptetmek, boyunduruk altına almak, zorlamak; azaltmak, hafifetmek (*ışık vs.*).

sub.head(.ing) ['sʌbhed(iŋ)] *n.* tâli (*veya* ikincil) başlık; bölüm başlığı.

sub.ja.cent [sʌb'dʒeisənt] *adj.* altındaki, alttaki.

sub.ject ['sʌbdʒikt] 1. *adj.* bağımlı olan (*to -e*), *b-nin* emri altında olan; maruz, karşı karşıya olan *ile*; *be* ~ *to* bşe meyletmek, temayül göstermek; ~ *to a fee veya duty* vergiye tabi; 2. *adv.* ~ *to bşin* kaydı ihtirazisi altında, ...koşulu ile; *to change without notice* ihbarsız değiştirilebilir; 3. *n.* tebaa, vatandaş, uyruk; PHLS, GR özne, fail; *a.* ~ *matter* esas fikir, konu, mevzu; MUS tem, esas makam; PAINT süje, resme konu olan şey; ders (konusu); denek; vesile, neden; 4. *v/t.* boyunduruk altına almak; ~ *to* maruz kılmak *-e*; sub'jec.tion *n.* hüküm altına alma; boyun eğme, itaat; sub.jec.tive □ sübjektif; öznel; kişisel.

sub.join [sʌb'dʒɔin] *v/t.* ilâve etm., katmak, eklemek.

sub.ju.gate ['sʌbdʒugeit] *v/t.* zaptetmek, boyunduruk altına almak; sub.ju'ga.tion *n.* boyunduruk altına alma.

sub.junc.tive GR [səb'dʒʌŋktiv] *n. a.* ~

mood şart kipi.

sub.lease ['sʌb'liːs], **sub.let** ['ˌ-'let] (*irr. **let***) *vb.* kiracının kiracısı olm.; kiralananı kira ile başkasına devretmek.

sub.li.mate CHEM **1.** ['sʌblimit] *n.* süblime, aksülümen; **2.** ['ˌ-meit] *v/t.* süblimleştirmek; arıtmak; **sub.li'ma.tion** *n.* süblimleş(tir)me; arıtma; **sub.lime** [sə'blaim] **1.** □ ulu, yüce, asil; **2.** *n.* ***the ~*** ulviyet; **3.** *v/t.* CHEM süblimleştirmek; *fig.* yüceleştirmek; **sub.lim.i.ty** [sə'blimiti] *n.* yücelik, asillik, ululuk.

sub-ma.chine gun ['sʌbmə'ʃiːngʌn] *n.* hafif makineli tüfek.

sub.ma.rine [sʌbmə'riːn] **1.** *adj.* denizaltı...; denizaltında yetişen; **2.** *n.* NAUT denizaltı.

sub.merge [səb'məːdʒ] *v/t.* & *v/i.* bat(ır)mak; (*bir yeri*) su basmak; **sub.mers.ibil.i.ty** [ˌ-sə'biliti] *n.* su altında kalabilme; **sub'mer.sion** *n.* dal(dır)ma; bat(ır)ma; su baskını.

sub.mis.sion [səb'miʃən] *n.* boyun eğme, itaat, teslim olma (***to*** -*e*); alçak gönüllülük, uysallık; arz, sunuş; **sub'mis.sive** □ boyun eğen, itaatkâr, alçakgönüllü.

sub.mit [səb'mit] *v/t.* teslim etm. (***to*** -*e*); takdirine bırakmak, sunmak -*e*; *part.* PARL ileri sürmek; *v/i. a.* ***~ o.s.*** boyun eğmek, itaat etm. (***to*** -*e*); *fig. k-ni bşe* hasretmek, adamak (***to***).

sub.or.di.nate 1. □ [sə'bɔːdnit] ikincil, alt, ast; tabi, bağlı; ***~ clause*** GR yan cümle, bağımlı cümlecik; **2.** *n.* ikinci derecede, ast memur; **sub.or.di'na.tion** *n.* ikincil olma (***to*** -*e*); itaat, boyun eğme.

sub.orn JUR [sʌ'bɔːn] *v/t.* yalancı tanıklığa teşvik etm., kışkırtmak, ayartmak (***to*** -*e*); **sub.or'na.tion** *n.* yalancı tanıklığa teşvik.

sub.p(o)e.na JUR [səb'piːnə] **1.** *n.* çağrı kâğıdı, celp, mahkemeye davet; **2.** *v/t.* mahkemeye davet etm. -*i*.

sub.scribe [səb'skraib] *v/t.* bağış olarak vermek, bağışlamak (*para*) (***to*** -*e*); imzalamak; altına adını yazmak (***to*** -*e*); *v/i.* (*gazete, dergi vs.*) abone olm. (***to*** -*e*); imzalayarak onaylamak; **sub'scriber** *n.* bağış veren (***for, to*** -*e*); abone (*a.* TELEPH) olan.

sub.scrip.tion [səb'skripʃən] *n.* imza; abone; üye aidatı.

sub.sec.tion ['sʌbsekʃən] *n.* şube, kol, dal.

sub.se.quence ['sʌbsikwəns] *n.* son-

radan gelme, arkası gelme; **sub.se.quent** □ sonra gelen, sonraki (***to***); ***~ly*** sonradan, arkadan.

sub.serve [səb'səːv] *vb.* hizmette bulunmak, işe yaramak, ilerlemesine yardım etm.; **sub'ser.vi.ence** [ˌ-vjəns] *n.* yararlılık; boyun eğme, itaatkârlık; **sub'servi.ent** □ boyun eğen, itaatkâr; faydalı, yararlı.

sub.side [səb'said] *v/i.* inmek, alçalmak; düşmek (*ateş*); (*toprağa*) yerleşmek, çökmek (*ev*); yatışmak, sakinleşmek; ***~ into*** *bşe* düşmek, gömülmek (*koltuğa*); çekilmek, hafiflemek (*sel, rüzgâr vs.*); **sub.sid.ence** ['sʌbsidəns] *n.* çökme; yatışma, hafifleme (*rüzgâr vs.*); **sub.sid.iar.y** [səb'sidjəri] **1.** □ yardımcı..., ek; bağlı, tabi, yardımcı olarak kullanılan (***to*** -*e*); ***be ~ to*** yardımcı olm., bütünleyici olm.; **2.** *n.* bayi, şube; muavin, yardımcı; *a.* ***~ company*** bağımlı ortaklık, yan kuruluş; **sub.si.dize** ['sʌbsidaiz] *v/t.* para vermek -*e*, tahsisat bağlamak -*e*, sübvansiyone etm. -*i*; **'sub.si.dy** *n.* devlet yardımı, tahsisat, sübvansiyon.

sub.sist [səb'sist] *v/i.* yaşamak, geçinmek, beslenmek (***on ile***; ***by ile***); *v/t.* *bşe.* bakmak, beslemek; **sub'sist.ence** *n.* geçinim, rızk, nafaka; ***~ wage*** en düşük geçinme ücreti.

sub.soil ['sʌbsɔil] *n.* toprakaltı.

sub.son.ic [sʌb'sɔnik] *adj.* ses hızından yavaş.

sub.stance ['sʌbstəns] *n.* madde, cevher, cisim; öz; *fig.* asıl mesele; içerik, esas; realite, gerçeklik; unsur; varlık, servet.

sub.stan.tial □ [səb'stænʃəl] gerçek; önemli, esaslı; dayanıklı, mukavim; zengin, varlıklı; **sub.stan.ti.al.i.ty** [ˌ-ʃi'æliti] *n.* gerçek varlık, öz, realite; dayanıklılık.

sub.stan.ti.ate [səb'stænʃieit] *v/t.* kanıtlamak, neden göstermek.

sub.stan.ti.val □ GR [sʌbstən'taivəl] isim, ad olarak kullanılan, isim niteliğinde; **sub.stan.tive** ['ˌ-tiv] **1.** □ bağımsız, müstakil; GR isim olarak kullanılan; dayanıklı; tözel; **2.** *n.* isim, ad.

sub.sti.tute ['sʌbstitjuːt] **1.** *v/i.* yerine geçmek (***for*** -*in*); *v/t.* yerine koymak (***for*** -*in*); **2.** *n.* vekil, mümessil; bedel; **sub.sti'tu.tion** *n.* ikame, yerine koyma, başka *bşin* yerine kullanma.

sub.stra.tum ['sʌb'stɑːtəm] *n.* esas, temel; MEC, GEOL alt tabaka; cevher, madde, töz.

sub.struc.ture ['sʌbstrʌktʃə] *n.* yapı temeli, toprak alt yapı.

sub.ten.ant ['sʌb'tenənt] *n.* kiracının kiracısı, ikinci kiracı.

sub.ter.fuge ['sʌbtəfjuːdʒ] *n.* kaçamak, kaçamaklı söz, bahane.

sub.ter.ra.ne.an □ [sʌbtə'reinjən] yeraltı; gizli.

sub.til.ize ['sʌtilaiz] *v/t.* inceltmek, düzeltmek; *v/i.* incelikle, ustalıkla kullanmak.

sub.ti.tle ['sʌbtaitl] *n.* ikincil başlık.

sub.tle □ ['sʌtl] ince (ruhlu); esrarengiz; çözümü zor, karışık; kurnaz, hilekâr; kılı kırk yaran; mahir, usta; '**sub-tle.ty** *n.* incelik, nazriklik; kurnazlık, cin fikirlilik.

sub.to.pia [sʌb'təupiə] *n.* şehir dışında geniş yerleşim bölgesi.

sub.tract [səb'trækt] *v/t.* MATH çıkarmak, hesaptan düşmek **sub'trac.tion** *n.* çıkarma, tarh.

sub.trop.i.cal ['sʌb'trɔpikəl] *adj.* astropikal.

sub.urb ['sʌbəːb] *n.* varoş, banliyö, dış mahalle; **sub.ur.ban** [sə'bəːbən] *adj.* kenar mahallede oturan; banliyö..., banliyö ile ilgili; **Sub'ur.bia** [‿bjə] *n.* dış mahalleler ve buralarda oturanların yaşamı.

sub.ven.tion [səb'venʃən] *n.* para yardımı, tahsisat, sübvansiyon, yardım.

sub.ver.sion [sʌb'vəːʃən] *n.* devirme, devrilme; yık(ıl)ma, tahrip; **sub'ver-sive** *adj.* yıkıcı, devirmeyi amaçlayan, tahripkâr (**of**).

sub.vert [sʌb'vəːt] *v/t.* devirmeye çalışmak (*hükümeti*); sarsmak, harap etm.; bozmak, ifsat etm.

sub.way ['sʌbwei] *n.* (*part. yaya*) tünel, yeraltı geçidi; *Am.* yeraltı metro, tünel.

suc.ceed [sək'siːd] *vb.* muvaffak olm.; başarmak (**in** -*i*); vâris olm. (**to** -*e*); -*in* yerine geçmek (*taht vs.*); başarıyla sonuçlanmak; izlemek, sonra gelmek -*den*; **he ~s in** -*de* başarılı oluyor.

suc.cess [sək'ses] *n.* başarı(lı sonuç), muvaffakiyet; başarılı kimse; **he was a great ~** çok başarılıydı; **suc'cess.ful** □ [‿ful] başarılı, muvaffakiyetli; **be ~** başarılı olm.; **suc.ces.sion** [‿'seʃən] *n.* ardıllık, silsile, sıra, seri; kalıtım; döl, zürriyet; **~ to the throne** tahta geçme hakkı, veliahat olma; **in ~** ardı ardına; **~ duty** veraset ve intikal vergisi; **suc'ces.sive** □ ardıl, müteakip, birbi-

rini izleyen; **suc'ces.sor** *n.* halef, ardıl, vâris; **~ to the throne** veliaht.

suc.cinct □ [sək'siŋkt] az ve özlü, kısa ve açık olarak.

suc.co.ry BOT ['sʌkəri] hindiba.

suc.co(u)r ['sʌkə] **1.** *n.* yardım, imdat; MIL kurtarmaya gelen kuvvetler; **2.** *v/t.* yardım etm. -*e*; MIL imdada yetişerek kuşat madan kurtarmak.

suc.cu.lence ['sʌkjuləns] *n.* körpelik, sulu olma, özlülük; **'suc.cu.lent** □ sulu, özlü; lezzetli; dolgun (*meyve*), etli, kalın (*bitki*).

suc.cumb [sə'kʌm] *v/i.* dayanamamak (**to** -*e*); yenik düşmek (**to** -*e*).

such [sʌtʃ] **1.** *adj.* böyle, şöyle, öyle, bu gibi; bu kadar, o kadar; **~ a man** böyle bir adam, öyle biri ki; *s.* **another, no ~ thing** böyle bir şey yoktur; **~ as** gibi, örneğin; **~ and ~** falan filân; **~ is life** hayat bu; **2.** *pron.* bu, şu, o gibi; **'such.like** *adj. & pron.* bu gibi, buna benzer, benzeri, böylesi.

suck [sʌk] **1.** *vb.* emmek, içine çekmek; meme emmek; **~ up to** *sl.* b-ne çanak yalayıcılığı, yaltaklık etm.; **~ s.o.'s brains** b-nin ağzını aramak, bilgi almaya çalışmak; **2.** *n.* emme, emiş, mas; **give ~** emzirmek; **'suck.er** *n.* emen b-i veya bş; MEC tulumba pistonu; *Am.* F saplı şeker; BOT kök filizi, fışkın; *Am.* budala, ahmak; **'suck.ing** *adj.* emici; **~ pig** henüz süt emen domuz yavrusu; **suck.le** ['‿l] *vb.* emzirmek, çocuğa meme vermek; **'suckling** *n.* memede çocuk, süt çocuğu.

suc.tion ['sʌkʃən] *n.* emme; *attr.* emici...; **~ cleaner, ~ sweeper** aspiratör.

sud.den □ ['sʌdn] ani, beklenilmeyen, birden; **on a ~, (all) of a ~** ansızın, birdenbire; **'sud.den.ness** *n.* birdenbire olma.

su.dor.if.ic [sjuːdə'rifik] *adj.* terletici (*ilâç*).

suds [sʌdz] *n. pl.* alkalik sıvı, sabun köpüğü; **'suds.y** *adj. Am.* köpüklü, sabunlu.

sue [sjuː] *v/t.* b-nin aleyhine dava açmak; **~ out** mahkemeden hüküm çıkartmak; *v/i.* istemek, talep etm. (**for** -*i*), dava açmak (**for**).

suède [sweid] *n.* (podü)süet.

su.et ['sjuit] *n.* içyağı, donyağı; **'su.et.y** *adj.* içyağlı.

suf.fer ['sʌfə] *v/i.* tutulmuş olm. (**from** -*e*), dert çekmek (**from** -*den*); *v/t.* katlanmak -*e*, dayanmak, sabretmek;

'suf.fer.ance *n.* müsamaha, göz yumma; **on ~** müsamaha yüzünden (*veya* dolayısıyle); **'suffer.er** *n.* dertli, ıstırap çeken kimse; hasta; kazazede; **suf.fer-ing** *n.* acı, ıstırap.

suf.fice [sə'fais] *vb.* kâfi gelmek, yet(iş)mek; **~ it to say** yalnız şu kadarını söyleyeyim ki.

suf.fi.cien.cy [sə'fiʃənsi] *n.* yeterlilik, kifayet; geçinecek kadar gelir; **a ~ of money** yeterli miktar para; **suf'fici.ent** □ kâfi, yeterli; **be~** kâfi gelmek, yetmek.

suf.fix GR ['sʌfiks] **1.** *v/t.* bir sözcüğün sonuna ek koymak; **2.** *n.* sonek, sontakı.

suf.fo.cate ['sʌfəkeit] *v/t. & v/i.* boğ(ul)mak; tıka(n)mak; sön(dür)-mek; **suf.fo'ca.tion** *n.* boğ(ul)ma; sön(dür)me; **suffo.ca.tive** □ ['-kətiv] boğucu.

suf.fra.gan ECCL ['sʌfrəgən] *n.* piskopos yardımcısı; **'suf.frage** *n.* oy kullanma (hakkı); onay, tasvip (oyu); **suf-fra.gette** [-ə-'dʒet] *n.* kadınların oy kullanma haklarını savunan kadın.

suf.fuse [sə'fju:z] *v/t.* dökmek, yayılıp örtmek, kaplamak (*renk, sıvı vs.*); **suf'fu.sion** [-ʒən] *n.* yay(ıl)ma; kızartı.

sug.ar ['ʃugə] **1.** *n.* şeker; *fig.* tatlı söz; **2.** *v/t.* şeker katmak *-e*; tatlı sözle yumuşatmak *-i*; **'~ba.sin** *n.* şekerlik, şeker kutusu; **'~beet** *n.* şeker pancarı; **'~bowl** *n.* Am. şekerlik, şeker kâsesi; **'~cane** *n.* şekerkamışı; **'~coat** *v/t.* şekerle kaplamak; tatlılaştırmak; **'~loaf** *n.* kelle şekeri; **'~plum** *n.* bonbon, şekerleme; **'~tongs** *n. pl.* (**a pair of**) şeker maşası; **sug.ar.y** *adj.* şekerli, şekere benzer, şeker gibi, bal gibi; yüze gülücü.

sug.gest [sə'dʒest] *v/t.* telkin etm.; teklif etm., önermek, sunmak; ileri sürmek, ortaya koymak; ima etm., sezdirmek; **sug'ges.tion** *n.* fikir, teklif; öneri, tavsiye; ima, işaret; telkin, ilham.

sug.ges.tive □ [sə'dʒestiv] manalı, telkin edici, imalı, fikir verici, manidar (**of**); açık saçık, müstehcen; **sug'gestive.ness** *n.* anlamlılık, manalılık; müstehcenlik.

su.i.cid.al □ [sjui'saidl] intiharla ilgili, intihar etme isteğiyle ilgili, intihara sürükleyen; **su.i.cide** ['-said] **1.** *n.* intihar; kendini öldüren kimse; **~ bomber** intihar bombacısı; **2.** *v/i.* Am. intihar

etm.

suit [sju:t] **1.** *n.* takım; erkek elbisesi; tayyör, kostüm; dilek, istek; evlenme teklifi; *iskambil:* takım; JUR dava; **follow ~** *iskambil:* takıma uymak; *fig.* aynı şeyi yapmak, taklit etm.; **2.** *v/t.* uygun gelmek, yaramak, iyi gelmek, uygun düşürmek, uydurmak; *b-ne* yakışmak, açmak, uymak (*elbise, renk vs.*); **~ oneself** kendi rahatını, gereksinimini, isteklerini sağlamak; **~ s.th. to** bşi uydurmak, intibak ettirmek; **be ~ed** uygun olm. (**for, to** *-e*); *v/i.* uymak, olmak; işine gelmek; **suita'bil.i.ty** *n.* uygunluk, elverişlilik; **'suit.able** □ uygun, elverişli (**for, to** *-e*); **'suita.ble-ness** = **suitability**; **'suit.case** *n.* bavul, valiz; **suite** [swi:t] *n.* maiyet; takım; MUS suit; *a.* **~ of rooms** daire, takım odalar (*otelde*); oda takımı (*bir kanepe, iki koltuk*); **suit.ing** COM ['sju:tiŋ] *n.* takım elbiselik kumaş; **'suit.or** *n.* âşık, bir kıza talip erkek; JUR davacı.

sulk [sʌlk] **1.** *v/i. a.* **be in the ~s** somurtmak, gücenmek, surat asmak; **2.** *n.* **sulks** *pl.*, **'sulk.i.ness** asık suratlılık, somurtkanlık; **'sulk.y 1.** □ somurtkan, asık suratlı, aksi, huysuz; **2.** *n. spor:* iki tekerlekli tek kişilik hafif atlı araba.

sul.len □ ['sʌlən] can sıkıcı, sinirlendirici, asık yüzlü, somurtkan; kapanık; **'sullen.ness** *n.* somurtkanlık.

sul.ly *mst fig.* ['sʌli] *v/t.* kirletmek, lekelemek.

sul.pha ['sʌlfə] *pl.* = **sulphonamides**. **sul.phate** CHEM ['sʌlfeit] *n.* asit sülfirik tuzu, sülfat; **sul.phide** CHEM ['-faid] *n.* sülfirik karışımı, sülfit.

sul.pho.na.mides MED [sʌl'fɔnə-maidz] *n. pl.* sülfonamid.

sul.phur CHEM ['sʌlfə] **1.** *n.* kükürt; **2.** *v/t.* kükürtlemek; **sul.phu.re.ous** [sʌl'fjuəriəs] *adj.* kükürtlü, kükürt gibi; **sul.phu.retted** hy.dro.gen ['-fjuretid'haidridʒən] *n.* sülfit hidrik; **sul-phu.ric** [-'fjuərik] *adj.* kükürtlü; **~ ac-id** sülfirik asit, zaç yağı; **'sul.phu.rize** *v/t.* MEC kükürtlemek, kükürt katmak, vulkanize etm.; **sul.phur.ous** ['-fərəs] *adj.* kükürtlü, kükürt gibi.

sul.tan ['sʌltən] *n.* sultan, padişah; **sul.tan.a** [sʌl'tɑːnə] *n.* sultan karısı, annesi *veya* kızı.

sul.tri.ness ['sʌltrinis] *n.* sıcak ve rutubetli oluş, boğucu oluş; **'sul.try** □ boğucu, bunaltıcı, sıkıntılı; *fig.* ateşli, hararetli, heyecanlı.

sum [sʌm] **1.** *n.* tutar, hesap; toplam, ye-kûn; miktar, meblağ; özet, hülâsa; *fig.* örnek; aritmetik problemi; **do ~s** bşin hesabını yapmak, saymak; **in ~** özetle, kısaca; **2.** *vb.* *mst ~* **up** özetlemek; *b-i* hakkında hüküm vermek; yekûn top-lamak.

su.mac(h) BOT ['su:mæk] *n.* sumak, so-mak.

sum.ma.rize ['sʌməraiz] *v/t.* özetle-mek; **sum.mar.y 1.** □ kısa, özet halin-de; JUR seri, basit ve kısa...; jürisiz; **2.** *n.* özet, hülâsa.

sum.mer¹ ['sʌmə] **1.** *n.* yaz (mevsimi); *~* **resort** sayfiye; **2.** *v/t.* & *v/i.* yazı geçir-mek; yazın beslemek; '~**-house** *n.* ka-meriye, çardak.

sum.mer² ARCH [~] *n.* tabanın ana kirişi, ta şıyıcı kiriş.

sum.mer.like ['sʌməlaik], '**sum.mer.ly** *adj.* yazlık, yaza ait, yaz gibi.

summer...: '~**-school** *n.* yaz okulu; '.**time** *n.* yaz mevsimi; '~'**time** *n.* yaz saati (*bir saat ileri*); '**sum.mer.y** *adj.* yaza ait, yaz gibi.

sum.mit ['sʌmit] *n.* tepe, zirve, doruk, en üst derece (*a. fig.*).

sum.mon ['sʌmən] *v/t.* çağır(t)mak, emirle davet etm.; JUR celp etm.; *fig.* *mst ~* **up** toplamak (*güç*); '**sum.mon.er** *n.* haberci, kurye, ulak; **sum.mons** ['~z] *n. pl.* JUR celpname, çağrı; JUR tes-lim ol çağrısı.

sump MOT [sʌmp] *n.* çirkef çukuru (*ma-dende*); MEC yağ haznesi.

sump.ter ['sʌmptə] *n. a.* '~**-horse**, '~**-mule** *obs.* yük beygiri.

sump.ter ['sʌmptjuəri] *adj.* sarfiyata ait.

sump.tu.ar.y ['sʌmptjuəri] *adj.* sarfi-yata ait, masrafla ilgili; masrafları sınırlayan; lüks...

sump.tu.ous □ ['sʌmptjuəs] kıymetli, mükellef, tantanalı, çok konforlu, muhteşem; '**sump.tu.ous.ness** *n.* gör-kem, ihtişam, tantana, lüks.

sun [sʌn] **1.** *n.* güneş; **2.** *v/t.* & *v/i.* güneş-len(dir)mek, güneşe sermek; güneş banyosu yapmak; '~**baked** *adj.* güneş-te kurutulup sertleştirilmiş; '~**bath** *n.* güneş banyosu; '~**bathe** *v/i.* güneşlen-mek, güneş banyosu yapmak; '~**beam** *n.* güneş ışını; '~**blind** *n.* güneşlik, gü-neş tentesi; '~**burn** *n.* güneşten yanma; güneş yanığı; '~**burnt** *adj.* güneşten es-merleşmiş.

sun.dae ['sʌndi] *n.* üstü ceviz meyve ve şurupla kaplanmış dondurma, peşmel-ba.

Sun.day ['sʌndi] *n.* pazar (günü); ~ **school** kilisede pazar günleri din ders-leri verilen okul.

sun.der *poet.* ['sʌndə] *vb.* birbirinden ayırmak, ayrılmak; kop(ar)mak.

sun-di.al ['sʌndaiəl] *n.* güneş saati.

sun.down ['sʌndaun] *n.* güneş batması, gurup.

sun.dry ['sʌndri] **1.** *adj.* çeşitli (şeyler); **2. sun.dries** *n. pl. part.* COM ['~driz] ufak tefek şeyler, muhtelif parça mal-lar.

sun.flow.er BOT ['sʌnflauə] *n.* ayçiçeği.

sung [sʌŋ] *pret.* & *p.p. of* **sing**.

sun...: '~**glass.es** *n. pl.* **(a. pair of)** gü-neş gözlüğü; '~**god** *n.* güneş tanrısı; '~**helmet** *n.* tropik güneş ışınından ko-ruyan şapka, kolonyal şapka.

sunk [sʌŋk] *pret.* & *p.p. of* **sink 1.**

sunk.en ['sʌŋkən] **1.** *rare p.p. of* **sink 1;** **2.** *adj.* batan, batmış; *fig.* çökmüş, zayıflamış (*yanak*); çukur (*göz*); MEC içine yerleştirilmiş, gömülmüş.

sun-lamp ['sʌnlæmp] *n.* MED ültraviyo-le lambası; *film:* jüpiter lambası.

sun.less ['sʌnlis] *adj.* güneş ışığı alma-yan, karanlık, kasvetli; '**sun.light** *n.* güneş ışığı; '**sun.lit** *adj.* güneşle aydın-lanmış.

sun.ni.ness ['sʌninis] *n.* güneşlilik, gü-neşli olma, parlak olma (*a. fig.*); '**sun-ny** □ güneşli, aydınlık (*a. fig.*); '**sun.ny** □ güneşli, aydınlık (*a. fig.*); neşeli.

sun...: '~**rise** *n.* gün doğuşu, tulu; '~**room** *n.* camekânlı taraça; '~**set** *n.* güneş batması; '~**shade** *n.* güneş şemsiyesi, parasol; '~**shine** *n.* güneş ışığı; ~ **roof** MOT açılır kapanır tavan; '~**shin.y** *adj.* güneşli, açık, bulutsuz; neşeli, keyifli; '~**spot** *n.* AST güneş le-kesi; '~**stroke** *n.* MED güneş çarpması; '~**-up** *n.* gündoğumu.

sup¹ [sʌp] *v/i.* akşam yemeğini yemek **(off** *veya* **on s.th.).**

sup² [~] *v/t.* & *v/i.* yudum yudum içmek, yudumlamak; kaşık kaşık içmek.

su.per¹ ['sju:pə] **1.** *n.* THEAT *sl.* figüran; **2.** *adj.* F birinci sınıf, süper, mükem-mel; büyük boyda.

su.per² [~] *prefix* üst, üstün(de); fazla.

su.per...: ~**.a'bound** *vb.* fazlasiyle bu-lunmak, *bş* çok bol miktarda bulun-mak **(in, with);** ~**.a'bun.dant** □ bol bol, pek çok, bitmez tükenmez; '~**.'add** *v/t.* daha da ilâve etm., eklemek; ~.an.nu.ate [-'rænjueit] v/t. emekliye ayırmak; ~d emekli, yaşlılık nedeniyle çalışamaz olmuş; eski kafalı; eskimiş, modası geçmiş; ~annu-'a.tion n. emeklilik; emekli maaşı; ~ fund emekli sandığı.

su.perb □ muhteşem, görkemli, harikulâde, enfes.

su.per...: '~.car.go n. NAUT geminin yük memuru veya armatör vekili; '~.charg.er n. MOT kompresör, üfleç; su.per.cil.i.ous □ [-'siliəs] kibirli, gururlu; su.per'cil.ious.ness n. kibir, gurur; su.per-'dreadnought n. ağır toplu deniz zırhlısı; super.er.o.ga.tion [-rero'geiʃən] n. vazifenin gereğinden fazla iş görme; su.per.erog.a.to.ry □ [-re'rogətəri] vazifesinden fazla olarak; su.per.fi.cial □ [-'fiʃəl] sathî, üstünkörü, yüzeysel; su.per.fi.ci.ali.ty [-fiʃi'æliti] n. sathîlik, üstünkörü oluş; su.per.fi.ci.es [-'fiʃiːz] n. satıh, yüz(ey); 'su.per'fine adj. fevkalâde güzel; çok zarif; pek ince; su.per.flu-i.ty [-'fluːiti] n. bolluk, fazlalık, çokluk (of); su'per.flu.ous □ [-fluəs] fazla, lüzumsuz, bol bol; su.per'heat v/t. MEC fazla ısıtmak; su.per.het ['-'het] n. radyo: gelen sinyali aynı sinyale karıştıran alıcı, cihaz.

su.per...: ~.'high.way n. Am. oto yolu, otoban; ~'hu.man □ insanüstü; ~.im-pose ['-rim'pəuz] v/t. bşin üzerine koymak veya birbiri üzerine koymak; ~.in.duce ['-rin'djuːs] v/t. katmak, eklemek (on, upon -e); ~.in.tend [-rin-'tend] v/t. kontrol etm., gözetmek; ~.in'tend.ence n. kontrol, gözetim; ~.in'tend.ent 1. n. müfettiş; müdür; 2. adj. yönetimsel, idarî; yöneten.

su.pe.ri.or [sjuː'piəriə] 1. □ üstün (to), daha yüksek, daha iyi; mükemmel, fevkalâde, olağanüstü; kibirli, üstünlük taslayan; ~ officer üst subay veya memur; 2. n. üst, amir; ECCL baş rahip; mst lady ~ başrahibe; su.pe.ri.or.i.ty [-'oriti] n. üstünlük.

su.per.la.tive [sjuː'pɔːlətiv] 1. □ en yüksek; mükemmel, eşsiz; fazla; GR enüstün (sıfat ve zarfların); 2. n. a. ~ de-gree GR enüstünlük (derecesi); su.per.man ['sjuː'pæmən] n. üst insan, fevkalbeşer; 'su.per.mar.ket n. büyük mağaza, süpermarket; su.per.nal [sjuː'pɔːnl] adj. göksel, semavî; ulu, yüce; ilâhi; su.per.natu.ral □ [sjuːpə-'nætʃrəl] doğaüstü, sürnatürel, hari-

kulâde; su.per.nu.mer.ar.y [-'njuː-mərəri] 1. adj. fazla, artakalan; 2. n. fazla b-i veya bş; THEAT figüran; 'su-per'pose vb. başka bşin üstüne koymak; birbiri üzerine koymak; su.per-po'si.tion n. üstüste koyma; GEOL katmanlaşma, tabakalaşma; 'su.per-'scribe vb. üstüne yazmak, başlığını koymak; adres yazmak, koymak; su.per.scrip.tion n. yazıt; adres; başlık; su.per.sede [-'siːd] v/t. yerine geçmek, yerine başka bşi (veya b-ni) geçirmek, b-nin ayağını kaydırarak yerine geçmek; fig. b-ni geçmek, geride bırakmak; su.per'ses.sion n. yerine geçme; su.per.son.ic PHYS [-'sɔnik] adj. sesten hızlı; su.per.sti.tion [-'sti-ʃən] n. bâtıl itikat, boş inan; hurafe; su.per.sti.tious □ [-'stiʃəs] boş şeylere inanan; su.per.struc.ture ['-strʌk-tʃə] n. üst yapı; temel üzerine yapılan bina; su.per.vene [-'viːn] v/i. b-ne iltihak etm., katılmak; eklenmek, ilâve olunmak (on, upon -e), ummadık anda dahil olm., katılmak; super.ven-tion [-'venʃən] n. iltihak, dahil olma, eklenme; su.per.vise ['-vaiz] v/t. nezaret etm. -e, denetlemek -i, gözetmek -i; idare etm. -i; su.per.vi.sion [-'vi-ʒən] n. nezaret, denetim, gözetim; idare, kontrol; su.per.vi.sor ['-vaizə] n. murakıp, denetçi, müfettiş; UNIV danışman.

su.pine 1. GR ['sjuːpain] n. Latince'de -i veya -den halindeki isim-fiil; 2. □ [-'pain] sırtüstü yatan, yüz yukarı duran, yatay (duran); kaygısız, üşengeç, miskin, lâkayt; su'pine.ness [-'lâ-kaytlık, miskinlik.

sup.per ['sʌpə] n. akşam yemeği; the (Lord's) ♀ ECCL Kudas.

sup.plant [sə'plɑːnt] v/t. b-nin ayağını kaydırıp yerine geçmek; fig. gölgede bırakmak, üstün gelmek.

sup.ple ['sʌpl] 1. □ kolayca eğilir, yumuşak, elâstiki; uysal, muti; 2. vb. yumuşatmak, kolay eğilir hale getirmek.

sup.ple.ment 1. ['sʌplimənt] n. ek, zeyil, ilâve (gazete vs.); 2. v/t. [-ment] ilâve etm., eklemek, tamamlamak (by, with ile) sup.ple'men.tal □, sup-ple'men.ta.ry adj. eklenen, ilâve...; bütünleyici, tamamlayıcı; ~ order ek sipariş.

sup.ple.ness ['sʌplnis] n. yumuşaklık, esneklik; fig. uysallık.

sup.pli.ant ['sʌpliənt] **1.** ☐ yalvarıp yakaran, rica eden; **2.** *n.* dilekçe sahibi; ricacı kimse.

sup.pli.cate ['sʌplikeit] *vb. b-ne* yalvarmak, rica etm.; yakarmak; **sup.pli'cation** *n.* yalvarış, niyaz; **sup.pli.cato.ry** ['..kətəri] *adj.* yalvarış kabilinden; niyaz eden.

sup.pli.er [sə'plaiə] *n.* gereksinimleri karşılayan kimse *veya* firma (*a.* COM).

sup.ply [sə'plai] **1.** *v/t.* bşi *b-ne* sağlamak, temin etm., ihtiyacı karşılamak (*with ile*); çare bulmak; tatmin etm., görevini yerine getirmek; *b-nin* yerini tutmak, telâfi etm.; teçhiz etm.; ikmal etm.; **2.** *n.* gereç, malzeme; tedarik, temin; stok, depo mevcudu; COM arz, sunu; mümessil, acenta; *mst* **supplies** *pl.* COM erzak, gereçler, levazım; PARL bütçe, tahsisat, ödenek; MIL ikmal; *in short ~* yetersiz, kıt, az; *on ~ b-ne* vekâleten, *b-nin* yerine; *Committee of ~* PARL bütçe komisyonu.

sup.port [sə'pɔːt] **1.** *n.* dayanak, destek (*a. fig.*); MEC mesnet, dayak, istinatgâh; destekleme, yardım, geçim; **2.** *v/t.* desteklemek (*a. fig.*); beslemek *-i*, bakmak, yardım etm. *-e* (*aile vs.*); ısrar etm., durmak (*münakaşa*); arka olm. *-e*, savunmak, müdafaa etm.; ileri sürmek, iddia etm. (*düşünce*); tahammül etm., dayanmak, katlanmak *-e*; *~ing actor* yardımcı oyuncu; *~ing programme* film: esas filmden başka gösterilen (küçük) film(ler); **sup'port.able** ☐ katlanılabilir, çekilir, tahammül edilebilir; dayanıklı; **sup'port.er** *n.* taraftar; yardımcı, muavin; jartiyer, askı, korse.

sup.pose [sə'pəuz] *v/t.* farzetmek, zannetmek; *he is ~d to do* yapması gerekir; *~ veya supposing* (*that*)... faraza, farzedelim ki...; *~ we go* gitsek nasıl olur?; *he is rich, I ~* sanırım zengindir.

sup.posed ☐ [sə'pəuzd] sözde, sözüm ona, farzedilen, denen; **sup'pos.ed.ly** [..idli] *adv.* güya, muhtemel.

sup.pos.ing [sə'pəuziŋ] *conj.* şayet, faraza.

sup.po.si.tion [sʌpə'ziʃən] *n.* farz, zan, tahmin; varsayım, ipotez, faraziye; **suppos.i.ti.tious** ☐ [səpɔzi'tiʃəs] değiştirilmiş, sahte; varsayılı, ipotetik, **sup'pos.ito.ry** [..təri] fitil, supozituvar.

sup.press [sə'pres] *v/t.* bastırmak, sindirmek; zaptetmek; basılıp yayınlanmasını önlemek; **sup.pres.sion** [sə'preʃən] *n.* bastırma, sindirme; baskı, tutma, önleme; örtbas etme; **sup'pres.sive** ☐ [..siv] bastıran, sindiren; tutan, zapteden; **sup'pres.sor** *n.* ELECT paraziti önleyici cihaz.

sup.pu.rate ['sʌpjuəreit] *v/i.* cerahat toplamak, irinlenmek; işlemek (*yara*); **suppu'ra.tion** *n.* cerahat, irin.

su.pra-na.tion.al ['sjuːprə'næʃənl] *adj.* devletlerüstü.

su.prem.a.cy [sju'preməsi] *n.* üstünlük, yücelik, ululuk; egemenlik; **supreme** ☐ [sjuː'priːm] en yüksek; en yüksek derecede; en yüksek mertebede; kritik; ♀ **Court** Anayasa Mahkemesi; Yargıtay.

sur.charge [səː'tʃɑːdʒ] **1.** *v/t.* fazla yüklemek, fazla doldurmak; sürşarj basmak *-e*; posta pulunun üzerine yeni fiyat bastırmak; **2.** *n.* sürşarj; fazla ağır yük; fazla navlun alma, sürtaks.

surd MATH [səːd] *adj.* asam, tamsayı ile ifade edilemeyen, irrasyonal (*sayı*).

sure ☐ [ʃuə] *com.* güvenilir, emin (*of -den*); kesin; sağlam; şüphesiz, muhakkak; *to be ~!,* F *~ enough!,* Am. *~!* elbette, muhakkak; *I'm ~ I don't know* vallahi bilmiyorum; *he is ~ to return* muhakkak geri gelir; *make ~* kanaat getirmek (*of*); temin, tasdik etm. (*of*); *'~-foot.ed* *adj.* ayağını sıkı basan, düşmez, kaymaz; **'sure.ly** *adv.* elbette, şüphesiz; emniyetle olarak, tehlikesizce; **'sure.ness** *n.* kesinlik; emin olma, güven; **'sure.ty** *n.* emniyet, güvenlik; güvence; kefil, rehine.

surf [səːf] *n.* çatlayan dalgalar; dalgaların kıyıya *veya* kayalara vurup çatlaması; *~ the net* internette gezinmek.

sur.face ['səːfis] **1.** *n.* yüz, düzey, satıh, dış görünüş yüzey; görünüş; AVIA kanatlar; *control ~* AVIA kontrol dümeni; *below the ~* MIN yeraltında; **2.** *v/i.* suyun üstüne çıkmak (*denizaltı*); kaplamak (*yol*); düz yapmak; '*~.man* *n.* RAIL hat amelesi.

surf...: '*~-board* *n. surfing:* kayak; '*~-boat* *n.* dalgaları aşabilen hafif kayık.

sur.feit ['səːfit] **1.** *n.* aşırı doyma; yemekte aşırılık, şişkinlik, tiksinti; **2.** *v/t. & v/i.* tıka basa dol(dur)mak; fazlasiyle doy(ur)mak (*on, with*); *fig.* bıktırmak, çatlayacak derecede ye(dir)mek.

surf-rid.ing ['səːfraidiŋ] *n. spor:* dalgalar üzerinde tahta ile kayarak yapılan bir tür su kayağı.

surge [səːdʒ] **1.** *n.* büyük dalga; dalgaların çatlaması; dalga gibi sürüklenme; **2.** *vb.* dalgalanmak; kabarmak; sahile *veya* kayalara vurup parçalanmak.

sur.geon [səːdʒən] *n.* cerrah, operatör; MIL askerî doktor; NAUT gemi doktoru; **surger.y** ['səːdʒəri] *n.* cerrahlık (ilmi), operatörlük; muayene(hane); ameliyat(hane); ~ *hours pl.* hasta kabul saati.

sur.gi.cal ☐ [səːdʒikəl] cerrahî, cerrahlığa ait, ameliyat...

sur.li.ness ['səːlinis] *n.* aksilik, huysuzluk, somurtkanlık; **'sur.ly** ☐ gülmez, ters, aksi, huysuz; sert (*arazi*).

sur.mise 1. ['səːmaiz] *n.* sanı, zan; kuşku, vesvese; **2.** [səː'maiz] *vb.* sanmak, zannetmek, kuşkulanmak; vesvese beslemek, şüphe etm.

sur.mount [səː'maunt] *v/t.* üstün gelmek *-e*, üstesinden gelmek *-in* (*güçlük vs.*); *b-ni* yenmek, galip gelmek; ~ed **by** *veya* **with** *bşin* üstünde olan, üstü ...ile örtülen; **sur'mount.a.ble** *adj.* üstesinden gelinebilir.

sur.name ['səːneim] **1.** *n.* soyadı, aile adı; lakap; **2.** *v/t.* soyadı vermek *-e*; ~d soyadlı.

sur.pass *fig.* [səː'paːs] *v/t.* geçmek, aşmak; üstün olm. *-e*; **sur'pass.ing** ☐ eşsiz, fevkalâde, harikulâde.

sur.plice ECCL ['səːpləs] katolik papazların kilisede giydikleri beyaz cüppe.

sur.plus ['səːpləs] **1.** *n.* fazla kısım, artan miktar; **2.** *adj.* artık, fazla(lık); ~ **population** nüfus fazlalığı; **'sur.plus-age** = **surplus 1**; gerektiğinden fazla olan şey.

sur.prise [sə'praiz] **1.** *n.* sürpriz, hayret, şaşkınlık; baskın; beklenmedik olay; MIL baskınla ele geçirme; **take by** ~ gafil avlamak; *attr.* sürpriz..., beklenmedik...; **2.** *v/t.* hayrete düşürmek, şaşırtmak; MIL baskın yapmak; **sur'pris.ing** ☐ hayret verici, şaşırtıcı.

sur.re.al.ism [sə'riəlizəm] *n. sanat:* sürrealizm, gerçeküstücülük; **sur're.al.ist** *n.* sürrealist, gerçeküstücü kimse.

sur.ren.der [sə'rendə] **1.** *n.* teslim(iyet), feragat; bırakma, terk; **2.** *v/t.* teslim etm.; terk etm. (*mülkiyet*); feragat etm., vermek; *v/i. a.* ~ **o.s.** teslim olm. (**to** *-e*); bir duygu ve fikrin esiri olm., kapılmak *-e*.

sur.rep.ti.tious ☐ [sʌrəp'tiʃəs] gizli, saklı, el altından.

sur.ro.gate ['sʌrogit] *n.* vekil, mümessil (*part. papaz*), yerine geçen *b-i veya bş*.

sur.round [sə'raund] *v/t.* etrafını sarmak, çevirmek; MIL kuşatmak, çember içine almak; **sur'round.ing** *adj.* civarında bulunan; **sur'round.ings** *n. pl.* çevre, muhit, etraf.

sur.tax ['səːtæks] *n.* munzam vergi, ek vergi, katma vergi.

sur.veil.lance [səː'veiləns] *n.* gözetim, gözaltı(nda tutma).

sur.vey 1. [səː'vei] *v/t.* teftiş, tetkik etm.; yoklamak, gözden geçirmek; mesaha etm., haritasını çıkarmak; dikkatle *bşin* tümüne göz gezdirmek; **2.** ['‿] *n.* teftiş, tetkik; gözden geçirme; *bşe* genel bakış; mesaha, yüzölçümü, yer ölçmesi; rapor, ekspertiz; **sur'vey.or** *n.* sürveyan; mesaha memuru, arazi mühendisi; müfettiş, bilirkişi.

sur.viv.al [sə'vaivəl] *n.* kalım, beka, hayatta kalma, artakalma; **sur'vive** *v/t.* fazla yaşamak *-den*, daha uzun ömürlü olm. *-den*; *v/i.* hayatta kalmak; **sur'vi.vor** *n.* hayatta kalan, kurtulan kimse.

sus.cep.ti.bil.i.ty [səseptə'biliti] *n.* alınganlık, hassasiyet (**to** *-e*); *oft.* **susceptibilities** *pl.* hassas nokta(lar); **sus'cep.ti.ble** ☐, **sus'cep.tive** hassas, alıngan (**to** *-e*); duygulu; **be** ~ **of** elverişli *-e*, kaldırır.

sus.pect 1. [səs'pekt] *v/t. b-den*, *bşden* şüphelenmek, kuşkulanmak, *bşe* ihtimal vermek, endişe etm., vesveselenmek; **2.** ['sʌspket] *n.* şüpheli, kuşkulu, zanlı *b-i veya bş*, sanık; **3.** = **sus'pect.ed** *adj.* şüpheli, kuşkulu, zanlı, güvenilmez.

sus.pend [səs'pend] *vb.* asmak; havada asılmış gibi durmak; ertelemek, tehir etm., askıya almak; tatil etm., geçici olarak durdurmak (*iş*); ertelemek, tecil etm. (*hüküm*); bir memura geçici işten el çektirmek; boykot etm. (*sporcu*); ~ed asılı, muallak; ~ed **animation** zâhirî ölüm, geçici olarak canlılığını kaybetme; **sus'pend.er** *n.* çorap askısı, jartiyer; ~s *pl. Am.* pantolon askısı.

sus.pense [səs'pens] *n.* muallak kalma, askıda kalış, şüpheli olma, kararsızlık, tereddüt; merak, heyecan; ~ **account** COM geçici, muvakkat hesap; **sus.pen.sion** [‿'penʃən] *n.* as(ıl)ma;

erteleme, sonraya bırakma, tehir, talik; geçici tatil, durdurma; geçici olarak memuriyetten ihraç; boykot (*spor vs.*); ödemeleri geçici durdurma; **sus.pen.sion bridge** *n.* asma köprü; **sus'pen.sive** □ erteleme kabilinden, geçici...; **sus.pen.so.ry** [-'pensəri] *adj.* asmaya yarayan; muallakta bırakan; **~ bandage** MED kasık bağı, suspensuvar; asıcı bağ.

sus.pi.cion [səs'piʃən] *n.* şüphe(lenme), kuşku(lanma), vehim; *fig.* iz, belirti; **sus'pi.cious** □ şüphelenen, şüpheci; şüphe verici, kuşkulu, vesveseli; şüpheli, güvenilmez; **sus'pi.cious.ness** *n.* şüpheli, kuşkulu oluş; vesveseli duygu *veya* karakter.

sus.tain [səs'tein] *v/t.* desteklemek, payanda vurmak; beslemek; dayanmak, katlanmak *-e*; MUS uzatmak; JUR teslim ve itiraf etm.; THEAT *b-nin* oyun gücünü takdir etm., hakkını teslim etm.; kuvvet vermek *-e*; **sus'tain.a.ble** *adj.* dayanıklı; onaylanabilir, kanıtlanabilir; **sus'tained** *adj.* sürekli, devamlı, aralıksız.

sus.te.nance ['sʌstinəns] *n.* besleme; gıda, yiyecek, içecek.

sut.ler MIL ['sʌtlə] *n.* kantinci, orduya gıda maddesi satan seyyar satıcı.

su.ture ['suːtʃə] **1.** *n.* BOT, ANAT, MED dikiş (yeri), sutur, derz; **2.** *vb.* dikişle birleştirmek, dikmek.

SUV [sʌv] *n.* (= *sports utility vehicle*) SUV.

su.ze.rain ['suːzərein] *n.* *k-ne* uyruk olunan *b-i veya* devlet; hükümdar.

svelte [svelt] *adj.* narin, ince yapılı, fidan gibi.

swab [swɔb] **1.** *n.* temizleme bezi, tahta bezi; NAUT denizci, tayfa; MED ilaçlı bez, tampon; **2.** *v/t. a.* **~ down** silmek, temizlemek.

Swa.bi.an ['sweibjən] **1.** *n.* Suebyalı (kadın); **2.** *adj.* Suebyalı, Suebya ile ilgili.

swad.dle ['swɔdl] *v/t.* kundaklamak, kundağa sarmak (*bebek*); **'swaddling-clothes** *n. pl.* kundak (takımı); *fig.* bebeklik çağı.

swag.ger ['swægə] **1.** *v/i.* caka satmak, azametle yürümek, horozlanmak; *bşle* övünmek, atıp tutmak; **2.** *adj.* F şık, modaya uygun; **3.** *n.* caka, kurum; kabadayılık, farfaralık; '**~cane** *n.* MIL süs için taşınan kamçı vs.

swain *poet. veya obs.* [swein] *n.* genç köylü, çoban; *co.* âşık.

swale *Am.* [sweil] *n.* çukur (yer); vadi, ova.

swal.low¹ ORN [swɔləu] *n.* kırlangıç.

swal.low² [-] **1.** *n.* yutma, yutuş; yudum; **2.** *v/t.* yutmak; içine çekmek, emmek; (*fig. mst* **~ up**) yutmak; tükürdüğünü yalamak, sözünü geri almak; sineye çekmek, tahammül etm.; *v/i.* yutkunmak.

swam [swæm] *pret. of* **swim 1.**

swamp [swɔmp] **1.** *n.* batak(lık); **2.** *vb.* batırmak (*a. fig.*); NAUT içine su doldurup batırmak; *fig.* başını kaşıyacak vakti olmamak; '**swamp.y** *adj.* bataklık.

swan [swɔn] *n.* ZOO kuğu.

swank *sl.* [swæŋk] **1.** *n.* caka, fiyaka, gösteriş; **2.** *v/i.* caka satmak, gösteriş yapmak; '**swank.y** *adj.* çalımlı, gösterişli, övünen.

swan-neck ['swɔnnek] *n.* kuğu boynu; '**swan.ner.y** *n.* kuğuların beslenip muhafaza edildiği yer; '**swan-song** *n.* efsaneye göre kuğunun ölmeden önceki son ötüşü; bir sanatçının son eseri.

swap F [swɔp] *vb.* değiş tokuş etm., trampa etm.

sward [swɔːd] *n.* çim, çimen(lik).

sware *obs.* [swɛə] *pret. of* **swear.**

swarm¹ [swɔːm] **1.** *n.* arı kümesi, oğul; *fig.* sürü, küme, kalabalık, kütle; **2.** *v/i.* toplanmak; (*oğul arıları*) kovanı terketmek; kaynaşmak (**with** ile).

swarm² [-] *v/t.:* **~ up** tırmanmak (*ip, ağaç vs.'ye*).

swarth.i.ness ['swɔːθinis] *n.* esmerlik, karalık; '**swarth.y** □ siyahımsı, siyahımtırak; esmer, yağız.

swash [swɔʃ] **1.** *v/i.* çalkalanmak; övünmek, caka satmak; *v/t.* su sıçratmak; çalkalamak; **2.** *n.* çalkantı (sesi); çalkalama (*su*); **~buck.ler** *n.* atılgan, cesur, dövüşken kimse (*part. film ve hikâyelerde*).

swas.ti.ka ['swɔstikə] *n.* gamalı haç, Nazilerin sembolü olan haç.

swat [swɔt] **1.** *v/t.* ezmek, şaklatmak (*sinek vs.*); **2.** *n.* vuruş, darbe, ezme.

swath AGR [swɔːθ] *n.* orakla biçilip yere serilmiş ekin.

swathe [sweið] **1.** *n.* kundak bağı; sargı; *s.* **swath**; **2.** *vb.* sarmak, çevrelemek, bürümek.

sway [swei] **1.** *n.* sallanma, dalgalanma; nüfuz, tesir, etki; makam, güç, otorite; **2.** *v/t.* sallamak; nüfuz ve etki altında bulundurmak; hükmetmek; *v/i.* sallanmak, sarsılmak.

swear [swɛə] **1.** (*irr.*) *v/i.* yemin etm., andiçmek (**by** F *b-ne veya bşe*), yeminle onaylamak (**to s.th.**); küfretmek, lânet etm. (**at** *-e*); *v/t.* yeminle işe başlatmak; **~ s.o.** *b-ne* yemin ettirmek; **2.** *n. a.* **~-word** F küfür, sövüp sayma; lânet.

sweat [swet] **1.** *n.* ter(leme); terletici iş, angarya; **old ~** *sl.* eski kurt; **by the ~ of one's brow** alnının teriyle; **2.** (*irr.*) *v/t. & v/i.* terle(t)mek; çok sıkı çalış(tır)-mak, ağır iş gör(dür)mek; düşük ücretle çalıştırmak, sömürmek; sızıntı yapmak; **MEC** kaynak yapmak (*kablo vs.*), '**sweat.ed** *adj.* az ücretle uzun süre çalışmaya zorlanan; '**sweat.er** *n.* kazak, süveter, pulover; işçilerini sömüren işveren; '**sweat-shop** *n.* az ücretle işçi çalıştıran işyeri; **sweat suit** antrenman elbisesi, eşofman; '**sweat.y** *adj.* terli, terlemiş, ter gibi; terletici, güç, ağır (*iş*).

Swede [swi:d] *n.* İsveçli; **Swed.ish** ['swi:diʃ] **1.** *adj.* İsveçli, İsveç ile ilgili; **2.** *n.* İsveç dili, İsveççe.

sweep [swi:p] **1.** (*irr.*) *v/t.* süpürmek, temizlemek; *fig.* (*mst* **with** *adv.*) silip süpürmek, ezici çoğunlukla kazanmak; taramak (*a.* MIL); sürüklemek; temizlemek, yok etm. (*suç vs.*); *v/i.* geçmek, çok hızla geçip gitmek, azametle geçip gitmek; kavis yaparak dönmek; şiddetle esmek (*rüzgâr*); sürmek, uzanmak; **be swept off one's feet** *fig.* üstüne fazla düşmek *-in*; heyecana kapılmak; **2.** *n.* süpürme; hızlı hareket, savlet; MUS farfar, üflemeli bakır çalgılardan kurulu mızıka takımı; bütün ödülleri kazanma; muhteşem zafer; kavis, dönemeç; alan, saha; etki alanı, hareket serbestliği; ocakçı, baca temizleyicisi; uzun kürek; tulumba kolu; **make a clean ~ of** bütün bütün temizlemek, ortadan kaldırmak; (*masayı*) silip süpürmek; *b-ni* kapı dışarı etm.; '**sweep.er** *n.* sokak süpürücüsü, çöpçü; '**sweep.ing** □ şümullü, geniş bir alanı kapsayan; umumî, genel (*iddia vs.*); '**sweep.ings** *n. pl.* süprüntü; **sweep.stakes** ['--steiks] *n. pl.* bahsimüşterek (*part. at yarışı*).

sweet [swi:t] **1.** □ tatlı, şekerli; sevimli, şirin, hoş; kolay, rahat; güzel kokulu; MEC sessiz, gürültüsüz; verimli (*toprak*); **have a ~ tooth** tatlı şeyleri sevmek; **2.** *n.* tatlı (şey); sevgili, gözde;

tatlılık; **~s** *pl.* bonbon, şekerleme; '**~.bread** *n.* (*part. dana*) uykuluk; '**~.bri.ar** *n.* BOT yaban gülü; '**sweet.en** *v/t. & v/i.* tatlılaş(tır)mak; *fig.* cazip hale getirmek *veya* gelmek; '**sweet.heart** *n.* sevgili, gözde; '**sweet.ish** *adj.* tatlımsı; aşırı tatlı; '**sweet.meat** *n.* şekerleme, bonbon; reçel; '**sweet-ness** *n.* tatlılık; sevimlilik, hoşluk; **sweet pea** BOT kokulu bezelye çiçeği; '**sweet.shop** *n.* şekerci dükkânı; pastane; '**sweet-'wil.liam** *n.* BOT hüsnüyusuf çiçeği.

swell [swel] **1.** (*irr.*) *v/i.* şişmek, kabarmak (**into** *-e*) (*a. fig. & yelken vs.*); *v/t.* şişirmek, kabartmak; büyütmek, yükseltmek; **2.** *adj.* F şık, züppe; *Am. sl.* fevkalâde, güzel, alâ, birinci sınıf; **3.** *n. part.* MUS kreşendo ve ardından diminuendo; şiddetlenme; şişme, kabarış; NAUT ölü dalga; yükseklik; tatlı meyil, tümseklik; F züppe, şık kimse; '**swell.ing 1.** *n.* kabarma, şişlik; **2.** □ şiş, kabarık; fazla süslü (*üslup vs.*).

swel.ter ['swelta] *v/i.* sıcaktan bunalmak, çok terlemek.

swept [swept] *pret. & p.p. of* **sweep 1.**

swerve [swəːv] *v/i.* yoldan sapmak; aniden direksiyonu kırmak, çevirmek; *v/t.* yolundan çevirmek, saptırmak; *spor:* kesmek, çelmek (*top*).

swift [swift] **1.** □ çabuk, hızlı, süratli, çevik, atik; **2.** *n.* ORN bir tür kırlangıç; '**swift.ness** *n.* sürat, hız, çeviklik, çabukluk.

swig F [swig] **1.** *n.* yudum; içme; **2.** *vb.* yutmak, bir dikişte içmek; *sl.* kafayı çekmek, çakıştırmak.

swill [swil] **1.** *n.* bulaşık suyu (*a. fig.*); sulu domuz yemi; *sl.* bir dikişte içilen içki; **2.** *vb.* sudan geçirmek, bol su ile yıkamak, çalkalamak *-i*; fazla içmek, kafayı çekmek.

swim [swim] **1.** (*irr.*) *v/i.* yüzmek, batmamak, su yüzünde durmak; dönmek; **my head ~s** başım dönüyor; *v/t.* yüzerek boydan boya geçmek *-i*; sürükleyip götürmek, yüzdürmek; **2.** *n.* yüzme (hareketi); **be in the ~** hayatta olup bitenden haberdar olm.; '**swim.mer** *n.* yüzücü.

swim.ming ['swimiŋ] **1.** *n.* yüzme; yüzücülük; baş dönmesi; **2.** *adj.* yüzmeye ait *veya* uygun (*elbise...*); dönen (*baş*); '**~-bath** *n.* yüzme yeri, üstü kapalı yüzme havuzu; '**~-cos.tume** *n.* mayo; '**swimming.ly** *adv.* kolaylıkla, rahatlıkla; **'swim.ming-pool** *n.* yüzme havuzu; **'swim-suit** *n.* mayo.

swin.dle ['swindl] **1.** *v/t.* dolandırmak, aldatmak (*out of*); *v/i.* dolandırıcılık etm., yalan söylemek, uydurmak; **'swin.dler** *n.* dolandırıcı.

swine *only* RHET, ZOO *veya fig. contp.* [swain] *n., pl.* ~ domuz; **'swine.herd** *n.* domuz çobanı.

swing [swiŋ] **1.** (*irr.*) *v/i.* sallanmak, salınmak; sendelemek; F darağacına çekilmiş olm.; sallana sallana yürümek; dönmek, deveran etm., devretmek (*eksen üzerinde*); ~ *into motion* harekete geçmek, işlemeğe başlamak; *v/t.* sallamak; asmak, sallandırmak; idare etm., işletmek; **2.** *n.* salla(n)ma; salıncak; rakkasın bir sallanma mesafesi; hareket sahası (*a. fig.*); MUS hızlı ritim; 1930'larda kuvvetli ritimli bir tür caz müziği; *boks*; sving; *in full* ~ en civcivli anında, tam faaliyette; *go with a* ~ herşey yolunda gitmek; *attr.* salla(n)ma..., sallanan...; ~ **bridge** açılır kapanır köprü; ~ **door** iki tarafa açılır kapanır kapı.

swinge.ing □ F ['swindʒiŋ] çok, pek, gayet, muazzam.

swing.ing □ ['swiŋiŋ] neşeli, canlı; ileri görüşlü, modern (*part. seks konusunda*).

swin.gle MEC ['swiŋgl] **1.** *v/t.* tokmakla döverek temizlemek (*keten*); **2.** *n.* keten bıçağı; ı **'~.tree** *n.* araba falakası.

swin.ish □ ['swainiʃ] domuz gibi, kaba.

swipe [swaip] **1.** *vb.* koluyla hızla vurmak, kuvvetli bir darbe indirmek; *sl.* aşırmak, çalmak; **2.** *n.* kuvvetli darbe; ~*s pl.* hafif bira.

swirl [swəːl] **1.** *vb.* şiddetle dön(dür)-mek, girdap gibi dön(dür)mek; **2.** *n.* girdap.

swish [swiʃ] **1.** *vb.* vız diye geçip gitmek; havada hareket ederken ıslık gibi ses çıkarmak, vızlamak, tıslamak (*tırpan*); hışırdamak; kırbaçlamak; **2.** *n.* hışırtı vs.; **3.** *adj.* F cazip, çekici.

Swiss [swis] **1.** *adj.* İsviçreli, İsviçre ile ilgili; **2.** *n.* İsviçreli; *the* ~ *pl.* İsviçre halkı.

switch [switʃ] **1.** *n.* ince ağaç dalı, değnek, çubuk; RAIL makas; ELECT şalter, düğme, anahtar; takma saç örgüsü; **2.** *vb.* değnekle vurmak, dövmek; sallamak, savurmak; RAIL makastan geçirmek; ELECT elektrik düğmesini çevir-

mek; (*rüzgâr*) yön değiştirmek; *fig.* değiş tokuş etm.; ~ *on* (*off*) ELECT elektrik düğmesini açmak (kapatmak); **'~.back** *n.* iniş çıkışlı tren yolu (*part. lunaparkta*); **'~.board** *n.* ELECT telefon santralı; anahtar tablosu, tevzi tablosu; ~ **box** ELECT anahtar kutusu, tablo.

swiv.el MEC ['swivl] *n.* fırdöndülü zincir halkası, fırdöndü; *attr.* döner...; ~ **chair** döner iskemle.

swol.len ['swəulən] *p.p. of* **swell** 1.

swoon [swuːn] **1.** *n.* bayılma, baygınlık; **2.** *v/i.* bayılmak.

swoop [swuːp] **1.** *v/i.* = *down* on *veya* *upon* üzerine atılmak, çullanmak; **2.** *n.* üstüne çullanma, ani saldırış.

swop F [swɔp] *vb.* değiş tokuş etm., trampa etm.

sword F [sɔːd] *n.* kılıç, pala; **'~.cane** *n.* kılıçlı baston; **'~.play** *n.* eskrim kılıç oyunu; *fig.* söz düellosu.

swords.man ['sɔːdzmən] *n.* eskrimci, kılıcı ustalıkla kullanan kimse; **'swords.manship** *n.* eskrimcilik, kılıç kullanmada ustalık.

swore [swɔː] *pret. of* **swear** 1.

sworn [swɔːn] **1.** *p.p. of* **swear** 1.; **2.** *adj.* JUR yeminli; ~ *expert* JUR yeminli bilirkişi.

swot *okul sl.* [swɔt] **1.** *n.* inekleme; inekleyen öğrenci; **2.** *v/i.* ineklemek.

swum [swʌm] *p.p. of* **swim** 1.

swung [swʌŋ] *pret. & p.p. of* **swing** 1.

syb.a.rite ['sibərait] *n.* lüks ve rahatlık içinde yaşayan kimse, muhallebi çocuğu.

syc.a.more BOT ['sikəmɔː] *n.* firavuninciri; *Am.* çınar ağacı.

syc.o.phant ['sikəfənt] *n.* dalkavuk, yaltakçı, parazit, asalak kimse; **syc.o-phantic** [.'fæntik] *adj.* (~*ally*) dalkavukluk kabilinden.

syl.lab.ic [si'læbik] *adj.* (~*ally*) hece itibariyle, hecelere ait, hecelerden ibaret, hece...; **syl.la.ble** ['siləbl] *n.* hece.

syl.la.bus ['siləbəs] *n.* müfredat proğramı, plan; hulasa, özet; liste, cetvel.

syl.lo.gism PHLS ['silədʒizəm] *n.* tasım, kıyas.

sylph [silf] *n.* havada yaşadığı farzedilen peri; ince ve zarif kadın.

syl.van ['silvən] *adj.* ormanlık; ormana ait, orman...

sym.bi.o.sis BIOL [simbi'əusis] *n.* birbirinden farklı canlıların ortak yaşayışı, ortak yaşama, sembiyoz.

sym.bol ['simbəl] *n.* sembol, simge, işaret, belirti, nişan, timsel, amblem; **symbol.ic, sym.bol.i.cal** □ [_'bɔl-ik(l)] sembolik, simgesel; **sym.bol.ism** ['_bɔlizəm] *n*. simgecilik, sembolizm; 'sym.bol.ize *vb*. temsil etm., sembolize etm.; sembolü olm.

sym.met.ri.cal □ [si'metrikəl] simetrik, bakışık; uygun, mütenasip; **symme.try** ['simitri] *n*. simetri, bakışım.

sym.pa.thet.ic [simpə'θetik] *adj*. (~al-ly) sempatik, sevimli, karşısındakinin duygularına katılan, sevgi ve acıma gösteren; uygun, ahenkli; ANAT sempatik; ~ **strike** dayanışma grevi; 'sym-pa.thize *v/i*. sempatizan olm., yakınlık duymak (**with** -*e*); 'sym.pa.thiz.er *n*. sempatizan, yandaş, taraftar; **sym.pa-thy** ['_θi] *n*. sempati; dert ortaklığı, aynı duyguları paylaşma, duygudaşlık, şefkat.

sym.phon.ic [sim'fɔnik] *adj*. senfonik; **sym.pho.ny** MUS ['_fəni] *n*. senfoni.

sym.po.sium [sim'pəuzjəm] *n*. sempozyum, belirli bir konunun tartışıldığı bilimsel toplantı; aynı konuda yazılmış bilimsel yazılar serisi.

symp.tom ['simptəm] *n*. araz, belirti, alâmet; **symp.to.mat.ic** [_'mætik] *adj*. (~ally) arazî; *bşe* delâlet eden, belirti niteliğinde, araz olan (**of**).

syn.a.gogue ['sinəgɔg] *n*. havra, sinagog.

Syn.chro.flash PHOT ['siŋkrəuflæʃ] *n*. senkronize mağnezyum ışığı.

syn.chro.mesh gear MOT ['siŋkrəu-meʃ'giə] *n*. dişlilerin kolay ve sessizce birleşmesini sağlayan vites tertibatı.

syn.chro.nism ['siŋkrənizəm] *n*. aynı anda olma, eşzamanlılık, zamandaşlık; 'syn.chro.nize *v/i*. aynı zamana uymak, aynı zamanda olm.; *v/t*. aynı zamana uydurmak; ayarlarını birbirine uydurmak (*saatler*); aynı tarihe tesadüf ettirmek; 'syn.chro.nous □ aynı zamanda olan, zamandaş, eşzaman, senkronize; aynı frekansta olan.

syn.chro.tron PHYS ['siŋkrəutrɔn] *n*. sinkrotron, elektronları çok hızlı hareket ettiren aygıt.

syn.co.pate ['siŋkəpeit] *v/t*. kısaltmak, sözcüğün ortasında bulunan bir fonemi düşürmek; MUS senkope etm.; **syn-co.pe** ['_pi] *n*. senkop, sözcüğün orta-

sında bulunan bir fonemin (*özellikle bir ünlünün*) düşmesi; MED beyine kan gitmemesinden olan baygınlık.

syn.dic ['sindik] *n*. mutemet, müşavir, vekil, savunucu; **syn.di.cate 1.** ['_kit] *n*. sendika; ticarî firmalar birliği, kartel; yazıları gazetelere satan kurum; **2.** ['_keit] *vb*. sendika oluşturmak; şirket *veya* kartel oluşturmak; şirket vasıtasiyle üretmek (*mal*); kurum aracılığı ile üretmek *veya* satmak (*yazı, seri vs.*); 'syn.di.cat.ed *adj*. pek çok gazetede birden yayımlanan.

syn.od ECCL ['sinəd] *n*. kilise meclisi; **synod.al** ['_dəl], **syn.od.ic, syn.od.i-cal** □ ECCL [si'nɔdik(l)] kilise meclisine ait.

syn.o.nym ['sinənim] *n*. GR eşanlam, anlamdaş sözcük; **syn.on.y.mous** □ [si'nɔniməs] anlamdaş, eş anlamlı.

syn.op.sis [si'nɔpsis] *n*., *pl*. **syn'op-ses** [_si:z] özet, hulasa.

syn.op.tic, syn.op.ti.cal □ [si'nɔp-tik(əl)] özet halinde olan.

syn.tac.tic, syn.tac.ti.cal □ GR [sin-'tæktik(əl)] sentaksik, sözdizimi kuralları ile ilgili; **syn.tax** GR ['sintæks] *n*. sözdizimi, sentaks.

syn.the.sis ['sinθisis] *n*., *pl*. **syn.the-ses** ['_si:z] bireşim, sentez; **syn.the-size** MEC ['_saiz] *v/t*. bireşim haline getirmek, sentez yapmak, sentez yoluyla ortaya çıkarmak.

syn.thet.ic, syn.thet.i.cal □ [sin'θet-ik(əl)] sentetik, yapay, suni.

syn.to.nize ['sintənaiz] *vb*. *radyo*: birbirine uydurmak (*frekans*); 'syn.to.ny *n*. birbirine uyma, seselim, rezonans.

syph.i.lis MED ['sifilis] *n*. frengi, sifilis.

syph.i.lit.ic MED [sifi'litik] *adj*. sifilitik, frengili.

sy.phon ['saifən] = **siphon**.

Syr.i.an ['siriən] **1.** *adj*. Suriyeli; **2.** *n*. Suriyeli kimse.

sy.rin.ga BOT [si'riŋgə] *n*. leylâk.

syr.inge ['sirindʒ] **1.** *n*. şırınga; **2.** *v/t*. şırınga etm. -*i*.

syr.up ['sirəp] *n*. şekerli sos, şurup.

sys.tem ['sistim] *n*. sistem, usul, düzen, kural, yol, kaide; bünye, organizma; evren, âlem, kâinat; **sys.tem.at.ic** [_'mætik] *adj*. (~ally) sistematik, sistemli, usul ve kurala göre *veya* uygun, planlı.

T

T [tiː]: *to a ~* F aynen, tıpatıp, tıpkı; mükemmel olarak.

tab [tæb] *n.* askı, brit; kayış, şerit, kaytan; etiket, yafta; ayakkabı bağındaki madenî parça; F hesap; *keep a ~ on, keep ~s on* hesabını tutmak *-in; fig.* kontrol etm. *-i.*

tab.ard ['tæbəd] *n.* şövalyelerin zırh üzerine giydikleri kolsuz ve kısa cüppe.

tab.by ['tæbi] *n., a.* '~-cat tekir kedi.

tab.er.nac.le ['tæbə:nækl] *n.* (taşınabilen) tapınak.

ta.ble ['teibl] **1.** *n.* masa; sofra, sofraya konan yemek; masada oturanların hepsi; liste, cetvel, tablo, çizelge; tarife; *İncil*: tablet, yazılı taş; *s. ~-land; at ~* sofrada; *lay s.th. on the ~* PARL bşi süresiz ertelemek; *turn the ~s* durumu aleyhine çevirmek (*on -in*); **2.** *v/t.* listeye geçirmek; masaya koymak; PARL tehir etm., ertelemek; müzakereye sunmak (*tasarı, teklif vs.*).

tab.leau ['tæbləu] *n., pl.* **tab.leaux** ['tæbləuz] canlı tablo.

ta.ble...: '~-cloth *n.* masa örtüsü, sofra bezi; '~-land *n.* plato, yayla; '~-lin.en *n.* masa örtüsü takımı; '~-spoon *n.* yemek kaşığı; '~.spoon.ful *n.* bir yemek kaşığı dolusu miktar.

tab.let ['tæblit] *n.* levha, kitabe, yazıt; yazı kâğıdı destesi, bloknot; PHARM tablet, komprime.

ta.ble...: '~-talk *n.* sofra sohbeti; '~-tennis *n.* masa tenisi, pingpong; '~-top *n.* masa üstü.

tab.loid ['tæbloid] *n.* resimli küçük gazete.

ta.boo [tə'buː] **1.** *adj.* yasak, tabu, dokunulmaz; **2.** *n.* tabu olan şey; **3.** *v/t.* yasaklamak.

ta.bor MUS ['teibə] *n.* dümbelek; zilli tef.

tab.u.lar □ ['tæbjulə] cetvel (*veya* çizelge) şeklindeki; masa şeklindeki; cetvele göre hesaplanmış; **tab.u.late** ['~leit] *v/t.* cetvel haline koymak; **tab.u'la.tion** *n.* cetvel haline koyma.

tac.it □ ['tæsit] söylenmeden anlaşılan, kapalı ifade olunan, zımnî; kontratsız yapılan; **tac.i.turn** □ ['~tə:n] az ko-

nuşur, sessiz, ağzı var dili yok; **tac.i-'tur.ni.ty** *n.* sessizlik, suskunluk.

tack [tæk] **1.** *n.* ufak çivi, pünez; teyel (dikiş); NAUT kuntra; *fig.* yol, usül; NAUT yelken durumuna göre gidilen yol; NAUT yiyecek, gıda; *on the wrong ~* yanlış yolda; **2.** *v/t.* çivi ile iliştirmek; teyellemek; *fig.* eklemek (*to, on -e*); *v/i.* NAUT orsa etm.; *fig.* bşi iyi kötü yoluna koymak.

tack.le ['tækl] **1.** *n.* tutma, zaptetme; NAUT halat takımı; NAUT palanga; MEC takım, cihaz; **2.** *v/t.* uğraşmak (*s.th. ile*), çaresine bakmak, üstesinden gelmek; tutmak, zaptetmek; *v/i. Am. futbol:* topu taşıyan rakibini tutup durdurmak.

tack.y ['tæki] *adj.* yapışkan, yapış yapış, henüz kurumamış (*boya vs.*); *Am.* F yırtık pırtık, pejmürde.

tact [tækt] *n.* incelik, nezaket, zarafet; **tact.ful** ['_ful] *adj.* ince(likli), nazik, zarif.

tac.ti.cal □ MIL ['tæktikəl] taktiğe ait, taktik...; **tac.ti.cian** [_'tiʃən] *n.* taktik veren kimse, tabiyeci; **tac.tics** ['_iks] *n. pl., a. sg.* taktik, manevra, tabiye.

tac.tile ['tæktail] *adj.* dokunma duyusuna ait, dokunma...

tact.less □ ['tæktlis] nezaketsiz, kaba, patavatsız.

tad.pole ZOO ['tædpəul] *n.* iribaş, tetari.

taf.fe.ta ['tæfitə] *n.* tafta.

taf.fy *Am.* ['tæfi] *n.* = *toffee*; F dalkavukluk, yağcılık.

tag [tæg] **1.** *n.* etiket, fiş; ayakkabı bağı demiri; meşhur söz; sarkık uç; «elim sende» oyunu; **2.** *v/t.* etiketlemek, etiket yapıştırmak (*to, onto -e*); *~ after* takılmak *-e*, peşinden gitmek *-in*; *~ together* birleştirmek, biraraya getirmek.

tail [teil] **1.** *n.* kuyruk; kuyruğa benzer şey; arka; son; maiyet; *sl.* kıç, popo; *sl.* cinsel ilişki; *sl. b-nin* peşine salınan kimse; sayfa altındaki boşluk; saç örgüsü; *~s pl.* paranın resimsiz tarafı, yazı; F frak; *from the ~ of one's eye* göz ucuyla; *turn ~* gerisin geriye kaçmak; *~s up* keyfi yerinde, keyfi kekâ; **2.** *v/t. ~ after s.o. b-ni* izlemek, takip etm.; ~ *s.o.* *Am.* *b-nin* peşini bırakmamak; *v/i.* ~ *off*, ~ *away* azalmak, küçülmek; geride kalmak, geride kalarak dağılmak; '~-board *n.* мот arka kapak; '~-coat *n.* frak; tailed *comb.* …kuyruklu; '~-'end *n.* arka kısım, kıç; son; 'tailless *adj.* kuyruksuz; 'tail-light *n.* stop lambası, kuyruk lambası.

tai.lor ['teilə] 1. *n.* terzi; 2. *vb.* terzilik yapmak; biçip dikmek; uydurmak, uyarlamak; ~*ed suit* ısmarlama elbise; '~-made *adj.* terzi elinden çıkmış, iyi dikilmiş; *fig.* uygun; ~ *costume* ısmarlama kostüm.

tail…: '~piece *n.* түр kitap sonundaki süslü şekil; '~-spin *n.* avıa kuyruk çevrintisi.

taint [teint] 1. *n.* leke, nokta, iz, eser; ayıp, kusur; sirayet, bulaşma; çürüme, bozulma; 2. *v/t. & v/i.* boz(ul)mak; lekelemek; мед bulaştırmak; ahlâkını bozmak.

take [teik] 1. (*irr.*) *v/t.* almak; tutmak, yakalamak, kapmak; zaptetmek; esir etm.; kazanmak (*ödül vs.*); kullanmak; çalmak; yararlanmak *-den*; götürmek; tuzağa düşürmek; yapmak; kiralamak; içmek (*çay vs.*); yemek; satın almak; kabul etm.; getirmek (*kazanç*); рнот çekmek (*resim*); F kavramak, anlamak; sanmak, zannetmek (*for*); üstlenmek, yüklenmek (*sorumluluk, görev vs.*); seçmek; uymak (*tavsiyeye vs.*); çıkarmak; *sl.* aldatmak, kandırmak; sürmek; uğramak *-e*; ihtiyacı olm. *-e*; *the devil ~ it!* Allah kahretsin!, kör şeytan!; *I ~ it that* sanıyorum ki; ~ *breath* nefes almak; ~ *comfort* teselli bulmak, avunmak; ~ *compassion on* acımak *-e*; *s.* *consideration*; ~ *counsel* danışmak; *s.* *decision*; ~ *a drive* araba ile gezmek; *s.* *effect*; *s.* *exercise*; ~ *fire* ateş almak; ~ *in hand* avucunun içine almak, idaresini ele almak; *s.* *heart*; ~ *hold of* tutmak, kapmak, yakalamak; ~ *it* F anlamak; katlanmak; *s.* *liberty*; *s.* *note*; *s.* *notice*; ~ *pity on* acımak *-e*; ~ *place* olmak, vuku bulmak; ~ *s.o.'s place* *b-nin* yerine geçmek, yerini almak; ~ *a rest* dinlenmek; *s.* *rise*; ~ *a seat* oturmak; ~ *a walk* yürüyüşe çıkmak; ~ *my word for it* bana inanın, sizi temin ederim; ~ *about* gezdirmek, dolaştırmak; ~ *along* beraberinde götürmek; ~ *down* yazmak, kaydetmek, dikte almak; indirmek; sökmek, parçalara ayırmak; yıkmak; ~ *for* sanmak,

zannetmek; ~ *from* alıp götürmek; çekip almak, çıkarmak; küçültmek, azaltmak; ~ *in* (içeriye) almak; daraltmak (*elbise vs.*); sarmak (*yelken*); kapsamak; zimmetine geçirmek; talep etm. (*hak*); anlamak, kavramak; görmek; heyecanla dinlemek *veya* izlemek; kabul etm.; F aldatmak, yutturmak; ~ *off* çıkarmak (*elbise vs.*); kesmek (*sakal, bıyık vs.*); seferden almak, kaldırmak (*tren, uçak vs.*); çekmek; indirmek (*fiyat*); götürmek, yol göstermek; kurtarmak; F taklit etm.; *be ~n off* RAIL servisten kalkmak; ~ *on* üstüne almak, üstlenmek, yüklenmek; işe almak; almak (*yolcu*); ~ *out* çıkar(t)mak; götürmek, eşlik etm., çekmek (*diş*); ~ *it out of s.o.* *fig.* bitkin düşürmek, halsiz bırakmak, perişan etm.; ~ *over* götürmek, taşımak; devralmak, *-in* idaresini ele almak; ~ *to* alışmak *-e*; başlamak *-e*; çare olarak kullanmak; sevmek, hoşlanmak; ~ *to pieces* sökmek, parçalara ayırmak, dağıtmak (*a. fig.*); ~ *up* kaldırmak; almak (*yolcu*); emmek (*sıvı*); eritmek; başlamak; işgal etm., kaplamak (*yer*); tutmak, almak (*zaman*); kabul etm.; arz etm., sunmak (*with -e*); *be ~n up with* *fig.* ilgilenmek *ile*, yakınlık duymak *-e*; çok hoşuna gitmek; ~ *upon o.s.* üzerine almak, yüklenmek; 2. (*irr.*) *v/i.* yola çıkmak, gitmek; işe yaramak; olmak; yakalanmak (*hastalığa vs.*); yapışmak; büyüleyici olm.; etkili olm.; ateş almak, tutuşmak; resim çektirmek; ~ *after* benzemek *-e*; ~ *from* itibarını bozmak, lekelemek; ~ *off* yola çıkmak, ayrılmak; avıa havalanmak, kalkmak; ~ *on* F rol yapmak; ~ *over* idareyi ele almak, yönetici olm.; ~ *to* bşe alışmak; bşe müracaat etm.; *fig.* k-ni bşe vermek; hoşuna gitmek; ~ *to ger.* bş yapmaya başlamak; ~ *up* F açılmak, düzelmek (*hava*); çekmek, küçülmek, kısalmak; ~ *up with* arkadaş olm. *ile*; *that won't ~ with me* o beni etkilemiyor; 3. *n.* hâsılat; *film:* çekim; alma, alış; tutma, tutuş; bir seferlik av miktarı; tutma (*aşı*).

take…: '~-home pay net maaş; '~-'in *n.* F aldatmaca, yutturmaca; 'tak.en *p.p.* of *take*; *be ~* ele geçmek; *be ~ with* bşe hayran olm., bayılmak; etkilenmek *-den*; *be ~ ill* hastalanmak; 'take-off *n.* taklit; karikatür; avıa kalkış, havalanma; başlama *veya* hareket noktası;

'**tak.er** *n.* bahse giren kimse.
tak.ing ['teikiŋ] **1.** □ F cazip, çekici, büyüleyici; **2.** *n.* alma, alış; kötü durum; F heyecan, telâş; **~s** *pl.* COM hâsılat, gelir.
talc MIN [tælk] *n.* talk; **tal.cum** ['_kəm] = *talc.*
tale [teil] *n.* masal, hikâye; rapor; dedi kodu; yalan; sayı, adet, toplam; *it tells its own* ~ kendini bizzat açıklıyor, başka *bş* söylemeğe gerek yok '**~bear.er** *n.* dedikoducu kimse.
tal.ent ['tælənt] *n.* kabiliyet, yetenek, hüner, Allah vergisi; '**tal.ent.ed** *adj.* kabiliyetli, hünerli, yetenekli.
ta.les JUR ['teili:z] *n. pl.* yedek jüri üyeleri.
tal.is.man ['tælizmən] *n.* tılsım.
talk [tɔ:k] **1.** *n.* konuşma; laf, söz, lakırdı; görüşme, müzakere; boş laf; konuşma şekli, ağız; dedikodu, söylenti; konferans; *give a* ~ konuşma yapmak; *have a* ~ konuşmak, görüşmek; **2.** *v/t.* konuşmak, söylemek; görüşmek, tartışmak, müzakere etm.; konuşarak etkilemek; *v/i.* konuşmak, laf (*veya* lakırdı) etm.; dedikodu etm.; ~ *to s.o.* F *b-ni* terslemek, azarlamak, haşlamak; '**talk.a.tive** □ ['_ətiv] konuşkan, çenesi düşük, geveze; '**talk.ee-talk.ee** F ['tɔ:ki'tɔ:ki] *n.* gevezelik, boş laf; '**talk.er** *n.* konuşkan, geveze, boşboğaz kimse; konuşan kimse; *he is a good* ~ iyi konuşur, iyi bir konuşmacıdır; **talk.ie** F ['_i] *n.* sesli film; '**talk.ing** *n.* konuşma; **talk.ing-to** F ['_tu:] *n.* azar(lama), paylama, haşlama.
tall [tɔ:l] *adj.* uzun (boylu); yüksek; F abartmalı; büyük, fahiş, fazla; *that's a* ~ *order* F yerine getirilmesi güç bir istek; '**tall.boy** *n.* şifoniyer, konsol; '**tallness** *n.* uzunluk, uzun boyluluk; yükseklik.
tal.low ['tæləu] *n.* donyağı; mum yağı; '**tal.low.y** *adj.* yağlı.
tal.ly ['tæli] **1.** *n.* çetele; karşılık, denk (*of* -*in*); etiket, fiş; çentik, kertik; hesap (tutma); **2.** *v/t. & v/i.* uy(dur)mak; çeteleye yazmak; sayı(m) yapmak.
tal.ly-ho ['tæli'həu] **1.** *int.* haydi!, yallah!; **2.** *n.* HUNT köpekleri ileri sürmek için avcının seslenmesi; **3.** *vb.* «Haydi!» diyerek köpekleri koşturmak.
tal.on ORN ['tælən] *n.* pençe.
ta.lus¹ ['teiləs] *n.* meyil; GEOL tepe *veya* uçurum dibinde biriken kaya parçaları, kayşat.
ta.lus² ANAT [_] *n.* aşık kemiği.

tam.a.ble ['teiməbl] *adj.* evcilleştirilebilir, ehlileştirilebilir.
tam.a.rind BOT ['tæmərind] *n.* demirhindi(ninmeyvesi).
tam.a.risk BOT ['tæmərisk] *n.* ılgın.
tam.bour ['tæmbuə] **1.** *n.* kasnak, gergef; trampet, ufak davul; ARCH kasnak işi; **2.** *v/t.* kasnağa gerip işlemek; **tam.bou.rine** MUS [_bə'ri:n] *n.* tef.
tame [teim] **1.** □ evcil, ehli; uysal, yumuşak başlı; tatsız, yavan, sıkıcı; zararsız; **2.** *v/t.* evcilleştirmek, ehlileştirmek, alıştırmak; uysallaştırmak; yumuşatmak; '**tame.ness** *n.* evcillik; uysallık; boyun eğme; '**tam.er** *n.* terbiyeci.
Tam.ma.ny *Am.* ['tæməni] *n.* New York'taki demokratik parti merkez kuruluşu.
tam-o'-shan.ter [tæmə'ʃæntə] *n.* İskoç beresi.
tamp [tæmp] *v/t.* MIN, MEC bastırıp sıkıştırmak.
tam.per ['tæmpə] *v/t. & v/i.:* ~ *with* karış(tır)mak, kurcalamak, oynamak; dokunmak; değiştirip bozmak.
tam.pon MED ['tæmpən] *n.* tampon.
tan [tæn] **1.** *n.* güneş yanığı; tanen, mazı tozu; **2.** *adj.* açık kahverengi; **3.** *v/t. & v/i.* karar(t)mak, esmerleş(tir)mek; tabaklamak (*deri*); F kamçılamak, dövmek.
tan.dem ['tændəm] *n.* iki kişilik bisiklet; ~ *connexion* ELECT seri bağlantı.
tang¹ [tæŋ] *n.* pırazvana, berazban, bıçağın maça giren kuyruğu; *fig.* ağızda kalan tat *veya* koku.
tang² [_] **1.** *n.* madenî ses, tangırtı; **2.** *v/i.* madenî ses çıkarmak, tangırdamak.
tan.gent MATH ['tændʒənt] *n.* teğet; tanjant; *go* (*a. fly*) *off at a* ~ birden fikir *veya* konu değiştirmek, daldan dala konmak; **tan.gen.tial** □ MATH [_'dʒenʃəl] teğet şeklinde, teğet halindeki..
tan.ger.ine BOT [tændʒə'ri:n] *n.* mandalina.
tan.gi.bil.i.ty [tændʒi'biliti] *n.* tutulabilme; **tan.gi.ble** □ ['_dʒəbl] dokunulur, tutulur; anlaşılır, açık; *fig.* gerçek; maddî; duyulur, hissedilir.
tan.gle ['tæŋgl] **1.** *n.* karışıklık; karmakarışık şey, arapsaçı; düğüm; **2.** *v/t. & v/i.* karış(tır)mak, dolaş(tır)mak, karmakarışık etm., arapsaçına çevirmek; tartışmak, münakaşa etm. (*with ile*).
tan.go ['tæŋgəu] *n.* tango.
tank [tæŋk] **1.** *n.* depo, sarnıç, tank; ha-

vuz, gölcük; MEC, MIL tank; **2.** *v/t.* depo *veya* sarnıca koymak; **~ up** arabanın deposunu doldurmak, yakıt almak; '**tankage** *n.* havuz *veya* depo istiap hacmi; havuz *veya* depoya doldurma; havuz doldurma ücreti.

tank.ard ['tæŋkəd] *n.* içki maşrapası.

tank-car RAIL ['tæŋkkɑ:] *n.* tanklı vagon; '**tank.er** *n.* tanker.

tan.ner[1] ['tænə] *n.* sepici, tabak.

tan.ner[2] *sl.* [_] *n.* altı penilik para.

tan.ner.y ['tænəri] *n.* tabakhane.

tan.nic ac.id CHEM ['tænik'æsid] *n.* tanen asidi.

tan.nin CHEM [tænin] *n.* tanen, mazı tozu.

tan.ta.lize ['tæntəlaiz] *v/t.* hayal kırıklığına uğratmak, boşuna ümit vermek, *bşi* gösterip vermemek, eziyet etm.

tan.ta.mount ['tæntəmaunt] *adj.* eşit, aynı (**to** -e, ile).

tan.trum F ['tæntrəm] *n.* hiddet (nöbeti), aksilik, terslik.

tap[1] [tæp] **1.** *n.* hafif vuruş; **2.** *v/t.* hafifçe vurmak -e.

tap[2] [_] **1.** *n.* musluk; fıçı tapası, tıkaç; F fıçıdan alınmış içki; MEC kılavuz, burgu; F *s.* **~-room**; ELECT bağlantı; **on ~** fıçıdan alınıp satılmaya hazır (*içki*); *fig.* hazır; **2.** *v/t.* akıtmak -*i*; delerek akıtmak (*kauçuk*); sızdırmak (*para, bilgi vs.*); **~ the wire(s)** ELECT gizli bağlantı kurmak; TELEPH gizlice dinlemek.

tap-dance ['tæpdɑ:ns] ayakları yere vurarak yapılan bir çeşit dans.

tape [teip] *n.* şerit, bant, kurdele; metre şeridi; *spor:* varış ipi; TEL kâğıt şerit; **red ~** bürokrasi, gereksiz resmî muamele, kırtasiyecilik; '**~-meas.ure** *n.* mezür, mezura, metre şeridi; **tape re.cord.er** *n.* teyp; **tape re.cord.ing** teybe alma.

ta.per [teipə] **1.** *n.* çok ince mum; **2.** *adj.* gittikçe incelen; **3.** *v/t.* & *v/i.* gittikçe incel(t)mek, sivril(t)mek; azalmak, eksilmek; **~ing** = **~ 2.**

tap.es.tried ['tæpistrid] *adj.* goblenle kaplı; '**tap.es.try** *n.* goblen, resim dokumalı duvar örtüsü.

tape.worm ['teipwə:m] *n.* bağırsak kurdu, şerit, tenya.

tap.i.o.ca [tæpi'əukə] *n.* tapyoka.

ta.pir ZOO ['teipə] *n.* tapir.

tap.pet MEC ['tæpit] *n.* kol, manivela.

tap-room ['tæprum] *n.* meyhane, bar.

tap-root BOT ['tæpru:t] *n.* ana kök.

taps *Am.* MIL [tæps] *n. pl.* yat borusu.

tap.ster ['tæpstə] *n.* barmen.

tar [tɑ:] **1.** *n.* katran; **Jack ~** F deniz kurdu, denizci, gemici; **2.** *v/t.* katranlamak.

ta.ran.tu.la ZOO [tə'ræntjulə] *n.* büyük örümcek.

tar-board ['tɑ:bɔ:d] *n.* katranlı mukavva.

tar.di.ness ['tɑ:dinis] *n.* gecikme; yavaşlık, ağırlık; '**tar.dy** □ yavaş, ağır; geç kalan *veya* gelen, geciken.

tare[1] BOT [tɛə] *n. mst* **~s** *pl.* delice.

tare[2] COM [_] **1.** *n.* dara; **2.** *v/t.* -*in* darasını düşmek.

tar.get ['tɑ:git] *n.* hedef, nişangâh; *fig.* eleştiriye hedef olan *bş veya b-i*; ulaşılmak istenilen miktar; amaç, gaye; **~ practice** atış talimi.

tar.iff ['tærif] *n.* gümrük tarifesi; fiyat listesi.

tar.mac ['tɑ:mæk] *n.* asfalt (*yol veya uçak iniş alanı*).

tarn [tɑ:n] *n.* dağ gölü.

tar.nish ['tɑ:niʃ] **1.** *v/t.* & *v/i.* MEC donuklaş(tır)mak, matlaş(tır)mak, karar(t)mak; *fig.* lekelemek, kirletmek (*şöhret vs.*); **2.** *n.* donukluk, matlık; leke, kir.

tar.pau.lin [tɑ:'pɔ:lin] *n.* NAUT gemici, denizci; su geçirmez muşamba *veya* örtü.

tar.ry[1] *lit.* ['tæri] *v/i.* kalmak, durmak; gecikmek, oyalanmak.

tar.ry[2] ['tɑ:ri] *adj.* katranlı.

tart [tɑ:t] **1.** □ ekşi, mayhoş; keskin, acı; *fig.* ters, sert (*davranış, huy vs.*); **2.** *n.* turta; *sl.* fahişe, orospu.

tar.tan ['tɑ:tən] *n.* kareli ve yünlü İskoç kumaşı; **~ plaid** İskoç şalı.

Tar.tar[1] ['tɑ:tə] *n.* Tatar; *fig.* düzenbaz kimse, baş belâsı kimse; **catch a ~** belâya çatmak, daha belâlısına çatmak.

tar.tar[2] [_] *n.* CHEM kefeki, pesek; şarap tortusu.

task [tɑ:sk] **1.** *n.* ödev; iş, görev, vazife; hizmet; külfet; **take to ~** (**for**) azarlamak, paylamak, haşlamak (-*den dolayı*); **2.** *v/t.* külfet yüklemek -*e*; görevlendirmek, vazifelendirmek; **task force** MIL geçici işbirliği; '**task.mas.ter** *n.* angaryacı.

tas.sel ['tæsəl] **1.** *n.* püskül; **2.** *v/t.* püsküllerle süslemek.

taste [teist] **1.** *n.* tat, lezzet, çeşni; tat alma duyusu; yudumluk, tadımlık miktar (**of** -*in*); hoşlanma, zevk, beğeni *(for -e karşı)*; **there is no accounting for~s** zevkler ve renkler tartışılmaz; **to** ~ zevkine uygun; **2.** *v/t. -in* tadına bakmak, tatmak; denemek *-i*; *v/i.* tadı olm., tat vermek **(of)**; **taste.ful** □ [-'ful] lezzetli; zevkli; uyumlu, zarif.

taste.less □ ['teistlis] tatsız, yavan; zevksiz; uygunsuz; **'taste.less.ness** *n.* tatsızlık; uygunsuzluk.

tas.ter ['teistə] *n.* çeşnici *(şarap, çay vs.).*

tast.y □ F ['teisti] tatlı, lezzetli, leziz; zevkli.

tat¹ [tæt] *s. tit¹.*

tat² [-] *v/i.* mekik oyası yapmak.

ta-ta ['tæ'ta:] *int.* F *(çocuk dilinde veya co.)* Allaha ısmarladık; güle güle.

tat.ter ['tætə] **1.** *v/t. & v/i.* parçala(n)-mak, parçalayıp paçavra yapmak; **2.** *n. ~s pl.* paçavra, çaput; **tat.ter.de.mal.ion** [-də'meiljən] *n.* pejmürde kimse, üstübaşı dökük kimse.

tat.tle ['tætl] **1.** *v/i.* gevezelik etm., çene çalmak, boşboğazlık etm.; *v/t. b.s.* fitlemek, gammazlamak; **2.** *n.* boşboğazlık, dedikodu, zevzeklik; *b.s.* fitnecilik, gammazlık; **'tat.tler** *n.* boşboğaz *(veya* zevzek, fitneci, gammaz) kimse.

tat.too¹ [tə'tu:] **1.** *n.* MIL koğuş borusu; **beat the devil's ~** *fig.* parmakları bir yere tıkır tıkır vurmak; **2.** *vb. fig.* tıkır tıkır vurmak, tıkırdatmak.

tat.too² [-] **1.** *v/t.* dövme yapmak *-e*; **2.** *n.* dövme.

taught [tɔːt] *prep & p.p. of* **teach.**

taunt [tɔːnt] **1.** *n.* hakaret, alay; iğneli söz; **2.** *v/t.* alay etm. *ile*, sataşmak *-e*; **~ s.o. with s.th.** *b-le* bş yüzünden alay etm., başına kakmak *-i*; **'taunt.ing** □ alaylı; iğneli *(söz).*

taut [tɔːt] *adj.* NAUT sıkı, gergin *(ip, halat vs.)*; *fig.* gergin *(sinir)*; **'taut.en** *v/t. & v/i.* gerginleş(tir)mek, sıkılaş(tır)mak; NAUT aganta etm.

tau.tol.o.gy [tɔː'tɔlədʒi] *n.* gereksiz tekrar(lanan ifade).

tav.ern ['tævən] *n.* meyhane, taverna; han.

taw¹ MEC [tɔː] *v/t.* şaplamak.

taw² [-] *n.* bilye (oyunu).

taw.dri.ness ['tɔːdrinis] *n.* zevksizlik, bayağılık; **'taw.dry** □ ucuz ve gösterişli, bayağı, zevksiz.

taw.ny ['tɔːni] *adj.* sarımsı kahverengi, esmer, koyu kumral.

tax [tæks] **1.** *n.* vergi, resim **(on** *üzerine)*; *fig.* külfet, yük **(on, upon** *-e)*; **~ eva-**

sion vergi kaçırma; **2.** *vb.* vergi koymak *-e*; *fig.* külfet olm., yük olm., tüketmek *(sabır)*; JUR mahkeme masrafını belirlemek; suçlamak; **~ s.o. with s.th.** *b-ni bşden* dolayı suçlamak; **'tax.a.ble** □ vergiye tabi; **tax'a.tion** *n.* vergi (tarhı); vergilendirme; *part.* JUR mahkeme masrafı; **'tax-col.lec.tor** *n.* vergici, tahsildar; **'tax-free** *adj.* vergiden muaf.

tax.i F ['tæksi] **1.** *n.* = '~-cab taksi; **2.** *v/t. & v/i.* taksi ile gitmek *veya* taşımak; AVIA taksile(t)mek; '~-danc.er *n.* dansetmek için tutulan kız; '~-driv.er *n.* taksi şoförü; '~.me.ter *n.* taksimetre.

tax.pay.er ['tækspeiə] *n.* vergi mükellefi.

tea [tiː] *n.* çay (fidanı); çay ziyafeti; akşam kahvaltısı; **high~, meat~** ikindi kahvaltısı, beş çayı; '~-cad.dy *n.* çay kutusu.

teach [tiːtʃ] *(irr.) v/t.* öğretmek, okutmak, eğitmek, yetiştirmek; ders vermek *-e*; göstermek; **I'll ~ you to come home late!** eve geç gelmeyi ben sana gösteririm!; *v/i.* öğretmenlik yapmak; **'teacha.ble** □ çabuk öğrenen, öğrenmeye hevesli; **'teach.er** *n.* öğretmen, hoca; **'teach.er-'train.ing col.lege** eğitim fakültesi; **'teach-'in** *n.* tartışma, münazara; **'teach.ing** *n.* öğretme, öğretim; öğretmenlik; **~s** *pl.* telkin, talim, öğretilen şey.

tea...: '~-co.sy *n.* çaydanlık külâhı; '~.cup *n.* çay fincanı; **storm in a ~** *fig.* bir bardak suda fırtına; '~-gown *n.* ikindide giyilen elbise.

teak BOT [tiːk] *n.* tik ağacı (kerestesi).

tea-ket.tle ['tiːketl] *n.* çaydanlık.

team [tiːm] *n.* ekip, grup; çift hayvan takımı; *part. spor:* takım; ~ spir.it ekip halinde çalışma ruhu; **~** team.ster ['-stə] *n.* çift hayvan süren kimse; *Am.* kamyon şoförü; **'team-work** *n.* takım halinde çalışma, ekip çalışması *(a. spor)*; THEAT piyesteki oyuncuların hepsi.

tea.pot ['tiːpɔt] *n.* demlik, çaydanlık.

tear¹ [tɛə] **1.** *(irr.) v/t. & v/i.* yırt(ıl)mak, kop(ar)mak, yar(ıl)mak, çok hırpala(n)mak; açmak *(delik)*; yolmak; F çılgın gibi koşmak; **2.** *n.* yırtık; *s. wear.*

tear² [tiə] *n.* gözyaşı.

tear.ful □ ['tiəful] gözleri yaşlı, ağlayan.

tear-gas ['tiəgæs] *n.* göz yaşartıcı gaz.

tear.ing *fig.* ['tɛəriŋ] *adj.* çılgınca, müthiş.

tear.less □ ['tiəlis] gözyaşsız, gözleri kurumuş.

tea.room ['tiːrum] *n.* kafeterya.

tease [tiːz] **1.** *v/t.* tedirgin etm., rahatsız etm., kızdırmak; *fig.* takılmak -*e*, alay etm. *ile*; liflere ayırmak; kabartmak (*saç*); **2.** *n.* takılmayı seven kimse, şakacı kimse; **tea.sel** BOT ['tiːzl] *n.* tarakotu; MEC hav kabartma tarağı; 'teas.er *n.* F *fig.* zor mesele, güç iş.

tea...: '~-spoon çay kaşığı; '~.spoon.ful *n.* çay kaşığı dolusu; '~.strain.er *n.* çay süzgeci.

teat [tiːt] *n.* meme, emcik.

tea...: '~-things *n. pl.* çay takımı; '~-urn *n.* semaver.

tech.nic ['teknik] *n. a.* ~**s** *pl. veya sg.* = *technique*; 'tech.ni.cal □ teknik..., meslekî..., ilmî; resmî; kurallara uygun; ~ *support* teknik destek; tech-ni.cal.i.ty [-'kæliti] *n.* teknik ayrıntı, incelik, ilmî nitelik; tech'ni.cian [-ʃən] *n.* teknisyen, teknikçi, tekniker.

Tech.ni.col.or ['teknikʌlə] **1.** *adj.* renkli film...; **2.** *n.* renkli film.

tech.nique [tek'niːk] *n.* teknik, yöntem, yordam, metod, yapma usulü.

tech.no.cra.cy [tek'nɔkrəsi] *n.* teknokrasi.

tech.nol.o.gy [tek'nɔlədʒi] *n.* teknoloji; *school of* ~ teknik üniversite.

tech.y ['tetʃi] = *testy*.

ted.der *Am.* ['tedə] *n.* yaş out harman makinesi.

ted.dy boy F ['tedibɔi] *n.* asi genç.

te.di.ous □ ['tiːdjəs] usandırıcı, can sıkıcı, yorucu; 'te.di.ous.ness *n.* sıkıcılık, usandırıcılık; can sıkıntısı; monotonluk.

te.di.um ['tiːdjəm] *n.* sıkıcılık; can sıkıntısı, bezginlik.

tee [tiː] **1.** *n. spor*: hedef; *golf*: topun konulduğu küçük kum yığını *veya* tahta çubuk; **2.** *vb.* ~ *off* topa kum yığınının üstünden vurarak oyuna başlamak.

teem [tiːm] *v/i.* dolu olm., kaynamak (*with ile*); boşanmak, çok yağmak (*yağmur*).

teen-ag.er ['tiːneidʒə] *n.* on üç on dokuz yaşlar arasındaki kimse, genç, delikanlı.

teens [tiːnz] *n. pl.* on üç ile on dokuz arasındaki yaşlar; *in one's* ~ 13-19 yaşları arasında.

tee.ny F ['tiːni] *adj.* ufak, ufacık, küçük, mini mini.

tee.ter F ['tiːtə] *v/i.* sendeleyerek yürümek, sallanmak, bocalamak.

teeth [tiːθ] *pl. of* **tooth**.

teethe [tiːð] *v/i.* diş çıkarmak; *teething troubles pl.* diş çıkardığı için bebeğin huysuzluğu.

tee.to.tal [tiː'təutl] *adj.* içki içmemeye ait; yeşilaycı; **tee'to.tal.(l)er** *n.* alkollü içki içmeyen kimse.

tee.to.tum ['tiːtəu'tʌm] *n.* el ile çevrilen topaç.

tel.e.cast ['telikɑːst] **1.** *n.* televizyon yayını; **2.** *v/t.* televizyonla yayınlamak.

tel.e.con.fer.ence [teli'kɔnfərəns] *n.* telekonferans.

tel.e.course *Am.* F ['telikɔːs] *n.* televizyonla öğretim.

tel.e.gram ['teligræm] *n.* telgraf(name).

tel.e.graph ['teligrɑːf] **1.** *n.* telgraf (makinesi); *attr.* telgraf...; **2.** *v/i.* telgraf çekmek; *v/t.* tellemek; **tel.e.graph.ic** [-'græfik] *adj.* (~*ally*) telgrafla ilgili, telgraf...; **te.leg.ra.phist** [ti'legrəfist] *n.* telgrafçı; **te'leg.ra.phy** *n.* telgraf sistemi, telgrafçılık.

tel.e.mar.ket.ing [teli'mɑːkitiŋ] *n.* telepazarlama.

te.lep.a.thy [ti'lepəθi] *n.* telepati, uzaduyum.

tel.e.phone ['telifəun] **1.** *n.* telefon; *by* ~ telefonla; *be on the* ~ telefonda olm.; **2.** *v/t.* telefon etm. -*e*; ~ *booth* telefon kulübesi; 'tel.e.phon.ic [-'fɔnik] *adj.* (~*ally*) telefona ait, telefon...; **te.leph.o.nist** [ti'lefənist] *n.* santral memuru, telefoncu; **te'leph.o.ny** *n.* telefonculuk.

tel.e.pho.to PHOT ['teli'fəutəu] *n. a.* ~ *lens* teleobjektif, teleskopik mercek; telefotografik resim.

tel.e.print.er ['teliprintə] *n.* teleks.

tel.e.scope ['teliskəup] **1.** *n.* OPT teleskop, ırakgörür; **2.** *v/t. & v/i.* içe içe geç(ir)mek; kısal(t)mak; iç içe girmek; **tel.escop.ic** [-'kɔpik] *adj.* teleskopa ait; teleskopik; teleskopla görülebilen; ~ *sight* nişan dürbünü (*tüfekte*).

tel.e.typ.er ['teli'taipə] *n.* teleks.

tel.e.vise ['telivaiz] *v/t.* televizyonla yayınlamak; **tel.e.vi.sion** ['-viʒən] *n.* televizyon, uzagörüm; *attr.* televizyon...; *watch* ~ televizyon seyretmek; ~ *set* televizyon cihazı; **tel.e.vi.sor** ['-vaizə] *n.* televizyon alıcısı.

telex ['teleks] *n.* teleks.

tell [tel] (*irr.*) *v/t.* söylemek -*e*, anlatmak -*e*, bildirmek -*e*, nakletmek -*e*; ifade etm., belirtmek; emretmek; anlamak; keşfetmek; haber vermek; temin etm.; itiraf etm.; **~ s.o. to do s.th.** *b-ne bş* yapmasını söylemek; **I have been told** bana söylendi; **~ off** sayıp ayırmak **(for s.th.** *bş için;* **to do bş** *yapmak için);* F paylamak; haşlamak; **~ the world** *sl.* yedi mahalleye duyurmak; *v/i.* bahsetmek **(of, about** *-den);* gammazlamak, ispiyonlamak **(on** *i-);* ifşa etm., yaymak **(on, of** *-i);* tesiri olm., tesir etm. *(darbe vs.);* **'tell.er** *n.* veznedar; anlatan kimse; mecliste oyları sayan kimse, sayıcı; **'tell.ing** □ etkili, tesirli; **tell.tale** ['⌐teil] **1.** *adj.* dedikoducu; belli eden; *fig.* ağzında bakla ıslanmayan; **2.** *n.* gammaz kimse, dedikoducu kimse; MEC sayaç; **~ clock** çalışanların işe gelip gitme zamanını kaydeden saat.

tel.ly F ['teli] *n.* televizyon.

tel.pher ['telfə] *n.* teleferik.

te.mer.i.ty ['ti'meriti] *n.* gözüpeklik, delice cesaret; aşırı cüret; küstahlık.

tem.per ['tempə] *v/t.* yumuşatmak, hafifletmek; ayarlamak; kıvama getirmek; su ile yoğurmak *(balçık);* MEC tavlamak, su vermek *(çelik);* MUS gam dizisine göre akort etm.; sertleştirmek; **2.** *n.* MEC kıvam, karar, terkip; tabiat, huy, mizaç; öfke, terslik, aksilik; **hot~** öfkelenme, köpürme; **lose one's ~** hiddetlenmek, tepesi atmak; **tem.per.a.ment** ['⌐rəmənt] *n.* mizaç, tabiat, huy, yaradılış; MUS akort; **tem.per.a.men.tal** [⌐'mentl] mizaca bağlı; limonî tabiatlı, değişken mizaçlı; çabuk kızan, öfkesi burnunda, **'tem.per.ance 1.** *n.* ölçülülük, ılımlılık; içkiden kaçınma; **2.** *adj.* içkiden kaçınan...; alkolsüz...; **tem.per.ate** ['⌐rit] ılımlı, mutedil; ılıman, ılık; içkiden kaçınan; **~ zone** ılıman bölge; **tem.per.a.ture** ['tempritʃə] *n.* sıcaklık, ısı, hararet; ısı derecesi; MED ateş; **have** *veya* **run a ~** ateşi olm.; **tempered** ['tempəd] *comb.* ... mizaçlı,... huylu; **hot~** sinirli, öfkeli.

tem.pest ['tempist] *n.* fırtına, bora; **tempes.tu.ous** □ [⌐'pestjuəs] fırtınalı; şiddetli, zorlu.

Tem.plar ['templə] *n.* HIST şövalye; ♀ UNIV Londra'da Temple'de oturan hukuk öğrencisi.

tem.ple¹ ['templ] *n.* mabet, tapınak.

tem.ple² ANAT [⌐] *n.* şakak.

tem.po ['tempəu] *n.* tempo; gidiş(at),

tarz.

tem.po.ral □ ['tempərəl] geçici; (şimdiki) zamana ait; dünyevî; cismanî; GR zaman belirten; **tem.po.ral.i.ties** [⌐'rælitiz] *n. pl.* dünyevî mülk; **tem.po.ra.ri.ness** ['⌐rərinis] *n.* geçicilik; **'tem.po.rar.y** □ geçici, muvakkat; **~ bridge** geçici köprü; **~ work** geçici iş; **'tem.po.rize** *v/i.* zamana ayak uydurmak; uzlaşmak; vakit kazanmaya çalışmak.

tempt [tempt] *v/t.* baştan çıkarmak, ayartmak, kandırmak; çekmek, cezbetmek; teşvik etm.; sinirlendirmek; **be ~ed** baştan çıkarılmak; **temp'ta.tion** *n.* günaha teşvik; ayartma, baştan çıkarma; cezbedici şey; **'tempt.er** *n.* ayartan kimse, baştan çıkaran kimse; şeytan; **'tempt-ing** □ cezbedici, çekici; **'temptress** *n.* baştan çıkaran kadın.

ten [ten] **1.** *adj.* on; **2.** *n.* on sayısı *veya* rakamı.

ten.a.ble ['tenəbl] *adj.* savunması kolay; elde tutulabilen; makûl.

te.na.cious □ [ti'neiʃəs] yapışkan; tutan, bırakmayan, vazgeçmez **(of** *-den);* kuvvetli *(hafıza);* inatçı, direngen; **te.nac.ity** [ti'næsiti] *n.* yapışkanlık; sebat, direnme; bırakmama, vazgeçmeme **(of** *-den);* sağlamlık.

ten.an.cy ['tenənsi] *n.* kiracılık, kullanım; kira süresi.

ten.ant ['tenənt] **1.** *n.* kiracı; *fig.* bir yerde oturan kimse, sakin; **~ right** kiracının kirayı ödedikçe kullanma hakkı; **2.** *v/t.* kiralamak; **'ten.ant.ry** *n.* kiracılar; kiracılık.

tench ICHTH [tenʃ] *n.* kilizbalığı.

tend¹ [tend] **1.** *v/i.* meyletmek, yönelmek, eğinmek **(to, towards** *-e);* **~ from** uzaklaşmaya çalışmak *-den;* **~ upwards** yükselmek *(fiyat).*

tend² [⌐] *v/t.* bakmak *-e,* dikkat etm. *-e,* göz kulak olm. *-e;* kullanmak *(makine);* **'tend.ance** *n.* bakım, bakma, göz kulak olma.

tend.en.cy ['tendənsi] *n.* meyil, eğilim, eğinme; yönseme; **ten.den.tious** [⌐'denʃəs] *adj.* belli bir amaç güden, davalı, tezli; meyilli, eğik.

ten.der¹ ['tendə] nazik, hassas, kolay incinir; müşfik, şefkatli, merhametli; ince, narin, cılız; olgunlaşmamış; sevecen; körpe, gevrek.

ten.der² ['tendənsi] **1.** *n.* teklif, arz; COM teklif; ihale; **legal ~** geçerli para; **2.** *v/t.* sunmak, teklif etm; *v/i.* teklif vermek.

ten.der³ [̣-] *n.* bakıcı; RAIL, NAUT tender.
ten.der.foot *Am.* F ['tendəfut] *n.* güçlüklere alışık olmayan kimse, acemi;
ten.derloin [' ̣-lɔin] *n. part. Am.* fileto; *Am.* her türlü karanlık işin yapıldığı bölge; 'tender.ness *n.* şefkat, yufka yüreklilik.
ten.don ANAT ['tendən] *n.* veter, kiriş, tendon.
ten.dril BOT ['tendril] *n.* asma *veya* sarmaşık filizi.
ten.e.ment ['tenimənt] *n.* çok kiracılı ucuz apartman; (kiralık) daire; JUR mülk olabilen herhangi *bş*; konut, mesken; ~ *house* ucuz apartman.
ten.et ['ti:net] *n.* inan, doktrin, akide, prensip, ilke, görüş.
ten.fold ['tenfəuld] *adv.* on kat, on misli.
ten.nis ['tenis] *n.* tenis; '~court *n.* tenis kortu.
ten.on MEC ['tenən] *n.* erkek geçme parçası; '~saw *n.* MEC zıvana testeresi.
ten.or ['tenə] *n.* gidiş(at), akış; yön; anlam, mana; MUS tenor (sesi), tenor çalgı.
tense¹ GR [tens] *n.* fiil zamanı.
tense² [̣-] *a.* gerili, gergin (*a. fig.*); sinirli; nazik; 'tense.ness gerginlik; tensile ['tensail] *adj.* geril(ebil)ir; gerilme...; ~ *strength* gerilme direnci; tension [' ̣-ʃən] *n.* gerginlik; ger(il)me; ELECT gerilim; *high* ~ ELECT yüksek gerilim; ~ *test* germe deneyi.
tent¹ [tent] *n.* çadır, otağ, oba; *pitch one's* ~*s* çadır kurmak; *fig.* bir yere yerleşmek.
tent² [̣-] *n.* bir çeşit siyah şarap.
ten.ta.cle ZOO ['tentəkl] *n.* kavrama uzvu; dokunaç.
ten.ta.tive ['tentətiv] **1.** ☐ deneme..., tecrübe olarak yapılan; ~*ly* deneme kabilinden; **2.** *n.* deneme, tecrübe.
ten.ter ['tentə] *n.* gergef, gergi; '~hook *n.* gergi kancası; *be on* ~*s fig.* endişe içinde olm.
tenth [tenθ] **1.** *adj.* onuncu; onda bir; **2.** *n.* onda bir kısım; onuncu gelen şey; ondalık; 'tenth.ly *adv.* onuncu olarak.
tent-peg ['tentpeg] *n.* çadır kazığı.
ten.u.ous ☐ ['tenjuəs] ince, narin; seyrek, hafif.
ten.ure ['tenjuə] *n.* tasarruf (hakkı); görev süresi; kullanım süresi; işinde kalabilme hakkı; ~ *of office* hizmet süresi.
te.pee ['ti:pi:] *n.* kızılderili çadırı.

tep.id ☐ ['tepid] ılık; **te'pid.i.ty**, 'tep.id.ness *n.* ılıklık.
ter.cen.te.nar.y [tə:sen'ti:nəri], **ter.cen.tenni.al** [̣-'tenjəl] **1.** *adj.* üç yüzyıla ait; **2.** *n.* üç yüzüncü yıldönümü.
ter.gi.ver.sa.tion [tə:dʒivə:'seifən] *n.* döneklik, değişkenlik.
term [tə:m] **1.** *n.* süre, müddet, vade; sömestr; dönem; MATH, PHLS had, terim; JUR toplantı devresi; anlatım, dil, söz, terim; ~*s pl.* koşullar, şartlar; ~*s pl.* ilişkiler; *in* ~*s of praise* överek, övgü ile; *be on good* (*bad*) ~*s with b-le* arası iyi (kötü) olm.; *come to* ~*s*, *make* ~*s* anlaşmak, uzlaşmak; **2.** *v/t.* isim vermek, adlandırmak, demek.
ter.ma.gant ['tə:məgənt] **1.** ☐ yaygaracı, şirret, cadaloz (*kadın*); **2.** *n.* şirret kadın, cadaloz kadın.
ter.mi.na.ble ☐ ['tə:minəbl] sınırlan(dırıl)abilir, süresi tayin edilebilir; **ter.mi.nal** [̣-nl] **1.** ☐ uçta bulunan, uç, son; döneme ait, dönem...; ölümcül, ölümle sonuçlanan; BOT dal *veya* sapın ucunda olan; ~*ly* ölümcül derecede; **2.** *n.* son, uç, nihayet; ELECT kutup, terminal; RAIL *etc.* terminal; **ter.mi.nate** [' ̣-neit] *v/t. & v/i.* bit(ir)mek, son vermek; sınırlamak; sona ermek; **ter.mi'na.tion** *n.* son, bit(ir)me; sonuç, netice; sınır; GR sonek, çekim eki.
ter.mi.nol.o.gy [tə:mi'nɔlədʒi] *n.* terminoloji; özel anlamlı terimler.
ter.mi.nus ['tə:minəs] *n., pl.* **ter.mi.ni** [' ̣-nai] son, nihayet, hudut, sınır; RAIL son istasyon; son durak; terminal.
ter.mite ZOO ['tə:mait] *n.* beyaz karınca, divik.
tern ORN [tə:n] *n.* balıkçın, deniz kırlangıcı.
ter.na.ry ['tə:nəri] *adj.* üçlü; üçer üçer giden; üç madenden oluşmuş (*alaşım*).
ter.race ['terəs] *n.* taraça, teras; set; sıra evler; 'ter.raced *adj.* teraslı; taraçalı...; ~ *house* sıra ev.
ter.ra-cot.ta ['terə'kɔtə] *n.* pişirilmiş tuğla *veya* çömlek.
ter.rain ['terein] *n.* arazi, alan, arsa, yer.
ter.res.tri.al ☐ [ti'restriəl] dünya ile ilgili, dünyasal; kara ile ilgili, karasal; karadan oluşan; *part.* ZOO, BOT karada yaşayan.
ter.ri.ble ☐ ['terəbl] korkunç, dehşetli; aşırı, çok, pek; berbat; 'ter.ri.ble.ness *n.* korkunçluk; aşırılık; berbatlık.
ter.ri.er ZOO ['teriə] *n.* teriyer.

ter.rif.ic [tə'rifik] *adj.* (*~ally*) korkunç, dehşetli, dehşet verici; aşırı, çok, pek; F fevkalâde, harika, çok güzel; **ter.ri.fy** ['terifai] *v/t.* korkutmak, dehşete düşürmek.

ter.ri.to.ri.al [teri'tɔːriəl] **1.** □ karaya ait; belirli bir bölgeye ait; *Am.* devlet teşkilâtına girmemiş bölgelere ait; ~ *waters pl.* kara suları; ⨯ *Army*, ⨯ *Force* yedek gönüllü ordusu, ana vatan ordusu; **2.** *n.* MIL ana vatan ordusu üyesi; **ter.ri.to.ry** ['_təri] *n.* toprak, arazi; memleket, ülke; bölge.

ter.ror ['terə] *n.* terör, tedhiş; korku, dehşet; baş belâsı kimse; çok yaramaz çocuk; '**ter.ror.ism** *n.* tedhişçilik, terörizm; '**ter.ror.ist** *n.* tedhişçi, terörist; '**ter.ror.ize** *v/t.* tedhiş etm., yıldırmak.

terse □ [tɔːs] kısa ve öz, veciz (*söz, konuşma*); '**terse.ness** *n.* kısa ve özlülük.

ter.tian MED ['tɔːʃən] *adj. & n.* günaşırı tutan (nöbet); '**ter.ti.ar.y** *adj.* üçüncü (dereceye ait); GEOL üçüncü zamana ait.

Tery.lene ['terəliːn] *n.* terilen.

tes.sel.late ['tesilet] *v/t.* mozaik taş *veya* parçalarla donatmak; **~d pavement** mozaik döşeli kaldırım.

test [test] **1.** *n.* test, imtihan; tecrübe, deney; test, muayene; *fig.* deneme; CHEM analiz, çözümleme, tahlil; ölçü, ayar; maden potası; *put to the ~* denemeye tabi tutmak, sınamak, tecrübe etm.; **2.** *v/t.* denemek, prova etm.; imtihan etm., tecrübe etm.; çözümlemek, tahlil etm.; kontrol etm.

tes.ta.ceous ZOO [tes'teiʃəs] *adj.* kabuklu...

tes.ta.ment *Mukaddes Kitap,* JUR ['testəmənt] *n.* ahit; vasiyetname; **tes.ta.menta.ry** [_'mentəri] *adj.* vasiyet kabilinden; vasiyetnamede olan.

tes.ta.tor [tes'teitə] *n.* vasiyetname sahibi, vasiyetçi.

tes.ta.trix [tes'teitriks] *n.* vasiyetname yapan kadın.

test case ['test'keis] *n.* deneme davası.

tes.ter[1] ['testə] *n.* yatak tentesi.

test.er[2] [_] *n.* muayene eden kimse *veya* alet.

tes.ti.cle ANAT ['testikl] *n.* testis, erbezi, husye, haya, taşak.

tes.ti.fi.er ['testifaiə] *n.* şahit, tanık (*to* -*e*); **tes.ti.fy** ['_fai] *v/t.* kanıtlamak, ispatlamak; açığa vurmak; *v/i.* şehadette bulunmak (*on üzerine*); şahitlik etm. (*for lehte*).

tes.ti.mo.ni.al [testi'məunjəl] *n.* bonservis, tavsiye mektubu; belge; takdirname; **tes.ti.mo.ny** ['_məni] *n.* tanıklık, şahadet, şahitlik (*to* -*e*); ifade.

tes.ti.ness ['testinis] *n.* terslik, hırçınlık.

test...: '**~-match** *n.* kriket: uluslararası kriket turnuva maçı; '**~-pa.per** *n.* CHEM turnusol kâğıdı; '**~-pi.lot** *n.* AVIA deney pilotu; '**~-print** *n.* PHOT prova; '**~-tube** *n.* CHEM deney tüpü.

tes.ty □ ['testi], **tetch.y** □ ['tetʃi] ters, hırçın, huysuz, sinirli, alıngan.

teth.er ['teðə] **1.** *n.* hayvanı bağlama ipi; *fig.* sınır, had; *at the end of one's ~ fig.* kuvvet *veya* sabrının son haddinde; **2.** *v/t.* iple bir yere bağlamak (*at vs.*).

tet.ra.gon MATH ['tetrəgən] *n.* dörtgen, dörtkenar; **te.trag.o.nal** [_'trægənl] *adj.* dört açılı.

tet.ter MED ['tetə] *n.* temriye.

Teu.ton ['tjuːtən] *n.* Germen kabile üyesi; **Teu.ton.ic** [_'tɔnik] *adj.* Germen halkına ait.

text [tekst] *n.* metin, parça; konu; asıl kitap *veya* yazı; TELEPH kısa mesaj; **2.** *v/t.* kısa mesaj göndermek; '**~.book** *n.* ders kitabı.

tex.tile ['tekstail] **1.** *adj.* dokumacılıkla ilgili, dokuma..., tekstil...; **2.** *n.* dokuma kumaş; **~s** *pl.* mensucat.

text-mes.sage ['tekstmesidʒ] *n.* kısa mesaj.

tex.tu.al □ ['tekstjuəl] metne ait, metin...

tex.ture ['tekstʃə] *n.* doku; dokum, dokunuş; bünye, yapı; teşekkül.

than [ðæn, ðən] *cj.* -den (daha), -dan, -e göre; -den başka, -den hariç.

thane HIST [θein] *n.* krala hizmet eden asılzade.

thank [θæŋk] **1.** *v/t.* teşekkür etm. -*e*; şükretmek -*e*; ~ *you* teşekkür ederim; *no,* ~ *you* hayır, teşekkür ederim; *I will thank you for* ... için size minnettar kalırım; ~ *you for nothing iro.* yine de sağol; **2.** *n.* ~*s pl.* teşekkür, şükran, şükür; ~*s!* teşekkürler!; *give* ~*s* şükretmek; ~*s to* -*in* sayesinde; **thank.ful** □ ['_ful] minnettar, müteşekkir, memnun; '**thankless** □ nankör, iyilik bilmez; değeri bilinmemiş; **thanks.giv.ing** ['_sgiviŋ] *n.* teşekkür, minnet; şükran duası; ⨯ (*Day*) *part. Am.* şükran yortusu; '**thank.worthy** *adj.* teşekküre lâyık.

that [ðæt, ðət] **1.** *pron.* (*pl. those*) o, şu;

ki o; **so ~'s ~!** hepsi bu kadar!, işte o kadar!; **... and ~** ve bu da; **at ~** bundan başka, hem de, artık; **2.** *cj.* ki; -sin diye; -si için; böylece.

thatch [θætʃ] **1.** *n.* dam örtüsü olarak kullanılan saman *veya* saz; **2.** *v/t.* sazla kaplamak *(dam vs.).*

thaw [θɔ:] **1.** *n.* erime, çözülme; ısınma; samimileşme; **2.** *v/t. & v/i.* eri(t)mek, buzları çözülmek; ısınmak, samimileşmek, kaynaşmak, açılmak.

the [ðə; ði:] **1.** *definite article, determiner (belirtme edatı)* bu, şu, o; **2.** *adv.* **~ ... ~** ne kadar... o kadar.

the.a.tre, *Am.* **the.a.ter** ['θiətə] *n.* tiyatro (binası); amfi(teatr); alan, sahne, meydan; **'~-go.er** *n.* tiyatro meraklısı; **the.at.ric, the.at.ri.cal** □ [θi'ætrik(əl)] tiyatroya ait, tiyatro...; yapmacık, sahte *(tavır vs.);* **the'at.ri.cals** *n. pl.* amatörlerce oynanan piyesler.

thee *obs. veya lit.* [ði:] *pron.* sen(i), sana.

theft [θeft] *n.* hırsızlık.

their [ðɛə] *adj.* onların; **theirs** [_z] *pron.* onların(ki).

the.ism ['θi:izəm] *n.* Allaha inanma; tektanrıcılık, monoteizm.

them [ðem, ðəm] *pron.* onları, onlara.

theme [θi:m] *n.* konu, mevzu, tema *(a.* MUS); *rare* vazife, ödev, görev; kompozisyon ödevi; GR kök, gövde; **~ song** müzikal oyunda sık tekrarlanan müzik parçası; film müziği.

them.selves [ðəm'selvz] *pron.* kendileri (ni, -ne, -nde), bizzat.

then [ðen] **1.** *adv.* o zaman, o vakit; o zamanın; (ondan) sonra, daha sonra; demek (ki); ayrıca, bundan başka; bunun için; sonuç olarak; **by ~** o zamana kadar; **every now and ~** bir, ara sıra; **there and ~** derhal, hemen; **now ~** şu halde, öyle ise; **2.** *cj.* öyle ise, o halde, şu halde; **3.** *adj.* o zaman olan.

thence *lit.* [ðens] *adv.* oradan; bundan dolayı; o zamandan.

thence.forth ['ðens'fɔ:θ] *adv.*, **thence.forward** ['_'fɔ:wəd] o zamandan beri.

the.oc.ra.cy [θi'ɔkrəsi] *n.* teokrasi, dincirki (ülke); papazlar idaresi; **the.o.cratic** [θiə'krætik] *adj.* **(~ally)** teokratik, dinerkine dayalı.

the.o.lo.gi.an [θiə'ləudʒjən] *n.* ilahiyatçı, tanrıbilimci; **the.o.log.i.cal** □

[_'lɔdʒikəl] ilahiyata ait, tanrıbilimle ilgili; **the.ol.ogy** [θi'ɔlədʒi] *n.* ilahiyat, tanrıbilim, teoloji.

the.o.rem ['θiərəm] *n.* teorem; **the.o.ret.ic, the.o.ret.i.cal** □ [_'retik(əl)] kuramsal, nazarî; **'the.o.rist** *n.* nazariyeci, kuramcı; **'the.o.rize** *v/i.* teori kurmak, nazariye yürütmek; **'the.o.ry** *n.* teori, kuram.

the.os.o.phy [θi'ɔsəfi] *n.* teosofi.

ther.a.peu.tic [θerə'pju:tik] **1.** *adj.* tedavi edici, iyileştirici, şifa verici; **2.** *n.* **~s** *mst sg.* terapi ilmi; **'ther.a.py** *n.* tedavi, terapi; **'ther.a.pist** *n.* terapist; **mental ~** psikoterapist.

there [ðɛə] **1.** *adv.* ora(sı); orada; oraya; o noktada, o hususta, o konuda; **~ is, ~ are** [ðə'riz, ðə'rɑ:] var; **~ you are!** demedim mi!, buyurun!; **2.** *int.* gördün mü?, işte!, haydi!

there...: '**~.a.bout(s)** *adv.* o civarda, oralarda, o sularda; **~'aft.er** *adv.* (ondan) sonra; '**~'by** *adv.* o suretle, o münasebetle; **~'for** *adv.* onun için, ona; '**~.fore** *adv.* onun için, bundan dolayı, bu yüzden; **~'from** *adv.* ondan, oradan; **~'in** *adv.* orada, onda, o hususta; **~'of** *adv.* ondan; bundan dolayı; **~'on** *adv.* onun üzerine; **~'to** *adv.* ona, oraya; ilâveten, ayrıca; '**~.up'on** *adv.* onun üzerin(d)e; bundan dolayı; hemen, derhal; **~'with** *adv.* onunla; **~.with'al** *adv.* ayrıca, bundan başka.

ther.mal ['θə:məl] **1.** □ termal, kaplıca kabiliyeti; PHYS sıcağa ait; **~ value** ısı değeri; **2.** *n.* yükselen sıcak hava kitlesi; '**ther.mic** *adj.* **(~ally)** ısıya ilişkin, termik...; **therm.i.on.ic** [_'ɔnik] *adj. radyo:* **~ valve** termiyonik lamba.

ther.mo-e.lec.tric cou.ple PHYS ['θə:-məui'lektrik'kʌpl] *n.* termoelektrik kuplesi; **ther.mom.e.ter** [θə'mɔmitə] *n.* termometre, sıcakölçer; **ther.mo.met.ric, ther.mo.met.ri.cal** □ [θə:-məu'metrik(əl)] termometreye ait, termometre...; **thermo.pile** PHYS ['_.məupail] *n.* termopil; **Ther.mos** ['_.mɔs] *n. a.* **~ flask, ~ bottle** termos; **ther.mo.stat** ['_.məstæt] *n.* termostat.

the.sau.rus [θi'sɔ:rəs] *n.* kavramlar dizini; kelime kitabı; hazine, ambar.

these [ði:z] *adj. & pron.* (*pl. of* **this**) bunlar; **~ three years** bu üç yıl.

the.sis ['θi:sis] *n., pl.* **the.ses** ['_-si:z] sav, dava, önerme, iddia; tez, inceleme, araştırma.

they [ðei] *pron.* onlar.

thick [θik] **1.** □ *com.* kalın; sık (*saç vs.*), çok; kesif (*hava vs.*); koyu (*sis, çorba vs.*); boğuk, kısık (*ses*); ahmak, kalın kafalı; samimî, senli benli; aşırı; *oft.* **as ~ as thieves** F *pred.* aralarından su sızmaz; **~ with** kesif, yoğun, dolu *ile*; **that's a bit ~!** *sl.* bu kadarı da fazla!; **2.** *n.* en kalabalık yer; *bşin* kalın kısmı; *fig. bşin* en yoğun yeri *veya* zamanı; **in the ~ of** ortasında, en şiddetli anında; **'thick.en** *v/t. & v/i.* kalınlaş(tır)mak; koyulaş(tır)mak; bulan(dır)mak; sıklaş(tır)mak; yoğunlaş(tır)mak; **thick.et** ['θikit] *n.* çalılık, ağaçlık; **'thick-head.ed** *adj.* kalın kafalı; **'thick.ness** *n.* kalınlık; sıklık; MEC, COM kat, tabaka; **'thick-'set** *adj.* tıknaz; sık dikilmiş (*bitkiler*); **'thick-'skinned** *adj. fig.* vurdumduymaz, duygusuz.

thief [θiːf] *n., pl.* **thieves** [θiːvz] hırsız; **thieve** [θiːv] *v/i.* hırsızlık yapmak; *v/t.* çalmak; **'thiev.er.y** *n.* hırsızlık.

thiev.ish □ ['θiːviʃ] hırsızlığa alışmış; hırsız gibi; **'thiev.ish.ness** *n.* hırsızlık alışkanlığı.

thigh [θai] *n.* uyluk, but.

thim.ble ['θimbl] *n.* yüksük; **thim.ble-ful** ['‿ful] *n.* yüksük dolusu miktar; azıcık şey.

thin [θin] **1.** □ *com.* ince, zayıf; seyrek; az; cılız, çelimsiz, kuvvetsiz; sulu, hafif (*içki vs.*); sudan (*bahane*); soğuk (*espri*); soluk, cansız; eksik, yetersiz; **he had a ~ time** F çok eziyet çekti, berbat vakit geçirdi; **2.** *v/t. & v/i.* incel(t)mek; seyrekleş(tir)mek, seyrelmek; zayıf-la(t)mak; dağılmak (*sis*).

thine *obs. veya poet.* [ðain] *pron.* se-nin(ki).

thing [θiŋ] *n.* şey, nesne; mesele, mevzu, konu; şart, durum; olay; mahlûk, ya-ratık; **~s** *pl.* giyecekler, eşya; **such a ~** böyle bir şey; **the ~** F doğru (*veya* mo-da, uygun, gerekli) olan şey; **the ~ is** mesele şu ki, önemli olan; **know a ~ or two** F çok iyi bilmek; **of all ~s** her şeyden evvel, evvelemirde; **~s are go-ing better** durum iyiye gidiyor; **I don't feel quite the ~** F biraz keyifsizim.

thing.um(.a).bob F ['θiŋəm(i)bɔb] *n.*, **thingum.my** F ['‿əmi] şey, zımbırtı, zırıltı.

think [θiŋk] (*irr.*) *v/i.* düşünmek (**of**, **about** *-i*; **to** *-inf. ...meyi*); düşünüp taşınmak (**about**, **over** *üzerinde*); hatırlamak, ileri sürmek, tavsiye etm. (**of** *-i*); *v/t.* düşünmek; zannetmek, san-

mak; niyet etm., tasarlamak; hatırla-mak; tasavvur etm., farz etm.; addet-mek; ummak; **~ much** *etc.* **of** çok kıymet vermek *-e*, değer vermek *-e*, sevmek *-i*; **~ out** düşünüp çıkarmak; ta-sarlamak; **~ s.th.** **over** *-in* üzerinde düşünmek; **'think.a.ble** *adj.* düşünüle-bilir, akla uygun; **'think.er** *n.* düşünür, filozof; **'think.ing** *adj.* düşünceli; akıllı; mantıklı...

thin.ness ['θinnis] *n.* incelik; zayıflık.

third [θəːd] **1.** *adj.* üçüncü; **~ degree** işkence ile yapılan sorgu; **2.** *n.* üçte bir; MUS üçlü; **'third.ly** *adv.* üçüncü ola-rak; **'third-'rate** *adj.* kalitesiz, adi.

thirst [θəːst] **1.** *n.* susuzluk; *fig.* özlem, tutku; **2.** *v/i.* susamak (**for, after** *-e*); **'thirst.y** □ susuz, susamış; *fig.* çok is-tekli; F kurak (*toprak vs.*).

thir.teen ['θəː'tiːn] *adj. & n.* on üç (sayı sı): **'thir'teenth** [-θ] **1.** *adj.* on üçüncü; **2.** *n.* on üçte bir; **thir.ti.eth** ['θəːtiiθ] **1.** *adj.* otuzuncu; **2.** *n.* otuzda bir; **'thir.ty** *adj. & n.* otuz (sayısı); **the thirties** *pl.* 30-39 yaşları arası.

this [ðis] *adj. & pron.* (*pl.* **these**) bu; COM cari; **in ~ country** bu ülkede; **~ morning** bu sabah; **~ day week** haftaya bugün.

this.tle BOT ['θisl] *n.* devedikeni; **'~-down** *n.* diken pamuğu.

thith.er(.ward) *obs. veya poet.* ['ðið-ə(wəd)] *adv.* oraya; o yöne.

tho' [ðəu] = **though.**

thole NAUT [θəul] *n.* kürek ıskarmozu; **'~-pin** *n. fig.* eksen.

thong [θɔŋ] *n.* sırım.

tho.rax ANAT ['θɔːræks] *n.* göğüs, to-raks.

thorn BOT [θɔːn] *n.* diken; *fig.* üzüntü, cefa; **'thorn.y** *adj.* dikenli; *fig.* sıkıntılı, cefalı.

thor.ough □ ['θʌrə] tam, mükemmel; çok dikkatli, titiz; baştan başa; ayrıntılı; **~ly** tamamen, adamakıllı; **'~-bred 1.** *adj.* saf kan; soylu; tam...; **2.** *n.* saf kan hayvan; *fig.* kültürlü kim-se; **'~-fare** *n.* cadde, yol, geçit; **'~-go.ing** *adj.* tam, adamakıllı; **'thor.ough.ness** *n.* kusursuzluk; dikkatlilik; **'thor-ough.paced** *adj.* her türlü yürüyüşe alışkın (*at*); tam, mükemmel.

those [ðəuz] *adj. & pron.* (*pl. of* **that 1.**) şunlar; onlar; **are ~ your parents?** şun-lar senin ebeveynin mi?

thou *obs. İncil, poet.* [ðau] *pron.* sen.

though [ðəu] *cj.* gerçi, her ne kadar, ise

de; -diği halde, olsa da; *as* ~ -miş gibi, sanki, güya.

thought [θɔːt] **1.** *pret. & p.p. of think*; **2.** *n.* düşünme; düşünce, fikir, görüş, kanaat; düşünce tarzı; endişe; niyet; ümit; *give* ~ *to* üzerinde enine boyuna düşünmek; *on second* ~*s* yeniden düşününce; *take* ~ *for -i* düşünmek, tartmak.

thought.ful □ ['θɔːtful] dalgın, düşünceli (*of*); saygılı, nazik (*of*); dikkatli; '**thoughtful.ness** *n.* düşüncelilik; saygı.

thought.less □ ['θɔːtlis] düşüncesiz (*of*), saygısız; dikkatsiz, pervasız; bencil; '**thought.less.ness** *n.* düşüncesizlik; dikkatsizlik.

thought-read.ing ['θɔːtriːdiŋ] *n.* düşünceleri okuma.

thou.sand ['θauzənd] **1.** *adj.* bin; **2.** *n.* bin sayısı; **thou.sandth** ['-zəntθ] **1.** *adj.* bininci; **2.** *n.* binde bir.

Thra.cian ['θreiʃjən] **1.** *n.* Trakyalı; **2.** *adj.* Trakya'ya özgü.

thral(l).dom ['θrɔːldəm] *n.* kölelik, esaret.

thrall [θrɔːl] *n.* esir, köle(lik), esaret.

thrash [θræʃ] *v/t.* dövmek, dayak atmak; kamçılamak, kırbaçlamak; F yenmek; tartışarak halletmek (*sorun*); tartışarak varmak (*karara, çözüme*); yapmak (*plan vs.*); *v/i. b-ni* pataklamak; kıvranmak (*acıdan vs.*); NAUT denize karşı seyretmek; = *thresh*; '**thrash.er** = *thresher*; '**thrashing** *n.* dayak, kötek; yenilgi; = *threshing*.

thread [θred] **1.** *n.* iplik, tire; tel; lif; ince çizgi; çok ince *bş*; MEC yiv; sıra, silsile; **2.** *v/t. -den* iplik geçirmek; ipliğe dizmek; yol bulup geçmek; arasına serpmek; takmak (*film vs.*); '~**.bare** *adj.* eskimiş, yıpranmış, pejmürde (*giyecek*); *fig.* bayatlamış (*espri vs.*); '**thread.y** *adj.* iplik gibi; tel tel.

threat [θret] *n.* tehdit, gözdağı; tehlike; '**threat.en** *v/t.* tehdit etm., gözdağı vermek, korkutmak; yıldırmak; *v/i.* kötü *bşe* işaret olm.; '**threat.en.ing** *adj.* tehdit edici; endişe verici.

three [θriː] **1.** *adj.* üç; **2.** *n.* üç rakamı; '~**'col.our** *adj.* üç renkli...; '~**.fold** *adv.* üç misli; ~**.pence** ['θrepəns] *n.* üç peni; '~**.pen.ny** *adj.* üç penilik...; *fig.* değersiz; ~**phase cur.rent** ELECT ['θriːfeiz'kʌrənt] *n.* trifaz akım; '~**'score** *adj. & n.* altmış (sayısı).

thresh [θreʃ] *v/t.* dövmek (*harman*); =

thrash; ~ *out fig.* inceden inceye görüşmek (*iş, mesele*).

thresh.er ['θreʃə] *n.* harman dövme makinesi; harmancı; sapanbalığı.

thresh.ing ['θreʃiŋ] *n.* harman dövme; '~**floor** *n.* harman yeri; '~**ma.chine** *n.* harman dövme makinesi.

thresh.old ['θreʃhəuld] *n.* eşik; *fig.* başlangıç.

threw [θruː] *pret. of throw* 1.

thrice *rare* [θrais] *adv.* üç kez, üç kere.

thrift, thrift.i.ness [θrift, '-inis] *n.* idare, tutum, tasarruf, ekonomi; verimlilik; '**thrift.less** □ müsrif, idaresiz, tutumsuz, savurgan; '**thrift.y** □ tutumlu, idareli; *poet.* verimli, başarılı, hızla büyüyen.

thrill [θril] **1.** *v/t. & v/i.* (heyecanla) titremek (*with ile*); heyecanlan(dır)mak; tesir etm., etkile(n)mek; **2.** *n.* titreme, titreşim; heyecan; '**thrill.er** *n.* F heyecanlı kitap *veya* piyes.

thrive [θraiv] (*irr.*) *v/i.* iyi gitmek, gelişmek, başarılı olm.; *fig.* zenginleşmek, refaha ermek; büyümek; **thriv.en** ['θrivn] *p.p. of thrive*; **thriv.ing** □ ['θraiviŋ] başarılı, gelişen, büyüyen.

thro' [θruː] *abbr. of through.*

throat [θrəut] *n. com.* boğaz, gırtlak; *clear one's* ~ hafifçe öksürmek, «öhö öhö» demek; '**throat.y** □ gırtlaktan çıkan (*ses*).

throb [θrɔb] **1.** *v/i.* vurmak, çarpmak, atmak (*nabız, kalp*); zonklamak (*baş*); titreşmek; **2.** *n.* nabız artması, kalp çarpması; çarpıntı; titreşme.

throe [θrəu] *n.* sancı, ağrı; elem, dert; ~*s pl.* doğum *veya* ölüm sancısı.

throm.bo.sis MED [θrɔm'bəusis] *n.* tromboz.

throne [θrəun] **1.** *n.* that; hâkimiyet, saltanat; kral, hükümdar; **2.** *v/t. & v/i.* tahta geç(ir)mek.

throng [θrɔŋ] **1.** *n.* kalabalık, izdiham; **2.** *v/t.* üşüşmek *-e*; *v/i.* toplanmak, kalabalık etm.

thros.tle ORN ['θrɔsl] *n.* ardıçkuşu.

throt.tle ['θrɔtl] **1.** *v/t.* boğmak; bastırmak; MEC kısmak; **2.** *n.* = '~**valve** MEC kısma valfı, kelebek.

through [θruː] **1.** *prp.* içinden, bir yandan diğer yana, bir başından diğer başına; başından sonuna kadar; sayesinde; -den (geçerek); her tarafında; her yerin(d)e; -den dolayı, yüzünden; **2.** *adv.* (başından) sonuna kadar; baştan başa; tamamen; **3.** *adj.* engelsiz, direkt (*yol*); aktarmasız (*tren*), ekspres; işi bitik; bitirmiş; ~'out **1.** *prp.* baştan başa, boyunca, -*in* her tarafında, her hususta; ~ **the year** yıl boyunca; **2.** *adv.* baştan başa, baştan aşağı.

throve [θrəuv] *pret. of* **thrive**.

throw [θrəu] **1.** (*irr.*) *v/t. com,* atmak, fırlatmak; üstünden atmak (*at*); kullanmak (*güç, nüfuz*); inşa etm., yapmak; şekillendirmek (*çömlek*); MEC büküp ibrişim yapmak (*ipek*); atmak, savurmak (*yumruk*); atmak (*zar*); *Am.* F yere sermek, düşürmek (*rakibini*); bırakmak, teı ketmek; giyivermek (*elbise*); meydana getirmek; şike yaparak kaybetmek (*oyun*); vermek (*parti*); çekmek (*ziyafet*); (*yılan*) değiştirmek (*deri*); yavrulamak (*hayvan*); sarsmak, perişan etm.; ~ *at* fırlatmak, savurmak -*e*; dikkatini vermek -*e*; ~ *away* kaçırmak (*fırsat*); ziyan etm., çarçur etm.; vaz geçmek; atmak; ~ *in* fazladan eklemek, parasız olarak ilâve etm.; birbirine geçirmek (*dişli*); katmak (*söze*); oyuna dahil etm. (*top*); ~ *off* çıkarmak, üstünden atmak; -*den* kurtulmak; atlatmak; başka tarafa saptu mak, yöneltmek; saçmak, yaymak; çabucak yapıvermek; ~ *out* söylemek (*söz*); savurmak (*tehdit*); *part.* PARL reddetmek, kabul etmemek (*tasarı*); inşa etm., yapmak; şaşırtmak, kafasını karıştırmak; dışarı atmak; işten kovmak; geçmek, geride bırakmak; yaymak, saçmak (*ışık, koku vs.*); altüst etm. (*plan*); MEC ayırmak, debreye etm. (*motor*); ~ *over* terketmek, (yüzüstü) bırakmak, vaz geçmek; ~ *up* yukarı atmak; kusmak; -*den* istifa etm., bırakmak (*işini*); ortaya çıkarmak; acele inşa etm.; yığıvermek; *s.* **sponge**; *v/i.* fırlatıp atmak, savurmak; ~ *off* ava başlamak; **2.** *n.* atış, atma; atım; MEC sia uzunluğu; risk, tehlike; örtü; atkı, eşarp; birim; '~*back n. part.* BIOL atavizm, atacılık; **thrown** [θrəun] *p.p. of* **throw**; 'throw- -'off *n.* ava başlama; başlangıç.

thru *Am.* [θru:] = **through**.

thrum[1] ORN [θrʌm] *n.* dokumacılık: kırpıntı; iplik saçağı *veya* püskülü.

thrum[2] [~] *v/t.* tıngırdatmak (*çalgı*); monoton bir şekilde söylemek.

thrush[1] ORN [θrʌʃ] *n.* ardıçkuşu.

thrush[2] [~] *n.* MED pamukçuk.

thrust [θrʌst] **1.** *n.* itme, itiş, dürtme; hamle; MIL taarruz; hücum; *fig.* çıkışma, sert çıkma; MEC itme kuvveti;

2. (*irr.*) *v/t.* itmek, dürtmek; saplamak (*bıçak, süngü vs.*); ite kaka sürmek; zorla getirmek (*bir mevkiye*); yüklemek (*sorumluluk vs.*); ~ *o.s.* **into** *k-ni* zorla kabul ettirmek -*e*, davetsiz olarak girmek -*e*; ~ *out* savurmak; uzatmak (*dil*); ~ *upon s.o. b-ne* zorla kabul ettirmek; *v/i.* saldırmak (*at* -*e*).

thud [θʌd] **1.** *v/i.* güm diye ses çıkarmak; **2.** *n.* gümbürtü.

thug [θʌg] *n.* katil, cani, eşkiya.

thumb [θʌm] **1.** *n.* başparmak; **Tom** ♎ parmak çocuk; **2.** *vb.* çevirmek (*sayfa*); başparmakla tuta tuta aşındırmak *veya* kirletmek (*sayfa*); ~ **one's nose at** *s.o. b-ne* nanik yapmak; ~ *a lift* otostop yapmak; '~-print *n.* parmak izi; '~screw *n.* parmakla döndürülen vida; MEC kelebek başlı civata; '~-stall *n.* başparmak kılıfı; '~tack *n. Am.* pünez, raptiye.

thump [θʌmp] **1.** *n.* vuruş; yumruk (sesi), darbe (sesi); güm; ağır düşüş (sesi); **2.** *v/t.* güm güm vurmak -*e*; yumruklamak, dövmek; *v/i.* küt küt atmak (*kalp*); gümbürdemek; 'thump.er *sl.* vurucu, katil; 'thump.ing *adj. sl.* iri, kocaman.

thun.der ['θʌndə] **1.** *n.* gök gürlemesi; *fig. oft.* ~*s pl.* gürültü, gümbürtü, tufan (*alkış vs.*); **2.** *v/i.* gürlemek, gümbürdemek; *v/t.* şiddetle söylemek; '~.bolt *n.* yıldırım; *fig.* beklenmedik olay; '~.clap *n.* gök gürlemesi; *fig.* kötü olay *veya* haber; '~.cloud *n.* fırtına bulutu. **thun.der...:** '~.head *n.* fırtına bulutu (*a. fig.*); 'thun.der.ing *adj. sl.* (kos)kocaman, muazzam; 'thun.der.ous □ *fig.* gürleyen; ~ **applause** alkış tufanı; 'thun.der.storm *n.* gök gürültülü yağmur fırtınası; 'thunder.struck *adj.* hayrete düşmüş, yıldırımla vurulmuşa dönmüş; 'thun.der.y *adj.* gök gürültülü (*hava*).

Thurs.day ['θə:zdi] *n.* perşembe.

thus [ðʌs] *adv.* böyle(ce), bu suretle, bunun için, bu nedenle, nitekim.

thwack [θwæk] = **whack**.

thwart [θwɔ:t] **1.** *v/t.* bozmak (*işini vs.*), önlemek, engellemek; hüsrana uğratmak; **2.** *n.* kürekçinin oturduğu tahta.

thy *Kutsal Kitap, poet.* [ðai] *adj.* senin.

thyme BOT [taim] *n.* kekik.

thy.roid ANAT ['θairɔid] **1.** *adj.* kalkansı... tiroid...; ~ **extract** kalkanbezi özü; **gland** = **2.** *n.* tiroid, kalkanbezi.

thy.self *Kutsal Kitap, poet.* [ðai'self]

pron. bizzat kendin.

ti.ar.a [ti'ɑːrə] *n.* papanın üç katlı tacı; taç.

tib.i.a ANAT ['tibiə] *n.* kaval kemiği; incik kemiği.

tic MED [tik] *n.* tik.

tick¹ ZOO [-] *n.* kene, sakırga.

tick² [-] *n.* kılıf.

tick³ F [-]: *on* ~ veresiye.

tick⁴ [-] **1.** *n.* tıkırtı; saatin tik tak sesi; doğru işareti (AGR); F an; *to the* ~ saatin çalması ile; **2.** *v/i.* tıkırdamak, tıklamak, tik tak etm. (*saat*); ~ *over* MOT rölantide çalışmak; *v/t.* işaret koymak, çetele çekmek; ~ *off* işaret koymak, işaretleyerek saymak; *sl.* azarlamak, haşlamak, paylamak.

tick.er ['tikə] *n.* özellikle borsa fiyatlarını şeride kaydeden alet; F saat; *sl.* kalp; *sl.* yürek, cesaret; '~-tape *n.* F eğlencelerde fırlatılan renkli kâğıt şerit.

tick.et ['tikit] **1.** *n.* bilet; etiket; POL aday listesi; (*trafik*) para cezası, karakol davetiyesi; ehliyet (kâğıdı); *the* ~ F doğru olan, münasip şey; ~ *of leave* JUR tahliye izni; **2.** *v/t.* etiketlemek; '~-col.lec.tor *n.* biletçi, kondüktör; '~-in.spec.tor *n.* bilet kontrolörü; '~-ma.chine *n.* bilet makinesi; '~-of.fice, '~-win.dow *n. part. Am.* bilet gişesi; '~-punch *n.* bilet zımbası.

tick.ing ['tikiŋ] *n.* kılıflık kumaş.

tick.le ['tikl] *v/t. & v/i.* gıdıkla(n)mak; *fig.* eğlendirmek; '**tick.ler** *n.* güç durum; *a.* ~ *coil* reaksiyon bobini; '**tick.lish** □ gıdıklanır; nazik, tehlikeli (*durum, sorun vs.*).

tid.al □ ['taidl] gelgite bağlı; ~ *wave* met dalgası; *fig.* galeyan.

tid.bit ['tidbit] = *titbit*.

tid.dly-winks ['tidliwiŋks] *n.* parmak gücüyle disk atma oyunu.

tide [taid] **1.** *n.* gelgit, meddücezir, (*low* ~) met ve (*high* ~) cezir; *fig.* akış, cereyan, eğilim, meyil; mevsim; zaman, vakit; *turn of the* ~ *fig.* durumun lehe dönmesi, şansın dönmesi; **2.** *v/t. & v/i.* akıntı ile yüz(dür)mek; ~ *over* *fig.* çıkarmak (*kışı vs.*), atlatmak (*krizi*), üstesinden gelmek.

ti.di.ness ['taidinis] *n.* düzen, tertip, intizam.

ti.dings ['taidiŋz] *n. pl. veya sg.* haber, havadis.

ti.dy ['taidi] **1.** *adj.* temiz, düzenli, tertipli, derli toplu, muntazam; F olduk-

ça, epey (*para*); **2.** *n.* kap; **3.** *vb. a.* ~ *up* düzeltmek, derleyip toplamak, çekidüzen vermek.

tie [tai] **1.** *n.* bağ (*a. fig.*), düğüm; fiyonk; kravat, boyunbağı; bağlantı; MUS bağlı nota işareti; ARCH kiriş, lata; *fig.* ayak bağı; *spor.* beraberlik, berabere kalma; PARL oy eşitliği; RAIL *Am.* travers; **2.** *v/t. com.* bağlamak (*a.* MUS), raptetmek; düğümlemek; ARCH tespit etm.; ~ *down fig.* bağlamak (*to -e*); ~ *up* bağlamak (*para vs.*); şarta bağlamak; *v/i. spor.* berabere kalmak (*with ile*).

tier [tiə] *n.* THEAT sıra, kat, dizi.

tierce [tiəs] *n.* FENC bir vaziyet şekli; *iskambil:* üçlü seri.

tie-up ['taiʌp] *n.* bağ(lantı); COM ortaklık; *part. Am.* işin durması, grev; birleşme; tıkanıklık (*trafik*); kesatlık, durgunluk (*iş*); ahır.

tiff F [tif] **1.** *n.* münakaşa, hafif tartışma; **2.** *v/i.* münakaşa etm., gücenmek, darılmak.

tif.fin ['tifin] *n.* hafif öğle yemeği.

ti.ger ['taigə] *n.* kaplan; *Am.* F kana susamış adam; '**ti.ger.ish** □ *fig.* vahşî, yırtıcı; kaplan gibi.

tight □ [tait] sıkı, gergin; su geçirmez, akmaz, sızmaz; zor, müşkül; dar, sıkışık; cimri, eli sıkı; tıkalı; ucu ucuna; kesat; F sarhoş, küfelik; *be in a* ~ *place veya corner* F zor *veya* tehlikeli durumda olm.; *hold* ~ sıkı tut(un)mak; *it is a* ~ *fit* dar, sıkı; '**tight.en** *v/t. & v/i. a.* ~ *up* sıkış(tır)mak; ger(ginleş)-mek; '~-'fisted *adj.* eli sıkı, cimri; '~-laced *adj.* sofu; '~-lipped *adj.* ağzı sıkı, ağzı pek; '**tight.ness** *n.* sıkılık, gerginlik; '**tight-rope** *n.* sıkı gerilmiş ip; **tights** [-s] *n. pl.* sıkı giysi; külotlu çorap; '**tight.wad** *n. sl.* cimri, pinti kimse.

ti.gress ['taigris] *n.* dişi kaplan.

tile [tail] **1.** *n.* kiremit; tuğla; çini; *sl.* silindir şapka; *he has a* ~ *loose sl.* kaçık, bir tahtası noksan; **2.** *v/t.* kiremit kaplamak *-e*; '~-lay.er, '**til.er** *n.* kiremitçi.

till¹ [til] *n.* para çekmecesi, kasa.

till² [-] *prp. & cj.* -e kadar, -e değin, -e gelinceye kadar, zamana kadar.

till³ AGR [-] *v/t.* işlemek (*toprak*); '**till.age** *n.* toprağı işleme, çiftçilik, ziraat; işlenmiş toprak.

till.er¹ ['tilə] *n.* çiftçi.

till.er² NAUT [-] *n.* dümen yekesi.

tilt¹ [tilt] *n.* tente.

tilt² [-] **1.** *n.* eğim, meyil, eğiklik; eğilme;

fig. çekişme, kavga, atışma; hız; at üstünde yapılan mızrak oyunu; **on the ~** meyilli, eğri, devrilmekte; **(at) full ~** son süratle, bütün hızı ile; **have a ~ at s.o.** *b-ne* saldırmak, itiraz etm.; **2.** *v/t. & v/i.* eğ(il)mek, devirmek; devrilmek; at üzerinde mızrakla saldırmak **(at -e)**; **~ against** koşarken çarpmak *e*; **'tilt.ing** *adj.* eğik..., meyilli...

tilth [tilθ] *n.* ziraat, çiftçilik, tarım; işlenmiş toprak.

tim.bal MUS ['timbəl] *n.* dümbelek.

tim.ber ['timbə] **1.** *n.* kereste(lik orman); NAUT gemi kaburgası (*veya* postası); **2.** *v/t.* kereste ile kaplamak *veya* desteklemek; **~ed** kerestelik, ağaçlık; ahşap (*ev*); **'~-line** *n.* orman sınırı; **'~-work** *n.* ahşap yapı; **'~-yard** *n.* kereste deposu.

time [taim] **1.** *n.* vakit, zaman; süre, müddet; kere, defa, kez; MUS tempo; saat, dakika; çağ, devir, devre; vade, mühlet; ecel; kat, misil; **~!** PARL paydos!; **~ and again** tekrar tekrar, defalarca; **at ~s** ara sıra, bazen, zaman zaman; **at a ~, at the same ~** aynı zamanda; yine de, bununla birlikte; **at one ~** bir zamanlar, vaktiyle, eskiden; **before one's ~** vakitsiz; **behind one's ~** gecikmiş, geç kalmış; **behind the ~s** eski kafalı, zamana ayak uyduramayan; çok eski; **by that ~** o zamana kadar; **do ~** F hapse girmek; **for the ~ being** şimdilik; **have a good ~** iyi vakit geçirmek, eğlenmek; **in (good)~** tam zamanında, vaktinde; **in no ~** bir an evvel; **in a month's ~** bir ay sonra; *s.* **mean²** 1; **on ~** tam zamanında, vaktinde; **out of ~** temposuz; **beat the ~** tempo tutmak; *s.* **keep**; **2.** *v/t.* ayarlamak; uydurmak; ölçmek; *a.* **take the ~ of** saat tutmak *için*; **the train is ~d to leave at 7** tren saat 7'de hareket edecektir; *v/i.* MUS tempo tutmak **(to -e)**; **'~-bar.gain** *n.* vadeli alışveriş, alivre satış; **'~-ex.po.sure** *n.* PHOT poz; uzun pozlu resim; **'~-hono(u)red** *adj.* eskiliğinden dolayı saygı duyulan; **'~.keep.er** *n.* çalışma saatlerini tutan kimse *veya* gösterge; saat hakemi; *part.* saat, kronometre; **'~-lag** *n.* ara; **'~-'lim.it** *n.* sınırlı zaman; zaman sınırı; **'time.ly** *adj.* yerinde olan, uygun; vakitli; **'time.piece** *n.* saat, kronometre; **'timer** *n.* *spor:* kronometre (tutan kimse), saat hakemi; PHOT deklanşör.

time...: **'~-serv.er** ['taimsə:və] *n.* ey-

yamcı, zaman adamı, çıkarcı; **'~-sheet** *n.* yoklama cetveli; **'~-sig.nal** *n. part.* *radyo:* saat ayarı; **'~-ta.ble** *n.* tarife; *okul:* ders programı.

tim.id □ ['timid] sıkılgan, ürkek, çekingen, mahçup, utangaç; **ti'mid.i.ty** *n.* utangaçlık, çekingenlik.

tim.ing ['taimiŋ] *n.* ayarlama, zamanlama.

tim.or.ous □ ['timərəs] = **timid**.

tin [tin] **1.** *n.* teneke (kutu); kalay; *sl.* mangır, mangiz; **2.** *adj.* tenekeden yapılmış, teneke...; kalay...; **~ solder** kalay lehimi; **3.** *v/t.* kalaylamak; teneke kutulara doldurmak; **~ned meat** konserve et.

tinc.ture ['tiŋktʃə] **1.** *n.* hafif renk; *fig.* görünüş, sahte tavır; PHARM ispirto eriyiği, ruh, mahlul; **2.** *v/t.* hafifçe boyamak; içine katmak; hafifçe etkilemek.

tin.der ['tində] *n.* kav.

tine [tain] *n.* çatal dişi; geyik boynuzunun çatalı.

tin.foil ['tin'fɔil] *n.* stanyol, kalay yaprağı.

ting F [tiŋ] = **tinkle**.

tinge [tindʒ] **1.** *n.* hafif renk, boya; *fig.* az miktar, nebze, cüz; iz, belirti; **2.** *v/t.* hafifçe boyamak; içine katmak; *fig.* hafifçe etkilemek.

tin.gle ['tiŋgl] *v/i.* sızlamak; karıncalanmak; çınlamak.

tin...: **~god** F put, sanem; **~ hat** *sl.* miğfer, çelik asker başlığı.

tink.er ['tiŋkə] **1.** *n.* tenekeci; lehimci; tamirci(lik); **2.** *v/t.* tamir etm.; *v/i.* üstünkörü çalışmak **(at** *üzerinde*); **~ up** amatörce çalışmak; kabaca tamir etm.

tin.kle ['tiŋkl] **1.** *v/t. & v/i.* çıngırda(t)-mak, çınlamak; **2.** *n.* çıngırtı.

tin.man ['tinmən] *n.* tenekeci; **'tin.ny** *adj.* teneke gibi, teneke sesli; teneke tadı veren; **'tin-o.pen.er** *n.* konserve açacağı; **'tin.plate** *n.* saç, demir levha.

tin.sel ['tinsl] **1.** *n.* gelin teli; *fig.* aldatıcı parlaklık, cicili bicili şey; **2.** *adj.* gösterişli fakat değersiz, cicili bicili...; aslı astarı olmayan; **3.** *v/t.* gelin teli ile süslemek; cicili bicili yapmak.

tint [tint] **1.** *n.* hafif renk; renk tonu; **2.** *v/t.* hafifçe boyamak, hafif renk vermek; **~ed paper** renkli kâğıt.

tin.tin.nab.u.la.tion ['tintinæbju'leiʃən] *n.* çıngırdama; çan çalınması; çan sesi.

tin.ware ['tinwɛə] *n.* teneke kaplar.

ti.ny □ ['taini] küçücük, ufacık, minicik, ufak tefek.

tip [tip] **1.** *n.* uç, burun; tepe, doruk; ağızlık; bahşiş, sadaka; tavsiye; tiyo; hafif vuruş; çöplük (*a. fig.*); *give* **s.th. a.** ~ *bşi* devirmek; **2.** *v/t. & v/i.* eğ(il)mek, bir yana yat(ır)mak; devirmek; devrilmek; ucuna *bş* takmak; dökmek, boşaltmak; hafifçe vurmak; bahşiş vermek *-e*; *a.* ~ *off* imada bulunmak *-e*; sır vermek *-e*; uyarmak *-i*; '~-**cart** *n.* atlı yük arabası; '~-**off** *n.* ima, ikaz, ihtar, uyarı.

tip.pet ['tipit] *n.* boyun atkısı.

tip.ple ['tipl] **1.** *vb.* içkiye düşkün olm.; **2.** *n.* içki; '**tip.pler** *n.* akşamcı, ayyaş.

tip.si.ness ['tipsinis] *n.* çakırkeyflik.

tip.staff ['tipstɑːf] *n.* şerif vekili; mübaşir, kavas.

tip.ster ['tipstə] *n.* yarış öncesi gizli bilgi veren kimse, tiyocu.

tip.sy ['tipsi] *adj.* çakırkeyf.

tip.toe ['tiptəu] **1.** *v/i.* ayaklarının ucuna basa basa yürümek; **2.** *n. on* ~ ayaklarının ucuna basarak.

tip.top F ['tip'tɔp] **1.** *n.* en iyi kalite; **2.** *adj.* birinci sınıf, en âlâ.

tip-up seat THEAT ['tipʌp'siːt] *n.* açılır kapanır koltuk.

ti.rade [tai'reid] *n.* tirad; azarlayıcı sert söz.

tire[1] ['taiə] *n.* dış lastik.

tire[2] [-] *v/t. & v/i.* yor(ul)mak; usan(dır)mak, bık(tır)mak (*of -den*).

tired ['taiəd] yorgun, bitkin, bitap; usanmış, bıkmış (*of -den*); '**tired.ness** *n.* yorgunluk.

tire.less □ ['taiəlis] dur durak bilmez, yorulmak bilmez, yorulmaz; bitmez tükenmez.

tire.some □ ['taiəsəm] yorucu, sıkıcı.

ti.ro ['taiərəu] *n.* acemi (*veya* yeni başlayan) kimse.

'**tis** [tiz] = *it is.*

tis.sue ['tiʃuː] *n.* doku; (ince tül) kumaş; kâğıt mendil; ince kâğıt; *fig.* ağ, şebeke; seri, silsile; COM dokuma; '~-'**pa.per** *n.* ince (ipek) kâğıt.

tit[1] [tit] *n.*: ~ *for tat* yumruğa yumruk; *fig.* kısasa kısas.

tit[2] *Am.* [-] = *teat*.

tit[3] ORN [-] *n.* baştankara.

Ti.tan ['taitən] *n.* Titan; '**Ti.tan.ess** *n.* süper güçleri olan kadın; **ti.ta.nic** [-'tænik] *adj.* (~*ally*) muazzam, koskocaman.

ti.ta.ni.um CHEM [tai'teinjəm] *n.* titan.

tit.bit ['titbit] *n.* lezzetli lokma, cazip kısım.

tithe[taið] *n.* ondalık, öşür; aşar vergisi; *mst fig.* onda bir.

tit.il.late ['titileit] *v/t.* gıcıklamak, gıdıklamak; **tit.il'la.tion** *n.* gıdıkla(n)-ma, gıcıkla(n)ma.

tit.i.vate F ['titiveit] *v/t. & v/i.* süsle(n)-mek, şıklaş(tır)mak.

ti.tle ['taitl] **1.** *n.* başlık; ünvan, isim, lakap; hak (*to -e*); senet, tapu; **2.** *v/t.* lakap *veya* ünvan vermek; isimlendirmek; ~*d part.* asil, asılzade; '~-**deed** *n.* JUR tapu senedi; '~-**hold.er** *n. part. spor.* ünvan sahibi kimse; '~-**page** *n.* baş sayfa; '~-**role** *n.* başrol.

tit.mouse ORN ['titmaus] *n., pl.* **tit.mice** ['-mais] baştankara.

ti.trate CHEM ['titreit] *vb.* titre etm., derecesini saptamak; **ti'tra.tion** *n.* titre, titrasyon.

tit.ter ['titə] **1.** *v/i.* kıkır kıkır gülmek, kıkırdamak; **2.** *n.* kıkırdama.

tit.tle ['titl] *n.* nokta; *fig.* zerre, cüz, nebze; '~-**tat.tle** **1.** *n.* dedikodu; **2.** *v/i.* dedikodu yapmak.

tit.u.lar □ ['titjulə] hak olarak elde tutulan; ismi var cismi yok; lakaba ait; ünvandan dolayı olan.

to [tuː; tə] **1.** *particle* -mek (için), -mak (için); **2.** *prp.* -e -a, -ye, -ya; *-e* doğru (*a. adv.*), yönüne doğru, tarafına; -e kadar, -e değin; ile; -e nispetle, -e nazaran, -e göre; -e dair, hakkında; için, maksadıyla; ~ *me*, ~ *you* bana, sana; *he gave it* ~ *his friend* onu arkadaşına verdi; *it happened* ~ *me* başıma geldi; *alive* ~ *s.th. bşin* farkında, bilincinde; *cousin* ~ *-in* kuzeni; *heir* ~ *-in* vârisi, mirasçısı; *secretary* ~ *-in* sekreteri; *I weep* ~ *think of it* onu düşününce ağlarım; *here's* ~ *you!* şerefinize!, sıhhatinize!; ~ *and fro* öteye beriye, öne ve arkaya.

toad ZOO [təud] *n.* kara kurbağa; '~-**stool** *n.* zehirli (*veya* şapkalı) mantar.

toad.y ['təudi] **1.** *n.* dalkavuk, yağcı; **2.** *v/i.* dalkavukluk etm., yağ çekmek, yaltaklanmak (*to -e*); '**toad.y.ism** *n.* dalkavukluk, yağcılık.

toast [təust] **1.** *n.* kızartılmış ekmek; sıhhatine içme; sıhhatine içilen kimse; **2.** *v/t. & v/i.* kızar(t)mak (*ekmek*); *fig.* ateşe tutup ısıtmak; çok ısınmak, yanmak; sıhhatine içmek *-in*; '**toast.er** ekmek kızartma makinesi.

to.bac.co [tə'bækəu] *n.* tütün; **to'bac-conist** [_kənist] *n.* tütüncü.

to.bog.gan [tə'bɔgən] **1.** *n.* kızak; **2.** *v/i.* kızakla kaymak.

toc.sin ['tɔksin] *n.* alarm zili; *fig.* tehlike işareti.

to.day [tə'dei] *n.* & *adv.* bugün; günümüz; bu günlerde, şimdi.

tod.dle ['tɔdl] *v/i.* sendeleyerek yürümek, tıpış tıpış yürümek; gitmek; **'tod.dler** *n.* yeni yürümeye başlayan çocuk.

tod.dy ['tɔdi] *n.* sıcak su ile karıştırılmış içki; bazı hurma ağaçlarından çıkarılan öz.

to-do F [tə'du:] *n.* gürültü, patırtı, telâş, kıyamet.

toe [təu] **1.** *n.* ayak parmağı; ayak ucu; uç; ayakkabı *veya* çorap burnu; *from top to* ~ tepeden tırnağa; *on one's* ~*s fig.* uyanık, tetikte, dikkatli; **2.** *v/t.* ayak parmakları ile vurmak, dokunmak *veya* ulaşmak; ~ *the line spor:* başlama çizgisinde dizilmek; POL söyleneni yapmak, verilen emirlere uymak.

toed [təud] *adj.* … parmaklı.

toff P [tɔf] *n.* iyi giyimli, şık kimse.

tof.fee, tof.fy ['tɔfi] *n.* bonbon, şekerleme.

tog F [tɔg] **1.** *v/t.* giydirmek; **2.** *s.* **togs**.

to.ga ['təugə] *n.* toga.

to.geth.er [tə'geðə] *adv.* beraber(ce), birlikte, hep bir yerde, hep bir arada; aralıksız, durmadan, devamlı.

tog.gle NAUT & MEC ['tɔgl] **1.** *n.* kasa çeliği; **2.** *v/t.* kasa çeliği ile bağlamak.

togs F [tɔgz] *n. pl.* elbise, giysi.

toil [tɔil] **1.** *n.* zahmet, emek, yorgunluk; uğraş; **2.** *v/i.* zahmet çekmek, didinmek, çalışmak, yorulmak; zar zor ilerlemek.

toil.er *fig.* ['tɔilə] *n.* ağır işçi.

toi.let ['tɔilit] *n.* tuvalet, apteshane; tuvalet, makyaj, giyinip kuşanma, süslenme; *Am.* banyo odası; *make one's* ~ giyinip kuşanmak; '~*-pa.per* *n.* tuvalet kâğıdı; '~*-set* *n.* tuvalet takımı; '~*-ta.ble* *n.* tuvalet masası.

toils [tɔilz] *n. pl.* tuzak, ağ (*a. fig.*).

toil.some □ ['tɔilsəm] zahmetli, yorucu, ağır (*iş vs.*).

toil-worn ['tɔilwɔ:n] *adj.* bitkin, yorgun.

to ken ['təukən] *n.* belirti, iz, işaret, nişan; hatıra, yadigâr, andaç; özellik, hususiyet; jeton; ~ *money* itibarî para; *in* ~ *of* -*in* belirtisi olarak.

told [təuld] *pret.* & *p.p. of tell; all* ~ toplam olarak, tümü.

tol.er.a.ble □ ['tɔlərəbl] dayanılabilir, çekilebilir, hoşgörülebilir, katlanılabilir; orta, ne iyi ne kötü, iyice; **'tol.er.ance** *n.* müsamaha, hoşgörü, tolerans, tahammül; **'tol.er.ant** □ müsamahakâr, hoşgörülü, toleranslı, hoşgörücü, hoşgörü sahibi, tahammüllü, sabırlı (*of* -e karşı); **tol.er.ate** ['_reit] *v/t.* müsamaha etm. -e, hoş görmek -i, tolerans göstermek -e; katlanmak -e, tahammül etm. -e; **tol.er'a.tion** *n.* müsamaha, hoşgörü, tolerans; müsaade; sabır, tahammül.

toll[1] [təul] *n.* yol *veya* köprü parası, resim, geçiş ücreti; giriş ücreti; şehirlerarası telefon ücreti; *fig.* haraç; ~ *call* TELEPH şehirlerarası telefon konuşması; ~ *of the road* trafik kazalarında ölen *veya* yaralananlar; '~*-bar,* '~*-gate* *n.* bariyer, paralı köprü *veya* yol girişi.

toll[2] [_] *v/t.* & *v/i.* çalmak (*çan vs.*).

tom.a.hawk ['tɔməhɔ:k] **1.** *n.* kızılderili baltası; **2.** *v/t.* bu balta ile vurmak, kesmek *veya* öldürmek.

to.ma.to BOT [tə:'mɑːtəu, *Am.* tə'meitəu] *n., pl.* **to'ma.toes** domates (fidanı).

tomb [tu:m] *n.* kabir, mezar, gömüt, sin; türbe.

tom.boy ['tɔmbɔi] *n.* erkek tavırlı kız, erkek Fatma.

tomb.stone ['tu:mstəun] *n.* mezar taşı.

tom.cat ['tɔm'kæt] *n.* erkek kedi.

tome [təum] *n.* cilt, büyük kitap.

tom.fool ['tɔm'fu:l] **1.** *n.* aptal kimse; **2.** *adj.* aptal; **tom'fool.er.y** *n.* aptallık; aptalca şaka, saçmalık.

tom.my *sl.* ['tɔmi] *n.* İngiliz eri, askeri; ~ *gun* hafif makineli tüfek; ~*rot* saçma.

to.mor.row [tə'mɔrəu] *n.* & *adv.* yarın.

tom-tom ['tɔmtɔm] *n.* tamtam.

ton [tʌn] ton (*1016 kilo, Am.* 907 *kilo*); ~*s pl.* F yığın, dünya kadar (*para vs.*).

to.nal.i.ty [təu'næliti] *n.* tonalite, tonculuk; PAINT renk uyumu.

tone [təun] **1.** *n.* ses, nitelik; MUS ton, perde; MED beden kuvveti; PAINT renk tonu; *fig.* tarz, tavır, hal, hava; *out of* ~ akortsuz, akordu bozuk; **2.** *v/t.* belirli bir ses (*veya* özellik) vermek; PAINT renk vermek; PHOT nüanslamak; ~ *down* tonunu hafifletmek -*in*, yumuşatmak; donuklaştırmak; *v/i.* uymak (*with* -e) (*part. renk*); ~ *down* yumuşamak; donuklaşmak.

tongs [tɒŋz] *n. pl.* (*a pair of* bir) maşa.
tongue [tʌŋ] *n. com.* dil; lisan; dil şeklinde *bş*; söz, konuşma (tarzı); broş iğnesi; araba oku; GEOGR dil; **hold one's ~** çenesini tutmak, susmak; **speak with one's ~ in one's cheek** alaylı ve gerçek niyetini aksettirmeyen türde konuşmak, yarım ağızla söylemek; 'tongue.less *adj.* dilsiz; *fig.* sessiz, suskun; 'tongue-tied *adj.* dili tutulmuş; *fig.* ağzı var dili yok; 'tongue-twist.er *n.* tekerleme.
ton.ic ['tɒnik] **1.** *adj.* (~*ally*) MUS sese ait; MED kuvvet verici; GR vurgulu; ~ **chord** MUS ses akordu; **2.** *n.* MUS ana *veya* baş nota; MED kuvvet ilacı, tonik; soda; GR vurgulu ses.
to.night [tə'nait] *n. & adv.* bu gece, bu akşam.
ton.ing so.lu.tion PHOT ['təuniŋ sə'lu:-ʃən] *n.* viraj (*veya* ton tespit) banyosu.
ton.nage NAUT ['tʌnidʒ] *n.* tonilato, tonaj, taşıma kapasitesi; bir memleketin tüm gemilerinin tonajı; tonaj ücreti.
ton.sil ANAT ['tɒnsl] *n.* bademcik; **ton-silli.tis** [˯si'laitis] *n.* bademcik iltihabı.
ton.sure ['tɒnʃə] **1.** *n.* başın tepesini traş etme; başın traş edilmiş tepe kısmı; **2.** *v/t.* -*in* tepesini traş etm.
ton.y *Am. sl.* ['təuni] *adj.* yüksek zümreye ait, lüks.
too [tu:] *adv.* dahi, keza, de, da, ilâveten, ek olarak, hem de, üstelik; (haddinden) fazla, çok.
took [tuk] *pret. of* **take**.
tool [tu:l] **1.** *n.* alet (*a. fig.*); **2.** *v/t.* aletle süslemek *veya* şekillendirmek; '~-bag, '~-kit *n.* takım çantası.
toot [tu:t] **1.** *v/t. & v/i.* öt(tür)mek, çalmak (*düdük, korna vs.*); **2.** *n.* düdük (*veya* boru) sesi.
tooth [tu:θ] *n.*, *pl.* **teeth** [ti:θ] diş; dişe benzer *bş*; etkin güç; ~ **and nail** canını dişine takarak, var gücüyle; **cast s.th. in s.o.'s teeth** *bş*i b-*nin* yüzüne vurmak, yüzüne karşı söylemek; '~ache *n.* diş ağrısı; '~-brush *n.* diş fırçası; **toothed** *comb.* …dişli; 'tooth.ing *n.* MEC dişleme, dişleme; 'tooth.less □ dişsiz; 'tooth-paste *n.* diş macunu; 'tooth.pick *n.* kürdan.
tooth.some □ ['tu:θsəm] lezzetli, leziz, tadı güzel (*yiyecek*).
too.tle ['tu:tl] *vb.* yavaş *veya* sürekli çalmak (*nefesli çalgı*).
top¹ [tɒp] **1.** *n.* üst, zirve, tepe, doruk;

baş; *fig.* en yüksek nokta, yer *veya* derece; MOT *Am.* kapak; NAUT çanaklık; **at the ~** üstünde, tepesinde, başında, zirvesinde; **at the ~ of** -*in* üstünde, tepesinde, başında, zirvesinde; **at the ~ of one's speed** azamî sürati ile; **at the ~ of one's voice** avazı çıktığı kadar, bar bar; **on ~** tepede, üstte; **on ~ of** -*in* üstün(d)e; -*e* ilâveten, üstelik, hem de, …yetmiyormuş gibi; **2.** *adj.* en yüksek, en üst; en iyi, birinci sınıf; önde gelen; **the ~ right corner** sağ üst köşe; **3.** *v/t.* kapamak, horul horul uyumak; *fig.* üstün gelmek -*den*, geçmek -*i*, üstesinden gelmek; -*in* birincisi olm., -*in* zirvesinde olm.; AGR tepesini kesmek; -*in* tepesine çıkmak; ~ **up** doldurmak, tamamlamak.
top² [˯] *n.* topaç; **sleep like a ~** kütük gibi uyumak, horul horul uyumak.
to.paz MIN ['təupæz] *n.* topaz.
top…: '~-boots *n. pl.* uzun çizme; ~ **dog** *sl.* galip, üstün gelen, fatih; efendi, lider, patron.
to.pee ['təupi] *n.* güneş başlığı, kolonyal şapka.
top.er ['təupə] *n.* akşamcı, ayyaş kimse.
top…: '~-flight *adj.* F birinci sınıf, üstün, seçkin; ~.gal.lant NAUT [˯'gælənt, NAUT tə'gælənt] **1.** *adj.* babafingo…; **2.** *n. a.* ~ **sail** babafingo; ~ **hat** silindir şapka; '~-'heav.y *adj.* havaleli, üstü çok yüklü; '~-'hole *adj. sl.* birinci sınıf, en iyi kalite, şahane.
top.ic ['tɒpik] *n.* konu, mevzu; 'top.i-cal □ güncel, aktüel; konuya ait; tartışmalı; yöresel; MED lokal.
top…: '~.knot *n.* saç topuzu; ORN sorguç, tepe, ibik; '~.mast *n.* NAUT gabya çubuğu; '~.most *adj.* en üstteki, en tepedeki; '~'notch *adj.* F birinci sınıf, en iyi kalite, seçkin.
to.pog.ra.pher [tə'pɒgrəfə] *n.* topografya uzmanı; **top.o.graph.ic, top.o-graph.i.cal** □ [tɒpə'græfik(əl)] topografik; **to.pog.ra.phy** [tə'pɒgrəfi] *n.* topografya.
top.per F ['tɒpə] *n.* silindir şapka; 'top-ping *adj.* F birinci sınıf, şahane, fevkalâde.
top.ple ['tɒpl] *v/t. & v/i.* mst ~ **over, ~ down** düş(ür)mek; devirmek; devrilmek; yık(ıl)mak.
top.sail NAUT ['tɒpsl] *n.* gabya yelkeni.
top.sy-tur.vy □ ['tɒpsi'tə:vi] altüst, baş aşağı; karmakarışık, karman çorman.
toque [təuk] *n.* sıkı ve kenarsız bir çeşit

kadın şapkası.

tor [tɔː] *n.* kayalık tepe (*veya* burun).

torch [tɔːtʃ] *n.* meşale; *a.* ***electric*** ~ cep feneri; *Am.* asetilen lambası; '~**light** *n.* meşale ışığı; ~ ***procession*** fener alayı.

tore [tɔː] *pret. of* ***tear¹*** 1.

tor.ment 1. ['tɔːment] *n.* cefa, eziyet, işkence, elem, azap, dert; 2. [tɔː'ment] *v/t.* eziyet etm. -*e*, işkence etm. -*e*, azap çektirmek -*e*; -*in* canını sıkmak, -*in* başını ağrıtmak; **tor'men.tor** *n.* eziyetçi kimse *veya* şey.

torn [tɔːn] *p.p. of* ***tear¹*** 1.

tor.na.do [tɔː'neidəu] *n.*, *pl.* **tor'nadoes** [-z] kasırga, hortum.

tor.pe.do [tɔː'piːdəu] *n.*, *pl.* **tor'pedoes** [-z] 1. *n.* NAUT, AVIA torpil; *a.* ***toy*** ~ eğlence fişeği; *a.* ~***-fish*** ICHTH torpilbalığı, uyuşturanbalığı; 2. *v/t.* NAUT torpillemek; *fig.* baltalamak, kösteklemek; ~***-boat*** *n.* NAUT torpido(bot); ~***-tube*** *n.* torpil kovanı.

tor.pid □ ['tɔːpid] uyuşuk, uyuşmuş; ölü gibi; duygusuz; *fig.* durgun, hareketsiz, atıl; **tor'pid.i.ty**, **'tor.pid.ness**, **tor.por** ['tɔːpə] *n.* uyuşukluk, hareketsizlik, cansızlık.

torque MEC [tɔːk] *n.* dönme momenti, tork; burma madenden gerdanlık.

tor.rent ['tɔrənt] *n.* sel (*a. fig.*); **tor.rential** □ [tɔ'renʃəl] sel gibi; selden oluşan; *fig.* sert, şiddetli.

tor.rid ['tɔrid] *adj.* çok sıcak, kızgın, yakıcı; tropikal; ~ ***zone*** tropikal kuşak, tropika, sıcak bölge.

tor.sion ['tɔːʃən] *n.* bur(ul)ma, bük(ül)me, kıvırma, kıvrılma; **tor.sion.al** ['-ʃənl] *adj.* bükülmeye ait, bükülmeme..., burulma...

tor.so ['tɔːsəu] *n.* insan *veya* heykel gövdesi.

tort JUR [tɔːt] *n.* haksız muamele (*veya* fiil), haksızlık.

tor.toise ZOO ['tɔːtəs] *n.* kaplumbağa; ~***-shell** ['tɔːtəʃel] *n.* bağa, kaplumbağa kabuğu.

tor.tu.os.i.ty [tɔːtjuˈɔsiti] *n.* eğri büğrülük, yılankavilik; **'tor.tu.ous** □ eğri büğrü, yılankavi, dolambaçlı (*a. fig.*); *fig.* çapraşık, hileli.

tor.ture ['tɔːtʃə] 1. *n.* işkence, eziyet, elem, azap; 2. *v/t.* işkence etm. -*e*, eziyet etm. -*e*, azap çektirmek -*e*; **'tor.turer** *n.* işkence (*veya* eziyet) eden kimse.

To.ry ['tɔːri] 1. *n.* tutucu (*veya* muhafazakâr) parti üyesi; 2. *adj.* tutucu..., muhafazakâr...; **'To.ry.ism** *n.* tutucu

luk.

tosh *sl.* [tɔʃ] *n.* saçma.

toss [tɔs] 1. *n.* atma, fırlatma; yazı tura için para atma; ***win the*** ~ yazı turada kazanmak; 2. *v/t. a.* ~ ***about*** atmak, fırlatmak, savurmak, çalkalamak; hafifçe karıştırmak; rahatsız etm.; *a.* ~ ***up*** yazı tura için atmak (*para*); ~ ***off*** bir dikişte içmek, yuvarlamak (*içki*); yapıvermek, kolayca yapmak; *v/i.* yatakta dönüp durmak; oraya buraya çarpmak; çalkalanmak, çalkanmak; silkinmek, sarsılmak; *a.* ~ ***up*** yazı tura atmak (*for* için); '~***-up** *n.* yazı tura için para atma (*fig.* şüpheli durum, düşeş, şans işi; ***it's a*** ~ şüphelidir.

tot¹ F [tɔt] *n.* minimini yavru, yavrucak, minicik çocuk; bir yudum içki.

tot² F [tɔt] 1. *n.* toplam, yekûn; 2. *v/t.* ~ ***up*** toplamak; *v/i.* tutmak, bulmak (***to*** -*i*).

to.tal ['təutl] 1. □ bütün, tam(am), tüm; top yekûn (*savaş*); 2. *n.* toplam, tutar, yekûn; top, hepsi; 3. *vb.* toplamak, hesaplamak, yekûnunu bulmak; tutmak, etmek; hurdalanış etm. (*araba*); **to.talitar.i.an** [-tæliˈteəriən] *adj.* totaliter, bütüncül; **to.tal.i'tar.i.an.ism** *n.* totalitercilik; **to'tal.i.ty** *n.* bütünlük, tümlük; **to.tali.zator** ['-təlaizeitə] *n.* at yarışlarında müşterek bahisleri hesaplayan makine; **to.tal.ize** ['-təlaiz] *v/t.* toplamak; özetlemek.

tote F [təut] *v/t.* taşımak (*part. silah*).

to.tem ['təutəm] *n.* totem (heykeli), ongun; '~***-pole** *n.* totem heykeli.

tot.ter ['tɔtə] *v/i.* sendelemek, yalpalamak; sendeleyerek kalkmak; sallanmak; '**tot.ter.ing** □, '**tot.ter.y** sarsak (sursak); sallantıdıa olan.

touch [tʌtʃ] 1. *v/t.* dokunmak -*e* (*a. fig.*), ellemek -*i*, el sürmek -*e*; koparmak, sızdırmak (*para*); bitiştirmek; erişmek -*e*, ulaşmak -*e*; teğet geçmek -*e*, değmek -*e*; etkilemek, tesir etm. -*e*; bozmak; *fig.* incitmek, kalbini kırmak; ~ ***one's hat to s.o.*** şapkasına dokunarak *b-ni* selamlamak; ~ ***bottom*** dibe değmek; çok düşmek (*fiyat*); *fig.* suya düşmek (*ümit*); ~ ***the spot*** F makbule geçmek; ~ ***s.o. for*** *sl. b-den* para dilenmek; ***a bit*** ~***ed** *fig.* kaçık, kafadan çatlak; ~ ***off*** ateşlemek (*top vs.*); *fig.* başlatmak; ~ ***up*** yenilemek; PHOT rötuş yapmak; *v/i.* temas etm.; ~ ***at*** NAUT uğramak; ~ **(up)on** *fig.* değinmek (*bir konuya*); 2. *n.* dokunma, dokunuş, temas, değme; iz; dokunma hissi, dokunum; üs-

lûp; rötuş; MUS tuşlayış; *spor*: taç; *k-den*
kolayca para sızdırılan kimse; **get in**
(*-to*) ~ **with** temas kurmak *ile*, temasa
geçmek *ile*; '~-**and-'go 1**. *n*. şüpheli durum; **it is** ~ şüphelidir, belli değil; **2**.
adj. tehlikeli, riskli, nazik, şüpheli;
'**touch.i.ness** *n*. alınganlık; titizlik;
'**touch.ing 1.** □ dokunaklı, acıklı; **2**.
prp. ...e dair, ...hususunda, ilgili olarak; '**touch-line** *n*. *futbol*: taç çizgisi;
'**touchstone** *n*. mihenk taşı, denektaşı
(*a. fig.*); '**touch.y** □ alıngan; = *testy*.
tough [tʌf] **1.** *adj*. sert; kopmaz,
kırılmaz, dayanıklı; kart; çetin, zor,
güç; kuvvetli, direşken, dirençli; belâlı;
inatçı, boyun eğmez; **a ~ customer** F
baş belâsı kimse; **2.** *n*. külhanbeyi,
bıçkın, kabadayı; '**tough.en** *v/t*. &
v/i. sertleş(tir)mek, katılaş(tır)mak;
'**tough.ie** F ['tʌfi] = *tough* **2**; '**toughness** *n*. dayanıklılık, sertlik; zorluk.
tour [tuə] **1.** *n*. gezi, tur, seyahat; devir;
dolaşma; nöbet; turne; *conducted* ~
rehberli gezi; **2.** *v/t*. & *v/i*. gezmek, seyahat etm.; turneye çıkmak; '**tour.ing**
adj. gezi..., tur..., seyahat...; ~ *car* MOT
büyük otomobil; '**tour.ist** *n*. turist; ~
agency, ~ *office*, ~ *bureau* seyahat
acentesi; ~ *industry* turizm sanayii; ~
season turizm mevsimi; ~ *ticket* tur
bileti.
tour.ma.line MIN ['tuəməlin] *n*. turma-
lin.
tour.na.ment ['tɔːnəmənt] *n*., **tour.ney**
['-ni] turnuva, yarışma; ortaçağda
mızrak oyunu.
tour.ni.quet MED ['tuənikei] *n*. sıkı
sargı.
tou.sle ['tauzl] *v/t*. karıştırmak (*saç*),
karmakarışık etm., arap saçına çevirmek.
tout [taut] **1.** *n*. tiyocu, karaborsacı, simsar; **2.** *v/i*. müşteri aramak, çığırtkanlık
etm., simsarlık etm.; tiyo vermek.
tow[1] NAUT [təu] **1.** *n*. yedekte çek(il)me;
take in ~ yedekte çekmek, yedeğe almak; **2.** *v/t*. (yedekte) çekmek.
tow[2] [-] *n*. kıtık.
tow.age NAUT ['təuidʒ] *n*. yedekte çekme (ücreti).
to.ward(s) [tə'wɔːd(z), tɔːd(z)] *prp*. -e
doğru, doğrultusunda, tarafına doğru,
yönün(d)e; -e karşı, -e yakın; için.
tow.el ['tauəl] **1.** *n*. havlu; **2.** *v/t*. havlu
ile kurulamak *veya* silmek; '~-**horse**
n. havlu asacağı; '~-**rack** = ~-*horse*.
tow.er ['tauə] **1.** *n*. kule, burç; kale, hi-

sar; *fig*. himaye, sığınak, siper; **2.** *v/i*.
yükselmek; ~ **above** *mst fig. b-den* daha üstün olm.; '**tow.er.ing** □ çok yüksek; *fig*. şiddetli (*öfke*).
tow(.**ing**)... ['təu(iŋ)]: '~-**line** *n*. çekme
halatı; '~-**path** *n*. kanal *veya* nehir
kıyısında gemi çeken atlara ait yol.
town [taun] *n*. şehir (merkezi), kasaba;
kasaba halkı; **man about** ~ sosyete
adamı, hovarda kimse; *attr*. şehir...,
kasaba...; ~ **cen.tre**, *Am*. ~ **cen.ter**
şehir merkezi; ~ **clerk** kasaba sicil memuru; ~ **coun.cil** belediye meclisi; ~
coun.cil.lor belediye meclis üyesi; ~
cri.er şehir tellâlı; ~ **hall** belediye binası; '~-'**plan.ning** *n*. şehir planlaması;
~.**scape** ['-skeip] *n*. şehir manzarası.
towns.folk ['taunzfəuk] *n*. şehir halkı.
town.ship ['taunʃip] *n*. kaza, ilçe.
towns.man ['taunzmən] *n*. şehirli, hemşeri; *fellow* ~ hemşeri; '**towns.peo-
ple** = *townsfolk*.
tow...: '~-**path** *n*. kanal *veya* nehir
kıyısında gemi çeken atlara ait yol;
'~-**rope** *n*. NAUT çekme (*veya* yedek)
halatı.
tox.ic, **tox.i.cal** □ ['tɔksik(əl)] zehirli,
zehirden oluşmuş; **tox.in** ['tɔksin] *n*.
toksin.
toy [tɔi] **1.** *n*. oyuncak; değersiz şey; ~**s**
pl. oyuncak eşya; **2.** *adj*. oyuncak gibi,
oyuncak...; küçük..., ufak...; **3.** *v/i*. oynamak (*mst fig.*), eğlenmek; önemsememek; '~-**book** *n*. resimli kitap;
'~-**box** *n*. oyuncak kutusu; '~.**shop** *n*.
oyuncakçı dükkânı.
trace[1] [treis] **1.** *n*. iz (*a. fig.*), eser, nişan;
zerre, azıcık miktar; işaret; kalıntı; **2.**
v/t. izlemek; kopya etm.; çizmek; dikkatle yazmak; keşfetmek; ~ *back* uzanmak, dayanmak (**to** *-e*); ~ *out* planını,
krokisini yapmak, yolunu çizmek.
trace[2] [-] *n*. koşum kayışı; *kick over the*
~**s** *fig*. gemi azıya almak, serkeşlik
etm.
trace.a.ble □ ['treisəbl] izlenebilir, izi
bulunabilir; '**trac.er** *n. a*. ~ **ammunition** havada iz bırakan mermi; *a*. ~ **element** (*teşhiste kullanılan*) radyoaktif
izotop; '**trac.er.y** *n*. ARCH ağ şeklinde
süs.
tra.che.a ANAT [trə'kiːə] *n*. nefes (*veya*
soluk) borusu.
trac.ing ['treisiŋ] *n*. kopya (etme);
'~-**paper** *n*. kopya (*veya* aydinger)
kâğıdı.
track [træk] **1.** *n*. iz (*a.* HUNT), eser,

nişan; RAIL ray, hat; dümen suyu; keçi yolu, patika; *part. spor.* pist; MEC palet, tırtıl; yol; dizi, seri; yörünge; ~ *events pl.* (*koşu pistinde yapılan*) atletizm karşılaşmaları; **2.** *v/t.* izlemek, takip etm., *-in* izini aramak; geçmek (*çöl vs.*); ayakla içeri taşımak (*çamur vs.*); ~ **down**, ~ **out** izleyerek bulmak; *v/i.* iz bırakmak *veya* yapmak; ˈtrack.er *n. part.* HUNT iz süren kimse; ˈtrackless *adj.* izsiz; yolsuz; MEC raysız giden.

tract¹ [trækt] *n.* saha, alan, arazi, toprak; ANAT bölge, nahiye, sistem.

tract² [-] *n.* risale, broşür.

trac.ta.bil.i.ty [træktəˈbiliti] *n.*, ˈtract.a.bleness uysallık, yumuşaklık; ˈtracta.ble □ uysal, yumuşak başlı, söz dinler; kolay işlenir.

trac.tion [ˈtrækʃən] *n.* çek(il)me, çekiş gücü; ~ **engine** yük çekme makinesi; ˈtractive *adj.* çekici…; ˈtrac.tor *n.* MEC traktör.

trade [treid] **1.** *n.* ticaret; alışveriş; meslek, iş, sanat; esnaf; müşteriler; değiş tokuş, takas, trampa; *Board of* Ω Ticaret Bakanlığı; *the* ~*s pl.* NAUT alize rüzgârları; **2.** *v/i.* ticaret yapmak (*with ile*; *in -de*); alışveriş etm.; iş yapmak; ~ *on* F *-den* faydalanmak, istifade etm.; *v/t.* takas etm., değiş tokuş etm. (*for ile*); ~ *s.th. in* fiyat farkı vererek eskisini yenisi ile değiştirmek; ~ cy.cle ticaret çarkı; ˈ~-fair *n.* COM ticaret fuarı; ~ mark alâmeti farika, marka; ~ name ticaret ünvanı; ~ price ticari (*veya* toptan) fiyat; ˈtrad.er *n.* tüccar, tacir; ticaret gemisi; trade school sanat okulu; trades.man [ˈ-zmən] *n.* dükkâncı, esnaf kimse; ˈtrades.peo.ple *n.* esnaf; trade uni.on sendika; trade-ˈun.ionism *n.* sendikacılık; trade-ˈun.ion.ist **1.** *n.* sendikacı; **2.** *adj.* sendika…, sendikal.

trade wind NAUT [ˈtreidˈwind] *n.* alize rüzgârı.

trad.ing [ˈtreidiŋ] *adj.* ticaretle ilgili, ticarî, alışveriş…

tra.di.tion [trəˈdiʃən] *n.* gelenek, anane, görenek, âdet; traˈdi.tion.al □ [-ʃənl], traˈdi.tion.ar.y [-ʃnəri] geleneksel, ananevî, göreneksel.

traf.fic [ˈtræfik] **1.** *n.* trafik, gidişgeliş; ticaret, trampa, alışveriş, değiş tokuş; yük; yolcu sayısı; iş, muamele; **2.** *v/i.* ticaret yapmak (*in ile*); traf.fi.ca.tor [ˈ-keitə] *n. mot* sinyal; ˈtraf.fick.er *n.* tüccar; *b.s.* kaçakçı; traf.fic jam trafik tıkanıklığı; traf.fic light trafik lambası (*veya* ışığı).

tra.ge.di.an [trəˈdʒiːdjən] *n.* trajedi yazarı *veya* aktörü; trag.e.dy [ˈtrædʒidi] *n.* trajedi (*a. fig.*); facia, felâket.

trag.ic, trag.i.cal □ [ˈtrædʒik(əl)] trajik (*a. fig.*); feci, korkunç, müthiş, hüzünlü, acıklı.

trag.i.com.e.dy [ˈtrædʒikɔmidi] *n.* trajikomedi, güldürülü trajedi; ˈtrag.i-ˈcom.ic *adj.* (~*ally*) hem ağlatıcı hem güldürücü.

trail [treil] **1.** *n. fig.* kuyruk; iz (*a. hunt*); yol, patika, keçiyolu; (bir) süre, (bir) yığın; ~ *of smoke* havada uzanan duman; **2.** *v/t. & v/i.* peşinden sürükle(n)mek; izlemek, takip etm.; yerde sürünmek (*a.* BOT); geri kalmak; iz bırakmak; ~ blaz.er *Am.* yol açan kimse; öncü; ˈtrail.er *n.* römork; treyler; BOT sürüngen bitki; *film:* fragman, (gelecek programla ilgili) reklâm filmi.

train [trein] **1.** *n. com.* tren, katar; maiyet, refakatçiler; sıra, silsile, dizi, zincir (*olaylar*); yerde sürünen uzun etek; barut serpintisi; **2.** *v/t. & v/i.* öğretmek, alıştırmak, talim et(tir)mek, yetiştirmek, eğitmek; ehlileştirmek; *spor:* antrenman (*veya* idman) yapmak; doğrultmak (*top vs.*); *a.* ~ *it* F trenle gitmek; ˈ~-acci.dent, ˈ~-dis.as.ter *n.* tren kazası (*veya* faciası); train'ee *n.* stajyer;

ˈtrain.er *n.* eğitici, antrenör; eğitim uçağı; ˈtrain-ˈfer.ry *n.* tren feribotu.

train.ing [ˈtreiniŋ] *n.* talim; *spor:* antrenman, idman; *physical* ~ beden eğitimi; ˈ~-col.lege *n.* öğretmen okulu, eğitim fakültesi; ˈ~-ship *n.* okul gemisi.

train-oil [ˈtreinɔil] *n.* balina yağı.

trait [treit] *n.* özellik.

trai.tor [ˈtreitə] *n.* hain, vatan haini (*to -e* karşı); ˈtrai.tor.ous □ haince.

trai.tress [ˈtreitris] *n.* hain kadın.

tra.jec.to.ry PHYS [ˈtrædʒiktəri] *n.* mermi yolu; yörünge.

tram [træm] *n.* MIN maden ocağı arabası, dekovil; ~ *-car*, ~ *way*; ˈ~-car *n.* tramvay (vagonu); ˈ~-line *n.* tramvay hattı.

tram.mel [ˈtræml] **1.** *n.* ağ; MEC elipsograf; ~*s pl. fig.* engel, mânia; **2.** *v/t.* engellemek; güçleştirmek; ağa düşürmek.

tramp [træmp] **1.** *n.* serseri, derbeder, avare (gezme); ağır adım ve sesi; uzun yürüyüş; sürtük; *a.* ~ *steamer* NAUT tarifesiz işleyen yük gemisi; **on the~** serserilik etmekte; **2.** v/i. avare (veya serserice) dolaşmak; ağır adımlarla yürümek; taban tepmek, yayan gitmek; v/t. ayak altında çiğnemek, tram.ple ['₋l] v/t. ayak altında çiğnemek, ezmek.

tram.way ['træmwei] n. tramvay (hattı).

trance [trɑːns] n. dalınç, kendinden geçme, esrime, vecit; (h)ipnotizma.

tran.quil □ ['træŋkwil] sakin, rahat, asude, sessiz, durgun; tran'quil.(l)i.ty n. sükûn, sessizlik; tran.quil.i.za.tion [₋lai'zeiʃən] n. yatıştırma, sakinleştirme; 'tran.quil.(l)ize v/t. & v/i. sakinleş(tir)mek, yatış(tır)mak; 'tranquil.(l)i.zer n. yatıştırıcı (ilaç), müsekkin.

trans.act [træn'zækt] v/t. bitirmek, görmek (iş); ~ **business** iş yapmak; trans'ac.tion n. iş (görme), muamele; ~**s** pl. bir kurumun tüm işlemlerini gösteren rapor veya kayıtlar.

trans.al.pine ['trænz'ælpain] n. & adj. Alplerin ötesinde yaşayan (kimse).

trans.at.lan.tic ['trænzət'læntik] adj. Atlantik aşırı (giden), transatlantik...

tran.scend [træn'send] v/t. geçmek, aşmak, -in ötesinde olm.; üstün gelmek; tran'scend.ence, tran'scenden.cy n. üstünlük; PHLS deneyüstülük; tran'scendent □ üstün, âlâ; a. = tran-scen.den.tal □ [₋'dentl] MATH üstün (fonksiyon); PHLS deneyüstü; P şüpheli, bellisiz, anlaşılması güç; doğaüstü.

trans.con.ti.nen.tal ['trænzkɔnti-'nentl] adj. kıtayı kateden.

tran.scribe [træns'kraib] v/t. kopya etm., suret çıkarmak; MUS uyarlamak; radyo: kaydetmek.

tran.script ['trænskript] n. ikinci nüsha, kopya, suret; tran'scrip.tion n. kopya etme; transkripsiyon; MUS uyarlama; radyo: kaydetme, kayıt.

tran.sept ARCH ['trænsept] n. haç şeklindeki kilisenin iki kanadı.

trans.fer 1. [træns'fəː] v/t. nakletmek, geçirmek (**to, in, into** -e); devretmek (part. JUR, **to** -e); havale etm.; baskı ile kopya etm.; v/i. aktarma yapmak; **2.** [₋'₋] n. taşıma, nakil, havale, geçirme, devir (part. JUR); COM transfer; aktarma bileti; spor: kulüp değiştirme, transfer; trans'fer.a.ble adj. devredilebilir, nakli mümkün, havale edilebilir; trans.fer.ee JUR [₋fəˈriː] n. k-ne bş devredilen kimse; trans.fer.ence

['₋fərəns] n. nakletme, nakledilme; 'trans.fer.or n. JUR devreden kimse; trans.fer-pic.ture ['₋fəːpiktʃə] n. çıkartma.

trans.fig.u.ra.tion [trænsfigjuəˈrei-ʃən] n. şekil değişimi; trans.fig.ure [₋'figə] v/t. şeklini değiştirmek, başkalaştırmak; yüceltmek.

trans.fix [træns'fiks] v/t. mıhlamak, delmek; kazığa oturtmak, kazıklamak; hareketsiz bırakmak; ~**ed** fig. donakalmış (**with** -den).

trans.form [træns'fɔːm] v/t. başka kalıba sokmak; -in şeklini değiştirmek, dönüştürmek; tahvil etm. -i; transfor.ma.tion [₋fəˈmeiʃən] n. dönüş(tür)üm, şekil değişmesi; trans.form.er ELECT [₋'fɔːmə] n. transformatör, trafo.

trans.fuse [træns'fjuːz] v/t. MED aktarmak, nakletmek (kan vs.) (**into** -e); fig. ilham etm., esinlemek (**with** ile); trans'fu.sion [₋ʒən] n. (part. MED kan) nakil, aktarma.

trans.gress [træns'gres] v/t. bozmak, ihlâl etm., çiğnemek, karşı gelmek (kanun vs.); aşmak; v/i. günah işlemek; sınırı aşmak; trans'gres.sion n. sınırı aşma; suç, günah; ihlâl, karşı gelme; trans'gres.sor [₋sə] n. tecavüz eden kimse, günahkâr kimse.

tran.sience, tran.sien.cy ['trænziəns(i)] n. geçicilik.

tran.sient ['trænziənt] **1.** adj. geçici, süreksiz, kısa; fani; kalımsız; **2.** n. Am. kısa zaman kalan misafir.

tran.sis.tor [træn'zistə] n. ELECT transistor.

trans.it ['trænsit] n. geçme; geçiş; taşı(n)ma, nakil; transit; **in** ~ nakledilirken; transit olarak; ~ **camp** transit kampı.

tran.si.tion [træn'siʒən] n. geçiş, intikal, değişim; tran'si.tion.al □ [₋ʒənl] geçişe ait, geçiş..., değişme...

tran.si.tive □ GR ['trænsitiv] geçişli, nesneli (fiil).

tran.si.to.ri.ness ['trænsitərinis] n. geçicilik; fanilik; 'tran.si.to.ry □ geçici, süreksiz; fani, kalımsız.

trans.lat.a.ble [træns'leitəbl] adj. tercüme edilebilir, çevrilebilir; trans'late v/t. çevirmek, tercüme etm.; ölmeden cennete göndermek; nakletmek; fig. dönüştürmek, değiştirmek (**into** -e); (başka kelimelerle) açıklamak; v/i. tercüme edilmek; tercümanlık yapmak; **trans'la.tion** *n.* çeviri, tercüme; nakil; **trans'la.tor** *n.* çevir(m)en, tercüman, mütercim.

trans.lu.cence, **trans.lu.cen.cy** [trænz'luːsns(i)] *n.* yarı şeffaflık; **trans'lu.cent** *adj.* yarı şeffaf; *fig.* açık, belli.

trans.ma.rine [trænzmə'riːn] *adj.* denizaşırı.

trans.mi.grant ['trænzmigrənt] *n.* göçmen; **trans.mi.grate** ['trænzmai'greit] *v/t. & v/i.* göç et(tir)mek, hicret et(tir)mek; *fig.* göçmek (*ruh*); **trans.mi'gra-tion** *n.* göç, hicret; **~ of souls** ruh göçü, başka bir varlığa geçme (*ruh*).

trans.mis.si.ble [trænz'misəbl] *adj.* geçirilebilir, nakledilebilir, gönderilebilir; **trans'mis.sion** *n.* geçirme, nakil, intikal, gönderme; BIOL kalıtım; PHYS iletme, taşıma; MEC transmisyon; MOT vites; *radyo*; yayım.

trans.mit [trænz'mit] *v/t.* geçirmek, TEL, *radyo*: yayımlamak, göndermek, nakletmek; BIOL kalıtımla geçirmek; PHYS iletmek (*ısı vs.*); **trans'mit.ter** *n.* yayım (*veya* verici) istasyonu; *tel, etc.* nakledici alet; **trans'mit.ting** *adj.* radyo: verici...; **~ station** verici istasyonu.

trans.mog.ri.fy F [trænz'mɔgrifai] *v/t.* şeklini değiştirmek, garip şekle sokmak.

trans.mut.a.ble □ [trænz'mjuːtəbl] değiştirilebilir; **trans.mu'ta.tion** *n.* değiştir(il)me; **trans'mute** *v/t.* şeklini değiştirmek, dönüştürmek (**into** -e).

trans.o.ce.an.ic ['trænzəuʃi'ænik] *adj.* okyanus aşırı (*veya* ötesi).

tran.som ARCH ['trænsəm] *n.* vasistas; çapraz kiriş; travers.

trans.par.en.cy [træns'peərənsi] *n.* şeffaflık, saydamlık; slayt; **trans'par-ent** □ şeffaf, saydam, berrak; *fig.* açık (seçik), apaçık, kolay anlaşılır.

tran.spi.ra.tion [trænspi'reiʃən] *n.* terleme; **tran.spire** [-'paiə] *v/i.* terlemek; *fig.* duyulmak, sızmak (*haber, sır vs.*); *sl.* olmak, meydana gelmek.

trans.plant [træns'plɑːnt] *v/t.* başka bir yere dikmek *veya* yerleştirmek; nakletmek (*organ vs.*); **trans.plan'ta.tion** *n.* nakil.

trans.port 1. [træns'pɔːt] *v/t.* götürmek, nakletmek, taşımak; *fig.* coşturmak, heyecanlandırmak; HIST sürgüne göndermek; **2.** ['-] *n.* nakil; taşı(n)ma; (askerî) araç, taşıt; ulaştırma, ulaşım; coşku; **Minister of** ♀ Ulaştırma Bakanı;

in **~s** coşku içinde; **trans'port.a.ble** *adj.* nakledilebilir, taşınabilir; **trans-por'ta.tion** *n.* nakil, ulaştırma; ulaşım; taşıt, araç; sürgün cezası.

trans.pose [træns'pəuz] *v/t.* sırasını (*veya* yerlerini) değiştirmek; MUS aktarmak, perdesini değiştirmek; **trans-po.si.tion** [-pə'zifən] *n.* yerlerini değiştirme; MUS aktarma.

trans-ship NAUT, RAIL [træns'ʃip] *v/t.* aktarmak; *v/i.* aktarma yapmak.

tran.sub.stan.ti.ate [trænsəb'stæn-ʃieit] *v/t.* başka bir cisme dönüştürmek; ECCL Hz. İsa'nın et ve kanına değiştirmek (*ekmek ve şarabı*); **tran-sub.stan.ti'a.tion** *n.* başka bir cisme dönüştürme; ECCL ekmek ve şarabın Hz. İsa'nın et ve kanına değiştirilmesi.

trans.ver.sal [trænz'vɔːsəl] **1.** □ yanal, çaprazvari, enine; **2.** *n.* MATH doğru çizgi; **'trans.verse** □ karşıdan karşıya, enine, çaprazvari...; **~ section** enine (*veya* profil) kesit; **~ strength** MEC çapraz kuvvet.

trap¹ [træp] **1.** *n.* tuzak (*a. fig.*), kapan(-ca); hile, oyun, dolap; küçük at arabası; *sl.* ağız, gaga; MEC boruda U şeklindeki kısım; = **~door; 2.** *v/t.* tuzağa düşürmek (*a. fig.*), yakalamak, tutmak.

trap² MIN [-] *n.* bir çeşit volkanik siyah taş.

trap.door ['træp'dɔː] *n.* kapak şeklinde kapı; THEAT sahne kapısı.

trapes F [treips] *v/i.* sürtmek, taban tepmek.

tra.peze [trə'piːz] *n.* sirk: trapez; **tra-'pezi.um** MATH [-zjəm] *n.* yamuk; **trap.e.zoid** MATH ['træpizɔid] *n.* ikizkenar yamuk.

trap.per ['træpə] *n.* tuzakçı, avcı.

trap.pings ['træpiŋz] *n. pl.* süslü koşum takımı; *fig.* süs, ziynet.

Trap.pist ECCL ['træpist] *n.* konuşmanın bile yasak olduğu Katolik manastırda rahip.

trap.py ['træpi] *adj.* fesatçı, kötü niyetli, enrikacı.

traps F [træps] *n. pl.* eşya, pılı pırtı.

trash [træʃ] *n.* çerçöp, süprüntü; *fig.* değersiz (*veya* eski püskü) şey, pılı pırtı; değersiz, ciğeri beş para etmez adam; ayaktakımı, avam; artık; saçma; **'trash.y** □ adi, değersiz, beş para etmez.

trav.ail *obs.* ['træveil] *n. pl.* doğum sancıları; zahmet.

trav.el ['trævl] **1.** *v/i.* seyahat etm., yolculuk etm. (*a.* COM); yol almak, gitmek;

v/t. (gezip) dolaşmak; **2.** *n.* yolculuk, seyahat; MEC işleme; **~s** *pl.* yolculuk, seyahat; **'trav.el(l)ed** *adj.* çok seyahat etmiş; işlek; **'trav.el.(l)er** *n.* yolcu, seyyah; COM satış elemanı, pazarlamacı; MEC transbordör; **~'s cheque** seyahat çeki; **'trav.el(l)ing** *adj.* seyahat…, yolculuk…; MEC hareketli…; **~ rug** yol battaniyesi.

trav.e.log(ue) ['trævəlɔg] *n.* bir seyahati anlatan film *veya* konferans.

trav.erse ['trævɜːs] **1.** *n.* çapraz (*veya* kateden) kısım; travers; galeri; engel, mâni(a); çapraz çizgi; MOUNT çapraz geçiş (yeri); JUR resmî red; MIL top yönünü değiştirme; MEC yanal hareket sahası; **2.** *v/t.* & *v/i.* karşıdan karşıya geç(ir)mek; taramak; geçmek, aşmak, katetmek; *fig.* karşı gelmek, engel olm.; resmen reddetmek (*iddia*); incelemek; sağa sola dön(dür)mek; MOUNT çaprazlama geçmek.

trav.es.ty ['trævisti] **1.** *n.* alay, hiciv, karikatür, hezel; **2.** *v/t.* taklit etm.; hicvetmek.

trawl [trɔːl] **1.** *n.* tarak ağı; sürtme ağı; **2.** *v/t.* & *v/i.* tarak ağı ile (balık) tutmak; **'trawl.er** *n.* tarak ağlı balıkçı (gemisi).

tray [trei] *n.* tepsi, sini; tabla; **pen~** kalemlik.

treach.er.ous □ ['tretʃərəs] hain, güvenilmez, emniyetsiz; aldatıcı; tehlikeli; **'treach.er.ous.ness, 'treach.er.y** *n.* hainlik, ihanet.

trea.cle ['triːkl] *n.* şeker pekmezi; **'trea.cly** *adj.* şeker pekmezi gibi ağdalı; *fig.* çok hoş.

tread [tred] **1.** (*irr.*) *v/i.* (ayakla) basmak (**on, upon** *-e*); yürümek; çiftleşmek; *v/t.* çiğnemek *-i*, ezmek *-i*; çiftleştirmek; yürüyerek yapmak (*yol vs.*); **2.** *n.* ayak basışı; yürüyüş; merdiven basamağı; ayak sesi; lastik tırtılı; **trea.dle** ['~dl] **1.** *n.* pedal, basarık, ayaklık; **2.** *v/t.* & *v/i.* pedalla çalış(tır)mak; **'tread.mill** *n.* ayak değirmeni; *fig.* sıkıcı iş.

trea.son ['triːzn] *n.* hainlik, hıyanet, ihanet; **'trea.son.a.ble** □ hainlik kabilinden (*part. devlete*).

treas.ure ['treʒə] **1.** *n.* hazine (*a. fig.*); **~s of the soil** yeraltı zenginlikleri; **~-house** hazine dairesi; **~ trove** define, gömü, hazine; **2.** *v/t. oft.* **~ up** biriktirmek; aklında tutmak; *fig.* değerli tutmak, çok değer vermek *-e*; **'treas.ur.er** *n.* haznedar, veznedar, kesedar.

treas.ur.y ['treʒəri] *n.* hazine; maliye dairesi; fon; bilgi hazinesi (*kimse, kitap vs*); ♀ (**Board**), *Am.* ♀ **Department** Maliye Bakanlığı; ♀ **Bench** PARL Avam Kamarası'nda bakanların oturduğu sıra; **~ bill** hazine bonosu; **~ note** hazinece çıkarılan kâğıt para, banknot.

treat [triːt] **1.** *v/t.* davranmak *-e*, muamele etm. *-e*; sunmak, *-e*, ikram etm. *-e*; ele almak; kullanmak; tedavi etm. *-i*; işlemden geçirmek; dikkate almak, düşünmek; **~ s.o. to s.th.** *b-ne* bş ısmarlamak, ikram etm.; **~ o.s. to s.th.** *k-ne* bş almak; *v/i.* **~-of** bahsetmek *-den*, söz etm. *-den*; **~ with** müzakereye girişmek (**for** için); **2.** *n.* zevk (verici şey); ikram; **it is my ~** F bu benden, benim ikramım; **stand ~** F ısmarlamak, ikram etm.; **treatise** ['~tiz] *n.* risale; bilimsel inceleme, tez; **'treat.ment** *n.* muamele, davranış; tedavi; **'trea.ty** *n.* antlaşma; **be in ~ with** anlaşmak *ile*; **~ port** antlaşma şartı ile dış ticarete açık olan liman, serbest liman.

tre.ble ['trebl] **1.** □ üç kat, üç misli; MUS tiz…; **2.** *n.* MUS soprano ses(li çalgı *veya* kimse); **3.** *v/t.* & *v/i.* üç misli art(ır)mak, üç kat etm.

tree [triː] **1.** *n.* ağaç; *s.* **family**; **at the top of the ~** *fig.* mesleğinin zirvesinde; **up a ~** F çıkmaza girmiş, şaşkın halde; **2.** *v/t.* ağaca çıkarmak; *fig.* çıkmaza sokmak; **'tree.less** *adj.* ağaçsız; **'tree.top** *n.* ağaç tepesi.

tre.foil ['trefɔil] *n.* BOT yonca; ARCH yonca şeklinde süs.

trek [trek] *Güney Afrika*: **1.** *v/i.* kağnı ile seyahat *veya* göç etm.; **2.** *n.* kağnı ile seyahat *veya* göç.

trel.lis ['trelis] **1.** *n.* AGR kafes işi; **2.** *v/t.* birbirine geçirmek; AGR dallarını kafese sarmak.

trem.ble ['trembl] **1.** *v/i.* titremek (**with** *-den*), sallanmak; ürpermek; endişe etm. (**for** *-den*); **2.** *n.* titreme; ürperme; **he was all of a ~** tir tir titriyordu.

tre.men.dous □ [tri'mendəs] (kos)kocaman, çok büyük, muazzam; heybetli; F şahane, görkemli, olağanüstü.

trem.or ['tremə] *n.* titreme; ürperme; sarsıntı.

trem.u.lous □ ['tremjuləs] titrek; ürkek, ödlek; sinirli; **'trem.u.lous.ness** *n.* titreklik; ödleklik.

trench [trentʃ] **1.** *n.* hendek, çukur; MIL siper; **~ warfare** siper savaşı; **2.** *v/t.* hendekle çevirmek; AGR bellemek;

v/i. MIL siper kazmak; ~ *(up)on* tecavüz etm. *-e; fig.* yakın gelmek; 'trench.ant □ kuvvetli, tesirli, etkin, acı, şiddetli, keskin *(dil vs.)*; trench coat trençkot, yağmurluk.

trench.er ['trentʃə] *n.* hendek kazıcısı; HIST büyük tahta tabak; ~ cap üniversite öğrencilerinin giydiği dört köşeli kasket.

trend [trend] **1.** *n.* yön; *fig.* eğilim, meyil *(towards -e)*; **2.** *v/i.* yönelmek, meyletmek *(towards -e)*.

tre.pan [tri'pæn] **1.** MED HIST yuvarlak, kafatası delme testeresi; **2.** *v/t.* MED cerrah testeresi ile delmek *(kafatası)*; MEC burgu ile delmek.

trep.i.da.tion [trepi'deiʃən] *n.* korku, dehşet; titreme; ürperme.

tres.pass ['trespəs] **1.** *n.* günah, suç; başkasının arazisine izinsiz girme; ihlâl; **2.** *v/i.* başkasının arazisine izinsiz girmek; tecavüz etm. *(on, upon -e)*; ihlâl etm. *-i*, bozmak *-i*, çiğnemek *-i*; günah işlemek; 'tres.pass.er *n.* başkasının arazisine izinsiz giren kimse; ~s will be prosecuted bu araziye girenler cezalandırılacaklardır.

tress [tres] *n.* saç (örgüsü), bukle, lüle.

tres.tle ['tresl] *n.* sehpa; ~ bridge sehpa köprü.

trey [trei] *n.* iskambil *veya* zar üçlüsü.

tri.ad ['traiəd] *n.* üçlü takım.

tri.al ['traiəl] *n.* tecrübe, deneme *(of -i)*; *fig.* test, imtihan; JUR muhakeme, duruşma, yargılama; baş belâsı kimse *veya* şey, dert; ~ match hazırlık maçı; on ~ deneme için; denenince; imtihan üzerine; yargılanmakta; prisoner on ~ yargılanan mahkûm, hükümlü; ~ of strength kuvvet denemesi; bring to ~ mahkemelik etm., mahkemeye vermek, dava etm. *-i*; give s.o. *veya* s.th. a ~ b-ni *veya* bşi bir denemek; send for ~ duruşmaya çağırmak; he is a ~ to his family ailesi için bir baş belasıdır; ~ run deneme, tecrübe.

tri.an.gle ['traiæŋgl] *n.* üçgen; üçlü grup; MUS üçköşe, triangel; tri.an.gu.lar □ [-'æŋgjulə] üçgen şeklinde, üç köşeli; üçlü; tri'an.gu.late *surv.* [-leit] *v/t.* nirengi yapmak; üçgenlere bölmek.

trib.al □ ['traibəl] kabileye ait, kabile…; tribe *n.* kabile, aşiret, boy, oymak, soy; *part. contp.* grup; BOT, ZOO takım, familya; tribes.man ['-zmən] *n.* kabile üyesi.

---

trib.u.la.tion [tribju'leiʃən] *n.* dert, keder, sıkıntı.

tri.bu.nal [tri'bju:nl] *n.* mahkeme; hâkimler kurulu; hâkim kürsüsü; 'trib.une *n.* halkı savunan kimse, halkın koruyucusu; kürsü, platform, tribün.

trib.u.tar.y ['tribjutəri] **1.** □ vergi veren; haraç olarak verilen; bağımlı; bir ırmağa karışan *(akarsu)*; **2.** *n.* haraç veren hükümet *veya* hükümdar; ırmak ayağı; trib.ute ['-bju:t] *n.* haraç, vergi; takdir, övme; hediye; saygı.

trice[1] [trais] *n.*: in a ~ bir anda, bir çırpıda.

trice[2] [-] *v/t.*: ~ up kaldırıp bağlamak, hisa etm.

tri.chi.na ZOO [tri'kainə] *n.* trişin.

trick [trik] **1.** *n.* oyun, hile, düzen, dolap, entrika; şeytanlık, yaramazlık, eşek şakası; marifet, hüner; hokkabazlık, el çabukluğu; garip huy; özellik; *iskambil:* el; NAUT nöbet; F şirin çocuk; güzel kadın; ~ film miki filmi; **2.** *v/t.* aldatmak, kandırmak, dolandırmak, aldatarak almak *(out of -i)*; faka bastırmak; ayartmak, kafeslemek *(into için)*; ~ out, ~ up süslemek, telleyip pullamak; 'trick.er, trickster ['-stə] *n.* hilekâr, düzenbaz, üçkâğıtçı kimse; 'trick.er.y *n.* hile(kârlık), düzenbazlık, üçkâğıtçılık; 'trick.ish □ hile kabilinden.

trick.le ['trikl] **1.** *v/t. & v/i.* damla damla ak(ıt)mak, damla(t)mak; F *fig.* yavaş yavaş çıkmak, gelmek; yavaş yavaş kaybolmak; **2.** *n.* damla(ma).

trick.si.ness ['triksinis] *n.* muziplik, yaramazlık; 'trick.sy □ muzip, yaramaz, haşarı; = 'trick.y □ hileli, aldatıcı, üçkâğıtçı; F beceri isteyen *(iş vs.)*; güç, zor; tehlikeli.

tri.col.o(u)r ['trikələ] *n.* üç renkli bayrak; the ♀ Fransız bayrağı.

tri.cy.cle ['traisikl] *n.* üç tekerlekli bisiklet.

tri.dent ['traidənt] *n.* üç çatallı mızrak.

tri.en.ni.al □ [trai'enjəl] üç yılda bir olan; üç yıl süren, üç yıllık.

tri.er ['traiə] *n.* deneyen kimse; elinden geleni yapan kimse; yargılayan kimse.

tri.fle ['traifl] **1.** *n.* önemsiz şey; az miktar, az para; bir çeşit tatlı; a ~ biraz, azıcık; **2.** *v/i.* oynamak; oyalanmak, vakit öldürmek; boş boş konuşmak; *v/t.* önemsememek, başına atmak, hafife almak; ~ away harcamak *(güç vs.)*, öldürmek *(vakit)*, çarçur etm. *(para vs.)*; 'tri.fler *n.* işini ciddiye almayan kimse.

tri.fling ['traifliŋ] □ önemsiz, değersiz, ufak tefek, az; saçma, manasız (*konuşma vs.*); yüzeysel, üstünkörü.

trig¹ [trig] **1.** *v/t.* takozlayarak hareketini engellemek; ~ **up** düzeltmek, çekidüzen vermek, güzelleştirmek, şıklaştırmak; **2.** *n.* takoz, köstek.

trig² [-] *adj.* şık, temiz giyimli; sağlam, dayanıklı, sıkı; emin; canlı, cıvıl cıvıl.

trig.ger ['trigǝ] **1.** *n.* tetik; PHOT deklanşör; **2.** *v/t.* ~ **off** *fig.* başlatmak, sebep olm.

trig.o.no.met.ric, **trig.o.no.met.ri.cal** MATH [trigǝnǝ'metrik(ǝl)] trigonometrik; **trigo.nom.e.try** MATH [-'nɔmitri] *n.* trigonometri.

tri.lat.er.al □ MATH ['trai'lætǝrǝl] üç yönlü, üç kenarlı, üç taraflı.

tril.by F ['trilbi] *n.* yumuşak keçeli erkek şapkası.

tri.lin.gual ['trai'liŋgwǝl] üç dil konuşan; üç dilli; üç dilde söylenen.

trill [tril] **1.** *n.* ses titremesi; titrek ses; 'r' sesinin titretilerek söylenmesi; **2.** *v/t. & v/i.* sesi titre(t)mek, titrek sesle söylemek *veya* çalmak; titrek sesle ötmek, şakımak (*kuş*).

tril.lion ['triljǝn] *n.* trilyon; *Am.* bilyon.

trim [trim] **1.** □ biçimli, şık; düzenli, tertipli, derli toplu; **2.** *n.* nizam, intizam, düzen, tertip; hal, durum, vaziyet; süs; kıyafet; kılık; NAUT geminin dengesi; *in* (*out of*) ~ iyi (kötü) durumda; dengeli (dengesiz) (*gemi*); idmanlı (idmansız); **3.** *v/t.* düzeltmek, budamak, kırkmak; süslemek; kısaltmak; AVIA, NAUT dengeleştirmek, ayar etm.; rüzgâra göre ayarlamak (*yelken*); azarlamak, paylamak; yenmek; aldatmak, kandırmak; *v/i. fig.* iki parti arasında her ikisine de taraftar görünmek; '**trim.mer** *n.* süslemeci, düzenleyici kimse; NAUT gemiyi dengeleyen kimse; POL çıkarcı politikacı; '**trim.ming** *n.* süsleme; dayak, yenilgi; *mst* ~ **s** *pl.* süs, garnitür, kırpıntı; '**trim.ness** *n.* düzgünlük, derli topluluk.

tri.mo.tor ['taimǝutǝ] *n.* üç motorlu uçak; '**tri.mo.tored** *adj.* üç motorlu...

Trin.i.ty ['triniti] *n.* teslis.

trin.ket ['triŋkit] *n.* değersiz süs, biblo; ~**s** *pl.* cici bici.

tri.o MUS ['tri:ǝu] *n.* üçlü, triyo.

trip [trip] **1.** *n.* gezi(nti), kısa seyahat; tur; takılma, tökezlenme; hata, yanlış; *sl.* uyuşturucu madde etkisi, keyif hali, dalga; *fig.* sürçme; ~ **of the tongue** dil

sürçmesi; **2.** *v/i.* sürçmek (*dil*); tökezlenmek, takılmak (**over** *-e*); seke seke yürümek, koşmak *veya* dans etm.; *fig.* hata yapmak, yanılmak; sekmek, sıçramak; seyahat etm.; uyuşturucu madde etkisinde olm.; *catch s.o.* ~**ing** *b-nin* hatasını yakalamak; *v/t. a.* ~ **up** çelme takmak, düşürmek; *fig.* yalanını yakalamak.

tri.par.tite ['trai'pɑːtait] *adj.* üçlü; üç partili; üç taraf arasında yapılmış (*antlaşma vs.*).

tripe [traip] *n.* işkembe; *sl.* saçma.

tri.phase ['trai'feiz] *adj.* üç fazlı; ~ **current** ELECT üç fazlı, trifaze akım.

tri.plane AVIA ['traiplein] *n.* üst üste üç kanatlı uçak.

tri.ple □ ['tripl] üç misli, üç kat, üçlü.

tri.plet ['triplit] *n.* üçlü takım; *poet.* üç mısralı şiir parçası; MUS triolet, üçlem; üçüzlerden biri, üçüz; ~**s** *pl.* üçüzler.

tri.plex ['tripleks] *adj.* üç kısımlı, üç katlı; üç kez; ~ **glass** tripleks, mikalı cam.

trip.li.cate 1. ['triplikit] *adj.* üç kopyadan oluşan; üç kat, üç misli; **2.** ['-keit] *v/t.* üç kopyasını çıkarmak; üç kat yapmak.

tri.pod ['traipɔd] *n.* üç ayaklı sehpa (*a.* PHOT).

tri.pos ['traipɔs] *n.* Cambridge Üniversitesinde şeref payesi imtihanı.

trip.per F ['tripǝ] *n.* gezenti, seyahat eden kimse; '**trip.ping 1.** □ çevik, kıvrak; **2.** *n.* seke seke yürüme.

trip.tych ['triptik] *n.* üç kez katlanan resim.

tri.sect ['trai'sekt] *v/t.* üç (eşit) kısma bölmek.

tris.yl.lab.ic ['traisi'læbik] *adj.* (~**ally**) üç heceden ibaret, üç heceli...; '**tri'syl.lable** *n.* üç heceli kelime.

trite □ [trait] basmakalıp, herkesçe bilinen; adi, bayağı; bayat, eski.

trit.u.rate ['tritjureit] *v/t.* ezip toz etm., öğütmek, ezmek; dövmek.

tri.umph ['traiǝmf] **1.** *n.* zafer, başarı, galebe, yengi (**over** *-e karşı*); zafer alayı; **2.** *v/i.* yenmek, zafer kazanmak, galip gelmek (**over** *-i, -e karşı*) (*a. fig.*); **tri.um.phal** [-'ʌmfǝl] *adj.* zafere ait, zafer...; ~ **arch** zafer takı; ~ **procession** zafer alayı; **tri'um.phant** □ muzaffer, galip, utkulu.

tri.um.vi.rate [trai'ʌmvirit] *n.* triumvirlik, üç kişiden oluşan yönetim şekli; üçlü grup.

tri.une ['traiju:n] *adj.* birde üç olan.

triv.et ['trivit] *n.* ayaklı destek; nihale, sahan altlığı; *as right as a* ~ iyi bir durumda, sağlığı yerinde.

triv.i.al □ ['triviəl] ufak tefek, önemsiz; yavan, monoton; bayağı, sıradan, alelade, olağan; üstünkörü, yarımyamalak; değersiz, işe yaramaz; saçma, abes; **triv.i.al.i.ty** [‿'æliti] *n.* önemsizlik; aleladelik; saçmalık.

tro.chee ['trəuki:] *n.* biri uzun ve biri kısa iki heceli vezin.

trod [trɔd], *pret.*, **'trod.den** *p.p. of* **tread 1**.

trog.lo.dyte ['trɔglədait] *n.* mağarada yaşayan kimse.

Tro.jan ['trəudʒən] **1.** *adj.* Truva şehrine *veya* halkına ait; **2.** *n.* Truvalı; *work like a* ~ çok çalışmak.

troll[1] [trəul] *v/t.* & *v/i.* suda oltayı çekerek (balık) tutmak; bağıra bağıra (şarkı) okumak; döndürmek; gezinmek.

troll[2] [‿] *n.* efsanevî cüce *veya* dev.

trol.l(e)y ['trɔli] *n.* el arabası, yük arabası; *a.* **tea**‿ tekerlekli servis masası; *Am.* tramvay (arabası); '~-**bus** *n.* troleybüs.

trol.lop *contp.* ['trɔləp] *n.* pasaklı kadın; fahişe, orospu, sürtük.

trom.bone MUS [trɔm'bəun] *n.* trombon.

troop [tru:p] **1.** *n.* takım, sürü, küme, grup; cemaat; süvari bölüğü; erkek izci grubu; MIL bölük, tabur, alay; ~*s pl.* askerler, askerî kuvvetler; **2.** *v/t.* & *v/i.* bir araya topla(n)mak; ~ *away*, ~ *off* yürüyüş yapmak, ilerlemek, gitmek, gidivermek; ~*ing the colour(s)* MIL bayrak taşıma töreni; '~-**carri.er** *n.* NAUT, AVIA asker taşıyan uçak *veya* gemi; '**troop.er** *n.* süvari askeri; atlı polis; F polis; *swear like a* ~ ağzına geleni söylemek.

trope [trəup] *n.* mecaz, kinaye.

tro.phy ['trəufi] *n.* ganimet; hatıra, andaç, yadigâr; ödül, kupa.

trop.ic ['trɔpik] *n.* tropika, dönence; ~*s pl.* sıcak ülkeler, tropical kuşak; '**trop.ic**, **'trop.i.cal** □ tropikal.

trot [trɔt] **1.** *n.* tırıs; hızlı gitme, koşuş; *be on the* ~ *fig.* koşuşturmak, koşturup durmak; *sl.* ishal olm.; **2.** *v/i.* tırıs gitmek; koşmak; yürümek, gitmek; ~ *out* F teşhir etm., göstermek; ~ *s.o. round b-ni* gezdirmek, dolaştırmak; *b-ni* beraberinde görürmek.

troth *obs.* [trəuθ] *n.* sadakat, bağlılık;

gerçek, hakikat; *plight one's* ~ yemin etm.; evlenmeye söz vermek.

trot.ter ['trɔtə] *n.* tırıs giden koşu atı; ~*s pl.* paça.

trou.ble ['trʌbl] **1.** *n.* sıkıntı, zahmet, üzüntü, ıstırap; dert, keder, belâ; rahatsızlık, hastalık; endişe; mutsuzluk; mesele; ~*s pl.* POL huzursuzluk, asayişsizlik, kargaşalık; *be in* ~ başı belâda *veya* dertte olm.; *ask veya look for* ~ belâ aramak, kaşınmak; *take (the)* ~ zahmete katlanmak, zahmet etm.; **2.** *v/t.* rahatsız etm., tedirgin etm., zahmet vermek, canını sıkmak; endişelendirmek; zahmet etm.; başını ağrıtmak, üzmek, eziyet vermek; ~ *s.o. for b-ne* zahmet vermek; *v/i.* F zahmet çekmek, üzülmek, telâşlanmak; '~.**man**, '~-**shoot.er** *n. Am.* F arabulucu, aracı, uzlaştırıcı kimse; makine bakımcısı; **trou.ble.some** ['‿səm] *adj.* zahmetli, sıkıntılı, belâlı, üzüntülü; baş belâsı, can sıkıcı; '**troub.lous** *adj.* karışık, kargaşalı, güç, sıkıntılı.

trough [trɔf] *n.* tekne, yalak; oluk; uçurum; ~ *of the sea* iki dalga arasındaki çukur.

trounce F [trauns] *v/t.* dövmek, pataklamak, dayak atmak; yenmek; azarlamak, haşlamak.

troupe [tru:p] *n.* trup, oyuncu grubu.

trou.sered ['trauzəd] *adj.* pantolonlu; **trou.sers** ['‿z] *n. pl.* (*a pair of* bir) pantolon.

trous.seau ['tru:səu] *n.* çeyiz.

trout ICHTH [traut] *n.* alabalık.

tro.ver JUR ['trəuvə] *n.* istirdat (*veya* istihkak) davası.

trow *obs. veya co.* [trau] *vb.* inanmak; sanmak, zannetmek.

trow.el ['trauəl] *n.* mala.

troy (weight) ['trɔi(weit)] *n.* kuyumcu tartısı.

tru.an.cy ['tru:ənsi] *n.* dersi asma, okulu kırma; '**tru.ant 1.** *adj.* kaçak, firarî; aylak; **2.** *n.* dersi asan, okulu kıran çocuk; *fig.* işten kaytaran kimse; avare, başıboş kimse; *play* ~ dersi asmak, okulu kırmak.

truce [tru:s] *n.* ateşkes, mütareke, anlaşma; *political* ~ siyasi anlaşma.

truck[1] [trʌk] *n.* kamyon; el arabası; üstü açık yük vagonu.

truck[2] [‿] **1.** *v/t.* değiş tokuş etm., takas etm., trampa etm.; **2.** *n.* değiş tokuş, takas, trampa; *mst* ~ *system* ücretlerin para yerine mal olarak ödenmesi sistemi; **garden** ~ *Am.* sebze ve meyve.

truck.le¹ ['trʌkl] *v/i.* boyun eğmek, yaltaklanmak (**to** -*e*).

truck.le² [_] *n. mst* **~-bed** karyolanın altına itilebilen tekerlekli portatif yatak.

truck.man ['trʌkmən] *n.* kamyon şoförü, kamyoncu.

truc.u.lence, **truc.u.len.cy** ['trʌkjuləns(i)] *n.* kavgacılık, saldırganlık, vahşîlik; **'truc.u.lent** ☐ kavgacı, saldırgan, vahşi, haşin, zalim, gaddar, insafsız.

trudge [trʌdʒ] *v/i.* zahmetle yürümek, yorgun argın yürümek.

true [tru:] *adj.* (*adv.* **truly**) doğru, gerçek, sahi, hakikî; halis, som, katkısız, safi; sadık, vefakâr, samimî, içten; tam, aynı; iyi yerleştirilmiş; **be~ of** gerçek, doğru olm.; **it is** ~ doğrudur, gerçektir; **come** ~ gerçekleşmek (*ümit, hayal vs.*); ~ **to life** (**nature**) gerçek hayatta olduğu gibi; **prove** ~ doğru çıkmak; '~'**blue** *fig.* **1.** *adj.* çok sadık, sözünün eri; **2.** *n.* sözünün eri kimse; '~-**bred** *adj.* soylu; safkan; '~-**love** *n.* sevgili, âşık; **'true.ness** *n.* doğruluk, hakikat, gerçeklik; bağlılık, sadakat, vefa; saflık.

truf.fle BOT ['trʌfl] *n.* yermantarı, domalan.

tru.ism ['tru:izəm] *n.* su götürmez gerçek, apaçıklık, bellilik.

tru.ly ['tru:li] *adv.* gerçekten, hakikaten, doğrulukla, sadakatle, içtenlikle, samimi olarak; tamamen, doğru olarak; **Yours** ~ saygılarımla.

trump [trʌmp] **1.** *n. iskambil:* koz; F yaman adam, iyi adam; **2.** *v/i.* koz çıkarmak, koz oynamak; ~ **up** uydurmak (*bahane, yalan vs.*); **'trump.er.y 1.** *n.* gösterişli fakat adi şey, pılı pırtı; saçma; **2.** *adj.* gösterişli fakat değersiz; uydurma, sudan (*bahane*).

trum.pet ['trʌmpit] **1.** *n.* MUS boru (sesi); borazan; **blow one's own** ~ *fig. k-ni* methetmek, övünmek; *s.* **ear~**, **speaking~**; **2.** *v/i.* (boru çalarak) ilan etm., bildirmek, yaymak; ~ **forth** *fig.* yedi mahalleye davul zurna ile duyurmak; *v/i.* boru çalmak; boru gibi ses çıkarmak; **'trumpet.er** *n.* boru çalan kimse, borazan; tellal.

trun.cate ['trʌŋkeit] *v/t.* kısaltmak, budamak, ucunu tepesini kesmek; **trun'ca.tion** *n.* ucunu *veya* tepesini kesme, kısaltma.

trun.cheon ['trʌntʃən] *n.* sopa, çomak; cop.

trun.dle ['trʌndl] **1.** *n.* çember; **2.** *v/t.* yuvarlamak, çevirmek (*çember*).

trunk [trʌŋk] *n.* bavul; gövde, beden; hortum (*fil*); ağaç gövdesi; otomobil bagajı; *Am.* kısa don; *s.* **~-line**; '~-**call** *n.* TELEPH şehirlerarası telefon; '~-**exchange** *n.* TELEPH şehirlerarası telefon santralı; '~-**line** *n.* RAIL demiryolu ana hattı; TELEPH şehirlerarası telefon hattı; **trunks** *n. pl.* erkek mayosu.

trun.nion MEC ['trʌnjən] *n.* top muylusu, mil, aks, şaft.

truss [trʌs] **1.** *n.* saman demeti; MED kasık bağı; ARCH kiriş, destek, makas, dayak **2.** *v/t.* sımsıkı bağlamak; ARCH kirişle desteklemek; '~-**bridge** *n.* çatkılı köprü.

trust [trʌst] **1.** *n.* güven, itimat, inanç (**in** -*e*); sorumluluk, mesuliyet; emanet; JUR mutemetlik; JUR vakıf, tesis; COM tröst; ~ **company** tröst şirketi; **in** ~ himayesinde, gözetiminde; **on** ~ güvenerek, güvenle, emniyetle; COM kredi ile, veresiye; **position of** ~ sorumluluk mevkii; **2.** *v/t.* güvenmek -*e*, itimat etm. -*e*; emanet etm., teslim etm., güvenerek vermek (**s.o. with s.th.**, **s.th. to s.o.** *bşi b-ne*); inanmak; ~ **s.o. to do s.th.** *b-nin bşi yapacağına güvenmek;* ümit etm., ummak; kredi vermek; *v/i.* inancı, güveni olm. (**in**, **to** -*e*).

trus.tee [trʌs'ti:] *n.* JUR mutemet, vekil, yediemin, mütevelli; ~ **security**, ~ **stock** mütevelli senedi (*veya* tahvili); **trus'teeship** *n.* vekillik, mutemetlik.

trust.ful ☐ ['trʌstful], **'trust.ing** ☐ güvenen.

trust.wor.thi.ness ['trʌstwɔ:ðinis] *n.* güvenilirlik; **'trust.wor.thy** *adj.* güvenilir, güvene lâyık; **'trust.y** *adj.* güvenilir, emniyetli.

truth [tru:θ] *n., pl.* **truths** [tru:ðz] doğruluk, hakikat, gerçek(lik); sadakat, vefa; samimiyet, içtenlik; dürüstlük; Tanrı; ~ **to life** hayata bağlılık; **to tell the** ~ doğruyu söylemek gerekirse, doğrusunu isterseniz.

truth.ful ☐ ['tru:θful] doğru, gerçek; doğru sözlü, doğrucu, içten; **'truth-ful.ness** *n.* doğru(cu)luk, gerçeklik.

try [trai] **1.** *v/t.* denemek (*a. fig.*), tecrübe etm., imtihan etm., sınamak; teşebbüs etm., kalkışmak; JUR yargılamak, muhakeme etm. (**for** -*den*); elde etmeye çalışmak (**for** -*i*); yormak; taşırmak (*sabrını*); göstermek, ispatlamak; arıtmak, tasfiye etm.; eritmek (*yağ*); araştırmak, tetkik etm.; ~ **on** prova etm. (*elbise*); ~ **it on with s.o.** F bşi b-*de* cüretle denemeye kalkışmak; ~ **one's hand at** bşe el atmak, bşi denemek; ~ **out** denemek; *v/i.* uğraşmak, çalışmak (*at* -*e*); **2.** *n.* F deneme, tecrübe; çalışma, uğraşma; *have a* ~ bir deneyivermek; 'try.ing □ yorucu, sıkıcı, sinirlendirici, sabır tüketici; 'try-'on *n.* prova; F cüretkâr teşebbüs; 'try--'out *n.* deneme; *spor*: yetenek denemesi; **try.sail** NAUT ['traisl] *n.* yan yelken.

tryst [traist] **1.** *n.* randevu, buluşma (yeri); **2.** *vb.* randevulaşmak.

Tsar [zɑː] *n.* çar.

T-shirt ['tiːʃəːt] *n.* tişört.

T-square ['tiːskwɛə] *n.* T cetveli.

tub [tʌb] **1.** *n.* tekne (dolusu), yayık, fıçı, leğen; banyo; F küvet; F co. tekne; *sl.* külüstür otomobil; **2.** *v/t. & v/i.* teknede yıkamak; fıçıya dikmek *veya* koymak; F yıka(n)mak, banyo yap(tır)mak; 'tub.by *adj.* fıçı gibi; bıdık, tıknaz; boğuk sesli.

tube [tjuːb] *n.* boru, tüp; MOT iç lastik; F metro (*part. Londra'da*); *sl.* televizyon; radyo lambası.

tu.ber BOT ['tjuːbə] *n.* yumru kök; **tuber.cle** ['-bəːkl] *n.* ANAT, ZOO yumrucuk, tümsecik, türberkül; MED küçük ur, kabarcık, şiş; **tu.ber.cu.lo.sis** MED [-bəːkjuˈləusis] *n.* tüberküloz, verem; **tu'ber.cu.lous** *adj.* MED veremli, tüberkülozlu; **tu.ber.ous** BOT ['-bərəs] *adj.* yumrulu.

tub.ing ['tjuːbiŋ] *n.* boru şeklinde dokuma; boru takımı.

tu.bu.lar □ ['tjuːbjulə] boru şeklinde; borulu...

tuck [tʌk] **1.** *n.* elbise kırması, pli; *sl.* yemek, börek çörek; **2.** *v/t.* katlamak, (içine) sokmak, (içine) tıkmak, altına kıvırmak; sıkıştırmak; ~ **in** iştahla yemek, tıkınmak; içeri sokmak; ~ **up** sıvamak, katlamak.

tuck.er HIST ['tʌkə] *n.* dantel şal.

tuck...: '~-**in** *n. sl.* yemek; '~-**shop** *n. sl.* pastane, kantin.

Tues.day ['tjuːzdi] *n.* salı.

tu.fa MIN ['tjuːfə] *n.*, **tuff** [tʌf] süngertaşı.

tuft [tʌft] *n.* küme, öbek, top; tepe, sorguç; püskül; '~-**hunt.er** *n.* otlakçı, bedavacı, asalak kimse; 'tuft.y □ öbek

öbek, püsküllü, küme küme.

tug [tʌg] **1.** *n.* kuvvetli çekiş; NAUT römorkör; *fig.* büyük güçlük, zorluk; ~ **of war** *spor*: halat çekme oyunu; *fig.* şiddetli rekabet; **2.** *v/t.* (şiddetle) çekmek, çekelemek (*at* -*i*); NAUT römorkörle çekmek; sıkıntı çekmek (*for* -*den*).

tu.i.tion [tjuːˈiʃən] *n.* eğitim, öğretim, ders; okul taksidi.

tu.lip BOT ['tjuːlip] *n.* lale.

tulle [tjuːl] *n.* tül.

tum.ble ['tʌmbl] **1.** *v/t. & v/i.* düş(ür)-mek, yık(ıl)mak, yuvarla(n)mak, devirmek; devrilmek; karıştırmak, karman çorman etm., altüst etm.; rastlamak, rast gelmek; ~ **to** F anlamak, kavramak; **2.** *n.* düşüş, yuvarlanma; karman çorman durum, karmakarışıklık; '~.**down** *adj.* yıkılacak gibi, yıkılmak üzere; 'tumbler *n.* bardak; MEC kilidin hareketli kısmı; ORN taklakçı güvercin; akrobat, cambaz.

tum.brel ['tʌmbrəl] *n.*, **tum.bril** ['-bril] suçluları idama götürmek için kullanılan araba.

tu.mid ['tjuːmid] *adj.* şişmiş, şişkin, kabarmış, kabarık; *fig.* abartmalı, şişirilmiş, tumturaklı; **tu'mid.i.ty** *n.* şişkinlik, kabarıklık.

tum.my F ['tʌmi] *n.* mide, karın, göbek.

tu.mo(u)r MED ['tjuːmə] *n.* tümör, ur, şiş, yumru.

tu.mult ['tjuːmʌlt] *n.* kargaşa(lık), gürültü, karışıklık; isyan, ayaklanma; *fig.* heyecan; **tu'mul.tu.ous** □ [-tjuəs] gürültülü, kargaşalı, patırdılı; düzensiz.

tu.mu.lus ['tjuːmjuləs] *n.* höyük; mezar üzerindeki toprak yığını.

tun [tʌn] *n.* büyük fıçı, varil; 950 litrelik sıvı ölçüsü.

tu.na ICHTH ['tuːnə] *n.* tonbalığı, orkinos.

tun.dra ['tʌndrə] *n.* tundura.

tune [tjuːn] **1.** *n.* nağme, melodi, beste, hava; mizaç, huy; MUS akort; *fig.* ahenk, düzen, uyum; **in** ~ akortlu; *fig.* uyumlu (*with* ile); **out of** ~ akortsuz; *fig.* uyumsuz, ahenksiz, düzensiz; **to the** ~ **of $ 200** $ 200'a kadar; *change* **one's** ~ *fig.* ağız değiştirmek; **2.** *v/t.* akort etm.; *fig.* ahenk vermek; ~ **in** radyo: frekansı ayarlamak (**to** -*e*); ~ **out** radyo: istasyonu düzeltmek; ~ **up** çalgıları akort etm.; *fig.* forma girmek; MOT ayarlamak; MUS şarkı söylemeye başlamak; **tune.ful** □ ['ˌful] ahenkli, hoş sesli; **'tune.less** □ ahenksiz, makamsız; sessiz, müziksiz; **'tun.er** *n.* MUS akortçu; *radyo*: amplifikatör ve hoparlörsüz radyo.

tung.sten CHEM ['tʌŋstən] *n.* tungsten, volfram.

tu.nic ['tjuːnik] *n.* tünik; MIL asker ceketi; ANAT tabaka, kılıf; BOT gömlek, zar, kılıf.

tun.ing…: '~-**coil** *n. radyo*: ayar bobini; '~-**fork** *n.* MUS diyapazon.

tun.nel ['tʌnl] **1.** *n.* tünel; MIN yatay yol; **2.** *vb.* tünel açmak.

tun.ny ICHTH ['tʌni] *n.* tonbalığı, orkinos.

tun.y F ['tjuːni] *adj.* ahenkli, hoş sesli.

tur.ban ['təːbən] *n.* sarık, turban.

tur.bid ['təːbid] *adj.* koyu, yoğun; çamurlu, bulanık; karmakarışık, allak bullak; **'tur.bid.i.ty** *n.* bulanıklık; koyuluk; karmakarışıklık.

tur.bine MEC ['təːbin] *n.* türbin; '~-'**pow.ered** *adj.* türbinle işleyen; **tur.bo-jet** ['təːbəu'dʒet] *n.* türbinli jet motoru ile işleyen uçak; **tur.bo--prop** ['ˌ-'prɔp] *n.* türbin pervaneli uçak.

tur.bot ICHTH ['təːbət] *n.* kalkan balığı.

tur.bu.lence ['təːbjuləns] *n.* karışıklık, kargaşalık, düzensizlik; **'tur.bu.lent** □ çalkantılı, dalgalı; serkeş, kavgacı, hır çıkaran; sert, şiddetli; karışık, düzensiz.

tu.reen [tjuˈriːn] *n.* derin çorba kâsesi.

turf [təːf] **1.** *n.* çimen(lik), çim; kesek; turba; *the* ~ hipodrom; at yarışçılığı; **2.** *v/t.* çimen döşemek -*e*, çimlendirmek; ~ *out sl.* kovmak, dışarı atmak; **turf.ite** ['ˌ-ait] *n.* at yarış meraklısı; **'turf.y** *adj.* kesekle kaplı, çimli; at yarışına ait.

tur.gid □ ['təːdʒid] şişkin, şiş(miş); *fig.* tumturaklı, şatafatlı; **tur'gid.i.ty** *n.* şişkinlik.

Turk [təːk] *n.* Türk.

tur.key ['təːki] **1.** *n.* ♀ *carpet* Türk halısı; **2.** *n.* ORN hindi; *Am. sl.* THEAT, *film:* fiyasko.

Turk.ish ['təːkiʃ] *adj.* Türk…; Türkçe…; ~ *bath* Türk hamamı; ~ *delight* lokum; ~ *towel* havlu.

tur.moil ['təːmɔil] *n.* kargaşa, gürültü, karışıklık.

turn [təːn] **1.** *v/t.* döndürmek, çevirmek; altüst etm., bozmak, bulandırmak, ekşitmek; erişmek, ulaşmak, gelmek;

torna tezgâhında şekillendirmek; tersyüz etm. (*elbise*); burkmak; kıvırmak; doğrultmak, yöneltmek; püskürtmek (*düşman vs.*); yönünü değiştirmek; adamak, vakfetmek; göndermek, nakletmek; takas etm., değiş tokuş etm.; körletmek (*bıçak vs.*); dönüştürmek (*into -e*); geri döndürmek, caydırmak (*from -den*); tercüme etm., çevirmek (*into English* İngilizceye); **he has** ~*ed 50, he is* ~*ed* (*of*) 50 ellisini aştı; ~ *s.o.'s brain* kafasını allak bullak etm., beynini bulandırmak; ~ *colour* renk değiştirmek; ~ *the corner* buhranı (*veya* krizi, tehlikeyi) atlatmak; *he can* ~ *his hand to anything* elinden herşey gelir, on parmağında on marifet; ~ *tail* F sıvışmak, tüymek, tabanları yağlamak; ~ *s.o. against* b-ni -e karşı kışkırtmak, düşman etm.; ~ *aside* bir tarafa çevirmek; ~ *away* döndürmek, geri çevirmek; kovmak; ~ *down* kıvırmak, bükmek, katlamak; kısmak; indirmek; reddetmek, geri çevirmek; ~ *in* içine kıvırmak; teslim etm. (*polise*); F geri vermek, iade etm.; ~ *off* kapatmak, kesmek, söndürmek; ~ *on* açmak; çevirmek; heyecanlandırmak, etkilemek; bağlı olm.; ~ *out* dışarı doğru döndürmek; söndürmek, kapatmak; boşaltmak; yapmak, üretmek, imal etm., meydana getirmek; toplamak, biraraya getirmek; yataktan kaldırmak; kovmak, defetmek; tersyüz etm.; ~ *over* çevirmek, devirmek; devretmek, bırakmak; teslim etm.; *fig.* altüst etm.; COM alıp satmak; üzerinde düşünmek; ~ *over a new leaf* yeni bir hayata başlamak; ~ *round* çevirmek, döndürmek; ~ *up* yukarı çevirmek, sıvamak; açmak, çevirmek; ortaya çıkarmak; AGR altüst etm. (*toprağı*); F kusturmak, iğrendirmek; *v/i.* dönmek; olmak; sersemlemek, başı dönmek; sapmak, yönelmek (*to -e*); bulanmak; başvurmak (*to -e*); *k-ni* adamak (*to -e*); değişmek, dönüşmek (*into -e*); *a.* ~ *sour* ekşimek, bozulmak; solmak, renk atmak; eğilmek, yamulmak; körelmek, körlenmek, körleşmek; ~ *about* diğer tarafa dönmek; MIL geriye dönmek; ~ *away* başka tarafa yönelmek; çekip gitmek; ~ *back* geri dönmek; ~ *in* içeri kıvrılmak; F yatmak; ~ *off* sapmak; ~ *on* zevk almak, heyecan duymak; düşman olm.; saldırmak; ~ *out* meydana çıkmak, olmak; yukarı doğru bakmak; toplanmak, biraraya gelmek; F yataktan kalkmak; MIL yola çıkmak, hareket etm.; ~ **over** devrilmek, dönmek, altüst olm.; ~ **round** dönmek, çevrilmek; ~ **to** işe koyulmak; başvurmak, müracaat etm., danışmak; koşmak; ~ **up** bulunmak, ortaya çıkmak; olmak; gelmek, görünmek; ~ **upon** saldırmak; **2.** *n.* dönme, dönüş, devir, deveran; sapma, yön değiştirme, yönelme; dönemeç, viraj; sıra; değişiklik, değişim; kabiliyet, yetenek; eğilim, meyil; amaç, gaye, maksat; gezme, dolaşma; nöbet; tarz, nevi; kısa piyes; F sarsıntı, şok; işlem, muamele; büklüm, kıvrım; *at every* ~ her defasında, her keresinde; *by veya in* ~s nöbetleşe, sıra ile, arka arkaya; *do s.o. a good (bad)* ~ *b-ne* iyilik (kötülük) etm., *b-ne* yardım et(me)mek; *in* ~ sıra ile, arka arkaya; *in my* ~ tarafımdan; *it is my* ~ sıra bende, sıra benim; *take a* ~ değişmek; tur atmak; *take a* ~ *at. s.th.* payına düşeni yapmak; *take a few* ~s gezinmek, dolaşmak; *take one's* ~ sırası gelmek; *take* ~s nöbetleşerek, sıra ile yapmak (*at -i*); *to a* ~ tam kararında, kıvamında; *does it serve your* ~? o işinizi görür mü?; '~**a.bout** *n.* atlıkarınca; '~**buck.le** *n.* MEC germe donanımı; '~**coat** *n.* dönek adam; '**turn.down collar** devrik yaka; '**turn.er** *n.* tornacı; bedeneğitimi uzmanı; '**turn.er.y** *n.* tornacılık; tornacı dükkânı.

turn.ing ['tə:niŋ] *n.* dönüş, dönme; dönen; dönemeç; *take a* ~ dönmek; '~**lathe** *n.* MEC torna tezgâhı; '~**point** *n. fig.* dönüm noktası.

tur.nip BOT ['tə:nip] *n.* şalgam.

turn.key ['tə:nki:] *n.* zindancı, gardiyan; '**turn-'out** *n.* COM ürün, verim, mahsül; katılanlar, toplantı mevcudu; RAIL, NAUT yan hat; grev(ci); sapak, dönemeç; malzeme, teçhizat; temizlik; giysi; '**turn.o.ver** *n.* COM satış; sermaye devri, ciro; devrilme; meyveli turta; '**turn.pike** *n.* bariyer; *Am.* geçiş parası alınan yol; '**turn-screw** *n.* tornavida; '**turn.spit** *n.* kebapçı, dönerci; '**turn-stile** *n.* turnike; '**turn-ta.ble** *n.* RAIL döner levha; '**turn-'up 1.** *adj.* katlı; kalkık (*burun, yaka vs.*); **2.** *n.* duble paça.

tur.pen.tine CHEM ['tə:pəntain] *n.* terebentin, neftyağı.

tur.pi.tude *lit.* ['tə:pidju:d] *n.* ahlaksızlık, günahkârlık, kötülük.

tur.quoise MIN ['tə:kwɑ:z] *n.* firuze,

türkuvaz.

tur.ret ['tʌrit] *n.* küçük kule; MIL, NAUT taret; AVIA uçağın baştarafı; ~ **lathe** MEC torna tezgâhı; '**tur.ret.ed** *adj.* kuleli, taretli; kule şeklindeki.

tur.tle[1] ZOO ['tə:tl] *n.* kaplumbağa; *turn* ~ alabora olm., devrilmek.

tur.tle[2] ORN [~] *n. mst* ~**-dove** kumru.

Tus.can ['tʌskən] **1.** *adj.* Toskana'ya ait; **2.** *n.* Toskanalı; Toskana lehçesi.

tush [tʌʃ] *int.* sus!, boş ver!

tusk [tʌsk] *n.* fildişi; azıdişi.

tus.sle ['tʌsl] **1.** *n.* itişip kakışma, çekişme, çetin mücadele, kavga; **2.** *v/i.* mücadele etm., uğraşmak, kavga etm.

tus.sock ['tʌsək] *n.* ot öbeği, çalı demeti.

tut [tʌt] *int.* yetti be!, kes sesini!, adam sen de!

tu.te.lage ['tju:tilidʒ] *n.* vasilik, vesayet.

tu.te.lar.y ['tju:tiləri] *adj.* vasi olan; vasiye ait, vasi...

tu.tor ['tju:tə] **1.** *n.* özel öğretmen; UNIV öğretmen; JUR vasi asistan öğretmen; JUR vasi, veli; **2.** *v/t.* -*e* özel ders vermek; *fig.* hükmetmek -*e*, hâkim olm. -*e*; **tu.tori.al** [~'tɔ:riəl] **1.** *adj.* özel öğretmene *veya* vasiye ait; özel öğretmenli...; özel öğretmen...; **2.** *n.* UNIV özel ders; **tu.tor.ship** ['~təʃip] *n.* özel öğretmenlik; JUR vesayet.

tux.e.do *Am.* [tʌk'si:dəu] *n.* smokin.

TV ['ti:'vi:] *n.* televizyon.

twad.dle ['twɔdl] **1.** *n.* saçma, boş laf; **2.** *v/i.* saçmalamak, boş boş konuşmak.

twain *obs.* [twein] *n.* iki.

twang [twæŋ] **1.** *n.* tıngırtı; *mst nasal* ~ genizden çıkan ses, genzel ses; **2.** *v/t. & v/i.* tıngırda(t)mak; genizden konuşmak.

'**twas** [twɔz, twəs] = *it was*.

tweak [twi:k] *v/t.* çimdikleyip çekmek, bükmek.

tweed [twi:d] *n.* tüvit.

'**tween** [twi:n] = *between*.

tween.y ['twi:ni] *n.* hizmetçi kız.

tweet [twi:t] *v/i.* cıvıldamak (*kuş*); '**tweet.er** *n. radyo:* tiz sesler için küçük hoparlör.

tweez.ers ['twi:zəs] *n. pl.* (*a pair of bir*) cımbız.

twelfth [twelfθ] **1.** *adj.* on ikinci; **2.** *n.* on ikide bir; '~**-night** *n.* Noelden on iki gün sonraki gece.

twelve [twelv] *n. & adj.* on iki; ~**fold** ['~-fəuld] *adj.* on iki misli; '~**month**

n. yıl, sene.

twen.ti.eth ['twentiiθ] **1.** *adj.* yirminci; **2.** *n.* yirmide bir.

twen.ty ['twenti] *n. & adj.* yirmi; **∼.fold** ['ˌ-fəuld] *adj.* yirmi misli; '**∼-four-seven** ['ˌ-fɔː'sevn] *her günde bütün gün*; 24 saat 7 gün.

'**twere** [twəː] = *It were.*

twerp *sl.* [twəːp] *n.* hergele, herifçioğlu.

twice [twais] *adv.* iki kere, iki defa, iki kez; ∼ **the sum** iki misli miktar; ∼ **as much** iki misli, iki katı.

twid.dle ['twidl] **1.** *v/t.* döndürmek, döndürüp durmak; *v/i.* oynayıp durmak; **2.** *n.* hafifçe döndürme.

twig[1] [twig] *n.* ince dal, sürgün, çubuk.

twig[2] F [ˌ-] *v/t.* anlamak, farkına varmak, kavramak, çakmak.

twi.light ['twailait] *n.* alaca karanlık; *fig.* karanlık devre; ∼ *of the gods* tanrılarla devlerin birbirlerini mahvettikleri savaş; *attr.* alaca karanlık…; ∼ *sleep* MED ağrıyı kesmek için yapılan hafif anestezi.

twill [twil] **1.** *n.* kabarık ve çapraz dokunmuş kumaş; **2.** *vb.* böyle kumaş dokumak.

'**twill** [ˌ-] = *it will.*

twin [twin] **1.** *adj.* çift(e)…; **2.** *n.* ikiz; **∼-en.gined** AVIA ['ˌ-endʒind] *adj.* çift motorlu.

twine [twain] **1.** *n.* sicim; sarma, bükme; **2.** *v/t. & v/i.* sar(ıl)mak, dola(n)mak, kıvrılmak; bükmek; *fig. b-ni* bir işe bulaştırmak; ∼ *o.s.* sarılmak, çöreklenmek, kıvrılmak.

twinge [twindʒ] *n.* ani ve şiddetli ağrı, sancı.

twin.kle ['twiŋkl] **1.** *v/i.* pırıldamak, parlamak; göz kırpıştırmak; *in the twinkling of an eye* göz açıp kapayıncaya kadar; **2.** *n.* pırıltı, parıltı; göz kırpıştırma; *in a* ∼ kaşla göz arasında.

twirl [twəːl] **1.** *n.* dönüş, kıvrılış; kıvrım, büklüm; **2.** *v/t. & v/i.* dön(dür)mek; çevirmek; fırıldatmak; fırıldanmak; burmak, kıvırmak.

twirp [twəːp] = *twerp.*

twist [twist] **1.** *n.* bük(ül)me, bur(kul)ma, sar(ıl)ma; sicim, ibrişim; dönüş; dönme; düğüm; kötülüğe eğilim, meyil; **2.** *v/t. & v/i.* bük(ül)mek, bur(ul)-mak, sar(ıl)mak; dolamak; burkmak; döndürmek, çevirmek; kıvırmak; ters anlam vermek, saptırmak, çarpıtmak; kıvrılmak; bozmak; '**twist.er** *n.* büken şey *veya* kimse; *spor:* yuvarlanarak gi-

den top; F sahtekâr kimse; F zor iş *veya* sorun; *Am.* kasırga, hortum.

twit *fig.* [twit] *v/t.* takılmak, kızdırmak, alaya almak (**with** *hakkında*).

twitch [twitʃ] **1.** *v/t. & v/i.* seğir(t)mek; birden çekmek, kapıvermek; **2.** *n.* seğirme, tik; birden çekme, kapıverme; VET yavaşa; = *twinge.*

twit.ter ['twitə] **1.** *v/i.* cıvıldamak; kıkırdamak, kıs kıs gülmek; titrek bir sesle konuşmak; **2.** *n.* cıvıltı; kıkırdama; heyecan; *be in a* ∼ titremek, heyecan içinde olm.

'**twixt** [twikst] = *betwixt.*

two [tuː] **1.** *adj.* iki, çift; *in* ∼ iki kısma, ikiye; *put* ∼ *and* ∼ *together* doğru tahmin etm., bağdaştırarak sonuç çıkarmak; **2.** *n.* iki rakamı; *in* ∼**s** ikişer ikişer; '**∼-bit** *adj.* 25 sentlik…; *fig.* ucuz, değersiz, önemsiz, ufak tefek…; '**∼-edged** *adj.* iki yüzü de keskin (*kılıç*); iki anlamlı; '**∼-faced** *adj.* ikiyüzlü, riyakâr; **∼.fold** ['ˌ-fəuld] *adj. & adv.* iki kat, iki misli; '**∼-hand.ed** *adj.* iki elle kullanılan (*kılıç*); iki kişi ile kullanılan (*testere vs.*); **∼.pence** ['tʌpəns] *n.* iki peni; **∼.pen.ny** ['tʌpəni] *adj.* iki penilik…; '**∼-phase** *adj.* ELECT çift fazlı; '**∼-'piece** *n.* iki parçalı giysi; '**∼-ply** *adj.* katmerli, iki katlı; '**∼-'seater** *n.* MOT iki kişilik araba; '**∼-'sid.ed** *adj.* iki taraflı, iki yanlı; '**∼-'step** *n.* bir çeşit dans; bu dansın müziği; '**∼-'sto.rey** *adj.* iki katlı; '**∼-stroke** *adj.* MOT iki zamanlı…; '**∼-'thirds** *adj.* üçte iki…; '**∼-way** *adj.* MEC çift taraflı; ∼ *adapter* ELECT çiftli adaptör; ∼ *traffic* iki yönlü *veya* yollu trafik.

'**twould** [twud] = *it would.*

ty.coon *Am.* F [tai'kuːn] *n.* büyük işadamı, sermayedar; kodaman.

tyke [taik] *n.* it, sokak köpeği; kaba saba adam, hödük.

tym.pa.num ['timpənəm] *n.* ANAT timpan, kulak davulu, orta kulak; ARCH alın.

type [taip] **1.** *n.* çeşit, tip, cins, nevi, tür, kategori, sınıf; örnek, numune; MEC model; TYP basma harf, hurufat; *in* ∼ baskıya hazır; ∼ *area* tertip dizisinin boyu; *true to* ∼ tipine uygun; *set in* ∼ dizmek; **2.** = *write;* '**∼-found.er** *n.* dizmen, diz(g)ici; '**∼-script** *n.* daktilo ile yazılmış yazı; '**∼-set.ter** *n.* diz(g)ici, dizmen; dizgi makinesi; '**∼.write** (*irr. write*) *v/t.* daktilo etm., daktilo ile yaz-

mak; v/i. daktilo yazmak; '~.writer n.
daktilo, yazı makinesi; ~ **face** daktilo
yazısı; ~ **ribbon** daktilo şeridi; '~writ-
ten adj. daktilo edilmiş, daktiloda
yazılmış.
ty.phoid MED ['taifɔid] **1.** adj. tifoya
benzer; ~ **fever** = **2.** n. tifo.
ty.phoon METEOR [tai'fuːn] n. tayfun.
ty.phus MED ['taifəs] n. tifüs.
typ.i.cal □ ['tipikəl] tipik; simgesel,
sembolik (**of**); typ.i.fy ['~fai] v/t. -in
simgesi, sembolü olm.; simgesel olarak
göstermek; typ.ist ['taipist] n. dakti-
lo(graf); **shorthand** ~ stenograf.
ty.pog.ra.pher [tai'pɔgrəfə] n. matbaacı, basımcı; ty.po.graph.ic, ty.po-
graph.i.cal □ [~pə'græfik(əl)] mat-
baacılığa ait; basımcılık...; ty.pog.ra-
phy [~'pɔgrəfi] n. matbaacılık,

basımcılık, tipografya.
ty.ran.nic, ty.ran.ni.cal □ [ti'rænik(əl)]
zalim(ce), gaddar(ca); ty'ran.ni.cide
[~said] n. zalimi öldürme; zalimi öldüren kimse; tyr.an.nize ['tirənaiz] vb.
eziyet etm. -e, işkence etm. -e; ~ **over**
zulmetmek -e; 'tyr.an.nous □ zalim(-
ce), gaddar(ca); 'tyr.an.ny n. zulüm,
gaddarlık, istibdat; zorba hükümet
(devresi).
ty.rant ['taiərənt] n. zalim, zorba, gaddar, acımasız, yıkıcı; zorba hükümdar,
tiran.
tyre ['taiə] s. **tire**[1].
ty.ro ['taiərəu] s. **tiro**.
Tyr.o.lese [tirə'liːz] **1.** n. Tirol halkı; Ti-
rollü; **2.** adj. Tirol eyalet veya halkına
ait.
Tzar [zɑː] n. çar.

U

u.biq.ui.tous □ [juː'bikwitəs] aynı anda her yerde olan, hazır ve nazır;
u'biq.ui.ty n. hazır ve nazırlık, aynı anda her yerde hazır olma.
U-boat NAUT ['juːbəut] n. Alman deni-
zaltısı.
ud.der ['ʌdə] n. inek memesi.
ugh [ʌx, uh, əːh] int. of!, öf!, ö!
ug.li.fy ['ʌglifai] v/t. çirkinleştirmek.
ug.li.ness ['ʌglinis] n. çirkinlik, iğrençlik.
ug.ly □ ['ʌgli] çirkin, iğrenç; korkunç,
berbat; ters, huysuz; nahoş; fırtınalı;
tehlikeli.
U.krain.i.an [juː'kreinjən] **1.** adj. Uk-
rayna veya Ukraynacaya ait; **2.** n. Ukraynalı; Ukraynaca, Rutenca.
u.ku.le.le MUS [juːkə'leili] n. Hawaii
adalarına ait dört telli gitar, kitara.
ul.cer MED ['ʌlsə] n. ülser, karha; ul-
cer.ate ['~reit] v/t. & v/i. ülsere dö-
nüş(tür)mek, ülser olm.; ülsere sebep
olm.; ulcer'a.tion n. ülser(leşme); 'ul-
cer.ous adj. ülserli, ülserleşmiş.
ul.lage COM ['ʌlidʒ] n. fıçıda boş kalan
kısım; fire.
ul.na ANAT ['ʌlnə] n., pl. ul.nae ['~niː]
ulna, dirsek kemiği.
ul.ster ['ʌlstə] n. bol ve uzun palto.
ul.te.ri.or [ʌl'tiəriə] ötedeki, öteyan-
daki; uzaktaki; fig. gizli; sonraki; ~ **motive** gizli maksat, art niyet.

ul.ti.mate □ ['ʌltimit] (en) son, nihaî,
en uzak; esas, temel, asıl; en yüksek,
en büyük; aşırı; çözümlenemeyen; 'ul-
timate.ly adj. (eninde) sonunda.
ul.ti.ma.tum [ʌlti'meitəm] n., pl. a. ul-
ti'mata [~tə] ültimatom.
ul.ti.mo COM ['ʌltiməu] adj. geçen
ayın..., geçen ayki, geçen ayda.
ul.tra ['ʌltrə] adj. aşırı, son derece, fazla; '~'fash.ion.a.ble adj. son derece
modaya uygun; ~.ma'rine **1.** adj. denizaşırı; **2.** n. CHEM, PAINT lâcivert (boya);
'~'mod.ern adj. çok modern; ~.mon-
tane ECCL, POL [~'mɔntein] **1.** adj. Papanın mutlak yetkisinden yana olan;
2. n. Papanın mutlak yetkisinden yana
kimse; '~'red adj. kızılötesi, enfraruj;
'~'short wave çok kısa dalga; '~'son-
ic adj. sesötesi, yüksek frekanslı (titreşim, ses); '~'vi.o.let adj. ültraviyole,
morötesi.
ul.u.late ['juːljuleit] v/i. ulumak; feryat,
figan etm.
um.bel BOT ['ʌmbəl] n. umbel, şemsiye
şeklinde çiçek durumu.
um.ber MIN, PAINT ['ʌmbə] n. ombra,
aşıboyası.
um.bil.i.cal □ [ʌm'bilikəl, MED ~'laikəl]
göbeğe ait, göbek...; ~ **cord** göbek kordonu.
um.brage ['ʌmbridʒ] n. gücenme, alınma, içerleme; poet. gölge; kuşku, şüp-

he; ima; **um.bra.geous** □ [‿'breidʒəs] gölgeli; *fig.* alıngan.

um.brel.la [ʌm'brelə] *n.* şemsiye; *fig.* himaye, koruma; MIL koruyucu avcı uçakları; **um'brel.la-stand** *n.* şemsiyelik.

um.pire ['ʌmpaiə] **1.** *n.* hakem; **2.** *v/t.* yönetmek (*maç vs.*); *v/i.* hakemlik yapmak.

ump.teen ['ʌmpti:n] *adj.*, **'ump.ty** *sl.* pek çok, bir sürü, sayısız.

un... [ʌn] *prefix* -siz, -sız, gayri.

'un F [ʌn, ən] = **one.**

un.a.bashed ['ʌnə'bæʃt] *adj.* küstah, arsız, utanmaz, yüzsüz.

un.a.bat.ed ['ʌnə'beitid] *adj.* şiddeti azalmayan, dinmemiş, şiddetini sürdüren (*fırtına vs.*).

un.a.ble ['ʌn'eibl] *adj.* gücü yetmez, yapamaz (**to** *inf.* -*meyi*), iktidarsız, âciz; beceriksiz.

un.a.bridged ['ʌnə'bridʒd] *adj.* kısaltılmamış, orijinal, tam.

un.ac.cept.a.ble ['ʌnək'septəbl] *adj.* kabul edilemez.

un.ac.com.mo.dat.ing ['ʌnə'kɔmə-deitiŋ] *adj.* rahatına düşkün.

un.ac.count.a.ble □ ['ʌnə'kauntəbl] anlatılmaz, açıklanamaz, garip; olağanüstü; sorumsuz.

un.ac.cus.tomed ['ʌnə'kʌstəmd] *adj.* alışılmamış, garip, tuhaf; **~ to** alışmamış -*e*, alışık olmayan -*e*.

un.ac.knowl.edged ['ʌnək'nɔlidʒd] *adj.* kabul edilmemiş, onaylanmamış, cevaplandırılmamış.

un.ac.quaint.ed ['ʌnə'kweintid] *adj.*; **~ with** tanışmayan *ile*, tanışık olmayan *ile*, bilmez.

un.a.dorned ['ʌnə'dɔːnd] *adj.* süslenmemiş, süssüz, sade, donatılmamış.

un.a.dul.ter.at.ed □ ['ʌnə'dʌltəreitid] saf(i), halis, katıksız.

un.ad.vis.a.ble □ ['ʌnəd'vaizəbl] tavsiye edilmez; **'un.ad'vised** □ [‿zd], *adv.* ‿zidli] danışmamış, nasihat almamış; düşüncesiz, patavatsız.

un.af.fect.ed □ ['ʌnə'fektid] etkilenmemiş, değişmemiş; *fig.* samimî, içten.

un.a.fraid ['ʌnə'freid] *adj.* korkusuz, cesur, gözü pek.

un.aid.ed ['ʌn'eidid] *adj.* yardım görmemiş, yardım edilmemiş, yardımsız.

un.al.ien.a.ble ['ʌn'eiljənəbl] *adj.* alınamaz, ayrılamaz, devredilemez.

un.al.loyed ['ʌnə'lɔid] *adj.* saf(i), halis, katışıksız; *fig.* tam.

un.al.ter.a.ble □ [ʌn'ɔ:ltərəbl] değiş-(tirile)mez, sabit; **un'al.tered** *adj.* değiştirilmemiş.

un.am.big.u.ous □ ['ʌnæm'bigjuəs] tam, kesin, açık, belli.

un.am.bi.tious □ ['ʌnæm'biʃəs] kanaatkâr, kanık, ihtirası olmayan, yetingen.

un.a.me.na.ble ['ʌnə'mi:nəbl] *adj.* dik başlı, asi; sorumsuz.

un-A.mer.i.can ['ʌnə'merikən] *adj.* Amerikan(vari) olmayan.

un.a.mi.a.ble □ ['ʌn'eimjəbl] sevimsiz, nahoş.

u.na.nim.i.ty [ju:nə'nimiti] *n.* oy birliği, ittifak; **u.nan.i.mous** □ [ju:'næniməs] aynı fikirde, hemfikir, oydaş.

un.an.nounced ['ʌnə'naunst] *adj.* duyurulmamış, anons edilmemiş, habersiz (gelen).

un.an.swer.a.ble □ [ʌn'ɑ:nsərəbl] cevaplandırılamaz, reddedilemez; **'un-'answered** *adj.* cevaplandırılmamış (*mektup vs.*); karşılıksız (*aşk*).

un.ap.palled ['ʌnə'pɔ:ld] *adj.* korkusuz, pervasız.

un.ap.peal.a.ble JUR ['ʌnə'pi:ləbl] *adj.* temyiz edilemez.

un.ap.peas.a.ble □ ['ʌnə'pi:zəbl] yatıştırılamaz, amansız.

un.ap.proach.a.ble □ ['ʌnə'prəutʃ-əbl] yanına varılamaz, yaklaşılamaz; uzak; çok üstün, eşsiz.

un.ap.pro.pri.at.ed ['ʌnə'prəuprieit-id] *adj.* sahipsiz.

un.apt □ ['ʌn'æpt] uygunsuz; kalın kafalı; **~ to** *inf.* -*meyi* yapacağa benzemeyen; **be ~ to learn** çarçabuk öğrenememek.

un.armed ['ʌn'ɑːmd] *adj.* silahsız.

un.a.shamed □ ['ʌnə'ʃeimd] utanmaz, arsız, yüzsüz.

un.asked ['ʌn'ɑ:skt] *adj.* sorulmamış; davetsiz; istenmemiş.

un.as.sail.a.ble □ [ʌnə'seiləbl] katî, kesin, muhakkak; saldırılamaz.

un.as.sist.ed □ ['ʌnə'sistid] yardım(cı)sız.

un.as.sum.ing ['ʌnə'sju:miŋ] *adj.* gösterişsiz, mütevazı, alçak gönüllü.

un.at.tached ['ʌnə'tætʃt] *adj.* bağımsız, bekâr.

un.at.tain.a.ble □ ['ʌnə'teinəbl] elde edilemez; ulaşılamaz.

un.at.tend.ed ['ʌnə'tendid] *adj.* yalnız, arkadaşsız; yapılmamış, bakılmamış (*iş vs.*); sahipsiz.

un.at.trac.tive □ [ʌnə'træktiv] gösterişsiz, sade, şatafatsız, cazibesiz, sevimsiz.

un.au.thor.ized ['ʌn'ɔ:θəraizd] adj. yetkisiz; gayri resmi.

un.a.vail.a.ble ['ʌnə'veiləbl] adj. mevcut olmayan; kullanılmaz, işe yaramaz; 'un.a'vail.ing adj. boşuna; başarısız; tesirsiz, faydasız.

un.a.void.a.ble □ [ʌnə'vɔidəbl] kaçınılmaz, çaresiz.

un.a.ware ['ʌnə'wɛə] adj. habersiz, farkında olmayan; önemsemeyen; be ~ of -in farkında olmamak, -den habersiz olm.; 'un.a'wares adv. beklenmedik bir anda, ansızın; farkında olmadan, bilinçsizce.

un.backed ['ʌn'bækt] adj. desteklenmeyen; üzerine bahse girilmemiş; arkasız; ~ horse üzerine binilmemiş at.

un.bal.ance ['ʌn'bæləns] n. dengesizlik; 'un'bal.anced adj. dengesiz; aklî dengesi bozuk; birbirini tutmayan.

un.bap.tized ['ʌnbæp'taizd] adj. vaftiz edilmemiş.

un.bar ['ʌn'bɑ:] v/t. -in sürgüsünü açmak.

un.bear.a.ble □ [ʌn'bɛərəbl] dayanılmaz, çekilmez, hoşgörülemez.

un.beat.en ['ʌn'bi:tn] adj. kırılmamış (rekor vs.); yenilmemiş (takım vs.); dövülmemiş; ayak basılmamış.

un.be.com.ing □ ['ʌnbi'kʌmiŋ] yakışmamış, yakışıksız, uygunsuz; münasip olmayan (to veya for s.o. b-i için).

un.be.friend.ed ['ʌnbi'frendid] adj. arkadaşsız, dostsuz.

un.be.known ['ʌnbi'nəun] adj. meçhul; habersiz; ~ to s.o. b-nin haberi olmadan.

un.be.lief ['ʌnbi'li:f] n. imansızlık, inançsızlık; un.be'liev.a.ble □ inanılmaz; 'unbe'liev.er n. imansız, dinsiz, kâfir; 'unbe'liev.ing □ imansız; şüpheci.

un.be.loved ['ʌnbi'lʌvd] adj. sevilmeyen.

un.bend ['ʌn'bend] (irr. bend) v/t. & v/i. gevşe(t)mek (a. fig.), yumuşa(t)mak; dinlen(dir)mek; MEC düzel(t)mek, doğrul(t)mak; 'un'bend.ing □ eğilmez; fig. kararlı, sabit, kararından dönmez; boyun eğmez.

un.be.seem.ing □ ['ʌnbi'si:miŋ] yakışıksız, uygunsuz.

un.bi.as(s)ed □ ['ʌn'baiəst] tarafsız, yansız, bitaraf.

un.bid(.den) ['ʌn'bid(n)] adj. davetsiz; kendiliğinden gelen.

un.bind ['ʌn'baind] (irr. bind) v/t. çözmek; gevşetmek; serbest bırakmak, salıvermek.

un.bleached ['ʌn'bli:tʃt] adj. ağartılmamış.

un.blem.ished [ʌn'blemiʃt] adj. lekesiz; hatasız, kusursuz.

un.blush.ing □ [ʌn'blʌʃiŋ] utanmaz, arsız, yüzsüz.

un.bolt ['ʌn'bəult] v/t. -in sürgüsünü açmak; 'un'bolt.ed adj. sürgülenmemiş; elenmemiş (un vs.).

un.born ['ʌn'bɔ:n] adj. henüz doğmamış; gelecek, müstakbel.

un.bos.om [ʌn'buzəm] v/t. açığa vurmak, ortaya dökmek; ~ o.s. içini dökmek (to s.o. b-ne).

un.bound ['ʌn'baund] adj. çözük, bağlı olmayan; ciltsiz (kitap).

un.bound.ed □ [ʌn'baundid] sınırsız, hudutsuz; sonsuz, ölçüsüz.

un.brace ['ʌn'breis] v/t. çözmek; gevşetmek; zayıflatmak.

un.break.a.ble ['ʌn'breikəbl] adj. kırılamaz.

un.bri.dled [ʌn'braidld] adj. gem vurulmamış (at); fig. azgın, dizginlenemeyen, önüne geçilmez (hırs vs.).

un.bro.ken ['ʌn'brəukən] adj. kırılmamış (rekor vs.); sürekli, aralıksız; ehlileştirilmemiş, alıştırılmamış (at); bütün, tam; bozulmamış; sürülmemiş (toprak).

un.buck.le ['ʌn'bʌkl] v/t. -in tokasını çözmek.

un.bur.den ['ʌn'bɔ:dn] v/t. mst fig. açığa vurmak, dökmek (içini, derdini).

un.bur.ied ['ʌn'berid] adj. gömülmemiş.

un.burned ['ʌn'bɔ:nd] adj., un.burnt ['ʌ'bɔ:nt] yanmamış.

un.busi.ness.like [ʌn'biznislaik] adj. iş düzenine aykırı.

un.but.ton ['ʌn'bʌtn] v/t. -in düğmelerini çözmek.

un.called ['ʌn'kɔ:ld] adj. çağrılmamış, davetsiz; COM talep edilmemiş; un'called-for adj. lüzumsuz, gereksiz, yersiz.

un.can.did □ ['ʌn'kændid] ikiyüzlü, dürüst olmayan.

un.can.ny □ [ʌn'kæni] tekin olmayan; esrarengiz, acayip, anlaşılmaz.

un.cared-for ['ʌn'kɛədfɔ:] adj. bakımsız, ihmal edilmiş.

un.case ['ʌn'keis] *v/t.* açmak, çözmek.

un.ceas.ing ☐ [ʌn'siːsiŋ] durmayan, aralıksız, sürekli, devamlı; sonsuz, ebedî.

un.cer.e.mo.ni.ous ☐ ['ʌnseri-'məunjəs] gayri resmî; teklifsiz, lâubali; kaba, nezaketsiz.

un.cer.tain ☐ [ʌn'səːtn] *com.* şüpheli; kararsız, belirsiz; güvenilmez; değişken, dönek; **be ~ of** *-den* emin olmamak; **un'cer.tain.ty** *n.* şüphe, tereddüt, kesin olmayış.

un.chain ['ʌn'tʃein] *v/t.* serbest bırakmak, salıvermek.

un.chal.lenge.a.ble ['ʌn'tʃælindʒəbl] *adj.* su götürmez, tartışılmaz; 'un-'chal.lenged *adj.* itiraz kabul etmez, tartışılmaz.

un.change.a.ble ☐ [ʌn'tʃeindʒəbl], un'chang.ing değişmez; 'un'changed *adj.* değişmemiş, eskisi gibi.

un.char.i.ta.ble ☐ [ʌn'tʃæritəbl] merhametsiz, katı, sert.

un.chart.ed ['ʌn'tʃɑːtid] *adj.* haritada olmayan; meçhul, bilinmeyen, keşfedilmemiş.

un.chaste ☐ ['ʌn'tʃeist] namussuz, iffetsiz; **un.chas.ti.ty** ['ʌn'tʃæstiti] *n.* namussuzluk.

un.checked ['ʌn'tʃekt] *adj.* durdurulmamış, serbest, kontrolsüz, dizginsiz.

un.chris.tian ☐ ['ʌn'kristjən] Hıristiyan olmayan; Hıristiyanlığa aykırı; medeniyetsiz; yersiz, uygunsuz.

un.civ.il ☐ ['ʌn'sivl] nezaketsiz, kaba; 'un'civ.i.lized [_vilaizd] *adj.* medeniyetsiz, medenileşmemiş.

un.claimed ['ʌn'kleimd] *adj.* sahibi çıkmamış.

un.clasp ['ʌn'klɑːsp] *v/t.* bırakmak (*sıkılan el vs.*), açmak (*toka vs.*).

un.cle ['ʌŋkl] *n.* amca, dayı, enişte; *sl.* tefeci.

un.clean ☐ ['ʌn'kliːn] pis, kirli; *fig.* ahlâksız.

un.clench ['ʌn'klentʃ] *v/t. & v/i.* aç(tır)mak.

un.cloak ['ʌn'kləuk] *v/t. -in* örtüsünü kaldırmak; *fig.* açığa vurmak, ortaya dökmek.

un.close ['ʌn'kləuz] *v/t. & v/i.* aç(ıl)mak; açığa vurmak.

un.clothe ['ʌn'kləuð] *v/t. -in* elbisesini çıkarmak, soymak.

un.cloud.ed ['ʌn'klaudid] *adj.* bulutsuz; berrak, parlak (*a. fig.*).

un.coil ['ʌn'kɔil] *v/t. & v/i.* çöz(ül)mek,

aç(ıl)mak.

un.col.lect.ed ['ʌnkə'lektid] *adj.* toplanmamış; *fig.* kendine hâkim olmayan.

un.col.o(u)red ['ʌn'kʌləd] *adj.* boyasız; *fig.* abartmasız.

un-come-at-a.ble F ['ʌnkʌm'ætəbl] *adj.* yanına varılmaz, erişilmez.

un.come.ly ['ʌn'kʌmli] *adj.* yakışık almaz, yersiz, uygunsuz.

un.com.fort.a.ble ☐ [ʌn'kʌmfətəbl] rahatsız (edici).

un.com.mit.ted [ʌnkə'mitid] *adj.* taahhüt altına girmemiş; POL bağımsız, hür.

un.com.mon ☐ [ʌn'kəmən] (*a.* F *adv.*) olağanüstü, görülmedik; nadir, seyrek.

un.com.mu.ni.ca.tive ['ʌnkə'mjuːnikətiv] *adj.* az konuşur, ağzı sıkı.

un.com.plain.ing ☐ ['ʌnkəm'pleiniŋ] şikâyet etmeyen, sabırlı.

un.com.pro.mis.ing ☐ [ʌn'kɔmprəmaiziŋ] uzlaşmaz, uyuşmaz; *fig.* eğilmez, sert.

un.con.cern ['ʌnkən'səːn] *n.* ilgisizlik, kayıtsızlık; 'un.con.'cerned ☐ [*adv.* _idli] endişesiz, kayıtsız, ilgisiz (**about** *hususunda*); duygusuz, hissiz (**with** *-e karşı*); ilgisi olmayan, karışmamış (**in** *-e*).

un.con.di.tion.al ☐ ['ʌnkən'diʃənl] (kayıtsız) şartsız.

un.con.fined ['ʌnkən'faind] kuşatılmamış; sınırsız, hudutsuz, serbest.

un.con.firmed ['ʌnkən'fəːmd] *adj.* doğrulanmamış; COM teyitsiz.

un.con.gen.ial ['ʌnkən'dʒiːnjəl] *adj.* sıkıcı; uygun olmayan.

un.con.nect.ed ☐ ['ʌnkə'nektid] ilgisiz, alâkasız; birbirini tutmaz.

un.con.quer.a.ble ☐ [ʌn'kɔŋkərəbl] zaptedilemez, fethedilemez; 'un'conquered *adj.* fethedilmemiş.

un.con.sci.en.tious ☐ ['ʌnkənʃi'enʃəs] vicdansız; mantıksız; aşırı, fazla.

un.con.scion.a.ble ☐ ['ʌn'kɔnʃnəbl] mantıksız; vicdansız; prensipsiz; F fahiş (*fiyat*).

un.con.scious [ʌn'kɔnʃəs] **1.** ☐ suursuz, bilinçsiz; baygın; **be ~ of** *-in* bilincinde olmamak; **2.** *n.* **the ~** PSYCH bilinçaltı; un'con.scious.ness *n.* şuursuzluk, bilinçsizlik.

un.con.se.crat.ed ['ʌn'kɔnsikreitid] *adj.* adanmamış; kutsanmamış.

un.con.sid.ered ['ʌnkən'sidəd] *adj.*

düşüncesizce söylenmiş (*söz*); önemsenmemiş.

un.con.sti.tu.tion.al ☐ ['ʌnkənsti-'tjuːʃənl] anayasaya aykırı.

un.con.strained ☐ ['ʌnkən'streind] serbest, kolay.

un.con.test.ed ☐ ['ʌnkən'testid] itiraza uğramamış.

un.con.tra.dict.ed ['ʌnkɔntrə'diktid] *adj.* yalanlanmamış.

un.con.trol.la.ble ☐ [ʌnkən'trəuləbl] idare edilemez, yönetilemez; önlenemez; '**un.con'trolled** *adj.* kontrolsüz, başıboş, idaresiz; *fig. k-ne* hâkim olamayan, dizginsiz.

un.con.ven.tion.al ☐ ['ʌnkən'venʃənl] göreneklere uymayan; garip, acayip; läubali.

un.con.vert.ed ['ʌnkən'vəːtid] *adj.* değiştirilmemiş; COM paraya çevrilmemiş.

un.con.vinced ['ʌnkən'vinst] *adj.* emin olmayan, inanmamış; '**un.con-'vinc.ing** *adj.* inandırıcı olmayan, inanılmaz.

un.cooked ['ʌn'kukt] *adj.* piş(iril)memiş.

un.cord ['ʌn'kɔːd] *v/t. -in* ipini çözmek.

un.cork ['ʌn'kɔːk] *v/t. -in* tapasını çıkarmak.

un.cor.rupt.ed ☐ ['ʌnkə'rʌptid] bozulmamış.

un.count.a.ble ['ʌn'kauntəbl] *adj.* sayılamayan; '**un'count.ed** *adj.* sayılmamış; hesapsız, sayılamayacak kadar çok.

un.cou.ple ['ʌn'kʌpl] *v/t.* çözmek, ayırmak.

un.couth ☐ [ʌn'kuːθ] kaba, nezaketsiz, kültürsüz; garip, acayip.

un.cov.er [ʌn'kʌvə] *v/t. -in* örtüsünü kaldırmak, açmak; ortaya, açığa çıkarmak; saldırmak; *v/i.* şapkasını çıkarmak.

un.crit.i.cal ☐ ['ʌn'kritikəl] eleştirmeyen, tenkit etmeyen.

un.crowned ['ʌn'kraund] *adj.* taç giymemiş; resmî sıfatı olmayan.

unc.tion ['ʌŋkʃən] *n.* yağ (sürme); *fig.* aşırı tatlı dillilik, yalancı nezaket; **ex-treme ~** ECCL Katoliklerde ölmekte olan birine yağ sürme ayini; **unc.tu-ous** ☐ ['ʌŋktjuəs] yağlı; *fig.* aşırı tatlı dilli, yalandan heyecanlı görünen.

un.cul.ti.vat.ed ['ʌn'kʌltiveitid] *adj.* işlenmemiş (*toprak*); *fig.* kültürsüz, yontulmamış.

un.cured ['ʌn'kjuəd] *adj.* iyileşmemiş; tedavi edilmemiş.

un.curl ['ʌn'kəːl] *v/t. & v/i.* aç(ıl)mak (*kıvrım*).

un.cut ['ʌn'kʌt] *adj.* kesilmemiş, makaslanmamış (*film*), kısaltılmamış (*kitap*); sayfa kenarları açılmamış (*kitap*); yontulmamış (*kıymetli taş*).

un.dam.aged ['ʌn'dæmidʒd] *adj.* zarar görmemiş, sağlam.

un.damped ['ʌn'dæmpt] *adj.* sindirilmemiş; gücenmemiş, kırılmamış.

un.dat.ed ['ʌn'deitid] *adj.* tarihsiz.

un.daunt.ed ☐ [ʌn'dɔːntid] korkusuz, gözü pek, yılmaz.

un.de.ceive ['ʌndi'siːv] *v/t.* aldatılmaktan kurtarmak, gözünü açmak (**of**).

un.de.cid.ed ☐ ['ʌndi'saidid] kararsız; kararlaştırılmamış; as(k)ıda, sallantıda.

un.de.ci.pher.a.ble ['ʌndi'saifərəbl] *adj.* okunamaz, çözülemez.

un.de.fend.ed ['ʌndi'fendid] *adj.* korunmamış, savunulmamış.

un.de.filed ['ʌndi'faild] *adj.* lekelenmemiş, kirlenmemiş, tertemiz.

un.de.fined ☐ ['ʌndi'faind, *adv.* _-nidli] tarif edilmemiş; bellisiz, belirsiz.

un.de.mon.stra.tive ☐ ['ʌndi'mɔn-strətiv] ağzı sıkı; duygularını belli etmeyen.

un.de.ni.a.ble ☐ [ʌndi'naiəbl] inkâr olunamaz; mükemmel.

un.de.nom.i.na.tion.al ☐ ['ʌndinɔmi-'neiʃənl] mezhepsiz, din ayrımı gözetmeyen.

un.der ['ʌndə] **1.** *adv. -in* altın(d)a, dibe; *-den* aşağı(da), altta; alt mevkide, daha aşağı derecede; **2.** *prp. -in* altın(d)a; *-in* altı; *-in* altından; *-in* aşağısın(d)a; *-den* eksik, *-den* düşük; *-den* küçük; *-in* himayesinde; *-in* kumandasında, emrinde; *-in* yetkisinde; **from ~ ... -in** altından; **~ sentence of ...** JUR ...hükmü altında, ...e mahkûm olmuş; **3.** *adj.* alt...; alt(taki), az...; yardımcı, ikinci; iç; '**~'act** *v/t. & v/i.* THEAT (rolü) cansız, isteksiz oynamak; '**~'bid** (*irr.* **bid**) *v/t. -den* daha düşük fiyat vermek; '**~'bred** *adj.* terbiyesiz, kaba; saf kan olmayan; '**~.brush** *n.* çalılık; '**~.car.riage** *n.* AVIA iniş takımı; MOT şasi; '**~'charge** *v/t. -den* az ücret istemek; '**~.clothes** *n. pl.*, '**~.cloth.ing** iç çamaşır; '**~.cov.er** *adj.* gizli...; '**~-cur.rent** *n.* dip akıntısı; *fig.* gizli eğilim; '**~'cut** *v/t. -den* daha ucuza fiyat teklif etm., kırmak (*fiyat*); *-in* altını kesmek; '~.dog *n.* ezilen kişi, haksızlığa uğramış zavallı kimse, biçare; '~'done *adj.* iyi piş(iril)memiş, az pişmiş; '~'dress *v/t. -in* altına giydirmek; *v/i. -in* altına giyinmek; '~'es.ti-mate *v/t.* gereğinden az değer vermek *-e*, küçümsemek *-i*; '~-ex'pose *v/t.* PHOT karanlık çıkarmak, düşük poza tutmak; '~'fed *adj.* gıdasız; '~'feed.ing *n.* yetersiz beslenme; ~'foot *adv.* ayak altında; yerde, yolda; ~'go (*irr.* **go**) *v/t.* katlanmak, uğramak *-e*, çekmek *-i*; geçirmek *-i*; ~'grad.u.ate *n.* UNIV üniversite öğrencisi; '~.ground **1.** *adj.* yeraltında olan, yeraltı...; gizli...; ~ *movement* yeraltı örgütü; *go* ~ saklanmak; **2.** *n. a.* ~ *railway* metro; yeraltı geçidi; '~-growth *n.* çalılık; '~.hand *adj. & adv.* el altından, gizlice, sinsi sinsi, kurnazca, alçakça; *spor:* aşağıdan atılan (*veya* vurulan); '~'hung *adj.* alt çenesi çıkık; ~.lay **1.** [ʌndə'lei] (*irr.* **lay**) *v/t. -in* altını kaplamak; *-in* altına koymak, beslemek; **2.** ['~] *n.* besleme maddesi (*keçe, lastik vs.*); '~'let (*irr.* **let**) *v/t.* düşük fiyata kiraya vermek; ~'lie (*irr.* **lie**) *vb. -in* altında olm.; *fig. -in* esasını oluşturmak; ~.line **1.** [ʌndə'lain] *v/t. -in* altını çizmek; *-in* önemini belirtmek; **2.** ['~] *n.* alt çizgi; '~.lin.en *n.* iç çamaşır.

un.der.ling ['ʌndəliŋ] *n.* ast, başkasının emrinde olan kimse; un.der'ly.ing *adj.* alttaki; temel, esas; un.der.manned ['~'mænd] *adj.* personeli yetersiz olan; un.der'mine *v/t. -in* altını kazmak (*veya* oymak); *fig. -in* temelini çürütmek, zayıflatmak, sarsmak (*otorite vs.*); 'un.dermost *adj. & adv.* en alttaki; un.der.neath [~'ni:θ] *prp. & adv. -in* altın(d)a; 'un.der'nour.ished *adj.* iyi beslenmemiş, gıdasız kalmış.

un.der...: '~.pass *n.* alt geçit; '~'pay (*irr.* **pay**) *v/t.* hakkından az ücret vermek *-e*; ~'pin *v/t.* MEC *-in* altını desteklemek, beslemek; *fig.* desteklemek, arka çıkmak; ~'pin.ning *n.* MEC destek, ayak; yapı temeli; '~.plot *n.* yan aksiyon; '~'print *v/t.* PHOT az basmak; '~'priv.i.leged *adj.* temel imkânları kıt olan; ~'rate *v/t.* gereğinden az değer vermek *-e*, küçümsemek *-i*; ~'score *v/t. -in* altını çizmek; *-in* üstünde durmak; '~-'sec.re.tar.y *n.* müsteşar, müşavir; '~'sell COM (*irr.* **sell**) *v/t.* fiyat kırarak satmak; '~'shoot (*irr.* **shoot**) *v/t.*: ~ *the runway* AVIA uçağı inişten önce pis-

te değdirerek yeniden havalandırmak; '~.shot *adj.* alt dişleri çıkıntılı olan; alttan geçen su ile işleyen; '~.side *n.* alt kısım; ~'signed *adj.* imza sahibi; '~'sized *adj.* normalden küçük; bodur, cücemsi; '~.slung MOT dingile alttan bağlı...; ~ *frame* alçak şasi; '~'staffed *adj.* personeli az olan; ~'stand (*irr.* **stand**) *v/t. com.* anlamak, kavramak, bilmek; öğrenmek; kestirmek; farz etm.; tahmin etm.; *v/i.* anlayışlı olm.; *b-nin* duygularını paylaşmak; *make o.s. understood* derdini anlatabilmek; *it is understood* demek (oluyor ki), anlaşılıyor ki; *that is understood* anlaşıldı; *an understood thing* anlaşılmış *bş*; ~'stand.a.ble *adj.* anlaşılır, kavranılır; ~'stand.ing **1.** *n.* anlayış, kavrama; anlaşma; açıklama, yorum; duygudaşlık, sempati; *on the* ~ *that* ...koşuluyla, ...şartıyla; **2.** *adj.* anlayışlı; '~'state *v/t.* olduğundan az *veya* hafif göstermek, küçültmek; '~'state.ment *n.* olduğundan hafif gösteren ifade, az gösterme.

un.der...: '~.strap.per = *underling*; '~.study THEAT **1.** *n.* yedek oyuncu, yardımcı oyuncu; **2.** *vb.* başka oyuncunun yerine geçebilmek için onun rolünü ezberlemek; ~'take (*irr.* **take**) *v/t.* üzerine almak, yüklenmek, üstlenmek (*to inf. -meyi*); girişmek, başlamak; ~ *that* ...meyi garanti etm., ...meye söz vermek; '~.tak.er *n.* cenaze işleri görevlisi, ölü kaldırıcısı; ~'tak.ing *n.* iş, teşebbüs, girişim; garanti, vaat, söz; cenaze işi; '~'ten.ant *n.* ikinci kiracı, kiracının kiracısı; '~.tone *n.* alçak ses tonu, fısıltı; donuk *veya* mat renk; *in an* ~ alçak sesle; '~'val.ue *v/t.* kıymetinden az değer vermek *-e*; küçümsemek, hafife almak; '~.wear *n.* iç çamaşır; '~-weight *n.* normalden hafif olan ağırlık; '~.wood *n.* çalılık; '~.world *n.* ölüler diyarı; kanunsuzlar âlemi, yeraltı dünyası; '~.write COM (*irr.* **write**) *v/t. -in* masrafını ödemeyi taahhüt etm.; sigorta etm.; imzalamak; '~.wri.ter *n.* sigortacı.

un.de.served □ ['ʌndi'zə:vd] lâyık olmayan, hak edilmemiş; 'un.de'serv-ing *adj.* hak etmeyen.

un.de.signed □ ['ʌndi'zaind] kasıtsız; önceden tasarlanmamış; önceden bilinmeyen.

un.de.sir.a.ble ['ʌndi'zaiərəbl] **1.** □ hosa gitmeyen, istenilmeyen; itiraz edilebilir, hoş karşılanmayan; **2.** *n.* istenilmeyen kimse.

un.de.terred ['ʌndi'tɜːd] *adj.* azimli, yılmayan.

un.de.vel.oped ['ʌndi'veləpt] *adj.* gelişmemiş; işlenmemiş (*toprak*).

un.de.vi.at.ing □ [ʌn'diːvieitiŋ] yolunu şaşmayan.

un.dies F ['ʌndiz] *n. pl.* kadın iç çamaşırı.

un.di.gest.ed ['ʌndi'dʒestid] *adj.* hazmedilmemiş.

un.dig.ni.fied □ [ʌn'dignifaid] onursuz, haysiyetsiz; beceriksiz, sakar.

un.di.min.ished ['ʌndi'miniʃt] *adj.* azalmamış, eksilmemiş.

un.di.rect.ed ['ʌndi'rektid] *adj.* idare altında olmayan; yönlendirilmemiş; adressiz (*mektup*).

un.dis.cerned □ ['ʌndi'sɜːnd] ayırt edilmemiş; **'un.dis'cern.ing** *adj.* anlayışsız.

un.dis.charged ['ʌndis'tʃɑːdʒd] *adj.* boşaltılmamış (*yük*); ödenmemiş (*borç*).

un.dis.ci.plined [ʌn'disiplind] *adj.* disiplinsiz, terbiye edilmemiş; afacan.

un.dis.cov.ered ['ʌndis'kʌvəd] *adj.* keşfedilmemiş, meçhul.

un.dis.crim.i.nat.ing □ ['ʌndis'krimineitiŋ] farkı ayırt edemeyen.

un.dis.guised □ ['ʌndis'gaizd] kılığını değiştirmemiş, gizlenmemiş; açık, içten.

un.dis.posed ['ʌndis'pəuzd] *adj.* isteksiz, gönülsüz (**to** -*e*); COM satılmamış, elde kalmış.

un.dis.put.ed □ ['ʌndis'pjuːtid] karşı gelinmeyen, tartışılmaz.

un.dis.tin.guished ['ʌndis'tiŋgwiʃt] *adj.* alelade, silik, önemsiz, hiçten; kaba.

un.dis.tort.ed ['ʌndis'tɔːtid] *adj.* bozulmamış, çarpıtılmamış.

un.dis.turbed □ ['ʌndis'tɜːbd] karıştırılmamış, rahatsız edilmemiş; rahat.

un.di.vid.ed □ ['ʌndi'vaidid] bölünmemiş; bütün; devamlı.

un.do ['ʌn'duː] (*irr. do*) *v/t.* açmak, çözmek, sökmek, gevşetmek; *rare* bozmak, mahvetmek; telâfi etm.; **'un'do.ing** *n.* çözme, açma; yıkım, felâket; feshetme.

un.do.mes.ti.cat.ed ['ʌndə'mestikeit-id] *adj.* ev işlerine alıştırılmamış, ev işlerine ilgi duymayan.

un.done ['ʌn'dʌn] *adj.* açık, bağı çözülmüş; bitirilmemiş, yapılmamış; mahvolmuş, perişan; **he is** ~ hapı yuttu, yandı; **come** ~ açılmak, çözülmek.

un.doubt.ed □ [ʌn'dautid] kesin, şüphesiz.

un.dreamt [ʌn'dremt] *adj.* ~-*of* akla hayale gelmez.

un.dress ['ʌn'dres] **1.** *v/t. & v/i.* soy(un)mak, elbiselerini çıkarmak; **2.** *n.* çıplaklık; MIL sivil elbise; 'un-'dressed *adj.* çıplak; işlenmemiş (*deri vs.*); bakımsız.

un.due ['ʌn'djuː] *adj.* uygunsuz, yakışık almaz; aşırı; kanunsuz; gereksiz, yersiz; COM vadesi gelmemiş.

un.du.late ['ʌndjuleit] *v/t. & v/i.* dalgalan(dır)mak; dalga dalga olm., inişli çıkışlı olm.; **'un.du.lat.ing** □ dalgalı; inişli çıkışlı; **un.du'la.tion** *n.* dalga(-lanma); **un.du.la.to.ry** ['‑lətəri] *adj.* dalgalanmaya ait; dalgalı…

un.du.ly ['ʌn'djuːli] *adv. of* **undue**.

un.du.ti.ful □ ['ʌn'djuːtiful] itaatsiz, saygısız; görevine bağlı olmayan, sorumluluk duygusu taşımayan.

un.dy.ing □ [ʌn'daiiŋ] ölmez, ölümsüz, sonsuz, ebedî.

un.earned ['ʌn'ɜːnd] *adj.* çalışarak kaza nılmamış; *fig.* hak edilmemiş; ~ *income* havadan gelen gelir.

un.earth ['ʌn'ɜːθ] *v/t.* topraktan çıkarmak; *fig.* ortaya çıkarmak, keşfetmek; **un'earth.ly** *adj.* doğaüstü; esrarengiz, korkunç, müthiş; F uygunsuz.

un.eas.i.ness [ʌn'iːzinis] *n.* huzursuzluk, rahatsızlık; endişe; **un'eas.y** □ huzursuz, rahatsız; üzgün; gergin; endişeli (**about** -*den*); rahatsız edici.

un.eat.a.ble ['ʌn'iːtəbl] *adj.* yen(il)-mez.

un.e.co.nom.ic, un.e.co.nom.i.cal □ ['ʌniːkə'nɔmik(əl)] ekonomik olmayan; savurgan.

un.ed.i.fy.ing □ ['ʌn'edifaiiŋ] eğitici olmayan.

un.ed.u.cat.ed ['ʌn'edjukeitid] *adj.* okumamış, cahil.

un.em.bar.rassed ['ʌnim'bærəst] *adj.* utanmaz, sıkılmaz.

un.e.mo.tion.al □ ['ʌni'məuʃənl] hissiz, duygusuz.

un.em.ployed ['ʌnim'plɔid] **1.** *adj.* işsiz (güçsüz); kullanılmayan; **2.** *n.* **the** ~ *pl.* işsizler; **'un.em'ploy.ment** *n.* işsizlik; ~ **benefit**, ~ **pay** işsizlik tazminatı.

un.en.cum.bered ['ʌnin'kʌmbəd] *adj.*

ipoteksiz; yüksüz; engelsiz.

un.end.ing □ [ʌn'endiŋ] sonsuz, bitmez tükenmez.

un.en.dowed ['ʌnin'daud] *adj.* bağışlanmamış; doğuştan yeteneksiz (*with*).

un.en.dur.a.ble ['ʌnin'djuərəbl] *adj.* dayanılmaz, çekilmez.

un.en.gaged ['ʌnin'geidʒd] *adj.* serbest, hür.

un-Eng.lish ['ʌn'iŋgliʃ] *adj.* İngiliz'e yakışmaz *veya* benzemez.

un.en.light.ened ['ʌnin'laitnd] *adj. fig.* okumamış; önyargılı; batıl inançlı.

un.en.ter.pris.ing ['ʌn'entəpraiziŋ] *adj.* uyanık olmayan, girişken olmayan.

un.en.vi.a.ble □ ['ʌn'enviəbl] kıskanılmaya değmez.

un.e.qual □ ['ʌn'iːkwəl] eşit olmayan; düzensiz; aynı nitelikte olmayan; haksız, adaletsiz; yetersiz (*to* -e); '**un.e.qual(l)ed** *adj.* eşsiz, eşi bulunmaz; üstün, rakipsiz.

un.e.quiv.o.cal □ ['ʌni'kwivəkəl] kesin, şüphesiz; tek anlamlı.

un.err.ing □ ['ʌn'əːriŋ] tam isabetli, doğru, kesin; yanılmaz, emin.

un.es.sen.tial □ ['ʌni'senʃəl] gereksiz, önemsiz (*to* -e).

un.e.ven □ ['ʌn'iːvən] düz olmayan, eğri büğrü, çarpık çurpuk; MATH tek (*sayı*); gayri muntazam, düzensiz, gelişigüzel; eşit olmayan, eşitsiz; değişken, dengesiz (*karakter vs.*).

un.e.vent.ful □ ['ʌni'ventful] olaysız, sakin; *be ~* olaysız geçmek.

un.ex.am.pled [ʌnig'zɑːmpld] *adj.* misli (*veya* eşi) görülmemiş, eşsiz.

un.ex.cep.tion.a.ble □ [ʌnik'sepʃnəbl] karşı çıkılmaz, itiraz kabul etmez; kusursuz.

un.ex.pect.ed ['ʌniks'pektid] beklenilmedik, umulmadık.

un.ex.pired ['ʌniks'paiəd] *adj.* süresi dolmamış, vadesi gelmemiş, günü geçmemiş.

un.ex.plained ['ʌniks'pleind] *adj.* açıklanmamış, anlaşılmamış.

un.ex.posed PHOT ['ʌniks'pəuzd] *adj.* poz verilmemiş.

un.ex.plored ['ʌniks'plɔːd] *adj.* keşfedilmemiş.

un.ex.pressed ['ʌniks'prest] *adj.* açıklanmamış.

un.fad.ing □ [ʌn'feidiŋ] solmaz, solmayan.

un.fail.ing □ [ʌn'feiliŋ] (bitmez) tüken-

mez, sonu gelmez; şaşmaz, doğru, güvenilir; yorulmaz; *fig.* sadık, vefalı.

un.fair □ ['ʌn'fɛə] haksız, adaletsiz; hileli; '**un'fair.ness** *n.* haksızlık.

un.faith.ful □ ['ʌn'feiθful] sadakatsiz, vefasız; güvenilmez; yanlış, hatalı; '**un'faith.ful.ness** *n.* sadakatsizlik.

un.fal.ter.ing □ [ʌn'fɔːltəriŋ] kararlı, azimli.

un.fa.mil.iar ['ʌnfə'miljə] *adj.* iyi bilmeyen, yabancı (*with* -i, -e); alışılmamış, garip.

un.fash.ion.a.ble □ ['ʌn'fæʃnəbl] modaya uymayan; eski moda.

un.fas.ten ['ʌn'fɑːsn] *v/t.* açmak, çözmek, gevşetmek.

un.fath.om.a.ble □ [ʌn'fæðəməbl] dibine ulaşılamaz; *fig.* anlaşılmaz, kavranılamaz, akıl ermez.

un.fa.vo(u)r.a.ble □ ['ʌn'feivərəbl] müsait olmayan; elverişsiz; zıt, ters, aksi; olumsuz; zararlı, sakıncalı.

un.feel.ing □ [ʌn'fiːliŋ] hissiz, duygusuz; katı yürekli, acımasız, merhametsiz.

un.feigned □ [ʌn'feind, *adv.* ˍnidli] yapmacıksız, samimî, içten; hakikî.

un.felt ['ʌn'felt] *adj.* hissedilmemiş.

un.fer.ment.ed ['ʌnfəː'mentid] *adj.* mayalandırılmamış.

un.fet.ter ['ʌn'fetə] *v/t.* kurtarmak, özgür kılmak; '**un'fet.tered** *adj. fig.* serbest, özgür.

un.fil.i.al □ ['ʌn'filjəl] evlada yakışmaz, saygısız.

un.fin.ished ['ʌn'finiʃt] *adj.* bitmemiş, tamamlanmamış.

un.fit 1. □ ['ʌn'fit] uymaz, uygunsuz (*for s.th.* bşe; *to inf.* -meye); yetersiz, ehliyetsiz; **2.** [ʌn'fit] *v/t.* işe yaramaz hale getirmek, kuvvetten düşürmek; '**un'fitness** *n.* uygunsuzluk; **un'fit.ted** *adj.* ehliyetsiz, uygun nitelikleri olmayan.

un.fix ['ʌn'fiks] *v/t.* çözmek, açmak, sökmek; kararsız kılmak; '**un'fixed** *adj.* kararlaştırılmamış.

un.flag.ging □ [ʌn'flægiŋ] yorulmaz; bitmez tükenmez.

un.flat.ter.ing □ ['ʌn'flætəriŋ] yerici, zemmedici.

un.fledged ['ʌn'fledʒd] *adj.* tüyleri bitmemiş, uçamayan (*kuş*); *fig.* toy, acemi çaylak, olgunlaşmamış.

un.flick.er.ing ['ʌn'flikəriŋ] *adj.* titrek yanmayan; *fig.* sabit.

un.flinch.ing □ [ʌn'flintʃiŋ] korkusuz,

yiğit, cesur, yılmaz.

un.fly.a.ble [ˈʌnˈflaiəbl] *adj.*; ~ *weather*
AVIA uçuşa elverişli olmayan hava.

un.fold [ˈʌnˈfəuld] *v/t. & v/i.* aç(ıl)mak,
yaymak; açıklamak, bildirmek, göz
önüne ser(il)mek; gelişmek (*hikâye
vs.*).

un.forced □ [ˈʌnˈfɔːst, *adv.* ˌsidli] tabiî.

un.fore.seen [ˈʌnfɔːˈsiːn] *adj.* beklenmedik, umulmadık.

un.for.get.ta.ble □ [ˈʌnfəˈgetəbl] unu-
tulmaz.

un.for.giv.ing [ˈʌnfəˈgiviŋ] *adj.* uzlaşmaz; affetmez, bağışlamaz, acımasız.

un.for.got, un.for.got.ten [ˈʌnfə-
ˈgɔt(n)] *adj.* unutulmamış.

un.for.ti.fied [ˈʌnˈfɔːtifaid] *adj.* kuv-
vetlendirilmemiş.

un.for.tu.nate [ʌnˈfɔːtʃnit] **1.** □ talihsiz, bahtsız, şanssız, bedbaht, biçare,
kimsesiz; pişmanlık duyulan; isabetsiz,
uygunsuz; **2.** *n.* şanssız kimse; **un'for-
tu.nate.ly** *adv.* maalesef, (ne) yazık ki.

un.found.ed □ [ˈʌnˈfaundid] temelsiz,
asılsız, boş, yalan.

un.fre.quent [ʌnˈfriːkwənt] *adj.* nadir,
ender, seyrek.

un.fre.quent.ed [ˈʌnfriˈkwentid] *adj.*
seyrek ziyaret edilen, sık sık gidilme-
yen; ıssız, tenha.

un.friend.ed [ˈʌnˈfrendid] *adj.* arkadaşsız, dostsuz; **un'friend.ly** *adj.* dostça olmayan, samimiyetsiz; düşmanca;
soğuk.

un.frock [ˈʌnˈfrɔk] *v/t.* papazlıktan
çıkarmak.

un.fruit.ful □ [ˈʌnˈfruːtful] verimsiz,
mahsulsüz; semeresiz, başarısız; kısır,
dölsüz.

un.ful.filled [ˈʌnfulˈfild] *adj.* yerine getirilmemiş.

un.furl [ˈʌnˈfəːl] *v/t.* açmak, yaymak,
sermek.

un.fur.nished [ˈʌnˈfəːniʃt] *adj.* mobilyasız, döşenmemiş; ~ *with* ile donatılmamış.

un.gain.li.ness [ʌnˈgeinlinis] *n.* hantallık, biçimsizlik; sakarlık; kabalık;
un'gain.ly *adj.* hantal, biçimsiz; sakar;
kaba, inceliksiz.

un.gal.lant □ [ˈʌnˈgælənt] kaba, nezaketsiz (**to** -e karşı).

un.gear MEC [ˈʌnˈgiə] *v/t.* birbirinden
ayırmak, avaraya almak; boşa almak
(*vites*).

un.gen.er.ous □ [ˈʌnˈdʒenərəs] cö-

mert olmayan, cimri, pinti; merhametsiz, gönlü yüce olmayan.

un.gen.ial □ [ˈʌnˈdʒiːnjəl] suratsız,
soğuk, nezaketsiz.

un.gen.tle □ [ˈʌnˈdʒentl] sert, haşin,
gaddar, kaba.

un.gen.tle.man.ly [ʌnˈdʒentlmənli]
adj. nezaketsiz, kaba.

un.get-at-able [ˈʌnget'ætəbl] *adj.*
erişilmez, yanına yaklaşılmaz.

un.glazed [ˈʌnˈgleizd] *adj.* sırlan-
mamış, perdahsız.

un.god.li.ness [ʌnˈgɔdlinis] *n.* dinsizlik, günahkârlık, Allahsızlık; **un'godly** □ Allahsız, dinsiz, günahkâr; F Allahın cezası, berbat, uygunsuz; F can
sıkıcı.

un.gov.ern.a.ble □ [ʌnˈgʌvənəbl] yönetilemez, hâkim olunmaz, asi; **'un-
'gov.erned** *adj. k-ne* hâkim olamayan.

un.grace.ful □ [ˈʌnˈgreisful] inceliksiz, kaba, nezaketsiz; beceriksiz, hantal.

un.gra.cious □ [ˈʌnˈgreiʃəs] nezaketsiz, kaba; hoşa gitmeyen, nahoş.

un.gram'mat.i.cal □ [ˈʌngrəˈmætikəl]
dilbilgisi kurallarına aykırı olan.

un.grate.ful □ [ʌnˈgreitful] nankör;
nahoş, tatsız (*iş*).

un.ground.ed [ʌnˈgraundid] *adj.*
asılsız, yersiz, boş; ELECT topraklan-
mamış.

un.grudg.ing □ [ˈʌnˈgrʌdʒiŋ] isteyerek, seve seve yapan; istekli.

un.gual ANAT [ˈʌŋgwəl] *adj.* toynak...,
pençe..., tırnak...

un.guard.ed □ [ˈʌnˈgɑːdid] koruyucu-
suz; dikkatsiz, tedbirsiz, gafil; MEC mu-
hafazasız.

un.guent [ˈʌŋgwənt] *n.* merhem, yağ.

un.guid.ed □ [ˈʌnˈgaidid] rehbersiz.

un.gu.late [ˈʌŋgjuleit] *n. a.* ~ *animal*
toynaklılar familyasından bir hayvan.

un.hal.lowed [ʌnˈhæləud] *adj.* takdis
edilmemiş, kutsanmamış; kötü,
hayırsız; kâfir; ahlâksız, edepsiz.

un.ham.pered [ʌnˈhæmpəd] *adj.* engellenmemiş, serbest.

un.hand.some □ [ʌnˈhænsəm]
yakışıklı olmayan, çirkin (*a. fig.*); uygunsuz, yakışıksız; kaba, nezaketsiz.

un.hand.y □ [ʌnˈhændi] kullanışsız, elverişsiz; acemi, sakar, eli işe yakışmaz.

un.hap.pi.ness [ʌnˈhæpinis] *n.* mutsuzluk, keder; **un'hap.py** □ mutsuz,
kederli, üzüntülü; uygunsuz, münasebetsiz; şanssız, talihsiz; uğursuz.

un.harmed [ʌn'hɑːmd] *adj.* zararsız, sağsalim.

un.har.mo.ni.ous □ ['ʌnhɑː'məunjəs] ahenksiz, uyumsuz.

un.har.ness ['ʌn'hɑːnis] *v/t. -den* koşum takımını çıkarmak.

un.health.y □ [ʌn'helθi] sıhhate zararlı; sıhhati bozuk, keyifsiz; tehlikeli; ahlâkı bozan.

un.heard ['ʌn'həːd] *adj.* duyulmamış, işitilmemiş; duyulmayan; **un.heard- -of** [ʌn'həːdɔv] *adj.* misli görülmemiş, olağanüstü.

un.heed.ed ['ʌn'hiːdid] *adj.* önemsenmeyen, aldırış edilmeyen; **'un'heeding** *adj.* dikkat etmeyen, önemsemeyen, kayıtsız.

un.hes.i.tat.ing □ [ʌn'heziteitiŋ] tereddüt etmeyen; **~ly** tereddüt etmeyerek.

un.hin.dered ['ʌn'hindəd] *adj.* engellenmeyen.

un.hinge [ʌn'hindʒ] *v/t.* menteşelerden çıkarmak (*kapı vs.*); *fig.* dengesini bozmak, oynatmak (*akıl*).

un.his.tor.ic , **un.his.tor.i.cal** □ ['ʌnhis'tɔrik(əl)] tarihî olmayan.

un.hitch ['ʌn'hitʃ] *v/t.* çözmek, açmak.

un.ho.ly [ʌn'həuli] *adj.* kutsal olmayan; kötücül, günahkâr; F berbat, iğrenç.

un.hon.o(u)red ['ʌn'ɔnəd] *adj.* şereflendirilmemiş; ödenmemiş (*çek vs.*).

un.hook ['ʌn'huk] *v/t. -in* çengellerini çıkarmak; çengelden çıkarmak.

un.hoped-for ['ʌn'həuptfɔː] *adj.* beklenmedik, umulmadık.

un.horse ['ʌn'hɔːs] *v/t.* attan düşürmek; üstünden atmak.

un.house ['ʌn'hauz] *v/t.* evden atmak, evsiz barksız bırakmak.

un.hung [ʌn'hʌŋ] *adj.* asılmamış.

un.hurt ['ʌn'həːt] *adj.* zarar görmemiş, incinmemiş, sağlam.

u.ni.corn ['juːnikɔːn] *n.* tek boynuzlu ata benzer hayalî bir hayvan.

u.ni.fi.ca.tion [juːnifi'keiʃən] *n.* birleş(tir)me.

u.ni.form ['juːnifɔːm] **1.** □ aynı, değişmez; düzenli; tekdüzen, yeknesak; **~ price** tek fiyat; **2.** *n.* üniforma, resmî elbise; **3.** *v/t.* üniforma giydirmek; aynı şekle sokmak, standartlaştırmak; **u.ni'form.i.ty** *n.* aynılık, değişmezlik; düzen; tekdüzenlik, monotonluk.

u.ni.fy ['juːnifai] *v/t.* birleştirmek.

u.ni.lat.er.al ['juːni'lætərəl] *adj.* tek taraflı, tek yanlı.

un.im.ag.i.na.ble □ [ʌni'mædʒinəbl] tasavvur edilemez; '**un.im'ag.i.na.tive** □ [ˌ-nətiv] yaratma kabiliyeti olmayan, hayal gücü dar.

un.im.paired ['ʌnim'pɛəd] *adj.* zarar görmemiş, bozulmamış.

un.im.peach.a.ble □ [ʌnim'piːtʃəbl] şüphe götürmez, güvenilir; kusursuz, suçsuz; çürütülemez.

un.im.ped.ed □ ['ʌnim'piːdid] engellenmemiş.

un.im.por.tant □ ['ʌnim'pɔːtənt] önemsiz.

un.im.proved ['ʌnim'pruːvd] *adj.* geliştirilmemiş; değerlendirilmemiş (*fırsat vs.*); sürülmemiş (*toprak*); iyileşmemiş.

un.in.flu.enced ['ʌn'influənst] *adj.* etkilenmemiş.

un.in.formed ['ʌnin'fɔːmd] *adj.* haberdar edilmemiş.

un.in.hab.it.a.ble ['ʌnin'hæbitəbl] *adj.* oturulamaz, yaşanılmaz; '**un.in'hab.it.ed** *adj.* oturulmamış; ıssız, tenha, boş.

un.in.jured ['ʌn'indʒəd] *adj.* yaralanmamış, incinmemiş.

un.in.struct.ed ['ʌnin'strʌktid] *adj.* talimat verilmemiş.

un.in.sured ['ʌnin'ʃuəd] *adj.* sigorta edilmemiş.

un.in.tel.li.gi.bil.i.ty ['ʌnintelidʒə'biliti] *n.* anlaşılmazlık; '**un.in'tel.li.gi.ble** □ anlaşılmaz.

un.in.tend.ed □ ['ʌnin'tendid] kasıtsız; niyet edilmemiş.

un.in.ten.tion.al □ ['ʌnin'tenʃənl] istemeyerek yapılan, kasıtsız.

un.in.ter.est.ing □ ['ʌn'intristiŋ] ilginç olmayan.

un.in.ter.rupt.ed □ ['ʌnintə'rʌptid] aralıksız, kesilmeyen, devamlı; **~ working hours** *pl.* devamlı çalışma saatleri.

un.in.vit.ed ['ʌnin'vaitid] *adj.* davet edilmemiş; '**un.in'vit.ing** □ davet edilmeyen.

un.ion ['juːnjən] *n.* birleş(tir)me; anlaşma; POL birlik, ittifak; dernek, sendika; darülaceze, güçsüzler yurdu; evlilik; MEC rakor, bilezik; '**un.ion.ism** *n.* POL *etc.* bir lik taraftarı olma; sendikacılık; '**un.ionist** *n.* POL birlik taraftarı; sendika yanlısı, sendikacı; '**un.ion.ize** *v/t.* birlik haline getirmek; sendikalaştırmak.

un.ion… :♀ **Jack** İngiliz bayrağı; **~ suit**

Am. kombinezon.

u.nique [juːˈniːk] □ tek, biricik, yegâne; eşsiz.

u.ni.son MUS & *fig.* [ˈjuːnizn] *n.* birlik, ahenk, uyum; *in* ~ hep bir ağızdan, hep beraber; **u.nis.o.nous** MUS [juːˈnisənəs] *adj.* aynı perdeden; birlikte.

u.nit [ˈjuːnit] *n.* birlik (*a.* MIL); MATH, MEC birim, ünite; ~ *furniture* mobilya ünitesi; **U.nitar.i.an** [ˌ-ˈtɛəriən] **1.** *n.* teslis doktrinini reddeden bir Hıristiyan mezhebi üyesi; **2.** *adj.* bu Hıristiyan mezhebine ait; **u.nitar.y** [ˈ-təri] *adj.* üniteye ait, birimsel..., ünite...; MATH bölünmez..., tek...; **u.nite** [juːˈnait] *v/t. & v/i.* birleş(tir)mek, bağlamak; bitişmek.

u.nit.ed [juːˈnaitid] *adj.* birleşmiş, birleşik; ahenkli, uyumlu; ♀ **King.dom** Britanya Krallığı; ♀ **Na.tions** *pl.* Birleşmiş Milletler; ♀ **States** *pl.* of America Amerika Birleşik Devletleri.

u.ni.ty [ˈjuːniti] *n.* birlik, ittifak; birleşme; MATH bir sayısı.

u.ni.ver.sal □ [juːniˈvəːsəl] genel, umumî; evrensel, dünya çapında; küllî, tümel; MEC üniversal; ~ *heir* tek vâris; ~ *joint* MEC üniversal kavrama; ~ *language* evrensel dil; ♀ *Postal Union* Milletlerarası Posta Birliği; ~ *suffrage* genel oy hakkı; **u.ni.ver.sal.i.ty** [ˌ-ˈsæliti] *n.* genellik, evrensellik; **u.ni.verse** [ˈjuːnivəːs] *n.* evren, kâinat, âlem; **u.ni'ver.si.ty** *n.* üniversite.

un.just □ [ˈʌnˈdʒʌst] haksız, adaletsiz; **un'jus.ti.fi.a.ble** □ [ˌ-tifaiəbl] gereksiz, yersiz.

un.kempt [ˈʌnˈkempt] *adj.* taranmamış (*saç*); *fig.* dağınık, düzensiz, derbeder, hırpani.

un.kind □ [ʌnˈkaind] dostça olmayan, sert, zalim, kalp kırıcı.

un.knit *part. fig.* [ˈʌnˈnit] (*irr. knit*) *v/t.* sökmek, çözmek.

un.knot [ˈʌnˈnɔt] *v/t. -in* düğümünü çözmek.

un.know.ing □ [ˈʌnˈnəuiŋ] habersiz; **'un'known 1.** *adj.* bilinmez, meçhul, yabancı; **2.** *adv.* ~ *to me* bana yabancı, benim bilmediğim; **3.** *n.* yabancı, meçhul kimse; MATH bilinmeyen.

un.lace [ʌnˈleis] *v/t. -in* bağlarını gevşetmek, çözmek, açmak.

un.lade [ʌnˈleid] (*irr. lade*) *v/t.* boşaltmak; *v/i.* NAUT yükünü boşaltmak.

un.la.dy.like [ʌnˈleidilaik] *adj.* hanıma yakışmaz.

un.laid [ʌnˈleid] *adj.* ipleri ayrılmış, örgüsü açılmış.

un.la.ment.ed [ˈʌnləˈmentid] *adj.* yası tutulmayan.

un.latch [ˈʌnˈlætʃ] *v/t. -in* mandalını açmak; *v/i.* açılmak.

un.law.ful □ [ˈʌnˈlɔːful] kanunsuz, gayri meşru, kanuna aykırı.

un.learn [ˈʌnˈləːn] (*irr. learn*) *v/t.* unutmak (*öğrendiğini*), bırakmak, vazgeçmek (*alışkanlık vs.*); **'un'learn.ed** □ [ˌ-nid] okuma yazma bilmez, cahil, bilgisiz; çalışarak öğrenilmeyen.

un.leash [ˈʌnˈliːʃ] *v/t.* tasmasını çıkarmak (*köpek*); *fig.* serbest bırakmak, koyvermek.

un.leav.ened [ˈʌnˈlevnd] *adj.* mayasız (*ekmek*).

un.less [ənˈles] *cj.* -medikçe, -mezse, meğerki.

un.let.tered [ˈʌnˈletəd] *adj.* okuma yazma bilmez, cahil, okumamış.

un.li.censed [ˈʌnˈlaisənst] *adj.* ehliyetsiz, ruhsatsız.

un.licked *mst fig.* [ˈʌnˈlikt] *adj.* şekilsiz, biçimsiz, yontulmamış; ~ *cub* acemi çaylak, ağzı süt kokan genç.

un.like □ [ˈʌnˈlaik] *-e* benzemeyen, farklı (*s.o. b-den*); **un'like.li.hood** [ˌ-lihud] *n.* olasısızlık; **un'like.ly** *adj.* umulmaz, olasısız, muhtemel olmayan.

un.lim.it.ed [ʌnˈlimitid] *adj.* sınırsız, sonsuz, sayısız; *fig.* kısıtsız, kayıtsız, şartsız.

un.lined [ˈʌnˈlaind] *adj.* çizgisiz.

un.liq.ui.dat.ed [ˈʌnˈlikwideitid] *adj.* tasfiye edilmemiş, ödenmemiş.

un.load [ˈʌnˈləud] *vb.* boşaltmak (*yük, silah*); başından savmak; dökmek (*derdini*); kurtarmak *-den*; rahatlatmak.

un.lock [ˈʌnˈlɔk] *v/t. -in* kilidini açmak; açmak (*kapı*); *fig.* çözmek, ortaya çıkarmak; **'un'locked** *adj.* açık.

un.looked-for [ʌnˈluktfɔː] *adj.* beklenmedik, umulmadık.

un.loose, un.loos.en [ʌnˈluːs(n)] *v/t.* çözmek; salıvermek, serbest bırakmak.

un.lov.a.ble [ˈʌnˈlʌvəbl] *adj.* sevilmeyen; **'un'love.ly** *adj.* sevimsiz; hoşa gitmeyen; **'un'lov.ing** □ hissiz, sevgisiz.

un.lucky □ [ʌnˈlʌki] talihsiz, şanssız, bahtsız; uğursuz.

un.made [ˈʌnˈmeid] *adj.* yapılmamış.

un.make [ˈʌnˈmeik] (*irr. make*) *v/t.* bozmak; harap etm.; parçalamak; değiştirmek.

un.man ['ʌn'mæn] *v/t.* cesaretini kırmak; yumuşatmak, gevşetmek; kısırlaştırmak; adamsız bırakmak.

un.man.age.a.ble □ [ʌn'mænidʒəbl] idare edilemez.

un.man.ly ['ʌn'mænli] *adj.* zayıf, korkak, ödlek; erkeğe yaraşmaz, kadınımsı, erkekçe olmayan.

un.manned ['ʌn'mænd] *adj.* insansız; mürettebatsız.

un.man.ner.ly [ʌn'mænəli] *adj.* kaba, terbiyesiz, saygısız.

un.marked ['ʌn'mɑːkt] *adj.* işaretsiz; çizgisiz; not verilmemiş.

un.mar.ried ['ʌn'mærid] *adj.* evlenmemiş, bekâr.

un.mask ['ʌn'mɑːsk] *v/t.* maskesini çıkartmak; *fig.* ortaya çıkarmak, maskesini düşürmek.

un.matched ['ʌn'mætʃt] *adj.* eşsiz, emsalsiz.

un.mean.ing □ [ʌn'miːniŋ] anlamsız; ifadesiz; **un.meant** ['ʌn'ment] *adj.* kasıtsız.

un.meas.ured [ʌn'meʒəd] *adj.* sonsuz, sınırsız.

un.meet ['ʌn'miːt] *adj.* uygunsuz, yakışıksız.

un.men.tion.a.ble [ʌn'menʃnəbl] **1.** *adj.* sözü edilmez, ağıza alınmaz; **2.** *n.* **~s** *pl.* F iç çamaşırları.

un.mer.ci.ful □ [ʌn'məːsiful] insafsız, merhametsiz, zalim.

un.mer.it.ed ['ʌn'meritid] *adj.* haksız.

un.me.thod.i.cal ['ʌnmiθɔdikəl] *adj.* sistemsiz, yöntemsiz.

un.mil.i.tar.y ['ʌn'militəri] *adj.* askerî olmayan.

un.mind.ful □ [ʌn'maindful] unutkan; dikkatsiz, düşüncesiz, kayıtsız, aldırmaz (*of -e*).

un.mis.tak.a.ble □ ['ʌnmis'teikəbl] açık, belli.

un.mit.i.gat.ed [ʌn'mitigeitid] *adj.* tam; *fig.* dinmeyen...

un.mixed ['ʌn'mikst] *adj.* karış(tırıl)- mamış, saf, halis.

un.mod.i.fied ['ʌn'mɔdifaid] *adj.* değiştirilmemiş.

un.mo.lest.ed ['ʌnmou'lestid] *adj.* rahatsız edilmemiş, rahat bırakılmış.

un.moor ['ʌn'muə] *v/i.* lenger çekmek.

un.mor.al ['ʌn'mɔrəl] *adj.* ahlâkî değerleri olmayan.

un.mort.gaged ['ʌn'mɔːgidʒd] *adj.* ipoteksiz.

un.mount.ed ['ʌn'mauntid] *adj.* atsız;

çerçevelenmemiş; oturtulmamış; monte edilmemiş.

un.mourned ['ʌn'mɔːnd] *adj.* yas tutulunamış.

un.moved □ ['ʌn'muːvd] *mst fig.* hissiz, duygusuz; sarsılmaz; kayıtsız, lâkayt; **un'mov.ing** *adj.* hareketsiz.

un.mu.si.cal □ ['ʌn'mjuːzikəl] ahenksiz, uyumsuz.

un.muz.zle ['ʌn'mʌzl] *v/t.* *-in* burunsalığını çıkarmak; **~d** burunsalıksız.

un.named ['ʌn'neimd] *adj.* isimsiz; bahsedilmeyen.

un.nat.u.ral □ [ʌn'nætʃrəl] tuhaf, garip, anormal; tabiata aykırı.

un.nav.i.ga.ble ['ʌn'nævigəbl] *adj.* gidiş gelişe elverişsiz.

un.nec.es.sar.y □ [ʌn'nesisəri] lüzumsuz, gereksiz; faydasız.

un.neigh.bo(u)r.ly ['ʌn'neibəli] *adj.* komşuya yakışmaz.

un.nerve ['ʌn'nəːv] *v/t.* cesaretini kırmak, güvenini sarsmak, sinirlendirmek.

un.not.ed ['ʌn'nəutid] *adj.* dikkate alınmamış.

un.no.ticed ['ʌn'nəutist] *adj.* gözden kaçmış.

un.num.bered ['ʌn'nʌmbəd] *adj.* numarasız; sayılamaz; sayılmamış; *poet.* sayısız.

un.ob.jec.tion.a.ble □ ['ʌnəb'dʒekʃnəbl] itiraz edilemez, kusursuz.

un.ob.serv.ant □ ['ʌnəb'zəːvənt] dikkatsiz, dikkat etmeyen (*of -e*); **'un.ob.'served** □ dikkat edilmemiş, gözden kaçmış.

un.ob.tain.a.ble ['ʌnəb'teinəbl] *adj.* elde edilemez, bulunamaz.

un.ob.tru.sive □ ['ʌnəb'truːsiv] göze çarpmaz; alçak gönüllü.

un.oc.cu.pied ['ʌn'ɔkjupaid] *adj.* boş, serbest; işsiz, boşta gezen.

un.of.fend.ing ['ʌnə'fendiŋ] *adj.* karıncayı ezmez, zararsız, kusursuz.

un.of.fi.cial □ ['ʌnə'fiʃəl] resmî olmayan, gayri resmî.

un.o.pened ['ʌn'əupənd] *adj.* açılmamış.

un.op.posed ['ʌnə'pəuzd] *adj.* karşı çıkılmamış; rakipsiz.

un.or.gan.ized ['ʌn'ɔːgənaizd] *adj.* örgütlenmemiş, düzenlenmemiş, organize edilmemiş; inorganik; sendikalaşmamış.

un.os.ten.ta.tious □ ['ʌnɔsten'teiʃəs] gösterişsiz, dikkati çekmeyen, sade.

un.owned ['ʌn'əund] *adj.* sahipsiz.

un.pack ['ʌn'pæk] *v/t.* boşaltmak; açmak (*bavul vs.*).

un.paid ['ʌn'peid] *adj.* ödenmemiş; alacaklı; ücretsiz; POST pulsuz.

un.pal.at.a.ble [ʌn'pælətəbl] *adj.* tatsız, yavan; *fig.* hoşa gitmeyen.

un.par.al.leled [ʌn'pærəleld] *adj.* eşsiz, emsalsiz.

un.par.don.a.ble [ʌn'pɑːdnəbl] affedilemez.

un.par.lia.men.ta.ry [ʌn'pɑːləˈmentəri] parlamento kaidelerine aykırı.

un.pat.ent.ed ['ʌn'peitəntid] *adj.* patentsiz

un.pa.tri.ot.ic ['ʌnpætri'ɔtik] *adj.* (**~al.ly**) vatanperver olmayan.

un.paved ['ʌn'peivd] *adj.* asfaltlanmamış.

un.per.ceived [ˈʌnpə'siːvd] kavranılmamış.

un.per.formed ['ʌnpə'fɔːmd] *adj.* yerine getirilmemiş.

un.per.plexed ['ʌnpə'plekst] *adj.* şaşırmamış, zihni karışmamış.

un.per.turbed ['ʌnpəːˈtəːbd] *adj.* sakin, soğukkanlı, tasasız.

un.phil.o.soph.i.cal ['ʌnfilə'sɔfikəl] felsefî olmayan.

un.pin ['ʌn'pin] *v/t.* -*in* iğnelerini çıkarmak; açmak, çözmek.

un.placed ['ʌn'pleist] *adj. yarışma*; ilk üçe girememiş.

un.pleas.ant [ʌn'pleznt] nahoş, hoşa gitmeyen; un'pleas.ant.ness *n.* nahoşluk, tatsızlık.

un.plumbed ['ʌn'plʌmd] *adj.* derinliği ölçülmemiş; su boruları tesisatı olmayan.

un.po.et.ic, un.po.et.i.cal ['ʌnpəu-'etik(əl)] şiirsel olmayan.

un.po.lished ['ʌn'pɔliʃt] *adj.* parlatılmamış; *fig.* kaba.

un.polled ['ʌn'pəuld] *adj.* seçmen olarak kaydedilmemiş.

un.pol.lut.ed ['ʌnpə'luːtid] *adj.* kirletilmemiş.

un.pop.u.lar ['ʌn'pɔpjulə] rağbet görmeyen, benimsenmeyen, tutulmayan; gözden düşmüş; un.pop.u.lar.i.ty ['ˌ-'læriti] *n.* tutulmama; gözden düşmüş olma.

un.pos.sessed ['ʌnpə'zest] *adj.*: **~ of s.th.** *bşi* olmayan.

un.prac.ti.cal ['ʌn'præktikəl] elverişli (*veya* kullanışlı) olmayan; 'un-'prac.ticed, 'un'prac.tised [ˌ-'tist]

adj. acemi, deneyimsiz.

un.prec.e.dent.ed [ʌn'presidəntid] emsali görülmemiş, eşsiz, yeni.

un.prej.u.diced [ʌn'predʒudist] önyargısız, peşin hükümsüz, tarafsız, yansız.

un.pre.med.i.tat.ed ['ʌnpri'mediteitid] kasıtsız; önceden tasarlanmamış.

un.pre.pared ['ʌnpri'pɛəd, *adv.* ˌ-ridli] hazırlıksız, tedbirsiz.

un.pre.pos.sess.ing ['ʌnpriːpə'zesiŋ] *adj.* cazibesiz, albenisiz, alımsız.

un.pre.sent.a.ble ['ʌnpri'zentəbl] *adj.* sunulamaz, insan içine çıkarılamaz.

un.pre.tend.ing ['ʌnpri'təndiŋ], 'un.pre'ten.tious alçak gönüllü, mütevazı.

un.prin.ci.pled [ʌn'prinsəpld] *adj.* karaktersiz, ahlâksız, prensipsiz.

un.print.a.ble ['ʌn'printəbl] *adj.* basılmaya elverişsiz.

un.priv.il.eged *Am.* [ʌn'privilidʒd] *adj.* ayrılacalıksız.

un.pro.duc.tive ['ʌnprə'dʌktiv] bereketsiz, kısır (*of*); COM verimsiz, randımansız, kâr getirmeyen.

un.pro.fes.sion.al ['ʌnprə'feʃənl] meslek kurallarına aykırı, mesleğine yakışmaz.

un.prof.it.a.ble [ʌn'prɔfitəbl] kârsız, kazançsız, verimsiz; boş, nafile; un-'profit.a.ble.ness *n.* kârsızlık, verimsizlik.

un.prom.is.ing ['ʌn'prɔmisiŋ] ümit vermeyen.

un.prompt.ed [ʌn'prɔmptid] *adj.* ihtiyari, istemli.

un.pro.nounce.a.ble ['ʌnprə-'naunsəbl] telaffuz edilemeyen.

un.pro.pi.tious ['ʌnprə'piʃəs] elverişsiz, uygunsuz.

un.pro.tect.ed ['ʌnprə'tektid] korunmamış, korunmasız; himaye görmeyen.

un.proved ['ʌnːpruːvd] *adj.* ispatlanmamış.

un.pro.vid.ed ['ʌnprə'vaidid] *adj.* yoksun (**with** -*den*); **~ for** ihtiyacı karşılanmamış.

un.pro.voked ['ʌnprə'vəukt] kışkırtılmamış, tahrik edilmemiş.

un.pub.lished ['ʌn'pʌbliʃt] *adj.* basılmamış, yayımlanmamış.

un.punc.tu.al ['ʌn'pʌŋktjuəl] dakik olmayan, tam zamanında gelmeyen; unpunc.tu.al.i.ty ['ˌ-'æliti] *n.* dakik olmayış.

un.pun.ished ['ʌn'pʌniʃt] *adj.* cezalandırılmamış; **go ~** cezasız kalmak.

un.qual.i.fied □ [ʌn'kwɔlifaid] ehliyetsiz, yetersiz; şartsız; sınırsız; F tam, kesin, müthiş.

un.quench.a.ble □ [ʌn'kwentʃəbl] söndürülemez, bastırılamaz (*a. fig.*).

un.ques.tion.a.ble □ [ʌn'kwestʃənəbl] şüphe götürmez, kesin, muhakkak; **un'questioned** *adj.* kesin, şüphesiz; sorgusuz; **un'ques.tion.ing** □ kayıtsız şartsız.

un.qui.et [ʌn'kwaiət] *adj.* rahatsız, huzursuz, endişeli.

un.quote ['ʌn'kwəut] *vb.* tırnak işaretini kapamak; **un'quot.ed** *adj. borsa*: kayıtlı olmayan.

un.rav.el [ʌn'rævəl] *v/t. & v/i.* sök(ül)mek, çöz(ül)mek.

un.read ['ʌn'red] *adj.* okunmamış; cahil; **un.read.a.ble** ['ʌn'ri:dəbl] *adj.* okunmaz, okunaksız.

un.read.i.ness ['ʌn'redinis] *n.* hazırlıksızlık; **'un'read.y** □ hazırlıksız, hazır olmayan; yavaş, ağır.

un.re.al ['ʌn'riəl] gerçek olmayan, gerçek dışı, hayalî, asılsız; **un.re.al.is.tic** ['ʌnriə'listik] *adj.* gerçekçi olmayan; gerçeğe uymayan; **un.re.al.i.ty** ['¸-'æliti] *n.* gerçeksizlik; **'un're.al.iz.a.ble** [¸-əlaizəbl] *adj.* gerçekleştirilemez; COM satılmaz.

un.rea.son ['ʌn'ri:zn] *n.* mantıksızlık; saçmalık; **un'rea.son.a.ble** □ makûl olmayan, mantıksız; aşırı.

un.re.claimed ['ʌnri'kleimd] *adj.* yeniden talep edilmemiş; işlenmemiş (*toprak*).

un.rec.og.niz.a.ble □ ['ʌn'rekəgnaizəbl] tanınmaz; **'un'rec.og.nized** □ tanınmamış.

un.rec.om.pensed ['ʌn'rekəmpenst] *adj.* mükâfatlandırılmamış.

un.rec.on.ciled ['ʌn'rekənsaild] *adj.* uzlaşmamış, barışmamış.

un.re.cord.ed ['ʌnri'kɔ:did] *adj.* kaydedilmemiş.

un.re.dee.med □ ['ʌnri'di:md] rehinden kurtarılmamış; *fig.* yerine getirilmemiş, tutulmamış (*söz vs.*).

un.re.dressed ['ʌnri'drest] *adj.* düzeltilmemiş.

un.reel ['ʌn'ri:l] *v/t. & v/i.* makaradan çöz(ül)mek.

un.re.fined ['ʌnri'faind] *adj.* tasfiye edilmemiş, ham; *fig.* inceliksiz, kaba.

un.re.flect.ing □ ['ʌnri'flektiŋ] yansımasız, aksetmeyen.

un.re.formed ['ʌnri'fɔ:md] *adj.* düzeltilmemiş; yola gelmemiş.

un.re.gard.ed ['ʌnri'gɑ:did] *adj.* önemsenmemiş; **'un.re'gard.ful** [¸-ful] *adj.* dikkatsiz (*of -e karşı*).

un.reg.is.tered ['ʌn'redʒistəd] *adj.* kaydedilmemiş; taahhütlü gönderilmemiş (*mektup*).

un.re.lat.ed ['ʌnri'leitid] *adj.* ilgisiz, alâkasız (*to -e karşı*).

un.re.lent.ing □ ['ʌnri'lentiŋ] acımasız, amansız, sert, şiddetli; gevşemeyen.

un.re.li.a.ble ['ʌnri'laiəbl] *adj.* güvenilmez, inanılmaz.

un.re.lieved □ ['ʌnri'li:vd] hafiflememiş, dinmemiş, rahatlamamış; monoton, tekdüzen.

un.re.mit.ting □ [ʌnri'mitiŋ] sürekli, devamlı, aralıksız.

un.re.mu.ner.a.tive □ ['ʌnri'mju:nərətiv] kârsız, kazançsız.

un.re.pealed ['ʌnri'pi:ld] *adj.* feshedilmemiş.

un.re.pent.ed ['ʌnri'pentid] *adj.* pişmanlık duymamış.

un.re.pin.ing □ ['ʌnri'painiŋ] halinden memnun.

un.re.quit.ed □ ['ʌnri'kwaitid] karşılıksız, karşılık görmeyen; ödüllendirilmemiş.

un.re.served □ ['ʌnri'zə:vd] *adv.* ¸-vidli] sınırlanmamış; samimî, açık sözlü, serbest.

un.re.sist.ing □ ['ʌnri'zistiŋ] karşı koymayan, dirençsiz.

un.re.spon.sive ['ʌnris'pɔnsiv] *adj.* tepki göstermeyen (*to -e*).

un.rest ['ʌn'rest] *n.* kargaşa, huzursuzluk; rahatsızlık; **'un'rest.ing** □ durdurak bilmeyen.

un.re.strained □ ['ʌnris'treind] frenlenmemiş, denetsiz, serbest.

un.re.strict.ed □ ['ʌnris'triktid] sınırsız, kısıtsız; hız sınırı olmayan (*yol*).

un.re.vealed ['ʌnri'vi:ld] *adj.* açıklanmamış.

un.re.ward.ed ['ʌnri'wɔ:did] *adj.* ödüllendirilmemiş.

un.rhymed ['ʌn'raimd] *adj.* kafiyesiz.

un.rid.dle ['ʌnridl] *v/t.* çözmek, halletmek.

un.rig NAUT ['ʌn'rig] *v/t. -den* donanımı çıkarmak.

un.right.eous □ [ʌn'raitʃəs] haksız, adaletsiz; günahkâr, kötü.

un.rip ['ʌn'rip] v/t. dikişlerini sökmek; parçalamak.

un.ripe ['ʌn'raip] adj. ham; erken gelişmiş; hazırlıksız.

un.ri.val(l)ed [ʌn'raivəld] adj. eşsiz, emsalsiz; rakipsiz.

un.roll ['ʌn'rəul] v/t. & v/i. aç(ıl)mak, yay(ıl)mak; göz önüne sermek.

un.roof ['ʌn'ruːf] v/t. -in çatısını veya üstünü açmak.

un.rope MOUNT ['ʌn'rəup] v/t. & v/i. çöz(ül)mek.

un.ruf.fled ['ʌn'rʌfld] adj. sakin, soğukkanlı.

un.ruled ['ʌn'ruːld] adj. k-ne hâkim olamayan; çizgisiz (kâğıt).

un.rul.y [ʌn'ruːli] adj. azılı; itaatsiz, asi; ele avuca sığmaz.

un.sad.dle ['ʌn'sædl] v/t. -in eyerini çıkarmak; eyerden düşürmek.

un.safe □ ['ʌn'seif] emniyetsiz, güvensiz, tehlikeli.

un.said ['ʌn'sed] adj. söylenmemiş, bahsedilmemiş.

un.sal(e).a.ble ['ʌn'seiləbl] adj. satılamaz.

un.salt.ed ['ʌn'sɔːltid] adj. tuzlanmamış.

un.sanc.tioned ['ʌn'sæŋkʃənd] adj. onaylanmamış.

un.san.i.tar.y ['ʌn'sænitəri] adj. sağlıkla ilgili olmayan.

un.sat.is.fac.to.ry □ ['ʌnsætis'fæktəri] memnuniyet vermeyen; yetersiz, tatmin etmeyen; 'un'sat.is.fied [-faid] adj. giderilmemiş; hoşnut kalmamış; 'un'satis.fy.ing □ [-faiiŋ] = **unsatisfactory**.

un.sa.vo(u).r.y □ ['ʌn'seivəri] tatsız, lezzetsiz, yavan; fig. çirkin, kötü, rezil.

un.say ['ʌn'sei] (irr. **say**) v/t. geri almak (sözünü).

un.scathed ['ʌn'skeiðd] adj. yaralanmamış; incinmemiş.

un.schooled ['ʌn'skuːld] adj. cahil, tahsilsiz; doğal.

un.sci.en.tif.ic ['ʌnsaiən'tifik] adj. (~ally) bilimsel olmayan; bilime aykırı.

un.screw ['ʌn'skruː] v/t. -in vidalarını sökmek; çevirerek açmak -i.

un.script.ur.al □ ['ʌn'skriptʃərəl] Kitabı Mukaddes'e aykırı.

un.scru.pu.lous □ [ʌn'skruːpjuləs] vicdansız; prensipsiz.

un.seal ['ʌn'siːl] v/t. -in mührünü bozmak veya açmak.

un.search.a.ble □ [ʌn'səːtʃəbl] anlaşılmaz; keşfedilmez.

un.sea.son.a.ble □ [ʌn'siːznəbl] mevsimsiz; fig. zamansız, vakitsiz; 'un'sea-soned adj. yaş (tahta); fig. olgunlaşmamış; baharatsız (yemek).

un.seat ['ʌn'siːt] v/t. görevden almak, azletmek; binicisini düşürmek (at); **be ~ed** görevden alınmak.

un.sea.wor.thy NAUT ['ʌn'siːwəːði] adj. denize çıkmaya elverişsiz.

un.seem.li.ness [ʌn'siːmlinis] n. uygunsuzluk; 'un'seem.ly adj. uygunsuz, yakışıksız, yakışık almaz (davranış vs.).

un.seen ['ʌn'siːn] 1. adj. görülmemiş; görünmez, gizli; 2. n. okul: tercüme, çeviri; **the ~** ahret, öbür dünya.

un.self.ish □ ['ʌn'selfiʃ] kendini düşünmeyen, bencil olmayan, özverili; 'un'self.ish.ness n. kendini düşünmeme, özveri.

un.sen.ti.men.tal ['ʌnsenti'mentl] adj. hissî olmayan, hissiz, duygusuz.

un.serv.ice.a.ble □ ['ʌn'səːvisəbl] işe yaramaz.

un.set.tle ['ʌn'setl] v/t. & v/i. yerinden çık(ar)mak; tedirgin etm.; düzenini bozmak; tedirgin olm.; 'un'set.tled adj. kararlaştırılmamış; henüz yerleş(il)memiş; belirsiz; boş; değişken, dönek (hava); сом ödenmemiş, kapanmamış (borç); kararsız; düzensiz.

un.sex ['ʌn'seks] v/t. cinsiyetinden yoksun kılmak.

un.shack.le ['ʌn'ʃækl] v/t. -in zincirlerini çıkarmak.

un.shak.en ['ʌn'ʃeikən] adj. sarsılmaz, metin; sabit.

un.shape.ly ['ʌn'ʃeipli] adj. biçimsiz, şekilsiz.

un.shav.en ['ʌn'ʃeivn] adj. tıraşı uzamış.

un.sheathe ['ʌn'ʃiːð] v/t. kınından çıkarmak.

un.shell ['ʌn'ʃel] v/t. -in kabuğunu soymak.

un.ship ['ʌn'ʃip] v/t. gemiden çıkarmak, boşaltmak; fora etm. (kürek); F fig. -den kurtulmak.

un.shod ['ʌn'ʃɔd] adj. yalınayak; nalsız.

un.shorn ['ʌn'ʃɔːn] adj. saçı kesilmemiş.

un.shrink.a.ble ['ʌn'ʃriŋkəbl] adj. çekmez, büzülmez; 'un'shrink.ing □ çekinmesiz, sarsılmaz; çekmeyen.

un.sight.ed [ʌn'saitid] *adj.* nişangâhsız,**un'sight.ly** *adj.* çirkin, göz zevkini bozan, göze batan.

un.signed ['ʌn'saind] *adj.* imzalanmamış.

un.skil(l).ful □ ['ʌn'skilful] beceriksiz, hünersiz, acemi;'**un'skilled** *adj.* beceriksiz, maharetsiz, ehliyetsiz; hüner gerektirmeyen (*iş*).

un.skimmed ['ʌn'skimd] *adj.* kaymağı alınmamış.

un.sleep.ing ['ʌn'sli:piŋ] *adj.* uykusuz.

un.so.cia.ble [ʌn'səuʃəbl] *adj.* çekingen, konuşmayan, kaçınık, çekilgen; **un'social** *adj.* insandan kaçan, kaçınık, yabani.

un.sold ['ʌn'səuld] *adj.* satılmamış.

un.sol.der ['ʌn'sɔldə] *v/t.* -*in* lehimini çıkarmak.

un.sol.dier.ly ['ʌn'səuldʒəli] *adj.* askere yakışmaz.

un.so.lic.it.ed ['ʌnsə'lisitid] *adj.* istenilmemiş; davetsiz.

un.solv.a.ble ['ʌn'sɔlvəbl] *adj.* çözülemez, halledilemez;'**un'solved** *adj.* çözülmemiş, halledilmemiş.

un.so.phis.ti.cat.ed ['ʌnsə'fistikeitid] *adj.* saf, bön, acemi, tecrübesiz; basit, sade; halis, katkısız.

un.sought ['ʌn'sɔːt] *adj.* araştırılmamış.

un.sound □ ['ʌn'saund] sağlam olmayan, çürük, derme çatma; hastalıklı, sıhhatsiz; hafif (*uyku*); gerçeksiz; geçersiz; *of ~ mind* şuuru bozuk.

un.spar.ing □ ['ʌn'spɛəriŋ] esirgemeyen (*of*, *in* -*i*); bol, çok (*of*-*i*); acımasız, zalim.

un.speak.a.ble □ [ʌn'spiːkəbl] kelimelerle anlatılamaz, tarife sığmaz; yakışıksız, ağıza alınmaz.

un.spec.i.fied ['ʌn'spesifaid] *adj.* kesinlikle belirtilmemiş.

un.spent ['ʌn'spent] *adj.* sarfedilmemiş, harcanmamış.

un.spoiled ['ʌn'spɔild] *adj.*,'**un'spoilt** [-t] bozulmamış; şımarmamış.

un.spo.ken ['ʌn'spəukən] *adj.* açığa vurulmamış, söylenmemiş.

un.sport.ing ['ʌn'spɔːtiŋ] *adj.*, **un-sportsman.like** ['ʌn'spɔːtsmənlaik] sportmence olmayan.

un.spot.ted ['ʌn'spɔtid] *adj.* lekesiz, beneksiz; *fig.* temiz, pak, arı.

un.sta.ble □ ['ʌn'steibl] sağlam olmayan; kararsız, dönek, gelgeç; düzensiz,

değişken.

un.stained *fig.* ['ʌn'steind] *adj.* lekesiz, kusursuz.

un.stamped ['ʌn'stæmpt] *adj.* damgalanmamış; ᴘᴏsᴛ pulsuz.

un.states.man.like ['ʌn'steitsmənlaik] *adj.* devlet adamına yakışmaz.

un.stead.y □ ['ʌn'stedi] sallanan, oynak; titrek; düzensiz; değişken, kararsız, güvenilmez.

un.stint.ed [ʌn'stintid] *adj.* kayıtsız şartsız, sınırsız.

un.stitch ['ʌn'stitʃ] *v/t.* -*in* dikişlerini sökmek.

un.stop ['ʌn'stɔp] *v/t.* açmak; -*in* tıkacını çıkarmak.

un.strained ['ʌn'streind] *adj.* süzülmemiş; *fig.* tabiî.

un.strap ['ʌn'stræp] *v/t.* -*in* kayışını çıkarmak *veya* gevşetmek.

un.stressed ['ʌn'strest] *adj.* vurgusuz.

un.string ['ʌn'striŋ] (*irr.* **string**) *v/t.* -*in* tellerini çıkarmak *veya* gevşetmek; zayıflatmak, bozmak (*sinir*); **un-strung** ['ʌn'strʌŋ] *adj.* gevşek; *fig.* sinirleri bozuk, sinirli.

un.stuck ['ʌn'stʌk] *adj.*: *come* ~ açılmak, ayrılmak; *sl.* başarısız olm.; suya düşmek (*plan vs.*).

un.stud.ied ['ʌn'stʌdid] *adj.* tabiî, doğal; çalışılmamış; çalışma ile öğrenilmemiş; plansız.

un.sub.dued ['ʌnsəb'djuːd] *adj.* boyun eğmemiş.

un.sub.mis.sive □ ['ʌnsəb'misiv] itaatsiz, boyun eğmez, serkeş, dik kafalı.

un.sub.stan.tial □ ['ʌnsəb'stænʃəl] cisimsiz; hayalî; asılsız.

un.suc.cess.ful □ ['ʌnsək'sesful] başarısız; '**un.suc'cess.ful.ness** *n.* başarısızlık.

un.suit.a.ble □ ['ʌn'sjuːtəbl] uygunsuz, yakışıksız; '**un'suit.ed** *adj.* uymamış, yakışmamış (*for*, *to* -*e*).

un.sul.lied ['ʌn'sʌlid] *adj.* lekesiz, (ter)temiz.

un.sup.port.ed ['ʌnsə'pɔːtid] *adj.* desteksiz.

un.sure ['ʌn'ʃuə] *adj.* emin olmayan; emniyetsiz.

un.sur.passed ['ʌnsəː'pɑːst] *adj.* geçilemez, üstün, eşsiz.

un.sus.pect.ed ['ʌnsəs'pektid] *adj.* şüphelenilmeyen; '**un.sus'pect.ing** *adj.* masum, saf; *pred.* kuşkulanmayan (*of* -*den*).

un.sus.pi.cious □ ['ʌnsəs'piʃəs] şüpheci olmayan, kalbi temiz, kuşkusuz.

un.swear ['ʌn'swɛə] (irr. **swear**) v/i. sözünden *veya* yemininden dönmek.

un.swerv.ing □ ['ʌn'swəːviŋ] değişmez; sapmaz.

un.sworn ['ʌn'swɔːn] adj. yeminli olmayan (*tanık*).

un.tack ['ʌn'tæk] v/t. çıkarmak, sökmek.

un.taint.ed □ ['ʌn'teintid] lekesiz; *fig.* namuslu.

un.tam(e).a.ble ['ʌn'teiməbl] adj. evcillestirilemez; 'un'tamed adj. evcilleştirilmemiş, yabanî.

un.tan.gle ['ʌn'tæŋgl] v/t. açmak, çözmek.

un.tanned ['ʌn'tænd] adj. tabaklanmamış.

un.tar.nished ['ʌn'tɑːniʃt] adj. lekesiz, kararmamış.

un.tast.ed ['ʌn'teistid] adj. tadılmamış.

un.taught ['ʌn'tɔːt] adj. cahil, tahsilsiz; doğal, doğuştan olan.

un.taxed ['ʌn'tækst] adj. vergilendirilmemiş.

un.teach.a.ble ['ʌn'tiːtʃəbl] adj. söz dinlemez (*kimse*); öğretilemez.

un.tem.per.a.men.tal ['ʌntempərə'mentl] adj. cansız, ruhsuz.

un.tem.pered ['ʌn'tempəd] adj. MEC tavlanmamış, su verilmemiş.

un.ten.ant.ed ['ʌn'tenəntid] adj. kiralanmamış, şenelmemiş, kiracısız, boş.

un.thank.ful □ ['ʌn'θæŋkful] nankör; istenmeyen, hoş karşılanmayan.

un.think.a.ble [ʌn'θiŋkəbl] adj. düşünülemez, akla gelmez, olanaksız; un-'thinking □ düsüncesiz; düşüncesizce yapılan.

un.thought ['ʌn'θɔːt] adj. düsünülmemis: **~of** beklenmedik, akla hayale gelmedik.

un.thread ['ʌn'θred] v/t. -*in* ipliğini çıkarmak; *fig.* yolunu bulmak, *k-ne* yol açmak.

un.thrift.y □ ['ʌn'θrifti] savurgan, tutumsuz.

un.ti.dy □ [ʌn'taidi] düzensiz, tertipsiz, dağınık, şapşal.

un.tie ['ʌn'tai] v/t. & v/i. çöz(ül)mek, aç(ıl)mak; halletmek.

un.til [ən'til] prp. & cj. -e kadar, -e değin, e- dek; **not ~** -den önce değil.

un.tilled ['ʌn'tild] adj. işlenmemiş (*top-*rak).

un.time.ly [ʌn'taimli] adj. vakitsiz, zamansız, mevsimsiz; uygunsuz, yersiz.

un.tir.ing □ [ʌn'taiəriŋ] yorulmak bilmez.

un.to ['ʌntu] = **to**.

un.told ['ʌn'təuld] adj. anlatılmamış; hesapsız sayısız, haddi hesabı olmayan, muazzam.

un.touched ['ʌn'tʌtʃt] adj. dokunulmamış; *fig.* etkilenmemiş; PHOT rötuşsuz.

un.to.ward [ʌn'təuəd] adj. uygunsuz, münasebetsiz; bahtsız, şanssız, aksi, ters, huysuz.

un.trained ['ʌn'treind] adj. eğitilmemiş; tecrübesiz, acemi.

un.tram.mel(l)ed [ʌn'træməld] adj. engellenmemiş, serbest.

un.trans.fer.a.ble ['ʌntræns'fəːrəbl] adj. nakledilemez; devredilemez.

un.trans.lat.a.ble ['ʌntræns'leitəbl] adj. tercüme edilemez, çevrilemez.

un.trav.el(l)ed ['ʌn'trævld] adj. kullanılmayan (*yol*); dar kafalı (*kimse*).

un.tried ['ʌn'traid] adj. denenmemiş; JUR yargılanmamış.

un.trimmed ['ʌn'trimd] adj. budanmamış; kesilip düzeltilmemiş (*saç vs.*).

un.trod, un.trod.den ['ʌn'trɔd(n)] adj. ayak basılmamış, bakir.

un.trou.bled ['ʌn'trʌbld] adj. sıkıntısız, dertsiz; durgun, sakin.

un.true □ ['ʌn'truː] yalan, sahte, yanlış; sadakatsiz, hakikatsiz, vefasız.

un.trust.wor.thy □ ['ʌn'trʌstwəːði] güvenilmez, dönek.

un.truth ['ʌn'truːθ] n. yalan; sahtelik; vefasızlık.

un.tu.tored ['ʌn'tjuːtəd] adj. eğitilmemiş, cahil, tahsilsiz, saf, bön.

un.twine ['ʌn'twain], un.twist ['ʌn'twist] v/t. & v/i. aç(ıl)mak, çöz(ül)mek.

un.used ['ʌn'juːzd] adj. kullanılmamış; ['ʌn'juːst] alışık olmayan (**to** -*e*); un.usu.al □ [ʌn'juːʒuəl] görülmedik, nadir; olağandışı, garip, acayip.

un.ut.ter.a.ble □ [ʌn'ʌtərəbl] ağıza alınmaz, söylenmez, anlatılamaz.

un.val.ued ['ʌn'væljuːd] adj. değer verilmemiş, önemsenmemiş; paha biçilmemiş.

un.var.ied [ʌn'vɛərid] adj. değişmemiş.

un.var.nished ['ʌn'vɑːniʃt] adj. cilasız; *fig.* sade, süssüz; dürüst; salt (*gerçek*).

un.var.y.ing □ [ʌn'vɛəriiŋ] değişmez.

un.veil [ʌn'veil] v/t. -in örtüsünü (veya peçesini) açmak; açığa vurmak, ortaya çıkarmak.

un.versed ['ʌn'vəːst] adj. deneyimsiz, acemi (in -de).

un.voiced ['ʌn'vɔist] adj. açıklanmamış, söylenmemiş; GR ünsüz, sessiz.

un.vouched ['ʌn'vautʃt] adj. a. ~-for doğrulanmamış.

un.want.ed ['ʌn'wɔntid] adj. istenilmez, istenmeyen.

un.war.i.ness [ʌn'wɛərinis] n. gaflet, tedbirsizlik.

un.war.like ['ʌn'wɔːlaik] adj. barışçı, barışsever.

un.war.rant.a.ble □ [ʌn'wɔrəntəbl] affedilemez, haklı sayılmaz; özürsüz; 'un'warrant.ed adj. haksız, özürsüz.

un.war.y □ ['ʌn'wɛəri] gafil, dikkatsiz, tedbirsiz.

un.washed ['ʌn'wɔʃt] adj. yıkanmamış.

un.wa.tered ['ʌn'wɔːtəd] adj. sulanmamış.

un.wa.ver.ing [ʌn'weivəriŋ] adj. değişmez, sabit, kararlı.

un.wea.ried [ʌn'wiərid], **un.wea.ry.ing** □ [ʌn'wiəriiŋ] yorulmak bilmez, usanmaz; yorulmamış.

un.wel.come [ʌn'welkəm] adj. hoş karşılanmayan, istenilmeyen; hoşa gitmeyen, tatsız.

un.well ['ʌn'wel] adj. rahatsız, keyifsiz, hasta.

un.whole.some ['ʌn'həulsəm] adj. sıhhate zararlı; sakat, sıhhatsiz; bozuk; iğrenç.

un.wield.y □ [ʌn'wiːldi] hantal, kaba, koskocaman; POST havaleli.

un.will.ing □ ['ʌn'wiliŋ] isteksiz, gönülsüz; istemeyerek yapılan veya verilen; **be ~ to do** bş yapmaya isteksiz olm.; **be ~ for s.th. to be done** bşin yapılmasına isteksiz olm.

un.wind ['ʌn'waind] (irr. **wind**) v/t. & v/i. çöz(ül)mek, aç(ıl)mak, gevşe(t)mek; rahatla(t)mak.

un.wis.dom ['ʌn'wizdəm] n. akılsızlık; **unwise** □ ['ʌn'waiz] akılsız; makûl olmayan.

un.wished [ʌn'wiʃt] adj. dileğinden vaz geçmiş; ~-for arzu edilmemiş.

un.wit.ting □ [ʌn'witiŋ] farkında olmayan, habersiz; kasıtsız.

un.wom.an.ly [ʌn'wumənli] adj. kadına yakışmaz, kadınca olmayan.

un.wont.ed □ [ʌn'wəuntid] alışıl-

mamış (to -e); nadir, olağandışı.

un.work.a.ble ['ʌn'wəːkəbl] adj. kullanışsız; MEC işlenemez.

un.world.ly ['ʌn'wəːldli] adj. tinsel, ruhanî, manevî.

un.wor.thy □ [ʌn'wəːði] değmez; yakışmaz, uygunsuz; lâyık olmayan (of -e); değersiz.

un.wrap ['ʌn'ræp] v/t. & v/i. aç(ıl)mak, çöz(ül)mek.

un.wrin.kle ['ʌn'riŋkl] v/t. -in kırışıklarını gidermek.

un.writ.ten ['ʌn'ritn] adj. yazılmamış; geleneksel; yazısız, boş.

un.wrought ['ʌn'rɔːt] adj. işlenmemiş, ham…

un.yield.ing □ [ʌn'jiːldiŋ] boyun eğmez, direngen; sert.

un.yoke ['ʌn'jəuk] v/t. boyunduruktan kurtarmak; ayırmak; v/i. boyunduruktan kurtulmak.

up [ʌp] 1. adv. yukarı(ya); yukarıda; yükseğe; yüksek mevkiye; öne, ileri(-ye); MUS tize doğru; -e kadar; tamamen; kuzeye doğru; **come ~ to s.o.** b-ne yaklaşmak; **~ and about** hastalıktan kurtulmuş, ayağa kalkmış; **be hard ~** eli darda olm.; **~ against a task** bir işle karşı karşıya olm.; **~ to** -e kadar; s. **date²** 1; **be ~ to s.th.** bşe eşit olm.; fig. dolap çevirmek, halt karıştırmak; **it is ~ to me to do** yapması bana kalmış; s. **mark** 1; **the time is ~** vakit doldu; **what are you ~ to there?** orada ne halt karıştırıyorsun?; **what's ~** sl. ne oluyor?, ne var?; **~ with** ile aynı hizada; **it's all ~ with him** hapı yuttu, yandı, ayvayı yedi; 2. int. kalk!; yukarı(ya)!; 3. prp. yukarıya, yukarıda; ileride; içeride; -e, -a; **~ the hill** tepeye; 4. adj. yükselmiş; yataktan kalkmış; ayakta; yüksek, kabarık; üstün; hazır, yapılmış; ata binmiş; haberdar; yargılanmakta; **~ train** şehir treni; 5. n. **the ~s and downs** pl. iniş çıkışlar, iyi ve kötü günler; 6. v/t. & v/i. F yüksel(t)mek; artırmak; ayağa kalkmak; kaldırmak.

up-and-com.ing Am. F ['ʌpən'kʌmiŋ] adj. ümit verici; başarı vadeden, girişken.

up.braid [ʌp'breid] v/t. azarlamak, paylamak, haşlamak (**s.o. with** veya **for s.th.** b-ni bşden dolayı).

up.bring.ing ['ʌpbriŋiŋ] n. yetiş(tir)-me, terbiye.

up.build ['ʌp'bild] (irr. **build**) v/t. inşa (veya bina) etm.

up.cast ['ʌpkɑːst] *n.* yukarıya at(ıl)ma, yukarıya çevirme *veya* çevrilme; *a.* ~ **shaft** MIL hava bacası.

up-coun.try ['ʌp'kʌntri] **1.** *adj.* sahilden uzak, iç taraftaki, iç kesimdeki; **2.** *adv.* iç kesimlere doğru.

up-cur.rent AVIA ['ʌpkʌrənt] yükselen hava akımı.

up.grade 1. ['ʌpgreid] *n.* yokuş; artış; **on the ~** *fig.* iyileşmekte; gelişmekte; artmakta; **2.** [ʌp'greid] *v/t.* -*in* kalitesini artırmak; -*in* rütbesini yükseltmek.

up.heav.al [ʌp'hiːvəl] *n.* GEOL yer kabuğunun kabarması; *fig.* karışıklık, ayaklanma, devrim.

up.hill ['ʌp'hil] *adj. & adv.* yokuş yukarı (giden); yükselen; *fig.* zor, güç, çetin.

up.hold [ʌp'həuld] (*irr.* **hold**) *v/t.* kaldırmak; tutmak, desteklemek; onaylamak; onamak, uygun bulmak; **up'hold.er** *n. fig.* destek, savunucu kimse, arka.

up.hol.ster [ʌp'həulstə] *v/t.* döşemek, kaplamak (*koltuk vs.*); **up'hol.ster.er** *n.* döşemeci; **up'hol.ster.y** *n.* döşemecilik; döşemelik eşya, mefruşat.

up.keep ['ʌpkiːp] *n.* bakım (masrafı).

up.land ['ʌplənd] **1.** *n. oft.* ~*s pl.* yüksek arazi, yayla; **2.** *adj.* yüksek.

up.lift 1. [ʌp'lift] *v/t. fig.* yüceltmek; **2.** ['ʌ] *n.* arazi çıkıntısı; sütyen; *fig.* yüceltme.

up.load IT ['ʌpləud] **1.** *v/t.* yüklemek; **2.** *n.* yüklenen dosya.

up.mar.ket *Brit.* ['ʌpmaːkit] *n.* seçkin (*otel v.b.*).

up.most ['ʌpməust] = **uppermost**.

up.on [ə'pɔn] = **on**.

up.per ['ʌpə] *n. adj.* üst(teki); yukarıdaki; **the ~ ten** (**thousand**) onbinden fazlası; **2.** *n. mst* ~*s pl.* saya, ayakkabı yüzü; **be** (**down**) **on one's** ~*s* F meteliğe kurşun atmak, cebi delik (*veya* züğürt) olm.; '~**.cut** *n. boks:* aparküt, aperkat; '~**.most** *adj.* en üst, en yukarıdaki; akla ilk gelen, başlıca.

up.pish □ F ['ʌpiʃ] kibirli, kendini beğenmiş.

up.pi.ty F ['ʌpiti] *adj.* kibirli, kendini beğenmiş.

up.raise [ʌp'reiz] *v/t.* yükseltmek, kaldırmak.

up.rear [ʌp'riə] *v/t. & v/i.* yüksel(t)mek; dikmek.

up.right 1. □ ['ʌp'rait] dik(ey); *fig.* ['ʌ'] dürüst, namuslu, âdil; **2.** ['ʌ] *n.* direk; dik duran şey; = ~ **pia.no** MUS dik (*veya*

düz) piyano.

up.ris.ing [ʌp'raiziŋ] *n.* ayaklanma, isyan.

up.roar *fig.* ['ʌprɔː] *n.* şamata, gürültü; kargaşa; **up'roar.i.ous** □ gürültülü; kahkahadan kırıp geçiren.

up.root [ʌp'ruːt] *v/t.* kökünden sökmek; yerini değiştirmek, uzaklaştırmak; kökünü kazımak, yok etm.

up.scale *Am.* ['ʌpskeil] *n.* seçkin (*otel v.b.*).

up.set [ʌp'set] **1.** (*irr.* **set**) *v/t.* devirmek, altüst etm. (*a. fig.*); bozmak; sinirlendirmek; hükümsüz kılmak; bozguna uğratmak; düzenini bozmak, karıştırmak; MEC döverek kısaltıp kalınlaştırmak; **be** ~ keyfi kaçmak; *v/i.* devrilmek, altüst olm.; **2.** *n.* devrilme, altüst olma; *spor:* bozguh, sürprizli yenilgi; bozukluk, bozulma; **stomach** ~ mide bozulması; sarsıntı, şok; ~ **price** açık arttırmada satıcının koyduğu en düşük fiyat.

up.shot ['ʌpʃɔt] *n.* netice, sonuç, son; **in the** ~ sonunda.

up.side *adv.* ['ʌpsaid]: ~ **down** tepetaklak, tepesi üstü, ters; *fig.* altüst; **turn** ~ **down** altüst etm., altını üstüne getirmek.

up.stage F *fig.* ['ʌp'steidʒ] *adj.* kibirli, kendini beğenmiş.

up.stairs ['ʌp'stɛəz] **1.** *adj.* üst kattaki, yukarıdaki; **2.** *adv.* üst kat(t)a, yukarıya, yukarıda; **3.** *n.* üst kat.

up.stand.ing [ʌp'stændiŋ] *adj.* dik; gürbüz, sağlıklı; dürüst.

up.start ['ʌpstaːt] **1.** *n.* birden zengin olan kimse; **2.** *adj.* türedi, sonradan görme.

up.state *Am.* ['ʌp'steit] *n.* taşra.

up.stream ['ʌp'striːm] *adv.* akıntıya karşı; nehrin yukarısına doğru.

up.stroke ['ʌpstrəuk] *n.* (*yazı*) yukarı doğru çekilen kuyruk.

up.surge ['ʌpsəːdʒ] *n.* kabarma, hızlı artış.

up.swing ['ʌpswiŋ] *n.* yukarıya sallanma; ilerleme, yükselme, iyileşme.

up.take ['ʌpteik] *n.* kavrama, anlama; **be slow** (**quick**) **in** *veya* **on the** ~ F yavaş (çabuk) kavramak, anlamak.

up.throw ['ʌpθrəu] *n.* yukarıya fırlatma.

up-to-date ['ʌptə'deit] *adj.* modern, asrî, çağcıl, güncel, çağdaş.

up-town ['ʌp'təun] *adj. & adv.* şehir merkezinin dışında(ki).

up.turn [ʌp'tə:n] *v/t.* & *v/i.* yukarı dön(dür)mek.

up.ward ['ʌpwəd] **1.** *adj.* yükselen, yukarı doğru giden; **2.** *adv.* = **up.wards** ['ˌ-z] yukarıya doğru, yukarı; **~ of** -den fazla.

u.ra.ni.um CHEM [juə'reinjəm] *n.* uranyum.

ur.ban ['ə:bən] *adj.* şehre ait, şehir...; **ur.bane** □ [ə:'bein] görgülü, nazik, kibar; **ur.ban.i.ty** [ə:'bæniti] *n.* nezaket, kibarlık; **ur.ban.i.za.tion** [ə:bənai-'zeiʃən] *n.* kentleşme, şehirleşme; **'ur.ban.ize** *v/t.* kentleştirmek, şehirleştirmek.

ur.chin ['ə:tʃin] *n.* afacan, haşarı çocuk.

urge [ə:dʒ] **1.** *v/t. oft.* **~ on** ileri sürmek, sevketmek, harekete geçirmek; *fig.* kışkırtmak (**to** -e); zorlamak (**to** *inf.* -meye); dürtmek; sıkıştırmak; **~ s.th. on s.o.** *b-ne bşi* ısrarla anlatmak; **2.** *n.* dürtü; zorlama; kışkırtma; özlem, arzu; **ur.gen.cy** ['ə:dʒənsi] *n.* acele; ısrar; sıkıştırma; zorunluluk; **'ur.gent** □ acele olan, âcil; zorunlu, kaçınılmaz; ısrar eden; **be ~ with s.o. to** *inf. b-ni bş* yapmaya zorlamak.

u.ric CHEM ['juərik] *adj.* idrara ait, idrar..., ürik...

u.ri.nal ['juərinl] *n.* idrar kabı, sürgü, ördek; pisuar; **'u.ri.nar.y** *adj.* idrara ait, sidik...; **u.ri.nate** ['ˌneit] *v/i.* işemek; **'urine** *n.* idrar, sidik.

urn [ə:n] *n.* kap; büyük kavanoz; sema ver.

us [ʌs, əs] *pron.* bizi, bize; **all of ~** hepimiz.

us.a.ble ['ju:zəbl] *adj.* kullanışlı, elverişli, kullanılabilir.

us.age ['ju:zidʒ] *n.* kullanış, kullanım; işlem; usûl; âdet, gelenek.

us.ance COM ['ju:zəns] *n.* yabancı tahvillerin ödenme vadesi; **bill at ~** vadeli senet.

use 1. [ju:s] *n.* fayda, yarar; kullanma, kullanım; alışıklık, âdet; amaç, gaye; kullanma hakkı; **be of ~** yararlı olm.; **it is (of) no ~** *ger. veya* **to** *inf. ...menin* yararı yok, ...mek bir işe yaramaz; **have no ~ for** -e hiç tahammülü olmamak; artık ihtiyacı olmamak; *Am.* F -den hiç hoşlanmamak; **put to ~** kullanmak; **2.** [ju:z] *v/t.* kullanmak; yararlanmak -*den;* davranmak -*e;* **~ up** tüketmek, sarfetmek, harcamak; **I ~d** ['ju:s(t)] **to do** eskiden yapardım; **used** ['ju:zd] kullanılmış; ['ju:st]

alışık, alışkın (**to** -*e);* **use.ful** □ ['ju:s-ful] faydalı, yararlı; MEC işe yarar; **'use.ful.ness** *n.* fayda, yarar, kullanışlılık; **'use.less** □ faydasız, yararsız, boş, nafile; bir işe yaramaz; **'use.less.ness** *n.* faydasızlık, yararsızlık; **us.er** ['ju:zə] *n.* kullanan.

ush.er ['ʌʃə] **1.** *n.* mübaşir; kapıcı; THEAT yer gösteren kimse; *contp.* yardımcı öğretmen; **2.** *v/t.* yer göstermek -*e; mst ~ **in** bildirmek, haber vermek; *fig.* açmak, başlatmak (*yeni bir devir);* **usher.ette** [ˌ-'ret] *n.* yer gösteren kadın.

u.su.al □ ['ju:ʒuəl] her zamanki, olağan, alışılagelmiş; **as ~** her zamanki gibi; **'u.su.al.iy** *adv.* çoğunlukla, ekseriya, çoğu kere.

u.su.fruct JUR ['ju:ʃju:frʌkt] *n.* yararlanma hakkı, intifa hakkı; **u.su'fruc.tu.ar.y** [ˌtjuəri] *n.* intifa hakkı olan kimse.

u.su.rer ['ju:ʒərə] *n.* tefeci; **u.su.ri.ous** □ [ju:'zjuəriəs] tefecilik kabilinden, aşırı faizli...

u.surp [ju:'zə:p] *v/t.* gaspetmek -*i,* zorla almak -*i,* el koymak -*e;* **u.sur'pa.tion** *n.* gasp, zorla alma, el koyma; **u'surp.er** *n.* gasp, zorla alan kimse.

u.su.ry ['ju:ʒuri] *n.* tefecilik; aşırı faiz.

u.ten.sil [ju:'tensl] *n.* kap; alet; **~s** *pl.* malzeme; alet edavat; kap kacak, mutfak takımı.

u.ter.ine ['ju:tərain] *adj.* rahme ait, rahim...; anası bir babası ayrı; **~ brother** üvey kardeş; **u.ter.us** ANAT ['ˌ-rəs] *n.* rahim, dölyatağı.

u.til.i.tar.i.an [ju:tili'tɛəriən] **1.** *n.* faydacıl kimse; **2.** *adj.* faydacıl; **u'til.i.ty** **1.** *n.* yarar(lık), fayda; işe yarar şey; kamu hizmeti yapan kuruluş; *a.* **public ~** kamu hizmeti; **public utilities** kamu kuruluşları; **2.** *adj.* kullanışlı.

u.ti.li.za.tion [ju:tilai'zeiʃən] *n.* kullanım, yararlanma; **'u.ti.lize** *v/t.* kullanmak; faydalanmak -*den.*

ut.most ['ʌtməust] *adj.* en uzak, en son; en büyük, olanca, en yüksek, en fazla; azamî, son derece.

U.to.pi.an [ju:'təupjən] **1.** *adj.* ülküsel, ideal, hayalî, ütopik; **2.** *n.* ütopyacı kimse.

ut.ter ['ʌtə] **1.** *fig.* tam(amen), bütün bütün; kesin, son; aşama kadar, su katılmadık; **2.** *v/t.* ağza almak, söylemek; ağızdan çıkarmak (*ses);* piyasaya sürmek (*sahte para vs.);* **'ut.ter.ance** *n.*

ifade; konuşma şekli; söz; söyleme; **give~ to** dile getirmek, kelimelerle ifade etm.; '**ut.ter.er** *n.* konuşan kimse; '**ut.ter.most** *adj.* azamî; en son, en uzak.

u.vu.la ANAT ['juːvjulə] *n.* küçükdil; 'u.vular *adj.* küçükdile ait.
ux.ori.ous [ʌk'sɔːriəs] *adj.* karısına çok düşkün.

V

vac F [væk] = **vacation**.
va.can.cy ['veikənsi] *n.* boşluk (*a. fig.*); açık kadro; boş yer, aralık; **gaze into ~** boşluğa dalıp bakmak; '**va.cant** □ boş (*a. fig.*); açık; münhal; bön, aptal; ifadesiz; terkedilmiş, sahipsiz; vârissiz.
va.cate [və'keit, *Am.* 'veikeit] *v/t.* tahliye etm., boşaltmak; boş bırakmak, terketmek; bırakmak; kalkmak (*yerinden*); lağvetmek, feshetmek; **va'ca-tion** 1. *n.* tatil; 2. *v/t. Am.* tatilini geçirmek (**at, in** -*de*); **va'ca.tion.ist** *n. Am.* tatile çıkan kimse.
vac.ci.nate ['væksineit] *v/t.* aşılamak, aşı yapmak; **vac.ci'na.tion** *n.* aşı(lama); '**vac.ci.na.tor** *n.* aşıcı; **vac.cine** ['ˍsiːn] *n.* aşı (maddesi).
vac.il.late ['væsileit] *v/i.* tereddüt etm., kararsız olm.; sallanmak, sendelemek; **vac.il.'la.tion** *n.* tereddüt; sendeleme.
va.cu.i.ty [ʌæ'kjuːiti] *n.* boşluk (*mst fig.*); aptallık; düşüncesizlik; budalaca konuşma; işsizlik; **vac.u.ous** □ ['vækjuəs] *fig.* boş, anlamsız; aptal; işsiz; **vac.u.um** ['ˍəm] 1. *n.* PHYS boşluk, vakum; **~ brake** vakum freni; **~ cleaner** elektrik süpürgesi; **~ flask, ~ bottle** termos; **~ tube** radyo lambası; 2. *v/i.* elektrik süpürgesi kullanmak.
va.de-me.cum ['veidi'miːkəm] *n.* her zaman yanda taşınılan elkitabı.
vag.a.bond ['vægəbɔnd] 1. *adj.* serseri, avare; ELECT kararsız (*akım*); 2. *n.* serseri kimse, avare kimse; '**vag.a.bond-age** *n.* serserilik.
va.gar.y ['veigəri] *n.* garip davranış *veya* fikir; kapris; delilik, çılgınlık.
va.gran.cy ['veigrənsi] *n.* serserilik; göçebelik; '**va.grant** 1. *adj.* serseri, avare; *fig.* göçebe, yersiz yurtsuz; 2. = **vaga-bond** 2.
vague □ [veig] belirsiz, müphem, bulanık, şüpheli, anlaşılmaz; '**vague-ness** *n.* belirsizlik, anlaşılmazlık.
vail *obs. veya poet.* [veil] *v/t.* indirmek (*bayrak*); çıkarmak (*şapka*).

vain □ [vein] boş, nafile; *fig.* kendini beğenmiş, kibirli, gururlu; değersiz, verimsiz; faydasız, anlamsız; **in ~** (boşu) boşuna, beyhude (yere); **~.glo-ri.ous** □ [ˍ'glɔːriəs] mağrur, gururlu; **~'glo.ry** *n.* kendini beğenmişlik, gurur.
val.ance ['væləns] *n.* saçak, farbala, fırfır.
vale [veil] *n. poet.* vadi, dere.
val.e.dic.tion [væli'dikʃən] *n.* veda; **val.e'dic.to.ry** [ˍtəri] 1. *adj.* veda...; 2. *n.* veda konuşması.
va.lence CHEM ['veiləns] *n.* valans, değerlik.
val.en.tine ['væləntain] *n.* 14 Şubat Valentine gününde seçilen sevgili(ye gönderilen kart).
va.le.ri.an BOT [və'liəriən] *n.* kediotu.
val.et ['vælit] 1. *n.* uşak, erkek oda hizmetçisi; 2. *v/t.* oda hizmetçiliği yapmak -*e*.
val.e.tu.di.nar.i.an ['vælitjuːdi'nɛəriən] 1. *adj.* sıhhatsiz, sağlığı bozuk; sağlığına çok düşkün; 2. *n.* hasta kimse; sağlığına çok düşkün kimse.
val.iant □ ['væljənt] yiğit, cesur, yürekli.
val.id □ ['vælid] geçerli, yürürlükte olan; doğru, sağlam; kanunî, yasal; **be ~** geçerli olm.; **val.i.date** ['ˍdeit] *v/t.* geçerli kılmak; onaylamak; **va.lid-i.ty** [və'liditi] *n.* geçerlik; yürürlük; sağlamlık, doğruluk.
va.lise [və'liːz] *n.* valiz, küçük bavul; MIL sırt çantası.
val.ley ['væli] *n.* vadi, dere.
val.or.i.za.tion [vælərai'zeiʃən] *n.* hükümetçe fiyat tespiti; '**val.or.ize** *vb.* hükümetçe fiyat tespit etm.
val.or.ous □ ['vælərəs] cesur, yiğit.
val.o(u)r ['vælə] *n.* yiğitlik, cesaret, kahramanlık.
val.u.a.ble ['væljuəbl] 1. □ değerli, kıymetli, pahalı; aziz; 2. *n.* **~s** *pl.* değerli şey, mücevherat.
val.u.a.tion [vælju'eiʃən] *n.* değer (biç-

me); kıymet; 'val.u.a.tor *n.* istimator, tahminci.

val.ue ['vælju:] 1. *n.* değer, kıymet (*a. fig.*); önem, itibar; gerçek değer; MUS değer; PAINT renk tonu; anlam, mana; mal; *give (get) good ~ (for one's money)* COM parasının tam karşılığını vermek (almak); *~-added tax* katma değer vergisi; 2. *v/t.* takdir etm., saymak, paha biçmek; *fig.* değer vermek -*e*; 'val.ued *adj.* değerlendirilmiş, değerli; 'val.ue.less *adj.* değersiz, beş para etmez.

valve [vælv] *n.* valf, supap, ventil; BOT çenet; ANAT kapacık; *radyo:* radyo lambası.

va.moose *Am. sl.* [væ'mu:s] *v/i.* defolmak, çekip gitmek, tüymek.

vamp¹ [væmp] 1. *n.* saya; 2. *v/t.* -*e* saya takmak; uydurmak (*bahane*); MUS eşlik etm.

vamp² F [-] 1. *n.* şuh kadın, fındıkçı kadın; 2. *v/t.* ayartmak (*erkeği*), baştan çıkarmak.

vam.pire ['væmpaiə] *n.* vampir, hortlak.

van¹ [væn] *n.* üstü kapalı yük arabası, karavan; RAIL furgon.

van² MIL *veya fig.* [-] *n.* keşif kolu, öncü.

Van.dal ['vændəl] *n.* HIST vandal; ♀ *fig.* barbar, yıkıcı, vahşî kimse; 'van.dal.ism *n.* yıkıcılık, vandalizm.

van.dyke [væn'daik] *n.* geniş oymalı yaka; keçisakal; *attr.* ♀ Van Dyck...

vane [vein] *n.* rüzgârgülü; fırıldak, yelkovan; pervane kanadı; yeldeğirmeni kanadı.

van.guard MIL ['vænɡɑːd] *n.* ileri kol, öncü kolu.

va.nil.la BOT [və'nilə] *n.* vanilya.

van.ish ['væniʃ] *v/i.* gözden kaybolmak, yok olmak, uçup gitmek; *~ into thin air* yer yarılıp içine girmek.

van.i.ty ['væniti] *n.* kendini beğenmişlik, kibirlilik; nafilelik; değersizlik; gösteriş, caka; *~ bag*, *~ case* makyaj çantası.

van.quish ['væŋkwiʃ] *v/t.* yenmek, altetmek, hakkından gelmek.

van.tage ['vɑːntidʒ] *n.* üstünlük; *tenis:* düsten sonra gelen puan, avantaj; '*~-ground* *n.* avantajlı alan.

vap.id ['væpid] ☐ sıkıcı; yavan; tatsız, sönük, cansız.

va.po(u)r.ize ['veipəraiz] *v/t. & v/i.* buharlaş(tır)mak; 'va.po(u)r.iz.er *n.* MEC püskürteç, vaporizatör (*a.* MED).

va.por.ous ☐ ['veipərəs] buharlı, dumanlı; *fig.* hayalperest; boş, asılsız.

va.po(u)r ['veipə] *n.* buhar, buğu, duman; *fig.* hayalî şey, kuruntu; *~ bath* buhar banyosu; 'va.po(u)r.y = *vaporous*.

var.i.a.bil.i.ty [vɛəriə'biliti] *n.* değişkenlik; 'var.i.a.ble ☐ değişken; kararsız; 'var.iance *n.* değişiklik; uyuşmazlık, çelişki, ayrılık; *be at ~* aykırı olm., araları bozuk olm., uyuşamamak (*with ile*); *set at ~* aralarını bozmak; 'var.i.ant 1. *adj.* farklı, değişik; 2. *n.* varyant; değişik biçim; var.i'a.tion *n.* değişme, dönme, dönüşme; değişiklik; MUS çeşitleme, varyasyon.

var.i.cose MED ['værikəus] *adj.* genişlemiş, varisli...; *~ vein* varisli damar.

var.ied ☐ ['vɛərid] çeşitli, farklı, türlü, değişik; var.i.e.gate ['~rigeit] *v/t.* renklendirmek; çeşitlemek; 'var.i.e-gat.ed *adj.* alaca(lı), rengârenk; var.i-e'ga.tion *n.* renklilik, alacalık; çeşitlilik; va.ri.e.ty [və'raiəti] *n.* değişiklik, farklılık; karışım; *part.* COM çeşit (*a.* BIOL); cins, nevi, tür; *~ show* varyete; *~ theatre* varyete tiyatrosu.

va.ri.o.la MED [və'raiələ] *n.* çiçek hastalığı.

var.i.ous ☐ ['vɛəriəs] çeşitli, birkaç, muhtelif; değişik, farklı.

var.let *obs.* ['vɑːlit] *n.* alçak adam; şövalye uşağı.

var.mint *sl., co.* ['vɑːmint] *n.* sefil adam, alçak adam.

var.nish ['vɑːniʃ] 1. *n.* vernik, cila; *fig.* yapmacıklık, dış güzellik; 2. *v/t.* verniklemek, cilalamak; *fig.* içyüzünü gizlemek, görünüşte süslemek.

var.si.ty F ['vɑːsiti] *n.* üniversite.

var.y ['vɛəri] *v/t. & v/i.* değiş(tir)mek; farklı olm. (*from -den*); *part.* MUS çeşitlemek; değişime uğramak.

vas.cu.lar BOT, ANAT ['væskjulə] *adj.* damara ait, damar(lı)...

vase [vɑːz, *Am.* veiz] *n.* vazo.

vas.sal ['væsəl] *n.* vasal; uyruk; köle, hizmetli; *attr.* vasal...; 'vas.sal.age *n.* vasallık; kölelik, kulluk (*to* -*e*).

vast ☐ [vɑːst] engin, geniş, vâsi; çok, dünya kadar; koskocaman; 'vast.ness *n.* enginlik; büyüklük; çokluk.

vat [væt] 1. *n.* tekne, fıçı; sarnıç; 2. *v/t.* fıçıya koymak, fıçılamak.

vat.ted ['vætid] *adj.* fıçılanmış (*şarap vs.*).

vaude.ville ['vəudəvil] *n. Am.* vodvil,

varyete.
vault[1] [vɔːlt] **1.** *n.* tonoz, kemer; mahzen; yeraltı mezarı; (*banka*) kasa dairesi; gök, sema; **2.** *v/t.* üstünü kemerle çevirmek.
vault[2] [-] **1.** *v/t.* atlamak, sıçramak; **2.** *n.* atlayış, atlama.
vault.ing ARCH ['vɔːltiŋ] *n.* tonozlu (*veya* kemerli) yapı.
vault.ing-horse ['vɔːltiŋhɔːs] *n.* jimnastik; kasa, atlama beygiri.
vaunt *lit.* [vɔːnt] **1.** *v/t.* & *v/i.* öv(ün)mek; **2.** *n.* övünme; '**vaunt.ing** ☐ övüngen, farfara.
veal [viːl] *n.* dana eti; *roast* ~ dana rostosu.
veer [viə] **1.** *v/t.* & *v/i.* dön(dür)mek, yön(ünü) değiştirmek; *fig.* caymak, fikrini değiştirmek; **2.** *n.* dönüş, dönme.
veg.e.ta.ble ['vedʒitəbl] **1.** *adj.* bitkilere ait, bitkisel...; **2.** *n.* bitki; *mst* ~**s** *pl.* sebze, zerzevat; **veg.e.tar.i.an** [-'teəriən] **1.** *n.* et yemez kimse, otobur; **2.** *adj.* etyemez; yalnız sebzeden oluşan, sebze...; **veg.e.tate** ['-teit] *v/i. fig.* ot gibi yaşamak; **veg.e'ta.tion** *n.* bitkiler, bitki örtüsü; **veg.e.ta.tive** ['-tətiv] bitkisel; bitek; ot gibi yaşayan, hareketsiz.
ve.he.mence ['viːiməns] *n.* şiddet, hiddet, ateşlilik; '**ve.he.ment** ☐ şiddetli, hiddetli, ateşli.
ve.hi.cle ['viːikl] *n.* taşıt, araç, vasıta (*a. fig.*); PHARM vehikül, vasıta; **ve.hic.u.lar** [-] [vi'hikjulə] taşıtlara ait, taşıt...
veil [veil] **1.** *n.* peçe, yaşmak, perde (*a.* PHOT); örtü, tül; *fig.* bahane, maske; **2.** *v/t.* & *v/i.* ört(ün)mek; *fig.* gizlemek, saklamak; '**veil.ing** *n.* peçelik ince kumaş (*a.* COM); PHOT donukluk, vual.
vein [vein] *n.* damar (*a. fig.*); huy, mizaç; oluk, oyuk; **veined** *adj.* damarlı; '**vein.ing** *n.* damar sistemi.
vel.le.i.ty [ve'liːiti] *n.* hafif heves, eğilim.
vel.lum ['veləm] *n.* parşömen, tirşe; *a.* ~ *paper* parşömen kâğıdı.
ve.loc.i.pede [vi'lɔsipiːd] *n. Am.* üç tekerlekli çocuk bisikleti, velespit; HIST ön tekerlekten pedallı bisiklet.
ve.loc.i.ty [vi'lɔsiti] *n.* hız, sürat (derecesi).
ve.lour(s) [və'luə] *n.* kadife taklidi.
vel.vet ['velvit] **1.** *n.* kadife, velur; HUNT kadifemsi deri; *sl.* kolay kazanç; **2.** *adj.* kadife...; kadife gibi; yumuşak; **vel.veteen** [-'tiːn] *n.* pamuklu kadife;

'**vel.vet.y** *adj.* kadife gibi; yumuşak.
ve.nal ['viːnl] *adj.* satın alınır, rüşvetle kandırılır, rüşvet alan, yiyici; **ve.nal.i.ty** [viː'næliti] *n.* rüşvet yeme.
vend [vend] *v/t.* satmak; '**vend.er**, '**vendor** *n.* satıcı, işportacı; '**vend.i.ble** *adj.* satılabilir; '**vend.ing ma.chine** para ile çalışan satıcı makine.
ven.det.ta [ven'detə] *n.* kan davası.
ve.neer [vi'niə] **1.** *n.* kaplama tahtası; *fig.* yapma tavır, gösteriş; **2.** *v/t.* kaplamak; *fig.* cilalamak, yaldızlamak.
ven.er.a.ble ☐ ['venərəbl] muhterem, saygıdeğer; **ven.er.ate** ['-reit] *v/t.* saygı göstermek *-e*, hürmet etm. *-e*; tapmak *-e*; **ven.er'a.tion** *n.* hürmet, saygı; '**ven.er.a.tor** *n.* hürmet eden (*veya* tapınan) kimse.
ve.ne.re.al [vi'niəriəl] *adj.* cinsel ilişkiye ait; *a.* MED zührevî; ~ *disease* zührevî hastalık.
Ve.ne.tian [vi'niːʃən] **1.** *adj.* Venedik'e ait; ~ *blind* jaluzi; **2.** *n.* Venedikli.
venge.ance ['vendʒəns] *n.* öç, intikam; *with a* ~ F son derecede, alabildiğine, şiddetle; '**venge.ful** ☐ ['-ful] intikamcı, kinci.
ve.ni.al ☐ ['viːnjəl] affedilir, önemsiz.
ven.i.son ['venzn] *n.* geyik *veya* karaca eti.
ven.om ['venəm] *n.* yılan *vs.* zehiri; *fig.* düşmanlık, kin, garez; '**ven.om.ous** ☐ zehirli; kinci, garezkâr, düşman.
ve.nous ['viːnəs] *adj.* toplardamara ait, toplardamar...; BOT damarlı...
vent [vent] **1.** *n.* delik, menfez, ağız; kıç; yırtmaç; yarık, çıkak, çıkıt; *give* ~ *to* -*i* açığa vurmak, *k-ni* tutamamak; **2.** *v/t.* dışarı salıvermek; *fig.* göstermek, ifade etm., çıkarmak (*öfkesini*) (*on* -*den*); '~*hole* *n.* hava deliği.
ven.ti.late ['ventileit] *v/t.* havalandırmak; *fig.* açığa vurmak, tartışmak; **ven.ti'lation** *n.* havalandırma (*a.* MI)N; *fig.* açığa vurma; '**ven.ti.la.tor** *n.* vantilatör.
ven.tral ['ventrəl] *adj.* karna ait, karın...
ven.tri.cle ANAT ['ventrikl] *n.* karıncık; beden *veya* organda boşluk.
ven.tril.o.quist [ven'triləkwist] *n.* vantrlok; **ven'tril.o.quize** *v/i.* vantrlokluk yapmak.
ven.ture ['ventʃə] **1.** *n.* tehlikeli iş, şans işi; risk, riziko; *at a* ~ rasgele; **2.** *v/t.* & *v/i.* tehlikeye atmak; göze almak (*to inf. -meyi*); şansa bırakmak; riske gir-

mek; ~ **(up)on** girişmek -*e*, atılmak -*e*;
cesaret etm.; *I ~ to say* diyebilirim ki;
ven.ture.some □ ['₋səm], 'ven-
tur.ous □ atılgan, cesur, atak; tehlikeli, riskli.
ven.ue ['venju:] *n.* olay yeri; yetki dairesi; *fig.* yarışma yeri; F buluşma yeri.
ve.ra.cious □ [və'reiʃəs] doğru (sözlü); gerçeğe sadık;**ve.rac.i.ty** [və'ræsi-
ti] *n.* gerçek(lik); dürüstlük.
ve.ran.da(h) [və'rændə] *n.* veranda,
camlı taraça.
verb GR [və:b] *n.* fiil;'**ver.bal** □ fiile ait,
fiil...; sözlü; kelimesi kelimesine, harfiyen; **ver.ba.tim** [₋'beitim] *adj.* kelimesi kelimesine; **ver.bi.age** ['₋biidʒ]
n. laf kalabalığı; **ver.bose** □ [₋'bəus]
ağzı kalabalık; gereksiz sözlerle dolu;
ver.bos.i.ty [₋'bɒsiti] *n.* laf kalabalığı.
ver.dan.cy ['və:dənsi] *n.* yeşillik, tazelik; *fig.* toyluk;'**ver.dant** □ yeşil, taze;
fig. toy, deneyimsiz.
ver.dict ['və:dikt] *n.* JUR jüri kurulu
hükmü; karar, hüküm; *fig.* fikir, ka-
naat (**on** -*de*); **bring in** *veya* **return a**
~ **of guilty** suçlu olduğu kararına varmak.
ver.di.gris ['və:digris] *n.* jengâr, zen-
car, bakır pası.
ver.dure ['və:dʒə] *n.* yeşillik, çimen.
verge¹ [və:dʒ] *n.* değnek, sopa, asa.
verge² [₋] **1.** *n. mst fig.* kenar, hudut,
sınır, eşik; **on the** ~ **of** eşiğinde, üzere;
2. *v/i.* yönelmek; ~ **(up)on** yaklaşmak
-*e*.
ver.ger ['və:dʒə] *n.* piskopos hizmetlisi;
zangoç.
ver.i.fi.a.ble ['verifaiəbl] *adj.* doğrula-
nabilir; tetkik edilebilir; **ver.i.fi.ca-**
tion [₋fi'keiʃən] *n.* tahkik, tetkik; doğrulama; **ver.i.fy** ['₋fai] *v/t.* doğrulamak, gerçeklemek; tahkik etm., tetkik
etm.;'**ver.i.ly** *adv. obs.* gerçekten, doğrusu; **ver.i.simil.i.tude** [₋si'militju:d]
n. gerçeğe benzeme; olasılık; **ver.i.ta-**
ble □ ['₋təbl] gerçek, hakikî; 'ver.i.ty
n. doğru(luk), gerçek(lik).
ver.mi.cel.li [və:mi'seli] *n.* tel şehriye;
ver.mi.cide PHARM ['₋said] *n.* solucan
ilacı; **ver'mic.u.lar** [₋kjulə] *adj.* solu-
cana benzer; **ver.mi.form** ['₋fɔ:m]
adj. solucan şeklindeki, kurda benzer;
ver.mifuge PHARM ['₋fju:dʒ] *n.* solucan ilacı.
ver.mil.ion [və'miljən] **1.** *n.* parlak
kırmızı; sülüğen; **2.** *adj.* zincifre
kırmızısı, al.

ver.min [və:min] *n.* haşarat; HUNT zararlı hayvanlar; *fig.* mikrop, ayaktakımı; '**ver.min.ous** *adj.* haşaratlı;
haşarattan olan; alçak, pis.
ver.m(o)uth ['və:məθ] *n.* vermut.
ver.nac.u.lar [və'nækjulə] **1.** □ bölgesel; ana diline ait; argoyla ilgili; yaygın;
2. *n.* günlük dil; anadil; lehçe; argo.
ver.nal ['və:nl] *adj.* ilkbaharda olan;
ilkbahar...; *fig.* gençliğe ait, taze.
ver.ni.er ['və:njə] *n.* MATH, MEC verniye.
ver.sa.tile □ ['və:sətail] çok iş bilen,
çok yönlü; çok kullanımlı; **ver.sa.til.i-**
ty [₋'tiliti] *n.* çok yönlülük; beceriklilik.
verse [və:s] *n.* dize, mısra; şiir, koşuk;
nazım; beyit, kıta; ayet;**versed** *adj.* bilgili, becerikli, usta (**in** -*de*).
ver.si.fi.ca.tion [və:sifi'keiʃən] *n.* şiir
yazma sanatı; şiir vezni; **ver.si.fy**
['₋fai] *v/t.* şiir haline koymak; *v/i.* şiir
yazmak.
ver.sion ['və:ʃən] *n.* tercüme, çeviri;
okunuş tarzı; yorum.
ver.sus *part.* JUR ['və:səs] *prp.* -*e* karşı,
-*in* aleyhinde.
vert F ECCL [və:t] *vb.* din değiştirmek.
ver.te.bra ANAT ['və:tibrə] *n.*, *pl.* **ver.te-**
brae ['₋bri:] omur(ga kemiği), verteb-
ra; **ver.te.bral** ['₋brəl] *adj.* vertebral,
omur...; **ver.te.brate** ['₋brit] **1.** *adj.*
omurgalı...; ~ **animal** = **2.** *n.* omurgalı
hayvan.
ver.tex ['və:teks] *n.*, *pl. mst* **ver.ti.ces**
['₋tisi:z] zirve, doruk, tepe; 'ver.ti.cal
□ dikey, düşey...
ver.tig.i.nous □ [və:'tidʒinəs] baş
döndürücü; **ver.ti.go** ['₋tigəu] *n.* baş
dönmesi.
verve [və:v] *n.* şevk, gayret, heves.
ver.y ['veri] **1.** *adv.* çok, pek, gayet, ziya-
desiyle; gerçekten; tam(amen); **2.** *adj.*
tam, ta kendisi; aynı, tıpkısı; bile, hatta; en; katî; belirli; *the* ~ *same* tıpkı
tıpkısına; *in the* ~ *act* suçüstü; *to the*
~ *bone* ta iliklerine kadar; *the* ~ *thing*
biçilmiş kaftan; *the* ~ *thought* düşüncesi bile; *the* ~ *stones* taşlar bile; *the*
veriest baby bebekler bile; *the veri-*
est rascal alçakların alçağı, köpoğlu
köpek.
ves.i.ca ['vesikə] *n.* torba; mesane, sidik torbası;**ves.i.cle** ['₋kl] *n.* kabarcık,
kese, kist.
ves.per ['vespə] *n. poet.* akşam; ~*s pl.*
ECCL akşam duası.
ves.sel ['vesl] *n.* kap, tas, leğen; NAUT

gemi, tekne; ANAT damar.
vest [vest] **1.** *n.* iç gömleği, fanila; COM
yelek; **2.** *v/t. mst fig. b-ne* vermek (*with
-i*); hak vermek (*in -e*); yetki vermek
(*in s.o. b-ne*); giydirmek (*cüppe*); *v/i.*
hakkı olm. (*in s.o. b-nin*); ∼*ed rights
pl.* kazanılmış haklar.
ves.tal ['vestl] **1.** *adj.* ocak tanrıçasına
ait; namuslu; **2.** *n.* ocak tanrıçasının rahibesi.
ves.ti.bule ['vestibju:l] *n.* giriş, antre;
RAIL *part. Am.* vagonlar arasındaki kapalı geçit.
ves.tige ['vestidʒ] *n.* iz, eser, işaret;
ves'tig.i.al [‿dʒiəl] *adj.* iz bırakmış; artakalan.
vest.ment ['vestmənt] *n.* giysi, resmî
elbise; cüppe.
vest-pock.et ['vest'pɔkit] *adj.* cebe
sığacak kadar küçük, küçücük…
ves.try ['vestri] *n.* ECCL giyinme odası;
yönetim kurulu; '∼.man *n.* kilise yönetim kurulu üyesi.
ves.ture *poet.* ['vestʃə] **1.** *n.* giysi, kılık
kıyafet; örtü; **2.** *v/t.* giydirmek.
vet F [vet] **1.** *n.* veteriner, baytar; *Am.*
MIL kıdemli asker; **2.** *v/t.* muayene
etm.; *fig.* dikkatle incelemek.
vetch BOT [vetʃ] *n.* baklagillerden herhangi bir bitki.
vet.er.an ['vetərən] **1.** *adj.* kıdemli, deneyimli; emekli; **2.** *n.* kıdemli asker;
emekli asker; deneyimli kimse.
vet.er.i.nar.y ['vetərinəri] **1.** *adj.* veteri-
nerliğe ait; **2.** *n. a.* ∼ *surgeon* veteriner,
baytar.
ve.to ['vi:təu] **1.** *n., pl.* **ve.toes** ['‿z] veto; *put a veya one's* ∼ (*up)on* = **2.** *v/t.*
veto etm., reddetmek.
vex [veks] *v/t.* kızdırmak, canını
sıkmak, sinirlendirmek; darıltmak; incitmek; rahatsız etm.; tartışmak; *part.*
JUR eziyet etm.; **vex'a.tion** *n.* kızma, sinirlenme; sıkıntı, üzüntü; **vex'a.tious**
□ gücendirici, üzücü, sinirlendirici,
can sıkıcı; **vexed** □ dargın, kızgın, canı
sıkkın (*at s.th. bşe, with s.o. b-ne*); ∼
question tartışmalı mesele; 'vex.ing
□ üzücü, can sıkıcı.
vi.a ['vaiə] *prp.* yolu ile, *-den* geçerek.
vi.a.ble ['vaiəbl] *adj.* yaşayabilir; uygulanabilir.
vi.a.duct ['vaiədʌkt] *n.* köprü, viyadük.
vi.al ['vaiəl] *n.* küçük şişe.
vi.and ['vaiənd] *n. mst* ∼*s pl.* yemek, yiyecek.
vi.at.i.cum ECCL [vai'ætikəm] *n.* ölüm

döşeğindeki kimseye verilen Aşai
Rabbani.
vi.brant ['vaibrənt] *adj.* titrek, titreşimli; canlı; coşkun; gür, tok, yankılı (*ses*).
vi.brate [vai'breit] *v/t. & v/i.* titre(t)-
mek, sallan(dır)mak; titreşmek; **vi-
'bra.tion** *n.* titreşim; titreme, sallanma;
vi'bra.tor *n.* titreten şey; titreşimli masaj aleti; elektrik zilinin dili; **vi.bra.to-
ry** ['‿brətəri] *adj.* titretici; titreşimli.
vic.ar ECCL ['vikə] *n.* papaz; vekil; ∼
general piskopos yardımcısı; 'vic.ar-
age *n.* papazın evi; **vi.car.i.ous** □
[vai'kɛəriəs] başkasının yerine
yapılmış; vekâleten yapılan.
vice[1] [vais] *n.* kötü huy, ayıp, kusur, leke.
vice[2] MEC [‿] *n.* mengene, sıkmaç.
vice[3] ['vaisi] *prp. -in* yerine.
vice[4] [vais] **1.** *adj.* muavin, yardımcı,
ikinci; **2.** *n.* F vekil, muavin; '∼'ad.mi-
ral *n.* koramiral; '∼'chair.man *n.* başkan yardımcısı; '∼'chan.cel.lor *n.* baş-
hâkim yardımcısı; UNIV rektör
yardımcısı; '∼'con.sul *n.* viskonsül,
konsolos yardımcısı; ∼.ge.rent
['‿'dʒerənt] *n.* vekil; '∼'pres.i.dent
n. ikinci başkan, başkan yardımcısı;
'∼'re.gal *adj.* genel valiye ait; ∼.reine
['‿'rein] *n.* genel vali karısı; kadın genel vali; ∼.roy ['‿rɔi] *n.* genel vali.
vi.ce ver.sa ['vaisi'və:sə] *adv.* tersine;
karşılıklı olarak.
vic.i.nage ['visinidʒ] *n.,* **vi'cin.i.ty** civar, çevre, havali, yöre, semt, mahalle;
yakınlık (*to -e*); *in the* ∼ *of 50* 50 civarında, 50 kadar.
vi.cious □ ['viʃəs] kötü; kinci, haince;
ahlâkı bozuk; huysuz, hırçın (*hayvan*);
kusurlu; bozuk; çirkin; şiddetli, sert; ∼
circle kısır döngü.
vi.cis.si.tude [vi'sisitju:d] *n.* değişiklik; ∼*s pl.* olaylar.
vic.tim ['viktim] *n.* kurban; mağdur
kimse; 'vic.tim.ize *v/t.* cezalandırmak;
fig. aldatmak, faka bastırmak.
vic.tor ['viktə] *n.* galip, fatih; **Vic.to.ri-
an** HIST [vik'tɔːriən] *adj.* Kraliçe Vik-
torya zamanına ait; **vic'to.ri.ous** □ galip, muzaffer; **vic.to.ry** ['‿təri] *n.* zafer,
yengi, utku, başarı.
vict.ual ['vitl] **1.** *v/t. -e* erzak tedarik
etm.; *v/i.* erzak almak; yemek yemek;
2. *n. mst* ∼*s pl.* yemek, erzak; **vict-
ual.(l)er** ['vitlə] *n.* erzakçı; lokantacı;
erzak gemisi; *licensed* ∼ meyhaneci,
ruhsatlı içki satıcısı.

vi.de ['vaidi:] *vb.* bakınız!

vi.de.li.cet [vi'di:liset] *adv.* (*abbr.* **viz.**) yani, demek oluyor ki.

vid.e.o ['vidiəu] *adj.* televizyonla resim nakline ait, video…;'~ con.fe.rence *n.* videokonferans.

vie [vai] *v/i.* yarışmak, çekişmek, rekabet etm. (**with** *ile*).

Vi.en.nese [vie'ni:z] **1.** *n.* Viyanalı; **2.** *adj.* Viyana'ya ait.

view [vju:] **1.** *n.* bakış, nazar; fikir, görüş (alanı); manzara, görünüm (*a.* PAINT, PHOT); görme fırsatı; amaç, maksat, gaye, emel; *at first* ~ ilk bakışta; *in* ~ görünürde; beklenen, umulan; *in* ~ *of* -*in* karşısında,… göz önüne alındığında; -den dolayı, …yüzünden; *in my* ~ kanımca, bence; *on* ~ sergilenmekte; *out of* ~ görünmez; *with a* ~ *to* ger., *with the* ~ *of* ger. amacıyle; ümidiyle, umarak; *come into* ~ görünmek, ortaya çıkmak; *have* (*keep*) *in* ~ gözü önünde olm. (*veya* tutmak); **2.** *v/t.* bakmak -*e*, görmek -*i*; tetkik etm. -*i*, incelemek -*i*; düşünmek -*i*; 'view.er *n.* seyirci; 'view-find.er *n.* PHOT vizör; 'view.less *adj.* fikirsiz; manzarasız; *poet.* görünmez; '~.point *n.* görüş noktası, bakış açısı; 'view.y □ F gösterişli; garip fikirli.

vig.il [vidʒil] *part.* ECCL ['vidʒil] *n.* yortu arifesi; uyanıklık; gece nöbet tutma; 'vig.i-lance *n.* uyanıklık, uyumama; ~ *committee* Am. HIST güvenliği sağlamak için kurulan yasadışı örgüt; 'vig.i.lant □ uyanık, tetikte, tedbirli; vig.i.lan.te Am. [-'lænti] *n.* «*vigil committee*» üyesi.

vi.gnette TYP, PHOT [vi'njet] **1.** *n.* süs; **2.** *v/t.* süslemek.

vig.or.ous □ ['vigərəs] dinç, kuvvetli, etkin; *fig.* gayretli, enerjik; 'vig.o(u)r *n.* kuvvet, dinçlik; *fig.* gayret, enerji.

Vi.king ['vaikiŋ] *n.* viking; korsan.

vile □ [vail] kötü, iğrenç, berbat, çirkin, pis, utanç verici; aşağılık, değersiz; alçak, rezil.

vil.i.fi.ca.tion [vilifi'keiʃən] *n.* iftira, yerme; vil.i.fy ['-fai] *v/i.* iftira etm.; alçaltmak, kötülemek, yermek.

vil.la ['vilə] *n.* villa, köşk.

vil.lage ['vilidʒ] *n.* köy; ~ green köy merası; 'vil.lag.er *n.* köylü.

vil.lain ['vilən] *n.* alçak *veya* çapkın adam (*a. co.*); 'vil.lain.ous □ çirkin, bozuk, habis; F çok fena, kötü; 'vil-lain.y *n.* kötülük, rezalet, alçaklık.

vil.lein HIST ['vilin] *n.* derebeyi idaresindeki köylü.

vim F [vim] *n.* enerji; gayret.

vin.di.cate ['vindikeit] *v/t.* -*in* doğruluğunu ispat etm., haklı çıkarmak; korumak -*i*, savunmak -*i* (*from* -*den*); vin.di'ca.tion *n.* koruma, doğrulama; vin.di.ca.to.ry □ ['-təri] koruma kabilinden.

vin.dic.tive □ [vin'diktiv] kinci; affetmeyen.

vine BOT [vain] *n.* asma (çubuğu); sarılgan herhangi bir bitki; '~-dress.er *n.* bağcı; vin.e.gar ['vinigə] *n.* sirke; hırçınlık, suratsızlık; gayret, enerji; 'vin.e.gar.y *adj. mst fig.* suratsız, asık suratlı; vine-grow.er ['vaingrəuə] *n.* bağcı; 'vine-grow.ing *n.* bağcılık; 'vine-louse *n.* asma biti; vine.yard ['vinjəd] *n.* bağ.

vi.nous ['vainəs] *adj.* şaraba ait, şarap…; şarap gibi.

vin.tage ['vintidʒ] **1.** *n.* bağ bozumu; bir mevsimin bağ ürünü; kaliteli şarap; **2.** *adj.* kaliteli…; eski, klasik, seçkin; demode; ~ *car* MOT eski araba; 'vin.tag.er *n.* üzüm toplayıcısı; vint.ner ['vintnə] *n.* şarap tüccarı.

vi.ol MUS ['vaiəl] *n.* viyol.

vi.o.la **1.** MUS [vi'əulə] *n.* viyola; **2.** BOT ['vaiələ] *n.* bir tür hercai menekşe.

vi.o.la.ble □ ['vaiələbl] bozulabilir, ihlal edilebilir.

vi.o.late ['vaiəleit] *v/t.* bozmak, ihlal etm., çiğnemek, karşı gelmek; tecavüz etm. -*e* (*a. fig.*), ırzına geçmek; vi.o'la-tion *n.* ihlal; tecavüz; 'vi.o.la.tor *n.* tecavüz *veya* ihlal eden kimse.

vi.o.lence ['vaiələns] *n.* zor(lama), şiddet, tecavüz; zorbalık; bozma; iğfal; *do veya offer* ~ *to* aykırı olm. -*e*, zorlamak -*i*; 'vi.o.lent □ şiddetli, sert, zorlu, kuvvetli; berbat.

vi.o.let ['vaiəlit] **1.** *n.* BOT menekşe; **2.** *adj.* mor.

vi.o.lin MUS [vaiə'lin] *n.* keman; 'vi.o-lin.ist *n.* kemancı.

vi.o.lon.cel.list MUS [vaiələn'tʃelist] *n.* viyolonsel çalan kimse; vi.o.lon'cel.lo [-'ləu] *n.* viyolonsel.

VIP *sl.* ['vi:ai'pi:] *n.* kodamanlar.

vi.per ZOO ['vaipə] *n.* engerek; *fig.* yılan; vi.per.ine ['-rain], 'vi.per.ous □ *mst fig.* zehirli, yılan…, hain…

vi.ra.go [vi'rɑːgəu] *n.* şirret kadın, eli maşalı kadın, cadaloz kadın.

vir.gin ['vəːdʒin] **1.** *n.* kız, bakire; **2.** □

bakire…; bakir, el değmemiş, balta girmemiş (*orman*); bozulmamış, doğal;
kullanılmamış; *fig.* & MEC işlenmemiş;
'**virgin.al** ['vəːdʒinl] **1.** ☐ bakireye yaraşır; bakireye ait, bakire…; **2.** *n.* MUS
virginal; **Vir.gin.ia** [vəˈdʒinjə] *n. a.* ~
tobacco Virjinya tütünü; ~ **creeper**
frenk asması; **Vir'gin.i.an** *adj.* Virjinya…; Virjinyalı; **vir.gin.i.ty** [vəːˈdʒini-
ti] *n.* kızlık, bakirelik, bekâret.
vir.ile ['virail] *adj.* erkekçe, yiğit, kuvvetli, enerjik; iktidarlı (*erkek*); **vi.ril.i-
ty** [vi'riliti] *n.* erkeklik, cinsel güç;
yiğitlik.
vir.tu [vəːˈtuː] *n.*: **article of ~** ince sanat
eseri; **vir.tu.al** ☐ ['‿tjuəl] gerçek kuvveti olan; fiilî, esas, asıl; '**vir.tu.al.ly**
adv. aslında; gerçekte; fiilen; **vir.tue**
['‿tjuː] *n.* fazilet, iffet, erdem; namus;
etki, tesir, yarar, fayda; avantaj, üstünlük; *in veya* **by ~ of** *-e* dayanarak, *-den*
dolayı, …sebebiyle; **make a ~ of necessity** zorunlu bir durumdan fazilet
hissesi çıkarmak; **vir.tu.os.i.ty** [vəː-
tjuˈositi] *n.* virtüözlük, büyük ustalık;
vir.tu.o.so [‿ˈəuzəu] *n. part.* MUS virtüöz; güzel sanatlardan anlayan kimse;
vir.tu.ous ☐ iffetli, erdemli; dürüst.
vir.u.lence ['viruləns] *n.* zehirlilik, teh-
likelilik, öldürücülük; aşırı sertlik; *fig.*
kötülük; '**vir.u.lent** ☐ kuvvetli (*zehir*);
öldürücü; zehirli (*hastalık vs.*); *fig.* kötücül; şiddetli.
vi.rus MED ['vaiərəs] *n.* virüs (*a. bilgisayar*); *fig.* zehir.
vi.sa ['viːzə] **1.** *n.* vize; **2.** *v/t. pret.* & *p.p.*
'**vi.saed** vize etm.
vis.age *lit.* ['vizidʒ] *n.* yüz, surat, sima,
çehre.
vis.cer.a ANAT ['visərə] *n.* iç organlar.
vis.cid ☐ ['visid] = **viscous**.
vis.cose CHEM ['viskəus] *n.* viskoz; ~
silk selüloz ipeği; **vis.cos.i.ty** [‿ˈkosi-
ti] *n.* yapışkanlık; yarı sıvılık, viskozite.
vis.count ['vaikaunt] *n.* vikont; '**viscountess** *n.* vikontes.
vis.cous ☐ ['viskəs] yapışkan; yarı sıvı,
lüzuci.
vise [vais] *Am. for* **vice²**.
vi.sé ['viːzei] = **visa**.
vis.i.bil.i.ty [vizi'biliti] *n.* görüş mesafesi (*veya* derecesi); görünürlük, görme
olanağı; '**vis.i.ble** ☐ görünebilir,
görülür; *fig.* belli, açık.
vi.sion ['viʒən] *n.* görme (gücü); görüş;
önsezi; *fig.* hayal, kuruntu, evham; **vi-
sion.ar.y** ['‿nəri] **1.** *adj.* hayalî; me-

raklı, kuruntulu; düşsel; **2.** *n.* hayalperest kimse.
vis.it ['vizit] **1.** *v/t.* ziyaret etm., görmeğe gitmek, uğramak; teftiş etm.; cezalandırmak, çektirmek (**upon** *-i*, *-e*);
v/i. ziyarette bulunmak; ~ **with** *Am.*
ile çene çalmak; kalmak; **2.** *n.* ziyaret,
uğrama (**to** *-e*), görüşmeye gitme;
(*doktor*) vizite; misafirlik; '**vis.it.ant**
n. ziyaretçi; ORN göçmen kuş; **vis.it'a-
tion** *n.* (resmî) ziyaret; *fig.* felâket; **vis-
it.a.to.ri.al** [‿təˈtɔːriəl] *adj.* teftişe ait,
teftiş…; '**vis.it.ing** *n.* & *adj.* ziyaret
(eden); ~ **card** kartvizit; '**vis.i.tor** *n.* ziyaretçi, misafir konuk (**to** *-e*); müfettiş;
turist; ~**s' book** ziyaretçi defteri.
vi.sor ['vaizə] *n.* miğfer siperliği; MOT
güneşlik.
vis.ta ['vistə] *n.* manzara; *fig.* olaylar
serisi.
vis.u.al ☐ ['vizjuəl] görmekle ilgili,
görme…; görülebilir; optik; '**vis.u.al-
ize** *v/t.* & *v/i.* gözünde canlan(dır)mak.
vi.tal ☐ ['vaitl] hayatî…; yaşam için gerekli; canlı, yaşayan, dirimsel; esaslı,
zarurî, önemli, elzem (**to** *için*); öldürücü, amansız; ~**s** *pl.*, ~ **parts** *pl.* yaşam
için gerekli olan organlar (*kalp*, *ciğer*,
beyin vs.); *s.* **statistics**; **vi.tal.i.ty** [‿-
ˈtæliti] *n.* dirilik, hayatiyet, canlılık;
dayanma gücü; **vi.tal.ize** ['‿təlaiz]
v/t. hayat vermek, canlandırmak (*a.
fig.*), diriltmek.
vi.ta.min(e) ['vitəmin] *n.* vitamin; **vi-
ta.minized** ['‿naizd] *adj.* vitaminli.
vi.ti.ate ['viʃieit] *v/t.* kirletmek; (tesirini) bozmak, etkisini azaltmak; iptal
etm.; JUR hükümsüz kılmak.
vit.i.cul.ture ['vitikʌltʃə] *n.* bağcılık.
vit.re.ous ☐ ['vitriəs] camdan yapılma,
cam…; cam gibi, camlı…
vit.ri.fac.tion [vitri'fækʃən] *n.* cam-
laştırma; **vit.ri.fy** ['‿fai] *v/t.* & *v/i.* cam-
laş(tır)mak.
vit.ri.ol CHEM ['vitriəl] *n.* sülfürik asit,
zaç yağı, karaboya.
vi.tu.per.ate [vi'tjuːpəreit] *vb.* küfretmek, sövmek; **vi.tu.per'a.tion** *n.* sövüp
sayma, küfretme, hakaret etme; **vi'tu-
per.a.tive** ☐ [‿rətiv] küfürbaz.
vi.va (vo.ce) ['vaivə('vəusi)] **1.** *adj.* sözlü; **2.** *n.* sözlü imtihan.
vi.va.cious ☐ [vi'veiʃəs] canlı, neşeli,
hayat dolu; **vi.vac.i.ty** [vi'væsiti] *n.*
canlılık, neşelilik.
viv.id ☐ ['vivid] canlı, berrak; parlak;
açık, belli; kuvvetli; hayat dolu; '**viv.id-**

ness *n.* canlılık, parlaklık.

viv.i.fy ['vivifai] *v/t.* canlandırmak, canlılık vermek; **vi'vip.a.rous** □ [-pərəs] doğurucu; **viv.i.sec.tion** [-'sekʃən] *n.* bilimsel araştırma için canlı hayvanlar üzerinde yapılan deney.

vix.en ['viksn] *n.* dişi tilki; cadaloz kadın.

viz. [viz] = *videlicet.*

vi.zier [vi'ziə] *n.* vezir.

vi.zor ['vaizə] = *visor.*

vo.cab.u.lar.y [vəu'kæbjuləri] *n.* kısa sözlük; kelime bilgisi (*veya* haznesi).

vo.cal □ ['vəukəl] sesle ilgili; ses...; sesli; ses gibi, sesle söylenen; kelimelerle açıklanmış; konuşkan, sözünü sakınmaz; MUS vokal...; GR ünlü, sesli; ~ *c(h)ord* ses teli; '**vo.cal.ist** *n.* şarkıcı, vokalist; **'vocal.ize** *v/t.* seslendirmek; söylemek; MUS vokallemek; **'vo.cal.ly** *adv.* sesli olarak.

vo.ca.tion [vəu'keiʃən] *n.* davet, çağırma; iş, meslek; yetenek, kabiliyet; **vo-'ca.tional** □ [-ʃənl] meslekle ilgili, meslekî...; ~ *guidance* meslek seçiminde rehberlik.

voc.a.tive GR ['vɔkətiv] *n.* bir ismin hitap şekli.

vo.cif.er.ate [vəu'sifəreit] *v/t.* bağıra bağıra söylemek; *v/i.* bağırmak, haykırmak; **vo.cif.er'a.tion** *n. a.* ~**s** *pl.* bağırma, haykırma, feryat; **vo'cifer.ous** □ gürültülü, bağırtkan, şamatalı.

vogue [vəug] *n.* moda; rağbet, itibar; *in* ~ moda halinde; rağbette.

voice [vɔis] **1.** *n.* ses; fikir; *active* (*passive*) ~ GR etken (edilgen) çatı; *in* (*good*) ~ şarkı söyleyebilir *veya* konuşabilir durumda; *give* ~ *to -i* ifade etm.; **2.** *v/t.* söylemek, ifade etm., belirtmek; GR telaf fuz etm.; MUS akort etm.; **'voice-ac.tiv.a.ted** *adj.* sesle çalışan; *insan sesine tepki göstererek işlemeye başlayan;* **voiced** *comb.* GR ...sesli; **'voice.less** □ *part.* GR sessiz; **'~ mail** telesekreter.

void [vɔid] **1.** *adj.* boş, ıssız; faydasız, yararsız; JUR hükümsüz; ~ *of -den* mahrum, *-den* yoksun, *-siz,* *-sız;* **2.** *n.* boşluk (*a. fig.*); **3.** *v/t.* hükümsüz kılmak; boşaltmak; çıkarmak; **'void.ness** *n.* boşluk.

voile [vɔil] *n.* ince kumaş, vual.

vol.a.tile ['vɔlətail] *adj.* CHEM buharlaşabilen, uçucu; *fig.* havaî; dönek;

vol.a.til.ity [-'tiliti] *n.* uçuculuk; **vol-a.til.ize** [vɔ'lætilaiz] *v/t. & v/i.* buharlaş(tır)mak.

vol.can.ic [vɔl'kænik] *adj.* (~*ally*) volkanik; **vol.ca.no** [vɔl'keinəu] *n., pl.* **vol'canoes** [-z] yanardağ, volkan.

vo.li.tion [vəu'liʃən] *n.* irade; *on one's own* ~ kendi iradesiyle.

vol.ley ['vɔli] **1.** *n.* yaylım ateş; *fig.* yağmur; *tenis;* topa yere değmeden geri vurma; vole; **2.** *v/t. mst* ~ *out* (*soru vs.*) yağmuruna tutmak; yere değmeden geri vurmak (*top*); *v/i.* yaylım ateş etm.; **'vol.ley.ball** *n. spor.* voleybol.

vol.plane AVIA ['vɔlplein] **1.** *n.* süzülme uçuş; **2.** *v/i.* süzülerek uçmak.

volt ELECT [vəult] *n.* volt; **'volt.age** *n.* ELECT voltaj, gerilim; **vol.ta.ic** ELECT [vɔl'teiik] *adj.* galvanik.

volte-face *fig.* ['vɔlt'fɑːs] *n.* tamamen geriye dönüş.

volt.me.ter ELECT ['vəultmiːtə] *n.* voltmetre.

vol.u.bil.i.ty [vɔlju'biliti] *n.* dillilik, konuşkanlık; **vol.u.ble** □ ['-bl] dilli, konuşkan, çenebaz.

vol.ume ['vɔljum] *n.* cilt; miktar; PHYS *etc.* hacim, oylum; ses şiddeti; ~ *of sound radyo:* ses şiddeti; ~ *control,* ~ *regulator* potansiyometre, ses (yükseltme) regülatörü; **vo.lu.mi.nous** □ [və'ljuːminəs] büyük, hacimli, koskocaman; ciltler doldurur; çok kitap yazan, verimli (*yazar*).

vol.un.tar.y ['vɔləntəri] **1.** □ gönüllü, ihtiyarî, istemli; PHYSIOL iradeli; iradeye bağlı, îradî; ~ *death* intihar; **2.** *n.* istemli hareket; MUS org solosu; **vol.un-teer** [-'tiə] **1.** *n.* gönüllü (asker); *attr.* gönüllü...; **2.** *v/i.* gönüllü yazılmak (*for -e*); *v/t.* kendi isteği ile teklif etm. *veya* vermek.

vo.lup.tu.ar.y [və'lʌptjuəri] *n.* şehvet düşkünü, şehvestperest kimse.

vo.lup.tu.ous □ [və'lʌptʃuəs] şehvetli; duygusal; zevk düşkünü; **vo'lup.tu-ousness** *n.* şehvete düşkünlük.

vo.lute ARCH [və'ljuːt] *n.* kıvrım, sarmal süs; **vo'lut.ed** *adj.* sarmal.

vom.it ['vɔmit] **1.** *v/t. & v/i.* kus(tur)-mak; *fig.* çıkarmak; (*yanardağ*) ağzından fışkırtmak (*lav*); **2.** *n.* kusmuk; kusma; kusturucu ilaç.

voo.doo ['vuːduː] **1.** *n.* zenci büyücü *veya* büyüsü; **2.** *vb.* büyülemek, büyü yapmak.

vo.ra.cious ☐ [vəˈreiʃəs] doymak bilmez, açgözlü, obur; çok istekli; voˈraciousness, vo.rac.i.ty [vəˈræsiti] n. açgözlülük; hırs (**of**).

vor.tex [ˈvɔːteks] n., pl. mst vor.ti.ces [ˈ-tisiːz] girdap (mst fig.).

vo.ta.ry [ˈvəutəri] n. kendini bşe adamış kimse, bşe düşkün kimse; hararetli taraftar.

vote [vəut] **1.** n. oy (hakkı), rey; oy toplamı; **~ of no confidence** güvensizlik oyu; **cast a ~** oy vermek; **put to the ~** oya sunmak; **take a ~ on s.th.** bşe oy vermek; **2.** v/t. seçmek; önermek; F söylemek, bildirmek; v/i. oy vermek; **~ for** -in lehine oy vermek; ˈvot.er n. seçmen.

vot.ing...: ~-booth [ˈvəutiŋbuːð] n. oy verme kulübesi; ˈ~-box n. oy sandığı; ˈ~-paper n. oy pusulası.

vo.tive [ˈvəutiv] adj. adak olarak verilen, adak...

vouch [vautʃ] v/t. temin etm., garanti etm.; doğrulamak (**for** -i); v/i. **~ for** -e kefil olm.; ˈvouch.er n. belgit, tanıt, vesika, senet, alındı, makbuz; kefil; ˈvouchˈsafe vb. lütfetmek, vermek; tenezzül etm.

vow [vau] **1.** n. adak, yemin, söz; **2.** v/t. yemin etm. -e; adamak, nezretmek -i; ahdetmek.

vow.el [ˈvauəl] n. sesli, ünlü harf, vokal.

voy.age [ˈvɔiidʒ] **1.** n. yolculuk, seyahat; **2.** v/i. yolculuk etm.; ˈvoy.ag.er [ˈvɔiədʒə] n. yolcu, gezmen.

vul.can.ite [ˈvʌlkənait] n. ebonit; vulkanit; vul.can.iˈza.tion. n. MEC ebonitleştirme, vulkanizasyon; ˈvul.can.ize v/t. MEC ebonitleştirmek, vulkanize etm.; ~d fibre vulkanize lif.

vul.gar [ˈvʌlgə] **1.** ☐ kaba, terbiyesiz; aşağılık; bayağı, adi; halka ait, halka özgü; **~ tongue** halk dili; **2.** n. **the ~** avam; ayaktakımı; ˈvul.gar.ism n. kabalık, adilik; argo; vul.gar.i.ty [ˈ-ˈgæriti] n. kabalık, terbiyesizlik; vul.gar.ize [ˈ-gəraiz] v/t. adileştirmek; genelleştirmek, herkesin anlayacağı şekle sokmak.

vul.ner.a.bil.i.ty [vʌlnərəˈbiliti] n. yaralanma olasılığı; ˈvul.ner.a.ble ☐ kolayca yaralanır, zedelenir, incinebilir; fig. zayıf (nokta); ˈvul.ner.ar.y **1.** adj. şifalı, yarayı iyileştiren; **2.** n. yarayı iyileştiren ilaç.

vul.pine [ˈvʌlpain] adj. tilki gibi (a. fig.); fig. kurnaz.

vul.ture ORN [ˈvʌltʃə] n. akbaba; fig. aç gözlü kimse; ˈvul.tur.ine [ˈ-tʃurain] adj. akbaba familyasından.

vy.ing [ˈvaiiŋ] adj. rekabet eden.

W

wab.ble [ˈwɔbl] = **wobble**.

wack.y Am. sl. [ˈwæki] adj. kaçık, sapık, manyak.

wad [wɔd] **1.** n. tıkaç, tampon; tutam, tomar, deste; çok miktar; bir tomar para; **2.** v/t. pamukla beslemek; tıkamak; ˈwad.ding n. tıkaç, tampon; pamuk vatkası.

wad.dle [ˈwɔdl] v/i. badi badi yürümek; paytak paytak yürümek.

wade [weid] v/i. su veya çamur içinde yürümek; fig. zorla bitirmek, güçlükle ilerlemek; v/t. yürüyerek geçmek; ˈwad.er n. su veya çamurda yürüyen kimse; ~s pl. su geçirmez uzun çizme.

wa.fer [ˈweifə] n. bisküvi, kâğıt helvası; a. **consecrated ~** ECCL mayasız ince ekmek.

waf.fle [ˈwɔfl] **1.** n. boş laf, saçma; **2.** v/i. F saçmalamak.

waft [wɑːft] **1.** v/t. sürüklemek, yavaşça götürmek; **2.** n. hafif koku, esinti; sürükleme.

wag¹ [wæg] **1.** v/t. & v/i. salla(n)mak; **2.** n. salla(n)ma.

wag² [-.] n. şakacı kimse; **play ~** sl. okulu kırmak.

wage [weidʒ] **1.** v/t. sürdürmek, yürütmek; **2.** n. mst ~s pl. ücret, maaş, haftalık; ~-earn.er [ˈ-əːnə] n. ücretli kimse, haftalıkçı kimse; ˈ~-sheet, ˈ~es sheet n. ücret bordrosu.

wa.ger lit. [ˈweidʒə] **1.** n. bahis; **2.** v/i. bahis tutuşmak (**on** üzerine).

wag.ger.y [ˈwægəri] n. şaka(cılık); ˈwaggish ☐ şakacı; şaka yollu yapılan.

wag.gle F [ˈwægl] = **wag¹ 1**; ˈwag.gly adj. F sallanan.

wag.(g)on [ˈwægən] n. yük arabası; yük vagonu, katar; devriye arabası; tekerlekli servis arabası; *be veya go on the* (*water*) ~ F artık ağzına içki koymamak; 'wag.(g)on.er *n.* arabacı.

wag.tail ORN ['wægteil] *n.* kuyruksallayan.

waif [weif] *n.* kimsesiz çocuk; başıboş hayvan; ~s and strays *pl.* evsiz barksız çocuklar.

wail [weil] 1. *n.* çığlık, figan, feryat; 2. *v/t.* feryat etm., figan etm.; *v/i.* hayıflanmak (*over -e*).

wain *poet.* [wein] *n.* yük arabası; *Charles's* ♀, *the* ♀ AST Büyükayı.

wain.scot ['weinskət] 1. *n.* tahta kaplama, lambri; 2. *v/t.* lambri kaplamak.

waist [weist] *n.* bel (*a.* NAUT); korsaj; bluz; '~band *n.* bel kuşağı; ~coat ['weiskəut] *n.* yelek; ~deep ['weist-'diːp] *adj. & adv.* yarı beline kadar (çıkan).

wait [weit] 1. *v/i.* beklemek; *a.* ~at (*Am.* on) *table -e* hizmetçilik (*veya* servis) yapmak; ~ *for -i* beklemek; ~ (*up*)on s.o. *b-ne* hizmet etm.; *b-ni* ziyaret etm.; *keep* ~ing bekletmek; ~ and see bekleyip görmek; ~ in line kuyrukta beklemek; *v/t.* ertelemek, bekletmek; 2. *n.* bekleme (süresi); gecikme; pusu; ~s *pl.* Noel'de sokaklarda ilâhiler söyleyen grup; *have a long* ~ uzun süre beklemek; *lie in* ~ *for s.o. b-i* için pusuya yatmak; 'wait.er *n.* garson.

wait.ing ['weitiŋ] *n.* bekleme; *in* ~ refakat eden; *no* ~ bekleme yapılmaz; '~maid *n.* hizmetçi kız; '~room *n.* bekleme salonu.

wait.ress ['weitris] *n.* kadın garson.

waive [weiv] *v/t.* vazgeçmek *-den*, feragat etm. *-den* (*a.* JUR); ertelemek; 'waiver *n.* JUR feragat(name).

wake¹ [weik] *n.* NAUT dümen suyu; AVIA hava çevrisi; *fig.* iz, eser; *in the* ~ *of -in* peşi sıra; *-in* sonucu olarak.

wake² [~] 1. (*irr.*) *v/t. & v/i. a.* ~ up uyan(dır)mak; *fig.* canlan(dır)mak; harekete getirmek; ölü başında beklemek; 2. *n.* ölüyü bekleme; ölüyü bekleme merasimi sırasında verilen ziyafet; wake.ful □ ['~ful] uyanık; uykusuz; 'wak.en *v/t. & v/i.* uyan(dır)mak; *fig.* uyarmak.

wale [weil] *part. Am. for weal².*

walk [woːk] 1. *v/t. & v/i.* yürü(t)mek, gez(dir)mek; yürüyerek (*veya* yaya) gitmek; yürüyüşe çık(ar)mak; hareket etm., davranmak; yürüyerek eşlik etm.; adımlamak; ~ *about* dolaşmak;

~ *into sl.* saldırmak; paylamak, haşlamak, azarlamak; açgözlülükle yemek; ~ *out* F grev yapmak; ~ *out on sl.* terketmek; ~ *the hospitals* (*tıp öğrencisi*) hastane stajı yapmak; 2. *n.* yürüyüş; gezme, yürüme; davranış, hareket, gidiş; yürüyüş yeri, kaldırım, yol; *go for* a ~ yürüyüşe çıkmak, dolaşmak, gezinmek; ~ *of life* sosyal durum, hayat yolu; meslek; 'walker *n.* gezen, yürüyen, yaya; *spor.* yürüyücü; *be a good* ~ ayağına sıkı olm.; 'walk.er-on *n.* THEAT figüran.

walk.ie-talk.ie MIL ['woːki'toːki] *n.* portatif telsiz telefon.

walk.ing ['woːkiŋ] *n.* gezme, yürüme; *attr.* yürüme..., yürüyüş...; ~ *pa.pers pl. Am.* F işten atılma kâğıdı; '~stick *n.* baston, asa; '~tour *n.* gezinti.

walk...: '~out *n. Am.* grev; (*toplantı vs.'yi*) terketme; '~over *n.* kolay yengi; '~up *adj.* asansörsüz (*bina*).

wall [woːl] 1. *n.* duvar; sur; *give s.o. the* ~ kibarca yol göstermek; *go to the* ~ *fig.* iflâs etm.; çıkmaza girmek; 2. *v/t.* duvarla çevirmek; *fig.* kapatmak, ayırmak; ~ *up* duvarla kapamak.

wal.la.by ZOO ['woləbi] *n.* küçük kanguru.

wal.let ['wolit] *n.* cüzdan; *obs.* sırt çantası.

wall...: '~eye *n.* VET akçıl gözbebeği; '~flow.er *n.* BOT bahçe şebboyu; *fig.* damsız olduğu için dans edemeyen kimse; '~fruit *n.* espalye ağacının meyvesi; '~map *n.* duvar haritası.

Wal.loon [wo'luːn] 1. *n.* Valon (dili), Valonca; 2. *adj.* Valon'a ait.

wal.lop F ['woləp] *v/i.* koşmak; *v/i.* bata çıka yürümek; ses çıkararak kaynamak; *v/t.* eşek sudan gelinceye kadar dövmek; 2. *n.* ağır darbe; *sl.* bira; 'wal.lop.ing *adj.* F koskocaman; kuyruklu (*yalan*).

wal.low ['woləu] 1. *v/i.* çamur içinde yuvarlanmak; *fig.* büyük zevk almak (*in -den*); 2. *n.* hayvanın yuvarlandığı çamurlu yer; çamurda yuvarlanma.

wall...: '~pa.per *n.* duvar kâğıdı; '~socket *n.* ELECT duvar prizi.

wal.nut BOT ['woːlnʌt] *n.* ceviz (ağacı).

wal.rus ZOO ['woːlrəs] *n.* mors.

waltz [woːls] 1. *n.* vals; 2. *v/t. & v/i.* vals yap(tır)mak.

wam.pum ['wompəm] *n.* para *veya* süs olarak Amerikan kızılderililerince kullanılan boncuklar; *sl.* mangır, mangiz.

wan □ [wɔn] solgun, soluk, beti benzi atmış, bitkin.

wand [wɔnd] *n.* değnek, çubuk; asa.

wan.der ['wɔndə] *v/i.* dolaşmak, gezmek; *a.* **~ about** aylak aylak dolanıp durmak; *fig.* ayrılmak **(from** *-den)*; abuk sabuk konuşmak, sayıklamak; **'wan.der.er** *n.* gayesizce dolaşan kimse, avare; **'wander.ing 1.** □ dolaşan, gezginci; *fig.* daldan dala konan; **2.** *n.* **~s** *pl.* seyahatler; sayıklama.

wane [wein] **1.** *v/i.* küçülmek *(ay)*; *fig.* azalmak, zayıflamak; solmak; **2.** *n.* azalma; **on the ~** azalmakta.

wan.gle *sl.* ['wæŋgl] *v/t.* sızdırmak, dalavereyle koparmak; **'wan.gler** *n.* hilekâr kimse.

wan.ness ['wɔnnis] *n.* solgunluk; bitkinlik.

want [wɔnt] **1.** *n.* yokluk, azlık, kıtlık **(of),** sıkıntı, zaruret, fakirlik; ihtiyaç, lüzum, gerek, hacet; arzu, istek; **for ~ of** …bulunmadığından,… yokluğundan; **2.** *v/i.* **be ~ing** eksik olm.; **be ~ing in** *-den* yoksun olm.; **he does not ~ for** *-e* ihtiyaç duymuyor, *-e* gereksinmesi yok; **it ~s** lâzım, gerek; *v/t.* istemek, arzulamak; gereksemek; gerektirmek; **it ~s** *s.th.* *bş* gerektiriyor; **he ~s energy** gayrete gereksinmesi var; **you ~ to be careful** dikkatli olmanız gerekir; **~** *s.o.* **to do** *b-den bş* yapmasını istemek; **~ed** aranan, istenen; **'~-ad** *n.* küçük ilan.

wan.ton ['wɔntən] **1.** □ zevk düşkünü; şehvet düşkünü, ahlâksız; amaçsız, gayesiz, nedensiz; acımasız, insanlık dışı; sorumsuz, başıboş; **2.** *n.* ahlâksız kadın; **3.** *v/i.* вот çok gelişmek; **'wan.ton.ness** *n.* şehvet.

war [wɔː] **1.** *n.* savaş, harp *(a. fig.)*; *attr.* savaş…; **at ~** savaşmakta, savaş halinde; **make ~** savaşmak **(upon** *ile)*; **~ criminal** savaş suçlusu; **2.** *v/i. lit.* savaşmak; *fig.* mücadele etm.

war.ble ['wɔːbl] **1.** *v/i.* ötmek, şakımak; **2.** *n.* ötme, şakıma; **'war.bler** *n.* ötücü kuş; şarkıcı.

war…: **'~-cry** *n.* savaş narası; *fig.* parola.

ward [wɔːd] **1.** *n.* vesayet (altında bulunan kimse); *(hastane, hapishane vs.)* koğuş; bölge, mıntıka; FENC çelme, parad; MEC kilit dili; **in ~** vesayet altında; **2.** *v/t.* **~ off** savuşturmak, geçiştirmek; **'warden** *n.* bekçi, koruyucu; müdür; UNIV rektör; **'ward.er** *n.* bekçi, koruyucu; gardiyan; **'ward.robe** *n.* giysi dolabı; gardırop; elbiseler; THEAT kostümler; **~ dealer** elbiseci; **~ trunk** gardırop bavul; **'wardroom** *n.* NAUT oyun salonu ve yemekhane; **'ward.ship** *n.* koruyuculuk; vasilik, vesayet.

ware [wɛə] *n.* mal, emtia, eşya.

ware.house 1. ['wɛəhaus] *n.* ambar; antrepo; eşya deposu; mağaza; **2.** ['~hauz] *v/t.* ambarda saklamak; **~.man** ['~hausmən] *n.* ambarcı; antrepocu; mağaza sahibi.

war…: '~.fare *n.* savaş(ma); mücadele; '~-grave *n.* asker mezarı; '~.head *n.* merminin patlayıcı kısmı, harp başlığı.

war.i.ness ['wɛərinis] *n.* uyanıklık, ihtiyat.

war.like ['wɔːlaik] *adj.* savaşçı; savaşla ilgili, savaş…; askerî.

war-loan ['wɔːləun] *n.* savaş borçlanması.

warm [wɔːm] **1.** □ sıcak *(a. fig.)*, hararetli, ılık; sıcak tutan, ısıtan; *fig.* gayretli, şevkli; *fig.* içten, candan; *fig.* sevimli, sempatik; yeni, taze; **make things ~ for** *s.o. b-nin* anasından emdiğini burnundan getirmek; **2.** *n.* F ısınma; **3.** *v/t. & v/i.* *a.* **~ up** ısıtmak; ısınmak; kız(dır)mak; *sl.* coş(tur)mak; şevkle sarılmak **(to** *-e)*; **'warm.ing** *n. sl.* pataklama.

war-mon.ger ['wɔːmʌŋgə] *n.* savaş kışkırtıcısı; **'war-mon.ger.ing,** **'war-mon.ger.y** *n.* savaş kışkırtıcılığı.

warmth [wɔːmθ] *n.* sıcaklık, ılıklık; coşkunluk; içtenlik.

warn [wɔːn] *v/t.* ikaz etm., uyarmak **(of, against** *-e karşı)*; tembihlemek **(to** *inf. -meyi)*; ihtar etm. *-e* **(of** *-i)*; öğütlemek **(of** *-i)*; **'warn.ing** *n.* ihtar, ikaz, uyarı; ihbar; **give ~** uyarmak, ikaz etm.; **take ~ from** *-den* ibret almak.

War Of.fice ['wɔːrɔfis] *n.* Millî Savunma Bakanlığı.

warp [wɔːp] **1.** *n.* çözgü, arış; NAUT palamar; *fig.* eğrilik, çarpıklık; **2.** *v/t. & v/i.* eğril(t)mek, yamul(t)mak; NAUT palamarı çekerek yürütmek; AVIA yesarilenmek; saptırmak **(from** *-den)*.

war-paint ['wɔːpeint] *n.* savaş işareti olarak vücuda sürülen boya; *fig.* resmî kıyafet; *sl.* kozmetik; **in full ~** resmî kıyafetli.

warp.ing AVIA ['wɔːpiŋ] *n.* yesarilenme.

war…: '~-plane *n.* savaş uçağı; '~-prof.it'eer *n.* savaş zengini.

war.rant ['wɔrənt] **1.** *n.* yetki; ruhsat; makbuz; teminat, garanti, kefalet; arama kâğıdı; JUR müzekkere; *a.* ~ *of apprehension veya* ~ *of arrest* tevkif müzekkeresi; **2.** *v/t.* temin etm.; izin (*veya* ruhsat) vermek *-e*; kefil olm. *-e*; *part.* COM garanti etm., teminat vermek; 'war.ranta.ble □ garanti edilebilir; HUNT avlanabilir; 'war.rant.a.bly *adv.* uygun bir şekilde; 'war.rant.ed *adj.* garantili; war.ran'tee *n.* JUR *k-ne* teminat verilen kimse; 'war.rant-offi-cer *n.* NAUT güverte subayı; MIL gedikli, erbaş; war.ran.tor JUR ['_-tɔː] *n.* kefil; 'war.ran.ty *n.* kefalet(name), garanti, teminat; yetki.

war.ren ['wɔrən] *n.* tavşanın bol olduğu yer.

war.ri.or ['wɔriə] *n.* savaşçı, cenkçi, asker.

war.ship ['wɔːʃip] *n.* savaş gemisi.

wart [wɔːt] *n.* siğil; *part.* BOT yumru, şiş; 'wart.y *adj.* siğilli.

war.time ['wɔːtaim] **1.** *n.* savaş zamanı; **2.** *adj.* savaştan doğan, savaş...

war.y □ ['wɛəri] uyanık, ihtiyatlı, açıkgöz.

was [wɔz, wəz] *pret. of* **be**; **he** ~ **to have come** gelmiş olmalıydı.

wash [wɔʃ] **1.** *v/t. & v/i.* yıka(n)mak, ıslatmak; yıkanmaya gelmek (*kumaş*); yalamak (*dalga*); aşındırarak açmak; ~**ed out** yağmur nedeniyle ertelenmiş *veya* kapanmış; solgun, soluk; F bitkin, yorgun; ~ **up** bulaşık yıkamak; elini yüzünü yıkamak; **2.** *n.* yıka(n)ma; çamaşır(hane); çalkantı; dalga sesi; losyon, şampuan; sulu mutfak artığı; NAUT dümen suyu; *contp.* saçmalık; **mouth-** ~ gargara; *s.* **white**~; 'wash.a.ble *adj.* yıkanabilir; 'wash-ba.sin *n.* lavabo; 'wash-cloth *n.* sabun bezi, havlu; 'wash-draw.ing *n.* sulu boya resim.

wash.er ['wɔʃə] *n.* yıkama makinesi; yıkayıcı; MEC pul, rondela; '~-wom.an *n.* çamaşırcı kadın.

wash.ing ['wɔʃiŋ] *n.* yıka(n)ma; ~**s** *pl.* çamaşır; *attr.* çamaşır...; '~-ma.chine *n.* çamaşır makinesi; ~ **pow.der** çamaşır tozu.

wash.ing-up ['wɔʃi'ŋʌp] *n.* bulaşık yıkama.

wash...: '~-'out *n. sl.* başarısız kimse; fiyasko; '~.rag *n. part. Am.* sabun bezi, havlu; '~-stand *n.* lavabo; '~-tub *n.* leğen; 'wash.y *adj.* sulu; soluk, solgun; cansız, sönük.

was.n't [wɔznt] = **was not**.

wasp [wɔsp] *n.* yabanarısı; 'wasp.ish

□ hırçın, huysuz, dik kafalı.

was.sail *obs.* ['wɔseil] *n.* içki âlemi; baharlı içki.

wast.age ['weistidʒ] *n.* israf, sarfiyat.

waste [weist] **1.** *adj.* boş, ıssız; çorak, kıraç; artık, işe yaramaz, atılmış; viran, harap; MEC kullanılmaz; **lay** ~ harap etm., viraneye çevirmek; ~ **paper** kullanılmış kâğıt; **2.** *n.* israf, çarçur, savurma, sarfiyat; artık, çöp, süprüntü; boş arazi, ıssız yer; yıkım; **go** *veya* **run to** ~ israf olm., ziyan olm., boşa gitmek; **3.** *v/t.* boşuna sarfetmek; israf etm., çarçur etm.; harap etm., viraneye çevirmek; aşındırmak; *v/i.* heba olm.; aşınmak; ~ **away** eriyip gitmek, günden güne zayıflamak; 'waste.ful □ ['_-ful] savurgan, ziyankâr; 'waste-pa.per bas-ket *n.* kâğıt sepeti; 'waste-pipe *n.* künk; 'wast.er *n.* savurgan kimse; = **wastrel.**

wast.rel ['weistrəl] *n.* savurgan kimse; bir işe yaramaz kimse.

watch [wɔtʃ] **1.** *n.* gözetleme, bekçilik; nöbet (*a.* NAUT); nöbetçi, bekçi; nöbetçilik; devriye; cep *veya* kol saati; uyanıklık; **be on the** ~ **for** *-i* gözlemek, yolunu beklemek; *-e* dikkat etm., için tetikte olm.; **2.** *v/i.* dikkat etm., göz kulak olm. (**with**, **over** *-e*); ~ **for** *-i* beklemek, gözlemek; ~ **out** F dikkat etm.; *v/t.* gözetlemek, seyretmek; ~ **one's time** uygun zamanı beklemek; '~.boat *n.* NAUT devriye botu; '~-brace.let *n.* saat bileziği; '~-case *n.* saat kutusu; '~.dog *n.* bekçi köpeği; 'watch.er *n.* muhafız, bekçi; bakıcı; gözlemci; watch.ful □ ['_-ful] uyanık, tetik; watch...: '~-mak.er *n.* saatçi; '~.man *n.* bekçi; '~-tow.er *n.* gözetleme kulesi; '~.word *n.* parola.

wa.ter ['wɔːtə] **1.** *n.* su; ~**s** *pl.* sular; ~**s** *pl.* kara suları; gölcük, gölet; gözyaşı; salya; (*kumaş*) hare, şanjan; ~ **supply** su rezervi; su kaynakları; **high** ~ met, kabarma; **low** ~ cezir, inme; **by** ~ deniz yoluyla; **drink** *veya* **take the** ~**s** kaplıcalara gidip şifalı su içmek; **of the first** ~ en iyi kalite, birinci sınıf; **be in hot** ~ F bası dertte olm., ayvayı yemiş olm., hapı yutmuş olm.; **be in low** ~ F meteliğe kurşun atmak, eli darda olm.; **hold** ~ *fig.* su kaldırmak, tutacak yanı olm.; **make** ~ su dökmek, işemek; **2.** *v/t. & v/i.* sulamak; sulan(dır)mak; suvar(ıl)-mak; *oft.* ~ **down** sulandırmak; *fig.* hafifletmek, yumuşatmak; MEC harelemek (*ipek*); AVIA denize inmek; *make s.o.'s mouth* ~ *b-nin* ağzını sulandırmak; '~-blis.ter *n.* MED su kabarcığı; '~-borne *adj.* deniz yoluyla nakledilen (*mal*); '~-bot.tle *n.* su şişesi; matara; '~-buf.fa.lo *n.* manda; '~-cart *n.* su arabası; '~-clos.et *n.* hela, tuvalet, apteshane; '~-col.o(u)r *n.* suluboya (resim); '~-cool.ing *n.* suyla soğutma; '~.course *n.* dere, çay; kanal; nehir yatağı; '~.cress *n.* BOT suteresi; '~.fall *n.* çağlayan, şelale; '~.fowl *n. pl.* su kuşu, su kuşları; '~-front *n.* sahil arsası; *part. Am.* liman bölgesi; '~.ga(u)ge *n.* MEC derinlik göstergesi; '~-glass *n.* CHEM sodyum silikat; '~-hose *n.* su hortumu; 'wa.ter.i.ness *n.* sululuk; lezzetsizlik; solgunluk.

wa.ter.ing ['wɔːtəriŋ] *n.* sulama; '~-can, '~-pot *n.* emzikli kova, sulama ibriği; '~-place *n.* içmeler; plaj; kaplıca; suvarma yeri.

water...: '~-jack.et *n.* MEC su soğutma gömleği; '~-lev.el *n.* su seviyesi; MEC tesviye ruhu; '~-lil.y BOT nilüfer; '~.logged *adj.* içi su dolu; '~-main *n.* yeraltı su hattı; '~.man *n.* kayıkçı; '~-mark *n.* filigran; '~-mel.on *n.* BOT karpuz; '~-pipe *n.* su borusu; '~-plane *n.* deniz uçağı; '~-po.lo *n.* su topu; '~-pow.er *n.* su gücü; ~ *station* hidroelektrik santralı; '~.proof 1. *adj.* sugeçirmez; 2. *n.* yağmurluk, muşamba; 3. *v/t.* sugeçirmez hale koymak; '~-re'pellent *adj.* su çekmez; '~.shed *n.* iki nehir havzası arasındaki set; sınır; '~.side 1. *n.* sahil, kıyı; 2. *adj.* sahilde olan; sahilde çalışan; sahile özgü, sahil...; '~-ski *n.* su kayağı; '~.spout *n.* oluk; deniz hortumu; '~-ta.ble *n.* yağmur etekliği; su tabakası (seviyesi); '~.tight *adj.* sugeçirmez, sızmaz, akmaz; *fig.* hata kabul etmez, göz açtırmaz; '~-wave 1. *n.* ondüle; 2. *vb.* ondüle yapmak; '~-way *n.* su yolu, kanal; '~.works *n. pl., a. sg.* su dağıtım tesisatı; gözyaşı; 'wa.ter.y *adj.* sulu (*a. fig.*); su gibi; soluk (*renk*); sudan, zayıf.

watt ELECT [wɔt] *n.* vat.

wat.tle ['wɔtl] 1. *n.* dal *veya* çubuklardan örülmüş yapı; ORN sarkık gerdan; BOT akasya; 2. *vb.* ince çubuklarla çit örmek.

waul [wɔːl] *v/i.* miyavlamak.

wave [weiv] 1. *n.* dalga (*a.* PHYS & *saç*); el sallama; dalgalanma; hare; 2. *v/t.* &

v/i. dalgalan(dır)mak; salla(n)mak; harelemek; el sallamak (*to s.o. b-ne*); elle işaret etm.; ondüle yapmak (*saç*); ~ *aside* bir kenara bırakmak; reddetmek; '~-length *n.* ELECT dalga boyu (*veya* uzunluğu).

wa.ver ['weivə] *v/i.* kararsızlık göstermek, tereddüt etm., duraksamak; sallanmak; sendelemek; titrek yanmak.

wave...: '~-range *n. radyo*: dalga gamı; '~-trap *n. radyo*: süzme (*veya* süzgeç) devresi.

wav.y ['weivi] *adj.* dalgalı, dalga dalga; titreyen, titreşen.

wax[1] [wæks] 1. *n.* balmumu, mum; parafin; kulak kiri; cila; kızgınlık; ~ *can.dle* mum; ~ *doll* balmumundan bebek; 2. *v/t.* mum sürmek -*e*, mumlamak; cilalamak.

wax[2] [_] (*irr.*) *v/i.* büyümek, artmak, yükselmek; *obs.* olmak.

wax.en ['wæksn] *adj.* mumdan yapılmış; mum gibi; *fig.* beti benzi atmış, solgun; 'wax.work *n.* balmumu işi; balmumundan yapılmış heykel; ~*s pl.*, ~ *show* balmumundan yapılmış heykeller (müzesi); 'wax.y □ mum gibi; mumlu; solgun; öfkeli.

way[wei] 1. *n. mst* yol; F yön, istikamet, taraf, yan, cihet; NAUT rota; *fig.* hal, durum, gidiş(at); mesafe; tarz, usül; şekil; çare, vasıta; yer; tutum, davranış, huy, âdet; ~ *in* giriş; ~ *out* çıkış; *fig.* çıkar yol; ~*s and means* para bulma (yolları); *right of* ~ JUR irtifak hakkı; *part.* MOT yol hakkı; ~ *of life* yaşam biçimi; yaşama tarzı; *this* ~ bu taraftan, buraya; *the wrong* ~ yanlış yol; *in some* ~, *in a* ~ bir bakıma; *in no* ~ hiç bir suretle, asla, katiyen; *go a great* ~ *towards* ger., *go a long* (*some*) ~ *to inf.* büyük katkıda bulunmak -*e*; *by the* ~ aklıma gelmişken, sırası gelmişken; *by* ~ *of* ...yolu ile, ...üzerinden; ...niyetiyle; *by* ~ *of excuse* özür mahiyetinde; *on the* ~, *on one's* ~ yol üstünde, yol(un)da, yoluna; *out of the* ~ alışılmışın dışında; sapa; yerinde olmayan; *under* ~ devam etmekte, hareket halinde, ilerlemekte; NAUT rotasında; *give* ~ geri çekilmek; kopmak; kırılmak; çökmek, yol vermek (*to* -*e*); öncelik vermek (*to* -*e*); *k-ni* vermek (*to* -*e*); küreklere asılmak; *have one's* ~ arzusuna kavuşmak, muradına ermek; *if I had my* ~ istediğim olsa; *have a* ~ *with* ikna kabiliyeti olm.; *lead the* ~ yol göstermek (*a.*

fig.); *s.* **make**; **pay one's** ~ kendi masrafını ödemek; kimseye borcu olmamak; **see one's** ~ **to** *ger. veya inf.* ...ceğini sanmak; ...i mümkün görmek; **2.** *adv.* uzak; yakın; '~**-bill** *n.* manifesto, nakliye senedi; '~**.far.er** *n.* yaya yolcu; ~'**lay** (*irr.* **lay**) *v/t. -in* yolunu kesmek, pusuya yatıp beklemek *-i*; '~**-leave** *n.* geçit hakkı; '~**.side 1.** *n.* yol kenarı; **by the** ~ yol kenarında; **2.** *adj.* yol kenarındaki; ~ **sta.tion** *Am.* ara istasyon; ~ **train** *Am.* dilenci postası, her istasyona uğrayan tren.

way.ward □ ['weiwəd] ters, inatçı, aksi, dik başlı; '**way.ward.ness** *n.* inatçılık, dik başlılık.

we [wi:, wi] *pron.* biz.

weak □ [wi:k] *com.* zayıf, kuvvetsiz, halsiz, takatsiz; dayanıksız; sulu, yavan (*çorba vs.*); GR vurgusuz; '**weak.en** *v/t. & v/i.* zayıfla(t)mak, kuvvetten düş(ür)mek, hafifle(t)mek; '**weak.ling** *n.* zayıf kimse *veya* hayvan; karaktersiz kimse; '**weak.ly 1.** *adv.* zayıf bir şekilde; **2.** *adj.* hastalıklı; '**weak--'mind.ed** *adj.* zayıf iradeli; '**weak.ness** *n.* zayıflık, kuvvetsizlik; zaaf; hata, kusur.

weal[1] [wi:l] *n.* refah, saadet.

weal[2] [_] *n.* iz, bere.

wealth [welθ] *n.* servet, zenginlik, varlık, para, mal; *fig.* bolluk; '**wealth.y** □ zengin, varlıklı.

wean [wi:n] *v/t.* sütten (*veya* memeden) kesmek; *fig.* ~ *s.o.* **from** *veya* **of s.th.** *b-ne bşi* bıraktırmak, *b-ni bşden* vazgeçirmek.

weap.on ['wepən] *n.* silah; '**weap.on.less** *adj.* silahsız.

wear [wɛə] **1.** (*irr.*) *v/t. & v/i.* giymek, tak(ın)mak; yıpratmak, yemek; taşımak; dayanmak *-e*; açmak (*delik, yol*); kabul etm., uygun görmek; kullanmak; yormak; yıpranmak; tükenmek; *a.* ~ **away**, ~ **down**, ~ **off**, ~ **out** aşın(dır)mak, eski(t)mek; ~ **away** azaltmak (*direnç*); tüketmek; tükenmek (*sabır*); zayıfla(t)mak; geç(ir)mek (*zaman*); ~ **off** yavaş yavaş yok olm.; yavaş yavaş geçmek (*ağrı*); ~ **on** yavaş geçmek (*zaman*); ~ **out** düzelmek (*kıvrım, kırışıklık*); yormak, tüketmek, yıpratmak; sıkıcı bir şekilde geç(ir)mek (*zaman*); tükenmek (*sabır*); giyip eskitmek (*elbise*); dövmek, pataklamak; kullanmak (*eski deyim*); **2.** *n.* giysi, elbise; aşınma, yıpran-

ma, eskime; dayanıklılık; **gentlemen's** ~ erkek elbiseleri; **for hard** ~ çok dayanıklı; *s.* **worse 1**; **there is plenty of** ~ **in it yet** daha giyilebilir, bu daha çok dayanır; '**wear.a.ble** *adj.* giyilebilir; **wear and tear** aşınma, yıpranma; zararlı etkiler; '**wearer** *n.* bş giyen (*veya* takan) kimse.

wea.ri.ness ['wiərinis] *n.* yorgunluk, bezginlik; *fig.* usanç, bıkkınlık.

wea.ri.some □ ['wiərisəm] usandırıcı, sıkıcı, yorucu, bıktırıcı.

wea.ry ['wiəri] **1.** □ yorgun, bitkin (**with**); yorucu, bıkkınlık verici, sıkıcı, usandırıcı; *fig.* bıkmış, usanmış (**of s.th.** *bşden*); **2.** *v/t. & v/i.* yor(ul)mak; bık(tır)mak, usan(dır)mak, bez(dir)-mek.

wea.sel ZOO ['wi:zl] *n.* gelincik, samur.

weath.er ['weðə] **1.** *n.* hava; *s.* **permit**; **2.** *adj.* NAUT rüzgâr yönündeki...; **3.** *v/t.* havaya göstermek; NAUT *-in* rüzgâr yönünden geçmek; *a.* ~ **out** geçiştirmek, savuşturmak (*fırtına*); *fig.* atlatmak (*güçlük*); ~**ed** yıpranmış; meyilli; *v/i.* aşınmak; solmak; ~**-beat.en** ['_-bi:tn] *adj.* fırtına yemiş; yanık (*yüz, cilt*); '~**-board** *n.* bindirme, siper tahtası; '~**-board.ing** = ~**-board**; '~**.bound** *adj.* kötü hava yüzünden evde kalmış *veya* gecikmiş; '~**-bureau** *n.* meteoroloji bürosu; '~**.chart** *n.* meteoroloji (*veya* hava) haritası; '~**.cock** *n.* rüzgârgülü, fırıldak, yelkovan '~**-forecast** *n.* hava raporu; '~**-proof**, '~**-tight** *adj.* rüzgâr (*veya* yağmur) geçirmez; '~**-sta.tion** *n.* meteoroloji istasyonu; '~**-strip** *n.* pencere bandı; '~**-vane** *n.* rüzgârgülü, fırıldak; '~**-worn** *adj.* hava etkisiyle bozulmuş *veya* aşınmış.

weave [wi:v] **1.** (*irr.*) *v/t.* dokumak; örmek (*sepet*); *fig.* yapmak, kurmak; *v/i.* zikzak yapmak; **2.** *n.* dokuma; örme; '**weav.er** *n.* dokumacı, çulha; '**weav.ing** *n.* dokuma; *attr.* dokuma...

wea.zen ['wi:zn] *adj.* buruşuk, kırışık.

web [web] *n.* ağ; örümcek ağı; dokuma; ORN perde; ANAT zar; doku; örgü; tomar; **webbed** *adj.* perde ayaklı; '**web.bing** *n.* kalın dokuma kayış; '**web.foot.ed** *adj.* perde ayaklı; '**web.page** IT *n.* web sayfası; '**web.site** IT ['_-sait] *n.* web sitesi.

wed [wed] *vb.* evlenmek *ile*, kocaya varmak, dünya evine girmek; *fig.* bağlanmak, birleşmek (**to** *-e*).

we'd F [wi:d] = **we had**; **we should**; **we**

would.

wed.ded ['wedid] *adj.* evli; ~ **to** *fig.*
bağlı -*e*, kendini adamış -*e*; '**wed.ding**
n. evlenme, düğün, nikâh; *attr.* nikâh..., evlilik...; ~ **ring** nikâh yüzüğü.

wedge [wedʒ] **1.** *n.* kıskı, kama, takoz,
çivi; **the thin end of the** ~ *fig.* büyük
değişikliklerin ilk adımı, atılan ilk sağlam adım; ~ **heel** sivri topuk; **2.** *v/t.*
kıskı ile sıkıştırmak; *a.* ~ **in**
sık(ıştır)mak; '**~-shaped** *adj.* kama
şeklinde.

wed.lock ['wedlɔk] *n.* evlilik; **out of** ~
evlilik dışı, gayri meşru.

Wednes.day ['wenzdi] *n.* çarşamba.

wee [wi:] *adj.* küçücük, minnacık, minimini, azıcık; **a** ~ **bit** biraz, oldukça.

weed [wi:d] **1.** *n.* yabanı ot, zararlı ot; F
tütün, sigara, puro; *sl.* haşiş; bir deri bir
kemik kimse; **2.** *v/t.* -*den* yabanî otları
temizlemek; ~ **out** ayıklamak, temizlemek, başından savmak; '**weed.er** *n.* yabanî ot temizleyen kimse *veya* alet;
'**weed-kill.er** *n.* yabanî otları öldür-
mekte kullanılan madde.

weeds [wi:dz] *n. pl. mst* widow's ~ matem elbisesi.

weed.y ['wi:di] *adj.* yabanî otlarla dolu;
fig. çiroz gibi, kara kuru, çelimsiz.

week [wi:k] *n.* hafta; **this day** ~ haftaya
bugün; '~-**day** *n.* iş günü, sair gün, hafta
günü; '~-'**end 1.** *n.* hafta sonu; ~ **ticket**
hafta sonu bileti; **2.** *v/i.* hafta sonunu
geçirmek; '~-'**end.er** *n.* hafta sonunu
evinden uzakta geçiren kimse; '**week-
ly 1.** *adj.* haftalık; **2.** *adv.* haftada bir,
her hafta; **3.** *n. a.* ~ **paper** haftalık gazete *veya* dergi.

weep [wi:p] (*irr.*) *vb.* ağlamak, göz yaşı
dökmek (**for** *için*); sızmak, damlamak;
'**weep.er** *n.* ağlayan kimse, ağıtçı; ~**s**
pl. uzun favori; '**weep.ing 1.** *adj.* gözleri yaşlı; yağmurlu; sarkık dallı; ~ **willow**
BOT salkımsöğüt; **2.** *n.* ağlama.

wee.vil ['wi:vil] *n.* buğday biti; pamuk
kurdu.

weft [weft] *n.* kumaş atkısı, argaç; *poet.*
dokuma, örgü.

weigh [wei] **1.** *v/t.* tartmak; *a.* ~ **up** *fig.*
ölçünmek, hesap etm.; anlamak; ~ **an-
chor** NAUT demir almak, vira etm.; ~
down yüklemek; üzmek, kederlendirmek; ~**ed down** yere eğilmiş; üzgün;
yüklü; *v/i.* ...ağırlığında olm., ...gel-
mek; *fig.* önem taşımak, etkilemek
(**with** -*e göre*, -*i*); ~ **in** (**out**) tartılmak;
~ **in with** ileri sürmek, ortaya koymak;

~ (**up**)**on** üzmek, kurcalamak (*zihin*);
2. *n.* **get under** ~ (= **way**) NAUT yola
çıkmak; '**weigh.a.ble** *adj.* tartılabilir;
'**weigh.bridge** *n.* kantar; '**weigh.er** *n.*
tartan kimse; '**weigh.ing-ma.chine** *n.*
kantar, baskül.

weight [weit] **1.** *n.* ağırlık (*a. fig.*), sıklet;
tartı; dirhem; ağır cisim; *fig.* önem, nü-
fuz, itibar, etki; *fig.* endişe, sıkıntı, yük;
carry great ~ *fig.* büyük önem taşımak;
give short ~ eksik gelmek; **putting the**
~ gülle atma; **2.** *v/t.* ağırlaştırmak; *fig.*
yüklemek; eklemek; '**weight.i.ness** *n.*
ağırlık; önemlilik; '**weight.y** □ ağır;
yüklü; sıkıntılı; önemli, etkili, nüfuzlu.

weir [wiə] *n.* su seddi, bent, büğet, bağ-
lağı.

weird [wiəd] *adj.* anlaşılmaz, esrarengiz, tekinsiz; F garip, acayip,
olağandışı.

wel.come ['welkəm] **1.** □ sevindirici, istenilen, hoşa giden, makbule geçen;
hoş karşılanan; **you are** ~ **to** *inf.* kuşkusuz ...ebilirsiniz; **you are** ~ **to it** buyurun, alın, denemesi bedava, buyurun-
uz; (**you are**) ~**l** bir şey değil!, rica
ederim!; **2.** *n.* karşılama; **3.** *v/t.* hoş
karşılamak; hoş geldiniz demek -*e*;
fig. karşılamak.

weld MEC [weld] **1.** *v/t. & v/i.* kayna(t)-
mak (**into** -*e*), kaynak yaparak birleştirmek; **2.** *n. a.* ~**ing seam** kaynak yeri;
'**weld.ing** *n.* MEC kaynak yapma; *attr.*
kaynak...

wel.fare ['welfɛə] *n.* refah, sıhhat, afiyet; (yoksullara) yardım; ~ **cen.tre**
yardım merkezi; ~ **state** refah devleti;
~ **work** sosyal yardım; ~ **work.er** sosyal
yardım uzmanı.

well[1] [wel] **1.** *n.* kuyu; memba, pınar;
fig. kaynak; MEC boru; MEC merdiven
boşluğu; **2.** *v/i.* kaynamak, fışkırmak.

well[2] [–] **1.** *adv.* iyi(ce), tamamıyle, oldukça, hayli; güzel, hoş; hakkıyle;
çok, pek; *s.* **as**; ~ **off** zengin, hali vakti
yerinde; şanslı, talihli; ~ **past fifty** ellisini hayli geçmiş; **2.** *pred. adj.* iyi, güzel;
sıhhatli, sağlıklı; uygun, yerinde; elverişli; **I am not** ~ rahatsızım, keyfim yok;
that's ~ iyi; **3.** *int.* iyi!; şey!; F pekâlâ!;
işte!; neyse!

we'll F [wi:l] = **we will**; **we shall**.

well...:'~-**ad'vised** *adj.* akıllı, sağgörülü;
inceden inceye düşünülmüş; '~-'**bal-
anced** *adj.* dengeli; '~-'**be.ing** *n.* saadet,
refah, iyilik; '~-'**born** *adj.* kibar, soylu,
iyi bir aileden gelmiş; '~-'**bred** *adj.* ter-

biyeli, kibar; '~-de'fined *adj.* açık seçik görülen, belirgin; '~-dis'posed *adj.* kibar, yardımseven (*to, towards-e karşı*); '~'fa.vo(u)red *adj.* güzel, yakışıklı; '~in'formed *adj.* çok bilgili, her şeyden haberi olan.

Wel.ling.tons ['weliŋtənz] *n. pl.* lastik çizme.

well...: '~-in'ten.tioned *adj.* iyi niyetli; '~'knit *adj.* adaleli, kuvvetli; ~ known; '~'known *adj.* tanınmış, meşhur, ünlü, bilinen; ~ *made* endamlı, boyu bosu yerinde; '~'man.nered *adj.* terbiyeli; '~-'marked *adj.* açık, belirgin; '~-nigh *adv.* hemen hemen; '~-'or.dered *adj.* derli toplu, düzenli; '~-'sea.soned *adj.* baharatlı; ~-timed *adj.* uygun, zamanlı; '~-to-'do *adj.* hali vakti yerinde, zengin; '~'trained *adj.* iyi eğitilmiş; ~ turned *fig.* güzel ifade edilmiş; '~-'wish.er *n.* iyiliksever kimse; '~-'worn *adj.* eskimiş; *fig.* bayatlamış, sıradan.

Welsh¹ [welʃ] **1.** *adj.* Gal eyaletine ait; Gallilere özgü; **2.** *n.* Gal dili; *the ~ pl.* Gallier.

welsh² [-] *v/i.* borcunu ödememek; sözünü tutmamak; 'welsh.er *n.* borcunu ödemeyen, sözünü tutmayan kimse.

Welsh...: '~.man *n.* Galli; ~ rab.bit kızarmış ekmeğe sürülen peynir; '~.wom.an *n.* Galli kadın.

welt [welt] **1.** *n.* MEC kösele şerit; elbisenin kenar şeridi; kamçı izi; **2.** *v/t.* şerit koymak; F vurup iz bırakmak; ~ed kösele şeritli (*ayakkabı*).

wel.ter ['weltə] **1.** *v/i.* yatıp yuvarlanmak, ağnamak; ~ in *fig.* içinde yüzmek (*kan vs.*); **2.** *n.* karışıklık, kargaşa; '~-weight *n. boks*; 62-67 kilo arasındaki boksör.

wen [wen] *n.* MED yağ kisti; *fig.* çok büyük şehir.

wench [wentʃ] *n.* kız, genç kadın; fahişe.

wend [wend] *v/t.*: ~ *one's way* yönelmek, gitmek (*to -e*).

went [went] *pret. of* **go 1.**

wept [wept] *pret. & p.p. of* **weep**.

were [wəː, wə] *pret. of* **be**.

we're F [wiə] = *we are*.

weren't F [wəːnt] = *were not*.

west [west] **1.** *n.* batı; **2.** *adj.* batı..., batıdaki...; batıya doğru olan; batıdan gelen (*rüzgâr*); *go ~ sl.* ölmek, gebermek; mahvolmak, bozulmak.

west.er.ly ['westəli] *adj.* batıya doğru

olan; batıdaki; batıdan gelen (*rüzgâr*).

west.ern ['westən] **1.** *adj.* batıya ait, batı...; **2.** *n.* kovboy filmi *veya* romanı; = 'west.ern.er *n.* batılı; *Am.* batı Amerikalı; 'west.ern.most *adj.* en batıdaki.

West In.dian ['west'indjən] **1.** *adj.* Batı Hint adalarına ait; **2.** *n.* Batı Hint adalarında yaşayan kimse.

west.ing NAUT ['westiŋ] *n.* batı rotası; batıya yönelme.

west.ward(s) ['westwəd(z)] *adv.* batıya doğru.

wet [wet] **1.** *adj.* ıslak, yaş, rutubetli; yağmurlu, yağışlı; *Am.* içki yasağı olmayan (*yer*); *sl.* isteksiz (*kimse*); *s.* **blanket 1.**; ~ **through** sır(ıl)sıklam; **2.** *n.* yağmur(luhava); ıslak yer; yaşlık, nem, rutubet; *sl.* içki; **3.** (*irr.*) *v/t.* ıslatmak; F içki içerek kutlamak; *v/i.* ıslanmak; ~ **through** sır(ıl)sıklam etm.

wet.back *Am. sl.* ['wetbæk] *n.* Amerika'ya kaçak giren Meksikalı.

weth.er ['weðə] *n.* iğdiş edilmiş koç.

wet-nurse ['wetnəːs] *n.* sütnine.

we've F [wiːv] = *we have*.

whack F [wæk] **1.** *v/t.* dövmek, pataklamak; küt diye vurmak; **2.** *n.* şaklama; deneme, tecrübe; *sl.* hisse, pay; *have veya take a ~ at* denemek -*i*; 'whack.er *n.* F koskocaman şey; kuyruklu yalan; 'whack.ing F **1.** *n.* dayak; **2.** *adj.* koskocaman; kuyruklu (*yalan*).

whale [weil] *n.* balina; *a ~ of* oldukça, hayli, büyük, çok; *a ~ at* F bir işin ehli, otorite; '~.bone *n.* balina (*elbisede*); '~-fish.er, '~.man, *mst* 'whal.er *n.* balina avcısı; balina avlama gemisi; 'whale-oil *n.* balina yağı.

whal.ing ['weiliŋ] *n.* balina avı.

whang F [wæŋ] **1.** *n.* şaplak; **2.** *v/t.* dövmek, şak diye vurmak.

wharf [wɔːf] **1.** *n., pl. a.* **wharves** [wɔːvz] iskele, rıhtım; **2.** *v/t.* rıhtıma boşaltmak; 'wharf.age *n.* iskele ücreti; **wharf.in.ger** ['-indʒə] *n.* rıhtım müdürü.

what [wɔt] **1.** *pron.* ne, hangi şey; -dığı şey; *know ~'s* neyin ne olduğunu bilmek; ~ *money I had* ne kadar param varsa, bendeki para; *... and ~ not* ve saire, falan filan; **2.** *int.* ne?, vay!; ~ *about ...?* ...den ne haber?, ya ...?, ...e ne dersin?; ~ *for?* niçin?; ~ *of it?* bana ne!, ne çıkar?, ne olmuş yani?; ~ *if ...?* ya ...ise?; ~ *though ...?*

...ise ne olmuş?; **what-d'you-call-him**, **~'s-his-name** adı her neyse, falanca; **~ next?** başka?; *iro.* daha neler!, yok canım!; **~ a blessing!** ne iyi!, çok şükür!; **~ impudence!** bu ne lâubalilik!; **3.** *adv.* **~ with ... ~ with...** ...ve ... yüzünden; what.e'er *poet.* [wɔt'ɛə], what'ever = **whatsoever**; 'what.not *n.* biblo rafı; falan; what.so.e'er *poet.* [wɔtsəu'ɛə], what.so'ever **1.** *pron.* her ne, her hangi; **2.** *adj.* ne, hangi.

wheat BOT [wi:t] *n.* buğday; 'wheat.en *adj.* buğdaydan yapılmış, buğday...

whee.dle ['wi:dl] *vb.* tatlılıkla ikna etm. (*into* -*e*); kandırıp elinden almak; **~ s.th. out of s.o.** tatlı sözlerle *b-den bş* almak.

wheel [wi:l] **1.** *n.* tekerlek; deveran, dönme; *part. Am.* F bisiklet; MIL çark; MOT direksiyon; **2.** *v/t. & v/i.* dön(dür)mek; sür(ül)mek; tekerlekli bir taşıtla götürmek; MIL çark etm.; '**~.bar.row** *n.* tekerlekli el arabası; **~ base** MOT dingil mesafesi; **~ chair** tekerlekli sandalye; 'wheeled *adj.* tekerlekli; 'wheelwright *n.* tekerlekçi, tekerlek tamircisi.

wheeze [wi:z] **1.** *v/i.* hırıltıyla solumak; **2.** *n.* hırıltılı ses; THEAT *sl.* espri; parlak fikir; 'wheez.y □ hırıltılı.

whelk ZOO [welk] *n.* bir tür deniz salyangozu.

whelp RHET [welp] **1.** *n.* yırtıcı hayvan yavrusu, en(c)ik; *com.* genç kız *veya* delikanlı; terbiyesiz genç; **2.** *v/i.* eniklemek, enciklemek.

when [wen] **1.** *adv.* ne zaman?; **2.** *cj.* -diği zaman; iken; sırasında; -mesine rağmen; eğer, şayet.

whence [wens] *adv.* nereden.

when.e'er *poet.* [wen'ɛə], when.(so.)ev.er [wen(səu)'evə] *adv. & cj.* her ne zaman.

where [wɛə] **1.** *adv.* nerede?; nereye?; **2.** *cj.* -diği yer(d)e; **~.a.bout**, *mst* **~.a.bouts 1.** ['wɛərə'baut(s)] *adv.* nereler(d)e; **2.** ['_] *n.* olduğu (*veya* bulunduğu) yer; **~'as** *cj.* halbuki, oysa; JUR mademki, ... dayanarak; **~'at 1.** *adv.* neye; **2.** *cj.* bunun üzerine; **~'by** *adv.* vasıtasiyle; mademki; '**~.fore** *adv.* niçin, neden; **~'in** *adv.* nerede, neyin için(d)e; hangi hususta; **~'of** *adv.* -den; **~'on** *adv.* üstünde; bunun üzerine; **~.so'ev.er** *adv.* her nerede, her nereye; **~.up'on** *adv. & cj.* bunun üzerine; wher'ev.er *adv. & cj.* her nereye; her

nerede; where'with *adv.* (ne) ile, nasıl; where.with.al **1.** [wɛəwi'ðɔːl] *adv.* ne ile, nasıl; **2.** F ['_] *n.* araçlar, gereçler; para.

wher.ry ['weri] *n.* küçük kayık.

whet [wet] **1.** *v/t.* bilemek; açmak (*iştah*); **2.** *n.* bile(n)me; iştah açıcı şey.

wheth.er ['weðə] *cj.* -ip -mediğini, -mi acaba; **~ or no** olsa da olmasa da.

whet.stone ['wetstəun] *n.* bileğitaşı.

whew [hwu:] *int.* pöf!, püf!, ya! vay be!

whey [wei] *n.* kesilmiş sütün suyu.

which [witʃ] **1.** *adj.* hangi(si) **2.** *pron.* hangisin(i); ki o, ki; ki onu, -dığım; **~'ev.er 1.** *pron.* her hangi(si); **2.** *adj.* (her)hangi, hangisi olursa olsun.

whiff [wif] **1.** *n.* esinti; koku; püf; küçük puro; **2.** *v/t.* ağızdan çıkarmak (*tütün dumanı*); *v/i.* kötü kokmak.

Whig [wig] **1.** *n.* İngiliz liberal partisi üyesi; **2.** *adj.* İngiliz liberal partisine ait.

while [wail] **1.** *n.* müddet, zaman, süre, vakit; *for a* **~** bir süre; *worth* **~** değer; **2.** *v/t. mst* **~ away** geçirmek (*vakit*); **3.** *cj.* **a. whilst** [wailst] iken; -diği halde, -e rağmen; süresince.

whim [wim] = **whimsy**.

whim.per ['wimpə] **1.** *v/i.* ağlamak, inlemek, sızlanmak; **2.** *n.* inleme, sızlanma.

whim.si.cal □ ['wimzikəl] tuhaf, acayip, kaprisli, saçma; garip fikirli; havaî; whim.si.cal.i.ty ['_kæliti], whim.si.cal.ness ['_kəlnis] *n.* tuhaflık, saçmalık; kapris.

whim.s(e)y ['wimzi] *n.* saçma arzu, kapris; tuhaflık; mizah.

whin BOT [win] *n.* katırtırnağına benzer bir bitki.

whine [wain] **1.** *v/i.* sızlanmak, mırıldanmak, zırıldamak; ağlamsamak, mızmızlanmak; **2.** *n.* sızlanma; mızmızlanma; zırıltı.

whin.ny ['wini] *v/i.* kişnemek.

whip [wip] **1.** *v/t.* kamçılamak; F dövmek, pataklamak; çalkamak, çırpmak (*uymurta*); yenmek; çalmak, aşırmak, araklamak; çıkarıvermek; sokuvermek; bastırmak (*kumaş*); döndürmek; çevirmek (*topaç*); fırlatmak; **~ away** aniden çekmek, çıkarmak; götürmek; **~ in** PARL bir araya toplamak (*parti üyesi*); **~ off** çıkarmak; uçurmak (*çatı vs.*); götürmek; gitmek; **~ on** yürütmek, kamçı ile dürtmek; **~ up** kışkırtmak; yapıvermek; çırpmak (*yumurta vs.*);

kapmak; arttırmak, toplamak; v/i. hızla hareket etm., fırlamak; **2.** *n.* kırbaç, kamçı; HUNT köpekleri idare eden kimse; PARL parti denetçisi; çırpılmış yumurta ile yapılan yiyecek; '~.cord *n.* sırım; kalın kumaş; '~'hand *n.* üstünlük, idare; **have the ~ of s.o.** *b-ne* oranla üstünlüğü olm.

whip.per... ['wipə]: '~'in *n.* HUNT köpekleri idare eden kimse; PARL parti denetçisi; '~-snap.per *n. k-ni bş* zanneden genç.

whip.pet ZOO ['wipit] *n.* tazı.

whip.ping ['wipiŋ] *n.* kamçılama, dövme; dayak; '~-boy *n.* başkalarının cezasını yüklenen kimse, şamar oğlanı; HIST bir soylunun çocuğunun yerine cezalandırılan çocuk; '~-post *n.* HIST kamçılamak üzere suçluların bağlandığı direk; '~-top *n.* topaç.

whip.poor.will ORN ['wippuəwil] *n.* çobanaldatana benzer bir kuş.

whip-saw MEC ['wipsɔ:] *n.* tomruk testeresi.

whir [wə:] = **whirr.**

whirl [wə:l] **1.** v/t. & v/i. hızla dön(dür)-mek; hızla götürmek; hızla geçmek; kafası karışmak; başı dönmek; **2.** *n.* hızla dönme; koşuşturma; whirl.i.gig ['ₐligig] *n.* topaç; fırıldak; atlıkarınca; *fig.* devir, dönüş; 'whirl.pool *n.* girdap, burgaç; 'whirl.wind *n.* kasırga, hortum.

whirr [wə:] **1.** v/i. vızlamak, pırlamak; **2.** *n.* vızıltı, pırlama sesi; zırıltı.

whisk [wisk] **1.** *n.* yumurta teli; tüy süpürge; **2.** v/t. & v/i. çalkamak; fırla(t)-mak; çırpmak (*yumurta*); hafifçe süpürmek; sallamak; götürmek; **~ away** ortadan kaldırmak; 'whis.ker *n.* ZOO hayvan bıyığı; *mst* (**a pair of**)**~s** *pl.* favori, bıyık; 'whis.kered *adj.* favorili.

whis.k(e)y ['wiski] *n.* viski.

whis.per ['wispə] **1.** v/i. fısıldamak; hışırdamak; v/t. gizlice söylemek; 'whis.perer *n.* dedikoducu kimse; whis.per.ing cam.paign *b-nin* aleyhinde dedikodu *veya* iftira yayma.

whist¹ [wist] *int.* sus!

whist² [-] *n.* vist, bir çeşit iskambil oyunu.

whis.tle ['wisl] **1.** v/i. ıslık çalmak; düdük çalmak; v/t. ıslıkla çalmak; ıslıkla çağırmak; **2.** *n.* ıslık; düdük; **~ stop** *Am.* işaret verildiğinde trenin durduğu istasyon; POL seçim gezisi.

whit¹ [wit] *n.:* **not a ~** hiç, asla.

Whit² [-] *n.* pantekot yortusunun pazar günü; **~ week** pantekot haftası.

white [wait] **1.** *adj. com.* beyaz, ak; soluk, solgun; sütlü (*kahve*); saf, lekesiz; F edepli, terbiyeli; boş, yazısız; **2.** *n.* beyaz renk; yumurta akı; beyaz tenli kimse; gözün beyaz kısmı; TYP beyaz aralık; **~ ant** ZOO beyaz karınca, divik; '~.bait *n.* ICHTH bir çeşit küçük balık; **~ book** POL resmî hükümet raporu; '~-caps *n. pl.* köpüklü dalgalar; 'white-col.lar(ed) *adj.* dairede çalışan, büro...; **~ workers** *pl.* masa başında çalışanlar, memur sınıfı; '~'faced *adj.* beti benzi atmış; '~'haired *adj.* ak saçlı; **~ heat** akkor; '~'hot *adj.* kızgın, akkor; **~ lie** zararsız yalan; '~-liv.ered *adj.* ödlek, korkak; **~ man** beyaz tenli adam; 'whit.en *v/t. & v/i.* ağar(t)mak, beyazlatmak; beyazlanmak; 'whiten.er *n.* beyazlatıcı madde; 'white.ness *n.* beyazlık; saflık; 'whiten.ing *n.* beyazlatıcı madde.

white...: **~ pa.per** POL resmî hükümet raporu; '~.smith *n.* tenekeci; kalaycı; '~.wash **1.** *n.* badana; örtbas etme; **2.** *v/t.* badana etm., badanalamak; *fig.* örtbas etm., temize çıkarmak; '~.wash.er *n.* badanacı.

whith.er *lit.* ['wiðə] *adv.* nereye; whither·so'ev.er *adv.* her nereye.

whit.ing ['waitiŋ] *n.* arıtılmış tebeşir tozu; ICHTH merlanos.

whit.ish ['waitiʃ] *adj.* beyazımsı, beyazımtırak, akça.

whit.low MED ['witləu] *n.* dolama.

Whit.sun ['witsn] *adj.* pantekot yortusuna ait;~.day ['wit'sʌndi] *n.* pantekot yortusunun pazar günü;~.tide ['witsn-taid] *n.* pantekot.

whit.tle ['witl] *v/t.* yontmak; **~ away** eksiltmek, azaltmak; **~ down** zayıflatmak; kesmek.

whiz(z) [wiz] **1.** v/i. vızıldamak, vızlamak; yıldırım gibi gitmek; **2.** *n.* vızıltı.

who [hu:] **1.** *cj.* o ki, onlar ki; **2.** *pron.* kim?; **Who's Who?** Kim Kimdir, ünlülerin kimliğini açıklayan yıllık ansiklopedi.

whoa [wəu] *int.* çüş!, dur!

who.dun.(n)it *sl.* [hu:'dʌnit] *n.* dedektif romanı.

who.ev.er [hu:'evə] *pron.* kim olursa olsun, her kim.

whole [həul] **1.** □ bütün, tam, tüm; *obs.* sağlıklı; iyi, sağlam; **made out of ~**

cloth *Am.* F uydurmasyon yapılmış; **2.** *n.* tam şey; toplam; tüm, bütün; *the* ~ *of London* Londra'nın tümü; *the* ~ *of them* onların hepsi; (*up*)*on the* ~ genellikle; çoğunlukla; '~-'**heart.ed** □ samimî, içten, candan; '~-'**hog.ger** *n.* *sl.* bir işi sonuna kadar götüren kimse; '~-'**length** *n.* *a.* ~ *portrait* tam boy portre; '~-**meal bread** kepekli buğday ekmeği; '~**.sale 1.** *n.* *mst* ~ *trade* toptan satış; **2.** *adj.* toptan...; *fig.* çok sayıda; ~ *dealer* = '~**.sal.er** *n.* toptancı; **whole.some** □ ['~-səm] sıhhate yararlı; sıhhatli; yararlı; '**whole.time** *adj.* tüm vakti alan...; '**whole.wheat** *adj.* kepekli buğdaydan yapılmış.

who'll F [hu:l] = *who will*; *who shall.*

whol.ly ['həulli] *adv.* tamamen, büsbütün, sırf.

whom [hu:m, hum] *acc. of* *who.*

whoop [wu:p] **1.** *n.* bağırma, çığlık; boğmaca öksürüğü sesi; **2.** *v/i.* bağırmak, haykırmak, çığlık atmak; ~ *it up* *Am.* *sl.* çılgınlar gibi eğlenmek; **whoop.ee** *Am.* F ['wupi:] *n.* şamata; *make* ~ şamata yapmak; **whoop.ing-cough** MED ['hu:piŋkɔf] *n.* boğmaca öksürüğü.

whop *sl.* [wɔp] *v/t.* vurmak, dövmek; yenmek; '**whop.per** *n.* *sl.* kocaman şey; *part.* kuyruklu yalan; '**whop.ping** *adj.* koskocaman; kuyruklu (*yalan*).

whore [hɔ:] *n.* fahişe, orospu.

whorl [wə:l] *n.* MEC ağırşak; BOT halkadizilişli yapraklar; ZOO, ANAT helezonî kabuğun bir halkası.

whor.tle.ber.ry BOT ['wə:tlberi] *n.* çayüzümü; *red* ~ kırmızı yabanmersini.

who's F [hu:z] = *who is.*

whose [hu:z] *gen. of* *who*; **who.so.** (**-ev.er**) ['hu:səu; hu:səu'evə] *pron.* her kim.

why [wai] **1.** *adv.* niçin?, niye?, neden?; ~ *so?* neden böyle?; *that is* ~ işte bu yüzden; **2.** *int.* demek öyle!, ya!, bak sen!

wick [wik] *n.* fitil.

wick.ed □ ['wikid] fena, kötü(cül), günahkâr; hayırsız; aşağılık; tehlikeli, şeytansı; kinci, hain; yaramaz; ahlâksız; '**wick.ed.ness** *n.* kötülük; günahkârlık.

wick.er ['wikə] *adj.* hasır...; ~ *basket* hasır sepet; ~ *chair* hasır koltuk; ~ *furniture* hasır mobilya; '~**.work 1.** *n.* sepet işi; **2.** = *wicker.*

wick.et ['wikit] *n.* ufak kapı; *kriket*; ka-

le; '~-**keep.er** *n.* top hedefinin arkasında duran oyuncu.

wide [waid] *a.* □ *& adv.* geniş, enli; açık, engin; ferah; uzak; *sl.* üçkâğıtçı; ~ *awake* tamamen uyanık; *3 feet* ~ 3 ayak genişliğinde; ~ *difference* büyük fark; '~-**an.gle** *adj.* PHOT geniş açılı...; ~-**awake** ['waidə'weik] *adj.* tamamen uyanık; F zeki, açıkgöz; '~-'**eyed** *adj.* gözleri faltaşı gibi açılmış; saf, masum; '**wid.en** *v/t.* & *v/i.* genişle(t)mek, aç(ıl)mak, bollaş(tır)mak; '**wide.ness** *n.* genişlik; '**wide-'o.pen** *adj.* ardına kadar açık; *Am.* *sl.* kanun yönünden gevşek (*şehir*); '**wide.spread** *adj.* yaygın.

wid.ow ['widəu] *n.* dul kadın; *attr.* dul...; '**wid.owed** *adj.* dul kalmış; *fig.* boş, tenha; '**wid.ow.er** *n.* dul erkek; **wid.ow.hood** ['~-hud] *n.* dulluk.

width [widθ] *n.* genişlik, en(lilik).

wield *lit.* [wi:ld] *v/t.* kullanmak.

wife [waif] *n.*, *pl.* **wives** [waivz] karı, eş, hanım; '**wife.ly** *adj.* eşe yaraşır.

wig [wig] *n.* peruka, takma saç; **wigged** *adj.* perukalı, takma saçlı; '**wig.ging** *n.* F azar, haşlama.

wig.gle ['wigl] *v/t.* & *v/i.* kıpırda(t)mak, kımılda(t)mak, kıpır kıpır oynamak.

wight *obs. veya co.* [wait] *n.* insan, kimse.

wig.wag F ['wigwæg] *vb.* işaretle (haber) vermek.

wig.wam ['wigwæm] *n.* Kuzey Amerika yerlilerinin çadır *veya* kulübesi.

wild [waild] **1.** □ *com.* yabanıl, vahşî; şiddetli; sert, fırtınalı; hiddetli, öfkeli; çılgın, deli gibi; düzensiz, dağınık; rasgele; terbiyesiz, arsız; çok hevesli, meraklı; zırzop; dönek; serseri (*kurşun*); iyi, hoş; kaba (*tahmin*); *run* ~ başıboş kalmak; BOT yabanîleşmek; *talk* ~ saçma sapan konuşmak; *be* ~ *for* *veya* *about s.th.* bşe bayılmak, bş için deli olm.; **2.** *n.* *mst the* ~*s* *pl.* çorak ve ıssız yer; '**wild.cat 1.** *n.* ZOO yaban kedisi; vaşak; *Am.* huysuz kimse; *part.* *Am.* verimsiz bir bölgede petrol veren kuyu; **2.** *adj.* *fig.* düzensiz; rizikolu, çürük (*iş*); kanun dışı; **wil.der.ness** ['wildənis] *n.* kır, sahra; el değmemiş bölge; boşluk; **wild.fire** ['waildfaiə] *n.*: *like* ~ hızla, süratle, çarçabuk; '**wild-goose chase** *fig.* boş iş, aptalca girişim; '**wild.ing** *n.* BOT yabanıl bitki; '**wild.ness** *n.* yabanîlik, vahşet.

wile [wail] **1.** *n.* *mst* ~*s* *pl.* oyun, hile,

kurnazlık; **2.** *v/t.* ayartmak, baştan çıkarmak, cezbetmek; ~ *away* = *while* **2.**

wil.ful □ ['wilful] inatçı; kasıtlı.

wil.i.ness ['wailinis] *n.* düzenbazlık.

will [wil] **1.** *n.* istek, arzu, dilek, murat; vasiyet(name), maksat, amaç; *at* ~ istediği zaman, canı nasıl isterse; *of one's own free* ~ kendi isteğiyle; **2.** (*irr.*) *v/aux.*: *he* ~ *come* gelecek; *I* ~ *do it* onu yapacağım; **3.** *v/t.* vasiyetle bırakmak; amaçlamak; niyet etm., karar vermek; arzulamak; emretmek; buyurmak (*Tanrı*); **willed** *comb.* ...iradeli.

will.ing □ ['wiliŋ] gönüllü; içten; *pred.* razı, istekli, hazır (*to inf.* -*meğe*); *I am* ~ *to believe* inanmak istiyorum; 'will-ingly *adv.* isteyerek, seve seve; 'will-ing.ness *n.* gönüllülük, isteyerek yapma.

will-o'-the-wisp ['wiləðəwisp] *n.* bataklık yakamozu.

wil.low ['wiləu] *n.* BOT söğüt; MEC hallaç makinesi; *attr.* söğüt...; '~-herb *n.* BOT yakı otu; 'wil.low.y *adj.* söğüdü çok; *fig.* narin, zarif.

wil.ly-nil.ly ['wili'nili] *adv.* ister istemez, istense de istenmese de.

wilt¹ *obs.* [wilt] *vb.* -eceksin.

wilt² [_] *v/t.* & *v/i.* sol(dur)mak; *fig.* bitkin düşmek.

Wil.ton car.pet ['wiltən'ka:pit] *n.* bir çeşit halı.

wil.y □ ['waili] düzenbaz, hilekâr, kurnaz.

wim.ple ['wimpl] *n.* rahibe başörtüsü.

win [win] **1.** (*irr.*) *v/t.* kazanmak, yenmek; elde etm., ele geçirmek; doğru tahmin etm.; erişmek, ulaşmak, varmak; çıkarmak (*maden, kömür*); MIL *sl.* organize etm.; ikna etm. (*to inf.* -*meğe*); ~ *s.o. over* b-ni ikna etm., kandırmak; *v/i.* haklı çıkmak; başarılı olm.; ~ *through to* tüm güçlükleri yenmek; **2.** *n. spor*: yengi, galibiyet, zafer, başarı.

wince [wins] **1.** *v/i.* birdenbire ürkmek, ürküp çekinmek; **2.** *n.* ürkme, çekinme.

winch [wintʃ] *n.* vinç, bocurgat.

wind¹ [wind, *poet. a.* waind] **1.** *n.* rüzgâr, yel; hava; *fig.* nefes, soluk; MED osuruk; MUS nefesli çalgılar; koku; boş laf, saçmalık; *be in the* ~ ortalıkta bir şeyler dönmek; *have a long* ~ nefesi kuvvetli olm.; *throw to the* ~*s fig.*

bşe kulak asmamak, aldırış etmemek; saçıp dağıtmak; *raise the* ~ *sl.* gerekli parayı sağlamak; *get veya have the* ~ *up sl.* korkmak, endişelenmek; **2.** *v/t.* HUNT koklayarak bulmak; nefes nefese bırakmak; nefesini kesmek; *be* ~*ed* nefesi kesilmek, nefes nefese kalmak.

wind² [waind] (*irr.*) *v/t.* & *v/i.* çevirmek, dola(ş)mak; döndürmek; sar(ıl)mak; eğrilmek, bükülmek, kıvrılmak; sokulmak; *a.* ~ *o.s.* sarınmak; ~ *one's way* kıvrıla kıvrıla uzanmak; ~ *up* çıkarmak, kaldırmak, açmak (*araba camı*); kurmak (*saat*); sarmak (*ip*); bitirmek, bağlamak (*konuşma vs.*); COM tasfiye (*veya* likide) etm.; olmak; gitmek, varmak; boylamak (*hapsi*); almak (*ödül vs.*).

wind... [wind]: '~.bag *n. contp.* geveze (*veya* çenesi düşük) kimse; '~-break *n.* rüzgâr çiti; '~-cheat.er *n.* parka, anorak; '~.fall *n.* ağaçtan düşmüş meyve; beklenmedik yerden gelen para *vs.*; '~-ga(u)ge *n.* rüzgârın gücünü ölçen alet; 'wind.i.ness *n.* rüzgârlılık; gevezelik.

wind.ing ['waindiŋ] **1.** *n.* dön(dür)me; sarmal sargı; sarmal, dönemeç; dolambaç; **2.** □ dolambaçlı; sarmal; ~ *staircase*, ~ *stairs pl.* döner merdiven; '~-sheet *n.* kefen; '~'up *n.* bit(ir)me, son, kapanış; COM tasfiye.

wind-in.stru.ment MUS ['windinstru-mənt] *n.* nefesli çalgı.

wind-jam.mer NAUT F ['winddʒæmə] *n.* yelkenli gemi; *Am.* geveze kimse.

wind.lass MEC ['windləs] *n.* ırgat, bocurgat.

wind.mill ['windmil] *n.* yeldeğirmeni.

win.dow ['windəu] *n.* pencere; vitrin; '~-dress.ing *n.* vitrin dekorasyonu; *fig.* göz boyama; 'win.dowed *adj.* pencereli.

win.dow...: ~ **en.ve.lope** adresin görüneceği kısmı şeffaf olan zarf, pencereli zarf; '~-frame *n.* pencere çerçevesi; '~-ledge *n.* pencere eşiği; '~-pane *n.* pencere camı; '~-shade *n. Am.* güneşlik; '~-shopping *n.* vitrin gezme; '~-shut.ter *n.* pancur, kepenk; '~.sill *n.* pencere eşiği.

wind... [wind]: '~.pipe *n.* nefes borusu; '~.screen, *Am.* '~-shield *n.* MOT ön cam; ~ *wiper* silecek, silgiç; '~-tun.nel *n.* AVIA hava deneme tüneli.

wind.ward ['windwəd] **1.** *adj.* rüzgâr üstü yönündeki; **2.** *n.* rüzgâr üstü.

wind.y □ ['windi] rüzgârlı; fırtınalı; *fig.*
geveze; *sl.* korkmuş; MED gaz yapan.

wine [wain] *n.* şarap; '~-grow.er *n.*
bağcı; '~-mer.chant *n.* şarap tüccarı;
'~.press *n.* üzüm cenderesi; '~-vault
n. şarap mahzeni.

wing [wiŋ] **1.** *n.* kanat (*a.* MIL, ARCH); F
co. kol; MOT çamurluk; AVIA kanat;
uçuş; AVIA, MIL kol; *futbol*: kanat (oyuncusu); ~**s** *pl.* THEAT kulis; ARCH ek bina;
take ~ uçup gitmek; kanatlanmak; *be*
on the ~ uçuyor olm.; *fig.* ayağı üzen-
gide olm.; **2.** *v/t. & v/i.* uç(ur)mak; kanat takmak; kanadından *veya* kolun-
dan yaralamak; kanatlanmak; '~-case,
'~-sheath *n.* zoo böcek kanadının kabuğu; '~-chair *n.* koltuk; **winged** *adj.*
kanatlı...

wink [wiŋk] **1.** *n.* göz kırpma; an; *not get*
a ~ *of sleep* gözünü kırpmamak, hiç
uyumamak; *tip s.o. the* ~ *sl.* b-ni gizlice
uyarmak, haber vermek; *s.* **forty**; **2.** *v/i.*
göz kırpmak; gözle işaret vermek (*at*
-e); *fig.* pırıldamak; ~ *at* göz yummak
-e, görmezlikten gelmek *-i*; 'wink.ing
light MOT yanıp sönen ışık.

win.ner ['winə] *n.* kazanan; *spor:* galip.

win.ning ['winiŋ] **1.** □ kazanan; cazip;
dostça, sevimli; **2.** *n.* ~**s** *pl.* kazanç;
'~-post *n. spor:* bitiş direği.

win.now ['winəu] *v/t.* savurup taneleri-
ni ayırmak (*buğday*); *fig.* ayırmak.

win.some ['winsəm] *adj.* güzel, çekici,
alımlı; hoş, sevimli; neşeli, şen.

win.ter ['wintə] **1.** *n.* kış; ~ *sports* kış
sporları; **2.** *v/i.* kışlamak, kışı geçirmek.

win.try ['wintri] *adj.* kış gibi; *fig.* pek
soğuk, buz gibi.

wipe [waip] **1.** *v/t.* silmek, silip kurutmak; ~ *off* silip gidermek, temizlemek,
silmek; ~ *out* silip yok etm., silmek, temizlemek; *fig.* ortadan kaldırmak; **2.** *n.*
silme, temizleme; F darbe, kötek; alay;
'wip.er *n.* silecek.

wire [waiə] **1.** *n.* tel; F telgraf; *attr.* tel...;
pull the ~**s** *fig.* torpil patlatmak; *s.* **live**
2; **2.** *v/t.* telle bağlamak; ELECT elektrik
tesisatı döşemek *-e*; *v/i.* telgraf çekmek
-e; '~.drawn *adj.* kılı kırk yaran;
'~-ga(u)ge *n.* MEC tel mastarı;
'~.haired *adj.* tel gibi tüyleri olan (*köpek*); 'wireless **1.** □ telsiz; ~ *phone* telsiz telefon; **2.** *n. a.* ~ *set* radyo; *on the* ~
radyoda; ~ *station* radyo istasyonu; **3.**
v/t. telsizle göndermek; 'wire'netting
n. tel örgü; 'wire-pull.er *n. fig.* torpil

patlatan kimse;'**wire-wove** *adj.* kaliteli...

wir.ing ['waiəriŋ] *n.* tel çekme; ELECT
tel bağlantı sistemi; ~ *diagram* ELECT
tel bağlantı şeması, şebeke planı;'**wir.y**
□ tel gibi; sırım gibi.

wis.dom ['wizdəm] *n.* akıl(lılık), hikmet; bilgece söz; ~ *tooth* akıl dişi, yirmi
yaş dişi.

wise[1] □ [waiz] akıllı; tedbirli; tecrübeli,
deneyimli; bilgili; mahir, usta; ~ *guy*
Am. sl. ukalâ dümbeleği; *put s.o.* ~
b-ne bilgi vermek (*to, on hakkında*).

wise[2] *obs.* [_] *n.* usûl, tarz, suret.

wise.a.cre ['waizeikə] *n.* ukalâ; 'wise-
crack F **1.** *n.* espri; **2.** *v/i.* espri yapmak.

wish [wiʃ] **1.** *v/t.* istemek, arzu etm., dilemek, temenni etm.; ~ *s.o. joy (of)*
b-ne bşden dolayı başarılar dilemek;
~ *for -i* çok arzulamak, *-e* can atmak;
~ *well (ill)* iyi şans dile(me)mek (*to*
-e); **2.** *n.* istek, arzu, dilek, emel; *good*
~*es pl.* tebrikler;'wish.ful □ ['_ful] arzulu, istekli (*to inf. -meğe*); ~ *thinking*
hüsnükuruntu; 'wish(.ing)-bone *n.* lades kemiği.

wish-wash F ['wiʃwɔʃ] *n.* yavan içki;
saçmalık;'wish.y-wash.y *adj.* F yavan,
sulu, hafif; karaktersiz; boş (*fikir*).

wisp [wisp] *n.* tutam; demet, deste.

wist.ful □ ['wistful] hasretli, arzulu, istekli, dalgın.

wit [wit] **1.** *n.* akıl; *a.* ~**s** *pl.* zekâ, anlayış;
nükte(ci); *be at one's* ~*'s end* apışıp
kalmak, tamamen şaşırmak, ne yapacağını bilememek; *have veya keep*
one's ~**s** *about one* paniğe kapılma-
mak, tetikte olm.; *live by one's* ~**s**
açıkgözlülüğe geçimini sağlamak;
out of one's ~**s** çileden çıkmış; **2.** *vb.*
to ~ yani, demek ki.

witch [witʃ] *n.* büyücü kadın; cadı, kocakarı; büyüleyici güzellikte kadın;
'~.craft, 'witch.er.y *n.* büyü(cülük);
witch *hunt Am.* düzene baş kaldıran-
ları sindirme avı.

with [wið] *prp.* ile; *-den; -e* karşı; *-e* rağmen; *-den* dolayı; *-in* yanında, *ile* birlikte; *it is just so* ~ *me* benim için öyle; ~ *it*
sl. zamane, modern.

with.al *obs.* [wi'ðɔːl] **1.** *adv.* bununla beraber; ayrıca; **2.** *prp.* ile.

with.draw [wið'drɔː] (*irr.* **draw**) *v/t. &*
v/i. geri çek(il)mek; geri almak; çekmek (*para*);'with'draw.al *n.* geri alma;
part. MIL geri çek(il)me.

withe [wiθ] *n.* söğüt çubuğu, saz.

with.er ['wiðə] v/t. & v/i. a. ~ **up**, ~ **away** kuru(t)mak, sol(dur)mak; çürü(t)-mek, boz(ul)mak; utandırmak, sustur-mak; fig. kaybolmak, yıkılmak (umut).
with.ers ['wiðəz] n. pl. cıdağı, cıdağu, atın iki omuzunun arası.
with.hold [wið'həuld] (irr. **hold**) v/t. tutmak, saklamak (**s.th. from s.o.** b-den bşi); vermemek; bırakmamak; kısıtlamak; **with'in 1.** lit. adv. içeri-de(n), içeriye; **from** ~ içeriden; **2.** prp. -in içinde, zarfında, dahilinde; ~ **doors** evde; ~ **a mile of** -e bir mil kala; ~ **call**, ~ **sight**, ~ **hearing** çağrılabile-cek, görülebilecek, duyulabilecek uzaklıkta; **with'out 1.** lit. adv. dışarıda; **from** ~ dışarıdan; **2.** prp. -siz, -sız, -meyerek, -meden, -meksizin; lit. ha-riç, -in dışında; **with'stand** (irr. **stand**) v/t. dayanmak -e, karşı koymak -e.
with.y ['wiði] = **withe**.
wit.less □ ['witlis] akılsız, kafasız, düşüncesiz.
wit.ness ['witnis] **1.** n. tanık, şahit; de-lil, tanıt; şahitlik, tanıklık; **bear** ~ tanıklık etm.; kanıtlamak (**to** -i); **in** ~ **of** -in kanıtı olarak; **marriage** ~ nikâh şahidi; **2.** v/t. şahit olm. -e, görmek -i; şehadet etm. -e; v/i. şahitlik (veya tanıklık) etm. (**for, to** lehte; **against** aleyhte); '~-**box**, Am. ~ **stand** tanık kürsüsü.
wit.ti.cism ['witisizəm] n. espri, şaka; 'wit.ti.ness n. espri yeteneği, hazırce-vaplık; 'wit.ting.ly adv. bile bile, kas-ten; 'wit.ty □ nükteli, esprili, hazırce-vap; nükteci, zeki.
wives [waivz] pl. of **wife**.
wiz Am. sl. [wiz] n. deha; **wiz.ard** ['-əd] **1.** n. büyücü, sihirbaz; fig. deha; **finan-cial** ~ çok kolay para kazanan kimse; **2.** adj. sl. mükemmel, şahane.
wiz.en(.ed) ['wizn (d)] adj. pörsümüş, pör sük.
wo(**a**) [wəu] int. atları durdurmak için kullanılan bir ünlem.
woad BOT, MEC [wəud] n. çivitotu.
wob.ble ['wɔbl] v/t. & v/i. salla(n)mak; titremek; tereddüt etm., bocalamak; sendelemek; MEC yalpalamak, yalpa vurmak.
wo(**e**) RHET veya co. [wəu] n. keder, dert, elem, acı; ~ **is me!** vah başıma ge-lenlere!, eyvahlar olsun; '~-**be.gone** adj. kederli, gamlı; wo(e).**ful** □ rhet, veya co. ['-ful] kederli, hüzünlü; üzü-cü; 'wo(e)**ful.ness** n. hüzün, keder.

woke [wəuk] pret. & p.p. of **wake²** 1.
wold [wəuld] n. yayla, bozkır.
wolf [wulf] n., pl. **wolves** [wulvz] **1.** n. zoo kurt; sl. zampara, çapkın; **cry** ~ ya-lan yere tehlike işareti vermek; **2.** v/t. F aç kurt gibi yemek, silip süpürmek (yemek); 'wolf.ish □ kurt gibi; F fig. aç kurt gibi.
wolf.ram MIN ['wulfrəm] n. tungsten, volfram.
wolves [wulvz] pl. of **wolf**.
wom.an ['wumən] n., pl. **wom.en** ['wimin] n. kadın; eş, karı; sevgili, me-tres; kadınlık; kadın cinsi; ~**'s rights** pl. kadın hakları; attr. kadın...; ~ **doctor** kadın doktor; ~ **student** kız öğrenci; ~ **suffrage** kadınların oy kullanma hakkı; 'wom.an-hat.er n. kadın düş-manı; 'wom.an.hood ['-hud] n. kadınlık; kadınlar; **reach** ~ kadın olm.; 'wom.an.ish □ kadın gibi, kadınsı; 'wom.an.kind n. kadınlar; 'woman.like adj. kadın gibi; 'wom-an.ly adj. kadına yakışır; kadın gibi.
womb [wu:m] n. ANAT rahim, dölyatağı; fig. menşe.
wom.en ['wimin] pl. of **woman**; ~**'s rights** kadın hakları; ~**'s team** spor: bayan takımı; wom.en.folk(s) ['-fəuk(s)], 'women.kind n. kadınlar, kadın kısmı; kadın akrabalar.
won [wʌn] pret. & p.p. of **win** 1.
won.der ['wʌndə] **1.** n. harika, şaşıla-cak şey, mucize; hayret, şaşkınlık; **for a** ~ hayret; **2.** vb. şaşmak, hayret etm. (**at** -e); hayrette kalmak, hayran olm.; merak etm. (**whether, if** -ip -me-diğini); düşünmek; şüphe etm.; won-der.**ful** □ ['-ful] hayret verici, harika, fevkalâde, şahane; şaşılacak, tuhaf; 'won.der.ing **1.** □ şaşkın, şaşırmış; **2.** n. hayret, şaşkınlık; 'won.der-land n. harikalar diyarı; 'won.der.ment n. hayret, şaşkınlık; merak; 'won.der--struck adj. hayretler içinde kalmış; 'won.der-work.er n. harikalar yaratan kimse.
won.drous □ lit. ['wʌndrəs] harikula-de, olağanüstü.
won.ky sl. ['wɔŋki] adj. çürük (a. fig.); halsiz, bitkin, zayıf.
won't [wəunt] = **will not**.
wont [wəunt] **1.** pred. alışmış, alışkanlık haline getirmiş; **be** ~ **to do** bşi yapmak âdetinde olm.; **2.** n. âdet, alışkanlık; 'wont.ed adj. alışılmış, her zamanki.
woo [wu:] v/t. kur yapmak -e; kazanma-

ya çalışmak; kendine çekmek.
wood [wud] *n.* orman, koru; odun, tahta, kereste, ağaç; MUS tahtadan yapılmış nefesli sazlar; **~s** *pl.* orman, koru; **touch ~!** şeytan kulağına kurşun!, nazar değmesin!; **out of the ~** *fig.* tehlikeden uzak, güçlükleri yenmiş; **from the ~** fıçıdan; **~.bine**, *a.* **~.bind** BOT ['_bain(d)] *n.* hanımeli; '**~-carv.ing** *n.* oymacılık; tahta oyma işi; '**~.chuck** *n.* zoo bir çeşit dağ sıçanı; '**~.cock** *n.* ORN çulluk; '**~.craft** *n.* ormancılık; oymacılık; '**~.cut** *n.* tahta basma kalıbı (ile basılmış desen *veya* resim); '**~.cut.ter** *n.* baltacı, oduncu; '**wood.ed** *adj.* ağaçlı; '**wood.en** *adj.* tahtadan yapılmış, tahta...; ahşap...; *fig.* odun gibi, sert; '**wood-en.grav.er** *n.* tahta oymacısı (*veya* hakkâkı); '**wood-en.grav.ing** *n.* ağaç oymacılığı; '**wood.i.ness** *n.* ağaçlık (*veya* ormanlık) olma; orman bolluğu.
wood...: '**~.land** **1.** *n.* ormanlık, ağaçlık; **2.** *adj.* ormanlık...; orman...; '**~.lark** *n.* ORN ağaççıl tarlakuşu; '**~-louse** *n.* zoo tespihböceği '**~.man** *n.* oduncu, baltacı; orman adamı; '**~.peck.er** *n.* ORN ağaçkakan; '**~.pile** *n.* odun yığını; '**~-pulp** *n.* kâğıt hamuru; '**~.ruff** *n.* BOT ince otu; '**~-shavings** *n. pl.* talaş; '**~.shed** *n.* odunluk; '**woods.man** *Am. for* **woodman**; '**wood-wind** *n.*, *a.* **~ instruments** *pl.* MUS tahtadan yapılmış nefesli sazlar; '**~-work** *n.* doğrama (cılık), dülgerlik (*part.* ARCH); '**~-work.ing ma.chine** marangoz tezgâhı; '**wood.y** *adj.* ormanlık, ağaçlık; ağaç cinsinden, ağaçsıl; '**wood.yard** *n.* kereste deposu.
woo.er ['wu:ə] *n.* âşık, kur yapan kimse.
woof [wu:f] *s.* **weft**.
woof.er ELECT ['wu:fə] *n.* alçak titreşimli ses hoparlörü.
wool [wul] *n.* yün, yapağı; kıvırcık saç; **dyed in the ~** dokunmadan önce boyanmış; *fig.* tam, halis muhlis; koyu; **pull the ~ over s.o.'s eyes** *b-ni* aldatmak, *b-nin* gözünü boyamak; **lose one's ~** F tepesi atmak, kızmak, sinirlenmek; '**~-gath.ering** **1.** *n.* aklı başka yerde olma, dalgınlık; **go ~** aklı başka yerde olm., dalgın olm.; **2.** *adj.* dalgın, aklı başka yerde olan; '**wool.(l)en** **1.** *adj.* yünden yapılmış, yünlü yün...; **2.** *n.* **~s** *pl.* yünlüler; '**wool.(l)y** **1.** *adj.* yünlü; yün gibi; yumuşak; PAINT &

fig. bulanık, dağınık; flu; **2.** *n.* **woollies** *pl.* F yünlü giyecek, *part.* kazak.
wool...: '**~.sack** *n.* Lortlar Kamarası başkanının meclisteki yün minderi; '**~-stapler** *n.* yün tüccarı; '**~-work** *n.* yün işi.
Wop *Am. sl.* [wɔp] *n.* İtalyan.
word [wə:d] **1.** *n. mst* kelime, söz(cük); laf; haber, bilgi; vaat, söz; emir, kumanda; MIL parola; **~s** *pl.* konuşma; *fig.* ağız kavgası, münakaşa; **by ~ of mouth** ağızdan, sözlü olarak, şifahen; **eat one's ~s** tükürdüğünü yalamak, sözünü geri almek; **have ~s** ağız kavgası (*veya* münakaşa) etm. (**with** *ile*) **leave ~** haber bırakmak; **send** (**bring**) **~** haber göndermek (getirmek); **be as good as one's ~** sözü nün eri olm.; **take s.o. at his ~** *b-nin* sözüne inanmak; **2.** *v/t.* ifade etm., söylemek; **~ed as follows** şöyle denilmiştir; '**~-book** *n.* sözlük; libretto; '**word.i.ness** *n.* çok kelimelilik; '**word.ing** *n.* yazılış tarzı, üslup; '**word.less** *adj.* kelimesiz, sessiz, suskun; '**word-'per.fect** *adj.* THEAT ezbere bilen; '**word-split.ting** *n.* bilgicilik, sofizm.
word.y □ [wə:di] çok kelimeli; kelimeye ait, kelime...
wore [wɔ:] *pret. of* **wear 1**.
work [wə:k] **1.** *n.* iş, çalışma; emek; vazife, görev; eser; **~s** *sg.* fabrika, tesis; **~s** *pl.* MEC mekanizma; MIL istihkâm; **pub.lic ~s** *pl.* bayındırlık; **~ of art** sanat eseri; **at ~** iş başında, işte; **be in ~** bir işi olm.; **be out of ~** işsiz, boşta olm.; **make sad ~ of** yüzüne gözüne bulaştırmak; **make short ~ of** çabucak bitirivermek, kısa kesmek; **put out of ~** işsiz bırakmak; **set to ~**, **set** *veya* **go about one's ~** işe koyulmak, başlamak; **~s council** yönetim kurulu; **2.** (*irr.*) *v/t.* & *v/i.* çalış(tır)mak; işle(t)mek; oyna(t)mak; çözmek, halletmek; etkilemek; yaratmak, yapmak; zorlamak (**in.to** *-e*); uğraşmak, emek sarf etm.; görevli olm.; yürümek; başarılı olm., iyi sonuç vermek; mayalanmak; **~ one's way** *k-ne* yol açmak; **he is ~ing his way through college** hem okuyup hem çalışıyor; **~ one's will** istediğini yaptırmak (**upon** *-e*); **~ it** *sl.* becermek, halletmek; **~ at** çalışmak, çabalamak; **~ off** çık(ar)mak; geç(ir)mek; bitirmek; COM çalışarak ödemek (*borç*); **~ out** çık(ar)mak; hesaplamak; halletmek, çöz(ül)mek, çözüm yolu bulmak; anla-

mak, kestirmek; sonuçlanmak; geliş-(tir)mek; başarılı olm., başarı kazanmak; bitirmek (*maden damarı*); idman yapmak; geçirmek (*vakit*); çalışarak ödemek (*borç*); gitmek; bulmak, keşfetmek; **~ up** geliş(tir)mek, ilerle(t)-mek; artırmak; heyecanlandırmak, kamçılamak, körüklemek; beslemek (*ümit*); bitirmek, tamamlamak, düzenlemek; sokmak (*into ... haline*).

work.a.ble □ ['wə:kəbl] işlenebilir; pratik, elverişli; işletilebilir; 'work.a day *adj.* sıradan, alelade, sıkıcı; work.a.hol.ic [wə:kə'hɒlık] *n. çalışmadan duramayan kimse*; işkolik; 'work.day *n.* işgünü; 'work.er *n.* işçi, amele; **~s** *pl.* işçi sınıfı; 'work.house *n.* darülaceze; *Am.* ıslahevi.

work.ing ['wə:kıŋ] **1.** *n.* çalışma; **2.** *adj.* iş gören, çalışan; işleyen; işe ait, iş...; **~ knowledge** yeterli bilgi; **in ~ order** çalışır vaziyette, işler durumda; **~ cap.i.tal** döner sermaye; '**~-class** *adj.* işçi sınıfı...; **~ day** işgünü; **~ draw.ing** ARCH çalışma projesi; **~ hours** *pl.* iş saatleri; **~ man** işçi; '**~-out** *n.* uygulama, tatbik; hesaplama; **~ plan** ARCH çalışma planı.

work.man ['wə:kmən] *n.* işçi; '**~.like** *adj.* ustaya yakışır; 'work.man.ship *n.* ustalık; usta işi; zanaat.

work...: '**~.out** *n. Am.* F *mst spor:* idman, antrenman; '**~.room** *n.* çalışma odası; '**~.shop** *n.* atelye; '**~-shy** *adj.* tembel, işten kaçan; '**~.wom.an** *n.* kadın işçi.

world [wə:ld] *n. com.* dünya, cihan, âlem; evren; uzay; yer(yüzü); gezegen; hayat, ömür; toplum; **a ~ of** dünya kadar, pek çok; **in the ~** dünyada; yahu, Allah aşkına; **what in the ~ are you doing?** ne yapıyorsun sen Allah aşkına?; **bring (come) into the ~** dünyaya getirmek (gelmek), doğ(ur)mak; **for all the ~ like** *veya* **as if** *ile* tıpatıp aynı, hık demiş burnundan düşmüş; **a ~ too wide** çok geniş; **think the ~ of** hayran olm. -*e*, çok sevmek -*i*; **man of the ~** dünya (*veya* hayat) adamı; world.li ness ['_linis] *n.* dünyevîlik, maddecilik; 'world.ling *n.* dünyaperest kimse.

world.ly ['wə:ldli] *adj.* dünyevî; maddî; **~ innocence** dünyadan haberi olmama; **~ wisdom** görmüş geçirmişlik; '**~'wise** *adj.* görmüş geçirmiş, bilgili.

world...: '**~-pow.er** *n.* POL önemli devlet; '**~-wear.y** *adj.* dünyadan bezmiş; '**~-wide** *adj.* dünya çapında, dünyaya

yaygın, âlemşümul.

worm [wə:m] **1.** *n.* kurt, solucan; *fig.* aşağılık (*veya* pısırık) kimse; MEC vidanın helezonî kısmı; MEC sonsuz vida; **2.** *v/t.* **~ a secret out of s.o.** *b-nin* ağzından ustalıkla laf almak; **~ o.s.** sokulmak; *fig.* girmek (**into** -*e*); '**~-drive** *n.* MEC helezonî dişli; '**~-eat.en** *adj.* kurt yemiş; *fig.* eski, demode; '**~-gear** *n.* MEC sonsuz dişli; = '**~-wheel** *n.* MEC helezonî tekerlek; '**~.wood** *n.* pelin; *fig.* acılık; acı veren şey; 'worm.y *adj.* kurtlu; kurt yemiş; kurt gibi.

worn [wɔ:n] *p.p.* of **wear** *1*; '**~'out** *adj.* bitkin, çok yorgun; eskimiş, aşınmış, yıpranmış.

wor.ri.ment F ['warimənt] *n.* üzüntü, endişe; **wor.rit** *sl.* ['wʌrit] *vb.* canını sıkmak; 'wor.ry **1.** *v/t. & v/i.* üz(ül)-mek, endişelen(dir)mek; rahatsız etm., canını sıkmak; ısırmak (*köpek*); merak etm., kaygılanmak, tasalanmak (**about**-*e*); **2.** *n.* üzüntü, endişe, merak, tasa, kaygı, sıkıntı; baş belâsı.

worse [wə:s] **1.** *adj.* daha fena, daha kötü, beter; MED daha hasta; **~ luck!** maalesef!, ne yazık ki!; **he is none the ~ for it** ondan ona bir zarar gelmez; **the ~ for wear** giyile giyile eskimiş; bitkin, çok yorgun; **2.** *n.* daha kötü şey, beteri; **from bad to ~** daha kötüye; 'wor.sen *v/t. & v/i.* fenalaş(tır)mak, kötüleş-(tir)mek.

wor.ship ['wə:ʃip] **1.** *n.* tapınma, ibadet; hayranlık, tapma; **Your ♀** zatıaliniz; **place of ~** ibadethane; **2.** *v/t.* tapmak, tapınmak, hayranlık duymak -*e*; *v/i.* ibadet etm.; wor.ship.ful □ ['_ful] saygıdeğer, muhterem; 'wor.ship.(-p)er *n.* tapan, ibadet eden kimse.

worst [wə:st] **1.** *adj.* en fena, en kötü; **2.** *n.* en kötü şey *veya* durum; **at (the) ~** en kötü olasılıkla; **do your ~!** elinden geleni ardına koyma!; **get the ~ of it** yenilmek; **if the ~ comes to the ~** başka çıkar yol kalmazsa, durum daha da kötü olursa; **3.** *v/t.* yenmek, mağlûp etm.

wor.sted ['wustid] *n.* bükme ün, yün ipliği; bükme yünden dokunmuş kumaş.

wort¹ ʙoʈ [wə:t] *n.* bitki, sebze, ot.

wort² [_] *n.* bira mayası.

worth [wə:θ] **1.** *adj.* değer, lâyık; ... değerinde, -lik, ...sahibi; **he is ~ a million** bir milyonu var; **~ reading** okumaya değer; **2.** *n.* değer, kıymet; servet, varlık; bedel, -lik; wor.thi.ness ['wə:-

ðinis] *n.* değer(lilik); **worth.less** □
['wəːθlis] değersiz, işe yaramaz; karaktersiz, ciğeri beş para etmez;
'worth-'while *adj.* (zahmetine) değer,
yapmaya değer; faydalı; wor.thy ['wəː-
ði] **1.** □ değerli; layık (*of -e*), reva, müstahak; uygun, yaraşır; *oft. co.* saygıdeğer, muhterem; ~ *of s.th.* bşe lâyık,
bşe değer; **2.** *n.* değerli kimse.
would [wud, wəd] *pret. of will*, -ecek(-
ti); istedi.
would-be ['wudbiː] *adj.* sözde, güya,
sözümona; ~ *aggressor* güya saldırgan; ~ *buyer* sözümona müşteri; ~
painter sözde ressam; ~ *poet* şair müsveddesi; ~ *politician* sözümona politikacı.
wouldn't ['wudnt] = *would not.*
wound[1] [wuːnd] **1.** *n.* yara, bere; *fig.* gönül yarası; **2.** *v/t.* yaralamak; *fig. -in*
gönlünü kırmak, incitmek.
wound[2] [waund] *pret. & p.p. of wind*[2].
wove *pret.*, **wo.ven** ['wəuv(ən)] *p.p. of*
weave **1**.
wow *Am.* [wau] **1.** *int.* hayret!, deme!; **2.**
n. THEAT *sl.* büyük başarı.
wrack[1] BOT [ræk] *n.* deniz yosunu.
wrack[2] [-] = *rack*[3].
wraith [reiθ] *n.* bir kimsenin ölümünden az önce görülen hayali, tayf; sıska
kimse.
wran.gle ['ræŋgl] **1.** *v/i.* kavga etm., çekişmek; ağız dalaşı yapmak, münakaşa
etm.; **2.** *n.* kavga, ağız dalaşı.
wrap [ræp] **1.** *v/t. & v/i.* ört(ün)mek; *oft.*
~ *up* sar(ıl)mak, sarmalamak, paketle-
mek; bürü(n)mek; bükmek, katlamak;
fig. bitirmek, bağlamak (*iş*); *be* ~*ped*
up in -e sarılmış, bürünmüş olm.; *-de*
gizli, saklı olm.; *fig. -e* dört elle
sarılmış, kendini vermiş, dalmış olm.;
2. *n.* örtü; atkı; giysi 'wrap.per *n.* sargı;
sabahlık; *a postal* ~ kitap kabı; 'wrapping *n.* ambalaj; sargı; ~ *paper* paket
(*veya* ambalaj) kâğıdı.
wrath *lit.* [rɔθ] *n.* öfke, hiddet, gazap;
wrath.ful □ ['-ful] öfkeli, küplere binmiş.
wreak [riːk] *v/t.* yapmak, çıkarmak
(*hınç, öfke vs.*) (*upon -den*).
wreath [riːθ] *n.*, *pl.* wreaths [riːðz] çelenk; **wreathe** [riːð] *v/t. & v/i.* sar(ıl)-
mak; kaplamak; çelenk yapmak; çöreklenmek (*yılan*); daireler halinde
hareket etm. (*duman vs.*).
wreck [rek] **1.** *n.* NAUT gemi enkazı; harabe, virane, yıkıntı, enkaz (*oft. fig.*);

kazaya uğrama; harabiyet, tahribat;
fig. harap olmuş kimse; **2.** *v/t.* kazaya
uğratmak; yıkmak, altüst etm.; *be*
~*ed* NAUT karaya oturmak; kazaya
uğramak; 'wreck.age *n.* enkaz, yıkıntı;
wrecked *adj.* kazaya uğramış; karaya
oturmuş; yıkılmış; 'wreck.er *n.* NAUT
enkaz temizleyen kimse; *fig.* sabotajcı;
Am. bina yıkıcısı; MOT kurtarıcı, çekici;
'wreck.ing *n.* enkaz hırsızlığı; ~ *com-*
pany eski binaları yıkan şirket; ~ *ser-*
vice MOT kurtarma (*veya* yedeğe alma)
servisi.
wren ORN [ren] *n.* çalıkuşu.
wrench [rentʃ] **1.** *v/t.* burkmak; burka-
rak koparmak; zorla almak (*from s.o.*
b-den); *fig.* çarpıtmak (*anlam*); ~ *open*
çekip açmak; ~ *out* çekip çıkarmak; **2.**
n. burk(ul)ma; bük(ül)me; *fig.* ayrılık
acısı; MEC İngiliz anahtarı.
wrest [rest] *v/t.* zorla elde etm., zorla almak (*from s.o. b-den*); çarpıtmak (*an-*
lam, gerçek).
wres.tle ['resl] **1.** *v/i.* güreşmek; *fig.*
uğraşmak, mücadele etm.; **2.** = *wres-*
tling; 'wres.tler *n.* pehlivan, güreşçi;
'wrestling *n.* güreş(me).
wretch [retʃ] *n.* sefil, biçare, zavallı
kimse; *co.* herif, alçak adam; *poor* ~
adamcağız.
wretch.ed □ ['retʃid] alçak, sefil; bitkin, bezgin, üzgün; perişan, acınacak
halde; acıklı; kötü, berbat; 'wretch-
ed.ness *n.* sefalet, perişanlık; bitkinlik.
wrick [rik] **1.** *v/t.* burkmak; **2.** *n.* bur-
k(ul)ma.
wrig.gle ['rigl] *v/t. & v/i.* kımılda(t)-
mak; sıyrılmak, sıyrılıp çıkmak;
kıvranmak, sallanmak; kıpır kıpır
kıpırdanmak; kıvrılmek; ~ *out of*
-den sıyrılıp çıkmak; *-den* yakayı
sıyırmak (*güçlük vs.*).
wright [rait] *n.* işçi; yapımcı; yazar; marangoz.
wring [riŋ] **1.** (*irr.*) *v/t.* burup sıkmak;
burmak, bükmek, sıkmak; ~ *s.th. from*
s.o. b-den bşi zorla almak; ~ *s.o.'s*
heart b-nin yüreğine işlemek; ~*ing*
wet sırılsıklam; **2.** *n.* burma, sıkma;
'wring.er, 'wring.ing-ma.chine *n.* çamaşır merdanesi.
wrin.kle[1] ['riŋkl] **1.** *n.* kırışık, buruşuk;
yöntem, teknik; **2.** *v/t. & v/i.*
kırış(tır)mak, buruş(tur)mak; ~*d*
kırışık, buruşuk.
wrin.kle[2] F [-] *n.* fikir, öğüt, çıtlatma.

wrist [rist] *n.* bilek; **~ watch** kol saati; **'wrist.band** *n.* kol ağzı, manşet; = **wristlet** ['~lit] *n.* kayış (*part. saat*); *spor*: bileklik.

writ [rit] *n.* yazı; ferman, ilâm, mahkeme emri; davetiye; **Holy ~** İncil; **~ of attachment** JUR haciz belgesi; **~ of execution** JUR icra emri.

write [rait] (*irr.*) *v/t.* yazmak; kaleme almak; ifade etm., kaydetmek; doldurmak (*form vs.*); **~ down** yazmak, kaydetmek; **~ in full** tam olarak (*veya* ayrıntılarıyla) yazmak; **~ off** derhal yazmak, yazıvermek; kapatmak, ödemek (*borç*); iptal etm.; hurdahaş etm.; COM zarara geçmek; **~ out** yazıya dökmek; yazmak (*çek vs.*); **~ up** yazıp tamamlamak; değerini yüksek göstermek (*hisse vs.*); *fig. -den* övgüyle bahsetmek; *v/i.* yazı yazmak; yazarlık yapmak; **~ for** ...hesabına yazı yazmak; beste yapmak; mektupla *bş* ısmarlamak; **~ home about** *fig.* bahsetmeye değer; **'~-off** *n.* COM zarar olarak kabul edilen miktar; **a complete ~** F hurdahaş olmuş şey.

writ.er ['raitə] *n.* yazar; kâtip; **~ to the signet** (*Iskoçya'da*) noter; **~'s cramp**, **~'s palsy** çok yazı yazmaktan ele giren kramp.

write-up ['raitʌp] *n.* makale; övücü yazı.

writhe [raið] *v/i.* kıvranmak; *fig.* acı çekmek.

writ.ing ['raitiŋ] *n.* yazı; el yazısı; yazı yaz(ıl)ma; yazarlık; **~s** *pl.* eser, kitap; *attr.* yazı...; **in ~** yazılı; **'~-block** *n.* bloknot; **'~-case** *n.* sumen; **'~-desk** *n.* yazı masası; **'~-pa.per** *n.* yazı kâğıdı.

writ.ten ['ritn] **1.** *p.p. of* **write**; **2.** *adj.* yazılı.

wrong [rɔŋ] **1.** ☐ yanlış, hatalı; ters; haksız; uygunsuz, yakışık almaz; bozuk; **be ~** yanılmak; hatalı, yanlış olm.; uygunsuz olm.; bozuk olm.; yanlış gitmek (*saat*); **go ~** yanılmak; kötü sonuçlanmak; bozulmak; *fig.* doğru yoldan sapmak; **there is something ~** bir bozukluk var; **what's ~ with ...?** F *-in* nesi var?; **on the ~ side of sixty** altmış yaşını geçmiş; **2.** *n.* hata, kusur; haksızlık; günah; yalan; **be in the ~** hatalı, haksız olm.; **put s.o. in the ~** *b-ni* haksız çıkarmak; **3.** *v/t.* haksız muamele etm. *-e*, haksızlık etm. *-e*; *-in* hakkını yemek; **'~-'do.er** *n.* haksızlık eden (*veya* günahkâr) kimse; **'~'do.ing** *n.* haksızlık; günah; **wrong.ful** ☐ ['~ful] haksız; kanunsuz; gayri meşru; **'wrong'head.ed** *adj.* inatçı, ters; yanlış; **'wrong.ness** *n.* haksızlık, yanlışlık.

wrote [rəut] *pret. of* **write**.

wroth *poet. veya co.* [rəuθ] *adj.* öfkeli, hiddetli.

wrought *lit.* [rɔːt] *pret. & p.p. of* **work 2**; **'~-'i.ron 1.** *n.* dövme demir; **2.** *adj.* dövme demirden yapılmış; **'~-up** *adj.* çok heyecanlı, sinirli.

wrung [rʌŋ] *pret. & p.p. of* **wring 1**.

wry ☐ [rai] eğri, çarpık.

X

X MATH & fig. [eks] *n.* «X» işareti.
Xe.rox ['ziərɔks] **1.** *n.* fotokopi; **2.** *vb.* fotokopi çekmek.
Xmas ['krisməs] = *Christmas.*
X-ray ['eks'rei] **1.** *n.* ∼*s pl.* röntgen ışını; *attr.* röntgen...; **2.** *v/t.* röntgen ışınları ile muayene *veya* tedavi etm.

X-shaped ['eksʃeipt] *adj.* «X» şeklindeki.
xy.log.ra.phy [zai'lɔgrəfi] *n.* tahta kalıptan resim basma sanatı.
xy.lo.nite ['zailənait] *n.* selüloyt.
xy.lo.phone MUS ['zailəfəun] *n.* ksilofon.

Y

yacht NAUT [jɔt] **1.** *n.* yat; **2.** *v/i.* yat ile gezmek *veya* yarışmak; '∼-club *n.* yat kulübü; 'yacht.er, yachts.man ['-smən] *n.* yat sahibi *veya* yat kullanan kimse; 'yachting *n.* yatçılık, kotracılık; *attr.* yat...
yah [jɑ:] ah!, ya!
ya.hoo [jə'hu:] *n.* hayvan gibi herif.
yam BOT [jæm] *n.* Hint yerelması.
yank¹ [jænk] **1.** *v/t.* birden çekmek; **2.** *n.* birden çekiş.
Yank² *sl.* [_] = *Yankee.*
Yan.kee F ['jænki] *n.* Amerikalı; ABD:'nin kuzey eyaletlerinde oturan kimse; ∼ *Doodle* Amerikan halk şarkısı.
yap [jæp] **1.** *v/i.* havlamak; F gevezelik etm.; **2.** *n.* havlama; F gevezelik.
yard¹ [jɑ:d] *n.* yarda *(0,914 m)*; NAUT seren.
yard² [_] *n.* avlu; *Am.* bahçe; *the* ♀ Londra Emniyet Müdürlüğü; *marshalling* ∼, *railway* ∼ manevra istasyonu.
yard...: '∼-arm *n.* NAUT seren cundası; '∼.man *n.* RAIL manevracı; '∼-measure, '∼.stick *n.* bir yardalık ölçü (çubuğu).
yarn [jɑ:n] **1.** *n.* iplik; NAUT gemici masalı; F masal, hikâye; *spin a* ∼ hikâye anlatmak; **2.** *v/i.* F hikâye anlatmak.
yar.row BOT [j'ærəu] *n.* civanperçemi.
yaw NAUT, AVIA [jɔ:] *v/i.* rotadan çıkmak.
yawl NAUT [jɔ:l] *n.* filika; iki yelkenli gemi.
yawn [jɔ:n] **1.** *v/i.* esnemek; açılmak; yarılmak; **2.** *n.* esneme.
ye *obs. veya poet.* veya *co.* [ji:, ji] *pron.*

siz(ler).
yea *obs. veya prov.* [jei] **1.** *adv.* evet; **2.** *n.* olumlu oy (veren kimse).
year [jiə, jə:] *n.* yıl, sene; yaş; ∼ *of arace* milâdî yıl; *he bears his* ∼*s well* yaşına göre çok dinç; 'year.ling *n.* bir yaşında hayvan yavrusu; 'year-long *adj.* bir yıllık, bir yıl süren; 'year.ly *adj. & adv.* yıllık, senelik, yılda bir (olan).
yearn [jə:n] *v/i.* arzulamak, çok istemek *(for, after* -i; *to inf.* -meği); 'yearn.ing **1.** *n.* arzu, hasret, özlem; **2.** ☐ hasretli, özlemli.
yeast [ji:st] *n.* maya; 'yeast.y ☐ mayalı, maya gibi; köpüklü; *fig.* önemsiz, boş, anlamsız.
yegg(.man) *Am. sl.* ['jeg(mən)] *n.* hırsız, kasa hırsızı.
yell [jel] **1.** *v/i.* çığlık koparmak, bağırmak, haykırmak, feryat etm.; **2.** *n.* çığlık, bağırma, haykırma.
yel.low ['jeləu] **1.** *adj.* sarı; F ödlek, korkak; *sl.* şoven; heyecan yaratan *(gazete)*; **2.** *n.* sarı renk; yumurta sarısı; **3.** *v/t. & v/i.* sarar(t)mak; ∼*ed* sararmış, solmuş; '∼-back *n.* değersiz eski kitap; ∼ fe.ver MED sarıhumma; '∼-ham.mer *n.* ORN sarıcık; 'yel.low.ish *adj.* sarımsı, sarımtırak; 'yel.low press olayları heyecanlı bir biçimde veren gazeteler.
yelp [jelp] **1.** *n.* kesik kesik havlama; **2.** *v/i.* kesik hesik havlamak.
yen *Am. sl.* [jen] *n.* hasret, özlem, arzu.
yeo.man ['jəumən] *n.* toprak sahibi; ∼ *of the guard* hassa askeri; 'yeo.man.ry *n.* küçük toprak sahipleri; MIL çiftçilerden oluşan gönüllü süvari alayı.
yep *Am.* F [jep] *adv.* evet.

yes [jes] **1.** *adv.* evet, hay hay; **2.** *n.* olumlu yanıt; olumlu oy (veren kimse); **~-man** *sl.* ['‿mæn] *n.* evet efendimci.

yes.ter.day ['jestədi] *n. & adv.* dün; **yester'year** *n. & adv.* geçen yıl.

yet [jet] **1.** *adv.* henüz, daha, hâlâ; bile; yine, nihayet; **as~** şimdiye kadar; **not~** henüz değil; **2.** *cj.* ancak; yine de, bununla birlikte, buna rağmen.

yew BOT [ju:] *n.* porsukağacı.

Yid.dish ['jidiʃ] *n.* Eskenazi dili.

yield [ji:ld] **1.** *v/t.* vermek, meydana çıkarmak; getirmek (*kâr*); sağlamak; **~ up the ghost** ruhunu teslim etm., ölmek; *v/i. part.* AGR mahsül vermek; razı olm., teslim olm., boyun eğmek (**to** *-e*); çökmek, kırılmak; **2.** *n.* mahsül, ürün, rekolte, hâsılat, gelir; **'yield.ing** □ bükülebilir, eğrilebilir; verimli, bereketli; *fig.* yumuşak, uysal.

yip *Am.* F [jip] *v/i.* acı acı havlamak.

yo.del, yo.dle ['jəudl] **1.** *n.* pesten tize anî geçişlerle söylenen şarkı; **2.** *vb.* böyle şarkı söylemek.

yo.gi ['jəugi] *n.* yogacı.

yo.gurt, yo.ghurt, yo.ghourt ['jɔgət] *n.* yoğurt.

yoicks HUNT [jɔiks] *int.* haydi!

yoke [jəuk] **1.** *n.* boyunduruk (*a. fig.*); çift; omuz sırığı; bağ; **2.** *v/t. & v/i.* boyunduruğa koşmak; boyunduruk vurmak; bağla(n)mak; *fig.* evlendirmek (**to** *ile*); **'~-fel.low** *n.* arkadaş, *part.* hayat arkadaşı, eş.

yo.kel F ['jəukəl] *n.* hödük, cahil taşralı.

yolk [jəuk] *n.* yumurta sarısı.

yon *obs. veya poet.* [jɔn], **yon.der** *lit.* ['jɔndə] **1.** *adj.* ötedeki, oradaki, şuradaki; **2.** *adv.* orada, şurada, ötede.

yore [jɔ:] *n.*: **of ~** eskiden olan.

you [ju:, ju] *pron.* sen; siz(ler); sana, seni; size, sizi.

you'd F [ju:d] = **you had**; **you would**; **you'll** F [ju:l] = **you will**; **you shall**.

young [jʌŋ] **1.** □ genç, küçük; taze, körpe, yeni; toy; **2.** *n.* yavru(lar); **with ~** hamile, gebe; **'young.ish** *adj.* gepegenç, oldukça genç; **young.ster** ['‿stə] *n.* çocuk, yavru, *part.* delikanlı.

your [jɔ:, jə] *adj.* senin; sizin; **you're** F [juə] = **you are**; **yours** [jɔ:z] *pron.* seninki; sizinki; **your'self**, *pl.* **yourselves** [‿'selvz] *pron.* kendin(iz); kendi kendinize.

youth [ju:θ] *n.*, *pl.* **youths** [ju:ðz] genç, delikanlı; gençlik; **~ hostel** gençlik yurdu, hostel; **go ~-hostelling** hostellerde gecelemek.

youth.ful □ ['ju:θful] genç, dinç, taze; **'youth.ful.ness** *n.* gençlik, dinçlik.

you've F [ju:v, juv] = **you have**.

yo-yo di.e.ting ['jəujəu'daiətiŋ] *rejim yapmaya bir başlayıp bir bırakarak sürekli olarak kilo alıp vermek.*

yuc.ca BOT ['jʌkə] *n.* avizeağacı.

Yu.go.slav ['ju:gəu'slɑ:v] *n. & adj.* Yugoslav(yalı).

Yule *lit.* [ju:l] *n.* Noel; **~ log** Noel gecesi yakılan kütük.

Z

za.ny ['zeini] *n.* soytarı, palyaço, maskara.

zap F [zæp] *vb. bilgisayar:* silmek; *bilgisayar oyununda:* öldürmek, vurmak; *TV* zapping yapmak.

zeal [zi:l] *n.* gayret, heves, istek, azim; **zeal.ot** ['zelət] *n.* gayretli kimse; *part.* ECCL fanatik kimse; **'zeal.ot.ry** *n.* fanatizm; **'zeal.ous** □ şevkli, gayretli (*for -e*; *to inf. -meğe*).

ze.bra ZOO ['zi:brə] *n.* zebra, zebîr; ~ **crossing** çizgili yaya geçidi.

ze.bu ZOO ['zi:bu:] *n.* hörgüçlü Hint sığırı.

ze.nith ['zeniθ] *n.* başucu; *fig.* zirve, doruk.

zeph.yr ['zefə] *n.* esinti, meltem; COM zefir (kumaş).

zep.pe.lin ['zepəlin] *n.* zeplin.

ze.ro ['ziərəu] *n.* sıfır; *fig.* hiç; ~ **hour** MIL saldırı saati.

zest [zest] **1.** *n.* tat, lezzet, çeşni; *fig.* zevk, haz, heyecan (*for için*); ~ **for life** yaşama coşkusu; **2.** *vb.* çeşni vermek.

zig.zag ['zigzæg] **1.** *n.* zikzak yol; *attr.* zigzag..., dolambaçlı, yılankavî; **2.** *v/i.* zikzak yapmak.

zinc [ziŋk] **1.** *n.* MIN çinko, tutya; **2.** *v/t.* çinko kaplamak, galvanizlemek.

Zi.on ['zaiən] *n.* İsrail kavmi; cennet; **'Zi.on.ism** *n.* siyonizm; **'Zi.on.ist** *n.*

& *adj.* siyonist.

zip [zip] **1.** *n.* vızıltı; F gayret, enerji; **2.** *vb.* fermuarı kapatmak; vızıldayarak geçmek (*kurşun*); **zip code** *Am.* posta bölgesi numarası; **'~-fas.ten.er** = **zipper 1**; **'zip.per 1.** *n.* fermuar; **2.** *vb.* fermuarlamak; **'zip.py** *adj.* F hareketli, enerjik.

zith.er MUS ['ziθə] *n.* kanuna benzer bir çalgı aleti.

zo.di.ac AST ['zəudiæk] *n.* zodyak; burçlar kuşağı; **zo.di.a.cal** [zəu'daiəkəl] *adj.* zodyaka ait, zodyak...

zon.al □ ['zəunl] kuşağa ait, kuşak...; **zone** *n.* kuşak; *fig.* bölge, mıntıka, yöre.

zoo F [zu:] *n.* hayvanat bahçesi.

zo.o.log.i.cal □ [zəuə'lɔdʒikəl] zoolojik; ~ **garden(s** *pl.*) hayvanat bahçesi; **zo.olo.gist** [-'ɔlədʒist] *n.* zoolog; **zo.'ol.o.gy** *n.* zooloji, hayvanlar bilimi.

zoom [zu:m] **1.** *v/i.* AVIA *sl.* dikine yükselmek; *fig.* fırlamak (*fiyat*); rüzgâr gibi gitmek (*araba*); PHOT zum yapmak, mesafeyi ayarlamak; **2.** *n.* dikine yükselme; ~ **lens** PHOT mesafeyi ayarlayan mercek.

Zu.lu ['zu:lu:] *n.* Zulu (dili).

zy.mot.ic [zai'mɔtik] *adj.* CHEM mayalamaya ait, mayalanmadan ileri gelen; MED bulaşıcı hastalığa ait.

Appendices

Cardinal Numbers
Asıl Sayılar

0 nought, zero, cipher; TELEPH 0 [əu] *sıfır*
1 one *bir*
2 two *iki*
3 three *üç*
4 four *dört*
5 five *beş*
6 six *altı*
7 seven *yedi*
8 eight *sekiz*
9 nine *dokuz*
10 ten *on*
11 eleven *on bir*
12 twelve *on iki*
13 thirteen *on üç*
14 fourteen *on dört*
15 fifteen *on beş*
16 sixteen *on altı*
17 seventeen *on yedi*
18 eighteen *on sekiz*
19 nineteen *on dokuz*
20 twenty *yirmi*
21 twenty-one *yirmi bir*
22 twenty-two *yirmi iki*
30 thirty *otuz*
31 thirty-one *otuz bir*
40 forty *kırk*

41 forty-one *kırk bir*
50 fifty *elli*
51 fifty-one *elli bir*
60 sixty *altmış*
61 sixty-one *altmış bir*
70 seventy *yetmiş*
71 seventy-one *yetmiş bir*
80 eighty *seksen*
81 eighty-one *seksen bir*
90 ninety *doksan*
91 ninety-one *doksan bir*
100 a *or* one hundred *yüz*
101 hundred and one *yüz bir*
200 two hundred *iki yüz*
300 three hundred *üç yüz*
572 five hundred and seventy-two *beş yüz yetmiş iki*
1000 a *or* one thousand *bin*
1066 ten sixty-six *bin altmış altı*
1971 nineteen (hundred and) seventy-one *bin dokuz yüz yetmiş bir*
2000 two thousand *iki bin*
1 000 000 a *or* one million *bir milyon*
2 000 000 two million *iki milyon*
1 000 000 000 a *or* one billion *bir milyar*

Ordinal Numbers
Sıra Sayıları

1st first *birinci*	**31st** thirty-first *otuz birinci*
2nd second *ikinci*	**40th** fortieth *kırkıncı*
3rd third *üçüncü*	**41st** forty-first *kırk birinci*
4th fourth *dördüncü*	**50th** fiftieth *ellinci*
5th fifth *beşinci*	**51st** fifty-first *elli birinci*
6th sixth *altıncı*	**60th** sixtieth *altmışıncı*
7th seventh *yedinci*	**61st** sixty-first *altmış birinci*
8th eighth *sekizinci*	**70th** seventieth *yetmişinci*
9th ninth *dokuzuncu*	**71st** seventy-first *yetmiş birinci*
10th tenth *onuncu*	**80th** eightieth *sekseninci*
11th eleventh *on birinci*	**81st** eighty-first *seksen birinci*
12th twelfth *on ikinci*	**90th** ninetieth *doksanıncı*
13th thirteenth *on üçüncü*	**100th** a *or* one hundredth *yüzüncü*
14th fourteenth *on dördüncü*	**101st** hundred and first *yüz birinci*
15th fifteenth *on beşinci*	**200th** two hundredth *iki yüzüncü*
16th sixteenth *on altıncı*	**300th** three hundredth *üç yüzüncü*
17th seventeenth *on yedinci*	**572nd** five hundred and seventy-second
18th eighteenth *on sekizinci*	*beş yüz yetmiş ikinci*
19th nineteenth *on dokuzuncu*	**1000th** a *or* one thousandth *bininci*
20th twentieth *yirminci*	**1950th** nineteen hundred and fiftieth
21st twenty-first *yirmi birinci*	*bin dokuz yüz ellinci*
22nd twenty-second *yirmi ikinci*	**2000th** two thousandth *iki bininci*
23rd twenty-third *yirmi üçüncü*	**1 000 000th** a *or* one millionth *bir milyonuncu*
30th thirtieth *otuzuncu*	**2 000 000th** two millionth *iki milyonuncu*

Fractions, decimals and mathematical calculation methods
Kesirli ve Diğer Sayılar

½ one *or* a half *yarım*
1½ one and a half *bir buçuk*
2½ two and a half *iki buçuk*
⅓ one *or* a third *üçte bir*
⅔ two thirds *üçte iki*
¼ one *or* a quarter, one fourth *çeyrek*, *dörtte bir*
¾ three quarters, three fourths *dörtte üç*
⅕ one *or* a fifth *beşte bir*
⅝ five eighths *sekizde beş*
2.5 two point five *iki onda beş*

once *bir kere*
twice *iki kere*
three times *üç kere*
7 + 8 = 15 seven and eight are fifteen *yedi sekiz daha on beş eder*
9 − 4 = 5 nine less four are five *dokuzdan dört çıkarsa beş kalır*
2 × 3 = 6 twice three are *or* make six *iki kere üç altı eder*
20 : 5 = 4 twenty divided by five make four *yirmide beş dört kere var*

Irregular Verbs
Kuraldışı Fiiller

INFINITIVE	PAST	PAST PARTICIPLE
abide	abode	abode
arise	arose	arisen
awake	awoke	awoke, awoken
be	was	been
bear	bore	borne, born
beat	beat	beaten
become	became	become
befall	befell	befallen
beget	begot	begotten
begin	began	begun
behold	beheld	beheld
bend	bent	bent, bended
bereave	bereft	bereft, bereaved
beseech	besought	besought
beset	beset	beset
bet	bet, betted	bet, betted
betake	betook	betaken
bethink	bethought	bethought
bid	bade, bid	bidden, bid
bide	bided	bided
bind	bound	bound
bite	bit	bitten, bit
bleed	bled	bled
blow	blew	blown
break	broke	broken
breed	bred	bred
bring	brought	brought
broadcast	broadcast	broadcast
build	built	built
burn	burnt, burned	burnt, burned
burst	burst	burst
buy	bought	bought
cast	cast	cast
catch	caught	caught
chide	chid	chidden, chid
choose	chose	chosen
cleave	clove, cleft	cloven, cleft
cling	clung	clung
clothe	clothed	clothed, clad
come	came	come
cost	cost	cost

creep	crept	crept
cut	cut	cut
deal	dealt	dealt
dig	dug	dug
do	did	done
draw	drew	drawn
dream	dreamt, dreamed	dreamt, dreamed
drink	drank	drunk, drunken
drive	drove	driven
dwell	dwelt	dwelt
eat	ate	eaten
fall	fell	fallen
feed	fed	fed
feel	felt	felt
fight	fought	fought
find	found	found
flee	fled	fled
fling	flung	flung
fly	flew	flown
forbear	forbore	forborne
forbid	forbade	forbidden
forecast	forecast	forecast
foreknow	foreknew	foreknown
foresee	foresaw	foreseen
foretell	foretold	foretold
forget	forgot	forgotten
forgive	forgave	forgiven
forsake	forsook	forsaken
forswear	forswore	forsworn
freeze	froze	frozen
gainsay	gainsaid	gainsaid
get	got	got
gild	gilded	gilded, gilt
gird	girded	girded, girt
give	gave	given
go	went	gone
grind	ground	ground
grow	grew	grown
hamstring	hamstrung	hamstrung
hang	hung	hung
have	had	had
hear	heard	heard
heave	heaved, hove	heaved
hew	hewed	hewn
hide	hid	hidden, hid
hit	hit	hit
hold	held	held
hurt	hurt	hurt
inlay	inlaid	inlaid
keep	kept	kept
kneel	knelt	knelt
knit	knitted, knit	knitted, knit
know	knew	known
lade	laded	laden
lay	laid	laid

lead	led	led
lean	leant, leaned	leant, leaned
leap	leapt, leaped	leapt, leaped
learn	learnt, learned	learnt, learned
leave	left	left
lend	lent	lent
let	let	let
lie	lay	lain
light	lighted, lit	lighted, lit
lose	lost	lost
make	made	made
mean	meant	meant
meet	met	met
melt	melted	melted, molten
miscast	miscast	miscast
misdeal	misdealt	misdealt
misgive	misgave	misgiven
mislay	mislaid	mislaid
mislead	misled	misled
misspell	misspelt	misspelt
misspend	misspent	misspent
mistake	mistook	mistaken
misunderstand	misunderstood	misunderstood
mow	mowed	mown
outbid	outbid	outbidden, outbid
outdo	outdid	outdone
outgo	outwent	outgone
outgrow	outgrew	outgrown
outride	outrode	outridden
outrun	outran	outrun
outshine	outshone	outshone
overbear	overbore	overborne
overcast	overcast	overcast
overcome	overcame	overcome
overdo	overdid	overdone
overhang	overhung	overhung
overhear	overheard	overheard
overlay	overlaid	overlaid
overleap	overleapt, overleaped	overleapt, overleaped
overlie	overlay	overlain
override	overrode	overridden
overrun	overran	overrun
oversee	oversaw	overseen
overset	overset	overset
overshoot	overshot	overshot
oversleep	overslept	overslept
overtake	overtook	overtaken
overthrow	overthrew	overthrown
partake	partook	partaken
pay	paid	paid
prove	proved	proved, proven
put	put	put
read	read	read
rebind	rebound	rebound
rebuild	rebuilt	rebuilt

recast	recast	recast
redo	redid	redone
relay	relaid	relaid
remake	remade	remade
rend	rent	rent
repay	repaid	repaid
rerun	reran	rerun
reset	reset	reset
retell	retold	retold
rewrite	rewrote	rewritten
rid	rid, ridded	rid, ridded
ride	rode	ridden
ring	rang	rung
rise	rose	risen
rive	rived	riven, rived
run	ran	run
saw	sawed	sawn, sawed
say	said	said
see	saw	seen
seek	sought	sought
sell	sold	sold
send	sent	sent
set	set	set
sew	sewed	sewn, sewed
shake	shook	shaken
shave	shaved	shaved, shaven
shear	sheared, shore	shorn, sheared
shed	shed	shed
shine	shone	shone
shoe	shod	shod
shoot	shot	shot
show	showed	shown, showed
shrink	shrank	shrunk, shrunken
shrive	shrived	shriven
shut	shut	shut
sing	sang	sung
sink	sank	sunk, sunken
sit	sat	sat
slay	slew	slain
sleep	slept	slept
slide	slid	slid, slidden
sling	slung	slung
slink	slunk	slunk
slit	slit	slit
smell	smelt, smelled	smelt, smelled
smite	smote	smitten
sow	sowed	sown, sowed
speak	spoke	spoken
speed	sped	sped
spell	spelt, spelled	spelt, spelled
spend	spent	spent
spill	spilt, spilled	spilt, spilled
spin	spun, span	spun
spit	spat	spat
split	split	split

spoil	spoilt, spoiled	spoilt, spoiled
spread	spread	spread
spring	sprang	sprung
stand	stood	stood
stave	staved, stove	staved, stove
steal	stole	stolen
stick	stuck	stuck
sting	stung	stung
stink	stank	stunk
strew	strewed	strewn, strewed
stride	strode	stridden, strid
strike	struck	struck, stricken
string	strung	strung
strive	strove	striven
sunburn	sunburnt, sunburned	sunburnt, sunburned
swear	swore	sworn
sweep	swept	swept
swell	swelled	swollen, swelled
swim	swam	swum
swing	swung	swung
take	took	taken
teach	taugh	taugh
tear	tore	torn
tell	told	told
think	thought	thought
thrive	throve, thrived	thriven, thrived
throw	threw	thrown
thrust	thrust	thrust
tread	trod	trodden, trod
unbend	unbent	unbent
unbind	unbound	unbound
underbid	underbid	underbidden, underbid
undergo	underwent	undergone
understand	understood	understood
undertake	undertook	undertaken
undo	undid	undone
upset	upset	upset
wake	woke, waked	woken, waked
waylay	waylaid	waylaid
wear	wore	worn
weave	wove	woven, wove
wed	wedded	wedded, wed
weep	wept	wept
wet	wet, wetted	wet, wetted
win	won	won
wind	wound	wound
withdraw	withdrew	withdrawn
withhold	withheld	withheld
withstand	withstood	withstood
wring	wrung	wrung
write	wrote	written